GOD SIGHTINGS:
THE ONE YEAR BIBLE
New International Version

GOD SIGHTINGS™

Learning to Experience God Every Day™

Group
Loveland, Colorado

NIV

Tyndale House Publishers, Inc.
Carol Stream, Illinois

Visit Group's exciting Web sites at www.MyGodSightings.com and www.group.com

Visit Tyndale's exciting Web site at www.tyndale.com

CONTENTS

ALPHABETICAL INDEX
to the Books of the Bible

GOD SIGHTINGS

Once you've seen God at work there's no turning back.
Not to a ho-hum, lukewarm faith.

Not to yet another half-hearted commitment to "do better."

You're about to be transformed, to see the world through new eyes. To see God working in his creation—and in your own life.

Nothing will ever be the same again.

Welcome to GOD SIGHTINGS . . .
You'll develop an ear for God's voice, an eye for seeing him move in the world. And as you explore Scripture, each word will spring to life—because it helps you know God even better.

Whether you've been a Christian for decades or just since yesterday, *God Sightings* will deepen your faith. That's because, in addition to the truth you'll find in God's Word, you'll build your faith on rock-solid experience.

And if you don't happen to be a Christian, no problem—you're invited along for the journey too.

God will meet you where you are.

Guaranteed.

Don't worry about missing a day
If you've read through the Bible in a year, you know the drill: you miss a day here or there and soon you're discouraged. So you cram a week's reading in a single setting.

Or you give up altogether.

With *God Sightings*, you'll read at your own pace. Want to finish in a year? Fine. Two years? Okay.

Remember: the goal isn't to complete a homework assignment. It's to let the living God of the universe reveal himself to you . . . and there's no stopwatch running.

GOD SIGHTINGS

Pick a page

Begin your adventure on Day 1. Or start on the current date. It's your choice.

You'll find daily readings for each day of the year. Every day there's an excerpt from the Old Testament, the New Testament, Psalms, and Proverbs.

Pause

Use *God Sightings: The One Year Companion Guide* during or after your reading to capture your feelings—and to reflect on the questions you'll find in the *Companion Guide*. Consider how God was active in your life that day.

Get and stay connected

To get the most out of *God Sightings: The One Year Bible*, connect with others. Invite a friend along on the experience. Form a face-to-face small group. Or join an online discussion at MyGodSightings.com. Or do them all. Again—it's your choice.

Share your God Sightings

Here's the thing: as you grow deeper in your faith, you can encourage others. Your accounts of God at work feed others who are hungry for encouragement . . . who are thirsty for inspiration . . . who are on the same journey you're on.

A journey further into God's love.

So be willing to share. To add your own God Sightings to the thousands reported in Scripture and the thousands more reported by current-day Christ-followers.

Begin your adventure—now

This Bible is an account of God's interactions with his people. People just like you. God's looking for a relationship with you—one that grows and deepens as you read his Word . . . experience his love . . . and join him in his ongoing work.

There's no greater adventure, no more satisfying life.

PUBLISHER'S NOTE

The One Year Bible has been prepared especially for regular Bible readers who wish to read through the entire Bible in one year.

Each day you will read a passage from the Old Testament and from the New Testament, along with short selections from Psalms and Proverbs. This will give variety and freshness to your daily reading.

Instead of following a Bible reading chart and experiencing the delay of turning from place to place, you will find the text here in sequence, ready for your quiet reading and meditation. This fulfills our goal at Tyndale to make the Bible as accessible as possible for people no matter what their background or walk of life.

May this year and every year be enriched as you enjoy daily portions from God's Word.

This edition of *The One Year Bible* contains the entire text of the *Holy Bible*, New International Version.

PREFACE

THE NEW INTERNATIONAL VERSION is a completely new translation of the Holy Bible made by over a hundred scholars working directly from the best available Hebrew, Aramaic and Greek texts. It had its beginning in 1965 when, after several years of exploratory study by committees from the Christian Reformed Church and the National Association of Evangelicals, a group of scholars met at Palos Heights, Illinois, and concurred in the need for a new translation of the Bible in contemporary English. This group, though not made up of official church representatives, was transdenominational. Its conclusion was endorsed by a large number of leaders from many denominations who met in Chicago in 1966.

Responsibility for the new version was delegated by the Palos Heights group to a self-governing body of fifteen, the Committee on Bible Translation, composed for the most part of biblical scholars from colleges, universities and seminaries. In 1967 the New York Bible Society (now the International Bible Society) generously undertook the financial sponsorship of the project—a sponsorship that made it possible to enlist the help of many distinguished scholars. The fact that participants from the United States, Great Britain, Canada, Australia and New Zealand worked together gave the project its international scope. That they were from many denominations—including Anglican, Assemblies of God, Baptist, Brethren, Christian Reformed, Church of Christ, Evangelical Free, Lutheran, Mennonite, Methodist, Nazarene, Presbyterian, Wesleyan and other churches—helped to safeguard the translation from sectarian bias.

How it was made helps to give the New International Version its distinctiveness. The translation of each book was assigned to a team of scholars. Next, one of the Intermediate Editorial Committees revised the initial translation, with constant reference to the Hebrew, Aramaic or Greek. Their work then went to one of the General Editorial Committees, which checked it in detail and made another thorough revision. This revision in turn was carefully reviewed by the Committee on Bible Translation, which made further changes and then released the final version for publication. In this way the entire Bible underwent three revisions, during each of which the translation was examined for its faithfulness to the original languages and for its English style.

All this involved many thousands of hours of research and discussion regarding the meaning of the texts and the precise way of putting them into English. It may well be that no other translation has been made by a more thorough process of review and revision from committee to committee than this one.

From the beginning of the project, the Committee on Bible Translation held to certain goals for the New International Version: that it would be an accurate translation and one that would have clarity and literary quality and so prove suitable for public and private reading, teaching, preaching, memorizing and liturgical use. The Committee also sought to preserve some measure of continuity with the long tradition of translating the Scriptures into English.

In working toward these goals, the translators were united in their commitment to the authority and infallibility of the Bible as God's Word in written form. They believe that it contains the divine answer to the deepest needs of humanity, that it sheds unique light on our path in a dark world, and that it sets forth the way to our eternal well-being.

The first concern of the translators has been the accuracy of the translation and its fidelity to the thought of the biblical writers. They have weighed the significance of the lexical and grammatical details of the Hebrew, Aramaic and Greek texts. At the same time, they have striven for more than a word-for-word translation. Because thought patterns and syntax differ from language to language, faithful communication of the meaning of the writers of the Bible demands frequent modifications in sentence structure and constant regard for the contextual meanings of words.

A sensitive feeling for style does not always accompany scholarship. Accordingly the Committee on Bible Translation submitted the developing version to a number of stylistic consultants. Two of them read every book of both Old and New Testaments twice—once before and once after the last major revision—and made invaluable suggestions. Samples of the translation were tested for clarity and ease of reading by various kinds of people—young and old, highly educated and less well educated, ministers and laymen.

Concern for clear and natural English—that the New International Version should be idiomatic but not idiosyncratic, contemporary but not dated—motivated the translators and consultants. At the same time, they tried to reflect the differing styles of the biblical writers. In view of the international use of English, the translators sought to avoid obvious Americanisms on the one hand and obvious Anglicisms on the other. A British edition reflects the comparatively few differences of significant idiom and of spelling.

As for the traditional pronouns "thou," "thee" and "thine" in reference to the Deity, the translators judged that to use these archaisms (along with the old verb forms such as "doest," "wouldest" and "hadst") would violate accuracy in translation. Neither Hebrew, Aramaic nor Greek uses special pronouns for the persons of the Godhead. A present-day translation is not enhanced by forms that in the time of the King James Version were used in everyday speech, whether referring to God or man.

For the Old Testament the standard Hebrew text, the Masoretic Text as published in the latest editions of *Biblia Hebraica,* was used throughout. The Dead Sea Scrolls contain material bearing on an earlier stage of the Hebrew text. They were consulted, as were the Samaritan Pentateuch and the ancient scribal traditions relating to textual changes. Sometimes a variant Hebrew reading in the margin of the Masoretic Text was followed instead of the text itself. Such instances, being variants within the Masoretic tradition, are not specified by footnotes. In rare cases, words in the consonantal text were divided differently from the way they appear in the Masoretic Text. Footnotes indicate this. The translators also consulted the more important early versions—the Septuagint; Aquila, Symmachus and Theodotion; the Vulgate; the Syriac Peshitta; the Targums; and for the Psalms the *Juxta Hebraica* of Jerome. Readings from these versions were occasionally followed where the Masoretic Text seemed doubtful and where accepted principles of textual criticism showed that one or more of these textual witnesses appeared to provide the correct reading. Such instances are footnoted. Sometimes vowel letters and vowel signs did not, in the judgment of the translators, represent the correct vowels for the original consonantal text. Accordingly some words were read with a different set of vowels. These instances are usually not indicated by footnotes.

The Greek text used in translating the New Testament was an eclectic one. No other piece of ancient literature has such an abundance of manuscript witnesses as does the New Testament. Where existing manuscripts differ, the translators made their choice of readings according to accepted principles of New Testament textual criticism. Footnotes call attention to places where there was uncertainty about what the original text was. The best current printed texts of the Greek New Testament were used.

There is a sense in which the work of translation is never wholly finished. This applies to all great literature and uniquely so to the Bible. In 1973 the New Testament in the New International Version was published. Since then, suggestions for corrections and revisions have been received from various sources. The Committee on Bible Translation carefully considered the suggestions and adopted a number of them. These were incorporated in the first printing of the entire Bible in 1978. Additional revisions were made by the Committee on Bible Translation in 1983 and appear in printings after that date.

As in other ancient documents, the precise meaning of the biblical texts is sometimes uncertain. This is more often the case with the Hebrew and Aramaic texts than with the Greek text. Although archaeological and linguistic discoveries in this century aid in understanding difficult passages, some uncertainties remain. The more significant of these have been called to the reader's attention in the footnotes.

In regard to the divine name *YHWH*, commonly referred to as the *Tetragrammaton*, the translators adopted the device used in most English versions of rendering that name as "LORD" in capital letters to distinguish it from *Adonai*, another Hebrew word rendered "Lord," for which small letters are used. Wherever the two names stand together in the Old Testament as a compound name of God, they are rendered "Sovereign LORD."

Because for most readers today the phrases "the LORD of hosts" and "God of hosts" have little meaning, this version renders them "the LORD Almighty" and "God Almighty." These renderings convey the sense of the Hebrew, namely, "he who is sovereign over all the 'hosts' (powers) in heaven and on earth, especially over the 'hosts' (armies) of Israel." For readers unacquainted with Hebrew this does not make clear the distinction between *Sabaoth* ("hosts" or "Almighty") and *Shaddai* (which can also be translated "Almighty"), but the latter occurs infrequently and is always footnoted. When *Adonai* and *YHWH Sabaoth* occur together, they are rendered "the Lord, the LORD Almighty."

As for other proper nouns, the familiar spellings of the King James Version are generally retained. Names traditionally spelled with "ch," except where it is final, are usually spelled in this translation with "k" or "c," since the biblical languages do not have the sound that "ch" frequently indicates in English—for example, in *chant*. For well-known names such as Zechariah, however, the traditional spelling has been retained. Variation in the spelling of names in the original languages has usually not been indicated. Where a person or place has two or more different names in the Hebrew, Aramaic or Greek texts, the more familiar one has generally been used, with footnotes where needed.

To achieve clarity the translators sometimes supplied words not in the original texts but required by the context. If there was uncertainty about such material, it is enclosed in brackets. Also for the sake of clarity or style, nouns, including some proper nouns, are sometimes substituted for pronouns, and vice versa. And though the Hebrew writers often shifted back and forth between first, second and third personal pronouns without change of antecedent, this translation often makes them uniform, in accordance with English style and without the use of footnotes.

Poetical passages are printed as poetry, that is, with indentation of lines and with separate stanzas. These are generally designed to reflect the structure of Hebrew poetry. This poetry is normally characterized by parallelism in balanced lines. Most of the poetry in the Bible is in the Old Testament, and scholars differ regarding the scansion of Hebrew lines. The translators determined the stanza divisions for the most part by analysis of the subject matter. The stanzas therefore serve as poetic paragraphs.

The footnotes in this version are of several kinds, most of which need no explanation. Those giving alternative translations begin with "Or" and generally introduce the alternative with the last word preceding it in the text, except when it is a single-word alternative; in poetry quoted in a footnote a slant mark indicates a line division. Footnotes introduced by "Or" do not have uniform significance. In some cases two possible translations were considered to have about equal validity. In other cases, though the translators were convinced that the translation in the text was correct, they judged that another interpretation was possible and of sufficient importance to be represented in a footnote.

In the New Testament, footnotes that refer to uncertainty regarding the original text are introduced by "Some manuscripts" or similar expressions. In the Old Testament, evidence for the reading chosen is given first and evidence for the alternative is added after a semicolon (for example: Septuagint; Hebrew *father*). In such notes the term "Hebrew" refers to the Masoretic Text.

It should be noted that minerals, flora and fauna, architectural details, articles of clothing and jewelry, musical instruments and other articles cannot always be identified with precision. Also measures of capacity in the biblical period are particularly uncertain.

Like all translations of the Bible, made as they are by imperfect man, this one undoubtedly falls short of its goals. Yet we are grateful to God for the extent to which he has enabled us to realize these goals and for the strength he has given us and our colleagues to complete our task. We offer this version of the Bible to him in whose name and for whose glory it has been made. We pray that it will lead many into a better understanding of the Holy Scriptures and a fuller knowledge of Jesus Christ the incarnate Word, of whom the Scriptures so faithfully testify.

The Committee on Bible Translation
June 1978 (Revised August 1983)

Names of the translators and editors may be secured from the International Bible Society, translation sponsors of the New International Version, 1820 Jet Stream Drive, Colorado Springs, Colorado 80921-3696 U.S.A.

□ DAY 1

January 1

GENESIS 1:1–2:25

In the beginning God created the heavens and the earth. ²Now the earth was^a formless and empty, darkness was over the surface of the deep, and the Spirit of God was hovering over the waters.

³ And God said, "Let there be light," and there was light. ⁴God saw that the light was good, and he separated the light from the darkness. ⁵God called the light "day," and the darkness he called "night." And there was evening, and there was morning—the first day.

⁶ And God said, "Let there be an expanse between the waters to separate water from water." ⁷So God made the expanse and separated the water under the expanse from the water above it. And it was so. ⁸God called the expanse "sky." And there was evening, and there was morning—the second day.

⁹ And God said, "Let the water under the sky be gathered to one place, and let dry ground appear." And it was so. ¹⁰God called the dry ground "land," and the gathered waters he called "seas." And God saw that it was good.

¹¹Then God said, "Let the land produce vegetation: seed-bearing plants and trees on the land that bear fruit with seed in it, according to their various kinds." And it was so. ¹²The land produced vegetation: plants bearing seed according to their kinds and trees bearing fruit with seed in it according to their kinds. And God saw that it was good. ¹³And there was eve-

ning, and there was morning—the third day.

¹⁴ And God said, "Let there be lights in the expanse of the sky to separate the day from the night, and let them serve as signs to mark seasons and days and years, ¹⁵and let them be lights in the expanse of the sky to give light on the earth." And it was so. ¹⁶God made two great lights—the greater light to govern the day and the lesser light to govern the night. He also made the stars. ¹⁷God set them in the expanse of the sky to give light on the earth, ¹⁸to govern the day and the night, and to separate light from darkness. And God saw that it was good. ¹⁹And there was evening, and there was morning—the fourth day.

²⁰ And God said, "Let the water teem with living creatures, and let birds fly above the earth across the expanse of the sky." ²¹So God created the great creatures of the sea and every living and moving thing with which the water teems, according to their kinds, and every winged bird according to its kind. And God saw that it was good. ²²God blessed them and said, "Be fruitful and increase in number and fill the water in the seas, and let the birds increase on the earth." ²³And there was evening, and there was morning—the fifth day.

²⁴ And God said, "Let the land produce living creatures according to their kinds: livestock, creatures that move along the ground, and wild animals, each according to its kind." And it was so. ²⁵God made the wild animals according to their kinds, the livestock according to their kinds, and all the creatures that move along the ground according to their kinds. And God saw that it was good.

26Then God said, "Let us make man in our image, in our likeness, and let them rule over the fish of the sea and the birds of the air, over the livestock, over all the earth,*b* and over all the creatures that move along the ground."

27So God created man in his
    own image,
  in the image of God he
    created him;
  male and female he created
    them.

28God blessed them and said to them, "Be fruitful and increase in number; fill the earth and subdue it. Rule over the fish of the sea and the birds of the air and over every living creature that moves on the ground."

29Then God said, "I give you every seed-bearing plant on the face of the whole earth and every tree that has fruit with seed in it. They will be yours for food. 30And to all the beasts of the earth and all the birds of the air and all the creatures that move on the ground—everything that has the breath of life in it—I give every green plant for food." And it was so.

31God saw all that he had made, and it was very good. And there was evening, and there was morning—the sixth day.

2:1Thus the heavens and the earth were completed in all their vast array.

2By the seventh day God had finished the work he had been doing; so on the seventh day he rested*c* from all his work. 3And God blessed the seventh day and made it holy, because on it he rested from all the work of creating that he had done.

4This is the account of the heavens and the earth when they were created.

When the Lord God made the earth and the heavens— 5and no shrub of the field had yet appeared on the earth*d* and no plant of the field had yet sprung up, for the Lord God had not sent rain on the earth*d* and there was no man to work the ground, 6but streams*e* came up from the earth and watered the whole surface of the ground— 7the Lord God formed the man*f* from the dust of the ground and breathed into his nostrils the breath of life, and the man became a living being.

8Now the Lord God had planted a garden in the east, in Eden; and there he put the man he had formed. 9And the Lord God made all kinds of trees grow out of the ground—trees that were pleasing to the eye and good for food. In the middle of the garden were the tree of life and the tree of the knowledge of good and evil.

10A river watering the garden flowed from Eden; from there it was separated into four headwaters. 11The name of the first is the Pishon; it winds through the entire land of Havilah, where there is gold. 12(The gold of that land is good; aromatic resin*g* and onyx are also there.) 13The name of the second river is the Gihon; it winds through the entire land of Cush.*h* 14The name of the third river is the Tigris; it runs along the east side of Asshur. And the fourth river is the Euphrates.

15The Lord God took the man and put him in the Garden of Eden to work it and take care of it. 16And the Lord God commanded the man, "You are free to eat from any tree in the garden; 17but you must not eat from the tree of the knowledge of good and evil, for when you eat of it you will surely die."

18The Lord God said, "It is not good for the man to be alone. I will make a helper suitable for him."

19Now the Lord God had formed out of the ground all the beasts of the field and all the birds of the air. He brought them to the man to see what he would name them; and whatever the man called each living creature, that was its name. 20So the man gave names to all the livestock, the birds of the air and all the beasts of the field.

But for Adam[j] no suitable helper was found. 21So the LORD God caused the man to fall into a deep sleep; and while he was sleeping, he took one of the man's ribs[j] and closed up the place with flesh. 22Then the LORD God made a woman from the rib[k] he had taken out of the man, and he brought her to the man.

23The man said,

"This is now bone of my bones
  and flesh of my flesh;
she shall be called 'woman,'[l]
  for she was taken out of man."

24For this reason a man will leave his father and mother and be united to his wife, and they will become one flesh. 25The man and his wife were both naked, and they felt no shame.

a2 Or possibly *became*   b26 Hebrew; Syriac *all the wild animals*   c2 Or *ceased*; also in verse 3   d5 Or *land*; also in verse 6   e6 Or *mist*   f7 The Hebrew for *man (adam)* sounds like and may be related to the Hebrew for *ground (adamah)*; it is also the name *Adam* (see Gen. 2:20).   g12 Or *good; pearls*   h13 Possibly southeast Mesopotamia   i20 Or *the man*   j21 Or *took part of the man's side*   k22 Or *part*   l23 The Hebrew for *woman* sounds like the Hebrew for *man.*

MATTHEW 1:1–2:12

A record of the genealogy of Jesus Christ the son of David, the son of Abraham:

2Abraham was the father of Isaac,
  Isaac the father of Jacob,
  Jacob the father of Judah and his brothers,
3Judah the father of Perez and Zerah, whose mother was Tamar,
  Perez the father of Hezron,
  Hezron the father of Ram,
4Ram the father of Amminadab,
  Amminadab the father of Nahshon,
  Nahshon the father of Salmon,
5Salmon the father of Boaz, whose mother was Rahab,
  Boaz the father of Obed, whose mother was Ruth,
  Obed the father of Jesse,
6and Jesse the father of King David.

David was the father of Solomon, whose mother had been Uriah's wife,
7Solomon the father of Rehoboam,
  Rehoboam the father of Abijah,
  Abijah the father of Asa,
8Asa the father of Jehoshaphat,
  Jehoshaphat the father of Jehoram,
  Jehoram the father of Uzziah,
9Uzziah the father of Jotham,
  Jotham the father of Ahaz,
  Ahaz the father of Hezekiah,
10Hezekiah the father of Manasseh,
  Manasseh the father of Amon,
  Amon the father of Josiah,
11and Josiah the father of Jeconiah[a] and his brothers at the time of the exile to Babylon.

12After the exile to Babylon:
  Jeconiah was the father of Shealtiel,
  Shealtiel the father of Zerubbabel,
13Zerubbabel the father of Abiud,
  Abiud the father of Eliakim,
  Eliakim the father of Azor,
14Azor the father of Zadok,
  Zadok the father of Akim,
  Akim the father of Eliud,
15Eliud the father of Eleazar,
  Eleazar the father of Matthan,
  Matthan the father of Jacob,
16and Jacob the father of Joseph, the husband of Mary, of whom was born Jesus, who is called Christ.

17Thus there were fourteen generations in all from Abraham to David, fourteen from David to the exile to Babylon, and fourteen from the exile to the Christ.[b]

18This is how the birth of Jesus Christ came about: His mother Mary was pledged to be married to Joseph, but before they came together, she was found to be with child through the Holy Spirit. 19Because Joseph her husband was a righteous man and did not want to expose her to public disgrace, he had in mind to divorce her quietly.

20But after he had considered this, an angel of the Lord appeared to him in a dream and said, "Joseph son of David, do not be afraid to take Mary home as your wife, because what is conceived in her is from the Holy Spirit. 21She will give birth to a son, and you are to give him the name Jesus,c because he will save his people from their sins."

22All this took place to fulfill what the Lord had said through the prophet: 23"The virgin will be with child and will give birth to a son, and they will call him Immanuel"d—which means, "God with us."

24When Joseph woke up, he did what the angel of the Lord had commanded him and took Mary home as his wife. 25But he had no union with her until she gave birth to a son. And he gave him the name Jesus.

2:1AFTER Jesus was born in Bethlehem in Judea, during the time of King Herod, Magie from the east came to Jerusalem 2and asked, "Where is the one who has been born king of the Jews? We saw his star in the eastf and have come to worship him."

3When King Herod heard this he was disturbed, and all Jerusalem with him. 4When he had called together all the people's chief priests and teachers of the law, he asked them where the Christg was to be born. 5"In Bethlehem in Judea," they replied, "for this is what the prophet has written:

6"'But you, Bethlehem, in the land of Judah,
    are by no means least among the rulers of Judah;
for out of you will come a ruler
    who will be the shepherd of my people Israel.'h"

7Then Herod called the Magi secretly and found out from them the exact time the star had appeared. 8He sent them to Bethlehem and said, "Go and make a careful search for the child. As soon as you find him, report to me, so that I too may go and worship him."

9After they had heard the king, they went on their way, and the star they had seen in the easti went ahead of them un-

til it stopped over the place where the child was. 10When they saw the star, they were overjoyed. 11On coming to the house, they saw the child with his mother Mary, and they bowed down and worshiped him. Then they opened their treasures and presented him with gifts of gold and of incense and of myrrh. 12And having been warned in a dream not to go back to Herod, they returned to their country by another route.

a11 That is, Jehoiachin; also in verse 12   b17Or Messiah. "The Christ" (Greek) and "the Messiah" (Hebrew) both mean "the Anointed One."   c21 Jesus is the Greek form of Joshua, which means the LORD saves.   d23 Isaiah 7:14 e1 Traditionally Wise Men   f2 Or star when it rose g4 Or Messiah   h6 Micah 5:2   i9 Or seen when it rose

PSALM 1:1-6

1 **B**lessed is the man
    who does not walk in the counsel
        of the wicked
or stand in the way of sinners
    or sit in the seat of mockers.
2 But his delight is in the law of
        the LORD,
    and on his law he meditates day
        and night.

3 He is like a tree planted by streams
        of water,
    which yields its fruit in season
and whose leaf does not wither.
    Whatever he does prospers.

4 Not so the wicked!
    They are like chaff
    that the wind blows away.
5 Therefore the wicked will not stand
        in the judgment,
    nor sinners in the assembly of
        the righteous.

6 For the LORD watches over the way
        of the righteous,
    but the way of the wicked will
        perish.

PROVERBS 1:1-6

The proverbs of Solomon son of David, king of Israel:

2 for attaining wisdom and discipline;
    for understanding words
        of insight;

³for acquiring a disciplined and
 prudent life,
  doing what is right and just
   and fair;
⁴for giving prudence to the simple,
 knowledge and discretion to
  the young—
⁵let the wise listen and add to
 their learning,
  and let the discerning get
   guidance—
⁶for understanding proverbs
 and parables,
  the sayings and riddles of
   the wise.

□ DAY 2

GOD SIGHTINGS

January 2

GENESIS 3:1–4:26

Now the serpent was more crafty than any of the wild animals the LORD God had made. He said to the woman, "Did God really say, 'You must not eat from any tree in the garden'?"

²The woman said to the serpent, "We may eat fruit from the trees in the garden, ³but God did say, 'You must not eat fruit from the tree that is in the middle of the garden, and you must not touch it, or you will die.'"

⁴"You will not surely die," the serpent said to the woman. ⁵"For God knows that when you eat of it your eyes will be opened, and you will be like God, knowing good and evil."

⁶When the woman saw that the fruit of the tree was good for food and pleasing to the eye, and also desirable for gaining wisdom, she took some and ate it. She also gave some to her husband, who was with her, and he ate it. ⁷Then the eyes of both of them were opened, and they realized they were naked; so they sewed fig leaves together and made coverings for themselves.

⁸Then the man and his wife heard the sound of the LORD God as he was walking in the garden in the cool of the day, and they hid from the LORD God among the trees of the garden. ⁹But the LORD God called to the man, "Where are you?"

¹⁰He answered, "I heard you in the garden, and I was afraid because I was naked; so I hid."

¹¹And he said, "Who told you that you were naked? Have you eaten from the tree that I commanded you not to eat from?"

¹²The man said, "The woman you put here with me—she gave me some fruit from the tree, and I ate it."

¹³Then the LORD God said to the woman, "What is this you have done?"

The woman said, "The serpent deceived me, and I ate."

¹⁴So the LORD God said to the serpent, "Because you have done this,

"Cursed are you above all the
  livestock
 and all the wild animals!
You will crawl on your belly
 and you will eat dust
  all the days of your life.
¹⁵And I will put enmity
 between you and the woman,
 and between your offspring^a
  and hers;
he will crush^b your head,
 and you will strike his heel."

¹⁶To the woman he said,

"I will greatly increase your pains
  in childbearing;
 with pain you will give birth
  to children.
Your desire will be for your husband,
 and he will rule over you."

¹⁷To Adam he said, "Because you listened to your wife and ate from the tree about which I commanded you, 'You must not eat of it,'

"Cursed is the ground because of you;
 through painful toil you will eat
  of it
 all the days of your life.

¹⁸It will produce thorns and thistles for
you,
and you will eat the plants of
the field.
¹⁹By the sweat of your brow
you will eat your food
until you return to the ground,
since from it you were taken;
for dust you are
and to dust you will return."

²⁰Adam*c* named his wife Eve,*d* because she would become the mother of
all the living.

²¹The Lᴏʀᴅ God made garments of
skin for Adam and his wife and clothed
them. ²²And the Lᴏʀᴅ God said, "The
man has now become like one of us,
knowing good and evil. He must not be
allowed to reach out his hand and take
also from the tree of life and eat, and live
forever." ²³So the Lᴏʀᴅ God banished
him from the Garden of Eden to work
the ground from which he had been
taken. ²⁴After he drove the man out, he
placed on the east side*e* of the Garden
of Eden cherubim and a flaming sword
flashing back and forth to guard the way
to the tree of life.

⁴:¹Aᴅᴀᴍ*c* lay with his wife Eve, and she
became pregnant and gave birth to
Cain.*f* She said, "With the help of the
Lᴏʀᴅ I have brought forth*g* a man."
²Later she gave birth to his brother
Abel.

Now Abel kept flocks, and Cain
worked the soil. ³In the course of time
Cain brought some of the fruits of the
soil as an offering to the Lᴏʀᴅ. ⁴But Abel
brought fat portions from some of the
firstborn of his flock. The Lᴏʀᴅ looked
with favor on Abel and his offering, ⁵but
on Cain and his offering he did not look
with favor. So Cain was very angry, and
his face was downcast.

⁶Then the Lᴏʀᴅ said to Cain, "Why
are you angry? Why is your face downcast? ⁷If you do what is right, will you
not be accepted? But if you do not do
what is right, sin is crouching at your

door; it desires to have you, but you
must master it."

⁸Now Cain said to his brother Abel,
"Let's go out to the field."*h* And while
they were in the field, Cain attacked his
brother Abel and killed him.

⁹Then the Lᴏʀᴅ said to Cain, "Where
is your brother Abel?"

"I don't know," he replied. "Am I my
brother's keeper?"

¹⁰The Lᴏʀᴅ said, "What have you
done? Listen! Your brother's blood
cries out to me from the ground. ¹¹Now
you are under a curse and driven from
the ground, which opened its mouth to
receive your brother's blood from your
hand. ¹²When you work the ground, it
will no longer yield its crops for you.
You will be a restless wanderer on the
earth."

¹³Cain said to the Lᴏʀᴅ, "My punishment is more than I can bear. ¹⁴Today
you are driving me from the land, and I
will be hidden from your presence; I will
be a restless wanderer on the earth, and
whoever finds me will kill me."

¹⁵But the Lᴏʀᴅ said to him, "Not so*i*; if
anyone kills Cain, he will suffer vengeance seven times over." Then the
Lᴏʀᴅ put a mark on Cain so that no one
who found him would kill him. ¹⁶So
Cain went out from the Lᴏʀᴅ's presence
and lived in the land of Nod,*j* east of
Eden.

¹⁷Cain lay with his wife, and she became pregnant and gave birth to Enoch.
Cain was then building a city, and he
named it after his son Enoch. ¹⁸To
Enoch was born Irad, and Irad was the
father of Mehujael, and Mehujael was
the father of Methushael, and Methushael was the father of Lamech.

¹⁹Lamech married two women, one
named Adah and the other Zillah.
²⁰Adah gave birth to Jabal; he was the father of those who live in tents and raise
livestock. ²¹His brother's name was Ju-
bal; he was the father of all who play the
harp and flute. ²²Zillah also had a son,
Tubal-Cain, who forged all kinds of tools
out of*k* bronze and iron. Tubal-Cain's
sister was Naamah.

[23]Lamech said to his wives,

"Adah and Zillah, listen to me;
    wives of Lamech, hear my words.
I have killed[i] a man for wounding me,
    a young man for injuring me.
[24]If Cain is avenged seven times,
    then Lamech seventy-seven times."

[25]Adam lay with his wife again, and she gave birth to a son and named him Seth,[m] saying, "God has granted me another child in place of Abel, since Cain killed him." [26]Seth also had a son, and he named him Enosh.

At that time men began to call on[n] the name of the LORD.

a15 Or *seed*   *b15* Or *strike*   *c20,1* Or *The man*   *d20 Eve* probably means *living.*   *e24* Or *placed in front*   *f1 Cain* sounds like the Hebrew for *brought forth* or *acquired.* *g1* Or *have acquired*   *h8* Samaritan Pentateuch, Septuagint, Vulgate and Syriac; Masoretic Text does not have *"Let's go out to the field."*   *i15* Septuagint, Vulgate and Syriac; Hebrew *Very well*   *i16 Nod* means *wandering* (see verses 12 and 14).   *k22* Or *who instructed all who work in* *l23* Or *I will kill*   *m25 Seth* probably means *granted.* *n26* Or *to proclaim*

MATTHEW 2:13–3:6

When they [the Magi] had gone, an angel of the Lord appeared to Joseph in a dream. "Get up," he said, "take the child and his mother and escape to Egypt. Stay there until I tell you, for Herod is going to search for the child to kill him." [14]So he got up, took the child and his mother during the night and left for Egypt, [15]where he stayed until the death of Herod. And so was fulfilled what the Lord had said through the prophet: "Out of Egypt I called my son."[a] [16]When Herod realized that he had been outwitted by the Magi, he was furious, and he gave orders to kill all the boys in Bethlehem and its vicinity who were two years old and under, in accordance with the time he had learned from the Magi. [17]Then what was said through the prophet Jeremiah was fulfilled:

[18]"A voice is heard in Ramah,
    weeping and great mourning,
Rachel weeping for her children
    and refusing to be comforted,
because they are no more."[b]

[19]After Herod died, an angel of the Lord appeared in a dream to Joseph in Egypt [20]and said, "Get up, take the child and his mother and go to the land of Israel, for those who were trying to take the child's life are dead."

[21]So he got up, took the child and his mother and went to the land of Israel. [22]But when he heard that Archelaus was reigning in Judea in place of his father Herod, he was afraid to go there. Having been warned in a dream, he withdrew to the district of Galilee, [23]and he went and lived in a town called Nazareth. So was fulfilled what was said through the prophets: "He will be called a Nazarene."

3:1In those days John the Baptist came, preaching in the Desert of Judea [2]and saying, "Repent, for the kingdom of heaven is near." [3]This is he who was spoken of through the prophet Isaiah:

"A voice of one calling in the desert,
'Prepare the way for the Lord,
    make straight paths for him.'"[c]

[4]John's clothes were made of camel's hair, and he had a leather belt around his waist. His food was locusts and wild honey. [5]People went out to him from Jerusalem and all Judea and the whole region of the Jordan. [6]Confessing their sins, they were baptized by him in the Jordan River.

a15 Hosea 11:1   *b18* Jer. 31:15   *c3* Isaiah 40:3

PSALM 2:1-12

[1]**W**hy do the nations conspire[a]
    and the peoples plot in vain?
[2]The kings of the earth take
        their stand
    and the rulers gather together
against the LORD
    and against his Anointed One.[b]
[3]"Let us break their chains," they say,
    "and throw off their fetters."

[4]The One enthroned in heaven
        laughs;
    the Lord scoffs at them.

5 Then he rebukes them in his anger
    and terrifies them in his wrath,
        saying,
6 "I have installed my King*c*
    on Zion, my holy hill."

7 I will proclaim the decree of the
Lord:

He said to me, "You are my Son*d*;
    today I have become your
        Father.*e*
8 Ask of me,
    and I will make the nations your
        inheritance,
    the ends of the earth your
        possession.
9 You will rule them with an iron
        scepter*f*;
    you will dash them to pieces like
        pottery."

10 Therefore, you kings, be wise;
    be warned, you rulers of
        the earth.
11 Serve the Lord with fear
    and rejoice with trembling.
12 Kiss the Son, lest he be angry
    and you be destroyed in your way,
    for his wrath can flare up in a
        moment.
        Blessed are all who take refuge
            in him.

*a1 Hebrew; Septuagint rage b2 Or anointed one
c6 Or king d7 Or son; also in verse 12 e7 Or have
begotten you f9 Or will break them with a rod of iron*

PROVERBS 1:7-9

7 The fear of the Lord is the beginning
        of knowledge,
    but fools*a* despise wisdom and
        discipline.
8 Listen, my son, to your father's
        instruction
    and do not forsake your mother's
        teaching.
9 They will be a garland to grace your
        head
    and a chain to adorn your neck.

*a7 The Hebrew words rendered fool in Proverbs, and often
elsewhere in the Old Testament, denote one who is morally
deficient.*

GOD SIGHTINGS

January 3

GENESIS 5:1–7:24
This is the written account of Adam's line.

When God created man, he made him in the likeness of God. 2 He created them male and female and blessed them. And when they were created, he called them "man.*a*"

3 When Adam had lived 130 years, he had a son in his own likeness, in his own image; and he named him Seth. 4 After Seth was born, Adam lived 800 years and had other sons and daughters. 5 Altogether, Adam lived 930 years, and then he died.

6 When Seth had lived 105 years, he became the father*b* of Enosh. 7 And after he became the father of Enosh, Seth lived 807 years and had other sons and daughters. 8 Altogether, Seth lived 912 years, and then he died.

9 When Enosh had lived 90 years, he became the father of Kenan. 10 And after he became the father of Kenan, Enosh lived 815 years and had other sons and daughters. 11 Altogether, Enosh lived 905 years, and then he died.

12 When Kenan had lived 70 years, he became the father of Mahalalel. 13 And after he became the father of Mahalalel, Kenan lived 840 years and had other sons and daughters. 14 Altogether, Kenan lived 910 years, and then he died.

15 When Mahalalel had lived 65 years, he became the father of Jared. 16 And after he became the father of Jared, Mahalalel lived 830 years and had other sons and daughters. 17 Altogether, Mahalalel lived 895 years, and then he died.

18 When Jared had lived 162 years, he became the father of Enoch. 19 And after he became the father of Enoch, Jared lived 800 years and had other sons

and daughters. ²⁰Altogether, Jared lived 962 years, and then he died.

²¹When Enoch had lived 65 years, he became the father of Methuselah. ²²And after he became the father of Methuselah, Enoch walked with God 300 years and had other sons and daughters. ²³Altogether, Enoch lived 365 years. ²⁴Enoch walked with God; then he was no more, because God took him away.

²⁵When Methuselah had lived 187 years, he became the father of Lamech. ²⁶And after he became the father of Lamech, Methuselah lived 782 years and had other sons and daughters. ²⁷Altogether, Methuselah lived 969 years, and then he died.

²⁸When Lamech had lived 182 years, he had a son. ²⁹He named him Noah[c] and said, "He will comfort us in the labor and painful toil of our hands caused by the ground the LORD has cursed." ³⁰After Noah was born, Lamech lived 595 years and had other sons and daughters. ³¹Altogether, Lamech lived 777 years, and then he died.

³²After Noah was 500 years old, he became the father of Shem, Ham and Japheth.

^{6:1}WHEN men began to increase in number on the earth and daughters were born to them, ²the sons of God saw that the daughters of men were beautiful, and they married any of them they chose. ³Then the LORD said, "My Spirit will not contend with[d] man forever, for he is mortal[e]; his days will be a hundred and twenty years."

⁴The Nephilim were on the earth in those days—and also afterward—when the sons of God went to the daughters of men and had children by them. They were the heroes of old, men of renown.

⁵The LORD saw how great man's wickedness on the earth had become, and that every inclination of the thoughts of his heart was only evil all the time. ⁶The LORD was grieved that he had made man on the earth, and his heart was filled with pain. ⁷So the LORD said, "I will wipe man-

kind, whom I have created, from the face of the earth—men and animals, and creatures that move along the ground, and birds of the air—for I am grieved that I have made them." ⁸But Noah found favor in the eyes of the LORD.

⁹This is the account of Noah.

Noah was a righteous man, blameless among the people of his time, and he walked with God. ¹⁰Noah had three sons: Shem, Ham and Japheth.

¹¹Now the earth was corrupt in God's sight and was full of violence. ¹²God saw how corrupt the earth had become, for all the people on earth had corrupted their ways. ¹³So God said to Noah, "I am going to put an end to all people, for the earth is filled with violence because of them. I am surely going to destroy both them and the earth. ¹⁴So make yourself an ark of cypress[f] wood; make rooms in it and coat it with pitch inside and out. ¹⁵This is how you are to build it: The ark is to be 450 feet long, 75 feet wide and 45 feet high.[g] ¹⁶Make a roof for it and finish[h] the ark to within 18 inches[i] of the top. Put a door in the side of the ark and make lower, middle and upper decks. ¹⁷I am going to bring floodwaters on the earth to destroy all life under the heavens, every creature that has the breath of life in it. Everything on earth will perish. ¹⁸But I will establish my covenant with you, and you will enter the ark—you and your sons and your wife and your sons' wives with you. ¹⁹You are to bring into the ark two of all living creatures, male and female, to keep them alive with you. ²⁰Two of every kind of bird, of every kind of animal and of every kind of creature that moves along the ground will come to you to be kept alive. ²¹You are to take every kind of food that is to be eaten and store it away as food for you and for them."

²²Noah did everything just as God commanded him.

^{7:1}THE LORD then said to Noah, "Go into the ark, you and your whole family, because I have found you righteous in this

generation. [2] Take with you seven[j] of every kind of clean animal, a male and its mate, and two of every kind of unclean animal, a male and its mate, [3] and also seven of every kind of bird, male and female, to keep their various kinds alive throughout the earth. [4] Seven days from now I will send rain on the earth for forty days and forty nights, and I will wipe from the face of the earth every living creature I have made."

[5] And Noah did all that the LORD commanded him.

[6] Noah was six hundred years old when the floodwaters came on the earth. [7] And Noah and his sons and his wife and his sons' wives entered the ark to escape the waters of the flood. [8] Pairs of clean and unclean animals, of birds and of all creatures that move along the ground, [9] male and female, came to Noah and entered the ark, as God had commanded Noah. [10] And after the seven days the floodwaters came on the earth.

[11] In the six hundredth year of Noah's life, on the seventeenth day of the second month—on that day all the springs of the great deep burst forth, and the floodgates of the heavens were opened. [12] And rain fell on the earth forty days and forty nights.

[13] On that very day Noah and his sons, Shem, Ham and Japheth, together with his wife and the wives of his three sons, entered the ark. [14] They had with them every wild animal according to its kind, all livestock according to their kinds, every creature that moves along the ground according to its kind and every bird according to its kind, everything with wings. [15] Pairs of all creatures that have the breath of life in them came to Noah and entered the ark. [16] The animals going in were male and female of every living thing, as God had commanded Noah. Then the LORD shut him in.

[17] For forty days the flood kept coming on the earth, and as the waters increased they lifted the ark high above the earth. [18] The waters rose and increased greatly on the earth, and the ark floated on the surface of the water.

[19] They rose greatly on the earth, and all the high mountains under the entire heavens were covered. [20] The waters rose and covered the mountains to a depth of more than twenty feet.[k,l] [21] Every living thing that moved on the earth perished—birds, livestock, wild animals, all the creatures that swarm over the earth, and all mankind. [22] Everything on dry land that had the breath of life in its nostrils died. [23] Every living thing on the face of the earth was wiped out; men and animals and the creatures that move along the ground and the birds of the air were wiped from the earth. Only Noah was left, and those with him in the ark.

[24] The waters flooded the earth for a hundred and fifty days.

a2 Hebrew adam b6 Father may mean ancestor; also in verses 7-26. c29 Noah sounds like the Hebrew for comfort. d3 Or My spirit will not remain in e3 Or corrupt f14 The meaning of the Hebrew for this word is uncertain. g15 Hebrew 300 cubits long, 50 cubits wide and 30 cubits high (about 140 meters long, 23 meters wide and 13.5 meters high) h16 Or Make an opening for light by finishing i16 Hebrew a cubit (about 0.5 meter) j2 Or seven pairs; also in verse 3 k20 Hebrew fifteen cubits (about 6.9 meters) l20 Or rose more than twenty feet, and the mountains were covered

MATTHEW 3:7–4:11

But when he [John the Baptist] saw many of the Pharisees and Sadducees coming to where he was baptizing, he said to them: "You brood of vipers! Who warned you to flee from the coming wrath? [8] Produce fruit in keeping with repentance. [9] And do not think you can say to yourselves, 'We have Abraham as our father.' I tell you that out of these stones God can raise up children for Abraham. [10] The ax is already at the root of the trees, and every tree that does not produce good fruit will be cut down and thrown into the fire.

[11] "I baptize you with[a] water for repentance. But after me will come one who is more powerful than I, whose sandals I am not fit to carry. He will baptize you with the Holy Spirit and with fire. [12] His winnowing fork is in his hand, and he will clear his threshing floor, gathering his wheat into the barn and burning up the chaff with unquenchable fire."

¹³Then Jesus came from Galilee to the Jordan to be baptized by John. ¹⁴But John tried to deter him, saying, "I need to be baptized by you, and do you come to me?"

¹⁵Jesus replied, "Let it be so now; it is proper for us to do this to fulfill all righteousness." Then John consented.

¹⁶As soon as Jesus was baptized, he went up out of the water. At that moment heaven was opened, and he saw the Spirit of God descending like a dove and lighting on him. ¹⁷And a voice from heaven said, "This is my Son, whom I love; with him I am well pleased."

⁴:¹THEN Jesus was led by the Spirit into the desert to be tempted by the devil. ²After fasting forty days and forty nights, he was hungry. ³The tempter came to him and said, "If you are the Son of God, tell these stones to become bread."

⁴Jesus answered, "It is written: 'Man does not live on bread alone, but on every word that comes from the mouth of God.'ᵇ"

⁵Then the devil took him to the holy city and had him stand on the highest point of the temple. ⁶"If you are the Son of God," he said, "throw yourself down. For it is written:

"'He will command his angels
    concerning you,
and they will lift you up in
    their hands,
so that you will not strike your foot
    against a stone.'ᶜ"

⁷Jesus answered him, "It is also written: 'Do not put the Lord your God to the test.'ᵈ"

⁸Again, the devil took him to a very high mountain and showed him all the kingdoms of the world and their splendor. ⁹"All this I will give you," he said, "if you will bow down and worship me."

¹⁰Jesus said to him, "Away from me, Satan! For it is written: 'Worship the Lord your God, and serve him only.'ᵉ"

¹¹Then the devil left him, and angels came and attended him.

a11 Or *in* *b4* Deut. 8:3 *c6* Psalm 91:11,12 *d7* Deut. 6:16 *e10* Deut. 6:13

PSALM 3:1-8

A psalm of David. When he fled from his son Absalom.

¹O Lᴏʀᴅ, how many are my foes!
    How many rise up against me!
²Many are saying of me,
    "God will not deliver him." *Selahᵃ*

³**But you are a shield around me,**
        O Lᴏʀᴅ;
    you bestow glory on me and liftᵇ
        up my head.

⁴To the Lᴏʀᴅ I cry aloud,
    and he answers me from his
        holy hill. *Selah*

⁵I lie down and sleep;
    I wake again, because the Lᴏʀᴅ
        sustains me.
⁶I will not fear the tens of thousands
    drawn up against me on every side.

⁷Arise, O Lᴏʀᴅ!
    Deliver me, O my God!
Strike all my enemies on the jaw;
    break the teeth of the wicked.

⁸From the Lᴏʀᴅ comes deliverance.
    May your blessing be on
        your people. *Selah*

a2 A word of uncertain meaning, occurring frequently in the Psalms; possibly a musical term *b3* Or *Lᴏʀᴅ, / my Glorious One, who lifts*

PROVERBS 1:10-19

¹⁰**M**y son, if sinners entice you,
    do not give in to them.
¹¹If they say, "Come along with us;
    let's lie in wait for someone's blood,
    let's waylay some harmless soul;
¹²let's swallow them alive, like the grave,ᵃ
    and whole, like those who go down
        to the pit;
¹³we will get all sorts of valuable things
    and fill our houses with plunder;
¹⁴throw in your lot with us,
    and we will share a common
        purse"—
¹⁵my son, do not go along with them,
    do not set foot on their paths;
¹⁶for their feet rush into sin,
    they are swift to shed blood.
¹⁷How useless to spread a net
    in full view of all the birds!

18These men lie in wait for their
        own blood;
    they waylay only themselves!
19Such is the end of all who go after
        ill-gotten gain;
    it takes away the lives of those who
        get it.

a 12 Hebrew *Sheol*

□ DAY 4

GOD SIGHTINGS

January 4

GENESIS 8:1–10:32

But God remembered Noah and all the wild animals and the livestock that were with him in the ark, and he sent a wind over the earth, and the waters receded. 2Now the springs of the deep and the floodgates of the heavens had been closed, and the rain had stopped falling from the sky. 3The water receded steadily from the earth. At the end of the hundred and fifty days the water had gone down, 4and on the seventeenth day of the seventh month the ark came to rest on the mountains of Ararat. 5The waters continued to recede until the tenth month, and on the first day of the tenth month the tops of the mountains became visible.

6After forty days Noah opened the window he had made in the ark 7and sent out a raven, and it kept flying back and forth until the water had dried up from the earth. 8Then he sent out a dove to see if the water had receded from the surface of the ground. 9But the dove could find no place to set its feet because there was water over all the surface of the earth; so it returned to Noah in the ark. He reached out his hand and took the dove and brought it back to himself in the ark. 10He waited seven more days and again sent out the dove from the ark. 11When the dove returned to him in the evening, there in its beak was a freshly

plucked olive leaf! Then Noah knew that the water had receded from the earth. 12He waited seven more days and sent the dove out again, but this time it did not return to him.

13By the first day of the first month of Noah's six hundred and first year, the water had dried up from the earth. Noah then removed the covering from the ark and saw that the surface of the ground was dry. 14By the twenty-seventh day of the second month the earth was completely dry.

15Then God said to Noah, 16"Come out of the ark, you and your wife and your sons and their wives. 17Bring out every kind of living creature that is with you— the birds, the animals, and all the creatures that move along the ground—so they can multiply on the earth and be fruitful and increase in number upon it."

18So Noah came out, together with his sons and his wife and his sons' wives. 19All the animals and all the creatures that move along the ground and all the birds—everything that moves on the earth—came out of the ark, one kind after another.

20Then Noah built an altar to the LORD and, taking some of all the clean animals and clean birds, he sacrificed burnt offerings on it. 21The LORD smelled the pleasing aroma and said in his heart: "Never again will I curse the ground because of man, even though*a* every inclination of his heart is evil from childhood. And never again will I destroy all living creatures, as I have done.

22"As long as the earth endures,
    seedtime and harvest,
    cold and heat,
    summer and winter,
    day and night
    will never cease."

9:1THEN God blessed Noah and his sons, saying to them, "Be fruitful and increase in number and fill the earth. 2The fear and dread of you will fall upon all the beasts of the earth and all the birds of the air, upon every creature that moves along the ground, and upon all the fish of the sea; they are given into your hands. ³Everything that lives and moves will be food for you. Just as I gave you the green plants, I now give you everything.

⁴"But you must not eat meat that has its lifeblood still in it. ⁵And for your lifeblood I will surely demand an accounting. I will demand an accounting from every animal. And from each man, too, I will demand an accounting for the life of his fellow man.

⁶"Whoever sheds the blood of man,
    by man shall his blood be shed;
for in the image of God
    has God made man.

⁷As for you, be fruitful and increase in number; multiply on the earth and increase upon it."

⁸Then God said to Noah and to his sons with him: ⁹"I now establish my covenant with you and with your descendants after you ¹⁰and with every living creature that was with you—the birds, the livestock and all the wild animals, all those that came out of the ark with you—every living creature on earth. ¹¹I establish my covenant with you: Never again will all life be cut off by the waters of a flood; never again will there be a flood to destroy the earth."

¹²And God said, "This is the sign of the covenant I am making between me and you and every living creature with you, a covenant for all generations to come: ¹³I have set my rainbow in the clouds, and it will be the sign of the covenant between me and the earth. ¹⁴Whenever I bring clouds over the earth and the rainbow appears in the clouds, ¹⁵I will remember my covenant between me and you and all living creatures of every kind. Never again will the waters become a flood to destroy all life. ¹⁶Whenever the rainbow appears in the clouds, I will see it and remember the everlasting covenant between God and all living creatures of every kind on the earth."

¹⁷So God said to Noah, "This is the sign of the covenant I have established between me and all life on the earth."

¹⁸The sons of Noah who came out of the ark were Shem, Ham and Japheth. (Ham was the father of Canaan.) ¹⁹These were the three sons of Noah, and from them came the people who were scattered over the earth.

²⁰Noah, a man of the soil, proceeded[b] to plant a vineyard. ²¹When he drank some of its wine, he became drunk and lay uncovered inside his tent. ²²Ham, the father of Canaan, saw his father's nakedness and told his two brothers outside. ²³But Shem and Japheth took a garment and laid it across their shoulders; then they walked in backward and covered their father's nakedness. Their faces were turned the other way so that they would not see their father's nakedness.

²⁴When Noah awoke from his wine and found out what his youngest son had done to him, ²⁵he said,

"Cursed be Canaan!
    The lowest of slaves
    will he be to his brothers."

²⁶He also said,

"Blessed be the LORD, the God of
    Shem!
    May Canaan be the slave of
    Shem.[c]
²⁷May God extend the territory of
    Japheth[d];
    may Japheth live in the tents of
    Shem,
    and may Canaan be his[e] slave."

²⁸After the flood Noah lived 350 years. ²⁹Altogether, Noah lived 950 years, and then he died.

10:1THIS is the account of Shem, Ham and Japheth, Noah's sons, who themselves had sons after the flood.

²The sons[f] of Japheth:
    Gomer, Magog, Madai, Javan,
    Tubal, Meshech and Tiras.
³The sons of Gomer:
    Ashkenaz, Riphath and To-
    garmah.

⁴The sons of Javan:

Elishah, Tarshish, the Kittim and the Rodanim.*g* ⁵(From these the maritime peoples spread out into their territories by their clans within their nations, each with its own language.)

⁶The sons of Ham:

Cush, Mizraim,*h* Put and Canaan.

⁷The sons of Cush:

Seba, Havilah, Sabtah, Raamah and Sabteca.

The sons of Raamah:

Sheba and Dedan.

⁸Cush was the father*i* of Nimrod, who grew to be a mighty warrior on the earth. ⁹He was a mighty hunter before the Lord; that is why it is said, "Like Nimrod, a mighty hunter before the Lord." ¹⁰The first centers of his kingdom were Babylon, Erech, Akkad and Calneh, in*j* Shinar.*k* ¹¹From that land he went to Assyria, where he built Nineveh, Rehoboth Ir,*l* Calah ¹²and Resen, which is between Nineveh and Calah; that is the great city.

¹³Mizraim was the father of

the Ludites, Anamites, Lehabites, Naphtuhites, ¹⁴Pathrusites, Casluhites (from whom the Philistines came) and Caphtorites.

¹⁵Canaan was the father of

Sidon his firstborn,*m* and of the Hittites, ¹⁶Jebusites, Amorites, Girgashites, ¹⁷Hivites, Arkites, Sinites, ¹⁸Arvadites, Zemarites and Hamathites.

Later the Canaanite clans scattered ¹⁹and the borders of Canaan reached from Sidon toward Gerar as far as Gaza, and then toward Sodom, Gomorrah, Admah and Zeboiim, as far as Lasha.

²⁰These are the sons of Ham by their clans and languages, in their territories and nations.

²¹Sons were also born to Shem, whose older brother was*n* Japheth; Shem was the ancestor of all the sons of Eber.

²²The sons of Shem:

Elam, Asshur, Arphaxad, Lud and Aram.

²³The sons of Aram:

Uz, Hul, Gether and Meshech.*o*

²⁴Arphaxad was the father of*p* Shelah,

and Shelah the father of Eber.

²⁵Two sons were born to Eber:

One was named Peleg,*q* because in his time the earth was divided; his brother was named Joktan.

²⁶Joktan was the father of

Almodad, Sheleph, Hazarmaveth, Jerah, ²⁷Hadoram, Uzal, Diklah, ²⁸Obal, Abimael, Sheba, ²⁹Ophir, Havilah and Jobab. All these were sons of Joktan.

³⁰The region where they lived stretched from Mesha toward Sephar, in the eastern hill country.

³¹These are the sons of Shem by their clans and languages, in their territories and nations.

³²These are the clans of Noah's sons, according to their lines of descent, within their nations. From these the nations spread out over the earth after the flood.

a21 Or *man, for* *b20* Or *soil, was the first* *c26* Or *be his slave* *d27* Japheth sounds like the Hebrew for *extend.* *e27* Or *their* *f2* Sons may mean *descendants* or *successors* or *nations;* also in verses 3, 4, 6, 7, 20-23, 29 and 31. *g4* Some manuscripts of the Masoretic Text and Samaritan Pentateuch (see also Septuagint and 1 Chron. 1:7); most manuscripts of the Masoretic Text *Dodanim* *h6* That is, Egypt; also in verse 13 *i8* Father may mean *ancestor* or *predecessor* or *founder;* also in verses 13, 15, 24 and 26. *j10* Or *Erech and Akkad—all of them in* *k10* That is, Babylonia *l11* Or *Nineveh with its city squares* *m15* Or *of the Sidonians, the foremost* *n21* Or *Shem, the older brother of* *o23* See Septuagint and 1 Chron. 1:17; Hebrew *Mash* *p24* Hebrew; Septuagint *father of Cainan, and Cainan was the father of* *q25* Peleg means *division.*

MATTHEW 4:12-25

When Jesus heard that John had been put in prison, he returned to Galilee. ¹³Leaving Nazareth, he went and lived in Capernaum, which was by the lake in the area of

Zebulun and Naphtali— [14]to fulfill what was said through the prophet Isaiah:

[15]"Land of Zebulun and land
    of Naphtali,
  the way to the sea, along
    the Jordan,
  Galilee of the Gentiles—
[16]the people living in darkness
    have seen a great light;
  on those living in the land of the
    shadow of death
  a light has dawned."[a]

[17]From that time on Jesus began to preach, "Repent, for the kingdom of heaven is near."

[18]As Jesus was walking beside the Sea of Galilee, he saw two brothers, Simon called Peter and his brother Andrew. They were casting a net into the lake, for they were fishermen. [19]**"Come, follow me," Jesus said, "and I will make you fishers of men." [20]At once they left their nets and followed him.**

[21]Going on from there, he saw two other brothers, James son of Zebedee and his brother John. They were in a boat with their father Zebedee, preparing their nets. Jesus called them, [22]and immediately they left the boat and their father and followed him.

[23]Jesus went throughout Galilee, teaching in their synagogues, preaching the good news of the kingdom, and healing every disease and sickness among the people. [24]News about him spread all over Syria, and people brought to him all who were ill with various diseases, those suffering severe pain, the demon-possessed, those having seizures, and the paralyzed, and he healed them. [25]Large crowds from Galilee, the Decapolis,[b] Jerusalem, Judea and the region across the Jordan followed him.

[a]16 Isaiah 9:1,2   [b]25 That is, the Ten Cities

PSALM 4:1-8
For the director of music. With stringed instruments. A psalm of David.

[1]**A**nswer me when I call to you,
    O my righteous God.

  Give me relief from my distress;
    be merciful to me and hear
      my prayer.

[2]How long, O men, will you turn my
    glory into shame[a]?
  How long will you love delusions
    and seek false gods[b]?   *Selah*
[3]Know that the LORD has set apart the
    godly for himself;
  the LORD will hear when I call to him.

[4]In your anger do not sin;
  when you are on your beds,
    search your hearts and be silent.
                                    Selah
[5]Offer right sacrifices
  and trust in the LORD.

[6]Many are asking, "Who can show us
    any good?"
  Let the light of your face shine
    upon us, O LORD.
[7]You have filled my heart with
    greater joy
  than when their grain and new
    wine abound.
[8]I will lie down and sleep in peace,
  for you alone, O LORD,
  make me dwell in safety.

[a]2 Or *you dishonor my Glorious One*   [b]2 Or *seek lies*

PROVERBS 1:20-23
[20]**W**isdom calls aloud in the street,
    she raises her voice in the public
      squares;
[21]at the head of the noisy streets[a] she
    cries out,
  in the gateways of the city she
    makes her speech:

[22]"How long will you simple ones[b] love
    your simple ways?
  How long will mockers delight in
    mockery
  and fools hate knowledge?
[23]If you had responded to my rebuke,
  I would have poured out my heart
    to you
  and made my thoughts known to
    you."

[a]21 Hebrew; Septuagint / *on the tops of the walls*   [b]22 The Hebrew word rendered *simple* in Proverbs generally denotes one without moral direction and inclined to evil.

☐ DAY 5

GOD SIGHTINGS

January 5

GENESIS 11:1–13:4

Now the whole world had one language and a common speech. ²As men moved eastward,ᵃ they found a plain in Shinarᵇ and settled there.

³They said to each other, "Come, let's make bricks and bake them thoroughly." They used brick instead of stone, and tar for mortar. ⁴Then they said, "Come, let us build ourselves a city, with a tower that reaches to the heavens, so that we may make a name for ourselves and not be scattered over the face of the whole earth."

⁵But the LORD came down to see the city and the tower that the men were building. ⁶The LORD said, "If as one people speaking the same language they have begun to do this, then nothing they plan to do will be impossible for them. ⁷Come, let us go down and confuse their language so they will not understand each other."

⁸So the LORD scattered them from there over all the earth, and they stopped building the city. ⁹That is why it was called Babelᶜ—because there the LORD confused the language of the whole world. From there the LORD scattered them over the face of the whole earth.

¹⁰This is the account of Shem.

Two years after the flood, when Shem was 100 years old, he became the fatherᵈ of Arphaxad. ¹¹And after he became the father of Arphaxad, Shem lived 500 years and had other sons and daughters.

¹²When Arphaxad had lived 35 years, he became the father of Shelah. ¹³And after he became the father of Shelah, Arphaxad lived 403 years and had other sons and daughters.ᵉ

¹⁴When Shelah had lived 30 years, he became the father of Eber. ¹⁵And after he became the father of Eber, Shelah lived 403 years and had other sons and daughters.

¹⁶When Eber had lived 34 years, he became the father of Peleg. ¹⁷And after he became the father of Peleg, Eber lived 430 years and had other sons and daughters.

¹⁸When Peleg had lived 30 years, he became the father of Reu. ¹⁹And after he became the father of Reu, Peleg lived 209 years and had other sons and daughters.

²⁰When Reu had lived 32 years, he became the father of Serug. ²¹And after he became the father of Serug, Reu lived 207 years and had other sons and daughters.

²²When Serug had lived 30 years, he became the father of Nahor. ²³And after he became the father of Nahor, Serug lived 200 years and had other sons and daughters.

²⁴When Nahor had lived 29 years, he became the father of Terah. ²⁵And after he became the father of Terah, Nahor lived 119 years and had other sons and daughters.

²⁶After Terah had lived 70 years, he became the father of Abram, Nahor and Haran.

²⁷This is the account of Terah.

Terah became the father of Abram, Nahor and Haran. And Haran became the father of Lot. ²⁸While his father Terah was still alive, Haran died in Ur of the Chaldeans, in the land of his birth. ²⁹Abram and Nahor both married. The name of Abram's wife was Sarai, and the name of Nahor's wife was Milcah; she was the daughter of Haran, the father of both Milcah and Iscah. ³⁰Now Sarai was barren; she had no children.

³¹Terah took his son Abram, his grandson Lot son of Haran, and his daughter-in-law Sarai, the wife of his son Abram, and together they set out from Ur of the Chaldeans to go to Canaan. But when they came to Haran, they settled there.

[32]Terah lived 205 years, and he died in Haran.

[12:1]THE LORD had said to Abram, "Leave your country, your people and your father's household and go to the land I will show you.

[2]"I will make you into a great nation
    and I will bless you;
I will make your name great,
    and you will be a blessing.
[3]I will bless those who bless you,
    and whoever curses you I will
        curse;
and all peoples on earth
    will be blessed through you."

[4]So Abram left, as the LORD had told him; and Lot went with him. Abram was seventy-five years old when he set out from Haran. [5]He took his wife Sarai, his nephew Lot, all the possessions they had accumulated and the people they had acquired in Haran, and they set out for the land of Canaan, and they arrived there.

[6]Abram traveled through the land as far as the site of the great tree of Moreh at Shechem. At that time the Canaanites were in the land. [7]The LORD appeared to Abram and said, "To your offspring[f] I will give this land." So he built an altar there to the LORD, who had appeared to him.

[8]From there he went on toward the hills east of Bethel and pitched his tent, with Bethel on the west and Ai on the east. There he built an altar to the LORD and called on the name of the LORD. [9]Then Abram set out and continued toward the Negev.

[10]Now there was a famine in the land, and Abram went down to Egypt to live there for a while because the famine was severe. [11]As he was about to enter Egypt, he said to his wife Sarai, "I know what a beautiful woman you are. [12]When the Egyptians see you, they will say, 'This is his wife.' Then they will kill me but will let you live. [13]Say you are my sister, so that I will be treated well for your sake and my life will be spared because of you."

[14]When Abram came to Egypt, the Egyptians saw that she was a very beautiful woman. [15]And when Pharaoh's officials saw her, they praised her to Pharaoh, and she was taken into his palace. [16]He treated Abram well for her sake, and Abram acquired sheep and cattle, male and female donkeys, menservants and maidservants, and camels.

[17]But the LORD inflicted serious diseases on Pharaoh and his household because of Abram's wife Sarai. [18]So Pharaoh summoned Abram. "What have you done to me?" he said. "Why didn't you tell me she was your wife? [19]Why did you say, 'She is my sister,' so that I took her to be my wife? Now then, here is your wife. Take her and go!" [20]Then Pharaoh gave orders about Abram to his men, and they sent him on his way, with his wife and everything he had.

[13:1]So Abram went up from Egypt to the Negev, with his wife and everything he had, and Lot went with him. [2]Abram had become very wealthy in livestock and in silver and gold.

[3]From the Negev he went from place to place until he came to Bethel, to the place between Bethel and Ai where his tent had been earlier [4]and where he had first built an altar. There Abram called on the name of the LORD.

---

[a]2 Or from the east; or in the east   [b]2 That is, Babylonia
[c]9 That is, Babylon; Babel sounds like the Hebrew for confused.
[d]10 Father may mean ancestor; also in verses 11-25.
[e]12,13 Hebrew; Septuagint (see also Luke 3:35, 36 and note at Gen. 10:24) 35 years, he became the father of Cainan. [13]And after he became the father of Cainan, Arphaxad lived 430 years and had other sons and daughters, and then he died. When Cainan had lived 130 years, he became the father of Shelah. And after he became the father of Shelah, Cainan lived 330 years and had other sons and daughters   [f]7 Or seed

MATTHEW 5:1-26

Now when he [Jesus] saw the crowds, he went up on a mountainside and sat down. His disciples came to him, [2]and he began to teach them, saying:

[3]"Blessed are the poor in spirit,
    for theirs is the kingdom
        of heaven.
[4]Blessed are those who mourn,
    for they will be comforted.
[5]Blessed are the meek,
    for they will inherit the earth.

⁶Blessed are those who hunger and
    thirst for righteousness,
  for they will be filled.
⁷Blessed are the merciful,
  for they will be shown mercy.
⁸Blessed are the pure in heart,
  for they will see God.
⁹Blessed are the peacemakers,
  for they will be called sons of God.
¹⁰Blessed are those who are persecuted
    because of righteousness,
  for theirs is the kingdom
    of heaven.

¹¹"Blessed are you when people insult you, persecute you and falsely say
all kinds of evil against you because of
me. ¹²Rejoice and be glad, because great
is your reward in heaven, for in the same
way they persecuted the prophets who
were before you.

¹³"You are the salt of the earth. But if
the salt loses its saltiness, how can it be
made salty again? It is no longer good
for anything, except to be thrown out
and trampled by men.

¹⁴"You are the light of the world. A
city on a hill cannot be hidden. ¹⁵Neither do people light a lamp and put it
under a bowl. Instead they put it on its
stand, and it gives light to everyone in
the house. ¹⁶**In the same way, let your
light shine before men, that they may
see your good deeds and praise your
Father in heaven.**

¹⁷"Do not think that I have come to
abolish the Law or the Prophets; I have not
come to abolish them but to fulfill them.
¹⁸I tell you the truth, until heaven and
earth disappear, not the smallest letter,
not the least stroke of a pen, will by any
means disappear from the Law until everything is accomplished. ¹⁹Anyone who
breaks one of the least of these commandments and teaches others to do the
same will be called least in the kingdom
of heaven, but whoever practices and
teaches these commands will be called
great in the kingdom of heaven. ²⁰For I tell
you that unless your righteousness surpasses that of the Pharisees and the

teachers of the law, you will certainly not
enter the kingdom of heaven.

²¹"You have heard that it was said to
the people long ago, 'Do not murder,ᵃ
and anyone who murders will be subject to judgment.' ²²But I tell you that
anyone who is angry with his brotherᵇ
will be subject to judgment. Again, anyone who says to his brother, 'Raca,ᶜ' is
answerable to the Sanhedrin. But anyone who says, 'You fool!' will be in danger of the fire of hell.

²³"Therefore, if you are offering
your gift at the altar and there remember that your brother has something
against you, ²⁴leave your gift there in
front of the altar. First go and be reconciled to your brother; then come and
offer your gift.

²⁵"Settle matters quickly with your
adversary who is taking you to court. Do
it while you are still with him on the way,
or he may hand you over to the judge,
and the judge may hand you over to the
officer, and you may be thrown into
prison. ²⁶I tell you the truth, you will not
get out until you have paid the last
penny.ᵈ"

ᵃ21 Exodus 20:13   ᵇ22 Some manuscripts *brother without
cause*   ᶜ22 An Aramaic term of contempt   ᵈ26 Greek
kodrantes

PSALM 5:1-12
For the director of music. For flutes. A
psalm of David.

¹ **G**ive ear to my words, O LORD,
    consider my sighing.
²Listen to my cry for help,
    my King and my God,
    for to you I pray.
³In the morning, O LORD, you hear
      my voice;
  in the morning I lay my requests
      before you
  and wait in expectation.

⁴You are not a God who takes pleasure
      in evil;
  with you the wicked cannot dwell.
⁵The arrogant cannot stand in your
      presence;
  you hate all who do wrong.

⁶You destroy those who tell lies;
  bloodthirsty and deceitful men
  the LORD abhors.

⁷But I, by your great mercy,
  will come into your house;
in reverence will I bow down
  toward your holy temple.
⁸Lead me, O LORD, in your
  righteousness
  because of my enemies—
  make straight your way
  before me.

⁹Not a word from their mouth can
  be trusted;
  their heart is filled with
  destruction.
Their throat is an open grave;
  with their tongue they speak
  deceit.
¹⁰Declare them guilty, O God!
  Let their intrigues be their
  downfall.
Banish them for their many sins,
  for they have rebelled against you.

¹¹But let all who take refuge in you
  be glad;
  let them ever sing for joy.
Spread your protection over them,
  that those who love your name
  may rejoice in you.
¹²For surely, O LORD, you bless the
  righteous;
  you surround them with your favor
  as with a shield.

PROVERBS 1:24-28
²⁴"But since you rejected me
  [Wisdom] when I called
  and no one gave heed when I
  stretched out my hand,
²⁵since you ignored all my advice
  and would not accept my rebuke,
²⁶I in turn will laugh at your disaster;
  I will mock when calamity
  overtakes you—
²⁷when calamity overtakes you like a
  storm,
  when disaster sweeps over you like
  a whirlwind,

when distress and trouble
  overwhelm you.
²⁸"Then they will call to me but I will
  not answer;
  they will look for me but will not
  find me."

□ DAY 6

GOD SIGHTINGS

January 6

GENESIS 13:5–15:21
Now Lot, who was moving about with Abram, also had flocks and herds and tents. ⁶But the land could not support them while they stayed together, for their possessions were so great that they were not able to stay together. ⁷And quarreling arose between Abram's herdsmen and the herdsmen of Lot. The Canaanites and Perizzites were also living in the land at that time.

⁸So Abram said to Lot, "Let's not have any quarreling between you and me, or between your herdsmen and mine, for we are brothers. ⁹Is not the whole land before you? Let's part company. If you go to the left, I'll go to the right; if you go to the right, I'll go to the left."

¹⁰Lot looked up and saw that the whole plain of the Jordan was well watered, like the garden of the LORD, like the land of Egypt, toward Zoar. (This was before the LORD destroyed Sodom and Gomorrah.) ¹¹So Lot chose for himself the whole plain of the Jordan and set out toward the east. The two men parted company: ¹²Abram lived in the land of Canaan, while Lot lived among the cities of the plain and pitched his tents near Sodom. ¹³Now the men of Sodom were wicked and were sinning greatly against the LORD.

¹⁴The LORD said to Abram after Lot had parted from him, "Lift up your eyes from where you are and look north and south, east and west. ¹⁵All the land that

you see I will give to you and your off-springᵃ forever. ¹⁶I will make your offspring like the dust of the earth, so that if anyone could count the dust, then your offspring could be counted. ¹⁷Go, walk through the length and breadth of the land, for I am giving it to you."

¹⁸So Abram moved his tents and went to live near the great trees of Mamre at Hebron, where he built an altar to the LORD.

¹⁴:¹At this time Amraphel king of Shinar,ᵇ Arioch king of Ellasar, Kedorlaomer king of Elam and Tidal king of Goiim ²went to war against Bera king of Sodom, Birsha king of Gomorrah, Shinab king of Admah, Shemeber king of Zeboiim, and the king of Bela (that is, Zoar). ³All these latter kings joined forces in the Valley of Siddim (the Salt Seaᶜ). ⁴For twelve years they had been subject to Kedorlaomer, but in the thirteenth year they rebelled.

⁵In the fourteenth year, Kedorlaomer and the kings allied with him went out and defeated the Rephaites in Ashteroth Karnaim, the Zuzites in Ham, the Emites in Shaveh Kiriathaim ⁶and the Horites in the hill country of Seir, as far as El Paran near the desert. ⁷Then they turned back and went to En Mishpat (that is, Kadesh), and they conquered the whole territory of the Amalekites, as well as the Amorites who were living in Hazazon Tamar.

⁸Then the king of Sodom, the king of Gomorrah, the king of Admah, the king of Zeboiim and the king of Bela (that is, Zoar) marched out and drew up their battle lines in the Valley of Siddim ⁹against Kedorlaomer king of Elam, Tidal king of Goiim, Amraphel king of Shinar and Arioch king of Ellasar—four kings against five. ¹⁰Now the Valley of Siddim was full of tar pits, and when the kings of Sodom and Gomorrah fled, some of the men fell into them and the rest fled to the hills. ¹¹The four kings seized all the goods of Sodom and Gomorrah and all their food; then they went away. ¹²They also carried off Abram's nephew Lot and his possessions, since he was living in Sodom.

¹³One who had escaped came and reported this to Abram the Hebrew. Now Abram was living near the great trees of Mamre the Amorite, a brotherᵈ of Eshcol and Aner, all of whom were allied with Abram. ¹⁴When Abram heard that his relative had been taken captive, he called out the 318 trained men born in his household and went in pursuit as far as Dan. ¹⁵During the night Abram divided his men to attack them and he routed them, pursuing them as far as Hobah, north of Damascus. ¹⁶He recovered all the goods and brought back his relative Lot and his possessions, together with the women and the other people.

¹⁷After Abram returned from defeating Kedorlaomer and the kings allied with him, the king of Sodom came out to meet him in the Valley of Shaveh (that is, the King's Valley).

¹⁸Then Melchizedek king of Salemᵉ brought out bread and wine. He was priest of God Most High, ¹⁹and he blessed Abram, saying,

"Blessed be Abram by God Most High,
    Creatorᶠ of heaven and earth.
²⁰And blessed beᵍ God Most High,
    who delivered your enemies into
    your hand."

Then Abram gave him a tenth of everything.

²¹The king of Sodom said to Abram, "Give me the people and keep the goods for yourself."

²²But Abram said to the king of Sodom, "I have raised my hand to the LORD, God Most High, Creator of heaven and earth, and have taken an oath ²³that I will accept nothing belonging to you, not even a thread or the thong of a sandal, so that you will never be able to say, 'I made Abram rich.' ²⁴I will accept nothing but what my men have eaten and the share that belongs to the men who went with me—to Aner, Eshcol and Mamre. Let them have their share."

15:1AFTER this, the word of the LORD came to Abram in a vision:

"Do not be afraid, Abram.
    I am your shield,*h*
    your very great reward.*i*"

2But Abram said, "O Sovereign LORD, what can you give me since I remain childless and the one who will inherit*j* my estate is Eliezer of Damascus?" 3And Abram said, "You have given me no children; so a servant in my household will be my heir." 4Then the word of the LORD came to him: "This man will not be your heir, but a son coming from your own body will be your heir." 5He took him outside and said, "Look up at the heavens and count the stars—if indeed you can count them." Then he said to him, "So shall your offspring be."

6Abram believed the LORD, and he credited it to him as righteousness.

7He also said to him, "I am the LORD, who brought you out of Ur of the Chaldeans to give you this land to take possession of it."

8But Abram said, "O Sovereign LORD, how can I know that I will gain possession of it?"

9So the LORD said to him, "Bring me a heifer, a goat and a ram, each three years old, along with a dove and a young pigeon."

10Abram brought all these to him, cut them in two and arranged the halves opposite each other; the birds, however, he did not cut in half. 11Then birds of prey came down on the carcasses, but Abram drove them away.

12As the sun was setting, Abram fell into a deep sleep, and a thick and dreadful darkness came over him. 13Then the LORD said to him, "Know for certain that your descendants will be strangers in a country not their own, and they will be enslaved and mistreated four hundred years. 14But I will punish the nation they serve as slaves, and afterward they will come out with great possessions. 15You, however, will go to your fathers in peace

and be buried at a good old age. 16In the fourth generation your descendants will come back here, for the sin of the Amorites has not yet reached its full measure."

17When the sun had set and darkness had fallen, a smoking firepot with a blazing torch appeared and passed between the pieces. 18On that day the LORD made a covenant with Abram and said, "To your descendants I give this land, from the river*k* of Egypt to the great river, the Euphrates— 19the land of the Kenites, Kenizzites, Kadmonites, 20Hittites, Perizzites, Rephaites, 21Amorites, Canaanites, Girgashites and Jebusites."

a15 Or *seed*; also in verse 16   *b1* That is, Babylonia; also in verse 9   *c3* That is, the Dead Sea   *d13* Or *a relative*; or *an ally*   *e18* That is, Jerusalem   *f19* Or *Possessor*; also in verse 22   *g20* Or *And praise be to*   *h1* Or *sovereign*   *i1* Or *shield; / your reward will be very great*   *j2* The meaning of the Hebrew for this phrase is uncertain.   *k18* Or *Wadi*

MATTHEW 5:27-48

"**Y**ou have heard that it was said, 'Do not commit adultery.'*a* 28But I [Jesus] tell you that anyone who looks at a woman lustfully has already committed adultery with her in his heart. 29If your right eye causes you to sin, gouge it out and throw it away. It is better for you to lose one part of your body than for your whole body to be thrown into hell. 30And if your right hand causes you to sin, cut it off and throw it away. It is better for you to lose one part of your body than for your whole body to go into hell.

31"It has been said, 'Anyone who divorces his wife must give her a certificate of divorce.'*b* 32But I tell you that anyone who divorces his wife, except for marital unfaithfulness, causes her to become an adulteress, and anyone who marries the divorced woman commits adultery.

33"Again, you have heard that it was said to the people long ago, 'Do not break your oath, but keep the oaths you have made to the Lord.' 34But I tell you, Do not swear at all: either by heaven, for it is God's throne; 35or by the earth, for it is his footstool; or by Jerusalem, for it is the city of the Great King. 36And do not swear by your head, for you cannot make even one hair white or black. [37]Simply let your 'Yes' be 'Yes,' and your 'No,' 'No'; anything beyond this comes from the evil one.

[38]"You have heard that it was said, 'Eye for eye, and tooth for tooth.'[c] [39]But I tell you, Do not resist an evil person. If someone strikes you on the right cheek, turn to him the other also. [40]And if someone wants to sue you and take your tunic, let him have your cloak as well. [41]If someone forces you to go one mile, go with him two miles. [42]Give to the one who asks you, and do not turn away from the one who wants to borrow from you.

[43]"You have heard that it was said, **'Love your neighbor[d] and hate your enemy.'** [44]But I tell you: Love your enemies[e] and pray for those who persecute you, [45]that you may be sons of your Father in heaven.** He causes his sun to rise on the evil and the good, and sends rain on the righteous and the unrighteous. [46]If you love those who love you, what reward will you get? Are not even the tax collectors doing that? [47]And if you greet only your brothers, what are you doing more than others? Do not even pagans do that? [48]Be perfect, therefore, as your heavenly Father is perfect."

*a27*Exodus 20:14   *b31*Deut. 24:1   *c38*Exodus 21:24; Lev. 24:20; Deut. 19:21   *d43*Lev. 19:18   *e44*Some late . manuscripts *enemies, bless those who curse you, do good to those who hate you*

PSALM 6:1-10

For the director of music. With stringed instruments. According to *sheminith*.[a] A psalm of David.

[1] O Lord, do not rebuke me in
        your anger
    or discipline me in your wrath.
[2]Be merciful to me, Lord, for
        I am faint;
    O Lord, heal me, for my bones
        are in agony.
[3]My soul is in anguish.
    How long, O Lord, how long?
[4]Turn, O Lord, and deliver me;
    save me because of your unfailing
        love.

[5]No one remembers you when he
        is dead.
    Who praises you from the grave[b]?

[6]I am worn out from groaning;
    all night long I flood my bed
        with weeping
    and drench my couch with tears.
[7]My eyes grow weak with sorrow;
    they fail because of all my foes.

[8]Away from me, all you who do evil,
    for the Lord has heard my weeping.
[9]The Lord has heard my cry for mercy;
    the Lord accepts my prayer.
[10]All my enemies will be ashamed
        and dismayed;
    they will turn back in sudden
        disgrace.

*a*Title: Probably a musical term   *b5*Hebrew *Sheol*

PROVERBS 1:29-33

[29]"**S**ince they hated knowledge
    and did not choose to fear
        the Lord,
[30]since they would not accept my
        [Wisdom's] advice
    and spurned my rebuke,
[31]they will eat the fruit of their ways
    and be filled with the fruit of
        their schemes.
[32]For the waywardness of the simple
        will kill them,
    and the complacency of fools will
        destroy them;
[33]but whoever listens to me will live
        in safety
    and be at ease, without fear
        of harm."

□ DAY 7

GOD SIGHTINGS

January 7

GENESIS 16:1–18:19
Now Sarai, Abram's wife, had borne him no children. But she had an Egyptian maidservant named Hagar; [2]so she

said to Abram, "The Lord has kept me from having children. Go, sleep with my maidservant; perhaps I can build a family through her."

Abram agreed to what Sarai said. [3] So after Abram had been living in Canaan ten years, Sarai his wife took her Egyptian maidservant Hagar and gave her to her husband to be his wife. [4] He slept with Hagar, and she conceived.

When she knew she was pregnant, she began to despise her mistress. [5] Then Sarai said to Abram, "You are responsible for the wrong I am suffering. I put my servant in your arms, and now that she knows she is pregnant, she despises me. May the Lord judge between you and me."

[6] "Your servant is in your hands," Abram said. "Do with her whatever you think best." Then Sarai mistreated Hagar; so she fled from her.

[7] The angel of the Lord found Hagar near a spring in the desert; it was the spring that is beside the road to Shur. [8] And he said, "Hagar, servant of Sarai, where have you come from, and where are you going?"

"I'm running away from my mistress Sarai," she answered.

[9] Then the angel of the Lord told her, "Go back to your mistress and submit to her." [10] The angel added, "I will so increase your descendants that they will be too numerous to count."

[11] The angel of the Lord also said to her:

"You are now with child
    and you will have a son.
You shall name him Ishmael,[a]
    for the Lord has heard of
        your misery.
[12] He will be a wild donkey of a man;
    his hand will be against everyone
    and everyone's hand against him,
and he will live in hostility
    toward[b] all his brothers."

[13] She gave this name to the Lord who spoke to her: "You are the God who sees me," for she said, "I have now seen[c] the

One who sees me." [14] That is why the well was called Beer Lahai Roi[d]; it is still there, between Kadesh and Bered.

[15] So Hagar bore Abram a son, and Abram gave the name Ishmael to the son she had borne. [16] Abram was eighty-six years old when Hagar bore him Ishmael.

[17:1] When Abram was ninety-nine years old, the Lord appeared to him and said, "I am God Almighty[e]; walk before me and be blameless. [2] I will confirm my covenant between me and you and will greatly increase your numbers."

[3] Abram fell facedown, and God said to him, [4] "As for me, this is my covenant with you: You will be the father of many nations. [5] No longer will you be called Abram[f]; your name will be Abraham,[g] for I have made you a father of many nations. [6] I will make you very fruitful; I will make nations of you, and kings will come from you. [7] I will establish my covenant as an everlasting covenant between me and you and your descendants after you for the generations to come, to be your God and the God of your descendants after you. [8] The whole land of Canaan, where you are now an alien, I will give as an everlasting possession to you and your descendants after you; and I will be their God."

[9] Then God said to Abraham, "As for you, you must keep my covenant, you and your descendants after you for the generations to come. [10] This is my covenant with you and your descendants after you, the covenant you are to keep: Every male among you shall be circumcised. [11] You are to undergo circumcision, and it will be the sign of the covenant between me and you. [12] For the generations to come every male among you who is eight days old must be circumcised, including those born in your household or bought with money from a foreigner—those who are not your offspring. [13] Whether born in your household or bought with your money, they must be circumcised. My covenant in your flesh is to be an everlasting

covenant. [14]Any uncircumcised male, who has not been circumcised in the flesh, will be cut off from his people; he has broken my covenant."

[15]God also said to Abraham, "As for Sarai your wife, you are no longer to call her Sarai; her name will be Sarah. [16]I will bless her and will surely give you a son by her. I will bless her so that she will be the mother of nations; kings of peoples will come from her."

[17]Abraham fell facedown; he laughed and said to himself, "Will a son be born to a man a hundred years old? Will Sarah bear a child at the age of ninety?" [18]And Abraham said to God, "If only Ishmael might live under your blessing!"

[19]Then God said, "Yes, but your wife Sarah will bear you a son, and you will call him Isaac.[h] I will establish my covenant with him as an everlasting covenant for his descendants after him. [20]And as for Ishmael, I have heard you: I will surely bless him; I will make him fruitful and will greatly increase his numbers. He will be the father of twelve rulers, and I will make him into a great nation. [21]But my covenant I will establish with Isaac, whom Sarah will bear to you by this time next year." [22]When he had finished speaking with Abraham, God went up from him.

[23]On that very day Abraham took his son Ishmael and all those born in his household or bought with his money, every male in his household, and circumcised them, as God told him. [24]Abraham was ninety-nine years old when he was circumcised, [25]and his son Ishmael was thirteen; [26]Abraham and his son Ishmael were both circumcised on that same day. [27]And every male in Abraham's household, including those born in his household or bought from a foreigner, was circumcised with him.

[18:1]THE LORD appeared to Abraham near the great trees of Mamre while he was sitting at the entrance to his tent in the heat of the day. [2]Abraham looked up and saw three men standing nearby. When he saw them, he hurried from the entrance of his tent to meet them and bowed low to the ground.

[3]He said, "If I have found favor in your eyes, my lord,[i] do not pass your servant by. [4]Let a little water be brought, and then you may all wash your feet and rest under this tree. [5]Let me get you something to eat, so you can be refreshed and then go on your way—now that you have come to your servant."

"Very well," they answered, "do as you say."

[6]So Abraham hurried into the tent to Sarah. "Quick," he said, "get three seahs[j] of fine flour and knead it and bake some bread."

[7]Then he ran to the herd and selected a choice, tender calf and gave it to a servant, who hurried to prepare it. [8]He then brought some curds and milk and the calf that had been prepared, and set these before them. While they ate, he stood near them under a tree.

[9]"Where is your wife Sarah?" they asked him.

"There, in the tent," he said.

[10]Then the LORD[k] said, "I will surely return to you about this time next year, and Sarah your wife will have a son."

Now Sarah was listening at the entrance to the tent, which was behind him. [11]Abraham and Sarah were already old and well advanced in years, and Sarah was past the age of childbearing. [12]So Sarah laughed to herself as she thought, "After I am worn out and my master[l] is old, will I now have this pleasure?"

[13]Then the LORD said to Abraham, "Why did Sarah laugh and say, 'Will I really have a child, now that I am old?' [14]Is anything too hard for the LORD? I will return to you at the appointed time next year and Sarah will have a son."

[15]Sarah was afraid, so she lied and said, "I did not laugh."

But he said, "Yes, you did laugh."

[16]When the men got up to leave, they looked down toward Sodom, and Abraham walked along with them to see them on their way. [17]Then the LORD said, "Shall I hide from Abraham what I am about to do? [18]Abraham will surely be-

come a great and powerful nation, and all nations on earth will be blessed through him. [19]For I have chosen him, so that he will direct his children and his household after him to keep the way of the LORD by doing what is right and just, so that the LORD will bring about for Abraham what he has promised him."

[a]11 Ishmael means *God hears.* [b]12 Or *live to the east / of*
[c]13 Or *seen the back of* [d]14 Beer Lahai Roi means *well of
the Living One who sees me.* [e]1 Hebrew *El-Shaddai*
[f]5 Abram means *exalted father.* [g]5 Abraham means *father
of many.* [h]19 Isaac means *he laughs.* [i]3 Or *O Lord* [j]6 That
is, probably about 20 quarts (about 22 liters) [k]10 Hebrew
Then he [l]12 Or *husband*

MATTHEW 6:1-24

"Be careful not to do your 'acts of righteousness' before men, to be seen by them. If you do, you will have no reward from your Father in heaven.

[2]"So when you give to the needy, do not announce it with trumpets, as the hypocrites do in the synagogues and on the streets, to be honored by men. I tell you the truth, they have received their reward in full. [3]But when you give to the needy, do not let your left hand know what your right hand is doing, [4]so that your giving may be in secret. Then your Father, who sees what is done in secret, will reward you.

[5]"And when you pray, do not be like the hypocrites, for they love to pray standing in the synagogues and on the street corners to be seen by men. I tell you the truth, they have received their reward in full. [6]But when you pray, go into your room, close the door and pray to your Father, who is unseen. Then your Father, who sees what is done in secret, will reward you. [7]And when you pray, do not keep on babbling like pagans, for they think they will be heard because of their many words. [8]Do not be like them, for your Father knows what you need before you ask him.

[9]"This, then, is how you should pray:

"'Our Father in heaven,
  hallowed be your name,
[10]your kingdom come,
  your will be done
    on earth as it is in heaven.
[11]Give us today our daily bread.
[12]Forgive us our debts,
    as we also have forgiven our
      debtors.
[13]And lead us not into temptation,
  but deliver us from the evil one.[a]'

[14]For if you forgive men when they sin against you, your heavenly Father will also forgive you. [15]But if you do not forgive men their sins, your Father will not forgive your sins.

[16]"When you fast, do not look somber as the hypocrites do, for they disfigure their faces to show men they are fasting. I tell you the truth, they have received their reward in full. [17]But when you fast, put oil on your head and wash your face, [18]so that it will not be obvious to men that you are fasting, but only to your Father, who is unseen; and your Father, who sees what is done in secret, will reward you.

[19]"Do not store up for yourselves treasures on earth, where moth and rust destroy, and where thieves break in and steal. [20]But store up for yourselves treasures in heaven, where moth and rust do not destroy, and where thieves do not break in and steal. [21]For where your treasure is, there your heart will be also.

[22]"The eye is the lamp of the body. If your eyes are good, your whole body will be full of light. [23]But if your eyes are bad, your whole body will be full of darkness. If then the light within you is darkness, how great is that darkness!

[24]"No one can serve two masters. Either he will hate the one and love the other, or he will be devoted to the one and despise the other. You cannot serve both God and Money."

[a]13 Or *from evil*; some late manuscripts *one, / for yours is
the kingdom and the power and the glory forever. Amen.*

PSALM 7:1-17

A *shiggaion*[a] of David, which he sang to the LORD concerning Cush, a Benjamite.

[1]O LORD my God, I take refuge
    in you;
  save and deliver me from all who
    pursue me,

2 or they will tear me like a lion
  and rip me to pieces with no one
    to rescue me.

3 O LORD my God, if I have done this
  and there is guilt on my hands—
4 if I have done evil to him who is at
    peace with me
  or without cause have robbed
    my foe—
5 then let my enemy pursue and
    overtake me;
  let him trample my life to
    the ground
  and make me sleep in the dust.
                                    Selah

6 Arise, O LORD, in your anger;
  rise up against the rage of my
    enemies.
  Awake, my God; decree justice.
7 Let the assembled peoples gather
    around you.
  Rule over them from on high;
8   let the LORD judge the peoples.
  Judge me, O LORD, according to
    my righteousness,
    according to my integrity,
      O Most High.
9 O righteous God,
  who searches minds and hearts,
  bring to an end the violence of
    the wicked
  and make the righteous secure.

10 My shield*b* is God Most High,
  who saves the upright in heart.
11 God is a righteous judge,
  a God who expresses his wrath
    every day.
12 If he does not relent,
  he*c* will sharpen his sword;
  he will bend and string his bow.
13 He has prepared his deadly weapons;
  he makes ready his flaming
    arrows.

14 He who is pregnant with evil
  and conceives trouble gives birth
    to disillusionment.
15 He who digs a hole and scoops
    it out
  falls into the pit he has made.

16 The trouble he causes recoils
    on himself;
  his violence comes down on
    his own head.

17 I will give thanks to the LORD because
    of his righteousness
  and will sing praise to the name
    of the LORD Most High.

*a*Title: Probably a literary or musical term   *b10* Or *sovereign*
c12 Or *If a man does not repent, / God*

PROVERBS 2:1-5

My son, if you accept my words
  and store up my commands within
    you,
2 turning your ear to wisdom
  and applying your heart to
    understanding,
3 and if you call out for insight
  and cry aloud for understanding,
4 and if you look for it as for silver
  and search for it as for hidden
    treasure,
5 then you will understand the fear of
    the LORD
  and find the knowledge of God.

□ D A Y 8

GOD SIGHTINGS

January 8

GENESIS 18:20–19:38

Then the LORD said, "The outcry against Sodom and Gomorrah is so great and their sin so grievous 21 that I will go down and see if what they have done is as bad as the outcry that has reached me. If not, I will know."

22 The men turned away and went toward Sodom, but Abraham remained standing before the LORD.*a* 23 Then Abraham approached him and said: "Will you sweep away the righteous with the wicked? 24 What if there are fifty righteous people in the city? Will you really sweep it away and not spare*b* the place for the sake of the fifty righ-

teous people in it? 25Far be it from you to do such a thing—to kill the righteous with the wicked, treating the righteous and the wicked alike. Far be it from you! Will not the Judge*c* of all the earth do right?"

26The Lord said, "If I find fifty righteous people in the city of Sodom, I will spare the whole place for their sake."

27Then Abraham spoke up again: "Now that I have been so bold as to speak to the Lord, though I am nothing but dust and ashes, 28what if the number of the righteous is five less than fifty? Will you destroy the whole city because of five people?"

"If I find forty-five there," he said, "I will not destroy it."

29Once again he spoke to him, "What if only forty are found there?"

He said, "For the sake of forty, I will not do it."

30Then he said, "May the Lord not be angry, but let me speak. What if only thirty can be found there?"

He answered, "I will not do it if I find thirty there."

31Abraham said, "Now that I have been so bold as to speak to the Lord, what if only twenty can be found there?"

He said, "For the sake of twenty, I will not destroy it."

32Then he said, "May the Lord not be angry, but let me speak just once more. What if only ten can be found there?"

He answered, "For the sake of ten, I will not destroy it."

33When the Lord had finished speaking with Abraham, he left, and Abraham returned home.

19:1THE two angels arrived at Sodom in the evening, and Lot was sitting in the gateway of the city. When he saw them, he got up to meet them and bowed down with his face to the ground. 2"My lords," he said, "please turn aside to your servant's house. You can wash your feet and spend the night and then go on your way early in the morning."

"No," they answered, "we will spend the night in the square."

3But he insisted so strongly that they did go with him and entered his house. He prepared a meal for them, baking bread without yeast, and they ate. 4Before they had gone to bed, all the men from every part of the city of Sodom—both young and old—surrounded the house. 5They called to Lot, "Where are the men who came to you tonight? Bring them out to us so that we can have sex with them."

6Lot went outside to meet them and shut the door behind him 7and said, "No, my friends. Don't do this wicked thing. 8Look, I have two daughters who have never slept with a man. Let me bring them out to you, and you can do what you like with them. But don't do anything to these men, for they have come under the protection of my roof."

9"Get out of our way," they replied. And they said, "This fellow came here as an alien, and now he wants to play the judge! We'll treat you worse than them." They kept bringing pressure on Lot and moved forward to break down the door.

10But the men inside reached out and pulled Lot back into the house and shut the door. 11Then they struck the men who were at the door of the house, young and old, with blindness so that they could not find the door.

12The two men said to Lot, "Do you have anyone else here—sons-in-law, sons or daughters, or anyone else in the city who belongs to you? Get them out of here, 13because we are going to destroy this place. The outcry to the Lord against its people is so great that he has sent us to destroy it."

14So Lot went out and spoke to his sons-in-law, who were pledged to marry*d* his daughters. He said, "Hurry and get out of this place, because the Lord is about to destroy the city!" But his sons-in-law thought he was joking.

15With the coming of dawn, the angels urged Lot, saying, "Hurry! Take your wife and your two daughters who are here, or you will be swept away when the city is punished."

16When he hesitated, the men grasped his hand and the hands of his wife and of his two daughters and led them safely out of the city, for the LORD was merciful to them. 17As soon as they had brought them out, one of them said, "Flee for your lives! Don't look back, and don't stop anywhere in the plain! Flee to the mountains or you will be swept away!"

18But Lot said to them, "No, my lords,e please! 19Yourf servant has found favor in yourf eyes, and youf have shown great kindness to me in sparing my life. But I can't flee to the mountains; this disaster will overtake me, and I'll die. 20Look, here is a town near enough to run to, and it is small. Let me flee to it—it is very small, isn't it? Then my life will be spared."

21He said to him, "Very well, I will grant this request too; I will not overthrow the town you speak of. 22But flee there quickly, because I cannot do anything until you reach it." (That is why the town was called Zoar.g)

23By the time Lot reached Zoar, the sun had risen over the land. 24Then the LORD rained down burning sulfur on Sodom and Gomorrah—from the LORD out of the heavens. 25Thus he overthrew those cities and the entire plain, including all those living in the cities—and also the vegetation in the land. 26But Lot's wife looked back, and she became a pillar of salt.

27Early the next morning Abraham got up and returned to the place where he had stood before the LORD. 28He looked down toward Sodom and Gomorrah, toward all the land of the plain, and he saw dense smoke rising from the land, like smoke from a furnace.

29So when God destroyed the cities of the plain, he remembered Abraham, and he brought Lot out of the catastrophe that overthrew the cities where Lot had lived.

30Lot and his two daughters left Zoar and settled in the mountains, for he was afraid to stay in Zoar. He and his two daughters lived in a cave. 31One day the older daughter said to the younger, "Our father is old, and there is no man around here to lie with us, as is the custom all over the earth. 32Let's get our father to drink wine and then lie with him and preserve our family line through our father."

33That night they got their father to drink wine, and the older daughter went in and lay with him. He was not aware of it when she lay down or when she got up.

34The next day the older daughter said to the younger, "Last night I lay with my father. Let's get him to drink wine again tonight, and you go in and lie with him so we can preserve our family line through our father." 35So they got their father to drink wine that night also, and the younger daughter went and lay with him. Again he was not aware of it when she lay down or when she got up.

36So both of Lot's daughters became pregnant by their father. 37The older daughter had a son, and she named him Moabh; he is the father of the Moabites of today. 38The younger daughter also had a son, and she named him Ben-Ammii; he is the father of the Ammonites of today.

a22 Masoretic Text; an ancient Hebrew scribal tradition *but the LORD remained standing before Abraham* b24 Or *forgive*; also in verse 26   c25 Or *Ruler*   d14 Or *were married to*   e18 Or *No, Lord*; or *No, my lord*   f19 The Hebrew is singular.   g22 *Zoar* means *small*.   h37 *Moab* sounds like the Hebrew for *from father*.   i38 *Ben-Ammi* means *son of my people*.

MATTHEW 6:25–7:14

"Therefore I [Jesus] tell you, do not worry about your life, what you will eat or drink; or about your body, what you will wear. Is not life more important than food, and the body more important than clothes? 26Look at the birds of the air; they do not sow or reap or store away in barns, and yet your heavenly Father feeds them. Are you not much more valuable than they? 27Who of you by worrying can add a single hour to his lifea?

28"And why do you worry about

clothes? See how the lilies of the field grow. They do not labor or spin. ²⁹Yet I tell you that not even Solomon in all his splendor was dressed like one of these. ³⁰If that is how God clothes the grass of the field, which is here today and tomorrow is thrown into the fire, will he not much more clothe you, O you of little faith? ³¹So do not worry, saying, 'What shall we eat?' or 'What shall we drink?' or 'What shall we wear?' ³²For the pagans run after all these things, and your heavenly Father knows that you need them. ³³But seek first his kingdom and his righteousness, and all these things will be given to you as well. ³⁴Therefore do not worry about tomorrow, for tomorrow will worry about itself. Each day has enough trouble of its own.

⁷:¹"Do not judge, or you too will be judged. ²For in the same way you judge others, you will be judged, and with the measure you use, it will be measured to you.

³"Why do you look at the speck of sawdust in your brother's eye and pay no attention to the plank in your own eye? ⁴How can you say to your brother, 'Let me take the speck out of your eye,' when all the time there is a plank in your own eye? ⁵You hypocrite, first take the plank out of your own eye, and then you will see clearly to remove the speck from your brother's eye.

⁶"Do not give dogs what is sacred; do not throw your pearls to pigs. If you do, they may trample them under their feet, and then turn and tear you to pieces.

⁷"Ask and it will be given to you; seek and you will find; knock and the door will be opened to you. ⁸For everyone who asks receives; he who seeks finds; and to him who knocks, the door will be opened.

⁹"Which of you, if his son asks for bread, will give him a stone? ¹⁰Or if he asks for a fish, will give him a snake? ¹¹If you, then, though you are evil, know how to give good gifts to your children, how much more will your Father in heaven give good gifts to those who ask

him! ¹²**So in everything, do to others what you would have them do to you, for this sums up the Law and the Prophets.**

¹³"Enter through the narrow gate. For wide is the gate and broad is the road that leads to destruction, and many enter through it. ¹⁴But small is the gate and narrow the road that leads to life, and only a few find it."

a27 Or single cubit to his height

PSALM 8:1-9
For the director of music. According to *gittith.ᵃ* A psalm of David.

¹ **O** Lᴏʀᴅ, our Lord,
 how majestic is your name in all
  the earth!

 You have set your glory
  above the heavens.
² From the lips of children and infants
  you have ordained praiseᵇ
 because of your enemies,
  to silence the foe and the avenger.

³ When I consider your heavens,
  the work of your fingers,
 the moon and the stars,
  which you have set in place,
⁴ what is man that you are mindful
   of him,
  the son of man that you care
   for him?
⁵ You made him a little lower than the
   heavenly beingsᶜ
  and crowned him with glory
   and honor.

⁶ You made him ruler over the works
   of your hands;
  you put everything under his feet:
⁷ all flocks and herds,
  and the beasts of the field,
⁸ the birds of the air,
  and the fish of the sea,
  all that swim the paths of the seas.

⁹ O Lᴏʀᴅ, our Lord,
  how majestic is your name in all
   the earth!

aTitle: Probably a musical term b2 Or strength c5 Or than God

PROVERBS 2:6-15

6 **F**or the LORD gives wisdom,
  and from his mouth come
    knowledge and
    understanding.
7 He holds victory in store for the
    upright,
  he is a shield to those whose walk
    is blameless,
8 for he guards the course of the just
  and protects the way of his faithful
    ones.

9 Then you will understand what is
    right and just
  and fair—every good path.
10 For wisdom will enter your heart,
  and knowledge will be pleasant to
    your soul.
11 Discretion will protect you,
  and understanding will guard you.

12 Wisdom will save you from the ways
    of wicked men,
  from men whose words are perverse,
13 who leave the straight paths
  to walk in dark ways,
14 who delight in doing wrong
  and rejoice in the perverseness
    of evil,
15 whose paths are crooked
  and who are devious in their ways.

□ DAY 9

GOD SIGHTINGS

January 9

GENESIS 20:1-22:24

Now Abraham moved on from there into the region of the Negev and lived between Kadesh and Shur. For a while he stayed in Gerar, 2 and there Abraham said of his wife Sarah, "She is my sister." Then Abimelech king of Gerar sent for Sarah and took her.

3 But God came to Abimelech in a dream one night and said to him, "You are as good as dead because of the woman you have taken; she is a married woman."

4 Now Abimelech had not gone near her, so he said, "Lord, will you destroy an innocent nation? 5 Did he not say to me, 'She is my sister,' and didn't she also say, 'He is my brother'? I have done this with a clear conscience and clean hands."

6 Then God said to him in the dream, "Yes, I know you did this with a clear conscience, and so I have kept you from sinning against me. That is why I did not let you touch her. 7 Now return the man's wife, for he is a prophet, and he will pray for you and you will live. But if you do not return her, you may be sure that you and all yours will die."

8 Early the next morning Abimelech summoned all his officials, and when he told them all that had happened, they were very much afraid. 9 Then Abimelech called Abraham in and said, "What have you done to us? How have I wronged you that you have brought such great guilt upon me and my kingdom? You have done things to me that should not be done." 10 And Abimelech asked Abraham, "What was your reason for doing this?"

11 Abraham replied, "I said to myself, 'There is surely no fear of God in this place, and they will kill me because of my wife.' 12 Besides, she really is my sister, the daughter of my father though not of my mother; and she became my wife. 13 And when God had me wander from my father's household, I said to her, 'This is how you can show your love to me: Everywhere we go, say of me, "He is my brother."'"

14 Then Abimelech brought sheep and cattle and male and female slaves and gave them to Abraham, and he returned Sarah his wife to him. 15 And Abimelech said, "My land is before you; live wherever you like."

16 To Sarah he said, "I am giving your brother a thousand shekels[a] of silver. This is to cover the offense against you before all who are with you; you are completely vindicated."

17 Then Abraham prayed to God, and

God healed Abimelech, his wife and his slave girls so they could have children again, 18 for the Lord had closed up every womb in Abimelech's household because of Abraham's wife Sarah.

21:1 Now the Lord was gracious to Sarah as he had said, and the Lord did for Sarah what he had promised. 2 Sarah became pregnant and bore a son to Abraham in his old age, at the very time God had promised him. 3 Abraham gave the name Isaac^b to the son Sarah bore him. 4 When his son Isaac was eight days old, Abraham circumcised him, as God commanded him. 5 Abraham was a hundred years old when his son Isaac was born to him.

6 Sarah said, "God has brought me laughter, and everyone who hears about this will laugh with me." 7 And she added, "Who would have said to Abraham that Sarah would nurse children? Yet I have borne him a son in his old age."

8 The child grew and was weaned, and on the day Isaac was weaned Abraham held a great feast. 9 But Sarah saw that the son whom Hagar the Egyptian had borne to Abraham was mocking, 10 and she said to Abraham, "Get rid of that slave woman and her son, for that slave woman's son will never share in the inheritance with my son Isaac."

11 The matter distressed Abraham greatly because it concerned his son. 12 But God said to him, "Do not be so distressed about the boy and your maidservant. Listen to whatever Sarah tells you, because it is through Isaac that your offspring^c will be reckoned. 13 I will make the son of the maidservant into a nation also, because he is your offspring."

14 Early the next morning Abraham took some food and a skin of water and gave them to Hagar. He set them on her shoulders and then sent her off with the boy. She went on her way and wandered in the desert of Beersheba.

15 When the water in the skin was gone, she put the boy under one of the bushes. 16 Then she went off and sat down nearby, about a bowshot away, for

she thought, "I cannot watch the boy die." And as she sat there nearby, she^d began to sob.

17 God heard the boy crying, and the angel of God called to Hagar from heaven and said to her, "What is the matter, Hagar? Do not be afraid; God has heard the boy crying as he lies there. 18 Lift the boy up and take him by the hand, for I will make him into a great nation."

19 Then God opened her eyes and she saw a well of water. So she went and filled the skin with water and gave the boy a drink.

20 God was with the boy as he grew up. He lived in the desert and became an archer. 21 While he was living in the Desert of Paran, his mother got a wife for him from Egypt.

22 At that time Abimelech and Phicol the commander of his forces said to Abraham, "God is with you in everything you do. 23 Now swear to me here before God that you will not deal falsely with me or my children or my descendants. Show to me and the country where you are living as an alien the same kindness I have shown to you."

24 Abraham said, "I swear it."

25 Then Abraham complained to Abimelech about a well of water that Abimelech's servants had seized. 26 But Abimelech said, "I don't know who has done this. You did not tell me, and I heard about it only today."

27 So Abraham brought sheep and cattle and gave them to Abimelech, and the two men made a treaty. 28 Abraham set apart seven ewe lambs from the flock, 29 and Abimelech asked Abraham, "What is the meaning of these seven ewe lambs you have set apart by themselves?"

30 He replied, "Accept these seven lambs from my hand as a witness that I dug this well."

31 So that place was called Beersheba,^e because the two men swore an oath there.

32 After the treaty had been made at Beersheba, Abimelech and Phicol the commander of his forces returned to

the land of the Philistines. [33]Abraham planted a tamarisk tree in Beersheba, and there he called upon the name of the LORD, the Eternal God. [34]And Abraham stayed in the land of the Philistines for a long time.

[22:1]SOME time later God tested Abraham. He said to him, "Abraham!"

"Here I am," he replied.

[2]Then God said, "Take your son, your only son, Isaac, whom you love, and go to the region of Moriah. Sacrifice him there as a burnt offering on one of the mountains I will tell you about."

[3]Early the next morning Abraham got up and saddled his donkey. He took with him two of his servants and his son Isaac. When he had cut enough wood for the burnt offering, he set out for the place God had told him about. [4]On the third day Abraham looked up and saw the place in the distance. [5]He said to his servants, "Stay here with the donkey while I and the boy go over there. We will worship and then we will come back to you."

[6]Abraham took the wood for the burnt offering and placed it on his son Isaac, and he himself carried the fire and the knife. As the two of them went on together, [7]Isaac spoke up and said to his father Abraham, "Father?"

"Yes, my son?" Abraham replied.

"The fire and wood are here," Isaac said, "but where is the lamb for the burnt offering?"

[8]Abraham answered, "God himself will provide the lamb for the burnt offering, my son." And the two of them went on together.

[9]When they reached the place God had told him about, Abraham built an altar there and arranged the wood on it. He bound his son Isaac and laid him on the altar, on top of the wood. [10]Then he reached out his hand and took the knife to slay his son. [11]But the angel of the LORD called out to him from heaven, "Abraham! Abraham!"

"Here I am," he replied.

[12]"Do not lay a hand on the boy," he said. "Do not do anything to him. Now I know that you fear God, because you have not withheld from me your son, your only son."

[13]Abraham looked up and there in a thicket he saw a ram[f] caught by its horns. He went over and took the ram and sacrificed it as a burnt offering instead of his son. [14]So Abraham called that place The LORD Will Provide. And to this day it is said, "On the mountain of the LORD it will be provided."

[15]The angel of the LORD called to Abraham from heaven a second time [16]and said, "I swear by myself, declares the LORD, that because you have done this and have not withheld your son, your only son, [17]I will surely bless you and make your descendants as numerous as the stars in the sky and as the sand on the seashore. Your descendants will take possession of the cities of their enemies, [18]and through your offspring[c] all nations on earth will be blessed, because you have obeyed me."

[19]Then Abraham returned to his servants, and they set off together for Beersheba. And Abraham stayed in Beersheba.

[20]Some time later Abraham was told, "Milcah is also a mother; she has borne sons to your brother Nahor: [21]Uz the firstborn, Buz his brother, Kemuel (the father of Aram), [22]Kesed, Hazo, Pildash, Jidlaph and Bethuel." [23]Bethuel became the father of Rebekah. Milcah bore these eight sons to Abraham's brother Nahor. [24]His concubine, whose name was Reumah, also had sons: Tebah, Gaham, Tahash and Maacah.

a16 That is, about 25 pounds (about 11.5 kilograms)
b3 Isaac means he laughs.   c12 Or seed   d16 Hebrew; Septuagint the child   e31 Beersheba can mean well of seven or well of the oath.   f13 Many manuscripts of the Masoretic Text, Samaritan Pentateuch, Septuagint and Syriac; most manuscripts of the Masoretic Text a ram behind ⌊him⌋

MATTHEW 7:15-29

"**W**atch out for false prophets. They come to you in sheep's clothing, but inwardly they are ferocious wolves. [16]By their fruit you will recognize them. Do people pick grapes from thornbushes, or figs from thistles? 17Likewise every good tree bears good fruit, but a bad tree bears bad fruit. 18A good tree cannot bear bad fruit, and a bad tree cannot bear good fruit. 19Every tree that does not bear good fruit is cut down and thrown into the fire. 20Thus, by their fruit you will recognize them.

21"Not everyone who says to me, 'Lord, Lord,' will enter the kingdom of heaven, but only he who does the will of my Father who is in heaven. 22Many will say to me on that day, 'Lord, Lord, did we not prophesy in your name, and in your name drive out demons and perform many miracles?' 23Then I will tell them plainly, 'I never knew you. Away from me, you evildoers!'

24"Therefore everyone who hears these words of mine and puts them into practice is like a wise man who built his house on the rock. 25The rain came down, the streams rose, and the winds blew and beat against that house; yet it did not fall, because it had its foundation on the rock. 26But everyone who hears these words of mine and does not put them into practice is like a foolish man who built his house on sand. 27The rain came down, the streams rose, and the winds blew and beat against that house, and it fell with a great crash."

28When Jesus had finished saying these things, the crowds were amazed at his teaching, 29because he taught as one who had authority, and not as their teachers of the law.

PSALM 9:1-12a

For the director of music. To the tune of "The Death of the Son." A psalm of David.

1 I will praise you, O Lord, with all my heart;
I will tell of all your wonders.
2 I will be glad and rejoice in you;
I will sing praise to your name, O Most High.

3 My enemies turn back;
they stumble and perish before you.

4 For you have upheld my right and my cause;
you have sat on your throne, judging righteously.
5 You have rebuked the nations and destroyed the wicked;
you have blotted out their name for ever and ever.
6 Endless ruin has overtaken the enemy,
you have uprooted their cities;
even the memory of them has perished.

7 The Lord reigns forever;
he has established his throne for judgment.
8 He will judge the world in righteousness;
he will govern the peoples with justice.
9 **The Lord is a refuge for the oppressed,
a stronghold in times of trouble.**
10 **Those who know your name will trust in you,
for you, Lord, have never forsaken those who seek you.**

11 Sing praises to the Lord, enthroned in Zion;
proclaim among the nations what he has done.
12 For he who avenges blood remembers;
he does not ignore the cry of the afflicted.

aPsalms 9 and 10 may have been originally a single acrostic poem, the stanzas of which begin with the successive letters of the Hebrew alphabet. In the Septuagint they constitute one psalm.

PROVERBS 2:16-22

16 It [wisdom] will save you also from the adulteress,
from the wayward wife with her seductive words,
17 who has left the partner of her youth and ignored the covenant she made before God.a
18 For her house leads down to death and her paths to the spirits of the dead.

¹⁹None who go to her return
    or attain the paths of life.

²⁰Thus you will walk in the ways of
        good men
    and keep to the paths of the
        righteous.
²¹For the upright will live in the land,
    and the blameless will remain
        in it;
²²but the wicked will be cut off from
        the land,
    and the unfaithful will be torn
        from it.

a17 Or covenant of her God

□ DAY 10

GOD SIGHTINGS

January 10

GENESIS 23:1–24:51

Sarah lived to be a hundred and twenty-seven years old. ²She died at Kiriath Arba (that is, Hebron) in the land of Canaan, and Abraham went to mourn for Sarah and to weep over her.

³Then Abraham rose from beside his dead wife and spoke to the Hittites.ᵃ He said, ⁴"I am an alien and a stranger among you. Sell me some property for a burial site here so I can bury my dead."

⁵The Hittites replied to Abraham, ⁶"Sir, listen to us. You are a mighty prince among us. Bury your dead in the choicest of our tombs. None of us will refuse you his tomb for burying your dead."

⁷Then Abraham rose and bowed down before the people of the land, the Hittites. ⁸He said to them, "If you are willing to let me bury my dead, then listen to me and intercede with Ephron son of Zohar on my behalf ⁹so he will sell me the cave of Machpelah, which belongs to him and is at the end of his field. Ask him to sell it to me for the full price as a burial site among you."

¹⁰Ephron the Hittite was sitting among his people and he replied to Abraham in the hearing of all the Hittites who had come to the gate of his city. ¹¹"No, my lord," he said. "Listen to me; I giveᵇ you the field, and I giveᵇ you the cave that is in it. I giveᵇ it to you in the presence of my people. Bury your dead."

¹²Again Abraham bowed down before the people of the land ¹³and he said to Ephron in their hearing, "Listen to me, if you will. I will pay the price of the field. Accept it from me so I can bury my dead there."

¹⁴Ephron answered Abraham, ¹⁵"Listen to me, my lord; the land is worth four hundred shekelsᶜ of silver, but what is that between me and you? Bury your dead."

¹⁶Abraham agreed to Ephron's terms and weighed out for him the price he had named in the hearing of the Hittites: four hundred shekels of silver, according to the weight current among the merchants.

¹⁷So Ephron's field in Machpelah near Mamre—both the field and the cave in it, and all the trees within the borders of the field—was deeded ¹⁸to Abraham as his property in the presence of all the Hittites who had come to the gate of the city. ¹⁹Afterward Abraham buried his wife Sarah in the cave in the field of Machpelah near Mamre (which is at Hebron) in the land of Canaan. ²⁰So the field and the cave in it were deeded to Abraham by the Hittites as a burial site.

²⁴:¹ABRAHAM was now old and well advanced in years, and the LORD had blessed him in every way. ²He said to the chiefᵈ servant in his household, the one in charge of all that he had, "Put your hand under my thigh. ³I want you to swear by the LORD, the God of heaven and the God of earth, that you will not get a wife for my son from the daughters of the Canaanites, among whom I am living, ⁴but will go to my country and my own relatives and get a wife for my son Isaac."

⁵The servant asked him, "What if the woman is unwilling to come back with

me to this land? Shall I then take your son back to the country you came from?"

6"Make sure that you do not take my son back there," Abraham said. 7"The LORD, the God of heaven, who brought me out of my father's household and my native land and who spoke to me and promised me on oath, saying, 'To your offspringᵉ I will give this land'—he will send his angel before you so that you can get a wife for my son from there. 8If the woman is unwilling to come back with you, then you will be released from this oath of mine. Only do not take my son back there." 9So the servant put his hand under the thigh of his master Abraham and swore an oath to him concerning this matter.

10Then the servant took ten of his master's camels and left, taking with him all kinds of good things from his master. He set out for Aram Naharaimᶠ and made his way to the town of Nahor. 11He had the camels kneel down near the well outside the town; it was toward evening, the time the women go out to draw water.

12Then he prayed, "O LORD, God of my master Abraham, give me success today, and show kindness to my master Abraham. 13See, I am standing beside this spring, and the daughters of the townspeople are coming out to draw water. 14May it be that when I say to a girl, 'Please let down your jar that I may have a drink,' and she says, 'Drink, and I'll water your camels too'—let her be the one you have chosen for your servant Isaac. By this I will know that you have shown kindness to my master."

15Before he had finished praying, Rebekah came out with her jar on her shoulder. She was the daughter of Bethuel son of Milcah, who was the wife of Abraham's brother Nahor. 16The girl was very beautiful, a virgin; no man had ever lain with her. She went down to the spring, filled her jar and came up again.

17The servant hurried to meet her and said, "Please give me a little water from your jar."

18"Drink, my lord," she said, and quickly lowered the jar to her hands and gave him a drink.

19After she had given him a drink, she said, "I'll draw water for your camels too, until they have finished drinking." 20So she quickly emptied her jar into the trough, ran back to the well to draw more water, and drew enough for all his camels. 21Without saying a word, the man watched her closely to learn whether or not the LORD had made his journey successful.

22When the camels had finished drinking, the man took out a gold nose ring weighing a bekaᵍ and two gold bracelets weighing ten shekels.ʰ 23Then he asked, "Whose daughter are you? Please tell me, is there room in your father's house for us to spend the night?"

24She answered him, "I am the daughter of Bethuel, the son that Milcah bore to Nahor." 25And she added, "We have plenty of straw and fodder, as well as room for you to spend the night."

26Then the man bowed down and worshiped the LORD, 27saying, "Praise be to the LORD, the God of my master Abraham, who has not abandoned his kindness and faithfulness to my master. As for me, the LORD has led me on the journey to the house of my master's relatives."

28The girl ran and told her mother's household about these things. 29Now Rebekah had a brother named Laban, and he hurried out to the man at the spring. 30As soon as he had seen the nose ring, and the bracelets on his sister's arms, and had heard Rebekah tell what the man said to her, he went out to the man and found him standing by the camels near the spring. 31"Come, you who are blessed by the LORD," he said. "Why are you standing out here? I have prepared the house and a place for the camels."

32So the man went to the house, and the camels were unloaded. Straw and fodder were brought for the camels, and water for him and his men to wash their feet. 33 Then food was set before him, but he said, "I will not eat until I have told you what I have to say."

"Then tell us," Laban said.

34 So he said, "I am Abraham's servant. 35 The LORD has blessed my master abundantly, and he has become wealthy. He has given him sheep and cattle, silver and gold, menservants and maidservants, and camels and donkeys. 36 My master's wife Sarah has borne him a son in her*i* old age, and he has given him everything he owns. 37 And my master made me swear an oath, and said, 'You must not get a wife for my son from the daughters of the Canaanites, in whose land I live, 38 but go to my father's family and to my own clan, and get a wife for my son.'

39 "Then I asked my master, 'What if the woman will not come back with me?'

40 "He replied, 'The LORD, before whom I have walked, will send his angel with you and make your journey a success, so that you can get a wife for my son from my own clan and from my father's family. 41 Then, when you go to my clan, you will be released from my oath even if they refuse to give her to you—you will be released from my oath.'

42 "When I came to the spring today, I said, 'O LORD, God of my master Abraham, if you will, please grant success to the journey on which I have come. 43 See, I am standing beside this spring; if a maiden comes out to draw water and I say to her, "Please let me drink a little water from your jar," 44 and if she says to me, "Drink, and I'll draw water for your camels too," let her be the one the LORD has chosen for my master's son.'

45 "Before I finished praying in my heart, Rebekah came out, with her jar on her shoulder. She went down to the spring and drew water, and I said to her, 'Please give me a drink.'

46 "She quickly lowered her jar from her shoulder and said, 'Drink, and I'll water your camels too.' So I drank, and she watered the camels also.

47 "I asked her, 'Whose daughter are you?'

"She said, 'The daughter of Bethuel son of Nahor, whom Milcah bore to him.'

"Then I put the ring in her nose and the bracelets on her arms, 48 and I bowed down and worshiped the LORD. I praised the LORD, the God of my master Abraham, who had led me on the right road to get the granddaughter of my master's brother for his son. 49 Now if you will show kindness and faithfulness to my master, tell me; and if not, tell me, so I may know which way to turn."

50 Laban and Bethuel answered, "This is from the LORD; we can say nothing to you one way or the other. 51 Here is Rebekah; take her and go, and let her become the wife of your master's son, as the LORD has directed."

a3 Or *the sons of Heth*; also in verses 5, 7, 10, 16, 18 and 20 *b11* Or *sell* *c15* That is, about 10 pounds (about 4.5 kilograms) *d2* Or *oldest* *e7* Or *seed* *f10* That is, Northwest Mesopotamia *g22* That is, about 1/5 ounce (about 5.5 grams) *h22* That is, about 4 ounces (about 110 grams) *i36* Or *his*

MATTHEW 8:1-17

When he [Jesus] came down from the mountainside, large crowds followed him. 2 A man with leprosy*a* came and knelt before him and said, "Lord, if you are willing, you can make me clean."

3 Jesus reached out his hand and touched the man. "I am willing," he said. "Be clean!" Immediately he was cured*b* of his leprosy. 4 Then Jesus said to him, "See that you don't tell anyone. But go, show yourself to the priest and offer the gift Moses commanded, as a testimony to them."

5 When Jesus had entered Capernaum, a centurion came to him, asking for help. 6 "Lord," he said, "my servant lies at home paralyzed and in terrible suffering."

7 Jesus said to him, "I will go and heal him."

8 The centurion replied, "Lord, I do not deserve to have you come under my roof. But just say the word, and my servant will be healed. 9 For I myself am a man under authority, with soldiers under me. I tell

this one, 'Go,' and he goes; and that one, 'Come,' and he comes. I say to my servant, 'Do this,' and he does it."

¹⁰When Jesus heard this, he was astonished and said to those following him, "I tell you the truth, I have not found anyone in Israel with such great faith. ¹¹**I say to you that many will come from the east and the west, and will take their places at the feast with Abraham, Isaac and Jacob in the kingdom of heaven.** ¹²But the subjects of the kingdom will be thrown outside, into the darkness, where there will be weeping and gnashing of teeth."

¹³Then Jesus said to the centurion, "Go! It will be done just as you believed it would." And his servant was healed at that very hour.

¹⁴When Jesus came into Peter's house, he saw Peter's mother-in-law lying in bed with a fever. ¹⁵He touched her hand and the fever left her, and she got up and began to wait on him.

¹⁶When evening came, many who were demon-possessed were brought to him, and he drove out the spirits with a word and healed all the sick. ¹⁷This was to fulfill what was spoken through the prophet Isaiah:

"He took up our infirmities
and carried our diseases."ᶜ

ᵃ2 The Greek word was used for various diseases affecting the skin—not necessarily leprosy. ᵇ3 Greek *made clean* ᶜ17 Isaiah 53:4

PSALM 9:13-20

¹³**O** Lᴏʀᴅ, see how my enemies
persecute me!
Have mercy and lift me up from
the gates of death,
¹⁴that I may declare your praises
in the gates of the Daughter of Zion
and there rejoice in your salvation.
¹⁵The nations have fallen into the pit
they have dug;
their feet are caught in the net
they have hidden.
¹⁶The Lᴏʀᴅ is known by his justice;
the wicked are ensnared by the
work of their hands.
*Higgaion.*ᵃ *Selah*

¹⁷The wicked return to the grave,ᵇ
all the nations that forget God.
¹⁸But the needy will not always be
forgotten,
nor the hope of the afflicted
ever perish.

¹⁹Arise, O Lᴏʀᴅ, let not man triumph;
let the nations be judged in your
presence.
²⁰Strike them with terror, O Lᴏʀᴅ;
let the nations know they are
but men.   *Selah*

ᵃ16 Or *Meditation*; possibly a musical notation
ᵇ17 Hebrew *Sheol*

PROVERBS 3:1-6

My son, do not forget my teaching,
but keep my commands in your
heart,
²for they will prolong your life
many years
and bring you prosperity.

³Let love and faithfulness never
leave you;
bind them around your neck,
write them on the tablet of
your heart.
⁴Then you will win favor and a
good name
in the sight of God and man.

⁵Trust in the Lᴏʀᴅ with all your heart
and lean not on your own
understanding;
⁶in all your ways acknowledge him,
and he will make your paths
straight.ᵃ

ᵃ6 Or *will direct your paths*

☐ DAY 11

GOD SIGHTINGS

January 11

GENESIS 24:52–26:16

When Abraham's servant heard what they said, he bowed down to the ground before the Lᴏʀᴅ. ⁵³Then the servant brought out gold and silver jewelry and articles of clothing and gave them to Rebekah; he also gave costly gifts to her brother and to her mother. 54Then he and the men who were with him ate and drank and spent the night there.

When they got up the next morning, he said, "Send me on my way to my master."

55 But her brother and her mother replied, "Let the girl remain with us ten days or so; then youª may go."

56 But he said to them, "Do not detain me, now that the LORD has granted success to my journey. Send me on my way so I may go to my master."

57 Then they said, "Let's call the girl and ask her about it." 58So they called Rebekah and asked her, "Will you go with this man?"

"I will go," she said.

59 So they sent their sister Rebekah on her way, along with her nurse and Abraham's servant and his men. 60And they blessed Rebekah and said to her,

"Our sister, may you increase
    to thousands upon thousands;
may your offspring possess
    the gates of their enemies."

61 Then Rebekah and her maids got ready and mounted their camels and went back with the man. So the servant took Rebekah and left.

62 Now Isaac had come from Beer Lahai Roi, for he was living in the Negev. 63He went out to the field one evening to meditate,ᵇ and as he looked up, he saw camels approaching. 64Rebekah also looked up and saw Isaac. She got down from her camel 65and asked the servant, "Who is that man in the field coming to meet us?"

"He is my master," the servant answered. So she took her veil and covered herself.

66 Then the servant told Isaac all he had done. 67Isaac brought her into the tent of his mother Sarah, and he married Rebekah. So she became his wife, and he loved her; and Isaac was comforted after his mother's death.

25:1ABRAHAM tookᶜ another wife, whose name was Keturah. 2She bore him Zimran, Jokshan, Medan, Midian, Ishbak and Shuah. 3Jokshan was the father of Sheba and Dedan; the descendants of Dedan were the Asshurites, the Letushites and the Leummites. 4The sons of Midian were Ephah, Epher, Hanoch, Abida and Eldaah. All these were descendants of Keturah.

5Abraham left everything he owned to Isaac. 6But while he was still living, he gave gifts to the sons of his concubines and sent them away from his son Isaac to the land of the east.

7Altogether, Abraham lived a hundred and seventy-five years. 8Then Abraham breathed his last and died at a good old age, an old man and full of years; and he was gathered to his people. 9His sons Isaac and Ishmael buried him in the cave of Machpelah near Mamre, in the field of Ephron son of Zohar the Hittite, 10the field Abraham had bought from the Hittites.ᵈ There Abraham was buried with his wife Sarah. 11After Abraham's death, God blessed his son Isaac, who then lived near Beer Lahai Roi.

12This is the account of Abraham's son Ishmael, whom Sarah's maidservant, Hagar the Egyptian, bore to Abraham.

13These are the names of the sons of Ishmael, listed in the order of their birth: Nebaioth the firstborn of Ishmael, Kedar, Adbeel, Mibsam, 14Mishma, Dumah, Massa, 15Hadad, Tema, Jetur, Naphish and Kedemah. 16These were the sons of Ishmael, and these are the names of the twelve tribal rulers according to their settlements and camps. 17Altogether, Ishmael lived a hundred and thirty-seven years. He breathed his last and died, and he was gathered to his people. 18His descendants settled in the area from Havilah to Shur, near the border of Egypt, as you go toward Asshur. And they lived in hostility towardᵉ all their brothers.

¹⁹This is the account of Abraham's son Isaac.

Abraham became the father of Isaac, ²⁰and Isaac was forty years old when he married Rebekah daughter of Bethuel the Aramean from Paddan Aram*f* and sister of Laban the Aramean.

²¹Isaac prayed to the LORD on behalf of his wife, because she was barren. The LORD answered his prayer, and his wife Rebekah became pregnant. ²²The babies jostled each other within her, and she said, "Why is this happening to me?" So she went to inquire of the LORD.

²³The LORD said to her,

"Two nations are in your womb,
    and two peoples from within you
        will be separated;
one people will be stronger than the
        other,
    and the older will serve the
        younger."

²⁴When the time came for her to give birth, there were twin boys in her womb. ²⁵The first to come out was red, and his whole body was like a hairy garment; so they named him Esau.*g* ²⁶After this, his brother came out, with his hand grasping Esau's heel; so he was named Jacob.*h* Isaac was sixty years old when Rebekah gave birth to them.

²⁷The boys grew up, and Esau became a skillful hunter, a man of the open country, while Jacob was a quiet man, staying among the tents. ²⁸Isaac, who had a taste for wild game, loved Esau, but Rebekah loved Jacob.

²⁹Once when Jacob was cooking some stew, Esau came in from the open country, famished. ³⁰He said to Jacob, "Quick, let me have some of that red stew! I'm famished!" (That is why he was also called Edom.*i*)

³¹Jacob replied, "First sell me your birthright."

³²"Look, I am about to die," Esau said. "What good is the birthright to me?"

³³But Jacob said, "Swear to me first." So he swore an oath to him, selling his birthright to Jacob.

³⁴Then Jacob gave Esau some bread and some lentil stew. He ate and drank, and then got up and left.

So Esau despised his birthright.

²⁶:¹Now there was a famine in the land—besides the earlier famine of Abraham's time—and Isaac went to Abimelech king of the Philistines in Gerar. ²The LORD appeared to Isaac and said, "Do not go down to Egypt; live in the land where I tell you to live. ³Stay in this land for a while, and I will be with you and will bless you. For to you and your descendants I will give all these lands and will confirm the oath I swore to your father Abraham. **⁴I will make your descendants as numerous as the stars in the sky and will give them all these lands, and through your offspring*j* all nations on earth will be blessed, ⁵because Abraham obeyed me and kept my requirements, my commands, my decrees and my laws."** ⁶So Isaac stayed in Gerar.

⁷When the men of that place asked him about his wife, he said, "She is my sister," because he was afraid to say, "She is my wife." He thought, "The men of this place might kill me on account of Rebekah, because she is beautiful."

⁸When Isaac had been there a long time, Abimelech king of the Philistines looked down from a window and saw Isaac caressing his wife Rebekah. ⁹So Abimelech summoned Isaac and said, "She is really your wife! Why did you say, 'She is my sister'?"

Isaac answered him, "Because I thought I might lose my life on account of her."

¹⁰Then Abimelech said, "What is this you have done to us? One of the men might well have slept with your wife, and you would have brought guilt upon us."

¹¹So Abimelech gave orders to all the people: "Anyone who molests this man or his wife shall surely be put to death."

¹²Isaac planted crops in that land and the same year reaped a hundredfold, because the LORD blessed him. ¹³The man became rich, and his wealth con-

tinued to grow until he became very wealthy. [14]He had so many flocks and herds and servants that the Philistines envied him. [15]So all the wells that his father's servants had dug in the time of his father Abraham, the Philistines stopped up, filling them with earth.

[16]Then Abimelech said to Isaac, "Move away from us; you have become too powerful for us."

MATTHEW 8:18-34

When Jesus saw the crowd around him, he gave orders to cross to the other side of the lake. [19]Then a teacher of the law came to him and said, "Teacher, I will follow you wherever you go."

[20]Jesus replied, "Foxes have holes and birds of the air have nests, but the Son of Man has no place to lay his head."

[21]Another disciple said to him, "Lord, first let me go and bury my father."

[22]But Jesus told him, "Follow me, and let the dead bury their own dead."

[23]Then he got into the boat and his disciples followed him. [24]Without warning, a furious storm came up on the lake, so that the waves swept over the boat. But Jesus was sleeping. [25]The disciples went and woke him, saying, "Lord, save us! We're going to drown!"

[26]He replied, "You of little faith, why are you so afraid?" Then he got up and rebuked the winds and the waves, and it was completely calm.

[27]The men were amazed and asked, "What kind of man is this? Even the winds and the waves obey him!"

[28]When he arrived at the other side in the region of the Gadarenes,*a* two demon-possessed men coming from the tombs met him. They were so violent that no one could pass that way. [29]"What do you want with us, Son of God?" they shouted. "Have you come here to torture us before the appointed time?"

[30]Some distance from them a large herd of pigs was feeding. [31]The demons begged Jesus, "If you drive us out, send us into the herd of pigs."

[32]He said to them, "Go!" So they came out and went into the pigs, and the whole herd rushed down the steep bank into the lake and died in the water. [33]Those tending the pigs ran off, went into the town and reported all this, including what had happened to the demon-possessed men. [34]Then the whole town went out to meet Jesus. And when they saw him, they pleaded with him to leave their region.

PSALM 10:1-15*a*

[1]**W**hy, O Lᴏʀᴅ, do you stand far off?
  Why do you hide yourself in times
    of trouble?

[2]In his arrogance the wicked man
    hunts down the weak,
  who are caught in the schemes
    he devises.

[3]He boasts of the cravings of
    his heart;
  he blesses the greedy and reviles
    the Lᴏʀᴅ.

[4]In his pride the wicked does not
    seek him;
  in all his thoughts there is no room
    for God.

[5]His ways are always prosperous;
  he is haughty and your laws are
    far from him;
  he sneers at all his enemies.

[6]He says to himself, "Nothing will
    shake me;
  I'll always be happy and never have
    trouble."

[7]His mouth is full of curses and lies
    and threats;
  trouble and evil are under his
    tongue.

[8]He lies in wait near the villages;
  from ambush he murders the
    innocent,
  watching in secret for his victims.

[9]He lies in wait like a lion in cover;
  he lies in wait to catch the
    helpless;

he catches the helpless and drags
   them off in his net.
¹⁰His victims are crushed, they
   collapse;
   they fall under his strength.
¹¹He says to himself, "God has
   forgotten;
   he covers his face and never sees."

¹²Arise, Lord! Lift up your hand,
   O God.
   Do not forget the helpless.
¹³Why does the wicked man revile
   God?
   Why does he say to himself,
   "He won't call me to account"?
¹⁴But you, O God, do see trouble
   and grief;
   you consider it to take it in hand.
   The victim commits himself to you;
   you are the helper of the
   fatherless.
¹⁵Break the arm of the wicked and
   evil man;
   call him to account for his
   wickedness
   that would not be found out.

ᵃPsalms 9 and 10 may have been originally a single acrostic
poem, the stanzas of which begin with the successive letters
of the Hebrew alphabet. In the Septuagint they constitute
one psalm.

PROVERBS 3:7-8

⁷Do not be wise in your own eyes;
   fear the Lord and shun evil.
⁸This will bring health to your body
   and nourishment to your bones.

□ DAY 12

GOD SIGHTINGS

January 12

GENESIS 26:17–27:46

So Isaac moved away from there and
encamped in the Valley of Gerar and
settled there. ¹⁸Isaac reopened the
wells that had been dug in the time of
his father Abraham, which the Philistines had stopped up after Abraham

died, and he gave them the same names
his father had given them.

¹⁹Isaac's servants dug in the valley
and discovered a well of fresh water
there. ²⁰But the herdsmen of Gerar
quarreled with Isaac's herdsmen and
said, "The water is ours!" So he named
the well Esek,ᵃ because they disputed
with him. ²¹Then they dug another well,
but they quarreled over that one also; so
he named it Sitnah.ᵇ ²²He moved on
from there and dug another well, and no
one quarreled over it. He named it Rehoboth,ᶜ saying, "Now the Lord has
given us room and we will flourish in
the land."

²³From there he went up to Beersheba. ²⁴That night the Lord appeared
to him and said, "I am the God of your
father Abraham. Do not be afraid, for I
am with you; I will bless you and will increase the number of your descendants
for the sake of my servant Abraham."

²⁵Isaac built an altar there and called
on the name of the Lord. There he
pitched his tent, and there his servants
dug a well.

²⁶Meanwhile, Abimelech had come to
him from Gerar, with Ahuzzath his personal adviser and Phicol the commander
of his forces. ²⁷Isaac asked them, "Why
have you come to me, since you were
hostile to me and sent me away?"

²⁸They answered, "We saw clearly
that the Lord was with you; so we said,
'There ought to be a sworn agreement
between us'—between us and you. Let
us make a treaty with you ²⁹that you will
do us no harm, just as we did not molest
you but always treated you well and sent
you away in peace. And now you are
blessed by the Lord."

³⁰Isaac then made a feast for them,
and they ate and drank. ³¹Early the next
morning the men swore an oath to each
other. Then Isaac sent them on their
way, and they left him in peace.

³²That day Isaac's servants came and
told him about the well they had dug.
They said, "We've found water!" ³³He
called it Shibah,ᵈ and to this day the
name of the town has been Beersheba.ᵉ

34When Esau was forty years old, he married Judith daughter of Beeri the Hittite, and also Basemath daughter of Elon the Hittite. 35 They were a source of grief to Isaac and Rebekah.

27:1WHEN Isaac was old and his eyes were so weak that he could no longer see, he called for Esau his older son and said to him, "My son."

"Here I am," he answered.

2Isaac said, "I am now an old man and don't know the day of my death. 3Now then, get your weapons—your quiver and bow—and go out to the open country to hunt some wild game for me. 4Prepare me the kind of tasty food I like and bring it to me to eat, so that I may give you my blessing before I die."

5Now Rebekah was listening as Isaac spoke to his son Esau. When Esau left for the open country to hunt game and bring it back, 6Rebekah said to her son Jacob, "Look, I overheard your father say to your brother Esau, 7'Bring me some game and prepare me some tasty food to eat, so that I may give you my blessing in the presence of the LORD before I die.' 8Now, my son, listen carefully and do what I tell you: 9Go out to the flock and bring me two choice young goats, so I can prepare some tasty food for your father, just the way he likes it. 10Then take it to your father to eat, so that he may give you his blessing before he dies."

11Jacob said to Rebekah his mother, "But my brother Esau is a hairy man, and I'm a man with smooth skin. 12What if my father touches me? I would appear to be tricking him and would bring down a curse on myself rather than a blessing."

13His mother said to him, "My son, let the curse fall on me. Just do what I say; go and get them for me."

14So he went and got them and brought them to his mother, and she prepared some tasty food, just the way his father liked it. 15Then Rebekah took the best clothes of Esau her older son, which she had in the house, and put them on her younger son Jacob. 16She also covered his hands and the smooth part of his neck with the goatskins. 17Then she handed to her son Jacob the tasty food and the bread she had made.

18He went to his father and said, "My father."

"Yes, my son," he answered. "Who is it?"

19Jacob said to his father, "I am Esau your firstborn. I have done as you told me. Please sit up and eat some of my game so that you may give me your blessing."

20Isaac asked his son, "How did you find it so quickly, my son?"

"The LORD your God gave me success," he replied.

21Then Isaac said to Jacob, "Come near so I can touch you, my son, to know whether you really are my son Esau or not."

22Jacob went close to his father Isaac, who touched him and said, "The voice is the voice of Jacob, but the hands are the hands of Esau." 23He did not recognize him, for his hands were hairy like those of his brother Esau; so he blessed him. 24"Are you really my son Esau?" he asked.

"I am," he replied.

25Then he said, "My son, bring me some of your game to eat, so that I may give you my blessing."

Jacob brought it to him and he ate; and he brought some wine and he drank. 26Then his father Isaac said to him, "Come here, my son, and kiss me."

27So he went to him and kissed him. When Isaac caught the smell of his clothes, he blessed him and said,

"Ah, the smell of my son
     is like the smell of a field
     that the LORD has blessed.
28May God give you of heaven's dew
     and of earth's richness—
     an abundance of grain and
          new wine.
29May nations serve you
     and peoples bow down to you.
Be lord over your brothers,
     and may the sons of your mother
          bow down to you.

May those who curse you be cursed
    and those who bless you be blessed."

³⁰After Isaac finished blessing him
and Jacob had scarcely left his father's
presence, his brother Esau came in from
hunting. ³¹He too prepared some tasty
food and brought it to his father. Then
he said to him, "My father, sit up and eat
some of my game, so that you may give
me your blessing."

³²His father Isaac asked him, "Who
are you?"

"I am your son," he answered, "your
firstborn, Esau."

³³Isaac trembled violently and said,
"Who was it, then, that hunted game
and brought it to me? I ate it just before
you came and I blessed him—and indeed he will be blessed!"

³⁴When Esau heard his father's
words, he burst out with a loud and bitter cry and said to his father, "Bless me—
me too, my father!"

³⁵But he said, "Your brother came deceitfully and took your blessing."

³⁶Esau said, "Isn't he rightly named Ja-
cobᶠ? He has deceived me these two
times: He took my birthright, and now
he's taken my blessing!" Then he asked,
"Haven't you reserved any blessing for
me?"

³⁷Isaac answered Esau, "I have made
him lord over you and have made all his
relatives his servants, and I have sustained him with grain and new wine. So
what can I possibly do for you, my son?"

³⁸Esau said to his father, "Do you
have only one blessing, my father? Bless
me too, my father!" Then Esau wept
aloud.

³⁹His father Isaac answered him,

"Your dwelling will be
    away from the earth's richness,
    away from the dew of heaven
      above.
⁴⁰You will live by the sword
    and you will serve your brother.
But when you grow restless,
    you will throw his yoke
    from off your neck."

⁴¹Esau held a grudge against Jacob
because of the blessing his father had
given him. He said to himself, "The days
of mourning for my father are near;
then I will kill my brother Jacob."

⁴²When Rebekah was told what her
older son Esau had said, she sent for her
younger son Jacob and said to him, "Your
brother Esau is consoling himself with
the thought of killing you. ⁴³Now then,
my son, do what I say: Flee at once to my
brother Laban in Haran. ⁴⁴Stay with him
for a while until your brother's fury sub-
sides. ⁴⁵When your brother is no longer
angry with you and forgets what you did
to him, I'll send word for you to come
back from there. Why should I lose both
of you in one day?"

⁴⁶Then Rebekah said to Isaac, "I'm
disgusted with living because of these
Hittite women. If Jacob takes a wife
from among the women of this land,
from Hittite women like these, my life
will not be worth living."

ᵃ20 Esek means dispute. ᵇ21 Sitnah means opposition.
ᶜ22 Rehoboth means room. ᵈ33 Shibah can mean oath
or seven. ᵉ33 Beersheba can mean well of the oath or well
of seven. ᶠ36 Jacob means he grasps the heel (figuratively,
he deceives).

MATTHEW 9:1-17

Jesus stepped into a boat, crossed over
and came to his own town. ²Some men
brought to him a paralytic, lying on a
mat. When Jesus saw their faith, he said
to the paralytic, "Take heart, son; your
sins are forgiven."

³At this, some of the teachers of the
law said to themselves, "This fellow is
blaspheming!"

⁴Knowing their thoughts, Jesus said,
"Why do you entertain evil thoughts in
your hearts? ⁵Which is easier: to say,
'Your sins are forgiven,' or to say, 'Get up
and walk'? ⁶But so that you may know
that the Son of Man has authority on
earth to forgive sins…" Then he said to
the paralytic, "Get up, take your mat and
go home." ⁷And the man got up and
went home. ⁸When the crowd saw this,
they were filled with awe; and they
praised God, who had given such authority to men.

9As Jesus went on from there, he saw a man named Matthew sitting at the tax collector's booth. "Follow me," he told him, and Matthew got up and followed him.

10While Jesus was having dinner at Matthew's house, many tax collectors and "sinners" came and ate with him and his disciples. 11When the Pharisees saw this, they asked his disciples, "Why does your teacher eat with tax collectors and 'sinners'?"

12On hearing this, Jesus said, "It is not the healthy who need a doctor, but the sick. 13But go and learn what this means: 'I desire mercy, not sacrifice.'a For I have not come to call the righteous, but sinners."

14Then John's disciples came and asked him, "How is it that we and the Pharisees fast, but your disciples do not fast?"

15Jesus answered, "How can the guests of the bridegroom mourn while he is with them? The time will come when the bridegroom will be taken from them; then they will fast.

16"No one sews a patch of unshrunk cloth on an old garment, for the patch will pull away from the garment, making the tear worse. 17Neither do men pour new wine into old wineskins. If they do, the skins will burst, the wine will run out and the wineskins will be ruined. No, they pour new wine into new wineskins, and both are preserved."

a 13 Hosea 6:6

PSALM 10:16-18

16The Lord is King for ever and ever;
    the nations will perish from
        his land.
17You hear, O Lord, the desire of
    the afflicted;
    you encourage them, and you
        listen to their cry,
18defending the fatherless and the
    oppressed,
    in order that man, who is of the
        earth, may terrify no more.

PROVERBS 3:9-10

9Honor the Lord with your wealth,
    with the firstfruits of all your crops;

10then your barns will be filled to
    overflowing,
    and your vats will brim over with
        new wine.

□ DAY 13

GOD SIGHTINGS

January 13

GENESIS 28:1–29:35

So Isaac called for Jacob and blesseda him and commanded him: "Do not marry a Canaanite woman. 2Go at once to Paddan Aram,b to the house of your mother's father Bethuel. Take a wife for yourself there, from among the daughters of Laban, your mother's brother. 3May God Almightyc bless you and make you fruitful and increase your numbers until you become a community of peoples. 4May he give you and your descendants the blessing given to Abraham, so that you may take possession of the land where you now live as an alien, the land God gave to Abraham." 5Then Isaac sent Jacob on his way, and he went to Paddan Aram, to Laban son of Bethuel the Aramean, the brother of Rebekah, who was the mother of Jacob and Esau.

6Now Esau learned that Isaac had blessed Jacob and had sent him to Paddan Aram to take a wife from there, and that when he blessed him he commanded him, "Do not marry a Canaanite woman," 7and that Jacob had obeyed his father and mother and had gone to Paddan Aram. 8Esau then realized how displeasing the Canaanite women were to his father Isaac; 9so he went to Ishmael and married Mahalath, the sister of Nebaioth and daughter of Ishmael son of Abraham, in addition to the wives he already had.

10Jacob left Beersheba and set out for Haran. 11When he reached a certain place, he stopped for the night because the sun had set. Taking one of the stones there, he put it under his head and lay down to sleep. 12He had a dream in which he saw a stairway*d* resting on the earth, with its top reaching to heaven, and the angels of God were ascending and descending on it. 13There above it*e* stood the Lord, and he said: "I am the Lord, the God of your father Abraham and the God of Isaac. I will give you and your descendants the land on which you are lying. 14Your descendants will be like the dust of the earth, and you will spread out to the west and to the east, to the north and to the south. All peoples on earth will be blessed through you and your offspring. 15I am with you and will watch over you wherever you go, and I will bring you back to this land. I will not leave you until I have done what I have promised you."

16When Jacob awoke from his sleep, he thought, "Surely the Lord is in this place, and I was not aware of it." 17He was afraid and said, "How awesome is this place! This is none other than the house of God; this is the gate of heaven."

18Early the next morning Jacob took the stone he had placed under his head and set it up as a pillar and poured oil on top of it. 19He called that place Bethel,*f* though the city used to be called Luz.

20Then Jacob made a vow, saying, "If God will be with me and will watch over me on this journey I am taking and will give me food to eat and clothes to wear 21so that I return safely to my father's house, then the Lord*g* will be my God 22and*h* this stone that I have set up as a pillar will be God's house, and of all that you give me I will give you a tenth."

29:1Then Jacob continued on his journey and came to the land of the eastern peoples. 2There he saw a well in the field, with three flocks of sheep lying near it because the flocks were watered from that well. The stone over the mouth of the well was large. 3When all the flocks were gathered there, the shepherds would roll the stone away from the well's mouth and water the sheep. Then they would return the stone to its place over the mouth of the well.

4Jacob asked the shepherds, "My brothers, where are you from?"

"We're from Haran," they replied.

5He said to them, "Do you know Laban, Nahor's grandson?"

"Yes, we know him," they answered.

6Then Jacob asked them, "Is he well?"

"Yes, he is," they said, "and here comes his daughter Rachel with the sheep."

7"Look," he said, "the sun is still high; it is not time for the flocks to be gathered. Water the sheep and take them back to pasture."

8"We can't," they replied, "until all the flocks are gathered and the stone has been rolled away from the mouth of the well. Then we will water the sheep."

9While he was still talking with them, Rachel came with her father's sheep, for she was a shepherdess. 10When Jacob saw Rachel daughter of Laban, his mother's brother, and Laban's sheep, he went over and rolled the stone away from the mouth of the well and watered his uncle's sheep. 11Then Jacob kissed Rachel and began to weep aloud. 12He had told Rachel that he was a relative of her father and a son of Rebekah. So she ran and told her father.

13As soon as Laban heard the news about Jacob, his sister's son, he hurried to meet him. He embraced him and kissed him and brought him to his home, and there Jacob told him all these things. 14Then Laban said to him, "You are my own flesh and blood."

After Jacob had stayed with him for a whole month, 15Laban said to him, "Just because you are a relative of mine, should you work for me for nothing? Tell me what your wages should be."

16Now Laban had two daughters; the name of the older was Leah, and the name of the younger was Rachel. 17Leah had weak*i* eyes, but Rachel was lovely in form, and beautiful. 18Jacob was in love with Rachel and said, "I'll work for you seven years in return for your younger daughter Rachel."

¹⁹Laban said, "It's better that I give her to you than to some other man. Stay here with me." ²⁰So Jacob served seven years to get Rachel, but they seemed like only a few days to him because of his love for her.

²¹Then Jacob said to Laban, "Give me my wife. My time is completed, and I want to lie with her."

²²So Laban brought together all the people of the place and gave a feast. ²³But when evening came, he took his daughter Leah and gave her to Jacob, and Jacob lay with her. ²⁴And Laban gave his servant girl Zilpah to his daughter as her maidservant.

²⁵When morning came, there was Leah! So Jacob said to Laban, "What is this you have done to me? I served you for Rachel, didn't I? Why have you deceived me?"

²⁶Laban replied, "It is not our custom here to give the younger daughter in marriage before the older one. ²⁷Finish this daughter's bridal week; then we will give you the younger one also, in return for another seven years of work."

²⁸And Jacob did so. He finished the week with Leah, and then Laban gave him his daughter Rachel to be his wife. ²⁹Laban gave his servant girl Bilhah to his daughter Rachel as her maidservant. ³⁰Jacob lay with Rachel also, and he loved Rachel more than Leah. And he worked for Laban another seven years.

³¹When the LORD saw that Leah was not loved, he opened her womb, but Rachel was barren. ³²Leah became pregnant and gave birth to a son. She named him Reuben,ʲ for she said, "It is because the LORD has seen my misery. Surely my husband will love me now."

³³She conceived again, and when she gave birth to a son she said, "Because the LORD heard that I am not loved, he gave me this one too." So she named him Simeon.ᵏ

³⁴Again she conceived, and when she gave birth to a son she said, "Now at last my husband will become attached to me, because I have borne him three sons." So he was named Levi.ˡ

³⁵She conceived again, and when she gave birth to a son she said, "This time I will praise the LORD." So she named him Judah.ᵐ Then she stopped having children.

a1 Or *greeted*   *b2* That is, Northwest Mesopotamia; also in verses 5, 6 and 7   *c3* Hebrew *El-Shaddai*   *d12* Or *ladder*   *e13* Or *There beside him*   *f19* *Bethel* means *house of God.*   *9*20,21 Or *Since God... father's house, the* LORD   *h*21,22 Or *house, and the* LORD *will be my God,* 22*then*   *i*17 Or *delicate*   *l32 Reuben* sounds like the Hebrew for *he has seen my misery*; the name means *see, a son.*   *k33 Simeon* probably means *one who hears.*   *l34 Levi* sounds like and may be derived from the Hebrew for *attached.*   *m35 Judah* sounds like and may be derived from the Hebrew for *praise.*

MATTHEW 9:18-38

While he [Jesus] was saying this, a ruler came and knelt before him and said, "My daughter has just died. But come and put your hand on her, and she will live." ¹⁹Jesus got up and went with him, and so did his disciples.

²⁰Just then a woman who had been subject to bleeding for twelve years came up behind him and touched the edge of his cloak. ²¹She said to herself, "If I only touch his cloak, I will be healed."

²²Jesus turned and saw her. "Take heart, daughter," he said, "your faith has healed you." And the woman was healed from that moment.

²³When Jesus entered the ruler's house and saw the flute players and the noisy crowd, ²⁴he said, "Go away. The girl is not dead but asleep." But they laughed at him. ²⁵After the crowd had been put outside, he went in and took the girl by the hand, and she got up. ²⁶News of this spread through all that region.

²⁷As Jesus went on from there, two blind men followed him, calling out, "Have mercy on us, Son of David!"

²⁸When he had gone indoors, the blind men came to him, and he asked them, "Do you believe that I am able to do this?"

"Yes, Lord," they replied.

²⁹Then he touched their eyes and said, "According to your faith will it be done to you"; ³⁰and their sight was restored. Jesus warned them sternly, "See that no one knows about this." ³¹But

they went out and spread the news about him all over that region.

32While they were going out, a man who was demon-possessed and could not talk was brought to Jesus. 33And when the demon was driven out, the man who had been mute spoke. The crowd was amazed and said, "Nothing like this has ever been seen in Israel."

34But the Pharisees said, "It is by the prince of demons that he drives out demons."

35Jesus went through all the towns and villages, teaching in their synagogues, preaching the good news of the kingdom and healing every disease and sickness. 36When he saw the crowds, he had compassion on them, because they were harassed and helpless, like sheep without a shepherd. 37Then he said to his disciples, "The harvest is plentiful but the workers are few. 38Ask the Lord of the harvest, therefore, to send out workers into his harvest field."

PSALM 11:1-7
For the director of music. Of David.

1 In the Lord I take refuge.
  How then can you say to me:
    "Flee like a bird to your mountain.
2 For look, the wicked bend their
      bows;
  they set their arrows against
      the strings
to shoot from the shadows
  at the upright in heart.
3 When the foundations are being
      destroyed,
  what can the righteous do*a*?"

4 The Lord is in his holy temple;
  the Lord is on his heavenly
      throne.
He observes the sons of men;
  his eyes examine them.
5 The Lord examines the righteous,
  but the wicked*b* and those who
      love violence
      his soul hates.
6 On the wicked he will rain
    fiery coals and burning sulfur;
  a scorching wind will be their lot.

7 For the Lord is righteous,
  he loves justice;
  upright men will see his face.

a3 Or *what is the Righteous One doing* *b5* Or *The Lord, the Righteous One, examines the wicked,/*

PROVERBS 3:11-12
11 My son, do not despise the Lord's
      discipline
  and do not resent his rebuke,
12 because the Lord disciplines those
      he loves,
  as a father*a* the son he delights in.

a12 Hebrew; Septuagint */ and he punishes*

□ DAY 14

GOD SIGHTINGS

January 14

GENESIS 30:1–31:16
When Rachel saw that she was not bearing Jacob any children, she became jealous of her sister. So she said to Jacob, "Give me children, or I'll die!"

2Jacob became angry with her and said, "Am I in the place of God, who has kept you from having children?"

3Then she said, "Here is Bilhah, my maidservant. Sleep with her so that she can bear children for me and that through her I too can build a family."

4So she gave him her servant Bilhah as a wife. Jacob slept with her, 5and she became pregnant and bore him a son. 6Then Rachel said, "God has vindicated me; he has listened to my plea and given me a son." Because of this she named him Dan.*a*

7Rachel's servant Bilhah conceived again and bore Jacob a second son. 8Then Rachel said, "I have had a great struggle with my sister, and I have won." So she named him Naphtali.*b*

9When Leah saw that she had stopped having children, she took her maidservant Zilpah and gave her to Jacob as a wife. 10Leah's servant Zilpah bore Jacob a son. ¹¹Then Leah said, "What good fortune!"^c So she named him Gad.^d

¹²Leah's servant Zilpah bore Jacob a second son. ¹³Then Leah said, "How happy I am! The women will call me happy." So she named him Asher.^e

¹⁴During wheat harvest, Reuben went out into the fields and found some mandrake plants, which he brought to his mother Leah. Rachel said to Leah, "Please give me some of your son's mandrakes."

¹⁵But she said to her, "Wasn't it enough that you took away my husband? Will you take my son's mandrakes too?"

"Very well," Rachel said, "he can sleep with you tonight in return for your son's mandrakes."

¹⁶So when Jacob came in from the fields that evening, Leah went out to meet him. "You must sleep with me," she said. "I have hired you with my son's mandrakes." So he slept with her that night.

¹⁷God listened to Leah, and she became pregnant and bore Jacob a fifth son. ¹⁸Then Leah said, "God has rewarded me for giving my maidservant to my husband." So she named him Issachar.^f

¹⁹Leah conceived again and bore Jacob a sixth son. ²⁰Then Leah said, "God has presented me with a precious gift. This time my husband will treat me with honor, because I have borne him six sons." So she named him Zebulun.^g

²¹Some time later she gave birth to a daughter and named her Dinah.

²²Then God remembered Rachel; he listened to her and opened her womb. ²³She became pregnant and gave birth to a son and said, "God has taken away my disgrace." ²⁴She named him Joseph,^h and said, "May the Lord add to me another son."

²⁵After Rachel gave birth to Joseph, Jacob said to Laban, "Send me on my way so I can go back to my own homeland. ²⁶Give me my wives and children, for whom I have served you, and I will

be on my way. You know how much work I've done for you."

²⁷But Laban said to him, "If I have found favor in your eyes, please stay. I have learned by divination thatⁱ the Lord has blessed me because of you." ²⁸He added, "Name your wages, and I will pay them."

²⁹Jacob said to him, "You know how I have worked for you and how your livestock has fared under my care. ³⁰The little you had before I came has increased greatly, and the Lord has blessed you wherever I have been. But now, when may I do something for my own household?"

³¹"What shall I give you?" he asked.

"Don't give me anything," Jacob replied. "But if you will do this one thing for me, I will go on tending your flocks and watching over them: ³²Let me go through all your flocks today and remove from them every speckled or spotted sheep, every dark-colored lamb and every spotted or speckled goat. They will be my wages. ³³And my honesty will testify for me in the future, whenever you check on the wages you have paid me. Any goat in my possession that is not speckled or spotted, or any lamb that is not dark-colored, will be considered stolen."

³⁴"Agreed," said Laban. "Let it be as you have said." ³⁵That same day he removed all the male goats that were streaked or spotted, and all the speckled or spotted female goats (all that had white on them) and all the dark-colored lambs, and he placed them in the care of his sons. ³⁶Then he put a three-day journey between himself and Jacob, while Jacob continued to tend the rest of Laban's flocks.

³⁷Jacob, however, took fresh-cut branches from poplar, almond and plane trees and made white stripes on them by peeling the bark and exposing the white inner wood of the branches. ³⁸Then he placed the peeled branches in all the watering troughs, so that they would be directly in front of the flocks when they came to drink. When the

flocks were in heat and came to drink, [39] they mated in front of the branches. And they bore young that were streaked or speckled or spotted. [40] Jacob set apart the young of the flock by themselves, but made the rest face the streaked and dark-colored animals that belonged to Laban. Thus he made separate flocks for himself and did not put them with Laban's animals. [41] Whenever the stronger females were in heat, Jacob would place the branches in the troughs in front of the animals so they would mate near the branches, [42] but if the animals were weak, he would not place them there. So the weak animals went to Laban and the strong ones to Jacob. [43] In this way the man grew exceedingly prosperous and came to own large flocks, and maidservants and menservants, and camels and donkeys.

[31:1] JACOB heard that Laban's sons were saying, "Jacob has taken everything our father owned and has gained all this wealth from what belonged to our father." [2] And Jacob noticed that Laban's attitude toward him was not what it had been.

[3] Then the LORD said to Jacob, "Go back to the land of your fathers and to your relatives, and I will be with you."

[4] So Jacob sent word to Rachel and Leah to come out to the fields where his flocks were. [5] He said to them, "I see that your father's attitude toward me is not what it was before, but the God of my father has been with me. [6] You know that I've worked for your father with all my strength, [7] yet your father has cheated me by changing my wages ten times. However, God has not allowed him to harm me. [8] If he said, 'The speckled ones will be your wages,' then all the flocks gave birth to speckled young; and if he said, 'The streaked ones will be your wages,' then all the flocks bore streaked young. [9] So God has taken away your father's livestock and has given them to me.

[10] "In breeding season I once had a dream in which I looked up and saw that the male goats mating with the flock were streaked, speckled or spotted. [11] The angel of God said to me in the dream, 'Jacob.' I answered, 'Here I am.' [12] And he said, 'Look up and see that all the male goats mating with the flock are streaked, speckled or spotted, for I have seen all that Laban has been doing to you. [13] I am the God of Bethel, where you anointed a pillar and where you made a vow to me. Now leave this land at once and go back to your native land.'"

[14] Then Rachel and Leah replied, "Do we still have any share in the inheritance of our father's estate? [15] Does he not regard us as foreigners? Not only has he sold us, but he has used up what was paid for us. [16] Surely all the wealth that God took away from our father belongs to us and our children. So do whatever God has told you."

a 6 Dan here means he has vindicated.   b 8 Naphtali means my struggle.   c 11 Or "A troop is coming!"   d 11 Gad can mean good fortune or a troop.   e 13 Asher means happy.   f 18 Issachar sounds like the Hebrew for reward.   g 20 Zebulun probably means honor.   h 24 Joseph means may he add.   i 27 Or possibly have become rich and

MATTHEW 10:1-25

He [Jesus] called his twelve disciples to him and gave them authority to drive out evil[a] spirits and to heal every disease and sickness.

[2] **These are the names of the twelve apostles: first, Simon (who is called Peter) and his brother Andrew; James son of Zebedee, and his brother John; [3] Philip and Bartholomew; Thomas and Matthew the tax collector; James son of Alphaeus, and Thaddaeus; [4] Simon the Zealot and Judas Iscariot, who betrayed him.**

[5] These twelve Jesus sent out with the following instructions: "Do not go among the Gentiles or enter any town of the Samaritans. [6] Go rather to the lost sheep of Israel. [7] As you go, preach this message: 'The kingdom of heaven is near.' [8] Heal the sick, raise the dead, cleanse those who have leprosy,[b] drive out demons. Freely you have received, freely give. [9] Do not take along any gold or silver or copper in your belts; [10] take

no bag for the journey, or extra tunic, or sandals or a staff; for the worker is worth his keep.

¹¹"Whatever town or village you enter, search for some worthy person there and stay at his house until you leave. ¹²As you enter the home, give it your greeting. ¹³If the home is deserving, let your peace rest on it; if it is not, let your peace return to you. ¹⁴If anyone will not welcome you or listen to your words, shake the dust off your feet when you leave that home or town. ¹⁵I tell you the truth, it will be more bearable for Sodom and Gomorrah on the day of judgment than for that town. ¹⁶I am sending you out like sheep among wolves. Therefore be as shrewd as snakes and as innocent as doves.

¹⁷"Be on your guard against men; they will hand you over to the local councils and flog you in their synagogues. ¹⁸On my account you will be brought before governors and kings as witnesses to them and to the Gentiles. ¹⁹But when they arrest you, do not worry about what to say or how to say it. At that time you will be given what to say, ²⁰for it will not be you speaking, but the Spirit of your Father speaking through you.

²¹"Brother will betray brother to death, and a father his child; children will rebel against their parents and have them put to death. ²²All men will hate you because of me, but he who stands firm to the end will be saved. ²³When you are persecuted in one place, flee to another. I tell you the truth, you will not finish going through the cities of Israel before the Son of Man comes.

²⁴"A student is not above his teacher, nor a servant above his master. ²⁵It is enough for the student to be like his teacher, and the servant like his master. If the head of the house has been called Beelzebub,c how much more the members of his household!"

a1 Greek *unclean*   b8 The Greek word was used for various diseases affecting the skin—not necessarily leprosy.
c25 Greek *Beezeboul* or *Beelzeboul*

PSALM 12:1-8

For the director of music. According to *sheminith.a* A psalm of David.

¹ **H**elp, LORD, for the godly are
        no more;
    the faithful have vanished from
        among men.
² Everyone lies to his neighbor;
    their flattering lips speak with
        deception.

³ May the LORD cut off all flattering
        lips
    and every boastful tongue
⁴ that says, "We will triumph with
        our tongues;
    we own our lipsb—who is our
        master?"

⁵ "Because of the oppression of
        the weak
    and the groaning of the needy,
    I will now arise," says the LORD.
    "I will protect them from those
        who malign them."
⁶ And the words of the LORD are
        flawless,
    like silver refined in a furnace
        of clay,
    purified seven times.

⁷ O LORD, you will keep us safe
    and protect us from such people
        forever.
⁸ The wicked freely strut about
    when what is vile is honored
        among men.

aTitle: Probably a musical term   b4 Or / *our lips are our plowshares*

PROVERBS 3:13-15

¹³ **B**lessed is the man who finds
        wisdom,
    the man who gains understanding,
¹⁴ for she is more profitable
        than silver
    and yields better returns than
        gold.
¹⁵ She is more precious than rubies;
    nothing you desire can compare
        with her.

□ DAY 15

GOD SIGHTINGS

January 15

GENESIS 31:17–32:12

Then Jacob put his children and his wives on camels, [18]and he drove all his livestock ahead of him, along with all the goods he had accumulated in Paddan Aram,[a] to go to his father Isaac in the land of Canaan.

[19]When Laban had gone to shear his sheep, Rachel stole her father's household gods. [20]Moreover, Jacob deceived Laban the Aramean by not telling him he was running away. [21]So he fled with all he had, and crossing the River,[b] he headed for the hill country of Gilead.

[22]On the third day Laban was told that Jacob had fled. [23]Taking his relatives with him, he pursued Jacob for seven days and caught up with him in the hill country of Gilead. [24]Then God came to Laban the Aramean in a dream at night and said to him, "Be careful not to say anything to Jacob, either good or bad."

[25]Jacob had pitched his tent in the hill country of Gilead when Laban overtook him, and Laban and his relatives camped there too. [26]Then Laban said to Jacob, "What have you done? You've deceived me, and you've carried off my daughters like captives in war. [27]Why did you run off secretly and deceive me? Why didn't you tell me, so I could send you away with joy and singing to the music of tambourines and harps? [28]You didn't even let me kiss my grandchildren and my daughters good-by. You have done a foolish thing. [29]I have the power to harm you; but last night the God of your father said to me, 'Be careful not to say anything to Jacob, either good or bad.' [30]Now you have gone off because you longed to return to your father's house. But why did you steal my gods?"

[31]Jacob answered Laban, "I was afraid, because I thought you would take your daughters away from me by force. [32]But

if you find anyone who has your gods, he shall not live. In the presence of our relatives, see for yourself whether there is anything of yours here with me; and if so, take it." Now Jacob did not know that Rachel had stolen the gods.

[33]So Laban went into Jacob's tent and into Leah's tent and into the tent of the two maidservants, but he found nothing. After he came out of Leah's tent, he entered Rachel's tent. [34]Now Rachel had taken the household gods and put them inside her camel's saddle and was sitting on them. Laban searched through everything in the tent but found nothing.

[35]Rachel said to her father, "Don't be angry, my lord, that I cannot stand up in your presence; I'm having my period." So he searched but could not find the household gods.

[36]Jacob was angry and took Laban to task. "What is my crime?" he asked Laban. "What sin have I committed that you hunt me down? [37]Now that you have searched through all my goods, what have you found that belongs to your household? Put it here in front of your relatives and mine, and let them judge between the two of us.

[38]"I have been with you for twenty years now. Your sheep and goats have not miscarried, nor have I eaten rams from your flocks. [39]I did not bring you animals torn by wild beasts; I bore the loss myself. And you demanded payment from me for whatever was stolen by day or night. [40]This was my situation: The heat consumed me in the daytime and the cold at night, and sleep fled from my eyes. [41]It was like this for the twenty years I was in your household. I worked for you fourteen years for your two daughters and six years for your flocks, and you changed my wages ten times. [42]If the God of my father, the God of Abraham and the Fear of Isaac, had not been with me, you would surely have sent me away empty-handed. But God has seen my hardship and the toil of my hands, and last night he rebuked you."

⁴³Laban answered Jacob, "The women are my daughters, the children are my children, and the flocks are my flocks. All you see is mine. Yet what can I do today about these daughters of mine, or about the children they have borne? ⁴⁴Come now, let's make a covenant, you and I, and let it serve as a witness between us."

⁴⁵So Jacob took a stone and set it up as a pillar. ⁴⁶He said to his relatives, "Gather some stones." So they took stones and piled them in a heap, and they ate there by the heap. ⁴⁷Laban called it Jegar Sahadutha,*c* and Jacob called it Galeed.*d*

⁴⁸Laban said, "This heap is a witness between you and me today." That is why it was called Galeed. ⁴⁹It was also called Mizpah,*e* because he said, "May the LORD keep watch between you and me when we are away from each other. ⁵⁰If you mistreat my daughters or if you take any wives besides my daughters, even though no one is with us, remember that God is a witness between you and me."

⁵¹Laban also said to Jacob, "Here is this heap, and here is this pillar I have set up between you and me. ⁵²This heap is a witness, and this pillar is a witness, that I will not go past this heap to your side to harm you and that you will not go past this heap and pillar to my side to harm me. ⁵³May the God of Abraham and the God of Nahor, the God of their father, judge between us."

So Jacob took an oath in the name of the Fear of his father Isaac. ⁵⁴He offered a sacrifice there in the hill country and invited his relatives to a meal. After they had eaten, they spent the night there.

⁵⁵Early the next morning Laban kissed his grandchildren and his daughters and blessed them. Then he left and returned home.

³²:¹Jacob also went on his way, and the angels of God met him. ²When Jacob saw them, he said, "This is the camp of God!" So he named that place Mahanaim.*f*

³Jacob sent messengers ahead of him to his brother Esau in the land of Seir, the country of Edom. ⁴He instructed them: "This is what you are to say to my master Esau: 'Your servant Jacob says, I have been staying with Laban and have remained there till now. ⁵I have cattle and donkeys, sheep and goats, menservants and maidservants. Now I am sending this message to my lord, that I may find favor in your eyes.'"

⁶When the messengers returned to Jacob, they said, "We went to your brother Esau, and now he is coming to meet you, and four hundred men are with him."

⁷In great fear and distress Jacob divided the people who were with him into two groups,*g* and the flocks and herds and camels as well. ⁸He thought, "If Esau comes and attacks one group,*h* the group*h* that is left may escape."

⁹Then Jacob prayed, "O God of my father Abraham, God of my father Isaac, O LORD, who said to me, 'Go back to your country and your relatives, and I will make you prosper,' ¹⁰I am unworthy of all the kindness and faithfulness you have shown your servant. I had only my staff when I crossed this Jordan, but now I have become two groups. ¹¹Save me, I pray, from the hand of my brother Esau, for I am afraid he will come and attack me, and also the mothers with their children. ¹²But you have said, 'I will surely make you prosper and will make your descendants like the sand of the sea, which cannot be counted.'"

a 18 That is, Northwest Mesopotamia   *b 21* That is, the Euphrates   *c 47* The Aramaic *Jegar Sahadutha* means *witness heap.*   *d 47* The Hebrew *Galeed* means *witness heap.*   *e 49* Mizpah means *watchtower.*   *f 2* Mahanaim means *two camps.*   *g 7* Or *camps;* also in verse 10   *h 8* Or *camp*

MATTHEW 10:26–11:6

"So do not be afraid of them [those who persecute you]. There is nothing concealed that will not be disclosed, or hidden that will not be made known. ²⁷What I tell you in the dark, speak in the daylight; what is whispered in your ear, proclaim from the roofs. 28Do not be afraid of those who kill the body but cannot kill the soul. Rather, be afraid of the One who can destroy both soul and body in hell. 29**Are not two sparrows sold for a penny**a**? Yet not one of them will fall to the ground apart from the will of your Father.** 30**And even the very hairs of your head are all numbered.** 31**So don't be afraid; you are worth more than many sparrows.**

32"Whoever acknowledges me before men, I will also acknowledge him before my Father in heaven. 33But whoever disowns me before men, I will disown him before my Father in heaven.

34"Do not suppose that I have come to bring peace to the earth. I did not come to bring peace, but a sword. 35For I have come to turn

"'a man against his father,
    a daughter against her mother,
a daughter-in-law against her
        mother-in-law—
36   a man's enemies will be the
        members of his own
        household.'b

37"Anyone who loves his father or mother more than me is not worthy of me; anyone who loves his son or daughter more than me is not worthy of me; 38and anyone who does not take his cross and follow me is not worthy of me. 39Whoever finds his life will lose it, and whoever loses his life for my sake will find it.

40"He who receives you receives me, and he who receives me receives the one who sent me. 41Anyone who receives a prophet because he is a prophet will receive a prophet's reward, and anyone who receives a righteous man because he is a righteous man will receive a righteous man's reward. 42And if anyone gives even a cup of cold water to one of these little ones because he is my disciple, I tell you the truth, he will certainly not lose his reward."

11:1AFTER Jesus had finished instructing his twelve disciples, he went on from

there to teach and preach in the towns of Galilee.c

2When John heard in prison what Christ was doing, he sent his disciples 3to ask him, "Are you the one who was to come, or should we expect someone else?"

4Jesus replied, "Go back and report to John what you hear and see: 5The blind receive sight, the lame walk, those who have leprosyd are cured, the deaf hear, the dead are raised, and the good news is preached to the poor. 6Blessed is the man who does not fall away on account of me."

a29 Greek an assarion   b36 Micah 7:6   c1 Greek in their towns   d5 The Greek word was used for various diseases affecting the skin—not necessarily leprosy.

PSALM 13:1-6
For the director of music. A psalm of David.

1 How long, O LORD? Will you forget
        me forever?
    How long will you hide your face
        from me?
2How long must I wrestle with my
        thoughts
    and every day have sorrow in my
        heart?
    How long will my enemy triumph
        over me?

3Look on me and answer, O LORD
        my God.
    Give light to my eyes, or I will sleep
        in death;
4my enemy will say, "I have
        overcome him,"
    and my foes will rejoice when
        I fall.

5But I trust in your unfailing love;
    my heart rejoices in your salvation.
6I will sing to the LORD,
    for he has been good to me.

PROVERBS 3:16-18
16Long life is in her [wisdom's] right
        hand;
    in her left hand are riches and
        honor.
17Her ways are pleasant ways,
    and all her paths are peace.

[18]She is a tree of life to those who
   embrace her;
   those who lay hold of her will
   be blessed.

☐ DAY 16

GOD SIGHTINGS

January 16

GENESIS 32:13–34:31

He [Jacob] spent the night there, and from what he had with him he selected a gift for his brother Esau: [14]two hundred female goats and twenty male goats, two hundred ewes and twenty rams, [15]thirty female camels with their young, forty cows and ten bulls, and twenty female donkeys and ten male donkeys. [16]He put them in the care of his servants, each herd by itself, and said to his servants, "Go ahead of me, and keep some space between the herds."

[17]He instructed the one in the lead: "When my brother Esau meets you and asks, 'To whom do you belong, and where are you going, and who owns all these animals in front of you?' [18]then you are to say, 'They belong to your servant Jacob. They are a gift sent to my lord Esau, and he is coming behind us.'"

[19]He also instructed the second, the third and all the others who followed the herds: "You are to say the same thing to Esau when you meet him. [20]And be sure to say, 'Your servant Jacob is coming behind us.'" For he thought, "I will pacify him with these gifts I am sending on ahead; later, when I see him, perhaps he will receive me." [21]So Jacob's gifts went on ahead of him, but he himself spent the night in the camp.

[22]That night Jacob got up and took his two wives, his two maidservants and his eleven sons and crossed the ford of the Jabbok. [23]After he had sent them across the stream, he sent over all his possessions. [24]So Jacob was left alone, and a man wrestled with him till daybreak. [25]When the man saw that he could not overpower him, he touched the socket of Jacob's hip so that his hip was wrenched as he wrestled with the man. [26]Then the man said, "Let me go, for it is daybreak."

But Jacob replied, "I will not let you go unless you bless me."

[27]The man asked him, "What is your name?"

"Jacob," he answered.

[28]Then the man said, "Your name will no longer be Jacob, but Israel,[a] because you have struggled with God and with men and have overcome."

[29]Jacob said, "Please tell me your name."

But he replied, "Why do you ask my name?" Then he blessed him there.

[30]So Jacob called the place Peniel,[b] saying, "It is because I saw God face to face, and yet my life was spared."

[31]The sun rose above him as he passed Peniel,[c] and he was limping because of his hip. [32]Therefore to this day the Israelites do not eat the tendon attached to the socket of the hip, because the socket of Jacob's hip was touched near the tendon.

[33:1]JACOB looked up and there was Esau, coming with his four hundred men; so he divided the children among Leah, Rachel and the two maidservants. [2]He put the maidservants and their children in front, Leah and her children next, and Rachel and Joseph in the rear. [3]He himself went on ahead and bowed down to the ground seven times as he approached his brother.

[4]But Esau ran to meet Jacob and embraced him; he threw his arms around his neck and kissed him. And they wept. [5]Then Esau looked up and saw the women and children. "Who are these with you?" he asked.

Jacob answered, "They are the children God has graciously given your servant."

6Then the maidservants and their children approached and bowed down. 7Next, Leah and her children came and bowed down. Last of all came Joseph and Rachel, and they too bowed down.

8Esau asked, "What do you mean by all these droves I met?"

"To find favor in your eyes, my lord," he said.

9But Esau said, "I already have plenty, my brother. Keep what you have for yourself."

10"No, please!" said Jacob. "If I have found favor in your eyes, accept this gift from me. For to see your face is like seeing the face of God, now that you have received me favorably. 11Please accept the present that was brought to you, for God has been gracious to me and I have all I need." And because Jacob insisted, Esau accepted it.

12Then Esau said, "Let us be on our way; I'll accompany you."

13But Jacob said to him, "My lord knows that the children are tender and that I must care for the ewes and cows that are nursing their young. If they are driven hard just one day, all the animals will die. 14So let my lord go on ahead of his servant, while I move along slowly at the pace of the droves before me and that of the children, until I come to my lord in Seir."

15Esau said, "Then let me leave some of my men with you."

"But why do that?" Jacob asked. "Just let me find favor in the eyes of my lord."

16So that day Esau started on his way back to Seir. 17Jacob, however, went to Succoth, where he built a place for himself and made shelters for his livestock. That is why the place is called Succoth.d

18After Jacob came from Paddan Aram,e he arrived safely at thef city of Shechem in Canaan and camped within sight of the city. 19For a hundred pieces of silver,g he bought from the sons of Hamor, the father of Shechem, the plot of ground where he pitched his tent. 20There he set up an altar and called it El Elohe Israel.h

34:1Now Dinah, the daughter Leah had borne to Jacob, went out to visit the women of the land. 2When Shechem son of Hamor the Hivite, the ruler of that area, saw her, he took her and violated her. 3His heart was drawn to Dinah daughter of Jacob, and he loved the girl and spoke tenderly to her. 4And Shechem said to his father Hamor, "Get me this girl as my wife."

5When Jacob heard that his daughter Dinah had been defiled, his sons were in the fields with his livestock; so he kept quiet about it until they came home.

6Then Shechem's father Hamor went out to talk with Jacob. 7Now Jacob's sons had come in from the fields as soon as they heard what had happened. They were filled with grief and fury, because Shechem had done a disgraceful thing inj Israel by lying with Jacob's daughter—a thing that should not be done.

8But Hamor said to them, "My son Shechem has his heart set on your daughter. Please give her to him as his wife. 9Intermarry with us; give us your daughters and take our daughters for yourselves. 10You can settle among us; the land is open to you. Live in it, tradej in it, and acquire property in it."

11Then Shechem said to Dinah's father and brothers, "Let me find favor in your eyes, and I will give you whatever you ask. 12Make the price for the bride and the gift I am to bring as great as you like, and I'll pay whatever you ask me. Only give me the girl as my wife."

13Because their sister Dinah had been defiled, Jacob's sons replied deceitfully as they spoke to Shechem and his father Hamor. 14They said to them, "We can't do such a thing; we can't give our sister to a man who is not circumcised. That would be a disgrace to us. 15We will give our consent to you on one condition only: that you become like us by circumcising all your males. 16Then we will give you our daughters and take your daughters for ourselves. We'll settle among you and become one people with you. [17]But if you will not agree to be circumcised, we'll take our sister[k] and go."

[18]Their proposal seemed good to Hamor and his son Shechem. [19]The young man, who was the most honored of all his father's household, lost no time in doing what they said, because he was delighted with Jacob's daughter. [20]So Hamor and his son Shechem went to the gate of their city to speak to their fellow townsmen. [21]"These men are friendly toward us," they said. "Let them live in our land and trade in it; the land has plenty of room for them. We can marry their daughters and they can marry ours. [22]But the men will consent to live with us as one people only on the condition that our males be circumcised, as they themselves are. [23]Won't their livestock, their property and all their other animals become ours? So let us give our consent to them, and they will settle among us."

[24]All the men who went out of the city gate agreed with Hamor and his son Shechem, and every male in the city was circumcised.

[25]Three days later, while all of them were still in pain, two of Jacob's sons, Simeon and Levi, Dinah's brothers, took their swords and attacked the unsuspecting city, killing every male. [26]They put Hamor and his son Shechem to the sword and took Dinah from Shechem's house and left. [27]The sons of Jacob came upon the dead bodies and looted the city where[l] their sister had been defiled. [28]They seized their flocks and herds and donkeys and everything else of theirs in the city and out in the fields. [29]They carried off all their wealth and all their women and children, taking as plunder everything in the houses.

[30]Then Jacob said to Simeon and Levi, "You have brought trouble on me by making me a stench to the Canaanites and Perizzites, the people living in this land. We are few in number, and if they join forces against me and attack me, I and my household will be destroyed."

[31]But they replied, "Should he have treated our sister like a prostitute?"

[a]28 Israel means he struggles with God. [b]30 Peniel means face of God. [c]31 Hebrew Penuel, a variant of Peniel [d]17 Succoth means shelters. [e]18 That is, Northwest Mesopotamia [f]18 Or arrived at Shalem, a [g]19 Hebrew hundred kesitahs; a kesitah was a unit of money of unknown weight and value. [h]20 El Elohe Israel can mean God, the God of Israel or mighty is the God of Israel. [i]7 Or against [j]10 Or move about freely; also in verse 21 [k]17 Hebrew daughter [l]27 Or because

MATTHEW 11:7-30

As John's disciples were leaving, Jesus began to speak to the crowd about John: "What did you go out into the desert to see? A reed swayed by the wind? [8]If not, what did you go out to see? A man dressed in fine clothes? No, those who wear fine clothes are in kings' palaces. [9]Then what did you go out to see? A prophet? Yes, I tell you, and more than a prophet. [10]This is the one about whom it is written:

> "'I will send my messenger ahead
>   of you,
>   who will prepare your way
>   before you.'[a]

[11]I tell you the truth: Among those born of women there has not risen anyone greater than John the Baptist; yet he who is least in the kingdom of heaven is greater than he. [12]From the days of John the Baptist until now, the kingdom of heaven has been forcefully advancing, and forceful men lay hold of it. [13]For all the Prophets and the Law prophesied until John. [14]And if you are willing to accept it, he is the Elijah who was to come. [15]He who has ears, let him hear.

[16]"To what can I compare this generation? They are like children sitting in the marketplaces and calling out to others:

> [17]"'We played the flute for you,
>   and you did not dance;
>   we sang a dirge,
>   and you did not mourn.'

[18]For John came neither eating nor drinking, and they say, 'He has a demon.' [19]The Son of Man came eating and drinking, and they say, 'Here is a glutton and a drunkard, a friend of tax

collectors and "sinners."' But wisdom is proved right by her actions."

20Then Jesus began to denounce the cities in which most of his miracles had been performed, because they did not repent. 21"Woe to you, Korazin! Woe to you, Bethsaida! If the miracles that were performed in you had been performed in Tyre and Sidon, they would have repented long ago in sackcloth and ashes. 22But I tell you, it will be more bearable for Tyre and Sidon on the day of judgment than for you. 23And you, Capernaum, will you be lifted up to the skies? No, you will go down to the depths.*b* If the miracles that were performed in you had been performed in Sodom, it would have remained to this day. 24But I tell you that it will be more bearable for Sodom on the day of judgment than for you."

25At that time Jesus said, "I praise you, Father, Lord of heaven and earth, because you have hidden these things from the wise and learned, and revealed them to little children. 26Yes, Father, for this was your good pleasure.

27"All things have been committed to me by my Father. No one knows the Son except the Father, and no one knows the Father except the Son and those to whom the Son chooses to reveal him.

28**"Come to me, all you who are weary and burdened, and I will give you rest. 29Take my yoke upon you and learn from me, for I am gentle and humble in heart, and you will find rest for your souls. 30For my yoke is easy and my burden is light."**

a10 Mal. 3:1   *b23* Greek *Hades*

PSALM 14:1-7
For the director of music. Of David.

¹**T**he fool*a* says in his heart,
   "There is no God."
 They are corrupt, their deeds are vile;
   there is no one who does good.

²The LORD looks down from heaven
   on the sons of men

to see if there are any who
      understand,
   any who seek God.
³All have turned aside,
   they have together become
      corrupt;
 there is no one who does good,
   not even one.

⁴Will evildoers never learn—
   those who devour my people as
      men eat bread
   and who do not call on
      the LORD?
⁵There they are, overwhelmed with
      dread,
   for God is present in the company
      of the righteous.
⁶You evildoers frustrate the plans of
      the poor,
   but the LORD is their refuge.

⁷Oh, that salvation for Israel would
      come out of Zion!
   When the LORD restores the
      fortunes of his people,
   let Jacob rejoice and Israel
      be glad!

a1 The Hebrew words rendered *fool* in Psalms denote one who is morally deficient.

PROVERBS 3:19-20
¹⁹**B**y wisdom the LORD laid the earth's
      foundations,
   by understanding he set the
      heavens in place;
²⁰by his knowledge the deeps were
      divided,
   and the clouds let drop the dew.

□ DAY 17

GOD SIGHTINGS

January 17

GENESIS 35:1–36:43
Then God said to Jacob, "Go up to Bethel and settle there, and build an altar there

to God, who appeared to you when you were fleeing from your brother Esau."

[2] So Jacob said to his household and to all who were with him, "Get rid of the foreign gods you have with you, and purify yourselves and change your clothes. [3] Then come, let us go up to Bethel, where I will build an altar to God, who answered me in the day of my distress and who has been with me wherever I have gone." [4] So they gave Jacob all the foreign gods they had and the rings in their ears, and Jacob buried them under the oak at Shechem. [5] Then they set out, and the terror of God fell upon the towns all around them so that no one pursued them.

[6] Jacob and all the people with him came to Luz (that is, Bethel) in the land of Canaan. [7] There he built an altar, and he called the place El Bethel,[a] because it was there that God revealed himself to him when he was fleeing from his brother.

[8] Now Deborah, Rebekah's nurse, died and was buried under the oak below Bethel. So it was named Allon Bacuth.[b]

[9] After Jacob returned from Paddan Aram,[c] God appeared to him again and blessed him. [10] God said to him, "Your name is Jacob,[d] but you will no longer be called Jacob; your name will be Israel.[e]" So he named him Israel.

[11] And God said to him, "I am God Almighty[f]; be fruitful and increase in number. A nation and a community of nations will come from you, and kings will come from your body. [12] The land I gave to Abraham and Isaac I also give to you, and I will give this land to your descendants after you." [13] Then God went up from him at the place where he had talked with him.

[14] Jacob set up a stone pillar at the place where God had talked with him, and he poured out a drink offering on it; he also poured oil on it. [15] Jacob called the place where God had talked with him Bethel.[g]

[16] Then they moved on from Bethel. While they were still some distance from Ephrath, Rachel began to give birth and had great difficulty. [17] And as she was having great difficulty in childbirth, the midwife said to her, "Don't be afraid, for you have another son." [18] As she breathed her last—for she was dying—she named her son Ben-Oni.[h] But his father named him Benjamin.[i]

[19] So Rachel died and was buried on the way to Ephrath (that is, Bethlehem). [20] Over her tomb Jacob set up a pillar, and to this day that pillar marks Rachel's tomb.

[21] Israel moved on again and pitched his tent beyond Migdal Eder. [22] While Israel was living in that region, Reuben went in and slept with his father's concubine Bilhah, and Israel heard of it.

Jacob had twelve sons:

[23] The sons of Leah:
   Reuben the firstborn of Jacob,
   Simeon, Levi, Judah, Issachar
   and Zebulun.
[24] The sons of Rachel:
   Joseph and Benjamin.
[25] The sons of Rachel's maidservant Bilhah:
   Dan and Naphtali.
[26] The sons of Leah's maidservant Zilpah:
   Gad and Asher.

These were the sons of Jacob, who were born to him in Paddan Aram.

[27] Jacob came home to his father Isaac in Mamre, near Kiriath Arba (that is, Hebron), where Abraham and Isaac had stayed. [28] Isaac lived a hundred and eighty years. [29] Then he breathed his last and died and was gathered to his people, old and full of years. And his sons Esau and Jacob buried him.

[36:1] THIS is the account of Esau (that is, Edom).

[2] Esau took his wives from the women of Canaan: Adah daughter of Elon the Hittite, and Oholi-

bamah daughter of Anah and granddaughter of Zibeon the Hivite— ³also Basemath daughter of Ishmael and sister of Nebaioth.

⁴Adah bore Eliphaz to Esau, Basemath bore Reuel, ⁵and Oholibamah bore Jeush, Jalam and Korah. These were the sons of Esau, who were born to him in Canaan.

⁶ Esau took his wives and sons and daughters and all the members of his household, as well as his livestock and all his other animals and all the goods he had acquired in Canaan, and moved to a land some distance from his brother Jacob. ⁷ Their possessions were too great for them to remain together; the land where they were staying could not support them both because of their livestock. ⁸So Esau (that is, Edom) settled in the hill country of Seir.

⁹This is the account of Esau the father of the Edomites in the hill country of Seir.

¹⁰These are the names of Esau's sons:
   Eliphaz, the son of Esau's wife Adah, and Reuel, the son of Esau's wife Basemath.
¹¹The sons of Eliphaz:
   Teman, Omar, Zepho, Gatam and Kenaz.
¹²Esau's son Eliphaz also had a concubine named Timna, who bore him Amalek. These were grandsons of Esau's wife Adah.
¹³The sons of Reuel:
   Nahath, Zerah, Shammah and Mizzah. These were grandsons of Esau's wife Basemath.
¹⁴The sons of Esau's wife Oholibamah daughter of Anah and granddaughter of Zibeon, whom she bore to Esau:
   Jeush, Jalam and Korah.

¹⁵These were the chiefs among Esau's descendants:

The sons of Eliphaz the firstborn of Esau:
   Chiefs Teman, Omar, Zepho, Kenaz, ¹⁶Korah,ʲ Gatam and Amalek. These were the chiefs descended from Eliphaz in Edom; they were grandsons of Adah.
¹⁷The sons of Esau's son Reuel:
   Chiefs Nahath, Zerah, Shammah and Mizzah. These were the chiefs descended from Reuel in Edom; they were grandsons of Esau's wife Basemath.
¹⁸The sons of Esau's wife Oholibamah:
   Chiefs Jeush, Jalam and Korah. These were the chiefs descended from Esau's wife Oholibamah daughter of Anah.

¹⁹These were the sons of Esau (that is, Edom), and these were their chiefs.

²⁰These were the sons of Seir the Horite, who were living in the region:
   Lotan, Shobal, Zibeon, Anah, ²¹Dishon, Ezer and Dishan. These sons of Seir in Edom were Horite chiefs.
²²The sons of Lotan:
   Hori and Homam.ᵏ Timna was Lotan's sister.
²³The sons of Shobal:
   Alvan, Manahath, Ebal, Shepho and Onam.
²⁴The sons of Zibeon:
   Aiah and Anah. This is the Anah who discovered the hot springsˡ in the desert while he was grazing the donkeys of his father Zibeon.
²⁵The children of Anah:
   Dishon and Oholibamah daughter of Anah.
²⁶The sons of Dishonᵐ:
   Hemdan, Eshban, Ithran and Keran.
²⁷The sons of Ezer:
   Bilhan, Zaavan and Akan.

28 The sons of Dishan:
Uz and Aran.

29 These were the Horite chiefs:
Lotan, Shobal, Zibeon, Anah, 30Dishon, Ezer and Dishan. These were the Horite chiefs, according to their divisions, in the land of Seir.

31 These were the kings who reigned in Edom before any Israelite king reigned[n]:

32 Bela son of Beor became king of Edom. His city was named Dinhabah.

33 When Bela died, Jobab son of Zerah from Bozrah succeeded him as king.

34 When Jobab died, Husham from the land of the Temanites succeeded him as king.

35 When Husham died, Hadad son of Bedad, who defeated Midian in the country of Moab, succeeded him as king. His city was named Avith.

36 When Hadad died, Samlah from Masrekah succeeded him as king.

37 When Samlah died, Shaul from Rehoboth on the river[o] succeeded him as king.

38 When Shaul died, Baal-Hanan son of Acbor succeeded him as king.

39 When Baal-Hanan son of Acbor died, Hadad[p] succeeded him as king. His city was named Pau, and his wife's name was Mehetabel daughter of Matred, the daughter of Me-Zahab.

40 These were the chiefs descended from Esau, by name, according to their clans and regions:
Timna, Alvah, Jetheth, 41Oholibamah, Elah, Pinon, 42Kenaz, Teman, Mibzar, 43Magdiel and Iram. These were the chiefs of Edom, according to their settlements in the land they occupied.

This was Esau the father of the Edomites.

a7 El Bethel means God of Bethel.   b8 Allon Bacuth means oak of weeping.   c9 That is, Northwest Mesopotamia; also in verse 26   d10 Jacob means he grasps the heel (figuratively, he deceives).   e10 Israel means he struggles with God.   f11 Hebrew El-Shaddai   g15 Bethel means house of God.   h18 Ben-Oni means son of my trouble.   i18 Benjamin means son of my right hand.   j16 Masoretic Text; Samaritan Pentateuch (see also Gen. 36:11 and 1 Chron. 1:36) does not have Korah.   k22 Hebrew Hemam, a variant of Homam (see 1 Chron. 1:39)   l24 Vulgate; Syriac discovered water; the meaning of the Hebrew for this word is uncertain.   m26 Hebrew Dishan, a variant of Dishon   n31 Or before an Israelite king reigned over them   o37 Possibly the Euphrates   p39 Many manuscripts of the Masoretic Text, Samaritan Pentateuch and Syriac (see also 1 Chron. 1:50); most manuscripts of the Masoretic Text Hadar

MATTHEW 12:1-21

At that time Jesus went through the grainfields on the Sabbath. His disciples were hungry and began to pick some heads of grain and eat them. 2 When the Pharisees saw this, they said to him, "Look! Your disciples are doing what is unlawful on the Sabbath."

3 He answered, "Haven't you read what David did when he and his companions were hungry? 4 He entered the house of God, and he and his companions ate the consecrated bread—which was not lawful for them to do, but only for the priests. 5 Or haven't you read in the Law that on the Sabbath the priests in the temple desecrate the day and yet are innocent? 6 **I tell you that one[a] greater than the temple is here.** 7 **If you had known what these words mean, 'I desire mercy, not sacrifice,'[b] you would not have condemned the innocent.** 8 **For the Son of Man is Lord of the Sabbath."**

9 Going on from that place, he went into their synagogue, 10 and a man with a shriveled hand was there. Looking for a reason to accuse Jesus, they asked him, "Is it lawful to heal on the Sabbath?"

11 He said to them, "If any of you has a sheep and it falls into a pit on the Sabbath, will you not take hold of it and lift it out? 12 How much more valuable is a man than a sheep! Therefore it is lawful to do good on the Sabbath."

13 Then he said to the man, "Stretch out your hand." So he stretched it out

and it was completely restored, just as sound as the other. ¹⁴But the Pharisees went out and plotted how they might kill Jesus.

¹⁵Aware of this, Jesus withdrew from that place. Many followed him, and he healed all their sick, ¹⁶warning them not to tell who he was. ¹⁷This was to fulfill what was spoken through the prophet Isaiah:

¹⁸"Here is my servant whom I have chosen,
>   the one I love, in whom I delight;
> I will put my Spirit on him,
>   and he will proclaim justice to the nations.
¹⁹He will not quarrel or cry out;
>   no one will hear his voice in the streets.
²⁰A bruised reed he will not break,
>   and a smoldering wick he will not snuff out,
> till he leads justice to victory.
²¹   In his name the nations will put their hope."^c

^a6 Or *something*; also in verses 41 and 42   ^b7 Hosea 6:6
^c21 Isaiah 42:1-4

PSALM 15:1-5
A psalm of David.

¹LORD, who may dwell in your sanctuary?
> Who may live on your holy hill?

²He whose walk is blameless
>   and who does what is righteous,
> who speaks the truth from his heart
³   and has no slander on his tongue,
> who does his neighbor no wrong
>   and casts no slur on his fellowman,
⁴who despises a vile man
>   but honors those who fear the LORD,
> who keeps his oath
>   even when it hurts,
⁵who lends his money without usury
>   and does not accept a bribe
>   against the innocent.

He who does these things
> will never be shaken.

PROVERBS 3:21-26
²¹My son, preserve sound judgment
>   and discernment,
> do not let them out of your sight;
²²they will be life for you,
>   an ornament to grace your neck.
²³Then you will go on your way in safety,
>   and your foot will not stumble;
²⁴when you lie down, you will not be afraid;
>   when you lie down, your sleep will be sweet.
²⁵Have no fear of sudden disaster
>   or of the ruin that overtakes the wicked,
²⁶for the LORD will be your confidence
>   and will keep your foot from being snared.

□ DAY 18

GOD SIGHTINGS

January 18

GENESIS 37:1-38:30
Jacob lived in the land where his father had stayed, the land of Canaan.

²This is the account of Jacob.

Joseph, a young man of seventeen, was tending the flocks with his brothers, the sons of Bilhah and the sons of Zilpah, his father's wives, and he brought their father a bad report about them.

³Now Israel loved Joseph more than any of his other sons, because he had been born to him in his old age; and he made a richly ornamented^a robe for him. ⁴When his brothers saw that their father loved him more than any of them, they hated him and could not speak a kind word to him.

⁵Joseph had a dream, and when he told it to his brothers, they hated him all the more. ⁶He said to them, "Listen to this dream I had: ⁷We were binding

sheaves of grain out in the field when suddenly my sheaf rose and stood upright, while your sheaves gathered around mine and bowed down to it."

8His brothers said to him, "Do you intend to reign over us? Will you actually rule us?" And they hated him all the more because of his dream and what he had said.

9Then he had another dream, and he told it to his brothers. "Listen," he said, "I had another dream, and this time the sun and moon and eleven stars were bowing down to me."

10When he told his father as well as his brothers, his father rebuked him and said, "What is this dream you had? Will your mother and I and your brothers actually come and bow down to the ground before you?" 11His brothers were jealous of him, but his father kept the matter in mind.

12Now his brothers had gone to graze their father's flocks near Shechem, 13and Israel said to Joseph, "As you know, your brothers are grazing the flocks near Shechem. Come, I am going to send you to them."

"Very well," he replied.

14So he said to him, "Go and see if all is well with your brothers and with the flocks, and bring word back to me." Then he sent him off from the Valley of Hebron.

When Joseph arrived at Shechem, 15a man found him wandering around in the fields and asked him, "What are you looking for?"

16He replied, "I'm looking for my brothers. Can you tell me where they are grazing their flocks?"

17"They have moved on from here," the man answered. "I heard them say, 'Let's go to Dothan.'"

So Joseph went after his brothers and found them near Dothan. 18But they saw him in the distance, and before he reached them, they plotted to kill him.

19"Here comes that dreamer!" they said to each other. 20"Come now, let's kill him and throw him into one of these cisterns and say that a ferocious animal devoured him. Then we'll see what comes of his dreams."

21When Reuben heard this, he tried to rescue him from their hands. "Let's not take his life," he said. 22"Don't shed any blood. Throw him into this cistern here in the desert, but don't lay a hand on him." Reuben said this to rescue him from them and take him back to his father.

23So when Joseph came to his brothers, they stripped him of his robe—the richly ornamented robe he was wearing— 24and they took him and threw him into the cistern. Now the cistern was empty; there was no water in it.

25As they sat down to eat their meal, they looked up and saw a caravan of Ishmaelites coming from Gilead. Their camels were loaded with spices, balm and myrrh, and they were on their way to take them down to Egypt.

26Judah said to his brothers, "What will we gain if we kill our brother and cover up his blood? 27Come, let's sell him to the Ishmaelites and not lay our hands on him; after all, he is our brother, our own flesh and blood." His brothers agreed.

28So when the Midianite merchants came by, his brothers pulled Joseph up out of the cistern and sold him for twenty shekels*b* of silver to the Ishmaelites, who took him to Egypt.

29When Reuben returned to the cistern and saw that Joseph was not there, he tore his clothes. 30He went back to his brothers and said, "The boy isn't there! Where can I turn now?"

31Then they got Joseph's robe, slaughtered a goat and dipped the robe in the blood. 32They took the ornamented robe back to their father and said, "We found this. Examine it to see whether it is your son's robe."

33He recognized it and said, "It is my son's robe! Some ferocious animal has devoured him. Joseph has surely been torn to pieces."

34Then Jacob tore his clothes, put on sackcloth and mourned for his son many days. 35All his sons and daughters came to comfort him, but he refused to be comforted. "No," he said, "in mourning will I go down to the grave[c] to my son." So his father wept for him.

[36]Meanwhile, the Midianites[d] sold Joseph in Egypt to Potiphar, one of Pharaoh's officials, the captain of the guard.

38:[1]AT that time, Judah left his brothers and went down to stay with a man of Adullam named Hirah. [2]There Judah met the daughter of a Canaanite man named Shua. He married her and lay with her; [3]she became pregnant and gave birth to a son, who was named Er. [4]She conceived again and gave birth to a son and named him Onan. [5]She gave birth to still another son and named him Shelah. It was at Kezib that she gave birth to him.

[6]Judah got a wife for Er, his firstborn, and her name was Tamar. [7]But Er, Judah's firstborn, was wicked in the LORD's sight; so the LORD put him to death.

[8]Then Judah said to Onan, "Lie with your brother's wife and fulfill your duty to her as a brother-in-law to produce offspring for your brother." [9]But Onan knew that the offspring would not be his; so whenever he lay with his brother's wife, he spilled his semen on the ground to keep from producing offspring for his brother. [10]What he did was wicked in the LORD's sight; so he put him to death also.

[11]Judah then said to his daughter-in-law Tamar, "Live as a widow in your father's house until my son Shelah grows up." For he thought, "He may die too, just like his brothers." So Tamar went to live in her father's house.

[12]After a long time Judah's wife, the daughter of Shua, died. When Judah had recovered from his grief, he went up to Timnah, to the men who were shearing his sheep, and his friend Hirah the Adullamite went with him. [13]When Tamar was told, "Your father-in-law is on his way to Timnah to shear his sheep," [14]she took off her widow's clothes, covered herself with a veil to disguise herself, and then sat down at the entrance to Enaim, which is on the road to Timnah. For she saw that, though Shelah had now grown up, she had not been given to him as his wife.

[15]When Judah saw her, he thought she was a prostitute, for she had covered her face. [16]Not realizing that she was his daughter-in-law, he went over to her by the roadside and said, "Come now, let me sleep with you."

"And what will you give me to sleep with you?" she asked.

[17]"I'll send you a young goat from my flock," he said.

"Will you give me something as a pledge until you send it?" she asked.

[18]He said, "What pledge should I give you?"

"Your seal and its cord, and the staff in your hand," she answered. So he gave them to her and slept with her, and she became pregnant by him. [19]After she left, she took off her veil and put on her widow's clothes again.

[20]Meanwhile Judah sent the young goat by his friend the Adullamite in order to get his pledge back from the woman, but he did not find her. [21]He asked the men who lived there, "Where is the shrine prostitute who was beside the road at Enaim?"

"There hasn't been any shrine prostitute here," they said.

[22]So he went back to Judah and said, "I didn't find her. Besides, the men who lived there said, 'There hasn't been any shrine prostitute here.'"

[23]Then Judah said, "Let her keep what she has, or we will become a laughingstock. After all, I did send her this young goat, but you didn't find her."

[24]About three months later Judah was told, "Your daughter-in-law Tamar is guilty of prostitution, and as a result she is now pregnant."

Judah said, "Bring her out and have her burned to death!"

[25]As she was being brought out, she sent a message to her father-in-law. "I am pregnant by the man who owns

these," she said. And she added, "See if you recognize whose seal and cord and staff these are."

26 Judah recognized them and said, "She is more righteous than I, since I wouldn't give her to my son Shelah." And he did not sleep with her again.

27 When the time came for her to give birth, there were twin boys in her womb. 28 As she was giving birth, one of them put out his hand; so the midwife took a scarlet thread and tied it on his wrist and said, "This one came out first." 29 But when he drew back his hand, his brother came out, and she said, "So this is how you have broken out!" And he was named Perez.*e* 30 Then his brother, who had the scarlet thread on his wrist, came out and he was given the name Zerah.*f*

a3 The meaning of the Hebrew for *richly ornamented* is uncertain; also in verses 23 and 32. *b28* That is, about 8 ounces (about 0.2 kilogram) *c35* Hebrew *Sheol* *d36* Samaritan Pentateuch, Septuagint, Vulgate and Syriac (see also verse 28); Masoretic Text *Medanites* *e29 Perez* means *breaking out.* *f30 Zerah* can mean *scarlet* or *brightness.*

MATTHEW 12:22-45

Then they [the crowds] brought him [Jesus] a demon-possessed man who was blind and mute, and Jesus healed him, so that he could both talk and see. 23 All the people were astonished and said, "Could this be the Son of David?"

24 But when the Pharisees heard this, they said, "It is only by Beelzebub,*a* the prince of demons, that this fellow drives out demons."

25 Jesus knew their thoughts and said to them, "Every kingdom divided against itself will be ruined, and every city or household divided against itself will not stand. 26 If Satan drives out Satan, he is divided against himself. How then can his kingdom stand? 27 And if I drive out demons by Beelzebub, by whom do your people drive them out? So then, they will be your judges. 28 But if I drive out demons by the Spirit of God, then the kingdom of God has come upon you.

29 "Or again, how can anyone enter a strong man's house and carry off his possessions unless he first ties up the strong man? Then he can rob his house.

30 "He who is not with me is against me, and he who does not gather with me scatters. 31 And so I tell you, every sin and blasphemy will be forgiven men, but the blasphemy against the Spirit will not be forgiven. 32 Anyone who speaks a word against the Son of Man will be forgiven, but anyone who speaks against the Holy Spirit will not be forgiven, either in this age or in the age to come.

33 "Make a tree good and its fruit will be good, or make a tree bad and its fruit will be bad, for a tree is recognized by its fruit. 34 You brood of vipers, how can you who are evil say anything good? For out of the overflow of the heart the mouth speaks. 35 **The good man brings good things out of the good stored up in him, and the evil man brings evil things out of the evil stored up in him.** 36 But I tell you that men will have to give account on the day of judgment for every careless word they have spoken. 37 For by your words you will be acquitted, and by your words you will be condemned."

38 Then some of the Pharisees and teachers of the law said to him, "Teacher, we want to see a miraculous sign from you."

39 He answered, "A wicked and adulterous generation asks for a miraculous sign! But none will be given it except the sign of the prophet Jonah. 40 For as Jonah was three days and three nights in the belly of a huge fish, so the Son of Man will be three days and three nights in the heart of the earth. 41 The men of Nineveh will stand up at the judgment with this generation and condemn it; for they repented at the preaching of Jonah, and now one*b* greater than Jonah is here. 42 The Queen of the South will rise at the judgment with this generation and condemn it; for she came from the ends of the earth to listen to Solomon's wisdom, and now one greater than Solomon is here.

43 "When an evil*c* spirit comes out of

a man, it goes through arid places seeking rest and does not find it. ⁴⁴Then it says, 'I will return to the house I left.' When it arrives, it finds the house unoccupied, swept clean and put in order. ⁴⁵Then it goes and takes with it seven other spirits more wicked than itself, and they go in and live there. And the final condition of that man is worse than the first. That is how it will be with this wicked generation."

a24 Greek *Beezeboul* or *Beelzeboul*; also in verse 27
b41 Or *something*; also in verse 42   *c43* Greek *unclean*

PSALM 16:1-11

A *miktam*ᵃ of David.

¹ **K**eep me safe, O God,
    for in you I take refuge.

² I said to the Lᴏʀᴅ, "You are my Lord;
    apart from you I have no good
        thing."
³ As for the saints who are in the land,
    they are the glorious ones in
        whom is all my delight.ᵇ
⁴ The sorrows of those will increase
    who run after other gods.
  I will not pour out their libations of
        blood
    or take up their names on my lips.

⁵ Lᴏʀᴅ, you have assigned me my
        portion and my cup;
    you have made my lot secure.
⁶ The boundary lines have fallen for
        me in pleasant places;
    surely I have a delightful
        inheritance.

⁷ I will praise the Lᴏʀᴅ, who counsels
        me;
    even at night my heart instructs
        me.
⁸ I have set the Lᴏʀᴅ always before me.
    Because he is at my right hand,
    I will not be shaken.

⁹ Therefore my heart is glad and my
        tongue rejoices;
    my body also will rest secure,
¹⁰ because you will not abandon me to
        the grave,ᶜ
    nor will you let your Holy Oneᵈ see
        decay.

¹¹ You have madeᵉ known to me the
        path of life;
    you will fill me with joy in your
        presence,
    with eternal pleasures at your right
        hand.

*a*Title: Probably a literary or musical term   *b3* Or *As for the pagan priests who are in the land / and the nobles in whom all delight, I said:*   *c10* Hebrew *Sheol*   *d10* Or *your faithful one*   *e11* Or *You will make*

PROVERBS 3:27-32

²⁷ **D**o not withhold good from those
        who deserve it,
    when it is in your power to act.
²⁸ Do not say to your neighbor,
    "Come back later; I'll give it
        tomorrow"—
    when you now have it with you.

²⁹ Do not plot harm against your
        neighbor,
    who lives trustfully near you.
³⁰ Do not accuse a man for no reason—
    when he has done you no harm.

³¹ Do not envy a violent man
    or choose any of his ways,
³² for the Lᴏʀᴅ detests a perverse man
    but takes the upright into his
        confidence.

☐ D A Y   1 9

GOD SIGHTINGS

January 19

GENESIS 39:1–41:16

Now Joseph had been taken down to Egypt. Potiphar, an Egyptian who was one of Pharaoh's officials, the captain of the guard, bought him from the Ishmaelites who had taken him there.

² The Lᴏʀᴅ was with Joseph and he prospered, and he lived in the house of his Egyptian master. ³ When his master saw that the Lᴏʀᴅ was with him and that the Lᴏʀᴅ gave him success in everything he did, ⁴ Joseph found favor in his eyes and became his attendant. Potiphar put

him in charge of his household, and he entrusted to his care everything he owned. 5From the time he put him in charge of his household and of all that he owned, the LORD blessed the household of the Egyptian because of Joseph. The blessing of the LORD was on everything Potiphar had, both in the house and in the field. 6So he left in Joseph's care everything he had; with Joseph in charge, he did not concern himself with anything except the food he ate.

Now Joseph was well-built and handsome, 7and after a while his master's wife took notice of Joseph and said, "Come to bed with me!"

8But he refused. "With me in charge," he told her, "my master does not concern himself with anything in the house; everything he owns he has entrusted to my care. 9No one is greater in this house than I am. My master has withheld nothing from me except you, because you are his wife. How then could I do such a wicked thing and sin against God?" 10And though she spoke to Joseph day after day, he refused to go to bed with her or even be with her.

11One day he went into the house to attend to his duties, and none of the household servants was inside. 12She caught him by his cloak and said, "Come to bed with me!" But he left his cloak in her hand and ran out of the house.

13When she saw that he had left his cloak in her hand and had run out of the house, 14she called her household servants. "Look," she said to them, "this Hebrew has been brought to us to make sport of us! He came in here to sleep with me, but I screamed. 15When he heard me scream for help, he left his cloak beside me and ran out of the house."

16She kept his cloak beside her until his master came home. 17Then she told him this story: "That Hebrew slave you brought us came to me to make sport of me. 18But as soon as I screamed for help, he left his cloak beside me and ran out of the house."

19When his master heard the story his wife told him, saying, " This is how

your slave treated me," he burned with anger. 20**Joseph's master took him and put him in prison, the place where the king's prisoners were confined.**

But while Joseph was there in the prison, 21the LORD was with him; he showed him kindness and granted him favor in the eyes of the prison warden. 22So the warden put Joseph in charge of all those held in the prison, and he was made responsible for all that was done there. 23The warden paid no attention to anything under Joseph's care, because the LORD was with Joseph and gave him success in whatever he did.

40:1SOME time later, the cupbearer and the baker of the king of Egypt offended their master, the king of Egypt. 2Pharaoh was angry with his two officials, the chief cupbearer and the chief baker, 3and put them in custody in the house of the captain of the guard, in the same prison where Joseph was confined. 4The captain of the guard assigned them to Joseph, and he attended them.

After they had been in custody for some time, 5each of the two men—the cupbearer and the baker of the king of Egypt, who were being held in prison—had a dream the same night, and each dream had a meaning of its own.

6When Joseph came to them the next morning, he saw that they were dejected. 7So he asked Pharaoh's officials who were in custody with him in his master's house, "Why are your faces so sad today?"

8"We both had dreams," they answered, "but there is no one to interpret them."

Then Joseph said to them, "Do not interpretations belong to God? Tell me your dreams."

9So the chief cupbearer told Joseph his dream. He said to him, "In my dream I saw a vine in front of me, 10and on the vine were three branches. As soon as it budded, it blossomed, and its clusters ripened into grapes. 11Pharaoh's cup was in my hand, and I took the grapes, squeezed them into Pharaoh's cup and put the cup in his hand."

12"This is what it means," Joseph said to him. "The three branches are three days. 13Within three days Pharaoh will lift up your head and restore you to your position, and you will put Pharaoh's cup in his hand, just as you used to do when you were his cupbearer. 14But when all goes well with you, remember me and show me kindness; mention me to Pharaoh and get me out of this prison. 15For I was forcibly carried off from the land of the Hebrews, and even here I have done nothing to deserve being put in a dungeon."

16When the chief baker saw that Joseph had given a favorable interpretation, he said to Joseph, "I too had a dream: On my head were three baskets of bread.a 17In the top basket were all kinds of baked goods for Pharaoh, but the birds were eating them out of the basket on my head."

18"This is what it means," Joseph said. "The three baskets are three days. 19Within three days Pharaoh will lift off your head and hang you on a tree.b And the birds will eat away your flesh."

20Now the third day was Pharaoh's birthday, and he gave a feast for all his officials. He lifted up the heads of the chief cupbearer and the chief baker in the presence of his officials: 21He restored the chief cupbearer to his position, so that he once again put the cup into Pharaoh's hand, 22but he hangedc the chief baker, just as Joseph had said to them in his interpretation.

23The chief cupbearer, however, did not remember Joseph; he forgot him.

41:1WHEN two full years had passed, Pharaoh had a dream: He was standing by the Nile, 2when out of the river there came up seven cows, sleek and fat, and they grazed among the reeds. 3After them, seven other cows, ugly and gaunt, came up out of the Nile and stood beside those on the riverbank. 4And the cows that were ugly and gaunt ate up the seven sleek, fat cows. Then Pharaoh woke up.

5He fell asleep again and had a second dream: Seven heads of grain, healthy and good, were growing on a single stalk. 6After them, seven other heads of grain sprouted—thin and scorched by the east wind. 7The thin heads of grain swallowed up the seven healthy, full heads. Then Pharaoh woke up; it had been a dream.

8In the morning his mind was troubled, so he sent for all the magicians and wise men of Egypt. Pharaoh told them his dreams, but no one could interpret them for him.

9Then the chief cupbearer said to Pharaoh, "Today I am reminded of my shortcomings. 10Pharaoh was once angry with his servants, and he imprisoned me and the chief baker in the house of the captain of the guard. 11Each of us had a dream the same night, and each dream had a meaning of its own. 12Now a young Hebrew was there with us, a servant of the captain of the guard. We told him our dreams, and he interpreted them for us, giving each man the interpretation of his dream. 13And things turned out exactly as he interpreted them to us: I was restored to my position, and the other man was hanged.c"

14So Pharaoh sent for Joseph, and he was quickly brought from the dungeon. When he had shaved and changed his clothes, he came before Pharaoh.

15Pharaoh said to Joseph, "I had a dream, and no one can interpret it. But I have heard it said of you that when you hear a dream you can interpret it."

16"I cannot do it," Joseph replied to Pharaoh, "but God will give Pharaoh the answer he desires."

a16 Or three wicker baskets   b19 Or and impale you on a pole   c22 Or impaled

MATTHEW 12:46–13:23

While Jesus was still talking to the crowd, his mother and brothers stood outside, wanting to speak to him. 47Someone told him, "Your mother and brothers are standing outside, wanting to speak to you."a

48He replied to him, "Who is my

mother, and who are my brothers?" [49]Pointing to his disciples, he said, "Here are my mother and my brothers. [50]For whoever does the will of my Father in heaven is my brother and sister and mother."

[13:1]THAT same day Jesus went out of the house and sat by the lake. [2]Such large crowds gathered around him that he got into a boat and sat in it, while all the people stood on the shore. [3]Then he told them many things in parables, saying: "A farmer went out to sow his seed. [4]As he was scattering the seed, some fell along the path, and the birds came and ate it up. [5]Some fell on rocky places, where it did not have much soil. It sprang up quickly, because the soil was shallow. [6]But when the sun came up, the plants were scorched, and they withered because they had no root. [7]Other seed fell among thorns, which grew up and choked the plants. [8]Still other seed fell on good soil, where it produced a crop— a hundred, sixty or thirty times what was sown. [9]He who has ears, let him hear."

[10]The disciples came to him and asked, "Why do you speak to the people in parables?"

[11]He replied, "The knowledge of the secrets of the kingdom of heaven has been given to you, but not to them. [12]Whoever has will be given more, and he will have an abundance. Whoever does not have, even what he has will be taken from him. [13]This is why I speak to them in parables:

"Though seeing, they do not see;
    though hearing, they do not hear
        or understand.

[14]In them is fulfilled the prophecy of Isaiah:

"'You will be ever hearing but never
        understanding;
    you will be ever seeing but never
        perceiving.
[15]For this people's heart has become
        calloused;
    they hardly hear with their ears,

and they have closed their eyes.
Otherwise they might see with
        their eyes,
    hear with their ears,
    understand with their hearts
and turn, and I would heal them.'[b]

[16]But blessed are your eyes because they see, and your ears because they hear. [17]For I tell you the truth, many prophets and righteous men longed to see what you see but did not see it, and to hear what you hear but did not hear it.

[18]"Listen then to what the parable of the sower means: [19]When anyone hears the message about the kingdom and does not understand it, the evil one comes and snatches away what was sown in his heart. This is the seed sown along the path. [20]The one who received the seed that fell on rocky places is the man who hears the word and at once receives it with joy. [21]But since he has no root, he lasts only a short time. When trouble or persecution comes because of the word, he quickly falls away. [22]The one who received the seed that fell among the thorns is the man who hears the word, but the worries of this life and the deceitfulness of wealth choke it, making it unfruitful. [23]But the one who received the seed that fell on good soil is the man who hears the word and understands it. He produces a crop, yielding a hundred, sixty or thirty times what was sown."

[a]47 Some manuscripts do not have verse 47.
[b]15 Isaiah 6:9,10

PSALM 17:1-15
A prayer of David.

[1]Hear, O LORD, my righteous plea;
    listen to my cry.
Give ear to my prayer—
    it does not rise from deceitful lips.
[2]May my vindication come
        from you;
    may your eyes see what is right.

[3]Though you probe my heart and
        examine me at night,
    though you test me, you will find
        nothing;

I have resolved that my mouth
    will not sin.
4 As for the deeds of men—
    by the word of your lips
I have kept myself
    from the ways of the violent.
5 My steps have held to your paths;
    my feet have not slipped.

6 I call on you, O God, for you will
    answer me;
    give ear to me and hear my prayer.
7 Show the wonder of your great love,
    you who save by your right hand
    those who take refuge in you from
        their foes.
8 Keep me as the apple of your eye;
    hide me in the shadow of your
        wings
9 from the wicked who assail me,
    from my mortal enemies who
        surround me.

10 They close up their callous hearts,
    and their mouths speak with
        arrogance.
11 They have tracked me down, they
        now surround me,
    with eyes alert, to throw me to
        the ground.
12 They are like a lion hungry for prey,
    like a great lion crouching in
        cover.

13 Rise up, O LORD, confront them, bring
        them down;
    rescue me from the wicked by
        your sword.
14 O LORD, by your hand save me from
        such men,
    from men of this world whose
        reward is in this life.

    You still the hunger of those you
        cherish;
    their sons have plenty,
    and they store up wealth for their
        children.
15 And I—in righteousness I will see
        your face;
    when I awake, I will be satisfied
        with seeing your likeness.

PROVERBS 3:33-35
33 The LORD's curse is on the house of
        the wicked,
    but he blesses the home of the
        righteous.
34 He mocks proud mockers
    but gives grace to the humble.
35 The wise inherit honor,
    but fools he holds up to shame.

□ DAY 20

GOD SIGHTINGS

January 20

GENESIS 41:17–42:17

Then Pharaoh said to Joseph, "In my dream I was standing on the bank of the Nile, 18 when out of the river there came up seven cows, fat and sleek, and they grazed among the reeds. 19 After them, seven other cows came up—scrawny and very ugly and lean. I had never seen such ugly cows in all the land of Egypt. 20 The lean, ugly cows ate up the seven fat cows that came up first. 21 But even after they ate them, no one could tell that they had done so; they looked just as ugly as before. Then I woke up.

22 "In my dreams I also saw seven heads of grain, full and good, growing on a single stalk. 23 After them, seven other heads sprouted—withered and thin and scorched by the east wind. 24 The thin heads of grain swallowed up the seven good heads. I told this to the magicians, but none could explain it to me."

25 Then Joseph said to Pharaoh, "The dreams of Pharaoh are one and the same. God has revealed to Pharaoh what he is about to do. 26 The seven good cows are seven years, and the seven good heads of grain are seven years; it is one and the same dream. 27 The seven lean, ugly cows that came up afterward are seven years, and so are the seven worthless heads of grain

scorched by the east wind: They are seven years of famine.

28 "It is just as I said to Pharaoh: God has shown Pharaoh what he is about to do. 29 Seven years of great abundance are coming throughout the land of Egypt, 30 but seven years of famine will follow them. Then all the abundance in Egypt will be forgotten, and the famine will ravage the land. 31 The abundance in the land will not be remembered, because the famine that follows it will be so severe. 32 The reason the dream was given to Pharaoh in two forms is that the matter has been firmly decided by God, and God will do it soon.

33 "And now let Pharaoh look for a discerning and wise man and put him in charge of the land of Egypt. 34 Let Pharaoh appoint commissioners over the land to take a fifth of the harvest of Egypt during the seven years of abundance. 35 They should collect all the food of these good years that are coming and store up the grain under the authority of Pharaoh, to be kept in the cities for food. 36 This food should be held in reserve for the country, to be used during the seven years of famine that will come upon Egypt, so that the country may not be ruined by the famine."

37 The plan seemed good to Pharaoh and to all his officials. 38 So Pharaoh asked them, "Can we find anyone like this man, one in whom is the spirit of God*a*?"

39 Then Pharaoh said to Joseph, "Since God has made all this known to you, there is no one so discerning and wise as you. 40 You shall be in charge of my palace, and all my people are to submit to your orders. Only with respect to the throne will I be greater than you."

41 So Pharaoh said to Joseph, "I hereby put you in charge of the whole land of Egypt." 42 Then Pharaoh took his signet ring from his finger and put it on Joseph's finger. He dressed him in robes of fine linen and put a gold chain around his neck. 43 He had him ride in a chariot as his second-in-command,*b* and men shouted before him, "Make

way*c*!" Thus he put him in charge of the whole land of Egypt.

44 Then Pharaoh said to Joseph, "I am Pharaoh, but without your word no one will lift hand or foot in all Egypt." 45 Pharaoh gave Joseph the name Zaphenath-Paneah and gave him Asenath daughter of Potiphera, priest of On,*d* to be his wife. And Joseph went throughout the land of Egypt.

46 Joseph was thirty years old when he entered the service of Pharaoh king of Egypt. And Joseph went out from Pharaoh's presence and traveled throughout Egypt. 47 During the seven years of abundance the land produced plentifully. 48 Joseph collected all the food produced in those seven years of abundance in Egypt and stored it in the cities. In each city he put the food grown in the fields surrounding it. 49 Joseph stored up huge quantities of grain, like the sand of the sea; it was so much that he stopped keeping records because it was beyond measure.

50 Before the years of famine came, two sons were born to Joseph by Asenath daughter of Potiphera, priest of On. 51 Joseph named his firstborn Manasseh*e* and said, "It is because God has made me forget all my trouble and all my father's household." 52 The second son he named Ephraim*f* and said, "It is because God has made me fruitful in the land of my suffering."

53 The seven years of abundance in Egypt came to an end, 54 and the seven years of famine began, just as Joseph had said. There was famine in all the other lands, but in the whole land of Egypt there was food. 55 When all Egypt began to feel the famine, the people cried to Pharaoh for food. Then Pharaoh told all the Egyptians, "Go to Joseph and do what he tells you."

56 When the famine had spread over the whole country, Joseph opened the storehouses and sold grain to the Egyptians, for the famine was severe throughout Egypt. 57 And all the countries came to Egypt to buy grain from

Joseph, because the famine was severe in all the world.

42:1WHEN Jacob learned that there was grain in Egypt, he said to his sons, "Why do you just keep looking at each other?" 2He continued, "I have heard that there is grain in Egypt. Go down there and buy some for us, so that we may live and not die."

3Then ten of Joseph's brothers went down to buy grain from Egypt. 4But Jacob did not send Benjamin, Joseph's brother, with the others, because he was afraid that harm might come to him. 5So Israel's sons were among those who went to buy grain, for the famine was in the land of Canaan also.

6Now Joseph was the governor of the land, the one who sold grain to all its people. So when Joseph's brothers arrived, they bowed down to him with their faces to the ground. 7As soon as Joseph saw his brothers, he recognized them, but he pretended to be a stranger and spoke harshly to them. "Where do you come from?" he asked.

"From the land of Canaan," they replied, "to buy food."

8Although Joseph recognized his brothers, they did not recognize him. 9Then he remembered his dreams about them and said to them, "You are spies! You have come to see where our land is unprotected."

10"No, my lord," they answered. "Your servants have come to buy food. 11We are all the sons of one man. Your servants are honest men, not spies."

12"No!" he said to them. "You have come to see where our land is unprotected."

13But they replied, "Your servants were twelve brothers, the sons of one man, who lives in the land of Canaan. The youngest is now with our father, and one is no more."

14Joseph said to them, "It is just as I told you: You are spies! 15And this is how you will be tested: As surely as Pharaoh lives, you will not leave this place unless your youngest brother comes

here. 16Send one of your number to get your brother; the rest of you will be kept in prison, so that your words may be tested to see if you are telling the truth. If you are not, then as surely as Pharaoh lives, you are spies!" 17And he put them all in custody for three days.

a38 Or of the gods b43 Or in the chariot of his second-in-command; or in his second chariot c43 Or Bow down d45 That is, Heliopolis; also in verse 50 e51 Manasseh sounds like and may be derived from the Hebrew for forget. f52 Ephraim sounds like the Hebrew for twice fruitful.

MATTHEW 13:24-46

Jesus told them [the disciples] another parable: "The kingdom of heaven is like a man who sowed good seed in his field. 25But while everyone was sleeping, his enemy came and sowed weeds among the wheat, and went away. 26When the wheat sprouted and formed heads, then the weeds also appeared.

27"The owner's servants came to him and said, 'Sir, didn't you sow good seed in your field? Where then did the weeds come from?'

28"'An enemy did this,' he replied.

"The servants asked him, 'Do you want us to go and pull them up?'

29"'No,' he answered, 'because while you are pulling the weeds, you may root up the wheat with them. 30Let both grow together until the harvest. At that time I will tell the harvesters: First collect the weeds and tie them in bundles to be burned; then gather the wheat and bring it into my barn.'"

31He told them another parable: "The kingdom of heaven is like a mustard seed, which a man took and planted in his field. 32Though it is the smallest of all your seeds, yet when it grows, it is the largest of garden plants and becomes a tree, so that the birds of the air come and perch in its branches."

33He told them still another parable: "The kingdom of heaven is like yeast that a woman took and mixed into a large amounta of flour until it worked all through the dough."

34Jesus spoke all these things to the crowd in parables; he did not say anything to them without using a parable.

³⁵So was fulfilled what was spoken through the prophet:

"I will open my mouth in parables,
I will utter things hidden since the creation of the world."ᵇ

³⁶Then he left the crowd and went into the house. His disciples came to him and said, "Explain to us the parable of the weeds in the field."

³⁷He answered, "The one who sowed the good seed is the Son of Man. ³⁸The field is the world, and the good seed stands for the sons of the kingdom. The weeds are the sons of the evil one, ³⁹and the enemy who sows them is the devil. The harvest is the end of the age, and the harvesters are angels.

⁴⁰"As the weeds are pulled up and burned in the fire, so it will be at the end of the age. ⁴¹The Son of Man will send out his angels, and they will weed out of his kingdom everything that causes sin and all who do evil. ⁴²They will throw them into the fiery furnace, where there will be weeping and gnashing of teeth. ⁴³Then the righteous will shine like the sun in the kingdom of their Father. He who has ears, let him hear.

⁴⁴"The kingdom of heaven is like treasure hidden in a field. When a man found it, he hid it again, and then in his joy went and sold all he had and bought that field.

⁴⁵"Again, the kingdom of heaven is like a merchant looking for fine pearls. ⁴⁶When he found one of great value, he went away and sold everything he had and bought it."

ᵃ33 Greek *three satas* (probably about 1/2 bushel or 22 liters)   ᵇ35 Psalm 78:2

PSALM 18:1-15

For the director of music. Of David the servant of the LORD. He sang to the LORD the words of this song when the LORD delivered him from the hand of all his enemies and from the hand of Saul. He said:

¹I love you, O LORD, my strength.

²The LORD is my rock, my fortress and
my deliverer;
my God is my rock, in whom I take
refuge.
He is my shield and the hornᵃ of
my salvation, my stronghold.
³I call to the LORD, who is worthy
of praise,
and I am saved from my enemies.

⁴The cords of death entangled me;
the torrents of destruction
overwhelmed me.
⁵The cords of the graveᵇ coiled
around me;
the snares of death
confronted me.
⁶In my distress I called to the LORD;
I cried to my God for help.
From his temple he heard my voice;
my cry came before him, into
his ears.

⁷The earth trembled and quaked,
and the foundations of the
mountains shook;
they trembled because he was
angry.
⁸Smoke rose from his nostrils;
consuming fire came from
his mouth,
burning coals blazed out of it.
⁹He parted the heavens and came
down;
dark clouds were under his feet.
¹⁰He mounted the cherubim and flew;
he soared on the wings of the wind.
¹¹He made darkness his covering, his
canopy around him—
the dark rain clouds of the sky.
¹²Out of the brightness of his presence
clouds advanced,
with hailstones and bolts of
lightning.
¹³The LORD thundered from heaven;
the voice of the Most High
resounded.ᶜ
¹⁴He shot his arrows and scattered the
enemies,
great bolts of lightning and
routed them.
¹⁵The valleys of the sea were exposed
and the foundations of the earth
laid bare

at your rebuke, O Lᴏʀᴅ,
　　at the blast of breath from your
　　　nostrils.

ᵃ2 *Horn* here symbolizes strength.　ᵇ5 Hebrew *Sheol*
ᶜ13 Some Hebrew manuscripts and Septuagint (see also
2 Samuel 22:14); most Hebrew manuscripts *resounded, /
amid hailstones and bolts of lightning*

PROVERBS 4:1-6

Listen, my sons, to a father's
　　instruction;
　　pay attention and gain
　　　understanding.
² I give you sound learning,
　　so do not forsake my teaching.
³ When I was a boy in my father's
　　house,
　　still tender, and an only child of
　　　my mother,
⁴ he taught me and said,
　　"Lay hold of my words with all
　　　your heart;
　　keep my commands and you
　　　will live.
⁵ Get wisdom, get understanding;
　　do not forget my words or swerve
　　　from them.
⁶ Do not forsake wisdom, and she will
　　protect you;
　　love her, and she will watch
　　　over you.

□ DAY 21

GOD SIGHTINGS

January 21

GENESIS 42:18–43:34

On the third day, Joseph said to them [his brothers], "Do this and you will live, for I fear God: ¹⁹ If you are honest men, let one of your brothers stay here in prison, while the rest of you go and take grain back for your starving households. ²⁰ But you must bring your youngest brother to me, so that your words may be verified and that you may not die." This they proceeded to do.

²¹ They said to one another, "Surely we are being punished because of our brother. We saw how distressed he was when he pleaded with us for his life, but we would not listen; that's why this distress has come upon us."

²² Reuben replied, "Didn't I tell you not to sin against the boy? But you wouldn't listen! Now we must give an accounting for his blood." ²³ They did not realize that Joseph could understand them, since he was using an interpreter.

²⁴ He turned away from them and began to weep, but then turned back and spoke to them again. He had Simeon taken from them and bound before their eyes.

²⁵ Joseph gave orders to fill their bags with grain, to put each man's silver back in his sack, and to give them provisions for their journey. After this was done for them, ²⁶ they loaded their grain on their donkeys and left.

²⁷ At the place where they stopped for the night one of them opened his sack to get feed for his donkey, and he saw his silver in the mouth of his sack. ²⁸ "My silver has been returned," he said to his brothers. "Here it is in my sack."

Their hearts sank and they turned to each other trembling and said, "What is this that God has done to us?"

²⁹ When they came to their father Jacob in the land of Canaan, they told him all that had happened to them. They said, ³⁰ "The man who is lord over the land spoke harshly to us and treated us as though we were spying on the land. ³¹ But we said to him, 'We are honest men; we are not spies. ³² We were twelve brothers, sons of one father. One is no more, and the youngest is now with our father in Canaan.'

³³ "Then the man who is lord over the land said to us, 'This is how I will know whether you are honest men: Leave one of your brothers here with me, and take food for your starving households and go. ³⁴ But bring your youngest brother to me so I will know that you are not spies but honest men. Then I will give your

brother back to you, and you can trade*a*
in the land.'"

35As they were emptying their sacks,
there in each man's sack was his pouch
of silver! When they and their father
saw the money pouches, they were
frightened. 36Their father Jacob said to
them, "You have deprived me of my
children. Joseph is no more and Simeon
is no more, and now you want to take
Benjamin. Everything is against me!"

37Then Reuben said to his father,
"You may put both of my sons to death if
I do not bring him back to you. Entrust
him to my care, and I will bring him
back."

38But Jacob said, "My son will not go
down there with you; his brother is dead
and he is the only one left. If harm
comes to him on the journey you are
taking, you will bring my gray head
down to the grave*b* in sorrow."

43:1Now the famine was still severe in
the land. 2So when they had eaten all
the grain they had brought from Egypt,
their father said to them, "Go back and
buy us a little more food."

3But Judah said to him, "The man
warned us solemnly, 'You will not see
my face again unless your brother is
with you.' 4If you will send our brother
along with us, we will go down and buy
food for you. 5But if you will not send
him, we will not go down, because the
man said to us, 'You will not see my face
again unless your brother is with you.'"

6Israel asked, "Why did you bring this
trouble on me by telling the man you
had another brother?"

7They replied, "The man questioned
us closely about ourselves and our family. 'Is your father still living?' he asked
us. 'Do you have another brother?' We
simply answered his questions. How
were we to know he would say, 'Bring
your brother down here'?"

8Then Judah said to Israel his father,
"Send the boy along with me and we will
go at once, so that we and you and our
children may live and not die. 9I myself
will guarantee his safety; you can hold

me personally responsible for him. If I
do not bring him back to you and set
him here before you, I will bear the
blame before you all my life. 10As it is, if
we had not delayed, we could have gone
and returned twice."

11Then their father Israel said to
them, "If it must be, then do this: Put
some of the best products of the land in
your bags and take them down to the
man as a gift—a little balm and a little
honey, some spices and myrrh, some
pistachio nuts and almonds. 12Take
double the amount of silver with you,
for you must return the silver that was
put back into the mouths of your sacks.
Perhaps it was a mistake. 13Take your
brother also and go back to the man at
once. 14And may God Almighty*c* grant
you mercy before the man so that he will
let your other brother and Benjamin
come back with you. As for me, if I am
bereaved, I am bereaved."

15So the men took the gifts and double the amount of silver, and Benjamin
also. They hurried down to Egypt and
presented themselves to Joseph.
16When Joseph saw Benjamin with
them, he said to the steward of his
house, "Take these men to my house,
slaughter an animal and prepare dinner;
they are to eat with me at noon."

17The man did as Joseph told him
and took the men to Joseph's house.
18Now the men were frightened when
they were taken to his house. They
thought, "We were brought here because of the silver that was put back into
our sacks the first time. He wants to attack us and overpower us and seize us as
slaves and take our donkeys."

19So they went up to Joseph's steward
and spoke to him at the entrance to the
house. 20"Please, sir," they said, "we
came down here the first time to buy
food. 21But at the place where we
stopped for the night we opened our
sacks and each of us found his silver—
the exact weight—in the mouth of his
sack. So we have brought it back with
us. 22We have also brought additional

silver with us to buy food. We don't know who put our silver in our sacks."

23"It's all right," he said. "Don't be afraid. Your God, the God of your father, has given you treasure in your sacks; I received your silver." Then he brought Simeon out to them.

24The steward took the men into Joseph's house, gave them water to wash their feet and provided fodder for their donkeys. 25They prepared their gifts for Joseph's arrival at noon, because they had heard that they were to eat there.

26When Joseph came home, they presented to him the gifts they had brought into the house, and they bowed down before him to the ground. 27He asked them how they were, and then he said, "How is your aged father you told me about? Is he still living?"

28They replied, "Your servant our father is still alive and well." And they bowed low to pay him honor.

29As he looked about and saw his brother Benjamin, his own mother's son, he asked, "Is this your youngest brother, the one you told me about?" And he said, "God be gracious to you, my son." 30Deeply moved at the sight of his brother, Joseph hurried out and looked for a place to weep. He went into his private room and wept there.

31After he had washed his face, he came out and, controlling himself, said, "Serve the food."

32They served him by himself, the brothers by themselves, and the Egyptians who ate with him by themselves, because Egyptians could not eat with Hebrews, for that is detestable to Egyptians. 33The men had been seated before him in the order of their ages, from the firstborn to the youngest; and they looked at each other in astonishment. 34When portions were served to them from Joseph's table, Benjamin's portion was five times as much as anyone else's. So they feasted and drank freely with him.

a34 Or move about freely b38 Hebrew Sheol c14 Hebrew
El-Shaddai

MATTHEW 13:47–14:12

"Once again, the kingdom of heaven is like a net that was let down into the lake and caught all kinds of fish. 48When it was full, the fishermen pulled it up on the shore. Then they sat down and collected the good fish in baskets, but threw the bad away. 49This is how it will be at the end of the age. The angels will come and separate the wicked from the righteous 50and throw them into the fiery furnace, where there will be weeping and gnashing of teeth.

51"Have you understood all these things?" Jesus asked.

"Yes," they replied.

52He said to them, "Therefore every teacher of the law who has been instructed about the kingdom of heaven is like the owner of a house who brings out of his storeroom new treasures as well as old."

53When Jesus had finished these parables, he moved on from there. 54Coming to his hometown, he began teaching the people in their synagogue, and they were amazed. "Where did this man get this wisdom and these miraculous powers?" they asked. 55"Isn't this the carpenter's son? Isn't his mother's name Mary, and aren't his brothers James, Joseph, Simon and Judas? 56Aren't all his sisters with us? Where then did this man get all these things?" 57And they took offense at him.

But Jesus said to them, "Only in his hometown and in his own house is a prophet without honor."

58And he did not do many miracles there because of their lack of faith.

14:1At that time Herod the tetrarch heard the reports about Jesus, 2and he said to his attendants, "This is John the Baptist; he has risen from the dead! That is why miraculous powers are at work in him."

3Now Herod had arrested John and bound him and put him in prison because of Herodias, his brother Philip's wife, 4for John had been saying to him: "It is not lawful for you to have her."

⁵Herod wanted to kill John, but he was afraid of the people, because they considered him a prophet.

⁶On Herod's birthday the daughter of Herodias danced for them and pleased Herod so much ⁷that he promised with an oath to give her whatever she asked. ⁸Prompted by her mother, she said, "Give me here on a platter the head of John the Baptist." ⁹The king was distressed, but because of his oaths and his dinner guests, he ordered that her request be granted ¹⁰and had John beheaded in the prison. ¹¹His head was brought in on a platter and given to the girl, who carried it to her mother. ¹²John's disciples came and took his body and buried it. Then they went and told Jesus.

PSALM 18:16-36

¹⁶He [the LORD] reached down from on high and took hold of me;
  he drew me out of deep waters.
¹⁷He rescued me from my powerful enemy,
  from my foes, who were too strong for me.
¹⁸They confronted me in the day of my disaster,
  but the LORD was my support.
¹⁹He brought me out into a spacious place;
  he rescued me because he delighted in me.

²⁰The LORD has dealt with me according to my righteousness;
  according to the cleanness of my hands he has rewarded me.
²¹For I have kept the ways of the LORD;
  I have not done evil by turning from my God.
²²All his laws are before me;
  I have not turned away from his decrees.
²³I have been blameless before him and have kept myself from sin.
²⁴The LORD has rewarded me according to my righteousness,
  according to the cleanness of my hands in his sight.

²⁵To the faithful you show yourself faithful,
  to the blameless you show yourself blameless,
²⁶to the pure you show yourself pure,
  but to the crooked you show yourself shrewd.
²⁷You save the humble
  but bring low those whose eyes are haughty.
²⁸You, O LORD, keep my lamp burning;
  my God turns my darkness into light.
²⁹With your help I can advance against a troopᵃ;
  with my God I can scale a wall.

³⁰As for God, his way is perfect;
  the word of the LORD is flawless.
 He is a shield
  for all who take refuge in him.
³¹For who is God besides the LORD?
  And who is the Rock except our God?
³²**It is God who arms me with strength
  and makes my way perfect.**
³³**He makes my feet like the feet of a deer;
  he enables me to stand on the heights.**
³⁴He trains my hands for battle;
  my arms can bend a bow of bronze.
³⁵You give me your shield of victory,
  and your right hand sustains me;
  you stoop down to make me great.
³⁶You broaden the path beneath me,
  so that my ankles do not turn.

ᵃ29 Or can run through a barricade

PROVERBS 4:7-10

⁷**W**isdom is supreme; therefore get wisdom.
  Though it cost all you have,ᵃ get understanding.
⁸Esteem her, and she will exalt you;
  embrace her, and she will honor you.

[9]She will set a garland of grace on
your head
and present you with a crown of
splendor."

[10]Listen, my son, accept what I say,
and the years of your life will be
many.

a 7 Or Whatever else you get

☐ D A Y 2 2

GOD SIGHTINGS

January 22

GENESIS 44:1–45:28

Now Joseph gave these instructions to the steward of his house: "Fill the men's sacks with as much food as they can carry, and put each man's silver in the mouth of his sack. [2]Then put my cup, the silver one, in the mouth of the youngest one's sack, along with the silver for his grain." And he did as Joseph said.

[3]As morning dawned, the men were sent on their way with their donkeys. [4]They had not gone far from the city when Joseph said to his steward, "Go after those men at once, and when you catch up with them, say to them, 'Why have you repaid good with evil? [5]Isn't this the cup my master drinks from and also uses for divination? This is a wicked thing you have done.'"

[6]When he caught up with them, he repeated these words to them. [7]But they said to him, "Why does my lord say such things? Far be it from your servants to do anything like that! [8]We even brought back to you from the land of Canaan the silver we found inside the mouths of our sacks. So why would we steal silver or gold from your master's house? [9]If any of your servants is found to have it, he will die; and the rest of us will become my lord's slaves."

[10]"Very well, then," he said, "let it be as you say. Whoever is found to have it

will become my slave; the rest of you will be free from blame."

[11]Each of them quickly lowered his sack to the ground and opened it. [12]Then the steward proceeded to search, beginning with the oldest and ending with the youngest. And the cup was found in Benjamin's sack. [13]At this, they tore their clothes. Then they all loaded their donkeys and returned to the city.

[14]Joseph was still in the house when Judah and his brothers came in, and they threw themselves to the ground before him. [15]Joseph said to them, "What is this you have done? Don't you know that a man like me can find things out by divination?"

[16]"What can we say to my lord?" Judah replied. "What can we say? How can we prove our innocence? God has uncovered your servants' guilt. We are now my lord's slaves—we ourselves and the one who was found to have the cup."

[17]But Joseph said, "Far be it from me to do such a thing! Only the man who was found to have the cup will become my slave. The rest of you, go back to your father in peace."

[18]Then Judah went up to him and said: "Please, my lord, let your servant speak a word to my lord. Do not be angry with your servant, though you are equal to Pharaoh himself. [19]My lord asked his servants, 'Do you have a father or a brother?' [20]And we answered, 'We have an aged father, and there is a young son born to him in his old age. His brother is dead, and he is the only one of his mother's sons left, and his father loves him.'

[21]"Then you said to your servants, 'Bring him down to me so I can see him for myself.' [22]And we said to my lord, 'The boy cannot leave his father; if he leaves him, his father will die.' [23]But you told your servants, 'Unless your youngest brother comes down with you, you will not see my face again.' [24]When we went back to your servant my father, we told him what my lord had said.

[25]"Then our father said, 'Go back and buy a little more food.' [26]But we said,

'We cannot go down. Only if our youngest brother is with us will we go. We cannot see the man's face unless our youngest brother is with us.'

27 "Your servant my father said to us, 'You know that my wife bore me two sons. 28One of them went away from me, and I said, "He has surely been torn to pieces." And I have not seen him since. 29If you take this one from me too and harm comes to him, you will bring my gray head down to the grave*a* in misery.'

30"So now, if the boy is not with us when I go back to your servant my father and if my father, whose life is closely bound up with the boy's life, 31sees that the boy isn't there, he will die. Your servants will bring the gray head of our father down to the grave in sorrow. 32Your servant guaranteed the boy's safety to my father. I said, 'If I do not bring him back to you, I will bear the blame before you, my father, all my life!'

33"Now then, please let your servant remain here as my lord's slave in place of the boy, and let the boy return with his brothers. 34How can I go back to my father if the boy is not with me? No! Do not let me see the misery that would come upon my father."

45:1THEN Joseph could no longer control himself before all his attendants, and he cried out, "Have everyone leave my presence!" So there was no one with Joseph when he made himself known to his brothers. 2And he wept so loudly that the Egyptians heard him, and Pharaoh's household heard about it.

3Joseph said to his brothers, "I am Joseph! Is my father still living?" But his brothers were not able to answer him, because they were terrified at his presence.

4Then Joseph said to his brothers, "Come close to me." When they had done so, he said, "I am your brother Joseph, the one you sold into Egypt! 5And now, do not be distressed and do not be angry with yourselves for selling me here, because it was to save lives

that God sent me ahead of you. 6For two years now there has been famine in the land, and for the next five years there will not be plowing and reaping. 7But God sent me ahead of you to preserve for you a remnant on earth and to save your lives by a great deliverance.*b*

8"So then, it was not you who sent me here, but God. He made me father to Pharaoh, lord of his entire household and ruler of all Egypt. 9Now hurry back to my father and say to him, 'This is what your son Joseph says: God has made me lord of all Egypt. Come down to me; don't delay. 10You shall live in the region of Goshen and be near me—you, your children and grandchildren, your flocks and herds, and all you have. 11I will provide for you there, because five years of famine are still to come. Otherwise you and your household and all who belong to you will become destitute.'

12"You can see for yourselves, and so can my brother Benjamin, that it is really I who am speaking to you. 13Tell my father about all the honor accorded me in Egypt and about everything you have seen. And bring my father down here quickly."

14Then he threw his arms around his brother Benjamin and wept, and Benjamin embraced him, weeping. 15And he kissed all his brothers and wept over them. Afterward his brothers talked with him.

16When the news reached Pharaoh's palace that Joseph's brothers had come, Pharaoh and all his officials were pleased. 17Pharaoh said to Joseph, "Tell your brothers, 'Do this: Load your animals and return to the land of Canaan, 18and bring your father and your families back to me. I will give you the best of the land of Egypt and you can enjoy the fat of the land.'

19"You are also directed to tell them, 'Do this: Take some carts from Egypt for your children and your wives, and get your father and come. 20Never mind about your belongings, because the best of all Egypt will be yours.'"

21So the sons of Israel did this. Joseph

gave them carts, as Pharaoh had commanded, and he also gave them provisions for their journey. 22To each of them he gave new clothing, but to Benjamin he gave three hundred shekels*c* of silver and five sets of clothes. 23And this is what he sent to his father: ten donkeys loaded with the best things of Egypt, and ten female donkeys loaded with grain and bread and other provisions for his journey. 24Then he sent his brothers away, and as they were leaving he said to them, "Don't quarrel on the way!"

25So they went up out of Egypt and came to their father Jacob in the land of Canaan. 26They told him, "Joseph is still alive! In fact, he is ruler of all Egypt." Jacob was stunned; he did not believe them. 27But when they told him everything Joseph had said to them, and when he saw the carts Joseph had sent to carry him back, the spirit of their father Jacob revived. 28And Israel said, "I'm convinced! My son Joseph is still alive. I will go and see him before I die."

a29 Hebrew *Sheol*; also in verse 31   *b7* Or *save you as a great band of survivors*   *c22* That is, about 7 1/2 pounds (about 3.5 kilograms)

MATTHEW 14:13-36

When Jesus heard what had happened, he withdrew by boat privately to a solitary place. Hearing of this, the crowds followed him on foot from the towns. 14When Jesus landed and saw a large crowd, he had compassion on them and healed their sick.

15As evening approached, the disciples came to him and said, "This is a remote place, and it's already getting late. Send the crowds away, so they can go to the villages and buy themselves some food."

16Jesus replied, "They do not need to go away. You give them something to eat."

17"We have here only five loaves of bread and two fish," they answered.

18"Bring them here to me," he said. 19And he directed the people to sit down on the grass. Taking the five loaves and the two fish and looking up

to heaven, he gave thanks and broke the loaves. Then he gave them to the disciples, and the disciples gave them to the people. 20They all ate and were satisfied, and the disciples picked up twelve basketfuls of broken pieces that were left over. 21The number of those who ate was about five thousand men, besides women and children.

22Immediately Jesus made the disciples get into the boat and go on ahead of him to the other side, while he dismissed the crowd. 23After he had dismissed them, he went up on a mountainside by himself to pray. When evening came, he was there alone, 24but the boat was already a considerable distance*a* from land, buffeted by the waves because the wind was against it.

25During the fourth watch of the night Jesus went out to them, walking on the lake. 26When the disciples saw him walking on the lake, they were terrified. "It's a ghost," they said, and cried out in fear.

27But Jesus immediately said to them: "Take courage! It is I. Don't be afraid."

28"Lord, if it's you," Peter replied, "tell me to come to you on the water."

29"Come," he said.

Then Peter got down out of the boat, walked on the water and came toward Jesus. 30But when he saw the wind, he was afraid and, beginning to sink, cried out, "Lord, save me!"

31Immediately Jesus reached out his hand and caught him. "You of little faith," he said, "why did you doubt?"

32And when they climbed into the boat, the wind died down. 33Then those who were in the boat worshiped him, saying, "Truly you are the Son of God."

34When they had crossed over, they landed at Gennesaret. 35And when the men of that place recognized Jesus, they sent word to all the surrounding country. People brought all their sick to him 36and begged him to let the sick just touch the edge of his cloak, and all who touched him were healed.

a24 Greek *many stadia*

PSALM 18:37-50

37 I pursued my enemies and
    overtook them;
  I did not turn back till they were
    destroyed.
38 I crushed them so that they could not
    rise;
  they fell beneath my feet.
39 You armed me with strength
    for battle;
  you made my adversaries bow at
    my feet.
40 You made my enemies turn their
    backs in flight,
  and I destroyed my foes.
41 They cried for help, but there was no
    one to save them—
  to the Lord, but he did not answer.
42 I beat them as fine as dust borne on
    the wind;
  I poured them out like mud in
    the streets.

43 You have delivered me from the
    attacks of the people;
  you have made me the head of
    nations;
  people I did not know are subject
    to me.
44 As soon as they hear me, they
    obey me;
  foreigners cringe before me.
45 They all lose heart;
  they come trembling from their
    strongholds.

46 The Lord lives! Praise be to
    my Rock!
  Exalted be God my Savior!
47 He is the God who avenges me,
  who subdues nations under me,
48   who saves me from my enemies.
  You exalted me above my foes;
  from violent men you rescued me.
49 Therefore I will praise you among the
    nations, O Lord;
  I will sing praises to your name.
50 He gives his king great victories;
  he shows unfailing kindness to his
    anointed,
  to David and his descendants
    forever.

PROVERBS 4:11-13

11 I guide you in the way of wisdom
  and lead you along straight paths.
12 When you walk, your steps will not
    be hampered;
  when you run, you will not stumble.
13 Hold on to instruction, do not let
    it go;
  guard it well, for it is your life.

□ DAY 23

GOD SIGHTINGS

January 23

GENESIS 46:1–47:31

So Israel set out with all that was his, and when he reached Beersheba, he offered sacrifices to the God of his father Isaac. 2 And God spoke to Israel in a vision at night and said, "Jacob! Jacob!"

"Here I am," he replied.

3 "I am God, the God of your father," he said. "Do not be afraid to go down to Egypt, for I will make you into a great nation there. 4 I will go down to Egypt with you, and I will surely bring you back again. And Joseph's own hand will close your eyes."

5 Then Jacob left Beersheba, and Israel's sons took their father Jacob and their children and their wives in the carts that Pharaoh had sent to transport him. 6 They also took with them their livestock and the possessions they had acquired in Canaan, and Jacob and all his offspring went to Egypt. 7 He took with him to Egypt his sons and grandsons and his daughters and granddaughters—all his offspring.

8 These are the names of the sons of Israel (Jacob and his descendants) who went to Egypt:

Reuben the firstborn of Jacob.
  9 The sons of Reuben:
    Hanoch, Pallu, Hezron and
    Carmi.

10 The sons of Simeon:

Jemuel, Jamin, Ohad, Jakin, Zohar and Shaul the son of a Canaanite woman.

11 The sons of Levi:

Gershon, Kohath and Merari.

12 The sons of Judah:

Er, Onan, Shelah, Perez and Zerah (but Er and Onan had died in the land of Canaan).

The sons of Perez:

Hezron and Hamul.

13 The sons of Issachar:

Tola, Puah,a Jashubb and Shimron.

14 The sons of Zebulun:

Sered, Elon and Jahleel.

15 These were the sons Leah bore to Jacob in Paddan Aram,c besides his daughter Dinah. These sons and daughters of his were thirty-three in all.

16 The sons of Gad:

Zephon,d Haggi, Shuni, Ezbon, Eri, Arodi and Areli.

17 The sons of Asher:

Imnah, Ishvah, Ishvi and Beriah.

Their sister was Serah.

The sons of Beriah:

Heber and Malkiel.

18 These were the children born to Jacob by Zilpah, whom Laban had given to his daughter Leah—sixteen in all.

19 The sons of Jacob's wife Rachel:

Joseph and Benjamin. 20 In Egypt, Manasseh and Ephraim were born to Joseph by Asenath daughter of Potiphera, priest of On.e

21 The sons of Benjamin:

Bela, Beker, Ashbel, Gera, Naaman, Ehi, Rosh, Muppim, Huppim and Ard.

22 These were the sons of Rachel who were born to Jacob—fourteen in all.

23 The son of Dan:

Hushim.

24 The sons of Naphtali:

Jahziel, Guni, Jezer and Shillem.

25 These were the sons born to Jacob by Bilhah, whom Laban had given to his daughter Rachel—seven in all.

26 All those who went to Egypt with Jacob—those who were his direct descendants, not counting his sons' wives—numbered sixty-six persons. 27 With the two sonsf who had been born to Joseph in Egypt, the members of Jacob's family, which went to Egypt, were seventyg in all.

28 Now Jacob sent Judah ahead of him to Joseph to get directions to Goshen. When they arrived in the region of Goshen, 29 Joseph had his chariot made ready and went to Goshen to meet his father Israel. As soon as Joseph appeared before him, he threw his arms around his fatherh and wept for a long time.

30 Israel said to Joseph, "Now I am ready to die, since I have seen for myself that you are still alive."

31 Then Joseph said to his brothers and to his father's household, "I will go up and speak to Pharaoh and will say to him, 'My brothers and my father's household, who were living in the land of Canaan, have come to me. 32 The men are shepherds; they tend livestock, and they have brought along their flocks and herds and everything they own.' 33 When Pharaoh calls you in and asks, 'What is your occupation?' 34 you should answer, 'Your servants have tended livestock from our boyhood on, just as our fathers did.' Then you will be allowed to settle in the region of Goshen, for all shepherds are detestable to the Egyptians."

47:1 JOSEPH went and told Pharaoh, "My father and brothers, with their flocks and herds and everything they own, have come from the land of Canaan and are now in Goshen." 2 He chose five of his brothers and presented them before Pharaoh.

3 Pharaoh asked the brothers, "What is your occupation?"

"Your servants are shepherds," they

replied to Pharaoh, "just as our fathers were." ⁴They also said to him, "We have come to live here awhile, because the famine is severe in Canaan and your servants' flocks have no pasture. So now, please let your servants settle in Goshen."

⁵Pharaoh said to Joseph, "Your father and your brothers have come to you, ⁶and the land of Egypt is before you; settle your father and your brothers in the best part of the land. Let them live in Goshen. And if you know of any among them with special ability, put them in charge of my own livestock."

⁷Then Joseph brought his father Jacob in and presented him before Pharaoh. After Jacob blessedʲ Pharaoh, ⁸Pharaoh asked him, "How old are you?"

⁹And Jacob said to Pharaoh, "The years of my pilgrimage are a hundred and thirty. My years have been few and difficult, and they do not equal the years of the pilgrimage of my fathers." ¹⁰Then Jacob blessedʲ Pharaoh and went out from his presence.

¹¹So Joseph settled his father and his brothers in Egypt and gave them property in the best part of the land, the district of Rameses, as Pharaoh directed. ¹²Joseph also provided his father and his brothers and all his father's household with food, according to the number of their children.

¹³There was no food, however, in the whole region because the famine was severe; both Egypt and Canaan wasted away because of the famine. ¹⁴Joseph collected all the money that was to be found in Egypt and Canaan in payment for the grain they were buying, and he brought it to Pharaoh's palace. ¹⁵When the money of the people of Egypt and Canaan was gone, all Egypt came to Joseph and said, "Give us food. Why should we die before your eyes? Our money is used up."

¹⁶"Then bring your livestock," said Joseph. "I will sell you food in exchange for your livestock, since your money is gone." ¹⁷So they brought their livestock to Joseph, and he gave them food in exchange for their horses, their sheep and goats, their cattle and donkeys. And he brought them through that year with food in exchange for all their livestock.

¹⁸When that year was over, they came to him the following year and said, "We cannot hide from our lord the fact that since our money is gone and our livestock belongs to you, there is nothing left for our lord except our bodies and our land. ¹⁹Why should we perish before your eyes—we and our land as well? Buy us and our land in exchange for food, and we with our land will be in bondage to Pharaoh. Give us seed so that we may live and not die, and that the land may not become desolate."

²⁰So Joseph bought all the land in Egypt for Pharaoh. The Egyptians, one and all, sold their fields, because the famine was too severe for them. The land became Pharaoh's, ²¹and Joseph reduced the people to servitude,ᵏ from one end of Egypt to the other. ²²However, he did not buy the land of the priests, because they received a regular allotment from Pharaoh and had food enough from the allotment Pharaoh gave them. That is why they did not sell their land.

²³Joseph said to the people, "Now that I have bought you and your land today for Pharaoh, here is seed for you so you can plant the ground. ²⁴But when the crop comes in, give a fifth of it to Pharaoh. The other four-fifths you may keep as seed for the fields and as food for yourselves and your households and your children."

²⁵"You have saved our lives," they said. "May we find favor in the eyes of our lord; we will be in bondage to Pharaoh."

²⁶So Joseph established it as a law concerning land in Egypt—still in force today—that a fifth of the produce belongs to Pharaoh. It was only the land of the priests that did not become Pharaoh's.

²⁷Now the Israelites settled in Egypt in the region of Goshen. They acquired

property there and were fruitful and increased greatly in number.

²⁸Jacob lived in Egypt seventeen years, and the years of his life were a hundred and forty-seven. ²⁹When the time drew near for Israel to die, he called for his son Joseph and said to him, "If I have found favor in your eyes, put your hand under my thigh and promise that you will show me kindness and faithfulness. Do not bury me in Egypt, ³⁰but when I rest with my fathers, carry me out of Egypt and bury me where they are buried."

"I will do as you say," he said.

³¹"Swear to me," he said. Then Joseph swore to him, and Israel worshiped as he leaned on the top of his staff.ʲ

a 13 Samaritan Pentateuch and Syriac (see also 1 Chron. 7:1); Masoretic Text Puvah b 13 Samaritan Pentateuch and some Septuagint manuscripts (see also Num. 26:24 and 1 Chron. 7:1); Masoretic Text Iob c 15 That is, Northwest Mesopotamia d 16 Samaritan Pentateuch and Septuagint (see also Num. 26:15); Masoretic Text Ziphion e 20 That is, Heliopolis f 27 Hebrew; Septuagint the nine children g 27 Hebrew (see also Exodus 1:5 and footnote); Septuagint (see also Acts 7:14) seventy-five h 29 Hebrew around him i 7 Or greeted j 10 Or said farewell to k 21 Samaritan Pentateuch and Septuagint (see also Vulgate); Masoretic Text and he moved the people into the cities l 31 Or Israel bowed down at the head of his bed

MATTHEW 15:1-28

Then some Pharisees and teachers of the law came to Jesus from Jerusalem and asked, ²"Why do your disciples break the tradition of the elders? They don't wash their hands before they eat!"

³Jesus replied, "And why do you break the command of God for the sake of your tradition? ⁴For God said, 'Honor your father and mother'ᵃ and 'Anyone who curses his father or mother must be put to death.'ᵇ ⁵But you say that if a man says to his father or mother, 'Whatever help you might otherwise have received from me is a gift devoted to God,' ⁶he is not to 'honor his fatherᶜ' with it. Thus you nullify the word of God for the sake of your tradition. ⁷You hypocrites! Isaiah was right when he prophesied about you:

⁸"'These people honor me with their lips,
    but their hearts are far from me.

⁹They worship me in vain;
    their teachings are but rules
        taught by men.'ᵈ"

¹⁰Jesus called the crowd to him and said, "Listen and understand. ¹¹What goes into a man's mouth does not make him 'unclean,' but what comes out of his mouth, that is what makes him 'unclean.'"

¹²Then the disciples came to him and asked, "Do you know that the Pharisees were offended when they heard this?"

¹³He replied, "Every plant that my heavenly Father has not planted will be pulled up by the roots. ¹⁴Leave them; they are blind guides.ᵉ If a blind man leads a blind man, both will fall into a pit."

¹⁵Peter said, "Explain the parable to us."

¹⁶"Are you still so dull?" Jesus asked them. ¹⁷"Don't you see that whatever enters the mouth goes into the stomach and then out of the body? ¹⁸But the things that come out of the mouth come from the heart, and these make a man 'unclean.' ¹⁹For out of the heart come evil thoughts, murder, adultery, sexual immorality, theft, false testimony, slander. ²⁰These are what make a man 'unclean'; but eating with unwashed hands does not make him 'unclean.'"

²¹Leaving that place, Jesus withdrew to the region of Tyre and Sidon. ²²A Canaanite woman from that vicinity came to him, crying out, "Lord, Son of David, have mercy on me! My daughter is suffering terribly from demon-possession."

²³Jesus did not answer a word. So his disciples came to him and urged him, "Send her away, for she keeps crying out after us."

²⁴He answered, "I was sent only to the lost sheep of Israel."

²⁵The woman came and knelt before him. "Lord, help me!" she said.

²⁶He replied, "It is not right to take the children's bread and toss it to their dogs."

²⁷"Yes, Lord," she said, "but even the

dogs eat the crumbs that fall from their masters' table."

28Then Jesus answered, "Woman, you have great faith! Your request is granted." And her daughter was healed from that very hour.

a4 Exodus 20:12; Deut. 5:16   *b4* Exodus 21:17; Lev. 20:9
c6 Some manuscripts *father or his mother*   *d9* Isaiah 29:13
e14 Some manuscripts *guides of the blind*

PSALM 19:1-14
For the director of music. A psalm of David.

1 The heavens declare the glory
      of God;
   the skies proclaim the work of
      his hands.
2 Day after day they pour forth speech;
   night after night they display
      knowledge.
3 There is no speech or language
   where their voice is not heard.*a*
4 Their voice*b* goes out into all the
      earth,
   their words to the ends of the world.

   In the heavens he has pitched a tent
      for the sun,
5   which is like a bridegroom coming
         forth from his pavilion,
   like a champion rejoicing to run
      his course.
6 It rises at one end of the heavens
   and makes its circuit to the other;
   nothing is hidden from its heat.

7 The law of the LORD is perfect,
   reviving the soul.
   The statutes of the LORD are
      trustworthy,
   making wise the simple.
8 The precepts of the LORD are right,
   giving joy to the heart.
   The commands of the LORD
      are radiant,
   giving light to the eyes.
9 The fear of the LORD is pure,
   enduring forever.
   The ordinances of the LORD are sure
   and altogether righteous.
10 They are more precious than gold,
   than much pure gold;
   they are sweeter than honey,
   than honey from the comb.

11 By them is your servant warned;
   in keeping them there is great
      reward.

12 Who can discern his errors?
   Forgive my hidden faults.
13 Keep your servant also from
      willful sins;
   may they not rule over me.
   Then will I be blameless,
      innocent of great transgression.

14 **May the words of my mouth and
      the meditation of my heart
   be pleasing in your sight,
   O LORD, my Rock and my
      Redeemer.**

a3 Or *They have no speech, there are no words; / no sound is
heard from them*   *b4* Septuagint, Jerome and Syriac;
Hebrew *line*

PROVERBS 4:14-19
14 Do not set foot on the path of the
      wicked
   or walk in the way of evil men.
15 Avoid it, do not travel on it;
   turn from it and go on your way.
16 For they cannot sleep till they do evil;
   they are robbed of slumber till
      they make someone fall.
17 They eat the bread of wickedness
   and drink the wine of violence.

18 The path of the righteous is like the
      first gleam of dawn,
   shining ever brighter till the full
      light of day.
19 But the way of the wicked is like deep
      darkness;
   they do not know what makes
      them stumble.

□ DAY 24

GOD SIGHTINGS

January 24

GENESIS 48:1–49:33
Some time later Joseph was told, "Your father is ill." So he took his two sons Ma-

nasseh and Ephraim along with him. ²When Jacob was told, "Your son Joseph has come to you," Israel rallied his strength and sat up on the bed.

³Jacob said to Joseph, "God Almighty*a* appeared to me at Luz in the land of Canaan, and there he blessed me ⁴and said to me, 'I am going to make you fruitful and will increase your numbers. I will make you a community of peoples, and I will give this land as an everlasting possession to your descendants after you.'

⁵"Now then, your two sons born to you in Egypt before I came to you here will be reckoned as mine; Ephraim and Manasseh will be mine, just as Reuben and Simeon are mine. ⁶Any children born to you after them will be yours; in the territory they inherit they will be reckoned under the names of their brothers. ⁷As I was returning from Paddan,*b* to my sorrow Rachel died in the land of Canaan while we were still on the way, a little distance from Ephrath. So I buried her there beside the road to Ephrath" (that is, Bethlehem).

⁸When Israel saw the sons of Joseph, he asked, "Who are these?"

⁹"They are the sons God has given me here," Joseph said to his father.

Then Israel said, "Bring them to me so I may bless them."

¹⁰Now Israel's eyes were failing because of old age, and he could hardly see. So Joseph brought his sons close to him, and his father kissed them and embraced them.

¹¹Israel said to Joseph, "I never expected to see your face again, and now God has allowed me to see your children too."

¹²Then Joseph removed them from Israel's knees and bowed down with his face to the ground. ¹³And Joseph took both of them, Ephraim on his right toward Israel's left hand and Manasseh on his left toward Israel's right hand, and brought them close to him. ¹⁴But Israel reached out his right hand and put it on Ephraim's head, though he was the younger, and crossing his arms, he put his left hand on Manasseh's head, even though Manasseh was the firstborn.

¹⁵Then he blessed Joseph and said,

"May the God before whom my
    fathers
   Abraham and Isaac walked,
the God who has been my shepherd
    all my life to this day,
¹⁶the Angel who has delivered me from
    all harm
   —may he bless these boys.
May they be called by my name
    and the names of my fathers
    Abraham and Isaac,
and may they increase greatly
    upon the earth."

¹⁷When Joseph saw his father placing his right hand on Ephraim's head he was displeased; so he took hold of his father's hand to move it from Ephraim's head to Manasseh's head. ¹⁸Joseph said to him, "No, my father, this one is the firstborn; put your right hand on his head."

¹⁹But his father refused and said, "I know, my son, I know. He too will become a people, and he too will become great. Nevertheless, his younger brother will be greater than he, and his descendants will become a group of nations." ²⁰He blessed them that day and said,

"In your*c* name will Israel pronounce
    this blessing:
   'May God make you like Ephraim
       and Manasseh.'"

So he put Ephraim ahead of Manasseh.

²¹Then Israel said to Joseph, "I am about to die, but God will be with you*c* and take you*c* back to the land of your*d* fathers. ²²And to you, as one who is over your brothers, I give the ridge of land*e* I took from the Amorites with my sword and my bow."

49:1THEN Jacob called for his sons and said: "Gather around so I can tell you what will happen to you in days to come.

²"Assemble and listen, sons of Jacob;
    listen to your father Israel.

3 "Reuben, you are my firstborn,
    my might, the first sign of my
        strength,
    excelling in honor, excelling
        in power.
4 Turbulent as the waters, you will no
        longer excel,
    for you went up onto your
        father's bed,
    onto my couch and defiled it.

5 "Simeon and Levi are brothers—
    their swords*f* are weapons
        of violence.
6 Let me not enter their council,
    let me not join their assembly,
    for they have killed men in their
        anger
    and hamstrung oxen as they
        pleased.
7 Cursed be their anger, so fierce,
    and their fury, so cruel!
    I will scatter them in Jacob
    and disperse them in Israel.

8 "Judah,*g* your brothers will praise
        you;
    your hand will be on the neck of
        your enemies;
    your father's sons will bow down
        to you.
9 You are a lion's cub, O Judah;
    you return from the prey,
        my son.
    Like a lion he crouches and lies down,
    like a lioness—who dares to rouse
        him?
10 The scepter will not depart from
        Judah,
    nor the ruler's staff from between
        his feet,
    until he comes to whom it belongs*h*
    and the obedience of the nations
        is his.
11 He will tether his donkey to a vine,
    his colt to the choicest branch;
    he will wash his garments in wine,
    his robes in the blood of grapes.
12 His eyes will be darker than wine,
    his teeth whiter than milk.*i*

13 "Zebulun will live by the seashore
    and become a haven for ships;

    his border will extend toward
        Sidon.

14 "Issachar is a rawboned*j* donkey
    lying down between two
        saddlebags.*k*
15 When he sees how good is his
        resting place
    and how pleasant is his land,
    he will bend his shoulder to
        the burden
    and submit to forced labor.

16 "Dan*l* will provide justice for
        his people
    as one of the tribes of Israel.
17 Dan will be a serpent by the
        roadside,
    a viper along the path,
    that bites the horse's heels
    so that its rider tumbles
        backward.

18 "I look for your deliverance,
    O LORD.

19 "Gad*m* will be attacked by a band
        of raiders,
    but he will attack them at their
        heels.

20 "Asher's food will be rich;
    he will provide delicacies fit for
        a king.

21 "Naphtali is a doe set free
    that bears beautiful fawns.*n*

22 "Joseph is a fruitful vine,
    a fruitful vine near a spring,
    whose branches climb over
        a wall.*o*
23 With bitterness archers attacked
        him;
    they shot at him with hostility.
24 But his bow remained steady,
    his strong arms stayed*p* limber,
    because of the hand of the Mighty
        One of Jacob,
    because of the Shepherd, the Rock
        of Israel,
25 because of your father's God, who
        helps you,
    because of the Almighty,*q* who
        blesses you

with blessings of the heavens above,
  blessings of the deep that lies
    below,
  blessings of the breast
    and womb.
26 Your father's blessings are greater
    than the blessings of the ancient
    mountains,
  than[r] the bounty of the age-old
    hills.
  Let all these rest on the head of
    Joseph,
  on the brow of the prince among[s]
    his brothers.

27 "Benjamin is a ravenous wolf;
  in the morning he devours
    the prey,
  in the evening he divides the
    plunder."

28 All these are the twelve tribes of Israel, and this is what their father said to them when he blessed them, giving each the blessing appropriate to him.

29 Then he gave them these instructions: "I am about to be gathered to my people. Bury me with my fathers in the cave in the field of Ephron the Hittite, 30 the cave in the field of Machpelah, near Mamre in Canaan, which Abraham bought as a burial place from Ephron the Hittite, along with the field. 31 There Abraham and his wife Sarah were buried, there Isaac and his wife Rebekah were buried, and there I buried Leah. 32 The field and the cave in it were bought from the Hittites.[t]"

33 When Jacob had finished giving instructions to his sons, he drew his feet up into the bed, breathed his last and was gathered to his people.

a 3 Hebrew *El-Shaddai*   b 7 That is, Northwest Mesopotamia
c 20,21 The Hebrew is singular.   d 21 The Hebrew is plural.
e 22 Or *And to you I give one portion more than to your brothers—the portion*   f 5 The meaning of the Hebrew for this word is uncertain.   g 8 *Judah* sounds like and may be derived from the Hebrew for *praise.*   h 10 Or *until Shiloh comes; or until he comes to whom tribute belongs*   i 12 Or *will be dull from wine, / his teeth white from milk*   j 14 Or *strong*   k 14 Or *campfires*   l 16 *Dan* here means *he provides justice.*   m 19 *Gad* can mean *attack* and *band of raiders.*   n 21 Or *free; / he utters beautiful words*   o 22 Or *Joseph is a wild colt, / a wild colt near a spring, / a wild donkey on a terraced hill*   p 23,24 Or *archers will attack... will shoot... will remain... will stay*   q 25 Hebrew *Shaddai*   r 26 Or *of my progenitors, / as great as*   s 26 Or *the one separated from*   t 32 Or *the sons of Heth*

MATTHEW 15:29–16:12
Jesus left there and went along the Sea of Galilee. Then he went up on a mountainside and sat down. 30 Great crowds came to him, bringing the lame, the blind, the crippled, the mute and many others, and laid them at his feet; and he healed them. 31 The people were amazed when they saw the mute speaking, the crippled made well, the lame walking and the blind seeing. And they praised the God of Israel.

32 Jesus called his disciples to him and said, "I have compassion for these people; they have already been with me three days and have nothing to eat. I do not want to send them away hungry, or they may collapse on the way."

33 His disciples answered, "Where could we get enough bread in this remote place to feed such a crowd?"

34 "How many loaves do you have?" Jesus asked.

"Seven," they replied, "and a few small fish."

35 He told the crowd to sit down on the ground. 36 Then he took the seven loaves and the fish, and when he had given thanks, he broke them and gave them to the disciples, and they in turn to the people. 37 They all ate and were satisfied. Afterward the disciples picked up seven basketfuls of broken pieces that were left over. 38 The number of those who ate was four thousand, besides women and children. 39 After Jesus had sent the crowd away, he got into the boat and went to the vicinity of Magadan.

16:1 THE Pharisees and Sadducees came to Jesus and tested him by asking him to show them a sign from heaven.

2 He replied,[a] "When evening comes, you say, 'It will be fair weather, for the sky is red,' 3 and in the morning, 'Today it will be stormy, for the sky is red and overcast.' You know how to interpret the appearance of the sky, but you cannot interpret the signs of the times. 4 A wicked and adulterous generation looks for a miraculous sign, but none will be

given it except the sign of Jonah." Jesus then left them and went away.

⁵When they went across the lake, the disciples forgot to take bread. ⁶"Be careful," Jesus said to them. "Be on your guard against the yeast of the Pharisees and Sadducees."

⁷They discussed this among themselves and said, "It is because we didn't bring any bread."

⁸Aware of their discussion, Jesus asked, "You of little faith, why are you talking among yourselves about having no bread? ⁹Do you still not understand? Don't you remember the five loaves for the five thousand, and how many basketfuls you gathered? ¹⁰Or the seven loaves for the four thousand, and how many basketfuls you gathered? ¹¹How is it you don't understand that I was not talking to you about bread? But be on your guard against the yeast of the Pharisees and Sadducees." ¹²Then they understood that he was not telling them to guard against the yeast used in bread, but against the teaching of the Pharisees and Sadducees.

a2 Some early manuscripts do not have the rest of verse 2 and all of verse 3.

PSALM 20:1-9

For the director of music. A psalm of David.

¹ May the LORD answer you when you
      are in distress;
   may the name of the God of Jacob
      protect you.
² May he send you help from the
      sanctuary
   and grant you support from Zion.
³ May he remember all your
      sacrifices
   and accept your burnt offerings.
                                        Selah
⁴ May he give you the desire of
      your heart
   and make all your plans succeed.
⁵ We will shout for joy when you are
      victorious
   and will lift up our banners in the
      name of our God.
   May the LORD grant all your
      requests.

⁶ Now I know that the LORD saves
      his anointed;
   he answers him from his holy
      heaven
   with the saving power of his
      right hand.
⁷ **Some trust in chariots and some
      in horses,
   but we trust in the name of the
      LORD our God.**
⁸ **They are brought to their knees
      and fall,
   but we rise up and stand firm.**

⁹ O LORD, save the king!
   Answer*a* us when we call!

a9 Or save! / O King, answer

PROVERBS 4:20-27

²⁰ **M**y son, pay attention to what I say;
   listen closely to my words.
²¹ Do not let them out of your sight,
   keep them within your heart;
²² for they are life to those who find
      them
   and health to a man's whole body.
²³ Above all else, guard your heart,
   for it is the wellspring of life.
²⁴ Put away perversity from your mouth;
   keep corrupt talk far from your
      lips.
²⁵ Let your eyes look straight ahead,
   fix your gaze directly before you.
²⁶ Make level*a* paths for your feet
   and take only ways that are firm.
²⁷ Do not swerve to the right or the left;
   keep your foot from evil.

a26 Or Consider the

□ DAY 25

GOD SIGHTINGS

January 25

GENESIS 50:1—EXODUS 2:10

Joseph threw himself upon his father and wept over him and kissed him. ²Then Joseph directed the physicians in his service to embalm his father Israel.

So the physicians embalmed him, ³taking a full forty days, for that was the time required for embalming. And the Egyptians mourned for him seventy days.

⁴When the days of mourning had passed, Joseph said to Pharaoh's court, "If I have found favor in your eyes, speak to Pharaoh for me. Tell him, ⁵'My father made me swear an oath and said, "I am about to die; bury me in the tomb I dug for myself in the land of Canaan." Now let me go up and bury my father; then I will return.'"

⁶Pharaoh said, "Go up and bury your father, as he made you swear to do."

⁷So Joseph went up to bury his father. All Pharaoh's officials accompanied him—the dignitaries of his court and all the dignitaries of Egypt— ⁸besides all the members of Joseph's household and his brothers and those belonging to his father's household. Only their children and their flocks and herds were left in Goshen. ⁹Chariots and horsemenᵃ also went up with him. It was a very large company.

¹⁰When they reached the threshing floor of Atad, near the Jordan, they lamented loudly and bitterly; and there Joseph observed a seven-day period of mourning for his father. ¹¹When the Canaanites who lived there saw the mourning at the threshing floor of Atad, they said, "The Egyptians are holding a solemn ceremony of mourning." That is why that place near the Jordan is called Abel Mizraim.ᵇ

¹²So Jacob's sons did as he had commanded them: ¹³They carried him to the land of Canaan and buried him in the cave in the field of Machpelah, near Mamre, which Abraham had bought as a burial place from Ephron the Hittite, along with the field. ¹⁴After burying his father, Joseph returned to Egypt, together with his brothers and all the others who had gone with him to bury his father.

¹⁵When Joseph's brothers saw that their father was dead, they said, "What if Joseph holds a grudge against us and pays us back for all the wrongs we did to him?" ¹⁶So they sent word to Joseph,

saying, "Your father left these instructions before he died: ¹⁷'This is what you are to say to Joseph: I ask you to forgive your brothers the sins and the wrongs they committed in treating you so badly.' Now please forgive the sins of the servants of the God of your father." When their message came to him, Joseph wept.

¹⁸His brothers then came and threw themselves down before him. "We are your slaves," they said.

¹⁹But Joseph said to them, "Don't be afraid. Am I in the place of God? ²⁰You intended to harm me, but God intended it for good to accomplish what is now being done, the saving of many lives. ²¹So then, don't be afraid. I will provide for you and your children." And he reassured them and spoke kindly to them.

²²Joseph stayed in Egypt, along with all his father's family. He lived a hundred and ten years ²³and saw the third generation of Ephraim's children. Also the children of Makir son of Manasseh were placed at birth on Joseph's knees.ᶜ

²⁴Then Joseph said to his brothers, "I am about to die. But God will surely come to your aid and take you up out of this land to the land he promised on oath to Abraham, Isaac and Jacob." ²⁵And Joseph made the sons of Israel swear an oath and said, "God will surely come to your aid, and then you must carry my bones up from this place."

²⁶So Joseph died at the age of a hundred and ten. And after they embalmed him, he was placed in a coffin in Egypt.

1:1THESE are the names of the sons of Israel who went to Egypt with Jacob, each with his family: ²Reuben, Simeon, Levi and Judah; ³Issachar, Zebulun and Benjamin; ⁴Dan and Naphtali; Gad and Asher. ⁵The descendants of Jacob numbered seventyᵈ in all; Joseph was already in Egypt.

⁶Now Joseph and all his brothers and all that generation died, ⁷but the Israelites were fruitful and multiplied greatly and became exceedingly numerous, so that the land was filled with them.

⁸Then a new king, who did not know about Joseph, came to power in Egypt. ⁹"Look," he said to his people, "the Israelites have become much too numerous for us. ¹⁰Come, we must deal shrewdly with them or they will become even more numerous and, if war breaks out, will join our enemies, fight against us and leave the country."

¹¹So they put slave masters over them to oppress them with forced labor, and they built Pithom and Rameses as store cities for Pharaoh. ¹²But the more they were oppressed, the more they multiplied and spread; so the Egyptians came to dread the Israelites ¹³and worked them ruthlessly. ¹⁴They made their lives bitter with hard labor in brick and mortar and with all kinds of work in the fields; in all their hard labor the Egyptians used them ruthlessly.

¹⁵The king of Egypt said to the Hebrew midwives, whose names were Shiphrah and Puah, ¹⁶"When you help the Hebrew women in childbirth and observe them on the delivery stool, if it is a boy, kill him; but if it is a girl, let her live." ¹⁷The midwives, however, feared God and did not do what the king of Egypt had told them to do; they let the boys live. ¹⁸Then the king of Egypt summoned the midwives and asked them, "Why have you done this? Why have you let the boys live?"

¹⁹The midwives answered Pharaoh, "Hebrew women are not like Egyptian women; they are vigorous and give birth before the midwives arrive."

²⁰So God was kind to the midwives and the people increased and became even more numerous. ²¹And because the midwives feared God, he gave them families of their own.

²²Then Pharaoh gave this order to all his people: "Every boy that is born𝑒 you must throw into the Nile, but let every girl live."

2:1Now a man of the house of Levi married a Levite woman, ²and she became pregnant and gave birth to a son. When she saw that he was a fine child, she hid him for three months. ³But when she could hide him no longer, she got a papyrus basket for him and coated it with tar and pitch. Then she placed the child in it and put it among the reeds along the bank of the Nile. ⁴His sister stood at a distance to see what would happen to him.

⁵Then Pharaoh's daughter went down to the Nile to bathe, and her attendants were walking along the river bank. She saw the basket among the reeds and sent her slave girl to get it. ⁶She opened it and saw the baby. He was crying, and she felt sorry for him. "This is one of the Hebrew babies," she said.

⁷Then his sister asked Pharaoh's daughter, "Shall I go and get one of the Hebrew women to nurse the baby for you?"

⁸"Yes, go," she answered. And the girl went and got the baby's mother. ⁹Pharaoh's daughter said to her, "Take this baby and nurse him for me, and I will pay you." So the woman took the baby and nursed him. ¹⁰When the child grew older, she took him to Pharaoh's daughter and he became her son. She named him Moses,𝑓 saying, "I drew him out of the water."

ᵃ9 Or *charioteers* ᵇ11 *Abel Mizraim* means *mourning of the Egyptians.* ᶜ23 That is, were counted as his ᵈ5 Masoretic Text (see also Gen. 46:27); Dead Sea Scrolls and Septuagint (see also Acts 7:14 and note at Gen. 46:27) *seventy-five* ᵉ22 Masoretic Text; Samaritan Pentateuch, Septuagint and Targums *born to the Hebrews* ᶠ10 *Moses* sounds like the Hebrew for *draw out.*

MATTHEW 16:13–17:9

When Jesus came to the region of Caesarea Philippi, he asked his disciples, "Who do people say the Son of Man is?"

¹⁴They replied, "Some say John the Baptist; others say Elijah; and still others, Jeremiah or one of the prophets."

¹⁵"But what about you?" he asked. "Who do you say I am?"

¹⁶Simon Peter answered, "You are the Christ,ᵃ the Son of the living God."

¹⁷Jesus replied, "Blessed are you, Simon son of Jonah, for this was not revealed to you by man, but by my Father in heaven. ¹⁸And I tell you that you are Peter,ᵇ and on this rock I will build my

church, and the gates of Hades*c* will not overcome it.*d* 19I will give you the keys of the kingdom of heaven; whatever you bind on earth will be*e* bound in heaven, and whatever you loose on earth will be*e* loosed in heaven." 20Then he warned his disciples not to tell anyone that he was the Christ.

21From that time on Jesus began to explain to his disciples that he must go to Jerusalem and suffer many things at the hands of the elders, chief priests and teachers of the law, and that he must be killed and on the third day be raised to life.

22Peter took him aside and began to rebuke him. "Never, Lord!" he said. "This shall never happen to you!"

23Jesus turned and said to Peter, "Get behind me, Satan! You are a stumbling block to me; you do not have in mind the things of God, but the things of men."

24**Then Jesus said to his disciples, "If anyone would come after me, he must deny himself and take up his cross and follow me.** 25**For whoever wants to save his life*f* will lose it, but whoever loses his life for me will find it.** 26What good will it be for a man if he gains the whole world, yet forfeits his soul? Or what can a man give in exchange for his soul? 27For the Son of Man is going to come in his Father's glory with his angels, and then he will reward each person according to what he has done. 28I tell you the truth, some who are standing here will not taste death before they see the Son of Man coming in his kingdom."

17:1AFTER six days Jesus took with him Peter, James and John the brother of James, and led them up a high mountain by themselves. 2There he was transfigured before them. His face shone like the sun, and his clothes became as white as the light. 3Just then there appeared before them Moses and Elijah, talking with Jesus.

4Peter said to Jesus, "Lord, it is good for us to be here. If you wish, I will put up three shelters—one for you, one for Moses and one for Elijah."

5While he was still speaking, a bright cloud enveloped them, and a voice from the cloud said, "This is my Son, whom I love; with him I am well pleased. Listen to him!"

6When the disciples heard this, they fell facedown to the ground, terrified. 7But Jesus came and touched them. "Get up," he said. "Don't be afraid." 8When they looked up, they saw no one except Jesus.

9As they were coming down the mountain, Jesus instructed them, "Don't tell anyone what you have seen, until the Son of Man has been raised from the dead."

a16 Or *Messiah*; also in verse 20   *b18* *Peter* means *rock.*
c18 Or *hell*   *d18* Or *not prove stronger than it*   *e19* Or *have been.*   *f25* The Greek word means either *life* or *soul*; also in verse 26.

PSALM 21:1-13
For the director of music. A psalm of David.

1 ● LORD, the king rejoices in your
        strength.
   How great is his joy in the victories
        you give!
2 You have granted him the desire of
        his heart
   and have not withheld the request
        of his lips.   *Selah*
3 You welcomed him with rich
        blessings
   and placed a crown of pure gold
        on his head.
4 He asked you for life, and you gave it
        to him—
   length of days, for ever and ever.
5 Through the victories you gave, his
        glory is great;
   you have bestowed on him
        splendor and majesty.
6 Surely you have granted him eternal
        blessings
   and made him glad with the joy of
        your presence.
7 For the king trusts in the LORD;
   through the unfailing love of the
        Most High
   he will not be shaken.

8 Your hand will lay hold on all your
enemies;
your right hand will seize
your foes.
9 At the time of your appearing
you will make them like a fiery
furnace.
In his wrath the LORD will swallow
them up,
and his fire will consume them.
10 You will destroy their descendants
from the earth,
their posterity from mankind.
11 Though they plot evil against you
and devise wicked schemes, they
cannot succeed;
12 for you will make them turn their
backs
when you aim at them with
drawn bow.

13 Be exalted, O LORD, in your
strength;
we will sing and praise your
might.

PROVERBS 5:1-6

My son, pay attention to my
wisdom,
listen well to my words of
insight,
2 that you may maintain discretion
and your lips may preserve
knowledge.
3 For the lips of an adulteress drip
honey,
and her speech is smoother
than oil;
4 but in the end she is bitter as gall,
sharp as a double-edged sword.
5 Her feet go down to death;
her steps lead straight to the
grave.a
6 She gives no thought to the way of
life;
her paths are crooked, but she
knows it not.

a5 Hebrew *Sheol*

GOD SIGHTINGS

January 26

EXODUS 2:11–3:22

One day, after Moses had grown up, he
went out to where his own people were
and watched them at their hard labor.
He saw an Egyptian beating a Hebrew,
one of his own people. 12 Glancing this
way and that and seeing no one, he
killed the Egyptian and hid him in the
sand. 13 The next day he went out and
saw two Hebrews fighting. He asked the
one in the wrong, "Why are you hitting
your fellow Hebrew?"

14 The man said, "Who made you
ruler and judge over us? Are you thinking of killing me as you killed the Egyptian?" Then Moses was afraid and
thought, "What I did must have become
known."

15 When Pharaoh heard of this, he tried
to kill Moses, but Moses fled from Pharaoh and went to live in Midian, where he
sat down by a well. 16 Now a priest of Midian had seven daughters, and they came
to draw water and fill the troughs to water
their father's flock. 17 Some shepherds
came along and drove them away, but Moses got up and came to their rescue and
watered their flock.

18 When the girls returned to Reuel
their father, he asked them, "Why have
you returned so early today?"

19 They answered, "An Egyptian rescued us from the shepherds. He even
drew water for us and watered the
flock."

20 "And where is he?" he asked his
daughters. "Why did you leave him? Invite him to have something to eat."

21 Moses agreed to stay with the man,
who gave his daughter Zipporah to Moses in marriage. 22 Zipporah gave birth
to a son, and Moses named him Gershom,a saying, "I have become an alien
in a foreign land."

23 During that long period, the king of

Egypt died. The Israelites groaned in their slavery and cried out, and their cry for help because of their slavery went up to God. 24God heard their groaning and he remembered his covenant with Abraham, with Isaac and with Jacob. 25So God looked on the Israelites and was concerned about them.

3:1Now Moses was tending the flock of Jethro his father-in-law, the priest of Midian, and he led the flock to the far side of the desert and came to Horeb, the mountain of God. 2There the angel of the LORD appeared to him in flames of fire from within a bush. Moses saw that though the bush was on fire it did not burn up. 3So Moses thought, "I will go over and see this strange sight—why the bush does not burn up."

4When the LORD saw that he had gone over to look, God called to him from within the bush, "Moses! Moses!"

And Moses said, "Here I am."

5"Do not come any closer," God said. "Take off your sandals, for the place where you are standing is holy ground." 6Then he said, "I am the God of your father, the God of Abraham, the God of Isaac and the God of Jacob." At this, Moses hid his face, because he was afraid to look at God.

7The LORD said, "I have indeed seen the misery of my people in Egypt. I have heard them crying out because of their slave drivers, and I am concerned about their suffering. 8So I have come down to rescue them from the hand of the Egyptians and to bring them up out of that land into a good and spacious land, a land flowing with milk and honey—the home of the Canaanites, Hittites, Amorites, Perizzites, Hivites and Jebusites. 9And now the cry of the Israelites has reached me, and I have seen the way the Egyptians are oppressing them. 10So now, go. I am sending you to Pharaoh to bring my people the Israelites out of Egypt."

11But Moses said to God, "Who am I, that I should go to Pharaoh and bring the Israelites out of Egypt?"

12And God said, "I will be with you. And this will be the sign to you that it is I who have sent you: When you have brought the people out of Egypt, youb will worship God on this mountain."

13Moses said to God, "Suppose I go to the Israelites and say to them, 'The God of your fathers has sent me to you,' and they ask me, 'What is his name?' Then what shall I tell them?"

14**God said to Moses, "I AM WHO I AM.c This is what you are to say to the Israelites: 'I AM has sent me to you.'"**

15God also said to Moses, "Say to the Israelites, 'The LORD,d the God of your fathers—the God of Abraham, the God of Isaac and the God of Jacob—has sent me to you.' This is my name forever, the name by which I am to be remembered from generation to generation.

16"Go, assemble the elders of Israel and say to them, 'The LORD, the God of your fathers—the God of Abraham, Isaac and Jacob—appeared to me and said: I have watched over you and have seen what has been done to you in Egypt. 17And I have promised to bring you up out of your misery in Egypt into the land of the Canaanites, Hittites, Amorites, Perizzites, Hivites and Jebusites—a land flowing with milk and honey.'

18"The elders of Israel will listen to you. Then you and the elders are to go to the king of Egypt and say to him, 'The LORD, the God of the Hebrews, has met with us. Let us take a three-day journey into the desert to offer sacrifices to the LORD our God.' 19But I know that the king of Egypt will not let you go unless a mighty hand compels him. 20So I will stretch out my hand and strike the Egyptians with all the wonders that I will perform among them. After that, he will let you go.

21"And I will make the Egyptians favorably disposed toward this people, so that when you leave you will not go empty-handed. 22Every woman is to ask her neighbor and any woman living in her house for articles of silver and gold and for clothing, which you will put on your sons and daughters. And so you will plunder the Egyptians."

a 22 Gershom sounds like the Hebrew for *an alien there.*
b 12 The Hebrew is plural.   c 14 Or *I WILL BE WHAT I WILL BE*
d 15 The Hebrew for LORD sounds like and may be derived from the Hebrew for *I AM* in verse 14.

MATTHEW 17:10-27

The disciples asked him [Jesus], "Why then do the teachers of the law say that Elijah must come first?"

11 Jesus replied, "To be sure, Elijah comes and will restore all things. 12 But I tell you, Elijah has already come, and they did not recognize him, but have done to him everything they wished. In the same way the Son of Man is going to suffer at their hands." 13 Then the disciples understood that he was talking to them about John the Baptist.

14 When they came to the crowd, a man approached Jesus and knelt before him. 15 "Lord, have mercy on my son," he said. "He has seizures and is suffering greatly. He often falls into the fire or into the water. 16 I brought him to your disciples, but they could not heal him."

17 "O unbelieving and perverse generation," Jesus replied, "how long shall I stay with you? How long shall I put up with you? Bring the boy here to me." 18 Jesus rebuked the demon, and it came out of the boy, and he was healed from that moment.

19 Then the disciples came to Jesus in private and asked, "Why couldn't we drive it out?"

20 He replied, "Because you have so little faith. I tell you the truth, if you have faith as small as a mustard seed, you can say to this mountain, 'Move from here to there' and it will move. Nothing will be impossible for you. a "

22 When they came together in Galilee, he said to them, "The Son of Man is going to be betrayed into the hands of men. 23 They will kill him, and on the third day he will be raised to life." And the disciples were filled with grief.

24 After Jesus and his disciples arrived in Capernaum, the collectors of the two-drachma tax came to Peter and asked, "Doesn't your teacher pay the temple tax b ?"

25 "Yes, he does," he replied.

When Peter came into the house, Jesus was the first to speak. "What do you think, Simon?" he asked. "From whom do the kings of the earth collect duty and taxes—from their own sons or from others?"

26 "From others," Peter answered.

"Then the sons are exempt," Jesus said to him. 27 "But so that we may not offend them, go to the lake and throw out your line. Take the first fish you catch; open its mouth and you will find a four-drachma coin. Take it and give it to them for my tax and yours."

a 20 Some manuscripts *you.* 21 But this kind does not go out except by prayer and fasting.   b 24 Greek *the two drachmas*

PSALM 22:1-18

For the director of music. To ⌊the tune of⌋ "The Doe of the Morning." A psalm of David.

1 **M**y God, my God, why have you
     forsaken me?
  Why are you so far from
     saving me,
  so far from the words of my
     groaning?
2 O my God, I cry out by day, but you
     do not answer,
  by night, and am not silent.

3 Yet you are enthroned as the Holy One;
  you are the praise of Israel. a
4 In you our fathers put their trust;
  they trusted and you delivered
     them.
5 They cried to you and were saved;
  in you they trusted and were not
     disappointed.

6 But I am a worm and not a man,
  scorned by men and despised by
     the people.
7 All who see me mock me;
  they hurl insults, shaking their
     heads:
8 "He trusts in the LORD;
  let the LORD rescue him.
  Let him deliver him,
  since he delights in him."

⁹ Yet you brought me out of the
        womb;
    you made me trust in you
    even at my mother's breast.
¹⁰ From birth I was cast upon you;
    from my mother's womb you have
        been my God.
¹¹ Do not be far from me,
    for trouble is near
    and there is no one to help.

¹² Many bulls surround me;
    strong bulls of Bashan
        encircle me.
¹³ Roaring lions tearing their prey
    open their mouths wide
        against me.
¹⁴ I am poured out like water,
    and all my bones are out of joint.
    My heart has turned to wax;
    it has melted away within me.
¹⁵ My strength is dried up like a
        potsherd,
    and my tongue sticks to the roof of
        my mouth;
    you lay me*b* in the dust of death.
¹⁶ Dogs have surrounded me;
    a band of evil men has encircled
        me,
    they have pierced*c* my hands and
        my feet.
¹⁷ I can count all my bones;
    people stare and gloat over me.
¹⁸ They divide my garments among
        them
    and cast lots for my clothing.

*a3 Or Yet you are holy, / enthroned on the praises of Israel
b15 Or / I am laid   c16 Some Hebrew manuscripts, Septuagint
and Syriac; most Hebrew manuscripts / like the lion,*

PROVERBS 5:7–14
⁷ Now then, my sons, listen to me;
    do not turn aside from what I say.
⁸ Keep to a path far from her,
    do not go near the door of
        her house,
⁹ lest you give your best strength
        to others
    and your years to one who
        is cruel,
¹⁰ lest strangers feast on your wealth
    and your toil enrich another
        man's house.

¹¹ At the end of your life you will groan,
    when your flesh and body
        are spent.
¹² You will say, "How I hated
        discipline!
    How my heart spurned correction!
¹³ I would not obey my teachers
    or listen to my instructors.
¹⁴ I have come to the brink of utter ruin
    in the midst of the whole
        assembly."

☐ DAY 27

GOD SIGHTINGS

January 27

EXODUS 4:1–5:21
Moses answered, "What if they [the Is-raelites] do not believe me or listen to me and say, 'The LORD did not appear to you'?"

² Then the LORD said to him, "What is that in your hand?"

"A staff," he replied.

³ The LORD said, "Throw it on the ground."

Moses threw it on the ground and it became a snake, and he ran from it. ⁴ Then the LORD said to him, "Reach out your hand and take it by the tail." So Moses reached out and took hold of the snake and it turned back into a staff in his hand. ⁵ "This," said the LORD, "is so that they may believe that the LORD, the God of their fathers—the God of Abraham, the God of Isaac and the God of Jacob—has appeared to you."

⁶ Then the LORD said, "Put your hand inside your cloak." So Moses put his hand into his cloak, and when he took it out, it was leprous,*a* like snow.

⁷ "Now put it back into your cloak," he said. So Moses put his hand back into his cloak, and when he took it out, it was restored, like the rest of his flesh.

⁸ Then the LORD said, "If they do not believe you or pay attention to the first

miraculous sign, they may believe the second. [9] But if they do not believe these two signs or listen to you, take some water from the Nile and pour it on the dry ground. The water you take from the river will become blood on the ground."

[10] Moses said to the LORD, "O Lord, I have never been eloquent, neither in the past nor since you have spoken to your servant. I am slow of speech and tongue."

[11] **The LORD said to him, "Who gave man his mouth? Who makes him deaf or mute? Who gives him sight or makes him blind? Is it not I, the LORD? [12] Now go; I will help you speak and will teach you what to say."**

[13] But Moses said, "O Lord, please send someone else to do it."

[14] Then the LORD's anger burned against Moses and he said, "What about your brother, Aaron the Levite? I know he can speak well. He is already on his way to meet you, and his heart will be glad when he sees you. [15] You shall speak to him and put words in his mouth; I will help both of you speak and will teach you what to do. [16] He will speak to the people for you, and it will be as if he were your mouth and as if you were God to him. [17] But take this staff in your hand so you can perform miraculous signs with it."

[18] Then Moses went back to Jethro his father-in-law and said to him, "Let me go back to my own people in Egypt to see if any of them are still alive."

Jethro said, "Go, and I wish you well."

[19] Now the LORD had said to Moses in Midian, "Go back to Egypt, for all the men who wanted to kill you are dead." [20] So Moses took his wife and sons, put them on a donkey and started back to Egypt. And he took the staff of God in his hand.

[21] The LORD said to Moses, "When you return to Egypt, see that you perform before Pharaoh all the wonders I have given you the power to do. But I will harden his heart so that he will not let the people go. [22] Then say to Pharaoh, 'This is what the LORD says: Israel is my firstborn son, [23] and I told you, "Let my son go, so he may worship me." But you refused to let him go; so I will kill your firstborn son.'"

[24] At a lodging place on the way, the LORD met ⌊Moses⌋ [b] and was about to kill him. [25] But Zipporah took a flint knife, cut off her son's foreskin and touched ⌊Moses'⌋ feet with it. [c] "Surely you are a bridegroom of blood to me," she said. [26] So the LORD let him alone. (At that time she said "bridegroom of blood," referring to circumcision.)

[27] The LORD said to Aaron, "Go into the desert to meet Moses." So he met Moses at the mountain of God and kissed him. [28] Then Moses told Aaron everything the LORD had sent him to say, and also about all the miraculous signs he had commanded him to perform.

[29] Moses and Aaron brought together all the elders of the Israelites, [30] and Aaron told them everything the LORD had said to Moses. He also performed the signs before the people, [31] and they believed. And when they heard that the LORD was concerned about them and had seen their misery, they bowed down and worshiped.

[5:1] AFTERWARD Moses and Aaron went to Pharaoh and said, "This is what the LORD, the God of Israel, says: 'Let my people go, so that they may hold a festival to me in the desert.'"

[2] Pharaoh said, "Who is the LORD, that I should obey him and let Israel go? I do not know the LORD and I will not let Israel go."

[3] Then they said, "The God of the Hebrews has met with us. Now let us take a three-day journey into the desert to offer sacrifices to the LORD our God, or he may strike us with plagues or with the sword."

[4] But the king of Egypt said, "Moses and Aaron, why are you taking the people away from their labor? Get back to your work!" [5] Then Pharaoh said, "Look, the people of the land are now numerous, and you are stopping them from working."

6That same day Pharaoh gave this order to the slave drivers and foremen in charge of the people: 7"You are no longer to supply the people with straw for making bricks; let them go and gather their own straw. 8But require them to make the same number of bricks as before; don't reduce the quota. They are lazy; that is why they are crying out, 'Let us go and sacrifice to our God.' 9Make the work harder for the men so that they keep working and pay no attention to lies."

10Then the slave drivers and the foremen went out and said to the people, "This is what Pharaoh says: 'I will not give you any more straw. 11Go and get your own straw wherever you can find it, but your work will not be reduced at all.'" 12So the people scattered all over Egypt to gather stubble to use for straw. 13The slave drivers kept pressing them, saying, "Complete the work required of you for each day, just as when you had straw." 14The Israelite foremen appointed by Pharaoh's slave drivers were beaten and were asked, "Why didn't you meet your quota of bricks yesterday or today, as before?"

15Then the Israelite foremen went and appealed to Pharaoh: "Why have you treated your servants this way? 16Your servants are given no straw, yet we are told, 'Make bricks!' Your servants are being beaten, but the fault is with your own people."

17Pharaoh said, "Lazy, that's what you are—lazy! That is why you keep saying, 'Let us go and sacrifice to the LORD.' 18Now get to work. You will not be given any straw, yet you must produce your full quota of bricks."

19The Israelite foremen realized they were in trouble when they were told, "You are not to reduce the number of bricks required of you for each day." 20When they left Pharaoh, they found Moses and Aaron waiting to meet them, 21and they said, "May the LORD look upon you and judge you! You have made us a stench to Pharaoh and his officials

and have put a sword in their hand to kill us."

a6 The Hebrew word was used for various diseases affecting the skin—not necessarily leprosy.   b24 Or ⌊Moses' son⌋; Hebrew him   c25 Or and drew near ⌊Moses'⌋ feet

MATTHEW 18:1-22

At that time the disciples came to Jesus and asked, "Who is the greatest in the kingdom of heaven?"

2He called a little child and had him stand among them. 3And he said: "I tell you the truth, unless you change and become like little children, you will never enter the kingdom of heaven. 4Therefore, whoever humbles himself like this child is the greatest in the kingdom of heaven.

5"And whoever welcomes a little child like this in my name welcomes me. 6But if anyone causes one of these little ones who believe in me to sin, it would be better for him to have a large millstone hung around his neck and to be drowned in the depths of the sea.

7"Woe to the world because of the things that cause people to sin! Such things must come, but woe to the man through whom they come! 8If your hand or your foot causes you to sin, cut it off and throw it away. It is better for you to enter life maimed or crippled than to have two hands or two feet and be thrown into eternal fire. 9And if your eye causes you to sin, gouge it out and throw it away. It is better for you to enter life with one eye than to have two eyes and be thrown into the fire of hell.

10"See that you do not look down on one of these little ones. For I tell you that their angels in heaven always see the face of my Father in heaven.a

12"What do you think? If a man owns a hundred sheep, and one of them wanders away, will he not leave the ninety-nine on the hills and go to look for the one that wandered off ? 13And if he finds it, I tell you the truth, he is happier about that one sheep than about the ninety-nine that did not wander off. 14In the same way your Father in heaven is not willing that any of these little ones should be lost.

15"If your brother sins against you,*b* go and show him his fault, just between the two of you. If he listens to you, you have won your brother over. 16But if he will not listen, take one or two others along, so that 'every matter may be established by the testimony of two or three witnesses.'*c* 17If he refuses to listen to them, tell it to the church; and if he refuses to listen even to the church, treat him as you would a pagan or a tax collector.

18"I tell you the truth, whatever you bind on earth will be*d* bound in heaven, and whatever you loose on earth will be*d* loosed in heaven.

19"Again, I tell you that if two of you on earth agree about anything you ask for, it will be done for you by my Father in heaven. 20For where two or three come together in my name, there am I with them."

21Then Peter came to Jesus and asked, "Lord, how many times shall I forgive my brother when he sins against me? Up to seven times?"

22Jesus answered, "I tell you, not seven times, but seventy-seven times.*e*"

a10 Some manuscripts *heaven.* *11The Son of Man came to save what was lost.* *b15* Some manuscripts do not have *against you.* *c16* Deut. 19:15 *d18* Or *have been* *e22* Or *seventy times seven*

PSALM 22:19-31

19But you, O Lord, be not far off;
  O my Strength, come quickly to
    help me.
20Deliver my life from the sword,
  my precious life from the power of
    the dogs.
21Rescue me from the mouth of the
    lions;
  save*a* me from the horns of the
    wild oxen.

22I will declare your name to my
    brothers;
  in the congregation I will praise
    you.
23You who fear the Lord, praise him!
  All you descendants of Jacob,
    honor him!
  Revere him, all you descendants
    of Israel!

24For he has not despised or disdained
  the suffering of the afflicted one;
 he has not hidden his face
    from him
  but has listened to his cry
    for help.

25From you comes the theme of my
    praise in the great assembly;
  before those who fear you*b* will
    I fulfill my vows.
26The poor will eat and be satisfied;
  they who seek the Lord will praise
    him—
  may your hearts live forever!
27All the ends of the earth
  will remember and turn to the
    Lord,
 and all the families of the nations
  will bow down before him,
28for dominion belongs to the Lord
  and he rules over the nations.

29All the rich of the earth will feast and
    worship;
  all who go down to the dust will
    kneel before him—
  those who cannot keep themselves
    alive.
30Posterity will serve him;
  future generations will be told
    about the Lord.
31They will proclaim his righteousness
  to a people yet unborn—
  for he has done it.

a21 Or */ you have heard* *b25* Hebrew *him*

PROVERBS 5:15-21

15Drink water from your own cistern,
  running water from your own well.
16Should your springs overflow in the
    streets,
  your streams of water in the public
    squares?
17Let them be yours alone,
  never to be shared with strangers.
18May your fountain be blessed,
  and may you rejoice in the wife of
    your youth.
19A loving doe, a graceful deer—
  may her breasts satisfy you always,
  may you ever be captivated by
    her love.

20Why be captivated, my son, by an
adulteress?
Why embrace the bosom of
another man's wife?

21For a man's ways are in full view of
the Lord,
and he examines all his paths.

□ DAY 28

GOD SIGHTINGS

January 28

EXODUS 5:22–7:24

Moses returned to the Lord and said,
"O Lord, why have you brought trouble
upon this people? Is this why you sent
me? 23Ever since I went to Pharaoh to
speak in your name, he has brought
trouble upon this people, and you have
not rescued your people at all."

6:1Then the Lord said to Moses, "Now
you will see what I will do to Pharaoh:
Because of my mighty hand he will let
them go; because of my mighty hand he
will drive them out of his country."

2God also said to Moses, "I am the
Lord. 3I appeared to Abraham, to Isaac
and to Jacob as God Almighty,a but by
my name the Lordb I did not make myself known to them.c 4I also established
my covenant with them to give them the
land of Canaan, where they lived as
aliens. 5Moreover, I have heard the
groaning of the Israelites, whom the
Egyptians are enslaving, and I have remembered my covenant.

6"Therefore, say to the Israelites: 'I
am the Lord, and I will bring you out
from under the yoke of the Egyptians. I
will free you from being slaves to them,
and I will redeem you with an outstretched arm and with mighty acts of
judgment. 7I will take you as my own
people, and I will be your God. Then you
will know that I am the Lord your God,
who brought you out from under the

yoke of the Egyptians. 8And I will bring
you to the land I swore with uplifted
hand to give to Abraham, to Isaac and to
Jacob. I will give it to you as a possession. I am the Lord.'"

9Moses reported this to the Israelites,
but they did not listen to him because of
their discouragement and cruel bondage.

10Then the Lord said to Moses, 11"Go,
tell Pharaoh king of Egypt to let the Israelites go out of his country."

12But Moses said to the Lord, "If the
Israelites will not listen to me, why
would Pharaoh listen to me, since I
speak with faltering lipsd?"

13Now the Lord spoke to Moses and
Aaron about the Israelites and Pharaoh
king of Egypt, and he commanded them
to bring the Israelites out of Egypt.

14These were the heads of their
familiese:

The sons of Reuben the firstborn son of Israel were Hanoch
and Pallu, Hezron and Carmi.
These were the clans of Reuben.

15The sons of Simeon were Jemuel, Jamin, Ohad, Jakin, Zohar
and Shaul the son of a Canaanite
woman. These were the clans of
Simeon.

16These were the names of the
sons of Levi according to their records: Gershon, Kohath and Merari.
Levi lived 137 years.

17The sons of Gershon, by clans,
were Libni and Shimei.

18The sons of Kohath were Amram, Izhar, Hebron and Uzziel. Kohath lived 133 years.

19The sons of Merari were
Mahli and Mushi.

These were the clans of Levi according to their records.

20Amram married his father's
sister Jochebed, who bore him
Aaron and Moses. Amram lived
137 years.

21The sons of Izhar were Korah,
Nepheg and Zicri.

22 The sons of Uzziel were Mishael, Elzaphan and Sithri.

23 Aaron married Elisheba, daughter of Amminadab and sister of Nahshon, and she bore him Nadab and Abihu, Eleazar and Ithamar.

24 The sons of Korah were Assir, Elkanah and Abiasaph. These were the Korahite clans.

25 Eleazar son of Aaron married one of the daughters of Putiel, and she bore him Phinehas.

These were the heads of the Levite families, clan by clan.

26 It was this same Aaron and Moses to whom the LORD said, "Bring the Israelites out of Egypt by their divisions." 27 They were the ones who spoke to Pharaoh king of Egypt about bringing the Israelites out of Egypt. It was the same Moses and Aaron.

28 Now when the LORD spoke to Moses in Egypt, 29 he said to him, "I am the LORD. Tell Pharaoh king of Egypt everything I tell you."

30 But Moses said to the LORD, "Since I speak with faltering lips, why would Pharaoh listen to me?"

7:1 THEN the LORD said to Moses, "See, I have made you like God to Pharaoh, and your brother Aaron will be your prophet. 2 You are to say everything I command you, and your brother Aaron is to tell Pharaoh to let the Israelites go out of his country. 3 But I will harden Pharaoh's heart, and though I multiply my miraculous signs and wonders in Egypt, 4 he will not listen to you. Then I will lay my hand on Egypt and with mighty acts of judgment I will bring out my divisions, my people the Israelites. 5 And the Egyptians will know that I am the LORD when I stretch out my hand against Egypt and bring the Israelites out of it."

6 Moses and Aaron did just as the LORD commanded them. 7 Moses was eighty years old and Aaron eighty-three when they spoke to Pharaoh.

8 The LORD said to Moses and Aaron, 9 "When Pharaoh says to you, 'Perform a miracle,' then say to Aaron, 'Take your staff and throw it down before Pharaoh,' and it will become a snake."

10 So Moses and Aaron went to Pharaoh and did just as the LORD commanded. Aaron threw his staff down in front of Pharaoh and his officials, and it became a snake. 11 Pharaoh then summoned wise men and sorcerers, and the Egyptian magicians also did the same things by their secret arts: 12 Each one threw down his staff and it became a snake. But Aaron's staff swallowed up their staffs. 13 Yet Pharaoh's heart became hard and he would not listen to them, just as the LORD had said.

14 Then the LORD said to Moses, "Pharaoh's heart is unyielding; he refuses to let the people go. 15 Go to Pharaoh in the morning as he goes out to the water. Wait on the bank of the Nile to meet him, and take in your hand the staff that was changed into a snake. 16 Then say to him, 'The LORD, the God of the Hebrews, has sent me to say to you: Let my people go, so that they may worship me in the desert. But until now you have not listened. 17 This is what the LORD says: By this you will know that I am the LORD: With the staff that is in my hand I will strike the water of the Nile, and it will be changed into blood. 18 The fish in the Nile will die, and the river will stink; the Egyptians will not be able to drink its water.'"

19 The LORD said to Moses, "Tell Aaron, 'Take your staff and stretch out your hand over the waters of Egypt—over the streams and canals, over the ponds and all the reservoirs'—and they will turn to blood. Blood will be everywhere in Egypt, even in the wooden buckets and stone jars."

20 Moses and Aaron did just as the LORD had commanded. He raised his staff in the presence of Pharaoh and his officials and struck the water of the Nile, and all the water was changed into blood. 21 The fish in the Nile died, and the river smelled so bad that the Egyp-

tians could not drink its water. Blood was everywhere in Egypt.

²²But the Egyptian magicians did the same things by their secret arts, and Pharaoh's heart became hard; he would not listen to Moses and Aaron, just as the Lᴏʀᴅ had said. ²³Instead, he turned and went into his palace, and did not take even this to heart. ²⁴And all the Egyptians dug along the Nile to get drinking water, because they could not drink the water of the river.

a3 Hebrew *El-Shaddai*   *b3* See note at Exodus 3:15.
c3 Or *Almighty, and by my name the Lᴏʀᴅ did I not let myself be known to them?*   *d12* Hebrew *I am uncircumcised of lips;* also in verse 30   *e14* The Hebrew for *families* here and in verse 25 refers to units larger than clans.

MATTHEW 18:23–19:12

"Therefore, the kingdom of heaven is like a king who wanted to settle accounts with his servants. ²⁴As he began the settlement, a man who owed him ten thousand talents*a* was brought to him. ²⁵Since he was not able to pay, the master ordered that he and his wife and his children and all that he had be sold to repay the debt.

²⁶"The servant fell on his knees before him. 'Be patient with me,' he begged, 'and I will pay back everything.' ²⁷The servant's master took pity on him, canceled the debt and let him go.

²⁸"But when that servant went out, he found one of his fellow servants who owed him a hundred denarii.*b* He grabbed him and began to choke him. 'Pay back what you owe me!' he demanded.

²⁹"His fellow servant fell to his knees and begged him, 'Be patient with me, and I will pay you back.'

³⁰"But he refused. Instead, he went off and had the man thrown into prison until he could pay the debt. ³¹When the other servants saw what had happened, they were greatly distressed and went and told their master everything that had happened.

³²"Then the master called the servant in. 'You wicked servant,' he said, 'I canceled all that debt of yours because you begged me to. ³³Shouldn't you have had mercy on your fellow servant just as I had on you?' ³⁴In anger his master turned him over to the jailers to be tortured, until he should pay back all he owed.

³⁵"This is how my heavenly Father will treat each of you unless you forgive your brother from your heart."

¹⁹:¹When Jesus had finished saying these things, he left Galilee and went into the region of Judea to the other side of the Jordan. ²Large crowds followed him, and he healed them there.

³Some Pharisees came to him to test him. They asked, "Is it lawful for a man to divorce his wife for any and every reason?"

⁴"Haven't you read," he replied, "that at the beginning the Creator 'made them male and female,'*c* ⁵and said, 'For this reason a man will leave his father and mother and be united to his wife, and the two will become one flesh'*d*? ⁶So they are no longer two, but one. Therefore what God has joined together, let man not separate."

⁷"Why then," they asked, "did Moses command that a man give his wife a certificate of divorce and send her away?"

⁸Jesus replied, "Moses permitted you to divorce your wives because your hearts were hard. But it was not this way from the beginning. ⁹I tell you that anyone who divorces his wife, except for marital unfaithfulness, and marries another woman commits adultery."

¹⁰The disciples said to him, "If this is the situation between a husband and wife, it is better not to marry."

¹¹Jesus replied, "Not everyone can accept this word, but only those to whom it has been given. ¹²For some are eunuchs because they were born that way; others were made that way by men; and others have renounced marriage*e* because of the kingdom of heaven. The one who can accept this should accept it."

a24 That is, millions of dollars   *b28* That is, a few dollars   *c4* Gen. 1:27   *d5* Gen. 2:24   *e12* Or *have made themselves eunuchs*

PSALM 23:1-6
A psalm of David.

1 The Lord is my shepherd, I shall
   not be in want.
2   He makes me lie down in green
      pastures,
   he leads me beside quiet waters,
3   he restores my soul.
   He guides me in paths of
      righteousness
      for his name's sake.
4 Even though I walk
      through the valley of the shadow
      of death,a
   I will fear no evil,
      for you are with me;
   your rod and your staff,
      they comfort me.

5 You prepare a table before me
      in the presence of my enemies.
   You anoint my head with oil;
      my cup overflows.
6 Surely goodness and love will
      follow me
      all the days of my life,
   and I will dwell in the house of
      the Lord
      forever.

a4 Or through the darkest valley

PROVERBS 5:22-23
22 The evil deeds of a wicked man
      ensnare him;
   the cords of his sin hold him fast.
23 He will die for lack of discipline,
   led astray by his own great folly.

☐ D A Y 2 9

GOD SIGHTINGS

January 29

EXODUS 7:25–9:35
Seven days passed after the Lord struck
the Nile.

8:1 Then the Lord said to Moses, "Go to
Pharaoh and say to him, 'This is what

the Lord says: Let my people go, so that
they may worship me. 2 If you refuse to
let them go, I will plague your whole
country with frogs. 3 The Nile will teem
with frogs. They will come up into your
palace and your bedroom and onto your
bed, into the houses of your officials
and on your people, and into your ovens
and kneading troughs. 4 The frogs will
go up on you and your people and all
your officials.'"

5 Then the Lord said to Moses, "Tell
Aaron, 'Stretch out your hand with your
staff over the streams and canals and
ponds, and make frogs come up on the
land of Egypt.'"

6 So Aaron stretched out his hand
over the waters of Egypt, and the frogs
came up and covered the land. 7 But the
magicians did the same things by their
secret arts; they also made frogs come
up on the land of Egypt.

8 Pharaoh summoned Moses and
Aaron and said, "Pray to the Lord to take
the frogs away from me and my people,
and I will let your people go to offer sacrifices to the Lord."

9 Moses said to Pharaoh, "I leave to
you the honor of setting the time for me
to pray for you and your officials and
your people that you and your houses
may be rid of the frogs, except for those
that remain in the Nile."

10 "Tomorrow," Pharaoh said.

Moses replied, "It will be as you say, so
that you may know there is no one like
the Lord our God. 11 The frogs will leave
you and your houses, your officials and
your people; they will remain only in the
Nile."

12 After Moses and Aaron left Pharaoh, Moses cried out to the Lord about
the frogs he had brought on Pharaoh.
13 And the Lord did what Moses asked.
The frogs died in the houses, in the
courtyards and in the fields. 14 They
were piled into heaps, and the land
reeked of them. 15 But when Pharaoh
saw that there was relief, he hardened
his heart and would not listen to Moses
and Aaron, just as the Lord had said.

16 Then the Lord said to Moses, "Tell

Aaron, 'Stretch out your staff and strike the dust of the ground,' and throughout the land of Egypt the dust will become gnats." 17They did this, and when Aaron stretched out his hand with the staff and struck the dust of the ground, gnats came upon men and animals. All the dust throughout the land of Egypt became gnats. 18But when the magicians tried to produce gnats by their secret arts, they could not. And the gnats were on men and animals.

19The magicians said to Pharaoh, "This is the finger of God." But Pharaoh's heart was hard and he would not listen, just as the LORD had said.

20Then the LORD said to Moses, "Get up early in the morning and confront Pharaoh as he goes to the water and say to him, 'This is what the LORD says: Let my people go, so that they may worship me. 21If you do not let my people go, I will send swarms of flies on you and your officials, on your people and into your houses. The houses of the Egyptians will be full of flies, and even the ground where they are.

22" 'But on that day I will deal differently with the land of Goshen, where my people live; no swarms of flies will be there, so that you will know that I, the LORD, am in this land. 23I will make a distinctiona between my people and your people. This miraculous sign will occur tomorrow.'"

24And the LORD did this. Dense swarms of flies poured into Pharaoh's palace and into the houses of his officials, and throughout Egypt the land was ruined by the flies.

25Then Pharaoh summoned Moses and Aaron and said, "Go, sacrifice to your God here in the land."

26But Moses said, "That would not be right. The sacrifices we offer the LORD our God would be detestable to the Egyptians. And if we offer sacrifices that are detestable in their eyes, will they not stone us? 27We must take a three-day journey into the desert to offer sacrifices to the LORD our God, as he commands us."

28Pharaoh said, "I will let you go to offer sacrifices to the LORD your God in the desert, but you must not go very far. Now pray for me."

29Moses answered, "As soon as I leave you, I will pray to the LORD, and tomorrow the flies will leave Pharaoh and his officials and his people. Only be sure that Pharaoh does not act deceitfully again by not letting the people go to offer sacrifices to the LORD."

30Then Moses left Pharaoh and prayed to the LORD, 31and the LORD did what Moses asked: The flies left Pharaoh and his officials and his people; not a fly remained. 32But this time also Pharaoh hardened his heart and would not let the people go.

9:1Then the LORD said to Moses, "Go to Pharaoh and say to him, 'This is what the LORD, the God of the Hebrews, says: "Let my people go, so that they may worship me." 2If you refuse to let them go and continue to hold them back, 3the hand of the LORD will bring a terrible plague on your livestock in the field—on your horses and donkeys and camels and on your cattle and sheep and goats. 4But the LORD will make a distinction between the livestock of Israel and that of Egypt, so that no animal belonging to the Israelites will die.'"

5The LORD set a time and said, "Tomorrow the LORD will do this in the land." 6And the next day the LORD did it: All the livestock of the Egyptians died, but not one animal belonging to the Israelites died. 7Pharaoh sent men to investigate and found that not even one of the animals of the Israelites had died. Yet his heart was unyielding and he would not let the people go.

8Then the LORD said to Moses and Aaron, "Take handfuls of soot from a furnace and have Moses toss it into the air in the presence of Pharaoh. 9It will become fine dust over the whole land of Egypt, and festering boils will break out on men and animals throughout the land."

10So they took soot from a furnace

and stood before Pharaoh. Moses tossed it into the air, and festering boils broke out on men and animals. [11] The magicians could not stand before Moses because of the boils that were on them and on all the Egyptians. [12] But the LORD hardened Pharaoh's heart and he would not listen to Moses and Aaron, just as the LORD had said to Moses.

[13] Then the LORD said to Moses, "Get up early in the morning, confront Pharaoh and say to him, 'This is what the LORD, the God of the Hebrews, says: Let my people go, so that they may worship me, [14] or this time I will send the full force of my plagues against you and against your officials and your people, so you may know that there is no one like me in all the earth. [15] For by now I could have stretched out my hand and struck you and your people with a plague that would have wiped you off the earth. [16] But I have raised you up[b] for this very purpose, that I might show you my power and that my name might be proclaimed in all the earth. [17] You still set yourself against my people and will not let them go. [18] Therefore, at this time tomorrow I will send the worst hailstorm that has ever fallen on Egypt, from the day it was founded till now. [19] Give an order now to bring your livestock and everything you have in the field to a place of shelter, because the hail will fall on every man and animal that has not been brought in and is still out in the field, and they will die.'"

[20] Those officials of Pharaoh who feared the word of the LORD hurried to bring their slaves and their livestock inside. [21] But those who ignored the word of the LORD left their slaves and livestock in the field.

[22] Then the LORD said to Moses, "Stretch out your hand toward the sky so that hail will fall all over Egypt—on men and animals and on everything growing in the fields of Egypt." [23] When Moses stretched out his staff toward the sky, the LORD sent thunder and hail, and lightning flashed down to the ground. So the LORD rained hail on the land of Egypt; [24] hail fell and lightning flashed back and forth. It was the worst storm in all the land of Egypt since it had become a nation. [25] Throughout Egypt hail struck everything in the fields—both men and animals; it beat down everything growing in the fields and stripped every tree. [26] The only place it did not hail was the land of Goshen, where the Israelites were.

[27] Then Pharaoh summoned Moses and Aaron. "This time I have sinned," he said to them. "The LORD is in the right, and I and my people are in the wrong. [28] Pray to the LORD, for we have had enough thunder and hail. I will let you go; you don't have to stay any longer."

[29] Moses replied, "When I have gone out of the city, I will spread out my hands in prayer to the LORD. The thunder will stop and there will be no more hail, so you may know that the earth is the LORD's. [30] But I know that you and your officials still do not fear the LORD God."

[31] (The flax and barley were destroyed, since the barley had headed and the flax was in bloom. [32] The wheat and spelt, however, were not destroyed, because they ripen later.)

[33] Then Moses left Pharaoh and went out of the city. He spread out his hands toward the LORD; the thunder and hail stopped, and the rain no longer poured down on the land. [34] When Pharaoh saw that the rain and hail and thunder had stopped, he sinned again: He and his officials hardened their hearts. [35] So Pharaoh's heart was hard and he would not let the Israelites go, just as the LORD had said through Moses.

a 23 Septuagint and Vulgate; Hebrew will put a deliverance
b 16 Or have spared you

MATTHEW 19:13-30

Then little children were brought to Jesus for him to place his hands on them and pray for them. But the disciples rebuked those who brought them. [14] Jesus said, "Let the little children come to me, and do not hinder them, for the kingdom of heaven belongs to such as these." [15]When he had placed his hands on them, he went on from there.

[16]Now a man came up to Jesus and asked, "Teacher, what good thing must I do to get eternal life?"

[17]"Why do you ask me about what is good?" Jesus replied. "There is only One who is good. If you want to enter life, obey the commandments."

[18]"Which ones?" the man inquired.

Jesus replied, "'Do not murder, do not commit adultery, do not steal, do not give false testimony, [19]honor your father and mother,'[a] and 'love your neighbor as yourself.'[b]"

[20]"All these I have kept," the young man said. "What do I still lack?"

[21]Jesus answered, "If you want to be perfect, go, sell your possessions and give to the poor, and you will have treasure in heaven. Then come, follow me."

[22]When the young man heard this, he went away sad, because he had great wealth.

[23]Then Jesus said to his disciples, "I tell you the truth, it is hard for a rich man to enter the kingdom of heaven. [24]Again I tell you, it is easier for a camel to go through the eye of a needle than for a rich man to enter the kingdom of God."

[25]When the disciples heard this, they were greatly astonished and asked, "Who then can be saved?"

[26]Jesus looked at them and said, "With man this is impossible, but with God all things are possible."

[27]Peter answered him, "We have left everything to follow you! What then will there be for us?"

[28]Jesus said to them, "I tell you the truth, at the renewal of all things, when the Son of Man sits on his glorious throne, you who have followed me will also sit on twelve thrones, judging the twelve tribes of Israel. [29]And everyone who has left houses or brothers or sisters or father or mother[c] or children or fields for my sake will receive a hundred times as much and will inherit eternal life.

[30]But many who are first will be last, and many who are last will be first."

[a]19 Exodus 20:12-16; Deut. 5:16-20   [b]19 Lev. 19:18
[c]29 Some manuscripts *mother or wife*

PSALM 24:1-10
Of David. A psalm.

[1]**T**he earth is the LORD's, and
   everything in it,
   the world, and all who live in it;
[2]for he founded it upon the seas
   and established it upon the
   waters.

[3]Who may ascend the hill of
   the LORD?
   Who may stand in his holy place?
[4]He who has clean hands and a pure
   heart,
   who does not lift up his soul to
   an idol
   or swear by what is false.[a]
[5]He will receive blessing from the
   LORD
   and vindication from God his
   Savior.
[6]Such is the generation of those who
   seek him,
   who seek your face, O God of
   Jacob.[b]   *Selah*

[7]Lift up your heads, O you gates;
   be lifted up, you ancient doors,
   that the King of glory may
   come in.
[8]Who is this King of glory?
   The LORD strong and mighty,
   the LORD mighty in battle.
[9]Lift up your heads, O you gates;
   lift them up, you ancient doors,
   that the King of glory may
   come in.
[10]Who is he, this King of glory?
   The LORD Almighty—
   he is the King of glory.   *Selah*

[a]4 Or *swear falsely*   [b]6 Two Hebrew manuscripts and Syriac
(see also Septuagint); most Hebrew manuscripts *face, Jacob*

PROVERBS 6:1-5
My son, if you have put up security
   for your neighbor,
   if you have struck hands in pledge
   for another,

2 if you have been trapped by what you
said,
ensnared by the words of your
mouth,
3 then do this, my son, to free yourself,
since you have fallen into your
neighbor's hands:
Go and humble yourself;
press your plea with your
neighbor!
4 Allow no sleep to your eyes,
no slumber to your eyelids.
5 Free yourself, like a gazelle from the
hand of the hunter,
like a bird from the snare of the
fowler.

☐ D A Y 3 0

GOD SIGHTINGS

January 30

EXODUS 10:1–12:13

Then the LORD said to Moses, "Go to
Pharaoh, for I have hardened his heart
and the hearts of his officials so that I
may perform these miraculous signs of
mine among them 2 that you may tell
your children and grandchildren how I
dealt harshly with the Egyptians and
how I performed my signs among them,
and that you may know that I am the
LORD.

3 So Moses and Aaron went to Pharaoh and said to him, "This is what the
LORD, the God of the Hebrews, says:
'How long will you refuse to humble
yourself before me? Let my people go, so
that they may worship me. 4 If you refuse
to let them go, I will bring locusts into
your country tomorrow. 5 They will
cover the face of the ground so that it
cannot be seen. They will devour what
little you have left after the hail, including every tree that is growing in your
fields. 6 They will fill your houses and
those of all your officials and all the
Egyptians—something neither your fa-

thers nor your forefathers have ever
seen from the day they settled in this
land till now.'" Then Moses turned and
left Pharaoh.

7 Pharaoh's officials said to him, "How
long will this man be a snare to us? Let
the people go, so that they may worship
the LORD their God. Do you not yet realize that Egypt is ruined?"

8 Then Moses and Aaron were
brought back to Pharaoh. "Go, worship
the LORD your God," he said. "But just
who will be going?"

9 Moses answered, "We will go with
our young and old, with our sons and
daughters, and with our flocks and
herds, because we are to celebrate a festival to the LORD."

10 Pharaoh said, "The LORD be with
you—if I let you go, along with your
women and children! Clearly you are
bent on evil.ᵃ 11 No! Have only the men
go; and worship the LORD, since that's
what you have been asking for." Then
Moses and Aaron were driven out of
Pharaoh's presence.

12 And the LORD said to Moses,
"Stretch out your hand over Egypt so
that locusts will swarm over the land
and devour everything growing in the
fields, everything left by the hail."

13 So Moses stretched out his staff
over Egypt, and the LORD made an east
wind blow across the land all that day
and all that night. By morning the wind
had brought the locusts; 14 they invaded
all Egypt and settled down in every area
of the country in great numbers. Never
before had there been such a plague of
locusts, nor will there ever be again.
15 They covered all the ground until it
was black. They devoured all that was
left after the hail—everything growing
in the fields and the fruit on the trees.
Nothing green remained on tree or
plant in all the land of Egypt.

16 Pharaoh quickly summoned Moses
and Aaron and said, "I have sinned
against the LORD your God and against
you. 17 Now forgive my sin once more
and pray to the LORD your God to take
this deadly plague away from me."

18Moses then left Pharaoh and prayed to the LORD. 19And the LORD changed the wind to a very strong west wind, which caught up the locusts and carried them into the Red Sea.*b* Not a locust was left anywhere in Egypt. 20But the LORD hardened Pharaoh's heart, and he would not let the Israelites go.

21Then the LORD said to Moses, "Stretch out your hand toward the sky so that darkness will spread over Egypt— darkness that can be felt." 22So Moses stretched out his hand toward the sky, and total darkness covered all Egypt for three days. 23No one could see anyone else or leave his place for three days. Yet all the Israelites had light in the places where they lived.

24Then Pharaoh summoned Moses and said, "Go, worship the LORD. Even your women and children may go with you; only leave your flocks and herds behind."

25But Moses said, "You must allow us to have sacrifices and burnt offerings to present to the LORD our God. 26Our livestock too must go with us; not a hoof is to be left behind. We have to use some of them in worshiping the LORD our God, and until we get there we will not know what we are to use to worship the LORD."

27But the LORD hardened Pharaoh's heart, and he was not willing to let them go. 28Pharaoh said to Moses, "Get out of my sight! Make sure you do not appear before me again! The day you see my face you will die."

29"Just as you say," Moses replied, "I will never appear before you again."

11:1Now the LORD had said to Moses, "I will bring one more plague on Pharaoh and on Egypt. After that, he will let you go from here, and when he does, he will drive you out completely. 2Tell the people that men and women alike are to ask their neighbors for articles of silver and gold." 3(The LORD made the Egyptians favorably disposed toward the people, and Moses himself was highly regarded in Egypt by Pharaoh's officials and by the people.)

4So Moses said, "This is what the LORD says: 'About midnight I will go throughout Egypt. 5Every firstborn son in Egypt will die, from the firstborn son of Pharaoh, who sits on the throne, to the firstborn son of the slave girl, who is at her hand mill, and all the firstborn of the cattle as well. 6There will be loud wailing throughout Egypt—worse than there has ever been or ever will be again. 7But among the Israelites not a dog will bark at any man or animal.' Then you will know that the LORD makes a distinction between Egypt and Israel. 8All these officials of yours will come to me, bowing down before me and saying, 'Go, you and all the people who follow you!' After that I will leave." Then Moses, hot with anger, left Pharaoh.

9The LORD had said to Moses, "Pharaoh will refuse to listen to you—so that my wonders may be multiplied in Egypt." 10Moses and Aaron performed all these wonders before Pharaoh, but the LORD hardened Pharaoh's heart, and he would not let the Israelites go out of his country.

12:1THE LORD said to Moses and Aaron in Egypt, 2"This month is to be for you the first month, the first month of your year. 3Tell the whole community of Israel that on the tenth day of this month each man is to take a lamb*c* for his family, one for each household. 4If any household is too small for a whole lamb, they must share one with their nearest neighbor, having taken into account the number of people there are. You are to determine the amount of lamb needed in accordance with what each person will eat. 5The animals you choose must be year-old males without defect, and you may take them from the sheep or the goats. 6Take care of them until the fourteenth day of the month, when all the people of the community of Israel must slaughter them at twilight. 7Then they are to take some of the blood and put it on the sides and tops of the doorframes of the houses where they eat the lambs. ⁸That same night they are to eat the meat roasted over the fire, along with bitter herbs, and bread made without yeast. ⁹Do not eat the meat raw or cooked in water, but roast it over the fire—head, legs and inner parts. ¹⁰Do not leave any of it till morning; if some is left till morning, you must burn it. ¹¹This is how you are to eat it: with your cloak tucked into your belt, your sandals on your feet and your staff in your hand. Eat it in haste; it is the LORD's Passover.

¹²"On that same night I will pass through Egypt and strike down every firstborn—both men and animals—and I will bring judgment on all the gods of Egypt. I am the LORD. ¹³The blood will be a sign for you on the houses where you are; and when I see the blood, I will pass over you. No destructive plague will touch you when I strike Egypt."

a10 Or Be careful, trouble is in store for you! *b19 Hebrew Yam Suph; that is, Sea of Reeds* *c3 The Hebrew word can mean lamb or kid; also in verse 4.*

MATTHEW 20:1-28

"For the kingdom of heaven is like a landowner who went out early in the morning to hire men to work in his vineyard. ²He agreed to pay them a denarius for the day and sent them into his vineyard.

³"About the third hour he went out and saw others standing in the marketplace doing nothing. ⁴He told them, 'You also go and work in my vineyard, and I will pay you whatever is right.' ⁵So they went.

"He went out again about the sixth hour and the ninth hour and did the same thing. ⁶About the eleventh hour he went out and found still others standing around. He asked them, 'Why have you been standing here all day long doing nothing?'

⁷"'Because no one has hired us,' they answered.

"He said to them, 'You also go and work in my vineyard.'

⁸"When evening came, the owner of the vineyard said to his foreman, 'Call the workers and pay them their wages, beginning with the last ones hired and going on to the first.'

⁹"The workers who were hired about the eleventh hour came and each received a denarius. ¹⁰So when those came who were hired first, they expected to receive more. But each one of them also received a denarius. ¹¹When they received it, they began to grumble against the landowner. ¹²'These men who were hired last worked only one hour,' they said, 'and you have made them equal to us who have borne the burden of the work and the heat of the day.'

¹³"But he answered one of them, 'Friend, I am not being unfair to you. Didn't you agree to work for a denarius? ¹⁴Take your pay and go. I want to give the man who was hired last the same as I gave you. ¹⁵Don't I have the right to do what I want with my own money? Or are you envious because I am generous?'

¹⁶"So the last will be first, and the first will be last."

¹⁷Now as Jesus was going up to Jerusalem, he took the twelve disciples aside and said to them, ¹⁸"We are going up to Jerusalem, and the Son of Man will be betrayed to the chief priests and the teachers of the law. They will condemn him to death ¹⁹and will turn him over to the Gentiles to be mocked and flogged and crucified. On the third day he will be raised to life!"

²⁰Then the mother of Zebedee's sons came to Jesus with her sons and, kneeling down, asked a favor of him.

²¹"What is it you want?" he asked.

She said, "Grant that one of these two sons of mine may sit at your right and the other at your left in your kingdom."

²²"You don't know what you are asking," Jesus said to them. "Can you drink the cup I am going to drink?"

"We can," they answered.

²³Jesus said to them, "You will indeed drink from my cup, but to sit at my right or left is not for me to grant. These

places belong to those for whom they have been prepared by my Father."

24When the ten heard about this, they were indignant with the two brothers. 25Jesus called them together and said, "You know that the rulers of the Gentiles lord it over them, and their high officials exercise authority over them. 26**Not so with you. Instead, whoever wants to become great among you must be your servant, 27and whoever wants to be first must be your slave— 28just as the Son of Man did not come to be served, but to serve, and to give his life as a ransom for many.**"

PSALM 25:1-15a
Of David.

1 To you, O Lᴏʀᴅ, I lift up my soul;
2   in you I trust, O my God.
  Do not let me be put to shame,
    nor let my enemies triumph
      over me.
3 No one whose hope is in you
    will ever be put to shame,
  but they will be put to shame
    who are treacherous without
      excuse.

4 Show me your ways, O Lᴏʀᴅ,
    teach me your paths;
5 guide me in your truth and teach me,
    for you are God my Savior,
    and my hope is in you all day long.
6 Remember, O Lᴏʀᴅ, your great mercy
      and love,
  for they are from of old.
7 Remember not the sins of my youth
    and my rebellious ways;
  according to your love remember me,
    for you are good, O Lᴏʀᴅ.

8 Good and upright is the Lᴏʀᴅ;
    therefore he instructs sinners in
      his ways.
9 He guides the humble in what
      is right
    and teaches them his way.
10 All the ways of the Lᴏʀᴅ are loving
      and faithful
    for those who keep the demands
      of his covenant.

11 For the sake of your name, O Lᴏʀᴅ,
    forgive my iniquity, though it
      is great.
12 Who, then, is the man that fears
      the Lᴏʀᴅ?
  He will instruct him in the way
    chosen for him.
13 He will spend his days in prosperity,
    and his descendants will inherit
      the land.
14 The Lᴏʀᴅ confides in those who
    fear him;
  he makes his covenant known
    to them.
15 My eyes are ever on the Lᴏʀᴅ,
    for only he will release my feet
      from the snare.

aThis psalm is an acrostic poem, the verses of which begin with the successive letters of the Hebrew alphabet.

PROVERBS 6:6-11
6 Go to the ant, you sluggard;
    consider its ways and be wise!
7 It has no commander,
    no overseer or ruler,
8 yet it stores its provisions in summer
    and gathers its food at harvest.

9 How long will you lie there, you
      sluggard?
  When will you get up from your
      sleep?
10 A little sleep, a little slumber,
    a little folding of the hands to
      rest—
11 and poverty will come on you like a
      bandit
    and scarcity like an armed man.a

a11 Or like a vagrant / and scarcity like a beggar

□ DAY 31

GOD SIGHTINGS

January 31

EXODUS 12:14–13:16
"This is a day you are to commemorate; for the generations to come you shall celebrate it as a festival to the Lᴏʀᴅ—a

lasting ordinance. 15For seven days you are to eat bread made without yeast. On the first day remove the yeast from your houses, for whoever eats anything with yeast in it from the first day through the seventh must be cut off from Israel. 16On the first day hold a sacred assembly, and another one on the seventh day. Do no work at all on these days, except to prepare food for everyone to eat— that is all you may do.

17"Celebrate the Feast of Unleavened Bread, because it was on this very day that I brought your divisions out of Egypt. Celebrate this day as a lasting ordinance for the generations to come. 18In the first month you are to eat bread made without yeast, from the evening of the fourteenth day until the evening of the twenty-first day. 19For seven days no yeast is to be found in your houses. And whoever eats anything with yeast in it must be cut off from the community of Israel, whether he is an alien or native-born. 20Eat nothing made with yeast. Wherever you live, you must eat unleavened bread."

21Then Moses summoned all the elders of Israel and said to them, "Go at once and select the animals for your families and slaughter the Passover lamb. 22Take a bunch of hyssop, dip it into the blood in the basin and put some of the blood on the top and on both sides of the doorframe. Not one of you shall go out the door of his house until morning. 23When the LORD goes through the land to strike down the Egyptians, he will see the blood on the top and sides of the doorframe and will pass over that doorway, and he will not permit the destroyer to enter your houses and strike you down.

24"Obey these instructions as a lasting ordinance for you and your descendants. 25When you enter the land that the LORD will give you as he promised, observe this ceremony. 26And when your children ask you, 'What does this ceremony mean to you?' 27then tell them, 'It is the Passover sacrifice to the LORD, who passed over the houses of the

Israelites in Egypt and spared our homes when he struck down the Egyptians.' " Then the people bowed down and worshiped. 28The Israelites did just what the LORD commanded Moses and Aaron.

29At midnight the LORD struck down all the firstborn in Egypt, from the firstborn of Pharaoh, who sat on the throne, to the firstborn of the prisoner, who was in the dungeon, and the firstborn of all the livestock as well. 30Pharaoh and all his officials and all the Egyptians got up during the night, and there was loud wailing in Egypt, for there was not a house without someone dead.

31During the night Pharaoh summoned Moses and Aaron and said, "Up! Leave my people, you and the Israelites! Go, worship the LORD as you have requested. 32Take your flocks and herds, as you have said, and go. And also bless me."

33The Egyptians urged the people to hurry and leave the country. "For otherwise," they said, "we will all die!" 34So the people took their dough before the yeast was added, and carried it on their shoulders in kneading troughs wrapped in clothing. 35The Israelites did as Moses instructed and asked the Egyptians for articles of silver and gold and for clothing. 36The LORD had made the Egyptians favorably disposed toward the people, and they gave them what they asked for; so they plundered the Egyptians.

37The Israelites journeyed from Rameses to Succoth. There were about six hundred thousand men on foot, besides women and children. 38Many other people went up with them, as well as large droves of livestock, both flocks and herds. 39With the dough they had brought from Egypt, they baked cakes of unleavened bread. The dough was without yeast because they had been driven out of Egypt and did not have time to prepare food for themselves.

40Now the length of time the Israelite people lived in Egypta was 430 years. 41At the end of the 430 years, to the very day, all the Lord's divisions left Egypt. [42]Because the Lord kept vigil that night to bring them out of Egypt, on this night all the Israelites are to keep vigil to honor the Lord for the generations to come.

[43]The Lord said to Moses and Aaron, "These are the regulations for the Passover:

"No foreigner is to eat of it. [44]Any slave you have bought may eat of it after you have circumcised him, [45]but a temporary resident and a hired worker may not eat of it.

[46]"It must be eaten inside one house; take none of the meat outside the house. Do not break any of the bones. [47]The whole community of Israel must celebrate it.

[48]"An alien living among you who wants to celebrate the Lord's Passover must have all the males in his household circumcised; then he may take part like one born in the land. No uncircumcised male may eat of it. [49]The same law applies to the native-born and to the alien living among you."

[50]All the Israelites did just what the Lord had commanded Moses and Aaron. [51]And on that very day the Lord brought the Israelites out of Egypt by their divisions.

[13:1]The Lord said to Moses, [2]"Consecrate to me every firstborn male. The first offspring of every womb among the Israelites belongs to me, whether man or animal."

[3]Then Moses said to the people, "Commemorate this day, the day you came out of Egypt, out of the land of slavery, because the Lord brought you out of it with a mighty hand. Eat nothing containing yeast. [4]Today, in the month of Abib, you are leaving. [5]When the Lord brings you into the land of the Canaanites, Hittites, Amorites, Hivites and Jebusites—the land he swore to your forefathers to give you, a land flowing with milk and honey—you are to observe this ceremony in this month: [6]For

seven days eat bread made without yeast and on the seventh day hold a festival to the Lord. [7]Eat unleavened bread during those seven days; nothing with yeast in it is to be seen among you, nor shall any yeast be seen anywhere within your borders. [8]On that day tell your son, 'I do this because of what the Lord did for me when I came out of Egypt.' [9]This observance will be for you like a sign on your hand and a reminder on your forehead that the law of the Lord is to be on your lips. For the Lord brought you out of Egypt with his mighty hand. [10]You must keep this ordinance at the appointed time year after year.

[11]"After the Lord brings you into the land of the Canaanites and gives it to you, as he promised on oath to you and your forefathers, [12]you are to give over to the Lord the first offspring of every womb. All the firstborn males of your livestock belong to the Lord. [13]Redeem with a lamb every firstborn donkey, but if you do not redeem it, break its neck. Redeem every firstborn among your sons.

[14]"In days to come, when your son asks you, 'What does this mean?' say to him, 'With a mighty hand the Lord brought us out of Egypt, out of the land of slavery. [15]When Pharaoh stubbornly refused to let us go, the Lord killed every firstborn in Egypt, both man and animal. This is why I sacrifice to the Lord the first male offspring of every womb and redeem each of my firstborn sons.' [16]And it will be like a sign on your hand and a symbol on your forehead that the Lord brought us out of Egypt with his mighty hand."

a40 Masoretic Text; Samaritan Pentateuch and Septuagint *Egypt and Canaan*

MATTHEW 20:29–21:22

As Jesus and his disciples were leaving Jericho, a large crowd followed him. [30]Two blind men were sitting by the roadside, and when they heard that Jesus was going by, they shouted, "Lord, Son of David, have mercy on us!"

[31]The crowd rebuked them and told

them to be quiet, but they shouted all the louder, "Lord, Son of David, have mercy on us!"

32 Jesus stopped and called them. "What do you want me to do for you?" he asked.

33 "Lord," they answered, "we want our sight."

34 Jesus had compassion on them and touched their eyes. Immediately they received their sight and followed him.

21:1 As they approached Jerusalem and came to Bethphage on the Mount of Olives, Jesus sent two disciples, 2 saying to them, "Go to the village ahead of you, and at once you will find a donkey tied there, with her colt by her. Untie them and bring them to me. 3 If anyone says anything to you, tell him that the Lord needs them, and he will send them right away."

4 This took place to fulfill what was spoken through the prophet:

5 "Say to the Daughter of Zion,
'See, your king comes to you,
gentle and riding on a donkey,
   on a colt, the foal of a donkey.'"*a*

6 The disciples went and did as Jesus had instructed them. 7 They brought the donkey and the colt, placed their cloaks on them, and Jesus sat on them. 8 A very large crowd spread their cloaks on the road, while others cut branches from the trees and spread them on the road. 9 The crowds that went ahead of him and those that followed shouted,

"Hosanna*b* to the Son of David!"

"Blessed is he who comes in the
   name of the Lord!"*c*

"Hosanna*b* in the highest!"

10 When Jesus entered Jerusalem, the whole city was stirred and asked, "Who is this?"

11 The crowds answered, "This is Jesus, the prophet from Nazareth in Galilee."

12 Jesus entered the temple area and drove out all who were buying and sell-

ing there. He overturned the tables of the money changers and the benches of those selling doves. 13 "It is written," he said to them, "'My house will be called a house of prayer,'*d* but you are making it a 'den of robbers.'*e*"

14 The blind and the lame came to him at the temple, and he healed them. 15 But when the chief priests and the teachers of the law saw the wonderful things he did and the children shouting in the temple area, "Hosanna to the Son of David," they were indignant.

16 "Do you hear what these children are saying?" they asked him.

"Yes," replied Jesus, "have you never read,

"'From the lips of children and
      infants
   you have ordained praise'*f*/?"

17 And he left them and went out of the city to Bethany, where he spent the night.

18 Early in the morning, as he was on his way back to the city, he was hungry. 19 Seeing a fig tree by the road, he went up to it but found nothing on it except leaves. Then he said to it, "May you never bear fruit again!" Immediately the tree withered.

20 When the disciples saw this, they were amazed. "How did the fig tree wither so quickly?" they asked.

21 Jesus replied, "I tell you the truth, if you have faith and do not doubt, not only can you do what was done to the fig tree, but also you can say to this mountain, 'Go, throw yourself into the sea,' and it will be done. 22 If you believe, you will receive whatever you ask for in prayer."

a5 Zech. 9:9   *b9* A Hebrew expression meaning "Save!" which became an exclamation of praise; also in verse 15   *c9* Psalm 118:26   *d13* Isaiah 56:7   *e13* Jer. 7:11   *f16* Psalm 8:2

PSALM 25:16-22

16 **Turn [Lord] to me and be gracious
      to me,
   for I am lonely and afflicted.**
17 **The troubles of my heart have
      multiplied;
   free me from my anguish.**

¹⁸Look upon my affliction and my
        distress
    and take away all my sins.
¹⁹See how my enemies have increased
    and how fiercely they hate me!
²⁰Guard my life and rescue me;
    let me not be put to shame,
    for I take refuge in you.
²¹May integrity and uprightness
        protect me,
    because my hope is in you.

²²Redeem Israel, O God,
    from all their troubles!

PROVERBS 6:12-15
¹²**A** scoundrel and villain,
    who goes about with a corrupt
        mouth,
¹³   who winks with his eye,
    signals with his feet
    and motions with his fingers,
¹⁴   who plots evil with deceit in his
        heart—
    he always stirs up dissension.
¹⁵Therefore disaster will overtake him
        in an instant;
    he will suddenly be destroyed—
        without remedy.

GOD SIGHTINGS

February 1

EXODUS 13:17–15:18

When Pharaoh let the people go, God did not lead them on the road through the Philistine country, though that was shorter. For God said, "If they face war, they might change their minds and return to Egypt." 18So God led the people around by the desert road toward the Red Sea.*a* The Israelites went up out of Egypt armed for battle.

19Moses took the bones of Joseph with him because Joseph had made the sons of Israel swear an oath. He had said, "God will surely come to your aid, and then you must carry my bones up with you from this place."*b*

20After leaving Succoth they camped at Etham on the edge of the desert. 21By day the LORD went ahead of them in a pillar of cloud to guide them on their way and by night in a pillar of fire to give them light, so that they could travel by day or night. 22Neither the pillar of cloud by day nor the pillar of fire by night left its place in front of the people.

14:1THEN the LORD said to Moses, 2"Tell the Israelites to turn back and encamp near Pi Hahiroth, between Migdol and the sea. They are to encamp by the sea, directly opposite Baal Zephon. 3Pharaoh will think, 'The Israelites are wandering around the land in confusion, hemmed in by the desert.' 4And I will harden Pharaoh's heart, and he will pursue them. But I will gain glory for myself through Pharaoh and all his army, and the Egyptians will know that I am the LORD." So the Israelites did this.

5When the king of Egypt was told that the people had fled, Pharaoh and his officials changed their minds about them and said, "What have we done? We have

let the Israelites go and have lost their services!" 6So he had his chariot made ready and took his army with him. 7He took six hundred of the best chariots, along with all the other chariots of Egypt, with officers over all of them. 8The LORD hardened the heart of Pharaoh king of Egypt, so that he pursued the Israelites, who were marching out boldly. 9The Egyptians—all Pharaoh's horses and chariots, horsemen*c* and troops—pursued the Israelites and overtook them as they camped by the sea near Pi Hahiroth, opposite Baal Zephon.

10As Pharaoh approached, the Israelites looked up, and there were the Egyptians, marching after them. They were terrified and cried out to the LORD. 11They said to Moses, "Was it because there were no graves in Egypt that you brought us to the desert to die? What have you done to us by bringing us out of Egypt? 12Didn't we say to you in Egypt, 'Leave us alone; let us serve the Egyptians'? It would have been better for us to serve the Egyptians than to die in the desert!"

13**Moses answered the people, "Do not be afraid. Stand firm and you will see the deliverance the LORD will bring you today. The Egyptians you see today you will never see again.** 14**The LORD will fight for you; you need only to be still."**

15Then the LORD said to Moses, "Why are you crying out to me? Tell the Israelites to move on. 16Raise your staff and stretch out your hand over the sea to divide the water so that the Israelites can go through the sea on dry ground. 17I will harden the hearts of the Egyptians so that they will go in after them. And I will gain glory through Pharaoh and all his army, through his chariots and his horsemen. 18The Egyptians will know that I am the LORD when I gain glory through Pharaoh, his chariots and his horsemen."

¹⁹Then the angel of God, who had been traveling in front of Israel's army, withdrew and went behind them. The pillar of cloud also moved from in front and stood behind them, ²⁰coming between the armies of Egypt and Israel. Throughout the night the cloud brought darkness to the one side and light to the other side; so neither went near the other all night long.

²¹Then Moses stretched out his hand over the sea, and all that night the Lord drove the sea back with a strong east wind and turned it into dry land. The waters were divided, ²²and the Israelites went through the sea on dry ground, with a wall of water on their right and on their left.

²³The Egyptians pursued them, and all Pharaoh's horses and chariots and horsemen followed them into the sea. ²⁴During the last watch of the night the Lord looked down from the pillar of fire and cloud at the Egyptian army and threw it into confusion. ²⁵He made the wheels of their chariots come off[d] so that they had difficulty driving. And the Egyptians said, "Let's get away from the Israelites! The Lord is fighting for them against Egypt."

²⁶Then the Lord said to Moses, "Stretch out your hand over the sea so that the waters may flow back over the Egyptians and their chariots and horsemen." ²⁷Moses stretched out his hand over the sea, and at daybreak the sea went back to its place. The Egyptians were fleeing toward[e] it, and the Lord swept them into the sea. ²⁸The water flowed back and covered the chariots and horsemen—the entire army of Pharaoh that had followed the Israelites into the sea. Not one of them survived.

²⁹But the Israelites went through the sea on dry ground, with a wall of water on their right and on their left. ³⁰That day the Lord saved Israel from the hands of the Egyptians, and Israel saw the Egyptians lying dead on the shore. ³¹And when the Israelites saw the great power the Lord displayed against the Egyptians, the people feared the Lord and put their trust in him and in Moses his servant.

15:1 Then Moses and the Israelites sang this song to the Lord:

"I will sing to the Lord,
  for he is highly exalted.
The horse and its rider
  he has hurled into the sea.
²The Lord is my strength and
    my song;
  he has become my salvation.
He is my God, and I will praise him,
  my father's God, and I will
    exalt him.
³The Lord is a warrior;
  the Lord is his name.
⁴Pharaoh's chariots and his army
  he has hurled into the sea.
The best of Pharaoh's officers
  are drowned in the Red Sea.[f]
⁵The deep waters have covered
    them;
  they sank to the depths like
    a stone.

⁶"Your right hand, O Lord,
  was majestic in power.
Your right hand, O Lord,
  shattered the enemy.
⁷In the greatness of your majesty
  you threw down those who
    opposed you.
You unleashed your burning anger;
  it consumed them like stubble.
⁸By the blast of your nostrils
  the waters piled up.
The surging waters stood firm like
    a wall;
  the deep waters congealed in the
    heart of the sea.

⁹"The enemy boasted,
  'I will pursue, I will overtake them.
I will divide the spoils;
  I will gorge myself on them.
I will draw my sword
  and my hand will destroy them.'
¹⁰But you blew with your breath,
  and the sea covered them.
They sank like lead
  in the mighty waters.

[11] "Who among the gods is like you,
       O Lord?
   Who is like you—
       majestic in holiness,
       awesome in glory,
       working wonders?
[12] You stretched out your right hand
       and the earth swallowed them.

[13] "In your unfailing love you will lead
       the people you have redeemed.
   In your strength you will guide them
       to your holy dwelling.
[14] The nations will hear and tremble;
       anguish will grip the people
       of Philistia.
[15] The chiefs of Edom will be terrified,
       the leaders of Moab will be seized
       with trembling,
   the people[g] of Canaan will melt
       away;
[16]   terror and dread will fall upon
       them.
   By the power of your arm
       they will be as still as a stone—
   until your people pass by, O Lord,
       until the people you bought[h]
       pass by.
[17] You will bring them in and plant
       them
       on the mountain of your
       inheritance—
   the place, O Lord, you made for your
       dwelling,
       the sanctuary, O Lord, your hands
       established.
[18] The Lord will reign
       for ever and ever."

[a]18 Hebrew *Yam Suph*; that is, Sea of Reeds   [b]19 See Gen.
50:25.   [c]9 Or *charioteers*; also in verses 17, 18, 23, 26
and 28   [d]25 Or *He jammed the wheels of their chariots*
(see Samaritan Pentateuch, Septuagint and Syriac)
[e]27 Or *from*   [f]4 Hebrew *Yam Suph*; that is, Sea of Reeds;
also in verse 22   [g]15 Or *rulers*   [h]16 Or *created*

MATTHEW 21:23-46

Jesus entered the temple courts, and, while he was teaching, the chief priests and the elders of the people came to him. "By what authority are you doing these things?" they asked. "And who gave you this authority?"

[24] Jesus replied, "I will also ask you one question. If you answer me, I will tell you by what authority I am doing these things. [25] John's baptism—where did it come from? Was it from heaven, or from men?"

They discussed it among themselves and said, "If we say, 'From heaven,' he will ask, 'Then why didn't you believe him?' [26] But if we say, 'From men'—we are afraid of the people, for they all hold that John was a prophet."

[27] So they answered Jesus, "We don't know."

Then he said, "Neither will I tell you by what authority I am doing these things.

[28] "What do you think? There was a man who had two sons. He went to the first and said, 'Son, go and work today in the vineyard.'

[29] "'I will not,' he answered, but later he changed his mind and went.

[30] "Then the father went to the other son and said the same thing. He answered, 'I will, sir,' but he did not go.

[31] "Which of the two did what his father wanted?"

"The first," they answered.

Jesus said to them, "I tell you the truth, the tax collectors and the prostitutes are entering the kingdom of God ahead of you. [32] For John came to you to show you the way of righteousness, and you did not believe him, but the tax collectors and the prostitutes did. And even after you saw this, you did not repent and believe him.

[33] "Listen to another parable: There was a landowner who planted a vineyard. He put a wall around it, dug a winepress in it and built a watchtower. Then he rented the vineyard to some farmers and went away on a journey. [34] When the harvest time approached, he sent his servants to the tenants to collect his fruit.

[35] "The tenants seized his servants; they beat one, killed another, and stoned a third. [36] Then he sent other servants to them, more than the first time, and the tenants treated them the same way. [37] Last of all, he sent his son to

them. 'They will respect my son,' he said.

38 "But when the tenants saw the son, they said to each other, 'This is the heir. Come, let's kill him and take his inheritance.' 39 So they took him and threw him out of the vineyard and killed him.

40 "Therefore, when the owner of the vineyard comes, what will he do to those tenants?"

41 "He will bring those wretches to a wretched end," they replied, "and he will rent the vineyard to other tenants, who will give him his share of the crop at harvest time."

42 Jesus said to them, "Have you never read in the Scriptures:

"'The stone the builders rejected
    has become the capstone*a*;
the Lord has done this,
    and it is marvelous in our eyes'*b*?

43 "Therefore I tell you that the kingdom of God will be taken away from you and given to a people who will produce its fruit. 44 He who falls on this stone will be broken to pieces, but he on whom it falls will be crushed."*c*

45 When the chief priests and the Pharisees heard Jesus' parables, they knew he was talking about them. 46 They looked for a way to arrest him, but they were afraid of the crowd because the people held that he was a prophet.

a42 Or cornerstone   b42 Psalm 118:22,23   c44 Some manuscripts do not have verse 44.

PSALM 26:1-12
Of David.

1 Vindicate me, O Lord,
    for I have led a blameless life;
I have trusted in the Lord
    without wavering.
2 Test me, O Lord, and try me,
    examine my heart and my mind;
3 for your love is ever before me,
    and I walk continually in your
        truth.
4 I do not sit with deceitful men,
    nor do I consort with hypocrites;
5 I abhor the assembly of evildoers

and refuse to sit with the wicked.
6 I wash my hands in innocence,
    and go about your altar, O Lord,
7 proclaiming aloud your praise
    and telling of all your wonderful
        deeds.
8 I love the house where you live,
    O Lord,
    the place where your glory dwells.

9 Do not take away my soul along with
        sinners,
    my life with bloodthirsty men,
10 in whose hands are wicked schemes,
    whose right hands are full of
        bribes.
11 But I lead a blameless life;
    redeem me and be merciful to me.

12 My feet stand on level ground;
    in the great assembly I will praise
        the Lord.

PROVERBS 6:16-19
16 There are six things the Lord hates,
    seven that are detestable to him:
17   haughty eyes,
        a lying tongue,
        hands that shed innocent blood,
18   a heart that devises wicked
            schemes,
        feet that are quick to rush into
            evil,
19   a false witness who pours out
            lies
        and a man who stirs up
            dissension among brothers.

□ DAY 33

GOD SIGHTINGS

February 2

EXODUS 15:19–17:7
When Pharaoh's horses, chariots and horsemen*a* went into the sea, the Lord brought the waters of the sea back over them, but the Israelites walked through the sea on dry ground. 20 Then Miriam

the prophetess, Aaron's sister, took a tambourine in her hand, and all the women followed her, with tambourines and dancing. 21Miriam sang to them:

"Sing to the Lᴏʀᴅ,
    for he is highly exalted.
The horse and its rider
    he has hurled into the sea."

22Then Moses led Israel from the Red Sea and they went into the Desert of Shur. For three days they traveled in the desert without finding water. 23When they came to Marah, they could not drink its water because it was bitter. (That is why the place is called Marah.*b*) 24So the people grumbled against Moses, saying, "What are we to drink?"

25Then Moses cried out to the Lᴏʀᴅ, and the Lᴏʀᴅ showed him a piece of wood. He threw it into the water, and the water became sweet.

There the Lᴏʀᴅ made a decree and a law for them, and there he tested them. 26He said, "If you listen carefully to the voice of the Lᴏʀᴅ your God and do what is right in his eyes, if you pay attention to his commands and keep all his decrees, I will not bring on you any of the diseases I brought on the Egyptians, for I am the Lᴏʀᴅ, who heals you."

27Then they came to Elim, where there were twelve springs and seventy palm trees, and they camped there near the water.

16:1THE whole Israelite community set out from Elim and came to the Desert of Sin, which is between Elim and Sinai, on the fifteenth day of the second month after they had come out of Egypt. 2In the desert the whole community grumbled against Moses and Aaron. 3The Israelites said to them, "If only we had died by the Lᴏʀᴅ's hand in Egypt! There we sat around pots of meat and ate all the food we wanted, but you have brought us out into this desert to starve this entire assembly to death."

4Then the Lᴏʀᴅ said to Moses, "I will rain down bread from heaven for you. The people are to go out each day and gather enough for that day. In this way I will test them and see whether they will follow my instructions. 5On the sixth day they are to prepare what they bring in, and that is to be twice as much as they gather on the other days."

6So Moses and Aaron said to all the Israelites, "In the evening you will know that it was the Lᴏʀᴅ who brought you out of Egypt, 7and in the morning you will see the glory of the Lᴏʀᴅ, because he has heard your grumbling against him. Who are we, that you should grumble against us?" 8Moses also said, "You will know that it was the Lᴏʀᴅ when he gives you meat to eat in the evening and all the bread you want in the morning, because he has heard your grumbling against him. Who are we? You are not grumbling against us, but against the Lᴏʀᴅ."

9Then Moses told Aaron, "Say to the entire Israelite community, 'Come before the Lᴏʀᴅ, for he has heard your grumbling.'"

10While Aaron was speaking to the whole Israelite community, they looked toward the desert, and there was the glory of the Lᴏʀᴅ appearing in the cloud.

11The Lᴏʀᴅ said to Moses, 12"I have heard the grumbling of the Israelites. Tell them, 'At twilight you will eat meat, and in the morning you will be filled with bread. Then you will know that I am the Lᴏʀᴅ your God.'"

13That evening quail came and covered the camp, and in the morning there was a layer of dew around the camp. 14When the dew was gone, thin flakes like frost on the ground appeared on the desert floor. 15When the Israelites saw it, they said to each other, "What is it?" For they did not know what it was.

Moses said to them, "It is the bread the Lᴏʀᴅ has given you to eat. 16This is what the Lᴏʀᴅ has commanded: 'Each one is to gather as much as he needs. Take an omer*c* for each person you have in your tent.'"

17The Israelites did as they were told;

some gathered much, some little. ¹⁸And when they measured it by the omer, he who gathered much did not have too much, and he who gathered little did not have too little. Each one gathered as much as he needed.

¹⁹Then Moses said to them, "No one is to keep any of it until morning."

²⁰However, some of them paid no attention to Moses; they kept part of it until morning, but it was full of maggots and began to smell. So Moses was angry with them.

²¹Each morning everyone gathered as much as he needed, and when the sun grew hot, it melted away. ²²On the sixth day, they gathered twice as much—two omers*d* for each person—and the leaders of the community came and reported this to Moses. ²³He said to them, "This is what the Lᴏʀᴅ commanded: 'Tomorrow is to be a day of rest, a holy Sabbath to the Lᴏʀᴅ. So bake what you want to bake and boil what you want to boil. Save whatever is left and keep it until morning.'"

²⁴So they saved it until morning, as Moses commanded, and it did not stink or get maggots in it. ²⁵"Eat it today," Moses said, "because today is a Sabbath to the Lᴏʀᴅ. You will not find any of it on the ground today. ²⁶Six days you are to gather it, but on the seventh day, the Sabbath, there will not be any."

²⁷Nevertheless, some of the people went out on the seventh day to gather it, but they found none. ²⁸Then the Lᴏʀᴅ said to Moses, "How long will you*e* refuse to keep my commands and my instructions? ²⁹Bear in mind that the Lᴏʀᴅ has given you the Sabbath; that is why on the sixth day he gives you bread for two days. Everyone is to stay where he is on the seventh day; no one is to go out." ³⁰So the people rested on the seventh day.

³¹The people of Israel called the bread manna.*f* It was white like coriander seed and tasted like wafers made with honey. ³²Moses said, "This is what the Lᴏʀᴅ has commanded: 'Take an omer of manna and keep it for the gen-

erations to come, so they can see the bread I gave you to eat in the desert when I brought you out of Egypt.'"

³³So Moses said to Aaron, "Take a jar and put an omer of manna in it. Then place it before the Lᴏʀᴅ to be kept for the generations to come."

³⁴As the Lᴏʀᴅ commanded Moses, Aaron put the manna in front of the Testimony, that it might be kept. ³⁵The Israelites ate manna forty years, until they came to a land that was settled; they ate manna until they reached the border of Canaan.

³⁶(An omer is one tenth of an ephah.)

¹⁷:¹Tʜᴇ whole Israelite community set out from the Desert of Sin, traveling from place to place as the Lᴏʀᴅ commanded. They camped at Rephidim, but there was no water for the people to drink. ²So they quarreled with Moses and said, "Give us water to drink."

Moses replied, "Why do you quarrel with me? Why do you put the Lᴏʀᴅ to the test?"

³But the people were thirsty for water there, and they grumbled against Moses. They said, "Why did you bring us up out of Egypt to make us and our children and livestock die of thirst?"

⁴Then Moses cried out to the Lᴏʀᴅ, "What am I to do with these people? They are almost ready to stone me."

⁵The Lᴏʀᴅ answered Moses, "Walk on ahead of the people. Take with you some of the elders of Israel and take in your hand the staff with which you struck the Nile, and go. ⁶I will stand there before you by the rock at Horeb. Strike the rock, and water will come out of it for the people to drink." So Moses did this in the sight of the elders of Israel. ⁷And he called the place Massah*g* and Meribah*h* because the Israelites quarreled and because they tested the Lᴏʀᴅ saying, "Is the Lᴏʀᴅ among us or not?"

a19 Or *charioteers*   *b23 Marah* means *bitter.*   *c16* That is, probably about 2 quarts (about 2 liters); also in verses 18, 32, 33 and 36   *d22* That is, probably about 4 quarts (about 4.5 liters)   *e28* The Hebrew is plural.   *f31 Manna* means *What is it?* (see verse 15).   *g7 Massah* means *testing.*   *h7 Meribah* means *quarreling.*

MATTHEW 22:1-33

Jesus spoke to them [the crowds] again in parables, saying: 2"The kingdom of heaven is like a king who prepared a wedding banquet for his son. 3He sent his servants to those who had been invited to the banquet to tell them to come, but they refused to come.

4"Then he sent some more servants and said, 'Tell those who have been invited that I have prepared my dinner: My oxen and fattened cattle have been butchered, and everything is ready. Come to the wedding banquet.'

5"But they paid no attention and went off—one to his field, another to his business. 6The rest seized his servants, mistreated them and killed them. 7The king was enraged. He sent his army and destroyed those murderers and burned their city.

8"Then he said to his servants, 'The wedding banquet is ready, but those I invited did not deserve to come. 9Go to the street corners and invite to the banquet anyone you find.' 10So the servants went out into the streets and gathered all the people they could find, both good and bad, and the wedding hall was filled with guests.

11"But when the king came in to see the guests, he noticed a man there who was not wearing wedding clothes. 12'Friend,' he asked, 'how did you get in here without wedding clothes?' The man was speechless.

13"Then the king told the attendants, 'Tie him hand and foot, and throw him outside, into the darkness, where there will be weeping and gnashing of teeth.'

14"For many are invited, but few are chosen."

15Then the Pharisees went out and laid plans to trap him in his words. 16They sent their disciples to him along with the Herodians. "Teacher," they said, "we know you are a man of integrity and that you teach the way of God in accordance with the truth. You aren't swayed by men, because you pay no attention to who they are. 17Tell us then, what is your opinion? Is it right to pay taxes to Caesar or not?"

18But Jesus, knowing their evil intent, said, "You hypocrites, why are you trying to trap me? 19Show me the coin used for paying the tax." They brought him a denarius, 20and he asked them, "Whose portrait is this? And whose inscription?"

21"Caesar's," they replied.

Then he said to them, "Give to Caesar what is Caesar's, and to God what is God's."

22When they heard this, they were amazed. So they left him and went away.

23That same day the Sadducees, who say there is no resurrection, came to him with a question. 24"Teacher," they said, "Moses told us that if a man dies without having children, his brother must marry the widow and have children for him. 25Now there were seven brothers among us. The first one married and died, and since he had no children, he left his wife to his brother. 26The same thing happened to the second and third brother, right on down to the seventh. 27Finally, the woman died. 28Now then, at the resurrection, whose wife will she be of the seven, since all of them were married to her?"

29Jesus replied, "You are in error because you do not know the Scriptures or the power of God. 30At the resurrection people will neither marry nor be given in marriage; they will be like the angels in heaven. 31But about the resurrection of the dead—have you not read what God said to you, 32'I am the God of Abraham, the God of Isaac, and the God of Jacob'*a*? He is not the God of the dead but of the living."

33When the crowds heard this, they were astonished at his teaching.

a32 Exodus 3:6

PSALM 27:1-6
Of David.

1**The Lord is my light and my salvation—
whom shall I fear?**

The LORD is the stronghold of
     my life—
  of whom shall I be afraid?
2 When evil men advance against me
     to devour my flesh,*a*
  when my enemies and my foes
       attack me,
     they will stumble and fall.
3 Though an army besiege me,
     my heart will not fear;
  though war break out against me,
     even then will I be confident.

4 One thing I ask of the LORD,
     this is what I seek:
  that I may dwell in the house of
       the LORD
     all the days of my life,
  to gaze upon the beauty of the
       LORD
     and to seek him in his temple.
5 For in the day of trouble
     he will keep me safe in his
       dwelling;
  he will hide me in the shelter of his
       tabernacle
     and set me high upon a rock.
6 Then my head will be exalted
     above the enemies who
       surround me;
  at his tabernacle will I sacrifice with
       shouts of joy;
     I will sing and make music to
       the LORD.

a2 Or to slander me

PROVERBS 6:20-26
20 **M**y son, keep your father's
       commands
     and do not forsake your mother's
       teaching.
21 Bind them upon your heart forever;
     fasten them around your neck.
22 When you walk, they will guide you;
     when you sleep, they will watch
       over you;
  when you awake, they will speak
       to you.
23 For these commands are a lamp,
     this teaching is a light,
  and the corrections of discipline
     are the way to life,

24 keeping you from the immoral
       woman,
  from the smooth tongue of the
       wayward wife.
25 Do not lust in your heart after her
       beauty
  or let her captivate you with
       her eyes,
26 for the prostitute reduces you to a
       loaf of bread,
  and the adulteress preys upon
       your very life.

☐ DAY 34

GOD SIGHTINGS

February 3

EXODUS 17:8–19:15
The Amalekites came and attacked the Israelites at Rephidim. 9Moses said to Joshua, "Choose some of our men and go out to fight the Amalekites. Tomorrow I will stand on top of the hill with the staff of God in my hands."

10 So Joshua fought the Amalekites as Moses had ordered, and Moses, Aaron and Hur went to the top of the hill. 11As long as Moses held up his hands, the Israelites were winning, but whenever he lowered his hands, the Amalekites were winning. 12 When Moses' hands grew tired, they took a stone and put it under him and he sat on it. Aaron and Hur held his hands up—one on one side, one on the other—so that his hands remained steady till sunset. 13 So Joshua overcame the Amalekite army with the sword.

14 Then the LORD said to Moses, "Write this on a scroll as something to be remembered and make sure that Joshua hears it, because I will completely blot out the memory of Amalek from under heaven."

15 Moses built an altar and called it The LORD is my Banner. 16He said, "For hands were lifted up to the throne of

the LORD. The[a] LORD will be at war against the Amalekites from generation to generation."

18:1 Now Jethro, the priest of Midian and father-in-law of Moses, heard of everything God had done for Moses and for his people Israel, and how the LORD had brought Israel out of Egypt.

2 After Moses had sent away his wife Zipporah, his father-in-law Jethro received her 3 and her two sons. One son was named Gershom,[b] for Moses said, "I have become an alien in a foreign land"; 4 and the other was named Eliezer,[c] for he said, "My father's God was my helper; he saved me from the sword of Pharaoh."

5 Jethro, Moses' father-in-law, together with Moses' sons and wife, came to him in the desert, where he was camped near the mountain of God. 6 Jethro had sent word to him, "I, your father-in-law Jethro, am coming to you with your wife and her two sons."

7 So Moses went out to meet his father-in-law and bowed down and kissed him. They greeted each other and then went into the tent. 8 Moses told his father-in-law about everything the LORD had done to Pharaoh and the Egyptians for Israel's sake and about all the hardships they had met along the way and how the LORD had saved them.

9 Jethro was delighted to hear about all the good things the LORD had done for Israel in rescuing them from the hand of the Egyptians. 10 He said, "Praise be to the LORD, who rescued you from the hand of the Egyptians and of Pharaoh, and who rescued the people from the hand of the Egyptians. 11 Now I know that the LORD is greater than all other gods, for he did this to those who had treated Israel arrogantly." 12 Then Jethro, Moses' father-in-law, brought a burnt offering and other sacrifices to God, and Aaron came with all the elders of Israel to eat bread with Moses' father-in-law in the presence of God.

13 The next day Moses took his seat to serve as judge for the people, and they stood around him from morning till evening. 14 When his father-in-law saw all that Moses was doing for the people, he said, "What is this you are doing for the people? Why do you alone sit as judge, while all these people stand around you from morning till evening?"

15 Moses answered him, "Because the people come to me to seek God's will. 16 Whenever they have a dispute, it is brought to me, and I decide between the parties and inform them of God's decrees and laws."

17 Moses' father-in-law replied, "What you are doing is not good. 18 You and these people who come to you will only wear yourselves out. The work is too heavy for you; you cannot handle it alone. 19 Listen now to me and I will give you some advice, and may God be with you. You must be the people's representative before God and bring their disputes to him. 20 Teach them the decrees and laws, and show them the way to live and the duties they are to perform. 21 But select capable men from all the people—men who fear God, trustworthy men who hate dishonest gain—and appoint them as officials over thousands, hundreds, fifties and tens. 22 Have them serve as judges for the people at all times, but have them bring every difficult case to you; the simple cases they can decide themselves. That will make your load lighter, because they will share it with you. 23 If you do this and God so commands, you will be able to stand the strain, and all these people will go home satisfied."

24 Moses listened to his father-in-law and did everything he said. 25 He chose capable men from all Israel and made them leaders of the people, officials over thousands, hundreds, fifties and tens. 26 They served as judges for the people at all times. The difficult cases they brought to Moses, but the simple ones they decided themselves.

27 Then Moses sent his father-in-law on his way, and Jethro returned to his own country.

19:1 IN the third month after the Israelites left Egypt—on the very day—they came to the Desert of Sinai. 2After they set out from Rephidim, they entered the Desert of Sinai, and Israel camped there in the desert in front of the mountain.

3 Then Moses went up to God, and the LORD called to him from the mountain and said, "This is what you are to say to the house of Jacob and what you are to tell the people of Israel: 4'You yourselves have seen what I did to Egypt, and how I carried you on eagles' wings and brought you to myself. 5Now if you obey me fully and keep my covenant, then out of all nations you will be my treasured possession. Although the whole earth is mine, 6you d will be for me a kingdom of priests and a holy nation.' These are the words you are to speak to the Israelites."

7So Moses went back and summoned the elders of the people and set before them all the words the LORD had commanded him to speak. 8The people all responded together, "We will do everything the LORD has said." So Moses brought their answer back to the LORD.

9The LORD said to Moses, "I am going to come to you in a dense cloud, so that the people will hear me speaking with you and will always put their trust in you." Then Moses told the LORD what the people had said.

10And the LORD said to Moses, "Go to the people and consecrate them today and tomorrow. Have them wash their clothes 11and be ready by the third day, because on that day the LORD will come down on Mount Sinai in the sight of all the people. 12Put limits for the people around the mountain and tell them, 'Be careful that you do not go up the mountain or touch the foot of it. Whoever touches the mountain shall surely be put to death. 13He shall surely be stoned or shot with arrows; not a hand is to be laid on him. Whether man or animal, he shall not be permitted to live.' Only when the ram's horn sounds a long blast may they go up to the mountain."

14After Moses had gone down the mountain to the people, he consecrated them, and they washed their clothes. 15Then he said to the people, "Prepare yourselves for the third day. Abstain from sexual relations."

a 16 Or "Because a hand was against the throne of the LORD, the
b 3 Gershom sounds like the Hebrew for an alien there.
c 4 Eliezer means my God is helper.   d 5,6 Or possession,
for the whole earth is mine.   e You

MATTHEW 22:34–23:12

Hearing that Jesus had silenced the Sadducees, the Pharisees got together. 35One of them, an expert in the law, tested him with this question: 36"Teacher, which is the greatest commandment in the Law?"

37Jesus replied: " 'Love the Lord your God with all your heart and with all your soul and with all your mind.' a 38This is the first and greatest commandment. 39And the second is like it: 'Love your neighbor as yourself.' b 40All the Law and the Prophets hang on these two commandments."

41While the Pharisees were gathered together, Jesus asked them, 42"What do you think about the Christ c? Whose son is he?"

"The son of David," they replied.

43He said to them, "How is it then that David, speaking by the Spirit, calls him 'Lord'? For he says,

44"'The Lord said to my Lord:
    "Sit at my right hand
    until I put your enemies
        under your feet."' d

45If then David calls him 'Lord,' how can he be his son?" 46No one could say a word in reply, and from that day on no one dared to ask him any more questions.

23:1 THEN Jesus said to the crowds and to his disciples: 2"The teachers of the law and the Pharisees sit in Moses' seat. 3So you must obey them and do everything they tell you. But do not do what they do, for they do not practice what they preach. 4They tie up heavy loads and put them on men's shoulders, but they themselves are not willing to lift a finger to move them.

5 "Everything they do is done for men to see: They make their phylacteries[e] wide and the tassels on their garments long; 6 they love the place of honor at banquets and the most important seats in the synagogues; 7 they love to be greeted in the marketplaces and to have men call them 'Rabbi.'

8 "But you are not to be called 'Rabbi,' for you have only one Master and you are all brothers. 9 And do not call anyone on earth 'father,' for you have one Father, and he is in heaven. 10 Nor are you to be called 'teacher,' for you have one Teacher, the Christ.[c] 11 The greatest among you will be your servant. 12 For whoever exalts himself will be humbled, and whoever humbles himself will be exalted."

a37 Deut. 6:5 b39 Lev. 19:18 c42, 10 Or *Messiah*
d44 Psalm 110:1 e5 That is, boxes containing Scripture verses, worn on forehead and arm

PSALM 27:7-14
7 **H**ear my voice when I call, O Lord;
    be merciful to me and answer me.
8 My heart says of you, "Seek his[a]
        face!"
    Your face, Lord, I will seek.
9 Do not hide your face from me,
    do not turn your servant away in
        anger;
    you have been my helper.
  Do not reject me or forsake me,
    O God my Savior.
10 Though my father and mother
        forsake me,
    the Lord will receive me.
11 Teach me your way, O Lord;
    lead me in a straight path
        because of my oppressors.
12 Do not turn me over to the desire of
        my foes,
    for false witnesses rise up
        against me,
    breathing out violence.

13 I am still confident of this:
    I will see the goodness of
        the Lord
    in the land of the living.

14 Wait for the Lord;
    be strong and take heart
    and wait for the Lord.

a8 Or *To you, O my heart, he has said, "Seek my*

PROVERBS 6:27-35
27 **C**an a man scoop fire into his lap
    without his clothes being burned?
28 Can a man walk on hot coals
    without his feet being scorched?
29 So is he who sleeps with another
        man's wife;
    no one who touches her will go
        unpunished.

30 Men do not despise a thief if he
        steals
    to satisfy his hunger when he is
        starving.
31 Yet if he is caught, he must pay
        sevenfold,
    though it costs him all the wealth
        of his house.
32 But a man who commits adultery
        lacks judgment;
    whoever does so destroys himself.
33 Blows and disgrace are his lot,
    and his shame will never be
        wiped away;
34 for jealousy arouses a husband's
        fury,
    and he will show no mercy when
        he takes revenge.
35 He will not accept any
        compensation;
    he will refuse the bribe, however
        great it is.

☐ DAY 35

GOD SIGHTINGS

February 4

EXODUS 19:16-21:21
On the morning of the third day there was thunder and lightning, with a thick cloud over the mountain, and a very loud trumpet blast. Everyone in the camp trembled. 17 Then Moses led the people

out of the camp to meet with God, and they stood at the foot of the mountain. [18]Mount Sinai was covered with smoke, because the LORD descended on it in fire. The smoke billowed up from it like smoke from a furnace, the whole mountain[a] trembled violently, [19]and the sound of the trumpet grew louder and louder. Then Moses spoke and the voice of God answered him.[b]

[20]The LORD descended to the top of Mount Sinai and called Moses to the top of the mountain. So Moses went up [21]and the LORD said to him, "Go down and warn the people so they do not force their way through to see the LORD and many of them perish. [22]Even the priests, who approach the LORD, must consecrate themselves, or the LORD will break out against them."

[23]Moses said to the LORD, "The people cannot come up Mount Sinai, because you yourself warned us, 'Put limits around the mountain and set it apart as holy.'"

[24]The LORD replied, "Go down and bring Aaron up with you. But the priests and the people must not force their way through to come up to the LORD, or he will break out against them."

[25]So Moses went down to the people and told them.

[20:1]AND God spoke all these words:

[2]**"I am the LORD your God, who brought you out of Egypt, out of the land of slavery.**

[3]**"You shall have no other gods before[c] me.**

[4]"You shall not make for yourself an idol in the form of anything in heaven above or on the earth beneath or in the waters below. [5]You shall not bow down to them or worship them; for I, the LORD your God, am a jealous God, punishing the children for the sin of the fathers to the third and fourth generation of those who hate me, [6]but showing love to a thousand generations of those who love me and keep my commandments.

[7]"You shall not misuse the name of the LORD your God, for the LORD will not hold anyone guiltless who misuses his name.

[8]"Remember the Sabbath day by keeping it holy. [9]Six days you shall labor and do all your work, [10]but the seventh day is a Sabbath to the LORD your God. On it you shall not do any work, neither you, nor your son or daughter, nor your manservant or maidservant, nor your animals, nor the alien within your gates. [11]For in six days the LORD made the heavens and the earth, the sea, and all that is in them, but he rested on the seventh day. Therefore the LORD blessed the Sabbath day and made it holy.

[12]"Honor your father and your mother, so that you may live long in the land the LORD your God is giving you.

[13]"You shall not murder.

[14]"You shall not commit adultery.

[15]"You shall not steal.

[16]"You shall not give false testimony against your neighbor.

[17]"You shall not covet your neighbor's house. You shall not covet your neighbor's wife, or his manservant or maidservant, his ox or donkey, or anything that belongs to your neighbor."

[18]When the people saw the thunder and lightning and heard the trumpet and saw the mountain in smoke, they trembled with fear. They stayed at a dis-

tance ¹⁹and said to Moses, "Speak to us yourself and we will listen. But do not have God speak to us or we will die."

²⁰Moses said to the people, "Do not be afraid. God has come to test you, so that the fear of God will be with you to keep you from sinning."

²¹The people remained at a distance, while Moses approached the thick darkness where God was.

²²Then the LORD said to Moses, "Tell the Israelites this: 'You have seen for yourselves that I have spoken to you from heaven: ²³Do not make any gods to be alongside me; do not make for yourselves gods of silver or gods of gold.

²⁴" 'Make an altar of earth for me and sacrifice on it your burnt offerings and fellowship offerings,ᵈ your sheep and goats and your cattle. Wherever I cause my name to be honored, I will come to you and bless you. ²⁵If you make an altar of stones for me, do not build it with dressed stones, for you will defile it if you use a tool on it. ²⁶And do not go up to my altar on steps, lest your nakedness be exposed on it.'

²¹:¹"THESE are the laws you are to set before them:

²"If you buy a Hebrew servant, he is to serve you for six years. But in the seventh year, he shall go free, without paying anything. ³If he comes alone, he is to go free alone; but if he has a wife when he comes, she is to go with him. ⁴If his master gives him a wife and she bears him sons or daughters, the woman and her children shall belong to her master, and only the man shall go free.

⁵"But if the servant declares, 'I love my master and my wife and children and do not want to go free,' ⁶then his master must take him before the judges.ᵉ He shall take him to the door or the doorpost and pierce his ear with an awl. Then he will be his servant for life.

⁷"If a man sells his daughter as a servant, she is not to go free as menservants do. ⁸If she does not please the master who has selected her for him-

self,ᶠ he must let her be redeemed. He has no right to sell her to foreigners, because he has broken faith with her. ⁹If he selects her for his son, he must grant her the rights of a daughter. ¹⁰If he marries another woman, he must not deprive the first one of her food, clothing and marital rights. ¹¹If he does not provide her with these three things, she is to go free, without any payment of money.

¹²"Anyone who strikes a man and kills him shall surely be put to death. ¹³However, if he does not do it intentionally, but God lets it happen, he is to flee to a place I will designate. ¹⁴But if a man schemes and kills another man deliberately, take him away from my altar and put him to death.

¹⁵"Anyone who attacksᵍ his father or his mother must be put to death.

¹⁶"Anyone who kidnaps another and either sells him or still has him when he is caught must be put to death.

¹⁷"Anyone who curses his father or mother must be put to death.

¹⁸"If men quarrel and one hits the other with a stone or with his fistʰ and he does not die but is confined to bed, ¹⁹the one who struck the blow will not be held responsible if the other gets up and walks around outside with his staff; however, he must pay the injured man for the loss of his time and see that he is completely healed.

²⁰"If a man beats his male or female slave with a rod and the slave dies as a direct result, he must be punished, ²¹but he is not to be punished if the slave gets up after a day or two, since the slave is his property."

ᵃ18 Most Hebrew manuscripts; a few Hebrew manuscripts and Septuagint *all the people* ᵇ19 Or *and God answered him with thunder* ᶜ3 Or *besides* ᵈ24 Traditionally *peace offerings* ᵉ6 Or *before God* ᶠ8 Or *master so that he does not choose her* ᵍ15 Or *kills* ʰ18 Or *with a tool*

MATTHEW 23:13-39

"**W**oe to you, teachers of the law and Pharisees, you hypocrites! You shut the kingdom of heaven in men's faces. You yourselves do not enter, nor will you let those enter who are trying to.ᵃ

¹⁵"Woe to you, teachers of the law and Pharisees, you hypocrites! You travel over land and sea to win a single convert, and when he becomes one, you make him twice as much a son of hell as you are.

¹⁶"Woe to you, blind guides! You say, 'If anyone swears by the temple, it means nothing; but if anyone swears by the gold of the temple, he is bound by his oath.' ¹⁷You blind fools! Which is greater: the gold, or the temple that makes the gold sacred? ¹⁸You also say, 'If anyone swears by the altar, it means nothing; but if anyone swears by the gift on it, he is bound by his oath.' ¹⁹You blind men! Which is greater: the gift, or the altar that makes the gift sacred? ²⁰Therefore, he who swears by the altar swears by it and by everything on it. ²¹And he who swears by the temple swears by it and by the one who dwells in it. ²²And he who swears by heaven swears by God's throne and by the one who sits on it.

²³"Woe to you, teachers of the law and Pharisees, you hypocrites! You give a tenth of your spices—mint, dill and cummin. But you have neglected the more important matters of the law—justice, mercy and faithfulness. You should have practiced the latter, without neglecting the former. ²⁴You blind guides! You strain out a gnat but swallow a camel.

²⁵"Woe to you, teachers of the law and Pharisees, you hypocrites! You clean the outside of the cup and dish, but inside they are full of greed and self-indulgence. ²⁶Blind Pharisee! First clean the inside of the cup and dish, and then the outside also will be clean.

²⁷"Woe to you, teachers of the law and Pharisees, you hypocrites! You are like whitewashed tombs, which look beautiful on the outside but on the inside are full of dead men's bones and everything unclean. ²⁸In the same way, on the outside you appear to people as righteous but on the inside you are full of hypocrisy and wickedness.

²⁹"Woe to you, teachers of the law and Pharisees, you hypocrites! You build tombs for the prophets and decorate the graves of the righteous. ³⁰And you say, 'If we had lived in the days of our forefathers, we would not have taken part with them in shedding the blood of the prophets.' ³¹So you testify against yourselves that you are the descendants of those who murdered the prophets. ³²Fill up, then, the measure of the sin of your forefathers!

³³"You snakes! You brood of vipers! How will you escape being condemned to hell? ³⁴Therefore I am sending you prophets and wise men and teachers. Some of them you will kill and crucify; others you will flog in your synagogues and pursue from town to town. ³⁵And so upon you will come all the righteous blood that has been shed on earth, from the blood of righteous Abel to the blood of Zechariah son of Berekiah, whom you murdered between the temple and the altar. ³⁶I tell you the truth, all this will come upon this generation.

³⁷"O Jerusalem, Jerusalem, you who kill the prophets and stone those sent to you, how often I have longed to gather your children together, as a hen gathers her chicks under her wings, but you were not willing. ³⁸Look, your house is left to you desolate. ³⁹For I tell you, you will not see me again until you say, 'Blessed is he who comes in the name of the Lord.'^b

^a*13* Some manuscripts to. *¹⁴Woe to you, teachers of the law and Pharisees, you hypocrites! You devour widows' houses and for a show make lengthy prayers. Therefore you will be punished more severely.* ^b*39* Psalm 118:26

PSALM 28:1-9
Of David.

¹To you I call, O Lord my Rock;
  do not turn a deaf ear to me.
For if you remain silent,
  I will be like those who have gone
    down to the pit.
²Hear my cry for mercy
  as I call to you for help,
as I lift up my hands
  toward your Most Holy Place.

³Do not drag me away with the
  wicked,

with those who do evil,
who speak cordially with their
    neighbors
but harbor malice in their hearts.
4 Repay them for their deeds
    and for their evil work;
repay them for what their hands
    have done
    and bring back upon them what
    they deserve.
5 Since they show no regard for the
    works of the LORD
    and what his hands have done,
he will tear them down
    and never build them up again.

6 Praise be to the LORD,
    for he has heard my cry for mercy.
7 The LORD is my strength and my
    shield;
    my heart trusts in him, and I am
    helped.
My heart leaps for joy
    and I will give thanks to him
    in song.

8 The LORD is the strength of his
    people,
    a fortress of salvation for his
    anointed one.
9 Save your people and bless your
    inheritance;
    be their shepherd and carry them
    forever.

PROVERBS 7:1-5

My son, keep my words
    and store up my commands
    within you.
2 Keep my commands and you will
    live;
    guard my teachings as the apple
    of your eye.
3 Bind them on your fingers;
    write them on the tablet of your
    heart.
4 Say to wisdom, "You are my sister,"
    and call understanding your
    kinsman;
5 they will keep you from the
    adulteress,

from the wayward wife with her
    seductive words.

☐ DAY 36

GOD SIGHTINGS

February 5

EXODUS 21:22–23:13

"If men who are fighting hit a pregnant woman and she gives birth prematurely[a] but there is no serious injury, the offender must be fined whatever the woman's husband demands and the court allows. 23 But if there is serious injury, you are to take life for life, 24 eye for eye, tooth for tooth, hand for hand, foot for foot, 25 burn for burn, wound for wound, bruise for bruise.

26 "If a man hits a manservant or maidservant in the eye and destroys it, he must let the servant go free to compensate for the eye. 27 And if he knocks out the tooth of a manservant or maidservant, he must let the servant go free to compensate for the tooth.

28 "If a bull gores a man or a woman to death, the bull must be stoned to death, and its meat must not be eaten. But the owner of the bull will not be held responsible. 29 If, however, the bull has had the habit of goring and the owner has been warned but has not kept it penned up and it kills a man or woman, the bull must be stoned and the owner also must be put to death. 30 However, if payment is demanded of him, he may redeem his life by paying whatever is demanded. 31 This law also applies if the bull gores a son or daughter. 32 If the bull gores a male or female slave, the owner must pay thirty shekels[b] of silver to the master of the slave, and the bull must be stoned.

33 "If a man uncovers a pit or digs one and fails to cover it and an ox or a donkey falls into it, 34 the owner of the pit

must pay for the loss; he must pay its owner, and the dead animal will be his.

35 "If a man's bull injures the bull of another and it dies, they are to sell the live one and divide both the money and the dead animal equally. 36However, if it was known that the bull had the habit of goring, yet the owner did not keep it penned up, the owner must pay, animal for animal, and the dead animal will be his.

22:1 "If a man steals an ox or a sheep and slaughters it or sells it, he must pay back five head of cattle for the ox and four sheep for the sheep.

2 "If a thief is caught breaking in and is struck so that he dies, the defender is not guilty of bloodshed; 3 but if it happens*c* after sunrise, he is guilty of bloodshed.

"A thief must certainly make restitution, but if he has nothing, he must be sold to pay for his theft.

4 "If the stolen animal is found alive in his possession—whether ox or donkey or sheep—he must pay back double.

5 "If a man grazes his livestock in a field or vineyard and lets them stray and they graze in another man's field, he must make restitution from the best of his own field or vineyard.

6 "If a fire breaks out and spreads into thornbushes so that it burns shocks of grain or standing grain or the whole field, the one who started the fire must make restitution.

7 "If a man gives his neighbor silver or goods for safekeeping and they are stolen from the neighbor's house, the thief, if he is caught, must pay back double. 8But if the thief is not found, the owner of the house must appear before the judges*d* to determine whether he has laid his hands on the other man's property. 9 In all cases of illegal possession of an ox, a donkey, a sheep, a garment, or any other lost property about which somebody says, 'This is mine,' both parties are to bring their cases before the judges. The one whom the judges declare*e* guilty must pay back double to his neighbor.

10 "If a man gives a donkey, an ox, a sheep or any other animal to his neighbor for safekeeping and it dies or is injured or is taken away while no one is looking, 11 the issue between them will be settled by the taking of an oath before the Lord that the neighbor did not lay hands on the other person's property. The owner is to accept this, and no restitution is required. 12But if the animal was stolen from the neighbor, he must make restitution to the owner. 13If it was torn to pieces by a wild animal, he shall bring in the remains as evidence and he will not be required to pay for the torn animal.

14 "If a man borrows an animal from his neighbor and it is injured or dies while the owner is not present, he must make restitution. 15But if the owner is with the animal, the borrower will not have to pay. If the animal was hired, the money paid for the hire covers the loss.

16 "If a man seduces a virgin who is not pledged to be married and sleeps with her, he must pay the bride-price, and she shall be his wife. 17If her father absolutely refuses to give her to him, he must still pay the bride-price for virgins.

18 "Do not allow a sorceress to live.

19 "Anyone who has sexual relations with an animal must be put to death.

20 "Whoever sacrifices to any god other than the Lord must be destroyed.*f*

21 "Do not mistreat an alien or oppress him, for you were aliens in Egypt.

22 **"Do not take advantage of a widow or an orphan.** 23**If you do and they cry out to me, I will certainly hear their cry.** 24My anger will be aroused, and I will kill you with the sword; your wives will become widows and your children fatherless.

25 "If you lend money to one of my people among you who is needy, do not be like a moneylender; charge him no interest.*g* 26If you take your neighbor's cloak as a pledge, return it to him by sunset, 27 because his cloak is the only covering he has for his body. What else

will he sleep in? When he cries out to me, I will hear, for I am compassionate.

28"Do not blaspheme God[h] or curse the ruler of your people.

29"Do not hold back offerings from your granaries or your vats.[i]

"You must give me the firstborn of your sons. 30Do the same with your cattle and your sheep. Let them stay with their mothers for seven days, but give them to me on the eighth day.

31"You are to be my holy people. So do not eat the meat of an animal torn by wild beasts; throw it to the dogs.

23:1"Do not spread false reports. Do not help a wicked man by being a malicious witness.

2"Do not follow the crowd in doing wrong. When you give testimony in a lawsuit, do not pervert justice by siding with the crowd, 3 and do not show favoritism to a poor man in his lawsuit.

4"If you come across your enemy's ox or donkey wandering off, be sure to take it back to him. 5If you see the donkey of someone who hates you fallen down under its load, do not leave it there; be sure you help him with it.

6"Do not deny justice to your poor people in their lawsuits. 7Have nothing to do with a false charge and do not put an innocent or honest person to death, for I will not acquit the guilty.

8"Do not accept a bribe, for a bribe blinds those who see and twists the words of the righteous.

9"Do not oppress an alien; you yourselves know how it feels to be aliens, because you were aliens in Egypt.

10"For six years you are to sow your fields and harvest the crops, 11 but during the seventh year let the land lie unplowed and unused. Then the poor among your people may get food from it, and the wild animals may eat what they leave. Do the same with your vineyard and your olive grove.

12"Six days do your work, but on the seventh day do not work, so that your ox and your donkey may rest and the slave

born in your household, and the alien as well, may be refreshed.

13"Be careful to do everything I have said to you. Do not invoke the names of other gods; do not let them be heard on your lips."

[a]22 Or she has a miscarriage [b]32 That is, about 12 ounces (about 0.3 kilogram) [c]3 Or if he strikes him [d]8 Or before God; also in verse 9 [e]9 Or whom God declares [f]20 The Hebrew term refers to the irrevocable giving over of things or persons to the LORD, often by totally destroying them. [g]25 Or excessive interest [h]28 Or Do not revile the judges [i]29 The meaning of the Hebrew for this phrase is uncertain.

MATTHEW 24:1-28

Jesus left the temple and was walking away when his disciples came up to him to call his attention to its buildings. 2"Do you see all these things?" he asked. "I tell you the truth, not one stone here will be left on another; every one will be thrown down."

3As Jesus was sitting on the Mount of Olives, the disciples came to him privately. "Tell us," they said, "when will this happen, and what will be the sign of your coming and of the end of the age?"

4Jesus answered: "Watch out that no one deceives you. 5For many will come in my name, claiming, 'I am the Christ,[a]' and will deceive many. 6You will hear of wars and rumors of wars, but see to it that you are not alarmed. Such things must happen, but the end is still to come. 7Nation will rise against nation, and kingdom against kingdom. There will be famines and earthquakes in various places. 8All these are the beginning of birth pains.

9"Then you will be handed over to be persecuted and put to death, and you will be hated by all nations because of me. 10At that time many will turn away from the faith and will betray and hate each other, 11and many false prophets will appear and deceive many people. 12Because of the increase of wickedness, the love of most will grow cold, 13but he who stands firm to the end will be saved. 14And this gospel of the kingdom will be preached in the whole world as a testimony to all nations, and then the end will come.

15"So when you see standing in the

holy place 'the abomination that causes desolation,'[b] spoken of through the prophet Daniel—let the reader understand— [16]then let those who are in Judea flee to the mountains. [17]Let no one on the roof of his house go down to take anything out of the house. [18]Let no one in the field go back to get his cloak. [19]How dreadful it will be in those days for pregnant women and nursing mothers! [20]Pray that your flight will not take place in winter or on the Sabbath. [21]For then there will be great distress, unequaled from the beginning of the world until now—and never to be equaled again. [22]If those days had not been cut short, no one would survive, but for the sake of the elect those days will be shortened. [23]At that time if anyone says to you, 'Look, here is the Christ!' or, 'There he is!' do not believe it. [24]For false Christs and false prophets will appear and perform great signs and miracles to deceive even the elect—if that were possible. [25]See, I have told you ahead of time.

[26]"So if anyone tells you, 'There he is, out in the desert,' do not go out; or, 'Here he is, in the inner rooms,' do not believe it. [27]For as lightning that comes from the east is visible even in the west, so will be the coming of the Son of Man. [28]Wherever there is a carcass, there the vultures will gather."

[a]5 Or *Messiah*; also in verse 23   [b]15 Daniel 9:27; 11:31; 12:11

PSALM 29:1-11

A psalm of David.

[1]Ascribe to the LORD, O mighty ones,
    ascribe to the LORD glory and
        strength.
[2]Ascribe to the LORD the glory due
        his name;
    worship the LORD in the splendor
        of his[a] holiness.

[3]The voice of the LORD is over the
        waters;
    the God of glory thunders,
    the LORD thunders over the
        mighty waters.
[4]The voice of the LORD is powerful;
    the voice of the LORD is majestic.

[5]The voice of the LORD breaks the
        cedars;
    the LORD breaks in pieces the
        cedars of Lebanon.
[6]He makes Lebanon skip like a calf,
    Sirion[b] like a young wild ox.
[7]The voice of the LORD strikes
    with flashes of lightning.
[8]The voice of the LORD shakes the
        desert;
    the LORD shakes the Desert of
        Kadesh.
[9]The voice of the LORD twists the
        oaks[c]
    and strips the forests bare.
And in his temple all cry, "Glory!"

[10]The LORD sits[d] enthroned over the
        flood;
    the LORD is enthroned as King
        forever.
[11]The LORD gives strength to his
        people;
    the LORD blesses his people with
        peace.

[a]2 Or LORD *with the splendor of*   [b]6 That is, Mount Hermon
[c]9 Or LORD *makes the deer give birth*   [d]10 Or *sat*

PROVERBS 7:6-23

[6]At the window of my house
    I looked out through the lattice.
[7]I saw among the simple,
    I noticed among the young men,
    a youth who lacked judgment.
[8]He was going down the street near
        her corner,
    walking along in the direction of
        her house
[9]at twilight, as the day was fading,
    as the dark of night set in.

[10]Then out came a woman to meet
        him,
    dressed like a prostitute and with
        crafty intent.
[11](She is loud and defiant,
    her feet never stay at home;
[12]now in the street, now in the
        squares,
    at every corner she lurks.)
[13]She took hold of him and kissed
        him
    and with a brazen face she said:

14"I have fellowship offerings*a* at
     home;
   today I fulfilled my vows.
15So I came out to meet you;
   I looked for you and have found
       you!
16I have covered my bed
   with colored linens from Egypt.
17I have perfumed my bed
   with myrrh, aloes and cinnamon.
18Come, let's drink deep of love till
       morning;
   let's enjoy ourselves with love!
19My husband is not at home;
   he has gone on a long journey.
20He took his purse filled with money
   and will not be home till full moon."

21With persuasive words she led him
       astray;
   she seduced him with her
       smooth talk.
22All at once he followed her
   like an ox going to the slaughter,
   like a deer*b* stepping into a noose*c*
23   till an arrow pierces his liver,
   like a bird darting into a snare,
       little knowing it will cost him
           his life.

a 14 Traditionally *peace offerings   b 22* Syriac (see also
Septuagint); Hebrew *fool   c 22* The meaning of the Hebrew
for this line is uncertain.

□ DAY 37

GOD SIGHTINGS

February 6

EXODUS 23:14–25:40
"Three times a year you [Israelites] are
to celebrate a festival to me [the LORD].

15"Celebrate the Feast of Unleavened
Bread; for seven days eat bread made
without yeast, as I commanded you. Do
this at the appointed time in the month
of Abib, for in that month you came out
of Egypt.
   "No one is to appear before me
empty-handed.

16"Celebrate the Feast of Harvest with
the firstfruits of the crops you sow in
your field.
   "Celebrate the Feast of Ingathering at
the end of the year, when you gather in
your crops from the field.
17"Three times a year all the men are
to appear before the Sovereign LORD.
18"Do not offer the blood of a sacrifice to me along with anything containing yeast.
   "The fat of my festival offerings must
not be kept until morning.
19"Bring the best of the firstfruits of
your soil to the house of the LORD your
God.
   "Do not cook a young goat in its
mother's milk.
20"See, I am sending an angel ahead of
you to guard you along the way and to
bring you to the place I have prepared.
21Pay attention to him and listen to what
he says. Do not rebel against him; he will
not forgive your rebellion, since my
Name is in him. 22If you listen carefully
to what he says and do all that I say, I will
be an enemy to your enemies and will
oppose those who oppose you. 23My angel will go ahead of you and bring you
into the land of the Amorites, Hittites,
Perizzites, Canaanites, Hivites and Jebusites, and I will wipe them out. 24Do not
bow down before their gods or worship
them or follow their practices. You must
demolish them and break their sacred
stones to pieces. 25Worship the LORD
your God, and his blessing will be on your
food and water. I will take away sickness
from among you, 26and none will miscarry or be barren in your land. I will give
you a full life span.
27"I will send my terror ahead of you
and throw into confusion every nation
you encounter. I will make all your enemies turn their backs and run. 28I will
send the hornet ahead of you to drive
the Hivites, Canaanites and Hittites out
of your way. 29But I will not drive them
out in a single year, because the land
would become desolate and the wild
animals too numerous for you. 30Little
by little I will drive them out before you,

until you have increased enough to take possession of the land.

31"I will establish your borders from the Red Sea*a* to the Sea of the Philistines,*b* and from the desert to the River.*c* I will hand over to you the people who live in the land and you will drive them out before you. 32Do not make a covenant with them or with their gods. 33Do not let them live in your land, or they will cause you to sin against me, because the worship of their gods will certainly be a snare to you."

24:1THEN he said to Moses, "Come up to the LORD, you and Aaron, Nadab and Abihu, and seventy of the elders of Israel. You are to worship at a distance, 2but Moses alone is to approach the LORD; the others must not come near. And the people may not come up with him."

3When Moses went and told the people all the LORD's words and laws, they responded with one voice, "Everything the LORD has said we will do." 4Moses then wrote down everything the LORD had said.

He got up early the next morning and built an altar at the foot of the mountain and set up twelve stone pillars representing the twelve tribes of Israel. 5Then he sent young Israelite men, and they offered burnt offerings and sacrificed young bulls as fellowship offerings*d* to the LORD. 6Moses took half of the blood and put it in bowls, and the other half he sprinkled on the altar. 7Then he took the Book of the Covenant and read it to the people. They responded, "We will do everything the LORD has said; we will obey."

8Moses then took the blood, sprinkled it on the people and said, "This is the blood of the covenant that the LORD has made with you in accordance with all these words."

9Moses and Aaron, Nadab and Abihu, and the seventy elders of Israel went up 10and saw the God of Israel. Under his feet was something like a pavement made of sapphire,*e* clear as the sky itself. 11But God did not raise his hand against these leaders of the Israelites; they saw God, and they ate and drank.

12The LORD said to Moses, "Come up to me on the mountain and stay here, and I will give you the tablets of stone, with the law and commands I have written for their instruction."

13Then Moses set out with Joshua his aide, and Moses went up on the mountain of God. 14He said to the elders, "Wait here for us until we come back to you. Aaron and Hur are with you, and anyone involved in a dispute can go to them."

15When Moses went up on the mountain, the cloud covered it, 16and the glory of the LORD settled on Mount Sinai. For six days the cloud covered the mountain, and on the seventh day the LORD called to Moses from within the cloud. 17To the Israelites the glory of the LORD looked like a consuming fire on top of the mountain. 18Then Moses entered the cloud as he went on up the mountain. And he stayed on the mountain forty days and forty nights.

25:1THE LORD said to Moses, 2"Tell the Israelites to bring me an offering. You are to receive the offering for me from each man whose heart prompts him to give. 3These are the offerings you are to receive from them: gold, silver and bronze; 4blue, purple and scarlet yarn and fine linen; goat hair; 5ram skins dyed red and hides of sea cows*f*; acacia wood; 6olive oil for the light; spices for the anointing oil and for the fragrant incense; 7and onyx stones and other gems to be mounted on the ephod and breastpiece.

8"Then have them make a sanctuary for me, and I will dwell among them. 9Make this tabernacle and all its furnishings exactly like the pattern I will show you.

10"Have them make a chest of acacia wood—two and a half cubits long, a cubit and a half wide, and a cubit and a half high.*g* 11Overlay it with pure gold, both inside and out, and make a gold molding around it. 12Cast four gold rings for it and fasten them to its four feet, with two rings on one side and two rings on the other. ¹³Then make poles of acacia wood and overlay them with gold. ¹⁴Insert the poles into the rings on the sides of the chest to carry it. ¹⁵The poles are to remain in the rings of this ark; they are not to be removed. ¹⁶Then put in the ark the Testimony, which I will give you.

¹⁷"Make an atonement cover*h* of pure gold—two and a half cubits long and a cubit and a half wide.*i* ¹⁸And make two cherubim out of hammered gold at the ends of the cover. ¹⁹Make one cherub on one end and the second cherub on the other; make the cherubim of one piece with the cover, at the two ends. ²⁰The cherubim are to have their wings spread upward, overshadowing the cover with them. The cherubim are to face each other, looking toward the cover. ²¹Place the cover on top of the ark and put in the ark the Testimony, which I will give you. ²²There, above the cover between the two cherubim that are over the ark of the Testimony, I will meet with you and give you all my commands for the Israelites.

²³"Make a table of acacia wood—two cubits long, a cubit wide and a cubit and a half high.*j* ²⁴Overlay it with pure gold and make a gold molding around it. ²⁵Also make around it a rim a handbreadth*k* wide and put a gold molding on the rim. ²⁶Make four gold rings for the table and fasten them to the four corners, where the four legs are. ²⁷The rings are to be close to the rim to hold the poles used in carrying the table. ²⁸Make the poles of acacia wood, overlay them with gold and carry the table with them. ²⁹And make its plates and dishes of pure gold, as well as its pitchers and bowls for the pouring out of offerings. ³⁰Put the bread of the Presence on this table to be before me at all times.

³¹"Make a lampstand of pure gold and hammer it out, base and shaft; its flowerlike cups, buds and blossoms shall be of one piece with it. ³²Six branches are to extend from the sides of the lamp-

stand—three on one side and three on the other. ³³Three cups shaped like almond flowers with buds and blossoms are to be on one branch, three on the next branch, and the same for all six branches extending from the lampstand. ³⁴And on the lampstand there are to be four cups shaped like almond flowers with buds and blossoms. ³⁵One bud shall be under the first pair of branches extending from the lampstand, a second bud under the second pair, and a third bud under the third pair—six branches in all. ³⁶The buds and branches shall all be of one piece with the lampstand, hammered out of pure gold.

³⁷"Then make its seven lamps and set them up on it so that they light the space in front of it. ³⁸Its wick trimmers and trays are to be of pure gold. ³⁹A talent*l* of pure gold is to be used for the lampstand and all these accessories. ⁴⁰See that you make them according to the pattern shown you on the mountain."

a31 Hebrew *Yam Suph;* that is, Sea of Reeds   *b31* That is, the Mediterranean   *c31* That is, the Euphrates   *d5* Traditionally *peace offerings*   *e10* Or *lapis lazuli*   *f5* That is, dugongs   *g10* That is, about 3 3/4 feet (about 1.1 meters) long and 2 1/4 feet (about 0.7 meter) wide and high   *h17* Traditionally *a mercy seat*   *i17* That is, about 3 3/4 feet (about 1.1 meters) long and 2 1/4 feet (about 0.7 meter) wide   *j23* That is, about 3 feet (about 0.9 meter) long and 1 1/2 feet (about 0.5 meter) wide and 2 1/4 feet (about 0.7 meter) high   *k25* That is, about 3 inches (about 8 centimeters)   *l39* That is, about 75 pounds (about 34 kilograms)

MATTHEW 24:29-51

"Immediately after the distress of those days

"'the sun will be darkened,
   and the moon will not give its
      light;
the stars will fall from the sky,
   and the heavenly bodies will be
      shaken.'*a*

³⁰"At that time the sign of the Son of Man will appear in the sky, and all the nations of the earth will mourn. They will see the Son of Man coming on the clouds of the sky, with power and great glory. ³¹And he will send his angels with a loud trumpet call, and they will gather his elect from the four winds, from one end of the heavens to the other.

32"Now learn this lesson from the fig tree: As soon as its twigs get tender and its leaves come out, you know that summer is near. 33Even so, when you see all these things, you know that it*b* is near, right at the door. 34I tell you the truth, this generation*c* will certainly not pass away until all these things have happened. 35Heaven and earth will pass away, but my words will never pass away.

36"No one knows about that day or hour, not even the angels in heaven, nor the Son,*d* but only the Father. 37As it was in the days of Noah, so it will be at the coming of the Son of Man. 38For in the days before the flood, people were eating and drinking, marrying and giving in marriage, up to the day Noah entered the ark; 39and they knew nothing about what would happen until the flood came and took them all away. That is how it will be at the coming of the Son of Man. 40Two men will be in the field; one will be taken and the other left. 41Two women will be grinding with a hand mill; one will be taken and the other left.

42"Therefore keep watch, because you do not know on what day your Lord will come. 43But understand this: If the owner of the house had known at what time of night the thief was coming, he would have kept watch and would not have let his house be broken into. 44So you also must be ready, because the Son of Man will come at an hour when you do not expect him.

45"Who then is the faithful and wise servant, whom the master has put in charge of the servants in his household to give them their food at the proper time? 46It will be good for that servant whose master finds him doing so when he returns. 47I tell you the truth, he will put him in charge of all his possessions. 48But suppose that servant is wicked and says to himself, 'My master is staying away a long time,' 49and he then begins to beat his fellow servants and to eat and drink with drunkards. 50The master of that servant will come on a day when he does not expect him and at an hour he is not aware of. 51He will cut

him to pieces and assign him a place with the hypocrites, where there will be weeping and gnashing of teeth."

a29 Isaiah 13:10; 34:4   *b33* Or he   *c34* Or race   *d36* Some manuscripts do not have *nor the Son.*

PSALM 30:1-12

A psalm. A song. For the dedication of the temple.*a* Of David.

1 I will exalt you, O LORD,
   for you lifted me out of the depths
   and did not let my enemies gloat over me.
2 O LORD my God, I called to you for help
   and you healed me.
3 O LORD, you brought me up from the grave*b*;
   you spared me from going down into the pit.

4 Sing to the LORD, you saints of his;
   praise his holy name.
5 For his anger lasts only a moment,
   but his favor lasts a lifetime;
 weeping may remain for a night,
   but rejoicing comes in the morning.

6 When I felt secure, I said,
   "I will never be shaken."
7 O LORD, when you favored me,
   you made my mountain*c* stand firm;
 but when you hid your face,
   I was dismayed.

8 To you, O LORD, I called;
   to the Lord I cried for mercy:
9 "What gain is there in my destruction,*d*
   in my going down into the pit?
 Will the dust praise you?
   Will it proclaim your faithfulness?
10 Hear, O LORD, and be merciful to me;
   O LORD, be my help."

11 You turned my wailing into dancing;
   you removed my sackcloth and clothed me with joy,

¹²that my heart may sing to you and
      not be silent.
   O Lord my God, I will give you
      thanks forever.

^aTitle: Or *palace*   ^b3 Hebrew *Sheol*   ^c7 Or *hill country*
^d9 Or *there if I am silenced*

PROVERBS 7:24-27

²⁴**N**ow then, my sons, listen to me;
      pay attention to what I say.
²⁵Do not let your heart turn to her ways
      or stray into her paths.
²⁶Many are the victims she has brought
      down;
   her slain are a mighty throng.
²⁷Her house is a highway to the grave,^a
      leading down to the chambers of
      death.

^a27 Hebrew *Sheol*

□ DAY 38

GOD SIGHTINGS

February 7

EXODUS 26:1–27:21

"**M**ake the tabernacle with ten curtains
of finely twisted linen and blue, purple
and scarlet yarn, with cherubim worked
into them by a skilled craftsman. ²All the
curtains are to be the same size—twenty-
eight cubits long and four cubits wide.^a
³Join five of the curtains together, and do
the same with the other five. ⁴Make
loops of blue material along the edge of
the end curtain in one set, and do the
same with the end curtain in the other
set. ⁵Make fifty loops on one curtain and
fifty loops on the end curtain of the
other set, with the loops opposite each
other. ⁶Then make fifty gold clasps and
use them to fasten the curtains together
so that the tabernacle is a unit.

⁷"Make curtains of goat hair for the
tent over the tabernacle—eleven alto-
gether. ⁸All eleven curtains are to be the
same size—thirty cubits long and four
cubits wide.^b ⁹Join five of the curtains

together into one set and the other six
into another set. Fold the sixth curtain
double at the front of the tent. ¹⁰Make
fifty loops along the edge of the end
curtain in one set and also along the
edge of the end curtain in the other set.
¹¹Then make fifty bronze clasps and
put them in the loops to fasten the tent
together as a unit. ¹²As for the additional length of the tent curtains, the
half curtain that is left over is to hang
down at the rear of the tabernacle.
¹³The tent curtains will be a cubit^c lon-
ger on both sides; what is left will hang
over the sides of the tabernacle so as to
cover it. ¹⁴Make for the tent a covering
of ram skins dyed red, and over that a
covering of hides of sea cows.^d

¹⁵"Make upright frames of acacia
wood for the tabernacle. ¹⁶Each frame is
to be ten cubits long and a cubit and a
half wide,^e ¹⁷with two projections set
parallel to each other. Make all the
frames of the tabernacle in this way.
¹⁸Make twenty frames for the south side
of the tabernacle ¹⁹and make forty silver
bases to go under them—two bases for
each frame, one under each projection.
²⁰For the other side, the north side of the
tabernacle, make twenty frames ²¹and
forty silver bases—two under each
frame. ²²Make six frames for the far end,
that is, the west end of the tabernacle,
²³and make two frames for the corners
at the far end. ²⁴At these two corners
they must be double from the bottom all
the way to the top, and fitted into a single
ring; both shall be like that. ²⁵So there
will be eight frames and sixteen silver
bases—two under each frame.

²⁶"Also make crossbars of acacia
wood: five for the frames on one side of
the tabernacle, ²⁷five for those on the
other side, and five for the frames on the
west, at the far end of the tabernacle.
²⁸The center crossbar is to extend from
end to end at the middle of the frames.
²⁹Overlay the frames with gold and make
gold rings to hold the crossbars. Also
overlay the crossbars with gold.

³⁰"Set up the tabernacle according to
the plan shown you on the mountain.

³¹"Make a curtain of blue, purple and scarlet yarn and finely twisted linen, with cherubim worked into it by a skilled craftsman. ³²Hang it with gold hooks on four posts of acacia wood overlaid with gold and standing on four silver bases. ³³Hang the curtain from the clasps and place the ark of the Testimony behind the curtain. The curtain will separate the Holy Place from the Most Holy Place. ³⁴Put the atonement cover on the ark of the Testimony in the Most Holy Place. ³⁵Place the table outside the curtain on the north side of the tabernacle and put the lampstand opposite it on the south side.

³⁶"For the entrance to the tent make a curtain of blue, purple and scarlet yarn and finely twisted linen—the work of an embroiderer. ³⁷Make gold hooks for this curtain and five posts of acacia wood overlaid with gold. And cast five bronze bases for them.

²⁷:¹"Build an altar of acacia wood, three cubitsᶠ high; it is to be square, five cubits long and five cubits wide.ᵍ ²Make a horn at each of the four corners, so that the horns and the altar are of one piece, and overlay the altar with bronze. ³Make all its utensils of bronze—its pots to remove the ashes, and its shovels, sprinkling bowls, meat forks and firepans. ⁴Make a grating for it, a bronze network, and make a bronze ring at each of the four corners of the network. ⁵Put it under the ledge of the altar so that it is halfway up the altar. ⁶Make poles of acacia wood for the altar and overlay them with bronze. ⁷The poles are to be inserted into the rings so they will be on two sides of the altar when it is carried. ⁸Make the altar hollow, out of boards. It is to be made just as you were shown on the mountain.

⁹"Make a courtyard for the tabernacle. The south side shall be a hundred cubitsʰ long and is to have curtains of finely twisted linen, ¹⁰with twenty posts and twenty bronze bases and with silver hooks and bands on the posts. ¹¹The north side shall also be a hundred cubits long and is to have curtains, with twenty posts and twenty bronze bases and with silver hooks and bands on the posts.

¹²"The west end of the courtyard shall be fifty cubitsⁱ wide and have curtains, with ten posts and ten bases. ¹³On the east end, toward the sunrise, the courtyard shall also be fifty cubits wide. ¹⁴Curtains fifteen cubitsʲ long are to be on one side of the entrance, with three posts and three bases, ¹⁵and curtains fifteen cubits long are to be on the other side, with three posts and three bases.

¹⁶"For the entrance to the courtyard, provide a curtain twenty cubitsᵏ long, of blue, purple and scarlet yarn and finely twisted linen—the work of an embroiderer—with four posts and four bases. ¹⁷All the posts around the courtyard are to have silver bands and hooks, and bronze bases. ¹⁸The courtyard shall be a hundred cubits long and fifty cubits wide,ˡ with curtains of finely twisted linen five cubitsᵐ high, and with bronze bases. ¹⁹All the other articles used in the service of the tabernacle, whatever their function, including all the tent pegs for it and those for the courtyard, are to be of bronze.

²⁰"Command the Israelites to bring you clear oil of pressed olives for the light so that the lamps may be kept burning. ²¹In the Tent of Meeting, outside the curtain that is in front of the Testimony, Aaron and his sons are to keep the lamps burning before the Lord from evening till morning. This is to be a lasting ordinance among the Israelites for the generations to come."

ᵃ2 That is, about 42 feet (about 12.5 meters) long and 6 feet (about 1.8 meters) wide   ᵇ8 That is, about 45 feet (about 13.5 meters) long and 6 feet (about 1.8 meters) wide   ᶜ13 That is, about 1 1/2 feet (about 0.5 meter)   ᵈ14 That is, dugongs   ᵉ16 That is, about 15 feet (about 4.5 meters) long and 2 1/4 feet (about 0.7 meter) wide   ᶠ1 That is, about 4 1/2 feet (about 1.3 meters)   ᵍ1 That is, about 7 1/2 feet (about 2.3 meters) long and wide   ʰ9 That is, about 150 feet (about 46 meters); also in verse 11   ⁱ12 That is, about 75 feet (about 23 meters); also in verse 13   ʲ14 That is, about 22 1/2 feet (about 6.9 meters); also in verse 15   ᵏ16 That is, about 30 feet (about 9 meters)   ˡ18 That is, about 150 feet (about 46 meters) long and 75 feet (about 23 meters) wide   ᵐ18 That is, about 7 1/2 feet (about 2.3 meters)

MATTHEW 25:1-30

"**A**t that time the kingdom of heaven will be like ten virgins who took their lamps and went out to meet the bridegroom. ²Five of them were foolish and five were wise. ³The foolish ones took their lamps but did not take any oil with them. ⁴The wise, however, took oil in jars along with their lamps. ⁵The bridegroom was a long time in coming, and they all became drowsy and fell asleep.

⁶"At midnight the cry rang out: 'Here's the bridegroom! Come out to meet him!'

⁷"Then all the virgins woke up and trimmed their lamps. ⁸The foolish ones said to the wise, 'Give us some of your oil; our lamps are going out.'

⁹"'No,' they replied, 'there may not be enough for both us and you. Instead, go to those who sell oil and buy some for yourselves.'

¹⁰"But while they were on their way to buy the oil, the bridegroom arrived. The virgins who were ready went in with him to the wedding banquet. And the door was shut.

¹¹"Later the others also came. 'Sir! Sir!' they said. 'Open the door for us!'

¹²"But he replied, 'I tell you the truth, I don't know you.'

¹³"Therefore keep watch, because you do not know the day or the hour.

¹⁴"Again, it will be like a man going on a journey, who called his servants and entrusted his property to them. ¹⁵To one he gave five talents*a* of money, to another two talents, and to another one talent, each according to his ability. Then he went on his journey. ¹⁶The man who had received the five talents went at once and put his money to work and gained five more. ¹⁷So also, the one with the two talents gained two more. ¹⁸But the man who had received the one talent went off, dug a hole in the ground and hid his master's money.

¹⁹"After a long time the master of those servants returned and settled accounts with them. ²⁰The man who had received the five talents brought the other five. 'Master,' he said, 'you entrusted me with five talents. See, I have gained five more.'

²¹"His master replied, 'Well done, good and faithful servant! You have been faithful with a few things; I will put you in charge of many things. Come and share your master's happiness!'

²²"The man with the two talents also came. 'Master,' he said, 'you entrusted me with two talents; see, I have gained two more.'

²³"His master replied, 'Well done, good and faithful servant! You have been faithful with a few things; I will put you in charge of many things. Come and share your master's happiness!'

²⁴"Then the man who had received the one talent came. 'Master,' he said, 'I knew that you are a hard man, harvesting where you have not sown and gathering where you have not scattered seed. ²⁵So I was afraid and went out and hid your talent in the ground. See, here is what belongs to you.'

²⁶"His master replied, 'You wicked, lazy servant! So you knew that I harvest where I have not sown and gather where I have not scattered seed? ²⁷Well then, you should have put my money on deposit with the bankers, so that when I returned I would have received it back with interest.

²⁸"'Take the talent from him and give it to the one who has the ten talents. ²⁹For everyone who has will be given more, and he will have an abundance. Whoever does not have, even what he has will be taken from him. ³⁰And throw that worthless servant outside, into the darkness, where there will be weeping and gnashing of teeth.'"

a 15 A talent was worth more than a thousand dollars.

PSALM 31:1-8

For the director of music. A psalm of David.

¹ **In you, O Lord, I have taken refuge;**
let me never be put to shame;
deliver me in your
righteousness.

2 Turn your ear to me,
 come quickly to my rescue;
 be my rock of refuge,
  a strong fortress to save me.
3 Since you are my rock and my
  fortress,
 for the sake of your name lead and
  guide me.
4 Free me from the trap that is set
  for me,
 for you are my refuge.
5 Into your hands I commit my spirit;
 redeem me, O Lord, the God of
  truth.

6 I hate those who cling to worthless
  idols;
 I trust in the Lord.
7 I will be glad and rejoice in your love,
 for you saw my affliction
 and knew the anguish of my soul.
8 You have not handed me over to the
  enemy
 but have set my feet in a spacious
  place.

PROVERBS 8:1-11

Does not wisdom call out?
 Does not understanding raise her
  voice?
2 On the heights along the way,
 where the paths meet, she takes
  her stand;
3 beside the gates leading into the city,
 at the entrances, she cries aloud:
4 "To you, O men, I call out;
 I raise my voice to all mankind.
5 You who are simple, gain prudence;
 you who are foolish, gain
  understanding.
6 Listen, for I have worthy things
  to say;
 I open my lips to speak what is right.
7 My mouth speaks what is true,
 for my lips detest wickedness.
8 All the words of my mouth are just;
 none of them is crooked or
  perverse.
9 To the discerning all of them are
  right;
 they are faultless to those who
  have knowledge.

10 Choose my instruction instead of
  silver,
 knowledge rather than choice
  gold,
11 for wisdom is more precious than
  rubies,
 and nothing you desire can
  compare with her.

□ DAY 39

GOD SIGHTINGS

February 8

EXODUS 28:1-43

"Have Aaron your [Moses'] brother brought to you from among the Israelites, along with his sons Nadab and Abihu, Eleazar and Ithamar, so they may serve me as priests. 2 Make sacred garments for your brother Aaron, to give him dignity and honor. 3 Tell all the skilled men to whom I have given wisdom in such matters that they are to make garments for Aaron, for his consecration, so he may serve me as priest. 4 These are the garments they are to make: a breastpiece, an ephod, a robe, a woven tunic, a turban and a sash. They are to make these sacred garments for your brother Aaron and his sons, so they may serve me as priests. 5 Have them use gold, and blue, purple and scarlet yarn, and fine linen.

6 "Make the ephod of gold, and of blue, purple and scarlet yarn, and of finely twisted linen—the work of a skilled craftsman. 7 It is to have two shoulder pieces attached to two of its corners, so it can be fastened. 8 Its skillfully woven waistband is to be like it—of one piece with the ephod and made with gold, and with blue, purple and scarlet yarn, and with finely twisted linen.

9 "Take two onyx stones and engrave on them the names of the sons of Israel 10 in the order of their birth—six names

on one stone and the remaining six on the other. [11]Engrave the names of the sons of Israel on the two stones the way a gem cutter engraves a seal. Then mount the stones in gold filigree settings [12]and fasten them on the shoulder pieces of the ephod as memorial stones for the sons of Israel. Aaron is to bear the names on his shoulders as a memorial before the LORD. [13]Make gold filigree settings [14]and two braided chains of pure gold, like a rope, and attach the chains to the settings.

[15]"Fashion a breastpiece for making decisions—the work of a skilled craftsman. Make it like the ephod: of gold, and of blue, purple and scarlet yarn, and of finely twisted linen. [16]It is to be square—a span[a] long and a span wide—and folded double. [17]Then mount four rows of precious stones on it. In the first row there shall be a ruby, a topaz and a beryl; [18]in the second row a turquoise, a sapphire[b] and an emerald; [19]in the third row a jacinth, an agate and an amethyst; [20]in the fourth row a chrysolite, an onyx and a jasper.[c] Mount them in gold filigree settings. [21]There are to be twelve stones, one for each of the names of the sons of Israel, each engraved like a seal with the name of one of the twelve tribes.

[22]"For the breastpiece make braided chains of pure gold, like a rope. [23]Make two gold rings for it and fasten them to two corners of the breastpiece. [24]Fasten the two gold chains to the rings at the corners of the breastpiece, [25]and the other ends of the chains to the two settings, attaching them to the shoulder pieces of the ephod at the front. [26]Make two gold rings and attach them to the other two corners of the breastpiece on the inside edge next to the ephod. [27]Make two more gold rings and attach them to the bottom of the shoulder pieces on the front of the ephod, close to the seam just above the waistband of the ephod. [28]The rings of the breastpiece are to be tied to the rings of the ephod with blue cord, connecting it to the waistband, so that the breastpiece will not swing out from the ephod.

[29]"Whenever Aaron enters the Holy Place, he will bear the names of the sons of Israel over his heart on the breastpiece of decision as a continuing memorial before the LORD. [30]Also put the Urim and the Thummim in the breastpiece, so they may be over Aaron's heart whenever he enters the presence of the LORD. Thus Aaron will always bear the means of making decisions for the Israelites over his heart before the LORD.

[31]"Make the robe of the ephod entirely of blue cloth, [32]with an opening for the head in its center. There shall be a woven edge like a collar[d] around this opening, so that it will not tear. [33]Make pomegranates of blue, purple and scarlet yarn around the hem of the robe, with gold bells between them. [34]The gold bells and the pomegranates are to alternate around the hem of the robe. [35]Aaron must wear it when he ministers. The sound of the bells will be heard when he enters the Holy Place before the LORD and when he comes out, so that he will not die.

[36]"Make a plate of pure gold and engrave on it as on a seal: HOLY TO THE LORD. [37]Fasten a blue cord to it to attach it to the turban; it is to be on the front of the turban. [38]It will be on Aaron's forehead, and he will bear the guilt involved in the sacred gifts the Israelites consecrate, whatever their gifts may be. It will be on Aaron's forehead continually so that they will be acceptable to the LORD.

[39]"Weave the tunic of fine linen and make the turban of fine linen. The sash is to be the work of an embroiderer. [40]Make tunics, sashes and headbands for Aaron's sons, to give them dignity and honor. [41]After you put these clothes on your brother Aaron and his sons, anoint and ordain them. Consecrate them so they may serve me as priests.

[42]"Make linen undergarments as a covering for the body, reaching from the waist to the thigh. [43]Aaron and his sons must wear them whenever they enter the Tent of Meeting or approach

the altar to minister in the Holy Place, so that they will not incur guilt and die.

"This is to be a lasting ordinance for Aaron and his descendants."

a16 That is, about 9 inches (about 22 centimeters)
b18 Or *lapis lazuli* *c20* The precise identification of some of these precious stones is uncertain. *d32* The meaning of the Hebrew for this word is uncertain.

MATTHEW 25:31–26:13

"**W**hen the Son of Man comes in his glory, and all the angels with him, he will sit on his throne in heavenly glory. 32All the nations will be gathered before him, and he will separate the people one from another as a shepherd separates the sheep from the goats. 33He will put the sheep on his right and the goats on his left.

34"Then the King will say to those on his right, 'Come, you who are blessed by my Father; take your inheritance, the kingdom prepared for you since the creation of the world. 35For I was hungry and you gave me something to eat, I was thirsty and you gave me something to drink, I was a stranger and you invited me in, 36I needed clothes and you clothed me, I was sick and you looked after me, I was in prison and you came to visit me.'

37"Then the righteous will answer him, 'Lord, when did we see you hungry and feed you, or thirsty and give you something to drink? 38When did we see you a stranger and invite you in, or needing clothes and clothe you? 39When did we see you sick or in prison and go to visit you?'

40**" The King will reply, 'I tell you the truth, whatever you did for one of the least of these brothers of mine, you did for me.'**

41"Then he will say to those on his left, 'Depart from me, you who are cursed, into the eternal fire prepared for the devil and his angels. 42For I was hungry and you gave me nothing to eat, I was thirsty and you gave me nothing to drink, 43I was a stranger and you did not invite me in, I needed clothes and you did not clothe me, I was sick and in prison and you did not look after me.'

44"They also will answer, 'Lord, when did we see you hungry or thirsty or a stranger or needing clothes or sick or in prison, and did not help you?'

45"He will reply, 'I tell you the truth, whatever you did not do for one of the least of these, you did not do for me.'

46"Then they will go away to eternal punishment, but the righteous to eternal life."

26:1WHEN Jesus had finished saying all these things, he said to his disciples, 2"As you know, the Passover is two days away—and the Son of Man will be handed over to be crucified."

3 Then the chief priests and the elders of the people assembled in the palace of the high priest, whose name was Caiaphas, 4and they plotted to arrest Jesus in some sly way and kill him. 5"But not during the Feast," they said, "or there may be a riot among the people."

6While Jesus was in Bethany in the home of a man known as Simon the Leper, 7a woman came to him with an alabaster jar of very expensive perfume, which she poured on his head as he was reclining at the table.

8When the disciples saw this, they were indignant. "Why this waste?" they asked. 9"This perfume could have been sold at a high price and the money given to the poor."

10Aware of this, Jesus said to them, "Why are you bothering this woman? She has done a beautiful thing to me. 11The poor you will always have with you, but you will not always have me. 12When she poured this perfume on my body, she did it to prepare me for burial. 13I tell you the truth, wherever this gospel is preached throughout the world, what she has done will also be told, in memory of her."

PSALM 31:9-18

9**B**e merciful to me, O LORD, for I am
  in distress;
  my eyes grow weak with sorrow,
  my soul and my body with grief.

10My life is consumed by anguish
   and my years by groaning;
my strength fails because of my
      affliction,*a*
   and my bones grow weak.
11Because of all my enemies,
   I am the utter contempt of my
      neighbors;
I am a dread to my friends—
   those who see me on the street
      flee from me.
12I am forgotten by them as though
   I were dead;
I have become like broken pottery.
13For I hear the slander of many;
   there is terror on every side;
they conspire against me
   and plot to take my life.

14But I trust in you, O Lord;
   I say, "You are my God."
15My times are in your hands;
   deliver me from my enemies
   and from those who pursue me.
16Let your face shine on your
      servant;
   save me in your unfailing love.
17Let me not be put to shame,
   O Lord,
   for I have cried out to you;
but let the wicked be put to shame
   and lie silent in the grave.*b*
18Let their lying lips be silenced,
   for with pride and contempt
   they speak arrogantly against the
      righteous.

a10 Or *guilt*   *b17* Hebrew *Sheol*

PROVERBS 8:12-13
12"I, wisdom, dwell together with
      prudence;
   I possess knowledge and
      discretion.
13To fear the Lord is to hate evil;
   I hate pride and arrogance,
   evil behavior and perverse
      speech."

☐ D A Y   4 0

GOD SIGHTINGS

February 9

EXODUS 29:1–30:10

"This is what you [Moses] are to do to consecrate them, so they may serve me as priests: Take a young bull and two rams without defect. 2And from fine wheat flour, without yeast, make bread, and cakes mixed with oil, and wafers spread with oil. 3Put them in a basket and present them in it—along with the bull and the two rams. 4Then bring Aaron and his sons to the entrance to the Tent of Meeting and wash them with water. 5Take the garments and dress Aaron with the tunic, the robe of the ephod, the ephod itself and the breastpiece. Fasten the ephod on him by its skillfully woven waistband. 6Put the turban on his head and attach the sacred diadem to the turban. 7Take the anointing oil and anoint him by pouring it on his head. 8Bring his sons and dress them in tunics 9and put headbands on them. Then tie sashes on Aaron and his sons.*a* The priesthood is theirs by a lasting ordinance. In this way you shall ordain Aaron and his sons.

10"Bring the bull to the front of the Tent of Meeting, and Aaron and his sons shall lay their hands on its head. 11Slaughter it in the Lord's presence at the entrance to the Tent of Meeting. 12Take some of the bull's blood and put it on the horns of the altar with your finger, and pour out the rest of it at the base of the altar. 13Then take all the fat around the inner parts, the covering of the liver, and both kidneys with the fat on them, and burn them on the altar. 14But burn the bull's flesh and its hide and its offal outside the camp. It is a sin offering.

15"Take one of the rams, and Aaron and his sons shall lay their hands on its head. 16Slaughter it and take the blood and sprinkle it against the altar on all sides. ¹⁷Cut the ram into pieces and wash the inner parts and the legs, putting them with the head and the other pieces. ¹⁸Then burn the entire ram on the altar. It is a burnt offering to the Lord, a pleasing aroma, an offering made to the Lord by fire.

¹⁹"Take the other ram, and Aaron and his sons shall lay their hands on its head. ²⁰Slaughter it, take some of its blood and put it on the lobes of the right ears of Aaron and his sons, on the thumbs of their right hands, and on the big toes of their right feet. Then sprinkle blood against the altar on all sides. ²¹And take some of the blood on the altar and some of the anointing oil and sprinkle it on Aaron and his garments and on his sons and their garments. Then he and his sons and their garments will be consecrated.

²²"Take from this ram the fat, the fat tail, the fat around the inner parts, the covering of the liver, both kidneys with the fat on them, and the right thigh. (This is the ram for the ordination.) ²³From the basket of bread made without yeast, which is before the Lord, take a loaf, and a cake made with oil, and a wafer. ²⁴Put all these in the hands of Aaron and his sons and wave them before the Lord as a wave offering. ²⁵Then take them from their hands and burn them on the altar along with the burnt offering for a pleasing aroma to the Lord, an offering made to the Lord by fire. ²⁶After you take the breast of the ram for Aaron's ordination, wave it before the Lord as a wave offering, and it will be your share.

²⁷"Consecrate those parts of the ordination ram that belong to Aaron and his sons: the breast that was waved and the thigh that was presented. ²⁸This is always to be the regular share from the Israelites for Aaron and his sons. It is the contribution the Israelites are to make to the Lord from their fellowship offerings.ᵇ

²⁹"Aaron's sacred garments will belong to his descendants so that they can be anointed and ordained in them.

³⁰The son who succeeds him as priest and comes to the Tent of Meeting to minister in the Holy Place is to wear them seven days.

³¹"Take the ram for the ordination and cook the meat in a sacred place. ³²At the entrance to the Tent of Meeting, Aaron and his sons are to eat the meat of the ram and the bread that is in the basket. ³³They are to eat these offerings by which atonement was made for their ordination and consecration. But no one else may eat them, because they are sacred. ³⁴And if any of the meat of the ordination ram or any bread is left over till morning, burn it up. It must not be eaten, because it is sacred.

³⁵"Do for Aaron and his sons everything I have commanded you, taking seven days to ordain them. ³⁶Sacrifice a bull each day as a sin offering to make atonement. Purify the altar by making atonement for it, and anoint it to consecrate it. ³⁷For seven days make atonement for the altar and consecrate it. Then the altar will be most holy, and whatever touches it will be holy.

³⁸"This is what you are to offer on the altar regularly each day: two lambs a year old. ³⁹Offer one in the morning and the other at twilight. ⁴⁰With the first lamb offer a tenth of an ephahᶜ of fine flour mixed with a quarter of a hinᵈ of oil from pressed olives, and a quarter of a hin of wine as a drink offering. ⁴¹Sacrifice the other lamb at twilight with the same grain offering and its drink offering as in the morning—a pleasing aroma, an offering made to the Lord by fire.

⁴²"For the generations to come this burnt offering is to be made regularly at the entrance to the Tent of Meeting before the Lord. There I will meet you and speak to you; ⁴³there also I will meet with the Israelites, and the place will be consecrated by my glory.

⁴⁴"So I will consecrate the Tent of Meeting and the altar and will consecrate Aaron and his sons to serve me as priests. ⁴⁵Then I will dwell among the Israelites and be their God. ⁴⁶They will

145

know that I am the LORD their God, who brought them out of Egypt so that I might dwell among them. I am the LORD their God.

30:1"MAKE an altar of acacia wood for burning incense. ²It is to be square, a cubit long and a cubit wide, and two cubits high*e*—its horns of one piece with it. ³Overlay the top and all the sides and the horns with pure gold, and make a gold molding around it. ⁴Make two gold rings for the altar below the molding—two on opposite sides—to hold the poles used to carry it. ⁵Make the poles of acacia wood and overlay them with gold. ⁶Put the altar in front of the curtain that is before the ark of the Testimony—before the atonement cover that is over the Testimony—where I will meet with you.

⁷"Aaron must burn fragrant incense on the altar every morning when he tends the lamps. ⁸He must burn incense again when he lights the lamps at twilight so incense will burn regularly before the LORD for the generations to come. ⁹Do not offer on this altar any other incense or any burnt offering or grain offering, and do not pour a drink offering on it. ¹⁰Once a year Aaron shall make atonement on its horns. This annual atonement must be made with the blood of the atoning sin offering for the generations to come. It is most holy to the LORD."

a9 Hebrew; Septuagint on them b28 Traditionally peace offerings c40 That is, probably about 2 quarts (about 2 liters) d40 That is, probably about 1 quart (about 1 liter) e2 That is, about 1 1/2 feet (about 0.5 meter) long and wide and about 3 feet (about 0.9 meter) high

MATTHEW 26:14-46

Then one of the Twelve—the one called Judas Iscariot—went to the chief priests ¹⁵and asked, "What are you willing to give me if I hand him over to you?" So they counted out for him thirty silver coins. ¹⁶From then on Judas watched for an opportunity to hand him over.

¹⁷On the first day of the Feast of Unleavened Bread, the disciples came to Jesus and asked, "Where do you want us to make preparations for you to eat the Passover?"

¹⁸He replied, "Go into the city to a certain man and tell him, 'The Teacher says: My appointed time is near. I am going to celebrate the Passover with my disciples at your house.'" ¹⁹So the disciples did as Jesus had directed them and prepared the Passover.

²⁰When evening came, Jesus was reclining at the table with the Twelve. ²¹And while they were eating, he said, "I tell you the truth, one of you will betray me."

²²They were very sad and began to say to him one after the other, "Surely not I, Lord?"

²³Jesus replied, "The one who has dipped his hand into the bowl with me will betray me. ²⁴The Son of Man will go just as it is written about him. But woe to that man who betrays the Son of Man! It would be better for him if he had not been born."

²⁵Then Judas, the one who would betray him, said, "Surely not I, Rabbi?"

Jesus answered, "Yes, it is you."*a*

²⁶While they were eating, Jesus took bread, gave thanks and broke it, and gave it to his disciples, saying, "Take and eat; this is my body."

²⁷Then he took the cup, gave thanks and offered it to them, saying, "Drink from it, all of you. ²⁸This is my blood of the*b* covenant, which is poured out for many for the forgiveness of sins. ²⁹I tell you, I will not drink of this fruit of the vine from now on until that day when I drink it anew with you in my Father's kingdom."

³⁰When they had sung a hymn, they went out to the Mount of Olives.

³¹Then Jesus told them, "This very night you will all fall away on account of me, for it is written:

"'I will strike the shepherd,
    and the sheep of the flock will be
        scattered.'*c*

³²But after I have risen, I will go ahead of you into Galilee."

³³Peter replied, "Even if all fall away on account of you, I never will."

34"I tell you the truth," Jesus answered, "this very night, before the rooster crows, you will disown me three times."

35But Peter declared, "Even if I have to die with you, I will never disown you." And all the other disciples said the same.

36Then Jesus went with his disciples to a place called Gethsemane, and he said to them, "Sit here while I go over there and pray." 37He took Peter and the two sons of Zebedee along with him, and he began to be sorrowful and troubled. 38Then he said to them, "My soul is overwhelmed with sorrow to the point of death. Stay here and keep watch with me."

39Going a little farther, he fell with his face to the ground and prayed, "My Father, if it is possible, may this cup be taken from me. Yet not as I will, but as you will."

40Then he returned to his disciples and found them sleeping. "Could you men not keep watch with me for one hour?" he asked Peter. 41"Watch and pray so that you will not fall into temptation. The spirit is willing, but the body is weak."

42He went away a second time and prayed, "My Father, if it is not possible for this cup to be taken away unless I drink it, may your will be done."

43When he came back, he again found them sleeping, because their eyes were heavy. 44So he left them and went away once more and prayed the third time, saying the same thing.

45Then he returned to the disciples and said to them, "Are you still sleeping and resting? Look, the hour is near, and the Son of Man is betrayed into the hands of sinners. 46Rise, let us go! Here comes my betrayer!"

a25 Or "You yourself have said it"   b28 Some manuscripts the new   c31 Zech. 13:7

PSALM 31:19-24

19How great is your [the LORD's]
    goodness,
  which you have stored up for those
    who fear you,

which you bestow in the sight
    of men
  on those who take refuge in you.
20In the shelter of your presence you
    hide them
  from the intrigues of men;
in your dwelling you keep them safe
    from accusing tongues.

21Praise be to the LORD,
  for he showed his wonderful love
    to me
  when I was in a besieged city.
22In my alarm I said,
  "I am cut off from your sight!"
Yet you heard my cry for mercy
  when I called to you for help.

23Love the LORD, all his saints!
  The LORD preserves the
    faithful,
  but the proud he pays back
    in full.
24Be strong and take heart,
  all you who hope in the LORD.

PROVERBS 8:14-26

14"Counsel and sound judgment are
    mine [wisdom's];
  I have understanding and power.
15By me kings reign
  and rulers make laws that are just;
16by me princes govern,
  and all nobles who rule on earth.a
17I love those who love me,
  and those who seek me find me.
18With me are riches and honor,
  enduring wealth and prosperity.
19My fruit is better than fine gold;
  what I yield surpasses choice
    silver.
20I walk in the way of righteousness,
  along the paths of justice,
21bestowing wealth on those who
    love me
  and making their treasuries full.

22"The LORD brought me forth as the
    first of his works,b, c
  before his deeds of old;
23I was appointedd from eternity,
  from the beginning, before the
    world began.

24When there were no oceans, I was
      given birth,
  when there were no springs
      abounding with water;
25before the mountains were settled
      in place,
  before the hills, I was given birth,
26before he made the earth or its fields
      or any of the dust of the world."

a16 Many Hebrew manuscripts and Septuagint; most
Hebrew manuscripts *and nobles—all righteous rulers*
b22 Or *way;* or *dominion*   c22 Or *The Lord possessed me
at the beginning of his work;* or *The Lord brought me forth
at the beginning of his work*   d23 Or *fashioned*

☐ D A Y   4 1

GOD SIGHTINGS

February 10

EXODUS 30:11–31:18

Then the Lord said to Moses, 12"When
you take a census of the Israelites to
count them, each one must pay the Lord
a ransom for his life at the time he is
counted. Then no plague will come on
them when you number them. 13Each
one who crosses over to those already
counted is to give a half shekel,a according to the sanctuary shekel, which
weighs twenty gerahs. This half shekel
is an offering to the Lord. 14All who
cross over, those twenty years old or
more, are to give an offering to the Lord.
15The rich are not to give more than a
half shekel and the poor are not to give
less when you make the offering to the
Lord to atone for your lives. 16Receive
the atonement money from the Israelites and use it for the service of the Tent
of Meeting. It will be a memorial for the
Israelites before the Lord, making
atonement for your lives."

17Then the Lord said to Moses,
18"Make a bronze basin, with its bronze
stand, for washing. Place it between the
Tent of Meeting and the altar, and put
water in it. 19Aaron and his sons are to
wash their hands and feet with water
from it. 20Whenever they enter the Tent

of Meeting, they shall wash with water so
that they will not die. Also, when they approach the altar to minister by presenting an offering made to the Lord by fire,
21they shall wash their hands and feet so
that they will not die. This is to be a lasting ordinance for Aaron and his descendants for the generations to come."

22Then the Lord said to Moses,
23"Take the following fine spices: 500
shekelsb of liquid myrrh, half as much
(that is, 250 shekels) of fragrant cinnamon, 250 shekels of fragrant cane,
24500 shekels of cassia—all according
to the sanctuary shekel—and a hinc of
olive oil. 25Make these into a sacred
anointing oil, a fragrant blend, the work
of a perfumer. It will be the sacred
anointing oil. 26Then use it to anoint the
Tent of Meeting, the ark of the Testimony, 27the table and all its articles, the
lampstand and its accessories, the altar
of incense, 28the altar of burnt offering
and all its utensils, and the basin with its
stand. 29You shall consecrate them so
they will be most holy, and whatever
touches them will be holy.

30"Anoint Aaron and his sons and
consecrate them so they may serve me
as priests. 31Say to the Israelites, 'This is
to be my sacred anointing oil for the
generations to come. 32Do not pour it
on men's bodies and do not make any oil
with the same formula. It is sacred, and
you are to consider it sacred. 33Who-
ever makes perfume like it and whoever
puts it on anyone other than a priest
must be cut off from his people.'"

34Then the Lord said to Moses, "Take
fragrant spices—gum resin, onycha and
galbanum—and pure frankincense, all
in equal amounts, 35and make a fragrant blend of incense, the work of a
perfumer. It is to be salted and pure and
sacred. 36Grind some of it to powder
and place it in front of the Testimony in
the Tent of Meeting, where I will meet
with you. It shall be most holy to you.
37Do not make any incense with this
formula for yourselves; consider it holy
to the Lord. 38Whoever makes any like

it to enjoy its fragrance must be cut off from his people."

31:1Then the Lord said to Moses, 2"See, I have chosen Bezalel son of Uri, the son of Hur, of the tribe of Judah, 3and I have filled him with the Spirit of God, with skill, ability and knowledge in all kinds of crafts— 4to make artistic designs for work in gold, silver and bronze, 5to cut and set stones, to work in wood, and to engage in all kinds of craftsmanship. 6Moreover, I have appointed Oholiab son of Ahisamach, of the tribe of Dan, to help him. Also I have given skill to all the craftsmen to make everything I have commanded you: 7the Tent of Meeting, the ark of the Testimony with the atonement cover on it, and all the other furnishings of the tent— 8the table and its articles, the pure gold lampstand and all its accessories, the altar of incense, 9the altar of burnt offering and all its utensils, the basin with its stand— 10and also the woven garments, both the sacred garments for Aaron the priest and the garments for his sons when they serve as priests, 11and the anointing oil and fragrant incense for the Holy Place. They are to make them just as I commanded you."

12Then the Lord said to Moses, 13"Say to the Israelites, 'You must observe my Sabbaths. This will be a sign between me and you for the generations to come, so you may know that I am the Lord, who makes you holy.d

14"'Observe the Sabbath, because it is holy to you. Anyone who desecrates it must be put to death; whoever does any work on that day must be cut off from his people. 15For six days, work is to be done, but the seventh day is a Sabbath of rest, holy to the Lord. Whoever does any work on the Sabbath day must be put to death. 16The Israelites are to observe the Sabbath, celebrating it for the generations to come as a lasting covenant. 17It will be a sign between me and the Israelites forever, for in six days the Lord made the heavens and the earth, and on the seventh day he abstained from work and rested.'"

18When the Lord finished speaking to Moses on Mount Sinai, he gave him the two tablets of the Testimony, the tablets of stone inscribed by the finger of God.

a 13 That is, about 1/5 ounce (about 6 grams); also in verse 15
b 23 That is, about 12 1/2 pounds (about 6 kilograms)
c 24 That is, probably about 4 quarts (about 4 liters)
d 13 Or who sanctifies you; or who sets you apart as holy

MATTHEW 26:47-68

While he [Jesus] was still speaking, Judas, one of the Twelve, arrived. With him was a large crowd armed with swords and clubs, sent from the chief priests and the elders of the people. 48Now the betrayer had arranged a signal with them: "The one I kiss is the man; arrest him." 49Going at once to Jesus, Judas said, "Greetings, Rabbi!" and kissed him.

50Jesus replied, "Friend, do what you came for."a

Then the men stepped forward, seized Jesus and arrested him. 51With that, one of Jesus' companions reached for his sword, drew it out and struck the servant of the high priest, cutting off his ear.

52"Put your sword back in its place," Jesus said to him, "for all who draw the sword will die by the sword. 53Do you think I cannot call on my Father, and he will at once put at my disposal more than twelve legions of angels? 54But how then would the Scriptures be fulfilled that say it must happen in this way?"

55At that time Jesus said to the crowd, "Am I leading a rebellion, that you have come out with swords and clubs to capture me? Every day I sat in the temple courts teaching, and you did not arrest me. 56But this has all taken place that the writings of the prophets might be fulfilled." Then all the disciples deserted him and fled.

57Those who had arrested Jesus took him to Caiaphas, the high priest, where the teachers of the law and the elders had assembled. 58But Peter followed him at a distance, right up to the courtyard of the high priest. He entered and sat down with the guards to see the outcome.

59 The chief priests and the whole Sanhedrin were looking for false evidence against Jesus so that they could put him to death. 60 But they did not find any, though many false witnesses came forward.

Finally two came forward 61 and declared, "This fellow said, 'I am able to destroy the temple of God and rebuild it in three days.'"

62 Then the high priest stood up and said to Jesus, "Are you not going to answer? What is this testimony that these men are bringing against you?" 63 But Jesus remained silent.

The high priest said to him, "I charge you under oath by the living God: Tell us if you are the Christ,b the Son of God."

64 "Yes, it is as you say," Jesus replied. "But I say to all of you: In the future you will see the Son of Man sitting at the right hand of the Mighty One and coming on the clouds of heaven."

65 Then the high priest tore his clothes and said, "He has spoken blasphemy! Why do we need any more witnesses? Look, now you have heard the blasphemy. 66 What do you think?"

"He is worthy of death," they answered.

67 Then they spit in his face and struck him with their fists. Others slapped him 68 and said, "Prophesy to us, Christ. Who hit you?"

a50 Or "Friend, why have you come?"   b63 Or Messiah; also in verse 68

PSALM 32:1-11
Of David. A maskil.a

1 Blessed is he
   whose transgressions are
      forgiven,
   whose sins are covered.
2 Blessed is the man
   whose sin the LORD does not
      count against him
   and in whose spirit is no deceit.

3 When I kept silent,
   my bones wasted away
   through my groaning all day long.

4 For day and night
   your hand was heavy upon me;
   my strength was sapped
      as in the heat of summer.   Selah
5 Then I acknowledged my sin to you
   and did not cover up my iniquity.
   I said, "I will confess
   my transgressions to the LORD"—
   and you forgave
      the guilt of my sin.   Selah

6 Therefore let everyone who is godly
      pray to you
   while you may be found;
   surely when the mighty waters rise,
      they will not reach him.
7 You are my hiding place;
   you will protect me from trouble
   and surround me with songs of
      deliverance.   Selah

8 I will instruct you and teach you in
      the way you should go;
   I will counsel you and watch over
      you.
9 Do not be like the horse or the mule,
   which have no understanding
   but must be controlled by bit and
      bridle
   or they will not come to you.
10 Many are the woes of the wicked,
   but the LORD's unfailing love
   surrounds the man who trusts
      in him.
11 Rejoice in the LORD and be glad, you
      righteous;
   sing, all you who are upright in
      heart!

aTitle: Probably a literary or musical term

PROVERBS 8:27-32
27 "I [wisdom] was there when he set
      the heavens in place,
   when he marked out the horizon
      on the face of the deep,
28 when he established the clouds
      above
   and fixed securely the fountains of
      the deep,
29 when he gave the sea its boundary
   so the waters would not overstep
      his command,

and when he marked out the
    foundations of the earth.
30   Then I was the craftsman at his
    side.
I was filled with delight day after
    day,
    rejoicing always in his presence,
31 rejoicing in his whole world
    and delighting in mankind.

32 "Now then, my sons, listen to me;
    blessed are those who keep my
    ways."

□ D A Y 4 2

GOD SIGHTINGS

February 11

EXODUS 32:1–33:23

When the people saw that Moses was
so long in coming down from the mountain, they gathered around Aaron and
said, "Come, make us gods*a* who will go
before us. As for this fellow Moses who
brought us up out of Egypt, we don't
know what has happened to him."

2 Aaron answered them, "Take off the
gold earrings that your wives, your sons
and your daughters are wearing, and
bring them to me." 3 So all the people
took off their earrings and brought
them to Aaron. 4 He took what they
handed him and made it into an idol
cast in the shape of a calf, fashioning it
with a tool. Then they said, "These are
your gods,*b* O Israel, who brought you
up out of Egypt."

5 When Aaron saw this, he built an altar in front of the calf and announced,
"Tomorrow there will be a festival to the
LORD." 6 So the next day the people rose
early and sacrificed burnt offerings and
presented fellowship offerings.*c* Afterward they sat down to eat and drink and
got up to indulge in revelry.

7 Then the LORD said to Moses, "Go
down, because your people, whom you
brought up out of Egypt, have become

corrupt. 8 They have been quick to turn
away from what I commanded them
and have made themselves an idol cast
in the shape of a calf. They have bowed
down to it and sacrificed to it and have
said, 'These are your gods, O Israel, who
brought you up out of Egypt.'

9 "I have seen these people," the LORD
said to Moses, "and they are a stiff-
necked people. 10 Now leave me alone so
that my anger may burn against them
and that I may destroy them. Then I will
make you into a great nation."

11 But Moses sought the favor of the
LORD his God. "O LORD," he said, "why
should your anger burn against your
people, whom you brought out of Egypt
with great power and a mighty hand?
12 Why should the Egyptians say, 'It was
with evil intent that he brought them
out, to kill them in the mountains and to
wipe them off the face of the earth'?
Turn from your fierce anger; relent and
do not bring disaster on your people.
13 Remember your servants Abraham,
Isaac and Israel, to whom you swore by
your own self: 'I will make your descendants as numerous as the stars in the sky
and I will give your descendants all this
land I promised them, and it will be
their inheritance forever.'" 14 Then the
LORD relented and did not bring on his
people the disaster he had threatened.

15 Moses turned and went down the
mountain with the two tablets of the
Testimony in his hands. They were inscribed on both sides, front and back.
16 The tablets were the work of God; the
writing was the writing of God, engraved on the tablets.

17 When Joshua heard the noise of
the people shouting, he said to Moses,
"There is the sound of war in the camp."

18 Moses replied:

"It is not the sound of victory,
    it is not the sound of defeat;
    it is the sound of singing that
        I hear."

19 When Moses approached the
camp and saw the calf and the dancing,

his anger burned and he threw the tablets out of his hands, breaking them to pieces at the foot of the mountain. [20]And he took the calf they had made and burned it in the fire; then he ground it to powder, scattered it on the water and made the Israelites drink it.

[21]He said to Aaron, "What did these people do to you, that you led them into such great sin?"

[22]"Do not be angry, my lord," Aaron answered. "You know how prone these people are to evil. [23]They said to me, 'Make us gods who will go before us. As for this fellow Moses who brought us up out of Egypt, we don't know what has happened to him.' [24]So I told them, 'Whoever has any gold jewelry, take it off.' Then they gave me the gold, and I threw it into the fire, and out came this calf!"

[25]Moses saw that the people were running wild and that Aaron had let them get out of control and so become a laughingstock to their enemies. [26]So he stood at the entrance to the camp and said, "Whoever is for the LORD, come to me." And all the Levites rallied to him. [27]Then he said to them, "This is what the LORD, the God of Israel, says: 'Each man strap a sword to his side. Go back and forth through the camp from one end to the other, each killing his brother and friend and neighbor.'" [28]The Levites did as Moses commanded, and that day about three thousand of the people died. [29]Then Moses said, "You have been set apart to the LORD today, for you were against your own sons and brothers, and he has blessed you this day."

[30]The next day Moses said to the people, "You have committed a great sin. But now I will go up to the LORD; perhaps I can make atonement for your sin." [31]So Moses went back to the LORD and said, "Oh, what a great sin these people have committed! They have made themselves gods of gold. [32]But now, please forgive their sin—but if not, then blot me out of the book you have written."

[33]The LORD replied to Moses, "Whoever has sinned against me I will blot out of my book. [34]Now go, lead the people to the place I spoke of, and my angel will go before you. However, when the time comes for me to punish, I will punish them for their sin."

[35]And the LORD struck the people with a plague because of what they did with the calf Aaron had made.

[33:1]THEN the LORD said to Moses, "Leave this place, you and the people you brought up out of Egypt, and go up to the land I promised on oath to Abraham, Isaac and Jacob, saying, 'I will give it to your descendants.' [2]I will send an angel before you and drive out the Canaanites, Amorites, Hittites, Perizzites, Hivites and Jebusites. [3]Go up to the land flowing with milk and honey. But I will not go with you, because you are a stiff-necked people and I might destroy you on the way."

[4]When the people heard these distressing words, they began to mourn and no one put on any ornaments. [5]For the LORD had said to Moses, "Tell the Israelites, 'You are a stiff-necked people. If I were to go with you even for a moment, I might destroy you. Now take off your ornaments and I will decide what to do with you.'" [6]So the Israelites stripped off their ornaments at Mount Horeb.

[7]Now Moses used to take a tent and pitch it outside the camp some distance away, calling it the "tent of meeting." Anyone inquiring of the LORD would go to the tent of meeting outside the camp. [8]And whenever Moses went out to the tent, all the people rose and stood at the entrances to their tents, watching Moses until he entered the tent. [9]As Moses went into the tent, the pillar of cloud would come down and stay at the entrance, while the LORD spoke with Moses. [10]Whenever the people saw the pillar of cloud standing at the entrance to the tent, they all stood and worshiped, each at the entrance to his tent. [11]The LORD would speak to Moses face to face, as a man speaks with his friend. Then Moses would return to the camp, but his young aide Joshua son of Nun did not leave the tent.

¹²Moses said to the LORD, "You have been telling me, 'Lead these people,' but you have not let me know whom you will send with me. You have said, 'I know you by name and you have found favor with me.' ¹³If you are pleased with me, teach me your ways so I may know you and continue to find favor with you. Remember that this nation is your people."

¹⁴The LORD replied, "My Presence will go with you, and I will give you rest."

¹⁵Then Moses said to him, "If your Presence does not go with us, do not send us up from here. ¹⁶How will anyone know that you are pleased with me and with your people unless you go with us? What else will distinguish me and your people from all the other people on the face of the earth?"

¹⁷And the LORD said to Moses, "I will do the very thing you have asked, because I am pleased with you and I know you by name."

¹⁸Then Moses said, "Now show me your glory."

¹⁹**And the LORD said, "I will cause all my goodness to pass in front of you, and I will proclaim my name, the LORD, in your presence. I will have mercy on whom I will have mercy, and I will have compassion on whom I will have compassion.** ²⁰But," he said, "you cannot see my face, for no one may see me and live."

²¹Then the LORD said, "There is a place near me where you may stand on a rock. ²²When my glory passes by, I will put you in a cleft in the rock and cover you with my hand until I have passed by. ²³Then I will remove my hand and you will see my back; but my face must not be seen."

a 1 Or a god; also in verses 23 and 31   b 4 Or This is your god; also in verse 8   c 6 Traditionally peace offerings

MATTHEW 26:69–27:14

Now Peter was sitting out in the courtyard, and a servant girl came to him. "You also were with Jesus of Galilee," she said.

⁷⁰But he denied it before them all. "I don't know what you're talking about," he said.

⁷¹Then he went out to the gateway, where another girl saw him and said to the people there, "This fellow was with Jesus of Nazareth."

⁷²He denied it again, with an oath: "I don't know the man!"

⁷³After a little while, those standing there went up to Peter and said, "Surely you are one of them, for your accent gives you away."

⁷⁴Then he began to call down curses on himself and he swore to them, "I don't know the man!"

Immediately a rooster crowed. ⁷⁵Then Peter remembered the word Jesus had spoken: "Before the rooster crows, you will disown me three times." And he went outside and wept bitterly.

²⁷:¹EARLY in the morning, all the chief priests and the elders of the people came to the decision to put Jesus to death. ²They bound him, led him away and handed him over to Pilate, the governor.

³When Judas, who had betrayed him, saw that Jesus was condemned, he was seized with remorse and returned the thirty silver coins to the chief priests and the elders. ⁴"I have sinned," he said, "for I have betrayed innocent blood."

"What is that to us?" they replied. "That's your responsibility."

⁵So Judas threw the money into the temple and left. Then he went away and hanged himself.

⁶The chief priests picked up the coins and said, "It is against the law to put this into the treasury, since it is blood money." ⁷So they decided to use the money to buy the potter's field as a burial place for foreigners. ⁸That is why it has been called the Field of Blood to this day. ⁹Then what was spoken by Jeremiah the prophet was fulfilled: "They took the thirty silver coins, the price set on him by the people of Israel, ¹⁰and they used them to buy the potter's field, as the Lord commanded me."*a*

¹¹Meanwhile Jesus stood before the

governor, and the governor asked him, "Are you the king of the Jews?"

"Yes, it is as you say," Jesus replied.

[12]When he was accused by the chief priests and the elders, he gave no answer. [13]Then Pilate asked him, "Don't you hear the testimony they are bringing against you?" [14]But Jesus made no reply, not even to a single charge—to the great amazement of the governor.

a10 See Zech. 11:12,13; Jer. 19:1-13; 32:6-9.

PSALM 33:1-11

[1]**S**ing joyfully to the LORD, you
    righteous;
  it is fitting for the upright to
    praise him.
[2]Praise the LORD with the harp;
  make music to him on the ten-
    stringed lyre.
[3]Sing to him a new song;
  play skillfully, and shout for joy.

[4]For the word of the LORD is right
    and true;
  he is faithful in all he does.
[5]The LORD loves righteousness and
    justice;
  the earth is full of his unfailing
    love.

[6]By the word of the LORD were the
    heavens made,
  their starry host by the breath of
    his mouth.
[7]He gathers the waters of the sea into
    jars*a*;
  he puts the deep into storehouses.
[8]Let all the earth fear the LORD;
  let all the people of the world
    revere him.
[9]For he spoke, and it came to be;
  he commanded, and it stood firm.
[10]The LORD foils the plans of the
    nations;
  he thwarts the purposes of the
    peoples.
[11]But the plans of the LORD stand firm
    forever,
  the purposes of his heart through
    all generations.

a7 Or *sea as into a heap*

PROVERBS 8:33-36

[33]"**L**isten to my [wisdom's] instruction
    and be wise;
  do not ignore it.
[34]Blessed is the man who listens to me,
  watching daily at my doors,
  waiting at my doorway.
[35]For whoever finds me finds life
  and receives favor from the LORD.
[36]But whoever fails to find me harms
    himself;
  all who hate me love death."

□ DAY 43

GOD SIGHTINGS

February 12

EXODUS 34:1–35:9

The LORD said to Moses, "Chisel out two stone tablets like the first ones, and I will write on them the words that were on the first tablets, which you broke. [2]Be ready in the morning, and then come up on Mount Sinai. Present yourself to me there on top of the mountain. [3]No one is to come with you or be seen anywhere on the mountain; not even the flocks and herds may graze in front of the mountain."

[4]So Moses chiseled out two stone tablets like the first ones and went up Mount Sinai early in the morning, as the LORD had commanded him; and he carried the two stone tablets in his hands. [5]Then the LORD came down in the cloud and stood there with him and proclaimed his name, the LORD. [6]And he passed in front of Moses, proclaiming, "The LORD, the LORD, the compassionate and gracious God, slow to anger, abounding in love and faithfulness, [7]maintaining love to thousands, and forgiving wickedness, rebellion and sin. Yet he does not leave the guilty unpunished; he punishes the children and their children for the sin of the fathers to the third and fourth generation."

8Moses bowed to the ground at once and worshiped. 9"O Lord, if I have found favor in your eyes," he said, "then let the Lord go with us. Although this is a stiff-necked people, forgive our wickedness and our sin, and take us as your inheritance."

10Then the Lord said: "I am making a covenant with you. Before all your people I will do wonders never before done in any nation in all the world. The people you live among will see how awesome is the work that I, the Lord, will do for you. 11Obey what I command you today. I will drive out before you the Amorites, Canaanites, Hittites, Perizzites, Hivites and Jebusites. 12Be careful not to make a treaty with those who live in the land where you are going, or they will be a snare among you. 13Break down their altars, smash their sacred stones and cut down their Asherah poles.a 14Do not worship any other god, for the Lord, whose name is Jealous, is a jealous God.

15"Be careful not to make a treaty with those who live in the land; for when they prostitute themselves to their gods and sacrifice to them, they will invite you and you will eat their sacrifices. 16And when you choose some of their daughters as wives for your sons and those daughters prostitute themselves to their gods, they will lead your sons to do the same.

17"Do not make cast idols.

18"Celebrate the Feast of Unleavened Bread. For seven days eat bread made without yeast, as I commanded you. Do this at the appointed time in the month of Abib, for in that month you came out of Egypt.

19"The first offspring of every womb belongs to me, including all the first-born males of your livestock, whether from herd or flock. 20Redeem the first-born donkey with a lamb, but if you do not redeem it, break its neck. Redeem all your firstborn sons.

"No one is to appear before me empty-handed.

21"Six days you shall labor, but on the seventh day you shall rest; even during the plowing season and harvest you must rest.

22"Celebrate the Feast of Weeks with the firstfruits of the wheat harvest, and the Feast of Ingathering at the turn of the year.b 23Three times a year all your men are to appear before the Sovereign Lord, the God of Israel. 24I will drive out nations before you and enlarge your territory, and no one will covet your land when you go up three times each year to appear before the Lord your God.

25"Do not offer the blood of a sacrifice to me along with anything containing yeast, and do not let any of the sacrifice from the Passover Feast remain until morning.

26"Bring the best of the firstfruits of your soil to the house of the Lord your God.

"Do not cook a young goat in its mother's milk."

27Then the Lord said to Moses, "Write down these words, for in accordance with these words I have made a covenant with you and with Israel." 28Moses was there with the Lord forty days and forty nights without eating bread or drinking water. And he wrote on the tablets the words of the covenant—the Ten Commandments.

29When Moses came down from Mount Sinai with the two tablets of the Testimony in his hands, he was not aware that his face was radiant because he had spoken with the Lord. 30When Aaron and all the Israelites saw Moses, his face was radiant, and they were afraid to come near him. 31But Moses called to them; so Aaron and all the leaders of the community came back to him, and he spoke to them. 32Afterward all the Israelites came near him, and he gave them all the commands the Lord had given him on Mount Sinai.

33When Moses finished speaking to them, he put a veil over his face. 34But whenever he entered the Lord's presence to speak with him, he removed the veil until he came out. And when he came out and told the Israelites what he had been commanded, 35they saw that his face was radiant. Then Moses would put the veil back over his face until he went in to speak with the Lord.

35:1 MOSES assembled the whole Israelite community and said to them, "These are the things the Lord has commanded you to do: 2For six days, work is to be done, but the seventh day shall be your holy day, a Sabbath of rest to the Lord. Whoever does any work on it must be put to death. 3Do not light a fire in any of your dwellings on the Sabbath day."

4Moses said to the whole Israelite community, "This is what the Lord has commanded: 5From what you have, take an offering for the Lord. Everyone who is willing is to bring to the Lord an offering of gold, silver and bronze; 6blue, purple and scarlet yarn and fine linen; goat hair; 7ram skins dyed red and hides of sea cowsᶜ; acacia wood; 8olive oil for the light; spices for the anointing oil and for the fragrant incense; 9and onyx stones and other gems to be mounted on the ephod and breastpiece."

a 13 That is, symbols of the goddess Asherah   *b 22* That is, in the fall   *c 7* That is, dugongs; also in verse 23

MATTHEW 27:15-31

Now it was the governor's custom at the Feast to release a prisoner chosen by the crowd. 16At that time they had a notorious prisoner, called Barabbas. 17So when the crowd had gathered, Pilate asked them, "Which one do you want me to release to you: Barabbas, or Jesus who is called Christ?" 18For he knew it was out of envy that they had handed Jesus over to him.

19While Pilate was sitting on the judge's seat, his wife sent him this message: "Don't have anything to do with that innocent man, for I have suffered a great deal today in a dream because of him."

20But the chief priests and the elders persuaded the crowd to ask for Barabbas and to have Jesus executed.

21"Which of the two do you want me to release to you?" asked the governor.

"Barabbas," they answered.

22"What shall I do, then, with Jesus who is called Christ?" Pilate asked.

They all answered, "Crucify him!"

23"Why? What crime has he committed?" asked Pilate.

But they shouted all the louder, "Crucify him!"

24When Pilate saw that he was getting nowhere, but that instead an uproar was starting, he took water and washed his hands in front of the crowd. "I am innocent of this man's blood," he said. "It is your responsibility!"

25All the people answered, "Let his blood be on us and on our children!"

26Then he released Barabbas to them. But he had Jesus flogged, and handed him over to be crucified.

27Then the governor's soldiers took Jesus into the Praetorium and gathered the whole company of soldiers around him. 28They stripped him and put a scarlet robe on him, 29and then twisted together a crown of thorns and set it on his head. They put a staff in his right hand and knelt in front of him and mocked him. "Hail, king of the Jews!" they said. 30They spit on him, and took the staff and struck him on the head again and again. 31After they had mocked him, they took off the robe and put his own clothes on him. Then they led him away to crucify him.

PSALM 33:12-22

12 Blessed is the nation whose God is
      the Lord,
   the people he chose for his
      inheritance.
13 From heaven the Lord looks down
      and sees all mankind;
14 from his dwelling place he watches
      all who live on earth—
15 he who forms the hearts of all,
   who considers everything they do.
16 No king is saved by the size of his
      army;
   no warrior escapes by his great
      strength.
17 A horse is a vain hope for
      deliverance;

despite all its great strength it
cannot save.
18 But the eyes of the Lord are on
those who fear him,
on those whose hope is in his
unfailing love,
19 to deliver them from death
and keep them alive in famine.

20 We wait in hope for the Lord;
he is our help and our shield.
21 In him our hearts rejoice,
for we trust in his holy name.
22 May your unfailing love rest upon us,
O Lord,
even as we put our hope in you.

PROVERBS 9:1-6

Wisdom has built her house;
she has hewn out its seven pillars.
2 She has prepared her meat and
mixed her wine;
she has also set her table.
3 She has sent out her maids, and
she calls
from the highest point of the city.
4 "Let all who are simple come in
here!"
she says to those who lack
judgment.
5 "Come, eat my food
and drink the wine I have mixed.
6 Leave your simple ways and you
will live;
walk in the way of understanding."

☐ DAY 44

GOD SIGHTINGS

February 13

EXODUS 35:10–36:38

"**A**ll who are skilled among you [the Is-
raelites] are to come and make everything the Lord has commanded: 11 the
tabernacle with its tent and its covering, clasps, frames, crossbars, posts
and bases; 12 the ark with its poles and
the atonement cover and the curtain

that shields it; 13 the table with its poles
and all its articles and the bread of the
Presence; 14 the lampstand that is for
light with its accessories, lamps and oil
for the light; 15 the altar of incense with
its poles, the anointing oil and the fragrant incense; the curtain for the doorway at the entrance to the tabernacle;
16 the altar of burnt offering with its
bronze grating, its poles and all its
utensils; the bronze basin with its
stand; 17 the curtains of the courtyard
with its posts and bases, and the curtain for the entrance to the courtyard;
18 the tent pegs for the tabernacle and
for the courtyard, and their ropes;
19 the woven garments worn for ministering in the sanctuary—both the sacred garments for Aaron the priest and
the garments for his sons when they
serve as priests."

20 Then the whole Israelite community withdrew from Moses' presence,
21 and everyone who was willing and
whose heart moved him came and
brought an offering to the Lord for the
work on the Tent of Meeting, for all its
service, and for the sacred garments.
22 All who were willing, men and women
alike, came and brought gold jewelry of
all kinds: brooches, earrings, rings and
ornaments. They all presented their gold
as a wave offering to the Lord. 23 Everyone who had blue, purple or scarlet yarn
or fine linen, or goat hair, ram skins dyed
red or hides of sea cows brought them.
24 Those presenting an offering of silver
or bronze brought it as an offering to the
Lord, and everyone who had acacia
wood for any part of the work brought it.
25 Every skilled woman spun with her
hands and brought what she had spun—
blue, purple or scarlet yarn or fine linen.
26 And all the women who were willing
and had the skill spun the goat hair.
27 The leaders brought onyx stones and
other gems to be mounted on the ephod
and breastpiece. 28 They also brought
spices and olive oil for the light and for
the anointing oil and for the fragrant incense. 29 All the Israelite men and
women who were willing brought to the

LORD freewill offerings for all the work the LORD through Moses had commanded them to do.

30Then Moses said to the Israelites, "See, the LORD has chosen Bezalel son of Uri, the son of Hur, of the tribe of Judah, 31and he has filled him with the Spirit of God, with skill, ability and knowledge in all kinds of crafts— 32to make artistic designs for work in gold, silver and bronze, 33to cut and set stones, to work in wood and to engage in all kinds of artistic craftsmanship. 34And he has given both him and Oholiab son of Ahisamach, of the tribe of Dan, the ability to teach others. 35He has filled them with skill to do all kinds of work as craftsmen, designers, embroiderers in blue, purple and scarlet yarn and fine linen, and weavers—all of them master craftsmen and designers.

36:1So Bezalel, Oholiab and every skilled person to whom the LORD has given skill and ability to know how to carry out all the work of constructing the sanctuary are to do the work just as the LORD has commanded."

2Then Moses summoned Bezalel and Oholiab and every skilled person to whom the LORD had given ability and who was willing to come and do the work. 3They received from Moses all the offerings the Israelites had brought to carry out the work of constructing the sanctuary. And the people continued to bring freewill offerings morning after morning. 4So all the skilled craftsmen who were doing all the work on the sanctuary left their work 5and said to Moses, "The people are bringing more than enough for doing the work the LORD commanded to be done."

6Then Moses gave an order and they sent this word throughout the camp: "No man or woman is to make anything else as an offering for the sanctuary." And so the people were restrained from bringing more, 7because what they already had was more than enough to do all the work.

8All the skilled men among the workmen made the tabernacle with ten curtains of finely twisted linen and blue, purple and scarlet yarn, with cherubim worked into them by a skilled craftsman. 9All the curtains were the same size—twenty-eight cubits long and four cubits wide.a 10They joined five of the curtains together and did the same with the other five. 11Then they made loops of blue material along the edge of the end curtain in one set, and the same was done with the end curtain in the other set. 12They also made fifty loops on one curtain and fifty loops on the end curtain of the other set, with the loops opposite each other. 13Then they made fifty gold clasps and used them to fasten the two sets of curtains together so that the tabernacle was a unit.

14They made curtains of goat hair for the tent over the tabernacle—eleven altogether. 15All eleven curtains were the same size—thirty cubits long and four cubits wide.b 16They joined five of the curtains into one set and the other six into another set. 17Then they made fifty loops along the edge of the end curtain in one set and also along the edge of the end curtain in the other set. 18They made fifty bronze clasps to fasten the tent together as a unit. 19Then they made for the tent a covering of ram skins dyed red, and over that a covering of hides of sea cows.c

20They made upright frames of acacia wood for the tabernacle. 21Each frame was ten cubits long and a cubit and a half wide,d 22with two projections set parallel to each other. They made all the frames of the tabernacle in this way. 23They made twenty frames for the south side of the tabernacle 24and made forty silver bases to go under them—two bases for each frame, one under each projection. 25For the other side, the north side of the tabernacle, they made twenty frames 26and forty silver bases—two under each frame. 27They made six frames for the far end, that is, the west end of the tabernacle, 28and two frames were made for the corners of the tabernacle at the far end. 29At these two corners the frames were double from the bottom all the way to the top and fitted into a single ring; both were made alike. 30So there were eight frames and sixteen silver bases—two under each frame.

31They also made crossbars of acacia wood: five for the frames on one side of the tabernacle, 32five for those on the other side, and five for the frames on the west, at the far end of the tabernacle. 33They made the center crossbar so that it extended from end to end at the middle of the frames. 34They overlaid the frames with gold and made gold rings to hold the crossbars. They also overlaid the crossbars with gold.

35They made the curtain of blue, purple and scarlet yarn and finely twisted linen, with cherubim worked into it by a skilled craftsman. 36They made four posts of acacia wood for it and overlaid them with gold. They made gold hooks for them and cast their four silver bases. 37For the entrance to the tent they made a curtain of blue, purple and scarlet yarn and finely twisted linen—the work of an embroiderer; 38and they made five posts with hooks for them. They overlaid the tops of the posts and their bands with gold and made their five bases of bronze.

a9 That is, about 42 feet (about 12.5 meters) long and 6 feet (about 1.8 meters) wide   b15 That is, about 45 feet (about 13.5 meters) long and 6 feet (about 1.8 meters) wide   c19 That is, dugongs   d21 That is, about 15 feet (about 4.5 meters) long and 2 1/4 feet (about 0.7 meter) wide

MATTHEW 27:32-66

As they [the soldiers and Jesus] were going out, they met a man from Cyrene, named Simon, and they forced him to carry the cross. 33They came to a place called Golgotha (which means The Place of the Skull). 34There they offered Jesus wine to drink, mixed with gall; but after tasting it, he refused to drink it. 35When they had crucified him, they divided up his clothes by casting lots.a 36And sitting down, they kept watch over him there. 37Above his head they placed the written charge against him: THIS IS JESUS, THE KING OF THE JEWS. 38Two robbers were crucified with him, one

on his right and one on his left. 39Those who passed by hurled insults at him, shaking their heads 40and saying, "You who are going to destroy the temple and build it in three days, save yourself! Come down from the cross, if you are the Son of God!"

41In the same way the chief priests, the teachers of the law and the elders mocked him. 42"He saved others," they said, "but he can't save himself! He's the King of Israel! Let him come down now from the cross, and we will believe in him. 43He trusts in God. Let God rescue him now if he wants him, for he said, 'I am the Son of God.'" 44In the same way the robbers who were crucified with him also heaped insults on him.

45From the sixth hour until the ninth hour darkness came over all the land. 46About the ninth hour Jesus cried out in a loud voice, "Eloi, Eloi,b lama sabachthani?"—which means, "My God, my God, why have you forsaken me?"c

47When some of those standing there heard this, they said, "He's calling Elijah."

48Immediately one of them ran and got a sponge. He filled it with wine vinegar, put it on a stick, and offered it to Jesus to drink. 49The rest said, "Now leave him alone. Let's see if Elijah comes to save him."

50And when Jesus had cried out again in a loud voice, he gave up his spirit.

51At that moment the curtain of the temple was torn in two from top to bottom. The earth shook and the rocks split. 52The tombs broke open and the bodies of many holy people who had died were raised to life. 53They came out of the tombs, and after Jesus' resurrection they went into the holy city and appeared to many people.

54**When the centurion and those with him who were guarding Jesus saw the earthquake and all that had happened, they were terrified, and exclaimed, "Surely he was the Son**d **of God!"**

55Many women were there, watching from a distance. They had followed

Jesus from Galilee to care for his needs.
⁵⁶Among them were Mary Magdalene,
Mary the mother of James and Joses,
and the mother of Zebedee's sons.

⁵⁷As evening approached, there came
a rich man from Arimathea, named Joseph, who had himself become a disciple
of Jesus. ⁵⁸Going to Pilate, he asked for
Jesus' body, and Pilate ordered that it be
given to him. ⁵⁹Joseph took the body,
wrapped it in a clean linen cloth, ⁶⁰and
placed it in his own new tomb that he
had cut out of the rock. He rolled a big
stone in front of the entrance to the
tomb and went away. ⁶¹Mary Magdalene
and the other Mary were sitting there opposite the tomb.

⁶²The next day, the one after Preparation Day, the chief priests and the Pharisees went to Pilate. ⁶³"Sir," they said, "we
remember that while he was still alive
that deceiver said, 'After three days I will
rise again.' ⁶⁴So give the order for the
tomb to be made secure until the third
day. Otherwise, his disciples may come
and steal the body and tell the people
that he has been raised from the dead.
This last deception will be worse than
the first."

⁶⁵"Take a guard," Pilate answered.
"Go, make the tomb as secure as you
know how." ⁶⁶So they went and made
the tomb secure by putting a seal on the
stone and posting the guard.

ª35 A few late manuscripts *lots that the word spoken by the
prophet might be fulfilled: "They divided my garments
among themselves and cast lots for my clothing"* (Psalm 22:18)
ᵇ46 Some manuscripts *Eli, Eli*   ᶜ46 Psalm 22:1   ᵈ54 Or *a son*

PSALM 34:1-10ª
Of David. When he pretended to be insane
before Abimelech, who drove him away, and
he left.

¹I will extol the LORD at all times;
    his praise will always be on my lips.
²My soul will boast in the LORD;
    let the afflicted hear and rejoice.
³Glorify the LORD with me;
    let us exalt his name together.

⁴I sought the LORD, and he
        answered me;
    he delivered me from all my fears.

⁵Those who look to him are radiant;
    their faces are never covered with
        shame.
⁶This poor man called, and the LORD
        heard him;
    he saved him out of all his
        troubles.
⁷The angel of the LORD encamps
        around those who fear him,
    and he delivers them.

⁸Taste and see that the LORD is good;
    blessed is the man who takes
        refuge in him.
⁹Fear the LORD, you his saints,
    for those who fear him lack
        nothing.
¹⁰The lions may grow weak and
        hungry,
    but those who seek the LORD lack
        no good thing.

ªThis psalm is an acrostic poem, the verses of which begin
with the successive letters of the Hebrew alphabet.

PROVERBS 9:7-8
⁷"**W**hoever corrects a mocker invites
        insult;
    whoever rebukes a wicked man
        incurs abuse.
⁸Do not rebuke a mocker or he will
        hate you;
    rebuke a wise man and he will
        love you."

☐ DAY 45

GOD SIGHTINGS

February 14

EXODUS 37:1–38:31
Bezalel made the ark of acacia wood—
two and a half cubits long, a cubit and a
half wide, and a cubit and a half high.ª
²He overlaid it with pure gold, both inside
and out, and made a gold molding
around it. ³He cast four gold rings for it
and fastened them to its four feet, with
two rings on one side and two rings
on the other. ⁴Then he made poles of aca-

cia wood and overlaid them with gold.
⁵And he inserted the poles into the rings
on the sides of the ark to carry it.

⁶He made the atonement cover of
pure gold—two and a half cubits long
and a cubit and a half wide.*ᵇ ⁷Then he
made two cherubim out of hammered
gold at the ends of the cover. ⁸He made
one cherub on one end and the second
cherub on the other; at the two ends he
made them of one piece with the cover.
⁹The cherubim had their wings spread
upward, overshadowing the cover with
them. The cherubim faced each other,
looking toward the cover.

¹⁰Theyᶜ made the table of acacia
wood—two cubits long, a cubit wide, and
a cubit and a half high.ᵈ ¹¹Then they
overlaid it with pure gold and made a
gold molding around it. ¹²They also
made around it a rim a handbreadthᵉ
wide and put a gold molding on the rim.
¹³They cast four gold rings for the table
and fastened them to the four corners,
where the four legs were. ¹⁴The rings
were put close to the rim to hold the
poles used in carrying the table. ¹⁵The
poles for carrying the table were made of
acacia wood and were overlaid with gold.
¹⁶And they made from pure gold the articles for the table—its plates and dishes
and bowls and its pitchers for the pouring out of drink offerings.

¹⁷They made the lampstand of pure
gold and hammered it out, base and
shaft; its flowerlike cups, buds and blossoms were of one piece with it. ¹⁸Six
branches extended from the sides of
the lampstand—three on one side and
three on the other. ¹⁹Three cups shaped
like almond flowers with buds and blossoms were on one branch, three on the
next branch and the same for all six
branches extending from the lampstand. ²⁰And on the lampstand were
four cups shaped like almond flowers
with buds and blossoms. ²¹One bud was
under the first pair of branches extending from the lampstand, a second bud
under the second pair, and a third bud
under the third pair—six branches in
all. ²²The buds and the branches were

all of one piece with the lampstand,
hammered out of pure gold.

²³They made its seven lamps, as well
as its wick trimmers and trays, of pure
gold. ²⁴They made the lampstand and
all its accessories from one talentᶠ of
pure gold.

²⁵They made the altar of incense out
of acacia wood. It was square, a cubit
long and a cubit wide, and two cubits
highᵍ—its horns of one piece with it.
²⁶They overlaid the top and all the sides
and the horns with pure gold, and made a
gold molding around it. ²⁷They made
two gold rings below the molding—two
on opposite sides—to hold the poles
used to carry it. ²⁸They made the poles of
acacia wood and overlaid them with
gold.

²⁹They also made the sacred anointing oil and the pure, fragrant incense—
the work of a perfumer.

38:1THEYʰ built the altar of burnt offering of acacia wood, three cubitsⁱ high; it
was square, five cubits long and five cubits wide.ʲ ²They made a horn at each of
the four corners, so that the horns and
the altar were of one piece, and they
overlaid the altar with bronze. ³They
made all its utensils of bronze—its pots,
shovels, sprinkling bowls, meat forks
and firepans. ⁴They made a grating for
the altar, a bronze network, to be under
its ledge, halfway up the altar. ⁵They
cast bronze rings to hold the poles for
the four corners of the bronze grating.
⁶They made the poles of acacia wood
and overlaid them with bronze. ⁷They
inserted the poles into the rings so they
would be on the sides of the altar for
carrying it. They made it hollow, out of
boards.

⁸They made the bronze basin and its
bronze stand from the mirrors of the
women who served at the entrance to
the Tent of Meeting.

⁹Next they made the courtyard. The
south side was a hundred cubitsᵏ long
and had curtains of finely twisted linen,
¹⁰with twenty posts and twenty bronze
bases, and with silver hooks and bands

on the posts. [11]The north side was also a hundred cubits long and had twenty posts and twenty bronze bases, with silver hooks and bands on the posts.

[12]The west end was fifty cubits[l] wide and had curtains, with ten posts and ten bases, with silver hooks and bands on the posts. [13]The east end, toward the sunrise, was also fifty cubits wide. [14]Curtains fifteen cubits[m] long were on one side of the entrance, with three posts and three bases, [15]and curtains fifteen cubits long were on the other side of the entrance to the courtyard, with three posts and three bases. [16]All the curtains around the courtyard were of finely twisted linen. [17]The bases for the posts were bronze. The hooks and bands on the posts were silver, and their tops were overlaid with silver; so all the posts of the courtyard had silver bands.

[18]The curtain for the entrance to the courtyard was of blue, purple and scarlet yarn and finely twisted linen—the work of an embroiderer. It was twenty cubits[n] long and, like the curtains of the courtyard, five cubits[o] high, [19]with four posts and four bronze bases. Their hooks and bands were silver, and their tops were overlaid with silver. [20]All the tent pegs of the tabernacle and of the surrounding courtyard were bronze.

[21]These are the amounts of the materials used for the tabernacle, the tabernacle of the Testimony, which were recorded at Moses' command by the Levites under the direction of Ithamar son of Aaron, the priest. [22](Bezalel son of Uri, the son of Hur, of the tribe of Judah, made everything the LORD commanded Moses; [23]with him was Oholiab son of Ahisamach, of the tribe of Dan—a craftsman and designer, and an embroiderer in blue, purple and scarlet yarn and fine linen.) [24]The total amount of the gold from the wave offering used for all the work on the sanctuary was 29 talents and 730 shekels,[p] according to the sanctuary shekel.

[25]The silver obtained from those of the community who were counted in the census was 100 talents and 1,775 shek-

els,[q] according to the sanctuary shekel—[26]one beka per person, that is, half a shekel,[r] according to the sanctuary shekel, from everyone who had crossed over to those counted, twenty years old or more, a total of 603,550 men. [27]The 100 talents[s] of silver were used to cast the bases for the sanctuary and for the curtain—100 bases from the 100 talents, one talent for each base. [28]They used the 1,775 shekels[t] to make the hooks for the posts, to overlay the tops of the posts, and to make their bands.

[29]The bronze from the wave offering was 70 talents and 2,400 shekels.[u] [30]They used it to make the bases for the entrance to the Tent of Meeting, the bronze altar with its bronze grating and all its utensils, [31]the bases for the surrounding courtyard and those for its entrance and all the tent pegs for the tabernacle and those for the surrounding courtyard.

a[1] That is, about 3 3/4 feet (about 1.1 meters) long and 2 1/4 feet (about 0.7 meter) wide and high   b[6] That is, about 3 3/4 feet (about 1.1 meters) long and 2 1/4 feet (about 0.7 meter) wide   c[10] Or *He*; also in verses 11-29   d[10] That is, about 3 feet (about 0.9 meter) long, 1 1/2 feet (about 0.5 meter) wide, and 2 1/4 feet (about 0.7 meter) high   e[12] That is, about 3 inches (about 8 centimeters)   f[24] That is, about 75 pounds (about 34 kilograms)   g[25] That is, about 1 1/2 feet (about 0.5 meter) long and wide, and about 3 feet (about 0.9 meter) high   h[1] Or *He*; also in verses 2-9   i[1] That is, about 4 1/2 feet (about 1.3 meters)   j[1] That is, about 7 1/2 feet (about 2.3 meters) long and wide   k[9] That is, about 150 feet (about 46 meters)   l[12] That is, about 75 feet (about 23 meters)   m[14] That is, about 22 1/2 feet (about 6.9 meters)   n[18] That is, about 30 feet (about 9 meters)   o[18] That is, about 7 1/2 feet (about 2.3 meters)   p[24] The weight of the gold was a little over one ton (about 1 metric ton).   q[25] The weight of the silver was a little over 3 3/4 tons (about 3.4 metric tons).   r[26] That is, about 1/5 ounce (about 5.5 grams)   s[27] That is, about 3 3/4 tons (about 3.4 metric tons)   t[28] That is, about 45 pounds (about 20 kilograms)   u[29] The weight of the bronze was about 2 1/2 tons (about 2.4 metric tons).

MATTHEW 28:1-20

After the Sabbath, at dawn on the first day of the week, Mary Magdalene and the other Mary went to look at the tomb.

[2]There was a violent earthquake, for an angel of the Lord came down from heaven and, going to the tomb, rolled back the stone and sat on it. [3]His appearance was like lightning, and his clothes were white as snow. [4]The guards were so afraid of him that they shook and became like dead men.

⁵The angel said to the women, "Do not be afraid, for I know that you are looking for Jesus, who was crucified. ⁶He is not here; he has risen, just as he said. Come and see the place where he lay. ⁷Then go quickly and tell his disciples: 'He has risen from the dead and is going ahead of you into Galilee. There you will see him.' Now I have told you."

⁸So the women hurried away from the tomb, afraid yet filled with joy, and ran to tell his disciples. ⁹Suddenly Jesus met them. "Greetings," he said. They came to him, clasped his feet and worshiped him. ¹⁰Then Jesus said to them, "Do not be afraid. Go and tell my brothers to go to Galilee; there they will see me."

¹¹While the women were on their way, some of the guards went into the city and reported to the chief priests everything that had happened. ¹²When the chief priests had met with the elders and devised a plan, they gave the soldiers a large sum of money, ¹³telling them, "You are to say, 'His disciples came during the night and stole him away while we were asleep.' ¹⁴If this report gets to the governor, we will satisfy him and keep you out of trouble." ¹⁵So the soldiers took the money and did as they were instructed. And this story has been widely circulated among the Jews to this very day.

¹⁶Then the eleven disciples went to Galilee, to the mountain where Jesus had told them to go. ¹⁷When they saw him, they worshiped him; but some doubted. ¹⁸Then Jesus came to them and said, "All authority in heaven and on earth has been given to me. ¹⁹Therefore go and make disciples of all nations, baptizing them in[a] the name of the Father and of the Son and of the Holy Spirit, ²⁰and teaching them to obey everything I have commanded you. And surely I am with you always, to the very end of the age."

a 19 Or into; see Acts 8:16; 19:5; Romans 6:3; 1 Cor. 1:13; 10:2 and Gal. 3:27.

PSALM 34:11-22

¹¹Come, my children, listen to me;
  I will teach you the fear of the
    LORD.
¹²Whoever of you loves life
  and desires to see many good days,
¹³keep your tongue from evil
  and your lips from speaking lies.
¹⁴Turn from evil and do good;
  seek peace and pursue it.

¹⁵The eyes of the LORD are on the
    righteous
  and his ears are attentive to
    their cry;
¹⁶the face of the LORD is against those
    who do evil,
  to cut off the memory of them
    from the earth.

¹⁷The righteous cry out, and the LORD
    hears them;
  he delivers them from all their
    troubles.
¹⁸The LORD is close to the
    brokenhearted
  and saves those who are crushed
    in spirit.

¹⁹A righteous man may have many
    troubles,
  but the LORD delivers him from
    them all;
²⁰he protects all his bones,
  not one of them will be broken.

²¹Evil will slay the wicked;
  the foes of the righteous will be
    condemned.
²²The LORD redeems his servants;
  no one will be condemned who
    takes refuge in him.

PROVERBS 9:9-10

⁹"Instruct a wise man and he will be
    wiser still;
  teach a righteous man and he will
    add to his learning.

¹⁰"The fear of the LORD is the
    beginning of wisdom,
  and knowledge of the Holy One is
    understanding."

GOD SIGHTINGS

February 15

EXODUS 39:1–40:38

From the blue, purple and scarlet yarn they [the skilled workers] made woven garments for ministering in the sanctuary. They also made sacred garments for Aaron, as the LORD commanded Moses.

2 They*a* made the ephod of gold, and of blue, purple and scarlet yarn, and of finely twisted linen. 3 They hammered out thin sheets of gold and cut strands to be worked into the blue, purple and scarlet yarn and fine linen—the work of a skilled craftsman. 4 They made shoulder pieces for the ephod, which were attached to two of its corners, so it could be fastened. 5 Its skillfully woven waistband was like it—of one piece with the ephod and made with gold, and with blue, purple and scarlet yarn, and with finely twisted linen, as the LORD commanded Moses.

6 They mounted the onyx stones in gold filigree settings and engraved them like a seal with the names of the sons of Israel. 7 Then they fastened them on the shoulder pieces of the ephod as memorial stones for the sons of Israel, as the LORD commanded Moses.

8 They fashioned the breastpiece—the work of a skilled craftsman. They made it like the ephod: of gold, and of blue, purple and scarlet yarn, and of finely twisted linen. 9 It was square—a span*b* long and a span wide—and folded double. 10 Then they mounted four rows of precious stones on it. In the first row there was a ruby, a topaz and a beryl; 11 in the second row a turquoise, a sapphire*c* and an emerald; 12 in the third row a jacinth, an agate and an amethyst; 13 in the fourth row a chrysolite, an onyx and a jasper.*d* They were mounted in gold filigree settings. 14 There were twelve stones, one for each of the names of the sons of Israel,

each engraved like a seal with the name of one of the twelve tribes.

15 For the breastpiece they made braided chains of pure gold, like a rope. 16 They made two gold filigree settings and two gold rings, and fastened the rings to two of the corners of the breastpiece. 17 They fastened the two gold chains to the rings at the corners of the breastpiece, 18 and the other ends of the chains to the two settings, attaching them to the shoulder pieces of the ephod at the front. 19 They made two gold rings and attached them to the other two corners of the breastpiece on the inside edge next to the ephod. 20 Then they made two more gold rings and attached them to the bottom of the shoulder pieces on the front of the ephod, close to the seam just above the waistband of the ephod. 21 They tied the rings of the breastpiece to the rings of the ephod with blue cord, connecting it to the waistband so that the breastpiece would not swing out from the ephod—as the LORD commanded Moses.

22 They made the robe of the ephod entirely of blue cloth—the work of a weaver— 23 with an opening in the center of the robe like the opening of a collar,*e* and a band around this opening, so that it would not tear. 24 They made pomegranates of blue, purple and scarlet yarn and finely twisted linen around the hem of the robe. 25 And they made bells of pure gold and attached them around the hem between the pomegranates. 26 The bells and pomegranates alternated around the hem of the robe to be worn for ministering, as the LORD commanded Moses.

27 For Aaron and his sons, they made tunics of fine linen—the work of a weaver— 28 and the turban of fine linen, the linen headbands and the undergarments of finely twisted linen. 29 The sash was of finely twisted linen and blue, purple and scarlet yarn—the work of an embroiderer—as the LORD commanded Moses.

30 They made the plate, the sacred diadem, out of pure gold and engraved on

it, like an inscription on a seal: HOLY TO THE LORD. ³¹Then they fastened a blue cord to it to attach it to the turban, as the LORD commanded Moses.

³²So all the work on the tabernacle, the Tent of Meeting, was completed. The Israelites did everything just as the LORD commanded Moses. ³³Then they brought the tabernacle to Moses: the tent and all its furnishings, its clasps, frames, crossbars, posts and bases; ³⁴the covering of ram skins dyed red, the covering of hides of sea cows*f* and the shielding curtain; ³⁵the ark of the Testimony with its poles and the atonement cover; ³⁶the table with all its articles and the bread of the Presence; ³⁷the pure gold lampstand with its row of lamps and all its accessories, and the oil for the light; ³⁸the gold altar, the anointing oil, the fragrant incense, and the curtain for the entrance to the tent; ³⁹the bronze altar with its bronze grating, its poles and all its utensils; the basin with its stand; ⁴⁰the curtains of the courtyard with its posts and bases, and the curtain for the entrance to the courtyard; the ropes and tent pegs for the courtyard; all the furnishings for the tabernacle, the Tent of Meeting; ⁴¹and the woven garments worn for ministering in the sanctuary, both the sacred garments for Aaron the priest and the garments for his sons when serving as priests.

⁴²The Israelites had done all the work just as the LORD had commanded Moses. ⁴³Moses inspected the work and saw that they had done it just as the LORD had commanded. So Moses blessed them.

40:1THEN the LORD said to Moses: ²"Set up the tabernacle, the Tent of Meeting, on the first day of the first month. ³Place the ark of the Testimony in it and shield the ark with the curtain. ⁴Bring in the table and set out what belongs on it. Then bring in the lampstand and set up its lamps. ⁵Place the gold altar of incense in front of the ark of the Testimony and put the curtain at the entrance to the tabernacle.

⁶"Place the altar of burnt offering in front of the entrance to the tabernacle, the Tent of Meeting; ⁷place the basin between the Tent of Meeting and the altar and put water in it. ⁸Set up the courtyard around it and put the curtain at the entrance to the courtyard.

⁹"Take the anointing oil and anoint the tabernacle and everything in it; consecrate it and all its furnishings, and it will be holy. ¹⁰Then anoint the altar of burnt offering and all its utensils; consecrate the altar, and it will be most holy. ¹¹Anoint the basin and its stand and consecrate them.

¹²"Bring Aaron and his sons to the entrance to the Tent of Meeting and wash them with water. ¹³Then dress Aaron in the sacred garments, anoint him and consecrate him so he may serve me as priest. ¹⁴Bring his sons and dress them in tunics. ¹⁵Anoint them just as you anointed their father, so they may serve me as priests. Their anointing will be to a priesthood that will continue for all generations to come." ¹⁶Moses did everything just as the LORD commanded him.

¹⁷So the tabernacle was set up on the first day of the first month in the second year. ¹⁸When Moses set up the tabernacle, he put the bases in place, erected the frames, inserted the crossbars and set up the posts. ¹⁹Then he spread the tent over the tabernacle and put the covering over the tent, as the LORD commanded him.

²⁰He took the Testimony and placed it in the ark, attached the poles to the ark and put the atonement cover over it. ²¹Then he brought the ark into the tabernacle and hung the shielding curtain and shielded the ark of the Testimony, as the LORD commanded him.

²²Moses placed the table in the Tent of Meeting on the north side of the tabernacle outside the curtain ²³and set out the bread on it before the LORD, as the LORD commanded him.

²⁴He placed the lampstand in the Tent of Meeting opposite the table on the south side of the tabernacle ²⁵and set up the lamps before the LORD, as the LORD commanded him.

26Moses placed the gold altar in the Tent of Meeting in front of the curtain 27and burned fragrant incense on it, as the LORD commanded him. 28Then he put up the curtain at the entrance to the tabernacle.

29He set the altar of burnt offering near the entrance to the tabernacle, the Tent of Meeting, and offered on it burnt offerings and grain offerings, as the LORD commanded him.

30He placed the basin between the Tent of Meeting and the altar and put water in it for washing, 31and Moses and Aaron and his sons used it to wash their hands and feet. 32They washed whenever they entered the Tent of Meeting or approached the altar, as the LORD commanded Moses.

33Then Moses set up the courtyard around the tabernacle and altar and put up the curtain at the entrance to the courtyard. And so Moses finished the work.

34Then the cloud covered the Tent of Meeting, and the glory of the LORD filled the tabernacle. 35Moses could not enter the Tent of Meeting because the cloud had settled upon it, and the glory of the LORD filled the tabernacle.

36In all the travels of the Israelites, whenever the cloud lifted from above the tabernacle, they would set out; 37but if the cloud did not lift, they did not set out—until the day it lifted. 38So the cloud of the LORD was over the tabernacle by day, and fire was in the cloud by night, in the sight of all the house of Israel during all their travels.

a2 Or He; also in verses 7, 8 and 22   b9 That is, about 9 inches (about 22 centimeters)   c11 Or lapis lazuli   d13 The precise identification of some of these precious stones is uncertain.   e23 The meaning of the Hebrew for this word is uncertain.   f34 That is, dugongs

MARK 1:1-28

The beginning of the gospel about Jesus Christ, the Son of God.a

2It is written in Isaiah the prophet:

"I will send my messenger ahead
    of you,
  who will prepare your way"b—
3"a voice of one calling in the desert,

'Prepare the way for the Lord,
    make straight paths for him.'"c

4And so John came, baptizing in the desert region and preaching a baptism of repentance for the forgiveness of sins. 5The whole Judean countryside and all the people of Jerusalem went out to him. Confessing their sins, they were baptized by him in the Jordan River. 6John wore clothing made of camel's hair, with a leather belt around his waist, and he ate locusts and wild honey. 7And this was his message: "After me will come one more powerful than I, the thongs of whose sandals I am not worthy to stoop down and untie. 8I baptize you withd water, but he will baptize you with the Holy Spirit."

9At that time Jesus came from Nazareth in Galilee and was baptized by John in the Jordan. 10**As Jesus was coming up out of the water, he saw heaven being torn open and the Spirit descending on him like a dove. 11And a voice came from heaven: " You are my Son, whom I love; with you I am well pleased."**

12At once the Spirit sent him out into the desert, 13and he was in the desert forty days, being tempted by Satan. He was with the wild animals, and angels attended him.

14After John was put in prison, Jesus went into Galilee, proclaiming the good news of God. 15"The time has come," he said. "The kingdom of God is near. Repent and believe the good news!"

16As Jesus walked beside the Sea of Galilee, he saw Simon and his brother Andrew casting a net into the lake, for they were fishermen. 17"Come, follow me," Jesus said, "and I will make you fishers of men." 18At once they left their nets and followed him.

19When he had gone a little farther, he saw James son of Zebedee and his brother John in a boat, preparing their nets. 20Without delay he called them, and they left their father Zebedee in the boat with the hired men and followed him.

21 They went to Capernaum, and when the Sabbath came, Jesus went into the synagogue and began to teach. 22 The people were amazed at his teaching, because he taught them as one who had authority, not as the teachers of the law. 23 Just then a man in their synagogue who was possessed by an evil*e* spirit cried out, 24 "What do you want with us, Jesus of Nazareth? Have you come to destroy us? I know who you are—the Holy One of God!"

25 "Be quiet!" said Jesus sternly. "Come out of him!" 26 The evil spirit shook the man violently and came out of him with a shriek.

27 The people were all so amazed that they asked each other, "What is this? A new teaching—and with authority! He even gives orders to evil spirits and they obey him." 28 News about him spread quickly over the whole region of Galilee.

a1 Some manuscripts do not have the Son of God.   b2 Mal. 3:1   c3 Isaiah 40:3   d8 Or in   e23 Greek unclean; also in verses 26 and 27

PSALM 35:1-16
Of David.

1 **C**ontend, O Lord, with those who
    contend with me;
    fight against those who fight
      against me.
2 Take up shield and buckler;
    arise and come to my aid.
3 Brandish spear and javelin*a*
    against those who pursue me.
  Say to my soul,
    "I am your salvation."

4 May those who seek my life
    be disgraced and put to shame;
  may those who plot my ruin
    be turned back in dismay.
5 May they be like chaff before the
    wind,
    with the angel of the Lord driving
      them away;
6 may their path be dark and slippery,
    with the angel of the Lord
      pursuing them.
7 Since they hid their net for me
    without cause

  and without cause dug a pit for me,
8 may ruin overtake them by surprise—
  may the net they hid entangle them,
  may they fall into the pit, to their
    ruin.
9 Then my soul will rejoice in the Lord
    and delight in his salvation.
10 My whole being will exclaim,
    "Who is like you, O Lord?
  You rescue the poor from those too
    strong for them,
    the poor and needy from those
      who rob them."

11 Ruthless witnesses come forward;
    they question me on things I know
      nothing about.
12 They repay me evil for good
    and leave my soul forlorn.
13 Yet when they were ill, I put on
    sackcloth
    and humbled myself with fasting.
  When my prayers returned to me
    unanswered,
14   I went about mourning
    as though for my friend or brother.
  I bowed my head in grief
    as though weeping for my mother.
15 But when I stumbled, they gathered
    in glee;
    attackers gathered against me
      when I was unaware.
  They slandered me without
    ceasing.
16 Like the ungodly they maliciously
    mocked*b*;
    they gnashed their teeth at me.

a3 Or and block the way   b16 Septuagint; Hebrew may mean ungodly circle of mockers.

PROVERBS 9:11-12
11 "**F**or through me [wisdom] your days
    will be many,
    and years will be added to your
      life.
12 If you are wise, your wisdom will
    reward you;
    if you are a mocker, you alone will
      suffer."

☐ DAY 47

GOD SIGHTINGS

February 16

LEVITICUS 1:1–3:17

The Lord called to Moses and spoke to him from the Tent of Meeting. He said, ²"Speak to the Israelites and say to them: 'When any of you brings an offering to the Lord, bring as your offering an animal from either the herd or the flock.

³" 'If the offering is a burnt offering from the herd, he is to offer a male without defect. He must present it at the entrance to the Tent of Meeting so that it*a* will be acceptable to the Lord. ⁴He is to lay his hand on the head of the burnt offering, and it will be accepted on his behalf to make atonement for him. ⁵He is to slaughter the young bull before the Lord, and then Aaron's sons the priests shall bring the blood and sprinkle it against the altar on all sides at the entrance to the Tent of Meeting. ⁶He is to skin the burnt offering and cut it into pieces. ⁷The sons of Aaron the priest are to put fire on the altar and arrange wood on the fire. ⁸Then Aaron's sons the priests shall arrange the pieces, including the head and the fat, on the burning wood that is on the altar. ⁹He is to wash the inner parts and the legs with water, and the priest is to burn all of it on the altar. It is a burnt offering, an offering made by fire, an aroma pleasing to the Lord.

¹⁰" 'If the offering is a burnt offering from the flock, from either the sheep or the goats, he is to offer a male without defect. ¹¹He is to slaughter it at the north side of the altar before the Lord, and Aaron's sons the priests shall sprinkle its blood against the altar on all sides. ¹²He is to cut it into pieces, and the priest shall arrange them, including the head and the fat, on the burning wood that is on the altar. ¹³He is to wash the inner parts and the legs with water,

and the priest is to bring all of it and burn it on the altar. It is a burnt offering, an offering made by fire, an aroma pleasing to the Lord.

¹⁴" 'If the offering to the Lord is a burnt offering of birds, he is to offer a dove or a young pigeon. ¹⁵The priest shall bring it to the altar, wring off the head and burn it on the altar; its blood shall be drained out on the side of the altar. ¹⁶He is to remove the crop with its contents*b* and throw it to the east side of the altar, where the ashes are. ¹⁷He shall tear it open by the wings, not severing it completely, and then the priest shall burn it on the wood that is on the fire on the altar. It is a burnt offering, an offering made by fire, an aroma pleasing to the Lord.

²:¹" 'When someone brings a grain offering to the Lord, his offering is to be of fine flour. He is to pour oil on it, put incense on it ²and take it to Aaron's sons the priests. The priest shall take a handful of the fine flour and oil, together with all the incense, and burn this as a memorial portion on the altar, an offering made by fire, an aroma pleasing to the Lord. ³The rest of the grain offering belongs to Aaron and his sons; it is a most holy part of the offerings made to the Lord by fire.

⁴" 'If you bring a grain offering baked in an oven, it is to consist of fine flour: cakes made without yeast and mixed with oil, or*c* wafers made without yeast and spread with oil. ⁵If your grain offering is prepared on a griddle, it is to be made of fine flour mixed with oil, and without yeast. ⁶Crumble it and pour oil on it; it is a grain offering. ⁷If your grain offering is cooked in a pan, it is to be made of fine flour and oil. ⁸Bring the grain offering made of these things to the Lord; present it to the priest, who shall take it to the altar. ⁹He shall take out the memorial portion from the grain offering and burn it on the altar as an offering made by fire, an aroma pleasing to the Lord. ¹⁰The rest of the grain offering belongs to Aaron and his

sons; it is a most holy part of the offerings made to the LORD by fire.

11" 'Every grain offering you bring to the LORD must be made without yeast, for you are not to burn any yeast or honey in an offering made to the LORD by fire. 12You may bring them to the LORD as an offering of the firstfruits, but they are not to be offered on the altar as a pleasing aroma. 13Season all your grain offerings with salt. Do not leave the salt of the covenant of your God out of your grain offerings; add salt to all your offerings.

14" 'If you bring a grain offering of firstfruits to the LORD, offer crushed heads of new grain roasted in the fire. 15Put oil and incense on it; it is a grain offering. 16The priest shall burn the memorial portion of the crushed grain and the oil, together with all the incense, as an offering made to the LORD by fire.

3:1"'IF someone's offering is a fellowship offering,d and he offers an animal from the herd, whether male or female, he is to present before the LORD an animal without defect. 2He is to lay his hand on the head of his offering and slaughter it at the entrance to the Tent of Meeting. Then Aaron's sons the priests shall sprinkle the blood against the altar on all sides. 3From the fellowship offering he is to bring a sacrifice made to the LORD by fire: all the fat that covers the inner parts or is connected to them, 4both kidneys with the fat on them near the loins, and the covering of the liver, which he will remove with the kidneys. 5Then Aaron's sons are to burn it on the altar on top of the burnt offering that is on the burning wood, as an offering made by fire, an aroma pleasing to the LORD.

6" 'If he offers an animal from the flock as a fellowship offering to the LORD, he is to offer a male or female without defect. 7If he offers a lamb, he is to present it before the LORD. 8He is to lay his hand on the head of his offering and slaughter it in front of the Tent of Meeting. Then Aaron's sons shall sprin-

kle its blood against the altar on all sides. 9From the fellowship offering he is to bring a sacrifice made to the LORD by fire: its fat, the entire fat tail cut off close to the backbone, all the fat that covers the inner parts or is connected to them, 10both kidneys with the fat on them near the loins, and the covering of the liver, which he will remove with the kidneys. 11The priest shall burn them on the altar as food, an offering made to the LORD by fire.

12" 'If his offering is a goat, he is to present it before the LORD. 13He is to lay his hand on its head and slaughter it in front of the Tent of Meeting. Then Aaron's sons shall sprinkle its blood against the altar on all sides. 14From what he offers he is to make this offering to the LORD by fire: all the fat that covers the inner parts or is connected to them, 15both kidneys with the fat on them near the loins, and the covering of the liver, which he will remove with the kidneys. 16The priest shall burn them on the altar as food, an offering made by fire, a pleasing aroma. All the fat is the LORD's.

17" 'This is a lasting ordinance for the generations to come, wherever you live: You must not eat any fat or any blood.'"

a3 Or he   b16 Or crop and the feathers; the meaning of the Hebrew for this word is uncertain.   c4 Or and   d1 Traditionally peace offering; also in verses 3, 6 and 9

MARK 1:29–2:12

As soon as they [Jesus and his disciples] left the synagogue, they went with James and John to the home of Simon and Andrew. 30Simon's mother-in-law was in bed with a fever, and they told Jesus about her. 31So he went to her, took her hand and helped her up. The fever left her and she began to wait on them.

32That evening after sunset the people brought to Jesus all the sick and demon-possessed. 33The whole town gathered at the door, 34and Jesus healed many who had various diseases. He also drove out many demons, but he would not let the demons speak because they knew who he was.

35 Very early in the morning, while it was still dark, Jesus got up, left the house and went off to a solitary place, where he prayed. 36 Simon and his companions went to look for him, 37 and when they found him, they exclaimed: "Everyone is looking for you!"

38 Jesus replied, "Let us go somewhere else—to the nearby villages—so I can preach there also. That is why I have come." 39 So he traveled throughout Galilee, preaching in their synagogues and driving out demons.

40 **A man with leprosy**ᵃ **came to him and begged him on his knees, "If you are willing, you can make me clean."** 41 **Filled with compassion, Jesus reached out his hand and touched the man. "I am willing," he said. "Be clean!"** 42 **Immediately the leprosy left him and he was cured.**

43 Jesus sent him away at once with a strong warning: 44 "See that you don't tell this to anyone. But go, show yourself to the priest and offer the sacrifices that Moses commanded for your cleansing, as a testimony to them." 45 Instead he went out and began to talk freely, spreading the news. As a result, Jesus could no longer enter a town openly but stayed outside in lonely places. Yet the people still came to him from everywhere.

2:1 A FEW days later, when Jesus again entered Capernaum, the people heard that he had come home. 2 So many gathered that there was no room left, not even outside the door, and he preached the word to them. 3 Some men came, bringing to him a paralytic, carried by four of them. 4 Since they could not get him to Jesus because of the crowd, they made an opening in the roof above Jesus and, after digging through it, lowered the mat the paralyzed man was lying on. 5 When Jesus saw their faith, he said to the paralytic, "Son, your sins are forgiven."

6 Now some teachers of the law were sitting there, thinking to themselves, 7 "Why does this fellow talk like that? He's blaspheming! Who can forgive sins but God alone?"

8 Immediately Jesus knew in his spirit that this was what they were thinking in their hearts, and he said to them, "Why are you thinking these things? 9 Which is easier: to say to the paralytic, 'Your sins are forgiven,' or to say, 'Get up, take your mat and walk'? 10 But that you may know that the Son of Man has authority on earth to forgive sins . . ." He said to the paralytic, 11 "I tell you, get up, take your mat and go home." 12 He got up, took his mat and walked out in full view of them all. This amazed everyone and they praised God, saying, "We have never seen anything like this!"

ᵃ40 The Greek word was used for various diseases affecting the skin—not necessarily leprosy.

PSALM 35:17-28

17 ⊙ Lord, how long will you look on?
　　Rescue my life from their ravages,
　　　my precious life from these lions.
18 I will give you thanks in the great assembly;
　　among throngs of people I will praise you.

19 Let not those gloat over me
　　who are my enemies without cause;
　　let not those who hate me without reason
　　maliciously wink the eye.
20 They do not speak peaceably,
　　but devise false accusations
　　against those who live quietly in the land.
21 They gape at me and say, "Aha! Aha!
　　With our own eyes we have seen it."

22 O LORD, you have seen this; be not silent.
　　Do not be far from me, O Lord.
23 Awake, and rise to my defense!
　　Contend for me, my God and Lord.
24 Vindicate me in your righteousness,
　　O LORD my God;
　　do not let them gloat over me.
25 Do not let them think, "Aha, just what we wanted!"
　　or say, "We have swallowed him up."

26 May all who gloat over my distress
    be put to shame and confusion;
  may all who exalt themselves
      over me
    be clothed with shame and
      disgrace.
27 May those who delight in my
      vindication
    shout for joy and gladness;
  may they always say, "The LORD be
      exalted,
    who delights in the well-being of
      his servant."
28 My tongue will speak of your
      righteousness
    and of your praises all day long.

PROVERBS 9:13-18

13 The woman Folly is loud;
    she is undisciplined and without
      knowledge.
14 She sits at the door of her house,
    on a seat at the highest point of
      the city,
15 calling out to those who pass by,
    who go straight on their way.
16 "Let all who are simple come in
      here!"
    she says to those who lack
      judgment.
17 "Stolen water is sweet;
    food eaten in secret is delicious!"
18 But little do they know that the dead
      are there,
    that her guests are in the depths of
      the grave.*a*

a18 Hebrew *Sheol*

□ D A Y 4 8

GOD SIGHTINGS

February 17

LEVITICUS 4:1–5:19

The LORD said to Moses, 2 "Say to the Israelites: 'When anyone sins unintentionally and does what is forbidden in
any of the LORD's commands—

3 "'If the anointed priest sins, bringing
guilt on the people, he must bring to the
LORD a young bull without defect as a sin
offering for the sin he has committed.
4 He is to present the bull at the entrance
to the Tent of Meeting before the LORD.
He is to lay his hand on its head and
slaughter it before the LORD. 5 Then the
anointed priest shall take some of the
bull's blood and carry it into the Tent of
Meeting. 6 He is to dip his finger into the
blood and sprinkle some of it seven
times before the LORD, in front of the curtain of the sanctuary. 7 The priest shall
then put some of the blood on the horns
of the altar of fragrant incense that is before the LORD in the Tent of Meeting. The
rest of the bull's blood he shall pour out
at the base of the altar of burnt offering
at the entrance to the Tent of Meeting.
8 He shall remove all the fat from the bull
of the sin offering—the fat that covers
the inner parts or is connected to them,
9 both kidneys with the fat on them near
the loins, and the covering of the liver,
which he will remove with the kidneys—
10 just as the fat is removed from the ox*a*
sacrificed as a fellowship offering.*b*
Then the priest shall burn them on the
altar of burnt offering. 11 But the hide of
the bull and all its flesh, as well as the
head and legs, the inner parts and offal—
12 that is, all the rest of the bull—he must
take outside the camp to a place ceremonially clean, where the ashes are thrown,
and burn it in a wood fire on the ash
heap.

13 "'If the whole Israelite community
sins unintentionally and does what is
forbidden in any of the LORD's commands, even though the community is
unaware of the matter, they are guilty.
14 When they become aware of the sin
they committed, the assembly must
bring a young bull as a sin offering and
present it before the Tent of Meeting.
15 The elders of the community are to lay
their hands on the bull's head before the
LORD, and the bull shall be slaughtered
before the LORD. 16 Then the anointed
priest is to take some of the bull's blood

into the Tent of Meeting. [17]He shall dip his finger into the blood and sprinkle it before the LORD seven times in front of the curtain. [18]He is to put some of the blood on the horns of the altar that is before the LORD in the Tent of Meeting. The rest of the blood he shall pour out at the base of the altar of burnt offering at the entrance to the Tent of Meeting. [19]He shall remove all the fat from it and burn it on the altar, [20]and do with this bull just as he did with the bull for the sin offering. In this way the priest will make atonement for them, and they will be forgiven. [21]Then he shall take the bull outside the camp and burn it as he burned the first bull. This is the sin offering for the community.

[22]" 'When a leader sins unintentionally and does what is forbidden in any of the commands of the LORD his God, he is guilty. [23]When he is made aware of the sin he committed, he must bring as his offering a male goat without defect. [24]He is to lay his hand on the goat's head and slaughter it at the place where the burnt offering is slaughtered before the LORD. It is a sin offering. [25]Then the priest shall take some of the blood of the sin offering with his finger and put it on the horns of the altar of burnt offering and pour out the rest of the blood at the base of the altar. [26]He shall burn all the fat on the altar as he burned the fat of the fellowship offering. In this way the priest will make atonement for the man's sin, and he will be forgiven.

[27]" 'If a member of the community sins unintentionally and does what is forbidden in any of the LORD's commands, he is guilty. [28]When he is made aware of the sin he committed, he must bring as his offering for the sin he committed a female goat without defect. [29]He is to lay his hand on the head of the sin offering and slaughter it at the place of the burnt offering. [30]Then the priest is to take some of the blood with his finger and put it on the horns of the altar of burnt offering and pour out the rest of

the blood at the base of the altar. [31]He shall remove all the fat, just as the fat is removed from the fellowship offering, and the priest shall burn it on the altar as an aroma pleasing to the LORD. In this way the priest will make atonement for him, and he will be forgiven.

[32]" 'If he brings a lamb as his sin offering, he is to bring a female without defect. [33]He is to lay his hand on its head and slaughter it for a sin offering at the place where the burnt offering is slaughtered. [34]Then the priest shall take some of the blood of the sin offering with his finger and put it on the horns of the altar of burnt offering and pour out the rest of the blood at the base of the altar. [35]He shall remove all the fat, just as the fat is removed from the lamb of the fellowship offering, and the priest shall burn it on the altar on top of the offerings made to the LORD by fire. In this way the priest will make atonement for him for the sin he has committed, and he will be forgiven.

[5:1]" 'If a person sins because he does not speak up when he hears a public charge to testify regarding something he has seen or learned about, he will be held responsible.

[2]" 'Or if a person touches anything ceremonially unclean—whether the carcasses of unclean wild animals or of unclean livestock or of unclean creatures that move along the ground—even though he is unaware of it, he has become unclean and is guilty.

[3]" 'Or if he touches human uncleanness—anything that would make him unclean—even though he is unaware of it, when he learns of it he will be guilty.

[4]" 'Or if a person thoughtlessly takes an oath to do anything, whether good or evil—in any matter one might carelessly swear about—even though he is unaware of it, in any case when he learns of it he will be guilty.

[5]" 'When anyone is guilty in any of these ways, he must confess in what way he has sinned [6]and, as a penalty for the sin he has committed, he must

bring to the LORD a female lamb or goat from the flock as a sin offering; and the priest shall make atonement for him for his sin.

7"'If he cannot afford a lamb, he is to bring two doves or two young pigeons to the LORD as a penalty for his sin—one for a sin offering and the other for a burnt offering. 8He is to bring them to the priest, who shall first offer the one for the sin offering. He is to wring its head from its neck, not severing it completely, 9and is to sprinkle some of the blood of the sin offering against the side of the altar; the rest of the blood must be drained out at the base of the altar. It is a sin offering. 10The priest shall then offer the other as a burnt offering in the prescribed way and make atonement for him for the sin he has committed, and he will be forgiven.

11"'If, however, he cannot afford two doves or two young pigeons, he is to bring as an offering for his sin a tenth of an ephah*c* of fine flour for a sin offering. He must not put oil or incense on it, because it is a sin offering. 12He is to bring it to the priest, who shall take a handful of it as a memorial portion and burn it on the altar on top of the offerings made to the LORD by fire. It is a sin offering. 13In this way the priest will make atonement for him for any of these sins he has committed, and he will be forgiven. The rest of the offering will belong to the priest, as in the case of the grain offering.'"

14The LORD said to Moses: 15"When a person commits a violation and sins unintentionally in regard to any of the LORD's holy things, he is to bring to the LORD as a penalty a ram from the flock, one without defect and of the proper value in silver, according to the sanctuary shekel.*d* It is a guilt offering. 16He must make restitution for what he has failed to do in regard to the holy things, add a fifth of the value to that and give it all to the priest, who will make atonement for him with the ram as a guilt offering, and he will be forgiven.

17"If a person sins and does what is forbidden in any of the LORD's commands, even though he does not know it, he is guilty and will be held responsible. 18He is to bring to the priest as a guilt offering a ram from the flock, one without defect and of the proper value. In this way the priest will make atonement for him for the wrong he has committed unintentionally, and he will be forgiven. 19It is a guilt offering; he has been guilty of*e* wrongdoing against the LORD."

a10 The Hebrew word can include both male and female.
b10 Traditionally *peace offering*; also in verses 26, 31 and 35 *c11* That is, probably about 2 quarts (about 2 liters) *d15* That is, about 2/5 ounce (about 11.5 grams)
e19 Or *has made full expiation for his*

MARK 2:13-3:6

❶nce again Jesus went out beside the lake. A large crowd came to him, and he began to teach them. 14As he walked along, he saw Levi son of Alphaeus sitting at the tax collector's booth. "Follow me," Jesus told him, and Levi got up and followed him.

15While Jesus was having dinner at Levi's house, many tax collectors and "sinners" were eating with him and his disciples, for there were many who followed him. 16When the teachers of the law who were Pharisees saw him eating with the "sinners" and tax collectors, they asked his disciples: "Why does he eat with tax collectors and 'sinners'?"

17On hearing this, Jesus said to them, "It is not the healthy who need a doctor, but the sick. I have not come to call the righteous, but sinners."

18Now John's disciples and the Pharisees were fasting. Some people came and asked Jesus, "How is it that John's disciples and the disciples of the Pharisees are fasting, but yours are not?"

19Jesus answered, "How can the guests of the bridegroom fast while he is with them? They cannot, so long as they have him with them. 20But the time will come when the bridegroom will be taken from them, and on that day they will fast.

21"No one sews a patch of unshrunk cloth on an old garment. If he does, the new piece will pull away from the old, making the tear worse. 22And no one pours new wine into old wineskins. If he does, the wine will burst the skins, and both the wine and the wineskins will be ruined. No, he pours new wine into new wineskins."

23One Sabbath Jesus was going through the grainfields, and as his disciples walked along, they began to pick some heads of grain. 24The Pharisees said to him, "Look, why are they doing what is unlawful on the Sabbath?"

25He answered, "Have you never read what David did when he and his companions were hungry and in need? 26In the days of Abiathar the high priest, he entered the house of God and ate the consecrated bread, which is lawful only for priests to eat. And he also gave some to his companions."

27Then he said to them, "The Sabbath was made for man, not man for the Sabbath. 28So the Son of Man is Lord even of the Sabbath."

3:1ANOTHER time he went into the synagogue, and a man with a shriveled hand was there. 2Some of them were looking for a reason to accuse Jesus, so they watched him closely to see if he would heal him on the Sabbath. 3Jesus said to the man with the shriveled hand, "Stand up in front of everyone."

4Then Jesus asked them, "Which is lawful on the Sabbath: to do good or to do evil, to save life or to kill?" But they remained silent.

5He looked around at them in anger and, deeply distressed at their stubborn hearts, said to the man, "Stretch out your hand." He stretched it out, and his hand was completely restored. 6Then the Pharisees went out and began to plot with the Herodians how they might kill Jesus.

PSALM 36:1-12

For the director of music. Of David the servant of the LORD.

1 An oracle is within my heart
    concerning the sinfulness of the
    wicked:a

There is no fear of God
    before his eyes.
2For in his own eyes he flatters
    himself
    too much to detect or hate his sin.
3The words of his mouth are wicked
    and deceitful;
    he has ceased to be wise and to do
    good.
4Even on his bed he plots evil;
    he commits himself to a sinful
    course
    and does not reject what is wrong.

5Your love, O LORD, reaches to the
    heavens,
    your faithfulness to the skies.
6Your righteousness is like the
    mighty mountains,
    your justice like the great deep.
O LORD, you preserve both man
    and beast.
7   How priceless is your unfailing
        love!
Both high and low among men
    findb refuge in the shadow of your
        wings.
8They feast on the abundance of your
        house;
    you give them drink from your
        river of delights.
9For with you is the fountain of life;
    in your light we see light.

10Continue your love to those who
        know you,
    your righteousness to the upright
        in heart.
11May the foot of the proud not come
        against me,
    nor the hand of the wicked drive
        me away.
12See how the evildoers lie fallen—
    thrown down, not able to rise!

a1 Or heart: / Sin proceeds from the wicked.   b7 Or love,
O God! / Men find; or love! / Both heavenly beings and men
/ find

PROVERBS 10:1-2

The proverbs of Solomon:

A wise son brings joy to his father,
    but a foolish son grief to his mother.

2 Ill-gotten treasures are of no value,
   but righteousness delivers from
   death.

□ DAY 49

February 18

LEVITICUS 6:1–7:27

The Lᴏʀᴅ said to Moses: 2"If anyone sins and is unfaithful to the Lᴏʀᴅ by deceiving his neighbor about something entrusted to him or left in his care or stolen, or if he cheats him, 3 or if he finds lost property and lies about it, or if he swears falsely, or if he commits any such sin that people may do— 4when he thus sins and becomes guilty, he must return what he has stolen or taken by extortion, or what was entrusted to him, or the lost property he found, 5 or whatever it was he swore falsely about. He must make restitution in full, add a fifth of the value to it and give it all to the owner on the day he presents his guilt offering. 6And as a penalty he must bring to the priest, that is, to the Lᴏʀᴅ, his guilt offering, a ram from the flock, one without defect and of the proper value. 7 In this way the priest will make atonement for him before the Lᴏʀᴅ, and he will be forgiven for any of these things he did that made him guilty."

8The Lᴏʀᴅ said to Moses: 9"Give Aaron and his sons this command: 'These are the regulations for the burnt offering: The burnt offering is to remain on the altar hearth throughout the night, till morning, and the fire must be kept burning on the altar. 10The priest shall then put on his linen clothes, with linen undergarments next to his body, and shall remove the ashes of the burnt offering that the fire has consumed on the altar and place them beside the altar. 11Then he is to take off these clothes and put on others, and carry the ashes

outside the camp to a place that is ceremonially clean. 12The fire on the altar must be kept burning; it must not go out. Every morning the priest is to add firewood and arrange the burnt offering on the fire and burn the fat of the fellowship offeringsª on it. 13The fire must be kept burning on the altar continuously; it must not go out.

14"'These are the regulations for the grain offering: Aaron's sons are to bring it before the Lᴏʀᴅ, in front of the altar. 15The priest is to take a handful of fine flour and oil, together with all the incense on the grain offering, and burn the memorial portion on the altar as an aroma pleasing to the Lᴏʀᴅ. 16Aaron and his sons shall eat the rest of it, but it is to be eaten without yeast in a holy place; they are to eat it in the courtyard of the Tent of Meeting. 17It must not be baked with yeast; I have given it as their share of the offerings made to me by fire. Like the sin offering and the guilt offering, it is most holy. 18Any male descendant of Aaron may eat it. It is his regular share of the offerings made to the Lᴏʀᴅ by fire for the generations to come. Whatever touches them will become holy.ᵇ'"

19The Lᴏʀᴅ also said to Moses, 20"This is the offering Aaron and his sons are to bring to the Lᴏʀᴅ on the day heᶜ is anointed: a tenth of an ephahᵈ of fine flour as a regular grain offering, half of it in the morning and half in the evening. 21Prepare it with oil on a griddle; bring it well-mixed and present the grain offering brokenᵉ in pieces as an aroma pleasing to the Lᴏʀᴅ. 22The son who is to succeed him as anointed priest shall prepare it. It is the Lᴏʀᴅ's regular share and is to be burned completely. 23Every grain offering of a priest shall be burned completely; it must not be eaten."

24The Lᴏʀᴅ said to Moses, 25"Say to Aaron and his sons: 'These are the regulations for the sin offering: The sin offering is to be slaughtered before the Lᴏʀᴅ in the place the burnt offering is slaughtered; it is most holy. 26The priest who offers it shall eat it; it is to be eaten in a holy place, in the courtyard of the Tent of Meeting. 27Whatever touches any of the flesh will become holy, and if any of the blood is spattered on a garment, you must wash it in a holy place. 28The clay pot the meat is cooked in must be broken; but if it is cooked in a bronze pot, the pot is to be scoured and rinsed with water. 29Any male in a priest's family may eat it; it is most holy. 30But any sin offering whose blood is brought into the Tent of Meeting to make atonement in the Holy Place must not be eaten; it must be burned.

7:1" 'THESE are the regulations for the guilt offering, which is most holy: 2The guilt offering is to be slaughtered in the place where the burnt offering is slaughtered, and its blood is to be sprinkled against the altar on all sides. 3All its fat shall be offered: the fat tail and the fat that covers the inner parts, 4both kidneys with the fat on them near the loins, and the covering of the liver, which is to be removed with the kidneys. 5The priest shall burn them on the altar as an offering made to the LORD by fire. It is a guilt offering. 6Any male in a priest's family may eat it, but it must be eaten in a holy place; it is most holy.

7" 'The same law applies to both the sin offering and the guilt offering: They belong to the priest who makes atonement with them. 8The priest who offers a burnt offering for anyone may keep its hide for himself. 9Every grain offering baked in an oven or cooked in a pan or on a griddle belongs to the priest who offers it, 10and every grain offering, whether mixed with oil or dry, belongs equally to all the sons of Aaron.

11" 'These are the regulations for the fellowship offeringf a person may present to the LORD:

12" 'If he offers it as an expression of thankfulness, then along with this thank offering he is to offer cakes of bread made without yeast and mixed with oil, wafers made without yeast and

spread with oil, and cakes of fine flour well-kneaded and mixed with oil. 13Along with his fellowship offering of thanksgiving he is to present an offering with cakes of bread made with yeast. 14He is to bring one of each kind as an offering, a contribution to the LORD; it belongs to the priest who sprinkles the blood of the fellowship offerings. 15The meat of his fellowship offering of thanksgiving must be eaten on the day it is offered; he must leave none of it till morning.

16" 'If, however, his offering is the result of a vow or is a freewill offering, the sacrifice shall be eaten on the day he offers it, but anything left over may be eaten on the next day. 17Any meat of the sacrifice left over till the third day must be burned up. 18If any meat of the fellowship offering is eaten on the third day, it will not be accepted. It will not be credited to the one who offered it, for it is impure; the person who eats any of it will be held responsible.

19" 'Meat that touches anything ceremonially unclean must not be eaten; it must be burned up. As for other meat, anyone ceremonially clean may eat it. 20But if anyone who is unclean eats any meat of the fellowship offering belonging to the LORD, that person must be cut off from his people. 21If anyone touches something unclean—whether human uncleanness or an unclean animal or any unclean, detestable thing—and then eats any of the meat of the fellowship offering belonging to the LORD, that person must be cut off from his people.'"

22The LORD said to Moses, 23"Say to the Israelites: 'Do not eat any of the fat of cattle, sheep or goats. 24The fat of an animal found dead or torn by wild animals may be used for any other purpose, but you must not eat it. 25Anyone who eats the fat of an animal from which an offering by fire may beg made to the LORD must be cut off from his people. 26And wherever you live, you must not eat the blood of any bird or animal. ²⁷If anyone eats blood, that person must be cut off from his people.'"

a12 Traditionally *peace offerings*   *b18* Or *Whoever touches them must be holy*; similarly in verse 27   *c20* Or *each*   *d20* That is, probably about 2 quarts (about 2 liters)   *e21* The meaning of the Hebrew for this word is uncertain.   *f11* Traditionally *peace offering*; also in verses 13-37   *g25* Or *fire is*

MARK 3:7-30

Jesus withdrew with his disciples to the lake, and a large crowd from Galilee followed. ⁸When they heard all he was doing, many people came to him from Judea, Jerusalem, Idumea, and the regions across the Jordan and around Tyre and Sidon. ⁹Because of the crowd he told his disciples to have a small boat ready for him, to keep the people from crowding him. ¹⁰For he had healed many, so that those with diseases were pushing forward to touch him. ¹¹Whenever the evil[a] spirits saw him, they fell down before him and cried out, "You are the Son of God." ¹²But he gave them strict orders not to tell who he was.

¹³Jesus went up on a mountainside and called to him those he wanted, and they came to him. ¹⁴He appointed twelve—designating them apostles[b]— that they might be with him and that he might send them out to preach ¹⁵and to have authority to drive out demons. ¹⁶These are the twelve he appointed: Simon (to whom he gave the name Peter); ¹⁷James son of Zebedee and his brother John (to them he gave the name Boanerges, which means Sons of Thunder); ¹⁸Andrew, Philip, Bartholomew, Matthew, Thomas, James son of Alphaeus, Thaddaeus, Simon the Zealot ¹⁹and Judas Iscariot, who betrayed him.

²⁰Then Jesus entered a house, and again a crowd gathered, so that he and his disciples were not even able to eat. ²¹When his family heard about this, they went to take charge of him, for they said, "He is out of his mind."

²²And the teachers of the law who came down from Jerusalem said, "He is possessed by Beelzebub[c]! By the prince of demons he is driving out demons."

²³So Jesus called them and spoke to them in parables: "How can Satan drive out Satan? ²⁴If a kingdom is divided against itself, that kingdom cannot stand. ²⁵If a house is divided against itself, that house cannot stand. ²⁶And if Satan opposes himself and is divided, he cannot stand; his end has come. ²⁷In fact, no one can enter a strong man's house and carry off his possessions unless he first ties up the strong man. Then he can rob his house. ²⁸I tell you the truth, all the sins and blasphemies of men will be forgiven them. ²⁹But whoever blasphemes against the Holy Spirit will never be forgiven; he is guilty of an eternal sin."

³⁰He said this because they were saying, "He has an evil spirit."

a11 Greek *unclean*; also in verse 30   *b14* Some manuscripts do not have *designating them apostles*.   *c22* Greek *Beezeboul* or *Beelzeboul*

PSALM 37:1-11[a]
Of David.

¹ **D**o not fret because of evil men
    or be envious of those who do
        wrong;
² for like the grass they will soon
        wither,
    like green plants they will soon
        die away.

³ **Trust in the Lord and do good;**
    dwell in the land and enjoy safe
        pasture.
⁴ **Delight yourself in the Lord**
    and he will give you the desires
        of your heart.

⁵ Commit your way to the Lord;
    trust in him and he will do this:
⁶ He will make your righteousness
        shine like the dawn,
    the justice of your cause like the
        noonday sun.

⁷ Be still before the Lord and wait
        patiently for him;
    do not fret when men succeed in
        their ways,
    when they carry out their wicked
        schemes.

8 Refrain from anger and turn from
   wrath;
   do not fret—it leads only to evil.
9 For evil men will be cut off,
   but those who hope in the LORD
   will inherit the land.

10 A little while, and the wicked will be
   no more;
   though you look for them, they
   will not be found.
11 But the meek will inherit the land
   and enjoy great peace.

a This psalm is an acrostic poem, the stanzas of which begin
with the successive letters of the Hebrew alphabet.

PROVERBS 10:3-4

3 The LORD does not let the righteous
   go hungry
   but he thwarts the craving of the
   wicked.

4 Lazy hands make a man poor,
   but diligent hands bring wealth.

☐ DAY 50

GOD SIGHTINGS

February 19

LEVITICUS 7:28–9:6

The LORD said to Moses, 29 "Say to the Israelites: 'Anyone who brings a fellowship offering to the LORD is to bring part
of it as his sacrifice to the LORD. 30 With
his own hands he is to bring the offering
made to the LORD by fire; he is to bring
the fat, together with the breast, and
wave the breast before the LORD as a
wave offering. 31 The priest shall burn
the fat on the altar, but the breast belongs to Aaron and his sons. 32 You are to
give the right thigh of your fellowship
offerings to the priest as a contribution.
33 The son of Aaron who offers the
blood and the fat of the fellowship offering shall have the right thigh as his
share. 34 From the fellowship offerings
of the Israelites, I have taken the breast

that is waved and the thigh that is presented and have given them to Aaron
the priest and his sons as their regular
share from the Israelites.'"
35 This is the portion of the offerings
made to the LORD by fire that were allotted to Aaron and his sons on the day they
were presented to serve the LORD as
priests. 36 On the day they were anointed,
the LORD commanded that the Israelites
give this to them as their regular share
for the generations to come.

37 These, then, are the regulations for
the burnt offering, the grain offering,
the sin offering, the guilt offering, the
ordination offering and the fellowship
offering, 38 which the LORD gave Moses
on Mount Sinai on the day he commanded the Israelites to bring their offerings to the LORD, in the Desert of
Sinai.

8:1 THE LORD said to Moses, 2 "Bring
Aaron and his sons, their garments, the
anointing oil, the bull for the sin offering, the two rams and the basket containing bread made without yeast, 3 and
gather the entire assembly at the entrance to the Tent of Meeting." 4 Moses
did as the LORD commanded him, and
the assembly gathered at the entrance
to the Tent of Meeting.

5 Moses said to the assembly, "This is
what the LORD has commanded to be
done." 6 Then Moses brought Aaron and
his sons forward and washed them with
water. 7 He put the tunic on Aaron, tied
the sash around him, clothed him with
the robe and put the ephod on him. He
also tied the ephod to him by its skillfully
woven waistband; so it was fastened on
him. 8 He placed the breastpiece on him
and put the Urim and Thummim in the
breastpiece. 9 Then he placed the turban
on Aaron's head and set the gold plate,
the sacred diadem, on the front of it, as
the LORD commanded Moses.

10 Then Moses took the anointing oil
and anointed the tabernacle and everything in it, and so consecrated them.
11 He sprinkled some of the oil on the altar seven times, anointing the altar and

all its utensils and the basin with its stand, to consecrate them. [12]He poured some of the anointing oil on Aaron's head and anointed him to consecrate him. [13]Then he brought Aaron's sons forward, put tunics on them, tied sashes around them and put headbands on them, as the Lord commanded Moses.

[14]He then presented the bull for the sin offering, and Aaron and his sons laid their hands on its head. [15]Moses slaughtered the bull and took some of the blood, and with his finger he put it on all the horns of the altar to purify the altar. He poured out the rest of the blood at the base of the altar. So he consecrated it to make atonement for it. [16]Moses also took all the fat around the inner parts, the covering of the liver, and both kidneys and their fat, and burned it on the altar. [17]But the bull with its hide and its flesh and its offal he burned up outside the camp, as the Lord commanded Moses.

[18]He then presented the ram for the burnt offering, and Aaron and his sons laid their hands on its head. [19]Then Moses slaughtered the ram and sprinkled the blood against the altar on all sides. [20]He cut the ram into pieces and burned the head, the pieces and the fat. [21]He washed the inner parts and the legs with water and burned the whole ram on the altar as a burnt offering, a pleasing aroma, an offering made to the Lord by fire, as the Lord commanded Moses.

[22]He then presented the other ram, the ram for the ordination, and Aaron and his sons laid their hands on its head. [23]Moses slaughtered the ram and took some of its blood and put it on the lobe of Aaron's right ear, on the thumb of his right hand and on the big toe of his right foot. [24]Moses also brought Aaron's sons forward and put some of the blood on the lobes of their right ears, on the thumbs of their right hands and on the big toes of their right feet. Then he sprinkled blood against the altar on all sides. [25]He took the fat, the fat tail, all the fat around the inner parts, the covering of the liver, both kidneys and their fat and

the right thigh. [26]Then from the basket of bread made without yeast, which was before the Lord, he took a cake of bread, and one made with oil, and a wafer; he put these on the fat portions and on the right thigh. [27]He put all these in the hands of Aaron and his sons and waved them before the Lord as a wave offering. [28]Then Moses took them from their hands and burned them on the altar on top of the burnt offering as an ordination offering, a pleasing aroma, an offering made to the Lord by fire. [29]He also took the breast—Moses' share of the ordination ram—and waved it before the Lord as a wave offering, as the Lord commanded Moses.

[30]Then Moses took some of the anointing oil and some of the blood from the altar and sprinkled them on Aaron and his garments and on his sons and their garments. So he consecrated Aaron and his garments and his sons and their garments.

[31]Moses then said to Aaron and his sons, "Cook the meat at the entrance to the Tent of Meeting and eat it there with the bread from the basket of ordination offerings, as I commanded, saying,[a] 'Aaron and his sons are to eat it.' [32]Then burn up the rest of the meat and the bread. [33]Do not leave the entrance to the Tent of Meeting for seven days, until the days of your ordination are completed, for your ordination will last seven days. [34]What has been done today was commanded by the Lord to make atonement for you. [35]You must stay at the entrance to the Tent of Meeting day and night for seven days and do what the Lord requires, so you will not die; for that is what I have been commanded." [36]So Aaron and his sons did everything the Lord commanded through Moses.

[9:1]On the eighth day Moses summoned Aaron and his sons and the elders of Israel. [2]He said to Aaron, "Take a bull calf for your sin offering and a ram for your burnt offering, both without defect, and present them before the Lord. [3]Then say to the Israelites: 'Take a male goat for a sin offering, a calf and a lamb—both a year old and without defect—for a burnt offering, [4]and an ox[b] and a ram for a fellowship offering[c] to sacrifice before the LORD, together with a grain offering mixed with oil. For today the LORD will appear to you.'"

[5]They took the things Moses commanded to the front of the Tent of Meeting, and the entire assembly came near and stood before the LORD. [6]Then Moses said, "This is what the LORD has commanded you to do, so that the glory of the LORD may appear to you."

[a]31 Or I was commanded: [b]4 The Hebrew word can include both male and female; also in verses 18 and 19.
[c]4 Traditionally peace offering; also in verses 18 and 22

MARK 3:31–4:25

Then Jesus' mother and brothers arrived. Standing outside, they sent someone in to call him. [32]A crowd was sitting around him, and they told him, "Your mother and brothers are outside looking for you."

[33]**"Who are my mother and my brothers?" he asked.**

[34]**Then he looked at those seated in a circle around him and said, "Here are my mother and my brothers!** [35]**Whoever does God's will is my brother and sister and mother."**

[4:1]AGAIN Jesus began to teach by the lake. The crowd that gathered around him was so large that he got into a boat and sat in it out on the lake, while all the people were along the shore at the water's edge. [2]He taught them many things by parables, and in his teaching said: [3]"Listen! A farmer went out to sow his seed. [4]As he was scattering the seed, some fell along the path, and the birds came and ate it up. [5]Some fell on rocky places, where it did not have much soil. It sprang up quickly, because the soil was shallow. [6]But when the sun came up, the plants were scorched, and they withered because they had no root. [7]Other seed fell among thorns, which grew up and choked the plants, so that they did not bear grain. [8]Still other seed fell on good soil. It came up, grew and produced a crop, multiplying thirty, sixty, or even a hundred times."

[9]Then Jesus said, "He who has ears to hear, let him hear."

[10]When he was alone, the Twelve and the others around him asked him about the parables. [11]He told them, "The secret of the kingdom of God has been given to you. But to those on the outside everything is said in parables [12]so that,

"'they may be ever seeing but never
        perceiving,
    and ever hearing but never
        understanding;
otherwise they might turn and be
        forgiven!'[a]"

[13]Then Jesus said to them, "Don't you understand this parable? How then will you understand any parable? [14]The farmer sows the word. [15]Some people are like seed along the path, where the word is sown. As soon as they hear it, Satan comes and takes away the word that was sown in them. [16]Others, like seed sown on rocky places, hear the word and at once receive it with joy. [17]But since they have no root, they last only a short time. When trouble or persecution comes because of the word, they quickly fall away. [18]Still others, like seed sown among thorns, hear the word; [19]but the worries of this life, the deceitfulness of wealth and the desires for other things come in and choke the word, making it unfruitful. [20]Others, like seed sown on good soil, hear the word, accept it, and produce a crop—thirty, sixty or even a hundred times what was sown."

[21]He said to them, "Do you bring in a lamp to put it under a bowl or a bed? Instead, don't you put it on its stand? [22]For whatever is hidden is meant to be disclosed, and whatever is concealed is meant to be brought out into the open. [23]If anyone has ears to hear, let him hear."

[24]"Consider carefully what you hear," he continued. "With the measure you use, it will be measured to you—and even more. [25]Whoever has will be given

more; whoever does not have, even what
he has will be taken from him."

a 12 Isaiah 6:9,10

PSALM 37:12-29
¹²The wicked plot against the
        righteous
    and gnash their teeth at them;
¹³but the Lord laughs at the wicked,
    for he knows their day is coming.

¹⁴The wicked draw the sword
    and bend the bow
  to bring down the poor and needy,
    to slay those whose ways are
        upright.
¹⁵But their swords will pierce their
        own hearts,
    and their bows will be broken.

¹⁶Better the little that the righteous
        have
    than the wealth of many wicked;
¹⁷for the power of the wicked will be
        broken,
    but the Lord upholds the
        righteous.

¹⁸The days of the blameless are known
        to the Lord,
    and their inheritance will endure
        forever.
¹⁹In times of disaster they will not
        wither;
    in days of famine they will enjoy
        plenty.

²⁰But the wicked will perish:
    The Lord's enemies will be like the
        beauty of the fields,
    they will vanish—vanish like
        smoke.

²¹The wicked borrow and do not repay,
    but the righteous give generously;
²²those the Lord blesses will inherit
        the land,
    but those he curses will be cut off.

²³If the Lord delights in a man's way,
    he makes his steps firm;
²⁴though he stumble, he will not fall,
    for the Lord upholds him with
        his hand.

²⁵I was young and now I am old,
    yet I have never seen the righteous
        forsaken
    or their children begging bread.
²⁶They are always generous and lend
        freely;
    their children will be blessed.

²⁷Turn from evil and do good;
    then you will dwell in the land
        forever.
²⁸For the Lord loves the just
    and will not forsake his faithful
        ones.

    They will be protected forever,
        but the offspring of the wicked
            will be cut off;
²⁹the righteous will inherit the land
    and dwell in it forever.

PROVERBS 10:5
⁵He who gathers crops in summer is a
        wise son,
    but he who sleeps during harvest
        is a disgraceful son.

□ DAY 51

GOD SIGHTINGS

February 20

LEVITICUS 9:7–10:20
Moses said to Aaron, "Come to the altar
and sacrifice your sin offering and your
burnt offering and make atonement for
yourself and the people; sacrifice the
offering that is for the people and make
atonement for them, as the Lord has
commanded."

⁸So Aaron came to the altar and
slaughtered the calf as a sin offering for
himself. ⁹His sons brought the blood to
him, and he dipped his finger into the
blood and put it on the horns of the altar; the rest of the blood he poured out
at the base of the altar. ¹⁰On the altar he
burned the fat, the kidneys and the covering of the liver from the sin offering,

as the Lord commanded Moses; [11]the flesh and the hide he burned up outside the camp.

[12]Then he slaughtered the burnt offering. His sons handed him the blood, and he sprinkled it against the altar on all sides. [13]They handed him the burnt offering piece by piece, including the head, and he burned them on the altar. [14]He washed the inner parts and the legs and burned them on top of the burnt offering on the altar.

[15]Aaron then brought the offering that was for the people. He took the goat for the people's sin offering and slaughtered it and offered it for a sin offering as he did with the first one.

[16]He brought the burnt offering and offered it in the prescribed way. [17]He also brought the grain offering, took a handful of it and burned it on the altar in addition to the morning's burnt offering.

[18]He slaughtered the ox and the ram as the fellowship offering for the people. His sons handed him the blood, and he sprinkled it against the altar on all sides. [19]But the fat portions of the ox and the ram—the fat tail, the layer of fat, the kidneys and the covering of the liver— [20]these they laid on the breasts, and then Aaron burned the fat on the altar. [21]Aaron waved the breasts and the right thigh before the Lord as a wave offering, as Moses commanded.

[22]Then Aaron lifted his hands toward the people and blessed them. And having sacrificed the sin offering, the burnt offering and the fellowship offering, he stepped down.

[23]Moses and Aaron then went into the Tent of Meeting. When they came out, they blessed the people; and the glory of the Lord appeared to all the people. [24]Fire came out from the presence of the Lord and consumed the burnt offering and the fat portions on the altar. And when all the people saw it, they shouted for joy and fell facedown.

[10:1]Aaron's sons Nadab and Abihu took their censers, put fire in them and added incense; and they offered unauthorized fire before the Lord, contrary to his command. [2]So fire came out from the presence of the Lord and consumed them, and they died before the Lord. [3]Moses then said to Aaron, "This is what the Lord spoke of when he said:

"'Among those who approach me
I will show myself holy;
in the sight of all the people
I will be honored.'"

Aaron remained silent.

[4]Moses summoned Mishael and Elzaphan, sons of Aaron's uncle Uzziel, and said to them, "Come here; carry your cousins outside the camp, away from the front of the sanctuary." [5]So they came and carried them, still in their tunics, outside the camp, as Moses ordered.

[6]Then Moses said to Aaron and his sons Eleazar and Ithamar, "Do not let your hair become unkempt,[a] and do not tear your clothes, or you will die and the Lord will be angry with the whole community. But your relatives, all the house of Israel, may mourn for those the Lord has destroyed by fire. [7]Do not leave the entrance to the Tent of Meeting or you will die, because the Lord's anointing oil is on you." So they did as Moses said.

[8]Then the Lord said to Aaron, [9]"You and your sons are not to drink wine or other fermented drink whenever you go into the Tent of Meeting, or you will die. This is a lasting ordinance for the generations to come. [10]You must distinguish between the holy and the common, between the unclean and the clean, [11]and you must teach the Israelites all the decrees the Lord has given them through Moses."

[12]Moses said to Aaron and his remaining sons, Eleazar and Ithamar, "Take the grain offering left over from the offerings made to the Lord by fire and eat it prepared without yeast beside the altar, for it is most holy. [13]Eat it in a holy place, because it is your share and your sons' share of the offerings made to the Lord by fire; for so I have been

commanded. [14]But you and your sons and your daughters may eat the breast that was waved and the thigh that was presented. Eat them in a ceremonially clean place; they have been given to you and your children as your share of the Israelites' fellowship offerings.[b] [15]The thigh that was presented and the breast that was waved must be brought with the fat portions of the offerings made by fire, to be waved before the Lord as a wave offering. This will be the regular share for you and your children, as the Lord has commanded."

[16]When Moses inquired about the goat of the sin offering and found that it had been burned up, he was angry with Eleazar and Ithamar, Aaron's remaining sons, and asked, [17]"Why didn't you eat the sin offering in the sanctuary area? It is most holy; it was given to you to take away the guilt of the community by making atonement for them before the Lord. [18]Since its blood was not taken into the Holy Place, you should have eaten the goat in the sanctuary area, as I commanded."

[19]Aaron replied to Moses, "Today they sacrificed their sin offering and their burnt offering before the Lord, but such things as this have happened to me. Would the Lord have been pleased if I had eaten the sin offering today?" [20]When Moses heard this, he was satisfied.

a 6 Or Do not uncover your heads   b 14 Traditionally peace offerings

MARK 4:26–5:20

He [Jesus] also said, "This is what the kingdom of God is like. A man scatters seed on the ground. [27]Night and day, whether he sleeps or gets up, the seed sprouts and grows, though he does not know how. [28]All by itself the soil produces grain—first the stalk, then the head, then the full kernel in the head. [29]As soon as the grain is ripe, he puts the sickle to it, because the harvest has come."

[30]Again he said, "What shall we say the kingdom of God is like, or what par-able shall we use to describe it? [31]It is like a mustard seed, which is the smallest seed you plant in the ground. [32]Yet when planted, it grows and becomes the largest of all garden plants, with such big branches that the birds of the air can perch in its shade."

[33]With many similar parables Jesus spoke the word to them, as much as they could understand. [34]He did not say anything to them without using a parable. But when he was alone with his own disciples, he explained everything.

[35]That day when evening came, he said to his disciples, "Let us go over to the other side." [36]Leaving the crowd behind, they took him along, just as he was, in the boat. There were also other boats with him. [37]A furious squall came up, and the waves broke over the boat, so that it was nearly swamped. [38]Jesus was in the stern, sleeping on a cushion. The disciples woke him and said to him, "Teacher, don't you care if we drown?"

[39]He got up, rebuked the wind and said to the waves, "Quiet! Be still!" Then the wind died down and it was completely calm.

[40]He said to his disciples, "Why are you so afraid? Do you still have no faith?"

[41]They were terrified and asked each other, "Who is this? Even the wind and the waves obey him!"

[5:1]They went across the lake to the region of the Gerasenes.[a] [2]When Jesus got out of the boat, a man with an evil[b] spirit came from the tombs to meet him. [3]This man lived in the tombs, and no one could bind him any more, not even with a chain. [4]For he had often been chained hand and foot, but he tore the chains apart and broke the irons on his feet. No one was strong enough to subdue him. [5]Night and day among the tombs and in the hills he would cry out and cut himself with stones.

[6]When he saw Jesus from a distance, he ran and fell on his knees in front of him. [7]He shouted at the top of his voice, "What do you want with me, Jesus, Son

of the Most High God? Swear to God that you won't torture me!" [8]For Jesus had said to him, "Come out of this man, you evil spirit!"

[9]Then Jesus asked him, "What is your name?"

"My name is Legion," he replied, "for we are many." [10]And he begged Jesus again and again not to send them out of the area.

[11]A large herd of pigs was feeding on the nearby hillside. [12]The demons begged Jesus, "Send us among the pigs; allow us to go into them." [13]He gave them permission, and the evil spirits came out and went into the pigs. The herd, about two thousand in number, rushed down the steep bank into the lake and were drowned.

[14]Those tending the pigs ran off and reported this in the town and countryside, and the people went out to see what had happened. [15]When they came to Jesus, they saw the man who had been possessed by the legion of demons, sitting there, dressed and in his right mind; and they were afraid. [16]Those who had seen it told the people what had happened to the demon-possessed man— and told about the pigs as well. [17]Then the people began to plead with Jesus to leave their region.

[18]As Jesus was getting into the boat, the man who had been demon-possessed begged to go with him. [19]Jesus did not let him, but said, "Go home to your family and tell them how much the Lord has done for you, and how he has had mercy on you." [20]So the man went away and began to tell in the Decapolis[c] how much Jesus had done for him. And all the people were amazed.

[a]1 Some manuscripts Gadarenes; other manuscripts Gergesenes   [b]2 Greek unclean; also in verses 8 and 13   [c]20 That is, the Ten Cities

PSALM 37:30-40

[30]The mouth of the righteous man
    utters wisdom,
  and his tongue speaks what is just.
[31]The law of his God is in his heart;
  his feet do not slip.

[32]The wicked lie in wait for the
    righteous,
  seeking their very lives;
[33]but the Lord will not leave them in
    their power
  or let them be condemned when
    brought to trial.

[34]Wait for the Lord
  and keep his way.
He will exalt you to inherit the land;
  when the wicked are cut off, you
    will see it.

[35]I have seen a wicked and ruthless
    man
  flourishing like a green tree in its
    native soil,
[36]but he soon passed away and was no
    more;
  though I looked for him, he could
    not be found.

[37]Consider the blameless, observe the
    upright;
  there is a future[a] for the man of
    peace.
[38]But all sinners will be destroyed;
  the future[b] of the wicked will be
    cut off.

[39]**The salvation of the righteous
    comes from the Lord;
  he is their stronghold in time of
    trouble.**
[40]**The Lord helps them and delivers
    them;
  he delivers them from the
    wicked and saves them,
  because they take refuge in him.**

[a]37 Or there will be posterity   [b]38 Or posterity

PROVERBS 10:6-7

[6]**B**lessings crown the head of the
    righteous,
  but violence overwhelms the
    mouth of the wicked.[a]

[7]The memory of the righteous will be
    a blessing,
  but the name of the wicked will
    rot.

[a]6 Or but the mouth of the wicked conceals violence; also in verse 11

GOD SIGHTINGS

February 21

LEVITICUS 11:1–12:8

The LORD said to Moses and Aaron, 2"Say to the Israelites: 'Of all the animals that live on land, these are the ones you may eat: 3You may eat any animal that has a split hoof completely divided and that chews the cud.

4"'There are some that only chew the cud or only have a split hoof, but you must not eat them. The camel, though it chews the cud, does not have a split hoof; it is ceremonially unclean for you. 5The coney,a though it chews the cud, does not have a split hoof; it is unclean for you. 6The rabbit, though it chews the cud, does not have a split hoof; it is unclean for you. 7And the pig, though it has a split hoof completely divided, does not chew the cud; it is unclean for you. 8You must not eat their meat or touch their carcasses; they are unclean for you.

9"'Of all the creatures living in the water of the seas and the streams, you may eat any that have fins and scales. 10But all creatures in the seas or streams that do not have fins and scales—whether among all the swarming things or among all the other living creatures in the water—you are to detest. 11And since you are to detest them, you must not eat their meat and you must detest their carcasses. 12Anything living in the water that does not have fins and scales is to be detestable to you.

13"'These are the birds you are to detest and not eat because they are detestable: the eagle, the vulture, the black vulture, 14the red kite, any kind of black kite, 15any kind of raven, 16the horned owl, the screech owl, the gull, any kind of hawk, 17the little owl, the cormorant, the great owl, 18the white owl, the desert owl, the osprey, 19the stork, any kind of heron, the hoopoe and the bat.b

20"'All flying insects that walk on all fours are to be detestable to you. 21There are, however, some winged creatures that walk on all fours that you may eat: those that have jointed legs for hopping on the ground. 22Of these you may eat any kind of locust, katydid, cricket or grasshopper. 23But all other winged creatures that have four legs you are to detest.

24"'You will make yourselves unclean by these; whoever touches their carcasses will be unclean till evening. 25Whoever picks up one of their carcasses must wash his clothes, and he will be unclean till evening.

26"'Every animal that has a split hoof not completely divided or that does not chew the cud is unclean for you; whoever touches ⌞the carcass of⌟ any of them will be unclean. 27Of all the animals that walk on all fours, those that walk on their paws are unclean for you; whoever touches their carcasses will be unclean till evening. 28Anyone who picks up their carcasses must wash his clothes, and he will be unclean till evening. They are unclean for you.

29"'Of the animals that move about on the ground, these are unclean for you: the weasel, the rat, any kind of great lizard, 30the gecko, the monitor lizard, the wall lizard, the skink and the chameleon. 31Of all those that move along the ground, these are unclean for you. Whoever touches them when they are dead will be unclean till evening. 32When one of them dies and falls on something, that article, whatever its use, will be unclean, whether it is made of wood, cloth, hide or sackcloth. Put it in water; it will be unclean till evening, and then it will be clean. 33If one of them falls into a clay pot, everything in it will be unclean, and you must break the pot. 34Any food that could be eaten but has water on it from such a pot is unclean, and any liquid that could be drunk from it is unclean. 35Anything that one of their carcasses falls on becomes unclean; an oven or cooking pot must be broken up. They are unclean, and you are to regard them as unclean. [36]A spring, however, or a cistern for collecting water remains clean, but anyone who touches one of these carcasses is unclean. [37]If a carcass falls on any seeds that are to be planted, they remain clean. [38]But if water has been put on the seed and a carcass falls on it, it is unclean for you.

[39]"'If an animal that you are allowed to eat dies, anyone who touches the carcass will be unclean till evening. [40]Anyone who eats some of the carcass must wash his clothes, and he will be unclean till evening. Anyone who picks up the carcass must wash his clothes, and he will be unclean till evening.

[41]"'Every creature that moves about on the ground is detestable; it is not to be eaten. [42]You are not to eat any creature that moves about on the ground, whether it moves on its belly or walks on all fours or on many feet; it is detestable. [43]Do not defile yourselves by any of these creatures. Do not make yourselves unclean by means of them or be made unclean by them. [44]I am the LORD your God; consecrate yourselves and be holy, because I am holy. Do not make yourselves unclean by any creature that moves about on the ground. [45]**I am the LORD who brought you up out of Egypt to be your God; therefore be holy, because I am holy.**

[46]"'These are the regulations concerning animals, birds, every living thing that moves in the water and every creature that moves about on the ground. [47]You must distinguish between the unclean and the clean, between living creatures that may be eaten and those that may not be eaten.'"

[12:1]THE LORD said to Moses, [2]"Say to the Israelites: 'A woman who becomes pregnant and gives birth to a son will be ceremonially unclean for seven days, just as she is unclean during her monthly period. [3]On the eighth day the boy is to be circumcised. [4]Then the woman must wait thirty-three days to be purified from her bleeding. She must not touch anything sacred or go to the sanctuary

until the days of her purification are over. [5]If she gives birth to a daughter, for two weeks the woman will be unclean, as during her period. Then she must wait sixty-six days to be purified from her bleeding.

[6]"'When the days of her purification for a son or daughter are over, she is to bring to the priest at the entrance to the Tent of Meeting a year-old lamb for a burnt offering and a young pigeon or a dove for a sin offering. [7]He shall offer them before the LORD to make atonement for her, and then she will be ceremonially clean from her flow of blood.

" 'These are the regulations for the woman who gives birth to a boy or a girl. [8]If she cannot afford a lamb, she is to bring two doves or two young pigeons, one for a burnt offering and the other for a sin offering. In this way the priest will make atonement for her, and she will be clean.'"

[a]5 That is, the hyrax or rock badger   [b]19 The precise identification of some of the birds, insects and animals in this chapter is uncertain.

MARK 5:21-43

When Jesus had again crossed over by boat to the other side of the lake, a large crowd gathered around him while he was by the lake. [22]Then one of the synagogue rulers, named Jairus, came there. Seeing Jesus, he fell at his feet [23]and pleaded earnestly with him, "My little daughter is dying. Please come and put your hands on her so that she will be healed and live." [24]So Jesus went with him.

A large crowd followed and pressed around him. [25]And a woman was there who had been subject to bleeding for twelve years. [26]She had suffered a great deal under the care of many doctors and had spent all she had, yet instead of getting better she grew worse. [27]When she heard about Jesus, she came up behind him in the crowd and touched his cloak, [28]because she thought, "If I just touch his clothes, I will be healed." [29]Immediately her bleeding stopped and she felt in her body that she was freed from her suffering.

³⁰At once Jesus realized that power had gone out from him. He turned around in the crowd and asked, "Who touched my clothes?"

³¹"You see the people crowding against you," his disciples answered, "and yet you can ask, 'Who touched me?'"

³²But Jesus kept looking around to see who had done it. ³³Then the woman, knowing what had happened to her, came and fell at his feet and, trembling with fear, told him the whole truth. ³⁴He said to her, "Daughter, your faith has healed you. Go in peace and be freed from your suffering."

³⁵While Jesus was still speaking, some men came from the house of Jairus, the synagogue ruler. "Your daughter is dead," they said. "Why bother the teacher any more?"

³⁶Ignoring what they said, Jesus told the synagogue ruler, "Don't be afraid; just believe."

³⁷He did not let anyone follow him except Peter, James and John the brother of James. ³⁸When they came to the home of the synagogue ruler, Jesus saw a commotion, with people crying and wailing loudly. ³⁹He went in and said to them, "Why all this commotion and wailing? The child is not dead but asleep." ⁴⁰But they laughed at him.

After he put them all out, he took the child's father and mother and the disciples who were with him, and went in where the child was. ⁴¹He took her by the hand and said to her, "*Talitha koum!*" (which means, "Little girl, I say to you, get up!"). ⁴²Immediately the girl stood up and walked around (she was twelve years old). At this they were completely astonished. ⁴³He gave strict orders not to let anyone know about this, and told them to give her something to eat.

PSALM 38:1-22
A psalm of David. A petition.

¹ **O** LORD, do not rebuke me in your anger
    or discipline me in your wrath.
²For your arrows have pierced me,
    and your hand has come down
        upon me.
³Because of your wrath there is no
        health in my body;
    my bones have no soundness
        because of my sin.
⁴My guilt has overwhelmed me
    like a burden too heavy to bear.

⁵My wounds fester and are loathsome
    because of my sinful folly.
⁶I am bowed down and brought
        very low;
    all day long I go about mourning.
⁷My back is filled with searing pain;
    there is no health in my body.
⁸I am feeble and utterly crushed;
    I groan in anguish of heart.

⁹All my longings lie open before you,
        O Lord;
    my sighing is not hidden
        from you.
¹⁰My heart pounds, my strength
        fails me;
    even the light has gone from
        my eyes.
¹¹My friends and companions avoid
        me because of my wounds;
    my neighbors stay far away.
¹²Those who seek my life set their
        traps,
    those who would harm me talk
        of my ruin;
    all day long they plot deception.

¹³I am like a deaf man, who cannot
        hear,
    like a mute, who cannot open his
        mouth;
¹⁴I have become like a man who does
        not hear,
    whose mouth can offer no reply.
¹⁵I wait for you, O LORD;
    you will answer, O Lord my God.
¹⁶For I said, "Do not let them gloat
    or exalt themselves over me when
        my foot slips."

¹⁷For I am about to fall,
    and my pain is ever with me.
¹⁸I confess my iniquity;
    I am troubled by my sin.

[19]Many are those who are my vigorous
    enemies;
      those who hate me without reason
      are numerous.
[20]Those who repay my good with evil
      slander me when I pursue what
      is good.

[21]O LORD, do not forsake me;
      be not far from me, O my God.
[22]Come quickly to help me,
      O Lord my Savior.

PROVERBS 10:8-9

[8]The wise in heart accept commands,
    but a chattering fool comes
    to ruin.

[9]The man of integrity walks securely,
    but he who takes crooked paths
    will be found out.

☐ D A Y   5 3

GOD SIGHTINGS

February 22

LEVITICUS 13:1-59

The LORD said to Moses and Aaron,
[2]"When anyone has a swelling or a rash
or a bright spot on his skin that may become an infectious skin disease,[a] he
must be brought to Aaron the priest or
to one of his sons[b] who is a priest. [3]The
priest is to examine the sore on his skin,
and if the hair in the sore has turned
white and the sore appears to be more
than skin deep,[c] it is an infectious skin
disease. When the priest examines him,
he shall pronounce him ceremonially
unclean. [4]If the spot on his skin is white
but does not appear to be more than
skin deep and the hair in it has not
turned white, the priest is to put the infected person in isolation for seven
days. [5]On the seventh day the priest is to
examine him, and if he sees that the
sore is unchanged and has not spread in
the skin, he is to keep him in isolation

another seven days. [6]On the seventh
day the priest is to examine him again,
and if the sore has faded and has not
spread in the skin, the priest shall pronounce him clean; it is only a rash. The
man must wash his clothes, and he will
be clean. [7]But if the rash does spread in
his skin after he has shown himself to
the priest to be pronounced clean, he
must appear before the priest again.
[8]The priest is to examine him, and if the
rash has spread in the skin, he shall pronounce him unclean; it is an infectious
disease.

[9]"When anyone has an infectious
skin disease, he must be brought to the
priest. [10]The priest is to examine him,
and if there is a white swelling in the
skin that has turned the hair white and
if there is raw flesh in the swelling, [11]it
is a chronic skin disease and the priest
shall pronounce him unclean. He is not
to put him in isolation, because he is already unclean.

[12]"If the disease breaks out all over his
skin and, so far as the priest can see, it
covers all the skin of the infected person
from head to foot, [13]the priest is to examine him, and if the disease has covered his whole body, he shall pronounce
that person clean. Since it has all turned
white, he is clean. [14]But whenever raw
flesh appears on him, he will be unclean.
[15]When the priest sees the raw flesh, he
shall pronounce him unclean. The raw
flesh is unclean; he has an infectious disease. [16]Should the raw flesh change and
turn white, he must go to the priest.
[17]The priest is to examine him, and if the
sores have turned white, the priest shall
pronounce the infected person clean;
then he will be clean.

[18]"When someone has a boil on his
skin and it heals, [19]and in the place
where the boil was, a white swelling or
reddish-white spot appears, he must
present himself to the priest. [20]The
priest is to examine it, and if it appears
to be more than skin deep and the hair
in it has turned white, the priest shall
pronounce him unclean. It is an infectious skin disease that has broken out

where the boil was. ²¹But if, when the priest examines it, there is no white hair in it and it is not more than skin deep and has faded, then the priest is to put him in isolation for seven days. ²²If it is spreading in the skin, the priest shall pronounce him unclean; it is infectious. ²³But if the spot is unchanged and has not spread, it is only a scar from the boil, and the priest shall pronounce him clean.

²⁴"When someone has a burn on his skin and a reddish-white or white spot appears in the raw flesh of the burn, ²⁵the priest is to examine the spot, and if the hair in it has turned white, and it appears to be more than skin deep, it is an infectious disease that has broken out in the burn. The priest shall pronounce him unclean; it is an infectious skin disease. ²⁶But if the priest examines it and there is no white hair in the spot and if it is not more than skin deep and has faded, then the priest is to put him in isolation for seven days. ²⁷On the seventh day the priest is to examine him, and if it is spreading in the skin, the priest shall pronounce him unclean; it is an infectious skin disease. ²⁸If, however, the spot is unchanged and has not spread in the skin but has faded, it is a swelling from the burn, and the priest shall pronounce him clean; it is only a scar from the burn.

²⁹"If a man or woman has a sore on the head or on the chin, ³⁰the priest is to examine the sore, and if it appears to be more than skin deep and the hair in it is yellow and thin, the priest shall pronounce that person unclean; it is an itch, an infectious disease of the head or chin. ³¹But if, when the priest examines this kind of sore, it does not seem to be more than skin deep and there is no black hair in it, then the priest is to put the infected person in isolation for seven days. ³²On the seventh day the priest is to examine the sore, and if the itch has not spread and there is no yellow hair in it and it does not appear to be more than skin deep, ³³he must be shaved except for the diseased area,

and the priest is to keep him in isolation another seven days. ³⁴On the seventh day the priest is to examine the itch, and if it has not spread in the skin and appears to be no more than skin deep, the priest shall pronounce him clean. He must wash his clothes, and he will be clean. ³⁵But if the itch does spread in the skin after he is pronounced clean, ³⁶the priest is to examine him, and if the itch has spread in the skin, the priest does not need to look for yellow hair; the person is unclean. ³⁷If, however, in his judgment it is unchanged and black hair has grown in it, the itch is healed. He is clean, and the priest shall pronounce him clean.

³⁸"When a man or woman has white spots on the skin, ³⁹the priest is to examine them, and if the spots are dull white, it is a harmless rash that has broken out on the skin; that person is clean.

⁴⁰"When a man has lost his hair and is bald, he is clean. ⁴¹If he has lost his hair from the front of his scalp and has a bald forehead, he is clean. ⁴²But if he has a reddish-white sore on his bald head or forehead, it is an infectious disease breaking out on his head or forehead. ⁴³The priest is to examine him, and if the swollen sore on his head or forehead is reddish-white like an infectious skin disease, ⁴⁴the man is diseased and is unclean. The priest shall pronounce him unclean because of the sore on his head.

⁴⁵"The person with such an infectious disease must wear torn clothes, let his hair be unkempt,ᵈ cover the lower part of his face and cry out, 'Unclean! Unclean!' ⁴⁶As long as he has the infection he remains unclean. He must live alone; he must live outside the camp.

⁴⁷"If any clothing is contaminated with mildew—any woolen or linen clothing, ⁴⁸any woven or knitted material of linen or wool, any leather or anything made of leather— ⁴⁹and if the contamination in the clothing, or leather, or woven or knitted material, or any leather article, is greenish or reddish, it is a spreading mildew and must

be shown to the priest. [50]The priest is to examine the mildew and isolate the affected article for seven days. [51]On the seventh day he is to examine it, and if the mildew has spread in the clothing, or the woven or knitted material, or the leather, whatever its use, it is a destructive mildew; the article is unclean. [52]He must burn up the clothing, or the woven or knitted material of wool or linen, or any leather article that has the contamination in it, because the mildew is destructive; the article must be burned up.

[53]"But if, when the priest examines it, the mildew has not spread in the clothing, or the woven or knitted material, or the leather article, [54]he shall order that the contaminated article be washed. Then he is to isolate it for another seven days. [55]After the affected article has been washed, the priest is to examine it, and if the mildew has not changed its appearance, even though it has not spread, it is unclean. Burn it with fire, whether the mildew has affected one side or the other. [56]If, when the priest examines it, the mildew has faded after the article has been washed, he is to tear the contaminated part out of the clothing, or the leather, or the woven or knitted material. [57]But if it reappears in the clothing, or in the woven or knitted material, or in the leather article, it is spreading, and whatever has the mildew must be burned with fire. [58]The clothing, or the woven or knitted material, or any leather article that has been washed and is rid of the mildew, must be washed again, and it will be clean."

[59]These are the regulations concerning contamination by mildew in woolen or linen clothing, woven or knitted material, or any leather article, for pronouncing them clean or unclean.

a2 Traditionally *leprosy*; the Hebrew word was used for various diseases affecting the skin—not necessarily leprosy; also elsewhere in this chapter. *b2* Or *descendants* *c3* Or *be lower than the rest of the skin*; also elsewhere in this chapter *d45* Or *clothes, uncover his head*

MARK 6:1-29

Jesus left there [the house of Jairus] and went to his hometown, accompanied by his disciples. [2]When the Sabbath came, he began to teach in the synagogue, and many who heard him were amazed.

"Where did this man get these things?" they asked. "What's this wisdom that has been given him, that he even does miracles! [3]Isn't this the carpenter? Isn't this Mary's son and the brother of James, Joseph,*a* Judas and Simon? Aren't his sisters here with us?" And they took offense at him.

[4]Jesus said to them, "Only in his hometown, among his relatives and in his own house is a prophet without honor." [5]He could not do any miracles there, except lay his hands on a few sick people and heal them. [6]And he was amazed at their lack of faith.

Then Jesus went around teaching from village to village. [7]Calling the Twelve to him, he sent them out two by two and gave them authority over evil*b* spirits.

[8]These were his instructions: "Take nothing for the journey except a staff— no bread, no bag, no money in your belts. [9]Wear sandals but not an extra tunic. [10]Whenever you enter a house, stay there until you leave that town. [11]And if any place will not welcome you or listen to you, shake the dust off your feet when you leave, as a testimony against them."

[12]They went out and preached that people should repent. [13]They drove out many demons and anointed many sick people with oil and healed them.

[14]King Herod heard about this, for Jesus' name had become well known. Some were saying,*c* "John the Baptist has been raised from the dead, and that is why miraculous powers are at work in him."

[15]Others said, "He is Elijah."

And still others claimed, "He is a prophet, like one of the prophets of long ago."

[16]But when Herod heard this, he said, "John, the man I beheaded, has been raised from the dead!"

[17]For Herod himself had given orders to have John arrested, and he had him

bound and put in prison. He did this because of Herodias, his brother Philip's wife, whom he had married. [18]For John had been saying to Herod, "It is not lawful for you to have your brother's wife." [19]So Herodias nursed a grudge against John and wanted to kill him. But she was not able to, [20]because Herod feared John and protected him, knowing him to be a righteous and holy man. When Herod heard John, he was greatly puzzled[d]; yet he liked to listen to him.

[21]Finally the opportune time came. On his birthday Herod gave a banquet for his high officials and military commanders and the leading men of Galilee. [22]When the daughter of Herodias came in and danced, she pleased Herod and his dinner guests.

The king said to the girl, "Ask me for anything you want, and I'll give it to you." [23]And he promised her with an oath, "Whatever you ask I will give you, up to half my kingdom."

[24]She went out and said to her mother, "What shall I ask for?"

"The head of John the Baptist," she answered.

[25]At once the girl hurried in to the king with the request: "I want you to give me right now the head of John the Baptist on a platter."

[26]The king was greatly distressed, but because of his oaths and his dinner guests, he did not want to refuse her. [27]So he immediately sent an executioner with orders to bring John's head. The man went, beheaded John in the prison, [28]and brought back his head on a platter. He presented it to the girl, and she gave it to her mother. [29]On hearing of this, John's disciples came and took his body and laid it in a tomb.

a3 Greek Joses, a variant of Joseph   b7 Greek unclean   c14 Some early manuscripts He was saying   d20 Some early manuscripts he did many things

PSALM 39:1-13
For the director of music. For Jeduthun. A psalm of David.

[1] I said, "I will watch my ways
    and keep my tongue from sin;

I will put a muzzle on my mouth
    as long as the wicked are in my
        presence."
[2] But when I was silent and still,
    not even saying anything good,
    my anguish increased.
[3] My heart grew hot within me,
    and as I meditated, the fire
        burned;
    then I spoke with my tongue:

[4] **"Show me, O Lord, my life's end
    and the number of my days;
    let me know how fleeting is
        my life.**
[5] **You have made my days a mere
        handbreadth;
    the span of my years is as
        nothing before you.
    Each man's life is but a breath.**
                                Selah
[6] Man is a mere phantom as he goes to
        and fro:
    He bustles about, but only in vain;
    he heaps up wealth, not knowing
        who will get it.

[7] "But now, Lord, what do I look for?
    My hope is in you.
[8] Save me from all my transgressions;
    do not make me the scorn of
        fools.
[9] I was silent; I would not open my
        mouth,
    for you are the one who has done
        this.
[10] Remove your scourge from me;
    I am overcome by the blow of your
        hand.
[11] You rebuke and discipline men for
        their sin;
    you consume their wealth like a
        moth—
    each man is but a breath.   *Selah*

[12] "Hear my prayer, O Lord,
    listen to my cry for help;
    be not deaf to my weeping.
For I dwell with you as an alien,
    a stranger, as all my fathers were.
[13] Look away from me, that I may
        rejoice again
    before I depart and am no more."

PROVERBS 10:10

¹⁰He who winks maliciously causes
   grief,
   and a chattering fool comes
      to ruin.

□ D A Y 5 4

GOD SIGHTINGS

February 23

LEVITICUS 14:1-57

The LORD said to Moses, ²"These are the
regulations for the diseased person at
the time of his ceremonial cleansing,
when he is brought to the priest: ³The
priest is to go outside the camp and examine him. If the person has been
healed of his infectious skin disease,ᵃ
⁴the priest shall order that two live clean
birds and some cedar wood, scarlet yarn
and hyssop be brought for the one to be
cleansed. ⁵Then the priest shall order
that one of the birds be killed over fresh
water in a clay pot. ⁶He is then to take the
live bird and dip it, together with the cedar wood, the scarlet yarn and the hyssop, into the blood of the bird that was
killed over the fresh water. ⁷Seven times
he shall sprinkle the one to be cleansed
of the infectious disease and pronounce
him clean. Then he is to release the live
bird in the open fields.

⁸"The person to be cleansed must
wash his clothes, shave off all his hair
and bathe with water; then he will be
ceremonially clean. After this he may
come into the camp, but he must stay
outside his tent for seven days. ⁹On the
seventh day he must shave off all his
hair; he must shave his head, his beard,
his eyebrows and the rest of his hair. He
must wash his clothes and bathe himself with water, and he will be clean.

¹⁰"On the eighth day he must bring
two male lambs and one ewe lamb a
year old, each without defect, along
with three-tenths of an ephahᵇ of fine
flour mixed with oil for a grain offering,
and one logᶜ of oil. ¹¹The priest who
pronounces him clean shall present
both the one to be cleansed and his offerings before the LORD at the entrance
to the Tent of Meeting.

¹²"Then the priest is to take one of
the male lambs and offer it as a guilt offering, along with the log of oil; he shall
wave them before the LORD as a wave offering. ¹³He is to slaughter the lamb in
the holy place where the sin offering
and the burnt offering are slaughtered.
Like the sin offering, the guilt offering
belongs to the priest; it is most holy.
¹⁴The priest is to take some of the blood
of the guilt offering and put it on the
lobe of the right ear of the one to be
cleansed, on the thumb of his right
hand and on the big toe of his right foot.
¹⁵The priest shall then take some of the
log of oil, pour it in the palm of his own
left hand, ¹⁶dip his right forefinger into
the oil in his palm, and with his finger
sprinkle some of it before the LORD
seven times. ¹⁷The priest is to put some
of the oil remaining in his palm on the
lobe of the right ear of the one to be
cleansed, on the thumb of his right
hand and on the big toe of his right foot,
on top of the blood of the guilt offering.
¹⁸The rest of the oil in his palm the
priest shall put on the head of the one to
be cleansed and make atonement for
him before the LORD.

¹⁹"Then the priest is to sacrifice the
sin offering and make atonement for
the one to be cleansed from his uncleanness. After that, the priest shall
slaughter the burnt offering ²⁰and offer
it on the altar, together with the grain offering, and make atonement for him,
and he will be clean.

²¹"If, however, he is poor and cannot
afford these, he must take one male
lamb as a guilt offering to be waved to
make atonement for him, together with
a tenth of an ephahᵈ of fine flour mixed
with oil for a grain offering, a log of oil,
²²and two doves or two young pigeons,
which he can afford, one for a sin offering and the other for a burnt offering.

23"On the eighth day he must bring them for his cleansing to the priest at the entrance to the Tent of Meeting, before the LORD. 24The priest is to take the lamb for the guilt offering, together with the log of oil, and wave them before the LORD as a wave offering. 25He shall slaughter the lamb for the guilt offering and take some of its blood and put it on the lobe of the right ear of the one to be cleansed, on the thumb of his right hand and on the big toe of his right foot. 26The priest is to pour some of the oil into the palm of his own left hand, 27and with his right forefinger sprinkle some of the oil from his palm seven times before the LORD. 28Some of the oil in his palm he is to put on the same places he put the blood of the guilt offering—on the lobe of the right ear of the one to be cleansed, on the thumb of his right hand and on the big toe of his right foot. 29The rest of the oil in his palm the priest shall put on the head of the one to be cleansed, to make atonement for him before the LORD. 30Then he shall sacrifice the doves or the young pigeons, which the person can afford, 31one*e* as a sin offering and the other as a burnt offering, together with the grain offering. In this way the priest will make atonement before the LORD on behalf of the one to be cleansed."

32These are the regulations for anyone who has an infectious skin disease and who cannot afford the regular offerings for his cleansing.

33The LORD said to Moses and Aaron, 34"When you enter the land of Canaan, which I am giving you as your possession, and I put a spreading mildew in a house in that land, 35the owner of the house must go and tell the priest, 'I have seen something that looks like mildew in my house.' 36The priest is to order the house to be emptied before he goes in to examine the mildew, so that nothing in the house will be pronounced unclean. After this the priest is to go in and inspect the house. 37He is to examine the mildew on the walls, and if it has greenish or reddish depressions that appear to be deeper than the surface of the wall, 38the priest shall go out the doorway of the house and close it up for seven days. 39On the seventh day the priest shall return to inspect the house. If the mildew has spread on the walls, 40he is to order that the contaminated stones be torn out and thrown into an unclean place outside the town. 41He must have all the inside walls of the house scraped and the material that is scraped off dumped into an unclean place outside the town. 42Then they are to take other stones to replace these and take new clay and plaster the house.

43"If the mildew reappears in the house after the stones have been torn out and the house scraped and plastered, 44the priest is to go and examine it and, if the mildew has spread in the house, it is a destructive mildew; the house is unclean. 45It must be torn down—its stones, timbers and all the plaster—and taken out of the town to an unclean place.

46"Anyone who goes into the house while it is closed up will be unclean till evening. 47Anyone who sleeps or eats in the house must wash his clothes.

48"But if the priest comes to examine it and the mildew has not spread after the house has been plastered, he shall pronounce the house clean, because the mildew is gone. 49To purify the house he is to take two birds and some cedar wood, scarlet yarn and hyssop. 50He shall kill one of the birds over fresh water in a clay pot. 51Then he is to take the cedar wood, the hyssop, the scarlet yarn and the live bird, dip them into the blood of the dead bird and the fresh water, and sprinkle the house seven times. 52He shall purify the house with the bird's blood, the fresh water, the live bird, the cedar wood, the hyssop and the scarlet yarn. 53Then he is to release the live bird in the open fields outside the town. In this way he will make atonement for the house, and it will be clean."

54These are the regulations for any infectious skin disease, for an itch, 55for mildew in clothing or in a house,

⁵⁶and for a swelling, a rash or a bright spot, ⁵⁷to determine when something is clean or unclean.

These are the regulations for infectious skin diseases and mildew.

a3 Traditionally *leprosy;* the Hebrew word was used for various diseases affecting the skin—not necessarily leprosy; also elsewhere in this chapter. *b10* That is, probably about 6 quarts (about 6.5 liters) *c10* That is, probably about 2/3 pint (about 0.3 liter); also in verses 12, 15, 21 and 24 *d21* That is, probably about 2 quarts (about 2 liters) *e31* Septuagint and Syriac; Hebrew *³¹such as the person can afford, one*

MARK 6:30-56

The apostles gathered around Jesus and reported to him all they had done and taught. ³¹Then, because so many people were coming and going that they did not even have a chance to eat, he said to them, "Come with me by yourselves to a quiet place and get some rest."

³²So they went away by themselves in a boat to a solitary place. ³³But many who saw them leaving recognized them and ran on foot from all the towns and got there ahead of them. ³⁴When Jesus landed and saw a large crowd, he had compassion on them, because they were like sheep without a shepherd. So he began teaching them many things.

³⁵By this time it was late in the day, so his disciples came to him. "This is a remote place," they said, "and it's already very late. ³⁶Send the people away so they can go to the surrounding countryside and villages and buy themselves something to eat."

³⁷But he answered, "You give them something to eat."

They said to him, "That would take eight months of a man's wages*a*! Are we to go and spend that much on bread and give it to them to eat?"

³⁸"How many loaves do you have?" he asked. "Go and see."

When they found out, they said, "Five—and two fish."

³⁹Then Jesus directed them to have all the people sit down in groups on the green grass. ⁴⁰So they sat down in groups of hundreds and fifties. ⁴¹Taking the five loaves and the two fish and looking up to heaven, he gave thanks

and broke the loaves. Then he gave them to his disciples to set before the people. He also divided the two fish among them all. ⁴²They all ate and were satisfied, ⁴³and the disciples picked up twelve basketfuls of broken pieces of bread and fish. ⁴⁴The number of the men who had eaten was five thousand.

⁴⁵Immediately Jesus made his disciples get into the boat and go on ahead of him to Bethsaida, while he dismissed the crowd. ⁴⁶After leaving them, he went up on a mountainside to pray.

⁴⁷When evening came, the boat was in the middle of the lake, and he was alone on land. ⁴⁸He saw the disciples straining at the oars, because the wind was against them. About the fourth watch of the night he went out to them, walking on the lake. He was about to pass by them, ⁴⁹but when they saw him walking on the lake, they thought he was a ghost. They cried out, ⁵⁰because they all saw him and were terrified.

Immediately he spoke to them and said, "Take courage! It is I. Don't be afraid." ⁵¹Then he climbed into the boat with them, and the wind died down. They were completely amazed, ⁵²for they had not understood about the loaves; their hearts were hardened.

⁵³When they had crossed over, they landed at Gennesaret and anchored there. ⁵⁴As soon as they got out of the boat, people recognized Jesus. ⁵⁵They ran throughout that whole region and carried the sick on mats to wherever they heard he was. ⁵⁶And wherever he went—into villages, towns or countryside—they placed the sick in the marketplaces. They begged him to let them touch even the edge of his cloak, and all who touched him were healed.

a37 Greek *take two hundred denarii*

PSALM 40:1-10
For the director of music. Of David. A psalm.

¹I waited patiently for the LORD;
  he turned to me and heard
  my cry.

²**He lifted me out of the slimy pit,**
    out of the mud and mire;
he set my feet on a rock
    and gave me a firm place to
        stand.
³He put a new song in my mouth,
    a hymn of praise to our God.
Many will see and fear
    and put their trust in the LORD.

⁴Blessed is the man
    who makes the LORD his trust,
who does not look to the proud,
    to those who turn aside to false
        gods.^a
⁵Many, O LORD my God,
    are the wonders you have done.
The things you planned for us
    no one can recount to you;
were I to speak and tell of them,
    they would be too many to
        declare.

⁶Sacrifice and offering you did not
        desire,
    but my ears you have pierced^{b, c};
burnt offerings and sin offerings
    you did not require.
⁷Then I said, "Here I am, I have
        come—
    it is written about me in the
        scroll.^d
⁸I desire to do your will, O my God;
    your law is within my heart."

⁹I proclaim righteousness in the great
        assembly;
    I do not seal my lips,
        as you know, O LORD.
¹⁰I do not hide your righteousness in
        my heart;
    I speak of your faithfulness and
        salvation.
    I do not conceal your love and your
        truth
        from the great assembly.

^a4 Or *to falsehood*   ^b6 Hebrew; Septuagint *but a body you
have prepared for me* (see also Symmachus and
Theodotion)   ^c6 Or *opened*   ^d7 Or *come / with the scroll
written for me*

PROVERBS 10:11-12
¹¹**T**he mouth of the righteous is a
    fountain of life,

but violence overwhelms the
    mouth of the wicked.

¹²Hatred stirs up dissension,
    but love covers over all wrongs.

☐ D A Y   5 5

GOD SIGHTINGS

February 24

LEVITICUS 15:1–16:28
The LORD said to Moses and Aaron,
²"Speak to the Israelites and say to
them: 'When any man has a bodily discharge, the discharge is unclean.
³Whether it continues flowing from his
body or is blocked, it will make him unclean. This is how his discharge will
bring about uncleanness:

⁴"'Any bed the man with a discharge
lies on will be unclean, and anything he
sits on will be unclean. ⁵Anyone who
touches his bed must wash his clothes
and bathe with water, and he will be unclean till evening. ⁶Whoever sits on anything that the man with a discharge sat
on must wash his clothes and bathe with
water, and he will be unclean till evening.

⁷"'Whoever touches the man who
has a discharge must wash his clothes
and bathe with water, and he will be unclean till evening.

⁸"'If the man with the discharge spits
on someone who is clean, that person
must wash his clothes and bathe with
water, and he will be unclean till evening.

⁹"'Everything the man sits on when
riding will be unclean, ¹⁰and whoever
touches any of the things that were under him will be unclean till evening;
whoever picks up those things must
wash his clothes and bathe with water,
and he will be unclean till evening.

¹¹"'Anyone the man with a discharge
touches without rinsing his hands with
water must wash his clothes and bathe
with water, and he will be unclean till
evening.

¹²"'A clay pot that the man touches must be broken, and any wooden article is to be rinsed with water.

¹³"'When a man is cleansed from his discharge, he is to count off seven days for his ceremonial cleansing; he must wash his clothes and bathe himself with fresh water, and he will be clean. ¹⁴On the eighth day he must take two doves or two young pigeons and come before the LORD to the entrance to the Tent of Meeting and give them to the priest. ¹⁵The priest is to sacrifice them, the one for a sin offering and the other for a burnt offering. In this way he will make atonement before the LORD for the man because of his discharge.

¹⁶"'When a man has an emission of semen, he must bathe his whole body with water, and he will be unclean till evening. ¹⁷Any clothing or leather that has semen on it must be washed with water, and it will be unclean till evening. ¹⁸When a man lies with a woman and there is an emission of semen, both must bathe with water, and they will be unclean till evening.

¹⁹"'When a woman has her regular flow of blood, the impurity of her monthly period will last seven days, and anyone who touches her will be unclean till evening.

²⁰"'Anything she lies on during her period will be unclean, and anything she sits on will be unclean. ²¹Whoever touches her bed must wash his clothes and bathe with water, and he will be unclean till evening. ²²Whoever touches anything she sits on must wash his clothes and bathe with water, and he will be unclean till evening. ²³Whether it is the bed or anything she was sitting on, when anyone touches it, he will be unclean till evening.

²⁴"'If a man lies with her and her monthly flow touches him, he will be unclean for seven days; any bed he lies on will be unclean.

²⁵"'When a woman has a discharge of blood for many days at a time other than her monthly period or has a discharge that continues beyond her period, she will be unclean as long as she has the discharge, just as in the days of her period. ²⁶Any bed she lies on while her discharge continues will be unclean, as is her bed during her monthly period, and anything she sits on will be unclean, as during her period. ²⁷Whoever touches them will be unclean; he must wash his clothes and bathe with water, and he will be unclean till evening.

²⁸"'When she is cleansed from her discharge, she must count off seven days, and after that she will be ceremonially clean. ²⁹On the eighth day she must take two doves or two young pigeons and bring them to the priest at the entrance to the Tent of Meeting. ³⁰The priest is to sacrifice one for a sin offering and the other for a burnt offering. In this way he will make atonement for her before the LORD for the uncleanness of her discharge.

³¹"'You must keep the Israelites separate from things that make them unclean, so they will not die in their uncleanness for defiling my dwelling place,ᵃ which is among them.'"

³²These are the regulations for a man with a discharge, for anyone made unclean by an emission of semen, ³³for a woman in her monthly period, for a man or a woman with a discharge, and for a man who lies with a woman who is ceremonially unclean.

¹⁶:¹THE LORD spoke to Moses after the death of the two sons of Aaron who died when they approached the LORD. ²The LORD said to Moses: "Tell your brother Aaron not to come whenever he chooses into the Most Holy Place behind the curtain in front of the atonement cover on the ark, or else he will die, because I appear in the cloud over the atonement cover.

³"This is how Aaron is to enter the sanctuary area: with a young bull for a sin offering and a ram for a burnt offering. ⁴He is to put on the sacred linen tunic, with linen undergarments next to his body; he is to tie the linen sash around him and put on the linen turban.

These are sacred garments; so he must bathe himself with water before he puts them on. 5From the Israelite community he is to take two male goats for a sin offering and a ram for a burnt offering.

6"Aaron is to offer the bull for his own sin offering to make atonement for himself and his household. 7Then he is to take the two goats and present them before the Lord at the entrance to the Tent of Meeting. 8He is to cast lots for the two goats—one lot for the Lord and the other for the scapegoat.b 9Aaron shall bring the goat whose lot falls to the Lord and sacrifice it for a sin offering. 10But the goat chosen by lot as the scapegoat shall be presented alive before the Lord to be used for making atonement by sending it into the desert as a scapegoat.

11"Aaron shall bring the bull for his own sin offering to make atonement for himself and his household, and he is to slaughter the bull for his own sin offering. 12He is to take a censer full of burning coals from the altar before the Lord and two handfuls of finely ground fragrant incense and take them behind the curtain. 13He is to put the incense on the fire before the Lord, and the smoke of the incense will conceal the atonement cover above the Testimony, so that he will not die. 14He is to take some of the bull's blood and with his finger sprinkle it on the front of the atonement cover; then he shall sprinkle some of it with his finger seven times before the atonement cover.

15"He shall then slaughter the goat for the sin offering for the people and take its blood behind the curtain and do with it as he did with the bull's blood: He shall sprinkle it on the atonement cover and in front of it. 16In this way he will make atonement for the Most Holy Place because of the uncleanness and rebellion of the Israelites, whatever their sins have been. He is to do the same for the Tent of Meeting, which is among them in the midst of their uncleanness. 17No one is to be in the Tent of Meeting from the time Aaron goes in

to make atonement in the Most Holy Place until he comes out, having made atonement for himself, his household and the whole community of Israel.

18"Then he shall come out to the altar that is before the Lord and make atonement for it. He shall take some of the bull's blood and some of the goat's blood and put it on all the horns of the altar. 19He shall sprinkle some of the blood on it with his finger seven times to cleanse it and to consecrate it from the uncleanness of the Israelites.

20"When Aaron has finished making atonement for the Most Holy Place, the Tent of Meeting and the altar, he shall bring forward the live goat. 21He is to lay both hands on the head of the live goat and confess over it all the wickedness and rebellion of the Israelites—all their sins—and put them on the goat's head. He shall send the goat away into the desert in the care of a man appointed for the task. 22The goat will carry on itself all their sins to a solitary place; and the man shall release it in the desert.

23"Then Aaron is to go into the Tent of Meeting and take off the linen garments he put on before he entered the Most Holy Place, and he is to leave them there. 24He shall bathe himself with water in a holy place and put on his regular garments. Then he shall come out and sacrifice the burnt offering for himself and the burnt offering for the people, to make atonement for himself and for the people. 25He shall also burn the fat of the sin offering on the altar.

26"The man who releases the goat as a scapegoat must wash his clothes and bathe himself with water; afterward he may come into the camp. 27The bull and the goat for the sin offerings, whose blood was brought into the Most Holy Place to make atonement, must be taken outside the camp; their hides, flesh and offal are to be burned up. 28The man who burns them must wash his clothes and bathe himself with water; afterward he may come into the camp."

a31 Or *my tabernacle*   b8 That is, the goat of removal; Hebrew *azazel*; also in verses 10 and 26

MARK 7:1-23

The Pharisees and some of the teachers of the law who had come from Jerusalem gathered around Jesus and ²saw some of his disciples eating food with hands that were "unclean," that is, unwashed. ³(The Pharisees and all the Jews do not eat unless they give their hands a ceremonial washing, holding to the tradition of the elders. ⁴When they come from the marketplace they do not eat unless they wash. And they observe many other traditions, such as the washing of cups, pitchers and kettles.ᵃ)

⁵So the Pharisees and teachers of the law asked Jesus, "Why don't your disciples live according to the tradition of the elders instead of eating their food with 'unclean' hands?"

⁶He replied, "Isaiah was right when he prophesied about you hypocrites; as it is written:

"'These people honor me with
        their lips,
    but their hearts are far from me.
⁷ They worship me in vain;
        their teachings are but rules
            taught by men.'ᵇ

⁸You have let go of the commands of God and are holding on to the traditions of men."

⁹And he said to them: "You have a fine way of setting aside the commands of God in order to observeᶜ your own traditions! ¹⁰For Moses said, 'Honor your father and your mother,'ᵈ and, 'Anyone who curses his father or mother must be put to death.'ᵉ ¹¹But you say that if a man says to his father or mother: 'Whatever help you might otherwise have received from me is Corban' (that is, a gift devoted to God), ¹²then you no longer let him do anything for his father or mother. ¹³Thus you nullify the word of God by your tradition that you have handed down. And you do many things like that."

¹⁴**Again Jesus called the crowd to him and said, "Listen to me, everyone, and understand this. ¹⁵Nothing**

outside a man can make him 'unclean' by going into him. Rather, it is what comes out of a man that makes him 'unclean.'ᶠ "

¹⁷After he had left the crowd and entered the house, his disciples asked him about this parable. ¹⁸"Are you so dull?" he asked. "Don't you see that nothing that enters a man from the outside can make him 'unclean'? ¹⁹For it doesn't go into his heart but into his stomach, and then out of his body." (In saying this, Jesus declared all foods "clean.")

²⁰He went on: "What comes out of a man is what makes him 'unclean.' ²¹For from within, out of men's hearts, come evil thoughts, sexual immorality, theft, murder, adultery, ²²greed, malice, deceit, lewdness, envy, slander, arrogance and folly. ²³All these evils come from inside and make a man 'unclean.'"

ᵃ4 Some early manuscripts *pitchers, kettles and dining couches*   ᵇ6,7 Isaiah 29:13   ᶜ9 Some manuscripts *set up*   ᵈ10 Exodus 20:12; Deut. 5:16   ᵉ10 Exodus 21:17; Lev. 20:9   ᶠ15 Some early manuscripts *'unclean.'* ¹⁶*If anyone has ears to hear, let him hear.*

PSALM 40:11-17

¹¹**D**o not withhold your mercy from
        me, O Lᴏʀᴅ;
    may your love and your truth
        always protect me.
¹²For troubles without number
        surround me;
    my sins have overtaken me, and
        I cannot see.
    They are more than the hairs of
        my head,
    and my heart fails within me.

¹³Be pleased, O Lᴏʀᴅ, to save me;
    O Lᴏʀᴅ, come quickly to help me.
¹⁴May all who seek to take my life
        be put to shame and confusion;
    may all who desire my ruin
        be turned back in disgrace.
¹⁵May those who say to me, "Aha! Aha!"
        be appalled at their own shame.
¹⁶But may all who seek you
        rejoice and be glad in you;
    may those who love your salvation
        always say,
    "The Lᴏʀᴅ be exalted!"

17 Yet I am poor and needy;
      may the Lord think of me.
   You are my help and my deliverer;
      O my God, do not delay.

PROVERBS 10:13-14

13 **W**isdom is found on the lips of the
      discerning,
   but a rod is for the back of him
      who lacks judgment.

14 Wise men store up knowledge,
      but the mouth of a fool invites
      ruin.

□ DAY 56

GOD SIGHTINGS

February 25

LEVITICUS 16:29–18:30

"**T**his is to be a lasting ordinance for you
[the Israelites]: On the tenth day of the
seventh month you must deny yourselves*a* and not do any work—whether
native-born or an alien living among
you— 30 because on this day atonement
will be made for you, to cleanse you.
Then, before the LORD, you will be clean
from all your sins. 31 It is a sabbath of rest,
and you must deny yourselves; it is a lasting ordinance. 32 The priest who is
anointed and ordained to succeed his father as high priest is to make atonement.
He is to put on the sacred linen garments
33 and make atonement for the Most
Holy Place, for the Tent of Meeting and
the altar, and for the priests and all the
people of the community.

34 "This is to be a lasting ordinance
for you: Atonement is to be made once a
year for all the sins of the Israelites."

   And it was done, as the LORD commanded Moses.

17:1 THE LORD said to Moses, 2 "Speak to
Aaron and his sons and to all the Israel-
ites and say to them: 'This is what the
LORD has commanded: 3 Any Israelite

who sacrifices an ox,*b* a lamb or a goat in
the camp or outside of it 4 instead of
bringing it to the entrance to the Tent of
Meeting to present it as an offering to
the LORD in front of the tabernacle of
the LORD—that man shall be considered
guilty of bloodshed; he has shed blood
and must be cut off from his people.
5 This is so the Israelites will bring to the
LORD the sacrifices they are now making
in the open fields. They must bring
them to the priest, that is, to the LORD, at
the entrance to the Tent of Meeting and
sacrifice them as fellowship offerings.*c*
6 The priest is to sprinkle the blood
against the altar of the LORD at the entrance to the Tent of Meeting and burn
the fat as an aroma pleasing to the LORD.
7 They must no longer offer any of their
sacrifices to the goat idols*d* to whom
they prostitute themselves. This is to be
a lasting ordinance for them and for the
generations to come.'

   8 "Say to them: 'Any Israelite or any
alien living among them who offers a
burnt offering or sacrifice 9 and does not
bring it to the entrance to the Tent of
Meeting to sacrifice it to the LORD—that
man must be cut off from his people.

   10 "Any Israelite or any alien living
among them who eats any blood—I will
set my face against that person who eats
blood and will cut him off from his people. 11 For the life of a creature is in the
blood, and I have given it to you to make
atonement for yourselves on the altar; it
is the blood that makes atonement for
one's life. 12 Therefore I say to the Israelites, "None of you may eat blood, nor
may an alien living among you eat
blood."

   13 "Any Israelite or any alien living
among you who hunts any animal or
bird that may be eaten must drain out
the blood and cover it with earth, 14 because the life of every creature is its
blood. That is why I have said to the Israelites, "You must not eat the blood of
any creature, because the life of every
creature is its blood; anyone who eats it
must be cut off."

   15 'Anyone, whether native-born or

alien, who eats anything found dead or torn by wild animals must wash his clothes and bathe with water, and he will be ceremonially unclean till evening; then he will be clean. ¹⁶But if he does not wash his clothes and bathe himself, he will be held responsible.'"

¹⁸:¹THE LORD said to Moses, ²"Speak to the Israelites and say to them: 'I am the LORD your God. ³You must not do as they do in Egypt, where you used to live, and you must not do as they do in the land of Canaan, where I am bringing you. Do not follow their practices. ⁴You must obey my laws and be careful to follow my decrees. I am the LORD your God. ⁵Keep my decrees and laws, for the man who obeys them will live by them. I am the LORD.

⁶" 'No one is to approach any close relative to have sexual relations. I am the LORD.

⁷" 'Do not dishonor your father by having sexual relations with your mother. She is your mother; do not have relations with her.

⁸" 'Do not have sexual relations with your father's wife; that would dishonor your father.

⁹" 'Do not have sexual relations with your sister, either your father's daughter or your mother's daughter, whether she was born in the same home or elsewhere.

¹⁰" 'Do not have sexual relations with your son's daughter or your daughter's daughter; that would dishonor you.

¹¹" 'Do not have sexual relations with the daughter of your father's wife, born to your father; she is your sister.

¹²" 'Do not have sexual relations with your father's sister; she is your father's close relative.

¹³" 'Do not have sexual relations with your mother's sister, because she is your mother's close relative.

¹⁴" 'Do not dishonor your father's brother by approaching his wife to have sexual relations; she is your aunt.

¹⁵" 'Do not have sexual relations with your daughter-in-law. She is your son's wife; do not have relations with her.

¹⁶" 'Do not have sexual relations with your brother's wife; that would dishonor your brother.

¹⁷" 'Do not have sexual relations with both a woman and her daughter. Do not have sexual relations with either her son's daughter or her daughter's daughter; they are her close relatives. That is wickedness.

¹⁸" 'Do not take your wife's sister as a rival wife and have sexual relations with her while your wife is living.

¹⁹" 'Do not approach a woman to have sexual relations during the uncleanness of her monthly period.

²⁰" 'Do not have sexual relations with your neighbor's wife and defile yourself with her.

²¹" 'Do not give any of your children to be sacrificedᵉ to Molech, for you must not profane the name of your God. I am the LORD.

²²" 'Do not lie with a man as one lies with a woman; that is detestable.

²³" 'Do not have sexual relations with an animal and defile yourself with it. A woman must not present herself to an animal to have sexual relations with it; that is a perversion.

²⁴" 'Do not defile yourselves in any of these ways, because this is how the nations that I am going to drive out before you became defiled. ²⁵Even the land was defiled; so I punished it for its sin, and the land vomited out its inhabitants. ²⁶But you must keep my decrees and my laws. The native-born and the aliens living among you must not do any of these detestable things, ²⁷for all these things were done by the people who lived in the land before you, and the land became defiled. ²⁸And if you defile the land, it will vomit you out as it vomited out the nations that were before you.

²⁹" 'Everyone who does any of these detestable things—such persons must be cut off from their people. ³⁰Keep my requirements and do not follow any of the detestable customs that were

practiced before you came and do not defile yourselves with them. I am the LORD your God.'"

a29 Or *must fast;* also in verse 31   *b3* The Hebrew word can include both male and female.   *c5* Traditionally *peace offerings*   *d7* Or *demons*   *e21* Or *to be passed through ⌊the fire⌋*

MARK 7:24–8:10

Jesus left that place and went to the vicinity of Tyre.*a* He entered a house and did not want anyone to know it; yet he could not keep his presence secret. 25 In fact, as soon as she heard about him, a woman whose little daughter was possessed by an evil*b* spirit came and fell at his feet. 26 The woman was a Greek, born in Syrian Phoenicia. She begged Jesus to drive the demon out of her daughter.

27 "First let the children eat all they want," he told her, "for it is not right to take the children's bread and toss it to their dogs."

28 "Yes, Lord," she replied, "but even the dogs under the table eat the children's crumbs."

29 Then he told her, "For such a reply, you may go; the demon has left your daughter."

30 She went home and found her child lying on the bed, and the demon gone.

31 Then Jesus left the vicinity of Tyre and went through Sidon, down to the Sea of Galilee and into the region of the Decapolis.*c* 32 There some people brought to him a man who was deaf and could hardly talk, and they begged him to place his hand on the man.

33 After he took him aside, away from the crowd, Jesus put his fingers into the man's ears. Then he spit and touched the man's tongue. 34 He looked up to heaven and with a deep sigh said to him, *"Ephphatha!"* (which means, "Be opened!"). 35 At this, the man's ears were opened, his tongue was loosened and he began to speak plainly.

36 Jesus commanded them not to tell anyone. But the more he did so, the more they kept talking about it. 37 People were overwhelmed with amazement. "He has done everything well," they said. "He even makes the deaf hear and the mute speak."

8:1 DURING those days another large crowd gathered. Since they had nothing to eat, Jesus called his disciples to him and said, 2 "I have compassion for these people; they have already been with me three days and have nothing to eat. 3 If I send them home hungry, they will collapse on the way, because some of them have come a long distance."

4 His disciples answered, "But where in this remote place can anyone get enough bread to feed them?"

5 "How many loaves do you have?" Jesus asked.

"Seven," they replied.

6 He told the crowd to sit down on the ground. When he had taken the seven loaves and given thanks, he broke them and gave them to his disciples to set before the people, and they did so. 7 They had a few small fish as well; he gave thanks for them also and told the disciples to distribute them. 8 The people ate and were satisfied. Afterward the disciples picked up seven basketfuls of broken pieces that were left over. 9 About four thousand men were present. And having sent them away, 10 he got into the boat with his disciples and went to the region of Dalmanutha.

a24 Many early manuscripts *Tyre and Sidon*   *b25* Greek *unclean*   *c31* That is, the Ten Cities

PSALM 41:1-13

For the director of music. A psalm of David.

1 Blessed is he who has regard for
    the weak;
  the LORD delivers him in times
    of trouble.
2 The LORD will protect him and
    preserve his life;
  he will bless him in the land
  and not surrender him to the
    desire of his foes.
3 The LORD will sustain him on his
    sickbed
  and restore him from his bed of
    illness.

⁴I said, "O LORD, have mercy on me;
    heal me, for I have sinned against
    you."
⁵My enemies say of me in malice,
    "When will he die and his name
    perish?"
⁶Whenever one comes to see me,
    he speaks falsely, while his heart
        gathers slander;
    then he goes out and spreads it
        abroad.

⁷All my enemies whisper together
        against me;
    they imagine the worst for me,
        saying,
⁸"A vile disease has beset him;
    he will never get up from the place
        where he lies."
⁹Even my close friend, whom I
        trusted,
    he who shared my bread,
    has lifted up his heel against me.

¹⁰But you, O LORD, have mercy on me;
    raise me up, that I may repay them.
¹¹I know that you are pleased with me,
    for my enemy does not triumph
        over me.
¹²In my integrity you uphold me
    and set me in your presence
        forever.

¹³Praise be to the LORD, the God of
        Israel,
    from everlasting to everlasting.
        Amen and Amen.

PROVERBS 10:15-16
¹⁵The wealth of the rich is their
        fortified city,
    but poverty is the ruin of
        the poor.

¹⁶The wages of the righteous bring
        them life,
    but the income of the wicked
        brings them punishment.

☐ DAY 57

GOD SIGHTINGS

February 26

LEVITICUS 19:1–20:21
The LORD said to Moses, ²"Speak to the entire assembly of Israel and say to them: 'Be holy because I, the LORD your God, am holy.

³" 'Each of you must respect his mother and father, and you must observe my Sabbaths. I am the LORD your God.

⁴" 'Do not turn to idols or make gods of cast metal for yourselves. I am the LORD your God.

⁵" 'When you sacrifice a fellowship offeringᵃ to the LORD, sacrifice it in such a way that it will be accepted on your behalf. ⁶It shall be eaten on the day you sacrifice it or on the next day; anything left over until the third day must be burned up. ⁷If any of it is eaten on the third day, it is impure and will not be accepted. ⁸Whoever eats it will be held responsible because he has desecrated what is holy to the LORD; that person must be cut off from his people.

⁹" 'When you reap the harvest of your land, do not reap to the very edges of your field or gather the gleanings of your harvest. ¹⁰Do not go over your vineyard a second time or pick up the grapes that have fallen. Leave them for the poor and the alien. I am the LORD your God.

¹¹" 'Do not steal.

" 'Do not lie.

" 'Do not deceive one another.

¹²" 'Do not swear falsely by my name and so profane the name of your God. I am the LORD.

¹³" 'Do not defraud your neighbor or rob him.

" 'Do not hold back the wages of a hired man overnight.

¹⁴" 'Do not curse the deaf or put a stumbling block in front of the blind, but fear your God. I am the LORD.

15 " 'Do not pervert justice; do not show partiality to the poor or favoritism to the great, but judge your neighbor fairly.

16 " 'Do not go about spreading slander among your people.

" 'Do not do anything that endangers your neighbor's life. I am the LORD.

17 " 'Do not hate your brother in your heart. Rebuke your neighbor frankly so you will not share in his guilt.

18 " 'Do not seek revenge or bear a grudge against one of your people, but love your neighbor as yourself. I am the LORD.

19 " 'Keep my decrees.

" 'Do not mate different kinds of animals.

" 'Do not plant your field with two kinds of seed.

" 'Do not wear clothing woven of two kinds of material.

20 " 'If a man sleeps with a woman who is a slave girl promised to another man but who has not been ransomed or given her freedom, there must be due punishment. Yet they are not to be put to death, because she had not been freed. 21 The man, however, must bring a ram to the entrance to the Tent of Meeting for a guilt offering to the LORD. 22 With the ram of the guilt offering the priest is to make atonement for him before the LORD for the sin he has committed, and his sin will be forgiven.

23 " 'When you enter the land and plant any kind of fruit tree, regard its fruit as forbidden.b For three years you are to consider it forbiddenb; it must not be eaten. 24 In the fourth year all its fruit will be holy, an offering of praise to the LORD. 25 But in the fifth year you may eat its fruit. In this way your harvest will be increased. I am the LORD your God.

26 " 'Do not eat any meat with the blood still in it.

" 'Do not practice divination or sorcery.

27 " 'Do not cut the hair at the sides of your head or clip off the edges of your beard.

28 " 'Do not cut your bodies for the dead or put tattoo marks on yourselves. I am the LORD.

29 " 'Do not degrade your daughter by making her a prostitute, or the land will turn to prostitution and be filled with wickedness.

30 " 'Observe my Sabbaths and have reverence for my sanctuary. I am the LORD.

31 " 'Do not turn to mediums or seek out spiritists, for you will be defiled by them. I am the LORD your God.

32 " 'Rise in the presence of the aged, show respect for the elderly and revere your God. I am the LORD.

33 " 'When an alien lives with you in your land, do not mistreat him. 34 The alien living with you must be treated as one of your native-born. Love him as yourself, for you were aliens in Egypt. I am the LORD your God.

35 " 'Do not use dishonest standards when measuring length, weight or quantity. 36 Use honest scales and honest weights, an honest ephahc and an honest hin.d I am the LORD your God, who brought you out of Egypt.

37 " 'Keep all my decrees and all my laws and follow them. I am the LORD.'"

20:1 THE LORD said to Moses, 2 "Say to the Israelites: 'Any Israelite or any alien living in Israel who givese any of his children to Molech must be put to death. The people of the community are to stone him. 3 I will set my face against that man and I will cut him off from his people; for by giving his children to Molech, he has defiled my sanctuary and profaned my holy name. 4 If the people of the community close their eyes when that man gives one of his children to Molech and they fail to put him to death, 5 I will set my face against that man and his family and will cut off from their people both him and all who follow him in prostituting themselves to Molech.

6 " 'I will set my face against the person who turns to mediums and spiritists to prostitute himself by following them, and I will cut him off from his people.

7 " 'Consecrate yourselves and be holy, because I am the LORD your God. 8Keep my decrees and follow them. I am the LORD, who makes you holy.*f*

9 " 'If anyone curses his father or mother, he must be put to death. He has cursed his father or his mother, and his blood will be on his own head.

10 " 'If a man commits adultery with another man's wife—with the wife of his neighbor—both the adulterer and the adulteress must be put to death.

11 " 'If a man sleeps with his father's wife, he has dishonored his father. Both the man and the woman must be put to death; their blood will be on their own heads.

12 " 'If a man sleeps with his daughter-in-law, both of them must be put to death. What they have done is a perversion; their blood will be on their own heads.

13 " 'If a man lies with a man as one lies with a woman, both of them have done what is detestable. They must be put to death; their blood will be on their own heads.

14 " 'If a man marries both a woman and her mother, it is wicked. Both he and they must be burned in the fire, so that no wickedness will be among you.

15 " 'If a man has sexual relations with an animal, he must be put to death, and you must kill the animal.

16 " 'If a woman approaches an animal to have sexual relations with it, kill both the woman and the animal. They must be put to death; their blood will be on their own heads.

17 " 'If a man marries his sister, the daughter of either his father or his mother, and they have sexual relations, it is a disgrace. They must be cut off before the eyes of their people. He has dishonored his sister and will be held responsible.

18 " 'If a man lies with a woman during her monthly period and has sexual relations with her, he has exposed the source of her flow, and she has also uncovered it. Both of them must be cut off from their people.

19 " 'Do not have sexual relations with the sister of either your mother or your father, for that would dishonor a close relative; both of you would be held responsible.

20 " 'If a man sleeps with his aunt, he has dishonored his uncle. They will be held responsible; they will die childless.

21 " 'If a man marries his brother's wife, it is an act of impurity; he has dishonored his brother. They will be childless.' "

a5 Traditionally *peace offering*   *b23* Hebrew *uncircumcised*   *c36* An ephah was a dry measure.   *d36* A hin was a liquid measure.   *e2* Or *sacrifices*; also in verses 3 and 4   *f8* Or *who sanctifies you*; or *who sets you apart as holy*

MARK 8:11-38

The Pharisees came and began to question Jesus. To test him, they asked him for a sign from heaven. 12He sighed deeply and said, "Why does this generation ask for a miraculous sign? I tell you the truth, no sign will be given to it." 13Then he left them, got back into the boat and crossed to the other side.

14The disciples had forgotten to bring bread, except for one loaf they had with them in the boat. 15"Be careful," Jesus warned them. "Watch out for the yeast of the Pharisees and that of Herod."

16They discussed this with one another and said, "It is because we have no bread."

17Aware of their discussion, Jesus asked them: "Why are you talking about having no bread? Do you still not see or understand? Are your hearts hardened? 18Do you have eyes but fail to see, and ears but fail to hear? And don't you remember? 19When I broke the five loaves for the five thousand, how many basketfuls of pieces did you pick up?"

"Twelve," they replied.

20"And when I broke the seven loaves for the four thousand, how many basketfuls of pieces did you pick up?"

They answered, "Seven."

21He said to them, "Do you still not understand?"

22They came to Bethsaida, and some people brought a blind man and begged

Jesus to touch him. ²³He took the blind man by the hand and led him outside the village. When he had spit on the man's eyes and put his hands on him, Jesus asked, "Do you see anything?"

²⁴He looked up and said, "I see people; they look like trees walking around."

²⁵Once more Jesus put his hands on the man's eyes. Then his eyes were opened, his sight was restored, and he saw everything clearly. ²⁶Jesus sent him home, saying, "Don't go into the village.ᵃ"

²⁷Jesus and his disciples went on to the villages around Caesarea Philippi. On the way he asked them, "Who do people say I am?"

²⁸They replied, "Some say John the Baptist; others say Elijah; and still others, one of the prophets."

²⁹"But what about you?" he asked. "Who do you say I am?"

Peter answered, "You are the Christ.ᵇ"

³⁰Jesus warned them not to tell anyone about him.

³¹He then began to teach them that the Son of Man must suffer many things and be rejected by the elders, chief priests and teachers of the law, and that he must be killed and after three days rise again. ³²He spoke plainly about this, and Peter took him aside and began to rebuke him.

³³But when Jesus turned and looked at his disciples, he rebuked Peter. "Get behind me, Satan!" he said. "You do not have in mind the things of God, but the things of men."

³⁴Then he called the crowd to him along with his disciples and said: "If anyone would come after me, he must deny himself and take up his cross and follow me. ³⁵For whoever wants to save his lifeᶜ will lose it, but whoever loses his life for me and for the gospel will save it. ³⁶What good is it for a man to gain the whole world, yet forfeit his soul? ³⁷Or what can a man give in exchange for his soul? ³⁸If anyone is ashamed of me and my words in this adulterous and sinful generation, the Son of Man will be ashamed of him

when he comes in his Father's glory with the holy angels."

ᵃ26 Some manuscripts *Don't go and tell anyone in the village*   ᵇ29 Or *Messiah*. "The Christ" (Greek) and "the Messiah" (Hebrew) both mean "the Anointed One."   ᶜ35 The Greek word means either *life* or *soul*; also in verse 36.

PSALM 42:1-11ᵃ

For the director of music. A *maskil*ᵇ of the Sons of Korah.

¹ **As the deer pants for streams of water,**
  so my soul pants for you,
    O God.
² **My soul thirsts for God, for the living God.**
  When can I go and meet with God?
³ My tears have been my food
    day and night,
  while men say to me all day long,
    "Where is your God?"
⁴ These things I remember
    as I pour out my soul:
  how I used to go with the multitude,
    leading the procession to the
      house of God,
  with shouts of joy and thanksgiving
    among the festive throng.

⁵ Why are you downcast, O my soul?
    Why so disturbed within me?
  Put your hope in God,
    for I will yet praise him,
    my Savior and ⁶my God.

Myᶜ soul is downcast within me;
    therefore I will remember you
  from the land of the Jordan,
    the heights of Hermon—from
      Mount Mizar.
⁷ Deep calls to deep
    in the roar of your waterfalls;
  all your waves and breakers
    have swept over me.

⁸ By day the LORD directs his love,
    at night his song is with me—
  a prayer to the God of my life.

⁹ I say to God my Rock,
    "Why have you forgotten me?
  Why must I go about mourning,
    oppressed by the enemy?"

¹⁰My bones suffer mortal agony
as my foes taunt me,
saying to me all day long,
"Where is your God?"

¹¹Why are you downcast, O my soul?
Why so disturbed within me?
Put your hope in God,
for I will yet praise him,
my Savior and my God.

^aIn many Hebrew manuscripts Psalms 42 and 43 constitute
one psalm. ^bTitle: Probably a literary or musical term
^c5,6 A few Hebrew manuscripts, Septuagint and Syriac;
most Hebrew manuscripts *praise him for his saving
help.* / ⁶O my God, my

PROVERBS 10:17

¹⁷He who heeds discipline shows the
way to life,
but whoever ignores correction
leads others astray.

□ DAY 58

GOD SIGHTINGS

February 27

LEVITICUS 20:22–22:16

" 'Keep all my [the Lord's] decrees and
laws and follow them, so that the land
where I am bringing you [the Israelites]
to live may not vomit you out. ²³You
must not live according to the customs
of the nations I am going to drive out before you. Because they did all these
things, I abhorred them. ²⁴But I said to
you, "You will possess their land; I will
give it to you as an inheritance, a land
flowing with milk and honey." I am the
Lord your God, who has set you apart
from the nations.

²⁵" 'You must therefore make a dis-
tinction between clean and unclean animals and between unclean and clean
birds. Do not defile yourselves by any
animal or bird or anything that moves
along the ground—those which I have
set apart as unclean for you. ²⁶You are to
be holy to me^a because I, the Lord, am

holy, and I have set you apart from the
nations to be my own.

²⁷" 'A man or woman who is a medium
or spiritist among you must be put to
death. You are to stone them; their
blood will be on their own heads.' "

^{21:1}The Lord said to Moses, "Speak to
the priests, the sons of Aaron, and say to
them: 'A priest must not make himself
ceremonially unclean for any of his peo-
ple who die, ²except for a close relative,
such as his mother or father, his son or
daughter, his brother, ³or an unmarried
sister who is dependent on him since
she has no husband—for her he may
make himself unclean. ⁴He must not
make himself unclean for people re-
lated to him by marriage,^b and so defile
himself.

⁵" 'Priests must not shave their heads
or shave off the edges of their beards or
cut their bodies. ⁶They must be holy to
their God and must not profane the
name of their God. Because they present the offerings made to the Lord by
fire, the food of their God, they are to be
holy.

⁷" 'They must not marry women de-
filed by prostitution or divorced from
their husbands, because priests are holy
to their God. ⁸Regard them as holy, because they offer up the food of your
God. Consider them holy, because I the
Lord am holy—I who make you holy.^c

⁹" 'If a priest's daughter defiles her-
self by becoming a prostitute, she disgraces her father; she must be burned in
the fire.

¹⁰" 'The high priest, the one among
his brothers who has had the anointing
oil poured on his head and who has
been ordained to wear the priestly garments, must not let his hair become un-
kempt^d or tear his clothes. ¹¹He must
not enter a place where there is a dead
body. He must not make himself unclean, even for his father or mother,
¹²nor leave the sanctuary of his God or
desecrate it, because he has been dedicated by the anointing oil of his God. I
am the Lord.

13"'The woman he marries must be a virgin. 14He must not marry a widow, a divorced woman, or a woman defiled by prostitution, but only a virgin from his own people, 15so he will not defile his offspring among his people. I am the LORD, who makes him holy.ᵉ'"

16The LORD said to Moses, 17"Say to Aaron: 'For the generations to come none of your descendants who has a defect may come near to offer the food of his God. 18No man who has any defect may come near: no man who is blind or lame, disfigured or deformed; 19no man with a crippled foot or hand, 20or who is hunchbacked or dwarfed, or who has any eye defect, or who has festering or running sores or damaged testicles. 21No descendant of Aaron the priest who has any defect is to come near to present the offerings made to the LORD by fire. He has a defect; he must not come near to offer the food of his God. 22He may eat the most holy food of his God, as well as the holy food; 23yet because of his defect, he must not go near the curtain or approach the altar, and so desecrate my sanctuary. I am the LORD, who makes them holy.ᶠ'"

24So Moses told this to Aaron and his sons and to all the Israelites.

22:1THE LORD said to Moses, 2"Tell Aaron and his sons to treat with respect the sacred offerings the Israelites consecrate to me, so they will not profane my holy name. I am the LORD.

3"Say to them: 'For the generations to come, if any of your descendants is ceremonially unclean and yet comes near the sacred offerings that the Israelites consecrate to the LORD, that person must be cut off from my presence. I am the LORD.

4"'If a descendant of Aaron has an infectious skin diseaseᵍ or a bodily discharge, he may not eat the sacred offerings until he is cleansed. He will also be unclean if he touches something defiled by a corpse or by anyone who has an emission of semen, 5or if he touches any crawling thing that makes

him unclean, or any person who makes him unclean, whatever the uncleanness may be. 6The one who touches any such thing will be unclean till evening. He must not eat any of the sacred offerings unless he has bathed himself with water. 7When the sun goes down, he will be clean, and after that he may eat the sacred offerings, for they are his food. 8He must not eat anything found dead or torn by wild animals, and so become unclean through it. I am the LORD.

9"'The priests are to keep my requirements so that they do not become guilty and die for treating them with contempt. I am the LORD, who makes them holy.ʰ

10"'No one outside a priest's family may eat the sacred offering, nor may the guest of a priest or his hired worker eat it. 11But if a priest buys a slave with money, or if a slave is born in his household, that slave may eat his food. 12If a priest's daughter marries anyone other than a priest, she may not eat any of the sacred contributions. 13But if a priest's daughter becomes a widow or is divorced, yet has no children, and she returns to live in her father's house as in her youth, she may eat of her father's food. No unauthorized person, however, may eat any of it.

14"'If anyone eats a sacred offering by mistake, he must make restitution to the priest for the offering and add a fifth of the value to it. 15The priests must not desecrate the sacred offerings the Israelites present to the LORD 16by allowing them to eat the sacred offerings and so bring upon them guilt requiring payment. I am the LORD, who makes them holy.'"

ᵃ26 Or be my holy ones   ᵇ4 Or unclean as a leader among his people   ᶜ8 Or who sanctify you; or who set you apart as holy   ᵈ10 Or not uncover his head   ᵉ15 Or who sanctifies him; or who sets him apart as holy   ᶠ23 Or who sanctifies them; or who sets them apart as holy   ᵍ4 Traditionally leprosy; the Hebrew word was used for various diseases affecting the skin—not necessarily leprosy.   ʰ9 Or who sanctifies them; or who sets them apart as holy; also in verse 16

MARK 9:1-29

And he [Jesus] said to them [his disciples], "I tell you the truth, some who are standing here will not taste death before they see the kingdom of God come with power."

[2] After six days Jesus took Peter, James and John with him and led them up a high mountain, where they were all alone. There he was transfigured before them. [3] His clothes became dazzling white, whiter than anyone in the world could bleach them. [4] And there appeared before them Elijah and Moses, who were talking with Jesus.

[5] Peter said to Jesus, "Rabbi, it is good for us to be here. Let us put up three shelters—one for you, one for Moses and one for Elijah." [6] (He did not know what to say, they were so frightened.)

[7] Then a cloud appeared and enveloped them, and a voice came from the cloud: "This is my Son, whom I love. Listen to him!"

[8] Suddenly, when they looked around, they no longer saw anyone with them except Jesus.

[9] As they were coming down the mountain, Jesus gave them orders not to tell anyone what they had seen until the Son of Man had risen from the dead. [10] They kept the matter to themselves, discussing what "rising from the dead" meant.

[11] And they asked him, "Why do the teachers of the law say that Elijah must come first?"

[12] Jesus replied, "To be sure, Elijah does come first, and restores all things. Why then is it written that the Son of Man must suffer much and be rejected? [13] But I tell you, Elijah has come, and they have done to him everything they wished, just as it is written about him."

[14] When they came to the other disciples, they saw a large crowd around them and the teachers of the law arguing with them. [15] As soon as all the people saw Jesus, they were overwhelmed with wonder and ran to greet him.

[16] "What are you arguing with them about?" he asked.

[17] A man in the crowd answered, "Teacher, I brought you my son, who is possessed by a spirit that has robbed him

of speech. [18] Whenever it seizes him, it throws him to the ground. He foams at the mouth, gnashes his teeth and becomes rigid. I asked your disciples to drive out the spirit, but they could not."

[19] "O unbelieving generation," Jesus replied, "how long shall I stay with you? How long shall I put up with you? Bring the boy to me."

[20] So they brought him. When the spirit saw Jesus, it immediately threw the boy into a convulsion. He fell to the ground and rolled around, foaming at the mouth.

[21] Jesus asked the boy's father, "How long has he been like this?"

"From childhood," he answered. [22] "It has often thrown him into fire or water to kill him. But if you can do anything, take pity on us and help us."

[23] "'If you can'?" said Jesus. "Everything is possible for him who believes."

[24] **Immediately the boy's father exclaimed, "I do believe; help me overcome my unbelief!"**

[25] When Jesus saw that a crowd was running to the scene, he rebuked the evil[a] spirit. "You deaf and mute spirit," he said, "I command you, come out of him and never enter him again."

[26] The spirit shrieked, convulsed him violently and came out. The boy looked so much like a corpse that many said, "He's dead." [27] But Jesus took him by the hand and lifted him to his feet, and he stood up.

[28] After Jesus had gone indoors, his disciples asked him privately, "Why couldn't we drive it out?"

[29] He replied, "This kind can come out only by prayer.[b]"

a25 Greek *unclean* b29 Some manuscripts *prayer and fasting*

PSALM 43:1-5[a]
[1] **V**indicate me, O God,
    and plead my cause against an
        ungodly nation;
    rescue me from deceitful and
        wicked men.
[2] You are God my stronghold.
    Why have you rejected me?

Why must I go about mourning,
  oppressed by the enemy?
[3] Send forth your light and your truth,
  let them guide me;
let them bring me to your holy
    mountain,
  to the place where you dwell.
[4] Then will I go to the altar of God,
  to God, my joy and my delight.
I will praise you with the harp,
  O God, my God.

[5] Why are you downcast, O my soul?
  Why so disturbed within me?
Put your hope in God,
  for I will yet praise him,
  my Savior and my God.

[a] In many Hebrew manuscripts Psalms 42 and 43 constitute
one psalm.

PROVERBS 10:18

[18] **H**e who conceals his hatred has lying
    lips,
  and whoever spreads slander is
    a fool.

☐ D A Y 5 9

GOD SIGHTINGS

February 28

LEVITICUS 22:17–23:44

The LORD said to Moses, [18]"Speak to
Aaron and his sons and to all the Israelites and say to them: 'If any of you—either an Israelite or an alien living in
Israel—presents a gift for a burnt offering to the LORD, either to fulfill a vow or
as a freewill offering, [19]you must present
a male without defect from the cattle,
sheep or goats in order that it may be accepted on your behalf. [20]Do not bring
anything with a defect, because it will not
be accepted on your behalf. [21]When
anyone brings from the herd or flock a
fellowship offering[a] to the LORD to fulfill
a special vow or as a freewill offering, it
must be without defect or blemish to be
acceptable. [22]Do not offer to the LORD

the blind, the injured or the maimed, or
anything with warts or festering or running sores. Do not place any of these on
the altar as an offering made to the LORD
by fire. [23]You may, however, present as a
freewill offering an ox[b] or a sheep that is
deformed or stunted, but it will not be
accepted in fulfillment of a vow. [24]You
must not offer to the LORD an animal
whose testicles are bruised, crushed,
torn or cut. You must not do this in your
own land, [25]and you must not accept
such animals from the hand of a foreigner and offer them as the food of your
God. They will not be accepted on your
behalf, because they are deformed and
have defects.'"

[26]The LORD said to Moses, [27]"When a
calf, a lamb or a goat is born, it is to remain with its mother for seven days.
From the eighth day on, it will be acceptable as an offering made to the LORD by
fire. [28]Do not slaughter a cow or a sheep
and its young on the same day.

[29]"When you sacrifice a thank offering to the LORD, sacrifice it in such a way
that it will be accepted on your behalf.
[30]It must be eaten that same day; leave
none of it till morning. I am the LORD.

[31]"Keep my commands and follow
them. I am the LORD. [32]Do not profane
my holy name. I must be acknowledged
as holy by the Israelites. I am the LORD,
who makes[c] you holy[d] [33]and who
brought you out of Egypt to be your God.
I am the LORD."

[23:1]THE LORD said to Moses, [2]"Speak to
the Israelites and say to them: 'These are
my appointed feasts, the appointed
feasts of the LORD, which you are to proclaim as sacred assemblies.

[3]"'There are six days when you may
work, but the seventh day is a Sabbath of
rest, a day of sacred assembly. You are
not to do any work; wherever you live, it
is a Sabbath to the LORD.

[4]"'These are the LORD's appointed
feasts, the sacred assemblies you are to
proclaim at their appointed times: [5]The
LORD's Passover begins at twilight on
the fourteenth day of the first month.

6 On the fifteenth day of that month the LORD's Feast of Unleavened Bread begins; for seven days you must eat bread made without yeast. 7 On the first day hold a sacred assembly and do no regular work. 8 For seven days present an offering made to the LORD by fire. And on the seventh day hold a sacred assembly and do no regular work.'"

9 The LORD said to Moses, 10 "Speak to the Israelites and say to them: 'When you enter the land I am going to give you and you reap its harvest, bring to the priest a sheaf of the first grain you harvest. 11 He is to wave the sheaf before the LORD so it will be accepted on your behalf; the priest is to wave it on the day after the Sabbath. 12 On the day you wave the sheaf, you must sacrifice as a burnt offering to the LORD a lamb a year old without defect, 13 together with its grain offering of two-tenths of an ephah[e] of fine flour mixed with oil—an offering made to the LORD by fire, a pleasing aroma—and its drink offering of a quarter of a hin[f] of wine. 14 You must not eat any bread, or roasted or new grain, until the very day you bring this offering to your God. This is to be a lasting ordinance for the generations to come, wherever you live.

15 "'From the day after the Sabbath, the day you brought the sheaf of the wave offering, count off seven full weeks. 16 Count off fifty days up to the day after the seventh Sabbath, and then present an offering of new grain to the LORD. 17 From wherever you live, bring two loaves made of two-tenths of an ephah of fine flour, baked with yeast, as a wave offering of firstfruits to the LORD. 18 Present with this bread seven male lambs, each a year old and without defect, one young bull and two rams. They will be a burnt offering to the LORD, together with their grain offerings and drink offerings—an offering made by fire, an aroma pleasing to the LORD. 19 Then sacrifice one male goat for a sin offering and two lambs, each a year old, for a fellowship offering.[a] 20 The priest is to wave the two lambs

before the LORD as a wave offering, together with the bread of the firstfruits. They are a sacred offering to the LORD for the priest. 21 On that same day you are to proclaim a sacred assembly and do no regular work. This is to be a lasting ordinance for the generations to come, wherever you live.

22 "'When you reap the harvest of your land, do not reap to the very edges of your field or gather the gleanings of your harvest. Leave them for the poor and the alien. I am the LORD your God.'"

23 The LORD said to Moses, 24 "Say to the Israelites: 'On the first day of the seventh month you are to have a day of rest, a sacred assembly commemorated with trumpet blasts. 25 Do no regular work, but present an offering made to the LORD by fire.'"

26 The LORD said to Moses, 27 "The tenth day of this seventh month is the Day of Atonement. Hold a sacred assembly and deny yourselves,[g] and present an offering made to the LORD by fire. 28 Do no work on that day, because it is the Day of Atonement, when atonement is made for you before the LORD your God. 29 Anyone who does not deny himself on that day must be cut off from his people. 30 I will destroy from among his people anyone who does any work on that day. 31 You shall do no work at all. This is to be a lasting ordinance for the generations to come, wherever you live. 32 It is a sabbath of rest for you, and you must deny yourselves. From the evening of the ninth day of the month until the following evening you are to observe your sabbath."

33 The LORD said to Moses, 34 "Say to the Israelites: 'On the fifteenth day of the seventh month the LORD's Feast of Tabernacles begins, and it lasts for seven days. 35 The first day is a sacred assembly; do no regular work. 36 For seven days present offerings made to the LORD by fire, and on the eighth day hold a sacred assembly and present an offering made to the LORD by fire. It is the closing assembly; do no regular work.

37 "'These are the LORD's appointed feasts, which you are to proclaim as sacred

assemblies for bringing offerings made to the LORD by fire—the burnt offerings and grain offerings, sacrifices and drink offerings required for each day. 38These offerings are in addition to those for the LORD's Sabbaths and*h* in addition to your gifts and whatever you have vowed and all the freewill offerings you give to the LORD.)

39"'So beginning with the fifteenth day of the seventh month, after you have gathered the crops of the land, celebrate the festival to the LORD for seven days; the first day is a day of rest, and the eighth day also is a day of rest. 40On the first day you are to take choice fruit from the trees, and palm fronds, leafy branches and poplars, and rejoice before the LORD your God for seven days. 41Celebrate this as a festival to the LORD for seven days each year. This is to be a lasting ordinance for the generations to come; celebrate it in the seventh month. 42Live in booths for seven days: All native-born Israelites are to live in booths 43so your descendants will know that I had the Israelites live in booths when I brought them out of Egypt. I am the LORD your God.'"

44So Moses announced to the Israelites the appointed feasts of the LORD.

a21,19 Traditionally *peace offering*   *b23* The Hebrew word can include both male and female.   *c32* Or *made*   *d32* Or *who sanctifies you;* or *who sets you apart as holy*   *e13* That is, probably about 4 quarts (about 4.5 liters); also in verse 17   *f13* That is, probably about 1 quart (about 1 liter)   *g27* Or *and fast;* also in verses 29 and 32   *h38* Or *These feasts are in addition to the LORD's Sabbaths, and these offerings are*

MARK 9:30–10:12

They [Jesus and his disciples] left that place and passed through Galilee. Jesus did not want anyone to know where they were, 31because he was teaching his disciples. He said to them, "The Son of Man is going to be betrayed into the hands of men. They will kill him, and after three days he will rise." 32But they did not understand what he meant and were afraid to ask him about it.

33They came to Capernaum. When he was in the house, he asked them, "What were you arguing about on the road?" 34But they kept quiet because on

the way they had argued about who was the greatest.

35**Sitting down, Jesus called the Twelve and said, "If anyone wants to be first, he must be the very last, and the servant of all."**

36He took a little child and had him stand among them. Taking him in his arms, he said to them, 37"Whoever welcomes one of these little children in my name welcomes me; and whoever welcomes me does not welcome me but the one who sent me."

38"Teacher," said John, "we saw a man driving out demons in your name and we told him to stop, because he was not one of us."

39"Do not stop him," Jesus said. "No one who does a miracle in my name can in the next moment say anything bad about me, 40for whoever is not against us is for us. 41I tell you the truth, anyone who gives you a cup of water in my name because you belong to Christ will certainly not lose his reward.

42"And if anyone causes one of these little ones who believe in me to sin, it would be better for him to be thrown into the sea with a large millstone tied around his neck. 43If your hand causes you to sin, cut it off. It is better for you to enter life maimed than with two hands to go into hell, where the fire never goes out.*a* 45And if your foot causes you to sin, cut it off. It is better for you to enter life crippled than to have two feet and be thrown into hell.*b* 47And if your eye causes you to sin, pluck it out. It is better for you to enter the kingdom of God with one eye than to have two eyes and be thrown into hell, 48where

"'their worm does not die,
    and the fire is not quenched.'*c*

49Everyone will be salted with fire.

50"Salt is good, but if it loses its saltiness, how can you make it salty again? Have salt in yourselves, and be at peace with each other."

10:1JESUS then left that place and went into the region of Judea and across the

Jordan. Again crowds of people came to him, and as was his custom, he taught them.

2 Some Pharisees came and tested him by asking, "Is it lawful for a man to divorce his wife?"

3 "What did Moses command you?" he replied.

4 They said, "Moses permitted a man to write a certificate of divorce and send her away."

5 "It was because your hearts were hard that Moses wrote you this law," Jesus replied. 6 "But at the beginning of creation God 'made them male and female.'*d* 7 'For this reason a man will leave his father and mother and be united to his wife,*e* 8 and the two will become one flesh.'*f* So they are no longer two, but one. 9 Therefore what God has joined together, let man not separate."

10 When they were in the house again, the disciples asked Jesus about this. 11 He answered, "Anyone who divorces his wife and marries another woman commits adultery against her. 12 And if she divorces her husband and marries another man, she commits adultery."

a43 Some manuscripts *out,* *44where / "their worm does not die, / and the fire is not quenched.'* *b45* Some manuscripts hell, *46where / "their worm does not die, / and the fire is not quenched.'* *c48* Isaiah 66:24   *d6* Gen. 1:27   *e7* Some early manuscripts do not have *and be united to his wife.* *f8* Gen. 2:24

PSALM 44:1-8
For the director of music. Of the Sons of Korah. A *maskil.*a

1 **W**e have heard with our ears, O God;
    our fathers have told us

what you did in their days,
    in days long ago.
2 With your hand you drove out the nations
    and planted our fathers;
you crushed the peoples
    and made our fathers flourish.
3 It was not by their sword that they won the land,
    nor did their arm bring them victory;
it was your right hand, your arm,
    and the light of your face, for you loved them.

4 You are my King and my God,
    who decrees*b* victories for Jacob.
5 Through you we push back our enemies;
    through your name we trample our foes.
6 I do not trust in my bow,
    my sword does not bring me victory;
7 but you give us victory over our enemies,
    you put our adversaries to shame.
8 In God we make our boast all day long,
    and we will praise your name forever.   *Selah*

a Title: Probably a literary or musical term   *b4* Septuagint, Aquila and Syriac; Hebrew *King, O God; / command*

PROVERBS 10:19
19 **W**hen words are many, sin is not absent,
    but he who holds his tongue is wise.

March 1

LEVITICUS 24:1–25:46

The LORD said to Moses, 2"Command the Israelites to bring you clear oil of pressed olives for the light so that the lamps may be kept burning continually. 3Outside the curtain of the Testimony in the Tent of Meeting, Aaron is to tend the lamps before the LORD from evening till morning, continually. This is to be a lasting ordinance for the generations to come. 4The lamps on the pure gold lampstand before the LORD must be tended continually.

5"Take fine flour and bake twelve loaves of bread, using two-tenths of an ephah[a] for each loaf. 6Set them in two rows, six in each row, on the table of pure gold before the LORD. 7Along each row put some pure incense as a memorial portion to represent the bread and to be an offering made to the LORD by fire. 8This bread is to be set out before the LORD regularly, Sabbath after Sabbath, on behalf of the Israelites, as a lasting covenant. 9It belongs to Aaron and his sons, who are to eat it in a holy place, because it is a most holy part of their regular share of the offerings made to the LORD by fire."

10Now the son of an Israelite mother and an Egyptian father went out among the Israelites, and a fight broke out in the camp between him and an Israelite. 11The son of the Israelite woman blasphemed the Name with a curse; so they brought him to Moses. (His mother's name was Shelomith, the daughter of Dibri the Danite.) 12They put him in custody until the will of the LORD should be made clear to them.

13Then the LORD said to Moses: 14"Take the blasphemer outside the camp. All those who heard him are to lay their hands on his head, and the entire assembly is to stone him. 15Say to the Israelites: 'If anyone curses his God, he will be held responsible; 16anyone who blasphemes the name of the LORD must be put to death. The entire assembly must stone him. Whether an alien or native-born, when he blasphemes the Name, he must be put to death.

17"'If anyone takes the life of a human being, he must be put to death. 18Anyone who takes the life of someone's animal must make restitution—life for life. 19If anyone injures his neighbor, whatever he has done must be done to him: 20fracture for fracture, eye for eye, tooth for tooth. As he has injured the other, so he is to be injured. 21Whoever kills an animal must make restitution, but whoever kills a man must be put to death. 22You are to have the same law for the alien and the native-born. I am the LORD your God.'"

23Then Moses spoke to the Israelites, and they took the blasphemer outside the camp and stoned him. The Israelites did as the LORD commanded Moses.

25:1THE LORD said to Moses on Mount Sinai, 2"Speak to the Israelites and say to them: 'When you enter the land I am going to give you, the land itself must observe a sabbath to the LORD. 3For six years sow your fields, and for six years prune your vineyards and gather their crops. 4But in the seventh year the land is to have a sabbath of rest, a sabbath to the LORD. Do not sow your fields or prune your vineyards. 5Do not reap what grows of itself or harvest the grapes of your untended vines. The land is to have a year of rest. 6Whatever the land yields during the sabbath year will be food for you—for yourself, your manservant and maidservant, and the hired worker and temporary resident who live among you, 7as well as for your livestock and the wild animals in your land. Whatever the land produces may be eaten.

8 " 'Count off seven sabbaths of years—seven times seven years—so that the seven sabbaths of years amount to a period of forty-nine years. 9Then have the trumpet sounded everywhere on the tenth day of the seventh month; on the Day of Atonement sound the trumpet throughout your land. 10Consecrate the fiftieth year and proclaim liberty throughout the land to all its inhabitants. It shall be a jubilee for you; each one of you is to return to his family property and each to his own clan. 11The fiftieth year shall be a jubilee for you; do not sow and do not reap what grows of itself or harvest the untended vines. 12For it is a jubilee and is to be holy for you; eat only what is taken directly from the fields.

13 " 'In this Year of Jubilee everyone is to return to his own property.

14 " 'If you sell land to one of your countrymen or buy any from him, do not take advantage of each other. 15You are to buy from your countryman on the basis of the number of years since the Jubilee. And he is to sell to you on the basis of the number of years left for harvesting crops. 16When the years are many, you are to increase the price, and when the years are few, you are to decrease the price, because what he is really selling you is the number of crops. 17Do not take advantage of each other, but fear your God. I am the LORD your God.

18 " 'Follow my decrees and be careful to obey my laws, and you will live safely in the land. 19Then the land will yield its fruit, and you will eat your fill and live there in safety. 20You may ask, "What will we eat in the seventh year if we do not plant or harvest our crops?" 21I will send you such a blessing in the sixth year that the land will yield enough for three years. 22While you plant during the eighth year, you will eat from the old crop and will continue to eat from it until the harvest of the ninth year comes in.

23 " 'The land must not be sold permanently, because the land is mine and you are but aliens and my tenants. 24Throughout the country that you hold as a possession, you must provide for the redemption of the land.

25 " 'If one of your countrymen becomes poor and sells some of his property, his nearest relative is to come and redeem what his countryman has sold. 26If, however, a man has no one to redeem it for him but he himself prospers and acquires sufficient means to redeem it, 27he is to determine the value for the years since he sold it and refund the balance to the man to whom he sold it; he can then go back to his own property. 28But if he does not acquire the means to repay him, what he sold will remain in the possession of the buyer until the Year of Jubilee. It will be returned in the Jubilee, and he can then go back to his property.

29 " 'If a man sells a house in a walled city, he retains the right of redemption a full year after its sale. During that time he may redeem it. 30If it is not redeemed before a full year has passed, the house in the walled city shall belong permanently to the buyer and his descendants. It is not to be returned in the Jubilee. 31But houses in villages without walls around them are to be considered as open country. They can be redeemed, and they are to be returned in the Jubilee.

32 " 'The Levites always have the right to redeem their houses in the Levitical towns, which they possess. 33So the property of the Levites is redeemable—that is, a house sold in any town they hold—and is to be returned in the Jubilee, because the houses in the towns of the Levites are their property among the Israelites. 34But the pastureland belonging to their towns must not be sold; it is their permanent possession.

35 " 'If one of your countrymen becomes poor and is unable to support himself among you, help him as you would an alien or a temporary resident, so he can continue to live among you. 36Do not take interest of any kind[b] from him, but fear your God, so that your countryman may continue to live

among you. [37] You must not lend him money at interest or sell him food at a profit. [38] I am the LORD your God, who brought you out of Egypt to give you the land of Canaan and to be your God.

[39] " 'If one of your countrymen becomes poor among you and sells himself to you, do not make him work as a slave. [40] He is to be treated as a hired worker or a temporary resident among you; he is to work for you until the Year of Jubilee. [41] Then he and his children are to be released, and he will go back to his own clan and to the property of his forefathers. [42] Because the Israelites are my servants, whom I brought out of Egypt, they must not be sold as slaves. [43] Do not rule over them ruthlessly, but fear your God.

[44] " 'Your male and female slaves are to come from the nations around you; from them you may buy slaves. [45] You may also buy some of the temporary residents living among you and members of their clans born in your country, and they will become your property. [46] You can will them to your children as inherited property and can make them slaves for life, but you must not rule over your fellow Israelites ruthlessly.' "

[a]5 That is, probably about 4 quarts (about 4.5 liters)
[b]36 Or take excessive interest; similarly in verse 37

MARK 10:13-31

People were bringing little children to Jesus to have him touch them, but the disciples rebuked them. [14] When Jesus saw this, he was indignant. He said to them, "Let the little children come to me, and do not hinder them, for the kingdom of God belongs to such as these. [15] I tell you the truth, anyone who will not receive the kingdom of God like a little child will never enter it." [16] And he took the children in his arms, put his hands on them and blessed them.

[17] As Jesus started on his way, a man ran up to him and fell on his knees before him. "Good teacher," he asked, "what must I do to inherit eternal life?"

[18] "Why do you call me good?" Jesus answered. "No one is good—except God alone. [19] You know the commandments: 'Do not murder, do not commit adultery, do not steal, do not give false testimony, do not defraud, honor your father and mother.'[a] "

[20] "Teacher," he declared, "all these I have kept since I was a boy."

[21] Jesus looked at him and loved him. "One thing you lack," he said. "Go, sell everything you have and give to the poor, and you will have treasure in heaven. Then come, follow me."

[22] At this the man's face fell. He went away sad, because he had great wealth.

[23] Jesus looked around and said to his disciples, "How hard it is for the rich to enter the kingdom of God!"

[24] The disciples were amazed at his words. But Jesus said again, "Children, how hard it is[b] to enter the kingdom of God! [25] It is easier for a camel to go through the eye of a needle than for a rich man to enter the kingdom of God."

[26] The disciples were even more amazed, and said to each other, "Who then can be saved?"

[27] Jesus looked at them and said, "With man this is impossible, but not with God; all things are possible with God."

[28] Peter said to him, "We have left everything to follow you!"

[29] "I tell you the truth," Jesus replied, "no one who has left home or brothers or sisters or mother or father or children or fields for me and the gospel [30] will fail to receive a hundred times as much in this present age (homes, brothers, sisters, mothers, children and fields—and with them, persecutions) and in the age to come, eternal life. [31] But many who are first will be last, and the last first."

[a]19 Exodus 20:12-16; Deut. 5:16-20   [b]24 Some manuscripts is for those who trust in riches

PSALM 44:9-26

[9] But now you [God] have rejected and humbled us;
    you no longer go out with our armies.

¹⁰You made us retreat before the
   enemy,
   and our adversaries have
      plundered us.
¹¹You gave us up to be devoured like
   sheep
   and have scattered us among the
      nations.
¹²You sold your people for a pittance,
   gaining nothing from their sale.

¹³You have made us a reproach to our
   neighbors,
   the scorn and derision of those
      around us.
¹⁴You have made us a byword among
   the nations;
   the peoples shake their heads at us.
¹⁵My disgrace is before me all day
   long,
   and my face is covered with
      shame
¹⁶at the taunts of those who reproach
   and revile me,
   because of the enemy, who is bent
      on revenge.

¹⁷All this happened to us,
   though we had not forgotten you
      or been false to your covenant.
¹⁸Our hearts had not turned back;
   our feet had not strayed from
      your path.
¹⁹But you crushed us and made us a
   haunt for jackals
   and covered us over with deep
      darkness.

²⁰If we had forgotten the name of
   our God
   or spread out our hands to a
      foreign god,
²¹would not God have discovered it,
   since he knows the secrets of the
      heart?
²²Yet for your sake we face death all
   day long;
   we are considered as sheep to be
      slaughtered.

²³Awake, O Lord! Why do you sleep?
   Rouse yourself! Do not reject us
      forever.

²⁴Why do you hide your face
   and forget our misery and
      oppression?

²⁵We are brought down to the dust;
   our bodies cling to the ground.
²⁶Rise up and help us;
   redeem us because of your
      unfailing love.

PROVERBS 10:20-21
²⁰The tongue of the righteous is
   choice silver,
   but the heart of the wicked is of
      little value.

²¹The lips of the righteous nourish
   many,
   but fools die for lack of judgment.

□ DAY 61

GOD SIGHTINGS

March 2

LEVITICUS 25:47–27:13

" 'If an alien or a temporary resident
among you becomes rich and one of
your countrymen becomes poor and
sells himself to the alien living among
you or to a member of the alien's clan,
⁴⁸he retains the right of redemption after he has sold himself. One of his relatives may redeem him: ⁴⁹An uncle or a
cousin or any blood relative in his clan
may redeem him. Or if he prospers, he
may redeem himself. ⁵⁰He and his
buyer are to count the time from the
year he sold himself up to the Year of Jubilee. The price for his release is to be
based on the rate paid to a hired man
for that number of years. ⁵¹If many
years remain, he must pay for his redemption a larger share of the price
paid for him. ⁵²If only a few years remain until the Year of Jubilee, he is to
compute that and pay for his redemption accordingly. ⁵³He is to be treated as
a man hired from year to year; you must

see to it that his owner does not rule over him ruthlessly.

54 " 'Even if he is not redeemed in any of these ways, he and his children are to be released in the Year of Jubilee, 55 for the Israelites belong to me as servants. They are my servants, whom I brought out of Egypt. I am the Lord your God.

26:1 " 'Do not make idols or set up an image or a sacred stone for yourselves, and do not place a carved stone in your land to bow down before it. I am the Lord your God.

2 " 'Observe my Sabbaths and have reverence for my sanctuary. I am the Lord.

3 " 'If you follow my decrees and are careful to obey my commands, 4 I will send you rain in its season, and the ground will yield its crops and the trees of the field their fruit. 5 Your threshing will continue until grape harvest and the grape harvest will continue until planting, and you will eat all the food you want and live in safety in your land.

6 " 'I will grant peace in the land, and you will lie down and no one will make you afraid. I will remove savage beasts from the land, and the sword will not pass through your country. 7 You will pursue your enemies, and they will fall by the sword before you. 8 Five of you will chase a hundred, and a hundred of you will chase ten thousand, and your enemies will fall by the sword before you.

9 " 'I will look on you with favor and make you fruitful and increase your numbers, and I will keep my covenant with you. 10 You will still be eating last year's harvest when you will have to move it out to make room for the new. 11 I will put my dwelling place a among you, and I will not abhor you. 12 I will walk among you and be your God, and you will be my people. 13 I am the Lord your God, who brought you out of Egypt so that you would no longer be slaves to the Egyptians; I broke the bars of your yoke and enabled you to walk with heads held high.

14 " 'But if you will not listen to me and carry out all these commands, 15 and if you reject my decrees and abhor my laws and fail to carry out all my commands and so violate my covenant, 16 then I will do this to you: I will bring upon you sudden terror, wasting diseases and fever that will destroy your sight and drain away your life. You will plant seed in vain, because your enemies will eat it. 17 I will set my face against you so that you will be defeated by your enemies; those who hate you will rule over you, and you will flee even when no one is pursuing you.

18 " 'If after all this you will not listen to me, I will punish you for your sins seven times over. 19 I will break down your stubborn pride and make the sky above you like iron and the ground beneath you like bronze. 20 Your strength will be spent in vain, because your soil will not yield its crops, nor will the trees of the land yield their fruit.

21 " 'If you remain hostile toward me and refuse to listen to me, I will multiply your afflictions seven times over, as your sins deserve. 22 I will send wild animals against you, and they will rob you of your children, destroy your cattle and make you so few in number that your roads will be deserted.

23 " 'If in spite of these things you do not accept my correction but continue to be hostile toward me, 24 I myself will be hostile toward you and will afflict you for your sins seven times over. 25 And I will bring the sword upon you to avenge the breaking of the covenant. When you withdraw into your cities, I will send a plague among you, and you will be given into enemy hands. 26 When I cut off your supply of bread, ten women will be able to bake your bread in one oven, and they will dole out the bread by weight. You will eat, but you will not be satisfied.

27 " 'If in spite of this you still do not listen to me but continue to be hostile toward me, 28 then in my anger I will be hostile toward you, and I myself will punish you for your sins seven times

over. ²⁹You will eat the flesh of your sons and the flesh of your daughters. ³⁰I will destroy your high places, cut down your incense altars and pile your dead bodies on the lifeless forms of your idols, and I will abhor you. ³¹I will turn your cities into ruins and lay waste your sanctuaries, and I will take no delight in the pleasing aroma of your offerings. ³²I will lay waste the land, so that your enemies who live there will be appalled. ³³I will scatter you among the nations and will draw out my sword and pursue you. Your land will be laid waste, and your cities will lie in ruins. ³⁴Then the land will enjoy its sabbath years all the time that it lies desolate and you are in the country of your enemies; then the land will rest and enjoy its sabbaths. ³⁵All the time that it lies desolate, the land will have the rest it did not have during the sabbaths you lived in it.

³⁶"As for those of you who are left, I will make their hearts so fearful in the lands of their enemies that the sound of a windblown leaf will put them to flight. They will run as though fleeing from the sword, and they will fall, even though no one is pursuing them. ³⁷They will stumble over one another as though fleeing from the sword, even though no one is pursuing them. So you will not be able to stand before your enemies. ³⁸You will perish among the nations; the land of your enemies will devour you. ³⁹Those of you who are left will waste away in the lands of their enemies because of their sins; also because of their fathers' sins they will waste away.

⁴⁰"But if they will confess their sins and the sins of their fathers—their treachery against me and their hostility toward me, ⁴¹which made me hostile toward them so that I sent them into the land of their enemies—then when their uncircumcised hearts are humbled and they pay for their sin, ⁴²I will remember my covenant with Jacob and my covenant with Isaac and my covenant with Abraham, and I will remember the land. ⁴³For the land will be deserted by them and will enjoy its sabbaths while it lies desolate without them. They will pay for their sins because they rejected my laws and abhorred my decrees. ⁴⁴Yet in spite of this, when they are in the land of their enemies, I will not reject them or abhor them so as to destroy them completely, breaking my covenant with them. I am the LORD their God. ⁴⁵But for their sake I will remember the covenant with their ancestors whom I brought out of Egypt in the sight of the nations to be their God. I am the LORD.'"

⁴⁶These are the decrees, the laws and the regulations that the LORD established on Mount Sinai between himself and the Israelites through Moses.

²⁷:¹THE LORD said to Moses, ²"Speak to the Israelites and say to them: 'If anyone makes a special vow to dedicate persons to the LORD by giving equivalent values, ³set the value of a male between the ages of twenty and sixty at fifty shekels^b of silver, according to the sanctuary shekel^c; ⁴and if it is a female, set her value at thirty shekels.^d ⁵If it is a person between the ages of five and twenty, set the value of a male at twenty shekels^e and of a female at ten shekels.^f ⁶If it is a person between one month and five years, set the value of a male at five shekels^g of silver and that of a female at three shekels^h of silver. ⁷If it is a person sixty years old or more, set the value of a male at fifteen shekels^i and of a female at ten shekels. ⁸If anyone making the vow is too poor to pay the specified amount, he is to present the person to the priest, who will set the value for him according to what the man making the vow can afford.

⁹"If what he vowed is an animal that is acceptable as an offering to the LORD, such an animal given to the LORD becomes holy. ¹⁰He must not exchange it or substitute a good one for a bad one, or a bad one for a good one; if he should substitute one animal for another, both it and the substitute become holy. ¹¹If what he vowed is a ceremonially unclean animal—one that is not acceptable as an offering to the LORD—the

animal must be presented to the priest, [12]who will judge its quality as good or bad. Whatever value the priest then sets, that is what it will be. [13]If the owner wishes to redeem the animal, he must add a fifth to its value.'"

[a]11 Or *my tabernacle*   [b]3 That is, about 1 1/4 pounds (about 0.6 kilogram); also in verse 16   [c]3 That is, about 2/5 ounce (about 11.5 grams); also in verse 25   [d]4 That is, about 12 ounces (about 0.3 kilogram)   [e]5 That is, about 8 ounces (about 0.2 kilogram)   [f]5 That is, about 4 ounces (about 110 grams); also in verse 7   [g]6 That is, about 2 ounces (about 55 grams)   [h]6 That is, about 1 1/4 ounces (about 35 grams)   [i]7 That is, about 6 ounces (about 170 grams)

MARK 10:32-52

They [Jesus and his followers] were on their way up to Jerusalem, with Jesus leading the way, and the disciples were astonished, while those who followed were afraid. Again he took the Twelve aside and told them what was going to happen to him. [33]"We are going up to Jerusalem," he said, "and the Son of Man will be betrayed to the chief priests and teachers of the law. They will condemn him to death and will hand him over to the Gentiles, [34]who will mock him and spit on him, flog him and kill him. Three days later he will rise."

[35]Then James and John, the sons of Zebedee, came to him. "Teacher," they said, "we want you to do for us whatever we ask."

[36]"What do you want me to do for you?" he asked.

[37]They replied, "Let one of us sit at your right and the other at your left in your glory."

[38]"You don't know what you are asking," Jesus said. "Can you drink the cup I drink or be baptized with the baptism I am baptized with?"

[39]"We can," they answered.

Jesus said to them, " You will drink the cup I drink and be baptized with the baptism I am baptized with, [40]but to sit at my right or left is not for me to grant. These places belong to those for whom they have been prepared."

[41]When the ten heard about this, they became indignant with James and John. [42]Jesus called them together and said,

"You know that those who are regarded as rulers of the Gentiles lord it over them, and their high officials exercise authority over them. [43]Not so with you. Instead, whoever wants to become great among you must be your servant, [44]and whoever wants to be first must be slave of all. [45]For even the Son of Man did not come to be served, but to serve, and to give his life as a ransom for many."

[46]Then they came to Jericho. As Jesus and his disciples, together with a large crowd, were leaving the city, a blind man, Bartimaeus (that is, the Son of Timaeus), was sitting by the roadside begging. [47]When he heard that it was Jesus of Nazareth, he began to shout, "Jesus, Son of David, have mercy on me!"

[48]Many rebuked him and told him to be quiet, but he shouted all the more, "Son of David, have mercy on me!"

[49]Jesus stopped and said, "Call him."

So they called to the blind man, "Cheer up! On your feet! He's calling you." [50]Throwing his cloak aside, he jumped to his feet and came to Jesus.

[51]"What do you want me to do for you?" Jesus asked him.

The blind man said, "Rabbi, I want to see."

[52]"Go," said Jesus, "your faith has healed you." Immediately he received his sight and followed Jesus along the road.

PSALM 45:1-17

For the director of music. To ⌊the tune of⌋ "Lilies." Of the Sons of Korah. A *maskil*.[a] A wedding song.

[1] **M**y heart is stirred by a noble theme
    as I recite my verses for the king;
    my tongue is the pen of a skillful
        writer.

[2] You are the most excellent of men
    and your lips have been anointed
        with grace,
    since God has blessed you forever.
[3] Gird your sword upon your side,
        O mighty one;
    clothe yourself with splendor and
        majesty.

⁴In your majesty ride forth
victoriously
in behalf of truth, humility and
righteousness;
let your right hand display
awesome deeds.
⁵Let your sharp arrows pierce the
hearts of the king's enemies;
let the nations fall beneath your
feet.
⁶Your throne, O God, will last for ever
and ever;
a scepter of justice will be the
scepter of your kingdom.
⁷You love righteousness and hate
wickedness;
therefore God, your God, has set
you above your companions
by anointing you with the oil
of joy.
⁸All your robes are fragrant with
myrrh and aloes and cassia;
from palaces adorned with ivory
the music of the strings makes you
glad.
⁹Daughters of kings are among your
honored women;
at your right hand is the royal
bride in gold of Ophir.

¹⁰Listen, O daughter, consider and
give ear:
Forget your people and your
father's house.
¹¹The king is enthralled by your
beauty;
honor him, for he is your lord.
¹²The Daughter of Tyre will come with
a gift,ᵇ
men of wealth will seek your
favor.

¹³All glorious is the princess within
⌊her chamber⌋;
her gown is interwoven with gold.
¹⁴In embroidered garments she is led
to the king;
her virgin companions follow her
and are brought to you.
¹⁵They are led in with joy and gladness;
they enter the palace of the king.

¹⁶Your sons will take the place of your
fathers;
you will make them princes
throughout the land.
¹⁷I will perpetuate your memory
through all generations;
therefore the nations will praise
you for ever and ever.

ᵃTitle: Probably a literary or musical term ᵇ12 Or *A Tyrian
robe is among the gifts*

PROVERBS 10:22
²²The blessing of the LORD brings
wealth,
and he adds no trouble to it.

☐ DAY 62

GOD SIGHTINGS

March 3

LEVITICUS 27:14—NUMBERS 1:54
"'If a man dedicates his house as something holy to the LORD, the priest will
judge its quality as good or bad. Whatever value the priest then sets, so it will
remain. ¹⁵If the man who dedicates his
house redeems it, he must add a fifth to
its value, and the house will again become his.

¹⁶" 'If a man dedicates to the LORD
part of his family land, its value is to be
set according to the amount of seed required for it—fifty shekels of silver to a
homerᵃ of barley seed. ¹⁷If he dedicates
his field during the Year of Jubilee, the
value that has been set remains. ¹⁸But if
he dedicates his field after the Jubilee,
the priest will determine the value according to the number of years that remain until the next Year of Jubilee, and
its set value will be reduced. ¹⁹If the
man who dedicates the field wishes to
redeem it, he must add a fifth to its
value, and the field will again become
his. ²⁰If, however, he does not redeem
the field, or if he has sold it to someone
else, it can never be redeemed. ²¹When

the field is released in the Jubilee, it will become holy, like a field devoted to the Lord; it will become the property of the priests.*b*

22 "'If a man dedicates to the Lord a field he has bought, which is not part of his family land, 23 the priest will determine its value up to the Year of Jubilee, and the man must pay its value on that day as something holy to the Lord. 24 In the Year of Jubilee the field will revert to the person from whom he bought it, the one whose land it was. 25 Every value is to be set according to the sanctuary shekel, twenty gerahs to the shekel.

26 "'No one, however, may dedicate the firstborn of an animal, since the firstborn already belongs to the Lord; whether an ox*c* or a sheep, it is the Lord's. 27 If it is one of the unclean animals, he may buy it back at its set value, adding a fifth of the value to it. If he does not redeem it, it is to be sold at its set value.

28 "'But nothing that a man owns and devotes*d* to the Lord—whether man or animal or family land—may be sold or redeemed; everything so devoted is most holy to the Lord.

29 "'No person devoted to destruction*e* may be ransomed; he must be put to death.

30 "'A tithe of everything from the land, whether grain from the soil or fruit from the trees, belongs to the Lord; it is holy to the Lord. 31 If a man redeems any of his tithe, he must add a fifth of the value to it. 32 The entire tithe of the herd and flock—every tenth animal that passes under the shepherd's rod—will be holy to the Lord. 33 He must not pick out the good from the bad or make any substitution. If he does make a substitution, both the animal and its substitute become holy and cannot be redeemed.'"

34 These are the commands the Lord gave Moses on Mount Sinai for the Israelites.

1:1 THE Lord spoke to Moses in the Tent of Meeting in the Desert of Sinai on the first day of the second month of the second year after the Israelites came out of Egypt. He said: 2 "Take a census of the whole Israelite community by their clans and families, listing every man by name, one by one. 3 You and Aaron are to number by their divisions all the men in Israel twenty years old or more who are able to serve in the army. 4 One man from each tribe, each the head of his family, is to help you. 5 These are the names of the men who are to assist you:

from Reuben, Elizur son of Shedeur;
6 from Simeon, Shelumiel son of Zurishaddai;
7 from Judah, Nahshon son of Amminadab;
8 from Issachar, Nethanel son of Zuar;
9 from Zebulun, Eliab son of Helon;
10 from the sons of Joseph:
from Ephraim, Elishama son of Ammihud;
from Manasseh, Gamaliel son of Pedahzur;
11 from Benjamin, Abidan son of Gideoni;
12 from Dan, Ahiezer son of Ammishaddai;
13 from Asher, Pagiel son of Ocran;
14 from Gad, Eliasaph son of Deuel;
15 from Naphtali, Ahira son of Enan."

16 These were the men appointed from the community, the leaders of their ancestral tribes. They were the heads of the clans of Israel.

17 Moses and Aaron took these men whose names had been given, 18 and they called the whole community together on the first day of the second month. The people indicated their ancestry by their clans and families, and the men twenty years old or more were listed by name, one by one, 19 as the Lord commanded Moses. And so he counted them in the Desert of Sinai:

20 From the descendants of Reuben the firstborn son of Israel:

All the men twenty years old or more who were able to serve in the army were listed by name, one by one, according to the records of their clans and families. 21The number from the tribe of Reuben was 46,500.

22From the descendants of Simeon:
All the men twenty years old or more who were able to serve in the army were counted and listed by name, one by one, according to the records of their clans and families. 23The number from the tribe of Simeon was 59,300.

24From the descendants of Gad:
All the men twenty years old or more who were able to serve in the army were listed by name, according to the records of their clans and families. 25The number from the tribe of Gad was 45,650.

26From the descendants of Judah:
All the men twenty years old or more who were able to serve in the army were listed by name, according to the records of their clans and families. 27The number from the tribe of Judah was 74,600.

28From the descendants of Issachar:
All the men twenty years old or more who were able to serve in the army were listed by name, according to the records of their clans and families. 29The number from the tribe of Issachar was 54,400.

30From the descendants of Zebulun:
All the men twenty years old or more who were able to serve in the army were listed by name, according to the records of their clans and fami-

lies. 31The number from the tribe of Zebulun was 57,400.

32From the sons of Joseph:
From the descendants of Ephraim:
All the men twenty years old or more who were able to serve in the army were listed by name, according to the records of their clans and families. 33The number from the tribe of Ephraim was 40,500.

34From the descendants of Manasseh:
All the men twenty years old or more who were able to serve in the army were listed by name, according to the records of their clans and families. 35The number from the tribe of Manasseh was 32,200.

36From the descendants of Benjamin:
All the men twenty years old or more who were able to serve in the army were listed by name, according to the records of their clans and families. 37The number from the tribe of Benjamin was 35,400.

38From the descendants of Dan:
All the men twenty years old or more who were able to serve in the army were listed by name, according to the records of their clans and families. 39The number from the tribe of Dan was 62,700.

40From the descendants of Asher:
All the men twenty years old or more who were able to serve in the army were listed by name, according to the records of their clans and families. 41The number from the tribe of Asher was 41,500.

42From the descendants of Naphtali:
All the men twenty years old or more who were able to serve in the army were listed by name, according to the rec-

ords of their clans and families. ⁴³The number from the tribe of Naphtali was 53,400.

⁴⁴These were the men counted by Moses and Aaron and the twelve leaders of Israel, each one representing his family. ⁴⁵All the Israelites twenty years old or more who were able to serve in Israel's army were counted according to their families. ⁴⁶The total number was 603,550.

⁴⁷The families of the tribe of Levi, however, were not counted along with the others. ⁴⁸The LORD had said to Moses: ⁴⁹"You must not count the tribe of Levi or include them in the census of the other Israelites. ⁵⁰Instead, appoint the Levites to be in charge of the tabernacle of the Testimony—over all its furnishings and everything belonging to it. They are to carry the tabernacle and all its furnishings; they are to take care of it and encamp around it. ⁵¹Whenever the tabernacle is to move, the Levites are to take it down, and whenever the tabernacle is to be set up, the Levites shall do it. Anyone else who goes near it shall be put to death. ⁵²The Israelites are to set up their tents by divisions, each man in his own camp under his own standard. ⁵³The Levites, however, are to set up their tents around the tabernacle of the Testimony so that wrath will not fall on the Israelite community. The Levites are to be responsible for the care of the tabernacle of the Testimony."

⁵⁴The Israelites did all this just as the LORD commanded Moses.

a 16 That is, probably about 6 bushels (about 220 liters)
b 21 Or priest   c 26 The Hebrew word can include both male and female.   d 28 The Hebrew term refers to the irrevocable giving over of things or persons to the LORD.   e 29 The Hebrew term refers to the irrevocable giving over of things or persons to the LORD, often by totally destroying them.

MARK 11:1-25

As they [Jesus and his disciples] approached Jerusalem and came to Bethphage and Bethany at the Mount of Olives, Jesus sent two of his disciples, ²saying to them, "Go to the village ahead of you, and just as you enter it, you will find a colt tied there, which no one has ever ridden. Untie it and bring it here. ³If anyone asks you, 'Why are you doing this?' tell him, 'The Lord needs it and will send it back here shortly.'"

⁴They went and found a colt outside in the street, tied at a doorway. As they untied it, ⁵some people standing there asked, "What are you doing, untying that colt?" ⁶They answered as Jesus had told them to, and the people let them go. ⁷When they brought the colt to Jesus and threw their cloaks over it, he sat on it. ⁸Many people spread their cloaks on the road, while others spread branches they had cut in the fields. ⁹Those who went ahead and those who followed shouted,

"Hosanna!ᵃ"

"Blessed is he who comes in the
    name of the Lord!"ᵇ

¹⁰"Blessed is the coming kingdom of
    our father David!"

"Hosanna in the highest!"

¹¹Jesus entered Jerusalem and went to the temple. He looked around at everything, but since it was already late, he went out to Bethany with the Twelve.

¹²The next day as they were leaving Bethany, Jesus was hungry. ¹³Seeing in the distance a fig tree in leaf, he went to find out if it had any fruit. When he reached it, he found nothing but leaves, because it was not the season for figs. ¹⁴Then he said to the tree, "May no one ever eat fruit from you again." And his disciples heard him say it.

¹⁵On reaching Jerusalem, Jesus entered the temple area and began driving out those who were buying and selling there. He overturned the tables of the money changers and the benches of those selling doves, ¹⁶and would not allow anyone to carry merchandise through the temple courts. ¹⁷And as he taught them, he said, "Is it not written:

"'My house will be called
    a house of prayer for all
        nations'ᶜ?

But you have made it 'a den of robbers.'*d*"

¹⁸The chief priests and the teachers
of the law heard this and began looking
for a way to kill him, for they feared him,
because the whole crowd was amazed at
his teaching.

¹⁹When evening came, they*e* went
out of the city.

²⁰In the morning, as they went along,
they saw the fig tree withered from the
roots. ²¹Peter remembered and said to
Jesus, "Rabbi, look! The fig tree you
cursed has withered!"

²²"Have*f* faith in God," Jesus answered. ²³"I tell you the truth, if anyone
says to this mountain, 'Go, throw yourself into the sea,' and does not doubt in
his heart but believes that what he says
will happen, it will be done for him.
²⁴Therefore I tell you, whatever you ask
for in prayer, believe that you have received it, and it will be yours. ²⁵And
when you stand praying, if you hold anything against anyone, forgive him, so
that your Father in heaven may forgive
you your sins.*g*"

a9 A Hebrew expression meaning "Save!" which became an
exclamation of praise; also in verse 10   *b9* Psalm 118:25,26
c17 Isaiah 56:7   *d17* Jer. 7:11   *e19* Some early manuscripts *he*
f22 Some early manuscripts *If you have*   *g25* Some
manuscripts *sins.* ²⁶*But if you do not forgive, neither
will your Father who is in heaven forgive your sins.*

PSALM 46:1-11

For the director of music. Of the Sons of
Korah. According to *alamoth.*ᵃ A song.

¹ **God is our refuge and strength,**
    an ever-present help in trouble.
² **Therefore we will not fear, though**
      the earth give way
 and the mountains fall into the
      heart of the sea,
³ **though its waters roar and foam**
 and the mountains quake with
      their surging.   *Selah*

⁴ There is a river whose streams make
    glad the city of God,
 the holy place where the Most
      High dwells.
⁵ God is within her, she will not fall;
 God will help her at break of day.

⁶ Nations are in uproar, kingdoms fall;
 he lifts his voice, the earth melts.

⁷ The LORD Almighty is with us;
 the God of Jacob is our fortress.
                                    Selah

⁸ Come and see the works of the LORD,
 the desolations he has brought on
      the earth.
⁹ He makes wars cease to the ends of
      the earth;
 he breaks the bow and shatters the
      spear,
 he burns the shields*b* with fire.
¹⁰ "Be still, and know that I am God;
 I will be exalted among the nations,
 I will be exalted in the earth."

¹¹ The LORD Almighty is with us;
 the God of Jacob is our fortress.
                                    Selah

a Title: Probably a musical term   *b9* Or *chariots*

PROVERBS 10:23

²³ **A** fool finds pleasure in evil conduct,
 but a man of understanding
      delights in wisdom.

☐ D A Y   6 3

GOD SIGHTINGS

March 4

NUMBERS 2:1-3:51

The LORD said to Moses and Aaron:
²"The Israelites are to camp around the
Tent of Meeting some distance from it,
each man under his standard with the
banners of his family."

³On the east, toward the sunrise,
the divisions of the camp of Judah
are to encamp under their standard.
The leader of the people of Judah is
Nahshon son of Amminadab. ⁴His
division numbers 74,600.

⁵The tribe of Issachar will camp
next to them. The leader of the
people of Issachar is Nethanel son

of Zuar. [6]His division numbers 54,400.

[7]The tribe of Zebulun will be next. The leader of the people of Zebulun is Eliab son of Helon. [8]His division numbers 57,400.

[9]All the men assigned to the camp of Judah, according to their divisions, number 186,400. They will set out first.

[10]On the south will be the divisions of the camp of Reuben under their standard. The leader of the people of Reuben is Elizur son of Shedeur. [11]His division numbers 46,500.

[12]The tribe of Simeon will camp next to them. The leader of the people of Simeon is Shelumiel son of Zurishaddai. [13]His division numbers 59,300.

[14]The tribe of Gad will be next. The leader of the people of Gad is Eliasaph son of Deuel.[a] [15]His division numbers 45,650.

[16]All the men assigned to the camp of Reuben, according to their divisions, number 151,450. They will set out second.

[17]Then the Tent of Meeting and the camp of the Levites will set out in the middle of the camps. They will set out in the same order as they encamp, each in his own place under his standard.

[18]On the west will be the divisions of the camp of Ephraim under their standard. The leader of the people of Ephraim is Elishama son of Ammihud. [19]His division numbers 40,500.

[20]The tribe of Manasseh will be next to them. The leader of the people of Manasseh is Gamaliel son of Pedahzur. [21]His division numbers 32,200.

[22]The tribe of Benjamin will be next. The leader of the people of Benjamin is Abidan son of Gideoni. [23]His division numbers 35,400.

[24]All the men assigned to the camp of Ephraim, according to their divisions, number 108,100. They will set out third.

[25]On the north will be the divisions of the camp of Dan, under their standard. The leader of the people of Dan is Ahiezer son of Ammishaddai. [26]His division numbers 62,700.

[27]The tribe of Asher will camp next to them. The leader of the people of Asher is Pagiel son of Ocran. [28]His division numbers 41,500.

[29]The tribe of Naphtali will be next. The leader of the people of Naphtali is Ahira son of Enan. [30]His division numbers 53,400.

[31]All the men assigned to the camp of Dan number 157,600. They will set out last, under their standards.

[32]These are the Israelites, counted according to their families. All those in the camps, by their divisions, number 603,550. [33]The Levites, however, were not counted along with the other Israelites, as the LORD commanded Moses.

[34]So the Israelites did everything the LORD commanded Moses; that is the way they encamped under their standards, and that is the way they set out, each with his clan and family.

[3:1]THIS is the account of the family of Aaron and Moses at the time the LORD talked with Moses on Mount Sinai.

[2]The names of the sons of Aaron were Nadab the firstborn and Abihu, Eleazar and Ithamar. [3]Those were the names of Aaron's sons, the anointed priests, who were ordained to serve as priests. [4]Nadab and Abihu, however, fell dead before the LORD when they made an offering with unauthorized fire before him in the Desert of Sinai. They had no sons; so only Eleazar and Ithamar served as priests during the lifetime of their father Aaron.

⁵The Lord said to Moses, ⁶"Bring the tribe of Levi and present them to Aaron the priest to assist him. ⁷They are to perform duties for him and for the whole community at the Tent of Meeting by doing the work of the tabernacle. ⁸They are to take care of all the furnishings of the Tent of Meeting, fulfilling the obligations of the Israelites by doing the work of the tabernacle. ⁹Give the Levites to Aaron and his sons; they are the Israelites who are to be given wholly to him.ᵇ ¹⁰Appoint Aaron and his sons to serve as priests; anyone else who approaches the sanctuary must be put to death."

¹¹The Lord also said to Moses, ¹²"I have taken the Levites from among the Israelites in place of the first male offspring of every Israelite woman. The Levites are mine, ¹³for all the firstborn are mine. When I struck down all the firstborn in Egypt, I set apart for myself every firstborn in Israel, whether man or animal. They are to be mine. I am the Lord."

¹⁴The Lord said to Moses in the Desert of Sinai, ¹⁵"Count the Levites by their families and clans. Count every male a month old or more." ¹⁶So Moses counted them, as he was commanded by the word of the Lord.

¹⁷These were the names of the sons of Levi:

Gershon, Kohath and Merari.

¹⁸These were the names of the Gershonite clans:

Libni and Shimei.

¹⁹The Kohathite clans:

Amram, Izhar, Hebron and Uzziel.

²⁰The Merarite clans:

Mahli and Mushi.

These were the Levite clans, according to their families.

²¹To Gershon belonged the clans of the Libnites and Shimeites; these were the Gershonite clans. ²²The number of all the males a month old or more who were counted was 7,500. ²³The Gershonite clans were to camp on the west, behind the tabernacle. ²⁴The leader of the families of the Gershonites was Eliasaph son of Lael. ²⁵At the Tent of Meeting the Gershonites were responsible for the care of the tabernacle and tent, its coverings, the curtain at the entrance to the Tent of Meeting, ²⁶the curtains of the courtyard, the curtain at the entrance to the courtyard surrounding the tabernacle and altar, and the ropes—and everything related to their use.

²⁷To Kohath belonged the clans of the Amramites, Izharites, Hebronites and Uzzielites; these were the Kohathite clans. ²⁸The number of all the males a month old or more was 8,600.ᶜ The Kohathites were responsible for the care of the sanctuary. ²⁹The Kohathite clans were to camp on the south side of the tabernacle. ³⁰The leader of the families of the Kohathite clans was Elizaphan son of Uzziel. ³¹They were responsible for the care of the ark, the table, the lampstand, the altars, the articles of the sanctuary used in ministering, the curtain, and everything related to their use. ³²The chief leader of the Levites was Eleazar son of Aaron, the priest. He was appointed over those who were responsible for the care of the sanctuary.

³³To Merari belonged the clans of the Mahlites and the Mushites; these were the Merarite clans. ³⁴The number of all the males a month old or more who were counted was 6,200. ³⁵The leader of the families of the Merarite clans was Zuriel son of Abihail; they were to camp on the north side of the tabernacle. ³⁶The Merarites were appointed to take care of the frames of the tabernacle, its crossbars, posts, bases, all its equipment, and everything related to their use, ³⁷as well as the posts of the surrounding courtyard with their bases, tent pegs and ropes.

³⁸Moses and Aaron and his sons were to camp to the east of the tabernacle, toward the sunrise, in front of the Tent of

Meeting. They were responsible for the care of the sanctuary on behalf of the Israelites. Anyone else who approached the sanctuary was to be put to death.

39 The total number of Levites counted at the Lord's command by Moses and Aaron according to their clans, including every male a month old or more, was 22,000.

40The Lord said to Moses, "Count all the firstborn Israelite males who are a month old or more and make a list of their names. 41Take the Levites for me in place of all the firstborn of the Israelites, and the livestock of the Levites in place of all the firstborn of the livestock of the Israelites. I am the Lord."

42So Moses counted all the firstborn of the Israelites, as the Lord commanded him. 43The total number of firstborn males a month old or more, listed by name, was 22,273.

44The Lord also said to Moses, 45"Take the Levites in place of all the firstborn of Israel, and the livestock of the Levites in place of their livestock. The Levites are to be mine. I am the Lord. 46To redeem the 273 firstborn Israelites who exceed the number of the Levites, 47collect five shekels*d* for each one, according to the sanctuary shekel, which weighs twenty gerahs. 48Give the money for the redemption of the additional Israelites to Aaron and his sons."

49So Moses collected the redemption money from those who exceeded the number redeemed by the Levites. 50From the firstborn of the Israelites he collected silver weighing 1,365 shekels,*e* according to the sanctuary shekel. 51Moses gave the redemption money to Aaron and his sons, as he was commanded by the word of the Lord.

a14 Many manuscripts of the Masoretic Text, Samaritan Pentateuch and Vulgate (see also Num. 1:14); most manuscripts of the Masoretic Text *Reuel*   *b9* Most manuscripts of the Masoretic Text; some manuscripts of the Masoretic Text, Samaritan Pentateuch and Septuagint (see also Num. 8:16) *to me*   *c28* Hebrew; some Septuagint manuscripts *8,300*   *d47* That is, about 2 ounces (about 55 grams)   *e50* That is, about 35 pounds (about 15.5 kilograms)

MARK 11:27–12:17

They [Jesus and his disciples] arrived again in Jerusalem, and while Jesus was walking in the temple courts, the chief priests, the teachers of the law and the elders came to him. 28"By what authority are you doing these things?" they asked. "And who gave you authority to do this?"

29Jesus replied, "I will ask you one question. Answer me, and I will tell you by what authority I am doing these things. 30John's baptism—was it from heaven, or from men? Tell me!"

31They discussed it among themselves and said, "If we say, 'From heaven,' he will ask, 'Then why didn't you believe him?' 32But if we say, 'From men' . . ." (They feared the people, for everyone held that John really was a prophet.)

33So they answered Jesus, "We don't know."

Jesus said, "Neither will I tell you by what authority I am doing these things."

12:1He then began to speak to them in parables: "A man planted a vineyard. He put a wall around it, dug a pit for the winepress and built a watchtower. Then he rented the vineyard to some farmers and went away on a journey. 2At harvest time he sent a servant to the tenants to collect from them some of the fruit of the vineyard. 3But they seized him, beat him and sent him away empty-handed. 4Then he sent another servant to them; they struck this man on the head and treated him shamefully. 5He sent still another, and that one they killed. He sent many others; some of them they beat, others they killed.

6"He had one left to send, a son, whom he loved. He sent him last of all, saying, 'They will respect my son.'

7"But the tenants said to one another, 'This is the heir. Come, let's kill him, and the inheritance will be ours.' 8So they took him and killed him, and threw him out of the vineyard.

9"What then will the owner of the vineyard do? He will come and kill those tenants and give the vineyard to others. ¹⁰Haven't you read this scripture:

"'The stone the builders rejected
has become the capstone*ᵃ*;
¹¹the Lord has done this,
and it is marvelous in our eyes'*ᵇ*?"

¹²Then they looked for a way to arrest him because they knew he had spoken the parable against them. But they were afraid of the crowd; so they left him and went away.

¹³Later they sent some of the Pharisees and Herodians to Jesus to catch him in his words. ¹⁴They came to him and said, "Teacher, we know you are a man of integrity. You aren't swayed by men, because you pay no attention to who they are; but you teach the way of God in accordance with the truth. Is it right to pay taxes to Caesar or not? ¹⁵Should we pay or shouldn't we?"

But Jesus knew their hypocrisy. "Why are you trying to trap me?" he asked. "Bring me a denarius and let me look at it." ¹⁶They brought the coin, and he asked them, "Whose portrait is this? And whose inscription?"

"Caesar's," they replied.

¹⁷**Then Jesus said to them, "Give to Caesar what is Caesar's and to God what is God's."**

And they were amazed at him.

a10 Or *cornerstone*   *b11* Psalm 118:22,23

PSALM 47:1-9
For the director of music. Of the Sons of Korah. A psalm.

¹**C**lap your hands, all you nations;
shout to God with cries of joy.
²How awesome is the Lᴏʀᴅ Most High,
the great King over all the earth!
³He subdued nations under us,
peoples under our feet.
⁴He chose our inheritance for us,
the pride of Jacob, whom he loved.
Selah

⁵God has ascended amid shouts
of joy,
the Lᴏʀᴅ amid the sounding of
trumpets.

⁶Sing praises to God, sing praises;
sing praises to our King, sing
praises.
⁷For God is the King of all the earth;
sing to him a psalm*ᵃ* of praise.
⁸God reigns over the nations;
God is seated on his holy throne.
⁹The nobles of the nations assemble
as the people of the God of
Abraham,
for the kings*ᵇ* of the earth belong
to God;
he is greatly exalted.

a7 Or *a maskil* (probably a literary or musical term)
b9 Or *shields*

PROVERBS 10:24-25
²⁴**W**hat the wicked dreads will
overtake him;
what the righteous desire will be
granted.

²⁵When the storm has swept by, the
wicked are gone,
but the righteous stand firm
forever.

□ DAY 64

GOD SIGHTINGS

March 5

NUMBERS 4:1-5:31
The Lᴏʀᴅ said to Moses and Aaron: ²"Take a census of the Kohathite branch of the Levites by their clans and families. ³Count all the men from thirty to fifty years of age who come to serve in the work in the Tent of Meeting.

⁴"This is the work of the Kohathites in the Tent of Meeting: the care of the most holy things. ⁵When the camp is to move, Aaron and his sons are to go in and take down the shielding curtain and cover the ark of the Testimony with it. ⁶Then they are to cover this with hides of sea cows,*ᵃ* spread a cloth of

solid blue over that and put the poles in place.

7 "Over the table of the Presence they are to spread a blue cloth and put on it the plates, dishes and bowls, and the jars for drink offerings; the bread that is continually there is to remain on it. 8Over these they are to spread a scarlet cloth, cover that with hides of sea cows and put its poles in place.

9 "They are to take a blue cloth and cover the lampstand that is for light, together with its lamps, its wick trimmers and trays, and all its jars for the oil used to supply it. 10Then they are to wrap it and all its accessories in a covering of hides of sea cows and put it on a carrying frame.

11 "Over the gold altar they are to spread a blue cloth and cover that with hides of sea cows and put its poles in place.

12 "They are to take all the articles used for ministering in the sanctuary, wrap them in a blue cloth, cover that with hides of sea cows and put them on a carrying frame.

13 "They are to remove the ashes from the bronze altar and spread a purple cloth over it. 14Then they are to place on it all the utensils used for ministering at the altar, including the firepans, meat forks, shovels and sprinkling bowls. Over it they are to spread a covering of hides of sea cows and put its poles in place.

15 "After Aaron and his sons have finished covering the holy furnishings and all the holy articles, and when the camp is ready to move, the Kohathites are to come to do the carrying. But they must not touch the holy things or they will die. The Kohathites are to carry those things that are in the Tent of Meeting.

16 "Eleazar son of Aaron, the priest, is to have charge of the oil for the light, the fragrant incense, the regular grain offering and the anointing oil. He is to be in charge of the entire tabernacle and everything in it, including its holy furnishings and articles."

17 The LORD said to Moses and Aaron, 18 "See that the Kohathite tribal clans are not cut off from the Levites. 19So that they may live and not die when they come near the most holy things, do this for them: Aaron and his sons are to go into the sanctuary and assign to each man his work and what he is to carry. 20But the Kohathites must not go in to look at the holy things, even for a moment, or they will die."

21The LORD said to Moses, 22 "Take a census also of the Gershonites by their families and clans. 23Count all the men from thirty to fifty years of age who come to serve in the work at the Tent of Meeting.

24 "This is the service of the Gershonite clans as they work and carry burdens: 25 They are to carry the curtains of the tabernacle, the Tent of Meeting, its covering and the outer covering of hides of sea cows, the curtains for the entrance to the Tent of Meeting, 26 the curtains of the courtyard surrounding the tabernacle and altar, the curtain for the entrance, the ropes and all the equipment used in its service. The Gershonites are to do all that needs to be done with these things. 27All their service, whether carrying or doing other work, is to be done under the direction of Aaron and his sons. You shall assign to them as their responsibility all they are to carry. 28This is the service of the Gershonite clans at the Tent of Meeting. Their duties are to be under the direction of Ithamar son of Aaron, the priest.

29 "Count the Merarites by their clans and families. 30Count all the men from thirty to fifty years of age who come to serve in the work at the Tent of Meeting. 31This is their duty as they perform service at the Tent of Meeting: to carry the frames of the tabernacle, its crossbars, posts and bases, 32 as well as the posts of the surrounding courtyard with their bases, tent pegs, ropes, all their equipment and everything related to their use. Assign to each man the specific things he is to carry. 33This

is the service of the Merarite clans as they work at the Tent of Meeting under the direction of Ithamar son of Aaron, the priest."

34 Moses, Aaron and the leaders of the community counted the Kohathites by their clans and families. 35 All the men from thirty to fifty years of age who came to serve in the work in the Tent of Meeting, 36 counted by clans, were 2,750. 37 This was the total of all those in the Kohathite clans who served in the Tent of Meeting. Moses and Aaron counted them according to the LORD's command through Moses.

38 The Gershonites were counted by their clans and families. 39 All the men from thirty to fifty years of age who came to serve in the work at the Tent of Meeting, 40 counted by their clans and families, were 2,630. 41 This was the total of those in the Gershonite clans who served at the Tent of Meeting. Moses and Aaron counted them according to the LORD's command.

42 The Merarites were counted by their clans and families. 43 All the men from thirty to fifty years of age who came to serve in the work at the Tent of Meeting, 44 counted by their clans, were 3,200. 45 This was the total of those in the Merarite clans. Moses and Aaron counted them according to the LORD's command through Moses.

46 So Moses, Aaron and the leaders of Israel counted all the Levites by their clans and families. 47 All the men from thirty to fifty years of age who came to do the work of serving and carrying the Tent of Meeting 48 numbered 8,580. 49 At the LORD's command through Moses, each was assigned his work and told what to carry.

Thus they were counted, as the LORD commanded Moses.

5:1 THE LORD said to Moses, 2 "Command the Israelites to send away from the camp anyone who has an infectious skin disease*b* or a discharge of any kind, or who is ceremonially unclean because of a dead body. 3 Send away male and fe-

male alike; send them outside the camp so they will not defile their camp, where I dwell among them." 4 The Israelites did this; they sent them outside the camp. They did just as the LORD had instructed Moses.

5 The LORD said to Moses, 6 "Say to the Israelites: 'When a man or woman wrongs another in any way*c* and so is unfaithful to the LORD, that person is guilty 7 and must confess the sin he has committed. He must make full restitution for his wrong, add one fifth to it and give it all to the person he has wronged. 8 But if that person has no close relative to whom restitution can be made for the wrong, the restitution belongs to the LORD and must be given to the priest, along with the ram with which atonement is made for him. 9 All the sacred contributions the Israelites bring to a priest will belong to him. 10 Each man's sacred gifts are his own, but what he gives to the priest will belong to the priest.'"

11 Then the LORD said to Moses, 12 "Speak to the Israelites and say to them: 'If a man's wife goes astray and is unfaithful to him 13 by sleeping with another man, and this is hidden from her husband and her impurity is undetected (since there is no witness against her and she has not been caught in the act), 14 and if feelings of jealousy come over her husband and he suspects his wife and she is impure—or if he is jealous and suspects her even though she is not impure— 15 then he is to take his wife to the priest. He must also take an offering of a tenth of an ephah*d* of barley flour on her behalf. He must not pour oil on it or put incense on it, because it is a grain offering for jealousy, a reminder offering to draw attention to guilt.

16 " 'The priest shall bring her and have her stand before the LORD. 17 Then he shall take some holy water in a clay jar and put some dust from the tabernacle floor into the water. 18 After the priest has had the woman stand before the LORD, he shall loosen her hair and

place in her hands the reminder offering, the grain offering for jealousy, while he himself holds the bitter water that brings a curse. [19]Then the priest shall put the woman under oath and say to her, "If no other man has slept with you and you have not gone astray and become impure while married to your husband, may this bitter water that brings a curse not harm you. [20]But if you have gone astray while married to your husband and you have defiled yourself by sleeping with a man other than your husband"— [21]here the priest is to put the woman under this curse of the oath—"may the Lord cause your people to curse and denounce you when he causes your thigh to waste away and your abdomen to swell.[e] [22]May this water that brings a curse enter your body so that your abdomen swells and your thigh wastes away.[f]"

"'Then the woman is to say, "Amen. So be it."

[23]"'The priest is to write these curses on a scroll and then wash them off into the bitter water. [24]He shall have the woman drink the bitter water that brings a curse, and this water will enter her and cause bitter suffering. [25]The priest is to take from her hands the grain offering for jealousy, wave it before the Lord and bring it to the altar. [26]The priest is then to take a handful of the grain offering as a memorial offering and burn it on the altar; after that, he is to have the woman drink the water. [27]If she has defiled herself and been unfaithful to her husband, then when she is made to drink the water that brings a curse, it will go into her and cause bitter suffering; her abdomen will swell and her thigh waste away,[g] and she will become accursed among her people. [28]If, however, the woman has not defiled herself and is free from impurity, she will be cleared of guilt and will be able to have children.

[29]"'This, then, is the law of jealousy when a woman goes astray and defiles herself while married to her husband, [30]or when feelings of jealousy come

over a man because he suspects his wife. The priest is to have her stand before the Lord and is to apply this entire law to her. [31]The husband will be innocent of any wrongdoing, but the woman will bear the consequences of her sin.'"

[a]6 That is, dugongs; also in verses 8, 10, 11, 12, 14 and 25
[b]2 Traditionally *leprosy*; the Hebrew word was used for various diseases affecting the skin—not necessarily leprosy.
[c]6 Or *woman commits any wrong common to mankind*
[d]15 That is, probably about 2 quarts (about 2 liters)
[e]21 Or *causes you to have a miscarrying womb and barrenness* [f]22 Or *body and cause you to be barren and have a miscarrying womb* [g]27 Or *suffering; she will have barrenness and a miscarrying womb*

MARK 12:18-37

Then the Sadducees, who say there is no resurrection, came to him [Jesus] with a question. [19]"Teacher," they said, "Moses wrote for us that if a man's brother dies and leaves a wife but no children, the man must marry the widow and have children for his brother. [20]Now there were seven brothers. The first one married and died without leaving any children. [21]The second one married the widow, but he also died, leaving no child. It was the same with the third. [22]In fact, none of the seven left any children. Last of all, the woman died too. [23]At the resurrection[a] whose wife will she be, since the seven were married to her?"

[24]Jesus replied, "Are you not in error because you do not know the Scriptures or the power of God? [25]When the dead rise, they will neither marry nor be given in marriage; they will be like the angels in heaven. [26]Now about the dead rising—have you not read in the book of Moses, in the account of the bush, how God said to him, 'I am the God of Abraham, the God of Isaac, and the God of Jacob'[b]? [27]He is not the God of the dead, but of the living. You are badly mistaken!"

[28]One of the teachers of the law came and heard them debating. Noticing that Jesus had given them a good answer, he asked him, "Of all the commandments, which is the most important?"

[29]"The most important one," answered Jesus, "is this: 'Hear, O Israel, the

Lord our God, the Lord is one.*c* 30Love the Lord your God with all your heart and with all your soul and with all your mind and with all your strength.'*d* 31The second is this: 'Love your neighbor as yourself.'*e* There is no commandment greater than these."

32"Well said, teacher," the man replied. "You are right in saying that God is one and there is no other but him. 33**To love him with all your heart, with all your understanding and with all your strength, and to love your neighbor as yourself is more important than all burnt offerings and sacrifices.**"

34When Jesus saw that he had answered wisely, he said to him, "You are not far from the kingdom of God." And from then on no one dared ask him any more questions.

35While Jesus was teaching in the temple courts, he asked, "How is it that the teachers of the law say that the Christ*f* is the son of David? 36David himself, speaking by the Holy Spirit, declared:

> "'The Lord said to my Lord:
> "Sit at my right hand
> until I put your enemies
> under your feet."'*g*

37David himself calls him 'Lord.' How then can he be his son?"

The large crowd listened to him with delight.

a23 Some manuscripts *resurrection, when men rise from the dead,* *b26* Exodus 3:6 *c29* Or *the Lord our God is one Lord* *d30* Deut. 6:4,5 *e31* Lev. 19:18 *f35* Or *Messiah* *g36* Psalm 110:1

PSALM 48:1-14
A song. A psalm of the Sons of Korah.

1 **G**reat is the LORD, and most worthy
of praise,
in the city of our God, his holy
mountain.
2 It is beautiful in its loftiness,
the joy of the whole earth.
Like the utmost heights of Zaphon*a*
is Mount Zion,
the*b* city of the Great King.

3 God is in her citadels;
he has shown himself to be her
fortress.

4 When the kings joined forces,
when they advanced together,
5 they saw ⌐her⌐ and were astounded;
they fled in terror.
6 Trembling seized them there,
pain like that of a woman
in labor.
7 You destroyed them like ships of
Tarshish
shattered by an east wind.

8 As we have heard,
so have we seen
in the city of the LORD Almighty,
in the city of our God:
God makes her secure forever.
Selah

9 Within your temple, O God,
we meditate on your unfailing
love.
10 Like your name, O God,
your praise reaches to the ends
of the earth;
your right hand is filled with
righteousness.
11 Mount Zion rejoices,
the villages of Judah are glad
because of your judgments.

12 Walk about Zion, go around her,
count her towers,
13 consider well her ramparts,
view her citadels,
that you may tell of them to the
next generation.
14 For this God is our God for ever and
ever;
he will be our guide even to the
end.

a2 Zaphon *can refer to a sacred mountain or the direction north.* *b2* Or *earth, / Mount Zion, on the northern side / of the*

PROVERBS 10:26
26 **A**s vinegar to the teeth and smoke
to the eyes,
so is a sluggard to those who
send him.

GOD SIGHTINGS

March 6

NUMBERS 6:1–7:89

The LORD said to Moses, [2]"Speak to the Israelites and say to them: 'If a man or woman wants to make a special vow, a vow of separation to the LORD as a Nazirite, [3]he must abstain from wine and other fermented drink and must not drink vinegar made from wine or from other fermented drink. He must not drink grape juice or eat grapes or raisins. [4]As long as he is a Nazirite, he must not eat anything that comes from the grapevine, not even the seeds or skins.

[5]" 'During the entire period of his vow of separation no razor may be used on his head. He must be holy until the period of his separation to the LORD is over; he must let the hair of his head grow long. [6]Throughout the period of his separation to the LORD he must not go near a dead body. [7]Even if his own father or mother or brother or sister dies, he must not make himself ceremonially unclean on account of them, because the symbol of his separation to God is on his head. [8]Throughout the period of his separation he is consecrated to the LORD.

[9]" 'If someone dies suddenly in his presence, thus defiling the hair he has dedicated, he must shave his head on the day of his cleansing—the seventh day. [10]Then on the eighth day he must bring two doves or two young pigeons to the priest at the entrance to the Tent of Meeting. [11]The priest is to offer one as a sin offering and the other as a burnt offering to make atonement for him because he sinned by being in the presence of the dead body. That same day he is to consecrate his head. [12]He must dedicate himself to the LORD for the period of his separation and must bring a year-old male lamb as a guilt offering. The previous days do not count, because he became defiled during his separation.

[13]" 'Now this is the law for the Nazirite when the period of his separation is over. He is to be brought to the entrance to the Tent of Meeting. [14]There he is to present his offerings to the LORD: a year-old male lamb without defect for a burnt offering, a year-old ewe lamb without defect for a sin offering, a ram without defect for a fellowship offering,[a] [15]together with their grain offerings and drink offerings, and a basket of bread made without yeast—cakes made of fine flour mixed with oil, and wafers spread with oil.

[16]" 'The priest is to present them before the LORD and make the sin offering and the burnt offering. [17]He is to present the basket of unleavened bread and is to sacrifice the ram as a fellowship offering to the LORD, together with its grain offering and drink offering.

[18]" 'Then at the entrance to the Tent of Meeting, the Nazirite must shave off the hair that he dedicated. He is to take the hair and put it in the fire that is under the sacrifice of the fellowship offering.

[19]" 'After the Nazirite has shaved off the hair of his dedication, the priest is to place in his hands a boiled shoulder of the ram, and a cake and a wafer from the basket, both made without yeast. [20]The priest shall then wave them before the LORD as a wave offering; they are holy and belong to the priest, together with the breast that was waved and the thigh that was presented. After that, the Nazirite may drink wine.

[21]" 'This is the law of the Nazirite who vows his offering to the LORD in accordance with his separation, in addition to whatever else he can afford. He must fulfill the vow he has made, according to the law of the Nazirite.'"

[22]The LORD said to Moses, [23]"Tell Aaron and his sons, 'This is how you are to bless the Israelites. Say to them:

[24]" ' " The LORD bless you
and keep you;

²⁵the LORD make his face shine upon
you
and be gracious to you;
²⁶the LORD turn his face toward you
and give you peace."'

²⁷"So they will put my name on the Israelites, and I will bless them."

⁷:¹WHEN Moses finished setting up the
tabernacle, he anointed it and consecrated it and all its furnishings. He also
anointed and consecrated the altar and
all its utensils. ²Then the leaders of Israel, the heads of families who were the
tribal leaders in charge of those who
were counted, made offerings. ³They
brought as their gifts before the LORD
six covered carts and twelve oxen—an
ox from each leader and a cart from every two. These they presented before
the tabernacle.

⁴The LORD said to Moses, ⁵"Accept
these from them, that they may be used
in the work at the Tent of Meeting. Give
them to the Levites as each man's work
requires."

⁶So Moses took the carts and oxen
and gave them to the Levites. ⁷He gave
two carts and four oxen to the Gershonites, as their work required, ⁸and he gave
four carts and eight oxen to the Merarites, as their work required. They were
all under the direction of Ithamar son of
Aaron, the priest. ⁹But Moses did not
give any to the Kohathites, because they
were to carry on their shoulders the
holy things, for which they were responsible.

¹⁰When the altar was anointed, the
leaders brought their offerings for its
dedication and presented them before
the altar. ¹¹For the LORD had said to Moses, "Each day one leader is to bring his
offering for the dedication of the altar."

¹²The one who brought his offering on
the first day was Nahshon son of Amminadab of the tribe of Judah.

¹³His offering was one silver plate
weighing a hundred and thirty
shekels,ᵇ and one silver sprinkling
bowl weighing seventy shekels,ᶜ

both according to the sanctuary
shekel, each filled with fine flour
mixed with oil as a grain offering;
¹⁴one gold dish weighing ten shekels,ᵈ filled with incense; ¹⁵one
young bull, one ram and one male
lamb a year old, for a burnt offering; ¹⁶one male goat for a sin offering; ¹⁷and two oxen, five rams, five
male goats and five male lambs a
year old, to be sacrificed as a fellowship offering.ᵉ This was the offering of Nahshon son of
Amminadab.

¹⁸On the second day Nethanel son of
Zuar, the leader of Issachar, brought his
offering.

¹⁹The offering he brought was one
silver plate weighing a hundred
and thirty shekels, and one silver
sprinkling bowl weighing seventy
shekels, both according to the
sanctuary shekel, each filled with
fine flour mixed with oil as a grain
offering; ²⁰one gold dish weighing
ten shekels, filled with incense;
²¹one young bull, one ram and one
male lamb a year old, for a burnt
offering; ²²one male goat for a sin
offering; ²³and two oxen, five
rams, five male goats and five male
lambs a year old, to be sacrificed as
a fellowship offering. This was the
offering of Nethanel son of Zuar.

²⁴On the third day, Eliab son of Helon,
the leader of the people of Zebulun,
brought his offering.

²⁵His offering was one silver plate
weighing a hundred and thirty
shekels, and one silver sprinkling
bowl weighing seventy shekels,
both according to the sanctuary
shekel, each filled with fine flour
mixed with oil as a grain offering;
²⁶one gold dish weighing ten shekels, filled with incense; ²⁷one
young bull, one ram and one male
lamb a year old, for a burnt offering; ²⁸one male goat for a sin offering; ²⁹and two oxen, five rams,

five male goats and five male lambs a year old, to be sacrificed as a fellowship offering. This was the offering of Eliab son of Helon.

³⁰On the fourth day Elizur son of Shedeur, the leader of the people of Reuben, brought his offering.

³¹His offering was one silver plate weighing a hundred and thirty shekels, and one silver sprinkling bowl weighing seventy shekels, both according to the sanctuary shekel, each filled with fine flour mixed with oil as a grain offering; ³²one gold dish weighing ten shekels, filled with incense; ³³one young bull, one ram and one male lamb a year old, for a burnt offering; ³⁴one male goat for a sin offering; ³⁵and two oxen, five rams, five male goats and five male lambs a year old, to be sacrificed as a fellowship offering. This was the offering of Elizur son of Shedeur.

³⁶On the fifth day Shelumiel son of Zurishaddai, the leader of the people of Simeon, brought his offering.

³⁷His offering was one silver plate weighing a hundred and thirty shekels, and one silver sprinkling bowl weighing seventy shekels, both according to the sanctuary shekel, each filled with fine flour mixed with oil as a grain offering; ³⁸one gold dish weighing ten shekels, filled with incense; ³⁹one young bull, one ram and one male lamb a year old, for a burnt offering; ⁴⁰one male goat for a sin offering; ⁴¹and two oxen, five rams, five male goats and five male lambs a year old, to be sacrificed as a fellowship offering. This was the offering of Shelumiel son of Zurishaddai.

⁴²On the sixth day Eliasaph son of Deuel, the leader of the people of Gad, brought his offering.

⁴³His offering was one silver plate weighing a hundred and thirty

shekels, and one silver sprinkling bowl weighing seventy shekels, both according to the sanctuary shekel, each filled with fine flour mixed with oil as a grain offering; ⁴⁴one gold dish weighing ten shekels, filled with incense; ⁴⁵one young bull, one ram and one male lamb a year old, for a burnt offering; ⁴⁶one male goat for a sin offering; ⁴⁷and two oxen, five rams, five male goats and five male lambs a year old, to be sacrificed as a fellowship offering. This was the offering of Eliasaph son of Deuel.

⁴⁸On the seventh day Elishama son of Ammihud, the leader of the people of Ephraim, brought his offering.

⁴⁹His offering was one silver plate weighing a hundred and thirty shekels, and one silver sprinkling bowl weighing seventy shekels, both according to the sanctuary shekel, each filled with fine flour mixed with oil as a grain offering; ⁵⁰one gold dish weighing ten shekels, filled with incense; ⁵¹one young bull, one ram and one male lamb a year old, for a burnt offering; ⁵²one male goat for a sin offering; ⁵³and two oxen, five rams, five male goats and five male lambs a year old, to be sacrificed as a fellowship offering. This was the offering of Elishama son of Ammihud.

⁵⁴On the eighth day Gamaliel son of Pedahzur, the leader of the people of Manasseh, brought his offering.

⁵⁵His offering was one silver plate weighing a hundred and thirty shekels, and one silver sprinkling bowl weighing seventy shekels, both according to the sanctuary shekel, each filled with fine flour mixed with oil as a grain offering; ⁵⁶one gold dish weighing ten shekels, filled with incense; ⁵⁷one young bull, one ram and one male lamb a year old, for a burnt offering; ⁵⁸one

male goat for a sin offering; ⁵⁹and two oxen, five rams, five male goats and five male lambs a year old, to be sacrificed as a fellowship offering. This was the offering of Gamaliel son of Pedahzur.

⁶⁰On the ninth day Abidan son of Gideoni, the leader of the people of Benjamin, brought his offering.

⁶¹His offering was one silver plate weighing a hundred and thirty shekels, and one silver sprinkling bowl weighing seventy shekels, both according to the sanctuary shekel, each filled with fine flour mixed with oil as a grain offering; ⁶²one gold dish weighing ten shekels, filled with incense; ⁶³one young bull, one ram and one male lamb a year old, for a burnt offering; ⁶⁴one male goat for a sin offering; ⁶⁵and two oxen, five rams, five male goats and five male lambs a year old, to be sacrificed as a fellowship offering. This was the offering of Abidan son of Gideoni.

⁶⁶On the tenth day Ahiezer son of Ammishaddai, the leader of the people of Dan, brought his offering.

⁶⁷His offering was one silver plate weighing a hundred and thirty shekels, and one silver sprinkling bowl weighing seventy shekels, both according to the sanctuary shekel, each filled with fine flour mixed with oil as a grain offering; ⁶⁸one gold dish weighing ten shekels, filled with incense; ⁶⁹one young bull, one ram and one male lamb a year old, for a burnt offering; ⁷⁰one male goat for a sin offering; ⁷¹and two oxen, five rams, five male goats and five male lambs a year old, to be sacrificed as a fellowship offering. This was the offering of Ahiezer son of Ammishaddai.

⁷²On the eleventh day Pagiel son of Ocran, the leader of the people of Asher, brought his offering.

⁷³His offering was one silver plate weighing a hundred and thirty shekels, and one silver sprinkling bowl weighing seventy shekels, both according to the sanctuary shekel, each filled with fine flour mixed with oil as a grain offering; ⁷⁴one gold dish weighing ten shekels, filled with incense; ⁷⁵one young bull, one ram and one male lamb a year old, for a burnt offering; ⁷⁶one male goat for a sin offering; ⁷⁷and two oxen, five rams, five male goats and five male lambs a year old, to be sacrificed as a fellowship offering. This was the offering of Pagiel son of Ocran.

⁷⁸On the twelfth day Ahira son of Enan, the leader of the people of Naphtali, brought his offering.

⁷⁹His offering was one silver plate weighing a hundred and thirty shekels, and one silver sprinkling bowl weighing seventy shekels, both according to the sanctuary shekel, each filled with fine flour mixed with oil as a grain offering; ⁸⁰one gold dish weighing ten shekels, filled with incense; ⁸¹one young bull, one ram and one male lamb a year old, for a burnt offering; ⁸²one male goat for a sin offering; ⁸³and two oxen, five rams, five male goats and five male lambs a year old, to be sacrificed as a fellowship offering. This was the offering of Ahira son of Enan.

⁸⁴These were the offerings of the Israelite leaders for the dedication of the altar when it was anointed: twelve silver plates, twelve silver sprinkling bowls and twelve gold dishes. ⁸⁵Each silver plate weighed a hundred and thirty shekels, and each sprinkling bowl seventy shekels. Altogether, the silver dishes weighed two thousand four hundred shekels,ᶠ according to the sanctuary shekel. ⁸⁶The twelve gold dishes filled with incense weighed ten shekels each, according to the sanctuary shekel. Alto-

gether, the gold dishes weighed a hundred and twenty shekels.*g* 87 The total number of animals for the burnt offering came to twelve young bulls, twelve rams and twelve male lambs a year old, together with their grain offering. Twelve male goats were used for the sin offering. 88 The total number of animals for the sacrifice of the fellowship offering came to twenty-four oxen, sixty rams, sixty male goats and sixty male lambs a year old. These were the offerings for the dedication of the altar after it was anointed.

89 When Moses entered the Tent of Meeting to speak with the LORD, he heard the voice speaking to him from between the two cherubim above the atonement cover on the ark of the Testimony. And he spoke with him.

a14 Traditionally *peace offering*; also in verses 17 and 18   *b13* That is, about 3 1/4 pounds (about 1.5 kilograms); also elsewhere in this chapter   *c13* That is, about 1 3/4 pounds (about 0.8 kilogram); also elsewhere in this chapter   *d14* That is, about 4 ounces (about 110 grams); also elsewhere in this chapter   *e17* Traditionally *peace offering*; also elsewhere in this chapter   *f85* That is, about 60 pounds (about 28 kilograms)   *986* That is, about 3 pounds (about 1.4 kilograms)

MARK 12:38–13:13

As he taught, Jesus said, "Watch out for the teachers of the law. They like to walk around in flowing robes and be greeted in the marketplaces, 39 and have the most important seats in the synagogues and the places of honor at banquets. 40 They devour widows' houses and for a show make lengthy prayers. Such men will be punished most severely."

41 Jesus sat down opposite the place where the offerings were put and watched the crowd putting their money into the temple treasury. Many rich people threw in large amounts. 42 But a poor widow came and put in two very small copper coins,*a* worth only a fraction of a penny.*b*

43 Calling his disciples to him, Jesus said, "I tell you the truth, this poor widow has put more into the treasury than all the others. 44 They all gave out of their wealth; but she, out of her poverty, put in everything—all she had to live on."

13:1 As he was leaving the temple, one of his disciples said to him, "Look, Teacher! What massive stones! What magnificent buildings!"

2 "Do you see all these great buildings?" replied Jesus. "Not one stone here will be left on another; every one will be thrown down."

3 As Jesus was sitting on the Mount of Olives opposite the temple, Peter, James, John and Andrew asked him privately, 4 "Tell us, when will these things happen? And what will be the sign that they are all about to be fulfilled?"

5 Jesus said to them: "Watch out that no one deceives you. 6 Many will come in my name, claiming, 'I am he,' and will deceive many. 7 When you hear of wars and rumors of wars, do not be alarmed. Such things must happen, but the end is still to come. 8 Nation will rise against nation, and kingdom against kingdom. There will be earthquakes in various places, and famines. These are the beginning of birth pains.

9 "You must be on your guard. You will be handed over to the local councils and flogged in the synagogues. On account of me you will stand before governors and kings as witnesses to them. 10 And the gospel must first be preached to all nations. 11 Whenever you are arrested and brought to trial, do not worry beforehand about what to say. Just say whatever is given you at the time, for it is not you speaking, but the Holy Spirit.

12 "Brother will betray brother to death, and a father his child. Children will rebel against their parents and have them put to death. 13 All men will hate you because of me, but he who stands firm to the end will be saved."

a42 Greek *two lepta*   *b42* Greek *kodrantes*

PSALM 49:1-20

For the director of music. Of the Sons of Korah. A psalm.

1 Hear this, all you peoples;
    listen, all who live in this world,
2 both low and high,
    rich and poor alike:

3 My mouth will speak words of
    wisdom;
  the utterance from my heart will
    give understanding.
4 I will turn my ear to a proverb;
  with the harp I will expound
    my riddle:

5 Why should I fear when evil days
    come,
  when wicked deceivers
    surround me—
6 those who trust in their wealth
  and boast of their great riches?
7 No man can redeem the life of
    another
  or give to God a ransom for him—
8 the ransom for a life is costly,
  no payment is ever enough—
9 that he should live on forever
  and not see decay.

10 For all can see that wise men die;
  the foolish and the senseless alike
    perish
  and leave their wealth to others.
11 Their tombs will remain their
    houses[a] forever,
  their dwellings for endless
    generations,
  though they had[b] named lands
    after themselves.

12 But man, despite his riches, does not
    endure;
  he is[c] like the beasts that perish.

13 This is the fate of those who trust in
    themselves,
  and of their followers, who
    approve their sayings.   *Selah*
14 Like sheep they are destined for the
    grave,[d]
  and death will feed on them.
  The upright will rule over them in
    the morning;
  their forms will decay in the
    grave,[d]
  far from their princely mansions.
15 But God will redeem my life[e] from
    the grave;
  he will surely take me to himself.
                    Selah

16 Do not be overawed when a man
    grows rich,
  when the splendor of his house
    increases;
17 for he will take nothing with him
    when he dies,
  his splendor will not descend
    with him.
18 Though while he lived he counted
    himself blessed—
  and men praise you when you
    prosper—
19 he will join the generation of his
    fathers,
  who will never see the light
    ⌊of life⌋.

20 A man who has riches without
    understanding
  is like the beasts that perish.

*a 11 Septuagint and Syriac; Hebrew In their thoughts their
houses will remain   b 11 Or /for they have   c 12 Hebrew;
Septuagint and Syriac read verse 12 the same as verse 20.
d 14 Hebrew Sheol; also in verse 15   e 15 Or soul*

PROVERBS 10:27-28

27 The fear of the LORD adds length
    to life,
  but the years of the wicked are
    cut short.

28 The prospect of the righteous is joy,
  but the hopes of the wicked come
    to nothing.

☐ D A Y   6 6

GOD SIGHTINGS

March 7

NUMBERS 8:1-9:23

The LORD said to Moses, 2 "Speak to
Aaron and say to him, 'When you set up
the seven lamps, they are to light the
area in front of the lampstand.'"

3 Aaron did so; he set up the lamps so
that they faced forward on the lampstand, just as the LORD commanded Moses. 4 This is how the lampstand was
made: It was made of hammered gold—

from its base to its blossoms. The lampstand was made exactly like the pattern the Lord had shown Moses.

5 The Lord said to Moses: 6 "Take the Levites from among the other Israelites and make them ceremonially clean. 7 To purify them, do this: Sprinkle the water of cleansing on them; then have them shave their whole bodies and wash their clothes, and so purify themselves. 8 Have them take a young bull with its grain offering of fine flour mixed with oil; then you are to take a second young bull for a sin offering. 9 Bring the Levites to the front of the Tent of Meeting and assemble the whole Israelite community. 10 You are to bring the Levites before the Lord, and the Israelites are to lay their hands on them. 11 Aaron is to present the Levites before the Lord as a wave offering from the Israelites, so that they may be ready to do the work of the Lord.

12 "After the Levites lay their hands on the heads of the bulls, use the one for a sin offering to the Lord and the other for a burnt offering, to make atonement for the Levites. 13 Have the Levites stand in front of Aaron and his sons and then present them as a wave offering to the Lord. 14 In this way you are to set the Levites apart from the other Israelites, and the Levites will be mine.

15 "After you have purified the Levites and presented them as a wave offering, they are to come to do their work at the Tent of Meeting. 16 They are the Israelites who are to be given wholly to me. I have taken them as my own in place of the firstborn, the first male offspring from every Israelite woman. 17 Every firstborn male in Israel, whether man or animal, is mine. When I struck down all the firstborn in Egypt, I set them apart for myself. 18 And I have taken the Levites in place of all the firstborn sons in Israel. 19 Of all the Israelites, I have given the Levites as gifts to Aaron and his sons to do the work at the Tent of Meeting on behalf of the Israelites and to make atonement for them so that no plague

will strike the Israelites when they go near the sanctuary."

20 Moses, Aaron and the whole Israelite community did with the Levites just as the Lord commanded Moses. 21 The Levites purified themselves and washed their clothes. Then Aaron presented them as a wave offering before the Lord and made atonement for them to purify them. 22 After that, the Levites came to do their work at the Tent of Meeting under the supervision of Aaron and his sons. They did with the Levites just as the Lord commanded Moses.

23 The Lord said to Moses, 24 "This applies to the Levites: Men twenty-five years old or more shall come to take part in the work at the Tent of Meeting, 25 but at the age of fifty, they must retire from their regular service and work no longer. 26 They may assist their brothers in performing their duties at the Tent of Meeting, but they themselves must not do the work. This, then, is how you are to assign the responsibilities of the Levites."

9:1 THE Lord spoke to Moses in the Desert of Sinai in the first month of the second year after they came out of Egypt. He said, 2 "Have the Israelites celebrate the Passover at the appointed time. 3 Celebrate it at the appointed time, at twilight on the fourteenth day of this month, in accordance with all its rules and regulations."

4 So Moses told the Israelites to celebrate the Passover, 5 and they did so in the Desert of Sinai at twilight on the fourteenth day of the first month. The Israelites did everything just as the Lord commanded Moses.

6 But some of them could not celebrate the Passover on that day because they were ceremonially unclean on account of a dead body. So they came to Moses and Aaron that same day 7 and said to Moses, "We have become unclean because of a dead body, but why should we be kept from presenting the Lord's offering with the other Israelites at the appointed time?"

8 Moses answered them, "Wait until I

find out what the LORD commands concerning you."

9 Then the LORD said to Moses, 10 "Tell the Israelites: 'When any of you or your descendants are unclean because of a dead body or are away on a journey, they may still celebrate the LORD's Passover. 11 They are to celebrate it on the fourteenth day of the second month at twilight. They are to eat the lamb, together with unleavened bread and bitter herbs. 12 They must not leave any of it till morning or break any of its bones. When they celebrate the Passover, they must follow all the regulations. 13 But if a man who is ceremonially clean and not on a journey fails to celebrate the Passover, that person must be cut off from his people because he did not present the LORD's offering at the appointed time. That man will bear the consequences of his sin.

14 " 'An alien living among you who wants to celebrate the LORD's Passover must do so in accordance with its rules and regulations. You must have the same regulations for the alien and the native-born.' "

15 On the day the tabernacle, the Tent of the Testimony, was set up, the cloud covered it. From evening till morning the cloud above the tabernacle looked like fire. 16 That is how it continued to be; the cloud covered it, and at night it looked like fire. 17 Whenever the cloud lifted from above the Tent, the Israelites set out; wherever the cloud settled, the Israelites encamped. 18 At the LORD's command the Israelites set out, and at his command they encamped. As long as the cloud stayed over the tabernacle, they remained in camp. 19 When the cloud remained over the tabernacle a long time, the Israelites obeyed the LORD's order and did not set out. 20 Sometimes the cloud was over the tabernacle only a few days; at the LORD's command they would encamp, and then at his command they would set out. 21 Sometimes the cloud stayed only from evening till morning, and when it lifted in the morning, they set out.

Whether by day or by night, whenever the cloud lifted, they set out. 22 Whether the cloud stayed over the tabernacle for two days or a month or a year, the Israelites would remain in camp and not set out; but when it lifted, they would set out. 23 At the LORD's command they encamped, and at the LORD's command they set out. They obeyed the LORD's order, in accordance with his command through Moses.

MARK 13:14-37

"When you see 'the abomination that causes desolation'a standing where itb does not belong—let the reader understand—then let those who are in Judea flee to the mountains. 15 Let no one on the roof of his house go down or enter the house to take anything out. 16 Let no one in the field go back to get his cloak. 17 How dreadful it will be in those days for pregnant women and nursing mothers! 18 Pray that this will not take place in winter, 19 because those will be days of distress unequaled from the beginning, when God created the world, until now— and never to be equaled again. 20 If the Lord had not cut short those days, no one would survive. But for the sake of the elect, whom he has chosen, he has shortened them. 21 At that time if anyone says to you, 'Look, here is the Christ c !' or, 'Look, there he is!' do not believe it. 22 For false Christs and false prophets will appear and perform signs and miracles to deceive the elect—if that were possible. 23 So be on your guard; I have told you everything ahead of time.

24 "But in those days, following that distress,

" 'the sun will be darkened,
    and the moon will not give its
        light;
25 the stars will fall from the sky,
    and the heavenly bodies will be
        shaken.' d

26 "At that time men will see the Son of Man coming in clouds with great power and glory. 27 And he will send his angels and gather his elect from the

four winds, from the ends of the earth to the ends of the heavens.

28"Now learn this lesson from the fig tree: As soon as its twigs get tender and its leaves come out, you know that summer is near. 29Even so, when you see these things happening, you know that it is near, right at the door. 30I tell you the truth, this generation[e] will certainly not pass away until all these things have happened. 31Heaven and earth will pass away, but my words will never pass away.

32**"No one knows about that day or hour, not even the angels in heaven, nor the Son, but only the Father. 33Be on guard! Be alert[f]! You do not know when that time will come. 34It's like a** man going away: He leaves his house and puts his servants in charge, each with his assigned task, and tells the one at the door to keep watch.

35"Therefore keep watch because you do not know when the owner of the house will come back—whether in the evening, or at midnight, or when the rooster crows, or at dawn. 36If he comes suddenly, do not let him find you sleeping. 37What I say to you, I say to everyone: 'Watch!'"

a14 Daniel 9:27; 11:31; 12:11   *b14* Or *he;* also in verse 29
c21 Or *Messiah*   *d25* Isaiah 13:10; 34:4   *e30* Or *race*
f33 Some manuscripts *alert and pray*

PSALM 50:1-23
A psalm of Asaph.

1The Mighty One, God, the LORD,
  speaks and summons the earth
  from the rising of the sun to the
    place where it sets.
2From Zion, perfect in beauty,
  God shines forth.
3Our God comes and will not be
    silent;
  a fire devours before him,
  and around him a tempest rages.
4He summons the heavens above,
  and the earth, that he may judge
    his people:
5"Gather to me my consecrated ones,
  who made a covenant with me by
    sacrifice."

6And the heavens proclaim his
    righteousness,
  for God himself is judge.   *Selah*

7"Hear, O my people, and I will speak,
  O Israel, and I will testify
    against you:
  I am God, your God.
8I do not rebuke you for your
    sacrifices
  or your burnt offerings, which are
    ever before me.
9I have no need of a bull from
    your stall
  or of goats from your pens,
10for every animal of the forest
    is mine,
  and the cattle on a thousand hills.
11I know every bird in the mountains,
  and the creatures of the field
    are mine.
12If I were hungry I would not tell you,
  for the world is mine, and all that
    is in it.
13Do I eat the flesh of bulls
  or drink the blood of goats?
14Sacrifice thank offerings to God,
  fulfill your vows to the Most High,
15and call upon me in the day of
    trouble;
  I will deliver you, and you will
    honor me."

16But to the wicked, God says:

"What right have you to recite
    my laws
  or take my covenant on your lips?
17You hate my instruction
  and cast my words behind you.
18When you see a thief, you join
    with him;
  you throw in your lot with
    adulterers.
19You use your mouth for evil
  and harness your tongue to deceit.
20You speak continually against your
    brother
  and slander your own mother's son.
21These things you have done and I
    kept silent;
  you thought I was altogether[a]
    like you.

But I will rebuke you
and accuse you to your face.

22"Consider this, you who forget God,
or I will tear you to pieces, with
none to rescue:
23He who sacrifices thank offerings
honors me,
and he prepares the way
so that I may show him*b* the
salvation of God."

*a21 Or thought the 'I AM' was   b23 Or and to him who
considers his way / I will show*

PROVERBS 10:29-30
29The way of the LORD is a refuge for
the righteous,
but it is the ruin of those who
do evil.

30The righteous will never be uprooted,
but the wicked will not remain in
the land.

□ DAY 67

GOD SIGHTINGS

March 8

NUMBERS 10:1-11:23
The LORD said to Moses: 2"Make two
trumpets of hammered silver, and use
them for calling the community together
and for having the camps set out. 3When
both are sounded, the whole community
is to assemble before you at the entrance
to the Tent of Meeting. 4If only one is
sounded, the leaders—the heads of the
clans of Israel—are to assemble before
you. 5When a trumpet blast is sounded,
the tribes camping on the east are to set
out. 6At the sounding of a second blast,
the camps on the south are to set out. The
blast will be the signal for setting out. 7To
gather the assembly, blow the trumpets,
but not with the same signal.

8"The sons of Aaron, the priests, are
to blow the trumpets. This is to be a lasting ordinance for you and the genera-

tions to come. 9When you go into battle
in your own land against an enemy who
is oppressing you, sound a blast on the
trumpets. Then you will be remembered by the LORD your God and rescued
from your enemies. 10Also at your times
of rejoicing—your appointed feasts and
New Moon festivals—you are to sound
the trumpets over your burnt offerings
and fellowship offerings,*a* and they will
be a memorial for you before your God. I
am the LORD your God."

11On the twentieth day of the second
month of the second year, the cloud
lifted from above the tabernacle of the
Testimony. 12Then the Israelites set out
from the Desert of Sinai and traveled
from place to place until the cloud came
to rest in the Desert of Paran. 13They set
out, this first time, at the LORD's command through Moses.

14The divisions of the camp of Judah
went first, under their standard. Nahshon son of Amminadab was in command. 15Nethanel son of Zuar was over
the division of the tribe of Issachar,
16and Eliab son of Helon was over the
division of the tribe of Zebulun. 17Then
the tabernacle was taken down, and the
Gershonites and Merarites, who carried
it, set out.

18The divisions of the camp of Reuben went next, under their standard.
Elizur son of Shedeur was in command.
19Shelumiel son of Zurishaddai was
over the division of the tribe of Simeon,
20and Eliasaph son of Deuel was over
the division of the tribe of Gad. 21Then
the Kohathites set out, carrying the holy
things. The tabernacle was to be set up
before they arrived.

22The divisions of the camp of
Ephraim went next, under their standard.
Elishama son of Ammihud was in command. 23Gamaliel son of Pedahzur was
over the division of the tribe of Manasseh,
24and Abidan son of Gideoni was over the
division of the tribe of Benjamin.

25Finally, as the rear guard for all the
units, the divisions of the camp of Dan
set out, under their standard. Ahiezer
son of Ammishaddai was in command.

26Pagiel son of Ocran was over the division of the tribe of Asher, 27and Ahira son of Enan was over the division of the tribe of Naphtali. 28This was the order of march for the Israelite divisions as they set out.

29Now Moses said to Hobab son of Reuel the Midianite, Moses' father-in-law, "We are setting out for the place about which the Lord said, 'I will give it to you.' Come with us and we will treat you well, for the Lord has promised good things to Israel."

30He answered, "No, I will not go; I am going back to my own land and my own people."

31But Moses said, "Please do not leave us. You know where we should camp in the desert, and you can be our eyes. 32If you come with us, we will share with you whatever good things the Lord gives us."

33So they set out from the mountain of the Lord and traveled for three days. The ark of the covenant of the Lord went before them during those three days to find them a place to rest. 34The cloud of the Lord was over them by day when they set out from the camp.

35Whenever the ark set out, Moses said,

"Rise up, O Lord!
    May your enemies be scattered;
    may your foes flee before you."

36Whenever it came to rest, he said,

"Return, O Lord,
    to the countless thousands of
        Israel."

11:1Now the people complained about their hardships in the hearing of the Lord, and when he heard them his anger was aroused. Then fire from the Lord burned among them and consumed some of the outskirts of the camp. 2When the people cried out to Moses, he prayed to the Lord and the fire died down. 3So that place was called Taberah,b because fire from the Lord had burned among them.

4The rabble with them began to crave other food, and again the Israelites started wailing and said, "If only we had meat to eat! 5We remember the fish we ate in Egypt at no cost—also the cucumbers, melons, leeks, onions and garlic. 6But now we have lost our appetite; we never see anything but this manna!"

7The manna was like coriander seed and looked like resin. 8The people went around gathering it, and then ground it in a handmill or crushed it in a mortar. They cooked it in a pot or made it into cakes. And it tasted like something made with olive oil. 9When the dew settled on the camp at night, the manna also came down.

10Moses heard the people of every family wailing, each at the entrance to his tent. The Lord became exceedingly angry, and Moses was troubled. 11He asked the Lord, "Why have you brought this trouble on your servant? What have I done to displease you that you put the burden of all these people on me? 12Did I conceive all these people? Did I give them birth? Why do you tell me to carry them in my arms, as a nurse carries an infant, to the land you promised on oath to their forefathers? 13Where can I get meat for all these people? They keep wailing to me, 'Give us meat to eat!' 14I cannot carry all these people by myself; the burden is too heavy for me. 15If this is how you are going to treat me, put me to death right now—if I have found favor in your eyes—and do not let me face my own ruin."

16The Lord said to Moses: "Bring me seventy of Israel's elders who are known to you as leaders and officials among the people. Have them come to the Tent of Meeting, that they may stand there with you. 17I will come down and speak with you there, and I will take of the Spirit that is on you and put the Spirit on them. They will help you carry the burden of the people so that you will not have to carry it alone.

18"Tell the people: 'Consecrate yourselves in preparation for tomorrow, when you will eat meat. The Lord heard you when you wailed, "If only we had meat to eat! We were better off in Egypt!" Now the Lord will give you meat, and you will eat it. ¹⁹You will not eat it for just one day, or two days, or five, ten or twenty days, ²⁰but for a whole month—until it comes out of your nostrils and you loathe it—because you have rejected the Lord, who is among you, and have wailed before him, saying, "Why did we ever leave Egypt?"'"

²¹But Moses said, "Here I am among six hundred thousand men on foot, and you say, 'I will give them meat to eat for a whole month!' ²²Would they have enough if flocks and herds were slaughtered for them? Would they have enough if all the fish in the sea were caught for them?"

²³The Lord answered Moses, "Is the Lord's arm too short? You will now see whether or not what I say will come true for you."

a 10 Traditionally peace offerings   b 3 Taberah means burning.

MARK 14:1-21

Now the Passover and the Feast of Unleavened Bread were only two days away, and the chief priests and the teachers of the law were looking for some sly way to arrest Jesus and kill him. ²"But not during the Feast," they said, "or the people may riot."

³While he was in Bethany, reclining at the table in the home of a man known as Simon the Leper, a woman came with an alabaster jar of very expensive perfume, made of pure nard. She broke the jar and poured the perfume on his head.

⁴Some of those present were saying indignantly to one another, "Why this waste of perfume? ⁵It could have been sold for more than a year's wages*a* and the money given to the poor." And they rebuked her harshly.

⁶"Leave her alone," said Jesus. "Why are you bothering her? She has done a beautiful thing to me. ⁷The poor you will always have with you, and you can help them any time you want. But you will not always have me. ⁸She did what she could. She poured perfume on my

body beforehand to prepare for my burial. ⁹I tell you the truth, wherever the gospel is preached throughout the world, what she has done will also be told, in memory of her."

¹⁰Then Judas Iscariot, one of the Twelve, went to the chief priests to betray Jesus to them. ¹¹They were delighted to hear this and promised to give him money. So he watched for an opportunity to hand him over.

¹²On the first day of the Feast of Unleavened Bread, when it was customary to sacrifice the Passover lamb, Jesus' disciples asked him, "Where do you want us to go and make preparations for you to eat the Passover?"

¹³So he sent two of his disciples, telling them, "Go into the city, and a man carrying a jar of water will meet you. Follow him. ¹⁴Say to the owner of the house he enters, 'The Teacher asks: Where is my guest room, where I may eat the Passover with my disciples?' ¹⁵He will show you a large upper room, furnished and ready. Make preparations for us there."

¹⁶The disciples left, went into the city and found things just as Jesus had told them. So they prepared the Passover.

¹⁷When evening came, Jesus arrived with the Twelve. ¹⁸While they were reclining at the table eating, he said, "I tell you the truth, one of you will betray me—one who is eating with me."

¹⁹They were saddened, and one by one they said to him, "Surely not I?"

²⁰"It is one of the Twelve," he replied, "one who dips bread into the bowl with me. ²¹The Son of Man will go just as it is written about him. But woe to that man who betrays the Son of Man! It would be better for him if he had not been born."

a 5 Greek than three hundred denarii

PSALM 51:1-19

For the director of music. A psalm of David. When the prophet Nathan came to him after David had committed adultery with Bathsheba.

¹Have mercy on me, O God,
  according to your unfailing love;

according to your great compassion
blot out my transgressions.
2 Wash away all my iniquity
and cleanse me from my sin.

3 For I know my transgressions,
and my sin is always before me.
4 Against you, you only, have I sinned
and done what is evil in your sight,
so that you are proved right when
you speak
and justified when you judge.
5 Surely I was sinful at birth,
sinful from the time my mother
conceived me.
6 Surely you desire truth in the inner
parts*a*;
you teach*b* me wisdom in the
inmost place.

7 Cleanse me with hyssop, and I will
be clean;
wash me, and I will be whiter
than snow.
8 Let me hear joy and gladness;
let the bones you have crushed
rejoice.
9 Hide your face from my sins
and blot out all my iniquity.

10 **Create in me a pure heart, O God,
and renew a steadfast spirit
within me.**
11 **Do not cast me from your
presence**
or take your Holy Spirit from me.
12 **Restore to me the joy of your
salvation**
**and grant me a willing spirit, to
sustain me.**

13 Then I will teach transgressors your
ways,
and sinners will turn back to you.
14 Save me from bloodguilt, O God,
the God who saves me,
and my tongue will sing of your
righteousness.
15 O Lord, open my lips,
and my mouth will declare your
praise.
16 You do not delight in sacrifice, or I
would bring it;

you do not take pleasure in burnt
offerings.
17 The sacrifices of God are*c* a broken
spirit;
a broken and contrite heart,
O God, you will not despise.

18 In your good pleasure make Zion
prosper;
build up the walls of Jerusalem.
19 Then there will be righteous
sacrifices,
whole burnt offerings to delight
you;
then bulls will be offered on
your altar.

*a6 The meaning of the Hebrew for this phrase is uncertain.
b6 Or you desired...; / you taught   c17 Or My sacrifice,
O God, is*

PROVERBS 10:31-32
31 **T**he mouth of the righteous brings
forth wisdom,
but a perverse tongue will be
cut out.

32 The lips of the righteous know what
is fitting,
but the mouth of the wicked only
what is perverse.

□ DAY 68

GOD SIGHTINGS

March 9

NUMBERS 11:24–13:33
So Moses went out and told the people
what the LORD had said. He brought together seventy of their elders and had
them stand around the Tent. 25 Then the
LORD came down in the cloud and spoke
with him, and he took of the Spirit that
was on him and put the Spirit on the
seventy elders. When the Spirit rested
on them, they prophesied, but they did
not do so again.*a*

26 However, two men, whose names
were Eldad and Medad, had remained in
the camp. They were listed among the

elders, but did not go out to the Tent. Yet the Spirit also rested on them, and they prophesied in the camp. 27A young man ran and told Moses, "Eldad and Medad are prophesying in the camp."

28Joshua son of Nun, who had been Moses' aide since youth, spoke up and said, "Moses, my lord, stop them!"

29But Moses replied, "Are you jealous for my sake? I wish that all the Lord's people were prophets and that the Lord would put his Spirit on them!" 30Then Moses and the elders of Israel returned to the camp.

31Now a wind went out from the Lord and drove quail in from the sea. It brought them*b* down all around the camp to about three feet*c* above the ground, as far as a day's walk in any direction. 32All that day and night and all the next day the people went out and gathered quail. No one gathered less than ten homers.*d* Then they spread them out all around the camp. 33But while the meat was still between their teeth and before it could be consumed, the anger of the Lord burned against the people, and he struck them with a severe plague. 34Therefore the place was named Kibroth Hattaavah,*e* because there they buried the people who had craved other food.

35From Kibroth Hattaavah the people traveled to Hazeroth and stayed there.

12:1MIRIAM and Aaron began to talk against Moses because of his Cushite wife, for he had married a Cushite. 2"Has the Lord spoken only through Moses?" they asked. "Hasn't he also spoken through us?" And the Lord heard this.

3(Now Moses was a very humble man, more humble than anyone else on the face of the earth.)

4At once the Lord said to Moses, Aaron and Miriam, "Come out to the Tent of Meeting, all three of you." So the three of them came out. 5Then the Lord came down in a pillar of cloud; he stood at the entrance to the Tent and sum-

moned Aaron and Miriam. When both of them stepped forward, 6he said, "Listen to my words:

> "When a prophet of the Lord is
>   among you,
>   I reveal myself to him in visions,
>   I speak to him in dreams.
> 7But this is not true of my servant
>   Moses;
>   he is faithful in all my house.
> 8With him I speak face to face,
>   clearly and not in riddles;
>   he sees the form of the Lord.
>   Why then were you not afraid
>   to speak against my servant
>   Moses?"

9The anger of the Lord burned against them, and he left them.

10When the cloud lifted from above the Tent, there stood Miriam—leprous,*f* like snow. Aaron turned toward her and saw that she had leprosy; 11and he said to Moses, "Please, my lord, do not hold against us the sin we have so foolishly committed. 12Do not let her be like a stillborn infant coming from its mother's womb with its flesh half eaten away."

13So Moses cried out to the Lord, "O God, please heal her!"

14The Lord replied to Moses, "If her father had spit in her face, would she not have been in disgrace for seven days? Confine her outside the camp for seven days; after that she can be brought back." 15So Miriam was confined outside the camp for seven days, and the people did not move on till she was brought back.

16After that, the people left Hazeroth and encamped in the Desert of Paran.

13:1THE LORD said to Moses, 2"Send some men to explore the land of Canaan, which I am giving to the Israelites. From each ancestral tribe send one of its leaders."

3So at the Lord's command Moses sent them out from the Desert of Paran. All of them were leaders of the Israelites. 4These are their names:

from the tribe of Reuben, Shammua son of Zaccur;
⁵from the tribe of Simeon, Shaphat son of Hori;
⁶from the tribe of Judah, Caleb son of Jephunneh;
⁷from the tribe of Issachar, Igal son of Joseph;
⁸from the tribe of Ephraim, Hoshea son of Nun;
⁹from the tribe of Benjamin, Palti son of Raphu;
¹⁰from the tribe of Zebulun, Gaddiel son of Sodi;
¹¹from the tribe of Manasseh (a tribe of Joseph), Gaddi son of Susi;
¹²from the tribe of Dan, Ammiel son of Gemalli;
¹³from the tribe of Asher, Sethur son of Michael;
¹⁴from the tribe of Naphtali, Nahbi son of Vophsi;
¹⁵from the tribe of Gad, Geuel son of Maki.

¹⁶These are the names of the men Moses sent to explore the land. (Moses gave Hoshea son of Nun the name Joshua.)

¹⁷When Moses sent them to explore Canaan, he said, "Go up through the Negev and on into the hill country. ¹⁸See what the land is like and whether the people who live there are strong or weak, few or many. ¹⁹What kind of land do they live in? Is it good or bad? What kind of towns do they live in? Are they unwalled or fortified? ²⁰How is the soil? Is it fertile or poor? Are there trees on it or not? Do your best to bring back some of the fruit of the land." (It was the season for the first ripe grapes.)

²¹So they went up and explored the land from the Desert of Zin as far as Rehob, toward Lebo⁹ Hamath. ²²They went up through the Negev and came to Hebron, where Ahiman, Sheshai and Talmai, the descendants of Anak, lived. (Hebron had been built seven years before Zoan in Egypt.) ²³When they reached the Valley of Eshcol,ʰ they cut off a branch bearing a single

cluster of grapes. Two of them carried it on a pole between them, along with some pomegranates and figs. ²⁴That place was called the Valley of Eshcol because of the cluster of grapes the Israelites cut off there. ²⁵At the end of forty days they returned from exploring the land.

²⁶They came back to Moses and Aaron and the whole Israelite community at Kadesh in the Desert of Paran. There they reported to them and to the whole assembly and showed them the fruit of the land. ²⁷They gave Moses this account: "We went into the land to which you sent us, and it does flow with milk and honey! Here is its fruit. ²⁸But the people who live there are powerful, and the cities are fortified and very large. We even saw descendants of Anak there. ²⁹The Amalekites live in the Negev; the Hittites, Jebusites and Amorites live in the hill country; and the Canaanites live near the sea and along the Jordan."

³⁰Then Caleb silenced the people before Moses and said, "We should go up and take possession of the land, for we can certainly do it."

³¹But the men who had gone up with him said, "We can't attack those people; they are stronger than we are." ³²And they spread among the Israelites a bad report about the land they had explored. They said, "The land we explored devours those living in it. All the people we saw there are of great size. ³³We saw the Nephilim there (the descendants of Anak come from the Nephilim). We seemed like grasshoppers in our own eyes, and we looked the same to them."

ᵃ25 Or prophesied and continued to do so   ᵇ31 Or They flew   ᶜ31 Hebrew two cubits (about 1 meter)   ᵈ32 That is, probably about 60 bushels (about 2.2 kiloliters)   ᵉ34 Kibroth Hattaavah means graves of craving.   ᶠ10 The Hebrew word was used for various diseases affecting the skin—not necessarily leprosy.   ᵍ21 Or toward the entrance to   ʰ23 Eshcol means cluster; also in verse 24.

MARK 14:22-52

While they [Jesus and his disciples] were eating, Jesus took bread, gave thanks and broke it, and gave it to his disciples, saying, "Take it; this is my body."

²³**Then he took the cup, gave thanks and offered it to them, and they all drank from it.**

²⁴**" This is my blood of the**[a] **covenant, which is poured out for many,"** he said to them. ²⁵"I tell you the truth, I will not drink again of the fruit of the vine until that day when I drink it anew in the kingdom of God."

²⁶When they had sung a hymn, they went out to the Mount of Olives.

²⁷"You will all fall away," Jesus told them, "for it is written:

"'I will strike the shepherd,
     and the sheep will be scattered.'[b]

²⁸But after I have risen, I will go ahead of you into Galilee."

²⁹Peter declared, "Even if all fall away, I will not."

³⁰"I tell you the truth," Jesus answered, "today—yes, tonight—before the rooster crows twice[c] you yourself will disown me three times."

³¹But Peter insisted emphatically, "Even if I have to die with you, I will never disown you." And all the others said the same.

³²They went to a place called Gethsemane, and Jesus said to his disciples, "Sit here while I pray." ³³He took Peter, James and John along with him, and he began to be deeply distressed and troubled. ³⁴"My soul is overwhelmed with sorrow to the point of death," he said to them. "Stay here and keep watch."

³⁵Going a little farther, he fell to the ground and prayed that if possible the hour might pass from him. ³⁶"Abba,[d] Father," he said, "everything is possible for you. Take this cup from me. Yet not what I will, but what you will."

³⁷Then he returned to his disciples and found them sleeping. "Simon," he said to Peter, "are you asleep? Could you not keep watch for one hour? ³⁸Watch and pray so that you will not fall into temptation. The spirit is willing, but the body is weak."

³⁹Once more he went away and prayed the same thing. ⁴⁰When he came back, he again found them sleeping, because their eyes were heavy. They did not know what to say to him.

⁴¹Returning the third time, he said to them, "Are you still sleeping and resting? Enough! The hour has come. Look, the Son of Man is betrayed into the hands of sinners. ⁴²Rise! Let us go! Here comes my betrayer!"

⁴³Just as he was speaking, Judas, one of the Twelve, appeared. With him was a crowd armed with swords and clubs, sent from the chief priests, the teachers of the law, and the elders.

⁴⁴Now the betrayer had arranged a signal with them: "The one I kiss is the man; arrest him and lead him away under guard." ⁴⁵Going at once to Jesus, Judas said, "Rabbi!" and kissed him. ⁴⁶The men seized Jesus and arrested him. ⁴⁷Then one of those standing near drew his sword and struck the servant of the high priest, cutting off his ear.

⁴⁸"Am I leading a rebellion," said Jesus, "that you have come out with swords and clubs to capture me? ⁴⁹Every day I was with you, teaching in the temple courts, and you did not arrest me. But the Scriptures must be fulfilled." ⁵⁰Then everyone deserted him and fled.

⁵¹A young man, wearing nothing but a linen garment, was following Jesus. When they seized him, ⁵²he fled naked, leaving his garment behind.

a24 Some manuscripts the new b27 Zech. 13:7 c30 Some early manuscripts do not have twice. d36 Aramaic for Father

PSALM 52:1-9

For the director of music. A *maskil*[a] of David. When Doeg the Edomite had gone to Saul and told him: "David has gone to the house of Ahimelech."

¹**W**hy do you boast of evil, you mighty man?
     Why do you boast all day long,
     you who are a disgrace in the eyes of God?
²Your tongue plots destruction;
     it is like a sharpened razor,
     you who practice deceit.

3 You love evil rather than good,
  falsehood rather than speaking
      the truth.   *Selah*
4 You love every harmful word,
  O you deceitful tongue!

5 Surely God will bring you down to
      everlasting ruin:
  He will snatch you up and tear you
      from your tent;
  he will uproot you from the land
      of the living.   *Selah*
6 The righteous will see and fear;
  they will laugh at him, saying,
7 "Here now is the man
  who did not make God his
      stronghold
  but trusted in his great wealth
  and grew strong by destroying
      others!"

8 But I am like an olive tree
  flourishing in the house of God;
I trust in God's unfailing love
  for ever and ever.
9 I will praise you forever for what you
      have done;
  in your name I will hope, for your
      name is good.
  I will praise you in the presence of
      your saints.

*a*Title: Probably a literary or musical term

PROVERBS 11:1-3

The LORD abhors dishonest scales,
  but accurate weights are his
      delight.

2 When pride comes, then comes
      disgrace,
  but with humility comes wisdom.

3 The integrity of the upright guides
      them,
  but the unfaithful are destroyed by
      their duplicity.

□ D A Y 6 9

GOD SIGHTINGS

March 10

NUMBERS 14:1–15:16

That night all the people of the community raised their voices and wept aloud.
2 All the Israelites grumbled against Moses and Aaron, and the whole assembly
said to them, "If only we had died in
Egypt! Or in this desert! 3 Why is the LORD
bringing us to this land only to let us fall
by the sword? Our wives and children
will be taken as plunder. Wouldn't it be
better for us to go back to Egypt?" 4 And
they said to each other, "We should
choose a leader and go back to Egypt."

5 Then Moses and Aaron fell facedown in front of the whole Israelite assembly gathered there. 6 Joshua son of
Nun and Caleb son of Jephunneh, who
were among those who had explored
the land, tore their clothes 7 and said to
the entire Israelite assembly, "The land
we passed through and explored is exceedingly good. 8 If the LORD is pleased
with us, he will lead us into that land, a
land flowing with milk and honey, and
will give it to us. 9 Only do not rebel
against the LORD. And do not be afraid
of the people of the land, because we
will swallow them up. Their protection
is gone, but the LORD is with us. Do not
be afraid of them."

10 But the whole assembly talked
about stoning them. Then the glory of
the LORD appeared at the Tent of Meeting to all the Israelites. 11 The LORD said
to Moses, "How long will these people
treat me with contempt? How long will
they refuse to believe in me, in spite of
all the miraculous signs I have performed among them? 12 I will strike
them down with a plague and destroy
them, but I will make you into a nation
greater and stronger than they."

13 Moses said to the LORD, "Then the
Egyptians will hear about it! By your
power you brought these people up

from among them. [14]And they will tell the inhabitants of this land about it. They have already heard that you, O Lord, are with these people and that you, O Lord, have been seen face to face, that your cloud stays over them, and that you go before them in a pillar of cloud by day and a pillar of fire by night. [15]If you put these people to death all at one time, the nations who have heard this report about you will say, [16]'The Lord was not able to bring these people into the land he promised them on oath; so he slaughtered them in the desert.'

[17]"Now may the Lord's strength be displayed, just as you have declared: [18]'The Lord is slow to anger, abounding in love and forgiving sin and rebellion. Yet he does not leave the guilty unpunished; he punishes the children for the sin of the fathers to the third and fourth generation.' [19]In accordance with your great love, forgive the sin of these people, just as you have pardoned them from the time they left Egypt until now."

[20]The Lord replied, "I have forgiven them, as you asked. [21]Nevertheless, as surely as I live and as surely as the glory of the Lord fills the whole earth, [22]not one of the men who saw my glory and the miraculous signs I performed in Egypt and in the desert but who disobeyed me and tested me ten times— [23]not one of them will ever see the land I promised on oath to their forefathers. No one who has treated me with contempt will ever see it. [24]But because my servant Caleb has a different spirit and follows me wholeheartedly, I will bring him into the land he went to, and his descendants will inherit it. [25]Since the Amalekites and Canaanites are living in the valleys, turn back tomorrow and set out toward the desert along the route to the Red Sea.[a]"

[26]The Lord said to Moses and Aaron: [27]"How long will this wicked community grumble against me? I have heard the complaints of these grumbling Israelites. [28]So tell them, 'As surely as I live, declares the Lord, I will do to you the very things I heard you say: [29]In this desert your bodies will fall—every one of you twenty years old or more who was counted in the census and who has grumbled against me. [30]Not one of you will enter the land I swore with uplifted hand to make your home, except Caleb son of Jephunneh and Joshua son of Nun. [31]As for your children that you said would be taken as plunder, I will bring them in to enjoy the land you have rejected. [32]But you—your bodies will fall in this desert. [33]Your children will be shepherds here for forty years, suffering for your unfaithfulness, until the last of your bodies lies in the desert. [34]For forty years—one year for each of the forty days you explored the land—you will suffer for your sins and know what it is like to have me against you.' [35]I, the Lord, have spoken, and I will surely do these things to this whole wicked community, which has banded together against me. They will meet their end in this desert; here they will die."

[36]So the men Moses had sent to explore the land, who returned and made the whole community grumble against him by spreading a bad report about it— [37]these men responsible for spreading the bad report about the land were struck down and died of a plague before the Lord. [38]Of the men who went to explore the land, only Joshua son of Nun and Caleb son of Jephunneh survived.

[39]When Moses reported this to all the Israelites, they mourned bitterly. [40]Early the next morning they went up toward the high hill country. "We have sinned," they said. "We will go up to the place the Lord promised."

[41]But Moses said, "Why are you disobeying the Lord's command? This will not succeed! [42]Do not go up, because the Lord is not with you. You will be defeated by your enemies, [43]for the Amalekites and Canaanites will face you there. Because you have turned away from the Lord, he will not be with you and you will fall by the sword."

[44]Nevertheless, in their presumption they went up toward the high hill coun-

try, though neither Moses nor the ark of the LORD's covenant moved from the camp. 45 Then the Amalekites and Canaanites who lived in that hill country came down and attacked them and beat them down all the way to Hormah.

15:1 THE LORD said to Moses, 2 "Speak to the Israelites and say to them: 'After you enter the land I am giving you as a home 3 and you present to the LORD offerings made by fire, from the herd or the flock, as an aroma pleasing to the LORD— whether burnt offerings or sacrifices, for special vows or freewill offerings or festival offerings— 4 then the one who brings his offering shall present to the LORD a grain offering of a tenth of an ephah[b] of fine flour mixed with a quarter of a hin[c] of oil. 5 With each lamb for the burnt offering or the sacrifice, prepare a quarter of a hin of wine as a drink offering.

6 "'With a ram prepare a grain offering of two-tenths of an ephah[d] of fine flour mixed with a third of a hin[e] of oil, 7 and a third of a hin of wine as a drink offering. Offer it as an aroma pleasing to the LORD.

8 "'When you prepare a young bull as a burnt offering or sacrifice, for a special vow or a fellowship offering[f] to the LORD, 9 bring with the bull a grain offering of three-tenths of an ephah[g] of fine flour mixed with half a hin[h] of oil. 10 Also bring half a hin of wine as a drink offering. It will be an offering made by fire, an aroma pleasing to the LORD. 11 Each bull or ram, each lamb or young goat, is to be prepared in this manner. 12 Do this for each one, for as many as you prepare.

13 "'Everyone who is native-born must do these things in this way when he brings an offering made by fire as an aroma pleasing to the LORD. 14 For the generations to come, whenever an alien or anyone else living among you presents an offering made by fire as an aroma pleasing to the LORD, he must do exactly as you do. 15 The community is to have the same rules for you and for the alien living among you; this is a lasting ordinance for the generations to come. You and the alien shall be the same before the LORD: 16 The same laws and regulations will apply both to you and to the alien living among you.'"

a25 Hebrew *Yam Suph*; that is, Sea of Reeds   *b4* That is, probably about 2 quarts (about 2 liters)   *c4* That is, probably about 1 quart (about 1 liter); also in verse 5   *d6* That is, probably about 4 quarts (about 4.5 liters)   *e6* That is, probably about 1 1/4 quarts (about 1.2 liters); also in verse 7   *f8* Traditionally *peace offering*   *g9* That is, probably about 6 quarts (about 6.5 liters)   *h9* That is, probably about 2 quarts (about 2 liters); also in verse 10

MARK 14:53-72

They [the soldiers] took Jesus to the high priest, and all the chief priests, elders and teachers of the law came together. 54 Peter followed him at a distance, right into the courtyard of the high priest. There he sat with the guards and warmed himself at the fire.

55 The chief priests and the whole Sanhedrin were looking for evidence against Jesus so that they could put him to death, but they did not find any. 56 Many testified falsely against him, but their statements did not agree.

57 Then some stood up and gave this false testimony against him: 58 "We heard him say, 'I will destroy this man-made temple and in three days will build another, not made by man.'" 59 Yet even then their testimony did not agree.

60 Then the high priest stood up before them and asked Jesus, "Are you not going to answer? What is this testimony that these men are bringing against you?" 61 **But Jesus remained silent and gave no answer.**

Again the high priest asked him, "Are you the Christ,[a] the Son of the Blessed One?"

62 **"I am," said Jesus. "And you will see the Son of Man sitting at the right hand of the Mighty One and coming on the clouds of heaven."**

63 The high priest tore his clothes. "Why do we need any more witnesses?" he asked. 64 "You have heard the blasphemy. What do you think?"

They all condemned him as worthy of death. 65 Then some began to spit at him; they blindfolded him, struck him with their fists, and said, "Prophesy!" And the guards took him and beat him.

66While Peter was below in the courtyard, one of the servant girls of the high priest came by. 67When she saw Peter warming himself, she looked closely at him.

"You also were with that Nazarene, Jesus," she said.

68But he denied it. "I don't know or understand what you're talking about," he said, and went out into the entryway.b

69When the servant girl saw him there, she said again to those standing around, "This fellow is one of them." 70Again he denied it.

After a little while, those standing near said to Peter, "Surely you are one of them, for you are a Galilean."

71He began to call down curses on himself, and he swore to them, "I don't know this man you're talking about."

72Immediately the rooster crowed the second time.c Then Peter remembered the word Jesus had spoken to him: "Before the rooster crows twiced you will disown me three times." And he broke down and wept.

a61 Or Messiah b68 Some early manuscripts entryway and the rooster crowed c72 Some early manuscripts do not have the second time. d72 Some early manuscripts do not have twice.

PSALM 53:1-6

For the director of music. According to mahalath.a A maskilb of David.

1 The fool says in his heart,
     "There is no God."
  They are corrupt, and their ways
     are vile;
     there is no one who does good.

2 God looks down from heaven
     on the sons of men
  to see if there are any who
     understand,
     any who seek God.
3 Everyone has turned away,
     they have together become
     corrupt;
  there is no one who does good,
     not even one.

4 Will the evildoers never learn—
     those who devour my people as
        men eat bread
     and who do not call on God?
5 There they were, overwhelmed with
        dread,
     where there was nothing to dread.
  God scattered the bones of those
        who attacked you;
     you put them to shame, for God
        despised them.

6 Oh, that salvation for Israel would
     come out of Zion!
  When God restores the fortunes of
     his people,
     let Jacob rejoice and Israel be glad!

aTitle: Probably a musical term bTitle: Probably a literary or musical term

PROVERBS 11:4

4 **W**ealth is worthless in the day of
     wrath,
     but righteousness delivers from
        death.

□ DAY 70

GOD SIGHTINGS

March 11

NUMBERS 15:17–16:40

The Lord said to Moses, 18"Speak to the Israelites and say to them: 'When you enter the land to which I am taking you 19and you eat the food of the land, present a portion as an offering to the Lord. 20Present a cake from the first of your ground meal and present it as an offering from the threshing floor. 21Throughout the generations to come you are to give this offering to the Lord from the first of your ground meal.

22"Now if you unintentionally fail to keep any of these commands the Lord gave Moses— 23any of the Lord's commands to you through him, from the day the Lord gave them and continuing through the generations to come—

24 and if this is done unintentionally without the community being aware of it, then the whole community is to offer a young bull for a burnt offering as an aroma pleasing to the Lord, along with its prescribed grain offering and drink offering, and a male goat for a sin offering. 25 The priest is to make atonement for the whole Israelite community, and they will be forgiven, for it was not intentional and they have brought to the Lord for their wrong an offering made by fire and a sin offering. 26 The whole Israelite community and the aliens living among them will be forgiven, because all the people were involved in the unintentional wrong.

27 " 'But if just one person sins unintentionally, he must bring a year-old female goat for a sin offering. 28 The priest is to make atonement before the Lord for the one who erred by sinning unintentionally, and when atonement has been made for him, he will be forgiven. 29 One and the same law applies to everyone who sins unintentionally, whether he is a native-born Israelite or an alien.

30 " 'But anyone who sins defiantly, whether native-born or alien, blasphemes the Lord, and that person must be cut off from his people. 31 Because he has despised the Lord's word and broken his commands, that person must surely be cut off; his guilt remains on him.' "

32 While the Israelites were in the desert, a man was found gathering wood on the Sabbath day. 33 Those who found him gathering wood brought him to Moses and Aaron and the whole assembly, 34 and they kept him in custody, because it was not clear what should be done to him. 35 Then the Lord said to Moses, "The man must die. The whole assembly must stone him outside the camp." 36 So the assembly took him outside the camp and stoned him to death, as the Lord commanded Moses.

37 The Lord said to Moses, 38 "Speak to the Israelites and say to them: 'Throughout the generations to come you are to make tassels on the corners of your garments, with a blue cord on each tassel. 39 You will have these tassels to look at and so you will remember all the commands of the Lord, that you may obey them and not prostitute yourselves by going after the lusts of your own hearts and eyes. 40 Then you will remember to obey all my commands and will be consecrated to your God. 41 I am the Lord your God, who brought you out of Egypt to be your God. I am the Lord your God.' "

16:1 Korah son of Izhar, the son of Kohath, the son of Levi, and certain Reubenites—Dathan and Abiram, sons of Eliab, and On son of Peleth—became insolent^a 2 and rose up against Moses. With them were 250 Israelite men, well-known community leaders who had been appointed members of the council. 3 They came as a group to oppose Moses and Aaron and said to them, "You have gone too far! The whole community is holy, every one of them, and the Lord is with them. Why then do you set yourselves above the Lord's assembly?"

4 When Moses heard this, he fell facedown. 5 Then he said to Korah and all his followers: "In the morning the Lord will show who belongs to him and who is holy, and he will have that person come near him. The man he chooses he will cause to come near him. 6 You, Korah, and all your followers are to do this: Take censers 7 and tomorrow put fire and incense in them before the Lord. The man the Lord chooses will be the one who is holy. You Levites have gone too far!"

8 Moses also said to Korah, "Now listen, you Levites! 9 Isn't it enough for you that the God of Israel has separated you from the rest of the Israelite community and brought you near himself to do the work at the Lord's tabernacle and to stand before the community and minister to them? 10 He has brought you and all your fellow Levites near himself, but now you are trying to get the priesthood

too. ¹¹It is against the LORD that you and all your followers have banded together. Who is Aaron that you should grumble against him?"

¹²Then Moses summoned Dathan and Abiram, the sons of Eliab. But they said, "We will not come! ¹³Isn't it enough that you have brought us up out of a land flowing with milk and honey to kill us in the desert? And now you also want to lord it over us? ¹⁴Moreover, you haven't brought us into a land flowing with milk and honey or given us an inheritance of fields and vineyards. Will you gouge out the eyes of*b* these men? No, we will not come!"

¹⁵Then Moses became very angry and said to the LORD, "Do not accept their offering. I have not taken so much as a donkey from them, nor have I wronged any of them."

¹⁶Moses said to Korah, "You and all your followers are to appear before the LORD tomorrow—you and they and Aaron. ¹⁷Each man is to take his censer and put incense in it—250 censers in all—and present it before the LORD. You and Aaron are to present your censers also." ¹⁸So each man took his censer, put fire and incense in it, and stood with Moses and Aaron at the entrance to the Tent of Meeting. ¹⁹When Korah had gathered all his followers in opposition to them at the entrance to the Tent of Meeting, the glory of the LORD appeared to the entire assembly. ²⁰The LORD said to Moses and Aaron, ²¹"Separate yourselves from this assembly so I can put an end to them at once."

²²But Moses and Aaron fell facedown and cried out, "O God, God of the spirits of all mankind, will you be angry with the entire assembly when only one man sins?"

²³Then the LORD said to Moses, ²⁴"Say to the assembly, 'Move away from the tents of Korah, Dathan and Abiram.'"

²⁵Moses got up and went to Dathan and Abiram, and the elders of Israel followed him. ²⁶He warned the assembly, "Move back from the tents of these wicked men! Do not touch anything belonging to them, or you will be swept away because of all their sins." ²⁷So they moved away from the tents of Korah, Dathan and Abiram. Dathan and Abiram had come out and were standing with their wives, children and little ones at the entrances to their tents.

²⁸Then Moses said, "This is how you will know that the LORD has sent me to do all these things and that it was not my idea: ²⁹If these men die a natural death and experience only what usually happens to men, then the LORD has not sent me. ³⁰But if the LORD brings about something totally new, and the earth opens its mouth and swallows them, with everything that belongs to them, and they go down alive into the grave,*c* then you will know that these men have treated the LORD with contempt."

³¹As soon as he finished saying all this, the ground under them split apart ³²and the earth opened its mouth and swallowed them, with their households and all Korah's men and all their possessions. ³³They went down alive into the grave, with everything they owned; the earth closed over them, and they perished and were gone from the community. ³⁴At their cries, all the Israelites around them fled, shouting, "The earth is going to swallow us too!"

³⁵And fire came out from the LORD and consumed the 250 men who were offering the incense.

³⁶The LORD said to Moses, ³⁷"Tell Eleazar son of Aaron, the priest, to take the censers out of the smoldering remains and scatter the coals some distance away, for the censers are holy— ³⁸the censers of the men who sinned at the cost of their lives. Hammer the censers into sheets to overlay the altar, for they were presented before the LORD and have become holy. Let them be a sign to the Israelites."

³⁹So Eleazar the priest collected the bronze censers brought by those who had been burned up, and he had them hammered out to overlay the altar, ⁴⁰as the LORD directed him through Moses. This was to remind the Israelites that no

one except a descendant of Aaron should come to burn incense before the LORD, or he would become like Korah and his followers.

*a*1 Or *Peleth—took ⌞men⌟ *b*14 Or *you make slaves of*; or *you deceive* *c*30 Hebrew *Sheol*; also in verse 33

MARK 15:1-47

Very early in the morning, the chief priests, with the elders, the teachers of the law and the whole Sanhedrin, reached a decision. They bound Jesus, led him away and handed him over to Pilate.

²"Are you the king of the Jews?" asked Pilate.

"Yes, it is as you say," Jesus replied.

³The chief priests accused him of many things. ⁴So again Pilate asked him, "Aren't you going to answer? See how many things they are accusing you of."

⁵But Jesus still made no reply, and Pilate was amazed.

⁶Now it was the custom at the Feast to release a prisoner whom the people requested. ⁷A man called Barabbas was in prison with the insurrectionists who had committed murder in the uprising. ⁸The crowd came up and asked Pilate to do for them what he usually did.

⁹"Do you want me to release to you the king of the Jews?" asked Pilate, ¹⁰knowing it was out of envy that the chief priests had handed Jesus over to him. ¹¹But the chief priests stirred up the crowd to have Pilate release Barabbas instead.

¹²"What shall I do, then, with the one you call the king of the Jews?" Pilate asked them.

¹³"Crucify him!" they shouted.

¹⁴"Why? What crime has he committed?" asked Pilate.

But they shouted all the louder, "Crucify him!"

¹⁵Wanting to satisfy the crowd, Pilate released Barabbas to them. He had Jesus flogged, and handed him over to be crucified.

¹⁶The soldiers led Jesus away into the palace (that is, the Praetorium) and called together the whole company of soldiers. ¹⁷They put a purple robe on him, then twisted together a crown of thorns and set it on him. ¹⁸And they began to call out to him, "Hail, king of the Jews!" ¹⁹Again and again they struck him on the head with a staff and spit on him. Falling on their knees, they paid homage to him. ²⁰And when they had mocked him, they took off the purple robe and put his own clothes on him. Then they led him out to crucify him.

²¹A certain man from Cyrene, Simon, the father of Alexander and Rufus, was passing by on his way in from the country, and they forced him to carry the cross. ²²They brought Jesus to the place called Golgotha (which means The Place of the Skull). ²³Then they offered him wine mixed with myrrh, but he did not take it. ²⁴And they crucified him. Dividing up his clothes, they cast lots to see what each would get.

²⁵**It was the third hour when they crucified him. ²⁶The written notice of the charge against him read: THE KING OF THE JEWS. ²⁷They crucified two robbers with him, one on his right and one on his left.***a* ²⁹Those who passed by hurled insults at him, shaking their heads and saying, "So! You who are going to destroy the temple and build it in three days, ³⁰come down from the cross and save yourself!"

³¹In the same way the chief priests and the teachers of the law mocked him among themselves. "He saved others," they said, "but he can't save himself! ³²Let this Christ,*b* this King of Israel, come down now from the cross, that we may see and believe." Those crucified with him also heaped insults on him.

³³At the sixth hour darkness came over the whole land until the ninth hour. ³⁴And at the ninth hour Jesus cried out in a loud voice, *"Eloi, Eloi, lama sabachthani?"*—which means, "My God, my God, why have you forsaken me?"*c*

³⁵When some of those standing near heard this, they said, "Listen, he's calling Elijah."

³⁶One man ran, filled a sponge with

wine vinegar, put it on a stick, and offered it to Jesus to drink. "Now leave him alone. Let's see if Elijah comes to take him down," he said.

³⁷ With a loud cry, Jesus breathed his last.

³⁸ The curtain of the temple was torn in two from top to bottom. ³⁹ And when the centurion, who stood there in front of Jesus, heard his cry and*d* saw how he died, he said, "Surely this man was the Son*e* of God!"

⁴⁰ Some women were watching from a distance. Among them were Mary Magdalene, Mary the mother of James the younger and of Joses, and Salome. ⁴¹ In Galilee these women had followed him and cared for his needs. Many other women who had come up with him to Jerusalem were also there.

⁴² It was Preparation Day (that is, the day before the Sabbath). So as evening approached, ⁴³ Joseph of Arimathea, a prominent member of the Council, who was himself waiting for the kingdom of God, went boldly to Pilate and asked for Jesus' body. ⁴⁴ Pilate was surprised to hear that he was already dead. Summoning the centurion, he asked him if Jesus had already died. ⁴⁵ When he learned from the centurion that it was so, he gave the body to Joseph. ⁴⁶ So Joseph bought some linen cloth, took down the body, wrapped it in the linen, and placed it in a tomb cut out of rock. Then he rolled a stone against the entrance of the tomb. ⁴⁷ Mary Magdalene and Mary the mother of Joses saw where he was laid.

a27 Some manuscripts *left,* *²⁸and the scripture was fulfilled which says, "He was counted with the lawless ones"* (Isaiah 53:12) *b32* Or *Messiah* *c34* Psalm 22:1 *d39* Some manuscripts do not have *heard his cry* and *e39* Or *a son*

PSALM 54:1-7
For the director of music. With stringed instruments. A *maskil*ᵃ of David. When the Ziphites had gone to Saul and said, "Is not David hiding among us?"

¹ **S**ave me, O God, by your name;
    vindicate me by your might.
² Hear my prayer, O God;
    listen to the words of my mouth.

³ Strangers are attacking me;
    ruthless men seek my life—
    men without regard for God. *Selah*

⁴ Surely God is my help;
    the Lord is the one who
        sustains me.

⁵ Let evil recoil on those who
        slander me;
    in your faithfulness destroy them.

⁶ I will sacrifice a freewill offering
        to you;
    I will praise your name, O LORD,
    for it is good.
⁷ For he has delivered me from all my
        troubles,
    and my eyes have looked in
        triumph on my foes.

*a*Title: Probably a literary or musical term

PROVERBS 11:5-6
⁵ **T**he righteousness of the blameless
        makes a straight way for them,
    but the wicked are brought down
        by their own wickedness.

⁶ The righteousness of the upright
        delivers them,
    but the unfaithful are trapped by
        evil desires.

□ DAY 71

GOD SIGHTINGS

March 12

NUMBERS 16:41–18:32
The next day the whole Israelite community grumbled against Moses and Aaron. "You have killed the LORD's people," they said.

⁴² But when the assembly gathered in opposition to Moses and Aaron and turned toward the Tent of Meeting, suddenly the cloud covered it and the glory of the LORD appeared. ⁴³ Then Moses and Aaron went to the front of the Tent of Meeting, ⁴⁴ and the LORD said to

Moses, 45"Get away from this assembly so I can put an end to them at once." And they fell facedown.

46Then Moses said to Aaron, "Take your censer and put incense in it, along with fire from the altar, and hurry to the assembly to make atonement for them. Wrath has come out from the LORD; the plague has started." 47So Aaron did as Moses said, and ran into the midst of the assembly. The plague had already started among the people, but Aaron offered the incense and made atonement for them. 48He stood between the living and the dead, and the plague stopped. 49But 14,700 people died from the plague, in addition to those who had died because of Korah. 50Then Aaron returned to Moses at the entrance to the Tent of Meeting, for the plague had stopped.

17:1THE LORD said to Moses, 2"Speak to the Israelites and get twelve staffs from them, one from the leader of each of their ancestral tribes. Write the name of each man on his staff. 3On the staff of Levi write Aaron's name, for there must be one staff for the head of each ancestral tribe. 4Place them in the Tent of Meeting in front of the Testimony, where I meet with you. 5The staff belonging to the man I choose will sprout, and I will rid myself of this constant grumbling against you by the Israelites."

6So Moses spoke to the Israelites, and their leaders gave him twelve staffs, one for the leader of each of their ancestral tribes, and Aaron's staff was among them. 7Moses placed the staffs before the LORD in the Tent of the Testimony.

8The next day Moses entered the Tent of the Testimony and saw that Aaron's staff, which represented the house of Levi, had not only sprouted but had budded, blossomed and produced almonds. 9Then Moses brought out all the staffs from the LORD's presence to all the Israelites. They looked at them, and each man took his own staff.

10The LORD said to Moses, "Put back Aaron's staff in front of the Testimony,

to be kept as a sign to the rebellious. This will put an end to their grumbling against me, so that they will not die." 11Moses did just as the LORD commanded him.

12The Israelites said to Moses, "We will die! We are lost, we are all lost! 13Anyone who even comes near the tabernacle of the LORD will die. Are we all going to die?"

18:1THE LORD said to Aaron, "You, your sons and your father's family are to bear the responsibility for offenses against the sanctuary, and you and your sons alone are to bear the responsibility for offenses against the priesthood. 2Bring your fellow Levites from your ancestral tribe to join you and assist you when you and your sons minister before the Tent of the Testimony. 3They are to be responsible to you and are to perform all the duties of the Tent, but they must not go near the furnishings of the sanctuary or the altar, or both they and you will die. 4They are to join you and be responsible for the care of the Tent of Meeting—all the work at the Tent—and no one else may come near where you are.

5"You are to be responsible for the care of the sanctuary and the altar, so that wrath will not fall on the Israelites again. 6I myself have selected your fellow Levites from among the Israelites as a gift to you, dedicated to the LORD to do the work at the Tent of Meeting. 7But only you and your sons may serve as priests in connection with everything at the altar and inside the curtain. I am giving you the service of the priesthood as a gift. Anyone else who comes near the sanctuary must be put to death."

8Then the LORD said to Aaron, "I myself have put you in charge of the offerings presented to me; all the holy offerings the Israelites give me I give to you and your sons as your portion and regular share. 9You are to have the part of the most holy offerings that is kept from the fire. From all the gifts they bring me as most holy offerings, whether grain or sin or guilt offerings, that part belongs to you and your sons. 10Eat it as something most holy; every male shall eat it. You must regard it as holy.

11"This also is yours: whatever is set aside from the gifts of all the wave offerings of the Israelites. I give this to you and your sons and daughters as your regular share. Everyone in your household who is ceremonially clean may eat it.

12"I give you all the finest olive oil and all the finest new wine and grain they give the Lord as the firstfruits of their harvest. 13All the land's firstfruits that they bring to the Lord will be yours. Everyone in your household who is ceremonially clean may eat it.

14"Everything in Israel that is devoteda to the Lord is yours. 15The first offspring of every womb, both man and animal, that is offered to the Lord is yours. But you must redeem every firstborn son and every firstborn male of unclean animals. 16When they are a month old, you must redeem them at the redemption price set at five shekelsb of silver, according to the sanctuary shekel, which weighs twenty gerahs.

17"But you must not redeem the firstborn of an ox, a sheep or a goat; they are holy. Sprinkle their blood on the altar and burn their fat as an offering made by fire, an aroma pleasing to the Lord. 18Their meat is to be yours, just as the breast of the wave offering and the right thigh are yours. 19Whatever is set aside from the holy offerings the Israelites present to the Lord I give to you and your sons and daughters as your regular share. It is an everlasting covenant of salt before the Lord for both you and your offspring."

20The Lord said to Aaron, "You will have no inheritance in their land, nor will you have any share among them; I am your share and your inheritance among the Israelites.

21"I give to the Levites all the tithes in Israel as their inheritance in return for the work they do while serving at the Tent of Meeting. 22From now on the Israelites must not go near the Tent of Meeting, or they will bear the consequences of their sin and will die. 23It is the Levites who are to do the work at the Tent of Meeting and bear the responsibility for offenses against it. This is a lasting ordinance for the generations to come. They will receive no inheritance among the Israelites. 24Instead, I give to the Levites as their inheritance the tithes that the Israelites present as an offering to the Lord. That is why I said concerning them: 'They will have no inheritance among the Israelites.'"

25The Lord said to Moses, 26"Speak to the Levites and say to them: 'When you receive from the Israelites the tithe I give you as your inheritance, you must present a tenth of that tithe as the Lord's offering. 27Your offering will be reckoned to you as grain from the threshing floor or juice from the winepress. 28In this way you also will present an offering to the Lord from all the tithes you receive from the Israelites. From these tithes you must give the Lord's portion to Aaron the priest. 29You must present as the Lord's portion the best and holiest part of everything given to you.'

30"Say to the Levites: 'When you present the best part, it will be reckoned to you as the product of the threshing floor or the winepress. 31You and your households may eat the rest of it anywhere, for it is your wages for your work at the Tent of Meeting. 32By presenting the best part of it you will not be guilty in this matter; then you will not defile the holy offerings of the Israelites, and you will not die.'"

a 14 The Hebrew term refers to the irrevocable giving over of things or persons to the Lord.   b 16 That is, about 2 ounces (about 55 grams)

MARK 16:1-20

When the Sabbath was over, Mary Magdalene, Mary the mother of James, and Salome bought spices so that they might go to anoint Jesus' body. 2Very early on the first day of the week, just after sunrise, they were on their way to the tomb 3and they asked each other,

"Who will roll the stone away from the entrance of the tomb?"

4But when they looked up, they saw that the stone, which was very large, had been rolled away. 5As they entered the tomb, they saw a young man dressed in a white robe sitting on the right side, and they were alarmed.

6"Don't be alarmed," he said. "You are looking for Jesus the Nazarene, who was crucified. He has risen! He is not here. See the place where they laid him. 7But go, tell his disciples and Peter, 'He is going ahead of you into Galilee. There you will see him, just as he told you.'"

8Trembling and bewildered, the women went out and fled from the tomb. They said nothing to anyone, because they were afraid.

[The earliest manuscripts and some other ancient witnesses do not have Mark 16:9-20.]

9When Jesus rose early on the first day of the week, he appeared first to Mary Magdalene, out of whom he had driven seven demons. 10She went and told those who had been with him and who were mourning and weeping. 11When they heard that Jesus was alive and that she had seen him, they did not believe it.

12Afterward Jesus appeared in a different form to two of them while they were walking in the country. 13These returned and reported it to the rest; but they did not believe them either.

14Later Jesus appeared to the Eleven as they were eating; he rebuked them for their lack of faith and their stubborn refusal to believe those who had seen him after he had risen.

15He said to them, "Go into all the world and preach the good news to all creation. 16Whoever believes and is baptized will be saved, but whoever does not believe will be condemned. 17And these signs will accompany those who believe: In my name they will drive out demons; they will speak in new tongues; 18they will pick up snakes with their hands; and when they drink deadly poison, it will not hurt them at all; they will place their hands on sick people, and they will get well."

19After the Lord Jesus had spoken to them, he was taken up into heaven and he sat at the right hand of God. 20Then the disciples went out and preached everywhere, and the Lord worked with them and confirmed his word by the signs that accompanied it.

PSALM 55:1-23
For the director of music. With stringed instruments. A maskila of David.

1 Listen to my prayer, O God,
    do not ignore my plea;
2   hear me and answer me.
My thoughts trouble me and I am
        distraught
3   at the voice of the enemy,
    at the stares of the wicked;
for they bring down suffering
        upon me
    and revile me in their anger.

4 My heart is in anguish within me;
    the terrors of death assail me.
5 Fear and trembling have beset me;
    horror has overwhelmed me.
6 I said, "Oh, that I had the wings of
        a dove!
    I would fly away and be at rest—
7 I would flee far away
    and stay in the desert;   Selah
8 I would hurry to my place of shelter,
    far from the tempest and storm."

9 Confuse the wicked, O Lord,
        confound their speech,
    for I see violence and strife in
        the city.
10 Day and night they prowl about on its
        walls;
    malice and abuse are within it.
11 Destructive forces are at work in
        the city;
    threats and lies never leave its
        streets.

12 If an enemy were insulting me,
    I could endure it;

if a foe were raising himself
    against me,
    I could hide from him.
¹³But it is you, a man like myself,
    my companion, my close friend,
¹⁴with whom I once enjoyed sweet
    fellowship
    as we walked with the throng at
    the house of God.

¹⁵Let death take my enemies by surprise;
    let them go down alive to the grave,*b*
    for evil finds lodging among them.

¹⁶But I call to God,
    and the LORD saves me.
¹⁷Evening, morning and noon
    I cry out in distress,
    and he hears my voice.
¹⁸He ransoms me unharmed
    from the battle waged against me,
    even though many oppose me.
¹⁹God, who is enthroned forever,
    will hear them and afflict them—
                  Selah
men who never change their ways
    and have no fear of God.

²⁰My companion attacks his friends;
    he violates his covenant.
²¹His speech is smooth as butter,
    yet war is in his heart;
his words are more soothing than oil,
    yet they are drawn swords.

²²**Cast your cares on the LORD**
    and he will sustain you;
    he will never let the righteous
    fall.
²³But you, O God, will bring down the
    wicked
    into the pit of corruption;
bloodthirsty and deceitful men
    will not live out half their days.

But as for me, I trust in you.

*aTitle: Probably a literary or musical term   b15 Hebrew
Sheol*

PROVERBS 11:7
⁷**W**hen a wicked man dies, his hope
    perishes;
    all he expected from his power
    comes to nothing.

☐ DAY 72

GOD SIGHTINGS

March 13

NUMBERS 19:1–20:29
The LORD said to Moses and Aaron: ²"This is a requirement of the law that the LORD has commanded: Tell the Israelites to bring you a red heifer without defect or blemish and that has never been under a yoke. ³Give it to Eleazar the priest; it is to be taken outside the camp and slaughtered in his presence. ⁴Then Eleazar the priest is to take some of its blood on his finger and sprinkle it seven times toward the front of the Tent of Meeting. ⁵While he watches, the heifer is to be burned—its hide, flesh, blood and offal. ⁶The priest is to take some cedar wood, hyssop and scarlet wool and throw them onto the burning heifer. ⁷After that, the priest must wash his clothes and bathe himself with water. He may then come into the camp, but he will be ceremonially unclean till evening. ⁸The man who burns it must also wash his clothes and bathe with water, and he too will be unclean till evening.

⁹"A man who is clean shall gather up the ashes of the heifer and put them in a ceremonially clean place outside the camp. They shall be kept by the Israelite community for use in the water of cleansing; it is for purification from sin. ¹⁰The man who gathers up the ashes of the heifer must also wash his clothes, and he too will be unclean till evening. This will be a lasting ordinance both for the Israelites and for the aliens living among them.

¹¹"Whoever touches the dead body of anyone will be unclean for seven days. ¹²He must purify himself with the water on the third day and on the seventh day; then he will be clean. But if he does not purify himself on the third and seventh days, he will not be clean. ¹³Whoever touches the dead body of anyone and fails to purify himself de-

files the Lord's tabernacle. That person must be cut off from Israel. Because the water of cleansing has not been sprinkled on him, he is unclean; his uncleanness remains on him.

[14]"This is the law that applies when a person dies in a tent: Anyone who enters the tent and anyone who is in it will be unclean for seven days, [15]and every open container without a lid fastened on it will be unclean.

[16]"Anyone out in the open who touches someone who has been killed with a sword or someone who has died a natural death, or anyone who touches a human bone or a grave, will be unclean for seven days.

[17]"For the unclean person, put some ashes from the burned purification offering into a jar and pour fresh water over them. [18]Then a man who is ceremonially clean is to take some hyssop, dip it in the water and sprinkle the tent and all the furnishings and the people who were there. He must also sprinkle anyone who has touched a human bone or a grave or someone who has been killed or someone who has died a natural death. [19]The man who is clean is to sprinkle the unclean person on the third and seventh days, and on the seventh day he is to purify him. The person being cleansed must wash his clothes and bathe with water, and that evening he will be clean. [20]But if a person who is unclean does not purify himself, he must be cut off from the community, because he has defiled the sanctuary of the Lord. The water of cleansing has not been sprinkled on him, and he is unclean. [21]This is a lasting ordinance for them.

"The man who sprinkles the water of cleansing must also wash his clothes, and anyone who touches the water of cleansing will be unclean till evening. [22]Anything that an unclean person touches becomes unclean, and anyone who touches it becomes unclean till evening."

[20:1]In the first month the whole Israelite community arrived at the Desert of Zin, and they stayed at Kadesh. There Miriam died and was buried.

[2]Now there was no water for the community, and the people gathered in opposition to Moses and Aaron. [3]They quarreled with Moses and said, "If only we had died when our brothers fell dead before the Lord! [4]Why did you bring the Lord's community into this desert, that we and our livestock should die here? [5]Why did you bring us up out of Egypt to this terrible place? It has no grain or figs, grapevines or pomegranates. And there is no water to drink!"

[6]Moses and Aaron went from the assembly to the entrance to the Tent of Meeting and fell facedown, and the glory of the Lord appeared to them. [7]The Lord said to Moses, [8]"Take the staff, and you and your brother Aaron gather the assembly together. Speak to that rock before their eyes and it will pour out its water. You will bring water out of the rock for the community so they and their livestock can drink."

[9]So Moses took the staff from the Lord's presence, just as he commanded him. [10]He and Aaron gathered the assembly together in front of the rock and Moses said to them, "Listen, you rebels, must we bring you water out of this rock?" [11]Then Moses raised his arm and struck the rock twice with his staff. Water gushed out, and the community and their livestock drank.

[12]But the Lord said to Moses and Aaron, "Because you did not trust in me enough to honor me as holy in the sight of the Israelites, you will not bring this community into the land I give them."

[13]These were the waters of Meribah,[a] where the Israelites quarreled with the Lord and where he showed himself holy among them.

[14]Moses sent messengers from Kadesh to the king of Edom, saying:

"This is what your brother Israel says: You know about all the hardships that have come upon us. [15]Our forefathers went down into Egypt, and we lived there many years. The Egyptians mistreated us and our fathers, [16]but when we cried out to the LORD, he heard our cry and sent an angel and brought us out of Egypt.

"Now we are here at Kadesh, a town on the edge of your territory. [17]Please let us pass through your country. We will not go through any field or vineyard, or drink water from any well. We will travel along the king's highway and not turn to the right or to the left until we have passed through your territory."

[18]But Edom answered:

"You may not pass through here; if you try, we will march out and attack you with the sword."

[19]The Israelites replied:

"We will go along the main road, and if we or our livestock drink any of your water, we will pay for it. We only want to pass through on foot—nothing else."

[20]Again they answered:

"You may not pass through."

Then Edom came out against them with a large and powerful army. [21]Since Edom refused to let them go through their territory, Israel turned away from them.

[22]The whole Israelite community set out from Kadesh and came to Mount Hor. [23]At Mount Hor, near the border of Edom, the LORD said to Moses and Aaron, [24]"Aaron will be gathered to his people. He will not enter the land I give the Israelites, because both of you rebelled against my command at the waters of Meribah. [25]Get Aaron and his son Eleazar and take them up Mount Hor. [26]Remove Aaron's garments and put them on his son Eleazar, for Aaron will be gathered to his people; he will die there."

[27]Moses did as the LORD commanded: They went up Mount Hor in the sight of the whole community.

[28]Moses removed Aaron's garments and put them on his son Eleazar. And Aaron died there on top of the mountain. Then Moses and Eleazar came down from the mountain, [29]and when the whole community learned that Aaron had died, the entire house of Israel mourned for him thirty days.

a13 Meribah means quarreling.

LUKE 1:1-25

Many have undertaken to draw up an account of the things that have been fulfilled[a] among us, [2]just as they were handed down to us by those who from the first were eyewitnesses and servants of the word. [3]**Therefore, since I myself have carefully investigated everything from the beginning, it seemed good also to me to write an orderly account for you, most excellent Theophilus, [4]so that you may know the certainty of the things you have been taught.**

[5]In the time of Herod king of Judea there was a priest named Zechariah, who belonged to the priestly division of Abijah; his wife Elizabeth was also a descendant of Aaron. [6]Both of them were upright in the sight of God, observing all the Lord's commandments and regulations blamelessly. [7]But they had no children, because Elizabeth was barren; and they were both well along in years.

[8]Once when Zechariah's division was on duty and he was serving as priest before God, [9]he was chosen by lot, according to the custom of the priesthood, to go into the temple of the Lord and burn incense. [10]And when the time for the burning of incense came, all the assembled worshipers were praying outside.

[11]Then an angel of the Lord appeared to him, standing at the right side of the altar of incense. [12]When Zechariah saw him, he was startled and was gripped with fear. [13]But the angel said to him: "Do not be afraid, Zechariah; your prayer has been heard. Your wife Elizabeth will bear you a son, and you are to give him the name John. [14]He will be a joy and delight to you, and many will re-

joice because of his birth, [15]for he will be great in the sight of the Lord. He is never to take wine or other fermented drink, and he will be filled with the Holy Spirit even from birth.[b] [16]Many of the people of Israel will he bring back to the Lord their God. [17]And he will go on before the Lord, in the spirit and power of Elijah, to turn the hearts of the fathers to their children and the disobedient to the wisdom of the righteous—to make ready a people prepared for the Lord."

[18]Zechariah asked the angel, "How can I be sure of this? I am an old man and my wife is well along in years."

[19]The angel answered, "I am Gabriel. I stand in the presence of God, and I have been sent to speak to you and to tell you this good news. [20]And now you will be silent and not able to speak until the day this happens, because you did not believe my words, which will come true at their proper time."

[21]Meanwhile, the people were waiting for Zechariah and wondering why he stayed so long in the temple. [22]When he came out, he could not speak to them. They realized he had seen a vision in the temple, for he kept making signs to them but remained unable to speak.

[23]When his time of service was completed, he returned home. [24]After this his wife Elizabeth became pregnant and for five months remained in seclusion. [25]"The Lord has done this for me," she said. "In these days he has shown his favor and taken away my disgrace among the people."

[a]1 Or been surely believed   [b]15 Or from his mother's womb

PSALM 56:1-13

For the director of music. To ⌊the tune of⌋ "A Dove on Distant Oaks." Of David. A *miktam*.[a] When the Philistines had seized him in Gath.

[1] **B**e merciful to me, O God, for men
        hotly pursue me;
    all day long they press their
        attack.

[2]My slanderers pursue me all day
        long;
    many are attacking me in their
        pride.

[3]When I am afraid,
    I will trust in you.
[4]In God, whose word I praise,
    in God I trust; I will not be afraid.
    What can mortal man do to me?

[5]All day long they twist my words;
    they are always plotting to
        harm me.
[6]They conspire, they lurk,
    they watch my steps,
    eager to take my life.

[7]On no account let them escape;
    in your anger, O God, bring down
        the nations.
[8]Record my lament;
    list my tears on your scroll[b]—
    are they not in your record?

[9]Then my enemies will turn back
    when I call for help.
    By this I will know that God is
        for me.
[10]In God, whose word I praise,
    in the LORD, whose word
        I praise—
[11]in God I trust; I will not be afraid.
    What can man do to me?

[12]I am under vows to you, O God;
    I will present my thank offerings
        to you.
[13]For you have delivered me[c] from
        death
    and my feet from stumbling,
    that I may walk before God
    in the light of life.[d]

[a]Title: Probably a literary or musical term   [b]8 Or / put my tears in your wineskin   [c]13 Or my soul   [d]13 Or the land of the living

PROVERBS 11:8

[8]**T**he righteous man is rescued from
        trouble,
    and it comes on the wicked
        instead.

GOD SIGHTINGS

March 14

NUMBERS 21:1–22:20

When the Canaanite king of Arad, who lived in the Negev, heard that Israel was coming along the road to Atharim, he attacked the Israelites and captured some of them. ²Then Israel made this vow to the LORD: "If you will deliver these people into our hands, we will totally destroy*a* their cities." ³The LORD listened to Israel's plea and gave the Canaanites over to them. They completely destroyed them and their towns; so the place was named Hormah.*b*

⁴They traveled from Mount Hor along the route to the Red Sea,*c* to go around Edom. But the people grew impatient on the way; ⁵they spoke against God and against Moses, and said, "Why have you brought us up out of Egypt to die in the desert? There is no bread! There is no water! And we detest this miserable food!"

⁶Then the LORD sent venomous snakes among them; they bit the people and many Israelites died. ⁷The people came to Moses and said, "We sinned when we spoke against the LORD and against you. Pray that the LORD will take the snakes away from us." So Moses prayed for the people.

⁸The LORD said to Moses, "Make a snake and put it up on a pole; anyone who is bitten can look at it and live." ⁹So Moses made a bronze snake and put it up on a pole. Then when anyone was bitten by a snake and looked at the bronze snake, he lived.

¹⁰The Israelites moved on and camped at Oboth. ¹¹Then they set out from Oboth and camped in Iye Abarim, in the desert that faces Moab toward the sunrise. ¹²From there they moved on and camped in the Zered Valley. ¹³They set out from there and camped alongside the Arnon, which is in the desert

extending into Amorite territory. The Arnon is the border of Moab, between Moab and the Amorites. ¹⁴That is why the Book of the Wars of the LORD says:

". . . Waheb in Suphah*d* and the
        ravines,
    the Arnon ¹⁵and*e* the slopes of the
        ravines
that lead to the site of Ar
    and lie along the border of Moab."

¹⁶From there they continued on to Beer, the well where the LORD said to Moses, "Gather the people together and I will give them water."

¹⁷Then Israel sang this song:

"Spring up, O well!
    Sing about it,
¹⁸about the well that the princes dug,
    that the nobles of the people
        sank—
    the nobles with scepters and
        staffs."

Then they went from the desert to Mattanah, ¹⁹from Mattanah to Nahaliel, from Nahaliel to Bamoth, ²⁰and from Bamoth to the valley in Moab where the top of Pisgah overlooks the wasteland.

²¹Israel sent messengers to say to Sihon king of the Amorites:

²²"Let us pass through your country. We will not turn aside into any field or vineyard, or drink water from any well. We will travel along the king's highway until we have passed through your territory."

²³But Sihon would not let Israel pass through his territory. He mustered his entire army and marched out into the desert against Israel. When he reached Jahaz, he fought with Israel. ²⁴Israel, however, put him to the sword and took over his land from the Arnon to the Jabbok, but only as far as the Ammonites, because their border was fortified. ²⁵Israel captured all the cities of the Amorites and occupied them, including Heshbon and all its surrounding settlements. ²⁶Heshbon was the city of Sihon

king of the Amorites, who had fought against the former king of Moab and had taken from him all his land as far as the Arnon. ²⁷That is why the poets say:

"Come to Heshbon and let it be
        rebuilt;
    let Sihon's city be restored.

²⁸"Fire went out from Heshbon,
    a blaze from the city of Sihon.
It consumed Ar of Moab,
    the citizens of Arnon's heights.
²⁹Woe to you, O Moab!
    You are destroyed, O people of
        Chemosh!
He has given up his sons as fugitives
    and his daughters as captives
to Sihon king of the Amorites.

³⁰"But we have overthrown them;
    Heshbon is destroyed all the way
        to Dibon.
We have demolished them as far as
        Nophah,
    which extends to Medeba."

³¹So Israel settled in the land of the Amorites.

³²After Moses had sent spies to Jazer, the Israelites captured its surrounding settlements and drove out the Amorites who were there. ³³Then they turned and went up along the road toward Bashan, and Og king of Bashan and his whole army marched out to meet them in battle at Edrei.

³⁴The LORD said to Moses, "Do not be afraid of him, for I have handed him over to you, with his whole army and his land. Do to him what you did to Sihon king of the Amorites, who reigned in Heshbon."

³⁵So they struck him down, together with his sons and his whole army, leaving them no survivors. And they took possession of his land.

22:1THEN the Israelites traveled to the plains of Moab and camped along the Jordan across from Jericho.ᶠ

²Now Balak son of Zippor saw all that Israel had done to the Amorites, ³and

Moab was terrified because there were so many people. Indeed, Moab was filled with dread because of the Israelites.

⁴The Moabites said to the elders of Midian, "This horde is going to lick up everything around us, as an ox licks up the grass of the field."

So Balak son of Zippor, who was king of Moab at that time, ⁵sent messengers to summon Balaam son of Beor, who was at Pethor, near the River,ᵍ in his native land. Balak said:

"A people has come out of Egypt; they cover the face of the land and have settled next to me. ⁶Now come and put a curse on these people, because they are too powerful for me. Perhaps then I will be able to defeat them and drive them out of the country. For I know that those you bless are blessed, and those you curse are cursed."

⁷The elders of Moab and Midian left, taking with them the fee for divination. When they came to Balaam, they told him what Balak had said.

⁸"Spend the night here," Balaam said to them, "and I will bring you back the answer the LORD gives me." So the Moabite princes stayed with him.

⁹God came to Balaam and asked, "Who are these men with you?"

¹⁰Balaam said to God, "Balak son of Zippor, king of Moab, sent me this message: ¹¹'A people that has come out of Egypt covers the face of the land. Now come and put a curse on them for me. Perhaps then I will be able to fight them and drive them away.'"

¹²But God said to Balaam, "Do not go with them. You must not put a curse on those people, because they are blessed."

¹³The next morning Balaam got up and said to Balak's princes, "Go back to your own country, for the LORD has refused to let me go with you."

¹⁴So the Moabite princes returned to Balak and said, "Balaam refused to come with us."

15 Then Balak sent other princes, more numerous and more distinguished than the first. 16 They came to Balaam and said:

"This is what Balak son of Zippor says: Do not let anything keep you from coming to me, 17 because I will reward you handsomely and do whatever you say. Come and put a curse on these people for me."

18 But Balaam answered them, "Even if Balak gave me his palace filled with silver and gold, I could not do anything great or small to go beyond the command of the LORD my God. 19 Now stay here tonight as the others did, and I will find out what else the LORD will tell me."

20 That night God came to Balaam and said, "Since these men have come to summon you, go with them, but do only what I tell you."

a 2 The Hebrew term refers to the irrevocable giving over of things or persons to the LORD, often by totally destroying them; also in verse 3.   b 3 Hormah means destruction.
c 4 Hebrew Yam Suph; that is, Sea of Reeds   d 14 The meaning of the Hebrew for this phrase is uncertain.
e 14,15 Or "I have been given from Suphah and the ravines / of the Arnon   15 to   f 1 Hebrew Jordan of Jericho; possibly an ancient name for the Jordan River   9 5 That is, the Euphrates

LUKE 1:26-56

In the sixth month, God sent the angel Gabriel to Nazareth, a town in Galilee, 27 to a virgin pledged to be married to a man named Joseph, a descendant of David. The virgin's name was Mary. 28 The angel went to her and said, "Greetings, you who are highly favored! The Lord is with you."

29 Mary was greatly troubled at his words and wondered what kind of greeting this might be. 30 But the angel said to her, "Do not be afraid, Mary, you have found favor with God. 31 You will be with child and give birth to a son, and you are to give him the name Jesus. 32 He will be great and will be called the Son of the Most High. The Lord God will give him the throne of his father David, 33 and he will reign over the house of Jacob forever; his kingdom will never end."

34 "How will this be," Mary asked the angel, "since I am a virgin?"

35 The angel answered, "The Holy Spirit will come upon you, and the power of the Most High will overshadow you. So the holy one to be born will be calleda the Son of God. 36 Even Elizabeth your relative is going to have a child in her old age, and she who was said to be barren is in her sixth month. 37 For nothing is impossible with God."

38 "I am the Lord's servant," Mary answered. "May it be to me as you have said." Then the angel left her.

39 At that time Mary got ready and hurried to a town in the hill country of Judea, 40 where she entered Zechariah's home and greeted Elizabeth. 41 When Elizabeth heard Mary's greeting, the baby leaped in her womb, and Elizabeth was filled with the Holy Spirit. 42 In a loud voice she exclaimed: "Blessed are you among women, and blessed is the child you will bear! 43 But why am I so favored, that the mother of my Lord should come to me? 44 As soon as the sound of your greeting reached my ears, the baby in my womb leaped for joy. 45 Blessed is she who has believed that what the Lord has said to her will be accomplished!"

46 And Mary said:

"My soul glorifies the Lord
47   and my spirit rejoices in God my
          Savior,
48 for he has been mindful
      of the humble state of his servant.
  From now on all generations will call
          me blessed,
49   for the Mighty One has done great
          things for me—
  holy is his name.
50 His mercy extends to those who fear
          him,
      from generation to generation.
51 He has performed mighty deeds with
          his arm;
      he has scattered those who are
          proud in their inmost
          thoughts.
52 He has brought down rulers from
          their thrones
      but has lifted up the humble.

53He has filled the hungry with good
   things
      but has sent the rich away empty.
54He has helped his servant Israel,
      remembering to be merciful
55to Abraham and his descendants
      forever,
      even as he said to our fathers."

56Mary stayed with Elizabeth for
about three months and then returned
home.

a35 Or *So the child to be born will be called holy,*

PSALM 57:1-11

For the director of music. ⌊To the tune of⌋
"Do Not Destroy." Of David. A *miktam.a*
When he had fled from Saul into the cave.

1**H**ave mercy on me, O God, have
   mercy on me,
      for in you my soul takes refuge.
   I will take refuge in the shadow of
      your wings
      until the disaster has passed.

2I cry out to God Most High,
   to God, who fulfills ⌊his purpose⌋
      for me.
3He sends from heaven and saves me,
   rebuking those who hotly pursue
      me;   *Selah*
   God sends his love and his
      faithfulness.

4I am in the midst of lions;
   I lie among ravenous beasts—
men whose teeth are spears and
   arrows,
   whose tongues are sharp swords.

5Be exalted, O God, above the
   heavens;
   let your glory be over all the
      earth.

6They spread a net for my feet—
   I was bowed down in distress.
They dug a pit in my path—
   but they have fallen into it
      themselves.   *Selah*

7My heart is steadfast, O God,
   my heart is steadfast;
   I will sing and make music.

8Awake, my soul!
   Awake, harp and lyre!
   I will awaken the dawn.

9I will praise you, O Lord, among
   the nations;
   I will sing of you among the
      peoples.
10For great is your love, reaching to
   the heavens;
   your faithfulness reaches to
      the skies.

11Be exalted, O God, above the
   heavens;
   let your glory be over all the
      earth.

*a*Title: Probably a literary or musical term

PROVERBS 11:9-11

9**W**ith his mouth the godless destroys
   his neighbor,
      but through knowledge the
         righteous escape.

10When the righteous prosper, the city
   rejoices;
      when the wicked perish, there are
         shouts of joy.

11Through the blessing of the upright a
   city is exalted,
      but by the mouth of the wicked it
         is destroyed.

□ D A Y 7 4

GOD SIGHTINGS

March 15

NUMBERS 22:21–23:30

Balaam got up in the morning, saddled
his donkey and went with the princes of
Moab. 22But God was very angry when
he went, and the angel of the LORD stood
in the road to oppose him. Balaam was
riding on his donkey, and his two servants were with him. 23When the donkey saw the angel of the LORD standing
in the road with a drawn sword in his

hand, she turned off the road into a field. Balaam beat her to get her back on the road.

24Then the angel of the LORD stood in a narrow path between two vineyards, with walls on both sides. 25When the donkey saw the angel of the LORD, she pressed close to the wall, crushing Balaam's foot against it. So he beat her again.

26Then the angel of the LORD moved on ahead and stood in a narrow place where there was no room to turn, either to the right or to the left. 27When the donkey saw the angel of the LORD, she lay down under Balaam, and he was angry and beat her with his staff. 28Then the LORD opened the donkey's mouth, and she said to Balaam, "What have I done to you to make you beat me these three times?"

29Balaam answered the donkey, "You have made a fool of me! If I had a sword in my hand, I would kill you right now."

30The donkey said to Balaam, "Am I not your own donkey, which you have always ridden, to this day? Have I been in the habit of doing this to you?"

"No," he said.

31Then the LORD opened Balaam's eyes, and he saw the angel of the LORD standing in the road with his sword drawn. So he bowed low and fell face-down.

32The angel of the LORD asked him, "Why have you beaten your donkey these three times? I have come here to oppose you because your path is a reckless one before me.ᵃ 33The donkey saw me and turned away from me these three times. If she had not turned away, I would certainly have killed you by now, but I would have spared her."

34Balaam said to the angel of the LORD, "I have sinned. I did not realize you were standing in the road to oppose me. Now if you are displeased, I will go back."

35The angel of the LORD said to Balaam, "Go with the men, but speak only what I tell you." So Balaam went with the princes of Balak.

36When Balak heard that Balaam was coming, he went out to meet him at the Moabite town on the Arnon border, at the edge of his territory. 37Balak said to Balaam, "Did I not send you an urgent summons? Why didn't you come to me? Am I really not able to reward you?"

38"Well, I have come to you now," Balaam replied. "But can I say just anything? I must speak only what God puts in my mouth."

39Then Balaam went with Balak to Kiriath Huzoth. 40Balak sacrificed cattle and sheep, and gave some to Balaam and the princes who were with him. 41The next morning Balak took Balaam up to Bamoth Baal, and from there he saw part of the people.

23:1BALAAM said, "Build me seven altars here, and prepare seven bulls and seven rams for me." 2Balak did as Balaam said, and the two of them offered a bull and a ram on each altar.

3Then Balaam said to Balak, "Stay here beside your offering while I go aside. Perhaps the LORD will come to meet with me. Whatever he reveals to me I will tell you." Then he went off to a barren height.

4God met with him, and Balaam said, "I have prepared seven altars, and on each altar I have offered a bull and a ram."

5The LORD put a message in Balaam's mouth and said, "Go back to Balak and give him this message."

6So he went back to him and found him standing beside his offering, with all the princes of Moab. 7Then Balaam uttered his oracle:

"Balak brought me from Aram,
    the king of Moab from the eastern
        mountains.
'Come,' he said, 'curse Jacob for me;
    come, denounce Israel.'
8How can I curse
    those whom God has not cursed?
How can I denounce
    those whom the LORD has not
        denounced?

[9]From the rocky peaks I see them,
   from the heights I view them.
I see a people who live apart
   and do not consider themselves
      one of the nations.
[10]Who can count the dust of Jacob
   or number the fourth part of
      Israel?
Let me die the death of the
      righteous,
   and may my end be like theirs!"

[11]Balak said to Balaam, "What have you done to me? I brought you to curse my enemies, but you have done nothing but bless them!"

[12]He answered, "Must I not speak what the LORD puts in my mouth?"

[13]Then Balak said to him, "Come with me to another place where you can see them; you will see only a part but not all of them. And from there, curse them for me." [14]So he took him to the field of Zophim on the top of Pisgah, and there he built seven altars and offered a bull and a ram on each altar.

[15]Balaam said to Balak, "Stay here beside your offering while I meet with him over there."

[16]The LORD met with Balaam and put a message in his mouth and said, "Go back to Balak and give him this message."

[17]So he went to him and found him standing beside his offering, with the princes of Moab. Balak asked him, "What did the LORD say?"

[18]Then he uttered his oracle:

"Arise, Balak, and listen;
   hear me, son of Zippor.
[19]God is not a man, that he should lie,
   nor a son of man, that he should
      change his mind.
Does he speak and then not act?
   Does he promise and not fulfill?
[20]I have received a command
      to bless;
   he has blessed, and I cannot
      change it.

[21]"No misfortune is seen in Jacob,[a]
   no misery observed in Israel.[b]

The LORD their God is with them;
   the shout of the King is among
      them.
[22]God brought them out of Egypt;
   they have the strength of a
      wild ox.
[23]There is no sorcery against Jacob,
   no divination against Israel.
It will now be said of Jacob
   and of Israel, 'See what God
      has done!'
[24]The people rise like a lioness;
   they rouse themselves like a lion
that does not rest till he devours
      his prey
   and drinks the blood of his
      victims."

[25]Then Balak said to Balaam, "Neither curse them at all nor bless them at all!"

[26]Balaam answered, "Did I not tell you I must do whatever the LORD says?"

[27]Then Balak said to Balaam, "Come, let me take you to another place. Perhaps it will please God to let you curse them for me from there." [28]And Balak took Balaam to the top of Peor, overlooking the wasteland.

[29]Balaam said, "Build me seven altars here, and prepare seven bulls and seven rams for me." [30]Balak did as Balaam had said, and offered a bull and a ram on each altar.

[a]32 The meaning of the Hebrew for this clause is uncertain.
[b]21 Or He has not looked on Jacob's offenses / or on the wrongs found in Israel.

LUKE 1:57-80

When it was time for Elizabeth to have her baby, she gave birth to a son. [58]Her neighbors and relatives heard that the Lord had shown her great mercy, and they shared her joy.

[59]On the eighth day they came to circumcise the child, and they were going to name him after his father Zechariah, [60]but his mother spoke up and said, "No! He is to be called John."

[61]They said to her, "There is no one among your relatives who has that name."

[62]Then they made signs to his father,

to find out what he would like to name the child. 63He asked for a writing tablet, and to everyone's astonishment he wrote, "His name is John." 64Immediately his mouth was opened and his tongue was loosed, and he began to speak, praising God. 65The neighbors were all filled with awe, and throughout the hill country of Judea people were talking about all these things. 66Everyone who heard this wondered about it, asking, "What then is this child going to be?" For the Lord's hand was with him.

67His father Zechariah was filled with the Holy Spirit and prophesied:

68**"Praise be to the Lord, the God of Israel,**
because he has come and has redeemed his people.
69He has raised up a horna of salvation for us
in the house of his servant David
70(as he said through his holy prophets of long ago),
71salvation from our enemies
and from the hand of all who hate us—
72to show mercy to our fathers
and to remember his holy covenant,
73   the oath he swore to our father Abraham:
74to rescue us from the hand of our enemies,
and to enable us to serve him without fear
75   in holiness and righteousness before him all our days.

76And you, my child, will be called a prophet of the Most High;
for you will go on before the Lord to prepare the way for him,
77to give his people the knowledge of salvation
through the forgiveness of their sins,
78because of the tender mercy of our God,
by which the rising sun will come to us from heaven

79to shine on those living in darkness and in the shadow of death,
to guide our feet into the path of peace."

80And the child grew and became strong in spirit; and he lived in the desert until he appeared publicly to Israel.

a69 Horn here symbolizes strength.

PSALM 58:1-11
For the director of music. ⌊To the tune of⌋ "Do Not Destroy." Of David. A *miktam.a*

1**D**o you rulers indeed speak justly?
Do you judge uprightly among men?
2No, in your heart you devise injustice,
and your hands mete out violence on the earth.
3Even from birth the wicked go astray;
from the womb they are wayward and speak lies.
4Their venom is like the venom of a snake,
like that of a cobra that has stopped its ears,
5that will not heed the tune of the charmer,
however skillful the enchanter may be.

6Break the teeth in their mouths, O God;
tear out, O LORD, the fangs of the lions!
7Let them vanish like water that flows away;
when they draw the bow, let their arrows be blunted.
8Like a slug melting away as it moves along,
like a stillborn child, may they not see the sun.

9Before your pots can feel ⌊the heat of⌋ the thorns—
whether they are green or dry—the wicked will be swept away.b
10The righteous will be glad when they are avenged,

when they bathe their feet in the
blood of the wicked.
11 Then men will say,
"Surely the righteous still are
rewarded;
surely there is a God who judges
the earth."

[a]Title: Probably a literary or musical term [b]9 The meaning of the Hebrew for this verse is uncertain.

PROVERBS 11:12-13

12 **A** man who lacks judgment derides
his neighbor,
but a man of understanding holds
his tongue.

13 A gossip betrays a confidence,
but a trustworthy man keeps
a secret.

☐ DAY 75

GOD SIGHTINGS

March 16

NUMBERS 24:1–25:18

Now when Balaam saw that it pleased the
LORD to bless Israel, he did not resort to
sorcery as at other times, but turned his
face toward the desert. 2 When Balaam
looked out and saw Israel encamped tribe
by tribe, the Spirit of God came upon him
3 and he uttered his oracle:

"The oracle of Balaam son of Beor,
the oracle of one whose eye sees
clearly,
4 the oracle of one who hears the
words of God,
who sees a vision from the
Almighty,[a]
who falls prostrate, and whose
eyes are opened:

5 "How beautiful are your tents,
O Jacob,
your dwelling places, O Israel!

6 "Like valleys they spread out,
like gardens beside a river,
like aloes planted by the LORD,
like cedars beside the waters.
7 Water will flow from their buckets;
their seed will have abundant
water.

"Their king will be greater than Agag;
their kingdom will be exalted.

8 "God brought them out of Egypt;
they have the strength of a wild ox.
They devour hostile nations
and break their bones in pieces;
with their arrows they pierce them.
9 Like a lion they crouch and lie down,
like a lioness—who dares to rouse
them?

"May those who bless you be blessed
and those who curse you be cursed!"

10 Then Balak's anger burned against
Balaam. He struck his hands together
and said to him, "I summoned you to
curse my enemies, but you have blessed
them these three times. 11 Now leave at
once and go home! I said I would reward
you handsomely, but the LORD has kept
you from being rewarded."

12 Balaam answered Balak, "Did I not
tell the messengers you sent me, 13 'Even if
Balak gave me his palace filled with silver
and gold, I could not do anything of my
own accord, good or bad, to go beyond
the command of the LORD—and I must
say only what the LORD says'? 14 Now I am
going back to my people, but come, let me
warn you of what this people will do to
your people in days to come."

15 Then he uttered his oracle:

"The oracle of Balaam son of Beor,
the oracle of one whose eye sees
clearly,
16 the oracle of one who hears the
words of God,
who has knowledge from the Most
High,
who sees a vision from the Almighty,
who falls prostrate, and whose
eyes are opened:

17 "I see him, but not now;
I behold him, but not near.

A star will come out of Jacob;
  a scepter will rise out of Israel.
He will crush the foreheads of Moab,
  the skulls[b] of[c] all the sons of
  Sheth.[d]
18 Edom will be conquered;
  Seir, his enemy, will be conquered,
  but Israel will grow strong.
19 A ruler will come out of Jacob
  and destroy the survivors of
  the city."

20 Then Balaam saw Amalek and uttered his oracle:

"Amalek was first among the nations,
  but he will come to ruin at last."

21 Then he saw the Kenites and uttered his oracle:

"Your dwelling place is secure,
  your nest is set in a rock;
22 yet you Kenites will be destroyed
  when Asshur takes you captive."

23 Then he uttered his oracle:

"Ah, who can live when God does
  this?[e]
24   Ships will come from the shores of
     Kittim;
  they will subdue Asshur and Eber,
  but they too will come to ruin."

25 Then Balaam got up and returned
home and Balak went his own way.

25:1 WHILE Israel was staying in Shittim,
the men began to indulge in sexual immorality with Moabite women, 2 who invited them to the sacrifices to their
gods. The people ate and bowed down
before these gods. 3 So Israel joined in
worshiping the Baal of Peor. And the
LORD's anger burned against them.

4 The LORD said to Moses, "Take all the
leaders of these people, kill them and
expose them in broad daylight before
the LORD, so that the LORD's fierce anger
may turn away from Israel."

5 So Moses said to Israel's judges,
"Each of you must put to death those of
your men who have joined in worshiping the Baal of Peor."

6 Then an Israelite man brought to his
family a Midianite woman right before
the eyes of Moses and the whole assembly of Israel while they were weeping at
the entrance to the Tent of Meeting.
7 When Phinehas son of Eleazar, the son
of Aaron, the priest, saw this, he left the
assembly, took a spear in his hand 8 and
followed the Israelite into the tent. He
drove the spear through both of them—
through the Israelite and into the woman's body. Then the plague against the
Israelites was stopped; 9 but those who
died in the plague numbered 24,000.

10 The LORD said to Moses, 11 "Phinehas son of Eleazar, the son of Aaron, the
priest, has turned my anger away from
the Israelites; for he was as zealous as I
am for my honor among them, so that in
my zeal I did not put an end to them.
12 Therefore tell him I am making my
covenant of peace with him. 13 He and
his descendants will have a covenant of
a lasting priesthood, because he was
zealous for the honor of his God and
made atonement for the Israelites."

14 The name of the Israelite who was
killed with the Midianite woman was
Zimri son of Salu, the leader of a Sime-
onite family. 15 And the name of the
Midianite woman who was put to death
was Cozbi daughter of Zur, a tribal chief
of a Midianite family.

16 The LORD said to Moses, 17 "Treat
the Midianites as enemies and kill
them, 18 because they treated you as enemies when they deceived you in the affair of Peor and their sister Cozbi, the
daughter of a Midianite leader, the
woman who was killed when the plague
came as a result of Peor."

a4 Hebrew *Shaddai*; also in verse 16   b17 Samaritan
Pentateuch (see also Jer. 48:45); the meaning of the word in
the Masoretic Text is uncertain.   c17 Or possibly *Moab, / batter*
d17 Or *all the noisy boasters*   e23 Masoretic Text; with a
different word division of the Hebrew *A people will gather
from the north.*

LUKE 2:1-35

In those days Caesar Augustus issued a
decree that a census should be taken of
the entire Roman world. 2 (This was the
first census that took place while Qui-

rinius was governor of Syria.) ³And everyone went to his own town to register.

⁴So Joseph also went up from the town of Nazareth in Galilee to Judea, to Bethlehem the town of David, because he belonged to the house and line of David. ⁵He went there to register with Mary, who was pledged to be married to him and was expecting a child. ⁶While they were there, the time came for the baby to be born, ⁷and she gave birth to her firstborn, a son. She wrapped him in cloths and placed him in a manger, because there was no room for them in the inn.

⁸And there were shepherds living out in the fields nearby, keeping watch over their flocks at night. ⁹An angel of the Lord appeared to them, and the glory of the Lord shone around them, and they were terrified. ¹⁰But the angel said to them, "Do not be afraid. I bring you good news of great joy that will be for all the people. ¹¹Today in the town of David a Savior has been born to you; he is Christ*a* the Lord. ¹²This will be a sign to you: You will find a baby wrapped in cloths and lying in a manger."

¹³Suddenly a great company of the heavenly host appeared with the angel, praising God and saying,

¹⁴"Glory to God in the highest,
   and on earth peace to men on
      whom his favor rests."

¹⁵When the angels had left them and gone into heaven, the shepherds said to one another, "Let's go to Bethlehem and see this thing that has happened, which the Lord has told us about."

¹⁶So they hurried off and found Mary and Joseph, and the baby, who was lying in the manger. ¹⁷When they had seen him, they spread the word concerning what had been told them about this child, ¹⁸and all who heard it were amazed at what the shepherds said to them. ¹⁹But Mary treasured up all these things and pondered them in her heart. ²⁰The shepherds returned, glorifying and praising God for all the things they had heard and seen, which were just as they had been told.

²¹On the eighth day, when it was time to circumcise him, he was named Jesus, the name the angel had given him before he had been conceived.

²²When the time of their purification according to the Law of Moses had been completed, Joseph and Mary took him to Jerusalem to present him to the Lord ²³(as it is written in the Law of the Lord, "Every firstborn male is to be consecrated to the Lord"*b*), ²⁴and to offer a sacrifice in keeping with what is said in the Law of the Lord: "a pair of doves or two young pigeons."*c*

²⁵Now there was a man in Jerusalem called Simeon, who was righteous and devout. He was waiting for the consolation of Israel, and the Holy Spirit was upon him. ²⁶It had been revealed to him by the Holy Spirit that he would not die before he had seen the Lord's Christ. ²⁷Moved by the Spirit, he went into the temple courts. When the parents brought in the child Jesus to do for him what the custom of the Law required, ²⁸Simeon took him in his arms and praised God, saying:

²⁹"Sovereign Lord, as you have
      promised,
   you now dismiss*d* your servant
      in peace.
³⁰For my eyes have seen your salvation,
³¹   which you have prepared in the
      sight of all people,
³²a light for revelation to the Gentiles
   and for glory to your people
      Israel."

³³The child's father and mother marveled at what was said about him. **³⁴Then Simeon blessed them and said to Mary, his mother: " This child is destined to cause the falling and rising of many in Israel, and to be a sign that will be spoken against, ³⁵so that the thoughts of many hearts will be revealed. And a sword will pierce your own soul too."**

a11 Or Messiah. "The Christ" (Greek) and "the Messiah" (Hebrew) both mean "the Anointed One"; also in verse 26. b23 Exodus 13:2,12 c24 Lev. 12:8 d29 Or promised, / now dismiss

PSALM 59:1-17

For the director of music. ⌐To the tune of⌐ "Do Not Destroy." Of David. A *miktam.ᵃ* When Saul had sent men to watch David's house in order to kill him.

¹ **D**eliver me from my enemies,
O God;
protect me from those who rise
up against me.
² Deliver me from evildoers
and save me from bloodthirsty
men.

³ See how they lie in wait for me!
Fierce men conspire against me
for no offense or sin of mine,
O Lᴏʀᴅ.
⁴ I have done no wrong, yet they are
ready to attack me.
Arise to help me; look on my
plight!
⁵ O Lᴏʀᴅ God Almighty, the God of
Israel,
rouse yourself to punish all the
nations;
show no mercy to wicked traitors.
                                    Selah

⁶ They return at evening,
snarling like dogs,
and prowl about the city.
⁷ See what they spew from their
mouths—
they spew out swords from their
lips,
and they say, "Who can hear us?"
⁸ But you, O Lᴏʀᴅ, laugh at them;
you scoff at all those nations.

⁹ O my Strength, I watch for you;
you, O God, are my fortress, ¹⁰ my
loving God.

God will go before me
and will let me gloat over those
who slander me.
¹¹ But do not kill them, O Lord our
shield,ᵇ
or my people will forget.
In your might make them wander
about,
and bring them down.
¹² For the sins of their mouths,

for the words of their lips,
let them be caught in their pride.
For the curses and lies they utter,
¹³   consume them in wrath,
consume them till they are no
more.
Then it will be known to the ends of
the earth
that God rules over Jacob.   *Selah*

¹⁴ They return at evening,
snarling like dogs,
and prowl about the city.
¹⁵ They wander about for food
and howl if not satisfied.
¹⁶ But I will sing of your strength,
in the morning I will sing of your
love;
for you are my fortress,
my refuge in times of trouble.

¹⁷ O my Strength, I sing praise to you;
you, O God, are my fortress, my
loving God.

ᵃTitle: Probably a literary or musical term   ᵇ11 Or *sovereign*

PROVERBS 11:14

¹⁴ **F**or lack of guidance a nation falls,
but many advisers make victory
sure.

☐ D A Y 7 6

GOD SIGHTINGS

March 17

NUMBERS 26:1-51

After the plague the Lᴏʀᴅ said to Moses and Eleazar son of Aaron, the priest, ²"Take a census of the whole Israelite community by families—all those twenty years old or more who are able to serve in the army of Israel." ³ So on the plains of Moab by the Jordan across from Jericho,ᵃ Moses and Eleazar the priest spoke with them and said, ⁴"Take a census of the men twenty years old or more, as the Lᴏʀᴅ commanded Moses."

These were the Israelites who came out of Egypt:

5 The descendants of Reuben, the first-born son of Israel, were:

    through Hanoch, the Hanochite clan;

    through Pallu, the Palluite clan;

    6 through Hezron, the Hezronite clan;

    through Carmi, the Carmite clan.

7 These were the clans of Reuben; those numbered were 43,730.

8 The son of Pallu was Eliab, 9 and the sons of Eliab were Nemuel, Dathan and Abiram. The same Dathan and Abiram were the community officials who rebelled against Moses and Aaron and were among Korah's followers when they rebelled against the LORD. 10 The earth opened its mouth and swallowed them along with Korah, whose followers died when the fire devoured the 250 men. And they served as a warning sign. 11 The line of Korah, however, did not die out.

12 The descendants of Simeon by their clans were:

    through Nemuel, the Nemuelite clan;

    through Jamin, the Jaminite clan;

    through Jakin, the Jakinite clan;

    13 through Zerah, the Zerahite clan;

    through Shaul, the Shaulite clan.

14 These were the clans of Simeon; there were 22,200 men.

15 The descendants of Gad by their clans were:

    through Zephon, the Zephonite clan;

    through Haggi, the Haggite clan;

    through Shuni, the Shunite clan;

    16 through Ozni, the Oznite clan;

    through Eri, the Erite clan;

    17 through Arodi,*b* the Arodite clan;

    through Areli, the Arelite clan.

18 These were the clans of Gad; those numbered were 40,500.

19 Er and Onan were sons of Judah, but they died in Canaan.

20 The descendants of Judah by their clans were:

    through Shelah, the Shelanite clan;

    through Perez, the Perezite clan;

    through Zerah, the Zerahite clan.

    21 The descendants of Perez were:

    through Hezron, the Hezronite clan;

    through Hamul, the Hamulite clan.

22 These were the clans of Judah; those numbered were 76,500.

23 The descendants of Issachar by their clans were:

    through Tola, the Tolaite clan;

    through Puah, the Puite*c* clan;

    24 through Jashub, the Jashubite clan;

    through Shimron, the Shimronite clan.

25 These were the clans of Issachar; those numbered were 64,300.

26 The descendants of Zebulun by their clans were:

    through Sered, the Seredite clan;

    through Elon, the Elonite clan;

    through Jahleel, the Jahleelite clan.

27 These were the clans of Zebulun; those numbered were 60,500.

28 The descendants of Joseph by their clans through Manasseh and Ephraim were:

29 The descendants of Manasseh:

    through Makir, the Makirite clan (Makir was the father of Gilead);

    through Gilead, the Gileadite clan.

    30 These were the descendants of Gilead:

    through Iezer, the Iezerite clan;

    through Helek, the Helekite clan;

31 through Asriel, the Asrielite clan;

through Shechem, the Shechemite clan;

32 through Shemida, the Shemidaite clan;

through Hepher, the Hepherite clan.

33 (Zelophehad son of Hepher had no sons; he had only daughters, whose names were Mahlah, Noah, Hoglah, Milcah and Tirzah.)

34 These were the clans of Manasseh; those numbered were 52,700.

35 These were the descendants of Ephraim by their clans:

through Shuthelah, the Shuthelahite clan;

through Beker, the Bekerite clan;

through Tahan, the Tahanite clan.

36 These were the descendants of Shuthelah:

through Eran, the Eranite clan.

37 These were the clans of Ephraim; those numbered were 32,500.

These were the descendants of Joseph by their clans.

38 The descendants of Benjamin by their clans were:

through Bela, the Belaite clan;

through Ashbel, the Ashbelite clan;

through Ahiram, the Ahiramite clan;

39 through Shupham,*d* the Shuphamite clan;

through Hupham, the Huphamite clan.

40 The descendants of Bela through Ard and Naaman were:

through Ard,*e* the Ardite clan;

through Naaman, the Naamite clan.

41 These were the clans of Benjamin; those numbered were 45,600.

42 These were the descendants of Dan by their clans:

through Shuham, the Shuhamite clan.

These were the clans of Dan: 43 All of them were Shuhamite clans; and those numbered were 64,400.

44 The descendants of Asher by their clans were:

through Imnah, the Imnite clan;

through Ishvi, the Ishvite clan;

through Beriah, the Beriite clan;

45 and through the descendants of Beriah:

through Heber, the Heberite clan;

through Malkiel, the Malkielite clan.

46 (Asher had a daughter named Serah.)

47 These were the clans of Asher; those numbered were 53,400.

48 The descendants of Naphtali by their clans were:

through Jahzeel, the Jahzeelite clan;

through Guni, the Gunite clan;

49 through Jezer, the Jezerite clan;

through Shillem, the Shillemite clan.

50 These were the clans of Naphtali; those numbered were 45,400.

51 The total number of the men of Israel was 601,730.

a3 Hebrew *Jordan of Jericho*; possibly an ancient name for the Jordan River; also in verse 63   *b17* Samaritan Pentateuch and Syriac (see also Gen. 46:16); Masoretic Text *Arod*   *c23* Samaritan Pentateuch, Septuagint, Vulgate and Syriac (see also 1 Chron. 7:1); Masoretic Text *through Puvah, the Punite*   *d39* A few manuscripts of the Masoretic Text, Samaritan Pentateuch, Vulgate and Syriac (see also Septuagint); most manuscripts of the Masoretic Text *Shephupham*   *e40* Samaritan Pentateuch and Vulgate (see also Septuagint); Masoretic Text does not have *through Ard*.

LUKE 2:36-52

There was also a prophetess, Anna, the daughter of Phanuel, of the tribe of Asher. She was very old; she had lived with her husband seven years after her marriage, 37 and then was a widow until she was eighty-four.*a* She never left the temple but worshiped night and day, fasting and praying. 38 Coming up to them at that very moment, she gave thanks to God and spoke about the child to all who were looking forward to the redemption of Jerusalem.

³⁹When Joseph and Mary had done everything required by the Law of the Lord, they returned to Galilee to their own town of Nazareth. ⁴⁰And the child grew and became strong; he was filled with wisdom, and the grace of God was upon him.

⁴¹Every year his parents went to Jerusalem for the Feast of the Passover. ⁴²When he was twelve years old, they went up to the Feast, according to the custom. ⁴³After the Feast was over, while his parents were returning home, the boy Jesus stayed behind in Jerusalem, but they were unaware of it. ⁴⁴Thinking he was in their company, they traveled on for a day. Then they began looking for him among their relatives and friends. ⁴⁵When they did not find him, they went back to Jerusalem to look for him. ⁴⁶After three days they found him in the temple courts, sitting among the teachers, listening to them and asking them questions. ⁴⁷Everyone who heard him was amazed at his understanding and his answers. ⁴⁸When his parents saw him, they were astonished. His mother said to him, "Son, why have you treated us like this? Your father and I have been anxiously searching for you."

⁴⁹"Why were you searching for me?" he asked. "Didn't you know I had to be in my Father's house?" ⁵⁰But they did not understand what he was saying to them.

⁵¹Then he went down to Nazareth with them and was obedient to them. But his mother treasured all these things in her heart. ⁵²And Jesus grew in wisdom and stature, and in favor with God and men.

a37 Or widow for eighty-four years

PSALM 60:1-12

For the director of music. To ⌊the tune of⌋ "The Lily of the Covenant." A miktam a of David. For teaching. When he fought Aram Naharaim b and Aram Zobah, c and when Joab returned and struck down twelve thousand Edomites in the Valley of Salt.

¹ You have rejected us, O God, and
  burst forth upon us;
  you have been angry—now
    restore us!
² You have shaken the land and torn
    it open;
  mend its fractures, for it is quaking.
³ You have shown your people
    desperate times;
  you have given us wine that makes
    us stagger.

⁴ But for those who fear you, you have
    raised a banner
  to be unfurled against the bow.
                                        Selah

⁵ Save us and help us with your right
    hand,
  that those you love may be delivered.
⁶ God has spoken from his sanctuary:
  "In triumph I will parcel out
    Shechem
  and measure off the Valley of
    Succoth.
⁷ Gilead is mine, and Manasseh
    is mine;
  Ephraim is my helmet,
  Judah my scepter.
⁸ Moab is my washbasin,
  upon Edom I toss my sandal;
  over Philistia I shout in triumph."

⁹ Who will bring me to the fortified
    city?
  Who will lead me to Edom?
¹⁰ Is it not you, O God, you who have
    rejected us
  and no longer go out with our
    armies?
¹¹ Give us aid against the enemy,
  for the help of man is worthless.
¹² With God we will gain the victory,
  and he will trample down our
    enemies.

aTitle: Probably a literary or musical term   bTitle: That is, Arameans of Northwest Mesopotamia   cTitle: That is, Arameans of central Syria

PROVERBS 11:15

¹⁵ He who puts up security for another
    will surely suffer,
  but whoever refuses to strike
    hands in pledge is safe.

GOD SIGHTINGS

March 18

NUMBERS 26:52–28:15

The LORD said to Moses, ⁵³"The land is to be allotted to them [the tribes of Israel] as an inheritance based on the number of names. ⁵⁴To a larger group give a larger inheritance, and to a smaller group a smaller one; each is to receive its inheritance according to the number of those listed. ⁵⁵Be sure that the land is distributed by lot. What each group inherits will be according to the names for its ancestral tribe. ⁵⁶Each inheritance is to be distributed by lot among the larger and smaller groups."

⁵⁷These were the Levites who were counted by their clans:

through Gershon, the Gershonite clan;

through Kohath, the Kohathite clan;

through Merari, the Merarite clan.

⁵⁸These also were Levite clans:

the Libnite clan,

the Hebronite clan,

the Mahlite clan,

the Mushite clan,

the Korahite clan.

(Kohath was the forefather of Amram; ⁵⁹the name of Amram's wife was Jochebed, a descendant of Levi, who was born to the Levitesᵃ in Egypt. To Amram she bore Aaron, Moses and their sister Miriam. ⁶⁰Aaron was the father of Nadab and Abihu, Eleazar and Ithamar. ⁶¹But Nadab and Abihu died when they made an offering before the LORD with unauthorized fire.)

⁶²All the male Levites a month old or more numbered 23,000. They were not counted along with the other Israelites because they received no inheritance among them.

⁶³These are the ones counted by Moses and Eleazar the priest when they counted the Israelites on the plains of Moab by the Jordan across from Jericho. ⁶⁴Not one of them was among those counted by Moses and Aaron the priest when they counted the Israelites in the Desert of Sinai. ⁶⁵For the LORD had told those Israelites they would surely die in the desert, and not one of them was left except Caleb son of Jephunneh and Joshua son of Nun.

27:1THE daughters of Zelophehad son of Hepher, the son of Gilead, the son of Makir, the son of Manasseh, belonged to the clans of Manasseh son of Joseph. The names of the daughters were Mahlah, Noah, Hoglah, Milcah and Tirzah. They approached ²the entrance to the Tent of Meeting and stood before Moses, Eleazar the priest, the leaders and the whole assembly, and said, ³"Our father died in the desert. He was not among Korah's followers, who banded together against the LORD, but he died for his own sin and left no sons. ⁴Why should our father's name disappear from his clan because he had no son? Give us property among our father's relatives."

⁵So Moses brought their case before the LORD ⁶and the LORD said to him, ⁷"What Zelophehad's daughters are saying is right. You must certainly give them property as an inheritance among their father's relatives and turn their father's inheritance over to them.

⁸"Say to the Israelites, 'If a man dies and leaves no son, turn his inheritance over to his daughter. ⁹If he has no daughter, give his inheritance to his brothers. ¹⁰If he has no brothers, give his inheritance to his father's brothers. ¹¹If his father had no brothers, give his inheritance to the nearest relative in his clan, that he may possess it. This is to be a legal requirement for the Israelites, as the LORD commanded Moses.'"

¹²Then the LORD said to Moses, "Go up this mountain in the Abarim range and see the land I have given the Israelites. ¹³After you have seen it, you too

will be gathered to your people, as your brother Aaron was, [14] for when the community rebelled at the waters in the Desert of Zin, both of you disobeyed my command to honor me as holy before their eyes." (These were the waters of Meribah Kadesh, in the Desert of Zin.)

[15]Moses said to the LORD, [16]"May the LORD, the God of the spirits of all mankind, appoint a man over this community [17]to go out and come in before them, one who will lead them out and bring them in, so the LORD's people will not be like sheep without a shepherd."

[18]So the LORD said to Moses, "Take Joshua son of Nun, a man in whom is the spirit,[b] and lay your hand on him. [19]Have him stand before Eleazar the priest and the entire assembly and commission him in their presence. [20]Give him some of your authority so the whole Israelite community will obey him. [21]He is to stand before Eleazar the priest, who will obtain decisions for him by inquiring of the Urim before the LORD. At his command he and the entire community of the Israelites will go out, and at his command they will come in."

[22]Moses did as the LORD commanded him. He took Joshua and had him stand before Eleazar the priest and the whole assembly. [23]Then he laid his hands on him and commissioned him, as the LORD instructed through Moses.

[28:1]THE LORD said to Moses, [2]"Give this command to the Israelites and say to them: 'See that you present to me at the appointed time the food for my offerings made by fire, as an aroma pleasing to me.' [3]Say to them: 'This is the offering made by fire that you are to present to the LORD: two lambs a year old without defect, as a regular burnt offering each day. [4]Prepare one lamb in the morning and the other at twilight, [5]together with a grain offering of a tenth of an ephah[c] of fine flour mixed with a quarter of a hin[d] of oil from pressed olives. [6]This is the regular burnt offering instituted at Mount Sinai as a pleasing aroma, an offering made to the LORD by

fire. [7]The accompanying drink offering is to be a quarter of a hin of fermented drink with each lamb. Pour out the drink offering to the LORD at the sanctuary. [8]Prepare the second lamb at twilight, along with the same kind of grain offering and drink offering that you prepare in the morning. This is an offering made by fire, an aroma pleasing to the LORD.

[9]"'On the Sabbath day, make an offering of two lambs a year old without defect, together with its drink offering and a grain offering of two-tenths of an ephah[e] of fine flour mixed with oil. [10]This is the burnt offering for every Sabbath, in addition to the regular burnt offering and its drink offering.

[11]"'On the first of every month, present to the LORD a burnt offering of two young bulls, one ram and seven male lambs a year old, all without defect. [12]With each bull there is to be a grain offering of three-tenths of an ephah[f] of fine flour mixed with oil; with the ram, a grain offering of two-tenths of an ephah of fine flour mixed with oil; [13]and with each lamb, a grain offering of a tenth of an ephah of fine flour mixed with oil. This is for a burnt offering, a pleasing aroma, an offering made to the LORD by fire. [14]With each bull there is to be a drink offering of half a hin[g] of wine; with the ram, a third of a hin[h]; and with each lamb, a quarter of a hin. This is the monthly burnt offering to be made at each new moon during the year. [15]Besides the regular burnt offering with its drink offering, one male goat is to be presented to the LORD as a sin offering.'"

a 59 Or Jochebed, a daughter of Levi, who was born to Levi b 18 Or Spirit c 5 That is, probably about 2 quarts (about 2 liters); also in verses 13, 21 and 29 d 5 That is, probably about 1 quart (about 1 liter); also in verses 7 and 14 e 9 That is, probably about 4 quarts (about 4.5 liters); also in verses 12, 20 and 28 f 12 That is, probably about 6 quarts (about 6.5 liters); also in verses 20 and 28 g 14 That is, probably about 2 quarts (about 2 liters) h 14 That is, probably about 1 1/4 quarts (about 1.2 liters)

LUKE 3:1-22

In the fifteenth year of the reign of Tiberius Caesar—when Pontius Pilate was governor of Judea, Herod tetrarch of Galilee, his brother Philip tetrarch of Iturea and Traconitis, and Lysanias tetrarch of Abilene— ²during the high priesthood of Annas and Caiaphas, the word of God came to John son of Zechariah in the desert. ³He went into all the country around the Jordan, preaching a baptism of repentance for the forgiveness of sins. ⁴As is written in the book of the words of Isaiah the prophet:

"A voice of one calling in the desert,
'Prepare the way for the Lord,
    make straight paths for him.
⁵Every valley shall be filled in,
    every mountain and hill made low.
The crooked roads shall become
        straight,
    the rough ways smooth.
⁶And all mankind will see God's
        salvation.'"ᵃ

⁷John said to the crowds coming out to be baptized by him, "You brood of vipers! Who warned you to flee from the coming wrath? ⁸Produce fruit in keeping with repentance. And do not begin to say to yourselves, 'We have Abraham as our father.' For I tell you that out of these stones God can raise up children for Abraham. ⁹The ax is already at the root of the trees, and every tree that does not produce good fruit will be cut down and thrown into the fire."

¹⁰"What should we do then?" the crowd asked.

¹¹John answered, "The man with two tunics should share with him who has none, and the one who has food should do the same."

¹²Tax collectors also came to be baptized. "Teacher," they asked, "what should we do?"

¹³"Don't collect any more than you are required to," he told them.

¹⁴Then some soldiers asked him, "And what should we do?"

He replied, "Don't extort money and don't accuse people falsely—be content with your pay."

¹⁵The people were waiting expectantly and were all wondering in their hearts if John might possibly be the Christ.ᵇ ¹⁶John answered them all, "I baptize you withᶜ water. But one more powerful than I will come, the thongs of whose sandals I am not worthy to untie. He will baptize you with the Holy Spirit and with fire. ¹⁷His winnowing fork is in his hand to clear his threshing floor and to gather the wheat into his barn, but he will burn up the chaff with unquenchable fire." ¹⁸And with many other words John exhorted the people and preached the good news to them.

¹⁹But when John rebuked Herod the tetrarch because of Herodias, his brother's wife, and all the other evil things he had done, ²⁰Herod added this to them all: He locked John up in prison.

²¹When all the people were being baptized, Jesus was baptized too. And as he was praying, heaven was opened ²²and the Holy Spirit descended on him in bodily form like a dove. And a voice came from heaven: "You are my Son, whom I love; with you I am well pleased."

ᵃ6 Isaiah 40:3-5   ᵇ15 Or Messiah   ᶜ16 Or in

PSALM 61:1-8
For the director of music. With stringed instruments. Of David.

¹**Hear my cry, O God;**
    listen to my prayer.

²**From the ends of the earth I call**
        to you,
    I call as my heart grows faint;
    lead me to the rock that is
        higher than I.
³For you have been my refuge,
    a strong tower against the foe.

⁴I long to dwell in your tent forever
    and take refuge in the shelter of
        your wings.   *Selah*
⁵For you have heard my vows, O God;
    you have given me the heritage of
        those who fear your name.

⁶Increase the days of the king's life,
    his years for many generations.
⁷May he be enthroned in God's
        presence forever;

appoint your love and faithfulness
   to protect him.

8 Then will I ever sing praise to your
   name
and fulfill my vows day after day.

PROVERBS 11:16-17
16 **A** kindhearted woman gains respect,
   but ruthless men gain only wealth.

17 A kind man benefits himself,
   but a cruel man brings trouble on
      himself.

□ DAY 78

GOD SIGHTINGS

March 19

NUMBERS 28:16–29:40
" 'On the fourteenth day of the first
month the Lord's Passover is to be held.
17 On the fifteenth day of this month
there is to be a festival; for seven days eat
bread made without yeast. 18 On the first
day hold a sacred assembly and do no
regular work. 19 Present to the Lord an
offering made by fire, a burnt offering of
two young bulls, one ram and seven male
lambs a year old, all without defect.
20 With each bull prepare a grain offering
of three-tenths of an ephah of fine flour
mixed with oil; with the ram, two-tenths;
21 and with each of the seven lambs, one-
tenth. 22 Include one male goat as a sin
offering to make atonement for you.
23 Prepare these in addition to the regular
morning burnt offering. 24 In this way
prepare the food for the offering made
by fire every day for seven days as an
aroma pleasing to the Lord; it is to be
prepared in addition to the regular burnt
offering and its drink offering. 25 On the
seventh day hold a sacred assembly and
do no regular work.

26 " 'On the day of firstfruits, when
you present to the Lord an offering of
new grain during the Feast of Weeks,

hold a sacred assembly and do no regular work. 27 Present a burnt offering of
two young bulls, one ram and seven
male lambs a year old as an aroma
pleasing to the Lord. 28 With each bull
there is to be a grain offering of three-
tenths of an ephah of fine flour mixed
with oil; with the ram, two-tenths; 29 and
with each of the seven lambs, one-
tenth. 30 Include one male goat to make
atonement for you. 31 Prepare these together with their drink offerings, in addition to the regular burnt offering and
its grain offering. Be sure the animals
are without defect.

29:1 " 'On the first day of the seventh
month hold a sacred assembly and do
no regular work. It is a day for you to
sound the trumpets. 2 As an aroma
pleasing to the Lord, prepare a burnt offering of one young bull, one ram and
seven male lambs a year old, all without
defect. 3 With the bull prepare a grain
offering of three-tenths of an ephah*a* of
fine flour mixed with oil; with the ram,
two-tenths*b*; 4 and with each of the
seven lambs, one-tenth.*c* 5 Include one
male goat as a sin offering to make
atonement for you. 6 These are in addition to the monthly and daily burnt offerings with their grain offerings and
drink offerings as specified. They are
offerings made to the Lord by fire—a
pleasing aroma.

7 " 'On the tenth day of this seventh
month hold a sacred assembly. You
must deny yourselves*d* and do no work.
8 Present as an aroma pleasing to the
Lord a burnt offering of one young bull,
one ram and seven male lambs a year
old, all without defect. 9 With the bull
prepare a grain offering of three-tenths
of an ephah of fine flour mixed with oil;
with the ram, two-tenths; 10 and with
each of the seven lambs, one-tenth.
11 Include one male goat as a sin offering, in addition to the sin offering for
atonement and the regular burnt offering with its grain offering, and their
drink offerings.

12 " 'On the fifteenth day of the seventh

month, hold a sacred assembly and do no regular work. Celebrate a festival to the LORD for seven days. [13]Present an offering made by fire as an aroma pleasing to the LORD, a burnt offering of thirteen young bulls, two rams and fourteen male lambs a year old, all without defect. [14]With each of the thirteen bulls prepare a grain offering of three-tenths of an ephah of fine flour mixed with oil; with each of the two rams, two-tenths; [15]and with each of the fourteen lambs, one-tenth. [16]Include one male goat as a sin offering, in addition to the regular burnt offering with its grain offering and drink offering.

[17]"'On the second day prepare twelve young bulls, two rams and fourteen male lambs a year old, all without defect. [18]With the bulls, rams and lambs, prepare their grain offerings and drink offerings according to the number specified. [19]Include one male goat as a sin offering, in addition to the regular burnt offering with its grain offering, and their drink offerings.

[20]"'On the third day prepare eleven bulls, two rams and fourteen male lambs a year old, all without defect. [21]With the bulls, rams and lambs, prepare their grain offerings and drink offerings according to the number specified. [22]Include one male goat as a sin offering, in addition to the regular burnt offering with its grain offering and drink offering.

[23]"'On the fourth day prepare ten bulls, two rams and fourteen male lambs a year old, all without defect. [24]With the bulls, rams and lambs, prepare their grain offerings and drink offerings according to the number specified. [25]Include one male goat as a sin offering, in addition to the regular burnt offering with its grain offering and drink offering.

[26]"'On the fifth day prepare nine bulls, two rams and fourteen male lambs a year old, all without defect. [27]With the bulls, rams and lambs, prepare their grain offerings and drink offerings according to the number

specified. [28]Include one male goat as a sin offering, in addition to the regular burnt offering with its grain offering and drink offering.

[29]"'On the sixth day prepare eight bulls, two rams and fourteen male lambs a year old, all without defect. [30]With the bulls, rams and lambs, prepare their grain offerings and drink offerings according to the number specified. [31]Include one male goat as a sin offering, in addition to the regular burnt offering with its grain offering and drink offering.

[32]"'On the seventh day prepare seven bulls, two rams and fourteen male lambs a year old, all without defect. [33]With the bulls, rams and lambs, prepare their grain offerings and drink offerings according to the number specified. [34]Include one male goat as a sin offering, in addition to the regular burnt offering with its grain offering and drink offering.

[35]"'On the eighth day hold an assembly and do no regular work. [36]Present an offering made by fire as an aroma pleasing to the LORD, a burnt offering of one bull, one ram and seven male lambs a year old, all without defect. [37]With the bull, the ram and the lambs, prepare their grain offerings and drink offerings according to the number specified. [38]Include one male goat as a sin offering, in addition to the regular burnt offering with its grain offering and drink offering.

[39]"'In addition to what you vow and your freewill offerings, prepare these for the LORD at your appointed feasts: your burnt offerings, grain offerings, drink offerings and fellowship offerings.[e]'"

[40]Moses told the Israelites all that the LORD commanded him.

a3 That is, probably about 6 quarts (about 6.5 liters); also in verses 9 and 14   b3 That is, probably about 4 quarts (about 4.5 liters); also in verses 9 and 14   c4 That is, probably about 2 quarts (about 2 liters); also in verses 10 and 15   d7 Or must fast   e39 Traditionally peace offerings

LUKE 3:23-38

Now Jesus himself was about thirty years old when he began his ministry.

He was the son, so it was thought, of Joseph,

the son of Heli, [24]the son of Matthat,
the son of Levi, the son of Melki,
the son of Jannai, the son of Joseph,
[25]the son of Mattathias, the son of Amos,
the son of Nahum, the son of Esli,
the son of Naggai, [26]the son of Maath,
the son of Mattathias, the son of Semein,
the son of Josech, the son of Joda,
[27]the son of Joanan, the son of Rhesa,
the son of Zerubbabel, the son of Shealtiel,
the son of Neri, [28]the son of Melki,
the son of Addi, the son of Cosam,
the son of Elmadam, the son of Er,
[29]the son of Joshua, the son of Eliezer,
the son of Jorim, the son of Matthat,
the son of Levi, [30]the son of Simeon,
the son of Judah, the son of Joseph,
the son of Jonam, the son of Eliakim,
[31]the son of Melea, the son of Menna,
the son of Mattatha, the son of Nathan,
the son of David, [32]the son of Jesse,
the son of Obed, the son of Boaz,
the son of Salmon,[a] the son of Nahshon,
[33]the son of Amminadab, the son of Ram,[b]
the son of Hezron, the son of Perez,
the son of Judah, [34]the son of Jacob,
the son of Isaac, the son of Abraham,
the son of Terah, the son of Nahor,
[35]the son of Serug, the son of Reu,
the son of Peleg, the son of Eber,
the son of Shelah, [36]the son of Cainan,
the son of Arphaxad, the son of Shem,
the son of Noah, the son of Lamech,
[37]the son of Methuselah, the son of Enoch,
the son of Jared, the son of Mahalalel,
the son of Kenan, [38]the son of Enosh,
the son of Seth, the son of Adam, the son of God.

[a]32 Some early manuscripts *Sala*   [b]33 Some manuscripts *Amminadab, the son of Admin, the son of Arni*; other manuscripts vary widely.

PSALM 62:1-12

For the director of music. For Jeduthun. A psalm of David.

[1] **M**y soul finds rest in God alone;
    my salvation comes from him.
[2] He alone is my rock and my salvation;
    he is my fortress, I will never be shaken.

[3] How long will you assault a man?
    Would all of you throw him down—
    this leaning wall, this tottering fence?
[4] They fully intend to topple him from his lofty place;
    they take delight in lies.
  With their mouths they bless,
    but in their hearts they curse.   *Selah*

[5] Find rest, O my soul, in God alone;
    my hope comes from him.
[6] He alone is my rock and my salvation;
    he is my fortress, I will not be shaken.

⁷My salvation and my honor
     depend on God*a*;
  he is my mighty rock, my
     refuge.
⁸Trust in him at all times, O people;
  pour out your hearts to him,
     for God is our refuge.   *Selah*

⁹Lowborn men are but a breath,
  the highborn are but a lie;
if weighed on a balance, they are
     nothing;
  together they are only a breath.
¹⁰Do not trust in extortion
  or take pride in stolen goods;
though your riches increase,
  do not set your heart on them.

¹¹One thing God has spoken,
  two things have I heard:
that you, O God, are strong,
¹²   and that you, O Lord, are loving.
  Surely you will reward each person
     according to what he has done.

a7 Or / God Most High is my salvation and my honor

PROVERBS 11:18-19
¹⁸The wicked man earns deceptive
     wages,
  but he who sows righteousness
     reaps a sure reward.

¹⁹The truly righteous man attains life,
  but he who pursues evil goes to his
     death.

☐ DAY 79

GOD SIGHTINGS

March 20

NUMBERS 30:1–31:54
Moses said to the heads of the tribes of Israel: "This is what the Lord commands: ²When a man makes a vow to the Lord or takes an oath to obligate himself by a pledge, he must not break his word but must do everything he said.

³"When a young woman still living in her father's house makes a vow to the

Lord or obligates herself by a pledge ⁴and her father hears about her vow or pledge but says nothing to her, then all her vows and every pledge by which she obligated herself will stand. ⁵But if her father forbids her when he hears about it, none of her vows or the pledges by which she obligated herself will stand; the Lord will release her because her father has forbidden her.

⁶"If she marries after she makes a vow or after her lips utter a rash promise by which she obligates herself ⁷and her husband hears about it but says nothing to her, then her vows or the pledges by which she obligated herself will stand. ⁸But if her husband forbids her when he hears about it, he nullifies the vow that obligates her or the rash promise by which she obligates herself, and the Lord will release her.

⁹"Any vow or obligation taken by a widow or divorced woman will be binding on her.

¹⁰"If a woman living with her husband makes a vow or obligates herself by a pledge under oath ¹¹and her husband hears about it but says nothing to her and does not forbid her, then all her vows or the pledges by which she obligated herself will stand. ¹²But if her husband nullifies them when he hears about them, then none of the vows or pledges that came from her lips will stand. Her husband has nullified them, and the Lord will release her. ¹³Her husband may confirm or nullify any vow she makes or any sworn pledge to deny herself. ¹⁴But if her husband says nothing to her about it from day to day, then he confirms all her vows or the pledges binding on her. He confirms them by saying nothing to her when he hears about them. ¹⁵If, however, he nullifies them some time after he hears about them, then he is responsible for her guilt."

¹⁶These are the regulations the Lord gave Moses concerning relationships between a man and his wife, and between a father and his young daughter still living in his house.

31:1THE LORD said to Moses, 2"Take vengeance on the Midianites for the Israelites. After that, you will be gathered to your people."

3So Moses said to the people, "Arm some of your men to go to war against the Midianites and to carry out the LORD's vengeance on them. 4Send into battle a thousand men from each of the tribes of Israel." 5So twelve thousand men armed for battle, a thousand from each tribe, were supplied from the clans of Israel. 6Moses sent them into battle, a thousand from each tribe, along with Phinehas son of Eleazar, the priest, who took with him articles from the sanctuary and the trumpets for signaling.

7They fought against Midian, as the LORD commanded Moses, and killed every man. 8Among their victims were Evi, Rekem, Zur, Hur and Reba—the five kings of Midian. They also killed Balaam son of Beor with the sword. 9The Israelites captured the Midianite women and children and took all the Midianite herds, flocks and goods as plunder. 10They burned all the towns where the Midianites had settled, as well as all their camps. 11They took all the plunder and spoils, including the people and animals, 12and brought the captives, spoils and plunder to Moses and Eleazar the priest and the Israelite assembly at their camp on the plains of Moab, by the Jordan across from Jericho.a

13Moses, Eleazar the priest and all the leaders of the community went to meet them outside the camp. 14Moses was angry with the officers of the army—the commanders of thousands and commanders of hundreds—who returned from the battle.

15"Have you allowed all the women to live?" he asked them. 16"They were the ones who followed Balaam's advice and were the means of turning the Israelites away from the LORD in what happened at Peor, so that a plague struck the LORD's people. 17Now kill all the boys. And kill every woman who has slept with a man, 18but save for yourselves every girl who has never slept with a man.

19"All of you who have killed anyone or touched anyone who was killed must stay outside the camp seven days. On the third and seventh days you must purify yourselves and your captives. 20Purify every garment as well as everything made of leather, goat hair or wood."

21Then Eleazar the priest said to the soldiers who had gone into battle, "This is the requirement of the law that the LORD gave Moses: 22Gold, silver, bronze, iron, tin, lead 23and anything else that can withstand fire must be put through the fire, and then it will be clean. But it must also be purified with the water of cleansing. And whatever cannot withstand fire must be put through that water. 24On the seventh day wash your clothes and you will be clean. Then you may come into the camp."

25The LORD said to Moses, 26"You and Eleazar the priest and the family heads of the community are to count all the people and animals that were captured. 27Divide the spoils between the soldiers who took part in the battle and the rest of the community. 28From the soldiers who fought in the battle, set apart as tribute for the LORD one out of every five hundred, whether persons, cattle, donkeys, sheep or goats. 29Take this tribute from their half share and give it to Eleazar the priest as the LORD's part. 30From the Israelites' half, select one out of every fifty, whether persons, cattle, donkeys, sheep, goats or other animals. Give them to the Levites, who are responsible for the care of the LORD's tabernacle." 31So Moses and Eleazar the priest did as the LORD commanded Moses.

32The plunder remaining from the spoils that the soldiers took was 675,000 sheep, 3372,000 cattle, 3461,000 donkeys 35and 32,000 women who had never slept with a man.

36The half share of those who fought in the battle was:

337,500 sheep, [37] of which the tribute for the LORD was 675;
[38] 36,000 cattle, of which the tribute for the LORD was 72;
[39] 30,500 donkeys, of which the tribute for the LORD was 61;
[40] 16,000 people, of which the tribute for the LORD was 32.

[41] Moses gave the tribute to Eleazar the priest as the LORD's part, as the LORD commanded Moses.

[42] The half belonging to the Israelites, which Moses set apart from that of the fighting men— [43] the community's half— was 337,500 sheep, [44] 36,000 cattle, [45] 30,500 donkeys [46] and 16,000 people. [47] From the Israelites' half, Moses selected one out of every fifty persons and animals, as the LORD commanded him, and gave them to the Levites, who were responsible for the care of the LORD's tabernacle.

[48] Then the officers who were over the units of the army—the commanders of thousands and commanders of hundreds—went to Moses [49] and said to him, "Your servants have counted the soldiers under our command, and not one is missing. [50] So we have brought as an offering to the LORD the gold articles each of us acquired—armlets, bracelets, signet rings, earrings and necklaces—to make atonement for ourselves before the LORD."

[51] Moses and Eleazar the priest accepted from them the gold—all the crafted articles. [52] All the gold from the commanders of thousands and commanders of hundreds that Moses and Eleazar presented as a gift to the LORD weighed 16,750 shekels.[b] [53] Each soldier had taken plunder for himself. [54] Moses and Eleazar the priest accepted the gold from the commanders of thousands and commanders of hundreds and brought it into the Tent of Meeting as a memorial for the Israelites before the LORD.

a 12 Hebrew *Jordan of Jericho*; possibly an ancient name for the Jordan River b 52 That is, about 420 pounds (about 190 kilograms)

LUKE 4:1-30

Jesus, full of the Holy Spirit, returned from the Jordan and was led by the Spirit in the desert, [2] where for forty days he was tempted by the devil. He ate nothing during those days, and at the end of them he was hungry.

[3] The devil said to him, "If you are the Son of God, tell this stone to become bread."

[4] Jesus answered, "It is written: 'Man does not live on bread alone.'[a]"

[5] The devil led him up to a high place and showed him in an instant all the kingdoms of the world. [6] And he said to him, "I will give you all their authority and splendor, for it has been given to me, and I can give it to anyone I want to. [7] So if you worship me, it will all be yours."

[8] Jesus answered, "It is written: 'Worship the Lord your God and serve him only.'[b]"

[9] The devil led him to Jerusalem and had him stand on the highest point of the temple. "If you are the Son of God," he said, "throw yourself down from here. [10] For it is written:

"'He will command his angels
concerning you
to guard you carefully;
[11] they will lift you up in their hands,
so that you will not strike your foot
against a stone.'[c]"

[12] Jesus answered, "It says: 'Do not put the Lord your God to the test.'[d]"

[13] When the devil had finished all this tempting, he left him until an opportune time.

[14] Jesus returned to Galilee in the power of the Spirit, and news about him spread through the whole countryside. [15] He taught in their synagogues, and everyone praised him.

[16] He went to Nazareth, where he had been brought up, and on the Sabbath day he went into the synagogue, as was his custom. And he stood up to read. [17] The scroll of the prophet Isaiah was handed to him. Unrolling it, he found the place where it is written:

18" The Spirit of the Lord is on me,
     because he has anointed me
     to preach good news to the
         poor.
 He has sent me to proclaim
         freedom for the prisoners
     and recovery of sight for the
         blind,
 to release the oppressed,
19   to proclaim the year of the
         Lord's favor."*e*

20Then he rolled up the scroll, gave it
back to the attendant and sat down. The
eyes of everyone in the synagogue were
fastened on him, 21and he began by saying to them, "Today this scripture is fulfilled in your hearing."

22All spoke well of him and were
amazed at the gracious words that came
from his lips. "Isn't this Joseph's son?"
they asked.

23Jesus said to them, "Surely you will
quote this proverb to me: 'Physician, heal
yourself ! Do here in your hometown
what we have heard that you did in Capernaum.'"

24"I tell you the truth," he continued,
"no prophet is accepted in his hometown. 25I assure you that there were
many widows in Israel in Elijah's time,
when the sky was shut for three and a
half years and there was a severe famine
throughout the land. 26Yet Elijah was
not sent to any of them, but to a widow
in Zarephath in the region of Sidon.
27And there were many in Israel with
leprosy*f* in the time of Elisha the
prophet, yet not one of them was
cleansed—only Naaman the Syrian."

28All the people in the synagogue
were furious when they heard this.
29They got up, drove him out of the
town, and took him to the brow of the
hill on which the town was built, in order to throw him down the cliff. 30But
he walked right through the crowd and
went on his way.

a4 Deut. 8:3   *b8* Deut. 6:13   *c11* Psalm 91:11,12
d12 Deut. 6:16   *e19* Isaiah 61:1,2   *f27* The Greek word
was used for various diseases affecting the skin—not
necessarily leprosy.

PSALM 63:1-11
A psalm of David. When he was in the
Desert of Judah.

1 ● God, you are my God,
     earnestly I seek you;
 my soul thirsts for you,
     my body longs for you,
 in a dry and weary land
     where there is no water.

2I have seen you in the sanctuary
     and beheld your power and your
         glory.
3Because your love is better than life,
     my lips will glorify you.
4I will praise you as long as I live,
     and in your name I will lift up my
         hands.
5My soul will be satisfied as with the
         richest of foods;
     with singing lips my mouth will
         praise you.

6On my bed I remember you;
     I think of you through the watches
         of the night.
7Because you are my help,
     I sing in the shadow of your wings.
8My soul clings to you;
     your right hand upholds me.

9They who seek my life will be
         destroyed;
     they will go down to the depths of
         the earth.
10They will be given over to the sword
     and become food for jackals.

11But the king will rejoice in God;
     all who swear by God's name will
         praise him,
 while the mouths of liars will be
         silenced.

PROVERBS 11:20-21
20The Lord detests men of perverse
         heart
     but he delights in those whose
         ways are blameless.

21Be sure of this: The wicked will not
         go unpunished,
     but those who are righteous will
         go free.

☐ D A Y 8 0

GOD SIGHTINGS

March 21

NUMBERS 32:1–33:39

The Reubenites and Gadites, who had very large herds and flocks, saw that the lands of Jazer and Gilead were suitable for livestock. ²So they came to Moses and Eleazar the priest and to the leaders of the community, and said, ³"Ataroth, Dibon, Jazer, Nimrah, Heshbon, Elealeh, Sebam, Nebo and Beon— ⁴the land the LORD subdued before the people of Israel—are suitable for livestock, and your servants have livestock. ⁵If we have found favor in your eyes," they said, "let this land be given to your servants as our possession. Do not make us cross the Jordan."

⁶Moses said to the Gadites and Reubenites, "Shall your countrymen go to war while you sit here? ⁷Why do you discourage the Israelites from going over into the land the LORD has given them? ⁸This is what your fathers did when I sent them from Kadesh Barnea to look over the land. ⁹After they went up to the Valley of Eshcol and viewed the land, they discouraged the Israelites from entering the land the LORD had given them. ¹⁰The LORD's anger was aroused that day and he swore this oath: ¹¹'Because they have not followed me wholeheartedly, not one of the men twenty years old or more who came up out of Egypt will see the land I promised on oath to Abraham, Isaac and Jacob— ¹²not one except Caleb son of Jephunneh the Kenizzite and Joshua son of Nun, for they followed the LORD wholeheartedly.' ¹³The LORD's anger burned against Israel and he made them wander in the desert forty years, until the whole generation of those who had done evil in his sight was gone.

¹⁴"And here you are, a brood of sinners, standing in the place of your fathers and making the LORD even more angry with Israel. ¹⁵If you turn away from following him, he will again leave all this people in the desert, and you will be the cause of their destruction."

¹⁶Then they came up to him and said, "We would like to build pens here for our livestock and cities for our women and children. ¹⁷But we are ready to arm ourselves and go ahead of the Israelites until we have brought them to their place. Meanwhile our women and children will live in fortified cities, for protection from the inhabitants of the land. ¹⁸We will not return to our homes until every Israelite has received his inheritance. ¹⁹We will not receive any inheritance with them on the other side of the Jordan, because our inheritance has come to us on the east side of the Jordan."

²⁰Then Moses said to them, "If you will do this—if you will arm yourselves before the LORD for battle, ²¹and if all of you will go armed over the Jordan before the LORD until he has driven his enemies out before him— ²²then when the land is subdued before the LORD, you may return and be free from your obligation to the LORD and to Israel. And this land will be your possession before the LORD.

²³"But if you fail to do this, you will be sinning against the LORD; and you may be sure that your sin will find you out. ²⁴Build cities for your women and children, and pens for your flocks, but do what you have promised."

²⁵The Gadites and Reubenites said to Moses, "We your servants will do as our lord commands. ²⁶Our children and wives, our flocks and herds will remain here in the cities of Gilead. ²⁷But your servants, every man armed for battle, will cross over to fight before the LORD, just as our lord says."

²⁸Then Moses gave orders about them to Eleazar the priest and Joshua son of Nun and to the family heads of the Israelite tribes. ²⁹He said to them, "If the Gadites and Reubenites, every man armed for battle, cross over the Jordan with you before the LORD, then

when the land is subdued before you, give them the land of Gilead as their possession. 30But if they do not cross over with you armed, they must accept their possession with you in Canaan."

31The Gadites and Reubenites answered, "Your servants will do what the LORD has said. 32We will cross over before the LORD into Canaan armed, but the property we inherit will be on this side of the Jordan."

33Then Moses gave to the Gadites, the Reubenites and the half-tribe of Manasseh son of Joseph the kingdom of Sihon king of the Amorites and the kingdom of Og king of Bashan—the whole land with its cities and the territory around them.

34The Gadites built up Dibon, Ataroth, Aroer, 35Atroth Shophan, Jazer, Jogbehah, 36Beth Nimrah and Beth Haran as fortified cities, and built pens for their flocks. 37And the Reubenites rebuilt Heshbon, Elealeh and Kiriathaim, 38as well as Nebo and Baal Meon (these names were changed) and Sibmah. They gave names to the cities they rebuilt.

39The descendants of Makir son of Manasseh went to Gilead, captured it and drove out the Amorites who were there. 40So Moses gave Gilead to the Makirites, the descendants of Manasseh, and they settled there. 41Jair, a descendant of Manasseh, captured their settlements and called them Havvoth Jair.a 42And Nobah captured Kenath and its surrounding settlements and called it Nobah after himself.

33:1HERE are the stages in the journey of the Israelites when they came out of Egypt by divisions under the leadership of Moses and Aaron. 2At the LORD's command Moses recorded the stages in their journey. This is their journey by stages:

3The Israelites set out from Rameses on the fifteenth day of the first month, the day after the Passover. They marched out boldly in full view of all the Egyptians,

4who were burying all their firstborn, whom the LORD had struck down among them; for the LORD had brought judgment on their gods.

5The Israelites left Rameses and camped at Succoth.

6They left Succoth and camped at Etham, on the edge of the desert.

7They left Etham, turned back to Pi Hahiroth, to the east of Baal Zephon, and camped near Migdol.

8They left Pi Hahirothb and passed through the sea into the desert, and when they had traveled for three days in the Desert of Etham, they camped at Marah.

9They left Marah and went to Elim, where there were twelve springs and seventy palm trees, and they camped there.

10They left Elim and camped by the Red Sea.c

11They left the Red Sea and camped in the Desert of Sin.

12They left the Desert of Sin and camped at Dophkah.

13They left Dophkah and camped at Alush.

14They left Alush and camped at Rephidim, where there was no water for the people to drink.

15They left Rephidim and camped in the Desert of Sinai.

16They left the Desert of Sinai and camped at Kibroth Hattaavah.

17They left Kibroth Hattaavah and camped at Hazeroth.

18They left Hazeroth and camped at Rithmah.

19They left Rithmah and camped at Rimmon Perez.

20They left Rimmon Perez and camped at Libnah.

21They left Libnah and camped at Rissah.

22They left Rissah and camped at Kehelathah.

23They left Kehelathah and camped at Mount Shepher.

24They left Mount Shepher and camped at Haradah.

25 They left Haradah and camped at Makheloth.

26 They left Makheloth and camped at Tahath.

27 They left Tahath and camped at Terah.

28 They left Terah and camped at Mithcah.

29 They left Mithcah and camped at Hashmonah.

30 They left Hashmonah and camped at Moseroth.

31 They left Moseroth and camped at Bene Jaakan.

32 They left Bene Jaakan and camped at Hor Haggidgad.

33 They left Hor Haggidgad and camped at Jotbathah.

34 They left Jotbathah and camped at Abronah.

35 They left Abronah and camped at Ezion Geber.

36 They left Ezion Geber and camped at Kadesh, in the Desert of Zin.

37 They left Kadesh and camped at Mount Hor, on the border of Edom. 38 At the LORD's command Aaron the priest went up Mount Hor, where he died on the first day of the fifth month of the fortieth year after the Israelites came out of Egypt. 39 Aaron was a hundred and twenty-three years old when he died on Mount Hor.

a41 Or them the settlements of Jair b8 Many manuscripts of the Masoretic Text, Samaritan Pentateuch and Vulgate; most manuscripts of the Masoretic Text left from before Hahiroth c10 Hebrew Yam Suph; that is, Sea of Reeds; also in verse 11

LUKE 4:31–5:11

Then he [Jesus] went down to Capernaum, a town in Galilee, and on the Sabbath began to teach the people. 32 They were amazed at his teaching, because his message had authority.

33 In the synagogue there was a man possessed by a demon, an evil*a* spirit. He cried out at the top of his voice, 34 "Ha! What do you want with us, Jesus of Nazareth? Have you come to destroy us? I know who you are—the Holy One of God!"

35 "Be quiet!" Jesus said sternly. "Come out of him!" Then the demon threw the man down before them all and came out without injuring him.

36 All the people were amazed and said to each other, "What is this teaching? With authority and power he gives orders to evil spirits and they come out!" 37 And the news about him spread throughout the surrounding area.

38 Jesus left the synagogue and went to the home of Simon. Now Simon's mother-in-law was suffering from a high fever, and they asked Jesus to help her. 39 So he bent over her and rebuked the fever, and it left her. She got up at once and began to wait on them.

40 When the sun was setting, the people brought to Jesus all who had various kinds of sickness, and laying his hands on each one, he healed them. 41 Moreover, demons came out of many people, shouting, "You are the Son of God!" But he rebuked them and would not allow them to speak, because they knew he was the Christ.*b*

42 At daybreak Jesus went out to a solitary place. The people were looking for him and when they came to where he was, they tried to keep him from leaving them. 43 But he said, "I must preach the good news of the kingdom of God to the other towns also, because that is why I was sent." 44 And he kept on preaching in the synagogues of Judea.*c*

5:1 One day as Jesus was standing by the Lake of Gennesaret,*d* with the people crowding around him and listening to the word of God, 2 he saw at the water's edge two boats, left there by the fishermen, who were washing their nets. 3 He got into one of the boats, the one belonging to Simon, and asked him to put out a little from shore. Then he sat down and taught the people from the boat.

4 When he had finished speaking, he said to Simon, "Put out into deep water, and let down*e* the nets for a catch."

5 Simon answered, "Master, we've

worked hard all night and haven't caught anything. But because you say so, I will let down the nets."

⁶When they had done so, they caught such a large number of fish that their nets began to break. ⁷So they signaled their partners in the other boat to come and help them, and they came and filled both boats so full that they began to sink.

⁸When Simon Peter saw this, he fell at Jesus' knees and said, "Go away from me, Lord; I am a sinful man!" ⁹For he and all his companions were astonished at the catch of fish they had taken, ¹⁰and so were James and John, the sons of Zebedee, Simon's partners.

Then Jesus said to Simon, "Don't be afraid; from now on you will catch men." ¹¹So they pulled their boats up on shore, left everything and followed him.

a33 Greek *unclean*; also in verse 36　*b41* Or *Messiah*
c44 Or *the land of the Jews*; some manuscripts *Galilee*
d1 That is, Sea of Galilee　*e4* The Greek verb is plural.

PSALM 64:1-10
For the director of music. A psalm of David.

¹ Hear me, O God, as I voice my complaint;
　protect my life from the threat of the enemy.
² Hide me from the conspiracy of the wicked,
　from that noisy crowd of evildoers.
³ They sharpen their tongues like swords
　and aim their words like deadly arrows.
⁴ They shoot from ambush at the innocent man;
　they shoot at him suddenly, without fear.
⁵ They encourage each other in evil plans,
　they talk about hiding their snares;
　they say, "Who will see them*a*?"
⁶ They plot injustice and say,
　"We have devised a perfect plan!"
　Surely the mind and heart of man are cunning.

⁷ But God will shoot them with arrows;
　suddenly they will be struck down.
⁸ He will turn their own tongues against them
　and bring them to ruin;
　all who see them will shake their heads in scorn.

⁹ All mankind will fear;
　they will proclaim the works of God
　and ponder what he has done.
¹⁰ Let the righteous rejoice in the LORD
　and take refuge in him;
　let all the upright in heart praise him!

a5 Or *us*

PROVERBS 11:22
²² Like a gold ring in a pig's snout
　is a beautiful woman who shows no discretion.

□ DAY 81

GOD SIGHTINGS

March 22

NUMBERS 33:40-35:34
The Canaanite king of Arad, who lived in the Negev of Canaan, heard that the Israelites were coming.

⁴¹They left Mount Hor and camped at Zalmonah.

⁴²They left Zalmonah and camped at Punon.

⁴³They left Punon and camped at Oboth.

⁴⁴They left Oboth and camped at Iye Abarim, on the border of Moab.

⁴⁵They left Iyim*a* and camped at Dibon Gad.

⁴⁶They left Dibon Gad and camped at Almon Diblathaim.

⁴⁷They left Almon Diblathaim and camped in the mountains of Abarim, near Nebo.

⁴⁸They left the mountains of Abarim and camped on the plains of Moab by the Jordan across from Jericho.ᵇ ⁴⁹There on the plains of Moab they camped along the Jordan from Beth Jeshimoth to Abel Shittim.

⁵⁰On the plains of Moab by the Jordan across from Jericho the LORD said to Moses, ⁵¹"Speak to the Israelites and say to them: 'When you cross the Jordan into Canaan, ⁵²drive out all the inhabitants of the land before you. Destroy all their carved images and their cast idols, and demolish all their high places. ⁵³Take possession of the land and settle in it, for I have given you the land to possess. ⁵⁴Distribute the land by lot, according to your clans. To a larger group give a larger inheritance, and to a smaller group a smaller one. Whatever falls to them by lot will be theirs. Distribute it according to your ancestral tribes.

⁵⁵"'But if you do not drive out the inhabitants of the land, those you allow to remain will become barbs in your eyes and thorns in your sides. They will give you trouble in the land where you will live. ⁵⁶And then I will do to you what I plan to do to them.'"

³⁴:¹THE LORD said to Moses, ²"Command the Israelites and say to them: 'When you enter Canaan, the land that will be allotted to you as an inheritance will have these boundaries:

³"'Your southern side will include some of the Desert of Zin along the border of Edom. On the east, your southern boundary will start from the end of the Salt Sea,ᶜ ⁴cross south of Scorpionᵈ Pass, continue on to Zin and go south of Kadesh Barnea. Then it will go to Hazar Addar and over to Azmon, ⁵where it will turn, join the Wadi of Egypt and end at the Sea.ᵉ

⁶"'Your western boundary will be the coast of the Great Sea. This will be your boundary on the west.

⁷"'For your northern boundary, run a line from the Great Sea to Mount Hor ⁸and from Mount Hor to Leboᶠ Hamath. Then the boundary will go to Zedad, ⁹continue to Ziphron and end at Hazar Enan. This will be your boundary on the north.

¹⁰"'For your eastern boundary, run a line from Hazar Enan to Shepham. ¹¹The boundary will go down from Shepham to Riblah on the east side of Ain and continue along the slopes east of the Sea of Kinnereth.ᵍ ¹²Then the boundary will go down along the Jordan and end at the Salt Sea.

"'This will be your land, with its boundaries on every side.'"

¹³Moses commanded the Israelites: "Assign this land by lot as an inheritance. The LORD has ordered that it be given to the nine and a half tribes, ¹⁴because the families of the tribe of Reuben, the tribe of Gad and the half-tribe of Manasseh have received their inheritance. ¹⁵These two and a half tribes have received their inheritance on the east side of the Jordan of Jericho,ʰ toward the sunrise."

¹⁶The LORD said to Moses, ¹⁷"These are the names of the men who are to assign the land for you as an inheritance: Eleazar the priest and Joshua son of Nun. ¹⁸And appoint one leader from each tribe to help assign the land. ¹⁹These are their names:

Caleb son of Jephunneh,
   from the tribe of Judah;
²⁰Shemuel son of Ammihud,
   from the tribe of Simeon;
²¹Elidad son of Kislon,
   from the tribe of Benjamin;
²²Bukki son of Jogli,
   the leader from the tribe of Dan;
²³Hanniel son of Ephod,
   the leader from the tribe of Manasseh son of Joseph;
²⁴Kemuel son of Shiphtan,
   the leader from the tribe of Ephraim son of Joseph;
²⁵Elizaphan son of Parnach,
   the leader from the tribe of Zebulun;

26 Paltiel son of Azzan,
    the leader from the tribe of Is-
    sachar;
27 Ahihud son of Shelomi,
    the leader from the tribe of
    Asher;
28 Pedahel son of Ammihud,
    the leader from the tribe of
    Naphtali."

29 These are the men the LORD commanded to assign the inheritance to the Israelites in the land of Canaan.

35:1 On the plains of Moab by the Jordan across from Jericho,ⁱ the LORD said to Moses, 2 "Command the Israelites to give the Levites towns to live in from the inheritance the Israelites will possess. And give them pasturelands around the towns. 3 Then they will have towns to live in and pasturelands for their cattle, flocks and all their other livestock.

4 "The pasturelands around the towns that you give the Levites will extend out fifteen hundred feetʲ from the town wall. 5 Outside the town, measure three thousand feetᵏ on the east side, three thousand on the south side, three thousand on the west and three thousand on the north, with the town in the center. They will have this area as pastureland for the towns.

6 "Six of the towns you give the Levites will be cities of refuge, to which a person who has killed someone may flee. In addition, give them forty-two other towns. 7 In all you must give the Levites forty-eight towns, together with their pasturelands. 8 The towns you give the Levites from the land the Israelites possess are to be given in proportion to the inheritance of each tribe: Take many towns from a tribe that has many, but few from one that has few."

9 Then the LORD said to Moses: 10 "Speak to the Israelites and say to them: 'When you cross the Jordan into Canaan, 11 select some towns to be your cities of refuge, to which a person who has killed someone accidentally may flee. 12 They will be places of refuge from the avenger, so that a person accused of murder may not die before he stands trial before the assembly. 13 These six towns you give will be your cities of refuge. 14 Give three on this side of the Jordan and three in Canaan as cities of refuge. 15 These six towns will be a place of refuge for Israelites, aliens and any other people living among them, so that anyone who has killed another accidentally can flee there.

16 "'If a man strikes someone with an iron object so that he dies, he is a murderer; the murderer shall be put to death. 17 Or if anyone has a stone in his hand that could kill, and he strikes someone so that he dies, he is a murderer; the murderer shall be put to death. 18 Or if anyone has a wooden object in his hand that could kill, and he hits someone so that he dies, he is a murderer; the murderer shall be put to death. 19 The avenger of blood shall put the murderer to death; when he meets him, he shall put him to death. 20 If anyone with malice aforethought shoves another or throws something at him intentionally so that he dies 21 or if in hostility he hits him with his fist so that he dies, that person shall be put to death; he is a murderer. The avenger of blood shall put the murderer to death when he meets him.

22 "'But if without hostility someone suddenly shoves another or throws something at him unintentionally 23 or, without seeing him, drops a stone on him that could kill him, and he dies, then since he was not his enemy and he did not intend to harm him, 24 the assembly must judge between him and the avenger of blood according to these regulations. 25 The assembly must protect the one accused of murder from the avenger of blood and send him back to the city of refuge to which he fled. He must stay there until the death of the high priest, who was anointed with the holy oil.

26 "'But if the accused ever goes outside the limits of the city of refuge to which he has fled 27 and the avenger of blood finds him outside the city, the

avenger of blood may kill the accused without being guilty of murder. 28The accused must stay in his city of refuge until the death of the high priest; only after the death of the high priest may he return to his own property.

29" 'These are to be legal requirements for you throughout the generations to come, wherever you live.

30"'Anyone who kills a person is to be put to death as a murderer only on the testimony of witnesses. But no one is to be put to death on the testimony of only one witness.

31"'Do not accept a ransom for the life of a murderer, who deserves to die. He must surely be put to death.

32" 'Do not accept a ransom for anyone who has fled to a city of refuge and so allow him to go back and live on his own land before the death of the high priest.

33"'Do not pollute the land where you are. Bloodshed pollutes the land, and atonement cannot be made for the land on which blood has been shed, except by the blood of the one who shed it. 34Do not defile the land where you live and where I dwell, for I, the LORD, dwell among the Israelites.'"

a45 That is, Iye Abarim   *b48* Hebrew *Jordan of Jericho*; possibly an ancient name for the Jordan River; also in verse 50   *c3* That is, the Dead Sea; also in verse 12   *d4* Hebrew *Akrabbim*   *e5* That is, the Mediterranean; also in verses 6 and 7   *f8* Or *to the entrance to*   *g11* That is, Galilee   *h15* *Jordan of Jericho* was possibly an ancient name for the Jordan River.   *i1* Hebrew *Jordan of Jericho*; possibly an ancient name for the Jordan River   *j4* Hebrew *a thousand cubits* (about 450 meters)   *k5* Hebrew *two thousand cubits* (about 900 meters)

LUKE 5:12-28

While Jesus was in one of the towns, a man came along who was covered with leprosy.*a* When he saw Jesus, he fell with his face to the ground and begged him, "Lord, if you are willing, you can make me clean."

13Jesus reached out his hand and touched the man. "I am willing," he said. "Be clean!" And immediately the leprosy left him.

14Then Jesus ordered him, "Don't tell anyone, but go, show yourself to the priest and offer the sacrifices that Mo-

ses commanded for your cleansing, as a testimony to them."

15Yet the news about him spread all the more, so that crowds of people came to hear him and to be healed of their sicknesses. 16But Jesus often withdrew to lonely places and prayed.

17One day as he was teaching, Pharisees and teachers of the law, who had come from every village of Galilee and from Judea and Jerusalem, were sitting there. And the power of the Lord was present for him to heal the sick. 18Some men came carrying a paralytic on a mat and tried to take him into the house to lay him before Jesus. 19When they could not find a way to do this because of the crowd, they went up on the roof and lowered him on his mat through the tiles into the middle of the crowd, right in front of Jesus.

20When Jesus saw their faith, he said, "Friend, your sins are forgiven."

21The Pharisees and the teachers of the law began thinking to themselves, "Who is this fellow who speaks blasphemy? Who can forgive sins but God alone?"

22Jesus knew what they were thinking and asked, "Why are you thinking these things in your hearts? 23Which is easier: to say, 'Your sins are forgiven,' or to say, 'Get up and walk'? 24But that you may know that the Son of Man has authority on earth to forgive sins . . ." He said to the paralyzed man, "I tell you, get up, take your mat and go home." 25Immediately he stood up in front of them, took what he had been lying on and went home praising God. 26Everyone was amazed and gave praise to God. They were filled with awe and said, "We have seen remarkable things today."

27After this, Jesus went out and saw a tax collector by the name of Levi sitting at his tax booth. "Follow me," Jesus said to him, 28and Levi got up, left everything and followed him.

a12 The Greek word was used for various diseases affecting the skin—not necessarily leprosy.

PSALM 65:1-13

For the director of music. A psalm of David.
A song.

¹ **P**raise awaits*a* you, O God, in Zion;
    to you our vows will be fulfilled.
² O you who hear prayer,
    to you all men will come.
³ When we were overwhelmed by sins,
    you forgave*b* our transgressions.
⁴ Blessed are those you choose
    and bring near to live in your
        courts!
  We are filled with the good things of
        your house,
    of your holy temple.

⁵ You answer us with awesome deeds
        of righteousness,
    O God our Savior,
  the hope of all the ends of the earth
    and of the farthest seas,
⁶ who formed the mountains by your
        power,
    having armed yourself with
        strength,
⁷ who stilled the roaring of the seas,
    the roaring of their waves,
    and the turmoil of the nations.
⁸ Those living far away fear your
        wonders;
    where morning dawns and
        evening fades
    you call forth songs of joy.

⁹ You care for the land and water it;
    you enrich it abundantly.
  The streams of God are filled with
        water
    to provide the people with grain,
    for so you have ordained it.*c*
¹⁰ You drench its furrows
    and level its ridges;
  you soften it with showers
    and bless its crops.
¹¹ You crown the year with your
        bounty,
    and your carts overflow with
        abundance.
¹² The grasslands of the desert
        overflow;
    the hills are clothed with gladness.

¹³ The meadows are covered with
        flocks
    and the valleys are mantled with
        grain;
    they shout for joy and sing.

a 1 Or befits; the meaning of the Hebrew for this word is
uncertain.   *b 3 Or made atonement for   c 9 Or for that is
how you prepare the land*

PROVERBS 11:23

²³ **T**he desire of the righteous ends only
        in good,
    but the hope of the wicked only in
        wrath.

☐ D A Y 8 2

GOD SIGHTINGS

March 23

NUMBERS 36:1—DEUTERONOMY 1:46

The family heads of the clan of Gilead
son of Makir, the son of Manasseh, who
were from the clans of the descendants
of Joseph, came and spoke before Moses and the leaders, the heads of the Israelite families. ²They said, "When the
LORD commanded my lord to give the
land as an inheritance to the Israelites
by lot, he ordered you to give the inheritance of our brother Zelophehad to his
daughters. ³Now suppose they marry
men from other Israelite tribes; then
their inheritance will be taken from our
ancestral inheritance and added to that
of the tribe they marry into. And so part
of the inheritance allotted to us will be
taken away. ⁴When the Year of Jubilee
for the Israelites comes, their inheritance will be added to that of the tribe
into which they marry, and their property will be taken from the tribal inheritance of our forefathers."

⁵Then at the LORD's command Moses
gave this order to the Israelites: "What
the tribe of the descendants of Joseph is
saying is right. ⁶This is what the LORD
commands for Zelophehad's daughters: They may marry anyone they

please as long as they marry within the tribal clan of their father. 7No inheritance in Israel is to pass from tribe to tribe, for every Israelite shall keep the tribal land inherited from his forefathers. 8Every daughter who inherits land in any Israelite tribe must marry someone in her father's tribal clan, so that every Israelite will possess the inheritance of his fathers. 9No inheritance may pass from tribe to tribe, for each Israelite tribe is to keep the land it inherits."

10So Zelophehad's daughters did as the Lord commanded Moses. 11Zelophehad's daughters—Mahlah, Tirzah, Hoglah, Milcah and Noah—married their cousins on their father's side. 12They married within the clans of the descendants of Manasseh son of Joseph, and their inheritance remained in their father's clan and tribe.

13These are the commands and regulations the Lord gave through Moses to the Israelites on the plains of Moab by the Jordan across from Jericho.a

1:1These are the words Moses spoke to all Israel in the desert east of the Jordan—that is, in the Arabah—opposite Suph, between Paran and Tophel, Laban, Hazeroth and Dizahab. 2(It takes eleven days to go from Horeb to Kadesh Barnea by the Mount Seir road.)

3In the fortieth year, on the first day of the eleventh month, Moses proclaimed to the Israelites all that the Lord had commanded him concerning them. 4This was after he had defeated Sihon king of the Amorites, who reigned in Heshbon, and at Edrei had defeated Og king of Bashan, who reigned in Ashtaroth.

5East of the Jordan in the territory of Moab, Moses began to expound this law, saying:

6The Lord our God said to us at Horeb, "You have stayed long enough at this mountain. 7Break camp and advance into the hill country of the Amorites; go to all the neighboring peoples in the Arabah, in the mountains, in the western foothills, in the Negev and along the coast, to the land of the Canaanites and to Lebanon, as far as the great river, the Euphrates. 8See, I have given you this land. Go in and take possession of the land that the Lord swore he would give to your fathers—to Abraham, Isaac and Jacob—and to their descendants after them."

9At that time I said to you, "You are too heavy a burden for me to carry alone. 10The Lord your God has increased your numbers so that today you are as many as the stars in the sky. 11May the Lord, the God of your fathers, increase you a thousand times and bless you as he has promised! 12But how can I bear your problems and your burdens and your disputes all by myself? 13Choose some wise, understanding and respected men from each of your tribes, and I will set them over you."

14You answered me, "What you propose to do is good."

15So I took the leading men of your tribes, wise and respected men, and appointed them to have authority over you—as commanders of thousands, of hundreds, of fifties and of tens and as tribal officials. 16And I charged your judges at that time: Hear the disputes between your brothers and judge fairly, whether the case is between brother Israelites or between one of them and an alien. 17Do not show partiality in judging; hear both small and great alike. Do not be afraid of any man, for judgment belongs to God. Bring me any case too hard for you, and I will hear it. 18And at that time I told you everything you were to do.

19Then, as the Lord our God commanded us, we set out from Horeb and went toward the hill country of the Amorites through all that vast and dreadful desert that you have seen, and so we reached Kadesh Barnea. 20Then I said to you, "You have reached the hill country of the Amorites, which the Lord our God is giving us. 21See, the Lord your God has given you the land. Go up and take possession of it as the LORD, the God of your fathers, told you. Do not be afraid; do not be discouraged."

22 Then all of you came to me and said, "Let us send men ahead to spy out the land for us and bring back a report about the route we are to take and the towns we will come to."

23 The idea seemed good to me; so I selected twelve of you, one man from each tribe. 24 They left and went up into the hill country, and came to the Valley of Eshcol and explored it. 25 Taking with them some of the fruit of the land, they brought it down to us and reported, "It is a good land that the LORD our God is giving us."

26 But you were unwilling to go up; you rebelled against the command of the LORD your God. 27 You grumbled in your tents and said, "The LORD hates us; so he brought us out of Egypt to deliver us into the hands of the Amorites to destroy us. 28 Where can we go? Our brothers have made us lose heart. They say, 'The people are stronger and taller than we are; the cities are large, with walls up to the sky. We even saw the Anakites there.'"

29 Then I said to you, "Do not be terrified; do not be afraid of them. 30 The LORD your God, who is going before you, will fight for you, as he did for you in Egypt, before your very eyes, 31 and in the desert. There you saw how the LORD your God carried you, as a father carries his son, all the way you went until you reached this place."

32 In spite of this, you did not trust in the LORD your God, 33 who went ahead of you on your journey, in fire by night and in a cloud by day, to search out places for you to camp and to show you the way you should go.

34 When the LORD heard what you said, he was angry and solemnly swore: 35 "Not a man of this evil generation shall see the good land I swore to give your forefathers, 36 except Caleb son of Jephunneh. He will see it, and I will give him and his descendants the land he set

his feet on, because he followed the LORD wholeheartedly."

37 Because of you the LORD became angry with me also and said, "You shall not enter it, either. 38 But your assistant, Joshua son of Nun, will enter it. Encourage him, because he will lead Israel to inherit it. 39 And the little ones that you said would be taken captive, your children who do not yet know good from bad—they will enter the land. I will give it to them and they will take possession of it. 40 But as for you, turn around and set out toward the desert along the route to the Red Sea.*b*"

41 Then you replied, "We have sinned against the LORD. We will go up and fight, as the LORD our God commanded us." So every one of you put on his weapons, thinking it easy to go up into the hill country.

42 But the LORD said to me, "Tell them, 'Do not go up and fight, because I will not be with you. You will be defeated by your enemies.'"

43 So I told you, but you would not listen. You rebelled against the LORD's command and in your arrogance you marched up into the hill country. 44 The Amorites who lived in those hills came out against you; they chased you like a swarm of bees and beat you down from Seir all the way to Hormah. 45 You came back and wept before the LORD, but he paid no attention to your weeping and turned a deaf ear to you. 46 And so you stayed in Kadesh many days—all the time you spent there.

a 13 Hebrew *Jordan of Jericho*; possibly an ancient name for the Jordan River   *b 40* Hebrew *Yam Suph*; that is, Sea of Reeds

LUKE 5:29–6:11

Then Levi held a great banquet for Jesus at his house, and a large crowd of tax collectors and others were eating with them. 30 But the Pharisees and the teachers of the law who belonged to their sect complained to his disciples, "Why do you eat and drink with tax collectors and 'sinners'?"

31 Jesus answered them, "It is not the healthy who need a doctor, but the sick.

32I have not come to call the righteous, but sinners to repentance."

33They said to him, "John's disciples often fast and pray, and so do the disciples of the Pharisees, but yours go on eating and drinking."

34Jesus answered, "Can you make the guests of the bridegroom fast while he is with them? 35But the time will come when the bridegroom will be taken from them; in those days they will fast."

36He told them this parable: "No one tears a patch from a new garment and sews it on an old one. If he does, he will have torn the new garment, and the patch from the new will not match the old. 37And no one pours new wine into old wineskins. If he does, the new wine will burst the skins, the wine will run out and the wineskins will be ruined. 38No, new wine must be poured into new wineskins. 39And no one after drinking old wine wants the new, for he says, 'The old is better.'"

6:1ONE Sabbath Jesus was going through the grainfields, and his disciples began to pick some heads of grain, rub them in their hands and eat the kernels. 2Some of the Pharisees asked, "Why are you doing what is unlawful on the Sabbath?"

3Jesus answered them, "Have you never read what David did when he and his companions were hungry? 4He entered the house of God, and taking the consecrated bread, he ate what is lawful only for priests to eat. And he also gave some to his companions." 5Then Jesus said to them, "The Son of Man is Lord of the Sabbath."

6On another Sabbath he went into the synagogue and was teaching, and a man was there whose right hand was shriveled. 7The Pharisees and the teachers of the law were looking for a reason to accuse Jesus, so they watched him closely to see if he would heal on the Sabbath. 8But Jesus knew what they were thinking and said to the man with the shriveled hand, "Get up and stand in front of everyone." So he got up and stood there.

9Then Jesus said to them, "I ask you, which is lawful on the Sabbath: to do good or to do evil, to save life or to destroy it?"

10He looked around at them all, and then said to the man, "Stretch out your hand." He did so, and his hand was completely restored. 11But they were furious and began to discuss with one another what they might do to Jesus.

PSALM 66:1-20

For the director of music. A song. A psalm.

1 **S**hout with joy to God, all the earth!
2   Sing the glory of his name;
    make his praise glorious!
3 Say to God, "How awesome are your
      deeds!
    So great is your power
    that your enemies cringe before
        you.
4 All the earth bows down to you;
    they sing praise to you,
    they sing praise to your name." *Selah*

5 **Come and see what God has done,
    how awesome his works in
      man's behalf !**
6 He turned the sea into dry land,
    they passed through the waters
        on foot—
  come, let us rejoice in him.
7 He rules forever by his power,
    his eyes watch the nations—
    let not the rebellious rise up
        against him.   *Selah*

8 Praise our God, O peoples,
    let the sound of his praise be heard;
9 he has preserved our lives
    and kept our feet from slipping.
10 For you, O God, tested us;
    you refined us like silver.
11 You brought us into prison
    and laid burdens on our backs.
12 You let men ride over our heads;
    we went through fire and water,
    but you brought us to a place of
      abundance.

13 I will come to your temple with burnt
      offerings
    and fulfill my vows to you—

14vows my lips promised and my
        mouth spoke
    when I was in trouble.
15I will sacrifice fat animals to you
    and an offering of rams;
    I will offer bulls and goats.   *Selah*

16Come and listen, all you who fear
        God;
    let me tell you what he has done
        for me.
17I cried out to him with my mouth;
    his praise was on my tongue.
18If I had cherished sin in my heart,
    the Lord would not have listened;
19but God has surely listened
    and heard my voice in prayer.
20Praise be to God,
    who has not rejected my prayer
        or withheld his love from me!

PROVERBS 11:24-26
24One man gives freely, yet gains even
        more;
    another withholds unduly, but
        comes to poverty.

25A generous man will prosper;
    he who refreshes others will
        himself be refreshed.

26People curse the man who hoards
        grain,
    but blessing crowns him who is
        willing to sell.

☐ D A Y 8 3

GOD SIGHTINGS

March 24

DEUTERONOMY 2:1–3:29
Then we [the Israelites] turned back and
set out toward the desert along the
route to the Red Sea,a as the Lord had
directed me. For a long time we made
our way around the hill country of Seir.
    2Then the Lord said to me, 3"You
have made your way around this hill
country long enough; now turn north.

4Give the people these orders: 'You are
about to pass through the territory of
your brothers the descendants of Esau,
who live in Seir. They will be afraid of
you, but be very careful. 5Do not provoke them to war, for I will not give you
any of their land, not even enough to put
your foot on. I have given Esau the hill
country of Seir as his own. 6You are to
pay them in silver for the food you eat
and the water you drink.'"
    7The Lord your God has blessed you
in all the work of your hands. He has
watched over your journey through this
vast desert. These forty years the Lord
your God has been with you, and you
have not lacked anything.
    8So we went on past our brothers the
descendants of Esau, who live in Seir.
We turned from the Arabah road, which
comes up from Elath and Ezion Geber,
and traveled along the desert road of
Moab.
    9Then the Lord said to me, "Do not
harass the Moabites or provoke them to
war, for I will not give you any part of
their land. I have given Ar to the descendants of Lot as a possession."
    10(The Emites used to live there—a
people strong and numerous, and as tall
as the Anakites. 11Like the Anakites,
they too were considered Rephaites, but
the Moabites called them Emites. 12Ho-
rites used to live in Seir, but the descendants of Esau drove them out. They
destroyed the Horites from before them
and settled in their place, just as Israel
did in the land the Lord gave them as
their possession.)
    13And the Lord said, "Now get up and
cross the Zered Valley." So we crossed
the valley.
    14Thirty-eight years passed from the
time we left Kadesh Barnea until we
crossed the Zered Valley. By then, that
entire generation of fighting men had
perished from the camp, as the Lord
had sworn to them. 15The Lord's hand
was against them until he had completely eliminated them from the camp.
    16Now when the last of these fighting
men among the people had died, 17the

Lord said to me, [18]"Today you are to pass by the region of Moab at Ar. [19]When you come to the Ammonites, do not harass them or provoke them to war, for I will not give you possession of any land belonging to the Ammonites. I have given it as a possession to the descendants of Lot."

[20](That too was considered a land of the Rephaites, who used to live there; but the Ammonites called them Zamzummites. [21]They were a people strong and numerous, and as tall as the Anakites. The Lord destroyed them from before the Ammonites, who drove them out and settled in their place. [22]The Lord had done the same for the descendants of Esau, who lived in Seir, when he destroyed the Horites from before them. They drove them out and have lived in their place to this day. [23]And as for the Avvites who lived in villages as far as Gaza, the Caphtorites coming out from Caphtor[b] destroyed them and settled in their place.)

[24]"Set out now and cross the Arnon Gorge. See, I have given into your hand Sihon the Amorite, king of Heshbon, and his country. Begin to take possession of it and engage him in battle. [25]This very day I will begin to put the terror and fear of you on all the nations under heaven. They will hear reports of you and will tremble and be in anguish because of you."

[26]From the desert of Kedemoth I sent messengers to Sihon king of Heshbon offering peace and saying, [27]"Let us pass through your country. We will stay on the main road; we will not turn aside to the right or to the left. [28]Sell us food to eat and water to drink for their price in silver. Only let us pass through on foot— [29]as the descendants of Esau, who live in Seir, and the Moabites, who live in Ar, did for us—until we cross the Jordan into the land the Lord our God is giving us." [30]But Sihon king of Heshbon refused to let us pass through. For the Lord your God had made his spirit stubborn and his heart obstinate in order to give him into your hands, as he has now done.

[31]The Lord said to me, "See, I have begun to deliver Sihon and his country over to you. Now begin to conquer and possess his land."

[32]When Sihon and all his army came out to meet us in battle at Jahaz, [33]the Lord our God delivered him over to us and we struck him down, together with his sons and his whole army. [34]At that time we took all his towns and completely destroyed[c] them—men, women and children. We left no survivors. [35]But the livestock and the plunder from the towns we had captured we carried off for ourselves. [36]From Aroer on the rim of the Arnon Gorge, and from the town in the gorge, even as far as Gilead, not one town was too strong for us. The Lord our God gave us all of them. [37]But in accordance with the command of the Lord our God, you did not encroach on any of the land of the Ammonites, neither the land along the course of the Jabbok nor that around the towns in the hills.

[3:1]NEXT we turned and went up along the road toward Bashan, and Og king of Bashan with his whole army marched out to meet us in battle at Edrei. [2]The Lord said to me, "Do not be afraid of him, for I have handed him over to you with his whole army and his land. Do to him what you did to Sihon king of the Amorites, who reigned in Heshbon."

[3]So the Lord our God also gave into our hands Og king of Bashan and all his army. We struck them down, leaving no survivors. [4]At that time we took all his cities. There was not one of the sixty cities that we did not take from them—the whole region of Argob, Og's kingdom in Bashan. [5]All these cities were fortified with high walls and with gates and bars, and there were also a great many unwalled villages. [6]We completely destroyed[c] them, as we had done with Sihon king of Heshbon, destroying[c] every city—men, women and children. [7]But all the livestock and the plunder from their cities we carried off for ourselves.

⁸So at that time we took from these two kings of the Amorites the territory east of the Jordan, from the Arnon Gorge as far as Mount Hermon. ⁹(Hermon is called Sirion by the Sidonians; the Amorites call it Senir.) ¹⁰We took all the towns on the plateau, and all Gilead, and all Bashan as far as Salecah and Edrei, towns of Og's kingdom in Bashan. ¹¹(Only Og king of Bashan was left of the remnant of the Rephaites. His bed*d* was made of iron and was more than thirteen feet long and six feet wide.*e* It is still in Rabbah of the Ammonites.)

¹²Of the land that we took over at that time, I gave the Reubenites and the Gadites the territory north of Aroer by the Arnon Gorge, including half the hill country of Gilead, together with its towns. ¹³The rest of Gilead and also all of Bashan, the kingdom of Og, I gave to the half-tribe of Manasseh. (The whole region of Argob in Bashan used to be known as a land of the Rephaites. ¹⁴Jair, a descendant of Manasseh, took the whole region of Argob as far as the border of the Geshurites and the Maacathites; it was named after him, so that to this day Bashan is called Havvoth Jair.*f*) ¹⁵And I gave Gilead to Makir. ¹⁶But to the Reubenites and the Gadites I gave the territory extending from Gilead down to the Arnon Gorge (the middle of the gorge being the border) and out to the Jabbok River, which is the border of the Ammonites. ¹⁷Its western border was the Jordan in the Arabah, from Kinnereth to the Sea of the Arabah (the Salt Sea*g*), below the slopes of Pisgah.

¹⁸I commanded you at that time: "The LORD your God has given you this land to take possession of it. But all your able-bodied men, armed for battle, must cross over ahead of your brother Israelites. ¹⁹However, your wives, your children and your livestock (I know you have much livestock) may stay in the towns I have given you, ²⁰until the LORD gives rest to your brothers as he has to you, and they too have taken over the land that the LORD your God is giving them, across the Jordan. After that, each

of you may go back to the possession I have given you."

²¹At that time I commanded Joshua: "You have seen with your own eyes all that the LORD your God has done to these two kings. The LORD will do the same to all the kingdoms over there where you are going. ²²Do not be afraid of them; the LORD your God himself will fight for you."

²³At that time I pleaded with the LORD: ²⁴"O Sovereign LORD, you have begun to show to your servant your greatness and your strong hand. For what god is there in heaven or on earth who can do the deeds and mighty works you do? ²⁵Let me go over and see the good land beyond the Jordan—that fine hill country and Lebanon."

²⁶But because of you the LORD was angry with me and would not listen to me. "That is enough," the LORD said. "Do not speak to me anymore about this matter. ²⁷Go up to the top of Pisgah and look west and north and south and east. Look at the land with your own eyes, since you are not going to cross this Jordan. ²⁸But commission Joshua, and encourage and strengthen him, for he will lead this people across and will cause them to inherit the land that you will see." ²⁹So we stayed in the valley near Beth Peor.

a 1 Hebrew *Yam Suph*; that is, Sea of Reeds   *b 23* That is, Crete   *c 34,6* The Hebrew term refers to the irrevocable giving over of things or persons to the LORD, often by totally destroying them.   *d 11* Or *sarcophagus*   *e 11* Hebrew *nine cubits long and four cubits wide* (about 4 meters long and 1.8 meters wide)   *f 14* Or *called the settlements of Jair*   *g 17* That is, the Dead Sea

LUKE 6:12-38

❶ne of those days Jesus went out to a mountainside to pray, and spent the night praying to God. ¹³When morning came, he called his disciples to him and chose twelve of them, whom he also designated apostles: ¹⁴Simon (whom he named Peter), his brother Andrew, James, John, Philip, Bartholomew, ¹⁵Matthew, Thomas, James son of Alphaeus, Simon who was called the Zealot, ¹⁶Judas son of James, and Judas Iscariot, who became a traitor.

¹⁷He went down with them and stood

on a level place. A large crowd of his disciples was there and a great number of people from all over Judea, from Jerusalem, and from the coast of Tyre and Sidon, [18] who had come to hear him and to be healed of their diseases. Those troubled by evil[a] spirits were cured, [19] and the people all tried to touch him, because power was coming from him and healing them all.

[20] Looking at his disciples, he said:

"Blessed are you who are poor,
  for yours is the kingdom of God.
[21] Blessed are you who hunger now,
  for you will be satisfied.
Blessed are you who weep now,
  for you will laugh.
[22] Blessed are you when men hate you,
  when they exclude you and
      insult you
  and reject your name as evil,
      because of the Son of Man.

[23] "Rejoice in that day and leap for joy, because great is your reward in heaven. For that is how their fathers treated the prophets.

[24] "But woe to you who are rich,
  for you have already received your
      comfort.
[25] Woe to you who are well fed now,
  for you will go hungry.
Woe to you who laugh now,
  for you will mourn and weep.
[26] Woe to you when all men speak well
      of you,
  for that is how their fathers
      treated the false prophets.

[27] **"But I tell you who hear me: Love your enemies, do good to those who hate you, [28] bless those who curse you, pray for those who mistreat you.** [29] If someone strikes you on one cheek, turn to him the other also. If someone takes your cloak, do not stop him from taking your tunic. [30] Give to everyone who asks you, and if anyone takes what belongs to you, do not demand it back. [31] Do to others as you would have them do to you.

[32] "If you love those who love you, what credit is that to you? Even 'sinners' love those who love them. [33] And if you do good to those who are good to you, what credit is that to you? Even 'sinners' do that. [34] And if you lend to those from whom you expect repayment, what credit is that to you? Even 'sinners' lend to 'sinners,' expecting to be repaid in full. [35] But love your enemies, do good to them, and lend to them without expecting to get anything back. Then your reward will be great, and you will be sons of the Most High, because he is kind to the ungrateful and wicked. [36] Be merciful, just as your Father is merciful.

[37] "Do not judge, and you will not be judged. Do not condemn, and you will not be condemned. Forgive, and you will be forgiven. [38] Give, and it will be given to you. A good measure, pressed down, shaken together and running over, will be poured into your lap. For with the measure you use, it will be measured to you."

a 18 Greek *unclean*

PSALM 67:1-7
For the director of music. With stringed instruments. A psalm. A song.

[1] **M**ay God be gracious to us and
      bless us
  and make his face shine upon us,
                                    Selah
[2] that your ways may be known on
      earth,
  your salvation among all nations.

[3] May the peoples praise you, O God;
  may all the peoples praise you.
[4] May the nations be glad and sing
      for joy,
  for you rule the peoples justly
  and guide the nations of the earth.
                                    Selah
[5] May the peoples praise you, O God;
  may all the peoples praise you.

[6] Then the land will yield its harvest,
  and God, our God, will bless us.
[7] God will bless us,
  and all the ends of the earth will
      fear him.

PROVERBS 11:27
²⁷ He who seeks good finds goodwill,
   but evil comes to him who
      searches for it.

☐ D A Y   8 4

GOD SIGHTINGS

March 25

DEUTERONOMY 4:1-49
Hear now, O Israel, the decrees and laws I am about to teach you. Follow them so that you may live and may go in and take possession of the land that the Lord, the God of your fathers, is giving you. ²Do not add to what I command you and do not subtract from it, but keep the commands of the Lord your God that I give you.

³ You saw with your own eyes what the Lord did at Baal Peor. The Lord your God destroyed from among you everyone who followed the Baal of Peor, ⁴ but all of you who held fast to the Lord your God are still alive today.

⁵ See, I have taught you decrees and laws as the Lord my God commanded me, so that you may follow them in the land you are entering to take possession of it. ⁶ Observe them carefully, for this will show your wisdom and understanding to the nations, who will hear about all these decrees and say, "Surely this great nation is a wise and understanding people." ⁷ What other nation is so great as to have their gods near them the way the Lord our God is near us whenever we pray to him? ⁸ And what other nation is so great as to have such righteous decrees and laws as this body of laws I am setting before you today?

⁹ Only be careful, and watch yourselves closely so that you do not forget the things your eyes have seen or let them slip from your heart as long as you live. Teach them to your children and to their children after them. ¹⁰ Remember the day you stood before the Lord your God at Horeb, when he said to me, "Assemble the people before me to hear my words so that they may learn to revere me as long as they live in the land and may teach them to their children." ¹¹ You came near and stood at the foot of the mountain while it blazed with fire to the very heavens, with black clouds and deep darkness. ¹² Then the Lord spoke to you out of the fire. You heard the sound of words but saw no form; there was only a voice. ¹³ He declared to you his covenant, the Ten Commandments, which he commanded you to follow and then wrote them on two stone tablets. ¹⁴ And the Lord directed me at that time to teach you the decrees and laws you are to follow in the land that you are crossing the Jordan to possess.

¹⁵ You saw no form of any kind the day the Lord spoke to you at Horeb out of the fire. Therefore watch yourselves very carefully, ¹⁶ so that you do not become corrupt and make for yourselves an idol, an image of any shape, whether formed like a man or a woman, ¹⁷ or like any animal on earth or any bird that flies in the air, ¹⁸ or like any creature that moves along the ground or any fish in the waters below. ¹⁹ And when you look up to the sky and see the sun, the moon and the stars—all the heavenly array—do not be enticed into bowing down to them and worshiping things the Lord your God has apportioned to all the nations under heaven. ²⁰ But as for you, the Lord took you and brought you out of the iron-smelting furnace, out of Egypt, to be the people of his inheritance, as you now are.

²¹ The Lord was angry with me because of you, and he solemnly swore that I would not cross the Jordan and enter the good land the Lord your God is giving you as your inheritance. ²² I will die in this land; I will not cross the Jordan; but you are about to cross over and take possession of that good land. ²³ Be careful not to forget the covenant of the Lord your God that he made with you;

do not make for yourselves an idol in the form of anything the Lord your God has forbidden. 24For the Lord your God is a consuming fire, a jealous God.

25After you have had children and grandchildren and have lived in the land a long time—if you then become corrupt and make any kind of idol, doing evil in the eyes of the Lord your God and provoking him to anger, 26I call heaven and earth as witnesses against you this day that you will quickly perish from the land that you are crossing the Jordan to possess. You will not live there long but will certainly be destroyed. 27The Lord will scatter you among the peoples, and only a few of you will survive among the nations to which the Lord will drive you. 28There you will worship man-made gods of wood and stone, which cannot see or hear or eat or smell. 29But if from there you seek the Lord your God, you will find him if you look for him with all your heart and with all your soul. 30When you are in distress and all these things have happened to you, then in later days you will return to the Lord your God and obey him. 31For the Lord your God is a merciful God; he will not abandon or destroy you or forget the covenant with your forefathers, which he confirmed to them by oath.

32Ask now about the former days, long before your time, from the day God created man on the earth; ask from one end of the heavens to the other. Has anything so great as this ever happened, or has anything like it ever been heard of? 33Has any other people heard the voice of God*a* speaking out of fire, as you have, and lived? 34Has any god ever tried to take for himself one nation out of another nation, by testings, by miraculous signs and wonders, by war, by a mighty hand and an outstretched arm, or by great and awesome deeds, like all the things the Lord your God did for you in Egypt before your very eyes?

35You were shown these things so that you might know that the Lord is God; besides him there is no other.

36From heaven he made you hear his voice to discipline you. On earth he showed you his great fire, and you heard his words from out of the fire. 37Because he loved your forefathers and chose their descendants after them, he brought you out of Egypt by his Presence and his great strength, 38to drive out before you nations greater and stronger than you and to bring you into their land to give it to you for your inheritance, as it is today.

39Acknowledge and take to heart this day that the Lord is God in heaven above and on the earth below. There is no other. 40Keep his decrees and commands, which I am giving you today, so that it may go well with you and your children after you and that you may live long in the land the Lord your God gives you for all time.

41Then Moses set aside three cities east of the Jordan, 42to which anyone who had killed a person could flee if he had unintentionally killed his neighbor without malice aforethought. He could flee into one of these cities and save his life. 43The cities were these: Bezer in the desert plateau, for the Reubenites; Ramoth in Gilead, for the Gadites; and Golan in Bashan, for the Manassites.

44This is the law Moses set before the Israelites. 45These are the stipulations, decrees and laws Moses gave them when they came out of Egypt 46and were in the valley near Beth Peor east of the Jordan, in the land of Sihon king of the Amorites, who reigned in Heshbon and was defeated by Moses and the Israelites as they came out of Egypt. 47They took possession of his land and the land of Og king of Bashan, the two Amorite kings east of the Jordan. 48This land extended from Aroer on the rim of the Arnon Gorge to Mount Siyon*b* (that is, Hermon), 49and included all the Arabah east of the Jordan, as far as the Sea of the Arabah,*c* below the slopes of Pisgah.

a33 Or *of a god*   *b48* Hebrew; Syriac (see also Deut. 3:9)
Sirion   *c49* That is, the Dead Sea

LUKE 6:39–7:10

He [Jesus] also told them this parable: "Can a blind man lead a blind man? Will they not both fall into a pit? ⁴⁰A student is not above his teacher, but everyone who is fully trained will be like his teacher.

⁴¹"Why do you look at the speck of sawdust in your brother's eye and pay no attention to the plank in your own eye? ⁴²How can you say to your brother, 'Brother, let me take the speck out of your eye,' when you yourself fail to see the plank in your own eye? You hypocrite, first take the plank out of your eye, and then you will see clearly to remove the speck from your brother's eye.

⁴³"No good tree bears bad fruit, nor does a bad tree bear good fruit. ⁴⁴Each tree is recognized by its own fruit. People do not pick figs from thornbushes, or grapes from briers. ⁴⁵**The good man brings good things out of the good stored up in his heart, and the evil man brings evil things out of the evil stored up in his heart. For out of the overflow of his heart his mouth speaks.**

⁴⁶"Why do you call me, 'Lord, Lord,' and do not do what I say? ⁴⁷I will show you what he is like who comes to me and hears my words and puts them into practice. ⁴⁸He is like a man building a house, who dug down deep and laid the foundation on rock. When a flood came, the torrent struck that house but could not shake it, because it was well built. ⁴⁹But the one who hears my words and does not put them into practice is like a man who built a house on the ground without a foundation. The moment the torrent struck that house, it collapsed and its destruction was complete."

⁷:¹WHEN Jesus had finished saying all this in the hearing of the people, he entered Capernaum. ²There a centurion's servant, whom his master valued highly, was sick and about to die. ³The centurion heard of Jesus and sent some elders of the Jews to him, asking him to come and heal his servant. ⁴When they came

to Jesus, they pleaded earnestly with him, "This man deserves to have you do this, ⁵because he loves our nation and has built our synagogue." ⁶So Jesus went with them.

He was not far from the house when the centurion sent friends to say to him: "Lord, don't trouble yourself, for I do not deserve to have you come under my roof. ⁷That is why I did not even consider myself worthy to come to you. But say the word, and my servant will be healed. ⁸For I myself am a man under authority, with soldiers under me. I tell this one, 'Go,' and he goes; and that one, 'Come,' and he comes. I say to my servant, 'Do this,' and he does it."

⁹When Jesus heard this, he was amazed at him, and turning to the crowd following him, he said, "I tell you, I have not found such great faith even in Israel." ¹⁰Then the men who had been sent returned to the house and found the servant well.

PSALM 68:1-18

For the director of music. Of David.
A psalm. A song.

¹ **M**ay God arise, may his enemies be
        scattered;
    may his foes flee before him.
² As smoke is blown away by the wind,
    may you blow them away;
  as wax melts before the fire,
    may the wicked perish before God.
³ But may the righteous be glad
    and rejoice before God;
    may they be happy and joyful.

⁴ Sing to God, sing praise to his name,
    extol him who rides on the
        clouds*a*—
  his name is the LORD—
    and rejoice before him.
⁵ A father to the fatherless, a defender
        of widows,
    is God in his holy dwelling.
⁶ God sets the lonely in families,*b*
    he leads forth the prisoners with
        singing;
    but the rebellious live in a sun-
        scorched land.

7 When you went out before your
   people, O God,
   when you marched through the
      wasteland,   *Selah*
8 the earth shook,
   the heavens poured down rain,
   before God, the One of Sinai,
   before God, the God of Israel.
9 You gave abundant showers, O God;
   you refreshed your weary
      inheritance.
10 Your people settled in it,
   and from your bounty, O God, you
      provided for the poor.

11 The Lord announced the word,
   and great was the company of
      those who proclaimed it:
12 "Kings and armies flee in haste;
   in the camps men divide the
      plunder.
13 Even while you sleep among the
      campfires,*c*
   the wings of ⌐my⌐ dove are
      sheathed with silver,
   its feathers with shining gold."
14 When the Almighty*d* scattered the
      kings in the land,
   it was like snow fallen on Zalmon.

15 The mountains of Bashan are
      majestic mountains;
   rugged are the mountains of Bashan.
16 Why gaze in envy, O rugged
      mountains,
   at the mountain where God
      chooses to reign,
   where the Lord himself will dwell
      forever?
17 The chariots of God are tens of
      thousands
   and thousands of thousands;
   the Lord ⌐has come⌐ from Sinai
      into his sanctuary.
18 When you ascended on high,
   you led captives in your train;
   you received gifts from men,
   even from*e* the rebellious—
   that you,*f* O Lord God, might dwell
      there.

a4 Or / prepare the way for him who rides through the deserts
b6 Or the desolate in a homeland   c13 Or saddlebags
d14 Hebrew Shaddai   e18 Or gifts for men, / even
f18 Or they

PROVERBS 11:28
28 **W**hoever trusts in his riches will fall,
   but the righteous will thrive like a
      green leaf.

☐ D A Y   8 5

GOD SIGHTINGS

March 26

DEUTERONOMY 5:1–6:25
Moses summoned all Israel and said:
   Hear, O Israel, the decrees and laws I
declare in your hearing today. Learn
them and be sure to follow them. 2 The
Lord our God made a covenant with us at
Horeb. 3 It was not with our fathers that
the Lord made this covenant, but with
us, with all of us who are alive here today.
4 The Lord spoke to you face to face out
of the fire on the mountain. 5 (At that
time I stood between the Lord and you to
declare to you the word of the Lord, because you were afraid of the fire and did
not go up the mountain.) And he said:

6 "I am the Lord your God,
   who brought you out of
   Egypt, out of the land of
   slavery.
7 "You shall have no other gods
   before*a* me.
8 "You shall not make for yourself
   an idol in the form of anything in heaven above or on
   the earth beneath or in the
   waters below. 9 You shall
   not bow down to them or
   worship them; for I, the
   Lord your God, am a jealous God, punishing the
   children for the sin of the
   fathers to the third and
   fourth generation of those
   who hate me, 10 but showing love to a thousand
   ⌐generations⌐ of those who
   love me and keep my commandments.

11 "You shall not misuse the name of the LORD your God, for the LORD will not hold anyone guiltless who misuses his name.

12 "Observe the Sabbath day by keeping it holy, as the LORD your God has commanded you. 13 Six days you shall labor and do all your work, 14 but the seventh day is a Sabbath to the LORD your God. On it you shall not do any work, neither you, nor your son or daughter, nor your manservant or maidservant, nor your ox, your donkey or any of your animals, nor the alien within your gates, so that your manservant and maidservant may rest, as you do. 15 Remember that you were slaves in Egypt and that the LORD your God brought you out of there with a mighty hand and an outstretched arm. Therefore the LORD your God has commanded you to observe the Sabbath day.

16 "Honor your father and your mother, as the LORD your God has commanded you, so that you may live long and that it may go well with you in the land the LORD your God is giving you.

17 "You shall not murder.

18 "You shall not commit adultery.

19 "You shall not steal.

20 "You shall not give false testimony against your neighbor.

21 "You shall not covet your neighbor's wife. You shall not set your desire on your neighbor's house or land, his manservant or maidservant, his ox or donkey, or anything that belongs to your neighbor."

22 These are the commandments the LORD proclaimed in a loud voice to your whole assembly there on the mountain from out of the fire, the cloud and the deep darkness; and he added nothing more. Then he wrote them on two stone tablets and gave them to me.

23 When you heard the voice out of the darkness, while the mountain was ablaze with fire, all the leading men of your tribes and your elders came to me. 24 And you said, "The LORD our God has shown us his glory and his majesty, and we have heard his voice from the fire. Today we have seen that a man can live even if God speaks with him. 25 But now, why should we die? This great fire will consume us, and we will die if we hear the voice of the LORD our God any longer. 26 For what mortal man has ever heard the voice of the living God speaking out of fire, as we have, and survived? 27 Go near and listen to all that the LORD our God says. Then tell us whatever the LORD our God tells you. We will listen and obey."

28 The LORD heard you when you spoke to me and the LORD said to me, "I have heard what this people said to you. Everything they said was good. 29 Oh, that their hearts would be inclined to fear me and keep all my commands always, so that it might go well with them and their children forever!

30 "Go, tell them to return to their tents. 31 But you stay here with me so that I may give you all the commands, decrees and laws you are to teach them to follow in the land I am giving them to possess."

32 So be careful to do what the LORD your God has commanded you; do not turn aside to the right or to the left. 33 Walk in all the way that the LORD your God has commanded you, so that you may live and prosper and prolong your days in the land that you will possess.

6:1 THESE are the commands, decrees and laws the LORD your God directed me to teach you to observe in the land that you are crossing the Jordan to possess,

[2]so that you, your children and their children after them may fear the LORD your God as long as you live by keeping all his decrees and commands that I give you, and so that you may enjoy long life. [3]Hear, O Israel, and be careful to obey so that it may go well with you and that you may increase greatly in a land flowing with milk and honey, just as the LORD, the God of your fathers, promised you.

[4]Hear, O Israel: The LORD our God, the LORD is one.[b] [5]Love the LORD your God with all your heart and with all your soul and with all your strength. [6]**These commandments that I give you today are to be upon your hearts.** [7]**Impress them on your children. Talk about them when you sit at home and when you walk along the road, when you lie down and when you get up.** [8]**Tie them as symbols on your hands and bind them on your foreheads.** [9]**Write them on the doorframes of your houses and on your gates.**

[10]When the LORD your God brings you into the land he swore to your fathers, to Abraham, Isaac and Jacob, to give you—a land with large, flourishing cities you did not build, [11]houses filled with all kinds of good things you did not provide, wells you did not dig, and vineyards and olive groves you did not plant—then when you eat and are satisfied, [12]be careful that you do not forget the LORD, who brought you out of Egypt, out of the land of slavery.

[13]Fear the LORD your God, serve him only and take your oaths in his name. [14]Do not follow other gods, the gods of the peoples around you; [15]for the LORD your God, who is among you, is a jealous God and his anger will burn against you, and he will destroy you from the face of the land. [16]Do not test the LORD your God as you did at Massah. [17]Be sure to keep the commands of the LORD your God and the stipulations and decrees he has given you. [18]Do what is right and good in the LORD's sight, so that it may go well with you and you may go in and take over the good land that the LORD

promised on oath to your forefathers, [19]thrusting out all your enemies before you, as the LORD said.

[20]In the future, when your son asks you, "What is the meaning of the stipulations, decrees and laws the LORD our God has commanded you?" [21]tell him: "We were slaves of Pharaoh in Egypt, but the LORD brought us out of Egypt with a mighty hand. [22]Before our eyes the LORD sent miraculous signs and wonders—great and terrible—upon Egypt and Pharaoh and his whole household. [23]But he brought us out from there to bring us in and give us the land that he promised on oath to our forefathers. [24]The LORD commanded us to obey all these decrees and to fear the LORD our God, so that we might always prosper and be kept alive, as is the case today. [25]And if we are careful to obey all this law before the LORD our God, as he has commanded us, that will be our righteousness."

a7 Or besides   b4 Or The LORD our God is one LORD; or The LORD is our God, the LORD is one; or The LORD is our God, the LORD alone

LUKE 7:11-35

Soon afterward, Jesus went to a town called Nain, and his disciples and a large crowd went along with him. [12]As he approached the town gate, a dead person was being carried out—the only son of his mother, and she was a widow. And a large crowd from the town was with her. [13]When the Lord saw her, his heart went out to her and he said, "Don't cry."

[14]Then he went up and touched the coffin, and those carrying it stood still. He said, "Young man, I say to you, get up!" [15]The dead man sat up and began to talk, and Jesus gave him back to his mother.

[16]They were all filled with awe and praised God. "A great prophet has appeared among us," they said. "God has come to help his people." [17]This news about Jesus spread throughout Judea[a] and the surrounding country.

[18]John's disciples told him about all these things. Calling two of them, [19]he

sent them to the Lord to ask, "Are you the one who was to come, or should we expect someone else?"

20When the men came to Jesus, they said, "John the Baptist sent us to you to ask, 'Are you the one who was to come, or should we expect someone else?'"

21At that very time Jesus cured many who had diseases, sicknesses and evil spirits, and gave sight to many who were blind. 22So he replied to the messengers, "Go back and report to John what you have seen and heard: The blind receive sight, the lame walk, those who have leprosy[b] are cured, the deaf hear, the dead are raised, and the good news is preached to the poor. 23Blessed is the man who does not fall away on account of me."

24After John's messengers left, Jesus began to speak to the crowd about John: "What did you go out into the desert to see? A reed swayed by the wind? 25If not, what did you go out to see? A man dressed in fine clothes? No, those who wear expensive clothes and indulge in luxury are in palaces. 26But what did you go out to see? A prophet? Yes, I tell you, and more than a prophet. 27This is the one about whom it is written:

"'I will send my messenger ahead of
    you,
  who will prepare your way before
    you.'[c]

28I tell you, among those born of women there is no one greater than John; yet the one who is least in the kingdom of God is greater than he."

29(All the people, even the tax collectors, when they heard Jesus' words, acknowledged that God's way was right, because they had been baptized by John. 30But the Pharisees and experts in the law rejected God's purpose for themselves, because they had not been baptized by John.)

31"To what, then, can I compare the people of this generation? What are they like? 32They are like children sitting in the marketplace and calling out to each other:

"'We played the flute for you,
    and you did not dance;
  we sang a dirge,
    and you did not cry.'

33For John the Baptist came neither eating bread nor drinking wine, and you say, 'He has a demon.' 34The Son of Man came eating and drinking, and you say, 'Here is a glutton and a drunkard, a friend of tax collectors and "sinners."' 35But wisdom is proved right by all her children."

a17 Or the land of the Jews b22 The Greek word was used for various diseases affecting the skin—not necessarily leprosy. c27 Mal. 3:1

PSALM 68:19-35

19Praise be to the Lord, to God our
    Savior,
  who daily bears our burdens.
                                            Selah
20Our God is a God who saves;
    from the Sovereign LORD comes
      escape from death.

21Surely God will crush the heads of
    his enemies,
  the hairy crowns of those who go
    on in their sins.
22The Lord says, "I will bring them
    from Bashan;
  I will bring them from the depths
    of the sea,
23that you may plunge your feet in the
    blood of your foes,
  while the tongues of your dogs
    have their share."

24Your procession has come into view,
    O God,
  the procession of my God and
    King into the sanctuary.
25In front are the singers, after them
    the musicians;
  with them are the maidens playing
    tambourines.
26Praise God in the great
    congregation;
  praise the LORD in the assembly
    of Israel.

27 There is the little tribe of Benjamin,
leading them,
there the great throng of Judah's
princes,
and there the princes of Zebulun
and of Naphtali.

28 Summon your power, O God[a];
show us your strength, O God, as
you have done before.
29 Because of your temple at Jerusalem
kings will bring you gifts.
30 Rebuke the beast among the reeds,
the herd of bulls among the calves
of the nations.
Humbled, may it bring bars of silver.
Scatter the nations who delight
in war.
31 Envoys will come from Egypt;
Cush[b] will submit herself to God.

32 Sing to God, O kingdoms of the
earth,
sing praise to the Lord,   *Selah*
33 to him who rides the ancient skies
above,
who thunders with mighty voice.
34 Proclaim the power of God,
whose majesty is over Israel,
whose power is in the skies.
35 You are awesome, O God, in your
sanctuary;
the God of Israel gives power and
strength to his people.

Praise be to God!

a28 Many Hebrew manuscripts, Septuagint and Syriac; most
Hebrew manuscripts *Your God has summoned power for
you*   *b31* That is, the upper Nile region

PROVERBS 11:29-31

29 He who brings trouble on his family
will inherit only wind,
and the fool will be servant to
the wise.

30 The fruit of the righteous is a tree
of life,
and he who wins souls is wise.

31 If the righteous receive their due
on earth,
how much more the ungodly and
the sinner!

□ DAY 86

GOD SIGHTINGS

March 27

DEUTERONOMY 7:1–8:20

When the Lord your [the Israelites']
God brings you into the land you are entering to possess and drives out before
you many nations—the Hittites, Girgashites, Amorites, Canaanites, Perizzites,
Hivites and Jebusites, seven nations
larger and stronger than you— 2 and
when the Lord your God has delivered
them over to you and you have defeated
them, then you must destroy them totally.[a] Make no treaty with them, and
show them no mercy. 3 Do not intermarry with them. Do not give your
daughters to their sons or take their
daughters for your sons, 4 for they will
turn your sons away from following me
to serve other gods, and the Lord's anger will burn against you and will
quickly destroy you. 5 This is what you
are to do to them: Break down their altars, smash their sacred stones, cut
down their Asherah poles[b] and burn
their idols in the fire. 6 For you are a people holy to the Lord your God. The Lord
your God has chosen you out of all the
peoples on the face of the earth to be his
people, his treasured possession.

7 The Lord did not set his affection on
you and choose you because you were
more numerous than other peoples, for
you were the fewest of all peoples. 8 But it
was because the Lord loved you and kept
the oath he swore to your forefathers
that he brought you out with a mighty
hand and redeemed you from the land of
slavery, from the power of Pharaoh king
of Egypt. 9 Know therefore that the Lord
your God is God; he is the faithful God,
keeping his covenant of love to a thousand generations of those who love him
and keep his commands. 10 But

those who hate him he will repay to
their face by destruction;

he will not be slow to repay to their face those who hate him.

[11] Therefore, take care to follow the commands, decrees and laws I give you today.

[12] If you pay attention to these laws and are careful to follow them, then the LORD your God will keep his covenant of love with you, as he swore to your forefathers. [13] He will love you and bless you and increase your numbers. He will bless the fruit of your womb, the crops of your land—your grain, new wine and oil—the calves of your herds and the lambs of your flocks in the land that he swore to your forefathers to give you. [14] You will be blessed more than any other people; none of your men or women will be childless, nor any of your livestock without young. [15] The LORD will keep you free from every disease. He will not inflict on you the horrible diseases you knew in Egypt, but he will inflict them on all who hate you. [16] You must destroy all the peoples the LORD your God gives over to you. Do not look on them with pity and do not serve their gods, for that will be a snare to you.

[17] You may say to yourselves, "These nations are stronger than we are. How can we drive them out?" [18] But do not be afraid of them; remember well what the LORD your God did to Pharaoh and to all Egypt. [19] You saw with your own eyes the great trials, the miraculous signs and wonders, the mighty hand and outstretched arm, with which the LORD your God brought you out. The LORD your God will do the same to all the peoples you now fear. [20] Moreover, the LORD your God will send the hornet among them until even the survivors who hide from you have perished. [21] Do not be terrified by them, for the LORD your God, who is among you, is a great and awesome God. [22] The LORD your God will drive out those nations before you, little by little. You will not be allowed to eliminate them all at once, or the wild animals will multiply around you. [23] But the LORD your God will deliver them over to you, throwing them into great confusion until they are destroyed. [24] He will give their kings into your hand, and you will wipe out their names from under heaven. No one will be able to stand up against you; you will destroy them. [25] The images of their gods you are to burn in the fire. Do not covet the silver and gold on them, and do not take it for yourselves, or you will be ensnared by it, for it is detestable to the LORD your God. [26] Do not bring a detestable thing into your house or you, like it, will be set apart for destruction. Utterly abhor and detest it, for it is set apart for destruction.

[8:1] BE careful to follow every command I am giving you today, so that you may live and increase and may enter and possess the land that the LORD promised on oath to your forefathers. [2] Remember how the LORD your God led you all the way in the desert these forty years, to humble you and to test you in order to know what was in your heart, whether or not you would keep his commands. [3] He humbled you, causing you to hunger and then feeding you with manna, which neither you nor your fathers had known, to teach you that man does not live on bread alone but on every word that comes from the mouth of the LORD. [4] Your clothes did not wear out and your feet did not swell during these forty years. [5] Know then in your heart that as a man disciplines his son, so the LORD your God disciplines you.

[6] Observe the commands of the LORD your God, walking in his ways and revering him. [7] For the LORD your God is bringing you into a good land—a land with streams and pools of water, with springs flowing in the valleys and hills; [8] a land with wheat and barley, vines and fig trees, pomegranates, olive oil and honey; [9] a land where bread will not be scarce and you will lack nothing; a land where the rocks are iron and you can dig copper out of the hills.

[10] **When you have eaten and are satisfied, praise the LORD your God for the good land he has given you.**

¹¹**Be careful that you do not forget the LORD your God, failing to observe his commands, his laws and his decrees that I am giving you this day.** ¹²Otherwise, when you eat and are satisfied, when you build fine houses and settle down, ¹³and when your herds and flocks grow large and your silver and gold increase and all you have is multiplied, ¹⁴then your heart will become proud and you will forget the LORD your God, who brought you out of Egypt, out of the land of slavery. ¹⁵He led you through the vast and dreadful desert, that thirsty and waterless land, with its venomous snakes and scorpions. He brought you water out of hard rock. ¹⁶He gave you manna to eat in the desert, something your fathers had never known, to humble and to test you so that in the end it might go well with you. ¹⁷You may say to yourself, "My power and the strength of my hands have produced this wealth for me." ¹⁸But remember the LORD your God, for it is he who gives you the ability to produce wealth, and so confirms his covenant, which he swore to your forefathers, as it is today.

¹⁹If you ever forget the LORD your God and follow other gods and worship and bow down to them, I testify against you today that you will surely be destroyed. ²⁰Like the nations the LORD destroyed before you, so you will be destroyed for not obeying the LORD your God.

a2 The Hebrew term refers to the irrevocable giving over of things or persons to the LORD, often by totally destroying them; also in verse 26.   *b5* That is, symbols of the goddess Asherah; here and elsewhere in Deuteronomy

LUKE 7:36–8:3

Now one of the Pharisees invited Jesus to have dinner with him, so he went to the Pharisee's house and reclined at the table. ³⁷When a woman who had lived a sinful life in that town learned that Jesus was eating at the Pharisee's house, she brought an alabaster jar of perfume, ³⁸and as she stood behind him at his feet weeping, she began to wet his feet with her tears. Then she wiped them with her hair, kissed them and poured perfume on them.

³⁹When the Pharisee who had invited him saw this, he said to himself, "If this man were a prophet, he would know who is touching him and what kind of woman she is—that she is a sinner."

⁴⁰Jesus answered him, "Simon, I have something to tell you."

"Tell me, teacher," he said.

⁴¹"Two men owed money to a certain moneylender. One owed him five hundred denarii,*a* and the other fifty. ⁴²Neither of them had the money to pay him back, so he canceled the debts of both. Now which of them will love him more?"

⁴³Simon replied, "I suppose the one who had the bigger debt canceled."

"You have judged correctly," Jesus said.

⁴⁴Then he turned toward the woman and said to Simon, "Do you see this woman? I came into your house. You did not give me any water for my feet, but she wet my feet with her tears and wiped them with her hair. ⁴⁵You did not give me a kiss, but this woman, from the time I entered, has not stopped kissing my feet. ⁴⁶You did not put oil on my head, but she has poured perfume on my feet. ⁴⁷Therefore, I tell you, her many sins have been forgiven—for she loved much. But he who has been forgiven little loves little."

⁴⁸Then Jesus said to her, "Your sins are forgiven."

⁴⁹The other guests began to say among themselves, "Who is this who even forgives sins?"

⁵⁰Jesus said to the woman, "Your faith has saved you; go in peace."

⁸:¹AFTER this, Jesus traveled about from one town and village to another, proclaiming the good news of the kingdom of God. The Twelve were with him, ²and also some women who had been cured of evil spirits and diseases: Mary (called Magdalene) from whom seven demons had come out; ³Joanna the wife of Cuza, the manager of Herod's household; Su-

sanna; and many others. These women were helping to support them out of their own means.

a41 A denarius was a coin worth about a day's wages.

PSALM 69:1-18

For the director of music. To ⌐the tune of⌐ "Lilies." Of David.

¹ **S**ave me, O God,
    for the waters have come up to
        my neck.
² I sink in the miry depths,
    where there is no foothold.
I have come into the deep waters;
    the floods engulf me.
³ I am worn out calling for help;
    my throat is parched.
My eyes fail,
    looking for my God.
⁴ Those who hate me without reason
    outnumber the hairs of my head;
many are my enemies without
        cause,
    those who seek to destroy me.
I am forced to restore
    what I did not steal.

⁵ You know my folly, O God;
    my guilt is not hidden from you.

⁶ May those who hope in you
    not be disgraced because of me,
    O Lord, the LORD Almighty;
may those who seek you
    not be put to shame because
        of me,
    O God of Israel.
⁷ For I endure scorn for your sake,
    and shame covers my face.
⁸ I am a stranger to my brothers,
    an alien to my own mother's sons;
⁹ for zeal for your house
        consumes me,
    and the insults of those who insult
        you fall on me.
¹⁰ When I weep and fast,
    I must endure scorn;
¹¹ when I put on sackcloth,
    people make sport of me.
¹² Those who sit at the gate mock me,
    and I am the song of the
        drunkards.

¹³ But I pray to you, O LORD,
    in the time of your favor;
in your great love, O God,
    answer me with your sure
        salvation.
¹⁴ Rescue me from the mire,
    do not let me sink;
deliver me from those who hate me,
    from the deep waters.
¹⁵ Do not let the floodwaters engulf me
    or the depths swallow me up
    or the pit close its mouth over me.
¹⁶ Answer me, O LORD, out of the
        goodness of your love;
    in your great mercy turn to me.
¹⁷ Do not hide your face from your
        servant;
    answer me quickly, for I am in
        trouble.
¹⁸ Come near and rescue me;
    redeem me because of my foes.

PROVERBS 12:1

Whoever loves discipline loves
        knowledge,
    but he who hates correction is
        stupid.

☐ D A Y 8 7

GOD SIGHTINGS

March 28

DEUTERONOMY 9:1-10:22

Hear, O Israel. You are now about to cross the Jordan to go in and dispossess nations greater and stronger than you, with large cities that have walls up to the sky. ² The people are strong and tall—Anakites! You know about them and have heard it said: "Who can stand up against the Anakites?" ³ But be assured today that the LORD your God is the one who goes across ahead of you like a devouring fire. He will destroy them; he will subdue them before you. And you will drive them out and annihilate them quickly, as the LORD has promised you.

⁴After the LORD your God has driven them out before you, do not say to yourself, "The LORD has brought me here to take possession of this land because of my righteousness." No, it is on account of the wickedness of these nations that the LORD is going to drive them out before you. ⁵It is not because of your righteousness or your integrity that you are going in to take possession of their land; but on account of the wickedness of these nations, the LORD your God will drive them out before you, to accomplish what he swore to your fathers, to Abraham, Isaac and Jacob. ⁶Understand, then, that it is not because of your righteousness that the LORD your God is giving you this good land to possess, for you are a stiff-necked people.

⁷Remember this and never forget how you provoked the LORD your God to anger in the desert. From the day you left Egypt until you arrived here, you have been rebellious against the LORD. ⁸At Horeb you aroused the LORD's wrath so that he was angry enough to destroy you. ⁹When I went up on the mountain to receive the tablets of stone, the tablets of the covenant that the LORD had made with you, I stayed on the mountain forty days and forty nights; I ate no bread and drank no water. ¹⁰The LORD gave me two stone tablets inscribed by the finger of God. On them were all the commandments the LORD proclaimed to you on the mountain out of the fire, on the day of the assembly.

¹¹At the end of the forty days and forty nights, the LORD gave me the two stone tablets, the tablets of the covenant. ¹²Then the LORD told me, "Go down from here at once, because your people whom you brought out of Egypt have become corrupt. They have turned away quickly from what I commanded them and have made a cast idol for themselves."

¹³And the LORD said to me, "I have seen this people, and they are a stiff-necked people indeed! ¹⁴Let me alone,

so that I may destroy them and blot out their name from under heaven. And I will make you into a nation stronger and more numerous than they."

¹⁵So I turned and went down from the mountain while it was ablaze with fire. And the two tablets of the covenant were in my hands.ᵃ ¹⁶When I looked, I saw that you had sinned against the LORD your God; you had made for yourselves an idol cast in the shape of a calf. You had turned aside quickly from the way that the LORD had commanded you. ¹⁷So I took the two tablets and threw them out of my hands, breaking them to pieces before your eyes.

¹⁸Then once again I fell prostrate before the LORD for forty days and forty nights; I ate no bread and drank no water, because of all the sin you had committed, doing what was evil in the LORD's sight and so provoking him to anger. ¹⁹I feared the anger and wrath of the LORD, for he was angry enough with you to destroy you. But again the LORD listened to me. ²⁰And the LORD was angry enough with Aaron to destroy him, but at that time I prayed for Aaron too. ²¹Also I took that sinful thing of yours, the calf you had made, and burned it in the fire. Then I crushed it and ground it to powder as fine as dust and threw the dust into a stream that flowed down the mountain.

²²You also made the LORD angry at Taberah, at Massah and at Kibroth Hattaavah.

²³And when the LORD sent you out from Kadesh Barnea, he said, "Go up and take possession of the land I have given you." But you rebelled against the command of the LORD your God. You did not trust him or obey him. ²⁴You have been rebellious against the LORD ever since I have known you.

²⁵I lay prostrate before the LORD those forty days and forty nights because the LORD had said he would destroy you. ²⁶I prayed to the LORD and said, "O Sovereign LORD, do not destroy your people, your own inheritance that you redeemed by your great power and

brought out of Egypt with a mighty hand. 27Remember your servants Abraham, Isaac and Jacob. Overlook the stubbornness of this people, their wickedness and their sin. 28Otherwise, the country from which you brought us will say, 'Because the LORD was not able to take them into the land he had promised them, and because he hated them, he brought them out to put them to death in the desert.' 29But they are your people, your inheritance that you brought out by your great power and your outstretched arm."

10:1At that time the LORD said to me, "Chisel out two stone tablets like the first ones and come up to me on the mountain. Also make a wooden chest.b 2I will write on the tablets the words that were on the first tablets, which you broke. Then you are to put them in the chest."

3So I made the ark out of acacia wood and chiseled out two stone tablets like the first ones, and I went up on the mountain with the two tablets in my hands. 4The LORD wrote on these tablets what he had written before, the Ten Commandments he had proclaimed to you on the mountain, out of the fire, on the day of the assembly. And the LORD gave them to me. 5Then I came back down the mountain and put the tablets in the ark I had made, as the LORD commanded me, and they are there now.

6(The Israelites traveled from the wells of the Jaakanites to Moserah. There Aaron died and was buried, and Eleazar his son succeeded him as priest. 7From there they traveled to Gudgodah and on to Jotbathah, a land with streams of water. 8At that time the LORD set apart the tribe of Levi to carry the ark of the covenant of the LORD, to stand before the LORD to minister and to pronounce blessings in his name, as they still do today. 9That is why the Levites have no share or inheritance among their brothers; the LORD is their inheritance, as the LORD your God told them.)

10Now I had stayed on the mountain forty days and nights, as I did the first time, and the LORD listened to me at this time also. It was not his will to destroy you. 11"Go," the LORD said to me, "and lead the people on their way, so that they may enter and possess the land that I swore to their fathers to give them."

12**And now, O Israel, what does the LORD your God ask of you but to fear the LORD your God, to walk in all his ways, to love him, to serve the LORD your God with all your heart and with all your soul, 13and to observe the LORD's commands and decrees that I am giving you today for your own good?**

14To the LORD your God belong the heavens, even the highest heavens, the earth and everything in it. 15Yet the LORD set his affection on your forefathers and loved them, and he chose you, their descendants, above all the nations, as it is today. 16Circumcise your hearts, therefore, and do not be stiff-necked any longer. 17For the LORD your God is God of gods and Lord of lords, the great God, mighty and awesome, who shows no partiality and accepts no bribes. 18He defends the cause of the fatherless and the widow, and loves the alien, giving him food and clothing. 19And you are to love those who are aliens, for you yourselves were aliens in Egypt. 20Fear the LORD your God and serve him. Hold fast to him and take your oaths in his name. 21He is your praise; he is your God, who performed for you those great and awesome wonders you saw with your own eyes. 22Your forefathers who went down into Egypt were seventy in all, and now the LORD your God has made you as numerous as the stars in the sky.

a15 Or And I had the two tablets of the covenant with me, one in each hand   b1 That is, an ark

LUKE 8:4-21
While a large crowd was gathering and people were coming to Jesus from town after town, he told this parable: 5"A farmer went out to sow his seed. As he

was scattering the seed, some fell along the path; it was trampled on, and the birds of the air ate it up. ⁶Some fell on rock, and when it came up, the plants withered because they had no moisture. ⁷Other seed fell among thorns, which grew up with it and choked the plants. ⁸Still other seed fell on good soil. It came up and yielded a crop, a hundred times more than was sown."

When he said this, he called out, "He who has ears to hear, let him hear."

⁹His disciples asked him what this parable meant. ¹⁰He said, "The knowledge of the secrets of the kingdom of God has been given to you, but to others I speak in parables, so that,

"'though seeing, they may not see;
   though hearing, they may not
      understand.'ᵃ

¹¹"This is the meaning of the parable: The seed is the word of God. ¹²Those along the path are the ones who hear, and then the devil comes and takes away the word from their hearts, so that they may not believe and be saved. ¹³Those on the rock are the ones who receive the word with joy when they hear it, but they have no root. They believe for a while, but in the time of testing they fall away. ¹⁴The seed that fell among thorns stands for those who hear, but as they go on their way they are choked by life's worries, riches and pleasures, and they do not mature. ¹⁵But the seed on good soil stands for those with a noble and good heart, who hear the word, retain it, and by persevering produce a crop.

¹⁶"No one lights a lamp and hides it in a jar or puts it under a bed. Instead, he puts it on a stand, so that those who come in can see the light. ¹⁷For there is nothing hidden that will not be disclosed, and nothing concealed that will not be known or brought out into the open. ¹⁸Therefore consider carefully how you listen. Whoever has will be given more; whoever does not have, even what he thinks he has will be taken from him."

¹⁹Now Jesus' mother and brothers came to see him, but they were not able to get near him because of the crowd. ²⁰Someone told him, "Your mother and brothers are standing outside, wanting to see you."

²¹He replied, "My mother and brothers are those who hear God's word and put it into practice."

ᵃ10 Isaiah 6:9

PSALM 69:19-36

¹⁹You [the Lord] know how I am scorned,
      disgraced and shamed;
   all my enemies are before you.
²⁰Scorn has broken my heart
      and has left me helpless;
   I looked for sympathy, but there was
      none,
   for comforters, but I found none.
²¹They put gall in my food
   and gave me vinegar for my thirst.

²²May the table set before them
      become a snare;
   may it become retribution andᵃ
      a trap.
²³May their eyes be darkened so they
      cannot see,
   and their backs be bent forever.
²⁴Pour out your wrath on them;
   let your fierce anger overtake
      them.
²⁵May their place be deserted;
   let there be no one to dwell in
      their tents.
²⁶For they persecute those you wound
   and talk about the pain of those
      you hurt.
²⁷Charge them with crime upon crime;
   do not let them share in your
      salvation.
²⁸May they be blotted out of the book
      of life
   and not be listed with the
      righteous.

²⁹I am in pain and distress;
   may your salvation, O God,
      protect me.
³⁰I will praise God's name in song
   and glorify him with thanksgiving.

³¹This will please the LORD more than
an ox,
more than a bull with its horns
and hoofs.
³²The poor will see and be glad—
you who seek God, may your
hearts live!
³³The LORD hears the needy
and does not despise his captive
people.

³⁴Let heaven and earth praise him,
the seas and all that move in them,
³⁵for God will save Zion
and rebuild the cities of Judah.
Then people will settle there and
possess it;
³⁶   the children of his servants will
inherit it,
and those who love his name will
dwell there.

a22 Or snare / and their fellowship become

PROVERBS 12:2-3

²**A** good man obtains favor from the
LORD,
but the LORD condemns a crafty
man.

³A man cannot be established
through wickedness,
but the righteous cannot be
uprooted.

☐ D A Y 8 8

GOD SIGHTINGS

March 29

DEUTERONOMY 11:1–12:32

Love the LORD your God and keep his requirements, his decrees, his laws and his
commands always. ²Remember today
that your children were not the ones who
saw and experienced the discipline of
the LORD your God: his majesty, his
mighty hand, his outstretched arm; ³the
signs he performed and the things he did
in the heart of Egypt, both to Pharaoh

king of Egypt and to his whole country;
⁴what he did to the Egyptian army, to its
horses and chariots, how he overwhelmed them with the waters of the
Red Seaᵃ as they were pursuing you, and
how the LORD brought lasting ruin on
them. ⁵It was not your children who saw
what he did for you in the desert until
you arrived at this place, ⁶and what he
did to Dathan and Abiram, sons of Eliab
the Reubenite, when the earth opened its
mouth right in the middle of all Israel
and swallowed them up with their
households, their tents and every living
thing that belonged to them. ⁷But it was
your own eyes that saw all these great
things the LORD has done.

⁸Observe therefore all the commands
I am giving you today, so that you may
have the strength to go in and take over
the land that you are crossing the Jordan
to possess, ⁹and so that you may live
long in the land that the LORD swore to
your forefathers to give to them and
their descendants, a land flowing with
milk and honey. ¹⁰The land you are entering to take over is not like the land of
Egypt, from which you have come,
where you planted your seed and irri-
gated it by foot as in a vegetable garden.
¹¹But the land you are crossing the Jordan to take possession of is a land of
mountains and valleys that drinks rain
from heaven. ¹²It is a land the LORD your
God cares for; the eyes of the LORD your
God are continually on it from the beginning of the year to its end.

¹³So if you faithfully obey the commands I am giving you today—to love
the LORD your God and to serve him with
all your heart and with all your soul—
¹⁴then I will send rain on your land in its
season, both autumn and spring rains,
so that you may gather in your grain,
new wine and oil. ¹⁵I will provide grass
in the fields for your cattle, and you will
eat and be satisfied.

¹⁶Be careful, or you will be enticed to
turn away and worship other gods and
bow down to them. ¹⁷Then the LORD's
anger will burn against you, and he will
shut the heavens so that it will not rain

and the ground will yield no produce, and you will soon perish from the good land the Lord is giving you. ¹⁸Fix these words of mine in your hearts and minds; tie them as symbols on your hands and bind them on your foreheads. ¹⁹Teach them to your children, talking about them when you sit at home and when you walk along the road, when you lie down and when you get up. ²⁰Write them on the doorframes of your houses and on your gates, ²¹so that your days and the days of your children may be many in the land that the Lord swore to give your forefathers, as many as the days that the heavens are above the earth.

²²If you carefully observe all these commands I am giving you to follow— to love the Lord your God, to walk in all his ways and to hold fast to him— ²³then the Lord will drive out all these nations before you, and you will dispossess nations larger and stronger than you. ²⁴Every place where you set your foot will be yours: Your territory will extend from the desert to Lebanon, and from the Euphrates River to the western sea.*b* ²⁵No man will be able to stand against you. The Lord your God, as he promised you, will put the terror and fear of you on the whole land, wherever you go.

²⁶See, I am setting before you today a blessing and a curse— ²⁷the blessing if you obey the commands of the Lord your God that I am giving you today; ²⁸the curse if you disobey the commands of the Lord your God and turn from the way that I command you today by following other gods, which you have not known. ²⁹When the Lord your God has brought you into the land you are entering to possess, you are to proclaim on Mount Gerizim the blessings, and on Mount Ebal the curses. ³⁰As you know, these mountains are across the Jordan, west of the road,*c* toward the setting sun, near the great trees of Moreh, in the territory of those Canaanites living in the Arabah in the vicinity of Gilgal. ³¹You are about to cross the Jordan to enter and

take possession of the land the Lord your God is giving you. When you have taken it over and are living there, ³²be sure that you obey all the decrees and laws I am setting before you today.

12:1THESE are the decrees and laws you must be careful to follow in the land that the Lord, the God of your fathers, has given you to possess—as long as you live in the land. ²Destroy completely all the places on the high mountains and on the hills and under every spreading tree where the nations you are dispossessing worship their gods. ³Break down their altars, smash their sacred stones and burn their Asherah poles in the fire; cut down the idols of their gods and wipe out their names from those places.

⁴You must not worship the Lord your God in their way. ⁵But you are to seek the place the Lord your God will choose from among all your tribes to put his Name there for his dwelling. To that place you must go; ⁶there bring your burnt offerings and sacrifices, your tithes and special gifts, what you have vowed to give and your freewill offerings, and the firstborn of your herds and flocks. ⁷There, in the presence of the Lord your God, you and your families shall eat and shall rejoice in everything you have put your hand to, because the Lord your God has blessed you.

⁸You are not to do as we do here today, everyone as he sees fit, ⁹since you have not yet reached the resting place and the inheritance the Lord your God is giving you. ¹⁰But you will cross the Jordan and settle in the land the Lord your God is giving you as an inheritance, and he will give you rest from all your enemies around you so that you will live in safety. ¹¹Then to the place the Lord your God will choose as a dwelling for his Name—there you are to bring everything I command you: your burnt offerings and sacrifices, your tithes and special gifts, and all the choice possessions you have vowed to the Lord. ¹²And there rejoice before the Lord

your God, you, your sons and daughters, your menservants and maidservants, and the Levites from your towns, who have no allotment or inheritance of their own. ¹³Be careful not to sacrifice your burnt offerings anywhere you please. ¹⁴Offer them only at the place the LORD will choose in one of your tribes, and there observe everything I command you.

¹⁵Nevertheless, you may slaughter your animals in any of your towns and eat as much of the meat as you want, as if it were gazelle or deer, according to the blessing the LORD your God gives you. Both the ceremonially unclean and the clean may eat it. ¹⁶But you must not eat the blood; pour it out on the ground like water. ¹⁷You must not eat in your own towns the tithe of your grain and new wine and oil, or the firstborn of your herds and flocks, or whatever you have vowed to give, or your freewill offerings or special gifts. ¹⁸Instead, you are to eat them in the presence of the LORD your God at the place the LORD your God will choose—you, your sons and daughters, your menservants and maidservants, and the Levites from your towns—and you are to rejoice before the LORD your God in everything you put your hand to. ¹⁹Be careful not to neglect the Levites as long as you live in your land.

²⁰When the LORD your God has enlarged your territory as he promised you, and you crave meat and say, "I would like some meat," then you may eat as much of it as you want. ²¹If the place where the LORD your God chooses to put his Name is too far away from you, you may slaughter animals from the herds and flocks the LORD has given you, as I have commanded you, and in your own towns you may eat as much of them as you want. ²²Eat them as you would gazelle or deer. Both the ceremonially unclean and the clean may eat. ²³But be sure you do not eat the blood, because the blood is the life, and you must not eat the life with the meat. ²⁴You must not eat the blood; pour it out on the

ground like water. ²⁵Do not eat it, so that it may go well with you and your children after you, because you will be doing what is right in the eyes of the LORD.

²⁶But take your consecrated things and whatever you have vowed to give, and go to the place the LORD will choose. ²⁷Present your burnt offerings on the altar of the LORD your God, both the meat and the blood. The blood of your sacrifices must be poured beside the altar of the LORD your God, but you may eat the meat. ²⁸Be careful to obey all these regulations I am giving you, so that it may always go well with you and your children after you, because you will be doing what is good and right in the eyes of the LORD your God.

²⁹The LORD your God will cut off before you the nations you are about to invade and dispossess. But when you have driven them out and settled in their land, ³⁰and after they have been destroyed before you, be careful not to be ensnared by inquiring about their gods, saying, "How do these nations serve their gods? We will do the same." ³¹You must not worship the LORD your God in their way, because in worshiping their gods, they do all kinds of detestable things the LORD hates. They even burn their sons and daughters in the fire as sacrifices to their gods.

³²See that you do all I command you; do not add to it or take away from it.

a4 Hebrew *Yam Suph*; that is, Sea of Reeds   *b24* That is, the Mediterranean   *c30* Or *Jordan, westward*

LUKE 8:22-39

One day Jesus said to his disciples, "Let's go over to the other side of the lake." So they got into a boat and set out. ²³As they sailed, he fell asleep. A squall came down on the lake, so that the boat was being swamped, and they were in great danger.

²⁴The disciples went and woke him, saying, "Master, Master, we're going to drown!"

He got up and rebuked the wind and the raging waters; the storm subsided, and all was calm. ²⁵"Where is your faith?" he asked his disciples.

In fear and amazement they asked one another, "Who is this? He commands even the winds and the water, and they obey him."

²⁶They sailed to the region of the Gerasenes,ᵃ which is across the lake from Galilee. ²⁷When Jesus stepped ashore, he was met by a demon-possessed man from the town. For a long time this man had not worn clothes or lived in a house, but had lived in the tombs. ²⁸When he saw Jesus, he cried out and fell at his feet, shouting at the top of his voice, "What do you want with me, Jesus, Son of the Most High God? I beg you, don't torture me!" ²⁹For Jesus had commanded the evilᵇ spirit to come out of the man. Many times it had seized him, and though he was chained hand and foot and kept under guard, he had broken his chains and had been driven by the demon into solitary places.

³⁰Jesus asked him, "What is your name?"

"Legion," he replied, because many demons had gone into him. ³¹And they begged him repeatedly not to order them to go into the Abyss.

³²A large herd of pigs was feeding there on the hillside. The demons begged Jesus to let them go into them, and he gave them permission. ³³When the demons came out of the man, they went into the pigs, and the herd rushed down the steep bank into the lake and was drowned.

³⁴When those tending the pigs saw what had happened, they ran off and reported this in the town and countryside, ³⁵and the people went out to see what had happened. When they came to Jesus, they found the man from whom the demons had gone out, sitting at Jesus' feet, dressed and in his right mind; and they were afraid. ³⁶Those who had seen it told the people how the demon-possessed man had been cured. ³⁷Then all the people of the region of the Gerasenes asked Jesus to leave them,

because they were overcome with fear. So he got into the boat and left.

³⁸The man from whom the demons had gone out begged to go with him, but Jesus sent him away, saying, ³⁹"Return home and tell how much God has done for you." So the man went away and told all over town how much Jesus had done for him.

ᵃ26 Some manuscripts *Gadarenes*; other manuscripts *Gergesenes*; also in verse 37   ᵇ29 Greek *unclean*

PSALM 70:1-5

For the director of music. Of David. A petition.

¹ **H**asten, O God, to save me;
  O Lᴏʀᴅ, come quickly to help me.
² May those who seek my life
  be put to shame and confusion;
  may all who desire my ruin
  be turned back in disgrace.
³ May those who say to me, "Aha! Aha!"
  turn back because of their shame.
⁴ But may all who seek you
  rejoice and be glad in you;
  may those who love your salvation
    always say,
  "Let God be exalted!"

⁵ Yet I am poor and needy;
  come quickly to me, O God.
You are my help and my deliverer;
  O Lᴏʀᴅ, do not delay.

PROVERBS 12:4

⁴ **A** wife of noble character is her
    husband's crown,
  but a disgraceful wife is like decay
    in his bones.

☐ DAY 89

GOD SIGHTINGS

March 30

DEUTERONOMY 13:1–15:23

If a prophet, or one who foretells by dreams, appears among you [Israel] and announces to you a miraculous sign or wonder, [2] and if the sign or wonder of which he has spoken takes place, and he says, "Let us follow other gods" (gods you have not known) "and let us worship them," [3] you must not listen to the words of that prophet or dreamer. The LORD your God is testing you to find out whether you love him with all your heart and with all your soul. [4] It is the LORD your God you must follow, and him you must revere. Keep his commands and obey him; serve him and hold fast to him. [5] That prophet or dreamer must be put to death, because he preached rebellion against the LORD your God, who brought you out of Egypt and redeemed you from the land of slavery; he has tried to turn you from the way the LORD your God commanded you to follow. You must purge the evil from among you.

[6] If your very own brother, or your son or daughter, or the wife you love, or your closest friend secretly entices you, saying, "Let us go and worship other gods" (gods that neither you nor your fathers have known, [7] gods of the peoples around you, whether near or far, from one end of the land to the other), [8] do not yield to him or listen to him. Show him no pity. Do not spare him or shield him. [9] You must certainly put him to death. Your hand must be the first in putting him to death, and then the hands of all the people. [10] Stone him to death, because he tried to turn you away from the LORD your God, who brought you out of Egypt, out of the land of slavery. [11] Then all Israel will hear and be afraid, and no one among you will do such an evil thing again.

[12] If you hear it said about one of the towns the LORD your God is giving you to live in [13] that wicked men have arisen among you and have led the people of their town astray, saying, "Let us go and worship other gods" (gods you have not known), [14] then you must inquire, probe and investigate it thoroughly. And if it is true and it has been proved that this detestable thing has been done among you, [15] you must certainly put to the

sword all who live in that town. Destroy it completely,[a] both its people and its livestock. [16] Gather all the plunder of the town into the middle of the public square and completely burn the town and all its plunder as a whole burnt offering to the LORD your God. It is to remain a ruin forever, never to be rebuilt. [17] None of those condemned things[a] shall be found in your hands, so that the LORD will turn from his fierce anger; he will show you mercy, have compassion on you, and increase your numbers, as he promised on oath to your forefathers, [18] because you obey the LORD your God, keeping all his commands that I am giving you today and doing what is right in his eyes.

[14:1] You are the children of the LORD your God. Do not cut yourselves or shave the front of your heads for the dead, [2] for you are a people holy to the LORD your God. Out of all the peoples on the face of the earth, the LORD has chosen you to be his treasured possession.

[3] Do not eat any detestable thing. [4] These are the animals you may eat: the ox, the sheep, the goat, [5] the deer, the gazelle, the roe deer, the wild goat, the ibex, the antelope and the mountain sheep.[b] [6] You may eat any animal that has a split hoof divided in two and that chews the cud. [7] However, of those that chew the cud or that have a split hoof completely divided you may not eat the camel, the rabbit or the coney.[c] Although they chew the cud, they do not have a split hoof; they are ceremonially unclean for you. [8] The pig is also unclean; although it has a split hoof, it does not chew the cud. You are not to eat their meat or touch their carcasses.

[9] Of all the creatures living in the water, you may eat any that has fins and scales. [10] But anything that does not have fins and scales you may not eat; for you it is unclean.

[11] You may eat any clean bird. [12] But these you may not eat: the eagle, the vulture, the black vulture, [13] the red kite, the black kite, any kind of falcon, [14] any

kind of raven, [15]the horned owl, the screech owl, the gull, any kind of hawk, [16]the little owl, the great owl, the white owl, [17]the desert owl, the osprey, the cormorant, [18]the stork, any kind of heron, the hoopoe and the bat.

[19]All flying insects that swarm are unclean to you; do not eat them. [20]But any winged creature that is clean you may eat.

[21]Do not eat anything you find already dead. You may give it to an alien living in any of your towns, and he may eat it, or you may sell it to a foreigner. But you are a people holy to the LORD your God.

Do not cook a young goat in its mother's milk.

[22]Be sure to set aside a tenth of all that your fields produce each year. [23]Eat the tithe of your grain, new wine and oil, and the firstborn of your herds and flocks in the presence of the LORD your God at the place he will choose as a dwelling for his Name, so that you may learn to revere the LORD your God always. [24]But if that place is too distant and you have been blessed by the LORD your God and cannot carry your tithe (because the place where the LORD will choose to put his Name is so far away), [25]then exchange your tithe for silver, and take the silver with you and go to the place the LORD your God will choose. [26]Use the silver to buy whatever you like: cattle, sheep, wine or other fermented drink, or anything you wish. Then you and your household shall eat there in the presence of the LORD your God and rejoice. [27]And do not neglect the Levites living in your towns, for they have no allotment or inheritance of their own.

[28]At the end of every three years, bring all the tithes of that year's produce and store it in your towns, [29]so that the Levites (who have no allotment or inheritance of their own) and the aliens, the fatherless and the widows who live in your towns may come and eat and be satisfied, and so that the LORD your God may bless you in all the work of your hands.

[15:1]At the end of every seven years you must cancel debts. [2]This is how it is to be done: Every creditor shall cancel the loan he has made to his fellow Israelite. He shall not require payment from his fellow Israelite or brother, because the LORD's time for canceling debts has been proclaimed. [3]You may require payment from a foreigner, but you must cancel any debt your brother owes you. [4]However, there should be no poor among you, for in the land the LORD your God is giving you to possess as your inheritance, he will richly bless you, [5]if only you fully obey the LORD your God and are careful to follow all these commands I am giving you today. [6]For the LORD your God will bless you as he has promised, and you will lend to many nations but will borrow from none. You will rule over many nations but none will rule over you.

[7]If there is a poor man among your brothers in any of the towns of the land that the LORD your God is giving you, do not be hardhearted or tightfisted toward your poor brother. [8]Rather be openhanded and freely lend him whatever he needs. [9]Be careful not to harbor this wicked thought: "The seventh year, the year for canceling debts, is near," so that you do not show ill will toward your needy brother and give him nothing. He may then appeal to the LORD against you, and you will be found guilty of sin. [10]Give generously to him and do so without a grudging heart; then because of this the LORD your God will bless you in all your work and in everything you put your hand to. [11]There will always be poor people in the land. Therefore I command you to be openhanded toward your brothers and toward the poor and needy in your land.

[12]If a fellow Hebrew, a man or a woman, sells himself to you and serves you six years, in the seventh year you must let him go free. [13]And when you release him, do not send him away empty-

handed. 14Supply him liberally from your flock, your threshing floor and your winepress. Give to him as the LORD your God has blessed you. 15Remember that you were slaves in Egypt and the LORD your God redeemed you. That is why I give you this command today.

16But if your servant says to you, "I do not want to leave you," because he loves you and your family and is well off with you, 17then take an awl and push it through his ear lobe into the door, and he will become your servant for life. Do the same for your maidservant.

18Do not consider it a hardship to set your servant free, because his service to you these six years has been worth twice as much as that of a hired hand. And the LORD your God will bless you in everything you do.

19Set apart for the LORD your God every firstborn male of your herds and flocks. Do not put the firstborn of your oxen to work, and do not shear the firstborn of your sheep. 20Each year you and your family are to eat them in the presence of the LORD your God at the place he will choose. 21If an animal has a defect, is lame or blind, or has any serious flaw, you must not sacrifice it to the LORD your God. 22You are to eat it in your own towns. Both the ceremonially unclean and the clean may eat it, as if it were gazelle or deer. 23But you must not eat the blood; pour it out on the ground like water.

a15,17 The Hebrew term refers to the irrevocable giving over of things or persons to the LORD, often by totally destroying them. b5 The precise identification of some of the birds and animals in this chapter is uncertain. c7 That is, the hyrax or rock badger

LUKE 8:40–9:6

Now when Jesus returned, a crowd welcomed him, for they were all expecting him. 41Then a man named Jairus, a ruler of the synagogue, came and fell at Jesus' feet, pleading with him to come to his house 42because his only daughter, a girl of about twelve, was dying.

As Jesus was on his way, the crowds almost crushed him. 43And a woman was there who had been subject to bleeding for twelve years,a but no one could heal her. 44She came up behind him and touched the edge of his cloak, and immediately her bleeding stopped.

45"Who touched me?" Jesus asked.

When they all denied it, Peter said, "Master, the people are crowding and pressing against you."

46But Jesus said, "Someone touched me; I know that power has gone out from me."

47Then the woman, seeing that she could not go unnoticed, came trembling and fell at his feet. In the presence of all the people, she told why she had touched him and how she had been instantly healed. 48Then he said to her, "Daughter, your faith has healed you. Go in peace."

49While Jesus was still speaking, someone came from the house of Jairus, the synagogue ruler. "Your daughter is dead," he said. "Don't bother the teacher any more."

50Hearing this, Jesus said to Jairus, "Don't be afraid; just believe, and she will be healed."

51When he arrived at the house of Jairus, he did not let anyone go in with him except Peter, John and James, and the child's father and mother. 52Meanwhile, all the people were wailing and mourning for her. "Stop wailing," Jesus said. "She is not dead but asleep."

53They laughed at him, knowing that she was dead. 54But he took her by the hand and said, "My child, get up!" 55Her spirit returned, and at once she stood up. Then Jesus told them to give her something to eat. 56Her parents were astonished, but he ordered them not to tell anyone what had happened.

9:1WHEN Jesus had called the Twelve together, he gave them power and authority to drive out all demons and to cure diseases, 2and he sent them out to preach the kingdom of God and to heal the sick. 3He told them: "Take nothing for the journey—no staff, no bag, no bread, no money, no extra tunic. 4Whatever house you enter, stay there until you leave that town. ⁵If people do not welcome you, shake the dust off your feet when you leave their town, as a testimony against them." ⁶So they set out and went from village to village, preaching the gospel and healing people everywhere.

a43 Many manuscripts years, and she had spent all she had on doctors

PSALM 71:1-24

¹In you, O Lord, I have taken refuge;
  let me never be put to shame.
²Rescue me and deliver me in your righteousness;
  turn your ear to me and save me.
³Be my rock of refuge,
  to which I can always go;
 give the command to save me,
  for you are my rock and my fortress.
⁴Deliver me, O my God, from the hand of the wicked,
  from the grasp of evil and cruel men.

⁵For you have been my hope,
  O Sovereign Lord,
  my confidence since my youth.
⁶From birth I have relied on you;
  you brought me forth from my mother's womb.
  I will ever praise you.
⁷I have become like a portent to many,
  but you are my strong refuge.
⁸My mouth is filled with your praise,
  declaring your splendor all day long.

⁹Do not cast me away when I am old;
  do not forsake me when my strength is gone.
¹⁰For my enemies speak against me;
  those who wait to kill me conspire together.
¹¹They say, "God has forsaken him;
  pursue him and seize him,
  for no one will rescue him."
¹²Be not far from me, O God;
  come quickly, O my God, to help me.
¹³May my accusers perish in shame;
  may those who want to harm me
  be covered with scorn and disgrace.

¹⁴But as for me, I will always have hope;
  I will praise you more and more.
¹⁵My mouth will tell of your righteousness,
  of your salvation all day long,
  though I know not its measure.
¹⁶I will come and proclaim your mighty acts, O Sovereign Lord;
  I will proclaim your righteousness, yours alone.
¹⁷Since my youth, O God, you have taught me,
  and to this day I declare your marvelous deeds.
¹⁸Even when I am old and gray,
  do not forsake me, O God,
 till I declare your power to the next generation,
  your might to all who are to come.

¹⁹Your righteousness reaches to the skies, O God,
  you who have done great things.
  Who, O God, is like you?
²⁰Though you have made me see troubles, many and bitter,
  you will restore my life again;
 from the depths of the earth
  you will again bring me up.
²¹You will increase my honor
  and comfort me once again.

²²I will praise you with the harp
  for your faithfulness, O my God;
 I will sing praise to you with the lyre,
  O Holy One of Israel.
²³My lips will shout for joy
  when I sing praise to you—
  I, whom you have redeemed.
²⁴My tongue will tell of your righteous acts
  all day long,
 for those who wanted to harm me
  have been put to shame and confusion.

PROVERBS 12:5-7

⁵The plans of the righteous are just,
  but the advice of the wicked is deceitful.

⁶The words of the wicked lie in wait
  for blood,
  but the speech of the upright
    rescues them.

⁷Wicked men are overthrown and are
  no more,
  but the house of the righteous
    stands firm.

□ D A Y   9 0

GOD SIGHTINGS

March 31

DEUTERONOMY 16:1–17:20

Observe the month of Abib and celebrate the Passover of the Lᴏʀᴅ your [Is-
rael's] God, because in the month of Abib
he brought you out of Egypt by night.
²Sacrifice as the Passover to the Lᴏʀᴅ
your God an animal from your flock or
herd at the place the Lᴏʀᴅ will choose as
a dwelling for his Name. ³Do not eat it
with bread made with yeast, but for
seven days eat unleavened bread, the
bread of affliction, because you left
Egypt in haste—so that all the days of
your life you may remember the time of
your departure from Egypt. ⁴Let no yeast
be found in your possession in all your
land for seven days. Do not let any of the
meat you sacrifice on the evening of the
first day remain until morning.

⁵You must not sacrifice the Passover
in any town the Lᴏʀᴅ your God gives you
⁶except in the place he will choose as a
dwelling for his Name. There you must
sacrifice the Passover in the evening,
when the sun goes down, on the anni-
versaryᵃ of your departure from Egypt.
⁷Roast it and eat it at the place the Lᴏʀᴅ
your God will choose. Then in the
morning return to your tents. ⁸For six
days eat unleavened bread and on the
seventh day hold an assembly to the
Lᴏʀᴅ your God and do no work.

⁹Count off seven weeks from the
time you begin to put the sickle to the
standing grain. ¹⁰Then celebrate the
Feast of Weeks to the Lᴏʀᴅ your God by
giving a freewill offering in proportion
to the blessings the Lᴏʀᴅ your God has
given you. ¹¹And rejoice before the
Lᴏʀᴅ your God at the place he will
choose as a dwelling for his Name—you,
your sons and daughters, your menservants and maidservants, the Levites in
your towns, and the aliens, the fatherless and the widows living among you.
¹²Remember that you were slaves in
Egypt, and follow carefully these decrees.

¹³Celebrate the Feast of Tabernacles
for seven days after you have gathered
the produce of your threshing floor and
your winepress. ¹⁴Be joyful at your
Feast—you, your sons and daughters,
your menservants and maidservants,
and the Levites, the aliens, the fatherless
and the widows who live in your towns.
¹⁵For seven days celebrate the Feast to
the Lᴏʀᴅ your God at the place the Lᴏʀᴅ
will choose. For the Lᴏʀᴅ your God will
bless you in all your harvest and in all
the work of your hands, and your joy will
be complete.

¹⁶Three times a year all your men
must appear before the Lᴏʀᴅ your God
at the place he will choose: at the Feast
of Unleavened Bread, the Feast of
Weeks and the Feast of Tabernacles. No
man should appear before the Lᴏʀᴅ
empty-handed: ¹⁷Each of you must
bring a gift in proportion to the way the
Lᴏʀᴅ your God has blessed you.

¹⁸Appoint judges and officials for
each of your tribes in every town the
Lᴏʀᴅ your God is giving you, and they
shall judge the people fairly. ¹⁹Do not
pervert justice or show partiality. Do not
accept a bribe, for a bribe blinds the eyes
of the wise and twists the words of the
righteous. ²⁰Follow justice and justice
alone, so that you may live and possess
the land the Lᴏʀᴅ your God is giving you.

²¹Do not set up any wooden Asherah
poleᵇ beside the altar you build to the
Lᴏʀᴅ your God, ²²and do not erect a sacred stone, for these the Lᴏʀᴅ your God
hates.

17:1Do not sacrifice to the LORD your God an ox or a sheep that has any defect or flaw in it, for that would be detestable to him.

2If a man or woman living among you in one of the towns the LORD gives you is found doing evil in the eyes of the LORD your God in violation of his covenant, 3and contrary to my command has worshiped other gods, bowing down to them or to the sun or the moon or the stars of the sky, 4and this has been brought to your attention, then you must investigate it thoroughly. If it is true and it has been proved that this detestable thing has been done in Israel, 5take the man or woman who has done this evil deed to your city gate and stone that person to death. 6On the testimony of two or three witnesses a man shall be put to death, but no one shall be put to death on the testimony of only one witness. 7The hands of the witnesses must be the first in putting him to death, and then the hands of all the people. You must purge the evil from among you.

8If cases come before your courts that are too difficult for you to judge—whether bloodshed, lawsuits or assaults—take them to the place the LORD your God will choose. 9Go to the priests, who are Levites, and to the judge who is in office at that time. Inquire of them and they will give you the verdict. 10You must act according to the decisions they give you at the place the LORD will choose. Be careful to do everything they direct you to do. 11Act according to the law they teach you and the decisions they give you. Do not turn aside from what they tell you, to the right or to the left. 12The man who shows contempt for the judge or for the priest who stands ministering there to the LORD your God must be put to death. You must purge the evil from Israel. 13All the people will hear and be afraid, and will not be contemptuous again.

14When you enter the land the LORD your God is giving you and have taken possession of it and settled in it, and you say, "Let us set a king over us like all the nations around us," 15be sure to appoint over you the king the LORD your God chooses. He must be from among your own brothers. Do not place a foreigner over you, one who is not a brother Israelite. 16The king, moreover, must not acquire great numbers of horses for himself or make the people return to Egypt to get more of them, for the LORD has told you, "You are not to go back that way again." 17He must not take many wives, or his heart will be led astray. He must not accumulate large amounts of silver and gold.

18**When he takes the throne of his kingdom, he is to write for himself on a scroll a copy of this law, taken from that of the priests, who are Levites.** 19**It is to be with him, and he is to read it all the days of his life so that he may learn to revere the LORD his God and follow carefully all the words of this law and these decrees** 20and not consider himself better than his brothers and turn from the law to the right or to the left. Then he and his descendants will reign a long time over his kingdom in Israel.

a6 Or down, at the time of day   b21 Or Do not plant any tree dedicated to Asherah

LUKE 9:7-27

Now Herod the tetrarch heard about all that was going on. And he was perplexed, because some were saying that John had been raised from the dead, 8others that Elijah had appeared, and still others that one of the prophets of long ago had come back to life. 9But Herod said, "I beheaded John. Who, then, is this I hear such things about?" And he tried to see him.

10When the apostles returned, they reported to Jesus what they had done. Then he took them with him and they withdrew by themselves to a town called Bethsaida, 11but the crowds learned about it and followed him. He welcomed them and spoke to them about the kingdom of God, and healed those who needed healing.

12Late in the afternoon the Twelve

came to him and said, "Send the crowd away so they can go to the surrounding villages and countryside and find food and lodging, because we are in a remote place here."

13He replied, "You give them something to eat."

They answered, "We have only five loaves of bread and two fish—unless we go and buy food for all this crowd." 14(About five thousand men were there.)

But he said to his disciples, "Have them sit down in groups of about fifty each." 15The disciples did so, and everybody sat down. 16Taking the five loaves and the two fish and looking up to heaven, he gave thanks and broke them. Then he gave them to the disciples to set before the people. 17They all ate and were satisfied, and the disciples picked up twelve basketfuls of broken pieces that were left over.

18Once when Jesus was praying in private and his disciples were with him, he asked them, "Who do the crowds say I am?"

19They replied, "Some say John the Baptist; others say Elijah; and still others, that one of the prophets of long ago has come back to life."

20"But what about you?" he asked. "Who do you say I am?"

Peter answered, "The Christa of God."

21Jesus strictly warned them not to tell this to anyone. 22And he said, "The Son of Man must suffer many things and be rejected by the elders, chief priests and teachers of the law, and he must be killed and on the third day be raised to life."

23Then he said to them all: "If anyone would come after me, he must deny himself and take up his cross daily and follow me. 24For whoever wants to save his life will lose it, but whoever loses his life for me will save it. 25What good is it for a man to gain the whole world, and yet lose or forfeit his very self? 26If anyone is ashamed of me and my words, the Son of Man will be ashamed of him when he comes in his glory and in the glory of the Father and of the holy angels. 27I tell you the truth, some who are standing here will not taste death before they see the kingdom of God."

a20 Or Messiah

PSALM 72:1-20
Of Solomon.

1 Endow the king with your justice,
O God,
  the royal son with your
    righteousness.
2 He willa judge your people in
    righteousness,
  your afflicted ones with justice.
3 The mountains will bring prosperity
    to the people,
  the hills the fruit of righteousness.
4 He will defend the afflicted among
    the people
  and save the children of the needy;
  he will crush the oppressor.

5 He will endureb as long as the sun,
  as long as the moon, through all
    generations.
6 He will be like rain falling on a mown
    field,
  like showers watering the earth.
7 In his days the righteous will
    flourish;
  prosperity will abound till the
    moon is no more.

8 He will rule from sea to sea
  and from the Riverc to the ends of
    the earth.d
9 The desert tribes will bow before
    him
  and his enemies will lick the dust.
10 The kings of Tarshish and of distant
    shores
  will bring tribute to him;
  the kings of Sheba and Seba
  will present him gifts.
11 All kings will bow down to him
  and all nations will serve him.

12 For he will deliver the needy who
    cry out,
  the afflicted who have no one
    to help.

13 He will take pity on the weak and the
needy
and save the needy from death.
14 He will rescue them from oppression
and violence,
for precious is their blood in his
sight.

15 Long may he live!
May gold from Sheba be given him.
May people ever pray for him
and bless him all day long.
16 Let grain abound throughout the
land;
on the tops of the hills may it sway.
Let its fruit flourish like Lebanon;
let it thrive like the grass of the
field.
17 May his name endure forever;
may it continue as long as the sun.

All nations will be blessed through
him,
and they will call him blessed.

18 Praise be to the LORD God, the God
of Israel,
who alone does marvelous deeds.
19 Praise be to his glorious name
forever;
may the whole earth be filled with
his glory.
Amen and Amen.

20 This concludes the prayers of David
son of Jesse.

a2 Or *May he*; similarly in verses 3-11 and 17   *b5* Septuagint;
Hebrew *You will be feared*   *c8* That is, the Euphrates
d8 Or *the end of the land*

PROVERBS 12:8-9
8 **A** man is praised according to his
wisdom,
but men with warped minds are
despised.

9 Better to be a nobody and yet have
a servant
than pretend to be somebody and
have no food.

GOD SIGHTINGS

April 1

DEUTERONOMY 18:1–20:20

The priests, who are Levites—indeed the whole tribe of Levi—are to have no allotment or inheritance with Israel. They shall live on the offerings made to the LORD by fire, for that is their inheritance. ²They shall have no inheritance among their brothers; the LORD is their inheritance, as he promised them.

³This is the share due the priests from the people who sacrifice a bull or a sheep: the shoulder, the jowls and the inner parts. ⁴You are to give them the firstfruits of your grain, new wine and oil, and the first wool from the shearing of your sheep, ⁵for the LORD your God has chosen them and their descendants out of all your tribes to stand and minister in the LORD's name always.

⁶If a Levite moves from one of your towns anywhere in Israel where he is living, and comes in all earnestness to the place the LORD will choose, ⁷he may minister in the name of the LORD his God like all his fellow Levites who serve there in the presence of the LORD. ⁸He is to share equally in their benefits, even though he has received money from the sale of family possessions.

⁹When you enter the land the LORD your God is giving you, do not learn to imitate the detestable ways of the nations there. ¹⁰Let no one be found among you who sacrifices his son or daughter in*a* the fire, who practices divination or sorcery, interprets omens, engages in witchcraft, ¹¹or casts spells, or who is a medium or spiritist or who consults the dead. ¹²Anyone who does these things is detestable to the LORD, and because of these detestable practices the LORD your God will drive out

those nations before you. ¹³You must be blameless before the LORD your God.

¹⁴The nations you will dispossess listen to those who practice sorcery or divination. But as for you, the LORD your God has not permitted you to do so. ¹⁵The LORD your God will raise up for you a prophet like me from among your own brothers. You must listen to him. ¹⁶For this is what you asked of the LORD your God at Horeb on the day of the assembly when you said, "Let us not hear the voice of the LORD our God nor see this great fire anymore, or we will die."

¹⁷The LORD said to me: "What they say is good. ¹⁸I will raise up for them a prophet like you from among their brothers; I will put my words in his mouth, and he will tell them everything I command him. ¹⁹If anyone does not listen to my words that the prophet speaks in my name, I myself will call him to account. ²⁰But a prophet who presumes to speak in my name anything I have not commanded him to say, or a prophet who speaks in the name of other gods, must be put to death."

²¹You may say to yourselves, "How can we know when a message has not been spoken by the LORD?" ²²If what a prophet proclaims in the name of the LORD does not take place or come true, that is a message the LORD has not spoken. That prophet has spoken presumptuously. Do not be afraid of him.

¹⁹:¹WHEN the LORD your God has destroyed the nations whose land he is giving you, and when you have driven them out and settled in their towns and houses, ²then set aside for yourselves three cities centrally located in the land the LORD your God is giving you to possess. ³Build roads to them and divide into three parts the land the LORD your God is giving you as an inheritance, so that anyone who kills a man may flee there.

⁴This is the rule concerning the man

who kills another and flees there to save his life—one who kills his neighbor unintentionally, without malice aforethought. [5]For instance, a man may go into the forest with his neighbor to cut wood, and as he swings his ax to fell a tree, the head may fly off and hit his neighbor and kill him. That man may flee to one of these cities and save his life. [6]Otherwise, the avenger of blood might pursue him in a rage, overtake him if the distance is too great, and kill him even though he is not deserving of death, since he did it to his neighbor without malice aforethought. [7]This is why I command you to set aside for yourselves three cities.

[8]If the Lord your God enlarges your territory, as he promised on oath to your forefathers, and gives you the whole land he promised them, [9]because you carefully follow all these laws I command you today—to love the Lord your God and to walk always in his ways—then you are to set aside three more cities. [10]Do this so that innocent blood will not be shed in your land, which the Lord your God is giving you as your inheritance, and so that you will not be guilty of bloodshed.

[11]But if a man hates his neighbor and lies in wait for him, assaults and kills him, and then flees to one of these cities, [12]the elders of his town shall send for him, bring him back from the city, and hand him over to the avenger of blood to die. [13]Show him no pity. You must purge from Israel the guilt of shedding innocent blood, so that it may go well with you.

[14]Do not move your neighbor's boundary stone set up by your predecessors in the inheritance you receive in the land the Lord your God is giving you to possess.

[15]One witness is not enough to convict a man accused of any crime or offense he may have committed. A matter must be established by the testimony of two or three witnesses.

[16]If a malicious witness takes the stand to accuse a man of a crime, [17]the two men involved in the dispute must stand in the presence of the Lord before the priests and the judges who are in office at the time. [18]The judges must make a thorough investigation, and if the witness proves to be a liar, giving false testimony against his brother, [19]then do to him as he intended to do to his brother. You must purge the evil from among you. [20]The rest of the people will hear of this and be afraid, and never again will such an evil thing be done among you. [21]Show no pity: life for life, eye for eye, tooth for tooth, hand for hand, foot for foot.

20:1When you go to war against your enemies and see horses and chariots and an army greater than yours, do not be afraid of them, because the Lord your God, who brought you up out of Egypt, will be with you. [2]When you are about to go into battle, the priest shall come forward and address the army. [3]He shall say: "Hear, O Israel, today you are going into battle against your enemies. Do not be fainthearted or afraid; do not be terrified or give way to panic before them. [4]For the Lord your God is the one who goes with you to fight for you against your enemies to give you victory."

[5]The officers shall say to the army: "Has anyone built a new house and not dedicated it? Let him go home, or he may die in battle and someone else may dedicate it. [6]Has anyone planted a vineyard and not begun to enjoy it? Let him go home, or he may die in battle and someone else enjoy it. [7]Has anyone become pledged to a woman and not married her? Let him go home, or he may die in battle and someone else marry her." [8]Then the officers shall add, "Is any man afraid or fainthearted? Let him go home so that his brothers will not become disheartened too." [9]When the officers have finished speaking to the army, they shall appoint commanders over it.

[10]When you march up to attack a city, make its people an offer of peace. [11]If they accept and open their gates, all the people in it shall be subject to forced la-

bor and shall work for you. [12]If they refuse to make peace and they engage you in battle, lay siege to that city. [13]When the LORD your God delivers it into your hand, put to the sword all the men in it. [14]As for the women, the children, the livestock and everything else in the city, you may take these as plunder for yourselves. And you may use the plunder the LORD your God gives you from your enemies. [15]This is how you are to treat all the cities that are at a distance from you and do not belong to the nations nearby.

[16]However, in the cities of the nations the LORD your God is giving you as an inheritance, do not leave alive anything that breathes. [17]Completely destroy[b] them—the Hittites, Amorites, Canaanites, Perizzites, Hivites and Jebusites—as the LORD your God has commanded you. [18]Otherwise, they will teach you to follow all the detestable things they do in worshiping their gods, and you will sin against the LORD your God.

[19]When you lay siege to a city for a long time, fighting against it to capture it, do not destroy its trees by putting an ax to them, because you can eat their fruit. Do not cut them down. Are the trees of the field people, that you should besiege them?[c] [20]However, you may cut down trees that you know are not fruit trees and use them to build siege works until the city at war with you falls.

[a]10 Or *who makes his son or daughter pass through*
[b]17 The Hebrew term refers to the irrevocable giving over of things or persons to the LORD, often by totally destroying them. [c]19 Or *down to use in the siege, for the fruit trees are for the benefit of man.*

LUKE 9:28-50

About eight days after Jesus said this, he took Peter, John and James with him and went up onto a mountain to pray. [29]As he was praying, the appearance of his face changed, and his clothes became as bright as a flash of lightning. [30]Two men, Moses and Elijah, [31]appeared in glorious splendor, talking with Jesus. They spoke about his departure, which he was about to bring to fulfillment at Jerusalem. [32]Peter and his companions were very sleepy, but when they became fully awake, they saw his glory and the two men standing with him. [33]As the men were leaving Jesus, Peter said to him, "Master, it is good for us to be here. Let us put up three shelters—one for you, one for Moses and one for Elijah." (He did not know what he was saying.)

[34]While he was speaking, a cloud appeared and enveloped them, and they were afraid as they entered the cloud. [35]A voice came from the cloud, saying, "This is my Son, whom I have chosen; listen to him." [36]When the voice had spoken, they found that Jesus was alone. The disciples kept this to themselves, and told no one at that time what they had seen.

[37]The next day, when they came down from the mountain, a large crowd met him. [38]A man in the crowd called out, "Teacher, I beg you to look at my son, for he is my only child. [39]A spirit seizes him and he suddenly screams; it throws him into convulsions so that he foams at the mouth. It scarcely ever leaves him and is destroying him. [40]I begged your disciples to drive it out, but they could not."

[41]"O unbelieving and perverse generation," Jesus replied, "how long shall I stay with you and put up with you? Bring your son here."

[42]Even while the boy was coming, the demon threw him to the ground in a convulsion. But Jesus rebuked the evil[a] spirit, healed the boy and gave him back to his father. [43]And they were all amazed at the greatness of God.

While everyone was marveling at all that Jesus did, he said to his disciples, [44]"Listen carefully to what I am about to tell you: The Son of Man is going to be betrayed into the hands of men." [45]But they did not understand what this meant. It was hidden from them, so that they did not grasp it, and they were afraid to ask him about it.

[46]An argument started among the disciples as to which of them would be the greatest. [47]Jesus, knowing their thoughts, took a little child and had him

stand beside him. **48Then he said to them, " Whoever welcomes this little child in my name welcomes me; and whoever welcomes me welcomes the one who sent me. For he who is least among you all—he is the greatest."**

49"Master," said John, "we saw a man driving out demons in your name and we tried to stop him, because he is not one of us."

50"Do not stop him," Jesus said, "for whoever is not against you is for you."

a42 Greek *unclean*

PSALM 73:1-28
A psalm of Asaph.

1 **S**urely God is good to Israel,
　　to those who are pure in heart.

2 But as for me, my feet had almost
　　slipped;
　　I had nearly lost my foothold.
3 For I envied the arrogant
　　when I saw the prosperity of the
　　wicked.

4 They have no struggles;
　　their bodies are healthy and
　　strong.a
5 They are free from the burdens
　　common to man;
　　they are not plagued by human
　　ills.
6 Therefore pride is their necklace;
　　they clothe themselves with
　　violence.
7 From their callous hearts comes
　　iniquityb;
　　the evil conceits of their minds
　　know no limits.
8 They scoff, and speak with malice;
　　in their arrogance they threaten
　　oppression.
9 Their mouths lay claim to heaven,
　　and their tongues take possession
　　of the earth.
10 Therefore their people turn to them
　　and drink up waters in
　　abundance.c
11 They say, "How can God know?
　　Does the Most High have
　　knowledge?"

12 This is what the wicked are like—
　　always carefree, they increase
　　in wealth.

13 Surely in vain have I kept my heart
　　pure;
　　in vain have I washed my hands
　　in innocence.
14 All day long I have been plagued;
　　I have been punished every
　　morning.

15 If I had said, "I will speak thus,"
　　I would have betrayed your
　　children.
16 When I tried to understand all this,
　　it was oppressive to me
17 till I entered the sanctuary of God;
　　then I understood their final
　　destiny.

18 Surely you place them on slippery
　　ground;
　　you cast them down to ruin.
19 How suddenly are they destroyed,
　　completely swept away
　　by terrors!
20 As a dream when one awakes,
　　so when you arise, O Lord,
　　you will despise them
　　as fantasies.

21 When my heart was grieved
　　and my spirit embittered,
22 I was senseless and ignorant;
　　I was a brute beast before you.

23 Yet I am always with you;
　　you hold me by my right hand.
24 You guide me with your counsel,
　　and afterward you will take me
　　into glory.
25 Whom have I in heaven but you?
　　And earth has nothing I desire
　　besides you.
26 My flesh and my heart may fail,
　　but God is the strength of my heart
　　and my portion forever.

27 Those who are far from you will
　　perish;
　　you destroy all who are unfaithful
　　to you.

28But as for me, it is good to be near
    God.
    I have made the Sovereign LORD
        my refuge;
    I will tell of all your deeds.

a4 With a different word division of the Hebrew; Masoretic
Text *struggles at their death; / their bodies are healthy*
b7 Syriac (see also Septuagint); Hebrew *Their eyes bulge*
with fat *c10* The meaning of the Hebrew for this verse
is uncertain.

PROVERBS 12:10
10 **A** righteous man cares for the needs
    of his animal,
    but the kindest acts of the wicked
    are cruel.

□ D A Y 9 2

GOD SIGHTINGS

April 2

DEUTERONOMY 21:1–22:30
If a man is found slain, lying in a field in
the land the LORD your [Israel's] God is
giving you to possess, and it is not
known who killed him, 2 your elders and
judges shall go out and measure the distance from the body to the neighboring
towns. 3 Then the elders of the town
nearest the body shall take a heifer that
has never been worked and has never
worn a yoke 4 and lead her down to a valley that has not been plowed or planted
and where there is a flowing stream.
There in the valley they are to break the
heifer's neck. 5 The priests, the sons of
Levi, shall step forward, for the LORD
your God has chosen them to minister
and to pronounce blessings in the name
of the LORD and to decide all cases of
dispute and assault. 6 Then all the elders
of the town nearest the body shall wash
their hands over the heifer whose neck
was broken in the valley, 7 and they shall
declare: "Our hands did not shed this
blood, nor did our eyes see it done. 8 Accept this atonement for your people Israel, whom you have redeemed, O LORD,

and do not hold your people guilty of
the blood of an innocent man." And the
bloodshed will be atoned for. 9 So you
will purge from yourselves the guilt of
shedding innocent blood, since you
have done what is right in the eyes of the
LORD.

10 When you go to war against your
enemies and the LORD your God delivers
them into your hands and you take captives, 11 if you notice among the captives
a beautiful woman and are attracted to
her, you may take her as your wife.
12 Bring her into your home and have
her shave her head, trim her nails 13 and
put aside the clothes she was wearing
when captured. After she has lived in
your house and mourned her father and
mother for a full month, then you may
go to her and be her husband and she
shall be your wife. 14 If you are not
pleased with her, let her go wherever
she wishes. You must not sell her or
treat her as a slave, since you have dishonored her.

15 If a man has two wives, and he loves
one but not the other, and both bear him
sons but the firstborn is the son of the
wife he does not love, 16 when he wills
his property to his sons, he must not
give the rights of the firstborn to the son
of the wife he loves in preference to his
actual firstborn, the son of the wife he
does not love. 17 He must acknowledge
the son of his unloved wife as the firstborn by giving him a double share of all
he has. That son is the first sign of his father's strength. The right of the firstborn belongs to him.

18 If a man has a stubborn and rebellious son who does not obey his father
and mother and will not listen to them
when they discipline him, 19 his father
and mother shall take hold of him and
bring him to the elders at the gate of his
town. 20 They shall say to the elders, "This
son of ours is stubborn and rebellious.
He will not obey us. He is a profligate and
a drunkard." 21 Then all the men of his
town shall stone him to death. You must
purge the evil from among you. All Israel
will hear of it and be afraid.

22 If a man guilty of a capital offense is put to death and his body is hung on a tree, 23 you must not leave his body on the tree overnight. Be sure to bury him that same day, because anyone who is hung on a tree is under God's curse. You must not desecrate the land the LORD your God is giving you as an inheritance.

22:1 IF you see your brother's ox or sheep straying, do not ignore it but be sure to take it back to him. 2 If the brother does not live near you or if you do not know who he is, take it home with you and keep it until he comes looking for it. Then give it back to him. 3 Do the same if you find your brother's donkey or his cloak or anything he loses. Do not ignore it.

4 If you see your brother's donkey or his ox fallen on the road, do not ignore it. Help him get it to its feet.

5 A woman must not wear men's clothing, nor a man wear women's clothing, for the LORD your God detests anyone who does this.

6 If you come across a bird's nest beside the road, either in a tree or on the ground, and the mother is sitting on the young or on the eggs, do not take the mother with the young. 7 You may take the young, but be sure to let the mother go, so that it may go well with you and you may have a long life.

8 When you build a new house, make a parapet around your roof so that you may not bring the guilt of bloodshed on your house if someone falls from the roof.

9 Do not plant two kinds of seed in your vineyard; if you do, not only the crops you plant but also the fruit of the vineyard will be defiled.*a*

10 Do not plow with an ox and a donkey yoked together.

11 Do not wear clothes of wool and linen woven together.

12 Make tassels on the four corners of the cloak you wear.

13 If a man takes a wife and, after lying with her, dislikes her 14 and slanders her and gives her a bad name, saying, "I married this woman, but when I approached her, I did not find proof of her virginity," 15 then the girl's father and mother shall bring proof that she was a virgin to the town elders at the gate. 16 The girl's father will say to the elders, "I gave my daughter in marriage to this man, but he dislikes her. 17 Now he has slandered her and said, 'I did not find your daughter to be a virgin.' But here is the proof of my daughter's virginity." Then her parents shall display the cloth before the elders of the town, 18 and the elders shall take the man and punish him. 19 They shall fine him a hundred shekels of silver*b* and give them to the girl's father, because this man has given an Israelite virgin a bad name. She shall continue to be his wife; he must not divorce her as long as he lives.

20 If, however, the charge is true and no proof of the girl's virginity can be found, 21 she shall be brought to the door of her father's house and there the men of her town shall stone her to death. She has done a disgraceful thing in Israel by being promiscuous while still in her father's house. You must purge the evil from among you.

22 If a man is found sleeping with another man's wife, both the man who slept with her and the woman must die. You must purge the evil from Israel.

23 If a man happens to meet in a town a virgin pledged to be married and he sleeps with her, 24 you shall take both of them to the gate of that town and stone them to death—the girl because she was in a town and did not scream for help, and the man because he violated another man's wife. You must purge the evil from among you.

25 But if out in the country a man happens to meet a girl pledged to be married and rapes her, only the man who has done this shall die. 26 Do nothing to the girl; she has committed no sin deserving death. This case is like that of someone who attacks and murders his neighbor, 27 for the man found the girl out in the country, and though the betrothed girl screamed, there was no one to rescue her.

²⁸If a man happens to meet a virgin who is not pledged to be married and rapes her and they are discovered, ²⁹he shall pay the girl's father fifty shekels of silver.ᶜ He must marry the girl, for he has violated her. He can never divorce her as long as he lives.

³⁰A man is not to marry his father's wife; he must not dishonor his father's bed.

ᵃ⁹ Or *be forfeited to the sanctuary*   ᵇ¹⁹ That is, about 2 1/2 pounds (about 1 kilogram)   ᶜ²⁹ That is, about 1 1/4 pounds (about 0.6 kilogram)

LUKE 9:51–10:12

As the time approached for him to be taken up to heaven, Jesus resolutely set out for Jerusalem. ⁵²And he sent messengers on ahead, who went into a Samaritan village to get things ready for him; ⁵³but the people there did not welcome him, because he was heading for Jerusalem. ⁵⁴When the disciples James and John saw this, they asked, "Lord, do you want us to call fire down from heaven to destroy themᵃ?" ⁵⁵But Jesus turned and rebuked them, ⁵⁶andᵇ they went to another village.

⁵⁷As they were walking along the road, a man said to him, "I will follow you wherever you go."

⁵⁸Jesus replied, "Foxes have holes and birds of the air have nests, but the Son of Man has no place to lay his head."

⁵⁹He said to another man, "Follow me."

But the man replied, "Lord, first let me go and bury my father."

⁶⁰Jesus said to him, "Let the dead bury their own dead, but you go and proclaim the kingdom of God."

⁶¹Still another said, "I will follow you, Lord; but first let me go back and say good-by to my family."

⁶²**Jesus replied, "No one who puts his hand to the plow and looks back is fit for service in the kingdom of God."**

¹⁰:¹Aꜰᴛᴇʀ this the Lord appointed seventy-twoᶜ others and sent them two by two ahead of him to every town and place where he was about to go. ²He told them, "The harvest is plentiful, but the

workers are few. Ask the Lord of the harvest, therefore, to send out workers into his harvest field. ³Go! I am sending you out like lambs among wolves. ⁴Do not take a purse or bag or sandals; and do not greet anyone on the road.

⁵"When you enter a house, first say, 'Peace to this house.' ⁶If a man of peace is there, your peace will rest on him; if not, it will return to you. ⁷Stay in that house, eating and drinking whatever they give you, for the worker deserves his wages. Do not move around from house to house.

⁸"When you enter a town and are welcomed, eat what is set before you. ⁹Heal the sick who are there and tell them, 'The kingdom of God is near you.' ¹⁰But when you enter a town and are not welcomed, go into its streets and say, ¹¹'Even the dust of your town that sticks to our feet we wipe off against you. Yet be sure of this: The kingdom of God is near.' ¹²I tell you, it will be more bearable on that day for Sodom than for that town."

ᵃ⁵⁴ Some manuscripts *them, even as Elijah did*
ᵇ⁵⁵,⁵⁶ Some manuscripts *them. And he said, "You do not know what kind of spirit you are of, for the Son of Man did not come to destroy men's lives, but to save them."*
⁵⁶And   ᶜ¹ Some manuscripts *seventy*; also in verse 17

PSALM 74:1-23

A *maskil*ᵃ of Asaph.

¹ **W**hy have you rejected us forever,
        O God?
    Why does your anger smolder
        against the sheep of your
        pasture?
² Remember the people you
        purchased of old,
    the tribe of your inheritance,
        whom you redeemed—
    Mount Zion, where you dwelt.
³ Turn your steps toward these
        everlasting ruins,
    all this destruction the enemy has
        brought on the sanctuary.

⁴ Your foes roared in the place where
        you met with us;
    they set up their standards
        as signs.

5 They behaved like men wielding
     axes
   to cut through a thicket of trees.
6 They smashed all the carved
     paneling
   with their axes and hatchets.
7 They burned your sanctuary to the
     ground;
   they defiled the dwelling place of
     your Name.
8 They said in their hearts, "We will
     crush them completely!"
   They burned every place where
     God was worshiped in the
     land.
9 We are given no miraculous signs;
   no prophets are left,
   and none of us knows how long
     this will be.

10 How long will the enemy mock you,
     O God?
   Will the foe revile your name
     forever?
11 Why do you hold back your hand,
     your right hand?
   Take it from the folds of your
     garment and destroy them!

12 But you, O God, are my king from
     of old;
   you bring salvation upon the
     earth.
13 It was you who split open the sea by
     your power;
   you broke the heads of the
     monster in the waters.
14 It was you who crushed the heads of
     Leviathan
   and gave him as food to the
     creatures of the desert.
15 It was you who opened up springs
     and streams;
   you dried up the ever flowing
     rivers.
16 The day is yours, and yours also the
     night;
   you established the sun and
     moon.
17 It was you who set all the boundaries
     of the earth;

   you made both summer and
     winter.
18 Remember how the enemy has
     mocked you, O LORD,
   how foolish people have reviled
     your name.
19 Do not hand over the life of your
     dove to wild beasts;
   do not forget the lives of your
     afflicted people forever.
20 Have regard for your covenant,
   because haunts of violence fill the
     dark places of the land.
21 Do not let the oppressed retreat in
     disgrace;
   may the poor and needy praise
     your name.
22 Rise up, O God, and defend your
     cause;
   remember how fools mock you all
     day long.
23 Do not ignore the clamor of your
     adversaries,
   the uproar of your enemies, which
     rises continually.

aTitle: Probably a literary or musical term

PROVERBS 12:11
11 He who works his land will have
     abundant food,
   but he who chases fantasies lacks
     judgment.

□ DAY 93

GOD SIGHTINGS

April 3

DEUTERONOMY 23:1–25:19
No one who has been emasculated by
crushing or cutting may enter the assembly of the LORD.
   2 No one born of a forbidden mar-
riagea nor any of his descendants may
enter the assembly of the LORD, even
down to the tenth generation.
   3 No Ammonite or Moabite or any of

his descendants may enter the assembly of the Lord, even down to the tenth generation. ⁴For they did not come to meet you with bread and water on your way when you came out of Egypt, and they hired Balaam son of Beor from Pethor in Aram Naharaim*b* to pronounce a curse on you. ⁵However, the Lord your God would not listen to Balaam but turned the curse into a blessing for you, because the Lord your God loves you. ⁶Do not seek a treaty of friendship with them as long as you live.

⁷Do not abhor an Edomite, for he is your brother. Do not abhor an Egyptian, because you lived as an alien in his country. ⁸The third generation of children born to them may enter the assembly of the Lord.

⁹When you are encamped against your enemies, keep away from everything impure. ¹⁰If one of your men is unclean because of a nocturnal emission, he is to go outside the camp and stay there. ¹¹But as evening approaches he is to wash himself, and at sunset he may return to the camp.

¹²Designate a place outside the camp where you can go to relieve yourself. ¹³As part of your equipment have something to dig with, and when you relieve yourself, dig a hole and cover up your excrement. ¹⁴For the Lord your God moves about in your camp to protect you and to deliver your enemies to you. Your camp must be holy, so that he will not see among you anything indecent and turn away from you.

¹⁵If a slave has taken refuge with you, do not hand him over to his master. ¹⁶Let him live among you wherever he likes and in whatever town he chooses. Do not oppress him.

¹⁷No Israelite man or woman is to become a shrine prostitute. ¹⁸You must not bring the earnings of a female prostitute or of a male prostitute*c* into the house of the Lord your God to pay any vow, because the Lord your God detests them both.

¹⁹Do not charge your brother interest, whether on money or food or any-

thing else that may earn interest. ²⁰You may charge a foreigner interest, but not a brother Israelite, so that the Lord your God may bless you in everything you put your hand to in the land you are entering to possess.

²¹If you make a vow to the Lord your God, do not be slow to pay it, for the Lord your God will certainly demand it of you and you will be guilty of sin. ²²But if you refrain from making a vow, you will not be guilty. ²³Whatever your lips utter you must be sure to do, because you made your vow freely to the Lord your God with your own mouth.

²⁴If you enter your neighbor's vineyard, you may eat all the grapes you want, but do not put any in your basket. ²⁵If you enter your neighbor's grainfield, you may pick kernels with your hands, but you must not put a sickle to his standing grain.

²⁴:¹If a man marries a woman who becomes displeasing to him because he finds something indecent about her, and he writes her a certificate of divorce, gives it to her and sends her from his house, ²and if after she leaves his house she becomes the wife of another man, ³and her second husband dislikes her and writes her a certificate of divorce, gives it to her and sends her from his house, or if he dies, ⁴then her first husband, who divorced her, is not allowed to marry her again after she has been defiled. That would be detestable in the eyes of the Lord. Do not bring sin upon the land the Lord your God is giving you as an inheritance.

⁵If a man has recently married, he must not be sent to war or have any other duty laid on him. For one year he is to be free to stay at home and bring happiness to the wife he has married.

⁶Do not take a pair of millstones—not even the upper one—as security for a debt, because that would be taking a man's livelihood as security.

⁷If a man is caught kidnapping one of his brother Israelites and treats him as a slave or sells him, the kidnapper

must die. You must purge the evil from among you.

8In cases of leprous[d] diseases be very careful to do exactly as the priests, who are Levites, instruct you. You must follow carefully what I have commanded them. 9Remember what the LORD your God did to Miriam along the way after you came out of Egypt.

10When you make a loan of any kind to your neighbor, do not go into his house to get what he is offering as a pledge. 11Stay outside and let the man to whom you are making the loan bring the pledge out to you. 12If the man is poor, do not go to sleep with his pledge in your possession. 13Return his cloak to him by sunset so that he may sleep in it. Then he will thank you, and it will be regarded as a righteous act in the sight of the LORD your God.

14Do not take advantage of a hired man who is poor and needy, whether he is a brother Israelite or an alien living in one of your towns. 15Pay him his wages each day before sunset, because he is poor and is counting on it. Otherwise he may cry to the LORD against you, and you will be guilty of sin.

16Fathers shall not be put to death for their children, nor children put to death for their fathers; each is to die for his own sin.

17Do not deprive the alien or the fatherless of justice, or take the cloak of the widow as a pledge. 18Remember that you were slaves in Egypt and the LORD your God redeemed you from there. That is why I command you to do this.

19When you are harvesting in your field and you overlook a sheaf, do not go back to get it. Leave it for the alien, the fatherless and the widow, so that the LORD your God may bless you in all the work of your hands. 20When you beat the olives from your trees, do not go over the branches a second time. Leave what remains for the alien, the fatherless and the widow. 21When you harvest the grapes in your vineyard, do not go over the vines again. Leave what remains for the alien, the fatherless and

the widow. 22Remember that you were slaves in Egypt. That is why I command you to do this.

25:1WHEN men have a dispute, they are to take it to court and the judges will decide the case, acquitting the innocent and condemning the guilty. 2If the guilty man deserves to be beaten, the judge shall make him lie down and have him flogged in his presence with the number of lashes his crime deserves, 3but he must not give him more than forty lashes. If he is flogged more than that, your brother will be degraded in your eyes.

4Do not muzzle an ox while it is treading out the grain.

5If brothers are living together and one of them dies without a son, his widow must not marry outside the family. Her husband's brother shall take her and marry her and fulfill the duty of a brother-in-law to her. 6The first son she bears shall carry on the name of the dead brother so that his name will not be blotted out from Israel.

7However, if a man does not want to marry his brother's wife, she shall go to the elders at the town gate and say, "My husband's brother refuses to carry on his brother's name in Israel. He will not fulfill the duty of a brother-in-law to me." 8Then the elders of his town shall summon him and talk to him. If he persists in saying, "I do not want to marry her," 9his brother's widow shall go up to him in the presence of the elders, take off one of his sandals, spit in his face and say, "This is what is done to the man who will not build up his brother's family line." 10That man's line shall be known in Israel as The Family of the Unsandaled.

11If two men are fighting and the wife of one of them comes to rescue her husband from his assailant, and she reaches out and seizes him by his private parts, 12you shall cut off her hand. Show her no pity.

13Do not have two differing weights in your bag—one heavy, one light. 14Do not have two differing measures in your house—one large, one small. 15 You must have accurate and honest weights and measures, so that you may live long in the land the LORD your God is giving you. 16 For the LORD your God detests anyone who does these things, anyone who deals dishonestly.

17 Remember what the Amalekites did to you along the way when you came out of Egypt. 18 When you were weary and worn out, they met you on your journey and cut off all who were lagging behind; they had no fear of God. 19 When the LORD your God gives you rest from all the enemies around you in the land he is giving you to possess as an inheritance, you shall blot out the memory of Amalek from under heaven. Do not forget!

a2 Or one of illegitimate birth b4 That is, Northwest Mesopotamia c18 Hebrew of a dog d8 The Hebrew word was used for various diseases affecting the skin—not necessarily leprosy.

LUKE 10:13-37

"Woe to you, Korazin! Woe to you, Bethsaida! For if the miracles that were performed in you had been performed in Tyre and Sidon, they would have repented long ago, sitting in sackcloth and ashes. 14 But it will be more bearable for Tyre and Sidon at the judgment than for you. 15 And you, Capernaum, will you be lifted up to the skies? No, you will go down to the depths.a

16 "He who listens to you listens to me; he who rejects you rejects me; but he who rejects me rejects him who sent me."

17 The seventy-two returned with joy and said, "Lord, even the demons submit to us in your name."

18 He replied, "I saw Satan fall like lightning from heaven. 19 I have given you authority to trample on snakes and scorpions and to overcome all the power of the enemy; nothing will harm you. 20 However, do not rejoice that the spirits submit to you, but rejoice that your names are written in heaven."

21 At that time Jesus, full of joy through the Holy Spirit, said, "I praise you, Father, Lord of heaven and earth, because you have hidden these things

from the wise and learned, and revealed them to little children. Yes, Father, for this was your good pleasure.

22 "All things have been committed to me by my Father. No one knows who the Son is except the Father, and no one knows who the Father is except the Son and those to whom the Son chooses to reveal him."

23 Then he turned to his disciples and said privately, "Blessed are the eyes that see what you see. 24 For I tell you that many prophets and kings wanted to see what you see but did not see it, and to hear what you hear but did not hear it."

25 On one occasion an expert in the law stood up to test Jesus. "Teacher," he asked, "what must I do to inherit eternal life?"

26 "What is written in the Law?" he replied. "How do you read it?"

27 He answered: " 'Love the Lord your God with all your heart and with all your soul and with all your strength and with all your mind'b; and, 'Love your neighbor as yourself.'c "

28 "You have answered correctly," Jesus replied. "Do this and you will live."

29 But he wanted to justify himself, so he asked Jesus, "And who is my neighbor?"

30 In reply Jesus said: "A man was going down from Jerusalem to Jericho, when he fell into the hands of robbers. They stripped him of his clothes, beat him and went away, leaving him half dead. 31 A priest happened to be going down the same road, and when he saw the man, he passed by on the other side. 32 So too, a Levite, when he came to the place and saw him, passed by on the other side. 33 But a Samaritan, as he traveled, came where the man was; and when he saw him, he took pity on him. 34 He went to him and bandaged his wounds, pouring on oil and wine. Then he put the man on his own donkey, took him to an inn and took care of him. 35 The next day he took out two silver coinsd and gave them to the innkeeper. 'Look after him,' he said, 'and when I

return, I will reimburse you for any extra expense you may have.'

36 "Which of these three do you think was a neighbor to the man who fell into the hands of robbers?"

37 The expert in the law replied, "The one who had mercy on him."

Jesus told him, "Go and do likewise."

a15 Greek *Hades* b27 Deut. 6:5 c27 Lev. 19:18
d35 Greek *two denarii*

PSALM 75:1-10

For the director of music. ⌐To the tune of⌐ "Do Not Destroy." A psalm of Asaph. A song.

1 **W**e give thanks to you, O God,
we give thanks, for your Name
is near;
men tell of your wonderful deeds.

2 You say, "I choose the appointed time;
it is I who judge uprightly.
3 When the earth and all its people
quake,
it is I who hold its pillars firm.
Selah

4 To the arrogant I say, 'Boast no more,'
and to the wicked, 'Do not lift up
your horns.
5 Do not lift your horns against heaven;
do not speak with outstretched
neck.'"

6 No one from the east or the west
or from the desert can exalt a man.
7 But it is God who judges:
He brings one down, he exalts
another.
8 In the hand of the LORD is a cup
full of foaming wine mixed with
spices;
he pours it out, and all the wicked
of the earth
drink it down to its very dregs.

9 As for me, I will declare this forever;
I will sing praise to the God of
Jacob.
10 I will cut off the horns of all the
wicked,
but the horns of the righteous will
be lifted up.

PROVERBS 12:12-14

12 **T**he wicked desire the plunder of evil
men,
but the root of the righteous
flourishes.

13 An evil man is trapped by his sinful
talk,
but a righteous man escapes trouble.

14 From the fruit of his lips a man is
filled with good things
as surely as the work of his hands
rewards him.

☐ D A Y 9 4

GOD SIGHTINGS

April 4

DEUTERONOMY 26:1–27:26

When you [Israel] have entered the land the LORD your God is giving you as an inheritance and have taken possession of it and settled in it, 2 take some of the firstfruits of all that you produce from the soil of the land the LORD your God is giving you and put them in a basket. Then go to the place the LORD your God will choose as a dwelling for his Name 3 and say to the priest in office at the time, "I declare today to the LORD your God that I have come to the land the LORD swore to our forefathers to give us." 4 The priest shall take the basket from your hands and set it down in front of the altar of the LORD your God. 5 Then you shall declare before the LORD your God: "My father was a wandering Aramean, and he went down into Egypt with a few people and lived there and became a great nation, powerful and numerous. 6 But the Egyptians mistreated us and made us suffer, putting us to hard labor. 7 Then we cried out to the LORD, the God of our fathers, and the LORD heard our voice and saw our misery, toil and oppression. 8 So the LORD brought us out of Egypt with a mighty hand and an outstretched arm, with great terror and with miraculous signs and wonders. [9]He brought us to this place and gave us this land, a land flowing with milk and honey; [10]and now I bring the firstfruits of the soil that you, O Lord, have given me." Place the basket before the Lord your God and bow down before him. [11]And you and the Levites and the aliens among you shall rejoice in all the good things the Lord your God has given to you and your household.

[12]When you have finished setting aside a tenth of all your produce in the third year, the year of the tithe, you shall give it to the Levite, the alien, the fatherless and the widow, so that they may eat in your towns and be satisfied. [13]Then say to the Lord your God: "I have removed from my house the sacred portion and have given it to the Levite, the alien, the fatherless and the widow, according to all you commanded. I have not turned aside from your commands nor have I forgotten any of them. [14]I have not eaten any of the sacred portion while I was in mourning, nor have I removed any of it while I was unclean, nor have I offered any of it to the dead. I have obeyed the Lord my God; I have done everything you commanded me. [15]Look down from heaven, your holy dwelling place, and bless your people Israel and the land you have given us as you promised on oath to our forefathers, a land flowing with milk and honey."

[16]The Lord your God commands you this day to follow these decrees and laws; carefully observe them with all your heart and with all your soul. [17]You have declared this day that the Lord is your God and that you will walk in his ways, that you will keep his decrees, commands and laws, and that you will obey him. [18]And the Lord has declared this day that you are his people, his treasured possession as he promised, and that you are to keep all his commands. [19]He has declared that he will set you in praise, fame and honor high above all the nations he has made and that you will be a people holy to the Lord your God, as he promised.

[27:1]Moses and the elders of Israel commanded the people: "Keep all these commands that I give you today. [2]When you have crossed the Jordan into the land the Lord your God is giving you, set up some large stones and coat them with plaster. [3]Write on them all the words of this law when you have crossed over to enter the land the Lord your God is giving you, a land flowing with milk and honey, just as the Lord, the God of your fathers, promised you. [4]And when you have crossed the Jordan, set up these stones on Mount Ebal, as I command you today, and coat them with plaster. [5]Build there an altar to the Lord your God, an altar of stones. Do not use any iron tool upon them. [6]Build the altar of the Lord your God with fieldstones and offer burnt offerings on it to the Lord your God. [7]Sacrifice fellowship offerings[a] there, eating them and rejoicing in the presence of the Lord your God. [8]And you shall write very clearly all the words of this law on these stones you have set up."

[9]Then Moses and the priests, who are Levites, said to all Israel, "Be silent, O Israel, and listen! You have now become the people of the Lord your God. [10]Obey the Lord your God and follow his commands and decrees that I give you today."

[11]On the same day Moses commanded the people:

[12]When you have crossed the Jordan, these tribes shall stand on Mount Gerizim to bless the people: Simeon, Levi, Judah, Issachar, Joseph and Benjamin. [13]And these tribes shall stand on Mount Ebal to pronounce curses: Reuben, Gad, Asher, Zebulun, Dan and Naphtali.

[14]The Levites shall recite to all the people of Israel in a loud voice:

[15]"Cursed is the man who carves an image or casts an idol—a thing detestable to the Lord, the work of the craftsman's hands—and sets it up in secret."

Then all the people shall say, "Amen!"

16"Cursed is the man who dishonors his father or his mother."

Then all the people shall say, "Amen!"

17"Cursed is the man who moves his neighbor's boundary stone."

Then all the people shall say, "Amen!"

18"Cursed is the man who leads the blind astray on the road."

Then all the people shall say, "Amen!"

19"Cursed is the man who withholds justice from the alien, the fatherless or the widow."

Then all the people shall say, "Amen!"

20"Cursed is the man who sleeps with his father's wife, for he dishonors his father's bed."

Then all the people shall say, "Amen!"

21"Cursed is the man who has sexual relations with any animal."

Then all the people shall say, "Amen!"

22"Cursed is the man who sleeps with his sister, the daughter of his father or the daughter of his mother."

Then all the people shall say, "Amen!"

23"Cursed is the man who sleeps with his mother-in-law."

Then all the people shall say, "Amen!"

24"Cursed is the man who kills his neighbor secretly."

Then all the people shall say, "Amen!"

25"Cursed is the man who accepts a bribe to kill an innocent person."

Then all the people shall say, "Amen!"

26"Cursed is the man who does not uphold the words of this law by carrying them out."

Then all the people shall say, "Amen!"

a 7 Traditionally *peace offerings*

LUKE 10:38–11:13

As Jesus and his disciples were on their way, he came to a village where a woman named Martha opened her home to him. 39She had a sister called Mary, who sat at the Lord's feet listening to what he said. 40But Martha was distracted by all the preparations that had to be made. She came to him and asked, "Lord, don't you care that my sister has left me to do the work by myself ? Tell her to help me!"

41"Martha, Martha," the Lord answered, "you are worried and upset about many things, 42but only one thing is needed.a Mary has chosen what is better, and it will not be taken away from her."

11:1ONE day Jesus was praying in a certain place. When he finished, one of his disciples said to him, "Lord, teach us to pray, just as John taught his disciples."

2He said to them, "When you pray, say:

"'Father,b
hallowed be your name,
your kingdom come.c
3Give us each day our daily bread.
4Forgive us our sins,
    for we also forgive everyone who
        sins against us.d
And lead us not into temptation.e'"

5Then he said to them, "Suppose one of you has a friend, and he goes to him at midnight and says, 'Friend, lend me three loaves of bread, 6because a friend of mine on a journey has come to me, and I have nothing to set before him.'

7"Then the one inside answers, 'Don't bother me. The door is already locked, and my children are with me in bed. I can't get up and give you anything.' 8I tell you, though he will not get up and give him the bread because he is his friend, yet because of the man's boldnessf he will get up and give him as much as he needs.

9**"So I say to you: Ask and it will be given to you; seek and you will find; knock and the door will be opened to** you. ¹⁰**For everyone who asks receives; he who seeks finds; and to him who knocks, the door will be opened.**

¹¹"Which of you fathers, if your son asks for*ᵍ* a fish, will give him a snake instead? ¹²Or if he asks for an egg, will give him a scorpion? ¹³If you then, though you are evil, know how to give good gifts to your children, how much more will your Father in heaven give the Holy Spirit to those who ask him!"

a42 Some manuscripts but few things are needed—or only one   b2 Some manuscripts Our Father in heaven   c2 Some manuscripts come. May your will be done on earth as it is in heaven.   d4 Greek everyone who is indebted to us   e4 Some manuscripts temptation but deliver us from the evil one   f8 Or persistence   g11 Some manuscripts for bread, will give him a stone; or if he asks for

PSALM 76:1-12
For the director of music. With stringed instruments. A psalm of Asaph. A song.

¹ In Judah God is known;
   his name is great in Israel.
² His tent is in Salem,
   his dwelling place in Zion.
³ There he broke the flashing arrows,
   the shields and the swords, the
      weapons of war.   *Selah*

⁴ You are resplendent with light,
   more majestic than mountains
      rich with game.
⁵ Valiant men lie plundered,
   they sleep their last sleep;
not one of the warriors
   can lift his hands.
⁶ At your rebuke, O God of Jacob,
   both horse and chariot lie still.
⁷ You alone are to be feared.
   Who can stand before you when
      you are angry?
⁸ From heaven you pronounced
      judgment,
   and the land feared and was
      quiet—
⁹ when you, O God, rose up to judge,
   to save all the afflicted of the land.
                                 Selah
¹⁰ Surely your wrath against men brings
      you praise,
   and the survivors of your wrath are
      restrained.*ᵃ*

¹¹ Make vows to the Lᴏʀᴅ your God and
      fulfill them;
   let all the neighboring lands
      bring gifts to the One to
      be feared.
¹² He breaks the spirit of rulers;
   he is feared by the kings of the
      earth.

a10 Or Surely the wrath of men brings you praise, / and with the remainder of wrath you arm yourself

PROVERBS 12:15-17
¹⁵ The way of a fool seems right to him,
   but a wise man listens to advice.

¹⁶ A fool shows his annoyance at once,
   but a prudent man overlooks an
      insult.

¹⁷ A truthful witness gives honest
      testimony,
   but a false witness tells lies.

□ D A Y 9 5

GOD SIGHTINGS

April 5

DEUTERONOMY 28:1-68
If you [Israel] fully obey the Lᴏʀᴅ your God and carefully follow all his commands I give you today, the Lᴏʀᴅ your God will set you high above all the nations on earth. ²All these blessings will come upon you and accompany you if you obey the Lᴏʀᴅ your God:

³ You will be blessed in the city and blessed in the country.

⁴ The fruit of your womb will be blessed, and the crops of your land and the young of your livestock— the calves of your herds and the lambs of your flocks.

⁵ Your basket and your kneading trough will be blessed.

⁶ You will be blessed when you come in and blessed when you go out.

⁷The Lord will grant that the enemies who rise up against you will be defeated before you. They will come at you from one direction but flee from you in seven.

⁸The Lord will send a blessing on your barns and on everything you put your hand to. The Lord your God will bless you in the land he is giving you.

⁹The Lord will establish you as his holy people, as he promised you on oath, if you keep the commands of the Lord your God and walk in his ways. ¹⁰Then all the peoples on earth will see that you are called by the name of the Lord, and they will fear you. ¹¹The Lord will grant you abundant prosperity—in the fruit of your womb, the young of your livestock and the crops of your ground—in the land he swore to your forefathers to give you.

¹²The Lord will open the heavens, the storehouse of his bounty, to send rain on your land in season and to bless all the work of your hands. You will lend to many nations but will borrow from none. ¹³The Lord will make you the head, not the tail. If you pay attention to the commands of the Lord your God that I give you this day and carefully follow them, you will always be at the top, never at the bottom. ¹⁴Do not turn aside from any of the commands I give you today, to the right or to the left, following other gods and serving them.

¹⁵However, if you do not obey the Lord your God and do not carefully follow all his commands and decrees I am giving you today, all these curses will come upon you and overtake you:

¹⁶You will be cursed in the city and cursed in the country.

¹⁷Your basket and your kneading trough will be cursed.

¹⁸The fruit of your womb will be cursed, and the crops of your land, and the calves of your herds and the lambs of your flocks.

¹⁹You will be cursed when you come in and cursed when you go out.

²⁰The Lord will send on you curses, confusion and rebuke in everything you put your hand to, until you are destroyed and come to sudden ruin because of the evil you have done in forsaking him.ᵃ ²¹The Lord will plague you with diseases until he has destroyed you from the land you are entering to possess. ²²The Lord will strike you with wasting disease, with fever and inflammation, with scorching heat and drought, with blight and mildew, which will plague you until you perish. ²³The sky over your head will be bronze, the ground beneath you iron. ²⁴The Lord will turn the rain of your country into dust and powder; it will come down from the skies until you are destroyed.

²⁵The Lord will cause you to be defeated before your enemies. You will come at them from one direction but flee from them in seven, and you will become a thing of horror to all the kingdoms on earth. ²⁶Your carcasses will be food for all the birds of the air and the beasts of the earth, and there will be no one to frighten them away. ²⁷The Lord will afflict you with the boils of Egypt and with tumors, festering sores and the itch, from which you cannot be cured. ²⁸The Lord will afflict you with madness, blindness and confusion of mind. ²⁹At midday you will grope about like a blind man in the dark. You will be unsuccessful in everything you do; day after day you will be oppressed and robbed, with no one to rescue you.

³⁰You will be pledged to be married to a woman, but another will take her and ravish her. You will build a house, but you will not live in it. You will plant a vineyard, but you will not even begin to enjoy its fruit. ³¹Your ox will be slaughtered before your eyes, but you will eat none of it. Your donkey will be forcibly taken from you and will not be returned. Your sheep will be given to your enemies, and no one will rescue them. ³²Your sons and daughters will be given to another nation, and you will wear out your eyes watching for them day after day, powerless to lift a hand. ³³A people that you do not know will eat what your land and labor produce, and you will

have nothing but cruel oppression all your days. ³⁴The sights you see will drive you mad. ³⁵The Lord will afflict your knees and legs with painful boils that cannot be cured, spreading from the soles of your feet to the top of your head.

³⁶The Lord will drive you and the king you set over you to a nation unknown to you or your fathers. There you will worship other gods, gods of wood and stone. ³⁷You will become a thing of horror and an object of scorn and ridicule to all the nations where the Lord will drive you.

³⁸You will sow much seed in the field but you will harvest little, because locusts will devour it. ³⁹You will plant vineyards and cultivate them but you will not drink the wine or gather the grapes, because worms will eat them. ⁴⁰You will have olive trees throughout your country but you will not use the oil, because the olives will drop off. ⁴¹You will have sons and daughters but you will not keep them, because they will go into captivity. ⁴²Swarms of locusts will take over all your trees and the crops of your land.

⁴³The alien who lives among you will rise above you higher and higher, but you will sink lower and lower. ⁴⁴He will lend to you, but you will not lend to him. He will be the head, but you will be the tail.

⁴⁵All these curses will come upon you. They will pursue you and overtake you until you are destroyed, because you did not obey the Lord your God and observe the commands and decrees he gave you. ⁴⁶They will be a sign and a wonder to you and your descendants forever. ⁴⁷Because you did not serve the Lord your God joyfully and gladly in the time of prosperity, ⁴⁸therefore in hunger and thirst, in nakedness and dire poverty, you will serve the enemies the Lord sends against you. He will put an iron yoke on your neck until he has destroyed you.

⁴⁹The Lord will bring a nation against you from far away, from the ends of the earth, like an eagle swooping down, a na-

tion whose language you will not understand, ⁵⁰a fierce-looking nation without respect for the old or pity for the young. ⁵¹They will devour the young of your livestock and the crops of your land until you are destroyed. They will leave you no grain, new wine or oil, nor any calves of your herds or lambs of your flocks until you are ruined. ⁵²They will lay siege to all the cities throughout your land until the high fortified walls in which you trust fall down. They will besiege all the cities throughout the land the Lord your God is giving you.

⁵³Because of the suffering that your enemy will inflict on you during the siege, you will eat the fruit of the womb, the flesh of the sons and daughters the Lord your God has given you. ⁵⁴Even the most gentle and sensitive man among you will have no compassion on his own brother or the wife he loves or his surviving children, ⁵⁵and he will not give to one of them any of the flesh of his children that he is eating. It will be all he has left because of the suffering your enemy will inflict on you during the siege of all your cities. ⁵⁶The most gentle and sensitive woman among you—so sensitive and gentle that she would not venture to touch the ground with the sole of her foot—will begrudge the husband she loves and her own son or daughter ⁵⁷the afterbirth from her womb and the children she bears. For she intends to eat them secretly during the siege and in the distress that your enemy will inflict on you in your cities.

⁵⁸If you do not carefully follow all the words of this law, which are written in this book, and do not revere this glorious and awesome name—the Lord your God— ⁵⁹the Lord will send fearful plagues on you and your descendants, harsh and prolonged disasters, and severe and lingering illnesses. ⁶⁰He will bring upon you all the diseases of Egypt that you dreaded, and they will cling to you. ⁶¹The Lord will also bring on you every kind of sickness and disaster not recorded in this Book of the Law, until you are destroyed. ⁶²You who were as

numerous as the stars in the sky will be left but few in number, because you did not obey the LORD your God. 63 Just as it pleased the LORD to make you prosper and increase in number, so it will please him to ruin and destroy you. You will be uprooted from the land you are entering to possess.

64 Then the LORD will scatter you among all nations, from one end of the earth to the other. There you will worship other gods—gods of wood and stone, which neither you nor your fathers have known. 65 Among those nations you will find no repose, no resting place for the sole of your foot. There the LORD will give you an anxious mind, eyes weary with longing, and a despairing heart. 66 You will live in constant suspense, filled with dread both night and day, never sure of your life. 67 In the morning you will say, "If only it were evening!" and in the evening, "If only it were morning!"—because of the terror that will fill your hearts and the sights that your eyes will see. 68 The LORD will send you back in ships to Egypt on a journey I said you should never make again. There you will offer yourselves for sale to your enemies as male and female slaves, but no one will buy you.

a 20 Hebrew me

LUKE 11:14-36

Jesus was driving out a demon that was mute. When the demon left, the man who had been mute spoke, and the crowd was amazed. 15 But some of them said, "By Beelzebub,a the prince of demons, he is driving out demons." 16 Others tested him by asking for a sign from heaven.

17 Jesus knew their thoughts and said to them: "Any kingdom divided against itself will be ruined, and a house divided against itself will fall. 18 If Satan is divided against himself, how can his kingdom stand? I say this because you claim that I drive out demons by Beelzebub. 19 Now if I drive out demons by Beelzebub, by whom do your followers drive them out? So then, they will be your

judges. 20 But if I drive out demons by the finger of God, then the kingdom of God has come to you.

21 "When a strong man, fully armed, guards his own house, his possessions are safe. 22 But when someone stronger attacks and overpowers him, he takes away the armor in which the man trusted and divides up the spoils.

23 "He who is not with me is against me, and he who does not gather with me, scatters.

24 "When an evilb spirit comes out of a man, it goes through arid places seeking rest and does not find it. Then it says, 'I will return to the house I left.' 25 When it arrives, it finds the house swept clean and put in order. 26 Then it goes and takes seven other spirits more wicked than itself, and they go in and live there. And the final condition of that man is worse than the first."

27 As Jesus was saying these things, a woman in the crowd called out, "Blessed is the mother who gave you birth and nursed you."

28 He replied, "Blessed rather are those who hear the word of God and obey it."

29 As the crowds increased, Jesus said, "This is a wicked generation. It asks for a miraculous sign, but none will be given it except the sign of Jonah. 30 For as Jonah was a sign to the Ninevites, so also will the Son of Man be to this generation. 31 The Queen of the South will rise at the judgment with the men of this generation and condemn them; for she came from the ends of the earth to listen to Solomon's wisdom, and now onec greater than Solomon is here. 32 The men of Nineveh will stand up at the judgment with this generation and condemn it; for they repented at the preaching of Jonah, and now one greater than Jonah is here.

33 "No one lights a lamp and puts it in a place where it will be hidden, or under a bowl. Instead he puts it on its stand, so that those who come in may see the light. 34 Your eye is the lamp of your body. When your eyes are good, your

whole body also is full of light. But when they are bad, your body also is full of darkness. [35] See to it, then, that the light within you is not darkness. [36] Therefore, if your whole body is full of light, and no part of it dark, it will be completely lighted, as when the light of a lamp shines on you."

a15 Greek *Beezeboul* or *Beelzeboul*; also in verses 18 and 19.
b24 Greek *unclean*   *c31* Or *something*; also in verse 32

PSALM 77:1-20

For the director of music. For Jeduthun. Of Asaph. A psalm.

[1] I cried out to God for help;
   I cried out to God to hear me.
[2] When I was in distress, I sought the Lord;
   at night I stretched out untiring hands
   and my soul refused to be comforted.

[3] I remembered you, O God, and I groaned;
   I mused, and my spirit grew faint.   *Selah*
[4] You kept my eyes from closing;
   I was too troubled to speak.
[5] I thought about the former days,
   the years of long ago;
[6] I remembered my songs in the night.
   My heart mused and my spirit inquired:

[7] "Will the Lord reject forever?
   Will he never show his favor again?
[8] Has his unfailing love vanished forever?
   Has his promise failed for all time?
[9] Has God forgotten to be merciful?
   Has he in anger withheld his compassion?"   *Selah*

[10] Then I thought, "To this I will appeal:
   the years of the right hand of the Most High."
[11] I will remember the deeds of the Lord;
   yes, I will remember your miracles of long ago.
[12] I will meditate on all your works

and consider all your mighty deeds.

[13] Your ways, O God, are holy.
   What god is so great as our God?
[14] You are the God who performs miracles;
   you display your power among the peoples.
[15] With your mighty arm you redeemed your people,
   the descendants of Jacob and Joseph.   *Selah*

[16] The waters saw you, O God,
   the waters saw you and writhed;
   the very depths were convulsed.
[17] The clouds poured down water,
   the skies resounded with thunder;
   your arrows flashed back and forth.
[18] Your thunder was heard in the whirlwind,
   your lightning lit up the world;
   the earth trembled and quaked.
[19] Your path led through the sea,
   your way through the mighty waters,
   though your footprints were not seen.

[20] You led your people like a flock
   by the hand of Moses and Aaron.

PROVERBS 12:18

[18] Reckless words pierce like a sword,
   but the tongue of the wise brings healing.

☐ DAY 96

GOD SIGHTINGS

April 6

DEUTERONOMY 29:1–30:20

These are the terms of the covenant the LORD commanded Moses to make with the Israelites in Moab, in addition to the covenant he had made with them at Horeb.

²Moses summoned all the Israelites and said to them:

Your eyes have seen all that the Lord did in Egypt to Pharoah, to all his officials and to all his land. ³With your own eyes you saw those great trials, those miraculous signs and great wonders. ⁴But to this day the Lord has not given you a mind that understands or eyes that see or ears that hear. ⁵During the forty years that I led you through the desert, your clothes did not wear out, nor did the sandals on your feet. ⁶You ate no bread and drank no wine or other fermented drink. I did this so that you might know that I am the Lord your God.

⁷When you reached this place, Sihon king of Heshbon and Og king of Bashan came out to fight against us, but we defeated them. ⁸We took their land and gave it as an inheritance to the Reubenites, the Gadites and the half-tribe of Manasseh.

⁹Carefully follow the terms of this covenant, so that you may prosper in everything you do. ¹⁰All of you are standing today in the presence of the Lord your God—your leaders and chief men, your elders and officials, and all the other men of Israel, ¹¹together with your children and your wives, and the aliens living in your camps who chop your wood and carry your water. ¹²You are standing here in order to enter into a covenant with the Lord your God, a covenant the Lord is making with you this day and sealing with an oath, ¹³to confirm you this day as his people, that he may be your God as he promised you and as he swore to your fathers, Abraham, Isaac and Jacob. ¹⁴I am making this covenant, with its oath, not only with you ¹⁵who are standing here with us today in the presence of the Lord our God but also with those who are not here today.

¹⁶You yourselves know how we lived in Egypt and how we passed through the countries on the way here. ¹⁷You saw among them their detestable images and idols of wood and stone, of silver and gold. ¹⁸Make sure there is no man or woman, clan or tribe among you today whose heart turns away from the Lord our God to go and worship the gods of those nations; make sure there is no root among you that produces such bitter poison.

¹⁹When such a person hears the words of this oath, he invokes a blessing on himself and therefore thinks, "I will be safe, even though I persist in going my own way." This will bring disaster on the watered land as well as the dry.ᵃ ²⁰The Lord will never be willing to forgive him; his wrath and zeal will burn against that man. All the curses written in this book will fall upon him, and the Lord will blot out his name from under heaven. ²¹The Lord will single him out from all the tribes of Israel for disaster, according to all the curses of the covenant written in this Book of the Law.

²²Your children who follow you in later generations and foreigners who come from distant lands will see the calamities that have fallen on the land and the diseases with which the Lord has afflicted it. ²³The whole land will be a burning waste of salt and sulfur—nothing planted, nothing sprouting, no vegetation growing on it. It will be like the destruction of Sodom and Gomorrah, Admah and Zeboiim, which the Lord overthrew in fierce anger. ²⁴All the nations will ask: "Why has the Lord done this to this land? Why this fierce, burning anger?"

²⁵And the answer will be: "It is because this people abandoned the covenant of the Lord, the God of their fathers, the covenant he made with them when he brought them out of Egypt. ²⁶They went off and worshiped other gods and bowed down to them, gods they did not know, gods he had not given them. ²⁷Therefore the Lord's anger burned against this land, so that he brought on it all the curses written in this book. ²⁸In furious anger and in great wrath the Lord uprooted them from their land and thrust them into another land, as it is now."

²⁹The secret things belong to the Lord

our God, but the things revealed belong to us and to our children forever, that we may follow all the words of this law.

30:1 When all these blessings and curses I have set before you come upon you and you take them to heart wherever the Lord your God disperses you among the nations, 2 and when you and your children return to the Lord your God and obey him with all your heart and with all your soul according to everything I command you today, 3 then the Lord your God will restore your fortunes[b] and have compassion on you and gather you again from all the nations where he scattered you. 4 Even if you have been banished to the most distant land under the heavens, from there the Lord your God will gather you and bring you back. 5 He will bring you to the land that belonged to your fathers, and you will take possession of it. He will make you more prosperous and numerous than your fathers. 6 The Lord your God will circumcise your hearts and the hearts of your descendants, so that you may love him with all your heart and with all your soul, and live. 7 The Lord your God will put all these curses on your enemies who hate and persecute you. 8 You will again obey the Lord and follow all his commands I am giving you today. 9 Then the Lord your God will make you most prosperous in all the work of your hands and in the fruit of your womb, the young of your livestock and the crops of your land. The Lord will again delight in you and make you prosperous, just as he delighted in your fathers, 10 if you obey the Lord your God and keep his commands and decrees that are written in this Book of the Law and turn to the Lord your God with all your heart and with all your soul.

11 Now what I am commanding you today is not too difficult for you or beyond your reach. 12 It is not up in heaven, so that you have to ask, "Who will ascend into heaven to get it and proclaim it to us so we may obey it?" 13 Nor is it beyond the sea, so that you have to ask,

"Who will cross the sea to get it and proclaim it to us so we may obey it?" 14 No, the word is very near you; it is in your mouth and in your heart so you may obey it.

15 See, I set before you today life and prosperity, death and destruction. 16 For I command you today to love the Lord your God, to walk in his ways, and to keep his commands, decrees and laws; then you will live and increase, and the Lord your God will bless you in the land you are entering to possess.

17 But if your heart turns away and you are not obedient, and if you are drawn away to bow down to other gods and worship them, 18 I declare to you this day that you will certainly be destroyed. You will not live long in the land you are crossing the Jordan to enter and possess.

19 **This day I call heaven and earth as witnesses against you that I have set before you life and death, blessings and curses. Now choose life, so that you and your children may live 20 and that you may love the Lord your God, listen to his voice, and hold fast to him. For the Lord is your life, and he will give you many years in the land he swore to give to your fathers, Abraham, Isaac and Jacob.**

a 19 Or way, in order to add drunkenness to thirst."
b 3 Or will bring you back from captivity

LUKE 11:37–12:7

When Jesus had finished speaking, a Pharisee invited him to eat with him; so he went in and reclined at the table. 38 But the Pharisee, noticing that Jesus did not first wash before the meal, was surprised.

39 Then the Lord said to him, "Now then, you Pharisees clean the outside of the cup and dish, but inside you are full of greed and wickedness. 40 You foolish people! Did not the one who made the outside make the inside also? 41 But give what is inside ⌜the dish⌝[a] to the poor, and everything will be clean for you.

42 "Woe to you Pharisees, because you give God a tenth of your mint, rue

and all other kinds of garden herbs, but you neglect justice and the love of God. You should have practiced the latter without leaving the former undone.

43 "Woe to you Pharisees, because you love the most important seats in the synagogues and greetings in the marketplaces.

44 "Woe to you, because you are like unmarked graves, which men walk over without knowing it."

45 One of the experts in the law answered him, "Teacher, when you say these things, you insult us also."

46 Jesus replied, "And you experts in the law, woe to you, because you load people down with burdens they can hardly carry, and you yourselves will not lift one finger to help them.

47 "Woe to you, because you build tombs for the prophets, and it was your forefathers who killed them. 48 So you testify that you approve of what your forefathers did; they killed the prophets, and you build their tombs. 49 Because of this, God in his wisdom said, 'I will send them prophets and apostles, some of whom they will kill and others they will persecute.' 50 Therefore this generation will be held responsible for the blood of all the prophets that has been shed since the beginning of the world, 51 from the blood of Abel to the blood of Zechariah, who was killed between the altar and the sanctuary. Yes, I tell you, this generation will be held responsible for it all.

52 "Woe to you experts in the law, because you have taken away the key to knowledge. You yourselves have not entered, and you have hindered those who were entering."

53 When Jesus left there, the Pharisees and the teachers of the law began to oppose him fiercely and to besiege him with questions, 54 waiting to catch him in something he might say.

12:1 MEANWHILE, when a crowd of many thousands had gathered, so that they were trampling on one another, Jesus began to speak first to his disciples, saying: "Be on your guard against the yeast of the Pharisees, which is hypocrisy. 2 There is nothing concealed that will not be disclosed, or hidden that will not be made known. 3 What you have said in the dark will be heard in the daylight, and what you have whispered in the ear in the inner rooms will be proclaimed from the roofs.

4 "I tell you, my friends, do not be afraid of those who kill the body and after that can do no more. 5 But I will show you whom you should fear: Fear him who, after the killing of the body, has power to throw you into hell. Yes, I tell you, fear him. 6 Are not five sparrows sold for two pennies b? Yet not one of them is forgotten by God. 7 Indeed, the very hairs of your head are all numbered. Don't be afraid; you are worth more than many sparrows."

a 41 Or *what you have*   b 6 Greek *two assaria*

PSALM 78:1-31

A *maskil* a of Asaph.

1 **O** my people, hear my teaching;
  listen to the words of my mouth.
2 I will open my mouth in parables,
  I will utter hidden things, things
    from of old—
3 what we have heard and known,
  what our fathers have told us.
4 We will not hide them from their
    children;
  we will tell the next generation
the praiseworthy deeds of the LORD,
  his power, and the wonders he
    has done.
5 He decreed statutes for Jacob
  and established the law in Israel,
which he commanded our
    forefathers
  to teach their children,
6 so the next generation would know
    them,
  even the children yet to be born,
  and they in turn would tell their
    children.
7 Then they would put their trust in
    God
  and would not forget his deeds
  but would keep his commands.

8 They would not be like their
    forefathers—
  a stubborn and rebellious
    generation,
  whose hearts were not loyal to God,
  whose spirits were not faithful
    to him.

9 The men of Ephraim, though armed
    with bows,
  turned back on the day of battle;
10 they did not keep God's covenant
  and refused to live by his law.
11 They forgot what he had done,
  the wonders he had shown them.
12 He did miracles in the sight of their
    fathers
  in the land of Egypt, in the region
    of Zoan.
13 He divided the sea and led them
    through;
  he made the water stand firm like
    a wall.
14 He guided them with the cloud
    by day
  and with light from the fire all
    night.
15 He split the rocks in the desert
  and gave them water as abundant
    as the seas;
16 he brought streams out of a rocky
    crag
  and made water flow down like
    rivers.

17 But they continued to sin against
    him,
  rebelling in the desert against the
    Most High.
18 They willfully put God to the test
  by demanding the food they
    craved.
19 They spoke against God, saying,
  "Can God spread a table in the
    desert?
20 When he struck the rock, water
    gushed out,
  and streams flowed abundantly.
  But can he also give us food?
  Can he supply meat for his
    people?"

21 When the LORD heard them, he was
    very angry;
  his fire broke out against Jacob,
  and his wrath rose against Israel,
22 for they did not believe in God
  or trust in his deliverance.
23 Yet he gave a command to the skies
    above
  and opened the doors of the
    heavens;
24 he rained down manna for the
    people to eat,
  he gave them the grain of heaven.
25 Men ate the bread of angels;
  he sent them all the food they
    could eat.
26 He let loose the east wind from the
    heavens
  and led forth the south wind by his
    power.
27 He rained meat down on them like
    dust,
  flying birds like sand on the
    seashore.
28 He made them come down inside
    their camp,
  all around their tents.
29 They ate till they had more than
    enough,
  for he had given them what they
    craved.
30 But before they turned from the food
    they craved,
  even while it was still in their
    mouths,
31 God's anger rose against them;
  he put to death the sturdiest
    among them,
  cutting down the young men of
    Israel.

aTitle: Probably a literary or musical term

PROVERBS 12:19-20
19 Truthful lips endure forever,
  but a lying tongue lasts only a
    moment.

20 There is deceit in the hearts of those
    who plot evil,
  but joy for those who promote
    peace.

☐ DAY 97

GOD SIGHTINGS

April 7

DEUTERONOMY 31:1–32:27

Then Moses went out and spoke these words to all Israel: ²"I am now a hundred and twenty years old and I am no longer able to lead you. The LORD has said to me, 'You shall not cross the Jordan.' ³The LORD your God himself will cross over ahead of you. He will destroy these nations before you, and you will take possession of their land. Joshua also will cross over ahead of you, as the LORD said. ⁴And the LORD will do to them what he did to Sihon and Og, the kings of the Amorites, whom he destroyed along with their land. ⁵The LORD will deliver them to you, and you must do to them all that I have commanded you. ⁶Be strong and courageous. Do not be afraid or terrified because of them, for the LORD your God goes with you; he will never leave you nor forsake you."

⁷Then Moses summoned Joshua and said to him in the presence of all Israel, "Be strong and courageous, for you must go with this people into the land that the LORD swore to their forefathers to give them, and you must divide it among them as their inheritance. ⁸The LORD himself goes before you and will be with you; he will never leave you nor forsake you. Do not be afraid; do not be discouraged."

⁹So Moses wrote down this law and gave it to the priests, the sons of Levi, who carried the ark of the covenant of the LORD, and to all the elders of Israel. ¹⁰Then Moses commanded them: "At the end of every seven years, in the year for canceling debts, during the Feast of Tabernacles, ¹¹when all Israel comes to appear before the LORD your God at the place he will choose, you shall read this law before them in their hearing. ¹²Assemble the people—men, women and children, and the aliens living in your towns—so they can listen and learn to fear the LORD your God and follow carefully all the words of this law. ¹³Their children, who do not know this law, must hear it and learn to fear the LORD your God as long as you live in the land you are crossing the Jordan to possess."

¹⁴The LORD said to Moses, "Now the day of your death is near. Call Joshua and present yourselves at the Tent of Meeting, where I will commission him." So Moses and Joshua came and presented themselves at the Tent of Meeting.

¹⁵Then the LORD appeared at the Tent in a pillar of cloud, and the cloud stood over the entrance to the Tent. ¹⁶And the LORD said to Moses: "You are going to rest with your fathers, and these people will soon prostitute themselves to the foreign gods of the land they are entering. They will forsake me and break the covenant I made with them. ¹⁷On that day I will become angry with them and forsake them; I will hide my face from them, and they will be destroyed. Many disasters and difficulties will come upon them, and on that day they will ask, 'Have not these disasters come upon us because our God is not with us?' ¹⁸And I will certainly hide my face on that day because of all their wickedness in turning to other gods.

¹⁹"Now write down for yourselves this song and teach it to the Israelites and have them sing it, so that it may be a witness for me against them. ²⁰When I have brought them into the land flowing with milk and honey, the land I promised on oath to their forefathers, and when they eat their fill and thrive, they will turn to other gods and worship them, rejecting me and breaking my covenant. ²¹And when many disasters and difficulties come upon them, this song will testify against them, because it will not be forgotten by their descendants. I know what they are disposed to do, even before I bring them into the land I promised them on oath." ²²So Moses wrote down this song that day and taught it to the Israelites.

23 The LORD gave this command to Joshua son of Nun: "Be strong and courageous, for you will bring the Israelites into the land I promised them on oath, and I myself will be with you."

24 After Moses finished writing in a book the words of this law from beginning to end, 25 he gave this command to the Levites who carried the ark of the covenant of the LORD: 26 "Take this Book of the Law and place it beside the ark of the covenant of the LORD your God. There it will remain as a witness against you. 27 For I know how rebellious and stiff-necked you are. If you have been rebellious against the LORD while I am still alive and with you, how much more will you rebel after I die! 28 Assemble before me all the elders of your tribes and all your officials, so that I can speak these words in their hearing and call heaven and earth to testify against them. 29 For I know that after my death you are sure to become utterly corrupt and to turn from the way I have commanded you. In days to come, disaster will fall upon you because you will do evil in the sight of the LORD and provoke him to anger by what your hands have made."

30 And Moses recited the words of this song from beginning to end in the hearing of the whole assembly of Israel:

32:1 LISTEN, O heavens, and I will speak;
    hear, O earth, the words of my
        mouth.
2 Let my teaching fall like rain
    and my words descend like dew,
  like showers on new grass,
    like abundant rain on tender
        plants.

3 I will proclaim the name of the LORD.
    Oh, praise the greatness of our
        God!
4 He is the Rock, his works are
        perfect,
    and all his ways are just.
  A faithful God who does no wrong,
    upright and just is he.

5 They have acted corruptly toward
        him;
    to their shame they are no longer
        his children,
    but a warped and crooked
        generation.*a*
6 Is this the way you repay the LORD,
    O foolish and unwise people?
  Is he not your Father, your Creator,*b*
    who made you and formed you?

7 Remember the days of old;
    consider the generations long
        past.
  Ask your father and he will tell you,
    your elders, and they will explain
        to you.
8 When the Most High gave the
        nations their inheritance,
    when he divided all mankind,
  he set up boundaries for the peoples
    according to the number of the
        sons of Israel.*c*
9 For the LORD's portion is his people,
    Jacob his allotted inheritance.

10 In a desert land he found him,
    in a barren and howling waste.
  He shielded him and cared for him;
    he guarded him as the apple of his
        eye,
11 like an eagle that stirs up its nest
    and hovers over its young,
  that spreads its wings to catch them
    and carries them on its pinions.
12 The LORD alone led him;
    no foreign god was with him.

13 He made him ride on the heights of
        the land
    and fed him with the fruit of the
        fields.
  He nourished him with honey from
        the rock,
    and with oil from the flinty crag,
14 with curds and milk from herd and
        flock
    and with fattened lambs and goats,
  with choice rams of Bashan
    and the finest kernels of wheat.
  You drank the foaming blood of the
        grape.

15 Jeshurun*d* grew fat and kicked;
    filled with food, he became heavy
        and sleek.
He abandoned the God who made
    him
    and rejected the Rock his Savior.
16 They made him jealous with their
        foreign gods
    and angered him with their
        detestable idols.
17 They sacrificed to demons, which are
        not God—
    gods they had not known,
    gods that recently appeared,
    gods your fathers did not fear.
18 You deserted the Rock, who fathered
        you;
    you forgot the God who gave you
        birth.

19 The LORD saw this and rejected them
    because he was angered by his
        sons and daughters.
20 "I will hide my face from them,"
    he said,
    "and see what their end will be;
for they are a perverse generation,
    children who are unfaithful.
21 They made me jealous by what is
        no god
    and angered me with their
        worthless idols.
I will make them envious by those
    who are not a people;
I will make them angry by a nation
    that has no understanding.
22 For a fire has been kindled by my
        wrath,
    one that burns to the realm of
        death*e* below.
It will devour the earth and its
        harvests
    and set afire the foundations of
        the mountains.

23 "I will heap calamities upon them
    and spend my arrows against
        them.
24 I will send wasting famine against
        them,
    consuming pestilence and deadly
        plague;

I will send against them the fangs of
        wild beasts,
    the venom of vipers that glide in
        the dust.
25 In the street the sword will make
        them childless;
    in their homes terror will reign.
Young men and young women will
        perish,
    infants and gray-haired men.
26 I said I would scatter them
    and blot out their memory from
        mankind,
27 but I dreaded the taunt of the enemy,
    lest the adversary misunderstand
and say, 'Our hand has triumphed;
    the LORD has not done all this.'"

*a5 Or Corrupt are they and not his children, / a generation
warped and twisted to their shame   b6 Or Father, who
bought you   c8 Masoretic Text; Dead Sea Scrolls (see also
Septuagint) sons of God   d15 Jeshurun means the upright
one, that is, Israel.   e22 Hebrew to Sheol*

LUKE 12:8-34

"I [Jesus] tell you, whoever acknowledges me before men, the Son of Man will also acknowledge him before the angels of God. 9 But he who disowns me before men will be disowned before the angels of God. 10 And everyone who speaks a word against the Son of Man will be forgiven, but anyone who blasphemes against the Holy Spirit will not be forgiven.

11 "When you are brought before synagogues, rulers and authorities, do not worry about how you will defend yourselves or what you will say, 12 for the Holy Spirit will teach you at that time what you should say."

13 Someone in the crowd said to him, "Teacher, tell my brother to divide the inheritance with me."

14 Jesus replied, "Man, who appointed me a judge or an arbiter between you?" 15 Then he said to them, "Watch out! Be on your guard against all kinds of greed; a man's life does not consist in the abundance of his possessions."

16 And he told them this parable: "The ground of a certain rich man produced a good crop. 17 He thought to

himself, 'What shall I do? I have no place to store my crops.'

18"Then he said, 'This is what I'll do. I will tear down my barns and build bigger ones, and there I will store all my grain and my goods. 19And I'll say to myself, "You have plenty of good things laid up for many years. Take life easy; eat, drink and be merry."'

20"But God said to him, 'You fool! This very night your life will be demanded from you. Then who will get what you have prepared for yourself?'

21"This is how it will be with anyone who stores up things for himself but is not rich toward God."

22Then Jesus said to his disciples: "Therefore I tell you, do not worry about your life, what you will eat; or about your body, what you will wear. 23Life is more than food, and the body more than clothes. 24Consider the ravens: They do not sow or reap, they have no storeroom or barn; yet God feeds them. And how much more valuable you are than birds! 25Who of you by worrying can add a single hour to his life*a*? 26Since you cannot do this very little thing, why do you worry about the rest?

27"Consider how the lilies grow. They do not labor or spin. Yet I tell you, not even Solomon in all his splendor was dressed like one of these. 28If that is how God clothes the grass of the field, which is here today, and tomorrow is thrown into the fire, how much more will he clothe you, O you of little faith! 29And do not set your heart on what you will eat or drink; do not worry about it. 30For the pagan world runs after all such things, and your Father knows that you need them. 31But seek his kingdom, and these things will be given to you as well.

32"Do not be afraid, little flock, for your Father has been pleased to give you the kingdom. 33Sell your possessions and give to the poor. Provide purses for yourselves that will not wear out, a treasure in heaven that will not be exhausted, where no thief comes near and no moth destroys. 34For where your

treasure is, there your heart will be also."

a25 Or single cubit to his height

PSALM 78:32-55

32In spite of all this, they [the men of
　　Ephraim] kept on sinning;
　　in spite of his [the LORD's]
　　wonders, they did not
　　believe.
33So he ended their days in futility
　　and their years in terror.
34Whenever God slew them, they
　　would seek him;
　　they eagerly turned to him again.
35They remembered that God was their
　　Rock,
　　that God Most High was their
　　Redeemer.
36But then they would flatter him with
　　their mouths,
　　lying to him with their tongues;
37their hearts were not loyal to him,
　　they were not faithful to his
　　covenant.
38Yet he was merciful;
　　he forgave their iniquities
　　and did not destroy them.
　　Time after time he restrained his
　　anger
　　and did not stir up his full wrath.
39He remembered that they were but
　　flesh,
　　a passing breeze that does not return.
40How often they rebelled against him
　　in the desert
　　and grieved him in the wasteland!
41Again and again they put God to the
　　test;
　　they vexed the Holy One of Israel.
42They did not remember his power—
　　the day he redeemed them from
　　the oppressor,
43the day he displayed his miraculous
　　signs in Egypt,
　　his wonders in the region of Zoan.
44He turned their rivers to blood;
　　they could not drink from their
　　streams.
45He sent swarms of flies that
　　devoured them,

and frogs that devastated them.
⁴⁶ He gave their crops to the
   grasshopper,
   their produce to the locust.
⁴⁷ He destroyed their vines with hail
   and their sycamore-figs with
      sleet.
⁴⁸ He gave over their cattle to the hail,
   their livestock to bolts of
      lightning.
⁴⁹ He unleashed against them his hot
      anger,
   his wrath, indignation and
      hostility—
   a band of destroying angels.
⁵⁰ He prepared a path for his anger;
   he did not spare them from death
   but gave them over to the plague.
⁵¹ He struck down all the firstborn of
      Egypt,
   the firstfruits of manhood in the
      tents of Ham.
⁵² But he brought his people out like a
      flock;
   he led them like sheep through the
      desert.
⁵³ He guided them safely, so they were
      unafraid;
   but the sea engulfed their enemies.
⁵⁴ Thus he brought them to the border
      of his holy land,
   to the hill country his right hand
      had taken.
⁵⁵ He drove out nations before them
   and allotted their lands to them as
      an inheritance;
   he settled the tribes of Israel in
      their homes.

PROVERBS 12:21-23
²¹ No harm befalls the righteous,
   but the wicked have their fill of
      trouble.

²² The Lord detests lying lips,
   but he delights in men who are
      truthful.

²³ A prudent man keeps his knowledge
      to himself,
   but the heart of fools blurts out
      folly.

☐ DAY 98

GOD SIGHTINGS

April 8

DEUTERONOMY 32:28-52
²⁸ They [the Lord's people] are a nation
      without sense,
   there is no discernment in them.
²⁹ If only they were wise and would
      understand this
   and discern what their end will be!
³⁰ How could one man chase a
      thousand,
   or two put ten thousand to flight,
   unless their Rock had sold them,
   unless the Lord had given them
      up?
³¹ For their rock is not like our Rock,
   as even our enemies concede.
³² Their vine comes from the vine of
      Sodom
   and from the fields of Gomorrah.
   Their grapes are filled with poison,
   and their clusters with bitterness.
³³ Their wine is the venom of serpents,
   the deadly poison of cobras.

³⁴ "Have I not kept this in reserve
   and sealed it in my vaults?
³⁵ It is mine to avenge; I will repay.
   In due time their foot will slip;
   their day of disaster is near
   and their doom rushes upon them."

³⁶ The Lord will judge his people
   and have compassion on his
      servants
   when he sees their strength is gone
   and no one is left, slave or free.
³⁷ He will say: "Now where are their
      gods,
   the rock they took refuge in,
³⁸ the gods who ate the fat of their
      sacrifices
   and drank the wine of their drink
      offerings?
   Let them rise up to help you!
   Let them give you shelter!

³⁹ "See now that I myself am He!
   There is no god besides me.

I put to death and I bring to life,
    I have wounded and I will heal,
    and no one can deliver out of my
        hand.

⁴⁰I lift my hand to heaven and declare:
    As surely as I live forever,
⁴¹when I sharpen my flashing sword
    and my hand grasps it in
        judgment,
    I will take vengeance on my
        adversaries
    and repay those who hate me.
⁴²I will make my arrows drunk with
        blood,
    while my sword devours flesh:
    the blood of the slain and the
        captives,
    the heads of the enemy leaders."

⁴³ Rejoice, O nations, with his
        people,ᵃ,ᵇ
    for he will avenge the blood of his
        servants;
    he will take vengeance on his
        enemies
    and make atonement for his land
        and people.

⁴⁴Moses came with Joshuaᶜ son of Nun and spoke all the words of this song in the hearing of the people. ⁴⁵When Moses finished reciting all these words to all Israel, ⁴⁶he said to them, "Take to heart all the words I have solemnly declared to you this day, so that you may command your children to obey carefully all the words of this law. ⁴⁷They are not just idle words for you—they are your life. By them you will live long in the land you are crossing the Jordan to possess."

⁴⁸On that same day the LORD told Moses, ⁴⁹"Go up into the Abarim Range to Mount Nebo in Moab, across from Jericho, and view Canaan, the land I am giving the Israelites as their own possession. ⁵⁰There on the mountain that you have climbed you will die and be gathered to your people, just as your brother Aaron died on Mount Hor and was gathered to his people. ⁵¹This is because both of you broke faith with me in the presence of the Israelites at the waters of Meribah Kadesh in the Desert of Zin and because you did not uphold my holiness among the Israelites. ⁵²Therefore, you will see the land only from a distance; you will not enter the land I am giving to the people of Israel."

ᵃ43 Or Make his people rejoice, O nations   ᵇ43 Masoretic Text; Dead Sea Scrolls (see also Septuagint) people, / and let all the angels worship him /   ᶜ44 Hebrew Hoshea, a variant of Joshua

LUKE 12:35-59

"**B**e dressed ready for service and keep your lamps burning, ³⁶like men waiting for their master to return from a wedding banquet, so that when he comes and knocks they can immediately open the door for him. ³⁷It will be good for those servants whose master finds them watching when he comes. I tell you the truth, he will dress himself to serve, will have them recline at the table and will come and wait on them. ³⁸It will be good for those servants whose master finds them ready, even if he comes in the second or third watch of the night. ³⁹**But understand this: If the owner of the house had known at what hour the thief was coming, he would not have let his house be broken into. ⁴⁰You also must be ready, because the Son of Man will come at an hour when you do not expect him."**

⁴¹Peter asked, "Lord, are you telling this parable to us, or to everyone?"

⁴²The Lord answered, "Who then is the faithful and wise manager, whom the master puts in charge of his servants to give them their food allowance at the proper time? ⁴³It will be good for that servant whom the master finds doing so when he returns. ⁴⁴I tell you the truth, he will put him in charge of all his possessions. ⁴⁵But suppose the servant says to himself, 'My master is taking a long time in coming,' and he then begins to beat the menservants and maidservants and to eat and drink and get drunk. ⁴⁶The master of that servant will come on a day when he does not expect him and at an hour he is not aware of. He will cut him to pieces and assign him a place with the unbelievers.

47"That servant who knows his master's will and does not get ready or does not do what his master wants will be beaten with many blows. 48But the one who does not know and does things deserving punishment will be beaten with few blows. From everyone who has been given much, much will be demanded; and from the one who has been entrusted with much, much more will be asked.

49"I have come to bring fire on the earth, and how I wish it were already kindled! 50But I have a baptism to undergo, and how distressed I am until it is completed! 51Do you think I came to bring peace on earth? No, I tell you, but division. 52From now on there will be five in one family divided against each other, three against two and two against three. 53They will be divided, father against son and son against father, mother against daughter and daughter against mother, mother-in-law against daughter-in-law and daughter-in-law against mother-in-law."

54He said to the crowd: "When you see a cloud rising in the west, immediately you say, 'It's going to rain,' and it does. 55And when the south wind blows, you say, 'It's going to be hot,' and it is. 56Hypocrites! You know how to interpret the appearance of the earth and the sky. How is it that you don't know how to interpret this present time?

57"Why don't you judge for yourselves what is right? 58As you are going with your adversary to the magistrate, try hard to be reconciled to him on the way, or he may drag you off to the judge, and the judge turn you over to the officer, and the officer throw you into prison. 59I tell you, you will not get out until you have paid the last penny.a"

a59 Greek lepton

PSALM 78:56-64
56But they [the Lord's people] put God to the test
    and rebelled against the Most High;
    they did not keep his statutes.
57Like their fathers they were disloyal and faithless,
    as unreliable as a faulty bow.
58They angered him with their high places;
    they aroused his jealousy with their idols.
59When God heard them, he was very angry;
    he rejected Israel completely.
60He abandoned the tabernacle of Shiloh,
    the tent he had set up among men.
61He sent ⌊the ark of⌋ his might into captivity,
    his splendor into the hands of the enemy.
62He gave his people over to the sword;
    he was very angry with his inheritance.
63Fire consumed their young men,
    and their maidens had no wedding songs;
64their priests were put to the sword,
    and their widows could not weep.

PROVERBS 12:24
24Diligent hands will rule,
    but laziness ends in slave labor.

□ DAY 99

GOD SIGHTINGS

April 9

DEUTERONOMY 33:1-29
This is the blessing that Moses the man of God pronounced on the Israelites before his death. 2He said:

"The Lord came from Sinai
    and dawned over them from Seir;
    he shone forth from Mount Paran.
He came witha myriads of holy ones
    from the south, from his mountain slopes.b
3Surely it is you who love the people;
    all the holy ones are in your hand.
At your feet they all bow down,
    and from you receive instruction,

⁴the law that Moses gave us,
the possession of the assembly of
Jacob.
⁵He was king over Jeshurunᶜ
when the leaders of the people
assembled,
along with the tribes of Israel.

⁶"Let Reuben live and not die,
norᵈ his men be few."

⁷And this he said about Judah:

"Hear, O Lᴏʀᴅ, the cry of Judah;
bring him to his people.
With his own hands he defends his
cause.
Oh, be his help against his foes!"

⁸About Levi he said:

"Your Thummim and Urim belong
to the man you favored.
You tested him at Massah;
you contended with him at the
waters of Meribah.
⁹He said of his father and mother,
'I have no regard for them.'
He did not recognize his brothers
or acknowledge his own children,
but he watched over your word
and guarded your covenant.
¹⁰He teaches your precepts to Jacob
and your law to Israel.
He offers incense before you
and whole burnt offerings on your
altar.
¹¹Bless all his skills, O Lᴏʀᴅ,
and be pleased with the work of
his hands.
Smite the loins of those who rise up
against him;
strike his foes till they rise no
more."

¹²About Benjamin he said:

"Let the beloved of the Lᴏʀᴅ rest
secure in him,
for he shields him all day long,
and the one the Lᴏʀᴅ loves rests
between his shoulders."

¹³About Joseph he said:

"May the Lᴏʀᴅ bless his land

with the precious dew from
heaven above
and with the deep waters that lie
below;
¹⁴with the best the sun brings forth
and the finest the moon can yield;
¹⁵with the choicest gifts of the ancient
mountains
and the fruitfulness of the
everlasting hills;
¹⁶with the best gifts of the earth and its
fullness
and the favor of him who dwelt in
the burning bush.
Let all these rest on the head of
Joseph,
on the brow of the prince amongᵉ
his brothers.
¹⁷In majesty he is like a firstborn bull;
his horns are the horns of a wild
ox.
With them he will gore the nations,
even those at the ends of the earth.
Such are the ten thousands of
Ephraim;
such are the thousands of
Manasseh."

¹⁸About Zebulun he said:

"Rejoice, Zebulun, in your going out,
and you, Issachar, in your tents.
¹⁹They will summon peoples to the
mountain
and there offer sacrifices of
righteousness;
they will feast on the abundance of
the seas,
on the treasures hidden in the
sand."

²⁰About Gad he said:

"Blessed is he who enlarges Gad's
domain!
Gad lives there like a lion,
tearing at arm or head.
²¹He chose the best land for himself;
the leader's portion was kept for
him.
When the heads of the people
assembled,

he carried out the LORD's righteous
   will,
and his judgments concerning
   Israel."

22About Dan he said:

"Dan is a lion's cub,
   springing out of Bashan."

23About Naphtali he said:

"Naphtali is abounding with the
      favor of the LORD
   and is full of his blessing;
he will inherit southward to the
   lake."

24About Asher he said:

"Most blessed of sons is Asher;
   let him be favored by his brothers,
   and let him bathe his feet in oil.
25The bolts of your gates will be iron
      and bronze,
   and your strength will equal your
      days.

26"There is no one like the God of
      Jeshurun,
   who rides on the heavens to help
      you
   and on the clouds in his majesty.
27The eternal God is your refuge,
   and underneath are the everlasting
      arms.
He will drive out your enemy before
   you,
   saying, 'Destroy him!'
28So Israel will live in safety alone;
   Jacob's spring is secure
in a land of grain and new wine,
   where the heavens drop dew.
29Blessed are you, O Israel!
   Who is like you,
   a people saved by the LORD?
He is your shield and helper
   and your glorious sword.
Your enemies will cower before you,
   and you will trample down their
      high places.'"

a2 Or from   b2 The meaning of the Hebrew for this phrase
is uncertain.   c5 Jeshurun means the upright one, that is,
Israel; also in verse 26.   d6 Or but let   e16 Or of the one
separated from   f29 Or will tread upon their bodies

LUKE 13:1-21

Now there were some present at that
time who told Jesus about the Galileans
whose blood Pilate had mixed with
their sacrifices. 2Jesus answered, "Do
you think that these Galileans were
worse sinners than all the other Galileans because they suffered this way? 3I
tell you, no! But unless you repent, you
too will all perish. 4Or those eighteen
who died when the tower in Siloam fell
on them—do you think they were more
guilty than all the others living in Jerusalem? 5I tell you, no! But unless you repent, you too will all perish."

6Then he told this parable: "A man
had a fig tree, planted in his vineyard,
and he went to look for fruit on it, but
did not find any. 7So he said to the man
who took care of the vineyard, 'For three
years now I've been coming to look for
fruit on this fig tree and haven't found
any. Cut it down! Why should it use up
the soil?'

8"'Sir,' the man replied, 'leave it alone
for one more year, and I'll dig around it
and fertilize it. 9If it bears fruit next
year, fine! If not, then cut it down.'"

10On a Sabbath Jesus was teaching in
one of the synagogues, 11and a woman
was there who had been crippled by a
spirit for eighteen years. She was bent
over and could not straighten up at all.
12When Jesus saw her, he called her
forward and said to her, "Woman, you
are set free from your infirmity."
13Then he put his hands on her, and
immediately she straightened up and
praised God.

14Indignant because Jesus had
healed on the Sabbath, the synagogue
ruler said to the people, "There are six
days for work. So come and be healed
on those days, not on the Sabbath."

15The Lord answered him, "You hypocrites! Doesn't each of you on the Sabbath untie his ox or donkey from the
stall and lead it out to give it water?
16Then should not this woman, a
daughter of Abraham, whom Satan has
kept bound for eighteen long years, be

set free on the Sabbath day from what bound her?"

¹⁷When he said this, all his opponents were humiliated, but the people were delighted with all the wonderful things he was doing.

¹⁸**Then Jesus asked, "What is the kingdom of God like? What shall I compare it to?** ¹⁹**It is like a mustard seed, which a man took and planted in his garden. It grew and became a tree, and the birds of the air perched in its branches."**

²⁰Again he asked, "What shall I compare the kingdom of God to? ²¹It is like yeast that a woman took and mixed into a large amount*a* of flour until it worked all through the dough."

a21 Greek three satas (probably about 1/2 bushel or 22 liters)

PSALM 78:65-72

⁶⁵**T**hen the Lord awoke as from sleep,
    as a man wakes from the stupor
        of wine.
⁶⁶He beat back his enemies;
    he put them to everlasting shame.
⁶⁷Then he rejected the tents of Joseph,
    he did not choose the tribe of
        Ephraim;
⁶⁸but he chose the tribe of Judah,
    Mount Zion, which he loved.
⁶⁹He built his sanctuary like the
        heights,
    like the earth that he established
        forever.
⁷⁰He chose David his servant
    and took him from the sheep
        pens;
⁷¹from tending the sheep he brought
        him
    to be the shepherd of his people
        Jacob,
    of Israel his inheritance.
⁷²And David shepherded them with
        integrity of heart;
    with skillful hands he led them.

PROVERBS 12:25

²⁵**A**n anxious heart weighs a man
        down,
    but a kind word cheers him up.

☐ D A Y 1 0 0

GOD SIGHTINGS

April 10

DEUTERONOMY 34:1—JOSHUA 2:24
Then Moses climbed Mount Nebo from the plains of Moab to the top of Pisgah, across from Jericho. There the LORD showed him the whole land—from Gilead to Dan, ²all of Naphtali, the territory of Ephraim and Manasseh, all the land of Judah as far as the western sea,*a* ³the Negev and the whole region from the Valley of Jericho, the City of Palms, as far as Zoar. ⁴Then the LORD said to him, "This is the land I promised on oath to Abraham, Isaac and Jacob when I said, 'I will give it to your descendants.' I have let you see it with your eyes, but you will not cross over into it."

⁵And Moses the servant of the LORD died there in Moab, as the LORD had said. ⁶He buried him*b* in Moab, in the valley opposite Beth Peor, but to this day no one knows where his grave is. ⁷Moses was a hundred and twenty years old when he died, yet his eyes were not weak nor his strength gone. ⁸The Israelites grieved for Moses in the plains of Moab thirty days, until the time of weeping and mourning was over.

⁹Now Joshua son of Nun was filled with the spirit*c* of wisdom because Moses had laid his hands on him. So the Israelites listened to him and did what the LORD had commanded Moses.

¹⁰**Since then, no prophet has risen in Israel like Moses, whom the LORD knew face to face,** ¹¹**who did all those miraculous signs and wonders the LORD sent him to do in Egypt—to Pharoah and to all his officials and to his whole land.** ¹²For no one has ever shown the mighty power or performed the awesome deeds that Moses did in the sight of all Israel.

¹:¹AFTER the death of Moses the servant of the LORD, the LORD said to Joshua son of Nun, Moses' aide: ²"Moses my

servant is dead. Now then, you and all these people, get ready to cross the Jordan River into the land I am about to give to them—to the Israelites. [3]I will give you every place where you set your foot, as I promised Moses. [4]Your territory will extend from the desert to Lebanon, and from the great river, the Euphrates—all the Hittite country—to the Great Sea*a* on the west. [5]No one will be able to stand up against you all the days of your life. As I was with Moses, so I will be with you; I will never leave you nor forsake you.

[6]"Be strong and courageous, because you will lead these people to inherit the land I swore to their forefathers to give them. [7]Be strong and very courageous. Be careful to obey all the law my servant Moses gave you; do not turn from it to the right or to the left, that you may be successful wherever you go. [8]Do not let this Book of the Law depart from your mouth; meditate on it day and night, so that you may be careful to do everything written in it. Then you will be prosperous and successful. [9]Have I not commanded you? Be strong and courageous. Do not be terrified; do not be discouraged, for the LORD your God will be with you wherever you go."

[10]So Joshua ordered the officers of the people: [11]"Go through the camp and tell the people, 'Get your supplies ready. Three days from now you will cross the Jordan here to go in and take possession of the land the LORD your God is giving you for your own.'"

[12]But to the Reubenites, the Gadites and the half-tribe of Manasseh, Joshua said, [13]"Remember the command that Moses the servant of the LORD gave you: 'The LORD your God is giving you rest and has granted you this land.' [14]Your wives, your children and your livestock may stay in the land that Moses gave you east of the Jordan, but all your fighting men, fully armed, must cross over ahead of your brothers. You are to help your brothers [15]until the LORD gives them rest, as he has done for you, and until they too have taken possession of the

land that the LORD your God is giving them. After that, you may go back and occupy your own land, which Moses the servant of the LORD gave you east of the Jordan toward the sunrise."

[16]Then they answered Joshua, "Whatever you have commanded us we will do, and wherever you send us we will go. [17]Just as we fully obeyed Moses, so we will obey you. Only may the LORD your God be with you as he was with Moses. [18]Whoever rebels against your word and does not obey your words, whatever you may command them, will be put to death. Only be strong and courageous!"

[2:1]THEN Joshua son of Nun secretly sent two spies from Shittim. "Go, look over the land," he said, "especially Jericho." So they went and entered the house of a prostitute*d* named Rahab and stayed there.

[2]The king of Jericho was told, "Look! Some of the Israelites have come here tonight to spy out the land." [3]So the king of Jericho sent this message to Rahab: "Bring out the men who came to you and entered your house, because they have come to spy out the whole land."

[4]But the woman had taken the two men and hidden them. She said, "Yes, the men came to me, but I did not know where they had come from. [5]At dusk, when it was time to close the city gate, the men left. I don't know which way they went. Go after them quickly. You may catch up with them." [6](But she had taken them up to the roof and hidden them under the stalks of flax she had laid out on the roof.) [7]So the men set out in pursuit of the spies on the road that leads to the fords of the Jordan, and as soon as the pursuers had gone out, the gate was shut.

[8]Before the spies lay down for the night, she went up on the roof [9]and said to them, "I know that the LORD has given this land to you and that a great fear of you has fallen on us, so that all who live in this country are melting in fear be-

cause of you. [10]We have heard how the Lord dried up the water of the Red Sea[e] for you when you came out of Egypt, and what you did to Sihon and Og, the two kings of the Amorites east of the Jordan, whom you completely destroyed.[f] [11]When we heard of it, our hearts melted and everyone's courage failed because of you, for the Lord your God is God in heaven above and on the earth below. [12]Now then, please swear to me by the Lord that you will show kindness to my family, because I have shown kindness to you. Give me a sure sign [13]that you will spare the lives of my father and mother, my brothers and sisters, and all who belong to them, and that you will save us from death."

[14]"Our lives for your lives!" the men assured her. "If you don't tell what we are doing, we will treat you kindly and faithfully when the Lord gives us the land."

[15]So she let them down by a rope through the window, for the house she lived in was part of the city wall. [16]Now she had said to them, "Go to the hills so the pursuers will not find you. Hide yourselves there three days until they return, and then go on your way."

[17]The men said to her, "This oath you made us swear will not be binding on us [18]unless, when we enter the land, you have tied this scarlet cord in the window through which you let us down, and unless you have brought your father and mother, your brothers and all your family into your house. [19]If anyone goes outside your house into the street, his blood will be on his own head; we will not be responsible. As for anyone who is in the house with you, his blood will be on our head if a hand is laid on him. [20]But if you tell what we are doing, we will be released from the oath you made us swear."

[21]"Agreed," she replied. "Let it be as you say." So she sent them away and they departed. And she tied the scarlet cord in the window.

[22]When they left, they went into the hills and stayed there three days, until the pursuers had searched all along the road and returned without finding them. [23]Then the two men started back. They went down out of the hills, forded the river and came to Joshua son of Nun and told him everything that had happened to them. [24]They said to Joshua, "The Lord has surely given the whole land into our hands; all the people are melting in fear because of us."

[a]2,4 That is, the Mediterranean [b]6 Or He was buried [c]9 Or Spirit [d]1 Or possibly an innkeeper [e]10 Hebrew Yam Suph; that is, Sea of Reeds [f]10 The Hebrew term refers to the irrevocable giving over of things or persons to the Lord, often by totally destroying them.

LUKE 13:22–14:6

Then Jesus went through the towns and villages, teaching as he made his way to Jerusalem. [23]Someone asked him, "Lord, are only a few people going to be saved?"

He said to them, [24]"Make every effort to enter through the narrow door, because many, I tell you, will try to enter and will not be able to. [25]Once the owner of the house gets up and closes the door, you will stand outside knocking and pleading, 'Sir, open the door for us.'

"But he will answer, 'I don't know you or where you come from.'

[26]"Then you will say, 'We ate and drank with you, and you taught in our streets.'

[27]"But he will reply, 'I don't know you or where you come from. Away from me, all you evildoers!'

[28]"There will be weeping there, and gnashing of teeth, when you see Abraham, Isaac and Jacob and all the prophets in the kingdom of God, but you yourselves thrown out. [29]People will come from east and west and north and south, and will take their places at the feast in the kingdom of God. [30]Indeed there are those who are last who will be first, and first who will be last."

[31]At that time some Pharisees came to Jesus and said to him, "Leave this place and go somewhere else. Herod wants to kill you."

[32]He replied, "Go tell that fox, 'I will drive out demons and heal people today

and tomorrow, and on the third day I will reach my goal.' ³³In any case, I must keep going today and tomorrow and the next day—for surely no prophet can die outside Jerusalem!

³⁴"O Jerusalem, Jerusalem, you who kill the prophets and stone those sent to you, how often I have longed to gather your children together, as a hen gathers her chicks under her wings, but you were not willing! ³⁵Look, your house is left to you desolate. I tell you, you will not see me again until you say, 'Blessed is he who comes in the name of the Lord.'ᵃ"

¹⁴:¹ONE Sabbath, when Jesus went to eat in the house of a prominent Pharisee, he was being carefully watched. ²There in front of him was a man suffering from dropsy. ³Jesus asked the Pharisees and experts in the law, "Is it lawful to heal on the Sabbath or not?" ⁴But they remained silent. So taking hold of the man, he healed him and sent him away.

⁵Then he asked them, "If one of you has a sonᵇ or an ox that falls into a well on the Sabbath day, will you not immediately pull him out?" ⁶And they had nothing to say.

ᵃ35 Psalm 118:26   ᵇ5 Some manuscripts *donkey*

PSALM 79:1-13
A psalm of Asaph.

¹ O God, the nations have invaded
   your inheritance;
   they have defiled your holy
      temple,
   they have reduced Jerusalem to
      rubble.
² They have given the dead bodies of
      your servants
   as food to the birds of the air,
   the flesh of your saints to the
      beasts of the earth.
³ They have poured out blood like
      water
   all around Jerusalem,
   and there is no one to bury the
      dead.
⁴ We are objects of reproach to our
      neighbors,

of scorn and derision to those
      around us.

⁵ How long, O LORD? Will you be angry
      forever?
   How long will your jealousy burn
      like fire?

⁶ Pour out your wrath on the nations
   that do not acknowledge you,
   on the kingdoms
   that do not call on your name;
⁷ for they have devoured Jacob
   and destroyed his homeland.
⁸ Do not hold against us the sins of the
      fathers;
   may your mercy come quickly to
      meet us,
   for we are in desperate need.

⁹ Help us, O God our Savior,
   for the glory of your name;
   deliver us and forgive our sins
   for your name's sake.
¹⁰ Why should the nations say,
   "Where is their God?"
   Before our eyes, make known among
      the nations
   that you avenge the outpoured
      blood of your servants.
¹¹ May the groans of the prisoners
      come before you;
   by the strength of your arm
   preserve those condemned to die.

¹² Pay back into the laps of our
      neighbors seven times
   the reproach they have hurled at
      you, O Lord.
¹³ Then we your people, the sheep of
      your pasture,
   will praise you forever;
   from generation to generation
   we will recount your praise.

PROVERBS 12:26

²⁶ A righteous man is cautious in
      friendship,ᵃ
   but the way of the wicked leads
      them astray.

ᵃ26 Or *man is a guide to his neighbor*

□ DAY 101

GOD SIGHTINGS

April 11

JOSHUA 3:1–4:24

Early in the morning Joshua and all the Israelites set out from Shittim and went to the Jordan, where they camped before crossing over. ²After three days the officers went throughout the camp, ³giving orders to the people: "When you see the ark of the covenant of the LORD your God, and the priests, who are Levites, carrying it, you are to move out from your positions and follow it. ⁴Then you will know which way to go, since you have never been this way before. But keep a distance of about a thousand yards*a* between you and the ark; do not go near it."

⁵Joshua told the people, "Consecrate yourselves, for tomorrow the LORD will do amazing things among you."

⁶Joshua said to the priests, "Take up the ark of the covenant and pass on ahead of the people." So they took it up and went ahead of them.

⁷And the LORD said to Joshua, "Today I will begin to exalt you in the eyes of all Israel, so they may know that I am with you as I was with Moses. ⁸Tell the priests who carry the ark of the covenant: 'When you reach the edge of the Jordan's waters, go and stand in the river.'"

⁹Joshua said to the Israelites, "Come here and listen to the words of the LORD your God. ¹⁰This is how you will know that the living God is among you and that he will certainly drive out before you the Canaanites, Hittites, Hivites, Perizzites, Girgashites, Amorites and Jebusites. ¹¹See, the ark of the covenant of the Lord of all the earth will go into the Jordan ahead of you. ¹²Now then, choose twelve men from the tribes of Israel, one from each tribe. ¹³And as soon as the priests who carry the ark of the LORD—the Lord of all the earth—set foot in the Jordan, its waters flowing down-

stream will be cut off and stand up in a heap."

¹⁴So when the people broke camp to cross the Jordan, the priests carrying the ark of the covenant went ahead of them. ¹⁵Now the Jordan is at flood stage all during harvest. Yet as soon as the priests who carried the ark reached the Jordan and their feet touched the water's edge, ¹⁶the water from upstream stopped flowing. It piled up in a heap a great distance away, at a town called Adam in the vicinity of Zarethan, while the water flowing down to the Sea of the Arabah (the Salt Sea*b*) was completely cut off. So the people crossed over opposite Jericho. ¹⁷The priests who carried the ark of the covenant of the LORD stood firm on dry ground in the middle of the Jordan, while all Israel passed by until the whole nation had completed the crossing on dry ground.

⁴:¹WHEN the whole nation had finished crossing the Jordan, the LORD said to Joshua, ²"Choose twelve men from among the people, one from each tribe, ³and tell them to take up twelve stones from the middle of the Jordan from right where the priests stood and to carry them over with you and put them down at the place where you stay tonight."

⁴So Joshua called together the twelve men he had appointed from the Israelites, one from each tribe, ⁵and said to them, "Go over before the ark of the LORD your God into the middle of the Jordan. Each of you is to take up a stone on his shoulder, according to the number of the tribes of the Israelites, ⁶to serve as a sign among you. In the future, when your children ask you, 'What do these stones mean?' ⁷tell them that the flow of the Jordan was cut off before the ark of the covenant of the LORD. When it crossed the Jordan, the waters of the Jordan were cut off. These stones are to be a memorial to the people of Israel forever."

⁸So the Israelites did as Joshua commanded them. They took twelve stones from the middle of the Jordan, according

to the number of the tribes of the Israel-ites, as the LORD had told Joshua; and they carried them over with them to their camp, where they put them down. [9]Joshua set up the twelve stones that had been[c] in the middle of the Jordan at the spot where the priests who carried the ark of the covenant had stood. And they are there to this day.

[10]Now the priests who carried the ark remained standing in the middle of the Jordan until everything the LORD had commanded Joshua was done by the people, just as Moses had directed Joshua. The people hurried over, [11]and as soon as all of them had crossed, the ark of the LORD and the priests came to the other side while the people watched. [12]The men of Reuben, Gad and the half-tribe of Manasseh crossed over, armed, in front of the Israelites, as Moses had directed them. [13]About forty thousand armed for battle crossed over before the LORD to the plains of Jericho for war.

[14]That day the LORD exalted Joshua in the sight of all Israel; and they revered him all the days of his life, just as they had revered Moses.

[15]Then the LORD said to Joshua, [16]"Command the priests carrying the ark of the Testimony to come up out of the Jordan."

[17]So Joshua commanded the priests, "Come up out of the Jordan."

[18]And the priests came up out of the river carrying the ark of the covenant of the LORD. No sooner had they set their feet on the dry ground than the waters of the Jordan returned to their place and ran at flood stage as before.

[19]On the tenth day of the first month the people went up from the Jordan and camped at Gilgal on the eastern border of Jericho. [20]And Joshua set up at Gilgal the twelve stones they had taken out of the Jordan. [21]He said to the Israelites, "In the future when your descendants ask their fathers, 'What do these stones mean?' [22]tell them, 'Israel crossed the Jordan on dry ground.' [23]For the LORD your God dried up the Jordan before

you until you had crossed over. The LORD your God did to the Jordan just what he had done to the Red Sea[d] when he dried it up before us until we had crossed over. [24]He did this so that all the peoples of the earth might know that the hand of the LORD is powerful and so that you might always fear the LORD your God."

a4 Hebrew *about two thousand cubits* (about 900 meters) b16 That is, the Dead Sea c9 Or *Joshua also set up twelve stones* d23 Hebrew *Yam Suph*; that is, Sea of Reeds

LUKE 14:7-35

When he [Jesus] noticed how the guests picked the places of honor at the table, he told them this parable: [8]"When someone invites you to a wedding feast, do not take the place of honor, for a person more distinguished than you may have been invited. [9]If so, the host who invited both of you will come and say to you, 'Give this man your seat.' Then, hu-miliated, you will have to take the least important place. [10]But when you are in-vited, take the lowest place, so that when your host comes, he will say to you, 'Friend, move up to a better place.' Then you will be honored in the presence of all your fellow guests. [11]For everyone who exalts himself will be humbled, and he who humbles himself will be ex-alted."

[12]Then Jesus said to his host, "When you give a luncheon or dinner, do not in-vite your friends, your brothers or rela-tives, or your rich neighbors; if you do, they may invite you back and so you will be repaid. [13]But when you give a ban-quet, invite the poor, the crippled, the lame, the blind, [14]and you will be blessed. Although they cannot repay you, you will be repaid at the resurrec-tion of the righteous."

[15]When one of those at the table with him heard this, he said to Jesus, "Blessed is the man who will eat at the feast in the kingdom of God."

[16]Jesus replied: "A certain man was preparing a great banquet and invited many guests. [17]At the time of the ban-quet he sent his servant to tell those

who had been invited, 'Come, for everything is now ready.'

¹⁸"But they all alike began to make excuses. The first said, 'I have just bought a field, and I must go and see it. Please excuse me.'

¹⁹"Another said, 'I have just bought five yoke of oxen, and I'm on my way to try them out. Please excuse me.'

²⁰"Still another said, 'I just got married, so I can't come.'

²¹"The servant came back and reported this to his master. Then the owner of the house became angry and ordered his servant, 'Go out quickly into the streets and alleys of the town and bring in the poor, the crippled, the blind and the lame.'

²²"'Sir,' the servant said, 'what you ordered has been done, but there is still room.'

²³"Then the master told his servant, 'Go out to the roads and country lanes and make them come in, so that my house will be full. ²⁴I tell you, not one of those men who were invited will get a taste of my banquet.'"

²⁵Large crowds were traveling with Jesus, and turning to them he said: ²⁶"If anyone comes to me and does not hate his father and mother, his wife and children, his brothers and sisters—yes, even his own life—he cannot be my disciple. ²⁷And anyone who does not carry his cross and follow me cannot be my disciple.

²⁸"Suppose one of you wants to build a tower. Will he not first sit down and estimate the cost to see if he has enough money to complete it? ²⁹For if he lays the foundation and is not able to finish it, everyone who sees it will ridicule him, ³⁰saying, 'This fellow began to build and was not able to finish.'

³¹"Or suppose a king is about to go to war against another king. Will he not first sit down and consider whether he is able with ten thousand men to oppose the one coming against him with twenty thousand? ³²If he is not able, he will send a delegation while the other is still a long way off and will ask for terms of peace. ³³**In the same way, any of you**

who does not give up everything he has cannot be my disciple.

³⁴"Salt is good, but if it loses its saltiness, how can it be made salty again? ³⁵It is fit neither for the soil nor for the manure pile; it is thrown out.

"He who has ears to hear, let him hear."

PSALM 80:1-19

For the director of music. To ⌊the tune of⌋ "The Lilies of the Covenant." Of Asaph. A psalm.

¹ **H**ear us, O Shepherd of Israel,
  you who lead Joseph like a flock;
 you who sit enthroned between the
    cherubim, shine forth
² before Ephraim, Benjamin and
    Manasseh.
 Awaken your might;
  come and save us.

³ Restore us, O God;
  make your face shine upon us,
  that we may be saved.

⁴ O Lᴏʀᴅ God Almighty,
  how long will your anger smolder
  against the prayers of your people?
⁵ You have fed them with the bread
    of tears;
  you have made them drink tears
    by the bowlful.
⁶ You have made us a source of
    contention to our neighbors,
  and our enemies mock us.

⁷ Restore us, O God Almighty;
  make your face shine upon us,
  that we may be saved.

⁸ You brought a vine out of Egypt;
  you drove out the nations and
    planted it.
⁹ You cleared the ground for it,
  and it took root and filled the land.
¹⁰ The mountains were covered with
    its shade,
  the mighty cedars with its branches.
¹¹ It sent out its boughs to the Sea,ᵃ
  its shoots as far as the River.ᵇ

¹² Why have you broken down its walls
  so that all who pass by pick its
    grapes?

13 Boars from the forest ravage it
   and the creatures of the field feed
      on it.
14 Return to us, O God Almighty!
   Look down from heaven and see!
   Watch over this vine,
15   the root your right hand has
         planted,
      the son*c* you have raised up for
         yourself.

16 Your vine is cut down, it is burned
      with fire;
   at your rebuke your people perish.
17 Let your hand rest on the man at your
      right hand,
   the son of man you have raised up
      for yourself.
18 Then we will not turn away from you;
   revive us, and we will call on your
      name.

19 Restore us, O Lord God Almighty;
   make your face shine upon us,
   that we may be saved.

*a11 Probably the Mediterranean   b11 That is, the
Euphrates   c15 Or branch*

PROVERBS 12:27-28

27 The lazy man does not roast*a* his
      game,
   but the diligent man prizes his
      possessions.

28 In the way of righteousness there
      is life;
   along that path is immortality.

a27 The meaning of the Hebrew for this word is uncertain.

□ DAY 102

GOD SIGHTINGS

April 12

JOSHUA 5:1–7:15

Now when all the Amorite kings west of
the Jordan and all the Canaanite kings
along the coast heard how the Lord had
dried up the Jordan before the Israelites
until we had crossed over, their hearts

melted and they no longer had the courage to face the Israelites.

2 At that time the Lord said to Joshua,
"Make flint knives and circumcise the
Israelites again." 3 So Joshua made flint
knives and circumcised the Israelites at
Gibeath Haaraloth.*a*

4 Now this is why he did so: All those
who came out of Egypt—all the men of
military age—died in the desert on the
way after leaving Egypt. 5 All the people
that came out had been circumcised,
but all the people born in the desert
during the journey from Egypt had not.
6 The Israelites had moved about in the
desert forty years until all the men who
were of military age when they left
Egypt had died, since they had not
obeyed the Lord. For the Lord had
sworn to them that they would not see
the land that he had solemnly promised
their fathers to give us, a land flowing
with milk and honey. 7 So he raised up
their sons in their place, and these were
the ones Joshua circumcised. They were
still uncircumcised because they had
not been circumcised on the way. 8 And
after the whole nation had been circumcised, they remained where they
were in camp until they were healed.

9 Then the Lord said to Joshua, "Today I have rolled away the reproach of
Egypt from you." So the place has been
called Gilgal*b* to this day.

10 On the evening of the fourteenth
day of the month, while camped at Gilgal
on the plains of Jericho, the Israelites celebrated the Passover. 11 The day after the
Passover, that very day, they ate some of
the produce of the land: unleavened
bread and roasted grain. 12 The manna
stopped the day after*c* they ate this food
from the land; there was no longer any
manna for the Israelites, but that year
they ate of the produce of Canaan.

13 Now when Joshua was near Jericho,
he looked up and saw a man standing in
front of him with a drawn sword in his
hand. Joshua went up to him and asked,
"Are you for us or for our enemies?"

14 "Neither," he replied, "but as commander of the army of the Lord I have

now come." Then Joshua fell facedown to the ground in reverence, and asked him, "What message does my Lord[d] have for his servant?"

15The commander of the LORD's army replied, "Take off your sandals, for the place where you are standing is holy." And Joshua did so.

6:1Now Jericho was tightly shut up because of the Israelites. No one went out and no one came in.

2Then the LORD said to Joshua, "See, I have delivered Jericho into your hands, along with its king and its fighting men. 3March around the city once with all the armed men. Do this for six days. 4Have seven priests carry trumpets of rams' horns in front of the ark. On the seventh day, march around the city seven times, with the priests blowing the trumpets. 5When you hear them sound a long blast on the trumpets, have all the people give a loud shout; then the wall of the city will collapse and the people will go up, every man straight in."

6So Joshua son of Nun called the priests and said to them, "Take up the ark of the covenant of the LORD and have seven priests carry trumpets in front of it." 7And he ordered the people, "Advance! March around the city, with the armed guard going ahead of the ark of the LORD."

8When Joshua had spoken to the people, the seven priests carrying the seven trumpets before the LORD went forward, blowing their trumpets, and the ark of the LORD's covenant followed them. 9The armed guard marched ahead of the priests who blew the trumpets, and the rear guard followed the ark. All this time the trumpets were sounding. 10But Joshua had commanded the people, "Do not give a war cry, do not raise your voices, do not say a word until the day I tell you to shout. Then shout!" 11So he had the ark of the LORD carried around the city, circling it once. Then the people returned to camp and spent the night there.

12Joshua got up early the next morn-ing and the priests took up the ark of the LORD. 13The seven priests carrying the seven trumpets went forward, marching before the ark of the LORD and blowing the trumpets. The armed men went ahead of them and the rear guard followed the ark of the LORD, while the trumpets kept sounding. 14So on the second day they marched around the city once and returned to the camp. They did this for six days.

15On the seventh day, they got up at daybreak and marched around the city seven times in the same manner, except that on that day they circled the city seven times. 16The seventh time around, when the priests sounded the trumpet blast, Joshua commanded the people, "Shout! For the LORD has given you the city! 17The city and all that is in it are to be devoted[e] to the LORD. Only Rahab the prostitute[f] and all who are with her in her house shall be spared, because she hid the spies we sent. 18But keep away from the devoted things, so that you will not bring about your own destruction by taking any of them. Otherwise you will make the camp of Israel liable to destruction and bring trouble on it. 19All the silver and gold and the articles of bronze and iron are sacred to the LORD and must go into his treasury."

20When the trumpets sounded, the people shouted, and at the sound of the trumpet, when the people gave a loud shout, the wall collapsed; so every man charged straight in, and they took the city. 21They devoted the city to the LORD and destroyed with the sword every living thing in it—men and women, young and old, cattle, sheep and donkeys.

22Joshua said to the two men who had spied out the land, "Go into the prostitute's house and bring her out and all who belong to her, in accordance with your oath to her." 23So the young men who had done the spying went in and brought out Rahab, her father and mother and brothers and all who belonged to her. They brought out her entire family and put them in a place outside the camp of Israel.

²⁴Then they burned the whole city and everything in it, but they put the silver and gold and the articles of bronze and iron into the treasury of the LORD's house. ²⁵But Joshua spared Rahab the prostitute, with her family and all who belonged to her, because she hid the men Joshua had sent as spies to Jericho—and she lives among the Israelites to this day.

²⁶At that time Joshua pronounced this solemn oath: "Cursed before the LORD is the man who undertakes to rebuild this city, Jericho:

"At the cost of his firstborn son
    will he lay its foundations;
at the cost of his youngest
    will he set up its gates."

²⁷So the LORD was with Joshua, and his fame spread throughout the land.

⁷:¹BUT the Israelites acted unfaithfully in regard to the devoted things*g*; Achan son of Carmi, the son of Zimri,*h* the son of Zerah, of the tribe of Judah, took some of them. So the LORD's anger burned against Israel.

²Now Joshua sent men from Jericho to Ai, which is near Beth Aven to the east of Bethel, and told them, "Go up and spy out the region." So the men went up and spied out Ai.

³When they returned to Joshua, they said, "Not all the people will have to go up against Ai. Send two or three thousand men to take it and do not weary all the people, for only a few men are there." ⁴So about three thousand men went up; but they were routed by the men of Ai, ⁵who killed about thirty-six of them. They chased the Israelites from the city gate as far as the stone quarries*i* and struck them down on the slopes. At this the hearts of the people melted and became like water.

⁶Then Joshua tore his clothes and fell facedown to the ground before the ark of the LORD, remaining there till evening. The elders of Israel did the same, and sprinkled dust on their heads. ⁷And Joshua said, "Ah, Sovereign LORD, why

did you ever bring this people across the Jordan to deliver us into the hands of the Amorites to destroy us? If only we had been content to stay on the other side of the Jordan! ⁸O Lord, what can I say, now that Israel has been routed by its enemies? ⁹The Canaanites and the other people of the country will hear about this and they will surround us and wipe out our name from the earth. What then will you do for your own great name?"

¹⁰The LORD said to Joshua, "Stand up! What are you doing down on your face? ¹¹Israel has sinned; they have violated my covenant, which I commanded them to keep. They have taken some of the devoted things; they have stolen, they have lied, they have put them with their own possessions. ¹²That is why the Israelites cannot stand against their enemies; they turn their backs and run because they have been made liable to destruction. I will not be with you anymore unless you destroy whatever among you is devoted to destruction.

¹³"Go, consecrate the people. Tell them, 'Consecrate yourselves in preparation for tomorrow; for this is what the LORD, the God of Israel, says: That which is devoted is among you, O Israel. You cannot stand against your enemies until you remove it.

¹⁴"'In the morning, present yourselves tribe by tribe. The tribe that the LORD takes shall come forward clan by clan; the clan that the LORD takes shall come forward family by family; and the family that the LORD takes shall come forward man by man. ¹⁵He who is caught with the devoted things shall be destroyed by fire, along with all that belongs to him. He has violated the covenant of the LORD and has done a disgraceful thing in Israel!'"

---

a3 Gibeath Haaraloth means *hill of foreskins.*   *b9* Gilgal sounds like the Hebrew for *roll.*   *c12* Or *the day*   *d14* Or *lord*   *e17* The Hebrew term refers to the irrevocable giving over of things or persons to the LORD, often by totally destroying them; also in verses 18 and 21.   *f17* Or possibly *innkeeper;* also in verses 22 and 25   *g1* The Hebrew term refers to the irrevocable giving over of things or persons to the LORD, often by totally destroying them; also in verses 11, 12, 13 and 15.   *h1* See Septuagint and 1 Chron. 2:6; Hebrew *Zabdi;* also in verses 17 and 18.   *i5* Or *as far as Shebarim*

LUKE 15:1-32

Now the tax collectors and "sinners" were all gathering around to hear him [Jesus]. ²But the Pharisees and the teachers of the law muttered, "This man welcomes sinners and eats with them."

³Then Jesus told them this parable: ⁴"Suppose one of you has a hundred sheep and loses one of them. Does he not leave the ninety-nine in the open country and go after the lost sheep until he finds it? ⁵And when he finds it, he joyfully puts it on his shoulders ⁶and goes home. Then he calls his friends and neighbors together and says, 'Rejoice with me; I have found my lost sheep.' ⁷**I tell you that in the same way there will be more rejoicing in heaven over one sinner who repents than over ninety-nine righteous persons who do not need to repent.**

⁸"Or suppose a woman has ten silver coins*a* and loses one. Does she not light a lamp, sweep the house and search carefully until she finds it? ⁹And when she finds it, she calls her friends and neighbors together and says, 'Rejoice with me; I have found my lost coin.' ¹⁰In the same way, I tell you, there is rejoicing in the presence of the angels of God over one sinner who repents."

¹¹Jesus continued: "There was a man who had two sons. ¹²The younger one said to his father, 'Father, give me my share of the estate.' So he divided his property between them.

¹³"Not long after that, the younger son got together all he had, set off for a distant country and there squandered his wealth in wild living. ¹⁴After he had spent everything, there was a severe famine in that whole country, and he began to be in need. ¹⁵So he went and hired himself out to a citizen of that country, who sent him to his fields to feed pigs. ¹⁶He longed to fill his stomach with the pods that the pigs were eating, but no one gave him anything.

¹⁷"When he came to his senses, he said, 'How many of my father's hired men have food to spare, and here I am

starving to death! ¹⁸I will set out and go back to my father and say to him: Father, I have sinned against heaven and against you. ¹⁹I am no longer worthy to be called your son; make me like one of your hired men.' ²⁰So he got up and went to his father.

"But while he was still a long way off, his father saw him and was filled with compassion for him; he ran to his son, threw his arms around him and kissed him.

²¹"The son said to him, 'Father, I have sinned against heaven and against you. I am no longer worthy to be called your son.*b*'

²²"But the father said to his servants, 'Quick! Bring the best robe and put it on him. Put a ring on his finger and sandals on his feet. ²³Bring the fattened calf and kill it. Let's have a feast and celebrate. ²⁴For this son of mine was dead and is alive again; he was lost and is found.' So they began to celebrate.

²⁵"Meanwhile, the older son was in the field. When he came near the house, he heard music and dancing. ²⁶So he called one of the servants and asked him what was going on. ²⁷'Your brother has come,' he replied, 'and your father has killed the fattened calf because he has him back safe and sound.'

²⁸"The older brother became angry and refused to go in. So his father went out and pleaded with him. ²⁹But he answered his father, 'Look! All these years I've been slaving for you and never disobeyed your orders. Yet you never gave me even a young goat so I could celebrate with my friends. ³⁰But when this son of yours who has squandered your property with prostitutes comes home, you kill the fattened calf for him!'

³¹"'My son,' the father said, 'you are always with me, and everything I have is yours. ³²But we had to celebrate and be glad, because this brother of yours was dead and is alive again; he was lost and is found.'"

---

a8 Greek *ten drachmas,* each worth about a day's wages
b21 Some early manuscripts *son. Make me like one of your hired men.*

PSALM 81:1-16

For the director of music. According to
*gittith.*ᵃ Of Asaph.

1 **S**ing for joy to God our strength;
   shout aloud to the God of Jacob!
2 Begin the music, strike the
   tambourine,
   play the melodious harp and lyre.

3 Sound the ram's horn at the New
   Moon,
   and when the moon is full, on the
   day of our Feast;
4 this is a decree for Israel,
   an ordinance of the God of Jacob.
5 He established it as a statute for
   Joseph
   when he went out against Egypt,
   where we heard a language we did
   not understand.ᵇ

6 He says, "I removed the burden from
   their shoulders;
   their hands were set free from the
   basket.
7 In your distress you called and I
   rescued you,
   I answered you out of a
   thundercloud;
   I tested you at the waters of
   Meribah.   *Selah*

8 "Hear, O my people, and I will warn
   you—
   if you would but listen to me,
   O Israel!
9 You shall have no foreign god among
   you;
   you shall not bow down to an
   alien god.
10 I am the LORD your God,
   who brought you up out of Egypt.
   Open wide your mouth and I will
   fill it.

11 "But my people would not listen
   to me;
   Israel would not submit to me.
12 So I gave them over to their stubborn
   hearts
   to follow their own devices.

13 "If my people would but listen to me,
   if Israel would follow my ways,

14 how quickly would I subdue their
   enemies
   and turn my hand against their
   foes!
15 Those who hate the LORD would
   cringe before him,
   and their punishment would last
   forever.
16 But you would be fed with the finest
   of wheat;
   with honey from the rock I would
   satisfy you."

ᵃTitle: Probably a musical term   ᵇ5 Or / and we heard a
voice we had not known

PROVERBS 13:1

A wise son heeds his father's
   instruction,
   but a mocker does not listen to
   rebuke.

☐ DAY 103

GOD SIGHTINGS

April 13

JOSHUA 7:16–9:2

Early the next morning Joshua had Israel come forward by tribes, and Judah
was taken. 17 The clans of Judah came
forward, and he took the Zerahites. He
had the clan of the Zerahites come forward by families, and Zimri was taken.
18 Joshua had his family come forward
man by man, and Achan son of Carmi,
the son of Zimri, the son of Zerah, of the
tribe of Judah, was taken.

19 Then Joshua said to Achan, "My
son, give glory to the LORD,ᵃ the God of
Israel, and give him the praise.ᵇ Tell me
what you have done; do not hide it from
me."

20 Achan replied, "It is true! I have
sinned against the LORD, the God of Israel. This is what I have done: 21 When I
saw in the plunder a beautiful robe from
Babylonia,ᶜ two hundred shekelsᵈ of silver and a wedge of gold weighing fifty

shekels,[e] I coveted them and took them. They are hidden in the ground inside my tent, with the silver underneath."

22 So Joshua sent messengers, and they ran to the tent, and there it was, hidden in his tent, with the silver underneath. 23 They took the things from the tent, brought them to Joshua and all the Israelites and spread them out before the LORD.

24 Then Joshua, together with all Israel, took Achan son of Zerah, the silver, the robe, the gold wedge, his sons and daughters, his cattle, donkeys and sheep, his tent and all that he had, to the Valley of Achor. 25 Joshua said, "Why have you brought this trouble on us? The LORD will bring trouble on you today."

Then all Israel stoned him, and after they had stoned the rest, they burned them. 26 Over Achan they heaped up a large pile of rocks, which remains to this day. Then the LORD turned from his fierce anger. Therefore that place has been called the Valley of Achor[f] ever since.

8:1 THEN the LORD said to Joshua, "Do not be afraid; do not be discouraged. Take the whole army with you, and go up and attack Ai. For I have delivered into your hands the king of Ai, his people, his city and his land. 2 You shall do to Ai and its king as you did to Jericho and its king, except that you may carry off their plunder and livestock for yourselves. Set an ambush behind the city."

3 So Joshua and the whole army moved out to attack Ai. He chose thirty thousand of his best fighting men and sent them out at night 4 with these orders: "Listen carefully. You are to set an ambush behind the city. Don't go very far from it. All of you be on the alert. 5 I and all those with me will advance on the city, and when the men come out against us, as they did before, we will flee from them. 6 They will pursue us until we have lured them away from the city, for they will say, 'They are running away from us as they did before.' So when we flee from them, 7 you are to rise up from ambush and take the city. The LORD your God will give it into your hand. 8 When you have taken the city, set it on fire. Do what the LORD has commanded. See to it; you have my orders."

9 Then Joshua sent them off, and they went to the place of ambush and lay in wait between Bethel and Ai, to the west of Ai—but Joshua spent that night with the people.

10 Early the next morning Joshua mustered his men, and he and the leaders of Israel marched before them to Ai. 11 The entire force that was with him marched up and approached the city and arrived in front of it. They set up camp north of Ai, with the valley between them and the city. 12 Joshua had taken about five thousand men and set them in ambush between Bethel and Ai, to the west of the city. 13 They had the soldiers take up their positions—all those in the camp to the north of the city and the ambush to the west of it. That night Joshua went into the valley.

14 When the king of Ai saw this, he and all the men of the city hurried out early in the morning to meet Israel in battle at a certain place overlooking the Arabah. But he did not know that an ambush had been set against him behind the city. 15 Joshua and all Israel let themselves be driven back before them, and they fled toward the desert. 16 All the men of Ai were called to pursue them, and they pursued Joshua and were lured away from the city. 17 Not a man remained in Ai or Bethel who did not go after Israel. They left the city open and went in pursuit of Israel.

18 Then the LORD said to Joshua, "Hold out toward Ai the javelin that is in your hand, for into your hand I will deliver the city." So Joshua held out his javelin toward Ai. 19 As soon as he did this, the men in the ambush rose quickly from their position and rushed forward. They entered the city and captured it and quickly set it on fire.

20 The men of Ai looked back and saw the smoke of the city rising against the sky, but they had no chance to escape in

any direction, for the Israelites who had been fleeing toward the desert had turned back against their pursuers. [21]For when Joshua and all Israel saw that the ambush had taken the city and that smoke was going up from the city, they turned around and attacked the men of Ai. [22]The men of the ambush also came out of the city against them, so that they were caught in the middle, with Israelites on both sides. Israel cut them down, leaving them neither survivors nor fugitives. [23]But they took the king of Ai alive and brought him to Joshua.

[24]When Israel had finished killing all the men of Ai in the fields and in the desert where they had chased them, and when every one of them had been put to the sword, all the Israelites returned to Ai and killed those who were in it. [25]Twelve thousand men and women fell that day—all the people of Ai. [26]For Joshua did not draw back the hand that held out his javelin until he had destroyed[g] all who lived in Ai. [27]But Israel did carry off for themselves the livestock and plunder of this city, as the LORD had instructed Joshua.

[28]So Joshua burned Ai and made it a permanent heap of ruins, a desolate place to this day. [29]He hung the king of Ai on a tree and left him there until evening. At sunset, Joshua ordered them to take his body from the tree and throw it down at the entrance of the city gate. And they raised a large pile of rocks over it, which remains to this day.

[30]Then Joshua built on Mount Ebal an altar to the LORD, the God of Israel, [31]as Moses the servant of the LORD had commanded the Israelites. He built it according to what is written in the Book of the Law of Moses—an altar of uncut stones, on which no iron tool had been used. On it they offered to the LORD burnt offerings and sacrificed fellowship offerings.[h] [32]There, in the presence of the Israelites, Joshua copied on stones the law of Moses, which he had written. [33]All Israel, aliens and citizens alike, with their elders, offi-

cials and judges, were standing on both sides of the ark of the covenant of the LORD, facing those who carried it—the priests, who were Levites. Half of the people stood in front of Mount Gerizim and half of them in front of Mount Ebal, as Moses the servant of the LORD had formerly commanded when he gave instructions to bless the people of Israel.

[34]Afterward, Joshua read all the words of the law—the blessings and the curses—just as it is written in the Book of the Law. [35]There was not a word of all that Moses had commanded that Joshua did not read to the whole assembly of Israel, including the women and children, and the aliens who lived among them.

[9:1]Now when all the kings west of the Jordan heard about these things—those in the hill country, in the western foothills, and along the entire coast of the Great Sea[i] as far as Lebanon (the kings of the Hittites, Amorites, Canaanites, Perizzites, Hivites and Jebusites)— [2]they came together to make war against Joshua and Israel.

a 19 A solemn charge to tell the truth   b 19 Or and confess to him   c 21 Hebrew Shinar   d 21 That is, about 5 pounds (about 2.3 kilograms)   e 21 That is, about 1 1/4 pounds (about 0.6 kilogram)   f 26 Achor means trouble.   g 26 The Hebrew term refers to the irrevocable giving over of things or persons to the LORD, often by totally destroying them.   h 31 Traditionally peace offerings   i 1 That is, the Mediterranean

LUKE 16:1-18

Jesus told his disciples: "There was a rich man whose manager was accused of wasting his possessions. [2]So he called him in and asked him, 'What is this I hear about you? Give an account of your management, because you cannot be manager any longer.'

[3]"The manager said to himself, 'What shall I do now? My master is taking away my job. I'm not strong enough to dig, and I'm ashamed to beg— [4]I know what I'll do so that, when I lose my job here, people will welcome me into their houses.'

[5]"So he called in each one of his mas-

ter's debtors. He asked the first, 'How much do you owe my master?'

⁶ "'Eight hundred gallons*a* of olive oil,' he replied.

"The manager told him, 'Take your bill, sit down quickly, and make it four hundred.'

⁷ "Then he asked the second, 'And how much do you owe?'

"'A thousand bushels*b* of wheat,' he replied.

"He told him, 'Take your bill and make it eight hundred.'

⁸ "The master commended the dishonest manager because he had acted shrewdly. For the people of this world are more shrewd in dealing with their own kind than are the people of the light. ⁹ I tell you, use worldly wealth to gain friends for yourselves, so that when it is gone, you will be welcomed into eternal dwellings.

¹⁰ "Whoever can be trusted with very little can also be trusted with much, and whoever is dishonest with very little will also be dishonest with much. ¹¹ So if you have not been trustworthy in handling worldly wealth, who will trust you with true riches? ¹² And if you have not been trustworthy with someone else's property, who will give you property of your own?

¹³ "No servant can serve two masters. Either he will hate the one and love the other, or he will be devoted to the one and despise the other. You cannot serve both God and Money."

¹⁴ The Pharisees, who loved money, heard all this and were sneering at Jesus. ¹⁵ He said to them, "You are the ones who justify yourselves in the eyes of men, but God knows your hearts. What is highly valued among men is detestable in God's sight.

¹⁶ "The Law and the Prophets were proclaimed until John. Since that time, the good news of the kingdom of God is being preached, and everyone is forcing his way into it. ¹⁷ It is easier for heaven and earth to disappear than for the least stroke of a pen to drop out of the Law.

¹⁸ "Anyone who divorces his wife and marries another woman commits adultery, and the man who marries a divorced woman commits adultery."

a6 Greek *one hundred batous* (probably about 3 kiloliters)
b7 Greek *one hundred korous* (probably about 35 kiloliters)

PSALM 82:1-8
A psalm of Asaph.

¹ **G**od presides in the great assembly;
  he gives judgment among the "gods":

² "How long will you*a* defend the unjust
  and show partiality to the wicked?
       Selah

³ Defend the cause of the weak and fatherless;
  maintain the rights of the poor and oppressed.

⁴ Rescue the weak and needy;
  deliver them from the hand of the wicked.

⁵ "They know nothing, they understand nothing.
  They walk about in darkness;
  all the foundations of the earth are shaken.

⁶ "I said, 'You are "gods";
  you are all sons of the Most High.'

⁷ But you will die like mere men;
  you will fall like every other ruler."

⁸ Rise up, O God, judge the earth,
  for all the nations are your inheritance.

a2 The Hebrew is plural.

PROVERBS 13:2-3

² **F**rom the fruit of his lips a man enjoys good things,
  but the unfaithful have a craving for violence.

³ He who guards his lips guards his life,
  but he who speaks rashly will come to ruin.

☐ D A Y   1 0 4

GOD SIGHTINGS

April 14

JOSHUA 9:3–10:43

However, when the people of Gibeon heard what Joshua had done to Jericho and Ai, ⁴they resorted to a ruse: They went as a delegation whose donkeys were loaded[a] with worn-out sacks and old wineskins, cracked and mended. ⁵The men put worn and patched sandals on their feet and wore old clothes. All the bread of their food supply was dry and moldy. ⁶Then they went to Joshua in the camp at Gilgal and said to him and the men of Israel, "We have come from a distant country; make a treaty with us."

⁷The men of Israel said to the Hivites, "But perhaps you live near us. How then can we make a treaty with you?"

⁸"We are your servants," they said to Joshua.

But Joshua asked, "Who are you and where do you come from?"

⁹They answered: "Your servants have come from a very distant country because of the fame of the Lord your God. For we have heard reports of him: all that he did in Egypt, ¹⁰and all that he did to the two kings of the Amorites east of the Jordan—Sihon king of Heshbon, and Og king of Bashan, who reigned in Ashtaroth. ¹¹And our elders and all those living in our country said to us, 'Take provisions for your journey; go and meet them and say to them, "We are your servants; make a treaty with us." ' ¹²This bread of ours was warm when we packed it at home on the day we left to come to you. But now see how dry and moldy it is. ¹³And these wineskins that we filled were new, but see how cracked they are. And our clothes and sandals are worn out by the very long journey."

¹⁴The men of Israel sampled their provisions but did not inquire of the Lord. ¹⁵Then Joshua made a treaty of peace with them to let them live, and the leaders of the assembly ratified it by oath.

¹⁶Three days after they made the treaty with the Gibeonites, the Israelites heard that they were neighbors, living near them. ¹⁷So the Israelites set out and on the third day came to their cities: Gibeon, Kephirah, Beeroth and Kiriath Jearim. ¹⁸But the Israelites did not attack them, because the leaders of the assembly had sworn an oath to them by the Lord, the God of Israel.

The whole assembly grumbled against the leaders, ¹⁹but all the leaders answered, "We have given them our oath by the Lord, the God of Israel, and we cannot touch them now. ²⁰This is what we will do to them: We will let them live, so that wrath will not fall on us for breaking the oath we swore to them." ²¹They continued, "Let them live, but let them be woodcutters and water carriers for the entire community." So the leaders' promise to them was kept.

²²Then Joshua summoned the Gibeonites and said, "Why did you deceive us by saying, 'We live a long way from you,' while actually you live near us? ²³You are now under a curse: You will never cease to serve as woodcutters and water carriers for the house of my God."

²⁴They answered Joshua, "Your servants were clearly told how the Lord your God had commanded his servant Moses to give you the whole land and to wipe out all its inhabitants from before you. So we feared for our lives because of you, and that is why we did this. ²⁵We are now in your hands. Do to us whatever seems good and right to you."

²⁶So Joshua saved them from the Israelites, and they did not kill them. ²⁷That day he made the Gibeonites woodcutters and water carriers for the community and for the altar of the Lord at the place the Lord would choose. And that is what they are to this day.

¹⁰:¹Now Adoni-Zedek king of Jerusalem heard that Joshua had taken Ai and to-

tally destroyed[b] it, doing to Ai and its king as he had done to Jericho and its king, and that the people of Gibeon had made a treaty of peace with Israel and were living near them. [2]He and his people were very much alarmed at this, because Gibeon was an important city, like one of the royal cities; it was larger than Ai, and all its men were good fighters. [3]So Adoni-Zedek king of Jerusalem appealed to Hoham king of Hebron, Piram king of Jarmuth, Japhia king of Lachish and Debir king of Eglon. [4]"Come up and help me attack Gibeon," he said, "because it has made peace with Joshua and the Israelites."

[5]Then the five kings of the Amorites—the kings of Jerusalem, Hebron, Jarmuth, Lachish and Eglon—joined forces. They moved up with all their troops and took up positions against Gibeon and attacked it.

[6]The Gibeonites then sent word to Joshua in the camp at Gilgal: "Do not abandon your servants. Come up to us quickly and save us! Help us, because all the Amorite kings from the hill country have joined forces against us."

[7]So Joshua marched up from Gilgal with his entire army, including all the best fighting men. [8]The LORD said to Joshua, "Do not be afraid of them; I have given them into your hand. Not one of them will be able to withstand you."

[9]After an all-night march from Gilgal, Joshua took them by surprise. [10]The LORD threw them into confusion before Israel, who defeated them in a great victory at Gibeon. Israel pursued them along the road going up to Beth Horon and cut them down all the way to Azekah and Makkedah. [11]As they fled before Israel on the road down from Beth Horon to Azekah, the LORD hurled large hailstones down on them from the sky, and more of them died from the hailstones than were killed by the swords of the Israelites.

[12]On the day the LORD gave the Amorites over to Israel, Joshua said to the LORD in the presence of Israel:

"O sun, stand still over Gibeon,
   O moon, over the Valley of
      Aijalon."
[13]So the sun stood still,
   and the moon stopped,
      till the nation avenged itself on[c] its
         enemies,

as it is written in the Book of Jashar.

The sun stopped in the middle of the sky and delayed going down about a full day. [14]There has never been a day like it before or since, a day when the LORD listened to a man. Surely the LORD was fighting for Israel!

[15]Then Joshua returned with all Israel to the camp at Gilgal.

[16]Now the five kings had fled and hidden in the cave at Makkedah. [17]When Joshua was told that the five kings had been found hiding in the cave at Makkedah, [18]he said, "Roll large rocks up to the mouth of the cave, and post some men there to guard it. [19]But don't stop! Pursue your enemies, attack them from the rear and don't let them reach their cities, for the LORD your God has given them into your hand."

[20]So Joshua and the Israelites destroyed them completely—almost to a man—but the few who were left reached their fortified cities. [21]The whole army then returned safely to Joshua in the camp at Makkedah, and no one uttered a word against the Israelites.

[22]Joshua said, "Open the mouth of the cave and bring those five kings out to me." [23]So they brought the five kings out of the cave—the kings of Jerusalem, Hebron, Jarmuth, Lachish and Eglon. [24]When they had brought these kings to Joshua, he summoned all the men of Israel and said to the army commanders who had come with him, "Come here and put your feet on the necks of these kings." So they came forward and placed their feet on their necks.

[25]Joshua said to them, "Do not be afraid; do not be discouraged. Be strong and courageous. This is what the LORD will do to all the enemies you are going to fight." [26]Then Joshua struck and

killed the kings and hung them on five trees, and they were left hanging on the trees until evening.

27 At sunset Joshua gave the order and they took them down from the trees and threw them into the cave where they had been hiding. At the mouth of the cave they placed large rocks, which are there to this day.

28 That day Joshua took Makkedah. He put the city and its king to the sword and totally destroyed everyone in it. He left no survivors. And he did to the king of Makkedah as he had done to the king of Jericho.

29 Then Joshua and all Israel with him moved on from Makkedah to Libnah and attacked it. 30 The LORD also gave that city and its king into Israel's hand. The city and everyone in it Joshua put to the sword. He left no survivors there. And he did to its king as he had done to the king of Jericho.

31 Then Joshua and all Israel with him moved on from Libnah to Lachish; he took up positions against it and attacked it. 32 The LORD handed Lachish over to Israel, and Joshua took it on the second day. The city and everyone in it he put to the sword, just as he had done to Libnah. 33 Meanwhile, Horam king of Gezer had come up to help Lachish, but Joshua defeated him and his army—until no survivors were left.

34 Then Joshua and all Israel with him moved on from Lachish to Eglon; they took up positions against it and attacked it. 35 They captured it that same day and put it to the sword and totally destroyed everyone in it, just as they had done to Lachish.

36 Then Joshua and all Israel with him went up from Eglon to Hebron and attacked it. 37 They took the city and put it to the sword, together with its king, its villages and everyone in it. They left no survivors. Just as at Eglon, they totally destroyed it and everyone in it.

38 Then Joshua and all Israel with him turned around and attacked Debir. 39 They took the city, its king and its villages, and put them to the sword. Every-

one in it they totally destroyed. They left no survivors. They did to Debir and its king as they had done to Libnah and its king and to Hebron.

40 So Joshua subdued the whole region, including the hill country, the Negev, the western foothills and the mountain slopes, together with all their kings. He left no survivors. He totally destroyed all who breathed, just as the LORD, the God of Israel, had commanded. 41 Joshua subdued them from Kadesh Barnea to Gaza and from the whole region of Goshen to Gibeon. 42 All these kings and their lands Joshua conquered in one campaign, because the LORD, the God of Israel, fought for Israel.

43 Then Joshua returned with all Israel to the camp at Gilgal.

a 4 Most Hebrew manuscripts; some Hebrew manuscripts, Vulgate and Syriac (see also Septuagint) *They prepared provisions and loaded their donkeys* b 1 The Hebrew term refers to the irrevocable giving over of things or persons to the LORD, often by totally destroying them; also in verses 28, 35, 37, 39 and 40. c 13 Or *nation triumphed over*

LUKE 16:19–17:10

"There was a rich man who was dressed in purple and fine linen and lived in luxury every day. 20 At his gate was laid a beggar named Lazarus, covered with sores 21 and longing to eat what fell from the rich man's table. Even the dogs came and licked his sores.

22 "The time came when the beggar died and the angels carried him to Abraham's side. The rich man also died and was buried. 23 In hell,a where he was in torment, he looked up and saw Abraham far away, with Lazarus by his side. 24 So he called to him, 'Father Abraham, have pity on me and send Lazarus to dip the tip of his finger in water and cool my tongue, because I am in agony in this fire.'

25 "But Abraham replied, 'Son, remember that in your lifetime you received your good things, while Lazarus received bad things, but now he is comforted here and you are in agony. 26 And besides all this, between us and you a great chasm has been fixed, so that those who want to go from here to you

cannot, nor can anyone cross over from there to us.'

27"He answered, 'Then I beg you, father, send Lazarus to my father's house, 28for I have five brothers. Let him warn them, so that they will not also come to this place of torment.'

29"Abraham replied, 'They have Moses and the Prophets; let them listen to them.'

30"'No, father Abraham,' he said, 'but if someone from the dead goes to them, they will repent.'

31"He said to him, 'If they do not listen to Moses and the Prophets, they will not be convinced even if someone rises from the dead.'"

17:1Jesus said to his disciples: "Things that cause people to sin are bound to come, but woe to that person through whom they come. 2It would be better for him to be thrown into the sea with a millstone tied around his neck than for him to cause one of these little ones to sin. 3So watch yourselves.

"If your brother sins, rebuke him, and if he repents, forgive him. 4If he sins against you seven times in a day, and seven times comes back to you and says, 'I repent,' forgive him."

5The apostles said to the Lord, "Increase our faith!"

6He replied, "If you have faith as small as a mustard seed, you can say to this mulberry tree, 'Be uprooted and planted in the sea,' and it will obey you.

7"Suppose one of you had a servant plowing or looking after the sheep. Would he say to the servant when he comes in from the field, 'Come along now and sit down to eat'? 8Would he not rather say, 'Prepare my supper, get yourself ready and wait on me while I eat and drink; after that you may eat and drink'? 9Would he thank the servant because he did what he was told to do? 10So you also, when you have done everything you were told to do, should say, ' We are unworthy servants; we have only done our duty.' "

a23 Greek Hades

PSALM 83:1-18

A song. A psalm of Asaph.

1 O God, do not keep silent;
   be not quiet, O God, be not still.
2 See how your enemies are astir,
   how your foes rear their heads.
3 With cunning they conspire against
      your people;
   they plot against those you
      cherish.
4 "Come," they say, "let us destroy them
      as a nation,
   that the name of Israel be
      remembered no more."

5 With one mind they plot together;
   they form an alliance against
      you—
6 the tents of Edom and the
      Ishmaelites,
   of Moab and the Hagrites,
7 Gebal,a Ammon and Amalek,
   Philistia, with the people of Tyre.
8 Even Assyria has joined them
   to lend strength to the
         descendants of Lot.   Selah

9 Do to them as you did to Midian,
   as you did to Sisera and Jabin at
      the river Kishon,
10 who perished at Endor
   and became like refuse on the
      ground.
11 Make their nobles like Oreb and
      Zeeb,
   all their princes like Zebah and
      Zalmunna,
12 who said, "Let us take possession
   of the pasturelands of God."

13 Make them like tumbleweed, O my
      God,
   like chaff before the wind.
14 As fire consumes the forest
   or a flame sets the mountains
      ablaze,
15 so pursue them with your tempest
   and terrify them with your storm.
16 Cover their faces with shame
   so that men will seek your name,
      O Lord.

17 May they ever be ashamed and
dismayed;
    may they perish in disgrace.
18 Let them know that you, whose name
is the LORD—
    that you alone are the Most High
    over all the earth.

a 7 That is, Byblos

PROVERBS 13:4
4 The sluggard craves and gets
nothing,
    but the desires of the diligent are
fully satisfied.

☐ DAY 105

GOD SIGHTINGS

April 15

JOSHUA 11:1–12:24

When Jabin king of Hazor heard of this
[Israel's victorious campaign], he sent
word to Jobab king of Madon, to the
kings of Shimron and Acshaph, 2 and to
the northern kings who were in the
mountains, in the Arabah south of Kinnereth, in the western foothills and in
Naphoth Dor*a* on the west; 3 to the Canaanites in the east and west; to the Amorites, Hittites, Perizzites and Jebusites
in the hill country; and to the Hivites below Hermon in the region of Mizpah.
4 They came out with all their troops and
a large number of horses and chariots—a
huge army, as numerous as the sand on
the seashore. 5 All these kings joined
forces and made camp together at the
Waters of Merom, to fight against Israel.

6 The LORD said to Joshua, "Do not be
afraid of them, because by this time tomorrow I will hand all of them over to
Israel, slain. You are to hamstring their
horses and burn their chariots."

7 So Joshua and his whole army came
against them suddenly at the Waters of
Merom and attacked them, 8 and the
LORD gave them into the hand of Israel.

They defeated them and pursued them
all the way to Greater Sidon, to Misrephoth Maim, and to the Valley of Mizpah on the east, until no survivors were
left. 9 Joshua did to them as the LORD
had directed: He hamstrung their
horses and burned their chariots.

10 At that time Joshua turned back and
captured Hazor and put its king to the
sword. (Hazor had been the head of all
these kingdoms.) 11 Everyone in it they
put to the sword. They totally destroyed*b*
them, not sparing anything that
breathed, and he burned up Hazor itself.

12 Joshua took all these royal cities
and their kings and put them to the
sword. He totally destroyed them, as
Moses the servant of the LORD had commanded. 13 Yet Israel did not burn any
of the cities built on their mounds—except Hazor, which Joshua burned.
14 The Israelites carried off for themselves all the plunder and livestock of
these cities, but all the people they put
to the sword until they completely destroyed them, not sparing anyone that
breathed. 15 As the LORD commanded
his servant Moses, so Moses commanded Joshua, and Joshua did it; he
left nothing undone of all that the LORD
commanded Moses.

16 So Joshua took this entire land: the
hill country, all the Negev, the whole region of Goshen, the western foothills,
the Arabah and the mountains of Israel
with their foothills, 17 from Mount Halak, which rises toward Seir, to Baal Gad
in the Valley of Lebanon below Mount
Hermon. He captured all their kings
and struck them down, putting them to
death. 18 Joshua waged war against all
these kings for a long time. 19 Except for
the Hivites living in Gibeon, not one city
made a treaty of peace with the Israelites, who took them all in battle. 20 For it
was the LORD himself who hardened
their hearts to wage war against Israel,
so that he might destroy them totally,
exterminating them without mercy, as
the LORD had commanded Moses.

21 At that time Joshua went and destroyed the Anakites from the hill coun-

try: from Hebron, Debir and Anab, from all the hill country of Judah, and from all the hill country of Israel. Joshua totally destroyed them and their towns. [22]No Anakites were left in Israelite territory; only in Gaza, Gath and Ashdod did any survive. [23]So Joshua took the entire land, just as the LORD had directed Moses, and he gave it as an inheritance to Israel according to their tribal divisions.

Then the land had rest from war.

[12:1]THESE are the kings of the land whom the Israelites had defeated and whose territory they took over east of the Jordan, from the Arnon Gorge to Mount Hermon, including all the eastern side of the Arabah:

[2]Sihon king of the Amorites,
   who reigned in Heshbon. He ruled from Aroer on the rim of the Arnon Gorge—from the middle of the gorge—to the Jabbok River, which is the border of the Ammonites. This included half of Gilead. [3]He also ruled over the eastern Arabah from the Sea of Kinnereth[c] to the Sea of the Arabah (the Salt Sea[d]), to Beth Jeshimoth, and then southward below the slopes of Pisgah.

[4]And the territory of Og king of Bashan, one of the last of the Rephaites, who reigned in Ashtaroth and Edrei. [5]He ruled over Mount Hermon, Salecah, all of Bashan to the border of the people of Geshur and Maacah, and half of Gilead to the border of Sihon king of Heshbon.

[6]Moses, the servant of the LORD, and the Israelites conquered them. And Moses the servant of the LORD gave their land to the Reubenites, the Gadites and the half-tribe of Manasseh to be their possession.

[7]These are the kings of the land that Joshua and the Israelites conquered on the west side of the Jordan, from Baal Gad in the Valley of Lebanon to Mount Halak, which rises toward Seir (their

lands Joshua gave as an inheritance to the tribes of Israel according to their tribal divisions— [8]the hill country, the western foothills, the Arabah, the mountain slopes, the desert and the Negev—the lands of the Hittites, Amorites, Canaanites, Perizzites, Hivites and Jebusites):

[9]the king of Jericho	one
the king of Ai (near Bethel)	one
[10]the king of Jerusalem	one
the king of Hebron	one
[11]the king of Jarmuth	one
the king of Lachish	one
[12]the king of Eglon	one
the king of Gezer	one
[13]the king of Debir	one
the king of Geder	one
[14]the king of Hormah	one
the king of Arad	one
[15]the king of Libnah	one
the king of Adullam	one
[16]the king of Makkedah	one
the king of Bethel	one
[17]the king of Tappuah	one
the king of Hepher	one
[18]the king of Aphek	one
the king of Lasharon	one
[19]the king of Madon	one
the king of Hazor	one
[20]the king of Shimron Meron	one
the king of Acshaph	one
[21]the king of Taanach	one
the king of Megiddo	one
[22]the king of Kedesh	one
the king of Jokneam in Carmel	one
[23]the king of Dor (in Naphoth Dor[a])	one
the king of Goyim in Gilgal	one
[24]the king of Tirzah	one

thirty-one kings in all.

[a]2,23 Or *in the heights of Dor*   [b]11 The Hebrew term refers to the irrevocable giving over of things or persons to the LORD, often by totally destroying them; also in verses 12, 20 and 21.   [c]3 That is, Galilee   [d]3 That is, the Dead Sea

LUKE 17:11-37

[N]ow on his way to Jerusalem, Jesus traveled along the border between Samaria and Galilee. [12]As he was going into a village, ten men who had leprosy[a]

met him. They stood at a distance [13] and called out in a loud voice, "Jesus, Master, have pity on us!"

[14]When he saw them, he said, "Go, show yourselves to the priests." And as they went, they were cleansed.

[15]One of them, when he saw he was healed, came back, praising God in a loud voice. [16]He threw himself at Jesus' feet and thanked him—and he was a Samaritan.

[17]Jesus asked, "Were not all ten cleansed? Where are the other nine? [18]Was no one found to return and give praise to God except this foreigner?" [19]Then he said to him, "Rise and go; your faith has made you well."

[20]**Once, having been asked by the Pharisees when the kingdom of God would come, Jesus replied, "The kingdom of God does not come with your careful observation, [21]nor will people say, 'Here it is,' or 'There it is,' because the kingdom of God is within[b] you."**

[22]Then he said to his disciples, "The time is coming when you will long to see one of the days of the Son of Man, but you will not see it. [23]Men will tell you, 'There he is!' or 'Here he is!' Do not go running off after them. [24]For the Son of Man in his day[c] will be like the lightning, which flashes and lights up the sky from one end to the other. [25]But first he must suffer many things and be rejected by this generation.

[26]"Just as it was in the days of Noah, so also will it be in the days of the Son of Man. [27]People were eating, drinking, marrying and being given in marriage up to the day Noah entered the ark. Then the flood came and destroyed them all.

[28]"It was the same in the days of Lot. People were eating and drinking, buying and selling, planting and building. [29]But the day Lot left Sodom, fire and sulfur rained down from heaven and destroyed them all.

[30]"It will be just like this on the day the Son of Man is revealed. [31]On that day no one who is on the roof of his house, with his goods inside, should go down to get them. Likewise, no one in the field should go back for anything. [32]Remember Lot's wife! [33]Whoever tries to keep his life will lose it, and whoever loses his life will preserve it. [34]I tell you, on that night two people will be in one bed; one will be taken and the other left. [35]Two women will be grinding grain together; one will be taken and the other left.[d] "

[37]"Where, Lord?" they asked.

He replied, "Where there is a dead body, there the vultures will gather."

a12 The Greek word was used for various diseases affecting the skin—not necessarily leprosy. b21 Or among c24 Some manuscripts do not have in his day. d35 Some manuscripts left. 36Two men will be in the field; one will be taken and the other left.

PSALM 84:1-12

For the director of music. According to *gittith.[a]* Of the Sons of Korah. A psalm.

[1] **H**ow lovely is your dwelling place,
    O Lord Almighty!
[2] My soul yearns, even faints,
    for the courts of the Lord;
my heart and my flesh cry out
    for the living God.

[3] Even the sparrow has found a home,
    and the swallow a nest for herself,
    where she may have her young—
a place near your altar,
    O Lord Almighty, my King and my
        God.
[4] Blessed are those who dwell in your
        house;
    they are ever praising you.   *Selah*

[5] Blessed are those whose strength is
        in you,
    who have set their hearts on
        pilgrimage.
[6] As they pass through the Valley of
        Baca,
    they make it a place of springs;
    the autumn rains also cover it with
        pools.[b]
[7] They go from strength to strength,
    till each appears before God in
        Zion.

[8] Hear my prayer, O Lord God Almighty;
    listen to me, O God of Jacob.   *Selah*

⁹Look upon our shield,ᶜ O God;
　　look with favor on your anointed
　　one.

¹⁰Better is one day in your courts
　　than a thousand elsewhere;
　I would rather be a doorkeeper in the
　　house of my God
　　than dwell in the tents of the
　　wicked.
¹¹For the Lᴏʀᴅ God is a sun and shield;
　　the Lᴏʀᴅ bestows favor and honor;
　no good thing does he withhold
　　from those whose walk is
　　blameless.

¹²O Lᴏʀᴅ Almighty,
　　blessed is the man who trusts
　　in you.

ᵃTitle: Probably a musical term　ᵇ6 Or *blessings*
ᶜ9 Or *sovereign*

PROVERBS 13:5-6

⁵The righteous hate what is false,
　　but the wicked bring shame and
　　disgrace.

⁶Righteousness guards the man of
　　integrity,
　　but wickedness overthrows the
　　sinner.

☐ D A Y　1 0 6

GOD SIGHTINGS

April 16

JOSHUA 13:1–14:15

When Joshua was old and well advanced in years, the Lᴏʀᴅ said to him,
"You are very old, and there are still very
large areas of land to be taken over.

²"This is the land that remains: all
the regions of the Philistines and
Geshurites: ³from the Shihor River
on the east of Egypt to the territory
of Ekron on the north, all of it
counted as Canaanite (the territory
of the five Philistine rulers in Gaza,
Ashdod, Ashkelon, Gath and Ek-

ron—that of the Avvites); ⁴from the
south, all the land of the Canaanites, from Arah of the Sidonians as
far as Aphek, the region of the Amorites, ⁵the area of the Gebalitesᵃ;
and all Lebanon to the east, from
Baal Gad below Mount Hermon to
Leboᵇ Hamath.

⁶"As for all the inhabitants of the
mountain regions from Lebanon to
Misrephoth Maim, that is, all the Sidonians, I myself will drive them out before
the Israelites. Be sure to allocate this
land to Israel for an inheritance, as I
have instructed you, ⁷and divide it as an
inheritance among the nine tribes and
half of the tribe of Manasseh."

⁸The other half of Manasseh,ᶜ the Reubenites and the Gadites had received
the inheritance that Moses had given
them east of the Jordan, as he, the servant of the Lᴏʀᴅ, had assigned it to
them.

⁹It extended from Aroer on the
rim of the Arnon Gorge, and from
the town in the middle of the
gorge, and included the whole plateau of Medeba as far as Dibon,
¹⁰and all the towns of Sihon king
of the Amorites, who ruled in
Heshbon, out to the border of the
Ammonites. ¹¹It also included Gilead, the territory of the people of
Geshur and Maacah, all of Mount
Hermon and all Bashan as far as
Salecah— ¹²that is, the whole kingdom of Og in Bashan, who had
reigned in Ashtaroth and Edrei and
had survived as one of the last of
the Rephaites. Moses had defeated
them and taken over their land.
¹³But the Israelites did not drive
out the people of Geshur and Maacah, so they continue to live among
the Israelites to this day.

¹⁴But to the tribe of Levi he gave no
inheritance, since the offerings made
by fire to the Lᴏʀᴅ, the God of Israel, are
their inheritance, as he promised them.

15 This is what Moses had given to the tribe of Reuben, clan by clan:

16 The territory from Aroer on the rim of the Arnon Gorge, and from the town in the middle of the gorge, and the whole plateau past Medeba 17 to Heshbon and all its towns on the plateau, including Dibon, Bamoth Baal, Beth Baal Meon, 18 Jahaz, Kedemoth, Mephaath, 19 Kiriathaim, Sibmah, Zereth Shahar on the hill in the valley, 20 Beth Peor, the slopes of Pisgah, and Beth Jeshimoth— 21 all the towns on the plateau and the entire realm of Sihon king of the Amorites, who ruled at Heshbon. Moses had defeated him and the Midianite chiefs, Evi, Rekem, Zur, Hur and Reba—princes allied with Sihon—who lived in that country. 22 In addition to those slain in battle, the Israelites had put to the sword Balaam son of Beor, who practiced divination. 23 The boundary of the Reubenites was the bank of the Jordan. These towns and their villages were the inheritance of the Reubenites, clan by clan.

24 This is what Moses had given to the tribe of Gad, clan by clan:

25 The territory of Jazer, all the towns of Gilead and half the Ammonite country as far as Aroer, near Rabbah; 26 and from Heshbon to Ramath Mizpah and Betonim, and from Mahanaim to the territory of Debir; 27 and in the valley, Beth Haram, Beth Nimrah, Succoth and Zaphon with the rest of the realm of Sihon king of Heshbon (the east side of the Jordan, the territory up to the end of the Sea of Kinne; 28 These towns and their villages were the inheritance of the Gadites, clan by clan.

29 This is what Moses had given to the half-tribe of Manasseh, that is, to half the family of the descendants of Manasseh, clan by clan:

30 The territory extending from Mahanaim and including all of Bashan, the entire realm of Og king of Bashan—all the settlements of Jair in Bashan, sixty towns, 31 half of Gilead, and Ashtaroth and Edrei (the royal cities of Og in Bashan). This was for the descendants of Makir son of Manasseh—for half of the sons of Makir, clan by clan.

32 This is the inheritance Moses had given when he was in the plains of Moab across the Jordan east of Jericho. 33 But to the tribe of Levi, Moses had given no inheritance; the LORD, the God of Israel, is their inheritance, as he promised them.

14:1 Now these are the areas the Israelites received as an inheritance in the land of Canaan, which Eleazar the priest, Joshua son of Nun and the heads of the tribal clans of Israel allotted to them. 2 Their inheritances were assigned by lot to the nine-and-a-half tribes, as the LORD had commanded through Moses. 3 Moses had granted the two-and-a-half tribes their inheritance east of the Jordan but had not granted the Levites an inheritance among the rest, 4 for the sons of Joseph had become two tribes—Manasseh and Ephraim. The Levites received no share of the land but only towns to live in, with pasturelands for their flocks and herds. 5 So the Israelites divided the land, just as the LORD had commanded Moses.

6 Now the men of Judah approached Joshua at Gilgal, and Caleb son of Jephunneh the Kenizzite said to him, "You know what the LORD said to Moses the man of God at Kadesh Barnea about you and me. 7 I was forty years old when Moses the servant of the LORD sent me from Kadesh Barnea to explore the land. And I brought him back a report according to my convictions, 8 but my

brothers who went up with me made the hearts of the people melt with fear. I, however, followed the LORD my God wholeheartedly. 9 So on that day Moses swore to me, 'The land on which your feet have walked will be your inheritance and that of your children forever, because you have followed the LORD my God wholeheartedly.'e

10 "Now then, just as the LORD promised, he has kept me alive for forty-five years since the time he said this to Moses, while Israel moved about in the desert. So here I am today, eighty-five years old! 11 I am still as strong today as the day Moses sent me out; I'm just as vigorous to go out to battle now as I was then. 12 Now give me this hill country that the LORD promised me that day. You yourself heard then that the Anakites were there and their cities were large and fortified, but, the LORD helping me, I will drive them out just as he said."

13 Then Joshua blessed Caleb son of Jephunneh and gave him Hebron as his inheritance. 14 So Hebron has belonged to Caleb son of Jephunneh the Kenizzite ever since, because he followed the LORD, the God of Israel, wholeheartedly. 15 (Hebron used to be called Kiriath Arba after Arba, who was the greatest man among the Anakites.)

Then the land had rest from war.

a5 That is, the area of Byblos   b5 Or to the entrance to   c8 Hebrew With it (that is, with the other half of Manasseh)   d27 That is, Galilee   e9 Deut. 1:36

LUKE 18:1-17

Then Jesus told his disciples a parable to show them that they should always pray and not give up. 2 He said: "In a certain town there was a judge who neither feared God nor cared about men. 3 And there was a widow in that town who kept coming to him with the plea, 'Grant me justice against my adversary.'

4 "For some time he refused. But finally he said to himself, 'Even though I don't fear God or care about men, 5 yet because this widow keeps bothering me, I will see that she gets justice, so that

she won't eventually wear me out with her coming!'"

6 And the Lord said, "Listen to what the unjust judge says. 7 And will not God bring about justice for his chosen ones, who cry out to him day and night? Will he keep putting them off? 8 I tell you, he will see that they get justice, and quickly. However, when the Son of Man comes, will he find faith on the earth?"

9 To some who were confident of their own righteousness and looked down on everybody else, Jesus told this parable: 10 "Two men went up to the temple to pray, one a Pharisee and the other a tax collector. 11 The Pharisee stood up and prayed abouta himself: 'God, I thank you that I am not like other men—robbers, evildoers, adulterers—or even like this tax collector. 12 I fast twice a week and give a tenth of all I get.'

13 "But the tax collector stood at a distance. He would not even look up to heaven, but beat his breast and said, 'God, have mercy on me, a sinner.'

14 "I tell you that this man, rather than the other, went home justified before God. For everyone who exalts himself will be humbled, and he who humbles himself will be exalted."

15 People were also bringing babies to Jesus to have him touch them. When the disciples saw this, they rebuked them. 16 But Jesus called the children to him and said, "Let the little children come to me, and do not hinder them, for the kingdom of God belongs to such as these. 17 I tell you the truth, anyone who will not receive the kingdom of God like a little child will never enter it."

a11 Or to

PSALM 85:1-13

For the director of music. Of the Sons of Korah. A psalm.

1 You showed favor to your land, O LORD;
    you restored the fortunes of Jacob.

2 You forgave the iniquity of your
      people
   and covered all their sins.   *Selah*
3 You set aside all your wrath
   and turned from your fierce anger.

4 Restore us again, O God our Savior,
   and put away your displeasure
      toward us.
5 Will you be angry with us forever?
   Will you prolong your anger
      through all generations?
6 Will you not revive us again,
   that your people may rejoice in
      you?
7 Show us your unfailing love,
      O LORD,
   and grant us your salvation.

8 I will listen to what God the LORD
      will say;
   he promises peace to his people,
      his saints—
   but let them not return to folly.
9 Surely his salvation is near those who
      fear him,
   that his glory may dwell in our
      land.

10 Love and faithfulness meet
      together;
   righteousness and peace kiss each
      other.
11 Faithfulness springs forth from the
      earth,
   and righteousness looks down
      from heaven.
12 The LORD will indeed give what is
      good,
   and our land will yield its harvest.
13 Righteousness goes before him
   and prepares the way for
      his steps.

PROVERBS 13:7-8
7 One man pretends to be rich, yet has
      nothing;
   another pretends to be poor, yet
      has great wealth.

8 A man's riches may ransom his life,
   but a poor man hears no threat.

□ DAY 107

GOD SIGHTINGS

April 17

JOSHUA 15:1-63

The allotment for the tribe of Judah, clan by clan, extended down to the territory of Edom, to the Desert of Zin in the extreme south.

2 Their southern boundary started from the bay at the southern end of the Salt Sea,ᵃ 3 crossed south of Scorpionᵇ Pass, continued on to Zin and went over to the south of Kadesh Barnea. Then it ran past Hezron up to Addar and curved around to Karka. 4 It then passed along to Azmon and joined the Wadi of Egypt, ending at the sea. This is theirᶜ southern boundary.

5 The eastern boundary is the Salt Sea as far as the mouth of the Jordan.

The northern boundary started from the bay of the sea at the mouth of the Jordan, 6 went up to Beth Hoglah and continued north of Beth Arabah to the Stone of Bohan son of Reuben. 7 The boundary then went up to Debir from the Valley of Achor and turned north to Gilgal, which faces the Pass of Adummim south of the gorge. It continued along to the waters of En Shemesh and came out at En Rogel. 8 Then it ran up the Valley of Ben Hinnom along the southern slope of the Jebusite city (that is, Jerusalem). From there it climbed to the top of the hill west of the Hinnom Valley at the northern end of the Valley of Rephaim. 9 From the hilltop the boundary headed toward the spring of the waters of Nephtoah, came out at the towns of Mount Ephron and went down toward Baalah (that is, Kiriath Jearim). 10 Then it curved westward from Baalah to Mount

Seir, ran along the northern slope of Mount Jearim (that is, Kesalon), continued down to Beth Shemesh and crossed to Timnah. [11]It went to the northern slope of Ekron, turned toward Shikkeron, passed along to Mount Baalah and reached Jabneel. The boundary ended at the sea.

[12]The western boundary is the coastline of the Great Sea.[d]

These are the boundaries around the people of Judah by their clans.

[13]In accordance with the LORD's command to him, Joshua gave to Caleb son of Jephunneh a portion in Judah—Kiriath Arba, that is, Hebron. (Arba was the forefather of Anak.) [14]From Hebron Caleb drove out the three Anakites—Sheshai, Ahiman and Talmai—descendants of Anak. [15]From there he marched against the people living in Debir (formerly called Kiriath Sepher). [16]And Caleb said, "I will give my daughter Acsah in marriage to the man who attacks and captures Kiriath Sepher." [17]Othniel son of Kenaz, Caleb's brother, took it; so Caleb gave his daughter Acsah to him in marriage.

[18]One day when she came to Othniel, she urged him[e] to ask her father for a field. When she got off her donkey, Caleb asked her, "What can I do for you?"

[19]She replied, "Do me a special favor. Since you have given me land in the Negev, give me also springs of water." So Caleb gave her the upper and lower springs.

[20]This is the inheritance of the tribe of Judah, clan by clan:

[21]The southernmost towns of the tribe of Judah in the Negev toward the boundary of Edom were:

Kabzeel, Eder, Jagur, [22]Kinah, Dimonah, Adadah, [23]Kedesh, Hazor, Ithnan, [24]Ziph, Telem, Bealoth, [25]Hazor Hadattah, Kerioth Hezron (that is, Hazor), [26]Amam, Shema, Moladah, [27]Hazar Gaddah, Heshmon, Beth Pelet, [28]Hazar Shual, Beersheba, Biziothiah, [29]Baalah, Iim, Ezem, [30]Eltolad, Kesil, Hormah, [31]Ziklag, Madmannah, Sansannah, [32]Lebaoth, Shilhim, Ain and Rimmon—a total of twenty-nine towns and their villages.

[33]In the western foothills:

Eshtaol, Zorah, Ashnah, [34]Zanoah, En Gannim, Tappuah, Enam, [35]Jarmuth, Adullam, Socoh, Azekah, [36]Shaaraim, Adithaim and Gederah (or Gederothaim)[f]—fourteen towns and their villages.

[37]Zenan, Hadashah, Migdal Gad, [38]Dilean, Mizpah, Joktheel, [39]Lachish, Bozkath, Eglon, [40]Cabbon, Lahmas, Kitlish, [41]Gederoth, Beth Dagon, Naamah and Makkedah—sixteen towns and their villages.

[42]Libnah, Ether, Ashan, [43]Iphtah, Ashnah, Nezib, [44]Keilah, Aczib and Mareshah—nine towns and their villages.

[45]Ekron, with its surrounding settlements and villages; [46]west of Ekron, all that were in the vicinity of Ashdod, together with their villages; [47]Ashdod, its surrounding settlements and villages; and Gaza, its settlements and villages, as far as the Wadi of Egypt and the coastline of the Great Sea.

[48]In the hill country:

Shamir, Jattir, Socoh, [49]Dannah, Kiriath Sannah (that is, Debir), [50]Anab, Eshtemoh, Anim, [51]Goshen, Holon and Giloh—eleven towns and their villages.

[52]Arab, Dumah, Eshan, [53]Janim, Beth Tappuah, Aphekah, [54]Humtah, Kiriath Arba (that is, Hebron) and Zior—nine towns and their villages.

[55]Maon, Carmel, Ziph, Juttah, [56]Jezreel, Jokdeam, Zanoah, [57]Kain, Gibeah and Timnah—ten towns and their villages.

[58]Halhul, Beth Zur, Gedor, [59]Maarath, Beth Anoth and Eltekon—six towns and their villages.

⁶⁰Kiriath Baal (that is, Kiriath Je-arim) and Rabbah—two towns and their villages.

⁶¹In the desert:

Beth Arabah, Middin, Secacah, ⁶²Nibshan, the City of Salt and En Gedi—six towns and their villages.

⁶³Judah could not dislodge the Jebu-sites, who were living in Jerusalem; to this day the Jebusites live there with the people of Judah.

a2 That is, the Dead Sea; also in verse 5   *b3* Hebrew *Akrabbim*   *c4* Hebrew *your*   *d12* That is, the Mediterranean; also in verse 47   *e18* Hebrew and some Septuagint manuscripts; other Septuagint manuscripts (see also note at Judges 1:14) *Othniel, he urged her*   *f36* Or *Gederah and Gederothaim*

LUKE 18:18-43

A certain ruler asked him [Jesus], "Good teacher, what must I do to inherit eter-nal life?"

¹⁹"Why do you call me good?" Jesus answered. "No one is good—except God alone. ²⁰You know the commandments: 'Do not commit adultery, do not murder, do not steal, do not give false testimony, honor your father and mother.'*a* "

²¹"All these I have kept since I was a boy," he said.

²²When Jesus heard this, he said to him, "You still lack one thing. Sell every-thing you have and give to the poor, and you will have treasure in heaven. Then come, follow me."

²³When he heard this, he became very sad, because he was a man of great wealth. ²⁴Jesus looked at him and said, "How hard it is for the rich to enter the kingdom of God! ²⁵Indeed, it is easier for a camel to go through the eye of a needle than for a rich man to enter the kingdom of God."

²⁶Those who heard this asked, "Who then can be saved?"

²⁷Jesus replied, "What is impossible with men is possible with God."

²⁸Peter said to him, "We have left all we had to follow you!"

²⁹"I tell you the truth," Jesus said to them, "no one who has left home or wife or brothers or parents or children for the sake of the kingdom of God ³⁰will

fail to receive many times as much in this age and, in the age to come, eternal life."

³¹Jesus took the Twelve aside and told them, "We are going up to Jerusa-lem, and everything that is written by the prophets about the Son of Man will be fulfilled. ³²He will be handed over to the Gentiles. They will mock him, insult him, spit on him, flog him and kill him. ³³On the third day he will rise again."

³⁴The disciples did not understand any of this. Its meaning was hidden from them, and they did not know what he was talking about.

³⁵As Jesus approached Jericho, a blind man was sitting by the roadside begging. ³⁶When he heard the crowd going by, he asked what was happening. ³⁷They told him, "Jesus of Nazareth is passing by."

³⁸He called out, "Jesus, Son of David, have mercy on me!"

³⁹Those who led the way rebuked him and told him to be quiet, but he shouted all the more, "Son of David, have mercy on me!"

⁴⁰Jesus stopped and ordered the man to be brought to him. When he came near, Jesus asked him, ⁴¹"What do you want me to do for you?"

"Lord, I want to see," he replied.

⁴²Jesus said to him, "Receive your sight; your faith has healed you." ⁴³Im-mediately he received his sight and fol-lowed Jesus, praising God. When all the people saw it, they also praised God.

a20 Exodus 20:12-16; Deut. 5:16-20

PSALM 86:1-17

A prayer of David.

¹ **H**ear, O LORD, and answer me,
   for I am poor and needy.
² Guard my life, for I am devoted to
      you.
   You are my God; save your servant
      who trusts in you.
³ Have mercy on me, O Lord,
   for I call to you all day long.
⁴ Bring joy to your servant,
   for to you, O Lord,
   I lift up my soul.

⁵You are forgiving and good, O Lord,
  abounding in love to all who call
    to you.
⁶Hear my prayer, O Lord;
  listen to my cry for mercy.
⁷In the day of my trouble I will call
    to you,
  for you will answer me.

⁸Among the gods there is none like
    you, O Lord;
  no deeds can compare with yours.
⁹All the nations you have made
  will come and worship before you,
    O Lord;
  they will bring glory to your
    name.
¹⁰For you are great and do marvelous
    deeds;
  you alone are God.

¹¹**Teach me your way, O Lord,**
  and I will walk in your truth;
give me an undivided heart,
  that I may fear your name.
¹²**I will praise you, O Lord my God,**
  with all my heart;
  I will glorify your name forever.
¹³For great is your love toward me;
  you have delivered me from the
    depths of the grave.ᵃ

¹⁴The arrogant are attacking me,
    O God;
  a band of ruthless men seeks my
    life—
  men without regard for you.
¹⁵But you, O Lord, are a compassionate
    and gracious God,
  slow to anger, abounding in love
    and faithfulness.
¹⁶Turn to me and have mercy on me;
  grant your strength to your
    servant
  and save the son of your
    maidservant.ᵇ
¹⁷Give me a sign of your goodness,
  that my enemies may see it and be
    put to shame,
  for you, O Lord, have helped me
    and comforted me.

ᵃ13 Hebrew Sheol   ᵇ16 Or save your faithful son

PROVERBS 13:9-10
⁹The light of the righteous shines
    brightly,
  but the lamp of the wicked is
    snuffed out.

¹⁰Pride only breeds quarrels,
  but wisdom is found in those who
    take advice.

□ D A Y   1 0 8

GOD SIGHTINGS

April 18

JOSHUA 16:1–18:28

The allotment for Joseph began at the Jordan of Jericho,ᵃ east of the waters of Jericho, and went up from there through the desert into the hill country of Bethel. ²It went on from Bethel (that is, Luz),ᵇ crossed over to the territory of the Arkites in Ataroth, ³descended westward to the territory of the Japhletites as far as the region of Lower Beth Horon and on to Gezer, ending at the sea.

⁴So Manasseh and Ephraim, the descendants of Joseph, received their inheritance.

⁵This was the territory of Ephraim, clan by clan:

The boundary of their inheritance went from Ataroth Addar in the east to Upper Beth Horon ⁶and continued to the sea. From Micmethath on the north it curved eastward to Taanath Shiloh, passing by it to Janoah on the east. ⁷Then it went down from Janoah to Ataroth and Naarah, touched Jericho and came out at the Jordan. ⁸From Tappuah the border went west to the Kanah Ravine and ended at the sea. This was the inheritance of the tribe of the Ephraimites, clan by clan. ⁹It also included all the towns and their villages that were set aside for the Ephraimites within the inheritance of the Manassites. [10]They did not dislodge the Canaanites living in Gezer; to this day the Canaanites live among the people of Ephraim but are required to do forced labor.

[17:1]THIS was the allotment for the tribe of Manasseh as Joseph's firstborn, that is, for Makir, Manasseh's firstborn. Makir was the ancestor of the Gileadites, who had received Gilead and Bashan because the Makirites were great soldiers. [2]So this allotment was for the rest of the people of Manasseh—the clans of Abiezer, Helek, Asriel, Shechem, Hepher and Shemida. These are the other male descendants of Manasseh son of Joseph by their clans.

[3]Now Zelophehad son of Hepher, the son of Gilead, the son of Makir, the son of Manasseh, had no sons but only daughters, whose names were Mahlah, Noah, Hoglah, Milcah and Tirzah. [4]They went to Eleazar the priest, Joshua son of Nun, and the leaders and said, "The LORD commanded Moses to give us an inheritance among our brothers." So Joshua gave them an inheritance along with the brothers of their father, according to the LORD's command. [5]Manasseh's share consisted of ten tracts of land besides Gilead and Bashan east of the Jordan, [6]because the daughters of the tribe of Manasseh received an inheritance among the sons. The land of Gilead belonged to the rest of the descendants of Manasseh.

[7]The territory of Manasseh extended from Asher to Micmethath east of Shechem. The boundary ran southward from there to include the people living at En Tappuah. [8](Manasseh had the land of Tappuah, but Tappuah itself, on the boundary of Manasseh, belonged to the Ephraimites.) [9]Then the boundary continued south to the Kanah Ravine. There were towns belonging to Ephraim lying among the towns of Manasseh, but the boundary of Manasseh was the northern side of the ravine and ended at the sea. [10]On the south the land belonged to Ephraim, on the north to Manasseh. The territory of Manasseh reached the sea and bordered Asher on the north and Issachar on the east.

[11]Within Issachar and Asher, Manasseh also had Beth Shan, Ibleam and the people of Dor, Endor, Taanach and Megiddo, together with their surrounding settlements (the third in the list is Naphoth[c]).

[12]Yet the Manassites were not able to occupy these towns, for the Canaanites were determined to live in that region. [13]However, when the Israelites grew stronger, they subjected the Canaanites to forced labor but did not drive them out completely.

[14]The people of Joseph said to Joshua, "Why have you given us only one allotment and one portion for an inheritance? We are a numerous people and the LORD has blessed us abundantly."

[15]"If you are so numerous," Joshua answered, "and if the hill country of Ephraim is too small for you, go up into the forest and clear land for yourselves there in the land of the Perizzites and Rephaites."

[16]The people of Joseph replied, "The hill country is not enough for us, and all the Canaanites who live in the plain have iron chariots, both those in Beth Shan and its settlements and those in the Valley of Jezreel."

[17]But Joshua said to the house of Joseph—to Ephraim and Manasseh—"You are numerous and very powerful. You will have not only one allotment [18]but the forested hill country as well. Clear it, and its farthest limits will be yours; though the Canaanites have iron chariots and though they are strong, you can drive them out."

[18:1]THE whole assembly of the Israelites gathered at Shiloh and set up the Tent of Meeting there. The country was brought under their control, [2]but there were still seven Israelite tribes who had not yet received their inheritance.

³So Joshua said to the Israelites: "How long will you wait before you begin to take possession of the land that the LORD, the God of your fathers, has given you? ⁴Appoint three men from each tribe. I will send them out to make a survey of the land and to write a description of it, according to the inheritance of each. Then they will return to me. ⁵You are to divide the land into seven parts. Judah is to remain in its territory on the south and the house of Joseph in its territory on the north. ⁶After you have written descriptions of the seven parts of the land, bring them here to me and I will cast lots for you in the presence of the LORD our God. ⁷The Levites, however, do not get a portion among you, because the priestly service of the LORD is their inheritance. And Gad, Reuben and the half-tribe of Manasseh have already received their inheritance on the east side of the Jordan. Moses the servant of the LORD gave it to them."

⁸As the men started on their way to map out the land, Joshua instructed them, "Go and make a survey of the land and write a description of it. Then return to me, and I will cast lots for you here at Shiloh in the presence of the LORD." ⁹So the men left and went through the land. They wrote its description on a scroll, town by town, in seven parts, and returned to Joshua in the camp at Shiloh. ¹⁰Joshua then cast lots for them in Shiloh in the presence of the LORD, and there he distributed the land to the Israelites according to their tribal divisions.

¹¹The lot came up for the tribe of Benjamin, clan by clan. Their allotted territory lay between the tribes of Judah and Joseph:

¹²On the north side their boundary began at the Jordan, passed the northern slope of Jericho and headed west into the hill country, coming out at the desert of Beth Aven. ¹³From there it crossed to the south slope of Luz (that is, Bethel) and went down to Ataroth Addar on the hill south of Lower Beth Horon.

¹⁴From the hill facing Beth Horon on the south the boundary turned south along the western side and came out at Kiriath Baal (that is, Kiriath Jearim), a town of the people of Judah. This was the western side.

¹⁵The southern side began at the outskirts of Kiriath Jearim on the west, and the boundary came out at the spring of the waters of Nephtoah. ¹⁶The boundary went down to the foot of the hill facing the Valley of Ben Hinnom, north of the Valley of Rephaim. It continued down the Hinnom Valley along the southern slope of the Jebusite city and so to En Rogel. ¹⁷It then curved north, went to En Shemesh, continued to Geliloth, which faces the Pass of Adummim, and ran down to the Stone of Bohan son of Reuben. ¹⁸It continued to the northern slope of Beth Arabah* and on down into the Arabah. ¹⁹It then went to the northern slope of Beth Hoglah and came out at the northern bay of the Salt Sea,* at the mouth of the Jordan in the south. This was the southern boundary.

²⁰The Jordan formed the boundary on the eastern side.

These were the boundaries that marked out the inheritance of the clans of Benjamin on all sides.

²¹The tribe of Benjamin, clan by clan, had the following cities:

Jericho, Beth Hoglah, Emek Keziz, ²²Beth Arabah, Zemaraim, Bethel, ²³Avvim, Parah, Ophrah, ²⁴Kephar Ammoni, Ophni and Geba—twelve towns and their villages.

²⁵Gibeon, Ramah, Beeroth, ²⁶Mizpah, Kephirah, Mozah, ²⁷Rekem, Irpeel, Taralah, ²⁸Zelah, Haeleph, the Jebusite city (that is, Jerusalem), Gibeah and Kiriath—fourteen towns and their villages.

This was the inheritance of Benjamin for its clans.

a 1 Jordan of Jericho was possibly an ancient name for the Jordan River. *b 2* Septuagint; Hebrew *Bethel to Luz* *c 11* That is, Naphoth Dor *d 18* Septuagint; Hebrew *slope facing the Arabah* *e 19* That is, the Dead Sea

LUKE 19:1-27

Jesus entered Jericho and was passing through. ²A man was there by the name of Zacchaeus; he was a chief tax collector and was wealthy. ³He wanted to see who Jesus was, but being a short man he could not, because of the crowd. ⁴So he ran ahead and climbed a sycamore-fig tree to see him, since Jesus was coming that way.

⁵When Jesus reached the spot, he looked up and said to him, "Zacchaeus, come down immediately. I must stay at your house today." ⁶So he came down at once and welcomed him gladly.

⁷All the people saw this and began to mutter, "He has gone to be the guest of a 'sinner.'"

⁸But Zacchaeus stood up and said to the Lord, "Look, Lord! Here and now I give half of my possessions to the poor, and if I have cheated anybody out of anything, I will pay back four times the amount."

⁹Jesus said to him, " Today salvation has come to this house, because this man, too, is a son of Abraham. ¹⁰For the Son of Man came to seek and to save what was lost."

¹¹While they were listening to this, he went on to tell them a parable, because he was near Jerusalem and the people thought that the kingdom of God was going to appear at once. ¹²He said: "A man of noble birth went to a distant country to have himself appointed king and then to return. ¹³So he called ten of his servants and gave them ten minas.*a* 'Put this money to work,' he said, 'until I come back.'

¹⁴"But his subjects hated him and sent a delegation after him to say, 'We don't want this man to be our king.'

¹⁵"He was made king, however, and returned home. Then he sent for the servants to whom he had given the money, in order to find out what they had gained with it.

¹⁶"The first one came and said, 'Sir, your mina has earned ten more.'

¹⁷"'Well done, my good servant!' his master replied. 'Because you have been trustworthy in a very small matter, take charge of ten cities.'

¹⁸"The second came and said, 'Sir, your mina has earned five more.'

¹⁹"His master answered, 'You take charge of five cities.'

²⁰"Then another servant came and said, 'Sir, here is your mina; I have kept it laid away in a piece of cloth. ²¹I was afraid of you, because you are a hard man. You take out what you did not put in and reap what you did not sow.'

²²"His master replied, 'I will judge you by your own words, you wicked servant! You knew, did you, that I am a hard man, taking out what I did not put in, and reaping what I did not sow? ²³Why then didn't you put my money on deposit, so that when I came back, I could have collected it with interest?'

²⁴"Then he said to those standing by, 'Take his mina away from him and give it to the one who has ten minas.'

²⁵"'Sir,' they said, 'he already has ten!'

²⁶"He replied, 'I tell you that to everyone who has, more will be given, but as for the one who has nothing, even what he has will be taken away. ²⁷But those enemies of mine who did not want me to be king over them—bring them here and kill them in front of me.'"

a 13 A mina was about three months' wages.

PSALM 87:1-7
Of the Sons of Korah. A psalm. A song.

¹ **H**e has set his foundation on the
holy mountain;
² the LORD loves the gates of Zion
more than all the dwellings of
Jacob.
³ Glorious things are said of you,
O city of God: *Selah*
⁴ "I will record Rahab*a* and Babylon
among those who acknowledge
me—

Philistia too, and Tyre, along with
  Cush[b]—
    and will say, 'This[c] one was born in
      Zion.'"

[5] Indeed, of Zion it will be said,
  "This one and that one were born
    in her,
  and the Most High himself will
    establish her."
[6] The LORD will write in the register of
  the peoples:
    "This one was born in Zion." *Selah*
[7] As they make music they will sing,
  "All my fountains are in you."

a4 A poetic name for Egypt   b4 That is, the upper Nile region   c4 Or "O Rahab and Babylon, / Philistia, Tyre and Cush, / I will record concerning those who acknowledge me: / 'This

PROVERBS 13:11
[11] **D**ishonest money dwindles away,
  but he who gathers money little by
    little makes it grow.

☐ D A Y 1 0 9

GOD SIGHTINGS

April 19

JOSHUA 19:1–20:9
The second lot came out for the tribe of
Simeon, clan by clan. Their inheritance
lay within the territory of Judah. [2] It included:
    Beersheba (or Sheba),[a] Mola-
dah, [3] Hazar Shual, Balah, Ezem,
[4] Eltolad, Bethul, Hormah, [5] Ziklag,
Beth Marcaboth, Hazar Susah,
[6] Beth Lebaoth and Sharuhen—
thirteen towns and their villages;
    [7] Ain, Rimmon, Ether and Ashan—
four towns and their villages— [8] and
all the villages around these towns
as far as Baalath Beer (Ramah in the
Negev).
This was the inheritance of the tribe of
the Simeonites, clan by clan. [9] The inheritance of the Simeonites was taken
from the share of Judah, because Ju-

dah's portion was more than they
needed. So the Simeonites received
their inheritance within the territory of
Judah.

[10] The third lot came up for Zebulun,
clan by clan:
    The boundary of their inheri-
tance went as far as Sarid. [11] Going
west it ran to Maralah, touched
Dabbesheth, and extended to the
ravine near Jokneam. [12] It turned
east from Sarid toward the sunrise
to the territory of Kisloth Tabor
and went on to Daberath and up to
Japhia. [13] Then it continued eastward to Gath Hepher and Eth Ka-
zin; it came out at Rimmon and
turned toward Neah. [14] There the
boundary went around on the
north to Hannathon and ended at
the Valley of Iphtah El. [15] Included
were Kattath, Nahalal, Shimron,
Idalah and Bethlehem. There were
twelve towns and their villages.
[16] These towns and their villages were
the inheritance of Zebulun, clan by
clan.

[17] The fourth lot came out for Issachar,
clan by clan. [18] Their territory included:
    Jezreel, Kesulloth, Shunem,
[19] Hapharaim, Shion, Anaharath,
[20] Rabbith, Kishion, Ebez, [21] Re-
meth, En Gannim, En Haddah and
Beth Pazzez. [22] The boundary
touched Tabor, Shahazumah and
Beth Shemesh, and ended at the
Jordan. There were sixteen towns
and their villages.
[23] These towns and their villages were
the inheritance of the tribe of Issachar,
clan by clan.

[24] The fifth lot came out for the tribe of
Asher, clan by clan. [25] Their territory included:
    Helkath, Hali, Beten, Acshaph,
[26] Allammelech, Amad and Mishal.
On the west the boundary touched
Carmel and Shihor Libnath. [27] It
then turned east toward Beth Dagon, touched Zebulun and the

Valley of Iphtah El, and went north to Beth Emek and Neiel, passing Cabul on the left. 28It went to Abdon,*b* Rehob, Hammon and Kanah, as far as Greater Sidon. 29The boundary then turned back toward Ramah and went to the fortified city of Tyre, turned toward Hosah and came out at the sea in the region of Aczib, 30Ummah, Aphek and Rehob. There were twenty-two towns and their villages.

31These towns and their villages were the inheritance of the tribe of Asher, clan by clan.

32The sixth lot came out for Naphtali, clan by clan:

33Their boundary went from Heleph and the large tree in Zaanannim, passing Adami Nekeb and Jabneel to Lakkum and ending at the Jordan. 34The boundary ran west through Aznoth Tabor and came out at Hukkok. It touched Zebulun on the south, Asher on the west and the Jordan*c* on the east. 35The fortified cities were Ziddim, Zer, Hammath, Rakkath, Kinnereth, 36Adamah, Ramah, Hazor, 37Kedesh, Edrei, En Hazor, 38Iron, Migdal El, Horem, Beth Anath and Beth Shemesh. There were nineteen towns and their villages.

39These towns and their villages were the inheritance of the tribe of Naphtali, clan by clan.

40The seventh lot came out for the tribe of Dan, clan by clan. 41The territory of their inheritance included:

Zorah, Eshtaol, Ir Shemesh, 42Shaalabbin, Aijalon, Ithlah, 43Elon, Timnah, Ekron, 44Eltekeh, Gibbethon, Baalath, 45Jehud, Bene Berak, Gath Rimmon, 46Me Jarkon and Rakkon, with the area facing Joppa.

47(But the Danites had difficulty taking possession of their territory, so they went up and attacked Leshem, took it, put it to the sword and occupied it. They settled in Leshem and named it Dan after their forefather.)

48These towns and their villages were the inheritance of the tribe of Dan, clan by clan.

49When they had finished dividing the land into its allotted portions, the Israelites gave Joshua son of Nun an inheritance among them, 50as the Lord had commanded. They gave him the town he asked for—Timnath Serah*d* in the hill country of Ephraim. And he built up the town and settled there.

51These are the territories that Eleazar the priest, Joshua son of Nun and the heads of the tribal clans of Israel assigned by lot at Shiloh in the presence of the Lord at the entrance to the Tent of Meeting. And so they finished dividing the land.

20:1Then the Lord said to Joshua: 2"Tell the Israelites to designate the cities of refuge, as I instructed you through Moses, 3so that anyone who kills a person accidentally and unintentionally may flee there and find protection from the avenger of blood.

4"When he flees to one of these cities, he is to stand in the entrance of the city gate and state his case before the elders of that city. Then they are to admit him into their city and give him a place to live with them. 5If the avenger of blood pursues him, they must not surrender the one accused, because he killed his neighbor unintentionally and without malice aforethought. 6He is to stay in that city until he has stood trial before the assembly and until the death of the high priest who is serving at that time. Then he may go back to his own home in the town from which he fled."

7So they set apart Kedesh in Galilee in the hill country of Naphtali, Shechem in the hill country of Ephraim, and Kiriath Arba (that is, Hebron) in the hill country of Judah. 8On the east side of the Jordan of Jericho*e* they designated Bezer in the desert on the plateau in the tribe of Reuben, Ramoth in Gilead in the tribe of Gad, and Golan in Bashan in the tribe of Manasseh. ⁹Any of the Israelites or any alien living among them who killed someone accidentally could flee to these designated cities and not be killed by the avenger of blood prior to standing trial before the assembly.

a2 Or Beersheba, Sheba; 1 Chron. 4:28 does not have Sheba. b28 Some Hebrew manuscripts (see also Joshua 21:30); most Hebrew manuscripts Ebron c34 Septuagint; Hebrew west, and Judah, the Jordan, d50 Also known as Timnath Heres (see Judges 2:9) e8 Jordan of Jericho was possibly an ancient name for the Jordan River.

LUKE 19:28-48

After Jesus had said this, he went on ahead, going up to Jerusalem. ²⁹As he approached Bethphage and Bethany at the hill called the Mount of Olives, he sent two of his disciples, saying to them, ³⁰"Go to the village ahead of you, and as you enter it, you will find a colt tied there, which no one has ever ridden. Untie it and bring it here. ³¹If anyone asks you, 'Why are you untying it?' tell him, 'The Lord needs it.'"

³²Those who were sent ahead went and found it just as he had told them. ³³As they were untying the colt, its owners asked them, "Why are you untying the colt?"

³⁴They replied, "The Lord needs it."

³⁵They brought it to Jesus, threw their cloaks on the colt and put Jesus on it. ³⁶As he went along, people spread their cloaks on the road.

³⁷When he came near the place where the road goes down the Mount of Olives, the whole crowd of disciples began joyfully to praise God in loud voices for all the miracles they had seen:

³⁸"Blessed is the king who comes in
  the name of the Lord!"a

"Peace in heaven and glory in the
  highest!"

³⁹Some of the Pharisees in the crowd said to Jesus, "Teacher, rebuke your disciples!"

⁴⁰"I tell you," he replied, "if they keep quiet, the stones will cry out."

⁴¹As he approached Jerusalem and saw the city, he wept over it ⁴²and said,

"If you, even you, had only known on this day what would bring you peace— but now it is hidden from your eyes. ⁴³The days will come upon you when your enemies will build an embankment against you and encircle you and hem you in on every side. ⁴⁴They will dash you to the ground, you and the children within your walls. They will not leave one stone on another, because you did not recognize the time of God's coming to you."

⁴⁵**Then he entered the temple area and began driving out those who were selling.** ⁴⁶**"It is written," he said to them, " 'My house will be a house of prayer'b; but you have made it 'a den of robbers.'c "**

⁴⁷Every day he was teaching at the temple. But the chief priests, the teachers of the law and the leaders among the people were trying to kill him. ⁴⁸Yet they could not find any way to do it, because all the people hung on his words.

a38 Psalm 118:26 b46 Isaiah 56:7 c46 Jer. 7:11

PSALM 88:1-18

A song. A psalm of the Sons of Korah. For the director of music. According to *mahalath leannoth.*a A *maskil*b of Heman the Ezrahite.

¹O LORD, the God who saves me,
  day and night I cry out before you.
²May my prayer come before you;
  turn your ear to my cry.

³For my soul is full of trouble
  and my life draws near the grave.c
⁴I am counted among those who go
    down to the pit;
  I am like a man without strength.
⁵I am set apart with the dead,
  like the slain who lie in the grave,
whom you remember no more,
  who are cut off from your care.

⁶You have put me in the lowest pit,
  in the darkest depths.
⁷Your wrath lies heavily upon me;
  you have overwhelmed me with all
    your waves.   *Selah*

⁸ You have taken from me my closest
friends
and have made me repulsive to them.
I am confined and cannot escape;
⁹   my eyes are dim with grief.

I call to you, O Lᴏʀᴅ, every day;
I spread out my hands to you.
¹⁰ Do you show your wonders to the
dead?
Do those who are dead rise up and
praise you?   *Selah*
¹¹ Is your love declared in the grave,
your faithfulness in Destruction*ᵈ*?
¹² Are your wonders known in the place
of darkness,
or your righteous deeds in the
land of oblivion?

¹³ But I cry to you for help, O Lᴏʀᴅ;
in the morning my prayer comes
before you.
¹⁴ Why, O Lᴏʀᴅ, do you reject me
and hide your face from me?

¹⁵ From my youth I have been afflicted
and close to death;
I have suffered your terrors and
am in despair.
¹⁶ Your wrath has swept over me;
your terrors have destroyed me.
¹⁷ All day long they surround me like a
flood;
they have completely engulfed me.
¹⁸ You have taken my companions and
loved ones from me;
the darkness is my closest friend.

*ᵃ*Title: Possibly a tune, "The Suffering of Affliction" *ᵇ*Title:
Probably a literary or musical term *ᶜ3* Hebrew
Sheol *ᵈ11* Hebrew *Abaddon*

PROVERBS 13:12-14

¹² **H**ope deferred makes the heart sick,
but a longing fulfilled is a tree of
life.

¹³ He who scorns instruction will pay
for it,
but he who respects a command is
rewarded.

¹⁴ The teaching of the wise is a fountain
of life,
turning a man from the snares of
death.

□ D A Y 1 1 0

GOD SIGHTINGS

April 20

JOSHUA 21:1–22:20

Now the family heads of the Levites approached Eleazar the priest, Joshua son of Nun, and the heads of the other tribal families of Israel ² at Shiloh in Canaan and said to them, "The Lᴏʀᴅ commanded through Moses that you give us towns to live in, with pasturelands for our livestock." ³ So, as the Lᴏʀᴅ had commanded, the Israelites gave the Levites the following towns and pasturelands out of their own inheritance:

⁴ The first lot came out for the Kohathites, clan by clan. The Levites who were descendants of Aaron the priest were allotted thirteen towns from the tribes of Judah, Simeon and Benjamin. ⁵ The rest of Kohath's descendants were allotted ten towns from the clans of the tribes of Ephraim, Dan and half of Manasseh.

⁶ The descendants of Gershon were allotted thirteen towns from the clans of the tribes of Issachar, Asher, Naphtali and the half-tribe of Manasseh in Bashan.

⁷ The descendants of Merari, clan by clan, received twelve towns from the tribes of Reuben, Gad and Zebulun.

⁸ So the Israelites allotted to the Levites these towns and their pasturelands, as the Lᴏʀᴅ had commanded through Moses.

⁹ From the tribes of Judah and Simeon they allotted the following towns by name ¹⁰ (these towns were assigned to the descendants of Aaron who were from the Kohathite clans of the Levites, because the first lot fell to them):

¹¹ They gave them Kiriath Arba (that is, Hebron), with its surrounding pastureland, in the hill country of Judah. (Arba was the forefather of Anak.) ¹² But the fields and villages around the city

they had given to Caleb son of Jephunneh as his possession.

¹³So to the descendants of Aaron the priest they gave Hebron (a city of refuge for one accused of murder), Libnah, ¹⁴Jattir, Eshtemoa, ¹⁵Holon, Debir, ¹⁶Ain, Juttah and Beth Shemesh, together with their pasturelands—nine towns from these two tribes.

¹⁷And from the tribe of Benjamin they gave them Gibeon, Geba, ¹⁸Anathoth and Almon, together with their pasturelands—four towns.

¹⁹All the towns for the priests, the descendants of Aaron, were thirteen, together with their pasturelands.

²⁰The rest of the Kohathite clans of the Levites were allotted towns from the tribe of Ephraim:

²¹In the hill country of Ephraim they were given Shechem (a city of refuge for one accused of murder) and Gezer, ²²Kibzaim and Beth Horon, together with their pasturelands—four towns.

²³Also from the tribe of Dan they received Eltekeh, Gibbethon, ²⁴Aijalon and Gath Rimmon, together with their pasturelands—four towns.

²⁵From half the tribe of Manasseh they received Taanach and Gath Rimmon, together with their pasturelands—two towns.

²⁶All these ten towns and their pasturelands were given to the rest of the Kohathite clans.

²⁷The Levite clans of the Gershonites were given:

from the half-tribe of Manasseh, Golan in Bashan (a city of refuge for one accused of murder) and Be Eshtarah, together with their pasturelands—two towns;

²⁸from the tribe of Issachar, Kishion, Daberath, ²⁹Jarmuth and En Gannim, together with their pasturelands—four towns;

³⁰from the tribe of Asher, Mishal, Abdon, ³¹Helkath and Rehob, together with their pasturelands—four towns;

³²from the tribe of Naphtali, Kedesh in Galilee (a city of refuge for one accused of murder), Hammoth Dor and Kartan, together with their pasturelands—three towns.

³³All the towns of the Gershonite clans were thirteen, together with their pasturelands.

³⁴The Merarite clans (the rest of the Levites) were given:

from the tribe of Zebulun, Jokneam, Kartah, ³⁵Dimnah and Nahalal, together with their pasturelands—four towns;

³⁶from the tribe of Reuben, Bezer, Jahaz, ³⁷Kedemoth and Mephaath, together with their pasturelands—four towns;

³⁸from the tribe of Gad, Ramoth in Gilead (a city of refuge for one accused of murder), Mahanaim, ³⁹Heshbon and Jazer, together with their pasturelands—four towns in all.

⁴⁰All the towns allotted to the Merarite clans, who were the rest of the Levites, were twelve.

⁴¹The towns of the Levites in the territory held by the Israelites were forty-eight in all, together with their pasturelands. ⁴²Each of these towns had pasturelands surrounding it; this was true for all these towns.

⁴³So the LORD gave Israel all the land he had sworn to give their forefathers, and they took possession of it and settled there. ⁴⁴The LORD gave them rest on every side, just as he had sworn to their forefathers. Not one of their enemies withstood them; the LORD handed all their enemies over to them. ⁴⁵Not one of all the LORD's good promises to the house of Israel failed; every one was fulfilled.

22:1THEN Joshua summoned the Reubenites, the Gadites and the half-tribe of Manasseh [2]and said to them, "You have done all that Moses the servant of the LORD commanded, and you have obeyed me in everything I commanded. [3]For a long time now—to this very day— you have not deserted your brothers but have carried out the mission the LORD your God gave you. [4]Now that the LORD your God has given your brothers rest as he promised, return to your homes in the land that Moses the servant of the LORD gave you on the other side of the Jordan. [5]But be very careful to keep the commandment and the law that Moses the servant of the LORD gave you: to love the LORD your God, to walk in all his ways, to obey his commands, to hold fast to him and to serve him with all your heart and all your soul."

[6]Then Joshua blessed them and sent them away, and they went to their homes. [7](To the half-tribe of Manasseh Moses had given land in Bashan, and to the other half of the tribe Joshua gave land on the west side of the Jordan with their brothers.) When Joshua sent them home, he blessed them, [8]saying, "Return to your homes with your great wealth—with large herds of livestock, with silver, gold, bronze and iron, and a great quantity of clothing—and divide with your brothers the plunder from your enemies."

[9]So the Reubenites, the Gadites and the half-tribe of Manasseh left the Israelites at Shiloh in Canaan to return to Gilead, their own land, which they had acquired in accordance with the command of the LORD through Moses.

[10]When they came to Geliloth near the Jordan in the land of Canaan, the Reubenites, the Gadites and the half-tribe of Manasseh built an imposing altar there by the Jordan. [11]And when the Israelites heard that they had built the altar on the border of Canaan at Geliloth near the Jordan on the Israelite side, [12]the whole assembly of Israel gathered at Shiloh to go to war against them.

[13]So the Israelites sent Phinehas son of Eleazar, the priest, to the land of Gilead—to Reuben, Gad and the half-tribe

of Manasseh. [14]With him they sent ten of the chief men, one for each of the tribes of Israel, each the head of a family division among the Israelite clans.

[15]When they went to Gilead—to Reuben, Gad and the half-tribe of Manasseh—they said to them: [16]"The whole assembly of the LORD says: 'How could you break faith with the God of Israel like this? How could you turn away from the LORD and build yourselves an altar in rebellion against him now? [17]Was not the sin of Peor enough for us? Up to this very day we have not cleansed ourselves from that sin, even though a plague fell on the community of the LORD! [18]And are you now turning away from the LORD?

"'If you rebel against the LORD today, tomorrow he will be angry with the whole community of Israel. [19]If the land you possess is defiled, come over to the LORD's land, where the LORD's tabernacle stands, and share the land with us. But do not rebel against the LORD or against us by building an altar for yourselves, other than the altar of the LORD our God. [20]When Achan son of Zerah acted unfaithfully regarding the devoted things,[a] did not wrath come upon the whole community of Israel? He was not the only one who died for his sin.'"

[a]20 The Hebrew term refers to the irrevocable giving over of things or persons to the LORD, often by totally destroying them.

LUKE 20:1-26

⏺ne day as he [Jesus] was teaching the people in the temple courts and preaching the gospel, the chief priests and the teachers of the law, together with the elders, came up to him. [2]"Tell us by what authority you are doing these things," they said. "Who gave you this authority?"

[3]He replied, "I will also ask you a question. Tell me, [4]John's baptism—was it from heaven, or from men?"

[5]They discussed it among themselves and said, "If we say, 'From heaven,' he will ask, 'Why didn't you believe him?' [6]But if we say, 'From men,' all

the people will stone us, because they are persuaded that John was a prophet."

⁷So they answered, "We don't know where it was from."

⁸Jesus said, "Neither will I tell you by what authority I am doing these things."

⁹He went on to tell the people this parable: "A man planted a vineyard, rented it to some farmers and went away for a long time. ¹⁰At harvest time he sent a servant to the tenants so they would give him some of the fruit of the vineyard. But the tenants beat him and sent him away empty-handed. ¹¹He sent another servant, but that one also they beat and treated shamefully and sent away empty-handed. ¹²He sent still a third, and they wounded him and threw him out.

¹³"Then the owner of the vineyard said, 'What shall I do? I will send my son, whom I love; perhaps they will respect him.'

¹⁴"But when the tenants saw him, they talked the matter over. 'This is the heir,' they said. 'Let's kill him, and the inheritance will be ours.' ¹⁵So they threw him out of the vineyard and killed him.

"What then will the owner of the vineyard do to them? ¹⁶He will come and kill those tenants and give the vineyard to others."

When the people heard this, they said, "May this never be!"

¹⁷Jesus looked directly at them and asked, " Then what is the meaning of that which is written:

" ' The stone the builders rejected has become the capstone*a *'b ?

¹⁸Everyone who falls on that stone will be broken to pieces, but he on whom it falls will be crushed."

¹⁹The teachers of the law and the chief priests looked for a way to arrest him immediately, because they knew he had spoken this parable against them. But they were afraid of the people.

²⁰Keeping a close watch on him, they sent spies, who pretended to be honest. They hoped to catch Jesus in something

he said so that they might hand him over to the power and authority of the governor. ²¹So the spies questioned him: "Teacher, we know that you speak and teach what is right, and that you do not show partiality but teach the way of God in accordance with the truth. ²²Is it right for us to pay taxes to Caesar or not?"

²³He saw through their duplicity and said to them, ²⁴"Show me a denarius. Whose portrait and inscription are on it?"

²⁵"Caesar's," they replied.

He said to them, "Then give to Caesar what is Caesar's, and to God what is God's."

²⁶They were unable to trap him in what he had said there in public. And astonished by his answer, they became silent.

a17 Or *cornerstone*   *b17* Psalm 118:22

PSALM 89:1-13
A *maskil*ᵃ of Ethan the Ezrahite.

¹ I will sing of the Lord's great love forever;
  with my mouth I will make your faithfulness known through all generations.
² I will declare that your love stands firm forever,
  that you established your faithfulness in heaven itself.

³ You said, "I have made a covenant with my chosen one,
  I have sworn to David my servant,
⁴ 'I will establish your line forever
  and make your throne firm through all generations.'"*Selah*

⁵ The heavens praise your wonders, O Lord,
  your faithfulness too, in the assembly of the holy ones.
⁶ For who in the skies above can compare with the Lord?
  Who is like the Lord among the heavenly beings?
⁷ In the council of the holy ones God is greatly feared;
  he is more awesome than all who surround him.

8 O LORD God Almighty, who is like
you?
You are mighty, O LORD, and your
faithfulness surrounds you.

9 You rule over the surging sea;
when its waves mount up, you still
them.
10 You crushed Rahab like one of the
slain;
with your strong arm you scattered
your enemies.
11 The heavens are yours, and yours also
the earth;
you founded the world and all that
is in it.
12 You created the north and the south;
Tabor and Hermon sing for joy at
your name.
13 Your arm is endued with power;
your hand is strong, your right
hand exalted.

aTitle: Probably a literary or musical term

PROVERBS 13:15-16

15 Good understanding wins favor,
but the way of the unfaithful is
hard.a

16 Every prudent man acts out of
knowledge,
but a fool exposes his folly.

a 15 Or unfaithful does not endure

□ D A Y 1 1 1

GOD SIGHTINGS

April 21

JOSHUA 22:21–23:16

Then Reuben, Gad and the half-tribe of
Manasseh replied to the heads of the
clans of Israel: 22 "The Mighty One, God,
the LORD! The Mighty One, God, the
LORD! He knows! And let Israel know! If
this has been in rebellion or disobedience to the LORD, do not spare us this
day. 23 If we have built our own altar to
turn away from the LORD and to offer

burnt offerings and grain offerings, or
to sacrifice fellowship offeringsa on it,
may the LORD himself call us to account.
24 "No! We did it for fear that some
day your descendants might say to ours,
'What do you have to do with the LORD,
the God of Israel? 25 The LORD has made
the Jordan a boundary between us and
you—you Reubenites and Gadites! You
have no share in the LORD.' So your descendants might cause ours to stop
fearing the LORD.
26 "That is why we said, 'Let us get
ready and build an altar—but not for
burnt offerings or sacrifices.' 27 On the
contrary, it is to be a witness between us
and you and the generations that follow,
that we will worship the LORD at his
sanctuary with our burnt offerings, sacrifices and fellowship offerings. Then in
the future your descendants will not be
able to say to ours, 'You have no share in
the LORD.'
28 "And we said, 'If they ever say this to
us, or to our descendants, we will answer: Look at the replica of the LORD's altar, which our fathers built, not for
burnt offerings and sacrifices, but as a
witness between us and you.'
29 "Far be it from us to rebel against
the LORD and turn away from him today
by building an altar for burnt offerings,
grain offerings and sacrifices, other
than the altar of the LORD our God that
stands before his tabernacle."
30 When Phinehas the priest and the
leaders of the community—the heads of
the clans of the Israelites—heard what
Reuben, Gad and Manasseh had to say,
they were pleased. 31 And Phinehas son
of Eleazar, the priest, said to Reuben,
Gad and Manasseh, "Today we know
that the LORD is with us, because you
have not acted unfaithfully toward the
LORD in this matter. Now you have rescued the Israelites from the LORD's
hand."
32 Then Phinehas son of Eleazar, the
priest, and the leaders returned to Canaan from their meeting with the Reubenites and Gadites in Gilead and
reported to the Israelites. 33 They were

glad to hear the report and praised God. And they talked no more about going to war against them to devastate the country where the Reubenites and the Gadites lived.

[34]And the Reubenites and the Gadites gave the altar this name: A Witness Between Us that the Lord is God.

[23:1]AFTER a long time had passed and the Lord had given Israel rest from all their enemies around them, Joshua, by then old and well advanced in years, [2]summoned all Israel—their elders, leaders, judges and officials—and said to them: "I am old and well advanced in years. [3]You yourselves have seen everything the Lord your God has done to all these nations for your sake; it was the Lord your God who fought for you. [4]Remember how I have allotted as an inheritance for your tribes all the land of the nations that remain—the nations I conquered—between the Jordan and the Great Sea[b] in the west. [5]The Lord your God himself will drive them out of your way. He will push them out before you, and you will take possession of their land, as the Lord your God promised you.

[6]"Be very strong; be careful to obey all that is written in the Book of the Law of Moses, without turning aside to the right or to the left. [7]Do not associate with these nations that remain among you; do not invoke the names of their gods or swear by them. You must not serve them or bow down to them. [8]But you are to hold fast to the Lord your God, as you have until now.

[9]"The Lord has driven out before you great and powerful nations; to this day no one has been able to withstand you. [10]One of you routs a thousand, because the Lord your God fights for you, just as he promised. [11]So be very careful to love the Lord your God.

[12]"But if you turn away and ally yourselves with the survivors of these nations that remain among you and if you intermarry with them and associate with them, [13]then you may be sure that the Lord your God will no longer drive

out these nations before you. Instead, they will become snares and traps for you, whips on your backs and thorns in your eyes, until you perish from this good land, which the Lord your God has given you.

[14]"Now I am about to go the way of all the earth. You know with all your heart and soul that not one of all the good promises the Lord your God gave you has failed. Every promise has been fulfilled; not one has failed. [15]But just as every good promise of the Lord your God has come true, so the Lord will bring on you all the evil he has threatened, until he has destroyed you from this good land he has given you. [16]If you violate the covenant of the Lord your God, which he commanded you, and go and serve other gods and bow down to them, the Lord's anger will burn against you, and you will quickly perish from the good land he has given you."

[a]23 Traditionally *peace offerings*; also in verse 27   [b]4 That is, the Mediterranean

LUKE 20:27-47

Some of the Sadducees, who say there is no resurrection, came to Jesus with a question. [28]"Teacher," they said, "Moses wrote for us that if a man's brother dies and leaves a wife but no children, the man must marry the widow and have children for his brother. [29]Now there were seven brothers. The first one married a woman and died childless. [30]The second [31]and then the third married her, and in the same way the seven died, leaving no children. [32]Finally, the woman died too. [33]Now then, at the resurrection whose wife will she be, since the seven were married to her?"

[34]Jesus replied, "The people of this age marry and are given in marriage. [35]But those who are considered worthy of taking part in that age and in the resurrection from the dead will neither marry nor be given in marriage, [36]and they can no longer die; for they are like the angels. They are God's children, since they are children of the resurrection. [37]But in the account of the bush,

even Moses showed that the dead rise, for he calls the Lord 'the God of Abraham, and the God of Isaac, and the God of Jacob.'[a] 38He is not the God of the dead, but of the living, for to him all are alive."

39Some of the teachers of the law responded, "Well said, teacher!" 40And no one dared to ask him any more questions.

41Then Jesus said to them, "How is it that they say the Christ[b] is the Son of David? 42David himself declares in the Book of Psalms:

"'The Lord said to my Lord:
"Sit at my right hand
43until I make your enemies
a footstool for your feet."'[c]

44David calls him 'Lord.' How then can he be his son?"

45While all the people were listening, Jesus said to his disciples, 46"Beware of the teachers of the law. They like to walk around in flowing robes and love to be greeted in the marketplaces and have the most important seats in the synagogues and the places of honor at banquets. 47They devour widows' houses and for a show make lengthy prayers. Such men will be punished most severely."

a37Exodus 3:6   b41Or Messiah   c43Psalm 110:1

PSALM 89:14-37

14Righteousness and justice are the
foundation of your [the
Lord's] throne;
love and faithfulness go before
you.
15Blessed are those who have
learned to acclaim you,
who walk in the light of your
presence, O Lord.
16They rejoice in your name all day
long;
they exult in your righteousness.
17For you are their glory and strength,
and by your favor you exalt our
horn.[a]
18Indeed, our shield[b] belongs to the
Lord,
our king to the Holy One of Israel.

19Once you spoke in a vision,
to your faithful people you said:
"I have bestowed strength on a
warrior;
I have exalted a young man from
among the people.
20I have found David my servant;
with my sacred oil I have anointed
him.
21My hand will sustain him;
surely my arm will strengthen him.
22No enemy will subject him to tribute;
no wicked man will oppress him.
23I will crush his foes before him
and strike down his adversaries.
24My faithful love will be with him,
and through my name his horn[c]
will be exalted.
25I will set his hand over the sea,
his right hand over the rivers.
26He will call out to me, 'You are my
Father,
my God, the Rock my Savior.'
27I will also appoint him my firstborn,
the most exalted of the kings of
the earth.
28I will maintain my love to him
forever,
and my covenant with him will
never fail.
29I will establish his line forever,
his throne as long as the heavens
endure.

30"If his sons forsake my law
and do not follow my statutes,
31if they violate my decrees
and fail to keep my commands,
32I will punish their sin with the rod,
their iniquity with flogging;
33but I will not take my love from him,
nor will I ever betray my
faithfulness.
34I will not violate my covenant
or alter what my lips have uttered.
35Once for all, I have sworn by my
holiness—
and I will not lie to David—
36that his line will continue forever
and his throne endure before me
like the sun;

37 it will be established forever like the
moon,
the faithful witness in the sky."

Selah

PROVERBS 13:17-19

17 **A** wicked messenger falls into
trouble,
but a trustworthy envoy brings
healing.

18 He who ignores discipline comes to
poverty and shame,
but whoever heeds correction is
honored.

19 A longing fulfilled is sweet to the
soul,
but fools detest turning from evil.

□ DAY 112

GOD SIGHTINGS

April 22

JOSHUA 24:1-33

Then Joshua assembled all the tribes of
Israel at Shechem. He summoned the
elders, leaders, judges and officials of
Israel, and they presented themselves
before God.

2 Joshua said to all the people, "This is
what the LORD, the God of Israel, says:
'Long ago your forefathers, including
Terah the father of Abraham and Nahor,
lived beyond the River*a* and worshiped
other gods. 3 But I took your father Abraham from the land beyond the River
and led him throughout Canaan and
gave him many descendants. I gave him
Isaac, 4 and to Isaac I gave Jacob and
Esau. I assigned the hill country of Seir
to Esau, but Jacob and his sons went
down to Egypt.

5 "'Then I sent Moses and Aaron, and I
afflicted the Egyptians by what I did
there, and I brought you out. 6 When I
brought your fathers out of Egypt, you

came to the sea, and the Egyptians pursued them with chariots and horsemen*b* as far as the Red Sea.*c* 7 But they
cried to the LORD for help, and he put
darkness between you and the Egyptians; he brought the sea over them and
covered them. You saw with your own
eyes what I did to the Egyptians. Then
you lived in the desert for a long time.

8 "'I brought you to the land of the
Amorites who lived east of the Jordan.
They fought against you, but I gave them
into your hands. I destroyed them from
before you, and you took possession of
their land. 9 When Balak son of Zippor,
the king of Moab, prepared to fight
against Israel, he sent for Balaam son of
Beor to put a curse on you. 10 But I would
not listen to Balaam, so he blessed you
again and again, and I delivered you out
of his hand.

11 "'Then you crossed the Jordan and
came to Jericho. The citizens of Jericho
fought against you, as did also the Amorites, Perizzites, Canaanites, Hittites,
Girgashites, Hivites and Jebusites, but I
gave them into your hands. 12 I sent the
hornet ahead of you, which drove them
out before you—also the two Amorite
kings. You did not do it with your own
sword and bow. 13 So I gave you a land on
which you did not toil and cities you did
not build; and you live in them and eat
from vineyards and olive groves that
you did not plant.'

14 "Now fear the LORD and serve him
with all faithfulness. Throw away the
gods your forefathers worshiped beyond the River and in Egypt, and serve
the LORD. 15 **But if serving the LORD
seems undesirable to you, then
choose for yourselves this day whom
you will serve, whether the gods your
forefathers served beyond the River,
or the gods of the Amorites, in whose
land you are living. But as for me and
my household, we will serve the
LORD."**

16 Then the people answered, "Far be
it from us to forsake the LORD to serve
other gods! 17 It was the LORD our God
himself who brought us and our fathers

up out of Egypt, from that land of slavery, and performed those great signs before our eyes. He protected us on our entire journey and among all the nations through which we traveled. [18]And the LORD drove out before us all the nations, including the Amorites, who lived in the land. We too will serve the LORD, because he is our God."

[19]Joshua said to the people, "You are not able to serve the LORD. He is a holy God; he is a jealous God. He will not forgive your rebellion and your sins. [20]If you forsake the LORD and serve foreign gods, he will turn and bring disaster on you and make an end of you, after he has been good to you."

[21]But the people said to Joshua, "No! We will serve the LORD."

[22]Then Joshua said, "You are witnesses against yourselves that you have chosen to serve the LORD."

"Yes, we are witnesses," they replied.

[23]"Now then," said Joshua, "throw away the foreign gods that are among you and yield your hearts to the LORD, the God of Israel."

[24]And the people said to Joshua, "We will serve the LORD our God and obey him."

[25]On that day Joshua made a covenant for the people, and there at Shechem he drew up for them decrees and laws. [26]And Joshua recorded these things in the Book of the Law of God. Then he took a large stone and set it up there under the oak near the holy place of the LORD.

[27]"See!" he said to all the people. "This stone will be a witness against us. It has heard all the words the LORD has said to us. It will be a witness against you if you are untrue to your God."

[28]Then Joshua sent the people away, each to his own inheritance.

[29]After these things, Joshua son of Nun, the servant of the LORD, died at the age of a hundred and ten. [30]And they buried him in the land of his inheritance, at Timnath Serah[d] in the hill country of Ephraim, north of Mount Gaash.

[31]Israel served the LORD throughout the lifetime of Joshua and of the elders who outlived him and who had experienced everything the LORD had done for Israel.

[32]And Joseph's bones, which the Israelites had brought up from Egypt, were buried at Shechem in the tract of land that Jacob bought for a hundred pieces of silver[e] from the sons of Hamor, the father of Shechem. This became the inheritance of Joseph's descendants.

[33]And Eleazar son of Aaron died and was buried at Gibeah, which had been allotted to his son Phinehas in the hill country of Ephraim.

[a]2 That is, the Euphrates; also in verses 3, 14 and 15
[b]6 Or *charioteers*   [c]6 Hebrew *Yam Suph*; that is, Sea of Reeds   [d]30 Also known as *Timnath Heres* (see Judges 2:9)
[e]32 Hebrew *hundred kesitahs*; a kesitah was a unit of money of unknown weight and value.

LUKE 21:1-28

As he looked up, Jesus saw the rich putting their gifts into the temple treasury. [2]He also saw a poor widow put in two very small copper coins.[a] [3]"I tell you the truth," he said, "this poor widow has put in more than all the others. [4]All these people gave their gifts out of their wealth; but she out of her poverty put in all she had to live on."

[5]Some of his disciples were remarking about how the temple was adorned with beautiful stones and with gifts dedicated to God. But Jesus said, [6]"As for what you see here, the time will come when not one stone will be left on another; every one of them will be thrown down."

[7]"Teacher," they asked, "when will these things happen? And what will be the sign that they are about to take place?"

[8]He replied: "Watch out that you are not deceived. For many will come in my name, claiming, 'I am he,' and, 'The time is near.' Do not follow them. [9]When you hear of wars and revolutions, do not be frightened. These things must happen first, but the end will not come right away."

[10]Then he said to them: "Nation will rise against nation, and kingdom against

kingdom. 11There will be great earthquakes, famines and pestilences in various places, and fearful events and great
signs from heaven.

12"But before all this, they will lay
hands on you and persecute you. They
will deliver you to synagogues and prisons, and you will be brought before
kings and governors, and all on account
of my name. 13This will result in your
being witnesses to them. 14But make up
your mind not to worry beforehand how
you will defend yourselves. 15For I will
give you words and wisdom that none of
your adversaries will be able to resist or
contradict. 16You will be betrayed even
by parents, brothers, relatives and
friends, and they will put some of you to
death. 17All men will hate you because
of me. 18But not a hair of your head will
perish. 19By standing firm you will gain
life.

20"When you see Jerusalem being
surrounded by armies, you will know
that its desolation is near. 21Then let
those who are in Judea flee to the mountains, let those in the city get out, and let
those in the country not enter the city.
22For this is the time of punishment in
fulfillment of all that has been written.
23How dreadful it will be in those days
for pregnant women and nursing mothers! There will be great distress in the
land and wrath against this people.
24They will fall by the sword and will be
taken as prisoners to all the nations. Jerusalem will be trampled on by the Gentiles until the times of the Gentiles are
fulfilled.

25"There will be signs in the sun,
moon and stars. On the earth, nations
will be in anguish and perplexity at the
roaring and tossing of the sea. 26Men will
faint from terror, apprehensive of what is
coming on the world, for the heavenly
bodies will be shaken. 27At that time they
will see the Son of Man coming in a cloud
with power and great glory. 28When
these things begin to take place, stand up
and lift up your heads, because your redemption is drawing near."

a2 Greek two lepta

PSALM 89:38-52

38But you [the LORD] have rejected, you
have spurned,
you have been very angry with
your anointed one.
39You have renounced the covenant
with your servant
and have defiled his crown in the
dust.
40You have broken through all his
walls
and reduced his strongholds to
ruins.
41All who pass by have plundered him;
he has become the scorn of his
neighbors.
42You have exalted the right hand of
his foes;
you have made all his enemies
rejoice.
43You have turned back the edge of his
sword
and have not supported him in
battle.
44You have put an end to his splendor
and cast his throne to the ground.
45You have cut short the days of his
youth;
you have covered him with a
mantle of shame.   Selah

46How long, O LORD? Will you hide
yourself forever?
How long will your wrath burn like
fire?
47Remember how fleeting is my life.
For what futility you have created
all men!
48What man can live and not see
death,
or save himself from the power of
the gravea?   Selah
49O Lord, where is your former great
love,
which in your faithfulness you
swore to David?
50Remember, Lord, how your servant
hasb been mocked,
how I bear in my heart the taunts
of all the nations,
51the taunts with which your enemies
have mocked, O LORD,

with which they have mocked
every step of your anointed
one.

52 Praise be to the LORD forever!
Amen and Amen.

a48 Hebrew *Sheol* *b50* Or *your servants have*

PROVERBS 13:20-23

20 **H**e who walks with the wise grows
wise,
but a companion of fools suffers
harm.

21 Misfortune pursues the sinner,
but prosperity is the reward of the
righteous.

22 A good man leaves an inheritance for
his children's children,
but a sinner's wealth is stored up
for the righteous.

23 A poor man's field may produce
abundant food,
but injustice sweeps it away.

□ DAY 113

GOD SIGHTINGS

April 23

JUDGES 1:1–2:9

After the death of Joshua, the Israelites
asked the LORD, "Who will be the first to
go up and fight for us against the Canaanites?"

2 The LORD answered, "Judah is to go; I
have given the land into their hands."

3 Then the men of Judah said to the
Simeonites their brothers, "Come up
with us into the territory allotted to us,
to fight against the Canaanites. We in
turn will go with you into yours." So the
Simeonites went with them.

4 When Judah attacked, the LORD gave
the Canaanites and Perizzites into their
hands and they struck down ten thousand men at Bezek. 5 It was there that
they found Adoni-Bezek and fought
against him, putting to rout the Canaan-

ites and Perizzites. 6 Adoni-Bezek fled,
but they chased him and caught him,
and cut off his thumbs and big toes.

7 Then Adoni-Bezek said, "Seventy
kings with their thumbs and big toes cut
off have picked up scraps under my table. Now God has paid me back for what
I did to them." They brought him to Jerusalem, and he died there.

8 The men of Judah attacked Jerusalem also and took it. They put the city to
the sword and set it on fire.

9 After that, the men of Judah went
down to fight against the Canaanites living in the hill country, the Negev and the
western foothills. 10 They advanced
against the Canaanites living in Hebron
(formerly called Kiriath Arba) and defeated Sheshai, Ahiman and Talmai.

11 From there they advanced against
the people living in Debir (formerly
called Kiriath Sepher). 12 And Caleb
said, "I will give my daughter Acsah in
marriage to the man who attacks and
captures Kiriath Sepher." 13 Othniel son
of Kenaz, Caleb's younger brother, took
it; so Caleb gave his daughter Acsah to
him in marriage.

14 One day when she came to Othniel,
she urged him*a* to ask her father for a
field. When she got off her donkey, Caleb asked her, "What can I do for you?"

15 She replied, "Do me a special favor.
Since you have given me land in the Negev, give me also springs of water." Then
Caleb gave her the upper and lower
springs.

16 The descendants of Moses' father-
in-law, the Kenite, went up from the City
of Palms*b* with the men of Judah to live
among the people of the Desert of Judah
in the Negev near Arad.

17 Then the men of Judah went with
the Simeonites their brothers and attacked the Canaanites living in Zephath,
and they totally destroyed*c* the city.
Therefore it was called Hormah.*d* 18 The
men of Judah also took*e* Gaza, Ashkelon
and Ekron—each city with its territory.

19 The LORD was with the men of Judah. They took possession of the hill
country, but they were unable to drive

the people from the plains, because they had iron chariots. 20As Moses had promised, Hebron was given to Caleb, who drove from it the three sons of Anak. 21The Benjamites, however, failed to dislodge the Jebusites, who were living in Jerusalem; to this day the Jebusites live there with the Benjamites.

22Now the house of Joseph attacked Bethel, and the LORD was with them. 23When they sent men to spy out Bethel (formerly called Luz), 24the spies saw a man coming out of the city and they said to him, "Show us how to get into the city and we will see that you are treated well." 25So he showed them, and they put the city to the sword but spared the man and his whole family. 26He then went to the land of the Hittites, where he built a city and called it Luz, which is its name to this day.

27But Manasseh did not drive out the people of Beth Shan or Taanach or Dor or Ibleam or Megiddo and their surrounding settlements, for the Canaanites were determined to live in that land. 28When Israel became strong, they pressed the Canaanites into forced labor but never drove them out completely. 29Nor did Ephraim drive out the Canaanites living in Gezer, but the Canaanites continued to live there among them. 30Neither did Zebulun drive out the Canaanites living in Kitron or Nahalol, who remained among them; but they did subject them to forced labor. 31Nor did Asher drive out those living in Acco or Sidon or Ahlab or Aczib or Helbah or Aphek or Rehob, 32and because of this the people of Asher lived among the Canaanite inhabitants of the land. 33Neither did Naphtali drive out those living in Beth Shemesh or Beth Anath; but the Naphtalites too lived among the Canaanite inhabitants of the land, and those living in Beth Shemesh and Beth Anath became forced laborers for them. 34The Amorites confined the Danites to the hill country, not allowing them to come down into the plain. 35And the Amorites were determined also to hold out in Mount Heres, Aijalon and Shaal-

bim, but when the power of the house of Joseph increased, they too were pressed into forced labor. 36The boundary of the Amorites was from Scorpion' Pass to Sela and beyond.

2:1THE angel of the LORD went up from Gilgal to Bokim and said, "I brought you up out of Egypt and led you into the land that I swore to give to your forefathers. I said, 'I will never break my covenant with you, 2and you shall not make a covenant with the people of this land, but you shall break down their altars.' Yet you have disobeyed me. Why have you done this? 3Now therefore I tell you that I will not drive them out before you; they will be ⌜thorns⌝ in your sides and their gods will be a snare to you."

4When the angel of the LORD had spoken these things to all the Israelites, the people wept aloud, 5and they called that place Bokim.g There they offered sacrifices to the LORD.

6After Joshua had dismissed the Israelites, they went to take possession of the land, each to his own inheritance. 7The people served the LORD throughout the lifetime of Joshua and of the elders who outlived him and who had seen all the great things the LORD had done for Israel.

8Joshua son of Nun, the servant of the LORD, died at the age of a hundred and ten. 9And they buried him in the land of his inheritance, at Timnath Heresh in the hill country of Ephraim, north of Mount Gaash.

a14 Hebrew; Septuagint and Vulgate Othniel, he urged her   b16 That is, Jericho   c17 The Hebrew term refers to the irrevocable giving over of things or persons to the LORD, often by totally destroying them.   d17 Hormah means destruction.   e18 Hebrew; Septuagint Judah did not take   f36 Hebrew Akrabbim   g5 Bokim means weepers.   h9 Also known as Timnath Serah (see Joshua 19:50 and 24:30)

LUKE 21:29–22:13

He [Jesus] told them [his disciples] this parable: "Look at the fig tree and all the trees. 30When they sprout leaves, you can see for yourselves and know that summer is near. 31Even so, when you see these things happening, you know that the kingdom of God is near.

32"I tell you the truth, this generation[a] will certainly not pass away until
all these things have happened.
33Heaven and earth will pass away, but
my words will never pass away.

34"Be careful, or your hearts will be
weighed down with dissipation, drunkenness and the anxieties of life, and that
day will close on you unexpectedly like a
trap. 35For it will come upon all those
who live on the face of the whole earth.
36Be always on the watch, and pray that
you may be able to escape all that is
about to happen, and that you may be
able to stand before the Son of Man."

37Each day Jesus was teaching at the
temple, and each evening he went out to
spend the night on the hill called the
Mount of Olives, 38and all the people
came early in the morning to hear him
at the temple.

22:1Now the Feast of Unleavened Bread,
called the Passover, was approaching,
2and the chief priests and the teachers of
the law were looking for some way to get
rid of Jesus, for they were afraid of the
people. 3Then Satan entered Judas, called
Iscariot, one of the Twelve. 4And Judas
went to the chief priests and the officers
of the temple guard and discussed with
them how he might betray Jesus. 5They
were delighted and agreed to give him
money. 6He consented, and watched for
an opportunity to hand Jesus over to them
when no crowd was present.

7Then came the day of Unleavened
Bread on which the Passover lamb had
to be sacrificed. 8Jesus sent Peter and
John, saying, "Go and make preparations
for us to eat the Passover."

9"Where do you want us to prepare
for it?" they asked.

10He replied, "As you enter the city, a
man carrying a jar of water will meet
you. Follow him to the house that he enters, 11and say to the owner of the
house, 'The Teacher asks: Where is the
guest room, where I may eat the Passover with my disciples?' 12He will show
you a large upper room, all furnished.
Make preparations there."

13They left and found things just as
Jesus had told them. So they prepared
the Passover.

[a]32 Or *race*

PSALMS 90:1–91:16

A prayer of Moses the man of God.

1 **L**ord, you have been our dwelling
place
    throughout all generations.
2 Before the mountains were born
    or you brought forth the earth and
        the world,
    from everlasting to everlasting you
        are God.

3 You turn men back to dust,
    saying, "Return to dust, O sons of
        men."
4 For a thousand years in your sight
    are like a day that has just
        gone by,
    or like a watch in the night.
5 You sweep men away in the sleep of
        death;
    they are like the new grass of the
        morning—
6 though in the morning it springs
        up new,
    by evening it is dry and withered.

7 We are consumed by your anger
    and terrified by your
        indignation.
8 You have set our iniquities before
        you,
    our secret sins in the light of your
        presence.
9 All our days pass away under your
        wrath;
    we finish our years with a moan.
10 The length of our days is seventy
        years—
    or eighty, if we have the strength;
    yet their span[a] is but trouble and
        sorrow,
    for they quickly pass, and we fly
        away.

11 Who knows the power of your
        anger?
    For your wrath is as great as the
        fear that is due you.

¹²Teach us to number our days aright,
that we may gain a heart of wisdom.

¹³Relent, O LORD! How long will it be?
Have compassion on your
servants.
¹⁴Satisfy us in the morning with your
unfailing love,
that we may sing for joy and be
glad all our days.
¹⁵Make us glad for as many days as you
have afflicted us,
for as many years as we have seen
trouble.
¹⁶May your deeds be shown to your
servants,
your splendor to their children.

¹⁷May the favor*b* of the Lord our God
rest upon us;
establish the work of our hands
for us—
yes, establish the work of our
hands.

**91:1He who dwells in the shelter of the
Most High
will rest in the shadow of the
Almighty.*c***
**²I will say*d* of the LORD, "He is my
refuge and my fortress,
my God, in whom I trust."**

³Surely he will save you from the
fowler's snare
and from the deadly pestilence.
⁴He will cover you with his feathers,
and under his wings you will find
refuge;
his faithfulness will be your shield
and rampart.
⁵You will not fear the terror of night,
nor the arrow that flies by day,
⁶nor the pestilence that stalks in the
darkness,
nor the plague that destroys at
midday.
⁷A thousand may fall at your side,
ten thousand at your right hand,
but it will not come near you.
⁸You will only observe with your eyes
and see the punishment of the
wicked.

⁹If you make the Most High your
dwelling—
even the LORD, who is my refuge—
¹⁰then no harm will befall you,
no disaster will come near your
tent.
¹¹For he will command his angels
concerning you
to guard you in all your ways;
¹²they will lift you up in their hands,
so that you will not strike your foot
against a stone.
¹³You will tread upon the lion and the
cobra;
you will trample the great lion and
the serpent.

¹⁴"Because he loves me," says the LORD,
"I will rescue him;
I will protect him, for he
acknowledges my name.
¹⁵He will call upon me, and I will
answer him;
I will be with him in trouble,
I will deliver him and honor him.
¹⁶With long life will I satisfy him
and show him my salvation."

*a10 Or yet the best of them   b17 Or beauty   c1 Hebrew
Shaddai   d2 Or He says*

PROVERBS 13:24-25
²⁴He who spares the rod hates his son,
but he who loves him is careful to
discipline him.

²⁵The righteous eat to their hearts'
content,
but the stomach of the wicked
goes hungry.

☐ DAY 114

GOD SIGHTINGS

April 24

JUDGES 2:10–3:31
After that whole generation had been
gathered to their fathers, another generation grew up, who knew neither the

LORD nor what he had done for Israel. [11]Then the Israelites did evil in the eyes of the LORD and served the Baals. [12]They forsook the LORD, the God of their fathers, who had brought them out of Egypt. They followed and worshiped various gods of the peoples around them. They provoked the LORD to anger [13]because they forsook him and served Baal and the Ashtoreths. [14]In his anger against Israel the LORD handed them over to raiders who plundered them. He sold them to their enemies all around, whom they were no longer able to resist. [15]Whenever Israel went out to fight, the hand of the LORD was against them to defeat them, just as he had sworn to them. They were in great distress.

[16]Then the LORD raised up judges,[a] who saved them out of the hands of these raiders. [17]Yet they would not listen to their judges but prostituted themselves to other gods and worshiped them. Unlike their fathers, they quickly turned from the way in which their fathers had walked, the way of obedience to the LORD's commands. [18]Whenever the LORD raised up a judge for them, he was with the judge and saved them out of the hands of their enemies as long as the judge lived; for the LORD had compassion on them as they groaned under those who oppressed and afflicted them. [19]But when the judge died, the people returned to ways even more corrupt than those of their fathers, following other gods and serving and worshiping them. They refused to give up their evil practices and stubborn ways.

[20]Therefore the LORD was very angry with Israel and said, "Because this nation has violated the covenant that I laid down for their forefathers and has not listened to me, [21]I will no longer drive out before them any of the nations Joshua left when he died. [22]I will use them to test Israel and see whether they will keep the way of the LORD and walk in it as their forefathers did." [23]The LORD had allowed those nations to remain; he did not drive them out at once by giving them into the hands of Joshua.

[3:1]THESE are the nations the LORD left to test all those Israelites who had not experienced any of the wars in Canaan [2](he did this only to teach warfare to the descendants of the Israelites who had not had previous battle experience): [3]the five rulers of the Philistines, all the Canaanites, the Sidonians, and the Hivites living in the Lebanon mountains from Mount Baal Hermon to Lebo[b] Hamath. [4]They were left to test the Israelites to see whether they would obey the LORD's commands, which he had given their forefathers through Moses.

[5]The Israelites lived among the Canaanites, Hittites, Amorites, Perizzites, Hivites and Jebusites. [6]They took their daughters in marriage and gave their own daughters to their sons, and served their gods.

[7]The Israelites did evil in the eyes of the LORD; they forgot the LORD their God and served the Baals and the Asherahs. [8]The anger of the LORD burned against Israel so that he sold them into the hands of Cushan-Rishathaim king of Aram Naharaim,[c] to whom the Israelites were subject for eight years. [9]But when they cried out to the LORD, he raised up for them a deliverer, Othniel son of Kenaz, Caleb's younger brother, who saved them. [10]The Spirit of the LORD came upon him, so that he became Israel's judge[d] and went to war. The LORD gave Cushan-Rishathaim king of Aram into the hands of Othniel, who overpowered him. [11]So the land had peace for forty years, until Othniel son of Kenaz died.

[12]Once again the Israelites did evil in the eyes of the LORD, and because they did this evil the LORD gave Eglon king of Moab power over Israel. [13]Getting the Ammonites and Amalekites to join him, Eglon came and attacked Israel, and they took possession of the City of Palms.[e] [14]The Israelites were subject to Eglon king of Moab for eighteen years.

[15]Again the Israelites cried out to the LORD, and he gave them a deliverer— Ehud, a left-handed man, the son of Gera the Benjamite. The Israelites sent

him with tribute to Eglon king of Moab. [16]Now Ehud had made a double-edged sword about a foot and a half[f] long, which he strapped to his right thigh under his clothing. [17]He presented the tribute to Eglon king of Moab, who was a very fat man. [18]After Ehud had presented the tribute, he sent on their way the men who had carried it. [19]At the idols[g] near Gilgal he himself turned back and said, "I have a secret message for you, O king."

The king said, "Quiet!" And all his attendants left him.

[20]Ehud then approached him while he was sitting alone in the upper room of his summer palace[h] and said, "I have a message from God for you." As the king rose from his seat, [21]Ehud reached with his left hand, drew the sword from his right thigh and plunged it into the king's belly. [22]Even the handle sank in after the blade, which came out his back. Ehud did not pull the sword out, and the fat closed in over it. [23]Then Ehud went out to the porch[i]; he shut the doors of the upper room behind him and locked them.

[24]After he had gone, the servants came and found the doors of the upper room locked. They said, "He must be relieving himself in the inner room of the house." [25]They waited to the point of embarrassment, but when he did not open the doors of the room, they took a key and unlocked them. There they saw their lord fallen to the floor, dead.

[26]While they waited, Ehud got away. He passed by the idols and escaped to Seirah. [27]When he arrived there, he blew a trumpet in the hill country of Ephraim, and the Israelites went down with him from the hills, with him leading them.

[28]"Follow me," he ordered, "for the Lord has given Moab, your enemy, into your hands." So they followed him down and, taking possession of the fords of the Jordan that led to Moab, they allowed no one to cross over. [29]At that time they struck down about ten thousand Moabites, all vigorous and strong; not a man escaped. [30]That day

Moab was made subject to Israel, and the land had peace for eighty years.

[31]After Ehud came Shamgar son of Anath, who struck down six hundred Philistines with an oxgoad. He too saved Israel.

[a]16 Or leaders; similarly in verses 17-19   [b]3 Or to the entrance to   [c]8 That is, Northwest Mesopotamia   [d]10 Or leader   [e]13 That is, Jericho   [f]16 Hebrew a cubit (about 0.5 meter)   [g]19 Or the stone quarries; also in verse 26   [h]20 The meaning of the Hebrew for this phrase is uncertain.   [i]23 The meaning of the Hebrew for this word is uncertain.

LUKE 22:14-34

When the hour came, Jesus and his apostles reclined at the table. [15]And he said to them, "I have eagerly desired to eat this Passover with you before I suffer. [16]For I tell you, I will not eat it again until it finds fulfillment in the kingdom of God."

[17]After taking the cup, he gave thanks and said, "Take this and divide it among you. [18]For I tell you I will not drink again of the fruit of the vine until the kingdom of God comes."

[19]And he took bread, gave thanks and broke it, and gave it to them, saying, "This is my body given for you; do this in remembrance of me."

[20]In the same way, after the supper he took the cup, saying, "This cup is the new covenant in my blood, which is poured out for you. [21]But the hand of him who is going to betray me is with mine on the table. [22]The Son of Man will go as it has been decreed, but woe to that man who betrays him." [23]They began to question among themselves which of them it might be who would do this.

[24]Also a dispute arose among them as to which of them was considered to be greatest. [25]Jesus said to them, "The kings of the Gentiles lord it over them; and those who exercise authority over them call themselves Benefactors. [26]But you are not to be like that. Instead, the greatest among you should be like the youngest, and the one who rules like the one who serves. [27]For who is greater, the one who is at the table or the one who serves? Is it not the one who is at the table? But I am among you

as one who serves. [28]You are those who have stood by me in my trials. [29]And I confer on you a kingdom, just as my Father conferred one on me, [30]so that you may eat and drink at my table in my kingdom and sit on thrones, judging the twelve tribes of Israel.

[31]"Simon, Simon, Satan has asked to sift you[a] as wheat. [32]But I have prayed for you, Simon, that your faith may not fail. And when you have turned back, strengthen your brothers."

[33]But he replied, "Lord, I am ready to go with you to prison and to death."

[34]Jesus answered, "I tell you, Peter, before the rooster crows today, you will deny three times that you know me."

[a]31 The Greek is plural.

PSALMS 92:1–93:5

A psalm. A song. For the Sabbath day.

[1]It is good to praise the Lord
    and make music to your name,
    O Most High,
[2]to proclaim your love in the
    morning
    and your faithfulness at night,
[3]to the music of the ten-stringed
    lyre
    and the melody of the harp.

[4]For you make me glad by your deeds,
    O Lord;
    I sing for joy at the works of your
    hands.
[5]How great are your works, O Lord,
    how profound your thoughts!
[6]The senseless man does not know,
    fools do not understand,
[7]that though the wicked spring up
    like grass
    and all evildoers flourish,
    they will be forever destroyed.

[8]But you, O Lord, are exalted forever.

[9]For surely your enemies, O Lord,
    surely your enemies will perish;
    all evildoers will be scattered.
[10]You have exalted my horn[a] like that
    of a wild ox;
    fine oils have been poured upon
    me.

[11]My eyes have seen the defeat of my
    adversaries;
    my ears have heard the rout of my
    wicked foes.

[12]The righteous will flourish like a
    palm tree,
    they will grow like a cedar of
    Lebanon;
[13]planted in the house of the Lord,
    they will flourish in the courts of
    our God.
[14]They will still bear fruit in old age,
    they will stay fresh and green,
[15]proclaiming, "The Lord is upright;
    he is my Rock, and there is no
    wickedness in him."

93:1The Lord reigns, he is robed in
    majesty;
    the Lord is robed in majesty
    and is armed with strength.
The world is firmly established;
    it cannot be moved.
[2]Your throne was established long
    ago;
    you are from all eternity.

[3]The seas have lifted up, O Lord,
    the seas have lifted up their
    voice;
    the seas have lifted up their
    pounding waves.
[4]Mightier than the thunder of the
    great waters,
    mightier than the breakers of the
    sea—
    the Lord on high is mighty.

[5]Your statutes stand firm;
    holiness adorns your house
    for endless days, O Lord.

[a]10 Horn here symbolizes strength.

PROVERBS 14:1-2

The wise woman builds her house,
    but with her own hands the
    foolish one tears hers down.

[2]He whose walk is upright fears the
    Lord,
    but he whose ways are devious
    despises him.

GOD SIGHTINGS

April 25

JUDGES 4:1–5:31

After Ehud died, the Israelites once again did evil in the eyes of the LORD. ²So the LORD sold them into the hands of Jabin, a king of Canaan, who reigned in Hazor. The commander of his army was Sisera, who lived in Harosheth Haggoyim. ³Because he had nine hundred iron chariots and had cruelly oppressed the Israelites for twenty years, they cried to the LORD for help.

⁴Deborah, a prophetess, the wife of Lappidoth, was leading*a* Israel at that time. ⁵She held court under the Palm of Deborah between Ramah and Bethel in the hill country of Ephraim, and the Israelites came to her to have their disputes decided. ⁶She sent for Barak son of Abinoam from Kedesh in Naphtali and said to him, "The LORD, the God of Israel, commands you: 'Go, take with you ten thousand men of Naphtali and Zebulun and lead the way to Mount Tabor. ⁷I will lure Sisera, the commander of Jabin's army, with his chariots and his troops to the Kishon River and give him into your hands.'"

⁸Barak said to her, "If you go with me, I will go; but if you don't go with me, I won't go."

⁹"Very well," Deborah said, "I will go with you. But because of the way you are going about this,*b* the honor will not be yours, for the LORD will hand Sisera over to a woman." So Deborah went with Barak to Kedesh, ¹⁰where he summoned Zebulun and Naphtali. Ten thousand men followed him, and Deborah also went with him.

¹¹Now Heber the Kenite had left the other Kenites, the descendants of Hobab, Moses' brother-in-law,*c* and pitched his tent by the great tree in Zaanannim near Kedesh.

¹²When they told Sisera that Barak son of Abinoam had gone up to Mount Tabor, ¹³Sisera gathered together his nine hundred iron chariots and all the men with him, from Harosheth Haggoyim to the Kishon River.

¹⁴Then Deborah said to Barak, "Go! This is the day the LORD has given Sisera into your hands. Has not the LORD gone ahead of you?" So Barak went down Mount Tabor, followed by ten thousand men. ¹⁵At Barak's advance, the LORD routed Sisera and all his chariots and army by the sword, and Sisera abandoned his chariot and fled on foot. ¹⁶But Barak pursued the chariots and army as far as Harosheth Haggoyim. All the troops of Sisera fell by the sword; not a man was left.

¹⁷Sisera, however, fled on foot to the tent of Jael, the wife of Heber the Kenite, because there were friendly relations between Jabin king of Hazor and the clan of Heber the Kenite.

¹⁸Jael went out to meet Sisera and said to him, "Come, my lord, come right in. Don't be afraid." So he entered her tent, and she put a covering over him.

¹⁹"I'm thirsty," he said. "Please give me some water." She opened a skin of milk, gave him a drink, and covered him up.

²⁰"Stand in the doorway of the tent," he told her. "If someone comes by and asks you, 'Is anyone here?' say 'No.'"

²¹But Jael, Heber's wife, picked up a tent peg and a hammer and went quietly to him while he lay fast asleep, exhausted. She drove the peg through his temple into the ground, and he died.

²²Barak came by in pursuit of Sisera, and Jael went out to meet him. "Come," she said, "I will show you the man you're looking for." So he went in with her, and there lay Sisera with the tent peg through his temple—dead.

²³On that day God subdued Jabin, the Canaanite king, before the Israelites. ²⁴And the hand of the Israelites grew stronger and stronger against Jabin, the Canaanite king, until they destroyed him.

5:1 ON that day Deborah and Barak son of Abinoam sang this song:

2 "When the princes in Israel take the
        lead,
    when the people willingly offer
        themselves—
    praise the LORD!

3 "Hear this, you kings! Listen, you
        rulers!
    I will sing to*d* the LORD, I will sing;
    I will make music to*e* the LORD, the
        God of Israel.

4 "O LORD, when you went out from
        Seir,
    when you marched from the land
        of Edom,
    the earth shook, the heavens poured,
        the clouds poured down water.
5 The mountains quaked before the
        LORD, the One of Sinai,
    before the LORD, the God of Israel.

6 "In the days of Shamgar son of
        Anath,
    in the days of Jael, the roads were
        abandoned;
    travelers took to winding paths.
7 Village life*f* in Israel ceased,
    ceased until I,*g* Deborah, arose,
    arose a mother in Israel.
8 When they chose new gods,
    war came to the city gates,
    and not a shield or spear was seen
        among forty thousand in Israel.
9 My heart is with Israel's princes,
    with the willing volunteers among
        the people.
    Praise the LORD!

10 "You who ride on white donkeys,
    sitting on your saddle blankets,
    and you who walk along the road,
    consider 11 the voice of the singers*h*
        at the watering places.
    They recite the righteous acts of
        the LORD,
    the righteous acts of his warriors*i*
        in Israel.

"Then the people of the LORD
    went down to the city gates.

12 'Wake up, wake up, Deborah!
    Wake up, wake up, break out in
        song!
    Arise, O Barak!
    Take captive your captives, O son
        of Abinoam.'

13 "Then the men who were left
    came down to the nobles;
    the people of the LORD
    came to me with the mighty.
14 Some came from Ephraim, whose
        roots were in Amalek;
    Benjamin was with the people who
        followed you.
    From Makir captains came down,
    from Zebulun those who bear a
        commander's staff.
15 The princes of Issachar were with
        Deborah;
    yes, Issachar was with Barak,
        rushing after him into the
        valley.
    In the districts of Reuben
    there was much searching of
        heart.
16 Why did you stay among the
        campfires*j*
    to hear the whistling for the
        flocks?
    In the districts of Reuben
    there was much searching of
        heart.
17 Gilead stayed beyond the Jordan.
    And Dan, why did he linger by the
        ships?
    Asher remained on the coast
    and stayed in his coves.
18 The people of Zebulun risked their
        very lives;
    so did Naphtali on the heights of
        the field.

19 "Kings came, they fought;
    the kings of Canaan fought
    at Taanach by the waters of
        Megiddo,
    but they carried off no silver, no
        plunder.
20 From the heavens the stars fought,
    from their courses they fought
        against Sisera.

²¹ The river Kishon swept them away,
     the age-old river, the river Kishon.
   March on, my soul; be strong!
²² Then thundered the horses' hoofs—
     galloping, galloping go his mighty
        steeds.
²³ 'Curse Meroz,' said the angel of the
        Lᴏʀᴅ.
   'Curse its people bitterly,
   because they did not come to help
        the Lᴏʀᴅ,
   to help the Lᴏʀᴅ against the mighty.'

²⁴ "Most blessed of women be Jael,
     the wife of Heber the Kenite,
   most blessed of tent-dwelling
        women.
²⁵ He asked for water, and she gave him
        milk;
   in a bowl fit for nobles she
        brought him curdled milk.
²⁶ Her hand reached for the tent peg,
     her right hand for the workman's
        hammer.
   She struck Sisera, she crushed his
        head,
     she shattered and pierced his
        temple.
²⁷ At her feet he sank,
     he fell; there he lay.
   At her feet he sank, he fell;
     where he sank, there he fell—dead.

²⁸ "Through the window peered
        Sisera's mother;
     behind the lattice she cried out,
   'Why is his chariot so long in
        coming?
   Why is the clatter of his chariots
        delayed?'
²⁹ The wisest of her ladies answer her;
     indeed, she keeps saying to
        herself,
³⁰ 'Are they not finding and dividing the
        spoils:
     a girl or two for each man,
     colorful garments as plunder for
        Sisera,
   colorful garments embroidered,
   highly embroidered garments for
        my neck—
   all this as plunder?'

³¹ "So may all your enemies perish,
        O Lᴏʀᴅ!
   But may they who love you be like
        the sun
   when it rises in its strength."

Then the land had peace forty years.

*a4 Traditionally judging   b9 Or But on the expedition you
are undertaking   c11 Or father-in-law   d3 Or of   e3 Or /
with song I will praise   f7 Or Warriors   g7 Or you   h11 Or
archers; the meaning of the Hebrew for this word is
uncertain.   i11 Or villagers   j16 Or saddlebags*

LUKE 22:35-53

Then Jesus asked them [his disciples],
"When I sent you without purse, bag or
sandals, did you lack anything?"

   "Nothing," they answered.

³⁶ He said to them, "But now if you
have a purse, take it, and also a bag; and
if you don't have a sword, sell your cloak
and buy one. ³⁷ It is written: 'And he was
numbered with the transgressors'*a*; and
I tell you that this must be fulfilled in
me. Yes, what is written about me is
reaching its fulfillment."

³⁸ The disciples said, "See, Lord, here
are two swords."

   "That is enough," he replied.

³⁹ Jesus went out as usual to the
Mount of Olives, and his disciples followed him. ⁴⁰ On reaching the place, he
said to them, "Pray that you will not fall
into temptation." **⁴¹ He withdrew
about a stone's throw beyond them,
knelt down and prayed, ⁴²"Father, if
you are willing, take this cup from
me; yet not my will, but yours be
done."** ⁴³ An angel from heaven appeared to him and strengthened him.
⁴⁴ And being in anguish, he prayed more
earnestly, and his sweat was like drops
of blood falling to the ground.*b*

⁴⁵ When he rose from prayer and
went back to the disciples, he found
them asleep, exhausted from sorrow.
⁴⁶ "Why are you sleeping?" he asked
them. "Get up and pray so that you will
not fall into temptation."

⁴⁷ While he was still speaking a crowd
came up, and the man who was called
Judas, one of the Twelve, was leading
them. He approached Jesus to kiss him,

48 but Jesus asked him, "Judas, are you betraying the Son of Man with a kiss?"

49 When Jesus' followers saw what was going to happen, they said, "Lord, should we strike with our swords?" 50 And one of them struck the servant of the high priest, cutting off his right ear.

51 But Jesus answered, "No more of this!" And he touched the man's ear and healed him.

52 Then Jesus said to the chief priests, the officers of the temple guard, and the elders, who had come for him, "Am I leading a rebellion, that you have come with swords and clubs? 53 Every day I was with you in the temple courts, and you did not lay a hand on me. But this is your hour—when darkness reigns."

a37 Isaiah 53:12   b44 Some early manuscripts do not have verses 43 and 44.

PSALM 94:1-23

1 ● LORD, the God who avenges,
   O God who avenges, shine forth.
2 Rise up, O Judge of the earth;
   pay back to the proud what they
      deserve.
3 How long will the wicked, O LORD,
   how long will the wicked be
      jubilant?

4 They pour out arrogant words;
   all the evildoers are full of
      boasting.
5 They crush your people, O LORD;
   they oppress your inheritance.
6 They slay the widow and the alien;
   they murder the fatherless.
7 They say, "The LORD does not see;
   the God of Jacob pays no heed."

8 Take heed, you senseless ones among
      the people;
   you fools, when will you become
      wise?
9 Does he who implanted the ear not
      hear?
   Does he who formed the eye not
      see?
10 Does he who disciplines nations not
      punish?
   Does he who teaches man lack
      knowledge?

11 The LORD knows the thoughts of
      man;
   he knows that they are futile.

12 Blessed is the man you discipline,
      O LORD,
   the man you teach from your law;
13 you grant him relief from days of
      trouble,
   till a pit is dug for the wicked.
14 For the LORD will not reject his
      people;
   he will never forsake his
      inheritance.
15 Judgment will again be founded on
      righteousness,
   and all the upright in heart will
      follow it.

16 Who will rise up for me against the
      wicked?
   Who will take a stand for me
      against evildoers?
17 Unless the LORD had given me help,
   I would soon have dwelt in the
      silence of death.
18 When I said, "My foot is slipping,"
   your love, O LORD, supported me.
19 When anxiety was great within me,
   your consolation brought joy to
      my soul.

20 Can a corrupt throne be allied with
      you—
   one that brings on misery by its
      decrees?
21 They band together against the
      righteous
   and condemn the innocent to
      death.
22 But the LORD has become my fortress,
   and my God the rock in whom I
      take refuge.
23 He will repay them for their sins
   and destroy them for their
      wickedness;
   the LORD our God will destroy them.

PROVERBS 14:3-4

3 A fool's talk brings a rod to his back,
   but the lips of the wise protect
      them.

4 Where there are no oxen, the manger
  is empty,
    but from the strength of an ox
      comes an abundant harvest.

□ DAY 116

GOD SIGHTINGS

April 26

JUDGES 6:1-40

Again the Israelites did evil in the eyes of the LORD, and for seven years he gave them into the hands of the Midianites. ²Because the power of Midian was so oppressive, the Israelites prepared shelters for themselves in mountain clefts, caves and strongholds. ³Whenever the Israelites planted their crops, the Midianites, Amalekites and other eastern peoples invaded the country. ⁴They camped on the land and ruined the crops all the way to Gaza and did not spare a living thing for Israel, neither sheep nor cattle nor donkeys. ⁵They came up with their livestock and their tents like swarms of locusts. It was impossible to count the men and their camels; they invaded the land to ravage it. ⁶Midian so impoverished the Israelites that they cried out to the LORD for help.

⁷When the Israelites cried to the LORD because of Midian, ⁸he sent them a prophet, who said, "This is what the LORD, the God of Israel, says: I brought you up out of Egypt, out of the land of slavery. ⁹I snatched you from the power of Egypt and from the hand of all your oppressors. I drove them from before you and gave you their land. ¹⁰I said to you, 'I am the LORD your God; do not worship the gods of the Amorites, in whose land you live.' But you have not listened to me."

¹¹The angel of the LORD came and sat down under the oak in Ophrah that belonged to Joash the Abiezrite, where his son Gideon was threshing wheat in a winepress to keep it from the Midianites. ¹²When the angel of the LORD appeared to Gideon, he said, "The LORD is with you, mighty warrior."

¹³"But sir," Gideon replied, "if the LORD is with us, why has all this happened to us? Where are all his wonders that our fathers told us about when they said, 'Did not the LORD bring us up out of Egypt?' But now the LORD has abandoned us and put us into the hand of Midian."

¹⁴The LORD turned to him and said, "Go in the strength you have and save Israel out of Midian's hand. Am I not sending you?"

¹⁵"But Lord,ᵃ " Gideon asked, "how can I save Israel? My clan is the weakest in Manasseh, and I am the least in my family."

¹⁶The LORD answered, "I will be with you, and you will strike down all the Midianites together."

¹⁷Gideon replied, "If now I have found favor in your eyes, give me a sign that it is really you talking to me. ¹⁸Please do not go away until I come back and bring my offering and set it before you."

And the LORD said, "I will wait until you return."

¹⁹Gideon went in, prepared a young goat, and from an ephahᵇ of flour he made bread without yeast. Putting the meat in a basket and its broth in a pot, he brought them out and offered them to him under the oak.

²⁰The angel of God said to him, "Take the meat and the unleavened bread, place them on this rock, and pour out the broth." And Gideon did so. ²¹With the tip of the staff that was in his hand, the angel of the LORD touched the meat and the unleavened bread. Fire flared from the rock, consuming the meat and the bread. And the angel of the LORD disappeared. ²²When Gideon realized that it was the angel of the LORD, he exclaimed, "Ah, Sovereign LORD! I have seen the angel of the LORD face to face!"

²³But the LORD said to him, "Peace! Do not be afraid. You are not going to die."

²⁴So Gideon built an altar to the LORD

there and called it The LORD is Peace. To this day it stands in Ophrah of the Abiezrites.

²⁵That same night the LORD said to him, "Take the second bull from your father's herd, the one seven years old.ᶜ Tear down your father's altar to Baal and cut down the Asherah poleᵈ beside it. ²⁶Then build a proper kind ofᵉ altar to the LORD your God on the top of this height. Using the wood of the Asherah pole that you cut down, offer the secondᶠ bull as a burnt offering."

²⁷So Gideon took ten of his servants and did as the LORD told him. But because he was afraid of his family and the men of the town, he did it at night rather than in the daytime.

²⁸In the morning when the men of the town got up, there was Baal's altar, demolished, with the Asherah pole beside it cut down and the second bull sacrificed on the newly built altar!

²⁹They asked each other, "Who did this?"

When they carefully investigated, they were told, "Gideon son of Joash did it."

³⁰The men of the town demanded of Joash, "Bring out your son. He must die, because he has broken down Baal's altar and cut down the Asherah pole beside it."

³¹But Joash replied to the hostile crowd around him, "Are you going to plead Baal's cause? Are you trying to save him? Whoever fights for him shall be put to death by morning! If Baal really is a god, he can defend himself when someone breaks down his altar." ³²So that day they called Gideon "Jerub-Baal,ᵍ" saying, "Let Baal contend with him," because he broke down Baal's altar.

³³Now all the Midianites, Amalekites and other eastern peoples joined forces and crossed over the Jordan and camped in the Valley of Jezreel. ³⁴Then the Spirit of the LORD came upon Gideon, and he blew a trumpet, summoning the Abiezrites to follow him. ³⁵He sent messengers throughout Manasseh, calling them to arms, and also into Asher, Zebulun and Naphtali, so that they too went up to meet them.

³⁶Gideon said to God, "If you will save Israel by my hand as you have promised— ³⁷look, I will place a wool fleece on the threshing floor. If there is dew only on the fleece and all the ground is dry, then I will know that you will save Israel by my hand, as you said." ³⁸And that is what happened. Gideon rose early the next day; he squeezed the fleece and wrung out the dew—a bowlful of water.

³⁹Then Gideon said to God, "Do not be angry with me. Let me make just one more request. Allow me one more test with the fleece. This time make the fleece dry and the ground covered with dew." ⁴⁰That night God did so. Only the fleece was dry; all the ground was covered with dew.

ᵃ15 Or sir ᵇ19 That is, probably about 3/5 bushel (about 22 liters) ᶜ25 Or Take a full-grown, mature bull from your father's herd ᵈ25 That is, a symbol of the goddess Asherah; here and elsewhere in Judges ᵉ26 Or build with layers of stone an ᶠ26 Or full-grown; also in verse 28 ᵍ32 Jerub-Baal means let Baal contend.

LUKE 22:54–23:12

Then seizing him [Jesus], they [the soldiers] led him away and took him into the house of the high priest. Peter followed at a distance. ⁵⁵But when they had kindled a fire in the middle of the courtyard and had sat down together, Peter sat down with them. ⁵⁶A servant girl saw him seated there in the firelight. She looked closely at him and said, "This man was with him."

⁵⁷But he denied it. "Woman, I don't know him," he said.

⁵⁸A little later someone else saw him and said, "You also are one of them."

"Man, I am not!" Peter replied.

⁵⁹About an hour later another asserted, "Certainly this fellow was with him, for he is a Galilean."

⁶⁰Peter replied, "Man, I don't know what you're talking about!" Just as he was speaking, the rooster crowed. ⁶¹The Lord turned and looked straight at Peter. Then Peter remembered the

word the Lord had spoken to him: "Before the rooster crows today, you will disown me three times." 62And he went outside and wept bitterly.

63The men who were guarding Jesus began mocking and beating him. 64They blindfolded him and demanded, "Prophesy! Who hit you?" 65And they said many other insulting things to him.

66At daybreak the council of the elders of the people, both the chief priests and teachers of the law, met together, and Jesus was led before them. 67"If you are the Christ,*a* " they said, "tell us."

Jesus answered, "If I tell you, you will not believe me, 68and if I asked you, you would not answer. 69But from now on, the Son of Man will be seated at the right hand of the mighty God."

70They all asked, "Are you then the Son of God?"

He replied, "You are right in saying I am."

71Then they said, "Why do we need any more testimony? We have heard it from his own lips."

23:1THEN the whole assembly rose and led him off to Pilate. 2And they began to accuse him, saying, "We have found this man subverting our nation. He opposes payment of taxes to Caesar and claims to be Christ,*b* a king."

3So Pilate asked Jesus, "Are you the king of the Jews?"

"Yes, it is as you say," Jesus replied.

4Then Pilate announced to the chief priests and the crowd, "I find no basis for a charge against this man."

5But they insisted, "He stirs up the people all over Judea*c* by his teaching. He started in Galilee and has come all the way here."

6On hearing this, Pilate asked if the man was a Galilean. 7When he learned that Jesus was under Herod's jurisdiction, he sent him to Herod, who was also in Jerusalem at that time.

8When Herod saw Jesus, he was greatly pleased, because for a long time he had been wanting to see him. From what he had heard about him, he hoped to see him perform some miracle. 9He plied him with many questions, but Jesus gave him no answer. 10The chief priests and the teachers of the law were standing there, vehemently accusing him. 11Then Herod and his soldiers ridiculed and mocked him. Dressing him in an elegant robe, they sent him back to Pilate. 12That day Herod and Pilate became friends—before this they had been enemies.

a67 Or *Messiah*   *b2* Or *Messiah*; also in verses 35 and 39
c5 Or *over the land of the Jews*

PSALMS 95:1–96:13

1 **C**ome, let us sing for joy to the LORD;
   let us shout aloud to the Rock of
      our salvation.
2 Let us come before him with
      thanksgiving
   and extol him with music and song.

3 For the LORD is the great God,
   the great King above all gods.
4 In his hand are the depths of the
      earth,
   and the mountain peaks belong
      to him.
5 The sea is his, for he made it,
   and his hands formed the dry land.

6 **Come, let us bow down in worship,**
   let us kneel before the LORD our
      Maker;
7 **for he is our God**
   and we are the people of his
      pasture,
   the flock under his care.

Today, if you hear his voice,
8   do not harden your hearts as you
         did at Meribah,*a*
      as you did that day at Massah*b* in
         the desert,
9 where your fathers tested and
         tried me,
      though they had seen what I did.
10 For forty years I was angry with that
         generation;
      I said, "They are a people whose
         hearts go astray,
      and they have not known my
         ways."

11 So I declared on oath in my anger,
"They shall never enter my rest."

96:1 SING to the LORD a new song;
sing to the LORD, all the earth.
2 Sing to the LORD, praise his name;
proclaim his salvation day after
day.
3 Declare his glory among the
nations,
his marvelous deeds among all
peoples.
4 For great is the LORD and most
worthy of praise;
he is to be feared above all gods.
5 For all the gods of the nations are
idols,
but the LORD made the heavens.
6 Splendor and majesty are before
him;
strength and glory are in his
sanctuary.
7 Ascribe to the LORD, O families of
nations,
ascribe to the LORD glory and
strength.
8 Ascribe to the LORD the glory due his
name;
bring an offering and come into
his courts.
9 Worship the LORD in the splendor of
his*c* holiness;
tremble before him, all the earth.
10 Say among the nations, "The LORD
reigns."
The world is firmly established, it
cannot be moved;
he will judge the peoples with
equity.
11 Let the heavens rejoice, let the earth
be glad;
let the sea resound, and all that is
in it;
12 let the fields be jubilant, and
everything in them.
Then all the trees of the forest will
sing for joy;
13 they will sing before the LORD, for
he comes,
he comes to judge the earth.

He will judge the world in
righteousness
and the peoples in his truth.

a8 Meribah means *quarreling.*   *b8 Massah* means
testing.   *c9* Or LORD *with the splendor of*

PROVERBS 14:5-6

5 **A** truthful witness does not deceive,
but a false witness pours out lies.

6 The mocker seeks wisdom and finds
none,
but knowledge comes easily to the
discerning.

□ DAY 117

GOD SIGHTINGS

April 27

JUDGES 7:1–8:17

Early in the morning, Jerub-Baal (that is,
Gideon) and all his men camped at the
spring of Harod. The camp of Midian
was north of them in the valley near the
hill of Moreh. 2 The LORD said to Gideon,
"You have too many men for me to deliver Midian into their hands. In order
that Israel may not boast against me that
her own strength has saved her, 3 announce now to the people, 'Anyone who
trembles with fear may turn back and
leave Mount Gilead.' " So twenty-two
thousand men left, while ten thousand
remained.

4 But the LORD said to Gideon, "There
are still too many men. Take them down
to the water, and I will sift them for you
there. If I say, 'This one shall go with
you,' he shall go; but if I say, 'This one
shall not go with you,' he shall not go."

5 So Gideon took the men down to the
water. There the LORD told him, "Separate those who lap the water with their
tongues like a dog from those who kneel
down to drink." 6 Three hundred men
lapped with their hands to their
mouths. All the rest got down on their
knees to drink.

7The Lord said to Gideon, "With the three hundred men that lapped I will save you and give the Midianites into your hands. Let all the other men go, each to his own place." 8So Gideon sent the rest of the Israelites to their tents but kept the three hundred, who took over the provisions and trumpets of the others.

Now the camp of Midian lay below him in the valley. 9During that night the Lord said to Gideon, "Get up, go down against the camp, because I am going to give it into your hands. 10If you are afraid to attack, go down to the camp with your servant Purah 11and listen to what they are saying. Afterward, you will be encouraged to attack the camp." So he and Purah his servant went down to the outposts of the camp. 12The Midianites, the Amalekites and all the other eastern peoples had settled in the valley, thick as locusts. Their camels could no more be counted than the sand on the seashore.

13Gideon arrived just as a man was telling a friend his dream. "I had a dream," he was saying. "A round loaf of barley bread came tumbling into the Midianite camp. It struck the tent with such force that the tent overturned and collapsed."

14His friend responded, "This can be nothing other than the sword of Gideon son of Joash, the Israelite. God has given the Midianites and the whole camp into his hands."

15When Gideon heard the dream and its interpretation, he worshiped God. He returned to the camp of Israel and called out, "Get up! The Lord has given the Midianite camp into your hands." 16Dividing the three hundred men into three companies, he placed trumpets and empty jars in the hands of all of them, with torches inside.

17"Watch me," he told them. "Follow my lead. When I get to the edge of the camp, do exactly as I do. 18When I and all who are with me blow our trumpets, then from all around the camp blow yours and shout, 'For the Lord and for Gideon.'"

19Gideon and the hundred men with him reached the edge of the camp at the beginning of the middle watch, just after they had changed the guard. They blew their trumpets and broke the jars that were in their hands. 20The three companies blew the trumpets and smashed the jars. Grasping the torches in their left hands and holding in their right hands the trumpets they were to blow, they shouted, "A sword for the Lord and for Gideon!" 21While each man held his position around the camp, all the Midianites ran, crying out as they fled.

22When the three hundred trumpets sounded, the Lord caused the men throughout the camp to turn on each other with their swords. The army fled to Beth Shittah toward Zererah as far as the border of Abel Meholah near Tabbath. 23Israelites from Naphtali, Asher and all Manasseh were called out, and they pursued the Midianites. 24Gideon sent messengers throughout the hill country of Ephraim, saying, "Come down against the Midianites and seize the waters of the Jordan ahead of them as far as Beth Barah."

So all the men of Ephraim were called out and they took the waters of the Jordan as far as Beth Barah. 25They also captured two of the Midianite leaders, Oreb and Zeeb. They killed Oreb at the rock of Oreb, and Zeeb at the winepress of Zeeb. They pursued the Midianites and brought the heads of Oreb and Zeeb to Gideon, who was by the Jordan.

8:1Now the Ephraimites asked Gideon, "Why have you treated us like this? Why didn't you call us when you went to fight Midian?" And they criticized him sharply.

2But he answered them, "What have I accomplished compared to you? Aren't the gleanings of Ephraim's grapes better than the full grape harvest of Abiezer? 3God gave Oreb and Zeeb, the Midianite leaders, into your hands. What was I able to do compared to you?" At this, their resentment against him subsided.

4Gideon and his three hundred men, exhausted yet keeping up the pursuit, came to the Jordan and crossed it. 5He said to the men of Succoth, "Give my troops some bread; they are worn out, and I am still pursuing Zebah and Zalmunna, the kings of Midian."

6But the officials of Succoth said, "Do you already have the hands of Zebah and Zalmunna in your possession? Why should we give bread to your troops?"

7Then Gideon replied, "Just for that, when the LORD has given Zebah and Zalmunna into my hand, I will tear your flesh with desert thorns and briers."

8From there he went up to Penielª and made the same request of them, but they answered as the men of Succoth had. 9So he said to the men of Peniel, "When I return in triumph, I will tear down this tower."

10Now Zebah and Zalmunna were in Karkor with a force of about fifteen thousand men, all that were left of the armies of the eastern peoples; a hundred and twenty thousand swordsmen had fallen. 11Gideon went up by the route of the nomads east of Nobah and Jogbehah and fell upon the unsuspecting army. 12Zebah and Zalmunna, the two kings of Midian, fled, but he pursued them and captured them, routing their entire army.

13Gideon son of Joash then returned from the battle by the Pass of Heres. 14He caught a young man of Succoth and questioned him, and the young man wrote down for him the names of the seventy-seven officials of Succoth, the elders of the town. 15Then Gideon came and said to the men of Succoth, "Here are Zebah and Zalmunna, about whom you taunted me by saying, 'Do you already have the hands of Zebah and Zalmunna in your possession? Why should we give bread to your exhausted men?' " 16He took the elders of the town and taught the men of Succoth a lesson by punishing them with desert thorns and briers. 17He also pulled down the tower of Peniel and killed the men of the town.

ª8 Hebrew *Penuel*, a variant of *Peniel*; also in verses 9 and 17

LUKE 23:13-43

Pilate called together the chief priests, the rulers and the people, 14and said to them, "You brought me this man as one who was inciting the people to rebellion. I have examined him in your presence and have found no basis for your charges against him. 15Neither has Herod, for he sent him back to us; as you can see, he has done nothing to deserve death. 16Therefore, I will punish him and then release him.ª "

18With one voice they cried out, "Away with this man! Release Barabbas to us!" 19(Barabbas had been thrown into prison for an insurrection in the city, and for murder.)

20Wanting to release Jesus, Pilate appealed to them again. 21But they kept shouting, "Crucify him! Crucify him!"

22For the third time he spoke to them: "Why? What crime has this man committed? I have found in him no grounds for the death penalty. Therefore I will have him punished and then release him."

23But with loud shouts they insistently demanded that he be crucified, and their shouts prevailed. 24So Pilate decided to grant their demand. 25He released the man who had been thrown into prison for insurrection and murder, the one they asked for, and surrendered Jesus to their will.

26As they led him away, they seized Simon from Cyrene, who was on his way in from the country, and put the cross on him and made him carry it behind Jesus. 27A large number of people followed him, including women who mourned and wailed for him. 28Jesus turned and said to them, "Daughters of Jerusalem, do not weep for me; weep for yourselves and for your children. 29For the time will come when you will say, 'Blessed are the barren women, the wombs that never bore and the breasts that never nursed!' 30Then

"'they will say to the mountains, "Fall on us!"
and to the hills, "Cover us!"'ᵇ

³¹For if men do these things when the tree is green, what will happen when it is dry?"

³²Two other men, both criminals, were also led out with him to be executed. ³³When they came to the place called the Skull, there they crucified him, along with the criminals—one on his right, the other on his left. ³⁴Jesus said, "Father, forgive them, for they do not know what they are doing."*c* And they divided up his clothes by casting lots.

³⁵The people stood watching, and the rulers even sneered at him. They said, "He saved others; let him save himself if he is the Christ of God, the Chosen One."

³⁶The soldiers also came up and mocked him. They offered him wine vinegar ³⁷and said, "If you are the king of the Jews, save yourself."

³⁸There was a written notice above him, which read: THIS IS THE KING OF THE JEWS.

³⁹One of the criminals who hung there hurled insults at him: "Aren't you the Christ? Save yourself and us!"

⁴⁰But the other criminal rebuked him. "Don't you fear God," he said, "since you are under the same sentence? ⁴¹We are punished justly, for we are getting what our deeds deserve. But this man has done nothing wrong."

⁴²Then he said, "Jesus, remember me when you come into your kingdom.*d*"

⁴³Jesus answered him, "I tell you the truth, today you will be with me in paradise."

a 16 Some manuscripts him." ¹⁷Now he was obliged to release one man to them at the Feast.   b 30 Hosea 10:8   c 34 Some early manuscripts do not have this sentence.   d 42 Some manuscripts come with your kingly power

PSALMS 97:1–98:9

¹The LORD reigns, let the earth be glad; let the distant shores rejoice.

²Clouds and thick darkness surround him;
    righteousness and justice are the foundation of his throne.
³Fire goes before him
    and consumes his foes on every side.

⁴His lightning lights up the world;
    the earth sees and trembles.
⁵The mountains melt like wax before the LORD,
    before the Lord of all the earth.
⁶The heavens proclaim his righteousness,
    and all the peoples see his glory.

⁷All who worship images are put to shame,
    those who boast in idols—
    worship him, all you gods!

⁸Zion hears and rejoices
    and the villages of Judah are glad
    because of your judgments,
        O LORD.
⁹For you, O LORD, are the Most High over all the earth;
    you are exalted far above all gods.

¹⁰Let those who love the LORD hate evil,
    for he guards the lives of his faithful ones
    and delivers them from the hand of the wicked.
¹¹Light is shed upon the righteous
    and joy on the upright in heart.
¹²Rejoice in the LORD, you who are righteous,
    and praise his holy name.

⁹⁸:¹SING to the LORD a new song,
    for he has done marvelous things;
his right hand and his holy arm
    have worked salvation for him.
²The LORD has made his salvation known
    and revealed his righteousness to the nations.
³He has remembered his love
    and his faithfulness to the house of Israel;
all the ends of the earth have seen
    the salvation of our God.

⁴**Shout for joy to the LORD, all the earth,
    burst into jubilant song with music;**
⁵**make music to the LORD with the harp,**

with the harp and the sound of
singing,
6 with trumpets and the blast of the
ram's horn—
shout for joy before the LORD,
the King.

7 Let the sea resound, and everything
in it,
the world, and all who live in it.
8 Let the rivers clap their hands,
let the mountains sing together for
joy;
9 let them sing before the LORD,
for he comes to judge the earth.
He will judge the world in
righteousness
and the peoples with equity.

PROVERBS 14:7-8

7 Stay away from a foolish man,
for you will not find knowledge on
his lips.

8 The wisdom of the prudent is to give
thought to their ways,
but the folly of fools is deception.

□ DAY 118

GOD SIGHTINGS

April 28

JUDGES 8:18–9:21

Then he [Gideon] asked Zebah and Zalmunna, "What kind of men did you kill
at Tabor?"

"Men like you," they answered, "each
one with the bearing of a prince."

19 Gideon replied, "Those were my
brothers, the sons of my own mother. As
surely as the LORD lives, if you had
spared their lives, I would not kill you."
20 Turning to Jether, his oldest son, he
said, "Kill them!" But Jether did not
draw his sword, because he was only a
boy and was afraid.

21 Zebah and Zalmunna said, "Come,
do it yourself. 'As is the man, so is his

strength.' " So Gideon stepped forward
and killed them, and took the ornaments off their camels' necks.

22 The Israelites said to Gideon, "Rule
over us—you, your son and your grandson—because you have saved us out of
the hand of Midian."

23 But Gideon told them, "I will not rule
over you, nor will my son rule over you.
The LORD will rule over you." 24 And he
said, "I do have one request, that each of
you give me an earring from your share
of the plunder." (It was the custom of the
Ishmaelites to wear gold earrings.)

25 They answered, "We'll be glad to
give them." So they spread out a garment,
and each man threw a ring from his
plunder onto it. 26 The weight of the gold
rings he asked for came to seventeen
hundred shekels,a not counting the ornaments, the pendants and the purple
garments worn by the kings of Midian or
the chains that were on their camels'
necks. 27 Gideon made the gold into an
ephod, which he placed in Ophrah, his
town. All Israel prostituted themselves
by worshiping it there, and it became a
snare to Gideon and his family.

28 Thus Midian was subdued before
the Israelites and did not raise its head
again. During Gideon's lifetime, the land
enjoyed peace forty years.

29 Jerub-Baal son of Joash went back
home to live. 30 He had seventy sons of
his own, for he had many wives. 31 His
concubine, who lived in Shechem, also
bore him a son, whom he named Abimelech. 32 Gideon son of Joash died at a
good old age and was buried in the
tomb of his father Joash in Ophrah of
the Abiezrites.

33 No sooner had Gideon died than the
Israelites again prostituted themselves
to the Baals. They set up Baal-Berith as
their god and 34 did not remember the
LORD their God, who had rescued them
from the hands of all their enemies on
every side. 35 They also failed to show
kindness to the family of Jerub-Baal (that
is, Gideon) for all the good things he had
done for them.

9:1ABIMELECH son of Jerub-Baal went to his mother's brothers in Shechem and said to them and to all his mother's clan, **2**"Ask all the citizens of Shechem, 'Which is better for you: to have all seventy of Jerub-Baal's sons rule over you, or just one man?' Remember, I am your flesh and blood."

3When the brothers repeated all this to the citizens of Shechem, they were inclined to follow Abimelech, for they said, "He is our brother." **4**They gave him seventy shekels*b* of silver from the temple of Baal-Berith, and Abimelech used it to hire reckless adventurers, who became his followers. **5**He went to his father's home in Ophrah and on one stone murdered his seventy brothers, the sons of Jerub-Baal. But Jotham, the youngest son of Jerub-Baal, escaped by hiding. **6**Then all the citizens of Shechem and Beth Millo gathered beside the great tree at the pillar in Shechem to crown Abimelech king.

7When Jotham was told about this, he climbed up on the top of Mount Gerizim and shouted to them, "Listen to me, citizens of Shechem, so that God may listen to you. **8**One day the trees went out to anoint a king for themselves. They said to the olive tree, 'Be our king.'

9"But the olive tree answered, 'Should I give up my oil, by which both gods and men are honored, to hold sway over the trees?'

10"Next, the trees said to the fig tree, 'Come and be our king.'

11"But the fig tree replied, 'Should I give up my fruit, so good and sweet, to hold sway over the trees?'

12"Then the trees said to the vine, 'Come and be our king.'

13"But the vine answered, 'Should I give up my wine, which cheers both gods and men, to hold sway over the trees?'

14"Finally all the trees said to the thornbush, 'Come and be our king.'

15"The thornbush said to the trees, 'If you really want to anoint me king over you, come and take refuge in my shade;

but if not, then let fire come out of the thornbush and consume the cedars of Lebanon!'

16"Now if you have acted honorably and in good faith when you made Abimelech king, and if you have been fair to Jerub-Baal and his family, and if you have treated him as he deserves— **17**and to think that my father fought for you, risked his life to rescue you from the hand of Midian **18**(but today you have revolted against my father's family, murdered his seventy sons on a single stone, and made Abimelech, the son of his slave girl, king over the citizens of Shechem because he is your brother)— **19**if then you have acted honorably and in good faith toward Jerub-Baal and his family today, may Abimelech be your joy, and may you be his, too! **20**But if you have not, let fire come out from Abimelech and consume you, citizens of Shechem and Beth Millo, and let fire come out from you, citizens of Shechem and Beth Millo, and consume Abimelech!"

21Then Jotham fled, escaping to Beer, and he lived there because he was afraid of his brother Abimelech.

a26 That is, about 43 pounds (about 19.5 kilograms)
b4 That is, about 1 3/4 pounds (about 0.8 kilogram)

LUKE 23:44–24:12

It was now about the sixth hour, and darkness came over the whole land until the ninth hour, **45**for the sun stopped shining. And the curtain of the temple was torn in two. **46**Jesus called out with a loud voice, "Father, into your hands I commit my spirit." When he had said this, he breathed his last.

47The centurion, seeing what had happened, praised God and said, "Surely this was a righteous man." **48**When all the people who had gathered to witness this sight saw what took place, they beat their breasts and went away. **49**But all those who knew him, including the women who had followed him from Galilee, stood at a distance, watching these things.

50Now there was a man named Joseph, a member of the Council, a good and upright man, [51] who had not consented to their decision and action. He came from the Judean town of Arimathea and he was waiting for the kingdom of God. [52]Going to Pilate, he asked for Jesus' body. [53]Then he took it down, wrapped it in linen cloth and placed it in a tomb cut in the rock, one in which no one had yet been laid. [54]It was Preparation Day, and the Sabbath was about to begin.

[55]The women who had come with Jesus from Galilee followed Joseph and saw the tomb and how his body was laid in it. [56]Then they went home and prepared spices and perfumes. But they rested on the Sabbath in obedience to the commandment.

[24:1]ON the first day of the week, very early in the morning, the women took the spices they had prepared and went to the tomb. [2]They found the stone rolled away from the tomb, [3]but when they entered, they did not find the body of the Lord Jesus. [4]While they were wondering about this, suddenly two men in clothes that gleamed like lightning stood beside them. [5]**In their fright the women bowed down with their faces to the ground, but the men said to them, " Why do you look for the living among the dead? [6]He is not here; he has risen! Remember how he told you, while he was still with you in Galilee: [7]'The Son of Man must be delivered into the hands of sinful men, be crucified and on the third day be raised again.'"** [8]Then they remembered his words.

[9]When they came back from the tomb, they told all these things to the Eleven and to all the others. [10]It was Mary Magdalene, Joanna, Mary the mother of James, and the others with them who told this to the apostles. [11]But they did not believe the women, because their words seemed to them like nonsense. [12]Peter, however, got up and ran to the tomb. Bending over, he saw the strips of linen lying by themselves,

and he went away, wondering to himself what had happened.

PSALM 99:1-9

[1]**T**he LORD reigns,
　let the nations tremble;
he sits enthroned between the
　　cherubim,
　let the earth shake.
[2]Great is the LORD in Zion;
　he is exalted over all the nations.
[3]Let them praise your great and
　　awesome name—
　he is holy.

[4]The King is mighty, he loves justice—
　you have established equity;
in Jacob you have done
　what is just and right.
[5]Exalt the LORD our God
　and worship at his footstool;
　he is holy.

[6]Moses and Aaron were among his
　　priests,
　Samuel was among those who
　　called on his name;
they called on the LORD
　and he answered them.
[7]He spoke to them from the pillar of
　　cloud;
　they kept his statutes and the
　　decrees he gave them.

[8]O LORD our God,
　you answered them;
you were to Israel[a] a forgiving God,
　though you punished their
　　misdeeds.[b]
[9]Exalt the LORD our God
　and worship at his holy mountain,
　for the LORD our God is holy.

a 8 Hebrew *them*　b 8 Or / *an avenger of the wrongs done to them*

PROVERBS 14:9-10

[9]**F**ools mock at making amends for
　　sin,
　　but goodwill is found among the
　　upright.

[10]Each heart knows its own bitterness,
　and no one else can share its joy.

GOD SIGHTINGS

April 29

JUDGES 9:22–10:18

After Abimelech had governed Israel three years, [23]God sent an evil spirit between Abimelech and the citizens of Shechem, who acted treacherously against Abimelech. [24]God did this in order that the crime against Jerub-Baal's seventy sons, the shedding of their blood, might be avenged on their brother Abimelech and on the citizens of Shechem, who had helped him murder his brothers. [25]In opposition to him these citizens of Shechem set men on the hilltops to ambush and rob everyone who passed by, and this was reported to Abimelech.

[26]Now Gaal son of Ebed moved with his brothers into Shechem, and its citizens put their confidence in him. [27]After they had gone out into the fields and gathered the grapes and trodden them, they held a festival in the temple of their god. While they were eating and drinking, they cursed Abimelech. [28]Then Gaal son of Ebed said, "Who is Abimelech, and who is Shechem, that we should be subject to him? Isn't he Jerub-Baal's son, and isn't Zebul his deputy? Serve the men of Hamor, Shechem's father! Why should we serve Abimelech? [29]If only this people were under my command! Then I would get rid of him. I would say to Abimelech, 'Call out your whole army!'"[a]

[30]When Zebul the governor of the city heard what Gaal son of Ebed said, he was very angry. [31]Under cover he sent messengers to Abimelech, saying, "Gaal son of Ebed and his brothers have come to Shechem and are stirring up the city against you. [32]Now then, during the night you and your men should come and lie in wait in the fields. [33]In the morning at sunrise, advance against the city. When Gaal and his men come

out against you, do whatever your hand finds to do."

[34]So Abimelech and all his troops set out by night and took up concealed positions near Shechem in four companies. [35]Now Gaal son of Ebed had gone out and was standing at the entrance to the city gate just as Abimelech and his soldiers came out from their hiding place.

[36]When Gaal saw them, he said to Zebul, "Look, people are coming down from the tops of the mountains!"

Zebul replied, "You mistake the shadows of the mountains for men."

[37]But Gaal spoke up again: "Look, people are coming down from the center of the land, and a company is coming from the direction of the soothsayers' tree."

[38]Then Zebul said to him, "Where is your big talk now, you who said, 'Who is Abimelech that we should be subject to him?' Aren't these the men you ridiculed? Go out and fight them!"

[39]So Gaal led out[b] the citizens of Shechem and fought Abimelech. [40]Abimelech chased him, and many fell wounded in the flight—all the way to the entrance to the gate. [41]Abimelech stayed in Arumah, and Zebul drove Gaal and his brothers out of Shechem.

[42]The next day the people of Shechem went out to the fields, and this was reported to Abimelech. [43]So he took his men, divided them into three companies and set an ambush in the fields. When he saw the people coming out of the city, he rose to attack them. [44]Abimelech and the companies with him rushed forward to a position at the entrance to the city gate. Then two companies rushed upon those in the fields and struck them down. [45]All that day Abimelech pressed his attack against the city until he had captured it and killed its people. Then he destroyed the city and scattered salt over it.

[46]On hearing this, the citizens in the tower of Shechem went into the stronghold of the temple of El-Berith. [47]When Abimelech heard that they had assembled there, [48]he and all his men went up Mount Zalmon. He took an ax and cut

off some branches, which he lifted to his shoulders. He ordered the men with him, "Quick! Do what you have seen me do!" ⁴⁹So all the men cut branches and followed Abimelech. They piled them against the stronghold and set it on fire over the people inside. So all the people in the tower of Shechem, about a thousand men and women, also died.

⁵⁰Next Abimelech went to Thebez and besieged it and captured it. ⁵¹Inside the city, however, was a strong tower, to which all the men and women—all the people of the city—fled. They locked themselves in and climbed up on the tower roof. ⁵²Abimelech went to the tower and stormed it. But as he approached the entrance to the tower to set it on fire, ⁵³a woman dropped an upper millstone on his head and cracked his skull.

⁵⁴Hurriedly he called to his armorbearer, "Draw your sword and kill me, so that they can't say, 'A woman killed him.'" So his servant ran him through, and he died. ⁵⁵When the Israelites saw that Abimelech was dead, they went home.

⁵⁶Thus God repaid the wickedness that Abimelech had done to his father by murdering his seventy brothers. ⁵⁷God also made the men of Shechem pay for all their wickedness. The curse of Jotham son of Jerub-Baal came on them.

¹⁰:¹AFTER the time of Abimelech a man of Issachar, Tola son of Puah, the son of Dodo, rose to save Israel. He lived in Shamir, in the hill country of Ephraim. ²He led*c* Israel twenty-three years; then he died, and was buried in Shamir.

³He was followed by Jair of Gilead, who led Israel twenty-two years. ⁴He had thirty sons, who rode thirty donkeys. They controlled thirty towns in Gilead, which to this day are called Havvoth Jair.*d* ⁵When Jair died, he was buried in Kamon.

⁶Again the Israelites did evil in the eyes of the LORD. They served the Baals and the Ashtoreths, and the gods of

Aram, the gods of Sidon, the gods of Moab, the gods of the Ammonites and the gods of the Philistines. And because the Israelites forsook the LORD and no longer served him, ⁷he became angry with them. He sold them into the hands of the Philistines and the Ammonites, ⁸who that year shattered and crushed them. For eighteen years they oppressed all the Israelites on the east side of the Jordan in Gilead, the land of the Amorites. ⁹The Ammonites also crossed the Jordan to fight against Judah, Benjamin and the house of Ephraim; and Israel was in great distress. ¹⁰Then the Israelites cried out to the LORD, "We have sinned against you, forsaking our God and serving the Baals."

¹¹The LORD replied, "When the Egyptians, the Amorites, the Ammonites, the Philistines, ¹²the Sidonians, the Amalekites and the Maonites*e* oppressed you and you cried to me for help, did I not save you from their hands? ¹³But you have forsaken me and served other gods, so I will no longer save you. ¹⁴Go and cry out to the gods you have chosen. Let them save you when you are in trouble!"

¹⁵But the Israelites said to the LORD, "We have sinned. Do with us whatever you think best, but please rescue us now." ¹⁶Then they got rid of the foreign gods among them and served the LORD. And he could bear Israel's misery no longer.

¹⁷When the Ammonites were called to arms and camped in Gilead, the Israelites assembled and camped at Mizpah. ¹⁸The leaders of the people of Gilead said to each other, "Whoever will launch the attack against the Ammonites will be the head of all those living in Gilead."

a29 Septuagint; Hebrew *him." Then he said to Abimelech, "Call out your whole army!"* *b39* Or *Gaal went out in the sight of* *c2* Traditionally *judged*; also in verse 3 *d4* Or *called the settlements of Jair* *e12* Hebrew; some Septuagint manuscripts *Midianites*

LUKE 24:13-53

Now that same day two of them [Jesus' followers] were going to a village called Emmaus, about seven miles*a* from Jerusalem. [14]They were talking with each other about everything that had happened. [15]As they talked and discussed these things with each other, Jesus himself came up and walked along with them; [16]but they were kept from recognizing him.

[17]He asked them, "What are you discussing together as you walk along?"

They stood still, their faces downcast. [18]One of them, named Cleopas, asked him, "Are you only a visitor to Jerusalem and do not know the things that have happened there in these days?"

[19]"What things?" he asked.

"About Jesus of Nazareth," they replied. "He was a prophet, powerful in word and deed before God and all the people. [20]The chief priests and our rulers handed him over to be sentenced to death, and they crucified him; [21]but we had hoped that he was the one who was going to redeem Israel. And what is more, it is the third day since all this took place. [22]In addition, some of our women amazed us. They went to the tomb early this morning [23]but didn't find his body. They came and told us that they had seen a vision of angels, who said he was alive. [24]Then some of our companions went to the tomb and found it just as the women had said, but him they did not see."

[25]He said to them, "How foolish you are, and how slow of heart to believe all that the prophets have spoken! [26]Did not the Christ[b] have to suffer these things and then enter his glory?" [27]And beginning with Moses and all the Prophets, he explained to them what was said in all the Scriptures concerning himself.

[28]As they approached the village to which they were going, Jesus acted as if he were going farther. [29]But they urged him strongly, "Stay with us, for it is nearly evening; the day is almost over." So he went in to stay with them.

[30]When he was at the table with them, he took bread, gave thanks, broke it and began to give it to them. [31]Then their eyes were opened and they recognized him, and he disappeared from their sight. [32]They asked each other, "Were not our hearts burning within us while he talked with us on the road and opened the Scriptures to us?"

[33]They got up and returned at once to Jerusalem. There they found the Eleven and those with them, assembled together [34]and saying, "It is true! The Lord has risen and has appeared to Simon." [35]Then the two told what had happened on the way, and how Jesus was recognized by them when he broke the bread.

[36]While they were still talking about this, Jesus himself stood among them and said to them, "Peace be with you."

[37]They were startled and frightened, thinking they saw a ghost. [38]He said to them, "Why are you troubled, and why do doubts rise in your minds? [39]Look at my hands and my feet. It is I myself! Touch me and see; a ghost does not have flesh and bones, as you see I have."

[40]When he had said this, he showed them his hands and feet. [41]And while they still did not believe it because of joy and amazement, he asked them, "Do you have anything here to eat?" [42]They gave him a piece of broiled fish, [43]and he took it and ate it in their presence.

[44]He said to them, "This is what I told you while I was still with you: Everything must be fulfilled that is written about me in the Law of Moses, the Prophets and the Psalms."

[45]Then he opened their minds so they could understand the Scriptures. [46]**He told them, "This is what is written: The Christ will suffer and rise from the dead on the third day, [47]and repentance and forgiveness of sins will be preached in his name to all nations, beginning at Jerusalem.** [48]You are witnesses of these things. [49]I am going to send you what my Father has promised; but stay in the city until you have been clothed with power from on high."

[50]When he had led them out to the vicinity of Bethany, he lifted up his hands and blessed them. [51]While he was blessing them, he left them and was

taken up into heaven. 52 Then they worshiped him and returned to Jerusalem with great joy. 53 And they stayed continually at the temple, praising God.

a 13 Greek *sixty stadia* (about 11 kilometers)   *b 26* Or *Messiah;* also in verse 46

PSALM 100:1-5
A psalm. For giving thanks.

1 Shout for joy to the LORD, all the
    earth.
2   Worship the LORD with gladness;
    come before him with joyful
      songs.
3 Know that the LORD is God.
    It is he who made us, and we are
      his*a*;
    we are his people, the sheep of his
      pasture.
4 Enter his gates with thanksgiving
    and his courts with praise;
    give thanks to him and praise his
      name.
5 For the LORD is good and his love
    endures forever;
    his faithfulness continues through
      all generations.

a 3 Or *and not we ourselves*

PROVERBS 14:11-12
11 The house of the wicked will be
    destroyed,
    but the tent of the upright will
      flourish.

12 There is a way that seems right to a
    man,
    but in the end it leads to death.

☐ DAY 120

GOD SIGHTINGS

April 30

JUDGES 11:1–12:5
Jephthah the Gileadite was a mighty warrior. His father was Gilead; his mother was a prostitute. 2 Gilead's wife

also bore him sons, and when they were grown up, they drove Jephthah away. "You are not going to get any inheritance in our family," they said, "because you are the son of another woman." 3 So Jephthah fled from his brothers and settled in the land of Tob, where a group of adventurers gathered around him and followed him.

4 Some time later, when the Ammonites made war on Israel, 5 the elders of Gilead went to get Jephthah from the land of Tob. 6 "Come," they said, "be our commander, so we can fight the Ammonites."

7 Jephthah said to them, "Didn't you hate me and drive me from my father's house? Why do you come to me now, when you're in trouble?"

8 The elders of Gilead said to him, "Nevertheless, we are turning to you now; come with us to fight the Ammonites, and you will be our head over all who live in Gilead."

9 Jephthah answered, "Suppose you take me back to fight the Ammonites and the LORD gives them to me—will I really be your head?"

10 The elders of Gilead replied, "The LORD is our witness; we will certainly do as you say." 11 So Jephthah went with the elders of Gilead, and the people made him head and commander over them. And he repeated all his words before the LORD in Mizpah.

12 Then Jephthah sent messengers to the Ammonite king with the question: "What do you have against us that you have attacked our country?"

13 The king of the Ammonites answered Jephthah's messengers, "When Israel came up out of Egypt, they took away my land from the Arnon to the Jabbok, all the way to the Jordan. Now give it back peaceably."

14 Jephthah sent back messengers to the Ammonite king, 15 saying:

"This is what Jephthah says: Israel
   did not take the land of Moab or
   the land of the Ammonites. 16 But
   when they came up out of Egypt,

Israel went through the desert to the Red Sea*a* and on to Kadesh. 17 Then Israel sent messengers to the king of Edom, saying, 'Give us permission to go through your country,' but the king of Edom would not listen. They sent also to the king of Moab, and he refused. So Israel stayed at Kadesh.

18 "Next they traveled through the desert, skirted the lands of Edom and Moab, passed along the eastern side of the country of Moab, and camped on the other side of the Arnon. They did not enter the territory of Moab, for the Arnon was its border.

19 "Then Israel sent messengers to Sihon king of the Amorites, who ruled in Heshbon, and said to him, 'Let us pass through your country to our own place.' 20 Sihon, however, did not trust Israel*b* to pass through his territory. He mustered all his men and encamped at Jahaz and fought with Israel.

21 "Then the LORD, the God of Israel, gave Sihon and all his men into Israel's hands, and they defeated them. Israel took over all the land of the Amorites who lived in that country, 22 capturing all of it from the Arnon to the Jabbok and from the desert to the Jordan.

23 "Now since the LORD, the God of Israel, has driven the Amorites out before his people Israel, what right have you to take it over? 24 Will you not take what your god Chemosh gives you? Likewise, whatever the LORD our God has given us, we will possess. 25 Are you better than Balak son of Zippor, king of Moab? Did he ever quarrel with Israel or fight with them? 26 For three hundred years Israel occupied Heshbon, Aroer, the surrounding settlements and all the towns along the Arnon. Why didn't you retake them during that time? 27 I have not wronged you, but you are doing me wrong by

waging war against me. Let the LORD, the Judge,*c* decide the dispute this day between the Israelites and the Ammonites."

28 The king of Ammon, however, paid no attention to the message Jephthah sent him.

29 Then the Spirit of the LORD came upon Jephthah. He crossed Gilead and Manasseh, passed through Mizpah of Gilead, and from there he advanced against the Ammonites. 30 And Jephthah made a vow to the LORD: "If you give the Ammonites into my hands, 31 whatever comes out of the door of my house to meet me when I return in triumph from the Ammonites will be the LORD's, and I will sacrifice it as a burnt offering."

32 Then Jephthah went over to fight the Ammonites, and the LORD gave them into his hands. 33 He devastated twenty towns from Aroer to the vicinity of Minnith, as far as Abel Keramim. Thus Israel subdued Ammon.

34 When Jephthah returned to his home in Mizpah, who should come out to meet him but his daughter, dancing to the sound of tambourines! She was an only child. Except for her he had neither son nor daughter. 35 When he saw her, he tore his clothes and cried, "Oh! My daughter! You have made me miserable and wretched, because I have made a vow to the LORD that I cannot break."

36 "My father," she replied, "you have given your word to the LORD. Do to me just as you promised, now that the LORD has avenged you of your enemies, the Ammonites. 37 But grant me this one request," she said. "Give me two months to roam the hills and weep with my friends, because I will never marry."

38 "You may go," he said. And he let her go for two months. She and the girls went into the hills and wept because she would never marry. 39 After the two months, she returned to her father and he did to her as he had vowed. And she was a virgin.

From this comes the Israelite custom

[40]that each year the young women of Israel go out for four days to commemorate the daughter of Jephthah the Gileadite.

12:1THE men of Ephraim called out their forces, crossed over to Zaphon and said to Jephthah, "Why did you go to fight the Ammonites without calling us to go with you? We're going to burn down your house over your head."

[2]Jephthah answered, "I and my people were engaged in a great struggle with the Ammonites, and although I called, you didn't save me out of their hands. [3]When I saw that you wouldn't help, I took my life in my hands and crossed over to fight the Ammonites, and the LORD gave me the victory over them. Now why have you come up today to fight me?"

[4]Jephthah then called together the men of Gilead and fought against Ephraim. The Gileadites struck them down because the Ephraimites had said, "You Gileadites are renegades from Ephraim and Manasseh." [5]The Gileadites captured the fords of the Jordan leading to Ephraim, and whenever a survivor of Ephraim said, "Let me cross over," the men of Gilead asked him, "Are you an Ephraimite?" If he replied, "No," [6]they said, "All right, say 'Shibboleth.'" If he said, "Sibboleth," because he could not pronounce the word correctly, they seized him and killed him at the fords of the Jordan. Forty-two thousand Ephraimites were killed at that time.

[7]Jephthah led[d] Israel six years. Then Jephthah the Gileadite died, and was buried in a town in Gilead.

[8]After him, Ibzan of Bethlehem led Israel. [9]He had thirty sons and thirty daughters. He gave his daughters away in marriage to those outside his clan, and for his sons he brought in thirty young women as wives from outside his clan. Ibzan led Israel seven years. [10]Then Ibzan died, and was buried in Bethlehem.

[11]After him, Elon the Zebulunite led Israel ten years. [12]Then Elon died, and was buried in Aijalon in the land of Zebulun.

[13]After him, Abdon son of Hillel, from Pirathon, led Israel. [14]He had forty sons and thirty grandsons, who rode on seventy donkeys. He led Israel eight years. [15]Then Abdon son of Hillel died, and was buried at Pirathon in Ephraim, in the hill country of the Amalekites.

a 16 Hebrew *Yam Suph;* that is, Sea of Reeds   *b 20* Or *however, would not make an agreement for Israel*   *c 27* Or *Ruler*   *d 7* Traditionally *judged;* also in verses 8-14

JOHN 1:1-28

In the beginning was the Word, and the Word was with God, and the Word was God. [2]He was with God in the beginning.

[3]Through him all things were made; without him nothing was made that has been made. [4]In him was life, and that life was the light of men. [5]The light shines in the darkness, but the darkness has not understood[a] it.

[6]There came a man who was sent from God; his name was John. [7]He came as a witness to testify concerning that light, so that through him all men might believe. [8]He himself was not the light; he came only as a witness to the light. [9]The true light that gives light to every man was coming into the world.[b]

[10]He was in the world, and though the world was made through him, the world did not recognize him. [11]He came to that which was his own, but his own did not receive him. [12]**Yet to all who received him, to those who believed in his name, he gave the right to become children of God—** [13]**children born not of natural descent,**[c] **nor of human decision or a husband's will, but born of God.**

[14]The Word became flesh and made his dwelling among us. We have seen his glory, the glory of the One and Only,[d] who came from the Father, full of grace and truth. [15]John testifies concerning him. He cries out, saying, "This was he of whom I said, 'He who comes after me has surpassed me because he was before me.'" [16]From the fullness of his grace we have all received one blessing after another.

[17] For the law was given through Moses; grace and truth came through Jesus Christ. [18] No one has ever seen God, but God the One and Only,[d, e] who is at the Father's side, has made him known.

[19] Now this was John's testimony when the Jews of Jerusalem sent priests and Levites to ask him who he was. [20] He did not fail to confess, but confessed freely, "I am not the Christ.[f]"

[21] They asked him, "Then who are you? Are you Elijah?"

He said, "I am not."

"Are you the Prophet?"

He answered, "No."

[22] Finally they said, "Who are you? Give us an answer to take back to those who sent us. What do you say about yourself?"

[23] John replied in the words of Isaiah the prophet, "I am the voice of one calling in the desert, 'Make straight the way for the Lord.'"[g]

[24] Now some Pharisees who had been sent [25] questioned him, "Why then do you baptize if you are not the Christ, nor Elijah, nor the Prophet?"

[26] "I baptize with[h] water," John replied, "but among you stands one you do not know. [27] He is the one who comes after me, the thongs of whose sandals I am not worthy to untie."

[28] This all happened at Bethany on the other side of the Jordan, where John was baptizing.

[a]5 Or darkness, and the darkness has not overcome   [b]9 Or This was the true light that gives light to every man who comes into the world   [c]13 Greek of bloods   [d]14,18 Or the Only Begotten   [e]18 Some manuscripts but the only (or only begotten) Son   [f]20 Or Messiah. "The Christ" (Greek) and "the Messiah" (Hebrew) both mean "the Anointed One"; also in verse 25.   [g]23 Isaiah 40:3   [h]26 Or in; also in verses 31 and 33

PSALM 101:1-8
Of David. A psalm.

[1] I will sing of your love and justice;
   to you, O Lord, I will sing praise.

[2] I will be careful to lead a blameless life—
   when will you come to me?

I will walk in my house
   with blameless heart.
[3] I will set before my eyes
   no vile thing.

The deeds of faithless men I hate;
   they will not cling to me.
[4] Men of perverse heart shall be far from me;
   I will have nothing to do with evil.

[5] Whoever slanders his neighbor in secret,
   him will I put to silence;
whoever has haughty eyes and a proud heart,
   him will I not endure.

[6] My eyes will be on the faithful in the land,
   that they may dwell with me;
he whose walk is blameless
   will minister to me.

[7] No one who practices deceit
   will dwell in my house;
no one who speaks falsely
   will stand in my presence.

[8] Every morning I will put to silence
   all the wicked in the land;
I will cut off every evildoer
   from the city of the Lord.

PROVERBS 14:13-14
[13] Even in laughter the heart may ache,
   and joy may end in grief.

[14] The faithless will be fully repaid for their ways,
   and the good man rewarded for his.

GOD SIGHTINGS

May 1

JUDGES 13:1–14:20

Again the Israelites did evil in the eyes of the LORD, so the LORD delivered them into the hands of the Philistines for forty years.

2A certain man of Zorah, named Manoah, from the clan of the Danites, had a wife who was sterile and remained childless. 3The angel of the LORD appeared to her and said, "You are sterile and childless, but you are going to conceive and have a son. 4Now see to it that you drink no wine or other fermented drink and that you do not eat anything unclean, 5because you will conceive and give birth to a son. No razor may be used on his head, because the boy is to be a Nazirite, set apart to God from birth, and he will begin the deliverance of Israel from the hands of the Philistines."

6Then the woman went to her husband and told him, "A man of God came to me. He looked like an angel of God, very awesome. I didn't ask him where he came from, and he didn't tell me his name. 7But he said to me, 'You will conceive and give birth to a son. Now then, drink no wine or other fermented drink and do not eat anything unclean, because the boy will be a Nazirite of God from birth until the day of his death.'"

8Then Manoah prayed to the LORD: "O Lord, I beg you, let the man of God you sent to us come again to teach us how to bring up the boy who is to be born."

9God heard Manoah, and the angel of God came again to the woman while she was out in the field; but her husband Manoah was not with her. 10The woman hurried to tell her husband, "He's here! The man who appeared to me the other day!"

11Manoah got up and followed his wife. When he came to the man, he said, "Are you the one who talked to my wife?"

"I am," he said.

12So Manoah asked him, "When your words are fulfilled, what is to be the rule for the boy's life and work?"

13The angel of the LORD answered, "Your wife must do all that I have told her. 14She must not eat anything that comes from the grapevine, nor drink any wine or other fermented drink nor eat anything unclean. She must do everything I have commanded her."

15Manoah said to the angel of the LORD, "We would like you to stay until we prepare a young goat for you."

16The angel of the LORD replied, "Even though you detain me, I will not eat any of your food. But if you prepare a burnt offering, offer it to the LORD." (Manoah did not realize that it was the angel of the LORD.)

17Then Manoah inquired of the angel of the LORD, "What is your name, so that we may honor you when your word comes true?"

18He replied, "Why do you ask my name? It is beyond understanding.a"

19Then Manoah took a young goat, together with the grain offering, and sacrificed it on a rock to the LORD. And the LORD did an amazing thing while Manoah and his wife watched: 20As the flame blazed up from the altar toward heaven, the angel of the LORD ascended in the flame. Seeing this, Manoah and his wife fell with their faces to the ground. 21When the angel of the LORD did not show himself again to Manoah and his wife, Manoah realized that it was the angel of the LORD.

22"We are doomed to die!" he said to his wife. "We have seen God!"

23But his wife answered, "If the LORD had meant to kill us, he would not have accepted a burnt offering and grain offering from our hands, nor shown us all these things or now told us this."

²⁴The woman gave birth to a boy and named him Samson. He grew and the LORD blessed him, ²⁵and the Spirit of the LORD began to stir him while he was in Mahaneh Dan, between Zorah and Eshtaol.

¹⁴:¹SAMSON went down to Timnah and saw there a young Philistine woman. ²When he returned, he said to his father and mother, "I have seen a Philistine woman in Timnah; now get her for me as my wife."

³His father and mother replied, "Isn't there an acceptable woman among your relatives or among all our people? Must you go to the uncircumcised Philistines to get a wife?"

But Samson said to his father, "Get her for me. She's the right one for me." ⁴(His parents did not know that this was from the LORD, who was seeking an occasion to confront the Philistines; for at that time they were ruling over Israel.) ⁵Samson went down to Timnah together with his father and mother. As they approached the vineyards of Timnah, suddenly a young lion came roaring toward him. ⁶The Spirit of the LORD came upon him in power so that he tore the lion apart with his bare hands as he might have torn a young goat. But he told neither his father nor his mother what he had done. ⁷Then he went down and talked with the woman, and he liked her.

⁸Some time later, when he went back to marry her, he turned aside to look at the lion's carcass. In it was a swarm of bees and some honey, ⁹which he scooped out with his hands and ate as he went along. When he rejoined his parents, he gave them some, and they too ate it. But he did not tell them that he had taken the honey from the lion's carcass.

¹⁰Now his father went down to see the woman. And Samson made a feast there, as was customary for bridegrooms. ¹¹When he appeared, he was given thirty companions.

¹²"Let me tell you a riddle," Samson said to them. "If you can give me the an-

swer within the seven days of the feast, I will give you thirty linen garments and thirty sets of clothes. ¹³If you can't tell me the answer, you must give me thirty linen garments and thirty sets of clothes."

"Tell us your riddle," they said. "Let's hear it."

¹⁴He replied,

"Out of the eater, something to eat;
    out of the strong, something
        sweet."

For three days they could not give the answer.

¹⁵On the fourthᵇ day, they said to Samson's wife, "Coax your husband into explaining the riddle for us, or we will burn you and your father's household to death. Did you invite us here to rob us?"

¹⁶Then Samson's wife threw herself on him, sobbing, "You hate me! You don't really love me. You've given my people a riddle, but you haven't told me the answer."

"I haven't even explained it to my father or mother," he replied, "so why should I explain it to you?" ¹⁷She cried the whole seven days of the feast. So on the seventh day he finally told her, because she continued to press him. She in turn explained the riddle to her people.

¹⁸Before sunset on the seventh day the men of the town said to him,

"What is sweeter than honey?
    What is stronger than a lion?"

Samson said to them,

"If you had not plowed with my
        heifer,
    you would not have solved my
        riddle."

¹⁹Then the Spirit of the LORD came upon him in power. He went down to Ashkelon, struck down thirty of their men, stripped them of their belongings and gave their clothes to those who had explained the riddle. Burning with anger, he went up to his father's house. ²⁰And Samson's wife was given to the

friend who had attended him at his wedding.

a18 Or *is wonderful*   b15 Some Septuagint manuscripts and Syriac; Hebrew *seventh*

JOHN 1:29-51

The next day John saw Jesus coming toward him and said, "Look, the Lamb of God, who takes away the sin of the world! 30This is the one I meant when I said, 'A man who comes after me has surpassed me because he was before me.' 31I myself did not know him, but the reason I came baptizing with water was that he might be revealed to Israel."

32 Then John gave this testimony: "I saw the Spirit come down from heaven as a dove and remain on him. 33I would not have known him, except that the one who sent me to baptize with water told me, 'The man on whom you see the Spirit come down and remain is he who will baptize with the Holy Spirit.' 34I have seen and I testify that this is the Son of God."

35 The next day John was there again with two of his disciples. 36When he saw Jesus passing by, he said, "Look, the Lamb of God!"

37 When the two disciples heard him say this, they followed Jesus. 38Turning around, Jesus saw them following and asked, "What do you want?"

They said, "Rabbi" (which means Teacher), "where are you staying?"

39"Come," he replied, "and you will see."

So they went and saw where he was staying, and spent that day with him. It was about the tenth hour.

40Andrew, Simon Peter's brother, was one of the two who heard what John had said and who had followed Jesus. 41The first thing Andrew did was to find his brother Simon and tell him, "We have found the Messiah" (that is, the Christ). 42And he brought him to Jesus.

Jesus looked at him and said, "You are Simon son of John. You will be called Cephas" (which, when translated, is Petera).

43 The next day Jesus decided to leave for Galilee. Finding Philip, he said to him, "Follow me."

44Philip, like Andrew and Peter, was from the town of Bethsaida. 45Philip found Nathanael and told him, "We have found the one Moses wrote about in the Law, and about whom the prophets also wrote—Jesus of Nazareth, the son of Joseph."

46 "Nazareth! Can anything good come from there?" Nathanael asked.

"Come and see," said Philip.

47 When Jesus saw Nathanael approaching, he said of him, "Here is a true Israelite, in whom there is nothing false."

48 "How do you know me?" Nathanael asked.

Jesus answered, "I saw you while you were still under the fig tree before Philip called you."

49 Then Nathanael declared, "Rabbi, you are the Son of God; you are the King of Israel."

50Jesus said, "You believeb because I told you I saw you under the fig tree. You shall see greater things than that." 51He then added, "I tell youc the truth, youc shall see heaven open, and the angels of God ascending and descending on the Son of Man."

a42 Both *Cephas* (Aramaic) and *Peter* (Greek) mean *rock.*   b50 Or *Do you believe…?*   c51 The Greek is plural.

PSALM 102:1-28

A prayer of an afflicted man. When he is faint and pours out his lament before the LORD.

1 **H**ear my prayer, O LORD;
  let my cry for help come to you.
2 Do not hide your face from me
  when I am in distress.
 Turn your ear to me;
  when I call, answer me quickly.

3 For my days vanish like smoke;
  my bones burn like glowing embers.
4 My heart is blighted and withered
  like grass;
 I forget to eat my food.
5 Because of my loud groaning
  I am reduced to skin and bones.

⁶I am like a desert owl,
   like an owl among the ruins.
⁷I lie awake; I have become
   like a bird alone on a roof.
⁸All day long my enemies taunt me;
   those who rail against me use my
      name as a curse.
⁹For I eat ashes as my food
   and mingle my drink with tears
¹⁰because of your great wrath,
   for you have taken me up and
      thrown me aside.
¹¹My days are like the evening shadow;
   I wither away like grass.

¹²But you, O Lord, sit enthroned
      forever;
   your renown endures through all
      generations.
¹³You will arise and have compassion
      on Zion,
   for it is time to show favor to her;
      the appointed time has come.
¹⁴For her stones are dear to your
      servants;
   her very dust moves them to pity.
¹⁵The nations will fear the name of
      the Lord,
   all the kings of the earth will
      revere your glory.
¹⁶For the Lord will rebuild Zion
   and appear in his glory.
¹⁷He will respond to the prayer of the
      destitute;
   he will not despise their plea.

¹⁸Let this be written for a future
      generation,
   that a people not yet created may
      praise the Lord:
¹⁹"The Lord looked down from his
      sanctuary on high,
   from heaven he viewed the earth,
²⁰to hear the groans of the prisoners
   and release those condemned
      to death."
²¹So the name of the Lord will be
      declared in Zion
   and his praise in Jerusalem
²²when the peoples and the kingdoms
   assemble to worship the Lord.

²³In the course of my life*a* he broke my
      strength;
   he cut short my days.
²⁴So I said:
   "Do not take me away, O my God,
      in the midst of my days;
   your years go on through all
      generations.
²⁵In the beginning you laid the
      foundations of the earth,
   and the heavens are the work of
      your hands.
²⁶They will perish, but you remain;
   they will all wear out like a
      garment.
   Like clothing you will change them
      and they will be discarded.
²⁷But you remain the same,
   and your years will never end.
²⁸The children of your servants will
      live in your presence;
   their descendants will be
      established before you."

a23 Or By his power

PROVERBS 14:15-16
¹⁵**A** simple man believes anything,
   but a prudent man gives thought
      to his steps.

¹⁶A wise man fears the Lord and
   shuns evil,
   but a fool is hotheaded and
      reckless.

□ DAY 122

GOD SIGHTINGS

May 2

JUDGES 15:1–16:31
Later on, at the time of wheat harvest,
Samson took a young goat and went to
visit his wife. He said, "I'm going to my
wife's room." But her father would not
let him go in.

²"I was so sure you thoroughly hated
her," he said, "that I gave her to your

friend. Isn't her younger sister more attractive? Take her instead."

³Samson said to them, "This time I have a right to get even with the Philistines; I will really harm them." ⁴So he went out and caught three hundred foxes and tied them tail to tail in pairs. He then fastened a torch to every pair of tails, ⁵lit the torches and let the foxes loose in the standing grain of the Philistines. He burned up the shocks and standing grain, together with the vineyards and olive groves.

⁶When the Philistines asked, "Who did this?" they were told, "Samson, the Timnite's son-in-law, because his wife was given to his friend."

So the Philistines went up and burned her and her father to death. ⁷Samson said to them, "Since you've acted like this, I won't stop until I get my revenge on you." ⁸He attacked them viciously and slaughtered many of them. Then he went down and stayed in a cave in the rock of Etam.

⁹The Philistines went up and camped in Judah, spreading out near Lehi. ¹⁰The men of Judah asked, "Why have you come to fight us?"

"We have come to take Samson prisoner," they answered, "to do to him as he did to us."

¹¹Then three thousand men from Judah went down to the cave in the rock of Etam and said to Samson, "Don't you realize that the Philistines are rulers over us? What have you done to us?"

He answered, "I merely did to them what they did to me."

¹²They said to him, "We've come to tie you up and hand you over to the Philistines."

Samson said, "Swear to me that you won't kill me yourselves."

¹³"Agreed," they answered. "We will only tie you up and hand you over to them. We will not kill you." So they bound him with two new ropes and led him up from the rock. ¹⁴As he approached Lehi, the Philistines came toward him shouting. The Spirit of the Lord came upon him in power. The ropes on his arms became like charred flax, and the bindings dropped from his hands. ¹⁵Finding a fresh jawbone of a donkey, he grabbed it and struck down a thousand men.

¹⁶Then Samson said,

"With a donkey's jawbone
    I have made donkeys of them.ᵃ
With a donkey's jawbone
    I have killed a thousand men."

¹⁷When he finished speaking, he threw away the jawbone; and the place was called Ramath Lehi.ᵇ

¹⁸Because he was very thirsty, he cried out to the Lord, "You have given your servant this great victory. Must I now die of thirst and fall into the hands of the uncircumcised?" ¹⁹Then God opened up the hollow place in Lehi, and water came out of it. When Samson drank, his strength returned and he revived. So the spring was called En Hakkore,ᶜ and it is still there in Lehi.

²⁰Samson ledᵈ Israel for twenty years in the days of the Philistines.

¹⁶:¹ONE day Samson went to Gaza, where he saw a prostitute. He went in to spend the night with her. ²The people of Gaza were told, "Samson is here!" So they surrounded the place and lay in wait for him all night at the city gate. They made no move during the night, saying, "At dawn we'll kill him."

³But Samson lay there only until the middle of the night. Then he got up and took hold of the doors of the city gate, together with the two posts, and tore them loose, bar and all. He lifted them to his shoulders and carried them to the top of the hill that faces Hebron.

⁴Some time later, he fell in love with a woman in the Valley of Sorek whose name was Delilah. ⁵The rulers of the Philistines went to her and said, "See if you can lure him into showing you the secret of his great strength and how we can overpower him so we may tie him up and subdue him. Each one of us will give you eleven hundred shekelsᵉ of silver."

⁶So Delilah said to Samson, "Tell me

the secret of your great strength and how you can be tied up and subdued."

[7]Samson answered her, "If anyone ties me with seven fresh thongs[f] that have not been dried, I'll become as weak as any other man."

[8]Then the rulers of the Philistines brought her seven fresh thongs that had not been dried, and she tied him with them. [9]With men hidden in the room, she called to him, "Samson, the Philistines are upon you!" But he snapped the thongs as easily as a piece of string snaps when it comes close to a flame. So the secret of his strength was not discovered.

[10]Then Delilah said to Samson, "You have made a fool of me; you lied to me. Come now, tell me how you can be tied."

[11]He said, "If anyone ties me securely with new ropes that have never been used, I'll become as weak as any other man."

[12]So Delilah took new ropes and tied him with them. Then, with men hidden in the room, she called to him, "Samson, the Philistines are upon you!" But he snapped the ropes off his arms as if they were threads.

[13]Delilah then said to Samson, "Until now, you have been making a fool of me and lying to me. Tell me how you can be tied."

He replied, "If you weave the seven braids of my head into the fabric ⌊on the loom⌋ and tighten it with the pin, I'll become as weak as any other man." So while he was sleeping, Delilah took the seven braids of his head, wove them into the fabric [14]and[g] tightened it with the pin.

Again she called to him, "Samson, the Philistines are upon you!" He awoke from his sleep and pulled up the pin and the loom, with the fabric.

[15]Then she said to him, "How can you say, 'I love you,' when you won't confide in me? This is the third time you have made a fool of me and haven't told me the secret of your great strength." [16]With such nagging she prodded him day after day until he was tired to death.

[17]So he told her everything. "No razor has ever been used on my head," he said, "because I have been a Nazirite set apart to God since birth. If my head were shaved, my strength would leave me, and I would become as weak as any other man."

[18]When Delilah saw that he had told her everything, she sent word to the rulers of the Philistines, "Come back once more; he has told me everything." So the rulers of the Philistines returned with the silver in their hands. [19]Having put him to sleep on her lap, she called a man to shave off the seven braids of his hair, and so began to subdue him.[h] And his strength left him.

[20]Then she called, "Samson, the Philistines are upon you!"

He awoke from his sleep and thought, "I'll go out as before and shake myself free." But he did not know that the Lord had left him.

[21]Then the Philistines seized him, gouged out his eyes and took him down to Gaza. Binding him with bronze shackles, they set him to grinding in the prison. [22]But the hair on his head began to grow again after it had been shaved.

[23]Now the rulers of the Philistines assembled to offer a great sacrifice to Dagon their god and to celebrate, saying, "Our god has delivered Samson, our enemy, into our hands."

[24]When the people saw him, they praised their god, saying,

"Our god has delivered our enemy
    into our hands,
the one who laid waste our land
    and multiplied our slain."

[25]While they were in high spirits, they shouted, "Bring out Samson to entertain us." So they called Samson out of the prison, and he performed for them.

When they stood him among the pillars, [26]Samson said to the servant who held his hand, "Put me where I can feel the pillars that support the temple, so that I may lean against them." [27]Now the temple was crowded with men and women; all the rulers of the Philistines were there, and on the roof were about three thousand men and women watching Samson perform. [28]Then Samson prayed to the LORD, "O Sovereign LORD, remember me. O God, please strengthen me just once more, and let me with one blow get revenge on the Philistines for my two eyes." [29]Then Samson reached toward the two central pillars on which the temple stood. Bracing himself against them, his right hand on the one and his left hand on the other, [30]Samson said, "Let me die with the Philistines!" Then he pushed with all his might, and down came the temple on the rulers and all the people in it. Thus he killed many more when he died than while he lived.

[31]Then his brothers and his father's whole family went down to get him. They brought him back and buried him between Zorah and Eshtaol in the tomb of Manoah his father. He had led[d] Israel twenty years.

a16 Or *made a heap or two*; the Hebrew for *donkey* sounds like the Hebrew for *heap*.   b17 *Ramath Lehi* means *jawbone hill*.   c19 *En Hakkore* means *caller's spring*.   d20,31 Traditionally *judged*   e5 That is, about 28 pounds (about 13 kilograms)   f7 Or *bowstrings*; also in verses 8 and 9   g13,14 Some Septuagint manuscripts; Hebrew "⌊*I can*⌋ *if you weave the seven braids of my head into the fabric* ⌊*on the loom*⌋." 14 So she   h19 Hebrew; some Septuagint manuscripts *and he began to weaken*

JOHN 2:1-25

On the third day a wedding took place at Cana in Galilee. Jesus' mother was there, [2]and Jesus and his disciples had also been invited to the wedding. [3]When the wine was gone, Jesus' mother said to him, "They have no more wine."

[4]"Dear woman, why do you involve me?" Jesus replied. "My time has not yet come."

[5]His mother said to the servants, "Do whatever he tells you."

[6]Nearby stood six stone water jars, the kind used by the Jews for ceremonial washing, each holding from twenty to thirty gallons.[a]

[7]Jesus said to the servants, "Fill the jars with water"; so they filled them to the brim.

[8]Then he told them, "Now draw some out and take it to the master of the banquet."

They did so, [9]and the master of the banquet tasted the water that had been turned into wine. He did not realize where it had come from, though the servants who had drawn the water knew. Then he called the bridegroom aside [10]and said, "Everyone brings out the choice wine first and then the cheaper wine after the guests have had too much to drink; but you have saved the best till now."

[11]This, the first of his miraculous signs, Jesus performed at Cana in Galilee. He thus revealed his glory, and his disciples put their faith in him.

[12]After this he went down to Capernaum with his mother and brothers and his disciples. There they stayed for a few days.

[13]When it was almost time for the Jewish Passover, Jesus went up to Jerusalem. [14]In the temple courts he found men selling cattle, sheep and doves, and others sitting at tables exchanging money. [15]So he made a whip out of cords, and drove all from the temple area, both sheep and cattle; he scattered the coins of the money changers and overturned their tables. [16]To those who sold doves he said, "Get these out of here! How dare you turn my Father's house into a market!"

[17]His disciples remembered that it is written: "Zeal for your house will consume me."[b]

[18]Then the Jews demanded of him, "What miraculous sign can you show us to prove your authority to do all this?"

[19]Jesus answered them, "Destroy this temple, and I will raise it again in three days."

[20]The Jews replied, "It has taken forty-six years to build this temple, and you are going to raise it in three days?" [21]But the temple he had spoken of was his body. [22]After he was raised from the dead, his disciples recalled what he had said. Then they believed the Scripture and the words that Jesus had spoken.

[23]Now while he was in Jerusalem at

the Passover Feast, many people saw the miraculous signs he was doing and believed in his name.*c* 24But Jesus would not entrust himself to them, for he knew all men. 25He did not need man's testimony about man, for he knew what was in a man.

a6 Greek two to three metretes (probably about 75 to 115 liters) b17 Psalm 69:9 c23 Or and believed in him

PSALM 103:1-22
Of David.

1 Praise the LORD, O my soul;
    all my inmost being, praise his
       holy name.
2 Praise the LORD, O my soul,
    and forget not all his benefits—
3 who forgives all your sins
    and heals all your diseases,
4 who redeems your life from the pit
    and crowns you with love and
       compassion,
5 who satisfies your desires with good
       things
    so that your youth is renewed like
       the eagle's.

6 The LORD works righteousness
    and justice for all the oppressed.

7 He made known his ways to Moses,
    his deeds to the people of Israel:
8 The LORD is compassionate and
       gracious,
    slow to anger, abounding in love.
9 He will not always accuse,
    nor will he harbor his anger
       forever;
10 he does not treat us as our sins
       deserve
    or repay us according to our
       iniquities.
11 For as high as the heavens are
       above the earth,
    so great is his love for those who
       fear him;
12 as far as the east is from the west,
    so far has he removed our
       transgressions from us.
13 As a father has compassion on his
       children,
    so the LORD has compassion on
       those who fear him;

14 for he knows how we are formed,
    he remembers that we are dust.
15 As for man, his days are like grass,
    he flourishes like a flower of the
       field;
16 the wind blows over it and it is gone,
    and its place remembers it no
       more.
17 But from everlasting to everlasting
    the LORD's love is with those who
       fear him,
    and his righteousness with their
       children's children—
18 with those who keep his covenant
    and remember to obey his
       precepts.

19 The LORD has established his throne
       in heaven,
    and his kingdom rules over all.

20 Praise the LORD, you his angels,
    you mighty ones who do his
       bidding,
    who obey his word.
21 Praise the LORD, all his heavenly
       hosts,
    you his servants who do his will.
22 Praise the LORD, all his works
    everywhere in his dominion.

    Praise the LORD, O my soul.

PROVERBS 14:17-19
17 A quick-tempered man does foolish
       things,
    and a crafty man is hated.

18 The simple inherit folly,
    but the prudent are crowned with
       knowledge.

19 Evil men will bow down in the
       presence of the good,
    and the wicked at the gates of the
       righteous.

GOD SIGHTINGS

May 3

JUDGES 17:1–18:31

Now a man named Micah from the hill country of Ephraim ²said to his mother, "The eleven hundred shekels*a* of silver that were taken from you and about which I heard you utter a curse—I have that silver with me; I took it."

Then his mother said, "The LORD bless you, my son!"

³When he returned the eleven hundred shekels of silver to his mother, she said, "I solemnly consecrate my silver to the LORD for my son to make a carved image and a cast idol. I will give it back to you."

⁴So he returned the silver to his mother, and she took two hundred shekels*b* of silver and gave them to a silversmith, who made them into the image and the idol. And they were put in Micah's house.

⁵Now this man Micah had a shrine, and he made an ephod and some idols and installed one of his sons as his priest. ⁶In those days Israel had no king; everyone did as he saw fit.

⁷A young Levite from Bethlehem in Judah, who had been living within the clan of Judah, ⁸left that town in search of some other place to stay. On his way*c* he came to Micah's house in the hill country of Ephraim.

⁹Micah asked him, "Where are you from?"

"I'm a Levite from Bethlehem in Judah," he said, "and I'm looking for a place to stay."

¹⁰Then Micah said to him, "Live with me and be my father and priest, and I'll give you ten shekels*d* of silver a year, your clothes and your food." ¹¹So the Levite agreed to live with him, and the young man was to him like one of his sons. ¹²Then Micah installed the Levite, and the young man became his priest and lived in his house. ¹³And Micah said, "Now I know that the LORD will be good to me, since this Levite has become my priest."

¹⁸:¹In those days Israel had no king.

And in those days the tribe of the Danites was seeking a place of their own where they might settle, because they had not yet come into an inheritance among the tribes of Israel. ²So the Danites sent five warriors from Zorah and Eshtaol to spy out the land and explore it. These men represented all their clans. They told them, "Go, explore the land."

The men entered the hill country of Ephraim and came to the house of Micah, where they spent the night. ³When they were near Micah's house, they recognized the voice of the young Levite; so they turned in there and asked him, "Who brought you here? What are you doing in this place? Why are you here?"

⁴He told them what Micah had done for him, and said, "He has hired me and I am his priest."

⁵Then they said to him, "Please inquire of God to learn whether our journey will be successful."

⁶The priest answered them, "Go in peace. Your journey has the LORD's approval."

⁷So the five men left and came to Laish, where they saw that the people were living in safety, like the Sidonians, unsuspecting and secure. And since their land lacked nothing, they were prosperous.*e* Also, they lived a long way from the Sidonians and had no relationship with anyone else.*f*

⁸When they returned to Zorah and Eshtaol, their brothers asked them, "How did you find things?"

⁹They answered, "Come on, let's attack them! We have seen that the land is very good. Aren't you going to do something? Don't hesitate to go there and take it over. ¹⁰When you get there, you will find an unsuspecting people and a spacious land that God has put into your

hands, a land that lacks nothing whatever."

¹¹Then six hundred men from the clan of the Danites, armed for battle, set out from Zorah and Eshtaol. ¹²On their way they set up camp near Kiriath Jearim in Judah. This is why the place west of Kiriath Jearim is called Mahaneh Dan*g* to this day. ¹³From there they went on to the hill country of Ephraim and came to Micah's house.

¹⁴Then the five men who had spied out the land of Laish said to their brothers, "Do you know that one of these houses has an ephod, other household gods, a carved image and a cast idol? Now you know what to do." ¹⁵So they turned in there and went to the house of the young Levite at Micah's place and greeted him. ¹⁶The six hundred Danites, armed for battle, stood at the entrance to the gate. ¹⁷The five men who had spied out the land went inside and took the carved image, the ephod, the other household gods and the cast idol while the priest and the six hundred armed men stood at the entrance to the gate.

¹⁸When these men went into Micah's house and took the carved image, the ephod, the other household gods and the cast idol, the priest said to them, "What are you doing?"

¹⁹They answered him, "Be quiet! Don't say a word. Come with us, and be our father and priest. Isn't it better that you serve a tribe and clan in Israel as priest rather than just one man's household?" ²⁰Then the priest was glad. He took the ephod, the other household gods and the carved image and went along with the people. ²¹Putting their little children, their livestock and their possessions in front of them, they turned away and left.

²²When they had gone some distance from Micah's house, the men who lived near Micah were called together and overtook the Danites. ²³As they shouted after them, the Danites turned and said to Micah, "What's the matter with you that you called out your men to fight?"

²⁴He replied, "You took the gods I made, and my priest, and went away. What else do I have? How can you ask, 'What's the matter with you?'"

²⁵The Danites answered, "Don't argue with us, or some hot-tempered men will attack you, and you and your family will lose your lives." ²⁶So the Danites went their way, and Micah, seeing that they were too strong for him, turned around and went back home.

²⁷Then they took what Micah had made, and his priest, and went on to Laish, against a peaceful and unsuspecting people. They attacked them with the sword and burned down their city. ²⁸There was no one to rescue them because they lived a long way from Sidon and had no relationship with anyone else. The city was in a valley near Beth Rehob.

The Danites rebuilt the city and settled there. ²⁹They named it Dan after their forefather Dan, who was born to Israel—though the city used to be called Laish. ³⁰There the Danites set up for themselves the idols, and Jonathan son of Gershom, the son of Moses,*h* and his sons were priests for the tribe of Dan until the time of the captivity of the land. ³¹They continued to use the idols Micah had made, all the time the house of God was in Shiloh.

a2 That is, about 28 pounds (about 13 kilograms)   *b4* That is, about 5 pounds (about 2.3 kilograms)   *c8* Or *To carry on his profession*   *d10* That is, about 4 ounces (about 110 grams)   *e7* The meaning of the Hebrew for this clause is uncertain.   *f7* Hebrew; some Septuagint manuscripts *with the Arameans*   *g12 Mahaneh Dan* means *Dan's camp.*   *h30* An ancient Hebrew scribal tradition, some Septuagint manuscripts and Vulgate; Masoretic Text *Manasseh*

JOHN 3:1-21

Now there was a man of the Pharisees named Nicodemus, a member of the Jewish ruling council. ²He came to Jesus at night and said, "Rabbi, we know you are a teacher who has come from God. For no one could perform the miraculous signs you are doing if God were not with him."

³In reply Jesus declared, "I tell you the truth, no one can see the kingdom of God unless he is born again.*a*"

4"How can a man be born when he is old?" Nicodemus asked. "Surely he cannot enter a second time into his mother's womb to be born!"

5 Jesus answered, "I tell you the truth, no one can enter the kingdom of God unless he is born of water and the Spirit. 6 Flesh gives birth to flesh, but the Spirit*b* gives birth to spirit. 7 You should not be surprised at my saying, 'You*c* must be born again.' 8 The wind blows wherever it pleases. You hear its sound, but you cannot tell where it comes from or where it is going. So it is with everyone born of the Spirit."

9 "How can this be?" Nicodemus asked.

10 "You are Israel's teacher," said Jesus, "and do you not understand these things? 11 I tell you the truth, we speak of what we know, and we testify to what we have seen, but still you people do not accept our testimony. 12 I have spoken to you of earthly things and you do not believe; how then will you believe if I speak of heavenly things? 13 No one has ever gone into heaven except the one who came from heaven—the Son of Man.*d* 14 Just as Moses lifted up the snake in the desert, so the Son of Man must be lifted up, 15 that everyone who believes in him may have eternal life.*e*

16 **"For God so loved the world that he gave his one and only Son,*f* that whoever believes in him shall not perish but have eternal life. 17 For God did not send his Son into the world to condemn the world, but to save the world through him. 18 Whoever believes in him is not condemned, but whoever does not believe stands condemned already because he has not believed in the name of God's one and only Son.*g*** 19 This is the verdict: Light has come into the world, but men loved darkness instead of light because their deeds were evil. 20 Everyone who does evil hates the light, and will not come into the light for fear that his deeds will be exposed. 21 But whoever lives by the truth comes into the light, so that it may be seen plainly that what he has done has been done through God."*h*

a3 Or *born from above*; also in verse 7   *b6* Or *but spirit*   *c7* The Greek is plural.   *d13* Some manuscripts *Man, who is in heaven*   *e15* Or *believes may have eternal life in him*   *f16* Or *his only begotten Son*   *g18* Or *God's only begotten Son*   *h21* Some interpreters end the quotation after verse 15.

PSALM 104:1-23

1 Praise the LORD, O my soul.

O LORD my God, you are very great;
   you are clothed with splendor and
     majesty.
2 He wraps himself in light as with a
   garment;
   he stretches out the heavens like
     a tent
3   and lays the beams of his upper
     chambers on their waters.
He makes the clouds his chariot
   and rides on the wings of the
     wind.
4 He makes winds his messengers,*a*
   flames of fire his servants.

5 He set the earth on its foundations;
   it can never be moved.
6 You covered it with the deep as with
     a garment;
   the waters stood above the
     mountains.
7 But at your rebuke the waters fled,
   at the sound of your thunder they
     took to flight;
8 they flowed over the mountains,
   they went down into the valleys,
   to the place you assigned for them.
9 You set a boundary they cannot
     cross;
   never again will they cover the
     earth.

10 He makes springs pour water into
     the ravines;
   it flows between the mountains.
11 They give water to all the beasts of
     the field;
   the wild donkeys quench their
     thirst.
12 The birds of the air nest by the
     waters;
   they sing among the branches.

13 He waters the mountains from his
  upper chambers;
    the earth is satisfied by the fruit of
    his work.
14 He makes grass grow for the cattle,
  and plants for man to cultivate—
    bringing forth food from the
    earth:
15 wine that gladdens the heart of
  man,
  oil to make his face shine,
  and bread that sustains his heart.
16 The trees of the LORD are well
  watered,
  the cedars of Lebanon that he
  planted.
17 There the birds make their nests;
  the stork has its home in the pine
  trees.
18 The high mountains belong to the
  wild goats;
  the crags are a refuge for the
  coneys.b

19 The moon marks off the seasons,
  and the sun knows when to go
  down.
20 You bring darkness, it becomes
  night,
  and all the beasts of the forest
  prowl.
21 The lions roar for their prey
  and seek their food from God.
22 The sun rises, and they steal away;
  they return and lie down in their
  dens.
23 Then man goes out to his work,
  to his labor until evening.

a4 Or *angels*   b18 That is, the hyrax or rock badger

PROVERBS 14:20-21
20 The poor are shunned even by their
  neighbors,
  but the rich have many friends.

21 He who despises his neighbor sins,
  but blessed is he who is kind to
  the needy.

□ D A Y   1 2 4

GOD SIGHTINGS

May 4

JUDGES 19:1–20:48
In those days Israel had no king.

Now a Levite who lived in a remote
area in the hill country of Ephraim took a
concubine from Bethlehem in Judah.
2 But she was unfaithful to him. She left
him and went back to her father's house
in Bethlehem, Judah. After she had been
there four months, 3 her husband went to
her to persuade her to return. He had
with him his servant and two donkeys.
She took him into her father's house, and
when her father saw him, he gladly welcomed him. 4 His father-in-law, the girl's
father, prevailed upon him to stay; so he
remained with him three days, eating
and drinking, and sleeping there.

5 On the fourth day they got up early
and he prepared to leave, but the girl's
father said to his son-in-law, "Refresh
yourself with something to eat; then you
can go." 6 So the two of them sat down to
eat and drink together. Afterward the
girl's father said, "Please stay tonight
and enjoy yourself." 7 And when the man
got up to go, his father-in-law persuaded him, so he stayed there that
night. 8 On the morning of the fifth day,
when he rose to go, the girl's father said,
"Refresh yourself. Wait till afternoon!"
So the two of them ate together.

9 Then when the man, with his concubine and his servant, got up to leave, his
father-in-law, the girl's father, said, "Now
look, it's almost evening. Spend the night
here; the day is nearly over. Stay and enjoy yourself. Early tomorrow morning
you can get up and be on your way
home." 10 But, unwilling to stay another
night, the man left and went toward Jebus (that is, Jerusalem), with his two saddled donkeys and his concubine.

11 When they were near Jebus and the
day was almost gone, the servant said to

his master, "Come, let's stop at this city of the Jebusites and spend the night."

¹²His master replied, "No. We won't go into an alien city, whose people are not Israelites. We will go on to Gibeah." ¹³He added, "Come, let's try to reach Gibeah or Ramah and spend the night in one of those places." ¹⁴So they went on, and the sun set as they neared Gibeah in Benjamin. ¹⁵There they stopped to spend the night. They went and sat in the city square, but no one took them into his home for the night.

¹⁶That evening an old man from the hill country of Ephraim, who was living in Gibeah (the men of the place were Benjamites), came in from his work in the fields. ¹⁷When he looked and saw the traveler in the city square, the old man asked, "Where are you going? Where did you come from?"

¹⁸He answered, "We are on our way from Bethlehem in Judah to a remote area in the hill country of Ephraim where I live. I have been to Bethlehem in Judah and now I am going to the house of the Lord. No one has taken me into his house. ¹⁹We have both straw and fodder for our donkeys and bread and wine for ourselves your servants—me, your maidservant, and the young man with us. We don't need anything."

²⁰"You are welcome at my house," the old man said. "Let me supply whatever you need. Only don't spend the night in the square." ²¹So he took him into his house and fed his donkeys. After they had washed their feet, they had something to eat and drink.

²²While they were enjoying themselves, some of the wicked men of the city surrounded the house. Pounding on the door, they shouted to the old man who owned the house, "Bring out the man who came to your house so we can have sex with him."

²³The owner of the house went outside and said to them, "No, my friends, don't be so vile. Since this man is my guest, don't do this disgraceful thing. ²⁴Look, here is my virgin daughter, and his concubine. I will bring them out to

you now, and you can use them and do to them whatever you wish. But to this man, don't do such a disgraceful thing."

²⁵But the men would not listen to him. So the man took his concubine and sent her outside to them, and they raped her and abused her throughout the night, and at dawn they let her go. ²⁶At daybreak the woman went back to the house where her master was staying, fell down at the door and lay there until daylight.

²⁷When her master got up in the morning and opened the door of the house and stepped out to continue on his way, there lay his concubine, fallen in the doorway of the house, with her hands on the threshold. ²⁸He said to her, "Get up; let's go." But there was no answer. Then the man put her on his donkey and set out for home.

²⁹When he reached home, he took a knife and cut up his concubine, limb by limb, into twelve parts and sent them into all the areas of Israel. ³⁰Everyone who saw it said, "Such a thing has never been seen or done, not since the day the Israelites came up out of Egypt. Think about it! Consider it! Tell us what to do!"

²⁰:¹Then all the Israelites from Dan to Beersheba and from the land of Gilead came out as one man and assembled before the Lord in Mizpah. ²The leaders of all the people of the tribes of Israel took their places in the assembly of the people of God, four hundred thousand soldiers armed with swords. ³(The Benjamites heard that the Israelites had gone up to Mizpah.) Then the Israelites said, "Tell us how this awful thing happened."

⁴So the Levite, the husband of the murdered woman, said, "I and my concubine came to Gibeah in Benjamin to spend the night. ⁵During the night the men of Gibeah came after me and surrounded the house, intending to kill me. They raped my concubine, and she died. ⁶I took my concubine, cut her into pieces and sent one piece to each region of Israel's inheritance, because they committed this lewd and disgraceful

act in Israel. ⁷Now, all you Israelites, speak up and give your verdict."

⁸All the people rose as one man, saying, "None of us will go home. No, not one of us will return to his house. ⁹But now this is what we'll do to Gibeah: We'll go up against it as the lot directs. ¹⁰We'll take ten men out of every hundred from all the tribes of Israel, and a hundred from a thousand, and a thousand from ten thousand, to get provisions for the army. Then, when the army arrives at Gibeahᵃ in Benjamin, it can give them what they deserve for all this vileness done in Israel." ¹¹So all the men of Israel got together and united as one man against the city.

¹²The tribes of Israel sent men throughout the tribe of Benjamin, saying, "What about this awful crime that was committed among you? ¹³Now surrender those wicked men of Gibeah so that we may put them to death and purge the evil from Israel."

But the Benjamites would not listen to their fellow Israelites. ¹⁴From their towns they came together at Gibeah to fight against the Israelites. ¹⁵At once the Benjamites mobilized twenty-six thousand swordsmen from their towns, in addition to seven hundred chosen men from those living in Gibeah. ¹⁶Among all these soldiers there were seven hundred chosen men who were left-handed, each of whom could sling a stone at a hair and not miss.

¹⁷Israel, apart from Benjamin, mustered four hundred thousand swordsmen, all of them fighting men.

¹⁸The Israelites went up to Bethelᵇ and inquired of God. They said, "Who of us shall go first to fight against the Benjamites?"

The Lᴏʀᴅ replied, "Judah shall go first."

¹⁹The next morning the Israelites got up and pitched camp near Gibeah. ²⁰The men of Israel went out to fight the Benjamites and took up battle positions against them at Gibeah. ²¹The Benjamites came out of Gibeah and cut down twenty-two thousand Israelites on the battlefield that day. ²²But the men of Israel encouraged one another and again took up their positions where they had stationed themselves the first day. ²³The Israelites went up and wept before the Lᴏʀᴅ until evening, and they inquired of the Lᴏʀᴅ. They said, "Shall we go up again to battle against the Benjamites, our brothers?"

The Lᴏʀᴅ answered, "Go up against them."

²⁴Then the Israelites drew near to Benjamin the second day. ²⁵This time, when the Benjamites came out from Gibeah to oppose them, they cut down another eighteen thousand Israelites, all of them armed with swords.

²⁶Then the Israelites, all the people, went up to Bethel, and there they sat weeping before the Lᴏʀᴅ. They fasted that day until evening and presented burnt offerings and fellowship offeringsᶜ to the Lᴏʀᴅ. ²⁷And the Israelites inquired of the Lᴏʀᴅ. (In those days the ark of the covenant of God was there, ²⁸with Phinehas son of Eleazar, the son of Aaron, ministering before it.) They asked, "Shall we go up again to battle with Benjamin our brother, or not?"

The Lᴏʀᴅ responded, "Go, for tomorrow I will give them into your hands."

²⁹Then Israel set an ambush around Gibeah. ³⁰They went up against the Benjamites on the third day and took up positions against Gibeah as they had done before. ³¹The Benjamites came out to meet them and were drawn away from the city. They began to inflict casualties on the Israelites as before, so that about thirty men fell in the open field and on the roads—the one leading to Bethel and the other to Gibeah.

³²While the Benjamites were saying, "We are defeating them as before," the Israelites were saying, "Let's retreat and draw them away from the city to the roads."

³³All the men of Israel moved from their places and took up positions at Baal Tamar, and the Israelite ambush charged out of its place on the westᵈ of Gibeah.ᵉ ³⁴Then ten thousand of Israel's

finest men made a frontal attack on Gibeah. The fighting was so heavy that the Benjamites did not realize how near disaster was. [35] The LORD defeated Benjamin before Israel, and on that day the Israelites struck down 25,100 Benjamites, all armed with swords. [36] Then the Benjamites saw that they were beaten.

Now the men of Israel had given way before Benjamin, because they relied on the ambush they had set near Gibeah. [37] The men who had been in ambush made a sudden dash into Gibeah, spread out and put the whole city to the sword. [38] The men of Israel had arranged with the ambush that they should send up a great cloud of smoke from the city, [39] and then the men of Israel would turn in the battle.

The Benjamites had begun to inflict casualties on the men of Israel (about thirty), and they said, "We are defeating them as in the first battle." [40] But when the column of smoke began to rise from the city, the Benjamites turned and saw the smoke of the whole city going up into the sky. [41] Then the men of Israel turned on them, and the men of Benjamin were terrified, because they realized that disaster had come upon them. [42] So they fled before the Israelites in the direction of the desert, but they could not escape the battle. And the men of Israel who came out of the towns cut them down there. [43] They surrounded the Benjamites, chased them and easily[f] overran them in the vicinity of Gibeah on the east. [44] Eighteen thousand Benjamites fell, all of them valiant fighters. [45] As they turned and fled toward the desert to the rock of Rimmon, the Israelites cut down five thousand men along the roads. They kept pressing after the Benjamites as far as Gidom and struck down two thousand more.

[46] On that day twenty-five thousand Benjamite swordsmen fell, all of them valiant fighters. [47] But six hundred men turned and fled into the desert to the rock of Rimmon, where they stayed four months. [48] The men of Israel went back to Benjamin and put all the towns to the

sword, including the animals and everything else they found. All the towns they came across they set on fire.

a10 One Hebrew manuscript; most Hebrew manuscripts *Geba,* a variant of *Gibeah* *b18* Or *to the house of God;* also in verse 26 *c26* Traditionally *peace offerings* *d33* Some Septuagint manuscripts and Vulgate; the meaning of the Hebrew for this word is uncertain. *e33* Hebrew *Geba,* a variant of *Gibeah* *f43* The meaning of the Hebrew for this word is uncertain.

JOHN 3:22–4:3

After this, Jesus and his disciples went out into the Judean countryside, where he spent some time with them, and baptized. [23] Now John also was baptizing at Aenon near Salim, because there was plenty of water, and people were constantly coming to be baptized. [24] (This was before John was put in prison.) [25] An argument developed between some of John's disciples and a certain Jew[a] over the matter of ceremonial washing. [26] They came to John and said to him, "Rabbi, that man who was with you on the other side of the Jordan—the one you testified about—well, he is baptizing, and everyone is going to him."

[27] To this John replied, "A man can receive only what is given him from heaven. [28] You yourselves can testify that I said, 'I am not the Christ[b] but am sent ahead of him.' [29] The bride belongs to the bridegroom. The friend who attends the bridegroom waits and listens for him, and is full of joy when he hears the bridegroom's voice. That joy is mine, and it is now complete. [30] He must become greater; I must become less.

[31] "The one who comes from above is above all; the one who is from the earth belongs to the earth, and speaks as one from the earth. The one who comes from heaven is above all. [32] He testifies to what he has seen and heard, but no one accepts his testimony. [33] The man who has accepted it has certified that God is truthful. [34] For the one whom God has sent speaks the words of God, for God[c] gives the Spirit without limit. **[35] The Father loves the Son and has placed everything in his hands. [36] Whoever believes in the Son has eternal life, but whoever rejects the**

Son will not see life, for God's wrath remains on him."d

4:1 THE Pharisees heard that Jesus was gaining and baptizing more disciples than John, 2although in fact it was not Jesus who baptized, but his disciples. 3When the Lord learned of this, he left Judea and went back once more to Galilee.

a25 Some manuscripts *and certain Jews*   b28 Or *Messiah*
c34 Greek *he*   d36 Some interpreters end the quotation after verse 30.

PSALM 104:24-35

24 **H**ow many are your works, O LORD!
In wisdom you made them all;
the earth is full of your creatures.
25 There is the sea, vast and spacious,
teeming with creatures beyond
number—
living things both large and small.
26 There the ships go to and fro,
and the leviathan, which you
formed to frolic there.

27 These all look to you
to give them their food at the
proper time.
28 When you give it to them,
they gather it up;
when you open your hand,
they are satisfied with good
things.
29 When you hide your face,
they are terrified;
when you take away their breath,
they die and return to the dust.
30 When you send your Spirit,
they are created,
and you renew the face of the
earth.

31 May the glory of the LORD endure
forever;
may the LORD rejoice in his
works—
32 he who looks at the earth, and it
trembles,
who touches the mountains, and
they smoke.

33 I will sing to the LORD all my life;
I will sing praise to my God as long
as I live.

34 May my meditation be pleasing to
him,
as I rejoice in the LORD.
35 But may sinners vanish from the
earth
and the wicked be no more.

Praise the LORD, O my soul.

Praise the LORD.a

a35 Hebrew *Hallelu Yah*; in the Septuagint this line stands at the beginning of Psalm 105.

PROVERBS 14:22-24

22 **D**o not those who plot evil go astray?
But those who plan what is good
finda love and faithfulness.

23 All hard work brings a profit,
but mere talk leads only to
poverty.

24 The wealth of the wise is their
crown,
but the folly of fools yields folly.

a22 Or *show*

☐ D A Y   1 2 5

GOD SIGHTINGS

May 5

JUDGES 21:1—RUTH 1:22

The men of Israel had taken an oath at Mizpah: "Not one of us will give his daughter in marriage to a Benjamite."

2 The people went to Bethel,a where they sat before God until evening, raising their voices and weeping bitterly. 3 "O LORD, the God of Israel," they cried, "why has this happened to Israel? Why should one tribe be missing from Israel today?"

4 Early the next day the people built an altar and presented burnt offerings and fellowship offerings.b

5 Then the Israelites asked, "Who from all the tribes of Israel has failed to assemble before the LORD?" For they had taken a solemn oath that anyone who failed to assemble before the LORD

at Mizpah should certainly be put to death.

⁶Now the Israelites grieved for their brothers, the Benjamites. "Today one tribe is cut off from Israel," they said. ⁷"How can we provide wives for those who are left, since we have taken an oath by the LORD not to give them any of our daughters in marriage?" ⁸Then they asked, "Which one of the tribes of Israel failed to assemble before the LORD at Mizpah?" They discovered that no one from Jabesh Gilead had come to the camp for the assembly. ⁹For when they counted the people, they found that none of the people of Jabesh Gilead were there.

¹⁰So the assembly sent twelve thousand fighting men with instructions to go to Jabesh Gilead and put to the sword those living there, including the women and children. ¹¹"This is what you are to do," they said. "Kill every male and every woman who is not a virgin." ¹²They found among the people living in Jabesh Gilead four hundred young women who had never slept with a man, and they took them to the camp at Shiloh in Canaan.

¹³Then the whole assembly sent an offer of peace to the Benjamites at the rock of Rimmon. ¹⁴So the Benjamites returned at that time and were given the women of Jabesh Gilead who had been spared. But there were not enough for all of them.

¹⁵The people grieved for Benjamin, because the LORD had made a gap in the tribes of Israel. ¹⁶And the elders of the assembly said, "With the women of Benjamin destroyed, how shall we provide wives for the men who are left? ¹⁷The Benjamite survivors must have heirs," they said, "so that a tribe of Israel will not be wiped out. ¹⁸We can't give them our daughters as wives, since we Israelites have taken this oath: 'Cursed be anyone who gives a wife to a Benjamite.' ¹⁹But look, there is the annual festival of the LORD in Shiloh, to the north of Bethel, and east of the road that goes

from Bethel to Shechem, and to the south of Lebonah."

²⁰So they instructed the Benjamites, saying, "Go and hide in the vineyards ²¹and watch. When the girls of Shiloh come out to join in the dancing, then rush from the vineyards and each of you seize a wife from the girls of Shiloh and go to the land of Benjamin. ²²When their fathers or brothers complain to us, we will say to them, 'Do us a kindness by helping them, because we did not get wives for them during the war, and you are innocent, since you did not give your daughters to them.'"

²³So that is what the Benjamites did. While the girls were dancing, each man caught one and carried her off to be his wife. Then they returned to their inheritance and rebuilt the towns and settled in them.

²⁴At that time the Israelites left that place and went home to their tribes and clans, each to his own inheritance.

²⁵In those days Israel had no king; everyone did as he saw fit.

¹:¹IN the days when the judges ruled,ᶜ there was a famine in the land, and a man from Bethlehem in Judah, together with his wife and two sons, went to live for a while in the country of Moab. ²The man's name was Elimelech, his wife's name Naomi, and the names of his two sons were Mahlon and Kilion. They were Ephrathites from Bethlehem, Judah. And they went to Moab and lived there.

³Now Elimelech, Naomi's husband, died, and she was left with her two sons. ⁴They married Moabite women, one named Orpah and the other Ruth. After they had lived there about ten years, ⁵both Mahlon and Kilion also died, and Naomi was left without her two sons and her husband.

⁶When she heard in Moab that the LORD had come to the aid of his people by providing food for them, Naomi and her daughters-in-law prepared to return home from there. ⁷With her two daughters-in-law she left the place

where she had been living and set out on the road that would take them back to the land of Judah.

8 Then Naomi said to her two daughters-in-law, "Go back, each of you, to your mother's home. May the Lord show kindness to you, as you have shown to your dead and to me. 9 May the Lord grant that each of you will find rest in the home of another husband."

Then she kissed them and they wept aloud 10 and said to her, "We will go back with you to your people."

11 But Naomi said, "Return home, my daughters. Why would you come with me? Am I going to have any more sons, who could become your husbands? 12 Return home, my daughters; I am too old to have another husband. Even if I thought there was still hope for me— even if I had a husband tonight and then gave birth to sons— 13 would you wait until they grew up? Would you remain unmarried for them? No, my daughters. It is more bitter for me than for you, because the Lord's hand has gone out against me!"

14 At this they wept again. Then Orpah kissed her mother-in-law good-by, but Ruth clung to her.

15 "Look," said Naomi, "your sister-in-law is going back to her people and her gods. Go back with her."

16 But Ruth replied, "Don't urge me to leave you or to turn back from you. Where you go I will go, and where you stay I will stay. Your people will be my people and your God my God. 17 Where you die I will die, and there I will be buried. May the Lord deal with me, be it ever so severely, if anything but death separates you and me." 18 When Naomi realized that Ruth was determined to go with her, she stopped urging her.

19 So the two women went on until they came to Bethlehem. When they arrived in Bethlehem, the whole town was stirred because of them, and the women exclaimed, "Can this be Naomi?"

20 "Don't call me Naomi,d " she told them. "Call me Mara,e because the Al-

mightyf has made my life very bitter. 21 I went away full, but the Lord has brought me back empty. Why call me Naomi? The Lord has afflictedg me; the Almighty has brought misfortune upon me."

22 So Naomi returned from Moab accompanied by Ruth the Moabitess, her daughter-in-law, arriving in Bethlehem as the barley harvest was beginning.

a2 Or to the house of God   b4 Traditionally peace offerings
c1 Traditionally judged   d20 Naomi means pleasant; also
in verse 21.   e20 Mara means bitter.   f20 Hebrew Shaddai;
also in verse 21   g21 Or has testified against

JOHN 4:4-42

Now he [Jesus] had to go through Samaria. 5 So he came to a town in Samaria called Sychar, near the plot of ground Jacob had given to his son Joseph. 6 Jacob's well was there, and Jesus, tired as he was from the journey, sat down by the well. It was about the sixth hour.

7 When a Samaritan woman came to draw water, Jesus said to her, "Will you give me a drink?" 8 (His disciples had gone into the town to buy food.)

9 The Samaritan woman said to him, "You are a Jew and I am a Samaritan woman. How can you ask me for a drink?" (For Jews do not associate with Samaritans.a)

10 Jesus answered her, "If you knew the gift of God and who it is that asks you for a drink, you would have asked him and he would have given you living water."

11 "Sir," the woman said, "you have nothing to draw with and the well is deep. Where can you get this living water? 12 Are you greater than our father Jacob, who gave us the well and drank from it himself, as did also his sons and his flocks and herds?"

13 Jesus answered, "Everyone who drinks this water will be thirsty again, 14 but whoever drinks the water I give him will never thirst. Indeed, the water I give him will become in him a spring of water welling up to eternal life."

15 The woman said to him, "Sir, give me this water so that I won't get thirsty and have to keep coming here to draw water."

¹⁶He told her, "Go, call your husband and come back."

¹⁷"I have no husband," she replied.

Jesus said to her, "You are right when you say you have no husband. ¹⁸The fact is, you have had five husbands, and the man you now have is not your husband. What you have just said is quite true."

¹⁹"Sir," the woman said, "I can see that you are a prophet. ²⁰Our fathers worshiped on this mountain, but you Jews claim that the place where we must worship is in Jerusalem."

²¹Jesus declared, "Believe me, woman, a time is coming when you will worship the Father neither on this mountain nor in Jerusalem. ²²You Samaritans worship what you do not know; we worship what we do know, for salvation is from the Jews. ²³Yet a time is coming and has now come when the true worshipers will worship the Father in spirit and truth, for they are the kind of worshipers the Father seeks. ²⁴God is spirit, and his worshipers must worship in spirit and in truth."

²⁵The woman said, "I know that Messiah" (called Christ) "is coming. When he comes, he will explain everything to us."

²⁶Then Jesus declared, "I who speak to you am he."

²⁷Just then his disciples returned and were surprised to find him talking with a woman. But no one asked, "What do you want?" or "Why are you talking with her?"

²⁸Then, leaving her water jar, the woman went back to the town and said to the people, ²⁹"Come, see a man who told me everything I ever did. Could this be the Christ^b?" ³⁰They came out of the town and made their way toward him.

³¹Meanwhile his disciples urged him, "Rabbi, eat something."

³²But he said to them, "I have food to eat that you know nothing about."

³³Then his disciples said to each other, "Could someone have brought him food?"

³⁴"My food," said Jesus, "is to do the will of him who sent me and to finish

his work. ³⁵Do you not say, 'Four months more and then the harvest'? I tell you, open your eyes and look at the fields! They are ripe for harvest. ³⁶Even now the reaper draws his wages, even now he harvests the crop for eternal life, so that the sower and the reaper may be glad together. ³⁷Thus the saying 'One sows and another reaps' is true. ³⁸I sent you to reap what you have not worked for. Others have done the hard work, and you have reaped the benefits of their labor."

³⁹Many of the Samaritans from that town believed in him because of the woman's testimony, "He told me everything I ever did." ⁴⁰So when the Samaritans came to him, they urged him to stay with them, and he stayed two days. ⁴¹And because of his words many more became believers.

⁴²They said to the woman, "We no longer believe just because of what you said; now we have heard for ourselves, and we know that this man really is the Savior of the world."

^a9 Or *do not use dishes Samaritans have used* ^b29 Or *Messiah*

PSALM 105:1-15

¹**G**ive thanks to the Lord, call on his name;
　make known among the nations what he has done.
²Sing to him, sing praise to him;
　tell of all his wonderful acts.
³Glory in his holy name;
　let the hearts of those who seek the Lord rejoice.
⁴Look to the Lord and his strength;
　seek his face always.

⁵Remember the wonders he has done,
　his miracles, and the judgments he pronounced,
⁶O descendants of Abraham his servant,
　O sons of Jacob, his chosen ones.
⁷He is the Lord our God;
　his judgments are in all the earth.

⁸He remembers his covenant forever,
　the word he commanded, for a thousand generations,

⁹the covenant he made with
      Abraham,
   the oath he swore to Isaac.
¹⁰He confirmed it to Jacob as a decree,
   to Israel as an everlasting
      covenant:
¹¹"To you I will give the land of
      Canaan
   as the portion you will inherit."

¹²When they were but few in number,
   few indeed, and strangers in it,
¹³they wandered from nation to
      nation,
   from one kingdom to another.
¹⁴He allowed no one to oppress them;
   for their sake he rebuked kings:
¹⁵"Do not touch my anointed ones;
   do my prophets no harm."

PROVERBS 14:25
²⁵**A** truthful witness saves lives,
   but a false witness is deceitful.

□ D A Y 1 2 6

GOD SIGHTINGS

May 6

RUTH 2:1–4:22
Now Naomi had a relative on her husband's side, from the clan of Elimelech,
a man of standing, whose name was
Boaz.

²And Ruth the Moabitess said to Naomi, "Let me go to the fields and pick up
the leftover grain behind anyone in
whose eyes I find favor."

Naomi said to her, "Go ahead, my
daughter." ³So she went out and began to
glean in the fields behind the harvesters.
As it turned out, she found herself working in a field belonging to Boaz, who was
from the clan of Elimelech.

⁴Just then Boaz arrived from Bethlehem and greeted the harvesters, "The
LORD be with you!"

"The LORD bless you!" they called back.

⁵Boaz asked the foreman of his harvesters, "Whose young woman is that?"

⁶The foreman replied, "She is the Moabitess who came back from Moab with
Naomi. ⁷She said, 'Please let me glean
and gather among the sheaves behind
the harvesters.' She went into the field
and has worked steadily from morning
till now, except for a short rest in the
shelter."

⁸So Boaz said to Ruth, "My daughter,
listen to me. Don't go and glean in another field and don't go away from here.
Stay here with my servant girls. ⁹Watch
the field where the men are harvesting,
and follow along after the girls. I have
told the men not to touch you. And
whenever you are thirsty, go and get a
drink from the water jars the men have
filled."

¹⁰At this, she bowed down with her
face to the ground. She exclaimed,
"Why have I found such favor in your
eyes that you notice me—a foreigner?"

¹¹Boaz replied, "I've been told all
about what you have done for your
mother-in-law since the death of your
husband—how you left your father and
mother and your homeland and came to
live with a people you did not know before. ¹²May the LORD repay you for what
you have done. May you be richly rewarded by the LORD, the God of Israel,
under whose wings you have come to
take refuge."

¹³"May I continue to find favor in your
eyes, my lord," she said. "You have given
me comfort and have spoken kindly to
your servant—though I do not have the
standing of one of your servant girls."

¹⁴At mealtime Boaz said to her,
"Come over here. Have some bread and
dip it in the wine vinegar."

When she sat down with the harvesters, he offered her some roasted grain.
She ate all she wanted and had some left
over. ¹⁵As she got up to glean, Boaz gave
orders to his men, "Even if she gathers
among the sheaves, don't embarrass her.
¹⁶Rather, pull out some stalks for her
from the bundles and leave them for her
to pick up, and don't rebuke her."

¹⁷So Ruth gleaned in the field until evening. Then she threshed the barley she had gathered, and it amounted to about an ephah.*a* ¹⁸She carried it back to town, and her mother-in-law saw how much she had gathered. Ruth also brought out and gave her what she had left over after she had eaten enough.

¹⁹Her mother-in-law asked her, "Where did you glean today? Where did you work? Blessed be the man who took notice of you!"

Then Ruth told her mother-in-law about the one at whose place she had been working. "The name of the man I worked with today is Boaz," she said.

²⁰"The Lᴏʀᴅ bless him!" Naomi said to her daughter-in-law. "He has not stopped showing his kindness to the living and the dead." She added, "That man is our close relative; he is one of our kinsman-redeemers."

²¹Then Ruth the Moabitess said, "He even said to me, 'Stay with my workers until they finish harvesting all my grain.'"

²²Naomi said to Ruth her daughter-in-law, "It will be good for you, my daughter, to go with his girls, because in someone else's field you might be harmed."

²³So Ruth stayed close to the servant girls of Boaz to glean until the barley and wheat harvests were finished. And she lived with her mother-in-law.

³:¹Oɴᴇ day Naomi her mother-in-law said to her, "My daughter, should I not try to find a home*b* for you, where you will be well provided for? ²Is not Boaz, with whose servant girls you have been, a kinsman of ours? Tonight he will be winnowing barley on the threshing floor. ³Wash and perfume yourself, and put on your best clothes. Then go down to the threshing floor, but don't let him know you are there until he has finished eating and drinking. ⁴When he lies down, note the place where he is lying. Then go and uncover his feet and lie down. He will tell you what to do."

⁵"I will do whatever you say," Ruth answered. ⁶So she went down to the threshing floor and did everything her mother-in-law told her to do.

⁷When Boaz had finished eating and drinking and was in good spirits, he went over to lie down at the far end of the grain pile. Ruth approached quietly, uncovered his feet and lay down. ⁸In the middle of the night something startled the man, and he turned and discovered a woman lying at his feet.

⁹"Who are you?" he asked.

"I am your servant Ruth," she said. "Spread the corner of your garment over me, since you are a kinsman-redeemer."

¹⁰"The Lᴏʀᴅ bless you, my daughter," he replied. "This kindness is greater than that which you showed earlier: You have not run after the younger men, whether rich or poor. ¹¹And now, my daughter, don't be afraid. I will do for you all you ask. All my fellow townsmen know that you are a woman of noble character. ¹²Although it is true that I am near of kin, there is a kinsman-redeemer nearer than I. ¹³Stay here for the night, and in the morning if he wants to redeem, good; let him redeem. But if he is not willing, as surely as the Lᴏʀᴅ lives I will do it. Lie here until morning."

¹⁴So she lay at his feet until morning, but got up before anyone could be recognized; and he said, "Don't let it be known that a woman came to the threshing floor."

¹⁵He also said, "Bring me the shawl you are wearing and hold it out." When she did so, he poured into it six measures of barley and put it on her. Then he*c* went back to town.

¹⁶When Ruth came to her mother-in-law, Naomi asked, "How did it go, my daughter?"

Then she told her everything Boaz had done for her ¹⁷and added, "He gave me these six measures of barley, saying, 'Don't go back to your mother-in-law empty-handed.'"

¹⁸Then Naomi said, "Wait, my daughter, until you find out what happens. For the man will not rest until the matter is settled today."

⁴:¹MEANWHILE Boaz went up to the town gate and sat there. When the kinsman-redeemer he had mentioned came along, Boaz said, "Come over here, my friend, and sit down." So he went over and sat down.

²Boaz took ten of the elders of the town and said, "Sit here," and they did so. ³Then he said to the kinsman-redeemer, "Naomi, who has come back from Moab, is selling the piece of land that belonged to our brother Elimelech. ⁴I thought I should bring the matter to your attention and suggest that you buy it in the presence of these seated here and in the presence of the elders of my people. If you will redeem it, do so. But if youᵈ will not, tell me, so I will know. For no one has the right to do it except you, and I am next in line."

"I will redeem it," he said.

⁵Then Boaz said, "On the day you buy the land from Naomi and from Ruth the Moabitess, you acquireᵉ the dead man's widow, in order to maintain the name of the dead with his property."

⁶At this, the kinsman-redeemer said, "Then I cannot redeem it because I might endanger my own estate. You redeem it yourself. I cannot do it."

⁷(Now in earlier times in Israel, for the redemption and transfer of property to become final, one party took off his sandal and gave it to the other. This was the method of legalizing transactions in Israel.)

⁸So the kinsman-redeemer said to Boaz, "Buy it yourself." And he removed his sandal.

⁹Then Boaz announced to the elders and all the people, "Today you are witnesses that I have bought from Naomi all the property of Elimelech, Kilion and Mahlon. ¹⁰I have also acquired Ruth the Moabitess, Mahlon's widow, as my wife, in order to maintain the name of the dead with his property, so that his name will not disappear from among his family or from the town records. Today you are witnesses!"

¹¹Then the elders and all those at the gate said, "We are witnesses. May the LORD make the woman who is coming into your home like Rachel and Leah, who together built up the house of Israel. May you have standing in Ephrathah and be famous in Bethlehem. ¹²Through the offspring the LORD gives you by this young woman, may your family be like that of Perez, whom Tamar bore to Judah."

¹³So Boaz took Ruth and she became his wife. Then he went to her, and the LORD enabled her to conceive, and she gave birth to a son. ¹⁴**The women said to Naomi: "Praise be to the LORD, who this day has not left you without a kinsman-redeemer. May he become famous throughout Israel! ¹⁵He will renew your life and sustain you in your old age. For your daughter-in-law, who loves you and who is better to you than seven sons, has given him birth."**

¹⁶Then Naomi took the child, laid him in her lap and cared for him. ¹⁷The women living there said, "Naomi has a son." And they named him Obed. He was the father of Jesse, the father of David.

¹⁸This, then, is the family line of Perez:

> Perez was the father of Hezron,
> ¹⁹Hezron the father of Ram,
>   Ram the father of Amminadab,
> ²⁰Amminadab the father of Nahshon,
>   Nahshon the father of Salmon,ᶠ
> ²¹Salmon the father of Boaz,
>   Boaz the father of Obed,
> ²²Obed the father of Jesse,
>   and Jesse the father of David.

ᵃ17 That is, probably about 3/5 bushel (about 22 liters)   ᵇ1 Hebrew *find rest* (see Ruth 1:9)   ᶜ15 Most Hebrew manuscripts; many Hebrew manuscripts, Vulgate and Syriac *she*   ᵈ4 Many Hebrew manuscripts, Septuagint, Vulgate and Syriac; most Hebrew manuscripts *he*   ᵉ5 Hebrew; Vulgate and Syriac *Naomi, you acquire Ruth the Moabitess*,   ᶠ20 A few Hebrew manuscripts, some Septuagint manuscripts and Vulgate (see also verse 21 and Septuagint of 1 Chron. 2:11); most Hebrew manuscripts *Salma*

JOHN 4:43-54

After the two days he [Jesus] left for Galilee. ⁴⁴(Now Jesus himself had pointed out that a prophet has no honor in his own country.) ⁴⁵When he arrived in Galilee, the Galileans welcomed him. They had seen all that he had done in Jerusalem at the Passover Feast, for they also had been there.

⁴⁶Once more he visited Cana in Galilee, where he had turned the water into wine. And there was a certain royal official whose son lay sick at Capernaum. ⁴⁷When this man heard that Jesus had arrived in Galilee from Judea, he went to him and begged him to come and heal his son, who was close to death.

⁴⁸"Unless you people see miraculous signs and wonders," Jesus told him, "you will never believe."

⁴⁹The royal official said, "Sir, come down before my child dies."

⁵⁰Jesus replied, "You may go. Your son will live."

The man took Jesus at his word and departed. ⁵¹While he was still on the way, his servants met him with the news that his boy was living. ⁵²When he inquired as to the time when his son got better, they said to him, "The fever left him yesterday at the seventh hour."

⁵³Then the father realized that this was the exact time at which Jesus had said to him, "Your son will live." So he and all his household believed.

⁵⁴This was the second miraculous sign that Jesus performed, having come from Judea to Galilee.

PSALM 105:16-36

¹⁶He [the LORD] called down famine on the land
  and destroyed all their supplies of food;
¹⁷and he sent a man before them—
  Joseph, sold as a slave.
¹⁸They bruised his feet with shackles,
  his neck was put in irons,
¹⁹till what he foretold came to pass,
  till the word of the LORD proved him true.
²⁰The king sent and released him,
  the ruler of peoples set him free.
²¹He made him master of his household,
  ruler over all he possessed,
²²to instruct his princes as he pleased
  and teach his elders wisdom.
²³Then Israel entered Egypt;
  Jacob lived as an alien in the land of Ham.
²⁴The LORD made his people very fruitful;
  he made them too numerous for their foes,
²⁵whose hearts he turned to hate his people,
  to conspire against his servants.
²⁶He sent Moses his servant,
  and Aaron, whom he had chosen.
²⁷They performed his miraculous signs among them,
  his wonders in the land of Ham.
²⁸He sent darkness and made the land dark—
  for had they not rebelled against his words?
²⁹He turned their waters into blood,
  causing their fish to die.
³⁰Their land teemed with frogs,
  which went up into the bedrooms of their rulers.
³¹He spoke, and there came swarms of flies,
  and gnats throughout their country.
³²He turned their rain into hail,
  with lightning throughout their land;
³³he struck down their vines and fig trees
  and shattered the trees of their country.
³⁴He spoke, and the locusts came,
  grasshoppers without number;
³⁵they ate up every green thing in their land,
  ate up the produce of their soil.
³⁶Then he struck down all the firstborn in their land,
  the firstfruits of all their manhood.

PROVERBS 14:26-27

²⁶He who fears the LORD has a secure fortress,
  and for his children it will be a refuge.

27 The fear of the LORD is a fountain
of life,
turning a man from the snares
of death.

☐ D A Y   1 2 7

GOD SIGHTINGS

May 7

1 SAMUEL 1:1–2:21

There was a certain man from Ramathaim, a Zuphite*a* from the hill country
of Ephraim, whose name was Elkanah
son of Jeroham, the son of Elihu, the son
of Tohu, the son of Zuph, an Ephraimite.
²He had two wives; one was called Hannah and the other Peninnah. Peninnah
had children, but Hannah had none.

³ Year after year this man went up
from his town to worship and sacrifice
to the LORD Almighty at Shiloh, where
Hophni and Phinehas, the two sons of
Eli, were priests of the LORD. ⁴Whenever
the day came for Elkanah to sacrifice, he
would give portions of the meat to his
wife Peninnah and to all her sons and
daughters. ⁵But to Hannah he gave a
double portion because he loved her,
and the LORD had closed her womb.
⁶And because the LORD had closed her
womb, her rival kept provoking her in
order to irritate her. ⁷This went on year
after year. Whenever Hannah went up
to the house of the LORD, her rival provoked her till she wept and would not
eat. ⁸Elkanah her husband would say to
her, "Hannah, why are you weeping?
Why don't you eat? Why are you down-
hearted? Don't I mean more to you than
ten sons?"

⁹Once when they had finished eating
and drinking in Shiloh, Hannah stood
up. Now Eli the priest was sitting on a
chair by the doorpost of the LORD's temple.*b* ¹⁰In bitterness of soul Hannah
wept much and prayed to the LORD.
¹¹And she made a vow, saying, "O LORD

Almighty, if you will only look upon your
servant's misery and remember me, and
not forget your servant but give her a
son, then I will give him to the LORD for
all the days of his life, and no razor will
ever be used on his head."

¹²As she kept on praying to the LORD,
Eli observed her mouth. ¹³Hannah was
praying in her heart, and her lips were
moving but her voice was not heard. Eli
thought she was drunk ¹⁴and said to
her, "How long will you keep on getting
drunk? Get rid of your wine."

¹⁵"Not so, my lord," Hannah replied,
"I am a woman who is deeply troubled. I
have not been drinking wine or beer; I
was pouring out my soul to the LORD.
¹⁶Do not take your servant for a wicked
woman; I have been praying here out of
my great anguish and grief."

¹⁷Eli answered, "Go in peace, and may
the God of Israel grant you what you
have asked of him."

¹⁸She said, "May your servant find favor in your eyes." Then she went her way
and ate something, and her face was no
longer downcast.

¹⁹Early the next morning they arose
and worshiped before the LORD and
then went back to their home at Ramah.
Elkanah lay with Hannah his wife, and
the LORD remembered her. ²⁰So in the
course of time Hannah conceived and
gave birth to a son. She named him
Samuel,*c* saying, "Because I asked the
LORD for him."

²¹When the man Elkanah went up
with all his family to offer the annual
sacrifice to the LORD and to fulfill his
vow, ²²Hannah did not go. She said to
her husband, "After the boy is weaned, I
will take him and present him before
the LORD, and he will live there always."

²³"Do what seems best to you," Elkanah her husband told her. "Stay here until you have weaned him; only may the
LORD make good his*d* word." So the
woman stayed at home and nursed her
son until she had weaned him.

²⁴After he was weaned, she took the
boy with her, young as he was, along with
a three-year-old bull,*e* an ephah*f* of flour

and a skin of wine, and brought him to the house of the LORD at Shiloh. 25 When they had slaughtered the bull, they brought the boy to Eli, 26 and she said to him, "As surely as you live, my lord, I am the woman who stood here beside you praying to the LORD. 27 I prayed for this child, and the LORD has granted me what I asked of him. 28 So now I give him to the LORD. For his whole life he will be given over to the LORD." And he worshiped the LORD there.

2:1 THEN Hannah prayed and said:

"My heart rejoices in the LORD;
  in the LORD my horn*g* is lifted high.
My mouth boasts over my enemies,
  for I delight in your deliverance.

2 "There is no one holy*h* like the LORD;
  there is no one besides you;
  there is no Rock like our God.

3 "Do not keep talking so proudly
  or let your mouth speak such
    arrogance,
for the LORD is a God who knows,
  and by him deeds are weighed.

4 "The bows of the warriors are broken,
  but those who stumbled are armed
    with strength.
5 Those who were full hire themselves
    out for food,
  but those who were hungry
    hunger no more.
She who was barren has borne seven
    children,
  but she who has had many sons
    pines away.

6 "The LORD brings death and makes
    alive;
  he brings down to the grave*i* and
    raises up.
7 The LORD sends poverty and wealth;
  he humbles and he exalts.
8 He raises the poor from the dust
  and lifts the needy from the ash
    heap;
he seats them with princes
  and has them inherit a throne of
    honor.

"For the foundations of the earth are
    the LORD's;
  upon them he has set the world.
9 He will guard the feet of his saints,
  but the wicked will be silenced in
    darkness.

"It is not by strength that one
    prevails;
10 those who oppose the LORD will be
    shattered.
He will thunder against them from
    heaven;
  the LORD will judge the ends of the
    earth.

"He will give strength to his king
  and exalt the horn of his
    anointed."

11 Then Elkanah went home to Ramah, but the boy ministered before the LORD under Eli the priest.

12 Eli's sons were wicked men; they had no regard for the LORD. 13 Now it was the practice of the priests with the people that whenever anyone offered a sacrifice and while the meat was being boiled, the servant of the priest would come with a three-pronged fork in his hand. 14 He would plunge it into the pan or kettle or caldron or pot, and the priest would take for himself whatever the fork brought up. This is how they treated all the Israelites who came to Shiloh. 15 But even before the fat was burned, the servant of the priest would come and say to the man who was sacrificing, "Give the priest some meat to roast; he won't accept boiled meat from you, but only raw."

16 If the man said to him, "Let the fat be burned up first, and then take whatever you want," the servant would then answer, "No, hand it over now; if you don't, I'll take it by force."

17 This sin of the young men was very great in the LORD's sight, for they*j* were treating the LORD's offering with contempt.

18 But Samuel was ministering before the LORD—a boy wearing a linen ephod. 19 Each year his mother made him a

little robe and took it to him when she went up with her husband to offer the annual sacrifice. [20]Eli would bless Elkanah and his wife, saying, "May the LORD give you children by this woman to take the place of the one she prayed for and gave to the LORD." Then they would go home. [21]And the LORD was gracious to Hannah; she conceived and gave birth to three sons and two daughters. Meanwhile, the boy Samuel grew up in the presence of the LORD.

*a1 Or from Ramathaim Zuphim   b9 That is, tabernacle
c20 Samuel sounds like the Hebrew for heard of God.
d23 Masoretic Text; Dead Sea Scrolls, Septuagint and
Syriac your   e24 Dead Sea Scrolls, Septuagint and Syriac;
Masoretic Text with three bulls   f24 That is, probably
about 3/5 bushel (about 22 liters)   g1 Horn here
symbolizes strength; also in verse 10.   h2 Or no Holy One
i6 Hebrew Sheol   j17 Or men*

JOHN 5:1-23

Some time later, Jesus went up to Jerusalem for a feast of the Jews. [2]Now there is in Jerusalem near the Sheep Gate a pool, which in Aramaic is called Bethesda[a] and which is surrounded by five covered colonnades. [3]Here a great number of disabled people used to lie—the blind, the lame, the paralyzed.[b] [5]One who was there had been an invalid for thirty-eight years. [6]When Jesus saw him lying there and learned that he had been in this condition for a long time, he asked him, "Do you want to get well?"

[7]"Sir," the invalid replied, "I have no one to help me into the pool when the water is stirred. While I am trying to get in, someone else goes down ahead of me."

[8]Then Jesus said to him, "Get up! Pick up your mat and walk." [9]At once the man was cured; he picked up his mat and walked.

The day on which this took place was a Sabbath, [10]and so the Jews said to the man who had been healed, "It is the Sabbath; the law forbids you to carry your mat."

[11]But he replied, "The man who made me well said to me, 'Pick up your mat and walk.'"

[12]So they asked him, "Who is this fellow who told you to pick it up and walk?"

[13]The man who was healed had no idea who it was, for Jesus had slipped away into the crowd that was there.

[14]Later Jesus found him at the temple and said to him, "See, you are well again. Stop sinning or something worse may happen to you." [15]The man went away and told the Jews that it was Jesus who had made him well.

[16]So, because Jesus was doing these things on the Sabbath, the Jews persecuted him. [17]Jesus said to them, "My Father is always at his work to this very day, and I, too, am working." [18]For this reason the Jews tried all the harder to kill him; not only was he breaking the Sabbath, but he was even calling God his own Father, making himself equal with God.

[19]**Jesus gave them this answer: "I tell you the truth, the Son can do nothing by himself; he can do only what he sees his Father doing, because whatever the Father does the Son also does.** [20]For the Father loves the Son and shows him all he does. Yes, to your amazement he will show him even greater things than these. [21]For just as the Father raises the dead and gives them life, even so the Son gives life to whom he is pleased to give it. [22]Moreover, the Father judges no one, but has entrusted all judgment to the Son, [23]that all may honor the Son just as they honor the Father. He who does not honor the Son does not honor the Father, who sent him."

*a2 Some manuscripts Bethzatha; other manuscripts
Bethsaida   b3 Some less important manuscripts
paralyzed—and they waited for the moving of the waters.
4From time to time an angel of the Lord would come down
and stir up the waters. The first one into the pool after each
such disturbance would be cured of whatever disease he had.*

PSALM 105:37-45

[37]**He** [the LORD] brought out Israel,
     laden with silver and gold,
   and from among their tribes no
     one faltered.
[38]Egypt was glad when they left,
     because dread of Israel had fallen
     on them.
[39]He spread out a cloud as a covering,
     and a fire to give light at night.

40 They asked, and he brought them
quail
and satisfied them with the bread
of heaven.
41 He opened the rock, and water
gushed out;
like a river it flowed in the desert.

42 For he remembered his holy promise
given to his servant Abraham.
43 He brought out his people with
rejoicing,
his chosen ones with shouts of joy;
44 he gave them the lands of the
nations,
and they fell heir to what others
had toiled for—
45 that they might keep his precepts
and observe his laws.

Praise the Lord.*a*

a45 Hebrew Hallelu Yah

PROVERBS 14:28-29
28 **A** large population is a king's glory,
but without subjects a prince is
ruined.

29 A patient man has great
understanding,
but a quick-tempered man
displays folly.

☐ D A Y 1 2 8

GOD SIGHTINGS

May 8

1 SAMUEL 2:22–4:22
Now Eli, who was very old, heard about
everything his sons were doing to all Israel and how they slept with the women
who served at the entrance to the Tent
of Meeting. 23 So he said to them, "Why
do you do such things? I hear from all
the people about these wicked deeds of
yours. 24 No, my sons; it is not a good report that I hear spreading among the
Lord's people. 25 If a man sins against
another man, God*a* may mediate for

him; but if a man sins against the Lord,
who will intercede for him?" His sons,
however, did not listen to their father's
rebuke, for it was the Lord's will to put
them to death.

26 And the boy Samuel continued to
grow in stature and in favor with the
Lord and with men.

27 Now a man of God came to Eli and
said to him, "This is what the Lord says:
'Did I not clearly reveal myself to your
father's house when they were in Egypt
under Pharaoh? 28 I chose your father
out of all the tribes of Israel to be my
priest, to go up to my altar, to burn incense, and to wear an ephod in my presence. I also gave your father's house all
the offerings made with fire by the Israelites. 29 Why do you*b* scorn my sacrifice and offering that I prescribed for
my dwelling? Why do you honor your
sons more than me by fattening yourselves on the choice parts of every offering made by my people Israel?'

30 "Therefore the Lord, the God of Israel, declares: 'I promised that your
house and your father's house would
minister before me forever.' But now the
Lord declares: 'Far be it from me! Those
who honor me I will honor, but those
who despise me will be disdained.
31 The time is coming when I will cut
short your strength and the strength of
your father's house, so that there will
not be an old man in your family line
32 and you will see distress in my dwelling. Although good will be done to Israel, in your family line there will never
be an old man. 33 Every one of you that I
do not cut off from my altar will be
spared only to blind your eyes with tears
and to grieve your heart, and all your descendants will die in the prime of life.

34 " 'And what happens to your two
sons, Hophni and Phinehas, will be a sign
to you—they will both die on the same
day. 35 I will raise up for myself a faithful
priest, who will do according to what is
in my heart and mind. I will firmly establish his house, and he will minister before my anointed one always. 36 Then
everyone left in your family line will

come and bow down before him for a piece of silver and a crust of bread and plead, "Appoint me to some priestly office so I can have food to eat."'"

3:1 THE boy Samuel ministered before the LORD under Eli. In those days the word of the LORD was rare; there were not many visions.

2 One night Eli, whose eyes were becoming so weak that he could barely see, was lying down in his usual place. 3 The lamp of God had not yet gone out, and Samuel was lying down in the temple*c* of the LORD, where the ark of God was. 4 Then the LORD called Samuel.

Samuel answered, "Here I am." 5 And he ran to Eli and said, "Here I am; you called me."

But Eli said, "I did not call; go back and lie down." So he went and lay down.

6 Again the LORD called, "Samuel!" And Samuel got up and went to Eli and said, "Here I am; you called me."

"My son," Eli said, "I did not call; go back and lie down."

7 Now Samuel did not yet know the LORD: The word of the LORD had not yet been revealed to him.

8 The LORD called Samuel a third time, and Samuel got up and went to Eli and said, "Here I am; you called me."

Then Eli realized that the LORD was calling the boy. 9 So Eli told Samuel, "Go and lie down, and if he calls you, say, 'Speak, LORD, for your servant is listening.'" So Samuel went and lay down in his place.

10 The LORD came and stood there, calling as at the other times, "Samuel! Samuel!"

Then Samuel said, "Speak, for your servant is listening."

11 And the LORD said to Samuel: "See, I am about to do something in Israel that will make the ears of everyone who hears of it tingle. 12 At that time I will carry out against Eli everything I spoke against his family—from beginning to end. 13 For I told him that I would judge his family forever because of the sin he knew about; his sons made themselves contemptible,*d* and he failed to restrain them. 14 Therefore, I swore to the house of Eli, 'The guilt of Eli's house will never be atoned for by sacrifice or offering.'"

15 Samuel lay down until morning and then opened the doors of the house of the LORD. He was afraid to tell Eli the vision, 16 but Eli called him and said, "Samuel, my son."

Samuel answered, "Here I am."

17 "What was it he said to you?" Eli asked. "Do not hide it from me. May God deal with you, be it ever so severely, if you hide from me anything he told you." 18 So Samuel told him everything, hiding nothing from him. Then Eli said, "He is the LORD; let him do what is good in his eyes."

19 The LORD was with Samuel as he grew up, and he let none of his words fall to the ground. 20 And all Israel from Dan to Beersheba recognized that Samuel was attested as a prophet of the LORD. 21 The LORD continued to appear at Shiloh, and there he revealed himself to Samuel through his word.

4:1 AND Samuel's word came to all Israel.

Now the Israelites went out to fight against the Philistines. The Israelites camped at Ebenezer, and the Philistines at Aphek. 2 The Philistines deployed their forces to meet Israel, and as the battle spread, Israel was defeated by the Philistines, who killed about four thousand of them on the battlefield. 3 When the soldiers returned to camp, the elders of Israel asked, "Why did the LORD bring defeat upon us today before the Philistines? Let us bring the ark of the LORD's covenant from Shiloh, so that it*e* may go with us and save us from the hand of our enemies."

4 So the people sent men to Shiloh, and they brought back the ark of the covenant of the LORD Almighty, who is enthroned between the cherubim. And Eli's two sons, Hophni and Phinehas, were there with the ark of the covenant of God.

5 When the ark of the LORD's covenant

came into the camp, all Israel raised such a great shout that the ground shook. [6]Hearing the uproar, the Philistines asked, "What's all this shouting in the Hebrew camp?"

When they learned that the ark of the Lord had come into the camp, [7]the Philistines were afraid. "A god has come into the camp," they said. "We're in trouble! Nothing like this has happened before. [8]Woe to us! Who will deliver us from the hand of these mighty gods? They are the gods who struck the Egyptians with all kinds of plagues in the desert. [9]Be strong, Philistines! Be men, or you will be subject to the Hebrews, as they have been to you. Be men, and fight!"

[10]So the Philistines fought, and the Israelites were defeated and every man fled to his tent. The slaughter was very great; Israel lost thirty thousand foot soldiers. [11]The ark of God was captured, and Eli's two sons, Hophni and Phinehas, died.

[12]That same day a Benjamite ran from the battle line and went to Shiloh, his clothes torn and dust on his head. [13]When he arrived, there was Eli sitting on his chair by the side of the road, watching, because his heart feared for the ark of God. When the man entered the town and told what had happened, the whole town sent up a cry.

[14]Eli heard the outcry and asked, "What is the meaning of this uproar?"

The man hurried over to Eli, [15]who was ninety-eight years old and whose eyes were set so that he could not see. [16]He told Eli, "I have just come from the battle line; I fled from it this very day."

Eli asked, "What happened, my son?"

[17]The man who brought the news replied, "Israel fled before the Philistines, and the army has suffered heavy losses. Also your two sons, Hophni and Phinehas, are dead, and the ark of God has been captured."

[18]When he mentioned the ark of God, Eli fell backward off his chair by the side of the gate. His neck was bro-

ken and he died, for he was an old man and heavy. He had led[f] Israel forty years.

[19]His daughter-in-law, the wife of Phinehas, was pregnant and near the time of delivery. When she heard the news that the ark of God had been captured and that her father-in-law and her husband were dead, she went into labor and gave birth, but was overcome by her labor pains. [20]As she was dying, the women attending her said, "Don't despair; you have given birth to a son." But she did not respond or pay any attention.

[21]She named the boy Ichabod,[g] saying, "The glory has departed from Israel"—because of the capture of the ark of God and the deaths of her father-in-law and her husband. [22]She said, "The glory has departed from Israel, for the ark of God has been captured."

a25 Or the judges   b29 The Hebrew is plural.   c3 That is, tabernacle   d13 Masoretic Text; an ancient Hebrew scribal tradition and Septuagint sons blasphemed God   e3 Or he   f18 Traditionally judged   g21 Ichabod means no glory.

JOHN 5:24-47

"I [Jesus] tell you the truth, whoever hears my word and believes him who sent me has eternal life and will not be condemned; he has crossed over from death to life. [25]I tell you the truth, a time is coming and has now come when the dead will hear the voice of the Son of God and those who hear will live. [26]For as the Father has life in himself, so he has granted the Son to have life in himself. [27]And he has given him authority to judge because he is the Son of Man.

[28]"Do not be amazed at this, for a time is coming when all who are in their graves will hear his voice [29]and come out—those who have done good will rise to live, and those who have done evil will rise to be condemned. [30]By myself I can do nothing; I judge only as I hear, and my judgment is just, for I seek not to please myself but him who sent me.

[31]"If I testify about myself, my testimony is not valid. [32]There is another who testifies in my favor, and I know that his testimony about me is valid.

33 "You have sent to John and he has testified to the truth. 34 Not that I accept human testimony; but I mention it that you may be saved. 35 John was a lamp that burned and gave light, and you chose for a time to enjoy his light.

36 "I have testimony weightier than that of John. For the very work that the Father has given me to finish, and which I am doing, testifies that the Father has sent me. 37 And the Father who sent me has himself testified concerning me. You have never heard his voice nor seen his form, 38 nor does his word dwell in you, for you do not believe the one he sent. 39 You diligently study*a* the Scriptures because you think that by them you possess eternal life. These are the Scriptures that testify about me, 40 yet you refuse to come to me to have life.

41 "I do not accept praise from men, 42 but I know you. I know that you do not have the love of God in your hearts. 43 I have come in my Father's name, and you do not accept me; but if someone else comes in his own name, you will accept him. 44 How can you believe if you accept praise from one another, yet make no effort to obtain the praise that comes from the only God*b*?

45 "But do not think I will accuse you before the Father. Your accuser is Moses, on whom your hopes are set. 46 If you believed Moses, you would believe me, for he wrote about me. 47 But since you do not believe what he wrote, how are you going to believe what I say?"

a39 Or *Study diligently* (the imperative)   *b44* Some early manuscripts *the Only One*

PSALM 106:1-12

1 **P**raise the LORD.*a*

Give thanks to the LORD, for he is good;
     his love endures forever.
2 Who can proclaim the mighty acts of the LORD
     or fully declare his praise?
3 Blessed are they who maintain justice,
     who constantly do what is right.

4 Remember me, O LORD, when you show favor to your people,
     come to my aid when you save them,
5 that I may enjoy the prosperity of your chosen ones,
     that I may share in the joy of your nation
     and join your inheritance in giving praise.

6 We have sinned, even as our fathers did;
     we have done wrong and acted wickedly.
7 When our fathers were in Egypt,
     they gave no thought to your miracles;
   they did not remember your many kindnesses,
     and they rebelled by the sea, the Red Sea.*b*
8 Yet he saved them for his name's sake,
     to make his mighty power known.
9 He rebuked the Red Sea, and it dried up;
     he led them through the depths as through a desert.
10 He saved them from the hand of the foe;
     from the hand of the enemy he redeemed them.
11 The waters covered their adversaries;
     not one of them survived.
12 Then they believed his promises and sang his praise.

a1 Hebrew *Hallelu Yah*; also in verse 48   *b7* Hebrew *Yam Suph*; that is, Sea of Reeds; also in verses 9 and 22

PROVERBS 14:30-31

30 **A** heart at peace gives life to the body,
     but envy rots the bones.

31 He who oppresses the poor shows contempt for their Maker,
     but whoever is kind to the needy honors God.

465

MAY 9

☐ DAY 129

GOD SIGHTINGS

May 9

1 SAMUEL 5:1–7:17

After the Philistines had captured the ark of God, they took it from Ebenezer to Ashdod. ²Then they carried the ark into Dagon's temple and set it beside Dagon. ³When the people of Ashdod rose early the next day, there was Dagon, fallen on his face on the ground before the ark of the LORD! They took Dagon and put him back in his place. ⁴But the following morning when they rose, there was Dagon, fallen on his face on the ground before the ark of the LORD! His head and hands had been broken off and were lying on the threshold; only his body remained. ⁵That is why to this day neither the priests of Dagon nor any others who enter Dagon's temple at Ashdod step on the threshold.

⁶The LORD's hand was heavy upon the people of Ashdod and its vicinity; he brought devastation upon them and afflicted them with tumors.ᵃ ⁷When the men of Ashdod saw what was happening, they said, "The ark of the god of Israel must not stay here with us, because his hand is heavy upon us and upon Dagon our god." ⁸So they called together all the rulers of the Philistines and asked them, "What shall we do with the ark of the god of Israel?"

They answered, "Have the ark of the god of Israel moved to Gath." So they moved the ark of the God of Israel.

⁹But after they had moved it, the LORD's hand was against that city, throwing it into a great panic. He afflicted the people of the city, both young and old, with an outbreak of tumors.ᵇ ¹⁰So they sent the ark of God to Ekron.

As the ark of God was entering Ekron, the people of Ekron cried out, "They have brought the ark of the god of Israel around to us to kill us and our people." ¹¹So they called together all the rulers

of the Philistines and said, "Send the ark of the god of Israel away; let it go back to its own place, or itᶜ will kill us and our people." For death had filled the city with panic; God's hand was very heavy upon it. ¹²Those who did not die were afflicted with tumors, and the outcry of the city went up to heaven.

⁶:¹WHEN the ark of the LORD had been in Philistine territory seven months, ²the Philistines called for the priests and the diviners and said, "What shall we do with the ark of the LORD? Tell us how we should send it back to its place."

³They answered, "If you return the ark of the god of Israel, do not send it away empty, but by all means send a guilt offering to him. Then you will be healed, and you will know why his hand has not been lifted from you."

⁴The Philistines asked, "What guilt offering should we send to him?"

They replied, "Five gold tumors and five gold rats, according to the number of the Philistine rulers, because the same plague has struck both you and your rulers. ⁵Make models of the tumors and of the rats that are destroying the country, and pay honor to Israel's god. Perhaps he will lift his hand from you and your gods and your land. ⁶Why do you harden your hearts as the Egyptians and Pharaoh did? When heᵈ treated them harshly, did they not send the Israelites out so they could go on their way?

⁷"Now then, get a new cart ready, with two cows that have calved and have never been yoked. Hitch the cows to the cart, but take their calves away and pen them up. ⁸Take the ark of the LORD and put it on the cart, and in a chest beside it put the gold objects you are sending back to him as a guilt offering. Send it on its way, ⁹but keep watching it. If it goes up to its own territory, toward Beth Shemesh, then the LORD has brought this great disaster on us. But if it does not, then we will know that it was not his hand that struck us and that it happened to us by chance."

10So they did this. They took two such cows and hitched them to the cart and penned up their calves. 11They placed the ark of the Lord on the cart and along with it the chest containing the gold rats and the models of the tumors. 12Then the cows went straight up toward Beth Shemesh, keeping on the road and lowing all the way; they did not turn to the right or to the left. The rulers of the Philistines followed them as far as the border of Beth Shemesh.

13Now the people of Beth Shemesh were harvesting their wheat in the valley, and when they looked up and saw the ark, they rejoiced at the sight. 14The cart came to the field of Joshua of Beth Shemesh, and there it stopped beside a large rock. The people chopped up the wood of the cart and sacrificed the cows as a burnt offering to the Lord. 15The Levites took down the ark of the Lord, together with the chest containing the gold objects, and placed them on the large rock. On that day the people of Beth Shemesh offered burnt offerings and made sacrifices to the Lord. 16The five rulers of the Philistines saw all this and then returned that same day to Ekron.

17These are the gold tumors the Philistines sent as a guilt offering to the Lord—one each for Ashdod, Gaza, Ashkelon, Gath and Ekron. 18And the number of the gold rats was according to the number of Philistine towns belonging to the five rulers—the fortified towns with their country villages. The large rock, on whiche they set the ark of the Lord, is a witness to this day in the field of Joshua of Beth Shemesh.

19But God struck down some of the men of Beth Shemesh, putting seventyf of them to death because they had looked into the ark of the Lord. The people mourned because of the heavy blow the Lord had dealt them, 20and the men of Beth Shemesh asked, "Who can stand in the presence of the Lord, this holy God? To whom will the ark go up from here?"

21Then they sent messengers to the people of Kiriath Jearim, saying, "The Philistines have returned the ark of the Lord. Come down and take it up to your place." 7:1So the men of Kiriath Jearim came and took up the ark of the Lord. They took it to Abinadab's house on the hill and consecrated Eleazar his son to guard the ark of the Lord.

2It was a long time, twenty years in all, that the ark remained at Kiriath Jearim, and all the people of Israel mourned and sought after the Lord. 3And Samuel said to the whole house of Israel, "If you are returning to the Lord with all your hearts, then rid yourselves of the foreign gods and the Ashtoreths and commit yourselves to the Lord and serve him only, and he will deliver you out of the hand of the Philistines." 4So the Israelites put away their Baals and Ashtoreths, and served the Lord only.

5Then Samuel said, "Assemble all Israel at Mizpah and I will intercede with the Lord for you." 6When they had assembled at Mizpah, they drew water and poured it out before the Lord. On that day they fasted and there they confessed, "We have sinned against the Lord." And Samuel was leaderg of Israel at Mizpah.

7When the Philistines heard that Israel had assembled at Mizpah, the rulers of the Philistines came up to attack them. And when the Israelites heard of it, they were afraid because of the Philistines. 8They said to Samuel, "Do not stop crying out to the Lord our God for us, that he may rescue us from the hand of the Philistines." 9Then Samuel took a suckling lamb and offered it up as a whole burnt offering to the Lord. He cried out to the Lord on Israel's behalf, and the Lord answered him.

10While Samuel was sacrificing the burnt offering, the Philistines drew near to engage Israel in battle. But that day the Lord thundered with loud thunder against the Philistines and threw them into such a panic that they were routed before the Israelites. 11The men of Israel rushed out of Mizpah and pursued the Philistines, slaughtering them along the way to a point below Beth Car.

¹²Then Samuel took a stone and set it up between Mizpah and Shen. He named it Ebenezer,ʰ saying, "Thus far has the Lᴏʀᴅ helped us." ¹³So the Philistines were subdued and did not invade Israelite territory again.

Throughout Samuel's lifetime, the hand of the Lᴏʀᴅ was against the Philistines. ¹⁴The towns from Ekron to Gath that the Philistines had captured from Israel were restored to her, and Israel delivered the neighboring territory from the power of the Philistines. And there was peace between Israel and the Amorites.

¹⁵Samuel continued as judge over Israel all the days of his life. ¹⁶From year to year he went on a circuit from Bethel to Gilgal to Mizpah, judging Israel in all those places. ¹⁷But he always went back to Ramah, where his home was, and there he also judged Israel. And he built an altar there to the Lᴏʀᴅ.

ᵃ6 Hebrew; Septuagint and Vulgate tumors. And rats appeared in their land, and death and destruction were throughout the city   ᵇ9 Or with tumors in the groin (see Septuagint)   ᶜ11 Or he   ᵈ6 That is, God   ᵉ18 A few Hebrew manuscripts (see also Septuagint); most Hebrew manuscripts villages as far as Greater Abel, where   ᶠ19 A few Hebrew manuscripts; most Hebrew manuscripts and Septuagint 50,070   ⁹⁶ Traditionally judge   ʰ12 Ebenezer means stone of help.

JOHN 6:1-21

Some time after this, Jesus crossed to the far shore of the Sea of Galilee (that is, the Sea of Tiberias), ²and a great crowd of people followed him because they saw the miraculous signs he had performed on the sick. ³Then Jesus went up on a mountainside and sat down with his disciples. ⁴The Jewish Passover Feast was near.

⁵When Jesus looked up and saw a great crowd coming toward him, he said to Philip, "Where shall we buy bread for these people to eat?" ⁶He asked this only to test him, for he already had in mind what he was going to do.

⁷Philip answered him, "Eight months' wagesᵃ would not buy enough bread for each one to have a bite!"

⁸Another of his disciples, Andrew, Si-mon Peter's brother, spoke up, ⁹"Here is a boy with five small barley loaves and two small fish, but how far will they go among so many?"

¹⁰Jesus said, "Have the people sit down." There was plenty of grass in that place, and the men sat down, about five thousand of them. ¹¹Jesus then took the loaves, gave thanks, and distributed to those who were seated as much as they wanted. He did the same with the fish.

¹²When they had all had enough to eat, he said to his disciples, "Gather the pieces that are left over. Let nothing be wasted." ¹³So they gathered them and filled twelve baskets with the pieces of the five barley loaves left over by those who had eaten.

¹⁴After the people saw the miraculous sign that Jesus did, they began to say, "Surely this is the Prophet who is to come into the world." ¹⁵Jesus, knowing that they intended to come and make him king by force, withdrew again to a mountain by himself.

¹⁶When evening came, his disciples went down to the lake, ¹⁷where they got into a boat and set off across the lake for Capernaum. By now it was dark, and Jesus had not yet joined them. ¹⁸A strong wind was blowing and the waters grew rough. ¹⁹When they had rowed three or three and a half miles,ᵇ they saw Jesus approaching the boat, walking on the water; and they were terrified. ²⁰But he said to them, "It is I; don't be afraid." ²¹Then they were willing to take him into the boat, and immediately the boat reached the shore where they were heading.

ᵃ7 Greek two hundred denarii   ᵇ19 Greek rowed twenty-five or thirty stadia (about 5 or 6 kilometers)

PSALM 106:13-31

¹³But they [the Israelites] soon
        forgot what he [the Lᴏʀᴅ]
        had done
    and did not wait for his counsel.
¹⁴In the desert they gave in to their
        craving;
    in the wasteland they put God to
        the test.

15 So he gave them what they asked for,
     but sent a wasting disease upon
     them.

16 In the camp they grew envious
     of Moses
     and of Aaron, who was
     consecrated to the LORD.
17 The earth opened up and swallowed
     Dathan;
     it buried the company of Abiram.
18 Fire blazed among their followers;
     a flame consumed the wicked.

19 At Horeb they made a calf
     and worshiped an idol cast from
     metal.
20 They exchanged their Glory
     for an image of a bull, which eats
     grass.
21 They forgot the God who saved them,
     who had done great things in
     Egypt,
22 miracles in the land of Ham
     and awesome deeds by the
     Red Sea.
23 So he said he would destroy them—
     had not Moses, his chosen one,
     stood in the breach before him
     to keep his wrath from destroying
     them.

24 Then they despised the pleasant land;
     they did not believe his promise.
25 They grumbled in their tents
     and did not obey the LORD.
26 So he swore to them with uplifted
     hand
     that he would make them fall in
     the desert,
27 make their descendants fall among
     the nations
     and scatter them throughout the
     lands.

28 They yoked themselves to the Baal
     of Peor
     and ate sacrifices offered to
     lifeless gods;
29 they provoked the LORD to anger by
     their wicked deeds,
     and a plague broke out among
     them.

30 But Phinehas stood up and
     intervened,
     and the plague was checked.
31 This was credited to him as
     righteousness
     for endless generations to come.

PROVERBS 14:32-33
32 When calamity comes, the wicked
     are brought down,
     but even in death the righteous
     have a refuge.

33 Wisdom reposes in the heart of the
     discerning
     and even among fools she lets
     herself be known.a

a33 Hebrew; Septuagint and Syriac / but in the heart of fools
she is not known

□ DAY 130

GOD SIGHTINGS

May 10

1 SAMUEL 8:1–9:27
When Samuel grew old, he appointed his sons as judges for Israel. 2 The name of his firstborn was Joel and the name of his second was Abijah, and they served at Beersheba. 3 But his sons did not walk in his ways. They turned aside after dishonest gain and accepted bribes and perverted justice.

4 So all the elders of Israel gathered together and came to Samuel at Ramah. 5 They said to him, "You are old, and your sons do not walk in your ways; now appoint a king to leada us, such as all the other nations have."

6 But when they said, "Give us a king to lead us," this displeased Samuel; so he prayed to the LORD. 7 And the LORD told him: "Listen to all that the people are saying to you; it is not you they have rejected, but they have rejected me as their king. 8 As they have done from the day I brought them up out of Egypt until this day, forsaking me and serving other

gods, so they are doing to you. ⁹Now listen to them; but warn them solemnly and let them know what the king who will reign over them will do."

¹⁰Samuel told all the words of the LORD to the people who were asking him for a king. ¹¹He said, "This is what the king who will reign over you will do: He will take your sons and make them serve with his chariots and horses, and they will run in front of his chariots. ¹²Some he will assign to be commanders of thousands and commanders of fifties, and others to plow his ground and reap his harvest, and still others to make weapons of war and equipment for his chariots. ¹³He will take your daughters to be perfumers and cooks and bakers. ¹⁴He will take the best of your fields and vineyards and olive groves and give them to his attendants. ¹⁵He will take a tenth of your grain and of your vintage and give it to his officials and attendants. ¹⁶Your menservants and maidservants and the best of your cattleᵇ and donkeys he will take for his own use. ¹⁷He will take a tenth of your flocks, and you yourselves will become his slaves. ¹⁸When that day comes, you will cry out for relief from the king you have chosen, and the LORD will not answer you in that day."

¹⁹But the people refused to listen to Samuel. "No!" they said. "We want a king over us. ²⁰Then we will be like all the other nations, with a king to lead us and to go out before us and fight our battles."

²¹When Samuel heard all that the people said, he repeated it before the LORD. ²²The LORD answered, "Listen to them and give them a king."

Then Samuel said to the men of Israel, "Everyone go back to his town."

⁹:¹THERE was a Benjamite, a man of standing, whose name was Kish son of Abiel, the son of Zeror, the son of Becorath, the son of Aphiah of Benjamin. ²He had a son named Saul, an impressive young man without equal among the Israelites—a head taller than any of the others.

³Now the donkeys belonging to Saul's father Kish were lost, and Kish said to his son Saul, "Take one of the servants with you and go and look for the donkeys." ⁴So he passed through the hill country of Ephraim and through the area around Shalisha, but they did not find them. They went on into the district of Shaalim, but the donkeys were not there. Then he passed through the territory of Benjamin, but they did not find them.

⁵When they reached the district of Zuph, Saul said to the servant who was with him, "Come, let's go back, or my father will stop thinking about the donkeys and start worrying about us."

⁶But the servant replied, "Look, in this town there is a man of God; he is highly respected, and everything he says comes true. Let's go there now. Perhaps he will tell us what way to take."

⁷Saul said to his servant, "If we go, what can we give the man? The food in our sacks is gone. We have no gift to take to the man of God. What do we have?"

⁸The servant answered him again. "Look," he said, "I have a quarter of a shekelᶜ of silver. I will give it to the man of God so that he will tell us what way to take." ⁹(Formerly in Israel, if a man went to inquire of God, he would say, "Come, let us go to the seer," because the prophet of today used to be called a seer.)

¹⁰"Good," Saul said to his servant. "Come, let's go." So they set out for the town where the man of God was.

¹¹As they were going up the hill to the town, they met some girls coming out to draw water, and they asked them, "Is the seer here?"

¹²"He is," they answered. "He's ahead of you. Hurry now; he has just come to our town today, for the people have a sacrifice at the high place. ¹³As soon as you enter the town, you will find him before he goes up to the high place to eat. The people will not begin eating

until he comes, because he must bless the sacrifice; afterward, those who are invited will eat. Go up now; you should find him about this time."

14They went up to the town, and as they were entering it, there was Samuel, coming toward them on his way up to the high place.

15Now the day before Saul came, the LORD had revealed this to Samuel: 16"About this time tomorrow I will send you a man from the land of Benjamin. Anoint him leader over my people Israel; he will deliver my people from the hand of the Philistines. I have looked upon my people, for their cry has reached me."

17When Samuel caught sight of Saul, the LORD said to him, "This is the man I spoke to you about; he will govern my people."

18Saul approached Samuel in the gateway and asked, "Would you please tell me where the seer's house is?"

19"I am the seer," Samuel replied. "Go up ahead of me to the high place, for today you are to eat with me, and in the morning I will let you go and will tell you all that is in your heart. 20As for the donkeys you lost three days ago, do not worry about them; they have been found. And to whom is all the desire of Israel turned, if not to you and all your father's family?"

21Saul answered, "But am I not a Benjamite, from the smallest tribe of Israel, and is not my clan the least of all the clans of the tribe of Benjamin? Why do you say such a thing to me?"

22Then Samuel brought Saul and his servant into the hall and seated them at the head of those who were invited—about thirty in number. 23Samuel said to the cook, "Bring the piece of meat I gave you, the one I told you to lay aside."

24So the cook took up the leg with what was on it and set it in front of Saul. Samuel said, "Here is what has been kept for you. Eat, because it was set aside for you for this occasion, from the time I said, 'I have invited guests.'" And Saul dined with Samuel that day.

25After they came down from the high place to the town, Samuel talked with Saul on the roof of his house. 26They rose about daybreak and Samuel called to Saul on the roof, "Get ready, and I will send you on your way." When Saul got ready, he and Samuel went outside together. 27As they were going down to the edge of the town, Samuel said to Saul, "Tell the servant to go on ahead of us"—and the servant did so—"but you stay here awhile, so that I may give you a message from God."

a5 Traditionally *judge*; also in verses 6 and 20   b16 Septuagint; Hebrew *young men*   c8 That is, about 1/10 ounce (about 3 grams)

JOHN 6:22-42

The next day the crowd that had stayed on the opposite shore of the lake realized that only one boat had been there, and that Jesus had not entered it with his disciples, but that they had gone away alone. 23Then some boats from Tiberias landed near the place where the people had eaten the bread after the Lord had given thanks. 24Once the crowd realized that neither Jesus nor his disciples were there, they got into the boats and went to Capernaum in search of Jesus.

25When they found him on the other side of the lake, they asked him, "Rabbi, when did you get here?"

26Jesus answered, "I tell you the truth, you are looking for me, not because you saw miraculous signs but because you ate the loaves and had your fill. 27Do not work for food that spoils, but for food that endures to eternal life, which the Son of Man will give you. On him God the Father has placed his seal of approval."

28Then they asked him, "What must we do to do the works God requires?"

29Jesus answered, "The work of God is this: to believe in the one he has sent."

30So they asked him, "What miraculous sign then will you give that we may see it and believe you? What will you do? 31Our forefathers ate the manna in the desert; as it is written: 'He gave them bread from heaven to eat.'a"

³²Jesus said to them, "I tell you the truth, it is not Moses who has given you the bread from heaven, but it is my Father who gives you the true bread from heaven. ³³For the bread of God is he who comes down from heaven and gives life to the world."

³⁴"Sir," they said, "from now on give us this bread."

³⁵Then Jesus declared, "I am the bread of life. He who comes to me will never go hungry, and he who believes in me will never be thirsty. ³⁶But as I told you, you have seen me and still you do not believe. ³⁷All that the Father gives me will come to me, and whoever comes to me I will never drive away. ³⁸For I have come down from heaven not to do my will but to do the will of him who sent me. ³⁹And this is the will of him who sent me, that I shall lose none of all that he has given me, but raise them up at the last day. ⁴⁰For my Father's will is that everyone who looks to the Son and believes in him shall have eternal life, and I will raise him up at the last day."

⁴¹At this the Jews began to grumble about him because he said, "I am the bread that came down from heaven." ⁴²They said, "Is this not Jesus, the son of Joseph, whose father and mother we know? How can he now say, 'I came down from heaven'?"

a31 Exodus 16:4; Neh. 9:15; Psalm 78:24,25

PSALM 106:32-48

³²By the waters of Meribah they [the Israelites] angered the LORD,
and trouble came to Moses because of them;
³³for they rebelled against the Spirit of God,
and rash words came from Moses' lips.*a*

³⁴They did not destroy the peoples as the LORD had commanded them,
³⁵but they mingled with the nations and adopted their customs.
³⁶They worshiped their idols, which became a snare to them.

³⁷They sacrificed their sons and their daughters to demons.
³⁸They shed innocent blood, the blood of their sons and daughters,
whom they sacrificed to the idols of Canaan,
and the land was desecrated by their blood.
³⁹They defiled themselves by what they did;
by their deeds they prostituted themselves.

⁴⁰Therefore the LORD was angry with his people
and abhorred his inheritance.
⁴¹He handed them over to the nations, and their foes ruled over them.
⁴²Their enemies oppressed them and subjected them to their power.
⁴³Many times he delivered them, but they were bent on rebellion
and they wasted away in their sin.

⁴⁴But he took note of their distress when he heard their cry;
⁴⁵for their sake he remembered his covenant
and out of his great love he relented.
⁴⁶He caused them to be pitied by all who held them captive.

⁴⁷Save us, O LORD our God, and gather us from the nations,
that we may give thanks to your holy name
and glory in your praise.

⁴⁸Praise be to the LORD, the God of Israel, from everlasting to everlasting.
Let all the people say, "Amen!"

Praise the LORD.

a33 Or *against his spirit, / and rash words came from his lips*

PROVERBS 14:34-35

³⁴Righteousness exalts a nation, but sin is a disgrace to any people.

³⁵A king delights in a wise servant, but a shameful servant incurs his wrath.

GOD SIGHTINGS

May 11

1 SAMUEL 10:1–11:15

Then Samuel took a flask of oil and poured it on Saul's head and kissed him, saying, "Has not the Lord anointed you leader over his inheritance?*a* ²When you leave me today, you will meet two men near Rachel's tomb, at Zelzah on the border of Benjamin. They will say to you, 'The donkeys you set out to look for have been found. And now your father has stopped thinking about them and is worried about you. He is asking, "What shall I do about my son?"'

³"Then you will go on from there until you reach the great tree of Tabor. Three men going up to God at Bethel will meet you there. One will be carrying three young goats, another three loaves of bread, and another a skin of wine. ⁴They will greet you and offer you two loaves of bread, which you will accept from them.

⁵"After that you will go to Gibeah of God, where there is a Philistine outpost. As you approach the town, you will meet a procession of prophets coming down from the high place with lyres, tambourines, flutes and harps being played before them, and they will be prophesying. ⁶The Spirit of the Lord will come upon you in power, and you will prophesy with them; and you will be changed into a different person. ⁷Once these signs are fulfilled, do whatever your hand finds to do, for God is with you.

⁸"Go down ahead of me to Gilgal. I will surely come down to you to sacrifice burnt offerings and fellowship offerings,*b* but you must wait seven days until I come to you and tell you what you are to do."

⁹As Saul turned to leave Samuel, God changed Saul's heart, and all these signs were fulfilled that day. ¹⁰When they arrived at Gibeah, a procession of prophets met him; the Spirit of God came

upon him in power, and he joined in their prophesying. ¹¹When all those who had formerly known him saw him prophesying with the prophets, they asked each other, "What is this that has happened to the son of Kish? Is Saul also among the prophets?"

¹²A man who lived there answered, "And who is their father?" So it became a saying: "Is Saul also among the prophets?" ¹³After Saul stopped prophesying, he went to the high place.

¹⁴Now Saul's uncle asked him and his servant, "Where have you been?"

"Looking for the donkeys," he said. "But when we saw they were not to be found, we went to Samuel."

¹⁵Saul's uncle said, "Tell me what Samuel said to you."

¹⁶Saul replied, "He assured us that the donkeys had been found." But he did not tell his uncle what Samuel had said about the kingship.

¹⁷Samuel summoned the people of Israel to the Lord at Mizpah ¹⁸and said to them, "This is what the Lord, the God of Israel, says: 'I brought Israel up out of Egypt, and I delivered you from the power of Egypt and all the kingdoms that oppressed you.' ¹⁹But you have now rejected your God, who saves you out of all your calamities and distresses. And you have said, 'No, set a king over us.' So now present yourselves before the Lord by your tribes and clans."

²⁰When Samuel brought all the tribes of Israel near, the tribe of Benjamin was chosen. ²¹Then he brought forward the tribe of Benjamin, clan by clan, and Matri's clan was chosen. Finally Saul son of Kish was chosen. But when they looked for him, he was not to be found. ²²So they inquired further of the Lord, "Has the man come here yet?"

And the Lord said, "Yes, he has hidden himself among the baggage."

²³They ran and brought him out, and as he stood among the people he was a head taller than any of the others. ²⁴Samuel said to all the people, "Do you see the man the Lord has chosen? There is no one like him among all the people."

Then the people shouted, "Long live the king!"

²⁵Samuel explained to the people the regulations of the kingship. He wrote them down on a scroll and deposited it before the Lord. Then Samuel dismissed the people, each to his own home.

²⁶Saul also went to his home in Gibeah, accompanied by valiant men whose hearts God had touched. ²⁷But some troublemakers said, "How can this fellow save us?" They despised him and brought him no gifts. But Saul kept silent.

¹¹:¹Nᴀʜᴀsʜ the Ammonite went up and besieged Jabesh Gilead. And all the men of Jabesh said to him, "Make a treaty with us, and we will be subject to you."

²But Nahash the Ammonite replied, "I will make a treaty with you only on the condition that I gouge out the right eye of every one of you and so bring disgrace on all Israel."

³The elders of Jabesh said to him, "Give us seven days so we can send messengers throughout Israel; if no one comes to rescue us, we will surrender to you."

⁴When the messengers came to Gibeah of Saul and reported these terms to the people, they all wept aloud. ⁵Just then Saul was returning from the fields, behind his oxen, and he asked, "What is wrong with the people? Why are they weeping?" Then they repeated to him what the men of Jabesh had said.

⁶When Saul heard their words, the Spirit of God came upon him in power, and he burned with anger. ⁷He took a pair of oxen, cut them into pieces, and sent the pieces by messengers throughout Israel, proclaiming, "This is what will be done to the oxen of anyone who does not follow Saul and Samuel." Then the terror of the Lord fell on the people, and they turned out as one man. ⁸When Saul mustered them at Bezek, the men of Israel numbered three hundred thousand and the men of Judah thirty thousand.

⁹They told the messengers who had come, "Say to the men of Jabesh Gilead, 'By the time the sun is hot tomorrow, you will be delivered.'" When the messengers went and reported this to the men of Jabesh, they were elated. ¹⁰They said to the Ammonites, "Tomorrow we will surrender to you, and you can do to us whatever seems good to you."

¹¹The next day Saul separated his men into three divisions; during the last watch of the night they broke into the camp of the Ammonites and slaughtered them until the heat of the day. Those who survived were scattered, so that no two of them were left together.

¹²The people then said to Samuel, "Who was it that asked, 'Shall Saul reign over us?' Bring these men to us and we will put them to death."

¹³But Saul said, "No one shall be put to death today, for this day the Lord has rescued Israel."

¹⁴Then Samuel said to the people, "Come, let us go to Gilgal and there reaffirm the kingship." ¹⁵So all the people went to Gilgal and confirmed Saul as king in the presence of the Lord. There they sacrificed fellowship offeringsᵇ before the Lord, and Saul and all the Israelites held a great celebration.

ᵃ1 Hebrew; Septuagint and Vulgate *over his people Israel? You will reign over the Lord's people and save them from the power of their enemies round about. And this will be a sign to you that the Lord has anointed you leader over his inheritance:*   ᵇ8,15 Traditionally *peace offerings*

JOHN 6:43-71

"Stop grumbling among yourselves," Jesus answered. ⁴⁴"No one can come to me unless the Father who sent me draws him, and I will raise him up at the last day. ⁴⁵It is written in the Prophets: 'They will all be taught by God.'ᵃ Everyone who listens to the Father and learns from him comes to me. ⁴⁶No one has seen the Father except the one who is from God; only he has seen the Father. ⁴⁷I tell you the truth, he who believes has everlasting life. ⁴⁸I am the bread of life. ⁴⁹Your forefathers ate the manna in the desert, yet they died. ⁵⁰But here is the bread that comes down from heaven, which a man may eat and not die. [51]I am the living bread that came down from heaven. If anyone eats of this bread, he will live forever. This bread is my flesh, which I will give for the life of the world."

[52]Then the Jews began to argue sharply among themselves, "How can this man give us his flesh to eat?"

[53]Jesus said to them, "I tell you the truth, unless you eat the flesh of the Son of Man and drink his blood, you have no life in you. [54]Whoever eats my flesh and drinks my blood has eternal life, and I will raise him up at the last day. [55]For my flesh is real food and my blood is real drink. [56]Whoever eats my flesh and drinks my blood remains in me, and I in him. [57]Just as the living Father sent me and I live because of the Father, so the one who feeds on me will live because of me. [58]This is the bread that came down from heaven. Your forefathers ate manna and died, but he who feeds on this bread will live forever." [59]He said this while teaching in the synagogue in Capernaum.

[60]On hearing it, many of his disciples said, "This is a hard teaching. Who can accept it?"

[61]Aware that his disciples were grumbling about this, Jesus said to them, "Does this offend you? [62]What if you see the Son of Man ascend to where he was before! [63]The Spirit gives life; the flesh counts for nothing. The words I have spoken to you are spirit[b] and they are life. [64]Yet there are some of you who do not believe." For Jesus had known from the beginning which of them did not believe and who would betray him. [65]He went on to say, "This is why I told you that no one can come to me unless the Father has enabled him."

[66]From this time many of his disciples turned back and no longer followed him.

[67]"You do not want to leave too, do you?" Jesus asked the Twelve.

[68]Simon Peter answered him, "Lord, to whom shall we go? You have the words of eternal life. [69]We believe and know that you are the Holy One of God."

[70]Then Jesus replied, "Have I not chosen you, the Twelve? Yet one of you is a devil!" [71](He meant Judas, the son of Simon Iscariot, who, though one of the Twelve, was later to betray him.)

a45 Isaiah 54:13   *b63* Or *Spirit*

PSALM 107:1-43

[1]Give thanks to the LORD, for he is
     good;
   his love endures forever.
[2]Let the redeemed of the LORD say
     this—
   those he redeemed from the hand
     of the foe,
[3]those he gathered from the lands,
   from east and west, from north
     and south.[a]

[4]Some wandered in desert wastelands,
   finding no way to a city where they
     could settle.
[5]They were hungry and thirsty,
   and their lives ebbed away.
[6]Then they cried out to the LORD in
     their trouble,
   and he delivered them from their
     distress.
[7]He led them by a straight way
   to a city where they could settle.
[8]Let them give thanks to the LORD for
     his unfailing love
   and his wonderful deeds for men,
[9]for he satisfies the thirsty
   and fills the hungry with good
     things.

[10]Some sat in darkness and the
     deepest gloom,
   prisoners suffering in iron chains,
[11]for they had rebelled against the
     words of God
   and despised the counsel of the
     Most High.
[12]So he subjected them to bitter labor;
   they stumbled, and there was no
     one to help.
[13]Then they cried to the LORD in their
     trouble,
   and he saved them from their
     distress.

14 He brought them out of darkness
and the deepest gloom
and broke away their chains.
15 Let them give thanks to the LORD for
his unfailing love
and his wonderful deeds for
men,
16 for he breaks down gates of bronze
and cuts through bars of iron.

17 Some became fools through their
rebellious ways
and suffered affliction because of
their iniquities.
18 They loathed all food
and drew near the gates of death.
19 Then they cried to the LORD in their
trouble,
and he saved them from their
distress.
20 He sent forth his word and healed
them;
he rescued them from the grave.
21 Let them give thanks to the LORD for
his unfailing love
and his wonderful deeds for men.
22 Let them sacrifice thank offerings
and tell of his works with songs
of joy.

23 Others went out on the sea in ships;
they were merchants on the
mighty waters.
24 They saw the works of the LORD,
his wonderful deeds in the deep.
25 For he spoke and stirred up a
tempest
that lifted high the waves.
26 They mounted up to the heavens and
went down to the depths;
in their peril their courage melted
away.
27 They reeled and staggered like
drunken men;
they were at their wits' end.
28 Then they cried out to the LORD in
their trouble,
and he brought them out of their
distress.
29 He stilled the storm to a whisper;
the waves of the sea were
hushed.

30 They were glad when it grew calm,
and he guided them to their
desired haven.
31 Let them give thanks to the LORD for
his unfailing love
and his wonderful deeds for
men.
32 Let them exalt him in the assembly
of the people
and praise him in the council of
the elders.

33 He turned rivers into a desert,
flowing springs into thirsty
ground,
34 and fruitful land into a salt waste,
because of the wickedness of
those who lived there.
35 He turned the desert into pools
of water
and the parched ground into
flowing springs;
36 there he brought the hungry to live,
and they founded a city where
they could settle.
37 They sowed fields and planted
vineyards
that yielded a fruitful harvest;
38 he blessed them, and their numbers
greatly increased,
and he did not let their herds
diminish.

39 Then their numbers decreased, and
they were humbled
by oppression, calamity and
sorrow;
40 he who pours contempt on nobles
made them wander in a trackless
waste.
41 But he lifted the needy out of their
affliction
and increased their families like
flocks.
42 The upright see and rejoice,
but all the wicked shut their
mouths.

43 Whoever is wise, let him heed these
things
and consider the great love of
the LORD.

a 3 Hebrew *north and the sea*

PROVERBS 15:1-3

A gentle answer turns away wrath,
but a harsh word stirs up anger.

2 The tongue of the wise commends
knowledge,
but the mouth of the fool gushes
folly.

3 The eyes of the Lord are everywhere,
keeping watch on the wicked and
the good.

☐ DAY 132

GOD SIGHTINGS

May 12

1 SAMUEL 12:1–13:22

Samuel said to all Israel, "I have listened
to everything you said to me and have
set a king over you. 2 Now you have a
king as your leader. As for me, I am old
and gray, and my sons are here with you.
I have been your leader from my youth
until this day. 3 Here I stand. Testify
against me in the presence of the Lord
and his anointed. Whose ox have I
taken? Whose donkey have I taken?
Whom have I cheated? Whom have I
oppressed? From whose hand have I accepted a bribe to make me shut my
eyes? If I have done any of these, I will
make it right."

4 "You have not cheated or oppressed
us," they replied. "You have not taken
anything from anyone's hand."

5 Samuel said to them, "The Lord is
witness against you, and also his
anointed is witness this day, that you
have not found anything in my hand."

"He is witness," they said.

6 Then Samuel said to the people, "It is
the Lord who appointed Moses and
Aaron and brought your forefathers up
out of Egypt. 7 Now then, stand here, because I am going to confront you with
evidence before the Lord as to all the
righteous acts performed by the Lord
for you and your fathers.

8 "After Jacob entered Egypt, they
cried to the Lord for help, and the Lord
sent Moses and Aaron, who brought
your forefathers out of Egypt and settled them in this place.

9 "But they forgot the Lord their God;
so he sold them into the hand of Sisera,
the commander of the army of Hazor,
and into the hands of the Philistines and
the king of Moab, who fought against
them. 10 They cried out to the Lord and
said, 'We have sinned; we have forsaken
the Lord and served the Baals and the
Ashtoreths. But now deliver us from the
hands of our enemies, and we will serve
you.' 11 Then the Lord sent Jerub-Baal,a
Barak,b Jephthah and Samuel,c and he
delivered you from the hands of your
enemies on every side, so that you lived
securely.

12 "But when you saw that Nahash
king of the Ammonites was moving
against you, you said to me, 'No, we want
a king to rule over us'—even though the
Lord your God was your king. 13 Now
here is the king you have chosen, the
one you asked for; see, the Lord has set a
king over you. 14 If you fear the Lord and
serve and obey him and do not rebel
against his commands, and if both you
and the king who reigns over you follow
the Lord your God—good! 15 But if you
do not obey the Lord, and if you rebel
against his commands, his hand will be
against you, as it was against your fathers.

16 "Now then, stand still and see this
great thing the Lord is about to do before your eyes! 17 Is it not wheat harvest
now? I will call upon the Lord to send
thunder and rain. And you will realize
what an evil thing you did in the eyes of
the Lord when you asked for a king."

18 Then Samuel called upon the Lord,
and that same day the Lord sent thunder and rain. So all the people stood in
awe of the Lord and of Samuel.

19 The people all said to Samuel, "Pray
to the Lord your God for your servants
so that we will not die, for we have

added to all our other sins the evil of asking for a king."

²⁰"Do not be afraid," Samuel replied. "You have done all this evil; yet do not turn away from the Lord, but serve the Lord with all your heart. ²¹Do not turn away after useless idols. They can do you no good, nor can they rescue you, because they are useless. ²²For the sake of his great name the Lord will not reject his people, because the Lord was pleased to make you his own. ²³As for me, far be it from me that I should sin against the Lord by failing to pray for you. And I will teach you the way that is good and right. ²⁴But be sure to fear the Lord and serve him faithfully with all your heart; consider what great things he has done for you. ²⁵Yet if you persist in doing evil, both you and your king will be swept away."

^{13:1}Saul was ⌞thirty⌟^d years old when he became king, and he reigned over Israel ⌞forty-⌟^e two years.

²Saul^f chose three thousand men from Israel; two thousand were with him at Micmash and in the hill country of Bethel, and a thousand were with Jonathan at Gibeah in Benjamin. The rest of the men he sent back to their homes.

³Jonathan attacked the Philistine outpost at Geba, and the Philistines heard about it. Then Saul had the trumpet blown throughout the land and said, "Let the Hebrews hear!" ⁴So all Israel heard the news: "Saul has attacked the Philistine outpost, and now Israel has become a stench to the Philistines." And the people were summoned to join Saul at Gilgal.

⁵The Philistines assembled to fight Israel, with three thousand^g chariots, six thousand charioteers, and soldiers as numerous as the sand on the seashore. They went up and camped at Micmash, east of Beth Aven. ⁶When the men of Israel saw that their situation was critical and that their army was hard pressed, they hid in caves and thickets, among the rocks, and in pits

and cisterns. ⁷Some Hebrews even crossed the Jordan to the land of Gad and Gilead.

Saul remained at Gilgal, and all the troops with him were quaking with fear. ⁸He waited seven days, the time set by Samuel; but Samuel did not come to Gilgal, and Saul's men began to scatter. ⁹So he said, "Bring me the burnt offering and the fellowship offerings.^h" And Saul offered up the burnt offering. ¹⁰Just as he finished making the offering, Samuel arrived, and Saul went out to greet him.

¹¹"What have you done?" asked Samuel.

Saul replied, "When I saw that the men were scattering, and that you did not come at the set time, and that the Philistines were assembling at Micmash, ¹²I thought, 'Now the Philistines will come down against me at Gilgal, and I have not sought the Lord's favor.' So I felt compelled to offer the burnt offering."

¹³"You acted foolishly," Samuel said. "You have not kept the command the Lord your God gave you; if you had, he would have established your kingdom over Israel for all time. ¹⁴But now your kingdom will not endure; the Lord has sought out a man after his own heart and appointed him leader of his people, because you have not kept the Lord's command."

¹⁵Then Samuel left Gilgalⁱ and went up to Gibeah in Benjamin, and Saul counted the men who were with him. They numbered about six hundred.

¹⁶Saul and his son Jonathan and the men with them were staying in Gibeah^j in Benjamin, while the Philistines camped at Micmash. ¹⁷Raiding parties went out from the Philistine camp in three detachments. One turned toward Ophrah in the vicinity of Shual, ¹⁸another toward Beth Horon, and the third toward the borderland overlooking the Valley of Zeboim facing the desert.

¹⁹Not a blacksmith could be found in the whole land of Israel, because the Philistines had said, "Otherwise the

Hebrews will make swords or spears!" [20]So all Israel went down to the Philistines to have their plowshares, mattocks, axes and sickles[k] sharpened. [21]The price was two thirds of a shekel[l] for sharpening plowshares and mattocks, and a third of a shekel[m] for sharpening forks and axes and for repointing goads.

[22]So on the day of the battle not a soldier with Saul and Jonathan had a sword or spear in his hand; only Saul and his son Jonathan had them.

a11 Also called Gideon   b11 Some Septuagint manuscripts and Syriac; Hebrew Bedan   c11 Hebrew; some Septuagint manuscripts and Syriac Samson   d1 A few late manuscripts of the Septuagint; Hebrew does not have thirty.   e1 See the round number in Acts 13:21; Hebrew does not have forty-.   f1,2 Or and when he had reigned over Israel two years, [2]he   g5 Some Septuagint manuscripts and Syriac; Hebrew thirty thousand   h9 Traditionally peace offerings   i15 Hebrew; Septuagint Gilgal and went his way; the rest of the people went after Saul to meet the army, and they went out of Gilgal   j16 Two Hebrew manuscripts; most Hebrew manuscripts Geba, a variant of Gibeah   k20 Septuagint; Hebrew plowshares   l21 Hebrew pim; that is, about 1/4 ounce (about 8 grams)   m21 That is, about 1/8 ounce (about 4 grams)

JOHN 7:1-29

After this, Jesus went around in Galilee, purposely staying away from Judea because the Jews there were waiting to take his life. [2]But when the Jewish Feast of Tabernacles was near, [3]Jesus' brothers said to him, "You ought to leave here and go to Judea, so that your disciples may see the miracles you do. [4]No one who wants to become a public figure acts in secret. Since you are doing these things, show yourself to the world." [5]For even his own brothers did not believe in him.

[6]Therefore Jesus told them, "The right time for me has not yet come; for you any time is right. [7]The world cannot hate you, but it hates me because I testify that what it does is evil. [8]You go to the Feast. I am not yet[a] going up to this Feast, because for me the right time has not yet come." [9]Having said this, he stayed in Galilee.

[10]However, after his brothers had left for the Feast, he went also, not publicly, but in secret. [11]Now at the Feast the Jews were watching for him and asking, "Where is that man?"

[12]Among the crowds there was widespread whispering about him. Some said, "He is a good man."

Others replied, "No, he deceives the people." [13]But no one would say anything publicly about him for fear of the Jews.

[14]Not until halfway through the Feast did Jesus go up to the temple courts and begin to teach. [15]The Jews were amazed and asked, "How did this man get such learning without having studied?"

[16]Jesus answered, "My teaching is not my own. It comes from him who sent me. [17]If anyone chooses to do God's will, he will find out whether my teaching comes from God or whether I speak on my own. [18]He who speaks on his own does so to gain honor for himself, but he who works for the honor of the one who sent him is a man of truth; there is nothing false about him. [19]Has not Moses given you the law? Yet not one of you keeps the law. Why are you trying to kill me?"

[20]"You are demon-possessed," the crowd answered. "Who is trying to kill you?"

[21]Jesus said to them, "I did one miracle, and you are all astonished. [22]Yet, because Moses gave you circumcision (though actually it did not come from Moses, but from the patriarchs), you circumcise a child on the Sabbath. [23]Now if a child can be circumcised on the Sabbath so that the law of Moses may not be broken, why are you angry with me for healing the whole man on the Sabbath? [24]Stop judging by mere appearances, and make a right judgment."

[25]At that point some of the people of Jerusalem began to ask, "Isn't this the man they are trying to kill? [26]Here he is, speaking publicly, and they are not saying a word to him. Have the authorities really concluded that he is the Christ[b]? [27]But we know where this man is from; when the Christ comes, no one will know where he is from."

[28]Then Jesus, still teaching in the temple courts, cried out, "Yes, you know me, and you know where I am from. I

---

am not here on my own, but he who sent me is true. You do not know him, ²⁹ but I know him because I am from him and he sent me."

a8 Some early manuscripts do not have yet. b26 Or Messiah; also in verses 27, 31, 41 and 42

PSALM 108:1-13

A song. A psalm of David.

¹ **M**y heart is steadfast, O God;
  I will sing and make music with all my soul.
² Awake, harp and lyre!
  I will awaken the dawn.
³ I will praise you, O LORD, among the nations;
  I will sing of you among the peoples.
⁴ For great is your love, higher than the heavens;
  your faithfulness reaches to the skies.
⁵ Be exalted, O God, above the heavens,
  and let your glory be over all the earth.

⁶ Save us and help us with your right hand,
  that those you love may be delivered.
⁷ God has spoken from his sanctuary:
  "In triumph I will parcel out Shechem
  and measure off the Valley of Succoth.
⁸ Gilead is mine, Manasseh is mine;
  Ephraim is my helmet,
  Judah my scepter.
⁹ Moab is my washbasin,
  upon Edom I toss my sandal;
  over Philistia I shout in triumph."

¹⁰ Who will bring me to the fortified city?
  Who will lead me to Edom?
¹¹ Is it not you, O God, you who have rejected us
  and no longer go out with our armies?
¹² Give us aid against the enemy,
  for the help of man is worthless.
¹³ With God we will gain the victory,
  and he will trample down our enemies.

PROVERBS 15:4

⁴ The tongue that brings healing is a tree of life,
  but a deceitful tongue crushes the spirit.

□ DAY 133

GOD SIGHTINGS

May 13

1 SAMUEL 13:23–14:52

Now a detachment of Philistines had gone out to the pass at Micmash. ¹⁴:¹ One day Jonathan son of Saul said to the young man bearing his armor, "Come, let's go over to the Philistine outpost on the other side." But he did not tell his father.

² Saul was staying on the outskirts of Gibeah under a pomegranate tree in Migron. With him were about six hundred men, ³ among whom was Ahijah, who was wearing an ephod. He was a son of Ichabod's brother Ahitub son of Phinehas, the son of Eli, the LORD's priest in Shiloh. No one was aware that Jonathan had left.

⁴ On each side of the pass that Jonathan intended to cross to reach the Philistine outpost was a cliff; one was called Bozez, and the other Seneh. ⁵ One cliff stood to the north toward Micmash, the other to the south toward Geba.

⁶ Jonathan said to his young armor-bearer, "Come, let's go over to the outpost of those uncircumcised fellows. Perhaps the LORD will act in our behalf. Nothing can hinder the LORD from saving, whether by many or by few."

⁷ "Do all that you have in mind," his armor-bearer said. "Go ahead; I am with you heart and soul."

⁸ Jonathan said, "Come, then; we will cross over toward the men and let them see us. ⁹ If they say to us, 'Wait there until we come to you,' we will stay where

we are and not go up to them. 10But if they say, 'Come up to us,' we will climb up, because that will be our sign that the LORD has given them into our hands."

11So both of them showed themselves to the Philistine outpost. "Look!" said the Philistines. "The Hebrews are crawling out of the holes they were hiding in." 12The men of the outpost shouted to Jonathan and his armor-bearer, "Come up to us and we'll teach you a lesson."

So Jonathan said to his armor-bearer, "Climb up after me; the LORD has given them into the hand of Israel."

13Jonathan climbed up, using his hands and feet, with his armor-bearer right behind him. The Philistines fell before Jonathan, and his armor-bearer followed and killed behind him. 14In that first attack Jonathan and his armor-bearer killed some twenty men in an area of about half an acre.*a*

15Then panic struck the whole army—those in the camp and field, and those in the outposts and raiding parties—and the ground shook. It was a panic sent by God.*b*

16Saul's lookouts at Gibeah in Benjamin saw the army melting away in all directions. 17Then Saul said to the men who were with him, "Muster the forces and see who has left us." When they did, it was Jonathan and his armor-bearer who were not there.

18Saul said to Ahijah, "Bring the ark of God." (At that time it was with the Israelites.)*c* 19While Saul was talking to the priest, the tumult in the Philistine camp increased more and more. So Saul said to the priest, "Withdraw your hand."

20Then Saul and all his men assembled and went to the battle. They found the Philistines in total confusion, striking each other with their swords. 21Those Hebrews who had previously been with the Philistines and had gone up with them to their camp went over to the Israelites who were with Saul and Jonathan. 22When all the Israelites who had hidden in the hill country of Ephraim heard that the Philistines were on the run, they joined the battle in hot pursuit. 23So the LORD rescued Israel that day, and the battle moved on beyond Beth Aven.

24Now the men of Israel were in distress that day, because Saul had bound the people under an oath, saying, "Cursed be any man who eats food before evening comes, before I have avenged myself on my enemies!" So none of the troops tasted food.

25The entire army*d* entered the woods, and there was honey on the ground. 26When they went into the woods, they saw the honey oozing out, yet no one put his hand to his mouth, because they feared the oath. 27But Jonathan had not heard that his father had bound the people with the oath, so he reached out the end of the staff that was in his hand and dipped it into the honeycomb. He raised his hand to his mouth, and his eyes brightened.*e* 28Then one of the soldiers told him, "Your father bound the army under a strict oath, saying, 'Cursed be any man who eats food today!' That is why the men are faint."

29Jonathan said, "My father has made trouble for the country. See how my eyes brightened*f* when I tasted a little of this honey. 30How much better it would have been if the men had eaten today some of the plunder they took from their enemies. Would not the slaughter of the Philistines have been even greater?"

31That day, after the Israelites had struck down the Philistines from Micmash to Aijalon, they were exhausted. 32They pounced on the plunder and, taking sheep, cattle and calves, they butchered them on the ground and ate them, together with the blood. 33Then someone said to Saul, "Look, the men are sinning against the LORD by eating meat that has blood in it."

"You have broken faith," he said. "Roll a large stone over here at once." 34Then he said, "Go out among the men and tell them, 'Each of you bring me your cattle and sheep, and slaughter them here and eat them. Do not sin against the Lord by eating meat with blood still in it.'"

So everyone brought his ox that night and slaughtered it there. [35]Then Saul built an altar to the Lord; it was the first time he had done this.

[36]Saul said, "Let us go down after the Philistines by night and plunder them till dawn, and let us not leave one of them alive."

"Do whatever seems best to you," they replied.

But the priest said, "Let us inquire of God here."

[37]So Saul asked God, "Shall I go down after the Philistines? Will you give them into Israel's hand?" But God did not answer him that day.

[38]Saul therefore said, "Come here, all you who are leaders of the army, and let us find out what sin has been committed today. [39]As surely as the Lord who rescues Israel lives, even if it lies with my son Jonathan, he must die." But not one of the men said a word.

[40]Saul then said to all the Israelites, "You stand over there; I and Jonathan my son will stand over here."

"Do what seems best to you," the men replied.

[41]Then Saul prayed to the Lord, the God of Israel, "Give me the right answer."[g] And Jonathan and Saul were taken by lot, and the men were cleared. [42]Saul said, "Cast the lot between me and Jonathan my son." And Jonathan was taken.

[43]Then Saul said to Jonathan, "Tell me what you have done."

So Jonathan told him, "I merely tasted a little honey with the end of my staff. And now must I die?"

[44]Saul said, "May God deal with me, be it ever so severely, if you do not die, Jonathan."

[45]But the men said to Saul, "Should Jonathan die—he who has brought about this great deliverance in Israel? Never! As surely as the Lord lives, not a hair of his head will fall to the ground, for he did this today with God's help."

So the men rescued Jonathan, and he was not put to death.

[46]Then Saul stopped pursuing the Philistines, and they withdrew to their own land.

[47]After Saul had assumed rule over Israel, he fought against their enemies on every side: Moab, the Ammonites, Edom, the kings[h] of Zobah, and the Philistines. Wherever he turned, he inflicted punishment on them.[i] [48]He fought valiantly and defeated the Amalekites, delivering Israel from the hands of those who had plundered them.

[49]Saul's sons were Jonathan, Ishvi and Malki-Shua. The name of his older daughter was Merab, and that of the younger was Michal. [50]His wife's name was Ahinoam daughter of Ahimaaz. The name of the commander of Saul's army was Abner son of Ner, and Ner was Saul's uncle. [51]Saul's father Kish and Abner's father Ner were sons of Abiel.

[52]All the days of Saul there was bitter war with the Philistines, and whenever Saul saw a mighty or brave man, he took him into his service.

[a]14 Hebrew half a yoke; a "yoke" was the land plowed by a yoke of oxen in one day.   [b]15 Or a terrible panic   [c]18 Hebrew; Septuagint "Bring the ephod." (At that time he wore the ephod before the Israelites.)   [d]25 Or Now all the people of the land   [e]27 Or his strength was renewed   [f]29 Or my strength was renewed   [g]41 Hebrew; Septuagint "Why have you not answered your servant today? If the fault is in me or my son Jonathan, respond with Urim, but if the men of Israel are at fault, respond with Thummim."   [h]47 Masoretic Text; Dead Sea Scrolls and Septuagint king   [i]47 Hebrew; Septuagint he was victorious

JOHN 7:30-53

At this they [the people of Jerusalem] tried to seize him [Jesus], but no one laid a hand on him, because his time had not yet come. [31]Still, many in the crowd put their faith in him. They said, "When the Christ comes, will he do more miraculous signs than this man?"

[32]The Pharisees heard the crowd whispering such things about him. Then the chief priests and the Pharisees sent temple guards to arrest him.

[33]Jesus said, "I am with you for only a short time, and then I go to the one who sent me. [34]You will look for me, but you

will not find me; and where I am, you cannot come."

35 The Jews said to one another, "Where does this man intend to go that we cannot find him? Will he go where our people live scattered among the Greeks, and teach the Greeks? 36What did he mean when he said, 'You will look for me, but you will not find me,' and 'Where I am, you cannot come'?"

37 On the last and greatest day of the Feast, Jesus stood and said in a loud voice, "If anyone is thirsty, let him come to me and drink. 38Whoever believes in me, as*a* the Scripture has said, streams of living water will flow from within him." 39 By this he meant the Spirit, whom those who believed in him were later to receive. Up to that time the Spirit had not been given, since Jesus had not yet been glorified.

40On hearing his words, some of the people said, "Surely this man is the Prophet."

41Others said, "He is the Christ."

Still others asked, "How can the Christ come from Galilee? 42Does not the Scripture say that the Christ will come from David's family*b* and from Bethlehem, the town where David lived?" 43 Thus the people were divided because of Jesus. 44Some wanted to seize him, but no one laid a hand on him.

45Finally the temple guards went back to the chief priests and Pharisees, who asked them, "Why didn't you bring him in?"

46"No one ever spoke the way this man does," the guards declared.

47"You mean he has deceived you also?" the Pharisees retorted. 48"Has any of the rulers or of the Pharisees believed in him? 49No! But this mob that knows nothing of the law—there is a curse on them."

50Nicodemus, who had gone to Jesus earlier and who was one of their own number, asked, 51"Does our law condemn anyone without first hearing him to find out what he is doing?"

52 They replied, "Are you from Galilee, too? Look into it, and you will find that a prophet*c* does not come out of Galilee."

_____

[The earliest manuscripts and many other ancient witnesses do not have John 7:53-8:11.]

53 Then each went to his own home.

a37,38 Or / *If anyone is thirsty, let him come to me. / And let him drink,* *38who believes in me.* / As   *b42* Greek *seed*
c52 Two early manuscripts *the Prophet*

PSALM 109:1-31
For the director of music. Of David. A psalm.

1 ⬤ God, whom I praise,
    do not remain silent,
2 for wicked and deceitful men
    have opened their mouths
        against me;
    they have spoken against me with
        lying tongues.
3 With words of hatred they
        surround me;
    they attack me without cause.
4 In return for my friendship they
        accuse me,
    but I am a man of prayer.
5 They repay me evil for good,
    and hatred for my friendship.

6 Appoint*a* an evil man*b* to oppose
        him;
    let an accuser*c* stand at his right
        hand.
7 When he is tried, let him be found
        guilty,
    and may his prayers condemn
        him.
8 May his days be few;
    may another take his place of
        leadership.
9 May his children be fatherless
    and his wife a widow.
10 May his children be wandering
        beggars;
    may they be driven*d* from their
        ruined homes.
11 May a creditor seize all he has;
    may strangers plunder the fruits of
        his labor.

¹²May no one extend kindness to him
    or take pity on his fatherless
    children.
¹³May his descendants be cut off,
    their names blotted out from the
    next generation.
¹⁴May the iniquity of his fathers be
    remembered before the Lord;
    may the sin of his mother never
    be blotted out.
¹⁵May their sins always remain before
    the Lord,
    that he may cut off the memory of
    them from the earth.

¹⁶For he never thought of doing a
    kindness,
    but hounded to death the poor
    and the needy and the
    brokenhearted.
¹⁷He loved to pronounce a curse—
    may it^e come on him;
    he found no pleasure in blessing—
    may it be^f far from him.
¹⁸He wore cursing as his garment;
    it entered into his body like water,
    into his bones like oil.
¹⁹May it be like a cloak wrapped about
    him,
    like a belt tied forever around him.
²⁰May this be the Lord's payment to
    my accusers,
    to those who speak evil of me.

²¹But you, O Sovereign Lord,
    deal well with me for your name's
    sake;
    out of the goodness of your love,
    deliver me.
²²For I am poor and needy,
    and my heart is wounded
    within me.
²³I fade away like an evening shadow;
    I am shaken off like a locust.
²⁴My knees give way from fasting;
    my body is thin and gaunt.
²⁵I am an object of scorn to my accusers;
    when they see me, they shake their
    heads.

²⁶Help me, O Lord my God;
    save me in accordance with your
    love.

²⁷Let them know that it is your hand,
    that you, O Lord, have done it.
²⁸They may curse, but you will bless;
    when they attack they will be put
    to shame,
    but your servant will rejoice.
²⁹My accusers will be clothed with
    disgrace
    and wrapped in shame as in a
    cloak.

³⁰**With my mouth I will greatly extol
    the Lord;**
    **in the great throng I will praise
    him.**
³¹**For he stands at the right hand of
    the needy one,**
    **to save his life from those who
    condemn him.**

^a6 Or ⌊They say:⌋ "Appoint (with quotation marks at the
end of verse 19)   ^b6 Or the Evil One   ^c6 Or let Satan
^d10 Septuagint; Hebrew sought   ^e17 Or curse, / and it has
^f17 Or blessing, / and it is

PROVERBS 15:5-7

⁵**A** fool spurns his father's discipline,
    but whoever heeds correction
        shows prudence.

⁶The house of the righteous contains
        great treasure,
    but the income of the wicked
        brings them trouble.

⁷The lips of the wise spread
        knowledge;
    not so the hearts of fools.

☐ D A Y 1 3 4

GOD SIGHTINGS

May 14

1 SAMUEL 15:1–16:23
Samuel said to Saul, "I am the one the
Lord sent to anoint you king over his
people Israel; so listen now to the mes-
sage from the Lord. ²This is what the
Lord Almighty says: 'I will punish the
Amalekites for what they did to Israel
when they waylaid them as they came

up from Egypt. ³Now go, attack the Amalekites and totally destroy^a everything that belongs to them. Do not spare them; put to death men and women, children and infants, cattle and sheep, camels and donkeys.'"

⁴So Saul summoned the men and mustered them at Telaim—two hundred thousand foot soldiers and ten thousand men from Judah. ⁵Saul went to the city of Amalek and set an ambush in the ravine. ⁶Then he said to the Kenites, "Go away, leave the Amalekites so that I do not destroy you along with them; for you showed kindness to all the Israelites when they came up out of Egypt." So the Kenites moved away from the Amalekites.

⁷Then Saul attacked the Amalekites all the way from Havilah to Shur, to the east of Egypt. ⁸He took Agag king of the Amalekites alive, and all his people he totally destroyed with the sword. ⁹But Saul and the army spared Agag and the best of the sheep and cattle, the fat calves^b and lambs—everything that was good. These they were unwilling to destroy completely, but everything that was despised and weak they totally destroyed.

¹⁰Then the word of the LORD came to Samuel: ¹¹"I am grieved that I have made Saul king, because he has turned away from me and has not carried out my instructions." Samuel was troubled, and he cried out to the LORD all that night.

¹²Early in the morning Samuel got up and went to meet Saul, but he was told, "Saul has gone to Carmel. There he has set up a monument in his own honor and has turned and gone on down to Gilgal."

¹³When Samuel reached him, Saul said, "The LORD bless you! I have carried out the LORD's instructions."

¹⁴But Samuel said, "What then is this bleating of sheep in my ears? What is this lowing of cattle that I hear?"

¹⁵Saul answered, "The soldiers brought them from the Amalekites; they spared the best of the sheep and cattle to sacrifice to the LORD your God, but we totally destroyed the rest."

¹⁶"Stop!" Samuel said to Saul. "Let me tell you what the LORD said to me last night."

"Tell me," Saul replied.

¹⁷Samuel said, "Although you were once small in your own eyes, did you not become the head of the tribes of Israel? The LORD anointed you king over Israel. ¹⁸And he sent you on a mission, saying, 'Go and completely destroy those wicked people, the Amalekites; make war on them until you have wiped them out.' ¹⁹Why did you not obey the LORD? Why did you pounce on the plunder and do evil in the eyes of the LORD?"

²⁰"But I did obey the LORD," Saul said. "I went on the mission the LORD assigned me. I completely destroyed the Amalekites and brought back Agag their king. ²¹The soldiers took sheep and cattle from the plunder, the best of what was devoted to God, in order to sacrifice them to the LORD your God at Gilgal."

²²But Samuel replied:

"Does the LORD delight in burnt
    offerings and sacrifices
  as much as in obeying the voice
    of the LORD?
To obey is better than sacrifice,
  and to heed is better than the fat
    of rams.
²³For rebellion is like the sin of
    divination,
  and arrogance like the evil of
    idolatry.
Because you have rejected the word
    of the LORD,
  he has rejected you as king."

²⁴Then Saul said to Samuel, "I have sinned. I violated the LORD's command and your instructions. I was afraid of the people and so I gave in to them. ²⁵Now I beg you, forgive my sin and come back with me, so that I may worship the LORD."

²⁶But Samuel said to him, "I will not go back with you. You have rejected the

word of the Lord, and the Lord has rejected you as king over Israel!"

27As Samuel turned to leave, Saul caught hold of the hem of his robe, and it tore. 28Samuel said to him, "The Lord has torn the kingdom of Israel from you today and has given it to one of your neighbors—to one better than you. 29He who is the Glory of Israel does not lie or change his mind; for he is not a man, that he should change his mind."

30Saul replied, "I have sinned. But please honor me before the elders of my people and before Israel; come back with me, so that I may worship the Lord your God." 31So Samuel went back with Saul, and Saul worshiped the Lord.

32Then Samuel said, "Bring me Agag king of the Amalekites."

Agag came to him confidently,c thinking, "Surely the bitterness of death is past."

33But Samuel said,

"As your sword has made women childless,
    so will your mother be childless among women."

And Samuel put Agag to death before the Lord at Gilgal.

34Then Samuel left for Ramah, but Saul went up to his home in Gibeah of Saul. 35Until the day Samuel died, he did not go to see Saul again, though Samuel mourned for him. And the Lord was grieved that he had made Saul king over Israel.

16:1The Lord said to Samuel, "How long will you mourn for Saul, since I have rejected him as king over Israel? Fill your horn with oil and be on your way; I am sending you to Jesse of Bethlehem. I have chosen one of his sons to be king."

2But Samuel said, "How can I go? Saul will hear about it and kill me."

The Lord said, "Take a heifer with you and say, 'I have come to sacrifice to the Lord.' 3Invite Jesse to the sacrifice, and I will show you what to do. You are to anoint for me the one I indicate."

4Samuel did what the Lord said.

When he arrived at Bethlehem, the elders of the town trembled when they met him. They asked, "Do you come in peace?"

5Samuel replied, "Yes, in peace; I have come to sacrifice to the Lord. Consecrate yourselves and come to the sacrifice with me." Then he consecrated Jesse and his sons and invited them to the sacrifice.

6When they arrived, Samuel saw Eliab and thought, "Surely the Lord's anointed stands here before the Lord."

7But the Lord said to Samuel, "Do not consider his appearance or his height, for I have rejected him. The Lord does not look at the things man looks at. Man looks at the outward appearance, but the Lord looks at the heart."

8Then Jesse called Abinadab and had him pass in front of Samuel. But Samuel said, "The Lord has not chosen this one either." 9Jesse then had Shammah pass by, but Samuel said, "Nor has the Lord chosen this one." 10Jesse had seven of his sons pass before Samuel, but Samuel said to him, "The Lord has not chosen these." 11So he asked Jesse, "Are these all the sons you have?"

"There is still the youngest," Jesse answered, "but he is tending the sheep."

Samuel said, "Send for him; we will not sit downd until he arrives."

12So he sent and had him brought in. He was ruddy, with a fine appearance and handsome features.

Then the Lord said, "Rise and anoint him; he is the one."

13So Samuel took the horn of oil and anointed him in the presence of his brothers, and from that day on the Spirit of the Lord came upon David in power. Samuel then went to Ramah.

14Now the Spirit of the Lord had departed from Saul, and an evile spirit from the Lord tormented him.

15Saul's attendants said to him, "See, an evil spirit from God is tormenting you. 16Let our lord command his servants here to search for someone who can play the harp. He will play when the evil spirit from God comes upon you, and you will feel better."

¹⁷So Saul said to his attendants, "Find someone who plays well and bring him to me."

¹⁸One of the servants answered, "I have seen a son of Jesse of Bethlehem who knows how to play the harp. He is a brave man and a warrior. He speaks well and is a fine-looking man. And the LORD is with him."

¹⁹Then Saul sent messengers to Jesse and said, "Send me your son David, who is with the sheep." ²⁰So Jesse took a donkey loaded with bread, a skin of wine and a young goat and sent them with his son David to Saul.

²¹David came to Saul and entered his service. Saul liked him very much, and David became one of his armor-bearers. ²²Then Saul sent word to Jesse, saying, "Allow David to remain in my service, for I am pleased with him."

²³Whenever the spirit from God came upon Saul, David would take his harp and play. Then relief would come to Saul; he would feel better, and the evil spirit would leave him.

^a3 The Hebrew term refers to the irrevocable giving over of things or persons to the LORD, often by totally destroying them; also in verses 8, 9, 15, 18, 20 and 21. ^b9 Or *the grown bulls*; the meaning of the Hebrew for this phrase is uncertain. ^c32 Or *him trembling, yet* ^d11 Some Septuagint manuscripts; Hebrew *not gather around* ^e14 Or *injurious*; also in verses 15, 16 and 23

JOHN 8:1-20

But Jesus went to the Mount of Olives. ²At dawn he appeared again in the temple courts, where all the people gathered around him, and he sat down to teach them. ³The teachers of the law and the Pharisees brought in a woman caught in adultery. They made her stand before the group ⁴and said to Jesus, "Teacher, this woman was caught in the act of adultery. ⁵In the Law Moses commanded us to stone such women. Now what do you say?" ⁶They were using this question as a trap, in order to have a basis for accusing him.

But Jesus bent down and started to write on the ground with his finger. ⁷When they kept on questioning him, he straightened up and said to them, "If any one of you is without sin, let him be the first to throw a stone at her." ⁸Again he stooped down and wrote on the ground.

⁹At this, those who heard began to go away one at a time, the older ones first, until only Jesus was left, with the woman still standing there. ¹⁰Jesus straightened up and asked her, "Woman, where are they? Has no one condemned you?"

¹¹"No one, sir," she said.

"Then neither do I condemn you," Jesus declared. "Go now and leave your life of sin."

---

¹²**When Jesus spoke again to the people, he said, "I am the light of the world. Whoever follows me will never walk in darkness, but will have the light of life."**

¹³The Pharisees challenged him, "Here you are, appearing as your own witness; your testimony is not valid."

¹⁴Jesus answered, "Even if I testify on my own behalf, my testimony is valid, for I know where I came from and where I am going. But you have no idea where I come from or where I am going. ¹⁵You judge by human standards; I pass judgment on no one. ¹⁶But if I do judge, my decisions are right, because I am not alone. I stand with the Father, who sent me. ¹⁷In your own Law it is written that the testimony of two men is valid. ¹⁸I am one who testifies for myself; my other witness is the Father, who sent me."

¹⁹Then they asked him, "Where is your father?"

"You do not know me or my Father," Jesus replied. "If you knew me, you would know my Father also." ²⁰He spoke these words while teaching in the temple area near the place where the offerings were put. Yet no one seized him, because his time had not yet come.

PSALM 110:1-7

Of David. A psalm.

¹**T**he LORD says to my Lord:
    "Sit at my right hand

until I make your enemies
    a footstool for your feet."

² The Lord will extend your mighty
        scepter from Zion;
    you will rule in the midst of your
        enemies.
³ Your troops will be willing
    on your day of battle.
  Arrayed in holy majesty,
    from the womb of the dawn
    you will receive the dew of your
        youth.ᵃ

⁴ The Lord has sworn
    and will not change his mind:
  "You are a priest forever,
    in the order of Melchizedek."

⁵ The Lord is at your right hand;
    he will crush kings on the day of
        his wrath.
⁶ He will judge the nations, heaping
        up the dead
    and crushing the rulers of the
        whole earth.
⁷ He will drink from a brook beside
        the wayᵇ;
    therefore he will lift up his head.

ᵃ 3 Or / your young men will come to you like the dew
ᵇ 7 Or / The One who grants succession will set him in
authority

PROVERBS 15:8-10

⁸ The Lord detests the sacrifice of the
        wicked,
    but the prayer of the upright
        pleases him.

⁹ The Lord detests the way of the
        wicked
    but he loves those who pursue
        righteousness.

¹⁰ Stern discipline awaits him who
        leaves the path;
    he who hates correction will die.

□ D A Y 1 3 5

GOD SIGHTINGS

May 15

1 SAMUEL 17:1–18:4

Now the Philistines gathered their forces for war and assembled at Socoh in Judah. They pitched camp at Ephes Dammim, between Socoh and Azekah. ² Saul and the Israelites assembled and camped in the Valley of Elah and drew up their battle line to meet the Philistines. ³ The Philistines occupied one hill and the Israelites another, with the valley between them.

⁴ A champion named Goliath, who was from Gath, came out of the Philistine camp. He was over nine feetᵃ tall. ⁵ He had a bronze helmet on his head and wore a coat of scale armor of bronze weighing five thousand shekelsᵇ; ⁶ on his legs he wore bronze greaves, and a bronze javelin was slung on his back. ⁷ His spear shaft was like a weaver's rod, and its iron point weighed six hundred shekels.ᶜ His shield bearer went ahead of him.

⁸ Goliath stood and shouted to the ranks of Israel, "Why do you come out and line up for battle? Am I not a Philistine, and are you not the servants of Saul? Choose a man and have him come down to me. ⁹ If he is able to fight and kill me, we will become your subjects; but if I overcome him and kill him, you will become our subjects and serve us." ¹⁰ Then the Philistine said, "This day I defy the ranks of Israel! Give me a man and let us fight each other." ¹¹ On hearing the Philistine's words, Saul and all the Israelites were dismayed and terrified.

¹² Now David was the son of an Ephrathite named Jesse, who was from Bethlehem in Judah. Jesse had eight sons, and in Saul's time he was old and well advanced in years. ¹³ Jesse's three oldest sons had followed Saul to the war: The firstborn was Eliab; the second, Abinadab; and the third, Shammah.

14David was the youngest. The three oldest followed Saul, 15but David went back and forth from Saul to tend his father's sheep at Bethlehem.

16For forty days the Philistine came forward every morning and evening and took his stand.

17Now Jesse said to his son David, "Take this ephah*d* of roasted grain and these ten loaves of bread for your brothers and hurry to their camp. 18Take along these ten cheeses to the commander of their unit.*e* See how your brothers are and bring back some assurance*f* from them. 19They are with Saul and all the men of Israel in the Valley of Elah, fighting against the Philistines."

20Early in the morning David left the flock with a shepherd, loaded up and set out, as Jesse had directed. He reached the camp as the army was going out to its battle positions, shouting the war cry. 21Israel and the Philistines were drawing up their lines facing each other. 22David left his things with the keeper of supplies, ran to the battle lines and greeted his brothers. 23As he was talking with them, Goliath, the Philistine champion from Gath, stepped out from his lines and shouted his usual defiance, and David heard it. 24When the Israelites saw the man, they all ran from him in great fear.

25Now the Israelites had been saying, "Do you see how this man keeps coming out? He comes out to defy Israel. The king will give great wealth to the man who kills him. He will also give him his daughter in marriage and will exempt his father's family from taxes in Israel."

26David asked the men standing near him, "What will be done for the man who kills this Philistine and removes this disgrace from Israel? Who is this uncircumcised Philistine that he should defy the armies of the living God?"

27They repeated to him what they had been saying and told him, "This is what will be done for the man who kills him."

28When Eliab, David's oldest brother, heard him speaking with the men, he burned with anger at him and asked, "Why have you come down here? And with whom did you leave those few sheep in the desert? I know how conceited you are and how wicked your heart is; you came down only to watch the battle."

29"Now what have I done?" said David. "Can't I even speak?" 30He then turned away to someone else and brought up the same matter, and the men answered him as before. 31What David said was overheard and reported to Saul, and Saul sent for him.

32David said to Saul, "Let no one lose heart on account of this Philistine; your servant will go and fight him."

33Saul replied, "You are not able to go out against this Philistine and fight him; you are only a boy, and he has been a fighting man from his youth."

34But David said to Saul, "Your servant has been keeping his father's sheep. When a lion or a bear came and carried off a sheep from the flock, 35I went after it, struck it and rescued the sheep from its mouth. When it turned on me, I seized it by its hair, struck it and killed it. 36Your servant has killed both the lion and the bear; this uncircumcised Philistine will be like one of them, because he has defied the armies of the living God. 37The Lord who delivered me from the paw of the lion and the paw of the bear will deliver me from the hand of this Philistine."

Saul said to David, "Go, and the Lord be with you."

38Then Saul dressed David in his own tunic. He put a coat of armor on him and a bronze helmet on his head. 39David fastened on his sword over the tunic and tried walking around, because he was not used to them.

"I cannot go in these," he said to Saul, "because I am not used to them." So he took them off. 40Then he took his staff in his hand, chose five smooth stones from the stream, put them in the pouch of his shepherd's bag and, with his sling in his hand, approached the Philistine.

41Meanwhile, the Philistine, with his

shield bearer in front of him, kept coming closer to David. ⁴²He looked David over and saw that he was only a boy, ruddy and handsome, and he despised him. ⁴³He said to David, "Am I a dog, that you come at me with sticks?" And the Philistine cursed David by his gods. ⁴⁴"Come here," he said, "and I'll give your flesh to the birds of the air and the beasts of the field!"

⁴⁵David said to the Philistine, "You come against me with sword and spear and javelin, but I come against you in the name of the LORD Almighty, the God of the armies of Israel, whom you have defied. ⁴⁶This day the LORD will hand you over to me, and I'll strike you down and cut off your head. Today I will give the carcasses of the Philistine army to the birds of the air and the beasts of the earth, and the whole world will know that there is a God in Israel. ⁴⁷All those gathered here will know that it is not by sword or spear that the LORD saves; for the battle is the LORD's, and he will give all of you into our hands."

⁴⁸As the Philistine moved closer to attack him, David ran quickly toward the battle line to meet him. ⁴⁹Reaching into his bag and taking out a stone, he slung it and struck the Philistine on the forehead. The stone sank into his forehead, and he fell facedown on the ground.

⁵⁰So David triumphed over the Philistine with a sling and a stone; without a sword in his hand he struck down the Philistine and killed him.

⁵¹David ran and stood over him. He took hold of the Philistine's sword and drew it from the scabbard. After he killed him, he cut off his head with the sword.

When the Philistines saw that their hero was dead, they turned and ran. ⁵²Then the men of Israel and Judah surged forward with a shout and pursued the Philistines to the entrance of Gath*g* and to the gates of Ekron. Their dead were strewn along the Shaaraim road to Gath and Ekron. ⁵³When the Israelites returned from chasing the Phi-

listines, they plundered their camp. ⁵⁴David took the Philistine's head and brought it to Jerusalem, and he put the Philistine's weapons in his own tent.

⁵⁵As Saul watched David going out to meet the Philistine, he said to Abner, commander of the army, "Abner, whose son is that young man?"

Abner replied, "As surely as you live, O king, I don't know."

⁵⁶The king said, "Find out whose son this young man is."

⁵⁷As soon as David returned from killing the Philistine, Abner took him and brought him before Saul, with David still holding the Philistine's head.

⁵⁸"Whose son are you, young man?" Saul asked him.

David said, "I am the son of your servant Jesse of Bethlehem."

¹⁸:¹AFTER David had finished talking with Saul, Jonathan became one in spirit with David, and he loved him as himself. ²From that day Saul kept David with him and did not let him return to his father's house. ³**And Jonathan made a covenant with David because he loved him as himself.** ⁴**Jonathan took off the robe he was wearing and gave it to David, along with his tunic, and even his sword, his bow and his belt.**

a4 Hebrew *was six cubits and a span* (about 3 meters)
b5 That is, about 125 pounds (about 57 kilograms)
c7 That is, about 15 pounds (about 7 kilograms)   *d17* That is, probably about 3/5 bushel (about 22 liters)   *e18* Hebrew *thousand*   *f18* Or *some token; or some pledge of spoils*
g52 Some Septuagint manuscripts; Hebrew *a valley*

JOHN 8:21-30

Once more Jesus said to them [the Jews], "I am going away, and you will look for me, and you will die in your sin. Where I go, you cannot come."

²²This made the Jews ask, "Will he kill himself? Is that why he says, 'Where I go, you cannot come'?"

²³But he continued, "You are from below; I am from above. You are of this world; I am not of this world. ²⁴I told you that you would die in your sins; if you do not believe that I am ˎthe one I

claim to be,*a* you will indeed die in your sins."

25 "Who are you?" they asked.

"Just what I have been claiming all along," Jesus replied. 26 "I have much to say in judgment of you. But he who sent me is reliable, and what I have heard from him I tell the world."

27 They did not understand that he was telling them about his Father. 28 So Jesus said, "When you have lifted up the Son of Man, then you will know that I am ⌊the one I claim to be⌋ and that I do nothing on my own but speak just what the Father has taught me. 29 The one who sent me is with me; he has not left me alone, for I always do what pleases him." 30 Even as he spoke, many put their faith in him.

a24 Or I am he; also in verse 28

PSALM 111:1-10*a*

1 **P**raise the LORD.*b*

I will extol the LORD with all my heart
　　in the council of the upright and
　　in the assembly.

2 Great are the works of the LORD;
　　they are pondered by all who
　　delight in them.
3 Glorious and majestic are his deeds,
　　and his righteousness endures
　　forever.
4 He has caused his wonders to be
　　remembered;
　　the LORD is gracious and
　　compassionate.
5 He provides food for those who fear
　　him;
　　he remembers his covenant
　　forever.
6 He has shown his people the power
　　of his works,
　　giving them the lands of other
　　nations.
7 The works of his hands are faithful
　　and just;
　　all his precepts are trustworthy.
8 They are steadfast for ever and ever,
　　done in faithfulness and
　　uprightness.

9 He provided redemption for his
　　people;
　　he ordained his covenant
　　forever—
　　holy and awesome is his name.

10 The fear of the LORD is the beginning
　　of wisdom;
　　all who follow his precepts have
　　good understanding.
　　To him belongs eternal praise.

aThis psalm is an acrostic poem, the lines of which begin with the successive letters of the Hebrew alphabet.
b1 Hebrew Hallelu Yah

PROVERBS 15:11

11 **D**eath and Destruction*a* lie open
　　before the LORD—
　　how much more the hearts of
　　men!

a11 Hebrew Sheol and Abaddon

□ DAY 136

GOD SIGHTINGS

May 16

1 SAMUEL 18:5-19:24

Whatever Saul sent him to do, David did it so successfully*a* that Saul gave him a high rank in the army. This pleased all the people, and Saul's officers as well.

6 When the men were returning home after David had killed the Philistine, the women came out from all the towns of Israel to meet King Saul with singing and dancing, with joyful songs and with tambourines and lutes. 7 As they danced, they sang:

"Saul has slain his thousands,
　　and David his tens of thousands."

8 Saul was very angry; this refrain galled him. "They have credited David with tens of thousands," he thought, "but me with only thousands. What more can he get but the kingdom?"

⁹And from that time on Saul kept a jealous eye on David.

¹⁰The next day an evil*ᵇ* spirit from God came forcefully upon Saul. He was prophesying in his house, while David was playing the harp, as he usually did. Saul had a spear in his hand ¹¹and he hurled it, saying to himself, "I'll pin David to the wall." But David eluded him twice.

¹²Saul was afraid of David, because the Lᴏʀᴅ was with David but had left Saul. ¹³So he sent David away from him and gave him command over a thousand men, and David led the troops in their campaigns. ¹⁴In everything he did he had great success,*ᶜ* because the Lᴏʀᴅ was with him. ¹⁵When Saul saw how successful*ᵈ* he was, he was afraid of him. ¹⁶But all Israel and Judah loved David, because he led them in their campaigns.

¹⁷Saul said to David, "Here is my older daughter Merab. I will give her to you in marriage; only serve me bravely and fight the battles of the Lᴏʀᴅ." For Saul said to himself, "I will not raise a hand against him. Let the Philistines do that!"

¹⁸But David said to Saul, "Who am I, and what is my family or my father's clan in Israel, that I should become the king's son-in-law?" ¹⁹So*ᵉ* when the time came for Merab, Saul's daughter, to be given to David, she was given in marriage to Adriel of Meholah.

²⁰Now Saul's daughter Michal was in love with David, and when they told Saul about it, he was pleased. ²¹"I will give her to him," he thought, "so that she may be a snare to him and so that the hand of the Philistines may be against him." So Saul said to David, "Now you have a second opportunity to become my son-in-law."

²²Then Saul ordered his attendants: "Speak to David privately and say, 'Look, the king is pleased with you, and his attendants all like you; now become his son-in-law.'"

²³They repeated these words to David. But David said, "Do you think it is a small matter to become the king's son-in-law? I'm only a poor man and little known."

²⁴When Saul's servants told him what David had said, ²⁵Saul replied, "Say to David, 'The king wants no other price for the bride than a hundred Philistine foreskins, to take revenge on his enemies.'" Saul's plan was to have David fall by the hands of the Philistines.

²⁶When the attendants told David these things, he was pleased to become the king's son-in-law. So before the allotted time elapsed, ²⁷David and his men went out and killed two hundred Philistines. He brought their foreskins and presented the full number to the king so that he might become the king's son-in-law. Then Saul gave him his daughter Michal in marriage.

²⁸When Saul realized that the Lᴏʀᴅ was with David and that his daughter Michal loved David, ²⁹Saul became still more afraid of him, and he remained his enemy the rest of his days.

³⁰The Philistine commanders continued to go out to battle, and as often as they did, David met with more success*ᶠ* than the rest of Saul's officers, and his name became well known.

19:1Sᴀᴜʟ told his son Jonathan and all the attendants to kill David. But Jonathan was very fond of David ²and warned him, "My father Saul is looking for a chance to kill you. Be on your guard tomorrow morning; go into hiding and stay there. ³I will go out and stand with my father in the field where you are. I'll speak to him about you and will tell you what I find out."

⁴Jonathan spoke well of David to Saul his father and said to him, "Let not the king do wrong to his servant David; he has not wronged you, and what he has done has benefited you greatly. ⁵He took his life in his hands when he killed the Philistine. The Lᴏʀᴅ won a great victory for all Israel, and you saw it and were glad. Why then would you do wrong to an innocent man like David by killing him for no reason?"

6Saul listened to Jonathan and took this oath: "As surely as the LORD lives, David will not be put to death."

7So Jonathan called David and told him the whole conversation. He brought him to Saul, and David was with Saul as before.

8Once more war broke out, and David went out and fought the Philistines. He struck them with such force that they fled before him.

9But an evil*b* spirit from the LORD came upon Saul as he was sitting in his house with his spear in his hand. While David was playing the harp, 10Saul tried to pin him to the wall with his spear, but David eluded him as Saul drove the spear into the wall. That night David made good his escape.

11Saul sent men to David's house to watch it and to kill him in the morning. But Michal, David's wife, warned him, "If you don't run for your life tonight, tomorrow you'll be killed." 12So Michal let David down through a window, and he fled and escaped. 13Then Michal took an idol*g* and laid it on the bed, covering it with a garment and putting some goats' hair at the head.

14When Saul sent the men to capture David, Michal said, "He is ill."

15Then Saul sent the men back to see David and told them, "Bring him up to me in his bed so that I may kill him." 16But when the men entered, there was the idol in the bed, and at the head was some goats' hair.

17Saul said to Michal, "Why did you deceive me like this and send my enemy away so that he escaped?"

Michal told him, "He said to me, 'Let me get away. Why should I kill you?'"

18When David had fled and made his escape, he went to Samuel at Ramah and told him all that Saul had done to him. Then he and Samuel went to Naioth and stayed there. 19Word came to Saul: "David is in Naioth at Ramah"; 20so he sent men to capture him. But when they saw a group of prophets prophesying, with Samuel standing there as their leader, the Spirit of God came upon Saul's men and they also prophesied. 21Saul was told about it, and he sent more men, and they prophesied too. Saul sent men a third time, and they also prophesied. 22Finally, he himself left for Ramah and went to the great cistern at Secu. And he asked, "Where are Samuel and David?"

"Over in Naioth at Ramah," they said.

23So Saul went to Naioth at Ramah. But the Spirit of God came even upon him, and he walked along prophesying until he came to Naioth. 24He stripped off his robes and also prophesied in Samuel's presence. He lay that way all that day and night. This is why people say, "Is Saul also among the prophets?"

a5 Or wisely   b10,9 Or injurious   c14 Or he was very wise   d15 Or wise   e19 Or However,   f30 Or David acted more wisely   g13 Hebrew teraphim; also in verse 16

JOHN 8:31-59

To the Jews who had believed him, Jesus said, "If you hold to my teaching, you are really my disciples. 32Then you will know the truth, and the truth will set you free."

33They answered him, "We are Abraham's descendants*a* and have never been slaves of anyone. How can you say that we shall be set free?"

34**Jesus replied, "I tell you the truth, everyone who sins is a slave to sin.** 35**Now a slave has no permanent place in the family, but a son belongs to it forever.** 36**So if the Son sets you free, you will be free indeed.** 37I know you are Abraham's descendants. Yet you are ready to kill me, because you have no room for my word. 38I am telling you what I have seen in the Father's presence, and you do what you have heard from your father.*b*"

39"Abraham is our father," they answered.

"If you were Abraham's children," said Jesus, "then you would*c* do the things Abraham did. 40As it is, you are determined to kill me, a man who has told you the truth that I heard from God. Abraham did not do such things.

⁴¹You are doing the things your own father does."

"We are not illegitimate children," they protested. "The only Father we have is God himself."

⁴²Jesus said to them, "If God were your Father, you would love me, for I came from God and now am here. I have not come on my own; but he sent me. ⁴³Why is my language not clear to you? Because you are unable to hear what I say. ⁴⁴You belong to your father, the devil, and you want to carry out your father's desire. He was a murderer from the beginning, not holding to the truth, for there is no truth in him. When he lies, he speaks his native language, for he is a liar and the father of lies. ⁴⁵Yet because I tell the truth, you do not believe me! ⁴⁶Can any of you prove me guilty of sin? If I am telling the truth, why don't you believe me? ⁴⁷He who belongs to God hears what God says. The reason you do not hear is that you do not belong to God."

⁴⁸The Jews answered him, "Aren't we right in saying that you are a Samaritan and demon-possessed?"

⁴⁹"I am not possessed by a demon," said Jesus, "but I honor my Father and you dishonor me. ⁵⁰I am not seeking glory for myself; but there is one who seeks it, and he is the judge. ⁵¹I tell you the truth, if anyone keeps my word, he will never see death."

⁵²At this the Jews exclaimed, "Now we know that you are demon-possessed! Abraham died and so did the prophets, yet you say that if anyone keeps your word, he will never taste death. ⁵³Are you greater than our father Abraham? He died, and so did the prophets. Who do you think you are?"

⁵⁴Jesus replied, "If I glorify myself, my glory means nothing. My Father, whom you claim as your God, is the one who glorifies me. ⁵⁵Though you do not know him, I know him. If I said I did not, I would be a liar like you, but I do know him and keep his word. ⁵⁶Your father Abraham rejoiced at the thought of seeing my day; he saw it and was glad."

⁵⁷"You are not yet fifty years old," the Jews said to him, "and you have seen Abraham!"

⁵⁸"I tell you the truth," Jesus answered, "before Abraham was born, I am!" ⁵⁹At this, they picked up stones to stone him, but Jesus hid himself, slipping away from the temple grounds.

a33 Greek *seed*; also in verse 37   *b38* Or *presence. Therefore do what you have heard from the Father.*   *c39* Some early manuscripts *"If you are Abraham's children," said Jesus, "then*

PSALM 112:1-10*a*

¹ **P**raise the LORD.*b*

Blessed is the man who fears the
　　LORD,
　　who finds great delight in his
　　　　commands.

²His children will be mighty in the
　　land;
　　the generation of the upright will
　　　　be blessed.

³Wealth and riches are in his house,
　　and his righteousness endures
　　　　forever.

⁴Even in darkness light dawns for the
　　upright,
　　for the gracious and
　　　　compassionate and righteous
　　　　man.*c*

⁵Good will come to him who is
　　generous and lends freely,
　　who conducts his affairs with
　　　　justice.

⁶Surely he will never be shaken;
　　a righteous man will be
　　　　remembered forever.

⁷He will have no fear of bad news;
　　his heart is steadfast, trusting in
　　　　the LORD.

⁸His heart is secure, he will have no
　　fear;
　　in the end he will look in triumph
　　　　on his foes.

⁹He has scattered abroad his gifts to
　　the poor,
　　his righteousness endures
　　　　forever;
　　his horn*d* will be lifted high in
　　　　honor.

10 The wicked man will see and be
　　vexed,
　　he will gnash his teeth and waste
　　　away;
　　the longings of the wicked will
　　　come to nothing.

*a This psalm is an acrostic poem, the lines of which begin
with the successive letters of the Hebrew alphabet.
b 1 Hebrew Hallelu Yah　c 4 Or / for ⌊the Lord⌋ is gracious
and compassionate and righteous　d 9 Horn here
symbolizes dignity.*

PROVERBS 15:12-14

12 A mocker resents correction;
　　he will not consult the wise.

13 A happy heart makes the face
　　cheerful,
　　but heartache crushes the spirit.

14 The discerning heart seeks
　　knowledge,
　　but the mouth of a fool feeds
　　　on folly.

□ DAY 137

GOD SIGHTINGS

May 17

1 SAMUEL 20:1–21:15

Then David fled from Naioth at Ramah and went to Jonathan and asked, "What have I done? What is my crime? How have I wronged your father, that he is trying to take my life?"

2 "Never!" Jonathan replied. "You are not going to die! Look, my father doesn't do anything, great or small, without confiding in me. Why would he hide this from me? It's not so!"

3 But David took an oath and said, "Your father knows very well that I have found favor in your eyes, and he has said to himself, 'Jonathan must not know this or he will be grieved.' Yet as surely as the Lord lives and as you live, there is only a step between me and death."

4 Jonathan said to David, "Whatever you want me to do, I'll do for you."

5 So David said, "Look, tomorrow is the New Moon festival, and I am supposed to dine with the king; but let me go and hide in the field until the evening of the day after tomorrow. 6 If your father misses me at all, tell him, 'David earnestly asked my permission to hurry to Bethlehem, his hometown, because an annual sacrifice is being made there for his whole clan.' 7 If he says, 'Very well,' then your servant is safe. But if he loses his temper, you can be sure that he is determined to harm me. 8 As for you, show kindness to your servant, for you have brought him into a covenant with you before the Lord. If I am guilty, then kill me yourself! Why hand me over to your father?"

9 "Never!" Jonathan said. "If I had the least inkling that my father was determined to harm you, wouldn't I tell you?"

10 David asked, "Who will tell me if your father answers you harshly?"

11 "Come," Jonathan said, "let's go out into the field." So they went there together.

12 Then Jonathan said to David: "By the Lord, the God of Israel, I will surely sound out my father by this time the day after tomorrow! If he is favorably disposed toward you, will I not send you word and let you know? 13 But if my father is inclined to harm you, may the Lord deal with me, be it ever so severely, if I do not let you know and send you away safely. May the Lord be with you as he has been with my father. 14 But show me unfailing kindness like that of the Lord as long as I live, so that I may not be killed, 15 and do not ever cut off your kindness from my family—not even when the Lord has cut off every one of David's enemies from the face of the earth."

16 So Jonathan made a covenant with the house of David, saying, "May the Lord call David's enemies to account." 17 And Jonathan had David reaffirm his oath out of love for him, because he loved him as he loved himself.

18 Then Jonathan said to David: "Tomorrow is the New Moon festival. You

will be missed, because your seat will be empty. ¹⁹The day after tomorrow, toward evening, go to the place where you hid when this trouble began, and wait by the stone Ezel. ²⁰I will shoot three arrows to the side of it, as though I were shooting at a target. ²¹Then I will send a boy and say, 'Go, find the arrows.' If I say to him, 'Look, the arrows are on this side of you; bring them here,' then come, because, as surely as the LORD lives, you are safe; there is no danger. ²²But if I say to the boy, 'Look, the arrows are beyond you,' then you must go, because the LORD has sent you away. ²³And about the matter you and I discussed—remember, the LORD is witness between you and me forever."

²⁴So David hid in the field, and when the New Moon festival came, the king sat down to eat. ²⁵He sat in his customary place by the wall, opposite Jonathan,ᵃ and Abner sat next to Saul, but David's place was empty. ²⁶Saul said nothing that day, for he thought, "Something must have happened to David to make him ceremonially unclean—surely he is unclean." ²⁷But the next day, the second day of the month, David's place was empty again. Then Saul said to his son Jonathan, "Why hasn't the son of Jesse come to the meal, either yesterday or today?"

²⁸Jonathan answered, "David earnestly asked me for permission to go to Bethlehem. ²⁹He said, 'Let me go, because our family is observing a sacrifice in the town and my brother has ordered me to be there. If I have found favor in your eyes, let me get away to see my brothers.' That is why he has not come to the king's table."

³⁰Saul's anger flared up at Jonathan and he said to him, "You son of a perverse and rebellious woman! Don't I know that you have sided with the son of Jesse to your own shame and to the shame of the mother who bore you? ³¹As long as the son of Jesse lives on this earth, neither you nor your kingdom will be established. Now send and bring him to me, for he must die!"

³²"Why should he be put to death? What has he done?" Jonathan asked his father. ³³But Saul hurled his spear at him to kill him. Then Jonathan knew that his father intended to kill David.

³⁴Jonathan got up from the table in fierce anger; on that second day of the month he did not eat, because he was grieved at his father's shameful treatment of David.

³⁵In the morning Jonathan went out to the field for his meeting with David. He had a small boy with him, ³⁶and he said to the boy, "Run and find the arrows I shoot." As the boy ran, he shot an arrow beyond him. ³⁷When the boy came to the place where Jonathan's arrow had fallen, Jonathan called out after him, "Isn't the arrow beyond you?" ³⁸Then he shouted, "Hurry! Go quickly! Don't stop!" The boy picked up the arrow and returned to his master. ³⁹(The boy knew nothing of all this; only Jonathan and David knew.) ⁴⁰Then Jonathan gave his weapons to the boy and said, "Go, carry them back to town."

⁴¹After the boy had gone, David got up from the south side ˌof the stoneˌ and bowed down before Jonathan three times, with his face to the ground. Then they kissed each other and wept together—but David wept the most.

⁴²Jonathan said to David, "Go in peace, for we have sworn friendship with each other in the name of the LORD, saying, 'The LORD is witness between you and me, and between your descendants and my descendants forever.' " Then David left, and Jonathan went back to the town.

²¹:¹DAVID went to Nob, to Ahimelech the priest. Ahimelech trembled when he met him, and asked, "Why are you alone? Why is no one with you?"

²David answered Ahimelech the priest, "The king charged me with a certain matter and said to me, 'No one is to know anything about your mission and your instructions.' As for my men, I have told them to meet me at a certain place. ³Now then, what do you have on

hand? Give me five loaves of bread, or whatever you can find."

4But the priest answered David, "I don't have any ordinary bread on hand; however, there is some consecrated bread here—provided the men have kept themselves from women."

5David replied, "Indeed women have been kept from us, as usual whenever*b* I set out. The men's things*c* are holy even on missions that are not holy. How much more so today!" 6So the priest gave him the consecrated bread, since there was no bread there except the bread of the Presence that had been removed from before the Lord and replaced by hot bread on the day it was taken away.

7Now one of Saul's servants was there that day, detained before the Lord; he was Doeg the Edomite, Saul's head shepherd.

8David asked Ahimelech, "Don't you have a spear or a sword here? I haven't brought my sword or any other weapon, because the king's business was urgent."

9The priest replied, "The sword of Goliath the Philistine, whom you killed in the Valley of Elah, is here; it is wrapped in a cloth behind the ephod. If you want it, take it; there is no sword here but that one."

David said, "There is none like it; give it to me."

10That day David fled from Saul and went to Achish king of Gath. 11But the servants of Achish said to him, "Isn't this David, the king of the land? Isn't he the one they sing about in their dances:

"'Saul has slain his thousands,
    and David his tens of thousands'?"

12David took these words to heart and was very much afraid of Achish king of Gath. 13So he pretended to be insane in their presence; and while he was in their hands he acted like a madman, making marks on the doors of the gate and letting saliva run down his beard.

14Achish said to his servants, "Look at the man! He is insane! Why bring him to me? 15Am I so short of madmen that you have to bring this fellow here to carry on like this in front of me? Must this man come into my house?"

a 25 Septuagint; Hebrew *wall. Jonathan arose*   *b 5* Or *from us in the past few days since*   *c 5* Or *bodies*

JOHN 9:1-41

As he [Jesus] went along, he saw a man blind from birth. 2**His disciples asked him, "Rabbi, who sinned, this man or his parents, that he was born blind?"**

3**"Neither this man nor his parents sinned," said Jesus, "but this happened so that the work of God might be displayed in his life. 4As long as it is day, we must do the work of him who sent me. Night is coming, when no one can work. 5While I am in the world, I am the light of the world."**

6Having said this, he spit on the ground, made some mud with the saliva, and put it on the man's eyes. 7"Go," he told him, "wash in the Pool of Siloam" (this word means Sent). So the man went and washed, and came home seeing.

8His neighbors and those who had formerly seen him begging asked, "Isn't this the same man who used to sit and beg?" 9Some claimed that he was.

Others said, "No, he only looks like him."

But he himself insisted, "I am the man."

10"How then were your eyes opened?" they demanded.

11He replied, "The man they call Jesus made some mud and put it on my eyes. He told me to go to Siloam and wash. So I went and washed, and then I could see."

12"Where is this man?" they asked him.

"I don't know," he said.

13They brought to the Pharisees the man who had been blind. 14Now the day on which Jesus had made the mud and opened the man's eyes was a Sabbath. 15Therefore the Pharisees also asked him how he had received his sight. "He put mud on my eyes," the man replied, "and I washed, and now I see."

¹⁶Some of the Pharisees said, "This man is not from God, for he does not keep the Sabbath."

But others asked, "How can a sinner do such miraculous signs?" So they were divided.

¹⁷Finally they turned again to the blind man, "What have you to say about him? It was your eyes he opened."

The man replied, "He is a prophet."

¹⁸The Jews still did not believe that he had been blind and had received his sight until they sent for the man's parents. ¹⁹"Is this your son?" they asked. "Is this the one you say was born blind? How is it that now he can see?"

²⁰"We know he is our son," the parents answered, "and we know he was born blind. ²¹But how he can see now, or who opened his eyes, we don't know. Ask him. He is of age; he will speak for himself." ²²His parents said this because they were afraid of the Jews, for already the Jews had decided that anyone who acknowledged that Jesus was the Christ*a* would be put out of the synagogue. ²³That was why his parents said, "He is of age; ask him."

²⁴A second time they summoned the man who had been blind. "Give glory to God,*b*" they said. "We know this man is a sinner."

²⁵He replied, "Whether he is a sinner or not, I don't know. One thing I do know. I was blind but now I see!"

²⁶Then they asked him, "What did he do to you? How did he open your eyes?"

²⁷He answered, "I have told you already and you did not listen. Why do you want to hear it again? Do you want to become his disciples, too?"

²⁸Then they hurled insults at him and said, "You are this fellow's disciple! We are disciples of Moses! ²⁹We know that God spoke to Moses, but as for this fellow, we don't even know where he comes from."

³⁰The man answered, "Now that is remarkable! You don't know where he

comes from, yet he opened my eyes. ³¹We know that God does not listen to sinners. He listens to the godly man who does his will. ³²Nobody has ever heard of opening the eyes of a man born blind. ³³If this man were not from God, he could do nothing."

³⁴To this they replied, "You were steeped in sin at birth; how dare you lecture us!" And they threw him out.

³⁵Jesus heard that they had thrown him out, and when he found him, he said, "Do you believe in the Son of Man?"

³⁶"Who is he, sir?" the man asked. "Tell me so that I may believe in him."

³⁷Jesus said, "You have now seen him; in fact, he is the one speaking with you."

³⁸Then the man said, "Lord, I believe," and he worshiped him.

³⁹Jesus said, "For judgment I have come into this world, so that the blind will see and those who see will become blind."

⁴⁰Some Pharisees who were with him heard him say this and asked, "What? Are we blind too?"

⁴¹Jesus said, "If you were blind, you would not be guilty of sin; but now that you claim you can see, your guilt remains."

a22 Or *Messiah*   *b24* A solemn charge to tell the truth (see Joshua 7:19)

PSALMS 113:1–114:8

¹Praise the LORD.*a*

Praise, O servants of the LORD,
    praise the name of the LORD.
²Let the name of the LORD be praised,
    both now and forevermore.
³From the rising of the sun to the
        place where it sets,
    the name of the LORD is to be
        praised.

⁴The LORD is exalted over all the
        nations,
    his glory above the heavens.
⁵Who is like the LORD our God,
    the One who sits enthroned
        on high,

⁶who stoops down to look
    on the heavens and the earth?

⁷He raises the poor from the dust
    and lifts the needy from the ash
      heap;
⁸he seats them with princes,
    with the princes of their people.
⁹He settles the barren woman in her
    home
    as a happy mother of children.

   Praise the LORD.

114:1 WHEN Israel came out of Egypt,
    the house of Jacob from a people
      of foreign tongue,
²Judah became God's sanctuary,
    Israel his dominion.

³The sea looked and fled,
    the Jordan turned back;
⁴the mountains skipped like rams,
    the hills like lambs.

⁵Why was it, O sea, that you fled,
    O Jordan, that you turned back,
⁶you mountains, that you skipped
      like rams,
    you hills, like lambs?

⁷Tremble, O earth, at the presence of
      the Lord,
    at the presence of the God of
      Jacob,
⁸who turned the rock into a pool,
    the hard rock into springs of
      water.

a 1 Hebrew Hallelu Yah; also in verse 9

PROVERBS 15:15-17

¹⁵All the days of the oppressed are
    wretched,
    but the cheerful heart has a
      continual feast.

¹⁶Better a little with the fear of the
    LORD
    than great wealth with turmoil.

¹⁷Better a meal of vegetables where
    there is love
    than a fattened calf with hatred.

☐ DAY 138

GOD SIGHTINGS

May 18

1 SAMUEL 22:1–23:29

David left Gath and escaped to the cave of Adullam. When his brothers and his father's household heard about it, they went down to him there. ²All those who were in distress or in debt or discontented gathered around him, and he became their leader. About four hundred men were with him.

³From there David went to Mizpah in Moab and said to the king of Moab, "Would you let my father and mother come and stay with you until I learn what God will do for me?" ⁴So he left them with the king of Moab, and they stayed with him as long as David was in the stronghold.

⁵But the prophet Gad said to David, "Do not stay in the stronghold. Go into the land of Judah." So David left and went to the forest of Hereth.

⁶Now Saul heard that David and his men had been discovered. And Saul, spear in hand, was seated under the tamarisk tree on the hill at Gibeah, with all his officials standing around him. ⁷Saul said to them, "Listen, men of Benjamin! Will the son of Jesse give all of you fields and vineyards? Will he make all of you commanders of thousands and commanders of hundreds? ⁸Is that why you have all conspired against me? No one tells me when my son makes a covenant with the son of Jesse. None of you is concerned about me or tells me that my son has incited my servant to lie in wait for me, as he does today."

⁹But Doeg the Edomite, who was standing with Saul's officials, said, "I saw the son of Jesse come to Ahimelech son of Ahitub at Nob. ¹⁰Ahimelech inquired of the LORD for him; he also gave him provisions and the sword of Goliath the Philistine."

¹¹Then the king sent for the priest

Ahimelech son of Ahitub and his father's whole family, who were the priests at Nob, and they all came to the king. ¹²Saul said, "Listen now, son of Ahitub."

"Yes, my lord," he answered.

¹³Saul said to him, "Why have you conspired against me, you and the son of Jesse, giving him bread and a sword and inquiring of God for him, so that he has rebelled against me and lies in wait for me, as he does today?"

¹⁴Ahimelech answered the king, "Who of all your servants is as loyal as David, the king's son-in-law, captain of your bodyguard and highly respected in your household? ¹⁵Was that day the first time I inquired of God for him? Of course not! Let not the king accuse your servant or any of his father's family, for your servant knows nothing at all about this whole affair."

¹⁶But the king said, "You will surely die, Ahimelech, you and your father's whole family."

¹⁷Then the king ordered the guards at his side: "Turn and kill the priests of the LORD, because they too have sided with David. They knew he was fleeing, yet they did not tell me."

But the king's officials were not willing to raise a hand to strike the priests of the LORD.

¹⁸The king then ordered Doeg, "You turn and strike down the priests." So Doeg the Edomite turned and struck them down. That day he killed eighty-five men who wore the linen ephod. ¹⁹He also put to the sword Nob, the town of the priests, with its men and women, its children and infants, and its cattle, donkeys and sheep.

²⁰But Abiathar, a son of Ahimelech son of Ahitub, escaped and fled to join David. ²¹He told David that Saul had killed the priests of the LORD. ²²Then David said to Abiathar: "That day, when Doeg the Edomite was there, I knew he would be sure to tell Saul. I am responsible for the death of your father's whole family. ²³Stay with me; don't be afraid; the man who is seeking your life is seeking mine also. You will be safe with me."

²³:¹WHEN David was told, "Look, the Philistines are fighting against Keilah and are looting the threshing floors," ²he inquired of the LORD, saying, "Shall I go and attack these Philistines?"

The LORD answered him, "Go, attack the Philistines and save Keilah."

³But David's men said to him, "Here in Judah we are afraid. How much more, then, if we go to Keilah against the Philistine forces!"

⁴Once again David inquired of the LORD, and the LORD answered him, "Go down to Keilah, for I am going to give the Philistines into your hand." ⁵So David and his men went to Keilah, fought the Philistines and carried off their livestock. He inflicted heavy losses on the Philistines and saved the people of Keilah. ⁶(Now Abiathar son of Ahimelech had brought the ephod down with him when he fled to David at Keilah.)

⁷Saul was told that David had gone to Keilah, and he said, "God has handed him over to me, for David has imprisoned himself by entering a town with gates and bars." ⁸And Saul called up all his forces for battle, to go down to Keilah to besiege David and his men.

⁹When David learned that Saul was plotting against him, he said to Abiathar the priest, "Bring the ephod." ¹⁰David said, "O LORD, God of Israel, your servant has heard definitely that Saul plans to come to Keilah and destroy the town on account of me. ¹¹Will the citizens of Keilah surrender me to him? Will Saul come down, as your servant has heard? O LORD, God of Israel, tell your servant."

And the LORD said, "He will."

¹²Again David asked, "Will the citizens of Keilah surrender me and my men to Saul?"

And the LORD said, "They will."

¹³So David and his men, about six hundred in number, left Keilah and kept moving from place to place. When Saul was told that David had escaped from Keilah, he did not go there.

¹⁴David stayed in the desert strongholds and in the hills of the Desert of Ziph. Day after day Saul searched for

him, but God did not give David into his hands.

15 While David was at Horesh in the Desert of Ziph, he learned that Saul had come out to take his life. 16 And Saul's son Jonathan went to David at Horesh and helped him find strength in God. 17 "Don't be afraid," he said. "My father Saul will not lay a hand on you. You will be king over Israel, and I will be second to you. Even my father Saul knows this." 18 The two of them made a covenant before the LORD. Then Jonathan went home, but David remained at Horesh.

19 The Ziphites went up to Saul at Gibeah and said, "Is not David hiding among us in the strongholds at Horesh, on the hill of Hakilah, south of Jeshimon? 20 Now, O king, come down whenever it pleases you to do so, and we will be responsible for handing him over to the king."

21 Saul replied, "The LORD bless you for your concern for me. 22 Go and make further preparation. Find out where David usually goes and who has seen him there. They tell me he is very crafty. 23 Find out about all the hiding places he uses and come back to me with definite information.a Then I will go with you; if he is in the area, I will track him down among all the clans of Judah."

24 So they set out and went to Ziph ahead of Saul. Now David and his men were in the Desert of Maon, in the Arabah south of Jeshimon. 25 Saul and his men began the search, and when David was told about it, he went down to the rock and stayed in the Desert of Maon. When Saul heard this, he went into the Desert of Maon in pursuit of David.

26 Saul was going along one side of the mountain, and David and his men were on the other side, hurrying to get away from Saul. As Saul and his forces were closing in on David and his men to capture them, 27 a messenger came to Saul, saying, "Come quickly! The Philistines are raiding the land." 28 Then Saul broke off his pursuit of David and went to meet the Philistines. That is why they call this place Sela Hammahlekoth.b

29 And David went up from there and lived in the strongholds of En Gedi.

a23 Or me at Nacon   b28 Sela Hammahlekoth means rock of parting.

JOHN 10:1-21

"I [Jesus] tell you the truth, the man who does not enter the sheep pen by the gate, but climbs in by some other way, is a thief and a robber. 2 The man who enters by the gate is the shepherd of his sheep. 3 The watchman opens the gate for him, and the sheep listen to his voice. He calls his own sheep by name and leads them out. 4 When he has brought out all his own, he goes on ahead of them, and his sheep follow him because they know his voice. 5 But they will never follow a stranger; in fact, they will run away from him because they do not recognize a stranger's voice." 6 Jesus used this figure of speech, but they did not understand what he was telling them.

7 Therefore Jesus said again, "I tell you the truth, I am the gate for the sheep. 8 All who ever came before me were thieves and robbers, but the sheep did not listen to them. 9 I am the gate; whoever enters through me will be saved.a He will come in and go out, and find pasture. 10 The thief comes only to steal and kill and destroy; I have come that they may have life, and have it to the full.

11 "I am the good shepherd. The good shepherd lays down his life for the sheep. 12 The hired hand is not the shepherd who owns the sheep. So when he sees the wolf coming, he abandons the sheep and runs away. Then the wolf attacks the flock and scatters it. 13 The man runs away because he is a hired hand and cares nothing for the sheep.

14 "I am the good shepherd; I know my sheep and my sheep know me— 15 just as the Father knows me and I know the Father—and I lay down my life for the sheep. 16 I have other sheep that are not of this sheep pen. I must bring them also. They too will listen to my voice, and there shall be one flock and

one shepherd. ¹⁷The reason my Father loves me is that I lay down my life—only to take it up again. ¹⁸No one takes it from me, but I lay it down of my own accord. I have authority to lay it down and authority to take it up again. This command I received from my Father."

¹⁹At these words the Jews were again divided. ²⁰Many of them said, "He is demon-possessed and raving mad. Why listen to him?"

²¹But others said, "These are not the sayings of a man possessed by a demon. Can a demon open the eyes of the blind?"

a9 Or *kept safe*

PSALM 115:1-18

¹**N**ot to us, O LORD, not to us
  but to your name be the glory,
  because of your love and
    faithfulness.

²Why do the nations say,
  "Where is their God?"
³Our God is in heaven;
  he does whatever pleases him.
⁴But their idols are silver and gold,
  made by the hands of men.
⁵They have mouths, but cannot speak,
  eyes, but they cannot see;
⁶they have ears, but they cannot hear,
  noses, but they cannot smell;
⁷they have hands, but they cannot feel,
  feet, but they cannot walk;
  nor can they utter a sound with
    their throats.
⁸Those who make them will be like
    them,
  and so will all who trust in them.

⁹O house of Israel, trust in the LORD—
  he is their help and shield.
¹⁰O house of Aaron, trust in the LORD—
  he is their help and shield.
¹¹You who fear him, trust in the LORD—
  he is their help and shield.

¹²The LORD remembers us and will
    bless us:
  He will bless the house of Israel,
  he will bless the house of Aaron,

¹³he will bless those who fear the
    LORD—
  small and great alike.

¹⁴May the LORD make you increase,
  both you and your children.
¹⁵May you be blessed by the LORD,
  the Maker of heaven and earth.

¹⁶The highest heavens belong to the
    LORD,
  but the earth he has given to man.
¹⁷It is not the dead who praise the
    LORD,
  those who go down to silence;
¹⁸it is we who extol the LORD,
  both now and forevermore.

Praise the LORD.*a*

a18 Hebrew *Hallelu Yah*

PROVERBS 15:18-19

¹⁸**A** hot-tempered man stirs up
    dissension,
  but a patient man calms a quarrel.

¹⁹The way of the sluggard is blocked
    with thorns,
  but the path of the upright is a
    highway.

□ D A Y 1 3 9

GOD SIGHTINGS

May 19

1 SAMUEL 24:1–25:44

After Saul returned from pursuing the Philistines, he was told, "David is in the Desert of En Gedi." ²So Saul took three thousand chosen men from all Israel and set out to look for David and his men near the Crags of the Wild Goats.

³He came to the sheep pens along the way; a cave was there, and Saul went in to relieve himself. David and his men were far back in the cave. ⁴The men said, "This is the day the LORD spoke of when he said*a* to you, 'I will give your enemy into your hands for you to deal with

as you wish.'" Then David crept up unnoticed and cut off a corner of Saul's robe.

5Afterward, David was conscience-stricken for having cut off a corner of his robe. 6He said to his men, "The Lord forbid that I should do such a thing to my master, the Lord's anointed, or lift my hand against him; for he is the anointed of the Lord." 7With these words David rebuked his men and did not allow them to attack Saul. And Saul left the cave and went his way.

8Then David went out of the cave and called out to Saul, "My lord the king!" When Saul looked behind him, David bowed down and prostrated himself with his face to the ground. 9He said to Saul, "Why do you listen when men say, 'David is bent on harming you'? 10This day you have seen with your own eyes how the Lord delivered you into my hands in the cave. Some urged me to kill you, but I spared you; I said, 'I will not lift my hand against my master, because he is the Lord's anointed.' 11See, my father, look at this piece of your robe in my hand! I cut off the corner of your robe but did not kill you. Now understand and recognize that I am not guilty of wrongdoing or rebellion. I have not wronged you, but you are hunting me down to take my life. 12May the Lord judge between you and me. And may the Lord avenge the wrongs you have done to me, but my hand will not touch you. 13As the old saying goes, 'From evildoers come evil deeds,' so my hand will not touch you.

14"Against whom has the king of Israel come out? Whom are you pursuing? A dead dog? A flea? 15May the Lord be our judge and decide between us. May he consider my cause and uphold it; may he vindicate me by delivering me from your hand."

16When David finished saying this, Saul asked, "Is that your voice, David my son?" And he wept aloud. 17"You are more righteous than I," he said. "You have treated me well, but I have treated you badly. 18You have just now told me

of the good you did to me; the Lord delivered me into your hands, but you did not kill me. 19When a man finds his enemy, does he let him get away unharmed? May the Lord reward you well for the way you treated me today. 20I know that you will surely be king and that the kingdom of Israel will be established in your hands. 21Now swear to me by the Lord that you will not cut off my descendants or wipe out my name from my father's family."

22So David gave his oath to Saul. Then Saul returned home, but David and his men went up to the stronghold.

25:1Now Samuel died, and all Israel assembled and mourned for him; and they buried him at his home in Ramah.

Then David moved down into the Desert of Maon.*b* 2A certain man in Maon, who had property there at Carmel, was very wealthy. He had a thousand goats and three thousand sheep, which he was shearing in Carmel. 3His name was Nabal and his wife's name was Abigail. She was an intelligent and beautiful woman, but her husband, a Calebite, was surly and mean in his dealings.

4While David was in the desert, he heard that Nabal was shearing sheep. 5So he sent ten young men and said to them, "Go up to Nabal at Carmel and greet him in my name. 6Say to him: 'Long life to you! Good health to you and your household! And good health to all that is yours!

7"'Now I hear that it is sheep-shearing time. When your shepherds were with us, we did not mistreat them, and the whole time they were at Carmel nothing of theirs was missing. 8Ask your own servants and they will tell you. Therefore be favorable toward my young men, since we come at a festive time. Please give your servants and your son David whatever you can find for them.'"

9When David's men arrived, they gave Nabal this message in David's name. Then they waited.

10Nabal answered David's servants, "Who is this David? Who is this son of Jesse? Many servants are breaking away from their masters these days. 11Why should I take my bread and water, and the meat I have slaughtered for my shearers, and give it to men coming from who knows where?"

12David's men turned around and went back. When they arrived, they reported every word. 13David said to his men, "Put on your swords!" So they put on their swords, and David put on his. About four hundred men went up with David, while two hundred stayed with the supplies.

14One of the servants told Nabal's wife Abigail: "David sent messengers from the desert to give our master his greetings, but he hurled insults at them. 15Yet these men were very good to us. They did not mistreat us, and the whole time we were out in the fields near them nothing was missing. 16Night and day they were a wall around us all the time we were herding our sheep near them. 17Now think it over and see what you can do, because disaster is hanging over our master and his whole household. He is such a wicked man that no one can talk to him."

18Abigail lost no time. She took two hundred loaves of bread, two skins of wine, five dressed sheep, five seahs*c* of roasted grain, a hundred cakes of raisins and two hundred cakes of pressed figs, and loaded them on donkeys. 19Then she told her servants, "Go on ahead; I'll follow you." But she did not tell her husband Nabal.

20As she came riding her donkey into a mountain ravine, there were David and his men descending toward her, and she met them. 21David had just said, "It's been useless—all my watching over this fellow's property in the desert so that nothing of his was missing. He has paid me back evil for good. 22May God deal with David,*d* be it ever so severely, if by morning I leave alive one male of all who belong to him!"

23When Abigail saw David, she quickly got off her donkey and bowed down before David with her face to the ground. 24She fell at his feet and said: "My lord, let the blame be on me alone. Please let your servant speak to you; hear what your servant has to say. 25May my lord pay no attention to that wicked man Nabal. He is just like his name—his name is Fool, and folly goes with him. But as for me, your servant, I did not see the men my master sent.

26"Now since the Lord has kept you, my master, from bloodshed and from avenging yourself with your own hands, as surely as the Lord lives and as you live, may your enemies and all who intend to harm my master be like Nabal. 27And let this gift, which your servant has brought to my master, be given to the men who follow you. 28Please forgive your servant's offense, for the Lord will certainly make a lasting dynasty for my master, because he fights the Lord's battles. Let no wrongdoing be found in you as long as you live. 29Even though someone is pursuing you to take your life, the life of my master will be bound securely in the bundle of the living by the Lord your God. But the lives of your enemies he will hurl away as from the pocket of a sling. 30When the Lord has done for my master every good thing he promised concerning him and has appointed him leader over Israel, 31my master will not have on his conscience the staggering burden of needless bloodshed or of having avenged himself. And when the Lord has brought my master success, remember your servant."

32David said to Abigail, "Praise be to the Lord, the God of Israel, who has sent you today to meet me. 33May you be blessed for your good judgment and for keeping me from bloodshed this day and from avenging myself with my own hands. 34Otherwise, as surely as the Lord, the God of Israel, lives, who has kept me from harming you, if you had not come quickly to meet me, not one male belonging to Nabal would have been left alive by daybreak."

35Then David accepted from her

hand what she had brought him and said, "Go home in peace. I have heard your words and granted your request."

36When Abigail went to Nabal, he was in the house holding a banquet like that of a king. He was in high spirits and very drunk. So she told him nothing until daybreak. 37Then in the morning, when Nabal was sober, his wife told him all these things, and his heart failed him and he became like a stone. 38About ten days later, the LORD struck Nabal and he died.

39When David heard that Nabal was dead, he said, "Praise be to the LORD, who has upheld my cause against Nabal for treating me with contempt. He has kept his servant from doing wrong and has brought Nabal's wrongdoing down on his own head."

Then David sent word to Abigail, asking her to become his wife. 40His servants went to Carmel and said to Abigail, "David has sent us to you to take you to become his wife."

41She bowed down with her face to the ground and said, "Here is your maidservant, ready to serve you and wash the feet of my master's servants." 42Abigail quickly got on a donkey and, attended by her five maids, went with David's messengers and became his wife. 43David had also married Ahinoam of Jezreel, and they both were his wives. 44But Saul had given his daughter Michal, David's wife, to Paltiele son of Laish, who was from Gallim.

a4 Or "Today the LORD is saying   b1 Some Septuagint manuscripts; Hebrew Paran   c18 That is, probably about a bushel (about 37 liters)   d22 Some Septuagint manuscripts; Hebrew with David's enemies   e44 Hebrew Palti, a variant of Paltiel

JOHN 10:22-42

Then came the Feast of Dedicationa at Jerusalem. It was winter, 23and Jesus was in the temple area walking in Solomon's Colonnade. 24The Jews gathered around him, saying, "How long will you keep us in suspense? If you are the Christ,b tell us plainly."

25Jesus answered, "I did tell you, but you do not believe. The miracles I do in my Father's name speak for me, 26but you do not believe because you are not my sheep. 27My sheep listen to my voice; I know them, and they follow me. 28I give them eternal life, and they shall never perish; no one can snatch them out of my hand. 29My Father, who has given them to me, is greater than allc; no one can snatch them out of my Father's hand. 30I and the Father are one."

31Again the Jews picked up stones to stone him, 32but Jesus said to them, "I have shown you many great miracles from the Father. For which of these do you stone me?"

33"We are not stoning you for any of these," replied the Jews, "but for blasphemy, because you, a mere man, claim to be God."

34Jesus answered them, "Is it not written in your Law, 'I have said you are gods'd ? 35If he called them 'gods,' to whom the word of God came—and the Scripture cannot be broken— 36what about the one whom the Father set apart as his very own and sent into the world? Why then do you accuse me of blasphemy because I said, 'I am God's Son'? 37Do not believe me unless I do what my Father does. 38But if I do it, even though you do not believe me, believe the miracles, that you may know and understand that the Father is in me, and I in the Father." 39Again they tried to seize him, but he escaped their grasp.

40Then Jesus went back across the Jordan to the place where John had been baptizing in the early days. Here he stayed 41and many people came to him. They said, "Though John never performed a miraculous sign, all that John said about this man was true." 42And in that place many believed in Jesus.

a22 That is, Hanukkah   b24 Or Messiah   c29 Many early manuscripts What my Father has given me is greater than all   d34 Psalm 82:6

PSALM 116:1-19

1 I love the LORD, for he heard my
        voice;
    he heard my cry for mercy.

²Because he turned his ear to me,
  I will call on him as long as I live.

³The cords of death entangled me,
  the anguish of the grave*a* came
    upon me;
  I was overcome by trouble and
    sorrow.
⁴Then I called on the name of the
    Lord:
  "O Lord, save me!"

⁵The Lord is gracious and righteous;
  our God is full of compassion.
⁶The Lord protects the
    simplehearted;
  when I was in great need, he
    saved me.

⁷Be at rest once more, O my soul,
  for the Lord has been good
    to you.

⁸For you, O Lord, have delivered my
    soul from death,
  my eyes from tears,
  my feet from stumbling,
⁹that I may walk before the Lord
  in the land of the living.
¹⁰I believed; therefore*b* I said,
  "I am greatly afflicted."
¹¹And in my dismay I said,
  "All men are liars."

¹²How can I repay the Lord
  for all his goodness to me?
¹³I will lift up the cup of salvation
  and call on the name of the Lord.
¹⁴I will fulfill my vows to the Lord
  in the presence of all his people.

¹⁵Precious in the sight of the Lord
  is the death of his saints.
¹⁶O Lord, truly I am your servant;
  I am your servant, the son of your
    maidservant*c*;
  you have freed me from my
    chains.

¹⁷I will sacrifice a thank offering to
    you
  and call on the name of the Lord.
¹⁸I will fulfill my vows to the Lord
  in the presence of all his people,

¹⁹in the courts of the house of the
    Lord—
  in your midst, O Jerusalem.

  Praise the Lord.*d*

a3 Hebrew *Sheol*   *b10* Or *believed even when*   *c16* Or
servant, your faithful son   *d19* Hebrew *Hallelu Yah*

PROVERBS 15:20-21
²⁰A wise son brings joy to his father,
  but a foolish man despises his
    mother.

²¹Folly delights a man who lacks
    judgment,
  but a man of understanding keeps
    a straight course.

☐ D A Y 1 4 0

GOD SIGHTINGS

May 20

1 SAMUEL 26:1–28:25
The Ziphites went to Saul at Gibeah and
said, "Is not David hiding on the hill of
Hakilah, which faces Jeshimon?"
²So Saul went down to the Desert of
Ziph, with his three thousand chosen
men of Israel, to search there for David.
³Saul made his camp beside the road on
the hill of Hakilah facing Jeshimon, but
David stayed in the desert. When he saw
that Saul had followed him there, ⁴he
sent out scouts and learned that Saul
had definitely arrived.*a*
⁵Then David set out and went to the
place where Saul had camped. He saw
where Saul and Abner son of Ner, the
commander of the army, had lain down.
Saul was lying inside the camp, with the
army encamped around him.
⁶David then asked Ahimelech the
Hittite and Abishai son of Zeruiah, Joab's brother, "Who will go down into the
camp with me to Saul?"
  "I'll go with you," said Abishai.
⁷So David and Abishai went to the
army by night, and there was Saul, lying

asleep inside the camp with his spear stuck in the ground near his head. Abner and the soldiers were lying around him.

⁸Abishai said to David, "Today God has delivered your enemy into your hands. Now let me pin him to the ground with one thrust of my spear; I won't strike him twice."

⁹But David said to Abishai, "Don't destroy him! Who can lay a hand on the Lord's anointed and be guiltless? ¹⁰As surely as the Lord lives," he said, "the Lord himself will strike him; either his time will come and he will die, or he will go into battle and perish. ¹¹But the Lord forbid that I should lay a hand on the Lord's anointed. Now get the spear and water jug that are near his head, and let's go."

¹²So David took the spear and water jug near Saul's head, and they left. No one saw or knew about it, nor did anyone wake up. They were all sleeping, because the Lord had put them into a deep sleep.

¹³Then David crossed over to the other side and stood on top of the hill some distance away; there was a wide space between them. ¹⁴He called out to the army and to Abner son of Ner, "Aren't you going to answer me, Abner?"

Abner replied, "Who are you who calls to the king?"

¹⁵David said, "You're a man, aren't you? And who is like you in Israel? Why didn't you guard your lord the king? Someone came to destroy your lord the king. ¹⁶What you have done is not good. As surely as the Lord lives, you and your men deserve to die, because you did not guard your master, the Lord's anointed. Look around you. Where are the king's spear and water jug that were near his head?"

¹⁷Saul recognized David's voice and said, "Is that your voice, David my son?"

David replied, "Yes it is, my lord the king." ¹⁸And he added, "Why is my lord pursuing his servant? What have I done, and what wrong am I guilty of? ¹⁹Now let my lord the king listen to his ser-

vant's words. If the Lord has incited you against me, then may he accept an offering. If, however, men have done it, may they be cursed before the Lord! They have now driven me from my share in the Lord's inheritance and have said, 'Go, serve other gods.' ²⁰Now do not let my blood fall to the ground far from the presence of the Lord. The king of Israel has come out to look for a flea—as one hunts a partridge in the mountains."

²¹Then Saul said, "I have sinned. Come back, David my son. Because you considered my life precious today, I will not try to harm you again. Surely I have acted like a fool and have erred greatly."

²²"Here is the king's spear," David answered. "Let one of your young men come over and get it. ²³The Lord rewards every man for his righteousness and faithfulness. The Lord delivered you into my hands today, but I would not lay a hand on the Lord's anointed. ²⁴As surely as I valued your life today, so may the Lord value my life and deliver me from all trouble."

²⁵Then Saul said to David, "May you be blessed, my son David; you will do great things and surely triumph."

So David went on his way, and Saul returned home.

²⁷:¹But David thought to himself, "One of these days I will be destroyed by the hand of Saul. The best thing I can do is to escape to the land of the Philistines. Then Saul will give up searching for me anywhere in Israel, and I will slip out of his hand."

²So David and the six hundred men with him left and went over to Achish son of Maoch king of Gath. ³David and his men settled in Gath with Achish. Each man had his family with him, and David had his two wives: Ahinoam of Jezreel and Abigail of Carmel, the widow of Nabal. ⁴When Saul was told that David had fled to Gath, he no longer searched for him.

⁵Then David said to Achish, "If I have found favor in your eyes, let a place be

assigned to me in one of the country towns, that I may live there. Why should your servant live in the royal city with you?"

⁶So on that day Achish gave him Ziklag, and it has belonged to the kings of Judah ever since. ⁷David lived in Philistine territory a year and four months.

⁸Now David and his men went up and raided the Geshurites, the Girzites and the Amalekites. (From ancient times these peoples had lived in the land extending to Shur and Egypt.) ⁹Whenever David attacked an area, he did not leave a man or woman alive, but took sheep and cattle, donkeys and camels, and clothes. Then he returned to Achish.

¹⁰When Achish asked, "Where did you go raiding today?" David would say, "Against the Negev of Judah" or "Against the Negev of Jerahmeel" or "Against the Negev of the Kenites." ¹¹He did not leave a man or woman alive to be brought to Gath, for he thought, "They might inform on us and say, 'This is what David did.'" And such was his practice as long as he lived in Philistine territory. ¹²Achish trusted David and said to himself, "He has become so odious to his people, the Israelites, that he will be my servant forever."

²⁸:¹In those days the Philistines gathered their forces to fight against Israel. Achish said to David, "You must understand that you and your men will accompany me in the army."

²David said, "Then you will see for yourself what your servant can do."

Achish replied, "Very well, I will make you my bodyguard for life."

³Now Samuel was dead, and all Israel had mourned for him and buried him in his own town of Ramah. Saul had expelled the mediums and spiritists from the land.

⁴The Philistines assembled and came and set up camp at Shunem, while Saul gathered all the Israelites and set up camp at Gilboa. ⁵When Saul saw the Philistine army, he was afraid; terror filled his heart. ⁶He inquired of the Lord, but the Lord did not answer him by dreams or Urim or prophets. ⁷Saul then said to his attendants, "Find me a woman who is a medium, so I may go and inquire of her."

"There is one in Endor," they said.

⁸So Saul disguised himself, putting on other clothes, and at night he and two men went to the woman. "Consult a spirit for me," he said, "and bring up for me the one I name."

⁹But the woman said to him, "Surely you know what Saul has done. He has cut off the mediums and spiritists from the land. Why have you set a trap for my life to bring about my death?"

¹⁰Saul swore to her by the Lord, "As surely as the Lord lives, you will not be punished for this."

¹¹Then the woman asked, "Whom shall I bring up for you?"

"Bring up Samuel," he said.

¹²When the woman saw Samuel, she cried out at the top of her voice and said to Saul, "Why have you deceived me? You are Saul!"

¹³The king said to her, "Don't be afraid. What do you see?"

The woman said, "I see a spirit*ᵇ* coming up out of the ground."

¹⁴"What does he look like?" he asked.

"An old man wearing a robe is coming up," she said.

Then Saul knew it was Samuel, and he bowed down and prostrated himself with his face to the ground.

¹⁵Samuel said to Saul, "Why have you disturbed me by bringing me up?"

"I am in great distress," Saul said. "The Philistines are fighting against me, and God has turned away from me. He no longer answers me, either by prophets or by dreams. So I have called on you to tell me what to do."

¹⁶Samuel said, "Why do you consult me, now that the Lord has turned away from you and become your enemy? ¹⁷The Lord has done what he predicted through me. The Lord has torn the kingdom out of your hands and given it to one of your neighbors—to David.

18Because you did not obey the Lord or carry out his fierce wrath against the Amalekites, the Lord has done this to you today. 19The Lord will hand over both Israel and you to the Philistines, and tomorrow you and your sons will be with me. The Lord will also hand over the army of Israel to the Philistines."

20Immediately Saul fell full length on the ground, filled with fear because of Samuel's words. His strength was gone, for he had eaten nothing all that day and night.

21When the woman came to Saul and saw that he was greatly shaken, she said, "Look, your maidservant has obeyed you. I took my life in my hands and did what you told me to do. 22Now please listen to your servant and let me give you some food so you may eat and have the strength to go on your way."

23He refused and said, "I will not eat."

But his men joined the woman in urging him, and he listened to them. He got up from the ground and sat on the couch.

24The woman had a fattened calf at the house, which she butchered at once. She took some flour, kneaded it and baked bread without yeast. 25Then she set it before Saul and his men, and they ate. That same night they got up and left.

a4 Or had come to Nacon   b13 Or see spirits; or see gods

JOHN 11:1-53

Now a man named Lazarus was sick. He was from Bethany, the village of Mary and her sister Martha. 2This Mary, whose brother Lazarus now lay sick, was the same one who poured perfume on the Lord and wiped his feet with her hair. 3So the sisters sent word to Jesus, "Lord, the one you love is sick."

4When he heard this, Jesus said, "This sickness will not end in death. No, it is for God's glory so that God's Son may be glorified through it." 5Jesus loved Martha and her sister and Lazarus. 6Yet when he heard that Lazarus was sick, he stayed where he was two more days.

7Then he said to his disciples, "Let us go back to Judea."

8"But Rabbi," they said, "a short while ago the Jews tried to stone you, and yet you are going back there?"

9Jesus answered, "Are there not twelve hours of daylight? A man who walks by day will not stumble, for he sees by this world's light. 10It is when he walks by night that he stumbles, for he has no light."

11After he had said this, he went on to tell them, "Our friend Lazarus has fallen asleep; but I am going there to wake him up."

12His disciples replied, "Lord, if he sleeps, he will get better." 13Jesus had been speaking of his death, but his disciples thought he meant natural sleep.

14So then he told them plainly, "Lazarus is dead, 15and for your sake I am glad I was not there, so that you may believe. But let us go to him."

16Then Thomas (called Didymus) said to the rest of the disciples, "Let us also go, that we may die with him."

17On his arrival, Jesus found that Lazarus had already been in the tomb for four days. 18Bethany was less than two milesa from Jerusalem, 19and many Jews had come to Martha and Mary to comfort them in the loss of their brother. 20When Martha heard that Jesus was coming, she went out to meet him, but Mary stayed at home.

21"Lord," Martha said to Jesus, "if you had been here, my brother would not have died. 22But I know that even now God will give you whatever you ask."

23Jesus said to her, "Your brother will rise again."

24Martha answered, "I know he will rise again in the resurrection at the last day."

25Jesus said to her, "I am the resurrection and the life. He who believes in me will live, even though he dies; 26and whoever lives and believes in me will never die. Do you believe this?"

27"Yes, Lord," she told him, "I believe

that you are the Christ,*b* the Son of God, who was to come into the world."

28And after she had said this, she went back and called her sister Mary aside. "The Teacher is here," she said, "and is asking for you." 29When Mary heard this, she got up quickly and went to him. 30Now Jesus had not yet entered the village, but was still at the place where Martha had met him. 31When the Jews who had been with Mary in the house, comforting her, noticed how quickly she got up and went out, they followed her, supposing she was going to the tomb to mourn there.

32When Mary reached the place where Jesus was and saw him, she fell at his feet and said, "Lord, if you had been here, my brother would not have died."

33When Jesus saw her weeping, and the Jews who had come along with her also weeping, he was deeply moved in spirit and troubled. 34"Where have you laid him?" he asked.

"Come and see, Lord," they replied.

35Jesus wept.

36Then the Jews said, "See how he loved him!"

37But some of them said, "Could not he who opened the eyes of the blind man have kept this man from dying?"

38Jesus, once more deeply moved, came to the tomb. It was a cave with a stone laid across the entrance. 39"Take away the stone," he said.

"But, Lord," said Martha, the sister of the dead man, "by this time there is a bad odor, for he has been there four days."

40Then Jesus said, "Did I not tell you that if you believed, you would see the glory of God?"

41So they took away the stone. Then Jesus looked up and said, "Father, I thank you that you have heard me. 42I knew that you always hear me, but I said this for the benefit of the people standing here, that they may believe that you sent me."

43When he had said this, Jesus called in a loud voice, "Lazarus, come out!" 44The dead man came out, his hands

and feet wrapped with strips of linen, and a cloth around his face.

Jesus said to them, "Take off the grave clothes and let him go."

45Therefore many of the Jews who had come to visit Mary, and had seen what Jesus did, put their faith in him. 46But some of them went to the Pharisees and told them what Jesus had done. 47Then the chief priests and the Pharisees called a meeting of the Sanhedrin.

"What are we accomplishing?" they asked. "Here is this man performing many miraculous signs. 48If we let him go on like this, everyone will believe in him, and then the Romans will come and take away both our place*c* and our nation."

49Then one of them, named Caiaphas, who was high priest that year, spoke up, "You know nothing at all! 50You do not realize that it is better for you that one man die for the people than that the whole nation perish."

51He did not say this on his own, but as high priest that year he prophesied that Jesus would die for the Jewish nation, 52and not only for that nation but also for the scattered children of God, to bring them together and make them one. 53So from that day on they plotted to take his life.

a18 Greek *fifteen stadia* (about 3 kilometers) *b27* Or *Messiah* *c48* Or *temple*

PSALM 117:1-2

1**P**raise the Lord, all you nations;
  extol him, all you peoples.
2For great is his love toward us,
  and the faithfulness of the Lord
    endures forever.

  Praise the Lord.*a*

a2 Hebrew *Hallelu Yah*

PROVERBS 15:22-23

22**P**lans fail for lack of counsel,
  but with many advisers they
    succeed.

23A man finds joy in giving an apt
    reply—
  and how good is a timely word!

□ D A Y 1 4 1

GOD SIGHTINGS

May 21

1 SAMUEL 29:1–31:13

The Philistines gathered all their forces at Aphek, and Israel camped by the spring in Jezreel. ²As the Philistine rulers marched with their units of hundreds and thousands, David and his men were marching at the rear with Achish. ³The commanders of the Philistines asked, "What about these Hebrews?"

Achish replied, "Is this not David, who was an officer of Saul king of Israel? He has already been with me for over a year, and from the day he left Saul until now, I have found no fault in him."

⁴But the Philistine commanders were angry with him and said, "Send the man back, that he may return to the place you assigned him. He must not go with us into battle, or he will turn against us during the fighting. How better could he regain his master's favor than by taking the heads of our own men? ⁵Isn't this the David they sang about in their dances:

"'Saul has slain his thousands,
  and David his tens of thousands'?"

⁶So Achish called David and said to him, "As surely as the LORD lives, you have been reliable, and I would be pleased to have you serve with me in the army. From the day you came to me until now, I have found no fault in you, but the rulers don't approve of you. ⁷Turn back and go in peace; do nothing to displease the Philistine rulers."

⁸"But what have I done?" asked David. "What have you found against your servant from the day I came to you until now? Why can't I go and fight against the enemies of my lord the king?"

⁹Achish answered, "I know that you have been as pleasing in my eyes as an angel of God; nevertheless, the Philistine commanders have said, 'He must not go up with us into battle.' ¹⁰Now get up

early, along with your master's servants who have come with you, and leave in the morning as soon as it is light."

¹¹So David and his men got up early in the morning to go back to the land of the Philistines, and the Philistines went up to Jezreel.

³⁰:¹DAVID and his men reached Ziklag on the third day. Now the Amalekites had raided the Negev and Ziklag. They had attacked Ziklag and burned it, ²and had taken captive the women and all who were in it, both young and old. They killed none of them, but carried them off as they went on their way.

³When David and his men came to Ziklag, they found it destroyed by fire and their wives and sons and daughters taken captive. ⁴So David and his men wept aloud until they had no strength left to weep. ⁵David's two wives had been captured—Ahinoam of Jezreel and Abigail, the widow of Nabal of Carmel. ⁶David was greatly distressed because the men were talking of stoning him; each one was bitter in spirit because of his sons and daughters. But David found strength in the LORD his God.

⁷Then David said to Abiathar the priest, the son of Ahimelech, "Bring me the ephod." Abiathar brought it to him, ⁸and David inquired of the LORD, "Shall I pursue this raiding party? Will I overtake them?"

"Pursue them," he answered. "You will certainly overtake them and succeed in the rescue."

⁹David and the six hundred men with him came to the Besor Ravine, where some stayed behind, ¹⁰for two hundred men were too exhausted to cross the ravine. But David and four hundred men continued the pursuit.

¹¹They found an Egyptian in a field and brought him to David. They gave him water to drink and food to eat— ¹²part of a cake of pressed figs and two cakes of raisins. He ate and was revived, for he had not eaten any food or drunk any water for three days and three nights.

¹³David asked him, "To whom do you belong, and where do you come from?"

He said, "I am an Egyptian, the slave of an Amalekite. My master abandoned me when I became ill three days ago. ¹⁴We raided the Negev of the Kerethites and the territory belonging to Judah and the Negev of Caleb. And we burned Ziklag."

¹⁵David asked him, "Can you lead me down to this raiding party?"

He answered, "Swear to me before God that you will not kill me or hand me over to my master, and I will take you down to them."

¹⁶He led David down, and there they were, scattered over the countryside, eating, drinking and reveling because of the great amount of plunder they had taken from the land of the Philistines and from Judah. ¹⁷David fought them from dusk until the evening of the next day, and none of them got away, except four hundred young men who rode off on camels and fled. ¹⁸David recovered everything the Amalekites had taken, including his two wives. ¹⁹Nothing was missing: young or old, boy or girl, plunder or anything else they had taken. David brought everything back. ²⁰He took all the flocks and herds, and his men drove them ahead of the other livestock, saying, "This is David's plunder."

²¹Then David came to the two hundred men who had been too exhausted to follow him and who were left behind at the Besor Ravine. They came out to meet David and the people with him. As David and his men approached, he greeted them. ²²But all the evil men and troublemakers among David's followers said, "Because they did not go out with us, we will not share with them the plunder we recovered. However, each man may take his wife and children and go."

²³David replied, "No, my brothers, you must not do that with what the LORD has given us. He has protected us and handed over to us the forces that came against us. ²⁴Who will listen to what you say? The share of the man who stayed with the supplies is to be the same as that of him who went down to the battle. All will share alike." ²⁵David made this a statute and ordinance for Israel from that day to this.

²⁶When David arrived in Ziklag, he sent some of the plunder to the elders of Judah, who were his friends, saying, "Here is a present for you from the plunder of the LORD's enemies."

²⁷He sent it to those who were in Bethel, Ramoth Negev and Jattir; ²⁸to those in Aroer, Siphmoth, Eshtemoa ²⁹and Racal; to those in the towns of the Jerahmeelites and the Kenites; ³⁰to those in Hormah, Bor Ashan, Athach ³¹and Hebron; and to those in all the other places where David and his men had roamed.

³¹:¹Now the Philistines fought against Israel; the Israelites fled before them, and many fell slain on Mount Gilboa. ²The Philistines pressed hard after Saul and his sons, and they killed his sons Jonathan, Abinadab and Malki-Shua. ³The fighting grew fierce around Saul, and when the archers overtook him, they wounded him critically.

⁴Saul said to his armor-bearer, "Draw your sword and run me through, or these uncircumcised fellows will come and run me through and abuse me."

But his armor-bearer was terrified and would not do it; so Saul took his own sword and fell on it. ⁵When the armor-bearer saw that Saul was dead, he too fell on his sword and died with him. ⁶So Saul and his three sons and his armor-bearer and all his men died together that same day.

⁷When the Israelites along the valley and those across the Jordan saw that the Israelite army had fled and that Saul and his sons had died, they abandoned their towns and fled. And the Philistines came and occupied them.

⁸The next day, when the Philistines came to strip the dead, they found Saul and his three sons fallen on Mount Gilboa. ⁹They cut off his head and stripped off his armor, and they sent messengers throughout the land of the Philistines to

proclaim the news in the temple of their idols and among their people. 10They put his armor in the temple of the Ashtoreths and fastened his body to the wall of Beth Shan.

11When the people of Jabesh Gilead heard of what the Philistines had done to Saul, 12all their valiant men journeyed through the night to Beth Shan. They took down the bodies of Saul and his sons from the wall of Beth Shan and went to Jabesh, where they burned them. 13Then they took their bones and buried them under a tamarisk tree at Jabesh, and they fasted seven days.

JOHN 11:54–12:19

Therefore Jesus no longer moved about publicly among the Jews. Instead he withdrew to a region near the desert, to a village called Ephraim, where he stayed with his disciples.

55When it was almost time for the Jewish Passover, many went up from the country to Jerusalem for their ceremonial cleansing before the Passover. 56They kept looking for Jesus, and as they stood in the temple area they asked one another, "What do you think? Isn't he coming to the Feast at all?" 57But the chief priests and Pharisees had given orders that if anyone found out where Jesus was, he should report it so that they might arrest him.

12:1Six days before the Passover, Jesus arrived at Bethany, where Lazarus lived, whom Jesus had raised from the dead. 2Here a dinner was given in Jesus' honor. Martha served, while Lazarus was among those reclining at the table with him. 3Then Mary took about a pinta of pure nard, an expensive perfume; she poured it on Jesus' feet and wiped his feet with her hair. And the house was filled with the fragrance of the perfume.

4But one of his disciples, Judas Iscariot, who was later to betray him, objected, 5"Why wasn't this perfume sold and the money given to the poor? It was worth a year's wages.b " 6He did not say this because he cared about the poor but because he was a thief; as keeper of the money bag, he used to help himself to what was put into it.

7"Leave her alone," Jesus replied. "ₗIt was intendedₗ that she should save this perfume for the day of my burial. 8You will always have the poor among you, but you will not always have me."

9Meanwhile a large crowd of Jews found out that Jesus was there and came, not only because of him but also to see Lazarus, whom he had raised from the dead. 10So the chief priests made plans to kill Lazarus as well, 11for on account of him many of the Jews were going over to Jesus and putting their faith in him.

12The next day the great crowd that had come for the Feast heard that Jesus was on his way to Jerusalem. 13They took palm branches and went out to meet him, shouting,

"Hosanna!c"

"Blessed is he who comes in the
     name of the Lord!"d

"Blessed is the King of Israel!"

14Jesus found a young donkey and sat upon it, as it is written,

15"Do not be afraid, O Daughter of Zion;
     see, your king is coming,
     seated on a donkey's colt."e

16At first his disciples did not understand all this. Only after Jesus was glorified did they realize that these things had been written about him and that they had done these things to him.

17Now the crowd that was with him when he called Lazarus from the tomb and raised him from the dead continued to spread the word. 18Many people, because they had heard that he had given this miraculous sign, went out to meet him. 19So the Pharisees said to one another, "See, this is getting us nowhere. Look how the whole world has gone after him!"

a3 Greek a litra (probably about 0.5 liter) b5 Greek three
hundred denarii c13 A Hebrew expression meaning
"Save!" which became an exclamation of praise
d13 Psalm 118:25,26 e15 Zech. 9:9

PSALM 118:1-18

¹ **G**ive thanks to the Lord, for he is
good;
his love endures forever.

² Let Israel say:
"His love endures forever."
³ Let the house of Aaron say:
"His love endures forever."
⁴ Let those who fear the Lord say:
"His love endures forever."

⁵ In my anguish I cried to the Lord,
and he answered by setting me
free.
⁶ The Lord is with me; I will not be
afraid.
What can man do to me?
⁷ The Lord is with me; he is my helper.
I will look in triumph on my
enemies.

⁸ **It is better to take refuge in the**
Lord
than to trust in man.
⁹ **It is better to take refuge in the**
Lord
than to trust in princes.

¹⁰ All the nations surrounded me,
but in the name of the Lord I cut
them off.
¹¹ They surrounded me on every side,
but in the name of the Lord I cut
them off.
¹² They swarmed around me like bees,
but they died out as quickly as
burning thorns;
in the name of the Lord I cut
them off.

¹³ I was pushed back and about to fall,
but the Lord helped me.
¹⁴ The Lord is my strength and my song;
he has become my salvation.

¹⁵ Shouts of joy and victory
resound in the tents of the
righteous:
"The Lord's right hand has done
mighty things!
¹⁶ The Lord's right hand is lifted high;
the Lord's right hand has done
mighty things!"

¹⁷ I will not die but live,
and will proclaim what the Lord
has done.
¹⁸ The Lord has chastened me severely,
but he has not given me over to
death.

PROVERBS 15:24-26

²⁴ **T**he path of life leads upward for the
wise
to keep him from going down to
the grave.ᵃ

²⁵ The Lord tears down the proud
man's house
but he keeps the widow's
boundaries intact.

²⁶ The Lord detests the thoughts of the
wicked,
but those of the pure are pleasing
to him.

ᵃ24 Hebrew *Sheol*

☐ DAY 142

GOD SIGHTINGS

May 22

2 SAMUEL 1:1–2:11

After the death of Saul, David returned
from defeating the Amalekites and
stayed in Ziklag two days. ²On the third
day a man arrived from Saul's camp,
with his clothes torn and with dust on
his head. When he came to David, he fell
to the ground to pay him honor.

³ "Where have you come from?" David asked him.

He answered, "I have escaped from
the Israelite camp."

⁴ "What happened?" David asked.
"Tell me."

He said, "The men fled from the battle. Many of them fell and died. And
Saul and his son Jonathan are dead."

⁵ Then David said to the young man
who brought him the report, "How do

you know that Saul and his son Jonathan are dead?"

⁶"I happened to be on Mount Gilboa," the young man said, "and there was Saul, leaning on his spear, with the chariots and riders almost upon him. ⁷When he turned around and saw me, he called out to me, and I said, 'What can I do?'

⁸"He asked me, 'Who are you?'

"'An Amalekite,' I answered.

⁹"Then he said to me, 'Stand over me and kill me! I am in the throes of death, but I'm still alive.'

¹⁰"So I stood over him and killed him, because I knew that after he had fallen he could not survive. And I took the crown that was on his head and the band on his arm and have brought them here to my lord."

¹¹Then David and all the men with him took hold of their clothes and tore them. ¹²They mourned and wept and fasted till evening for Saul and his son Jonathan, and for the army of the LORD and the house of Israel, because they had fallen by the sword.

¹³David said to the young man who brought him the report, "Where are you from?"

"I am the son of an alien, an Amalekite," he answered.

¹⁴David asked him, "Why were you not afraid to lift your hand to destroy the LORD's anointed?"

¹⁵Then David called one of his men and said, "Go, strike him down!" So he struck him down, and he died. ¹⁶For David had said to him, "Your blood be on your own head. Your own mouth testified against you when you said, 'I killed the LORD's anointed.'"

¹⁷David took up this lament concerning Saul and his son Jonathan, ¹⁸and ordered that the men of Judah be taught this lament of the bow (it is written in the Book of Jashar):

¹⁹"Your glory, O Israel, lies slain on
        your heights.
    How the mighty have fallen!

²⁰"Tell it not in Gath,
    proclaim it not in the streets of
        Ashkelon,
lest the daughters of the Philistines
        be glad,
    lest the daughters of the
        uncircumcised rejoice.

²¹"O mountains of Gilboa,
    may you have neither dew nor
        rain,
    nor fields that yield offerings ⌊of
        grain⌋.
For there the shield of the mighty
        was defiled,
    the shield of Saul—no longer
        rubbed with oil.
²²From the blood of the slain,
    from the flesh of the mighty,
the bow of Jonathan did not turn
        back,
    the sword of Saul did not return
        unsatisfied.

²³"Saul and Jonathan—
    in life they were loved and
        gracious,
    and in death they were not parted.
They were swifter than eagles,
    they were stronger than lions.

²⁴"O daughters of Israel,
    weep for Saul,
who clothed you in scarlet and
        finery,
    who adorned your garments with
        ornaments of gold.

²⁵"How the mighty have fallen in
        battle!
    Jonathan lies slain on your heights.
²⁶I grieve for you, Jonathan my brother;
    you were very dear to me.
Your love for me was wonderful,
    more wonderful than that of
        women.

²⁷"How the mighty have fallen!
    The weapons of war have
        perished!"

²:¹IN the course of time, David inquired of the LORD. "Shall I go up to one of the towns of Judah?" he asked.

The LORD said, "Go up."

David asked, "Where shall I go?"

"To Hebron," the LORD answered.

² So David went up there with his two wives, Ahinoam of Jezreel and Abigail, the widow of Nabal of Carmel. ³David also took the men who were with him, each with his family, and they settled in Hebron and its towns. ⁴Then the men of Judah came to Hebron and there they anointed David king over the house of Judah.

When David was told that it was the men of Jabesh Gilead who had buried Saul, ⁵he sent messengers to the men of Jabesh Gilead to say to them, "The LORD bless you for showing this kindness to Saul your master by burying him. ⁶May the LORD now show you kindness and faithfulness, and I too will show you the same favor because you have done this. ⁷Now then, be strong and brave, for Saul your master is dead, and the house of Judah has anointed me king over them."

⁸Meanwhile, Abner son of Ner, the commander of Saul's army, had taken Ish-Bosheth son of Saul and brought him over to Mahanaim. ⁹He made him king over Gilead, Ashuri*a* and Jezreel, and also over Ephraim, Benjamin and all Israel.

¹⁰Ish-Bosheth son of Saul was forty years old when he became king over Israel, and he reigned two years. The house of Judah, however, followed David. ¹¹The length of time David was king in Hebron over the house of Judah was seven years and six months.

a9 Or *Asher*

JOHN 12:20-50

Now there were some Greeks among those who went up to worship at the Feast. ²¹They came to Philip, who was from Bethsaida in Galilee, with a request. "Sir," they said, "we would like to see Jesus." ²²Philip went to tell Andrew; Andrew and Philip in turn told Jesus.

²³**Jesus replied, " The hour has come for the Son of Man to be glorified. ²⁴I tell you the truth, unless a kernel of wheat falls to the ground and dies, it remains only a single seed. But if it dies, it produces many seeds.** ²⁵The man who loves his life will lose it, while the man who hates his life in this world will keep it for eternal life. ²⁶Whoever serves me must follow me; and where I am, my servant also will be. My Father will honor the one who serves me.

²⁷"Now my heart is troubled, and what shall I say? 'Father, save me from this hour'? No, it was for this very reason I came to this hour. ²⁸Father, glorify your name!"

Then a voice came from heaven, "I have glorified it, and will glorify it again." ²⁹The crowd that was there and heard it said it had thundered; others said an angel had spoken to him.

³⁰Jesus said, "This voice was for your benefit, not mine. ³¹Now is the time for judgment on this world; now the prince of this world will be driven out. ³²But I, when I am lifted up from the earth, will draw all men to myself." ³³He said this to show the kind of death he was going to die.

³⁴The crowd spoke up, "We have heard from the Law that the Christ*a* will remain forever, so how can you say, 'The Son of Man must be lifted up'? Who is this 'Son of Man'?"

³⁵Then Jesus told them, "You are going to have the light just a little while longer. Walk while you have the light, before darkness overtakes you. The man who walks in the dark does not know where he is going. ³⁶Put your trust in the light while you have it, so that you may become sons of light." When he had finished speaking, Jesus left and hid himself from them.

³⁷Even after Jesus had done all these miraculous signs in their presence, they still would not believe in him. ³⁸This was to fulfill the word of Isaiah the prophet:

"Lord, who has believed our message
    and to whom has the arm of the
        Lord been revealed?"*b*

[39] For this reason they could not believe, because, as Isaiah says elsewhere:

[40] "He has blinded their eyes
and deadened their hearts,
so they can neither see with their
eyes,
nor understand with their hearts,
nor turn—and I would heal
them."[c]

[41] Isaiah said this because he saw Jesus' glory and spoke about him.

[42] Yet at the same time many even among the leaders believed in him. But because of the Pharisees they would not confess their faith for fear they would be put out of the synagogue; [43] for they loved praise from men more than praise from God.

[44] Then Jesus cried out, "When a man believes in me, he does not believe in me only, but in the one who sent me. [45] When he looks at me, he sees the one who sent me. [46] I have come into the world as a light, so that no one who believes in me should stay in darkness.

[47] "As for the person who hears my words but does not keep them, I do not judge him. For I did not come to judge the world, but to save it. [48] There is a judge for the one who rejects me and does not accept my words; that very word which I spoke will condemn him at the last day. [49] For I did not speak of my own accord, but the Father who sent me commanded me what to say and how to say it. [50] I know that his command leads to eternal life. So whatever I say is just what the Father has told me to say."

a34 Or Messiah   b38 Isaiah 53:1   c40 Isaiah 6:10

PSALM 118:19-29
[19] Open for me the gates of
righteousness;
I will enter and give thanks to the
Lord.
[20] This is the gate of the Lord
through which the righteous may
enter.
[21] I will give you thanks, for you
answered me;
you have become my salvation.

[22] The stone the builders rejected
has become the capstone;
[23] the Lord has done this,
and it is marvelous in our eyes.
[24] This is the day the Lord has made;
let us rejoice and be glad in it.

[25] O Lord, save us;
O Lord, grant us success.
[26] Blessed is he who comes in the name
of the Lord.
From the house of the Lord we
bless you.[a]
[27] The Lord is God,
and he has made his light shine
upon us.
With boughs in hand, join in the
festal procession
up[b] to the horns of the altar.

[28] You are my God, and I will give you
thanks;
you are my God, and I will exalt
you.

[29] Give thanks to the Lord, for he is
good;
his love endures forever.

a26 The Hebrew is plural.   b27 Or Bind the festal sacrifice with ropes / and take it

PROVERBS 15:27-28
[27] A greedy man brings trouble to his
family,
but he who hates bribes will live.

[28] The heart of the righteous weighs its
answers,
but the mouth of the wicked
gushes evil.

☐ DAY 143

GOD SIGHTINGS

May 23

2 SAMUEL 2:12–3:39
Abner son of Ner, together with the men of Ish-Bosheth son of Saul, left Mahanaim and went to Gibeon. [13] Joab son

of Zeruiah and David's men went out and met them at the pool of Gibeon. One group sat down on one side of the pool and one group on the other side.

¹⁴Then Abner said to Joab, "Let's have some of the young men get up and fight hand to hand in front of us."

"All right, let them do it," Joab said.

¹⁵So they stood up and were counted off—twelve men for Benjamin and Ish-Bosheth son of Saul, and twelve for David. ¹⁶Then each man grabbed his opponent by the head and thrust his dagger into his opponent's side, and they fell down together. So that place in Gibeon was called Helkath Hazzurim.ᵃ

¹⁷The battle that day was very fierce, and Abner and the men of Israel were defeated by David's men.

¹⁸The three sons of Zeruiah were there: Joab, Abishai and Asahel. Now Asahel was as fleet-footed as a wild gazelle. ¹⁹He chased Abner, turning neither to the right nor to the left as he pursued him. ²⁰Abner looked behind him and asked, "Is that you, Asahel?"

"It is," he answered.

²¹Then Abner said to him, "Turn aside to the right or to the left; take on one of the young men and strip him of his weapons." But Asahel would not stop chasing him.

²²Again Abner warned Asahel, "Stop chasing me! Why should I strike you down? How could I look your brother Joab in the face?"

²³But Asahel refused to give up the pursuit; so Abner thrust the butt of his spear into Asahel's stomach, and the spear came out through his back. He fell there and died on the spot. And every man stopped when he came to the place where Asahel had fallen and died.

²⁴But Joab and Abishai pursued Abner, and as the sun was setting, they came to the hill of Ammah, near Giah on the way to the wasteland of Gibeon. ²⁵Then the men of Benjamin rallied behind Abner. They formed themselves into a group and took their stand on top of a hill.

²⁶Abner called out to Joab, "Must the

sword devour forever? Don't you realize that this will end in bitterness? How long before you order your men to stop pursuing their brothers?"

²⁷Joab answered, "As surely as God lives, if you had not spoken, the men would have continued the pursuit of their brothers until morning.ᵇ"

²⁸So Joab blew the trumpet, and all the men came to a halt; they no longer pursued Israel, nor did they fight anymore.

²⁹All that night Abner and his men marched through the Arabah. They crossed the Jordan, continued through the whole Bithronᶜ and came to Mahanaim.

³⁰Then Joab returned from pursuing Abner and assembled all his men. Besides Asahel, nineteen of David's men were found missing. ³¹But David's men had killed three hundred and sixty Benjamites who were with Abner. ³²They took Asahel and buried him in his father's tomb at Bethlehem. Then Joab and his men marched all night and arrived at Hebron by daybreak.

³:¹THE war between the house of Saul and the house of David lasted a long time. David grew stronger and stronger, while the house of Saul grew weaker and weaker.

²Sons were born to David in Hebron:
His firstborn was Amnon the son of Ahinoam of Jezreel;
³his second, Kileab the son of Abigail the widow of Nabal of Carmel;
the third, Absalom the son of Maacah daughter of Talmai king of Geshur;
⁴the fourth, Adonijah the son of Haggith;
the fifth, Shephatiah the son of Abital;
⁵and the sixth, Ithream the son of David's wife Eglah.
These were born to David in Hebron.

⁶During the war between the house of Saul and the house of David, Abner had been strengthening his own position in the house of Saul. ⁷Now Saul had had a concubine named Rizpah daughter of Aiah. And Ish-Bosheth said to Abner, "Why did you sleep with my father's concubine?"

⁸Abner was very angry because of what Ish-Bosheth said and he answered, "Am I a dog's head—on Judah's side? This very day I am loyal to the house of your father Saul and to his family and friends. I haven't handed you over to David. Yet now you accuse me of an offense involving this woman! ⁹May God deal with Abner, be it ever so severely, if I do not do for David what the Lord promised him on oath ¹⁰and transfer the kingdom from the house of Saul and establish David's throne over Israel and Judah from Dan to Beersheba." ¹¹Ish-Bosheth did not dare to say another word to Abner, because he was afraid of him.

¹²Then Abner sent messengers on his behalf to say to David, "Whose land is it? Make an agreement with me, and I will help you bring all Israel over to you."

¹³"Good," said David. "I will make an agreement with you. But I demand one thing of you: Do not come into my presence unless you bring Michal daughter of Saul when you come to see me." ¹⁴Then David sent messengers to Ish-Bosheth son of Saul, demanding, "Give me my wife Michal, whom I betrothed to myself for the price of a hundred Philistine foreskins."

¹⁵So Ish-Bosheth gave orders and had her taken away from her husband Paltiel son of Laish. ¹⁶Her husband, however, went with her, weeping behind her all the way to Bahurim. Then Abner said to him, "Go back home!" So he went back.

¹⁷Abner conferred with the elders of Israel and said, "For some time you have wanted to make David your king. ¹⁸Now do it! For the Lord promised David, 'By my servant David I will rescue my people Israel from the hand of the Philis-

tines and from the hand of all their enemies.'"

¹⁹Abner also spoke to the Benjamites in person. Then he went to Hebron to tell David everything that Israel and the whole house of Benjamin wanted to do. ²⁰When Abner, who had twenty men with him, came to David at Hebron, David prepared a feast for him and his men. ²¹Then Abner said to David, "Let me go at once and assemble all Israel for my lord the king, so that they may make a compact with you, and that you may rule over all that your heart desires." So David sent Abner away, and he went in peace.

²²Just then David's men and Joab returned from a raid and brought with them a great deal of plunder. But Abner was no longer with David in Hebron, because David had sent him away, and he had gone in peace. ²³When Joab and all the soldiers with him arrived, he was told that Abner son of Ner had come to the king and that the king had sent him away and that he had gone in peace.

²⁴So Joab went to the king and said, "What have you done? Look, Abner came to you. Why did you let him go? Now he is gone! ²⁵You know Abner son of Ner; he came to deceive you and observe your movements and find out everything you are doing."

²⁶Joab then left David and sent messengers after Abner, and they brought him back from the well of Sirah. But David did not know it. ²⁷Now when Abner returned to Hebron, Joab took him aside into the gateway, as though to speak with him privately. And there, to avenge the blood of his brother Asahel, Joab stabbed him in the stomach, and he died.

²⁸Later, when David heard about this, he said, "I and my kingdom are forever innocent before the Lord concerning the blood of Abner son of Ner. ²⁹May his blood fall upon the head of Joab and upon all his father's house! May Joab's house never be without someone who has a running sore or leprosy*d* or who leans on a crutch or who falls by the sword or who lacks food."

30(Joab and his brother Abishai murdered Abner because he had killed their brother Asahel in the battle at Gibeon.) 31Then David said to Joab and all the people with him, "Tear your clothes and put on sackcloth and walk in mourning in front of Abner." King David himself walked behind the bier. 32They buried Abner in Hebron, and the king wept aloud at Abner's tomb. All the people wept also.

33The king sang this lament for Abner:

"Should Abner have died as the
        lawless die?
34   Your hands were not bound,
        your feet were not fettered.
You fell as one falls before wicked
        men."

And all the people wept over him again.

35Then they all came and urged David to eat something while it was still day; but David took an oath, saying, "May God deal with me, be it ever so severely, if I taste bread or anything else before the sun sets!"

36All the people took note and were pleased; indeed, everything the king did pleased them. 37So on that day all the people and all Israel knew that the king had no part in the murder of Abner son of Ner.

38Then the king said to his men, "Do you not realize that a prince and a great man has fallen in Israel this day? 39And today, though I am the anointed king, I am weak, and these sons of Zeruiah are too strong for me. May the Lord repay the evildoer according to his evil deeds!"

a 16 Helkath Hazzurim means field of daggers or field of hostilities.   b27 Or spoken this morning, the men would not have taken up the pursuit of their brothers; or spoken, the men would have given up the pursuit of their brothers by morning   c29 Or morning; or ravine; the meaning of the Hebrew for this word is uncertain.   d29 The Hebrew word was used for various diseases affecting the skin—not necessarily leprosy.

JOHN 13:1-30

It was just before the Passover Feast. Jesus knew that the time had come for him to leave this world and go to the Father. Having loved his own who were in the world, he now showed them the full extent of his love.a

2The evening meal was being served, and the devil had already prompted Judas Iscariot, son of Simon, to betray Jesus. 3Jesus knew that the Father had put all things under his power, and that he had come from God and was returning to God; 4so he got up from the meal, took off his outer clothing, and wrapped a towel around his waist. 5After that, he poured water into a basin and began to wash his disciples' feet, drying them with the towel that was wrapped around him.

6He came to Simon Peter, who said to him, "Lord, are you going to wash my feet?"

7Jesus replied, "You do not realize now what I am doing, but later you will understand."

8"No," said Peter, "you shall never wash my feet."

Jesus answered, "Unless I wash you, you have no part with me."

9"Then, Lord," Simon Peter replied, "not just my feet but my hands and my head as well!"

10Jesus answered, "A person who has had a bath needs only to wash his feet; his whole body is clean. And you are clean, though not every one of you." 11For he knew who was going to betray him, and that was why he said not every one was clean.

12When he had finished washing their feet, he put on his clothes and returned to his place. "Do you understand what I have done for you?" he asked them. 13"You call me 'Teacher' and 'Lord,' and rightly so, for that is what I am. 14Now that I, your Lord and Teacher, have washed your feet, you also should wash one another's feet. 15I have set you an example that you should do as I have done for you. 16I tell you the truth, no servant is greater than his master, nor is a messenger greater than the one who sent him.

17Now that you know these things, you will be blessed if you do them.

18"I am not referring to all of you; I know those I have chosen. But this is to fulfill the scripture: 'He who shares my bread has lifted up his heel against me.'b

19"I am telling you now before it happens, so that when it does happen you will believe that I am He. 20I tell you the truth, whoever accepts anyone I send accepts me; and whoever accepts me accepts the one who sent me."

21After he had said this, Jesus was troubled in spirit and testified, "I tell you the truth, one of you is going to betray me."

22His disciples stared at one another, at a loss to know which of them he meant. 23One of them, the disciple whom Jesus loved, was reclining next to him. 24Simon Peter motioned to this disciple and said, "Ask him which one he means."

25Leaning back against Jesus, he asked him, "Lord, who is it?"

26Jesus answered, "It is the one to whom I will give this piece of bread when I have dipped it in the dish." Then, dipping the piece of bread, he gave it to Judas Iscariot, son of Simon. 27As soon as Judas took the bread, Satan entered into him.

"What you are about to do, do quickly," Jesus told him, 28but no one at the meal understood why Jesus said this to him. 29Since Judas had charge of the money, some thought Jesus was telling him to buy what was needed for the Feast, or to give something to the poor. 30As soon as Judas had taken the bread, he went out. And it was night.

a1 Or he loved them to the last   b18 Psalm 41:9

PSALM 119:1-16a

א   Aleph

1Blessed are they whose ways are blameless,
   who walk according to the law of the LORD.

2Blessed are they who keep his statutes
   and seek him with all their heart.
3They do nothing wrong;
   they walk in his ways.
4You have laid down precepts
   that are to be fully obeyed.
5Oh, that my ways were steadfast
   in obeying your decrees!
6Then I would not be put to shame
   when I consider all your commands.
7I will praise you with an upright heart
   as I learn your righteous laws.
8I will obey your decrees;
   do not utterly forsake me.

ב   Beth

9How can a young man keep his way pure?
   By living according to your word.
10I seek you with all my heart;
   do not let me stray from your commands.
11I have hidden your word in my heart
   that I might not sin against you.
12Praise be to you, O LORD;
   teach me your decrees.
13With my lips I recount
   all the laws that come from your mouth.
14I rejoice in following your statutes
   as one rejoices in great riches.
15I meditate on your precepts
   and consider your ways.
16I delight in your decrees;
   I will not neglect your word.

aThis psalm is an acrostic poem; the verses of each stanza begin with the same letter of the Hebrew alphabet.

PROVERBS 15:29-30

29The LORD is far from the wicked
   but he hears the prayer of the righteous.

30A cheerful look brings joy to the heart,
   and good news gives health to the bones.

□ DAY 144

GOD SIGHTINGS

May 24

2 SAMUEL 4:1–6:23

When Ish-Bosheth son of Saul heard that Abner had died in Hebron, he lost courage, and all Israel became alarmed. ²Now Saul's son had two men who were leaders of raiding bands. One was named Baanah and the other Recab; they were sons of Rimmon the Beerothite from the tribe of Benjamin—Beeroth is considered part of Benjamin, ³because the people of Beeroth fled to Gittaim and have lived there as aliens to this day.

⁴(Jonathan son of Saul had a son who was lame in both feet. He was five years old when the news about Saul and Jonathan came from Jezreel. His nurse picked him up and fled, but as she hurried to leave, he fell and became crippled. His name was Mephibosheth.)

⁵Now Recab and Baanah, the sons of Rimmon the Beerothite, set out for the house of Ish-Bosheth, and they arrived there in the heat of the day while he was taking his noonday rest. ⁶They went into the inner part of the house as if to get some wheat, and they stabbed him in the stomach. Then Recab and his brother Baanah slipped away.

⁷They had gone into the house while he was lying on the bed in his bedroom. After they stabbed and killed him, they cut off his head. Taking it with them, they traveled all night by way of the Arabah. ⁸They brought the head of Ish-Bosheth to David at Hebron and said to the king, "Here is the head of Ish-Bosheth son of Saul, your enemy, who tried to take your life. This day the LORD has avenged my lord the king against Saul and his offspring."

⁹David answered Recab and his brother Baanah, the sons of Rimmon the Beerothite, "As surely as the LORD lives, who has delivered me out of all trouble, ¹⁰when a man told me, 'Saul is dead,' and thought he was bringing good news, I seized him and put him to death in Ziklag. That was the reward I gave him for his news! ¹¹How much more—when wicked men have killed an innocent man in his own house and on his own bed—should I not now demand his blood from your hand and rid the earth of you!"

¹²So David gave an order to his men, and they killed them. They cut off their hands and feet and hung the bodies by the pool in Hebron. But they took the head of Ish-Bosheth and buried it in Abner's tomb at Hebron.

⁵:¹ALL the tribes of Israel came to David at Hebron and said, "We are your own flesh and blood. ²In the past, while Saul was king over us, you were the one who led Israel on their military campaigns. And the LORD said to you, 'You will shepherd my people Israel, and you will become their ruler.'"

³When all the elders of Israel had come to King David at Hebron, the king made a compact with them at Hebron before the LORD, and they anointed David king over Israel.

⁴David was thirty years old when he became king, and he reigned forty years. ⁵In Hebron he reigned over Judah seven years and six months, and in Jerusalem he reigned over all Israel and Judah thirty-three years.

⁶The king and his men marched to Jerusalem to attack the Jebusites, who lived there. The Jebusites said to David, "You will not get in here; even the blind and the lame can ward you off." They thought, "David cannot get in here." ⁷Nevertheless, David captured the fortress of Zion, the City of David.

⁸On that day, David said, "Anyone who conquers the Jebusites will have to use the water shaft*a* to reach those 'lame and blind' who are David's enemies.*b*" That is why they say, "The 'blind and lame' will not enter the palace."

⁹David then took up residence in the fortress and called it the City of David. He built up the area around it, from the

supporting terraces*c* inward. [10]And he became more and more powerful, because the Lord God Almighty was with him.

[11]Now Hiram king of Tyre sent messengers to David, along with cedar logs and carpenters and stonemasons, and they built a palace for David. [12]And David knew that the Lord had established him as king over Israel and had exalted his kingdom for the sake of his people Israel.

[13]After he left Hebron, David took more concubines and wives in Jerusalem, and more sons and daughters were born to him. [14]These are the names of the children born to him there: Shammua, Shobab, Nathan, Solomon, [15]Ibhar, Elishua, Nepheg, Japhia, [16]Elishama, Eliada and Eliphelet.

[17]When the Philistines heard that David had been anointed king over Israel, they went up in full force to search for him, but David heard about it and went down to the stronghold. [18]Now the Philistines had come and spread out in the Valley of Rephaim; [19]so David inquired of the Lord, "Shall I go and attack the Philistines? Will you hand them over to me?"

The Lord answered him, "Go, for I will surely hand the Philistines over to you."

[20]So David went to Baal Perazim, and there he defeated them. He said, "As waters break out, the Lord has broken out against my enemies before me." So that place was called Baal Perazim.*d* [21]The Philistines abandoned their idols there, and David and his men carried them off.

[22]Once more the Philistines came up and spread out in the Valley of Rephaim; [23]so David inquired of the Lord, and he answered, "Do not go straight up, but circle around behind them and attack them in front of the balsam trees. [24]As soon as you hear the sound of marching in the tops of the balsam trees, move quickly, because that will mean the Lord has gone out in front of you to strike the Philistine army." [25]So David

did as the Lord commanded him, and he struck down the Philistines all the way from Gibeon*e* to Gezer.

[6:1]David again brought together out of Israel chosen men, thirty thousand in all. [2]He and all his men set out from Baalah of Judah*f* to bring up from there the ark of God, which is called by the Name,*g* the name of the Lord Almighty, who is enthroned between the cherubim that are on the ark. [3]They set the ark of God on a new cart and brought it from the house of Abinadab, which was on the hill. Uzzah and Ahio, sons of Abinadab, were guiding the new cart [4]with the ark of God on it,*h* and Ahio was walking in front of it. [5]David and the whole house of Israel were celebrating with all their might before the Lord, with songs*i* and with harps, lyres, tambourines, sistrums and cymbals.

[6]When they came to the threshing floor of Nacon, Uzzah reached out and took hold of the ark of God, because the oxen stumbled. [7]The Lord's anger burned against Uzzah because of his irreverent act; therefore God struck him down and he died there beside the ark of God.

[8]Then David was angry because the Lord's wrath had broken out against Uzzah, and to this day that place is called Perez Uzzah.*j*

[9]David was afraid of the Lord that day and said, "How can the ark of the Lord ever come to me?" [10]He was not willing to take the ark of the Lord to be with him in the City of David. Instead, he took it aside to the house of Obed-Edom the Gittite. [11]The ark of the Lord remained in the house of Obed-Edom the Gittite for three months, and the Lord blessed him and his entire household.

[12]Now King David was told, "The Lord has blessed the household of Obed-Edom and everything he has, because of the ark of God." So David went down and brought up the ark of God from the house of Obed-Edom to the City of David with rejoicing. [13]When those who were carrying the ark of the Lord had taken six steps, he sacrificed a

bull and a fattened calf. [14]David, wearing a linen ephod, danced before the Lord with all his might, [15]while he and the entire house of Israel brought up the ark of the Lord with shouts and the sound of trumpets.

[16]As the ark of the Lord was entering the City of David, Michal daughter of Saul watched from a window. And when she saw King David leaping and dancing before the Lord, she despised him in her heart.

[17]They brought the ark of the Lord and set it in its place inside the tent that David had pitched for it, and David sacrificed burnt offerings and fellowship offerings[k] before the Lord. [18]After he had finished sacrificing the burnt offerings and fellowship offerings, he blessed the people in the name of the Lord Almighty. [19]Then he gave a loaf of bread, a cake of dates and a cake of raisins to each person in the whole crowd of Israelites, both men and women. And all the people went to their homes.

[20]When David returned home to bless his household, Michal daughter of Saul came out to meet him and said, "How the king of Israel has distinguished himself today, disrobing in the sight of the slave girls of his servants as any vulgar fellow would!"

[21]David said to Michal, "It was before the Lord, who chose me rather than your father or anyone from his house when he appointed me ruler over the Lord's people Israel—I will celebrate before the Lord. [22]I will become even more undignified than this, and I will be humiliated in my own eyes. But by these slave girls you spoke of, I will be held in honor."

[23]And Michal daughter of Saul had no children to the day of her death.

a8 Or use scaling hooks   b8 Or are hated by David   c9 Or the Millo   d20 Baal Perazim means the lord who breaks out. e25 Septuagint (see also 1 Chron. 14:16); Hebrew Geba f2 That is, Kiriath Jearim; Hebrew Baale Judah, a variant of Baalah of Judah   g2 Hebrew; Septuagint and Vulgate do not have the Name.   h3,4 Dead Sea Scrolls and some Septuagint manuscripts; Masoretic Text cart   i4and they brought it with the ark of God from the house of Abinadab, which was on the hill   j5 See Dead Sea Scrolls, Septuagint and 1 Chronicles 13:8; Masoretic Text celebrating before the Lord with all kinds of instruments made of pine.   j8 Perez Uzzah means outbreak against Uzzah.   k17 Traditionally peace offerings; also in verse 18

JOHN 13:31–14:14

When he [Judas] was gone, Jesus said, "Now is the Son of Man glorified and God is glorified in him. [32]If God is glorified in him,[a] God will glorify the Son in himself, and will glorify him at once.

[33]"My children, I will be with you only a little longer. You will look for me, and just as I told the Jews, so I tell you now: Where I am going, you cannot come.

[34]**"A new command I give you: Love one another. As I have loved you, so you must love one another. [35]By this all men will know that you are my disciples, if you love one another."**

[36]Simon Peter asked him, "Lord, where are you going?"

Jesus replied, "Where I am going, you cannot follow now, but you will follow later."

[37]Peter asked, "Lord, why can't I follow you now? I will lay down my life for you."

[38]Then Jesus answered, "Will you really lay down your life for me? I tell you the truth, before the rooster crows, you will disown me three times!

[14:1]"Do not let your hearts be troubled. Trust in God[b]; trust also in me. [2]In my Father's house are many rooms; if it were not so, I would have told you. I am going there to prepare a place for you. [3]And if I go and prepare a place for you, I will come back and take you to be with me that you also may be where I am. [4]You know the way to the place where I am going."

[5]Thomas said to him, "Lord, we don't know where you are going, so how can we know the way?"

[6]Jesus answered, "I am the way and the truth and the life. No one comes to the Father except through me. [7]If you really knew me, you would know[c] my Father as well. From now on, you do know him and have seen him."

[8]Philip said, "Lord, show us the Father and that will be enough for us."

[9]Jesus answered: "Don't you know me, Philip, even after I have been among you such a long time? Anyone who has seen me has seen the Father. How can you say, 'Show us the Father'? [10]Don't

you believe that I am in the Father, and that the Father is in me? The words I say to you are not just my own. Rather, it is the Father, living in me, who is doing his work. ¹¹Believe me when I say that I am in the Father and the Father is in me; or at least believe on the evidence of the miracles themselves. ¹²I tell you the truth, anyone who has faith in me will do what I have been doing. He will do even greater things than these, because I am going to the Father. ¹³And I will do whatever you ask in my name, so that the Son may bring glory to the Father. ¹⁴You may ask me for anything in my name, and I will do it."

PSALM 119:17-32

∂ Gimel

¹⁷**D**o good to your servant, and I will live;
  I will obey your word.
¹⁸Open my eyes that I may see
  wonderful things in your law.
¹⁹I am a stranger on earth;
  do not hide your commands
    from me.
²⁰My soul is consumed with longing
  for your laws at all times.
²¹You rebuke the arrogant, who are
    cursed
  and who stray from your commands.
²²Remove from me scorn and contempt,
  for I keep your statutes.
²³Though rulers sit together and
    slander me,
  your servant will meditate on your
    decrees.
²⁴Your statutes are my delight;
  they are my counselors.

ㄱ Daleth

²⁵I am laid low in the dust;
  preserve my life according to your
    word.
²⁶I recounted my ways and you
    answered me;
  teach me your decrees.

²⁷Let me understand the teaching of
    your precepts;
  then I will meditate on your
    wonders.
²⁸My soul is weary with sorrow;
  strengthen me according to your
    word.
²⁹Keep me from deceitful ways;
  be gracious to me through your
    law.
³⁰I have chosen the way of truth;
  I have set my heart on your laws.
³¹I hold fast to your statutes, O LORD;
  do not let me be put to shame.
³²I run in the path of your commands,
  for you have set my heart free.

PROVERBS 15:31-32

³¹**H**e who listens to a life-giving
    rebuke
  will be at home among the wise.

³²He who ignores discipline despises
    himself,
  but whoever heeds correction
    gains understanding.

□ D A Y 1 4 5

GOD SIGHTINGS

May 25

2 SAMUEL 7:1-8:18

After the king was settled in his palace and the LORD had given him rest from all his enemies around him, ²he said to Nathan the prophet, "Here I am, living in a palace of cedar, while the ark of God remains in a tent."

³Nathan replied to the king, "Whatever you have in mind, go ahead and do it, for the LORD is with you."

⁴That night the word of the LORD came to Nathan, saying:

⁵"Go and tell my servant David, 'This is what the LORD says: Are you the one to build me a house to dwell in? ⁶I have not dwelt in a

house from the day I brought the Israelites up out of Egypt to this day. I have been moving from place to place with a tent as my dwelling. [7] Wherever I have moved with all the Israelites, did I ever say to any of their rulers whom I commanded to shepherd my people Israel, "Why have you not built me a house of cedar?"'

[8] "Now then, tell my servant David, 'This is what the LORD Almighty says: I took you from the pasture and from following the flock to be ruler over my people Israel. [9] I have been with you wherever you have gone, and I have cut off all your enemies from before you. Now I will make your name great, like the names of the greatest men of the earth. [10] And I will provide a place for my people Israel and will plant them so that they can have a home of their own and no longer be disturbed. Wicked people will not oppress them anymore, as they did at the beginning [11] and have done ever since the time I appointed leaders[a] over my people Israel. I will also give you rest from all your enemies.

"'The LORD declares to you that the LORD himself will establish a house for you: [12] When your days are over and you rest with your fathers, I will raise up your offspring to succeed you, who will come from your own body, and I will establish his kingdom. [13] He is the one who will build a house for my Name, and I will establish the throne of his kingdom forever. [14] I will be his father, and he will be my son. When he does wrong, I will punish him with the rod of men, with floggings inflicted by men. [15] But my love will never be taken away from him, as I took it away from Saul, whom I removed from before you. [16] Your house and your kingdom will endure forever before me[b]; your throne will be established forever.'"

[17] Nathan reported to David all the words of this entire revelation.

[18] Then King David went in and sat before the LORD, and he said:

"Who am I, O Sovereign LORD, and what is my family, that you have brought me this far? [19] And as if this were not enough in your sight, O Sovereign LORD, you have also spoken about the future of the house of your servant. Is this your usual way of dealing with man, O Sovereign LORD?

[20] "What more can David say to you? For you know your servant, O Sovereign LORD. [21] For the sake of your word and according to your will, you have done this great thing and made it known to your servant.

[22] "How great you are, O Sovereign LORD! There is no one like you, and there is no God but you, as we have heard with our own ears. [23] And who is like your people Israel—the one nation on earth that God went out to redeem as a people for himself, and to make a name for himself, and to perform great and awesome wonders by driving out nations and their gods from before your people, whom you redeemed from Egypt?[c] [24] You have established your people Israel as your very own forever, and you, O LORD, have become their God.

[25] "And now, LORD God, keep forever the promise you have made concerning your servant and his house. Do as you promised, [26] so that your name will be great forever. Then men will say, 'The LORD Almighty is God over Israel!' And the house of your servant David will be established before you.

[27] "O LORD Almighty, God of Israel, you have revealed this to your servant, saying, 'I will build a house for you.' So your servant has found courage to offer you this prayer. [28] O Sovereign LORD, you are God!

Your words are trustworthy, and you have promised these good things to your servant. 29Now be pleased to bless the house of your servant, that it may continue forever in your sight; for you, O Sovereign LORD, have spoken, and with your blessing the house of your servant will be blessed forever."

8:1IN the course of time, David defeated the Philistines and subdued them, and he took Metheg Ammah from the control of the Philistines.

2David also defeated the Moabites. He made them lie down on the ground and measured them off with a length of cord. Every two lengths of them were put to death, and the third length was allowed to live. So the Moabites became subject to David and brought tribute.

3Moreover, David fought Hadadezer son of Rehob, king of Zobah, when he went to restore his control along the Euphrates River. 4David captured a thousand of his chariots, seven thousand charioteers*d* and twenty thousand foot soldiers. He hamstrung all but a hundred of the chariot horses.

5When the Arameans of Damascus came to help Hadadezer king of Zobah, David struck down twenty-two thousand of them. 6He put garrisons in the Aramean kingdom of Damascus, and the Arameans became subject to him and brought tribute. The LORD gave David victory wherever he went.

7David took the gold shields that belonged to the officers of Hadadezer and brought them to Jerusalem. 8From Tebah*e* and Berothai, towns that belonged to Hadadezer, King David took a great quantity of bronze.

9When Tou*f* king of Hamath heard that David had defeated the entire army of Hadadezer, 10he sent his son Joram*g* to King David to greet him and congratulate him on his victory in battle over Hadadezer, who had been at war with Tou. Joram brought with him articles of silver and gold and bronze.

11King David dedicated these articles

to the LORD, as he had done with the silver and gold from all the nations he had subdued: 12Edom*h* and Moab, the Ammonites and the Philistines, and Amalek. He also dedicated the plunder taken from Hadadezer son of Rehob, king of Zobah.

13And David became famous after he returned from striking down eighteen thousand Edomites*i* in the Valley of Salt.

14He put garrisons throughout Edom, and all the Edomites became subject to David. The LORD gave David victory wherever he went.

15David reigned over all Israel, doing what was just and right for all his people. 16Joab son of Zeruiah was over the army; Jehoshaphat son of Ahilud was recorder; 17Zadok son of Ahitub and Ahimelech son of Abiathar were priests; Seraiah was secretary; 18Benaiah son of Jehoiada was over the Kerethites and Pelethites; and David's sons were royal advisers.*j*

a11 Traditionally *judges*   *b16* Some Hebrew manuscripts and Septuagint; most Hebrew manuscripts *you*   *c23* See Septuagint and 1 Chron. 17:21; Hebrew *wonders for your land and before your people, whom you redeemed from Egypt, from the nations and their gods.*   *d4* Septuagint (see also Dead Sea Scrolls and 1 Chron. 18:4); Masoretic Text *captured seventeen hundred of his charioteers*   *e8* See some Septuagint manuscripts (see also 1 Chron. 18:8); Hebrew *Betah.*   *f9* Hebrew *Toi,* a variant of *Tou;* also in verse 10   *g10* A variant of *Hadoram*   *h12* Some Hebrew manuscripts, Septuagint and Syriac (see also 1 Chron. 18:11); most Hebrew manuscripts *Aram*   *i13* A few Hebrew manuscripts, Septuagint and Syriac (see also 1 Chron. 18:12); most Hebrew manuscripts *Aram* (that is, Arameans)   *j18* Or *were priests*

JOHN 14:15-31

"If you [Jesus' disciples] love me [Jesus], you will obey what I command. 16And I will ask the Father, and he will give you another Counselor to be with you forever— 17the Spirit of truth. The world cannot accept him, because it neither sees him nor knows him. But you know him, for he lives with you and will be*a* in you. 18I will not leave you as orphans; I will come to you. 19Before long, the world will not see me anymore, but you will see me. Because I live, you also will live. 20On that day you will realize that I am in my Father, and you are in me, and I am in you. 21Whoever has my commands and obeys them, he is the one who loves me. He who loves me will be loved by my Father, and I too will love him and show myself to him."

22 Then Judas (not Judas Iscariot) said, "But, Lord, why do you intend to show yourself to us and not to the world?"

23 Jesus replied, "If anyone loves me, he will obey my teaching. My Father will love him, and we will come to him and make our home with him. 24 He who does not love me will not obey my teaching. These words you hear are not my own; they belong to the Father who sent me.

25 "All this I have spoken while still with you. 26 But the Counselor, the Holy Spirit, whom the Father will send in my name, will teach you all things and will remind you of everything I have said to you. 27 Peace I leave with you; my peace I give you. I do not give to you as the world gives. Do not let your hearts be troubled and do not be afraid.

28 "You heard me say, 'I am going away and I am coming back to you.' If you loved me, you would be glad that I am going to the Father, for the Father is greater than I. 29 I have told you now before it happens, so that when it does happen you will believe. 30 I will not speak with you much longer, for the prince of this world is coming. He has no hold on me, 31 but the world must learn that I love the Father and that I do exactly what my Father has commanded me.

"Come now; let us leave."

a17 Some early manuscripts *and is*

PSALM 119:33-48

ה   He

33 Teach me, O Lord, to follow your decrees;
    then I will keep them to the end.
34 Give me understanding, and I will keep your law
    and obey it with all my heart.
35 Direct me in the path of your commands,
    for there I find delight.
36 Turn my heart toward your statutes

and not toward selfish gain.
37 Turn my eyes away from worthless things;
    preserve my life according to your word.*a*
38 Fulfill your promise to your servant,
    so that you may be feared.
39 Take away the disgrace I dread,
    for your laws are good.
40 How I long for your precepts!
    Preserve my life in your righteousness.

ו   Waw

41 May your unfailing love come to me, O Lord,
    your salvation according to your promise;
42 then I will answer the one who taunts me,
    for I trust in your word.
43 Do not snatch the word of truth from my mouth,
    for I have put my hope in your laws.
44 I will always obey your law,
    for ever and ever.
45 I will walk about in freedom,
    for I have sought out your precepts.
46 I will speak of your statutes before kings
    and will not be put to shame,
47 for I delight in your commands because I love them.
48 I lift up my hands to*b* your commands, which I love,
    and I meditate on your decrees.

a37 Two manuscripts of the Masoretic Text and Dead Sea Scrolls; most manuscripts of the Masoretic Text *life in your way*   *b48* Or *for*

PROVERBS 15:33

33 The fear of the Lord teaches a man wisdom,*a*
    and humility comes before honor.

a33 Or *Wisdom teaches the fear of the Lord*

□ DAY 146

GOD SIGHTINGS

May 26

2 SAMUEL 9:1–11:27

David asked, "Is there anyone still left of the house of Saul to whom I can show kindness for Jonathan's sake?"

2 Now there was a servant of Saul's household named Ziba. They called him to appear before David, and the king said to him, "Are you Ziba?"

"Your servant," he replied.

3 The king asked, "Is there no one still left of the house of Saul to whom I can show God's kindness?"

Ziba answered the king, "There is still a son of Jonathan; he is crippled in both feet."

4 "Where is he?" the king asked.

Ziba answered, "He is at the house of Makir son of Ammiel in Lo Debar."

5 So King David had him brought from Lo Debar, from the house of Makir son of Ammiel.

6 When Mephibosheth son of Jonathan, the son of Saul, came to David, he bowed down to pay him honor.

David said, "Mephibosheth!"

"Your servant," he replied.

7 "Don't be afraid," David said to him, "for I will surely show you kindness for the sake of your father Jonathan. I will restore to you all the land that belonged to your grandfather Saul, and you will always eat at my table."

8 Mephibosheth bowed down and said, "What is your servant, that you should notice a dead dog like me?"

9 Then the king summoned Ziba, Saul's servant, and said to him, "I have given your master's grandson everything that belonged to Saul and his family. 10 You and your sons and your servants are to farm the land for him and bring in the crops, so that your master's grandson may be provided for. And Mephibosheth, grandson of your master, will always eat at my table." (Now Ziba had fifteen sons and twenty servants.)

11 Then Ziba said to the king, "Your servant will do whatever my lord the king commands his servant to do." So Mephibosheth ate at David's*a* table like one of the king's sons.

12 Mephibosheth had a young son named Mica, and all the members of Ziba's household were servants of Mephibosheth. 13 And Mephibosheth lived in Jerusalem, because he always ate at the king's table, and he was crippled in both feet.

10:1 In the course of time, the king of the Ammonites died, and his son Hanun succeeded him as king. 2 David thought, "I will show kindness to Hanun son of Nahash, just as his father showed kindness to me." So David sent a delegation to express his sympathy to Hanun concerning his father.

When David's men came to the land of the Ammonites, 3 the Ammonite nobles said to Hanun their lord, "Do you think David is honoring your father by sending men to you to express sympathy? Hasn't David sent them to you to explore the city and spy it out and overthrow it?" 4 So Hanun seized David's men, shaved off half of each man's beard, cut off their garments in the middle at the buttocks, and sent them away.

5 When David was told about this, he sent messengers to meet the men, for they were greatly humiliated. The king said, "Stay at Jericho till your beards have grown, and then come back."

6 When the Ammonites realized that they had become a stench in David's nostrils, they hired twenty thousand Aramean foot soldiers from Beth Rehob and Zobah, as well as the king of Maacah with a thousand men, and also twelve thousand men from Tob.

7 On hearing this, David sent Joab out with the entire army of fighting men. 8 The Ammonites came out and drew up in battle formation at the entrance to their city gate, while the Arameans of Zobah and Rehob and the men of Tob

and Maacah were by themselves in the open country.

⁹Joab saw that there were battle lines in front of him and behind him; so he selected some of the best troops in Israel and deployed them against the Arameans. ¹⁰He put the rest of the men under the command of Abishai his brother and deployed them against the Ammonites. ¹¹Joab said, "If the Arameans are too strong for me, then you are to come to my rescue; but if the Ammonites are too strong for you, then I will come to rescue you. ¹²Be strong and let us fight bravely for our people and the cities of our God. The LORD will do what is good in his sight."

¹³Then Joab and the troops with him advanced to fight the Arameans, and they fled before him. ¹⁴When the Ammonites saw that the Arameans were fleeing, they fled before Abishai and went inside the city. So Joab returned from fighting the Ammonites and came to Jerusalem.

¹⁵After the Arameans saw that they had been routed by Israel, they regrouped. ¹⁶Hadadezer had Arameans brought from beyond the River[b]; they went to Helam, with Shobach the commander of Hadadezer's army leading them.

¹⁷When David was told of this, he gathered all Israel, crossed the Jordan and went to Helam. The Arameans formed their battle lines to meet David and fought against him. ¹⁸But they fled before Israel, and David killed seven hundred of their charioteers and forty thousand of their foot soldiers.[c] He also struck down Shobach the commander of their army, and he died there. ¹⁹When all the kings who were vassals of Hadadezer saw that they had been defeated by Israel, they made peace with the Israelites and became subject to them.

So the Arameans were afraid to help the Ammonites anymore.

¹¹:¹IN the spring, at the time when kings go off to war, David sent Joab out with the king's men and the whole Israelite army. They destroyed the Ammonites and besieged Rabbah. But David remained in Jerusalem.

²One evening David got up from his bed and walked around on the roof of the palace. From the roof he saw a woman bathing. The woman was very beautiful, ³and David sent someone to find out about her. The man said, "Isn't this Bathsheba, the daughter of Eliam and the wife of Uriah the Hittite?" ⁴Then David sent messengers to get her. She came to him, and he slept with her. (She had purified herself from her uncleanness.) Then[d] she went back home. ⁵The woman conceived and sent word to David, saying, "I am pregnant."

⁶So David sent this word to Joab: "Send me Uriah the Hittite." And Joab sent him to David. ⁷When Uriah came to him, David asked him how Joab was, how the soldiers were and how the war was going. ⁸Then David said to Uriah, "Go down to your house and wash your feet." So Uriah left the palace, and a gift from the king was sent after him. ⁹But Uriah slept at the entrance to the palace with all his master's servants and did not go down to his house.

¹⁰When David was told, "Uriah did not go home," he asked him, "Haven't you just come from a distance? Why didn't you go home?"

¹¹Uriah said to David, "The ark and Israel and Judah are staying in tents, and my master Joab and my lord's men are camped in the open fields. How could I go to my house to eat and drink and lie with my wife? As surely as you live, I will not do such a thing!"

¹²Then David said to him, "Stay here one more day, and tomorrow I will send you back." So Uriah remained in Jerusalem that day and the next. ¹³At David's invitation, he ate and drank with him, and David made him drunk. But in the evening Uriah went out to sleep on his mat among his master's servants; he did not go home.

¹⁴In the morning David wrote a letter to Joab and sent it with Uriah. ¹⁵In it he wrote, "Put Uriah in the front line where

the fighting is fiercest. Then withdraw from him so he will be struck down and die."

16So while Joab had the city under siege, he put Uriah at a place where he knew the strongest defenders were. 17When the men of the city came out and fought against Joab, some of the men in David's army fell; moreover, Uriah the Hittite died.

18Joab sent David a full account of the battle. 19He instructed the messenger: "When you have finished giving the king this account of the battle, 20the king's anger may flare up, and he may ask you, 'Why did you get so close to the city to fight? Didn't you know they would shoot arrows from the wall? 21Who killed Abimelech son of Jerub-Beshethe? Didn't a woman throw an upper millstone on him from the wall, so that he died in Thebez? Why did you get so close to the wall?' If he asks you this, then say to him, 'Also, your servant Uriah the Hittite is dead.'"

22The messenger set out, and when he arrived he told David everything Joab had sent him to say. 23The messenger said to David, "The men overpowered us and came out against us in the open, but we drove them back to the entrance to the city gate. 24Then the archers shot arrows at your servants from the wall, and some of the king's men died. Moreover, your servant Uriah the Hittite is dead."

25David told the messenger, "Say this to Joab: 'Don't let this upset you; the sword devours one as well as another. Press the attack against the city and destroy it.' Say this to encourage Joab."

26When Uriah's wife heard that her husband was dead, she mourned for him. 27After the time of mourning was over, David had her brought to his house, and she became his wife and bore him a son. But the thing David had done displeased the LORD.

a11 Septuagint; Hebrew my   b16 That is, the Euphrates
c18 Some Septuagint manuscripts (see also 1 Chron. 19:18);
Hebrew horsemen   d4 Or with her. When she purified
herself from her uncleanness,   e21 Also known as Jerub-
Baal (that is, Gideon)

JOHN 15:1-27

"I [Jesus] am the true vine, and my Father is the gardener. 2He cuts off every branch in me that bears no fruit, while every branch that does bear fruit he prunesa so that it will be even more fruitful. 3You are already clean because of the word I have spoken to you. 4Remain in me, and I will remain in you. No branch can bear fruit by itself; it must remain in the vine. Neither can you bear fruit unless you remain in me.

5**"I am the vine; you are the branches. If a man remains in me and I in him, he will bear much fruit; apart from me you can do nothing.** 6If anyone does not remain in me, he is like a branch that is thrown away and withers; such branches are picked up, thrown into the fire and burned. 7If you remain in me and my words remain in you, ask whatever you wish, and it will be given you. 8This is to my Father's glory, that you bear much fruit, showing yourselves to be my disciples.

9"As the Father has loved me, so have I loved you. Now remain in my love. 10If you obey my commands, you will remain in my love, just as I have obeyed my Father's commands and remain in his love. 11I have told you this so that my joy may be in you and that your joy may be complete. 12My command is this: Love each other as I have loved you. 13Greater love has no one than this, that he lay down his life for his friends. 14You are my friends if you do what I command. 15I no longer call you servants, because a servant does not know his master's business. Instead, I have called you friends, for everything that I learned from my Father I have made known to you. 16You did not choose me, but I chose you and appointed you to go and bear fruit—fruit that will last. Then the Father will give you whatever you ask in my name. 17This is my command: Love each other.

18"If the world hates you, keep in mind that it hated me first. 19If you belonged to the world, it would love you as its own. As it is, you do not belong to the world, but I have chosen you out of the world. That is why the world hates you. 20Remember the words I spoke to you: 'No servant is greater than his master.'*b* If they persecuted me, they will persecute you also. If they obeyed my teaching, they will obey yours also. 21They will treat you this way because of my name, for they do not know the One who sent me. 22If I had not come and spoken to them, they would not be guilty of sin. Now, however, they have no excuse for their sin. 23He who hates me hates my Father as well. 24If I had not done among them what no one else did, they would not be guilty of sin. But now they have seen these miracles, and yet they have hated both me and my Father. 25But this is to fulfill what is written in their Law: 'They hated me without reason.'*c*

26"When the Counselor comes, whom I will send to you from the Father, the Spirit of truth who goes out from the Father, he will testify about me. 27And you also must testify, for you have been with me from the beginning."

a2 The Greek for *prunes* also means *cleans.*   *b20* John 13:16   *c25* Psalms 35:19; 69:4

PSALM 119:49-64

ז Zayin

49Remember your [the LORD's] word to your servant,
    for you have given me hope.
50My comfort in my suffering is this:
    Your promise preserves my life.
51The arrogant mock me without restraint,
    but I do not turn from your law.
52I remember your ancient laws,
    O LORD,
    and I find comfort in them.
53Indignation grips me because of the wicked,
    who have forsaken your law.
54Your decrees are the theme of my song
    wherever I lodge.
55In the night I remember your name,
    O LORD,
    and I will keep your law.

56This has been my practice:
    I obey your precepts.

ח Heth

57You are my portion, O LORD;
    I have promised to obey your words.
58I have sought your face with all my heart;
    be gracious to me according to your promise.
59I have considered my ways
    and have turned my steps to your statutes.
60I will hasten and not delay
    to obey your commands.
61Though the wicked bind me with ropes,
    I will not forget your law.
62At midnight I rise to give you thanks
    for your righteous laws.
63I am a friend to all who fear you,
    to all who follow your precepts.
64The earth is filled with your love,
    O LORD;
    teach me your decrees.

PROVERBS 16:1-3

To man belong the plans of the heart,
    but from the LORD comes the reply of the tongue.

2All a man's ways seem innocent to him,
    but motives are weighed by the LORD.

3Commit to the LORD whatever you do,
    and your plans will succeed.

□ DAY 147

GOD SIGHTINGS

May 27

2 SAMUEL 12:1-31

The LORD sent Nathan to David. When he came to him, he said, "There were two men in a certain town, one rich and the other poor. 2The rich man had a very large number of sheep and cattle,

3 but the poor man had nothing except one little ewe lamb he had bought. He raised it, and it grew up with him and his children. It shared his food, drank from his cup and even slept in his arms. It was like a daughter to him.

4 "Now a traveler came to the rich man, but the rich man refrained from taking one of his own sheep or cattle to prepare a meal for the traveler who had come to him. Instead, he took the ewe lamb that belonged to the poor man and prepared it for the one who had come to him."

5 David burned with anger against the man and said to Nathan, "As surely as the LORD lives, the man who did this deserves to die! 6 He must pay for that lamb four times over, because he did such a thing and had no pity."

7 Then Nathan said to David, "You are the man! This is what the LORD, the God of Israel, says: 'I anointed you king over Israel, and I delivered you from the hand of Saul. 8 I gave your master's house to you, and your master's wives into your arms. I gave you the house of Israel and Judah. And if all this had been too little, I would have given you even more. 9 Why did you despise the word of the LORD by doing what is evil in his eyes? You struck down Uriah the Hittite with the sword and took his wife to be your own. You killed him with the sword of the Ammonites. 10 Now, therefore, the sword will never depart from your house, because you despised me and took the wife of Uriah the Hittite to be your own.'

11 "This is what the LORD says: 'Out of your own household I am going to bring calamity upon you. Before your very eyes I will take your wives and give them to one who is close to you, and he will lie with your wives in broad daylight. 12 You did it in secret, but I will do this thing in broad daylight before all Israel.'"

13 Then David said to Nathan, "I have sinned against the LORD."

Nathan replied, "The LORD has taken away your sin. You are not going to die. 14 But because by doing this you have made the enemies of the LORD show utter contempt,[a] the son born to you will die."

15 After Nathan had gone home, the LORD struck the child that Uriah's wife had borne to David, and he became ill. 16 David pleaded with God for the child. He fasted and went into his house and spent the nights lying on the ground. 17 The elders of his household stood beside him to get him up from the ground, but he refused, and he would not eat any food with them.

18 On the seventh day the child died. David's servants were afraid to tell him that the child was dead, for they thought, "While the child was still living, we spoke to David but he would not listen to us. How can we tell him the child is dead? He may do something desperate."

19 David noticed that his servants were whispering among themselves and he realized the child was dead. "Is the child dead?" he asked.

"Yes," they replied, "he is dead."

20 Then David got up from the ground. After he had washed, put on lotions and changed his clothes, he went into the house of the LORD and worshiped. Then he went to his own house, and at his request they served him food, and he ate.

21 His servants asked him, "Why are you acting this way? While the child was alive, you fasted and wept, but now that the child is dead, you get up and eat!"

22 He answered, "While the child was still alive, I fasted and wept. I thought, 'Who knows? The LORD may be gracious to me and let the child live.' 23 But now that he is dead, why should I fast? Can I bring him back again? I will go to him, but he will not return to me."

24 Then David comforted his wife Bathsheba, and he went to her and lay with her. She gave birth to a son, and they named him Solomon. The LORD loved him; 25 and because the LORD loved him, he sent word through Nathan the prophet to name him Jedidiah.[b]

26 Meanwhile Joab fought against Rabbah of the Ammonites and captured the royal citadel. 27 Joab then sent

messengers to David, saying, "I have fought against Rabbah and taken its water supply. [28]Now muster the rest of the troops and besiege the city and capture it. Otherwise I will take the city, and it will be named after me."

[29]So David mustered the entire army and went to Rabbah, and attacked and captured it. [30]He took the crown from the head of their king[c]—its weight was a talent[d] of gold, and it was set with precious stones—and it was placed on David's head. He took a great quantity of plunder from the city [31]and brought out the people who were there, consigning them to labor with saws and with iron picks and axes, and he made them work at brickmaking.[e] He did this to all the Ammonite towns. Then David and his entire army returned to Jerusalem.

[a]14 Masoretic Text; an ancient Hebrew scribal tradition *this you have shown utter contempt for the LORD*   [b]25 *Jedidiah* means *loved by the LORD*.   [c]30 Or *of Milcom* (that is, Molech)   [d]30 That is, about 75 pounds (about 34 kilograms)   [e]31 The meaning of the Hebrew for this clause is uncertain.

JOHN 16:1-33

"All this I [Jesus] have told you [Jesus' disciples] so that you will not go astray. [2]They will put you out of the synagogue; in fact, a time is coming when anyone who kills you will think he is offering a service to God. [3]They will do such things because they have not known the Father or me. [4]I have told you this, so that when the time comes you will remember that I warned you. I did not tell you this at first because I was with you.

[5]"Now I am going to him who sent me, yet none of you asks me, 'Where are you going?' [6]Because I have said these things, you are filled with grief. [7]But I tell you the truth: It is for your good that I am going away. Unless I go away, the Counselor will not come to you; but if I go, I will send him to you. [8]When he comes, he will convict the world of guilt[a] in regard to sin and righteousness and judgment: [9]in regard to sin, because men do not believe in me; [10]in regard to righteousness, because I am going to the Father, where you can see me no longer; [11]and in regard to judg-

ment, because the prince of this world now stands condemned.

[12]"I have much more to say to you, more than you can now bear. [13]But when he, the Spirit of truth, comes, he will guide you into all truth. He will not speak on his own; he will speak only what he hears, and he will tell you what is yet to come. [14]He will bring glory to me by taking from what is mine and making it known to you. [15]All that belongs to the Father is mine. That is why I said the Spirit will take from what is mine and make it known to you.

[16]"In a little while you will see me no more, and then after a little while you will see me."

[17]Some of his disciples said to one another, "What does he mean by saying, 'In a little while you will see me no more, and then after a little while you will see me,' and 'Because I am going to the Father'?" [18]They kept asking, "What does he mean by 'a little while'? We don't understand what he is saying."

[19]Jesus saw that they wanted to ask him about this, so he said to them, "Are you asking one another what I meant when I said, 'In a little while you will see me no more, and then after a little while you will see me'? [20]I tell you the truth, you will weep and mourn while the world rejoices. You will grieve, but your grief will turn to joy. [21]A woman giving birth to a child has pain because her time has come; but when her baby is born she forgets the anguish because of her joy that a child is born into the world. [22]So with you: Now is your time of grief, but I will see you again and you will rejoice, and no one will take away your joy. [23]In that day you will no longer ask me anything. I tell you the truth, my Father will give you whatever you ask in my name. [24]Until now you have not asked for anything in my name. Ask and you will receive, and your joy will be complete.

[25]"Though I have been speaking figuratively, a time is coming when I will no longer use this kind of language but will tell you plainly about my Father. [26]In that day you will ask in my name. I

am not saying that I will ask the Father on your behalf. 27No, the Father himself loves you because you have loved me and have believed that I came from God. 28I came from the Father and entered the world; now I am leaving the world and going back to the Father."

29Then Jesus' disciples said, "Now you are speaking clearly and without figures of speech. 30Now we can see that you know all things and that you do not even need to have anyone ask you questions. This makes us believe that you came from God."

31"You believe at last!"b Jesus answered. 32"But a time is coming, and has come, when you will be scattered, each to his own home. You will leave me all alone. Yet I am not alone, for my Father is with me.

33**"I have told you these things, so that in me you may have peace. In this world you will have trouble. But take heart! I have overcome the world."**

a8 Or *will expose the guilt of the world*   b31 Or *"Do you now believe?"*

PSALM 119:65-80

ט   Teth

65 **D**o good to your servant
   according to your word, O LORD.
66 Teach me knowledge and good
      judgment,
   for I believe in your commands.
67 Before I was afflicted I went astray,
   but now I obey your word.
68 You are good, and what you do is good;
   teach me your decrees.
69 Though the arrogant have smeared
      me with lies,
   I keep your precepts with all my
      heart.
70 Their hearts are callous and
      unfeeling,
   but I delight in your law.
71 It was good for me to be afflicted
   so that I might learn your decrees.
72 The law from your mouth is more
      precious to me
   than thousands of pieces of silver
      and gold.

י   Yodh

73 Your hands made me and formed me;
   give me understanding to learn
      your commands.
74 May those who fear you rejoice when
      they see me,
   for I have put my hope in your
      word.
75 I know, O LORD, that your laws are
      righteous,
   and in faithfulness you have
      afflicted me.
76 May your unfailing love be my comfort,
   according to your promise to your
      servant.
77 Let your compassion come to me
      that I may live,
   for your law is my delight.
78 May the arrogant be put to shame for
      wronging me without cause;
   but I will meditate on your precepts.
79 May those who fear you turn to me,
   those who understand your
      statutes.
80 May my heart be blameless toward
      your decrees,
   that I may not be put to shame.

PROVERBS 16:4-5

4 **T**he LORD works out everything for
      his own ends—
   even the wicked for a day of
      disaster.

5 The LORD detests all the proud of
      heart.
   Be sure of this: They will not go
      unpunished.

☐ D A Y   1 4 8

GOD SIGHTINGS

May 28

2 SAMUEL 13:1-39

In the course of time, Amnon son of David fell in love with Tamar, the beautiful sister of Absalom son of David.

[2] Amnon became frustrated to the point of illness on account of his sister Tamar, for she was a virgin, and it seemed impossible for him to do anything to her.

[3] Now Amnon had a friend named Jonadab son of Shimeah, David's brother. Jonadab was a very shrewd man. [4] He asked Amnon, "Why do you, the king's son, look so haggard morning after morning? Won't you tell me?"

Amnon said to him, "I'm in love with Tamar, my brother Absalom's sister."

[5] "Go to bed and pretend to be ill," Jonadab said. "When your father comes to see you, say to him, 'I would like my sister Tamar to come and give me something to eat. Let her prepare the food in my sight so I may watch her and then eat it from her hand.'"

[6] So Amnon lay down and pretended to be ill. When the king came to see him, Amnon said to him, "I would like my sister Tamar to come and make some special bread in my sight, so I may eat from her hand."

[7] David sent word to Tamar at the palace: "Go to the house of your brother Amnon and prepare some food for him." [8] So Tamar went to the house of her brother Amnon, who was lying down. She took some dough, kneaded it, made the bread in his sight and baked it. [9] Then she took the pan and served him the bread, but he refused to eat.

"Send everyone out of here," Amnon said. So everyone left him. [10] Then Amnon said to Tamar, "Bring the food here into my bedroom so I may eat from your hand." And Tamar took the bread she had prepared and brought it to her brother Amnon in his bedroom. [11] But when she took it to him to eat, he grabbed her and said, "Come to bed with me, my sister."

[12] "Don't, my brother!" she said to him. "Don't force me. Such a thing should not be done in Israel! Don't do this wicked thing. [13] What about me? Where could I get rid of my disgrace? And what about you? You would be like one of the wicked fools in Israel. Please

speak to the king; he will not keep me from being married to you." [14] But he refused to listen to her, and since he was stronger than she, he raped her.

[15] Then Amnon hated her with intense hatred. In fact, he hated her more than he had loved her. Amnon said to her, "Get up and get out!"

[16] "No!" she said to him. "Sending me away would be a greater wrong than what you have already done to me."

But he refused to listen to her. [17] He called his personal servant and said, "Get this woman out of here and bolt the door after her." [18] So his servant put her out and bolted the door after her. She was wearing a richly ornamented[a] robe, for this was the kind of garment the virgin daughters of the king wore. [19] Tamar put ashes on her head and tore the ornamented[b] robe she was wearing. She put her hand on her head and went away, weeping aloud as she went.

[20] Her brother Absalom said to her, "Has that Amnon, your brother, been with you? Be quiet now, my sister; he is your brother. Don't take this thing to heart." And Tamar lived in her brother Absalom's house, a desolate woman.

[21] When King David heard all this, he was furious. [22] Absalom never said a word to Amnon, either good or bad; he hated Amnon because he had disgraced his sister Tamar.

[23] Two years later, when Absalom's sheepshearers were at Baal Hazor near the border of Ephraim, he invited all the king's sons to come. [24] Absalom went to the king and said, "Your servant has had shearers come. Will the king and his officials please join me?"

[25] "No, my son," the king replied. "All of us should not go; we would only be a burden to you." Although Absalom urged him, he still refused to go, but gave him his blessing.

[26] Then Absalom said, "If not, please let my brother Amnon come with us."

The king asked him, "Why should he go with you?" [27] But Absalom urged him, so he sent with him Amnon and the rest of the king's sons.

28Absalom ordered his men, "Listen! When Amnon is in high spirits from drinking wine and I say to you, 'Strike Amnon down,' then kill him. Don't be afraid. Have not I given you this order? Be strong and brave." 29So Absalom's men did to Amnon what Absalom had ordered. Then all the king's sons got up, mounted their mules and fled.

30While they were on their way, the report came to David: "Absalom has struck down all the king's sons; not one of them is left." 31The king stood up, tore his clothes and lay down on the ground; and all his servants stood by with their clothes torn.

32But Jonadab son of Shimeah, David's brother, said, "My lord should not think that they killed all the princes; only Amnon is dead. This has been Absalom's expressed intention ever since the day Amnon raped his sister Tamar. 33My lord the king should not be concerned about the report that all the king's sons are dead. Only Amnon is dead."

34Meanwhile, Absalom had fled.

Now the man standing watch looked up and saw many people on the road west of him, coming down the side of the hill. The watchman went and told the king, "I see men in the direction of Horonaim, on the side of the hill."c

35Jonadab said to the king, "See, the king's sons are here; it has happened just as your servant said."

36As he finished speaking, the king's sons came in, wailing loudly. The king, too, and all his servants wept very bitterly.

37Absalom fled and went to Talmai son of Ammihud, the king of Geshur. But King David mourned for his son every day.

38After Absalom fled and went to Geshur, he stayed there three years. 39And the spirit of the kingd longed to go to Absalom, for he was consoled concerning Amnon's death.

a18 The meaning of the Hebrew for this phrase is uncertain.
b19 The meaning of the Hebrew for this word is uncertain.
c34 Septuagint; Hebrew does not have this sentence.
d39 Dead Sea Scrolls and some Septuagint manuscripts; Masoretic Text But ⌊the spirit of⌋ David the king

JOHN 17:1-26

After Jesus said this, he looked toward heaven and prayed:

"Father, the time has come. Glorify your Son, that your Son may glorify you. 2For you granted him authority over all people that he might give eternal life to all those you have given him. 3Now this is eternal life: that they may know you, the only true God, and Jesus Christ, whom you have sent. 4I have brought you glory on earth by completing the work you gave me to do. 5And now, Father, glorify me in your presence with the glory I had with you before the world began.

6"I have revealed youa to those whom you gave me out of the world. They were yours; you gave them to me and they have obeyed your word. 7Now they know that everything you have given me comes from you. 8For I gave them the words you gave me and they accepted them. They knew with certainty that I came from you, and they believed that you sent me. 9I pray for them. I am not praying for the world, but for those you have given me, for they are yours. 10All I have is yours, and all you have is mine. And glory has come to me through them. 11I will remain in the world no longer, but they are still in the world, and I am coming to you. Holy Father, protect them by the power of your name—the name you gave me—so that they may be one as we are one. 12While I was with them, I protected them and kept them safe by that name you gave me. None has been lost except the one doomed to destruction so that Scripture would be fulfilled.

13"I am coming to you now, but I say these things while I am still in the world, so that they may have the full measure of my joy within them. 14I have given them your word and the world has hated them, for they are not of the world any more than I am of the world. 15My prayer is not that you take them out of the world but that you protect them from the evil one. 16They are not of the world, even as I am not of it. 17Sanctify[b] them by the truth; your word is truth. 18As you sent me into the world, I have sent them into the world. 19For them I sanctify myself, that they too may be truly sanctified.

20"My prayer is not for them alone. I pray also for those who will believe in me through their message, 21that all of them may be one, Father, just as you are in me and I am in you. May they also be in us so that the world may believe that you have sent me. 22I have given them the glory that you gave me, that they may be one as we are one: 23I in them and you in me. May they be brought to complete unity to let the world know that you sent me and have loved them even as you have loved me.

24"Father, I want those you have given me to be with me where I am, and to see my glory, the glory you have given me because you loved me before the creation of the world.

25"Righteous Father, though the world does not know you, I know you, and they know that you have sent me. 26I have made you known to them, and will continue to make you known in order that the love you have for me may be in them and that I myself may be in them."

a6 Greek *your name*; also in verse 26   b17 Greek *hagiazo*
(*set apart for sacred use* or *make holy*); also in verse 19

PSALM 119:81-96

 כ Kaph

81 **M**y soul faints with longing for your [the Lord's] salvation,
  but I have put my hope in your word.
82 My eyes fail, looking for your promise;
  I say, "When will you comfort me?"

83 Though I am like a wineskin in the smoke,
  I do not forget your decrees.
84 How long must your servant wait?
  When will you punish my persecutors?
85 The arrogant dig pitfalls for me,
  contrary to your law.
86 All your commands are trustworthy;
  help me, for men persecute me without cause.
87 They almost wiped me from the earth,
  but I have not forsaken your precepts.
88 Preserve my life according to your love,
  and I will obey the statutes of your mouth.

ל Lamedh

89 Your word, O Lord, is eternal;
  it stands firm in the heavens.
90 Your faithfulness continues through all generations;
  you established the earth, and it endures.
91 Your laws endure to this day,
  for all things serve you.
92 If your law had not been my delight,
  I would have perished in my affliction.
93 I will never forget your precepts,
  for by them you have preserved my life.
94 Save me, for I am yours;
  I have sought out your precepts.
95 The wicked are waiting to destroy me,
  but I will ponder your statutes.
96 To all perfection I see a limit;
  but your commands are boundless.

PROVERBS 16:6-7

6 **T**hrough love and faithfulness sin is atoned for;
  through the fear of the Lord a man avoids evil.

7 When a man's ways are pleasing to the Lord,
  he makes even his enemies live at peace with him.

GOD SIGHTINGS

May 29

2 SAMUEL 14:1–15:22

Joab son of Zeruiah knew that the king's heart longed for Absalom. [2] So Joab sent someone to Tekoa and had a wise woman brought from there. He said to her, "Pretend you are in mourning. Dress in mourning clothes, and don't use any cosmetic lotions. Act like a woman who has spent many days grieving for the dead. [3] Then go to the king and speak these words to him." And Joab put the words in her mouth.

[4] When the woman from Tekoa went[a] to the king, she fell with her face to the ground to pay him honor, and she said, "Help me, O king!"

[5] The king asked her, "What is troubling you?"

She said, "I am indeed a widow; my husband is dead. [6] I your servant had two sons. They got into a fight with each other in the field, and no one was there to separate them. One struck the other and killed him. [7] Now the whole clan has risen up against your servant; they say, 'Hand over the one who struck his brother down, so that we may put him to death for the life of his brother whom he killed; then we will get rid of the heir as well.' They would put out the only burning coal I have left, leaving my husband neither name nor descendant on the face of the earth."

[8] The king said to the woman, "Go home, and I will issue an order in your behalf."

[9] But the woman from Tekoa said to him, "My lord the king, let the blame rest on me and on my father's family, and let the king and his throne be without guilt."

[10] The king replied, "If anyone says anything to you, bring him to me, and he will not bother you again."

[11] She said, "Then let the king invoke the LORD his God to prevent the avenger of blood from adding to the destruction, so that my son will not be destroyed."

"As surely as the LORD lives," he said, "not one hair of your son's head will fall to the ground."

[12] Then the woman said, "Let your servant speak a word to my lord the king."

"Speak," he replied.

[13] The woman said, "Why then have you devised a thing like this against the people of God? When the king says this, does he not convict himself, for the king has not brought back his banished son? [14] Like water spilled on the ground, which cannot be recovered, so we must die. But God does not take away life; instead, he devises ways so that a banished person may not remain estranged from him.

[15] "And now I have come to say this to my lord the king because the people have made me afraid. Your servant thought, 'I will speak to the king; perhaps he will do what his servant asks. [16] Perhaps the king will agree to deliver his servant from the hand of the man who is trying to cut off both me and my son from the inheritance God gave us.'

[17] "And now your servant says, 'May the word of my lord the king bring me rest, for my lord the king is like an angel of God in discerning good and evil. May the LORD your God be with you.'"

[18] Then the king said to the woman, "Do not keep from me the answer to what I am going to ask you."

"Let my lord the king speak," the woman said.

[19] The king asked, "Isn't the hand of Joab with you in all this?"

The woman answered, "As surely as you live, my lord the king, no one can turn to the right or to the left from anything my lord the king says. Yes, it was your servant Joab who instructed me to do this and who put all these words into the mouth of your servant. [20] Your servant Joab did this to change the present situation. My lord has wisdom like that of an angel of God—he knows everything that happens in the land."

21 The king said to Joab, "Very well, I will do it. Go, bring back the young man Absalom."

22 Joab fell with his face to the ground to pay him honor, and he blessed the king. Joab said, "Today your servant knows that he has found favor in your eyes, my lord the king, because the king has granted his servant's request."

23 Then Joab went to Geshur and brought Absalom back to Jerusalem. 24 But the king said, "He must go to his own house; he must not see my face." So Absalom went to his own house and did not see the face of the king.

25 In all Israel there was not a man so highly praised for his handsome appearance as Absalom. From the top of his head to the sole of his foot there was no blemish in him. 26 Whenever he cut the hair of his head—he used to cut his hair from time to time when it became too heavy for him—he would weigh it, and its weight was two hundred shekels[b] by the royal standard.

27 Three sons and a daughter were born to Absalom. The daughter's name was Tamar, and she became a beautiful woman.

28 Absalom lived two years in Jerusalem without seeing the king's face. 29 Then Absalom sent for Joab in order to send him to the king, but Joab refused to come to him. So he sent a second time, but he refused to come. 30 Then he said to his servants, "Look, Joab's field is next to mine, and he has barley there. Go and set it on fire." So Absalom's servants set the field on fire.

31 Then Joab did go to Absalom's house and he said to him, "Why have your servants set my field on fire?"

32 Absalom said to Joab, "Look, I sent word to you and said, 'Come here so I can send you to the king to ask, "Why have I come from Geshur? It would be better for me if I were still there!"' Now then, I want to see the king's face, and if I am guilty of anything, let him put me to death."

33 So Joab went to the king and told him this. Then the king summoned Absalom, and he came in and bowed down with his face to the ground before the king. And the king kissed Absalom.

15:1 In the course of time, Absalom provided himself with a chariot and horses and with fifty men to run ahead of him. 2 He would get up early and stand by the side of the road leading to the city gate. Whenever anyone came with a complaint to be placed before the king for a decision, Absalom would call out to him, "What town are you from?" He would answer, "Your servant is from one of the tribes of Israel." 3 Then Absalom would say to him, "Look, your claims are valid and proper, but there is no representative of the king to hear you." 4 And Absalom would add, "If only I were appointed judge in the land! Then everyone who has a complaint or case could come to me and I would see that he gets justice."

5 Also, whenever anyone approached him to bow down before him, Absalom would reach out his hand, take hold of him and kiss him. 6 Absalom behaved in this way toward all the Israelites who came to the king asking for justice, and so he stole the hearts of the men of Israel.

7 At the end of four[c] years, Absalom said to the king, "Let me go to Hebron and fulfill a vow I made to the LORD. 8 While your servant was living at Geshur in Aram, I made this vow: 'If the LORD takes me back to Jerusalem, I will worship the LORD in Hebron.[d]'"

9 The king said to him, "Go in peace." So he went to Hebron.

10 Then Absalom sent secret messengers throughout the tribes of Israel to say, "As soon as you hear the sound of the trumpets, then say, 'Absalom is king in Hebron.'" 11 Two hundred men from Jerusalem had accompanied Absalom. They had been invited as guests and went quite innocently, knowing nothing about the matter. 12 While Absalom was offering sacrifices, he also sent for Ahithophel the Gilonite, David's

counselor, to come from Giloh, his hometown. And so the conspiracy gained strength, and Absalom's following kept on increasing.

¹³A messenger came and told David, "The hearts of the men of Israel are with Absalom."

¹⁴Then David said to all his officials who were with him in Jerusalem, "Come! We must flee, or none of us will escape from Absalom. We must leave immediately, or he will move quickly to overtake us and bring ruin upon us and put the city to the sword."

¹⁵The king's officials answered him, "Your servants are ready to do whatever our lord the king chooses."

¹⁶The king set out, with his entire household following him; but he left ten concubines to take care of the palace. ¹⁷So the king set out, with all the people following him, and they halted at a place some distance away. ¹⁸All his men marched past him, along with all the Kerethites and Pelethites; and all the six hundred Gittites who had accompanied him from Gath marched before the king.

¹⁹The king said to Ittai the Gittite, "Why should you come along with us? Go back and stay with King Absalom. You are a foreigner, an exile from your homeland. ²⁰You came only yesterday. And today shall I make you wander about with us, when I do not know where I am going? Go back, and take your countrymen. May kindness and faithfulness be with you."

²¹But Ittai replied to the king, "As surely as the LORD lives, and as my lord the king lives, wherever my lord the king may be, whether it means life or death, there will your servant be."

²²David said to Ittai, "Go ahead, march on." So Ittai the Gittite marched on with all his men and the families that were with him.

a4 Many Hebrew manuscripts, Septuagint, Vulgate and Syriac; most Hebrew manuscripts *spoke*   b26 That is, about 5 pounds (about 2.3 kilograms)   c7 Some Septuagint manuscripts, Syriac and Josephus; Hebrew *forty*   d8 Some Septuagint manuscripts; Hebrew does not have *in Hebron.*

JOHN 18:1-24

When he had finished praying, Jesus left with his disciples and crossed the Kidron Valley. On the other side there was an olive grove, and he and his disciples went into it.

²Now Judas, who betrayed him, knew the place, because Jesus had often met there with his disciples. ³So Judas came to the grove, guiding a detachment of soldiers and some officials from the chief priests and Pharisees. They were carrying torches, lanterns and weapons.

⁴Jesus, knowing all that was going to happen to him, went out and asked them, "Who is it you want?"

⁵"Jesus of Nazareth," they replied.

"I am he," Jesus said. (And Judas the traitor was standing there with them.) ⁶When Jesus said, "I am he," they drew back and fell to the ground.

⁷Again he asked them, "Who is it you want?"

And they said, "Jesus of Nazareth."

⁸"I told you that I am he," Jesus answered. "If you are looking for me, then let these men go." ⁹This happened so that the words he had spoken would be fulfilled: "I have not lost one of those you gave me."ᵃ

¹⁰Then Simon Peter, who had a sword, drew it and struck the high priest's servant, cutting off his right ear. (The servant's name was Malchus.)

¹¹Jesus commanded Peter, "Put your sword away! Shall I not drink the cup the Father has given me?"

¹²Then the detachment of soldiers with its commander and the Jewish officials arrested Jesus. They bound him ¹³and brought him first to Annas, who was the father-in-law of Caiaphas, the high priest that year. ¹⁴Caiaphas was the one who had advised the Jews that it would be good if one man died for the people.

¹⁵Simon Peter and another disciple were following Jesus. Because this disciple was known to the high priest, he went with Jesus into the high priest's courtyard, ¹⁶but Peter had to wait outside at the door. The other disciple, who

was known to the high priest, came back, spoke to the girl on duty there and brought Peter in.

17 "You are not one of his disciples, are you?" the girl at the door asked Peter.

He replied, "I am not."

18 It was cold, and the servants and officials stood around a fire they had made to keep warm. Peter also was standing with them, warming himself.

19 Meanwhile, the high priest questioned Jesus about his disciples and his teaching.

20 "I have spoken openly to the world," Jesus replied. "I always taught in synagogues or at the temple, where all the Jews come together. I said nothing in secret. 21 Why question me? Ask those who heard me. Surely they know what I said."

22 When Jesus said this, one of the officials nearby struck him in the face. "Is this the way you answer the high priest?" he demanded.

23 "If I said something wrong," Jesus replied, "testify as to what is wrong. But if I spoke the truth, why did you strike me?" 24 Then Annas sent him, still bound, to Caiaphas the high priest.*b*

a9 John 6:39 *b24* Or (Now Annas had sent him, still bound, to Caiaphas the high priest.)

PSALM 119:97-112

מ Mem

97 **O**h, how I love your [the LORD's] law!
  I meditate on it all day long.
98 Your commands make me wiser
    than my enemies,
  for they are ever with me.
99 I have more insight than all my teachers,
  for I meditate on your statutes.
100 I have more understanding than the
    elders,
  for I obey your precepts.
101 I have kept my feet from every evil
    path
  so that I might obey your word.
102 I have not departed from your laws,
  for you yourself have taught me.
103 How sweet are your words to my
    taste,
  sweeter than honey to my mouth!

104 I gain understanding from your
    precepts;
  therefore I hate every wrong path.

נ Nun

105 **Your word is a lamp to my feet
  and a light for my path.**
106 **I have taken an oath and
    confirmed it,
  that I will follow your righteous
    laws.**
107 I have suffered much;
  preserve my life, O LORD, according
    to your word.
108 Accept, O LORD, the willing praise of
    my mouth,
  and teach me your laws.
109 Though I constantly take my life in
    my hands,
  I will not forget your law.
110 The wicked have set a snare for me,
  but I have not strayed from your
    precepts.
111 Your statutes are my heritage forever;
  they are the joy of my heart.
112 My heart is set on keeping your
    decrees
  to the very end.

PROVERBS 16:8-9

8 **B**etter a little with righteousness
  than much gain with injustice.

9 In his heart a man plans his course,
  but the LORD determines his steps.

□ DAY 150

GOD SIGHTINGS

May 30

2 SAMUEL 15:23-16:23

The whole countryside wept aloud as all the people passed by. The king also crossed the Kidron Valley, and all the people moved on toward the desert.

24 Zadok was there, too, and all the Levites who were with him were carrying the ark of the covenant of God. They set

down the ark of God, and Abiathar offered sacrifices[a] until all the people had finished leaving the city.

25 Then the king said to Zadok, "Take the ark of God back into the city. If I find favor in the LORD's eyes, he will bring me back and let me see it and his dwelling place again. 26 But if he says, 'I am not pleased with you,' then I am ready; let him do to me whatever seems good to him."

27 The king also said to Zadok the priest, "Aren't you a seer? Go back to the city in peace, with your son Ahimaaz and Jonathan son of Abiathar. You and Abiathar take your two sons with you. 28 I will wait at the fords in the desert until word comes from you to inform me." 29 So Zadok and Abiathar took the ark of God back to Jerusalem and stayed there.

30 But David continued up the Mount of Olives, weeping as he went; his head was covered and he was barefoot. All the people with him covered their heads too and were weeping as they went up. 31 Now David had been told, "Ahithophel is among the conspirators with Absalom." So David prayed, "O LORD, turn Ahithophel's counsel into foolishness."

32 When David arrived at the summit, where people used to worship God, Hushai the Arkite was there to meet him, his robe torn and dust on his head. 33 David said to him, "If you go with me, you will be a burden to me. 34 But if you return to the city and say to Absalom, 'I will be your servant, O king; I was your father's servant in the past, but now I will be your servant,' then you can help me by frustrating Ahithophel's advice. 35 Won't the priests Zadok and Abiathar be there with you? Tell them anything you hear in the king's palace. 36 Their two sons, Ahimaaz son of Zadok and Jonathan son of Abiathar, are there with them. Send them to me with anything you hear."

37 So David's friend Hushai arrived at Jerusalem as Absalom was entering the city.

16:1 When David had gone a short distance beyond the summit, there was Ziba, the steward of Mephibosheth, waiting to meet him. He had a string of donkeys saddled and loaded with two hundred loaves of bread, a hundred cakes of raisins, a hundred cakes of figs and a skin of wine.

2 The king asked Ziba, "Why have you brought these?"

Ziba answered, "The donkeys are for the king's household to ride on, the bread and fruit are for the men to eat, and the wine is to refresh those who become exhausted in the desert."

3 The king then asked, "Where is your master's grandson?"

Ziba said to him, "He is staying in Jerusalem, because he thinks, 'Today the house of Israel will give me back my grandfather's kingdom.'"

4 Then the king said to Ziba, "All that belonged to Mephibosheth is now yours."

"I humbly bow," Ziba said. "May I find favor in your eyes, my lord the king."

5 As King David approached Bahurim, a man from the same clan as Saul's family came out from there. His name was Shimei son of Gera, and he cursed as he came out. 6 He pelted David and all the king's officials with stones, though all the troops and the special guard were on David's right and left. 7 As he cursed, Shimei said, "Get out, get out, you man of blood, you scoundrel! 8 The LORD has repaid you for all the blood you shed in the household of Saul, in whose place you have reigned. The LORD has handed the kingdom over to your son Absalom. You have come to ruin because you are a man of blood!"

9 Then Abishai son of Zeruiah said to the king, "Why should this dead dog curse my lord the king? Let me go over and cut off his head."

10 But the king said, "What do you and I have in common, you sons of Zeruiah? If he is cursing because the LORD said to him, 'Curse David,' who can ask, 'Why do you do this?'"

11 David then said to Abishai and all

his officials, "My son, who is of my own flesh, is trying to take my life. How much more, then, this Benjamite! Leave him alone; let him curse, for the LORD has told him to. [12]It may be that the LORD will see my distress and repay me with good for the cursing I am receiving today."

[13]So David and his men continued along the road while Shimei was going along the hillside opposite him, cursing as he went and throwing stones at him and showering him with dirt. [14]The king and all the people with him arrived at their destination exhausted. And there he refreshed himself.

[15]Meanwhile, Absalom and all the men of Israel came to Jerusalem, and Ahithophel was with him. [16]Then Hushai the Arkite, David's friend, went to Absalom and said to him, "Long live the king! Long live the king!"

[17]Absalom asked Hushai, "Is this the love you show your friend? Why didn't you go with your friend?"

[18]Hushai said to Absalom, "No, the one chosen by the LORD, by these people, and by all the men of Israel—his I will be, and I will remain with him. [19]Furthermore, whom should I serve? Should I not serve the son? Just as I served your father, so I will serve you."

[20]Absalom said to Ahithophel, "Give us your advice. What should we do?"

[21]Ahithophel answered, "Lie with your father's concubines whom he left to take care of the palace. Then all Israel will hear that you have made yourself a stench in your father's nostrils, and the hands of everyone with you will be strengthened." [22]So they pitched a tent for Absalom on the roof, and he lay with his father's concubines in the sight of all Israel.

[23]Now in those days the advice Ahithophel gave was like that of one who inquires of God. That was how both David and Absalom regarded all of Ahithophel's advice.

[a]24 Or *Abiathar went up*

JOHN 18:25–19:22

As Simon Peter stood warming himself, he was asked, "You are not one of his disciples, are you?"

He denied it, saying, "I am not."

[26]One of the high priest's servants, a relative of the man whose ear Peter had cut off, challenged him, "Didn't I see you with him in the olive grove?" [27]Again Peter denied it, and at that moment a rooster began to crow.

[28]Then the Jews led Jesus from Caiaphas to the palace of the Roman governor. By now it was early morning, and to avoid ceremonial uncleanness the Jews did not enter the palace; they wanted to be able to eat the Passover. [29]So Pilate came out to them and asked, "What charges are you bringing against this man?"

[30]"If he were not a criminal," they replied, "we would not have handed him over to you."

[31]Pilate said, "Take him yourselves and judge him by your own law."

"But we have no right to execute anyone," the Jews objected. [32]This happened so that the words Jesus had spoken indicating the kind of death he was going to die would be fulfilled.

[33]Pilate then went back inside the palace, summoned Jesus and asked him, "Are you the king of the Jews?"

[34]"Is that your own idea," Jesus asked, "or did others talk to you about me?"

[35]"Am I a Jew?" Pilate replied. "It was your people and your chief priests who handed you over to me. What is it you have done?"

[36]**Jesus said, "My kingdom is not of this world. If it were, my servants would fight to prevent my arrest by the Jews. But now my kingdom is from another place."**

[37]"You are a king, then!" said Pilate.

Jesus answered, "You are right in saying I am a king. In fact, for this reason I was born, and for this I came into the world, to testify to the truth. Everyone on the side of truth listens to me."

[38]"What is truth?" Pilate asked. With this he went out again to the Jews and said, "I find no basis for a charge against

him. 39 But it is your custom for me to release to you one prisoner at the time of the Passover. Do you want me to release 'the king of the Jews'?"

40 They shouted back, "No, not him! Give us Barabbas!" Now Barabbas had taken part in a rebellion.

19:1 THEN Pilate took Jesus and had him flogged. 2 The soldiers twisted together a crown of thorns and put it on his head. They clothed him in a purple robe 3 and went up to him again and again, saying, "Hail, king of the Jews!" And they struck him in the face.

4 Once more Pilate came out and said to the Jews, "Look, I am bringing him out to you to let you know that I find no basis for a charge against him." 5 When Jesus came out wearing the crown of thorns and the purple robe, Pilate said to them, "Here is the man!"

6 As soon as the chief priests and their officials saw him, they shouted, "Crucify! Crucify!"

But Pilate answered, "You take him and crucify him. As for me, I find no basis for a charge against him."

7 The Jews insisted, "We have a law, and according to that law he must die, because he claimed to be the Son of God."

8 When Pilate heard this, he was even more afraid, 9 and he went back inside the palace. "Where do you come from?" he asked Jesus, but Jesus gave him no answer. 10 "Do you refuse to speak to me?" Pilate said. "Don't you realize I have power either to free you or to crucify you?"

11 Jesus answered, "You would have no power over me if it were not given to you from above. Therefore the one who handed me over to you is guilty of a greater sin."

12 From then on, Pilate tried to set Jesus free, but the Jews kept shouting, "If you let this man go, you are no friend of Caesar. Anyone who claims to be a king opposes Caesar."

13 When Pilate heard this, he brought Jesus out and sat down on the judge's seat at a place known as the Stone Pavement (which in Aramaic is Gabbatha). 14 It was the day of Preparation of Passover Week, about the sixth hour.

"Here is your king," Pilate said to the Jews.

15 But they shouted, "Take him away! Take him away! Crucify him!"

"Shall I crucify your king?" Pilate asked.

"We have no king but Caesar," the chief priests answered.

16 Finally Pilate handed him over to them to be crucified.

So the soldiers took charge of Jesus. 17 Carrying his own cross, he went out to the place of the Skull (which in Aramaic is called Golgotha). 18 Here they crucified him, and with him two others—one on each side and Jesus in the middle.

19 Pilate had a notice prepared and fastened to the cross. It read: JESUS OF NAZARETH, THE KING OF THE JEWS. 20 Many of the Jews read this sign, for the place where Jesus was crucified was near the city, and the sign was written in Aramaic, Latin and Greek. 21 The chief priests of the Jews protested to Pilate, "Do not write 'The King of the Jews,' but that this man claimed to be king of the Jews."

22 Pilate answered, "What I have written, I have written."

PSALM 119:113-128

ם   Samekh

113 I hate double-minded men,
    but I love your [the LORD's] law.
114 You are my refuge and my shield;
    I have put my hope in your word.
115 Away from me, you evildoers,
    that I may keep the commands of
        my God!
116 Sustain me according to your
        promise, and I will live;
    do not let my hopes be dashed.
117 Uphold me, and I will be delivered;
    I will always have regard for your
        decrees.
118 You reject all who stray from your
        decrees,
    for their deceitfulness is in vain.

119All the wicked of the earth you
    discard like dross;
    therefore I love your statutes.
120My flesh trembles in fear of you;
    I stand in awe of your laws.

צ Ayin

121I have done what is righteous and
    just;
    do not leave me to my oppressors.
122Ensure your servant's well-being;
    let not the arrogant oppress me.
123My eyes fail, looking for your
    salvation,
    looking for your righteous
    promise.
124Deal with your servant according to
    your love
    and teach me your decrees.
125I am your servant; give me
    discernment
    that I may understand your statutes.
126It is time for you to act, O LORD;
    your law is being broken.
127Because I love your commands
    more than gold, more than pure
    gold,
128and because I consider all your
    precepts right,
    I hate every wrong path.

PROVERBS 16:10-11

10The lips of a king speak as an oracle,
    and his mouth should not betray
    justice.

11Honest scales and balances are from
    the LORD;
    all the weights in the bag are of his
    making.

☐ DAY 151

GOD SIGHTINGS

May 31

2 SAMUEL 17:1-29

Ahithophel said to Absalom, "I woulda
choose twelve thousand men and set out
tonight in pursuit of David. 2I wouldb attack him while he is weary and weak. I
wouldb strike him with terror, and then
all the people with him will flee. I wouldb
strike down only the king 3and bring all
the people back to you. The death of the
man you seek will mean the return of all;
all the people will be unharmed." 4This
plan seemed good to Absalom and to all
the elders of Israel.

5But Absalom said, "Summon also
Hushai the Arkite, so we can hear what
he has to say." 6When Hushai came to
him, Absalom said, "Ahithophel has
given this advice. Should we do what he
says? If not, give us your opinion."

7Hushai replied to Absalom, "The advice Ahithophel has given is not good
this time. 8You know your father and his
men; they are fighters, and as fierce as a
wild bear robbed of her cubs. Besides,
your father is an experienced fighter; he
will not spend the night with the troops.
9Even now, he is hidden in a cave or
some other place. If he should attack
your troops first,c whoever hears about
it will say, 'There has been a slaughter
among the troops who follow Absalom.'
10Then even the bravest soldier, whose
heart is like the heart of a lion, will melt
with fear, for all Israel knows that your
father is a fighter and that those with
him are brave.

11"So I advise you: Let all Israel, from
Dan to Beersheba—as numerous as the
sand on the seashore—be gathered to
you, with you yourself leading them into
battle. 12Then we will attack him wherever he may be found, and we will fall on
him as dew settles on the ground. Neither he nor any of his men will be left
alive. 13If he withdraws into a city, then
all Israel will bring ropes to that city, and
we will drag it down to the valley until not
even a piece of it can be found."

14Absalom and all the men of Israel
said, "The advice of Hushai the Arkite is
better than that of Ahithophel." For the
LORD had determined to frustrate the
good advice of Ahithophel in order to
bring disaster on Absalom.

15Hushai told Zadok and Abiathar,

the priests, "Ahithophel has advised Absalom and the elders of Israel to do such and such, but I have advised them to do so and so. [16]Now send a message immediately and tell David, 'Do not spend the night at the fords in the desert; cross over without fail, or the king and all the people with him will be swallowed up.'"

[17]Jonathan and Ahimaaz were staying at En Rogel. A servant girl was to go and inform them, and they were to go and tell King David, for they could not risk being seen entering the city. [18]But a young man saw them and told Absalom. So the two of them left quickly and went to the house of a man in Bahurim. He had a well in his courtyard, and they climbed down into it. [19]His wife took a covering and spread it out over the opening of the well and scattered grain over it. No one knew anything about it.

[20]When Absalom's men came to the woman at the house, they asked, "Where are Ahimaaz and Jonathan?"

The woman answered them, "They crossed over the brook."[d] The men searched but found no one, so they returned to Jerusalem.

[21]After the men had gone, the two climbed out of the well and went to inform King David. They said to him, "Set out and cross the river at once; Ahithophel has advised such and such against you." [22]So David and all the people with him set out and crossed the Jordan. By daybreak, no one was left who had not crossed the Jordan.

[23]When Ahithophel saw that his advice had not been followed, he saddled his donkey and set out for his house in his hometown. He put his house in order and then hanged himself. So he died and was buried in his father's tomb.

[24]David went to Mahanaim, and Absalom crossed the Jordan with all the men of Israel. [25]Absalom had appointed Amasa over the army in place of Joab. Amasa was the son of a man named Jether,[e] an Israelite[f] who had married Abigail,[g] the daughter of Nahash and sister of Zeruiah the mother

of Joab. [26]The Israelites and Absalom camped in the land of Gilead.

[27]When David came to Mahanaim, Shobi son of Nahash from Rabbah of the Ammonites, and Makir son of Ammiel from Lo Debar, and Barzillai the Gileadite from Rogelim [28]brought bedding and bowls and articles of pottery. They also brought wheat and barley, flour and roasted grain, beans and lentils,[h] [29]honey and curds, sheep, and cheese from cows' milk for David and his people to eat. For they said, "The people have become hungry and tired and thirsty in the desert."

a1 Or Let me   b2 Or will   c9 Or When some of the men fall at the first attack   d20 Or "They passed by the sheep pen toward the water."   e25 Hebrew Ithra, a variant of Jether   f25 Hebrew and some Septuagint manuscripts; other Septuagint manuscripts (see also 1 Chron. 2:17) Ishmaelite or Jezreelite   g25 Hebrew Abigal, a variant of Abigail   h28 Most Septuagint manuscripts and Syriac; Hebrew lentils, and roasted grain

JOHN 19:23-42

When the soldiers crucified Jesus, they took his clothes, dividing them into four shares, one for each of them, with the undergarment remaining. This garment was seamless, woven in one piece from top to bottom.

[24]"Let's not tear it," they said to one another. "Let's decide by lot who will get it."

This happened that the scripture might be fulfilled which said,

"They divided my garments among them
and cast lots for my clothing."[a]

So this is what the soldiers did.

[25]Near the cross of Jesus stood his mother, his mother's sister, Mary the wife of Clopas, and Mary Magdalene. [26]When Jesus saw his mother there, and the disciple whom he loved standing nearby, he said to his mother, "Dear woman, here is your son," [27]and to the disciple, "Here is your mother." From that time on, this disciple took her into his home.

[28]Later, knowing that all was now completed, and so that the Scripture would be fulfilled, Jesus said, "I am

thirsty." [29]A jar of wine vinegar was there, so they soaked a sponge in it, put the sponge on a stalk of the hyssop plant, and lifted it to Jesus' lips. [30]When he had received the drink, Jesus said, "It is finished." With that, he bowed his head and gave up his spirit.

[31]Now it was the day of Preparation, and the next day was to be a special Sabbath. Because the Jews did not want the bodies left on the crosses during the Sabbath, they asked Pilate to have the legs broken and the bodies taken down. [32]The soldiers therefore came and broke the legs of the first man who had been crucified with Jesus, and then those of the other. [33]But when they came to Jesus and found that he was already dead, they did not break his legs. [34]Instead, one of the soldiers pierced Jesus' side with a spear, bringing a sudden flow of blood and water. [35]The man who saw it has given testimony, and his testimony is true. He knows that he tells the truth, and he testifies so that you also may believe. [36]These things happened so that the scripture would be fulfilled: "Not one of his bones will be broken,"[b] [37]and, as another scripture says, "They will look on the one they have pierced."[c]

[38]Later, Joseph of Arimathea asked Pilate for the body of Jesus. Now Joseph was a disciple of Jesus, but secretly because he feared the Jews. With Pilate's permission, he came and took the body away. [39]He was accompanied by Nicodemus, the man who earlier had visited Jesus at night. Nicodemus brought a mixture of myrrh and aloes, about seventy-five pounds.[d] [40]Taking Jesus' body, the two of them wrapped it, with the spices, in strips of linen. This was in accordance with Jewish burial customs. [41]At the place where Jesus was crucified, there was a garden, and in the garden a new tomb, in which no one had ever been laid. [42]Because it was the Jewish day of Preparation and since the tomb was nearby, they laid Jesus there.

a24 Psalm 22:18 b36 Exodus 12:46; Num. 9:12; Psalm 34:20 c37 Zech. 12:10 d39 Greek *a hundred litrai* (about 34 kilograms)

PSALM 119:129-152

⅌ Pe

[129]**Y**our [the LORD's] statutes are
wonderful;
therefore I obey them.
[130]The unfolding of your words gives
light;
it gives understanding to the
simple.
[131]I open my mouth and pant,
longing for your commands.
[132]Turn to me and have mercy on me,
as you always do to those who love
your name.
[133]Direct my footsteps according to
your word;
let no sin rule over me.
[134]Redeem me from the oppression of
men,
that I may obey your precepts.
[135]Make your face shine upon your
servant
and teach me your decrees.
[136]Streams of tears flow from my
eyes,
for your law is not obeyed.

צ Tsadhe

[137]**Righteous are you, O LORD,**
and your laws are right.
[138]**The statutes you have laid down**
are righteous;
they are fully trustworthy.
[139]My zeal wears me out,
for my enemies ignore your
words.
[140]Your promises have been
thoroughly tested,
and your servant loves them.
[141]Though I am lowly and despised,
I do not forget your precepts.
[142]Your righteousness is everlasting
and your law is true.
[143]Trouble and distress have come
upon me,
but your commands are my
delight.
[144]Your statutes are forever right;
give me understanding that I may
live.

ק Qoph

145I call with all my heart; answer me,
O Lord,
and I will obey your decrees.
146I call out to you; save me
and I will keep your statutes.
147I rise before dawn and cry for
help;
I have put my hope in your
word.
148My eyes stay open through the
watches of the night,
that I may meditate on your
promises.
149Hear my voice in accordance with
your love;
preserve my life, O Lord, according
to your laws.

150Those who devise wicked schemes
are near,
but they are far from your law.
151Yet you are near, O Lord,
and all your commands are true.
152Long ago I learned from your
statutes
that you established them to last
forever.

PROVERBS 16:12-13
12Kings detest wrongdoing,
for a throne is established through
righteousness.

13Kings take pleasure in honest lips;
they value a man who speaks the
truth.

GOD SIGHTINGS

June 1

2 SAMUEL 18:1–19:10

David mustered the men who were with him and appointed over them commanders of thousands and commanders of hundreds. ²David sent the troops out—a third under the command of Joab, a third under Joab's brother Abishai son of Zeruiah, and a third under Ittai the Gittite. The king told the troops, "I myself will surely march out with you."

³But the men said, "You must not go out; if we are forced to flee, they won't care about us. Even if half of us die, they won't care; but you are worth ten thousand of us.ᵃ It would be better now for you to give us support from the city."

⁴The king answered, "I will do whatever seems best to you."

So the king stood beside the gate while all the men marched out in units of hundreds and of thousands. ⁵The king commanded Joab, Abishai and Ittai, "Be gentle with the young man Absalom for my sake." And all the troops heard the king giving orders concerning Absalom to each of the commanders.

⁶The army marched into the field to fight Israel, and the battle took place in the forest of Ephraim. ⁷There the army of Israel was defeated by David's men, and the casualties that day were great— twenty thousand men. ⁸The battle spread out over the whole countryside, and the forest claimed more lives that day than the sword.

⁹Now Absalom happened to meet David's men. He was riding his mule, and as the mule went under the thick branches of a large oak, Absalom's head got caught in the tree. He was left hanging in midair, while the mule he was riding kept on going.

¹⁰When one of the men saw this, he told Joab, "I just saw Absalom hanging in an oak tree."

¹¹Joab said to the man who had told him this, "What! You saw him? Why didn't you strike him to the ground right there? Then I would have had to give you ten shekelsᵇ of silver and a warrior's belt."

¹²But the man replied, "Even if a thousand shekelsᶜ were weighed out into my hands, I would not lift my hand against the king's son. In our hearing the king commanded you and Abishai and Ittai, 'Protect the young man Absalom for my sake.ᵈ' ¹³And if I had put my life in jeopardyᵉ—and nothing is hidden from the king—you would have kept your distance from me."

¹⁴Joab said, "I'm not going to wait like this for you." So he took three javelins in his hand and plunged them into Absalom's heart while Absalom was still alive in the oak tree. ¹⁵And ten of Joab's armor-bearers surrounded Absalom, struck him and killed him.

¹⁶Then Joab sounded the trumpet, and the troops stopped pursuing Israel, for Joab halted them. ¹⁷They took Absalom, threw him into a big pit in the forest and piled up a large heap of rocks over him. Meanwhile, all the Israelites fled to their homes.

¹⁸During his lifetime Absalom had taken a pillar and erected it in the King's Valley as a monument to himself, for he thought, "I have no son to carry on the memory of my name." He named the pillar after himself, and it is called Absalom's Monument to this day.

¹⁹Now Ahimaaz son of Zadok said, "Let me run and take the news to the king that the LORD has delivered him from the hand of his enemies."

²⁰"You are not the one to take the news today," Joab told him. "You may take the news another time, but you

must not do so today, because the king's son is dead."

²¹Then Joab said to a Cushite, "Go, tell the king what you have seen." The Cushite bowed down before Joab and ran off.

²²Ahimaaz son of Zadok again said to Joab, "Come what may, please let me run behind the Cushite."

But Joab replied, "My son, why do you want to go? You don't have any news that will bring you a reward."

²³He said, "Come what may, I want to run."

So Joab said, "Run!" Then Ahimaaz ran by way of the plain[f] and outran the Cushite.

²⁴While David was sitting between the inner and outer gates, the watchman went up to the roof of the gateway by the wall. As he looked out, he saw a man running alone. ²⁵The watchman called out to the king and reported it.

The king said, "If he is alone, he must have good news." And the man came closer and closer.

²⁶Then the watchman saw another man running, and he called down to the gatekeeper, "Look, another man running alone!"

The king said, "He must be bringing good news, too."

²⁷The watchman said, "It seems to me that the first one runs like Ahimaaz son of Zadok."

"He's a good man," the king said. "He comes with good news."

²⁸Then Ahimaaz called out to the king, "All is well!" He bowed down before the king with his face to the ground and said, "Praise be to the Lord your God! He has delivered up the men who lifted their hands against my lord the king."

²⁹The king asked, "Is the young man Absalom safe?"

Ahimaaz answered, "I saw great confusion just as Joab was about to send the king's servant and me, your servant, but I don't know what it was."

³⁰The king said, "Stand aside and wait here." So he stepped aside and stood there.

³¹Then the Cushite arrived and said,

"My lord the king, hear the good news! The Lord has delivered you today from all who rose up against you."

³²The king asked the Cushite, "Is the young man Absalom safe?"

The Cushite replied, "May the enemies of my lord the king and all who rise up to harm you be like that young man."

³³The king was shaken. He went up to the room over the gateway and wept. As he went, he said: "O my son Absalom! My son, my son Absalom! If only I had died instead of you—O Absalom, my son, my son!"

19:1 Joab was told, "The king is weeping and mourning for Absalom." ²And for the whole army the victory that day was turned into mourning, because on that day the troops heard it said, "The king is grieving for his son." ³The men stole into the city that day as men steal in who are ashamed when they flee from battle. ⁴The king covered his face and cried aloud, "O my son Absalom! O Absalom, my son, my son!"

⁵Then Joab went into the house to the king and said, "Today you have humiliated all your men, who have just saved your life and the lives of your sons and daughters and the lives of your wives and concubines. ⁶You love those who hate you and hate those who love you. You have made it clear today that the commanders and their men mean nothing to you. I see that you would be pleased if Absalom were alive today and all of us were dead. ⁷Now go out and encourage your men. I swear by the Lord that if you don't go out, not a man will be left with you by nightfall. This will be worse for you than all the calamities that have come upon you from your youth till now."

⁸So the king got up and took his seat in the gateway. When the men were told, "The king is sitting in the gateway," they all came before him.

Meanwhile, the Israelites had fled to their homes. ⁹Throughout the tribes of Israel, the people were all arguing with each other, saying, "The king delivered us from the hand of our enemies; he is the one who rescued us from the hand of the Philistines. But now he has fled the country because of Absalom; [10]and Absalom, whom we anointed to rule over us, has died in battle. So why do you say nothing about bringing the king back?"

a3 Two Hebrew manuscripts, some Septuagint manuscripts and Vulgate; most Hebrew manuscripts care; for now there are ten thousand like us b11 That is, about 4 ounces (about 115 grams) c12 That is, about 25 pounds (about 11 kilograms) d12 A few Hebrew manuscripts, Septuagint, Vulgate and Syriac; most Hebrew manuscripts may be translated Absalom, whoever you may be. e13 Or Otherwise, if I had acted treacherously toward him f23 That is, the plain of the Jordan

JOHN 20:1-31

Early on the first day of the week, while it was still dark, Mary Magdalene went to the tomb and saw that the stone had been removed from the entrance. [2]So she came running to Simon Peter and the other disciple, the one Jesus loved, and said, "They have taken the Lord out of the tomb, and we don't know where they have put him!"

[3]So Peter and the other disciple started for the tomb. [4]Both were running, but the other disciple outran Peter and reached the tomb first. [5]He bent over and looked in at the strips of linen lying there but did not go in. [6]Then Simon Peter, who was behind him, arrived and went into the tomb. He saw the strips of linen lying there, [7]as well as the burial cloth that had been around Jesus' head. The cloth was folded up by itself, separate from the linen. [8]Finally the other disciple, who had reached the tomb first, also went inside. He saw and believed. [9](They still did not understand from Scripture that Jesus had to rise from the dead.)

[10]Then the disciples went back to their homes, [11]but Mary stood outside the tomb crying. As she wept, she bent over to look into the tomb [12]and saw two angels in white, seated where Jesus' body had been, one at the head and the other at the foot.

[13]They asked her, "Woman, why are you crying?"

"They have taken my Lord away," she said, "and I don't know where they have put him." [14]At this, she turned around and saw Jesus standing there, but she did not realize that it was Jesus.

[15]"Woman," he said, "why are you crying? Who is it you are looking for?"

Thinking he was the gardener, she said, "Sir, if you have carried him away, tell me where you have put him, and I will get him."

[16]Jesus said to her, "Mary."

She turned toward him and cried out in Aramaic, "Rabboni!" (which means Teacher).

[17]Jesus said, "Do not hold on to me, for I have not yet returned to the Father. Go instead to my brothers and tell them, 'I am returning to my Father and your Father, to my God and your God.'"

[18]Mary Magdalene went to the disciples with the news: "I have seen the Lord!" And she told them that he had said these things to her.

[19]On the evening of that first day of the week, when the disciples were together, with the doors locked for fear of the Jews, Jesus came and stood among them and said, "Peace be with you!" [20]After he said this, he showed them his hands and side. The disciples were overjoyed when they saw the Lord.

[21]Again Jesus said, "Peace be with you! As the Father has sent me, I am sending you." [22]And with that he breathed on them and said, "Receive the Holy Spirit. [23]If you forgive anyone his sins, they are forgiven; if you do not forgive them, they are not forgiven."

[24]Now Thomas (called Didymus), one of the Twelve, was not with the disciples when Jesus came. [25]So the other disciples told him, "We have seen the Lord!"

But he said to them, "Unless I see the nail marks in his hands and put my finger where the nails were, and put my hand into his side, I will not believe it."

[26]A week later his disciples were in the house again, and Thomas was with them. Though the doors were locked, Jesus came and stood among them and said, "Peace be with you!" [27]Then he said to Thomas, "Put your finger here; see my hands. Reach out your hand and

put it into my side. Stop doubting and believe."

²⁸Thomas said to him, "My Lord and my God!"

²⁹Then Jesus told him, "Because you have seen me, you have believed; blessed are those who have not seen and yet have believed."

³⁰**Jesus did many other miraculous signs in the presence of his disciples, which are not recorded in this book.** ³¹**But these are written that you may**ᵃ **believe that Jesus is the Christ, the Son of God, and that by believing you may have life in his name.**

a31 Some manuscripts may continue to

PSALM 119:153-176

ר Resh

¹⁵³**L**ook upon my suffering and deliver me,
    for I have not forgotten your [the LORD's] law.
¹⁵⁴Defend my cause and redeem me;
    preserve my life according to your promise.
¹⁵⁵Salvation is far from the wicked,
    for they do not seek out your decrees.
¹⁵⁶Your compassion is great, O LORD;
    preserve my life according to your laws.
¹⁵⁷Many are the foes who persecute me,
    but I have not turned from your statutes.
¹⁵⁸I look on the faithless with loathing,
    for they do not obey your word.
¹⁵⁹See how I love your precepts;
    preserve my life, O LORD, according to your love.
¹⁶⁰All your words are true;
    all your righteous laws are eternal.

ש Sin and Shin

¹⁶¹Rulers persecute me without cause,
    but my heart trembles at your word.
¹⁶²I rejoice in your promise

like one who finds great spoil.
¹⁶³I hate and abhor falsehood
    but I love your law.
¹⁶⁴Seven times a day I praise you
    for your righteous laws.
¹⁶⁵Great peace have they who love your law,
    and nothing can make them stumble.
¹⁶⁶I wait for your salvation, O LORD,
    and I follow your commands.
¹⁶⁷I obey your statutes,
    for I love them greatly.
¹⁶⁸I obey your precepts and your statutes,
    for all my ways are known to you.

ת Taw

¹⁶⁹May my cry come before you,
        O LORD;
    give me understanding according to your word.
¹⁷⁰May my supplication come before you;
    deliver me according to your promise.
¹⁷¹May my lips overflow with praise,
    for you teach me your decrees.
¹⁷²May my tongue sing of your word,
    for all your commands are righteous.
¹⁷³May your hand be ready to help me,
    for I have chosen your precepts.
¹⁷⁴I long for your salvation, O LORD,
    and your law is my delight.
¹⁷⁵Let me live that I may praise you,
    and may your laws sustain me.
¹⁷⁶I have strayed like a lost sheep.
    Seek your servant,
    for I have not forgotten your commands.

PROVERBS 16:14-15

¹⁴**A** king's wrath is a messenger of death,
    but a wise man will appease it.

¹⁵When a king's face brightens, it means life;
    his favor is like a rain cloud in spring.

□ DAY 153

June 2

2 SAMUEL 19:11–20:13

King David sent this message to Zadok and Abiathar, the priests: "Ask the elders of Judah, 'Why should you be the last to bring the king back to his palace, since what is being said throughout Israel has reached the king at his quarters? 12 You are my brothers, my own flesh and blood. So why should you be the last to bring back the king?' 13 And say to Amasa, 'Are you not my own flesh and blood? May God deal with me, be it ever so severely, if from now on you are not the commander of my army in place of Joab.'"

14 He won over the hearts of all the men of Judah as though they were one man. They sent word to the king, "Return, you and all your men." 15 Then the king returned and went as far as the Jordan.

Now the men of Judah had come to Gilgal to go out and meet the king and bring him across the Jordan. 16 Shimei son of Gera, the Benjamite from Bahurim, hurried down with the men of Judah to meet King David. 17 With him were a thousand Benjamites, along with Ziba, the steward of Saul's household, and his fifteen sons and twenty servants. They rushed to the Jordan, where the king was. 18 They crossed at the ford to take the king's household over and to do whatever he wished.

When Shimei son of Gera crossed the Jordan, he fell prostrate before the king 19 and said to him, "May my lord not hold me guilty. Do not remember how your servant did wrong on the day my lord the king left Jerusalem. May the king put it out of his mind. 20 For I your servant know that I have sinned, but today I have come here as the first of the whole house of Joseph to come down and meet my lord the king."

21 Then Abishai son of Zeruiah said, "Shouldn't Shimei be put to death for this? He cursed the LORD's anointed."

22 David replied, "What do you and I have in common, you sons of Zeruiah? This day you have become my adversaries! Should anyone be put to death in Israel today? Do I not know that today I am king over Israel?" 23 So the king said to Shimei, "You shall not die." And the king promised him on oath.

24 Mephibosheth, Saul's grandson, also went down to meet the king. He had not taken care of his feet or trimmed his mustache or washed his clothes from the day the king left until the day he returned safely. 25 When he came from Jerusalem to meet the king, the king asked him, "Why didn't you go with me, Mephibosheth?"

26 He said, "My lord the king, since I your servant am lame, I said, 'I will have my donkey saddled and will ride on it, so I can go with the king.' But Ziba my servant betrayed me. 27 And he has slandered your servant to my lord the king. My lord the king is like an angel of God; so do whatever pleases you. 28 All my grandfather's descendants deserved nothing but death from my lord the king, but you gave your servant a place among those who eat at your table. So what right do I have to make any more appeals to the king?"

29 The king said to him, "Why say more? I order you and Ziba to divide the fields."

30 Mephibosheth said to the king, "Let him take everything, now that my lord the king has arrived home safely."

31 Barzillai the Gileadite also came down from Rogelim to cross the Jordan with the king and to send him on his way from there. 32 Now Barzillai was a very old man, eighty years of age. He had provided for the king during his stay in Mahanaim, for he was a very wealthy man. 33 The king said to Barzillai, "Cross over with me and stay with me in Jerusalem, and I will provide for you."

34 But Barzillai answered the king, "How many more years will I live, that I

should go up to Jerusalem with the king? [35] I am now eighty years old. Can I tell the difference between what is good and what is not? Can your servant taste what he eats and drinks? Can I still hear the voices of men and women singers? Why should your servant be an added burden to my lord the king? [36] Your servant will cross over the Jordan with the king for a short distance, but why should the king reward me in this way? [37] Let your servant return, that I may die in my own town near the tomb of my father and mother. But here is your servant Kimham. Let him cross over with my lord the king. Do for him whatever pleases you."

[38] The king said, "Kimham shall cross over with me, and I will do for him whatever pleases you. And anything you desire from me I will do for you."

[39] So all the people crossed the Jordan, and then the king crossed over. The king kissed Barzillai and gave him his blessing, and Barzillai returned to his home.

[40] When the king crossed over to Gilgal, Kimham crossed with him. All the troops of Judah and half the troops of Israel had taken the king over.

[41] Soon all the men of Israel were coming to the king and saying to him, "Why did our brothers, the men of Judah, steal the king away and bring him and his household across the Jordan, together with all his men?"

[42] All the men of Judah answered the men of Israel, "We did this because the king is closely related to us. Why are you angry about it? Have we eaten any of the king's provisions? Have we taken anything for ourselves?"

[43] Then the men of Israel answered the men of Judah, "We have ten shares in the king; and besides, we have a greater claim on David than you have. So why do you treat us with contempt? Were we not the first to speak of bringing back our king?"

But the men of Judah responded even more harshly than the men of Israel.

[20:1] Now a troublemaker named Sheba son of Bicri, a Benjamite, happened to be there. He sounded the trumpet and shouted,

"We have no share in David,
    no part in Jesse's son!
Every man to his tent, O Israel!"

[2] So all the men of Israel deserted David to follow Sheba son of Bicri. But the men of Judah stayed by their king all the way from the Jordan to Jerusalem.

[3] When David returned to his palace in Jerusalem, he took the ten concubines he had left to take care of the palace and put them in a house under guard. He provided for them, but did not lie with them. They were kept in confinement till the day of their death, living as widows.

[4] Then the king said to Amasa, "Summon the men of Judah to come to me within three days, and be here yourself." [5] But when Amasa went to summon Judah, he took longer than the time the king had set for him.

[6] David said to Abishai, "Now Sheba son of Bicri will do us more harm than Absalom did. Take your master's men and pursue him, or he will find fortified cities and escape from us." [7] So Joab's men and the Kerethites and Pelethites and all the mighty warriors went out under the command of Abishai. They marched out from Jerusalem to pursue Sheba son of Bicri.

[8] While they were at the great rock in Gibeon, Amasa came to meet them. Joab was wearing his military tunic, and strapped over it at his waist was a belt with a dagger in its sheath. As he stepped forward, it dropped out of its sheath.

[9] Joab said to Amasa, "How are you, my brother?" Then Joab took Amasa by the beard with his right hand to kiss him. [10] Amasa was not on his guard against the dagger in Joab's hand, and Joab plunged it into his belly, and his intestines spilled out on the ground. Without being stabbed again, Amasa

died. Then Joab and his brother Abishai pursued Sheba son of Bicri.

¹¹One of Joab's men stood beside Amasa and said, "Whoever favors Joab, and whoever is for David, let him follow Joab!" ¹²Amasa lay wallowing in his blood in the middle of the road, and the man saw that all the troops came to a halt there. When he realized that everyone who came up to Amasa stopped, he dragged him from the road into a field and threw a garment over him. ¹³After Amasa had been removed from the road, all the men went on with Joab to pursue Sheba son of Bicri.

JOHN 21:1-25

Afterward Jesus appeared again to his disciples, by the Sea of Tiberias.ᵃ It happened this way: ²Simon Peter, Thomas (called Didymus), Nathanael from Cana in Galilee, the sons of Zebedee, and two other disciples were together. ³"I'm going out to fish," Simon Peter told them, and they said, "We'll go with you." So they went out and got into the boat, but that night they caught nothing.

⁴Early in the morning, Jesus stood on the shore, but the disciples did not realize that it was Jesus.

⁵He called out to them, "Friends, haven't you any fish?"

"No," they answered.

⁶He said, "Throw your net on the right side of the boat and you will find some." When they did, they were unable to haul the net in because of the large number of fish.

⁷Then the disciple whom Jesus loved said to Peter, "It is the Lord!" As soon as Simon Peter heard him say, "It is the Lord," he wrapped his outer garment around him (for he had taken it off) and jumped into the water. ⁸The other disciples followed in the boat, towing the net full of fish, for they were not far from shore, about a hundred yards.ᵇ ⁹When they landed, they saw a fire of burning coals there with fish on it, and some bread.

¹⁰Jesus said to them, "Bring some of the fish you have just caught."

¹¹Simon Peter climbed aboard and dragged the net ashore. It was full of large fish, 153, but even with so many the net was not torn. ¹²Jesus said to them, "Come and have breakfast." None of the disciples dared ask him, "Who are you?" They knew it was the Lord. ¹³Jesus came, took the bread and gave it to them, and did the same with the fish. ¹⁴This was now the third time Jesus appeared to his disciples after he was raised from the dead.

¹⁵When they had finished eating, Jesus said to Simon Peter, "Simon son of John, do you truly love me more than these?"

"Yes, Lord," he said, "you know that I love you."

Jesus said, "Feed my lambs."

¹⁶Again Jesus said, "Simon son of John, do you truly love me?"

He answered, "Yes, Lord, you know that I love you."

Jesus said, "Take care of my sheep."

¹⁷The third time he said to him, "Simon son of John, do you love me?"

Peter was hurt because Jesus asked him the third time, "Do you love me?" He said, "Lord, you know all things; you know that I love you."

Jesus said, "Feed my sheep. ¹⁸I tell you the truth, when you were younger you dressed yourself and went where you wanted; but when you are old you will stretch out your hands, and someone else will dress you and lead you where you do not want to go." ¹⁹Jesus said this to indicate the kind of death by which Peter would glorify God. Then he said to him, "Follow me!"

²⁰Peter turned and saw that the disciple whom Jesus loved was following them. (This was the one who had leaned back against Jesus at the supper and had said, "Lord, who is going to betray you?") ²¹When Peter saw him, he asked, "Lord, what about him?"

²²Jesus answered, "If I want him to remain alive until I return, what is that to you? You must follow me." ²³Because of this, the rumor spread among the brothers that this disciple would not

die. But Jesus did not say that he would not die; he only said, "If I want him to remain alive until I return, what is that to you?"

24This is the disciple who testifies to these things and who wrote them down. We know that his testimony is true.

25**Jesus did many other things as well. If every one of them were written down, I suppose that even the whole world would not have room for the books that would be written.**

a 1 That is, Sea of Galilee   b 8 Greek *about two hundred cubits* (about 90 meters)

PSALM 120:1-7

A song of ascents.

1 **I** call on the Lord in my distress,
    and he answers me.
2 Save me, O Lord, from lying lips
    and from deceitful tongues.

3 What will he do to you,
    and what more besides,
        O deceitful tongue?
4 He will punish you with a warrior's
        sharp arrows,
    with burning coals of the broom
        tree.

5 Woe to me that I dwell in Meshech,
    that I live among the tents of
        Kedar!
6 Too long have I lived
    among those who hate peace.
7 I am a man of peace;
    but when I speak, they are
        for war.

PROVERBS 16:16-17

16 **H**ow much better to get wisdom
    than gold,
    to choose understanding rather
        than silver!

17 The highway of the upright avoids
    evil;
    he who guards his way guards
        his life.

□ DAY 154

GOD SIGHTINGS

June 3

2 SAMUEL 20:14–22:20

Sheba passed through all the tribes of Israel to Abel Beth Maacaha and through the entire region of the Berites, who gathered together and followed him. 15All the troops with Joab came and besieged Sheba in Abel Beth Maacah. They built a siege ramp up to the city, and it stood against the outer fortifications. While they were battering the wall to bring it down, 16a wise woman called from the city, "Listen! Listen! Tell Joab to come here so I can speak to him." 17He went toward her, and she asked, "Are you Joab?"

"I am," he answered.

She said, "Listen to what your servant has to say."

"I'm listening," he said.

18She continued, "Long ago they used to say, 'Get your answer at Abel,' and that settled it. 19We are the peaceful and faithful in Israel. You are trying to destroy a city that is a mother in Israel. Why do you want to swallow up the Lord's inheritance?"

20"Far be it from me!" Joab replied, "Far be it from me to swallow up or destroy! 21That is not the case. A man named Sheba son of Bicri, from the hill country of Ephraim, has lifted up his hand against the king, against David. Hand over this one man, and I'll withdraw from the city."

The woman said to Joab, "His head will be thrown to you from the wall."

22Then the woman went to all the people with her wise advice, and they cut off the head of Sheba son of Bicri and threw it to Joab. So he sounded the trumpet, and his men dispersed from the city, each returning to his home. And Joab went back to the king in Jerusalem.

23Joab was over Israel's entire army; Benaiah son of Jehoiada was over the

Kerethites and Pelethites; [24]Adoniram[b] was in charge of forced labor; Jehoshaphat son of Ahilud was recorder; [25]Sheva was secretary; Zadok and Abiathar were priests; [26]and Ira the Jairite was David's priest.

[21:1]DURING the reign of David, there was a famine for three successive years; so David sought the face of the LORD. The LORD said, "It is on account of Saul and his blood-stained house; it is because he put the Gibeonites to death."

[2]The king summoned the Gibeonites and spoke to them. (Now the Gibeonites were not a part of Israel but were survivors of the Amorites; the Israelites had sworn to ⌊spare⌋ them, but Saul in his zeal for Israel and Judah had tried to annihilate them.) [3]David asked the Gibeonites, "What shall I do for you? How shall I make amends so that you will bless the LORD's inheritance?"

[4]The Gibeonites answered him, "We have no right to demand silver or gold from Saul or his family, nor do we have the right to put anyone in Israel to death."

"What do you want me to do for you?" David asked.

[5]They answered the king, "As for the man who destroyed us and plotted against us so that we have been decimated and have no place anywhere in Israel, [6]let seven of his male descendants be given to us to be killed and exposed before the LORD at Gibeah of Saul—the LORD's chosen one."

So the king said, "I will give them to you."

[7]The king spared Mephibosheth son of Jonathan, the son of Saul, because of the oath before the LORD between David and Jonathan son of Saul. [8]But the king took Armoni and Mephibosheth, the two sons of Aiah's daughter Rizpah, whom she had borne to Saul, together with the five sons of Saul's daughter Merab,[c] whom she had borne to Adriel son of Barzillai the Meholathite. [9]He handed them over to the Gibeonites, who killed and exposed them on a hill

before the LORD. All seven of them fell together; they were put to death during the first days of the harvest, just as the barley harvest was beginning.

[10]Rizpah daughter of Aiah took sackcloth and spread it out for herself on a rock. From the beginning of the harvest till the rain poured down from the heavens on the bodies, she did not let the birds of the air touch them by day or the wild animals by night. [11]When David was told what Aiah's daughter Rizpah, Saul's concubine, had done, [12]he went and took the bones of Saul and his son Jonathan from the citizens of Jabesh Gilead. (They had taken them secretly from the public square at Beth Shan, where the Philistines had hung them after they struck Saul down on Gilboa.) [13]David brought the bones of Saul and his son Jonathan from there, and the bones of those who had been killed and exposed were gathered up.

[14]They buried the bones of Saul and his son Jonathan in the tomb of Saul's father Kish, at Zela in Benjamin, and did everything the king commanded. After that, God answered prayer in behalf of the land.

[15]Once again there was a battle between the Philistines and Israel. David went down with his men to fight against the Philistines, and he became exhausted. [16]And Ishbi-Benob, one of the descendants of Rapha, whose bronze spearhead weighed three hundred shekels[d] and who was armed with a new ⌊sword⌋, said he would kill David. [17]But Abishai son of Zeruiah came to David's rescue; he struck the Philistine down and killed him. Then David's men swore to him, saying, "Never again will you go out with us to battle, so that the lamp of Israel will not be extinguished."

[18]In the course of time, there was another battle with the Philistines, at Gob. At that time Sibbecai the Hushathite killed Saph, one of the descendants of Rapha.

[19]In another battle with the Philistines at Gob, Elhanan son of Jaare-

Oregim*e* the Bethlehemite killed Goliath*f* the Gittite, who had a spear with a shaft like a weaver's rod.

²⁰In still another battle, which took place at Gath, there was a huge man with six fingers on each hand and six toes on each foot—twenty-four in all. He also was descended from Rapha. ²¹When he taunted Israel, Jonathan son of Shimeah, David's brother, killed him.

²²These four were descendants of Rapha in Gath, and they fell at the hands of David and his men.

²²:¹DAVID sang to the LORD the words of this song when the LORD delivered him from the hand of all his enemies and from the hand of Saul. ²He said:

"The LORD is my rock, my fortress
    and my deliverer;
³   my God is my rock, in whom I take
        refuge,
    my shield and the horn*g* of my
        salvation.
He is my stronghold, my refuge and
    my savior—
    from violent men you save me.
⁴I call to the LORD, who is worthy of
    praise,
    and I am saved from my enemies.

⁵"The waves of death swirled about
    me;
    the torrents of destruction
        overwhelmed me.
⁶The cords of the grave*h* coiled
        around me;
    the snares of death confronted me.
⁷In my distress I called to the LORD;
    I called out to my God.
From his temple he heard my voice;
    my cry came to his ears.

⁸"The earth trembled and quaked,
    the foundations of the heavens*i*
        shook;
    they trembled because he was
        angry.
⁹Smoke rose from his nostrils;
    consuming fire came from his
        mouth,
    burning coals blazed out of it.

¹⁰He parted the heavens and came
        down;
    dark clouds were under his feet.
¹¹He mounted the cherubim and flew;
    he soared*j* on the wings of the
        wind.
¹²He made darkness his canopy
        around him—
    the dark*k* rain clouds of the sky.
¹³Out of the brightness of his presence
    bolts of lightning blazed forth.
¹⁴The LORD thundered from heaven;
    the voice of the Most High
        resounded.
¹⁵He shot arrows and scattered ⌞the
    enemies⌟,
    bolts of lightning and routed them.
¹⁶The valleys of the sea were exposed
    and the foundations of the earth
        laid bare
at the rebuke of the LORD,
    at the blast of breath from his
        nostrils.

¹⁷"He reached down from on high and
    took hold of me;
    he drew me out of deep waters.
¹⁸He rescued me from my powerful
        enemy,
    from my foes, who were too strong
        for me.
¹⁹They confronted me in the day of my
        disaster,
    but the LORD was my support.
²⁰He brought me out into a spacious
        place;
    he rescued me because he
        delighted in me."

a14 Or *Abel, even Beth Maacah*; also in verse 15   *b24* Some
Septuagint manuscripts (see also 1 Kings 4:6 and 5:14);
Hebrew *Adoram*   *c8* Two Hebrew manuscripts, some
Septuagint manuscripts and Syriac (see also 1 Samuel
18:19); most Hebrew and Septuagint manuscripts *Michal*
d16 That is, about 7 1/2 pounds (about 3.5 kilograms)
e19 Or *son of Jair the weaver*   *f19* Hebrew and Septuagint;
1 Chron. 20:5 *son of Jair killed Lahmi the brother of Goliath*
g3 Horn here symbolizes strength.   *h6* Hebrew *Sheol*
i8 Hebrew; Vulgate and Syriac (see also Psalm 18:7)
mountains   *j11* Many Hebrew manuscripts (see also
Psalm 18:10); most Hebrew manuscripts *appeared*
k12 Septuagint and Vulgate (see also Psalm 18:11);
Hebrew *massed*

ACTS 1:1-26

In my former book, Theophilus, I wrote
about all that Jesus began to do and to

teach ²until the day he was taken up to heaven, after giving instructions through the Holy Spirit to the apostles he had chosen. ³After his suffering, he showed himself to these men and gave many convincing proofs that he was alive. He appeared to them over a period of forty days and spoke about the kingdom of God. ⁴On one occasion, while he was eating with them, he gave them this command: "Do not leave Jerusalem, but wait for the gift my Father promised, which you have heard me speak about. ⁵For John baptized with[a] water, but in a few days you will be baptized with the Holy Spirit."

⁶So when they met together, they asked him, "Lord, are you at this time going to restore the kingdom to Israel?"

⁷He said to them: "It is not for you to know the times or dates the Father has set by his own authority. ⁸But you will receive power when the Holy Spirit comes on you; and you will be my witnesses in Jerusalem, and in all Judea and Samaria, and to the ends of the earth."

⁹After he said this, he was taken up before their very eyes, and a cloud hid him from their sight.

¹⁰They were looking intently up into the sky as he was going, when suddenly two men dressed in white stood beside them. ¹¹"Men of Galilee," they said, "why do you stand here looking into the sky? This same Jesus, who has been taken from you into heaven, will come back in the same way you have seen him go into heaven."

¹²Then they returned to Jerusalem from the hill called the Mount of Olives, a Sabbath day's walk[b] from the city. ¹³When they arrived, they went upstairs to the room where they were staying. Those present were Peter, John, James and Andrew; Philip and Thomas, Bartholomew and Matthew; James son of Alphaeus and Simon the Zealot, and Judas son of James. ¹⁴They all joined together constantly in prayer, along with the women and Mary the mother of Jesus, and with his brothers.

¹⁵In those days Peter stood up among the believers[c] (a group numbering about a hundred and twenty) ¹⁶and said, "Brothers, the Scripture had to be fulfilled which the Holy Spirit spoke long ago through the mouth of David concerning Judas, who served as guide for those who arrested Jesus— ¹⁷he was one of our number and shared in this ministry."

¹⁸(With the reward he got for his wickedness, Judas bought a field; there he fell headlong, his body burst open and all his intestines spilled out. ¹⁹Everyone in Jerusalem heard about this, so they called that field in their language Akeldama, that is, Field of Blood.)

²⁰"For," said Peter, "it is written in the book of Psalms,

"'May his place be deserted;
    let there be no one to dwell in it,'[d]

and,

"'May another take his place of
    leadership.'[e]

²¹Therefore it is necessary to choose one of the men who have been with us the whole time the Lord Jesus went in and out among us, ²²beginning from John's baptism to the time when Jesus was taken up from us. For one of these must become a witness with us of his resurrection."

²³So they proposed two men: Joseph called Barsabbas (also known as Justus) and Matthias. ²⁴Then they prayed, "Lord, you know everyone's heart. Show us which of these two you have chosen ²⁵to take over this apostolic ministry, which Judas left to go where he belongs." ²⁶Then they cast lots, and the lot fell to Matthias; so he was added to the eleven apostles.

---

a5 Or in   b12 That is, about 3/4 mile (about 1,100 meters)   c15 Greek brothers   d20 Psalm 69:25   e20 Psalm 109:8

PSALM 121:1-8
A song of ascents.

1 I lift up my eyes to the hills—
    where does my help come from?
2 My help comes from the LORD,
    the Maker of heaven and earth.

³He will not let your foot slip—
  he who watches over you will
    not slumber;
⁴indeed, he who watches over Israel
  will neither slumber nor sleep.

⁵The LORD watches over you—
  the LORD is your shade at your
    right hand;
⁶the sun will not harm you by day,
  nor the moon by night.

⁷The LORD will keep you from all harm—
  he will watch over your life;
⁸the LORD will watch over your
    coming and going
  both now and forevermore.

PROVERBS 16:18
¹⁸**P**ride goes before destruction,
  a haughty spirit before a fall.

☐ DAY 155

GOD SIGHTINGS

June 4

2 SAMUEL 22:21–23:23
²¹"**T**he LORD has dealt with me
    according to my
    righteousness;
  according to the cleanness of my
    hands he has rewarded me.
²²For I have kept the ways of the LORD;
  I have not done evil by turning
    from my God.
²³All his laws are before me;
  I have not turned away from his
    decrees.
²⁴I have been blameless before him
  and have kept myself from sin.
²⁵The LORD has rewarded me
    according to my
    righteousness,
  according to my cleanness*ᵃ* in his
    sight.
²⁶"To the faithful you show yourself
    faithful,

to the blameless you show yourself
    blameless,
²⁷to the pure you show yourself pure,
  but to the crooked you show
    yourself shrewd.
²⁸You save the humble,
  but your eyes are on the haughty
    to bring them low.
²⁹You are my lamp, O LORD;
  the LORD turns my darkness into
    light.
³⁰With your help I can advance against
    a troop*ᵇ*;
  with my God I can scale a wall.

³¹"As for God, his way is perfect;
  the word of the LORD is flawless.
  He is a shield
    for all who take refuge in him.
³²For who is God besides the LORD?
  And who is the Rock except our
    God?
³³**It is God who arms me with
    strength*ᶜ*
  and makes my way perfect.**
³⁴**He makes my feet like the feet of
    a deer;
  he enables me to stand on the
    heights.**
³⁵He trains my hands for battle;
  my arms can bend a bow of
    bronze.
³⁶You give me your shield of victory;
  you stoop down to make me great.
³⁷You broaden the path beneath me,
  so that my ankles do not turn.

³⁸"I pursued my enemies and crushed
    them;
  I did not turn back till they were
    destroyed.
³⁹I crushed them completely, and they
    could not rise;
  they fell beneath my feet.
⁴⁰You armed me with strength for
    battle;
  you made my adversaries bow at
    my feet.
⁴¹You made my enemies turn their
    backs in flight,
  and I destroyed my foes.

⁴²They cried for help, but there was no
      one to save them—
   to the LORD, but he did not
      answer.
⁴³I beat them as fine as the dust of the
      earth;
   I pounded and trampled them like
      mud in the streets.

⁴⁴"You have delivered me from the
      attacks of my people;
   you have preserved me as the head
      of nations.
People I did not know are subject
      to me,
⁴⁵   and foreigners come cringing
      to me;
   as soon as they hear me, they
      obey me.
⁴⁶They all lose heart;
   they come trembling*d* from their
      strongholds.

⁴⁷"The LORD lives! Praise be to my
      Rock!
   Exalted be God, the Rock, my
      Savior!
⁴⁸He is the God who avenges me,
   who puts the nations under me,
⁴⁹   who sets me free from my
      enemies.
You exalted me above my foes;
   from violent men you rescued me.
⁵⁰Therefore I will praise you, O LORD,
      among the nations;
   I will sing praises to your name.
⁵¹He gives his king great victories;
   he shows unfailing kindness to his
      anointed,
   to David and his descendants
      forever."

²³:¹THESE are the last words of David:

"The oracle of David son of Jesse,
   the oracle of the man exalted by
      the Most High,
the man anointed by the God of
      Jacob,
   Israel's singer of songs*e*:

²"The Spirit of the LORD spoke
      through me;
   his word was on my tongue.

³The God of Israel spoke,
   the Rock of Israel said to me:
'When one rules over men in
      righteousness,
   when he rules in the fear of God,
⁴he is like the light of morning at
      sunrise
   on a cloudless morning,
like the brightness after rain
   that brings the grass from the
      earth.'

⁵"Is not my house right with God?
   Has he not made with me an
      everlasting covenant,
   arranged and secured in every
      part?
Will he not bring to fruition my
      salvation
   and grant me my every desire?
⁶But evil men are all to be cast aside
      like thorns,
   which are not gathered with the
      hand.
⁷Whoever touches thorns
   uses a tool of iron or the shaft of
      a spear;
   they are burned up where they
      lie."

⁸These are the names of David's
mighty men:

Josheb-Basshebeth,*f* a Tahkemonite,*g*
was chief of the Three; he raised his
spear against eight hundred men,
whom he killed*h* in one encounter.

⁹Next to him was Eleazar son of Dodai
the Ahohite. As one of the three mighty
men, he was with David when they
taunted the Philistines gathered ₗat Pas
Dammim,*i* for battle. Then the men of
Israel retreated, ¹⁰but he stood his
ground and struck down the Philistines
till his hand grew tired and froze to the
sword. The LORD brought about a great
victory that day. The troops returned to
Eleazar, but only to strip the dead.

¹¹Next to him was Shammah son of
Agee the Hararite. When the Philistines
banded together at a place where there
was a field full of lentils, Israel's troops
fled from them. ¹²But Shammah took

his stand in the middle of the field. He defended it and struck the Philistines down, and the Lord brought about a great victory.

¹³During harvest time, three of the thirty chief men came down to David at the cave of Adullam, while a band of Philistines was encamped in the Valley of Rephaim. ¹⁴At that time David was in the stronghold, and the Philistine garrison was at Bethlehem. ¹⁵David longed for water and said, "Oh, that someone would get me a drink of water from the well near the gate of Bethlehem!" ¹⁶So the three mighty men broke through the Philistine lines, drew water from the well near the gate of Bethlehem and carried it back to David. But he refused to drink it; instead, he poured it out before the Lord. ¹⁷"Far be it from me, O Lord, to do this!" he said. "Is it not the blood of men who went at the risk of their lives?" And David would not drink it.

Such were the exploits of the three mighty men.

¹⁸Abishai the brother of Joab son of Zeruiah was chief of the Three.ʲ He raised his spear against three hundred men, whom he killed, and so he became as famous as the Three. ¹⁹Was he not held in greater honor than the Three? He became their commander, even though he was not included among them.

²⁰Benaiah son of Jehoiada was a valiant fighter from Kabzeel, who performed great exploits. He struck down two of Moab's best men. He also went down into a pit on a snowy day and killed a lion. ²¹And he struck down a huge Egyptian. Although the Egyptian had a spear in his hand, Benaiah went against him with a club. He snatched the spear from the Egyptian's hand and killed him with his own spear. ²²Such were the exploits of Benaiah son of Jehoiada; he too was as famous as the three mighty men. ²³He was held in greater honor than any of the Thirty, but he was not included among the Three.

And David put him in charge of his bodyguard.

ᵃ25 Hebrew; Septuagint and Vulgate (see also Psalm 18:24) to the cleanness of my hands   ᵇ30 Or can run through a barricade   ᶜ33 Dead Sea Scrolls, some Septuagint manuscripts, Vulgate and Syriac (see also Psalm 18:32); Masoretic Text who is my strong refuge   ᵈ46 Some Septuagint manuscripts and Vulgate (see also Psalm 18:45); Masoretic Text they arm themselves.   ᵉ1 Or Israel's beloved singer   ᶠ8 Hebrew; some Septuagint manuscripts suggest Ish-Bosheth, that is, Esh-Baal (see also 1 Chron. 11:11 Jashobeam).   ᵍ8 Probably a variant of Hacmonite (see 1 Chron. 11:11)   ʰ8 Some Septuagint manuscripts (see also 1 Chron. 11:11); Hebrew and other Septuagint manuscripts Three; it was Adino the Eznite who killed eight hundred men   ⁱ9 See 1 Chron. 11:13; Hebrew gathered there.   ʲ18 Most Hebrew manuscripts (see also 1 Chron. 11:20); two Hebrew manuscripts and Syriac Thirty

ACTS 2:1-47

When the day of Pentecost came, they [Jesus' disciples] were all together in one place. ²Suddenly a sound like the blowing of a violent wind came from heaven and filled the whole house where they were sitting. ³They saw what seemed to be tongues of fire that separated and came to rest on each of them. ⁴All of them were filled with the Holy Spirit and began to speak in other tonguesᵃ as the Spirit enabled them.

⁵Now there were staying in Jerusalem God-fearing Jews from every nation under heaven. ⁶When they heard this sound, a crowd came together in bewilderment, because each one heard them speaking in his own language. ⁷Utterly amazed, they asked: "Are not all these men who are speaking Galileans? ⁸Then how is it that each of us hears them in his own native language? ⁹Parthians, Medes and Elamites; residents of Mesopotamia, Judea and Cappadocia, Pontus and Asia, ¹⁰Phrygia and Pamphylia, Egypt and the parts of Libya near Cyrene; visitors from Rome ¹¹(both Jews and converts to Judaism); Cretans and Arabs—we hear them declaring the wonders of God in our own tongues!" ¹²Amazed and perplexed, they asked one another, "What does this mean?"

¹³Some, however, made fun of them and said, "They have had too much wine.ᵇ"

¹⁴Then Peter stood up with the Eleven, raised his voice and addressed the crowd: "Fellow Jews and all of you

who live in Jerusalem, let me explain this to you; listen carefully to what I say. 15These men are not drunk, as you suppose. It's only nine in the morning! 16No, this is what was spoken by the prophet Joel:

17"'In the last days, God says,
    I will pour out my Spirit on all
        people.
Your sons and daughters will
        prophesy,
    your young men will see visions,
    your old men will dream dreams.
18Even on my servants, both men and
        women,
    I will pour out my Spirit in those
        days,
    and they will prophesy.
19I will show wonders in the heaven
        above
    and signs on the earth below,
    blood and fire and billows of
        smoke.
20The sun will be turned to darkness
    and the moon to blood
    before the coming of the great and
        glorious day of the Lord.
21And everyone who calls
    on the name of the Lord will be
        saved.'c

22"Men of Israel, listen to this: Jesus of Nazareth was a man accredited by God to you by miracles, wonders and signs, which God did among you through him, as you yourselves know. 23This man was handed over to you by God's set purpose and foreknowledge; and you, with the help of wicked men,d put him to death by nailing him to the cross. 24But God raised him from the dead, freeing him from the agony of death, because it was impossible for death to keep its hold on him. 25David said about him:

"'I saw the Lord always before me.
    Because he is at my right hand,
    I will not be shaken.
26Therefore my heart is glad and my
        tongue rejoices;
    my body also will live in hope,

27because you will not abandon me to
        the grave,
    nor will you let your Holy One see
        decay.
28You have made known to me the
        paths of life;
    you will fill me with joy in your
        presence.'e

29"Brothers, I can tell you confidently that the patriarch David died and was buried, and his tomb is here to this day. 30But he was a prophet and knew that God had promised him on oath that he would place one of his descendants on his throne. 31Seeing what was ahead, he spoke of the resurrection of the Christ,f that he was not abandoned to the grave, nor did his body see decay. 32God has raised this Jesus to life, and we are all witnesses of the fact. 33Exalted to the right hand of God, he has received from the Father the promised Holy Spirit and has poured out what you now see and hear. 34For David did not ascend to heaven, and yet he said,

"'The Lord said to my Lord:
    "Sit at my right hand
35until I make your enemies
    a footstool for your feet."'g

36"Therefore let all Israel be assured of this: God has made this Jesus, whom you crucified, both Lord and Christ."

37When the people heard this, they were cut to the heart and said to Peter and the other apostles, "Brothers, what shall we do?"

38Peter replied, "Repent and be baptized, every one of you, in the name of Jesus Christ for the forgiveness of your sins. And you will receive the gift of the Holy Spirit. 39The promise is for you and your children and for all who are far off—for all whom the Lord our God will call."

40With many other words he warned them; and he pleaded with them, "Save yourselves from this corrupt generation." 41Those who accepted his message were baptized, and about three thousand were added to their number that day.

⁴²They devoted themselves to the apostles' teaching and to the fellowship, to the breaking of bread and to prayer. ⁴³Everyone was filled with awe, and many wonders and miraculous signs were done by the apostles. ⁴⁴All the believers were together and had everything in common. ⁴⁵Selling their possessions and goods, they gave to anyone as he had need. ⁴⁶Every day they continued to meet together in the temple courts. They broke bread in their homes and ate together with glad and sincere hearts, ⁴⁷praising God and enjoying the favor of all the people. And the Lord added to their number daily those who were being saved.

a4 Or *languages;* also in verse 11   *b13* Or *sweet wine*
c21 Joel 2:28-32   *d23* Or *of those not having the law* (that is, Gentiles)   *e28* Psalm 16:8-11   *f31* Or *Messiah.* "The Christ" (Greek) and "the Messiah" (Hebrew) both mean "the Anointed One"; also in verse 36.   *g35* Psalm 110:1

PSALM 122:1-9
A song of ascents. Of David.

¹ I rejoiced with those who said to me,
   "Let us go to the house of the
      LORD."
² Our feet are standing
   in your gates, O Jerusalem.

³ Jerusalem is built like a city
   that is closely compacted
      together.
⁴ That is where the tribes go up,
   the tribes of the LORD,
   to praise the name of the LORD
      according to the statute given to
         Israel.
⁵ There the thrones for judgment
      stand,
   the thrones of the house of David.

⁶ Pray for the peace of Jerusalem:
   "May those who love you be
      secure.
⁷ May there be peace within your walls
   and security within your citadels."
⁸ For the sake of my brothers and
      friends,
   I will say, "Peace be within you."

⁹ For the sake of the house of the LORD
   our God,
   I will seek your prosperity.

PROVERBS 16:19-20
¹⁹ Better to be lowly in spirit and
      among the oppressed
   than to share plunder with the
      proud.

²⁰ Whoever gives heed to instruction
      prospers,
   and blessed is he who trusts in the
      LORD.

☐ DAY 156

GOD SIGHTINGS

June 5

2 SAMUEL 23:24–24:25
²⁴ Among the Thirty were:
   Asahel the brother of Joab,
   Elhanan son of Dodo from Bethlehem,
²⁵ Shammah the Harodite,
   Elika the Harodite,
²⁶ Helez the Paltite,
   Ira son of Ikkesh from Tekoa,
²⁷ Abiezer from Anathoth,
   Mebunnai*a* the Hushathite,
²⁸ Zalmon the Ahohite,
   Maharai the Netophathite,
²⁹ Heled*b* son of Baanah the Netophathite,
   Ithai son of Ribai from Gibeah in
      Benjamin,
³⁰ Benaiah the Pirathonite,
   Hiddai*c* from the ravines of Gaash,
³¹ Abi-Albon the Arbathite,
   Azmaveth the Barhumite,
³² Eliahba the Shaalbonite,
   the sons of Jashen,
   Jonathan ³³son of*d* Shammah the
      Hararite,
   Ahiam son of Sharar*e* the Hararite,
³⁴ Eliphelet son of Ahasbai the Maacathite,

Eliam son of Ahithophel the Gilonite,

35 Hezro the Carmelite,
Paarai the Arbite,

36 Igal son of Nathan from Zobah,
the son of Hagri,*f*

37 Zelek the Ammonite,
Naharai the Beerothite, the armor-
bearer of Joab son of Zeruiah,

38 Ira the Ithrite,
Gareb the Ithrite

39 and Uriah the Hittite.
There were thirty-seven in all.

24:1 AGAIN the anger of the Lord burned
against Israel, and he incited David
against them, saying, "Go and take a census of Israel and Judah."

2 So the king said to Joab and the
army commanders*g* with him, "Go
throughout the tribes of Israel from
Dan to Beersheba and enroll the fighting men, so that I may know how many
there are."

3 But Joab replied to the king, "May
the Lord your God multiply the troops
a hundred times over, and may the eyes
of my lord the king see it. But why does
my lord the king want to do such a
thing?"

4 The king's word, however, overruled
Joab and the army commanders; so they
left the presence of the king to enroll
the fighting men of Israel.

5 After crossing the Jordan, they
camped near Aroer, south of the town in
the gorge, and then went through Gad
and on to Jazer. 6 They went to Gilead
and the region of Tahtim Hodshi, and on
to Dan Jaan and around toward Sidon.
7 Then they went toward the fortress of
Tyre and all the towns of the Hivites and
Canaanites. Finally, they went on to Beersheba in the Negev of Judah.

8 After they had gone through the entire land, they came back to Jerusalem at
the end of nine months and twenty
days.

9 Joab reported the number of the
fighting men to the king: In Israel there
were eight hundred thousand able-
bodied men who could handle a sword,
and in Judah five hundred thousand.

10 David was conscience-stricken after he had counted the fighting men,
and he said to the Lord, "I have sinned
greatly in what I have done. Now,
O Lord, I beg you, take away the guilt of
your servant. I have done a very foolish
thing."

11 Before David got up the next morning, the word of the Lord had come to
Gad the prophet, David's seer: 12 "Go and
tell David, 'This is what the Lord says: I
am giving you three options. Choose
one of them for me to carry out against
you.'"

13 So Gad went to David and said to
him, "Shall there come upon you three*h*
years of famine in your land? Or three
months of fleeing from your enemies
while they pursue you? Or three days of
plague in your land? Now then, think it
over and decide how I should answer
the one who sent me."

14 David said to Gad, "I am in deep distress. Let us fall into the hands of the
Lord, for his mercy is great; but do not
let me fall into the hands of men."

15 So the Lord sent a plague on Israel
from that morning until the end of the
time designated, and seventy thousand
of the people from Dan to Beersheba
died. 16 When the angel stretched out
his hand to destroy Jerusalem, the Lord
was grieved because of the calamity
and said to the angel who was afflicting
the people, "Enough! Withdraw your
hand." The angel of the Lord was then
at the threshing floor of Araunah the
Jebusite.

17 When David saw the angel who was
striking down the people, he said to the
Lord, "I am the one who has sinned and
done wrong. These are but sheep. What
have they done? Let your hand fall upon
me and my family."

18 On that day Gad went to David and
said to him, "Go up and build an altar to
the Lord on the threshing floor of Araunah the Jebusite." 19 So David went up,
as the Lord had commanded through
Gad. 20 When Araunah looked and saw

the king and his men coming toward him, he went out and bowed down before the king with his face to the ground.

²¹Araunah said, "Why has my lord the king come to his servant?"

"To buy your threshing floor," David answered, "so I can build an altar to the LORD, that the plague on the people may be stopped."

²²Araunah said to David, "Let my lord the king take whatever pleases him and offer it up. Here are oxen for the burnt offering, and here are threshing sledges and ox yokes for the wood. ²³O king, Araunah gives all this to the king." Araunah also said to him, "May the LORD your God accept you."

²⁴But the king replied to Araunah, "No, I insist on paying you for it. I will not sacrifice to the LORD my God burnt offerings that cost me nothing."

So David bought the threshing floor and the oxen and paid fifty shekels*ⁱ* of silver for them. ²⁵David built an altar to the LORD there and sacrificed burnt offerings and fellowship offerings.*ʲ* Then the LORD answered prayer in behalf of the land, and the plague on Israel was stopped.

a27 Hebrew; some Septuagint manuscripts (see also 1 Chron. 11:29) *Sibbecai*   *b29* Some Hebrew manuscripts and Vulgate (see also 1 Chron. 11:30); most Hebrew manuscripts *Heleb*   *c30* Hebrew; some Septuagint manuscripts (see also 1 Chron. 11:32) *Hurai*   *d33* Some Septuagint manuscripts (see also 1 Chron. 11:34); Hebrew does not have *son of.*   *e33* Hebrew; some Septuagint manuscripts (see also 1 Chron. 11:35) *Sacar*   *f36* Some Septuagint manuscripts (see also 1 Chron. 11:38); Hebrew *Haggadi*   *g2* Septuagint (see also verse 4 and 1 Chron. 21:2); Hebrew *Joab the army commander*   *h13* Septuagint (see also 1 Chron. 21:12); Hebrew *seven*   *i24* That is, about 1 1/4 pounds (about 0.6 kilogram)   *j25* Traditionally *peace offerings*

ACTS 3:1-26

One day Peter and John were going up to the temple at the time of prayer—at three in the afternoon. ²Now a man crippled from birth was being carried to the temple gate called Beautiful, where he was put every day to beg from those going into the temple courts. ³When he saw Peter and John about to enter, he asked them for money. ⁴Peter looked straight at him, as did John.

Then Peter said, "Look at us!" ⁵So the man gave them his attention, expecting to get something from them.

⁶Then Peter said, "Silver or gold I do not have, but what I have I give you. In the name of Jesus Christ of Nazareth, walk." ⁷Taking him by the right hand, he helped him up, and instantly the man's feet and ankles became strong. ⁸He jumped to his feet and began to walk. Then he went with them into the temple courts, walking and jumping, and praising God. ⁹When all the people saw him walking and praising God, ¹⁰they recognized him as the same man who used to sit begging at the temple gate called Beautiful, and they were filled with wonder and amazement at what had happened to him.

¹¹While the beggar held on to Peter and John, all the people were astonished and came running to them in the place called Solomon's Colonnade. ¹²When Peter saw this, he said to them: "Men of Israel, why does this surprise you? Why do you stare at us as if by our own power or godliness we had made this man walk? ¹³The God of Abraham, Isaac and Jacob, the God of our fathers, has glorified his servant Jesus. You handed him over to be killed, and you disowned him before Pilate, though he had decided to let him go. ¹⁴You disowned the Holy and Righteous One and asked that a murderer be released to you. ¹⁵You killed the author of life, but God raised him from the dead. We are witnesses of this. ¹⁶By faith in the name of Jesus, this man whom you see and know was made strong. It is Jesus' name and the faith that comes through him that has given this complete healing to him, as you can all see.

¹⁷"Now, brothers, I know that you acted in ignorance, as did your leaders. ¹⁸But this is how God fulfilled what he had foretold through all the prophets, saying that his Christ*ᵃ* would suffer. ¹⁹Repent, then, and turn to God, so that your sins may be wiped out, that times of refreshing may come from the Lord, ²⁰and that he may send the Christ, who

has been appointed for you—even Jesus. 21He must remain in heaven until the time comes for God to restore everything, as he promised long ago through his holy prophets. 22For Moses said, 'The Lord your God will raise up for you a prophet like me from among your own people; you must listen to everything he tells you. 23Anyone who does not listen to him will be completely cut off from among his people.'b

24"Indeed, all the prophets from Samuel on, as many as have spoken, have foretold these days. 25And you are heirs of the prophets and of the covenant God made with your fathers. He said to Abraham, 'Through your offspring all peoples on earth will be blessed.'c 26When God raised up his servant, he sent him first to you to bless you by turning each of you from your wicked ways."

a18 Or *Messiah*; also in verse 20   b23 Deut. 18:15,18,19
c25 Gen. 22:18; 26:4

PSALM 123:1-4
A song of ascents.

1 I lift up my eyes to you,
    to you whose throne is in heaven.
2 As the eyes of slaves look to the
        hand of their master,
    as the eyes of a maid look to the
        hand of her mistress,
    so our eyes look to the Lord our
        God,
    till he shows us his mercy.

3 Have mercy on us, O Lord, have
        mercy on us,
    for we have endured much
        contempt.
4 We have endured much ridicule
        from the proud,
    much contempt from the
        arrogant.

PROVERBS 16:21-23
21 The wise in heart are called
        discerning,
    and pleasant words promote
        instruction.a

22 Understanding is a fountain of life to
        those who have it,
    but folly brings punishment to
        fools.

23 A wise man's heart guides his mouth,
    and his lips promote instruction.b

a21 Or *words make a man persuasive*   b23 Or *mouth / and
makes his lips persuasive*

□ DAY 157

GOD SIGHTINGS

June 6

1 KINGS 1:1-53
When King David was old and well advanced in years, he could not keep warm even when they put covers over him. 2So his servants said to him, "Let us look for a young virgin to attend the king and take care of him. She can lie beside him so that our lord the king may keep warm."

3Then they searched throughout Israel for a beautiful girl and found Abishag, a Shunammite, and brought her to the king. 4The girl was very beautiful; she took care of the king and waited on him, but the king had no intimate relations with her.

5Now Adonijah, whose mother was Haggith, put himself forward and said, "I will be king." So he got chariots and horsesa ready, with fifty men to run ahead of him. 6(His father had never interfered with him by asking, "Why do you behave as you do?" He was also very handsome and was born next after Absalom.)

7Adonijah conferred with Joab son of Zeruiah and with Abiathar the priest, and they gave him their support. 8But Zadok the priest, Benaiah son of Jehoiada, Nathan the prophet, Shimei and Reib and David's special guard did not join Adonijah.

9Adonijah then sacrificed sheep, cattle and fattened calves at the Stone of

Zoheleth near En Rogel. He invited all his brothers, the king's sons, and all the men of Judah who were royal officials, 10 but he did not invite Nathan the prophet or Benaiah or the special guard or his brother Solomon.

11 Then Nathan asked Bathsheba, Solomon's mother, "Have you not heard that Adonijah, the son of Haggith, has become king without our lord David's knowing it? 12 Now then, let me advise you how you can save your own life and the life of your son Solomon. 13 Go in to King David and say to him, 'My lord the king, did you not swear to me your servant: "Surely Solomon your son shall be king after me, and he will sit on my throne"? Why then has Adonijah become king?' 14 While you are still there talking to the king, I will come in and confirm what you have said."

15 So Bathsheba went to see the aged king in his room, where Abishag the Shunammite was attending him. 16 Bathsheba bowed low and knelt before the king.

"What is it you want?" the king asked.

17 She said to him, "My lord, you yourself swore to me your servant by the LORD your God: 'Solomon your son shall be king after me, and he will sit on my throne.' 18 But now Adonijah has become king, and you, my lord the king, do not know about it. 19 He has sacrificed great numbers of cattle, fattened calves, and sheep, and has invited all the king's sons, Abiathar the priest and Joab the commander of the army, but he has not invited Solomon your servant. 20 My lord the king, the eyes of all Israel are on you, to learn from you who will sit on the throne of my lord the king after him. 21 Otherwise, as soon as my lord the king is laid to rest with his fathers, I and my son Solomon will be treated as criminals."

22 While she was still speaking with the king, Nathan the prophet arrived. 23 And they told the king, "Nathan the prophet is here." So he went before the king and bowed with his face to the ground.

24 Nathan said, "Have you, my lord the king, declared that Adonijah shall be king after you, and that he will sit on your throne? 25 Today he has gone down and sacrificed great numbers of cattle, fattened calves, and sheep. He has invited all the king's sons, the commanders of the army and Abiathar the priest. Right now they are eating and drinking with him and saying, 'Long live King Adonijah!' 26 But me your servant, and Zadok the priest, and Benaiah son of Jehoiada, and your servant Solomon he did not invite. 27 Is this something my lord the king has done without letting his servants know who should sit on the throne of my lord the king after him?"

28 Then King David said, "Call in Bathsheba." So she came into the king's presence and stood before him.

29 The king then took an oath: "As surely as the LORD lives, who has delivered me out of every trouble, 30 I will surely carry out today what I swore to you by the LORD, the God of Israel: Solomon your son shall be king after me, and he will sit on my throne in my place."

31 Then Bathsheba bowed low with her face to the ground and, kneeling before the king, said, "May my lord King David live forever!"

32 King David said, "Call in Zadok the priest, Nathan the prophet and Benaiah son of Jehoiada." When they came before the king, 33 he said to them: "Take your lord's servants with you and set Solomon my son on my own mule and take him down to Gihon. 34 There have Zadok the priest and Nathan the prophet anoint him king over Israel. Blow the trumpet and shout, 'Long live King Solomon!' 35 Then you are to go up with him, and he is to come and sit on my throne and reign in my place. I have appointed him ruler over Israel and Judah."

36 Benaiah son of Jehoiada answered the king, "Amen! May the LORD, the God of my lord the king, so declare it. 37 As the LORD was with my lord the king, so may he be with Solomon to make his throne even greater than the throne of my lord King David!"

[38]So Zadok the priest, Nathan the prophet, Benaiah son of Jehoiada, the Kerethites and the Pelethites went down and put Solomon on King David's mule and escorted him to Gihon. [39]Zadok the priest took the horn of oil from the sacred tent and anointed Solomon. Then they sounded the trumpet and all the people shouted, "Long live King Solomon!" [40]And all the people went up after him, playing flutes and rejoicing greatly, so that the ground shook with the sound.

[41]Adonijah and all the guests who were with him heard it as they were finishing their feast. On hearing the sound of the trumpet, Joab asked, "What's the meaning of all the noise in the city?"

[42]Even as he was speaking, Jonathan son of Abiathar the priest arrived. Adonijah said, "Come in. A worthy man like you must be bringing good news."

[43]"Not at all!" Jonathan answered. "Our lord King David has made Solomon king. [44]The king has sent with him Zadok the priest, Nathan the prophet, Benaiah son of Jehoiada, the Kerethites and the Pelethites, and they have put him on the king's mule, [45]and Zadok the priest and Nathan the prophet have anointed him king at Gihon. From there they have gone up cheering, and the city resounds with it. That's the noise you hear. [46]Moreover, Solomon has taken his seat on the royal throne. [47]Also, the royal officials have come to congratulate our lord King David, saying, 'May your God make Solomon's name more famous than yours and his throne greater than yours!' And the king bowed in worship on his bed [48]and said, 'Praise be to the LORD, the God of Israel, who has allowed my eyes to see a successor on my throne today.'"

[49]At this, all Adonijah's guests rose in alarm and dispersed. [50]But Adonijah, in fear of Solomon, went and took hold of the horns of the altar. [51]Then Solomon was told, "Adonijah is afraid of King Solomon and is clinging to the horns of the altar. He says, 'Let King Solomon swear to me today that he will not put his servant to death with the sword.'"

[52]Solomon replied, "If he shows himself to be a worthy man, not a hair of his head will fall to the ground; but if evil is found in him, he will die." [53]Then King Solomon sent men, and they brought him down from the altar. And Adonijah came and bowed down to King Solomon, and Solomon said, "Go to your home."

a5 Or *charioteers* *b8* Or *and his friends*

ACTS 4:1-37

The priests and the captain of the temple guard and the Sadducees came up to Peter and John while they were speaking to the people. [2]They were greatly disturbed because the apostles were teaching the people and proclaiming in Jesus the resurrection of the dead. [3]They seized Peter and John, and because it was evening, they put them in jail until the next day. [4]But many who heard the message believed, and the number of men grew to about five thousand.

[5]The next day the rulers, elders and teachers of the law met in Jerusalem. [6]Annas the high priest was there, and so were Caiaphas, John, Alexander and the other men of the high priest's family. [7]They had Peter and John brought before them and began to question them: "By what power or what name did you do this?"

[8]Then Peter, filled with the Holy Spirit, said to them: "Rulers and elders of the people! [9]If we are being called to account today for an act of kindness shown to a cripple and are asked how he was healed, [10]then know this, you and all the people of Israel: It is by the name of Jesus Christ of Nazareth, whom you crucified but whom God raised from the dead, that this man stands before you healed. [11]He is

> "'the stone you builders rejected,
> which has become the
> capstone.*a'b*

[12]Salvation is found in no one else, for there is no other name under heaven given to men by which we must be saved."

13 When they saw the courage of Peter and John and realized that they were unschooled, ordinary men, they were astonished and they took note that these men had been with Jesus. 14 But since they could see the man who had been healed standing there with them, there was nothing they could say. 15 So they ordered them to withdraw from the Sanhedrin and then conferred together. 16 "What are we going to do with these men?" they asked. "Everybody living in Jerusalem knows they have done an outstanding miracle, and we cannot deny it. 17 But to stop this thing from spreading any further among the people, we must warn these men to speak no longer to anyone in this name."

18 Then they called them in again and commanded them not to speak or teach at all in the name of Jesus. 19 But Peter and John replied, "Judge for yourselves whether it is right in God's sight to obey you rather than God. 20 For we cannot help speaking about what we have seen and heard."

21 After further threats they let them go. They could not decide how to punish them, because all the people were praising God for what had happened. 22 For the man who was miraculously healed was over forty years old.

23 On their release, Peter and John went back to their own people and reported all that the chief priests and elders had said to them. 24 When they heard this, they raised their voices together in prayer to God. "Sovereign Lord," they said, "you made the heaven and the earth and the sea, and everything in them. 25 You spoke by the Holy Spirit through the mouth of your servant, our father David:

"'Why do the nations rage
    and the peoples plot in vain?
26 The kings of the earth take their
        stand
    and the rulers gather together
against the Lord
    and against his Anointed One.c'd

27 Indeed Herod and Pontius Pilate met together with the Gentiles and the peoplee of Israel in this city to conspire against your holy servant Jesus, whom you anointed. 28 They did what your power and will had decided beforehand should happen. 29 Now, Lord, consider their threats and enable your servants to speak your word with great boldness. 30 Stretch out your hand to heal and perform miraculous signs and wonders through the name of your holy servant Jesus."

31 After they prayed, the place where they were meeting was shaken. And they were all filled with the Holy Spirit and spoke the word of God boldly.

32 All the believers were one in heart and mind. No one claimed that any of his possessions was his own, but they shared everything they had. 33 With great power the apostles continued to testify to the resurrection of the Lord Jesus, and much grace was upon them all. 34 There were no needy persons among them. For from time to time those who owned lands or houses sold them, brought the money from the sales 35 and put it at the apostles' feet, and it was distributed to anyone as he had need.

36 Joseph, a Levite from Cyprus, whom the apostles called Barnabas (which means Son of Encouragement), 37 sold a field he owned and brought the money and put it at the apostles' feet.

a 11 Or cornerstone   b 11 Psalm 118:22   c 26 That is, Christ or Messiah   d 26 Psalm 2:1,2   e 27 The Greek is plural.

PSALM 124:1-8
A song of ascents. Of David.

1 If the Lord had not been on our
        side—
    let Israel say—
2 if the Lord had not been on our side
    when men attacked us,
3 when their anger flared against us,
    they would have swallowed us
        alive;
4 the flood would have engulfed us,
    the torrent would have swept
        over us,
5 the raging waters
    would have swept us away.

6 Praise be to the LORD,
  who has not let us be torn by
    their teeth.
7 We have escaped like a bird
  out of the fowler's snare;
 the snare has been broken,
   and we have escaped.
8 Our help is in the name of the LORD,
  the Maker of heaven and earth.

PROVERBS 16:24

24 Pleasant words are a honeycomb,
   sweet to the soul and healing to
     the bones.

☐ D A Y 1 5 8

GOD SIGHTINGS

June 7

1 KINGS 2:1–3:3

When the time drew near for David to die, he gave a charge to Solomon his son.

2 "I am about to go the way of all the earth," he said. "So be strong, show yourself a man, 3 and observe what the LORD your God requires: Walk in his ways, and keep his decrees and commands, his laws and requirements, as written in the Law of Moses, so that you may prosper in all you do and wherever you go, 4 and that the LORD may keep his promise to me: 'If your descendants watch how they live, and if they walk faithfully before me with all their heart and soul, you will never fail to have a man on the throne of Israel.'

5 "Now you yourself know what Joab son of Zeruiah did to me—what he did to the two commanders of Israel's armies, Abner son of Ner and Amasa son of Jether. He killed them, shedding their blood in peacetime as if in battle, and with that blood stained the belt around his waist and the sandals on his feet. 6 Deal with him according to your wisdom, but do not let his gray head go down to the gravea in peace.

7 "But show kindness to the sons of Barzillai of Gilead and let them be among those who eat at your table. They stood by me when I fled from your brother Absalom.

8 "And remember, you have with you Shimei son of Gera, the Benjamite from Bahurim, who called down bitter curses on me the day I went to Mahanaim. When he came down to meet me at the Jordan, I swore to him by the LORD: 'I will not put you to death by the sword.' 9 But now, do not consider him innocent. You are a man of wisdom; you will know what to do to him. Bring his gray head down to the grave in blood."

10 Then David rested with his fathers and was buried in the City of David. 11 He had reigned forty years over Israel—seven years in Hebron and thirty-three in Jerusalem. 12 So Solomon sat on the throne of his father David, and his rule was firmly established.

13 Now Adonijah, the son of Haggith, went to Bathsheba, Solomon's mother. Bathsheba asked him, "Do you come peacefully?"

He answered, "Yes, peacefully." 14 Then he added, "I have something to say to you."

"You may say it," she replied.

15 "As you know," he said, "the kingdom was mine. All Israel looked to me as their king. But things changed, and the kingdom has gone to my brother; for it has come to him from the LORD. 16 Now I have one request to make of you. Do not refuse me."

"You may make it," she said.

17 So he continued, "Please ask King Solomon—he will not refuse you—to give me Abishag the Shunammite as my wife."

18 "Very well," Bathsheba replied, "I will speak to the king for you."

19 When Bathsheba went to King Solomon to speak to him for Adonijah, the king stood up to meet her, bowed down to her and sat down on his throne. He had a throne brought for the king's mother, and she sat down at his right hand.

²⁰"I have one small request to make of you," she said. "Do not refuse me."

The king replied, "Make it, my mother; I will not refuse you."

²¹So she said, "Let Abishag the Shunammite be given in marriage to your brother Adonijah."

²²King Solomon answered his mother, "Why do you request Abishag the Shunammite for Adonijah? You might as well request the kingdom for him—after all, he is my older brother—yes, for him and for Abiathar the priest and Joab son of Zeruiah!"

²³Then King Solomon swore by the LORD: "May God deal with me, be it ever so severely, if Adonijah does not pay with his life for this request! ²⁴And now, as surely as the LORD lives—he who has established me securely on the throne of my father David and has founded a dynasty for me as he promised—Adonijah shall be put to death today!" ²⁵So King Solomon gave orders to Benaiah son of Jehoiada, and he struck down Adonijah and he died.

²⁶To Abiathar the priest the king said, "Go back to your fields in Anathoth. You deserve to die, but I will not put you to death now, because you carried the ark of the Sovereign LORD before my father David and shared all my father's hardships." ²⁷So Solomon removed Abiathar from the priesthood of the LORD, fulfilling the word the LORD had spoken at Shiloh about the house of Eli.

²⁸When the news reached Joab, who had conspired with Adonijah though not with Absalom, he fled to the tent of the LORD and took hold of the horns of the altar. ²⁹King Solomon was told that Joab had fled to the tent of the LORD and was beside the altar. Then Solomon ordered Benaiah son of Jehoiada, "Go, strike him down!"

³⁰So Benaiah entered the tent of the LORD and said to Joab, "The king says, 'Come out!'"

But he answered, "No, I will die here."

Benaiah reported to the king, "This is how Joab answered me."

³¹Then the king commanded Bena-iah, "Do as he says. Strike him down and bury him, and so clear me and my father's house of the guilt of the innocent blood that Joab shed. ³²The LORD will repay him for the blood he shed, because without the knowledge of my father David he attacked two men and killed them with the sword. Both of them—Abner son of Ner, commander of Israel's army, and Amasa son of Jether, commander of Judah's army—were better men and more upright than he. ³³May the guilt of their blood rest on the head of Joab and his descendants forever. But on David and his descendants, his house and his throne, may there be the LORD's peace forever."

³⁴So Benaiah son of Jehoiada went up and struck down Joab and killed him, and he was buried on his own land*b* in the desert. ³⁵The king put Benaiah son of Jehoiada over the army in Joab's position and replaced Abiathar with Zadok the priest.

³⁶Then the king sent for Shimei and said to him, "Build yourself a house in Jerusalem and live there, but do not go anywhere else. ³⁷The day you leave and cross the Kidron Valley, you can be sure you will die; your blood will be on your own head."

³⁸Shimei answered the king, "What you say is good. Your servant will do as my lord the king has said." And Shimei stayed in Jerusalem for a long time.

³⁹But three years later, two of Shimei's slaves ran off to Achish son of Maacah, king of Gath, and Shimei was told, "Your slaves are in Gath." ⁴⁰At this, he saddled his donkey and went to Achish at Gath in search of his slaves. So Shimei went away and brought the slaves back from Gath.

⁴¹When Solomon was told that Shimei had gone from Jerusalem to Gath and had returned, ⁴²the king summoned Shimei and said to him, "Did I not make you swear by the LORD and warn you, 'On the day you leave to go anywhere else, you can be sure you will die'? At that time you said to me, 'What you say is good. I will obey.' ⁴³Why then did you not keep

your oath to the Lord and obey the command I gave you?"

44The king also said to Shimei, "You know in your heart all the wrong you did to my father David. Now the Lord will repay you for your wrongdoing. 45But King Solomon will be blessed, and David's throne will remain secure before the Lord forever."

46Then the king gave the order to Benaiah son of Jehoiada, and he went out and struck Shimei down and killed him.

The kingdom was now firmly established in Solomon's hands.

3:1Solomon made an alliance with Pharaoh king of Egypt and married his daughter. He brought her to the City of David until he finished building his palace and the temple of the Lord, and the wall around Jerusalem. 2The people, however, were still sacrificing at the high places, because a temple had not yet been built for the Name of the Lord. 3Solomon showed his love for the Lord by walking according to the statutes of his father David, except that he offered sacrifices and burned incense on the high places.

a6 Hebrew Sheol; also in verse 9   b34 Or buried in his tomb

ACTS 5:1-42
Now a man named Ananias, together with his wife Sapphira, also sold a piece of property. 2With his wife's full knowledge he kept back part of the money for himself, but brought the rest and put it at the apostles' feet.

3Then Peter said, "Ananias, how is it that Satan has so filled your heart that you have lied to the Holy Spirit and have kept for yourself some of the money you received for the land? 4Didn't it belong to you before it was sold? And after it was sold, wasn't the money at your disposal? What made you think of doing such a thing? You have not lied to men but to God."

5When Ananias heard this, he fell down and died. And great fear seized all who heard what had happened. 6Then the young men came forward, wrapped

up his body, and carried him out and buried him.

7About three hours later his wife came in, not knowing what had happened. 8Peter asked her, "Tell me, is this the price you and Ananias got for the land?"

"Yes," she said, "that is the price."

9Peter said to her, "How could you agree to test the Spirit of the Lord? Look! The feet of the men who buried your husband are at the door, and they will carry you out also."

10At that moment she fell down at his feet and died. Then the young men came in and, finding her dead, carried her out and buried her beside her husband. 11Great fear seized the whole church and all who heard about these events.

12The apostles performed many miraculous signs and wonders among the people. And all the believers used to meet together in Solomon's Colonnade. 13No one else dared join them, even though they were highly regarded by the people. 14Nevertheless, more and more men and women believed in the Lord and were added to their number. 15As a result, people brought the sick into the streets and laid them on beds and mats so that at least Peter's shadow might fall on some of them as he passed by. 16Crowds gathered also from the towns around Jerusalem, bringing their sick and those tormented by evila spirits, and all of them were healed.

17Then the high priest and all his associates, who were members of the party of the Sadducees, were filled with jealousy. 18They arrested the apostles and put them in the public jail. 19But during the night an angel of the Lord opened the doors of the jail and brought them out. 20"Go, stand in the temple courts," he said, "and tell the people the full message of this new life."

21At daybreak they entered the temple courts, as they had been told, and began to teach the people.

When the high priest and his associates arrived, they called together the Sanhedrin—the full assembly of the elders of Israel—and sent to the jail for the apostles. 22But on arriving at the jail, the officers did not find them there. So they went back and reported, 23"We found the jail securely locked, with the guards standing at the doors; but when we opened them, we found no one inside." 24On hearing this report, the captain of the temple guard and the chief priests were puzzled, wondering what would come of this.

25Then someone came and said, "Look! The men you put in jail are standing in the temple courts teaching the people." 26At that, the captain went with his officers and brought the apostles. They did not use force, because they feared that the people would stone them.

27Having brought the apostles, they made them appear before the Sanhedrin to be questioned by the high priest. 28"We gave you strict orders not to teach in this name," he said. "Yet you have filled Jerusalem with your teaching and are determined to make us guilty of this man's blood."

29Peter and the other apostles replied: "We must obey God rather than men! 30The God of our fathers raised Jesus from the dead—whom you had killed by hanging him on a tree. 31God exalted him to his own right hand as Prince and Savior that he might give repentance and forgiveness of sins to Israel. 32We are witnesses of these things, and so is the Holy Spirit, whom God has given to those who obey him."

33When they heard this, they were furious and wanted to put them to death. 34But a Pharisee named Gamaliel, a teacher of the law, who was honored by all the people, stood up in the Sanhedrin and ordered that the men be put outside for a little while. 35Then he addressed them: "Men of Israel, consider carefully what you intend to do to these men. 36Some time ago Theudas appeared, claiming to be somebody, and about four hundred men rallied to him. He was killed, all his followers were dispersed, and it all came to nothing.

37After him, Judas the Galilean appeared in the days of the census and led a band of people in revolt. He too was killed, and all his followers were scattered. 38Therefore, in the present case I advise you: Leave these men alone! Let them go! For if their purpose or activity is of human origin, it will fail. 39But if it is from God, you will not be able to stop these men; you will only find yourselves fighting against God."

40His speech persuaded them. They called the apostles in and had them flogged. Then they ordered them not to speak in the name of Jesus, and let them go.

41The apostles left the Sanhedrin, rejoicing because they had been counted worthy of suffering disgrace for the Name. 42Day after day, in the temple courts and from house to house, they never stopped teaching and proclaiming the good news that Jesus is the Christ.b

a16 Greek unclean   b42 Or Messiah

PSALM 125:1-5
A song of ascents.

1Those who trust in the LORD are like Mount Zion,
which cannot be shaken but endures forever.
2As the mountains surround Jerusalem,
so the LORD surrounds his people both now and forevermore.

3The scepter of the wicked will not remain
over the land allotted to the righteous,
for then the righteous might use their hands to do evil.

4Do good, O LORD, to those who are good,
to those who are upright in heart.
5But those who turn to crooked ways the LORD will banish with the evildoers.

Peace be upon Israel.

PROVERBS 16:25

25There is a way that seems right to a
man,
but in the end it leads to death.

☐ D A Y 1 5 9

GOD SIGHTINGS

June 8

1 KINGS 3:4–4:34

The king went to Gibeon to offer sacrifices, for that was the most important
high place, and Solomon offered a thousand burnt offerings on that altar. 5At
Gibeon the LORD appeared to Solomon
during the night in a dream, and God
said, "Ask for whatever you want me to
give you."

6Solomon answered, "You have
shown great kindness to your servant,
my father David, because he was faithful to you and righteous and upright in
heart. You have continued this great
kindness to him and have given him a
son to sit on his throne this very day.

7"Now, O LORD my God, you have
made your servant king in place of my
father David. But I am only a little child
and do not know how to carry out my
duties. 8Your servant is here among the
people you have chosen, a great people,
too numerous to count or number. 9So
give your servant a discerning heart
to govern your people and to distinguish between right and wrong. For
who is able to govern this great people of yours?"

10The Lord was pleased that Solomon had asked for this. 11So God said
to him, "Since you have asked for this
and not for long life or wealth for yourself, nor have asked for the death of your
enemies but for discernment in administering justice, 12I will do what you have
asked. I will give you a wise and discerning heart, so that there will never have
been anyone like you, nor will there ever

be. 13Moreover, I will give you what you
have not asked for—both riches and
honor—so that in your lifetime you will
have no equal among kings. 14And if you
walk in my ways and obey my statutes
and commands as David your father did,
I will give you a long life." 15Then Solomon awoke—and he realized it had
been a dream.

He returned to Jerusalem, stood before the ark of the Lord's covenant and
sacrificed burnt offerings and fellowship offerings.a Then he gave a feast for
all his court.

16Now two prostitutes came to the
king and stood before him. 17One of
them said, "My lord, this woman and I
live in the same house. I had a baby
while she was there with me. 18The
third day after my child was born, this
woman also had a baby. We were alone;
there was no one in the house but the
two of us.

19"During the night this woman's son
died because she lay on him. 20So she
got up in the middle of the night and
took my son from my side while I your
servant was asleep. She put him by her
breast and put her dead son by my
breast. 21The next morning, I got up to
nurse my son—and he was dead! But
when I looked at him closely in the
morning light, I saw that it wasn't the
son I had borne."

22The other woman said, "No! The living one is my son; the dead one is yours."

But the first one insisted, "No! The
dead one is yours; the living one is mine."
And so they argued before the king.

23The king said, "This one says, 'My
son is alive and your son is dead,' while
that one says, 'No! Your son is dead and
mine is alive.'"

24Then the king said, "Bring me a
sword." So they brought a sword for the
king. 25He then gave an order: "Cut the
living child in two and give half to one
and half to the other."

26The woman whose son was alive
was filled with compassion for her son
and said to the king, "Please, my lord,
give her the living baby! Don't kill him!"

But the other said, "Neither I nor you shall have him. Cut him in two!"

27 Then the king gave his ruling: "Give the living baby to the first woman. Do not kill him; she is his mother."

28When all Israel heard the verdict the king had given, they held the king in awe, because they saw that he had wisdom from God to administer justice.

4:1So King Solomon ruled over all Israel. 2And these were his chief officials:

Azariah son of Zadok—the priest;
3 Elihoreph and Ahijah, sons of Shisha—secretaries;
Jehoshaphat son of Ahilud—recorder;
4 Benaiah son of Jehoiada—commander in chief;
Zadok and Abiathar—priests;
5 Azariah son of Nathan—in charge of the district officers;
Zabud son of Nathan—a priest and personal adviser to the king;
6 Ahishar—in charge of the palace;
Adoniram son of Abda—in charge of forced labor.

7Solomon also had twelve district governors over all Israel, who supplied provisions for the king and the royal household. Each one had to provide supplies for one month in the year. 8These are their names:

Ben-Hur—in the hill country of Ephraim;
9 Ben-Deker—in Makaz, Shaalbim, Beth Shemesh and Elon Bethhanan;
10 Ben-Hesed—in Arubboth (Socoh and all the land of Hepher were his);
11 Ben-Abinadab—in Naphoth Dor[b] (he was married to Taphath daughter of Solomon);
12 Baana son of Ahilud—in Taanach and Megiddo, and in all of Beth Shan next to Zarethan below Jezreel, from Beth Shan to Abel Meholah across to Jokmeam;
13 Ben-Geber—in Ramoth Gilead (the settlements of Jair son of Manasseh in Gilead were his, as well as the district of Argob in Bashan and its sixty large walled cities with bronze gate bars);
14 Ahinadab son of Iddo—in Mahanaim;
15 Ahimaaz—in Naphtali (he had married Basemath daughter of Solomon);
16 Baana son of Hushai—in Asher and in Aloth;
17 Jehoshaphat son of Paruah—in Issachar;
18 Shimei son of Ela—in Benjamin;
19 Geber son of Uri—in Gilead (the country of Sihon king of the Amorites and the country of Og king of Bashan). He was the only governor over the district.

20The people of Judah and Israel were as numerous as the sand on the seashore; they ate, they drank and they were happy. 21And Solomon ruled over all the kingdoms from the River[c] to the land of the Philistines, as far as the border of Egypt. These countries brought tribute and were Solomon's subjects all his life.

22Solomon's daily provisions were thirty cors[d] of fine flour and sixty cors[e] of meal, 23ten head of stall-fed cattle, twenty of pasture-fed cattle and a hundred sheep and goats, as well as deer, gazelles, roebucks and choice fowl. 24For he ruled over all the kingdoms west of the River, from Tiphsah to Gaza, and had peace on all sides. 25During Solomon's lifetime Judah and Israel, from Dan to Beersheba, lived in safety, each man under his own vine and fig tree.

26Solomon had four[f] thousand stalls for chariot horses, and twelve thousand horses.[g]

27 The district officers, each in his

month, supplied provisions for King Solomon and all who came to the king's table. They saw to it that nothing was lacking. 28They also brought to the proper place their quotas of barley and straw for the chariot horses and the other horses.

29God gave Solomon wisdom and very great insight, and a breadth of understanding as measureless as the sand on the seashore. 30Solomon's wisdom was greater than the wisdom of all the men of the East, and greater than all the wisdom of Egypt. 31He was wiser than any other man, including Ethan the Ezrahite—wiser than Heman, Calcol and Darda, the sons of Mahol. And his fame spread to all the surrounding nations. 32He spoke three thousand proverbs and his songs numbered a thousand and five. 33He described plant life, from the cedar of Lebanon to the hyssop that grows out of walls. He also taught about animals and birds, reptiles and fish. 34Men of all nations came to listen to Solomon's wisdom, sent by all the kings of the world, who had heard of his wisdom.

a15 Traditionally *peace offerings*   b11 Or *in the heights of Dor*   c21 That is, the Euphrates; also in verse 24   d22 That is, probably about 185 bushels (about 6.6 kiloliters)   e22 That is, probably about 375 bushels (about 13.2 kiloliters)   f26 Some Septuagint manuscripts (see also 2 Chron. 9:25); Hebrew *forty*   g26 Or *charioteers*

ACTS 6:1-15

In those days when the number of disciples was increasing, the Grecian Jews among them complained against the Hebraic Jews because their widows were being overlooked in the daily distribution of food. 2So the Twelve gathered all the disciples together and said, "It would not be right for us to neglect the ministry of the word of God in order to wait on tables. 3Brothers, choose seven men from among you who are known to be full of the Spirit and wisdom. We will turn this responsibility over to them 4and will give our attention to prayer and the ministry of the word."

5This proposal pleased the whole group. They chose Stephen, a man full of faith and of the Holy Spirit; also

Philip, Procorus, Nicanor, Timon, Parmenas, and Nicolas from Antioch, a convert to Judaism. 6They presented these men to the apostles, who prayed and laid their hands on them.

7So the word of God spread. The number of disciples in Jerusalem increased rapidly, and a large number of priests became obedient to the faith.

8Now Stephen, a man full of God's grace and power, did great wonders and miraculous signs among the people. 9Opposition arose, however, from members of the Synagogue of the Freedmen (as it was called)—Jews of Cyrene and Alexandria as well as the provinces of Cilicia and Asia. These men began to argue with Stephen, 10but they could not stand up against his wisdom or the Spirit by whom he spoke.

11Then they secretly persuaded some men to say, "We have heard Stephen speak words of blasphemy against Moses and against God."

12So they stirred up the people and the elders and the teachers of the law. They seized Stephen and brought him before the Sanhedrin. 13They produced false witnesses, who testified, "This fellow never stops speaking against this holy place and against the law. 14For we have heard him say that this Jesus of Nazareth will destroy this place and change the customs Moses handed down to us."

15All who were sitting in the Sanhedrin looked intently at Stephen, and they saw that his face was like the face of an angel.

PSALM 126:1-6

A song of ascents.

1When the LORD brought back the
       captives toa Zion,
    we were like men who dreamed.b
2Our mouths were filled with
       laughter,
    our tongues with songs of joy.
Then it was said among the nations,
    "The LORD has done great things
       for them."

³The Lᴏʀᴅ has done great things
for us,
and we are filled with joy.

⁴Restore our fortunes,ᶜ O Lᴏʀᴅ,
like streams in the Negev.
⁵Those who sow in tears
will reap with songs of joy.
⁶He who goes out weeping,
carrying seed to sow,
will return with songs of joy,
carrying sheaves with him.

ᵃ1 Or Lᴏʀᴅ restored the fortunes of   ᵇ1 Or men restored to
health   ᶜ4 Or Bring back our captives

PROVERBS 16:26-27

²⁶The laborer's appetite works for
him;
his hunger drives him on.

²⁷A scoundrel plots evil,
and his speech is like a scorching
fire.

☐ D A Y 1 6 0

GOD SIGHTINGS

June 9

1 KINGS 5:1–6:38

When Hiram king of Tyre heard that
Solomon had been anointed king to
succeed his father David, he sent his
envoys to Solomon, because he had always been on friendly terms with David. ²Solomon sent back this message
to Hiram:

³"You know that because of the
wars waged against my father David from all sides, he could not
build a temple for the Name of the
Lᴏʀᴅ his God until the Lᴏʀᴅ put his
enemies under his feet. ⁴But now
the Lᴏʀᴅ my God has given me rest
on every side, and there is no adversary or disaster. ⁵I intend,
therefore, to build a temple for the
Name of the Lᴏʀᴅ my God, as the
Lᴏʀᴅ told my father David, when

he said, 'Your son whom I will put
on the throne in your place will
build the temple for my Name.'

⁶"So give orders that cedars of
Lebanon be cut for me. My men
will work with yours, and I will pay
you for your men whatever wages
you set. You know that we have no
one so skilled in felling timber as
the Sidonians."

⁷When Hiram heard Solomon's message, he was greatly pleased and said,
"Praise be to the Lᴏʀᴅ today, for he has
given David a wise son to rule over this
great nation."

⁸So Hiram sent word to Solomon:

"I have received the message
you sent me and will do all you
want in providing the cedar and
pine logs. ⁹My men will haul them
down from Lebanon to the sea, and
I will float them in rafts by sea to
the place you specify. There I will
separate them and you can take
them away. And you are to grant my
wish by providing food for my
royal household."

¹⁰In this way Hiram kept Solomon
supplied with all the cedar and pine logs
he wanted, ¹¹and Solomon gave Hiram
twenty thousand corsᵃ of wheat as food
for his household, in addition to twenty
thousand bathsᵇ,ᶜ of pressed olive oil.
Solomon continued to do this for Hiram
year after year. ¹²The Lᴏʀᴅ gave Solomon wisdom, just as he had promised
him. There were peaceful relations between Hiram and Solomon, and the two
of them made a treaty.

¹³King Solomon conscripted laborers from all Israel—thirty thousand
men. ¹⁴He sent them off to Lebanon in
shifts of ten thousand a month, so that
they spent one month in Lebanon and
two months at home. Adoniram was in
charge of the forced labor. ¹⁵Solomon
had seventy thousand carriers and
eighty thousand stonecutters in the
hills, ¹⁶as well as thirty-three hundredᵈ
foremen who supervised the project

and directed the workmen. 17At the king's command they removed from the quarry large blocks of quality stone to provide a foundation of dressed stone for the temple. 18The craftsmen of Solomon and Hiram and the men of Gebal*e* cut and prepared the timber and stone for the building of the temple.

6:1IN the four hundred and eightieth*f* year after the Israelites had come out of Egypt, in the fourth year of Solomon's reign over Israel, in the month of Ziv, the second month, he began to build the temple of the Lord.

2 The temple that King Solomon built for the Lord was sixty cubits long, twenty wide and thirty high.*g* 3 The portico at the front of the main hall of the temple extended the width of the temple, that is twenty cubits,*h* and projected ten cubits*i* from the front of the temple. 4He made narrow clerestory windows in the temple. 5Against the walls of the main hall and inner sanctuary he built a structure around the building, in which there were side rooms. 6The lowest floor was five cubits*j* wide, the middle floor six cubits*k* and the third floor seven.*l* He made offset ledges around the outside of the temple so that nothing would be inserted into the temple walls.

7 In building the temple, only blocks dressed at the quarry were used, and no hammer, chisel or any other iron tool was heard at the temple site while it was being built.

8The entrance to the lowest*m* floor was on the south side of the temple; a stairway led up to the middle level and from there to the third. 9 So he built the temple and completed it, roofing it with beams and cedar planks. 10And he built the side rooms all along the temple. The height of each was five cubits, and they were attached to the temple by beams of cedar.

11The word of the Lord came to Solomon: 12"As for this temple you are building, if you follow my decrees, carry out my regulations and keep all my commands and obey them, I will fulfill through you the promise I gave to David your father. 13And I will live among the Israelites and will not abandon my people Israel."

14So Solomon built the temple and completed it. 15He lined its interior walls with cedar boards, paneling them from the floor of the temple to the ceiling, and covered the floor of the temple with planks of pine. 16He partitioned off twenty cubits*h* at the rear of the temple with cedar boards from floor to ceiling to form within the temple an inner sanctuary, the Most Holy Place. 17The main hall in front of this room was forty cubits*n* long. 18The inside of the temple was cedar, carved with gourds and open flowers. Everything was cedar; no stone was to be seen.

19He prepared the inner sanctuary within the temple to set the ark of the covenant of the Lord there. 20The inner sanctuary was twenty cubits long, twenty wide and twenty high.*o* He overlaid the inside with pure gold, and he also overlaid the altar of cedar. 21Solomon covered the inside of the temple with pure gold, and he extended gold chains across the front of the inner sanctuary, which was overlaid with gold. 22So he overlaid the whole interior with gold. He also overlaid with gold the altar that belonged to the inner sanctuary.

23In the inner sanctuary he made a pair of cherubim of olive wood, each ten cubits*i* high. 24One wing of the first cherub was five cubits long, and the other wing five cubits—ten cubits from wing tip to wing tip. 25The second cherub also measured ten cubits, for the two cherubim were identical in size and shape. 26The height of each cherub was ten cubits. 27He placed the cherubim inside the innermost room of the temple, with their wings spread out. The wing of one cherub touched one wall, while the wing of the other touched the other wall, and their wings touched each other in the middle of the room. 28He overlaid the cherubim with gold.

29On the walls all around the temple, in both the inner and outer rooms, he carved cherubim, palm trees and open flowers. 30He also covered the floors of both the inner and outer rooms of the temple with gold.

31For the entrance of the inner sanctuary he made doors of olive wood with five-sided jambs. 32And on the two olive wood doors he carved cherubim, palm trees and open flowers, and overlaid the cherubim and palm trees with beaten gold. 33In the same way he made four-sided jambs of olive wood for the entrance to the main hall. 34He also made two pine doors, each having two leaves that turned in sockets. 35He carved cherubim, palm trees and open flowers on them and overlaid them with gold hammered evenly over the carvings.

36And he built the inner courtyard of three courses of dressed stone and one course of trimmed cedar beams.

37The foundation of the temple of the LORD was laid in the fourth year, in the month of Ziv. 38In the eleventh year in the month of Bul, the eighth month, the temple was finished in all its details according to its specifications. He had spent seven years building it.

a11 That is, probably about 125,000 bushels (about 4,400 kiloliters)   b11 Septuagint (see also 2 Chron. 2:10); Hebrew twenty cors   c11 That is, about 115,000 gallons (about 440 kiloliters)   d16 Hebrew; some Septuagint manuscripts (see also 2 Chron. 2:2, 18) thirty-six hundred   e18 That is, Byblos   f1 Hebrew; Septuagint four hundred and fortieth   g2 That is, about 90 feet (about 27 meters) long and 30 feet (about 9 meters) wide and 45 feet (about 13.5 meters) high   h3,16 That is, about 30 feet (about 9 meters)   i3,23 That is, about 15 feet (about 4.5 meters)   j6 That is, about 7 1/2 feet (about 2.3 meters); also in verses 10 and 24   k6 That is, about 9 feet (about 2.7 meters)   l6 That is, about 10 1/2 feet (about 3.1 meters)   m8 Septuagint; Hebrew middle   n17 That is, about 60 feet (about 18 meters)   o20 That is, about 30 feet (about 9 meters) long, wide and high

ACTS 7:1-29

Then the high priest asked him [Stephen], "Are these charges true?"

2To this he replied: "Brothers and fathers, listen to me! The God of glory appeared to our father Abraham while he was still in Mesopotamia, before he lived in Haran. 3'Leave your country and your people,' God said, 'and go to the land I will show you.'a

4"So he left the land of the Chaldeans and settled in Haran. After the death of his father, God sent him to this land where you are now living. 5He gave him no inheritance here, not even a foot of ground. But God promised him that he and his descendants after him would possess the land, even though at that time Abraham had no child. 6God spoke to him in this way: 'Your descendants will be strangers in a country not their own, and they will be enslaved and mistreated four hundred years. 7But I will punish the nation they serve as slaves,' God said, 'and afterward they will come out of that country and worship me in this place.'b 8Then he gave Abraham the covenant of circumcision. And Abraham became the father of Isaac and circumcised him eight days after his birth. Later Isaac became the father of Jacob, and Jacob became the father of the twelve patriarchs.

9"Because the patriarchs were jealous of Joseph, they sold him as a slave into Egypt. But God was with him 10and rescued him from all his troubles. He gave Joseph wisdom and enabled him to gain the goodwill of Pharaoh king of Egypt; so he made him ruler over Egypt and all his palace.

11"Then a famine struck all Egypt and Canaan, bringing great suffering, and our fathers could not find food. 12When Jacob heard that there was grain in Egypt, he sent our fathers on their first visit. 13On their second visit, Joseph told his brothers who he was, and Pharaoh learned about Joseph's family. 14After this, Joseph sent for his father Jacob and his whole family, seventy-five in all. 15Then Jacob went down to Egypt, where he and our fathers died. 16Their bodies were brought back to Shechem and placed in the tomb that Abraham had bought from the sons of Hamor at Shechem for a certain sum of money.

17"As the time drew near for God to fulfill his promise to Abraham, the number of our people in Egypt greatly increased. [18]Then another king, who knew nothing about Joseph, became ruler of Egypt. [19]He dealt treacherously with our people and oppressed our forefathers by forcing them to throw out their newborn babies so that they would die.

[20]"At that time Moses was born, and he was no ordinary child.[c] For three months he was cared for in his father's house. [21]When he was placed outside, Pharaoh's daughter took him and brought him up as her own son. [22]Moses was educated in all the wisdom of the Egyptians and was powerful in speech and action.

[23]"When Moses was forty years old, he decided to visit his fellow Israelites. [24]He saw one of them being mistreated by an Egyptian, so he went to his defense and avenged him by killing the Egyptian. [25]Moses thought that his own people would realize that God was using him to rescue them, but they did not. [26]The next day Moses came upon two Israelites who were fighting. He tried to reconcile them by saying, 'Men, you are brothers; why do you want to hurt each other?'

[27]"But the man who was mistreating the other pushed Moses aside and said, 'Who made you ruler and judge over us? [28]Do you want to kill me as you killed the Egyptian yesterday?'[d] [29]When Moses heard this, he fled to Midian, where he settled as a foreigner and had two sons."

[a]3 Gen. 12:1 [b]7 Gen. 15:13,14 [c]20 Or *was fair in the sight of God* [d]28 Exodus 2:14

PSALM 127:1-5
A song of ascents. Of Solomon.

[1]**U**nless the Lord builds the
    house,
  its builders labor in vain.
Unless the Lord watches over the
    city,
  the watchmen stand guard in
    vain.
[2]In vain you rise early
  and stay up late,

toiling for food to eat—
  for he grants sleep to[a] those he
    loves.

[3]Sons are a heritage from the Lord,
  children a reward from him.
[4]Like arrows in the hands of a warrior
  are sons born in one's youth.
[5]Blessed is the man
  whose quiver is full of them.
They will not be put to shame
  when they contend with their
    enemies in the gate.

[a]2 Or *eat— / for while they sleep he provides for*

PROVERBS 16:28-30
[28]**A** perverse man stirs up dissension,
  and a gossip separates close
    friends.

[29]A violent man entices his neighbor
  and leads him down a path that is
    not good.

[30]He who winks with his eye is plotting
    perversity;
  he who purses his lips is bent on
    evil.

□ DAY 161

GOD SIGHTINGS

June 10

1 KINGS 7:1-51
It took Solomon thirteen years, however, to complete the construction of his palace. [2]He built the Palace of the Forest of Lebanon a hundred cubits long, fifty wide and thirty high,[a] with four rows of cedar columns supporting trimmed cedar beams. [3]It was roofed with cedar above the beams that rested on the columns—forty-five beams, fifteen to a row. [4]Its windows were placed high in sets of three, facing each other. [5]All the doorways had rectangular frames; they were in the front part in sets of three, facing each other.[b] [6]He made a colonnade fifty cubits

long and thirty wide.*c* In front of it was a portico, and in front of that were pillars and an overhanging roof.

⁷He built the throne hall, the Hall of Justice, where he was to judge, and he covered it with cedar from floor to ceiling.*d* ⁸And the palace in which he was to live, set farther back, was similar in design. Solomon also made a palace like this hall for Pharaoh's daughter, whom he had married.

⁹All these structures, from the outside to the great courtyard and from foundation to eaves, were made of blocks of high-grade stone cut to size and trimmed with a saw on their inner and outer faces. ¹⁰The foundations were laid with large stones of good quality, some measuring ten cubits*e* and some eight.*f* ¹¹Above were high-grade stones, cut to size, and cedar beams. ¹²The great courtyard was surrounded by a wall of three courses of dressed stone and one course of trimmed cedar beams, as was the inner courtyard of the temple of the LORD with its portico.

¹³King Solomon sent to Tyre and brought Huram,*g* ¹⁴whose mother was a widow from the tribe of Naphtali and whose father was a man of Tyre and a craftsman in bronze. Huram was highly skilled and experienced in all kinds of bronze work. He came to King Solomon and did all the work assigned to him.

¹⁵He cast two bronze pillars, each eighteen cubits high and twelve cubits around,*h* by line. ¹⁶He also made two capitals of cast bronze to set on the tops of the pillars; each capital was five cubits*i* high. ¹⁷A network of interwoven chains festooned the capitals on top of the pillars, seven for each capital. ¹⁸He made pomegranates in two rows*j* encircling each network to decorate the capitals on top of the pillars.*k* He did the same for each capital. ¹⁹The capitals on top of the pillars in the portico were in the shape of lilies, four cubits*l* high. ²⁰On the capitals of both pillars, above the bowl-shaped part next to the network, were the two hundred pomegranates in rows all around. ²¹He erected the pillars at the portico of the temple. The pillar to the south he named Jakin*m* and the one to the north Boaz.*n* ²²The capitals on top were in the shape of lilies. And so the work on the pillars was completed.

²³He made the Sea of cast metal, circular in shape, measuring ten cubits*e* from rim to rim and five cubits high. It took a line of thirty cubits*o* to measure around it. ²⁴Below the rim, gourds encircled it—ten to a cubit. The gourds were cast in two rows in one piece with the Sea.

²⁵The Sea stood on twelve bulls, three facing north, three facing west, three facing south and three facing east. The Sea rested on top of them, and their hindquarters were toward the center. ²⁶It was a handbreadth*p* in thickness, and its rim was like the rim of a cup, like a lily blossom. It held two thousand baths.*q*

²⁷He also made ten movable stands of bronze; each was four cubits long, four wide and three high.*r* ²⁸This is how the stands were made: They had side panels attached to uprights. ²⁹On the panels between the uprights were lions, bulls and cherubim—and on the uprights as well. Above and below the lions and bulls were wreaths of hammered work. ³⁰Each stand had four bronze wheels with bronze axles, and each had a basin resting on four supports, cast with wreaths on each side. ³¹On the inside of the stand there was an opening that had a circular frame one cubit*s* deep. This opening was round, and with its basework it measured a cubit and a half.*t* Around its opening there was engraving. The panels of the stands were square, not round. ³²The four wheels were under the panels, and the axles of the wheels were attached to the stand. The diameter of each wheel was a cubit and a half. ³³The wheels were made like chariot wheels; the axles, rims, spokes and hubs were all of cast metal.

³⁴Each stand had four handles, one on each corner, projecting from the stand. ³⁵At the top of the stand there was a circular band half a cubit*u* deep. The supports and panels were attached

to the top of the stand. [36]He engraved cherubim, lions and palm trees on the surfaces of the supports and on the panels, in every available space, with wreaths all around. [37]This is the way he made the ten stands. They were all cast in the same molds and were identical in size and shape.

[38]He then made ten bronze basins, each holding forty baths[v] and measuring four cubits across, one basin to go on each of the ten stands. [39]He placed five of the stands on the south side of the temple and five on the north. He placed the Sea on the south side, at the southeast corner of the temple. [40]He also made the basins and shovels and sprinkling bowls.

So Huram finished all the work he had undertaken for King Solomon in the temple of the LORD:

  [41]the two pillars;

    the two bowl-shaped capitals on top of the pillars;

    the two sets of network decorating the two bowl-shaped capitals on top of the pillars;

  [42]the four hundred pomegranates for the two sets of network (two rows of pomegranates for each network, decorating the bowl-shaped capitals on top of the pillars);

  [43]the ten stands with their ten basins;

  [44]the Sea and the twelve bulls under it;

  [45]the pots, shovels and sprinkling bowls.

All these objects that Huram made for King Solomon for the temple of the LORD were of burnished bronze. [46]The king had them cast in clay molds in the plain of the Jordan between Succoth and Zarethan. [47]Solomon left all these things unweighed, because there were so many; the weight of the bronze was not determined.

[48]Solomon also made all the furnishings that were in the LORD's temple:

the golden altar;

the golden table on which was the bread of the Presence;

  [49]the lampstands of pure gold (five on the right and five on the left, in front of the inner sanctuary);

the gold floral work and lamps and tongs;

  [50]the pure gold basins, wick trimmers, sprinkling bowls, dishes and censers;

and the gold sockets for the doors of the innermost room, the Most Holy Place, and also for the doors of the main hall of the temple.

[51]When all the work King Solomon had done for the temple of the LORD was finished, he brought in the things his father David had dedicated—the silver and gold and the furnishings—and he placed them in the treasuries of the LORD's temple.

a2 That is, about 150 feet (about 46 meters) long, 75 feet (about 23 meters) wide and 45 feet (about 13.5 meters) high b5 The meaning of the Hebrew for this verse is uncertain. c6 That is, about 75 feet (about 23 meters) long and 45 feet (about 13.5 meters) wide d7 Vulgate and Syriac; Hebrew floor e10,23 That is, about 15 feet (about 4.5 meters) f10 That is, about 12 feet (about 3.6 meters) g13 Hebrew Hiram, a variant of Huram; also in verses 40 and 45 h15 That is, about 27 feet (about 8.1 meters) high and 18 feet (about 5.4 meters) around i16 That is, about 7 1/2 feet (about 2.3 meters); also in verse 23 j18 Two Hebrew manuscripts and Septuagint; most Hebrew manuscripts made the pillars, and there were two rows k18 Many Hebrew manuscripts and Syriac; most Hebrew manuscripts pomegranates l19 That is, about 6 feet (about 1.8 meters); also in verse 38 m21 Jakin probably means he establishes. n21 Boaz probably means in him is strength. o23 That is, about 45 feet (about 13.5 meters) p26 That is, about 3 inches (about 8 centimeters) q26 That is, probably about 11,500 gallons (about 44 kiloliters); the Septuagint does not have this sentence. r27 That is, about 6 feet (about 1.8 meters) long and wide and about 4 1/2 feet (about 1.3 meters) high s31 That is, about 1 1/2 feet (about 0.5 meter) t31 That is, about 2 1/4 feet (about 0.7 meter); also in verse 32 u35 That is, about 3/4 foot (about 0.2 meter) v38 That is, about 230 gallons (about 880 liters)

ACTS 7:30-50

"After forty years had passed, an angel appeared to Moses in the flames of a burning bush in the desert near Mount Sinai. [31]When he saw this, he was amazed at the sight. As he went over to look more closely, he heard the Lord's voice: [32]'I am the God of your fathers,

the God of Abraham, Isaac and Jacob.'*a*
Moses trembled with fear and did not
dare to look.

33"Then the Lord said to him, 'Take off
your sandals; the place where you are
standing is holy ground. 34I have indeed
seen the oppression of my people in
Egypt. I have heard their groaning and
have come down to set them free. Now
come, I will send you back to Egypt.'*b*

35"This is the same Moses whom they
had rejected with the words, 'Who
made you ruler and judge?' He was sent
to be their ruler and deliverer by God
himself, through the angel who appeared to him in the bush. 36He led
them out of Egypt and did wonders and
miraculous signs in Egypt, at the Red
Sea*c* and for forty years in the desert.

37"This is that Moses who told the Israelites, 'God will send you a prophet
like me from your own people.'*d* 38He
was in the assembly in the desert, with
the angel who spoke to him on Mount
Sinai, and with our fathers; and he received living words to pass on to us.

39"But our fathers refused to obey
him. Instead, they rejected him and in
their hearts turned back to Egypt.
40They told Aaron, 'Make us gods who
will go before us. As for this fellow Moses who led us out of Egypt—we don't
know what has happened to him!'*e*
41That was the time they made an idol in
the form of a calf. They brought sacrifices to it and held a celebration in
honor of what their hands had made.
42But God turned away and gave them
over to the worship of the heavenly bodies. This agrees with what is written in
the book of the prophets:

"'Did you bring me sacrifices and
        offerings
    forty years in the desert, O house
        of Israel?
43You have lifted up the shrine of
        Molech
    and the star of your god Rephan,
        the idols you made to worship.
Therefore I will send you into exile'*f*
    beyond Babylon.

44"Our forefathers had the tabernacle
of the Testimony with them in the desert. It had been made as God directed
Moses, according to the pattern he had
seen. 45Having received the tabernacle,
our fathers under Joshua brought it
with them when they took the land
from the nations God drove out before
them. It remained in the land until the
time of David, 46who enjoyed God's favor and asked that he might provide a
dwelling place for the God of Jacob.*g*
47But it was Solomon who built the
house for him.

48"However, the Most High does not
live in houses made by men. As the
prophet says:

49"'Heaven is my throne,
        and the earth is my footstool.
    What kind of house will you build
            for me?
                        says the Lord.
    Or where will my resting place be?
50Has not my hand made all these
            things?'*h*"

a32 Exodus 3:6 *b34* Exodus 3:5,7,8,10 *c36* That is, Sea
of Reeds *d37* Deut. 18:15 *e40* Exodus 32:1 *f43* Amos
5:25-27 *g46* Some early manuscripts *the house of Jacob*
h50 Isaiah 66:1,2

PSALM 128:1-6
A song of ascents.

1 **B**lessed are all who fear the LORD,
    who walk in his ways.
2 You will eat the fruit of your labor;
    blessings and prosperity will be
        yours.
3 Your wife will be like a fruitful vine
        within your house;
    your sons will be like olive shoots
        around your table.
4 Thus is the man blessed
    who fears the LORD.

5 May the LORD bless you from Zion
    all the days of your life;
    may you see the prosperity of
        Jerusalem,
6   and may you live to see your
        children's children.

Peace be upon Israel.

PROVERBS 16:31-33

³¹Gray hair is a crown of splendor;
      it is attained by a righteous life.

³²Better a patient man than a warrior,
      a man who controls his temper
            than one who takes a city.

³³The lot is cast into the lap,
      but its every decision is from the
            LORD.

□ DAY 162

GOD SIGHTINGS

June 11

1 KINGS 8:1-66

Then King Solomon summoned into
his presence at Jerusalem the elders of
Israel, all the heads of the tribes and the
chiefs of the Israelite families, to bring
up the ark of the LORD's covenant from
Zion, the City of David. ²All the men of
Israel came together to King Solomon at
the time of the festival in the month of
Ethanim, the seventh month.

³When all the elders of Israel had arrived, the priests took up the ark, ⁴and
they brought up the ark of the LORD and
the Tent of Meeting and all the sacred
furnishings in it. The priests and Levites
carried them up, ⁵and King Solomon
and the entire assembly of Israel that
had gathered about him were before the
ark, sacrificing so many sheep and cattle that they could not be recorded or
counted.

⁶The priests then brought the ark of
the LORD's covenant to its place in the
inner sanctuary of the temple, the Most
Holy Place, and put it beneath the wings
of the cherubim. ⁷The cherubim spread
their wings over the place of the ark and
overshadowed the ark and its carrying
poles. ⁸These poles were so long that
their ends could be seen from the Holy
Place in front of the inner sanctuary, but
not from outside the Holy Place; and

they are still there today. ⁹There was
nothing in the ark except the two stone
tablets that Moses had placed in it at
Horeb, where the LORD made a covenant
with the Israelites after they came out of
Egypt.

¹⁰When the priests withdrew from
the Holy Place, the cloud filled the temple of the LORD. ¹¹And the priests could
not perform their service because of the
cloud, for the glory of the LORD filled his
temple.

¹²Then Solomon said, "The LORD has
said that he would dwell in a dark
cloud; ¹³I have indeed built a magnificent temple for you, a place for you to
dwell forever."

¹⁴While the whole assembly of Israel
was standing there, the king turned
around and blessed them. ¹⁵Then he
said:

"Praise be to the LORD, the God
of Israel, who with his own hand
has fulfilled what he promised
with his own mouth to my father
David. For he said, ¹⁶'Since the day
I brought my people Israel out of
Egypt, I have not chosen a city in
any tribe of Israel to have a temple
built for my Name to be there, but I
have chosen David to rule my people Israel.'

¹⁷"My father David had it in his
heart to build a temple for the
Name of the LORD, the God of Israel.
¹⁸But the LORD said to my father David, 'Because it was in your heart to
build a temple for my Name, you
did well to have this in your heart.
¹⁹Nevertheless, you are not the one
to build the temple, but your son,
who is your own flesh and blood—
he is the one who will build the
temple for my Name.'

²⁰"The LORD has kept the promise he made: I have succeeded David my father and now I sit on the
throne of Israel, just as the LORD
promised, and I have built the temple for the Name of the LORD, the
God of Israel. ²¹I have provided a

place there for the ark, in which is the covenant of the LORD that he made with our fathers when he brought them out of Egypt."

22 Then Solomon stood before the altar of the LORD in front of the whole assembly of Israel, spread out his hands toward heaven 23 and said:

"O LORD, God of Israel, there is no God like you in heaven above or on earth below—you who keep your covenant of love with your servants who continue whole-heartedly in your way. 24 You have kept your promise to your servant David my father; with your mouth you have promised and with your hand you have fulfilled it—as it is today.

25 "Now LORD, God of Israel, keep for your servant David my father the promises you made to him when you said, 'You shall never fail to have a man to sit before me on the throne of Israel, if only your sons are careful in all they do to walk before me as you have done.' 26 And now, O God of Israel, let your word that you promised your servant David my father come true.

27 "But will God really dwell on earth? The heavens, even the highest heaven, cannot contain you. How much less this temple I have built! 28 Yet give attention to your servant's prayer and his plea for mercy, O LORD my God. Hear the cry and the prayer that your servant is praying in your presence this day. 29 May your eyes be open toward this temple night and day, this place of which you said, 'My Name shall be there,' so that you will hear the prayer your servant prays toward this place. 30 Hear the supplication of your servant and of your people Israel when they pray toward this place. Hear from heaven, your dwelling place, and when you hear, forgive.

31 "When a man wrongs his neighbor and is required to take an oath and he comes and swears the oath before your altar in this temple, 32 then hear from heaven and act. Judge between your servants, condemning the guilty and bringing down on his own head what he has done. Declare the innocent not guilty, and so establish his innocence.

33 "When your people Israel have been defeated by an enemy because they have sinned against you, and when they turn back to you and confess your name, praying and making supplication to you in this temple, 34 then hear from heaven and forgive the sin of your people Israel and bring them back to the land you gave to their fathers.

35 "When the heavens are shut up and there is no rain because your people have sinned against you, and when they pray toward this place and confess your name and turn from their sin because you have afflicted them, 36 then hear from heaven and forgive the sin of your servants, your people Israel. Teach them the right way to live, and send rain on the land you gave your people for an inheritance.

37 "When famine or plague comes to the land, or blight or mildew, locusts or grasshoppers, or when an enemy besieges them in any of their cities, whatever disaster or disease may come, 38 and when a prayer or plea is made by any of your people Israel—each one aware of the afflictions of his own heart, and spreading out his hands toward this temple— 39 then hear from heaven, your dwelling place. Forgive and act; deal with each man according to all he does, since you know his heart (for you alone know the hearts of all men), 40 so that they will fear you all the

time they live in the land you gave our fathers.

41"As for the foreigner who does not belong to your people Israel but has come from a distant land because of your name— 42for men will hear of your great name and your mighty hand and your outstretched arm—when he comes and prays toward this temple, 43then hear from heaven, your dwelling place, and do whatever the foreigner asks of you, so that all the peoples of the earth may know your name and fear you, as do your own people Israel, and may know that this house I have built bears your Name.

44"When your people go to war against their enemies, wherever you send them, and when they pray to the Lord toward the city you have chosen and the temple I have built for your Name, 45then hear from heaven their prayer and their plea, and uphold their cause.

46"When they sin against you— for there is no one who does not sin—and you become angry with them and give them over to the enemy, who takes them captive to his own land, far away or near; 47and if they have a change of heart in the land where they are held captive, and repent and plead with you in the land of their conquerors and say, 'We have sinned, we have done wrong, we have acted wickedly'; 48and if they turn back to you with all their heart and soul in the land of their enemies who took them captive, and pray to you toward the land you gave their fathers, toward the city you have chosen and the temple I have built for your Name; 49then from heaven, your dwelling place, hear their prayer and their plea, and uphold their cause. 50And forgive your people, who have sinned against you; forgive all the offenses they have committed against you, and cause their con-

querors to show them mercy; 51for they are your people and your inheritance, whom you brought out of Egypt, out of that iron-smelting furnace.

52"May your eyes be open to your servant's plea and to the plea of your people Israel, and may you listen to them whenever they cry out to you. 53For you singled them out from all the nations of the world to be your own inheritance, just as you declared through your servant Moses when you, O Sovereign Lord, brought our fathers out of Egypt."

54When Solomon had finished all these prayers and supplications to the Lord, he rose from before the altar of the Lord, where he had been kneeling with his hands spread out toward heaven. 55He stood and blessed the whole assembly of Israel in a loud voice, saying:

56"Praise be to the Lord, who has given rest to his people Israel just as he promised. Not one word has failed of all the good promises he gave through his servant Moses. 57**May the Lord our God be with us as he was with our fathers; may he never leave us nor forsake us.** 58**May he turn our hearts to him, to walk in all his ways and to keep the commands, decrees and regulations he gave our fathers.** 59And may these words of mine, which I have prayed before the Lord, be near to the Lord our God day and night, that he may uphold the cause of his servant and the cause of his people Israel according to each day's need, 60so that all the peoples of the earth may know that the Lord is God and that there is no other. 61But your hearts must be fully committed to the Lord our God, to live by his decrees and obey his commands, as at this time."

62Then the king and all Israel with him offered sacrifices before the Lord.

63 Solomon offered a sacrifice of fellowship offerings[a] to the LORD: twenty-two thousand cattle and a hundred and twenty thousand sheep and goats. So the king and all the Israelites dedicated the temple of the LORD.

64 On that same day the king consecrated the middle part of the courtyard in front of the temple of the LORD, and there he offered burnt offerings, grain offerings and the fat of the fellowship offerings, because the bronze altar before the LORD was too small to hold the burnt offerings, the grain offerings and the fat of the fellowship offerings.

65 So Solomon observed the festival at that time, and all Israel with him—a vast assembly, people from Lebo[b] Hamath to the Wadi of Egypt. They celebrated it before the LORD our God for seven days and seven days more, fourteen days in all. 66 On the following day he sent the people away. They blessed the king and then went home, joyful and glad in heart for all the good things the LORD had done for his servant David and his people Israel.

a63 Traditionally *peace offerings*; also in verse 64
b65 Or *from the entrance to*

ACTS 7:51–8:13

"You stiff-necked people, with uncircumcised hearts and ears! You are just like your fathers: You always resist the Holy Spirit! 52 Was there ever a prophet your fathers did not persecute? They even killed those who predicted the coming of the Righteous One. And now you have betrayed and murdered him— 53 you who have received the law that was put into effect through angels but have not obeyed it."

54 When they heard this, they were furious and gnashed their teeth at him. 55 But Stephen, full of the Holy Spirit, looked up to heaven and saw the glory of God, and Jesus standing at the right hand of God. 56 "Look," he said, "I see heaven open and the Son of Man standing at the right hand of God."

57 At this they covered their ears and, yelling at the top of their voices, they all rushed at him, 58 dragged him out of the city and began to stone him. Meanwhile, the witnesses laid their clothes at the feet of a young man named Saul.

59 While they were stoning him, Stephen prayed, "Lord Jesus, receive my spirit." 60 Then he fell on his knees and cried out, "Lord, do not hold this sin against them." When he had said this, he fell asleep.

8:1 AND Saul was there, giving approval to his death.

On that day a great persecution broke out against the church at Jerusalem, and all except the apostles were scattered throughout Judea and Samaria. 2 Godly men buried Stephen and mourned deeply for him. 3 But Saul began to destroy the church. Going from house to house, he dragged off men and women and put them in prison.

4 Those who had been scattered preached the word wherever they went. 5 Philip went down to a city in Samaria and proclaimed the Christ[a] there. 6 When the crowds heard Philip and saw the miraculous signs he did, they all paid close attention to what he said. 7 With shrieks, evil[b] spirits came out of many, and many paralytics and cripples were healed. 8 So there was great joy in that city.

9 Now for some time a man named Simon had practiced sorcery in the city and amazed all the people of Samaria. He boasted that he was someone great, 10 and all the people, both high and low, gave him their attention and exclaimed, "This man is the divine power known as the Great Power." 11 They followed him because he had amazed them for a long time with his magic. 12 But when they believed Philip as he preached the good news of the kingdom of God and the name of Jesus Christ, they were baptized, both men and women. 13 Simon himself believed and was baptized. And he followed Philip everywhere, astonished by the great signs and miracles he saw.

a5 Or *Messiah*   b7 Greek *unclean*

PSALM 129:1-8
A song of ascents.

[1] They have greatly oppressed me
        from my youth—
    let Israel say—
[2] they have greatly oppressed me from
        my youth,
    but they have not gained the
        victory over me.
[3] Plowmen have plowed my back
    and made their furrows long.
[4] But the LORD is righteous;
    he has cut me free from the cords
        of the wicked.

[5] May all who hate Zion
    be turned back in shame.
[6] May they be like grass on the roof,
    which withers before it can grow;
[7] with it the reaper cannot fill his
        hands,
    nor the one who gathers fill his
        arms.
[8] May those who pass by not say,
    "The blessing of the LORD be upon
        you;
    we bless you in the name of the
        LORD."

PROVERBS 17:1
[1] Better a dry crust with peace and
        quiet
    than a house full of feasting,[a] with
        strife.

[a] 1 Hebrew *sacrifices*

☐ D A Y   1 6 3

GOD SIGHTINGS

June 12

1 KINGS 9:1–10:29

[1] When Solomon had finished building
the temple of the LORD and the royal palace, and had achieved all he had desired
to do, [2] the LORD appeared to him a second time, as he had appeared to him at
Gibeon. [3] The LORD said to him:

"I have heard the prayer and
plea you have made before me; I
have consecrated this temple,
which you have built, by putting
my Name there forever. My eyes
and my heart will always be there.

[4] "As for you, if you walk before
me in integrity of heart and uprightness, as David your father did,
and do all I command and observe
my decrees and laws, [5] I will establish your royal throne over Israel
forever, as I promised David your
father when I said, 'You shall never
fail to have a man on the throne of
Israel.'

[6] "But if you[a] or your sons turn
away from me and do not observe
the commands and decrees I have
given you[a] and go off to serve
other gods and worship them,
[7] then I will cut off Israel from the
land I have given them and will reject this temple I have consecrated
for my Name. Israel will then become a byword and an object of
ridicule among all peoples. [8] And
though this temple is now imposing, all who pass by will be appalled and will scoff and say, 'Why
has the LORD done such a thing to
this land and to this temple?' [9] People will answer, 'Because they have
forsaken the LORD their God, who
brought their fathers out of Egypt,
and have embraced other gods,
worshiping and serving them—
that is why the LORD brought all
this disaster on them.'"

[10] At the end of twenty years, during
which Solomon built these two buildings—the temple of the LORD and the
royal palace— [11] King Solomon gave
twenty towns in Galilee to Hiram king
of Tyre, because Hiram had supplied
him with all the cedar and pine and gold
he wanted. [12] But when Hiram went
from Tyre to see the towns that Solomon had given him, he was not pleased
with them. [13] "What kind of towns are
these you have given me, my brother?"

he asked. And he called them the Land of Cabul,*b* a name they have to this day. 14Now Hiram had sent to the king 120 talents*c* of gold.

15Here is the account of the forced labor King Solomon conscripted to build the LORD's temple, his own palace, the supporting terraces,*d* the wall of Jerusalem, and Hazor, Megiddo and Gezer. 16(Pharaoh king of Egypt had attacked and captured Gezer. He had set it on fire. He killed its Canaanite inhabitants and then gave it as a wedding gift to his daughter, Solomon's wife. 17And Solomon rebuilt Gezer.) He built up Lower Beth Horon, 18Baalath, and Tadmor*e* in the desert, within his land, 19as well as all his store cities and the towns for his chariots and for his horses*f*—whatever he desired to build in Jerusalem, in Lebanon and throughout all the territory he ruled.

20All the people left from the Amorites, Hittites, Perizzites, Hivites and Jebusites (these peoples were not Israelites), 21that is, their descendants remaining in the land, whom the Israelites could not exterminate*g*—these Solomon conscripted for his slave labor force, as it is to this day. 22But Solomon did not make slaves of any of the Israelites; they were his fighting men, his government officials, his officers, his captains, and the commanders of his chariots and charioteers. 23They were also the chief officials in charge of Solomon's projects—550 officials supervising the men who did the work.

24After Pharaoh's daughter had come up from the City of David to the palace Solomon had built for her, he constructed the supporting terraces.

25Three times a year Solomon sacrificed burnt offerings and fellowship offerings*h* on the altar he had built for the LORD, burning incense before the LORD along with them, and so fulfilled the temple obligations.

26King Solomon also built ships at Ezion Geber, which is near Elath in Edom, on the shore of the Red Sea.*i* 27And Hiram sent his men—sailors who knew the sea—to serve in the fleet with Solomon's men. 28They sailed to Ophir and brought back 420 talents*j* of gold, which they delivered to King Solomon.

10:1WHEN the queen of Sheba heard about the fame of Solomon and his relation to the name of the LORD, she came to test him with hard questions. 2Arriving at Jerusalem with a very great caravan—with camels carrying spices, large quantities of gold, and precious stones—she came to Solomon and talked with him about all that she had on her mind. 3Solomon answered all her questions; nothing was too hard for the king to explain to her. 4When the queen of Sheba saw all the wisdom of Solomon and the palace he had built, 5the food on his table, the seating of his officials, the attending servants in their robes, his cupbearers, and the burnt offerings he made at*k* the temple of the LORD, she was overwhelmed.

6She said to the king, "The report I heard in my own country about your achievements and your wisdom is true. 7But I did not believe these things until I came and saw with my own eyes. Indeed, not even half was told me; in wisdom and wealth you have far exceeded the report I heard. 8How happy your men must be! How happy your officials, who continually stand before you and hear your wisdom! 9Praise be to the LORD your God, who has delighted in you and placed you on the throne of Israel. Because of the LORD's eternal love for Israel, he has made you king, to maintain justice and righteousness."

10And she gave the king 120 talents*c* of gold, large quantities of spices, and precious stones. Never again were so many spices brought in as those the queen of Sheba gave to King Solomon.

11(Hiram's ships brought gold from Ophir; and from there they brought great cargoes of almugwood*l* and precious stones. 12The king used the almugwood to make supports for the temple of the LORD and for the royal palace, and to make harps and lyres for the

musicians. So much almugwood has
never been imported or seen since that
day.)
13King Solomon gave the queen of
Sheba all she desired and asked for, besides what he had given her out of his
royal bounty. Then she left and returned
with her retinue to her own country.
14The weight of the gold that Solomon
received yearly was 666 talents,[m] 15not
including the revenues from merchants
and traders and from all the Arabian
kings and the governors of the land.
16King Solomon made two hundred
large shields of hammered gold; six
hundred bekas[n] of gold went into each
shield. 17He also made three hundred
small shields of hammered gold, with
three minas[o] of gold in each shield. The
king put them in the Palace of the Forest
of Lebanon.
18Then the king made a great throne
inlaid with ivory and overlaid with fine
gold. 19The throne had six steps, and its
back had a rounded top. On both sides of
the seat were armrests, with a lion standing beside each of them. 20Twelve lions
stood on the six steps, one at either end
of each step. Nothing like it had ever
been made for any other kingdom. 21All
King Solomon's goblets were gold, and
all the household articles in the Palace of
the Forest of Lebanon were pure gold.
Nothing was made of silver, because silver was considered of little value in Solomon's days. 22The king had a fleet of
trading ships[p] at sea along with the ships
of Hiram. Once every three years it returned, carrying gold, silver and ivory,
and apes and baboons.
23King Solomon was greater in riches
and wisdom than all the other kings of
the earth. 24The whole world sought audience with Solomon to hear the wisdom God had put in his heart. 25Year
after year, everyone who came brought a
gift—articles of silver and gold, robes,
weapons and spices, and horses and
mules.
26Solomon accumulated chariots
and horses; he had fourteen hundred
chariots and twelve thousand horses,[f]
which he kept in the chariot cities and
also with him in Jerusalem. 27The king
made silver as common in Jerusalem as
stones, and cedar as plentiful as sycamore-fig trees in the foothills. 28Solo-
mon's horses were imported from
Egypt[r] and from Kue[s]—the royal merchants purchased them from Kue.
29They imported a chariot from Egypt
for six hundred shekels[v] of silver, and a
horse for a hundred and fifty.[o] They also
exported them to all the kings of the
Hittites and of the Arameans.

[a]*6* The Hebrew is plural. [b]*13* *Cabul* sounds like the Hebrew for *good-for-nothing.* [c]*14* That is, about 4 1/2 tons (about 4 metric tons) [d]*15* Or *the Millo*; also in verse 24 [e]*18,26* The Hebrew may also be read *Tamar.* [f]*19* Or *charioteers* [g]*21* The Hebrew term refers to the irrevocable giving over of things or persons to the LORD, often by totally destroying them. [h]*25* Traditionally *peace offerings* [i]*26* Hebrew *Yam Suph*; that is, Sea of Reeds [j]*28* That is, about 16 tons (about 14.5 metric tons) [k]*5* Or *the ascent by which he went up to* [l]*11* Probably a variant of *algumwood*; also in verse 12 [m]*14* That is, about 25 tons (about 23 metric tons) [n]*16* That is, about 7 1/2 pounds (about 3.5 kilograms) [o]*17,29* That is, about 3 3/4 pounds (about 1.7 kilograms) [p]*22* Hebrew *of ships of Tarshish* q*28* Or possibly *Muzur*, a region in Cilicia; also in verse 29 [r]*28* Probably *Cilicia* [s]*29* That is, about 15 pounds (about 7 kilograms)

ACTS 8:14-40

When the apostles in Jerusalem heard
that Samaria had accepted the word of
God, they sent Peter and John to them.
15When they arrived, they prayed for
them that they might receive the Holy
Spirit, 16because the Holy Spirit had not
yet come upon any of them; they had
simply been baptized into[a] the name of
the Lord Jesus. 17Then Peter and John
placed their hands on them, and they received the Holy Spirit.
18When Simon saw that the Spirit
was given at the laying on of the apostles' hands, he offered them money
19and said, "Give me also this ability so
that everyone on whom I lay my hands
may receive the Holy Spirit."
20Peter answered: "May your money
perish with you, because you thought you
could buy the gift of God with money!
21You have no part or share in this ministry, because your heart is not right before
God. 22Repent of this wickedness and
pray to the Lord. Perhaps he will forgive
you for having such a thought in your

heart. 23For I see that you are full of bitterness and captive to sin."

24Then Simon answered, "Pray to the Lord for me so that nothing you have said may happen to me."

25When they had testified and proclaimed the word of the Lord, Peter and John returned to Jerusalem, preaching the gospel in many Samaritan villages.

26Now an angel of the Lord said to Philip, "Go south to the road—the desert road—that goes down from Jerusalem to Gaza." 27So he started out, and on his way he met an Ethiopian[b] eunuch, an important official in charge of all the treasury of Candace, queen of the Ethiopians. This man had gone to Jerusalem to worship, 28and on his way home was sitting in his chariot reading the book of Isaiah the prophet. 29The Spirit told Philip, "Go to that chariot and stay near it."

30Then Philip ran up to the chariot and heard the man reading Isaiah the prophet. "Do you understand what you are reading?" Philip asked.

31"How can I," he said, "unless someone explains it to me?" So he invited Philip to come up and sit with him.

32The eunuch was reading this passage of Scripture:

"He was led like a sheep to the slaughter,
and as a lamb before the shearer is silent,
so he did not open his mouth.
33In his humiliation he was deprived of justice.
Who can speak of his descendants?
For his life was taken from the earth."[c]

34The eunuch asked Philip, "Tell me, please, who is the prophet talking about, himself or someone else?" 35Then Philip began with that very passage of Scripture and told him the good news about Jesus.

36As they traveled along the road, they came to some water and the eunuch said, "Look, here is water. Why shouldn't I be baptized?"[d] 38And he gave orders to stop the chariot. Then both Philip and the eunuch went down into the water and Philip baptized him. 39When they came up out of the water, the Spirit of the Lord suddenly took Philip away, and the eunuch did not see him again, but went on his way rejoicing. 40Philip, however, appeared at Azotus and traveled about, preaching the gospel in all the towns until he reached Caesarea.

a16 Or in b27 That is, from the upper Nile region
c33 Isaiah 53:7,8 d36 Some late manuscripts baptized?"
37Philip said, "If you believe with all your heart, you may."
The eunuch answered, "I believe that Jesus Christ is the
Son of God."

PSALM 130:1-8
A song of ascents.

1 Out of the depths I cry to you,
O LORD;
2 O Lord, hear my voice.
Let your ears be attentive
to my cry for mercy.

3 If you, O LORD, kept a record of sins,
O Lord, who could stand?
4 But with you there is forgiveness;
therefore you are feared.

5 I wait for the LORD, my soul waits,
and in his word I put my hope.
6 My soul waits for the Lord
more than watchmen wait for the morning,
more than watchmen wait for the morning.

7 O Israel, put your hope in the LORD,
for with the LORD is unfailing love
and with him is full redemption.
8 He himself will redeem Israel
from all their sins.

PROVERBS 17:2-3
2 A wise servant will rule over a disgraceful son,
and will share the inheritance as one of the brothers.

3 The crucible for silver and the furnace for gold,
but the LORD tests the heart.

□ DAY 164

GOD SIGHTINGS

June 13

1 KINGS 11:1–12:19

King Solomon, however, loved many foreign women besides Pharaoh's daughter—Moabites, Ammonites, Edomites, Sidonians and Hittites. 2 They were from nations about which the LORD had told the Israelites, "You must not intermarry with them, because they will surely turn your hearts after their gods." Nevertheless, Solomon held fast to them in love. 3 He had seven hundred wives of royal birth and three hundred concubines, and his wives led him astray. 4 As Solomon grew old, his wives turned his heart after other gods, and his heart was not fully devoted to the LORD his God, as the heart of David his father had been. 5 He followed Ashtoreth the goddess of the Sidonians, and Molech*a* the detestable god of the Ammonites. 6 So Solomon did evil in the eyes of the LORD; he did not follow the LORD completely, as David his father had done.

7 On a hill east of Jerusalem, Solomon built a high place for Chemosh the detestable god of Moab, and for Molech the detestable god of the Ammonites. 8 He did the same for all his foreign wives, who burned incense and offered sacrifices to their gods.

9 The LORD became angry with Solomon because his heart had turned away from the LORD, the God of Israel, who had appeared to him twice. 10 Although he had forbidden Solomon to follow other gods, Solomon did not keep the LORD's command. 11 So the LORD said to Solomon, "Since this is your attitude and you have not kept my covenant and my decrees, which I commanded you, I will most certainly tear the kingdom away from you and give it to one of your subordinates. 12 Nevertheless, for the sake of David your father, I will not do it

during your lifetime. I will tear it out of the hand of your son. 13 Yet I will not tear the whole kingdom from him, but will give him one tribe for the sake of David my servant and for the sake of Jerusalem, which I have chosen."

14 Then the LORD raised up against Solomon an adversary, Hadad the Edomite, from the royal line of Edom. 15 Earlier when David was fighting with Edom, Joab the commander of the army, who had gone up to bury the dead, had struck down all the men in Edom. 16 Joab and all the Israelites stayed there for six months, until they had destroyed all the men in Edom. 17 But Hadad, still only a boy, fled to Egypt with some Edomite officials who had served his father. 18 They set out from Midian and went to Paran. Then taking men from Paran with them, they went to Egypt, to Pharaoh king of Egypt, who gave Hadad a house and land and provided him with food.

19 Pharaoh was so pleased with Hadad that he gave him a sister of his own wife, Queen Tahpenes, in marriage. 20 The sister of Tahpenes bore him a son named Genubath, whom Tahpenes brought up in the royal palace. There Genubath lived with Pharaoh's own children.

21 While he was in Egypt, Hadad heard that David rested with his fathers and that Joab the commander of the army was also dead. Then Hadad said to Pharaoh, "Let me go, that I may return to my own country."

22 "What have you lacked here that you want to go back to your own country?" Pharaoh asked.

"Nothing," Hadad replied, "but do let me go!"

23 And God raised up against Solomon another adversary, Rezon son of Eliada, who had fled from his master, Hadadezer king of Zobah. 24 He gathered men around him and became the leader of a band of rebels when David destroyed the forces*b* ⌊of Zobah⌋; the rebels went to Damascus, where they settled and took control. 25 Rezon was

Israel's adversary as long as Solomon lived, adding to the trouble caused by Hadad. So Rezon ruled in Aram and was hostile toward Israel.

26Also, Jeroboam son of Nebat rebelled against the king. He was one of Solomon's officials, an Ephraimite from Zeredah, and his mother was a widow named Zeruah.

27Here is the account of how he rebelled against the king: Solomon had built the supporting terracesᶜ and had filled in the gap in the wall of the city of David his father. 28Now Jeroboam was a man of standing, and when Solomon saw how well the young man did his work, he put him in charge of the whole labor force of the house of Joseph.

29About that time Jeroboam was going out of Jerusalem, and Ahijah the prophet of Shiloh met him on the way, wearing a new cloak. The two of them were alone out in the country, 30and Ahijah took hold of the new cloak he was wearing and tore it into twelve pieces. 31Then he said to Jeroboam, "Take ten pieces for yourself, for this is what the LORD, the God of Israel, says: 'See, I am going to tear the kingdom out of Solomon's hand and give you ten tribes. 32But for the sake of my servant David and the city of Jerusalem, which I have chosen out of all the tribes of Israel, he will have one tribe. 33I will do this because theyᵈ forsaken me and worshiped Ashtoreth the goddess of the Sidonians, Chemosh the god of the Moabites, and Molech the god of the Ammonites, and have not walked in my ways, nor done what is right in my eyes, nor kept my statutes and laws as David, Solomon's father, did.

34" 'But I will not take the whole kingdom out of Solomon's hand; I have made him ruler all the days of his life for the sake of David my servant, whom I chose and who observed my commands and statutes. 35I will take the kingdom from his son's hands and give you ten tribes. 36I will give one tribe to his son so that David my servant may always have a lamp before me in Jerusa-

lem, the city where I chose to put my Name. 37However, as for you, I will take you, and you will rule over all that your heart desires; you will be king over Israel. 38If you do whatever I command you and walk in my ways and do what is right in my eyes by keeping my statutes and commands, as David my servant did, I will be with you. I will build you a dynasty as enduring as the one I built for David and will give Israel to you. 39I will humble David's descendants because of this, but not forever.' "

40Solomon tried to kill Jeroboam, but Jeroboam fled to Egypt, to Shishak the king, and stayed there until Solomon's death.

41As for the other events of Solomon's reign—all he did and the wisdom he displayed—are they not written in the book of the annals of Solomon? 42Solomon reigned in Jerusalem over all Israel forty years. 43Then he rested with his fathers and was buried in the city of David his father. And Rehoboam his son succeeded him as king.

12:1REHOBOAM went to Shechem, for all the Israelites had gone there to make him king. 2When Jeroboam son of Nebat heard this (he was still in Egypt, where he had fled from King Solomon), he returned fromᵉ Egypt. 3So they sent for Jeroboam, and he and the whole assembly of Israel went to Rehoboam and said to him: 4"Your father put a heavy yoke on us, but now lighten the harsh labor and the heavy yoke he put on us, and we will serve you."

5Rehoboam answered, "Go away for three days and then come back to me." So the people went away.

6Then King Rehoboam consulted the elders who had served his father Solomon during his lifetime. "How would you advise me to answer these people?" he asked.

7They replied, "If today you will be a servant to these people and serve them and give them a favorable answer, they will always be your servants."

8But Rehoboam rejected the advice

the elders gave him and consulted the young men who had grown up with him and were serving him. [9]He asked them, "What is your advice? How should we answer these people who say to me, 'Lighten the yoke your father put on us'?"

[10]The young men who had grown up with him replied, "Tell these people who have said to you, 'Your father put a heavy yoke on us, but make our yoke lighter'—tell them, 'My little finger is thicker than my father's waist. [11]My father laid on you a heavy yoke; I will make it even heavier. My father scourged you with whips; I will scourge you with scorpions.'"

[12]Three days later Jeroboam and all the people returned to Rehoboam, as the king had said, "Come back to me in three days." [13]The king answered the people harshly. Rejecting the advice given him by the elders, [14]he followed the advice of the young men and said, "My father made your yoke heavy; I will make it even heavier. My father scourged you with whips; I will scourge you with scorpions." [15]So the king did not listen to the people, for this turn of events was from the LORD, to fulfill the word the LORD had spoken to Jeroboam son of Nebat through Ahijah the Shilonite.

[16]When all Israel saw that the king refused to listen to them, they answered the king:

"What share do we have in David,
    what part in Jesse's son?
To your tents, O Israel!
    Look after your own house, O
        David!"

So the Israelites went home. [17]But as for the Israelites who were living in the towns of Judah, Rehoboam still ruled over them.

[18]King Rehoboam sent out Adoniram,[f] who was in charge of forced labor, but all Israel stoned him to death. King Rehoboam, however, managed to get into his chariot and escape to Jerusa-

lem. [19]So Israel has been in rebellion against the house of David to this day.

[a]5 Hebrew *Milcom*; also in verse 33   [b]24 Hebrew *destroyed them*   [c]27 Or *the Millo*   [d]33 Hebrew; Septuagint, Vulgate and Syriac *because he has*   [e]2 Or *he remained in*   [f]18 Some Septuagint manuscripts and Syriac (see also 1 Kings 4:6 and 5:14); Hebrew *Adoram*

ACTS 9:1-25

Meanwhile, Saul was still breathing out murderous threats against the Lord's disciples. He went to the high priest [2]and asked him for letters to the synagogues in Damascus, so that if he found any there who belonged to the Way, whether men or women, he might take them as prisoners to Jerusalem. [3]As he neared Damascus on his journey, suddenly a light from heaven flashed around him. [4]He fell to the ground and heard a voice say to him, "Saul, Saul, why do you persecute me?"

[5]"Who are you, Lord?" Saul asked.

"I am Jesus, whom you are persecuting," he replied. [6]"Now get up and go into the city, and you will be told what you must do."

[7]The men traveling with Saul stood there speechless; they heard the sound but did not see anyone. [8]Saul got up from the ground, but when he opened his eyes he could see nothing. So they led him by the hand into Damascus. [9]For three days he was blind, and did not eat or drink anything.

[10]In Damascus there was a disciple named Ananias. The Lord called to him in a vision, "Ananias!"

"Yes, Lord," he answered.

[11]The Lord told him, "Go to the house of Judas on Straight Street and ask for a man from Tarsus named Saul, for he is praying. [12]In a vision he has seen a man named Ananias come and place his hands on him to restore his sight."

[13]"Lord," Ananias answered, "I have heard many reports about this man and all the harm he has done to your saints in Jerusalem. [14]And he has come here with authority from the chief priests to arrest all who call on your name."

[15]**But the Lord said to Ananias, "Go! This man is my chosen instrument**

to carry my name before the Gentiles and their kings and before the people of Israel. ¹⁶I will show him how much he must suffer for my name."

¹⁷Then Ananias went to the house and entered it. Placing his hands on Saul, he said, "Brother Saul, the Lord—Jesus, who appeared to you on the road as you were coming here—has sent me so that you may see again and be filled with the Holy Spirit." ¹⁸Immediately, something like scales fell from Saul's eyes, and he could see again. He got up and was baptized, ¹⁹and after taking some food, he regained his strength.

Saul spent several days with the disciples in Damascus. ²⁰At once he began to preach in the synagogues that Jesus is the Son of God. ²¹All those who heard him were astonished and asked, "Isn't he the man who raised havoc in Jerusalem among those who call on this name? And hasn't he come here to take them as prisoners to the chief priests?" ²²Yet Saul grew more and more powerful and baffled the Jews living in Damascus by proving that Jesus is the Christ.^a

²³After many days had gone by, the Jews conspired to kill him, ²⁴but Saul learned of their plan. Day and night they kept close watch on the city gates in order to kill him. ²⁵But his followers took him by night and lowered him in a basket through an opening in the wall.

^a22 Or *Messiah*

PSALM 131:1-3
A song of ascents. Of David.

¹ My heart is not proud, O Lord,
    my eyes are not haughty;
  I do not concern myself with great
      matters
    or things too wonderful for me.
² But I have stilled and quieted my
      soul;
    like a weaned child with its mother,
    like a weaned child is my soul
      within me.

³ O Israel, put your hope in the Lord
    both now and forevermore.

PROVERBS 17:4-5
⁴ A wicked man listens to evil lips;
    a liar pays attention to a malicious
      tongue.

⁵ He who mocks the poor shows
      contempt for their Maker;
    whoever gloats over disaster will
      not go unpunished.

□ DAY 165

GOD SIGHTINGS

June 14

1 KINGS 12:20–13:34
When all the Israelites heard that Jeroboam had returned, they sent and called him to the assembly and made him king over all Israel. Only the tribe of Judah remained loyal to the house of David.

²¹When Rehoboam arrived in Jerusalem, he mustered the whole house of Judah and the tribe of Benjamin—a hundred and eighty thousand fighting men—to make war against the house of Israel and to regain the kingdom for Rehoboam son of Solomon.

²²But this word of God came to Shemaiah the man of God: ²³"Say to Rehoboam son of Solomon king of Judah, to the whole house of Judah and Benjamin, and to the rest of the people, ²⁴'This is what the Lord says: Do not go up to fight against your brothers, the Israelites. Go home, every one of you, for this is my doing.'" So they obeyed the word of the Lord and went home again, as the Lord had ordered.

²⁵Then Jeroboam fortified Shechem in the hill country of Ephraim and lived there. From there he went out and built up Peniel.^a

²⁶Jeroboam thought to himself, "The kingdom will now likely revert to the house of David. ²⁷If these people go up to offer sacrifices at the temple of the Lord in Jerusalem, they will again give their allegiance to their lord, Rehoboam

king of Judah. They will kill me and return to King Rehoboam."

²⁸After seeking advice, the king made two golden calves. He said to the people, "It is too much for you to go up to Jerusalem. Here are your gods, O Israel, who brought you up out of Egypt." ²⁹One he set up in Bethel, and the other in Dan. ³⁰And this thing became a sin; the people went even as far as Dan to worship the one there.

³¹Jeroboam built shrines on high places and appointed priests from all sorts of people, even though they were not Levites. ³²He instituted a festival on the fifteenth day of the eighth month, like the festival held in Judah, and offered sacrifices on the altar. This he did in Bethel, sacrificing to the calves he had made. And at Bethel he also installed priests at the high places he had made. ³³On the fifteenth day of the eighth month, a month of his own choosing, he offered sacrifices on the altar he had built at Bethel. So he instituted the festival for the Israelites and went up to the altar to make offerings.

¹³:¹By the word of the Lord a man of God came from Judah to Bethel, as Jeroboam was standing by the altar to make an offering. ²He cried out against the altar by the word of the Lord: "O altar, altar! This is what the Lord says: 'A son named Josiah will be born to the house of David. On you he will sacrifice the priests of the high places who now make offerings here, and human bones will be burned on you.' " ³That same day the man of God gave a sign: "This is the sign the Lord has declared: The altar will be split apart and the ashes on it will be poured out."

⁴When King Jeroboam heard what the man of God cried out against the altar at Bethel, he stretched out his hand from the altar and said, "Seize him!" But the hand he stretched out toward the man shriveled up, so that he could not pull it back. ⁵Also, the altar was split apart and its ashes poured out accord-

ing to the sign given by the man of God by the word of the Lord.

⁶Then the king said to the man of God, "Intercede with the Lord your God and pray for me that my hand may be restored." So the man of God interceded with the Lord, and the king's hand was restored and became as it was before.

⁷The king said to the man of God, "Come home with me and have something to eat, and I will give you a gift."

⁸But the man of God answered the king, "Even if you were to give me half your possessions, I would not go with you, nor would I eat bread or drink water here. ⁹For I was commanded by the word of the Lord: 'You must not eat bread or drink water or return by the way you came.' " ¹⁰So he took another road and did not return by the way he had come to Bethel.

¹¹Now there was a certain old prophet living in Bethel, whose sons came and told him all that the man of God had done there that day. They also told their father what he had said to the king. ¹²Their father asked them, "Which way did he go?" And his sons showed him which road the man of God from Judah had taken. ¹³So he said to his sons, "Saddle the donkey for me." And when they had saddled the donkey for him, he mounted it ¹⁴and rode after the man of God. He found him sitting under an oak tree and asked, "Are you the man of God who came from Judah?"

"I am," he replied.

¹⁵So the prophet said to him, "Come home with me and eat."

¹⁶The man of God said, "I cannot turn back and go with you, nor can I eat bread or drink water with you in this place. ¹⁷I have been told by the word of the Lord: 'You must not eat bread or drink water there or return by the way you came.'"

¹⁸The old prophet answered, "I too am a prophet, as you are. And an angel said to me by the word of the Lord: 'Bring him back with you to your house so that he may eat bread and drink

water.'" (But he was lying to him.) ¹⁹So the man of God returned with him and ate and drank in his house.

²⁰While they were sitting at the table, the word of the LORD came to the old prophet who had brought him back. ²¹He cried out to the man of God who had come from Judah, "This is what the LORD says: 'You have defied the word of the LORD and have not kept the command the LORD your God gave you. ²²You came back and ate bread and drank water in the place where he told you not to eat or drink. Therefore your body will not be buried in the tomb of your fathers.'"

²³When the man of God had finished eating and drinking, the prophet who had brought him back saddled his donkey for him. ²⁴As he went on his way, a lion met him on the road and killed him, and his body was thrown down on the road, with both the donkey and the lion standing beside it. ²⁵Some people who passed by saw the body thrown down there, with the lion standing beside the body, and they went and reported it in the city where the old prophet lived.

²⁶When the prophet who had brought him back from his journey heard of it, he said, "It is the man of God who defied the word of the LORD. The LORD has given him over to the lion, which has mauled him and killed him, as the word of the LORD had warned him."

²⁷The prophet said to his sons, "Saddle the donkey for me," and they did so. ²⁸Then he went out and found the body thrown down on the road, with the donkey and the lion standing beside it. The lion had neither eaten the body nor mauled the donkey. ²⁹So the prophet picked up the body of the man of God, laid it on the donkey, and brought it back to his own city to mourn for him and bury him. ³⁰Then he laid the body in his own tomb, and they mourned over him and said, "Oh, my brother!"

³¹After burying him, he said to his sons, "When I die, bury me in the grave where the man of God is buried; lay my bones beside his bones. ³²For the message he declared by the word of the LORD against the altar in Bethel and against all the shrines on the high places in the towns of Samaria will certainly come true."

³³Even after this, Jeroboam did not change his evil ways, but once more appointed priests for the high places from all sorts of people. Anyone who wanted to become a priest he consecrated for the high places. ³⁴This was the sin of the house of Jeroboam that led to its downfall and to its destruction from the face of the earth.

^a25 Hebrew *Penuel*, a variant of *Peniel*

ACTS 9:26-43

When he [Saul] came to Jerusalem, he tried to join the disciples, but they were all afraid of him, not believing that he really was a disciple. ²⁷But Barnabas took him and brought him to the apostles. He told them how Saul on his journey had seen the Lord and that the Lord had spoken to him, and how in Damascus he had preached fearlessly in the name of Jesus. ²⁸So Saul stayed with them and moved about freely in Jerusalem, speaking boldly in the name of the Lord. ²⁹He talked and debated with the Grecian Jews, but they tried to kill him. ³⁰When the brothers learned of this, they took him down to Caesarea and sent him off to Tarsus.

³¹**Then the church throughout Judea, Galilee and Samaria enjoyed a time of peace. It was strengthened; and encouraged by the Holy Spirit, it grew in numbers, living in the fear of the Lord.**

³²As Peter traveled about the country, he went to visit the saints in Lydda. ³³There he found a man named Aeneas, a paralytic who had been bedridden for eight years. ³⁴"Aeneas," Peter said to him, "Jesus Christ heals you. Get up and take care of your mat." Immediately Aeneas got up. ³⁵All those who lived in Lydda and Sharon saw him and turned to the Lord.

³⁶In Joppa there was a disciple

named Tabitha (which, when translated, is Dorcas*a*), who was always doing good and helping the poor. ³⁷About that time she became sick and died, and her body was washed and placed in an upstairs room. ³⁸Lydda was near Joppa; so when the disciples heard that Peter was in Lydda, they sent two men to him and urged him, "Please come at once!"

³⁹Peter went with them, and when he arrived he was taken upstairs to the room. All the widows stood around him, crying and showing him the robes and other clothing that Dorcas had made while she was still with them.

⁴⁰Peter sent them all out of the room; then he got down on his knees and prayed. Turning toward the dead woman, he said, "Tabitha, get up." She opened her eyes, and seeing Peter she sat up. ⁴¹He took her by the hand and helped her to her feet. Then he called the believers and the widows and presented her to them alive. ⁴²This became known all over Joppa, and many people believed in the Lord. ⁴³Peter stayed in Joppa for some time with a tanner named Simon.

a36 Both *Tabitha* (Aramaic) and *Dorcas* (Greek) mean *gazelle*.

PSALM 132:1-18
A song of ascents.

¹ ⦿ Lᴏʀᴅ, remember David
    and all the hardships he endured.

²He swore an oath to the Lᴏʀᴅ
    and made a vow to the Mighty One
        of Jacob:
³"I will not enter my house
    or go to my bed—
⁴I will allow no sleep to my eyes,
    no slumber to my eyelids,
⁵till I find a place for the Lᴏʀᴅ,
    a dwelling for the Mighty One of
        Jacob."

⁶We heard it in Ephrathah,
    we came upon it in the fields of
        Jaar*a:b*
⁷"Let us go to his dwelling place;
    let us worship at his footstool—

⁸arise, O Lᴏʀᴅ, and come to your
        resting place,
    you and the ark of your might.
⁹May your priests be clothed with
        righteousness;
    may your saints sing for joy."

¹⁰For the sake of David your servant,
    do not reject your anointed one.

¹¹The Lᴏʀᴅ swore an oath to David,
    a sure oath that he will not
        revoke:
"One of your own descendants
    I will place on your throne—
¹²if your sons keep my covenant
    and the statutes I teach them,
then their sons will sit
    on your throne for ever and
        ever."

¹³For the Lᴏʀᴅ has chosen Zion,
    he has desired it for his dwelling:
¹⁴"This is my resting place for ever and
        ever;
    here I will sit enthroned, for I have
        desired it—
¹⁵I will bless her with abundant
        provisions;
    her poor will I satisfy with food.
¹⁶I will clothe her priests with
        salvation,
    and her saints will ever sing for joy.

¹⁷"Here I will make a horn*c* grow for
        David
    and set up a lamp for my anointed
        one.
¹⁸I will clothe his enemies with
        shame,
    but the crown on his head will be
        resplendent."

a6 That is, Kiriath Jearim   *b6* Or *heard of it in Ephrathah, / we found it in the fields of Jaar.* (And no quotes around verses 7-9)   *c17 Horn* here symbolizes strong one, that is, king.

PROVERBS 17:6
⁶Children's children are a crown to
        the aged,
    and parents are the pride of their
        children.

GOD SIGHTINGS

June 15

1 KINGS 14:1–15:24

At that time Abijah son of Jeroboam became ill, [2] and Jeroboam said to his wife, "Go, disguise yourself, so you won't be recognized as the wife of Jeroboam. Then go to Shiloh. Ahijah the prophet is there—the one who told me I would be king over this people. [3] Take ten loaves of bread with you, some cakes and a jar of honey, and go to him. He will tell you what will happen to the boy." [4] So Jeroboam's wife did what he said and went to Ahijah's house in Shiloh.

Now Ahijah could not see; his sight was gone because of his age. [5] But the LORD had told Ahijah, "Jeroboam's wife is coming to ask you about her son, for he is ill, and you are to give her such and such an answer. When she arrives, she will pretend to be someone else."

[6] So when Ahijah heard the sound of her footsteps at the door, he said, "Come in, wife of Jeroboam. Why this pretense? I have been sent to you with bad news. [7] Go, tell Jeroboam that this is what the LORD, the God of Israel, says: 'I raised you up from among the people and made you a leader over my people Israel. [8] I tore the kingdom away from the house of David and gave it to you, but you have not been like my servant David, who kept my commands and followed me with all his heart, doing only what was right in my eyes. [9] You have done more evil than all who lived before you. You have made for yourself other gods, idols made of metal; you have provoked me to anger and thrust me behind your back.

[10] " 'Because of this, I am going to bring disaster on the house of Jeroboam. I will cut off from Jeroboam every last male in Israel—slave or free. I will burn up the house of Jeroboam as one burns up dung, until it is all gone.

[11] Dogs will eat those belonging to Jeroboam who die in the city, and the birds of the air will feed on those who die in the country. The LORD has spoken!'

[12] "As for you, go back home. When you set foot in your city, the boy will die. [13] All Israel will mourn for him and bury him. He is the only one belonging to Jeroboam who will be buried, because he is the only one in the house of Jeroboam in whom the LORD, the God of Israel, has found anything good.

[14] "The LORD will raise up for himself a king over Israel who will cut off the family of Jeroboam. This is the day! What? Yes, even now.[a] [15] And the LORD will strike Israel, so that it will be like a reed swaying in the water. He will uproot Israel from this good land that he gave to their forefathers and scatter them beyond the River,[b] because they provoked the LORD to anger by making Asherah poles.[c] [16] And he will give Israel up because of the sins Jeroboam has committed and has caused Israel to commit."

[17] Then Jeroboam's wife got up and left and went to Tirzah. As soon as she stepped over the threshold of the house, the boy died. [18] They buried him, and all Israel mourned for him, as the LORD had said through his servant the prophet Ahijah.

[19] The other events of Jeroboam's reign, his wars and how he ruled, are written in the book of the annals of the kings of Israel. [20] He reigned for twenty-two years and then rested with his fathers. And Nadab his son succeeded him as king.

[21] Rehoboam son of Solomon was king in Judah. He was forty-one years old when he became king, and he reigned seventeen years in Jerusalem, the city the LORD had chosen out of all the tribes of Israel in which to put his Name. His mother's name was Naamah; she was an Ammonite.

[22] Judah did evil in the eyes of the LORD. By the sins they committed they stirred up his jealous anger more than their fathers had done. [23] They also set up for themselves high places, sacred

stones and Asherah poles on every high hill and under every spreading tree. 24There were even male shrine prostitutes in the land; the people engaged in all the detestable practices of the nations the Lord had driven out before the Israelites.

25In the fifth year of King Rehoboam, Shishak king of Egypt attacked Jerusalem. 26He carried off the treasures of the temple of the Lord and the treasures of the royal palace. He took everything, including all the gold shields Solomon had made. 27So King Rehoboam made bronze shields to replace them and assigned these to the commanders of the guard on duty at the entrance to the royal palace. 28Whenever the king went to the Lord's temple, the guards bore the shields, and afterward they returned them to the guardroom.

29As for the other events of Rehoboam's reign, and all he did, are they not written in the book of the annals of the kings of Judah? 30There was continual warfare between Rehoboam and Jeroboam. 31And Rehoboam rested with his fathers and was buried with them in the City of David. His mother's name was Naamah; she was an Ammonite. And Abijah*d* his son succeeded him as king.

15:1In the eighteenth year of the reign of Jeroboam son of Nebat, Abijah*e* became king of Judah, 2and he reigned in Jerusalem three years. His mother's name was Maacah daughter of Abishalom.*f*

3He committed all the sins his father had done before him; his heart was not fully devoted to the Lord his God, as the heart of David his forefather had been. 4Nevertheless, for David's sake the Lord his God gave him a lamp in Jerusalem by raising up a son to succeed him and by making Jerusalem strong. 5For David had done what was right in the eyes of the Lord and had not failed to keep any of the Lord's commands all the days of his life—except in the case of Uriah the Hittite.

6There was war between Rehoboam*g* and Jeroboam throughout ⌊Abijah's⌋

lifetime. 7As for the other events of Abijah's reign, and all he did, are they not written in the book of the annals of the kings of Judah? There was war between Abijah and Jeroboam. 8And Abijah rested with his fathers and was buried in the City of David. And Asa his son succeeded him as king.

9In the twentieth year of Jeroboam king of Israel, Asa became king of Judah, 10and he reigned in Jerusalem forty-one years. His grandmother's name was Maacah daughter of Abishalom.

11Asa did what was right in the eyes of the Lord, as his father David had done. 12He expelled the male shrine prostitutes from the land and got rid of all the idols his fathers had made. 13He even deposed his grandmother Maacah from her position as queen mother, because she had made a repulsive Asherah pole. Asa cut the pole down and burned it in the Kidron Valley. 14Although he did not remove the high places, Asa's heart was fully committed to the Lord all his life. 15He brought into the temple of the Lord the silver and gold and the articles that he and his father had dedicated.

16There was war between Asa and Baasha king of Israel throughout their reigns. 17Baasha king of Israel went up against Judah and fortified Ramah to prevent anyone from leaving or entering the territory of Asa king of Judah.

18Asa then took all the silver and gold that was left in the treasuries of the Lord's temple and of his own palace. He entrusted it to his officials and sent them to Ben-Hadad son of Tabrimmon, the son of Hezion, the king of Aram, who was ruling in Damascus. 19"Let there be a treaty between me and you," he said, "as there was between my father and your father. See, I am sending you a gift of silver and gold. Now break your treaty with Baasha king of Israel so he will withdraw from me."

20Ben-Hadad agreed with King Asa and sent the commanders of his forces against the towns of Israel. He conquered Ijon, Dan, Abel Beth Maacah and all Kinnereth in addition to Naphtali.

21When Baasha heard this, he stopped building Ramah and withdrew to Tirzah. 22Then King Asa issued an order to all Judah—no one was exempt—and they carried away from Ramah the stones and timber Baasha had been using there. With them King Asa built up Geba in Benjamin, and also Mizpah.

23As for all the other events of Asa's reign, all his achievements, all he did and the cities he built, are they not written in the book of the annals of the kings of Judah? In his old age, however, his feet became diseased. 24Then Asa rested with his fathers and was buried with them in the city of his father David. And Jehoshaphat his son succeeded him as king.

a 14 The meaning of the Hebrew for this sentence is uncertain. b 15 That is, the Euphrates   c 15 That is, symbols of the goddess Asherah; here and elsewhere in 1 Kings   d 31 Some Hebrew manuscripts and Septuagint (see also 2 Chron. 12:16); most Hebrew manuscripts Abijam   e 1 Some Hebrew manuscripts and Septuagint (see also 2 Chron. 12:16); most Hebrew manuscripts Abijam; also in verses 7 and 8   f 2 A variant of Absalom; also in verse 10   g 6 Most Hebrew manuscripts; some Hebrew manuscripts and Syriac Abijam (that is, Abijah)

ACTS 10:1–23A

At Caesarea there was a man named Cornelius, a centurion in what was known as the Italian Regiment. 2He and all his family were devout and God-fearing; he gave generously to those in need and prayed to God regularly. 3One day at about three in the afternoon he had a vision. He distinctly saw an angel of God, who came to him and said, "Cornelius!"

4Cornelius stared at him in fear. "What is it, Lord?" he asked.

The angel answered, "Your prayers and gifts to the poor have come up as a memorial offering before God. 5Now send men to Joppa to bring back a man named Simon who is called Peter. 6He is staying with Simon the tanner, whose house is by the sea."

7When the angel who spoke to him had gone, Cornelius called two of his servants and a devout soldier who was one of his attendants. 8He told them everything that had happened and sent them to Joppa.

9About noon the following day as they were on their journey and approaching the city, Peter went up on the roof to pray. 10He became hungry and wanted something to eat, and while the meal was being prepared, he fell into a trance. 11He saw heaven opened and something like a large sheet being let down to earth by its four corners. 12It contained all kinds of four-footed animals, as well as reptiles of the earth and birds of the air. 13Then a voice told him, "Get up, Peter. Kill and eat."

14"Surely not, Lord!" Peter replied. "I have never eaten anything impure or unclean."

15The voice spoke to him a second time, "Do not call anything impure that God has made clean."

16This happened three times, and immediately the sheet was taken back to heaven.

17While Peter was wondering about the meaning of the vision, the men sent by Cornelius found out where Simon's house was and stopped at the gate. 18They called out, asking if Simon who was known as Peter was staying there.

19While Peter was still thinking about the vision, the Spirit said to him, "Simon, threea men are looking for you. 20So get up and go downstairs. Do not hesitate to go with them, for I have sent them."

21Peter went down and said to the men, "I'm the one you're looking for. Why have you come?"

22The men replied, "We have come from Cornelius the centurion. He is a righteous and God-fearing man, who is respected by all the Jewish people. A holy angel told him to have you come to his house so that he could hear what you have to say." 23Then Peter invited the men into the house to be his guests.

a 19 One early manuscript two; other manuscripts do not have the number.

PSALM 133:1-3

A song of ascents. Of David.

1 **How good and pleasant it is
when brothers live together in
unity!**

²**It is like precious oil poured on the head,**
running down on the beard,
running down on Aaron's beard,
down upon the collar of his robes.
³It is as if the dew of Hermon
were falling on Mount Zion.
For there the Lᴏʀᴅ bestows his blessing,
even life forevermore.

PROVERBS 17:7-8
⁷**A**rroganta lips are unsuited to a fool—
how much worse lying lips to a ruler!

⁸A bribe is a charm to the one who gives it;
wherever he turns, he succeeds.

a7 Or Eloquent

□ DAY 167

GOD SIGHTINGS

June 16

1 KINGS 15:25–17:24
Nadab son of Jeroboam became king of Israel in the second year of Asa king of Judah, and he reigned over Israel two years. ²⁶He did evil in the eyes of the Lᴏʀᴅ, walking in the ways of his father and in his sin, which he had caused Israel to commit.

²⁷Baasha son of Ahijah of the house of Issachar plotted against him, and he struck him down at Gibbethon, a Philistine town, while Nadab and all Israel were besieging it. ²⁸Baasha killed Nadab in the third year of Asa king of Judah and succeeded him as king.

²⁹As soon as he began to reign, he killed Jeroboam's whole family. He did not leave Jeroboam anyone that breathed, but destroyed them all, according to the word of the Lᴏʀᴅ given through his servant Ahijah the Shilonite— ³⁰because of the sins Jeroboam had committed and had caused Israel to commit, and because he provoked the Lᴏʀᴅ, the God of Israel, to anger.

³¹As for the other events of Nadab's reign, and all he did, are they not written in the book of the annals of the kings of Israel? ³²There was war between Asa and Baasha king of Israel throughout their reigns.

³³In the third year of Asa king of Judah, Baasha son of Ahijah became king of all Israel in Tirzah, and he reigned twenty-four years. ³⁴He did evil in the eyes of the Lᴏʀᴅ, walking in the ways of Jeroboam and in his sin, which he had caused Israel to commit.

¹⁶:¹THEN the word of the Lᴏʀᴅ came to Jehu son of Hanani against Baasha: ²"I lifted you up from the dust and made you leader of my people Israel, but you walked in the ways of Jeroboam and caused my people Israel to sin and to provoke me to anger by their sins. ³So I am about to consume Baasha and his house, and I will make your house like that of Jeroboam son of Nebat. ⁴Dogs will eat those belonging to Baasha who die in the city, and the birds of the air will feed on those who die in the country."

⁵As for the other events of Baasha's reign, what he did and his achievements, are they not written in the book of the annals of the kings of Israel? ⁶Baasha rested with his fathers and was buried in Tirzah. And Elah his son succeeded him as king.

⁷Moreover, the word of the Lᴏʀᴅ came through the prophet Jehu son of Hanani to Baasha and his house, because of all the evil he had done in the eyes of the Lᴏʀᴅ, provoking him to anger by the things he did, and becoming like the house of Jeroboam—and also because he destroyed it.

⁸In the twenty-sixth year of Asa king of Judah, Elah son of Baasha became king of Israel, and he reigned in Tirzah two years.

⁹Zimri, one of his officials, who had command of half his chariots, plotted

against him. Elah was in Tirzah at the time, getting drunk in the home of Arza, the man in charge of the palace at Tirzah. ¹⁰Zimri came in, struck him down and killed him in the twenty-seventh year of Asa king of Judah. Then he succeeded him as king.

¹¹As soon as he began to reign and was seated on the throne, he killed off Baasha's whole family. He did not spare a single male, whether relative or friend. ¹²So Zimri destroyed the whole family of Baasha, in accordance with the word of the LORD spoken against Baasha through the prophet Jehu— ¹³because of all the sins Baasha and his son Elah had committed and had caused Israel to commit, so that they provoked the LORD, the God of Israel, to anger by their worthless idols.

¹⁴As for the other events of Elah's reign, and all he did, are they not written in the book of the annals of the kings of Israel?

¹⁵In the twenty-seventh year of Asa king of Judah, Zimri reigned in Tirzah seven days. The army was encamped near Gibbethon, a Philistine town. ¹⁶When the Israelites in the camp heard that Zimri had plotted against the king and murdered him, they proclaimed Omri, the commander of the army, king over Israel that very day there in the camp. ¹⁷Then Omri and all the Israelites with him withdrew from Gibbethon and laid siege to Tirzah. ¹⁸When Zimri saw that the city was taken, he went into the citadel of the royal palace and set the palace on fire around him. So he died, ¹⁹because of the sins he had committed, doing evil in the eyes of the LORD and walking in the ways of Jeroboam and in the sin he had committed and had caused Israel to commit.

²⁰As for the other events of Zimri's reign, and the rebellion he carried out, are they not written in the book of the annals of the kings of Israel?

²¹Then the people of Israel were split into two factions; half supported Tibni son of Ginath for king, and the other half supported Omri. ²²But Omri's fol-

lowers proved stronger than those of Tibni son of Ginath. So Tibni died and Omri became king.

²³In the thirty-first year of Asa king of Judah, Omri became king of Israel, and he reigned twelve years, six of them in Tirzah. ²⁴He bought the hill of Samaria from Shemer for two talents[a] of silver and built a city on the hill, calling it Samaria, after Shemer, the name of the former owner of the hill.

²⁵But Omri did evil in the eyes of the LORD and sinned more than all those before him. ²⁶He walked in all the ways of Jeroboam son of Nebat and in his sin, which he had caused Israel to commit, so that they provoked the LORD, the God of Israel, to anger by their worthless idols.

²⁷As for the other events of Omri's reign, what he did and the things he achieved, are they not written in the book of the annals of the kings of Israel? ²⁸Omri rested with his fathers and was buried in Samaria. And Ahab his son succeeded him as king.

²⁹In the thirty-eighth year of Asa king of Judah, Ahab son of Omri became king of Israel, and he reigned in Samaria over Israel twenty-two years. ³⁰Ahab son of Omri did more evil in the eyes of the LORD than any of those before him. ³¹He not only considered it trivial to commit the sins of Jeroboam son of Nebat, but he also married Jezebel daughter of Ethbaal king of the Sidonians, and began to serve Baal and worship him. ³²He set up an altar for Baal in the temple of Baal that he built in Samaria. ³³Ahab also made an Asherah pole and did more to provoke the LORD, the God of Israel, to anger than did all the kings of Israel before him.

³⁴In Ahab's time, Hiel of Bethel rebuilt Jericho. He laid its foundations at the cost of his firstborn son Abiram, and he set up its gates at the cost of his youngest son Segub, in accordance with the word of the LORD spoken by Joshua son of Nun.

¹⁷:¹Now Elijah the Tishbite, from Tishbe[b] in Gilead, said to Ahab, "As the LORD, the

God of Israel, lives, whom I serve, there will be neither dew nor rain in the next few years except at my word."

2 Then the word of the LORD came to Elijah: 3 "Leave here, turn eastward and hide in the Kerith Ravine, east of the Jordan. 4 You will drink from the brook, and I have ordered the ravens to feed you there."

5 So he did what the LORD had told him. He went to the Kerith Ravine, east of the Jordan, and stayed there. 6 The ravens brought him bread and meat in the morning and bread and meat in the evening, and he drank from the brook.

7 Some time later the brook dried up because there had been no rain in the land. 8 Then the word of the LORD came to him: 9 "Go at once to Zarephath of Sidon and stay there. I have commanded a widow in that place to supply you with food." 10 So he went to Zarephath. When he came to the town gate, a widow was there gathering sticks. He called to her and asked, "Would you bring me a little water in a jar so I may have a drink?" 11 As she was going to get it, he called, "And bring me, please, a piece of bread."

12 "As surely as the LORD your God lives," she replied, "I don't have any bread—only a handful of flour in a jar and a little oil in a jug. I am gathering a few sticks to take home and make a meal for myself and my son, that we may eat it—and die."

13 Elijah said to her, "Don't be afraid. Go home and do as you have said. But first make a small cake of bread for me from what you have and bring it to me, and then make something for yourself and your son. 14 For this is what the LORD, the God of Israel, says: 'The jar of flour will not be used up and the jug of oil will not run dry until the day the LORD gives rain on the land.'"

15 She went away and did as Elijah had told her. So there was food every day for Elijah and for the woman and her family. 16 For the jar of flour was not used up and the jug of oil did not run dry, in keeping with the word of the LORD spoken by Elijah.

17 Some time later the son of the woman who owned the house became ill. He grew worse and worse, and finally stopped breathing. 18 She said to Elijah, "What do you have against me, man of God? Did you come to remind me of my sin and kill my son?"

19 "Give me your son," Elijah replied. He took him from her arms, carried him to the upper room where he was staying, and laid him on his bed. 20 Then he cried out to the LORD, "O LORD my God, have you brought tragedy also upon this widow I am staying with, by causing her son to die?" 21 Then he stretched himself out on the boy three times and cried to the LORD, "O LORD my God, let this boy's life return to him!"

22 The LORD heard Elijah's cry, and the boy's life returned to him, and he lived. 23 Elijah picked up the child and carried him down from the room into the house. He gave him to his mother and said, "Look, your son is alive!"

24 Then the woman said to Elijah, "Now I know that you are a man of God and that the word of the LORD from your mouth is the truth."

a 24 That is, about 150 pounds (about 70 kilograms)
b 1 Or Tishbite, of the settlers

ACTS 10:23B–48

The next day Peter started out with them [the men sent by Cornelius], and some of the brothers from Joppa went along. 24 The following day he arrived in Caesarea. Cornelius was expecting them and had called together his relatives and close friends. 25 As Peter entered the house, Cornelius met him and fell at his feet in reverence. 26 But Peter made him get up. "Stand up," he said, "I am only a man myself."

27 Talking with him, Peter went inside and found a large gathering of people. 28 He said to them: "You are well aware that it is against our law for a Jew to associate with a Gentile or visit him. But God has shown me that I should not call any man impure or unclean. 29 So when I was sent for, I came without raising

any objection. May I ask why you sent for me?"

³⁰Cornelius answered: "Four days ago I was in my house praying at this hour, at three in the afternoon. Suddenly a man in shining clothes stood before me ³¹and said, 'Cornelius, God has heard your prayer and remembered your gifts to the poor. ³²Send to Joppa for Simon who is called Peter. He is a guest in the home of Simon the tanner, who lives by the sea.' ³³So I sent for you immediately, and it was good of you to come. Now we are all here in the presence of God to listen to everything the Lord has commanded you to tell us."

³⁴**Then Peter began to speak: "I now realize how true it is that God does not show favoritism ³⁵but accepts men from every nation who fear him and do what is right.** ³⁶You know the message God sent to the people of Israel, telling the good news of peace through Jesus Christ, who is Lord of all. ³⁷You know what has happened throughout Judea, beginning in Galilee after the baptism that John preached— ³⁸how God anointed Jesus of Nazareth with the Holy Spirit and power, and how he went around doing good and healing all who were under the power of the devil, because God was with him.

³⁹"We are witnesses of everything he did in the country of the Jews and in Jerusalem. They killed him by hanging him on a tree, ⁴⁰but God raised him from the dead on the third day and caused him to be seen. ⁴¹He was not seen by all the people, but by witnesses whom God had already chosen—by us who ate and drank with him after he rose from the dead. ⁴²He commanded us to preach to the people and to testify that he is the one whom God appointed as judge of the living and the dead. ⁴³All the prophets testify about him that everyone who believes in him receives forgiveness of sins through his name."

⁴⁴While Peter was still speaking these words, the Holy Spirit came on all who heard the message. ⁴⁵The circumcised believers who had come with Pe-

ter were astonished that the gift of the Holy Spirit had been poured out even on the Gentiles. ⁴⁶For they heard them speaking in tongues*ᵃ* and praising God.

Then Peter said, ⁴⁷"Can anyone keep these people from being baptized with water? They have received the Holy Spirit just as we have." ⁴⁸So he ordered that they be baptized in the name of Jesus Christ. Then they asked Peter to stay with them for a few days.

a 46 Or other languages

PSALM 134:1-3
A song of ascents.

¹**P**raise the LORD, all you servants of
    the LORD
  who minister by night in the house
    of the LORD.
²Lift up your hands in the sanctuary
    and praise the LORD.

³May the LORD, the Maker of heaven
    and earth,
  bless you from Zion.

PROVERBS 17:9-11
⁹**H**e who covers over an offense
    promotes love,
  but whoever repeats the matter
    separates close friends.

¹⁰A rebuke impresses a man of
    discernment
  more than a hundred lashes a fool.

¹¹An evil man is bent only on rebellion;
  a merciless official will be sent
    against him.

☐ D A Y   1 6 8

GOD SIGHTINGS

June 17

1 KINGS 18:1-46
After a long time, in the third year, the word of the LORD came to Elijah: "Go and present yourself to Ahab, and I will

send rain on the land." [2] So Elijah went to present himself to Ahab.

Now the famine was severe in Samaria, [3] and Ahab had summoned Obadiah, who was in charge of his palace. (Obadiah was a devout believer in the LORD. [4] While Jezebel was killing off the LORD's prophets, Obadiah had taken a hundred prophets and hidden them in two caves, fifty in each, and had supplied them with food and water.) [5] Ahab had said to Obadiah, "Go through the land to all the springs and valleys. Maybe we can find some grass to keep the horses and mules alive so we will not have to kill any of our animals." [6] So they divided the land they were to cover, Ahab going in one direction and Obadiah in another.

[7] As Obadiah was walking along, Elijah met him. Obadiah recognized him, bowed down to the ground, and said, "Is it really you, my lord Elijah?"

[8] "Yes," he replied. "Go tell your master, 'Elijah is here.'"

[9] "What have I done wrong," asked Obadiah, "that you are handing your servant over to Ahab to be put to death? [10] As surely as the LORD your God lives, there is not a nation or kingdom where my master has not sent someone to look for you. And whenever a nation or kingdom claimed you were not there, he made them swear they could not find you. [11] But now you tell me to go to my master and say, 'Elijah is here.' [12] I don't know where the Spirit of the LORD may carry you when I leave you. If I go and tell Ahab and he doesn't find you, he will kill me. Yet I your servant have worshiped the LORD since my youth. [13] Haven't you heard, my lord, what I did while Jezebel was killing the prophets of the LORD? I hid a hundred of the LORD's prophets in two caves, fifty in each, and supplied them with food and water. [14] And now you tell me to go to my master and say, 'Elijah is here.' He will kill me!"

[15] Elijah said, "As the LORD Almighty lives, whom I serve, I will surely present myself to Ahab today."

[16] So Obadiah went to meet Ahab and told him, and Ahab went to meet Elijah. [17] When he saw Elijah, he said to him, "Is that you, you troubler of Israel?"

[18] "I have not made trouble for Israel," Elijah replied. "But you and your father's family have. You have abandoned the LORD's commands and have followed the Baals. [19] Now summon the people from all over Israel to meet me on Mount Carmel. And bring the four hundred and fifty prophets of Baal and the four hundred prophets of Asherah, who eat at Jezebel's table."

[20] So Ahab sent word throughout all Israel and assembled the prophets on Mount Carmel. [21] Elijah went before the people and said, "How long will you waver between two opinions? If the LORD is God, follow him; but if Baal is God, follow him."

But the people said nothing.

[22] Then Elijah said to them, "I am the only one of the LORD's prophets left, but Baal has four hundred and fifty prophets. [23] Get two bulls for us. Let them choose one for themselves, and let them cut it into pieces and put it on the wood but not set fire to it. I will prepare the other bull and put it on the wood but not set fire to it. [24] Then you call on the name of your god, and I will call on the name of the LORD. The god who answers by fire—he is God."

Then all the people said, "What you say is good."

[25] Elijah said to the prophets of Baal, "Choose one of the bulls and prepare it first, since there are so many of you. Call on the name of your god, but do not light the fire." [26] So they took the bull given them and prepared it.

Then they called on the name of Baal from morning till noon. "O Baal, answer us!" they shouted. But there was no response; no one answered. And they danced around the altar they had made.

[27] At noon Elijah began to taunt them. "Shout louder!" he said. "Surely he is a god! Perhaps he is deep in thought, or busy, or traveling. Maybe he is sleeping and must be awakened." [28] So they

shouted louder and slashed themselves with swords and spears, as was their custom, until their blood flowed. [29]Midday passed, and they continued their frantic prophesying until the time for the evening sacrifice. But there was no response, no one answered, no one paid attention.

[30]Then Elijah said to all the people, "Come here to me." They came to him, and he repaired the altar of the Lord, which was in ruins. [31]Elijah took twelve stones, one for each of the tribes descended from Jacob, to whom the word of the Lord had come, saying, "Your name shall be Israel." [32]With the stones he built an altar in the name of the Lord, and he dug a trench around it large enough to hold two seahs[a] of seed. [33]He arranged the wood, cut the bull into pieces and laid it on the wood. Then he said to them, "Fill four large jars with water and pour it on the offering and on the wood."

[34]"Do it again," he said, and they did it again.

"Do it a third time," he ordered, and they did it the third time. [35]The water ran down around the altar and even filled the trench.

[36]At the time of sacrifice, the prophet Elijah stepped forward and prayed: "O Lord, God of Abraham, Isaac and Israel, let it be known today that you are God in Israel and that I am your servant and have done all these things at your command. [37]Answer me, O Lord, answer me, so these people will know that you, O Lord, are God, and that you are turning their hearts back again."

[38]Then the fire of the Lord fell and burned up the sacrifice, the wood, the stones and the soil, and also licked up the water in the trench.

[39]When all the people saw this, they fell prostrate and cried, "The Lord—he is God! The Lord—he is God!"

[40]Then Elijah commanded them, "Seize the prophets of Baal. Don't let anyone get away!" They seized them, and Elijah had them brought down to the Kishon Valley and slaughtered there.

[41]And Elijah said to Ahab, "Go, eat and drink, for there is the sound of a heavy rain." [42]So Ahab went off to eat and drink, but Elijah climbed to the top of Carmel, bent down to the ground and put his face between his knees.

[43]"Go and look toward the sea," he told his servant. And he went up and looked.

"There is nothing there," he said.

Seven times Elijah said, "Go back."

[44]The seventh time the servant reported, "A cloud as small as a man's hand is rising from the sea."

So Elijah said, "Go and tell Ahab, 'Hitch up your chariot and go down before the rain stops you.'"

[45]Meanwhile, the sky grew black with clouds, the wind rose, a heavy rain came on and Ahab rode off to Jezreel. [46]The power of the Lord came upon Elijah and, tucking his cloak into his belt, he ran ahead of Ahab all the way to Jezreel.

[a]32 That is, probably about 13 quarts (about 15 liters)

ACTS 11:1-30

The apostles and the brothers throughout Judea heard that the Gentiles also had received the word of God. [2]So when Peter went up to Jerusalem, the circumcised believers criticized him [3]and said, "You went into the house of uncircumcised men and ate with them."

[4]Peter began and explained everything to them precisely as it had happened: [5]"I was in the city of Joppa praying, and in a trance I saw a vision. I saw something like a large sheet being let down from heaven by its four corners, and it came down to where I was. [6]I looked into it and saw four-footed animals of the earth, wild beasts, reptiles, and birds of the air. [7]Then I heard a voice telling me, 'Get up, Peter. Kill and eat.'

[8]"I replied, 'Surely not, Lord! Nothing impure or unclean has ever entered my mouth.'

[9]"The voice spoke from heaven a second time, 'Do not call anything impure

that God has made clean.' ¹⁰This happened three times, and then it was all pulled up to heaven again.

¹¹"Right then three men who had been sent to me from Caesarea stopped at the house where I was staying. ¹²The Spirit told me to have no hesitation about going with them. These six brothers also went with me, and we entered the man's house. ¹³He told us how he had seen an angel appear in his house and say, 'Send to Joppa for Simon who is called Peter. ¹⁴He will bring you a message through which you and all your household will be saved.'

¹⁵"As I began to speak, the Holy Spirit came on them as he had come on us at the beginning. ¹⁶Then I remembered what the Lord had said: 'John baptized with[a] water, but you will be baptized with the Holy Spirit.' ¹⁷So if God gave them the same gift as he gave us, who believed in the Lord Jesus Christ, who was I to think that I could oppose God?"

¹⁸When they heard this, they had no further objections and praised God, saying, "So then, God has granted even the Gentiles repentance unto life."

¹⁹Now those who had been scattered by the persecution in connection with Stephen traveled as far as Phoenicia, Cyprus and Antioch, telling the message only to Jews. ²⁰Some of them, however, men from Cyprus and Cyrene, went to Antioch and began to speak to Greeks also, telling them the good news about the Lord Jesus. ²¹The Lord's hand was with them, and a great number of people believed and turned to the Lord.

²²News of this reached the ears of the church at Jerusalem, and they sent Barnabas to Antioch. ²³When he arrived and saw the evidence of the grace of God, he was glad and encouraged them all to remain true to the Lord with all their hearts. ²⁴He was a good man, full of the Holy Spirit and faith, and a great number of people were brought to the Lord.

²⁵Then Barnabas went to Tarsus to look for Saul, ²⁶and when he found him, he brought him to Antioch. So for a whole year Barnabas and Saul met with the church and taught great numbers of people. The disciples were called Christians first at Antioch.

²⁷During this time some prophets came down from Jerusalem to Antioch. ²⁸One of them, named Agabus, stood up and through the Spirit predicted that a severe famine would spread over the entire Roman world. (This happened during the reign of Claudius.) ²⁹The disciples, each according to his ability, decided to provide help for the brothers living in Judea. ³⁰This they did, sending their gift to the elders by Barnabas and Saul.

a 16 Or in

PSALM 135:1-21

¹ Praise the LORD.[a]

Praise the name of the LORD;
  praise him, you servants of the LORD,
² you who minister in the house of the LORD,
  in the courts of the house of our God.

³ Praise the LORD, for the LORD is good;
  sing praise to his name, for that is pleasant.
⁴ For the LORD has chosen Jacob to be his own,
  Israel to be his treasured possession.

⁵ I know that the LORD is great,
  that our Lord is greater than all gods.
⁶ The LORD does whatever pleases him,
  in the heavens and on the earth,
  in the seas and all their depths.
⁷ He makes clouds rise from the ends of the earth;
  he sends lightning with the rain
  and brings out the wind from his storehouses.

⁸ He struck down the firstborn of Egypt,
  the firstborn of men and animals.
⁹ He sent his signs and wonders into your midst, O Egypt,

against Pharaoh and all his
servants.
¹⁰He struck down many nations
and killed mighty kings—
¹¹Sihon king of the Amorites,
Og king of Bashan
and all the kings of Canaan—
¹²and he gave their land as an
inheritance,
an inheritance to his people
Israel.

¹³Your name, O LORD, endures
forever,
your renown, O LORD, through
all generations.
¹⁴For the LORD will vindicate his
people
and have compassion on his
servants.

¹⁵The idols of the nations are silver
and gold,
made by the hands of men.
¹⁶They have mouths, but cannot
speak,
eyes, but they cannot see;
¹⁷they have ears, but cannot hear,
nor is there breath in their
mouths.
¹⁸Those who make them will be like
them,
and so will all who trust in them.

¹⁹O house of Israel, praise the LORD;
O house of Aaron, praise the
LORD;
²⁰O house of Levi, praise the LORD;
you who fear him, praise the
LORD.
²¹Praise be to the LORD from Zion,
to him who dwells in Jerusalem.

Praise the LORD.

ᵃ1 Hebrew *Hallelu Yah*; also in verses 3 and 21

PROVERBS 17:12-13
¹²Better to meet a bear robbed of her
cubs
than a fool in his folly.

¹³If a man pays back evil for good,
evil will never leave his house.

GOD SIGHTINGS

June 18

1 KINGS 19:1-21
Now Ahab told Jezebel everything Elijah
had done and how he had killed all the
prophets with the sword. ²So Jezebel
sent a messenger to Elijah to say, "May
the gods deal with me, be it ever so severely, if by this time tomorrow I do not
make your life like that of one of them."

³Elijah was afraidᵃ and ran for his life.
When he came to Beersheba in Judah,
he left his servant there, ⁴while he himself went a day's journey into the desert.
He came to a broom tree, sat down under it and prayed that he might die. "I
have had enough, LORD," he said. "Take
my life; I am no better than my ancestors." ⁵Then he lay down under the tree
and fell asleep.

All at once an angel touched him and
said, "Get up and eat." ⁶He looked
around, and there by his head was a cake
of bread baked over hot coals, and a jar
of water. He ate and drank and then lay
down again.

⁷The angel of the LORD came back a
second time and touched him and said,
"Get up and eat, for the journey is too
much for you." ⁸So he got up and ate
and drank. Strengthened by that food,
he traveled forty days and forty nights
until he reached Horeb, the mountain of
God. ⁹There he went into a cave and
spent the night.

And the word of the LORD came to
him: "What are you doing here, Elijah?"

¹⁰He replied, "I have been very zealous for the LORD God Almighty. The Israelites have rejected your covenant,
broken down your altars, and put your
prophets to death with the sword. I am
the only one left, and now they are trying to kill me too."

¹¹The LORD said, "Go out and stand on
the mountain in the presence of the
LORD, for the LORD is about to pass by."

Then a great and powerful wind tore the mountains apart and shattered the rocks before the LORD, but the LORD was not in the wind. After the wind there was an earthquake, but the LORD was not in the earthquake. 12After the earthquake came a fire, but the LORD was not in the fire. And after the fire came a gentle whisper. 13When Elijah heard it, he pulled his cloak over his face and went out and stood at the mouth of the cave.

Then a voice said to him, "What are you doing here, Elijah?"

14He replied, "I have been very zealous for the LORD God Almighty. The Israelites have rejected your covenant, broken down your altars, and put your prophets to death with the sword. I am the only one left, and now they are trying to kill me too."

15The LORD said to him, "Go back the way you came, and go to the Desert of Damascus. When you get there, anoint Hazael king over Aram. 16Also, anoint Jehu son of Nimshi king over Israel, and anoint Elisha son of Shaphat from Abel Meholah to succeed you as prophet. 17Jehu will put to death any who escape the sword of Hazael, and Elisha will put to death any who escape the sword of Jehu. 18Yet I reserve seven thousand in Israel—all whose knees have not bowed down to Baal and all whose mouths have not kissed him."

19So Elijah went from there and found Elisha son of Shaphat. He was plowing with twelve yoke of oxen, and he himself was driving the twelfth pair. Elijah went up to him and threw his cloak around him. 20Elisha then left his oxen and ran after Elijah. "Let me kiss my father and mother good-by," he said, "and then I will come with you."

"Go back," Elijah replied. "What have I done to you?"

21So Elisha left him and went back. He took his yoke of oxen and slaughtered them. He burned the plowing equipment to cook the meat and gave it to the people, and they ate. Then he set out to follow Elijah and became his attendant.

a3 Or Elijah saw

ACTS 12:1-23

It was about this time that King Herod arrested some who belonged to the church, intending to persecute them. 2He had James, the brother of John, put to death with the sword. 3When he saw that this pleased the Jews, he proceeded to seize Peter also. This happened during the Feast of Unleavened Bread. 4After arresting him, he put him in prison, handing him over to be guarded by four squads of four soldiers each. Herod intended to bring him out for public trial after the Passover.

5So Peter was kept in prison, but the church was earnestly praying to God for him.

6The night before Herod was to bring him to trial, Peter was sleeping between two soldiers, bound with two chains, and sentries stood guard at the entrance. 7Suddenly an angel of the Lord appeared and a light shone in the cell. He struck Peter on the side and woke him up. "Quick, get up!" he said, and the chains fell off Peter's wrists.

8Then the angel said to him, "Put on your clothes and sandals." And Peter did so. "Wrap your cloak around you and follow me," the angel told him. 9Peter followed him out of the prison, but he had no idea that what the angel was doing was really happening; he thought he was seeing a vision. 10They passed the first and second guards and came to the iron gate leading to the city. It opened for them by itself, and they went through it. When they had walked the length of one street, suddenly the angel left him.

11Then Peter came to himself and said, "Now I know without a doubt that the Lord sent his angel and rescued me from Herod's clutches and from everything the Jewish people were anticipating."

12When this had dawned on him, he went to the house of Mary the mother of John, also called Mark, where many people had gathered and were praying. [13]Peter knocked at the outer entrance, and a servant girl named Rhoda came to answer the door. [14]When she recognized Peter's voice, she was so overjoyed she ran back without opening it and exclaimed, "Peter is at the door!"

[15]"You're out of your mind," they told her. When she kept insisting that it was so, they said, "It must be his angel."

[16]But Peter kept on knocking, and when they opened the door and saw him, they were astonished. [17]Peter motioned with his hand for them to be quiet and described how the Lord had brought him out of prison. "Tell James and the brothers about this," he said, and then he left for another place.

[18]In the morning, there was no small commotion among the soldiers as to what had become of Peter. [19]After Herod had a thorough search made for him and did not find him, he cross-examined the guards and ordered that they be executed.

Then Herod went from Judea to Caesarea and stayed there a while. [20]He had been quarreling with the people of Tyre and Sidon; they now joined together and sought an audience with him. Having secured the support of Blastus, a trusted personal servant of the king, they asked for peace, because they depended on the king's country for their food supply.

[21]On the appointed day Herod, wearing his royal robes, sat on his throne and delivered a public address to the people. [22]They shouted, "This is the voice of a god, not of a man." [23]Immediately, because Herod did not give praise to God, an angel of the Lord struck him down, and he was eaten by worms and died.

PSALM 136:1-26

[1]Give thanks to the LORD, for he is good.
  His love endures forever.
[2]Give thanks to the God of gods.
  His love endures forever.

[3]Give thanks to the Lord of lords:
  His love endures forever.

[4]to him who alone does great wonders,
  His love endures forever.
[5]who by his understanding made the heavens,
  His love endures forever.
[6]who spread out the earth upon the waters,
  His love endures forever.
[7]who made the great lights—
  His love endures forever.
[8]the sun to govern the day,
  His love endures forever.
[9]the moon and stars to govern the night;
  His love endures forever.

[10]to him who struck down the firstborn of Egypt
  His love endures forever.
[11]and brought Israel out from among them
  His love endures forever.
[12]with a mighty hand and outstretched arm;
  His love endures forever.

[13]to him who divided the Red Sea[a] asunder
  His love endures forever.
[14]and brought Israel through the midst of it,
  His love endures forever.
[15]but swept Pharaoh and his army into the Red Sea;
  His love endures forever.

[16]to him who led his people through the desert,
  His love endures forever.
[17]who struck down great kings,
  His love endures forever.
[18]and killed mighty kings—
  His love endures forever.
[19]Sihon king of the Amorites
  His love endures forever.
[20]and Og king of Bashan—
  His love endures forever.
[21]and gave their land as an inheritance,
  His love endures forever.

22 an inheritance to his servant Israel;
   His love endures forever.

23 to the One who remembered us in
  our low estate
   His love endures forever.
24 and freed us from our enemies,
   His love endures forever.
25 and who gives food to every creature.
   His love endures forever.

26 Give thanks to the God of heaven.
   His love endures forever.

a 13 Hebrew *Yam Suph*; that is, Sea of Reeds; also in verse 15

PROVERBS 17:14-15

14 Starting a quarrel is like breaching
  a dam;
 so drop the matter before a
  dispute breaks out.

15 Acquitting the guilty and
  condemning the innocent—
 the LORD detests them both.

□ DAY 170

GOD SIGHTINGS

June 19

1 KINGS 20:1–21:29

Now Ben-Hadad king of Aram mustered his entire army. Accompanied by thirty-two kings with their horses and chariots, he went up and besieged Samaria and attacked it. 2 He sent messengers into the city to Ahab king of Israel, saying, "This is what Ben-Hadad says: 3 'Your silver and gold are mine, and the best of your wives and children are mine.'"

4 The king of Israel answered, "Just as you say, my lord the king. I and all I have are yours."

5 The messengers came again and said, "This is what Ben-Hadad says: 'I sent to demand your silver and gold, your wives and your children. 6 But about this time tomorrow I am going to send my officials to search your palace and the houses of your officials. They

will seize everything you value and carry it away.'"

7 The king of Israel summoned all the elders of the land and said to them, "See how this man is looking for trouble! When he sent for my wives and my children, my silver and my gold, I did not refuse him."

8 The elders and the people all answered, "Don't listen to him or agree to his demands."

9 So he replied to Ben-Hadad's messengers, "Tell my lord the king, 'Your servant will do all you demanded the first time, but this demand I cannot meet.'" They left and took the answer back to Ben-Hadad.

10 Then Ben-Hadad sent another message to Ahab: "May the gods deal with me, be it ever so severely, if enough dust remains in Samaria to give each of my men a handful."

11 The king of Israel answered, "Tell him: 'One who puts on his armor should not boast like one who takes it off.'"

12 Ben-Hadad heard this message while he and the kings were drinking in their tents,*a* and he ordered his men: "Prepare to attack." So they prepared to attack the city.

13 Meanwhile a prophet came to Ahab king of Israel and announced, "This is what the LORD says: 'Do you see this vast army? I will give it into your hand today, and then you will know that I am the LORD.'"

14 "But who will do this?" asked Ahab.

The prophet replied, "This is what the LORD says: 'The young officers of the provincial commanders will do it.'"

"And who will start the battle?" he asked.

The prophet answered, "You will."

15 So Ahab summoned the young officers of the provincial commanders, 232 men. Then he assembled the rest of the Israelites, 7,000 in all. 16 They set out at noon while Ben-Hadad and the 32 kings allied with him were in their tents getting drunk. 17 The young officers of the provincial commanders went out first.

Now Ben-Hadad had dispatched scouts, who reported, "Men are advancing from Samaria."

[18]He said, "If they have come out for peace, take them alive; if they have come out for war, take them alive."

[19]The young officers of the provincial commanders marched out of the city with the army behind them [20]and each one struck down his opponent. At that, the Arameans fled, with the Israelites in pursuit. But Ben-Hadad king of Aram escaped on horseback with some of his horsemen. [21]The king of Israel advanced and overpowered the horses and chariots and inflicted heavy losses on the Arameans.

[22]Afterward, the prophet came to the king of Israel and said, "Strengthen your position and see what must be done, because next spring the king of Aram will attack you again."

[23]Meanwhile, the officials of the king of Aram advised him, "Their gods are gods of the hills. That is why they were too strong for us. But if we fight them on the plains, surely we will be stronger than they. [24]Do this: Remove all the kings from their commands and replace them with other officers. [25]You must also raise an army like the one you lost—horse for horse and chariot for chariot—so we can fight Israel on the plains. Then surely we will be stronger than they." He agreed with them and acted accordingly.

[26]The next spring Ben-Hadad mustered the Arameans and went up to Aphek to fight against Israel. [27]When the Israelites were also mustered and given provisions, they marched out to meet them. The Israelites camped opposite them like two small flocks of goats, while the Arameans covered the countryside.

[28]The man of God came up and told the king of Israel, "This is what the LORD says: 'Because the Arameans think the LORD is a god of the hills and not a god of the valleys, I will deliver this vast army into your hands, and you will know that I am the LORD.'"

[29]For seven days they camped opposite each other, and on the seventh day the battle was joined. The Israelites inflicted a hundred thousand casualties on the Aramean foot soldiers in one day. [30]The rest of them escaped to the city of Aphek, where the wall collapsed on twenty-seven thousand of them. And Ben-Hadad fled to the city and hid in an inner room.

[31]His officials said to him, "Look, we have heard that the kings of the house of Israel are merciful. Let us go to the king of Israel with sackcloth around our waists and ropes around our heads. Perhaps he will spare your life."

[32]Wearing sackcloth around their waists and ropes around their heads, they went to the king of Israel and said, "Your servant Ben-Hadad says: 'Please let me live.'"

The king answered, "Is he still alive? He is my brother."

[33]The men took this as a good sign and were quick to pick up his word. "Yes, your brother Ben-Hadad!" they said.

"Go and get him," the king said. When Ben-Hadad came out, Ahab had him come up into his chariot.

[34]"I will return the cities my father took from your father," Ben-Hadad offered. "You may set up your own market areas in Damascus, as my father did in Samaria."

⌊Ahab said,⌋ "On the basis of a treaty I will set you free." So he made a treaty with him, and let him go.

[35]By the word of the LORD one of the sons of the prophets said to his companion, "Strike me with your weapon," but the man refused.

[36]So the prophet said, "Because you have not obeyed the LORD, as soon as you leave me a lion will kill you." And after the man went away, a lion found him and killed him.

[37]The prophet found another man and said, "Strike me, please." So the man struck him and wounded him. [38]Then the prophet went and stood by the road waiting for the king. He disguised himself with his headband down over his eyes. [39]As the king passed by,

the prophet called out to him, "Your servant went into the thick of the battle, and someone came to me with a captive and said, 'Guard this man. If he is missing, it will be your life for his life, or you must pay a talent*b* of silver.' 40While your servant was busy here and there, the man disappeared."

"That is your sentence," the king of Israel said. "You have pronounced it yourself."

41Then the prophet quickly removed the headband from his eyes, and the king of Israel recognized him as one of the prophets. 42He said to the king, "This is what the LORD says: 'You have set free a man I had determined should die.*c* Therefore it is your life for his life, your people for his people.' " 43Sullen and angry, the king of Israel went to his palace in Samaria.

21:1SOME time later there was an incident involving a vineyard belonging to Naboth the Jezreelite. The vineyard was in Jezreel, close to the palace of Ahab king of Samaria. 2Ahab said to Naboth, "Let me have your vineyard to use for a vegetable garden, since it is close to my palace. In exchange I will give you a better vineyard or, if you prefer, I will pay you whatever it is worth."

3But Naboth replied, "The LORD forbid that I should give you the inheritance of my fathers."

4So Ahab went home, sullen and angry because Naboth the Jezreelite had said, "I will not give you the inheritance of my fathers." He lay on his bed sulking and refused to eat.

5His wife Jezebel came in and asked him, "Why are you so sullen? Why won't you eat?"

6He answered her, "Because I said to Naboth the Jezreelite, 'Sell me your vineyard; or if you prefer, I will give you another vineyard in its place.' But he said, 'I will not give you my vineyard.'"

7Jezebel his wife said, "Is this how you act as king over Israel? Get up and eat! Cheer up. I'll get you the vineyard of Naboth the Jezreelite."

8So she wrote letters in Ahab's name, placed his seal on them, and sent them to the elders and nobles who lived in Naboth's city with him. 9In those letters she wrote:

"Proclaim a day of fasting and seat Naboth in a prominent place among the people. 10But seat two scoundrels opposite him and have them testify that he has cursed both God and the king. Then take him out and stone him to death."

11So the elders and nobles who lived in Naboth's city did as Jezebel directed in the letters she had written to them. 12They proclaimed a fast and seated Naboth in a prominent place among the people. 13Then two scoundrels came and sat opposite him and brought charges against Naboth before the people, saying, "Naboth has cursed both God and the king." So they took him outside the city and stoned him to death. 14Then they sent word to Jezebel: "Naboth has been stoned and is dead."

15As soon as Jezebel heard that Naboth had been stoned to death, she said to Ahab, "Get up and take possession of the vineyard of Naboth the Jezreelite that he refused to sell you. He is no longer alive, but dead." 16When Ahab heard that Naboth was dead, he got up and went down to take possession of Naboth's vineyard.

17Then the word of the LORD came to Elijah the Tishbite: 18"Go down to meet Ahab king of Israel, who rules in Samaria. He is now in Naboth's vineyard, where he has gone to take possession of it. 19Say to him, 'This is what the LORD says: Have you not murdered a man and seized his property?' Then say to him, 'This is what the LORD says: In the place where dogs licked up Naboth's blood, dogs will lick up your blood—yes, yours!'"

20Ahab said to Elijah, "So you have found me, my enemy!"

"I have found you," he answered, "because you have sold yourself to do evil in the eyes of the LORD. 21'I am going to bring disaster on you. I will consume your descendants and cut off from Ahab every last male in Israel—slave or free. 22I will make your house like that of Jeroboam son of Nebat and that of Baasha son of Ahijah, because you have provoked me to anger and have caused Israel to sin.'

23"And also concerning Jezebel the LORD says: 'Dogs will devour Jezebel by the wall of[d] Jezreel.'

24"Dogs will eat those belonging to Ahab who die in the city, and the birds of the air will feed on those who die in the country."

25(There was never a man like Ahab, who sold himself to do evil in the eyes of the LORD, urged on by Jezebel his wife. 26He behaved in the vilest manner by going after idols, like the Amorites the LORD drove out before Israel.)

27When Ahab heard these words, he tore his clothes, put on sackcloth and fasted. He lay in sackcloth and went around meekly.

28Then the word of the LORD came to Elijah the Tishbite: 29"Have you noticed how Ahab has humbled himself before me? Because he has humbled himself, I will not bring this disaster in his day, but I will bring it on his house in the days of his son."

a12 Or in Succoth; also in verse 16   b39 That is, about 75 pounds (about 34 kilograms)   c42 The Hebrew term refers to the irrevocable giving over of things or persons to the LORD, often by totally destroying them.   d23 Most Hebrew manuscripts; a few Hebrew manuscripts, Vulgate and Syriac (see also 2 Kings 9:26) the plot of ground at

ACTS 12:24–13:15

But the word of God continued to increase and spread.

25When Barnabas and Saul had finished their mission, they returned from[a] Jerusalem, taking with them John, also called Mark.

13:1In the church at Antioch there were prophets and teachers: Barnabas, Simeon called Niger, Lucius of Cyrene, Manaen (who had been brought up with Herod the tetrarch) and Saul. 2While they were worshiping the Lord and fasting, the Holy Spirit said, "Set apart for me Barnabas and Saul for the work to which I have called them." 3So after they had fasted and prayed, they placed their hands on them and sent them off.

4The two of them, sent on their way by the Holy Spirit, went down to Seleucia and sailed from there to Cyprus. 5When they arrived at Salamis, they proclaimed the word of God in the Jewish synagogues. John was with them as their helper.

6They traveled through the whole island until they came to Paphos. There they met a Jewish sorcerer and false prophet named Bar-Jesus, 7who was an attendant of the proconsul, Sergius Paulus. The proconsul, an intelligent man, sent for Barnabas and Saul because he wanted to hear the word of God. 8But Elymas the sorcerer (for that is what his name means) opposed them and tried to turn the proconsul from the faith. 9Then Saul, who was also called Paul, filled with the Holy Spirit, looked straight at Elymas and said, 10"You are a child of the devil and an enemy of everything that is right! You are full of all kinds of deceit and trickery. Will you never stop perverting the right ways of the Lord? 11Now the hand of the Lord is against you. You are going to be blind, and for a time you will be unable to see the light of the sun."

Immediately mist and darkness came over him, and he groped about, seeking someone to lead him by the hand. 12When the proconsul saw what had happened, he believed, for he was amazed at the teaching about the Lord.

13From Paphos, Paul and his companions sailed to Perga in Pamphylia, where John left them to return to Jerusalem. 14From Perga they went on to Pisidian Antioch. On the Sabbath they entered the synagogue and sat down. 15After the reading from the Law and the Prophets, the synagogue rulers sent word to them, saying, "Brothers, if you have a message of encouragement for the people, please speak."

a25 Some manuscripts to

PSALM 137:1-9

¹ By the rivers of Babylon we sat and
    wept
  when we remembered Zion.
² There on the poplars
  we hung our harps,
³ for there our captors asked us for songs,
  our tormentors demanded songs
    of joy;
  they said, "Sing us one of the songs
    of Zion!"

⁴ How can we sing the songs of the LORD
  while in a foreign land?
⁵ If I forget you, O Jerusalem,
  may my right hand forget ⸤its skill⸥.
⁶ May my tongue cling to the roof of
    my mouth
  if I do not remember you,
  if I do not consider Jerusalem
    my highest joy.

⁷ Remember, O LORD, what the
    Edomites did
  on the day Jerusalem fell.
  "Tear it down," they cried,
    "tear it down to its foundations!"

⁸ O Daughter of Babylon, doomed to
    destruction,
  happy is he who repays you
    for what you have done to us—
⁹ he who seizes your infants
  and dashes them against the rocks.

PROVERBS 17:16

¹⁶ Of what use is money in the hand of
    a fool,
  since he has no desire to get
    wisdom?

□ D A Y 1 7 1

GOD SIGHTINGS

June 20

1 KINGS 22:1-53

For three years there was no war between Aram and Israel. ²But in the third year Jehoshaphat king of Judah went down to see the king of Israel. ³The king of Israel had said to his officials, "Don't you know that Ramoth Gilead belongs to us and yet we are doing nothing to retake it from the king of Aram?"

⁴So he asked Jehoshaphat, "Will you go with me to fight against Ramoth Gilead?"

Jehoshaphat replied to the king of Israel, "I am as you are, my people as your people, my horses as your horses." ⁵But Jehoshaphat also said to the king of Israel, "First seek the counsel of the LORD."

⁶So the king of Israel brought together the prophets—about four hundred men—and asked them, "Shall I go to war against Ramoth Gilead, or shall I refrain?"

"Go," they answered, "for the Lord will give it into the king's hand."

⁷But Jehoshaphat asked, "Is there not a prophet of the LORD here whom we can inquire of?"

⁸The king of Israel answered Jehoshaphat, "There is still one man through whom we can inquire of the LORD, but I hate him because he never prophesies anything good about me, but always bad. He is Micaiah son of Imlah."

"The king should not say that," Jehoshaphat replied.

⁹So the king of Israel called one of his officials and said, "Bring Micaiah son of Imlah at once."

¹⁰Dressed in their royal robes, the king of Israel and Jehoshaphat king of Judah were sitting on their thrones at the threshing floor by the entrance of the gate of Samaria, with all the prophets prophesying before them. ¹¹Now Zedekiah son of Kenaanah had made iron horns and he declared, "This is what the LORD says: 'With these you will gore the Arameans until they are destroyed.'"

¹²All the other prophets were prophesying the same thing. "Attack Ramoth Gilead and be victorious," they said, "for the LORD will give it into the king's hand."

¹³The messenger who had gone to summon Micaiah said to him, "Look, as one man the other prophets are predicting success for the king. Let your

word agree with theirs, and speak favorably."

14But Micaiah said, "As surely as the LORD lives, I can tell him only what the LORD tells me."

15When he arrived, the king asked him, "Micaiah, shall we go to war against Ramoth Gilead, or shall I refrain?"

"Attack and be victorious," he answered, "for the LORD will give it into the king's hand."

16The king said to him, "How many times must I make you swear to tell me nothing but the truth in the name of the LORD?"

17Then Micaiah answered, "I saw all Israel scattered on the hills like sheep without a shepherd, and the LORD said, 'These people have no master. Let each one go home in peace.'"

18The king of Israel said to Jehoshaphat, "Didn't I tell you that he never prophesies anything good about me, but only bad?"

19Micaiah continued, "Therefore hear the word of the LORD: I saw the LORD sitting on his throne with all the host of heaven standing around him on his right and on his left. 20And the LORD said, 'Who will entice Ahab into attacking Ramoth Gilead and going to his death there?'

"One suggested this, and another that. 21Finally, a spirit came forward, stood before the LORD and said, 'I will entice him.'

22"'By what means?' the LORD asked.

"'I will go out and be a lying spirit in the mouths of all his prophets,' he said.

"'You will succeed in enticing him,' said the LORD. 'Go and do it.'

23"So now the LORD has put a lying spirit in the mouths of all these prophets of yours. The LORD has decreed disaster for you."

24Then Zedekiah son of Kenaanah went up and slapped Micaiah in the face. "Which way did the spirit froma the LORD go when he went from me to speak to you?" he asked.

25Micaiah replied, "You will find out on the day you go to hide in an inner room."

26The king of Israel then ordered, "Take Micaiah and send him back to Amon the ruler of the city and to Joash the king's son 27and say, 'This is what the king says: Put this fellow in prison and give him nothing but bread and water until I return safely.'"

28Micaiah declared, "If you ever return safely, the LORD has not spoken through me." Then he added, "Mark my words, all you people!"

29So the king of Israel and Jehoshaphat king of Judah went up to Ramoth Gilead. 30The king of Israel said to Jehoshaphat, "I will enter the battle in disguise, but you wear your royal robes." So the king of Israel disguised himself and went into battle.

31Now the king of Aram had ordered his thirty-two chariot commanders, "Do not fight with anyone, small or great, except the king of Israel." 32When the chariot commanders saw Jehoshaphat, they thought, "Surely this is the king of Israel." So they turned to attack him, but when Jehoshaphat cried out, 33the chariot commanders saw that he was not the king of Israel and stopped pursuing him.

34But someone drew his bow at random and hit the king of Israel between the sections of his armor. The king told his chariot driver, "Wheel around and get me out of the fighting. I've been wounded." 35All day long the battle raged, and the king was propped up in his chariot facing the Arameans. The blood from his wound ran onto the floor of the chariot, and that evening he died. 36As the sun was setting, a cry spread through the army: "Every man to his town; everyone to his land!"

37So the king died and was brought to Samaria, and they buried him there. 38They washed the chariot at a pool in Samaria (where the prostitutes bathed),b and the dogs licked up his blood, as the word of the LORD had declared.

39As for the other events of Ahab's reign, including all he did, the palace he built and inlaid with ivory, and the cities he fortified, are they not written in the book of the annals of the kings of Israel? ⁴⁰Ahab rested with his fathers. And Ahaziah his son succeeded him as king.

⁴¹Jehoshaphat son of Asa became king of Judah in the fourth year of Ahab king of Israel. ⁴²Jehoshaphat was thirty-five years old when he became king, and he reigned in Jerusalem twenty-five years. His mother's name was Azubah daughter of Shilhi. ⁴³In everything he walked in the ways of his father Asa and did not stray from them; he did what was right in the eyes of the LORD. The high places, however, were not removed, and the people continued to offer sacrifices and burn incense there. ⁴⁴Jehoshaphat was also at peace with the king of Israel.

⁴⁵As for the other events of Jehoshaphat's reign, the things he achieved and his military exploits, are they not written in the book of the annals of the kings of Judah? ⁴⁶He rid the land of the rest of the male shrine prostitutes who remained there even after the reign of his father Asa. ⁴⁷There was then no king in Edom; a deputy ruled.

⁴⁸Now Jehoshaphat built a fleet of trading shipsᶜ to go to Ophir for gold, but they never set sail—they were wrecked at Ezion Geber. ⁴⁹At that time Ahaziah son of Ahab said to Jehoshaphat, "Let my men sail with your men," but Jehoshaphat refused.

⁵⁰Then Jehoshaphat rested with his fathers and was buried with them in the city of David his father. And Jehoram his son succeeded him.

⁵¹Ahaziah son of Ahab became king of Israel in Samaria in the seventeenth year of Jehoshaphat king of Judah, and he reigned over Israel two years. ⁵²He did evil in the eyes of the LORD, because he walked in the ways of his father and mother and in the ways of Jeroboam son of Nebat, who caused Israel to sin. ⁵³He served and worshiped Baal and provoked the LORD, the God of Israel, to anger, just as his father had done.

ᵃ24 Or Spirit of   ᵇ38 Or Samaria and cleaned the weapons   ᶜ48 Hebrew of ships of Tarshish

ACTS 13:16-41

Standing up, Paul motioned with his hand and said: "Men of Israel and you Gentiles who worship God, listen to me! ¹⁷The God of the people of Israel chose our fathers; he made the people prosper during their stay in Egypt, with mighty power he led them out of that country, ¹⁸he endured their conductᵃ for about forty years in the desert, ¹⁹he overthrew seven nations in Canaan and gave their land to his people as their inheritance. ²⁰All this took about 450 years.

"After this, God gave them judges until the time of Samuel the prophet. ²¹Then the people asked for a king, and he gave them Saul son of Kish, of the tribe of Benjamin, who ruled forty years. ²²After removing Saul, he made David their king. He testified concerning him: 'I have found David son of Jesse a man after my own heart; he will do everything I want him to do.'

²³"From this man's descendants God has brought to Israel the Savior Jesus, as he promised. ²⁴Before the coming of Jesus, John preached repentance and baptism to all the people of Israel. ²⁵As John was completing his work, he said: 'Who do you think I am? I am not that one. No, but he is coming after me, whose sandals I am not worthy to untie.'

²⁶"Brothers, children of Abraham, and you God-fearing Gentiles, it is to us that this message of salvation has been sent. ²⁷The people of Jerusalem and their rulers did not recognize Jesus, yet in condemning him they fulfilled the words of the prophets that are read every Sabbath. ²⁸Though they found no proper ground for a death sentence, they asked Pilate to have him executed. ²⁹When they had carried out all that was written about him, they took him down from the tree and laid him in a tomb. ³⁰But God raised him from the dead, ³¹and for many days he was seen by those who had traveled with him from Galilee to Jerusalem. They are now his witnesses to our people.

³²"We tell you the good news: What God promised our fathers ³³he has

fulfilled for us, their children, by raising up Jesus. As it is written in the second Psalm:

"'You are my Son;
today I have become your
Father.[b'c]

34 The fact that God raised him from the dead, never to decay, is stated in these words:

"'I will give you the holy and sure
blessings promised to
David.'[d]

35 So it is stated elsewhere:

"'You will not let your Holy One see
decay.'[e]

36 "For when David had served God's purpose in his own generation, he fell asleep; he was buried with his fathers and his body decayed. 37 But the one whom God raised from the dead did not see decay.

38 " Therefore, my brothers, I want you to know that through Jesus the forgiveness of sins is proclaimed to you. 39 Through him everyone who believes is justified from everything you could not be justified from by the law of Moses. 40 Take care that what the prophets have said does not happen to you:

41 "'Look, you scoffers,
wonder and perish,
for I am going to do something in
your days
that you would never believe,
even if someone told you.'[f]"

a 18 Some manuscripts *and cared for them*   *b 33* Or *have begotten you*   *c 33* Psalm 2:7   *d 34* Isaiah 55:3   *e 35* Psalm 16:10   *f 41* Hab. 1:5

PSALM 138:1-8
Of David.

1 I will praise you, O Lord, with all my
heart;
before the "gods" I will sing your
praise.
2 I will bow down toward your holy
temple

and will praise your name
for your love and your
faithfulness,
for you have exalted above all things
your name and your word.
3 When I called, you answered me;
you made me bold and
stouthearted.

4 May all the kings of the earth praise
you, O Lord,
when they hear the words of your
mouth.
5 May they sing of the ways of the Lord,
for the glory of the Lord is great.

6 Though the Lord is on high, he looks
upon the lowly,
but the proud he knows from afar.
7 Though I walk in the midst of trouble,
you preserve my life;
you stretch out your hand against the
anger of my foes,
with your right hand you save me.
8 The Lord will fulfill ⌞his purpose⌟ for
me;
your love, O Lord, endures
forever—
do not abandon the works of your
hands.

PROVERBS 17:17-18
17 A friend loves at all times,
and a brother is born for
adversity.

18 A man lacking in judgment strikes
hands in pledge
and puts up security for his
neighbor.

☐ DAY 172

GOD SIGHTINGS

June 21

2 KINGS 1:1–2:25
After Ahab's death, Moab rebelled against Israel. 2 Now Ahaziah had fallen through the lattice of his upper room in

Samaria and injured himself. So he sent messengers, saying to them, "Go and consult Baal-Zebub, the god of Ekron, to see if I will recover from this injury."

³But the angel of the LORD said to Elijah the Tishbite, "Go up and meet the messengers of the king of Samaria and ask them, 'Is it because there is no God in Israel that you are going off to consult Baal-Zebub, the god of Ekron?' ⁴Therefore this is what the LORD says: 'You will not leave the bed you are lying on. You will certainly die!'" So Elijah went.

⁵When the messengers returned to the king, he asked them, "Why have you come back?"

⁶"A man came to meet us," they replied. "And he said to us, 'Go back to the king who sent you and tell him, "This is what the LORD says: Is it because there is no God in Israel that you are sending men to consult Baal-Zebub, the god of Ekron? Therefore you will not leave the bed you are lying on. You will certainly die!"'"

⁷The king asked them, "What kind of man was it who came to meet you and told you this?"

⁸They replied, "He was a man with a garment of hair and with a leather belt around his waist."

The king said, "That was Elijah the Tishbite."

⁹Then he sent to Elijah a captain with his company of fifty men. The captain went up to Elijah, who was sitting on the top of a hill, and said to him, "Man of God, the king says, 'Come down!'"

¹⁰Elijah answered the captain, "If I am a man of God, may fire come down from heaven and consume you and your fifty men!" Then fire fell from heaven and consumed the captain and his men.

¹¹At this the king sent to Elijah another captain with his fifty men. The captain said to him, "Man of God, this is what the king says, 'Come down at once!'"

¹²"If I am a man of God," Elijah replied, "may fire come down from heaven and consume you and your fifty men!" Then the fire of God fell from heaven and consumed him and his fifty men.

¹³So the king sent a third captain with his fifty men. This third captain went up and fell on his knees before Elijah. "Man of God," he begged, "please have respect for my life and the lives of these fifty men, your servants! ¹⁴See, fire has fallen from heaven and consumed the first two captains and all their men. But now have respect for my life!"

¹⁵The angel of the LORD said to Elijah, "Go down with him; do not be afraid of him." So Elijah got up and went down with him to the king.

¹⁶He told the king, "This is what the LORD says: Is it because there is no God in Israel for you to consult that you have sent messengers to consult Baal-Zebub, the god of Ekron? Because you have done this, you will never leave the bed you are lying on. You will certainly die!" ¹⁷So he died, according to the word of the LORD that Elijah had spoken.

Because Ahaziah had no son, Joramᵃ succeeded him as king in the second year of Jehoram son of Jehoshaphat king of Judah. ¹⁸As for all the other events of Ahaziah's reign, and what he did, are they not written in the book of the annals of the kings of Israel?

2:1WHEN the LORD was about to take Elijah up to heaven in a whirlwind, Elijah and Elisha were on their way from Gilgal. ²Elijah said to Elisha, "Stay here; the LORD has sent me to Bethel."

But Elisha said, "As surely as the LORD lives and as you live, I will not leave you." So they went down to Bethel.

³The company of the prophets at Bethel came out to Elisha and asked, "Do you know that the LORD is going to take your master from you today?"

"Yes, I know," Elisha replied, "but do not speak of it."

⁴Then Elijah said to him, "Stay here, Elisha; the LORD has sent me to Jericho."

And he replied, "As surely as the LORD

lives and as you live, I will not leave you." So they went to Jericho.

⁵The company of the prophets at Jericho went up to Elisha and asked him, "Do you know that the LORD is going to take your master from you today?"

"Yes, I know," he replied, "but do not speak of it."

⁶Then Elijah said to him, "Stay here; the LORD has sent me to the Jordan."

And he replied, "As surely as the LORD lives and as you live, I will not leave you." So the two of them walked on.

⁷Fifty men of the company of the prophets went and stood at a distance, facing the place where Elijah and Elisha had stopped at the Jordan. ⁸Elijah took his cloak, rolled it up and struck the water with it. The water divided to the right and to the left, and the two of them crossed over on dry ground.

⁹When they had crossed, Elijah said to Elisha, "Tell me, what can I do for you before I am taken from you?"

"Let me inherit a double portion of your spirit," Elisha replied.

¹⁰"You have asked a difficult thing," Elijah said, "yet if you see me when I am taken from you, it will be yours—otherwise not."

¹¹As they were walking along and talking together, suddenly a chariot of fire and horses of fire appeared and separated the two of them, and Elijah went up to heaven in a whirlwind. ¹²Elisha saw this and cried out, "My father! My father! The chariots and horsemen of Israel!" And Elisha saw him no more. Then he took hold of his own clothes and tore them apart.

¹³He picked up the cloak that had fallen from Elijah and went back and stood on the bank of the Jordan. ¹⁴Then he took the cloak that had fallen from him and struck the water with it. "Where now is the LORD, the God of Elijah?" he asked. When he struck the water, it divided to the right and to the left, and he crossed over.

¹⁵The company of the prophets from Jericho, who were watching, said, "The spirit of Elijah is resting on Elisha." And they went to meet him and bowed to the ground before him. ¹⁶"Look," they said, "we your servants have fifty able men. Let them go and look for your master. Perhaps the Spirit of the LORD has picked him up and set him down on some mountain or in some valley."

"No," Elisha replied, "do not send them."

¹⁷But they persisted until he was too ashamed to refuse. So he said, "Send them." And they sent fifty men, who searched for three days but did not find him. ¹⁸When they returned to Elisha, who was staying in Jericho, he said to them, "Didn't I tell you not to go?"

¹⁹The men of the city said to Elisha, "Look, our lord, this town is well situated, as you can see, but the water is bad and the land is unproductive."

²⁰"Bring me a new bowl," he said, "and put salt in it." So they brought it to him.

²¹Then he went out to the spring and threw the salt into it, saying, "This is what the LORD says: 'I have healed this water. Never again will it cause death or make the land unproductive.' " ²²And the water has remained wholesome to this day, according to the word Elisha had spoken.

²³From there Elisha went up to Bethel. As he was walking along the road, some youths came out of the town and jeered at him. "Go on up, you baldhead!" they said. "Go on up, you baldhead!" ²⁴He turned around, looked at them and called down a curse on them in the name of the LORD. Then two bears came out of the woods and mauled forty-two of the youths. ²⁵And he went on to Mount Carmel and from there returned to Samaria.

a 17 Hebrew *Jehoram,* a variant of *Joram*

ACTS 13:42–14:7

As Paul and Barnabas were leaving the synagogue, the people invited them to speak further about these things on the next Sabbath. ⁴³When the congregation was dismissed, many of the Jews and devout converts to Judaism followed Paul and Barnabas, who talked with them and urged them to continue in the grace of God.

⁴⁴On the next Sabbath almost the whole city gathered to hear the word of the Lord. ⁴⁵When the Jews saw the crowds, they were filled with jealousy and talked abusively against what Paul was saying.

⁴⁶Then Paul and Barnabas answered them boldly: "We had to speak the word of God to you first. Since you reject it and do not consider yourselves worthy of eternal life, we now turn to the Gentiles. ⁴⁷For this is what the Lord has commanded us:

"'I have made you[a] a light for the
        Gentiles,
    that you[a] may bring salvation to
        the ends of the earth.'[b]"

⁴⁸When the Gentiles heard this, they were glad and honored the word of the Lord; and all who were appointed for eternal life believed.

⁴⁹The word of the Lord spread through the whole region. ⁵⁰But the Jews incited the God-fearing women of high standing and the leading men of the city. They stirred up persecution against Paul and Barnabas, and expelled them from their region. ⁵¹So they shook the dust from their feet in protest against them and went to Iconium. ⁵²And the disciples were filled with joy and with the Holy Spirit.

14:1 At Iconium Paul and Barnabas went as usual into the Jewish synagogue. There they spoke so effectively that a great number of Jews and Gentiles believed. ²But the Jews who refused to believe stirred up the Gentiles and poisoned their minds against the brothers. ³So Paul and Barnabas spent considerable time there, speaking boldly for the Lord, who confirmed the message of his grace by enabling them to do miraculous signs and wonders. ⁴The people of the city were divided; some sided with the Jews, others with the apostles. ⁵There was a plot afoot among the Gentiles and Jews, together with their leaders, to mistreat them and stone them. ⁶But they found out about it and fled to the Lycaonian cities of Lystra and Derbe and to the surrounding country, ⁷where they continued to preach the good news.

a47 The Greek is singular.   *b47* Isaiah 49:6

PSALM 139:1-24

For the director of music. Of David. A psalm.

¹ O Lᴏʀᴅ, you have searched me
    and you know me.
² You know when I sit and when I rise;
    you perceive my thoughts from
        afar.
³ You discern my going out and my
        lying down;
    you are familiar with all my ways.
⁴ Before a word is on my tongue
    you know it completely, O Lᴏʀᴅ.

⁵ You hem me in—behind and before;
    you have laid your hand upon me.
⁶ Such knowledge is too wonderful
        for me,
    too lofty for me to attain.

⁷ Where can I go from your Spirit?
    Where can I flee from your
        presence?
⁸ If I go up to the heavens, you are
        there;
    if I make my bed in the depths,[a]
        you are there.
⁹ If I rise on the wings of the dawn,
    if I settle on the far side of the sea,
¹⁰ even there your hand will guide me,
    your right hand will hold me fast.

¹¹ If I say, "Surely the darkness will hide
        me
    and the light become night around
        me,"
¹² even the darkness will not be dark
        to you;
    the night will shine like the day,
    for darkness is as light to you.

¹³ **For you created my inmost being;**
    you knit me together in my
        mother's womb.

¹⁴**I praise you because I am fearfully
      and wonderfully made;
   your works are wonderful,
   I know that full well.**
¹⁵My frame was not hidden from you
      when I was made in the secret
      place.
   When I was woven together in the
      depths of the earth,
¹⁶   your eyes saw my unformed body.
   All the days ordained for me
      were written in your book
      before one of them came to be.

¹⁷How precious to*b* me are your
      thoughts, O God!
   How vast is the sum of them!
¹⁸Were I to count them,
      they would outnumber the grains
      of sand.
   When I awake,
      I am still with you.

¹⁹If only you would slay the wicked,
      O God!
   Away from me, you bloodthirsty
      men!
²⁰They speak of you with evil intent;
      your adversaries misuse your
      name.
²¹Do I not hate those who hate you,
      O LORD,
   and abhor those who rise up
      against you?
²²I have nothing but hatred for them;
   I count them my enemies.

²³Search me, O God, and know my
      heart;
   test me and know my anxious
      thoughts.
²⁴See if there is any offensive way in
      me,
   and lead me in the way
      everlasting.

a8 Hebrew *Sheol* *b17* Or *concerning*

PROVERBS 17:19-21
¹⁹**H**e who loves a quarrel loves sin;
   he who builds a high gate invites
      destruction.

²⁰A man of perverse heart does not
      prosper;
   he whose tongue is deceitful falls
      into trouble.

²¹To have a fool for a son brings grief;
   there is no joy for the father of
      a fool.

□ D A Y   1 7 3

GOD SIGHTINGS

June 22

2 KINGS 3:1–4:17
Joram*a* son of Ahab became king of Israel in Samaria in the eighteenth year of Jehoshaphat king of Judah, and he reigned twelve years. ²He did evil in the eyes of the LORD, but not as his father and mother had done. He got rid of the sacred stone of Baal that his father had made. ³Nevertheless he clung to the sins of Jeroboam son of Nebat, which he had caused Israel to commit; he did not turn away from them.

⁴Now Mesha king of Moab raised sheep, and he had to supply the king of Israel with a hundred thousand lambs and with the wool of a hundred thousand rams. ⁵But after Ahab died, the king of Moab rebelled against the king of Israel. ⁶So at that time King Joram set out from Samaria and mobilized all Israel. ⁷He also sent this message to Jehoshaphat king of Judah: "The king of Moab has rebelled against me. Will you go with me to fight against Moab?"

"I will go with you," he replied. "I am as you are, my people as your people, my horses as your horses."

⁸"By what route shall we attack?" he asked.

"Through the Desert of Edom," he answered.

⁹So the king of Israel set out with the king of Judah and the king of Edom. After a roundabout march of seven days,

the army had no more water for them-selves or for the animals with them.

¹⁰"What!" exclaimed the king of Is-rael. "Has the Lᴏʀᴅ called us three kings together only to hand us over to Moab?"

¹¹But Jehoshaphat asked, "Is there no prophet of the Lᴏʀᴅ here, that we may inquire of the Lᴏʀᴅ through him?"

An officer of the king of Israel an-swered, "Elisha son of Shaphat is here. He used to pour water on the hands of Elijah.ᵇ"

¹²Jehoshaphat said, "The word of the Lᴏʀᴅ is with him." So the king of Israel and Jehoshaphat and the king of Edom went down to him.

¹³Elisha said to the king of Israel, "What do we have to do with each other? Go to the prophets of your father and the prophets of your mother."

"No," the king of Israel answered, "be-cause it was the Lᴏʀᴅ who called us three kings together to hand us over to Moab."

¹⁴Elisha said, "As surely as the Lᴏʀᴅ Almighty lives, whom I serve, if I did not have respect for the presence of Jehosh-aphat king of Judah, I would not look at you or even notice you. ¹⁵But now bring me a harpist."

While the harpist was playing, the hand of the Lᴏʀᴅ came upon Elisha ¹⁶and he said, "This is what the Lᴏʀᴅ says: Make this valley full of ditches. ¹⁷For this is what the Lᴏʀᴅ says: You will see neither wind nor rain, yet this valley will be filled with water, and you, your cattle and your other animals will drink. ¹⁸This is an easy thing in the eyes of the Lᴏʀᴅ; he will also hand Moab over to you. ¹⁹You will overthrow every forti-fied city and every major town. You will cut down every good tree, stop up all the springs, and ruin every good field with stones."

²⁰The next morning, about the time for offering the sacrifice, there it was—water flowing from the direction of Edom! And the land was filled with water.

²¹Now all the Moabites had heard that the kings had come to fight against them; so every man, young and old, who

could bear arms was called up and sta-tioned on the border. ²²When they got up early in the morning, the sun was shining on the water. To the Moabites across the way, the water looked red—like blood. ²³"That's blood!" they said. "Those kings must have fought and slaughtered each other. Now to the plunder, Moab!"

²⁴But when the Moabites came to the camp of Israel, the Israelites rose up and fought them until they fled. And the Isra-elites invaded the land and slaughtered the Moabites. ²⁵They destroyed the towns, and each man threw a stone on every good field until it was covered. They stopped up all the springs and cut down every good tree. Only Kir Hareseth was left with its stones in place, but men armed with slings surrounded it and at-tacked it as well.

²⁶When the king of Moab saw that the battle had gone against him, he took with him seven hundred swordsmen to break through to the king of Edom, but they failed. ²⁷Then he took his firstborn son, who was to succeed him as king, and offered him as a sacrifice on the city wall. The fury against Israel was great; they withdrew and returned to their own land.

4:¹THE wife of a man from the company of the prophets cried out to Elisha, "Your servant my husband is dead, and you know that he revered the Lᴏʀᴅ. But now his creditor is coming to take my two boys as his slaves."

²Elisha replied to her, "How can I help you? Tell me, what do you have in your house?"

"Your servant has nothing there at all," she said, "except a little oil."

³Elisha said, "Go around and ask all your neighbors for empty jars. Don't ask for just a few. ⁴Then go inside and shut the door behind you and your sons. Pour oil into all the jars, and as each is filled, put it to one side."

⁵She left him and afterward shut the door behind her and her sons. They brought the jars to her and she kept

pouring. [6]When all the jars were full, she said to her son, "Bring me another one."

But he replied, "There is not a jar left." Then the oil stopped flowing.

[7]She went and told the man of God, and he said, "Go, sell the oil and pay your debts. You and your sons can live on what is left."

[8]One day Elisha went to Shunem. And a well-to-do woman was there, who urged him to stay for a meal. So whenever he came by, he stopped there to eat. [9]She said to her husband, "I know that this man who often comes our way is a holy man of God. [10]Let's make a small room on the roof and put in it a bed and a table, a chair and a lamp for him. Then he can stay there whenever he comes to us."

[11]One day when Elisha came, he went up to his room and lay down there. [12]He said to his servant Gehazi, "Call the Shunammite." So he called her, and she stood before him. [13]Elisha said to him, "Tell her, 'You have gone to all this trouble for us. Now what can be done for you? Can we speak on your behalf to the king or the commander of the army?'"

She replied, "I have a home among my own people."

[14]"What can be done for her?" Elisha asked.

Gehazi said, "Well, she has no son and her husband is old."

[15]Then Elisha said, "Call her." So he called her, and she stood in the doorway. [16]"About this time next year," Elisha said, "you will hold a son in your arms."

"No, my lord," she objected. "Don't mislead your servant, O man of God!"

[17]But the woman became pregnant, and the next year about that same time she gave birth to a son, just as Elisha had told her.

a 1 Hebrew *Jehoram*, a variant of *Joram*; also in verse 6
b 11 That is, he was Elijah's personal servant.

ACTS 14:8-28

[I]n Lystra there sat a man crippled in his feet, who was lame from birth and had never walked. [9]He listened to Paul as he was speaking. Paul looked directly at him, saw that he had faith to be healed [10]and called out, "Stand up on your feet!" At that, the man jumped up and began to walk.

[11]When the crowd saw what Paul had done, they shouted in the Lycaonian language, "The gods have come down to us in human form!" [12]Barnabas they called Zeus, and Paul they called Hermes because he was the chief speaker. [13]The priest of Zeus, whose temple was just outside the city, brought bulls and wreaths to the city gates because he and the crowd wanted to offer sacrifices to them.

[14]But when the apostles Barnabas and Paul heard of this, they tore their clothes and rushed out into the crowd, shouting: [15]"Men, why are you doing this? We too are only men, human like you. We are bringing you good news, telling you to turn from these worthless things to the living God, who made heaven and earth and sea and everything in them. [16]In the past, he let all nations go their own way. [17]Yet he has not left himself without testimony: He has shown kindness by giving you rain from heaven and crops in their seasons; he provides you with plenty of food and fills your hearts with joy." [18]Even with these words, they had difficulty keeping the crowd from sacrificing to them.

[19]Then some Jews came from Antioch and Iconium and won the crowd over. They stoned Paul and dragged him outside the city, thinking he was dead. [20]But after the disciples had gathered around him, he got up and went back into the city. The next day he and Barnabas left for Derbe.

[21]They preached the good news in that city and won a large number of disciples. Then they returned to Lystra, Iconium and Antioch, [22]strengthening the disciples and encouraging them to remain true to the faith. "We must go through many hardships to enter the kingdom of God," they said. [23]Paul and Barnabas appointed elders[a] for them in

each church and, with prayer and fasting, committed them to the Lord, in whom they had put their trust. 24After going through Pisidia, they came into Pamphylia, 25 and when they had preached the word in Perga, they went down to Attalia.

26 From Attalia they sailed back to Antioch, where they had been committed to the grace of God for the work they had now completed. 27On arriving there, they gathered the church together and reported all that God had done through them and how he had opened the door of faith to the Gentiles. 28And they stayed there a long time with the disciples.

a23 Or Barnabas ordained elders; or Barnabas had elders elected

PSALM 140:1-13
For the director of music. A psalm of David.

1 Rescue me, O Lord, from evil men;
    protect me from men of violence,
2who devise evil plans in their hearts
    and stir up war every day.
3They make their tongues as sharp as
        a serpent's;
    the poison of vipers is on their
        lips.   Selah

4Keep me, O Lord, from the hands of
        the wicked;
    protect me from men of violence
    who plan to trip my feet.
5Proud men have hidden a snare for
        me;
    they have spread out the cords of
        their net
    and have set traps for me along my
        path.   Selah

6O Lord, I say to you, "You are my
        God."
    Hear, O Lord, my cry for mercy.
7O Sovereign Lord, my strong
        deliverer,
    who shields my head in the day
        of battle—
8do not grant the wicked their desires,
        O Lord;
    do not let their plans succeed,
        or they will become proud.   Selah

9Let the heads of those who surround
        me
    be covered with the trouble their
        lips have caused.
10Let burning coals fall upon them;
    may they be thrown into the fire,
        into miry pits, never to rise.
11Let slanderers not be established in
        the land;
    may disaster hunt down men of
        violence.

12I know that the Lord secures
        justice for the poor
    and upholds the cause of the
        needy.
13Surely the righteous will praise
        your name
    and the upright will live before
        you.

PROVERBS 17:22
22A cheerful heart is good medicine,
    but a crushed spirit dries up the
        bones.

□ DAY 174

GOD SIGHTINGS

June 23

2 KINGS 4:18–5:27
The child [of the woman from Shunem] grew, and one day he went out to his father, who was with the reapers. 19"My head! My head!" he said to his father.

His father told a servant, "Carry him to his mother." 20After the servant had lifted him up and carried him to his mother, the boy sat on her lap until noon, and then he died. 21She went up and laid him on the bed of the man of God, then shut the door and went out.

22She called her husband and said, "Please send me one of the servants and a donkey so I can go to the man of God quickly and return."

23"Why go to him today?" he asked. "It's not the New Moon or the Sabbath."

"It's all right," she said.

24She saddled the donkey and said to her servant, "Lead on; don't slow down for me unless I tell you." 25So she set out and came to the man of God at Mount Carmel.

When he saw her in the distance, the man of God said to his servant Gehazi, "Look! There's the Shunammite! 26Run to meet her and ask her, 'Are you all right? Is your husband all right? Is your child all right?'"

"Everything is all right," she said.

27When she reached the man of God at the mountain, she took hold of his feet. Gehazi came over to push her away, but the man of God said, "Leave her alone! She is in bitter distress, but the LORD has hidden it from me and has not told me why."

28"Did I ask you for a son, my lord?" she said. "Didn't I tell you, 'Don't raise my hopes'?"

29Elisha said to Gehazi, "Tuck your cloak into your belt, take my staff in your hand and run. If you meet anyone, do not greet him, and if anyone greets you, do not answer. Lay my staff on the boy's face."

30But the child's mother said, "As surely as the LORD lives and as you live, I will not leave you." So he got up and followed her.

31Gehazi went on ahead and laid the staff on the boy's face, but there was no sound or response. So Gehazi went back to meet Elisha and told him, "The boy has not awakened."

32When Elisha reached the house, there was the boy lying dead on his couch. 33He went in, shut the door on the two of them and prayed to the LORD. 34Then he got on the bed and lay upon the boy, mouth to mouth, eyes to eyes, hands to hands. As he stretched himself out upon him, the boy's body grew warm. 35Elisha turned away and walked back and forth in the room and then got on the bed and stretched out upon him once more. The boy sneezed seven times and opened his eyes.

36Elisha summoned Gehazi and said, "Call the Shunammite." And he did. When she came, he said, "Take your son." 37She came in, fell at his feet and bowed to the ground. Then she took her son and went out.

38Elisha returned to Gilgal and there was a famine in that region. While the company of the prophets was meeting with him, he said to his servant, "Put on the large pot and cook some stew for these men."

39One of them went out into the fields to gather herbs and found a wild vine. He gathered some of its gourds and filled the fold of his cloak. When he returned, he cut them up into the pot of stew, though no one knew what they were. 40The stew was poured out for the men, but as they began to eat it, they cried out, "O man of God, there is death in the pot!" And they could not eat it.

41Elisha said, "Get some flour." He put it into the pot and said, "Serve it to the people to eat." And there was nothing harmful in the pot.

42A man came from Baal Shalishah, bringing the man of God twenty loaves of barley bread baked from the first ripe grain, along with some heads of new grain. "Give it to the people to eat," Elisha said.

43"How can I set this before a hundred men?" his servant asked.

But Elisha answered, "Give it to the people to eat. For this is what the LORD says: 'They will eat and have some left over.'" 44Then he set it before them, and they ate and had some left over, according to the word of the LORD.

5:1Now Naaman was commander of the army of the king of Aram. He was a great man in the sight of his master and highly regarded, because through him the LORD had given victory to Aram. He was a valiant soldier, but he had leprosy.a

2Now bands from Aram had gone out and had taken captive a young girl from Israel, and she served Naaman's wife. 3She said to her mistress, "If only my master would see the prophet who is in

Samaria! He would cure him of his leprosy."

⁴Naaman went to his master and told him what the girl from Israel had said. ⁵"By all means, go," the king of Aram replied. "I will send a letter to the king of Israel." So Naaman left, taking with him ten talentsᵇ of silver, six thousand shekelsᶜ of gold and ten sets of clothing. ⁶The letter that he took to the king of Israel read: "With this letter I am sending my servant Naaman to you so that you may cure him of his leprosy."

⁷As soon as the king of Israel read the letter, he tore his robes and said, "Am I God? Can I kill and bring back to life? Why does this fellow send someone to me to be cured of his leprosy? See how he is trying to pick a quarrel with me!"

⁸When Elisha the man of God heard that the king of Israel had torn his robes, he sent him this message: "Why have you torn your robes? Have the man come to me and he will know that there is a prophet in Israel." ⁹So Naaman went with his horses and chariots and stopped at the door of Elisha's house. ¹⁰Elisha sent a messenger to say to him, "Go, wash yourself seven times in the Jordan, and your flesh will be restored and you will be cleansed."

¹¹But Naaman went away angry and said, "I thought that he would surely come out to me and stand and call on the name of the LORD his God, wave his hand over the spot and cure me of my leprosy. ¹²Are not Abana and Pharpar, the rivers of Damascus, better than any of the waters of Israel? Couldn't I wash in them and be cleansed?" So he turned and went off in a rage.

¹³Naaman's servants went to him and said, "My father, if the prophet had told you to do some great thing, would you not have done it? How much more, then, when he tells you, 'Wash and be cleansed'!" ¹⁴So he went down and dipped himself in the Jordan seven times, as the man of God had told him, and his flesh was restored and became clean like that of a young boy.

¹⁵Then Naaman and all his atten-

dants went back to the man of God. He stood before him and said, "Now I know that there is no God in all the world except in Israel. Please accept now a gift from your servant."

¹⁶The prophet answered, "As surely as the LORD lives, whom I serve, I will not accept a thing." And even though Naaman urged him, he refused.

¹⁷"If you will not," said Naaman, "please let me, your servant, be given as much earth as a pair of mules can carry, for your servant will never again make burnt offerings and sacrifices to any other god but the LORD. ¹⁸But may the LORD forgive your servant for this one thing: When my master enters the temple of Rimmon to bow down and he is leaning on my arm and I bow there also—when I bow down in the temple of Rimmon, may the LORD forgive your servant for this."

¹⁹"Go in peace," Elisha said.

After Naaman had traveled some distance, ²⁰Gehazi, the servant of Elisha the man of God, said to himself, "My master was too easy on Naaman, this Aramean, by not accepting from him what he brought. As surely as the LORD lives, I will run after him and get something from him."

²¹So Gehazi hurried after Naaman. When Naaman saw him running toward him, he got down from the chariot to meet him. "Is everything all right?" he asked.

²²"Everything is all right," Gehazi answered. "My master sent me to say, 'Two young men from the company of the prophets have just come to me from the hill country of Ephraim. Please give them a talentᵈ of silver and two sets of clothing.'"

²³"By all means, take two talents," said Naaman. He urged Gehazi to accept them, and then tied up the two talents of silver in two bags, with two sets of clothing. He gave them to two of his servants, and they carried them ahead of Gehazi. ²⁴When Gehazi came to the hill, he took the things from the servants and put them away in the house.

He sent the men away and they left. 25 Then he went in and stood before his master Elisha.

"Where have you been, Gehazi?" Elisha asked.

"Your servant didn't go anywhere," Gehazi answered.

26 But Elisha said to him, "Was not my spirit with you when the man got down from his chariot to meet you? Is this the time to take money, or to accept clothes, olive groves, vineyards, flocks, herds, or menservants and maidservants? 27 Naaman's leprosy will cling to you and to your descendants forever." Then Gehazi went from Elisha's presence and he was leprous, as white as snow.

a 1 The Hebrew word was used for various diseases affecting the skin—not necessarily leprosy; also in verses 3, 6, 7, 11 and 27.   b 5 That is, about 750 pounds (about 340 kilograms)
c 5 That is, about 150 pounds (about 70 kilograms)
d 22 That is, about 75 pounds (about 34 kilograms)

ACTS 15:1-35

Some men came down from Judea to Antioch and were teaching the brothers: "Unless you are circumcised, according to the custom taught by Moses, you cannot be saved." 2 This brought Paul and Barnabas into sharp dispute and debate with them. So Paul and Barnabas were appointed, along with some other believers, to go up to Jerusalem to see the apostles and elders about this question. 3 The church sent them on their way, and as they traveled through Phoenicia and Samaria, they told how the Gentiles had been converted. This news made all the brothers very glad. 4 When they came to Jerusalem, they were welcomed by the church and the apostles and elders, to whom they reported everything God had done through them.

5 Then some of the believers who belonged to the party of the Pharisees stood up and said, "The Gentiles must be circumcised and required to obey the law of Moses."

6 The apostles and elders met to consider this question. 7 After much discussion, Peter got up and addressed them: "Brothers, you know that some time ago God made a choice among you that the Gentiles might hear from my lips the message of the gospel and believe. 8 God, who knows the heart, showed that he accepted them by giving the Holy Spirit to them, just as he did to us. 9 He made no distinction between us and them, for he purified their hearts by faith. 10 Now then, why do you try to test God by putting on the necks of the disciples a yoke that neither we nor our fathers have been able to bear? 11 No! We believe it is through the grace of our Lord Jesus that we are saved, just as they are."

12 The whole assembly became silent as they listened to Barnabas and Paul telling about the miraculous signs and wonders God had done among the Gentiles through them. 13 When they finished, James spoke up: "Brothers, listen to me. 14 Simon a has described to us how God at first showed his concern by taking from the Gentiles a people for himself. 15 The words of the prophets are in agreement with this, as it is written:

16 "'After this I will return
    and rebuild David's fallen tent.
  Its ruins I will rebuild,
    and I will restore it,
17 that the remnant of men may seek
      the Lord,
  and all the Gentiles who bear my
      name,
  says the Lord, who does these
      things'b
18 that have been known for ages.c

19 "It is my judgment, therefore, that we should not make it difficult for the Gentiles who are turning to God. 20 Instead we should write to them, telling them to abstain from food polluted by idols, from sexual immorality, from the meat of strangled animals and from blood. 21 For Moses has been preached in every city from the earliest times and is read in the synagogues on every Sabbath."

22 Then the apostles and elders, with the whole church, decided to choose some of their own men and send them to Antioch with Paul and Barnabas.

They chose Judas (called Barsabbas) and Silas, two men who were leaders among the brothers. [23] With them they sent the following letter:

The apostles and elders, your brothers,

To the Gentile believers in Antioch, Syria and Cilicia:

Greetings.

[24] We have heard that some went out from us without our authorization and disturbed you, troubling your minds by what they said. [25] So we all agreed to choose some men and send them to you with our dear friends Barnabas and Paul— [26] men who have risked their lives for the name of our Lord Jesus Christ. [27] Therefore we are sending Judas and Silas to confirm by word of mouth what we are writing. [28] It seemed good to the Holy Spirit and to us not to burden you with anything beyond the following requirements: [29] You are to abstain from food sacrificed to idols, from blood, from the meat of strangled animals and from sexual immorality. You will do well to avoid these things.

Farewell.

[30] The men were sent off and went down to Antioch, where they gathered the church together and delivered the letter. [31] The people read it and were glad for its encouraging message. [32] Judas and Silas, who themselves were prophets, said much to encourage and strengthen the brothers. [33] After spending some time there, they were sent off by the brothers with the blessing of peace to return to those who had sent them.[d] [35] But Paul and Barnabas remained in Antioch, where they and many others taught and preached the word of the Lord.

a14 Greek Simeon, a variant of Simon; that is, Peter b17 Amos 9:11,12 c17,18 Some manuscripts things'—/ 18known to the Lord for ages is his work d33 Some manuscripts them, 34but Silas decided to remain there

PSALM 141:1-10
A psalm of David.

[1] O LORD, I call to you; come quickly to me.
Hear my voice when I call to you.
[2] May my prayer be set before you like incense;
may the lifting up of my hands be like the evening sacrifice.

[3] Set a guard over my mouth, O LORD;
keep watch over the door of my lips.
[4] Let not my heart be drawn to what is evil,
to take part in wicked deeds with men who are evildoers;
let me not eat of their delicacies.

[5] Let a righteous man[a] strike me—it is a kindness;
let him rebuke me—it is oil on my head.
My head will not refuse it.

Yet my prayer is ever against the deeds of evildoers;
[6] their rulers will be thrown down from the cliffs,
and the wicked will learn that my words were well spoken.
[7] They will say, "As one plows and breaks up the earth,
so our bones have been scattered at the mouth of the grave.[b]"

[8] But my eyes are fixed on you, O Sovereign LORD;
in you I take refuge—do not give me over to death.
[9] Keep me from the snares they have laid for me,
from the traps set by evildoers.
[10] Let the wicked fall into their own nets, while I pass by in safety.

a5 Or Let the Righteous One b7 Hebrew Sheol

PROVERBS 17:23
[23] A wicked man accepts a bribe in secret
to pervert the course of justice.

GOD SIGHTINGS

June 24

2 KINGS 6:1–7:20

The company of the prophets said to Elisha, "Look, the place where we meet with you is too small for us. ²Let us go to the Jordan, where each of us can get a pole; and let us build a place there for us to live."

And he said, "Go."

³Then one of them said, "Won't you please come with your servants?"

"I will," Elisha replied. ⁴And he went with them.

They went to the Jordan and began to cut down trees. ⁵As one of them was cutting down a tree, the iron axhead fell into the water. "Oh, my lord," he cried out, "it was borrowed!"

⁶The man of God asked, "Where did it fall?" When he showed him the place, Elisha cut a stick and threw it there, and made the iron float. ⁷"Lift it out," he said. Then the man reached out his hand and took it.

⁸Now the king of Aram was at war with Israel. After conferring with his officers, he said, "I will set up my camp in such and such a place."

⁹The man of God sent word to the king of Israel: "Beware of passing that place, because the Arameans are going down there." ¹⁰So the king of Israel checked on the place indicated by the man of God. Time and again Elisha warned the king, so that he was on his guard in such places.

¹¹This enraged the king of Aram. He summoned his officers and demanded of them, "Will you not tell me which of us is on the side of the king of Israel?"

¹²"None of us, my lord the king," said one of his officers, "but Elisha, the prophet who is in Israel, tells the king of Israel the very words you speak in your bedroom."

¹³"Go, find out where he is," the king ordered, "so I can send men and capture him." The report came back: "He is in Dothan." ¹⁴Then he sent horses and chariots and a strong force there. They went by night and surrounded the city.

¹⁵When the servant of the man of God got up and went out early the next morning, an army with horses and chariots had surrounded the city. "Oh, my lord, what shall we do?" the servant asked.

¹⁶"Don't be afraid," the prophet answered. "Those who are with us are more than those who are with them."

¹⁷And Elisha prayed, "O Lord, open his eyes so he may see." Then the Lord opened the servant's eyes, and he looked and saw the hills full of horses and chariots of fire all around Elisha.

¹⁸As the enemy came down toward him, Elisha prayed to the Lord, "Strike these people with blindness." So he struck them with blindness, as Elisha had asked.

¹⁹Elisha told them, "This is not the road and this is not the city. Follow me, and I will lead you to the man you are looking for." And he led them to Samaria.

²⁰After they entered the city, Elisha said, "Lord, open the eyes of these men so they can see." Then the Lord opened their eyes and they looked, and there they were, inside Samaria.

²¹When the king of Israel saw them, he asked Elisha, "Shall I kill them, my father? Shall I kill them?"

²²"Do not kill them," he answered. "Would you kill men you have captured with your own sword or bow? Set food and water before them so that they may eat and drink and then go back to their master." ²³So he prepared a great feast for them, and after they had finished eating and drinking, he sent them away, and they returned to their master. So the bands from Aram stopped raiding Israel's territory.

²⁴Some time later, Ben-Hadad king of Aram mobilized his entire army and marched up and laid siege to Samaria. ²⁵There was a great famine in the city; the siege lasted so long that a donkey's

head sold for eighty shekels*a* of silver, and a quarter of a cab*b* of seed pods*c* for five shekels.*d*

26 As the king of Israel was passing by on the wall, a woman cried to him, "Help me, my lord the king!"

27 The king replied, "If the Lord does not help you, where can I get help for you? From the threshing floor? From the winepress?" 28 Then he asked her, "What's the matter?"

She answered, "This woman said to me, 'Give up your son so we may eat him today, and tomorrow we'll eat my son.' 29 So we cooked my son and ate him. The next day I said to her, 'Give up your son so we may eat him,' but she had hidden him."

30 When the king heard the woman's words, he tore his robes. As he went along the wall, the people looked, and there, underneath, he had sackcloth on his body. 31 He said, "May God deal with me, be it ever so severely, if the head of Elisha son of Shaphat remains on his shoulders today!"

32 Now Elisha was sitting in his house, and the elders were sitting with him. The king sent a messenger ahead, but before he arrived, Elisha said to the elders, "Don't you see how this murderer is sending someone to cut off my head? Look, when the messenger comes, shut the door and hold it shut against him. Is not the sound of his master's footsteps behind him?"

33 While he was still talking to them, the messenger came down to him. And ⌊the king⌋ said, "This disaster is from the Lord. Why should I wait for the Lord any longer?"

7:1 Elisha said, "Hear the word of the Lord. This is what the Lord says: About this time tomorrow, a seah*e* of flour will sell for a shekel*f* and two seahs*g* of barley for a shekel at the gate of Samaria."

2 The officer on whose arm the king was leaning said to the man of God, "Look, even if the Lord should open the floodgates of the heavens, could this happen?"

"You will see it with your own eyes," answered Elisha, "but you will not eat any of it!"

3 Now there were four men with leprosy*h* at the entrance of the city gate. They said to each other, "Why stay here until we die? 4 If we say, 'We'll go into the city'—the famine is there, and we will die. And if we stay here, we will die. So let's go over to the camp of the Arameans and surrender. If they spare us, we live; if they kill us, then we die."

5 At dusk they got up and went to the camp of the Arameans. When they reached the edge of the camp, not a man was there, 6 for the Lord had caused the Arameans to hear the sound of chariots and horses and a great army, so that they said to one another, "Look, the king of Israel has hired the Hittite and Egyptian kings to attack us!" 7 So they got up and fled in the dusk and abandoned their tents and their horses and donkeys. They left the camp as it was and ran for their lives.

8 The men who had leprosy reached the edge of the camp and entered one of the tents. They ate and drank, and carried away silver, gold and clothes, and went off and hid them. They returned and entered another tent and took some things from it and hid them also.

9 Then they said to each other, "We're not doing right. This is a day of good news and we are keeping it to ourselves. If we wait until daylight, punishment will overtake us. Let's go at once and report this to the royal palace."

10 So they went and called out to the city gatekeepers and told them, "We went into the Aramean camp and not a man was there—not a sound of anyone—only tethered horses and donkeys, and the tents left just as they were." 11 The gatekeepers shouted the news, and it was reported within the palace.

12 The king got up in the night and said to his officers, "I will tell you what the Arameans have done to us. They know we are starving; so they have left the camp to hide in the countryside,

thinking, 'They will surely come out, and then we will take them alive and get into the city.'"

[13]One of his officers answered, "Have some men take five of the horses that are left in the city. Their plight will be like that of all the Israelites left here— yes, they will only be like all these Israelites who are doomed. So let us send them to find out what happened."

[14]So they selected two chariots with their horses, and the king sent them after the Aramean army. He commanded the drivers, "Go and find out what has happened." [15]They followed them as far as the Jordan, and they found the whole road strewn with the clothing and equipment the Arameans had thrown away in their headlong flight. So the messengers returned and reported to the king. [16]Then the people went out and plundered the camp of the Arameans. So a seah of flour sold for a shekel, and two seahs of barley sold for a shekel, as the Lord had said.

[17]Now the king had put the officer on whose arm he leaned in charge of the gate, and the people trampled him in the gateway, and he died, just as the man of God had foretold when the king came down to his house. [18]It happened as the man of God had said to the king: "About this time tomorrow, a seah of flour will sell for a shekel and two seahs of barley for a shekel at the gate of Samaria."

[19]The officer had said to the man of God, "Look, even if the Lord should open the floodgates of the heavens, could this happen?" The man of God had replied, "You will see it with your own eyes, but you will not eat any of it!" [20]And that is exactly what happened to him, for the people trampled him in the gateway, and he died.

a25 That is, about 2 pounds (about 1 kilogram) b25 That is, probably about 1/2 pint (about 0.3 liter) c25 Or of doves' dung d25 That is, about 2 ounces (about 55 grams) e1 That is, probably about 7 quarts (about 7.3 liters); also in verses 16 and 18 f1 That is, about 2/5 ounce (about 11 grams); also in verses 16 and 18 g1 That is, probably about 13 quarts (about 15 liters); also in verses 16 and 18 h3 The Hebrew word is used for various diseases affecting the skin—not necessarily leprosy; also in verse 8.

ACTS 15:36–16:15

Some time later Paul said to Barnabas, "Let us go back and visit the brothers in all the towns where we preached the word of the Lord and see how they are doing." [37]Barnabas wanted to take John, also called Mark, with them, [38]but Paul did not think it wise to take him, because he had deserted them in Pamphylia and had not continued with them in the work. [39]They had such a sharp disagreement that they parted company. Barnabas took Mark and sailed for Cyprus, [40]but Paul chose Silas and left, commended by the brothers to the grace of the Lord. [41]He went through Syria and Cilicia, strengthening the churches.

[16:1]HE came to Derbe and then to Lystra, where a disciple named Timothy lived, whose mother was a Jewess and a believer, but whose father was a Greek. [2]The brothers at Lystra and Iconium spoke well of him. [3]Paul wanted to take him along on the journey, so he circumcised him because of the Jews who lived in that area, for they all knew that his father was a Greek. [4]As they traveled from town to town, they delivered the decisions reached by the apostles and elders in Jerusalem for the people to obey. [5]So the churches were strengthened in the faith and grew daily in numbers.

[6]Paul and his companions traveled throughout the region of Phrygia and Galatia, having been kept by the Holy Spirit from preaching the word in the province of Asia. [7]When they came to the border of Mysia, they tried to enter Bithynia, but the Spirit of Jesus would not allow them to. [8]So they passed by Mysia and went down to Troas. [9]During the night Paul had a vision of a man of Macedonia standing and begging him, "Come over to Macedonia and help us." [10]After Paul had seen the vision, we got ready at once to leave for Macedonia, concluding that God had called us to preach the gospel to them.

[11]From Troas we put out to sea and sailed straight for Samothrace, and the next day on to Neapolis. [12]From there we

traveled to Philippi, a Roman colony and the leading city of that district of Macedonia. And we stayed there several days. ¹³On the Sabbath we went outside the city gate to the river, where we expected to find a place of prayer. We sat down and began to speak to the women who had gathered there. ¹⁴One of those listening was a woman named Lydia, a dealer in purple cloth from the city of Thyatira, who was a worshiper of God. The Lord opened her heart to respond to Paul's message. ¹⁵When she and the members of her household were baptized, she invited us to her home. "If you consider me a believer in the Lord," she said, "come and stay at my house." And she persuaded us.

PSALM 142:1-7

A *maskil*[a] of David. When he was in the cave. A prayer.

¹ I cry aloud to the LORD;
    I lift up my voice to the LORD for mercy.
² I pour out my complaint before him;
    before him I tell my trouble.

³ When my spirit grows faint within me,
    it is you who know my way.
  In the path where I walk
    men have hidden a snare for me.
⁴ Look to my right and see;
    no one is concerned for me.
  I have no refuge;
    no one cares for my life.

⁵ I cry to you, O LORD;
    I say, "You are my refuge,
    my portion in the land of the living."
⁶ Listen to my cry,
    for I am in desperate need;
  rescue me from those who pursue me,
    for they are too strong for me.
⁷ Set me free from my prison,
    that I may praise your name.

  Then the righteous will gather about me
    because of your goodness to me.

ᵃTitle: Probably a literary or musical term

PROVERBS 17:24-25

²⁴ A discerning man keeps wisdom in view,
    but a fool's eyes wander to the ends of the earth.

²⁵ A foolish son brings grief to his father
    and bitterness to the one who bore him.

☐ D A Y   1 7 6

GOD SIGHTINGS

June 25

2 KINGS 8:1-9:13

Now Elisha had said to the woman whose son he had restored to life, "Go away with your family and stay for a while wherever you can, because the LORD has decreed a famine in the land that will last seven years." ²The woman proceeded to do as the man of God said. She and her family went away and stayed in the land of the Philistines seven years.

³At the end of the seven years she came back from the land of the Philistines and went to the king to beg for her house and land. ⁴The king was talking to Gehazi, the servant of the man of God, and had said, "Tell me about all the great things Elisha has done." ⁵Just as Gehazi was telling the king how Elisha had restored the dead to life, the woman whose son Elisha had brought back to life came to beg the king for her house and land.

Gehazi said, "This is the woman, my lord the king, and this is her son whom Elisha restored to life." ⁶The king asked the woman about it, and she told him.

Then he assigned an official to her case and said to him, "Give back everything that belonged to her, including all the income from her land from the day she left the country until now."

⁷Elisha went to Damascus, and Ben-

Hadad king of Aram was ill. When the king was told, "The man of God has come all the way up here," ⁸he said to Hazael, "Take a gift with you and go to meet the man of God. Consult the Lord through him; ask him, 'Will I recover from this illness?'"

⁹Hazael went to meet Elisha, taking with him as a gift forty camel-loads of all the finest wares of Damascus. He went in and stood before him, and said, "Your son Ben-Hadad king of Aram has sent me to ask, 'Will I recover from this illness?'"

¹⁰Elisha answered, "Go and say to him, 'You will certainly recover'; but*a* the Lord has revealed to me that he will in fact die." ¹¹He stared at him with a fixed gaze until Hazael felt ashamed. Then the man of God began to weep.

¹²"Why is my lord weeping?" asked Hazael.

"Because I know the harm you will do to the Israelites," he answered. "You will set fire to their fortified places, kill their young men with the sword, dash their little children to the ground, and rip open their pregnant women."

¹³Hazael said, "How could your servant, a mere dog, accomplish such a feat?"

"The Lord has shown me that you will become king of Aram," answered Elisha.

¹⁴Then Hazael left Elisha and returned to his master. When Ben-Hadad asked, "What did Elisha say to you?" Hazael replied, "He told me that you would certainly recover." ¹⁵But the next day he took a thick cloth, soaked it in water and spread it over the king's face, so that he died. Then Hazael succeeded him as king.

¹⁶In the fifth year of Joram son of Ahab king of Israel, when Jehoshaphat was king of Judah, Jehoram son of Jehoshaphat began his reign as king of Judah. ¹⁷He was thirty-two years old when he became king, and he reigned in Jerusalem eight years. ¹⁸He walked in the ways of the kings of Israel, as the house of Ahab had done, for he married a daughter of Ahab. He did evil in the eyes of the Lord. ¹⁹Nevertheless, for the sake of his servant David, the Lord was not willing to destroy Judah. He had promised to maintain a lamp for David and his descendants forever.

²⁰In the time of Jehoram, Edom rebelled against Judah and set up its own king. ²¹So Jehoram*b* went to Zair with all his chariots. The Edomites surrounded him and his chariot commanders, but he rose up and broke through by night; his army, however, fled back home. ²²To this day Edom has been in rebellion against Judah. Libnah revolted at the same time.

²³As for the other events of Jehoram's reign, and all he did, are they not written in the book of the annals of the kings of Judah? ²⁴Jehoram rested with his fathers and was buried with them in the City of David. And Ahaziah his son succeeded him as king.

²⁵In the twelfth year of Joram son of Ahab king of Israel, Ahaziah son of Jehoram king of Judah began to reign. ²⁶Ahaziah was twenty-two years old when he became king, and he reigned in Jerusalem one year. His mother's name was Athaliah, a granddaughter of Omri king of Israel. ²⁷He walked in the ways of the house of Ahab and did evil in the eyes of the Lord, as the house of Ahab had done, for he was related by marriage to Ahab's family.

²⁸Ahaziah went with Joram son of Ahab to war against Hazael king of Aram at Ramoth Gilead. The Arameans wounded Joram; ²⁹so King Joram returned to Jezreel to recover from the wounds the Arameans had inflicted on him at Ramoth*c* in his battle with Hazael king of Aram.

Then Ahaziah son of Jehoram king of Judah went down to Jezreel to see Joram son of Ahab, because he had been wounded.

⁹:¹The prophet Elisha summoned a man from the company of the prophets and said to him, "Tuck your cloak into your belt, take this flask of oil with you and

go to Ramoth Gilead. [2] When you get there, look for Jehu son of Jehoshaphat, the son of Nimshi. Go to him, get him away from his companions and take him into an inner room. [3] Then take the flask and pour the oil on his head and declare, 'This is what the LORD says: I anoint you king over Israel.' Then open the door and run; don't delay!"

[4] So the young man, the prophet, went to Ramoth Gilead. [5] When he arrived, he found the army officers sitting together. "I have a message for you, commander," he said.

"For which of us?" asked Jehu.

"For you, commander," he replied.

[6] Jehu got up and went into the house. Then the prophet poured the oil on Jehu's head and declared, "This is what the LORD, the God of Israel, says: 'I anoint you king over the LORD's people Israel. [7] You are to destroy the house of Ahab your master, and I will avenge the blood of my servants the prophets and the blood of all the LORD's servants shed by Jezebel. [8] The whole house of Ahab will perish. I will cut off from Ahab every last male in Israel—slave or free. [9] I will make the house of Ahab like the house of Jeroboam son of Nebat and like the house of Baasha son of Ahijah. [10] As for Jezebel, dogs will devour her on the plot of ground at Jezreel, and no one will bury her.'" Then he opened the door and ran.

[11] When Jehu went out to his fellow officers, one of them asked him, "Is everything all right? Why did this madman come to you?"

"You know the man and the sort of things he says," Jehu replied.

[12] "That's not true!" they said. "Tell us." Jehu said, "Here is what he told me: 'This is what the LORD says: I anoint you king over Israel.'"

[13] They hurried and took their cloaks and spread them under him on the bare steps. Then they blew the trumpet and shouted, "Jehu is king!"

a10 The Hebrew may also be read Go and say, 'You will certainly not recover,' for.   b21 Hebrew Joram, a variant of Jehoram; also in verses 23 and 24   c29 Hebrew Ramah, a variant of Ramoth

ACTS 16:16-40

Once when we [Paul and his coworkers] were going to the place of prayer, we were met by a slave girl who had a spirit by which she predicted the future. She earned a great deal of money for her owners by fortune-telling. [17] This girl followed Paul and the rest of us, shouting, "These men are servants of the Most High God, who are telling you the way to be saved." [18] She kept this up for many days. Finally Paul became so troubled that he turned around and said to the spirit, "In the name of Jesus Christ I command you to come out of her!" At that moment the spirit left her.

[19] When the owners of the slave girl realized that their hope of making money was gone, they seized Paul and Silas and dragged them into the marketplace to face the authorities. [20] They brought them before the magistrates and said, "These men are Jews, and are throwing our city into an uproar [21] by advocating customs unlawful for us Romans to accept or practice."

[22] The crowd joined in the attack against Paul and Silas, and the magistrates ordered them to be stripped and beaten. [23] After they had been severely flogged, they were thrown into prison, and the jailer was commanded to guard them carefully. [24] Upon receiving such orders, he put them in the inner cell and fastened their feet in the stocks.

[25] **About midnight Paul and Silas were praying and singing hymns to God, and the other prisoners were listening to them.** [26] Suddenly there was such a violent earthquake that the foundations of the prison were shaken. At once all the prison doors flew open, and everybody's chains came loose. [27] The jailer woke up, and when he saw the prison doors open, he drew his sword and was about to kill himself because he thought the prisoners had escaped. [28] But Paul shouted, "Don't harm yourself! We are all here!"

[29] The jailer called for lights, rushed in and fell trembling before Paul and Silas. [30] He then brought them out and

asked, "Sirs, what must I do to be saved?"

³¹They replied, "Believe in the Lord Jesus, and you will be saved—you and your household." ³²Then they spoke the word of the Lord to him and to all the others in his house. ³³At that hour of the night the jailer took them and washed their wounds; then immediately he and all his family were baptized. ³⁴The jailer brought them into his house and set a meal before them; he was filled with joy because he had come to believe in God—he and his whole family.

³⁵When it was daylight, the magistrates sent their officers to the jailer with the order: "Release those men." ³⁶The jailer told Paul, "The magistrates have ordered that you and Silas be released. Now you can leave. Go in peace."

³⁷But Paul said to the officers: "They beat us publicly without a trial, even though we are Roman citizens, and threw us into prison. And now do they want to get rid of us quietly? No! Let them come themselves and escort us out."

³⁸The officers reported this to the magistrates, and when they heard that Paul and Silas were Roman citizens, they were alarmed. ³⁹They came to appease them and escorted them from the prison, requesting them to leave the city. ⁴⁰After Paul and Silas came out of the prison, they went to Lydia's house, where they met with the brothers and encouraged them. Then they left.

PSALM 143:1-12
A psalm of David.

¹O LORD, hear my prayer,
    listen to my cry for mercy;
  in your faithfulness and
      righteousness
    come to my relief.
²Do not bring your servant into
      judgment,
    for no one living is righteous
      before you.

³The enemy pursues me,
    he crushes me to the ground;
  he makes me dwell in darkness
    like those long dead.
⁴So my spirit grows faint within me;
    my heart within me is dismayed.

⁵I remember the days of long ago;
    I meditate on all your works
    and consider what your hands
      have done.
⁶I spread out my hands to you;
    my soul thirsts for you like a
      parched land.   *Selah*

⁷Answer me quickly, O LORD;
    my spirit fails.
  Do not hide your face from me
    or I will be like those who go down
      to the pit.
⁸Let the morning bring me word of
      your unfailing love,
    for I have put my trust in you.
  Show me the way I should go,
    for to you I lift up my soul.
⁹Rescue me from my enemies, O LORD,
    for I hide myself in you.
¹⁰Teach me to do your will,
    for you are my God;
  may your good Spirit
    lead me on level ground.

¹¹For your name's sake, O LORD,
      preserve my life;
    in your righteousness, bring me
      out of trouble.
¹²In your unfailing love, silence my
      enemies;
    destroy all my foes,
    for I am your servant.

PROVERBS 17:26
²⁶It is not good to punish an innocent
      man,
    or to flog officials for their
      integrity.

GOD SIGHTINGS

June 26

2 KINGS 9:14–10:31

So Jehu son of Jehoshaphat, the son of Nimshi, conspired against Joram. (Now Joram and all Israel had been defending Ramoth Gilead against Hazael king of Aram, [15] but King Joram*a* had returned to Jezreel to recover from the wounds the Arameans had inflicted on him in the battle with Hazael king of Aram.) Jehu said, "If this is the way you feel, don't let anyone slip out of the city to go and tell the news in Jezreel." [16] Then he got into his chariot and rode to Jezreel, because Joram was resting there and Ahaziah king of Judah had gone down to see him.

[17] When the lookout standing on the tower in Jezreel saw Jehu's troops approaching, he called out, "I see some troops coming."

"Get a horseman," Joram ordered. "Send him to meet them and ask, 'Do you come in peace?'"

[18] The horseman rode off to meet Jehu and said, "This is what the king says: 'Do you come in peace?'"

"What do you have to do with peace?" Jehu replied. "Fall in behind me."

The lookout reported, "The messenger has reached them, but he isn't coming back."

[19] So the king sent out a second horseman. When he came to them he said, "This is what the king says: 'Do you come in peace?'"

Jehu replied, "What do you have to do with peace? Fall in behind me."

[20] The lookout reported, "He has reached them, but he isn't coming back either. The driving is like that of Jehu son of Nimshi—he drives like a madman."

[21] "Hitch up my chariot," Joram ordered. And when it was hitched up, Jo-

ram king of Israel and Ahaziah king of Judah rode out, each in his own chariot, to meet Jehu. They met him at the plot of ground that had belonged to Naboth the Jezreelite. [22] When Joram saw Jehu he asked, "Have you come in peace, Jehu?"

"How can there be peace," Jehu replied, "as long as all the idolatry and witchcraft of your mother Jezebel abound?"

[23] Joram turned about and fled, calling out to Ahaziah, "Treachery, Ahaziah!"

[24] Then Jehu drew his bow and shot Joram between the shoulders. The arrow pierced his heart and he slumped down in his chariot. [25] Jehu said to Bidkar, his chariot officer, "Pick him up and throw him on the field that belonged to Naboth the Jezreelite. Remember how you and I were riding together in chariots behind Ahab his father when the LORD made this prophecy about him: [26] 'Yesterday I saw the blood of Naboth and the blood of his sons, declares the LORD, and I will surely make you pay for it on this plot of ground, declares the LORD.'*b* Now then, pick him up and throw him on that plot, in accordance with the word of the LORD."

[27] When Ahaziah king of Judah saw what had happened, he fled up the road to Beth Haggan.*c* Jehu chased him, shouting, "Kill him too!" They wounded him in his chariot on the way up to Gur near Ibleam, but he escaped to Megiddo and died there. [28] His servants took him by chariot to Jerusalem and buried him with his fathers in his tomb in the City of David. [29] (In the eleventh year of Joram son of Ahab, Ahaziah had become king of Judah.)

[30] Then Jehu went to Jezreel. When Jezebel heard about it, she painted her eyes, arranged her hair and looked out of a window. [31] As Jehu entered the gate, she asked, "Have you come in peace, Zimri, you murderer of your master?"*d*

[32] He looked up at the window and called out, "Who is on my side? Who?" Two or three eunuchs looked down at him. [33] "Throw her down!" Jehu said. So

they threw her down, and some of her blood spattered the wall and the horses as they trampled her underfoot.

34Jehu went in and ate and drank. "Take care of that cursed woman," he said, "and bury her, for she was a king's daughter." 35But when they went out to bury her, they found nothing except her skull, her feet and her hands. 36They went back and told Jehu, who said, "This is the word of the LORD that he spoke through his servant Elijah the Tishbite: On the plot of ground at Jezreel dogs will devour Jezebel's flesh.*e* 37Jezebel's body will be like refuse on the ground in the plot at Jezreel, so that no one will be able to say, 'This is Jezebel.'"

10:1Now there were in Samaria seventy sons of the house of Ahab. So Jehu wrote letters and sent them to Samaria: to the officials of Jezreel,*f* to the elders and to the guardians of Ahab's children. He said, 2"As soon as this letter reaches you, since your master's sons are with you and you have chariots and horses, a fortified city and weapons, 3choose the best and most worthy of your master's sons and set him on his father's throne. Then fight for your master's house."

4But they were terrified and said, "If two kings could not resist him, how can we?"

5So the palace administrator, the city governor, the elders and the guardians sent this message to Jehu: "We are your servants and we will do anything you say. We will not appoint anyone as king; you do whatever you think best."

6Then Jehu wrote them a second letter, saying, "If you are on my side and will obey me, take the heads of your master's sons and come to me in Jezreel by this time tomorrow."

Now the royal princes, seventy of them, were with the leading men of the city, who were rearing them. 7When the letter arrived, these men took the princes and slaughtered all seventy of them. They put their heads in baskets and sent them to Jehu in Jezreel. 8When the messenger arrived, he told Jehu,

"They have brought the heads of the princes."

Then Jehu ordered, "Put them in two piles at the entrance of the city gate until morning."

9The next morning Jehu went out. He stood before all the people and said, "You are innocent. It was I who conspired against my master and killed him, but who killed all these? 10Know then, that not a word the LORD has spoken against the house of Ahab will fail. The LORD has done what he promised through his servant Elijah." 11So Jehu killed everyone in Jezreel who remained of the house of Ahab, as well as all his chief men, his close friends and his priests, leaving him no survivor.

12Jehu then set out and went toward Samaria. At Beth Eked of the Shepherds, 13he met some relatives of Ahaziah king of Judah and asked, "Who are you?"

They said, "We are relatives of Ahaziah, and we have come down to greet the families of the king and of the queen mother."

14"Take them alive!" he ordered. So they took them alive and slaughtered them by the well of Beth Eked—forty-two men. He left no survivor.

15After he left there, he came upon Jehonadab son of Recab, who was on his way to meet him. Jehu greeted him and said, "Are you in accord with me, as I am with you?"

"I am," Jehonadab answered.

"If so," said Jehu, "give me your hand." So he did, and Jehu helped him up into the chariot. 16Jehu said, "Come with me and see my zeal for the LORD." Then he had him ride along in his chariot.

17When Jehu came to Samaria, he killed all who were left there of Ahab's family; he destroyed them, according to the word of the LORD spoken to Elijah.

18Then Jehu brought all the people together and said to them, "Ahab served Baal a little; Jehu will serve him much. 19Now summon all the prophets of Baal, all his ministers and all his priests. See that no one is missing, because I am going to hold a great sacrifice for Baal. Anyone who fails to come will no longer live." But Jehu was acting deceptively in order to destroy the ministers of Baal.

20Jehu said, "Call an assembly in honor of Baal." So they proclaimed it. 21Then he sent word throughout Israel, and all the ministers of Baal came; not one stayed away. They crowded into the temple of Baal until it was full from one end to the other. 22And Jehu said to the keeper of the wardrobe, "Bring robes for all the ministers of Baal." So he brought out robes for them.

23Then Jehu and Jehonadab son of Recab went into the temple of Baal. Jehu said to the ministers of Baal, "Look around and see that no servants of the LORD are here with you—only ministers of Baal." 24So they went in to make sacrifices and burnt offerings. Now Jehu had posted eighty men outside with this warning: "If one of you lets any of the men I am placing in your hands escape, it will be your life for his life."

25As soon as Jehu had finished making the burnt offering, he ordered the guards and officers: "Go in and kill them; let no one escape." So they cut them down with the sword. The guards and officers threw the bodies out and then entered the inner shrine of the temple of Baal. 26They brought the sacred stone out of the temple of Baal and burned it. 27They demolished the sacred stone of Baal and tore down the temple of Baal, and people have used it for a latrine to this day.

28So Jehu destroyed Baal worship in Israel. 29However, he did not turn away from the sins of Jeroboam son of Nebat, which he had caused Israel to commit— the worship of the golden calves at Bethel and Dan.

30The LORD said to Jehu, "Because you have done well in accomplishing what is right in my eyes and have done to the house of Ahab all I had in mind to do, your descendants will sit on the throne of Israel to the fourth generation." 31Yet Jehu was not careful to keep the law of the LORD, the God of Israel, with all his heart. He did not turn away from the sins of Jeroboam, which he had caused Israel to commit.

a15 Hebrew Jehoram, a variant of Joram; also in verses 17 and 21-24   b26 See 1 Kings 21:19.   c27 Or fled by way of the garden house   d31 Or "Did Zimri have peace, who murdered his master?"   e36 See 1 Kings 21:23.   f1 Hebrew; some Septuagint manuscripts and Vulgate of the city

ACTS 17:1-34

When they [Paul and his coworkers] had passed through Amphipolis and Apollonia, they came to Thessalonica, where there was a Jewish synagogue. 2As his custom was, Paul went into the synagogue, and on three Sabbath days he reasoned with them from the Scriptures, 3explaining and proving that the Christa had to suffer and rise from the dead. "This Jesus I am proclaiming to you is the Christ,a" he said. 4Some of the Jews were persuaded and joined Paul and Silas, as did a large number of God-fearing Greeks and not a few prominent women.

5But the Jews were jealous; so they rounded up some bad characters from the marketplace, formed a mob and started a riot in the city. They rushed to Jason's house in search of Paul and Silas in order to bring them out to the crowd.b 6But when they did not find them, they dragged Jason and some other brothers before the city officials, shouting: "These men who have caused trouble all over the world have now come here, 7and Jason has welcomed them into his house. They are all defying Caesar's decrees, saying that there is another king, one called Jesus." 8When they heard this, the crowd and the city officials were thrown into turmoil. 9Then they made Jason and the others post bond and let them go.

10As soon as it was night, the brothers sent Paul and Silas away to Berea. On arriving there, they went to the Jewish synagogue. 11Now the Bereans were of more noble character than the Thessalonians, for they received the message with great eagerness and examined the Scriptures every day to see if what Paul said was true. 12Many of the Jews believed, as did also a number of prominent Greek women and many Greek men.

13 When the Jews in Thessalonica learned that Paul was preaching the word of God at Berea, they went there too, agitating the crowds and stirring them up. 14 The brothers immediately sent Paul to the coast, but Silas and Timothy stayed at Berea. 15 The men who escorted Paul brought him to Athens and then left with instructions for Silas and Timothy to join him as soon as possible.

16 While Paul was waiting for them in Athens, he was greatly distressed to see that the city was full of idols. 17 So he reasoned in the synagogue with the Jews and the God-fearing Greeks, as well as in the marketplace day by day with those who happened to be there. 18 A group of Epicurean and Stoic philosophers began to dispute with him. Some of them asked, "What is this babbler trying to say?" Others remarked, "He seems to be advocating foreign gods." They said this because Paul was preaching the good news about Jesus and the resurrection. 19 Then they took him and brought him to a meeting of the Areopagus, where they said to him, "May we know what this new teaching is that you are presenting? 20 You are bringing some strange ideas to our ears, and we want to know what they mean." 21 (All the Athenians and the foreigners who lived there spent their time doing nothing but talking about and listening to the latest ideas.)

22 Paul then stood up in the meeting of the Areopagus and said: "Men of Athens! I see that in every way you are very religious. 23 For as I walked around and looked carefully at your objects of worship, I even found an altar with this inscription: TO AN UNKNOWN GOD. Now what you worship as something unknown I am going to proclaim to you.

24 "The God who made the world and everything in it is the Lord of heaven and earth and does not live in temples built by hands. 25 And he is not served by human hands, as if he needed anything, because he himself gives all men life and breath and everything else. 26 From one man he made every nation of men, that they should inhabit the whole

earth; and he determined the times set for them and the exact places where they should live. 27 God did this so that men would seek him and perhaps reach out for him and find him, though he is not far from each one of us. 28 'For in him we live and move and have our being.' As some of your own poets have said, 'We are his offspring.'

29 "Therefore since we are God's offspring, we should not think that the divine being is like gold or silver or stone—an image made by man's design and skill. 30 In the past God overlooked such ignorance, but now he commands all people everywhere to repent. 31 For he has set a day when he will judge the world with justice by the man he has appointed. He has given proof of this to all men by raising him from the dead."

32 When they heard about the resurrection of the dead, some of them sneered, but others said, "We want to hear you again on this subject." 33 At that, Paul left the Council. 34 A few men became followers of Paul and believed. Among them was Dionysius, a member of the Areopagus, also a woman named Damaris, and a number of others.

a 3 Or Messiah   b 5 Or the assembly of the people

PSALM 144:1-15
Of David.

1 Praise be to the LORD my Rock,
    who trains my hands for war,
    my fingers for battle.
2 He is my loving God and my fortress,
    my stronghold and my deliverer,
  my shield, in whom I take refuge,
    who subdues peoples[a] under me.

3 O LORD, what is man that you care
    for him,
    the son of man that you think
    of him?
4 Man is like a breath;
    his days are like a fleeting shadow.

5 Part your heavens, O LORD, and come
    down;
    touch the mountains, so that they
    smoke.

⁶Send forth lightning and scatter ⌐the
enemies⌐;
shoot your arrows and rout them.
⁷Reach down your hand from on high;
deliver me and rescue me
from the mighty waters,
from the hands of foreigners
⁸whose mouths are full of lies,
whose right hands are deceitful.

⁹I will sing a new song to you, O God;
on the ten-stringed lyre I will
make music to you,
¹⁰to the One who gives victory to kings,
who delivers his servant David
from the deadly sword.

¹¹Deliver me and rescue me
from the hands of foreigners
whose mouths are full of lies,
whose right hands are deceitful.

¹²Then our sons in their youth
will be like well-nurtured plants,
and our daughters will be like pillars
carved to adorn a palace.
¹³Our barns will be filled
with every kind of provision.
Our sheep will increase by
thousands,
by tens of thousands in our fields;
¹⁴   our oxen will draw heavy loads.ᵇ
There will be no breaching of walls,
no going into captivity,
no cry of distress in our streets.

¹⁵Blessed are the people of whom this
is true;
blessed are the people whose God
is the Lord.

ᵃ2 Many manuscripts of the Masoretic Text, Dead Sea
Scrolls, Aquila, Jerome and Syriac; most manuscripts of the
Masoretic Text *subdues my people*   ᵇ14 Or *our chieftains
will be firmly established*

PROVERBS 17:27-28
²⁷A man of knowledge uses words
with restraint,
and a man of understanding is
even-tempered.

²⁸Even a fool is thought wise if he
keeps silent,
and discerning if he holds his
tongue.

☐ DAY 178

GOD SIGHTINGS

June 27

2 KINGS 10:32–12:21
In those days the Lord began to reduce
the size of Israel. Hazael overpowered
the Israelites throughout their territory
³³east of the Jordan in all the land of Gilead (the region of Gad, Reuben and Manasseh), from Aroer by the Arnon Gorge
through Gilead to Bashan.

³⁴As for the other events of Jehu's
reign, all he did, and all his achievements, are they not written in the book
of the annals of the kings of Israel?

³⁵Jehu rested with his fathers and
was buried in Samaria. And Jehoahaz
his son succeeded him as king. ³⁶The
time that Jehu reigned over Israel in Samaria was twenty-eight years.

¹¹:¹WHEN Athaliah the mother of Ahaziah saw that her son was dead, she proceeded to destroy the whole royal
family. ²But Jehosheba, the daughter of
King Jehoramᵃ and sister of Ahaziah,
took Joash son of Ahaziah and stole him
away from among the royal princes,
who were about to be murdered. She
put him and his nurse in a bedroom to
hide him from Athaliah; so he was not
killed. ³He remained hidden with his
nurse at the temple of the Lord for six
years while Athaliah ruled the land.

⁴In the seventh year Jehoiada sent for
the commanders of units of a hundred,
the Carites and the guards and had
them brought to him at the temple of
the Lord. He made a covenant with
them and put them under oath at the
temple of the Lord. Then he showed
them the king's son. ⁵He commanded
them, saying, "This is what you are to do:
You who are in the three companies that
are going on duty on the Sabbath—a
third of you guarding the royal palace,
⁶a third at the Sur Gate, and a third at
the gate behind the guard, who take
turns guarding the temple— ⁷and you

who are in the other two companies that normally go off Sabbath duty are all to guard the temple for the king. 8Station yourselves around the king, each man with his weapon in his hand. Anyone who approaches your ranksᵇ must be put to death. Stay close to the king wherever he goes."

9The commanders of units of a hundred did just as Jehoiada the priest ordered. Each one took his men—those who were going on duty on the Sabbath and those who were going off duty—and came to Jehoiada the priest. 10Then he gave the commanders the spears and shields that had belonged to King David and that were in the temple of the LORD. 11The guards, each with his weapon in his hand, stationed themselves around the king—near the altar and the temple, from the south side to the north side of the temple.

12Jehoiada brought out the king's son and put the crown on him; he presented him with a copy of the covenant and proclaimed him king. They anointed him, and the people clapped their hands and shouted, "Long live the king!"

13When Athaliah heard the noise made by the guards and the people, she went to the people at the temple of the LORD. 14She looked and there was the king, standing by the pillar, as the custom was. The officers and the trumpeters were beside the king, and all the people of the land were rejoicing and blowing trumpets. Then Athaliah tore her robes and called out, "Treason! Treason!"

15Jehoiada the priest ordered the commanders of units of a hundred, who were in charge of the troops: "Bring her out between the ranksᶜ and put to the sword anyone who follows her." For the priest had said, "She must not be put to death in the temple of the LORD." 16So they seized her as she reached the place where the horses enter the palace grounds, and there she was put to death.

17Jehoiada then made a covenant between the LORD and the king and people that they would be the LORD's people. He also made a covenant between the king and the people. 18All the people of the land went to the temple of Baal and tore it down. They smashed the altars and idols to pieces and killed Mattan the priest of Baal in front of the altars.

Then Jehoiada the priest posted guards at the temple of the LORD. 19He took with him the commanders of hundreds, the Carites, the guards and all the people of the land, and together they brought the king down from the temple of the LORD and went into the palace, entering by way of the gate of the guards. The king then took his place on the royal throne, 20and all the people of the land rejoiced. And the city was quiet, because Athaliah had been slain with the sword at the palace.

21Joashᵈ was seven years old when he began to reign.

12:1In the seventh year of Jehu, Joashᵉ became king, and he reigned in Jerusalem forty years. His mother's name was Zibiah; she was from Beersheba. 2Joash did what was right in the eyes of the LORD all the years Jehoiada the priest instructed him. 3The high places, however, were not removed; the people continued to offer sacrifices and burn incense there.

4Joash said to the priests, "Collect all the money that is brought as sacred offerings to the temple of the LORD—the money collected in the census, the money received from personal vows and the money brought voluntarily to the temple. 5Let every priest receive the money from one of the treasurers, and let it be used to repair whatever damage is found in the temple."

6But by the twenty-third year of King Joash the priests still had not repaired the temple. 7Therefore King Joash summoned Jehoiada the priest and the other priests and asked them, "Why aren't you repairing the damage done to the temple? Take no more money from your treasurers, but hand it over for repairing the temple." 8The priests agreed that they would not collect any more money from the people and that they would not repair the temple themselves.

9Jehoiada the priest took a chest and bored a hole in its lid. He placed it beside the altar, on the right side as one enters the temple of the LORD. The priests who guarded the entrance put into the chest all the money that was brought to the temple of the LORD. 10Whenever they saw that there was a large amount of money in the chest, the royal secretary and the high priest came, counted the money that had been brought into the temple of the LORD and put it into bags. 11When the amount had been determined, they gave the money to the men appointed to supervise the work on the temple. With it they paid those who worked on the temple of the LORD—the carpenters and builders, 12the masons and stonecutters. They purchased timber and dressed stone for the repair of the temple of the LORD, and met all the other expenses of restoring the temple.

13The money brought into the temple was not spent for making silver basins, wick trimmers, sprinkling bowls, trumpets or any other articles of gold or silver for the temple of the LORD; 14it was paid to the workmen, who used it to repair the temple. 15They did not require an accounting from those to whom they gave the money to pay the workers, because they acted with complete honesty. 16The money from the guilt offerings and sin offerings was not brought into the temple of the LORD; it belonged to the priests.

17About this time Hazael king of Aram went up and attacked Gath and captured it. Then he turned to attack Jerusalem. 18But Joash king of Judah took all the sacred objects dedicated by his fathers—Jehoshaphat, Jehoram and Ahaziah, the kings of Judah—and the gifts he himself had dedicated and all the gold found in the treasuries of the temple of the LORD and of the royal palace, and he sent them to Hazael king of Aram, who then withdrew from Jerusalem.

19As for the other events of the reign of Joash, and all he did, are they not written in the book of the annals of the kings of Judah? 20His officials conspired against him and assassinated him at Beth Millo, on the road down to Silla. 21The officials who murdered him were Jozabad son of Shimeath and Jehozabad son of Shomer. He died and was buried with his fathers in the City of David. And Amaziah his son succeeded him as king.

a2 Hebrew *Joram*, a variant of *Jehoram*   b8 Or *approaches the precincts*   c15 Or *out from the precincts*   d21 Hebrew *Jehoash*, a variant of *Joash*   e1 Hebrew *Jehoash*, a variant of *Joash*; also in verses 2, 4, 6, 7 and 18

ACTS 18:1-22

After this, Paul left Athens and went to Corinth. 2There he met a Jew named Aquila, a native of Pontus, who had recently come from Italy with his wife Priscilla, because Claudius had ordered all the Jews to leave Rome. Paul went to see them, 3and because he was a tentmaker as they were, he stayed and worked with them. 4Every Sabbath he reasoned in the synagogue, trying to persuade Jews and Greeks.

5When Silas and Timothy came from Macedonia, Paul devoted himself exclusively to preaching, testifying to the Jews that Jesus was the Christ.a 6But when the Jews opposed Paul and became abusive, he shook out his clothes in protest and said to them, "Your blood be on your own heads! I am clear of my responsibility. From now on I will go to the Gentiles."

7Then Paul left the synagogue and went next door to the house of Titius Justus, a worshiper of God. 8Crispus, the synagogue ruler, and his entire household believed in the Lord; and many of the Corinthians who heard him believed and were baptized.

9One night the Lord spoke to Paul in a vision: "Do not be afraid; keep on speaking, do not be silent. 10For I am with you, and no one is going to attack and harm you, because I have many people in this city." 11So Paul stayed for a year and a half, teaching them the word of God.

¹²While Gallio was proconsul of Achaia, the Jews made a united attack on Paul and brought him into court. ¹³"This man," they charged, "is persuading the people to worship God in ways contrary to the law."

¹⁴Just as Paul was about to speak, Gallio said to the Jews, "If you Jews were making a complaint about some misdemeanor or serious crime, it would be reasonable for me to listen to you. ¹⁵But since it involves questions about words and names and your own law—settle the matter yourselves. I will not be a judge of such things." ¹⁶So he had them ejected from the court. ¹⁷Then they all turned on Sosthenes the synagogue ruler and beat him in front of the court. But Gallio showed no concern whatever.

¹⁸Paul stayed on in Corinth for some time. Then he left the brothers and sailed for Syria, accompanied by Priscilla and Aquila. Before he sailed, he had his hair cut off at Cenchrea because of a vow he had taken. ¹⁹They arrived at Ephesus, where Paul left Priscilla and Aquila. He himself went into the synagogue and reasoned with the Jews. ²⁰When they asked him to spend more time with them, he declined. ²¹But as he left, he promised, "I will come back if it is God's will." Then he set sail from Ephesus. ²²When he landed at Caesarea, he went up and greeted the church and then went down to Antioch.

a5 Or Messiah; also in verse 28

PSALM 145:1-21ᵃ
A psalm of praise. Of David.

¹ I will exalt you, my God the King;
  I will praise your name for ever
    and ever.
² Every day I will praise you
  and extol your name for ever and
    ever.

³ Great is the Lᴏʀᴅ and most worthy
    of praise;
  his greatness no one can fathom.

⁴ One generation will commend your
    works to another;
  they will tell of your mighty acts.
⁵ They will speak of the glorious
    splendor of your majesty,
  and I will meditate on your
    wonderful works.ᵇ
⁶ They will tell of the power of your
    awesome works,
  and I will proclaim your great
    deeds.
⁷ They will celebrate your abundant
    goodness
  and joyfully sing of your
    righteousness.

⁸ **The Lᴏʀᴅ is gracious and
    compassionate,
  slow to anger and rich in love.**
⁹ **The Lᴏʀᴅ is good to all;
  he has compassion on all he has
    made.**
¹⁰ All you have made will praise you,
    O Lᴏʀᴅ;
  your saints will extol you.
¹¹ They will tell of the glory of your
    kingdom
  and speak of your might,
¹² so that all men may know of your
    mighty acts
  and the glorious splendor of your
    kingdom.
¹³ Your kingdom is an everlasting
    kingdom,
  and your dominion endures
    through all generations.

  The Lᴏʀᴅ is faithful to all his
    promises
  and loving toward all he has
    made.ᶜ
¹⁴ The Lᴏʀᴅ upholds all those who fall
  and lifts up all who are bowed
    down.
¹⁵ The eyes of all look to you,
  and you give them their food at
    the proper time.
¹⁶ You open your hand
  and satisfy the desires of every
    living thing.

¹⁷ The Lᴏʀᴅ is righteous in all his ways
  and loving toward all he has made.

18 The LORD is near to all who call on
  him,
  to all who call on him in truth.
19 He fulfills the desires of those who
  fear him;
  he hears their cry and saves them.
20 The LORD watches over all who love
  him,
  but all the wicked he will destroy.
21 My mouth will speak in praise of the
  LORD.
  Let every creature praise his holy
  name
  for ever and ever.

aThis psalm is an acrostic poem, the verses of which
(including verse 13b) begin with the successive letters of the
Hebrew alphabet.   b5 Dead Sea Scrolls and Syriac (see also
Septuagint); Masoretic Text *On the glorious splendor of your
majesty / and on your wonderful works I will meditate*
c13 One manuscript of the Masoretic Text, Dead Sea Scrolls
and Syriac (see also Septuagint); most manuscripts of the
Masoretic Text do not have the last two lines of verse 13.

PROVERBS 18:1
An unfriendly man pursues selfish
  ends;
  he defies all sound judgment.

☐ D A Y 1 7 9

GOD SIGHTINGS

June 28

2 KINGS 13:1–14:29

In the twenty-third year of Joash son of
Ahaziah king of Judah, Jehoahaz son of
Jehu became king of Israel in Samaria,
and he reigned seventeen years. 2 He did
evil in the eyes of the LORD by following
the sins of Jeroboam son of Nebat,
which he had caused Israel to commit,
and he did not turn away from them.
3 So the LORD's anger burned against Israel, and for a long time he kept them
under the power of Hazael king of Aram
and Ben-Hadad his son.

4 Then Jehoahaz sought the LORD's favor, and the LORD listened to him, for he
saw how severely the king of Aram was
oppressing Israel. 5 The LORD provided a

deliverer for Israel, and they escaped
from the power of Aram. So the Israelites
lived in their own homes as they had before. 6 But they did not turn away from
the sins of the house of Jeroboam, which
he had caused Israel to commit; they
continued in them. Also, the Asherah
pole a remained standing in Samaria.

7 Nothing had been left of the army of
Jehoahaz except fifty horsemen, ten
chariots and ten thousand foot soldiers,
for the king of Aram had destroyed the
rest and made them like the dust at
threshing time.

8 As for the other events of the reign of
Jehoahaz, all he did and his achievements, are they not written in the book
of the annals of the kings of Israel? 9 Jehoahaz rested with his fathers and was
buried in Samaria. And Jehoash b his son
succeeded him as king.

10 In the thirty-seventh year of Joash
king of Judah, Jehoash son of Jehoahaz
became king of Israel in Samaria, and he
reigned sixteen years. 11 He did evil in
the eyes of the LORD and did not turn
away from any of the sins of Jeroboam
son of Nebat, which he had caused Israel to commit; he continued in them.

12 As for the other events of the reign
of Jehoash, all he did and his achievements, including his war against Amaziah king of Judah, are they not written
in the book of the annals of the kings of
Israel? 13 Jehoash rested with his fathers, and Jeroboam succeeded him on
the throne. Jehoash was buried in Samaria with the kings of Israel.

14 Now Elisha was suffering from the
illness from which he died. Jehoash
king of Israel went down to see him and
wept over him. "My father! My father!"
he cried. "The chariots and horsemen
of Israel!"

15 Elisha said, "Get a bow and some arrows," and he did so. 16 "Take the bow in
your hands," he said to the king of Israel.
When he had taken it, Elisha put his
hands on the king's hands.

17 "Open the east window," he said, and
he opened it. "Shoot!" Elisha said, and
he shot. "The LORD's arrow of victory,

the arrow of victory over Aram!" Elisha declared. "You will completely destroy the Arameans at Aphek."

18Then he said, "Take the arrows," and the king took them. Elisha told him, "Strike the ground." He struck it three times and stopped. 19The man of God was angry with him and said, "You should have struck the ground five or six times; then you would have defeated Aram and completely destroyed it. But now you will defeat it only three times."

20Elisha died and was buried.

Now Moabite raiders used to enter the country every spring. 21Once while some Israelites were burying a man, suddenly they saw a band of raiders; so they threw the man's body into Elisha's tomb. When the body touched Elisha's bones, the man came to life and stood up on his feet.

22Hazael king of Aram oppressed Israel throughout the reign of Jehoahaz. 23But the LORD was gracious to them and had compassion and showed concern for them because of his covenant with Abraham, Isaac and Jacob. To this day he has been unwilling to destroy them or banish them from his presence.

24Hazael king of Aram died, and Ben-Hadad his son succeeded him as king. 25Then Jehoash son of Jehoahaz recaptured from Ben-Hadad son of Hazael the towns he had taken in battle from his father Jehoahaz. Three times Jehoash defeated him, and so he recovered the Israelite towns.

14:1In the second year of Jehoash*c* son of Jehoahaz king of Israel, Amaziah son of Joash king of Judah began to reign. 2He was twenty-five years old when he became king, and he reigned in Jerusalem twenty-nine years. His mother's name was Jehoaddin; she was from Jerusalem. 3He did what was right in the eyes of the LORD, but not as his father David had done. In everything he followed the example of his father Joash. 4The high places, however, were not removed; the people continued to offer sacrifices and burn incense there.

5After the kingdom was firmly in his grasp, he executed the officials who had murdered his father the king. 6Yet he did not put the sons of the assassins to death, in accordance with what is written in the Book of the Law of Moses where the LORD commanded: "Fathers shall not be put to death for their children, nor children put to death for their fathers; each is to die for his own sins."*d*

7He was the one who defeated ten thousand Edomites in the Valley of Salt and captured Sela in battle, calling it Joktheel, the name it has to this day.

8Then Amaziah sent messengers to Jehoash son of Jehoahaz, the son of Jehu, king of Israel, with the challenge: "Come, meet me face to face."

9But Jehoash king of Israel replied to Amaziah king of Judah: "A thistle in Lebanon sent a message to a cedar in Lebanon, 'Give your daughter to my son in marriage.' Then a wild beast in Lebanon came along and trampled the thistle underfoot. 10You have indeed defeated Edom and now you are arrogant. Glory in your victory, but stay at home! Why ask for trouble and cause your own downfall and that of Judah also?"

11Amaziah, however, would not listen, so Jehoash king of Israel attacked. He and Amaziah king of Judah faced each other at Beth Shemesh in Judah. 12Judah was routed by Israel, and every man fled to his home. 13Jehoash king of Israel captured Amaziah king of Judah, the son of Joash, the son of Ahaziah, at Beth Shemesh. Then Jehoash went to Jerusalem and broke down the wall of Jerusalem from the Ephraim Gate to the Corner Gate—a section about six hundred feet long.*e* 14He took all the gold and silver and all the articles found in the temple of the LORD and in the treasuries of the royal palace. He also took hostages and returned to Samaria.

15As for the other events of the reign of Jehoash, what he did and his achievements, including his war against Amaziah king of Judah, are they not written in the book of the annals of the kings of Israel? 16Jehoash rested with his fathers and was buried in Samaria with the kings of Israel. And Jeroboam his son succeeded him as king.

[17] Amaziah son of Joash king of Judah lived for fifteen years after the death of Jehoash son of Jehoahaz king of Israel. [18] As for the other events of Amaziah's reign, are they not written in the book of the annals of the kings of Judah?

[19] They conspired against him in Jerusalem, and he fled to Lachish, but they sent men after him to Lachish and killed him there. [20] He was brought back by horse and was buried in Jerusalem with his fathers, in the City of David.

[21] Then all the people of Judah took Azariah,[f] who was sixteen years old, and made him king in place of his father Amaziah. [22] He was the one who rebuilt Elath and restored it to Judah after Amaziah rested with his fathers.

[23] In the fifteenth year of Amaziah son of Joash king of Judah, Jeroboam son of Jehoash king of Israel became king in Samaria, and he reigned forty-one years. [24] He did evil in the eyes of the LORD and did not turn away from any of the sins of Jeroboam son of Nebat, which he had caused Israel to commit. [25] He was the one who restored the boundaries of Israel from Lebo[g] Hamath to the Sea of the Arabah,[h] in accordance with the word of the LORD, the God of Israel, spoken through his servant Jonah son of Amittai, the prophet from Gath Hepher.

[26] The LORD had seen how bitterly everyone in Israel, whether slave or free, was suffering; there was no one to help them. [27] And since the LORD had not said he would blot out the name of Israel from under heaven, he saved them by the hand of Jeroboam son of Jehoash.

[28] As for the other events of Jeroboam's reign, all he did, and his military achievements, including how he recovered for Israel both Damascus and Hamath, which had belonged to Yaudi,[i] are they not written in the book of the annals of the kings of Israel? [29] Jeroboam rested with his fathers, the kings of Israel. And Zechariah his son succeeded him as king.

ACTS 18:23–19:12

After spending some time in Antioch, Paul set out from there and traveled from place to place throughout the region of Galatia and Phrygia, strengthening all the disciples.

[24] Meanwhile a Jew named Apollos, a native of Alexandria, came to Ephesus. He was a learned man, with a thorough knowledge of the Scriptures. [25] He had been instructed in the way of the Lord, and he spoke with great fervor[a] and taught about Jesus accurately, though he knew only the baptism of John. [26] He began to speak boldly in the synagogue. When Priscilla and Aquila heard him, they invited him to their home and explained to him the way of God more adequately.

[27] When Apollos wanted to go to Achaia, the brothers encouraged him and wrote to the disciples there to welcome him. On arriving, he was a great help to those who by grace had believed. [28] For he vigorously refuted the Jews in public debate, proving from the Scriptures that Jesus was the Christ.

[19:1] WHILE Apollos was at Corinth, Paul took the road through the interior and arrived at Ephesus. There he found some disciples [2] and asked them, "Did you receive the Holy Spirit when[b] you believed?"

They answered, "No, we have not even heard that there is a Holy Spirit."

[3] So Paul asked, "Then what baptism did you receive?"

"John's baptism," they replied.

[4] Paul said, "John's baptism was a baptism of repentance. He told the people to believe in the one coming after him, that is, in Jesus." [5] On hearing this, they were baptized into[c] the name of the

Lord Jesus. ⁶When Paul placed his hands on them, the Holy Spirit came on them, and they spoke in tongues*d* and prophesied. ⁷There were about twelve men in all.

⁸Paul entered the synagogue and spoke boldly there for three months, arguing persuasively about the kingdom of God. ⁹But some of them became obstinate; they refused to believe and publicly maligned the Way. So Paul left them. He took the disciples with him and had discussions daily in the lecture hall of Tyrannus. ¹⁰This went on for two years, so that all the Jews and Greeks who lived in the province of Asia heard the word of the Lord.

¹¹God did extraordinary miracles through Paul, ¹²so that even handkerchiefs and aprons that had touched him were taken to the sick, and their illnesses were cured and the evil spirits left them.

a25 Or *with fervor in the Spirit*   *b2* Or *after*   *c5* Or *in*   *d6* Or *other languages*

PSALM 146:1-10
¹Praise the Lord.*a*

Praise the Lord, O my soul.
²   I will praise the Lord all my life;
    I will sing praise to my God as long
        as I live.

³Do not put your trust in princes,
    in mortal men, who cannot save.
⁴When their spirit departs, they
        return to the ground;
    on that very day their plans come
        to nothing.

⁵Blessed is he whose help is the
        God of Jacob,
    whose hope is in the Lord his
        God,
⁶the Maker of heaven and earth,
    the sea, and everything in them—
    the Lord, who remains faithful
        forever.
⁷He upholds the cause of the
        oppressed
    and gives food to the hungry.
The Lord sets prisoners free,

⁸   the Lord gives sight to the blind,
    the Lord lifts up those who are
        bowed down,
    the Lord loves the righteous.
⁹The Lord watches over the alien
    and sustains the fatherless and the
        widow,
    but he frustrates the ways of the
        wicked.

¹⁰The Lord reigns forever,
    your God, O Zion, for all
        generations.

Praise the Lord.

a 1 Hebrew *Hallelu Yah*; also in verse 10

PROVERBS 18:2-3
²A fool finds no pleasure in
        understanding
    but delights in airing his own
        opinions.

³When wickedness comes, so does
        contempt,
    and with shame comes disgrace.

□ DAY 180

GOD SIGHTINGS

June 29

2 KINGS 15:1-16:20
In the twenty-seventh year of Jeroboam king of Israel, Azariah son of Amaziah king of Judah began to reign. ²He was sixteen years old when he became king, and he reigned in Jerusalem fifty-two years. His mother's name was Jecoliah; she was from Jerusalem. ³He did what was right in the eyes of the Lord, just as his father Amaziah had done. ⁴The high places, however, were not removed; the people continued to offer sacrifices and burn incense there.

⁵The Lord afflicted the king with leprosy*a* until the day he died, and he lived in a separate house.*b* Jotham the king's son had charge of the palace and governed the people of the land.

⁶As for the other events of Azariah's reign, and all he did, are they not written in the book of the annals of the kings of Judah? ⁷Azariah rested with his fathers and was buried near them in the City of David. And Jotham his son succeeded him as king.

⁸In the thirty-eighth year of Azariah king of Judah, Zechariah son of Jeroboam became king of Israel in Samaria, and he reigned six months. ⁹He did evil in the eyes of the LORD, as his fathers had done. He did not turn away from the sins of Jeroboam son of Nebat, which he had caused Israel to commit.

¹⁰Shallum son of Jabesh conspired against Zechariah. He attacked him in front of the people,ᶜ assassinated him and succeeded him as king. ¹¹The other events of Zechariah's reign are written in the book of the annals of the kings of Israel. ¹²So the word of the LORD spoken to Jehu was fulfilled: "Your descendants will sit on the throne of Israel to the fourth generation."ᵈ

¹³Shallum son of Jabesh became king in the thirty-ninth year of Uzziah king of Judah, and he reigned in Samaria one month. ¹⁴Then Menahem son of Gadi went from Tirzah up to Samaria. He attacked Shallum son of Jabesh in Samaria, assassinated him and succeeded him as king.

¹⁵The other events of Shallum's reign, and the conspiracy he led, are written in the book of the annals of the kings of Israel.

¹⁶At that time Menahem, starting out from Tirzah, attacked Tiphsah and everyone in the city and its vicinity, because they refused to open their gates. He sacked Tiphsah and ripped open all the pregnant women.

¹⁷In the thirty-ninth year of Azariah king of Judah, Menahem son of Gadi became king of Israel, and he reigned in Samaria ten years. ¹⁸He did evil in the eyes of the LORD. During his entire reign he did not turn away from the sins of Jeroboam son of Nebat, which he had caused Israel to commit.

¹⁹Then Pulᵉ king of Assyria invaded the land, and Menahem gave him a thousand talentsᶠ of silver to gain his support and strengthen his own hold on the kingdom. ²⁰Menahem exacted this money from Israel. Every wealthy man had to contribute fifty shekelsᵍ of silver to be given to the king of Assyria. So the king of Assyria withdrew and stayed in the land no longer.

²¹As for the other events of Menahem's reign, and all he did, are they not written in the book of the annals of the kings of Israel? ²²Menahem rested with his fathers. And Pekahiah his son succeeded him as king.

²³In the fiftieth year of Azariah king of Judah, Pekahiah son of Menahem became king of Israel in Samaria, and he reigned two years. ²⁴Pekahiah did evil in the eyes of the LORD. He did not turn away from the sins of Jeroboam son of Nebat, which he had caused Israel to commit. ²⁵One of his chief officers, Pekah son of Remaliah, conspired against him. Taking fifty men of Gilead with him, he assassinated Pekahiah, along with Argob and Arieh, in the citadel of the royal palace at Samaria. So Pekah killed Pekahiah and succeeded him as king.

²⁶The other events of Pekahiah's reign, and all he did, are written in the book of the annals of the kings of Israel.

²⁷In the fifty-second year of Azariah king of Judah, Pekah son of Remaliah became king of Israel in Samaria, and he reigned twenty years. ²⁸He did evil in the eyes of the LORD. He did not turn away from the sins of Jeroboam son of Nebat, which he had caused Israel to commit.

²⁹In the time of Pekah king of Israel, Tiglath-Pileser king of Assyria came and took Ijon, Abel Beth Maacah, Janoah, Kedesh and Hazor. He took Gilead and Galilee, including all the land of Naphtali, and deported the people to Assyria. ³⁰Then Hoshea son of Elah conspired against Pekah son of Remaliah. He attacked and assassinated him, and then succeeded him as king in the twentieth year of Jotham son of Uzziah.

31As for the other events of Pekah's reign, and all he did, are they not written in the book of the annals of the kings of Israel?

32In the second year of Pekah son of Remaliah king of Israel, Jotham son of Uzziah king of Judah began to reign. 33He was twenty-five years old when he became king, and he reigned in Jerusalem sixteen years. His mother's name was Jerusha daughter of Zadok. 34He did what was right in the eyes of the LORD, just as his father Uzziah had done. 35The high places, however, were not removed; the people continued to offer sacrifices and burn incense there. Jotham rebuilt the Upper Gate of the temple of the LORD.

36As for the other events of Jotham's reign, and what he did, are they not written in the book of the annals of the kings of Judah? 37(In those days the LORD began to send Rezin king of Aram and Pekah son of Remaliah against Judah.) 38Jotham rested with his fathers and was buried with them in the City of David, the city of his father. And Ahaz his son succeeded him as king.

16:1In the seventeenth year of Pekah son of Remaliah, Ahaz son of Jotham king of Judah began to reign. 2Ahaz was twenty years old when he became king, and he reigned in Jerusalem sixteen years. Unlike David his father, he did not do what was right in the eyes of the LORD his God. 3He walked in the ways of the kings of Israel and even sacrificed his son inh the fire, following the detestable ways of the nations the LORD had driven out before the Israelites. 4He offered sacrifices and burned incense at the high places, on the hilltops and under every spreading tree.

5Then Rezin king of Aram and Pekah son of Remaliah king of Israel marched up to fight against Jerusalem and besieged Ahaz, but they could not overpower him. 6At that time, Rezin king of Aram recovered Elath for Aram by driving out the men of Judah. Edomites then moved into Elath and have lived there to this day.

7Ahaz sent messengers to say to Tiglath-Pileser king of Assyria, "I am your servant and vassal. Come up and save me out of the hand of the king of Aram and of the king of Israel, who are attacking me." 8And Ahaz took the silver and gold found in the temple of the LORD and in the treasuries of the royal palace and sent it as a gift to the king of Assyria. 9The king of Assyria complied by attacking Damascus and capturing it. He deported its inhabitants to Kir and put Rezin to death.

10Then King Ahaz went to Damascus to meet Tiglath-Pileser king of Assyria. He saw an altar in Damascus and sent to Uriah the priest a sketch of the altar, with detailed plans for its construction. 11So Uriah the priest built an altar in accordance with all the plans that King Ahaz had sent from Damascus and finished it before King Ahaz returned. 12When the king came back from Damascus and saw the altar, he approached it and presented offeringsi on it. 13He offered up his burnt offering and grain offering, poured out his drink offering, and sprinkled the blood of his fellowship offeringsj on the altar. 14The bronze altar that stood before the LORD he brought from the front of the temple—from between the new altar and the temple of the LORD—and put it on the north side of the new altar.

15King Ahaz then gave these orders to Uriah the priest: "On the large new altar, offer the morning burnt offering and the evening grain offering, the king's burnt offering and his grain offering, and the burnt offering of all the people of the land, and their grain offering and their drink offering. Sprinkle on the altar all the blood of the burnt offerings and sacrifices. But I will use the bronze altar for seeking guidance." 16And Uriah the priest did just as King Ahaz had ordered.

17King Ahaz took away the side panels and removed the basins from the movable stands. He removed the Sea from the bronze bulls that supported it and set it on a stone base. [18]He took away the Sabbath canopy[k] that had been built at the temple and removed the royal entryway outside the temple of the Lord, in deference to the king of Assyria.

[19]As for the other events of the reign of Ahaz, and what he did, are they not written in the book of the annals of the kings of Judah? [20]Ahaz rested with his fathers and was buried with them in the City of David. And Hezekiah his son succeeded him as king.

[a]5 The Hebrew word was used for various diseases affecting the skin—not necessarily leprosy. [b]5 Or in a house where he was relieved of responsibility [c]10 Hebrew; some Septuagint manuscripts in Ibleam [d]12 2 Kings 10:30 [e]19 Also called Tiglath-Pileser [f]19 That is, about 37 tons (about 34 metric tons) [g]20 That is, about 1 1/4 pounds (about 0.6 kilogram) [h]3 Or even made his son pass through [i]12 Or and went up [j]13 Traditionally peace offerings [k]18 Or the dais of his throne (see Septuagint)

ACTS 19:13-41

Some Jews who went around driving out evil spirits tried to invoke the name of the Lord Jesus over those who were demon-possessed. They would say, "In the name of Jesus, whom Paul preaches, I command you to come out." [14]Seven sons of Sceva, a Jewish chief priest, were doing this. [15]One day the evil spirit answered them, "Jesus I know, and I know about Paul, but who are you?" [16]Then the man who had the evil spirit jumped on them and overpowered them all. He gave them such a beating that they ran out of the house naked and bleeding.

[17]When this became known to the Jews and Greeks living in Ephesus, they were all seized with fear, and the name of the Lord Jesus was held in high honor. [18]Many of those who believed now came and openly confessed their evil deeds. [19]A number who had practiced sorcery brought their scrolls together and burned them publicly. When they calculated the value of the scrolls, the total came to fifty thousand drachmas.[a] [20]In this way the word of the Lord spread widely and grew in power.

[21]After all this had happened, Paul decided to go to Jerusalem, passing through Macedonia and Achaia. "After I have been there," he said, "I must visit Rome also." [22]He sent two of his helpers, Timothy and Erastus, to Macedonia, while he stayed in the province of Asia a little longer.

[23]About that time there arose a great disturbance about the Way. [24]A silversmith named Demetrius, who made silver shrines of Artemis, brought in no little business for the craftsmen. [25]He called them together, along with the workmen in related trades, and said: "Men, you know we receive a good income from this business. [26]And you see and hear how this fellow Paul has convinced and led astray large numbers of people here in Ephesus and in practically the whole province of Asia. He says that man-made gods are no gods at all. [27]There is danger not only that our trade will lose its good name, but also that the temple of the great goddess Artemis will be discredited, and the goddess herself, who is worshiped throughout the province of Asia and the world, will be robbed of her divine majesty."

[28]When they heard this, they were furious and began shouting: "Great is Artemis of the Ephesians!" [29]Soon the whole city was in an uproar. The people seized Gaius and Aristarchus, Paul's traveling companions from Macedonia, and rushed as one man into the theater. [30]Paul wanted to appear before the crowd, but the disciples would not let him. [31]Even some of the officials of the province, friends of Paul, sent him a message begging him not to venture into the theater.

[32]The assembly was in confusion: Some were shouting one thing, some another. Most of the people did not even know why they were there. [33]The Jews pushed Alexander to the front, and some of the crowd shouted instructions to him. He motioned for silence in order to make a defense before the people. [34]But when they realized he was a Jew, they all shouted in unison for about two hours: "Great is Artemis of the Ephesians!"

[35]The city clerk quieted the crowd

and said: "Men of Ephesus, doesn't all the world know that the city of Ephesus is the guardian of the temple of the great Artemis and of her image, which fell from heaven? 36Therefore, since these facts are undeniable, you ought to be quiet and not do anything rash. 37You have brought these men here, though they have neither robbed temples nor blasphemed our goddess. 38If, then, Demetrius and his fellow craftsmen have a grievance against anybody, the courts are open and there are proconsuls. They can press charges. 39If there is anything further you want to bring up, it must be settled in a legal assembly. 40As it is, we are in danger of being charged with rioting because of today's events. In that case we would not be able to account for this commotion, since there is no reason for it." 41After he had said this, he dismissed the assembly.

a 19 A drachma was a silver coin worth about a day's wages.

PSALM 147:1-20

1 Praise the LORD.a

How good it is to sing praises to our
    God,
  how pleasant and fitting to praise
    him!

2 The LORD builds up Jerusalem;
  he gathers the exiles of Israel.
3 He heals the brokenhearted
  and binds up their wounds.

4 He determines the number of the
    stars
  and calls them each by name.
5 Great is our Lord and mighty in
    power;
  his understanding has no limit.
6 The LORD sustains the humble
  but casts the wicked to the
    ground.

7 Sing to the LORD with thanksgiving;
  make music to our God on the
    harp.
8 He covers the sky with clouds;
  he supplies the earth with rain
  and makes grass grow on the hills.

9 He provides food for the cattle
  and for the young ravens when
    they call.

10 His pleasure is not in the strength
    of the horse,
  nor his delight in the legs of a
    man;
11 the LORD delights in those who
    fear him,
  who put their hope in his
    unfailing love.

12 Extol the LORD, O Jerusalem;
  praise your God, O Zion,
13 for he strengthens the bars of your
    gates
  and blesses your people within
    you.
14 He grants peace to your borders
  and satisfies you with the finest
    of wheat.

15 He sends his command to the earth;
  his word runs swiftly.
16 He spreads the snow like wool
  and scatters the frost like ashes.
17 He hurls down his hail like pebbles.
  Who can withstand his icy blast?
18 He sends his word and melts them;
  he stirs up his breezes, and the
    waters flow.

19 He has revealed his word to Jacob,
  his laws and decrees to Israel.
20 He has done this for no other
    nation;
  they do not know his laws.

Praise the LORD.

a 1 Hebrew Hallelu Yah; also in verse 20

PROVERBS 18:4-5

4 The words of a man's mouth are
    deep waters,
  but the fountain of wisdom is a
    bubbling brook.

5 It is not good to be partial to the
    wicked
  or to deprive the innocent of
    justice.

GOD SIGHTINGS

June 30

2 KINGS 17:1–18:12

In the twelfth year of Ahaz king of Judah, Hoshea son of Elah became king of Israel in Samaria, and he reigned nine years. ²He did evil in the eyes of the Lord, but not like the kings of Israel who preceded him.

³Shalmaneser king of Assyria came up to attack Hoshea, who had been Shalmaneser's vassal and had paid him tribute. ⁴But the king of Assyria discovered that Hoshea was a traitor, for he had sent envoys to So[a] king of Egypt, and he no longer paid tribute to the king of Assyria, as he had done year by year. Therefore Shalmaneser seized him and put him in prison. ⁵The king of Assyria invaded the entire land, marched against Samaria and laid siege to it for three years. ⁶In the ninth year of Hoshea, the king of Assyria captured Samaria and deported the Israelites to Assyria. He settled them in Halah, in Gozan on the Habor River and in the towns of the Medes.

⁷All this took place because the Israelites had sinned against the Lord their God, who had brought them up out of Egypt from under the power of Pharaoh king of Egypt. They worshiped other gods ⁸and followed the practices of the nations the Lord had driven out before them, as well as the practices that the kings of Israel had introduced. ⁹The Israelites secretly did things against the Lord their God that were not right. From watchtower to fortified city they built themselves high places in all their towns. ¹⁰They set up sacred stones and Asherah poles on every high hill and under every spreading tree. ¹¹At every high place they burned incense, as the nations whom the Lord had driven out before them had done. They did wicked things that provoked the Lord to anger. ¹²They worshiped idols, though the Lord had said,

"You shall not do this."[b] ¹³The Lord warned Israel and Judah through all his prophets and seers: "Turn from your evil ways. Observe my commands and decrees, in accordance with the entire Law that I commanded your fathers to obey and that I delivered to you through my servants the prophets."

¹⁴But they would not listen and were as stiff-necked as their fathers, who did not trust in the Lord their God. ¹⁵They rejected his decrees and the covenant he had made with their fathers and the warnings he had given them. They followed worthless idols and themselves became worthless. They imitated the nations around them although the Lord had ordered them, "Do not do as they do," and they did the things the Lord had forbidden them to do.

¹⁶They forsook all the commands of the Lord their God and made for themselves two idols cast in the shape of calves, and an Asherah pole. They bowed down to all the starry hosts, and they worshiped Baal. ¹⁷They sacrificed their sons and daughters in[c] the fire. They practiced divination and sorcery and sold themselves to do evil in the eyes of the Lord, provoking him to anger.

¹⁸So the Lord was very angry with Israel and removed them from his presence. Only the tribe of Judah was left, ¹⁹and even Judah did not keep the commands of the Lord their God. They followed the practices Israel had introduced. ²⁰Therefore the Lord rejected all the people of Israel; he afflicted them and gave them into the hands of plunderers, until he thrust them from his presence.

²¹When he tore Israel away from the house of David, they made Jeroboam son of Nebat their king. Jeroboam enticed Israel away from following the Lord and caused them to commit a great sin. ²²The Israelites persisted in all the sins of Jeroboam and did not turn away from them ²³until the Lord removed them from his presence, as he had warned through all his servants the prophets. So the people of Israel were

taken from their homeland into exile in Assyria, and they are still there.

²⁴The king of Assyria brought people from Babylon, Cuthah, Avva, Hamath and Sepharvaim and settled them in the towns of Samaria to replace the Israelites. They took over Samaria and lived in its towns. ²⁵When they first lived there, they did not worship the LORD; so he sent lions among them and they killed some of the people. ²⁶It was reported to the king of Assyria: "The people you deported and resettled in the towns of Samaria do not know what the god of that country requires. He has sent lions among them, which are killing them off, because the people do not know what he requires."

²⁷Then the king of Assyria gave this order: "Have one of the priests you took captive from Samaria go back to live there and teach the people what the god of the land requires." ²⁸So one of the priests who had been exiled from Samaria came to live in Bethel and taught them how to worship the LORD.

²⁹Nevertheless, each national group made its own gods in the several towns where they settled, and set them up in the shrines the people of Samaria had made at the high places. ³⁰The men from Babylon made Succoth Benoth, the men from Cuthah made Nergal, and the men from Hamath made Ashima; ³¹the Avites made Nibhaz and Tartak, and the Sepharvites burned their children in the fire as sacrifices to Adrammelech and Anammelech, the gods of Sepharvaim. ³²They worshiped the LORD, but they also appointed all sorts of their own people to officiate for them as priests in the shrines at the high places. ³³They worshiped the LORD, but they also served their own gods in accordance with the customs of the nations from which they had been brought.

³⁴To this day they persist in their former practices. They neither worship the LORD nor adhere to the decrees and ordinances, the laws and commands that the LORD gave the descendants of Jacob, whom he named Israel. ³⁵When the LORD made a covenant with the Israelites, he commanded them: "Do not worship any other gods or bow down to them, serve them or sacrifice to them. ³⁶But the LORD, who brought you up out of Egypt with mighty power and outstretched arm, is the one you must worship. To him you shall bow down and to him offer sacrifices. ³⁷You must always be careful to keep the decrees and ordinances, the laws and commands he wrote for you. Do not worship other gods. ³⁸Do not forget the covenant I have made with you, and do not worship other gods. ³⁹Rather, worship the LORD your God; it is he who will deliver you from the hand of all your enemies."

⁴⁰They would not listen, however, but persisted in their former practices. ⁴¹Even while these people were worshiping the LORD, they were serving their idols. To this day their children and grandchildren continue to do as their fathers did.

18:1In the third year of Hoshea son of Elah king of Israel, Hezekiah son of Ahaz king of Judah began to reign. ²He was twenty-five years old when he became king, and he reigned in Jerusalem twenty-nine years. His mother's name was Abijahᵈ daughter of Zechariah. ³He did what was right in the eyes of the LORD, just as his father David had done. ⁴He removed the high places, smashed the sacred stones and cut down the Asherah poles. He broke into pieces the bronze snake Moses had made, for up to that time the Israelites had been burning incense to it. (It was calledᵉ Nehushtan.ᶠ)

⁵Hezekiah trusted in the LORD, the God of Israel. There was no one like him among all the kings of Judah, either before him or after him. ⁶He held fast to the LORD and did not cease to follow him; he kept the commands the LORD had given Moses. ⁷And the LORD was with him; he was successful in whatever he undertook. He rebelled against the king of Assyria and did not serve him. ⁸From watchtower to fortified city, he

defeated the Philistines, as far as Gaza and its territory.

9 In King Hezekiah's fourth year, which was the seventh year of Hoshea son of Elah king of Israel, Shalmaneser king of Assyria marched against Samaria and laid siege to it. 10At the end of three years the Assyrians took it. So Samaria was captured in Hezekiah's sixth year, which was the ninth year of Hoshea king of Israel. 11The king of Assyria deported Israel to Assyria and settled them in Halah, in Gozan on the Habor River and in towns of the Medes. 12This happened because they had not obeyed the LORD their God, but had violated his covenant—all that Moses the servant of the LORD commanded. They neither listened to the commands nor carried them out.

a4 Or to Sais, to the; So is possibly an abbreviation for Osorkon.   b12 Exodus 20:4,5   c17 Or They made their sons and daughters pass through   d2 Hebrew Abi, a variant of Abijah   e4 Or He called it   f4 Nehushtan sounds like the Hebrew for bronze and snake and unclean thing.

ACTS 20:1-38

When the uproar had ended, Paul sent for the disciples and, after encouraging them, said good-by and set out for Macedonia. 2He traveled through that area, speaking many words of encouragement to the people, and finally arrived in Greece, 3where he stayed three months. Because the Jews made a plot against him just as he was about to sail for Syria, he decided to go back through Macedonia. 4He was accompanied by Sopater son of Pyrrhus from Berea, Aristarchus and Secundus from Thessalonica, Gaius from Derbe, Timothy also, and Tychicus and Trophimus from the province of Asia. 5These men went on ahead and waited for us at Troas. 6But we sailed from Philippi after the Feast of Unleavened Bread, and five days later joined the others at Troas, where we stayed seven days.

7On the first day of the week we came together to break bread. Paul spoke to the people and, because he intended to leave the next day, kept on talking until midnight. 8There were many lamps in the upstairs room where we were meeting. 9Seated in a window was a young man named Eutychus, who was sinking into a deep sleep as Paul talked on and on. When he was sound asleep, he fell to the ground from the third story and was picked up dead. 10Paul went down, threw himself on the young man and put his arms around him. "Don't be alarmed," he said. "He's alive!" 11Then he went upstairs again and broke bread and ate. After talking until daylight, he left. 12The people took the young man home alive and were greatly comforted.

13 We went on ahead to the ship and sailed for Assos, where we were going to take Paul aboard. He had made this arrangement because he was going there on foot. 14When he met us at Assos, we took him aboard and went on to Mitylene. 15The next day we set sail from there and arrived off Kios. The day after that we crossed over to Samos, and on the following day arrived at Miletus. 16Paul had decided to sail past Ephesus to avoid spending time in the province of Asia, for he was in a hurry to reach Jerusalem, if possible, by the day of Pentecost.

17 From Miletus, Paul sent to Ephesus for the elders of the church. 18When they arrived, he said to them: "You know how I lived the whole time I was with you, from the first day I came into the province of Asia. 19I served the Lord with great humility and with tears, although I was severely tested by the plots of the Jews. 20You know that I have not hesitated to preach anything that would be helpful to you but have taught you publicly and from house to house. 21I have declared to both Jews and Greeks that they must turn to God in repentance and have faith in our Lord Jesus.

22 "And now, compelled by the Spirit, I am going to Jerusalem, not knowing what will happen to me there. 23I only know that in every city the Holy Spirit warns me that prison and hardships are facing me. 24However, I consider my life worth nothing to me, if only I may finish the race and complete the task

the Lord Jesus has given me—the task of testifying to the gospel of God's grace.

25 "Now I know that none of you among whom I have gone about preaching the kingdom will ever see me again. 26 Therefore, I declare to you today that I am innocent of the blood of all men. 27 For I have not hesitated to proclaim to you the whole will of God. 28 Keep watch over yourselves and all the flock of which the Holy Spirit has made you overseers.a Be shepherds of the church of God,b which he bought with his own blood. 29 I know that after I leave, savage wolves will come in among you and will not spare the flock. 30 Even from your own number men will arise and distort the truth in order to draw away disciples after them. 31 So be on your guard! Remember that for three years I never stopped warning each of you night and day with tears.

32 "Now I commit you to God and to the word of his grace, which can build you up and give you an inheritance among all those who are sanctified. 33 I have not coveted anyone's silver or gold or clothing. 34 You yourselves know that these hands of mine have supplied my own needs and the needs of my companions. 35 In everything I did, I showed you that by this kind of hard work we must help the weak, remembering the words the Lord Jesus himself said: 'It is more blessed to give than to receive.'"

36 When he had said this, he knelt down with all of them and prayed. 37 They all wept as they embraced him and kissed him. 38 What grieved them most was his statement that they would never see his face again. Then they accompanied him to the ship.

a28 Traditionally bishops   b28 Many manuscripts of the Lord

PSALM 148:1-14
1 **P**raise the Lord.a

Praise the Lord from the heavens,
    praise him in the heights above.

2 Praise him, all his angels,
    praise him, all his heavenly hosts.
3 Praise him, sun and moon,
    praise him, all you shining stars.
4 Praise him, you highest heavens
    and you waters above the skies.
5 Let them praise the name of the
        Lord,
    for he commanded and they were
        created.
6 He set them in place for ever and
        ever;
    he gave a decree that will never
        pass away.

7 Praise the Lord from the earth,
    you great sea creatures and all
        ocean depths,
8 lightning and hail, snow and clouds,
    stormy winds that do his bidding,
9 you mountains and all hills,
    fruit trees and all cedars,
10 wild animals and all cattle,
    small creatures and flying birds,
11 kings of the earth and all nations,
    you princes and all rulers on
        earth,
12 young men and maidens,
    old men and children.

13 **Let them praise the name of the
        Lord,
    for his name alone is exalted;
    his splendor is above the earth
        and the heavens.**
14 He has raised up for his people a
        horn,b
    the praise of all his saints,
    of Israel, the people close to his
        heart.

Praise the Lord.

a1 Hebrew Hallelu Yah; also in verse 14   b14 Horn here symbolizes strong one, that is, king.

PROVERBS 18:6-7
6 **A** fool's lips bring him strife,
    and his mouth invites a beating.

7 A fool's mouth is his undoing,
    and his lips are a snare to his soul.

July 1

2 KINGS 18:13–19:37

In the fourteenth year of King Hezekiah's reign, Sennacherib king of Assyria attacked all the fortified cities of Judah and captured them. [14]So Hezekiah king of Judah sent this message to the king of Assyria at Lachish: "I have done wrong. Withdraw from me, and I will pay whatever you demand of me." The king of Assyria exacted from Hezekiah king of Judah three hundred talents[a] of silver and thirty talents[b] of gold. [15]So Hezekiah gave him all the silver that was found in the temple of the LORD and in the treasuries of the royal palace.

[16]At this time Hezekiah king of Judah stripped off the gold with which he had covered the doors and doorposts of the temple of the LORD, and gave it to the king of Assyria.

[17]The king of Assyria sent his supreme commander, his chief officer and his field commander with a large army, from Lachish to King Hezekiah at Jerusalem. They came up to Jerusalem and stopped at the aqueduct of the Upper Pool, on the road to the Washerman's Field. [18]They called for the king; and Eliakim son of Hilkiah the palace administrator, Shebna the secretary, and Joah son of Asaph the recorder went out to them.

[19]The field commander said to them, "Tell Hezekiah:

"'This is what the great king, the king of Assyria, says: On what are you basing this confidence of yours? [20]You say you have strategy and military strength—but you speak only empty words. On whom are you depending, that you rebel against me? [21]Look now, you are depending on Egypt, that splintered reed of a staff, which pierces a man's hand and wounds him if he leans on it! Such is Pharaoh king of Egypt to all who depend on him. [22]And if you say to me, "We are depending on the LORD our God"—isn't he the one whose high places and altars Hezekiah removed, saying to Judah and Jerusalem, "You must worship before this altar in Jerusalem"?

[23]"'Come now, make a bargain with my master, the king of Assyria: I will give you two thousand horses—if you can put riders on them! [24]How can you repulse one officer of the least of my master's officials, even though you are depending on Egypt for chariots and horsemen[c]? [25]Furthermore, have I come to attack and destroy this place without word from the LORD? The LORD himself told me to march against this country and destroy it.'"

[26]Then Eliakim son of Hilkiah, and Shebna and Joah said to the field commander, "Please speak to your servants in Aramaic, since we understand it. Don't speak to us in Hebrew in the hearing of the people on the wall."

[27]But the commander replied, "Was it only to your master and you that my master sent me to say these things, and not to the men sitting on the wall—who, like you, will have to eat their own filth and drink their own urine?"

[28]Then the commander stood and called out in Hebrew: "Hear the word of the great king, the king of Assyria! [29]This is what the king says: Do not let Hezekiah deceive you. He cannot deliver you from my hand. [30]Do not let Hezekiah persuade you to trust in the LORD when he says, 'The LORD will surely deliver us; this city will not be given into the hand of the king of Assyria.'

³¹"Do not listen to Hezekiah. This is what the king of Assyria says: Make peace with me and come out to me. Then every one of you will eat from his own vine and fig tree and drink water from his own cistern, ³²until I come and take you to a land like your own, a land of grain and new wine, a land of bread and vineyards, a land of olive trees and honey. Choose life and not death!

"Do not listen to Hezekiah, for he is misleading you when he says, 'The LORD will deliver us.' ³³Has the god of any nation ever delivered his land from the hand of the king of Assyria? ³⁴Where are the gods of Hamath and Arpad? Where are the gods of Sepharvaim, Hena and Ivvah? Have they rescued Samaria from my hand? ³⁵Who of all the gods of these countries has been able to save his land from me? How then can the LORD deliver Jerusalem from my hand?"

³⁶But the people remained silent and said nothing in reply, because the king had commanded, "Do not answer him."

³⁷Then Eliakim son of Hilkiah the palace administrator, Shebna the secretary and Joah son of Asaph the recorder went to Hezekiah, with their clothes torn, and told him what the field commander had said.

¹⁹:¹WHEN King Hezekiah heard this, he tore his clothes and put on sackcloth and went into the temple of the LORD. ²He sent Eliakim the palace administrator, Shebna the secretary and the leading priests, all wearing sackcloth, to the prophet Isaiah son of Amoz. ³They told him, "This is what Hezekiah says: This day is a day of distress and rebuke and disgrace, as when children come to the point of birth and there is no strength to deliver them. ⁴It may be that the LORD your God will hear all the words of the field commander, whom his master, the king of Assyria, has sent to ridicule the living God, and that he will rebuke him for the words the LORD your God has heard. Therefore pray for the remnant that still survives."

⁵When King Hezekiah's officials came to Isaiah, ⁶Isaiah said to them, "Tell your master, 'This is what the LORD says: Do not be afraid of what you have heard—those words with which the underlings of the king of Assyria have blasphemed me. ⁷Listen! I am going to put such a spirit in him that when he hears a certain report, he will return to his own country, and there I will have him cut down with the sword.'"

⁸When the field commander heard that the king of Assyria had left Lachish, he withdrew and found the king fighting against Libnah.

⁹Now Sennacherib received a report that Tirhakah, the Cushite[d] king ˌof Egyptˌ, was marching out to fight against him. So he again sent messengers to Hezekiah with this word: ¹⁰"Say to Hezekiah king of Judah: Do not let the god you depend on deceive you when he says, 'Jerusalem will not be handed over to the king of Assyria.' ¹¹Surely you have heard what the kings of Assyria have done to all the countries, destroying them completely. And will you be delivered? ¹²Did the gods of the nations that were destroyed by my forefathers deliver them: the gods of Gozan, Haran, Rezeph and the people of Eden who were in Tel Assar? ¹³Where is the king of Hamath, the king of Arpad, the king of the city of Sepharvaim, or of Hena or Ivvah?"

¹⁴Hezekiah received the letter from the messengers and read it. Then he went up to the temple of the LORD and spread it out before the LORD. ¹⁵And Hezekiah prayed to the LORD: "O LORD, God of Israel, enthroned between the cherubim, you alone are God over all the kingdoms of the earth. You have made heaven and earth. ¹⁶Give ear, O LORD, and hear; open your eyes, O LORD, and see; listen to the words Sennacherib has sent to insult the living God.

¹⁷"It is true, O LORD, that the Assyrian kings have laid waste these nations and their lands. ¹⁸They have thrown their gods into the fire and destroyed them, for they were not gods but only wood and stone, fashioned by men's hands. ¹⁹Now, O LORD our God, deliver us from his hand,

so that all kingdoms on earth may know that you alone, O LORD, are God."

²⁰Then Isaiah son of Amoz sent a message to Hezekiah: "This is what the LORD, the God of Israel, says: I have heard your prayer concerning Sennacherib king of Assyria. ²¹This is the word that the LORD has spoken against him:

"'The Virgin Daughter of Zion
    despises you and mocks you.
The Daughter of Jerusalem
    tosses her head as you flee.
²²Who is it you have insulted and
        blasphemed?
    Against whom have you raised
        your voice
and lifted your eyes in pride?
    Against the Holy One of Israel!
²³By your messengers
    you have heaped insults on the
        Lord.
And you have said,
    "With my many chariots
I have ascended the heights of the
        mountains,
    the utmost heights of Lebanon.
I have cut down its tallest cedars,
    the choicest of its pines.
I have reached its remotest parts,
    the finest of its forests.
²⁴I have dug wells in foreign lands
    and drunk the water there.
With the soles of my feet
    I have dried up all the streams of
        Egypt."

²⁵"'Have you not heard?
    Long ago I ordained it.
In days of old I planned it;
    now I have brought it to pass,
that you have turned fortified cities
    into piles of stone.
²⁶Their people, drained of power,
    are dismayed and put to shame.
They are like plants in the field,
    like tender green shoots,
like grass sprouting on the roof,
    scorched before it grows up.
²⁷"'But I know where you stay
    and when you come and go
    and how you rage against me.

²⁸Because you rage against me
    and your insolence has reached
        my ears,
I will put my hook in your nose
    and my bit in your mouth,
and I will make you return
    by the way you came.'

²⁹"This will be the sign for you, O Hezekiah:

"This year you will eat what grows by
        itself,
    and the second year what springs
        from that.
But in the third year sow and reap,
    plant vineyards and eat their fruit.
³⁰Once more a remnant of the house of
        Judah
    will take root below and bear fruit
        above.
³¹For out of Jerusalem will come a
        remnant,
    and out of Mount Zion a band of
        survivors.

The zeal of the LORD Almighty will accomplish this.

³²"Therefore this is what the LORD says concerning the king of Assyria:

"He will not enter this city
    or shoot an arrow here.
He will not come before it with
        shield
    or build a siege ramp against it.
³³By the way that he came he will
        return;
    he will not enter this city,
                declares the LORD.
³⁴I will defend this city and save it,
    for my sake and for the sake of
        David my servant."

³⁵That night the angel of the LORD went out and put to death a hundred and eighty-five thousand men in the Assyrian camp. When the people got up the next morning—there were all the dead bodies! ³⁶So Sennacherib king of Assyria broke camp and withdrew. He returned to Nineveh and stayed there.

³⁷One day, while he was worshiping

in the temple of his god Nisroch, his sons Adrammelech and Sharezer cut him down with the sword, and they escaped to the land of Ararat. And Esarhaddon his son succeeded him as king.

a14 That is, about 11 tons (about 10 metric tons) *b14* That is, about 1 ton (about 1 metric ton) *c24* Or *charioteers* *d9* That is, from the upper Nile region

ACTS 21:1-16

After we [Paul and those with him] had torn ourselves away from them, we put out to sea and sailed straight to Cos. The next day we went to Rhodes and from there to Patara. ²We found a ship crossing over to Phoenicia, went on board and set sail. ³After sighting Cyprus and passing to the south of it, we sailed on to Syria. We landed at Tyre, where our ship was to unload its cargo. ⁴Finding the disciples there, we stayed with them seven days. Through the Spirit they urged Paul not to go on to Jerusalem. ⁵But when our time was up, we left and continued on our way. All the disciples and their wives and children accompanied us out of the city, and there on the beach we knelt to pray. ⁶After saying good-by to each other, we went aboard the ship, and they returned home.

⁷We continued our voyage from Tyre and landed at Ptolemais, where we greeted the brothers and stayed with them for a day. ⁸Leaving the next day, we reached Caesarea and stayed at the house of Philip the evangelist, one of the Seven. ⁹He had four unmarried daughters who prophesied.

¹⁰After we had been there a number of days, a prophet named Agabus came down from Judea. ¹¹Coming over to us, he took Paul's belt, tied his own hands and feet with it and said, "The Holy Spirit says, 'In this way the Jews of Jerusalem will bind the owner of this belt and will hand him over to the Gentiles.'"

¹²When we heard this, we and the people there pleaded with Paul not to go up to Jerusalem. ¹³Then Paul answered, "Why are you weeping and breaking my heart? I am ready not only to be bound, but also to die in Jerusalem for the name of the Lord Jesus." ¹⁴When he would not be dissuaded, we gave up and said, "The Lord's will be done."

¹⁵After this, we got ready and went up to Jerusalem. ¹⁶Some of the disciples from Caesarea accompanied us and brought us to the home of Mnason, where we were to stay. He was a man from Cyprus and one of the early disciples.

PSALM 149:1-9

¹ **P**raise the LORD.*a*

Sing to the LORD a new song,
　　his praise in the assembly of the
　　　saints.

² Let Israel rejoice in their Maker;
　　let the people of Zion be glad in
　　　their King.
³ **Let them praise his name with
　　dancing**
**and make music to him with
　　tambourine and harp.**
⁴ **For the LORD takes delight in his
　　people;**
**he crowns the humble with
　　salvation.**
⁵ Let the saints rejoice in this honor
　　and sing for joy on their beds.

⁶ May the praise of God be in their
　　mouths
　　and a double-edged sword in their
　　　hands,
⁷ to inflict vengeance on the nations
　　and punishment on the peoples,
⁸ to bind their kings with fetters,
　　their nobles with shackles of iron,
⁹ to carry out the sentence written
　　against them.
　　This is the glory of all his saints.

Praise the LORD.

a1 Hebrew *Hallelu Yah*; also in verse 9

PROVERBS 18:8

⁸ **T**he words of a gossip are like choice
　　morsels;
　　they go down to a man's inmost
　　　parts.

☐ DAY 183

GOD SIGHTINGS

July 2

2 KINGS 20:1–22:2

In those days Hezekiah became ill and was at the point of death. The prophet Isaiah son of Amoz went to him and said, "This is what the LORD says: Put your house in order, because you are going to die; you will not recover."

2Hezekiah turned his face to the wall and prayed to the LORD, 3"Remember, O LORD, how I have walked before you faithfully and with wholehearted devotion and have done what is good in your eyes." And Hezekiah wept bitterly.

4Before Isaiah had left the middle court, the word of the LORD came to him: 5"Go back and tell Hezekiah, the leader of my people, 'This is what the LORD, the God of your father David, says: I have heard your prayer and seen your tears; I will heal you. On the third day from now you will go up to the temple of the LORD. 6I will add fifteen years to your life. And I will deliver you and this city from the hand of the king of Assyria. I will defend this city for my sake and for the sake of my servant David.'"

7Then Isaiah said, "Prepare a poultice of figs." They did so and applied it to the boil, and he recovered.

8Hezekiah had asked Isaiah, "What will be the sign that the LORD will heal me and that I will go up to the temple of the LORD on the third day from now?"

9Isaiah answered, "This is the LORD's sign to you that the LORD will do what he has promised: Shall the shadow go forward ten steps, or shall it go back ten steps?"

10"It is a simple matter for the shadow to go forward ten steps," said Hezekiah. "Rather, have it go back ten steps."

11Then the prophet Isaiah called upon the LORD, and the LORD made the shadow go back the ten steps it had gone down on the stairway of Ahaz.

12At that time Merodach-Baladan son of Baladan king of Babylon sent Hezekiah letters and a gift, because he had heard of Hezekiah's illness. 13Hezekiah received the messengers and showed them all that was in his storehouses—the silver, the gold, the spices and the fine oil—his armory and everything found among his treasures. There was nothing in his palace or in all his kingdom that Hezekiah did not show them.

14Then Isaiah the prophet went to King Hezekiah and asked, "What did those men say, and where did they come from?"

"From a distant land," Hezekiah replied. "They came from Babylon."

15The prophet asked, "What did they see in your palace?"

"They saw everything in my palace," Hezekiah said. "There is nothing among my treasures that I did not show them."

16Then Isaiah said to Hezekiah, "Hear the word of the LORD: 17The time will surely come when everything in your palace, and all that your fathers have stored up until this day, will be carried off to Babylon. Nothing will be left, says the LORD. 18And some of your descendants, your own flesh and blood, that will be born to you, will be taken away, and they will become eunuchs in the palace of the king of Babylon."

19"The word of the LORD you have spoken is good," Hezekiah replied. For he thought, "Will there not be peace and security in my lifetime?"

20As for the other events of Hezekiah's reign, all his achievements and how he made the pool and the tunnel by which he brought water into the city, are they not written in the book of the annals of the kings of Judah? 21Hezekiah rested with his fathers. And Manasseh his son succeeded him as king.

21:1MANASSEH was twelve years old when he became king, and he reigned in Jerusalem fifty-five years. His mother's name was Hephzibah. 2He did evil in the eyes of the LORD, following the detestable practices of the nations the

LORD had driven out before the Israelites. ³He rebuilt the high places his father Hezekiah had destroyed; he also erected altars to Baal and made an Asherah pole, as Ahab king of Israel had done. He bowed down to all the starry hosts and worshiped them. ⁴He built altars in the temple of the LORD, of which the LORD had said, "In Jerusalem I will put my Name." ⁵In both courts of the temple of the LORD, he built altars to all the starry hosts. ⁶He sacrificed his own son ina the fire, practiced sorcery and divination, and consulted mediums and spiritists. He did much evil in the eyes of the LORD, provoking him to anger.

⁷He took the carved Asherah pole he had made and put it in the temple, of which the LORD had said to David and to his son Solomon, "In this temple and in Jerusalem, which I have chosen out of all the tribes of Israel, I will put my Name forever. ⁸I will not again make the feet of the Israelites wander from the land I gave their forefathers, if only they will be careful to do everything I commanded them and will keep the whole Law that my servant Moses gave them." ⁹But the people did not listen. Manasseh led them astray, so that they did more evil than the nations the LORD had destroyed before the Israelites.

¹⁰The LORD said through his servants the prophets: ¹¹"Manasseh king of Judah has committed these detestable sins. He has done more evil than the Amorites who preceded him and has led Judah into sin with his idols. ¹²Therefore this is what the LORD, the God of Israel, says: I am going to bring such disaster on Jerusalem and Judah that the ears of everyone who hears of it will tingle. ¹³I will stretch out over Jerusalem the measuring line used against Samaria and the plumb line used against the house of Ahab. I will wipe out Jerusalem as one wipes a dish, wiping it and turning it upside down. ¹⁴I will forsake the remnant of my inheritance and hand them over to their enemies. They will be looted and plundered by all their foes, ¹⁵because they have

done evil in my eyes and have provoked me to anger from the day their forefathers came out of Egypt until this day."

¹⁶Moreover, Manasseh also shed so much innocent blood that he filled Jerusalem from end to end—besides the sin that he had caused Judah to commit, so that they did evil in the eyes of the LORD.

¹⁷As for the other events of Manasseh's reign, and all he did, including the sin he committed, are they not written in the book of the annals of the kings of Judah? ¹⁸Manasseh rested with his fathers and was buried in his palace garden, the garden of Uzza. And Amon his son succeeded him as king.

¹⁹Amon was twenty-two years old when he became king, and he reigned in Jerusalem two years. His mother's name was Meshullemeth daughter of Haruz; she was from Jotbah. ²⁰He did evil in the eyes of the LORD, as his father Manasseh had done. ²¹He walked in all the ways of his father; he worshiped the idols his father had worshiped, and bowed down to them. ²²He forsook the LORD, the God of his fathers, and did not walk in the way of the LORD.

²³Amon's officials conspired against him and assassinated the king in his palace. ²⁴Then the people of the land killed all who had plotted against King Amon, and they made Josiah his son king in his place.

²⁵As for the other events of Amon's reign, and what he did, are they not written in the book of the annals of the kings of Judah? ²⁶He was buried in his grave in the garden of Uzza. And Josiah his son succeeded him as king.

22:1JOSIAH was eight years old when he became king, and he reigned in Jerusalem thirty-one years. His mother's name was Jedidah daughter of Adaiah; she was from Bozkath. ²He did what was right in the eyes of the LORD and walked in all the ways of his father David, not turning aside to the right or to the left.

a6 Or He made his own son pass through

ACTS 21:17-36

When we [Paul and those with him] arrived at Jerusalem, the brothers received us warmly. [18]The next day Paul and the rest of us went to see James, and all the elders were present. [19]Paul greeted them and reported in detail what God had done among the Gentiles through his ministry.

[20]When they heard this, they praised God. Then they said to Paul: "You see, brother, how many thousands of Jews have believed, and all of them are zealous for the law. [21]They have been informed that you teach all the Jews who live among the Gentiles to turn away from Moses, telling them not to circumcise their children or live according to our customs. [22]What shall we do? They will certainly hear that you have come, [23]so do what we tell you. There are four men with us who have made a vow. [24]Take these men, join in their purification rites and pay their expenses, so that they can have their heads shaved. Then everybody will know there is no truth in these reports about you, but that you yourself are living in obedience to the law. [25]As for the Gentile believers, we have written to them our decision that they should abstain from food sacrificed to idols, from blood, from the meat of strangled animals and from sexual immorality."

[26]The next day Paul took the men and purified himself along with them. Then he went to the temple to give notice of the date when the days of purification would end and the offering would be made for each of them.

[27]When the seven days were nearly over, some Jews from the province of Asia saw Paul at the temple. They stirred up the whole crowd and seized him, [28]shouting, "Men of Israel, help us! This is the man who teaches all men everywhere against our people and our law and this place. And besides, he has brought Greeks into the temple area and defiled this holy place." [29](They had previously seen Trophimus the Ephesian in the city with Paul and as-

sumed that Paul had brought him into the temple area.)

[30]The whole city was aroused, and the people came running from all directions. Seizing Paul, they dragged him from the temple, and immediately the gates were shut. [31]While they were trying to kill him, news reached the commander of the Roman troops that the whole city of Jerusalem was in an uproar. [32]He at once took some officers and soldiers and ran down to the crowd. When the rioters saw the commander and his soldiers, they stopped beating Paul.

[33]The commander came up and arrested him and ordered him to be bound with two chains. Then he asked who he was and what he had done. [34]Some in the crowd shouted one thing and some another, and since the commander could not get at the truth because of the uproar, he ordered that Paul be taken into the barracks. [35]When Paul reached the steps, the violence of the mob was so great he had to be carried by the soldiers. [36]The crowd that followed kept shouting, "Away with him!"

PSALM 150:1-6

[1] **P**raise the LORD.[a]

Praise God in his sanctuary;
   praise him in his mighty
      heavens.
[2]Praise him for his acts of power;
   praise him for his surpassing
      greatness.
[3]Praise him with the sounding of the
      trumpet,
   praise him with the harp and lyre,
[4]praise him with tambourine and
      dancing,
   praise him with the strings and
      flute,
[5]praise him with the clash of cymbals,
   praise him with resounding
      cymbals.

[6]Let everything that has breath praise
      the LORD.

Praise the LORD.

a 1 Hebrew *Hallelu Yah*; also in verse 6

PROVERBS 18:9-10

⁹ **O**ne who is slack in his work
  is brother to one who destroys.

¹⁰ The name of the LORD is a strong
  tower;
  the righteous run to it and are
  safe.

□ DAY 184

GOD SIGHTINGS

July 3

2 KINGS 22:3–23:30

In the eighteenth year of his reign, King Josiah sent the secretary, Shaphan son of Azaliah, the son of Meshullam, to the temple of the LORD. He said: ⁴"Go up to Hilkiah the high priest and have him get ready the money that has been brought into the temple of the LORD, which the doorkeepers have collected from the people. ⁵Have them entrust it to the men appointed to supervise the work on the temple. And have these men pay the workers who repair the temple of the LORD— ⁶the carpenters, the builders and the masons. Also have them purchase timber and dressed stone to repair the temple. ⁷But they need not account for the money entrusted to them, because they are acting faithfully."

⁸Hilkiah the high priest said to Shaphan the secretary, "I have found the Book of the Law in the temple of the LORD." He gave it to Shaphan, who read it. ⁹Then Shaphan the secretary went to the king and reported to him: "Your officials have paid out the money that was in the temple of the LORD and have entrusted it to the workers and supervisors at the temple." ¹⁰Then Shaphan the secretary informed the king, "Hilkiah the priest has given me a book." And Shaphan read from it in the presence of the king.

¹¹When the king heard the words of the Book of the Law, he tore his robes.

¹²He gave these orders to Hilkiah the priest, Ahikam son of Shaphan, Acbor son of Micaiah, Shaphan the secretary and Asaiah the king's attendant: ¹³"Go and inquire of the LORD for me and for the people and for all Judah about what is written in this book that has been found. Great is the LORD's anger that burns against us because our fathers have not obeyed the words of this book; they have not acted in accordance with all that is written there concerning us."

¹⁴Hilkiah the priest, Ahikam, Acbor, Shaphan and Asaiah went to speak to the prophetess Huldah, who was the wife of Shallum son of Tikvah, the son of Harhas, keeper of the wardrobe. She lived in Jerusalem, in the Second District.

¹⁵She said to them, "This is what the LORD, the God of Israel, says: Tell the man who sent you to me, ¹⁶'This is what the LORD says: I am going to bring disaster on this place and its people, according to everything written in the book the king of Judah has read. ¹⁷Because they have forsaken me and burned incense to other gods and provoked me to anger by all the idols their hands have made,ᵃ my anger will burn against this place and will not be quenched.' ¹⁸Tell the king of Judah, who sent you to inquire of the LORD, 'This is what the LORD, the God of Israel, says concerning the words you heard: ¹⁹Because your heart was responsive and you humbled yourself before the LORD when you heard what I have spoken against this place and its people, that they would become accursed and laid waste, and because you tore your robes and wept in my presence, I have heard you, declares the LORD. ²⁰Therefore I will gather you to your fathers, and you will be buried in peace. Your eyes will not see all the disaster I am going to bring on this place.'"

So they took her answer back to the king.

²³:¹THEN the king called together all the elders of Judah and Jerusalem. ²He went up to the temple of the LORD with the men of Judah, the people of Jerusalem,

the priests and the prophets—all the people from the least to the greatest. He read in their hearing all the words of the Book of the Covenant, which had been found in the temple of the Lord. ³The king stood by the pillar and renewed the covenant in the presence of the Lord—to follow the Lord and keep his commands, regulations and decrees with all his heart and all his soul, thus confirming the words of the covenant written in this book. Then all the people pledged themselves to the covenant.

⁴The king ordered Hilkiah the high priest, the priests next in rank and the doorkeepers to remove from the temple of the Lord all the articles made for Baal and Asherah and all the starry hosts. He burned them outside Jerusalem in the fields of the Kidron Valley and took the ashes to Bethel. ⁵He did away with the pagan priests appointed by the kings of Judah to burn incense on the high places of the towns of Judah and on those around Jerusalem—those who burned incense to Baal, to the sun and moon, to the constellations and to all the starry hosts. ⁶He took the Asherah pole from the temple of the Lord to the Kidron Valley outside Jerusalem and burned it there. He ground it to powder and scattered the dust over the graves of the common people. ⁷He also tore down the quarters of the male shrine prostitutes, which were in the temple of the Lord and where women did weaving for Asherah.

⁸Josiah brought all the priests from the towns of Judah and desecrated the high places, from Geba to Beersheba, where the priests had burned incense. He broke down the shrines*b* at the gates—at the entrance to the Gate of Joshua, the city governor, which is on the left of the city gate. ⁹Although the priests of the high places did not serve at the altar of the Lord in Jerusalem, they ate unleavened bread with their fellow priests.

¹⁰He desecrated Topheth, which was in the Valley of Ben Hinnom, so no one could use it to sacrifice his son or daughter in*c* the fire to Molech. ¹¹He removed from the entrance to the temple of the Lord the horses that the kings of Judah had dedicated to the sun. They were in the court near the room of an official named Nathan-Melech. Josiah then burned the chariots dedicated to the sun.

¹²He pulled down the altars the kings of Judah had erected on the roof near the upper room of Ahaz, and the altars Manasseh had built in the two courts of the temple of the Lord. He removed them from there, smashed them to pieces and threw the rubble into the Kidron Valley. ¹³The king also desecrated the high places that were east of Jerusalem on the south of the Hill of Corruption—the ones Solomon king of Israel had built for Ashtoreth the vile goddess of the Sidonians, for Chemosh the vile god of Moab, and for Molech*d* the detestable god of the people of Ammon. ¹⁴Josiah smashed the sacred stones and cut down the Asherah poles and covered the sites with human bones.

¹⁵Even the altar at Bethel, the high place made by Jeroboam son of Nebat, who had caused Israel to sin—even that altar and high place he demolished. He burned the high place and ground it to powder, and burned the Asherah pole also. ¹⁶Then Josiah looked around, and when he saw the tombs that were there on the hillside, he had the bones removed from them and burned on the altar to defile it, in accordance with the word of the Lord proclaimed by the man of God who foretold these things.

¹⁷The king asked, "What is that tombstone I see?"

The men of the city said, "It marks the tomb of the man of God who came from Judah and pronounced against the altar of Bethel the very things you have done to it."

¹⁸"Leave it alone," he said. "Don't let anyone disturb his bones." So they spared his bones and those of the prophet who had come from Samaria.

¹⁹Just as he had done at Bethel, Josiah removed and defiled all the shrines at

the high places that the kings of Israel had built in the towns of Samaria that had provoked the LORD to anger. [20]Josiah slaughtered all the priests of those high places on the altars and burned human bones on them. Then he went back to Jerusalem.

[21]The king gave this order to all the people: "Celebrate the Passover to the LORD your God, as it is written in this Book of the Covenant." [22]Not since the days of the judges who led Israel, nor throughout the days of the kings of Israel and the kings of Judah, had any such Passover been observed. [23]But in the eighteenth year of King Josiah, this Passover was celebrated to the LORD in Jerusalem.

[24]Furthermore, Josiah got rid of the mediums and spiritists, the household gods, the idols and all the other detestable things seen in Judah and Jerusalem. This he did to fulfill the requirements of the law written in the book that Hilkiah the priest had discovered in the temple of the LORD. [25]Neither before nor after Josiah was there a king like him who turned to the LORD as he did—with all his heart and with all his soul and with all his strength, in accordance with all the Law of Moses.

[26]Nevertheless, the LORD did not turn away from the heat of his fierce anger, which burned against Judah because of all that Manasseh had done to provoke him to anger. [27]So the LORD said, "I will remove Judah also from my presence as I removed Israel, and I will reject Jerusalem, the city I chose, and this temple, about which I said, 'There shall my Name be.'[e]"

[28]As for the other events of Josiah's reign, and all he did, are they not written in the book of the annals of the kings of Judah?

[29]While Josiah was king, Pharaoh Neco king of Egypt went up to the Euphrates River to help the king of Assyria. King Josiah marched out to meet him in battle, but Neco faced him and killed him at Megiddo. [30]Josiah's servants brought his body in a chariot from Megiddo to Jerusalem and buried him in his own tomb. And the people of the land took Jehoahaz son of Josiah and anointed him and made him king in place of his father.

[a]17 Or by everything they have done   [b]8 Or high places   [c]10 Or to make his son or daughter pass through   [d]13 Hebrew Milcom   [e]27 1 Kings 8:29

ACTS 21:37–22:16

As the soldiers were about to take Paul into the barracks, he asked the commander, "May I say something to you?"

"Do you speak Greek?" he replied. [38]"Aren't you the Egyptian who started a revolt and led four thousand terrorists out into the desert some time ago?"

[39]Paul answered, "I am a Jew, from Tarsus in Cilicia, a citizen of no ordinary city. Please let me speak to the people."

[40]Having received the commander's permission, Paul stood on the steps and motioned to the crowd. When they were all silent, he said to them in Aramaic[a]: [22:1]"BROTHERS and fathers, listen now to my defense."

[2]When they heard him speak to them in Aramaic, they became very quiet.

Then Paul said: [3]"I am a Jew, born in Tarsus of Cilicia, but brought up in this city. Under Gamaliel I was thoroughly trained in the law of our fathers and was just as zealous for God as any of you are today. [4]I persecuted the followers of this Way to their death, arresting both men and women and throwing them into prison, [5]as also the high priest and all the Council can testify. I even obtained letters from them to their brothers in Damascus, and went there to bring these people as prisoners to Jerusalem to be punished.

[6]"About noon as I came near Damascus, suddenly a bright light from heaven flashed around me. [7]I fell to the ground and heard a voice say to me, 'Saul! Saul! Why do you persecute me?'

[8]"'Who are you, Lord?' I asked.

"'I am Jesus of Nazareth, whom you are persecuting,' he replied. [9]My companions saw the light, but they did not understand the voice of him who was speaking to me.

¹⁰"'What shall I do, Lord?' I asked.

"'Get up,' the Lord said, 'and go into Damascus. There you will be told all that you have been assigned to do.' ¹¹My companions led me by the hand into Damascus, because the brilliance of the light had blinded me.

¹²"A man named Ananias came to see me. He was a devout observer of the law and highly respected by all the Jews living there. ¹³He stood beside me and said, 'Brother Saul, receive your sight!' And at that very moment I was able to see him.

¹⁴"Then he said: 'The God of our fathers has chosen you to know his will and to see the Righteous One and to hear words from his mouth. ¹⁵You will be his witness to all men of what you have seen and heard. ¹⁶And now what are you waiting for? Get up, be baptized and wash your sins away, calling on his name.'"

a40 Or possibly *Hebrew*; also in 22:2

PSALM 1:1-6
¹ Blessed is the man
   who does not walk in the
      counsel of the wicked
or stand in the way of sinners
   or sit in the seat of mockers.
² But his delight is in the law of the
      LORD,
   and on his law he meditates day
      and night.
³ He is like a tree planted by streams of
      water,
   which yields its fruit in season
and whose leaf does not wither.
   Whatever he does prospers.

⁴ Not so the wicked!
   They are like chaff
      that the wind blows away.
⁵ Therefore the wicked will not stand
      in the judgment,
   nor sinners in the assembly of the
      righteous.

⁶ For the LORD watches over the way of
      the righteous,
   but the way of the wicked will
      perish.

PROVERBS 18:11-12
¹¹ The wealth of the rich is their
      fortified city;
   they imagine it an unscalable wall.

¹² Before his downfall a man's heart is
      proud,
   but humility comes before honor.

□ DAY 185

GOD SIGHTINGS

July 4

2 KINGS 23:31–25:30

Jehoahaz was twenty-three years old when he became king, and he reigned in Jerusalem three months. His mother's name was Hamutal daughter of Jeremiah; she was from Libnah. ³²He did evil in the eyes of the LORD, just as his fathers had done. ³³Pharaoh Neco put him in chains at Riblah in the land of Hamath*a* so that he might not reign in Jerusalem, and he imposed on Judah a levy of a hundred talents*b* of silver and a talent*c* of gold. ³⁴Pharaoh Neco made Eliakim son of Josiah king in place of his father Josiah and changed Eliakim's name to Jehoiakim. But he took Jehoahaz and carried him off to Egypt, and there he died. ³⁵Jehoiakim paid Pharaoh Neco the silver and gold he demanded. In order to do so, he taxed the land and exacted the silver and gold from the people of the land according to their assessments.

³⁶Jehoiakim was twenty-five years old when he became king, and he reigned in Jerusalem eleven years. His mother's name was Zebidah daughter of Pedaiah; she was from Rumah. ³⁷And he did evil in the eyes of the LORD, just as his fathers had done.

²⁴:¹DURING Jehoiakim's reign, Nebuchadnezzar king of Babylon invaded the land, and Jehoiakim became his vassal for three years. But then he changed his mind and rebelled against Nebuchadnezzar.

²The Lord sent Babylonian,ᵈ Aramean, Moabite and Ammonite raiders against him. He sent them to destroy Judah, in accordance with the word of the Lord proclaimed by his servants the prophets. ³Surely these things happened to Judah according to the Lord's command, in order to remove them from his presence because of the sins of Manasseh and all he had done, ⁴including the shedding of innocent blood. For he had filled Jerusalem with innocent blood, and the Lord was not willing to forgive.

⁵As for the other events of Jehoiakim's reign, and all he did, are they not written in the book of the annals of the kings of Judah? ⁶Jehoiakim rested with his fathers. And Jehoiachin his son succeeded him as king.

⁷The king of Egypt did not march out from his own country again, because the king of Babylon had taken all his territory, from the Wadi of Egypt to the Euphrates River.

⁸Jehoiachin was eighteen years old when he became king, and he reigned in Jerusalem three months. His mother's name was Nehushta daughter of Elnathan; she was from Jerusalem. ⁹He did evil in the eyes of the Lord, just as his father had done.

¹⁰At that time the officers of Nebuchadnezzar king of Babylon advanced on Jerusalem and laid siege to it, ¹¹and Nebuchadnezzar himself came up to the city while his officers were besieging it. ¹²Jehoiachin king of Judah, his mother, his attendants, his nobles and his officials all surrendered to him.

In the eighth year of the reign of the king of Babylon, he took Jehoiachin prisoner. ¹³As the Lord had declared, Nebuchadnezzar removed all the treasures from the temple of the Lord and from the royal palace, and took away all the gold articles that Solomon king of Israel had made for the temple of the Lord. ¹⁴He carried into exile all Jerusalem: all the officers and fighting men, and all the craftsmen and artisans—a total of ten thousand. Only the poorest people of the land were left.

¹⁵Nebuchadnezzar took Jehoiachin captive to Babylon. He also took from Jerusalem to Babylon the king's mother, his wives, his officials and the leading men of the land. ¹⁶The king of Babylon also deported to Babylon the entire force of seven thousand fighting men, strong and fit for war, and a thousand craftsmen and artisans. ¹⁷He made Mattaniah, Jehoiachin's uncle, king in his place and changed his name to Zedekiah.

¹⁸Zedekiah was twenty-one years old when he became king, and he reigned in Jerusalem eleven years. His mother's name was Hamutal daughter of Jeremiah; she was from Libnah. ¹⁹He did evil in the eyes of the Lord, just as Jehoiakim had done. ²⁰It was because of the Lord's anger that all this happened to Jerusalem and Judah, and in the end he thrust them from his presence.

Now Zedekiah rebelled against the king of Babylon.

²⁵:¹So in the ninth year of Zedekiah's reign, on the tenth day of the tenth month, Nebuchadnezzar king of Babylon marched against Jerusalem with his whole army. He encamped outside the city and built siege works all around it. ²The city was kept under siege until the eleventh year of King Zedekiah. ³By the ninth day of the ₍fourth₎ᵉ month the famine in the city had become so severe that there was no food for the people to eat. ⁴Then the city wall was broken through, and the whole army fled at night through the gate between the two walls near the king's garden, though the Babyloniansᶠ were surrounding the city. They fled toward the Arabah,ᵍ ⁵but the Babylonianʰ army pursued the king and overtook him in the plains of Jericho. All his soldiers were separated from him and scattered, ⁶and he was captured. He was taken to the king of Babylon at Riblah, where sentence was pronounced on him. ⁷They killed the sons of Zedekiah before his eyes. Then they put out his eyes, bound him with bronze shackles and took him to Babylon.

⁸On the seventh day of the fifth

month, in the nineteenth year of Nebuchadnezzar king of Babylon, Nebuzaradan commander of the imperial guard, an official of the king of Babylon, came to Jerusalem. [9]He set fire to the temple of the LORD, the royal palace and all the houses of Jerusalem. Every important building he burned down. [10]The whole Babylonian army, under the commander of the imperial guard, broke down the walls around Jerusalem. [11]Nebuzaradan the commander of the guard carried into exile the people who remained in the city, along with the rest of the populace and those who had gone over to the king of Babylon. [12]But the commander left behind some of the poorest people of the land to work the vineyards and fields.

[13]The Babylonians broke up the bronze pillars, the movable stands and the bronze Sea that were at the temple of the LORD and they carried the bronze to Babylon. [14]They also took away the pots, shovels, wick trimmers, dishes and all the bronze articles used in the temple service. [15]The commander of the imperial guard took away the censers and sprinkling bowls—all that were made of pure gold or silver.

[16]The bronze from the two pillars, the Sea and the movable stands, which Solomon had made for the temple of the LORD, was more than could be weighed. [17]Each pillar was twenty-seven feet[i] high. The bronze capital on top of one pillar was four and a half feet[j] high and was decorated with a network and pomegranates of bronze all around. The other pillar, with its network, was similar.

[18]The commander of the guard took as prisoners Seraiah the chief priest, Zephaniah the priest next in rank and the three doorkeepers. [19]Of those still in the city, he took the officer in charge of the fighting men and five royal advisers. He also took the secretary who was chief officer in charge of conscripting the people of the land and sixty of his men who were found in the city. [20]Nebuzaradan the commander took them all

and brought them to the king of Babylon at Riblah. [21]There at Riblah, in the land of Hamath, the king had them executed.

So Judah went into captivity, away from her land.

[22]Nebuchadnezzar king of Babylon appointed Gedaliah son of Ahikam, the son of Shaphan, to be over the people he had left behind in Judah. [23]When all the army officers and their men heard that the king of Babylon had appointed Gedaliah as governor, they came to Gedaliah at Mizpah—Ishmael son of Nethaniah, Johanan son of Kareah, Seraiah son of Tanhumeth the Netophathite, Jaazaniah the son of the Maacathite, and their men. [24]Gedaliah took an oath to reassure them and their men. "Do not be afraid of the Babylonian officials," he said. "Settle down in the land and serve the king of Babylon, and it will go well with you."

[25]In the seventh month, however, Ishmael son of Nethaniah, the son of Elishama, who was of royal blood, came with ten men and assassinated Gedaliah and also the men of Judah and the Babylonians who were with him at Mizpah. [26]At this, all the people from the least to the greatest, together with the army officers, fled to Egypt for fear of the Babylonians.

[27]In the thirty-seventh year of the exile of Jehoiachin king of Judah, in the year Evil-Merodach[k] became king of Babylon, he released Jehoiachin from prison on the twenty-seventh day of the twelfth month. [28]He spoke kindly to him and gave him a seat of honor higher than those of the other kings who were with him in Babylon. [29]So Jehoiachin put aside his prison clothes and for the rest of his life ate regularly at the king's table. [30]Day by day the king gave Jehoiachin a regular allowance as long as he lived.

a33 Hebrew; Septuagint (see also 2 Chron. 36:3) Neco at Riblah in Hamath removed him   b33 That is, about 3 3/4 tons (about 3.4 metric tons)   c33 That is, about 75 pounds (about 34 kilograms)   d2 Or Chaldean   e3 See Jer. 52:6.   f4 Or Chaldeans; also in verses 13, 25 and 26   g4 Or the Jordan Valley   h5 Or Chaldean; also in verses 10 and 24   i17 Hebrew eighteen cubits (about 8.1 meters)   j17 Hebrew three cubits (about 1.3 meters)   k27 Also called Amel-Marduk

ACTS 22:17–23:10

"**W**hen I [Paul] returned to Jerusalem and was praying at the temple, I fell into a trance [18] and saw the Lord speaking. 'Quick!' he said to me. 'Leave Jerusalem immediately, because they will not accept your testimony about me.'

[19]"'Lord,' I replied, 'these men know that I went from one synagogue to another to imprison and beat those who believe in you. [20] And when the blood of your martyr[a] Stephen was shed, I stood there giving my approval and guarding the clothes of those who were killing him.'

[21]"Then the Lord said to me, 'Go; I will send you far away to the Gentiles.'"

[22] The crowd listened to Paul until he said this. Then they raised their voices and shouted, "Rid the earth of him! He's not fit to live!"

[23] As they were shouting and throwing off their cloaks and flinging dust into the air, [24] the commander ordered Paul to be taken into the barracks. He directed that he be flogged and questioned in order to find out why the people were shouting at him like this. [25] As they stretched him out to flog him, Paul said to the centurion standing there, "Is it legal for you to flog a Roman citizen who hasn't even been found guilty?"

[26] When the centurion heard this, he went to the commander and reported it. "What are you going to do?" he asked. "This man is a Roman citizen."

[27] The commander went to Paul and asked, "Tell me, are you a Roman citizen?"

"Yes, I am," he answered.

[28] Then the commander said, "I had to pay a big price for my citizenship."

"But I was born a citizen," Paul replied.

[29] Those who were about to question him withdrew immediately. The commander himself was alarmed when he realized that he had put Paul, a Roman citizen, in chains.

[30] The next day, since the commander wanted to find out exactly why Paul was being accused by the Jews, he released him and ordered the chief priests and all the Sanhedrin to assemble. Then he brought Paul and had him stand before them.

[23:1] PAUL looked straight at the Sanhedrin and said, "My brothers, I have fulfilled my duty to God in all good conscience to this day." [2] At this the high priest Ananias ordered those standing near Paul to strike him on the mouth. [3] Then Paul said to him, "God will strike you, you whitewashed wall! You sit there to judge me according to the law, yet you yourself violate the law by commanding that I be struck!"

[4] Those who were standing near Paul said, "You dare to insult God's high priest?"

[5] Paul replied, "Brothers, I did not realize that he was the high priest; for it is written: 'Do not speak evil about the ruler of your people.'[b]"

[6] Then Paul, knowing that some of them were Sadducees and the others Pharisees, called out in the Sanhedrin, "My brothers, I am a Pharisee, the son of a Pharisee. I stand on trial because of my hope in the resurrection of the dead." [7] When he said this, a dispute broke out between the Pharisees and the Sadducees, and the assembly was divided. [8] (The Sadducees say that there is no resurrection, and that there are neither angels nor spirits, but the Pharisees acknowledge them all.)

[9] There was a great uproar, and some of the teachers of the law who were Pharisees stood up and argued vigorously. "We find nothing wrong with this man," they said. "What if a spirit or an angel has spoken to him?" [10] The dispute became so violent that the commander was afraid Paul would be torn to pieces by them. He ordered the troops to go down and take him away from them by force and bring him into the barracks.

[a] 20 Or *witness*   [b] 5 Exodus 22:28

PSALM 2:1-12

[1] **W**hy do the nations conspire[a]
   and the peoples plot in vain?

² The kings of the earth take their
   stand
   and the rulers gather together
   against the LORD
   and against his Anointed One.ᵇ
³ "Let us break their chains," they say,
   "and throw off their fetters."

⁴ The One enthroned in heaven
   laughs;
   the Lord scoffs at them.
⁵ Then he rebukes them in his anger
   and terrifies them in his wrath,
   saying,
⁶ "I have installed my Kingᶜ
   on Zion, my holy hill."

⁷ I will proclaim the decree of the
LORD:

   He said to me, "You are my Sonᵈ;
   today I have become your
   Father.ᵉ
⁸ Ask of me,
   and I will make the nations your
   inheritance,
   the ends of the earth your
   possession.
⁹ You will rule them with an iron
   scepterᶠ;
   you will dash them to pieces like
   pottery."

¹⁰ Therefore, you kings, be wise;
   be warned, you rulers of the
   earth.
¹¹ Serve the LORD with fear
   and rejoice with trembling.
¹² Kiss the Son, lest he be angry
   and you be destroyed in
   your way,
   for his wrath can flare up in a
   moment.
   Blessed are all who take refuge in
   him.

a 1 Hebrew; Septuagint *rage*   b 2 Or *anointed one*   c 6 Or
king   d 7 Or *son*; also in verse 12   e 7 Or *have begotten
you*   f 9 Or *will break them with a rod of iron*

PROVERBS 18:13
¹³ He who answers before listening—
   that is his folly and his shame.

□ DAY 186

GOD SIGHTINGS

July 5

1 CHRONICLES 1:1–2:17
Adam, Seth, Enosh, ²Kenan, Mahalalel,
Jared, ³Enoch, Methuselah, Lamech,
Noah.

⁴ The sons of Noah:ᵃ
   Shem, Ham and Japheth.

⁵ The sonsᵇ of Japheth:
   Gomer, Magog, Madai, Javan,
   Tubal, Meshech and Tiras.
⁶ The sons of Gomer:
   Ashkenaz, Riphathᶜ and Togarmah.
⁷ The sons of Javan:
   Elishah, Tarshish, the Kittim
   and the Rodanim.

⁸ The sons of Ham:
   Cush, Mizraim,ᵈ Put and Canaan.
⁹ The sons of Cush:
   Seba, Havilah, Sabta, Raamah
   and Sabteca.
   The sons of Raamah:
   Sheba and Dedan.
¹⁰ Cush was the fatherᵉ of
   Nimrod, who grew to be a
   mighty warrior on earth.
¹¹ Mizraim was the father of
   the Ludites, Anamites, Lehabites, Naphtuhites, ¹²Pathru-
   sites, Casluhites (from whom
   the Philistines came) and
   Caphtorites.
¹³ Canaan was the father of
   Sidon his firstborn,ᶠ and of
   the Hittites, ¹⁴Jebusites, Amorites, Girgashites, ¹⁵Hivites,
   Arkites, Sinites, ¹⁶Arvadites,
   Zemarites and Hamathites.

¹⁷ The sons of Shem:
   Elam, Asshur, Arphaxad, Lud
   and Aram.
   The sons of Aram:ᵍ
   Uz, Hul, Gether and Meshech.

18 Arphaxad was the father of Shelah,
and Shelah the father of Eber.
19 Two sons were born to Eber:
One was named Peleg,*h* because in his time the earth was
divided; his brother was
named Joktan.
20 Joktan was the father of
Almodad, Sheleph, Hazarmaveth, Jerah, 21 Hadoram, Uzal,
Diklah, 22 Obal,*i* Abimael, Sheba,
23 Ophir, Havilah and Jobab. All
these were sons of Joktan.

24 Shem, Arphaxad,*j* Shelah,
25 Eber, Peleg, Reu,
26 Serug, Nahor, Terah
27 and Abram (that is, Abraham).

28 The sons of Abraham:
Isaac and Ishmael.
29 These were their descendants:
Nebaioth the firstborn of Ishmael, Kedar, Adbeel, Mibsam,
30 Mishma, Dumah, Massa,
Hadad, Tema, 31 Jetur, Naphish and Kedemah. These
were the sons of Ishmael.

32 The sons born to Keturah, Abra-
ham's concubine:
Zimran, Jokshan, Medan, Mid-
ian, Ishbak and Shuah.
The sons of Jokshan:
Sheba and Dedan.
33 The sons of Midian:
Ephah, Epher, Hanoch, Abida
and Eldaah.
All these were descendants of
Keturah.

34 Abraham was the father of Isaac.
The sons of Isaac:
Esau and Israel.

35 The sons of Esau:
Eliphaz, Reuel, Jeush, Jalam
and Korah.
36 The sons of Eliphaz:
Teman, Omar, Zepho,*k* Gatam
and Kenaz;
by Timna: Amalek.*l*

37 The sons of Reuel:
Nahath, Zerah, Shammah and
Mizzah.

38 The sons of Seir:
Lotan, Shobal, Zibeon, Anah,
Dishon, Ezer and Dishan.
39 The sons of Lotan:
Hori and Homam. Timna was
Lotan's sister.
40 The sons of Shobal:
Alvan,*m* Manahath, Ebal, She-
pho and Onam.
The sons of Zibeon:
Aiah and Anah.
41 The son of Anah:
Dishon.
The sons of Dishon:
Hemdan,*n* Eshban, Ithran and
Keran.
42 The sons of Ezer:
Bilhan, Zaavan and Akan.*o*
The sons of Dishan*p*:
Uz and Aran.

43 These were the kings who reigned
in Edom before any Israelite
king reigned*q*:
Bela son of Beor, whose city
was named Dinhabah.
44 When Bela died, Jobab son of
Zerah from Bozrah succeeded
him as king.
45 When Jobab died, Husham from
the land of the Temanites succeeded him as king.
46 When Husham died, Hadad son
of Bedad, who defeated Midian in the country of Moab,
succeeded him as king. His
city was named Avith.
47 When Hadad died, Samlah from
Masrekah succeeded him as
king.
48 When Samlah died, Shaul from
Rehoboth on the river*r* succeeded him as king.
49 When Shaul died, Baal-Hanan
son of Acbor succeeded him
as king.
50 When Baal-Hanan died, Hadad
succeeded him as king. His

city was named Pau,[s] and his wife's name was Mehetabel daughter of Matred, the daughter of Me-Zahab. [51]Hadad also died.

The chiefs of Edom were:
Timna, Alvah, Jetheth, [52]Oholibamah, Elah, Pinon, [53]Kenaz, Teman, Mibzar, [54]Magdiel and Iram. These were the chiefs of Edom.

[2:1]THESE were the sons of Israel:
Reuben, Simeon, Levi, Judah, Issachar, Zebulun, [2]Dan, Joseph, Benjamin, Naphtali, Gad and Asher.

[3] The sons of Judah:
Er, Onan and Shelah. These three were born to him by a Canaanite woman, the daughter of Shua. Er, Judah's firstborn, was wicked in the LORD's sight; so the LORD put him to death. [4]Tamar, Judah's daughter-in-law, bore him Perez and Zerah. Judah had five sons in all.

[5] The sons of Perez:
Hezron and Hamul.

[6] The sons of Zerah:
Zimri, Ethan, Heman, Calcol and Darda[t]—five in all.

[7] The son of Carmi:
Achar,[u] who brought trouble on Israel by violating the ban on taking devoted things.[v]

[8] The son of Ethan:
Azariah.

[9] The sons born to Hezron were:
Jerahmeel, Ram and Caleb.[w]

[10] Ram was the father of Amminadab, and Amminadab the father of Nahshon, the leader of the people of Judah. [11]Nahshon was the father of Salmon,[x] Salmon the father of Boaz, [12]Boaz the father of Obed and Obed the father of Jesse.

[13] Jesse was the father of Eliab his firstborn; the second son was Abinadab, the third Shimea, [14]the fourth Nethanel, the fifth Raddai, [15]the sixth Ozem and the seventh David. [16]Their sisters were Zeruiah and Abigail. Zeruiah's three sons were Abishai, Joab and Asahel. [17]Abigail was the mother of Amasa, whose father was Jether the Ishmaelite.

a4 Septuagint; Hebrew does not have this line.   *b5 Sons* may mean *descendants* or *successors* or *nations*; also in verses 6-10, 17 and 20.   *c6* Many Hebrew manuscripts and Vulgate (see also Septuagint and Gen. 10:3); most Hebrew manuscripts *Diphath*   *d8* That is, Egypt; also in verse 11   *e10 Father* may mean *ancestor* or *predecessor* or *founder*; also in verses 11, 13, 18 and 20.   *f13* Or *of the Sidonians, the foremost*   *g17* One Hebrew manuscript and some Septuagint manuscripts (see also Gen. 10:23); most Hebrew manuscripts do not have this line.   *h19 Peleg* means *division*.   *i22* Some Hebrew manuscripts and Syriac (see also Gen. 10:28); most Hebrew manuscripts *Ebal*   *j24* Hebrew; some Septuagint manuscripts *Arphaxad, Cainan* (see also note at Gen. 11:10)   *k36* Many Hebrew manuscripts, some Septuagint manuscripts and Syriac (see also Gen. 36:11); most Hebrew manuscripts *Zephi*   *l36* Some Septuagint manuscripts (see also Gen. 36:12); Hebrew *Gatam, Kenaz, Timna and Amalek*   *m40* Many Hebrew manuscripts and some Septuagint manuscripts (see also Gen. 36:23); most Hebrew manuscripts *Alian*   *n41* Many Hebrew manuscripts and some Septuagint manuscripts (see also Gen. 36:26); most Hebrew manuscripts *Hamran*   *o42* Many Hebrew and Septuagint manuscripts (see also Gen. 36:27); most Hebrew manuscripts *Zaavan, Jaakan*   *p42* Hebrew *Dishon,* a variant of *Dishan*   *q43* Or *before an Israelite king reigned over them*   *r48* Possibly the Euphrates   *s50* Many Hebrew manuscripts, some Septuagint manuscripts, Vulgate and Syriac (see also Gen. 36:39); most Hebrew manuscripts *Pai*   *t6* Many Hebrew manuscripts, some Septuagint manuscripts and Syriac (see also 1 Kings 4:31); most Hebrew manuscripts *Dara*   *u7 Achar* means *trouble; Achar* is called *Achan* in Joshua.   *v7* The Hebrew term refers to the irrevocable giving over of things or persons to the LORD, often by totally destroying them.   *w9* Hebrew *Kelubai,* a variant of *Caleb*   *x11* Septuagint (see also Ruth 4:21); Hebrew *Salma*

ACTS 23:11-35

The following night the Lord stood near Paul and said, "Take courage! As you have testified about me in Jerusalem, so you must also testify in Rome."

[12]The next morning the Jews formed a conspiracy and bound themselves with an oath not to eat or drink until they had killed Paul. [13]More than forty men were involved in this plot. [14]They went to the chief priests and elders and said, "We have taken a solemn oath not to eat anything until we have killed Paul. [15]Now then, you and the Sanhedrin petition the commander to bring him

before you on the pretext of wanting more accurate information about his case. We are ready to kill him before he gets here."

16 But when the son of Paul's sister heard of this plot, he went into the barracks and told Paul.

17 Then Paul called one of the centurions and said, "Take this young man to the commander; he has something to tell him." 18 So he took him to the commander.

The centurion said, "Paul, the prisoner, sent for me and asked me to bring this young man to you because he has something to tell you."

19 The commander took the young man by the hand, drew him aside and asked, "What is it you want to tell me?"

20 He said: "The Jews have agreed to ask you to bring Paul before the Sanhedrin tomorrow on the pretext of wanting more accurate information about him. 21 Don't give in to them, because more than forty of them are waiting in ambush for him. They have taken an oath not to eat or drink until they have killed him. They are ready now, waiting for your consent to their request."

22 The commander dismissed the young man and cautioned him, "Don't tell anyone that you have reported this to me."

23 Then he called two of his centurions and ordered them, "Get ready a detachment of two hundred soldiers, seventy horsemen and two hundred spearmen*a* to go to Caesarea at nine tonight. 24 Provide mounts for Paul so that he may be taken safely to Governor Felix."

25 He wrote a letter as follows:

26 Claudius Lysias,

To His Excellency, Governor Felix:

Greetings.

27 This man was seized by the Jews and they were about to kill him, but I came with my troops and rescued him, for I had learned

that he is a Roman citizen. 28 I wanted to know why they were accusing him, so I brought him to their Sanhedrin. 29 I found that the accusation had to do with questions about their law, but there was no charge against him that deserved death or imprisonment. 30 When I was informed of a plot to be carried out against the man, I sent him to you at once. I also ordered his accusers to present to you their case against him.

31 So the soldiers, carrying out their orders, took Paul with them during the night and brought him as far as Antipatris. 32 The next day they let the cavalry go on with him, while they returned to the barracks. 33 When the cavalry arrived in Caesarea, they delivered the letter to the governor and handed Paul over to him. 34 The governor read the letter and asked what province he was from. Learning that he was from Cilicia, 35 he said, "I will hear your case when your accusers get here." Then he ordered that Paul be kept under guard in Herod's palace.

a23 The meaning of the Greek for this word is uncertain.

PSALM 3:1-8

A psalm of David. When he fled from his son Absalom.

1 O LORD, how many are my foes!
  How many rise up against me!
2 Many are saying of me,
  "God will not deliver him." *Selaha*

3 But you are a shield around me,
    O LORD;
  you bestow glory on me and
    lift*b* up my head.
4 To the LORD I cry aloud,
  and he answers me from his
    holy hill. *Selah*

5 I lie down and sleep;
  I wake again, because the LORD
    sustains me.
6 I will not fear the tens of thousands
  drawn up against me on every
    side.

⁷Arise, O Lᴏʀᴅ!
    Deliver me, O my God!
    Strike all my enemies on the jaw;
    break the teeth of the wicked.

⁸From the Lᴏʀᴅ comes deliverance.
    May your blessing be on your
        people.   *Selah*

a2 A word of uncertain meaning, occurring frequently in the Psalms; possibly a musical term   *b3* Or Lᴏʀᴅ, / my Glorious One, who lifts

PROVERBS 18:14-15

¹⁴**A** man's spirit sustains him in
    sickness,
    but a crushed spirit who can bear?

¹⁵The heart of the discerning acquires
    knowledge;
    the ears of the wise seek it out.

□ DAY 187

GOD SIGHTINGS

July 6

1 CHRONICLES 2:18–4:4

¹⁸**C**aleb son of Hezron had children by his wife Azubah (and by Jerioth). These were her sons: Jesher, Shobab and Ardon. ¹⁹When Azubah died, Caleb married Ephrath, who bore him Hur. ²⁰Hur was the father of Uri, and Uri the father of Bezalel.

²¹Later, Hezron lay with the daughter of Makir the father of Gilead (he had married her when he was sixty years old), and she bore him Segub. ²²Segub was the father of Jair, who controlled twenty-three towns in Gilead. ²³(But Geshur and Aram captured Havvoth Jair,*a* as well as Kenath with its surrounding settlements—sixty towns.) All these were descendants of Makir the father of Gilead.

²⁴After Hezron died in Caleb Ephrathah, Abijah the wife of Hezron bore him Ashhur the father*b* of Tekoa.

²⁵The sons of Jerahmeel the firstborn of Hezron:
    Ram his firstborn, Bunah, Oren, Ozem and*c* Ahijah. ²⁶Jerahmeel had another wife, whose name was Atarah; she was the mother of Onam.

²⁷The sons of Ram the firstborn of Jerahmeel:
    Maaz, Jamin and Eker.

²⁸The sons of Onam:
    Shammai and Jada.
  The sons of Shammai:
    Nadab and Abishur.

²⁹Abishur's wife was named Abihail, who bore him Ahban and Molid.

³⁰The sons of Nadab:
    Seled and Appaim. Seled died without children.

³¹The son of Appaim:
    Ishi, who was the father of Sheshan.
    Sheshan was the father of Ahlai.

³²The sons of Jada, Shammai's brother:
    Jether and Jonathan. Jether died without children.

³³The sons of Jonathan:
    Peleth and Zaza.
  These were the descendants of Jerahmeel.

³⁴Sheshan had no sons—only daughters.
    He had an Egyptian servant named Jarha. ³⁵Sheshan gave his daughter in marriage to his servant Jarha, and she bore him Attai.

³⁶Attai was the father of Nathan, Nathan the father of Zabad,
³⁷Zabad the father of Ephlal, Ephlal the father of Obed,
³⁸Obed the father of Jehu, Jehu the father of Azariah,
³⁹Azariah the father of Helez, Helez the father of Eleasah,

⁴⁰ Eleasah the father of Sismai,
Sismai the father of Shallum,
⁴¹ Shallum the father of Jekamiah,
and Jekamiah the father of
Elishama.

⁴² The sons of Caleb the brother of
Jerahmeel:
Mesha his firstborn, who was
the father of Ziph, and his son
Mareshah,ᵈ who was the father of Hebron.
⁴³ The sons of Hebron:
Korah, Tappuah, Rekem and
Shema. ⁴⁴Shema was the father of Raham, and Raham the
father of Jorkeam. Rekem was
the father of Shammai. ⁴⁵The
son of Shammai was Maon,
and Maon was the father of
Beth Zur.
⁴⁶ Caleb's concubine Ephah was
the mother of Haran, Moza
and Gazez. Haran was the father of Gazez.
⁴⁷ The sons of Jahdai:
Regem, Jotham, Geshan, Pelet,
Ephah and Shaaph.
⁴⁸ Caleb's concubine Maacah was
the mother of Sheber and Tir-
hanah. ⁴⁹She also gave birth to
Shaaph the father of Madmannah and to Sheva the father of
Macbenah and Gibea. Caleb's
daughter was Acsah. ⁵⁰These
were the descendants of Caleb.

The sons of Hur the firstborn of
Ephrathah:
Shobal the father of Kiriath
Jearim, ⁵¹Salma the father of
Bethlehem, and Hareph the
father of Beth Gader.
⁵² The descendants of Shobal the
father of Kiriath Jearim were:
Haroeh, half the Manahath-
ites, ⁵³and the clans of Kiriath
Jearim: the Ithrites, Puthites,
Shumathites and Mishraites.
From these descended the Zo-
rathites and Eshtaolites.

⁵⁴ The descendants of Salma:
Bethlehem, the Netophathites,
Atroth Beth Joab, half the Ma-
nahathites, the Zorites, ⁵⁵and
the clans of scribesᵉ who lived
at Jabez: the Tirathites, Shime-
athites and Sucathites. These
are the Kenites who came
from Hammath, the father of
the house of Recab.ᶠ

3:1 THESE were the sons of David born to
him in Hebron:
The firstborn was Amnon the
son of Ahinoam of Jezreel;
the second, Daniel the son of
Abigail of Carmel;
² the third, Absalom the son of
Maacah daughter of Talmai
king of Geshur;
the fourth, Adonijah the son
of Haggith;
³ the fifth, Shephatiah the son
of Abital;
and the sixth, Ithream, by his
wife Eglah.
⁴ These six were born to David
in Hebron, where he reigned
seven years and six months.
David reigned in Jerusalem thirty-three
years, ⁵and these were the children
born to him there:
Shammua,ᵍ Shobab, Nathan and
Solomon. These four were by
Bathshebaʰ daughter of Ammiel. ⁶There were also Ibhar, Elishua,ʲ Eliphelet, ⁷Nogah, Nepheg,
Japhia, ⁸Elishama, Eliada and
Eliphelet—nine in all. ⁹All these
were the sons of David, besides
his sons by his concubines. And
Tamar was their sister.

¹⁰ Solomon's son was Rehoboam,
Abijah his son,
Asa his son,
Jehoshaphat his son,
¹¹ Jehoramʲ his son,
Ahaziah his son,
Joash his son,
¹² Amaziah his son,
Azariah his son,
Jotham his son,

13 Ahaz his son,
Hezekiah his son,
Manasseh his son,
14 Amon his son,
Josiah his son.
15 The sons of Josiah:
Johanan the firstborn,
Jehoiakim the second son,
Zedekiah the third,
Shallum the fourth.
16 The successors of Jehoiakim:
Jehoiachin[k] his son,
and Zedekiah.

17 The descendants of Jehoiachin
the captive:
Shealtiel his son, 18 Malkiram,
Pedaiah, Shenazzar, Jeka-
miah, Hoshama and Neda-
biah.
19 The sons of Pedaiah:
Zerubbabel and Shimei.
The sons of Zerubbabel:
Meshullam and Hananiah.
Shelomith was their sister.
20 There were also five others:
Hashubah, Ohel, Berekiah,
Hasadiah and Jushab-Hesed.
21 The descendants of Hananiah:
Pelatiah and Jeshaiah, and the
sons of Rephaiah, of Arnan, of
Obadiah and of Shecaniah.
22 The descendants of Shecaniah:
Shemaiah and his sons:
Hattush, Igal, Bariah, Neariah
and Shaphat—six in all.
23 The sons of Neariah:
Elioenai, Hizkiah and Azri-
kam—three in all.
24 The sons of Elioenai:
Hodaviah, Eliashib, Pelaiah,
Akkub, Johanan, Delaiah and
Anani—seven in all.

4:1 THE descendants of Judah:
Perez, Hezron, Carmi, Hur and
Shobal.
2 Reaiah son of Shobal was the fa-
ther of Jahath, and Jahath the
father of Ahumai and Lahad.
These were the clans of the
Zorathites.

3 These were the sons[l] of Etam:
Jezreel, Ishma and Idbash.
Their sister was named Haz-
zelelponi. 4 Penuel was the father of Gedor, and Ezer the
father of Hushah.

These were the descendants of
Hur, the firstborn of Ephrathah
and father[m] of Bethlehem.

a23 Or captured the settlements of Jair b24 Father may
mean civic leader or military leader; also in verses 42, 45,
49-52 and possibly elsewhere. c25 Or Oren and Ozem, by
d42 The meaning of the Hebrew for this phrase is uncertain.
e55 Or of the Sopherites f55 Or father of Beth Recab
g5 Hebrew Shimea, a variant of Shammua h5 One Hebrew
manuscript and Vulgate (see also Septuagint and 2 Samuel
11:3); most Hebrew manuscripts Bathshua i6 Two Hebrew
manuscripts (see also 2 Samuel 5:15 and 1 Chron. 14:5);
most Hebrew manuscripts Elishama j11 Hebrew Joram,
a variant of Jehoram k16 Hebrew Jeconiah, a variant of
Jehoiachin; also in verse 17 l3 Some Septuagint manuscripts
(see also Vulgate); Hebrew father m4 Father may mean
civic leader or military leader; also in verses 12, 14, 17, 18
and possibly elsewhere.

ACTS 24:1-27

Five days later the high priest Ananias went down to Caesarea with some of the elders and a lawyer named Tertullus, and they brought their charges against Paul before the governor. 2 When Paul was called in, Tertullus presented his case before Felix: "We have enjoyed a long period of peace under you, and your foresight has brought about reforms in this nation. 3 Everywhere and in every way, most excellent Felix, we acknowledge this with profound gratitude. 4 But in order not to weary you further, I would request that you be kind enough to hear us briefly.

5 "We have found this man to be a troublemaker, stirring up riots among the Jews all over the world. He is a ringleader of the Nazarene sect 6 and even tried to desecrate the temple; so we seized him. 8 By[a] examining him yourself you will be able to learn the truth about all these charges we are bringing against him."

9 The Jews joined in the accusation, asserting that these things were true.

10 When the governor motioned for him to speak, Paul replied: "I know that for a number of years you have been a judge over this nation; so I gladly make

my defense. ¹¹You can easily verify that no more than twelve days ago I went up to Jerusalem to worship. ¹²My accusers did not find me arguing with anyone at the temple, or stirring up a crowd in the synagogues or anywhere else in the city. ¹³And they cannot prove to you the charges they are now making against me. ¹⁴However, I admit that I worship the God of our fathers as a follower of the Way, which they call a sect. I believe everything that agrees with the Law and that is written in the Prophets, ¹⁵and I have the same hope in God as these men, that there will be a resurrection of both the righteous and the wicked. ¹⁶So I strive always to keep my conscience clear before God and man.

¹⁷"After an absence of several years, I came to Jerusalem to bring my people gifts for the poor and to present offerings. ¹⁸I was ceremonially clean when they found me in the temple courts doing this. There was no crowd with me, nor was I involved in any disturbance. ¹⁹But there are some Jews from the province of Asia, who ought to be here before you and bring charges if they have anything against me. ²⁰Or these who are here should state what crime they found in me when I stood before the Sanhedrin— ²¹unless it was this one thing I shouted as I stood in their presence: 'It is concerning the resurrection of the dead that I am on trial before you today.'"

²²Then Felix, who was well acquainted with the Way, adjourned the proceedings. "When Lysias the commander comes," he said, "I will decide your case." ²³He ordered the centurion to keep Paul under guard but to give him some freedom and permit his friends to take care of his needs.

²⁴Several days later Felix came with his wife Drusilla, who was a Jewess. He sent for Paul and listened to him as he spoke about faith in Christ Jesus. ²⁵As Paul discoursed on righteousness, self-control and the judgment to come, Felix was afraid and said, "That's enough for now! You may leave. When I find it convenient, I will send for you." ²⁶At the same time he was hoping that Paul would offer him a bribe, so he sent for him frequently and talked with him.

²⁷When two years had passed, Felix was succeeded by Porcius Festus, but because Felix wanted to grant a favor to the Jews, he left Paul in prison.

a6-8 Some manuscripts him and wanted to judge him according to our law. 7But the commander, Lysias, came and with the use of much force snatched him from our hands 8and ordered his accusers to come before you. By

PSALM 4:1-8

For the director of music. With stringed instruments. A psalm of David.

¹**A**nswer me when I call to you,
  O my righteous God.
Give me relief from my distress;
  be merciful to me and hear my prayer.

²How long, O men, will you turn my glory into shame*a*?
  How long will you love delusions and seek false gods*b*?   *Selah*

³**Know that the Lord has set apart the godly for himself;
  the Lord will hear when I call to him.**

⁴In your anger do not sin;
  when you are on your beds,
  search your hearts and be silent.
                              Selah

⁵Offer right sacrifices
  and trust in the Lord.

⁶Many are asking, "Who can show us any good?"
  Let the light of your face shine upon us, O Lord.

⁷You have filled my heart with greater joy
  than when their grain and new wine abound.

⁸I will lie down and sleep in peace,
  for you alone, O Lord,
  make me dwell in safety.

a2 Or you dishonor my Glorious One   b2 Or seek lies

PROVERBS 18:16-18

¹⁶**A** gift opens the way for the giver
  and ushers him into the presence of the great.

¹⁷The first to present his case seems
right,
till another comes forward and
questions him.

¹⁸Casting the lot settles disputes
and keeps strong opponents apart.

□ D A Y   1 8 8

GOD SIGHTINGS

July 7

1 CHRONICLES 4:5–5:17

⁵**A**shhur the father of Tekoa had
two wives, Helah and Naarah.
⁶Naarah bore him Ahuzzam, He-
pher, Temeni and Haahashtari.
These were the descendants of
Naarah.
⁷The sons of Helah:
Zereth, Zohar, Ethnan, ⁸and
Koz, who was the father of
Anub and Hazzobebah and of
the clans of Aharhel son of
Harum.

⁹Jabez was more honorable than his
brothers. His mother had named him
Jabez,^a saying, "I gave birth to him in
pain." ¹⁰Jabez cried out to the God of Israel, "Oh, that you would bless me and
enlarge my territory! Let your hand be
with me, and keep me from harm so that
I will be free from pain." And God
granted his request.

¹¹Kelub, Shuhah's brother, was the
father of Mehir, who was the
father of Eshton. ¹²Eshton
was the father of Beth Rapha,
Paseah and Tehinnah the father of Ir Nahash.^b These
were the men of Recah.

¹³The sons of Kenaz:
Othniel and Seraiah.
The sons of Othniel:
Hathath and Meonothai.^c

¹⁴Meonothai was the father of
Ophrah.
Seraiah was the father of Joab,
the father of Ge Harashim.^d It
was called this because its
people were craftsmen.
¹⁵The sons of Caleb son of Jephun-
neh:
Iru, Elah and Naam.
The son of Elah:
Kenaz.
¹⁶The sons of Jehallelel:
Ziph, Ziphah, Tiria and Asarel.
¹⁷The sons of Ezrah:
Jether, Mered, Epher and Jalon.
One of Mered's wives gave birth
to Miriam, Shammai and Ish-
bah the father of Eshtemoa.
¹⁸(His Judean wife gave birth to
Jered the father of Gedor, He-
ber the father of Soco and Je-
kuthiel the father of Zanoah.)
These were the children of Pharaoh's daughter Bithiah, whom
Mered had married.
¹⁹The sons of Hodiah's wife, the
sister of Naham:
the father of Keilah the Gar-
mite, and Eshtemoa the Maacathite.
²⁰The sons of Shimon:
Amnon, Rinnah, Ben-Hanan
and Tilon.
The descendants of Ishi:
Zoheth and Ben-Zoheth.
²¹The sons of Shelah son of Judah:
Er the father of Lecah, Laadah
the father of Mareshah and
the clans of the linen workers
at Beth Ashbea, ²²Jokim, the
men of Cozeba, and Joash and
Saraph, who ruled in Moab
and Jashubi Lehem. (These records are from ancient times.)
²³They were the potters who
lived at Netaim and Gederah;
they stayed there and worked
for the king.

²⁴The descendants of Simeon:
Nemuel, Jamin, Jarib, Zerah
and Shaul;

25 Shallum was Shaul's son, Mibsam his son and Mishma his son.

26 The descendants of Mishma:
Hammuel his son, Zaccur his son and Shimei his son.

27 Shimei had sixteen sons and six daughters, but his brothers did not have many children; so their entire clan did not become as numerous as the people of Judah. 28 They lived in Beersheba, Moladah, Hazar Shual, 29 Bilhah, Ezem, Tolad, 30 Bethuel, Hormah, Ziklag, 31 Beth Marcaboth, Hazar Susim, Beth Biri and Shaaraim. These were their towns until the reign of David. 32 Their surrounding villages were Etam, Ain, Rimmon, Token and Ashan—five towns— 33 and all the villages around these towns as far as Baalath.e These were their settlements. And they kept a genealogical record.

34 Meshobab, Jamlech, Joshah son of Amaziah, 35 Joel, Jehu son of Joshibiah, the son of Seraiah, the son of Asiel, 36 also Elioenai, Jaakobah, Jeshohaiah, Asaiah, Adiel, Jesimiel, Benaiah, 37 and Ziza son of Shiphi, the son of Allon, the son of Jedaiah, the son of Shimri, the son of Shemaiah.

38 The men listed above by name were leaders of their clans. Their families increased greatly, 39 and they went to the outskirts of Gedor to the east of the valley in search of pasture for their flocks. 40 They found rich, good pasture, and the land was spacious, peaceful and quiet. Some Hamites had lived there formerly.

41 The men whose names were listed came in the days of Hezekiah king of Judah. They attacked the Hamites in their dwellings and also the Meunites who were there and completely destroyedf them, as is evident to this day. Then they settled in their place, because there was pasture for their flocks. 42 And five hundred of these Simeonites, led by Pelatiah, Neariah, Rephaiah and Uzziel, the sons of Ishi, invaded the hill country of Seir. 43 They killed the remaining Amalekites who had escaped, and they have lived there to this day.

5:1 THE sons of Reuben the firstborn of Israel (he was the firstborn, but when he defiled his father's marriage bed, his rights as firstborn were given to the sons of Joseph son of Israel; so he could not be listed in the genealogical record in accordance with his birthright, 2 and though Judah was the strongest of his brothers and a ruler came from him, the rights of the firstborn belonged to Joseph)— 3 the sons of Reuben the firstborn of Israel:

Hanoch, Pallu, Hezron and Carmi.

4 The descendants of Joel:
Shemaiah his son, Gog his son, Shimei his son, 5 Micah his son, Reaiah his son, Baal his son,
6 and Beerah his son, whom Tiglath-Pileserg king of Assyria took into exile. Beerah was a leader of the Reubenites.

7 Their relatives by clans, listed according to their genealogical records:
Jeiel the chief, Zechariah, 8 and Bela son of Azaz, the son of Shema, the son of Joel. They settled in the area from Aroer to Nebo and Baal Meon. 9 To the east they occupied the land up to the edge of the desert that extends to the Euphrates River, because their livestock had increased in Gilead.

10 During Saul's reign they waged war against the Hagrites, who were defeated at their hands; they occupied the dwellings of the Hagrites throughout the entire region east of Gilead.

11 The Gadites lived next to them in Bashan, as far as Salecah:
12 Joel was the chief, Shapham the second, then Janai and Shaphat, in Bashan.
13 Their relatives, by families, were:
Michael, Meshullam, Sheba,

Jorai, Jacan, Zia and Eber—
seven in all.

14 These were the sons of Abihail
son of Huri, the son of Jaroah,
the son of Gilead, the son of Michael, the son of Jeshishai, the
son of Jahdo, the son of Buz.

15 Ahi son of Abdiel, the son of
Guni, was head of their family.

16 The Gadites lived in Gilead, in
Bashan and its outlying villages, and on all the pasturelands of Sharon as far as they
extended.

17 All these were entered in the genealogical records during the reigns of Jotham king of Judah and Jeroboam king
of Israel.

a 9 Jabez sounds like the Hebrew for pain.   b 12 Or of
the city of Nahash   c 13 Some Septuagint manuscripts
and Vulgate; Hebrew does not have and Meonothai.
d 14 Ge Harashim means valley of craftsmen.   e 33 Some
Septuagint manuscripts (see also Joshua 19:8); Hebrew Baal
f 41 The Hebrew term refers to the irrevocable giving over
of things or persons to the LORD, often by totally destroying
them.   96 Hebrew Tilgath-Pilneser, a variant of Tiglath-
Pileser; also in verse 26

ACTS 25:1-27

Three days after arriving in the province,
Festus went up from Caesarea to Jerusalem, 2 where the chief priests and Jewish
leaders appeared before him and presented the charges against Paul. 3 They
urgently requested Festus, as a favor to
them, to have Paul transferred to Jerusalem, for they were preparing an ambush
to kill him along the way. 4 Festus answered, "Paul is being held at Caesarea,
and I myself am going there soon. 5 Let
some of your leaders come with me and
press charges against the man there, if he
has done anything wrong."

6 After spending eight or ten days
with them, he went down to Caesarea,
and the next day he convened the court
and ordered that Paul be brought before
him. 7 When Paul appeared, the Jews
who had come down from Jerusalem
stood around him, bringing many serious charges against him, which they
could not prove.

8 Then Paul made his defense: "I have
done nothing wrong against the law of

the Jews or against the temple or against
Caesar."

9 Festus, wishing to do the Jews a favor, said to Paul, "Are you willing to go up
to Jerusalem and stand trial before me
there on these charges?"

10 Paul answered: "I am now standing
before Caesar's court, where I ought to
be tried. I have not done any wrong to
the Jews, as you yourself know very well.
11 If, however, I am guilty of doing anything deserving death, I do not refuse to
die. But if the charges brought against
me by these Jews are not true, no one
has the right to hand me over to them. I
appeal to Caesar!"

12 After Festus had conferred with his
council, he declared: "You have appealed to Caesar. To Caesar you will go!"

13 A few days later King Agrippa and
Bernice arrived at Caesarea to pay their
respects to Festus. 14 Since they were
spending many days there, Festus discussed Paul's case with the king. He
said: "There is a man here whom Felix
left as a prisoner. 15 When I went to Jerusalem, the chief priests and elders of the
Jews brought charges against him and
asked that he be condemned.

16 "I told them that it is not the Roman
custom to hand over any man before he
has faced his accusers and has had an
opportunity to defend himself against
their charges. 17 When they came here
with me, I did not delay the case, but convened the court the next day and ordered
the man to be brought in. 18 When his accusers got up to speak, they did not
charge him with any of the crimes I had
expected. 19 Instead, they had some
points of dispute with him about their
own religion and about a dead man
named Jesus who Paul claimed was alive.
20 I was at a loss how to investigate such
matters; so I asked if he would be willing
to go to Jerusalem and stand trial there
on these charges. 21 When Paul made his
appeal to be held over for the Emperor's
decision, I ordered him held until I could
send him to Caesar."

22 Then Agrippa said to Festus, "I
would like to hear this man myself."

He replied, "Tomorrow you will hear him."

²³The next day Agrippa and Bernice came with great pomp and entered the audience room with the high ranking officers and the leading men of the city. At the command of Festus, Paul was brought in. ²⁴Festus said: "King Agrippa, and all who are present with us, you see this man! The whole Jewish community has petitioned me about him in Jerusalem and here in Caesarea, shouting that he ought not to live any longer. ²⁵I found he had done nothing deserving of death, but because he made his appeal to the Emperor I decided to send him to Rome. ²⁶But I have nothing definite to write to His Majesty about him. Therefore I have brought him before all of you, and especially before you, King Agrippa, so that as a result of this investigation I may have something to write. ²⁷For I think it is unreasonable to send on a prisoner without specifying the charges against him."

PSALM 5:1-12
For the director of music. For flutes.
A psalm of David.

¹ **Give ear to my words, O Lord,
consider my sighing.**
² **Listen to my cry for help,
my King and my God,
for to you I pray.**
³ In the morning, O Lord, you hear
my voice;
in the morning I lay my requests
before you
and wait in expectation.

⁴ You are not a God who takes pleasure
in evil;
with you the wicked cannot
dwell.
⁵ The arrogant cannot stand in your
presence;
you hate all who do wrong.
⁶ You destroy those who tell lies;
bloodthirsty and deceitful men
the Lord abhors.
⁷ But I, by your great mercy,
will come into your house;

in reverence will I bow down
toward your holy temple.
⁸ Lead me, O Lord, in your
righteousness
because of my enemies—
make straight your way before me.

⁹ Not a word from their mouth can be
trusted;
their heart is filled with
destruction.
Their throat is an open grave;
with their tongue they speak
deceit.
¹⁰ Declare them guilty, O God!
Let their intrigues be their downfall.
Banish them for their many sins,
for they have rebelled against you.

¹¹ But let all who take refuge in you
be glad;
let them ever sing for joy.
Spread your protection over them,
that those who love your name
may rejoice in you.
¹² For surely, O Lord, you bless the
righteous;
you surround them with your favor
as with a shield.

PROVERBS 18:19
¹⁹ **An** offended brother is more
unyielding than a fortified
city,
and disputes are like the barred
gates of a citadel.

☐ DAY 189

GOD SIGHTINGS

July 8

1 CHRONICLES 5:18–6:81
The Reubenites, the Gadites and the half-tribe of Manasseh had 44,760 men ready for military service—able-bodied men who could handle shield and sword, who could use a bow, and who were trained for battle. ¹⁹They

waged war against the Hagrites, Jetur, Naphish and Nodab. ²⁰They were helped in fighting them, and God handed the Hagrites and all their allies over to them, because they cried out to him during the battle. He answered their prayers, because they trusted in him. ²¹They seized the livestock of the Hagrites—fifty thousand camels, two hundred fifty thousand sheep and two thousand donkeys. They also took one hundred thousand people captive, ²²and many others fell slain, because the battle was God's. And they occupied the land until the exile.

²³The people of the half-tribe of Manasseh were numerous; they settled in the land from Bashan to Baal Hermon, that is, to Senir (Mount Hermon).

²⁴These were the heads of their families: Epher, Ishi, Eliel, Azriel, Jeremiah, Hodaviah and Jahdiel. They were brave warriors, famous men, and heads of their families. ²⁵But they were unfaithful to the God of their fathers and prostituted themselves to the gods of the peoples of the land, whom God had destroyed before them. ²⁶So the God of Israel stirred up the spirit of Pul king of Assyria (that is, Tiglath-Pileser king of Assyria), who took the Reubenites, the Gadites and the half-tribe of Manasseh into exile. He took them to Halah, Habor, Hara and the river of Gozan, where they are to this day.

⁶:¹THE sons of Levi:
    Gershon, Kohath and Merari.
²The sons of Kohath:
    Amram, Izhar, Hebron and Uzziel.
³The children of Amram:
    Aaron, Moses and Miriam.
The sons of Aaron:
    Nadab, Abihu, Eleazar and Ithamar.
⁴Eleazar was the father of Phinehas,
    Phinehas the father of Abishua,
⁵Abishua the father of Bukki,
    Bukki the father of Uzzi,

⁶Uzzi the father of Zerahiah,
    Zerahiah the father of Meraioth,
⁷Meraioth the father of Amariah,
    Amariah the father of Ahitub,
⁸Ahitub the father of Zadok,
    Zadok the father of Ahimaaz,
⁹Ahimaaz the father of Azariah,
    Azariah the father of Johanan,
¹⁰Johanan the father of Azariah
    (it was he who served as priest in the temple Solomon built in Jerusalem),
¹¹Azariah the father of Amariah,
    Amariah the father of Ahitub,
¹²Ahitub the father of Zadok,
    Zadok the father of Shallum,
¹³Shallum the father of Hilkiah,
    Hilkiah the father of Azariah,
¹⁴Azariah the father of Seraiah,
    and Seraiah the father of Jehozadak.
¹⁵Jehozadak was deported when the LORD sent Judah and Jerusalem into exile by the hand of Nebuchadnezzar.

¹⁶The sons of Levi:
    Gershon,ᵃ Kohath and Merari.
¹⁷These are the names of the sons of Gershon:
    Libni and Shimei.
¹⁸The sons of Kohath:
    Amram, Izhar, Hebron and Uzziel.
¹⁹The sons of Merari:
    Mahli and Mushi.
These are the clans of the Levites listed according to their fathers:
²⁰Of Gershon:
    Libni his son, Jehath his son, Zimmah his son, ²¹Joah his son,
    Iddo his son, Zerah his son and Jeatherai his son.
²²The descendants of Kohath:
    Amminadab his son, Korah his son,
    Assir his son, ²³Elkanah his son, Ebiasaph his son, Assir his son,
²⁴Tahath his son, Uriel his son,

Uzziah his son and Shaul his son.

25 The descendants of Elkanah:
Amasai, Ahimoth,
26 Elkanah his son,*b* Zophai his son,
Nahath his son, 27 Eliab his son,
Jeroham his son, Elkanah his son
and Samuel his son.*c*
28 The sons of Samuel:
Joel*d* the firstborn
and Abijah the second son.
29 The descendants of Merari:
Mahli, Libni his son,
Shimei his son, Uzzah his son,
30 Shimea his son, Haggiah his son
and Asaiah his son.

31 These are the men David put in charge of the music in the house of the LORD after the ark came to rest there. 32 They ministered with music before the tabernacle, the Tent of Meeting, until Solomon built the temple of the LORD in Jerusalem. They performed their duties according to the regulations laid down for them.
33 Here are the men who served, together with their sons:

From the Kohathites:
Heman, the musician,
the son of Joel, the son of Samuel,
34 the son of Elkanah, the son of Jeroham,
the son of Eliel, the son of Toah,
35 the son of Zuph, the son of Elkanah,
the son of Mahath, the son of Amasai,
36 the son of Elkanah, the son of Joel,
the son of Azariah, the son of Zephaniah,
37 the son of Tahath, the son of Assir,
the son of Ebiasaph, the son of Korah,
38 the son of Izhar, the son of Kohath,
the son of Levi, the son of Israel;

39 and Heman's associate Asaph, who served at his right hand:
Asaph son of Berekiah, the son of Shimea,
40 the son of Michael, the son of Baaseiah,*e*
the son of Malkijah, 41 the son of Ethni,
the son of Zerah, the son of Adaiah,
42 the son of Ethan, the son of Zimmah,
the son of Shimei, 43 the son of Jahath,
the son of Gershon, the son of Levi;
44 and from their associates, the Merarites, at his left hand:
Ethan son of Kishi, the son of Abdi,
the son of Malluch, 45 the son of Hashabiah,
the son of Amaziah, the son of Hilkiah,
46 the son of Amzi, the son of Bani,
the son of Shemer, 47 the son of Mahli,
the son of Mushi, the son of Merari,
the son of Levi.

48 Their fellow Levites were assigned to all the other duties of the tabernacle, the house of God. 49 But Aaron and his descendants were the ones who presented offerings on the altar of burnt offering and on the altar of incense in connection with all that was done in the Most Holy Place, making atonement for Israel, in accordance with all that Moses the servant of God had commanded.

50 These were the descendants of Aaron:
Eleazar his son, Phinehas his son,
Abishua his son, 51 Bukki his son,
Uzzi his son, Zerahiah his son,
52 Meraioth his son, Amariah his son,
Ahitub his son, 53 Zadok his son
and Ahimaaz his son.

⁵⁴These were the locations of their settlements allotted as their territory (they were assigned to the descendants of Aaron who were from the Kohathite clan, because the first lot was for them):

⁵⁵They were given Hebron in Judah with its surrounding pasturelands. ⁵⁶But the fields and villages around the city were given to Caleb son of Jephunneh.

⁵⁷So the descendants of Aaron were given Hebron (a city of refuge), and Libnah,^f Jattir, Eshtemoa, ⁵⁸Hilen, Debir, ⁵⁹Ashan, Juttah^g and Beth Shemesh, together with their pasturelands. ⁶⁰And from the tribe of Benjamin they were given Gibeon,^h Geba, Alemeth and Anathoth, together with their pasturelands.

These towns, which were distributed among the Kohathite clans, were thirteen in all.

⁶¹The rest of Kohath's descendants were allotted ten towns from the clans of half the tribe of Manasseh.

⁶²The descendants of Gershon, clan by clan, were allotted thirteen towns from the tribes of Issachar, Asher and Naphtali, and from the part of the tribe of Manasseh that is in Bashan.

⁶³The descendants of Merari, clan by clan, were allotted twelve towns from the tribes of Reuben, Gad and Zebulun.

⁶⁴So the Israelites gave the Levites these towns and their pasturelands. ⁶⁵From the tribes of Judah, Simeon and Benjamin they allotted the previously named towns.

⁶⁶Some of the Kohathite clans were given as their territory towns from the tribe of Ephraim.

⁶⁷In the hill country of Ephraim they were given Shechem (a city of refuge), and Gezer,ⁱ ⁶⁸Jokmeam, Beth Horon, ⁶⁹Aijalon and Gath Rimmon, together with their pasturelands.

⁷⁰And from half the tribe of Manasseh the Israelites gave Aner and Bileam, together with their pasturelands, to the rest of the Kohathite clans.

⁷¹The Gershonites received the following:
From the clan of the half-tribe of Manasseh
they received Golan in Bashan and also Ashtaroth, together with their pasturelands;
⁷²from the tribe of Issachar
they received Kedesh, Daberath, ⁷³Ramoth and Anem, together with their pasturelands;
⁷⁴from the tribe of Asher
they received Mashal, Abdon, ⁷⁵Hukok and Rehob, together with their pasturelands;
⁷⁶and from the tribe of Naphtali
they received Kedesh in Galilee, Hammon and Kiriathaim, together with their pasturelands.

⁷⁷The Merarites (the rest of the Levites) received the following:
From the tribe of Zebulun
they received Jokneam, Kartah,^j Rimmono and Tabor, together with their pasturelands;
⁷⁸from the tribe of Reuben across the Jordan east of Jericho
they received Bezer in the desert, Jahzah, ⁷⁹Kedemoth and Mephaath, together with their pasturelands;
⁸⁰and from the tribe of Gad
they received Ramoth in Gilead, Mahanaim, ⁸¹Heshbon and Jazer, together with their pasturelands.

^a16 Hebrew *Gershom*, a variant of *Gershon*; also in verses 17, 20, 43, 62 and 71 ^b26 Some Hebrew manuscripts, Septuagint and Syriac; most Hebrew manuscripts *Ahimoth* ²⁶*and Elkanah. The sons of Elkanah:* ^c27 Some Septuagint manuscripts (see also 1 Samuel 1:19,20 and 1 Chron. 6:33,34); Hebrew does not have *and Samuel his son.* ^d28 Some Septuagint manuscripts and Syriac (see also 1 Samuel 8:2 and 1 Chron. 6:33); Hebrew does not have *Joel.* ^e40 Most Hebrew manuscripts; some Hebrew manuscripts, one Septuagint manuscript and Syriac *Maaseiah* ^f57 See Joshua 21:13; Hebrew *given the cities of refuge: Hebron, Libnah.* ^g59 Syriac (see also Septuagint and Joshua 21:16); Hebrew does not have *Juttah.* ^h60 See Joshua 21:17; Hebrew does not have *Gibeon.* ⁱ67 See Joshua 21:21; Hebrew *given the cities of refuge: Shechem, Gezer.* ^j77 See Septuagint and Joshua 21:34; Hebrew does not have *Jokneam, Kartah.*

ACTS 26:1-32

Then Agrippa said to Paul, "You have permission to speak for yourself."

So Paul motioned with his hand and began his defense: 2"King Agrippa, I consider myself fortunate to stand before you today as I make my defense against all the accusations of the Jews, 3and especially so because you are well acquainted with all the Jewish customs and controversies. Therefore, I beg you to listen to me patiently.

4"The Jews all know the way I have lived ever since I was a child, from the beginning of my life in my own country, and also in Jerusalem. 5They have known me for a long time and can testify, if they are willing, that according to the strictest sect of our religion, I lived as a Pharisee. 6And now it is because of my hope in what God has promised our fathers that I am on trial today. 7This is the promise our twelve tribes are hoping to see fulfilled as they earnestly serve God day and night. O king, it is because of this hope that the Jews are accusing me. 8Why should any of you consider it incredible that God raises the dead?

9"I too was convinced that I ought to do all that was possible to oppose the name of Jesus of Nazareth. 10And that is just what I did in Jerusalem. On the authority of the chief priests I put many of the saints in prison, and when they were put to death, I cast my vote against them. 11Many a time I went from one synagogue to another to have them punished, and I tried to force them to blaspheme. In my obsession against them, I even went to foreign cities to persecute them.

12"On one of these journeys I was going to Damascus with the authority and commission of the chief priests. 13About noon, O king, as I was on the road, I saw a light from heaven, brighter than the sun, blazing around me and my companions. 14We all fell to the ground, and I heard a voice saying to me in Aramaic,a 'Saul, Saul, why do you persecute me? It is hard for you to kick against the goads.'

15"Then I asked, 'Who are you, Lord?'

"'I am Jesus, whom you are persecuting,' the Lord replied. 16'Now get up and stand on your feet. I have appeared to you to appoint you as a servant and as a witness of what you have seen of me and what I will show you. 17I will rescue you from your own people and from the Gentiles. I am sending you to them 18to open their eyes and turn them from darkness to light, and from the power of Satan to God, so that they may receive forgiveness of sins and a place among those who are sanctified by faith in me.'

19"So then, King Agrippa, I was not disobedient to the vision from heaven. 20First to those in Damascus, then to those in Jerusalem and in all Judea, and to the Gentiles also, I preached that they should repent and turn to God and prove their repentance by their deeds. 21That is why the Jews seized me in the temple courts and tried to kill me. 22But I have had God's help to this very day, and so I stand here and testify to small and great alike. **I am saying nothing beyond what the prophets and Moses said would happen— 23that the Christ**b **would suffer and, as the first to rise from the dead, would proclaim light to his own people and to the Gentiles."**

24At this point Festus interrupted Paul's defense. "You are out of your mind, Paul!" he shouted. "Your great learning is driving you insane."

25"I am not insane, most excellent Festus," Paul replied. "What I am saying is true and reasonable. 26The king is familiar with these things, and I can speak freely to him. I am convinced that none of this has escaped his notice, because it was not done in a corner. 27King Agrippa, do you believe the prophets? I know you do."

28Then Agrippa said to Paul, "Do you think that in such a short time you can persuade me to be a Christian?"

29Paul replied, "Short time or long—I pray God that not only you but all who are listening to me today may become what I am, except for these chains."

30The king rose, and with him the

governor and Bernice and those sitting with them. 31They left the room, and while talking with one another, they said, "This man is not doing anything that deserves death or imprisonment."

32Agrippa said to Festus, "This man could have been set free if he had not appealed to Caesar."

a14 Or *Hebrew*   *b23* Or *Messiah*

PSALM 6:1-10
For the director of music. With stringed instruments. According to *sheminith.a* A psalm of David.

1 O Lord, do not rebuke me in your anger
    or discipline me in your wrath.
2 Be merciful to me, Lord, for I am faint;
    O Lord, heal me, for my bones are in agony.
3 My soul is in anguish.
    How long, O Lord, how long?

4 Turn, O Lord, and deliver me;
    save me because of your unfailing love.
5 No one remembers you when he is dead.
    Who praises you from the graveb?

6 I am worn out from groaning;
    all night long I flood my bed with weeping
    and drench my couch with tears.
7 My eyes grow weak with sorrow;
    they fail because of all my foes.

8 Away from me, all you who do evil,
    for the Lord has heard my weeping.
9 The Lord has heard my cry for mercy;
    the Lord accepts my prayer.
10 All my enemies will be ashamed and dismayed;
    they will turn back in sudden disgrace.

aTitle: Probably a musical term   b5 Hebrew Sheol

PROVERBS 18:20-21
20 From the fruit of his mouth a man's stomach is filled;
    with the harvest from his lips he is satisfied.

21 The tongue has the power of life and death,
    and those who love it will eat its fruit.

□ DAY 190

GOD SIGHTINGS

July 9

1 CHRONICLES 7:1–8:40
The sons of Issachar:
    Tola, Puah, Jashub and Shimron—four in all.
2 The sons of Tola:
    Uzzi, Rephaiah, Jeriel, Jahmai, Ibsam and Samuel—heads of their families. During the reign of David, the descendants of Tola listed as fighting men in their genealogy numbered 22,600.
3 The son of Uzzi:
    Izrahiah.
    The sons of Izrahiah:
    Michael, Obadiah, Joel and Isshiah. All five of them were chiefs. 4According to their family genealogy, they had 36,000 men ready for battle, for they had many wives and children.
5 The relatives who were fighting men belonging to all the clans of Issachar, as listed in their genealogy, were 87,000 in all.

6 Three sons of Benjamin:
    Bela, Beker and Jediael.
7 The sons of Bela:
    Ezbon, Uzzi, Uzziel, Jerimoth and Iri, heads of families—five in all. Their genealogical record listed 22,034 fighting men.
8 The sons of Beker:
    Zemirah, Joash, Eliezer, Elioenai, Omri, Jeremoth, Abijah, Anathoth and Alemeth. All these were the sons of Beker.

⁹Their genealogical record listed the heads of families and 20,200 fighting men.
¹⁰The son of Jediael:
Bilhan.

The sons of Bilhan:
Jeush, Benjamin, Ehud, Kenaanah, Zethan, Tarshish and Ahishahar. ¹¹All these sons of Jediael were heads of families. There were 17,200 fighting men ready to go out to war.
¹²The Shuppites and Huppites were the descendants of Ir, and the Hushites the descendants of Aher.

¹³The sons of Naphtali:
Jahziel, Guni, Jezer and Shillem*a*—the descendants of Bilhah.

¹⁴The descendants of Manasseh:
Asriel was his descendant through his Aramean concubine. She gave birth to Makir the father of Gilead. ¹⁵Makir took a wife from among the Huppites and Shuppites. His sister's name was Maacah.

Another descendant was named Zelophehad, who had only daughters.
¹⁶Makir's wife Maacah gave birth to a son and named him Peresh. His brother was named Sheresh, and his sons were Ulam and Rakem.
¹⁷The son of Ulam:
Bedan.

These were the sons of Gilead son of Makir, the son of Manasseh.
¹⁸His sister Hammoleketh gave birth to Ishhod, Abiezer and Mahlah.
¹⁹The sons of Shemida were:
Ahian, Shechem, Likhi and Aniam.

²⁰The descendants of Ephraim:
Shuthelah, Bered his son, Tahath his son, Eleadah his son, Tahath his son, ²¹Zabad his son and Shuthelah his son.

Ezer and Elead were killed by the native-born men of Gath, when they went down to seize their livestock. ²²Their father Ephraim mourned for them many days, and his relatives came to comfort him. ²³Then he lay with his wife again, and she became pregnant and gave birth to a son. He named him Beriah,*b* because there had been misfortune in his family. ²⁴His daughter was Sheerah, who built Lower and Upper Beth Horon as well as Uzzen Sheerah.
²⁵Rephah was his son, Resheph his son,*c*
Telah his son, Tahan his son,
²⁶Ladan his son, Ammihud his son,
Elishama his son, ²⁷Nun his son and Joshua his son.

²⁸Their lands and settlements included Bethel and its surrounding villages, Naaran to the east, Gezer and its villages to the west, and Shechem and its villages all the way to Ayyah and its villages. ²⁹Along the borders of Manasseh were Beth Shan, Taanach, Megiddo and Dor, together with their villages. The descendants of Joseph son of Israel lived in these towns.

³⁰The sons of Asher:
Imnah, Ishvah, Ishvi and Beriah. Their sister was Serah.
³¹The sons of Beriah:
Heber and Malkiel, who was the father of Birzaith.
³²Heber was the father of Japhlet, Shomer and Hotham and of their sister Shua.
³³The sons of Japhlet:
Pasach, Bimhal and Ashvath. These were Japhlet's sons.
³⁴The sons of Shomer:
Ahi, Rohgah,*d* Hubbah and Aram.
³⁵The sons of his brother Helem:
Zophah, Imna, Shelesh and Amal.
³⁶The sons of Zophah:
Suah, Harnepher, Shual, Beri, Imrah, ³⁷Bezer, Hod, Shamma, Shilshah, Ithran*e* and Beera.

38 The sons of Jether:

Jephunneh, Pispah and Ara.

39 The sons of Ulla:

Arah, Hanniel and Rizia.

40 All these were descendants of Asher—heads of families, choice men, brave warriors and outstanding leaders. The number of men ready for battle, as listed in their genealogy, was 26,000.

8:1 BENJAMIN was the father of Bela his firstborn,

Ashbel the second son, Aharah the third,

2 Nohah the fourth and Rapha the fifth.

3 The sons of Bela were:

Addar, Gera, Abihud,ᶠ 4 Abishua, Naaman, Ahoah, 5 Gera, She-phuphan and Huram.

6 These were the descendants of Ehud, who were heads of fami-lies of those living in Geba and were deported to Manahath:

7 Naaman, Ahijah, and Gera, who deported them and who was the father of Uzza and Ahihud.

8 Sons were born to Shaharaim in Moab after he had divorced his wives Hushim and Baara. 9 By his wife Hodesh he had Jobab, Zibia, Mesha, Malcam, 10 Jeuz, Sakia and Mirmah. These were his sons, heads of families. 11 By Hushim he had Abitub and El-paal.

12 The sons of Elpaal:

Eber, Misham, Shemed (who built Ono and Lod with its sur-rounding villages), 13 and Be-riah and Shema, who were heads of families of those liv-ing in Aijalon and who drove out the inhabitants of Gath.

14 Ahio, Shashak, Jeremoth, 15 Zeba-diah, Arad, Eder, 16 Michael, Ish-pah and Joha were the sons of Beriah.

17 Zebadiah, Meshullam, Hizki, He-ber, 18 Ishmerai, Izliah and Jo-bab were the sons of Elpaal.

19 Jakim, Zicri, Zabdi, 20 Elienai, Zil-lethai, Eliel, 21 Adaiah, Beraiah and Shimrath were the sons of Shimei.

22 Ishpan, Eber, Eliel, 23 Abdon, Zicri, Hanan, 24 Hananiah, Elam, An-thothijah, 25 Iphdeiah and Pe-nuel were the sons of Shashak.

26 Shamsherai, Shehariah, Athaliah, 27 Jareshiah, Elijah and Zicri were the sons of Jeroham.

28 All these were heads of families, chiefs as listed in their genealogy, and they lived in Jerusalem.

29 Jeielᵍ the fatherʰ of Gibeon lived in Gibeon.

His wife's name was Maacah, 30 and his firstborn son was Abdon, followed by Zur, Kish, Baal, Ner,ⁱ Nadab, 31 Gedor, Ahio, Zeker 32 and Mikloth, who was the father of Shim-eah. They too lived near their relatives in Jerusalem.

33 Ner was the father of Kish, Kish the father of Saul, and Saul the father of Jonathan, Malki-Shua, Abinadab and Esh-Baal.ʲ

34 The son of Jonathan:

Merib-Baal,ᵏ who was the fa-ther of Micah.

35 The sons of Micah:

Pithon, Melech, Tarea and Ahaz.

36 Ahaz was the father of Jeho-addah, Jehoaddah was the fa-ther of Alemeth, Azmaveth and Zimri, and Zimri was the father of Moza. 37 Moza was the father of Binea; Raphah was his son, Eleasah his son and Azel his son.

38 Azel had six sons, and these were their names:

Azrikam, Bokeru, Ishmael, Sheariah, Obadiah and Hanan. All these were the sons of Azel.

39 The sons of his brother Eshek:

Ulam his firstborn, Jeush the second son and Eliphelet the third. 40 The sons of Ulam were brave warriors who could handle the bow. They had many sons and grandsons— 150 in all.

All these were the descendants of Benjamin.

a13 Some Hebrew and Septuagint manuscripts (see also Gen. 46:24 and Num. 26:49); most Hebrew manuscripts *Shallum*   *b23 Beriah* sounds like the Hebrew for *misfortune.*   *c25* Some Septuagint manuscripts; Hebrew does not have *his son.*   *d34* Or *of his brother Shomer; Rohgah*   *e37* Possibly a variant of *Jether*   *f30* Or *Gera the father of Ehud*   *g29* Some Septuagint manuscripts (see also 1 Chron. 9:35); Hebrew does not have *Jeiel.*   *h29 Father* may mean *civic leader* or *military leader.*   *i30* Some Septuagint manuscripts (see also 1 Chron. 9:36); Hebrew does not have *Ner.*   *j33* Also known as *Ish-Bosheth*   *k34* Also known as *Mephibosheth*

ACTS 27:1-20

When it was decided that we [Paul and those with him] would sail for Italy, Paul and some other prisoners were handed over to a centurion named Julius, who belonged to the Imperial Regiment. ²We boarded a ship from Adramyttium about to sail for ports along the coast of the province of Asia, and we put out to sea. Aristarchus, a Macedonian from Thessalonica, was with us.

³The next day we landed at Sidon; and Julius, in kindness to Paul, allowed him to go to his friends so they might provide for his needs. ⁴From there we put out to sea again and passed to the lee of Cyprus because the winds were against us. ⁵When we had sailed across the open sea off the coast of Cilicia and Pamphylia, we landed at Myra in Lycia. ⁶There the centurion found an Alexandrian ship sailing for Italy and put us on board. ⁷We made slow headway for many days and had difficulty arriving off Cnidus. When the wind did not allow us to hold our course, we sailed to the lee of Crete, opposite Salmone. ⁸We moved along the coast with difficulty and came to a place called Fair Havens, near the town of Lasea.

⁹Much time had been lost, and sailing had already become dangerous because by now it was after the Fast.ᵃ So Paul warned them, ¹⁰"Men, I can see that our voyage is going to be disastrous and bring great loss to ship and cargo, and to our own lives also." ¹¹But the centurion,

instead of listening to what Paul said, followed the advice of the pilot and of the owner of the ship. ¹²Since the harbor was unsuitable to winter in, the majority decided that we should sail on, hoping to reach Phoenix and winter there. This was a harbor in Crete, facing both southwest and northwest.

¹³When a gentle south wind began to blow, they thought they had obtained what they wanted; so they weighed anchor and sailed along the shore of Crete. ¹⁴Before very long, a wind of hurricane force, called the "northeaster," swept down from the island. ¹⁵The ship was caught by the storm and could not head into the wind; so we gave way to it and were driven along. ¹⁶As we passed to the lee of a small island called Cauda, we were hardly able to make the lifeboat secure. ¹⁷When the men had hoisted it aboard, they passed ropes under the ship itself to hold it together. Fearing that they would run aground on the sandbars of Syrtis, they lowered the sea anchor and let the ship be driven along. ¹⁸We took such a violent battering from the storm that the next day they began to throw the cargo overboard. ¹⁹On the third day, they threw the ship's tackle overboard with their own hands. ²⁰When neither sun nor stars appeared for many days and the storm continued raging, we finally gave up all hope of being saved.

a9 That is, the Day of Atonement (Yom Kippur)

PSALM 7:1-17

A *shiggaion*ᵃ of David, which he sang to the LORD concerning Cush, a Benjamite.

¹ **O** LORD my God, I take refuge in you;
   save and deliver me from all who
      pursue me,
² or they will tear me like a lion
   and rip me to pieces with no one
      to rescue me.

³ O LORD my God, if I have done this
   and there is guilt on my hands—
⁴ if I have done evil to him who is at
   peace with me

or without cause have robbed my
    foe—
⁵then let my enemy pursue and
    overtake me;
let him trample my life to the
    ground
and make me sleep in the dust.
                                    Selah

⁶Arise, O Lᴏʀᴅ, in your anger;
    rise up against the rage of my
        enemies.
Awake, my God; decree justice.
⁷Let the assembled peoples gather
        around you.
Rule over them from on high;
⁸   let the Lᴏʀᴅ judge the peoples.
Judge me, O Lᴏʀᴅ, according to my
        righteousness,
according to my integrity, O Most
        High.
⁹O righteous God,
    who searches minds and hearts,
    bring to an end the violence of the
        wicked
    and make the righteous secure.

¹⁰My shieldᵇ is God Most High,
    who saves the upright in heart.
¹¹God is a righteous judge,
    a God who expresses his wrath
        every day.
¹²If he does not relent,
    heᶜ will sharpen his sword;
    he will bend and string his bow.
¹³He has prepared his deadly weapons;
    he makes ready his flaming arrows.

¹⁴He who is pregnant with evil
    and conceives trouble gives birth
        to disillusionment.
¹⁵He who digs a hole and scoops it out
    falls into the pit he has made.
¹⁶The trouble he causes recoils on
        himself;
    his violence comes down on his
        own head.

¹⁷I will give thanks to the Lᴏʀᴅ because
        of his righteousness
    and will sing praise to the name of
        the Lᴏʀᴅ Most High.

ᵃTitle: Probably a literary or musical term   ᵇ10 Or
sovereign   ᶜ12 Or *If a man does not repent, / God*

PROVERBS 18:22
²²He who finds a wife finds what is
        good
    and receives favor from the Lᴏʀᴅ.

☐ DAY 191

GOD SIGHTINGS

July 10

1 CHRONICLES 9:1–10:14
All Israel was listed in the genealogies
recorded in the book of the kings of Israel.

The people of Judah were taken captive to Babylon because of their unfaithfulness. ²Now the first to resettle on
their own property in their own towns
were some Israelites, priests, Levites
and temple servants.

³Those from Judah, from Benjamin,
and from Ephraim and Manasseh who
lived in Jerusalem were:
⁴Uthai son of Ammihud, the son
    of Omri, the son of Imri, the
    son of Bani, a descendant of
    Perez son of Judah.
⁵Of the Shilonites:
Asaiah the firstborn and his
    sons.
⁶Of the Zerahites:
Jeuel.
The people from Judah num-
    bered 690.
⁷Of the Benjamites:
Sallu son of Meshullam, the
    son of Hodaviah, the son of
    Hassenuah;
⁸Ibneiah son of Jeroham; Elah
    son of Uzzi, the son of Micri;
    and Meshullam son of Sheph-
    atiah, the son of Reuel, the son
    of Ibnijah.
⁹The people from Benjamin, as
    listed in their genealogy, num-
    bered 956. All these men
    were heads of their families.

¹⁰ Of the priests:
Jedaiah; Jehoiarib; Jakin;

¹¹ Azariah son of Hilkiah, the son of Meshullam, the son of Zadok, the son of Meraioth, the son of Ahitub, the official in charge of the house of God;

¹² Adaiah son of Jeroham, the son of Pashhur, the son of Malkijah; and Maasai son of Adiel, the son of Jahzerah, the son of Meshullam, the son of Meshillemith, the son of Immer.

¹³ The priests, who were heads of families, numbered 1,760. They were able men, responsible for ministering in the house of God.

¹⁴ Of the Levites:
Shemaiah son of Hasshub, the son of Azrikam, the son of Hashabiah, a Merarite; ¹⁵ Bakbakkar, Heresh, Galal and Mattaniah son of Mica, the son of Zicri, the son of Asaph; ¹⁶ Obadiah son of Shemaiah, the son of Galal, the son of Jeduthun; and Berekiah son of Asa, the son of Elkanah, who lived in the villages of the Netophathites.

¹⁷ The gatekeepers:
Shallum, Akkub, Talmon, Ahiman and their brothers, Shallum their chief ¹⁸ being stationed at the King's Gate on the east, up to the present time. These were the gatekeepers belonging to the camp of the Levites. ¹⁹ Shallum son of Kore, the son of Ebiasaph, the son of Korah, and his fellow gatekeepers from his family (the Korahites) were responsible for guarding the thresholds of the Tentᵃ just as their fathers had been responsible for guarding the entrance to the dwelling of the LORD. ²⁰ In earlier times Phinehas son of Eleazar was in charge of the gatekeepers, and the LORD was with him. ²¹ Zechariah son of Meshelemiah was the gatekeeper at the entrance to the Tent of Meeting.

²² Altogether, those chosen to be gatekeepers at the thresholds numbered 212. They were registered by genealogy in their villages. The gatekeepers had been assigned to their positions of trust by David and Samuel the seer. ²³ They and their descendants were in charge of guarding the gates of the house of the LORD—the house called the Tent. ²⁴ The gatekeepers were on the four sides: east, west, north and south. ²⁵ Their brothers in their villages had to come from time to time and share their duties for seven-day periods. ²⁶ But the four principal gatekeepers, who were Levites, were entrusted with the responsibility for the rooms and treasuries in the house of God. ²⁷ They would spend the night stationed around the house of God, because they had to guard it; and they had charge of the key for opening it each morning.

²⁸ Some of them were in charge of the articles used in the temple service; they counted them when they were brought in and when they were taken out. ²⁹ Others were assigned to take care of the furnishings and all the other articles of the sanctuary, as well as the flour and wine, and the oil, incense and spices. ³⁰ But some of the priests took care of mixing the spices. ³¹ A Levite named Mattithiah, the firstborn son of Shallum the Korahite, was entrusted with the responsibility for baking the offering bread. ³² Some of their Kohathite brothers were in charge of preparing for every Sabbath the bread set out on the table.

³³ Those who were musicians, heads of Levite families, stayed in the rooms of the temple and were exempt from other duties because they were responsible for the work day and night.

³⁴ All these were heads of Levite families, chiefs as listed in their genealogy, and they lived in Jerusalem.

³⁵ Jeiel the fatherᵇ of Gibeon lived in Gibeon.
His wife's name was Maacah,

36and his firstborn son was Abdon, followed by Zur, Kish, Baal, Ner, Nadab, 37Gedor, Ahio, Zechariah and Mikloth. 38Mikloth was the father of Shimeam. They too lived near their relatives in Jerusalem.

39Ner was the father of Kish, Kish the father of Saul, and Saul the father of Jonathan, Malki-Shua, Abinadab and Esh-Baal.c

40The son of Jonathan:

Merib-Baal,d who was the father of Micah.

41The sons of Micah:

Pithon, Melech, Tahrea and Ahaz.e

42 Ahaz was the father of Jadah, Jadahf was the father of Alemeth, Azmaveth and Zimri, and Zimri was the father of Moza.

43Moza was the father of Binea; Rephaiah was his son, Eleasah his son and Azel his son.

44 Azel had six sons, and these were their names:

Azrikam, Bokeru, Ishmael, Sheariah, Obadiah and Hanan. These were the sons of Azel.

10:1Now the Philistines fought against Israel; the Israelites fled before them, and many fell slain on Mount Gilboa. 2The Philistines pressed hard after Saul and his sons, and they killed his sons Jonathan, Abinadab and Malki-Shua. 3The fighting grew fierce around Saul, and when the archers overtook him, they wounded him.

4Saul said to his armor-bearer, "Draw your sword and run me through, or these uncircumcised fellows will come and abuse me."

But his armor-bearer was terrified and would not do it; so Saul took his own sword and fell on it. 5When the armor-bearer saw that Saul was dead, he too fell on his sword and died. 6So Saul and his three sons died, and all his house died together.

7When all the Israelites in the valley saw that the army had fled and that Saul

and his sons had died, they abandoned their towns and fled. And the Philistines came and occupied them.

8The next day, when the Philistines came to strip the dead, they found Saul and his sons fallen on Mount Gilboa. 9They stripped him and took his head and his armor, and sent messengers throughout the land of the Philistines to proclaim the news among their idols and their people. 10They put his armor in the temple of their gods and hung up his head in the temple of Dagon.

11When all the inhabitants of Jabesh Gilead heard of everything the Philistines had done to Saul, 12all their valiant men went and took the bodies of Saul and his sons and brought them to Jabesh. Then they buried their bones under the great tree in Jabesh, and they fasted seven days.

13Saul died because he was unfaithful to the LORD; he did not keep the word of the LORD and even consulted a medium for guidance, 14and did not inquire of the LORD. So the LORD put him to death and turned the kingdom over to David son of Jesse.

a19 That is, the temple; also in verses 21 and 23   b35 Father may mean civic leader or military leader.   c39 Also known as Ish-Bosheth   d40 Also known as Mephibosheth   e41 Vulgate and Syriac (see also Septuagint and 1 Chron. 8:35); Hebrew does not have and Ahaz.   f42 Some Hebrew manuscripts and Septuagint (see also 1 Chron. 8:36); most Hebrew manuscripts Jarah, Jarah

ACTS 27:21-44

After the men [those on the ship with Paul] had gone a long time without food, Paul stood up before them and said: "Men, you should have taken my advice not to sail from Crete; then you would have spared yourselves this damage and loss. 22But now I urge you to keep up your courage, because not one of you will be lost; only the ship will be destroyed. 23Last night an angel of the God whose I am and whom I serve stood beside me 24and said, 'Do not be afraid, Paul. You must stand trial before Caesar; and God has graciously given you the lives of all who sail with you.' 25So keep up your courage, men, for I have faith in God that it will happen just as he told me. [26]Nevertheless, we must run aground on some island."

[27]On the fourteenth night we were still being driven across the Adriatic[a] Sea, when about midnight the sailors sensed they were approaching land. [28]They took soundings and found that the water was a hundred and twenty feet[b] deep. A short time later they took soundings again and found it was ninety feet[c] deep. [29]Fearing that we would be dashed against the rocks, they dropped four anchors from the stern and prayed for daylight. [30]In an attempt to escape from the ship, the sailors let the lifeboat down into the sea, pretending they were going to lower some anchors from the bow. [31]Then Paul said to the centurion and the soldiers, "Unless these men stay with the ship, you cannot be saved." [32]So the soldiers cut the ropes that held the lifeboat and let it fall away.

[33]Just before dawn Paul urged them all to eat. "For the last fourteen days," he said, "you have been in constant suspense and have gone without food—you haven't eaten anything. [34]Now I urge you to take some food. You need it to survive. Not one of you will lose a single hair from his head." [35]After he said this, he took some bread and gave thanks to God in front of them all. Then he broke it and began to eat. [36]They were all encouraged and ate some food themselves. [37]Altogether there were 276 of us on board. [38]When they had eaten as much as they wanted, they lightened the ship by throwing the grain into the sea.

[39]When daylight came, they did not recognize the land, but they saw a bay with a sandy beach, where they decided to run the ship aground if they could. [40]Cutting loose the anchors, they left them in the sea and at the same time untied the ropes that held the rudders. Then they hoisted the foresail to the wind and made for the beach. [41]But the ship struck a sandbar and ran aground. The bow stuck fast and would not move, and the stern was broken to pieces by the pounding of the surf.

[42]The soldiers planned to kill the prisoners to prevent any of them from swimming away and escaping. [43]But the centurion wanted to spare Paul's life and kept them from carrying out their plan. He ordered those who could swim to jump overboard first and get to land. [44]The rest were to get there on planks or on pieces of the ship. In this way everyone reached land in safety.

[a]27 In ancient times the name referred to an area extending well south of Italy.   [b]28 Greek *twenty orguias* (about 37 meters)   [c]28 Greek *fifteen orguias* (about 27 meters)

PSALM 8:1-9

For the director of music. According to *gittith*.[a] A psalm of David.

[1] **O** LORD, our Lord,
   how majestic is your name in all
       the earth!

You have set your glory
   above the heavens.
[2] From the lips of children and infants
   you have ordained praise[b]
because of your enemies,
   to silence the foe and the avenger.

[3] **When I consider your heavens,**
   the work of your fingers,
the moon and the stars,
   which you have set in place,
[4] **what is man that you are mindful**
       of him,
   the son of man that you care for
       him?
[5] You made him a little lower than the
       heavenly beings[c]
   and crowned him with glory and
       honor.

[6] You made him ruler over the works
       of your hands;
   you put everything under his feet:
[7] all flocks and herds,
   and the beasts of the field,
[8] the birds of the air,
   and the fish of the sea,
   all that swim the paths of the seas.

[9] O LORD, our Lord,
   how majestic is your name in all
       the earth!

[a]Title: Probably a musical term   [b]2 Or *strength*
[c]5 Or *than God*

PROVERBS 18:23-24

²³A poor man pleads for mercy,
  but a rich man answers harshly.

²⁴A man of many companions may
    come to ruin,
  but there is a friend who sticks
    closer than a brother.

☐ D A Y   1 9 2

GOD SIGHTINGS

July 11

1 CHRONICLES 11:1–12:18

All Israel came together to David at Hebron and said, "We are your own flesh
and blood. ²In the past, even while Saul
was king, you were the one who led Israel on their military campaigns. And
the LORD your God said to you, 'You will
shepherd my people Israel, and you will
become their ruler.'"

³When all the elders of Israel had
come to King David at Hebron, he made
a compact with them at Hebron before
the LORD, and they anointed David king
over Israel, as the LORD had promised
through Samuel.

⁴David and all the Israelites marched
to Jerusalem (that is, Jebus). The Jebu-
sites who lived there ⁵said to David,
"You will not get in here." Nevertheless,
David captured the fortress of Zion, the
City of David.

⁶David had said, "Whoever leads the
attack on the Jebusites will become
commander-in-chief." Joab son of Zeruiah went up first, and so he received
the command.

⁷David then took up residence in the
fortress, and so it was called the City of
David. ⁸He built up the city around it,
from the supporting terracesª to the
surrounding wall, while Joab restored
the rest of the city. ⁹And David became
more and more powerful, because the
LORD Almighty was with him.

¹⁰These were the chiefs of David's

mighty men—they, together with all Israel, gave his kingship strong support to
extend it over the whole land, as the
LORD had promised— ¹¹this is the list of
David's mighty men:

Jashobeam,ᵇ a Hacmonite, was chief
of the officersᶜ; he raised his spear
against three hundred men, whom he
killed in one encounter.

¹²Next to him was Eleazar son of Dodai the Ahohite, one of the three mighty
men. ¹³He was with David at Pas Dammim when the Philistines gathered
there for battle. At a place where there
was a field full of barley, the troops fled
from the Philistines. ¹⁴But they took
their stand in the middle of the field.
They defended it and struck the Philistines down, and the LORD brought about
a great victory.

¹⁵Three of the thirty chiefs came
down to David to the rock at the cave of
Adullam, while a band of Philistines was
encamped in the Valley of Rephaim.
¹⁶At that time David was in the stronghold, and the Philistine garrison was at
Bethlehem. ¹⁷David longed for water
and said, "Oh, that someone would get
me a drink of water from the well near
the gate of Bethlehem!" ¹⁸So the Three
broke through the Philistine lines, drew
water from the well near the gate of
Bethlehem and carried it back to David.
But he refused to drink it; instead, he
poured it out before the LORD. ¹⁹"God
forbid that I should do this!" he said.
"Should I drink the blood of these men
who went at the risk of their lives?" Because they risked their lives to bring it
back, David would not drink it.

Such were the exploits of the three
mighty men.

²⁰Abishai the brother of Joab was
chief of the Three. He raised his spear
against three hundred men, whom he
killed, and so he became as famous as
the Three. ²¹He was doubly honored
above the Three and became their commander, even though he was not included among them.

²²Benaiah son of Jehoiada was a valiant
fighter from Kabzeel, who performed

great exploits. He struck down two of Moab's best men. He also went down into a pit on a snowy day and killed a lion. 23And he struck down an Egyptian who was seven and a half feet*d* tall. Although the Egyptian had a spear like a weaver's rod in his hand, Benaiah went against him with a club. He snatched the spear from the Egyptian's hand and killed him with his own spear. 24Such were the exploits of Benaiah son of Jehoiada; he too was as famous as the three mighty men. 25He was held in greater honor than any of the Thirty, but he was not included among the Three. And David put him in charge of his bodyguard.

26The mighty men were:
  Asahel the brother of Joab,
  Elhanan son of Dodo from Bethlehem,
27 Shammoth the Harorite,
  Helez the Pelonite,
28 Ira son of Ikkesh from Tekoa,
  Abiezer from Anathoth,
29 Sibbecai the Hushathite,
  Ilai the Ahohite,
30 Maharai the Netophathite,
  Heled son of Baanah the Netophathite,
31 Ithai son of Ribai from Gibeah in Benjamin,
  Benaiah the Pirathonite,
32 Hurai from the ravines of Gaash,
  Abiel the Arbathite,
33 Azmaveth the Baharumite,
  Eliahba the Shaalbonite,
34 the sons of Hashem the Gizonite,
  Jonathan son of Shagee the Hararite,
35 Ahiam son of Sacar the Hararite,
  Eliphal son of Ur,
36 Hepher the Mekerathite,
  Ahijah the Pelonite,
37 Hezro the Carmelite,
  Naarai son of Ezbai,
38 Joel the brother of Nathan,
  Mibhar son of Hagri,
39 Zelek the Ammonite,
  Naharai the Berothite, the armor-bearer of Joab son of Zeruiah,
40 Ira the Ithrite,
  Gareb the Ithrite,
41 Uriah the Hittite,
  Zabad son of Ahlai,
42 Adina son of Shiza the Reubenite, who was chief of the Reubenites, and the thirty with him,
43 Hanan son of Maacah,
  Joshaphat the Mithnite,
44 Uzzia the Ashterathite,
  Shama and Jeiel the sons of Hotham the Aroerite,
45 Jediael son of Shimri,
  his brother Joha the Tizite,
46 Eliel the Mahavite,
  Jeribai and Joshaviah the sons of Elnaam,
  Ithmah the Moabite,
47 Eliel, Obed and Jaasiel the Mezobaite.

12:1THESE were the men who came to David at Ziklag, while he was banished from the presence of Saul son of Kish (they were among the warriors who helped him in battle; 2 they were armed with bows and were able to shoot arrows or to sling stones right-handed or left-handed; they were kinsmen of Saul from the tribe of Benjamin):

3Ahiezer their chief and Joash the sons of Shemaah the Gibeathite; Jeziel and Pelet the sons of Azmaveth; Beracah, Jehu the Anathothite, 4and Ishmaiah the Gibeonite, a mighty man among the Thirty, who was a leader of the Thirty; Jeremiah, Jahaziel, Johanan, Jozabad the Gederathite, 5Eluzai, Jerimoth, Bealiah, Shemariah and Shephatiah the Haruphite; 6Elkanah, Isshiah, Azarel, Joezer and Jashobeam the Korahites; 7and Joelah and Zebadiah the sons of Jeroham from Gedor.

8Some Gadites defected to David at his stronghold in the desert. They were brave warriors, ready for battle and able to handle the shield and spear. Their faces were the faces of lions, and they were as swift as gazelles in the mountains.

⁹Ezer was the chief,
    Obadiah the second in command,
        Eliab the third,
¹⁰Mishmannah the fourth, Jere-
    miah the fifth,
¹¹Attai the sixth, Eliel the seventh,
¹²Johanan the eighth, Elzabad the
    ninth,
¹³Jeremiah the tenth and Macban-
    nai the eleventh.

¹⁴These Gadites were army commanders; the least was a match for a
hundred, and the greatest for a thousand. ¹⁵It was they who crossed the Jordan in the first month when it was
overflowing all its banks, and they put
to flight everyone living in the valleys, to
the east and to the west.

¹⁶Other Benjamites and some men
from Judah also came to David in his
stronghold. ¹⁷David went out to meet
them and said to them, "If you have
come to me in peace, to help me, I am
ready to have you unite with me. But if
you have come to betray me to my enemies when my hands are free from violence, may the God of our fathers see it
and judge you."

¹⁸Then the Spirit came upon Amasai,
chief of the Thirty, and he said:

"We are yours, O David!
    We are with you, O son of Jesse!
Success, success to you,
    and success to those who help you,
        for your God will help you."

So David received them and made
them leaders of his raiding bands.

a8 Or the Millo   b11 Possibly a variant of Jashob-Baal
c11 Or Thirty; some Septuagint manuscripts Three (see also
2 Samuel 23:8)   d23 Hebrew five cubits (about 2.3 meters)

ACTS 28:1-31

Once safely on shore, we [Paul and
those with him] found out that the island was called Malta. ²The islanders
showed us unusual kindness. They built
a fire and welcomed us all because it
was raining and cold. ³Paul gathered a
pile of brushwood and, as he put it on
the fire, a viper, driven out by the heat,
fastened itself on his hand. ⁴When the
islanders saw the snake hanging from
his hand, they said to each other, "This
man must be a murderer; for though he
escaped from the sea, Justice has not allowed him to live." ⁵But Paul shook the
snake off into the fire and suffered no ill
effects. ⁶The people expected him to
swell up or suddenly fall dead, but after
waiting a long time and seeing nothing
unusual happen to him, they changed
their minds and said he was a god.

⁷There was an estate nearby that belonged to Publius, the chief official of the
island. He welcomed us to his home and
for three days entertained us hospitably.
⁸His father was sick in bed, suffering
from fever and dysentery. Paul went in to
see him and, after prayer, placed his
hands on him and healed him. ⁹When
this had happened, the rest of the sick on
the island came and were cured. ¹⁰They
honored us in many ways and when we
were ready to sail, they furnished us with
the supplies we needed.

¹¹After three months we put out to
sea in a ship that had wintered in the island. It was an Alexandrian ship with
the figurehead of the twin gods Castor
and Pollux. ¹²We put in at Syracuse and
stayed there three days. ¹³From there we
set sail and arrived at Rhegium. The
next day the south wind came up, and
on the following day we reached Puteoli.
¹⁴There we found some brothers who
invited us to spend a week with them.
And so we came to Rome. ¹⁵The brothers there had heard that we were coming, and they traveled as far as the
Forum of Appius and the Three Taverns
to meet us. At the sight of these men
Paul thanked God and was encouraged.
¹⁶When we got to Rome, Paul was allowed to live by himself, with a soldier to
guard him.

¹⁷Three days later he called together
the leaders of the Jews. When they had
assembled, Paul said to them: "My
brothers, although I have done nothing
against our people or against the customs of our ancestors, I was arrested in
Jerusalem and handed over to the Romans. ¹⁸They examined me and wanted

to release me, because I was not guilty of any crime deserving death. ¹⁹But when the Jews objected, I was compelled to appeal to Caesar—not that I had any charge to bring against my own people. ²⁰For this reason I have asked to see you and talk with you. It is because of the hope of Israel that I am bound with this chain."

²¹They replied, "We have not received any letters from Judea concerning you, and none of the brothers who have come from there has reported or said anything bad about you. ²²But we want to hear what your views are, for we know that people everywhere are talking against this sect."

²³They arranged to meet Paul on a certain day, and came in even larger numbers to the place where he was staying. From morning till evening he explained and declared to them the kingdom of God and tried to convince them about Jesus from the Law of Moses and from the Prophets. ²⁴Some were convinced by what he said, but others would not believe. ²⁵They disagreed among themselves and began to leave after Paul had made this final statement: "The Holy Spirit spoke the truth to your forefathers when he said through Isaiah the prophet:

²⁶"'Go to this people and say,
"You will be ever hearing but never understanding;
    you will be ever seeing but never perceiving.'
²⁷For this people's heart has become calloused;
    they hardly hear with their ears,
    and they have closed their eyes.
Otherwise they might see with their eyes,
    hear with their ears,
    understand with their hearts
and turn, and I would heal them.'ᵃ

²⁸"Therefore I want you to know that God's salvation has been sent to the Gentiles, and they will listen!"ᵇ

³⁰For two whole years Paul stayed

there in his own rented house and welcomed all who came to see him. ³¹Boldly and without hindrance he preached the kingdom of God and taught about the Lord Jesus Christ.

ᵃ27 Isaiah 6:9,10   ᵇ28 Some manuscripts listen!" ²⁹After he said this, the Jews left, arguing vigorously among themselves.

PSALM 9:1-12ᵃ
For the director of music. To ⌊the tune of⌋ "The Death of the Son." A psalm of David.

¹ I will praise you, O Lord, with all my heart;
    I will tell of all your wonders.
² I will be glad and rejoice in you;
    I will sing praise to your name,
        O Most High.

³ My enemies turn back;
    they stumble and perish before you.
⁴ For you have upheld my right and my cause;
    you have sat on your throne,
        judging righteously.
⁵ You have rebuked the nations and destroyed the wicked;
    you have blotted out their name for ever and ever.
⁶ Endless ruin has overtaken the enemy,
    you have uprooted their cities;
    even the memory of them has perished.

⁷ The Lord reigns forever;
    he has established his throne for judgment.
⁸ He will judge the world in righteousness;
    he will govern the peoples with justice.
⁹ The Lord is a refuge for the oppressed,
    a stronghold in times of trouble.
¹⁰ Those who know your name will trust in you,
    for you, Lord, have never forsaken those who seek you.

¹¹ Sing praises to the Lord, enthroned in Zion;
    proclaim among the nations what he has done.

[12] For he who avenges blood
        remembers;
    he does not ignore the cry of the
        afflicted.

[a] Psalms 9 and 10 may have been originally a single acrostic poem, the stanzas of which begin with the successive letters of the Hebrew alphabet. In the Septuagint they constitute one psalm.

PROVERBS 19:1-3

Better a poor man whose walk is
        blameless
    than a fool whose lips are
        perverse.

[2] It is not good to have zeal without
        knowledge,
    nor to be hasty and miss the way.

[3] A man's own folly ruins his life,
    yet his heart rages against the LORD.

□ DAY 193

GOD SIGHTINGS

July 12

1 CHRONICLES 12:19–14:17

Some of the men of Manasseh defected to David when he went with the Philistines to fight against Saul. (He and his men did not help the Philistines because, after consultation, their rulers sent him away. They said, "It will cost us our heads if he deserts to his master Saul.") [20] When David went to Ziklag, these were the men of Manasseh who defected to him: Adnah, Jozabad, Jediael, Michael, Jozabad, Elihu and Zillethai, leaders of units of a thousand in Manasseh. [21] They helped David against raiding bands, for all of them were brave warriors, and they were commanders in his army. [22] Day after day men came to help David, until he had a great army, like the army of God.[a]

[23] These are the numbers of the men armed for battle who came to David at Hebron to turn Saul's kingdom over to him, as the LORD had said:

[24] men of Judah, carrying shield and spear—6,800 armed for battle;
[25] men of Simeon, warriors ready for battle—7,100;
[26] men of Levi—4,600, [27] including Jehoiada, leader of the family of Aaron, with 3,700 men, [28] and Zadok, a brave young warrior, with 22 officers from his family;
[29] men of Benjamin, Saul's kinsmen—3,000, most of whom had remained loyal to Saul's house until then;
[30] men of Ephraim, brave warriors, famous in their own clans— 20,800;
[31] men of half the tribe of Manasseh, designated by name to come and make David king— 18,000;
[32] men of Issachar, who understood the times and knew what Israel should do—200 chiefs, with all their relatives under their command;
[33] men of Zebulun, experienced soldiers prepared for battle with every type of weapon, to help David with undivided loyalty—50,000;
[34] men of Naphtali—1,000 officers, together with 37,000 men carrying shields and spears;
[35] men of Dan, ready for battle— 28,600;
[36] men of Asher, experienced soldiers prepared for battle— 40,000;
[37] and from east of the Jordan, men of Reuben, Gad and the half-tribe of Manasseh, armed with every type of weapon— 120,000.

[38] All these were fighting men who volunteered to serve in the ranks. They came to Hebron fully determined to make David king over all Israel. All the rest of the Israelites were also of one mind to make David king. [39] The men spent three days there with David,

eating and drinking, for their families had supplied provisions for them. ⁴⁰Also, their neighbors from as far away as Issachar, Zebulun and Naphtali came bringing food on donkeys, camels, mules and oxen. There were plentiful supplies of flour, fig cakes, raisin cakes, wine, oil, cattle and sheep, for there was joy in Israel.

¹³:¹DAVID conferred with each of his officers, the commanders of thousands and commanders of hundreds. ²He then said to the whole assembly of Israel, "If it seems good to you and if it is the will of the LORD our God, let us send word far and wide to the rest of our brothers throughout the territories of Israel, and also to the priests and Levites who are with them in their towns and pasturelands, to come and join us. ³Let us bring the ark of our God back to us, for we did not inquire ofᵇ itᶜ during the reign of Saul." ⁴The whole assembly agreed to do this, because it seemed right to all the people.

⁵So David assembled all the Israelites, from the Shihor River in Egypt to Leboᵈ Hamath, to bring the ark of God from Kiriath Jearim. ⁶David and all the Israelites with him went to Baalah of Judah (Kiriath Jearim) to bring up from there the ark of God the LORD, who is enthroned between the cherubim—the ark that is called by the Name.

⁷They moved the ark of God from Abinadab's house on a new cart, with Uzzah and Ahio guiding it. ⁸David and all the Israelites were celebrating with all their might before God, with songs and with harps, lyres, tambourines, cymbals and trumpets.

⁹When they came to the threshing floor of Kidon, Uzzah reached out his hand to steady the ark, because the oxen stumbled. ¹⁰The LORD's anger burned against Uzzah, and he struck him down because he had put his hand on the ark. So he died there before God.

¹¹Then David was angry because the LORD's wrath had broken out against

Uzzah, and to this day that place is called Perez Uzzah.ᵉ

¹²David was afraid of God that day and asked, "How can I ever bring the ark of God to me?" ¹³He did not take the ark to be with him in the City of David. Instead, he took it aside to the house of Obed-Edom the Gittite. ¹⁴The ark of God remained with the family of Obed-Edom in his house for three months, and the LORD blessed his household and everything he had.

¹⁴:¹Now Hiram king of Tyre sent messengers to David, along with cedar logs, stonemasons and carpenters to build a palace for him. ²And David knew that the LORD had established him as king over Israel and that his kingdom had been highly exalted for the sake of his people Israel.

³In Jerusalem David took more wives and became the father of more sons and daughters. ⁴These are the names of the children born to him there: Shammua, Shobab, Nathan, Solomon, ⁵Ibhar, Elishua, Elpelet, ⁶Nogah, Nepheg, Japhia, ⁷Elishama, Beeliadaᶠ and Eliphelet.

⁸When the Philistines heard that David had been anointed king over all Israel, they went up in full force to search for him, but David heard about it and went out to meet them. ⁹Now the Philistines had come and raided the Valley of Rephaim; ¹⁰so David inquired of God: "Shall I go and attack the Philistines? Will you hand them over to me?"

The LORD answered him, "Go, I will hand them over to you."

¹¹So David and his men went up to Baal Perazim, and there he defeated them. He said, "As waters break out, God has broken out against my enemies by my hand." So that place was called Baal Perazim.ᵍ ¹²The Philistines had abandoned their gods there, and David gave orders to burn them in the fire.

¹³Once more the Philistines raided the valley; ¹⁴so David inquired of God again, and God answered him, "Do not go straight up, but circle around them and attack them in front of the balsam

trees. [15]As soon as you hear the sound of marching in the tops of the balsam trees, move out to battle, because that will mean God has gone out in front of you to strike the Philistine army." [16]So David did as God commanded him, and they struck down the Philistine army, all the way from Gibeon to Gezer.

[17]So David's fame spread throughout every land, and the LORD made all the nations fear him.

a22 Or *a great and mighty army* *b3* Or *we neglected* *c3* Or *him* *d5* Or *to the entrance to* *e11 Perez Uzzah* means *outbreak against Uzzah.* *f7* A variant of *Eliada* *g11 Baal Perazim* means *the lord who breaks out.*

ROMANS 1:1-17

Paul, a servant of Christ Jesus, called to be an apostle and set apart for the gospel of God— [2]the gospel he promised beforehand through his prophets in the Holy Scriptures [3]regarding his Son, who as to his human nature was a descendant of David, [4]and who through the Spirit*a* of holiness was declared with power to be the Son of God*b* by his resurrection from the dead: Jesus Christ our Lord. [5]Through him and for his name's sake, we received grace and apostleship to call people from among all the Gentiles to the obedience that comes from faith. [6]And you also are among those who are called to belong to Jesus Christ.

[7]To all in Rome who are loved by God and called to be saints:

Grace and peace to you from God our Father and from the Lord Jesus Christ.

[8]First, I thank my God through Jesus Christ for all of you, because your faith is being reported all over the world. [9]God, whom I serve with my whole heart in preaching the gospel of his Son, is my witness how constantly I remember you [10]in my prayers at all times; and I pray that now at last by God's will the way may be opened for me to come to you. [11]I long to see you so that I may impart to you some spiritual gift to make you strong— [12]that is, that you and I may be mutually encouraged by each other's faith. [13]I do not want you to be unaware,

brothers, that I planned many times to come to you (but have been prevented from doing so until now) in order that I might have a harvest among you, just as I have had among the other Gentiles.

[14]I am obligated both to Greeks and non-Greeks, both to the wise and the foolish. [15]That is why I am so eager to preach the gospel also to you who are at Rome.

[16]**I am not ashamed of the gospel, because it is the power of God for the salvation of everyone who believes: first for the Jew, then for the Gentile.** [17]For in the gospel a righteousness from God is revealed, a righteousness that is by faith from first to last,*c* just as it is written: "The righteous will live by faith."*d*

a4 Or *who as to his spirit* *b4* Or *was appointed to be the Son of God with power* *c17* Or *is from faith to faith* *d17* Hab. 2:4

PSALM 9:13-20

[13]**O** LORD, see how my enemies persecute me!
Have mercy and lift me up from the gates of death,
[14]that I may declare your praises in the gates of the Daughter of Zion and there rejoice in your salvation.
[15]The nations have fallen into the pit they have dug;
their feet are caught in the net they have hidden.
[16]The LORD is known by his justice;
the wicked are ensnared by the work of their hands.
Higgaion.a Selah
[17]The wicked return to the grave,*b*
all the nations that forget God.
[18]But the needy will not always be forgotten,
nor the hope of the afflicted ever perish.

[19]Arise, O LORD, let not man triumph;
let the nations be judged in your presence.
[20]Strike them with terror, O LORD;
let the nations know they are but men. *Selah*

a16 Or *Meditation;* possibly a musical notation
b17 Hebrew *Sheol*

PROVERBS 19:4-5

4 **W**ealth brings many friends,
but a poor man's friend deserts
him.

5 A false witness will not go unpunished,
and he who pours out lies will not
go free.

☐ DAY 194

GOD SIGHTINGS

July 13

1 CHRONICLES 15:1–16:36

After David had constructed buildings
for himself in the City of David, he prepared a place for the ark of God and
pitched a tent for it. 2 Then David said,
"No one but the Levites may carry the
ark of God, because the LORD chose
them to carry the ark of the LORD and to
minister before him forever."

3 David assembled all Israel in Jerusalem to bring up the ark of the LORD to
the place he had prepared for it. 4 He
called together the descendants of
Aaron and the Levites:

5 From the descendants of Kohath,
Uriel the leader and 120 relatives;
6 from the descendants of Merari,
Asaiah the leader and 220 relatives;
7 from the descendants of Gershon,[a]
Joel the leader and 130 relatives;
8 from the descendants of Elizaphan,
Shemaiah the leader and 200
relatives;
9 from the descendants of Hebron,
Eliel the leader and 80 relatives;
10 from the descendants of Uzziel,
Amminadab the leader and
112 relatives.

11 Then David summoned Zadok and
Abiathar the priests, and Uriel, Asaiah,
Joel, Shemaiah, Eliel and Amminadab
the Levites. 12 He said to them, "You are
the heads of the Levitical families; you
and your fellow Levites are to consecrate yourselves and bring up the ark of
the LORD, the God of Israel, to the place I
have prepared for it. 13 It was because
you, the Levites, did not bring it up the
first time that the LORD our God broke
out in anger against us. We did not inquire of him about how to do it in the
prescribed way." 14 So the priests and
Levites consecrated themselves in order to bring up the ark of the LORD, the
God of Israel. 15 And the Levites carried
the ark of God with the poles on their
shoulders, as Moses had commanded in
accordance with the word of the LORD.

16 David told the leaders of the Levites
to appoint their brothers as singers to
sing joyful songs, accompanied by musical instruments: lyres, harps and cymbals.

17 So the Levites appointed Heman son
of Joel; from his brothers, Asaph son of
Berekiah; and from their brothers the
Merarites, Ethan son of Kushaiah; 18 and
with them their brothers next in rank:
Zechariah,[b] Jaaziel, Shemiramoth, Jehiel,
Unni, Eliab, Benaiah, Maaseiah, Matti-
thiah, Eliphelehu, Mikneiah, Obed-
Edom and Jeiel,[c] the gatekeepers.

19 The musicians Heman, Asaph and
Ethan were to sound the bronze cymbals; 20 Zechariah, Aziel, Shemiramoth,
Jehiel, Unni, Eliab, Maaseiah and Benaiah were to play the lyres according to
alamoth,[d] 21 and Mattithiah, Eliphelehu, Mikneiah, Obed-Edom, Jeiel and
Azaziah were to play the harps, direct-
ing according to *sheminith*.[d] 22 Kenaniah the head Levite was in charge of
the singing; that was his responsibility
because he was skillful at it.

23 Berekiah and Elkanah were to be
doorkeepers for the ark. 24 Shebaniah,
Joshaphat, Nethanel, Amasai, Zechariah, Benaiah and Eliezer the priests
were to blow trumpets before the ark of

God. Obed-Edom and Jehiah were also to be doorkeepers for the ark.

25 So David and the elders of Israel and the commanders of units of a thousand went to bring up the ark of the covenant of the LORD from the house of Obed-Edom, with rejoicing. 26 Because God had helped the Levites who were carrying the ark of the covenant of the LORD, seven bulls and seven rams were sacrificed. 27 Now David was clothed in a robe of fine linen, as were all the Levites who were carrying the ark, and as were the singers, and Kenaniah, who was in charge of the singing of the choirs. David also wore a linen ephod. 28 So all Israel brought up the ark of the covenant of the LORD with shouts, with the sounding of rams' horns and trumpets, and of cymbals, and the playing of lyres and harps.

29 As the ark of the covenant of the LORD was entering the City of David, Michal daughter of Saul watched from a window. And when she saw King David dancing and celebrating, she despised him in her heart.

16:1 THEY brought the ark of God and set it inside the tent that David had pitched for it, and they presented burnt offerings and fellowship offerings*e* before God. 2 After David had finished sacrificing the burnt offerings and fellowship offerings, he blessed the people in the name of the LORD. 3 Then he gave a loaf of bread, a cake of dates and a cake of raisins to each Israelite man and woman.

4 He appointed some of the Levites to minister before the ark of the LORD, to make petition, to give thanks, and to praise the LORD, the God of Israel: 5 Asaph was the chief, Zechariah second, then Jeiel, Shemiramoth, Jehiel, Mattithiah, Eliab, Benaiah, Obed-Edom and Jeiel. They were to play the lyres and harps, Asaph was to sound the cymbals, 6 and Benaiah and Jahaziel the priests were to blow the trumpets regularly before the ark of the covenant of God.

7 That day David first committed to Asaph and his associates this psalm of thanks to the LORD:

8 Give thanks to the LORD, call on his name;
    make known among the nations
        what he has done.
9 Sing to him, sing praise to him;
    tell of all his wonderful acts.
10 Glory in his holy name;
    let the hearts of those who seek
        the LORD rejoice.
11 Look to the LORD and his strength;
    seek his face always.
12 Remember the wonders he has done,
    his miracles, and the judgments he
        pronounced,
13 O descendants of Israel his servant,
    O sons of Jacob, his chosen ones.

14 He is the LORD our God;
    his judgments are in all the earth.
15 He remembers*f* his covenant
        forever,
    the word he commanded, for a
        thousand generations,
16 the covenant he made with Abraham,
    the oath he swore to Isaac.
17 He confirmed it to Jacob as a decree,
    to Israel as an everlasting
        covenant:
18 "To you I will give the land of Canaan
    as the portion you will inherit."

19 When they were but few in number,
    few indeed, and strangers in it,
20 they*g* wandered from nation to
        nation,
    from one kingdom to another.
21 He allowed no man to oppress them;
    for their sake he rebuked kings:
22 "Do not touch my anointed ones;
    do my prophets no harm."

23 Sing to the LORD, all the earth;
    proclaim his salvation day after
        day.
24 Declare his glory among the nations,
    his marvelous deeds among all
        peoples.
25 For great is the LORD and most
        worthy of praise;
    he is to be feared above all gods.
26 For all the gods of the nations are
        idols,
    but the LORD made the heavens.

^{27} Splendor and majesty are before him;
  strength and joy in his dwelling
    place.
^{28} Ascribe to the LORD, O families of
    nations,
  ascribe to the LORD glory and
    strength,
^{29} ascribe to the LORD the glory due
    his name.
  Bring an offering and come before
    him;
  worship the LORD in the splendor
    of his^h holiness.
^{30} Tremble before him, all the earth!
  The world is firmly established; it
    cannot be moved.
^{31} Let the heavens rejoice, let the earth
    be glad;
  let them say among the nations,
    "The LORD reigns!"
^{32} Let the sea resound, and all that is
    in it;
  let the fields be jubilant, and
    everything in them!
^{33} Then the trees of the forest will sing,
  they will sing for joy before the
    LORD,
  for he comes to judge the earth.

^{34} Give thanks to the LORD, for he is
    good;
  his love endures forever.
^{35} Cry out, "Save us, O God our Savior;
  gather us and deliver us from the
    nations,
  that we may give thanks to your holy
    name,
  that we may glory in your praise."
^{36} Praise be to the LORD, the God of
    Israel,
  from everlasting to everlasting.

Then all the people said "Amen" and
"Praise the LORD."

^{a}7 Hebrew *Gershom*, a variant of *Gershon* ^{b}18 Three
Hebrew manuscripts and most Septuagint manuscripts (see
also verse 20 and 1 Chron. 16:5); most Hebrew manuscripts
Zechariah son and or *Zechariah, Ben and* ^{c}18 Hebrew;
Septuagint (see also verse 21) *Jeiel and Azaziah* ^{d}20,21 Probably
a musical term ^{e}1 Traditionally *peace offerings*; also in
verse 2 ^{f}15 Some Septuagint manuscripts (see also
Psalm 105:8); Hebrew *Remember* ^{g}18-20 One Hebrew
manuscript, Septuagint and Vulgate (see also Psalm 105:12);
most Hebrew manuscripts *inherit*, / ^{19}*though you are but
few in number,* / *few indeed, and strangers in it."* / ^{20}*They*
^{h}29 Or LORD *with the splendor of*

ROMANS 1:18-32

The wrath of God is being revealed from
heaven against all the godlessness and
wickedness of men who suppress the
truth by their wickedness, ^{19} since what
may be known about God is plain to
them, because God has made it plain to
them. ^{20}**For since the creation of the
world God's invisible qualities—his
eternal power and divine nature—
have been clearly seen, being understood from what has been made, so
that men are without excuse.**

^{21} For although they knew God, they
neither glorified him as God nor gave
thanks to him, but their thinking became
futile and their foolish hearts were darkened. ^{22} Although they claimed to be
wise, they became fools ^{23} and exchanged the glory of the immortal God
for images made to look like mortal man
and birds and animals and reptiles.

^{24} Therefore God gave them over in
the sinful desires of their hearts to sexual impurity for the degrading of their
bodies with one another. ^{25} They exchanged the truth of God for a lie, and
worshiped and served created things
rather than the Creator—who is forever
praised. Amen.

^{26} Because of this, God gave them over
to shameful lusts. Even their women exchanged natural relations for unnatural
ones. ^{27} In the same way the men also
abandoned natural relations with
women and were inflamed with lust for
one another. Men committed indecent
acts with other men, and received in
themselves the due penalty for their
perversion.

^{28} Furthermore, since they did not
think it worthwhile to retain the knowledge of God, he gave them over to a depraved mind, to do what ought not to be
done. ^{29} They have become filled with
every kind of wickedness, evil, greed
and depravity. They are full of envy,
murder, strife, deceit and malice. They
are gossips, ^{30} slanderers, God-haters,
insolent, arrogant and boastful; they in-
vent ways of doing evil; they disobey
their parents; ^{31} they are senseless,

faithless, heartless, ruthless. ³²Although they know God's righteous decree that those who do such things deserve death, they not only continue to do these very things but also approve of those who practice them.

PSALM 10:1-15a

¹ **W**hy, O LORD, do you stand far off?
  Why do you hide yourself in times of trouble?

²In his arrogance the wicked man hunts down the weak,
  who are caught in the schemes he devises.
³He boasts of the cravings of his heart;
  he blesses the greedy and reviles the LORD.
⁴In his pride the wicked does not seek him;
  in all his thoughts there is no room for God.
⁵His ways are always prosperous;
  he is haughty and your laws are far from him;
  he sneers at all his enemies.
⁶He says to himself, "Nothing will shake me;
  I'll always be happy and never have trouble."
⁷His mouth is full of curses and lies and threats;
  trouble and evil are under his tongue.
⁸He lies in wait near the villages;
  from ambush he murders the innocent,
  watching in secret for his victims.
⁹He lies in wait like a lion in cover;
  he lies in wait to catch the helpless;
  he catches the helpless and drags them off in his net.
¹⁰His victims are crushed, they collapse;
  they fall under his strength.
¹¹He says to himself, "God has forgotten;
  he covers his face and never sees."

¹²Arise, LORD! Lift up your hand, O God.
  Do not forget the helpless.
¹³Why does the wicked man revile God?
  Why does he say to himself,
  "He won't call me to account"?
¹⁴But you, O God, do see trouble and grief;
  you consider it to take it in hand.
The victim commits himself to you;
  you are the helper of the fatherless.
¹⁵Break the arm of the wicked and evil man;
  call him to account for his wickedness
  that would not be found out.

aPsalms 9 and 10 may have been originally a single acrostic poem, the stanzas of which begin with the successive letters of the Hebrew alphabet. In the Septuagint they constitute one psalm.

PROVERBS 19:6-7

⁶ **M**any curry favor with a ruler,
  and everyone is the friend of a man who gives gifts.

⁷A poor man is shunned by all his relatives—
  how much more do his friends avoid him!
Though he pursues them with pleading,
  they are nowhere to be found.a

a7 The meaning of the Hebrew for this sentence is uncertain.

□ D A Y 1 9 5

GOD SIGHTINGS

July 14

1 CHRONICLES 16:37–18:17

David left Asaph and his associates before the ark of the covenant of the LORD to minister there regularly, according to each day's requirements. ³⁸He also left Obed-Edom and his sixty-eight associates to minister with them. Obed-Edom son of Jeduthun, and also Hosah, were gatekeepers.

³⁹David left Zadok the priest and his fellow priests before the tabernacle of the LORD at the high place in Gibeon ⁴⁰to present burnt offerings to the LORD on the altar of burnt offering regularly, morning and evening, in accordance with everything written in the Law of the LORD, which he had given Israel. ⁴¹With them were Heman and Jeduthun and the rest of those chosen and designated by name to give thanks to the LORD, "for his love endures forever." ⁴²Heman and Jeduthun were responsible for the sounding of the trumpets and cymbals and for the playing of the other instruments for sacred song. The sons of Jeduthun were stationed at the gate.

⁴³ Then all the people left, each for his own home, and David returned home to bless his family.

¹⁷:¹AFTER David was settled in his palace, he said to Nathan the prophet, "Here I am, living in a palace of cedar, while the ark of the covenant of the LORD is under a tent."

²Nathan replied to David, "Whatever you have in mind, do it, for God is with you."

³ That night the word of God came to Nathan, saying:

⁴"Go and tell my servant David, 'This is what the LORD says: You are not the one to build me a house to dwell in. ⁵I have not dwelt in a house from the day I brought Israel up out of Egypt to this day. I have moved from one tent site to another, from one dwelling place to another. ⁶Wherever I have moved with all the Israelites, did I ever say to any of their leadersª whom I commanded to shepherd my people, "Why have you not built me a house of cedar?"'

⁷"Now then, tell my servant David, 'This is what the LORD Almighty says: I took you from the pasture and from following the flock, to be ruler over my people Israel. ⁸I have

been with you wherever you have gone, and I have cut off all your enemies from before you. Now I will make your name like the names of the greatest men of the earth. ⁹And I will provide a place for my people Israel and will plant them so that they can have a home of their own and no longer be disturbed. Wicked people will not oppress them anymore, as they did at the beginning ¹⁰and have done ever since the time I appointed leaders over my people Israel. I will also subdue all your enemies.

" 'I declare to you that the LORD will build a house for you: ¹¹When your days are over and you go to be with your fathers, I will raise up your offspring to succeed you, one of your own sons, and I will establish his kingdom. ¹²He is the one who will build a house for me, and I will establish his throne forever. ¹³I will be his father, and he will be my son. I will never take my love away from him, as I took it away from your predecessor. ¹⁴I will set him over my house and my kingdom forever; his throne will be established forever.'"

¹⁵Nathan reported to David all the words of this entire revelation.

¹⁶Then King David went in and sat before the LORD, and he said:

"Who am I, O LORD God, and what is my family, that you have brought me this far? ¹⁷And as if this were not enough in your sight, O God, you have spoken about the future of the house of your servant. You have looked on me as though I were the most exalted of men, O LORD God.

¹⁸"What more can David say to you for honoring your servant? For you know your servant, ¹⁹O LORD. For the sake of your servant and according to your will, you have done this great thing and made known all these great promises.

20"There is no one like you, O LORD, and there is no God but you, as we have heard with our own ears. 21And who is like your people Israel—the one nation on earth whose God went out to redeem a people for himself, and to make a name for yourself, and to perform great and awesome wonders by driving out nations from before your people, whom you redeemed from Egypt? 22You made your people Israel your very own forever, and you, O LORD, have become their God.

23"And now, LORD, let the promise you have made concerning your servant and his house be established forever. Do as you promised, 24so that it will be established and that your name will be great forever. Then men will say, 'The LORD Almighty, the God over Israel, is Israel's God!' And the house of your servant David will be established before you.

25"You, my God, have revealed to your servant that you will build a house for him. So your servant has found courage to pray to you. 26O LORD, you are God! You have promised these good things to your servant. 27Now you have been pleased to bless the house of your servant, that it may continue forever in your sight; for you, O LORD, have blessed it, and it will be blessed forever."

18:1IN the course of time, David defeated the Philistines and subdued them, and he took Gath and its surrounding villages from the control of the Philistines.

2David also defeated the Moabites, and they became subject to him and brought tribute.

3Moreover, David fought Hadadezer king of Zobah, as far as Hamath, when he went to establish his control along the Euphrates River. 4David captured a thousand of his chariots, seven thousand charioteers and twenty thousand foot soldiers. He hamstrung all but a hundred of the chariot horses.

5When the Arameans of Damascus came to help Hadadezer king of Zobah, David struck down twenty-two thousand of them. 6He put garrisons in the Aramean kingdom of Damascus, and the Arameans became subject to him and brought tribute. The LORD gave David victory everywhere he went.

7David took the gold shields carried by the officers of Hadadezer and brought them to Jerusalem. 8From Tebah[b] and Cun, towns that belonged to Hadadezer, David took a great quantity of bronze, which Solomon used to make the bronze Sea, the pillars and various bronze articles.

9When Tou king of Hamath heard that David had defeated the entire army of Hadadezer king of Zobah, 10he sent his son Hadoram to King David to greet him and congratulate him on his victory in battle over Hadadezer, who had been at war with Tou. Hadoram brought all kinds of articles of gold and silver and bronze.

11King David dedicated these articles to the LORD, as he had done with the silver and gold he had taken from all these nations: Edom and Moab, the Ammonites and the Philistines, and Amalek.

12Abishai son of Zeruiah struck down eighteen thousand Edomites in the Valley of Salt. 13He put garrisons in Edom, and all the Edomites became subject to David. The LORD gave David victory everywhere he went.

14David reigned over all Israel, doing what was just and right for all his people. 15Joab son of Zeruiah was over the army; Jehoshaphat son of Ahilud was recorder; 16Zadok son of Ahitub and Ahimelech[c] son of Abiathar were priests; Shavsha was secretary; 17Benaiah son of Jehoiada was over the Kerethites and Pelethites; and David's sons were chief officials at the king's side.

a6 Traditionally *judges*; also in verse 10   b8 Hebrew *Tibhath*, a variant of *Tebah*   c16 Some Hebrew manuscripts, Vulgate and Syriac (see also 2 Samuel 8:17); most Hebrew manuscripts *Abimelech*

ROMANS 2:1-24

You, therefore, have no excuse, you who pass judgment on someone else, for at whatever point you judge the other, you are condemning yourself, because you who pass judgment do the same things. [2]Now we know that God's judgment against those who do such things is based on truth. [3]So when you, a mere man, pass judgment on them and yet do the same things, do you think you will escape God's judgment? [4]Or do you show contempt for the riches of his kindness, tolerance and patience, not realizing that God's kindness leads you toward repentance?

[5]But because of your stubbornness and your unrepentant heart, you are storing up wrath against yourself for the day of God's wrath, when his righteous judgment will be revealed. [6]God "will give to each person according to what he has done."[a] [7]To those who by persistence in doing good seek glory, honor and immortality, he will give eternal life. [8]But for those who are self-seeking and who reject the truth and follow evil, there will be wrath and anger. [9]There will be trouble and distress for every human being who does evil: first for the Jew, then for the Gentile; [10]but glory, honor and peace for everyone who does good: first for the Jew, then for the Gentile. [11]For God does not show favoritism.

[12]All who sin apart from the law will also perish apart from the law, and all who sin under the law will be judged by the law. [13]For it is not those who hear the law who are righteous in God's sight, but it is those who obey the law who will be declared righteous. [14](Indeed, when Gentiles, who do not have the law, do by nature things required by the law, they are a law for themselves, even though they do not have the law, [15]since they show that the requirements of the law are written on their hearts, their consciences also bearing witness, and their thoughts now accusing, now even defending them.) [16]This will take place on the day when God will judge men's secrets through Jesus Christ, as my gospel declares.

[17]Now you, if you call yourself a Jew; if you rely on the law and brag about your relationship to God; [18]if you know his will and approve of what is superior because you are instructed by the law; [19]if you are convinced that you are a guide for the blind, a light for those who are in the dark, [20]an instructor of the foolish, a teacher of infants, because you have in the law the embodiment of knowledge and truth— [21]you, then, who teach others, do you not teach yourself? You who preach against stealing, do you steal? [22]You who say that people should not commit adultery, do you commit adultery? You who abhor idols, do you rob temples? [23]You who brag about the law, do you dishonor God by breaking the law? [24]As it is written: "God's name is blasphemed among the Gentiles because of you."[b]

[a]6 Psalm 62:12; Prov. 24:12   [b]24 Isaiah 52:5; Ezek. 36:22

PSALM 10:16-18

[16]**T**he LORD is King for ever and ever;
the nations will perish from his
land.
[17]**You hear, O LORD, the desire of the
afflicted;
you encourage them, and you
listen to their cry,**
[18]**defending the fatherless and the
oppressed,
in order that man, who is of the
earth, may terrify no more.**

PROVERBS 19:8-9

[8]**H**e who gets wisdom loves his own
soul;
he who cherishes understanding
prospers.

[9]A false witness will not go
unpunished,
and he who pours out lies will
perish.

☐ DAY 196

GOD SIGHTINGS

July 15

1 CHRONICLES 19:1–21:30

In the course of time, Nahash king of the Ammonites died, and his son succeeded him as king. ²David thought, "I will show kindness to Hanun son of Nahash, because his father showed kindness to me." So David sent a delegation to express his sympathy to Hanun concerning his father.

When David's men came to Hanun in the land of the Ammonites to express sympathy to him, ³ the Ammonite nobles said to Hanun, "Do you think David is honoring your father by sending men to you to express sympathy? Haven't his men come to you to explore and spy out the country and overthrow it?" ⁴So Hanun seized David's men, shaved them, cut off their garments in the middle at the buttocks, and sent them away.

⁵When someone came and told David about the men, he sent messengers to meet them, for they were greatly humiliated. The king said, "Stay at Jericho till your beards have grown, and then come back."

⁶When the Ammonites realized that they had become a stench in David's nostrils, Hanun and the Ammonites sent a thousand talents^a of silver to hire chariots and charioteers from Aram Naharaim,^b Aram Maacah and Zobah. ⁷They hired thirty-two thousand chariots and charioteers, as well as the king of Maacah with his troops, who came and camped near Medeba, while the Ammonites were mustered from their towns and moved out for battle.

⁸On hearing this, David sent Joab out with the entire army of fighting men. ⁹The Ammonites came out and drew up in battle formation at the entrance to their city, while the kings who had come were by themselves in the open country. ¹⁰Joab saw that there were battle lines

in front of him and behind him; so he selected some of the best troops in Israel and deployed them against the Arameans. ¹¹He put the rest of the men under the command of Abishai his brother, and they were deployed against the Ammonites. ¹²Joab said, "If the Arameans are too strong for me, then you are to rescue me; but if the Ammonites are too strong for you, then I will rescue you. ¹³Be strong and let us fight bravely for our people and the cities of our God. The Lord will do what is good in his sight."

¹⁴Then Joab and the troops with him advanced to fight the Arameans, and they fled before him. ¹⁵When the Ammonites saw that the Arameans were fleeing, they too fled before his brother Abishai and went inside the city. So Joab went back to Jerusalem.

¹⁶After the Arameans saw that they had been routed by Israel, they sent messengers and had Arameans brought from beyond the River,^c with Shophach the commander of Hadadezer's army leading them.

¹⁷When David was told of this, he gathered all Israel and crossed the Jordan; he advanced against them and formed his battle lines opposite them. David formed his lines to meet the Arameans in battle, and they fought against him. ¹⁸But they fled before Israel, and David killed seven thousand of their charioteers and forty thousand of their foot soldiers. He also killed Shophach the commander of their army.

¹⁹When the vassals of Hadadezer saw that they had been defeated by Israel, they made peace with David and became subject to him.

So the Arameans were not willing to help the Ammonites anymore.

²⁰:¹In the spring, at the time when kings go off to war, Joab led out the armed forces. He laid waste the land of the Ammonites and went to Rabbah and besieged it, but David remained in Jerusalem. Joab attacked Rabbah and left it in ruins. ²David took the crown from the head of their king^d—its weight was

found to be a talent[e] of gold, and it was set with precious stones—and it was placed on David's head. He took a great quantity of plunder from the city [3]and brought out the people who were there, consigning them to labor with saws and with iron picks and axes. David did this to all the Ammonite towns. Then David and his entire army returned to Jerusalem.

[4]In the course of time, war broke out with the Philistines, at Gezer. At that time Sibbecai the Hushathite killed Sippai, one of the descendants of the Rephaites, and the Philistines were subjugated.

[5]In another battle with the Philistines, Elhanan son of Jair killed Lahmi the brother of Goliath the Gittite, who had a spear with a shaft like a weaver's rod.

[6]In still another battle, which took place at Gath, there was a huge man with six fingers on each hand and six toes on each foot—twenty-four in all. He also was descended from Rapha. [7]When he taunted Israel, Jonathan son of Shimea, David's brother, killed him.

[8]These were descendants of Rapha in Gath, and they fell at the hands of David and his men.

21:1 Satan rose up against Israel and incited David to take a census of Israel. [2]So David said to Joab and the commanders of the troops, "Go and count the Israelites from Beersheba to Dan. Then report back to me so that I may know how many there are."

[3]But Joab replied, "May the Lord multiply his troops a hundred times over. My lord the king, are they not all my lord's subjects? Why does my lord want to do this? Why should he bring guilt on Israel?"

[4]The king's word, however, overruled Joab; so Joab left and went throughout Israel and then came back to Jerusalem. [5]Joab reported the number of the fighting men to David: In all Israel there were one million one hundred thousand men who could handle a sword, including four hundred and seventy thousand in Judah.

[6]But Joab did not include Levi and Benjamin in the numbering, because the king's command was repulsive to him. [7]This command was also evil in the sight of God; so he punished Israel.

[8]Then David said to God, "I have sinned greatly by doing this. Now, I beg you, take away the guilt of your servant. I have done a very foolish thing."

[9]The Lord said to Gad, David's seer, [10]"Go and tell David, 'This is what the Lord says: I am giving you three options. Choose one of them for me to carry out against you.'"

[11]So Gad went to David and said to him, "This is what the Lord says: 'Take your choice: [12]three years of famine, three months of being swept away[f] before your enemies, with their swords overtaking you, or three days of the sword of the Lord—days of plague in the land, with the angel of the Lord ravaging every part of Israel.' Now then, decide how I should answer the one who sent me."

[13]David said to Gad, "I am in deep distress. Let me fall into the hands of the Lord, for his mercy is very great; but do not let me fall into the hands of men."

[14]So the Lord sent a plague on Israel, and seventy thousand men of Israel fell dead. [15]And God sent an angel to destroy Jerusalem. But as the angel was doing so, the Lord saw it and was grieved because of the calamity and said to the angel who was destroying the people, "Enough! Withdraw your hand." The angel of the Lord was then standing at the threshing floor of Araunah[g] the Jebusite.

[16]David looked up and saw the angel of the Lord standing between heaven and earth, with a drawn sword in his hand extended over Jerusalem. Then David and the elders, clothed in sackcloth, fell facedown.

[17]David said to God, "Was it not I who ordered the fighting men to be counted? I am the one who has sinned and done wrong. These are but sheep. What have they done? O Lord my God, let your hand fall upon me and my family, but do not let this plague remain on your people."

[18]Then the angel of the Lord ordered Gad to tell David to go up and build an al-

tar to the LORD on the threshing floor of
Araunah the Jebusite. 19So David went
up in obedience to the word that Gad
had spoken in the name of the LORD.
20While Araunah was threshing
wheat, he turned and saw the angel; his
four sons who were with him hid themselves. 21Then David approached, and
when Araunah looked and saw him, he
left the threshing floor and bowed down
before David with his face to the ground.
22David said to him, "Let me have the
site of your threshing floor so I can
build an altar to the LORD, that the
plague on the people may be stopped.
Sell it to me at the full price."
23Araunah said to David, "Take it! Let
my lord the king do whatever pleases
him. Look, I will give the oxen for the
burnt offerings, the threshing sledges
for the wood, and the wheat for the
grain offering. I will give all this."
24But King David replied to Araunah,
"No, I insist on paying the full price. I
will not take for the LORD what is yours,
or sacrifice a burnt offering that costs
me nothing."
25So David paid Araunah six hundred
shekels[h] of gold for the site. 26David
built an altar to the LORD there and sacrificed burnt offerings and fellowship offerings.[i] He called on the LORD, and the
LORD answered him with fire from
heaven on the altar of burnt offering.
27Then the LORD spoke to the angel,
and he put his sword back into its sheath.
28At that time, when David saw that the
LORD had answered him on the threshing
floor of Araunah the Jebusite, he offered
sacrifices there. 29The tabernacle of the
LORD, which Moses had made in the desert, and the altar of burnt offering were at
that time on the high place at Gibeon.
30But David could not go before it to inquire of God, because he was afraid of the
sword of the angel of the LORD.

[a]6 That is, about 37 tons (about 34 metric tons) [b]6 That is, Northwest Mesopotamia [c]16 That is, the Euphrates [d]2 Or *of Milcom,* that is, Molech [e]2 That is, about 75 pounds (about 34 kilograms) [f]12 Hebrew; Septuagint and Vulgate (see also 2 Samuel 24:13) *of fleeing* [g]15 Hebrew *Ornan,* a variant of *Araunah;* also in verses 18-28 [h]25 That is, about 15 pounds (about 7 kilograms) [i]26 Traditionally *peace offerings*

ROMANS 2:25–3:8

Circumcision has value if you observe
the law, but if you break the law, you
have become as though you had not
been circumcised. 26If those who are
not circumcised keep the law's requirements, will they not be regarded as
though they were circumcised? 27The
one who is not circumcised physically
and yet obeys the law will condemn you
who, even though you have the[a] written
code and circumcision, are a lawbreaker.
28A man is not a Jew if he is only one
outwardly, nor is circumcision merely
outward and physical. 29**No, a man is a
Jew if he is one inwardly; and circumcision is circumcision of the heart, by
the Spirit, not by the written code.
Such a man's praise is not from men,
but from God.**

3:1WHAT advantage, then, is there in being a Jew, or what value is there in circumcision? 2Much in every way! First of
all, they have been entrusted with the
very words of God.
3What if some did not have faith? Will
their lack of faith nullify God's faithfulness? 4Not at all! Let God be true, and every man a liar. As it is written:

"So that you may be proved right
when you speak
and prevail when you judge."[b]

5But if our unrighteousness brings
out God's righteousness more clearly,
what shall we say? That God is unjust in
bringing his wrath on us? (I am using a
human argument.) 6Certainly not! If
that were so, how could God judge the
world? 7Someone might argue, "If my
falsehood enhances God's truthfulness
and so increases his glory, why am I still
condemned as a sinner?" 8Why not
say—as we are being slanderously reported as saying and as some claim that
we say—"Let us do evil that good may
result"? Their condemnation is deserved.

[a]27 Or *who, by means of a* [b]4 Psalm 51:4

PSALM 11:1-7

For the director of music. Of David.

¹ In the LORD I take refuge.
  How then can you say to me:
  "Flee like a bird to your
    mountain.
² For look, the wicked bend their
    bows;
  they set their arrows against the
    strings
to shoot from the shadows
  at the upright in heart.
³ When the foundations are being
    destroyed,
  what can the righteous do*a*?"

⁴ The LORD is in his holy temple;
  the LORD is on his heavenly
    throne.
He observes the sons of men;
  his eyes examine them.
⁵ The LORD examines the righteous,
  but the wicked*b* and those who
    love violence
  his soul hates.
⁶ On the wicked he will rain
  fiery coals and burning sulfur;
  a scorching wind will be their lot.

⁷ For the LORD is righteous,
  he loves justice;
  upright men will see his face.

a 3 Or what is the Righteous One doing   b 5 Or The LORD, the Righteous One, examines the wicked, /

PROVERBS 19:10-12

¹⁰ It is not fitting for a fool to live in
    luxury—
  how much worse for a slave to rule
    over princes!

¹¹ A man's wisdom gives him patience;
  it is to his glory to overlook an
    offense.

¹² A king's rage is like the roar of a
    lion,
  but his favor is like dew on the
    grass.

GOD SIGHTINGS

July 16

1 CHRONICLES 22:1–23:32

Then David said, "The house of the LORD God is to be here, and also the altar of burnt offering for Israel."

² So David gave orders to assemble the aliens living in Israel, and from among them he appointed stonecutters to prepare dressed stone for building the house of God. ³ He provided a large amount of iron to make nails for the doors of the gateways and for the fittings, and more bronze than could be weighed. ⁴ He also provided more cedar logs than could be counted, for the Sidonians and Tyrians had brought large numbers of them to David.

⁵ David said, "My son Solomon is young and inexperienced, and the house to be built for the LORD should be of great magnificence and fame and splendor in the sight of all the nations. Therefore I will make preparations for it." So David made extensive preparations before his death.

⁶ Then he called for his son Solomon and charged him to build a house for the LORD, the God of Israel. ⁷ David said to Solomon: "My son, I had it in my heart to build a house for the Name of the LORD my God. ⁸ But this word of the LORD came to me: 'You have shed much blood and have fought many wars. You are not to build a house for my Name, because you have shed much blood on the earth in my sight. ⁹ But you will have a son who will be a man of peace and rest, and I will give him rest from all his enemies on every side. His name will be Solomon,*a* and I will grant Israel peace and quiet during his reign. ¹⁰ He is the one who will build a house for my Name. He will be my son, and I will be his father. And I will establish the throne of his kingdom over Israel forever.'

¹¹ "Now, my son, the LORD be with you,

and may you have success and build the house of the Lord your God, as he said you would. 12May the Lord give you discretion and understanding when he puts you in command over Israel, so that you may keep the law of the Lord your God. 13Then you will have success if you are careful to observe the decrees and laws that the Lord gave Moses for Israel. Be strong and courageous. Do not be afraid or discouraged.

14"I have taken great pains to provide for the temple of the Lord a hundred thousand talents*b* of gold, a million talents*c* of silver, quantities of bronze and iron too great to be weighed, and wood and stone. And you may add to them. 15You have many workmen: stonecutters, masons and carpenters, as well as men skilled in every kind of work 16in gold and silver, bronze and iron—craftsmen beyond number. Now begin the work, and the Lord be with you."

17Then David ordered all the leaders of Israel to help his son Solomon. 18He said to them, "Is not the Lord your God with you? And has he not granted you rest on every side? For he has handed the inhabitants of the land over to me, and the land is subject to the Lord and to his people. 19Now devote your heart and soul to seeking the Lord your God. Begin to build the sanctuary of the Lord God, so that you may bring the ark of the covenant of the Lord and the sacred articles belonging to God into the temple that will be built for the Name of the Lord."

23:1WHEN David was old and full of years, he made his son Solomon king over Israel.

2He also gathered together all the leaders of Israel, as well as the priests and Levites. 3The Levites thirty years old or more were counted, and the total number of men was thirty-eight thousand. 4David said, "Of these, twenty-four thousand are to supervise the work of the temple of the Lord and six thousand are to be officials and judges. 5Four thousand are to be gatekeepers and four thousand are to praise the Lord with

the musical instruments I have provided for that purpose."

6David divided the Levites into groups corresponding to the sons of Levi: Gershon, Kohath and Merari.

7Belonging to the Gershonites:
Ladan and Shimei.

8The sons of Ladan:
Jehiel the first, Zetham and Joel—three in all.

9The sons of Shimei:
Shelomoth, Haziel and Haran—three in all.
These were the heads of the families of Ladan.

10And the sons of Shimei:
Jahath, Ziza,*d* Jeush and Beriah.
These were the sons of Shimei—four in all.

11Jahath was the first and Ziza the second, but Jeush and Beriah did not have many sons; so they were counted as one family with one assignment.

12The sons of Kohath:
Amram, Izhar, Hebron and Uzziel—four in all.

13The sons of Amram:
Aaron and Moses.
Aaron was set apart, he and his descendants forever, to consecrate the most holy things, to offer sacrifices before the Lord, to minister before him and to pronounce blessings in his name forever. 14The sons of Moses the man of God were counted as part of the tribe of Levi.

15The sons of Moses:
Gershom and Eliezer.

16The descendants of Gershom:
Shubael was the first.

17The descendants of Eliezer:
Rehabiah was the first.
Eliezer had no other sons, but the sons of Rehabiah were very numerous.

18The sons of Izhar:
Shelomith was the first.

19 The sons of Hebron:
Jeriah the first, Amariah the
second, Jahaziel the third and
Jekameam the fourth.

20 The sons of Uzziel:
Micah the first and Isshiah
the second.

21 The sons of Merari:
Mahli and Mushi.
The sons of Mahli:
Eleazar and Kish.

22 Eleazar died without having
sons: he had only daughters.
Their cousins, the sons of Kish,
married them.

23 The sons of Mushi:
Mahli, Eder and Jerimoth—
three in all.

24 These were the descendants of Levi
by their families—the heads of families
as they were registered under their
names and counted individually, that is,
the workers twenty years old or more
who served in the temple of the LORD.
25 For David had said, "Since the LORD,
the God of Israel, has granted rest to his
people and has come to dwell in Jerusalem forever, 26 the Levites no longer
need to carry the tabernacle or any of
the articles used in its service." 27 According to the last instructions of David,
the Levites were counted from those
twenty years old or more.

28 The duty of the Levites was to help
Aaron's descendants in the service of
the temple of the LORD: to be in charge
of the courtyards, the side rooms, the
purification of all sacred things and the
performance of other duties at the
house of God. 29 They were in charge of
the bread set out on the table, the flour
for the grain offerings, the unleavened
wafers, the baking and the mixing, and
all measurements of quantity and size.
30 They were also to stand every morning to thank and praise the LORD. They
were to do the same in the evening
31 and whenever burnt offerings were
presented to the LORD on Sabbaths and
at New Moon festivals and at appointed

feasts. They were to serve before the
LORD regularly in the proper number
and in the way prescribed for them.

32 And so the Levites carried out their
responsibilities for the Tent of Meeting,
for the Holy Place and, under their
brothers the descendants of Aaron, for
the service of the temple of the LORD.

a 9 Solomon sounds like and may be derived from the
Hebrew for peace. b 14 That is, about 3,750 tons (about
3,450 metric tons) c 14 That is, about 37,500 tons (about
34,500 metric tons) d 10 One Hebrew manuscript,
Septuagint and Vulgate (see also verse 11); most Hebrew
manuscripts Zina

ROMANS 3:9-31

What shall we conclude then? Are we
any better a? Not at all! We have already
made the charge that Jews and Gentiles
alike are all under sin. 10 As it is written:

"There is no one righteous, not even
one;
11   there is no one who understands,
no one who seeks God.
12 All have turned away,
they have together become
worthless;
there is no one who does good,
not even one." b
13 "Their throats are open graves;
their tongues practice deceit." c
"The poison of vipers is on their
lips." d
14   "Their mouths are full of cursing
and bitterness." e
15 "Their feet are swift to shed blood;
16   ruin and misery mark their ways,
17 and the way of peace they do not
know." f
18   "There is no fear of God before
their eyes." g

19 Now we know that whatever the law
says, it says to those who are under the
law, so that every mouth may be silenced and the whole world held accountable to God. 20 Therefore no one
will be declared righteous in his sight by
observing the law; rather, through the
law we become conscious of sin.

21 But now a righteousness from
God, apart from law, has been made
known, to which the Law and the

Prophets testify. 22**This righteousness from God comes through faith in Jesus Christ to all who believe.** There is no difference, 23for all have sinned and fall short of the glory of God, 24and are justified freely by his grace through the redemption that came by Christ Jesus. 25God presented him as a sacrifice of atonement,*h* through faith in his blood. He did this to demonstrate his justice, because in his forbearance he had left the sins committed beforehand unpunished— 26he did it to demonstrate his justice at the present time, so as to be just and the one who justifies those who have faith in Jesus.

27Where, then, is boasting? It is excluded. On what principle? On that of observing the law? No, but on that of faith. 28For we maintain that a man is justified by faith apart from observing the law. 29Is God the God of Jews only? Is he not the God of Gentiles too? Yes, of Gentiles too, 30since there is only one God, who will justify the circumcised by faith and the uncircumcised through that same faith. 31Do we, then, nullify the law by this faith? Not at all! Rather, we uphold the law.

a9 Or worse   *b12 Psalms 14:1-3; 53:1-3; Eccles. 7:20*
c13 Psalm 5:9   *d13 Psalm 140:3*   *e14 Psalm 10:7*
f17 Isaiah 59:7,8   *g18 Psalm 36:1*   *h25 Or as the one who would turn aside his wrath, taking away sin*

PSALM 12:1-8
For the director of music. According to *sheminith.*a A psalm of David.

1**H**elp, LORD, for the godly are no more;
  the faithful have vanished from among men.
2Everyone lies to his neighbor;
  their flattering lips speak with deception.

3May the LORD cut off all flattering lips
  and every boastful tongue
4that says, "We will triumph with our tongues;
  we own our lips*b*—who is our master?"

5"Because of the oppression of the weak
  and the groaning of the needy,
I will now arise," says the LORD.
  "I will protect them from those who malign them."
6And the words of the LORD are flawless,
  like silver refined in a furnace of clay,
  purified seven times.

7O LORD, you will keep us safe
  and protect us from such people forever.
8The wicked freely strut about
  when what is vile is honored among men.

aTitle: Probably a musical term   *b4 Or / our lips are our plowshares*

PROVERBS 19:13-14
13**A** foolish son is his father's ruin,
  and a quarrelsome wife is like a constant dripping.

14Houses and wealth are inherited from parents,
  but a prudent wife is from the LORD.

□ DAY 198

GOD SIGHTINGS

July 17

1 CHRONICLES 24:1–26:11
These were the divisions of the sons of Aaron:

The sons of Aaron were Nadab, Abihu, Eleazar and Ithamar. 2But Nadab and Abihu died before their father did, and they had no sons; so Eleazar and Ithamar served as the priests. 3With the help of Zadok a descendant of Eleazar and Ahimelech a descendant of Ithamar, David separated them into divisions for their appointed order of ministering. 4A larger number of leaders were found among Eleazar's descendants than among Ithamar's, and they were divided accordingly: sixteen heads of families from Eleazar's descendants and eight heads of families from Ithamar's descendants. ⁵ They divided them impartially by drawing lots, for there were officials of the sanctuary and officials of God among the descendants of both Eleazar and Ithamar.

⁶ The scribe Shemaiah son of Nethanel, a Levite, recorded their names in the presence of the king and of the officials: Zadok the priest, Ahimelech son of Abiathar and the heads of families of the priests and of the Levites—one family being taken from Eleazar and then one from Ithamar.

⁷ The first lot fell to Jehoiarib,
  the second to Jedaiah,
⁸ the third to Harim,
  the fourth to Seorim,
⁹ the fifth to Malkijah,
  the sixth to Mijamin,
¹⁰ the seventh to Hakkoz,
  the eighth to Abijah,
¹¹ the ninth to Jeshua,
  the tenth to Shecaniah,
¹² the eleventh to Eliashib,
  the twelfth to Jakim,
¹³ the thirteenth to Huppah,
  the fourteenth to Jeshebeab,
¹⁴ the fifteenth to Bilgah,
  the sixteenth to Immer,
¹⁵ the seventeenth to Hezir,
  the eighteenth to Happizzez,
¹⁶ the nineteenth to Pethahiah,
  the twentieth to Jehezkel,
¹⁷ the twenty-first to Jakin,
  the twenty-second to Gamul,
¹⁸ the twenty-third to Delaiah
  and the twenty-fourth to Maaziah.

¹⁹ This was their appointed order of ministering when they entered the temple of the LORD, according to the regulations prescribed for them by their forefather Aaron, as the LORD, the God of Israel, had commanded him.

²⁰ As for the rest of the descendants of Levi:
  from the sons of Amram: Shubael;
  from the sons of Shubael: Jehdeiah.
²¹ As for Rehabiah, from his sons:
  Isshiah was the first.
²² From the Izharites: Shelomoth;
  from the sons of Shelomoth:
  Jahath.
²³ The sons of Hebron: Jeriah the first,ᵃ Amariah the second, Jahaziel the third and Jekameam the fourth.
²⁴ The son of Uzziel: Micah;
  from the sons of Micah: Shamir.
²⁵ The brother of Micah: Isshiah;
  from the sons of Isshiah:
  Zechariah.
²⁶ The sons of Merari: Mahli and Mushi.
  The son of Jaaziah: Beno.
²⁷ The sons of Merari:
  from Jaaziah: Beno, Shoham,
  Zaccur and Ibri.
²⁸ From Mahli: Eleazar, who had no sons.
²⁹ From Kish: the son of Kish:
  Jerahmeel.
³⁰ And the sons of Mushi: Mahli,
  Eder and Jerimoth.

These were the Levites, according to their families. ³¹ They also cast lots, just as their brothers the descendants of Aaron did, in the presence of King David and of Zadok, Ahimelech, and the heads of families of the priests and of the Levites. The families of the oldest brother were treated the same as those of the youngest.

²⁵:¹ DAVID, together with the commanders of the army, set apart some of the sons of Asaph, Heman and Jeduthun for the ministry of prophesying, accompanied by harps, lyres and cymbals. Here is the list of the men who performed this service:

² From the sons of Asaph:
  Zaccur, Joseph, Nethaniah and As-

arelah. The sons of Asaph were under the supervision of Asaph, who prophesied under the king's supervision.

³As for Jeduthun, from his sons:

Gedaliah, Zeri, Jeshaiah, Shimei,*b* Hashabiah and Mattithiah, six in all, under the supervision of their father Jeduthun, who prophesied, using the harp in thanking and praising the LORD.

⁴As for Heman, from his sons:

Bukkiah, Mattaniah, Uzziel, Shubael and Jerimoth; Hananiah, Hanani, Eliathah, Giddalti and Romamti-Ezer; Joshbekashah, Mallothi, Hothir and Mahazioth. ⁵All these were sons of Heman the king's seer. They were given him through the promises of God to exalt him.*c* God gave Heman fourteen sons and three daughters.

⁶All these men were under the supervision of their fathers for the music of the temple of the LORD, with cymbals, lyres and harps, for the ministry at the house of God. Asaph, Jeduthun and Heman were under the supervision of the king. ⁷Along with their relatives—all of them trained and skilled in music for the LORD—they numbered 288. ⁸Young and old alike, teacher as well as student, cast lots for their duties.

⁹The first lot, which was for Asaph, fell to Joseph,
his sons and relatives,*d*   12*e*
the second to Gedaliah,
he and his relatives and
sons,   12
¹⁰the third to Zaccur,
his sons and relatives,   12
¹¹the fourth to Izri,*f*
his sons and relatives,   12
¹²the fifth to Nethaniah,
his sons and relatives,   12
¹³the sixth to Bukkiah,
his sons and relatives,   12

¹⁴the seventh to Jesarelah,*g*
his sons and relatives,   12
¹⁵the eighth to Jeshaiah,
his sons and relatives,   12
¹⁶the ninth to Mattaniah,
his sons and relatives,   12
¹⁷the tenth to Shimei,
his sons and relatives,   12
¹⁸the eleventh to Azarel,*h*
his sons and relatives,   12
¹⁹the twelfth to Hashabiah,
his sons and relatives,   12
²⁰the thirteenth to Shubael,
his sons and relatives,   12
²¹the fourteenth to Mattithiah,
his sons and relatives,   12
²²the fifteenth to Jerimoth,
his sons and relatives,   12
²³the sixteenth to Hananiah,
his sons and relatives,   12
²⁴the seventeenth to
Joshbekashah,
his sons and relatives,   12
²⁵the eighteenth to Hanani,
his sons and relatives,   12
²⁶the nineteenth to Mallothi,
his sons and relatives,   12
²⁷the twentieth to Eliathah,
his sons and relatives,   12
²⁸the twenty-first to Hothir,
his sons and relatives,   12
²⁹the twenty-second to Giddalti,
his sons and relatives,   12
³⁰the twenty-third to Mahazioth,
his sons and relatives,   12
³¹the twenty-fourth to
Romamti-Ezer,
his sons and relatives,   12

²⁶:¹THE divisions of the gatekeepers:

From the Korahites: Meshelemiah son of Kore, one of the sons of Asaph.

²Meshelemiah had sons:
Zechariah the firstborn,
Jediael the second,
Zebadiah the third,
Jathniel the fourth,
³Elam the fifth,
Jehohanan the sixth
and Eliehoenai the seventh.

4 Obed-Edom also had sons:
Shemaiah the firstborn,
Jehozabad the second,
Joah the third,
Sacar the fourth,
Nethanel the fifth,
5 Ammiel the sixth,
Issachar the seventh
and Peullethai the eighth.
(For God had blessed Obed-
Edom.)

6 His son Shemaiah also had
sons, who were leaders in
their father's family because
they were very capable men.
7 The sons of Shemaiah:
Othni, Rephael, Obed and Elzabad; his relatives Elihu and
Semakiah were also able
men. 8 All these were descendants of Obed-Edom; they
and their sons and their relatives were capable men with
the strength to do the work—
descendants of Obed-Edom,
62 in all.
9 Meshelemiah had sons and relatives, who were able men—18
in all.

10 Hosah the Merarite had sons:
Shimri the first (although he
was not the firstborn, his father had appointed him the
first), 11 Hilkiah the second,
Tabaliah the third and Zechariah the fourth. The sons and
relatives of Hosah were 13 in
all.

a23 Two Hebrew manuscripts and some Septuagint
manuscripts (see also 1 Chron. 23:19); most Hebrew
manuscripts *The sons of Jeriah.*   b3 One Hebrew
manuscript and some Septuagint manuscripts (see also
verse 17); most Hebrew manuscripts do not have *Shimei.*
c5 Hebrew *exalt the horn*   d9 See Septuagint; Hebrew does
not have *his sons and relatives.*   e9 See the total in verse 7;
Hebrew does not have *twelve.*   f11 A variant of *Zeri*
g14 A variant of *Asarelah*   h18 A variant of *Uzziel*

ROMANS 4:1-12
What then shall we say that Abraham,
our forefather, discovered in this matter? 2 **If, in fact, Abraham was justified by works, he had something to**
boast about—**but not before God.**
3 **What does the Scripture say?
"Abraham believed God, and it was
credited to him as righteousness."**[a]

4 Now when a man works, his wages
are not credited to him as a gift, but as
an obligation. 5 However, to the man
who does not work but trusts God who
justifies the wicked, his faith is credited as righteousness. 6 David says the
same thing when he speaks of the
blessedness of the man to whom God
credits righteousness apart from
works:

7 "Blessed are they
whose transgressions are
forgiven,
whose sins are covered.
8 Blessed is the man
whose sin the Lord will never
count against him."[b]

9 Is this blessedness only for the circumcised, or also for the uncircumcised? We have been saying that
Abraham's faith was credited to him as
righteousness. 10 Under what circumstances was it credited? Was it after he
was circumcised, or before? It was not
after, but before! 11 And he received
the sign of circumcision, a seal of the
righteousness that he had by faith
while he was still uncircumcised. So
then, he is the father of all who believe
but have not been circumcised, in order that righteousness might be credited to them. 12 And he is also the
father of the circumcised who not
only are circumcised but who also
walk in the footsteps of the faith that
our father Abraham had before he was
circumcised.

a3 Gen. 15:6; also in verse 22   b8 Psalm 32:1,2

PSALM 13:1-6
For the director of music. A psalm of David.

1 **H**ow long, O Lord? Will you forget
me forever?
How long will you hide your face
from me?

2How long must I wrestle with my
        thoughts
   and every day have sorrow in my
        heart?
   How long will my enemy triumph
        over me?

3Look on me and answer, O Lᴏʀᴅ my
        God.
   Give light to my eyes, or I will sleep
        in death;
4my enemy will say, "I have overcome
        him,"
   and my foes will rejoice when
        I fall.

5But I trust in your unfailing love;
   my heart rejoices in your
        salvation.
6I will sing to the Lᴏʀᴅ,
   for he has been good to me.

PROVERBS 19:15-16

15Laziness brings on deep sleep,
   and the shiftless man goes
        hungry.

16He who obeys instructions guards
        his life,
   but he who is contemptuous of his
        ways will die.

☐ DAY 199

GOD SIGHTINGS

July 18

1 CHRONICLES 26:12–27:34

These divisions of the gatekeepers,
through their chief men, had duties for
ministering in the temple of the Lᴏʀᴅ,
just as their relatives had. 13Lots were
cast for each gate, according to their
families, young and old alike.
14The lot for the East Gate fell to
Shelemiah.*a* Then lots were cast for
his son Zechariah, a wise counselor,
and the lot for the North Gate fell to
him. 15The lot for the South Gate fell
to Obed-Edom, and the lot for the

storehouse fell to his sons. 16The lots
for the West Gate and the Shalleketh
Gate on the upper road fell to Shup-
pim and Hosah.
   Guard was alongside of guard:
17There were six Levites a day on the
east, four a day on the north, four a day
on the south and two at a time at the
storehouse. 18As for the court to the
west, there were four at the road and two
at the court itself.
19These were the divisions of the
gatekeepers who were descendants of
Korah and Merari.

20Their fellow Levites were*b* in
charge of the treasuries of the house of
God and the treasuries for the dedicated
things.
21The descendants of Ladan, who
were Gershonites through Ladan and
who were heads of families belonging
to Ladan the Gershonite, were Jehieli,
22the sons of Jehieli, Zetham and his
brother Joel. They were in charge of the
treasuries of the temple of the Lᴏʀᴅ.
23From the Amramites, the Izharites,
the Hebronites and the Uzzielites:

24Shubael, a descendant of Ger-
       shom son of Moses, was the
       officer in charge of the trea-
       suries. 25His relatives through
       Eliezer: Rehabiah his son, Je-
       shaiah his son, Joram his son,
       Zicri his son and Shelomith
       his son. 26Shelomith and his
       relatives were in charge of all
       the treasuries for the things
       dedicated by King David, by
       the heads of families who
       were the commanders of
       thousands and commanders
       of hundreds, and by the other
       army commanders. 27Some of
       the plunder taken in battle
       they dedicated for the repair
       of the temple of the Lᴏʀᴅ.
       28And everything dedicated
       by Samuel the seer and by
       Saul son of Kish, Abner son of
       Ner and Joab son of Zeruiah,
       and all the other dedicated

things were in the care of Shelomith and his relatives.
29 From the Izharites: Kenaniah
and his sons were assigned
duties away from the temple,
as officials and judges over Israel.
30 From the Hebronites: Hashabiah
and his relatives—seventeen
hundred able men—were re-
sponsible in Israel west of the
Jordan for all the work of the
LORD and for the king's service. 31 As for the Hebronites,
Jeriah was their chief according to the genealogical records
of their families. In the fortieth year of David's reign a
search was made in the records, and capable men were
found among the Hebronites
were found at Jazer in Gilead.
32 Jeriah had twenty-seven
hundred relatives, who were
able men and heads of families,
and King David put them in
charge of the Reubenites, the
Gadites and the half-tribe of
Manasseh for every matter per-
taining to God and for the affairs of the king.

27:1 THIS is the list of the Israelites—
heads of families, commanders of thousands and commanders of hundreds,
and their officers, who served the king
in all that concerned the army divisions
that were on duty month by month
throughout the year. Each division consisted of 24,000 men.

2 In charge of the first division, for the
first month, was Jashobeam son of
Zabdiel. There were 24,000 men in
his division. 3 He was a descendant
of Perez and chief of all the army
officers for the first month.
4 In charge of the division for the second month was Dodai the Ahohite;
Mikloth was the leader of his division. There were 24,000 men in his
division.

5 The third army commander, for the
third month, was Benaiah son of Jehoiada the priest. He was chief and
there were 24,000 men in his division. 6 This was the Benaiah who
was a mighty man among the
Thirty and was over the Thirty. His
son Ammizabad was in charge of
his division.
7 The fourth, for the fourth month, was
Asahel the brother of Joab; his son
Zebadiah was his successor. There
were 24,000 men in his division.
8 The fifth, for the fifth month, was the
commander Shamhuth the Izra-
hite. There were 24,000 men in his
division.
9 The sixth, for the sixth month, was Ira
the son of Ikkesh the Tekoite. There
were 24,000 men in his division.
10 The seventh, for the seventh month,
was Helez the Pelonite, an Ephraimite. There were 24,000 men in
his division.
11 The eighth, for the eighth month, was
Sibbecai the Hushathite, a Zera-
hite. There were 24,000 men in his
division.
12 The ninth, for the ninth month, was
Abiezer the Anathothite, a Benjamite. There were 24,000 men in
his division.
13 The tenth, for the tenth month, was
Maharai the Netophathite, a Zera-
hite. There were 24,000 men in his
division.
14 The eleventh, for the eleventh month,
was Benaiah the Pirathonite, an
Ephraimite. There were 24,000
men in his division.
15 The twelfth, for the twelfth month,
was Heldai the Netophathite, from
the family of Othniel. There were
24,000 men in his division.

16 The officers over the tribes of Israel:

over the Reubenites: Eliezer son
of Zicri;
over the Simeonites: Shephatiah
son of Maacah;

[17] over Levi: Hashabiah son of Kemuel;

over Aaron: Zadok;

[18] over Judah: Elihu, a brother of David;

over Issachar: Omri son of Michael;

[19] over Zebulun: Ishmaiah son of Obadiah;

over Naphtali: Jerimoth son of Azriel;

[20] over the Ephraimites: Hoshea son of Azaziah;

over half the tribe of Manasseh: Joel son of Pedaiah;

[21] over the half-tribe of Manasseh in Gilead: Iddo son of Zechariah;

over Benjamin: Jaasiel son of Abner;

[22] over Dan: Azarel son of Jeroham.

These were the officers over the tribes of Israel.

[23] David did not take the number of the men twenty years old or less, because the LORD had promised to make Israel as numerous as the stars in the sky. [24] Joab son of Zeruiah began to count the men but did not finish. Wrath came on Israel on account of this numbering, and the number was not entered in the book[c] of the annals of King David.

[25] Azmaveth son of Adiel was in charge of the royal storehouses.

Jonathan son of Uzziah was in charge of the storehouses in the outlying districts, in the towns, the villages and the watchtowers.

[26] Ezri son of Kelub was in charge of the field workers who farmed the land.

[27] Shimei the Ramathite was in charge of the vineyards.

Zabdi the Shiphmite was in charge of the produce of the vineyards for the wine vats.

[28] Baal-Hanan the Gederite was in charge of the olive and sycamore-fig trees in the western foothills.

Joash was in charge of the supplies of olive oil.

[29] Shitrai the Sharonite was in charge of the herds grazing in Sharon.

Shaphat son of Adlai was in charge of the herds in the valleys.

[30] Obil the Ishmaelite was in charge of the camels.

Jehdeiah the Meronothite was in charge of the donkeys.

[31] Jaziz the Hagrite was in charge of the flocks.

All these were the officials in charge of King David's property.

[32] Jonathan, David's uncle, was a counselor, a man of insight and a scribe. Jehiel son of Hacmoni took care of the king's sons.

[33] Ahithophel was the king's counselor.

Hushai the Arkite was the king's friend. [34] Ahithophel was succeeded by Jehoiada son of Benaiah and by Abiathar.

Joab was the commander of the royal army.

a14 A variant of Meshelemiah   b20 Septuagint; Hebrew As for the Levites, Ahijah was   c24 Septuagint; Hebrew number

ROMANS 4:13–5:5

It was not through law that Abraham and his offspring received the promise that he would be heir of the world, but through the righteousness that comes by faith. [14] For if those who live by law are heirs, faith has no value and the promise is worthless, [15] because law brings wrath. And where there is no law there is no transgression.

[16] Therefore, the promise comes by faith, so that it may be by grace and may be guaranteed to all Abraham's offspring—not only to those who are of the law but also to those who are of the faith of Abraham. He is the father of us all. [17] As it is written: "I have made you a father of many nations."[a] He is our father in the sight of God, in whom he believed—the God who gives life to the dead and calls things that are not as though they were.

[18] Against all hope, Abraham in hope believed and so became the father of

many nations, just as it had been said to him, "So shall your offspring be."[b] [19]Without weakening in his faith, he faced the fact that his body was as good as dead—since he was about a hundred years old—and that Sarah's womb was also dead. [20]Yet he did not waver through unbelief regarding the promise of God, but was strengthened in his faith and gave glory to God, [21]being fully persuaded that God had power to do what he had promised. [22]This is why "it was credited to him as righteousness." [23]The words "it was credited to him" were written not for him alone, [24]but also for us, to whom God will credit righteousness—for us who believe in him who raised Jesus our Lord from the dead. [25]He was delivered over to death for our sins and was raised to life for our justification.

[5:1]THEREFORE, since we have been justified through faith, we[c] have peace with God through our Lord Jesus Christ, [2]through whom we have gained access by faith into this grace in which we now stand. And we[c] rejoice in the hope of the glory of God. [3]Not only so, but we[c] also rejoice in our sufferings, because we know that suffering produces perseverance; [4]perseverance, character; and character, hope. [5]And hope does not disappoint us, because God has poured out his love into our hearts by the Holy Spirit, whom he has given us.

[a]17 Gen. 17:5 [b]18 Gen. 15:5 [c]1,2,3 Or let us

PSALM 14:1-7
For the director of music. Of David.

[1]The fool[a] says in his heart,
  "There is no God."
They are corrupt, their deeds
    are vile;
  there is no one who does good.

[2]The Lord looks down from heaven
    on the sons of men
to see if there are any who
    understand,
  any who seek God.

[3]All have turned aside,
  they have together become corrupt;
there is no one who does good,
  not even one.

[4]Will evildoers never learn—
  those who devour my people as
    men eat bread
  and who do not call on the Lord?

[5]There they are, overwhelmed with
    dread,
  for God is present in the company
    of the righteous.

[6]You evildoers frustrate the plans of
    the poor,
  but the Lord is their refuge.

[7]Oh, that salvation for Israel would
    come out of Zion!
When the Lord restores the
    fortunes of his people,
  let Jacob rejoice and Israel be glad!

[a]1 The Hebrew words rendered fool in Psalms denote one who is morally deficient.

PROVERBS 19:17
[17]He who is kind to the poor lends to
    the Lord,
  and he will reward him for what he
    has done.

☐ DAY 200

GOD SIGHTINGS

July 19

1 CHRONICLES 28:1–29:30
David summoned all the officials of Israel to assemble at Jerusalem: the officers over the tribes, the commanders of the divisions in the service of the king, the commanders of thousands and commanders of hundreds, and the officials in charge of all the property and livestock belonging to the king and his sons, together with the palace officials, the mighty men and all the brave warriors.

[2]King David rose to his feet and said: "Listen to me, my brothers and my peo-

ple. I had it in my heart to build a house as a place of rest for the ark of the covenant of the LORD, for the footstool of our God, and I made plans to build it. ³But God said to me, 'You are not to build a house for my Name, because you are a warrior and have shed blood.'

⁴"Yet the LORD, the God of Israel, chose me from my whole family to be king over Israel forever. He chose Judah as leader, and from the house of Judah he chose my family, and from my father's sons he was pleased to make me king over all Israel. ⁵Of all my sons—and the LORD has given me many—he has chosen my son Solomon to sit on the throne of the kingdom of the LORD over Israel. ⁶He said to me: 'Solomon your son is the one who will build my house and my courts, for I have chosen him to be my son, and I will be his father. ⁷I will establish his kingdom forever if he is unswerving in carrying out my commands and laws, as is being done at this time.'

⁸"So now I charge you in the sight of all Israel and of the assembly of the LORD, and in the hearing of our God: Be careful to follow all the commands of the LORD your God, that you may possess this good land and pass it on as an inheritance to your descendants forever.

⁹"And you, my son Solomon, acknowledge the God of your father, and serve him with wholehearted devotion and with a willing mind, for the LORD searches every heart and understands every motive behind the thoughts. If you seek him, he will be found by you; but if you forsake him, he will reject you forever. ¹⁰Consider now, for the LORD has chosen you to build a temple as a sanctuary. Be strong and do the work."

¹¹Then David gave his son Solomon the plans for the portico of the temple, its buildings, its storerooms, its upper parts, its inner rooms and the place of atonement. ¹²He gave him the plans of all that the Spirit had put in his mind for the courts of the temple of the LORD and all the surrounding rooms, for the treasuries of the temple of God and for the treasuries for the dedicated things.

¹³He gave him instructions for the divisions of the priests and Levites, and for all the work of serving in the temple of the LORD, as well as for all the articles to be used in its service. ¹⁴He designated the weight of gold for all the gold articles to be used in various kinds of service, and the weight of silver for all the silver articles to be used in various kinds of service: ¹⁵the weight of gold for the gold lampstands and their lamps, with the weight for each lampstand and its lamps; and the weight of silver for each silver lampstand and its lamps, according to the use of each lampstand; ¹⁶the weight of gold for each table for consecrated bread; the weight of silver for the silver tables; ¹⁷the weight of pure gold for the forks, sprinkling bowls and pitchers; the weight of gold for each gold dish; the weight of silver for each silver dish; ¹⁸and the weight of the refined gold for the altar of incense. He also gave him the plan for the chariot, that is, the cherubim of gold that spread their wings and shelter the ark of the covenant of the LORD.

¹⁹"All this," David said, "I have in writing from the hand of the LORD upon me, and he gave me understanding in all the details of the plan."

²⁰David also said to Solomon his son, "Be strong and courageous, and do the work. Do not be afraid or discouraged, for the LORD God, my God, is with you. He will not fail you or forsake you until all the work for the service of the temple of the LORD is finished. ²¹The divisions of the priests and Levites are ready for all the work on the temple of God, and every willing man skilled in any craft will help you in all the work. The officials and all the people will obey your every command."

²⁹:¹THEN King David said to the whole assembly: "My son Solomon, the one whom God has chosen, is young and inexperienced. The task is great, because this palatial structure is not for man but for the LORD God. ²With all my resources I have provided for the temple

of my God—gold for the gold work, silver for the silver, bronze for the bronze, iron for the iron and wood for the wood, as well as onyx for the settings, turquoise,*a* stones of various colors, and all kinds of fine stone and marble—all of these in large quantities. [3]Besides, in my devotion to the temple of my God I now give my personal treasures of gold and silver for the temple of my God, over and above everything I have provided for this holy temple: [4]three thousand talents*b* of gold (gold of Ophir) and seven thousand talents*c* of refined silver, for the overlaying of the walls of the buildings, [5]for the gold work and the silver work, and for all the work to be done by the craftsmen. Now, who is willing to consecrate himself today to the LORD?"

[6]Then the leaders of families, the officers of the tribes of Israel, the commanders of thousands and commanders of hundreds, and the officials in charge of the king's work gave willingly. [7]They gave toward the work on the temple of God five thousand talents*d* and ten thousand darics*e* of gold, ten thousand talents*f* of silver, eighteen thousand talents*g* of bronze and a hundred thousand talents*h* of iron. [8]Any who had precious stones gave them to the treasury of the temple of the LORD in the custody of Jehiel the Gershonite. [9]The people rejoiced at the willing response of their leaders, for they had given freely and wholeheartedly to the LORD. David the king also rejoiced greatly.

[10]David praised the LORD in the presence of the whole assembly, saying,

"Praise be to you, O LORD,
    God of our father Israel,
    from everlasting to everlasting.
[11]Yours, O LORD, is the greatness and
        the power
    and the glory and the majesty and
        the splendor,
    for everything in heaven and earth
        is yours.
Yours, O LORD, is the kingdom;
    you are exalted as head over all.

[12]Wealth and honor come from you;
    you are the ruler of all things.
In your hands are strength and
        power
    to exalt and give strength to all.
[13]Now, our God, we give you thanks,
    and praise your glorious name.

[14]"But who am I, and who are my people, that we should be able to give as generously as this? Everything comes from you, and we have given you only what comes from your hand. [15]We are aliens and strangers in your sight, as were all our forefathers. Our days on earth are like a shadow, without hope. [16]O LORD our God, as for all this abundance that we have provided for building you a temple for your Holy Name, it comes from your hand, and all of it belongs to you. [17]I know, my God, that you test the heart and are pleased with integrity. All these things have I given willingly and with honest intent. And now I have seen with joy how willingly your people who are here have given to you. [18]O LORD, God of our fathers Abraham, Isaac and Israel, keep this desire in the hearts of your people forever, and keep their hearts loyal to you. [19]And give my son Solomon the wholehearted devotion to keep your commands, requirements and decrees and to do everything to build the palatial structure for which I have provided."

[20]Then David said to the whole assembly, "Praise the LORD your God." So they all praised the LORD, the God of their fathers; they bowed low and fell prostrate before the LORD and the king.

[21]The next day they made sacrifices to the LORD and presented burnt offerings to him: a thousand bulls, a thousand rams and a thousand male lambs, together with their drink offerings, and other sacrifices in abundance for all Israel. [22]They ate and drank with great joy in the presence of the LORD that day.

Then they acknowledged Solomon son of David as king a second time, anointing him before the LORD to be ruler and Zadok to be priest. [23]So Solomon sat on the throne of the Lord as king in place of his father David. He prospered and all Israel obeyed him. [24]All the officers and mighty men, as well as all of King David's sons, pledged their submission to King Solomon.

[25]The Lord highly exalted Solomon in the sight of all Israel and bestowed on him royal splendor such as no king over Israel ever had before.

[26]David son of Jesse was king over all Israel. [27]He ruled over Israel forty years—seven in Hebron and thirty-three in Jerusalem. [28]He died at a good old age, having enjoyed long life, wealth and honor. His son Solomon succeeded him as king.

[29]As for the events of King David's reign, from beginning to end, they are written in the records of Samuel the seer, the records of Nathan the prophet and the records of Gad the seer, [30]together with the details of his reign and power, and the circumstances that surrounded him and Israel and the kingdoms of all the other lands.

a2 The meaning of the Hebrew for this word is uncertain.
b4 That is, about 110 tons (about 100 metric tons)
c4 That is, about 260 tons (about 240 metric tons)
d7 That is, about 190 tons (about 170 metric tons)
e7 That is, about 185 pounds (about 84 kilograms)
f7 That is, about 375 tons (about 345 metric tons)
g7 That is, about 675 tons (about 610 metric tons)
h7 That is, about 3,750 tons (about 3,450 metric tons)

ROMANS 5:6-21

You see, at just the right time, when we were still powerless, Christ died for the ungodly. [7]Very rarely will anyone die for a righteous man, though for a good man someone might possibly dare to die. [8]But God demonstrates his own love for us in this: While we were still sinners, Christ died for us.

[9]Since we have now been justified by his blood, how much more shall we be saved from God's wrath through him! [10]For if, when we were God's enemies, we were reconciled to him through the death of his Son, how much more, having been reconciled, shall we be saved through his life! [11]Not only is this so, but we also rejoice in God through our Lord Jesus Christ, through whom we have now received reconciliation.

[12]Therefore, just as sin entered the world through one man, and death through sin, and in this way death came to all men, because all sinned— [13]for before the law was given, sin was in the world. But sin is not taken into account when there is no law. [14]Nevertheless, death reigned from the time of Adam to the time of Moses, even over those who did not sin by breaking a command, as did Adam, who was a pattern of the one to come.

[15]But the gift is not like the trespass. For if the many died by the trespass of the one man, how much more did God's grace and the gift that came by the grace of the one man, Jesus Christ, overflow to the many! [16]Again, the gift of God is not like the result of the one man's sin: The judgment followed one sin and brought condemnation, but the gift followed many trespasses and brought justification. [17]For if, by the trespass of the one man, death reigned through that one man, how much more will those who receive God's abundant provision of grace and of the gift of righteousness reign in life through the one man, Jesus Christ.

[18]Consequently, just as the result of one trespass was condemnation for all men, so also the result of one act of righteousness was justification that brings life for all men. [19]**For just as through the disobedience of the one man the many were made sinners, so also through the obedience of the one man the many will be made righteous.**

[20]The law was added so that the trespass might increase. But where sin increased, grace increased all the more, [21]so that, just as sin reigned in death, so also grace might reign through righteousness to bring eternal life through Jesus Christ our Lord.

PSALM 15:1-5
A psalm of David.

[1]Lord, who may dwell in your
        sanctuary?
    Who may live on your holy hill?

2 He whose walk is blameless
  and who does what is righteous,
who speaks the truth from his heart
3   and has no slander on his tongue,
who does his neighbor no wrong
  and casts no slur on his
    fellowman,
4 who despises a vile man
  but honors those who fear the
    Lord,
who keeps his oath
  even when it hurts,
5 who lends his money without usury
  and does not accept a bribe
    against the innocent.

He who does these things
  will never be shaken.

PROVERBS 19:18-19

18 Discipline your son, for in that there
    is hope;
  do not be a willing party to his
    death.

19 A hot-tempered man must pay the
    penalty;
  if you rescue him, you will have to
    do it again.

☐ D A Y   2 0 1

GOD SIGHTINGS

July 20

2 CHRONICLES 1:1–3:17

Solomon son of David established himself firmly over his kingdom, for the
Lord his God was with him and made
him exceedingly great.

2 Then Solomon spoke to all Israel—to
the commanders of thousands and commanders of hundreds, to the judges and
to all the leaders in Israel, the heads of
families— 3 and Solomon and the whole
assembly went to the high place at Gibeon, for God's Tent of Meeting was there,
which Moses the Lord's servant had
made in the desert. 4 Now David had

brought up the ark of God from Kiriath
Jearim to the place he had prepared for it,
because he had pitched a tent for it in Jerusalem. 5 But the bronze altar that Bezalel son of Uri, the son of Hur, had made
was in Gibeon in front of the tabernacle
of the Lord; so Solomon and the assembly inquired of him there. 6 Solomon
went up to the bronze altar before the
Lord in the Tent of Meeting and offered
a thousand burnt offerings on it.

7 That night God appeared to Solomon and said to him, "Ask for whatever
you want me to give you."

8 Solomon answered God, "You have
shown great kindness to David my father and have made me king in his
place. 9 Now, Lord God, let your promise
to my father David be confirmed, for
you have made me king over a people
who are as numerous as the dust of the
earth. 10 Give me wisdom and knowledge, that I may lead this people, for
who is able to govern this great people
of yours?"

11 God said to Solomon, "Since this is
your heart's desire and you have not
asked for wealth, riches or honor, nor
for the death of your enemies, and since
you have not asked for a long life but for
wisdom and knowledge to govern my
people over whom I have made you
king, 12 therefore wisdom and knowledge will be given you. And I will also
give you wealth, riches and honor, such
as no king who was before you ever had
and none after you will have."

13 Then Solomon went to Jerusalem
from the high place at Gibeon, from before the Tent of Meeting. And he
reigned over Israel.

14 Solomon accumulated chariots and
horses; he had fourteen hundred chariots and twelve thousand horses,[a] which
he kept in the chariot cities and also with
him in Jerusalem. 15 The king made silver
and gold as common in Jerusalem as
stones, and cedar as plentiful as sycamore-fig trees in the foothills. 16 Solomon's horses were imported from
Egypt[b] and from Kue[c]—the royal merchants purchased them from Kue.

17 They imported a chariot from Egypt for six hundred shekels*d* of silver, and a horse for a hundred and fifty.*e* They also exported them to all the kings of the Hittites and of the Arameans.

2:1 SOLOMON gave orders to build a temple for the Name of the LORD and a royal palace for himself. 2 He conscripted seventy thousand men as carriers and eighty thousand as stonecutters in the hills and thirty-six hundred as foremen over them.

3 Solomon sent this message to Hiram*f* king of Tyre:

"Send me cedar logs as you did for my father David when you sent him cedar to build a palace to live in. 4 Now I am about to build a temple for the Name of the LORD my God and to dedicate it to him for burning fragrant incense before him, for setting out the consecrated bread regularly, and for making burnt offerings every morning and evening and on Sabbaths and New Moons and at the appointed feasts of the LORD our God. This is a lasting ordinance for Israel.

5 "The temple I am going to build will be great, because our God is greater than all other gods. 6 But who is able to build a temple for him, since the heavens, even the highest heavens, cannot contain him? Who then am I to build a temple for him, except as a place to burn sacrifices before him?

7 "Send me, therefore, a man skilled to work in gold and silver, bronze and iron, and in purple, crimson and blue yarn, and experienced in the art of engraving, to work in Judah and Jerusalem with my skilled craftsmen, whom my father David provided.

8 "Send me also cedar, pine and algum*g* logs from Lebanon, for I know that your men are skilled in cutting timber there. My men will work with yours 9 to provide me with plenty of lumber, because the temple I build must be large and magnificent. 10 I will give your servants, the woodsmen who cut the timber, twenty thousand cors*h* of ground wheat, twenty thousand cors of barley, twenty thousand baths*i* of wine and twenty thousand baths of olive oil."

11 Hiram king of Tyre replied by letter to Solomon:

"Because the LORD loves his people, he has made you their king."

12 And Hiram added:

"Praise be to the LORD, the God of Israel, who made heaven and earth! He has given King David a wise son, endowed with intelligence and discernment, who will build a temple for the LORD and a palace for himself.

13 "I am sending you Huram-Abi, a man of great skill, 14 whose mother was from Dan and whose father was from Tyre. He is trained to work in gold and silver, bronze and iron, stone and wood, and with purple and blue and crimson yarn and fine linen. He is experienced in all kinds of engraving and can execute any design given to him. He will work with your craftsmen and with those of my lord, David your father.

15 "Now let my lord send his servants the wheat and barley and the olive oil and wine he promised, 16 and we will cut all the logs from Lebanon that you need and will float them in rafts by sea down to Joppa. You can then take them up to Jerusalem."

17 Solomon took a census of all the aliens who were in Israel, after the census his father David had taken; and they were found to be 153,600. 18 He assigned 70,000 of them to be carriers and 80,000 to be stonecutters in the hills, with 3,600 foremen over them to keep the people working.

3:1THEN Solomon began to build the
temple of the LORD in Jerusalem on
Mount Moriah, where the LORD had appeared to his father David. It was on the
threshing floor of Araunah[j] the Jebusite,
the place provided by David. 2He began
building on the second day of the second
month in the fourth year of his reign.
3The foundation Solomon laid for
building the temple of God was sixty cubits long and twenty cubits wide[k] (using
the cubit of the old standard). 4The portico at the front of the temple was
twenty cubits[l] long across the width of
the building and twenty cubits[m] high.
He overlaid the inside with pure gold.
5He paneled the main hall with pine and
covered it with fine gold and decorated
it with palm tree and chain designs. 6He
adorned the temple with precious
stones. And the gold he used was gold of
Parvaim. 7He overlaid the ceiling
beams, doorframes, walls and doors of
the temple with gold, and he carved
cherubim on the walls.
8He built the Most Holy Place, its
length corresponding to the width of
the temple—twenty cubits long and
twenty cubits wide. He overlaid the inside with six hundred talents[n] of fine
gold. 9The gold nails weighed fifty shekels.[o] He also overlaid the upper parts
with gold.
10In the Most Holy Place he made a
pair of sculptured cherubim and overlaid them with gold. 11The total wing-
span of the cherubim was twenty cubits.
One wing of the first cherub was five cubits[p] long and touched the temple wall,
while its other wing, also five cubits
long, touched the wing of the other
cherub. 12Similarly one wing of the second cherub was five cubits long and
touched the other temple wall, and its
other wing, also five cubits long,
touched the wing of the first cherub.
13The wings of these cherubim extended twenty cubits. They stood on
their feet, facing the main hall.[q]
14He made the curtain of blue, purple
and crimson yarn and fine linen, with
cherubim worked into it.
15In the front of the temple he made
two pillars, which ⌊together⌋ were
thirty-five cubits[r] long, each with a capital on top measuring five cubits. 16He
made interwoven chains[s] and put them
on top of the pillars. He also made a
hundred pomegranates and attached
them to the chains. 17He erected the pillars in the front of the temple, one to the
south and one to the north. The one to
the south he named Jakin[t] and the one
to the north Boaz.[u]

[a]14 Or *charioteers* [b]16 Or possibly *Muzur,* a region in Cilicia; also in verse 17 [c]16 Probably Cilicia [d]17 That is, about 15 pounds (about 7 kilograms) [e]17 That is, about 3 3/4 pounds (about 1.7 kilograms) [f]3 Hebrew *Huram,* a variant of *Hiram*; also in verses 11 and 12 [g]8 Probably a variant of *almug*; possibly juniper [h]10 That is, probably about 125,000 bushels (about 4,400 kiloliters) [i]10 That is, probably about 115,000 gallons (about 440 kiloliters) [j]1 Hebrew *Ornan,* a variant of *Araunah* [k]3 That is, about 90 feet (about 27 meters) long and 30 feet (about 9 meters) wide [l]4 That is, about 30 feet (about 9 meters); also in verses 8, 11 and 13 [m]4 Some Septuagint and Syriac manuscripts; Hebrew *and a hundred and twenty* [n]8 That is, about 23 tons (about 21 metric tons) [o]9 That is, about 1 1/4 pounds (about 0.6 kilogram) [p]11 That is, about 7 1/2 feet (about 2.3 meters); also in verse 15 [q]13 Or *facing inward* [r]15 That is, about 52 feet (about 16 meters) [s]16 Or possibly *made chains in the inner sanctuary*; the meaning of the Hebrew for this phrase is uncertain. [t]17 *Jakin* probably means *he establishes.* [u]17 *Boaz* probably means *in him is strength.*

ROMANS 6:1-23

What shall we say, then? Shall we go on
sinning so that grace may increase? 2By
no means! We died to sin; how can we
live in it any longer? 3Or don't you know
that all of us who were baptized into
Christ Jesus were baptized into his
death? 4We were therefore buried with
him through baptism into death in order that, just as Christ was raised from
the dead through the glory of the Father,
we too may live a new life.
5If we have been united with him like
this in his death, we will certainly also
be united with him in his resurrection.
6For we know that our old self was crucified with him so that the body of sin
might be done away with,[a] that we
should no longer be slaves to sin— 7be-
cause anyone who has died has been
freed from sin.
8Now if we died with Christ, we believe that we will also live with him. 9For
we know that since Christ was raised

from the dead, he cannot die again; death no longer has mastery over him. [10]The death he died, he died to sin once for all; but the life he lives, he lives to God.

[11]In the same way, count yourselves dead to sin but alive to God in Christ Jesus. [12]Therefore do not let sin reign in your mortal body so that you obey its evil desires. [13]Do not offer the parts of your body to sin, as instruments of wickedness, but rather offer yourselves to God, as those who have been brought from death to life; and offer the parts of your body to him as instruments of righteousness. [14]For sin shall not be your master, because you are not under law, but under grace.

[15]What then? Shall we sin because we are not under law but under grace? By no means! [16]Don't you know that when you offer yourselves to someone to obey him as slaves, you are slaves to the one whom you obey—whether you are slaves to sin, which leads to death, or to obedience, which leads to righteousness? [17]But thanks be to God that, though you used to be slaves to sin, you wholeheartedly obeyed the form of teaching to which you were entrusted. [18]You have been set free from sin and have become slaves to righteousness.

[19]I put this in human terms because you are weak in your natural selves. Just as you used to offer the parts of your body in slavery to impurity and to ever-increasing wickedness, so now offer them in slavery to righteousness leading to holiness. [20]When you were slaves to sin, you were free from the control of righteousness. [21]What benefit did you reap at that time from the things you are now ashamed of? Those things result in death! [22]**But now that you have been set free from sin and have become slaves to God, the benefit you reap leads to holiness, and the result is eternal life.** [23]**For the wages of sin is death, but the gift of God is eternal life in**[b] **Christ Jesus our Lord.**

[a]6 Or *be rendered powerless*   [b]23 Or *through*

PSALM 16:1-11

A *miktam*[a] of David.

[1] **K**eep me safe, O God,
for in you I take refuge.

[2] I said to the LORD, "You are my Lord;
apart from you I have no good
thing."
[3] As for the saints who are in the land,
they are the glorious ones in
whom is all my delight.[b]
[4] The sorrows of those will increase
who run after other gods.
I will not pour out their libations of
blood
or take up their names on my lips.

[5] LORD, you have assigned me my
portion and my cup;
you have made my lot secure.
[6] The boundary lines have fallen for
me in pleasant places;
surely I have a delightful
inheritance.

[7] I will praise the LORD, who counsels
me;
even at night my heart instructs me.
[8] I have set the LORD always before me.
Because he is at my right hand,
I will not be shaken.

[9] Therefore my heart is glad and my
tongue rejoices;
my body also will rest secure,
[10] because you will not abandon me to
the grave,[c]
nor will you let your Holy One[d] see
decay.
[11] You have made[e] known to me the
path of life;
you will fill me with joy in your
presence,
with eternal pleasures at your right
hand.

[a]Title: Probably a literary or musical term   [b]3 Or *As for the pagan priests who are in the land / and the nobles in whom all delight, I said:*   [c]10 Hebrew *Sheol*   [d]10 Or *your faithful one*   [e]11 Or *You will make*

PROVERBS 19:20-21

[20] **L**isten to advice and accept
instruction,
and in the end you will be wise.

21 Many are the plans in a man's heart,
    but it is the LORD's purpose that
    prevails.

□ DAY 202

GOD SIGHTINGS

July 21

2 CHRONICLES 4:1–6:11

He [Solomon] made a bronze altar twenty cubits long, twenty cubits wide and ten cubits high.*a* ²He made the Sea of cast metal, circular in shape, measuring ten cubits from rim to rim and five cubits*b* high. It took a line of thirty cubits*c* to measure around it. ³Below the rim, figures of bulls encircled it—ten to a cubit.*d* The bulls were cast in two rows in one piece with the Sea.

⁴The Sea stood on twelve bulls, three facing north, three facing west, three facing south and three facing east. The Sea rested on top of them, and their hindquarters were toward the center. ⁵It was a handbreadth*e* in thickness, and its rim was like the rim of a cup, like a lily blossom. It held three thousand baths.*f*

⁶He then made ten basins for washing and placed five on the south side and five on the north. In them the things to be used for the burnt offerings were rinsed, but the Sea was to be used by the priests for washing.

⁷He made ten gold lampstands according to the specifications for them and placed them in the temple, five on the south side and five on the north.

⁸He made ten tables and placed them in the temple, five on the south side and five on the north. He also made a hundred gold sprinkling bowls.

⁹He made the courtyard of the priests, and the large court and the doors for the court, and overlaid the doors with bronze. ¹⁰He placed the Sea on the south side, at the southeast corner.

¹¹He also made the pots and shovels and sprinkling bowls.

So Huram finished the work he had undertaken for King Solomon in the temple of God:

¹² the two pillars;
    the two bowl-shaped capitals on
      top of the pillars;
    the two sets of network decorating
      the two bowl-shaped capitals on
      top of the pillars;
¹³ the four hundred pomegranates
    for the two sets of network
    (two rows of pomegranates
    for each network, decorating
    the bowl-shaped capitals on
    top of the pillars);
¹⁴ the stands with their basins;
¹⁵ the Sea and the twelve bulls under it;
¹⁶ the pots, shovels, meat forks and
    all related articles.

All the objects that Huram-Abi made for King Solomon for the temple of the LORD were of polished bronze. ¹⁷ The king had them cast in clay molds in the plain of the Jordan between Succoth and Zarethan.*g* ¹⁸All these things that Solomon made amounted to so much that the weight of the bronze was not determined.

¹⁹ Solomon also made all the furnishings that were in God's temple:

the golden altar;
    the tables on which was the
      bread of the Presence;
²⁰ the lampstands of pure gold with
    their lamps, to burn in front of
    the inner sanctuary as prescribed;
²¹ the gold floral work and lamps
    and tongs (they were solid
    gold);
²² the pure gold wick trimmers,
    sprinkling bowls, dishes and
    censers; and the gold doors of
    the temple: the inner doors to
    the Most Holy Place and the
    doors of the main hall.

⁵:¹WHEN all the work Solomon had done for the temple of the LORD was finished, he brought in the things his father David had dedicated—the silver and gold and all the furnishings—and he placed them in the treasuries of God's temple.

² Then Solomon summoned to Jerusalem the elders of Israel, all the heads of the tribes and the chiefs of the Israelite families, to bring up the ark of the LORD's covenant from Zion, the City of David. ³And all the men of Israel came together to the king at the time of the festival in the seventh month.

⁴When all the elders of Israel had arrived, the Levites took up the ark, ⁵and they brought up the ark and the Tent of Meeting and all the sacred furnishings in it. The priests, who were Levites, carried them up; ⁶and King Solomon and the entire assembly of Israel that had gathered about him were before the ark, sacrificing so many sheep and cattle that they could not be recorded or counted.

⁷ The priests then brought the ark of the LORD's covenant to its place in the inner sanctuary of the temple, the Most Holy Place, and put it beneath the wings of the cherubim. ⁸The cherubim spread their wings over the place of the ark and covered the ark and its carrying poles. ⁹These poles were so long that their ends, extending from the ark, could be seen from in front of the inner sanctuary, but not from outside the Holy Place; and they are still there today. ¹⁰There was nothing in the ark except the two tablets that Moses had placed in it at Horeb, where the LORD made a covenant with the Israelites after they came out of Egypt.

¹¹The priests then withdrew from the Holy Place. All the priests who were there had consecrated themselves, regardless of their divisions. ¹²All the Levites who were musicians—Asaph, Heman, Jeduthun and their sons and relatives—stood on the east side of the altar, dressed in fine linen and playing cymbals, harps and lyres. They were ac-

companied by 120 priests sounding trumpets. ¹³The trumpeters and singers joined in unison, as with one voice, to give praise and thanks to the LORD. Accompanied by trumpets, cymbals and other instruments, they raised their voices in praise to the LORD and sang:

"He is good;
    his love endures forever."

Then the temple of the LORD was filled with a cloud, ¹⁴and the priests could not perform their service because of the cloud, for the glory of the LORD filled the temple of God.

⁶:¹THEN Solomon said, "The LORD has said that he would dwell in a dark cloud; ²I have built a magnificent temple for you, a place for you to dwell forever."

³While the whole assembly of Israel was standing there, the king turned around and blessed them. ⁴Then he said:

"Praise be to the LORD, the God of Israel, who with his hands has fulfilled what he promised with his mouth to my father David. For he said, ⁵'Since the day I brought my people out of Egypt, I have not chosen a city in any tribe of Israel to have a temple built for my Name to be there, nor have I chosen anyone to be the leader over my people Israel. ⁶But now I have chosen Jerusalem for my Name to be there, and I have chosen David to rule my people Israel.'

⁷"My father David had it in his heart to build a temple for the Name of the LORD, the God of Israel. ⁸But the LORD said to my father David, 'Because it was in your heart to build a temple for my Name, you did well to have this in your heart. ⁹Nevertheless, you are not the one to build the temple, but your son, who is your own flesh and blood—he is the one who will build the temple for my Name.'

¹⁰"The LORD has kept the promise he made. I have succeeded

David my father and now I sit on the throne of Israel, just as the LORD promised, and I have built the temple for the Name of the LORD, the God of Israel. [11]There I have placed the ark, in which is the covenant of the LORD that he made with the people of Israel."

a1 That is, about 30 feet (about 9 meters) long and wide, and about 15 feet (about 4.5 meters) high b2 That is, about 7 1/2 feet (about 2.3 meters) c2 That is, about 45 feet (about 13.5 meters) d3 That is, about 1 1/2 feet (about 0.5 meter) e5 That is, about 3 inches (about 8 centimeters) f5 That is, about 17,500 gallons (about 66 kiloliters) g17 Hebrew Zeredatha, a variant of Zarethan

ROMANS 7:1-13

Do you not know, brothers—for I am speaking to men who know the law—that the law has authority over a man only as long as he lives? [2]For example, by law a married woman is bound to her husband as long as he is alive, but if her husband dies, she is released from the law of marriage. [3]So then, if she marries another man while her husband is still alive, she is called an adulteress. But if her husband dies, she is released from that law and is not an adulteress, even though she marries another man.

[4]So, my brothers, you also died to the law through the body of Christ, that you might belong to another, to him who was raised from the dead, in order that we might bear fruit to God. [5]For when we were controlled by the sinful nature,[a] the sinful passions aroused by the law were at work in our bodies, so that we bore fruit for death. [6]**But now, by dying to what once bound us, we have been released from the law so that we serve in the new way of the Spirit, and not in the old way of the written code.**

[7]What shall we say, then? Is the law sin? Certainly not! Indeed I would not have known what sin was except through the law. For I would not have known what coveting really was if the law had not said, "Do not covet."[b] [8]But sin, seizing the opportunity afforded by the commandment, produced in me every kind of covetous desire. For apart from law, sin is dead. [9]Once I was alive apart from law; but when the com-

mandment came, sin sprang to life and I died. [10]I found that the very commandment that was intended to bring life actually brought death. [11]For sin, seizing the opportunity afforded by the commandment, deceived me, and through the commandment put me to death. [12]So then, the law is holy, and the commandment is holy, righteous and good.

[13]Did that which is good, then, become death to me? By no means! But in order that sin might be recognized as sin, it produced death in me through what was good, so that through the commandment sin might become utterly sinful.

a5 Or the flesh; also in verse 25 b7 Exodus 20:17; Deut. 5:21

PSALM 17:1-15
A prayer of David.

[1]**H**ear, O LORD, my righteous plea;
　　listen to my cry.
　Give ear to my prayer—
　　it does not rise from deceitful lips.
[2]May my vindication come from you;
　　may your eyes see what is right.

[3]Though you probe my heart and
　　　　examine me at night,
　　though you test me, you will find
　　　　nothing;
　　I have resolved that my mouth will
　　　　not sin.
[4]As for the deeds of men—
　　　by the word of your lips
　I have kept myself
　　from the ways of the violent.
[5]My steps have held to your paths;
　　my feet have not slipped.

[6]I call on you, O God, for you will
　　　answer me;
　　give ear to me and hear my prayer.
[7]Show the wonder of your great love,
　　you who save by your right hand
　　those who take refuge in you from
　　　their foes.
[8]Keep me as the apple of your eye;
　　hide me in the shadow of your wings
[9]from the wicked who assail me,
　　from my mortal enemies who
　　　surround me.

10 They close up their callous hearts,
   and their mouths speak with
      arrogance.
11 They have tracked me down, they
      now surround me,
   with eyes alert, to throw me to the
      ground.
12 They are like a lion hungry for prey,
   like a great lion crouching in
      cover.

13 Rise up, O Lord, confront them, bring
      them down;
   rescue me from the wicked by
      your sword.
14 O Lord, by your hand save me from
      such men,
   from men of this world whose
      reward is in this life.

   You still the hunger of those you
      cherish;
   their sons have plenty,
   and they store up wealth for their
      children.
15 And I—in righteousness I will see
      your face;
   when I awake, I will be satisfied
      with seeing your likeness.

PROVERBS 19:22-23
22 **W**hat a man desires is unfailing
      love*a*;
   better to be poor than a liar.

23 The fear of the Lord leads to life:
   Then one rests content, untouched
      by trouble.

a22 Or A man's greed is his shame

□ DAY 203

GOD SIGHTINGS

July 22

2 CHRONICLES 6:12–8:10
Then Solomon stood before the altar of
the Lord in front of the whole assembly
of Israel and spread out his hands.
13 Now he had made a bronze platform,

five cubits*a* long, five cubits wide and
three cubits*b* high, and had placed it in
the center of the outer court. He stood
on the platform and then knelt down
before the whole assembly of Israel and
spread out his hands toward heaven.
14 He said:

   "O Lord, God of Israel, there is
no God like you in heaven or on
earth—you who keep your covenant of love with your servants
who continue wholeheartedly in
your way. 15 You have kept your
promise to your servant David my
father; with your mouth you have
promised and with your hand you
have fulfilled it—as it is today.

   16 "Now Lord, God of Israel, keep
for your servant David my father
the promises you made to him
when you said, 'You shall never fail
to have a man to sit before me on
the throne of Israel, if only your
sons are careful in all they do to
walk before me according to my
law, as you have done.' 17 And now,
O Lord, God of Israel, let your word
that you promised your servant
David come true.

   18 "But will God really dwell on
earth with men? The heavens, even
the highest heavens, cannot contain you. How much less this temple I have built! 19 Yet give
attention to your servant's prayer
and his plea for mercy, O Lord my
God. Hear the cry and the prayer
that your servant is praying in your
presence. 20 May your eyes be open
toward this temple day and night,
this place of which you said you
would put your Name there. May
you hear the prayer your servant
prays toward this place. 21 Hear the
supplications of your servant and
of your people Israel when they
pray toward this place. Hear from
heaven, your dwelling place; and
when you hear, forgive.

   22 "When a man wrongs his
neighbor and is required to take an

oath and he comes and swears the oath before your altar in this temple, 23then hear from heaven and act. Judge between your servants, repaying the guilty by bringing down on his own head what he has done. Declare the innocent not guilty and so establish his innocence.

24"When your people Israel have been defeated by an enemy because they have sinned against you and when they turn back and confess your name, praying and making supplication before you in this temple, 25then hear from heaven and forgive the sin of your people Israel and bring them back to the land you gave to them and their fathers.

26"When the heavens are shut up and there is no rain because your people have sinned against you, and when they pray toward this place and confess your name and turn from their sin because you have afflicted them, 27then hear from heaven and forgive the sin of your servants, your people Israel. Teach them the right way to live, and send rain on the land you gave your people for an inheritance.

28"When famine or plague comes to the land, or blight or mildew, locusts or grasshoppers, or when enemies besiege them in any of their cities, whatever disaster or disease may come, 29and when a prayer or plea is made by any of your people Israel—each one aware of his afflictions and pains, and spreading out his hands toward this temple— 30then hear from heaven, your dwelling place. Forgive, and deal with each man according to all he does, since you know his heart (for you alone know the hearts of men), 31so that they will fear you and walk in your ways all the time they live in the land you gave our fathers.

32"As for the foreigner who does not belong to your people Israel but

has come from a distant land because of your great name and your mighty hand and your outstretched arm—when he comes and prays toward this temple, 33then hear from heaven, your dwelling place, and do whatever the foreigner asks of you, so that all the peoples of the earth may know your name and fear you, as do your own people Israel, and may know that this house I have built bears your Name.

34"When your people go to war against their enemies, wherever you send them, and when they pray to you toward this city you have chosen and the temple I have built for your Name, 35then hear from heaven their prayer and their plea, and uphold their cause.

36"When they sin against you— for there is no one who does not sin—and you become angry with them and give them over to the enemy, who takes them captive to a land far away or near; 37and if they have a change of heart in the land where they are held captive, and repent and plead with you in the land of their captivity and say, 'We have sinned, we have done wrong and acted wickedly'; 38and if they turn back to you with all their heart and soul in the land of their captivity where they were taken, and pray toward the land you gave their fathers, toward the city you have chosen and toward the temple I have built for your Name; 39then from heaven, your dwelling place, hear their prayer and their pleas, and uphold their cause. And forgive your people, who have sinned against you.

40"Now, my God, may your eyes be open and your ears attentive to the prayers offered in this place.

41 "Now arise, O LORD God, and
       come to your resting place,
    you and the ark of your might.

May your priests, O Lᴏʀᴅ God, be
    clothed with salvation,
  may your saints rejoice in your
    goodness.
⁴²O Lᴏʀᴅ God, do not reject your
  anointed one.
  Remember the great love
    promised to David your
    servant."

⁷:¹Wʜᴇɴ Solomon finished praying, fire
came down from heaven and consumed
the burnt offering and the sacrifices,
and the glory of the Lᴏʀᴅ filled the temple. ²The priests could not enter the
temple of the Lᴏʀᴅ because the glory of
the Lᴏʀᴅ filled it. ³When all the Israelites saw the fire coming down and the
glory of the Lᴏʀᴅ above the temple, they
knelt on the pavement with their faces
to the ground, and they worshiped and
gave thanks to the Lᴏʀᴅ, saying,

"He is good;
  his love endures forever."

⁴Then the king and all the people offered sacrifices before the Lᴏʀᴅ. ⁵And
King Solomon offered a sacrifice of
twenty-two thousand head of cattle and
a hundred and twenty thousand sheep
and goats. So the king and all the people
dedicated the temple of God. ⁶The
priests took their positions, as did the
Levites with the Lᴏʀᴅ's musical instruments, which King David had made for
praising the Lᴏʀᴅ and which were used
when he gave thanks, saying, "His love
endures forever." Opposite the Levites,
the priests blew their trumpets, and all
the Israelites were standing.

⁷Solomon consecrated the middle
part of the courtyard in front of the temple of the Lᴏʀᴅ, and there he offered
burnt offerings and the fat of the fellowship offerings,ᶜ because the bronze altar he had made could not hold the
burnt offerings, the grain offerings and
the fat portions.

⁸So Solomon observed the festival at
that time for seven days, and all Israel
with him—a vast assembly, people from
Leboᵈ Hamath to the Wadi of Egypt. ⁹On

the eighth day they held an assembly, for
they had celebrated the dedication of the
altar for seven days and the festival for
seven days more. ¹⁰On the twenty-third
day of the seventh month he sent the
people to their homes, joyful and glad in
heart for the good things the Lᴏʀᴅ had
done for David and Solomon and for his
people Israel.

¹¹When Solomon had finished the
temple of the Lᴏʀᴅ and the royal palace,
and had succeeded in carrying out all he
had in mind to do in the temple of the
Lᴏʀᴅ and in his own palace, ¹²the Lᴏʀᴅ
appeared to him at night and said:

"I have heard your prayer and
have chosen this place for myself
as a temple for sacrifices.
  ¹³"When I shut up the heavens
so that there is no rain, or command locusts to devour the land or
send a plague among my people,
¹⁴if my people, who are called by
my name, will humble themselves
and pray and seek my face and
turn from their wicked ways, then
will I hear from heaven and will
forgive their sin and will heal their
land. ¹⁵Now my eyes will be open
and my ears attentive to the
prayers offered in this place. ¹⁶I
have chosen and consecrated this
temple so that my Name may be
there forever. My eyes and my
heart will always be there.
  ¹⁷"As for you, if you walk before
me as David your father did, and do
all I command, and observe my decrees and laws, ¹⁸I will establish
your royal throne, as I covenanted
with David your father when I said,
'You shall never fail to have a man
to rule over Israel.'
  ¹⁹"But if youᵉ turn away and forsake the decrees and commands I
have given youᵉ and go off to serve
other gods and worship them,
²⁰then I will uproot Israel from my
land, which I have given them, and
will reject this temple I have consecrated for my Name. I will make it a

byword and an object of ridicule among all peoples. 21And though this temple is now so imposing, all who pass by will be appalled and say, 'Why has the LORD done such a thing to this land and to this temple?' 22People will answer, 'Because they have forsaken the LORD, the God of their fathers, who brought them out of Egypt, and have embraced other gods, worshiping and serving them—that is why he brought all this disaster on them.'"

8:1At the end of twenty years, during which Solomon built the temple of the LORD and his own palace, 2Solomon rebuilt the villages that Hiram[f] had given him, and settled Israelites in them. 3Solomon then went to Hamath Zobah and captured it. 4He also built up Tadmor in the desert and all the store cities he had built in Hamath. 5He rebuilt Upper Beth Horon and Lower Beth Horon as fortified cities, with walls and with gates and bars, 6as well as Baalath and all his store cities, and all the cities for his chariots and for his horses[g]—whatever he desired to build in Jerusalem, in Lebanon and throughout all the territory he ruled.

7All the people left from the Hittites, Amorites, Perizzites, Hivites and Jebusites (these peoples were not Israelites), 8that is, their descendants remaining in the land, whom the Israelites had not destroyed—these Solomon conscripted for his slave labor force, as it is to this day. 9But Solomon did not make slaves of the Israelites for his work; they were his fighting men, commanders of his captains, and commanders of his chariots and charioteers. 10They were also King Solomon's chief officials—two hundred and fifty officials supervising the men.

a13 That is, about 7 1/2 feet (about 2.3 meters)   b13 That is, about 4 1/2 feet (about 1.3 meters)   c7 Traditionally peace offerings   d8 Or from the entrance to   e19 The Hebrew is plural.   f2 Hebrew Huram, a variant of Hiram; also in verse 18   96 Or charioteers

ROMANS 7:14–8:8
We know that the law is spiritual; but I am unspiritual, sold as a slave to sin. 15I

do not understand what I do. For what I want to do I do not do, but what I hate I do. 16And if I do what I do not want to do, I agree that the law is good. 17As it is, it is no longer I myself who do it, but it is sin living in me. 18I know that nothing good lives in me, that is, in my sinful nature.[a] For I have the desire to do what is good, but I cannot carry it out. 19For what I do is not the good I want to do; no, the evil I do not want to do—this I keep on doing. 20Now if I do what I do not want to do, it is no longer I who do it, but it is sin living in me that does it.

21So I find this law at work: When I want to do good, evil is right there with me. 22For in my inner being I delight in God's law; 23but I see another law at work in the members of my body, waging war against the law of my mind and making me a prisoner of the law of sin at work within my members. 24What a wretched man I am! Who will rescue me from this body of death? 25Thanks be to God—through Jesus Christ our Lord!

So then, I myself in my mind am a slave to God's law, but in the sinful nature a slave to the law of sin.

8:1THEREFORE, there is now no condemnation for those who are in Christ Jesus,[b] 2because through Christ Jesus the law of the Spirit of life set me free from the law of sin and death. 3For what the law was powerless to do in that it was weakened by the sinful nature,[c] God did by sending his own Son in the likeness of sinful man to be a sin offering.[d] And so he condemned sin in sinful man,[e] 4in order that the righteous requirements of the law might be fully met in us, who do not live according to the sinful nature but according to the Spirit.

5Those who live according to the sinful nature have their minds set on what that nature desires; but those who live in accordance with the Spirit have their minds set on what the Spirit desires. 6The mind of sinful man[f] is death, but the mind controlled by the Spirit is life and peace; 7the sinful mind[g] is hostile to God. It does not submit to God's law, nor can it do so. [8]Those controlled by the sinful nature cannot please God.

a18Or my flesh   b1Some later manuscripts Jesus, who do not live according to the sinful nature but according to the Spirit,   c3Or the flesh; also in verses 4, 5, 8, 9, 12 and 13   d3Or man, for sin   e3Or in the flesh   f6Or mind set on the flesh   g7Or the mind set on the flesh

PSALM 18:1-15

For the director of music. Of David the servant of the LORD. He sang to the LORD the words of this song when the LORD delivered him from the hand of all his enemies and from the hand of Saul. He said:

[1]I love you, O LORD, my strength.

[2]The LORD is my rock, my fortress and my deliverer;
    my God is my rock, in whom I take refuge.
    He is my shield and the horn[a] of my salvation, my stronghold.

[3]I call to the LORD, who is worthy of praise,
    and I am saved from my enemies.

[4]The cords of death entangled me;
    the torrents of destruction overwhelmed me.

[5]The cords of the grave[b] coiled around me;
    the snares of death confronted me.

[6]In my distress I called to the LORD;
    I cried to my God for help.
    From his temple he heard my voice;
    my cry came before him, into his ears.

[7]The earth trembled and quaked,
    and the foundations of the mountains shook;
    they trembled because he was angry.

[8]Smoke rose from his nostrils;
    consuming fire came from his mouth,
    burning coals blazed out of it.

[9]He parted the heavens and came down;
    dark clouds were under his feet.

[10]He mounted the cherubim and flew;
    he soared on the wings of the wind.

[11]He made darkness his covering, his canopy around him—
    the dark rain clouds of the sky.

[12]Out of the brightness of his presence clouds advanced,
    with hailstones and bolts of lightning.

[13]The LORD thundered from heaven;
    the voice of the Most High resounded.[c]

[14]He shot his arrows and scattered the enemies,
    great bolts of lightning and routed them.

[15]The valleys of the sea were exposed
    and the foundations of the earth laid bare
    at your rebuke, O LORD,
    at the blast of breath from your nostrils.

a2Horn here symbolizes strength.   b5Hebrew Sheol   c13Some Hebrew manuscripts and Septuagint (see also 2 Samuel 22:14); most Hebrew manuscripts resounded, / amid hailstones and bolts of lightning

PROVERBS 19:24-25

[24]The sluggard buries his hand in the dish;
    he will not even bring it back to his mouth!

[25]Flog a mocker, and the simple will learn prudence;
    rebuke a discerning man, and he will gain knowledge.

□ D A Y   2 0 4

GOD SIGHTINGS

July 23

2 CHRONICLES 8:11-10:19

Solomon brought Pharaoh's daughter up from the City of David to the palace he had built for her, for he said, "My wife must not live in the palace of David king of Israel, because the places the ark of the LORD has entered are holy."

[12]On the altar of the LORD that he had built in front of the portico, Solomon

sacrificed burnt offerings to the LORD, [13]according to the daily requirement for offerings commanded by Moses for Sabbaths, New Moons and the three annual feasts—the Feast of Unleavened Bread, the Feast of Weeks and the Feast of Tabernacles. [14]In keeping with the ordinance of his father David, he appointed the divisions of the priests for their duties, and the Levites to lead the praise and to assist the priests according to each day's requirement. He also appointed the gatekeepers by divisions for the various gates, because this was what David the man of God had ordered. [15]They did not deviate from the king's commands to the priests or to the Levites in any matter, including that of the treasuries.

[16]All Solomon's work was carried out, from the day the foundation of the temple of the LORD was laid until its completion. So the temple of the LORD was finished.

[17]Then Solomon went to Ezion Geber and Elath on the coast of Edom. [18]And Hiram sent him ships commanded by his own officers, men who knew the sea. These, with Solomon's men, sailed to Ophir and brought back four hundred and fifty talents[a] of gold, which they delivered to King Solomon.

[9:1]WHEN the queen of Sheba heard of Solomon's fame, she came to Jerusalem to test him with hard questions. Arriving with a very great caravan—with camels carrying spices, large quantities of gold, and precious stones—she came to Solomon and talked with him about all she had on her mind. [2]Solomon answered all her questions; nothing was too hard for him to explain to her. [3]When the queen of Sheba saw the wisdom of Solomon, as well as the palace he had built, [4]the food on his table, the seating of his officials, the attending servants in their robes, the cupbearers in their robes and the burnt offerings he made at[b] the temple of the LORD, she was overwhelmed.

[5]She said to the king, "The report I heard in my own country about your achievements and your wisdom is true. [6]But I did not believe what they said until I came and saw with my own eyes. Indeed, not even half the greatness of your wisdom was told me; you have far exceeded the report I heard. [7]How happy your men must be! How happy your officials, who continually stand before you and hear your wisdom! [8]Praise be to the LORD your God, who has delighted in you and placed you on his throne as king to rule for the LORD your God. Because of the love of your God for Israel and his desire to uphold them forever, he has made you king over them, to maintain justice and righteousness."

[9]Then she gave the king 120 talents[c] of gold, large quantities of spices, and precious stones. There had never been such spices as those the queen of Sheba gave to King Solomon.

[10](The men of Hiram and the men of Solomon brought gold from Ophir; they also brought algumwood[d] and precious stones. [11]The king used the algumwood to make steps for the temple of the LORD and for the royal palace, and to make harps and lyres for the musicians. Nothing like them had ever been seen in Judah.)

[12]King Solomon gave the queen of Sheba all she desired and asked for; he gave her more than she had brought to him. Then she left and returned with her retinue to her own country.

[13]The weight of the gold that Solomon received yearly was 666 talents,[e] [14]not including the revenues brought in by merchants and traders. Also all the kings of Arabia and the governors of the land brought gold and silver to Solomon.

[15]King Solomon made two hundred large shields of hammered gold; six hundred bekas[f] of hammered gold went into each shield. [16]He also made three hundred small shields of hammered gold, with three hundred bekas[g] of gold in each shield. The king put them in the Palace of the Forest of Lebanon.

[17]Then the king made a great throne inlaid with ivory and overlaid with pure

gold. [18]The throne had six steps, and a footstool of gold was attached to it. On both sides of the seat were armrests, with a lion standing beside each of them. [19]Twelve lions stood on the six steps, one at either end of each step. Nothing like it had ever been made for any other kingdom. [20]All King Solomon's goblets were gold, and all the household articles in the Palace of the Forest of Lebanon were pure gold. Nothing was made of silver, because silver was considered of little value in Solomon's day. [21]The king had a fleet of trading ships[h] manned by Hiram's[i] men. Once every three years it returned, carrying gold, silver and ivory, and apes and baboons.

[22]King Solomon was greater in riches and wisdom than all the other kings of the earth. [23]All the kings of the earth sought audience with Solomon to hear the wisdom God had put in his heart. [24]Year after year, everyone who came brought a gift—articles of silver and gold, and robes, weapons and spices, and horses and mules.

[25]Solomon had four thousand stalls for horses and chariots, and twelve thousand horses,[j] which he kept in the chariot cities and also with him in Jerusalem. [26]He ruled over all the kings from the River[k] to the land of the Philistines, as far as the border of Egypt. [27]The king made silver as common in Jerusalem as stones, and cedar as plentiful as sycamore-fig trees in the foothills. [28]Solomon's horses were imported from Egypt[l] and from all other countries.

[29]As for the other events of Solomon's reign, from beginning to end, are they not written in the records of Nathan the prophet, in the prophecy of Ahijah the Shilonite and in the visions of Iddo the seer concerning Jeroboam son of Nebat? [30]Solomon reigned in Jerusalem over all Israel forty years. [31]Then he rested with his fathers and was buried in the city of David his father. And Rehoboam his son succeeded him as king.

[10:1]REHOBOAM went to Shechem, for all the Israelites had gone there to make him king. [2]When Jeroboam son of Nebat heard this (he was in Egypt, where he had fled from King Solomon), he returned from Egypt. [3]So they sent for Jeroboam, and he and all Israel went to Rehoboam and said to him: [4]"Your father put a heavy yoke on us, but now lighten the harsh labor and the heavy yoke he put on us, and we will serve you."

[5]Rehoboam answered, "Come back to me in three days." So the people went away.

[6]Then King Rehoboam consulted the elders who had served his father Solomon during his lifetime. "How would you advise me to answer these people?" he asked.

[7]They replied, "If you will be kind to these people and please them and give them a favorable answer, they will always be your servants."

[8]But Rehoboam rejected the advice the elders gave him and consulted the young men who had grown up with him and were serving him. [9]He asked them, "What is your advice? How should we answer these people who say to me, 'Lighten the yoke your father put on us'?"

[10]The young men who had grown up with him replied, "Tell the people who have said to you, 'Your father put a heavy yoke on us, but make our yoke lighter'— tell them, 'My little finger is thicker than my father's waist. [11]My father laid on you a heavy yoke; I will make it even heavier. My father scourged you with whips; I will scourge you with scorpions.'"

[12]Three days later Jeroboam and all the people returned to Rehoboam, as the king had said, "Come back to me in three days." [13]The king answered them harshly. Rejecting the advice of the elders, [14]he followed the advice of the young men and said, "My father made your yoke heavy; I will make it even heavier. My father scourged you with whips; I will scourge you with scorpions." [15]So the king did not listen to the people, for this turn of events was from

God, to fulfill the word the Lord had spoken to Jeroboam son of Nebat through Ahijah the Shilonite.

¹⁶When all Israel saw that the king refused to listen to them, they answered the king:

"What share do we have in David,
    what part in Jesse's son?
To your tents, O Israel!
    Look after your own house, O David!"

So all the Israelites went home. ¹⁷But as for the Israelites who were living in the towns of Judah, Rehoboam still ruled over them.

¹⁸King Rehoboam sent out Adoniram,^m who was in charge of forced labor, but the Israelites stoned him to death. King Rehoboam, however, managed to get into his chariot and escape to Jerusalem. ¹⁹So Israel has been in rebellion against the house of David to this day.

^a18 That is, about 17 tons (about 16 metric tons)   ^b4 Or the ascent by which he went up to   ^c9 That is, about 4 1/2 tons (about 4 metric tons)   ^d10 Probably a variant of almugwood   ^e13 That is, about 25 tons (about 23 metric tons)   ^f15 That is, about 7 1/2 pounds (about 3.5 kilograms)   ^g16 That is, about 3 3/4 pounds (about 1.7 kilograms)   ^h21 Hebrew of ships that could go to Tarshish   ⁱ21 Hebrew Huram, a variant of Hiram   ^j25 Or charioteers   ^k26 That is, the Euphrates   ^l28 Or possibly Muzur, a region in Cilicia   ^m18 Hebrew Hadoram, a variant of Adoniram

ROMANS 8:9-21

You, however, are controlled not by the sinful nature but by the Spirit, if the Spirit of God lives in you. And if anyone does not have the Spirit of Christ, he does not belong to Christ. ¹⁰But if Christ is in you, your body is dead because of sin, yet your spirit is alive because of righteousness. ¹¹**And if the Spirit of him who raised Jesus from the dead is living in you, he who raised Christ from the dead will also give life to your mortal bodies through his Spirit, who lives in you.**

¹²Therefore, brothers, we have an obligation—but it is not to the sinful nature, to live according to it. ¹³For if you live according to the sinful nature, you will die; but if by the Spirit you put to death the misdeeds of the body, you will live, ¹⁴because those who are led by the

Spirit of God are sons of God. ¹⁵For you did not receive a spirit that makes you a slave again to fear, but you received the Spirit of sonship.^a And by him we cry, "Abba,^b Father." ¹⁶The Spirit himself testifies with our spirit that we are God's children. ¹⁷Now if we are children, then we are heirs—heirs of God and co-heirs with Christ, if indeed we share in his sufferings in order that we may also share in his glory.

¹⁸I consider that our present sufferings are not worth comparing with the glory that will be revealed in us. ¹⁹The creation waits in eager expectation for the sons of God to be revealed. ²⁰For the creation was subjected to frustration, not by its own choice, but by the will of the one who subjected it, in hope ²¹that^c the creation itself will be liberated from its bondage to decay and brought into the glorious freedom of the children of God.

^a15 Or adoption   ^b15 Aramaic for Father   ^c20,21 Or subjected it in hope. ²¹For

PSALM 18:16-36

¹⁶**H**e [the Lord] reached down from on
        high and took hold of me;
    he drew me out of deep waters.
¹⁷He rescued me from my powerful
        enemy,
    from my foes, who were too strong
        for me.
¹⁸They confronted me in the day of
        my disaster,
    but the Lord was my support.
¹⁹He brought me out into a spacious
        place;
    he rescued me because he
        delighted in me.

²⁰The Lord has dealt with me according
        to my righteousness;
    according to the cleanness of my
        hands he has rewarded me.
²¹For I have kept the ways of the Lord;
    I have not done evil by turning
        from my God.
²²All his laws are before me;
    I have not turned away from his
        decrees.

²³I have been blameless before him
and have kept myself from sin.
²⁴The Lord has rewarded me
according to my
righteousness,
according to the cleanness of my
hands in his sight.

²⁵To the faithful you show yourself
faithful,
to the blameless you show yourself
blameless,
²⁶to the pure you show yourself pure,
but to the crooked you show
yourself shrewd.
²⁷You save the humble
but bring low those whose eyes are
haughty.
²⁸You, O Lord, keep my lamp burning;
my God turns my darkness into
light.
²⁹With your help I can advance against
a troop*ᵃ*;
with my God I can scale a wall.

³⁰As for God, his way is perfect;
the word of the Lord is flawless.
He is a shield
for all who take refuge in him.
³¹For who is God besides the Lord?
And who is the Rock except our
God?
³²It is God who arms me with strength
and makes my way perfect.
³³He makes my feet like the feet of
a deer;
he enables me to stand on the
heights.
³⁴He trains my hands for battle;
my arms can bend a bow of
bronze.
³⁵You give me your shield of victory,
and your right hand sustains me;
you stoop down to make me great.
³⁶You broaden the path beneath me,
so that my ankles do not turn.

ᵃ29 Or can run through a barricade

PROVERBS 19:26
²⁶He who robs his father and drives
out his mother
is a son who brings shame and
disgrace.

□ DAY 205

GOD SIGHTINGS

July 24

2 CHRONICLES 11:1–13:22

When Rehoboam arrived in Jerusalem, he mustered the house of Judah and Benjamin—a hundred and eighty thousand fighting men—to make war against Israel and to regain the kingdom for Rehoboam.

²But this word of the Lord came to Shemaiah the man of God: ³"Say to Rehoboam son of Solomon king of Judah and to all the Israelites in Judah and Benjamin, ⁴'This is what the Lord says: Do not go up to fight against your brothers. Go home, every one of you, for this is my doing.'" So they obeyed the words of the Lord and turned back from marching against Jeroboam.

⁵Rehoboam lived in Jerusalem and built up towns for defense in Judah: ⁶Bethlehem, Etam, Tekoa, ⁷Beth Zur, Soco, Adullam, ⁸Gath, Mareshah, Ziph, ⁹Adoraim, Lachish, Azekah, ¹⁰Zorah, Aijalon and Hebron. These were fortified cities in Judah and Benjamin. ¹¹He strengthened their defenses and put commanders in them, with supplies of food, olive oil and wine. ¹²He put shields and spears in all the cities, and made them very strong. So Judah and Benjamin were his.

¹³The priests and Levites from all their districts throughout Israel sided with him. ¹⁴The Levites even abandoned their pasturelands and property, and came to Judah and Jerusalem because Jeroboam and his sons had rejected them as priests of the Lord. ¹⁵And he appointed his own priests for the high places and for the goat and calf idols he had made. ¹⁶Those from every tribe of Israel who set their hearts on seeking the Lord, the God of Israel, followed the Levites to Jerusalem to offer sacrifices to the Lord, the God of their fathers. ¹⁷They strengthened the

kingdom of Judah and supported Rehoboam son of Solomon three years, walking in the ways of David and Solomon
during this time.

[18]Rehoboam married Mahalath, who
was the daughter of David's son Jerimoth and of Abihail, the daughter of
Jesse's son Eliab. [19]She bore him sons:
Jeush, Shemariah and Zaham. [20]Then
he married Maacah daughter of Absalom, who bore him Abijah, Attai, Ziza
and Shelomith. [21]Rehoboam loved Maacah daughter of Absalom more than
any of his other wives and concubines.
In all, he had eighteen wives and sixty
concubines, twenty-eight sons and sixty
daughters.

[22]Rehoboam appointed Abijah son of
Maacah to be the chief prince among his
brothers, in order to make him king.
[23]He acted wisely, dispersing some of his
sons throughout the districts of Judah
and Benjamin, and to all the fortified cities. He gave them abundant provisions
and took many wives for them.

[12:1]AFTER Rehoboam's position as king
was established and he had become
strong, he and all Israel[a] with him abandoned the law of the LORD. [2]Because
they had been unfaithful to the LORD,
Shishak king of Egypt attacked Jerusalem in the fifth year of King Rehoboam.
[3]With twelve hundred chariots and
sixty thousand horsemen and the innu-
merable troops of Libyans, Sukkites and
Cushites[b] that came with him from
Egypt, [4]he captured the fortified cities
of Judah and came as far as Jerusalem.

[5]Then the prophet Shemaiah came to
Rehoboam and to the leaders of Judah
who had assembled in Jerusalem for
fear of Shishak, and he said to them,
"This is what the LORD says, 'You have
abandoned me; therefore, I now abandon you to Shishak.'"

[6]The leaders of Israel and the king
humbled themselves and said, "The
LORD is just."

[7]When the LORD saw that they humbled themselves, this word of the LORD
came to Shemaiah: "Since they have

humbled themselves, I will not destroy
them but will soon give them deliverance. My wrath will not be poured out
on Jerusalem through Shishak. [8]They
will, however, become subject to him, so
that they may learn the difference between serving me and serving the kings
of other lands."

[9]When Shishak king of Egypt attacked Jerusalem, he carried off the
treasures of the temple of the LORD and
the treasures of the royal palace. He
took everything, including the gold
shields Solomon had made. [10]So King
Rehoboam made bronze shields to replace them and assigned these to the
commanders of the guard on duty at the
entrance to the royal palace. [11]When-
ever the king went to the LORD's temple,
the guards went with him, bearing the
shields, and afterward they returned
them to the guardroom.

[12]Because Rehoboam humbled himself, the LORD's anger turned from him,
and he was not totally destroyed. Indeed, there was some good in Judah.

[13]King Rehoboam established himself firmly in Jerusalem and continued as
king. He was forty-one years old when he
became king, and he reigned seventeen
years in Jerusalem, the city the LORD had
chosen out of all the tribes of Israel in
which to put his Name. His mother's
name was Naamah; she was an Ammonite. [14]He did evil because he had not set
his heart on seeking the LORD.

[15]As for the events of Rehoboam's
reign, from beginning to end, are they
not written in the records of Shemaiah
the prophet and of Iddo the seer that
deal with genealogies? There was continual warfare between Rehoboam and
Jeroboam. [16]Rehoboam rested with his
fathers and was buried in the City of David. And Abijah his son succeeded him
as king.

[13:1]IN the eighteenth year of the reign of
Jeroboam, Abijah became king of Judah,
[2]and he reigned in Jerusalem three
years. His mother's name was Maacah,[c]
a daughter[d] of Uriel of Gibeah.

There was war between Abijah and Jeroboam. [3]Abijah went into battle with a force of four hundred thousand able fighting men, and Jeroboam drew up a battle line against him with eight hundred thousand able troops.

[4]Abijah stood on Mount Zemaraim, in the hill country of Ephraim, and said, "Jeroboam and all Israel, listen to me! [5]Don't you know that the LORD, the God of Israel, has given the kingship of Israel to David and his descendants forever by a covenant of salt? [6]Yet Jeroboam son of Nebat, an official of Solomon son of David, rebelled against his master. [7]Some worthless scoundrels gathered around him and opposed Rehoboam son of Solomon when he was young and indecisive and not strong enough to resist them.

[8]"And now you plan to resist the kingdom of the LORD, which is in the hands of David's descendants. You are indeed a vast army and have with you the golden calves that Jeroboam made to be your gods. [9]But didn't you drive out the priests of the LORD, the sons of Aaron, and the Levites, and make priests of your own as the peoples of other lands do? Whoever comes to consecrate himself with a young bull and seven rams may become a priest of what are not gods.

[10]"As for us, the LORD is our God, and we have not forsaken him. The priests who serve the LORD are sons of Aaron, and the Levites assist them. [11]Every morning and evening they present burnt offerings and fragrant incense to the LORD. They set out the bread on the ceremonially clean table and light the lamps on the gold lampstand every evening. We are observing the requirements of the LORD our God. But you have forsaken him. [12]God is with us; he is our leader. His priests with their trumpets will sound the battle cry against you. Men of Israel, do not fight against the LORD, the God of your fathers, for you will not succeed."

[13]Now Jeroboam had sent troops around to the rear, so that while he was in front of Judah the ambush was behind them. [14]Judah turned and saw that they were being attacked at both front and rear. Then they cried out to the LORD. The priests blew their trumpets [15]and the men of Judah raised the battle cry. At the sound of their battle cry, God routed Jeroboam and all Israel before Abijah and Judah. [16]The Israelites fled before Judah, and God delivered them into their hands. [17]Abijah and his men inflicted heavy losses on them, so that there were five hundred thousand casualties among Israel's able men. [18]The men of Israel were subdued on that occasion, and the men of Judah were victorious because they relied on the LORD, the God of their fathers.

[19]Abijah pursued Jeroboam and took from him the towns of Bethel, Jeshanah and Ephron, with their surrounding villages. [20]Jeroboam did not regain power during the time of Abijah. And the LORD struck him down and he died.

[21]But Abijah grew in strength. He married fourteen wives and had twenty-two sons and sixteen daughters.

[22]The other events of Abijah's reign, what he did and what he said, are written in the annotations of the prophet Iddo.

[a]1 That is, Judah, as frequently in 2 Chronicles   [b]3 That is, people from the upper Nile region   [c]2 Most Septuagint manuscripts and Syriac (see also 2 Chron. 11:20 and 1 Kings 15:2); Hebrew *Micaiah*   [d]2 Or *granddaughter*

ROMANS 8:22-39

We know that the whole creation has been groaning as in the pains of childbirth right up to the present time. [23]Not only so, but we ourselves, who have the firstfruits of the Spirit, groan inwardly as we wait eagerly for our adoption as sons, the redemption of our bodies. [24]For in this hope we were saved. But hope that is seen is no hope at all. Who hopes for what he already has? [25]But if we hope for what we do not yet have, we wait for it patiently.

[26]In the same way, the Spirit helps us in our weakness. We do not know what we ought to pray for, but the Spirit himself intercedes for us with groans that words cannot express. [27]And he who searches our hearts knows the mind of the Spirit,

because the Spirit intercedes for the saints in accordance with God's will.

28And we know that in all things God works for the good of those who love him,*a* who*b* have been called according to his purpose. 29For those God foreknew he also predestined to be conformed to the likeness of his Son, that he might be the firstborn among many brothers. 30And those he predestined, he also called; those he called, he also justified; those he justified, he also glorified.

31What, then, shall we say in response to this? If God is for us, who can be against us? 32He who did not spare his own Son, but gave him up for us all— how will he not also, along with him, graciously give us all things? 33Who will bring any charge against those whom God has chosen? It is God who justifies. 34Who is he that condemns? Christ Jesus, who died—more than that, who was raised to life—is at the right hand of God and is also interceding for us. 35Who shall separate us from the love of Christ? Shall trouble or hardship or persecution or famine or nakedness or danger or sword? 36As it is written:

"For your sake we face death all day
        long;
    we are considered as sheep to be
        slaughtered."*c*

37No, in all these things we are more than conquerors through him who loved us. 38**For I am convinced that neither death nor life, neither angels nor demons,*d* neither the present nor the future, nor any powers, 39neither height nor depth, nor anything else in all creation, will be able to separate us from the love of God that is in Christ Jesus our Lord.**

a28 Some manuscripts And we know that all things work together for good to those who love God   b28 Or works together with those who love him to bring about what is good— with those who   c36 Psalm 44:22   d38 Or nor heavenly rulers

PSALM 18:37-50

37 I pursued my enemies and overtook
        them;
    I did not turn back till they were
        destroyed.

38I crushed them so that they could not
        rise;
    they fell beneath my feet.
39You armed me with strength for
        battle;
    you made my adversaries bow at
        my feet.
40You made my enemies turn their
        backs in flight,
    and I destroyed my foes.
41They cried for help, but there was no
        one to save them—
    to the LORD, but he did not answer.
42I beat them as fine as dust borne on
        the wind;
    I poured them out like mud in the
        streets.

43You have delivered me from the
        attacks of the people;
    you have made me the head of
        nations;
    people I did not know are subject
        to me.
44As soon as they hear me, they obey
        me;
    foreigners cringe before me.
45They all lose heart;
    they come trembling from their
        strongholds.

46The LORD lives! Praise be to my Rock!
    Exalted be God my Savior!
47He is the God who avenges me,
    who subdues nations under me,
48   who saves me from my enemies.
You exalted me above my foes;
    from violent men you rescued me.
49Therefore I will praise you among the
        nations, O LORD;
    I will sing praises to your name.
50He gives his king great victories;
    he shows unfailing kindness to his
        anointed,
    to David and his descendants
        forever.

PROVERBS 19:27-29

27Stop listening to instruction,
        my son,
    and you will stray from the words
        of knowledge.

28 A corrupt witness mocks at justice,
    and the mouth of the wicked gulps
        down evil.

29 Penalties are prepared for mockers,
    and beatings for the backs of
        fools.

☐ DAY 206

GOD SIGHTINGS

July 25

2 CHRONICLES 14:1–16:14

And Abijah rested with his fathers and
was buried in the City of David. Asa his
son succeeded him as king, and in his
days the country was at peace for ten
years.

2 Asa did what was good and right in
the eyes of the LORD his God. 3 He removed the foreign altars and the high
places, smashed the sacred stones and
cut down the Asherah poles.*a* 4 He commanded Judah to seek the LORD, the God
of their fathers, and to obey his laws and
commands. 5 He removed the high
places and incense altars in every town
in Judah, and the kingdom was at peace
under him. 6 He built up the fortified cities of Judah, since the land was at peace.
No one was at war with him during those
years, for the LORD gave him rest.

7 "Let us build up these towns," he
said to Judah, "and put walls around
them, with towers, gates and bars. The
land is still ours, because we have
sought the LORD our God; we sought him
and he has given us rest on every side."
So they built and prospered.

8 Asa had an army of three hundred
thousand men from Judah, equipped
with large shields and with spears, and
two hundred and eighty thousand from
Benjamin, armed with small shields and
with bows. All these were brave fighting
men.

9 Zerah the Cushite marched out
against them with a vast army*b* and three

hundred chariots, and came as far as Mareshah. 10 Asa went out to meet him, and
they took up battle positions in the Valley of Zephathah near Mareshah.

11 Then Asa called to the LORD his God
and said, "LORD, there is no one like you
to help the powerless against the
mighty. Help us, O LORD our God, for we
rely on you, and in your name we have
come against this vast army. O LORD, you
are our God; do not let man prevail
against you."

12 The LORD struck down the Cushites
before Asa and Judah. The Cushites fled,
13 and Asa and his army pursued them
as far as Gerar. Such a great number of
Cushites fell that they could not recover;
they were crushed before the LORD and
his forces. The men of Judah carried off
a large amount of plunder. 14 They destroyed all the villages around Gerar, for
the terror of the LORD had fallen upon
them. They plundered all these villages,
since there was much booty there.
15 They also attacked the camps of the
herdsmen and carried off droves of
sheep and goats and camels. Then they
returned to Jerusalem.

15:1 THE Spirit of God came upon Azariah
son of Oded. 2 He went out to meet Asa
and said to him, "Listen to me, Asa and all
Judah and Benjamin. The LORD is with
you when you are with him. If you seek
him, he will be found by you, but if you
forsake him, he will forsake you. 3 For a
long time Israel was without the true
God, without a priest to teach and without the law. 4 But in their distress they
turned to the LORD, the God of Israel, and
sought him, and he was found by them.
5 In those days it was not safe to travel
about, for all the inhabitants of the lands
were in great turmoil. 6 One nation was
being crushed by another and one city by
another, because God was troubling
them with every kind of distress. 7 But as
for you, be strong and do not give up, for
your work will be rewarded."

8 When Asa heard these words and the
prophecy of Azariah son of*c* Oded the
prophet, he took courage. He removed

the detestable idols from the whole land of Judah and Benjamin and from the towns he had captured in the hills of Ephraim. He repaired the altar of the LORD that was in front of the portico of the LORD's temple.

⁹Then he assembled all Judah and Benjamin and the people from Ephraim, Manasseh and Simeon who had settled among them, for large numbers had come over to him from Israel when they saw that the LORD his God was with him.

¹⁰They assembled at Jerusalem in the third month of the fifteenth year of Asa's reign. ¹¹At that time they sacrificed to the LORD seven hundred head of cattle and seven thousand sheep and goats from the plunder they had brought back. ¹²They entered into a covenant to seek the LORD, the God of their fathers, with all their heart and soul. ¹³All who would not seek the LORD, the God of Israel, were to be put to death, whether small or great, man or woman. ¹⁴They took an oath to the LORD with loud acclamation, with shouting and with trumpets and horns. ¹⁵All Judah rejoiced about the oath because they had sworn it wholeheartedly. They sought God eagerly, and he was found by them. So the LORD gave them rest on every side.

¹⁶King Asa also deposed his grandmother Maacah from her position as queen mother, because she had made a repulsive Asherah pole. Asa cut the pole down, broke it up and burned it in the Kidron Valley. ¹⁷Although he did not remove the high places from Israel, Asa's heart was fully committed ₍to the LORD₎ all his life. ¹⁸He brought into the temple of God the silver and gold and the articles that he and his father had dedicated.

¹⁹There was no more war until the thirty-fifth year of Asa's reign.

16:1In the thirty-sixth year of Asa's reign Baasha king of Israel went up against Judah and fortified Ramah to prevent anyone from leaving or entering the territory of Asa king of Judah.

²Asa then took the silver and gold out of the treasuries of the LORD's temple and of his own palace and sent it to Ben-Hadad king of Aram, who was ruling in Damascus. ³"Let there be a treaty between me and you," he said, "as there was between my father and your father. See, I am sending you silver and gold. Now break your treaty with Baasha king of Israel so he will withdraw from me."

⁴Ben-Hadad agreed with King Asa and sent the commanders of his forces against the towns of Israel. They conquered Ijon, Dan, Abel Maim*d* and all the store cities of Naphtali. ⁵When Baasha heard this, he stopped building Ramah and abandoned his work. ⁶Then King Asa brought all the men of Judah, and they carried away from Ramah the stones and timber Baasha had been using. With them he built up Geba and Mizpah.

⁷At that time Hanani the seer came to Asa king of Judah and said to him: "Because you relied on the king of Aram and not on the LORD your God, the army of the king of Aram has escaped from your hand. ⁸Were not the Cushites*e* and Libyans a mighty army with great numbers of chariots and horsemen*f*? Yet when you relied on the LORD, he delivered them into your hand. ⁹**For the eyes of the LORD range throughout the earth to strengthen those whose hearts are fully committed to him.** You have done a foolish thing, and from now on you will be at war."

¹⁰Asa was angry with the seer because of this; he was so enraged that he put him in prison. At the same time Asa brutally oppressed some of the people.

¹¹The events of Asa's reign, from beginning to end, are written in the book of the kings of Judah and Israel. ¹²In the thirty-ninth year of his reign Asa was afflicted with a disease in his feet. Though his disease was severe, even in his illness he did not seek help from the LORD, but only from the physicians. ¹³Then in the forty-first year of his reign Asa died and rested with his fathers. ¹⁴They buried him in the tomb that he had cut out

for himself in the City of David. They laid him on a bier covered with spices and various blended perfumes, and they made a huge fire in his honor.

a3 That is, symbols of the goddess Asherah; here and elsewhere in 2 Chronicles   *b9* Hebrew *with an army of a thousand thousands* or *with an army of thousands upon thousands*   *c8* Vulgate and Syriac (see also Septuagint and verse 1); Hebrew does not have *Azariah son of.*   *d4* Also known as *Abel Beth Maacah*   *e8* That is, people from the upper Nile region   *f8* Or *charioteers*

ROMANS 9:1-21

I speak the truth in Christ—I am not lying, my conscience confirms it in the Holy Spirit— ²I have great sorrow and unceasing anguish in my heart. ³For I could wish that I myself were cursed and cut off from Christ for the sake of my brothers, those of my own race, ⁴the people of Israel. Theirs is the adoption as sons; theirs the divine glory, the covenants, the receiving of the law, the temple worship and the promises. ⁵Theirs are the patriarchs, and from them is traced the human ancestry of Christ, who is God over all, forever praised!*a* Amen.

⁶It is not as though God's word had failed. For not all who are descended from Israel are Israel. ⁷Nor because they are his descendants are they all Abraham's children. On the contrary, "It is through Isaac that your offspring will be reckoned."*b* ⁸In other words, it is not the natural children who are God's children, but it is the children of the promise who are regarded as Abraham's offspring. ⁹For this was how the promise was stated: "At the appointed time I will return, and Sarah will have a son."*c*

¹⁰Not only that, but Rebekah's children had one and the same father, our father Isaac. ¹¹Yet, before the twins were born or had done anything good or bad—in order that God's purpose in election might stand: ¹²not by works but by him who calls—she was told, "The older will serve the younger."*d* ¹³Just as it is written: "Jacob I loved, but Esau I hated."*e*

¹⁴What then shall we say? Is God unjust? Not at all! ¹⁵For he says to Moses,

"I will have mercy on whom I have
    mercy,
and I will have compassion on
    whom I have compassion."*f*

¹⁶It does not, therefore, depend on man's desire or effort, but on God's mercy. ¹⁷For the Scripture says to Pharaoh: "I raised you up for this very purpose, that I might display my power in you and that my name might be proclaimed in all the earth."*g* ¹⁸Therefore God has mercy on whom he wants to have mercy, and he hardens whom he wants to harden.

¹⁹One of you will say to me: "Then why does God still blame us? For who resists his will?" ²⁰But who are you, O man, to talk back to God? "Shall what is formed say to him who formed it, 'Why did you make me like this?'"*h* ²¹Does not the potter have the right to make out of the same lump of clay some pottery for noble purposes and some for common use?

a5 Or *Christ, who is over all. God be forever praised!* Or *Christ. God who is over all be forever praised!*   *b7* Gen. 21:12   *c9* Gen. 18:10,14   *d12* Gen. 25:23   *e13* Mal. 1:2,3   *f15* Exodus 33:19   *g17* Exodus 9:16   *h20* Isaiah 29:16; 45:9

PSALM 19:1-14
For the director of music. A psalm of David.

¹The heavens declare the glory of
    God;
    the skies proclaim the work of his
        hands.
²Day after day they pour forth
    speech;
    night after night they display
        knowledge.
³There is no speech or language
    where their voice is not heard.*a*
⁴Their voice*b* goes out into all the
    earth,
    their words to the ends of the
        world.

In the heavens he has pitched a tent
    for the sun,
5   which is like a bridegroom coming
        forth from his pavilion,
    like a champion rejoicing to run
        his course.

⁶It rises at one end of the heavens
and makes its circuit to the
other;
nothing is hidden from its heat.

⁷The law of the LORD is perfect,
reviving the soul.
The statutes of the LORD are
trustworthy,
making wise the simple.
⁸The precepts of the LORD are right,
giving joy to the heart.
The commands of the LORD are
radiant,
giving light to the eyes.
⁹The fear of the LORD is pure,
enduring forever.
The ordinances of the LORD are
sure
and altogether righteous.
¹⁰They are more precious than gold,
than much pure gold;
they are sweeter than honey,
than honey from the comb.
¹¹By them is your servant warned;
in keeping them there is great
reward.

¹²Who can discern his errors?
Forgive my hidden faults.
¹³Keep your servant also from willful
sins;
may they not rule over me.
Then will I be blameless,
innocent of great transgression.

¹⁴May the words of my mouth and the
meditation of my heart
be pleasing in your sight,
O LORD, my Rock and my
Redeemer.

a3 Or They have no speech, there are no words; / no sound is
heard from them   b4 Septuagint, Jerome and Syriac;
Hebrew line

PROVERBS 20:1
Wine is a mocker and beer a
brawler;
whoever is led astray by them is
not wise.

□ DAY 207

GOD SIGHTINGS

July 26

2 CHRONICLES 17:1–18:34
Jehoshaphat his son succeeded him as king and strengthened himself against Israel. ²He stationed troops in all the fortified cities of Judah and put garrisons in Judah and in the towns of Ephraim that his father Asa had captured.

³The LORD was with Jehoshaphat because in his early years he walked in the ways his father David had followed. He did not consult the Baals ⁴but sought the God of his father and followed his commands rather than the practices of Israel. ⁵The LORD established the kingdom under his control; and all Judah brought gifts to Jehoshaphat, so that he had great wealth and honor. ⁶His heart was devoted to the ways of the LORD; furthermore, he removed the high places and the Asherah poles from Judah.

⁷In the third year of his reign he sent his officials Ben-Hail, Obadiah, Zechariah, Nethanel and Micaiah to teach in the towns of Judah. ⁸With them were certain Levites—Shemaiah, Nethaniah, Zebadiah, Asahel, Shemiramoth, Jehonathan, Adonijah, Tobijah and Tob-Adonijah—and the priests Elishama and Jehoram. ⁹They taught throughout Judah, taking with them the Book of the Law of the LORD; they went around to all the towns of Judah and taught the people.

¹⁰The fear of the LORD fell on all the kingdoms of the lands surrounding Judah, so that they did not make war with Jehoshaphat. ¹¹Some Philistines brought Jehoshaphat gifts and silver as tribute, and the Arabs brought him flocks: seven thousand seven hundred rams and seven thousand seven hundred goats.

¹²Jehoshaphat became more and more powerful; he built forts and store cities in Judah ¹³and had large supplies in the towns of Judah. He also kept ex-

perienced fighting men in Jerusalem. [14]Their enrollment by families was as follows:

From Judah, commanders of units of 1,000:
Adnah the commander, with 300,000 fighting men;
[15] next, Jehohanan the commander, with 280,000;
[16] next, Amasiah son of Zicri, who volunteered himself for the service of the Lord, with 200,000.

[17]From Benjamin:
Eliada, a valiant soldier, with 200,000 men armed with bows and shields;
[18] next, Jehozabad, with 180,000 men armed for battle.

[19]These were the men who served the king, besides those he stationed in the fortified cities throughout Judah.

[18:1]Now Jehoshaphat had great wealth and honor, and he allied himself with Ahab by marriage. [2]Some years later he went down to visit Ahab in Samaria. Ahab slaughtered many sheep and cattle for him and the people with him and urged him to attack Ramoth Gilead. [3]Ahab king of Israel asked Jehoshaphat king of Judah, "Will you go with me against Ramoth Gilead?"

Jehoshaphat replied, "I am as you are, and my people as your people; we will join you in the war." [4]But Jehoshaphat also said to the king of Israel, "First seek the counsel of the Lord."

[5]So the king of Israel brought together the prophets—four hundred men—and asked them, "Shall we go to war against Ramoth Gilead, or shall I refrain?"

"Go," they answered, "for God will give it into the king's hand."

[6]But Jehoshaphat asked, "Is there not a prophet of the Lord here whom we can inquire of?"

[7]The king of Israel answered Jehoshaphat, "There is still one man through whom we can inquire of the Lord, but I hate him because he never prophesies

anything good about me, but always bad. He is Micaiah son of Imlah."

"The king should not say that," Jehoshaphat replied.

[8]So the king of Israel called one of his officials and said, "Bring Micaiah son of Imlah at once."

[9]Dressed in their royal robes, the king of Israel and Jehoshaphat king of Judah were sitting on their thrones at the threshing floor by the entrance to the gate of Samaria, with all the prophets prophesying before them. [10]Now Zedekiah son of Kenaanah had made iron horns, and he declared, "This is what the Lord says: 'With these you will gore the Arameans until they are destroyed.'"

[11]All the other prophets were prophesying the same thing. "Attack Ramoth Gilead and be victorious," they said, "for the Lord will give it into the king's hand."

[12]The messenger who had gone to summon Micaiah said to him, "Look, as one man the other prophets are predicting success for the king. Let your word agree with theirs, and speak favorably."

[13]But Micaiah said, "As surely as the Lord lives, I can tell him only what my God says."

[14]When he arrived, the king asked him, "Micaiah, shall we go to war against Ramoth Gilead, or shall I refrain?"

"Attack and be victorious," he answered, "for they will be given into your hand."

[15]The king said to him, "How many times must I make you swear to tell me nothing but the truth in the name of the Lord?"

[16]Then Micaiah answered, "I saw all Israel scattered on the hills like sheep without a shepherd, and the Lord said, 'These people have no master. Let each one go home in peace.'"

[17]The king of Israel said to Jehoshaphat, "Didn't I tell you that he never prophesies anything good about me, but only bad?"

[18]Micaiah continued, "Therefore hear the word of the Lord: I saw the Lord sitting on his throne with all the

host of heaven standing on his right and on his left. ¹⁹And the Lᴏʀᴅ said, 'Who will entice Ahab king of Israel into attacking Ramoth Gilead and going to his death there?'

"One suggested this, and another that. ²⁰Finally, a spirit came forward, stood before the Lᴏʀᴅ and said, 'I will entice him.'

"'By what means?' the Lᴏʀᴅ asked.

²¹"'I will go and be a lying spirit in the mouths of all his prophets,' he said.

"'You will succeed in enticing him,' said the Lᴏʀᴅ. 'Go and do it.'

²²"So now the Lᴏʀᴅ has put a lying spirit in the mouths of these prophets of yours. The Lᴏʀᴅ has decreed disaster for you."

²³Then Zedekiah son of Kenaanah went up and slapped Micaiah in the face. "Which way did the spirit from[a] the Lᴏʀᴅ go when he went from me to speak to you?" he asked.

²⁴Micaiah replied, "You will find out on the day you go to hide in an inner room."

²⁵The king of Israel then ordered, "Take Micaiah and send him back to Amon the ruler of the city and to Joash the king's son, ²⁶and say, 'This is what the king says: Put this fellow in prison and give him nothing but bread and water until I return safely.'"

²⁷Micaiah declared, "If you ever return safely, the Lᴏʀᴅ has not spoken through me." Then he added, "Mark my words, all you people!"

²⁸So the king of Israel and Jehoshaphat king of Judah went up to Ramoth Gilead. ²⁹The king of Israel said to Jehoshaphat, "I will enter the battle in disguise, but you wear your royal robes." So the king of Israel disguised himself and went into battle.

³⁰Now the king of Aram had ordered his chariot commanders, "Do not fight with anyone, small or great, except the king of Israel." ³¹When the chariot commanders saw Jehoshaphat, they thought, "This is the king of Israel." So they turned to attack him, but Jehoshaphat cried out, and the Lᴏʀᴅ helped

him. God drew them away from him, ³²for when the chariot commanders saw that he was not the king of Israel, they stopped pursuing him.

³³But someone drew his bow at random and hit the king of Israel between the sections of his armor. The king told the chariot driver, "Wheel around and get me out of the fighting. I've been wounded." ³⁴All day long the battle raged, and the king of Israel propped himself up in his chariot facing the Arameans until evening. Then at sunset he died.

a23 Or *Spirit of*

ROMANS 9:22–10:13

What if God, choosing to show his wrath and make his power known, bore with great patience the objects of his wrath—prepared for destruction? ²³What if he did this to make the riches of his glory known to the objects of his mercy, whom he prepared in advance for glory— ²⁴even us, whom he also called, not only from the Jews but also from the Gentiles? ²⁵As he says in Hosea:

> "I will call them 'my people' who are
>   not my people;
>   and I will call her 'my loved one'
>   who is not my loved one,"[a]

²⁶and,

> "It will happen that in the very place
>   where it was said to them,
>   'You are not my people,'
>   they will be called 'sons of the living
>   God.'"[b]

²⁷Isaiah cries out concerning Israel:

> "Though the number of the
>   Israelites be like the sand by
>   the sea,
>   only the remnant will be saved.
> ²⁸For the Lord will carry out
>   his sentence on earth with speed
>   and finality."[c]

²⁹It is just as Isaiah said previously:

> "Unless the Lord Almighty
>   had left us descendants,
>   we would have become like Sodom,

we would have been like
Gomorrah."ᵈ

³⁰What then shall we say? That the
Gentiles, who did not pursue righteousness, have obtained it, a righteousness
that is by faith; ³¹but Israel, who pursued a law of righteousness, has not attained it. ³²Why not? Because they
pursued it not by faith but as if it were
by works. They stumbled over the
"stumbling stone." ³³As it is written:

"See, I lay in Zion a stone that causes
    men to stumble
and a rock that makes them fall,
and the one who trusts in him will
    never be put to shame."ᵉ

¹⁰:¹BROTHERS, my heart's desire and
prayer to God for the Israelites is that
they may be saved. ²For I can testify
about them that they are zealous for
God, but their zeal is not based on
knowledge. ³Since they did not know
the righteousness that comes from God
and sought to establish their own, they
did not submit to God's righteousness.
⁴Christ is the end of the law so that there
may be righteousness for everyone who
believes.

⁵Moses describes in this way the righteousness that is by the law: "The man
who does these things will live by them."ᶠ
⁶But the righteousness that is by faith
says: "Do not say in your heart, 'Who will
ascend into heaven?'ᵍ" (that is, to bring
Christ down) ⁷"or 'Who will descend into
the deep?'ʰ" (that is, to bring Christ up
from the dead). ⁸But what does it say?
"The word is near you; it is in your mouth
and in your heart,"ⁱ that is, the word of
faith we are proclaiming: ⁹**That if you
confess with your mouth, "Jesus is
Lord," and believe in your heart that
God raised him from the dead, you will
be saved.** ¹⁰For it is with your heart that
you believe and are justified, and it is with
your mouth that you confess and are
saved. ¹¹As the Scripture says, "Anyone
who trusts in him will never be put to
shame."ʲ ¹²For there is no difference between Jew and Gentile—the same Lord is

Lord of all and richly blesses all who call
on him, ¹³for, "Everyone who calls on the
name of the Lord will be saved."ᵏ

a25 Hosea 2:23   b26 Hosea 1:10   c28 Isaiah 10:22,23
d29 Isaiah 1:9   e33 Isaiah 8:14; 28:16   f5 Lev. 18:5
g6 Deut. 30:12   h7 Deut. 30:13   i8 Deut. 30:14   j11 Isaiah 28:16
k13 Joel 2:32

PSALM 20:1-9
For the director of music. A psalm of David.

¹**M**ay the LORD answer you when you
        are in distress;
    may the name of the God of Jacob
        protect you.
²May he send you help from the
        sanctuary
    and grant you support from Zion.
³May he remember all your sacrifices
    and accept your burnt offerings.
                                              Selah
⁴May he give you the desire of your
        heart
    and make all your plans succeed.
⁵We will shout for joy when you are
        victorious
    and will lift up our banners in the
        name of our God.
May the LORD grant all your requests.

⁶Now I know that the LORD saves his
        anointed;
    he answers him from his holy
        heaven
    with the saving power of his right
        hand.
⁷Some trust in chariots and some in
        horses,
    but we trust in the name of the
        LORD our God.
⁸They are brought to their knees and
        fall,
    but we rise up and stand firm.

⁹O LORD, save the king!
    Answerᵃ us when we call!

PROVERBS 20:2-3
²**A** king's wrath is like the roar of a
        lion;
    he who angers him forfeits his life.

³It is to a man's honor to avoid strife,
    but every fool is quick to quarrel.

□ DAY 208

GOD SIGHTINGS

July 27

2 CHRONICLES 19:1–20:37

When Jehoshaphat king of Judah returned safely to his palace in Jerusalem, ²Jehu the seer, the son of Hanani, went out to meet him and said to the king, "Should you help the wicked and love*a* those who hate the LORD? Because of this, the wrath of the LORD is upon you. ³There is, however, some good in you, for you have rid the land of the Asherah poles and have set your heart on seeking God."

⁴Jehoshaphat lived in Jerusalem, and he went out again among the people from Beersheba to the hill country of Ephraim and turned them back to the LORD, the God of their fathers. ⁵He appointed judges in the land, in each of the fortified cities of Judah. ⁶He told them, "Consider carefully what you do, because you are not judging for man but for the LORD, who is with you whenever you give a verdict. ⁷Now let the fear of the LORD be upon you. Judge carefully, for with the LORD our God there is no injustice or partiality or bribery."

⁸In Jerusalem also, Jehoshaphat appointed some of the Levites, priests and heads of Israelite families to administer the law of the LORD and to settle disputes. And they lived in Jerusalem. ⁹He gave them these orders: "You must serve faithfully and wholeheartedly in the fear of the LORD. ¹⁰In every case that comes before you from your fellow countrymen who live in the cities—whether bloodshed or other concerns of the law, commands, decrees or ordinances—you are to warn them not to sin against the LORD; otherwise his wrath will come on you and your brothers. Do this, and you will not sin.

¹¹"Amariah the chief priest will be over you in any matter concerning the LORD, and Zebadiah son of Ishmael, the leader of the tribe of Judah, will be over you in any matter concerning the king, and the Levites will serve as officials before you. Act with courage, and may the LORD be with those who do well."

²⁰:¹AFTER this, the Moabites and Ammonites with some of the Meunites*b* came to make war on Jehoshaphat.

²Some men came and told Jehoshaphat, "A vast army is coming against you from Edom,*c* from the other side of the Sea.*d* It is already in Hazazon Tamar" (that is, En Gedi). ³Alarmed, Jehoshaphat resolved to inquire of the LORD, and he proclaimed a fast for all Judah. ⁴The people of Judah came together to seek help from the LORD; indeed, they came from every town in Judah to seek him.

⁵Then Jehoshaphat stood up in the assembly of Judah and Jerusalem at the temple of the LORD in the front of the new courtyard ⁶and said:

"O LORD, God of our fathers, are you not the God who is in heaven? You rule over all the kingdoms of the nations. Power and might are in your hand, and no one can withstand you. ⁷O our God, did you not drive out the inhabitants of this land before your people Israel and give it forever to the descendants of Abraham your friend? ⁸They have lived in it and have built in it a sanctuary for your Name, saying, ⁹'If calamity comes upon us, whether the sword of judgment, or plague or famine, we will stand in your presence before this temple that bears your Name and will cry out to you in our distress, and you will hear us and save us.'

¹⁰"But now here are men from Ammon, Moab and Mount Seir, whose territory you would not allow Israel to invade when they came from Egypt; so they turned away from them and did not destroy them. ¹¹See how they are repaying us by coming to drive us out of the possession you gave us as an inheri-

tance. ¹²O our God, will you not judge them? For we have no power to face this vast army that is attacking us. We do not know what to do, but our eyes are upon you."

¹³All the men of Judah, with their wives and children and little ones, stood there before the LORD.

¹⁴Then the Spirit of the LORD came upon Jahaziel son of Zechariah, the son of Benaiah, the son of Jeiel, the son of Mattaniah, a Levite and descendant of Asaph, as he stood in the assembly.

¹⁵He said: "Listen, King Jehoshaphat and all who live in Judah and Jerusalem! This is what the LORD says to you: 'Do not be afraid or discouraged because of this vast army. For the battle is not yours, but God's. ¹⁶Tomorrow march down against them. They will be climbing up by the Pass of Ziz, and you will find them at the end of the gorge in the Desert of Jeruel. ¹⁷You will not have to fight this battle. Take up your positions; stand firm and see the deliverance the LORD will give you, O Judah and Jerusalem. Do not be afraid; do not be discouraged. Go out to face them tomorrow, and the LORD will be with you.'"

¹⁸Jehoshaphat bowed with his face to the ground, and all the people of Judah and Jerusalem fell down in worship before the LORD. ¹⁹Then some Levites from the Kohathites and Korahites stood up and praised the LORD, the God of Israel, with a very loud voice.

²⁰Early in the morning they left for the Desert of Tekoa. As they set out, Jehoshaphat stood and said, "Listen to me, Judah and people of Jerusalem! Have faith in the LORD your God and you will be upheld; have faith in his prophets and you will be successful." ²¹After consulting the people, Jehoshaphat appointed men to sing to the LORD and to praise him for the splendor of hisᵉ holiness as they went out at the head of the army, saying:

"Give thanks to the LORD,
   for his love endures forever."

²²As they began to sing and praise, the LORD set ambushes against the men of Ammon and Moab and Mount Seir who were invading Judah, and they were defeated. ²³The men of Ammon and Moab rose up against the men from Mount Seir to destroy and annihilate them. After they finished slaughtering the men from Seir, they helped to destroy one another.

²⁴When the men of Judah came to the place that overlooks the desert and looked toward the vast army, they saw only dead bodies lying on the ground; no one had escaped. ²⁵So Jehoshaphat and his men went to carry off their plunder, and they found among them a great amount of equipment and clothingᶠ and also articles of value—more than they could take away. There was so much plunder that it took three days to collect it. ²⁶On the fourth day they assembled in the Valley of Beracah, where they praised the LORD. This is why it is called the Valley of Beracahᵍ to this day.

²⁷Then, led by Jehoshaphat, all the men of Judah and Jerusalem returned joyfully to Jerusalem, for the LORD had given them cause to rejoice over their enemies. ²⁸They entered Jerusalem and went to the temple of the LORD with harps and lutes and trumpets.

²⁹The fear of God came upon all the kingdoms of the countries when they heard how the LORD had fought against the enemies of Israel. ³⁰And the kingdom of Jehoshaphat was at peace, for his God had given him rest on every side.

³¹So Jehoshaphat reigned over Judah. He was thirty-five years old when he became king of Judah, and he reigned in Jerusalem twenty-five years. His mother's name was Azubah daughter of Shilhi. ³²He walked in the ways of his father Asa and did not stray from them; he did what was right in the eyes of the LORD. ³³The high places, however, were not removed, and the people still had not set their hearts on the God of their fathers.

³⁴The other events of Jehoshaphat's reign, from beginning to end, are written in the annals of Jehu son of Hanani,

which are recorded in the book of the kings of Israel.

35Later, Jehoshaphat king of Judah made an alliance with Ahaziah king of Israel, who was guilty of wickedness. 36He agreed with him to construct a fleet of trading ships.*h* After these were built at Ezion Geber, 37Eliezer son of Dodavahu of Mareshah prophesied against Jehoshaphat, saying, "Because you have made an alliance with Ahaziah, the LORD will destroy what you have made." The ships were wrecked and were not able to set sail to trade.*i*

a2 Or *and make alliances with* *b1* Some Septuagint manuscripts; Hebrew *Ammonites* *c2* One Hebrew manuscript; most Hebrew manuscripts, Septuagint and Vulgate *Aram* *d2* That is, the Dead Sea *e21* Or *him with the splendor of* *f25* Some Hebrew manuscripts and Vulgate; most Hebrew manuscripts *corpses* *926 Beracah* means *praise.* *h36* Hebrew *of ships that could go to Tarshish* *i37* Hebrew *sail for Tarshish*

ROMANS 10:14–11:12

How, then, can they call on the one they have not believed in? And how can they believe in the one of whom they have not heard? And how can they hear without someone preaching to them? 15And how can they preach unless they are sent? As it is written, "How beautiful are the feet of those who bring good news!"*a*

16But not all the Israelites accepted the good news. For Isaiah says, "Lord, who has believed our message?"*b* 17**Consequently, faith comes from hearing the message, and the message is heard through the word of Christ.** 18But I ask: Did they not hear? Of course they did:

"Their voice has gone out into all the
        earth,
    their words to the ends of the
        world."*c*

19Again I ask: Did Israel not understand? First, Moses says,

"I will make you envious by those
        who are not a nation;
    I will make you angry by a
        nation that has no
        understanding."*d*

20And Isaiah boldly says,

"I was found by those who did not
        seek me;
    I revealed myself to those who did
        not ask for me."*e*

21But concerning Israel he says,

"All day long I have held out my
        hands
    to a disobedient and obstinate
        people."*f*

11:1I ASK then: Did God reject his people? By no means! I am an Israelite myself, a descendant of Abraham, from the tribe of Benjamin. 2God did not reject his people, whom he foreknew. Don't you know what the Scripture says in the passage about Elijah—how he appealed to God against Israel: 3"Lord, they have killed your prophets and torn down your altars; I am the only one left, and they are trying to kill me"*g*? 4And what was God's answer to him? "I have reserved for myself seven thousand who have not bowed the knee to Baal."*h* 5So too, at the present time there is a remnant chosen by grace. 6And if by grace, then it is no longer by works; if it were, grace would no longer be grace.*i*

7What then? What Israel sought so earnestly it did not obtain, but the elect did. The others were hardened, 8as it is written:

"God gave them a spirit of stupor,
    eyes so that they could not see
    and ears so that they could not
        hear,
to this very day."*j*

9And David says:

"May their table become a snare and
        a trap,
    a stumbling block and a
        retribution for them.
10May their eyes be darkened so they
        cannot see,
    and their backs be bent forever."*k*

11Again I ask: Did they stumble so as to fall beyond recovery? Not at all!

Rather, because of their transgression, salvation has come to the Gentiles to make Israel envious. [12]But if their transgression means riches for the world, and their loss means riches for the Gentiles, how much greater riches will their fullness bring!

*a15*Isaiah 52:7   *b16*Isaiah 53:1   *c18*Psalm 19:4 *d19*Deut. 32:21   *e20*Isaiah 65:1   *f21*Isaiah 65:2 *g3*1 Kings 19:10,14   *h4*1 Kings 19:18   *i6*Some manuscripts *be grace. But if by works, then it is no longer grace; if it were, work would no longer be work.* *j8*Deut. 29:4; Isaiah 29:10   *k10*Psalm 69:22,23

PSALM 21:1-13

For the director of music. A psalm of David.

[1] **O** LORD, the king rejoices in your strength.
How great is his joy in the victories you give!
[2] You have granted him the desire of his heart
and have not withheld the request of his lips.   *Selah*
[3] You welcomed him with rich blessings
and placed a crown of pure gold on his head.
[4] He asked you for life, and you gave it to him—
length of days, for ever and ever.
[5] Through the victories you gave, his glory is great;
you have bestowed on him splendor and majesty.
[6] Surely you have granted him eternal blessings
and made him glad with the joy of your presence.
[7] For the king trusts in the LORD;
through the unfailing love of the Most High
he will not be shaken.

[8] Your hand will lay hold on all your enemies;
your right hand will seize your foes.
[9] At the time of your appearing
you will make them like a fiery furnace.
In his wrath the LORD will swallow them up,
and his fire will consume them.

[10] You will destroy their descendants from the earth,
their posterity from mankind.
[11] Though they plot evil against you
and devise wicked schemes, they cannot succeed;
[12] for you will make them turn their backs
when you aim at them with drawn bow.

[13] Be exalted, O LORD, in your strength;
we will sing and praise your might.

PROVERBS 20:4-6

[4] **A** sluggard does not plow in season;
so at harvest time he looks but finds nothing.

[5] The purposes of a man's heart are deep waters,
but a man of understanding draws them out.

[6] Many a man claims to have unfailing love,
but a faithful man who can find?

□ DAY 209

GOD SIGHTINGS

July 28

2 CHRONICLES 21:1-23:21

Then Jehoshaphat rested with his fathers and was buried with them in the City of David. And Jehoram his son succeeded him as king. [2]Jehoram's brothers, the sons of Jehoshaphat, were Azariah, Jehiel, Zechariah, Azariahu, Michael and Shephatiah. All these were sons of Jehoshaphat king of Israel.[a] [3]Their father had given them many gifts of silver and gold and articles of value, as well as fortified cities in Judah, but he had given the kingdom to Jehoram because he was his firstborn son.

[4]When Jehoram established himself firmly over his father's kingdom, he put all his brothers to the sword along with

some of the princes of Israel. ⁵Jehoram was thirty-two years old when he became king, and he reigned in Jerusalem eight years. ⁶He walked in the ways of the kings of Israel, as the house of Ahab had done, for he married a daughter of Ahab. He did evil in the eyes of the LORD. ⁷Nevertheless, because of the covenant the LORD had made with David, the LORD was not willing to destroy the house of David. He had promised to maintain a lamp for him and his descendants forever.

⁸In the time of Jehoram, Edom rebelled against Judah and set up its own king. ⁹So Jehoram went there with his officers and all his chariots. The Edomites surrounded him and his chariot commanders, but he rose up and broke through by night. ¹⁰To this day Edom has been in rebellion against Judah.

Libnah revolted at the same time, because Jehoram had forsaken the LORD, the God of his fathers. ¹¹He had also built high places on the hills of Judah and had caused the people of Jerusalem to prostitute themselves and had led Judah astray.

¹²Jehoram received a letter from Elijah the prophet, which said:

"This is what the LORD, the God of your father David, says: 'You have not walked in the ways of your father Jehoshaphat or of Asa king of Judah. ¹³But you have walked in the ways of the kings of Israel, and you have led Judah and the people of Jerusalem to prostitute themselves, just as the house of Ahab did. You have also murdered your own brothers, members of your father's house, men who were better than you. ¹⁴So now the LORD is about to strike your people, your sons, your wives and everything that is yours, with a heavy blow. ¹⁵You yourself will be very ill with a lingering disease of the bowels, until the disease causes your bowels to come out.'"

¹⁶The LORD aroused against Jehoram the hostility of the Philistines and of the Arabs who lived near the Cushites. ¹⁷They attacked Judah, invaded it and carried off all the goods found in the king's palace, together with his sons and wives. Not a son was left to him except Ahaziah,ᵇ the youngest.

¹⁸After all this, the LORD afflicted Jehoram with an incurable disease of the bowels. ¹⁹In the course of time, at the end of the second year, his bowels came out because of the disease, and he died in great pain. His people made no fire in his honor, as they had for his fathers.

²⁰Jehoram was thirty-two years old when he became king, and he reigned in Jerusalem eight years. He passed away, to no one's regret, and was buried in the City of David, but not in the tombs of the kings.

22:1THE people of Jerusalem made Ahaziah, Jehoram's youngest son, king in his place, since the raiders, who came with the Arabs into the camp, had killed all the older sons. So Ahaziah son of Jehoram king of Judah began to reign.

²Ahaziah was twenty-twoᶜ years old when he became king, and he reigned in Jerusalem one year. His mother's name was Athaliah, a granddaughter of Omri.

³He too walked in the ways of the house of Ahab, for his mother encouraged him in doing wrong. ⁴He did evil in the eyes of the LORD, as the house of Ahab had done, for after his father's death they became his advisers, to his undoing. ⁵He also followed their counsel when he went with Joramᵈ son of Ahab king of Israel to war against Hazael king of Aram at Ramoth Gilead. The Arameans wounded Joram; ⁶so he returned to Jezreel to recover from the wounds they had inflicted on him at Ramothᵉ in his battle with Hazael king of Aram.

Then Ahaziahᶠ son of Jehoram king of Judah went down to Jezreel to see Joram son of Ahab because he had been wounded.

⁷Through Ahaziah's visit to Joram, God brought about Ahaziah's downfall.

When Ahaziah arrived, he went out with Joram to meet Jehu son of Nimshi, whom the Lord had anointed to destroy the house of Ahab. ⁸While Jehu was executing judgment on the house of Ahab, he found the princes of Judah and the sons of Ahaziah's relatives, who had been attending Ahaziah, and he killed them. ⁹He then went in search of Ahaziah, and his men captured him while he was hiding in Samaria. He was brought to Jehu and put to death. They buried him, for they said, "He was a son of Jehoshaphat, who sought the Lord with all his heart." So there was no one in the house of Ahaziah powerful enough to retain the kingdom.

¹⁰When Athaliah the mother of Ahaziah saw that her son was dead, she proceeded to destroy the whole royal family of the house of Judah. ¹¹But Jehosheba,*g* the daughter of King Jehoram, took Joash son of Ahaziah and stole him away from among the royal princes who were about to be murdered and put him and his nurse in a bedroom. Because Jehosheba,*g* the daughter of King Jehoram and wife of the priest Jehoiada, was Ahaziah's sister, she hid the child from Athaliah so she could not kill him. ¹²He remained hidden with them at the temple of God for six years while Athaliah ruled the land.

²³:¹In the seventh year Jehoiada showed his strength. He made a covenant with the commanders of units of a hundred: Azariah son of Jeroham, Ishmael son of Jehohanan, Azariah son of Obed, Maaseiah son of Adaiah, and Elishaphat son of Zicri. ²They went throughout Judah and gathered the Levites and the heads of Israelite families from all the towns. When they came to Jerusalem, ³the whole assembly made a covenant with the king at the temple of God.

Jehoiada said to them, "The king's son shall reign, as the Lord promised concerning the descendants of David. ⁴Now this is what you are to do: A third of you priests and Levites who are going on duty on the Sabbath are to keep watch at the doors, ⁵a third of you at the royal palace and a third at the Foundation Gate, and all the other men are to be in the courtyards of the temple of the Lord. ⁶No one is to enter the temple of the Lord except the priests and Levites on duty; they may enter because they are consecrated, but all the other men are to guard what the Lord has assigned to them.*h* ⁷The Levites are to station themselves around the king, each man with his weapons in his hand. Anyone who enters the temple must be put to death. Stay close to the king wherever he goes."

⁸The Levites and all the men of Judah did just as Jehoiada the priest ordered. Each one took his men—those who were going on duty on the Sabbath and those who were going off duty—for Jehoiada the priest had not released any of the divisions. ⁹Then he gave the commanders of units of a hundred the spears and the large and small shields that had belonged to King David and that were in the temple of God. ¹⁰He stationed all the men, each with his weapon in his hand, around the king—near the altar and the temple, from the south side to the north side of the temple.

¹¹Jehoiada and his sons brought out the king's son and put the crown on him; they presented him with a copy of the covenant and proclaimed him king. They anointed him and shouted, "Long live the king!"

¹²When Athaliah heard the noise of the people running and cheering the king, she went to them at the temple of the Lord. ¹³She looked, and there was the king, standing by his pillar at the entrance. The officers and the trumpeters were beside the king, and all the people of the land were rejoicing and blowing trumpets, and singers with musical instruments were leading the praises. Then Athaliah tore her robes and shouted, "Treason! Treason!"

¹⁴Jehoiada the priest sent out the commanders of units of a hundred, who were in charge of the troops, and said to them: "Bring her out between the ranks*i* and put to the sword anyone

who follows her." For the priest had said, "Do not put her to death at the temple of the LORD." ¹⁵So they seized her as she reached the entrance of the Horse Gate on the palace grounds, and there they put her to death.

¹⁶Jehoiada then made a covenant that he and the people and the king*j* would be the LORD's people. ¹⁷All the people went to the temple of Baal and tore it down. They smashed the altars and idols and killed Mattan the priest of Baal in front of the altars.

¹⁸Then Jehoiada placed the oversight of the temple of the LORD in the hands of the priests, who were Levites, to whom David had made assignments in the temple, to present the burnt offerings of the LORD as written in the Law of Moses, with rejoicing and singing, as David had ordered. ¹⁹He also stationed doorkeepers at the gates of the LORD's temple so that no one who was in any way unclean might enter.

²⁰He took with him the commanders of hundreds, the nobles, the rulers of the people and all the people of the land and brought the king down from the temple of the LORD. They went into the palace through the Upper Gate and seated the king on the royal throne, ²¹and all the people of the land rejoiced. And the city was quiet, because Athaliah had been slain with the sword.

a2 That is, Judah, as frequently in 2 Chronicles   *b17* Hebrew *Jehoahaz*, a variant of *Ahaziah*   *c2* Some Septuagint manuscripts and Syriac (see also 2 Kings 8:26); Hebrew *forty-two*   *d5* Hebrew *Jehoram*, a variant of *Joram*; also in verses 6 and 7   *e6* Hebrew *Ramah*, a variant of *Ramoth*   *f6* Some Hebrew manuscripts, Septuagint, Vulgate and Syriac (see also 2 Kings 8:29); most Hebrew manuscripts *Azariah*   *g11* Hebrew *Jehoshabeath*, a variant of *Jehosheba*   *h6* Or *to observe the LORD's command* ⌞*not to enter*⌟   *i14* Or *out from the precincts*   *j16* Or *covenant between* ⌞*the LORD*⌟ *and the people and the king that they* (see 2 Kings 11:17)

ROMANS 11:13-36

❚ am talking to you Gentiles. Inasmuch as I am the apostle to the Gentiles, I make much of my ministry ¹⁴in the hope that I may somehow arouse my own people to envy and save some of them. ¹⁵For if their rejection is the reconciliation of the world, what will their acceptance be but

life from the dead? ¹⁶If the part of the dough offered as firstfruits is holy, then the whole batch is holy; if the root is holy, so are the branches.

¹⁷If some of the branches have been broken off, and you, though a wild olive shoot, have been grafted in among the others and now share in the nourishing sap from the olive root, ¹⁸do not boast over those branches. If you do, consider this: You do not support the root, but the root supports you. ¹⁹You will say then, "Branches were broken off so that I could be grafted in." ²⁰Granted. But they were broken off because of unbelief, and you stand by faith. Do not be arrogant, but be afraid. ²¹For if God did not spare the natural branches, he will not spare you either.

²²Consider therefore the kindness and sternness of God: sternness to those who fell, but kindness to you, provided that you continue in his kindness. Otherwise, you also will be cut off. ²³And if they do not persist in unbelief, they will be grafted in, for God is able to graft them in again. ²⁴After all, if you were cut out of an olive tree that is wild by nature, and contrary to nature were grafted into a cultivated olive tree, how much more readily will these, the natural branches, be grafted into their own olive tree!

²⁵I do not want you to be ignorant of this mystery, brothers, so that you may not be conceited: Israel has experienced a hardening in part until the full number of the Gentiles has come in. ²⁶And so all Israel will be saved, as it is written:

" The deliverer will come from Zion;
    he will turn godlessness away from Jacob.
²⁷ And this is*a* my covenant with them
    when I take away their sins."*b*

²⁸As far as the gospel is concerned, they are enemies on your account; but as far as election is concerned, they are loved on account of the patriarchs, ²⁹for God's gifts and his call are irrevocable. ³⁰Just as you who were at one

time disobedient to God have now received mercy as a result of their disobedience, ³¹ so they too have now become disobedient in order that they too may now^c receive mercy as a result of God's mercy to you. ³²For God has bound all men over to disobedience so that he may have mercy on them all.

³³ **Oh, the depth of the riches of the wisdom and^d knowledge of God!**

How unsearchable his judgments,

and his paths beyond tracing out!

³⁴"Who has known the mind of the Lord?

Or who has been his counselor?"^e

³⁵"Who has ever given to God,

that God should repay him?"^f

³⁶For from him and through him and to him are all things.

To him be the glory forever! Amen.

a27 Or will be   b27 Isaiah 59:20,21; 27:9; Jer. 31:33,34
c31 Some manuscripts do not have now.   d33 Or riches
and the wisdom and the   e34 Isaiah 40:13   f35 Job 41:11

PSALM 22:1-18

For the director of music. To ⌊the tune of⌋ "The Doe of the Morning." A psalm of David.

¹ **M**y God, my God, why have you forsaken me?

Why are you so far from saving me,

so far from the words of my groaning?

²O my God, I cry out by day, but you do not answer,

by night, and am not silent.

³Yet you are enthroned as the Holy One;

you are the praise of Israel.^a

⁴In you our fathers put their trust;

they trusted and you delivered them.

⁵They cried to you and were saved;

in you they trusted and were not disappointed.

⁶But I am a worm and not a man,

scorned by men and despised by the people.

⁷All who see me mock me;

they hurl insults, shaking their heads:

⁸"He trusts in the LORD;

let the LORD rescue him.

Let him deliver him,

since he delights in him."

⁹Yet you brought me out of the womb;

you made me trust in you

even at my mother's breast.

¹⁰From birth I was cast upon you;

from my mother's womb you have been my God.

¹¹Do not be far from me,

for trouble is near

and there is no one to help.

¹²Many bulls surround me;

strong bulls of Bashan encircle me.

¹³Roaring lions tearing their prey

open their mouths wide against me.

¹⁴I am poured out like water,

and all my bones are out of joint.

My heart has turned to wax;

it has melted away within me.

¹⁵My strength is dried up like a potsherd,

and my tongue sticks to the roof of my mouth;

you lay me^b in the dust of death.

¹⁶Dogs have surrounded me;

a band of evil men has encircled me,

they have pierced^c my hands and my feet.

¹⁷I can count all my bones;

people stare and gloat over me.

¹⁸They divide my garments among them

and cast lots for my clothing.

a3 Or Yet you are holy, / enthroned on the praises of
Israel   b15 Or / I am laid   c16 Some Hebrew manuscripts,
Septuagint and Syriac; most Hebrew manuscripts / like the
lion,

PROVERBS 20:7

⁷**T**he righteous man leads a blameless life;

blessed are his children after him.

☐ D A Y   2 1 0

GOD SIGHTINGS

July 29

2 CHRONICLES 24:1–25:28

Joash was seven years old when he became king, and he reigned in Jerusalem forty years. His mother's name was Zibiah; she was from Beersheba. 2 Joash did what was right in the eyes of the Lord all the years of Jehoiada the priest. 3 Jehoiada chose two wives for him, and he had sons and daughters.

4 Some time later Joash decided to restore the temple of the Lord. 5 He called together the priests and Levites and said to them, "Go to the towns of Judah and collect the money due annually from all Israel, to repair the temple of your God. Do it now." But the Levites did not act at once.

6 Therefore the king summoned Jehoiada the chief priest and said to him, "Why haven't you required the Levites to bring in from Judah and Jerusalem the tax imposed by Moses the servant of the Lord and by the assembly of Israel for the Tent of the Testimony?"

7 Now the sons of that wicked woman Athaliah had broken into the temple of God and had used even its sacred objects for the Baals.

8 At the king's command, a chest was made and placed outside, at the gate of the temple of the Lord. 9 A proclamation was then issued in Judah and Jerusalem that they should bring to the Lord the tax that Moses the servant of God had required of Israel in the desert. 10 All the officials and all the people brought their contributions gladly, dropping them into the chest until it was full. 11 Whenever the chest was brought in by the Levites to the king's officials and they saw that there was a large amount of money, the royal secretary and the officer of the chief priest would come and empty the chest and carry it back to its place. They did this regularly and collected a great amount of money. 12 The king and Jehoiada gave it to the men who carried out the work required for the temple of the Lord. They hired masons and carpenters to restore the Lord's temple, and also workers in iron and bronze to repair the temple.

13 The men in charge of the work were diligent, and the repairs progressed under them. They rebuilt the temple of God according to its original design and reinforced it. 14 When they had finished, they brought the rest of the money to the king and Jehoiada, and with it were made articles for the Lord's temple: articles for the service and for the burnt offerings, and also dishes and other objects of gold and silver. As long as Jehoiada lived, burnt offerings were presented continually in the temple of the Lord.

15 Now Jehoiada was old and full of years, and he died at the age of a hundred and thirty. 16 He was buried with the kings in the City of David, because of the good he had done in Israel for God and his temple.

17 After the death of Jehoiada, the officials of Judah came and paid homage to the king, and he listened to them. 18 They abandoned the temple of the Lord, the God of their fathers, and worshiped Asherah poles and idols. Because of their guilt, God's anger came upon Judah and Jerusalem. 19 Although the Lord sent prophets to the people to bring them back to him, and though they testified against them, they would not listen.

20 Then the Spirit of God came upon Zechariah son of Jehoiada the priest. He stood before the people and said, "This is what God says: 'Why do you disobey the Lord's commands? You will not prosper. Because you have forsaken the Lord, he has forsaken you.'"

21 But they plotted against him, and by order of the king they stoned him to death in the courtyard of the Lord's temple. 22 King Joash did not remember the kindness Zechariah's father Jehoiada had shown him but killed his son,

who said as he lay dying, "May the Lord see this and call you to account."

23 At the turn of the year,*a* the army of Aram marched against Joash; it invaded Judah and Jerusalem and killed all the leaders of the people. They sent all the plunder to their king in Damascus. 24 Although the Aramean army had come with only a few men, the Lord delivered into their hands a much larger army. Because Judah had forsaken the Lord, the God of their fathers, judgment was executed on Joash. 25 When the Arameans withdrew, they left Joash severely wounded. His officials conspired against him for murdering the son of Jehoiada the priest, and they killed him in his bed. So he died and was buried in the City of David, but not in the tombs of the kings.

26 Those who conspired against him were Zabad,*b* son of Shimeath an Ammonite woman, and Jehozabad, son of Shimrith*c* a Moabite woman. 27 The account of his sons, the many prophecies about him, and the record of the restoration of the temple of God are written in the annotations on the book of the kings. And Amaziah his son succeeded him as king.

25:1 Amaziah was twenty-five years old when he became king, and he reigned in Jerusalem twenty-nine years. His mother's name was Jehoaddin*d*; she was from Jerusalem. 2 He did what was right in the eyes of the Lord, but not wholeheartedly. 3 After the kingdom was firmly in his control, he executed the officials who had murdered his father the king. 4 Yet he did not put their sons to death, but acted in accordance with what is written in the Law, in the Book of Moses, where the Lord commanded: "Fathers shall not be put to death for their children, nor children put to death for their fathers; each is to die for his own sins."*e*

5 Amaziah called the people of Judah together and assigned them according to their families to commanders of thousands and commanders of hundreds for all Judah and Benjamin. He then mustered those twenty years old or more and found that there were three hundred thousand men ready for military service, able to handle the spear and shield. 6 He also hired a hundred thousand fighting men from Israel for a hundred talents*f* of silver.

7 But a man of God came to him and said, "O king, these troops from Israel must not march with you, for the Lord is not with Israel—not with any of the people of Ephraim. 8 Even if you go and fight courageously in battle, God will overthrow you before the enemy, for God has the power to help or to overthrow."

9 Amaziah asked the man of God, "But what about the hundred talents I paid for these Israelite troops?"

The man of God replied, "The Lord can give you much more than that."

10 So Amaziah dismissed the troops who had come to him from Ephraim and sent them home. They were furious with Judah and left for home in a great rage.

11 Amaziah then marshaled his strength and led his army to the Valley of Salt, where he killed ten thousand men of Seir. 12 The army of Judah also captured ten thousand men alive, took them to the top of a cliff and threw them down so that all were dashed to pieces.

13 Meanwhile the troops that Amaziah had sent back and had not allowed to take part in the war raided Judean towns from Samaria to Beth Horon. They killed three thousand people and carried off great quantities of plunder.

14 When Amaziah returned from slaughtering the Edomites, he brought back the gods of the people of Seir. He set them up as his own gods, bowed down to them and burned sacrifices to them. 15 The anger of the Lord burned against Amaziah, and he sent a prophet to him, who said, "Why do you consult this people's gods, which could not save their own people from your hand?"

16 While he was still speaking, the king said to him, "Have we appointed you an adviser to the king? Stop! Why be struck down?"

So the prophet stopped but said, "I

know that God has determined to destroy you, because you have done this and have not listened to my counsel."

¹⁷After Amaziah king of Judah consulted his advisers, he sent this challenge to Jehoash*g* son of Jehoahaz, the son of Jehu, king of Israel: "Come, meet me face to face."

¹⁸But Jehoash king of Israel replied to Amaziah king of Judah: "A thistle in Lebanon sent a message to a cedar in Lebanon, 'Give your daughter to my son in marriage.' Then a wild beast in Lebanon came along and trampled the thistle underfoot. ¹⁹You say to yourself that you have defeated Edom, and now you are arrogant and proud. But stay at home! Why ask for trouble and cause your own downfall and that of Judah also?"

²⁰Amaziah, however, would not listen, for God so worked that he might hand them over to ⌊Jehoash⌋, because they sought the gods of Edom. ²¹So Jehoash king of Israel attacked. He and Amaziah king of Judah faced each other at Beth Shemesh in Judah. ²²Judah was routed by Israel, and every man fled to his home. ²³Jehoash king of Israel captured Amaziah king of Judah, the son of Joash, the son of Ahaziah,*h* at Beth Shemesh. Then Jehoash brought him to Jerusalem and broke down the wall of Jerusalem from the Ephraim Gate to the Corner Gate—a section about six hundred feet*i* long. ²⁴He took all the gold and silver and all the articles found in the temple of God that had been in the care of Obed-Edom, together with the palace treasures and the hostages, and returned to Samaria.

²⁵Amaziah son of Joash king of Judah lived for fifteen years after the death of Jehoash son of Jehoahaz king of Israel. ²⁶As for the other events of Amaziah's reign, from beginning to end, are they not written in the book of the kings of Judah and Israel? ²⁷From the time that Amaziah turned away from following the LORD, they conspired against him in Jerusalem and he fled to Lachish, but they sent men after him to Lachish and killed him there. ²⁸He was brought back

by horse and was buried with his fathers in the City of Judah.

a23 Probably in the spring   *b26* A variant of *Jozabad*   *c26* A variant of *Shomer*   *d1* Hebrew *Jehoaddan,* a variant of *Jehoaddin*   *e4* Deut. 24:16   *f6* That is, about 3 3/4 tons (about 3.4 metric tons); also in verse 9   *g17* Hebrew *Joash,* a variant of *Jehoash*; also in verses 18, 21, 23 and 25   *h23* Hebrew *Jehoahaz,* a variant of *Ahaziah*   *i23* Hebrew *four hundred cubits* (about 180 meters)

ROMANS 12:1-21

Therefore, I urge you, brothers, in view of God's mercy, to offer your bodies as living sacrifices, holy and pleasing to God—this is your spiritual*a* act of worship. ²Do not conform any longer to the pattern of this world, but be transformed by the renewing of your mind. Then you will be able to test and approve what God's will is—his good, pleasing and perfect will.

³For by the grace given me I say to every one of you: Do not think of yourself more highly than you ought, but rather think of yourself with sober judgment, in accordance with the measure of faith God has given you. ⁴Just as each of us has one body with many members, and these members do not all have the same function, ⁵so in Christ we who are many form one body, and each member belongs to all the others. ⁶We have different gifts, according to the grace given us. If a man's gift is prophesying, let him use it in proportion to his*b* faith. ⁷If it is serving, let him serve; if it is teaching, let him teach; ⁸if it is encouraging, let him encourage; if it is contributing to the needs of others, let him give generously; if it is leadership, let him govern diligently; if it is showing mercy, let him do it cheerfully.

⁹Love must be sincere. Hate what is evil; cling to what is good. ¹⁰Be devoted to one another in brotherly love. Honor one another above yourselves. ¹¹Never be lacking in zeal, but keep your spiritual fervor, serving the Lord. ¹²Be joyful in hope, patient in affliction, faithful in prayer. ¹³Share with God's people who are in need. Practice hospitality.

¹⁴Bless those who persecute you; bless and do not curse. ¹⁵Rejoice with those who rejoice; mourn with those

who mourn. [16]Live in harmony with one another. Do not be proud, but be willing to associate with people of low position.[c] Do not be conceited.

[17]Do not repay anyone evil for evil. Be careful to do what is right in the eyes of everybody. [18]If it is possible, as far as it depends on you, live at peace with everyone. [19]Do not take revenge, my friends, but leave room for God's wrath, for it is written: "It is mine to avenge; I will repay,"[d] says the Lord. [20]On the contrary:

"If your enemy is hungry, feed him;
    if he is thirsty, give him something
    to drink.
In doing this, you will heap burning
    coals on his head."[e]

[21]Do not be overcome by evil, but overcome evil with good.

[a]1 Or reasonable [b]6 Or in agreement with the
[c]16 Or willing to do menial work [d]19 Deut. 32:35
[e]20 Prov. 25:21,22

PSALM 22:19-31

[19]**B**ut you, O Lord, be not far off;
    O my Strength, come quickly to
    help me.
[20]Deliver my life from the sword,
    my precious life from the power of
    the dogs.
[21]Rescue me from the mouth of the
    lions;
    save[a] me from the horns of the
    wild oxen.

[22]I will declare your name to my
    brothers;
    in the congregation I will praise you.
[23]You who fear the Lord, praise him!
    All you descendants of Jacob,
    honor him!
    Revere him, all you descendants
    of Israel!
[24]For he has not despised or disdained
    the suffering of the afflicted one;
he has not hidden his face from him
    but has listened to his cry for help.

[25]From you comes the theme of my
    praise in the great assembly;
    before those who fear you[b] will I
    fulfill my vows.

[26]The poor will eat and be satisfied;
    they who seek the Lord will praise
    him—
    may your hearts live forever!
[27]All the ends of the earth
    will remember and turn to the
    Lord,
and all the families of the nations
    will bow down before him,
[28]for dominion belongs to the Lord
    and he rules over the nations.

[29]All the rich of the earth will feast and
    worship;
    all who go down to the dust will
    kneel before him—
    those who cannot keep themselves
    alive.
[30]Posterity will serve him;
    future generations will be told
    about the Lord.
[31]They will proclaim his righteousness
    to a people yet unborn—
    for he has done it.

[a]21 Or / you have heard [b]25 Hebrew him

PROVERBS 20:8-10

[8]**W**hen a king sits on his throne to
    judge,
    he winnows out all evil with his
    eyes.

[9]Who can say, "I have kept my heart
    pure;
    I am clean and without sin"?

[10]Differing weights and differing
    measures—
    the Lord detests them both.

☐ D A Y 2 1 1

GOD SIGHTINGS

July 30

2 CHRONICLES 26:1–28:27

Then all the people of Judah took Uzziah,[a] who was sixteen years old, and made him king in place of his father Amaziah. [2]He was the one who rebuilt

Elath and restored it to Judah after Amaziah rested with his fathers.

³Uzziah was sixteen years old when he became king, and he reigned in Jerusalem fifty-two years. His mother's name was Jecoliah; she was from Jerusalem. ⁴He did what was right in the eyes of the Lord, just as his father Amaziah had done. ⁵He sought God during the days of Zechariah, who instructed him in the fear[b] of God. As long as he sought the Lord, God gave him success.

⁶He went to war against the Philistines and broke down the walls of Gath, Jabneh and Ashdod. He then rebuilt towns near Ashdod and elsewhere among the Philistines. ⁷God helped him against the Philistines and against the Arabs who lived in Gur Baal and against the Meunites. ⁸The Ammonites brought tribute to Uzziah, and his fame spread as far as the border of Egypt, because he had become very powerful.

⁹Uzziah built towers in Jerusalem at the Corner Gate, at the Valley Gate and at the angle of the wall, and he fortified them. ¹⁰He also built towers in the desert and dug many cisterns, because he had much livestock in the foothills and in the plain. He had people working his fields and vineyards in the hills and in the fertile lands, for he loved the soil.

¹¹Uzziah had a well-trained army, ready to go out by divisions according to their numbers as mustered by Jeiel the secretary and Maaseiah the officer under the direction of Hananiah, one of the royal officials. ¹²The total number of family leaders over the fighting men was 2,600. ¹³Under their command was an army of 307,500 men trained for war, a powerful force to support the king against his enemies. ¹⁴Uzziah provided shields, spears, helmets, coats of armor, bows and slingstones for the entire army. ¹⁵In Jerusalem he made machines designed by skillful men for use on the towers and on the corner defenses to shoot arrows and hurl large stones. His fame spread far and wide, for he was greatly helped until he became powerful.

¹⁶But after Uzziah became powerful, his pride led to his downfall. He was unfaithful to the Lord his God, and entered the temple of the Lord to burn incense on the altar of incense. ¹⁷Azariah the priest with eighty other courageous priests of the Lord followed him in. ¹⁸They confronted him and said, "It is not right for you, Uzziah, to burn incense to the Lord. That is for the priests, the descendants of Aaron, who have been consecrated to burn incense. Leave the sanctuary, for you have been unfaithful; and you will not be honored by the Lord God."

¹⁹Uzziah, who had a censer in his hand ready to burn incense, became angry. While he was raging at the priests in their presence before the incense altar in the Lord's temple, leprosy[c] broke out on his forehead. ²⁰When Azariah the chief priest and all the other priests looked at him, they saw that he had leprosy on his forehead, so they hurried him out. Indeed, he himself was eager to leave, because the Lord had afflicted him.

²¹King Uzziah had leprosy until the day he died. He lived in a separate house[d]—leprous, and excluded from the temple of the Lord. Jotham his son had charge of the palace and governed the people of the land.

²²The other events of Uzziah's reign, from beginning to end, are recorded by the prophet Isaiah son of Amoz. ²³Uzziah rested with his fathers and was buried near them in a field for burial that belonged to the kings, for people said, "He had leprosy." And Jotham his son succeeded him as king.

²⁷:¹Jotham was twenty-five years old when he became king, and he reigned in Jerusalem sixteen years. His mother's name was Jerusha daughter of Zadok. ²He did what was right in the eyes of the Lord, just as his father Uzziah had done, but unlike him he did not enter the temple of the Lord. The people, however, continued their corrupt practices. ³Jotham rebuilt the Upper Gate of the tem-

ple of the Lord and did extensive work on the wall at the hill of Ophel. 4He built towns in the Judean hills and forts and towers in the wooded areas.

5 Jotham made war on the king of the Ammonites and conquered them. That year the Ammonites paid him a hundred talents*e* of silver, ten thousand cors*f* of wheat and ten thousand cors of barley. The Ammonites brought him the same amount also in the second and third years.

6 Jotham grew powerful because he walked steadfastly before the Lord his God.

7 The other events in Jotham's reign, including all his wars and the other things he did, are written in the book of the kings of Israel and Judah. 8He was twenty-five years old when he became king, and he reigned in Jerusalem sixteen years. 9Jotham rested with his fathers and was buried in the City of David. And Ahaz his son succeeded him as king.

28:1Ahaz was twenty years old when he became king, and he reigned in Jerusalem sixteen years. Unlike David his father, he did not do what was right in the eyes of the Lord. 2He walked in the ways of the kings of Israel and also made cast idols for worshiping the Baals. 3He burned sacrifices in the Valley of Ben Hinnom and sacrificed his sons in the fire, following the detestable ways of the nations the Lord had driven out before the Israelites. 4He offered sacrifices and burned incense at the high places, on the hilltops and under every spreading tree.

5 Therefore the Lord his God handed him over to the king of Aram. The Arameans defeated him and took many of his people as prisoners and brought them to Damascus.

He was also given into the hands of the king of Israel, who inflicted heavy casualties on him. 6In one day Pekah son of Remaliah killed a hundred and twenty thousand soldiers in Judah—because Judah had forsaken the Lord, the God of their fathers. 7Zicri, an Ephraim-

ite warrior, killed Maaseiah the king's son, Azrikam the officer in charge of the palace, and Elkanah, second to the king. 8The Israelites took captive from their kinsmen two hundred thousand wives, sons and daughters. They also took a great deal of plunder, which they carried back to Samaria.

9 But a prophet of the Lord named Oded was there, and he went out to meet the army when it returned to Samaria. He said to them, "Because the Lord, the God of your fathers, was angry with Judah, he gave them into your hand. But you have slaughtered them in a rage that reaches to heaven. 10And now you intend to make the men and women of Judah and Jerusalem your slaves. But aren't you also guilty of sins against the Lord your God? 11Now listen to me! Send back your fellow countrymen you have taken as prisoners, for the Lord's fierce anger rests on you."

12 Then some of the leaders in Ephraim—Azariah son of Jehohanan, Berekiah son of Meshillemoth, Jehizkiah son of Shallum, and Amasa son of Hadlai—confronted those who were arriving from the war. 13"You must not bring those prisoners here," they said, "or we will be guilty before the Lord. Do you intend to add to our sin and guilt? For our guilt is already great, and his fierce anger rests on Israel."

14 So the soldiers gave up the prisoners and plunder in the presence of the officials and all the assembly. 15The men designated by name took the prisoners, and from the plunder they clothed all who were naked. They provided them with clothes and sandals, food and drink, and healing balm. All those who were weak they put on donkeys. So they took them back to their fellow countrymen at Jericho, the City of Palms, and returned to Samaria.

16 At that time King Ahaz sent to the king*g* of Assyria for help. 17The Edomites had again come and attacked Judah and carried away prisoners, 18while the Philistines had raided towns in the foothills and in the Negev of Judah. They

captured and occupied Beth Shemesh, Aijalon and Gederoth, as well as Soco, Timnah and Gimzo, with their surrounding villages. [19] The LORD had humbled Judah because of Ahaz king of Israel,[h] for he had promoted wickedness in Judah and had been most unfaithful to the LORD. [20] Tiglath-Pileser[i] king of Assyria came to him, but he gave him trouble instead of help. [21] Ahaz took some of the things from the temple of the LORD and from the royal palace and from the princes and presented them to the king of Assyria, but that did not help him.

[22] In his time of trouble King Ahaz became even more unfaithful to the LORD. [23] He offered sacrifices to the gods of Damascus, who had defeated him; for he thought, "Since the gods of the kings of Aram have helped them, I will sacrifice to them so they will help me." But they were his downfall and the downfall of all Israel.

[24] Ahaz gathered together the furnishings from the temple of God and took them away.[j] He shut the doors of the LORD's temple and set up altars at every street corner in Jerusalem. [25] In every town in Judah he built high places to burn sacrifices to other gods and provoked the LORD, the God of his fathers, to anger.

[26] The other events of his reign and all his ways, from beginning to end, are written in the book of the kings of Judah and Israel. [27] Ahaz rested with his fathers and was buried in the city of Jerusalem, but he was not placed in the tombs of the kings of Israel. And Hezekiah his son succeeded him as king.

a 1 Also called Azariah b 5 Many Hebrew manuscripts, Septuagint and Syriac; other Hebrew manuscripts vision c 19 The Hebrew word was used for various diseases affecting the skin—not necessarily leprosy; also in verses 20, 21 and 23. d 21 Or in a house where he was relieved of responsibilities e 5 That is, about 3 3/4 tons (about 3.4 metric tons) f 5 That is, probably about 62,000 bushels (about 2,200 kiloliters) g 16 One Hebrew manuscript, Septuagint and Vulgate (see also 2 Kings 16:7); most Hebrew manuscripts kings h 19 That is, Judah, as frequently in 2 Chronicles i 20 Hebrew Tilgath-Pilneser, a variant of Tiglath-Pileser j 24 Or and cut them up

ROMANS 13:1-14

Everyone must submit himself to the governing authorities, for there is no authority except that which God has established. The authorities that exist have been established by God. [2] Consequently, he who rebels against the authority is rebelling against what God has instituted, and those who do so will bring judgment on themselves. [3] For rulers hold no terror for those who do right, but for those who do wrong. Do you want to be free from fear of the one in authority? Then do what is right and he will commend you. [4] For he is God's servant to do you good. But if you do wrong, be afraid, for he does not bear the sword for nothing. He is God's servant, an agent of wrath to bring punishment on the wrongdoer. [5] Therefore, it is necessary to submit to the authorities, not only because of possible punishment but also because of conscience.

[6] This is also why you pay taxes, for the authorities are God's servants, who give their full time to governing. [7] Give everyone what you owe him: If you owe taxes, pay taxes; if revenue, then revenue; if respect, then respect; if honor, then honor.

[8] Let no debt remain outstanding, except the continuing debt to love one another, for he who loves his fellowman has fulfilled the law. [9] The commandments, "Do not commit adultery," "Do not murder," "Do not steal," "Do not covet,"[a] and whatever other commandment there may be, are summed up in this one rule: "Love your neighbor as yourself."[b] [10] Love does no harm to its neighbor. Therefore love is the fulfillment of the law.

[11] And do this, understanding the present time. The hour has come for you to wake up from your slumber, because our salvation is nearer now than when we first believed. [12] **The night is nearly over; the day is almost here. So let us put aside the deeds of darkness and put on the armor of light.** [13] Let us behave decently, as in the day-

time, not in orgies and drunkenness, not in sexual immorality and debauchery, not in dissension and jealousy. [14]Rather, clothe yourselves with the Lord Jesus Christ, and do not think about how to gratify the desires of the sinful nature.[c]

[a]9 Exodus 20:13-15,17; Deut. 5:17-19,21   [b]9 Lev. 19:18
[c]14 Or *the flesh*

PSALM 23:1-6
A psalm of David.

[1] **T**he Lord is my shepherd, I shall not
     be in want.
[2]   He makes me lie down in green
         pastures,
     he leads me beside quiet waters,
[3]   he restores my soul.
     He guides me in paths of
         righteousness
     for his name's sake.
[4] Even though I walk
         through the valley of the shadow
         of death,[a]
     I will fear no evil,
         for you are with me;
     your rod and your staff,
         they comfort me.

[5] You prepare a table before me
     in the presence of my enemies.
   You anoint my head with oil;
     my cup overflows.
[6] Surely goodness and love will
         follow me
     all the days of my life,
   and I will dwell in the house of the
         Lord
     forever.

[a]4 Or *through the darkest valley*

PROVERBS 20:11
[11] **E**ven a child is known by his actions,
     by whether his conduct is pure
         and right.

GOD SIGHTINGS

July 31

2 CHRONICLES 29:1-36
Hezekiah was twenty-five years old when he became king, and he reigned in Jerusalem twenty-nine years. His mother's name was Abijah daughter of Zechariah. [2]He did what was right in the eyes of the Lord, just as his father David had done.

[3]In the first month of the first year of his reign, he opened the doors of the temple of the Lord and repaired them. [4]He brought in the priests and the Levites, assembled them in the square on the east side [5]and said: "Listen to me, Levites! Consecrate yourselves now and consecrate the temple of the Lord, the God of your fathers. Remove all defilement from the sanctuary. [6]Our fathers were unfaithful; they did evil in the eyes of the Lord our God and forsook him. They turned their faces away from the Lord's dwelling place and turned their backs on him. [7]They also shut the doors of the portico and put out the lamps. They did not burn incense or present any burnt offerings at the sanctuary to the God of Israel. [8]Therefore, the anger of the Lord has fallen on Judah and Jerusalem; he has made them an object of dread and horror and scorn, as you can see with your own eyes. [9]This is why our fathers have fallen by the sword and why our sons and daughters and our wives are in captivity. [10]Now I intend to make a covenant with the Lord, the God of Israel, so that his fierce anger will turn away from us. [11]My sons, do not be negligent now, for the Lord has chosen you to stand before him and serve him, to minister before him and to burn incense."
[12]Then these Levites set to work:
   from the Kohathites,
     Mahath son of Amasai and Joel son
         of Azariah;
   from the Merarites,

Kish son of Abdi and Azariah son of
 Jehallelel;
from the Gershonites,
 Joah son of Zimmah and Eden son
 of Joah;
13from the descendants of Elizaphan,
 Shimri and Jeiel;
from the descendants of Asaph,
 Zechariah and Mattaniah;
14from the descendants of Heman,
 Jehiel and Shimei;
from the descendants of Jeduthun,
 Shemaiah and Uzziel.

15When they had assembled their
brothers and consecrated themselves,
they went in to purify the temple of the
LORD, as the king had ordered, following
the word of the LORD. 16The priests went
into the sanctuary of the LORD to purify
it. They brought out to the courtyard of
the LORD's temple everything unclean
that they found in the temple of the
LORD. The Levites took it and carried it
out to the Kidron Valley. 17They began
the consecration on the first day of the
first month, and by the eighth day of
the month they reached the portico of
the LORD. For eight more days they consecrated the temple of the LORD itself,
finishing on the sixteenth day of the
first month.

18Then they went in to King Hezekiah and reported: "We have purified
the entire temple of the LORD, the altar
of burnt offering with all its utensils,
and the table for setting out the consecrated bread, with all its articles. 19We
have prepared and consecrated all the
articles that King Ahaz removed in his
unfaithfulness while he was king. They
are now in front of the LORD's altar."

20Early the next morning King Hezekiah gathered the city officials together
and went up to the temple of the LORD.
21They brought seven bulls, seven rams,
seven male lambs and seven male goats
as a sin offering for the kingdom, for the
sanctuary and for Judah. The king commanded the priests, the descendants of
Aaron, to offer these on the altar of the
LORD. 22So they slaughtered the bulls,
and the priests took the blood and

sprinkled it on the altar; next they
slaughtered the rams and sprinkled
their blood on the altar; then they
slaughtered the lambs and sprinkled
their blood on the altar. 23The goats for
the sin offering were brought before the
king and the assembly, and they laid
their hands on them. 24The priests then
slaughtered the goats and presented
their blood on the altar for a sin offering
to atone for all Israel, because the king
had ordered the burnt offering and the
sin offering for all Israel.

25He stationed the Levites in the temple of the LORD with cymbals, harps and
lyres in the way prescribed by David and
Gad the king's seer and Nathan the
prophet; this was commanded by the
LORD through his prophets. 26So the Levites stood ready with David's instruments, and the priests with their
trumpets.

27Hezekiah gave the order to sacrifice the burnt offering on the altar. As
the offering began, singing to the LORD
began also, accompanied by trumpets
and the instruments of David king of Israel. 28The whole assembly bowed in
worship, while the singers sang and the
trumpeters played. All this continued
until the sacrifice of the burnt offering
was completed.

29When the offerings were finished,
the king and everyone present with him
knelt down and worshiped. 30King Hezekiah and his officials ordered the Levites to praise the LORD with the words
of David and of Asaph the seer. So they
sang praises with gladness and bowed
their heads and worshiped.

31Then Hezekiah said, "You have now
dedicated yourselves to the LORD. Come
and bring sacrifices and thank offerings
to the temple of the LORD." So the assembly brought sacrifices and thank offerings, and all whose hearts were
willing brought burnt offerings.

32The number of burnt offerings the
assembly brought was seventy bulls, a
hundred rams and two hundred male
lambs—all of them for burnt offerings
to the LORD. 33The animals consecrated

as sacrifices amounted to six hundred bulls and three thousand sheep and goats. [34]The priests, however, were too few to skin all the burnt offerings; so their kinsmen the Levites helped them until the task was finished and until other priests had been consecrated, for the Levites had been more conscientious in consecrating themselves than the priests had been. [35]There were burnt offerings in abundance, together with the fat of the fellowship offerings[a] and the drink offerings that accompanied the burnt offerings.

So the service of the temple of the LORD was reestablished. [36]Hezekiah and all the people rejoiced at what God had brought about for his people, because it was done so quickly.

[a]35 Traditionally *peace offerings*

ROMANS 14:1-23

Accept him whose faith is weak, without passing judgment on disputable matters. [2]One man's faith allows him to eat everything, but another man, whose faith is weak, eats only vegetables. [3]The man who eats everything must not look down on him who does not, and the man who does not eat everything must not condemn the man who does, for God has accepted him. [4]Who are you to judge someone else's servant? To his own master he stands or falls. And he will stand, for the Lord is able to make him stand.

[5]One man considers one day more sacred than another; another man considers every day alike. Each one should be fully convinced in his own mind. [6]He who regards one day as special, does so to the Lord. He who eats meat, eats to the Lord, for he gives thanks to God; and he who abstains, does so to the Lord and gives thanks to God. [7]For none of us lives to himself alone and none of us dies to himself alone. [8]If we live, we live to the Lord; and if we die, we die to the Lord. So, whether we live or die, we belong to the Lord.

[9]For this very reason, Christ died and returned to life so that he might be the Lord of both the dead and the living. [10]You, then, why do you judge your brother? Or why do you look down on your brother? For we will all stand before God's judgment seat. [11]It is written:

"'As surely as I live,' says the Lord,
'every knee will bow before me;
    every tongue will confess to God.'"[a]

[12]So then, each of us will give an account of himself to God.

[13]Therefore let us stop passing judgment on one another. Instead, make up your mind not to put any stumbling block or obstacle in your brother's way. [14]As one who is in the Lord Jesus, I am fully convinced that no food[b] is unclean in itself. But if anyone regards something as unclean, then for him it is unclean. [15]If your brother is distressed because of what you eat, you are no longer acting in love. Do not by your eating destroy your brother for whom Christ died. [16]Do not allow what you consider good to be spoken of as evil. [17]For the kingdom of God is not a matter of eating and drinking, but of righteousness, peace and joy in the Holy Spirit, [18]because anyone who serves Christ in this way is pleasing to God and approved by men.

[19]**Let us therefore make every effort to do what leads to peace and to mutual edification. [20]Do not destroy the work of God for the sake of food. All food is clean, but it is wrong for a man to eat anything that causes someone else to stumble.** [21]It is better not to eat meat or drink wine or to do anything else that will cause your brother to fall.

[22]So whatever you believe about these things keep between yourself and God. Blessed is the man who does not condemn himself by what he approves. [23]But the man who has doubts is condemned if he eats, because his eating is not from faith; and everything that does not come from faith is sin.

[a]11 Isaiah 45:23   [b]14 Or *that nothing*

PSALM 24:1-10
Of David. A psalm.

1 The earth is the LORD's, and
    everything in it,
  the world, and all who live in it;
2 for he founded it upon the seas
  and established it upon the
    waters.

3 Who may ascend the hill of the
    LORD?
  Who may stand in his holy place?
4 He who has clean hands and a pure
    heart,
  who does not lift up his soul to an
    idol
  or swear by what is false.*a*
5 He will receive blessing from the
    LORD
  and vindication from God his
    Savior.
6 Such is the generation of those who
    seek him,

who seek your face, O God of
    Jacob.*b*   *Selah*

7 Lift up your heads, O you gates;
  be lifted up, you ancient doors,
  that the King of glory may
    come in.
8 Who is this King of glory?
  The LORD strong and mighty,
  the LORD mighty in battle.
9 Lift up your heads, O you gates;
  lift them up, you ancient doors,
  that the King of glory may
    come in.
10 Who is he, this King of glory?
  The LORD Almighty—
  he is the King of glory.   *Selah*

a4 Or *swear falsely   b6* Two Hebrew manuscripts and
Syriac (see also Septuagint); most Hebrew manuscripts *face,
Jacob*

PROVERBS 20:12
12 Ears that hear and eyes that see—
  the LORD has made them both.

GOD SIGHTINGS

August 1

2 CHRONICLES 30:1–31:21

Hezekiah sent word to all Israel and Judah and also wrote letters to Ephraim and Manasseh, inviting them to come to the temple of the Lord in Jerusalem and celebrate the Passover to the Lord, the God of Israel. ² The king and his officials and the whole assembly in Jerusalem decided to celebrate the Passover in the second month. ³ They had not been able to celebrate it at the regular time because not enough priests had consecrated themselves and the people had not assembled in Jerusalem. ⁴ The plan seemed right both to the king and to the whole assembly. ⁵ They decided to send a proclamation throughout Israel, from Beersheba to Dan, calling the people to come to Jerusalem and celebrate the Passover to the Lord, the God of Israel. It had not been celebrated in large numbers according to what was written.

⁶ At the king's command, couriers went throughout Israel and Judah with letters from the king and from his officials, which read:

"People of Israel, return to the Lord, the God of Abraham, Isaac and Israel, that he may return to you who are left, who have escaped from the hand of the kings of Assyria. ⁷ Do not be like your fathers and brothers, who were unfaithful to the Lord, the God of their fathers, so that he made them an object of horror, as you see. ⁸ Do not be stiff-necked, as your fathers were; submit to the Lord. Come to the sanctuary, which he has consecrated forever. Serve the Lord your God, so that his fierce anger will turn away from you. ⁹ If you return to the Lord, then your brothers and your children will be shown compassion by their captors and will come back to this land, for the Lord your God is gracious and compassionate. He will not turn his face from you if you return to him."

¹⁰ The couriers went from town to town in Ephraim and Manasseh, as far as Zebulun, but the people scorned and ridiculed them. ¹¹ Nevertheless, some men of Asher, Manasseh and Zebulun humbled themselves and went to Jerusalem. ¹² Also in Judah the hand of God was on the people to give them unity of mind to carry out what the king and his officials had ordered, following the word of the Lord.

¹³ A very large crowd of people assembled in Jerusalem to celebrate the Feast of Unleavened Bread in the second month. ¹⁴ They removed the altars in Jerusalem and cleared away the incense altars and threw them into the Kidron Valley.

¹⁵ They slaughtered the Passover lamb on the fourteenth day of the second month. The priests and the Levites were ashamed and consecrated themselves and brought burnt offerings to the temple of the Lord. ¹⁶ Then they took up their regular positions as prescribed in the Law of Moses the man of God. The priests sprinkled the blood handed to them by the Levites. ¹⁷ Since many in the crowd had not consecrated themselves, the Levites had to kill the Passover lambs for all those who were not ceremonially clean and could not consecrate ⌊their lambs⌋ to the Lord. ¹⁸ Although most of the many people who came from Ephraim, Manasseh, Issachar and Zebulun had not purified themselves, yet they ate the Passover, contrary to what was written. But Hezekiah prayed for them, saying, "May the

LORD, who is good, pardon everyone
[19]who sets his heart on seeking God—
the LORD, the God of his fathers—even if
he is not clean according to the rules of
the sanctuary." [20]And the LORD heard
Hezekiah and healed the people.

[21]The Israelites who were present in
Jerusalem celebrated the Feast of Unleavened Bread for seven days with great
rejoicing, while the Levites and priests
sang to the LORD every day, accompanied by the LORD's instruments of
praise.[a]

[22]Hezekiah spoke encouragingly to
all the Levites, who showed good understanding of the service of the LORD. For
the seven days they ate their assigned
portion and offered fellowship offerings[b] and praised the LORD, the God of
their fathers.

[23]The whole assembly then agreed to
celebrate the festival seven more days;
so for another seven days they celebrated joyfully. [24]Hezekiah king of Judah provided a thousand bulls and
seven thousand sheep and goats for the
assembly, and the officials provided
them with a thousand bulls and ten
thousand sheep and goats. A great number of priests consecrated themselves.
[25]The entire assembly of Judah rejoiced, along with the priests and Levites and all who had assembled from
Israel, including the aliens who had
come from Israel and those who lived in
Judah. [26]There was great joy in Jerusalem, for since the days of Solomon son
of David king of Israel there had been
nothing like this in Jerusalem. [27]The
priests and the Levites stood to bless the
people, and God heard them, for their
prayer reached heaven, his holy dwelling place.

[31:1]WHEN all this had ended, the Israelites who were there went out to the
towns of Judah, smashed the sacred
stones and cut down the Asherah poles.
They destroyed the high places and the
altars throughout Judah and Benjamin
and in Ephraim and Manasseh. After
they had destroyed all of them, the Isra-

elites returned to their own towns and
to their own property.

[2]Hezekiah assigned the priests and
Levites to divisions—each of them according to their duties as priests or Levites—to offer burnt offerings and
fellowship offerings,[b] to minister, to
give thanks and to sing praises at the
gates of the LORD's dwelling. [3]The king
contributed from his own possessions
for the morning and evening burnt offerings and for the burnt offerings on
the Sabbaths, New Moons and appointed feasts as written in the Law of
the LORD. [4]He ordered the people living
in Jerusalem to give the portion due the
priests and Levites so they could devote
themselves to the Law of the LORD. [5]As
soon as the order went out, the Israelites
generously gave the firstfruits of their
grain, new wine, oil and honey and all
that the fields produced. They brought
a great amount, a tithe of everything.
[6]The men of Israel and Judah who lived
in the towns of Judah also brought a
tithe of their herds and flocks and a
tithe of the holy things dedicated to the
LORD their God, and they piled them in
heaps. [7]They began doing this in the
third month and finished in the seventh
month. [8]When Hezekiah and his officials came and saw the heaps, they
praised the LORD and blessed his people
Israel.

[9]Hezekiah asked the priests and Levites about the heaps; [10]and Azariah the
chief priest, from the family of Zadok,
answered, "Since the people began to
bring their contributions to the temple
of the LORD, we have had enough to eat
and plenty to spare, because the LORD
has blessed his people, and this great
amount is left over."

[11]Hezekiah gave orders to prepare
storerooms in the temple of the LORD,
and this was done. [12]Then they faithfully brought in the contributions,
tithes and dedicated gifts. Conaniah, a
Levite, was in charge of these things,
and his brother Shimei was next in
rank. [13]Jehiel, Azaziah, Nahath, Asahel,
Jerimoth, Jozabad, Eliel, Ismakiah, Ma-

hath and Benaiah were supervisors under Conaniah and Shimei his brother, by appointment of King Hezekiah and Azariah the official in charge of the temple of God.

[14] Kore son of Imnah the Levite, keeper of the East Gate, was in charge of the freewill offerings given to God, distributing the contributions made to the LORD and also the consecrated gifts. [15] Eden, Miniamin, Jeshua, Shemaiah, Amariah and Shecaniah assisted him faithfully in the towns of the priests, distributing to their fellow priests according to their divisions, old and young alike.

[16] In addition, they distributed to the males three years old or more whose names were in the genealogical records—all who would enter the temple of the LORD to perform the daily duties of their various tasks, according to their responsibilities and their divisions. [17] And they distributed to the priests enrolled by their families in the genealogical records and likewise to the Levites twenty years old or more, according to their responsibilities and their divisions. [18] They included all the little ones, the wives, and the sons and daughters of the whole community listed in these genealogical records. For they were faithful in consecrating themselves.

[19] As for the priests, the descendants of Aaron, who lived on the farm lands around their towns or in any other towns, men were designated by name to distribute portions to every male among them and to all who were recorded in the genealogies of the Levites.

[20] This is what Hezekiah did throughout Judah, doing what was good and right and faithful before the LORD his God. [21] In everything that he undertook in the service of God's temple and in obedience to the law and the commands, he sought his God and worked wholeheartedly. And so he prospered.

a21 Or priests praised the LORD every day with resounding instruments belonging to the LORD   b22,2 Traditionally peace offerings

ROMANS 15:1-22

We who are strong ought to bear with the failings of the weak and not to please ourselves. [2] Each of us should please his neighbor for his good, to build him up. [3] For even Christ did not please himself but, as it is written: "The insults of those who insult you have fallen on me."*a* [4] For everything that was written in the past was written to teach us, so that through endurance and the encouragement of the Scriptures we might have hope.

[5] **May the God who gives endurance and encouragement give you a spirit of unity among yourselves as you follow Christ Jesus, [6] so that with one heart and mouth you may glorify the God and Father of our Lord Jesus Christ.**

[7] Accept one another, then, just as Christ accepted you, in order to bring praise to God. [8] For I tell you that Christ has become a servant of the Jews*b* on behalf of God's truth, to confirm the promises made to the patriarchs [9] so that the Gentiles may glorify God for his mercy, as it is written:

"Therefore I will praise you among
    the Gentiles;
  I will sing hymns to your name."*c*

[10] Again, it says,

"Rejoice, O Gentiles, with his
    people."*d*

[11] And again,

"Praise the Lord, all you Gentiles,
  and sing praises to him, all you
    peoples."*e*

[12] And again, Isaiah says,

"The Root of Jesse will spring up,
  one who will arise to rule over the
    nations;
the Gentiles will hope in him."*f*

[13] May the God of hope fill you with all joy and peace as you trust in him, so that you may overflow with hope by the power of the Holy Spirit.

¹⁴I myself am convinced, my brothers, that you yourselves are full of goodness, complete in knowledge and competent to instruct one another. ¹⁵I have written you quite boldly on some points, as if to remind you of them again, because of the grace God gave me ¹⁶to be a minister of Christ Jesus to the Gentiles with the priestly duty of proclaiming the gospel of God, so that the Gentiles might become an offering acceptable to God, sanctified by the Holy Spirit.

¹⁷Therefore I glory in Christ Jesus in my service to God. ¹⁸I will not venture to speak of anything except what Christ has accomplished through me in leading the Gentiles to obey God by what I have said and done—¹⁹by the power of signs and miracles, through the power of the Spirit. So from Jerusalem all the way around to Illyricum, I have fully proclaimed the gospel of Christ. ²⁰It has always been my ambition to preach the gospel where Christ was not known, so that I would not be building on someone else's foundation. ²¹Rather, as it is written:

"Those who were not told about him
    will see,
  and those who have not heard will
    understand."ᵍ

²²This is why I have often been hindered from coming to you.

a3 Psalm 69:9 *b8* Greek *circumcision* *c9* 2 Samuel 22:50; Psalm 18:49 *d10* Deut. 32:43 *e11* Psalm 117:1 *f12* Isaiah 11:10 *g21* Isaiah 52:15

PSALM 25:1-15ᵃ
Of David.

¹ To you, O LORD, I lift up my soul;
²   in you I trust, O my God.
  Do not let me be put to shame,
    nor let my enemies triumph
      over me.
³ No one whose hope is in you
    will ever be put to shame,
  but they will be put to shame
    who are treacherous without
      excuse.

⁴ Show me your ways, O LORD,
    teach me your paths;

⁵ guide me in your truth and teach me,
    for you are God my Savior,
  and my hope is in you all day long.
⁶ Remember, O LORD, your great mercy
    and love,
  for they are from of old.
⁷ Remember not the sins of my youth
    and my rebellious ways;
  according to your love remember me,
    for you are good, O LORD.

⁸ Good and upright is the LORD;
    therefore he instructs sinners in
      his ways.
⁹ He guides the humble in what is
    right
  and teaches them his way.
¹⁰ All the ways of the LORD are loving
    and faithful
  for those who keep the demands
    of his covenant.
¹¹ For the sake of your name, O LORD,
    forgive my iniquity, though it is
      great.
¹² Who, then, is the man that fears the
    LORD?
  He will instruct him in the way
    chosen for him.
¹³ He will spend his days in prosperity,
    and his descendants will inherit
      the land.
¹⁴ The LORD confides in those who fear
    him;
  he makes his covenant known to
    them.
¹⁵ My eyes are ever on the LORD,
    for only he will release my feet
      from the snare.

ᵃThis psalm is an acrostic poem, the verses of which begin with the successive letters of the Hebrew alphabet.

PROVERBS 20:13-15
¹³ Do not love sleep or you will grow
    poor;
  stay awake and you will have food
    to spare.

¹⁴ "It's no good, it's no good!" says the
    buyer;
  then off he goes and boasts about
    his purchase.

¹⁵Gold there is, and rubies in
     abundance,
  but lips that speak knowledge are
     a rare jewel.

☐ D A Y   2 1 4

GOD SIGHTINGS

August 2

2 CHRONICLES 32:1–33:13

After all that Hezekiah had so faithfully done, Sennacherib king of Assyria came and invaded Judah. He laid siege to the fortified cities, thinking to conquer them for himself. ²When Hezekiah saw that Sennacherib had come and that he intended to make war on Jerusalem, ³he consulted with his officials and military staff about blocking off the water from the springs outside the city, and they helped him. ⁴A large force of men assembled, and they blocked all the springs and the stream that flowed through the land. "Why should the kings*a* of Assyria come and find plenty of water?" they said. ⁵Then he worked hard repairing all the broken sections of the wall and building towers on it. He built another wall outside that one and reinforced the supporting terraces*b* of the City of David. He also made large numbers of weapons and shields.

⁶He appointed military officers over the people and assembled them before him in the square at the city gate and encouraged them with these words: ⁷"Be strong and courageous. Do not be afraid or discouraged because of the king of Assyria and the vast army with him, for there is a greater power with us than with him. ⁸With him is only the arm of flesh, but with us is the LORD our God to help us and to fight our battles." And the people gained confidence from what Hezekiah the king of Judah said.

⁹Later, when Sennacherib king of Assyria and all his forces were laying siege

to Lachish, he sent his officers to Jerusalem with this message for Hezekiah king of Judah and for all the people of Judah who were there:

¹⁰"This is what Sennacherib king of Assyria says: On what are you basing your confidence, that you remain in Jerusalem under siege? ¹¹When Hezekiah says, 'The LORD our God will save us from the hand of the king of Assyria,' he is misleading you, to let you die of hunger and thirst. ¹²Did not Hezekiah himself remove this god's high places and altars, saying to Judah and Jerusalem, 'You must worship before one altar and burn sacrifices on it'?

¹³"Do you not know what I and my fathers have done to all the peoples of the other lands? Were the gods of those nations ever able to deliver their land from my hand? ¹⁴Who of all the gods of these nations that my fathers destroyed has been able to save his people from me? How then can your god deliver you from my hand? ¹⁵Now do not let Hezekiah deceive you and mislead you like this. Do not believe him, for no god of any nation or kingdom has been able to deliver his people from my hand or the hand of my fathers. How much less will your god deliver you from my hand!"

¹⁶Sennacherib's officers spoke further against the LORD God and against his servant Hezekiah. ¹⁷The king also wrote letters insulting the LORD, the God of Israel, and saying this against him: "Just as the gods of the peoples of the other lands did not rescue their people from my hand, so the god of Hezekiah will not rescue his people from my hand." ¹⁸Then they called out in Hebrew to the people of Jerusalem who were on the wall, to terrify them and make them afraid in order to capture the city. ¹⁹They spoke about the God of Jerusalem as they did about the gods of

the other peoples of the world—the work of men's hands.

20King Hezekiah and the prophet Isaiah son of Amoz cried out in prayer to heaven about this. 21And the LORD sent an angel, who annihilated all the fighting men and the leaders and officers in the camp of the Assyrian king. So he withdrew to his own land in disgrace. And when he went into the temple of his god, some of his sons cut him down with the sword.

22So the LORD saved Hezekiah and the people of Jerusalem from the hand of Sennacherib king of Assyria and from the hand of all others. He took care of them*c* on every side. 23Many brought offerings to Jerusalem for the LORD and valuable gifts for Hezekiah king of Judah. From then on he was highly regarded by all the nations.

24In those days Hezekiah became ill and was at the point of death. He prayed to the LORD, who answered him and gave him a miraculous sign. 25But Hezekiah's heart was proud and he did not respond to the kindness shown him; therefore the LORD's wrath was on him and on Judah and Jerusalem. 26Then Hezekiah repented of the pride of his heart, as did the people of Jerusalem; therefore the LORD's wrath did not come upon them during the days of Hezekiah.

27Hezekiah had very great riches and honor, and he made treasuries for his silver and gold and for his precious stones, spices, shields and all kinds of valuables. 28He also made buildings to store the harvest of grain, new wine and oil; and he made stalls for various kinds of cattle, and pens for the flocks. 29He built villages and acquired great numbers of flocks and herds, for God had given him very great riches.

30It was Hezekiah who blocked the upper outlet of the Gihon spring and channeled the water down to the west side of the City of David. He succeeded in everything he undertook. 31But when envoys were sent by the rulers of Babylon to ask him about the miraculous sign that had occurred in the land, God

left him to test him and to know everything that was in his heart.

32The other events of Hezekiah's reign and his acts of devotion are written in the vision of the prophet Isaiah son of Amoz in the book of the kings of Judah and Israel. 33Hezekiah rested with his fathers and was buried on the hill where the tombs of David's descendants are. All Judah and the people of Jerusalem honored him when he died. And Manasseh his son succeeded him as king.

33:1Manasseh was twelve years old when he became king, and he reigned in Jerusalem fifty-five years. 2He did evil in the eyes of the LORD, following the detestable practices of the nations the LORD had driven out before the Israelites. 3He rebuilt the high places his father Hezekiah had demolished; he also erected altars to the Baals and made Asherah poles. He bowed down to all the starry hosts and worshiped them. 4He built altars in the temple of the LORD, of which the LORD had said, "My Name will remain in Jerusalem forever." 5In both courts of the temple of the LORD, he built altars to all the starry hosts. 6He sacrificed his sons in*d* the fire in the Valley of Ben Hinnom, practiced sorcery, divination and witchcraft, and consulted mediums and spiritists. He did much evil in the eyes of the LORD, provoking him to anger.

7He took the carved image he had made and put it in God's temple, of which God had said to David and to his son Solomon, "In this temple and in Jerusalem, which I have chosen out of all the tribes of Israel, I will put my Name forever. 8I will not again make the feet of the Israelites leave the land I assigned to your forefathers, if only they will be careful to do everything I commanded them concerning all the laws, decrees and ordinances given through Moses." 9But Manasseh led Judah and the people of Jerusalem astray, so that they did more evil than the nations the LORD had destroyed before the Israelites.

10The LORD spoke to Manasseh and

his people, but they paid no attention. [11]So the LORD brought against them the army commanders of the king of Assyria, who took Manasseh prisoner, put a hook in his nose, bound him with bronze shackles and took him to Babylon. [12]In his distress he sought the favor of the LORD his God and humbled himself greatly before the God of his fathers. [13]And when he prayed to him, the LORD was moved by his entreaty and listened to his plea; so he brought him back to Jerusalem and to his kingdom. Then Manasseh knew that the LORD is God.

a4 Hebrew; Septuagint and Syriac *king*   *b5* Or *the Millo*
c22 Hebrew; Septuagint and Vulgate *He gave them rest*
d6 Or *He made his sons pass through*

ROMANS 15:23–16:7

But now that there is no more place for me to work in these regions, and since I have been longing for many years to see you, [24]I plan to do so when I go to Spain. I hope to visit you while passing through and to have you assist me on my journey there, after I have enjoyed your company for a while. [25]Now, however, I am on my way to Jerusalem in the service of the saints there. [26]For Macedonia and Achaia were pleased to make a contribution for the poor among the saints in Jerusalem. [27]They were pleased to do it, and indeed they owe it to them. For if the Gentiles have shared in the Jews' spiritual blessings, they owe it to the Jews to share with them their material blessings. [28]So after I have completed this task and have made sure that they have received this fruit, I will go to Spain and visit you on the way. [29]I know that when I come to you, I will come in the full measure of the blessing of Christ.

[30]I urge you, brothers, by our Lord Jesus Christ and by the love of the Spirit, to join me in my struggle by praying to God for me. [31]Pray that I may be rescued from the unbelievers in Judea and that my service in Jerusalem may be acceptable to the saints there, [32]so that by God's will I may come to you with joy and together with you be refreshed. [33]The God of peace be with you all. Amen.

[16:1]I commend to you our sister Phoebe, a servant*a* of the church in Cenchrea. [2]I ask you to receive her in the Lord in a way worthy of the saints and to give her any help she may need from you, for she has been a great help to many people, including me.

[3]Greet Priscilla*b* and Aquila, my fellow workers in Christ Jesus. [4]They risked their lives for me. Not only I but all the churches of the Gentiles are grateful to them.

[5]Greet also the church that meets at their house.

Greet my dear friend Epenetus, who was the first convert to Christ in the province of Asia.

[6]Greet Mary, who worked very hard for you.

[7]Greet Andronicus and Junias, my relatives who have been in prison with me. They are outstanding among the apostles, and they were in Christ before I was.

a1 Or *deaconess*   *b3* Greek *Prisca*, a variant of *Priscilla*

PSALM 25:16-22

[16]**T**urn [LORD] to me and be gracious to me,
  for I am lonely and afflicted.
[17]The troubles of my heart have multiplied;
  free me from my anguish.
[18]Look upon my affliction and my distress
  and take away all my sins.
[19]See how my enemies have increased
  and how fiercely they hate me!
[20]**Guard my life and rescue me;**
  let me not be put to shame,
  for I take refuge in you.
[21]**May integrity and uprightness protect me,**
  because my hope is in you.

[22]Redeem Israel, O God,
  from all their troubles!

PROVERBS 20:16-18

[16]**T**ake the garment of one who puts up security for a stranger;

hold it in pledge if he does it for a wayward woman.

[17] Food gained by fraud tastes sweet to a man,
but he ends up with a mouth full of gravel.

[18] Make plans by seeking advice;
if you wage war, obtain guidance.

☐ DAY 215

GOD SIGHTINGS

August 3

2 CHRONICLES 33:14–34:33

Afterward he [Manasseh] rebuilt the outer wall of the City of David, west of the Gihon spring in the valley, as far as the entrance of the Fish Gate and encircling the hill of Ophel; he also made it much higher. He stationed military commanders in all the fortified cities in Judah.

[15] He got rid of the foreign gods and removed the image from the temple of the LORD, as well as all the altars he had built on the temple hill and in Jerusalem; and he threw them out of the city. [16] Then he restored the altar of the LORD and sacrificed fellowship offerings[a] and thank offerings on it, and told Judah to serve the LORD, the God of Israel. [17] The people, however, continued to sacrifice at the high places, but only to the LORD their God.

[18] The other events of Manasseh's reign, including his prayer to his God and the words the seers spoke to him in the name of the LORD, the God of Israel, are written in the annals of the kings of Israel.[b] [19] His prayer and how God was moved by his entreaty, as well as all his sins and unfaithfulness, and the sites where he built high places and set up Asherah poles and idols before he humbled himself—all are written in the records of the seers.[c] [20] Manasseh rested

with his fathers and was buried in his palace. And Amon his son succeeded him as king.

[21] Amon was twenty-two years old when he became king, and he reigned in Jerusalem two years. [22] He did evil in the eyes of the LORD, as his father Manasseh had done. Amon worshiped and offered sacrifices to all the idols Manasseh had made. [23] But unlike his father Manasseh, he did not humble himself before the LORD; Amon increased his guilt.

[24] Amon's officials conspired against him and assassinated him in his palace. [25] Then the people of the land killed all who had plotted against King Amon, and they made Josiah his son king in his place.

[34:1] JOSIAH was eight years old when he became king, and he reigned in Jerusalem thirty-one years. [2] He did what was right in the eyes of the LORD and walked in the ways of his father David, not turning aside to the right or to the left.

[3] In the eighth year of his reign, while he was still young, he began to seek the God of his father David. In his twelfth year he began to purge Judah and Jerusalem of high places, Asherah poles, carved idols and cast images. [4] Under his direction the altars of the Baals were torn down; he cut to pieces the incense altars that were above them, and smashed the Asherah poles, the idols and the images. These he broke to pieces and scattered over the graves of those who had sacrificed to them. [5] He burned the bones of the priests on their altars, and so he purged Judah and Jerusalem. [6] In the towns of Manasseh, Ephraim and Simeon, as far as Naphtali, and in the ruins around them, [7] he tore down the altars and the Asherah poles and crushed the idols to powder and cut to pieces all the incense altars throughout Israel. Then he went back to Jerusalem.

[8] In the eighteenth year of Josiah's reign, to purify the land and the temple, he sent Shaphan son of Azaliah and Maaseiah the ruler of the city, with Joah

son of Joahaz, the recorder, to repair the temple of the Lord his God.

⁹They went to Hilkiah the high priest and gave him the money that had been brought into the temple of God, which the Levites who were the doorkeepers had collected from the people of Manasseh, Ephraim and the entire remnant of Israel and from all the people of Judah and Benjamin and the inhabitants of Jerusalem. ¹⁰Then they entrusted it to the men appointed to supervise the work on the Lord's temple. These men paid the workers who repaired and restored the temple. ¹¹They also gave money to the carpenters and builders to purchase dressed stone, and timber for joists and beams for the buildings that the kings of Judah had allowed to fall into ruin.

¹²The men did the work faithfully. Over them to direct them were Jahath and Obadiah, Levites descended from Merari, and Zechariah and Meshullam, descended from Kohath. The Levites—all who were skilled in playing musical instruments— ¹³had charge of the laborers and supervised all the workers from job to job. Some of the Levites were secretaries, scribes and doorkeepers.

¹⁴While they were bringing out the money that had been taken into the temple of the Lord, Hilkiah the priest found the Book of the Law of the Lord that had been given through Moses. ¹⁵Hilkiah said to Shaphan the secretary, "I have found the Book of the Law in the temple of the Lord." He gave it to Shaphan.

¹⁶Then Shaphan took the book to the king and reported to him: "Your officials are doing everything that has been committed to them. ¹⁷They have paid out the money that was in the temple of the Lord and have entrusted it to the supervisors and workers." ¹⁸Then Shaphan the secretary informed the king, "Hilkiah the priest has given me a book." And Shaphan read from it in the presence of the king.

¹⁹When the king heard the words of the Law, he tore his robes. ²⁰He gave these orders to Hilkiah, Ahikam son of

Shaphan, Abdon son of Micah,ᵈ Shaphan the secretary and Asaiah the king's attendant: ²¹"Go and inquire of the Lord for me and for the remnant in Israel and Judah about what is written in this book that has been found. Great is the Lord's anger that is poured out on us because our fathers have not kept the word of the Lord; they have not acted in accordance with all that is written in this book."

²²Hilkiah and those the king had sent with himᵉ went to speak to the prophetess Huldah, who was the wife of Shallum son of Tokhath,ᶠ the son of Hasrah,ᵍ keeper of the wardrobe. She lived in Jerusalem, in the Second District.

²³She said to them, "This is what the Lord, the God of Israel, says: Tell the man who sent you to me, ²⁴'This is what the Lord says: I am going to bring disaster on this place and its people—all the curses written in the book that has been read in the presence of the king of Judah. ²⁵Because they have forsaken me and burned incense to other gods and provoked me to anger by all that their hands have made,ʰ my anger will be poured out on this place and will not be quenched.' ²⁶Tell the king of Judah, who sent you to inquire of the Lord, 'This is what the Lord, the God of Israel, says concerning the words you heard: ²⁷Because your heart was responsive and you humbled yourself before God when you heard what he spoke against this place and its people, and because you humbled yourself before me and tore your robes and wept in my presence, I have heard you, declares the Lord. ²⁸Now I will gather you to your fathers, and you will be buried in peace. Your eyes will not see all the disaster I am going to bring on this place and on those who live here.'"

So they took her answer back to the king.

²⁹Then the king called together all the elders of Judah and Jerusalem. ³⁰He went up to the temple of the Lord with the men of Judah, the people of Jerusalem, the priests and the Levites—all the

people from the least to the greatest. He read in their hearing all the words of the Book of the Covenant, which had been found in the temple of the LORD. ³¹The king stood by his pillar and renewed the covenant in the presence of the LORD—to follow the LORD and keep his commands, regulations and decrees with all his heart and all his soul, and to obey the words of the covenant written in this book.

³²Then he had everyone in Jerusalem and Benjamin pledge themselves to it; the people of Jerusalem did this in accordance with the covenant of God, the God of their fathers.

³³Josiah removed all the detestable idols from all the territory belonging to the Israelites, and he had all who were present in Israel serve the LORD their God. As long as he lived, they did not fail to follow the LORD, the God of their fathers.

a16 Traditionally *peace offerings*   *b18* That is, Judah, as frequently in 2 Chronicles   *c19* One Hebrew manuscript and Septuagint; most Hebrew manuscripts *of Hozai*   *d20* Also called *Acbor son of Micaiah*   *e22* One Hebrew manuscript, Vulgate and Syriac; most Hebrew manuscripts do not have *had sent with him.*   *f22* Also called *Tikvah*   *g22* Also called *Harhas*   *h25* Or by *everything they have done*

ROMANS 16:8-27

⁸ Greet Ampliatus, whom I love in the Lord.

⁹ Greet Urbanus, our fellow worker in Christ, and my dear friend Stachys.

¹⁰ Greet Apelles, tested and approved in Christ.

Greet those who belong to the household of Aristobulus.

¹¹ Greet Herodion, my relative.

Greet those in the household of Narcissus who are in the Lord.

¹² Greet Tryphena and Tryphosa, those women who work hard in the Lord.

Greet my dear friend Persis, another woman who has worked very hard in the Lord.

¹³ Greet Rufus, chosen in the Lord, and his mother, who has been a mother to me, too.

¹⁴ Greet Asyncritus, Phlegon, Hermes, Patrobas, Hermas and the brothers with them.

¹⁵ Greet Philologus, Julia, Nereus and his sister, and Olympas and all the saints with them.

¹⁶ Greet one another with a holy kiss.

All the churches of Christ send greetings.

¹⁷ I urge you, brothers, to watch out for those who cause divisions and put obstacles in your way that are contrary to the teaching you have learned. Keep away from them. ¹⁸For such people are not serving our Lord Christ, but their own appetites. By smooth talk and flattery they deceive the minds of naive people. ¹⁹Everyone has heard about your obedience, so I am full of joy over you; but I want you to be wise about what is good, and innocent about what is evil.

²⁰The God of peace will soon crush Satan under your feet.

The grace of our Lord Jesus be with you.

²¹Timothy, my fellow worker, sends his greetings to you, as do Lucius, Jason and Sosipater, my relatives.

²²I, Tertius, who wrote down this letter, greet you in the Lord.

²³Gaius, whose hospitality I and the whole church here enjoy, sends you his greetings.

Erastus, who is the city's director of public works, and our brother Quartus send you their greetings.*a*

²⁵Now to him who is able to establish you by my gospel and the proclamation of Jesus Christ, according to the revelation of the mystery hidden for long ages past, ²⁶but now revealed and made known through the prophetic writings by the command of the eternal God, so that all nations might believe and obey him— ²⁷to the only wise God be glory forever through Jesus Christ! Amen.

a23 Some manuscripts *their greetings.* ²⁴*May the grace of our Lord Jesus Christ be with all of you. Amen.*

PSALM 26:1-12
Of David.

¹ Vindicate me, O LORD,
    for I have led a blameless life;
I have trusted in the LORD
    without wavering.

2 Test me, O LORD, and try me,
 examine my heart and my mind;
3 for your love is ever before me,
 and I walk continually in your
 truth.
4 I do not sit with deceitful men,
 nor do I consort with hypocrites;
5 I abhor the assembly of evildoers
 and refuse to sit with the wicked.
6 I wash my hands in innocence,
 and go about your altar, O LORD,
7 proclaiming aloud your praise
 and telling of all your wonderful
 deeds.
8 I love the house where you live,
 O LORD,
 the place where your glory dwells.

9 Do not take away my soul along with
 sinners,
 my life with bloodthirsty men,
10 in whose hands are wicked schemes,
 whose right hands are full of
 bribes.
11 But I lead a blameless life;
 redeem me and be merciful to me.

12 My feet stand on level ground;
 in the great assembly I will praise
 the LORD.

PROVERBS 20:19
19 **A** gossip betrays a confidence;
 so avoid a man who talks too
 much.

☐ D A Y 2 1 6

GOD SIGHTINGS

August 4

2 CHRONICLES 35:1–36:23
Josiah celebrated the Passover to the
LORD in Jerusalem, and the Passover
lamb was slaughtered on the fourteenth
day of the first month. 2 He appointed
the priests to their duties and encouraged them in the service of the LORD's
temple. 3 He said to the Levites, who instructed all Israel and who had been
consecrated to the LORD: "Put the sacred
ark in the temple that Solomon son of
David king of Israel built. It is not to be
carried about on your shoulders. Now
serve the LORD your God and his people
Israel. 4 Prepare yourselves by families
in your divisions, according to the directions written by David king of Israel and
by his son Solomon.

5 "Stand in the holy place with a group
of Levites for each subdivision of the
families of your fellow countrymen, the
lay people. 6 Slaughter the Passover
lambs, consecrate yourselves and prepare the lambs for your fellow countrymen, doing what the LORD commanded
through Moses."

7 Josiah provided for all the lay people
who were there a total of thirty thousand sheep and goats for the Passover
offerings, and also three thousand cattle—all from the king's own possessions.

8 His officials also contributed voluntarily to the people and the priests and
Levites. Hilkiah, Zechariah and Jehiel,
the administrators of God's temple, gave
the priests twenty-six hundred Passover
offerings and three hundred cattle.
9 Also Conaniah along with Shemaiah
and Nethanel, his brothers, and Hashabiah, Jeiel and Jozabad, the leaders of
the Levites, provided five thousand
Passover offerings and five hundred
head of cattle for the Levites.

10 The service was arranged and the
priests stood in their places with the Levites in their divisions as the king had
ordered. 11 The Passover lambs were
slaughtered, and the priests sprinkled
the blood handed to them, while the Levites skinned the animals. 12 They set
aside the burnt offerings to give them to
the subdivisions of the families of the
people to offer to the LORD, as is written
in the Book of Moses. They did the same
with the cattle. 13 They roasted the Passover animals over the fire as prescribed,
and boiled the holy offerings in pots,
caldrons and pans and served them
quickly to all the people. 14 After this,

they made preparations for themselves and for the priests, because the priests, the descendants of Aaron, were sacrificing the burnt offerings and the fat portions until nightfall. So the Levites made preparations for themselves and for the Aaronic priests.

15 The musicians, the descendants of Asaph, were in the places prescribed by David, Asaph, Heman and Jeduthun the king's seer. The gatekeepers at each gate did not need to leave their posts, because their fellow Levites made the preparations for them.

16 So at that time the entire service of the LORD was carried out for the celebration of the Passover and the offering of burnt offerings on the altar of the LORD, as King Josiah had ordered. 17 The Israelites who were present celebrated the Passover at that time and observed the Feast of Unleavened Bread for seven days. 18 The Passover had not been observed like this in Israel since the days of the prophet Samuel; and none of the kings of Israel had ever celebrated such a Passover as did Josiah, with the priests, the Levites and all Judah and Israel who were there with the people of Jerusalem. 19 This Passover was celebrated in the eighteenth year of Josiah's reign.

20 After all this, when Josiah had set the temple in order, Neco king of Egypt went up to fight at Carchemish on the Euphrates, and Josiah marched out to meet him in battle. 21 But Neco sent messengers to him, saying, "What quarrel is there between you and me, O king of Judah? It is not you I am attacking at this time, but the house with which I am at war. God has told me to hurry; so stop opposing God, who is with me, or he will destroy you."

22 Josiah, however, would not turn away from him, but disguised himself to engage him in battle. He would not listen to what Neco had said at God's command but went to fight him on the plain of Megiddo.

23 Archers shot King Josiah, and he told his officers, "Take me away; I am badly wounded." 24 So they took him out of his chariot, put him in the other char-iot he had and brought him to Jerusalem, where he died. He was buried in the tombs of his fathers, and all Judah and Jerusalem mourned for him.

25 Jeremiah composed laments for Josiah, and to this day all the men and women singers commemorate Josiah in the laments. These became a tradition in Israel and are written in the Laments.

26 The other events of Josiah's reign and his acts of devotion, according to what is written in the Law of the LORD— 27 all the events, from beginning to end, are written in the book of the kings of Israel and Judah.

36:1 AND the people of the land took Jehoahaz son of Josiah and made him king in Jerusalem in place of his father.

2 Jehoahaz[a] was twenty-three years old when he became king, and he reigned in Jerusalem three months. 3 The king of Egypt dethroned him in Jerusalem and imposed on Judah a levy of a hundred talents[b] of silver and a talent[c] of gold. 4 The king of Egypt made Eliakim, a brother of Jehoahaz, king over Judah and Jerusalem and changed Eliakim's name to Jehoiakim. But Neco took Eliakim's brother Jehoahaz and carried him off to Egypt.

5 Jehoiakim was twenty-five years old when he became king, and he reigned in Jerusalem eleven years. He did evil in the eyes of the LORD his God. 6 Nebuchadnezzar king of Babylon attacked him and bound him with bronze shackles to take him to Babylon. 7 Nebuchadnezzar also took to Babylon articles from the temple of the LORD and put them in his temple[d] there.

8 The other events of Jehoiakim's reign, the detestable things he did and all that was found against him, are written in the book of the kings of Israel and Judah. And Jehoiachin his son succeeded him as king.

9 Jehoiachin was eighteen[e] years old when he became king, and he reigned in Jerusalem three months and ten days. He did evil in the eyes of the LORD. 10 In the spring, King Nebuchadnezzar sent

for him and brought him to Babylon, together with articles of value from the temple of the Lord, and he made Jehoiachin's uncle,[f] Zedekiah, king over Judah and Jerusalem.

[11]Zedekiah was twenty-one years old when he became king, and he reigned in Jerusalem eleven years. [12]He did evil in the eyes of the Lord his God and did not humble himself before Jeremiah the prophet, who spoke the word of the Lord. [13]He also rebelled against King Nebuchadnezzar, who had made him take an oath in God's name. He became stiff-necked and hardened his heart and would not turn to the Lord, the God of Israel. [14]Furthermore, all the leaders of the priests and the people became more and more unfaithful, following all the detestable practices of the nations and defiling the temple of the Lord, which he had consecrated in Jerusalem.

[15]The Lord, the God of their fathers, sent word to them through his messengers again and again, because he had pity on his people and on his dwelling place. [16]But they mocked God's messengers, despised his words and scoffed at his prophets until the wrath of the Lord was aroused against his people and there was no remedy. [17]He brought up against them the king of the Babylonians,[g] who killed their young men with the sword in the sanctuary, and spared neither young man nor young woman, old man or aged. God handed all of them over to Nebuchadnezzar. [18]He carried to Babylon all the articles from the temple of God, both large and small, and the treasures of the Lord's temple and the treasures of the king and his officials. [19]They set fire to God's temple and broke down the wall of Jerusalem; they burned all the palaces and destroyed everything of value there.

[20]He carried into exile to Babylon the remnant, who escaped from the sword, and they became servants to him and his sons until the kingdom of Persia came to power. [21]The land enjoyed its sabbath rests; all the time of its desolation it rested, until the seventy years

were completed in fulfillment of the word of the Lord spoken by Jeremiah.

[22]In the first year of Cyrus king of Persia, in order to fulfill the word of the Lord spoken by Jeremiah, the Lord moved the heart of Cyrus king of Persia to make a proclamation throughout his realm and to put it in writing:

[23]"This is what Cyrus king of Persia says:

"'The Lord, the God of heaven, has given me all the kingdoms of the earth and he has appointed me to build a temple for him at Jerusalem in Judah. Anyone of his people among you—may the Lord his God be with him, and let him go up.'"

[a]2 Hebrew *Joahaz,* a variant of *Jehoahaz*; also in verse 4 [b]3 That is, about 3 3/4 tons (about 3.4 metric tons) [c]3 That is, about 75 pounds (about 34 kilograms) [d]7 Or *palace* [e]9 One Hebrew manuscript, some Septuagint manuscripts and Syriac (see also 2 Kings 24:8); most Hebrew manuscripts *eight* [f]10 Hebrew *brother,* that is, relative (see 2 Kings 24:17) [g]17 Or *Chaldeans*

1 CORINTHIANS 1:1-17

Paul, called to be an apostle of Christ Jesus by the will of God, and our brother Sosthenes,

[2]To the church of God in Corinth, to those sanctified in Christ Jesus and called to be holy, together with all those everywhere who call on the name of our Lord Jesus Christ—their Lord and ours:

[3]Grace and peace to you from God our Father and the Lord Jesus Christ.

[4]I always thank God for you because of his grace given you in Christ Jesus. [5]For in him you have been enriched in every way—in all your speaking and in all your knowledge— [6]because our testimony about Christ was confirmed in you. [7]**Therefore you do not lack any spiritual gift as you eagerly wait for our Lord Jesus Christ to be revealed. [8]He will keep you strong to the end, so that you will be blameless on the day of our Lord Jesus Christ.** [9]God, who has called you into fellowship with his Son Jesus Christ our Lord, is faithful.

[10]I appeal to you, brothers, in the

name of our Lord Jesus Christ, that all of you agree with one another so that there may be no divisions among you and that you may be perfectly united in mind and thought. ¹¹My brothers, some from Chloe's household have informed me that there are quarrels among you. ¹²What I mean is this: One of you says, "I follow Paul"; another, "I follow Apollos"; another, "I follow Cephas*"; still another, "I follow Christ."

¹³Is Christ divided? Was Paul crucified for you? Were you baptized into*b the name of Paul? ¹⁴I am thankful that I did not baptize any of you except Crispus and Gaius, ¹⁵so no one can say that you were baptized into my name. ¹⁶(Yes, I also baptized the household of Stephanas; beyond that, I don't remember if I baptized anyone else.) ¹⁷For Christ did not send me to baptize, but to preach the gospel—not with words of human wisdom, lest the cross of Christ be emptied of its power.

*a12 That is, Peter   *b13 Or in; also in verse 15*

PSALM 27:1-6
Of David.

¹ The Lᴏʀᴅ is my light and my
      salvation—
   whom shall I fear?
 The Lᴏʀᴅ is the stronghold of my
      life—
   of whom shall I be afraid?
² When evil men advance against me
      to devour my flesh,*a
   when my enemies and my foes attack
      me,
   they will stumble and fall.
³ Though an army besiege me,
      my heart will not fear;
   though war break out against me,
      even then will I be confident.

⁴ One thing I ask of the Lᴏʀᴅ,
      this is what I seek:
   that I may dwell in the house of the
      Lᴏʀᴅ
   all the days of my life,
   to gaze upon the beauty of the
      Lᴏʀᴅ
   and to seek him in his temple.

⁵ For in the day of trouble
      he will keep me safe in his
         dwelling;
   he will hide me in the shelter of his
      tabernacle
   and set me high upon a rock.
⁶ Then my head will be exalted
      above the enemies who
         surround me;
   at his tabernacle will I sacrifice with
      shouts of joy;
   I will sing and make music to the
      Lᴏʀᴅ.

a2 Or to slander me

PROVERBS 20:20-21
²⁰ ▌If a man curses his father or mother,
      his lamp will be snuffed out in
         pitch darkness.

²¹ An inheritance quickly gained at the
      beginning
   will not be blessed at the end.

□ D A Y   2 1 7

GOD SIGHTINGS

August 5

EZRA 1:1–2:70

▌In the first year of Cyrus king of Persia, in order to fulfill the word of the Lᴏʀᴅ spoken by Jeremiah, the Lᴏʀᴅ moved the heart of Cyrus king of Persia to make a proclamation throughout his realm and to put it in writing:

² "This is what Cyrus king of Persia says:

" 'The Lᴏʀᴅ, the God of heaven, has given me all the kingdoms of the earth and he has appointed me to build a temple for him at Jerusalem in Judah. ³Anyone of his people among you—may his God be with him, and let him go up to Jerusalem in Judah and build the temple of the Lᴏʀᴅ, the God of Israel, the God who is in Jerusalem. ⁴And the people of any place where survivors may now be living are to provide him with silver and gold, with goods and livestock, and with freewill offerings for the temple of God in Jerusalem.'"

[5] Then the family heads of Judah and Benjamin, and the priests and Levites—everyone whose heart God had moved—prepared to go up and build the house of the LORD in Jerusalem. [6] All their neighbors assisted them with articles of silver and gold, with goods and livestock, and with valuable gifts, in addition to all the freewill offerings. [7] Moreover, King Cyrus brought out the articles belonging to the temple of the LORD, which Nebuchadnezzar had carried away from Jerusalem and had placed in the temple of his god.[a] [8] Cyrus king of Persia had them brought by Mithredath the treasurer, who counted them out to Sheshbazzar the prince of Judah.

[9] This was the inventory:

gold dishes	30
silver dishes	1,000
silver pans[b]	29
[10] gold bowls	30
matching silver bowls	410
other articles	1,000

[11] In all, there were 5,400 articles of gold and of silver. Sheshbazzar brought all these along when the exiles came up from Babylon to Jerusalem.

[2:1] Now these are the people of the province who came up from the captivity of the exiles, whom Nebuchadnezzar king of Babylon had taken captive to Babylon (they returned to Jerusalem and Judah, each to his own town, [2] in company with Zerubbabel, Jeshua, Nehemiah, Seraiah, Reelaiah, Mordecai, Bilshan, Mispar, Bigvai, Rehum and Baanah):

The list of the men of the people of Israel:

[3] the descendants of Parosh	2,172
[4] of Shephatiah	372
[5] of Arah	775
[6] of Pahath-Moab (through the line of Jeshua and Joab)	2,812
[7] of Elam	1,254
[8] of Zattu	945
[9] of Zaccai	760
[10] of Bani	642
[11] of Bebai	623
[12] of Azgad	1,222
[13] of Adonikam	666
[14] of Bigvai	2,056
[15] of Adin	454
[16] of Ater (through Hezekiah)	98
[17] of Bezai	323
[18] of Jorah	112
[19] of Hashum	223
[20] of Gibbar	95
[21] the men of Bethlehem	123
[22] of Netophah	56
[23] of Anathoth	128
[24] of Azmaveth	42
[25] of Kiriath Jearim,[c] Kephirah and Beeroth	743
[26] of Ramah and Geba	621
[27] of Micmash	122
[28] of Bethel and Ai	223
[29] of Nebo	52
[30] of Magbish	156
[31] of the other Elam	1,254
[32] of Harim	320
[33] of Lod, Hadid and Ono	725
[34] of Jericho	345
[35] of Senaah	3,630

[36] The priests:

the descendants of Jedaiah (through the family of Jeshua)	973
[37] of Immer	1,052
[38] of Pashhur	1,247
[39] of Harim	1,017

[40] The Levites:

the descendants of Jeshua and Kadmiel (through the line of Hodaviah)	74

[41] The singers:

the descendants of Asaph	128

42 The gatekeepers of the temple:

the descendants of
   Shallum, Ater, Talmon,
   Akkub, Hatita and Shobai   139

43 The temple servants:

the descendants of
   Ziha, Hasupha, Tabbaoth,
44 Keros, Siaha, Padon,
45 Lebanah, Hagabah, Akkub,
46 Hagab, Shalmai, Hanan,
47 Giddel, Gahar, Reaiah,
48 Rezin, Nekoda, Gazzam,
49 Uzza, Paseah, Besai,
50 Asnah, Meunim, Nephusim,
51 Bakbuk, Hakupha, Harhur,
52 Bazluth, Mehida, Harsha,
53 Barkos, Sisera, Temah,
54 Neziah and Hatipha

55 The descendants of the servants
of Solomon:

the descendants of
   Sotai, Hassophereth, Peruda,
56 Jaala, Darkon, Giddel,
57 Shephatiah, Hattil,
   Pokereth-Hazzebaim
   and Ami

58 The temple servants and
the descendants of the
servants of Solomon   392

59 The following came up from
the towns of Tel Melah, Tel Harsha,
Kerub, Addon and Immer, but they
could not show that their families
were descended from Israel:

60 The descendants of
Delaiah, Tobiah
and Nekoda   652

61 And from among the priests:

The descendants of Hobaiah,
   Hakkoz and Barzillai (a man
   who had married a daughter
   of Barzillai the Gileadite and
   was called by that name).
62 These searched for their family records, but they could not find
them and so were excluded from
the priesthood as unclean. 63 The
governor ordered them not to eat
any of the most sacred food until
there was a priest ministering with
the Urim and Thummim.

64 The whole company num-
bered 42,360, 65 besides their 7,337
menservants and maidservants;
and they also had 200 men and
women singers. 66 They had 736
horses, 245 mules, 67 435 camels
and 6,720 donkeys.

68 When they arrived at the house of
the LORD in Jerusalem, some of the
heads of the families gave freewill offerings toward the rebuilding of the house
of God on its site. 69 According to their
ability they gave to the treasury for this
work 61,000 drachmas^d of gold, 5,000
minas^e of silver and 100 priestly garments.

70 The priests, the Levites, the singers,
the gatekeepers and the temple servants
settled in their own towns, along with
some of the other people, and the rest of
the Israelites settled in their towns.

a7 Or gods   b9 The meaning of the Hebrew for this word
is uncertain.   c25 See Septuagint (see also Neh. 7:29);
Hebrew Kiriath Arim.   d69 That is, about 1,100 pounds
(about 500 kilograms)   e69 That is, about 3 tons (about
2.9 metric tons)

1 CORINTHIANS 1:18–2:5

For the message of the cross is foolishness to those who are perishing,
but to us who are being saved it is the
power of God. 19 For it is written:

"I will destroy the wisdom of the
   wise;
   the intelligence of the intelligent
   I will frustrate."^a

20 Where is the wise man? Where is
the scholar? Where is the philosopher
of this age? Has not God made foolish
the wisdom of the world? 21 For since in
the wisdom of God the world through
its wisdom did not know him, God was
pleased through the foolishness of
what was preached to save those who
believe. 22 Jews demand miraculous
signs and Greeks look for wisdom,

23 but we preach Christ crucified: a stumbling block to Jews and foolishness to Gentiles, 24 but to those whom God has called, both Jews and Greeks, Christ the power of God and the wisdom of God. 25 For the foolishness of God is wiser than man's wisdom, and the weakness of God is stronger than man's strength.

26 Brothers, think of what you were when you were called. Not many of you were wise by human standards; not many were influential; not many were of noble birth. 27 But God chose the foolish things of the world to shame the wise; God chose the weak things of the world to shame the strong. 28 He chose the lowly things of this world and the despised things—and the things that are not—to nullify the things that are, 29 so that no one may boast before him. 30 It is because of him that you are in Christ Jesus, who has become for us wisdom from God—that is, our righteousness, holiness and redemption. 31 Therefore, as it is written: "Let him who boasts boast in the Lord."[b]

2:1 WHEN I came to you, brothers, I did not come with eloquence or superior wisdom as I proclaimed to you the testimony about God.[c] 2 For I resolved to know nothing while I was with you except Jesus Christ and him crucified. 3 I came to you in weakness and fear, and with much trembling. 4 My message and my preaching were not with wise and persuasive words, but with a demonstration of the Spirit's power, 5 so that your faith might not rest on men's wisdom, but on God's power.

a 19 Isaiah 29:14   b 31 Jer. 9:24   c 1 Some manuscripts as I proclaimed to you God's mystery

PSALM 27:7-14

7 **H**ear my voice when I call, O Lord;
   be merciful to me and
      answer me.
8 My heart says of you, "Seek his[a]
      face!"
   Your face, Lord, I will seek.

9 Do not hide your face from me,
   do not turn your servant away in
      anger;
   you have been my helper.
Do not reject me or forsake me,
   O God my Savior.
10 Though my father and mother
      forsake me,
   the Lord will receive me.
11 Teach me your way, O Lord;
   lead me in a straight path
   because of my oppressors.
12 Do not turn me over to the desire of
      my foes,
   for false witnesses rise up
      against me,
   breathing out violence.

13 I am still confident of this:
   I will see the goodness of the Lord
   in the land of the living.
14 Wait for the Lord;
   be strong and take heart
   and wait for the Lord.

a 8 Or To you, O my heart, he has said, "Seek my

PROVERBS 20:22-23

22 **D**o not say, "I'll pay you back for this
      wrong!"
   Wait for the Lord, and he will
      deliver you.

23 The Lord detests differing weights,
   and dishonest scales do not please
      him.

□ DAY 218

GOD SIGHTINGS

August 6

EZRA 3:1–4:24

When the seventh month came and the Israelites had settled in their towns, the people assembled as one man in Jerusalem. 2 Then Jeshua son of Jozadak and his fellow priests and Zerubbabel son of Shealtiel and his associates began to build the altar of the God of Israel to sacrifice burnt offerings on it, in accordance with what is written in the Law of Moses the man of God. ³Despite their fear of the peoples around them, they built the altar on its foundation and sacrificed burnt offerings on it to the Lᴏʀᴅ, both the morning and evening sacrifices. ⁴Then in accordance with what is written, they celebrated the Feast of Tabernacles with the required number of burnt offerings prescribed for each day. ⁵After that, they presented the regular burnt offerings, the New Moon sacrifices and the sacrifices for all the appointed sacred feasts of the Lᴏʀᴅ, as well as those brought as freewill offerings to the Lᴏʀᴅ. ⁶On the first day of the seventh month they began to offer burnt offerings to the Lᴏʀᴅ, though the foundation of the Lᴏʀᴅ's temple had not yet been laid.

⁷Then they gave money to the masons and carpenters, and gave food and drink and oil to the people of Sidon and Tyre, so that they would bring cedar logs by sea from Lebanon to Joppa, as authorized by Cyrus king of Persia.

⁸In the second month of the second year after their arrival at the house of God in Jerusalem, Zerubbabel son of Shealtiel, Jeshua son of Jozadak and the rest of their brothers (the priests and the Levites and all who had returned from the captivity to Jerusalem) began the work, appointing Levites twenty years of age and older to supervise the building of the house of the Lᴏʀᴅ. ⁹Jeshua and his sons and brothers and Kadmiel and his sons (descendants of Hodaviah*ᵃ*) and the sons of Henadad and their sons and brothers—all Levites—joined together in supervising those working on the house of God.

¹⁰When the builders laid the foundation of the temple of the Lᴏʀᴅ, the priests in their vestments and with trumpets, and the Levites (the sons of Asaph) with cymbals, took their places to praise the Lᴏʀᴅ, as prescribed by David king of Israel. ¹¹With praise and thanksgiving they sang to the Lᴏʀᴅ:

"He is good;
    his love to Israel endures forever."

And all the people gave a great shout of praise to the Lᴏʀᴅ, because the foundation of the house of the Lᴏʀᴅ was laid. ¹²But many of the older priests and Levites and family heads, who had seen the former temple, wept aloud when they saw the foundation of this temple being laid, while many others shouted for joy. ¹³No one could distinguish the sound of the shouts of joy from the sound of weeping, because the people made so much noise. And the sound was heard far away.

4:1Wʜᴇɴ the enemies of Judah and Benjamin heard that the exiles were building a temple for the Lᴏʀᴅ, the God of Israel, ²they came to Zerubbabel and to the heads of the families and said, "Let us help you build because, like you, we seek your God and have been sacrificing to him since the time of Esarhaddon king of Assyria, who brought us here."

³But Zerubbabel, Jeshua and the rest of the heads of the families of Israel answered, "You have no part with us in building a temple to our God. We alone will build it for the Lᴏʀᴅ, the God of Israel, as King Cyrus, the king of Persia, commanded us."

⁴Then the peoples around them set out to discourage the people of Judah and make them afraid to go on building.*ᵇ* ⁵They hired counselors to work against them and frustrate their plans during the entire reign of Cyrus king of Persia and down to the reign of Darius king of Persia.

⁶At the beginning of the reign of Xerxes,*ᶜ* they lodged an accusation against the people of Judah and Jerusalem.

⁷And in the days of Artaxerxes king of Persia, Bishlam, Mithredath, Tabeel and the rest of his associates wrote a letter to Artaxerxes. The letter was written in Aramaic script and in the Aramaic language.*ᵈ,ᵉ*

⁸Rehum the commanding officer and Shimshai the secretary wrote a let-

ter against Jerusalem to Artaxerxes the king as follows:

9Rehum the commanding officer and Shimshai the secretary, together with the rest of their associates—the judges and officials over the men from Tripolis, Persia,*f* Erech and Babylon, the Elamites of Susa, 10and the other people whom the great and honorable Ashurbanipal*g* deported and settled in the city of Samaria and elsewhere in Trans-Euphrates.

11(This is a copy of the letter they sent him.)

To King Artaxerxes,

From your servants, the men of Trans-Euphrates:

12The king should know that the Jews who came up to us from you have gone to Jerusalem and are rebuilding that rebellious and wicked city. They are restoring the walls and repairing the foundations. 13Furthermore, the king should know that if this city is built and its walls are restored, no more taxes, tribute or duty will be paid, and the royal revenues will suffer. 14Now since we are under obligation to the palace and it is not proper for us to see the king dishonored, we are sending this message to inform the king, 15so that a search may be made in the archives of your predecessors. In these records you will find that this city is a rebellious city, troublesome to kings and provinces, a place of rebellion from ancient times. That is why this city was destroyed. 16We inform the king that if this city is built and its walls are restored, you will be left with nothing in Trans-Euphrates.

17The king sent this reply:

To Rehum the commanding officer, Shimshai the secretary and the rest of their associates living in Samaria and elsewhere in Trans-Euphrates:

Greetings.

18The letter you sent us has been read and translated in my presence. 19I issued an order and a search was made, and it was found that this city has a long history of revolt against kings and has been a place of rebellion and sedition. 20Jerusalem has had powerful kings ruling over the whole of Trans-Euphrates, and taxes, tribute and duty were paid to them. 21Now issue an order to these men to stop work, so that this city will not be rebuilt until I so order. 22Be careful not to neglect this matter. Why let this threat grow, to the detriment of the royal interests?

23As soon as the copy of the letter of King Artaxerxes was read to Rehum and Shimshai the secretary and their associates, they went immediately to the Jews in Jerusalem and compelled them by force to stop.

24Thus the work on the house of God in Jerusalem came to a standstill until the second year of the reign of Darius king of Persia.

a9 Hebrew *Yehudah,* probably a variant of *Hodaviah*
b4 Or *and troubled them as they built*   *c6* Hebrew *Ahasuerus,*
a variant of Xerxes' Persian name   *d7* Or *written in Aramaic
and translated*   *e7* The text of Ezra 4:8—6:18 is in Aramaic.
f9 Or *officials, magistrates and governors over the men from*
g10 Aramaic *Osnappar,* a variant of *Ashurbanipal*

1 CORINTHIANS 2:6–3:4

We do, however, speak a message of wisdom among the mature, but not the wisdom of this age or of the rulers of this age, who are coming to nothing. 7No, we speak of God's secret wisdom, a wisdom that has been hidden and that God destined for our glory before time began. 8None of the rulers of this age understood it, for if they had, they would not have crucified the Lord of glory. 9However, as it is written:

"No eye has seen,
  no ear has heard,
no mind has conceived
  what God has prepared for those
    who love him"*a*—

10but God has revealed it to us by his Spirit.

The Spirit searches all things, even the deep things of God. 11For who among men knows the thoughts of a man except the man's spirit within him? In the same way no one knows the thoughts of God except the Spirit of God. 12**We have not received the spirit of the world but the Spirit who is from God, that we may understand what God has freely given us.** 13This is what we speak, not in words taught us by human wisdom but in words taught by the Spirit, expressing spiritual truths in spiritual words.*b* 14The man without the Spirit does not accept the things that come from the Spirit of God, for they are foolishness to him, and he cannot understand them, because they are spiritually discerned. 15The spiritual man makes judgments about all things, but he himself is not subject to any man's judgment:

16"For who has known the mind of the Lord
  that he may instruct him?"*c*

But we have the mind of Christ.

3:1BROTHERS, I could not address you as spiritual but as worldly—mere infants in Christ. 2I gave you milk, not solid food, for you were not yet ready for it. Indeed, you are still not ready. 3You are still worldly. For since there is jealousy and quarreling among you, are you not worldly? Are you not acting like mere men? 4For when one says, "I follow Paul," and another, "I follow Apollos," are you not mere men?

a9 Isaiah 64:4   *b13* Or *Spirit, interpreting spiritual truths to spiritual men*   *c16* Isaiah 40:13

PSALM 28:1-9
Of David.

1To you I call, O LORD my Rock;
  do not turn a deaf ear to me.

For if you remain silent,
  I will be like those who have gone
    down to the pit.
2Hear my cry for mercy
  as I call to you for help,
as I lift up my hands
  toward your Most Holy Place.

3Do not drag me away with the wicked,
  with those who do evil,
who speak cordially with their
    neighbors
  but harbor malice in their hearts.
4Repay them for their deeds
  and for their evil work;
repay them for what their hands have
    done
  and bring back upon them what
    they deserve.
5Since they show no regard for the
    works of the LORD
  and what his hands have done,
he will tear them down
  and never build them up again.

6Praise be to the LORD,
  for he has heard my cry for mercy.
7The LORD is my strength and my
    shield;
  my heart trusts in him, and I am
    helped.
My heart leaps for joy
  and I will give thanks to him in
    song.

8The LORD is the strength of his people,
  a fortress of salvation for his
    anointed one.
9Save your people and bless your
    inheritance;
  be their shepherd and carry them
    forever.

PROVERBS 20:24-25
24**A** man's steps are directed by the
    LORD.
  How then can anyone understand
    his own way?
25It is a trap for a man to dedicate
    something rashly
  and only later to consider his
    vows.

☐ DAY 219

August 7

EZRA 5:1–6:22

Now Haggai the prophet and Zechariah the prophet, a descendant of Iddo, prophesied to the Jews in Judah and Jerusalem in the name of the God of Israel, who was over them. ²Then Zerubbabel son of Shealtiel and Jeshua son of Jozadak set to work to rebuild the house of God in Jerusalem. And the prophets of God were with them, helping them.

³At that time Tattenai, governor of Trans-Euphrates, and Shethar-Bozenai and their associates went to them and asked, "Who authorized you to rebuild this temple and restore this structure?" ⁴They also asked, "What are the names of the men constructing this building?"ᵃ ⁵But the eye of their God was watching over the elders of the Jews, and they were not stopped until a report could go to Darius and his written reply be received.

⁶This is a copy of the letter that Tattenai, governor of Trans-Euphrates, and Shethar-Bozenai and their associates, the officials of Trans-Euphrates, sent to King Darius. ⁷The report they sent him read as follows:

To King Darius:

Cordial greetings.

⁸The king should know that we went to the district of Judah, to the temple of the great God. The people are building it with large stones and placing the timbers in the walls. The work is being carried on with diligence and is making rapid progress under their direction.

⁹We questioned the elders and asked them, "Who authorized you to rebuild this temple and restore this structure?" ¹⁰We also asked them their names, so that we could write down the names of their leaders for your information.

¹¹This is the answer they gave us:

"We are the servants of the God of heaven and earth, and we are rebuilding the temple that was built many years ago, one that a great king of Israel built and finished. ¹²But because our fathers angered the God of heaven, he handed them over to Nebuchadnezzar the Chaldean, king of Babylon, who destroyed this temple and deported the people to Babylon.

¹³"However, in the first year of Cyrus king of Babylon, King Cyrus issued a decree to rebuild this house of God. ¹⁴He even removed from the templeᵇ of Babylon the gold and silver articles of the house of God, which Nebuchadnezzar had taken from the temple in Jerusalem and brought to the templeᵇ in Babylon.

"Then King Cyrus gave them to a man named Sheshbazzar, whom he had appointed governor, ¹⁵and he told him, 'Take these articles and go and deposit them in the temple in Jerusalem. And rebuild the house of God on its site.' ¹⁶So this Sheshbazzar came and laid the foundations of the house of God in Jerusalem. From that day to the present it has been under construction but is not yet finished."

¹⁷Now if it pleases the king, let a search be made in the royal archives of Babylon to see if King Cyrus did in fact issue a decree to rebuild this house of God in Jerusalem. Then let the king send us his decision in this matter.

⁶:¹King Darius then issued an order, and they searched in the archives stored in the treasury at Babylon. ²A scroll was found in the citadel of Ecbatana in the province of Media, and this was written on it:

Memorandum:

3In the first year of King Cyrus, the king issued a decree concerning the temple of God in Jerusalem:

Let the temple be rebuilt as a place to present sacrifices, and let its foundations be laid. It is to be ninety feetᶜ high and ninety feet wide, 4with three courses of large stones and one of timbers. The costs are to be paid by the royal treasury. 5Also, the gold and silver articles of the house of God, which Nebuchadnezzar took from the temple in Jerusalem and brought to Babylon, are to be returned to their places in the temple in Jerusalem; they are to be deposited in the house of God.

6Now then, Tattenai, governor of Trans-Euphrates, and Shethar-Bozenai and you, their fellow officials of that province, stay away from there. 7Do not interfere with the work on this temple of God. Let the governor of the Jews and the Jewish elders rebuild this house of God on its site.

8Moreover, I hereby decree what you are to do for these elders of the Jews in the construction of this house of God:

The expenses of these men are to be fully paid out of the royal treasury, from the revenues of Trans-Euphrates, so that the work will not stop. 9Whatever is needed—young bulls, rams, male lambs for burnt offerings to the God of heaven, and wheat, salt, wine and oil, as requested by the priests in Jerusalem—must be given them daily without fail, 10so that they may offer sacrifices pleasing to the God of heaven and pray for the well-being of the king and his sons.

11Furthermore, I decree that if anyone changes this edict, a beam is to be pulled from his house and

he is to be lifted up and impaled on it. And for this crime his house is to be made a pile of rubble. 12May God, who has caused his Name to dwell there, overthrow any king or people who lifts a hand to change this decree or to destroy this temple in Jerusalem.

I Darius have decreed it. Let it be carried out with diligence.

13Then, because of the decree King Darius had sent, Tattenai, governor of Trans-Euphrates, and Shethar-Bozenai and their associates carried it out with diligence. 14So the elders of the Jews continued to build and prosper under the preaching of Haggai the prophet and Zechariah, a descendant of Iddo. They finished building the temple according to the command of the God of Israel and the decrees of Cyrus, Darius and Artaxerxes, kings of Persia. 15The temple was completed on the third day of the month Adar, in the sixth year of the reign of King Darius.

16Then the people of Israel—the priests, the Levites and the rest of the exiles—celebrated the dedication of the house of God with joy. 17For the dedication of this house of God they offered a hundred bulls, two hundred rams, four hundred male lambs and, as a sin offering for all Israel, twelve male goats, one for each of the tribes of Israel. 18And they installed the priests in their divisions and the Levites in their groups for the service of God at Jerusalem, according to what is written in the Book of Moses.

19On the fourteenth day of the first month, the exiles celebrated the Passover. 20The priests and Levites had purified themselves and were all ceremonially clean. The Levites slaughtered the Passover lamb for all the exiles, for their brothers the priests and for themselves. 21So the Israelites who had returned from the exile ate it, together with all who had separated themselves from the unclean practices of their Gentile neighbors in order to seek the LORD, the God of Israel. [22]For seven days they celebrated with joy the Feast of Unleavened Bread, because the Lord had filled them with joy by changing the attitude of the king of Assyria, so that he assisted them in the work on the house of God, the God of Israel.

[a]4 See Septuagint; Aramaic [d]*We told them the names of the men constructing this building*. [b]14 Or *palace* [c]3 Aramaic *sixty cubits* (about 27 meters)

1 CORINTHIANS 3:5-23

What, after all, is Apollos? And what is Paul? Only servants, through whom you came to believe—as the Lord has assigned to each his task. [6]I planted the seed, Apollos watered it, but God made it grow. [7]**So neither he who plants nor he who waters is anything, but only God, who makes things grow.** [8]**The man who plants and the man who waters have one purpose, and each will be rewarded according to his own labor.** [9]For we are God's fellow workers; you are God's field, God's building.

[10]By the grace God has given me, I laid a foundation as an expert builder, and someone else is building on it. But each one should be careful how he builds. [11]For no one can lay any foundation other than the one already laid, which is Jesus Christ. [12]If any man builds on this foundation using gold, silver, costly stones, wood, hay or straw, [13]his work will be shown for what it is, because the Day will bring it to light. It will be revealed with fire, and the fire will test the quality of each man's work. [14]If what he has built survives, he will receive his reward. [15]If it is burned up, he will suffer loss; he himself will be saved, but only as one escaping through the flames.

[16]Don't you know that you yourselves are God's temple and that God's Spirit lives in you? [17]If anyone destroys God's temple, God will destroy him; for God's temple is sacred, and you are that temple.

[18]Do not deceive yourselves. If any one of you thinks he is wise by the standards of this age, he should become a "fool" so that he may become wise. [19]For

the wisdom of this world is foolishness in God's sight. As it is written: "He catches the wise in their craftiness"[a]; [20]and again, "The Lord knows that the thoughts of the wise are futile."[b] [21]So then, no more boasting about men! All things are yours, [22]whether Paul or Apollos or Cephas[c] or the world or life or death or the present or the future—all are yours, [23]and you are of Christ, and Christ is of God.

[a]19 Job 5:13 [b]20 Psalm 94:11 [c]22 That is, Peter

PSALM 29:1-11
A psalm of David.

[1] **A**scribe to the Lord, O mighty ones,
   ascribe to the Lord glory and
      strength.
[2] Ascribe to the Lord the glory due his
      name;
   worship the Lord in the splendor
      of his[a] holiness.

[3] The voice of the Lord is over the
      waters;
   the God of glory thunders,
   the Lord thunders over the mighty
      waters.
[4] The voice of the Lord is powerful;
   the voice of the Lord is majestic.
[5] The voice of the Lord breaks the
      cedars;
   the Lord breaks in pieces the
      cedars of Lebanon.
[6] He makes Lebanon skip like a calf,
   Sirion[b] like a young wild ox.
[7] The voice of the Lord strikes
   with flashes of lightning.
[8] The voice of the Lord shakes the
      desert;
   the Lord shakes the Desert of
      Kadesh.
[9] The voice of the Lord twists the
      oaks[c]
   and strips the forests bare.
   And in his temple all cry, "Glory!"

[10] The Lord sits[d] enthroned over the
      flood;
   the Lord is enthroned as King
      forever.

11 The LORD gives strength to his
people;
the LORD blesses his people with
peace.

a2 Or LORD *with the splendor of*   b6 That is, Mount Hermon
c9 Or LORD *makes the deer give birth*   d10 Or *sat*

PROVERBS 20:26-27

26 **A** wise king winnows out the
wicked;
he drives the threshing wheel over
them.

27 The lamp of the LORD searches the
spirit of a man*a*;
it searches out his inmost being.

a27 Or *The spirit of man is the LORD's lamp*

□ D A Y   2 2 0

GOD SIGHTINGS

August 8

EZRA 7:1–8:20

After these things, during the reign of
Artaxerxes king of Persia, Ezra son of Se-
raiah, the son of Azariah, the son of Hil-
kiah, 2 the son of Shallum, the son of
Zadok, the son of Ahitub, 3 the son of
Amariah, the son of Azariah, the son of
Meraioth, 4 the son of Zerahiah, the son
of Uzzi, the son of Bukki, 5 the son of
Abishua, the son of Phinehas, the son of
Eleazar, the son of Aaron the chief
priest— 6 this Ezra came up from Babylon. He was a teacher well versed in the
Law of Moses, which the LORD, the God of
Israel, had given. The king had granted
him everything he asked, for the hand of
the LORD his God was on him. 7 Some of
the Israelites, including priests, Levites,
singers, gatekeepers and temple servants, also came up to Jerusalem in the
seventh year of King Artaxerxes.

8 Ezra arrived in Jerusalem in the fifth
month of the seventh year of the king.
9 He had begun his journey from Babylon
on the first day of the first month, and he
arrived in Jerusalem on the first day of

the fifth month, for the gracious hand of
his God was on him. 10 For Ezra had devoted himself to the study and observance of the Law of the LORD, and to
teaching its decrees and laws in Israel.

11 This is a copy of the letter King Artaxerxes had given to Ezra the priest and
teacher, a man learned in matters concerning the commands and decrees of
the LORD for Israel:

12a Artaxerxes, king of kings,

To Ezra the priest, a teacher of the
Law of the God of heaven:

Greetings.

13 Now I decree that any of the Israelites in my kingdom, including
priests and Levites, who wish to go
to Jerusalem with you, may go.
14 You are sent by the king and his
seven advisers to inquire about Judah and Jerusalem with regard to
the Law of your God, which is in
your hand. 15 Moreover, you are to
take with you the silver and gold
that the king and his advisers have
freely given to the God of Israel,
whose dwelling is in Jerusalem,
16 together with all the silver and
gold you may obtain from the province of Babylon, as well as the freewill offerings of the people and
priests for the temple of their God
in Jerusalem. 17 With this money be
sure to buy bulls, rams and male
lambs, together with their grain offerings and drink offerings, and
sacrifice them on the altar of the
temple of your God in Jerusalem.
18 You and your brother Jews
may then do whatever seems best
with the rest of the silver and gold,
in accordance with the will of your
God. 19 Deliver to the God of Jerusalem all the articles entrusted to
you for worship in the temple of
your God. 20 And anything else
needed for the temple of your God
that you may have occasion to supply, you may provide from the royal
treasury.

²¹Now I, King Artaxerxes, order all the treasurers of Trans-Euphrates to provide with diligence whatever Ezra the priest, a teacher of the Law of the God of heaven, may ask of you—²²up to a hundred talents*b* of silver, a hundred cors*c* of wheat, a hundred baths*d* of wine, a hundred baths*d* of olive oil, and salt without limit. ²³Whatever the God of heaven has prescribed, let it be done with diligence for the temple of the God of heaven. Why should there be wrath against the realm of the king and of his sons? ²⁴You are also to know that you have no authority to impose taxes, tribute or duty on any of the priests, Levites, singers, gatekeepers, temple servants or other workers at this house of God.

²⁵And you, Ezra, in accordance with the wisdom of your God, which you possess, appoint magistrates and judges to administer justice to all the people of Trans-Euphrates—all who know the laws of your God. And you are to teach any who do not know them. ²⁶Whoever does not obey the law of your God and the law of the king must surely be punished by death, banishment, confiscation of property, or imprisonment.

²⁷Praise be to the LORD, the God of our fathers, who has put it into the king's heart to bring honor to the house of the LORD in Jerusalem in this way ²⁸and who has extended his good favor to me before the king and his advisers and all the king's powerful officials. Because the hand of the LORD my God was on me, I took courage and gathered leading men from Israel to go up with me.

8:1THESE are the family heads and those registered with them who came up with me from Babylon during the reign of King Artaxerxes:

²of the descendants of Phinehas, Gershom;

of the descendants of Ithamar, Daniel;

of the descendants of David, Hattush ³of the descendants of Shecaniah;

of the descendants of Parosh, Zechariah, and with him were registered 150 men;

⁴of the descendants of Pahath-Moab, Eliehoenai son of Zerahiah, and with him 200 men;

⁵of the descendants of Zattu,*e* Shecaniah son of Jahaziel, and with him 300 men;

⁶of the descendants of Adin, Ebed son of Jonathan, and with him 50 men;

⁷of the descendants of Elam, Jeshaiah son of Athaliah, and with him 70 men;

⁸of the descendants of Shephatiah, Zebadiah son of Michael, and with him 80 men;

⁹of the descendants of Joab, Obadiah son of Jehiel, and with him 218 men;

¹⁰of the descendants of Bani,*f* Shelomith son of Josiphiah, and with him 160 men;

¹¹of the descendants of Bebai, Zechariah son of Bebai, and with him 28 men;

¹²of the descendants of Azgad, Johanan son of Hakkatan, and with him 110 men;

¹³of the descendants of Adonikam, the last ones, whose names were Eliphelet, Jeuel and Shemaiah, and with them 60 men;

¹⁴of the descendants of Bigvai, Uthai and Zaccur, and with them 70 men.

¹⁵I assembled them at the canal that flows toward Ahava, and we camped there three days. When I checked among the people and the priests, I found no Levites there. ¹⁶So I summoned Eliezer, Ariel, Shemaiah, Elnathan, Jarib, Elnathan, Nathan, Zechariah

and Meshullam, who were leaders, and Joiarib and Elnathan, who were men of learning, [17]and I sent them to Iddo, the leader in Casiphia. I told them what to say to Iddo and his kinsmen, the temple servants in Casiphia, so that they might bring attendants to us for the house of our God. [18]Because the gracious hand of our God was on us, they brought us Sherebiah, a capable man, from the descendants of Mahli son of Levi, the son of Israel, and Sherebiah's sons and brothers, 18 men; [19]and Hashabiah, together with Jeshaiah from the descendants of Merari, and his brothers and nephews, 20 men. [20]They also brought 220 of the temple servants—a body that David and the officials had established to assist the Levites. All were registered by name.

[a]12 The text of Ezra 7:12-26 is in Aramaic. [b]22 That is, about 3 3/4 tons (about 3.4 metric tons) [c]22 That is, probably about 600 bushels (about 22 kiloliters) [d]22 That is, probably about 600 gallons (about 2.2 kiloliters) [e]5 Some Septuagint manuscripts (also 1 Esdras 8:32); Hebrew does not have Zattu. [f]10 Some Septuagint manuscripts (also 1 Esdras 8:36); Hebrew does not have Bani.

1 CORINTHIANS 4:1-21

So then, men ought to regard us [the apostles] as servants of Christ and as those entrusted with the secret things of God. [2]Now it is required that those who have been given a trust must prove faithful. [3]I care very little if I am judged by you or by any human court; indeed, I do not even judge myself. [4]My conscience is clear, but that does not make me innocent. It is the Lord who judges me. [5]Therefore judge nothing before the appointed time; wait till the Lord comes. He will bring to light what is hidden in darkness and will expose the motives of men's hearts. At that time each will receive his praise from God.

[6]Now, brothers, I have applied these things to myself and Apollos for your benefit, so that you may learn from us the meaning of the saying, "Do not go beyond what is written." Then you will not take pride in one man over against another. [7]For who makes you different from anyone else? What do you have that you did not receive? And if you did receive it, why do you boast as though you did not?

[8]Already you have all you want! Already you have become rich! You have become kings—and that without us! How I wish that you really had become kings so that we might be kings with you! [9]For it seems to me that God has put us apostles on display at the end of the procession, like men condemned to die in the arena. We have been made a spectacle to the whole universe, to angels as well as to men. [10]We are fools for Christ, but you are so wise in Christ! We are weak, but you are strong! You are honored, we are dishonored! [11]To this very hour we go hungry and thirsty, we are in rags, we are brutally treated, we are homeless. [12]We work hard with our own hands. When we are cursed, we bless; when we are persecuted, we endure it; [13]when we are slandered, we answer kindly. Up to this moment we have become the scum of the earth, the refuse of the world.

[14]I am not writing this to shame you, but to warn you, as my dear children. [15]Even though you have ten thousand guardians in Christ, you do not have many fathers, for in Christ Jesus I became your father through the gospel. [16]Therefore I urge you to imitate me. [17]For this reason I am sending to you Timothy, my son whom I love, who is faithful in the Lord. He will remind you of my way of life in Christ Jesus, which agrees with what I teach everywhere in every church.

[18]Some of you have become arrogant, as if I were not coming to you. [19]But I will come to you very soon, if the Lord is willing, and then I will find out not only how these arrogant people are talking, but what power they have. [20]For the kingdom of God is not a matter of talk but of power. [21]What do you prefer? Shall I come to you with a whip, or in love and with a gentle spirit?

PSALM 30:1-12

A psalm. A song. For the dedication of the temple.*a* Of David.

1 I will exalt you, O LORD,
   for you lifted me out of the
      depths
   and did not let my enemies gloat
      over me.
2 O LORD my God, I called to you for
      help
   and you healed me.
3 O LORD, you brought me up from
      the grave*b*;
   you spared me from going down
      into the pit.

4 Sing to the LORD, you saints of his;
   praise his holy name.
5 For his anger lasts only a moment,
   but his favor lasts a lifetime;
   weeping may remain for a night,
   but rejoicing comes in the
      morning.

6 When I felt secure, I said,
   "I will never be shaken."
7 O LORD, when you favored me,
   you made my mountain*c* stand
      firm;
   but when you hid your face,
   I was dismayed.

8 To you, O LORD, I called;
   to the Lord I cried for mercy:
9 "What gain is there in my
      destruction,*d*
   in my going down into the pit?
   Will the dust praise you?
   Will it proclaim your
      faithfulness?
10 Hear, O LORD, and be merciful to me;
    O LORD, be my help."

11 You turned my wailing into dancing;
    you removed my sackcloth and
       clothed me with joy,
12 that my heart may sing to you and
       not be silent.
    O LORD my God, I will give you
       thanks forever.

*aTitle: Or palace   b3 Hebrew Sheol   c7 Or hill country
d9 Or there if I am silenced*

PROVERBS 20:28-30

28 Love and faithfulness keep a king
      safe;
   through love his throne is made
      secure.

29 The glory of young men is their
      strength,
   gray hair the splendor of the old.

30 Blows and wounds cleanse away evil,
   and beatings purge the inmost
      being.

☐ D A Y   2 2 1

GOD SIGHTINGS

August 9

EZRA 8:21–9:15

There, by the Ahava Canal, I [Ezra] proclaimed a fast, so that we [returning Jews] might humble ourselves before our God and ask him for a safe journey for us and our children, with all our possessions. 22I was ashamed to ask the king for soldiers and horsemen to protect us from enemies on the road, because we had told the king, "The gracious hand of our God is on everyone who looks to him, but his great anger is against all who forsake him." 23So we fasted and petitioned our God about this, and he answered our prayer.

24Then I set apart twelve of the leading priests, together with Sherebiah, Hashabiah and ten of their brothers, 25and I weighed out to them the offering of silver and gold and the articles that the king, his advisers, his officials and all Israel present there had donated for the house of our God. 26I weighed out to them 650 talents*a* of silver, silver articles weighing 100 talents,*b* 100 talents*b* of gold, 2720 bowls of gold valued at 1,000 darics,*c* and two fine articles of polished bronze, as precious as gold.

28I said to them, "You as well as these articles are consecrated to the LORD.

The silver and gold are a freewill offering to the LORD, the God of your fathers. ²⁹Guard them carefully until you weigh them out in the chambers of the house of the LORD in Jerusalem before the leading priests and the Levites and the family heads of Israel." ³⁰Then the priests and Levites received the silver and gold and sacred articles that had been weighed out to be taken to the house of our God in Jerusalem.

³¹On the twelfth day of the first month we set out from the Ahava Canal to go to Jerusalem. The hand of our God was on us, and he protected us from enemies and bandits along the way. ³²So we arrived in Jerusalem, where we rested three days.

³³On the fourth day, in the house of our God, we weighed out the silver and gold and the sacred articles into the hands of Meremoth son of Uriah, the priest. Eleazar son of Phinehas was with him, and so were the Levites Jozabad son of Jeshua and Noadiah son of Binnui. ³⁴Everything was accounted for by number and weight, and the entire weight was recorded at that time.

³⁵Then the exiles who had returned from captivity sacrificed burnt offerings to the God of Israel: twelve bulls for all Israel, ninety-six rams, seventy-seven male lambs and, as a sin offering, twelve male goats. All this was a burnt offering to the LORD. ³⁶They also delivered the king's orders to the royal satraps and to the governors of Trans-Euphrates, who then gave assistance to the people and to the house of God.

^{9:1}AFTER these things had been done, the leaders came to me and said, "The people of Israel, including the priests and the Levites, have not kept themselves separate from the neighboring peoples with their detestable practices, like those of the Canaanites, Hittites, Perizzites, Jebusites, Ammonites, Moabites, Egyptians and Amorites. ²They have taken some of their daughters as wives for themselves and their sons, and have mingled the holy race with the

peoples around them. And the leaders and officials have led the way in this unfaithfulness."

³When I heard this, I tore my tunic and cloak, pulled hair from my head and beard and sat down appalled. ⁴Then everyone who trembled at the words of the God of Israel gathered around me because of this unfaithfulness of the exiles. And I sat there appalled until the evening sacrifice.

⁵Then, at the evening sacrifice, I rose from my self-abasement, with my tunic and cloak torn, and fell on my knees with my hands spread out to the LORD my God ⁶and prayed:

"O my God, I am too ashamed and disgraced to lift up my face to you, my God, because our sins are higher than our heads and our guilt has reached to the heavens. ⁷From the days of our forefathers until now, our guilt has been great. Because of our sins, we and our kings and our priests have been subjected to the sword and captivity, to pillage and humiliation at the hand of foreign kings, as it is today.

⁸"But now, for a brief moment, the LORD our God has been gracious in leaving us a remnant and giving us a firm place in his sanctuary, and so our God gives light to our eyes and a little relief in our bondage. ⁹Though we are slaves, our God has not deserted us in our bondage. He has shown us kindness in the sight of the kings of Persia: He has granted us new life to rebuild the house of our God and repair its ruins, and he has given us a wall of protection in Judah and Jerusalem.

¹⁰"But now, O our God, what can we say after this? For we have disregarded the commands ¹¹you gave through your servants the prophets when you said: 'The land you are entering to possess is a land polluted by the corruption of its peoples. By their detestable

practices they have filled it with their impurity from one end to the other. [12]Therefore, do not give your daughters in marriage to their sons or take their daughters for your sons. Do not seek a treaty of friendship with them at any time, that you may be strong and eat the good things of the land and leave it to your children as an everlasting inheritance.'

[13]"What has happened to us is a result of our evil deeds and our great guilt, and yet, our God, you have punished us less than our sins have deserved and have given us a remnant like this. [14]Shall we again break your commands and intermarry with the peoples who commit such detestable practices? Would you not be angry enough with us to destroy us, leaving us no remnant or survivor? [15]O LORD, God of Israel, you are righteous! We are left this day as a remnant. Here we are before you in our guilt, though because of it not one of us can stand in your presence."

[a]26 That is, about 25 tons (about 22 metric tons)   [b]26 That is, about 3 3/4 tons (about 3.4 metric tons)   [c]27 That is, about 19 pounds (about 8.5 kilograms)

1 CORINTHIANS 5:1-13

It is actually reported that there is sexual immorality among you, and of a kind that does not occur even among pagans: A man has his father's wife. [2]And you are proud! Shouldn't you rather have been filled with grief and have put out of your fellowship the man who did this? [3]Even though I am not physically present, I am with you in spirit. And I have already passed judgment on the one who did this, just as if I were present. [4]When you are assembled in the name of our Lord Jesus and I am with you in spirit, and the power of our Lord Jesus is present, [5]hand this man over to Satan, so that the sinful nature[a] may be destroyed and his spirit saved on the day of the Lord.

[6]Your boasting is not good. Don't you

know that a little yeast works through the whole batch of dough? [7]Get rid of the old yeast that you may be a new batch without yeast—as you really are. For Christ, our Passover lamb, has been sacrificed. [8]Therefore let us keep the Festival, not with the old yeast, the yeast of malice and wickedness, but with bread without yeast, the bread of sincerity and truth.

[9]I have written you in my letter not to associate with sexually immoral people— [10]not at all meaning the people of this world who are immoral, or the greedy and swindlers, or idolaters. In that case you would have to leave this world. [11]But now I am writing you that you must not associate with anyone who calls himself a brother but is sexually immoral or greedy, an idolater or a slanderer, a drunkard or a swindler. With such a man do not even eat.

[12]**What business is it of mine to judge those outside the church? Are you not to judge those inside? [13]God will judge those outside. "Expel the wicked man from among you."[b]**

[a]5 Or that his body; or that the flesh   [b]13 Deut. 17:7; 19:19; 21:21; 22:21,24; 24:7

PSALM 31:1-8
For the director of music. A psalm of David.

[1]In you, O LORD, I have taken refuge;
    let me never be put to shame;
    deliver me in your righteousness.
[2]Turn your ear to me,
    come quickly to my rescue;
be my rock of refuge,
    a strong fortress to save me.
[3]Since you are my rock and my
        fortress,
    for the sake of your name lead and
        guide me.
[4]Free me from the trap that is set
        for me,
    for you are my refuge.
[5]Into your hands I commit my spirit;
    redeem me, O LORD, the God of
        truth.
[6]I hate those who cling to worthless
        idols;

I trust in the LORD.

7 I will be glad and rejoice in your love,
for you saw my affliction
and knew the anguish of my soul.

8 You have not handed me over to the
enemy
but have set my feet in a spacious
place.

PROVERBS 21:1-2

The king's heart is in the hand of the
LORD;
he directs it like a watercourse
wherever he pleases.

2 All a man's ways seem right to him,
but the LORD weighs the heart.

☐ D A Y   2 2 2

GOD SIGHTINGS

August 10

EZRA 10:1-44

While Ezra was praying and confessing, weeping and throwing himself down before the house of God, a large crowd of Israelites—men, women and children—gathered around him. They too wept bitterly. 2 Then Shecaniah son of Jehiel, one of the descendants of Elam, said to Ezra, "We have been unfaithful to our God by marrying foreign women from the peoples around us. But in spite of this, there is still hope for Israel. 3 Now let us make a covenant before our God to send away all these women and their children, in accordance with the counsel of my lord and of those who fear the commands of our God. Let it be done according to the Law. 4 Rise up; this matter is in your hands. We will support you, so take courage and do it."

5 So Ezra rose up and put the leading priests and Levites and all Israel under oath to do what had been suggested. And they took the oath. 6 Then Ezra withdrew from before the house of God

and went to the room of Jehohanan son of Eliashib. While he was there, he ate no food and drank no water, because he continued to mourn over the unfaithfulness of the exiles.

7 A proclamation was then issued throughout Judah and Jerusalem for all the exiles to assemble in Jerusalem. 8 Anyone who failed to appear within three days would forfeit all his property, in accordance with the decision of the officials and elders, and would himself be expelled from the assembly of the exiles.

9 Within the three days, all the men of Judah and Benjamin had gathered in Jerusalem. And on the twentieth day of the ninth month, all the people were sitting in the square before the house of God, greatly distressed by the occasion and because of the rain. 10 Then Ezra the priest stood up and said to them, "You have been unfaithful; you have married foreign women, adding to Israel's guilt. 11 Now make confession to the LORD, the God of your fathers, and do his will. Separate yourselves from the peoples around you and from your foreign wives."

12 The whole assembly responded with a loud voice: "You are right! We must do as you say. 13 But there are many people here and it is the rainy season; so we cannot stand outside. Besides, this matter cannot be taken care of in a day or two, because we have sinned greatly in this thing. 14 Let our officials act for the whole assembly. Then let everyone in our towns who has married a foreign woman come at a set time, along with the elders and judges of each town, until the fierce anger of our God in this matter is turned away from us." 15 Only Jonathan son of Asahel and Jahzeiah son of Tikvah, supported by Meshullam and Shabbethai the Levite, opposed this.

16 So the exiles did as was proposed. Ezra the priest selected men who were family heads, one from each family division, and all of them designated by

name. On the first day of the tenth month they sat down to investigate the cases, [17] and by the first day of the first month they finished dealing with all the men who had married foreign women.

[18] Among the descendants of the priests, the following had married foreign women:

From the descendants of Jeshua son of Jozadak, and his brothers: Maaseiah, Eliezer, Jarib and Gedaliah. [19] (They all gave their hands in pledge to put away their wives, and for their guilt they each presented a ram from the flock as a guilt offering.)

[20] From the descendants of Immer: Hanani and Zebadiah.

[21] From the descendants of Harim: Maaseiah, Elijah, Shemaiah, Jehiel and Uzziah.

[22] From the descendants of Pashhur: Elioenai, Maaseiah, Ishmael, Nethanel, Jozabad and Elasah.

[23] Among the Levites:

Jozabad, Shimei, Kelaiah (that is, Kelita), Pethahiah, Judah and Eliezer.

[24] From the singers: Eliashib.

From the gatekeepers: Shallum, Telem and Uri.

[25] And among the other Israelites:

From the descendants of Parosh: Ramiah, Izziah, Malkijah, Mijamin, Eleazar, Malkijah and Benaiah.

[26] From the descendants of Elam: Mattaniah, Zechariah, Jehiel, Abdi, Jeremoth and Elijah.

[27] From the descendants of Zattu: Elioenai, Eliashib, Mattaniah, Jeremoth, Zabad and Aziza.

[28] From the descendants of Bebai: Jehohanan, Hananiah, Zabbai and Athlai.

[29] From the descendants of Bani: Meshullam, Malluch, Adaiah, Jashub, Sheal and Jeremoth.

[30] From the descendants of Pahath-Moab: Adna, Kelal, Benaiah, Maaseiah, Mattaniah, Bezalel, Binnui and Manasseh.

[31] From the descendants of Harim: Eliezer, Ishijah, Malkijah, Shemaiah, Shimeon, [32] Benjamin, Malluch and Shemariah.

[33] From the descendants of Hashum: Mattenai, Mattattah, Zabad, Eliphelet, Jeremai, Manasseh and Shimei.

[34] From the descendants of Bani: Maadai, Amram, Uel, [35] Benaiah, Bedeiah, Keluhi, [36] Vaniah, Meremoth, Eliashib, [37] Mattaniah, Mattenai and Jaasu.

[38] From the descendants of Binnui:[a] Shimei, [39] Shelemiah, Nathan, Adaiah, [40] Macnadebai, Shashai, Sharai, [41] Azarel, Shelemiah, Shemariah, [42] Shallum, Amariah and Joseph.

[43] From the descendants of Nebo: Jeiel, Mattithiah, Zabad, Zebina, Jaddai, Joel and Benaiah.

[44] All these had married foreign women, and some of them had children by these wives.[b]

[a] 37,38 See Septuagint (also 1 Esdras 9:34); Hebrew Jaasu [38] and Bani and Binnui.   [b] 44 Or and they sent them away with their children

1 CORINTHIANS 6:1-20

If any of you has a dispute with another, dare he take it before the ungodly for judgment instead of before the saints? [2] Do you not know that the saints will judge the world? And if you are to judge the world, are you not competent to judge trivial cases? [3] Do you not know that we will judge angels? How much more the things of this life! [4] Therefore, if you have disputes about such matters, appoint as judges even men of little account in the church![a] [5] I say this to shame you. Is it possible that there is nobody among you wise enough to judge a dispute between believers? 6But instead, one brother goes to law against another—and this in front of unbelievers!

7The very fact that you have lawsuits among you means you have been completely defeated already. Why not rather be wronged? Why not rather be cheated? 8Instead, you yourselves cheat and do wrong, and you do this to your brothers.

9Do you not know that the wicked will not inherit the kingdom of God? Do not be deceived: Neither the sexually immoral nor idolaters nor adulterers nor male prostitutes nor homosexual offenders 10nor thieves nor the greedy nor drunkards nor slanderers nor swindlers will inherit the kingdom of God. 11And that is what some of you were. But you were washed, you were sanctified, you were justified in the name of the Lord Jesus Christ and by the Spirit of our God.

12"Everything is permissible for me"—but not everything is beneficial. "Everything is permissible for me"—but I will not be mastered by anything. 13"Food for the stomach and the stomach for food"—but God will destroy them both. The body is not meant for sexual immorality, but for the Lord, and the Lord for the body. 14By his power God raised the Lord from the dead, and he will raise us also. 15Do you not know that your bodies are members of Christ himself? Shall I then take the members of Christ and unite them with a prostitute? Never! 16Do you not know that he who unites himself with a prostitute is one with her in body? For it is said, "The two will become one flesh."b 17But he who unites himself with the Lord is one with him in spirit.

18Flee from sexual immorality. All other sins a man commits are outside his body, but he who sins sexually sins against his own body. 19**Do you not know that your body is a temple of the Holy Spirit, who is in you, whom you have received from God? You are not your own;** 20**you were bought at a price. Therefore honor God with your body.**

a4 Or matters, do you appoint as judges men of little account in the church?   b16 Gen. 2:24

PSALM 31:9-18

9 **Be** merciful to me, O Lord, for I am in distress;
my eyes grow weak with sorrow,
my soul and my body with grief.
10 My life is consumed by anguish
and my years by groaning;
my strength fails because of my affliction,a
and my bones grow weak.
11 Because of all my enemies,
I am the utter contempt of my neighbors;
I am a dread to my friends—
those who see me on the street flee from me.
12 I am forgotten by them as though I were dead;
I have become like broken pottery.
13 For I hear the slander of many;
there is terror on every side;
they conspire against me
and plot to take my life.

14 But I trust in you, O Lord;
I say, "You are my God."
15 My times are in your hands;
deliver me from my enemies
and from those who pursue me.
16 Let your face shine on your servant;
save me in your unfailing love.
17 Let me not be put to shame, O Lord,
for I have cried out to you;
but let the wicked be put to shame
and lie silent in the grave.b
18 Let their lying lips be silenced,
for with pride and contempt
they speak arrogantly against the righteous.

a10 Or guilt   b17 Hebrew Sheol

PROVERBS 21:3

3 **To** do what is right and just
is more acceptable to the Lord
than sacrifice.

GOD SIGHTINGS

August 11

NEHEMIAH 1:1–3:14

The words of Nehemiah son of Haca-liah:

In the month of Kislev in the twenti-eth year, while I was in the citadel of Susa, ²Hanani, one of my brothers, came from Judah with some other men, and I questioned them about the Jewish rem-nant that survived the exile, and also about Jerusalem.

³They said to me, "Those who sur-vived the exile and are back in the prov-ince are in great trouble and disgrace. The wall of Jerusalem is broken down, and its gates have been burned with fire."

⁴When I heard these things, I sat down and wept. For some days I mourned and fasted and prayed before the God of heaven. ⁵Then I said:

"O Lord, God of heaven, the great and awesome God, who keeps his covenant of love with those who love him and obey his commands, ⁶let your ear be atten-tive and your eyes open to hear the prayer your servant is praying be-fore you day and night for your ser-vants, the people of Israel. I confess the sins we Israelites, in-cluding myself and my father's house, have committed against you. ⁷We have acted very wickedly toward you. We have not obeyed the commands, decrees and laws you gave your servant Moses.

⁸"Remember the instruction you gave your servant Moses, saying, 'If you are unfaithful, I will scatter you among the nations, ⁹but if you re-turn to me and obey my com-mands, then even if your exiled people are at the farthest horizon, I will gather them from there and bring them to the place I have cho-sen as a dwelling for my Name.'

¹⁰"They are your servants and your people, whom you redeemed by your great strength and your mighty hand. ¹¹O Lord, let your ear be attentive to the prayer of this your servant and to the prayer of your servants who delight in rever-ing your name. Give your servant success today by granting him fa-vor in the presence of this man."

I was cupbearer to the king.

²:¹In the month of Nisan in the twenti-eth year of King Artaxerxes, when wine was brought for him, I took the wine and gave it to the king. I had not been sad in his presence before; ²so the king asked me, "Why does your face look so sad when you are not ill? This can be noth-ing but sadness of heart."

I was very much afraid, ³but I said to the king, "May the king live forever! Why should my face not look sad when the city where my fathers are buried lies in ruins, and its gates have been de-stroyed by fire?"

⁴The king said to me, "What is it you want?"

Then I prayed to the God of heaven, ⁵and I answered the king, "If it pleases the king and if your servant has found favor in his sight, let him send me to the city in Judah where my fathers are bur-ied so that I can rebuild it."

⁶Then the king, with the queen sit-ting beside him, asked me, "How long will your journey take, and when will you get back?" It pleased the king to send me; so I set a time.

⁷I also said to him, "If it pleases the king, may I have letters to the governors of Trans-Euphrates, so that they will provide me safe-conduct until I arrive in Judah? ⁸And may I have a letter to Asaph, keeper of the king's forest, so he will give me timber to make beams for the gates of the citadel by the temple and for the city wall and for the resi-dence I will occupy?" And because the gracious hand of my God was upon me,

the king granted my requests. ⁹So I went to the governors of Trans-Euphrates and gave them the king's letters. The king had also sent army officers and cavalry with me.

¹⁰When Sanballat the Horonite and Tobiah the Ammonite official heard about this, they were very much disturbed that someone had come to promote the welfare of the Israelites.

¹¹I went to Jerusalem, and after staying there three days ¹²I set out during the night with a few men. I had not told anyone what my God had put in my heart to do for Jerusalem. There were no mounts with me except the one I was riding on.

¹³By night I went out through the Valley Gate toward the Jackalᵃ Well and the Dung Gate, examining the walls of Jerusalem, which had been broken down, and its gates, which had been destroyed by fire. ¹⁴Then I moved on toward the Fountain Gate and the King's Pool, but there was not enough room for my mount to get through; ¹⁵so I went up the valley by night, examining the wall. Finally, I turned back and reentered through the Valley Gate. ¹⁶The officials did not know where I had gone or what I was doing, because as yet I had said nothing to the Jews or the priests or nobles or officials or any others who would be doing the work.

¹⁷Then I said to them, "You see the trouble we are in: Jerusalem lies in ruins, and its gates have been burned with fire. Come, let us rebuild the wall of Jerusalem, and we will no longer be in disgrace." ¹⁸I also told them about the gracious hand of my God upon me and what the king had said to me.

They replied, "Let us start rebuilding." So they began this good work.

¹⁹But when Sanballat the Horonite, Tobiah the Ammonite official and Geshem the Arab heard about it, they mocked and ridiculed us. "What is this you are doing?" they asked. "Are you rebelling against the king?"

²⁰I answered them by saying, "The God of heaven will give us success. We his servants will start rebuilding, but as for you, you have no share in Jerusalem or any claim or historic right to it."

3:1ELIASHIB the high priest and his fellow priests went to work and rebuilt the Sheep Gate. They dedicated it and set its doors in place, building as far as the Tower of the Hundred, which they dedicated, and as far as the Tower of Hananel. ²The men of Jericho built the adjoining section, and Zaccur son of Imri built next to them.

³The Fish Gate was rebuilt by the sons of Hassenaah. They laid its beams and put its doors and bolts and bars in place. ⁴Meremoth son of Uriah, the son of Hakkoz, repaired the next section. Next to him Meshullam son of Berekiah, the son of Meshezabel, made repairs, and next to him Zadok son of Baana also made repairs. ⁵The next section was repaired by the men of Tekoa, but their nobles would not put their shoulders to the work under their supervisors.ᵇ

⁶The Jeshanahᶜ Gate was repaired by Joiada son of Paseah and Meshullam son of Besodeiah. They laid its beams and put its doors and bolts and bars in place. ⁷Next to them, repairs were made by men from Gibeon and Mizpah—Melatiah of Gibeon and Jadon of Meronoth—places under the authority of the governor of Trans-Euphrates. ⁸Uzziel son of Harhaiah, one of the goldsmiths, repaired the next section; and Hananiah, one of the perfume-makers, made repairs next to that. They restoredᵈ Jerusalem as far as the Broad Wall. ⁹Rephaiah son of Hur, ruler of a half-district of Jerusalem, repaired the next section. ¹⁰Adjoining this, Jedaiah son of Harumaph made repairs opposite his house, and Hattush son of Hashabneiah made repairs next to him. ¹¹Malkijah son of Harim and Hasshub son of Pahath-Moab repaired another section and the Tower of the Ovens. ¹²Shallum son of Hallohesh, ruler of a half-district of

Jerusalem, repaired the next section with the help of his daughters.

¹³The Valley Gate was repaired by Hanun and the residents of Zanoah. They rebuilt it and put its doors and bolts and bars in place. They also repaired five hundred yards^e of the wall as far as the Dung Gate.

¹⁴The Dung Gate was repaired by Malkijah son of Recab, ruler of the district of Beth Hakkerem. He rebuilt it and put its doors and bolts and bars in place.

a13 Or *Serpent* or *Fig*   *b5* Or *their Lord* or *the governor*   *c6* Or *Old*   *d8* Or *They left out part of*   *e13* Hebrew *a thousand cubits* (about 450 meters)

1 CORINTHIANS 7:1-24

Now for the matters you wrote about: It is good for a man not to marry.^a ²But since there is so much immorality, each man should have his own wife, and each woman her own husband. ³The husband should fulfill his marital duty to his wife, and likewise the wife to her husband. ⁴The wife's body does not belong to her alone but also to her husband. In the same way, the husband's body does not belong to him alone but also to his wife. ⁵Do not deprive each other except by mutual consent and for a time, so that you may devote yourselves to prayer. Then come together again so that Satan will not tempt you because of your lack of self-control. ⁶I say this as a concession, not as a command. ⁷I wish that all men were as I am. But each man has his own gift from God; one has this gift, another has that.

⁸Now to the unmarried and the widows I say: It is good for them to stay unmarried, as I am. ⁹But if they cannot control themselves, they should marry, for it is better to marry than to burn with passion.

¹⁰To the married I give this command (not I, but the Lord): A wife must not separate from her husband. ¹¹But if she does, she must remain unmarried or else be reconciled to her husband. And a husband must not divorce his wife.

¹²To the rest I say this (I, not the Lord): If any brother has a wife who is not a believer and she is willing to live with him, he must not divorce her. ¹³And if a woman has a husband who is not a believer and he is willing to live with her, she must not divorce him. ¹⁴For the unbelieving husband has been sanctified through his wife, and the unbelieving wife has been sanctified through her believing husband. Otherwise your children would be unclean, but as it is, they are holy.

¹⁵But if the unbeliever leaves, let him do so. A believing man or woman is not bound in such circumstances; God has called us to live in peace. ¹⁶How do you know, wife, whether you will save your husband? Or, how do you know, husband, whether you will save your wife?

¹⁷Nevertheless, each one should retain the place in life that the Lord assigned to him and to which God has called him. This is the rule I lay down in all the churches. ¹⁸Was a man already circumcised when he was called? He should not become uncircumcised. Was a man uncircumcised when he was called? He should not be circumcised. ¹⁹Circumcision is nothing and uncircumcision is nothing. Keeping God's commands is what counts. ²⁰Each one should remain in the situation which he was in when God called him. ²¹Were you a slave when you were called? Don't let it trouble you—although if you can gain your freedom, do so. ²²For he who was a slave when he was called by the Lord is the Lord's freedman; similarly, he who was a free man when he was called is Christ's slave. ²³You were bought at a price; do not become slaves of men. ²⁴Brothers, each man, as responsible to God, should remain in the situation God called him to.

a1 Or *"It is good for a man not to have sexual relations with a woman."*

PSALM 31:19-24

¹⁹**H**ow great is your [the LORD's] goodness,
    which you have stored up for
        those who fear you,

which you bestow in the sight of
men
on those who take refuge in you.
20 In the shelter of your presence you
hide them
from the intrigues of men;
in your dwelling you keep them safe
from accusing tongues.

21 Praise be to the LORD,
for he showed his wonderful love
to me
when I was in a besieged city.
22 In my alarm I said,
"I am cut off from your sight!"
Yet you heard my cry for mercy
when I called to you for help.

23 Love the LORD, all his saints!
The LORD preserves the faithful,
but the proud he pays back in
full.
24 Be strong and take heart,
all you who hope in the LORD.

PROVERBS 21:4
4 Haughty eyes and a proud heart,
the lamp of the wicked, are sin!

□ DAY 224

GOD SIGHTINGS

August 12

NEHEMIAH 3:15–5:13
The Fountain Gate was repaired by
Shallun son of Col-Hozeh, ruler of the
district of Mizpah. He rebuilt it, roofing
it over and putting its doors and bolts
and bars in place. He also repaired the
wall of the Pool of Siloam,*a* by the King's
Garden, as far as the steps going down
from the City of David. 16 Beyond him,
Nehemiah son of Azbuk, ruler of a half-
district of Beth Zur, made repairs up to a
point opposite the tombs*b* of David, as
far as the artificial pool and the House
of the Heroes.
    17 Next to him, the repairs were made

by the Levites under Rehum son of Bani.
Beside him, Hashabiah, ruler of half the
district of Keilah, carried out repairs for
his district. 18 Next to him, the repairs
were made by their countrymen under
Binnui*c* son of Henadad, ruler of the
other half-district of Keilah. 19 Next to
him, Ezer son of Jeshua, ruler of Mizpah,
repaired another section, from a point
facing the ascent to the armory as far as
the angle. 20 Next to him, Baruch son of
Zabbai zealously repaired another section, from the angle to the entrance of
the house of Eliashib the high priest.
21 Next to him, Meremoth son of Uriah,
the son of Hakkoz, repaired another
section, from the entrance of Eliashib's
house to the end of it.
    22 The repairs next to him were made
by the priests from the surrounding region. 23 Beyond them, Benjamin and
Hasshub made repairs in front of their
house; and next to them, Azariah son of
Maaseiah, the son of Ananiah, made repairs beside his house. 24 Next to him,
Binnui son of Henadad repaired another section, from Azariah's house to
the angle and the corner, 25 and Palal son
of Uzai worked opposite the angle and
the tower projecting from the upper
palace near the court of the guard. Next
to him, Pedaiah son of Parosh 26 and the
temple servants living on the hill of
Ophel made repairs up to a point opposite the Water Gate toward the east and
the projecting tower. 27 Next to them,
the men of Tekoa repaired another section, from the great projecting tower to
the wall of Ophel.

    28 Above the Horse Gate, the priests
made repairs, each in front of his own
house. 29 Next to them, Zadok son of Immer made repairs opposite his house.
Next to him, Shemaiah son of Shecaniah, the guard at the East Gate, made
repairs. 30 Next to him, Hananiah son of
Shelemiah, and Hanun, the sixth son of
Zalaph, repaired another section. Next
to them, Meshullam son of Berekiah
made repairs opposite his living quarters. 31 Next to him, Malkijah, one of the

goldsmiths, made repairs as far as the house of the temple servants and the merchants, opposite the Inspection Gate, and as far as the room above the corner; 32 and between the room above the corner and the Sheep Gate the goldsmiths and merchants made repairs.

4:1 WHEN Sanballat heard that we were rebuilding the wall, he became angry and was greatly incensed. He ridiculed the Jews, 2 and in the presence of his associates and the army of Samaria, he said, "What are those feeble Jews doing? Will they restore their wall? Will they offer sacrifices? Will they finish in a day? Can they bring the stones back to life from those heaps of rubble—burned as they are?"

3 Tobiah the Ammonite, who was at his side, said, "What they are building—if even a fox climbed up on it, he would break down their wall of stones!"

4 Hear us, O our God, for we are despised. Turn their insults back on their own heads. Give them over as plunder in a land of captivity. 5 Do not cover up their guilt or blot out their sins from your sight, for they have thrown insults in the face of*d* the builders.

6 So we rebuilt the wall till all of it reached half its height, for the people worked with all their heart.

7 But when Sanballat, Tobiah, the Arabs, the Ammonites and the men of Ashdod heard that the repairs to Jerusalem's walls had gone ahead and that the gaps were being closed, they were very angry. 8 They all plotted together to come and fight against Jerusalem and stir up trouble against it. 9 But we prayed to our God and posted a guard day and night to meet this threat.

10 Meanwhile, the people in Judah said, "The strength of the laborers is giving out, and there is so much rubble that we cannot rebuild the wall."

11 Also our enemies said, "Before they know it or see us, we will be right there among them and will kill them and put an end to the work."

12 Then the Jews who lived near them came and told us ten times over, "Wherever you turn, they will attack us."

13 Therefore I stationed some of the people behind the lowest points of the wall at the exposed places, posting them by families, with their swords, spears and bows. 14 After I looked things over, I stood up and said to the nobles, the officials and the rest of the people, "Don't be afraid of them. Remember the Lord, who is great and awesome, and fight for your brothers, your sons and your daughters, your wives and your homes."

15 When our enemies heard that we were aware of their plot and that God had frustrated it, we all returned to the wall, each to his own work.

16 From that day on, half of my men did the work, while the other half were equipped with spears, shields, bows and armor. The officers posted themselves behind all the people of Judah 17 who were building the wall. Those who carried materials did their work with one hand and held a weapon in the other, 18 and each of the builders wore his sword at his side as he worked. But the man who sounded the trumpet stayed with me.

19 Then I said to the nobles, the officials and the rest of the people, "The work is extensive and spread out, and we are widely separated from each other along the wall. 20 Wherever you hear the sound of the trumpet, join us there. Our God will fight for us!"

21 So we continued the work with half the men holding spears, from the first light of dawn till the stars came out. 22 At that time I also said to the people, "Have every man and his helper stay inside Jerusalem at night, so they can serve us as guards by night and workmen by day." 23 Neither I nor my brothers nor my men nor the guards with me took off our clothes; each had his weapon, even when he went for water.*e*

5:1 Now the men and their wives raised a great outcry against their Jewish brothers. [2] Some were saying, "We and our sons and daughters are numerous; in order for us to eat and stay alive, we must get grain."

[3] Others were saying, "We are mortgaging our fields, our vineyards and our homes to get grain during the famine."

[4] Still others were saying, "We have had to borrow money to pay the king's tax on our fields and vineyards. [5] Although we are of the same flesh and blood as our countrymen and though our sons are as good as theirs, yet we have to subject our sons and daughters to slavery. Some of our daughters have already been enslaved, but we are powerless, because our fields and our vineyards belong to others."

[6] When I heard their outcry and these charges, I was very angry. [7] I pondered them in my mind and then accused the nobles and officials. I told them, "You are exacting usury from your own countrymen!" So I called together a large meeting to deal with them [8] and said: "As far as possible, we have bought back our Jewish brothers who were sold to the Gentiles. Now you are selling your brothers, only for them to be sold back to us!" They kept quiet, because they could find nothing to say.

[9] So I continued, "What you are doing is not right. Shouldn't you walk in the fear of our God to avoid the reproach of our Gentile enemies? [10] I and my brothers and my men are also lending the people money and grain. But let the exacting of usury stop! [11] Give back to them immediately their fields, vineyards, olive groves and houses, and also the usury you are charging them—the hundredth part of the money, grain, new wine and oil."

[12] "We will give it back," they said. "And we will not demand anything more from them. We will do as you say."

Then I summoned the priests and made the nobles and officials take an oath to do what they had promised. [13] I also shook out the folds of my robe and said, "In this way may God shake out of his house and possessions every man who does not keep this promise. So may such a man be shaken out and emptied!"

At this the whole assembly said, "Amen," and praised the LORD. And the people did as they had promised.

[a] 15 Hebrew *Shelah*, a variant of *Shiloah*, that is, Siloam   [b] 16 Hebrew; Septuagint, some Vulgate manuscripts and Syriac *tomb*   [c] 18 Two Hebrew manuscripts and Syriac (see also Septuagint and verse 24); most Hebrew manuscripts *Bavvai*   [d] 5 Or *have provoked you to anger before*   [e] 23 The meaning of the Hebrew for this clause is uncertain.

1 CORINTHIANS 7:25-40

Now about virgins: I have no command from the Lord, but I give a judgment as one who by the Lord's mercy is trustworthy. [26] Because of the present crisis, I think that it is good for you to remain as you are. [27] Are you married? Do not seek a divorce. Are you unmarried? Do not look for a wife. [28] But if you do marry, you have not sinned; and if a virgin marries, she has not sinned. But those who marry will face many troubles in this life, and I want to spare you this.

[29] What I mean, brothers, is that the time is short. From now on those who have wives should live as if they had none; [30] those who mourn, as if they did not; those who are happy, as if they were not; those who buy something, as if it were not theirs to keep; [31] those who use the things of the world, as if not engrossed in them. For this world in its present form is passing away.

[32] I would like you to be free from concern. An unmarried man is concerned about the Lord's affairs—how he can please the Lord. [33] But a married man is concerned about the affairs of this world—how he can please his wife—[34] and his interests are divided. An unmarried woman or virgin is concerned about the Lord's affairs: Her aim is to be devoted to the Lord in both body and spirit. But a married woman is concerned about the affairs of this world—how she can please her husband. [35] I am saying this for your own good, not to restrict you, but that you may live in a right way in undivided devotion to the Lord.

³⁶If anyone thinks he is acting improperly toward the virgin he is engaged to, and if she is getting along in years and he feels he ought to marry, he should do as he wants. He is not sinning. They should get married. ³⁷But the man who has settled the matter in his own mind, who is under no compulsion but has control over his own will, and who has made up his mind not to marry the virgin—this man also does the right thing. ³⁸So then, he who marries the virgin does right, but he who does not marry her does even better.ᵃ

³⁹A woman is bound to her husband as long as he lives. But if her husband dies, she is free to marry anyone she wishes, but he must belong to the Lord. ⁴⁰In my judgment, she is happier if she stays as she is—and I think that I too have the Spirit of God.

a36-38 Or *³⁶If anyone thinks he is not treating his daughter properly, and if she is getting along in years, and he feels she ought to marry, he should do as he wants. He is not sinning. He should let her get married. ³⁷But the man who has settled the matter in his own mind, who is under no compulsion but has control over his own will, and who has made up his mind to keep the virgin unmarried—this man also does the right thing. ³⁸So then, he who gives his virgin in marriage does right, but he who does not give her in marriage does even better.*

PSALM 32:1-11
Of David. A *maskil.ᵃ*

¹ **B**lessed is he
      whose transgressions are
         forgiven,
      whose sins are covered.
² Blessed is the man
      whose sin the Lord does not count
         against him
      and in whose spirit is no deceit.

³ When I kept silent,
      my bones wasted away
         through my groaning all day long.
⁴ For day and night
      your hand was heavy upon me;
   my strength was sapped
      as in the heat of summer.   *Selah*
⁵ Then I acknowledged my sin to you
      and did not cover up my iniquity.
   I said, "I will confess
      my transgressions to the Lord"—

and you forgave
      the guilt of my sin.   *Selah*

⁶ **Therefore let everyone who is**
         godly pray to you
      while you may be found;
   surely when the mighty waters
         rise,
      they will not reach him.
⁷ **You are my hiding place;**
      you will protect me from
         trouble
   and surround me with songs of
         deliverance.   *Selah*

⁸ I will instruct you and teach you in
         the way you should go;
      I will counsel you and watch over
         you.
⁹ Do not be like the horse or the
         mule,
      which have no understanding
   but must be controlled by bit and
         bridle
      or they will not come to you.
¹⁰ Many are the woes of the wicked,
      but the Lord's unfailing love
   surrounds the man who trusts in
         him.

¹¹ Rejoice in the Lord and be glad, you
         righteous;
      sing, all you who are upright in
         heart!

*a*Title: Probably a literary or musical term

PROVERBS 21:5-7

⁵ **T**he plans of the diligent lead to
         profit
      as surely as haste leads to
         poverty.

⁶ A fortune made by a lying tongue
      is a fleeting vapor and a deadly
         snare.ᵃ

⁷ The violence of the wicked will drag
         them away,
      for they refuse to do what is
         right.

a6 Some Hebrew manuscripts, Septuagint and Vulgate; most Hebrew manuscripts *vapor for those who seek death*

☐ DAY 225

GOD SIGHTINGS

August 13

NEHEMIAH 5:14–7:60

Moreover, from the twentieth year of King Artaxerxes, when I was appointed to be their governor in the land of Judah, until his thirty-second year—twelve years—neither I nor my brothers ate the food allotted to the governor. ¹⁵But the earlier governors—those preceding me—placed a heavy burden on the people and took forty shekels*a* of silver from them in addition to food and wine. Their assistants also lorded it over the people. But out of reverence for God I did not act like that. ¹⁶Instead, I devoted myself to the work on this wall. All my men were assembled there for the work; we*b* did not acquire any land.

¹⁷Furthermore, a hundred and fifty Jews and officials ate at my table, as well as those who came to us from the surrounding nations. ¹⁸Each day one ox, six choice sheep and some poultry were prepared for me, and every ten days an abundant supply of wine of all kinds. In spite of all this, I never demanded the food allotted to the governor, because the demands were heavy on these people.

¹⁹Remember me with favor, O my God, for all I have done for these people.

⁶:¹WHEN word came to Sanballat, Tobiah, Geshem the Arab and the rest of our enemies that I had rebuilt the wall and not a gap was left in it—though up to that time I had not set the doors in the gates— ²Sanballat and Geshem sent me this message: "Come, let us meet together in one of the villages*c* on the plain of Ono."

But they were scheming to harm me; ³so I sent messengers to them with this reply: "I am carrying on a great project and cannot go down. Why should the work stop while I leave it and go down to

you?" ⁴Four times they sent me the same message, and each time I gave them the same answer.

⁵Then, the fifth time, Sanballat sent his aide to me with the same message, and in his hand was an unsealed letter ⁶in which was written:

"It is reported among the nations—and Geshem*d* says it is true—that you and the Jews are plotting to revolt, and therefore you are building the wall. Moreover, according to these reports you are about to become their king ⁷and have even appointed prophets to make this proclamation about you in Jerusalem: 'There is a king in Judah!' Now this report will get back to the king; so come, let us confer together."

⁸I sent him this reply: "Nothing like what you are saying is happening; you are just making it up out of your head."

⁹They were all trying to frighten us, thinking, "Their hands will get too weak for the work, and it will not be completed."

⌐But I prayed,⌐ "Now strengthen my hands."

¹⁰One day I went to the house of Shemaiah son of Delaiah, the son of Mehetabel, who was shut in at his home. He said, "Let us meet in the house of God, inside the temple, and let us close the temple doors, because men are coming to kill you—by night they are coming to kill you."

¹¹But I said, "Should a man like me run away? Or should one like me go into the temple to save his life? I will not go!" ¹²I realized that God had not sent him, but that he had prophesied against me because Tobiah and Sanballat had hired him. ¹³He had been hired to intimidate me so that I would commit a sin by doing this, and then they would give me a bad name to discredit me.

¹⁴Remember Tobiah and Sanballat, O my God, because of what they have done; remember also the prophetess

Noadiah and the rest of the prophets who have been trying to intimidate me.

[15]So the wall was completed on the twenty-fifth of Elul, in fifty-two days. [16]When all our enemies heard about this, all the surrounding nations were afraid and lost their self-confidence, because they realized that this work had been done with the help of our God.

[17]Also, in those days the nobles of Judah were sending many letters to Tobiah, and replies from Tobiah kept coming to them. [18]For many in Judah were under oath to him, since he was son-in-law to Shecaniah son of Arah, and his son Jehohanan had married the daughter of Meshullam son of Berekiah. [19]Moreover, they kept reporting to me his good deeds and then telling him what I said. And Tobiah sent letters to intimidate me.

[7:1]AFTER the wall had been rebuilt and I had set the doors in place, the gatekeepers and the singers and the Levites were appointed. [2]I put in charge of Jerusalem my brother Hanani, along with[e] Hananiah the commander of the citadel, because he was a man of integrity and feared God more than most men do. [3]I said to them, "The gates of Jerusalem are not to be opened until the sun is hot. While the gatekeepers are still on duty, have them shut the doors and bar them. Also appoint residents of Jerusalem as guards, some at their posts and some near their own houses."

[4]Now the city was large and spacious, but there were few people in it, and the houses had not yet been rebuilt. [5]So my God put it into my heart to assemble the nobles, the officials and the common people for registration by families. I found the genealogical record of those who had been the first to return. This is what I found written there:

[6]These are the people of the province who came up from the captivity of the exiles whom Nebuchadnezzar king of Babylon had taken captive (they returned to Jerusalem and Judah, each to his own

town, [7]in company with Zerubbabel, Jeshua, Nehemiah, Azariah, Raamiah, Nahamani, Mordecai, Bilshan, Mispereth, Bigvai, Nehum and Baanah):

The list of the men of Israel:

[8]the descendants of Parosh	2,172
[9]of Shephatiah	372
[10]of Arah	652
[11]of Pahath-Moab (through the line of Jeshua and Joab)	2,818
[12]of Elam	1,254
[13]of Zattu	845
[14]of Zaccai	760
[15]of Binnui	648
[16]of Bebai	628
[17]of Azgad	2,322
[18]of Adonikam	667
[19]of Bigvai	2,067
[20]of Adin	655
[21]of Ater (through Hezekiah)	98
[22]of Hashum	328
[23]of Bezai	324
[24]of Hariph	112
[25]of Gibeon	95
[26]the men of Bethlehem and Netophah	188
[27]of Anathoth	128
[28]of Beth Azmaveth	42
[29]of Kiriath Jearim, Kephirah and Beeroth	743
[30]of Ramah and Geba	621
[31]of Micmash	122
[32]of Bethel and Ai	123
[33]of the other Nebo	52
[34]of the other Elam	1,254
[35]of Harim	320
[36]of Jericho	345
[37]of Lod, Hadid and Ono	721
[38]of Senaah	3,930

[39]The priests:

the descendants of Jedaiah (through the family of Jeshua)	973
[40]of Immer	1,052
[41]of Pashhur	1,247

⁴²of Harim   1,017

⁴³The Levites:

the descendants of Jeshua
(through Kadmiel through
the line of Hodaviah)   74

⁴⁴The singers:

the descendants of Asaph   148

⁴⁵The gatekeepers:

the descendants of
Shallum, Ater, Talmon,
Akkub, Hatita and Shobai 138

⁴⁶The temple servants:

the descendants of
Ziha, Hasupha, Tabbaoth,
⁴⁷Keros, Sia, Padon,
⁴⁸Lebana, Hagaba, Shalmai,
⁴⁹Hanan, Giddel, Gahar,
⁵⁰Reaiah, Rezin, Nekoda,
⁵¹Gazzam, Uzza, Paseah,
⁵²Besai, Meunim, Nephusim,
⁵³Bakbuk, Hakupha, Harhur,
⁵⁴Bazluth, Mehida, Harsha,
⁵⁵Barkos, Sisera, Temah,
⁵⁶Neziah and Hatipha

⁵⁷The descendants of the servants
of Solomon:

the descendants of Sotai,
Sophereth, Perida,
⁵⁸Jaala, Darkon, Giddel,
⁵⁹Shephatiah, Hattil, Pokereth-
Hazzebaim and Amon

⁶⁰The temple servants and the
descendants of the servants
of Solomon   392

a 15 That is, about 1 pound (about 0.5 kilogram)   b 16 Most
Hebrew manuscripts; some Hebrew manuscripts, Septuagint,
Vulgate and Syriac I   c 2 Or in Kephirim   d 6 Hebrew
Gashmu, a variant of Geshem   e 2 Or Hanani, that is,

1 CORINTHIANS 8:1-13

Now about food sacrificed to idols: We
know that we all possess knowledge.ᵃ
Knowledge puffs up, but love builds up.
²The man who thinks he knows something does not yet know as he ought to
know. ³But the man who loves God is
known by God.

⁴So then, about eating food sacrificed
to idols: We know that an idol is nothing
at all in the world and that there is no
God but one. ⁵For even if there are so-
called gods, whether in heaven or on
earth (as indeed there are many "gods"
and many "lords"), ⁶yet for us there is
but one God, the Father, from whom all
things came and for whom we live; and
there is but one Lord, Jesus Christ,
through whom all things came and
through whom we live.

⁷But not everyone knows this. Some
people are still so accustomed to idols
that when they eat such food they think
of it as having been sacrificed to an idol,
and since their conscience is weak, it is
defiled. ⁸But food does not bring us
near to God; we are no worse if we do
not eat, and no better if we do.

⁹Be careful, however, that the exercise of your freedom does not become a
stumbling block to the weak. ¹⁰For if
anyone with a weak conscience sees you
who have this knowledge eating in an
idol's temple, won't he be emboldened
to eat what has been sacrificed to idols?
¹¹So this weak brother, for whom Christ
died, is destroyed by your knowledge.
¹²When you sin against your brothers in
this way and wound their weak conscience, you sin against Christ. ¹³Therefore, if what I eat causes my brother to
fall into sin, I will never eat meat again,
so that I will not cause him to fall.

a 1 Or "We all possess knowledge," as you say

PSALM 33:1-11

¹Sing joyfully to the LORD, you
righteous;
it is fitting for the upright to praise
him.
²Praise the LORD with the harp;
make music to him on the ten-
stringed lyre.
³Sing to him a new song;
play skillfully, and shout for joy.

⁴For the word of the LORD is right and
true;
he is faithful in all he does.

5 The Lᴏʀᴅ loves righteousness and
     justice;
  the earth is full of his unfailing
     love.

6 By the word of the Lᴏʀᴅ were the
     heavens made,
  their starry host by the breath of
     his mouth.
7 He gathers the waters of the sea into
     jars*a*;
  he puts the deep into storehouses.
8 Let all the earth fear the Lᴏʀᴅ;
  let all the people of the world
     revere him.
9 For he spoke, and it came to be;
  he commanded, and it stood firm.
10 The Lᴏʀᴅ foils the plans of the
     nations;
  he thwarts the purposes of the
     peoples.
11 But the plans of the Lᴏʀᴅ stand firm
     forever,
  the purposes of his heart through
     all generations.

a7 Or sea as into a heap

PROVERBS 21:8-10

8 The way of the guilty is devious,
  but the conduct of the innocent is
     upright.

9 Better to live on a corner of the roof
  than share a house with a
     quarrelsome wife.

10 The wicked man craves evil;
  his neighbor gets no mercy from
     him.

☐ DAY 226

GOD SIGHTINGS

August 14

NEHEMIAH 7:61–9:21

The following came up from the towns
of Tel Melah, Tel Harsha, Kerub, Addon
and Immer, but they could not show

that their families were descended from
Israel:

62 the descendants of
     Delaiah, Tobiah
     and Nekoda   642

63 And from among the priests:

  the descendants of Hobaiah,
     Hakkoz and Barzillai (a man
     who had married a daughter
     of Barzillai the Gileadite
     and was called by that
     name).

64 These searched for their family records, but they could not find them and so were excluded from the priesthood as unclean. 65 The governor, therefore, ordered them not to eat any of the most sacred food until there should be a priest ministering with the Urim and Thummim.

66 The whole company numbered 42,360, 67 besides their 7,337 menservants and maidservants; and they also had 245 men and women singers. 68 There were 736 horses, 245 mules,*a* 69 435 camels and 6,720 donkeys.

70 Some of the heads of the families contributed to the work. The governor gave to the treasury 1,000 drachmas*b* of gold, 50 bowls and 530 garments for priests. 71 Some of the heads of the families gave to the treasury for the work 20,000 drachmas*c* of gold and 2,200 minas*d* of silver. 72 The total given by the rest of the people was 20,000 drachmas of gold, 2,000 minas*e* of silver and 67 garments for priests.

73 The priests, the Levites, the gatekeepers, the singers and the temple servants, along with certain of the people and the rest of the Israelites, settled in their own towns.

When the seventh month came and the Israelites had settled in their towns, 8:1 all the people assembled as one man in the square before the Water Gate. They told Ezra the scribe to bring out the Book of the Law of Moses, which the Lord had commanded for Israel.

²So on the first day of the seventh month Ezra the priest brought the Law before the assembly, which was made up of men and women and all who were able to understand. ³He read it aloud from daybreak till noon as he faced the square before the Water Gate in the presence of the men, women and others who could understand. And all the people listened attentively to the Book of the Law.

⁴Ezra the scribe stood on a high wooden platform built for the occasion. Beside him on his right stood Mattithiah, Shema, Anaiah, Uriah, Hilkiah and Maaseiah; and on his left were Pedaiah, Mishael, Malkijah, Hashum, Hashbaddanah, Zechariah and Meshullam.

⁵Ezra opened the book. All the people could see him because he was standing above them; and as he opened it, the people all stood up. ⁶Ezra praised the Lord, the great God; and all the people lifted their hands and responded, "Amen! Amen!" Then they bowed down and worshiped the Lord with their faces to the ground.

⁷The Levites—Jeshua, Bani, Sherebiah, Jamin, Akkub, Shabbethai, Hodiah, Maaseiah, Kelita, Azariah, Jozabad, Hanan and Pelaiah—instructed the people in the Law while the people were standing there. ⁸They read from the Book of the Law of God, making it clear*f* and giving the meaning so that the people could understand what was being read.

⁹Then Nehemiah the governor, Ezra the priest and scribe, and the Levites who were instructing the people said to them all, "This day is sacred to the Lord your God. Do not mourn or weep." For all the people had been weeping as they listened to the words of the Law.

¹⁰Nehemiah said, "Go and enjoy choice food and sweet drinks, and send some to those who have nothing prepared. This day is sacred to our Lord. Do not grieve, for the joy of the Lord is your strength."

¹¹The Levites calmed all the people, saying, "Be still, for this is a sacred day. Do not grieve."

¹²Then all the people went away to eat and drink, to send portions of food and to celebrate with great joy, because they now understood the words that had been made known to them.

¹³On the second day of the month, the heads of all the families, along with the priests and the Levites, gathered around Ezra the scribe to give attention to the words of the Law. ¹⁴They found written in the Law, which the Lord had commanded through Moses, that the Israelites were to live in booths during the feast of the seventh month ¹⁵and that they should proclaim this word and spread it throughout their towns and in Jerusalem: "Go out into the hill country and bring back branches from olive and wild olive trees, and from myrtles, palms and shade trees, to make booths"—as it is written.*g*

¹⁶So the people went out and brought back branches and built themselves booths on their own roofs, in their courtyards, in the courts of the house of God and in the square by the Water Gate and the one by the Gate of Ephraim. ¹⁷The whole company that had returned from exile built booths and lived in them. From the days of Joshua son of Nun until that day, the Israelites had not celebrated it like this. And their joy was very great.

¹⁸Day after day, from the first day to the last, Ezra read from the Book of the Law of God. They celebrated the feast for seven days, and on the eighth day, in accordance with the regulation, there was an assembly.

9:1 On the twenty-fourth day of the same month, the Israelites gathered together, fasting and wearing sackcloth and having dust on their heads. ²Those of Israelite descent had separated themselves from all foreigners. They stood in their places and confessed their sins and the wickedness of their fathers. ³They stood where they were and read from the Book of the Law of the LORD their God for a quarter of the day, and spent another quarter in confession and in worshiping the LORD their God. ⁴Standing on the stairs were the Levites—Jeshua, Bani, Kadmiel, Shebaniah, Bunni, Sherebiah, Bani and Kenani—who called with loud voices to the LORD their God. ⁵And the Levites—Jeshua, Kadmiel, Bani, Hashabneiah, Sherebiah, Hodiah, Shebaniah and Pethahiah—said: "Stand up and praise the LORD your God, who is from everlasting to everlasting.ʰ"

"Blessed be your glorious name, and may it be exalted above all blessing and praise. ⁶You alone are the LORD. You made the heavens, even the highest heavens, and all their starry host, the earth and all that is on it, the seas and all that is in them. You give life to everything, and the multitudes of heaven worship you.

⁷"You are the LORD God, who chose Abram and brought him out of Ur of the Chaldeans and named him Abraham. ⁸You found his heart faithful to you, and you made a covenant with him to give to his descendants the land of the Canaanites, Hittites, Amorites, Perizzites, Jebusites and Girgashites. You have kept your promise because you are righteous.

⁹"You saw the suffering of our forefathers in Egypt; you heard their cry at the Red Sea.ⁱ ¹⁰You sent miraculous signs and wonders against Pharaoh, against all his officials and all the people of his land, for you knew how arrogantly the Egyptians treated them. You made a name for yourself, which remains to this day. ¹¹You divided the sea before them, so that they passed through it on dry ground, but you hurled their pursuers into the depths, like a stone into mighty waters. ¹²By day you led them with a pillar of cloud, and by night with a pillar of fire to give them light on the way they were to take.

¹³"You came down on Mount Sinai; you spoke to them from heaven. You gave them regulations and laws that are just and right, and decrees and commands that are good. ¹⁴You made known to them your holy Sabbath and gave them commands, decrees and laws through your servant Moses. ¹⁵In their hunger you gave them bread from heaven and in their thirst you brought them water from the rock; you told them to go in and take possession of the land you had sworn with uplifted hand to give them.

¹⁶"But they, our forefathers, became arrogant and stiff-necked, and did not obey your commands. ¹⁷They refused to listen and failed to remember the miracles you performed among them. They became stiff-necked and in their rebellion appointed a leader in order to return to their slavery. But you are a forgiving God, gracious and compassionate, slow to anger and abounding in love. Therefore you did not desert them, ¹⁸even when they cast for themselves an image of a calf and said, 'This is your god, who brought you up out of Egypt,' or when they committed awful blasphemies.

¹⁹"Because of your great compassion you did not abandon them in the desert. By day the pillar of cloud did not cease to guide them on their path, nor the pillar of fire by night to shine on the way they were to take. ²⁰You gave your good Spirit to instruct them. You did not withhold your manna from their mouths, and you gave them water for their thirst. ²¹For forty years you sustained them in the desert; they lacked nothing, their clothes

did not wear out nor did their feet become swollen."

a68 Some Hebrew manuscripts (see also Ezra 2:66); most Hebrew manuscripts do not have this verse. b70 That is, about 19 pounds (about 8.5 kilograms) c71 That is, about 375 pounds (about 170 kilograms); also in verse 72 d71 That is, about 1 1/3 tons (about 1.2 metric tons) e72 That is, about 1 1/4 tons (about 1.1 metric tons) f8 Or God, translating it g15 See Lev. 23:37-40. h5 Or God for ever and ever i9 Hebrew Yam Suph; that is, Sea of Reeds

1 CORINTHIANS 9:1-18

Am I not free? Am I not an apostle? Have I not seen Jesus our Lord? Are you not the result of my work in the Lord? [2]Even though I may not be an apostle to others, surely I am to you! For you are the seal of my apostleship in the Lord.

[3]This is my defense to those who sit in judgment on me. [4]Don't we have the right to food and drink? [5]Don't we have the right to take a believing wife along with us, as do the other apostles and the Lord's brothers and Cephas[a]? [6]Or is it only I and Barnabas who must work for a living?

[7]Who serves as a soldier at his own expense? Who plants a vineyard and does not eat of its grapes? Who tends a flock and does not drink of the milk? [8]Do I say this merely from a human point of view? Doesn't the Law say the same thing? [9]For it is written in the Law of Moses: "Do not muzzle an ox while it is treading out the grain."[b] Is it about oxen that God is concerned? [10]Surely he says this for us, doesn't he? Yes, this was written for us, because when the plowman plows and the thresher threshes, they ought to do so in the hope of sharing in the harvest. [11]If we have sown spiritual seed among you, is it too much if we reap a material harvest from you? [12]If others have this right of support from you, shouldn't we have it all the more?

But we did not use this right. On the contrary, we put up with anything rather than hinder the gospel of Christ. [13]Don't you know that those who work in the temple get their food from the temple, and those who serve at the altar share in what is offered on the altar? [14]In the same way, the Lord has commanded that those who preach the gospel should receive their living from the gospel.

[15]But I have not used any of these rights. And I am not writing this in the hope that you will do such things for me. I would rather die than have anyone deprive me of this boast. [16]Yet when I preach the gospel, I cannot boast, for I am compelled to preach. Woe to me if I do not preach the gospel! [17]If I preach voluntarily, I have a reward; if not voluntarily, I am simply discharging the trust committed to me. [18]What then is my reward? Just this: that in preaching the gospel I may offer it free of charge, and so not make use of my rights in preaching it.

a5 That is, Peter b9 Deut. 25:4

PSALM 33:12-22

[12]**B**lessed is the nation whose God is the LORD,
the people he chose for his inheritance.
[13]From heaven the LORD looks down and sees all mankind;
[14]from his dwelling place he watches all who live on earth—
[15]he who forms the hearts of all, who considers everything they do.
[16]No king is saved by the size of his army;
no warrior escapes by his great strength.
[17]A horse is a vain hope for deliverance;
despite all its great strength it cannot save.
[18]But the eyes of the LORD are on those who fear him,
on those whose hope is in his unfailing love,
[19]to deliver them from death and keep them alive in famine.

[20]**We wait in hope for the LORD; he is our help and our shield.**
[21]**In him our hearts rejoice, for we trust in his holy name.**
[22]**May your unfailing love rest upon us, O LORD, even as we put our hope in you.**

PROVERBS 21:11-12

11 **W**hen a mocker is punished, the
     simple gain wisdom;
   when a wise man is instructed, he
     gets knowledge.

12 The Righteous One[a] takes note of
     the house of the wicked
   and brings the wicked to ruin.

[a] 12 Or *The righteous man*

□ DAY 227

GOD SIGHTINGS

August 15

NEHEMIAH 9:22–10:39

"**Y**ou [the LORD] gave them [the Isra-
elites] kingdoms and nations, allot-
ting to them even the remotest
frontiers. They took over the country of Sihon[a] king of Heshbon and
the country of Og king of Bashan.
23 You made their sons as numerous
as the stars in the sky, and you
brought them into the land that you
told their fathers to enter and possess. 24 Their sons went in and took
possession of the land. You subdued
before them the Canaanites, who
lived in the land; you handed the Canaanites over to them, along with
their kings and the peoples of the
land, to deal with them as they
pleased. 25 They captured fortified
cities and fertile land; they took possession of houses filled with all
kinds of good things, wells already
dug, vineyards, olive groves and fruit
trees in abundance. They ate to the
full and were well-nourished; they
reveled in your great goodness.

26 "But they were disobedient and
rebelled against you; they put your
law behind their backs. They killed
your prophets, who had admon-
ished them in order to turn them
back to you; they committed awful
blasphemies. 27 So you handed them

over to their enemies, who oppressed them. But when they were
oppressed they cried out to you.
From heaven you heard them, and in
your great compassion you gave
them deliverers, who rescued them
from the hand of their enemies.

28 "But as soon as they were at
rest, they again did what was evil in
your sight. Then you abandoned
them to the hand of their enemies
so that they ruled over them. And
when they cried out to you again,
you heard from heaven, and in
your compassion you delivered
them time after time.

29 "You warned them to return to
your law, but they became arrogant
and disobeyed your commands.
They sinned against your ordinances, by which a man will live if he
obeys them. Stubbornly they turned
their backs on you, became stiff-
necked and refused to listen. 30 For
many years you were patient with
them. By your Spirit you admon-
ished them through your prophets.
Yet they paid no attention, so you
handed them over to the neighboring peoples. 31 But in your great
mercy you did not put an end to
them or abandon them, for you are a
gracious and merciful God.

32 "Now therefore, O our God,
the great, mighty and awesome
God, who keeps his covenant of
love, do not let all this hardship
seem trifling in your eyes—the
hardship that has come upon us,
upon our kings and leaders, upon
our priests and prophets, upon our
fathers and all your people, from
the days of the kings of Assyria until today. 33 In all that has happened
to us, you have been just; you have
acted faithfully, while we did
wrong. 34 Our kings, our leaders,
our priests and our fathers did not
follow your law; they did not pay
attention to your commands or
the warnings you gave them. 35 Even while they were in their

kingdom, enjoying your great goodness to them in the spacious and fertile land you gave them, they did not serve you or turn from their evil ways.

36"But see, we are slaves today, slaves in the land you gave our forefathers so they could eat its fruit and the other good things it produces. 37 Because of our sins, its abundant harvest goes to the kings you have placed over us. They rule over our bodies and our cattle as they please. We are in great distress.

38"In view of all this, we are making a binding agreement, putting it in writing, and our leaders, our Levites and our priests are affixing their seals to it."

10:1THOSE who sealed it were:

Nehemiah the governor, the son of Hacaliah.

Zedekiah, 2Seraiah, Azariah, Jeremiah, 3Pashhur, Amariah, Malkijah, 4Hattush, Shebaniah, Malluch, 5Harim, Meremoth, Obadiah, 6Daniel, Ginnethon, Baruch, 7Meshullam, Abijah, Mijamin, 8Maaziah, Bilgai and Shemaiah.
These were the priests.

9The Levites:

Jeshua son of Azaniah, Binnui of the sons of Henadad, Kadmiel, 10and their associates: Shebaniah, Hodiah, Kelita, Pelaiah, Hanan, 11Mica, Rehob, Hashabiah, 12Zaccur, Sherebiah, Shebaniah, 13Hodiah, Bani and Beninu.

14The leaders of the people:

Parosh, Pahath-Moab, Elam, Zattu, Bani, 15Bunni, Azgad, Bebai, 16Adonijah, Bigvai, Adin, 17Ater, Hezekiah, Azzur, 18Hodiah, Hashum, Bezai, 19Hariph, Anathoth, Nebai, 20Magpiash, Meshullam, Hezir, 21Meshezabel, Zadok, Jaddua,

22Pelatiah, Hanan, Anaiah, 23Hoshea, Hananiah, Hasshub, 24Hallohesh, Pilha, Shobek, 25Rehum, Hashabnah, Maaseiah, 26Ahiah, Hanan, Anan, 27Malluch, Harim and Baanah.

28"The rest of the people—priests, Levites, gatekeepers, singers, temple servants and all who separated themselves from the neighboring peoples for the sake of the Law of God, together with their wives and all their sons and daughters who are able to understand—29all these now join their brothers the nobles, and bind themselves with a curse and an oath to follow the Law of God given through Moses the servant of God and to obey carefully all the commands, regulations and decrees of the LORD our Lord.

30"We promise not to give our daughters in marriage to the peoples around us or take their daughters for our sons.

31"When the neighboring peoples bring merchandise or grain to sell on the Sabbath, we will not buy from them on the Sabbath or on any holy day. Every seventh year we will forgo working the land and will cancel all debts.

32"We assume the responsibility for carrying out the commands to give a third of a shekelᵇ each year for the service of the house of our God: 33for the bread set out on the table; for the regular grain offerings and burnt offerings; for the offerings on the Sabbaths, New Moon festivals and appointed feasts; for the holy offerings; for sin offerings to make atonement for Israel; and for all the duties of the house of our God.

34"We—the priests, the Levites and the people—have cast lots to determine when each of our families is to bring to the house of our God at set times each year a contribution of wood to burn on the altar

821

of the LORD our God, as it is written in the Law.

35 "We also assume responsibility for bringing to the house of the LORD each year the firstfruits of our crops and of every fruit tree.

36 "As it is also written in the Law, we will bring the firstborn of our sons and of our cattle, of our herds and of our flocks to the house of our God, to the priests ministering there.

37 "Moreover, we will bring to the storerooms of the house of our God, to the priests, the first of our ground meal, of our ⌊grain⌋ offerings, of the fruit of all our trees and of our new wine and oil. And we will bring a tithe of our crops to the Levites, for it is the Levites who collect the tithes in all the towns where we work. 38 A priest descended from Aaron is to accompany the Levites when they receive the tithes, and the Levites are to bring a tenth of the tithes up to the house of our God, to the storerooms of the treasury. 39 The people of Israel, including the Levites, are to bring their contributions of grain, new wine and oil to the storerooms where the articles for the sanctuary are kept and where the ministering priests, the gatekeepers and the singers stay.

"We will not neglect the house of our God."

a22 One Hebrew manuscript and Septuagint; most Hebrew manuscripts Sihon, that is, the country of the   b32 That is, about 1/8 ounce (about 4 grams)

1 CORINTHIANS 9:19–10:13

Though I am free and belong to no man, I make myself a slave to everyone, to win as many as possible. 20 To the Jews I became like a Jew, to win the Jews. To those under the law I became like one under the law (though I myself am not under the law), so as to win those under the law. 21 To those not having the law I became like one not having the law (though I am not free from God's law but

am under Christ's law), so as to win those not having the law. 22 To the weak I became weak, to win the weak. I have become all things to all men so that by all possible means I might save some. 23 I do all this for the sake of the gospel, that I may share in its blessings.

24 Do you not know that in a race all the runners run, but only one gets the prize? Run in such a way as to get the prize. 25 Everyone who competes in the games goes into strict training. They do it to get a crown that will not last; but we do it to get a crown that will last forever. 26 Therefore I do not run like a man running aimlessly; I do not fight like a man beating the air. 27 No, I beat my body and make it my slave so that after I have preached to others, I myself will not be disqualified for the prize.

10:1 FOR I do not want you to be ignorant of the fact, brothers, that our forefathers were all under the cloud and that they all passed through the sea. 2 They were all baptized into Moses in the cloud and in the sea. 3 They all ate the same spiritual food 4 and drank the same spiritual drink; for they drank from the spiritual rock that accompanied them, and that rock was Christ. 5 Nevertheless, God was not pleased with most of them; their bodies were scattered over the desert.

6 Now these things occurred as examplesa to keep us from setting our hearts on evil things as they did. 7 Do not be idolaters, as some of them were; as it is written: "The people sat down to eat and drink and got up to indulge in pagan revelry."b 8 We should not commit sexual immorality, as some of them did—and in one day twenty-three thousand of them died. 9 We should not test the Lord, as some of them did—and were killed by snakes. 10 And do not grumble, as some of them did—and were killed by the destroying angel.

11 These things happened to them as examples and were written down as warnings for us, on whom the fulfillment of the ages has come. 12 So, if you

think you are standing firm, be careful that you don't fall! 13**No temptation has seized you except what is common to man. And God is faithful; he will not let you be tempted beyond what you can bear. But when you are tempted, he will also provide a way out so that you can stand up under it.**

a6 Or *types*; also in verse 11   b7 Exodus 32:6

PSALM 34:1-10ª

Of David. When he pretended to be insane before Abimelech, who drove him away, and he left.

1 I will extol the LORD at all times;
  his praise will always be on my lips.
2 My soul will boast in the LORD;
  let the afflicted hear and rejoice.
3 Glorify the LORD with me;
  let us exalt his name together.

4 I sought the LORD, and he answered me;
  he delivered me from all my fears.
5 Those who look to him are radiant;
  their faces are never covered with shame.
6 This poor man called, and the LORD heard him;
  he saved him out of all his troubles.
7 The angel of the LORD encamps around those who fear him,
  and he delivers them.

8 Taste and see that the LORD is good;
  blessed is the man who takes refuge in him.
9 Fear the LORD, you his saints,
  for those who fear him lack nothing.
10 The lions may grow weak and hungry,
  but those who seek the LORD lack no good thing.

a This psalm is an acrostic poem, the verses of which begin with the successive letters of the Hebrew alphabet.

PROVERBS 21:13

13 If a man shuts his ears to the cry of the poor,
  he too will cry out and not be answered.

☐ DAY 228

GOD SIGHTINGS

August 16

NEHEMIAH 11:1-12:26

Now the leaders of the people settled in Jerusalem, and the rest of the people cast lots to bring one out of every ten to live in Jerusalem, the holy city, while the remaining nine were to stay in their own towns. 2 The people commended all the men who volunteered to live in Jerusalem.

3 These are the provincial leaders who settled in Jerusalem (now some Israelites, priests, Levites, temple servants and descendants of Solomon's servants lived in the towns of Judah, each on his own property in the various towns, 4 while other people from both Judah and Benjamin lived in Jerusalem):

From the descendants of Judah:

Athaiah son of Uzziah, the son of Zechariah, the son of Amariah, the son of Shephatiah, the son of Mahalalel, a descendant of Perez; 5 and Maaseiah son of Baruch, the son of Col-Hozeh, the son of Hazaiah, the son of Adaiah, the son of Joiarib, the son of Zechariah, a descendant of Shelah. 6 The descendants of Perez who lived in Jerusalem totaled 468 able men.

7 From the descendants of Benjamin:

Sallu son of Meshullam, the son of Joed, the son of Pedaiah, the son of Kolaiah, the son of Maaseiah, the son of Ithiel, the son of Jeshaiah, 8 and his followers, Gabbai and Sallai—928 men. 9 Joel son of Zicri was their chief officer, and Judah son of Hassenuah was over the Second District of the city.

10 From the priests:

Jedaiah; the son of Joiarib; Jakin; 11 Seraiah son of Hilkiah, the son of

Meshullam, the son of Zadok, the son of Meraioth, the son of Ahitub, supervisor in the house of God, [12]and their associates, who carried on work for the temple—822 men; Adaiah son of Jeroham, the son of Pelaliah, the son of Amzi, the son of Zechariah, the son of Pashhur, the son of Malkijah, [13]and his associates, who were heads of families—242 men; Amashsai son of Azarel, the son of Ahzai, the son of Meshillemoth, the son of Immer, [14]and his[a] associates, who were able men—128. Their chief officer was Zabdiel son of Haggedolim.

[15]From the Levites:

Shemaiah son of Hasshub, the son of Azrikam, the son of Hashabiah, the son of Bunni; [16]Shabbethai and Jozabad, two of the heads of the Levites, who had charge of the outside work of the house of God; [17]Mattaniah son of Mica, the son of Zabdi, the son of Asaph, the director who led in thanksgiving and prayer; Bakbukiah, second among his associates; and Abda son of Shammua, the son of Galal, the son of Jeduthun. [18]The Levites in the holy city totaled 284.

[19]The gatekeepers:

Akkub, Talmon and their associates, who kept watch at the gates—172 men.

[20]The rest of the Israelites, with the priests and Levites, were in all the towns of Judah, each on his ancestral property.

[21]The temple servants lived on the hill of Ophel, and Ziha and Gishpa were in charge of them.

[22]The chief officer of the Levites in Jerusalem was Uzzi son of Bani, the son of Hashabiah, the son of Mattaniah, the son of Mica. Uzzi was one of Asaph's descendants, who were the singers responsible for the service of the house of God. [23]The singers were under the king's orders, which regulated their daily activity.

[24]Pethahiah son of Meshezabel, one of the descendants of Zerah son of Judah, was the king's agent in all affairs relating to the people.

[25]As for the villages with their fields, some of the people of Judah lived in Kiriath Arba and its surrounding settlements, in Dibon and its settlements, in Jekabzeel and its villages, [26]in Jeshua, in Moladah, in Beth Pelet, [27]in Hazar Shual, in Beersheba and its settlements, [28]in Ziklag, in Meconah and its settlements, [29]in En Rimmon, in Zorah, in Jarmuth, [30]Zanoah, Adullam and their villages, in Lachish and its fields, and in Azekah and its settlements. So they were living all the way from Beersheba to the Valley of Hinnom.

[31]The descendants of the Benjamites from Geba lived in Micmash, Aija, Bethel and its settlements, [32]in Anathoth, Nob and Ananiah, [33]in Hazor, Ramah and Gittaim, [34]in Hadid, Zeboim and Neballat, [35]in Lod and Ono, and in the Valley of the Craftsmen.

[36]Some of the divisions of the Levites of Judah settled in Benjamin.

[12:1]THESE were the priests and Levites who returned with Zerubbabel son of Shealtiel and with Jeshua:

Seraiah, Jeremiah, Ezra,
[2]Amariah, Malluch, Hattush,
[3]Shecaniah, Rehum, Meremoth,
[4]Iddo, Ginnethon,[b] Abijah,
[5]Mijamin,[c] Moadiah, Bilgah,
[6]Shemaiah, Joiarib, Jedaiah,
[7]Sallu, Amok, Hilkiah and Jedaiah.

These were the leaders of the priests and their associates in the days of Jeshua.

[8]The Levites were Jeshua, Binnui, Kadmiel, Sherebiah, Judah, and also Mattaniah, who, together with his associates, was in charge of the songs of thanksgiving. [9]Bakbukiah and Unni, their associates, stood opposite them in the services.

[10]Jeshua was the father of Joiakim, Joiakim the father of Eliashib, Eliashib the father of Joiada, [11]Joiada the father

824

of Jonathan, and Jonathan the father of
Jaddua.

¹²In the days of Joiakim, these were
the heads of the priestly families:

of Seraiah's family, Meraiah;
of Jeremiah's, Hananiah;
¹³of Ezra's, Meshullam;
of Amariah's, Jehohanan;
¹⁴of Malluch's, Jonathan;
of Shecaniah's,ᵈ Joseph;
¹⁵of Harim's, Adna;
of Meremoth's,ᵉ Helkai;
¹⁶of Iddo's, Zechariah;
of Ginnethon's, Meshullam;
¹⁷of Abijah's, Zicri;
of Miniamin's and of Moadiah's,
Piltai;
¹⁸of Bilgah's, Shammua;
of Shemaiah's, Jehonathan;
¹⁹of Joiarib's, Mattenai;
of Jedaiah's, Uzzi;
²⁰of Sallu's, Kallai;
of Amok's, Eber;
²¹of Hilkiah's, Hashabiah;
of Jedaiah's, Nethanel.

²²The family heads of the Levites in
the days of Eliashib, Joiada, Johanan and
Jaddua, as well as those of the priests,
were recorded in the reign of Darius the
Persian. ²³The family heads among the
descendants of Levi up to the time of Johanan son of Eliashib were recorded in
the book of the annals. ²⁴And the leaders of the Levites were Hashabiah, Sherebiah, Jeshua son of Kadmiel, and their
associates, who stood opposite them to
give praise and thanksgiving, one section responding to the other, as prescribed by David the man of God.

²⁵Mattaniah, Bakbukiah, Obadiah, Meshullam, Talmon and Akkub were gatekeepers who guarded the storerooms at
the gates. ²⁶They served in the days of Joiakim son of Jeshua, the son of Jozadak,
and in the days of Nehemiah the governor
and of Ezra the priest and scribe.

ᵃ14 Most Septuagint manuscripts; Hebrew their
ᵇ4 Many Hebrew manuscripts and Vulgate (see also
Neh. 12:16); most Hebrew manuscripts Ginnethoi
ᶜ5 A variant of Miniamin   ᵈ14 Very many Hebrew
manuscripts, some Septuagint manuscripts and Syriac
(see also Neh. 12:3); most Hebrew manuscripts Shebaniah's
ᵉ15 Some Septuagint manuscripts (see also Neh. 12:3);
Hebrew Meraioth's

1 CORINTHIANS 10:14–11:2

Therefore, my dear friends, flee from
idolatry. ¹⁵I speak to sensible people;
judge for yourselves what I say. ¹⁶Is not
the cup of thanksgiving for which we
give thanks a participation in the blood
of Christ? And is not the bread that we
break a participation in the body of
Christ? ¹⁷Because there is one loaf, we,
who are many, are one body, for we all
partake of the one loaf.

¹⁸Consider the people of Israel: Do not
those who eat the sacrifices participate in
the altar? ¹⁹Do I mean then that a sacrifice
offered to an idol is anything, or that an
idol is anything? ²⁰No, but the sacrifices
of pagans are offered to demons, not to
God, and I do not want you to be participants with demons. ²¹You cannot drink
the cup of the Lord and the cup of demons too; you cannot have a part in both
the Lord's table and the table of demons.
²²Are we trying to arouse the Lord's jealousy? Are we stronger than he?

²³"Everything is permissible"—but
not everything is beneficial. "Everything
is permissible"—but not everything is
constructive. ²⁴Nobody should seek his
own good, but the good of others.

²⁵Eat anything sold in the meat market without raising questions of conscience, ²⁶for, "The earth is the Lord's,
and everything in it."ᵃ

²⁷If some unbeliever invites you to a
meal and you want to go, eat whatever is
put before you without raising questions of conscience. ²⁸But if anyone says
to you, "This has been offered in sacrifice," then do not eat it, both for the sake
of the man who told you and for conscience' sakeᵇ— ²⁹the other man's conscience, I mean, not yours. For why
should my freedom be judged by another's conscience? ³⁰If I take part in the
meal with thankfulness, why am I denounced because of something I thank
God for?

³¹**So whether you eat or drink or
whatever you do, do it all for the glory
of God.** ³²**Do not cause anyone to
stumble, whether Jews, Greeks or the
church of God—** ³³**even as I try to**

please everybody in every way. For I am not seeking my own good but the good of many, so that they may be saved.

11:1 FOLLOW my example, as I follow the example of Christ.

2 I praise you for remembering me in everything and for holding to the teachings,*c* just as I passed them on to you.

a26 Psalm 24:1 *b28* Some manuscripts *conscience' sake,* for "the earth is the Lord's and everything in it" *c2* Or *traditions*

PSALM 34:11-22

11 Come, my children, listen to me;
   I will teach you the fear of the
      LORD.
12 Whoever of you loves life
   and desires to see many good days,
13 keep your tongue from evil
   and your lips from speaking lies.
14 Turn from evil and do good;
   seek peace and pursue it.

15 The eyes of the LORD are on the
      righteous
   and his ears are attentive to their
      cry;
16 the face of the LORD is against those
      who do evil,
   to cut off the memory of them
      from the earth.

17 The righteous cry out, and the LORD
      hears them;
   he delivers them from all their
      troubles.
18 The LORD is close to the
      brokenhearted
   and saves those who are crushed
      in spirit.

19 A righteous man may have many
      troubles,
   but the LORD delivers him from
      them all;
20 he protects all his bones,
   not one of them will be broken.

21 Evil will slay the wicked;
   the foes of the righteous will be
      condemned.
22 The LORD redeems his servants;
   no one will be condemned who
      takes refuge in him.

PROVERBS 21:14-16

14 A gift given in secret soothes anger,
   and a bribe concealed in the cloak
      pacifies great wrath.

15 When justice is done, it brings joy to
      the righteous
   but terror to evildoers.

16 A man who strays from the path of
      understanding
   comes to rest in the company of
      the dead.

□ DAY 229

GOD SIGHTINGS

August 17

NEHEMIAH 12:27–13:31

At the dedication of the wall of Jerusalem, the Levites were sought out from where they lived and were brought to Jerusalem to celebrate joyfully the dedication with songs of thanksgiving and with the music of cymbals, harps and lyres. 28 The singers also were brought together from the region around Jerusalem—from the villages of the Netophathites, 29 from Beth Gilgal, and from the area of Geba and Azmaveth, for the singers had built villages for themselves around Jerusalem. 30 When the priests and Levites had purified themselves ceremonially, they purified the people, the gates and the wall.

31 I had the leaders of Judah go up on top*a* of the wall. I also assigned two large choirs to give thanks. One was to proceed on top*b* of the wall to the right, toward the Dung Gate. 32 Hoshaiah and half the leaders of Judah followed them, 33 along with Azariah, Ezra, Meshullam, 34 Judah, Benjamin, Shemaiah, Jeremiah, 35 as well as some priests with trumpets, and also Zechariah son of Jonathan, the son of Shemaiah, the son of Mattaniah, the son of Micaiah, the son of Zaccur, the son of Asaph, 36 and

his associates—Shemaiah, Azarel, Milalai, Gilalai, Maai, Nethanel, Judah and Hanani—with musical instruments ⌞prescribed by⌟ David the man of God. Ezra the scribe led the procession. [37] At the Fountain Gate they continued directly up the steps of the City of David on the ascent to the wall and passed above the house of David to the Water Gate on the east.

[38] The second choir proceeded in the opposite direction. I followed them on top[c] of the wall, together with half the people—past the Tower of the Ovens to the Broad Wall, [39] over the Gate of Ephraim, the Jeshanah[d] Gate, the Fish Gate, the Tower of Hananel and the Tower of the Hundred, as far as the Sheep Gate. At the Gate of the Guard they stopped.

[40] The two choirs that gave thanks then took their places in the house of God; so did I, together with half the officials, [41] as well as the priests—Eliakim, Maaseiah, Miniamin, Micaiah, Elioenai, Zechariah and Hananiah with their trumpets— [42] and also Maaseiah, Shemaiah, Eleazar, Uzzi, Jehohanan, Malkijah, Elam and Ezer. The choirs sang under the direction of Jezrahiah. [43] And on that day they offered great sacrifices, rejoicing because God had given them great joy. The women and children also rejoiced. The sound of rejoicing in Jerusalem could be heard far away.

[44] At that time men were appointed to be in charge of the storerooms for the contributions, firstfruits and tithes. From the fields around the towns they were to bring into the storerooms the portions required by the Law for the priests and the Levites, for Judah was pleased with the ministering priests and Levites. [45] They performed the service of their God and the service of purification, as did also the singers and gatekeepers, according to the commands of David and his son Solomon. [46] For long ago, in the days of David and Asaph, there had been directors for the singers and for the songs of praise and thanksgiving to God. [47] So in the days of Zerubbabel and of Nehemiah, all Israel contributed the daily portions for the singers and gatekeepers. They also set aside the portion for the other Levites, and the Levites set aside the portion for the descendants of Aaron.

[13:1] ON that day the Book of Moses was read aloud in the hearing of the people and there it was found written that no Ammonite or Moabite should ever be admitted into the assembly of God, [2] because they had not met the Israelites with food and water but had hired Balaam to call a curse down on them. (Our God, however, turned the curse into a blessing.) [3] When the people heard this law, they excluded from Israel all who were of foreign descent.

[4] Before this, Eliashib the priest had been put in charge of the storerooms of the house of our God. He was closely associated with Tobiah, [5] and he had provided him with a large room formerly used to store the grain offerings and incense and temple articles, and also the tithes of grain, new wine and oil prescribed for the Levites, singers and gatekeepers, as well as the contributions for the priests.

[6] But while all this was going on, I was not in Jerusalem, for in the thirty-second year of Artaxerxes king of Babylon I had returned to the king. Some time later I asked his permission [7] and came back to Jerusalem. Here I learned about the evil thing Eliashib had done in providing Tobiah a room in the courts of the house of God. [8] I was greatly displeased and threw all Tobiah's household goods out of the room. [9] I gave orders to purify the rooms, and then I put back into them the equipment of the house of God, with the grain offerings and the incense.

[10] I also learned that the portions assigned to the Levites had not been given to them, and that all the Levites and singers responsible for the service had gone back to their own fields. [11] So I rebuked the officials and asked them, "Why is the house of God neglected?"

Then I called them together and stationed them at their posts.

[12]All Judah brought the tithes of grain, new wine and oil into the storerooms. [13]I put Shelemiah the priest, Zadok the scribe, and a Levite named Pedaiah in charge of the storerooms and made Hanan son of Zaccur, the son of Mattaniah, their assistant, because these men were considered trustworthy. They were made responsible for distributing the supplies to their brothers.

[14]Remember me for this, O my God, and do not blot out what I have so faithfully done for the house of my God and its services.

[15]In those days I saw men in Judah treading winepresses on the Sabbath and bringing in grain and loading it on donkeys, together with wine, grapes, figs and all other kinds of loads. And they were bringing all this into Jerusalem on the Sabbath. Therefore I warned them against selling food on that day. [16]Men from Tyre who lived in Jerusalem were bringing in fish and all kinds of merchandise and selling them in Jerusalem on the Sabbath to the people of Judah. [17]I rebuked the nobles of Judah and said to them, "What is this wicked thing you are doing—desecrating the Sabbath day? [18]Didn't your forefathers do the same things, so that our God brought all this calamity upon us and upon this city? Now you are stirring up more wrath against Israel by desecrating the Sabbath."

[19]When evening shadows fell on the gates of Jerusalem before the Sabbath, I ordered the doors to be shut and not opened until the Sabbath was over. I stationed some of my own men at the gates so that no load could be brought in on the Sabbath day. [20]Once or twice the merchants and sellers of all kinds of goods spent the night outside Jerusalem. [21]But I warned them and said, "Why do you spend the night by the wall? If you do this again, I will lay hands on you." From that time on they no longer came on the Sabbath. [22]Then I commanded the Levites to purify themselves and go and guard the gates in order to keep the Sabbath day holy.

Remember me for this also, O my God, and show mercy to me according to your great love.

[23]Moreover, in those days I saw men of Judah who had married women from Ashdod, Ammon and Moab. [24]Half of their children spoke the language of Ashdod or the language of one of the other peoples, and did not know how to speak the language of Judah. [25]I rebuked them and called curses down on them. I beat some of the men and pulled out their hair. I made them take an oath in God's name and said: "You are not to give your daughters in marriage to their sons, nor are you to take their daughters in marriage for your sons or for yourselves. [26]Was it not because of marriages like these that Solomon king of Israel sinned? Among the many nations there was no king like him. He was loved by his God, and God made him king over all Israel, but even he was led into sin by foreign women. [27]Must we hear now that you too are doing all this terrible wickedness and are being unfaithful to our God by marrying foreign women?"

[28]One of the sons of Joiada son of Eliashib the high priest was son-in-law to Sanballat the Horonite. And I drove him away from me.

[29]Remember them, O my God, because they defiled the priestly office and the covenant of the priesthood and of the Levites.

[30]So I purified the priests and the Levites of everything foreign, and assigned them duties, each to his own task. [31]I also made provision for contributions of wood at designated times, and for the firstfruits.

Remember me with favor, O my God.

a31 Or go alongside   b31 Or proceed alongside
c38 Or them alongside   d39 Or Old

1 CORINTHIANS 11:3-16

Now I want you to realize that the head of every man is Christ, and the head of the woman is man, and the head of Christ is God. [4]Every man who prays or prophesies with his head covered dishonors his head. [5]And every woman who prays or prophesies with her head uncovered dishonors her head—it is just as though her head were shaved. [6]If a woman does not cover her head, she should have her hair cut off; and if it is a disgrace for a woman to have her hair cut or shaved off, she should cover her head. [7]A man ought not to cover his head,[a] since he is the image and glory of God; but the woman is the glory of man. [8]For man did not come from woman, but woman from man; [9]neither was man created for woman, but woman for man. [10]For this reason, and because of the angels, the woman ought to have a sign of authority on her head.

[11]**In the Lord, however, woman is not independent of man, nor is man independent of woman.** [12]**For as woman came from man, so also man is born of woman. But everything comes from God.** [13]Judge for yourselves: Is it proper for a woman to pray to God with her head uncovered? [14]Does not the very nature of things teach you that if a man has long hair, it is a disgrace to him, [15]but that if a woman has long hair, it is her glory? For long hair is given to her as a covering. [16]If anyone wants to be contentious about this, we have no other practice—nor do the churches of God.

a 4-7 Or [4]*Every man who prays or prophesies with long hair dishonors his head. [5]And every woman who prays or prophesies with no covering ⌊of hair⌋ on her head dishonors her head—she is just like one of the "shorn women." [6]If a woman has no covering, let her be for now with short hair, but since it is a disgrace for a woman to have her hair shorn or shaved, she should grow it again. [7]A man ought not to have long hair*

PSALM 35:1-16

Of David.

[1] Contend, O LORD, with those who
      contend with me;
   fight against those who fight
      against me.

[2] Take up shield and buckler;
      arise and come to my aid.
[3] Brandish spear and javelin[a]
      against those who pursue me.
   Say to my soul,
      "I am your salvation."

[4] May those who seek my life
      be disgraced and put to shame;
   may those who plot my ruin
      be turned back in dismay.
[5] May they be like chaff before the
      wind,
   with the angel of the LORD driving
      them away;
[6] may their path be dark and slippery,
   with the angel of the LORD
      pursuing them.
[7] Since they hid their net for me
      without cause
   and without cause dug a pit
      for me,
[8] may ruin overtake them by
      surprise—
   may the net they hid entangle
      them,
   may they fall into the pit, to their
      ruin.
[9] Then my soul will rejoice in the LORD
   and delight in his salvation.
[10] My whole being will exclaim,
      "Who is like you, O LORD?
   You rescue the poor from those too
      strong for them,
   the poor and needy from those
      who rob them."

[11] Ruthless witnesses come forward;
      they question me on things I know
         nothing about.
[12] They repay me evil for good
      and leave my soul forlorn.
[13] Yet when they were ill, I put on
         sackcloth
   and humbled myself with fasting.
   When my prayers returned to me
      unanswered,
[14]   I went about mourning
      as though for my friend or brother.
   I bowed my head in grief
      as though weeping for my mother.

15 But when I stumbled, they gathered
      in glee;
   attackers gathered against me
      when I was unaware.
   They slandered me without
      ceasing.
16 Like the ungodly they maliciously
      mocked*b*;
   they gnashed their teeth at me.

a3 Or *and block the way*   *b16* Septuagint; Hebrew may
mean *ungodly circle of mockers.*

PROVERBS 21:17-18

17 **H**e who loves pleasure will become
      poor;
   whoever loves wine and oil will
      never be rich.

18 The wicked become a ransom for the
      righteous,
   and the unfaithful for the upright.

□ DAY 230

GOD SIGHTINGS

August 18

ESTHER 1:1–3:15

This is what happened during the time
of Xerxes,*a* the Xerxes who ruled over
127 provinces stretching from India to
Cush*b*: 2 At that time King Xerxes reigned
from his royal throne in the citadel of
Susa, 3 and in the third year of his reign
he gave a banquet for all his nobles and
officials. The military leaders of Persia
and Media, the princes, and the nobles of
the provinces were present.

4 For a full 180 days he displayed the
vast wealth of his kingdom and the
splendor and glory of his majesty.
5 When these days were over, the king
gave a banquet, lasting seven days, in the
enclosed garden of the king's palace, for
all the people from the least to the
greatest, who were in the citadel of Susa.
6 The garden had hangings of white and
blue linen, fastened with cords of white
linen and purple material to silver rings

on marble pillars. There were couches
of gold and silver on a mosaic pavement
of porphyry, marble, mother-of-pearl
and other costly stones. 7 Wine was
served in goblets of gold, each one different from the other, and the royal wine
was abundant, in keeping with the
king's liberality. 8 By the king's command each guest was allowed to drink
in his own way, for the king instructed
all the wine stewards to serve each man
what he wished.

9 Queen Vashti also gave a banquet for
the women in the royal palace of King
Xerxes.

10 On the seventh day, when King Xerxes was in high spirits from wine, he
commanded the seven eunuchs who
served him—Mehuman, Biztha, Harbona, Bigtha, Abagtha, Zethar and Car-
cas—11 to bring before him Queen
Vashti, wearing her royal crown, in order to display her beauty to the people
and nobles, for she was lovely to look at.
12 But when the attendants delivered the
king's command, Queen Vashti refused
to come. Then the king became furious
and burned with anger.

13 Since it was customary for the king
to consult experts in matters of law and
justice, he spoke with the wise men who
understood the times 14 and were closest
to the king—Carshena, Shethar, Adma-
tha, Tarshish, Meres, Marsena and Memucan, the seven nobles of Persia and
Media who had special access to the king
and were highest in the kingdom.

15 "According to law, what must be done
to Queen Vashti?" he asked. "She has not
obeyed the command of King Xerxes that
the eunuchs have taken to her."

16 Then Memucan replied in the presence of the king and the nobles, "Queen
Vashti has done wrong, not only against
the king but also against all the nobles
and the peoples of all the provinces of
King Xerxes. 17 For the queen's conduct
will become known to all the women,
and so they will despise their husbands
and say, 'King Xerxes commanded
Queen Vashti to be brought before him,
but she would not come.' 18 This very day

the Persian and Median women of the nobility who have heard about the queen's conduct will respond to all the king's nobles in the same way. There will be no end of disrespect and discord.

19"Therefore, if it pleases the king, let him issue a royal decree and let it be written in the laws of Persia and Media, which cannot be repealed, that Vashti is never again to enter the presence of King Xerxes. Also let the king give her royal position to someone else who is better than she. 20Then when the king's edict is proclaimed throughout all his vast realm, all the women will respect their husbands, from the least to the greatest."

21The king and his nobles were pleased with this advice, so the king did as Memucan proposed. 22He sent dispatches to all parts of the kingdom, to each province in its own script and to each people in its own language, proclaiming in each people's tongue that every man should be ruler over his own household.

2:1LATER when the anger of King Xerxes had subsided, he remembered Vashti and what she had done and what he had decreed about her. 2Then the king's personal attendants proposed, "Let a search be made for beautiful young virgins for the king. 3Let the king appoint commissioners in every province of his realm to bring all these beautiful girls into the harem at the citadel of Susa. Let them be placed under the care of Hegai, the king's eunuch, who is in charge of the women; and let beauty treatments be given to them. 4Then let the girl who pleases the king be queen instead of Vashti." This advice appealed to the king, and he followed it.

5Now there was in the citadel of Susa a Jew of the tribe of Benjamin, named Mordecai son of Jair, the son of Shimei, the son of Kish, 6who had been carried into exile from Jerusalem by Nebuchadnezzar king of Babylon, among those taken captive with Jehoiachin*c* king of Judah. 7Mordecai had a cousin named Hadassah, whom he had brought up be-

cause she had neither father nor mother. This girl, who was also known as Esther, was lovely in form and features, and Mordecai had taken her as his own daughter when her father and mother died.

8When the king's order and edict had been proclaimed, many girls were brought to the citadel of Susa and put under the care of Hegai. Esther also was taken to the king's palace and entrusted to Hegai, who had charge of the harem. 9The girl pleased him and won his favor. Immediately he provided her with her beauty treatments and special food. He assigned to her seven maids selected from the king's palace and moved her and her maids into the best place in the harem.

10Esther had not revealed her nationality and family background, because Mordecai had forbidden her to do so. 11Every day he walked back and forth near the courtyard of the harem to find out how Esther was and what was happening to her.

12Before a girl's turn came to go in to King Xerxes, she had to complete twelve months of beauty treatments prescribed for the women, six months with oil of myrrh and six with perfumes and cosmetics. 13And this is how she would go to the king: Anything she wanted was given her to take with her from the harem to the king's palace. 14In the evening she would go there and in the morning return to another part of the harem to the care of Shaashgaz, the king's eunuch who was in charge of the concubines. She would not return to the king unless he was pleased with her and summoned her by name.

15When the turn came for Esther (the girl Mordecai had adopted, the daughter of his uncle Abihail) to go to the king, she asked for nothing other than what Hegai, the king's eunuch who was in charge of the harem, suggested. And Esther won the favor of everyone who saw her. 16She was taken to King Xerxes in the royal residence in the tenth month, the month of Tebeth, in the seventh year of his reign.

¹⁷Now the king was attracted to Esther more than to any of the other women, and she won his favor and approval more than any of the other virgins. So he set a royal crown on her head and made her queen instead of Vashti. ¹⁸And the king gave a great banquet, Esther's banquet, for all his nobles and officials. He proclaimed a holiday throughout the provinces and distributed gifts with royal liberality.

¹⁹When the virgins were assembled a second time, Mordecai was sitting at the king's gate. ²⁰But Esther had kept secret her family background and nationality just as Mordecai had told her to do, for she continued to follow Mordecai's instructions as she had done when he was bringing her up.

²¹During the time Mordecai was sitting at the king's gate, Bigthana*d* and Teresh, two of the king's officers who guarded the doorway, became angry and conspired to assassinate King Xerxes. ²²But Mordecai found out about the plot and told Queen Esther, who in turn reported it to the king, giving credit to Mordecai. ²³And when the report was investigated and found to be true, the two officials were hanged on a gallows.*e* All this was recorded in the book of the annals in the presence of the king.

³:¹AFTER these events, King Xerxes honored Haman son of Hammedatha, the Agagite, elevating him and giving him a seat of honor higher than that of all the other nobles. ²All the royal officials at the king's gate knelt down and paid honor to Haman, for the king had commanded this concerning him. But Mordecai would not kneel down or pay him honor.

³Then the royal officials at the king's gate asked Mordecai, "Why do you disobey the king's command?" ⁴Day after day they spoke to him but he refused to comply. Therefore they told Haman about it to see whether Mordecai's be-

havior would be tolerated, for he had told them he was a Jew.

⁵When Haman saw that Mordecai would not kneel down or pay him honor, he was enraged. ⁶Yet having learned who Mordecai's people were, he scorned the idea of killing only Mordecai. Instead Haman looked for a way to destroy all Mordecai's people, the Jews, throughout the whole kingdom of Xerxes.

⁷In the twelfth year of King Xerxes, in the first month, the month of Nisan, they cast the *pur* (that is, the lot) in the presence of Haman to select a day and month. And the lot fell on*f* the twelfth month, the month of Adar.

⁸Then Haman said to King Xerxes, "There is a certain people dispersed and scattered among the peoples in all the provinces of your kingdom whose customs are different from those of all other people and who do not obey the king's laws; it is not in the king's best interest to tolerate them. ⁹If it pleases the king, let a decree be issued to destroy them, and I will put ten thousand talents*g* of silver into the royal treasury for the men who carry out this business."

¹⁰So the king took his signet ring from his finger and gave it to Haman son of Hammedatha, the Agagite, the enemy of the Jews. ¹¹"Keep the money," the king said to Haman, "and do with the people as you please."

¹²Then on the thirteenth day of the first month the royal secretaries were summoned. They wrote out in the script of each province and in the language of each people all Haman's orders to the king's satraps, the governors of the various provinces and the nobles of the various peoples. These were written in the name of King Xerxes himself and sealed with his own ring. ¹³Dispatches were sent by couriers to all the king's provinces with the order to destroy, kill and annihilate all the Jews—young and old, women and little children—on a single day, the thirteenth day of the twelfth month, the month of Adar, and to plunder their goods. ¹⁴A copy of the

text of the edict was to be issued as law in every province and made known to the people of every nationality so they would be ready for that day.

¹⁵Spurred on by the king's command, the couriers went out, and the edict was issued in the citadel of Susa. The king and Haman sat down to drink, but the city of Susa was bewildered.

a1 Hebrew *Ahasuerus,* a variant of Xerxes' Persian name; here and throughout Esther   *b1* That is, the upper Nile region   *c6* Hebrew *Jeconiah,* a variant of *Jehoiachin*   *d21* Hebrew *Bigthan,* a variant of *Bigthana*   *e23* Or *were hung* (or *impaled*) *on poles;* similarly elsewhere in Esther   *17* Septuagint; Hebrew does not have *And the lot fell on.*   *g9* That is, about 375 tons (about 345 metric tons)

1 CORINTHIANS 11:17-34

In the following directives I have no praise for you, for your meetings do more harm than good. ¹⁸In the first place, I hear that when you come together as a church, there are divisions among you, and to some extent I believe it. ¹⁹No doubt there have to be differences among you to show which of you have God's approval. ²⁰When you come together, it is not the Lord's Supper you eat, ²¹for as you eat, each of you goes ahead without waiting for anybody else. One remains hungry, another gets drunk. ²²Don't you have homes to eat and drink in? Or do you despise the church of God and humiliate those who have nothing? What shall I say to you? Shall I praise you for this? Certainly not!

²³For I received from the Lord what I also passed on to you: The Lord Jesus, on the night he was betrayed, took bread, ²⁴and when he had given thanks, he broke it and said, "This is my body, which is for you; do this in remembrance of me." ²⁵In the same way, after supper he took the cup, saying, "This cup is the new covenant in my blood; do this, whenever you drink it, in remembrance of me." ²⁶For whenever you eat this bread and drink this cup, you proclaim the Lord's death until he comes.

²⁷Therefore, whoever eats the bread or drinks the cup of the Lord in an unworthy manner will be guilty of sinning against the body and blood of the Lord. ²⁸A man ought to examine himself before he eats of the bread and drinks of the cup. ²⁹For anyone who eats and drinks without recognizing the body of the Lord eats and drinks judgment on himself. ³⁰That is why many among you are weak and sick, and a number of you have fallen asleep. ³¹But if we judged ourselves, we would not come under judgment. ³²When we are judged by the Lord, we are being disciplined so that we will not be condemned with the world.

³³So then, my brothers, when you come together to eat, wait for each other. ³⁴If anyone is hungry, he should eat at home, so that when you meet together it may not result in judgment.

And when I come I will give further directions.

PSALM 35:17-28

¹⁷❂ Lord, how long will you look on?
　　Rescue my life from their ravages,
　　my precious life from these lions.
¹⁸I will give you thanks in the great
　　assembly;
　　among throngs of people I will
　　praise you.

¹⁹Let not those gloat over me
　　who are my enemies without cause;
　let not those who hate me without
　　reason
　　maliciously wink the eye.
²⁰They do not speak peaceably,
　　but devise false accusations
　　against those who live quietly in
　　the land.
²¹They gape at me and say, "Aha! Aha!
　　With our own eyes we have seen it."

²²O LORD, you have seen this; be not
　　silent.
　　Do not be far from me, O Lord.
²³Awake, and rise to my defense!
　　Contend for me, my God and Lord.
²⁴Vindicate me in your righteousness,
　　O LORD my God;
　　do not let them gloat over me.
²⁵Do not let them think, "Aha, just what
　　we wanted!"
　　or say, "We have swallowed
　　him up."

26 May all who gloat over my distress
    be put to shame and confusion;
  may all who exalt themselves over me
    be clothed with shame and
    disgrace.
27 May those who delight in my
    vindication
    shout for joy and gladness;
  may they always say, "The Lord be
    exalted,
  who delights in the well-being
    of his servant."
28 My tongue will speak of your
    righteousness
  and of your praises all day long.

PROVERBS 21:19-20
19 Better to live in a desert
    than with a quarrelsome and ill-
    tempered wife.

20 In the house of the wise are stores
    of choice food and oil,
  but a foolish man devours all he
    has.

□ DAY 231

GOD SIGHTINGS

August 19

ESTHER 4:1–7:10
When Mordecai learned of all that had
been done, he tore his clothes, put on
sackcloth and ashes, and went out into
the city, wailing loudly and bitterly. 2 But
he went only as far as the king's gate, because no one clothed in sackcloth was allowed to enter it. 3 In every province to
which the edict and order of the king
came, there was great mourning among
the Jews, with fasting, weeping and wailing. Many lay in sackcloth and ashes.

4 When Esther's maids and eunuchs
came and told her about Mordecai, she
was in great distress. She sent clothes
for him to put on instead of his sackcloth, but he would not accept them.
5 Then Esther summoned Hathach, one

of the king's eunuchs assigned to attend
her, and ordered him to find out what
was troubling Mordecai and why.

6 So Hathach went out to Mordecai in
the open square of the city in front of
the king's gate. 7 Mordecai told him everything that had happened to him, including the exact amount of money
Haman had promised to pay into the
royal treasury for the destruction of the
Jews. 8 He also gave him a copy of the
text of the edict for their annihilation,
which had been published in Susa, to
show to Esther and explain it to her, and
he told him to urge her to go into the
king's presence to beg for mercy and
plead with him for her people.

9 Hathach went back and reported to
Esther what Mordecai had said. 10 Then
she instructed him to say to Mordecai,
11 "All the king's officials and the people
of the royal provinces know that for any
man or woman who approaches the
king in the inner court without being
summoned the king has but one law:
that he be put to death. The only excep-
tion to this is for the king to extend the
gold scepter to him and spare his life.
But thirty days have passed since I was
called to go to the king."

12 When Esther's words were reported to Mordecai, 13 he sent back this
answer: "Do not think that because you
are in the king's house you alone of all
the Jews will escape. 14 For if you remain
silent at this time, relief and deliverance
for the Jews will arise from another
place, but you and your father's family
will perish. And who knows but that you
have come to royal position for such a
time as this?"

15 Then Esther sent this reply to Mordecai: 16 "Go, gather together all the Jews
who are in Susa, and fast for me. Do not
eat or drink for three days, night or day. I
and my maids will fast as you do. When
this is done, I will go to the king, even
though it is against the law. And if I perish, I perish."

17 So Mordecai went away and carried
out all of Esther's instructions.

5:1ON the third day Esther put on her royal robes and stood in the inner court of the palace, in front of the king's hall. The king was sitting on his royal throne in the hall, facing the entrance. 2When he saw Queen Esther standing in the court, he was pleased with her and held out to her the gold scepter that was in his hand. So Esther approached and touched the tip of the scepter.

3Then the king asked, "What is it, Queen Esther? What is your request? Even up to half the kingdom, it will be given you."

4"If it pleases the king," replied Esther, "let the king, together with Haman, come today to a banquet I have prepared for him."

5"Bring Haman at once," the king said, "so that we may do what Esther asks."

So the king and Haman went to the banquet Esther had prepared. 6As they were drinking wine, the king again asked Esther, "Now what is your petition? It will be given you. And what is your request? Even up to half the kingdom, it will be granted."

7Esther replied, "My petition and my request is this: 8If the king regards me with favor and if it pleases the king to grant my petition and fulfill my request, let the king and Haman come tomorrow to the banquet I will prepare for them. Then I will answer the king's question."

9Haman went out that day happy and in high spirits. But when he saw Mordecai at the king's gate and observed that he neither rose nor showed fear in his presence, he was filled with rage against Mordecai. 10Nevertheless, Haman restrained himself and went home.

Calling together his friends and Zeresh, his wife, 11Haman boasted to them about his vast wealth, his many sons, and all the ways the king had honored him and how he had elevated him above the other nobles and officials. 12"And that's not all," Haman added. "I'm the only person Queen Esther invited to accompany the king to the banquet she gave. And she has invited me along with the king tomorrow. 13But all this gives me no satisfaction as long as I see that Jew Mordecai sitting at the king's gate."

14His wife Zeresh and all his friends said to him, "Have a gallows built, seventy-five feeta high, and ask the king in the morning to have Mordecai hanged on it. Then go with the king to the dinner and be happy." This suggestion delighted Haman, and he had the gallows built.

6:1THAT night the king could not sleep; so he ordered the book of the chronicles, the record of his reign, to be brought in and read to him. 2It was found recorded there that Mordecai had exposed Bigthana and Teresh, two of the king's officers who guarded the doorway, who had conspired to assassinate King Xerxes.

3"What honor and recognition has Mordecai received for this?" the king asked.

"Nothing has been done for him," his attendants answered.

4The king said, "Who is in the court?" Now Haman had just entered the outer court of the palace to speak to the king about hanging Mordecai on the gallows he had erected for him.

5His attendants answered, "Haman is standing in the court."

"Bring him in," the king ordered.

6When Haman entered, the king asked him, "What should be done for the man the king delights to honor?"

Now Haman thought to himself, "Who is there that the king would rather honor than me?" 7So he answered the king, "For the man the king delights to honor, 8have them bring a royal robe the king has worn and a horse the king has ridden, one with a royal crest placed on its head. 9Then let the robe and horse be entrusted to one of the king's most noble princes. Let them robe the man the king delights to honor, and lead him on the horse through the city streets, proclaiming before him, 'This is what is done for the man the king delights to honor!'"

10"Go at once," the king commanded Haman. "Get the robe and the horse and

---

do just as you have suggested for Mordecai the Jew, who sits at the king's gate. Do not neglect anything you have recommended."

¹¹So Haman got the robe and the horse. He robed Mordecai, and led him on horseback through the city streets, proclaiming before him, "This is what is done for the man the king delights to honor!"

¹²Afterward Mordecai returned to the king's gate. But Haman rushed home, with his head covered in grief, ¹³and told Zeresh his wife and all his friends everything that had happened to him.

His advisers and his wife Zeresh said to him, "Since Mordecai, before whom your downfall has started, is of Jewish origin, you cannot stand against him—you will surely come to ruin!" ¹⁴While they were still talking with him, the king's eunuchs arrived and hurried Haman away to the banquet Esther had prepared.

⁷:¹So the king and Haman went to dine with Queen Esther, ²and as they were drinking wine on that second day, the king again asked, "Queen Esther, what is your petition? It will be given you. What is your request? Even up to half the kingdom, it will be granted."

³Then Queen Esther answered, "If I have found favor with you, O king, and if it pleases your majesty, grant me my life—this is my petition. And spare my people—this is my request. ⁴For I and my people have been sold for destruction and slaughter and annihilation. If we had merely been sold as male and female slaves, I would have kept quiet, because no such distress would justify disturbing the king.ᵇ"

⁵King Xerxes asked Queen Esther, "Who is he? Where is the man who has dared to do such a thing?"

⁶Esther said, "The adversary and enemy is this vile Haman."

Then Haman was terrified before the king and queen. ⁷The king got up in a rage, left his wine and went out into the palace garden. But Haman, realizing that the king had already decided his fate, stayed behind to beg Queen Esther for his life.

⁸Just as the king returned from the palace garden to the banquet hall, Haman was falling on the couch where Esther was reclining.

The king exclaimed, "Will he even molest the queen while she is with me in the house?"

As soon as the word left the king's mouth, they covered Haman's face. ⁹Then Harbona, one of the eunuchs attending the king, said, "A gallows seventy-five feetᶜ high stands by Haman's house. He had it made for Mordecai, who spoke up to help the king."

The king said, "Hang him on it!" ¹⁰So they hanged Haman on the gallows he had prepared for Mordecai. Then the king's fury subsided.

ᵃ14 Hebrew fifty cubits (about 23 meters) ᵇ4 Or quiet, but the compensation our adversary offers cannot be compared with the loss the king would suffer ᶜ9 Hebrew fifty cubits (about 23 meters)

1 CORINTHIANS 12:1-26

Now about spiritual gifts, brothers, I do not want you to be ignorant. ²You know that when you were pagans, somehow or other you were influenced and led astray to mute idols. ³Therefore I tell you that no one who is speaking by the Spirit of God says, "Jesus be cursed," and no one can say, "Jesus is Lord," except by the Holy Spirit.

⁴There are different kinds of gifts, but the same Spirit. ⁵There are different kinds of service, but the same Lord. ⁶There are different kinds of working, but the same God works all of them in all men.

⁷Now to each one the manifestation of the Spirit is given for the common good. ⁸To one there is given through the Spirit the message of wisdom, to another the message of knowledge by means of the same Spirit, ⁹to another faith by the same Spirit, to another gifts of healing by that one Spirit, ¹⁰to another miraculous powers, to another prophecy, to another distinguishing between spirits, to another speaking in

different kinds of tongues,[a] and to still another the interpretation of tongues.[b] [11]All these are the work of one and the same Spirit, and he gives them to each one, just as he determines.

[12]**The body is a unit, though it is made up of many parts; and though all its parts are many, they form one body. So it is with Christ.** [13]**For we were all baptized by[b] one Spirit into one body—whether Jews or Greeks, slave or free—and we were all given the one Spirit to drink.**

[14]Now the body is not made up of one part but of many. [15]If the foot should say, "Because I am not a hand, I do not belong to the body," it would not for that reason cease to be part of the body. [16]And if the ear should say, "Because I am not an eye, I do not belong to the body," it would not for that reason cease to be part of the body. [17]If the whole body were an eye, where would the sense of hearing be? If the whole body were an ear, where would the sense of smell be? [18]But in fact God has arranged the parts in the body, every one of them, just as he wanted them to be. [19]If they were all one part, where would the body be? [20]As it is, there are many parts, but one body.

[21]The eye cannot say to the hand, "I don't need you!" And the head cannot say to the feet, "I don't need you!" [22]On the contrary, those parts of the body that seem to be weaker are indispensable, [23]and the parts that we think are less honorable we treat with special honor. And the parts that are unpresentable are treated with special modesty, [24]while our presentable parts need no special treatment. But God has combined the members of the body and has given greater honor to the parts that lacked it, [25]so that there should be no division in the body, but that its parts should have equal concern for each other. [26]If one part suffers, every part suffers with it; if one part is honored, every part rejoices with it.

a 10 Or languages; also in verse 28   b 13 Or with; or in

PSALM 36:1-12

For the director of music. Of David the servant of the LORD.

[1] **A**n oracle is within my heart
   concerning the sinfulness of the
      wicked:[a]
There is no fear of God
   before his eyes.
[2] For in his own eyes he flatters
      himself
   too much to detect or hate his sin.
[3] The words of his mouth are wicked
      and deceitful;
   he has ceased to be wise and to
      do good.
[4] Even on his bed he plots evil;
   he commits himself to a sinful
      course
   and does not reject what is wrong.

[5] Your love, O LORD, reaches to the
      heavens,
   your faithfulness to the skies.
[6] Your righteousness is like the mighty
      mountains,
   your justice like the great deep.
O LORD, you preserve both man and
      beast.
[7]   How priceless is your unfailing
         love!
Both high and low among men
   find[b] refuge in the shadow of your
      wings.
[8] They feast on the abundance of your
      house;
   you give them drink from your
      river of delights.
[9] For with you is the fountain of life;
   in your light we see light.

[10] Continue your love to those who
      know you,
   your righteousness to the upright
      in heart.
[11] May the foot of the proud not come
      against me,
   nor the hand of the wicked drive
      me away.
[12] See how the evildoers lie fallen—
   thrown down, not able to rise!

a 1 Or heart: / Sin proceeds from the wicked.   b 7 Or love,
O God! / Men find; or love! / Both heavenly beings and
men / find

PROVERBS 21:21-22
²¹He who pursues righteousness and
        love
    finds life, prosperityª and honor.

²²A wise man attacks the city of the
        mighty
    and pulls down the stronghold in
        which they trust.

ª21 Or *righteousness*

□ D A Y   2 3 2

GOD SIGHTINGS

August 20

ESTHER 8:1–10:3
That same day King Xerxes gave Queen
Esther the estate of Haman, the enemy
of the Jews. And Mordecai came into
the presence of the king, for Esther had
told how he was related to her. ²The
king took off his signet ring, which he
had reclaimed from Haman, and presented it to Mordecai. And Esther appointed him over Haman's estate.

³Esther again pleaded with the king,
falling at his feet and weeping. She
begged him to put an end to the evil plan
of Haman the Agagite, which he had devised against the Jews. ⁴Then the king
extended the gold scepter to Esther and
she arose and stood before him.

⁵"If it pleases the king," she said, "and
if he regards me with favor and thinks it
the right thing to do, and if he is pleased
with me, let an order be written overrul-
ing the dispatches that Haman son of
Hammedatha, the Agagite, devised and
wrote to destroy the Jews in all the king's
provinces. ⁶For how can I bear to see disaster fall on my people? How can I bear
to see the destruction of my family?"

⁷King Xerxes replied to Queen Esther
and to Mordecai the Jew, "Because Haman attacked the Jews, I have given his
estate to Esther, and they have hanged
him on the gallows. ⁸Now write another
decree in the king's name in behalf of

the Jews as seems best to you, and seal it
with the king's signet ring—for no docu-
ment written in the king's name and
sealed with his ring can be revoked."

⁹At once the royal secretaries were
summoned—on the twenty-third day of
the third month, the month of Sivan.
They wrote out all Mordecai's orders to
the Jews, and to the satraps, governors
and nobles of the 127 provinces
stretching from India to Cush.ª These
orders were written in the script of each
province and the language of each people and also to the Jews in their own
script and language. ¹⁰Mordecai wrote
in the name of King Xerxes, sealed the
dispatches with the king's signet ring,
and sent them by mounted couriers,
who rode fast horses especially bred for
the king.

¹¹The king's edict granted the Jews in
every city the right to assemble and protect themselves; to destroy, kill and annihilate any armed force of any
nationality or province that might attack them and their women and children; and to plunder the property of
their enemies. ¹²The day appointed for
the Jews to do this in all the provinces of
King Xerxes was the thirteenth day of
the twelfth month, the month of Adar.
¹³A copy of the text of the edict was to
be issued as law in every province and
made known to the people of every nationality so that the Jews would be ready
on that day to avenge themselves on
their enemies.

¹⁴The couriers, riding the royal
horses, raced out, spurred on by the
king's command. And the edict was also
issued in the citadel of Susa.

¹⁵Mordecai left the king's presence
wearing royal garments of blue and
white, a large crown of gold and a purple robe of fine linen. And the city of
Susa held a joyous celebration. ¹⁶For
the Jews it was a time of happiness and
joy, gladness and honor. ¹⁷In every
province and in every city, wherever the
edict of the king went, there was joy and
gladness among the Jews, with feasting
and celebrating. And many people of

other nationalities became Jews because fear of the Jews had seized them.

9:1On the thirteenth day of the twelfth month, the month of Adar, the edict commanded by the king was to be carried out. On this day the enemies of the Jews had hoped to overpower them, but now the tables were turned and the Jews got the upper hand over those who hated them. 2The Jews assembled in their cities in all the provinces of King Xerxes to attack those seeking their destruction. No one could stand against them, because the people of all the other nationalities were afraid of them. 3And all the nobles of the provinces, the satraps, the governors and the king's administrators helped the Jews, because fear of Mordecai had seized them. 4Mordecai was prominent in the palace; his reputation spread throughout the provinces, and he became more and more powerful.

5The Jews struck down all their enemies with the sword, killing and destroying them, and they did what they pleased to those who hated them. 6In the citadel of Susa, the Jews killed and destroyed five hundred men. 7They also killed Parshandatha, Dalphon, Aspatha, 8Poratha, Adalia, Aridatha, 9Parmashta, Arisai, Aridai and Vaizatha, 10the ten sons of Haman son of Hammedatha, the enemy of the Jews. But they did not lay their hands on the plunder.

11The number of those slain in the citadel of Susa was reported to the king that same day. 12The king said to Queen Esther, "The Jews have killed and destroyed five hundred men and the ten sons of Haman in the citadel of Susa. What have they done in the rest of the king's provinces? Now what is your petition? It will be given you. What is your request? It will also be granted."

13"If it pleases the king," Esther answered, "give the Jews in Susa permission to carry out this day's edict tomorrow also, and let Haman's ten sons be hanged on gallows."

14So the king commanded that this be done. An edict was issued in Susa, and they hanged the ten sons of Haman. 15The Jews in Susa came together on the fourteenth day of the month of Adar, and they put to death in Susa three hundred men, but they did not lay their hands on the plunder.

16Meanwhile, the remainder of the Jews who were in the king's provinces also assembled to protect themselves and get relief from their enemies. They killed seventy-five thousand of them but did not lay their hands on the plunder. 17This happened on the thirteenth day of the month of Adar, and on the fourteenth they rested and made it a day of feasting and joy.

18The Jews in Susa, however, had assembled on the thirteenth and fourteenth, and then on the fifteenth they rested and made it a day of feasting and joy.

19That is why rural Jews—those living in villages—observe the fourteenth of the month of Adar as a day of joy and feasting, a day for giving presents to each other.

20Mordecai recorded these events, and he sent letters to all the Jews throughout the provinces of King Xerxes, near and far, 21to have them celebrate annually the fourteenth and fifteenth days of the month of Adar 22as the time when the Jews got relief from their enemies, and as the month when their sorrow was turned into joy and their mourning into a day of celebration. He wrote them to observe the days as days of feasting and joy and giving presents of food to one another and gifts to the poor.

23So the Jews agreed to continue the celebration they had begun, doing what Mordecai had written to them. 24For Haman son of Hammedatha, the Agagite, the enemy of all the Jews, had plotted against the Jews to destroy them and had cast the *pur* (that is, the lot) for their ruin and destruction. 25But when the plot came to the king's attention,*b* he issued written orders that the evil scheme Haman had devised against the Jews should come back onto his own head, and that he and his sons should be hanged on the gallows. 26(Therefore these days were called Purim, from the word *pur.*) Because of everything written in this letter and because of what they had seen and what had happened to them, 27the Jews took it upon themselves to establish the custom that they and their descendants and all who join them should without fail observe these two days every year, in the way prescribed and at the time appointed. 28These days should be remembered and observed in every generation by every family, and in every province and in every city. And these days of Purim should never cease to be celebrated by the Jews, nor should the memory of them die out among their descendants.

29So Queen Esther, daughter of Abihail, along with Mordecai the Jew, wrote with full authority to confirm this second letter concerning Purim. 30And Mordecai sent letters to all the Jews in the 127 provinces of the kingdom of Xerxes—words of goodwill and assurance—31to establish these days of Purim at their designated times, as Mordecai the Jew and Queen Esther had decreed for them, and as they had established for themselves and their descendants in regard to their times of fasting and lamentation. 32Esther's decree confirmed these regulations about Purim, and it was written down in the records.

10:1KING Xerxes imposed tribute throughout the empire, to its distant shores. 2And all his acts of power and might, together with a full account of the greatness of Mordecai to which the king had raised him, are they not written in the book of the annals of the kings of Media and Persia? 3Mordecai the Jew was second in rank to King Xerxes, preeminent among the Jews, and held in high esteem by his many fellow Jews, because he worked for the good of his people and spoke up for the welfare of all the Jews.

a9 That is, the upper Nile region   *b25* Or *when Esther came before the king*

1 CORINTHIANS 12:27–13:13

Now you are the body of Christ, and each one of you is a part of it. 28And in the church God has appointed first of all apostles, second prophets, third teachers, then workers of miracles, also those having gifts of healing, those able to help others, those with gifts of administration, and those speaking in different kinds of tongues. 29Are all apostles? Are all prophets? Are all teachers? Do all work miracles? 30Do all have gifts of healing? Do all speak in tongues*a*? Do all interpret? 31But eagerly desire*b* the greater gifts.

And now I will show you the most excellent way.

13:1If I speak in the tongues*c* of men and of angels, but have not love, I am only a resounding gong or a clanging cymbal. 2If I have the gift of prophecy and can fathom all mysteries and all knowledge, and if I have a faith that can move mountains, but have not love, I am nothing. 3If I give all I possess to the poor and surrender my body to the flames,*d* but have not love, I gain nothing.

4Love is patient, love is kind. It does not envy, it does not boast, it is not proud. 5It is not rude, it is not self-seeking, it is not easily angered, it keeps no record of wrongs. 6Love does not delight in evil but rejoices with the truth. 7It always protects, always trusts, always hopes, always perseveres.

8Love never fails. But where there are prophecies, they will cease; where there are tongues, they will be stilled; where there is knowledge, it will pass away. 9For we know in part and we prophesy in part, 10but when perfection comes, the imperfect disappears. 11When I was a child, I talked like a child, I thought like a child, I reasoned like a child. When I became a man, I put childish ways behind me. 12Now we see but a poor reflection as in a mirror; then we shall see face to face. Now I know in part; then I shall know fully, even as I am fully known.

13And now these three remain:

faith, hope and love. But the greatest of these is love.

*a30 Or other languages b31 Or But you are eagerly desiring
c1 Or languages d3 Some early manuscripts body that
I may boast*

PSALM 37:1-11*a*
Of David.

¹ **D**o not fret because of evil men
　　or be envious of those who do
　　　　wrong;
² for like the grass they will soon
　　wither,
　　like green plants they will soon die
　　　　away.

³ Trust in the LORD and do good;
　　dwell in the land and enjoy safe
　　　　pasture.
⁴ Delight yourself in the LORD
　　and he will give you the desires of
　　　　your heart.

⁵ Commit your way to the LORD;
　　trust in him and he will do this:
⁶ He will make your righteousness
　　shine like the dawn,
　　the justice of your cause like the
　　　　noonday sun.

⁷ Be still before the LORD and wait
　　patiently for him;
　　do not fret when men succeed in
　　　　their ways,
　　when they carry out their wicked
　　　　schemes.

⁸ Refrain from anger and turn from
　　wrath;
　　do not fret—it leads only to evil.
⁹ For evil men will be cut off,
　　but those who hope in the LORD
　　　　will inherit the land.

¹⁰ A little while, and the wicked will be
　　no more;
　　though you look for them, they
　　　　will not be found.
¹¹ But the meek will inherit the land
　　and enjoy great peace.

*aThis psalm is an acrostic poem, the stanzas of which begin
with the successive letters of the Hebrew alphabet.*

PROVERBS 21:23-24
²³ **H**e who guards his mouth and his
　　tongue
　　keeps himself from calamity.

²⁴ The proud and arrogant man—
　　"Mocker" is his name;
　　he behaves with overweening
　　　　pride.

□ D A Y 2 3 3

GOD SIGHTINGS

August 21

JOB 1:1–3:26
In the land of Uz there lived a man whose name was Job. This man was blameless and upright; he feared God and shunned evil. ²He had seven sons and three daughters, ³and he owned seven thousand sheep, three thousand camels, five hundred yoke of oxen and five hundred donkeys, and had a large number of servants. He was the greatest man among all the people of the East.

⁴His sons used to take turns holding feasts in their homes, and they would invite their three sisters to eat and drink with them. ⁵When a period of feasting had run its course, Job would send and have them purified. Early in the morning he would sacrifice a burnt offering for each of them, thinking, "Perhaps my children have sinned and cursed God in their hearts." This was Job's regular custom.

⁶One day the angels*a* came to present themselves before the LORD, and Satan*b* also came with them. ⁷The LORD said to Satan, "Where have you come from?"

Satan answered the LORD, "From roaming through the earth and going back and forth in it."

⁸Then the LORD said to Satan, "Have you considered my servant Job? There is no one on earth like him; he is blameless and upright, a man who fears God and shuns evil."

⁹"Does Job fear God for nothing?" Sa-

tan replied. ¹⁰"Have you not put a hedge around him and his household and everything he has? You have blessed the work of his hands, so that his flocks and herds are spread throughout the land. ¹¹But stretch out your hand and strike everything he has, and he will surely curse you to your face."

¹²The Lord said to Satan, "Very well, then, everything he has is in your hands, but on the man himself do not lay a finger."

Then Satan went out from the presence of the Lord.

¹³One day when Job's sons and daughters were feasting and drinking wine at the oldest brother's house, ¹⁴a messenger came to Job and said, "The oxen were plowing and the donkeys were grazing nearby, ¹⁵and the Sabeans attacked and carried them off. They put the servants to the sword, and I am the only one who has escaped to tell you!"

¹⁶While he was still speaking, another messenger came and said, "The fire of God fell from the sky and burned up the sheep and the servants, and I am the only one who has escaped to tell you!"

¹⁷While he was still speaking, another messenger came and said, "The Chaldeans formed three raiding parties and swept down on your camels and carried them off. They put the servants to the sword, and I am the only one who has escaped to tell you!"

¹⁸While he was still speaking, yet another messenger came and said, "Your sons and daughters were feasting and drinking wine at the oldest brother's house, ¹⁹when suddenly a mighty wind swept in from the desert and struck the four corners of the house. It collapsed on them and they are dead, and I am the only one who has escaped to tell you!"

²⁰At this, Job got up and tore his robe and shaved his head. Then he fell to the ground in worship ²¹and said:

"Naked I came from my mother's
    womb,
  and naked I will depart.ᶜ

The Lord gave and the Lord has
    taken away;
  may the name of the Lord be
    praised."

²²In all this, Job did not sin by charging God with wrongdoing.

2:1On another day the angelsᵃ came to present themselves before the Lord, and Satan also came with them to present himself before him. ²And the Lord said to Satan, "Where have you come from?"

Satan answered the Lord, "From roaming through the earth and going back and forth in it."

³Then the Lord said to Satan, "Have you considered my servant Job? There is no one on earth like him; he is blameless and upright, a man who fears God and shuns evil. And he still maintains his integrity, though you incited me against him to ruin him without any reason."

⁴"Skin for skin!" Satan replied. "A man will give all he has for his own life. ⁵But stretch out your hand and strike his flesh and bones, and he will surely curse you to your face."

⁶The Lord said to Satan, "Very well, then, he is in your hands; but you must spare his life."

⁷So Satan went out from the presence of the Lord and afflicted Job with painful sores from the soles of his feet to the top of his head. ⁸Then Job took a piece of broken pottery and scraped himself with it as he sat among the ashes.

⁹His wife said to him, "Are you still holding on to your integrity? Curse God and die!"

¹⁰He replied, "You are talking like a foolishᵈ woman. Shall we accept good from God, and not trouble?"

In all this, Job did not sin in what he said.

¹¹When Job's three friends, Eliphaz the Temanite, Bildad the Shuhite and Zophar the Naamathite, heard about all the troubles that had come upon him, they set out from their homes and met together by agreement to go and sympathize with him and comfort him.

12 When they saw him from a distance, they could hardly recognize him; they began to weep aloud, and they tore their robes and sprinkled dust on their heads. 13 Then they sat on the ground with him for seven days and seven nights. No one said a word to him, because they saw how great his suffering was.

3:1 AFTER this, Job opened his mouth and cursed the day of his birth. 2 He said:

3 "May the day of my birth perish,
   and the night it was said, 'A boy is
   born!'
4 That day—may it turn to darkness;
   may God above not care about it;
   may no light shine upon it.
5 May darkness and deep shadow*e*
   claim it once more;
   may a cloud settle over it;
   may blackness overwhelm its light.
6 That night—may thick darkness
   seize it;
   may it not be included among the
   days of the year
   nor be entered in any of the
   months.
7 May that night be barren;
   may no shout of joy be heard in it.
8 May those who curse days*f* curse that
   day,
   those who are ready to rouse
   Leviathan.
9 May its morning stars become dark;
   may it wait for daylight in vain
   and not see the first rays of dawn,
10 for it did not shut the doors of the
   womb on me
   to hide trouble from my eyes.

11 "Why did I not perish at birth,
   and die as I came from the womb?
12 Why were there knees to receive me
   and breasts that I might be nursed?
13 For now I would be lying down in
   peace;
   I would be asleep and at rest
14 with kings and counselors of the earth,
   who built for themselves places
   now lying in ruins,
15 with rulers who had gold,
   who filled their houses with silver.

16 Or why was I not hidden in the
   ground like a stillborn child,
   like an infant who never saw the
   light of day?
17 There the wicked cease from
   turmoil,
   and there the weary are at rest.
18 Captives also enjoy their ease;
   they no longer hear the slave
   driver's shout.
19 The small and the great are there,
   and the slave is freed from his
   master.

20 "Why is light given to those in
   misery,
   and life to the bitter of soul,
21 to those who long for death that does
   not come,
   who search for it more than for
   hidden treasure,
22 who are filled with gladness
   and rejoice when they reach the
   grave?
23 Why is life given to a man
   whose way is hidden,
   whom God has hedged in?
24 For sighing comes to me instead of
   food;
   my groans pour out like water.
25 What I feared has come upon me;
   what I dreaded has happened
   to me.
26 I have no peace, no quietness;
   I have no rest, but only turmoil."

*a 6,1 Hebrew the sons of God   b 6 Satan means accuser.
c 21 Or will return there   d 10 The Hebrew word rendered
foolish denotes moral deficiency.   e 5 Or and the shadow of
death   f 8 Or the sea*

1 CORINTHIANS 14:1-17

Follow the way of love and eagerly desire spiritual gifts, especially the gift of prophecy. 2 For anyone who speaks in a tongue*a* does not speak to men but to God. Indeed, no one understands him; he utters mysteries with his spirit.*b* 3 But everyone who prophesies speaks to men for their strengthening, encouragement and comfort. 4 He who speaks in a tongue edifies himself, but he who prophesies edifies the church. 5 I would like every one of you to speak in tongues,*c* but I would rather have you prophesy. He who prophesies is greater than one who speaks in tongues,c unless he interprets, so that the church may be edified.

6Now, brothers, if I come to you and speak in tongues, what good will I be to you, unless I bring you some revelation or knowledge or prophecy or word of instruction? 7Even in the case of lifeless things that make sounds, such as the flute or harp, how will anyone know what tune is being played unless there is a distinction in the notes? 8Again, if the trumpet does not sound a clear call, who will get ready for battle? 9So it is with you. Unless you speak intelligible words with your tongue, how will anyone know what you are saying? You will just be speaking into the air. 10Undoubtedly there are all sorts of languages in the world, yet none of them is without meaning. 11If then I do not grasp the meaning of what someone is saying, I am a foreigner to the speaker, and he is a foreigner to me. 12So it is with you. Since you are eager to have spiritual gifts, try to excel in gifts that build up the church.

13For this reason anyone who speaks in a tongue should pray that he may interpret what he says. 14For if I pray in a tongue, my spirit prays, but my mind is unfruitful. 15So what shall I do? I will pray with my spirit, but I will also pray with my mind; I will sing with my spirit, but I will also sing with my mind. 16If you are praising God with your spirit, how can one who finds himself among those who do not understandd say "Amen" to your thanksgiving, since he does not know what you are saying? 17You may be giving thanks well enough, but the other man is not edified.

a2 Or another language; also in verses 4, 13, 14, 19, 26 and 27   b2 Or by the Spirit   c5 Or other languages; also in verses 6, 18, 22, 23 and 39   d16 Or among the inquirers

PSALM 37:12-29
12The wicked plot against the righteous
and gnash their teeth at them;
13but the Lord laughs at the wicked,
for he knows their day is coming.

14The wicked draw the sword
and bend the bow
to bring down the poor and needy,
to slay those whose ways are upright.
15But their swords will pierce their own hearts,
and their bows will be broken.

16Better the little that the righteous have
than the wealth of many wicked;
17for the power of the wicked will be broken,
but the Lord upholds the righteous.

18The days of the blameless are known to the Lord,
and their inheritance will endure forever.
19In times of disaster they will not wither;
in days of famine they will enjoy plenty.

20But the wicked will perish:
The Lord's enemies will be like the beauty of the fields,
they will vanish—vanish like smoke.

21The wicked borrow and do not repay,
but the righteous give generously;
22those the Lord blesses will inherit the land,
but those he curses will be cut off.

23If the Lord delights in a man's way,
he makes his steps firm;
24though he stumble, he will not fall,
for the Lord upholds him with his hand.

25I was young and now I am old,
yet I have never seen the righteous forsaken
or their children begging bread.
26They are always generous and lend freely;
their children will be blessed.

27Turn from evil and do good;
then you will dwell in the land forever.

28 For the LORD loves the just
    and will not forsake his faithful
        ones.

They will be protected forever,
    but the offspring of the wicked
        will be cut off;
29 the righteous will inherit the land
    and dwell in it forever.

PROVERBS 21:25-26
25 The sluggard's craving will be the
        death of him,
    because his hands refuse to work.
26 All day long he craves for more,
    but the righteous give without
        sparing.

□ DAY 234

GOD SIGHTINGS

August 22

JOB 4:1–7:21
Then Eliphaz the Temanite replied:

2 "If someone ventures a word with
        you, will you be impatient?
    But who can keep from speaking?
3 Think how you have instructed many,
    how you have strengthened feeble
        hands.
4 Your words have supported those
        who stumbled;
    you have strengthened faltering
        knees.
5 But now trouble comes to you, and
        you are discouraged;
    it strikes you, and you are
        dismayed.
6 Should not your piety be your
        confidence
    and your blameless ways your
        hope?

7 "Consider now: Who, being innocent,
        has ever perished?
    Where were the upright ever
        destroyed?

8 As I have observed, those who plow
        evil
    and those who sow trouble reap it.
9 At the breath of God they are
        destroyed;
    at the blast of his anger they perish.
10 The lions may roar and growl,
    yet the teeth of the great lions are
        broken.
11 The lion perishes for lack of prey,
    and the cubs of the lioness are
        scattered.

12 "A word was secretly brought to me,
    my ears caught a whisper of it.
13 Amid disquieting dreams in the night,
    when deep sleep falls on men,
14 fear and trembling seized me
    and made all my bones shake.
15 A spirit glided past my face,
    and the hair on my body stood
        on end.
16 It stopped,
    but I could not tell what it was.
A form stood before my eyes,
    and I heard a hushed voice:
17 'Can a mortal be more righteous than
        God?
    Can a man be more pure than his
        Maker?
18 If God places no trust in his servants,
    if he charges his angels with error,
19 how much more those who live in
        houses of clay,
    whose foundations are in the dust,
    who are crushed more readily than
        a moth!
20 Between dawn and dusk they are
        broken to pieces;
    unnoticed, they perish forever.
21 Are not the cords of their tent
        pulled up,
    so that they die without wisdom?'*a*

5:1 "CALL if you will, but who will answer
        you?
    To which of the holy ones will you
        turn?
2 Resentment kills a fool,
    and envy slays the simple.
3 I myself have seen a fool taking root,
    but suddenly his house was cursed.

4 His children are far from safety,
   crushed in court without a
   defender.
5 The hungry consume his harvest,
   taking it even from among thorns,
   and the thirsty pant after his
   wealth.
6 For hardship does not spring from
   the soil,
   nor does trouble sprout from the
   ground.
7 Yet man is born to trouble
   as surely as sparks fly upward.

8 "But if it were I, I would appeal to
   God;
   I would lay my cause before him.
9 He performs wonders that cannot be
   fathomed,
   miracles that cannot be counted.
10 He bestows rain on the earth;
   he sends water upon the
   countryside.
11 The lowly he sets on high,
   and those who mourn are lifted to
   safety.
12 He thwarts the plans of the crafty,
   so that their hands achieve no
   success.
13 He catches the wise in their
   craftiness,
   and the schemes of the wily are
   swept away.
14 Darkness comes upon them in the
   daytime;
   at noon they grope as in the night.
15 He saves the needy from the sword in
   their mouth;
   he saves them from the clutches of
   the powerful.
16 So the poor have hope,
   and injustice shuts its mouth.

17 "Blessed is the man whom God
   corrects;
   so do not despise the discipline of
   the Almighty.b
18 For he wounds, but he also binds up;
   he injures, but his hands also heal.
19 From six calamities he will rescue
   you;
   in seven no harm will befall you.

20 In famine he will ransom you from
   death,
   and in battle from the stroke of
   the sword.
21 You will be protected from the lash
   of the tongue,
   and need not fear when
   destruction comes.
22 You will laugh at destruction and
   famine,
   and need not fear the beasts of the
   earth.
23 For you will have a covenant with the
   stones of the field,
   and the wild animals will be at
   peace with you.
24 You will know that your tent is
   secure;
   you will take stock of your
   property and find nothing
   missing.
25 You will know that your children will
   be many,
   and your descendants like the
   grass of the earth.
26 You will come to the grave in full
   vigor,
   like sheaves gathered in season.

27 "We have examined this, and it is
   true.
   So hear it and apply it to yourself."

6:1 THEN Job replied:

2 "If only my anguish could be weighed
   and all my misery be placed on the
   scales!
3 It would surely outweigh the sand of
   the seas—
   no wonder my words have been
   impetuous.
4 The arrows of the Almighty are in me,
   my spirit drinks in their poison;
   God's terrors are marshaled
   against me.
5 Does a wild donkey bray when it has
   grass,
   or an ox bellow when it has
   fodder?
6 Is tasteless food eaten without salt,
   or is there flavor in the white of
   an eggc?

⁷I refuse to touch it;
    such food makes me ill.

⁸"Oh, that I might have my request,
    that God would grant what I hope
        for,
⁹that God would be willing to crush
        me,
    to let loose his hand and cut me off!
¹⁰Then I would still have this
        consolation—
    my joy in unrelenting pain—
    that I had not denied the words of
        the Holy One.

¹¹"What strength do I have, that I
        should still hope?
    What prospects, that I should be
        patient?
¹²Do I have the strength of stone?
    Is my flesh bronze?
¹³Do I have any power to help myself,
    now that success has been driven
        from me?

¹⁴"A despairing man should have the
        devotion of his friends,
    even though he forsakes the fear
        of the Almighty.
¹⁵But my brothers are as
        undependable as
        intermittent streams,
    as the streams that overflow
¹⁶when darkened by thawing ice
    and swollen with melting snow,
¹⁷but that cease to flow in the dry
        season,
    and in the heat vanish from their
        channels.
¹⁸Caravans turn aside from their routes;
    they go up into the wasteland and
        perish.
¹⁹The caravans of Tema look for water,
    the traveling merchants of Sheba
        look in hope.
²⁰They are distressed, because they
        had been confident;
    they arrive there, only to be
        disappointed.
²¹Now you too have proved to be of
        no help;
    you see something dreadful and
        are afraid.

²²Have I ever said, 'Give something on
        my behalf,
    pay a ransom for me from your
        wealth,
²³deliver me from the hand of the
        enemy,
    ransom me from the clutches of
        the ruthless'?

²⁴"Teach me, and I will be quiet;
    show me where I have been wrong.
²⁵How painful are honest words!
    But what do your arguments
        prove?
²⁶Do you mean to correct what I say,
    and treat the words of a despairing
        man as wind?
²⁷You would even cast lots for the
        fatherless
    and barter away your friend.

²⁸"But now be so kind as to look at me.
    Would I lie to your face?
²⁹Relent, do not be unjust;
    reconsider, for my integrity is at
        stake.ᵈ
³⁰Is there any wickedness on my lips?
    Can my mouth not discern malice?

7:1"Does not man have hard service on
        earth?
    Are not his days like those of a
        hired man?
²Like a slave longing for the evening
        shadows,
    or a hired man waiting eagerly for
        his wages,
³so I have been allotted months of
        futility,
    and nights of misery have been
        assigned to me.
⁴When I lie down I think, 'How long
        before I get up?'
    The night drags on, and I toss till
        dawn.
⁵My body is clothed with worms and
        scabs,
    my skin is broken and festering.

⁶"My days are swifter than a weaver's
        shuttle,
    and they come to an end without
        hope.

[7] Remember, O God, that my life is but
    a breath;
  my eyes will never see happiness
    again.
[8] The eye that now sees me will see me
    no longer;
  you will look for me, but I will be
    no more.
[9] As a cloud vanishes and is gone,
  so he who goes down to the grave[e]
    does not return.
[10] He will never come to his house
    again;
  his place will know him no more.

[11] "Therefore I will not keep silent;
  I will speak out in the anguish of
    my spirit,
  I will complain in the bitterness of
    my soul.
[12] Am I the sea, or the monster of the
    deep,
  that you put me under guard?
[13] When I think my bed will comfort me
  and my couch will ease my
    complaint,
[14] even then you frighten me with
    dreams
  and terrify me with visions,
[15] so that I prefer strangling and death,
  rather than this body of mine.
[16] I despise my life; I would not live
    forever.
  Let me alone; my days have no
    meaning.

[17] "What is man that you make so
    much of him,
  that you give him so much
    attention,
[18] that you examine him every morning
  and test him every moment?
[19] Will you never look away from me,
  or let me alone even for an
    instant?
[20] If I have sinned, what have I done to
    you,
  O watcher of men?
  Why have you made me your target?
  Have I become a burden to you?[f]
[21] Why do you not pardon my offenses
  and forgive my sins?

For I will soon lie down in the dust;
  you will search for me, but I will be
    no more."

[a]21 Some interpreters end the quotation after verse 17.
[b]17 Hebrew *Shaddai*; here and throughout Job   [c]6 The
meaning of the Hebrew for this phrase is uncertain.
[d]29 Or *my righteousness still stands*   [e]9 Hebrew *Sheol*
[f]20 A few manuscripts of the Masoretic Text, an ancient
Hebrew scribal tradition and Septuagint; most manuscripts
of the Masoretic Text *I have become a burden to myself.*

1 CORINTHIANS 14:18-40

I thank God that I speak in tongues
more than all of you. [19] But in the church
I would rather speak five intelligible
words to instruct others than ten thousand words in a tongue.

[20] Brothers, stop thinking like children. In regard to evil be infants, but in
your thinking be adults. [21] In the Law it
is written:

" Through men of strange tongues
  and through the lips of foreigners
I will speak to this people,
  but even then they will not listen
    to me,"[a]

                              says the Lord.

[22] Tongues, then, are a sign, not for
believers but for unbelievers; prophecy,
however, is for believers, not for unbelievers. [23] So if the whole church comes
together and everyone speaks in
tongues, and some who do not understand[b] or some unbelievers come in,
will they not say that you are out of your
mind? [24] But if an unbeliever or someone who does not understand[c] comes in
while everybody is prophesying, he will
be convinced by all that he is a sinner
and will be judged by all, [25] and the secrets of his heart will be laid bare. So he
will fall down and worship God, ex-
claiming, "God is really among you!"

[26] What then shall we say, brothers?
When you come together, everyone has
a hymn, or a word of instruction, a revelation, a tongue or an interpretation. All
of these must be done for the strengthening of the church. [27] If anyone speaks
in a tongue, two—or at the most three—
should speak, one at a time, and someone must interpret. [28] If there is no
interpreter, the speaker should keep

quiet in the church and speak to himself and God.

^{29} Two or three prophets should speak, and the others should weigh carefully what is said. ^{30} And if a revelation comes to someone who is sitting down, the first speaker should stop. ^{31} For you can all prophesy in turn so that everyone may be instructed and encouraged. ^{32} The spirits of prophets are subject to the control of prophets. ^{33} For God is not a God of disorder but of peace.

As in all the congregations of the saints, ^{34} women should remain silent in the churches. They are not allowed to speak, but must be in submission, as the Law says. ^{35} If they want to inquire about something, they should ask their own husbands at home; for it is disgraceful for a woman to speak in the church.

^{36} Did the word of God originate with you? Or are you the only people it has reached? ^{37} If anybody thinks he is a prophet or spiritually gifted, let him acknowledge that what I am writing to you is the Lord's command. ^{38} If he ignores this, he himself will be ignored.^{d}

^{39} Therefore, my brothers, be eager to prophesy, and do not forbid speaking in tongues. ^{40} But everything should be done in a fitting and orderly way.

a21 Isaiah 28:11,12   *b23* Or *some inquirers*   *c24* Or *or some inquirer*   *d38* Some manuscripts *If he is ignorant of this, let him be ignorant*

PSALM 37:30-40

^{30} **The mouth of the righteous man utters wisdom,**
   and his tongue speaks what is just.
^{31} **The law of his God is in his heart;**
   his feet do not slip.

^{32} The wicked lie in wait for the righteous,
   seeking their very lives;
^{33} but the LORD will not leave them in their power
   or let them be condemned when brought to trial.

^{34} Wait for the LORD
   and keep his way.

He will exalt you to inherit the land;
   when the wicked are cut off, you will see it.

^{35} I have seen a wicked and ruthless man flourishing like a green tree in its native soil,
^{36} but he soon passed away and was no more;
   though I looked for him, he could not be found.

^{37} Consider the blameless, observe the upright;
   there is a future^a for the man of peace.
^{38} But all sinners will be destroyed;
   the future^b of the wicked will be cut off.

^{39} The salvation of the righteous comes from the LORD;
   he is their stronghold in time of trouble.
^{40} The LORD helps them and delivers them;
   he delivers them from the wicked and saves them,
   because they take refuge in him.

a37 Or *there will be posterity*   *b38* Or *posterity*

PROVERBS 21:27

^{27} **T**he sacrifice of the wicked is detestable—
   how much more so when brought with evil intent!

☐ DAY 235

GOD SIGHTINGS

August 23

JOB 8:1–11:20

Then Bildad the Shuhite replied:

^{2} "How long will you say such things?
   Your words are a blustering wind.
^{3} Does God pervert justice?
   Does the Almighty pervert what is right?

⁴When your children sinned against
    him,
  he gave them over to the penalty
        of their sin.
⁵But if you will look to God
  and plead with the Almighty,
⁶if you are pure and upright,
  even now he will rouse himself on
        your behalf
  and restore you to your rightful
        place.
⁷Your beginnings will seem humble,
  so prosperous will your future be.

⁸"Ask the former generations
  and find out what their fathers
        learned,
⁹for we were born only yesterday and
        know nothing,
  and our days on earth are but a
        shadow.
¹⁰Will they not instruct you and tell
        you?
  Will they not bring forth words
        from their understanding?
¹¹Can papyrus grow tall where there is
        no marsh?
  Can reeds thrive without water?
¹²While still growing and uncut,
  they wither more quickly than
        grass.
¹³Such is the destiny of all who forget
        God;
  so perishes the hope of the godless.
¹⁴What he trusts in is fragile[a];
  what he relies on is a spider's web.
¹⁵He leans on his web, but it gives way;
  he clings to it, but it does not hold.
¹⁶He is like a well-watered plant in the
        sunshine,
  spreading its shoots over the
        garden;
¹⁷it entwines its roots around a pile of
        rocks
  and looks for a place among the
        stones.
¹⁸But when it is torn from its spot,
  that place disowns it and says, 'I
        never saw you.'
¹⁹Surely its life withers away,
  and[b] from the soil other plants
        grow.

²⁰"Surely God does not reject a
        blameless man
  or strengthen the hands of
        evildoers.
²¹He will yet fill your mouth with
        laughter
  and your lips with shouts of joy.
²²Your enemies will be clothed in
        shame,
  and the tents of the wicked will be
        no more."

^{9:1}THEN Job replied:

²"Indeed, I know that this is true.
  But how can a mortal be righteous
        before God?
³Though one wished to dispute with
        him,
  he could not answer him one time
        out of a thousand.
⁴His wisdom is profound, his power
        is vast.
  Who has resisted him and come
        out unscathed?
⁵He moves mountains without their
        knowing it
  and overturns them in his anger.
⁶He shakes the earth from its place
  and makes its pillars tremble.
⁷He speaks to the sun and it does not
        shine;
  he seals off the light of the stars.
⁸He alone stretches out the heavens
  and treads on the waves of the sea.
⁹He is the Maker of the Bear and Orion,
  the Pleiades and the constellations
        of the south.
¹⁰He performs wonders that cannot be
        fathomed,
  miracles that cannot be counted.
¹¹When he passes me, I cannot see
        him;
  when he goes by, I cannot perceive
        him.
¹²If he snatches away, who can stop
        him?
  Who can say to him, 'What are you
        doing?'
¹³God does not restrain his anger;
  even the cohorts of Rahab
        cowered at his feet.

14"How then can I dispute with him?
How can I find words to argue
with him?
15Though I were innocent, I could not
answer him;
I could only plead with my Judge
for mercy.
16Even if I summoned him and he
responded,
I do not believe he would give me
a hearing.
17He would crush me with a storm
and multiply my wounds for no
reason.
18He would not let me regain my breath
but would overwhelm me with
misery.
19If it is a matter of strength, he is
mighty!
And if it is a matter of justice, who
will summon him*c*?
20Even if I were innocent, my mouth
would condemn me;
if I were blameless, it would
pronounce me guilty.

21"Although I am blameless,
I have no concern for myself;
I despise my own life.
22It is all the same; that is why I say,
'He destroys both the blameless
and the wicked.'
23When a scourge brings sudden death,
he mocks the despair of the
innocent.
24When a land falls into the hands of
the wicked,
he blindfolds its judges.
If it is not he, then who is it?

25"My days are swifter than a runner;
they fly away without a glimpse of
joy.
26They skim past like boats of papyrus,
like eagles swooping down on
their prey.
27If I say, 'I will forget my complaint,
I will change my expression, and
smile,'
28I still dread all my sufferings,
for I know you will not hold me
innocent.

29Since I am already found guilty,
why should I struggle in vain?
30Even if I washed myself with soap*d*
and my hands with washing soda,
31you would plunge me into a slime pit
so that even my clothes would
detest me.

32"He is not a man like me that I might
answer him,
that we might confront each other
in court.
33If only there were someone to
arbitrate between us,
to lay his hand upon us both,
34someone to remove God's rod from me,
so that his terror would frighten
me no more.
35Then I would speak up without fear
of him,
but as it now stands with me,
I cannot.

10:1"I loathe my very life;
therefore I will give free rein to my
complaint
and speak out in the bitterness of
my soul.
2I will say to God: Do not condemn me,
but tell me what charges you have
against me.
3Does it please you to oppress me,
to spurn the work of your hands,
while you smile on the schemes of
the wicked?
4Do you have eyes of flesh?
Do you see as a mortal sees?
5Are your days like those of a mortal
or your years like those of a man,
6that you must search out my faults
and probe after my sin—
7though you know that I am not guilty
and that no one can rescue me
from your hand?

8"Your hands shaped me and
made me.
Will you now turn and destroy me?
9Remember that you molded me like
clay.
Will you now turn me to dust again?
10Did you not pour me out like milk
and curdle me like cheese,

11 clothe me with skin and flesh
    and knit me together with bones
        and sinews?
12 You gave me life and showed me
        kindness,
    and in your providence watched
        over my spirit.
13 "But this is what you concealed in
        your heart,
    and I know that this was in your
        mind:
14 If I sinned, you would be watching me
    and would not let my offense go
        unpunished.
15 If I am guilty—woe to me!
    Even if I am innocent, I cannot lift
        my head,
  for I am full of shame
    and drowned in*e* my affliction.
16 If I hold my head high, you stalk me
        like a lion
    and again display your awesome
        power against me.
17 You bring new witnesses against me
    and increase your anger toward me;
    your forces come against me wave
        upon wave.

18 "Why then did you bring me out of
        the womb?
    I wish I had died before any eye
        saw me.
19 If only I had never come into being,
    or had been carried straight from
        the womb to the grave!
20 Are not my few days almost over?
    Turn away from me so I can have a
        moment's joy
21 before I go to the place of no return,
    to the land of gloom and deep
        shadow,*f*
22 to the land of deepest night,
    of deep shadow and disorder,
    where even the light is like
        darkness."

11:1 THEN Zophar the Naamathite replied:

2 "Are all these words to go
        unanswered?
    Is this talker to be vindicated?
3 Will your idle talk reduce men to
        silence?
    Will no one rebuke you when you
        mock?
4 You say to God, 'My beliefs are
        flawless
    and I am pure in your sight.'
5 Oh, how I wish that God would speak,
    that he would open his lips against
        you
6 and disclose to you the secrets of
        wisdom,
    for true wisdom has two sides.
    Know this: God has even forgotten
        some of your sin.

7 "Can you fathom the mysteries
        of God?
    Can you probe the limits of the
        Almighty?
8 They are higher than the heavens—
        what can you do?
    They are deeper than the depths
        of the grave*g*—what can you
        know?
9 Their measure is longer than the
        earth
    and wider than the sea.

10 "If he comes along and confines you
        in prison
    and convenes a court, who can
        oppose him?
11 Surely he recognizes deceitful men;
    and when he sees evil, does he not
        take note?
12 But a witless man can no more
        become wise
    than a wild donkey's colt can be
        born a man.*h*

13 "Yet if you devote your heart to him
    and stretch out your hands to him,
14 if you put away the sin that is in your
        hand
    and allow no evil to dwell in your
        tent,
15 then you will lift up your face
        without shame;
    you will stand firm and without
        fear.
16 You will surely forget your trouble,
    recalling it only as waters gone by.

17 Life will be brighter than noonday,
 and darkness will become like
  morning.
18 You will be secure, because there is
  hope;
 you will look about you and take
  your rest in safety.
19 You will lie down, with no one to
  make you afraid,
 and many will court your favor.
20 But the eyes of the wicked will fail,
 and escape will elude them;
 their hope will become a dying
  gasp."

a 14 The meaning of the Hebrew for this word is uncertain.
b 19 Or *Surely all the joy it has / is that*   c 19 See Septuagint;
Hebrew *me*.   d 30 Or *snow*   e 15 Or *and aware of*   f 21 Or *and
the shadow of death*; also in verse 22   9 8 Hebrew *than Sheol*
h 12 Or *wild donkey can be born tame*

1 CORINTHIANS 15:1-28

Now, brothers, I want to remind you of the gospel I preached to you, which you received and on which you have taken your stand. 2 By this gospel you are saved, if you hold firmly to the word I preached to you. Otherwise, you have believed in vain.

3 For what I received I passed on to you as of first importance*a*: that Christ died for our sins according to the Scriptures, 4 that he was buried, that he was raised on the third day according to the Scriptures, 5 and that he appeared to Peter,*b* and then to the Twelve. 6 After that, he appeared to more than five hundred of the brothers at the same time, most of whom are still living, though some have fallen asleep. 7 Then he appeared to James, then to all the apostles, 8 and last of all he appeared to me also, as to one abnormally born.

9 For I am the least of the apostles and do not even deserve to be called an apostle, because I persecuted the church of God. 10 But by the grace of God I am what I am, and his grace to me was not without effect. No, I worked harder than all of them—yet not I, but the grace of God that was with me. 11 Whether, then, it was I or they, this is what we preach, and this is what you believed.

12 But if it is preached that Christ has been raised from the dead, how can some of you say that there is no resurrection of the dead? 13 If there is no resurrection of the dead, then not even Christ has been raised. 14 And if Christ has not been raised, our preaching is useless and so is your faith. 15 More than that, we are then found to be false witnesses about God, for we have testified about God that he raised Christ from the dead. But he did not raise him if in fact the dead are not raised. 16 For if the dead are not raised, then Christ has not been raised either. 17 And if Christ has not been raised, your faith is futile; you are still in your sins. 18 Then those also who have fallen asleep in Christ are lost. 19 If only for this life we have hope in Christ, we are to be pitied more than all men.

20 But Christ has indeed been raised from the dead, the firstfruits of those who have fallen asleep. 21 **For since death came through a man, the resurrection of the dead comes also through a man.** 22 For as in Adam all die, so in Christ all will be made alive. 23 But each in his own turn: Christ, the firstfruits; then, when he comes, those who belong to him. 24 Then the end will come, when he hands over the kingdom to God the Father after he has destroyed all dominion, authority and power. 25 For he must reign until he has put all his enemies under his feet. 26 The last enemy to be destroyed is death. 27 For he "has put everything under his feet."*c* Now when it says that "everything" has been put under him, it is clear that this does not include God himself, who put everything under Christ. 28 When he has done this, then the Son himself will be made subject to him who put everything under him, so that God may be all in all.

a 3 Or *you at the first*   b 5 Greek *Cephas*   c 27 Psalm 8:6

PSALM 38:1-22

A psalm of David. A petition.

1 O LORD, do not rebuke me in your
  anger
 or discipline me in your wrath.

² For your arrows have pierced me,
   and your hand has come down
      upon me.
³ Because of your wrath there is no
      health in my body;
   my bones have no soundness
      because of my sin.
⁴ My guilt has overwhelmed me
   like a burden too heavy to bear.

⁵ My wounds fester and are loathsome
   because of my sinful folly.
⁶ I am bowed down and brought very
      low;
   all day long I go about mourning.
⁷ My back is filled with searing pain;
   there is no health in my body.
⁸ I am feeble and utterly crushed;
   I groan in anguish of heart.

⁹ All my longings lie open before you,
      O Lord;
   my sighing is not hidden from you.
¹⁰ My heart pounds, my strength fails
      me;
   even the light has gone from my
      eyes.
¹¹ My friends and companions avoid
      me because of my wounds;
   my neighbors stay far away.
¹² Those who seek my life set their
      traps,
   those who would harm me talk of
      my ruin;
   all day long they plot deception.

¹³ I am like a deaf man, who cannot
      hear,
   like a mute, who cannot open his
      mouth;
¹⁴ I have become like a man who does
      not hear,
   whose mouth can offer no reply.
¹⁵ I wait for you, O Lord;
   you will answer, O Lord my God.
¹⁶ For I said, "Do not let them gloat
   or exalt themselves over me when
      my foot slips."

¹⁷ For I am about to fall,
   and my pain is ever with me.
¹⁸ I confess my iniquity;
   I am troubled by my sin.

¹⁹ Many are those who are my vigorous
      enemies;
   those who hate me without reason
      are numerous.
²⁰ Those who repay my good with evil
   slander me when I pursue what is
      good.

²¹ O Lord, do not forsake me;
   be not far from me, O my God.
²² Come quickly to help me,
   O Lord my Savior.

PROVERBS 21:28-29
²⁸ A false witness will perish,
   and whoever listens to him will be
      destroyed forever.ᵃ

²⁹ A wicked man puts up a bold front,
   but an upright man gives thought
      to his ways.

ᵃ28 Or / but the words of an obedient man will live on

□ DAY 236

GOD SIGHTINGS

August 24

JOB 12:1–15:35
Then Job replied:

² "Doubtless you are the people,
   and wisdom will die with you!
³ But I have a mind as well as you;
   I am not inferior to you.
   Who does not know all these
      things?

⁴ "I have become a laughingstock to
      my friends,
   though I called upon God and he
      answered—
   a mere laughingstock, though
      righteous and blameless!
⁵ Men at ease have contempt for
      misfortune
   as the fate of those whose feet are
      slipping.
⁶ The tents of marauders are
      undisturbed,

and those who provoke God are
secure—
those who carry their god in their
hands.[a]

7 "But ask the animals, and they will
teach you,
or the birds of the air, and they will
tell you;
8 or speak to the earth, and it will
teach you,
or let the fish of the sea inform
you.
9 Which of all these does not know
that the hand of the LORD has done
this?
10 In his hand is the life of every
creature
and the breath of all mankind.
11 Does not the ear test words
as the tongue tastes food?
12 Is not wisdom found among the aged?
Does not long life bring
understanding?

13 "To God belong wisdom and power;
counsel and understanding are
his.
14 What he tears down cannot be
rebuilt;
the man he imprisons cannot be
released.
15 If he holds back the waters, there is
drought;
if he lets them loose, they
devastate the land.
16 To him belong strength and victory;
both deceived and deceiver are
his.
17 He leads counselors away stripped
and makes fools of judges.
18 He takes off the shackles put on by
kings
and ties a loincloth[b] around their
waist.
19 He leads priests away stripped
and overthrows men long
established.
20 He silences the lips of trusted
advisers
and takes away the discernment of
elders.

21 He pours contempt on nobles
and disarms the mighty.
22 He reveals the deep things of
darkness
and brings deep shadows into the
light.
23 He makes nations great, and destroys
them;
he enlarges nations, and disperses
them.
24 He deprives the leaders of the earth
of their reason;
he sends them wandering through
a trackless waste.
25 They grope in darkness with no light;
he makes them stagger like
drunkards.

13:1 "MY eyes have seen all this,
my ears have heard and
understood it.
2 What you know, I also know;
I am not inferior to you.
3 But I desire to speak to the Almighty
and to argue my case with God.
4 You, however, smear me with lies;
you are worthless physicians, all
of you!
5 If only you would be altogether
silent!
For you, that would be wisdom.
6 Hear now my argument;
listen to the plea of my lips.
7 Will you speak wickedly on God's
behalf?
Will you speak deceitfully for him?
8 Will you show him partiality?
Will you argue the case for God?
9 Would it turn out well if he
examined you?
Could you deceive him as you
might deceive men?
10 He would surely rebuke you
if you secretly showed partiality.
11 Would not his splendor terrify you?
Would not the dread of him fall on
you?
12 Your maxims are proverbs of ashes;
your defenses are defenses of clay.

13 "Keep silent and let me speak;
then let come to me what may.

¹⁴Why do I put myself in jeopardy
  and take my life in my hands?
¹⁵Though he slay me, yet will I hope
    in him;
  I will surely*c* defend my ways to
    his face.
¹⁶Indeed, this will turn out for my
    deliverance,
  for no godless man would dare
    come before him!
¹⁷Listen carefully to my words;
  let your ears take in what I say.
¹⁸Now that I have prepared my case,
  I know I will be vindicated.
¹⁹Can anyone bring charges against
    me?
  If so, I will be silent and die.

²⁰"Only grant me these two things,
    O God,
  and then I will not hide from you:
²¹Withdraw your hand far from me,
  and stop frightening me with your
    terrors.
²²Then summon me and I will answer,
  or let me speak, and you reply.
²³How many wrongs and sins have I
    committed?
  Show me my offense and my sin.
²⁴Why do you hide your face
  and consider me your enemy?
²⁵Will you torment a windblown leaf?
  Will you chase after dry chaff?
²⁶For you write down bitter things
    against me
  and make me inherit the sins of
    my youth.
²⁷You fasten my feet in shackles;
  you keep close watch on all my
    paths
  by putting marks on the soles of
    my feet.

²⁸"So man wastes away like something
    rotten,
  like a garment eaten by moths.

¹⁴:¹"Man born of woman
  is of few days and full of trouble.
²He springs up like a flower and
    withers away;
  like a fleeting shadow, he does not
    endure.

³Do you fix your eye on such a one?
  Will you bring him*d* before you for
    judgment?
⁴Who can bring what is pure from the
    impure?
  No one!
⁵Man's days are determined;
  you have decreed the number of
    his months
  and have set limits he cannot
    exceed.
⁶So look away from him and let him
    alone,
  till he has put in his time like a
    hired man.

⁷"At least there is hope for a tree:
  If it is cut down, it will sprout
    again,
  and its new shoots will not fail.
⁸Its roots may grow old in the ground
  and its stump die in the soil,
⁹yet at the scent of water it will bud
  and put forth shoots like a plant.
¹⁰But man dies and is laid low;
  he breathes his last and is no
    more.
¹¹As water disappears from the sea
  or a riverbed becomes parched
    and dry,
¹²so man lies down and does not rise;
  till the heavens are no more, men
    will not awake
  or be roused from their sleep.

¹³"If only you would hide me in the
    grave*e*
  and conceal me till your anger has
    passed!
  If only you would set me a time
  and then remember me!
¹⁴If a man dies, will he live again?
  All the days of my hard service
  I will wait for my renewal*f* to come.
¹⁵You will call and I will answer you;
  you will long for the creature your
    hands have made.
¹⁶Surely then you will count my steps
  but not keep track of my sin.
¹⁷My offenses will be sealed up in
    a bag;
  you will cover over my sin.

18"But as a mountain erodes and
    crumbles
    and as a rock is moved from its
      place,
19as water wears away stones
    and torrents wash away the soil,
    so you destroy man's hope.
20You overpower him once for all, and
    he is gone;
    you change his countenance and
      send him away.
21If his sons are honored, he does not
    know it;
    if they are brought low, he does
      not see it.
22He feels but the pain of his own body
    and mourns only for himself."

15:1THEN Eliphaz the Temanite replied:

2"Would a wise man answer with
    empty notions
    or fill his belly with the hot east
      wind?
3Would he argue with useless words,
    with speeches that have no value?
4But you even undermine piety
    and hinder devotion to God.
5Your sin prompts your mouth;
    you adopt the tongue of the crafty.
6Your own mouth condemns you, not
    mine;
    your own lips testify against you.

7"Are you the first man ever born?
    Were you brought forth before the
      hills?
8Do you listen in on God's council?
    Do you limit wisdom to yourself?
9What do you know that we do not
    know?
    What insights do you have that we
      do not have?
10The gray-haired and the aged are on
    our side,
    men even older than your father.
11Are God's consolations not enough
    for you,
    words spoken gently to you?
12Why has your heart carried you
    away,
    and why do your eyes flash,

13so that you vent your rage against
    God
    and pour out such words from
      your mouth?

14"What is man, that he could be pure,
    or one born of woman, that he
      could be righteous?
15If God places no trust in his holy
    ones,
    if even the heavens are not pure in
      his eyes,
16how much less man, who is vile and
    corrupt,
    who drinks up evil like water!

17"Listen to me and I will explain
    to you;
    let me tell you what I have seen,
18what wise men have declared,
    hiding nothing received from their
      fathers
19(to whom alone the land was given
    when no alien passed among
      them):
20All his days the wicked man suffers
    torment,
    the ruthless through all the years
      stored up for him.
21Terrifying sounds fill his ears;
    when all seems well, marauders
      attack him.
22He despairs of escaping the darkness;
    he is marked for the sword.
23He wanders about—food for
    vultures*g*;
    he knows the day of darkness is
      at hand.
24Distress and anguish fill him with
    terror;
    they overwhelm him, like a king
      poised to attack,
25because he shakes his fist at God
    and vaunts himself against the
      Almighty,
26defiantly charging against him
    with a thick, strong shield.

27"Though his face is covered with fat
    and his waist bulges with flesh,
28he will inhabit ruined towns
    and houses where no one lives,
    houses crumbling to rubble.

²⁹He will no longer be rich and his
wealth will not endure,
nor will his possessions spread
over the land.
³⁰He will not escape the darkness;
a flame will wither his shoots,
and the breath of God's mouth will
carry him away.
³¹Let him not deceive himself by
trusting what is worthless,
for he will get nothing in return.
³²Before his time he will be paid in
full,
and his branches will not flourish.
³³He will be like a vine stripped of its
unripe grapes,
like an olive tree shedding its
blossoms.
³⁴For the company of the godless will
be barren,
and fire will consume the tents of
those who love bribes.
³⁵They conceive trouble and give birth
to evil;
their womb fashions deceit."

*a6 Or secure / in what God's hand brings them   b18 Or shackles
of kings / and ties a belt   c15 Or He will surely slay me;
I have no hope — / yet I will   d3 Septuagint, Vulgate and
Syriac; Hebrew me   e13 Hebrew Sheol   f14 Or release
g23 Or about, looking for food*

1 CORINTHIANS 15:29-58

Now if there is no resurrection, what will
those do who are baptized for the dead?
If the dead are not raised at all, why are
people baptized for them? ³⁰And as for
us, why do we endanger ourselves every
hour? ³¹I die every day—I mean that,
brothers—just as surely as I glory over
you in Christ Jesus our Lord. ³²If I fought
wild beasts in Ephesus for merely human
reasons, what have I gained? If the dead
are not raised,

"Let us eat and drink,
for tomorrow we die."*a*

³³Do not be misled: "Bad company corrupts good character." ³⁴Come back to
your senses as you ought, and stop sinning; for there are some who are ignorant of God—I say this to your shame.

³⁵But someone may ask, "How are the
dead raised? With what kind of body

will they come?" ³⁶How foolish! What
you sow does not come to life unless it
dies. ³⁷When you sow, you do not plant
the body that will be, but just a seed, perhaps of wheat or of something else.
³⁸But God gives it a body as he has determined, and to each kind of seed he gives
its own body. ³⁹All flesh is not the same:
Men have one kind of flesh, animals
have another, birds another and fish another. ⁴⁰There are also heavenly bodies
and there are earthly bodies; but the
splendor of the heavenly bodies is one
kind, and the splendor of the earthly
bodies is another. ⁴¹The sun has one
kind of splendor, the moon another and
the stars another; and star differs from
star in splendor.

⁴²So will it be with the resurrection of
the dead. The body that is sown is perishable, it is raised imperishable; ⁴³it is
sown in dishonor, it is raised in glory; it
is sown in weakness, it is raised in
power; ⁴⁴it is sown a natural body, it is
raised a spiritual body.

If there is a natural body, there is also
a spiritual body. ⁴⁵So it is written: "The
first man Adam became a living being"*b*; the last Adam, a life-giving spirit.
⁴⁶The spiritual did not come first, but
the natural, and after that the spiritual.
⁴⁷The first man was of the dust of the
earth, the second man from heaven.
⁴⁸As was the earthly man, so are those
who are of the earth; and as is the man
from heaven, so also are those who are
of heaven. ⁴⁹And just as we have borne
the likeness of the earthly man, so shall
we*c* bear the likeness of the man from
heaven.

⁵⁰I declare to you, brothers, that flesh
and blood cannot inherit the kingdom
of God, nor does the perishable inherit
the imperishable. ⁵¹Listen, I tell you a
mystery: We will not all sleep, but we
will all be changed— ⁵²in a flash, in the
twinkling of an eye, at the last trumpet.
For the trumpet will sound, the dead
will be raised imperishable, and we will
be changed. ⁵³For the perishable must
clothe itself with the imperishable, and
the mortal with immortality. ⁵⁴When

the perishable has been clothed with the imperishable, and the mortal with immortality, then the saying that is written will come true: **"Death has been swallowed up in victory."**[d]

⁵⁵**" Where, O death, is your victory?**
    Where, O death, is your sting?"[e]

⁵⁶**The sting of death is sin, and the power of sin is the law. ⁵⁷But thanks be to God! He gives us the victory through our Lord Jesus Christ.**

⁵⁸Therefore, my dear brothers, stand firm. Let nothing move you. Always give yourselves fully to the work of the Lord, because you know that your labor in the Lord is not in vain.

a32 Isaiah 22:13 b45 Gen. 2:7 c49 Some early manuscripts so let us d54 Isaiah 25:8 e55 Hosea 13:14

PSALM 39:1-13
For the director of music. For Jeduthun. A psalm of David.

¹ I said, "I will watch my ways
        and keep my tongue from sin;
    I will put a muzzle on my mouth
        as long as the wicked are in my
            presence."
² But when I was silent and still,
        not even saying anything good,
        my anguish increased.
³ My heart grew hot within me,
        and as I meditated, the fire burned;
    then I spoke with my tongue:

⁴ "Show me, O LORD, my life's end
        and the number of my days;
    let me know how fleeting is my life.
⁵ You have made my days a mere
            handbreadth;
        the span of my years is as nothing
            before you.
    Each man's life is but a breath. *Selah*
⁶ Man is a mere phantom as he goes to
            and fro:
        He bustles about, but only in vain;
        he heaps up wealth, not knowing
            who will get it.

⁷ "But now, Lord, what do I look for?
        My hope is in you.
⁸ Save me from all my transgressions;
        do not make me the scorn of fools.

⁹ I was silent; I would not open my
            mouth,
        for you are the one who has done
            this.
¹⁰ Remove your scourge from me;
        I am overcome by the blow of
            your hand.
¹¹ You rebuke and discipline men for
            their sin;
        you consume their wealth like
            a moth—
        each man is but a breath.   *Selah*

¹² "Hear my prayer, O LORD,
        listen to my cry for help;
        be not deaf to my weeping.
    For I dwell with you as an alien,
        a stranger, as all my fathers were.
¹³ Look away from me, that I may
            rejoice again
        before I depart and am no more."

PROVERBS 21:30-31
³⁰ There is no wisdom, no insight, no
            plan
        that can succeed against the LORD.

³¹ The horse is made ready for the day
            of battle,
        but victory rests with the LORD.

☐ D A Y 2 3 7

GOD SIGHTINGS

August 25

JOB 16:1–19:29
Then Job replied:

² "I have heard many things like these;
        miserable comforters are you all!
³ Will your long-winded speeches
            never end?
        What ails you that you keep on
            arguing?
⁴ I also could speak like you,
        if you were in my place;
    I could make fine speeches against
            you
        and shake my head at you.

5 But my mouth would encourage you;
   comfort from my lips would bring
      you relief.

6 "Yet if I speak, my pain is not relieved;
   and if I refrain, it does not go away.
7 Surely, O God, you have worn me out;
   you have devastated my entire
      household.
8 You have bound me—and it has
      become a witness;
   my gauntness rises up and testifies
      against me.
9 God assails me and tears me in his
      anger
   and gnashes his teeth at me;
   my opponent fastens on me his
      piercing eyes.
10 Men open their mouths to jeer at me;
   they strike my cheek in scorn
   and unite together against me.
11 God has turned me over to evil men
   and thrown me into the clutches
      of the wicked.
12 All was well with me, but he
      shattered me;
   he seized me by the neck and
      crushed me.
   He has made me his target;
13   his archers surround me.
   Without pity, he pierces my kidneys
   and spills my gall on the ground.
14 Again and again he bursts upon me;
   he rushes at me like a warrior.

15 "I have sewed sackcloth over my skin
   and buried my brow in the dust.
16 My face is red with weeping,
   deep shadows ring my eyes;
17 yet my hands have been free of
      violence
   and my prayer is pure.

18 "O earth, do not cover my blood;
   may my cry never be laid to rest!
19 Even now my witness is in heaven;
   my advocate is on high.
20 My intercessor is my friend*a*
   as my eyes pour out tears to God;
21 on behalf of a man he pleads
      with God
   as a man pleads for his friend.

22 "Only a few years will pass
   before I go on the journey of no
      return.
17:1 My spirit is broken,
   my days are cut short,
   the grave awaits me.
2 Surely mockers surround me;
   my eyes must dwell on their hostility.

3 "Give me, O God, the pledge you
      demand.
   Who else will put up security for
      me?
4 You have closed their minds to
      understanding;
   therefore you will not let them
      triumph.
5 If a man denounces his friends for
      reward,
   the eyes of his children will fail.

6 "God has made me a byword to
      everyone,
   a man in whose face people spit.
7 My eyes have grown dim with grief;
   my whole frame is but a shadow.
8 Upright men are appalled at this;
   the innocent are aroused against
      the ungodly.
9 Nevertheless, the righteous will hold
      to their ways,
   and those with clean hands will
      grow stronger.

10 "But come on, all of you, try again!
   I will not find a wise man among
      you.
11 My days have passed, my plans are
      shattered,
   and so are the desires of my heart.
12 These men turn night into day;
   in the face of darkness they say,
      'Light is near.'
13 If the only home I hope for is the
      grave,*b*
   if I spread out my bed in darkness,
14 if I say to corruption, 'You are my
      father,'
   and to the worm, 'My mother' or
      'My sister,'
15 where then is my hope?
   Who can see any hope for me?

16 Will it go down to the gates of
      death[b]?
    Will we descend together into the
      dust?"

18:1 THEN Bildad the Shuhite replied:

2 "When will you end these speeches?
    Be sensible, and then we can talk.
3 Why are we regarded as cattle
    and considered stupid in your
      sight?
4 You who tear yourself to pieces in
      your anger,
    is the earth to be abandoned for
      your sake?
    Or must the rocks be moved from
      their place?

5 "The lamp of the wicked is snuffed
      out;
    the flame of his fire stops burning.
6 The light in his tent becomes dark;
    the lamp beside him goes out.
7 The vigor of his step is weakened;
    his own schemes throw him down.
8 His feet thrust him into a net
    and he wanders into its mesh.
9 A trap seizes him by the heel;
    a snare holds him fast.
10 A noose is hidden for him on the
      ground;
    a trap lies in his path.
11 Terrors startle him on every side
    and dog his every step.
12 Calamity is hungry for him;
    disaster is ready for him when he
      falls.
13 It eats away parts of his skin;
    death's firstborn devours his
      limbs.
14 He is torn from the security of his
      tent
    and marched off to the king of
      terrors.
15 Fire resides[c] in his tent;
    burning sulfur is scattered over his
      dwelling.
16 His roots dry up below
    and his branches wither above.
17 The memory of him perishes from
      the earth;
    he has no name in the land.

18 He is driven from light into
      darkness
    and is banished from the world.
19 He has no offspring or descendants
      among his people,
    no survivor where once he lived.
20 Men of the west are appalled at his
      fate;
    men of the east are seized with
      horror.
21 Surely such is the dwelling of an evil
      man;
    such is the place of one who
      knows not God."

19:1 THEN Job replied:

2 "How long will you torment me
    and crush me with words?
3 Ten times now you have reproached
      me;
    shamelessly you attack me.
4 If it is true that I have gone astray,
    my error remains my concern
      alone.
5 If indeed you would exalt yourselves
      above me
    and use my humiliation against
      me,
6 then know that God has wronged
      me
    and drawn his net around me.

7 "Though I cry, 'I've been wronged!' I
      get no response;
    though I call for help, there is no
      justice.
8 He has blocked my way so I cannot
      pass;
    he has shrouded my paths in
      darkness.
9 He has stripped me of my honor
    and removed the crown from my
      head.
10 He tears me down on every side till I
      am gone;
    he uproots my hope like a tree.
11 His anger burns against me;
    he counts me among his enemies.
12 His troops advance in force;
    they build a siege ramp against
      me
    and encamp around my tent.

¹³"He has alienated my brothers
    from me;
  my acquaintances are completely
    estranged from me.
¹⁴My kinsmen have gone away;
  my friends have forgotten me.
¹⁵My guests and my maidservants
    count me a stranger;
  they look upon me as an alien.
¹⁶I summon my servant, but he does
    not answer,
  though I beg him with my own
    mouth.
¹⁷My breath is offensive to my wife;
  I am loathsome to my own
    brothers.
¹⁸Even the little boys scorn me;
  when I appear, they ridicule me.
¹⁹All my intimate friends detest me;
  those I love have turned against
    me.
²⁰I am nothing but skin and bones;
  I have escaped with only the skin
    of my teeth.ᵈ

²¹"Have pity on me, my friends, have
    pity,
  for the hand of God has struck
    me.
²²Why do you pursue me as God does?
  Will you never get enough of my
    flesh?

²³"Oh, that my words were recorded,
    that they were written on a scroll,
²⁴that they were inscribed with an iron
    tool onᵉ lead,
  or engraved in rock forever!
²⁵I know that my Redeemerᶠ lives,
  and that in the end he will stand
    upon the earth.ᵍ
²⁶And after my skin has been
    destroyed,
  yetʰ inⁱ my flesh I will see God;
²⁷I myself will see him
  with my own eyes—I, and not
    another.
  How my heart yearns within me!

²⁸"If you say, 'How we will hound him,
  since the root of the trouble lies in
    him,ʲ'

²⁹you should fear the sword
    yourselves;
  for wrath will bring punishment
    by the sword,
  and then you will know that there
    is judgment.ᵏ"

*a20 Or My friends treat me with scorn b13,16 Hebrew Sheol
c15 Or Nothing he had remains d20 Or only my gums
e24 Or and f25 Or defender g25 Or upon my grave
h26 Or And after I awake, / though this ⌊body⌋ has been
destroyed, / then i26 Or / apart from j28 Many Hebrew
manuscripts, Septuagint and Vulgate; most Hebrew
manuscripts me k29 Or / that you may come to know
the Almighty*

1 CORINTHIANS 16:1-24

Now about the collection for God's people: Do what I told the Galatian churches to do. ²On the first day of every week, each one of you should set aside a sum of money in keeping with his income, saving it up, so that when I come no collections will have to be made. ³Then, when I arrive, I will give letters of introduction to the men you approve and send them with your gift to Jerusalem. ⁴If it seems advisable for me to go also, they will accompany me.

⁵After I go through Macedonia, I will come to you—for I will be going through Macedonia. ⁶Perhaps I will stay with you awhile, or even spend the winter, so that you can help me on my journey, wherever I go. ⁷I do not want to see you now and make only a passing visit; I hope to spend some time with you, if the Lord permits. ⁸But I will stay on at Ephesus until Pentecost, ⁹because a great door for effective work has opened to me, and there are many who oppose me.

¹⁰If Timothy comes, see to it that he has nothing to fear while he is with you, for he is carrying on the work of the Lord, just as I am. ¹¹No one, then, should refuse to accept him. Send him on his way in peace so that he may return to me. I am expecting him along with the brothers.

¹²Now about our brother Apollos: I strongly urged him to go to you with the brothers. He was quite unwilling to go now, but he will go when he has the opportunity.

¹³Be on your guard; stand firm in the

faith; be men of courage; be strong. [14]Do everything in love.

[15]You know that the household of Stephanas were the first converts in Achaia, and they have devoted themselves to the service of the saints. I urge you, brothers, [16]to submit to such as these and to everyone who joins in the work, and labors at it. [17]I was glad when Stephanas, Fortunatus and Achaicus arrived, because they have supplied what was lacking from you. [18]For they refreshed my spirit and yours also. Such men deserve recognition.

[19]The churches in the province of Asia send you greetings. Aquila and Priscilla[a] greet you warmly in the Lord, and so does the church that meets at their house. [20]All the brothers here send you greetings. Greet one another with a holy kiss.

[21]I, Paul, write this greeting in my own hand.

[22]If anyone does not love the Lord—a curse be on him. Come, O Lord[b]!

[23]The grace of the Lord Jesus be with you.

[24]My love to all of you in Christ Jesus. Amen.[c]

a19 Greek *Prisca*, a variant of *Priscilla* *b22* In Aramaic the expression *Come, O Lord* is *Marana tha.* *c24* Some manuscripts do not have *Amen.*

PSALM 40:1-10
For the director of music. Of David. A psalm.

[1]I waited patiently for the Lord;
   he turned to me and heard my cry.
[2]He lifted me out of the slimy pit,
   out of the mud and mire;
he set my feet on a rock
   and gave me a firm place to stand.
[3]He put a new song in my mouth,
   a hymn of praise to our God.
Many will see and fear
   and put their trust in the Lord.

[4]Blessed is the man
   who makes the Lord his trust,
who does not look to the proud,
   to those who turn aside to false
      gods.[a]

[5]Many, O Lord my God,
   are the wonders you have done.
The things you planned for us
   no one can recount to you;
were I to speak and tell of them,
   they would be too many to
      declare.

[6]Sacrifice and offering you did not
      desire,
   but my ears you have pierced[b, c];
burnt offerings and sin offerings
   you did not require.
[7]Then I said, "Here I am, I have come—
   it is written about me in the scroll.[d]
[8]I desire to do your will, O my God;
   your law is within my heart."

[9]I proclaim righteousness in the great
      assembly;
   I do not seal my lips,
      as you know, O Lord.
[10]I do not hide your righteousness in
      my heart;
   I speak of your faithfulness and
      salvation.
I do not conceal your love and your
      truth
   from the great assembly.

a4 Or *to falsehood* *b6* Hebrew; Septuagint *but a body you have prepared for me* (see also Symmachus and Theodotion) *c6* Or *opened* *d7* Or *come / with the scroll written for me*

PROVERBS 22:1
A good name is more desirable than
      great riches;
   to be esteemed is better than
      silver or gold.

□ DAY 238

GOD SIGHTINGS

August 26

JOB 20:1–22:30
Then Zophar the Naamathite replied:

[2]"My troubled thoughts prompt me to
      answer
   because I am greatly disturbed.

3 I hear a rebuke that dishonors me,
   and my understanding inspires me
      to reply.

4 "Surely you know how it has been
      from of old,
   ever since man*a* was placed on the
      earth,
5 that the mirth of the wicked is brief,
   the joy of the godless lasts but a
      moment.
6 Though his pride reaches to the
      heavens
   and his head touches the clouds,
7 he will perish forever, like his own
      dung;
   those who have seen him will say,
      'Where is he?'
8 Like a dream he flies away, no more
      to be found,
   banished like a vision of the night.
9 The eye that saw him will not see
      him again;
   his place will look on him no more.
10 His children must make amends to
      the poor;
   his own hands must give back his
      wealth.
11 The youthful vigor that fills his bones
   will lie with him in the dust.

12 "Though evil is sweet in his mouth
   and he hides it under his tongue,
13 though he cannot bear to let it go
   and keeps it in his mouth,
14 yet his food will turn sour in his
      stomach;
   it will become the venom of
      serpents within him.
15 He will spit out the riches he
      swallowed;
   God will make his stomach vomit
      them up.
16 He will suck the poison of serpents;
   the fangs of an adder will kill him.
17 He will not enjoy the streams,
   the rivers flowing with honey and
      cream.
18 What he toiled for he must give back
      uneaten;
   he will not enjoy the profit from
      his trading.

19 For he has oppressed the poor and
      left them destitute;
   he has seized houses he did not
      build.

20 "Surely he will have no respite from
      his craving;
   he cannot save himself by his
      treasure.
21 Nothing is left for him to devour;
   his prosperity will not endure.
22 In the midst of his plenty, distress
      will overtake him;
   the full force of misery will come
      upon him.
23 When he has filled his belly,
   God will vent his burning anger
      against him
   and rain down his blows upon him.
24 Though he flees from an iron
      weapon,
   a bronze-tipped arrow pierces him.
25 He pulls it out of his back,
   the gleaming point out of his liver.
   Terrors will come over him;
26   total darkness lies in wait for his
         treasures.
   A fire unfanned will consume him
   and devour what is left in his tent.
27 The heavens will expose his guilt;
   the earth will rise up against him.
28 A flood will carry off his house,
   rushing waters*b* on the day of
      God's wrath.
29 Such is the fate God allots the wicked,
   the heritage appointed for them
      by God."

21:1 THEN Job replied:

2 "Listen carefully to my words;
   let this be the consolation you
      give me.
3 Bear with me while I speak,
   and after I have spoken, mock on.

4 "Is my complaint directed to man?
   Why should I not be impatient?
5 Look at me and be astonished;
   clap your hand over your mouth.
6 When I think about this, I am
      terrified;
   trembling seizes my body.

7 Why do the wicked live on,
    growing old and increasing in
    power?
8 They see their children established
    around them,
    their offspring before their eyes.
9 Their homes are safe and free from
    fear;
    the rod of God is not upon them.
10 Their bulls never fail to breed;
    their cows calve and do not
    miscarry.
11 They send forth their children as a
    flock;
    their little ones dance about.
12 They sing to the music of
    tambourine and harp;
    they make merry to the sound of
    the flute.
13 They spend their years in prosperity
    and go down to the grave*c* in
    peace.*d*
14 Yet they say to God, 'Leave us
    alone!
    We have no desire to know your
    ways.
15 Who is the Almighty, that we should
    serve him?
    What would we gain by praying to
    him?'
16 But their prosperity is not in their
    own hands,
    so I stand aloof from the counsel
    of the wicked.

17 "Yet how often is the lamp of the
    wicked snuffed out?
    How often does calamity come
    upon them,
    the fate God allots in his anger?
18 How often are they like straw before
    the wind,
    like chaff swept away by a gale?
19 It is said, 'God stores up a man's
    punishment for his sons.'
    Let him repay the man himself, so
    that he will know it!
20 Let his own eyes see his
    destruction;
    let him drink of the wrath of the
    Almighty.*e*

21 For what does he care about the
    family he leaves behind
    when his allotted months come to
    an end?
22 "Can anyone teach knowledge to God,
    since he judges even the highest?
23 One man dies in full vigor,
    completely secure and at ease,
24 his body*f* well nourished,
    his bones rich with marrow.
25 Another man dies in bitterness of
    soul,
    never having enjoyed anything
    good.
26 Side by side they lie in the dust,
    and worms cover them both.

27 "I know full well what you are
    thinking,
    the schemes by which you would
    wrong me.
28 You say, 'Where now is the great
    man's house,
    the tents where wicked men
    lived?'
29 Have you never questioned those
    who travel?
    Have you paid no regard to their
    accounts—
30 that the evil man is spared from the
    day of calamity,
    that he is delivered from*g* the day
    of wrath?
31 Who denounces his conduct to his
    face?
    Who repays him for what he has
    done?
32 He is carried to the grave,
    and watch is kept over his tomb.
33 The soil in the valley is sweet to him;
    all men follow after him,
    and a countless throng goes*h*
    before him.

34 "So how can you console me with
    your nonsense?
    Nothing is left of your answers but
    falsehood!"

22:1 THEN Eliphaz the Temanite replied:

2 "Can a man be of benefit to God?
    Can even a wise man benefit him?

3 What pleasure would it give the
    Almighty if you were righteous?
  What would he gain if your ways
    were blameless?

4 "Is it for your piety that he rebukes
    you
  and brings charges against you?
5 Is not your wickedness great?
  Are not your sins endless?
6 You demanded security from your
    brothers for no reason;
  you stripped men of their
    clothing, leaving them naked.
7 You gave no water to the weary
  and you withheld food from the
    hungry,
8 though you were a powerful man,
    owning land—
  an honored man, living on it.
9 And you sent widows away empty-
    handed
  and broke the strength of the
    fatherless.
10 That is why snares are all around you,
  why sudden peril terrifies you,
11 why it is so dark you cannot see,
  and why a flood of water covers
    you.

12 "Is not God in the heights of heaven?
  And see how lofty are the highest
    stars!
13 Yet you say, 'What does God know?
  Does he judge through such
    darkness?
14 Thick clouds veil him, so he does not
    see us
  as he goes about in the vaulted
    heavens.'
15 Will you keep to the old path
  that evil men have trod?
16 They were carried off before their
    time,
  their foundations washed away by
    a flood.
17 They said to God, 'Leave us alone!
  What can the Almighty do to us?'
18 Yet it was he who filled their houses
    with good things,
  so I stand aloof from the counsel
    of the wicked.

19 "The righteous see their ruin and
    rejoice;
  the innocent mock them, saying,
20 'Surely our foes are destroyed,
  and fire devours their wealth.'

21 "Submit to God and be at peace with
    him;
  in this way prosperity will come
    to you.
22 Accept instruction from his mouth
  and lay up his words in your heart.
23 If you return to the Almighty, you will
    be restored:
  If you remove wickedness far from
    your tent
24 and assign your nuggets to the dust,
  your gold of Ophir to the rocks in
    the ravines,
25 then the Almighty will be your gold,
  the choicest silver for you.
26 Surely then you will find delight in
    the Almighty
  and will lift up your face to God.
27 You will pray to him, and he will
    hear you,
  and you will fulfill your vows.
28 What you decide on will be done,
  and light will shine on your ways.
29 When men are brought low and you
    say, 'Lift them up!'
  then he will save the downcast.
30 He will deliver even one who is not
    innocent,
  who will be delivered through the
    cleanness of your hands."

a4 Or *Adam*   b28 Or *The possessions in his house will be
carried off,/ washed away*   c13 Hebrew *Sheol*   d13 Or *in
an instant*   e17-20 Verses 17 and 18 may be taken as
exclamations and 19 and 20 as declarations.   f24 The meaning
of the Hebrew for this word is uncertain.   g30 Or *man is
reserved for the day of calamity,/ that he is brought forth to*
h33 Or */ as a countless throng went*

2 CORINTHIANS 1:1-11

Paul, an apostle of Christ Jesus by the
will of God, and Timothy our brother,

To the church of God in Corinth, together with all the saints throughout
Achaia:

2 Grace and peace to you from God
our Father and the Lord Jesus Christ.

³Praise be to the God and Father of our Lord Jesus Christ, the Father of compassion and the God of all comfort, ⁴who comforts us in all our troubles, so that we can comfort those in any trouble with the comfort we ourselves have received from God. ⁵For just as the sufferings of Christ flow over into our lives, so also through Christ our comfort overflows. ⁶If we are distressed, it is for your comfort and salvation; if we are comforted, it is for your comfort, which produces in you patient endurance of the same sufferings we suffer. ⁷And our hope for you is firm, because we know that just as you share in our sufferings, so also you share in our comfort.

⁸We do not want you to be uninformed, brothers, about the hardships we suffered in the province of Asia. We were under great pressure, far beyond our ability to endure, so that we despaired even of life. ⁹Indeed, in our hearts we felt the sentence of death. But this happened that we might not rely on ourselves but on God, who raises the dead. ¹⁰He has delivered us from such a deadly peril, and he will deliver us. On him we have set our hope that he will continue to deliver us, ¹¹as you help us by your prayers. Then many will give thanks on our*a* behalf for the gracious favor granted us in answer to the prayers of many.

a11 Many manuscripts your

PSALM 40:11-17

¹¹ **D**o not withhold your mercy from
 me, O LORD;
  may your love and your truth
   always protect me.
¹²For troubles without number
  surround me;
  my sins have overtaken me, and I
   cannot see.
 They are more than the hairs of my
  head,
  and my heart fails within me.

¹³Be pleased, O LORD, to save me;
  O LORD, come quickly to help me.
¹⁴May all who seek to take my life
  be put to shame and confusion;

 may all who desire my ruin
  be turned back in disgrace.
¹⁵May those who say to me, "Aha! Aha!"
  be appalled at their own shame.
¹⁶But may all who seek you
  rejoice and be glad in you;
 may those who love your salvation
   always say,
  "The LORD be exalted!"

¹⁷Yet I am poor and needy;
  may the Lord think of me.
 You are my help and my deliverer;
  O my God, do not delay.

PROVERBS 22:2-4

² **R**ich and poor have this in common:
  The LORD is the Maker of them all.

³A prudent man sees danger and
   takes refuge,
  but the simple keep going and
   suffer for it.

⁴Humility and the fear of the LORD
  bring wealth and honor and life.

□ DAY 239

GOD SIGHTINGS

August 27

JOB 23:1–27:23
Then Job replied:

²"Even today my complaint is bitter;
  his hand*a* is heavy in spite of*b* my
   groaning.
³If only I knew where to find him;
  if only I could go to his dwelling!
⁴I would state my case before him
  and fill my mouth with arguments.
⁵I would find out what he would
    answer me,
  and consider what he would say.
⁶Would he oppose me with great
    power?
  No, he would not press charges
   against me.

7 There an upright man could present
his case before him,
and I would be delivered forever
from my judge.

8 "But if I go to the east, he is not there;
if I go to the west, I do not find
him.
9 When he is at work in the north, I do
not see him;
when he turns to the south, I catch
no glimpse of him.
10 But he knows the way that I take;
when he has tested me, I will come
forth as gold.
11 My feet have closely followed his
steps;
I have kept to his way without
turning aside.
12 I have not departed from the
commands of his lips;
I have treasured the words of his
mouth more than my daily
bread.

13 "But he stands alone, and who can
oppose him?
He does whatever he pleases.
14 He carries out his decree against me,
and many such plans he still has in
store.
15 That is why I am terrified before
him;
when I think of all this, I fear him.
16 God has made my heart faint;
the Almighty has terrified me.
17 Yet I am not silenced by the
darkness,
by the thick darkness that covers
my face.

24:1 "WHY does the Almighty not set
times for judgment?
Why must those who know him
look in vain for such days?
2 Men move boundary stones;
they pasture flocks they have
stolen.
3 They drive away the orphan's donkey
and take the widow's ox in pledge.
4 They thrust the needy from the path
and force all the poor of the land
into hiding.

5 Like wild donkeys in the desert,
the poor go about their labor of
foraging food;
the wasteland provides food for
their children.
6 They gather fodder in the fields
and glean in the vineyards of the
wicked.
7 Lacking clothes, they spend the night
naked;
they have nothing to cover
themselves in the cold.
8 They are drenched by mountain
rains
and hug the rocks for lack of
shelter.
9 The fatherless child is snatched from
the breast;
the infant of the poor is seized for
a debt.
10 Lacking clothes, they go about naked;
they carry the sheaves, but still go
hungry.
11 They crush olives among the
terraces[c];
they tread the winepresses, yet
suffer thirst.
12 The groans of the dying rise from the
city,
and the souls of the wounded cry
out for help.
But God charges no one with
wrongdoing.

13 "There are those who rebel against
the light,
who do not know its ways
or stay in its paths.
14 When daylight is gone, the murderer
rises up
and kills the poor and needy;
in the night he steals forth like a
thief.
15 The eye of the adulterer watches for
dusk;
he thinks, 'No eye will see me,'
and he keeps his face concealed.
16 In the dark, men break into houses,
but by day they shut themselves in;
they want nothing to do with the
light.

17 For all of them, deep darkness is
       their morning*d*;
     they make friends with the terrors
       of darkness.*e*

18 "Yet they are foam on the surface of
       the water;
     their portion of the land is cursed,
     so that no one goes to the
       vineyards.
19 As heat and drought snatch away the
       melted snow,
     so the grave*f* snatches away those
       who have sinned.
20 The womb forgets them,
       the worm feasts on them;
     evil men are no longer remembered
       but are broken like a tree.
21 They prey on the barren and
       childless woman,
     and to the widow show no
       kindness.
22 But God drags away the mighty by his
       power;
     though they become established,
       they have no assurance of
       life.
23 He may let them rest in a feeling of
       security,
     but his eyes are on their ways.
24 For a little while they are exalted, and
       then they are gone;
     they are brought low and gathered
       up like all others;
     they are cut off like heads of grain.

25 "If this is not so, who can prove me
       false
     and reduce my words to nothing?"

25:1 THEN Bildad the Shuhite replied:

2 "Dominion and awe belong to God;
     he establishes order in the heights
       of heaven.
3 Can his forces be numbered?
     Upon whom does his light not rise?
4 How then can a man be righteous
       before God?
     How can one born of woman be
       pure?
5 If even the moon is not bright

and the stars are not pure in his
       eyes,
6 how much less man, who is but a
       maggot—
     a son of man, who is only a worm!"

26:1 THEN Job replied:

2 "How you have helped the powerless!
     How you have saved the arm that
       is feeble!
3 What advice you have offered to one
       without wisdom!
     And what great insight you have
       displayed!
4 Who has helped you utter these
       words?
     And whose spirit spoke from your
       mouth?

5 "The dead are in deep anguish,
     those beneath the waters and all
       that live in them.
6 Death*f* is naked before God;
     Destruction*g* lies uncovered.
7 He spreads out the northern ⌊skies⌋
       over empty space;
     he suspends the earth over
       nothing.
8 He wraps up the waters in his
       clouds,
     yet the clouds do not burst under
       their weight.
9 He covers the face of the full moon,
     spreading his clouds over it.
10 He marks out the horizon on the face
       of the waters
     for a boundary between light and
       darkness.
11 The pillars of the heavens quake,
     aghast at his rebuke.
12 By his power he churned up the sea;
     by his wisdom he cut Rahab to
       pieces.
13 By his breath the skies became fair;
     his hand pierced the gliding
       serpent.
14 And these are but the outer fringe of
       his works;
     how faint the whisper we hear of
       him!
     Who then can understand the
       thunder of his power?"

27:1 AND Job continued his discourse:

2 "As surely as God lives, who has
    denied me justice,
  the Almighty, who has made me
    taste bitterness of soul,
3 as long as I have life within me,
  the breath of God in my nostrils,
4 my lips will not speak wickedness,
  and my tongue will utter no deceit.
5 I will never admit you are in the right;
  till I die, I will not deny my
    integrity.
6 I will maintain my righteousness and
    never let go of it;
  my conscience will not reproach
    me as long as I live.

7 "May my enemies be like the wicked,
  my adversaries like the unjust!
8 For what hope has the godless when
    he is cut off,
  when God takes away his life?
9 Does God listen to his cry
  when distress comes upon him?
10 Will he find delight in the Almighty?
  Will he call upon God at all times?

11 "I will teach you about the power
    of God;
  the ways of the Almighty I will not
    conceal.
12 You have all seen this yourselves.
  Why then this meaningless talk?

13 "Here is the fate God allots to the
    wicked,
  the heritage a ruthless man
    receives from the Almighty:
14 However many his children, their
    fate is the sword;
  his offspring will never have
    enough to eat.
15 The plague will bury those who
    survive him,
  and their widows will not weep for
    them.
16 Though he heaps up silver like dust
  and clothes like piles of clay,
17 what he lays up the righteous will
    wear,
  and the innocent will divide his
    silver.

18 The house he builds is like a moth's
    cocoon,
  like a hut made by a watchman.
19 He lies down wealthy, but will do so
    no more;
  when he opens his eyes, all is
    gone.
20 Terrors overtake him like a flood;
  a tempest snatches him away in
    the night.
21 The east wind carries him off, and he
    is gone;
  it sweeps him out of his place.
22 It hurls itself against him without
    mercy
  as he flees headlong from its
    power.
23 It claps its hands in derision
  and hisses him out of his place."

a2 Septuagint and Syriac; Hebrew / *the hand on me*
b2 Or *heavy on me in*   *c11* Or *olives between the millstones;*
the meaning of the Hebrew for this word is uncertain.
d17 Or *them, their morning is like the shadow of death*
e17 Or *of the shadow of death*   *f19,6* Hebrew *Sheol*
96 Hebrew *Abaddon*

2 CORINTHIANS 1:12–2:11

Now this is our boast: Our conscience
testifies that we have conducted ourselves in the world, and especially in our
relations with you, in the holiness and
sincerity that are from God. We have
done so not according to worldly wisdom but according to God's grace. 13 For
we do not write you anything you cannot read or understand. And I hope that,
14 as you have understood us in part, you
will come to understand fully that you
can boast of us just as we will boast of
you in the day of the Lord Jesus.

15 Because I was confident of this, I
planned to visit you first so that you
might benefit twice. 16 I planned to visit
you on my way to Macedonia and to
come back to you from Macedonia, and
then to have you send me on my way to
Judea. 17 When I planned this, did I do it
lightly? Or do I make my plans in a
worldly manner so that in the same
breath I say, "Yes, yes" and "No, no"?

18 But as surely as God is faithful, our
message to you is not "Yes" and "No."
19 For the Son of God, Jesus Christ, who

was preached among you by me and Silas[a] and Timothy, was not "Yes" and "No," but in him it has always been "Yes." [20]For no matter how many promises God has made, they are "Yes" in Christ. And so through him the "Amen" is spoken by us to the glory of God. [21]**Now it is God who makes both us and you stand firm in Christ. He anointed us,** [22]**set his seal of ownership on us, and put his Spirit in our hearts as a deposit, guaranteeing what is to come.**

[23]I call God as my witness that it was in order to spare you that I did not return to Corinth. [24]Not that we lord it over your faith, but we work with you for your joy, because it is by faith you stand firm. [2:1]So I made up my mind that I would not make another painful visit to you. [2]For if I grieve you, who is left to make me glad but you whom I have grieved? [3]I wrote as I did so that when I came I should not be distressed by those who ought to make me rejoice. I had confidence in all of you, that you would all share my joy. [4]For I wrote you out of great distress and anguish of heart and with many tears, not to grieve you but to let you know the depth of my love for you.

[5]If anyone has caused grief, he has not so much grieved me as he has grieved all of you, to some extent—not to put it too severely. [6]The punishment inflicted on him by the majority is sufficient for him. [7]Now instead, you ought to forgive and comfort him, so that he will not be overwhelmed by excessive sorrow. [8]I urge you, therefore, to reaffirm your love for him. [9]The reason I wrote you was to see if you would stand the test and be obedient in everything. [10]If you forgive anyone, I also forgive him. And what I have forgiven—if there was anything to forgive—I have forgiven in the sight of Christ for your sake, [11]in order that Satan might not outwit us. For we are not unaware of his schemes.

a 19 Greek *Silvanus*, a variant of *Silas*

PSALM 41:1-13

For the director of music. A psalm of David.

[1]**B**lessed is he who has regard for the weak;
　　the Lord delivers him in times of trouble.
[2]The Lord will protect him and preserve his life;
　　he will bless him in the land
　　and not surrender him to the desire of his foes.
[3]The Lord will sustain him on his sickbed
　　and restore him from his bed of illness.

[4]I said, "O Lord, have mercy on me;
　　heal me, for I have sinned against you."
[5]My enemies say of me in malice,
　　"When will he die and his name perish?"
[6]Whenever one comes to see me,
　　he speaks falsely, while his heart gathers slander;
　　then he goes out and spreads it abroad.

[7]All my enemies whisper together against me;
　　they imagine the worst for me, saying,
[8]"A vile disease has beset him;
　　he will never get up from the place where he lies."
[9]Even my close friend, whom I trusted,
　　he who shared my bread,
　　has lifted up his heel against me.

[10]But you, O Lord, have mercy on me;
　　raise me up, that I may repay them.
[11]I know that you are pleased with me,
　　for my enemy does not triumph over me.
[12]In my integrity you uphold me
　　and set me in your presence forever.

[13]Praise be to the Lord, the God of Israel,
　　from everlasting to everlasting.
　　Amen and Amen.

PROVERBS 22:5-6

5 In the paths of the wicked lie thorns
  and snares,
    but he who guards his soul stays
    far from them.

6 Train*a* a child in the way he should go,
    and when he is old he will not turn
    from it.

a6 Or Start

□ DAY 240

GOD SIGHTINGS

August 28

JOB 28:1–30:31

"There is a mine for silver
  and a place where gold is refined.
2 Iron is taken from the earth,
  and copper is smelted from ore.
3 Man puts an end to the darkness;
  he searches the farthest recesses
    for ore in the blackest darkness.
4 Far from where people dwell he cuts
    a shaft,
  in places forgotten by the foot of
    man;
  far from men he dangles and sways.
5 The earth, from which food comes,
  is transformed below as by fire;
6 sapphires*a* come from its rocks,
  and its dust contains nuggets of
    gold.
7 No bird of prey knows that hidden
    path,
  no falcon's eye has seen it.
8 Proud beasts do not set foot on it,
  and no lion prowls there.
9 Man's hand assaults the flinty rock
  and lays bare the roots of the
    mountains.
10 He tunnels through the rock;
  his eyes see all its treasures.
11 He searches*b* the sources of the rivers
  and brings hidden things to light.

12 "But where can wisdom be found?
  Where does understanding dwell?

13 Man does not comprehend its worth;
  it cannot be found in the land of
    the living.
14 The deep says, 'It is not in me';
  the sea says, 'It is not with me.'
15 It cannot be bought with the finest
    gold,
  nor can its price be weighed in
    silver.
16 It cannot be bought with the gold of
    Ophir,
  with precious onyx or sapphires.
17 Neither gold nor crystal can compare
    with it,
  nor can it be had for jewels of gold.
18 Coral and jasper are not worthy of
    mention;
  the price of wisdom is beyond
    rubies.
19 The topaz of Cush cannot compare
    with it;
  it cannot be bought with pure gold.

20 "Where then does wisdom come
    from?
  Where does understanding dwell?
21 It is hidden from the eyes of every
    living thing,
  concealed even from the birds of
    the air.
22 Destruction*c* and Death say,
  'Only a rumor of it has reached our
    ears.'
23 God understands the way to it
  and he alone knows where it
    dwells,
24 for he views the ends of the earth
  and sees everything under the
    heavens.
25 When he established the force of the
    wind
  and measured out the waters,
26 when he made a decree for the rain
  and a path for the thunderstorm,
27 then he looked at wisdom and
    appraised it;
  he confirmed it and tested it.
28 And he said to man,
  'The fear of the Lord—that is
    wisdom,
  and to shun evil is
    understanding.'"

29:1 JOB continued his discourse:

2 "How I long for the months gone by,
  for the days when God watched
     over me,
3 when his lamp shone upon my head
  and by his light I walked through
     darkness!
4 Oh, for the days when I was in my
     prime,
  when God's intimate friendship
     blessed my house,
5 when the Almighty was still with me
  and my children were around me,
6 when my path was drenched with
     cream
  and the rock poured out for me
     streams of olive oil.

7 "When I went to the gate of the city
  and took my seat in the public
     square,
8 the young men saw me and stepped
     aside
  and the old men rose to their feet;
9 the chief men refrained from
     speaking
  and covered their mouths with
     their hands;
10 the voices of the nobles were hushed,
  and their tongues stuck to the roof
     of their mouths.
11 Whoever heard me spoke well of me,
  and those who saw me
     commended me,
12 because I rescued the poor who
     cried for help,
  and the fatherless who had none
     to assist him.
13 The man who was dying blessed me;
  I made the widow's heart sing.
14 I put on righteousness as my
     clothing;
  justice was my robe and my
     turban.
15 I was eyes to the blind
  and feet to the lame.
16 I was a father to the needy;
  I took up the case of the stranger.
17 I broke the fangs of the wicked
  and snatched the victims from
     their teeth.

18 "I thought, 'I will die in my own
     house,
  my days as numerous as the grains
     of sand.
19 My roots will reach to the water,
  and the dew will lie all night on my
     branches.
20 My glory will remain fresh in me,
  the bow ever new in my hand.'

21 "Men listened to me expectantly,
  waiting in silence for my counsel.
22 After I had spoken, they spoke no
     more;
  my words fell gently on their ears.
23 They waited for me as for showers
  and drank in my words as the
     spring rain.
24 When I smiled at them, they scarcely
     believed it;
  the light of my face was precious
     to them.*d*
25 I chose the way for them and sat as
     their chief;
  I dwelt as a king among his troops;
  I was like one who comforts
     mourners.

30:1 "BUT now they mock me,
  men younger than I,
  whose fathers I would have
     disdained
  to put with my sheep dogs.
2 Of what use was the strength of their
     hands to me,
  since their vigor had gone from
     them?
3 Haggard from want and hunger,
  they roamed*e* the parched land
  in desolate wastelands at night.
4 In the brush they gathered salt herbs,
  and their food*f* was the root of the
     broom tree.
5 They were banished from their
     fellow men,
  shouted at as if they were thieves.
6 They were forced to live in the dry
     stream beds,
  among the rocks and in holes in
     the ground.
7 They brayed among the bushes
  and huddled in the undergrowth.

8 A base and nameless brood,
  they were driven out of the land.

9 "And now their sons mock me in
    song;
  I have become a byword among
    them.

10 They detest me and keep their
    distance;
  they do not hesitate to spit in my
    face.

11 Now that God has unstrung my bow
    and afflicted me,
  they throw off restraint in my
    presence.

12 On my right the tribe*g* attacks;
  they lay snares for my feet,
  they build their siege ramps
    against me.

13 They break up my road;
  they succeed in destroying me—
  without anyone's helping them.*h*

14 They advance as through a gaping
    breach;
  amid the ruins they come
    rolling in.

15 Terrors overwhelm me;
  my dignity is driven away as by the
    wind,
  my safety vanishes like a cloud.

16 "And now my life ebbs away;
  days of suffering grip me.

17 Night pierces my bones;
  my gnawing pains never rest.

18 In his great power ⌊God⌋ becomes
    like clothing to me*i*;
  he binds me like the neck of my
    garment.

19 He throws me into the mud,
  and I am reduced to dust and
    ashes.

20 "I cry out to you, O God, but you do
    not answer;
  I stand up, but you merely look
    at me.

21 You turn on me ruthlessly;
  with the might of your hand you
    attack me.

22 You snatch me up and drive me
    before the wind;
  you toss me about in the storm.

23 I know you will bring me down to
    death,
  to the place appointed for all the
    living.

24 "Surely no one lays a hand on a
    broken man
  when he cries for help in his
    distress.

25 Have I not wept for those in trouble?
  Has not my soul grieved for the
    poor?

26 Yet when I hoped for good, evil
    came;
  when I looked for light, then came
    darkness.

27 The churning inside me never stops;
  days of suffering confront me.

28 I go about blackened, but not by the
    sun;
  I stand up in the assembly and cry
    for help.

29 I have become a brother of jackals,
  a companion of owls.

30 My skin grows black and peels;
  my body burns with fever.

31 My harp is tuned to mourning,
  and my flute to the sound of
    wailing."

a6 Or *lapis lazuli*; also in verse 16   *b11* Septuagint, Aquila
and Vulgate; Hebrew *He dams up*   *c22* Hebrew *Abaddon*
d24 The meaning of the Hebrew for this clause is uncertain.
e3 Or *gnawed*   *f4* Or *fuel*   *g12* The meaning of the Hebrew
for this word is uncertain.   *h13* Or *me. / 'No one can help
him,' ⌊they say⌋*.   *i18* Hebrew; Septuagint ⌊God⌋ grasps my
clothing

2 CORINTHIANS 2:12-17

Now when I went to Troas to preach the
gospel of Christ and found that the Lord
had opened a door for me, 13 I still had
no peace of mind, because I did not find
my brother Titus there. So I said good-
by to them and went on to Macedonia.
  14 **But thanks be to God, who always
leads us in triumphal procession in
Christ and through us spreads everywhere the fragrance of the knowledge of him.** 15 For we are to God the
aroma of Christ among those who are
being saved and those who are perishing. 16 To the one we are the smell of
death; to the other, the fragrance of
life. And who is equal to such a task?

17 Unlike so many, we do not peddle the word of God for profit. On the contrary, in Christ we speak before God with sincerity, like men sent from God.

PSALM 42:1-11*a*

For the director of music. A *maskil*b of the Sons of Korah.

1 **A**s the deer pants for streams of water,
    so my soul pants for you, O God.
2 My soul thirsts for God, for the living God.
    When can I go and meet with God?
3 My tears have been my food
    day and night,
while men say to me all day long,
    "Where is your God?"
4 These things I remember
    as I pour out my soul:
how I used to go with the multitude,
    leading the procession to the
        house of God,
with shouts of joy and thanksgiving
    among the festive throng.

5 Why are you downcast, O my soul?
    Why so disturbed within me?
Put your hope in God,
    for I will yet praise him,
    my Savior and 6 my God.

My*c* soul is downcast within me;
    therefore I will remember you
from the land of the Jordan,
    the heights of Hermon—from
        Mount Mizar.
7 Deep calls to deep
    in the roar of your waterfalls;
all your waves and breakers
    have swept over me.

8 By day the LORD directs his love,
    at night his song is with me—
    a prayer to the God of my life.

9 I say to God my Rock,
    "Why have you forgotten me?
Why must I go about mourning,
    oppressed by the enemy?"
10 My bones suffer mortal agony
    as my foes taunt me,
saying to me all day long,
    "Where is your God?"

11 Why are you downcast, O my soul?
    Why so disturbed within me?
Put your hope in God,
    for I will yet praise him,
    my Savior and my God.

*a*In many Hebrew manuscripts Psalms 42 and 43 constitute one psalm.   *b*Title: Probably a literary or musical term   *c*5,6 A few Hebrew manuscripts, Septuagint and Syriac; most Hebrew manuscripts *praise him for his saving help. / 6O my God, my*

PROVERBS 22:7

7 **T**he rich rule over the poor,
    and the borrower is servant to the
        lender.

□ DAY 241

GOD SIGHTINGS

August 29

JOB 31:1-33:33

"**I** made a covenant with my eyes
    not to look lustfully at a girl.
2 For what is man's lot from God above,
    his heritage from the Almighty on
        high?
3 Is it not ruin for the wicked,
    disaster for those who do wrong?
4 Does he not see my ways
    and count my every step?

5 "If I have walked in falsehood
    or my foot has hurried after
        deceit—
6 let God weigh me in honest scales
    and he will know that I am
        blameless—
7 if my steps have turned from the path,
    if my heart has been led by my
        eyes,
    or if my hands have been defiled,
8 then may others eat what I have
        sown,
    and may my crops be uprooted.

9 "If my heart has been enticed by a
        woman,
    or if I have lurked at my
        neighbor's door,

¹⁰then may my wife grind another
man's grain,
and may other men sleep with her.
¹¹For that would have been shameful,
a sin to be judged.
¹²It is a fire that burns to Destruction*ᵃ;
it would have uprooted my
harvest.

¹³"If I have denied justice to my
menservants and
maidservants
when they had a grievance against
me,
¹⁴what will I do when God confronts
me?
What will I answer when called to
account?
¹⁵Did not he who made me in the
womb make them?
Did not the same one form us both
within our mothers?

¹⁶"If I have denied the desires of the
poor
or let the eyes of the widow grow
weary,
¹⁷if I have kept my bread to myself,
not sharing it with the fatherless—
¹⁸but from my youth I reared him as
would a father,
and from my birth I guided the
widow—
¹⁹if I have seen anyone perishing for
lack of clothing,
or a needy man without a garment,
²⁰and his heart did not bless me
for warming him with the fleece
from my sheep,
²¹if I have raised my hand against the
fatherless,
knowing that I had influence in
court,
²²then let my arm fall from the
shoulder,
let it be broken off at the joint.
²³For I dreaded destruction from God,
and for fear of his splendor I could
not do such things.

²⁴"If I have put my trust in gold
or said to pure gold, 'You are my
security,'

²⁵if I have rejoiced over my great
wealth,
the fortune my hands had gained,
²⁶if I have regarded the sun in its
radiance
or the moon moving in splendor,
²⁷so that my heart was secretly enticed
and my hand offered them a kiss
of homage,
²⁸then these also would be sins to be
judged,
for I would have been unfaithful to
God on high.

²⁹"If I have rejoiced at my enemy's
misfortune
or gloated over the trouble that
came to him—
³⁰I have not allowed my mouth to sin
by invoking a curse against his
life—
³¹if the men of my household have
never said,
'Who has not had his fill of Job's
meat?'—
³²but no stranger had to spend the
night in the street,
for my door was always open to
the traveler—
³³if I have concealed my sin as men do,ᵇ
by hiding my guilt in my heart
³⁴because I so feared the crowd
and so dreaded the contempt of
the clans
that I kept silent and would not go
outside—

³⁵("Oh, that I had someone to hear me!
I sign now my defense—let the
Almighty answer me;
let my accuser put his indictment
in writing.
³⁶Surely I would wear it on my
shoulder,
I would put it on like a crown.
³⁷I would give him an account of my
every step;
like a prince I would approach
him.)—

³⁸"if my land cries out against me
and all its furrows are wet with
tears,

39 if I have devoured its yield without
      payment
   or broken the spirit of its tenants,
40 then let briers come up instead of
      wheat
   and weeds instead of barley."

The words of Job are ended.

32:1 So these three men stopped answering Job, because he was righteous in his
own eyes. 2 But Elihu son of Barakel the
Buzite, of the family of Ram, became
very angry with Job for justifying himself rather than God. 3 He was also angry
with the three friends, because they had
found no way to refute Job, and yet had
condemned him.c 4 Now Elihu had
waited before speaking to Job because
they were older than he. 5 But when he
saw that the three men had nothing
more to say, his anger was aroused.

6 So Elihu son of Barakel the Buzite
said:

"I am young in years,
   and you are old;
that is why I was fearful,
   not daring to tell you what I know.
7 I thought, 'Age should speak;
   advanced years should teach
      wisdom.'
8 But it is the spiritd in a man,
   the breath of the Almighty, that
      gives him understanding.
9 It is not only the olde who are wise,
   not only the aged who
      understand what is right.

10 "Therefore I say: Listen to me;
   I too will tell you what I know.
11 I waited while you spoke,
   I listened to your reasoning;
   while you were searching for words,
12   I gave you my full attention.
   But not one of you has proved Job
      wrong;
   none of you has answered his
      arguments.
13 Do not say, 'We have found wisdom;
   let God refute him, not man.'
14 But Job has not marshaled his words
      against me,

and I will not answer him with
   your arguments.

15 "They are dismayed and have no
      more to say;
   words have failed them.
16 Must I wait, now that they are silent,
   now that they stand there with no
      reply?
17 I too will have my say;
   I too will tell what I know.
18 For I am full of words,
   and the spirit within me compels
      me;
19 inside I am like bottled-up wine,
   like new wineskins ready to burst.
20 I must speak and find relief;
   I must open my lips and reply.
21 I will show partiality to no one,
   nor will I flatter any man;
22 for if I were skilled in flattery,
   my Maker would soon take me
      away.

33:1 "But now, Job, listen to my words;
   pay attention to everything I say.
2 I am about to open my mouth;
   my words are on the tip of my
      tongue.
3 My words come from an upright
      heart;
   my lips sincerely speak what I
      know.
4 The Spirit of God has made me;
   the breath of the Almighty gives
      me life.
5 Answer me then, if you can;
   prepare yourself and confront me.
6 I am just like you before God;
   I too have been taken from clay.
7 No fear of me should alarm you,
   nor should my hand be heavy
      upon you.

8 "But you have said in my hearing—
   I heard the very words—
9 'I am pure and without sin;
   I am clean and free from guilt.
10 Yet God has found fault with me;
   he considers me his enemy.
11 He fastens my feet in shackles;
   he keeps close watch on all my
      paths.'

12"But I tell you, in this you are not
        right,
    for God is greater than man.
13 Why do you complain to him
        that he answers none of man's
        words*?
14 For God does speak—now one way,
        now another—
    though man may not perceive it.
15 In a dream, in a vision of the night,
        when deep sleep falls on men
        as they slumber in their beds,
16 he may speak in their ears
        and terrify them with warnings,
17 to turn man from wrongdoing
        and keep him from pride,
18 to preserve his soul from the pit,*g*
        his life from perishing by the
        sword.*h*
19 Or a man may be chastened on a bed
        of pain
    with constant distress in his
        bones,
20 so that his very being finds food
        repulsive
    and his soul loathes the choicest
        meal.
21 His flesh wastes away to nothing,
        and his bones, once hidden, now
        stick out.
22 His soul draws near to the pit,*i*
        and his life to the messengers of
        death.*j*

23 "Yet if there is an angel on his side
        as a mediator, one out of a
        thousand,
    to tell a man what is right for him,
24 to be gracious to him and say,
        'Spare him from going down to the
        pit*k*;
    I have found a ransom for him'—
25 then his flesh is renewed like a
        child's;
    it is restored as in the days of his
        youth.
26 He prays to God and finds favor with
        him,
    he sees God's face and shouts for
        joy;
    he is restored by God to his
        righteous state.

27 Then he comes to men and says,
        'I sinned, and perverted what was
        right,
    but I did not get what I deserved.
28 He redeemed my soul from going
        down to the pit,*l*
    and I will live to enjoy the light.'

29 "God does all these things to a man—
        twice, even three times—
30 to turn back his soul from the pit,*m*
    that the light of life may shine
        on him.

31 "Pay attention, Job, and listen to me;
        be silent, and I will speak.
32 If you have anything to say, answer
        me;
    speak up, for I want you to be
        cleared.
33 But if not, then listen to me;
        be silent, and I will teach you
        wisdom."

a12 Hebrew *Abaddon*   *b33* Or *as Adam did*   *c3* Masoretic
Text; an ancient Hebrew scribal tradition *Job, and so had
condemned God*   *d8* Or *Spirit*; also in verse 18   *e9* Or *many;*
or *great*   *f13* Or *that he does not answer for any of his
actions*   *g18* Or *preserve him from the grave*   *h18* Or *from
crossing the River*   *i22* Or *He draws near to the grave*
j22 Or *to the dead*   *k24* Or *grave*   *l28* Or *redeemed me
from going down to the grave*   *m30* Or *turn him back
from the grave*

2 CORINTHIANS 3:1-18

Are we beginning to commend ourselves again? Or do we need, like some
people, letters of recommendation to
you or from you? 2 You yourselves are
our letter, written on our hearts, known
and read by everybody. 3 You show that
you are a letter from Christ, the result of
our ministry, written not with ink but
with the Spirit of the living God, not on
tablets of stone but on tablets of human
hearts.

4 Such confidence as this is ours
through Christ before God. 5 Not that we
are competent in ourselves to claim anything for ourselves, but our competence
comes from God. 6 He has made us competent as ministers of a new covenant—
not of the letter but of the Spirit; for the
letter kills, but the Spirit gives life.

7 Now if the ministry that brought
death, which was engraved in letters on

stone, came with glory, so that the Israelites could not look steadily at the face of Moses because of its glory, fading though it was, 8 will not the ministry of the Spirit be even more glorious? 9 If the ministry that condemns men is glorious, how much more glorious is the ministry that brings righteousness! 10 For what was glorious has no glory now in comparison with the surpassing glory. 11 And if what was fading away came with glory, how much greater is the glory of that which lasts!

12 Therefore, since we have such a hope, we are very bold. 13 We are not like Moses, who would put a veil over his face to keep the Israelites from gazing at it while the radiance was fading away. 14 But their minds were made dull, for to this day the same veil remains when the old covenant is read. It has not been removed, because only in Christ is it taken away. 15 Even to this day when Moses is read, a veil covers their hearts. 16 But whenever anyone turns to the Lord, the veil is taken away. 17 Now the Lord is the Spirit, and where the Spirit of the Lord is, there is freedom. 18 And we, who with unveiled faces all reflect*a* the Lord's glory, are being transformed into his likeness with ever-increasing glory, which comes from the Lord, who is the Spirit.

a 18 Or contemplate

PSALM 43:1-5*a*

1 **V**indicate me, O God,
    and plead my cause against an
        ungodly nation;
    rescue me from deceitful and
        wicked men.
2 You are God my stronghold.
    Why have you rejected me?
Why must I go about mourning,
    oppressed by the enemy?
3 Send forth your light and your truth,
    let them guide me;
let them bring me to your holy
        mountain,
    to the place where you dwell.
4 Then will I go to the altar of God,
    to God, my joy and my delight.

I will praise you with the harp,
    O God, my God.

5 Why are you downcast, O my soul?
    Why so disturbed within me?
Put your hope in God,
    for I will yet praise him,
    my Savior and my God.

a In many Hebrew manuscripts Psalms 42 and 43 constitute one psalm.

PROVERBS 22:8-9

8 **H**e who sows wickedness reaps
        trouble,
    and the rod of his fury will be
        destroyed.

9 A generous man will himself be
        blessed,
    for he shares his food with the poor.

☐ DAY 242

GOD SIGHTINGS

August 30

JOB 34:1–36:33

Then Elihu said:

2 "Hear my words, you wise men;
    listen to me, you men of learning.
3 For the ear tests words
    as the tongue tastes food.
4 Let us discern for ourselves what is
        right;
    let us learn together what is good.

5 "Job says, 'I am innocent,
    but God denies me justice.
6 Although I am right,
    I am considered a liar;
although I am guiltless,
    his arrow inflicts an incurable
        wound.'
7 What man is like Job,
    who drinks scorn like water?
8 He keeps company with evildoers;
    he associates with wicked men.
9 For he says, 'It profits a man nothing
    when he tries to please God.'

¹⁰"So listen to me, you men of
         understanding.
      Far be it from God to do evil,
      from the Almighty to do wrong.
¹¹He repays a man for what he has done;
      he brings upon him what his
         conduct deserves.
¹²It is unthinkable that God would do
         wrong,
      that the Almighty would pervert
         justice.
¹³Who appointed him over the earth?
      Who put him in charge of the
         whole world?
¹⁴If it were his intention
      and he withdrew his spirit*a* and
         breath,
¹⁵all mankind would perish together
      and man would return to the dust.

¹⁶"If you have understanding, hear this;
      listen to what I say.
¹⁷Can he who hates justice govern?
      Will you condemn the just and
         mighty One?
¹⁸Is he not the One who says to kings,
         'You are worthless,'
      and to nobles, 'You are wicked,'
¹⁹who shows no partiality to princes
      and does not favor the rich over
         the poor,
      for they are all the work of his
         hands?
²⁰They die in an instant, in the middle
         of the night;
      the people are shaken and they
         pass away;
      the mighty are removed without
         human hand.

²¹"His eyes are on the ways of men;
      he sees their every step.
²²There is no dark place, no deep
         shadow,
      where evildoers can hide.
²³God has no need to examine men
         further,
      that they should come before him
         for judgment.
²⁴Without inquiry he shatters the
         mighty
      and sets up others in their place.

²⁵Because he takes note of their deeds,
      he overthrows them in the night
         and they are crushed.
²⁶He punishes them for their
         wickedness
      where everyone can see them,
²⁷because they turned from following
         him
      and had no regard for any of his
         ways.
²⁸They caused the cry of the poor to
         come before him,
      so that he heard the cry of the needy.
²⁹But if he remains silent, who can
         condemn him?
      If he hides his face, who can see
         him?
      Yet he is over man and nation alike,
³⁰   to keep a godless man from ruling,
      from laying snares for the people.

³¹"Suppose a man says to God,
      'I am guilty but will offend no more.
³²Teach me what I cannot see;
      if I have done wrong, I will not do
         so again.'
³³Should God then reward you on your
         terms,
      when you refuse to repent?
      You must decide, not I;
      so tell me what you know.

³⁴"Men of understanding declare,
      wise men who hear me say to me,
³⁵'Job speaks without knowledge;
      his words lack insight.'
³⁶Oh, that Job might be tested to the
         utmost
      for answering like a wicked man!
³⁷To his sin he adds rebellion;
      scornfully he claps his hands
         among us
      and multiplies his words against
         God."

³⁵:¹THEN Elihu said:

²"Do you think this is just?
      You say, 'I will be cleared by God.*b*'
³Yet you ask him, 'What profit is it
         to me,*c*
      and what do I gain by not sinning?'

4"I would like to reply to you
and to your friends with you.
5Look up at the heavens and see;
gaze at the clouds so high above you.
6If you sin, how does that affect him?
If your sins are many, what does
that do to him?
7If you are righteous, what do you give
to him,
or what does he receive from your
hand?
8Your wickedness affects only a man
like yourself,
and your righteousness only the
sons of men.

9"Men cry out under a load of
oppression;
they plead for relief from the arm
of the powerful.
10But no one says, 'Where is God my
Maker,
who gives songs in the night,
11who teaches more to us than to*d* the
beasts of the earth
and makes us wiser than*e* the
birds of the air?'
12He does not answer when men cry out
because of the arrogance of the
wicked.
13Indeed, God does not listen to their
empty plea;
the Almighty pays no attention to it.
14How much less, then, will he listen
when you say that you do not see
him,
that your case is before him
and you must wait for him,
15and further, that his anger never
punishes
and he does not take the least
notice of wickedness.*f*
16So Job opens his mouth with empty
talk;
without knowledge he multiplies
words."

36:1Elihu continued:

2"Bear with me a little longer and I
will show you
that there is more to be said in
God's behalf.

3I get my knowledge from afar;
I will ascribe justice to my Maker.
4Be assured that my words are not
false;
one perfect in knowledge is with
you.

5"God is mighty, but does not despise
men;
he is mighty, and firm in his
purpose.
6He does not keep the wicked alive
but gives the afflicted their
rights.
7He does not take his eyes off the
righteous;
he enthrones them with kings
and exalts them forever.
8But if men are bound in chains,
held fast by cords of affliction,
9he tells them what they have
done—
that they have sinned arrogantly.
10He makes them listen to correction
and commands them to repent of
their evil.
11If they obey and serve him,
they will spend the rest of their
days in prosperity
and their years in contentment.
12But if they do not listen,
they will perish by the sword*g*
and die without knowledge.

13"The godless in heart harbor
resentment;
even when he fetters them, they
do not cry for help.
14They die in their youth,
among male prostitutes of the
shrines.
15But those who suffer he delivers in
their suffering;
he speaks to them in their
affliction.

16"He is wooing you from the jaws of
distress
to a spacious place free from
restriction,
to the comfort of your table laden
with choice food.

[17] But now you are laden with the
            judgment due the wicked;
    judgment and justice have taken
            hold of you.
[18] Be careful that no one entices you by
            riches;
    do not let a large bribe turn you
            aside.
[19] Would your wealth
    or even all your mighty efforts
    sustain you so you would not be in
            distress?
[20] Do not long for the night,
    to drag people away from their
            homes.[h]
[21] Beware of turning to evil,
    which you seem to prefer to
            affliction.

[22] "God is exalted in his power.
    Who is a teacher like him?
[23] Who has prescribed his ways for
            him,
    or said to him, 'You have done
            wrong'?
[24] Remember to extol his work,
    which men have praised in song.
[25] All mankind has seen it;
    men gaze on it from afar.
[26] How great is God—beyond our
            understanding!
    The number of his years is past
            finding out.

[27] "He draws up the drops of water,
    which distill as rain to the
            streams[i];
[28] the clouds pour down their
            moisture
    and abundant showers fall on
            mankind.
[29] Who can understand how he spreads
            out the clouds,
    how he thunders from his
            pavilion?
[30] See how he scatters his lightning
            about him,
    bathing the depths of the sea.
[31] This is the way he governs[j] the
            nations
    and provides food in
            abundance.

[32] He fills his hands with lightning
    and commands it to strike its
            mark.
[33] His thunder announces the coming
            storm;
    even the cattle make known its
            approach.[k]"

[a]14 Or *Spirit*   [b]2 Or *My righteousness is more than God's*
[c]3 Or *you*   [d]11 Or *teaches us by*   [e]11 Or *us wise by*
[f]15 Symmachus, Theodotion and Vulgate; the meaning of
the Hebrew for this word is uncertain.   [g]12 Or *will cross
the River*   [h]20 The meaning of the Hebrew for verses 18-20
is uncertain.   [i]27 Or *distill from the mist as rain*
[j]31 Or *nourishes*   [k]33 Or *announces his coming— /
the One zealous against evil*

2 CORINTHIANS 4:1-12

Therefore, since through God's mercy we
have this ministry, we do not lose heart.
[2] Rather, we have renounced secret and
shameful ways; we do not use deception,
nor do we distort the word of God. On
the contrary, by setting forth the truth
plainly we commend ourselves to every
man's conscience in the sight of God.
[3] And even if our gospel is veiled, it is
veiled to those who are perishing. [4] The
god of this age has blinded the minds of
unbelievers, so that they cannot see the
light of the gospel of the glory of Christ,
who is the image of God. [5] For we do not
preach ourselves, but Jesus Christ as
Lord, and ourselves as your servants for
Jesus' sake. [6] For God, who said, "Let light
shine out of darkness,"[a] made his light
shine in our hearts to give us the light of
the knowledge of the glory of God in the
face of Christ.

[7] **But we have this treasure in jars of
clay to show that this all-surpassing
power is from God and not from us.**
[8] We are hard pressed on every side, but
not crushed; perplexed, but not in despair; [9] persecuted, but not abandoned;
struck down, but not destroyed. [10] We
always carry around in our body the
death of Jesus, so that the life of Jesus
may also be revealed in our body. [11] For
we who are alive are always being given
over to death for Jesus' sake, so that his
life may be revealed in our mortal body.
[12] So then, death is at work in us, but life
is at work in you.

[a]6 Gen. 1:3

PSALM 44:1-8

For the director of music. Of the Sons of Korah. A *maskil.ᵃ*

¹ **W**e have heard with our ears, O God;
  our fathers have told us
what you did in their days,
  in days long ago.
² With your hand you drove out the
    nations
  and planted our fathers;
you crushed the peoples
  and made our fathers flourish.
³ It was not by their sword that they
    won the land,
  nor did their arm bring them
    victory;
it was your right hand, your arm,
  and the light of your face, for you
    loved them.

⁴ You are my King and my God,
  who decreesᵇ victories for Jacob.
⁵ Through you we push back our
    enemies;
  through your name we trample
    our foes.
⁶ I do not trust in my bow,
  my sword does not bring me
    victory;
⁷ but you give us victory over our
    enemies,
  you put our adversaries to shame.
⁸ In God we make our boast all day
    long,
  and we will praise your name
    forever.   *Selah*

ᵃTitle: Probably a literary or musical term   ᵇ4 Septuagint,
Aquila and Syriac; Hebrew *King, O God; / command*

PROVERBS 22:10-12

¹⁰ **D**rive out the mocker, and out goes
    strife;
  quarrels and insults are ended.

¹¹ He who loves a pure heart and whose
    speech is gracious
  will have the king for his friend.

¹² The eyes of the Lᴏʀᴅ keep watch over
    knowledge,
  but he frustrates the words of the
    unfaithful.

GOD SIGHTINGS

August 31

JOB 37:1–39:30
  "**A**t this my heart pounds
    and leaps from its place.
² Listen! Listen to the roar of his voice,
    to the rumbling that comes from
      his mouth.
³ He unleashes his lightning beneath
      the whole heaven
    and sends it to the ends of the
      earth.
⁴ After that comes the sound of his
      roar;
    he thunders with his majestic
      voice.
  When his voice resounds,
    he holds nothing back.
⁵ God's voice thunders in marvelous
      ways;
    he does great things beyond our
      understanding.
⁶ He says to the snow, 'Fall on the
      earth,'
    and to the rain shower, 'Be a
      mighty downpour.'
⁷ So that all men he has made may
      know his work,
    he stops every man his labor.ᵃ
⁸ The animals take cover;
    they remain in their dens.
⁹ The tempest comes out from its
      chamber,
    the cold from the driving winds.
¹⁰ The breath of God produces ice,
    and the broad waters become
      frozen.
¹¹ He loads the clouds with moisture;
    he scatters his lightning through
      them.
¹² At his direction they swirl around
    over the face of the whole earth
    to do whatever he commands
      them.
¹³ He brings the clouds to punish men,
    or to water his earthᵇ and show
      his love.

14"Listen to this, Job;
  stop and consider God's wonders.
15Do you know how God controls the
    clouds
  and makes his lightning flash?
16Do you know how the clouds hang
    poised,
  those wonders of him who is
    perfect in knowledge?
17You who swelter in your clothes
  when the land lies hushed under
    the south wind,
18can you join him in spreading out the
    skies,
  hard as a mirror of cast bronze?

19"Tell us what we should say to him;
  we cannot draw up our case
    because of our darkness.
20Should he be told that I want to speak?
  Would any man ask to be
    swallowed up?
21Now no one can look at the sun,
  bright as it is in the skies
  after the wind has swept them clean.
22Out of the north he comes in golden
    splendor;
  God comes in awesome majesty.
23The Almighty is beyond our reach
    and exalted in power;
  in his justice and great
    righteousness, he does not
    oppress.
24Therefore, men revere him,
  for does he not have regard for all
    the wise in heart?c"

38:1THEN the LORD answered Job out of
the storm. He said:

2"Who is this that darkens my counsel
  with words without knowledge?
3Brace yourself like a man;
  I will question you,
  and you shall answer me.

4"Where were you when I laid the
    earth's foundation?
  Tell me, if you understand.
5Who marked off its dimensions?
    Surely you know!
  Who stretched a measuring line
    across it?

6On what were its footings set,
  or who laid its cornerstone—
7while the morning stars sang
    together
  and all the angelsd shouted for
    joy?

8"Who shut up the sea behind doors
  when it burst forth from the
    womb,
9when I made the clouds its garment
  and wrapped it in thick darkness,
10when I fixed limits for it
  and set its doors and bars in place,
11when I said, 'This far you may come
    and no farther;
  here is where your proud waves
    halt'?

12"Have you ever given orders to the
    morning,
  or shown the dawn its place,
13that it might take the earth by the
    edges
  and shake the wicked out of it?
14The earth takes shape like clay under
    a seal;
  its features stand out like those of
    a garment.
15The wicked are denied their light,
  and their upraised arm is broken.

16"Have you journeyed to the springs
    of the sea
  or walked in the recesses of the
    deep?
17Have the gates of death been shown
    to you?
  Have you seen the gates of the
    shadow of deathe?
18Have you comprehended the vast
    expanses of the earth?
  Tell me, if you know all this.

19"What is the way to the abode of
    light?
  And where does darkness reside?
20Can you take them to their places?
  Do you know the paths to their
    dwellings?
21Surely you know, for you were already
    born!
  You have lived so many years!

22"Have you entered the storehouses of
        the snow
    or seen the storehouses of the hail,
23which I reserve for times of trouble,
        for days of war and battle?
24What is the way to the place where
        the lightning is dispersed,
    or the place where the east winds
        are scattered over the earth?
25Who cuts a channel for the torrents
        of rain,
    and a path for the thunderstorm,
26to water a land where no man lives,
        a desert with no one in it,
27to satisfy a desolate wasteland
    and make it sprout with grass?
28Does the rain have a father?
    Who fathers the drops of dew?
29From whose womb comes the ice?
    Who gives birth to the frost from
        the heavens
30when the waters become hard as
        stone,
    when the surface of the deep is
        frozen?

31"Can you bind the beautiful*f*
        Pleiades?
    Can you loose the cords of Orion?
32Can you bring forth the
        constellations in their
        seasons*g*
    or lead out the Bear*h* with its cubs?
33Do you know the laws of the
        heavens?
    Can you set up ˻God's*i*˼ dominion
        over the earth?

34"Can you raise your voice to the clouds
        and cover yourself with a flood of
        water?
35Do you send the lightning bolts on
        their way?
    Do they report to you, 'Here we are'?
36Who endowed the heart*j* with
        wisdom
    or gave understanding to the
        mind*j*?
37Who has the wisdom to count the
        clouds?
    Who can tip over the water jars of
        the heavens

38when the dust becomes hard
        and the clods of earth stick
        together?

39"Do you hunt the prey for the lioness
        and satisfy the hunger of the lions
40when they crouch in their dens
        or lie in wait in a thicket?
41Who provides food for the raven
        when its young cry out to God
    and wander about for lack of
        food?

39:1"Do you know when the mountain
        goats give birth?
    Do you watch when the doe bears
        her fawn?
2Do you count the months till they
        bear?
    Do you know the time they give
        birth?
3They crouch down and bring forth
        their young;
    their labor pains are ended.
4Their young thrive and grow strong
        in the wilds;
    they leave and do not return.

5"Who let the wild donkey go free?
    Who untied his ropes?
6I gave him the wasteland as his home,
        the salt flats as his habitat.
7He laughs at the commotion in the
        town;
    he does not hear a driver's shout.
8He ranges the hills for his pasture
        and searches for any green thing.

9"Will the wild ox consent to serve
        you?
    Will he stay by your manger at
        night?
10Can you hold him to the furrow with
        a harness?
    Will he till the valleys behind you?
11Will you rely on him for his great
        strength?
    Will you leave your heavy work to
        him?
12Can you trust him to bring in your
        grain
    and gather it to your threshing
        floor?

13 "The wings of the ostrich flap
  joyfully,
  but they cannot compare with the
    pinions and feathers of the
    stork.
14 She lays her eggs on the ground
  and lets them warm in the sand,
15 unmindful that a foot may crush
    them,
  that some wild animal may
    trample them.
16 She treats her young harshly, as if
    they were not hers;
  she cares not that her labor was in
    vain,
17 for God did not endow her with
    wisdom
  or give her a share of good sense.
18 Yet when she spreads her feathers to
    run,
  she laughs at horse and rider.

19 "Do you give the horse his strength
  or clothe his neck with a flowing
    mane?
20 Do you make him leap like a locust,
  striking terror with his proud
    snorting?
21 He paws fiercely, rejoicing in his
    strength,
  and charges into the fray.
22 He laughs at fear, afraid of nothing;
  he does not shy away from the
    sword.
23 The quiver rattles against his side,
  along with the flashing spear and
    lance.
24 In frenzied excitement he eats up the
    ground;
  he cannot stand still when the
    trumpet sounds.
25 At the blast of the trumpet he snorts,
    'Aha!'
  He catches the scent of battle
    from afar,
  the shout of commanders and the
    battle cry.

26 "Does the hawk take flight by your
    wisdom
  and spread his wings toward the
    south?

27 Does the eagle soar at your
    command
  and build his nest on high?
28 He dwells on a cliff and stays there
    at night;
  a rocky crag is his stronghold.
29 From there he seeks out his food;
  his eyes detect it from afar.
30 His young ones feast on blood,
  and where the slain are, there
    is he."

a 7 Or / he fills all men with fear by his power   *b* 13 Or to
favor them   *c* 24 Or for he does not have regard for any who
think they are wise.   *d* 7 Hebrew the sons of God
e 17 Or gates of deep shadows   *f* 31 Or the twinkling; or
the chains of the   *g* 32 Or the morning star in its season
h 32 Or out Leo   *i* 33 Or his; or their   *j* 36 The meaning of
the Hebrew for this word is uncertain.

2 CORINTHIANS 4:13–5:10

It is written: "I believed; therefore I have
spoken."*a* With that same spirit of faith
we also believe and therefore speak,
14 because we know that the one who
raised the Lord Jesus from the dead will
also raise us with Jesus and present us
with you in his presence. 15 All this is for
your benefit, so that the grace that is
reaching more and more people may
cause thanksgiving to overflow to the
glory of God.

16 Therefore we do not lose heart.
Though outwardly we are wasting away,
yet inwardly we are being renewed day
by day. 17 **For our light and momentary
troubles are achieving for us an eternal glory that far outweighs them all.**
18 **So we fix our eyes not on what is
seen, but on what is unseen. For what
is seen is temporary, but what is unseen is eternal.**

5:1 Now we know that if the earthly tent
we live in is destroyed, we have a building from God, an eternal house in
heaven, not built by human hands.
2 Meanwhile we groan, longing to be
clothed with our heavenly dwelling,
3 because when we are clothed, we will
not be found naked. 4 For while we are in
this tent, we groan and are burdened,
because we do not wish to be unclothed
but to be clothed with our heavenly
dwelling, so that what is mortal may be

swallowed up by life. [5]Now it is God who has made us for this very purpose and has given us the Spirit as a deposit, guaranteeing what is to come.

[6]Therefore we are always confident and know that as long as we are at home in the body we are away from the Lord. [7]We live by faith, not by sight. [8]We are confident, I say, and would prefer to be away from the body and at home with the Lord. [9]So we make it our goal to please him, whether we are at home in the body or away from it. [10]For we must all appear before the judgment seat of Christ, that each one may receive what is due him for the things done while in the body, whether good or bad.

a13 Psalm 116:10

PSALM 44:9-26

[9]But now you [God] have rejected and humbled us;
  you no longer go out with our
    armies.
[10]You made us retreat before the
    enemy,
  and our adversaries have
    plundered us.
[11]You gave us up to be devoured like
    sheep
  and have scattered us among the
    nations.
[12]You sold your people for a pittance,
  gaining nothing from their sale.

[13]You have made us a reproach to our
    neighbors,
  the scorn and derision of those
    around us.
[14]You have made us a byword among
    the nations;
  the peoples shake their heads
    at us.
[15]My disgrace is before me all day long,
  and my face is covered with shame
[16]at the taunts of those who reproach
    and revile me,
  because of the enemy, who is bent
    on revenge.

[17]All this happened to us,
  though we had not forgotten you
    or been false to your covenant.
[18]Our hearts had not turned back;
  our feet had not strayed from your
    path.
[19]But you crushed us and made us a
    haunt for jackals
  and covered us over with deep
    darkness.

[20]If we had forgotten the name of our
    God
  or spread out our hands to a
    foreign god,
[21]would not God have discovered it,
  since he knows the secrets of the
    heart?
[22]Yet for your sake we face death all
    day long;
  we are considered as sheep to be
    slaughtered.

[23]Awake, O Lord! Why do you sleep?
  Rouse yourself! Do not reject us
    forever.
[24]Why do you hide your face
  and forget our misery and
    oppression?

[25]We are brought down to the dust;
  our bodies cling to the ground.
[26]Rise up and help us;
  redeem us because of your
    unfailing love.

PROVERBS 22:13

[13]The sluggard says, "There is a lion
    outside!"
  or, "I will be murdered in the
    streets!"

GOD SIGHTINGS

September 1

JOB 40:1–42:17

The LORD said to Job:

2 "Will the one who contends with the
Almighty correct him?
Let him who accuses God answer
him!"

3 Then Job answered the LORD:

4 "I am unworthy—how can I reply
to you?
I put my hand over my mouth.
5 I spoke once, but I have no answer—
twice, but I will say no more."

6 Then the LORD spoke to Job out of
the storm:

7 "Brace yourself like a man;
I will question you,
and you shall answer me.

8 "Would you discredit my justice?
Would you condemn me to justify
yourself?
9 Do you have an arm like God's,
and can your voice thunder like
his?
10 Then adorn yourself with glory and
splendor,
and clothe yourself in honor and
majesty.
11 Unleash the fury of your wrath,
look at every proud man and bring
him low,
12 look at every proud man and humble
him,
crush the wicked where they
stand.
13 Bury them all in the dust together;
shroud their faces in the grave.
14 Then I myself will admit to you
that your own right hand can save
you.

15 "Look at the behemoth,a
which I made along with you
and which feeds on grass like an ox.
16 What strength he has in his loins,
what power in the muscles of his
belly!
17 His tailb sways like a cedar;
the sinews of his thighs are close-
knit.
18 His bones are tubes of bronze,
his limbs like rods of iron.
19 He ranks first among the works of
God,
yet his Maker can approach him
with his sword.
20 The hills bring him their produce,
and all the wild animals play
nearby.
21 Under the lotus plants he lies,
hidden among the reeds in the
marsh.
22 The lotuses conceal him in their
shadow;
the poplars by the stream
surround him.
23 When the river rages, he is not
alarmed;
he is secure, though the Jordan
should surge against his
mouth.
24 Can anyone capture him by the eyes,c
or trap him and pierce his nose?

41:1 "Can you pull in the leviathand with a
fishhook
or tie down his tongue with a
rope?
2 Can you put a cord through his nose
or pierce his jaw with a hook?
3 Will he keep begging you for mercy?
Will he speak to you with gentle
words?
4 Will he make an agreement with you
for you to take him as your slave
for life?
5 Can you make a pet of him like a bird
or put him on a leash for your
girls?

6 Will traders barter for him?
   Will they divide him up among the
      merchants?
7 Can you fill his hide with harpoons
   or his head with fishing spears?
8 If you lay a hand on him,
   you will remember the struggle
      and never do it again!
9 Any hope of subduing him is false;
   the mere sight of him is
      overpowering.
10 No one is fierce enough to rouse him.
   Who then is able to stand against
      me?
11 Who has a claim against me that I
      must pay?
   Everything under heaven belongs
      to me.

12 "I will not fail to speak of his limbs,
   his strength and his graceful form.
13 Who can strip off his outer coat?
   Who would approach him with a
      bridle?
14 Who dares open the doors of his
      mouth,
   ringed about with his fearsome
      teeth?
15 His back hasᵉ rows of shields
   tightly sealed together;
16 each is so close to the next
   that no air can pass between.
17 They are joined fast to one another;
   they cling together and cannot be
      parted.
18 His snorting throws out flashes of
      light;
   his eyes are like the rays of dawn.
19 Firebrands stream from his mouth;
   sparks of fire shoot out.
20 Smoke pours from his nostrils
   as from a boiling pot over a fire of
      reeds.
21 His breath sets coals ablaze,
   and flames dart from his mouth.
22 Strength resides in his neck;
   dismay goes before him.
23 The folds of his flesh are tightly
      joined;
   they are firm and immovable.
24 His chest is hard as rock,
   hard as a lower millstone.

25 When he rises up, the mighty are
      terrified;
   they retreat before his thrashing.
26 The sword that reaches him has no
      effect,
   nor does the spear or the dart or
      the javelin.
27 Iron he treats like straw
   and bronze like rotten wood.
28 Arrows do not make him flee;
   slingstones are like chaff to him.
29 A club seems to him but a piece of
      straw;
   he laughs at the rattling of the
      lance.
30 His undersides are jagged potsherds,
   leaving a trail in the mud like a
      threshing sledge.
31 He makes the depths churn like a
      boiling caldron
   and stirs up the sea like a pot of
      ointment.
32 Behind him he leaves a glistening
      wake;
   one would think the deep had
      white hair.
33 Nothing on earth is his equal—
   a creature without fear.
34 He looks down on all that are
      haughty;
   he is king over all that are proud."

42:1 THEN Job replied to the LORD:

2 "I know that you can do all things;
   no plan of yours can be thwarted.
3 ⌊You asked,⌋ 'Who is this that
      obscures my counsel without
      knowledge?'
   Surely I spoke of things I did not
      understand,
   things too wonderful for me to
      know.

4 ⌊"You said,⌋ 'Listen now, and I will
      speak;
   I will question you,
      and you shall answer me.'
5 My ears had heard of you
   but now my eyes have seen you.
6 Therefore I despise myself
   and repent in dust and ashes."

7After the Lord had said these things to Job, he said to Eliphaz the Temanite, "I am angry with you and your two friends, because you have not spoken of me what is right, as my servant Job has. 8So now take seven bulls and seven rams and go to my servant Job and sacrifice a burnt offering for yourselves. My servant Job will pray for you, and I will accept his prayer and not deal with you according to your folly. You have not spoken of me what is right, as my servant Job has." 9So Eliphaz the Temanite, Bildad the Shuhite and Zophar the Naamathite did what the Lord told them; and the Lord accepted Job's prayer.

10After Job had prayed for his friends, the Lord made him prosperous again and gave him twice as much as he had before. 11All his brothers and sisters and everyone who had known him before came and ate with him in his house. They comforted and consoled him over all the trouble the Lord had brought upon him, and each one gave him a piece of silver*f* and a gold ring.

12The Lord blessed the latter part of Job's life more than the first. He had fourteen thousand sheep, six thousand camels, a thousand yoke of oxen and a thousand donkeys. 13And he also had seven sons and three daughters. 14The first daughter he named Jemimah, the second Keziah and the third Keren-Happuch. 15Nowhere in all the land were there found women as beautiful as Job's daughters, and their father granted them an inheritance along with their brothers.

16After this, Job lived a hundred and forty years; he saw his children and their children to the fourth generation. 17And so he died, old and full of years.

*a15 Possibly the hippopotamus or the elephant
b17 Possibly trunk   c24 Or by a water hole   d1 Possibly the crocodile   e15 Or His pride is his   f11 Hebrew him a kesitah; a kesitah was a unit of money of unknown weight and value.*

2 CORINTHIANS 5:11-21

Since, then, we know what it is to fear the Lord, we try to persuade men. What we are is plain to God, and I hope it is also plain to your conscience. 12We are not trying to commend ourselves to you again, but are giving you an opportunity to take pride in us, so that you can answer those who take pride in what is seen rather than in what is in the heart. 13If we are out of our mind, it is for the sake of God; if we are in our right mind, it is for you. 14**For Christ's love compels us, because we are convinced that one died for all, and therefore all died.** 15And he died for all, that those who live should no longer live for themselves but for him who died for them and was raised again.

16So from now on we regard no one from a worldly point of view. Though we once regarded Christ in this way, we do so no longer. 17Therefore, if anyone is in Christ, he is a new creation; the old has gone, the new has come! 18All this is from God, who reconciled us to himself through Christ and gave us the ministry of reconciliation: 19that God was reconciling the world to himself in Christ, not counting men's sins against them. And he has committed to us the message of reconciliation. 20We are therefore Christ's ambassadors, as though God were making his appeal through us. We implore you on Christ's behalf: Be reconciled to God. 21God made him who had no sin to be sin*a* for us, so that in him we might become the righteousness of God.

a21 Or be a sin offering

PSALM 45:1-17

For the director of music. To ⌊the tune of⌋ "Lilies." Of the Sons of Korah. A *maskil.*a
A wedding song.

1 **M**y heart is stirred by a noble theme
    as I recite my verses for the king;
    my tongue is the pen of a skillful
        writer.

2 You are the most excellent of men
    and your lips have been anointed
        with grace,
    since God has blessed you forever.
3 Gird your sword upon your side,
    O mighty one;
    clothe yourself with splendor and
        majesty.

⁴In your majesty ride forth
    victoriously
  in behalf of truth, humility and
      righteousness;
  let your right hand display
      awesome deeds.
⁵Let your sharp arrows pierce the
      hearts of the king's enemies;
  let the nations fall beneath your
      feet.
⁶Your throne, O God, will last for ever
      and ever;
  a scepter of justice will be the
      scepter of your kingdom.
⁷You love righteousness and hate
      wickedness;
  therefore God, your God, has set
      you above your companions
  by anointing you with the oil of
      joy.
⁸All your robes are fragrant with
      myrrh and aloes and cassia;
  from palaces adorned with ivory
  the music of the strings makes you
      glad.
⁹Daughters of kings are among your
      honored women;
  at your right hand is the royal
      bride in gold of Ophir.
¹⁰Listen, O daughter, consider and give
      ear:
  Forget your people and your
      father's house.
¹¹The king is enthralled by your
      beauty;
  honor him, for he is your lord.
¹²The Daughter of Tyre will come with
      a gift,ᵇ
  men of wealth will seek your favor.
¹³All glorious is the princess within
      ⌊her chamber⌋;
  her gown is interwoven with
      gold.
¹⁴In embroidered garments she is led
      to the king;
  her virgin companions follow her
      and are brought to you.
¹⁵They are led in with joy and gladness;
  they enter the palace of the king.

¹⁶Your sons will take the place of your
      fathers;
  you will make them princes
      throughout the land.
¹⁷I will perpetuate your memory
      through all generations;
  therefore the nations will praise
      you for ever and ever.

ᵃTitle: Probably a literary or musical term   ᵇ12 Or A Tyrian
robe is among the gifts

PROVERBS 22:14
¹⁴The mouth of an adulteress is a
      deep pit;
  he who is under the Lᴏʀᴅ's wrath
      will fall into it.

□ DAY 245

GOD SIGHTINGS

September 2

ECCLESIASTES 1:1–3:22
The words of the Teacher,ᵃ son of David,
king in Jerusalem:

²"Meaningless! Meaningless!"
    says the Teacher.
  "Utterly meaningless!
    Everything is meaningless."

³What does man gain from all his
      labor
  at which he toils under the sun?
⁴Generations come and generations
      go,
  but the earth remains forever.
⁵The sun rises and the sun sets,
  and hurries back to where it rises.
⁶The wind blows to the south
  and turns to the north;
  round and round it goes,
    ever returning on its course.
⁷All streams flow into the sea,
  yet the sea is never full.
  To the place the streams come from,
    there they return again.
⁸All things are wearisome,
  more than one can say.

The eye never has enough of seeing,
nor the ear its fill of hearing.
⁹What has been will be again,
what has been done will be done
again;
there is nothing new under the
sun.
¹⁰Is there anything of which one can
say,
"Look! This is something new"?
It was here already, long ago;
it was here before our time.
¹¹There is no remembrance of men
of old,
and even those who are yet to
come
will not be remembered
by those who follow.

¹²I, the Teacher, was king over Israel
in Jerusalem. ¹³I devoted myself to
study and to explore by wisdom all that
is done under heaven. What a heavy
burden God has laid on men! ¹⁴I have
seen all the things that are done under
the sun; all of them are meaningless, a
chasing after the wind.

¹⁵What is twisted cannot be
straightened;
what is lacking cannot be counted.

¹⁶I thought to myself, "Look, I have
grown and increased in wisdom more
than anyone who has ruled over Jerusalem before me; I have experienced
much of wisdom and knowledge."
¹⁷Then I applied myself to the understanding of wisdom, and also of madness and folly, but I learned that this, too,
is a chasing after the wind.

¹⁸For with much wisdom comes much
sorrow;
the more knowledge, the more
grief.

²:¹I THOUGHT in my heart, "Come now, I
will test you with pleasure to find out
what is good." But that also proved to be
meaningless. ²"Laughter," I said, "is
foolish. And what does pleasure accomplish?" ³I tried cheering myself with
wine, and embracing folly—my mind

still guiding me with wisdom. I wanted
to see what was worthwhile for men to
do under heaven during the few days of
their lives.

⁴I undertook great projects: I built
houses for myself and planted vineyards. ⁵I made gardens and parks and
planted all kinds of fruit trees in them.
⁶I made reservoirs to water groves of
flourishing trees. ⁷I bought male and female slaves and had other slaves who
were born in my house. I also owned
more herds and flocks than anyone in
Jerusalem before me. ⁸I amassed silver
and gold for myself, and the treasure of
kings and provinces. I acquired men
and women singers, and a harem*ᵇ* as
well—the delights of the heart of man.
⁹I became greater by far than anyone in
Jerusalem before me. In all this my wisdom stayed with me.

¹⁰I denied myself nothing my eyes
desired;
I refused my heart no pleasure.
My heart took delight in all my work,
and this was the reward for all my
labor.
¹¹Yet when I surveyed all that my
hands had done
and what I had toiled to achieve,
everything was meaningless, a
chasing after the wind;
nothing was gained under the
sun.

¹²Then I turned my thoughts to
consider wisdom,
and also madness and folly.
What more can the king's successor
do
than what has already been done?
¹³I saw that wisdom is better than
folly,
just as light is better than
darkness.
¹⁴The wise man has eyes in his head,
while the fool walks in the
darkness;
but I came to realize
that the same fate overtakes them
both.

15Then I thought in my heart,

"The fate of the fool will overtake me
also.
What then do I gain by being
wise?"
I said in my heart,
"This too is meaningless."
16For the wise man, like the fool, will
not be long remembered;
in days to come both will be
forgotten.
Like the fool, the wise man too must
die!

17So I hated life, because the work
that is done under the sun was grievous
to me. All of it is meaningless, a chasing
after the wind. 18I hated all the things I
had toiled for under the sun, because I
must leave them to the one who comes
after me. 19And who knows whether he
will be a wise man or a fool? Yet he will
have control over all the work into
which I have poured my effort and skill
under the sun. This too is meaningless.
20So my heart began to despair over all
my toilsome labor under the sun. 21For
a man may do his work with wisdom,
knowledge and skill, and then he must
leave all he owns to someone who has
not worked for it. This too is meaningless and a great misfortune. 22What
does a man get for all the toil and anxious striving with which he labors under
the sun? 23All his days his work is pain
and grief; even at night his mind does
not rest. This too is meaningless.

24A man can do nothing better than
to eat and drink and find satisfaction in
his work. This too, I see, is from the hand
of God, 25for without him, who can eat
or find enjoyment? 26To the man who
pleases him, God gives wisdom, knowledge and happiness, but to the sinner he
gives the task of gathering and storing
up wealth to hand it over to the one who
pleases God. This too is meaningless, a
chasing after the wind.

3:1THERE is a time for everything,
and a season for every activity
under heaven:

2   a time to be born and a time to die,
a time to plant and a time to
uproot,
3   a time to kill and a time to heal,
a time to tear down and a time to
build,
4   a time to weep and a time to laugh,
a time to mourn and a time to
dance,
5   a time to scatter stones and a time
to gather them,
a time to embrace and a time to
refrain,
6   a time to search and a time to give
up,
a time to keep and a time to throw
away,
7   a time to tear and a time to mend,
a time to be silent and a time to
speak,
8   a time to love and a time to hate,
a time for war and a time for
peace.

9What does the worker gain from
his toil? 10I have seen the burden God
has laid on men. 11He has made everything beautiful in its time. He has also
set eternity in the hearts of men; yet
they cannot fathom what God has done
from beginning to end. 12I know that
there is nothing better for men than to
be happy and do good while they live.
13That everyone may eat and drink,
and find satisfaction in all his toil—this
is the gift of God. 14I know that everything God does will endure forever;
nothing can be added to it and nothing
taken from it. God does it so that men
will revere him.

15Whatever is has already been,
and what will be has been before;
and God will call the past to
account.c

16And I saw something else under the
sun:

In the place of judgment—
wickedness was there,
in the place of justice—
wickedness was there.

¹⁷I thought in my heart,

"God will bring to judgment
  both the righteous and the wicked,
for there will be a time for every
      activity,
  a time for every deed."

¹⁸I also thought, "As for men, God tests
them so that they may see that they are
like the animals. ¹⁹Man's fate is like that
of the animals; the same fate awaits them
both: As one dies, so dies the other. All
have the same breath*d*; man has no advantage over the animal. Everything is
meaningless. ²⁰All go to the same place;
all come from dust, and to dust all return.
²¹Who knows if the spirit of man rises
upward and if the spirit of the animal*e*
goes down into the earth?"
²²So I saw that there is nothing better
for a man than to enjoy his work, because that is his lot. For who can bring
him to see what will happen after him?

a1 Or *leader of the assembly*; also in verses 2 and 12
b8 The meaning of the Hebrew for this phrase is uncertain.
c15 Or *God calls back the past*   *d19* Or *spirit*   *e21* Or *Who
knows the spirit of man, which rises upward, or the spirit
of the animal, which*

2 CORINTHIANS 6:1-13

As God's fellow workers we urge you
not to receive God's grace in vain. ²For
he says,

"In the time of my favor I heard you,
  and in the day of salvation I helped
  you."*a*

I tell you, now is the time of God's favor,
now is the day of salvation.
³We put no stumbling block in anyone's path, so that our ministry will not
be discredited. ⁴Rather, as servants of
God we commend ourselves in every
way: in great endurance; in troubles,
hardships and distresses; ⁵in beatings,
imprisonments and riots; in hard work,
sleepless nights and hunger; ⁶in purity,
understanding, patience and kindness;
in the Holy Spirit and in sincere love;
⁷in truthful speech and in the power of
God; with weapons of righteousness in
the right hand and in the left; ⁸through
glory and dishonor, bad report and

good report; genuine, yet regarded as
impostors; ⁹known, yet regarded as unknown; dying, and yet we live on;
beaten, and yet not killed; ¹⁰sorrowful,
yet always rejoicing; poor, yet making
many rich; having nothing, and yet pos-
sessing everything.
¹¹We have spoken freely to you, Corinthians, and opened wide our hearts
to you. ¹²We are not withholding our affection from you, but you are withholding yours from us. ¹³As a fair
exchange—I speak as to my children—
open wide your hearts also.

a2 Isaiah 49:8

PSALM 46:1-11
For the director of music. Of the Sons of
Korah. According to *alamoth*.*a* A song.

¹**G**od is our refuge and strength,
    an ever-present help in trouble.
²**Therefore we will not fear, though
    the earth give way
  and the mountains fall into the
    heart of the sea,**
³though its waters roar and foam
  and the mountains quake with
      their surging.   *Selah*

⁴There is a river whose streams make
    glad the city of God,
  the holy place where the Most
    High dwells.
⁵God is within her, she will not fall;
  God will help her at break of day.
⁶Nations are in uproar, kingdoms fall;
  he lifts his voice, the earth melts.

⁷The Lᴏʀᴅ Almighty is with us;
  the God of Jacob is our fortress.
                                        Selah

⁸Come and see the works of the Lᴏʀᴅ,
  the desolations he has brought on
    the earth.
⁹He makes wars cease to the ends of
    the earth;
  he breaks the bow and shatters the
    spear,
  he burns the shields*b* with fire.
¹⁰"Be still, and know that I am God;
  I will be exalted among the nations,
  I will be exalted in the earth."

11 The Lord Almighty is with us;
  the God of Jacob is our fortress.

Selah

^aTitle: Probably a musical term   ^b9 Or *chariots*

PROVERBS 22:15

15 **F**olly is bound up in the heart of a
  child,
    but the rod of discipline will drive
      it far from him.

□ DAY 246

GOD SIGHTINGS

September 3

ECCLESIASTES 4:1–6:12

Again I looked and saw all the oppression that was taking place under the sun:

I saw the tears of the oppressed—
  and they have no comforter;
power was on the side of their
  oppressors—
and they have no comforter.
2 And I declared that the dead,
  who had already died,
are happier than the living,
  who are still alive.
3 But better than both
  is he who has not yet been,
who has not seen the evil
  that is done under the sun.

4 And I saw that all labor and all achievement spring from man's envy of his neighbor. This too is meaningless, a chasing after the wind.

5 The fool folds his hands
  and ruins himself.
6 Better one handful with tranquillity
  than two handfuls with toil
  and chasing after the wind.

7 Again I saw something meaningless under the sun:

8 There was a man all alone;
  he had neither son nor brother.

There was no end to his toil,
  yet his eyes were not content with
    his wealth.
"For whom am I toiling," he asked,
  "and why am I depriving myself of
    enjoyment?"
This too is meaningless—
  a miserable business!

9 Two are better than one,
  because they have a good return
    for their work:
10 If one falls down,
  his friend can help him up.
But pity the man who falls
  and has no one to help him up!
11 Also, if two lie down together, they
    will keep warm.
  But how can one keep warm alone?
12 Though one may be overpowered,
  two can defend themselves.
A cord of three strands is not quickly
  broken.

13 Better a poor but wise youth than an old but foolish king who no longer knows how to take warning. 14 The youth may have come from prison to the kingship, or he may have been born in poverty within his kingdom. 15 I saw that all who lived and walked under the sun followed the youth, the king's successor. 16 There was no end to all the people who were before them. But those who came later were not pleased with the successor. This too is meaningless, a chasing after the wind.

5:1 Guard your steps when you go to the house of God. Go near to listen rather than to offer the sacrifice of fools, who do not know that they do wrong.

2 Do not be quick with your mouth,
  do not be hasty in your heart
    to utter anything before God.
God is in heaven
  and you are on earth,
    so let your words be few.
3 As a dream comes when there are
    many cares,
  so the speech of a fool when there
    are many words.

⁴When you make a vow to God, do not delay in fulfilling it. He has no pleasure in fools; fulfill your vow. ⁵It is better not to vow than to make a vow and not fulfill it. ⁶Do not let your mouth lead you into sin. And do not protest to the ⌐temple⌐ messenger, "My vow was a mistake." Why should God be angry at what you say and destroy the work of your hands? ⁷Much dreaming and many words are meaningless. Therefore stand in awe of God.

⁸If you see the poor oppressed in a district, and justice and rights denied, do not be surprised at such things; for one official is eyed by a higher one, and over them both are others higher still. ⁹The increase from the land is taken by all; the king himself profits from the fields.

¹⁰Whoever loves money never has
        money enough;
    whoever loves wealth is never
        satisfied with his income.
    This too is meaningless.

¹¹As goods increase,
    so do those who consume them.
    And what benefit are they to the
        owner
        except to feast his eyes on
            them?

¹²The sleep of a laborer is sweet,
    whether he eats little or much,
    but the abundance of a rich man
        permits him no sleep.

¹³I have seen a grievous evil under the sun:

    wealth hoarded to the harm of its
        owner,
¹⁴   or wealth lost through some
        misfortune,
    so that when he has a son
    there is nothing left for him.
¹⁵Naked a man comes from his
        mother's womb,
    and as he comes, so he departs.
    He takes nothing from his labor
    that he can carry in his hand.

¹⁶This too is a grievous evil:

    As a man comes, so he departs,
        and what does he gain,
    since he toils for the wind?
¹⁷All his days he eats in darkness,
        with great frustration, affliction
            and anger.

¹⁸Then I realized that it is good and proper for a man to eat and drink, and to find satisfaction in his toilsome labor under the sun during the few days of life God has given him—for this is his lot. ¹⁹Moreover, when God gives any man wealth and possessions, and enables him to enjoy them, to accept his lot and be happy in his work—this is a gift of God. ²⁰He seldom reflects on the days of his life, because God keeps him occupied with gladness of heart.

6:1I HAVE seen another evil under the sun, and it weighs heavily on men: ²God gives a man wealth, possessions and honor, so that he lacks nothing his heart desires, but God does not enable him to enjoy them, and a stranger enjoys them instead. This is meaningless, a grievous evil.

³A man may have a hundred children and live many years; yet no matter how long he lives, if he cannot enjoy his prosperity and does not receive proper burial, I say that a stillborn child is better off than he. ⁴It comes without meaning, it departs in darkness, and in darkness its name is shrouded. ⁵Though it never saw the sun or knew anything, it has more rest than does that man— ⁶even if he lives a thousand years twice over but fails to enjoy his prosperity. Do not all go to the same place?

⁷All man's efforts are for his mouth,
    yet his appetite is never satisfied.
⁸What advantage has a wise man
    over a fool?
    What does a poor man gain
    by knowing how to conduct
        himself before others?
⁹Better what the eye sees
    than the roving of the appetite.

This too is meaningless,
a chasing after the wind.

[10]Whatever exists has already been
named,
and what man is has been known;
no man can contend
with one who is stronger than he.
[11]The more the words,
the less the meaning,
and how does that profit anyone?

[12]For who knows what is good for a
man in life, during the few and meaningless days he passes through like a
shadow? Who can tell him what will
happen under the sun after he is gone?

2 CORINTHIANS 6:14–7:7

**Do not be yoked together with unbe-
lievers. For what do righteousness
and wickedness have in common? Or
what fellowship can light have with
darkness?** [15]What harmony is there
between Christ and Belial[a]? What does
a believer have in common with an unbeliever? [16]What agreement is there between the temple of God and idols? For
we are the temple of the living God. As
God has said: "I will live with them and
walk among them, and I will be their
God, and they will be my people."[b]

[17]"Therefore come out from them
and be separate,
says the Lord.
Touch no unclean thing,
and I will receive you."[c]
[18]"I will be a Father to you,
and you will be my sons and
daughters,
says the Lord Almighty."[d]

[7:1]SINCE we have these promises, dear
friends, let us purify ourselves from everything that contaminates body and
spirit, perfecting holiness out of reverence for God.

[2]Make room for us in your hearts. We
have wronged no one, we have corrupted no one, we have exploited no
one. [3]I do not say this to condemn you; I
have said before that you have such a

place in our hearts that we would live or
die with you. [4]I have great confidence in
you; I take great pride in you. I am
greatly encouraged; in all our troubles
my joy knows no bounds.

[5]For when we came into Macedonia,
this body of ours had no rest, but we
were harassed at every turn—conflicts
on the outside, fears within. [6]But God,
who comforts the downcast, comforted
us by the coming of Titus, [7]and not only
by his coming but also by the comfort
you had given him. He told us about
your longing for me, your deep sorrow,
your ardent concern for me, so that my
joy was greater than ever.

a 15 Greek *Beliar,* a variant of *Belial*   b 16 Lev. 26:12;
Jer. 32:38; Ezek. 37:27   c 17 Isaiah 52:11; Ezek. 20:34,41
d 18 2 Samuel 7:14; 7:8

PSALM 47:1–9
For the director of music. Of the Sons of
Korah. A psalm.

[1]Clap your hands, all you nations;
shout to God with cries of joy.
[2]How awesome is the LORD Most High,
the great King over all the earth!
[3]He subdued nations under us,
peoples under our feet.
[4]He chose our inheritance for us,
the pride of Jacob, whom he loved.
Selah

[5]God has ascended amid shouts of joy,
the LORD amid the sounding of
trumpets.
[6]Sing praises to God, sing praises;
sing praises to our King, sing
praises.

[7]For God is the King of all the earth;
sing to him a psalm[a] of praise.
[8]God reigns over the nations;
God is seated on his holy throne.
[9]The nobles of the nations assemble
as the people of the God of
Abraham,
for the kings[b] of the earth belong to
God;
he is greatly exalted.

a 7 Or *a maskil* (probably a literary or musical term)
b 9 Or *shields*

PROVERBS 22:16

16 **H**e who oppresses the poor to increase his wealth
and he who gives gifts to the rich—
both come to poverty.

□ D A Y   2 4 7

GOD SIGHTINGS

September 4

ECCLESIASTES 7:1–9:18

A good name is better than fine perfume,
and the day of death better than the day of birth.
2 It is better to go to a house of mourning
than to go to a house of feasting,
for death is the destiny of every man;
the living should take this to heart.
3 Sorrow is better than laughter,
because a sad face is good for the heart.
4 The heart of the wise is in the house of mourning,
but the heart of fools is in the house of pleasure.
5 It is better to heed a wise man's rebuke
than to listen to the song of fools.
6 Like the crackling of thorns under the pot,
so is the laughter of fools.
This too is meaningless.

7 Extortion turns a wise man into a fool,
and a bribe corrupts the heart.

8 The end of a matter is better than its beginning,
and patience is better than pride.
9 Do not be quickly provoked in your spirit,
for anger resides in the lap of fools.

10 Do not say, "Why were the old days better than these?"
For it is not wise to ask such questions.

11 Wisdom, like an inheritance, is a good thing
and benefits those who see the sun.
12 Wisdom is a shelter
as money is a shelter,
but the advantage of knowledge is this:
that wisdom preserves the life of its possessor.

13 Consider what God has done:

Who can straighten
what he has made crooked?
14 When times are good, be happy;
but when times are bad, consider:
God has made the one
as well as the other.
Therefore, a man cannot discover anything about his future.

15 In this meaningless life of mine I have seen both of these:

a righteous man perishing in his righteousness,
and a wicked man living long in his wickedness.
16 Do not be overrighteous,
neither be overwise—
why destroy yourself?
17 Do not be overwicked,
and do not be a fool—
why die before your time?
18 It is good to grasp the one
and not let go of the other.
The man who fears God will avoid all extremes.ᵃ

19 Wisdom makes one wise man more powerful
than ten rulers in a city.

20 There is not a righteous man on earth
who does what is right and never sins.

21 Do not pay attention to every word people say,
or you may hear your servant cursing you—
22 for you know in your heart
that many times you yourself have cursed others.

23All this I tested by wisdom and I said,

"I am determined to be wise"—
but this was beyond me.
24Whatever wisdom may be,
it is far off and most profound—
who can discover it?
25So I turned my mind to understand,
to investigate and to search out
wisdom and the scheme of
things
and to understand the stupidity of
wickedness
and the madness of folly.

26I find more bitter than death
the woman who is a snare,
whose heart is a trap
and whose hands are chains.
The man who pleases God will
escape her,
but the sinner she will ensnare.

27"Look," says the Teacher,b "this is what I have discovered:

"Adding one thing to another to
discover the scheme of
things—
28   while I was still searching
but not finding—
I found one ⌞upright⌟ man among a
thousand,
but not one ⌞upright⌟ woman
among them all.
29This only have I found:
God made mankind upright,
but men have gone in search of
many schemes."

8:1WHO is like the wise man?
Who knows the explanation of
things?
Wisdom brightens a man's face
and changes its hard appearance.

2Obey the king's command, I say, because you took an oath before God. 3Do not be in a hurry to leave the king's presence. Do not stand up for a bad cause, for he will do whatever he pleases. 4Since a king's word is supreme, who can say to him, "What are you doing?"

5Whoever obeys his command will
come to no harm,
and the wise heart will know the
proper time and procedure.
6For there is a proper time and
procedure for every matter,
though a man's misery weighs
heavily upon him.

7Since no man knows the future,
who can tell him what is to come?
8No man has power over the wind to
contain itc;
so no one has power over the day
of his death.
As no one is discharged in time of war,
so wickedness will not release
those who practice it.

9All this I saw, as I applied my mind to everything done under the sun. There is a time when a man lords it over others to his ownd hurt. 10Then too, I saw the wicked buried—those who used to come and go from the holy place and receive praisee in the city where they did this. This too is meaningless.

11When the sentence for a crime is not quickly carried out, the hearts of the people are filled with schemes to do wrong. 12Although a wicked man commits a hundred crimes and still lives a long time, I know that it will go better with God-fearing men, who are reverent before God. 13Yet because the wicked do not fear God, it will not go well with them, and their days will not lengthen like a shadow.

14There is something else meaningless that occurs on earth: righteous men who get what the wicked deserve, and wicked men who get what the righteous deserve. This too, I say, is meaningless. 15So I commend the enjoyment of life, because nothing is better for a man under the sun than to eat and drink and be glad. Then joy will accompany him in his work all the days of the life God has given him under the sun.

16When I applied my mind to know wisdom and to observe man's labor on earth—his eyes not seeing sleep day or night—[17]then I saw all that God has done. No one can comprehend what goes on under the sun. Despite all his efforts to search it out, man cannot discover its meaning. Even if a wise man claims he knows, he cannot really comprehend it.

[9:1]So I reflected on all this and concluded that the righteous and the wise and what they do are in God's hands, but no man knows whether love or hate awaits him. [2]All share a common destiny—the righteous and the wicked, the good and the bad,[f] the clean and the unclean, those who offer sacrifices and those who do not.

As it is with the good man,
　　so with the sinner;
as it is with those who take oaths,
　　so with those who are afraid to
　　　　take them.

[3]This is the evil in everything that happens under the sun: The same destiny overtakes all. The hearts of men, moreover, are full of evil and there is madness in their hearts while they live, and afterward they join the dead. [4]Anyone who is among the living has hope[g]—even a live dog is better off than a dead lion!

[5]For the living know that they will die,
　　but the dead know nothing;
they have no further reward,
　　and even the memory of them is
　　　　forgotten.
[6]Their love, their hate
　　and their jealousy have long since
　　　　vanished;
never again will they have a part
　　in anything that happens under
　　　　the sun.

[7]Go, eat your food with gladness, and drink your wine with a joyful heart, for it is now that God favors what you do. [8]Always be clothed in white, and always anoint your head with oil. [9]Enjoy life with your wife, whom you love, all the days of this meaningless life that God has given you under the sun—all your

meaningless days. For this is your lot in life and in your toilsome labor under the sun. [10]Whatever your hand finds to do, do it with all your might, for in the grave,[h] where you are going, there is neither working nor planning nor knowledge nor wisdom.

[11]I have seen something else under the sun:

The race is not to the swift
　　or the battle to the strong,
nor does food come to the wise
　　or wealth to the brilliant
　　or favor to the learned;
but time and chance happen to
　　them all.

[12]Moreover, no man knows when his hour will come:

As fish are caught in a cruel net,
　　or birds are taken in a snare,
so men are trapped by evil times
　　that fall unexpectedly upon them.

[13]I also saw under the sun this example of wisdom that greatly impressed me: [14]There was once a small city with only a few people in it. And a powerful king came against it, surrounded it and built huge siegeworks against it. [15]Now there lived in that city a man poor but wise, and he saved the city by his wisdom. But nobody remembered that poor man. [16]So I said, "Wisdom is better than strength." But the poor man's wisdom is despised, and his words are no longer heeded.

[17]The quiet words of the wise are more
　　to be heeded
　　than the shouts of a ruler of fools.
[18]Wisdom is better than weapons of
　　war,
　　but one sinner destroys much
　　　　good.

---

a18 Or *will follow them both*　*b27* Or *leader of the assembly*
c8 Or *over his spirit to retain it*　*d9* Or *to their*　*e10* Some
Hebrew manuscripts and Septuagint (Aquila); most Hebrew
manuscripts *and are forgotten*　*f2* Septuagint (Aquila),
Vulgate and Syriac; Hebrew does not have *and the bad.*
g4 Or *What then is to be chosen? With all who live, there
is hope*　*h10* Hebrew *Sheol*

2 CORINTHIANS 7:8-16

Even if I caused you sorrow by my letter, I do not regret it. Though I did regret it—I see that my letter hurt you, but only for a little while— [9]yet now I am happy, not because you were made sorry, but because your sorrow led you to repentance. For you became sorrowful as God intended and so were not harmed in any way by us. [10]**Godly sorrow brings repentance that leads to salvation and leaves no regret, but worldly sorrow brings death.** [11]See what this godly sorrow has produced in you: what earnestness, what eagerness to clear yourselves, what indignation, what alarm, what longing, what concern, what readiness to see justice done. At every point you have proved yourselves to be innocent in this matter. [12]So even though I wrote to you, it was not on account of the one who did the wrong or of the injured party, but rather that before God you could see for yourselves how devoted to us you are. [13]By all this we are encouraged.

In addition to our own encouragement, we were especially delighted to see how happy Titus was, because his spirit has been refreshed by all of you. [14]I had boasted to him about you, and you have not embarrassed me. But just as everything we said to you was true, so our boasting about you to Titus has proved to be true as well. [15]And his affection for you is all the greater when he remembers that you were all obedient, receiving him with fear and trembling. [16]I am glad I can have complete confidence in you.

PSALM 48:1-14

A song. A psalm of the Sons of Korah.

[1]**G**reat is the LORD, and most worthy of praise,
　in the city of our God, his holy mountain.
[2]It is beautiful in its loftiness,
　the joy of the whole earth.
Like the utmost heights of Zaphon[a]
　is Mount Zion,
　the[b] city of the Great King.

[3]God is in her citadels;
　he has shown himself to be her fortress.

[4]When the kings joined forces,
　when they advanced together,
[5]they saw ˻her˼ and were astounded;
　they fled in terror.
[6]Trembling seized them there,
　pain like that of a woman in labor.
[7]You destroyed them like ships of Tarshish
　shattered by an east wind.

[8]As we have heard,
　so have we seen
in the city of the LORD Almighty,
　in the city of our God:
God makes her secure forever.
　　　　　　　　　　Selah

[9]Within your temple, O God,
　we meditate on your unfailing love.
[10]Like your name, O God,
　your praise reaches to the ends of the earth;
　your right hand is filled with righteousness.
[11]Mount Zion rejoices,
　the villages of Judah are glad
　because of your judgments.

[12]Walk about Zion, go around her,
　count her towers,
[13]consider well her ramparts,
　view her citadels,
　that you may tell of them to the next generation.
[14]For this God is our God for ever and ever;
　he will be our guide even to the end.

[a]2 Zaphon can refer to a sacred mountain or the direction north.　[b]Or earth, / Mount Zion, on the northern side / of the

PROVERBS 22:17-19

[17]**P**ay attention and listen to the sayings of the wise;
　apply your heart to what I teach,
[18]for it is pleasing when you keep them in your heart
　and have all of them ready on your lips.

¹⁹So that your trust may be in the Lᴏʀᴅ,
   I teach you today, even you.

☐ D A Y 2 4 8

GOD SIGHTINGS

September 5

ECCLESIASTES 10:1–12:14
   As dead flies give perfume a bad
      smell,
         so a little folly outweighs wisdom
            and honor.
   ²The heart of the wise inclines to the
      right,
         but the heart of the fool to the left.
   ³Even as he walks along the road,
         the fool lacks sense
      and shows everyone how stupid he
         is.
   ⁴If a ruler's anger rises against you,
      do not leave your post;
         calmness can lay great errors to
            rest.

   ⁵There is an evil I have seen under the
      sun,
         the sort of error that arises from a
            ruler:
   ⁶Fools are put in many high positions,
      while the rich occupy the low ones.
   ⁷I have seen slaves on horseback,
      while princes go on foot like
         slaves.

   ⁸Whoever digs a pit may fall into it;
      whoever breaks through a wall
         may be bitten by a snake.
   ⁹Whoever quarries stones may be
      injured by them;
         whoever splits logs may be
            endangered by them.

   ¹⁰If the ax is dull
      and its edge unsharpened,
   more strength is needed
      but skill will bring success.

   ¹¹If a snake bites before it is charmed,
      there is no profit for the charmer.

¹²Words from a wise man's mouth are
      gracious,
         but a fool is consumed by his own
            lips.
¹³At the beginning his words are folly;
      at the end they are wicked
         madness—
¹⁴   and the fool multiplies words.

   No one knows what is coming—
      who can tell him what will happen
         after him?

¹⁵A fool's work wearies him;
      he does not know the way to
         town.

¹⁶Woe to you, O land whose king was a
      servantª
         and whose princes feast in the
            morning.
¹⁷Blessed are you, O land whose king is
      of noble birth
         and whose princes eat at a proper
            time—
      for strength and not for
         drunkenness.

¹⁸If a man is lazy, the rafters sag;
      if his hands are idle, the house
         leaks.

¹⁹A feast is made for laughter,
      and wine makes life merry,
         but money is the answer for
            everything.

²⁰Do not revile the king even in your
      thoughts,
         or curse the rich in your bedroom,
   because a bird of the air may carry
         your words,
      and a bird on the wing may report
         what you say.

¹¹:¹Cᴀsᴛ your bread upon the waters,
      for after many days you will find it
         again.
   ²Give portions to seven, yes to eight,
      for you do not know what
         disaster may come upon
            the land.

   ³If clouds are full of water,
      they pour rain upon the earth.

Whether a tree falls to the south or
to the north,
    in the place where it falls, there
    will it lie.
[4] Whoever watches the wind will not
plant;
    whoever looks at the clouds will
    not reap.

[5] As you do not know the path of the
wind,
    or how the body is formed[b] in a
    mother's womb,
so you cannot understand the work
of God,
    the Maker of all things.

[6] Sow your seed in the morning,
    and at evening let not your hands
    be idle,
for you do not know which will
succeed,
    whether this or that,
    or whether both will do equally
    well.

[7] Light is sweet,
    and it pleases the eyes to see the
    sun.
[8] However many years a man may live,
let him enjoy them all.
But let him remember the days of
darkness,
    for they will be many.
    Everything to come is
    meaningless.

[9] Be happy, young man, while you are
young,
    and let your heart give you joy in
    the days of your youth.
Follow the ways of your heart
and whatever your eyes see,
but know that for all these things
God will bring you to judgment.
[10] So then, banish anxiety from your
heart
    and cast off the troubles of your
    body,
    for youth and vigor are
    meaningless.

[12:1] REMEMBER your Creator
in the days of your youth,

before the days of trouble come
and the years approach when
you will say,
"I find no pleasure in them"—
[2] before the sun and the light
    and the moon and the stars grow
    dark,
    and the clouds return after the
    rain;
[3] when the keepers of the house
    tremble,
    and the strong men stoop,
when the grinders cease because
    they are few,
    and those looking through the
    windows grow dim;
[4] when the doors to the street are
    closed
    and the sound of grinding fades;
when men rise up at the sound of
    birds,
    but all their songs grow faint;
[5] when men are afraid of heights
    and of dangers in the streets;
when the almond tree blossoms
    and the grasshopper drags himself
    along
    and desire no longer is stirred.
Then man goes to his eternal home
and mourners go about the streets.

[6] Remember him—before the silver
    cord is severed,
    or the golden bowl is broken;
before the pitcher is shattered at the
    spring,
    or the wheel broken at the well,
[7] and the dust returns to the ground it
    came from,
    and the spirit returns to God who
    gave it.

[8] "Meaningless! Meaningless!" says the
    Teacher.[c]
    "Everything is meaningless!"

[9] Not only was the Teacher wise, but
also he imparted knowledge to the people. He pondered and searched out and
set in order many proverbs. [10] The
Teacher searched to find just the right
words, and what he wrote was upright
and true.

11The words of the wise are like goads, their collected sayings like firmly embedded nails—given by one Shepherd. 12Be warned, my son, of anything in addition to them.

Of making many books there is no end, and much study wearies the body.

13Now all has been heard;
    here is the conclusion of the matter:
Fear God and keep his
        commandments,
    for this is the whole ⌞duty⌟ of man.
14For God will bring every deed into
        judgment,
    including every hidden thing,
        whether it is good or evil.

a 16 Or king is a child b 5 Or know how life (or the spirit) / enters the body being formed c 8 Or the leader of the assembly; also in verses 9 and 10

2 CORINTHIANS 8:1-15

And now, brothers, we want you to know about the grace that God has given the Macedonian churches. 2Out of the most severe trial, their overflowing joy and their extreme poverty welled up in rich generosity. 3For I testify that they gave as much as they were able, and even beyond their ability. Entirely on their own, 4they urgently pleaded with us for the privilege of sharing in this service to the saints. 5And they did not do as we expected, but they gave themselves first to the Lord and then to us in keeping with God's will. 6So we urged Titus, since he had earlier made a beginning, to bring also to completion this act of grace on your part. 7But just as you excel in everything—in faith, in speech, in knowledge, in complete earnestness and in your love for usa—see that you also excel in this grace of giving.

8I am not commanding you, but I want to test the sincerity of your love by comparing it with the earnestness of others. 9For you know the grace of our Lord Jesus Christ, that though he was rich, yet for your sakes he became poor, so that you through his poverty might become rich.

10And here is my advice about what is best for you in this matter: Last year you

were the first not only to give but also to have the desire to do so. 11Now finish the work, so that your eager willingness to do it may be matched by your completion of it, according to your means. 12For if the willingness is there, the gift is acceptable according to what one has, not according to what he does not have.

13Our desire is not that others might be relieved while you are hard pressed, but that there might be equality. 14At the present time your plenty will supply what they need, so that in turn their plenty will supply what you need. Then there will be equality, 15as it is written: "He who gathered much did not have too much, and he who gathered little did not have too little."b

a 7 Some manuscripts in our love for you b 15 Exodus 16:18

PSALM 49:1-20

For the director of music. Of the Sons of Korah. A psalm.

1 Hear this, all you peoples;
    listen, all who live in this world,
2 both low and high,
    rich and poor alike:
3 My mouth will speak words of wisdom;
    the utterance from my heart will
        give understanding.
4 I will turn my ear to a proverb;
    with the harp I will expound my
        riddle:

5 Why should I fear when evil days
        come,
    when wicked deceivers surround
        me—
6 those who trust in their wealth
    and boast of their great riches?
7 No man can redeem the life of
        another
    or give to God a ransom for him—
8 the ransom for a life is costly,
    no payment is ever enough—
9 that he should live on forever
    and not see decay.

10 For all can see that wise men die;
    the foolish and the senseless alike
        perish
    and leave their wealth to others.

11 Their tombs will remain their
houses[a] forever,
their dwellings for endless
generations,
though they had[b] named lands
after themselves.

12 But man, despite his riches, does not
endure;
he is[c] like the beasts that perish.

13 This is the fate of those who trust in
themselves,
and of their followers, who
approve their sayings.   *Selah*

14 Like sheep they are destined for the
grave,[d]
and death will feed on them.
The upright will rule over them in
the morning;
their forms will decay in the grave,[d]
far from their princely mansions.

15 But God will redeem my life[e] from
the grave;
he will surely take me to himself.
Selah

16 Do not be overawed when a man
grows rich,
when the splendor of his house
increases;

17 for he will take nothing with him
when he dies,
his splendor will not descend with
him.

18 Though while he lived he counted
himself blessed—
and men praise you when you
prosper—

19 he will join the generation of his
fathers,
who will never see the light ⌊of life⌋.

20 A man who has riches without
understanding
is like the beasts that perish.

*a11 Septuagint and Syriac; Hebrew In their thoughts their
houses will remain   b11 Or / for they have   c12 Hebrew;
Septuagint and Syriac read verse 12 the same as verse 20.
d14 Hebrew Sheol; also in verse 15   e15 Or soul*

PROVERBS 22:20-21

20 Have I not written thirty[a] sayings for
you,
sayings of counsel and knowledge,

21 teaching you true and reliable words,
so that you can give sound answers
to him who sent you?

a20 Or not formerly written; or not written excellent

□ D A Y   2 4 9

GOD SIGHTINGS

September 6

SONG OF SONGS 1:1-4:16
Solomon's Song of Songs.

Beloved[a]

2 Let him kiss me with the kisses of his
mouth—
for your love is more delightful
than wine.

3 Pleasing is the fragrance of your
perfumes;
your name is like perfume poured
out.
No wonder the maidens love you!

4 Take me away with you—let us hurry!
Let the king bring me into his
chambers.

Friends

We rejoice and delight in you[b];
we will praise your love more than
wine.

Beloved

How right they are to adore you!

5 Dark am I, yet lovely,
O daughters of Jerusalem,
dark like the tents of Kedar,
like the tent curtains of Solomon.[c]

6 Do not stare at me because I am dark,
because I am darkened by the sun.
My mother's sons were angry with me
and made me take care of the
vineyards;
my own vineyard I have neglected.

7 Tell me, you whom I love, where you
graze your flock
and where you rest your sheep at
midday.

Why should I be like a veiled woman
  beside the flocks of your friends?

Friends

⁸ If you do not know, most beautiful of
    women,
  follow the tracks of the sheep
and graze your young goats
  by the tents of the shepherds.

Lover

⁹ I liken you, my darling, to a mare
  harnessed to one of the chariots of
    Pharaoh.
¹⁰ Your cheeks are beautiful with
    earrings,
  your neck with strings of jewels.
¹¹ We will make you earrings of gold,
  studded with silver.

Beloved

¹² While the king was at his table,
  my perfume spread its fragrance.
¹³ My lover is to me a sachet of myrrh
  resting between my breasts.
¹⁴ My lover is to me a cluster of henna
    blossoms
  from the vineyards of En Gedi.

Lover

¹⁵ How beautiful you are, my darling!
  Oh, how beautiful!
  Your eyes are doves.

Beloved

¹⁶ How handsome you are, my lover!
  Oh, how charming!
  And our bed is verdant.

Lover

¹⁷ The beams of our house are cedars;
  our rafters are firs.

*Beloved*ᵈ

2:1 I AM a roseᵉ of Sharon,
  a lily of the valleys.

Lover

² Like a lily among thorns
  is my darling among the maidens.

Beloved

³ Like an apple tree among the trees of
    the forest
  is my lover among the young men.
I delight to sit in his shade,
  and his fruit is sweet to my taste.
⁴ He has taken me to the banquet hall,
  and his banner over me is love.
⁵ Strengthen me with raisins,
  refresh me with apples,
  for I am faint with love.
⁶ His left arm is under my head,
  and his right arm embraces me.
⁷ Daughters of Jerusalem, I charge you
  by the gazelles and by the does of
    the field:
Do not arouse or awaken love
  until it so desires.

⁸ Listen! My lover!
  Look! Here he comes,
leaping across the mountains,
  bounding over the hills.
⁹ My lover is like a gazelle or a young
    stag.
  Look! There he stands behind our
    wall,
gazing through the windows,
  peering through the lattice.
¹⁰ My lover spoke and said to me,
  "Arise, my darling,
  my beautiful one, and come with
    me.
¹¹ See! The winter is past;
  the rains are over and gone.
¹² Flowers appear on the earth;
  the season of singing has come,
the cooing of doves
  is heard in our land.
¹³ The fig tree forms its early fruit;
  the blossoming vines spread their
    fragrance.
Arise, come, my darling;
  my beautiful one, come with me."

Lover

¹⁴ My dove in the clefts of the rock,
  in the hiding places on the
    mountainside,
show me your face,
  let me hear your voice;

for your voice is sweet,
    and your face is lovely.
15 Catch for us the foxes,
    the little foxes
that ruin the vineyards,
    our vineyards that are in bloom.

Beloved

16 My lover is mine and I am his;
    he browses among the lilies.
17 Until the day breaks
    and the shadows flee,
turn, my lover,
    and be like a gazelle
or like a young stag
    on the rugged hills.*f*

3:1 ALL night long on my bed
    I looked for the one my heart loves;
    I looked for him but did not find
        him.
2 I will get up now and go about the city,
    through its streets and squares;
I will search for the one my heart
    loves.
    So I looked for him but did not
        find him.
3 The watchmen found me
    as they made their rounds in the
        city.
    "Have you seen the one my heart
        loves?"
4 Scarcely had I passed them
    when I found the one my heart
        loves.
I held him and would not let him go
    till I had brought him to my
        mother's house,
    to the room of the one who
        conceived me.
5 Daughters of Jerusalem, I charge you
    by the gazelles and by the does of
        the field:
Do not arouse or awaken love
    until it so desires.

6 Who is this coming up from the
        desert
    like a column of smoke,
perfumed with myrrh and incense
    made from all the spices of the
        merchant?

7 Look! It is Solomon's carriage,
    escorted by sixty warriors,
    the noblest of Israel,
8 all of them wearing the sword,
    all experienced in battle,
each with his sword at his side,
    prepared for the terrors of the night.
9 King Solomon made for himself the
        carriage;
    he made it of wood from Lebanon.
10 Its posts he made of silver,
    its base of gold.
Its seat was upholstered with purple,
    its interior lovingly inlaid
    by*g* the daughters of Jerusalem.
11 Come out, you daughters of Zion,
    and look at King Solomon wearing
        the crown,
    the crown with which his mother
        crowned him
on the day of his wedding,
    the day his heart rejoiced.

Lover

4:1 How beautiful you are, my darling!
    Oh, how beautiful!
    Your eyes behind your veil are
        doves.
Your hair is like a flock of goats
    descending from Mount Gilead.
2 Your teeth are like a flock of sheep
    just shorn,
    coming up from the washing.
Each has its twin;
    not one of them is alone.
3 Your lips are like a scarlet ribbon;
    your mouth is lovely.
Your temples behind your veil
    are like the halves of a
        pomegranate.
4 Your neck is like the tower of David,
    built with elegance*h*;
    on it hang a thousand shields,
    all of them shields of warriors.
5 Your two breasts are like two fawns,
    like twin fawns of a gazelle
    that browse among the lilies.
6 Until the day breaks
    and the shadows flee,
I will go to the mountain of myrrh
    and to the hill of incense.

7 All beautiful you are, my darling;
  there is no flaw in you.

8 Come with me from Lebanon, my
  bride,
  come with me from Lebanon.
  Descend from the crest of Amana,
  from the top of Senir, the summit
  of Hermon,
  from the lions' dens
  and the mountain haunts of the
  leopards.
9 You have stolen my heart, my sister,
  my bride;
  you have stolen my heart
  with one glance of your eyes,
  with one jewel of your necklace.
10 How delightful is your love, my sister,
  my bride!
  How much more pleasing is your
  love than wine,
  and the fragrance of your perfume
  than any spice!
11 Your lips drop sweetness as the
  honeycomb, my bride;
  milk and honey are under your
  tongue.
  The fragrance of your garments is
  like that of Lebanon.
12 You are a garden locked up, my sister,
  my bride;
  you are a spring enclosed, a sealed
  fountain.
13 Your plants are an orchard of
  pomegranates
  with choice fruits,
  with henna and nard,
14   nard and saffron,
  calamus and cinnamon,
  with every kind of incense tree,
  with myrrh and aloes
  and all the finest spices.
15 You are^i a garden fountain,
  a well of flowing water
  streaming down from Lebanon.

Beloved

16 Awake, north wind,
  and come, south wind!
  Blow on my garden,
  that its fragrance may spread
  abroad.

Let my lover come into his garden
  and taste its choice fruits.

a Primarily on the basis of the gender of the Hebrew pronouns
used, male and female speakers are indicated in the margins
by the captions *Lover* and *Beloved* respectively. The words of
others are marked *Friends*. In some instances the divisions
and their captions are debatable.   b 4 The Hebrew is
masculine singular.   c 5 Or *Salma*   d Or *Lover*   e 1 Possibly
a member of the crocus family   f 17 Or *the hills of Bether*
g 10 Or *its inlaid interior a gift of love / from*   h 4 The meaning
of the Hebrew for this word is uncertain.   i 15 Or *I am*
(spoken by the *Beloved*)

2 CORINTHIANS 8:16-24

I thank God, who put into the heart of
Titus the same concern I have for you.
17 For Titus not only welcomed our appeal, but he is coming to you with much
enthusiasm and on his own initiative.
18 And we are sending along with him
the brother who is praised by all the
churches for his service to the gospel.
19 What is more, he was chosen by the
churches to accompany us as we carry
the offering, which we administer in order to honor the Lord himself and to
show our eagerness to help. 20 We want
to avoid any criticism of the way we administer this liberal gift. 21 For we are
taking pains to do what is right, not only
in the eyes of the Lord but also in the
eyes of men.

22 In addition, we are sending with
them our brother who has often proved
to us in many ways that he is zealous,
and now even more so because of his
great confidence in you. 23 As for Titus,
he is my partner and fellow worker
among you; as for our brothers, they are
representatives of the churches and an
honor to Christ. 24 Therefore show these
men the proof of your love and the reason for our pride in you, so that the
churches can see it.

PSALM 50:1-23
A psalm of Asaph.

1 **The Mighty One, God, the LORD,
  speaks and summons the earth
  from the rising of the sun to the
  place where it sets.**
2 **From Zion, perfect in beauty,
  God shines forth.**

3 Our God comes and will not be
      silent;
   a fire devours before him,
   and around him a tempest rages.
4 He summons the heavens above,
   and the earth, that he may judge
      his people:
5 "Gather to me my consecrated ones,
   who made a covenant with me by
      sacrifice."
6 And the heavens proclaim his
      righteousness,
   for God himself is judge.   *Selah*

7 "Hear, O my people, and I will speak,
   O Israel, and I will testify against
      you:
   I am God, your God.
8 I do not rebuke you for your
      sacrifices
   or your burnt offerings, which are
      ever before me.
9 I have no need of a bull from your
      stall
   or of goats from your pens,
10 for every animal of the forest is mine,
   and the cattle on a thousand hills.
11 I know every bird in the mountains,
   and the creatures of the field are
      mine.
12 If I were hungry I would not tell you,
   for the world is mine, and all that
      is in it.
13 Do I eat the flesh of bulls
   or drink the blood of goats?
14 Sacrifice thank offerings to God,
   fulfill your vows to the Most High,
15 and call upon me in the day of
      trouble;
   I will deliver you, and you will
      honor me."

16 But to the wicked, God says:

"What right have you to recite my
      laws
   or take my covenant on your lips?
17 You hate my instruction
   and cast my words behind you.
18 When you see a thief, you join with
      him;
   you throw in your lot with
      adulterers.

19 You use your mouth for evil
   and harness your tongue to deceit.
20 You speak continually against your
      brother
   and slander your own mother's
      son.
21 These things you have done and I
      kept silent;
   you thought I was altogether[a] like
      you.
   But I will rebuke you
   and accuse you to your face.

22 "Consider this, you who forget God,
   or I will tear you to pieces, with
      none to rescue:
23 He who sacrifices thank offerings
      honors me,
   and he prepares the way
   so that I may show him[b] the
      salvation of God."

[a]21 Or thought the 'I AM' was [b]23 Or and to him who
considers his way / I will show

PROVERBS 22:22-23
22 **D**o not exploit the poor because they
      are poor
   and do not crush the needy in
      court,
23 for the LORD will take up their case
   and will plunder those who
      plunder them.

□ D A Y 2 5 0

GOD SIGHTINGS

September 7

SONG OF SONGS 5:1–8:14

Lover

I have come into my garden, my
      sister, my bride;
   I have gathered my myrrh with my
      spice.
I have eaten my honeycomb and my
      honey;
   I have drunk my wine and my
      milk.

Friends

Eat, O friends, and drink;
    drink your fill, O lovers.

Beloved

² I slept but my heart was awake.
    Listen! My lover is knocking:
"Open to me, my sister, my darling,
    my dove, my flawless one.
My head is drenched with dew,
    my hair with the dampness of the
        night."
³ I have taken off my robe—
    must I put it on again?
I have washed my feet—
    must I soil them again?
⁴ My lover thrust his hand through the
        latch-opening;
    my heart began to pound for him.
⁵ I arose to open for my lover,
    and my hands dripped with myrrh,
my fingers with flowing myrrh,
    on the handles of the lock.
⁶ I opened for my lover,
    but my lover had left; he was gone.
    My heart sank at his departure.ᵃ
I looked for him but did not find him.
    I called him but he did not answer.
⁷ The watchmen found me
    as they made their rounds in the
        city.
They beat me, they bruised me;
    they took away my cloak,
    those watchmen of the walls!
⁸ O daughters of Jerusalem, I charge
        you—
    if you find my lover,
what will you tell him?
    Tell him I am faint with love.

Friends

⁹ How is your beloved better than
        others,
    most beautiful of women?
How is your beloved better than
        others,
    that you charge us so?

Beloved

¹⁰ My lover is radiant and ruddy,
    outstanding among ten thousand.
¹¹ His head is purest gold;
    his hair is wavy
    and black as a raven.
¹² His eyes are like doves
    by the water streams,
washed in milk,
    mounted like jewels.
¹³ His cheeks are like beds of spice
    yielding perfume.
His lips are like lilies
    dripping with myrrh.
¹⁴ His arms are rods of gold
    set with chrysolite.
His body is like polished ivory
    decorated with sapphires.ᵇ
¹⁵ His legs are pillars of marble
    set on bases of pure gold.
His appearance is like Lebanon,
    choice as its cedars.
¹⁶ His mouth is sweetness itself;
    he is altogether lovely.
This is my lover, this my friend,
    O daughters of Jerusalem.

Friends

⁶:¹ WHERE has your lover gone,
    most beautiful of women?
Which way did your lover turn,
    that we may look for him with you?

Beloved

² My lover has gone down to his garden,
    to the beds of spices,
to browse in the gardens
    and to gather lilies.
³ I am my lover's and my lover is mine;
    he browses among the lilies.

Lover

⁴ You are beautiful, my darling, as
        Tirzah,
    lovely as Jerusalem,
    majestic as troops with banners.
⁵ Turn your eyes from me;
    they overwhelm me.
Your hair is like a flock of goats
    descending from Gilead.
⁶ Your teeth are like a flock of sheep
    coming up from the washing.
Each has its twin,
    not one of them is alone.

7 Your temples behind your veil
   are like the halves of a
      pomegranate.
8 Sixty queens there may be,
   and eighty concubines,
   and virgins beyond number;
9 but my dove, my perfect one, is
      unique,
   the only daughter of her mother,
   the favorite of the one who bore
      her.
The maidens saw her and called her
      blessed;
   the queens and concubines
      praised her.

Friends

10 Who is this that appears like the
      dawn,
   fair as the moon, bright as the sun,
      majestic as the stars in
         procession?

Lover

11 I went down to the grove of nut trees
   to look at the new growth in the
      valley,
   to see if the vines had budded
   or if the pomegranates were in bloom.
12 Before I realized it,
   my desire set me among the royal
      chariots of my people.*c*

Friends

13 Come back, come back,
      O Shulammite;
   come back, come back, that we
      may gaze on you!

Lover

Why would you gaze on the
      Shulammite
   as on the dance of Mahanaim?

7:1 How beautiful your sandaled feet,
      O prince's daughter!
   Your graceful legs are like jewels,
      the work of a craftsman's hands.
2 Your navel is a rounded goblet
   that never lacks blended wine.
   Your waist is a mound of wheat
      encircled by lilies.

3 Your breasts are like two fawns,
   twins of a gazelle.
4 Your neck is like an ivory tower.
   Your eyes are the pools of Heshbon
      by the gate of Bath Rabbim.
   Your nose is like the tower of
      Lebanon
      looking toward Damascus.
5 Your head crowns you like Mount
      Carmel.
   Your hair is like royal tapestry;
      the king is held captive by its
         tresses.
6 How beautiful you are and how
      pleasing,
   O love, with your delights!
7 Your stature is like that of the
      palm,
   and your breasts like clusters of
      fruit.
8 I said, "I will climb the palm tree;
   I will take hold of its fruit."
May your breasts be like the clusters
      of the vine,
   the fragrance of your breath like
      apples,
9   and your mouth like the best wine.

Beloved

May the wine go straight to my
      lover,
   flowing gently over lips and
      teeth.*d*
10 I belong to my lover,
   and his desire is for me.
11 Come, my lover, let us go to the
      countryside,
   let us spend the night in the
      villages.*e*
12 Let us go early to the vineyards
   to see if the vines have budded,
   if their blossoms have opened,
   and if the pomegranates are in
      bloom—
   there I will give you my love.
13 The mandrakes send out their
      fragrance,
   and at our door is every delicacy,
both new and old,
   that I have stored up for you, my
      lover.

8:1If only you were to me like a brother,
    who was nursed at my mother's
        breasts!
Then, if I found you outside,
    I would kiss you,
    and no one would despise me.
²I would lead you
    and bring you to my mother's
        house—
    she who has taught me.
I would give you spiced wine to drink,
    the nectar of my pomegranates.
³His left arm is under my head
    and his right arm embraces me.
⁴Daughters of Jerusalem, I charge you:
    Do not arouse or awaken love
        until it so desires.

Friends

⁵Who is this coming up from the
        desert
    leaning on her lover?

Beloved

Under the apple tree I roused you;
    there your mother conceived you,
    there she who was in labor gave
        you birth.
⁶Place me like a seal over your heart,
    like a seal on your arm;
for love is as strong as death,
    its jealousy*f* unyielding as the grave.*g*
It burns like blazing fire,
    like a mighty flame.*h*
⁷Many waters cannot quench love;
    rivers cannot wash it away.
If one were to give
    all the wealth of his house for love,
    it*i* would be utterly scorned.

Friends

⁸We have a young sister,
    and her breasts are not yet grown.
What shall we do for our sister
    for the day she is spoken for?
⁹If she is a wall,
    we will build towers of silver on
        her.
If she is a door,
    we will enclose her with panels
        of cedar.

Beloved

¹⁰I am a wall,
    and my breasts are like towers.
Thus I have become in his eyes
    like one bringing contentment.
¹¹Solomon had a vineyard in Baal
        Hamon;
    he let out his vineyard to tenants.
Each was to bring for its fruit
    a thousand shekels*j* of silver.
¹²But my own vineyard is mine to give;
    the thousand shekels are for you,
        O Solomon,
    and two hundred*k* are for those
        who tend its fruit.

Lover

¹³You who dwell in the gardens
    with friends in attendance,
    let me hear your voice!

Beloved

¹⁴Come away, my lover,
    and be like a gazelle
or like a young stag
    on the spice-laden mountains.

a6 Or *heart had gone out to him when he spoke*   *b14* Or *lapis
lazuli*   *c12* Or *among the chariots of Amminadab;* or *among
the chariots of the people of the prince*   *d9* Septuagint,
Aquila, Vulgate and Syriac; Hebrew *lips of sleepers*
e11 Or *henna bushes*   *f6* Or *ardor*   *g6* Hebrew *Sheol*
h6 Or */ like the very flame of the* Lᴏʀᴅ   *i7* Or *he*   *j11* That is,
about 25 pounds (about 11.5 kilograms); also in verse 12
k12 That is, about 5 pounds (about 2.3 kilograms)

2 CORINTHIANS 9:1-15

There is no need for me to write to you
about this service to the saints. ²For I
know your eagerness to help, and I have
been boasting about it to the Macedonians, telling them that since last year you
in Achaia were ready to give; and your
enthusiasm has stirred most of them to
action. ³But I am sending the brothers
in order that our boasting about you in
this matter should not prove hollow, but
that you may be ready, as I said you
would be. ⁴For if any Macedonians
come with me and find you unprepared,
we—not to say anything about you—
would be ashamed of having been so
confident. ⁵So I thought it necessary to
urge the brothers to visit you in advance

and finish the arrangements for the generous gift you had promised. Then it will be ready as a generous gift, not as one grudgingly given.

⁶Remember this: Whoever sows sparingly will also reap sparingly, and whoever sows generously will also reap generously. ⁷Each man should give what he has decided in his heart to give, not reluctantly or under compulsion, for God loves a cheerful giver. ⁸And God is able to make all grace abound to you, so that in all things at all times, having all that you need, you will abound in every good work. ⁹As it is written:

"He has scattered abroad his gifts to the poor;
   his righteousness endures forever."ᵃ

¹⁰Now he who supplies seed to the sower and bread for food will also supply and increase your store of seed and will enlarge the harvest of your righteousness. ¹¹You will be made rich in every way so that you can be generous on every occasion, and through us your generosity will result in thanksgiving to God.

¹²This service that you perform is not only supplying the needs of God's people but is also overflowing in many expressions of thanks to God. ¹³Because of the service by which you have proved yourselves, men will praise God for the obedience that accompanies your confession of the gospel of Christ, and for your generosity in sharing with them and with everyone else. ¹⁴And in their prayers for you their hearts will go out to you, because of the surpassing grace God has given you. ¹⁵Thanks be to God for his indescribable gift!

ᵃ9 Psalm 112:9

PSALM 51:1-19

For the director of music. A psalm of David. When the prophet Nathan came to him after David had committed adultery with Bathsheba.

¹**Have mercy on me, O God,
   according to your unfailing
   love;**
according to your great
   compassion
blot out my transgressions.
²**Wash away all my iniquity
   and cleanse me from my sin.**

³For I know my transgressions,
   and my sin is always before me.
⁴Against you, you only, have I sinned
   and done what is evil in your
      sight,
so that you are proved right when
      you speak
   and justified when you judge.
⁵Surely I was sinful at birth,
   sinful from the time my mother
      conceived me.
⁶Surely you desire truth in the inner
      partsᵃ;
   you teachᵇ me wisdom in the
      inmost place.

⁷Cleanse me with hyssop, and I will
      be clean;
   wash me, and I will be whiter than
      snow.
⁸Let me hear joy and gladness;
   let the bones you have crushed
      rejoice.
⁹Hide your face from my sins
   and blot out all my iniquity.

¹⁰Create in me a pure heart, O God,
   and renew a steadfast spirit
      within me.
¹¹Do not cast me from your presence
   or take your Holy Spirit from me.
¹²Restore to me the joy of your
      salvation
   and grant me a willing spirit, to
      sustain me.

¹³Then I will teach transgressors your
      ways,
   and sinners will turn back to you.
¹⁴Save me from bloodguilt, O God,
   the God who saves me,
   and my tongue will sing of your
      righteousness.
¹⁵O Lord, open my lips,
   and my mouth will declare your
      praise.

¹⁶You do not delight in sacrifice, or I
     would bring it;
     you do not take pleasure in burnt
         offerings.
¹⁷The sacrifices of God are*c* a broken
     spirit;
     a broken and contrite heart,
     O God, you will not despise.

¹⁸In your good pleasure make Zion
     prosper;
     build up the walls of Jerusalem.
¹⁹Then there will be righteous
     sacrifices,
     whole burnt offerings to delight
         you;
     then bulls will be offered on your
         altar.

a6 The meaning of the Hebrew for this phrase is uncertain.
b6 Or *you desired…; / you taught*   *c17* Or *My sacrifice,
O God, is*

PROVERBS 22:24-25
²⁴Do not make friends with a hot-
     tempered man,
     do not associate with one easily
         angered,
²⁵or you may learn his ways
     and get yourself ensnared.

☐ DAY 251

GOD SIGHTINGS

September 8

ISAIAH 1:1–2:22
The vision concerning Judah and Jerusalem that Isaiah son of Amoz saw during the reigns of Uzziah, Jotham, Ahaz
and Hezekiah, kings of Judah.

²Hear, O heavens! Listen, O earth!
     For the LORD has spoken:
"I reared children and brought them
     up,
     but they have rebelled against me.
³The ox knows his master,
     the donkey his owner's manger,
     but Israel does not know,
     my people do not understand."

⁴Ah, sinful nation,
     a people loaded with guilt,
     a brood of evildoers,
     children given to corruption!
They have forsaken the LORD;
     they have spurned the Holy One
         of Israel
     and turned their backs on him.

⁵Why should you be beaten anymore?
     Why do you persist in rebellion?
Your whole head is injured,
     your whole heart afflicted.
⁶From the sole of your foot to the top
         of your head
     there is no soundness—
     only wounds and welts
         and open sores,
     not cleansed or bandaged
         or soothed with oil.

⁷Your country is desolate,
     your cities burned with fire;
     your fields are being stripped by
         foreigners
     right before you,
     laid waste as when overthrown by
         strangers.
⁸The Daughter of Zion is left
     like a shelter in a vineyard,
     like a hut in a field of melons,
     like a city under siege.
⁹Unless the LORD Almighty
     had left us some survivors,
     we would have become like Sodom,
     we would have been like
         Gomorrah.

¹⁰Hear the word of the LORD,
     you rulers of Sodom;
     listen to the law of our God,
     you people of Gomorrah!
¹¹"The multitude of your sacrifices—
     what are they to me?" says the
         LORD.
"I have more than enough of burnt
     offerings,
     of rams and the fat of fattened
         animals;
I have no pleasure
     in the blood of bulls and lambs
         and goats.

12 When you come to appear before
      me,
   who has asked this of you,
   this trampling of my courts?
13 Stop bringing meaningless offerings!
   Your incense is detestable to me.
   New Moons, Sabbaths and
      convocations—
   I cannot bear your evil assemblies.
14 Your New Moon festivals and your
      appointed feasts
   my soul hates.
   They have become a burden to me;
   I am weary of bearing them.
15 When you spread out your hands in
      prayer,
   I will hide my eyes from you;
   even if you offer many prayers,
   I will not listen.
   Your hands are full of blood;
16   wash and make yourselves clean.
   Take your evil deeds
      out of my sight!
   Stop doing wrong,
17   learn to do right!
   Seek justice,
      encourage the oppressed.*a*
   Defend the cause of the fatherless,
      plead the case of the widow.

18 **"Come now, let us reason
      together,"**
   says the LORD.
   " Though your sins are like scarlet,
      they shall be as white as snow;
   though they are red as crimson,
      they shall be like wool.
19 If you are willing and obedient,
      you will eat the best from the land;
20 but if you resist and rebel,
      you will be devoured by the sword."
   For the mouth of the LORD
      has spoken.

21 See how the faithful city
      has become a harlot!
   She once was full of justice;
      righteousness used to dwell in her—
      but now murderers!
22 Your silver has become dross,
      your choice wine is diluted with
      water.

23 Your rulers are rebels,
      companions of thieves;
   they all love bribes
      and chase after gifts.
   They do not defend the cause of the
      fatherless;
      the widow's case does not come
      before them.
24 Therefore the Lord, the LORD
      Almighty,
      the Mighty One of Israel, declares:
   "Ah, I will get relief from my foes
      and avenge myself on my enemies.
25 I will turn my hand against you;
      I will thoroughly purge away your
      dross
      and remove all your impurities.
26 I will restore your judges as in days of
      old,
      your counselors as at the beginning.
   Afterward you will be called
      the City of Righteousness,
      the Faithful City."

27 Zion will be redeemed with justice,
      her penitent ones with
      righteousness.
28 But rebels and sinners will both be
      broken,
      and those who forsake the LORD
      will perish.

29 "You will be ashamed because of the
      sacred oaks
      in which you have delighted;
   you will be disgraced because of the
      gardens
      that you have chosen.
30 You will be like an oak with fading
      leaves,
      like a garden without water.
31 The mighty man will become tinder
      and his work a spark;
   both will burn together,
      with no one to quench the fire."

2:1 THIS is what Isaiah son of Amoz saw
concerning Judah and Jerusalem:

2 In the last days

   the mountain of the LORD's temple
      will be established
      as chief among the mountains;

it will be raised above the hills,
   and all nations will stream to it.

³Many peoples will come and say,

"Come, let us go up to the mountain
   of the LORD,
to the house of the God of Jacob.
He will teach us his ways,
   so that we may walk in his paths."
The law will go out from Zion,
   the word of the LORD from
      Jerusalem.
⁴He will judge between the nations
   and will settle disputes for many
      peoples.
They will beat their swords into
      plowshares
   and their spears into pruning hooks.
Nation will not take up sword against
      nation,
   nor will they train for war anymore.

⁵Come, O house of Jacob,
   let us walk in the light of the LORD.

⁶You have abandoned your people,
   the house of Jacob.
They are full of superstitions from
      the East;
   they practice divination like the
      Philistines
   and clasp hands with pagans.
⁷Their land is full of silver and gold;
   there is no end to their treasures.
Their land is full of horses;
   there is no end to their chariots.
⁸Their land is full of idols;
   they bow down to the work of
      their hands,
to what their fingers have made.
⁹So man will be brought low
   and mankind humbled—
   do not forgive them.ᵇ

¹⁰Go into the rocks,
   hide in the ground
from dread of the LORD
   and the splendor of his majesty!
¹¹The eyes of the arrogant man will be
      humbled
   and the pride of men brought low;
the LORD alone will be exalted in
      that day.

¹²The LORD Almighty has a day in store
   for all the proud and lofty,
   for all that is exalted
   (and they will be humbled),
¹³for all the cedars of Lebanon, tall
      and lofty,
   and all the oaks of Bashan,
¹⁴for all the towering mountains
   and all the high hills,
¹⁵for every lofty tower
   and every fortified wall,
¹⁶for every trading shipᶜ
   and every stately vessel.
¹⁷The arrogance of man will be
      brought low
   and the pride of men humbled;
the LORD alone will be exalted in
      that day,
¹⁸   and the idols will totally
      disappear.

¹⁹Men will flee to caves in the rocks
   and to holes in the ground
from dread of the LORD
   and the splendor of his majesty,
   when he rises to shake the earth.
²⁰In that day men will throw away
   to the rodents and bats
their idols of silver and idols of gold,
   which they made to worship.
²¹They will flee to caverns in the rocks
   and to the overhanging crags
from dread of the LORD
   and the splendor of his majesty,
   when he rises to shake the earth.

²²Stop trusting in man,
   who has but a breath in his
      nostrils.
Of what account is he?

ᵃ17 Or / rebuke the oppressor   ᵇ9 Or not raise them up
ᶜ16 Hebrew every ship of Tarshish

2 CORINTHIANS 10:1-18

By the meekness and gentleness of
Christ, I appeal to you—I, Paul, who am
"timid" when face to face with you, but
"bold" when away! ²I beg you that when
I come I may not have to be as bold as I
expect to be toward some people who
think that we live by the standards of
this world. ³For though we live in the
world, we do not wage war as the world

does. ⁴The weapons we fight with are not the weapons of the world. On the contrary, they have divine power to demolish strongholds. ⁵We demolish arguments and every pretension that sets itself up against the knowledge of God, and we take captive every thought to make it obedient to Christ. ⁶And we will be ready to punish every act of disobedience, once your obedience is complete.

⁷You are looking only on the surface of things.ᵃ If anyone is confident that he belongs to Christ, he should consider again that we belong to Christ just as much as he. ⁸For even if I boast somewhat freely about the authority the Lord gave us for building you up rather than pulling you down, I will not be ashamed of it. ⁹I do not want to seem to be trying to frighten you with my letters. ¹⁰For some say, "His letters are weighty and forceful, but in person he is unimpressive and his speaking amounts to nothing." ¹¹Such people should realize that what we are in our letters when we are absent, we will be in our actions when we are present.

¹²We do not dare to classify or compare ourselves with some who commend themselves. When they measure themselves by themselves and compare themselves with themselves, they are not wise. ¹³We, however, will not boast beyond proper limits, but will confine our boasting to the field God has assigned to us, a field that reaches even to you. ¹⁴We are not going too far in our boasting, as would be the case if we had not come to you, for we did get as far as you with the gospel of Christ. ¹⁵Neither do we go beyond our limits by boasting of work done by others.ᵇ Our hope is that, as your faith continues to grow, our area of activity among you will greatly expand, ¹⁶so that we can preach the gospel in the regions beyond you. For we do not want to boast about work already done in another man's territory. ¹⁷But, "Let him who boasts boast in the Lord."ᶜ ¹⁸For it is not the one who commends himself who is approved, but the one whom the Lord commends.

ᵃ7 Or Look at the obvious facts   ᵇ13-15 Or ¹³We, however, will not boast about things that cannot be measured, but we will boast according to the standard of measurement that the God of measure has assigned us—a measurement that relates even to you. ¹⁴… ¹⁵Neither do we boast about things that cannot be measured in regard to the work done by others. ᶜ17 Jer. 9:24

PSALM 52:1-9

For the director of music. A maskilᵃ of David. When Doeg the Edomite had gone to Saul and told him: "David has gone to the house of Ahimelech."

¹ **W**hy do you boast of evil, you mighty man?
  Why do you boast all day long,
    you who are a disgrace in the eyes of God?
² Your tongue plots destruction;
    it is like a sharpened razor,
    you who practice deceit.
³ You love evil rather than good,
    falsehood rather than speaking the truth.   *Selah*
⁴ You love every harmful word,
    O you deceitful tongue!

⁵ Surely God will bring you down to everlasting ruin:
  He will snatch you up and tear you from your tent;
  he will uproot you from the land of the living.   *Selah*
⁶ The righteous will see and fear;
    they will laugh at him, saying,
⁷ "Here now is the man
    who did not make God his stronghold
  but trusted in his great wealth
  and grew strong by destroying others!"

⁸ But I am like an olive tree
    flourishing in the house of God;
  I trust in God's unfailing love
    for ever and ever.
⁹ I will praise you forever for what you have done;
    in your name I will hope, for your name is good.
  I will praise you in the presence of your saints.

ᵃTitle: Probably a literary or musical term

PROVERBS 22:26-27

26 Do not be a man who strikes hands
        in pledge
    or puts up security for debts;
27 if you lack the means to pay,
    your very bed will be snatched
        from under you.

□ DAY 252

GOD SIGHTINGS

September 9

ISAIAH 3:1–5:30

See now, the Lord,
    the LORD Almighty,
is about to take from Jerusalem and
        Judah
    both supply and support:
all supplies of food and all supplies
        of water,
2   the hero and warrior,
    the judge and prophet,
    the soothsayer and elder,
3 the captain of fifty and man of rank,
    the counselor, skilled craftsman
        and clever enchanter.

4 I will make boys their officials;
    mere children will govern them.
5 People will oppress each other—
    man against man, neighbor
        against neighbor.
The young will rise up against the
        old,
    the base against the honorable.

6 A man will seize one of his brothers
    at his father's home, and say,
"You have a cloak, you be our
        leader;
    take charge of this heap of
        ruins!"
7 But in that day he will cry out,
    "I have no remedy.
I have no food or clothing in my
        house;
    do not make me the leader of the
        people."

8 Jerusalem staggers,
    Judah is falling;
their words and deeds are against
        the LORD,
    defying his glorious presence.
9 The look on their faces testifies
        against them;
    they parade their sin like Sodom;
        they do not hide it.
Woe to them!
    They have brought disaster upon
        themselves.

10 Tell the righteous it will be well with
        them,
    for they will enjoy the fruit of
        their deeds.
11 Woe to the wicked! Disaster is upon
        them!
    They will be paid back for what their
        hands have done.

12 Youths oppress my people,
    women rule over them.
O my people, your guides lead you
        astray;
    they turn you from the path.

13 The LORD takes his place in court;
    he rises to judge the people.
14 The LORD enters into judgment
    against the elders and leaders of
        his people:
"It is you who have ruined my
        vineyard;
    the plunder from the poor is in
        your houses.
15 What do you mean by crushing my
        people
    and grinding the faces of the
        poor?"
                        declares the Lord,
                        the LORD Almighty.

16 The LORD says,
    "The women of Zion are
        haughty,
walking along with outstretched
        necks,
    flirting with their eyes,
tripping along with mincing steps,
    with ornaments jingling on their
        ankles.

¹⁷Therefore the Lord will bring sores
　　on the heads of the women of
　　Zion;
　the LORD will make their scalps
　　bald."

¹⁸In that day the Lord will snatch away
their finery: the bangles and headbands
and crescent necklaces, ¹⁹the earrings
and bracelets and veils, ²⁰the head-
dresses and ankle chains and sashes, the
perfume bottles and charms, ²¹the signet rings and nose rings, ²²the fine robes
and the capes and cloaks, the purses
²³and mirrors, and the linen garments
and tiaras and shawls.

²⁴Instead of fragrance there will be a
　　stench;
　instead of a sash, a rope;
　instead of well-dressed hair, baldness;
　instead of fine clothing, sackcloth;
　instead of beauty, branding.
²⁵Your men will fall by the sword,
　your warriors in battle.
²⁶The gates of Zion will lament and
　　mourn;
　destitute, she will sit on the
　　ground.

⁴:¹IN that day seven women
　will take hold of one man
and say, "We will eat our own food
　and provide our own clothes;
only let us be called by your name.
Take away our disgrace!"

²In that day the Branch of the LORD
will be beautiful and glorious, and the
fruit of the land will be the pride and
glory of the survivors in Israel. ³Those
who are left in Zion, who remain in Jerusalem, will be called holy, all who are recorded among the living in Jerusalem.
⁴The Lord will wash away the filth of the
women of Zion; he will cleanse the
bloodstains from Jerusalem by a spiritᵃ
of judgment and a spiritᵃ of fire. ⁵Then
the LORD will create over all of Mount
Zion and over those who assemble
there a cloud of smoke by day and a
glow of flaming fire by night; over all
the glory will be a canopy. ⁶It will be a
shelter and shade from the heat of the
day, and a refuge and hiding place from
the storm and rain.

⁵:¹I WILL sing for the one I love
　a song about his vineyard:
My loved one had a vineyard
　on a fertile hillside.
²He dug it up and cleared it of stones
　and planted it with the choicest
　　vines.
He built a watchtower in it
　and cut out a winepress as well.
Then he looked for a crop of good
　　grapes,
　but it yielded only bad fruit.

³"Now you dwellers in Jerusalem and
　　men of Judah,
　judge between me and my
　　vineyard.
⁴What more could have been done for
　　my vineyard
　than I have done for it?
When I looked for good grapes,
　why did it yield only bad?
⁵Now I will tell you
　what I am going to do to my
　　vineyard:
I will take away its hedge,
　and it will be destroyed;
I will break down its wall,
　and it will be trampled.
⁶I will make it a wasteland,
　neither pruned nor cultivated,
　and briers and thorns will grow
　　there.
I will command the clouds
　not to rain on it."

⁷The vineyard of the LORD Almighty
　is the house of Israel,
and the men of Judah
　are the garden of his delight.
And he looked for justice, but saw
　　bloodshed;
　for righteousness, but heard cries
　　of distress.

⁸Woe to you who add house to house
　and join field to field
till no space is left
　and you live alone in the land.

⁹The LORD Almighty has declared in my hearing:

"Surely the great houses will become
  desolate,
the fine mansions left without
  occupants.
¹⁰A ten-acreᵇ vineyard will produce
  only a bathᶜ of wine,
a homerᵈ of seed only an ephahᵉ
  of grain."

¹¹Woe to those who rise early in the
  morning
  to run after their drinks,
who stay up late at night
  till they are inflamed with wine.
¹²They have harps and lyres at their
  banquets,
  tambourines and flutes and wine,
but they have no regard for the deeds
  of the LORD,
  no respect for the work of his
  hands.
¹³Therefore my people will go into
  exile
  for lack of understanding;
their men of rank will die of hunger
  and their masses will be parched
  with thirst.
¹⁴Therefore the graveᶠ enlarges its
  appetite
  and opens its mouth without limit;
into it will descend their nobles and
  masses
  with all their brawlers and
  revelers.
¹⁵So man will be brought low
  and mankind humbled,
  the eyes of the arrogant humbled.
¹⁶But the LORD Almighty will be
  exalted by his justice,
  and the holy God will show
  himself holy by his
  righteousness.
¹⁷Then sheep will graze as in their own
  pasture;
  lambs will feedᵍ among the ruins
  of the rich.

¹⁸Woe to those who draw sin along
  with cords of deceit,
  and wickedness as with cart ropes,

¹⁹to those who say, "Let God hurry,
  let him hasten his work
  so we may see it.
Let it approach,
  let the plan of the Holy One of
  Israel come,
  so we may know it."

²⁰Woe to those who call evil good
  and good evil,
who put darkness for light
  and light for darkness,
who put bitter for sweet
  and sweet for bitter.

²¹Woe to those who are wise in their
  own eyes
  and clever in their own sight.

²²Woe to those who are heroes at
  drinking wine
  and champions at mixing drinks,
²³who acquit the guilty for a bribe,
  but deny justice to the innocent.
²⁴Therefore, as tongues of fire lick up
  straw
  and as dry grass sinks down in the
  flames,
so their roots will decay
  and their flowers blow away like
  dust;
for they have rejected the law of the
  LORD Almighty
  and spurned the word of the Holy
  One of Israel.
²⁵Therefore the LORD's anger burns
  against his people;
  his hand is raised and he strikes
  them down.
The mountains shake,
  and the dead bodies are like refuse
  in the streets.

Yet for all this, his anger is not turned
  away,
  his hand is still upraised.

²⁶He lifts up a banner for the distant
  nations,
  he whistles for those at the ends of
  the earth.
Here they come,
  swiftly and speedily!

27 Not one of them grows tired or
   stumbles,
   not one slumbers or sleeps;
   not a belt is loosened at the waist,
   not a sandal thong is broken.
28 Their arrows are sharp,
   all their bows are strung;
   their horses' hoofs seem like flint,
   their chariot wheels like a
   whirlwind.
29 Their roar is like that of the lion,
   they roar like young lions;
   they growl as they seize their prey
   and carry it off with no one to
   rescue.
30 In that day they will roar over it
   like the roaring of the sea.
   And if one looks at the land,
   he will see darkness and distress;
   even the light will be darkened by
   the clouds.

a4 Or *the Spirit*   *b10* Hebrew *ten-yoke,* that is, the land
plowed by 10 yoke of oxen in one day   *c10* That is, probably
about 6 gallons (about 22 liters)   *d10* That is, probably
about 6 bushels (about 220 liters)   *e0* That is, probably
about 3/5 bushel (about 22 liters)   *f14* Hebrew
Sheol   *h17* Septuagint; Hebrew */ strangers will eat*

2 CORINTHIANS 11:1-15

I hope you will put up with a little of my
foolishness; but you are already doing
that. ²I am jealous for you with a godly
jealousy. I promised you to one husband, to Christ, so that I might present
you as a pure virgin to him. ³But I am
afraid that just as Eve was deceived by
the serpent's cunning, your minds may
somehow be led astray from your sincere and pure devotion to Christ. ⁴For if
someone comes to you and preaches a
Jesus other than the Jesus we preached,
or if you receive a different spirit from
the one you received, or a different gospel from the one you accepted, you put
up with it easily enough. ⁵But I do not
think I am in the least inferior to those
"super-apostles." ⁶I may not be a trained
speaker, but I do have knowledge. We
have made this perfectly clear to you in
every way.

   ⁷Was it a sin for me to lower myself in
order to elevate you by preaching the
gospel of God to you free of charge? ⁸I

robbed other churches by receiving
support from them so as to serve you.
⁹And when I was with you and needed
something, I was not a burden to anyone, for the brothers who came from
Macedonia supplied what I needed. I
have kept myself from being a burden
to you in any way, and will continue to
do so. ¹⁰As surely as the truth of Christ is
in me, nobody in the regions of Achaia
will stop this boasting of mine. ¹¹Why?
Because I do not love you? God knows I
do! ¹²And I will keep on doing what I am
doing in order to cut the ground from
under those who want an opportunity
to be considered equal with us in the
things they boast about.

   ¹³For such men are false apostles, deceitful workmen, masquerading as
apostles of Christ. ¹⁴**And no wonder,
for Satan himself masquerades as an
angel of light.** ¹⁵**It is not surprising,
then, if his servants masquerade as
servants of righteousness. Their end
will be what their actions deserve.**

PSALM 53:1-6
For the director of music. According to
mahalath.ᵃ A *maskilᵇ* of David.

¹ The fool says in his heart,
   "There is no God."
   They are corrupt, and their ways are
      vile;
      there is no one who does good.

² God looks down from heaven
      on the sons of men
   to see if there are any who
      understand,
      any who seek God.
³ Everyone has turned away,
      they have together become corrupt;
   there is no one who does good,
      not even one.

⁴ Will the evildoers never learn—
      those who devour my people as
         men eat bread
      and who do not call on God?
⁵ There they were, overwhelmed with
      dread,
      where there was nothing to dread.

God scattered the bones of those
  who attacked you;
you put them to shame, for God
  despised them.

6 Oh, that salvation for Israel would
  come out of Zion!
When God restores the fortunes of
  his people,
let Jacob rejoice and Israel be glad!

*a*Title: Probably a musical term   *b*Title: Probably a literary
or musical term

PROVERBS 22:28-29

28 Do not move an ancient boundary
  stone
set up by your forefathers.

29 Do you see a man skilled in his work?
  He will serve before kings;
he will not serve before obscure
  men.

□ D A Y 2 5 3

GOD SIGHTINGS

September 10

ISAIAH 6:1–7:25

In the year that King Uzziah died, I
[Isaiah] saw the Lord seated on a
throne, high and exalted, and the
train of his robe filled the temple.
2 Above him were seraphs, each with six
wings: With two wings they covered
their faces, with two they covered their
feet, and with two they were flying. 3 And
they were calling to one another:

  "Holy, holy, holy is the LORD Almighty;
    the whole earth is full of his glory."

4 At the sound of their voices the doorposts and thresholds shook and the
temple was filled with smoke.
5 "Woe to me!" I cried. "I am ruined!
For I am a man of unclean lips, and I live
among a people of unclean lips, and my
eyes have seen the King, the LORD Almighty."

6 Then one of the seraphs flew to me
with a live coal in his hand, which he had
taken with tongs from the altar. 7 With it
he touched my mouth and said, "See, this
has touched your lips; your guilt is taken
away and your sin atoned for."
8 Then I heard the voice of the Lord
saying, "Whom shall I send? And who
will go for us?"
  And I said, "Here am I. Send me!"
9 He said, "Go and tell this people:

  "'Be ever hearing, but never
    understanding;
  be ever seeing, but never
    perceiving.'
10 Make the heart of this people
  calloused;
  make their ears dull
  and close their eyes.*a*
Otherwise they might see with their
  eyes,
  hear with their ears,
  understand with their hearts,
and turn and be healed."

11 Then I said, "For how long, O Lord?"
  And he answered:

  "Until the cities lie ruined
    and without inhabitant,
  until the houses are left deserted
    and the fields ruined and ravaged,
12 until the LORD has sent everyone far
    away
    and the land is utterly forsaken.
13 And though a tenth remains in the
    land,
    it will again be laid waste.
  But as the terebinth and oak
    leave stumps when they are cut
      down,
    so the holy seed will be the stump
      in the land."

7:1 WHEN Ahaz son of Jotham, the son of
Uzziah, was king of Judah, King Rezin
of Aram and Pekah son of Remaliah
king of Israel marched up to fight
against Jerusalem, but they could not
overpower it.
2 Now the house of David was told,
"Aram has allied itself with*b* Ephraim";

so the hearts of Ahaz and his people were shaken, as the trees of the forest are shaken by the wind.

³Then the Lord said to Isaiah, "Go out, you and your son Shear-Jashub,ᶜ to meet Ahaz at the end of the aqueduct of the Upper Pool, on the road to the Washerman's Field. ⁴Say to him, 'Be careful, keep calm and don't be afraid. Do not lose heart because of these two smoldering stubs of firewood—because of the fierce anger of Rezin and Aram and of the son of Remaliah. ⁵Aram, Ephraim and Remaliah's son have plotted your ruin, saying, ⁶"Let us invade Judah; let us tear it apart and divide it among ourselves, and make the son of Tabeel king over it." ⁷Yet this is what the Sovereign Lord says:

"'It will not take place,
    it will not happen,
⁸for the head of Aram is Damascus,
    and the head of Damascus is only
        Rezin.
Within sixty-five years
    Ephraim will be too shattered to
        be a people.
⁹The head of Ephraim is Samaria,
    and the head of Samaria is only
        Remaliah's son.
If you do not stand firm in your faith,
    you will not stand at all.'"

¹⁰Again the Lord spoke to Ahaz, ¹¹"Ask the Lord your God for a sign, whether in the deepest depths or in the highest heights."

¹²But Ahaz said, "I will not ask; I will not put the Lord to the test."

¹³Then Isaiah said, "Hear now, you house of David! Is it not enough to try the patience of men? Will you try the patience of my God also? ¹⁴Therefore the Lord himself will give youᵈ a sign: The virgin will be with child and will give birth to a son, andᵉ will call him Immanuel.ᶠ ¹⁵He will eat curds and honey when he knows enough to reject the wrong and choose the right. ¹⁶But before the boy knows enough to reject the wrong and choose the right, the land of

the two kings you dread will be laid waste. ¹⁷The Lord will bring on you and on your people and on the house of your father a time unlike any since Ephraim broke away from Judah—he will bring the king of Assyria."

¹⁸In that day the Lord will whistle for flies from the distant streams of Egypt and for bees from the land of Assyria. ¹⁹They will all come and settle in the steep ravines and in the crevices in the rocks, on all the thornbushes and at all the water holes. ²⁰In that day the Lord will use a razor hired from beyond the Riverᵍ—the king of Assyria—to shave your head and the hair of your legs, and to take off your beards also. ²¹In that day, a man will keep alive a young cow and two goats. ²²And because of the abundance of the milk they give, he will have curds to eat. All who remain in the land will eat curds and honey. ²³In that day, in every place where there were a thousand vines worth a thousand silver shekels,ʰ there will be only briers and thorns. ²⁴Men will go there with bow and arrow, for the land will be covered with briers and thorns. ²⁵As for all the hills once cultivated by the hoe, you will no longer go there for fear of the briers and thorns; they will become places where cattle are turned loose and where sheep run.

a9,10 Hebrew; Septuagint 'You will be ever hearing, but never understanding; / you will be ever seeing, but never perceiving.' / ¹⁰This people's heart has become calloused; / they hardly hear with their ears, / and they have closed their eyes   b2 Or has set up camp in   c3 Shear-Jashub means a remnant will return.   d14 The Hebrew is plural.   e14 Masoretic Text; Dead Sea Scrolls and he or and they   f14 Immanuel means God with us.   g20 That is, the Euphrates   h23 That is, about 25 pounds (about 11.5 kilograms)

2 CORINTHIANS 11:16-33

I repeat: Let no one take me for a fool. But if you do, then receive me just as you would a fool, so that I may do a little boasting. ¹⁷In this self-confident boasting I am not talking as the Lord would, but as a fool. ¹⁸Since many are boasting in the way the world does, I too will boast. ¹⁹You gladly put up with fools since you are so wise! ²⁰In fact, you even put up with anyone who enslaves you or exploits you or takes advantage of you or pushes himself forward or slaps you in the face. 21To my shame I admit that we were too weak for that!

What anyone else dares to boast about—I am speaking as a fool—I also dare to boast about. 22Are they Hebrews? So am I. Are they Israelites? So am I. Are they Abraham's descendants? So am I. 23Are they servants of Christ? (I am out of my mind to talk like this.) I am more. I have worked much harder, been in prison more frequently, been flogged more severely, and been exposed to death again and again. 24Five times I received from the Jews the forty lashes minus one. 25Three times I was beaten with rods, once I was stoned, three times I was shipwrecked, I spent a night and a day in the open sea, 26I have been constantly on the move. I have been in danger from rivers, in danger from bandits, in danger from my own countrymen, in danger from Gentiles; in danger in the city, in danger in the country, in danger at sea; and in danger from false brothers. 27I have labored and toiled and have often gone without sleep; I have known hunger and thirst and have often gone without food; I have been cold and naked. 28Besides everything else, I face daily the pressure of my concern for all the churches. 29Who is weak, and I do not feel weak? Who is led into sin, and I do not inwardly burn?

30If I must boast, I will boast of the things that show my weakness. 31The God and Father of the Lord Jesus, who is to be praised forever, knows that I am not lying. 32In Damascus the governor under King Aretas had the city of the Damascenes guarded in order to arrest me. 33But I was lowered in a basket from a window in the wall and slipped through his hands.

PSALM 54:1-7
For the director of music. With stringed instruments. A *maskil*a of David. When the Ziphites had gone to Saul and said, "Is not David hiding among us?"

¹Save me, O God, by your name;
    vindicate me by your might.

²Hear my prayer, O God;
    listen to the words of my mouth.

³Strangers are attacking me;
    ruthless men seek my life—
    men without regard for God. *Selah*

⁴Surely God is my help;
    the Lord is the one who sustains
    me.

⁵Let evil recoil on those who slander
    me;
    in your faithfulness destroy them.

⁶I will sacrifice a freewill offering to
    you;
    I will praise your name, O LORD,
    for it is good.
⁷For he has delivered me from all my
    troubles,
    and my eyes have looked in
    triumph on my foes.

aTitle: Probably a literary or musical term

PROVERBS 23:1-3
When you sit to dine with a ruler,
    note well whata is before you,
²and put a knife to your throat
    if you are given to gluttony.
³Do not crave his delicacies,
    for that food is deceptive.

a1 Or who

□ DAY 254

GOD SIGHTINGS

September 11

ISAIAH 8:1–9:21
The LORD said to me [Isaiah], "Take a large scroll and write on it with an ordinary pen: Maher-Shalal-Hash-Baz.a ²And I will call in Uriah the priest and Zechariah son of Jeberekiah as reliable witnesses for me."

³Then I went to the prophetess, and she conceived and gave birth to a son. And the LORD said to me, "Name him Maher-Shalal-Hash-Baz. ⁴Before the

boy knows how to say 'My father' or 'My mother,' the wealth of Damascus and the plunder of Samaria will be carried off by the king of Assyria."

⁵ The Lord spoke to me again:

⁶ "Because this people has rejected
  the gently flowing waters of Shiloah
and rejoices over Rezin
  and the son of Remaliah,
⁷ therefore the Lord is about to bring
    against them
  the mighty floodwaters of the
    River*b*—
  the king of Assyria with all his
    pomp.
It will overflow all its channels,
  run over all its banks
⁸ and sweep on into Judah, swirling
    over it,
  passing through it and reaching up
    to the neck.
Its outspread wings will cover the
    breadth of your land,
  O Immanuel*c*!"

⁹ Raise the war cry,*d* you nations, and
    be shattered!
  Listen, all you distant lands.
Prepare for battle, and be shattered!
Prepare for battle, and be shattered!
¹⁰ Devise your strategy, but it will be
    thwarted;
  propose your plan, but it will not
    stand,
  for God is with us.*e*

¹¹ The Lord spoke to me with his strong hand upon me, warning me not to follow the way of this people. He said:

¹² "Do not call conspiracy
  everything that these people call
    conspiracy*f*;
do not fear what they fear,
  and do not dread it.
¹³ The Lord Almighty is the one you are
    to regard as holy,
  he is the one you are to fear,
  he is the one you are to dread,
¹⁴ and he will be a sanctuary;
  but for both houses of Israel he
    will be

a stone that causes men to stumble
  and a rock that makes them fall.
And for the people of Jerusalem he
    will be
  a trap and a snare.
¹⁵ Many of them will stumble;
  they will fall and be broken,
  they will be snared and
    captured."

¹⁶ Bind up the testimony
  and seal up the law among my
    disciples.
¹⁷ I will wait for the Lord,
  who is hiding his face from the
    house of Jacob.
  I will put my trust in him.

¹⁸ Here am I, and the children the Lord has given me. We are signs and symbols in Israel from the Lord Almighty, who dwells on Mount Zion.

¹⁹ When men tell you to consult mediums and spiritists, who whisper and mutter, should not a people inquire of their God? Why consult the dead on behalf of the living? ²⁰ To the law and to the testimony! If they do not speak according to this word, they have no light of dawn. ²¹ Distressed and hungry, they will roam through the land; when they are famished, they will become enraged and, looking upward, will curse their king and their God. ²² Then they will look toward the earth and see only distress and darkness and fearful gloom, and they will be thrust into utter darkness.

⁹:¹ Nevertheless, there will be no more gloom for those who were in distress. In the past he humbled the land of Zebulun and the land of Naphtali, but in the future he will honor Galilee of the Gentiles, by the way of the sea, along the Jordan—

² The people walking in darkness
  have seen a great light;
on those living in the land of the
    shadow of death*g*
  a light has dawned.
³ You have enlarged the nation
  and increased their joy;

they rejoice before you
  as people rejoice at the harvest,
as men rejoice
  when dividing the plunder.
4 For as in the day of Midian's defeat,
  you have shattered
the yoke that burdens them,
  the bar across their shoulders,
  the rod of their oppressor.
5 Every warrior's boot used in battle
  and every garment rolled in
    blood
will be destined for burning,
  will be fuel for the fire.
6 **For to us a child is born,**
  to us a son is given,
  and the government will be on
    his shoulders.
And he will be called
  Wonderful Counselor,[h] **Mighty**
    God,
  Everlasting Father, Prince of
    Peace.
7 Of the increase of his government
    and peace
  there will be no end.
He will reign on David's throne
  and over his kingdom,
establishing and upholding it
  with justice and righteousness
  from that time on and forever.
The zeal of the LORD Almighty
  will accomplish this.

8 The Lord has sent a message against
    Jacob;
  it will fall on Israel.
9 All the people will know it—
  Ephraim and the inhabitants of
    Samaria—
who say with pride
  and arrogance of heart,
10 "The bricks have fallen down,
  but we will rebuild with dressed
    stone;
the fig trees have been felled,
  but we will replace them with
    cedars."
11 But the LORD has strengthened
    Rezin's foes against them
  and has spurred their enemies on.

12 Arameans from the east and
    Philistines from the west
  have devoured Israel with open
    mouth.

Yet for all this, his anger is not turned
    away,
  his hand is still upraised.

13 But the people have not returned to
    him who struck them,
  nor have they sought the LORD
    Almighty.
14 So the LORD will cut off from Israel
    both head and tail,
  both palm branch and reed in a
    single day;
15 the elders and prominent men are
    the head,
  the prophets who teach lies are
    the tail.
16 Those who guide this people mislead
    them,
  and those who are guided are led
    astray.
17 Therefore the Lord will take no
    pleasure in the young men,
  nor will he pity the fatherless and
    widows,
for everyone is ungodly and wicked,
  every mouth speaks vileness.

Yet for all this, his anger is not turned
    away,
  his hand is still upraised.

18 Surely wickedness burns like a fire;
  it consumes briers and thorns,
it sets the forest thickets ablaze,
  so that it rolls upward in a column
    of smoke.
19 By the wrath of the LORD Almighty
  the land will be scorched
and the people will be fuel for the
    fire;
  no one will spare his brother.
20 On the right they will devour,
  but still be hungry;
on the left they will eat,
  but not be satisfied.
Each will feed on the flesh of his
  own offspring[i]:

21 Manasseh will feed on Ephraim,
    and Ephraim on Manasseh;
  together they will turn against
      Judah.

  Yet for all this, his anger is not turned
      away,
    his hand is still upraised.

a1 *Maher-Shalal-Hash-Baz* means *quick to the plunder,
swift to the spoil;* also in verse 3.   b7 That is, the Euphrates
c8 *Immanuel* means *God with us.*   d9 Or *Do your worst*
e10 Hebrew *Immanuel*   f12 Or *Do not call for a treaty /
every time these people call for a treaty*   92 Or *land of
darkness*   h6 Or *Wonderful, Counselor*   i20 Or *arm*

2 CORINTHIANS 12:1-10

I must go on boasting. Although there is
nothing to be gained, I will go on to visions and revelations from the Lord. ²I
know a man in Christ who fourteen
years ago was caught up to the third
heaven. Whether it was in the body or
out of the body I do not know—God
knows. ³And I know that this man—
whether in the body or apart from the
body I do not know, but God knows—
⁴was caught up to paradise. He heard
inexpressible things, things that man is
not permitted to tell. ⁵I will boast about
a man like that, but I will not boast about
myself, except about my weaknesses.
⁶Even if I should choose to boast, I
would not be a fool, because I would be
speaking the truth. But I refrain, so no
one will think more of me than is war-
ranted by what I do or say.

⁷To keep me from becoming conceited because of these surpassing
great revelations, there was given me a
thorn in my flesh, a messenger of Satan,
to torment me. ⁸Three times I pleaded
with the Lord to take it away from me.
⁹But he said to me, "My grace is sufficient for you, for my power is made perfect in weakness." Therefore I will boast
all the more gladly about my weaknesses, so that Christ's power may rest
on me. ¹⁰That is why, for Christ's sake, I
delight in weaknesses, in insults, in
hardships, in persecutions, in difficulties. For when I am weak, then I am
strong.

PSALM 55:1-23

For the director of music. With stringed
instruments. A *maskil*a of David.

¹ Listen to my prayer, O God,
    do not ignore my plea;
² hear me and answer me.
  My thoughts trouble me and I am
      distraught
³ at the voice of the enemy,
    at the stares of the wicked;
  for they bring down suffering
      upon me
    and revile me in their anger.

⁴ My heart is in anguish within me;
    the terrors of death assail me.
⁵ Fear and trembling have beset me;
    horror has overwhelmed me.
⁶ I said, "Oh, that I had the wings of
      a dove!
    I would fly away and be at rest—
⁷ I would flee far away
    and stay in the desert;   *Selah*
⁸ I would hurry to my place of shelter,
    far from the tempest and storm."

⁹ Confuse the wicked, O Lord,
      confound their speech,
    for I see violence and strife in
        the city.
¹⁰ Day and night they prowl about on its
      walls;
    malice and abuse are within it.
¹¹ Destructive forces are at work in
        the city;
    threats and lies never leave its streets.

¹² If an enemy were insulting me,
    I could endure it;
  if a foe were raising himself against
      me,
    I could hide from him.
¹³ But it is you, a man like myself,
    my companion, my close friend,
¹⁴ with whom I once enjoyed sweet
        fellowship
    as we walked with the throng at
        the house of God.

¹⁵ Let death take my enemies by
      surprise;
    let them go down alive to the grave,b
  for evil finds lodging among them.

16 But I call to God,
   and the LORD saves me.
17 Evening, morning and noon
   I cry out in distress,
   and he hears my voice.
18 He ransoms me unharmed
   from the battle waged against
   me,
   even though many oppose me.
19 God, who is enthroned forever,
   will hear them and afflict them—
                                    Selah

   men who never change their ways
   and have no fear of God.

20 My companion attacks his friends;
   he violates his covenant.
21 His speech is smooth as butter,
   yet war is in his heart;
   his words are more soothing than
   oil,
   yet they are drawn swords.

22 Cast your cares on the LORD
   and he will sustain you;
   he will never let the righteous
   fall.
23 But you, O God, will bring down the
   wicked
   into the pit of corruption;
   bloodthirsty and deceitful men
   will not live out half their days.

   But as for me, I trust in you.

*a*Title: Probably a literary or musical term   *b15* Hebrew
Sheol

PROVERBS 23:4-5

4 Do not wear yourself out to get
  rich;
  have the wisdom to show
  restraint.
5 Cast but a glance at riches, and they
  are gone,
  for they will surely sprout wings
  and fly off to the sky like an
  eagle.

GOD SIGHTINGS

September 12

ISAIAH 10:1–11:16
   Woe to those who make unjust
   laws,
   to those who issue oppressive
   decrees,
2 to deprive the poor of their rights
   and withhold justice from the
   oppressed of my people,
   making widows their prey
   and robbing the fatherless.
3 What will you do on the day of
   reckoning,
   when disaster comes from afar?
   To whom will you run for help?
   Where will you leave your
   riches?
4 Nothing will remain but to cringe
   among the captives
   or fall among the slain.

   Yet for all this, his anger is not turned
   away,
   his hand is still upraised.

5 "Woe to the Assyrian, the rod of my
   anger,
   in whose hand is the club of my
   wrath!
6 I send him against a godless nation,
   I dispatch him against a people
   who anger me,
   to seize loot and snatch plunder,
   and to trample them down like
   mud in the streets.
7 But this is not what he intends,
   this is not what he has in mind;
   his purpose is to destroy,
   to put an end to many nations.
8 'Are not my commanders all kings?'
   he says.
9   'Has not Calno fared like
       Carchemish?
   Is not Hamath like Arpad,
   and Samaria like Damascus?
10 As my hand seized the kingdoms of
   the idols,

kingdoms whose images
    excelled those of Jerusalem
    and Samaria—
11 shall I not deal with Jerusalem and
    her images
    as I dealt with Samaria and her
    idols?'"

12 When the Lord has finished all his
work against Mount Zion and Jerusalem, he will say, "I will punish the king of
Assyria for the willful pride of his heart
and the haughty look in his eyes. 13 For
he says:

"'By the strength of my hand I have
    done this,
    and by my wisdom, because I have
    understanding.
I removed the boundaries of
    nations,
    I plundered their treasures;
    like a mighty one I subdued[a] their
    kings.
14 As one reaches into a nest,
    so my hand reached for the wealth
    of the nations;
as men gather abandoned eggs,
    so I gathered all the countries;
not one flapped a wing,
    or opened its mouth to chirp.'"

15 Does the ax raise itself above him
    who swings it,
    or the saw boast against him who
    uses it?
As if a rod were to wield him who
    lifts it up,
    or a club brandish him who is not
    wood!
16 Therefore, the Lord, the LORD
    Almighty,
    will send a wasting disease upon
    his sturdy warriors;
under his pomp a fire will be kindled
    like a blazing flame.
17 The Light of Israel will become a
    fire,
    their Holy One a flame;
in a single day it will burn and
    consume
    his thorns and his briers.

18 The splendor of his forests and
    fertile fields
    it will completely destroy,
    as when a sick man wastes away.
19 And the remaining trees of his
    forests will be so few
    that a child could write them down.

20 In that day the remnant of Israel,
    the survivors of the house of
    Jacob,
will no longer rely on him
    who struck them down
but will truly rely on the LORD,
    the Holy One of Israel.
21 A remnant will return,[b] a remnant of
    Jacob
    will return to the Mighty God.
22 Though your people, O Israel, be like
    the sand by the sea,
    only a remnant will return.
Destruction has been decreed,
    overwhelming and righteous.
23 The Lord, the LORD Almighty, will
    carry out
    the destruction decreed upon the
    whole land.

24 Therefore, this is what the Lord, the
LORD Almighty, says:

"O my people who live in Zion,
    do not be afraid of the Assyrians,
who beat you with a rod
    and lift up a club against you, as
    Egypt did.
25 Very soon my anger against you will
    end
    and my wrath will be directed to
    their destruction."

26 The LORD Almighty will lash them
    with a whip,
    as when he struck down Midian at
    the rock of Oreb;
and he will raise his staff over the
    waters,
    as he did in Egypt.
27 In that day their burden will be lifted
    from your shoulders,
    their yoke from your neck;
the yoke will be broken
    because you have grown so fat.[c]

28 They enter Aiath;
  they pass through Migron;
  they store supplies at Micmash.
29 They go over the pass, and say,
  "We will camp overnight at Geba."
  Ramah trembles;
  Gibeah of Saul flees.
30 Cry out, O Daughter of Gallim!
  Listen, O Laishah!
  Poor Anathoth!
31 Madmenah is in flight;
  the people of Gebim take cover.
32 This day they will halt at Nob;
  they will shake their fist
  at the mount of the Daughter of Zion,
  at the hill of Jerusalem.

33 See, the Lord, the LORD Almighty,
  will lop off the boughs with great
    power.
  The lofty trees will be felled,
    the tall ones will be brought low.
34 He will cut down the forest thickets
    with an ax;
  Lebanon will fall before the
    Mighty One.

11:1 A SHOOT will come up from the stump
    of Jesse;
  from his roots a Branch will bear
    fruit.
2 The Spirit of the LORD will rest on
    him—
  the Spirit of wisdom and of
    understanding,
  the Spirit of counsel and of power,
  the Spirit of knowledge and of the
    fear of the LORD—
3 and he will delight in the fear of the
    LORD.

He will not judge by what he sees
    with his eyes,
  or decide by what he hears with
    his ears;
4 but with righteousness he will judge
    the needy,
  with justice he will give decisions
    for the poor of the earth.
He will strike the earth with the rod
    of his mouth;
  with the breath of his lips he will
    slay the wicked.

5 Righteousness will be his belt
  and faithfulness the sash
    around his waist.

6 The wolf will live with the lamb,
  the leopard will lie down with
    the goat,
  the calf and the lion and the
    yearling[d] together;
  and a little child will lead them.
7 The cow will feed with the bear,
  their young will lie down together,
  and the lion will eat straw like the
    ox.
8 The infant will play near the hole of
    the cobra,
  and the young child put his hand
    into the viper's nest.
9 They will neither harm nor destroy
  on all my holy mountain,
for the earth will be full of the
    knowledge of the LORD
  as the waters cover the sea.

10 In that day the Root of Jesse will
stand as a banner for the peoples; the
nations will rally to him, and his place of
rest will be glorious. 11 In that day the
Lord will reach out his hand a second
time to reclaim the remnant that is left
of his people from Assyria, from Lower
Egypt, from Upper Egypt,[e] from Cush,[f]
from Elam, from Babylonia,[g] from Hamath and from the islands of the sea.

12 He will raise a banner for the nations
  and gather the exiles of Israel;
he will assemble the scattered people
    of Judah
  from the four quarters of the earth.
13 Ephraim's jealousy will vanish,
  and Judah's enemies[h] will be cut
    off;
Ephraim will not be jealous of Judah,
  nor Judah hostile toward Ephraim.
14 They will swoop down on the slopes
    of Philistia to the west;
  together they will plunder the
    people to the east.
They will lay hands on Edom and
    Moab,
  and the Ammonites will be subject
    to them.

15 The LORD will dry up
　　the gulf of the Egyptian sea;
　with a scorching wind he will sweep
　　　his hand
　　over the Euphrates River.[i]
　He will break it up into seven
　　　streams
　　so that men can cross over in
　　　sandals.
16 There will be a highway for the
　　　remnant of his people
　　that is left from Assyria,
　as there was for Israel
　　when they came up from Egypt.

a13 Or / *I subdued the mighty,*   *b21* Hebrew *shear-jashub;*
also in verse 22   *c27* Hebrew; Septuagint *broken / from
your shoulders*   *d6* Hebrew; Septuagint *lion will feed*
e11 Hebrew *from Pathros*   *f11* That is, the upper Nile region
g11 Hebrew *Shinar*   *h13* Or *hostility*   *i15* Hebrew *the River*

2 CORINTHIANS 12:11-21

I have made a fool of myself, but you
drove me to it. I ought to have been
commended by you, for I am not in the
least inferior to the "super-apostles,"
even though I am nothing. 12 The things
that mark an apostle—signs, wonders
and miracles—were done among you
with great perseverance. 13 How were
you inferior to the other churches, except that I was never a burden to you?
Forgive me this wrong!

14 Now I am ready to visit you for the
third time, and I will not be a burden to
you, because what I want is not your
possessions but you. After all, children
should not have to save up for their parents, but parents for their children. 15 So
I will very gladly spend for you everything I have and expend myself as well.
If I love you more, will you love me less?
16 Be that as it may, I have not been a burden to you. Yet, crafty fellow that I am, I
caught you by trickery! 17 Did I exploit
you through any of the men I sent you?
18 I urged Titus to go to you and I sent
our brother with him. Titus did not exploit you, did he? Did we not act in the
same spirit and follow the same course?

19 Have you been thinking all along
that we have been defending ourselves
to you? We have been speaking in the
sight of God as those in Christ; and

everything we do, dear friends, is for
your strengthening. 20 For I am afraid
that when I come I may not find you as I
want you to be, and you may not find me
as you want me to be. I fear that there
may be quarreling, jealousy, outbursts
of anger, factions, slander, gossip, arrogance and disorder. 21 I am afraid that
when I come again my God will humble
me before you, and I will be grieved over
many who have sinned earlier and have
not repented of the impurity, sexual sin
and debauchery in which they have in-
dulged.

PSALM 56:1-13

For the director of music. To ⌊the tune of⌋
"A Dove on Distant Oaks." Of David. A
miktam.[a] When the Philistines had seized
him in Gath.

1 Be merciful to me, O God, for men
　　　hotly pursue me;
　all day long they press their attack.
2 My slanderers pursue me all day long;
　　many are attacking me in their
　　　pride.

3 When I am afraid,
　I will trust in you.
4 In God, whose word I praise,
　　in God I trust; I will not be afraid.
　What can mortal man do to me?

5 All day long they twist my words;
　　they are always plotting to harm
　　　me.
6 They conspire, they lurk,
　　they watch my steps,
　　eager to take my life.

7 On no account let them escape;
　　in your anger, O God, bring down
　　　the nations.
8 Record my lament;
　　list my tears on your scroll[b]—
　　are they not in your record?

9 Then my enemies will turn back
　　when I call for help.
　By this I will know that God is for
　　　me.
10 In God, whose word I praise,
　　in the LORD, whose word I praise—

¹¹ in God I trust; I will not be afraid.
  What can man do to me?

¹² I am under vows to you, O God;
  I will present my thank offerings
    to you.
¹³ For you have delivered me^c from
    death
  and my feet from stumbling,
  that I may walk before God
    in the light of life.^d

^aTitle: Probably a literary or musical term   ^b8 Or / put my
tears in your wineskin   ^c13 Or my soul   ^d13 Or the land
of the living

PROVERBS 23:6-8

⁶ Do not eat the food of a stingy man,
  do not crave his delicacies;
⁷ for he is the kind of man
  who is always thinking about the
    cost.^a
"Eat and drink," he says to you,
  but his heart is not with you.
⁸ You will vomit up the little you have
    eaten
  and will have wasted your
    compliments.

^a7 Or for as he thinks within himself, / so he is; or for as he
puts on a feast, / so he is

☐ D A Y 2 5 6

GOD SIGHTINGS

September 13

ISAIAH 12:1–14:32

In that day you [the remnant of the
Lord's people] will say:

"I will praise you, O Lord.
  Although you were angry with me,
  your anger has turned away
    and you have comforted me.
² Surely God is my salvation;
  I will trust and not be afraid.
The Lord, the Lord, is my strength
    and my song;
  he has become my salvation."
³ With joy you will draw water
  from the wells of salvation.

⁴ In that day you will say:

"Give thanks to the Lord, call on his
    name;
  make known among the nations
    what he has done,
  and proclaim that his name is
    exalted.
⁵ Sing to the Lord, for he has done
    glorious things;
  let this be known to all the world.
⁶ Shout aloud and sing for joy, people
    of Zion,
  for great is the Holy One of Israel
    among you."

^{13:1} An oracle concerning Babylon that
Isaiah son of Amoz saw:

² Raise a banner on a bare hilltop,
  shout to them;
beckon to them
  to enter the gates of the nobles.
³ I have commanded my holy ones;
  I have summoned my warriors to
    carry out my wrath—
  those who rejoice in my triumph.

⁴ Listen, a noise on the mountains,
  like that of a great multitude!
Listen, an uproar among the
    kingdoms,
  like nations massing together!
The Lord Almighty is mustering
  an army for war.
⁵ They come from faraway lands,
  from the ends of the heavens—
the Lord and the weapons of his
    wrath—
  to destroy the whole country.

⁶ Wail, for the day of the Lord is near;
  it will come like destruction from
    the Almighty.^a
⁷ Because of this, all hands will go
    limp,
  every man's heart will melt.
⁸ Terror will seize them,
  pain and anguish will grip them;
  they will writhe like a woman in
    labor.
They will look aghast at each other,
  their faces aflame.

⁹See, the day of the LORD is coming
    —a cruel day, with wrath and fierce
        anger—
to make the land desolate
    and destroy the sinners within it.
¹⁰The stars of heaven and their
        constellations
    will not show their light.
The rising sun will be darkened
    and the moon will not give its
        light.
¹¹I will punish the world for its evil,
    the wicked for their sins.
I will put an end to the arrogance of
        the haughty
    and will humble the pride of the
        ruthless.
¹²I will make man scarcer than pure
        gold,
    more rare than the gold of Ophir.
¹³Therefore I will make the heavens
        tremble;
    and the earth will shake from its
        place
at the wrath of the LORD Almighty,
    in the day of his burning anger.

¹⁴Like a hunted gazelle,
    like sheep without a shepherd,
each will return to his own people,
    each will flee to his native land.
¹⁵Whoever is captured will be thrust
        through;
    all who are caught will fall by the
        sword.
¹⁶Their infants will be dashed to pieces
        before their eyes;
    their houses will be looted and
        their wives ravished.

¹⁷See, I will stir up against them the
        Medes,
    who do not care for silver
    and have no delight in gold.
¹⁸Their bows will strike down the
        young men;
    they will have no mercy on infants
    nor will they look with
        compassion on children.
¹⁹Babylon, the jewel of kingdoms,
    the glory of the Babylonians'ᵇ
        pride,

will be overthrown by God
    like Sodom and Gomorrah.
²⁰She will never be inhabited
    or lived in through all generations;
no Arab will pitch his tent there,
    no shepherd will rest his flocks
        there.
²¹But desert creatures will lie there,
    jackals will fill her houses;
there the owls will dwell,
    and there the wild goats will leap
        about.
²²Hyenas will howl in her strongholds,
    jackals in her luxurious palaces.
Her time is at hand,
    and her days will not be
        prolonged.

¹⁴:¹THE LORD will have compassion on
        Jacob;
    once again he will choose Israel
    and will settle them in their own
        land.
Aliens will join them
    and unite with the house of Jacob.
²Nations will take them
    and bring them to their own place.
And the house of Israel will possess
        the nations
    as menservants and maidservants
        in the LORD's land.
They will make captives of their
        captors
    and rule over their oppressors.

³On the day the LORD gives you relief
from suffering and turmoil and cruel
bondage, ⁴you will take up this taunt
against the king of Babylon:

How the oppressor has come to an
        end!
    How his furyᶜ has ended!
⁵The LORD has broken the rod of the
        wicked,
    the scepter of the rulers,
⁶which in anger struck down peoples
    with unceasing blows,
and in fury subdued nations
    with relentless aggression.
⁷All the lands are at rest and at peace;
    they break into singing.

⁸Even the pine trees and the cedars
      of Lebanon
   exult over you and say,
   "Now that you have been laid low,
      no woodsman comes to cut us
      down."

⁹The grave*ᵈ* below is all astir
      to meet you at your coming;
   it rouses the spirits of the departed
      to greet you—
   all those who were leaders in the
      world;
   it makes them rise from their
      thrones—
   all those who were kings over the
      nations.
¹⁰They will all respond,
      they will say to you,
   "You also have become weak, as we
      are;
      you have become like us."
¹¹All your pomp has been brought
      down to the grave,
   along with the noise of your harps;
   maggots are spread out beneath you
      and worms cover you.

¹²How you have fallen from heaven,
      O morning star, son of the dawn!
   You have been cast down to the
      earth,
      you who once laid low the nations!
¹³You said in your heart,
   "I will ascend to heaven;
   I will raise my throne
      above the stars of God;
   I will sit enthroned on the mount of
      assembly,
      on the utmost heights of the
      sacred mountain.*ᵉ*
¹⁴I will ascend above the tops of the
      clouds;
   I will make myself like the Most
      High."
¹⁵But you are brought down to the
      grave,
      to the depths of the pit.

¹⁶Those who see you stare at you,
   they ponder your fate:
   "Is this the man who shook the earth
      and made kingdoms tremble,

¹⁷the man who made the world a
      desert,
   who overthrew its cities
   and would not let his captives go
      home?"

¹⁸All the kings of the nations lie in
      state,
      each in his own tomb.
¹⁹But you are cast out of your tomb
      like a rejected branch;
   you are covered with the slain,
      with those pierced by the sword,
   those who descend to the stones
      of the pit.
   Like a corpse trampled underfoot,
²⁰   you will not join them in burial,
   for you have destroyed your land
      and killed your people.

   The offspring of the wicked
      will never be mentioned again.
²¹Prepare a place to slaughter his sons
      for the sins of their forefathers;
   they are not to rise to inherit the land
      and cover the earth with their
      cities.

²²"I will rise up against them,"
      declares the LORD Almighty.
   "I will cut off from Babylon her name
      and survivors,
   her offspring and descendants,"
                        declares the LORD.
²³"I will turn her into a place for owls
      and into swampland;
   I will sweep her with the broom of
      destruction,"
      declares the LORD Almighty.

²⁴The LORD Almighty has sworn,

   "Surely, as I have planned, so it will
      be,
   and as I have purposed, so it will
      stand.
²⁵I will crush the Assyrian in my land;
      on my mountains I will trample
      him down.
   His yoke will be taken from my
      people,
      and his burden removed from
      their shoulders."

²⁶This is the plan determined for the
 whole world;
 this is the hand stretched out over
 all nations.
²⁷For the LORD Almighty has purposed,
 and who can thwart him?
 His hand is stretched out, and who
 can turn it back?

²⁸This oracle came in the year King
Ahaz died:

²⁹Do not rejoice, all you Philistines,
 that the rod that struck you is
 broken;
 from the root of that snake will
 spring up a viper,
 its fruit will be a darting,
 venomous serpent.
³⁰The poorest of the poor will find
 pasture,
 and the needy will lie down in
 safety.
 But your root I will destroy by famine;
 it will slay your survivors.

³¹Wail, O gate! Howl, O city!
 Melt away, all you Philistines!
 A cloud of smoke comes from the
 north,
 and there is not a straggler in its
 ranks.
³²What answer shall be given
 to the envoys of that nation?
 "The LORD has established Zion,
 and in her his afflicted people will
 find refuge."

a6 Hebrew *Shaddai*   *b19* Or *Chaldeans'*   *c4* Dead Sea
Scrolls, Septuagint and Syriac; the meaning of the word in
the Masoretic Text is uncertain.   *d9* Hebrew *Sheol*; also in
verses 11 and 15   *e13* Or *the north*; Hebrew *Zaphon*

2 CORINTHIANS 13:1-14

This will be my third visit to you. "Every
matter must be established by the testimony of two or three witnesses."ᵃ ²I already gave you a warning when I was
with you the second time. I now repeat
it while absent: On my return I will not
spare those who sinned earlier or any of
the others, ³since you are demanding
proof that Christ is speaking through
me. He is not weak in dealing with you,
but is powerful among you. ⁴For to be

sure, he was crucified in weakness, yet
he lives by God's power. Likewise, we are
weak in him, yet by God's power we will
live with him to serve you.

⁵Examine yourselves to see whether
you are in the faith; test yourselves. Do
you not realize that Christ Jesus is in
you—unless, of course, you fail the test?
⁶And I trust that you will discover that
we have not failed the test. ⁷Now we
pray to God that you will not do anything wrong. Not that people will see
that we have stood the test but that you
will do what is right even though we may
seem to have failed. ⁸For we cannot do
anything against the truth, but only for
the truth. ⁹We are glad whenever we are
weak but you are strong; and our prayer
is for your perfection. ¹⁰This is why I
write these things when I am absent,
that when I come I may not have to be
harsh in my use of authority—the authority the Lord gave me for building
you up, not for tearing you down.

¹¹Finally, brothers, good-by. Aim for
perfection, listen to my appeal, be of
one mind, live in peace. And the God of
love and peace will be with you.

¹²Greet one another with a holy kiss.
¹³All the saints send their greetings.

¹⁴May the grace of the Lord Jesus
Christ, and the love of God, and the fellowship of the Holy Spirit be with you all.

a1 Deut. 19:15

PSALM 57:1-11

For the director of music. ⌊To the tune of⌋
"Do Not Destroy." Of David. A *miktam.ᵃ*
When he had fled from Saul into the cave.

¹Have mercy on me, O God, have
 mercy on me,
 for in you my soul takes refuge.
 I will take refuge in the shadow of
 your wings
 until the disaster has passed.

²I cry out to God Most High,
 to God, who fulfills ⌊his purpose⌋
 for me.
³He sends from heaven and saves me,
 rebuking those who hotly pursue
 me;   *Selah*

God sends his love and his
faithfulness.

[4] I am in the midst of lions;
I lie among ravenous beasts—
men whose teeth are spears and
arrows,
whose tongues are sharp swords.

[5] Be exalted, O God, above the heavens;
let your glory be over all the earth.

[6] They spread a net for my feet—
I was bowed down in distress.
They dug a pit in my path—
but they have fallen into it
themselves.   *Selah*

[7] **My heart is steadfast, O God,**
my heart is steadfast;
I will sing and make music.
[8] **Awake, my soul!**
Awake, harp and lyre!
I will awaken the dawn.

[9] I will praise you, O Lord, among the
nations;
I will sing of you among the
peoples.
[10] For great is your love, reaching to the
heavens;
your faithfulness reaches to the
skies.

[11] Be exalted, O God, above the heavens;
let your glory be over all the earth.

[a] Title: Probably a literary or musical term

PROVERBS 23:9-11

[9] **D**o not speak to a fool,
for he will scorn the wisdom of
your words.

[10] Do not move an ancient boundary
stone
or encroach on the fields of the
fatherless,
[11] for their Defender is strong;
he will take up their case against
you.

GOD SIGHTINGS

September 14

ISAIAH 15:1-18:7
An oracle concerning Moab:

Ar in Moab is ruined,
destroyed in a night!
Kir in Moab is ruined,
destroyed in a night!
[2] Dibon goes up to its temple,
to its high places to weep;
Moab wails over Nebo and
Medeba.
Every head is shaved
and every beard cut off.
[3] In the streets they wear sackcloth;
on the roofs and in the public
squares
they all wail,
prostrate with weeping.
[4] Heshbon and Elealeh cry out,
their voices are heard all the way
to Jahaz.
Therefore the armed men of Moab
cry out,
and their hearts are faint.

[5] My heart cries out over Moab;
her fugitives flee as far as Zoar,
as far as Eglath Shelishiyah.
They go up the way to Luhith,
weeping as they go;
on the road to Horonaim
they lament their destruction.
[6] The waters of Nimrim are dried up
and the grass is withered;
the vegetation is gone
and nothing green is left.
[7] So the wealth they have acquired and
stored up
they carry away over the Ravine of
the Poplars.
[8] Their outcry echoes along the border
of Moab;
their wailing reaches as far as
Eglaim,
their lamentation as far as Beer
Elim.

⁹Dimon's[a] waters are full of blood,
  but I will bring still more upon
    Dimon[a]—
a lion upon the fugitives of Moab
  and upon those who remain in the
    land.

16:1Send lambs as tribute
    to the ruler of the land,
from Sela, across the desert,
    to the mount of the Daughter of
      Zion.
²Like fluttering birds
    pushed from the nest,
so are the women of Moab
    at the fords of the Arnon.

³"Give us counsel,
    render a decision.
Make your shadow like night—
    at high noon.
Hide the fugitives,
    do not betray the refugees.
⁴Let the Moabite fugitives stay with
      you;
    be their shelter from the destroyer."

The oppressor will come to an end,
    and destruction will cease;
  the aggressor will vanish from the
      land.
⁵In love a throne will be established;
    in faithfulness a man will sit on it—
  one from the house[b] of David—
one who in judging seeks justice
    and speeds the cause of
      righteousness.

⁶We have heard of Moab's pride—
    her overweening pride and conceit,
  her pride and her insolence—
    but her boasts are empty.
⁷Therefore the Moabites wail,
    they wail together for Moab.
  Lament and grieve
    for the men[c] of Kir Haraseth.
⁸The fields of Heshbon wither,
    the vines of Sibmah also.
  The rulers of the nations
    have trampled down the choicest
      vines,
  which once reached Jazer
    and spread toward the desert.

Their shoots spread out
    and went as far as the sea.
⁹So I weep, as Jazer weeps,
    for the vines of Sibmah.
O Heshbon, O Elealeh,
    I drench you with tears!
The shouts of joy over your ripened
      fruit
    and over your harvests have been
      stilled.
¹⁰Joy and gladness are taken away from
      the orchards;
    no one sings or shouts in the
      vineyards;
  no one treads out wine at the presses,
    for I have put an end to the
      shouting.
¹¹My heart laments for Moab like a
      harp,
    my inmost being for Kir Hareseth.
¹²When Moab appears at her high
      place,
    she only wears herself out;
  when she goes to her shrine to pray,
    it is to no avail.

¹³This is the word the Lord has already spoken concerning Moab. ¹⁴But
now the Lord says: "Within three years,
as a servant bound by contract would
count them, Moab's splendor and all her
many people will be despised, and her
survivors will be very few and feeble."

17:1An oracle concerning Damascus:

"See, Damascus will no longer be a
      city
    but will become a heap of ruins.
²The cities of Aroer will be deserted
    and left to flocks, which will lie
      down,
  with no one to make them afraid.
³The fortified city will disappear from
      Ephraim,
    and royal power from Damascus;
  the remnant of Aram will be
    like the glory of the Israelites,"
        declares the Lord Almighty.

⁴"In that day the glory of Jacob will
      fade;
    the fat of his body will waste away.

⁵It will be as when a reaper gathers
　　the standing grain
　and harvests the grain with his
　　arm—
　as when a man gleans heads of grain
　　in the Valley of Rephaim.
⁶Yet some gleanings will remain,
　　as when an olive tree is beaten,
　leaving two or three olives on the
　　topmost branches,
　　four or five on the fruitful
　　　boughs,"
　declares the LORD, the God of Israel.

⁷In that day men will look to their
　　Maker
　and turn their eyes to the Holy
　　One of Israel.
⁸They will not look to the altars,
　　the work of their hands,
　and they will have no regard for the
　　Asherah poles*ᵈ*
　and the incense altars their fingers
　　have made.

⁹In that day their strong cities, which
they left because of the Israelites, will be
like places abandoned to thickets and
undergrowth. And all will be desolation.

¹⁰You have forgotten God your Savior;
　　you have not remembered the
　　Rock, your fortress.
　Therefore, though you set out the
　　finest plants
　and plant imported vines,
¹¹though on the day you set them out,
　　you make them grow,
　and on the morning when you
　　plant them, you bring them
　　to bud,
　yet the harvest will be as nothing
　　in the day of disease and incurable
　　pain.

¹²Oh, the raging of many nations—
　　they rage like the raging sea!
　Oh, the uproar of the peoples—
　　they roar like the roaring of great
　　waters!
¹³Although the peoples roar like the
　　roar of surging waters,

　when he rebukes them they flee
　　far away,
　driven before the wind like chaff on
　　the hills,
　like tumbleweed before a gale.
¹⁴In the evening, sudden terror!
　Before the morning, they are
　　gone!
　This is the portion of those who loot
　　us,
　　the lot of those who plunder us.

18:1WOE to the land of whirring wings*ᵉ*
　　along the rivers of Cush,*ᶠ*
　²which sends envoys by sea
　　in papyrus boats over the water.

　Go, swift messengers,
　to a people tall and smooth-skinned,
　　to a people feared far and wide,
　an aggressive nation of strange
　　speech,
　　whose land is divided by rivers.

³All you people of the world,
　　you who live on the earth,
　when a banner is raised on the
　　mountains,
　　you will see it,
　and when a trumpet sounds,
　　you will hear it.
⁴This is what the LORD says to me:
　"I will remain quiet and will look
　　on from my dwelling place,
　like shimmering heat in the
　　sunshine,
　　like a cloud of dew in the heat of
　　　harvest."
⁵For, before the harvest, when the
　　blossom is gone
　and the flower becomes a ripening
　　grape,
　he will cut off the shoots with
　　pruning knives,
　and cut down and take away the
　　spreading branches.
⁶They will all be left to the mountain
　　birds of prey
　and to the wild animals;
　the birds will feed on them all
　　summer,
　　the wild animals all winter.

⁷At that time gifts will be brought to the LORD Almighty

from a people tall and smooth-skinned,
from a people feared far and wide,
an aggressive nation of strange speech,
whose land is divided by rivers—

the gifts will be brought to Mount Zion, the place of the Name of the LORD Almighty.

a9 Masoretic Text; Dead Sea Scrolls, some Septuagint manuscripts and Vulgate *Dibon*   *b5* Hebrew *tent*   *c7* Or "*raisin cakes*," a wordplay   *d8* That is, symbols of the goddess Asherah   *e1* Or *of locusts*   *f1* That is, the upper Nile region

GALATIANS 1:1-24

Paul, an apostle—sent not from men nor by man, but by Jesus Christ and God the Father, who raised him from the dead— ²and all the brothers with me,

To the churches in Galatia:

³**Grace and peace to you from God our Father and the Lord Jesus Christ, ⁴who gave himself for our sins to rescue us from the present evil age, according to the will of our God and Father, ⁵to whom be glory for ever and ever. Amen.**

⁶I am astonished that you are so quickly deserting the one who called you by the grace of Christ and are turning to a different gospel— ⁷which is really no gospel at all. Evidently some people are throwing you into confusion and are trying to pervert the gospel of Christ. ⁸But even if we or an angel from heaven should preach a gospel other than the one we preached to you, let him be eternally condemned! ⁹As we have already said, so now I say again: If anybody is preaching to you a gospel other than what you accepted, let him be eternally condemned!

¹⁰Am I now trying to win the approval of men, or of God? Or am I trying to please men? If I were still trying to please men, I would not be a servant of Christ.

¹¹I want you to know, brothers, that the gospel I preached is not something that man made up. ¹²I did not receive it from any man, nor was I taught it; rather, I received it by revelation from Jesus Christ.

¹³For you have heard of my previous way of life in Judaism, how intensely I persecuted the church of God and tried to destroy it. ¹⁴I was advancing in Judaism beyond many Jews of my own age and was extremely zealous for the traditions of my fathers. ¹⁵But when God, who set me apart from birth*a* and called me by his grace, was pleased ¹⁶to reveal his Son in me so that I might preach him among the Gentiles, I did not consult any man, ¹⁷nor did I go up to Jerusalem to see those who were apostles before I was, but I went immediately into Arabia and later returned to Damascus.

¹⁸Then after three years, I went up to Jerusalem to get acquainted with Peter*b* and stayed with him fifteen days. ¹⁹I saw none of the other apostles—only James, the Lord's brother. ²⁰I assure you before God that what I am writing you is no lie. ²¹Later I went to Syria and Cilicia. ²²I was personally unknown to the churches of Judea that are in Christ. ²³They only heard the report: "The man who formerly persecuted us is now preaching the faith he once tried to destroy." ²⁴And they praised God because of me.

a15 Or *from my mother's womb*   *b18* Greek *Cephas*

PSALM 58:1-11

For the director of music. ⌊To the tune of⌋ "Do Not Destroy." Of David. A *miktam.a*

¹**D**o you rulers indeed speak justly?
    Do you judge uprightly among men?
²No, in your heart you devise injustice,
    and your hands mete out violence on the earth.
³Even from birth the wicked go astray;
    from the womb they are wayward and speak lies.
⁴Their venom is like the venom of a snake,
    like that of a cobra that has stopped its ears,

5 that will not heed the tune of the
     charmer,
        however skillful the enchanter
           may be.

6 Break the teeth in their mouths,
        O God;
        tear out, O LORD, the fangs of the
           lions!
7 Let them vanish like water that flows
        away;
        when they draw the bow, let their
           arrows be blunted.
8 Like a slug melting away as it moves
        along,
        like a stillborn child, may they not
           see the sun.

9 Before your pots can feel ⌐the heat
     of⌐ the thorns—
        whether they be green or dry—
           the wicked will be swept
              away.b
10 The righteous will be glad when they
        are avenged,
        when they bathe their feet in the
           blood of the wicked.
11 Then men will say,
        "Surely the righteous still are
           rewarded;
        surely there is a God who judges
           the earth."

a Title: Probably a literary or musical term   b9 The meaning
of the Hebrew for this verse is uncertain.

PROVERBS 23:12
12 **A**pply your heart to instruction
        and your ears to words of
           knowledge.

☐ D A Y   2 5 8

September 15

ISAIAH 19:1–21:17
An oracle concerning Egypt:

   See, the LORD rides on a swift cloud
        and is coming to Egypt.

The idols of Egypt tremble before him,
        and the hearts of the Egyptians
           melt within them.

2 "I will stir up Egyptian against
        Egyptian—
        brother will fight against brother,
        neighbor against neighbor,
        city against city,
        kingdom against kingdom.
3 The Egyptians will lose heart,
        and I will bring their plans to
           nothing;
        they will consult the idols and the
           spirits of the dead,
        the mediums and the spiritists.
4 I will hand the Egyptians over
        to the power of a cruel master,
        and a fierce king will rule over them,"
           declares the Lord, the LORD Almighty.

5 The waters of the river will dry up,
        and the riverbed will be parched
           and dry.
6 The canals will stink;
        the streams of Egypt will dwindle
           and dry up.
   The reeds and rushes will wither,
7   also the plants along the Nile,
        at the mouth of the river.
   Every sown field along the Nile
        will become parched, will blow
           away and be no more.
8 The fishermen will groan and
        lament,
        all who cast hooks into the Nile;
        those who throw nets on the water
           will pine away.
9 Those who work with combed flax
        will despair,
        the weavers of fine linen will lose
           hope.
10 The workers in cloth will be dejected,
        and all the wage earners will be
           sick at heart.

11 The officials of Zoan are nothing but
        fools;
        the wise counselors of Pharaoh
           give senseless advice.
   How can you say to Pharaoh,
        "I am one of the wise men,
        a disciple of the ancient kings"?

¹²Where are your wise men now?
    Let them show you and make
        known
    what the LORD Almighty
        has planned against Egypt.
¹³The officials of Zoan have become
        fools,
    the leaders of Memphis*a* are
        deceived;
    the cornerstones of her peoples
        have led Egypt astray.
¹⁴The LORD has poured into them
    a spirit of dizziness;
    they make Egypt stagger in all that
        she does,
    as a drunkard staggers around in
        his vomit.
¹⁵There is nothing Egypt can do—
    head or tail, palm branch or reed.

¹⁶In that day the Egyptians will be like women. They will shudder with fear at the uplifted hand that the LORD Almighty raises against them. ¹⁷And the land of Judah will bring terror to the Egyptians; everyone to whom Judah is mentioned will be terrified, because of what the LORD Almighty is planning against them.

¹⁸In that day five cities in Egypt will speak the language of Canaan and swear allegiance to the LORD Almighty. One of them will be called the City of Destruction.*b*

¹⁹In that day there will be an altar to the LORD in the heart of Egypt, and a monument to the LORD at its border. ²⁰It will be a sign and witness to the LORD Almighty in the land of Egypt. When they cry out to the LORD because of their oppressors, he will send them a savior and defender, and he will rescue them. ²¹So the LORD will make himself known to the Egyptians, and in that day they will acknowledge the LORD. They will worship with sacrifices and grain offerings; they will make vows to the LORD and keep them. ²²The LORD will strike Egypt with a plague; he will strike them and heal them. They will turn to the LORD, and he will respond to their pleas and heal them.

²³In that day there will be a highway from Egypt to Assyria. The Assyrians will go to Egypt and the Egyptians to Assyria. The Egyptians and Assyrians will worship together. ²⁴In that day Israel will be the third, along with Egypt and Assyria, a blessing on the earth. ²⁵The LORD Almighty will bless them, saying, "Blessed be Egypt my people, Assyria my handiwork, and Israel my inheritance."

20:¹IN the year that the supreme commander, sent by Sargon king of Assyria, came to Ashdod and attacked and captured it—²at that time the LORD spoke through Isaiah son of Amoz. He said to him, "Take off the sackcloth from your body and the sandals from your feet." And he did so, going around stripped and barefoot.

³Then the LORD said, "Just as my servant Isaiah has gone stripped and barefoot for three years, as a sign and portent against Egypt and Cush,*c* ⁴so the king of Assyria will lead away stripped and barefoot the Egyptian captives and Cushite exiles, young and old, with buttocks bared—to Egypt's shame. ⁵Those who trusted in Cush and boasted in Egypt will be afraid and put to shame. ⁶In that day the people who live on this coast will say, 'See what has happened to those we relied on, those we fled to for help and deliverance from the king of Assyria! How then can we escape?'"

21:¹AN oracle concerning the Desert by the Sea:

Like whirlwinds sweeping through
        the southland,
    an invader comes from the desert,
        from a land of terror.

²A dire vision has been shown to me:
    The traitor betrays, the looter
        takes loot.
Elam, attack! Media, lay siege!
    I will bring to an end all the
        groaning she caused.

³At this my body is racked with pain,
    pangs seize me, like those of a
        woman in labor;

I am staggered by what I hear,
I am bewildered by what I see.
⁴My heart falters,
fear makes me tremble;
the twilight I longed for
has become a horror to me.

⁵They set the tables,
they spread the rugs,
they eat, they drink!
Get up, you officers,
oil the shields!

⁶This is what the Lord says to me:

"Go, post a lookout
and have him report what he
sees.
⁷When he sees chariots
with teams of horses,
riders on donkeys
or riders on camels,
let him be alert,
fully alert."

⁸And the lookout*d* shouted,

"Day after day, my lord, I stand on the
watchtower;
every night I stay at my post.
⁹Look, here comes a man in a chariot
with a team of horses.
And he gives back the answer:
'Babylon has fallen, has fallen!
All the images of its gods
lie shattered on the ground!'"

¹⁰O my people, crushed on the
threshing floor,
I tell you what I have heard
from the Lord Almighty,
from the God of Israel.

¹¹An oracle concerning Dumah*e*:

Someone calls to me from Seir,
"Watchman, what is left of the
night?
Watchman, what is left of the
night?"
¹²The watchman replies,
"Morning is coming, but also the
night.
If you would ask, then ask;
and come back yet again."

¹³An oracle concerning Arabia:

You caravans of Dedanites,
who camp in the thickets of Arabia,
¹⁴   bring water for the thirsty;
you who live in Tema,
bring food for the fugitives.
¹⁵They flee from the sword,
from the drawn sword,
from the bent bow
and from the heat of battle.

¹⁶This is what the Lord says to me:
"Within one year, as a servant bound by
contract would count it, all the pomp of
Kedar will come to an end. ¹⁷The survivors of the bowmen, the warriors of Kedar, will be few." The Lord, the God of
Israel, has spoken.

a 13 Hebrew *Noph*   *b 18* Most manuscripts of the Masoretic
Text; some manuscripts of the Masoretic Text, Dead Sea
Scrolls and Vulgate *City of the Sun* (that is, Heliopolis)
c 3 That is, the upper Nile region; also in verse 5   *d 8* Dead
Sea Scrolls and Syriac; Masoretic Text *A lion*   *e 11* Dumah
means *silence* or *stillness*, a wordplay on *Edom*.

GALATIANS 2:1-16

Fourteen years later I went up again to
Jerusalem, this time with Barnabas. I
took Titus along also. ²I went in response to a revelation and set before
them the gospel that I preach among
the Gentiles. But I did this privately to
those who seemed to be leaders, for
fear that I was running or had run my
race in vain. ³Yet not even Titus, who
was with me, was compelled to be circumcised, even though he was a Greek.
⁴⌐This matter arose⌐ because some
false brothers had infiltrated our ranks
to spy on the freedom we have in Christ
Jesus and to make us slaves. ⁵We did
not give in to them for a moment, so
that the truth of the gospel might remain with you.

⁶As for those who seemed to be important—whatever they were makes no
difference to me; God does not judge by
external appearance—those men added
nothing to my message. ⁷On the contrary, they saw that I had been entrusted
with the task of preaching the gospel to
the Gentiles,*a* just as Peter had been to
the Jews.*b* ⁸For God, who was at work in

the ministry of Peter as an apostle to the Jews, was also at work in my ministry as an apostle to the Gentiles. [9]James, Peter[c] and John, those reputed to be pillars, gave me and Barnabas the right hand of fellowship when they recognized the grace given to me. They agreed that we should go to the Gentiles, and they to the Jews. [10]All they asked was that we should continue to remember the poor, the very thing I was eager to do.

[11]When Peter came to Antioch, I opposed him to his face, because he was clearly in the wrong. [12]Before certain men came from James, he used to eat with the Gentiles. But when they arrived, he began to draw back and separate himself from the Gentiles because he was afraid of those who belonged to the circumcision group. [13]The other Jews joined him in his hypocrisy, so that by their hypocrisy even Barnabas was led astray.

[14]When I saw that they were not acting in line with the truth of the gospel, I said to Peter in front of them all, "You are a Jew, yet you live like a Gentile and not like a Jew. How is it, then, that you force Gentiles to follow Jewish customs?

[15]"**We who are Jews by birth and not 'Gentile sinners'** [16]**know that a man is not justified by observing the law, but by faith in Jesus Christ.** So we, too, have put our faith in Christ Jesus that we may be justified by faith in Christ and not by observing the law, because by observing the law no one will be justified."

a7 Greek *uncircumcised*   *b7* Greek *circumcised*; also in verses 8 and 9   *c9* Greek *Cephas*; also in verses 11 and 14

PSALM 59:1-17

For the director of music. ⌞To the tune of⌟ "Do Not Destroy." Of David. A *miktam.a*
When Saul had sent men to watch David's house in order to kill him.

> [1] **D**eliver me from my enemies, O God;
>   protect me from those who rise up
>   against me.
> [2] Deliver me from evildoers
>   and save me from bloodthirsty men.

[3] See how they lie in wait for me!
    Fierce men conspire against me
    for no offense or sin of mine,
        O LORD.
[4] I have done no wrong, yet they are
        ready to attack me.
    Arise to help me; look on my
        plight!
[5] O LORD God Almighty, the God of
        Israel,
    rouse yourself to punish all the
        nations;
    show no mercy to wicked traitors.
                                    Selah

[6] They return at evening,
    snarling like dogs,
    and prowl about the city.
[7] See what they spew from their
        mouths—
    they spew out swords from their
        lips,
    and they say, "Who can hear us?"
[8] But you, O LORD, laugh at them;
    you scoff at all those nations.

[9] O my Strength, I watch for you;
    you, O God, are my fortress, [10]my
        loving God.

God will go before me
    and will let me gloat over those
        who slander me.
[11] But do not kill them, O Lord our
        shield,[b]
    or my people will forget.
In your might make them wander
        about,
    and bring them down.
[12] For the sins of their mouths,
    for the words of their lips,
    let them be caught in their pride.
For the curses and lies they utter,
[13]   consume them in wrath,
    consume them till they are no
        more.
Then it will be known to the ends of
        the earth
    that God rules over Jacob.   *Selah*

[14] They return at evening,
    snarling like dogs,
    and prowl about the city.

15 They wander about for food
    and howl if not satisfied.
16 But I will sing of your strength,
    in the morning I will sing of your
        love;
    for you are my fortress,
        my refuge in times of trouble.

17 O my Strength, I sing praise to you;
    you, O God, are my fortress, my
        loving God.

aTitle: Probably a literary or musical term   b11 Or sovereign

PROVERBS 23:13-14

13 Do not withhold discipline from a
        child;
    if you punish him with the rod, he
        will not die.
14 Punish him with the rod
    and save his soul from death.a

a14 Hebrew Sheol

□ DAY 259

GOD SIGHTINGS

September 16

ISAIAH 22:1–24:23

An oracle concerning the Valley of Vision:

    What troubles you now,
        that you have all gone up on the
            roofs,
2 O town full of commotion,
    O city of tumult and revelry?
    Your slain were not killed by the
        sword,
    nor did they die in battle.
3 All your leaders have fled together;
    they have been captured without
        using the bow.
    All you who were caught were taken
        prisoner together,
    having fled while the enemy was
        still far away.
4 Therefore I said, "Turn away from me;
    let me weep bitterly.

    Do not try to console me
        over the destruction of my
            people."

5 The Lord, the LORD Almighty, has
        a day
    of tumult and trampling and terror
        in the Valley of Vision,
    a day of battering down walls
    and of crying out to the
        mountains.
6 Elam takes up the quiver,
    with her charioteers and horses;
    Kir uncovers the shield.
7 Your choicest valleys are full of
        chariots,
    and horsemen are posted at the
        city gates;
8   the defenses of Judah are stripped
        away.

    And you looked in that day
        to the weapons in the Palace of the
            Forest;
9 you saw that the City of David
    had many breaches in its defenses;
    you stored up water
        in the Lower Pool.
10 You counted the buildings in
        Jerusalem
    and tore down houses to
        strengthen the wall.
11 You built a reservoir between the two
        walls
    for the water of the Old Pool,
    but you did not look to the One who
        made it,
    or have regard for the One who
        planned it long ago.

12 The Lord, the LORD Almighty,
    called you on that day
    to weep and to wail,
        to tear out your hair and put on
            sackcloth.
13 But see, there is joy and revelry,
    slaughtering of cattle and killing
        of sheep,
    eating of meat and drinking of
        wine!
    "Let us eat and drink," you say,
        "for tomorrow we die!"

¹⁴The LORD Almighty has revealed this in my hearing: "Till your dying day this sin will not be atoned for," says the Lord, the LORD Almighty.

¹⁵This is what the Lord, the LORD Almighty, says:

"Go, say to this steward,
  to Shebna, who is in charge of the palace:
¹⁶What are you doing here and who gave you permission
  to cut out a grave for yourself here,
hewing your grave on the height
  and chiseling your resting place in the rock?

¹⁷"Beware, the LORD is about to take firm hold of you
  and hurl you away, O you mighty man.
¹⁸He will roll you up tightly like a ball
  and throw you into a large country.
There you will die
  and there your splendid chariots will remain—
  you disgrace to your master's house!
¹⁹I will depose you from your office,
  and you will be ousted from your position.

²⁰"In that day I will summon my servant, Eliakim son of Hilkiah. ²¹I will clothe him with your robe and fasten your sash around him and hand your authority over to him. He will be a father to those who live in Jerusalem and to the house of Judah. ²²I will place on his shoulder the key to the house of David; what he opens no one can shut, and what he shuts no one can open. ²³I will drive him like a peg into a firm place; he will be a seat^a of honor for the house of his father. ²⁴All the glory of his family will hang on him: its offspring and offshoots—all its lesser vessels, from the bowls to all the jars.

²⁵"In that day," declares the LORD Almighty, "the peg driven into the firm place will give way; it will be sheared off and will fall, and the load hanging on it will be cut down." The LORD has spoken.

^{23:1}AN oracle concerning Tyre:

Wail, O ships of Tarshish!
  For Tyre is destroyed
  and left without house or harbor.
From the land of Cyprus^b
  word has come to them.

²Be silent, you people of the island
  and you merchants of Sidon,
  whom the seafarers have enriched.
³On the great waters
  came the grain of the Shihor;
the harvest of the Nile^c was the revenue of Tyre,
  and she became the marketplace of the nations.

⁴Be ashamed, O Sidon, and you,
  O fortress of the sea,
  for the sea has spoken:
"I have neither been in labor nor given birth;
  I have neither reared sons nor brought up daughters."
⁵When word comes to Egypt,
  they will be in anguish at the report from Tyre.

⁶Cross over to Tarshish;
  wail, you people of the island.
⁷Is this your city of revelry,
  the old, old city,
whose feet have taken her
  to settle in far-off lands?
⁸Who planned this against Tyre,
  the bestower of crowns,
whose merchants are princes,
  whose traders are renowned in the earth?
⁹The LORD Almighty planned it,
  to bring low the pride of all glory
  and to humble all who are renowned on the earth.

¹⁰Till^d your land as along the Nile,
  O Daughter of Tarshish,
  for you no longer have a harbor.

¹¹ The Lord has stretched out his hand
    over the sea
  and made its kingdoms tremble.
  He has given an order concerning
    Phoenicia*e*
  that her fortresses be destroyed.
¹² He said, "No more of your reveling,
    O Virgin Daughter of Sidon, now
      crushed!

  "Up, cross over to Cyprus*b*;
    even there you will find no rest."
¹³ Look at the land of the Babylonians,*f*
    this people that is now of no
      account!
  The Assyrians have made it
    a place for desert creatures;
  they raised up their siege towers,
    they stripped its fortresses bare
    and turned it into a ruin.

¹⁴ Wail, you ships of Tarshish;
    your fortress is destroyed!

¹⁵ At that time Tyre will be forgotten
for seventy years, the span of a king's
life. But at the end of these seventy
years, it will happen to Tyre as in the
song of the prostitute:

¹⁶ "Take up a harp, walk through the
      city,
    O prostitute forgotten;
  play the harp well, sing many a
      song,
    so that you will be remembered."

¹⁷ At the end of seventy years, the
Lord will deal with Tyre. She will return
to her hire as a prostitute and will ply
her trade with all the kingdoms on the
face of the earth. ¹⁸ Yet her profit and
her earnings will be set apart for the
Lord; they will not be stored up or
hoarded. Her profits will go to those
who live before the Lord, for abundant
food and fine clothes.

24:1 See, the Lord is going to lay waste
      the earth
    and devastate it;
  he will ruin its face
    and scatter its inhabitants—
² it will be the same

  for priest as for people,
    for master as for servant,
    for mistress as for maid,
    for seller as for buyer,
    for borrower as for lender,
    for debtor as for creditor.
³ The earth will be completely laid
      waste
    and totally plundered.
      The Lord has spoken this word.

⁴ The earth dries up and withers,
    the world languishes and withers,
    the exalted of the earth languish.
⁵ The earth is defiled by its people;
    they have disobeyed the laws,
  violated the statutes
    and broken the everlasting
      covenant.
⁶ Therefore a curse consumes the
      earth;
    its people must bear their guilt.
  Therefore earth's inhabitants are
      burned up,
    and very few are left.
⁷ The new wine dries up and the vine
      withers;
    all the merrymakers groan.
⁸ The gaiety of the tambourines is
      stilled,
    the noise of the revelers has
      stopped,
    the joyful harp is silent.
⁹ No longer do they drink wine with
      a song;
    the beer is bitter to its drinkers.
¹⁰ The ruined city lies desolate;
    the entrance to every house is
      barred.
¹¹ In the streets they cry out for wine;
    all joy turns to gloom,
    all gaiety is banished from the
      earth.
¹² The city is left in ruins,
    its gate is battered to pieces.
¹³ So will it be on the earth
    and among the nations,
  as when an olive tree is beaten,
    or as when gleanings are left after
      the grape harvest.

14 They raise their voices, they shout for
        joy;
    from the west they acclaim the
        LORD's majesty.
15 Therefore in the east give glory to the
        LORD;
    exalt the name of the LORD, the
        God of Israel,
    in the islands of the sea.
16 From the ends of the earth we hear
        singing:
    "Glory to the Righteous One."

    But I said, "I waste away, I waste
        away!
    Woe to me!
    The treacherous betray!
        With treachery the treacherous
            betray!"
17 Terror and pit and snare await you,
        O people of the earth.
18 Whoever flees at the sound of
        terror
    will fall into a pit;
    whoever climbs out of the pit
    will be caught in a snare.

    The floodgates of the heavens are
        opened,
    the foundations of the earth
        shake.
19 The earth is broken up,
    the earth is split asunder,
    the earth is thoroughly shaken.
20 The earth reels like a drunkard,
    it sways like a hut in the wind;
    so heavy upon it is the guilt of its
        rebellion
    that it falls—never to rise again.

21 In that day the LORD will punish
    the powers in the heavens above
    and the kings on the earth
        below.
22 They will be herded together
    like prisoners bound in a
        dungeon;
    they will be shut up in prison
    and be punished*g* after many
        days.
23 The moon will be abashed, the sun
        ashamed;
    for the LORD Almighty will reign

on Mount Zion and in Jerusalem,
    and before its elders, gloriously.

a23 Or *throne*   *b1,12* Hebrew *Kittim*   *c2,3* Masoretic Text;
one Dead Sea Scroll *Sidon, / who cross over the sea; / your
envoys* 3*are on the great waters. / The grain of the Shihor, /
the harvest of the Nile,*   *d10* Dead Sea Scrolls and some
Septuagint manuscripts; Masoretic Text *Go through*
e11 Hebrew *Canaan*   *f13* Or *Chaldeans*   *g22* Or *released*

GALATIANS 2:17–3:9

"**I**f, while we seek to be justified in Christ,
it becomes evident that we ourselves are
sinners, does that mean that Christ pro-
motes sin? Absolutely not! 18 If I rebuild
what I destroyed, I prove that I am a lawbreaker. 19 For through the law I died to
the law so that I might live for God. 20 **I
have been crucified with Christ and I
no longer live, but Christ lives in me.
The life I live in the body, I live by faith
in the Son of God, who loved me and
gave himself for me.** 21 I do not set aside
the grace of God, for if righteousness
could be gained through the law, Christ
died for nothing!"*a*

3:1 You foolish Galatians! Who has be-
witched you? Before your very eyes
Jesus Christ was clearly portrayed as
crucified. 2 I would like to learn just one
thing from you: Did you receive the
Spirit by observing the law, or by believing what you heard? 3 Are you so foolish?
After beginning with the Spirit, are you
now trying to attain your goal by human
effort? 4 Have you suffered so much for
nothing—if it really was for nothing?
5 Does God give you his Spirit and work
miracles among you because you observe the law, or because you believe
what you heard?

6 Consider Abraham: "He believed God,
and it was credited to him as righteousness."*b* 7 Understand, then, that those who
believe are children of Abraham. 8 The
Scripture foresaw that God would justify
the Gentiles by faith, and announced the
gospel in advance to Abraham: "All nations will be blessed through you."*c* 9 So
those who have faith are blessed along
with Abraham, the man of faith.

a21 Some interpreters end the quotation after verse 14.
b6 Gen. 15:6   *c8* Gen. 12:3; 18:18; 22:18

PSALM 60:1-12

For the director of music. To ⌊the tune of⌋
"The Lily of the Covenant." A *miktam*[a] of
David. For teaching. When he fought Aram
Naharaim[b] and Aram Zobah,[c] and when
Joab returned and struck down twelve
thousand Edomites in the Valley of Salt.

¹ You have rejected us, O God, and
　　burst forth upon us;
　　you have been angry—now restore
　　　us!
² You have shaken the land and torn it
　　open;
　　mend its fractures, for it is quaking.
³ You have shown your people
　　desperate times;
　　you have given us wine that makes
　　us stagger.

⁴ But for those who fear you, you have
　　raised a banner
　　to be unfurled against the bow. *Selah*

⁵ Save us and help us with your right
　　hand,
　　that those you love may be
　　delivered.
⁶ God has spoken from his sanctuary:
　　"In triumph I will parcel out
　　　Shechem
　　and measure off the Valley of
　　　Succoth.
⁷ Gilead is mine, and Manasseh is mine;
　　Ephraim is my helmet,
　　Judah my scepter.
⁸ Moab is my washbasin,
　　upon Edom I toss my sandal;
　　over Philistia I shout in triumph."

⁹ Who will bring me to the fortified
　　city?
　　Who will lead me to Edom?
¹⁰ Is it not you, O God, you who have
　　rejected us
　　and no longer go out with our
　　armies?
¹¹ Give us aid against the enemy,
　　for the help of man is worthless.
¹² With God we will gain the victory,
　　and he will trample down our
　　enemies.

[a]Title: Probably a literary or musical term　[b]Title: That is,
Arameans of Northwest Mesopotamia　[c]Title: That is,
Arameans of central Syria

PROVERBS 23:15-16

¹⁵ My son, if your heart is wise,
　　then my heart will be glad;
¹⁶ my inmost being will rejoice
　　when your lips speak what is right.

□ DAY 260

GOD SIGHTINGS

September 17

ISAIAH 25:1–28:13

O Lord, you are my God;
　　I will exalt you and praise your
　　　name,
for in perfect faithfulness
　　you have done marvelous things,
　　things planned long ago.
² You have made the city a heap of
　　rubble,
　　the fortified town a ruin,
　　the foreigners' stronghold a city no
　　　more;
　　it will never be rebuilt.
³ Therefore strong peoples will honor
　　you;
　　cities of ruthless nations will
　　revere you.
⁴ You have been a refuge for the poor,
　　a refuge for the needy in his
　　distress,
a shelter from the storm
　　and a shade from the heat.
For the breath of the ruthless
　　is like a storm driving against
　　　a wall
⁵　　and like the heat of the desert.
You silence the uproar of foreigners;
　　as heat is reduced by the shadow
　　　of a cloud,
　　so the song of the ruthless is
　　　stilled.

⁶ On this mountain the Lord Almighty
　　will prepare
　　a feast of rich food for all peoples,
a banquet of aged wine—
　　the best of meats and the finest
　　of wines.

7 On this mountain he will destroy
     the shroud that enfolds all
          peoples,
   the sheet that covers all nations;
8   he will swallow up death forever.
   The Sovereign LORD will wipe away
          the tears
     from all faces;
   he will remove the disgrace of his
          people
     from all the earth.
                    The LORD has spoken.

9 In that day they will say,

   "Surely this is our God;
     we trusted in him, and he saved
          us.
   This is the LORD, we trusted in him;
     let us rejoice and be glad in his
          salvation."

10 The hand of the LORD will rest on this
          mountain;
     but Moab will be trampled under
          him
     as straw is trampled down in the
          manure.
11 They will spread out their hands in it,
     as a swimmer spreads out his
          hands to swim.
   God will bring down their pride
     despite the cleverness*a* of their
          hands.
12 He will bring down your high
          fortified walls
     and lay them low;
   he will bring them down to the
          ground,
     to the very dust.

26:1 IN that day this song will be sung in
the land of Judah:

   We have a strong city;
     God makes salvation
        its walls and ramparts.
2 Open the gates
     that the righteous nation may
          enter,
     the nation that keeps faith.
3 You will keep in perfect peace
     him whose mind is steadfast,
     because he trusts in you.

4 Trust in the LORD forever,
     for the LORD, the LORD, is the Rock
          eternal.
5 He humbles those who dwell on high,
     he lays the lofty city low;
   he levels it to the ground
     and casts it down to the dust.
6 Feet trample it down—
     the feet of the oppressed,
     the footsteps of the poor.

7 The path of the righteous is level;
     O upright One, you make the way
          of the righteous smooth.
8 Yes, LORD, walking in the way of your
          laws,*b*
     we wait for you;
   your name and renown
     are the desire of our hearts.
9 My soul yearns for you in the night;
     in the morning my spirit longs for
          you.
   When your judgments come upon
          the earth,
     the people of the world learn
          righteousness.
10 Though grace is shown to the wicked,
     they do not learn righteousness;
   even in a land of uprightness they go
          on doing evil
     and regard not the majesty of the
          LORD.
11 O LORD, your hand is lifted high,
     but they do not see it.
   Let them see your zeal for your
          people and be put to shame;
     let the fire reserved for your
          enemies consume them.

12 LORD, you establish peace for us;
     all that we have accomplished you
          have done for us.
13 O LORD, our God, other lords besides
          you have ruled over us,
     but your name alone do we honor.
14 They are now dead, they live no
          more;
     those departed spirits do not rise.
   You punished them and brought
          them to ruin;
     you wiped out all memory of
          them.

¹⁵ You have enlarged the nation,
    O Lord;
  you have enlarged the nation.
  You have gained glory for yourself;
    you have extended all the borders
      of the land.

¹⁶ Lord, they came to you in their
    distress;
  when you disciplined them,
  they could barely whisper a
    prayer.^c
¹⁷ As a woman with child and about to
    give birth
  writhes and cries out in her pain,
  so were we in your presence,
    O Lord.
¹⁸ We were with child, we writhed in
    pain,
  but we gave birth to wind.
  We have not brought salvation to the
    earth;
  we have not given birth to people
    of the world.

¹⁹ But your dead will live;
    their bodies will rise.
  You who dwell in the dust,
    wake up and shout for joy.
  Your dew is like the dew of the
    morning;
  the earth will give birth to her dead.

²⁰ Go, my people, enter your rooms
    and shut the doors behind you;
  hide yourselves for a little while
    until his wrath has passed by.
²¹ See, the Lord is coming out of his
    dwelling
  to punish the people of the earth
    for their sins.
  The earth will disclose the blood
    shed upon her;
  she will conceal her slain no
    longer.

^{27:1} In that day,

  the Lord will punish with his sword,
    his fierce, great and powerful
      sword,
  Leviathan the gliding serpent,
  Leviathan the coiling serpent;
  he will slay the monster of the sea.

² In that day—

  "Sing about a fruitful vineyard:
³ I, the Lord, watch over it;
    I water it continually.
  I guard it day and night
    so that no one may harm it.
⁴ I am not angry.
  If only there were briers and thorns
    confronting me!
  I would march against them in
    battle;
  I would set them all on fire.
⁵ Or else let them come to me for
    refuge;
  let them make peace with me,
  yes, let them make peace
    with me."

⁶ In days to come Jacob will take root,
  Israel will bud and blossom
  and fill all the world with fruit.

⁷ Has ⌊the Lord⌋ struck her
  as he struck down those who
    struck her?
  Has she been killed
  as those were killed who killed
    her?
⁸ By warfare^d and exile you contend
    with her—
  with his fierce blast he drives her
    out,
  as on a day the east wind blows.
⁹ By this, then, will Jacob's guilt be
    atoned for,
  and this will be the full fruitage of
    the removal of his sin:
  When he makes all the altar stones
    to be like chalk stones crushed to
      pieces,
  no Asherah poles^e or incense altars
    will be left standing.
¹⁰ The fortified city stands desolate,
  an abandoned settlement,
    forsaken like the desert;
  there the calves graze,
    there they lie down;
  they strip its branches bare.
¹¹ When its twigs are dry, they are
    broken off
  and women come and make fires
    with them.

For this is a people without
    understanding;
  so their Maker has no compassion
    on them,
  and their Creator shows them no
    favor.

¹²In that day the LORD will thresh
from the flowing Euphrates*f* to the
Wadi of Egypt, and you, O Israelites, will
be gathered up one by one. ¹³And in that
day a great trumpet will sound. Those
who were perishing in Assyria and those
who were exiled in Egypt will come and
worship the LORD on the holy mountain
in Jerusalem.

²⁸:¹WOE to that wreath, the pride of
    Ephraim's drunkards,
  to the fading flower, his glorious
    beauty,
  set on the head of a fertile valley—
    to that city, the pride of those laid
    low by wine!
²See, the Lord has one who is
    powerful and strong.
  Like a hailstorm and a destructive
    wind,
  like a driving rain and a flooding
    downpour,
  he will throw it forcefully to the
    ground.
³That wreath, the pride of Ephraim's
    drunkards,
  will be trampled underfoot.
⁴That fading flower, his glorious
    beauty,
  set on the head of a fertile valley,
  will be like a fig ripe before harvest—
    as soon as someone sees it and
    takes it in his hand,
  he swallows it.

⁵In that day the LORD Almighty
  will be a glorious crown,
  a beautiful wreath
    for the remnant of his people.
⁶He will be a spirit of justice
  to him who sits in judgment,
  a source of strength
    to those who turn back the battle
    at the gate.

⁷And these also stagger from wine
  and reel from beer:
Priests and prophets stagger from
    beer
  and are befuddled with wine;
they reel from beer,
  they stagger when seeing visions,
  they stumble when rendering
    decisions.
⁸All the tables are covered with
    vomit
  and there is not a spot without
    filth.

⁹"Who is it he is trying to teach?
  To whom is he explaining his
    message?
To children weaned from their milk,
  to those just taken from the
    breast?
¹⁰For it is:
  Do and do, do and do,
  rule on rule, rule on rule*g*;
  a little here, a little there."

¹¹Very well then, with foreign lips and
    strange tongues
  God will speak to this people,
¹²to whom he said,
  "This is the resting place, let the
    weary rest";
  and, "This is the place of repose"—
  but they would not listen.
¹³So then, the word of the LORD to
    them will become:
  Do and do, do and do,
  rule on rule, rule on rule;
  a little here, a little there—
  so that they will go and fall
    backward,
  be injured and snared and
    captured.

a11 The meaning of the Hebrew for this word is uncertain.
b8 Or *judgments*   *c16* The meaning of the Hebrew for this
clause is uncertain.   *d8* See Septuagint; the meaning of the
Hebrew for this word is uncertain.   *e9* That is, symbols of
the goddess Asherah   *f12* Hebrew *River*   *g10* Hebrew / *sav
lasav sav lasav / kav lakav kav lakav* (possibly meaningless
sounds; perhaps a mimicking of the prophet's words); also in
verse 13

GALATIANS 3:10-22

All who rely on observing the law are under a curse, for it is written: "Cursed is everyone who does not continue to do

everything written in the Book of the Law."ᵃ ¹¹Clearly no one is justified before God by the law, because, "The righteous will live by faith."ᵇ ¹²The law is not based on faith; on the contrary, "The man who does these things will live by them."ᶜ ¹³Christ redeemed us from the curse of the law by becoming a curse for us, for it is written: "Cursed is everyone who is hung on a tree."ᵈ ¹⁴He redeemed us in order that the blessing given to Abraham might come to the Gentiles through Christ Jesus, so that by faith we might receive the promise of the Spirit.

¹⁵Brothers, let me take an example from everyday life. Just as no one can set aside or add to a human covenant that has been duly established, so it is in this case. ¹⁶The promises were spoken to Abraham and to his seed. The Scripture does not say "and to seeds," meaning many people, but "and to your seed,"ᵉ meaning one person, who is Christ. ¹⁷What I mean is this: The law, introduced 430 years later, does not set aside the covenant previously established by God and thus do away with the promise. ¹⁸For if the inheritance depends on the law, then it no longer depends on a promise; but God in his grace gave it to Abraham through a promise.

¹⁹What, then, was the purpose of the law? It was added because of transgressions until the Seed to whom the promise referred had come. The law was put into effect through angels by a mediator. ²⁰A mediator, however, does not represent just one party; but God is one.

²¹Is the law, therefore, opposed to the promises of God? Absolutely not! For if a law had been given that could impart life, then righteousness would certainly have come by the law. ²²**But the Scripture declares that the whole world is a prisoner of sin, so that what was promised, being given through faith in Jesus Christ, might be given to those who believe.**

ᵃ10 Deut. 27:26   ᵇ11 Hab. 2:4   ᶜ12 Lev. 18:5   ᵈ13 Deut. 21:23
ᵉ16 Gen. 12:7; 13:15; 24:7

PSALM 61:1-8

For the director of music. With stringed instruments. Of David.

¹ **H**ear my cry, O God;
　　listen to my prayer.

² From the ends of the earth I call to you,
　　I call as my heart grows faint;
　　lead me to the rock that is higher than I.
³ For you have been my refuge,
　　a strong tower against the foe.

⁴ I long to dwell in your tent forever
　　and take refuge in the shelter of your wings.　　*Selah*
⁵ For you have heard my vows, O God;
　　you have given me the heritage of those who fear your name.

⁶ Increase the days of the king's life,
　　his years for many generations.
⁷ May he be enthroned in God's presence forever;
　　appoint your love and faithfulness to protect him.

⁸ Then will I ever sing praise to your name
　　and fulfill my vows day after day.

PROVERBS 23:17-18

¹⁷ **D**o not let your heart envy sinners,
　　but always be zealous for the fear of the LORD.
¹⁸ There is surely a future hope for you,
　　and your hope will not be cut off.

□ DAY 261

GOD SIGHTINGS

September 18

ISAIAH 28:14–30:11

¹⁴ **T**herefore hear the word of the LORD, you scoffers
　　who rule this people in Jerusalem.
¹⁵ You boast, "We have entered into a covenant with death,

with the grave*a* we have made an
agreement.
When an overwhelming scourge
sweeps by,
it cannot touch us,
for we have made a lie our refuge
and falsehood*b* our hiding place."

¹⁶So this is what the Sovereign LORD
says:

"See, I lay a stone in Zion,
a tested stone,
a precious cornerstone for a sure
foundation;
the one who trusts will never be
dismayed.
¹⁷I will make justice the measuring
line
and righteousness the plumb line;
hail will sweep away your refuge, the
lie,
and water will overflow your
hiding place.
¹⁸Your covenant with death will be
annulled;
your agreement with the grave will
not stand.
When the overwhelming scourge
sweeps by,
you will be beaten down by it.
¹⁹As often as it comes it will carry you
away;
morning after morning, by day
and by night,
it will sweep through."

The understanding of this message
will bring sheer terror.
²⁰The bed is too short to stretch out on,
the blanket too narrow to wrap
around you.
²¹The LORD will rise up as he did at
Mount Perazim,
he will rouse himself as in the
Valley of Gibeon—
to do his work, his strange work,
and perform his task, his alien
task.
²²Now stop your mocking,
or your chains will become
heavier;

the Lord, the LORD Almighty, has told
me
of the destruction decreed against
the whole land.

²³Listen and hear my voice;
pay attention and hear what I say.
²⁴When a farmer plows for planting,
does he plow continually?
Does he keep on breaking up and
harrowing the soil?
²⁵When he has leveled the surface,
does he not sow caraway and
scatter cummin?
Does he not plant wheat in its place,*c*
barley in its plot,*c*
and spelt in its field?
²⁶His God instructs him
and teaches him the right way.

²⁷Caraway is not threshed with a
sledge,
nor is a cartwheel rolled over
cummin;
caraway is beaten out with a rod,
and cummin with a stick.
²⁸Grain must be ground to make
bread;
so one does not go on threshing it
forever.
Though he drives the wheels of his
threshing cart over it,
his horses do not grind it.
²⁹All this also comes from the LORD
Almighty,
wonderful in counsel and
magnificent in wisdom.

²⁹:¹WOE to you, Ariel, Ariel,
the city where David settled!
Add year to year
and let your cycle of festivals
go on.
²Yet I will besiege Ariel;
she will mourn and lament,
she will be to me like an altar
hearth.*d*
³I will encamp against you all
around;
I will encircle you with towers
and set up my siege works against
you.

⁴Brought low, you will speak from the
    ground;
  your speech will mumble out of
      the dust.
  Your voice will come ghostlike from
      the earth;
  out of the dust your speech will
      whisper.

⁵But your many enemies will become
    like fine dust,
  the ruthless hordes like blown
      chaff.
  Suddenly, in an instant,
⁶   the LORD Almighty will come
  with thunder and earthquake and
      great noise,
  with windstorm and tempest and
      flames of a devouring fire.
⁷Then the hordes of all the nations
    that fight against Ariel,
  that attack her and her fortress
      and besiege her,
  will be as it is with a dream,
  with a vision in the night—
⁸as when a hungry man dreams that
    he is eating,
  but he awakens, and his hunger
      remains;
  as when a thirsty man dreams that he
      is drinking,
  but he awakens faint, with his
      thirst unquenched.
  So will it be with the hordes of all the
      nations
  that fight against Mount Zion.

⁹Be stunned and amazed,
  blind yourselves and be sightless;
  be drunk, but not from wine,
  stagger, but not from beer.
¹⁰The LORD has brought over you a
    deep sleep:
  He has sealed your eyes (the
      prophets);
  he has covered your heads (the
      seers).

¹¹For you this whole vision is nothing
but words sealed in a scroll. And if you
give the scroll to someone who can
read, and say to him, "Read this, please,"
he will answer, "I can't; it is sealed." ¹²Or
if you give the scroll to someone who
cannot read, and say, "Read this, please,"
he will answer, "I don't know how to
read."

¹³The Lord says:

"These people come near to me with
    their mouth
  and honor me with their lips,
  but their hearts are far from me.
  Their worship of me
  is made up only of rules taught by
      men.ᵉ
¹⁴Therefore once more I will astound
    these people
  with wonder upon wonder;
  the wisdom of the wise will perish,
  the intelligence of the intelligent
      will vanish."
¹⁵Woe to those who go to great depths
    to hide their plans from the LORD,
  who do their work in darkness and
      think,
  "Who sees us? Who will know?"
¹⁶You turn things upside down,
  as if the potter were thought to be
      like the clay!
  Shall what is formed say to him who
      formed it,
  "He did not make me"?
  Can the pot say of the potter,
  "He knows nothing"?

¹⁷In a very short time, will not
    Lebanon be turned into a
      fertile field
  and the fertile field seem like a
      forest?
¹⁸In that day the deaf will hear the
    words of the scroll,
  and out of gloom and darkness
  the eyes of the blind will see.
¹⁹Once more the humble will rejoice in
    the LORD;
  the needy will rejoice in the Holy
      One of Israel.
²⁰The ruthless will vanish,
  the mockers will disappear,
  and all who have an eye for evil
      will be cut down—
²¹those who with a word make a man
    out to be guilty,

who ensnare the defender in court
and with false testimony deprive
the innocent of justice.

22 Therefore this is what the LORD,
who redeemed Abraham, says to the
house of Jacob:

"No longer will Jacob be ashamed;
no longer will their faces grow
pale.
23 When they see among them their
children,
the work of my hands,
they will keep my name holy;
they will acknowledge the holiness
of the Holy One of Jacob,
and will stand in awe of the God of
Israel.
24 Those who are wayward in spirit will
gain understanding;
those who complain will accept
instruction."

30:1 "WOE to the obstinate children,"
declares the LORD,
"to those who carry out plans that are
not mine,
forming an alliance, but not by my
Spirit,
heaping sin upon sin;
2 who go down to Egypt
without consulting me;
who look for help to Pharaoh's
protection,
to Egypt's shade for refuge.
3 But Pharaoh's protection will be to
your shame,
Egypt's shade will bring you
disgrace.
4 Though they have officials in Zoan
and their envoys have arrived in
Hanes,
5 everyone will be put to shame
because of a people useless to
them,
who bring neither help nor
advantage,
but only shame and disgrace."

6 An oracle concerning the animals of
the Negev:

Through a land of hardship and
distress,
of lions and lionesses,
of adders and darting snakes,
the envoys carry their riches on
donkeys' backs,
their treasures on the humps of
camels,
to that unprofitable nation,
7   to Egypt, whose help is utterly
useless.
Therefore I call her
Rahab the Do-Nothing.

8 Go now, write it on a tablet for them,
inscribe it on a scroll,
that for the days to come
it may be an everlasting witness.
9 These are rebellious people,
deceitful children,
children unwilling to listen to the
LORD's instruction.
10 They say to the seers,
"See no more visions!"
and to the prophets,
"Give us no more visions of what is
right!
Tell us pleasant things,
prophesy illusions.
11 Leave this way,
get off this path,
and stop confronting us
with the Holy One of Israel!"

a 15 Hebrew Sheol; also in verse 18   b 15 Or false gods
c 25 The meaning of the Hebrew for this word is uncertain.
d 2 The Hebrew for altar hearth sounds like the Hebrew
for Ariel.   e 13 Hebrew; Septuagint They worship me in
vain; / their teachings are but rules taught by men

GALATIANS 3:23–4:31

Before this faith came, we were held
prisoners by the law, locked up until
faith should be revealed. 24 So the law
was put in charge to lead us to Christ[a]
that we might be justified by faith.
25 Now that faith has come, we are no
longer under the supervision of the law.
26 You are all sons of God through
faith in Christ Jesus, 27 for all of you
who were baptized into Christ have
clothed yourselves with Christ.
28 There is neither Jew nor Greek, slave
nor free, male nor female, for you are

all one in Christ Jesus. [29]**If you belong to Christ, then you are Abraham's seed, and heirs according to the promise.**

[4:1]WHAT I am saying is that as long as the heir is a child, he is no different from a slave, although he owns the whole estate. [2]He is subject to guardians and trustees until the time set by his father. [3]So also, when we were children, we were in slavery under the basic principles of the world. [4]But when the time had fully come, God sent his Son, born of a woman, born under law, [5]to redeem those under law, that we might receive the full rights of sons. [6]Because you are sons, God sent the Spirit of his Son into our hearts, the Spirit who calls out, "Abba,[b] Father." [7]So you are no longer a slave, but a son; and since you are a son, God has made you also an heir.

[8]Formerly, when you did not know God, you were slaves to those who by nature are not gods. [9]But now that you know God—or rather are known by God—how is it that you are turning back to those weak and miserable principles? Do you wish to be enslaved by them all over again? [10]You are observing special days and months and seasons and years! [11]I fear for you, that somehow I have wasted my efforts on you.

[12]I plead with you, brothers, become like me, for I became like you. You have done me no wrong. [13]As you know, it was because of an illness that I first preached the gospel to you. [14]Even though my illness was a trial to you, you did not treat me with contempt or scorn. Instead, you welcomed me as if I were an angel of God, as if I were Christ Jesus himself. [15]What has happened to all your joy? I can testify that, if you could have done so, you would have torn out your eyes and given them to me. [16]Have I now become your enemy by telling you the truth?

[17]Those people are zealous to win you over, but for no good. What they want is to alienate you ⌊from us⌋, so that you may be zealous for them. [18]It is fine to be zealous, provided the purpose is good, and to be so always and not just when I am with you. [19]My dear children, for whom I am again in the pains of childbirth until Christ is formed in you, [20]how I wish I could be with you now and change my tone, because I am perplexed about you!

[21]Tell me, you who want to be under the law, are you not aware of what the law says? [22]For it is written that Abraham had two sons, one by the slave woman and the other by the free woman. [23]His son by the slave woman was born in the ordinary way; but his son by the free woman was born as the result of a promise.

[24]These things may be taken figuratively, for the women represent two covenants. One covenant is from Mount Sinai and bears children who are to be slaves: This is Hagar. [25]Now Hagar stands for Mount Sinai in Arabia and corresponds to the present city of Jerusalem, because she is in slavery with her children. [26]But the Jerusalem that is above is free, and she is our mother. [27]For it is written:

"Be glad, O barren woman,
    who bears no children;
break forth and cry aloud,
    you who have no labor pains;
because more are the children of the desolate woman
    than of her who has a husband."[c]

[28]Now you, brothers, like Isaac, are children of promise. [29]At that time the son born in the ordinary way persecuted the son born by the power of the Spirit. It is the same now. [30]But what does the Scripture say? "Get rid of the slave woman and her son, for the slave woman's son will never share in the inheritance with the free woman's son."[d] [31]Therefore, brothers, we are not children of the slave woman, but of the free woman.

a24 Or *charge until Christ came*   *b6* Aramaic for *Father*
c27 Isaiah 54:1   *d30* Gen. 21:10

PSALM 62:1-12
For the director of music. For Jeduthun. A psalm of David.

[1]**M**y soul finds rest in God alone;
    my salvation comes from him.

2 He alone is my rock and my
   salvation;
   he is my fortress, I will never be
   shaken.

3 How long will you assault a man?
   Would all of you throw him down—
   this leaning wall, this tottering
   fence?
4 They fully intend to topple him
   from his lofty place;
   they take delight in lies.
 With their mouths they bless,
   but in their hearts they curse.   *Selah*

5 Find rest, O my soul, in God alone;
   my hope comes from him.
6 He alone is my rock and my
   salvation;
   he is my fortress, I will not be
   shaken.
7 My salvation and my honor depend
   on God*a*;
   he is my mighty rock, my refuge.
8 Trust in him at all times, O people;
   pour out your hearts to him,
   for God is our refuge.   *Selah*

9 Lowborn men are but a breath,
   the highborn are but a lie;
 if weighed on a balance, they are
   nothing;
   together they are only a breath.
10 Do not trust in extortion
   or take pride in stolen goods;
 though your riches increase,
   do not set your heart on them.

11 One thing God has spoken,
   two things have I heard:
 that you, O God, are strong,
12   and that you, O Lord, are loving.
 Surely you will reward each person
   according to what he has done.

a 7 Or / God Most High is my salvation and my honor

PROVERBS 23:19-21
19 Listen, my son, and be wise,
   and keep your heart on the right
   path.
20 Do not join those who drink too
   much wine
   or gorge themselves on meat,

21 for drunkards and gluttons become
   poor,
   and drowsiness clothes them in
   rags.

□ DAY 262

GOD SIGHTINGS

September 19

ISAIAH 30:12–33:12
Therefore, this is what the Holy One of
Israel says:

 "Because you [those who rebel
   against the LORD] have
   rejected this message,
   relied on oppression
   and depended on deceit,
13 this sin will become for you
   like a high wall, cracked and
   bulging,
   that collapses suddenly, in an
   instant.
14 It will break in pieces like pottery,
   shattered so mercilessly
 that among its pieces not a fragment
   will be found
   for taking coals from a hearth
   or scooping water out of a
   cistern."

15 This is what the Sovereign LORD, the
Holy One of Israel, says:

 "In repentance and rest is your
   salvation,
   in quietness and trust is your
   strength,
   but you would have none of it.
16 You said, 'No, we will flee on horses.'
   Therefore you will flee!
 You said, 'We will ride off on swift
   horses.'
   Therefore your pursuers will be
   swift!
17 A thousand will flee
   at the threat of one;
 at the threat of five
   you will all flee away,

till you are left
    like a flagstaff on a mountaintop,
    like a banner on a hill."

18 Yet the LORD longs to be gracious to
    you;
    he rises to show you compassion.
For the LORD is a God of justice.
    Blessed are all who wait for him!

19 O people of Zion, who live in Jerusalem, you will weep no more. How gracious he will be when you cry for help! As soon as he hears, he will answer you. 20 Although the Lord gives you the bread of adversity and the water of affliction, your teachers will be hidden no more; with your own eyes you will see them. 21 Whether you turn to the right or to the left, your ears will hear a voice behind you, saying, "This is the way; walk in it." 22 Then you will defile your idols overlaid with silver and your images covered with gold; you will throw them away like a menstrual cloth and say to them, "Away with you!"

23 He will also send you rain for the seed you sow in the ground, and the food that comes from the land will be rich and plentiful. In that day your cattle will graze in broad meadows. 24 The oxen and donkeys that work the soil will eat fodder and mash, spread out with fork and shovel. 25 In the day of great slaughter, when the towers fall, streams of water will flow on every high mountain and every lofty hill. 26 The moon will shine like the sun, and the sunlight will be seven times brighter, like the light of seven full days, when the LORD binds up the bruises of his people and heals the wounds he inflicted.

27 See, the Name of the LORD comes
    from afar,
    with burning anger and dense
        clouds of smoke;
his lips are full of wrath,
    and his tongue is a consuming
        fire.
28 His breath is like a rushing torrent,
    rising up to the neck.

He shakes the nations in the sieve of
    destruction;
    he places in the jaws of the
        peoples
    a bit that leads them astray.
29 And you will sing
    as on the night you celebrate a
        holy festival;
your hearts will rejoice
    as when people go up with flutes
to the mountain of the LORD,
    to the Rock of Israel.
30 The LORD will cause men to hear his
        majestic voice
    and will make them see his arm
        coming down
with raging anger and consuming
    fire,
    with cloudburst, thunderstorm
        and hail.
31 The voice of the LORD will shatter
        Assyria;
    with his scepter he will strike
        them down.
32 Every stroke the LORD lays on them
    with his punishing rod
will be to the music of tambourines
        and harps,
    as he fights them in battle with the
        blows of his arm.
33 Topheth has long been prepared;
    it has been made ready for the
        king.
Its fire pit has been made deep and
        wide,
    with an abundance of fire and
        wood;
the breath of the LORD,
    like a stream of burning sulfur,
    sets it ablaze.

31:1 WOE to those who go down to Egypt
        for help,
    who rely on horses,
who trust in the multitude of their
        chariots
    and in the great strength of their
        horsemen,
but do not look to the Holy One of
        Israel,
    or seek help from the LORD.

2 Yet he too is wise and can bring
    disaster;
  he does not take back his words.
He will rise up against the house of
    the wicked,
  against those who help evildoers.
3 But the Egyptians are men and not
    God;
  their horses are flesh and not spirit.
When the LORD stretches out his hand,
  he who helps will stumble,
  he who is helped will fall;
  both will perish together.

4 This is what the LORD says to me:

"As a lion growls,
  a great lion over his prey—
and though a whole band of shepherds
  is called together against him,
he is not frightened by their shouts
  or disturbed by their clamor—
so the LORD Almighty will come down
  to do battle on Mount Zion and on
    its heights.
5 Like birds hovering overhead,
  the LORD Almighty will shield
    Jerusalem;
he will shield it and deliver it,
  he will 'pass over' it and will
    rescue it."

6 Return to him you have so greatly revolted against, O Israelites. 7 For in that
day every one of you will reject the idols
of silver and gold your sinful hands have
made.

8 "Assyria will fall by a sword that is not
    of man;
  a sword, not of mortals, will
    devour them.
They will flee before the sword
  and their young men will be put to
    forced labor.
9 Their stronghold will fall because of
    terror;
  at sight of the battle standard
    their commanders will
    panic,"
declares the LORD,
  whose fire is in Zion,
  whose furnace is in Jerusalem.

32:1 SEE, a king will reign in righteousness
  and rulers will rule with justice.
2 Each man will be like a shelter from
    the wind
  and a refuge from the storm,
like streams of water in the desert
  and the shadow of a great rock in a
    thirsty land.

3 Then the eyes of those who see will
    no longer be closed,
  and the ears of those who hear will
    listen.
4 The mind of the rash will know and
    understand,
  and the stammering tongue will be
    fluent and clear.
5 No longer will the fool be called
    noble
  nor the scoundrel be highly
    respected.
6 For the fool speaks folly,
  his mind is busy with evil:
He practices ungodliness
  and spreads error concerning the
    LORD;
the hungry he leaves empty
  and from the thirsty he withholds
    water.
7 The scoundrel's methods are wicked,
  he makes up evil schemes
to destroy the poor with lies,
  even when the plea of the needy
    is just.
8 But the noble man makes noble plans,
  and by noble deeds he stands.

9 You women who are so complacent,
  rise up and listen to me;
you daughters who feel secure,
  hear what I have to say!
10 In little more than a year
  you who feel secure will tremble;
the grape harvest will fail,
  and the harvest of fruit will not
    come.
11 Tremble, you complacent women;
  shudder, you daughters who feel
    secure!
Strip off your clothes,
  put sackcloth around your waists.

¹²Beat your breasts for the pleasant
      fields,
   for the fruitful vines
¹³and for the land of my people,
      a land overgrown with thorns and
         briers—
   yes, mourn for all houses of
         merriment
   and for this city of revelry.
¹⁴The fortress will be abandoned,
      the noisy city deserted;
   citadel and watchtower will become
         a wasteland forever,
      the delight of donkeys, a pasture
         for flocks,
¹⁵till the Spirit is poured upon us from
      on high,
   and the desert becomes a fertile
         field,
   and the fertile field seems like a
         forest.
¹⁶Justice will dwell in the desert
      and righteousness live in the
         fertile field.
¹⁷The fruit of righteousness will be
      peace;
   the effect of righteousness will be
      quietness and confidence
         forever.
¹⁸My people will live in peaceful
      dwelling places,
   in secure homes,
   in undisturbed places of rest.
¹⁹Though hail flattens the forest
      and the city is leveled completely,
²⁰how blessed you will be,
      sowing your seed by every stream,
      and letting your cattle and
         donkeys range free.

³³:¹Woe to you, O destroyer,
      you who have not been
         destroyed!
   Woe to you, O traitor,
      you who have not been betrayed!
   When you stop destroying,
      you will be destroyed;
   when you stop betraying,
      you will be betrayed.

²O Lord, be gracious to us;
      we long for you.

Be our strength every morning,
      our salvation in time of distress.
³At the thunder of your voice, the
      peoples flee;
   when you rise up, the nations
         scatter.
⁴Your plunder, O nations, is harvested
      as by young locusts;
   like a swarm of locusts men
         pounce on it.

⁵The Lord is exalted, for he dwells on
      high;
   he will fill Zion with justice and
         righteousness.
⁶He will be the sure foundation for
      your times,
   a rich store of salvation and
         wisdom and knowledge;
   the fear of the Lord is the key to
         this treasure.ᵃ

⁷Look, their brave men cry aloud in
      the streets;
   the envoys of peace weep bitterly.
⁸The highways are deserted,
      no travelers are on the roads.
   The treaty is broken,
      its witnessesᵇ are despised,
      no one is respected.
⁹The land mournsᶜ and wastes away,
      Lebanon is ashamed and withers;
   Sharon is like the Arabah,
      and Bashan and Carmel drop their
         leaves.

¹⁰"Now will I arise," says the Lord.
   "Now will I be exalted;
      now will I be lifted up.
¹¹You conceive chaff,
      you give birth to straw;
   your breath is a fire that consumes
         you.
¹²The peoples will be burned as if to
      lime;
   like cut thornbushes they will be
         set ablaze."

ᵃ6 Or is a treasure from him   ᵇ8 Dead Sea Scrolls; Masoretic
Text / the cities   ᶜ9 Or dries up

GALATIANS 5:1-12
▌t is for freedom that Christ has set us
free. Stand firm, then, and do not let

yourselves be burdened again by a yoke of slavery.

2Mark my words! I, Paul, tell you that if you let yourselves be circumcised, Christ will be of no value to you at all. 3Again I declare to every man who lets himself be circumcised that he is obligated to obey the whole law. 4You who are trying to be justified by law have been alienated from Christ; you have fallen away from grace. 5**But by faith we eagerly await through the Spirit the righteousness for which we hope.** 6**For in Christ Jesus neither circumcision nor uncircumcision has any value. The only thing that counts is faith expressing itself through love.**

7You were running a good race. Who cut in on you and kept you from obeying the truth? 8That kind of persuasion does not come from the one who calls you. 9"A little yeast works through the whole batch of dough." 10I am confident in the Lord that you will take no other view. The one who is throwing you into confusion will pay the penalty, whoever he may be. 11Brothers, if I am still preaching circumcision, why am I still being persecuted? In that case the offense of the cross has been abolished. 12As for those agitators, I wish they would go the whole way and emasculate themselves!

PSALM 63:1-11

A psalm of David. When he was in the Desert of Judah.

1 ⦿ God, you are my God,
    earnestly I seek you;
my soul thirsts for you,
    my body longs for you,
in a dry and weary land
    where there is no water.

2I have seen you in the sanctuary
    and beheld your power and your
        glory.
3Because your love is better than life,
    my lips will glorify you.
4I will praise you as long as I live,
    and in your name I will lift up my
        hands.

5My soul will be satisfied as with the
        richest of foods;
with singing lips my mouth will
        praise you.

6On my bed I remember you;
    I think of you through the watches
        of the night.
7Because you are my help,
    I sing in the shadow of your wings.
8My soul clings to you;
    your right hand upholds me.

9They who seek my life will be
        destroyed;
    they will go down to the depths of
        the earth.
10They will be given over to the sword
    and become food for jackals.

11But the king will rejoice in God;
    all who swear by God's name will
        praise him,
    while the mouths of liars will be
        silenced.

PROVERBS 23:22

22**L**isten to your father, who gave you
        life,
    and do not despise your mother
        when she is old.

□ D A Y   2 6 3

GOD SIGHTINGS

September 20

ISAIAH 33:13–36:22

13**Y**ou who are far away, hear what I
        [the LORD] have done;
    you who are near, acknowledge my
        power!
14The sinners in Zion are terrified;
    trembling grips the godless:
"Who of us can dwell with the
        consuming fire?
    Who of us can dwell with
        everlasting burning?"
15He who walks righteously
    and speaks what is right,

who rejects gain from extortion
and keeps his hand from
accepting bribes,
who stops his ears against plots of
murder
and shuts his eyes against
contemplating evil—
¹⁶this is the man who will dwell on the
heights,
whose refuge will be the mountain
fortress.
His bread will be supplied,
and water will not fail him.

¹⁷Your eyes will see the king in his
beauty
and view a land that stretches afar.
¹⁸In your thoughts you will ponder the
former terror:
"Where is that chief officer?
Where is the one who took the
revenue?
Where is the officer in charge of
the towers?"
¹⁹You will see those arrogant people no
more,
those people of an obscure
speech,
with their strange,
incomprehensible tongue.

²⁰Look upon Zion, the city of our
festivals;
your eyes will see Jerusalem,
a peaceful abode, a tent that will
not be moved;
its stakes will never be pulled up,
nor any of its ropes broken.
²¹There the LORD will be our Mighty
One.
It will be like a place of broad
rivers and streams.
No galley with oars will ride them,
no mighty ship will sail them.
²²For the LORD is our judge,
the LORD is our lawgiver,
the LORD is our king;
it is he who will save us.

²³Your rigging hangs loose:
The mast is not held secure,
the sail is not spread.

Then an abundance of spoils will be
divided
and even the lame will carry off
plunder.
²⁴No one living in Zion will say, "I am
ill";
and the sins of those who dwell
there will be forgiven.

^{34:1}COME near, you nations, and listen;
pay attention, you peoples!
Let the earth hear, and all that is in it,
the world, and all that comes out
of it!
²The LORD is angry with all nations;
his wrath is upon all their armies.
He will totally destroy^a them,
he will give them over to
slaughter.
³Their slain will be thrown out,
their dead bodies will send up a
stench;
the mountains will be soaked with
their blood.
⁴All the stars of the heavens will be
dissolved
and the sky rolled up like a scroll;
all the starry host will fall
like withered leaves from the vine,
like shriveled figs from the fig
tree.

⁵My sword has drunk its fill in the
heavens;
see, it descends in judgment on
Edom,
the people I have totally
destroyed.
⁶The sword of the LORD is bathed in
blood,
it is covered with fat—
the blood of lambs and goats,
fat from the kidneys of rams.
For the LORD has a sacrifice in Bozrah
and a great slaughter in Edom.
⁷And the wild oxen will fall with
them,
the bull calves and the great bulls.
Their land will be drenched with
blood,
and the dust will be soaked with
fat.

8 For the LORD has a day of vengeance,
a year of retribution, to uphold
Zion's cause.
9 Edom's streams will be turned into
pitch,
her dust into burning sulfur;
her land will become blazing pitch!
10 It will not be quenched night and day;
its smoke will rise forever.
From generation to generation it will
lie desolate;
no one will ever pass through it
again.
11 The desert owlᵇ and screech owlᵇ
will possess it;
the great owlᵇ and the raven will
nest there.
God will stretch out over Edom
the measuring line of chaos
and the plumb line of desolation.
12 Her nobles will have nothing there to
be called a kingdom,
all her princes will vanish away.
13 Thorns will overrun her citadels,
nettles and brambles her
strongholds.
She will become a haunt for jackals,
a home for owls.
14 Desert creatures will meet with
hyenas,
and wild goats will bleat to each
other;
there the night creatures will also
repose
and find for themselves places of
rest.
15 The owl will nest there and lay eggs,
she will hatch them, and care for
her young under the shadow
of her wings;
there also the falcons will gather,
each with its mate.

16 Look in the scroll of the LORD and
read:

None of these will be missing,
not one will lack her mate.
For it is his mouth that has given the
order,
and his Spirit will gather them
together.

17 He allots their portions;
his hand distributes them by
measure.
They will possess it forever
and dwell there from generation to
generation.

35:1 THE desert and the parched land will
be glad;
the wilderness will rejoice and
blossom.
Like the crocus, 2 it will burst into
bloom;
it will rejoice greatly and shout for
joy.
The glory of Lebanon will be given
to it,
the splendor of Carmel and
Sharon;
they will see the glory of the LORD,
the splendor of our God.

3 Strengthen the feeble hands,
steady the knees that give way;
4 say to those with fearful hearts,
"Be strong, do not fear;
your God will come,
he will come with vengeance;
with divine retribution
he will come to save you."

5 Then will the eyes of the blind be
opened
and the ears of the deaf unstopped.
6 Then will the lame leap like a deer,
and the mute tongue shout for joy.
Water will gush forth in the
wilderness
and streams in the desert.
7 The burning sand will become a
pool,
the thirsty ground bubbling springs.
In the haunts where jackals once lay,
grass and reeds and papyrus will
grow.

8 And a highway will be there;
it will be called the Way of Holiness.
The unclean will not journey on it;
it will be for those who walk in
that Way;
wicked fools will not go about
on it.ᶜ

⁹No lion will be there,
  nor will any ferocious beast get up
    on it;
  they will not be found there.
But only the redeemed will walk
    there,
¹⁰   and the ransomed of the LORD will
    return.
They will enter Zion with singing;
  everlasting joy will crown their
    heads.
Gladness and joy will overtake them,
  and sorrow and sighing will flee
    away.

³⁶:¹In the fourteenth year of King Hezekiah's reign, Sennacherib king of Assyria attacked all the fortified cities of
Judah and captured them. ²Then the
king of Assyria sent his field commander with a large army from Lachish
to King Hezekiah at Jerusalem. When
the commander stopped at the aqueduct of the Upper Pool, on the road to
the Washerman's Field, ³Eliakim son of
Hilkiah the palace administrator,
Shebna the secretary, and Joah son of
Asaph the recorder went out to him.

⁴The field commander said to them,
"Tell Hezekiah,

"'This is what the great king, the
king of Assyria, says: On what are
you basing this confidence of
yours? ⁵You say you have strategy
and military strength—but you
speak only empty words. On whom
are you depending, that you rebel
against me? ⁶Look now, you are depending on Egypt, that splintered
reed of a staff, which pierces a
man's hand and wounds him if he
leans on it! Such is Pharaoh king of
Egypt to all who depend on him.
⁷And if you say to me, "We are depending on the LORD our God"—
isn't he the one whose high places
and altars Hezekiah removed, saying to Judah and Jerusalem, "You
must worship before this altar"?

⁸"'Come now, make a bargain
with my master, the king of Assyria: I

will give you two thousand horses—
if you can put riders on them! ⁹How
then can you repulse one officer of
the least of my master's officials,
even though you are depending on
Egypt for chariots and horsemen?
¹⁰Furthermore, have I come to attack and destroy this land without
the LORD? The LORD himself told me
to march against this country and
destroy it.'"

¹¹Then Eliakim, Shebna and Joah said
to the field commander, "Please speak
to your servants in Aramaic, since we
understand it. Don't speak to us in Hebrew in the hearing of the people on the
wall."

¹²But the commander replied, "Was
it only to your master and you that my
master sent me to say these things, and
not to the men sitting on the wall—who,
like you, will have to eat their own filth
and drink their own urine?"

¹³Then the commander stood and
called out in Hebrew, "Hear the words of
the great king, the king of Assyria!
¹⁴This is what the king says: Do not let
Hezekiah deceive you. He cannot deliver you! ¹⁵Do not let Hezekiah persuade you to trust in the LORD when he
says, 'The LORD will surely deliver us;
this city will not be given into the hand
of the king of Assyria.'

¹⁶"Do not listen to Hezekiah. This is
what the king of Assyria says: Make
peace with me and come out to me.
Then every one of you will eat from his
own vine and fig tree and drink water
from his own cistern, ¹⁷until I come and
take you to a land like your own—a land
of grain and new wine, a land of bread
and vineyards.

¹⁸"Do not let Hezekiah mislead you
when he says, 'The LORD will deliver us.'
Has the god of any nation ever delivered
his land from the hand of the king of Assyria? ¹⁹Where are the gods of Hamath
and Arpad? Where are the gods of
Sepharvaim? Have they rescued Samaria from my hand? ²⁰Who of all the
gods of these countries has been able to

save his land from me? How then can the LORD deliver Jerusalem from my hand?"

²¹But the people remained silent and said nothing in reply, because the king had commanded, "Do not answer him."

²²Then Eliakim son of Hilkiah the palace administrator, Shebna the secretary, and Joah son of Asaph the recorder went to Hezekiah, with their clothes torn, and told him what the field commander had said.

a2 The Hebrew term refers to the irrevocable giving over of things or persons to the LORD, often by totally destroying them; also in verse 5. *b11* The precise identification of these birds is uncertain. *c8* Or / *the simple will not stray from it*

GALATIANS 5:13-26

You, my brothers, were called to be free. But do not use your freedom to indulge the sinful nature*a*; rather, serve one another in love. ¹⁴The entire law is summed up in a single command: "Love your neighbor as yourself."*b* ¹⁵If you keep on biting and devouring each other, watch out or you will be destroyed by each other.

¹⁶So I say, live by the Spirit, and you will not gratify the desires of the sinful nature. ¹⁷For the sinful nature desires what is contrary to the Spirit, and the Spirit what is contrary to the sinful nature. They are in conflict with each other, so that you do not do what you want. ¹⁸But if you are led by the Spirit, you are not under law.

¹⁹The acts of the sinful nature are obvious: sexual immorality, impurity and debauchery; ²⁰idolatry and witchcraft; hatred, discord, jealousy, fits of rage, selfish ambition, dissensions, factions ²¹and envy; drunkenness, orgies, and the like. I warn you, as I did before, that those who live like this will not inherit the kingdom of God.

²²**But the fruit of the Spirit is love, joy, peace, patience, kindness, goodness, faithfulness, ²³gentleness and self-control. Against such things there is no law.** ²⁴Those who belong to Christ Jesus have crucified the sinful nature with its passions and desires.

²⁵Since we live by the Spirit, let us keep in step with the Spirit. ²⁶Let us not become conceited, provoking and envying each other.

a13 Or *the flesh*; also in verses 16, 17, 19 and 24
b14 Lev. 19:18

PSALM 64:1-10
For the director of music. A psalm of David.

¹**H**ear me, O God, as I voice my
　　complaint;
　protect my life from the threat of
　　the enemy.
²Hide me from the conspiracy of the
　　wicked,
　from that noisy crowd of evildoers.

³They sharpen their tongues like
　　swords
　and aim their words like deadly
　　arrows.
⁴They shoot from ambush at the
　　innocent man;
　they shoot at him suddenly,
　　without fear.

⁵They encourage each other in evil
　　plans,
　they talk about hiding their snares;
　they say, "Who will see them*a*?"
⁶They plot injustice and say,
　"We have devised a perfect plan!"
　Surely the mind and heart of man
　　are cunning.

⁷But God will shoot them with arrows;
　suddenly they will be struck down.
⁸He will turn their own tongues
　　against them
　and bring them to ruin;
　all who see them will shake their
　　heads in scorn.

⁹All mankind will fear;
　they will proclaim the works of
　　God
　and ponder what he has done.
¹⁰Let the righteous rejoice in the LORD
　and take refuge in him;
　let all the upright in heart praise
　　him!

a5 Or *us*

PROVERBS 23:23

23 **B**uy the truth and do not sell it;
   get wisdom, discipline and
      understanding.

☐ D A Y   2 6 4

GOD SIGHTINGS

September 21

ISAIAH 37:1–38:22

When King Hezekiah heard this [what the Assyrian field commander said], he tore his clothes and put on sackcloth and went into the temple of the LORD. 2He sent Eliakim the palace administrator, Shebna the secretary, and the leading priests, all wearing sackcloth, to the prophet Isaiah son of Amoz. 3They told him, "This is what Hezekiah says: This day is a day of distress and rebuke and disgrace, as when children come to the point of birth and there is no strength to deliver them. 4It may be that the LORD your God will hear the words of the field commander, whom his master, the king of Assyria, has sent to ridicule the living God, and that he will rebuke him for the words the LORD your God has heard. Therefore pray for the remnant that still survives."

5When King Hezekiah's officials came to Isaiah, 6Isaiah said to them, "Tell your master, 'This is what the LORD says: Do not be afraid of what you have heard—those words with which the underlings of the king of Assyria have blasphemed me. 7Listen! I am going to put a spirit in him so that when he hears a certain report, he will return to his own country, and there I will have him cut down with the sword.'"

8When the field commander heard that the king of Assyria had left Lachish, he withdrew and found the king fighting against Libnah.

9Now Sennacherib received a report that Tirhakah, the Cushite*a* king of

Egypt, was marching out to fight against him. When he heard it, he sent messengers to Hezekiah with this word: 10"Say to Hezekiah king of Judah: Do not let the god you depend on deceive you when he says, 'Jerusalem will not be handed over to the king of Assyria.' 11Surely you have heard what the kings of Assyria have done to all the countries, destroying them completely. And will you be delivered? 12Did the gods of the nations that were destroyed by my forefathers deliver them—the gods of Gozan, Haran, Rezeph and the people of Eden who were in Tel Assar? 13Where is the king of Hamath, the king of Arpad, the king of the city of Sepharvaim, or of Hena or Ivvah?"

14Hezekiah received the letter from the messengers and read it. Then he went up to the temple of the LORD and spread it out before the LORD. 15And Hezekiah prayed to the LORD: 16"O LORD Almighty, God of Israel, enthroned between the cherubim, you alone are God over all the kingdoms of the earth. You have made heaven and earth. 17Give ear, O LORD, and hear; open your eyes, O LORD, and see; listen to all the words Sennacherib has sent to insult the living God.

18"It is true, O LORD, that the Assyrian kings have laid waste all these peoples and their lands. 19They have thrown their gods into the fire and destroyed them, for they were not gods but only wood and stone, fashioned by human hands. 20Now, O LORD our God, deliver us from his hand, so that all kingdoms on earth may know that you alone, O LORD, are God.*b*"

21Then Isaiah son of Amoz sent a message to Hezekiah: "This is what the LORD, the God of Israel, says: Because you have prayed to me concerning Sennacherib king of Assyria, 22this is the word the LORD has spoken against him:

"The Virgin Daughter of Zion
   despises and mocks you.
The Daughter of Jerusalem
   tosses her head as you flee.

²³ Who is it you have insulted and
    blasphemed?
  Against whom have you raised
    your voice
and lifted your eyes in pride?
  Against the Holy One of Israel!
²⁴ By your messengers
  you have heaped insults on the
    Lord.
And you have said,
  'With my many chariots
I have ascended the heights of the
    mountains,
  the utmost heights of Lebanon.
I have cut down its tallest cedars,
  the choicest of its pines.
I have reached its remotest heights,
  the finest of its forests.
²⁵ I have dug wells in foreign lands*c*
  and drunk the water there.
With the soles of my feet
  I have dried up all the streams of
    Egypt.'

²⁶ "Have you not heard?
  Long ago I ordained it.
In days of old I planned it;
  now I have brought it to pass,
that you have turned fortified cities
  into piles of stone.
²⁷ Their people, drained of power,
  are dismayed and put to shame.
They are like plants in the field,
  like tender green shoots,
like grass sprouting on the roof,
  scorched*d* before it grows up.

²⁸ "But I know where you stay
  and when you come and go
  and how you rage against me.
²⁹ Because you rage against me
  and because your insolence has
    reached my ears,
I will put my hook in your nose
  and my bit in your mouth,
and I will make you return
  by the way you came.

³⁰ "This will be the sign for you,
O Hezekiah:

"This year you will eat what grows by
  itself,

and the second year what springs
  from that.
But in the third year sow and reap,
  plant vineyards and eat their fruit.
³¹ Once more a remnant of the house of
    Judah
  will take root below and bear fruit
    above.
³² For out of Jerusalem will come a
    remnant,
  and out of Mount Zion a band of
    survivors.
The zeal of the LORD Almighty
  will accomplish this.

³³ "Therefore this is what the LORD
says concerning the king of Assyria:

"He will not enter this city
  or shoot an arrow here.
He will not come before it with
    shield
  or build a siege ramp against it.
³⁴ By the way that he came he will return;
  he will not enter this city,"
                    declares the LORD.
³⁵ "I will defend this city and save it,
  for my sake and for the sake of
    David my servant!"

³⁶ Then the angel of the LORD went out
and put to death a hundred and eighty-
five thousand men in the Assyrian
camp. When the people got up the next
morning—there were all the dead bodies! ³⁷ So Sennacherib king of Assyria
broke camp and withdrew. He returned
to Nineveh and stayed there.

³⁸ One day, while he was worshiping
in the temple of his god Nisroch, his
sons Adrammelech and Sharezer cut
him down with the sword, and they escaped to the land of Ararat. And Esarhaddon his son succeeded him as king.

³⁸:¹ IN those days Hezekiah became ill
and was at the point of death. The
prophet Isaiah son of Amoz went to him
and said, "This is what the LORD says: Put
your house in order, because you are going to die; you will not recover."
² Hezekiah turned his face to the wall
and prayed to the LORD, ³ "Remember,

O Lord, how I have walked before you faithfully and with wholehearted devotion and have done what is good in your eyes." And Hezekiah wept bitterly.

[4]Then the word of the Lord came to Isaiah: [5]"Go and tell Hezekiah, 'This is what the Lord, the God of your father David, says: I have heard your prayer and seen your tears; I will add fifteen years to your life. [6]And I will deliver you and this city from the hand of the king of Assyria. I will defend this city.

[7]"'This is the Lord's sign to you that the Lord will do what he has promised: [8]I will make the shadow cast by the sun go back the ten steps it has gone down on the stairway of Ahaz.'" So the sunlight went back the ten steps it had gone down.

[9]A writing of Hezekiah king of Judah after his illness and recovery:

[10]I said, "In the prime of my life
    must I go through the gates of
        death[e]
    and be robbed of the rest of my
        years?"
[11]I said, "I will not again see the Lord,
    the Lord, in the land of the living;
no longer will I look on mankind,
    or be with those who now dwell in
        this world.[f]
[12]Like a shepherd's tent my house
    has been pulled down and taken
        from me.
Like a weaver I have rolled up my
        life,
    and he has cut me off from the
        loom;
    day and night you made an end of
        me.
[13]I waited patiently till dawn,
    but like a lion he broke all my bones;
    day and night you made an end of
        me.
[14]I cried like a swift or thrush,
    I moaned like a mourning dove.
My eyes grew weak as I looked to the
        heavens.
I am troubled; O Lord, come to my
        aid!"

[15]But what can I say?
    He has spoken to me, and he
        himself has done this.
I will walk humbly all my years
    because of this anguish of my soul.
[16]Lord, by such things men live;
    and my spirit finds life in them too.
You restored me to health
    and let me live.
[17]Surely it was for my benefit
    that I suffered such anguish.
In your love you kept me
    from the pit of destruction;
you have put all my sins
    behind your back.
[18]For the grave[e] cannot praise you,
    death cannot sing your praise;
those who go down to the pit
    cannot hope for your faithfulness.
[19]The living, the living—they praise you,
    as I am doing today;
fathers tell their children
    about your faithfulness.

[20]The Lord will save me,
    and we will sing with stringed
        instruments
all the days of our lives
    in the temple of the Lord.

[21]Isaiah had said, "Prepare a poultice of figs and apply it to the boil, and he will recover."
[22]Hezekiah had asked, "What will be the sign that I will go up to the temple of the Lord?"

[a]9 That is, from the upper Nile region   [b]20 Dead Sea Scrolls (see also 2 Kings 19:19); Masoretic Text *alone are the Lord*   [c]25 Dead Sea Scrolls (see also 2 Kings 19:24); Masoretic Text does not have *in foreign lands*.   [d]27 Some manuscripts of the Masoretic Text, Dead Sea Scrolls and some Septuagint manuscripts (see also 2 Kings 19:26); most manuscripts of the Masoretic Text *roof / and terraced fields*   [e]10,18 Hebrew *Sheol*   [f]11 A few Hebrew manuscripts; most Hebrew manuscripts *in the place of cessation*

GALATIANS 6:1-18

Brothers, if someone is caught in a sin, you who are spiritual should restore him gently. But watch yourself, or you also may be tempted. [2]Carry each other's burdens, and in this way you will fulfill the law of Christ. [3]If anyone thinks he is something when he is nothing, he deceives himself. [4]Each one should test his own actions. Then he can take pride in himself, without comparing himself to somebody else, [5]for each one should carry his own load.

[6]Anyone who receives instruction in the word must share all good things with his instructor.

[7]Do not be deceived: God cannot be mocked. A man reaps what he sows. [8]The one who sows to please his sinful nature, from that nature[a] will reap destruction; the one who sows to please the Spirit, from the Spirit will reap eternal life. [9]**Let us not become weary in doing good, for at the proper time we will reap a harvest if we do not give up.** [10]**Therefore, as we have opportunity, let us do good to all people, especially to those who belong to the family of believers.**

[11]See what large letters I use as I write to you with my own hand!

[12]Those who want to make a good impression outwardly are trying to compel you to be circumcised. The only reason they do this is to avoid being persecuted for the cross of Christ. [13]Not even those who are circumcised obey the law, yet they want you to be circumcised that they may boast about your flesh. [14]May I never boast except in the cross of our Lord Jesus Christ, through which[b] the world has been crucified to me, and I to the world. [15]Neither circumcision nor uncircumcision means anything; what counts is a new creation. [16]Peace and mercy to all who follow this rule, even to the Israel of God.

[17]Finally, let no one cause me trouble, for I bear on my body the marks of Jesus.

[18]The grace of our Lord Jesus Christ be with your spirit, brothers. Amen.

a8 Or his flesh, from the flesh   b14 Or whom

PSALM 65:1-13

For the director of music. A psalm of David. A song.

[1]**P**raise awaits[a] you, O God, in Zion;
　　to you our vows will be fulfilled.
[2]O you who hear prayer,
　　to you all men will come.

[3]When we were overwhelmed by sins,
　　you forgave[b] our transgressions.
[4]Blessed are those you choose
　　and bring near to live in your
　　　courts!
We are filled with the good things of
　　your house,
　　of your holy temple.

[5]You answer us with awesome deeds
　　of righteousness,
　　O God our Savior,
the hope of all the ends of the earth
　　and of the farthest seas,
[6]who formed the mountains by your
　　power,
　　having armed yourself with
　　　strength,
[7]who stilled the roaring of the seas,
　　the roaring of their waves,
　　and the turmoil of the nations.
[8]Those living far away fear your
　　wonders;
　　where morning dawns and
　　　evening fades
　　you call forth songs of joy.

[9]You care for the land and water it;
　　you enrich it abundantly.
The streams of God are filled with
　　water
　　to provide the people with grain,
　　for so you have ordained it.[c]
[10]You drench its furrows
　　and level its ridges;
　　you soften it with showers
　　and bless its crops.
[11]You crown the year with your bounty,
　　and your carts overflow with
　　　abundance.
[12]The grasslands of the desert
　　overflow;
　　the hills are clothed with gladness.
[13]The meadows are covered with
　　flocks
　　and the valleys are mantled with
　　　grain;
　　they shout for joy and sing.

a1 Or befits; the meaning of the Hebrew for this word is uncertain.   b3 Or made atonement for   c9 Or for that is how you prepare the land

PROVERBS 23:24
²⁴The father of a righteous man has
    great joy;
  he who has a wise son delights in
    him.

□ DAY 265

GOD SIGHTINGS

September 22

ISAIAH 39:1–41:16
At that time Merodach-Baladan son of
Baladan king of Babylon sent Hezekiah
letters and a gift, because he had heard
of his illness and recovery. ²Hezekiah
received the envoys gladly and showed
them what was in his storehouses—the
silver, the gold, the spices, the fine oil,
his entire armory and everything found
among his treasures. There was nothing
in his palace or in all his kingdom that
Hezekiah did not show them.

³Then Isaiah the prophet went to
King Hezekiah and asked, "What did
those men say, and where did they come
from?"

"From a distant land," Hezekiah replied. "They came to me from Babylon."

⁴The prophet asked, "What did they
see in your palace?"

"They saw everything in my palace,"
Hezekiah said. "There is nothing
among my treasures that I did not show
them."

⁵Then Isaiah said to Hezekiah, "Hear
the word of the LORD Almighty: ⁶The
time will surely come when everything
in your palace, and all that your fathers
have stored up until this day, will be carried off to Babylon. Nothing will be left,
says the LORD. ⁷And some of your descendants, your own flesh and blood
who will be born to you, will be taken
away, and they will become eunuchs in
the palace of the king of Babylon."

⁸"The word of the LORD you have
spoken is good," Hezekiah replied. For

he thought, "There will be peace and security in my lifetime."

⁴⁰:¹**COMFORT, comfort my people,**
    says your God.
  ²**Speak tenderly to Jerusalem,**
    and proclaim to her
  that her hard service has been
    completed,
    that her sin has been paid for,
  that she has received from the
    LORD's hand
    double for all her sins.

³A voice of one calling:
"In the desert prepare
  the way for the LORD*ᵃ*;
make straight in the wilderness
  a highway for our God.*ᵇ*
⁴Every valley shall be raised up,
  every mountain and hill made low;
the rough ground shall become level,
  the rugged places a plain.
⁵And the glory of the LORD will be
    revealed,
  and all mankind together will
    see it.
      For the mouth of the LORD
        has spoken."

⁶A voice says, "Cry out."
  And I said, "What shall I cry?"

"All men are like grass,
  and all their glory is like the
    flowers of the field.
⁷The grass withers and the flowers
    fall,
  because the breath of the LORD
    blows on them.
Surely the people are grass.
⁸The grass withers and the flowers
    fall,
  but the word of our God stands
    forever."

⁹You who bring good tidings to Zion,
  go up on a high mountain.
You who bring good tidings to
    Jerusalem,*ᶜ*
  lift up your voice with a shout,
lift it up, do not be afraid;
  say to the towns of Judah,
  "Here is your God!"

¹⁰See, the Sovereign LORD comes with
    power,
  and his arm rules for him.
 See, his reward is with him,
  and his recompense accompanies
    him.
¹¹He tends his flock like a shepherd:
  He gathers the lambs in his arms
 and carries them close to his heart;
  he gently leads those that have
    young.

¹²Who has measured the waters in the
    hollow of his hand,
  or with the breadth of his hand
    marked off the heavens?
 Who has held the dust of the earth in
    a basket,
  or weighed the mountains on the
    scales
 and the hills in a balance?
¹³Who has understood the mind*d* of
    the LORD,
  or instructed him as his
    counselor?
¹⁴Whom did the LORD consult to
    enlighten him,
  and who taught him the right way?
 Who was it that taught him
    knowledge
  or showed him the path of
    understanding?

¹⁵Surely the nations are like a drop in
    a bucket;
  they are regarded as dust on the
    scales;
 he weighs the islands as though
    they were fine dust.
¹⁶Lebanon is not sufficient for altar
    fires,
  nor its animals enough for burnt
    offerings.
¹⁷Before him all the nations are as
    nothing;
  they are regarded by him as
    worthless
 and less than nothing.

¹⁸To whom, then, will you compare
    God?
  What image will you compare
    him to?

¹⁹As for an idol, a craftsman casts it,
  and a goldsmith overlays it with
    gold
 and fashions silver chains for it.
²⁰A man too poor to present such an
    offering
  selects wood that will not rot.
 He looks for a skilled craftsman
  to set up an idol that will not topple.

²¹Do you not know?
  Have you not heard?
 Has it not been told you from the
    beginning?
  Have you not understood since the
    earth was founded?
²²He sits enthroned above the circle of
    the earth,
  and its people are like
    grasshoppers.
 He stretches out the heavens like a
    canopy,
  and spreads them out like a tent to
    live in.
²³He brings princes to naught
  and reduces the rulers of this
    world to nothing.
²⁴No sooner are they planted,
  no sooner are they sown,
  no sooner do they take root in the
    ground,
 than he blows on them and they
    wither,
  and a whirlwind sweeps them
    away like chaff.

²⁵"To whom will you compare me?
  Or who is my equal?" says the Holy
    One.
²⁶Lift your eyes and look to the heavens:
  Who created all these?
 He who brings out the starry host
    one by one,
  and calls them each by name.
 Because of his great power and
    mighty strength,
  not one of them is missing.

²⁷Why do you say, O Jacob,
  and complain, O Israel,
 "My way is hidden from the LORD;
  my cause is disregarded by my
    God"?

²⁸ Do you not know?
  Have you not heard?
  The LORD is the everlasting God,
    the Creator of the ends of the
    earth.
  He will not grow tired or weary,
    and his understanding no one can
    fathom.
²⁹ He gives strength to the weary
    and increases the power of the
    weak.
³⁰ Even youths grow tired and weary,
    and young men stumble and fall;
³¹ but those who hope in the LORD
    will renew their strength.
  They will soar on wings like eagles;
    they will run and not grow weary,
    they will walk and not be faint.

⁴¹:¹ "BE silent before me, you islands!
  Let the nations renew their
    strength!
  Let them come forward and speak;
    let us meet together at the place of
    judgment.

² "Who has stirred up one from the
    east,
    calling him in righteousness to his
    serviceᵉ?
  He hands nations over to him
    and subdues kings before him.
  He turns them to dust with his
    sword,
    to windblown chaff with his bow.
³ He pursues them and moves on
    unscathed,
    by a path his feet have not traveled
    before.
⁴ Who has done this and carried it
    through,
    calling forth the generations from
    the beginning?
  I, the LORD—with the first of them
    and with the last—I am he."

⁵ The islands have seen it and fear;
    the ends of the earth tremble.
  They approach and come forward;
⁶   each helps the other
    and says to his brother, "Be
    strong!"

⁷ The craftsman encourages the
    goldsmith,
    and he who smooths with the
    hammer
    spurs on him who strikes the anvil.
  He says of the welding, "It is good."
  He nails down the idol so it will
    not topple.

⁸ "But you, O Israel, my servant,
    Jacob, whom I have chosen,
    you descendants of Abraham my
    friend,
⁹ I took you from the ends of the earth,
    from its farthest corners I called
    you.
  I said, 'You are my servant';
    I have chosen you and have not
    rejected you.
¹⁰ So do not fear, for I am with you;
    do not be dismayed, for I am your
    God.
  I will strengthen you and help you;
    I will uphold you with my
    righteous right hand.

¹¹ "All who rage against you
    will surely be ashamed and
    disgraced;
  those who oppose you
    will be as nothing and perish.
¹² Though you search for your enemies,
    you will not find them.
  Those who wage war against you
    will be as nothing at all.
¹³ For I am the LORD, your God,
    who takes hold of your right hand
  and says to you, Do not fear;
    I will help you.
¹⁴ Do not be afraid, O worm Jacob,
    O little Israel,
  for I myself will help you," declares
    the LORD,
    your Redeemer, the Holy One of
    Israel.
¹⁵ "See, I will make you into a threshing
    sledge,
    new and sharp, with many teeth.
  You will thresh the mountains and
    crush them,
    and reduce the hills to chaff.

16 You will winnow them, the wind will
   pick them up,
   and a gale will blow them away.
But you will rejoice in the LORD
   and glory in the Holy One of
   Israel."

*a3 Or A voice of one calling in the desert: / "Prepare the
way for the LORD   b3 Hebrew; Septuagint make straight the
paths of our God   c9 Or O Zion, bringer of good tidings,
/ go up on a high mountain. / O Jerusalem, bringer of good
tidings   d13 Or Spirit; or spirit   e2 Or / whom victory
meets at every step*

EPHESIANS 1:1-23

Paul, an apostle of Christ Jesus by the
will of God,

To the saints in Ephesus,a the faith-
fulb in Christ Jesus:

2 Grace and peace to you from God
our Father and the Lord Jesus Christ.

3 Praise be to the God and Father of our
Lord Jesus Christ, who has blessed us in
the heavenly realms with every spiritual
blessing in Christ. 4 For he chose us in
him before the creation of the world to
be holy and blameless in his sight. In love
5 hec predestined us to be adopted as his
sons through Jesus Christ, in accordance
with his pleasure and will— 6 to the
praise of his glorious grace, which he has
freely given us in the One he loves. 7 In
him we have redemption through his
blood, the forgiveness of sins, in accordance with the riches of God's grace
8 that he lavished on us with all wisdom
and understanding. 9 And hed made
known to us the mystery of his will according to his good pleasure, which he
purposed in Christ, 10 to be put into effect when the times will have reached
their fulfillment—to bring all things in
heaven and on earth together under one
head, even Christ.

11 In him we were also chosen,e having been predestined according to the
plan of him who works out everything
in conformity with the purpose of his
will, 12 in order that we, who were the
first to hope in Christ, might be for the
praise of his glory. 13 And you also were
included in Christ when you heard the
word of truth, the gospel of your salvation. Having believed, you were marked
in him with a seal, the promised Holy
Spirit, 14 who is a deposit guaranteeing
our inheritance until the redemption of
those who are God's possession—to the
praise of his glory.

15 For this reason, ever since I heard
about your faith in the Lord Jesus and
your love for all the saints, 16 I have not
stopped giving thanks for you, remembering you in my prayers. 17 I keep asking
that the God of our Lord Jesus Christ, the
glorious Father, may give you the Spiritf of
wisdom and revelation, so that you may
know him better. 18 I pray also that the
eyes of your heart may be enlightened in
order that you may know the hope to
which he has called you, the riches of his
glorious inheritance in the saints, 19 and
his incomparably great power for us who
believe. That power is like the working of
his mighty strength, 20 which he exerted
in Christ when he raised him from the
dead and seated him at his right hand in
the heavenly realms, 21 far above all rule
and authority, power and dominion, and
every title that can be given, not only in
the present age but also in the one to
come. 22 And God placed all things under
his feet and appointed him to be head
over everything for the church, 23 which is
his body, the fullness of him who fills everything in every way.

*a1 Some early manuscripts do not have in Ephesus.
b1 Or believers who are   c4,5 Or sight in love. 5 He
d8,9 Or us. With all wisdom and understanding, 9 he
e11 Or were made heirs   f17 Or a spirit*

PSALM 66:1-20

For the director of music. A song. A psalm.

1 Shout with joy to God, all the earth!
2   Sing the glory of his name;
     make his praise glorious!
3 Say to God, "How awesome are your
        deeds!
     So great is your power
     that your enemies cringe before
        you.
4 All the earth bows down to you;
     they sing praise to you,
     they sing praise to your name."
                                    Selah

⁵Come and see what God has done,
how awesome his works in man's
behalf!
⁶He turned the sea into dry land,
they passed through the waters on
foot—
come, let us rejoice in him.
⁷He rules forever by his power,
his eyes watch the nations—
let not the rebellious rise up
against him.   *Selah*

⁸Praise our God, O peoples,
let the sound of his praise be
heard;
⁹he has preserved our lives
and kept our feet from slipping.
¹⁰For you, O God, tested us;
you refined us like silver.
¹¹You brought us into prison
and laid burdens on our backs.
¹²You let men ride over our heads;
we went through fire and water,
but you brought us to a place of
abundance.

¹³I will come to your temple with burnt
offerings
and fulfill my vows to you—
¹⁴vows my lips promised and my
mouth spoke
when I was in trouble.
¹⁵I will sacrifice fat animals to you
and an offering of rams;
I will offer bulls and goats.   *Selah*

¹⁶Come and listen, all you who fear God;
let me tell you what he has done
for me.
¹⁷I cried out to him with my mouth;
his praise was on my tongue.
¹⁸If I had cherished sin in my heart,
the Lord would not have listened;
¹⁹but God has surely listened
and heard my voice in prayer.
²⁰Praise be to God,
who has not rejected my prayer
or withheld his love from me!

PROVERBS 23:25-28
²⁵May your father and mother be glad;
may she who gave you birth
rejoice!

²⁶My son, give me your heart
and let your eyes keep to my ways,
²⁷for a prostitute is a deep pit
and a wayward wife is a narrow
well.
²⁸Like a bandit she lies in wait,
and multiplies the unfaithful
among men.

□ DAY 266

GOD SIGHTINGS

September 23

ISAIAH 41:17–43:13
¹⁷"The poor and needy search for water,
but there is none;
their tongues are parched with
thirst.
But I the Lord will answer them;
I, the God of Israel, will not forsake
them.
¹⁸I will make rivers flow on barren
heights,
and springs within the valleys.
I will turn the desert into pools of
water,
and the parched ground into springs.
¹⁹I will put in the desert
the cedar and the acacia, the
myrtle and the olive.
I will set pines in the wasteland,
the fir and the cypress together,
²⁰so that people may see and know,
may consider and understand,
that the hand of the Lord has done
this,
that the Holy One of Israel has
created it.

²¹"Present your case," says the Lord.
"Set forth your arguments," says
Jacob's King.
²²"Bring in ˻your idols˼ to tell us
what is going to happen.
Tell us what the former things were,
so that we may consider them
and know their final outcome.
Or declare to us the things to come,

23 tell us what the future holds,
    so we may know that you are gods.
Do something, whether good or bad,
    so that we will be dismayed and
        filled with fear.
24 But you are less than nothing
    and your works are utterly
        worthless;
    he who chooses you is detestable.

25 "I have stirred up one from the north,
        and he comes—
    one from the rising sun who calls
        on my name.
He treads on rulers as if they were
        mortar,
    as if he were a potter treading the
        clay.
26 Who told of this from the beginning,
        so we could know,
    or beforehand, so we could say, 'He
        was right'?
No one told of this,
    no one foretold it,
    no one heard any words from you.
27 I was the first to tell Zion, 'Look, here
        they are!'
    I gave to Jerusalem a messenger of
        good tidings.
28 I look but there is no one—
    no one among them to give
        counsel,
    no one to give answer when I ask
        them.
29 See, they are all false!
    Their deeds amount to nothing;
    their images are but wind and
        confusion.

42:1 "HERE is my servant, whom I
        uphold,
    my chosen one in whom I delight;
I will put my Spirit on him
    and he will bring justice to the
        nations.
2 He will not shout or cry out,
    or raise his voice in the streets.
3 A bruised reed he will not break,
    and a smoldering wick he will not
        snuff out.
In faithfulness he will bring forth
        justice;

4 he will not falter or be discouraged
    till he establishes justice on earth.
    In his law the islands will put their
        hope."

5 This is what God the LORD says—
    he who created the heavens and
        stretched them out,
    who spread out the earth and all
        that comes out of it,
who gives breath to its people,
    and life to those who walk on it:
6 "I, the LORD, have called you in
        righteousness;
    I will take hold of your hand.
I will keep you and will make you
    to be a covenant for the people
    and a light for the Gentiles,
7 to open eyes that are blind,
    to free captives from prison
    and to release from the dungeon
        those who sit in darkness.

8 "I am the LORD; that is my name!
    I will not give my glory to another
    or my praise to idols.
9 See, the former things have taken
        place,
    and new things I declare;
before they spring into being
    I announce them to you."

10 Sing to the LORD a new song,
    his praise from the ends of the
        earth,
you who go down to the sea, and all
        that is in it,
    you islands, and all who live in
        them.
11 Let the desert and its towns raise
        their voices;
    let the settlements where Kedar
        lives rejoice.
Let the people of Sela sing for joy;
    let them shout from the
        mountaintops.
12 Let them give glory to the LORD
    and proclaim his praise in the
        islands.
13 The LORD will march out like a
        mighty man,
    like a warrior he will stir up his
        zeal;

with a shout he will raise the battle
cry
and will triumph over his enemies.

14"For a long time I have kept silent,
I have been quiet and held myself
back.
But now, like a woman in childbirth,
I cry out, I gasp and pant.
15 I will lay waste the mountains and
hills
and dry up all their vegetation;
I will turn rivers into islands
and dry up the pools.
16 I will lead the blind by ways they
have not known,
along unfamiliar paths I will guide
them;
I will turn the darkness into light
before them
and make the rough places
smooth.
These are the things I will do;
I will not forsake them.
17 But those who trust in idols,
who say to images, 'You are our
gods,'
will be turned back in utter shame.

18"Hear, you deaf;
look, you blind, and see!
19 Who is blind but my servant,
and deaf like the messenger I send?
Who is blind like the one committed
to me,
blind like the servant of the LORD?
20 You have seen many things, but have
paid no attention;
your ears are open, but you hear
nothing."
21 It pleased the LORD
for the sake of his righteousness
to make his law great and glorious.
22 But this is a people plundered and
looted,
all of them trapped in pits
or hidden away in prisons.
They have become plunder,
with no one to rescue them;
they have been made loot,
with no one to say, "Send them
back."

23 Which of you will listen to this
or pay close attention in time to
come?
24 Who handed Jacob over to become
loot,
and Israel to the plunderers?
Was it not the LORD,
against whom we have sinned?
For they would not follow his ways;
they did not obey his law.
25 So he poured out on them his
burning anger,
the violence of war.
It enveloped them in flames, yet they
did not understand;
it consumed them, but they did
not take it to heart.

43:1 BUT now, this is what the LORD says—
he who created you, O Jacob,
he who formed you, O Israel:
"Fear not, for I have redeemed you;
I have summoned you by name;
you are mine.
2 When you pass through the waters,
I will be with you;
and when you pass through the
rivers,
they will not sweep over you.
When you walk through the fire,
you will not be burned;
the flames will not set you ablaze.
3 For I am the LORD, your God,
the Holy One of Israel, your Savior;
I give Egypt for your ransom,
Cush*a* and Seba in your stead.
4 Since you are precious and honored
in my sight,
and because I love you,
I will give men in exchange for you,
and people in exchange for your
life.
5 Do not be afraid, for I am with you;
I will bring your children from the
east
and gather you from the west.
6 I will say to the north, 'Give them up!'
and to the south, 'Do not hold
them back.'
Bring my sons from afar
and my daughters from the ends
of the earth—

7 everyone who is called by my name,
  whom I created for my glory,
  whom I formed and made."

8 Lead out those who have eyes but are
    blind,
  who have ears but are deaf.
9 All the nations gather together
  and the peoples assemble.
  Which of them foretold this
  and proclaimed to us the former
    things?
  Let them bring in their witnesses to
    prove they were right,
  so that others may hear and say, "It
    is true."
10 "You are my witnesses," declares the
    LORD,
  "and my servant whom I have
    chosen,
  so that you may know and believe me
  and understand that I am he.
  Before me no god was formed,
  nor will there be one after me.
11 I, even I, am the LORD,
  and apart from me there is no
    savior.
12 I have revealed and saved and
    proclaimed—
  I, and not some foreign god among
    you.
  You are my witnesses," declares the
    LORD, "that I am God.
13   Yes, and from ancient days I am
    he.
  No one can deliver out of my hand.
  When I act, who can reverse it?"

a3 That is, the upper Nile region

EPHESIANS 2:1-22

As for you, you were dead in your transgressions and sins, 2 in which you used to
live when you followed the ways of this
world and of the ruler of the kingdom of
the air, the spirit who is now at work in
those who are disobedient. 3 All of us also
lived among them at one time, gratifying
the cravings of our sinful nature a and
following its desires and thoughts. Like
the rest, we were by nature objects of
wrath. 4 But because of his great love for
us, God, who is rich in mercy, 5 made us

alive with Christ even when we were
dead in transgressions—it is by grace you
have been saved. 6 And God raised us up
with Christ and seated us with him in the
heavenly realms in Christ Jesus, 7 in order
that in the coming ages he might show
the incomparable riches of his grace, expressed in his kindness to us in Christ
Jesus. 8 **For it is by grace you have been
saved, through faith—and this not
from yourselves, it is the gift of God—
9 not by works, so that no one can
boast.** 10 For we are God's workmanship,
created in Christ Jesus to do good works,
which God prepared in advance for us to
do.

11 Therefore, remember that formerly
you who are Gentiles by birth and called
"uncircumcised" by those who call
themselves "the circumcision" (that
done in the body by the hands of men)—
12 remember that at that time you were
separate from Christ, excluded from citizenship in Israel and foreigners to the
covenants of the promise, without hope
and without God in the world. 13 But
now in Christ Jesus you who once were
far away have been brought near
through the blood of Christ.

14 For he himself is our peace, who has
made the two one and has destroyed the
barrier, the dividing wall of hostility,
15 by abolishing in his flesh the law with
its commandments and regulations. His
purpose was to create in himself one
new man out of the two, thus making
peace, 16 and in this one body to reconcile both of them to God through the
cross, by which he put to death their
hostility. 17 He came and preached
peace to you who were far away and
peace to those who were near. 18 For
through him we both have access to the
Father by one Spirit.

19 Consequently, you are no longer
foreigners and aliens, but fellow citizens with God's people and members of
God's household, 20 built on the foundation of the apostles and prophets, with
Christ Jesus himself as the chief cornerstone. 21 In him the whole building is
joined together and rises to become a

holy temple in the Lord. ²²And in him
you too are being built together to become a dwelling in which God lives by
his Spirit.

a3 Or our flesh

PSALM 67:1-7

For the director of music. With stringed
instruments. A psalm. A song.

¹ **M**ay God be gracious to us and bless
us
and make his face shine upon us,
Selah
² that your ways may be known on
earth,
your salvation among all nations.

³ May the peoples praise you, O God;
may all the peoples praise you.
⁴ May the nations be glad and sing for
joy,
for you rule the peoples justly
and guide the nations of the earth.
Selah
⁵ May the peoples praise you, O God;
may all the peoples praise you.

⁶ Then the land will yield its harvest,
and God, our God, will bless us.
⁷ God will bless us,
and all the ends of the earth will
fear him.

PROVERBS 23:29-35

²⁹ **W**ho has woe? Who has sorrow?
Who has strife? Who has complaints?
Who has needless bruises? Who
has bloodshot eyes?
³⁰ Those who linger over wine,
who go to sample bowls of mixed
wine.
³¹ Do not gaze at wine when it is red,
when it sparkles in the cup,
when it goes down smoothly!
³² In the end it bites like a snake
and poisons like a viper.
³³ Your eyes will see strange sights
and your mind imagine confusing
things.
³⁴ You will be like one sleeping on the
high seas,
lying on top of the rigging.

³⁵ "They hit me," you will say, "but I'm
not hurt!
They beat me, but I don't feel it!
When will I wake up
so I can find another drink?"

☐ D A Y 2 6 7

GOD SIGHTINGS

September 24

ISAIAH 43:14-45:10

¹⁴ **T**his is what the LORD says—
your Redeemer, the Holy One of
Israel:
"For your sake I will send to Babylon
and bring down as fugitives all the
Babylonians,*a*
in the ships in which they took
pride.
¹⁵ I am the LORD, your Holy One,
Israel's Creator, your King."

¹⁶ This is what the LORD says—
he who made a way through the
sea,
a path through the mighty waters,
¹⁷ who drew out the chariots and
horses,
the army and reinforcements
together,
and they lay there, never to rise again,
extinguished, snuffed out like a
wick:
¹⁸ "Forget the former things;
do not dwell on the past.
¹⁹ See, I am doing a new thing!
Now it springs up; do you not
perceive it?
I am making a way in the desert
and streams in the wasteland.
²⁰ The wild animals honor me,
the jackals and the owls,
because I provide water in the desert
and streams in the wasteland,
to give drink to my people, my
chosen,
²¹   the people I formed for myself
that they may proclaim my praise.

22"Yet you have not called upon me,
  O Jacob,
    you have not wearied yourselves
      for me, O Israel.
23You have not brought me sheep for
  burnt offerings,
    nor honored me with your
      sacrifices.
  I have not burdened you with grain
    offerings
    nor wearied you with demands for
      incense.
24You have not bought any fragrant
  calamus for me,
    or lavished on me the fat of your
      sacrifices.
  But you have burdened me with your
    sins
    and wearied me with your
      offenses.

25"I, even I, am he who blots out
  your transgressions, for my own
    sake,
    and remembers your sins no more.
26Review the past for me,
    let us argue the matter together;
    state the case for your innocence.
27Your first father sinned;
    your spokesmen rebelled against
      me.
28So I will disgrace the dignitaries of
  your temple,
    and I will consign Jacob to
      destruction*b*
    and Israel to scorn.

44:1"BUT now listen, O Jacob, my servant,
  Israel, whom I have chosen.
2This is what the LORD says—
  he who made you, who formed you
    in the womb,
    and who will help you:
  Do not be afraid, O Jacob, my servant,
    Jeshurun, whom I have chosen.
3For I will pour water on the thirsty
  land,
    and streams on the dry ground;
  I will pour out my Spirit on your
    offspring,
    and my blessing on your
      descendants.

4They will spring up like grass in a
  meadow,
    like poplar trees by flowing
      streams.
5One will say, 'I belong to the LORD';
    another will call himself by the
      name of Jacob;
  still another will write on his hand,
    'The LORD's,'
    and will take the name Israel.

6"This is what the LORD says—
  Israel's King and Redeemer, the
    LORD Almighty:
  I am the first and I am the last;
    apart from me there is no God.
7Who then is like me? Let him
    proclaim it.
  Let him declare and lay out before
    me
  what has happened since I
      established my ancient
        people,
    and what is yet to come—
    yes, let him foretell what will
      come.
8Do not tremble, do not be afraid.
    Did I not proclaim this and foretell
      it long ago?
  You are my witnesses. Is there any
    God besides me?
    No, there is no other Rock; I know
      not one."

9All who make idols are nothing,
    and the things they treasure are
      worthless.
  Those who would speak up for them
    are blind;
    they are ignorant, to their own
      shame.
10Who shapes a god and casts an idol,
    which can profit him nothing?
11He and his kind will be put to shame;
    craftsmen are nothing but men.
  Let them all come together and take
    their stand;
    they will be brought down to
      terror and infamy.

12The blacksmith takes a tool
    and works with it in the coals;
  he shapes an idol with hammers,

he forges it with the might of his
arm.
He gets hungry and loses his
strength;
he drinks no water and grows
faint.
¹³The carpenter measures with a line
and makes an outline with a
marker;
he roughs it out with chisels
and marks it with compasses.
He shapes it in the form of man,
of man in all his glory,
that it may dwell in a shrine.
¹⁴He cut down cedars,
or perhaps took a cypress or oak.
He let it grow among the trees of the
forest,
or planted a pine, and the rain
made it grow.
¹⁵It is man's fuel for burning;
some of it he takes and warms
himself,
he kindles a fire and bakes bread.
But he also fashions a god and
worships it;
he makes an idol and bows down
to it.
¹⁶Half of the wood he burns in the fire;
over it he prepares his meal,
he roasts his meat and eats his fill.
He also warms himself and says,
"Ah! I am warm; I see the fire."
¹⁷From the rest he makes a god, his
idol;
he bows down to it and worships.
He prays to it and says,
"Save me; you are my god."
¹⁸They know nothing, they understand
nothing;
their eyes are plastered over so
they cannot see,
and their minds closed so they
cannot understand.
¹⁹No one stops to think,
no one has the knowledge or
understanding to say,
"Half of it I used for fuel;
I even baked bread over its coals,
I roasted meat and I ate.
Shall I make a detestable thing from
what is left?

Shall I bow down to a block of
wood?"
²⁰He feeds on ashes, a deluded heart
misleads him;
he cannot save himself, or say,
"Is not this thing in my right hand
a lie?"

²¹"Remember these things, O Jacob,
for you are my servant, O Israel.
I have made you, you are my servant;
O Israel, I will not forget you.
²²I have swept away your offenses like
a cloud,
your sins like the morning mist.
Return to me,
for I have redeemed you."

²³Sing for joy, O heavens, for the LORD
has done this;
shout aloud, O earth beneath.
Burst into song, you mountains,
you forests and all your trees,
for the LORD has redeemed Jacob,
he displays his glory in Israel.

²⁴"This is what the LORD says—
your Redeemer, who formed you
in the womb:

I am the LORD,
who has made all things,
who alone stretched out the heavens,
who spread out the earth by myself,

²⁵who foils the signs of false prophets
and makes fools of diviners,
who overthrows the learning of the
wise
and turns it into nonsense,
²⁶who carries out the words of his
servants
and fulfills the predictions of his
messengers,

who says of Jerusalem, 'It shall be
inhabited,'
of the towns of Judah, 'They shall
be built,'
and of their ruins, 'I will restore
them,'
²⁷who says to the watery deep, 'Be dry,
and I will dry up your streams,'

[28] who says of Cyrus, 'He is my
        shepherd
     and will accomplish all that I please;
     he will say of Jerusalem, "Let it be
        rebuilt,"
     and of the temple, "Let its
        foundations be laid."'

45:1 "This is what the LORD says to his
         anointed,
      to Cyrus, whose right hand I take
         hold of
   to subdue nations before him
      and to strip kings of their armor,
   to open doors before him
      so that gates will not be shut:
[2] I will go before you
      and will level the mountains[c];
   I will break down gates of bronze
      and cut through bars of iron.
[3] I will give you the treasures of
         darkness,
      riches stored in secret places,
   so that you may know that I am the
         LORD,
      the God of Israel, who summons
         you by name.
[4] For the sake of Jacob my servant,
      of Israel my chosen,
   I summon you by name
      and bestow on you a title of honor,
      though you do not acknowledge
         me.
[5] I am the LORD, and there is no other;
      apart from me there is no God.
   I will strengthen you,
      though you have not
         acknowledged me,
[6] so that from the rising of the sun
      to the place of its setting
   men may know there is none besides
      me.
   I am the LORD, and there is no
      other.
[7] I form the light and create darkness,
      I bring prosperity and create
         disaster;
   I, the LORD, do all these things.

[8] "You heavens above, rain down
      righteousness;
      let the clouds shower it down.

   Let the earth open wide,
      let salvation spring up,
   let righteousness grow with it;
      I, the LORD, have created it.

[9] "Woe to him who quarrels with his
         Maker,
      to him who is but a potsherd
         among the potsherds on the
         ground.
   Does the clay say to the potter,
      'What are you making?'
   Does your work say,
      'He has no hands'?
[10] Woe to him who says to his father,
      'What have you begotten?'
   or to his mother,
      'What have you brought to
         birth?'"

a14 Or Chaldeans   b28 The Hebrew term refers to the
irrevocable giving over of things or persons to the LORD,
often by totally destroying them.   c2 Dead Sea Scrolls and
Septuagint; the meaning of the word in the Masoretic Text is
uncertain.

EPHESIANS 3:1-21

For this reason I, Paul, the prisoner of
Christ Jesus for the sake of you Gentiles—

[2] Surely you have heard about the administration of God's grace that was
given to me for you, [3] that is, the mystery
made known to me by revelation, as I
have already written briefly. [4] In reading
this, then, you will be able to understand
my insight into the mystery of Christ,
[5] which was not made known to men in
other generations as it has now been revealed by the Spirit to God's holy apostles and prophets. [6] This mystery is that
through the gospel the Gentiles are
heirs together with Israel, members together of one body, and sharers together
in the promise in Christ Jesus.

[7] I became a servant of this gospel by
the gift of God's grace given me through
the working of his power. [8] Although I
am less than the least of all God's people,
this grace was given me: to preach to the
Gentiles the unsearchable riches of
Christ, [9] and to make plain to everyone
the administration of this mystery,
which for ages past was kept hidden in

God, who created all things. [10]His intent was that now, through the church, the manifold wisdom of God should be made known to the rulers and authorities in the heavenly realms, [11]according to his eternal purpose which he accomplished in Christ Jesus our Lord. [12]In him and through faith in him we may approach God with freedom and confidence. [13]I ask you, therefore, not to be discouraged because of my sufferings for you, which are your glory.

[14]For this reason I kneel before the Father, [15]from whom his whole family[a] in heaven and on earth derives its name. [16]I pray that out of his glorious riches he may strengthen you with power through his Spirit in your inner being, [17]so that Christ may dwell in your hearts through faith. And I pray that you, being rooted and established in love, [18]may have power, together with all the saints, to grasp how wide and long and high and deep is the love of Christ, [19]and to know this love that surpasses knowledge—that you may be filled to the measure of all the fullness of God.

[20]Now to him who is able to do immeasurably more than all we ask or imagine, according to his power that is at work within us, [21]to him be glory in the church and in Christ Jesus throughout all generations, for ever and ever! Amen.

[a]15 Or *whom all fatherhood*

PSALM 68:1-18

For the director of music. Of David. A psalm. A song.

[1] **M**ay God arise, may his enemies be
    scattered;
   may his foes flee before him.
[2] As smoke is blown away by the wind,
    may you blow them away;
   as wax melts before the fire,
    may the wicked perish before
       God.
[3] But may the righteous be glad
    and rejoice before God;
   may they be happy and joyful.

[4] Sing to God, sing praise to his name,
    extol him who rides on the
       clouds[a]—
   his name is the LORD—
    and rejoice before him.
[5] A father to the fatherless, a defender
    of widows,
   is God in his holy dwelling.
[6] God sets the lonely in families,[b]
    he leads forth the prisoners with
       singing;
   but the rebellious live in a sun-
       scorched land.

[7] When you went out before your
    people, O God,
   when you marched through the
       wasteland,   *Selah*
[8] the earth shook,
    the heavens poured down rain,
   before God, the One of Sinai,
    before God, the God of Israel.
[9] You gave abundant showers, O God;
    you refreshed your weary
       inheritance.
[10] Your people settled in it,
    and from your bounty, O God, you
       provided for the poor.

[11] The Lord announced the word,
    and great was the company of
       those who proclaimed it:
[12] "Kings and armies flee in haste;
    in the camps men divide the
       plunder.
[13] Even while you sleep among the
    campfires,[c]
   the wings of ⌐my⌐ dove are
       sheathed with silver,
   its feathers with shining gold."
[14] When the Almighty[d] scattered the
    kings in the land,
   it was like snow fallen on Zalmon.

[15] The mountains of Bashan are
    majestic mountains;
   rugged are the mountains of
       Bashan.
[16] Why gaze in envy, O rugged
    mountains,
   at the mountain where God
       chooses to reign,

where the LORD himself will dwell
forever?
17 The chariots of God are tens of
thousands
and thousands of thousands;
the Lord ⌊has come⌋ from Sinai
into his sanctuary.
18 When you ascended on high,
you led captives in your train;
you received gifts from men,
even from[e] the rebellious—
that you,[f] O LORD God, might dwell
there.

a4 Or / prepare the way for him who rides through the deserts
b6 Or the desolate in a homeland   c13 Or saddlebags
d14 Hebrew Shaddai   e18 Or gifts for men, / even
f18 Or they

PROVERBS 24:1-2

Do not envy wicked men,
do not desire their company;
2 for their hearts plot violence,
and their lips talk about making
trouble.

☐ DAY 268

GOD SIGHTINGS

September 25

ISAIAH 45:11–48:11
11 "This is what the LORD says—
the Holy One of Israel, and its
Maker:
Concerning things to come,
do you question me about my
children,
or give me orders about the work
of my hands?
12 It is I who made the earth
and created mankind upon it.
My own hands stretched out the
heavens;
I marshaled their starry hosts.
13 I will raise up Cyrus[a] in my
righteousness:
I will make all his ways straight.
He will rebuild my city
and set my exiles free,

but not for a price or reward,
says the LORD Almighty."

14 This is what the LORD says:

"The products of Egypt and the
merchandise of Cush,[b]
and those tall Sabeans—
they will come over to you
and will be yours;
they will trudge behind you,
coming over to you in chains.
They will bow down before you
and plead with you, saying,
'Surely God is with you, and there is
no other;
there is no other god.'"

15 Truly you are a God who hides
himself,
O God and Savior of Israel.
16 All the makers of idols will be put to
shame and disgraced;
they will go off into disgrace
together.
17 But Israel will be saved by the LORD
with an everlasting salvation;
you will never be put to shame or
disgraced,
to ages everlasting.

18 For this is what the LORD says—
he who created the heavens,
he is God;
he who fashioned and made the
earth,
he founded it;
he did not create it to be empty,
but formed it to be inhabited—
he says:
"I am the LORD,
and there is no other.
19 I have not spoken in secret,
from somewhere in a land of
darkness;
I have not said to Jacob's
descendants,
'Seek me in vain.'
I, the LORD, speak the truth;
I declare what is right.

20 "Gather together and come;
assemble, you fugitives from the
nations.

Ignorant are those who carry about
    idols of wood,
  who pray to gods that cannot
    save.
21 Declare what is to be, present it—
    let them take counsel together.
  Who foretold this long ago,
    who declared it from the distant
      past?
  Was it not I, the LORD?
    And there is no God apart from
      me,
  a righteous God and a Savior;
    there is none but me.

22 "Turn to me and be saved,
    all you ends of the earth;
    for I am God, and there is no
      other.
23 By myself I have sworn,
    my mouth has uttered in all
      integrity
    a word that will not be revoked:
  Before me every knee will bow;
    by me every tongue will swear.
24 They will say of me, 'In the LORD
      alone
    are righteousness and strength.'"
  All who have raged against him
    will come to him and be put to
      shame.
25 But in the LORD all the descendants
      of Israel
    will be found righteous and will
      exult.

46:1 BEL bows down, Nebo stoops low;
    their idols are borne by beasts of
      burden.c
  The images that are carried about are
      burdensome,
    a burden for the weary.
2 They stoop and bow down together;
    unable to rescue the burden,
    they themselves go off into
      captivity.

3 "Listen to me, O house of Jacob,
    all you who remain of the house of
      Israel,
  you whom I have upheld since you
      were conceived,
    and have carried since your birth.

4 Even to your old age and gray hairs
    I am he, I am he who will sustain
      you.
  I have made you and I will carry you;
    I will sustain you and I will rescue
      you.

5 "To whom will you compare me or
      count me equal?
    To whom will you liken me that we
      may be compared?
6 Some pour out gold from their bags
    and weigh out silver on the scales;
  they hire a goldsmith to make it into
      a god,
    and they bow down and worship it.
7 They lift it to their shoulders and
      carry it;
    they set it up in its place, and there
      it stands.
    From that spot it cannot move.
  Though one cries out to it, it does not
      answer;
    it cannot save him from his
      troubles.

8 "Remember this, fix it in mind,
    take it to heart, you rebels.
9 Remember the former things, those
      of long ago;
    I am God, and there is no other;
    I am God, and there is none like
      me.
10 I make known the end from the
      beginning,
    from ancient times, what is still to
      come.
  I say: My purpose will stand,
    and I will do all that I please.
11 From the east I summon a bird of
      prey;
    from a far-off land, a man to fulfill
      my purpose.
  What I have said, that will I bring
      about;
    what I have planned, that will I do.
12 Listen to me, you stubborn-hearted,
    you who are far from
      righteousness.
13 I am bringing my righteousness near,
    it is not far away;
    and my salvation will not be delayed.

I will grant salvation to Zion,
my splendor to Israel.

47:1"Go down, sit in the dust,
Virgin Daughter of Babylon;
sit on the ground without a throne,
Daughter of the Babylonians.*d*
No more will you be called
tender or delicate.
2 Take millstones and grind flour;
take off your veil.
Lift up your skirts, bare your legs,
and wade through the streams.
3 Your nakedness will be exposed
and your shame uncovered.
I will take vengeance;
I will spare no one."

4 Our Redeemer—the LORD Almighty is
his name—
is the Holy One of Israel.

5 "Sit in silence, go into darkness,
Daughter of the Babylonians;
no more will you be called
queen of kingdoms.
6 I was angry with my people
and desecrated my inheritance;
I gave them into your hand,
and you showed them no mercy.
Even on the aged
you laid a very heavy yoke.
7 You said, 'I will continue forever—
the eternal queen!'
But you did not consider these
things
or reflect on what might happen.

8 "Now then, listen, you wanton
creature,
lounging in your security
and saying to yourself,
'I am, and there is none besides
me.
I will never be a widow
or suffer the loss of children.'
9 Both of these will overtake you
in a moment, on a single day:
loss of children and widowhood.
They will come upon you in full
measure,
in spite of your many sorceries
and all your potent spells.

10 You have trusted in your wickedness
and have said, 'No one sees me.'
Your wisdom and knowledge
mislead you
when you say to yourself,
'I am, and there is none besides
me.'
11 Disaster will come upon you,
and you will not know how to
conjure it away.
A calamity will fall upon you
that you cannot ward off with a
ransom;
a catastrophe you cannot foresee
will suddenly come upon you.

12 "Keep on, then, with your magic
spells
and with your many sorceries,
which you have labored at since
childhood.
Perhaps you will succeed,
perhaps you will cause terror.
13 All the counsel you have received has
only worn you out!
Let your astrologers come forward,
those stargazers who make
predictions month by month,
let them save you from what is
coming upon you.
14 Surely they are like stubble;
the fire will burn them up.
They cannot even save themselves
from the power of the flame.
Here are no coals to warm anyone;
here is no fire to sit by.
15 That is all they can do for you—
these you have labored with
and trafficked with since
childhood.
Each of them goes on in his error;
there is not one that can save you.

48:1"LISTEN to this, O house of Jacob,
you who are called by the name of
Israel
and come from the line of Judah,
you who take oaths in the name of
the LORD
and invoke the God of Israel—
but not in truth or righteousness—

2you who call yourselves citizens of
  the holy city
 and rely on the God of Israel—
 the LORD Almighty is his name:
3I foretold the former things long
  ago,
 my mouth announced them and I
  made them known;
 then suddenly I acted, and they
  came to pass.
4For I knew how stubborn you were;
 the sinews of your neck were
  iron,
 your forehead was bronze.
5Therefore I told you these things
  long ago;
 before they happened I
  announced them to you
 so that you could not say,
 'My idols did them;
 my wooden image and metal god
  ordained them.'
6You have heard these things; look at
  them all.
 Will you not admit them?

 "From now on I will tell you of new
  things,
 of hidden things unknown to you.
7They are created now, and not long
  ago;
 you have not heard of them before
  today.
 So you cannot say,
 'Yes, I knew of them.'
8You have neither heard nor
  understood;
 from of old your ear has not been
  open.
 Well do I know how treacherous you
  are;
 you were called a rebel from birth.
9For my own name's sake I delay my
  wrath;
 for the sake of my praise I hold it
  back from you,
 so as not to cut you off.
10See, I have refined you, though not as
  silver;
 I have tested you in the furnace of
  affliction.

11For my own sake, for my own sake, I
  do this.
 How can I let myself be defamed?
 I will not yield my glory to
  another."

a13 Hebrew him   b14 That is, the upper Nile region
c1 Or are but beasts and cattle   d1 Or Chaldeans; also
in verse 5

EPHESIANS 4:1-16

As a prisoner for the Lord, then, I urge
you to live a life worthy of the calling
you have received. 2Be completely humble and gentle; be patient, bearing with
one another in love. 3Make every effort
to keep the unity of the Spirit through
the bond of peace. 4There is one body
and one Spirit—just as you were called
to one hope when you were called—
5one Lord, one faith, one baptism; 6one
God and Father of all, who is over all and
through all and in all.

7But to each one of us grace has been
given as Christ apportioned it. 8This is
why ita says:

 "When he ascended on high,
  he led captives in his train
  and gave gifts to men."b

9(What does "he ascended" mean except
that he also descended to the lower,
earthly regionsc? 10He who descended is
the very one who ascended higher than
all the heavens, in order to fill the whole
universe.) 11It was he who gave some to
be apostles, some to be prophets, some
to be evangelists, and some to be pastors
and teachers, 12to prepare God's people
for works of service, so that the body of
Christ may be built up 13until we all
reach unity in the faith and in the knowledge of the Son of God and become mature, attaining to the whole measure of
the fullness of Christ.

14Then we will no longer be infants,
tossed back and forth by the waves, and
blown here and there by every wind of
teaching and by the cunning and craftiness of men in their deceitful scheming. 15**Instead, speaking the truth in
love, we will in all things grow up into
him who is the Head, that is, Christ.**

16**From him the whole body, joined and held together by every supporting ligament, grows and builds itself up in love, as each part does its work.**

a8 Or *God*   *b8* Psalm 68:18   *c9* Or *the depths of the earth*

PSALM 68:19-35

19 Praise be to the Lord, to God our Savior,
who daily bears our burdens. *Selah*
20 Our God is a God who saves;
from the Sovereign LORD comes escape from death.

21 Surely God will crush the heads of his enemies,
the hairy crowns of those who go on in their sins.
22 The Lord says, "I will bring them from Bashan;
I will bring them from the depths of the sea,
23 that you may plunge your feet in the blood of your foes,
while the tongues of your dogs have their share."

24 Your procession has come into view, O God,
the procession of my God and King into the sanctuary.
25 In front are the singers, after them the musicians;
with them are the maidens playing tambourines.
26 Praise God in the great congregation;
praise the LORD in the assembly of Israel.
27 There is the little tribe of Benjamin, leading them,
there the great throng of Judah's princes,
and there the princes of Zebulun and of Naphtali.

28 Summon your power, O God*a*;
show us your strength, O God, as you have done before.
29 Because of your temple at Jerusalem kings will bring you gifts.
30 Rebuke the beast among the reeds, the herd of bulls among the calves of the nations.

Humbled, may it bring bars of silver.
Scatter the nations who delight in war.
31 Envoys will come from Egypt;
Cush*b* will submit herself to God.

32 Sing to God, O kingdoms of the earth,
sing praise to the Lord,   *Selah*
33 to him who rides the ancient skies above,
who thunders with mighty voice.
34 Proclaim the power of God,
whose majesty is over Israel,
whose power is in the skies.
35 You are awesome, O God, in your sanctuary;
the God of Israel gives power and strength to his people.

Praise be to God!

a28 Many Hebrew manuscripts, Septuagint and Syriac; most Hebrew manuscripts *Your God has summoned power for you*   *b31* That is, the upper Nile region

PROVERBS 24:3-4

3 By wisdom a house is built,
and through understanding it is established;
4 through knowledge its rooms are filled
with rare and beautiful treasures.

□ DAY 269

GOD SIGHTINGS

September 26

ISAIAH 48:12–50:11

12 "Listen to me [the LORD], O Jacob, Israel, whom I have called:
I am he;
I am the first and I am the last.
13 My own hand laid the foundations of the earth,
and my right hand spread out the heavens;
when I summon them,
they all stand up together.

14 "Come together, all of you, and listen:
   Which of the idols has foretold
      these things?
The LORD's chosen ally
   will carry out his purpose against
      Babylon;
   his arm will be against the
      Babylonians.*a*
15 I, even I, have spoken;
   yes, I have called him.
I will bring him,
   and he will succeed in his mission.

16 "Come near me and listen to this:

"From the first announcement I have
   not spoken in secret;
   at the time it happens, I am there."

And now the Sovereign LORD has sent
   me,
   with his Spirit.

17 This is what the LORD says—
   your Redeemer, the Holy One of
      Israel:
"I am the LORD your God,
   who teaches you what is best for
      you,
   who directs you in the way you
      should go.
18 If only you had paid attention to my
      commands,
   your peace would have been like a
      river,
   your righteousness like the waves
      of the sea.
19 Your descendants would have been
      like the sand,
   your children like its numberless
      grains;
   their name would never be cut off
      nor destroyed from before me."

20 Leave Babylon,
   flee from the Babylonians!
Announce this with shouts of joy
   and proclaim it.
Send it out to the ends of the earth;
   say, "The LORD has redeemed his
      servant Jacob."
21 They did not thirst when he led them
      through the deserts;

he made water flow for them from
      the rock;
he split the rock
   and water gushed out.

22 "There is no peace," says the LORD,
   "for the wicked."

49:1 LISTEN to me, you islands;
   hear this, you distant nations:
Before I was born the LORD called me;
   from my birth he has made
      mention of my name.
2 He made my mouth like a sharpened
      sword,
   in the shadow of his hand he hid
      me;
he made me into a polished arrow
   and concealed me in his quiver.
3 He said to me, "You are my servant,
   Israel, in whom I will display my
      splendor."
4 But I said, "I have labored to no
      purpose;
   I have spent my strength in vain
      and for nothing.
Yet what is due me is in the LORD's
      hand,
   and my reward is with my God."

5 And now the LORD says—
   he who formed me in the womb to
      be his servant
to bring Jacob back to him
   and gather Israel to himself,
for I am honored in the eyes of the
      LORD
   and my God has been my
      strength—
6 he says:
"It is too small a thing for you to be
      my servant
   to restore the tribes of Jacob
   and bring back those of Israel I
      have kept.
I will also make you a light for the
      Gentiles,
   that you may bring my salvation to
      the ends of the earth."

7 This is what the LORD says—
   the Redeemer and Holy One of
      Israel—

to him who was despised and
   abhorred by the nation,
to the servant of rulers:
"Kings will see you and rise up,
   princes will see and bow down,
because of the LORD, who is faithful,
   the Holy One of Israel, who has
      chosen you."

⁸This is what the LORD says:

"In the time of my favor I will answer
      you,
   and in the day of salvation I will
      help you;
I will keep you and will make you
   to be a covenant for the people,
to restore the land
   and to reassign its desolate
      inheritances,
⁹to say to the captives, 'Come out,'
   and to those in darkness, 'Be free!'

"They will feed beside the roads
   and find pasture on every barren
      hill.
¹⁰They will neither hunger nor thirst,
   nor will the desert heat or the sun
      beat upon them.
He who has compassion on them will
      guide them
   and lead them beside springs of
      water.
¹¹I will turn all my mountains into
      roads,
   and my highways will be raised up.
¹²See, they will come from afar—
   some from the north, some from
      the west,
   some from the region of Aswan.ᵇ"

¹³Shout for joy, O heavens;
   rejoice, O earth;
   burst into song, O mountains!
For the LORD comforts his people
   and will have compassion on his
      afflicted ones.

¹⁴But Zion said, "The LORD has
      forsaken me,
   the Lord has forgotten me."

¹⁵"Can a mother forget the baby at her
      breast

and have no compassion on the
      child she has borne?
Though she may forget,
   I will not forget you!
¹⁶See, I have engraved you on the
      palms of my hands;
   your walls are ever before me.
¹⁷Your sons hasten back,
   and those who laid you waste
      depart from you.
¹⁸Lift up your eyes and look around;
   all your sons gather and come to
      you.
As surely as I live," declares the LORD,
   "you will wear them all as
      ornaments;
   you will put them on, like a bride.

¹⁹"Though you were ruined and made
      desolate
   and your land laid waste,
now you will be too small for your
      people,
   and those who devoured you will
      be far away.
²⁰The children born during your
      bereavement
   will yet say in your hearing,
'This place is too small for us;
   give us more space to live in.'
²¹Then you will say in your heart,
   'Who bore me these?
I was bereaved and barren;
   I was exiled and rejected.
   Who brought these up?
I was left all alone,
   but these—where have they come
      from?'"

²²This is what the Sovereign LORD
says:

"See, I will beckon to the Gentiles,
   I will lift up my banner to the
      peoples;
they will bring your sons in their
      arms
   and carry your daughters on their
      shoulders.
²³Kings will be your foster fathers,
   and their queens your nursing
      mothers.

They will bow down before you with
  their faces to the ground;
    they will lick the dust at your feet.
Then you will know that I am the
  LORD;
    those who hope in me will not be
      disappointed."

²⁴Can plunder be taken from warriors,
  or captives rescued from the
    fierce^c?

²⁵But this is what the LORD says:

"Yes, captives will be taken from
  warriors,
    and plunder retrieved from the
      fierce;
I will contend with those who
  contend with you,
    and your children I will save.
²⁶I will make your oppressors eat their
  own flesh;
    they will be drunk on their own
      blood, as with wine.
Then all mankind will know
  that I, the LORD, am your Savior,
    your Redeemer, the Mighty One of
      Jacob."

^{50:1}THIS is what the LORD says:

"Where is your mother's certificate
  of divorce
    with which I sent her away?
Or to which of my creditors
  did I sell you?
Because of your sins you were sold;
  because of your transgressions
    your mother was sent away.
²When I came, why was there no one?
  When I called, why was there no
    one to answer?
Was my arm too short to ransom
  you?
    Do I lack the strength to rescue
      you?
By a mere rebuke I dry up the sea,
  I turn rivers into a desert;
    their fish rot for lack of water
      and die of thirst.
³I clothe the sky with darkness
  and make sackcloth its covering."

⁴The Sovereign LORD has given me an
  instructed tongue,
    to know the word that sustains the
      weary.
He wakens me morning by morning,
  wakens my ear to listen like one
    being taught.
⁵The Sovereign LORD has opened my
  ears,
    and I have not been rebellious;
      I have not drawn back.
⁶I offered my back to those who beat
  me,
    my cheeks to those who pulled out
      my beard;
I did not hide my face
  from mocking and spitting.
⁷Because the Sovereign LORD helps me,
  I will not be disgraced.
Therefore have I set my face like
  flint,
    and I know I will not be put to
      shame.
⁸He who vindicates me is near.
  Who then will bring charges
    against me?
Let us face each other!
Who is my accuser?
Let him confront me!
⁹It is the Sovereign LORD who helps me.
  Who is he that will condemn me?
They will all wear out like a garment;
  the moths will eat them up.

¹⁰Who among you fears the LORD
  and obeys the word of his servant?
Let him who walks in the dark,
  who has no light,
trust in the name of the LORD
  and rely on his God.
¹¹But now, all you who light fires
  and provide yourselves with
    flaming torches,
go, walk in the light of your fires
  and of the torches you have set
    ablaze.
This is what you shall receive from
  my hand:
    You will lie down in torment.

^a14 Or *Chaldeans*; also in verse 20   ^b12 Dead Sea Scrolls;
Masoretic Text *Sinim*   ^c24 Dead Sea Scrolls, Vulgate and
Syriac (see also Septuagint and verse 25); Masoretic Text
righteous

EPHESIANS 4:17-32

So I tell you this, and insist on it in the Lord, that you must no longer live as the Gentiles do, in the futility of their thinking. 18They are darkened in their understanding and separated from the life of God because of the ignorance that is in them due to the hardening of their hearts. 19Having lost all sensitivity, they have given themselves over to sensuality so as to indulge in every kind of impurity, with a continual lust for more.

20You, however, did not come to know Christ that way. 21Surely you heard of him and were taught in him in accordance with the truth that is in Jesus. 22You were taught, with regard to your former way of life, to put off your old self, which is being corrupted by its deceitful desires; 23to be made new in the attitude of your minds; 24and to put on the new self, created to be like God in true righteousness and holiness.

25Therefore each of you must put off falsehood and speak truthfully to his neighbor, for we are all members of one body. 26"In your anger do not sin"*a*: Do not let the sun go down while you are still angry, 27and do not give the devil a foothold. 28He who has been stealing must steal no longer, but must work, doing something useful with his own hands, that he may have something to share with those in need.

29**Do not let any unwholesome talk come out of your mouths, but only what is helpful for building others up according to their needs, that it may benefit those who listen.** 30And do not grieve the Holy Spirit of God, with whom you were sealed for the day of redemption. 31Get rid of all bitterness, rage and anger, brawling and slander, along with every form of malice. 32Be kind and compassionate to one another, forgiving each other, just as in Christ God forgave you.

a26 Psalm 4:4

PSALM 69:1-18

For the director of music. To ⌊the tune of⌋ "Lilies." Of David.

1 Save me, O God,
    for the waters have come up to my
        neck.
2 I sink in the miry depths,
    where there is no foothold.
I have come into the deep waters;
    the floods engulf me.
3 I am worn out calling for help;
    my throat is parched.
My eyes fail,
    looking for my God.
4 Those who hate me without reason
    outnumber the hairs of my head;
many are my enemies without cause,
    those who seek to destroy me.
I am forced to restore
    what I did not steal.

5 You know my folly, O God;
    my guilt is not hidden from you.

6 May those who hope in you
    not be disgraced because of me,
    O Lord, the LORD Almighty;
may those who seek you
    not be put to shame because of me,
    O God of Israel.
7 For I endure scorn for your sake,
    and shame covers my face.
8 I am a stranger to my brothers,
    an alien to my own mother's sons;
9 for zeal for your house consumes me,
    and the insults of those who insult
        you fall on me.
10 When I weep and fast,
    I must endure scorn;
11 when I put on sackcloth,
    people make sport of me.
12 Those who sit at the gate mock me,
    and I am the song of the drunkards.

13 But I pray to you, O LORD,
    in the time of your favor;
in your great love, O God,
    answer me with your sure
        salvation.
14 Rescue me from the mire,
    do not let me sink;
deliver me from those who hate me,
    from the deep waters.

15 Do not let the floodwaters engulf me
   or the depths swallow me up
   or the pit close its mouth over me.
16 Answer me, O LORD, out of the
     goodness of your love;
   in your great mercy turn to me.
17 Do not hide your face from your
     servant;
   answer me quickly, for I am in
     trouble.
18 Come near and rescue me;
   redeem me because of my foes.

PROVERBS 24:5-6

5 A wise man has great power,
   and a man of knowledge increases
     strength;
6 for waging war you need guidance,
   and for victory many advisers.

☐ D A Y   2 7 0

GOD SIGHTINGS

September 27

ISAIAH 51:1–53:12

  "Listen to me [the LORD], you who
     pursue righteousness
   and who seek the LORD:
Look to the rock from which you
     were cut
   and to the quarry from which you
     were hewn;
2 look to Abraham, your father,
   and to Sarah, who gave you birth.
When I called him he was but one,
   and I blessed him and made him
     many.
3 The LORD will surely comfort Zion
   and will look with compassion on
     all her ruins;
he will make her deserts like Eden,
   her wastelands like the garden of
     the LORD.
Joy and gladness will be found in
     her,
   thanksgiving and the sound of
     singing.

4 "Listen to me, my people;
   hear me, my nation:
The law will go out from me;
   my justice will become a light to
     the nations.
5 My righteousness draws near
     speedily,
   my salvation is on the way,
   and my arm will bring justice to
     the nations.
The islands will look to me
   and wait in hope for my arm.
6 Lift up your eyes to the heavens,
   look at the earth beneath;
the heavens will vanish like smoke,
   the earth will wear out like a
     garment
   and its inhabitants die like flies.
But my salvation will last forever,
   my righteousness will never fail.

7 "Hear me, you who know what is
     right,
   you people who have my law in
     your hearts:
Do not fear the reproach of men
   or be terrified by their insults.
8 For the moth will eat them up like a
     garment;
   the worm will devour them like
     wool.
But my righteousness will last
     forever,
   my salvation through all
     generations."

9 Awake, awake! Clothe yourself with
     strength,
   O arm of the LORD;
awake, as in days gone by,
   as in generations of old.
Was it not you who cut Rahab to
     pieces,
   who pierced that monster
     through?
10 Was it not you who dried up the sea,
   the waters of the great deep,
who made a road in the depths of the
     sea
   so that the redeemed might cross
     over?

11 The ransomed of the LORD will
        return.
    They will enter Zion with singing;
        everlasting joy will crown their
        heads.
    Gladness and joy will overtake them,
        and sorrow and sighing will flee
        away.

12 "I, even I, am he who comforts you.
    Who are you that you fear mortal
        men,
        the sons of men, who are but
        grass,
13 that you forget the LORD your Maker,
        who stretched out the heavens
        and laid the foundations of the
        earth,
    that you live in constant terror every
        day
        because of the wrath of the
        oppressor,
        who is bent on destruction?
    For where is the wrath of the
        oppressor?
14   The cowering prisoners will soon
        be set free;
    they will not die in their dungeon,
        nor will they lack bread.
15 For I am the LORD your God,
        who churns up the sea so that its
        waves roar—
        the LORD Almighty is his name.
16 I have put my words in your mouth
        and covered you with the shadow
        of my hand—
    I who set the heavens in place,
        who laid the foundations of the
        earth,
        and who say to Zion, 'You are my
        people.'"

17 Awake, awake!
    Rise up, O Jerusalem,
    you who have drunk from the hand
        of the LORD
        the cup of his wrath,
    you who have drained to its dregs
        the goblet that makes men
        stagger.
18 Of all the sons she bore
        there was none to guide her;

of all the sons she reared
        there was none to take her by the
        hand.
19 These double calamities have come
        upon you—
    who can comfort you?—
    ruin and destruction, famine and
        sword—
    who cana console you?
20 Your sons have fainted;
        they lie at the head of every street,
        like antelope caught in a net.
    They are filled with the wrath of the
        LORD
        and the rebuke of your God.

21 Therefore hear this, you afflicted
        one,
        made drunk, but not with wine.
22 This is what your Sovereign LORD
        says,
        your God, who defends his people:
    "See, I have taken out of your hand
        the cup that made you stagger;
    from that cup, the goblet of my wrath,
        you will never drink again.
23 I will put it into the hands of your
        tormentors,
        who said to you,
        'Fall prostrate that we may walk
        over you.'
    And you made your back like the
        ground,
        like a street to be walked over."

52:1 Awake, awake, O Zion,
        clothe yourself with strength.
    Put on your garments of splendor,
        O Jerusalem, the holy city.
    The uncircumcised and defiled
        will not enter you again.
2 Shake off your dust;
        rise up, sit enthroned,
        O Jerusalem.
    Free yourself from the chains on
        your neck,
        O captive Daughter of Zion.

3 For this is what the LORD says:

    "You were sold for nothing,
        and without money you will be
        redeemed."

4For this is what the Sovereign LORD says:

"At first my people went down to
      Egypt to live;
   lately, Assyria has oppressed
      them.

5"And now what do I have here?" declares the LORD.

"For my people have been taken away
      for nothing,
   and those who rule them mock,b"
                           declares the LORD.
"And all day long
   my name is constantly
      blasphemed.
6Therefore my people will know my
      name;
   therefore in that day they will
      know
that it is I who foretold it.
   Yes, it is I."

7How beautiful on the mountains
   are the feet of those who bring
      good news,
who proclaim peace,
   who bring good tidings,
   who proclaim salvation,
who say to Zion,
   "Your God reigns!"
8Listen! Your watchmen lift up their
      voices;
   together they shout for joy.
When the LORD returns to Zion,
   they will see it with their own
      eyes.
9Burst into songs of joy together,
   you ruins of Jerusalem,
for the LORD has comforted his
      people,
   he has redeemed Jerusalem.
10The LORD will lay bare his holy arm
   in the sight of all the nations,
and all the ends of the earth will see
   the salvation of our God.

11Depart, depart, go out from there!
   Touch no unclean thing!
Come out from it and be pure,
   you who carry the vessels of the
      LORD.

12But you will not leave in haste
   or go in flight;
for the LORD will go before you,
   the God of Israel will be your rear
      guard.

13See, my servant will act wiselyc;
   he will be raised and lifted up and
      highly exalted.
14Just as there were many who were
      appalled at himd—
   his appearance was so disfigured
      beyond that of any man
   and his form marred beyond
      human likeness—
15so will he sprinkle many nations,e
   and kings will shut their mouths
      because of him.
For what they were not told, they will
      see,
   and what they have not heard, they
      will understand.

53:1WHO has believed our message
   and to whom has the arm of the
      LORD been revealed?
2He grew up before him like a tender
      shoot,
   and like a root out of dry ground.
He had no beauty or majesty to
      attract us to him,
   nothing in his appearance that we
      should desire him.
3He was despised and rejected by
      men,
   a man of sorrows, and familiar
      with suffering.
Like one from whom men hide their
      faces
   he was despised, and we esteemed
      him not.

4Surely he took up our infirmities
   and carried our sorrows,
yet we considered him stricken by
      God,
   smitten by him, and afflicted.
5But he was pierced for our
      transgressions,
   he was crushed for our
      iniquities;
the punishment that brought us
      peace was upon him,

**and by his wounds we are
    healed.**
6 We all, like sheep, have gone astray,
    each of us has turned to his own
        way;
and the LORD has laid on him
    the iniquity of us all.

7 He was oppressed and afflicted,
    yet he did not open his mouth;
he was led like a lamb to the
        slaughter,
    and as a sheep before her shearers
        is silent,
    so he did not open his mouth.
8 By oppression*f* and judgment he was
        taken away.
    And who can speak of his
        descendants?
For he was cut off from the land of
        the living;
    for the transgression of my people
        he was stricken.*g*
9 He was assigned a grave with the
        wicked,
    and with the rich in his death,
though he had done no violence,
    nor was any deceit in his mouth.

10 Yet it was the LORD's will to crush him
        and cause him to suffer,
    and though the LORD makes*h* his
        life a guilt offering,
he will see his offspring and prolong
        his days,
    and the will of the LORD will
        prosper in his hand.
11 After the suffering of his soul,
    he will see the light ⌊of life⌋*i* and
        be satisfied*j*;
by his knowledge*k* my righteous
        servant will justify many,
    and he will bear their iniquities.
12 Therefore I will give him a portion
        among the great,*l*
    and he will divide the spoils with
        the strong,*m*
because he poured out his life unto
        death,
    and was numbered with the
        transgressors.
For he bore the sin of many,

and made intercession for the
    transgressors.

a 19 Dead Sea Scrolls, Septuagint, Vulgate and Syriac;
Masoretic Text / *how can I*   *b 5* Dead Sea Scrolls and
Vulgate; Masoretic Text *wail*   *c 13* Or *will prosper*
d 14 Hebrew *you*   *e 15* Hebrew; Septuagint *so will many
nations marvel at him*   *f 8* Or *From arrest*   *g 8* Or *away. /
Yet who of his generation considered / that he was cut off
from the land of the living / for the transgression of my
people, / to whom the blow was due?*   *h 10* Hebrew *though
you make*   *i 11* Dead Sea Scrolls (see also Septuagint);
Masoretic Text does not have *the light* ⌊*of life*⌋.   *j 11* Or (with
Masoretic Text) *11 He will see the result of the suffering of
his soul / and be satisfied*   *k 11* Or *by knowledge of him*
l 12 Or *many*   *m 12* Or *numerous*

EPHESIANS 5:1-33

Be imitators of God, therefore, as dearly
loved children 2 and live a life of love,
just as Christ loved us and gave himself
up for us as a fragrant offering and sacrifice to God.

3 But among you there must not be even
a hint of sexual immorality, or of any kind
of impurity, or of greed, because these are
improper for God's holy people. 4 Nor
should there be obscenity, foolish talk or
coarse joking, which are out of place, but
rather thanksgiving. 5 For of this you can
be sure: No immoral, impure or greedy
person—such a man is an idolater—has
any inheritance in the kingdom of Christ
and of God.*a* 6 Let no one deceive you with
empty words, for because of such things
God's wrath comes on those who are disobedient. 7 Therefore do not be partners
with them.

8 For you were once darkness, but now
you are light in the Lord. Live as children
of light 9 (for the fruit of the light consists in all goodness, righteousness and
truth) 10 and find out what pleases the
Lord. 11 Have nothing to do with the
fruitless deeds of darkness, but rather
expose them. 12 For it is shameful even
to mention what the disobedient do in
secret. 13 But everything exposed by the
light becomes visible, 14 for it is light
that makes everything visible. This is
why it is said:

"Wake up, O sleeper,
    rise from the dead,
and Christ will shine on you."

15 Be very careful, then, how you
live—not as unwise but as wise, 16 mak-

ing the most of every opportunity, because the days are evil. [17]Therefore do not be foolish, but understand what the Lord's will is. [18]Do not get drunk on wine, which leads to debauchery. Instead, be filled with the Spirit. [19]Speak to one another with psalms, hymns and spiritual songs. Sing and make music in your heart to the Lord, [20]always giving thanks to God the Father for everything, in the name of our Lord Jesus Christ.

[21]Submit to one another out of reverence for Christ.

[22]Wives, submit to your husbands as to the Lord. [23]For the husband is the head of the wife as Christ is the head of the church, his body, of which he is the Savior. [24]Now as the church submits to Christ, so also wives should submit to their husbands in everything.

[25]Husbands, love your wives, just as Christ loved the church and gave himself up for her [26]to make her holy, cleansing[b] her by the washing with water through the word, [27]and to present her to himself as a radiant church, without stain or wrinkle or any other blemish, but holy and blameless. [28]In this same way, husbands ought to love their wives as their own bodies. He who loves his wife loves himself. [29]After all, no one ever hated his own body, but he feeds and cares for it, just as Christ does the church— [30]for we are members of his body. [31]"For this reason a man will leave his father and mother and be united to his wife, and the two will become one flesh."[c] [32]This is a profound mystery— but I am talking about Christ and the church. [33]However, each one of you also must love his wife as he loves himself, and the wife must respect her husband.

a5 Or kingdom of the Christ and God   b26 Or having cleansed   c31 Gen. 2:24

PSALM 69:19-36

[19]You [LORD] know how I am scorned, disgraced and shamed;
all my enemies are before you.
[20]Scorn has broken my heart
and has left me helpless;

I looked for sympathy, but there was none,
for comforters, but I found none.
[21]They put gall in my food
and gave me vinegar for my thirst.

[22]May the table set before them
become a snare;
may it become retribution and[a] a trap.
[23]May their eyes be darkened so they cannot see,
and their backs be bent forever.
[24]Pour out your wrath on them;
let your fierce anger overtake them.
[25]May their place be deserted;
let there be no one to dwell in their tents.
[26]For they persecute those you wound
and talk about the pain of those you hurt.
[27]Charge them with crime upon crime;
do not let them share in your salvation.
[28]May they be blotted out of the book of life
and not be listed with the righteous.

[29]I am in pain and distress;
may your salvation, O God, protect me.

[30]I will praise God's name in song
and glorify him with thanksgiving.
[31]This will please the LORD more than an ox,
more than a bull with its horns and hoofs.
[32]The poor will see and be glad—
you who seek God, may your hearts live!
[33]The LORD hears the needy
and does not despise his captive people.

[34]Let heaven and earth praise him,
the seas and all that move in them,
[35]for God will save Zion
and rebuild the cities of Judah.
Then people will settle there and possess it;

36   the children of his servants will
            inherit it,
       and those who love his name will
            dwell there.

a22 Or snare / and their fellowship become

PROVERBS 24:7
7 **W**isdom is too high for a fool;
       in the assembly at the gate he has
            nothing to say.

□ DAY 271

GOD SIGHTINGS

September 28

ISAIAH 54:1–57:13
    "**S**ing, O barren woman,
       you who never bore a child;
    burst into song, shout for joy,
       you who were never in labor;
    because more are the children of the
            desolate woman
       than of her who has a husband,"
                                    says the LORD.
2 "Enlarge the place of your tent,
       stretch your tent curtains wide,
       do not hold back;
    lengthen your cords,
       strengthen your stakes.
3 For you will spread out to the right
            and to the left;
       your descendants will dispossess
            nations
       and settle in their desolate cities.

4 "Do not be afraid; you will not suffer
            shame.
       Do not fear disgrace; you will not
            be humiliated.
    You will forget the shame of your youth
       and remember no more the
            reproach of your widowhood.
5 For your Maker is your husband—
       the LORD Almighty is his name—
    the Holy One of Israel is your
            Redeemer;
       he is called the God of all the
            earth.

6 The LORD will call you back
       as if you were a wife deserted and
            distressed in spirit—
    a wife who married young,
       only to be rejected," says your God.
7 "For a brief moment I abandoned
            you,
       but with deep compassion I will
            bring you back.
8 In a surge of anger
       I hid my face from you for a
            moment,
    but with everlasting kindness
       I will have compassion on you,"
       says the LORD your Redeemer.

9 "To me this is like the days of Noah,
       when I swore that the waters of
            Noah would never again
            cover the earth.
    So now I have sworn not to be angry
            with you,
       never to rebuke you again.
10 Though the mountains be shaken
            and the hills be removed,
       yet my unfailing love for you will not
            be shaken
    nor my covenant of peace be
            removed,"
       says the LORD, who has
            compassion on you.

11 "O afflicted city, lashed by storms
            and not comforted,
       I will build you with stones of
            turquoise,*a*
       your foundations with sapphires.*b*
12 I will make your battlements of
            rubies,
       your gates of sparkling jewels,
       and all your walls of precious
            stones.
13 All your sons will be taught by the
            LORD,
       and great will be your children's
            peace.
14 In righteousness you will be
            established:
       Tyranny will be far from you;
       you will have nothing to fear.
    Terror will be far removed;
       it will not come near you.

¹⁵ If anyone does attack you, it will not
    be my doing;
  whoever attacks you will
    surrender to you.

¹⁶ "See, it is I who created the blacksmith
    who fans the coals into flame
  and forges a weapon fit for its work.
  And it is I who have created the
    destroyer to work havoc;
¹⁷ no weapon forged against you will
    prevail,
  and you will refute every tongue
    that accuses you.
  This is the heritage of the servants of
    the LORD,
  and this is their vindication from
    me,"
                    declares the LORD.

⁵⁵:¹ "COME, all you who are thirsty,
    come to the waters;
  and you who have no money,
    come, buy and eat!
  Come, buy wine and milk
    without money and without cost.
² Why spend money on what is not
    bread,
  and your labor on what does not
    satisfy?
  Listen, listen to me, and eat what is
    good,
  and your soul will delight in the
    richest of fare.
³ Give ear and come to me;
    hear me, that your soul may live.
  I will make an everlasting covenant
    with you,
  my faithful love promised to
    David.
⁴ See, I have made him a witness to the
    peoples,
  a leader and commander of the
    peoples.
⁵ Surely you will summon nations you
    know not,
  and nations that do not know you
    will hasten to you,
  because of the LORD your God,
    the Holy One of Israel,
  for he has endowed you with
    splendor."

⁶ Seek the LORD while he may be found;
    call on him while he is near.
⁷ Let the wicked forsake his way
    and the evil man his thoughts.
  Let him turn to the LORD, and he will
    have mercy on him,
  and to our God, for he will freely
    pardon.

⁸ "For my thoughts are not your
    thoughts,
  neither are your ways my ways,"
                    declares the LORD.
⁹ "As the heavens are higher than the
    earth,
  so are my ways higher than your
    ways
  and my thoughts than your
    thoughts.
¹⁰ As the rain and the snow
    come down from heaven,
  and do not return to it
    without watering the earth
  and making it bud and flourish,
    so that it yields seed for the sower
      and bread for the eater,
¹¹ so is my word that goes out from my
    mouth:
  It will not return to me empty,
    but will accomplish what I desire
  and achieve the purpose for which
    I sent it.
¹² You will go out in joy
    and be led forth in peace;
  the mountains and hills
    will burst into song before you,
  and all the trees of the field
    will clap their hands.
¹³ Instead of the thornbush will grow
    the pine tree,
  and instead of briers the myrtle
    will grow.
  This will be for the LORD's renown,
    for an everlasting sign,
  which will not be destroyed."

⁵⁶:¹ THIS is what the LORD says:

  "Maintain justice
    and do what is right,
  for my salvation is close at hand
    and my righteousness will soon be
      revealed.

² Blessed is the man who does this,
    the man who holds it fast,
who keeps the Sabbath without
        desecrating it,
    and keeps his hand from doing
        any evil."

³ Let no foreigner who has bound
        himself to the Lᴏʀᴅ say,
    "The Lᴏʀᴅ will surely exclude me
        from his people."
And let not any eunuch complain,
    "I am only a dry tree."

⁴ For this is what the Lᴏʀᴅ says:

"To the eunuchs who keep my
        Sabbaths,
    who choose what pleases me
    and hold fast to my covenant—
⁵ to them I will give within my temple
        and its walls
    a memorial and a name
    better than sons and daughters;
I will give them an everlasting name
    that will not be cut off.
⁶ And foreigners who bind themselves
        to the Lᴏʀᴅ
    to serve him,
to love the name of the Lᴏʀᴅ,
    and to worship him,
all who keep the Sabbath without
        desecrating it
    and who hold fast to my
        covenant—
⁷ these I will bring to my holy
        mountain
    and give them joy in my house of
        prayer.
Their burnt offerings and
        sacrifices
    will be accepted on my altar;
for my house will be called
    a house of prayer for all nations."
⁸ The Sovereign Lᴏʀᴅ declares—
    he who gathers the exiles of
        Israel:
"I will gather still others to them
    besides those already gathered."

⁹ Come, all you beasts of the field,
    come and devour, all you beasts of
        the forest!

¹⁰ Israel's watchmen are blind,
    they all lack knowledge;
they are all mute dogs,
    they cannot bark;
they lie around and dream,
    they love to sleep.
¹¹ They are dogs with mighty appetites;
    they never have enough.
They are shepherds who lack
        understanding;
    they all turn to their own way,
    each seeks his own gain.
¹² "Come," each one cries, "let me get
        wine!
    Let us drink our fill of beer!
And tomorrow will be like today,
    or even far better."

⁵⁷:¹ Tʜᴇ righteous perish,
    and no one ponders it in his heart;
devout men are taken away,
    and no one understands
that the righteous are taken away
    to be spared from evil.
² Those who walk uprightly
    enter into peace;
    they find rest as they lie in death.

³ "But you—come here, you sons of a
        sorceress,
    you offspring of adulterers and
        prostitutes!
⁴ Whom are you mocking?
    At whom do you sneer
    and stick out your tongue?
Are you not a brood of rebels,
    the offspring of liars?
⁵ You burn with lust among the oaks
    and under every spreading tree;
you sacrifice your children in the
        ravines
    and under the overhanging crags.
⁶ ⌞The idols⌟ among the smooth
        stones of the ravines are
        your portion;
    they, they are your lot.
Yes, to them you have poured out
        drink offerings
    and offered grain offerings.
    In the light of these things, should
        I relent?

7 You have made your bed on a high
    and lofty hill;
  there you went up to offer your
    sacrifices.
8 Behind your doors and your
    doorposts
  you have put your pagan symbols.
  Forsaking me, you uncovered your
    bed,
  you climbed into it and opened it
    wide;
  you made a pact with those whose
    beds you love,
  and you looked on their
    nakedness.
9 You went to Molech[c] with olive oil
    and increased your perfumes.
  You sent your ambassadors[d] far
    away;
  you descended to the grave[e] itself!
10 You were wearied by all your ways,
    but you would not say, 'It is
    hopeless.'
  You found renewal of your strength,
    and so you did not faint.

11 "Whom have you so dreaded and
    feared
  that you have been false to me,
  and have neither remembered me
    nor pondered this in your hearts?
  Is it not because I have long been
    silent
  that you do not fear me?
12 I will expose your righteousness and
    your works,
  and they will not benefit you.
13 When you cry out for help,
  let your collection ⌊of idols⌋ save
    you!
  The wind will carry all of them off,
    a mere breath will blow them away.
  But the man who makes me his
    refuge
  will inherit the land
    and possess my holy mountain."

a 11 The meaning of the Hebrew for this word is uncertain.
b 11 Or lapis lazuli c 9 Or to the king d 9 Or idols
e 9 Hebrew Sheol

EPHESIANS 6:1-24

Children, obey your parents in the Lord,
for this is right. 2 "Honor your father
and mother"—which is the first commandment with a promise— 3 "that it
may go well with you and that you may
enjoy long life on the earth."[a]

4 Fathers, do not exasperate your children; instead, bring them up in the
training and instruction of the Lord.

5 Slaves, obey your earthly masters
with respect and fear, and with sincerity
of heart, just as you would obey Christ.
6 Obey them not only to win their favor
when their eye is on you, but like slaves
of Christ, doing the will of God from
your heart. 7 Serve wholeheartedly, as if
you were serving the Lord, not men, 8 because you know that the Lord will reward everyone for whatever good he
does, whether he is slave or free.

9 And masters, treat your slaves in the
same way. Do not threaten them, since
you know that he who is both their Master and yours is in heaven, and there is
no favoritism with him.

10 Finally, be strong in the Lord and in
his mighty power. 11 Put on the full armor of God so that you can take your
stand against the devil's schemes.
12 **For our struggle is not against
flesh and blood, but against the rulers, against the authorities, against
the powers of this dark world and
against the spiritual forces of evil in
the heavenly realms.** 13 Therefore put
on the full armor of God, so that when
the day of evil comes, you may be able
to stand your ground, and after you
have done everything, to stand. 14 Stand
firm then, with the belt of truth buck-
led around your waist, with the breastplate of righteousness in place, 15 and
with your feet fitted with the readiness
that comes from the gospel of peace.
16 In addition to all this, take up the
shield of faith, with which you can ex-
tinguish all the flaming arrows of the
evil one. 17 Take the helmet of salvation
and the sword of the Spirit, which is the
word of God. 18 And pray in the Spirit
on all occasions with all kinds of
prayers and requests. With this in
mind, be alert and always keep on praying for all the saints.

¹⁹Pray also for me, that whenever I open my mouth, words may be given me so that I will fearlessly make known the mystery of the gospel, ²⁰for which I am an ambassador in chains. Pray that I may declare it fearlessly, as I should.

²¹Tychicus, the dear brother and faithful servant in the Lord, will tell you everything, so that you also may know how I am and what I am doing. ²²I am sending him to you for this very purpose, that you may know how we are, and that he may encourage you.

²³Peace to the brothers, and love with faith from God the Father and the Lord Jesus Christ. ²⁴Grace to all who love our Lord Jesus Christ with an undying love.

a3 Deut. 5:16

PSALM 70:1-5

For the director of music. Of David. A petition.

¹ **H**asten, O God, to save me;
    O Lᴏʀᴅ, come quickly to help me.
² May those who seek my life
    be put to shame and confusion;
  may all who desire my ruin
    be turned back in disgrace.
³ May those who say to me, "Aha! Aha!"
    turn back because of their shame.
⁴ But may all who seek you
    rejoice and be glad in you;
  may those who love your salvation
    always say,
    "Let God be exalted!"

⁵ Yet I am poor and needy;
    come quickly to me, O God.
  You are my help and my deliverer;
    O Lᴏʀᴅ, do not delay.

PROVERBS 24:8

⁸ **H**e who plots evil
    will be known as a schemer.

GOD SIGHTINGS

September 29

ISAIAH 57:14–59:21

And it will be said:

"Build up, build up, prepare the
        road!
    Remove the obstacles out of the
        way of my [the Lᴏʀᴅ's] people."
¹⁵ For this is what the high and lofty
        One says—
    he who lives forever, whose name
        is holy:
"I live in a high and holy place,
    but also with him who is contrite
        and lowly in spirit,
  to revive the spirit of the lowly
    and to revive the heart of the
        contrite.
¹⁶ I will not accuse forever,
    nor will I always be angry,
  for then the spirit of man would
        grow faint before me—
    the breath of man that I have
        created.
¹⁷ I was enraged by his sinful greed;
    I punished him, and hid my face in
        anger,
    yet he kept on in his willful ways.
¹⁸ I have seen his ways, but I will heal
        him;
    I will guide him and restore
        comfort to him,
¹⁹   creating praise on the lips of the
        mourners in Israel.
  Peace, peace, to those far and near,"
    says the Lᴏʀᴅ. "And I will heal
        them."
²⁰ But the wicked are like the tossing
        sea,
    which cannot rest,
    whose waves cast up mire and
        mud.
²¹ "There is no peace," says my God,
    "for the wicked."

⁵⁸:¹ "Sʜᴏᴜᴛ it aloud, do not hold back.
    Raise your voice like a trumpet.

Declare to my people their rebellion
 and to the house of Jacob their
  sins.
² For day after day they seek me out;
 they seem eager to know my ways,
as if they were a nation that does
  what is right
 and has not forsaken the
  commands of its God.
They ask me for just decisions
 and seem eager for God to come
  near them.
³ 'Why have we fasted,' they say,
 'and you have not seen it?
Why have we humbled ourselves,
 and you have not noticed?'

"Yet on the day of your fasting, you
  do as you please
 and exploit all your workers.
⁴ Your fasting ends in quarreling and
  strife,
 and in striking each other with
  wicked fists.
You cannot fast as you do today
 and expect your voice to be heard
  on high.
⁵ Is this the kind of fast I have chosen,
 only a day for a man to humble
  himself?
Is it only for bowing one's head like a
  reed
 and for lying on sackcloth and
  ashes?
Is that what you call a fast,
 a day acceptable to the LORD?

⁶ "Is not this the kind of fasting I have
  chosen:
to loose the chains of injustice
 and untie the cords of the yoke,
to set the oppressed free
 and break every yoke?
⁷ Is it not to share your food with the
  hungry
 and to provide the poor wanderer
  with shelter—
when you see the naked, to clothe
  him,
 and not to turn away from your
  own flesh and blood?

⁸ Then your light will break forth like
  the dawn,
 and your healing will quickly
  appear;
then your righteousness*a* will go
  before you,
 and the glory of the LORD will be
  your rear guard.
⁹ Then you will call, and the LORD will
  answer;
 you will cry for help, and he will
  say: Here am I.

"If you do away with the yoke of
  oppression,
 with the pointing finger and
  malicious talk,
¹⁰ and if you spend yourselves in behalf
  of the hungry
 and satisfy the needs of the
  oppressed,
then your light will rise in the
  darkness,
 and your night will become like
  the noonday.
¹¹ The LORD will guide you always;
 he will satisfy your needs in a sun-
  scorched land
 and will strengthen your frame.
You will be like a well-watered
  garden,
 like a spring whose waters never
  fail.
¹² Your people will rebuild the ancient
  ruins
 and will raise up the age-old
  foundations;
you will be called Repairer of Broken
  Walls,
 Restorer of Streets with Dwellings.

¹³ "If you keep your feet from breaking
  the Sabbath
 and from doing as you please on
  my holy day,
if you call the Sabbath a delight
 and the LORD's holy day honorable,
and if you honor it by not going your
  own way
 and not doing as you please or
  speaking idle words,

¹⁴then you will find your joy in the
  LORD,
    and I will cause you to ride on the
      heights of the land
    and to feast on the inheritance of
      your father Jacob."
  The mouth of the LORD has spoken.

^{59:1}SURELY the arm of the LORD is not
    too short to save,
  nor his ear too dull to hear.
²But your iniquities have separated
    you from your God;
  your sins have hidden his face from
    you,
    so that he will not hear.
³For your hands are stained with
    blood,
  your fingers with guilt.
Your lips have spoken lies,
  and your tongue mutters wicked
    things.
⁴No one calls for justice;
  no one pleads his case with
    integrity.
They rely on empty arguments and
    speak lies;
  they conceive trouble and give
    birth to evil.
⁵They hatch the eggs of vipers
  and spin a spider's web.
Whoever eats their eggs will die,
  and when one is broken, an adder
    is hatched.
⁶Their cobwebs are useless for
    clothing;
  they cannot cover themselves with
    what they make.
Their deeds are evil deeds,
  and acts of violence are in their
    hands.
⁷Their feet rush into sin;
  they are swift to shed innocent
    blood.
Their thoughts are evil thoughts;
  ruin and destruction mark their
    ways.
⁸The way of peace they do not know;
  there is no justice in their paths.
They have turned them into crooked
    roads;

no one who walks in them will
    know peace.

⁹So justice is far from us,
  and righteousness does not reach
    us.
We look for light, but all is darkness;
  for brightness, but we walk in
    deep shadows.
¹⁰Like the blind we grope along the
    wall,
  feeling our way like men without
    eyes.
At midday we stumble as if it were
    twilight;
  among the strong, we are like the
    dead.
¹¹We all growl like bears;
  we moan mournfully like doves.
We look for justice, but find none;
  for deliverance, but it is far away.

¹²For our offenses are many in your
    sight,
  and our sins testify against us.
Our offenses are ever with us,
  and we acknowledge our
    iniquities:
¹³rebellion and treachery against the
    LORD,
  turning our backs on our God,
fomenting oppression and revolt,
  uttering lies our hearts have
    conceived.
¹⁴So justice is driven back,
  and righteousness stands at a
    distance;
truth has stumbled in the streets,
  honesty cannot enter.
¹⁵Truth is nowhere to be found,
  and whoever shuns evil becomes a
    prey.

The LORD looked and was displeased
  that there was no justice.
¹⁶He saw that there was no one,
  he was appalled that there was no
    one to intervene;
so his own arm worked salvation for
    him,
  and his own righteousness
    sustained him.

17 He put on righteousness as his
        breastplate,
    and the helmet of salvation on his
        head;
    he put on the garments of vengeance
        and wrapped himself in zeal as in
        a cloak.
18 According to what they have done,
        so will he repay
    wrath to his enemies
        and retribution to his foes;
    he will repay the islands their due.
19 From the west, men will fear the
        name of the LORD,
    and from the rising of the sun,
        they will revere his glory.
    For he will come like a pent-up flood
        that the breath of the LORD drives
        along.b

20 "The Redeemer will come to Zion,
        to those in Jacob who repent of
        their sins,"
                                        declares the LORD.

21 "As for me, this is my covenant with
them," says the LORD. "My Spirit, who is
on you, and my words that I have put in
your mouth will not depart from your
mouth, or from the mouths of your children, or from the mouths of their descendants from this time on and
forever," says the LORD.

a 8 Or your righteous One   b 19 Or When the enemy comes
in like a flood, / the Spirit of the LORD will put him to flight

PHILIPPIANS 1:1-26

Paul and Timothy, servants of Christ
Jesus,

    To all the saints in Christ Jesus at Phi-
lippi, together with the overseersa and
deacons:

    2 Grace and peace to you from God
our Father and the Lord Jesus Christ.

    3 I thank my God every time I remem-
ber you. 4 In all my prayers for all of you, I
always pray with joy 5 because of your
partnership in the gospel from the first
day until now, 6 being confident of this,
that he who began a good work in you

will carry it on to completion until the
day of Christ Jesus.

    7 It is right for me to feel this way
about all of you, since I have you in my
heart; for whether I am in chains or defending and confirming the gospel, all
of you share in God's grace with me.
8 God can testify how I long for all of you
with the affection of Christ Jesus.

    9 And this is my prayer: that your love
may abound more and more in knowledge and depth of insight, 10 so that you
may be able to discern what is best and
may be pure and blameless until the
day of Christ, 11 filled with the fruit of
righteousness that comes through
Jesus Christ—to the glory and praise of
God.

    12 Now I want you to know, brothers,
that what has happened to me has really
served to advance the gospel. 13 As a result, it has become clear throughout the
whole palace guardb and to everyone
else that I am in chains for Christ. 14 Because of my chains, most of the brothers
in the Lord have been encouraged to
speak the word of God more courageously and fearlessly.

    15 It is true that some preach Christ
out of envy and rivalry, but others out of
goodwill. 16 The latter do so in love,
knowing that I am put here for the defense of the gospel. 17 The former
preach Christ out of selfish ambition,
not sincerely, supposing that they can
stir up trouble for me while I am in
chains.c 18 But what does it matter? The
important thing is that in every way,
whether from false motives or true,
Christ is preached. And because of this I
rejoice.

    Yes, and I will continue to rejoice,
19 for I know that through your prayers
and the help given by the Spirit of Jesus
Christ, what has happened to me will
turn out for my deliverance.d 20 **I eagerly expect and hope that I will in no
way be ashamed, but will have sufficient courage so that now as always
Christ will be exalted in my body,
whether by life or by death. 21 For to
me, to live is Christ and to die is gain.**

22If I am to go on living in the body, this will mean fruitful labor for me. Yet what shall I choose? I do not know! 23I am torn between the two: I desire to depart and be with Christ, which is better by far; 24but it is more necessary for you that I remain in the body. 25Convinced of this, I know that I will remain, and I will continue with all of you for your progress and joy in the faith, 26so that through my being with you again your joy in Christ Jesus will overflow on account of me.

*a*1 Traditionally *bishops*   *b*13 Or *whole palace*   *c*16,17 Some late manuscripts have verses 16 and 17 in reverse order. *d*19 Or *salvation*

PSALM 71:1-24

1 In you, O Lord, I have taken refuge;
    let me never be put to shame.
2 Rescue me and deliver me in your
        righteousness;
    turn your ear to me and save me.
3 Be my rock of refuge,
        to which I can always go;
    give the command to save me,
        for you are my rock and my
            fortress.
4 Deliver me, O my God, from the hand
        of the wicked,
    from the grasp of evil and cruel
        men.

5 For you have been my hope,
        O Sovereign Lord,
    my confidence since my youth.
6 From birth I have relied on you;
    you brought me forth from my
        mother's womb.
    I will ever praise you.
7 I have become like a portent to
        many,
    but you are my strong refuge.
8 My mouth is filled with your praise,
    declaring your splendor all day
        long.

9 Do not cast me away when I am old;
    do not forsake me when my
        strength is gone.
10 For my enemies speak against me;
    those who wait to kill me conspire
        together.

11 They say, "God has forsaken him;
    pursue him and seize him,
    for no one will rescue him."
12 Be not far from me, O God;
    come quickly, O my God, to help
        me.
13 May my accusers perish in shame;
    may those who want to harm me
        be covered with scorn and
            disgrace.

14 But as for me, I will always have hope;
    I will praise you more and more.
15 My mouth will tell of your
        righteousness,
    of your salvation all day long,
        though I know not its measure.
16 I will come and proclaim your mighty
        acts, O Sovereign Lord;
    I will proclaim your righteousness,
        yours alone.
17 Since my youth, O God, you have
        taught me,
    and to this day I declare your
        marvelous deeds.
18 Even when I am old and gray,
        do not forsake me, O God,
    till I declare your power to the next
        generation,
    your might to all who are to come.

19 Your righteousness reaches to the
        skies, O God,
    you who have done great things.
    Who, O God, is like you?
20 Though you have made me see
            troubles, many and bitter,
    you will restore my life again;
    from the depths of the earth
        you will again bring me up.
21 You will increase my honor
    and comfort me once again.

22 I will praise you with the harp
        for your faithfulness, O my God;
    I will sing praise to you with the lyre,
        O Holy One of Israel.
23 My lips will shout for joy
        when I sing praise to you—
    I, whom you have redeemed.
24 My tongue will tell of your righteous
        acts
    all day long,

for those who wanted to harm me
have been put to shame and
confusion.

PROVERBS 24:9-10
⁹The schemes of folly are sin,
and men detest a mocker.

¹⁰If you falter in times of trouble,
how small is your strength!

☐ DAY 273

GOD SIGHTINGS

September 30

ISAIAH 60:1–62:5
"Arise, shine, for your [the Lord's
peoples'] light has come,
and the glory of the Lord rises
upon you.
²See, darkness covers the earth
and thick darkness is over the
peoples,
but the Lord rises upon you
and his glory appears over you.
³Nations will come to your light,
and kings to the brightness of your
dawn.

⁴"Lift up your eyes and look about you:
All assemble and come to you;
your sons come from afar,
and your daughters are carried on
the arm.
⁵Then you will look and be radiant,
your heart will throb and swell
with joy;
the wealth on the seas will be
brought to you,
to you the riches of the nations
will come.
⁶Herds of camels will cover your land,
young camels of Midian and
Ephah.
And all from Sheba will come,
bearing gold and incense
and proclaiming the praise of the
Lord.

⁷All Kedar's flocks will be gathered to
you,
the rams of Nebaioth will serve
you;
they will be accepted as offerings on
my altar,
and I will adorn my glorious temple.

⁸"Who are these that fly along like
clouds,
like doves to their nests?
⁹Surely the islands look to me;
in the lead are the ships of
Tarshish,ᵃ
bringing your sons from afar,
with their silver and gold,
to the honor of the Lord your God,
the Holy One of Israel,
for he has endowed you with
splendor.

¹⁰"Foreigners will rebuild your walls,
and their kings will serve you.
Though in anger I struck you,
in favor I will show you
compassion.
¹¹Your gates will always stand open,
they will never be shut, day or night,
so that men may bring you the
wealth of the nations—
their kings led in triumphal
procession.
¹²For the nation or kingdom that will
not serve you will perish;
it will be utterly ruined.

¹³"The glory of Lebanon will come to
you,
the pine, the fir and the cypress
together,
to adorn the place of my sanctuary;
and I will glorify the place of my
feet.
¹⁴The sons of your oppressors will
come bowing before you;
all who despise you will bow down
at your feet
and will call you the City of the Lord,
Zion of the Holy One of Israel.

¹⁵"Although you have been forsaken
and hated,
with no one traveling through,

I will make you the everlasting pride
and the joy of all generations.
16 You will drink the milk of nations
and be nursed at royal breasts.
Then you will know that I, the LORD,
am your Savior,
your Redeemer, the Mighty One of
Jacob.
17 Instead of bronze I will bring you
gold,
and silver in place of iron.
Instead of wood I will bring you
bronze,
and iron in place of stones.
I will make peace your governor
and righteousness your ruler.
18 No longer will violence be heard in
your land,
nor ruin or destruction within
your borders,
but you will call your walls Salvation
and your gates Praise.
19 The sun will no more be your light by
day,
nor will the brightness of the
moon shine on you,
for the LORD will be your everlasting
light,
and your God will be your glory.
20 Your sun will never set again,
and your moon will wane no more;
the LORD will be your everlasting
light,
and your days of sorrow will end.
21 Then will all your people be
righteous
and they will possess the land
forever.
They are the shoot I have planted,
the work of my hands,
for the display of my splendor.
22 The least of you will become a
thousand,
the smallest a mighty nation.
I am the LORD;
in its time I will do this swiftly."

61:1 THE Spirit of the Sovereign LORD is
on me,
because the LORD has anointed me
to preach good news to the poor.

He has sent me to bind up the
brokenhearted,
to proclaim freedom for the
captives
and release from darkness for the
prisoners,*b*
2 to proclaim the year of the LORD's
favor
and the day of vengeance of our
God,
to comfort all who mourn,
3   and provide for those who grieve
in Zion—
to bestow on them a crown of beauty
instead of ashes,
the oil of gladness
instead of mourning,
and a garment of praise
instead of a spirit of despair.
They will be called oaks of
righteousness,
a planting of the LORD
for the display of his splendor.

4 They will rebuild the ancient ruins
and restore the places long
devastated;
they will renew the ruined cities
that have been devastated for
generations.
5 Aliens will shepherd your flocks;
foreigners will work your fields
and vineyards.
6 And you will be called priests of the
LORD,
you will be named ministers of our
God.
You will feed on the wealth of
nations,
and in their riches you will boast.

7 Instead of their shame
my people will receive a double
portion,
and instead of disgrace
they will rejoice in their
inheritance;
and so they will inherit a double
portion in their land,
and everlasting joy will be theirs.

8 "For I, the LORD, love justice;
I hate robbery and iniquity.

In my faithfulness I will reward them
   and make an everlasting covenant
      with them.
⁹Their descendants will be known
      among the nations
   and their offspring among the
      peoples.
All who see them will acknowledge
   that they are a people the LORD has
      blessed."

¹⁰I delight greatly in the LORD;
   my soul rejoices in my God.
For he has clothed me with garments
      of salvation
   and arrayed me in a robe of
      righteousness,
as a bridegroom adorns his head like
      a priest,
   and as a bride adorns herself with
      her jewels.
¹¹For as the soil makes the sprout
      come up
   and a garden causes seeds to
      grow,
so the Sovereign LORD will make
      righteousness and praise
   spring up before all nations.

⁶²:¹For Zion's sake I will not keep silent,
   for Jerusalem's sake I will not
      remain quiet,
till her righteousness shines out like
      the dawn,
   her salvation like a blazing torch.
²The nations will see your
      righteousness,
   and all kings your glory;
you will be called by a new name
   that the mouth of the LORD will
      bestow.
³You will be a crown of splendor in
      the LORD's hand,
   a royal diadem in the hand of your
      God.
⁴No longer will they call you
      Deserted,
   or name your land Desolate.
But you will be called Hephzibah,ᶜ
   and your land Beulahᵈ;
for the LORD will take delight in you,
   and your land will be married.

⁵As a young man marries a maiden,
   so will your sonsᵉ marry you;
as a bridegroom rejoices over his bride,
   so will your God rejoice over you.

ᵃ9 Or the trading ships   ᵇ1 Hebrew; Septuagint the blind
ᶜ4 Hephzibah means my delight is in her.   ᵈ4 Beulah means
married.   ᵉ5 Or Builder

PHILIPPIANS 1:27–2:18

Whatever happens, conduct yourselves
in a manner worthy of the gospel of
Christ. Then, whether I come and see
you or only hear about you in my ab-
sence, I will know that you stand firm in
one spirit, contending as one man for
the faith of the gospel ²⁸without being
frightened in any way by those who oppose you. This is a sign to them that they
will be destroyed, but that you will be
saved—and that by God. ²⁹For it has
been granted to you on behalf of Christ
not only to believe on him, but also to
suffer for him, ³⁰since you are going
through the same struggle you saw I
had, and now hear that I still have.

²:¹If you have any encouragement from
being united with Christ, if any comfort
from his love, if any fellowship with the
Spirit, if any tenderness and compassion, ²then make my joy complete by
being like-minded, having the same
love, being one in spirit and purpose.
³**Do nothing out of selfish ambition
or vain conceit, but in humility consider others better than yourselves.
⁴Each of you should look not only to
your own interests, but also to the interests of others.**
   ⁵Your attitude should be the same as
that of Christ Jesus:

⁶Who, being in very natureᵃ God,
   did not consider equality with God
      something to be grasped,
⁷but made himself nothing,
   taking the very natureᵇ of a servant,
   being made in human likeness.
⁸And being found in appearance as a
      man,
   he humbled himself
   and became obedient to death—
      even death on a cross!

9 Therefore God exalted him to the
highest place
and gave him the name that is
above every name,
10 that at the name of Jesus every knee
should bow,
in heaven and on earth and under
the earth,
11 and every tongue confess that Jesus
Christ is Lord,
to the glory of God the Father.

12 Therefore, my dear friends, as you
have always obeyed—not only in my
presence, but now much more in my ab-
sence—continue to work out your salvation with fear and trembling, 13 for it is
God who works in you to will and to act
according to his good purpose.

14 Do everything without complain-
ing or arguing, 15 so that you may become blameless and pure, children of
God without fault in a crooked and depraved generation, in which you shine
like stars in the universe 16 as you hold
out*c* the word of life—in order that I
may boast on the day of Christ that I did
not run or labor for nothing. 17 But even
if I am being poured out like a drink offering on the sacrifice and service coming from your faith, I am glad and
rejoice with all of you. 18 So you too
should be glad and rejoice with me.

a6 Or in the form of   b7 Or the form   c16 Or hold on to

PSALM 72:1-20
Of Solomon.

1 **E**ndow the king with your justice,
O God,
the royal son with your
righteousness.
2 He will*a* judge your people in
righteousness,
your afflicted ones with justice.
3 The mountains will bring prosperity
to the people,
the hills the fruit of righteousness.
4 He will defend the afflicted among
the people
and save the children of the needy;
he will crush the oppressor.

5 He will endure*b* as long as the sun,
as long as the moon, through all
generations.
6 He will be like rain falling on a mown
field,
like showers watering the earth.
7 In his days the righteous will
flourish;
prosperity will abound till the
moon is no more.

8 He will rule from sea to sea
and from the River*c* to the ends of
the earth.*d*
9 The desert tribes will bow before him
and his enemies will lick the dust.
10 The kings of Tarshish and of distant
shores
will bring tribute to him;
the kings of Sheba and Seba
will present him gifts.
11 All kings will bow down to him
and all nations will serve him.

12 For he will deliver the needy who cry
out,
the afflicted who have no one to
help.
13 He will take pity on the weak and the
needy
and save the needy from death.
14 He will rescue them from oppression
and violence,
for precious is their blood in his
sight.

15 Long may he live!
May gold from Sheba be given him.
May people ever pray for him
and bless him all day long.
16 Let grain abound throughout the
land;
on the tops of the hills may it sway.
Let its fruit flourish like Lebanon;
let it thrive like the grass of the
field.
17 May his name endure forever;
may it continue as long as the sun.

All nations will be blessed through
him,
and they will call him blessed.

¹⁸ Praise be to the Lord God, the God of
  Israel,
  who alone does marvelous deeds.
¹⁹ Praise be to his glorious name
  forever;
  may the whole earth be filled with
  his glory.
      Amen and Amen.

²⁰ This concludes the prayers of David
  son of Jesse.

^a2 Or *May he*; similarly in verses 3-11 and 17
^b5 Septuagint; Hebrew *You will be feared*   ^c8 That is,
the Euphrates   ^d8 Or *the end of the land*

PROVERBS 24:11-12

¹¹ **R**escue those being led away to
  death;
  hold back those staggering toward
  slaughter.
¹² If you say, "But we knew nothing
  about this,"
  does not he who weighs the heart
  perceive it?
Does not he who guards your life
  know it?
  Will he not repay each person
  according to what he has done?

GOD SIGHTINGS

October 1

ISAIAH 62:6–65:25

6 ❚ [the LORD] have posted watchmen
on your walls, O Jerusalem;
they will never be silent day or
night.
You who call on the LORD,
give yourselves no rest,
7 and give him no rest till he
establishes Jerusalem
and makes her the praise of the
earth.

8 The LORD has sworn by his right
hand
and by his mighty arm:
"Never again will I give your grain
as food for your enemies,
and never again will foreigners drink
the new wine
for which you have toiled;
9 but those who harvest it will eat it
and praise the LORD,
and those who gather the grapes will
drink it
in the courts of my sanctuary."

10 Pass through, pass through the gates!
Prepare the way for the people.
Build up, build up the highway!
Remove the stones.
Raise a banner for the nations.

11 The LORD has made proclamation
to the ends of the earth:
"Say to the Daughter of Zion,
'See, your Savior comes!
See, his reward is with him,
and his recompense accompanies
him.'"
12 They will be called the Holy People,
the Redeemed of the LORD;
and you will be called Sought After,
the City No Longer Deserted.

63:1 Who is this coming from Edom,
from Bozrah, with his garments
stained crimson?
Who is this, robed in splendor,
striding forward in the greatness
of his strength?

"It is I, speaking in righteousness,
mighty to save."

2 Why are your garments red,
like those of one treading the
winepress?

3 "I have trodden the winepress alone;
from the nations no one was with
me.
I trampled them in my anger
and trod them down in my wrath;
their blood spattered my garments,
and I stained all my clothing.
4 For the day of vengeance was in my
heart,
and the year of my redemption has
come.
5 I looked, but there was no one to help,
I was appalled that no one gave
support;
so my own arm worked salvation for
me,
and my own wrath sustained me.
6 I trampled the nations in my anger;
in my wrath I made them drunk
and poured their blood on the
ground."

7 I will tell of the kindnesses of the
LORD,
the deeds for which he is to be
praised,
according to all the LORD has done
for us—
yes, the many good things he has done
for the house of Israel,
according to his compassion and
many kindnesses.
8 He said, "Surely they are my people,
sons who will not be false to me";
and so he became their Savior.

9 In all their distress he too was
  distressed,
    and the angel of his presence
      saved them.
  In his love and mercy he redeemed
    them;
    he lifted them up and carried
      them
    all the days of old.
10 Yet they rebelled
    and grieved his Holy Spirit.
  So he turned and became their enemy
    and he himself fought against
      them.

11 Then his people recalled*a* the days of
    old,
    the days of Moses and his
      people—
  where is he who brought them
    through the sea,
    with the shepherd of his flock?
  Where is he who set
    his Holy Spirit among them,
12 who sent his glorious arm of power
    to be at Moses' right hand,
  who divided the waters before them,
    to gain for himself everlasting
      renown,
13 who led them through the depths?
  Like a horse in open country,
    they did not stumble;
14 like cattle that go down to the plain,
    they were given rest by the Spirit
      of the LORD.
  This is how you guided your people
    to make for yourself a glorious
      name.

15 Look down from heaven and see
    from your lofty throne, holy and
      glorious.
  Where are your zeal and your might?
    Your tenderness and compassion
      are withheld from us.
16 But you are our Father,
    though Abraham does not know us
      or Israel acknowledge us;
  you, O LORD, are our Father,
    our Redeemer from of old is your
      name.

17 Why, O LORD, do you make us wander
    from your ways
    and harden our hearts so we do
      not revere you?
  Return for the sake of your servants,
    the tribes that are your
      inheritance.
18 For a little while your people
    possessed your holy place,
  but now our enemies have
    trampled down your
      sanctuary.
19 We are yours from of old;
    but you have not ruled over them,
    they have not been called by your
      name.*b*

64:1 OH, that you would rend the heavens
    and come down,
    that the mountains would tremble
      before you!
2 As when fire sets twigs ablaze
    and causes water to boil,
  come down to make your name
      known to your enemies
    and cause the nations to quake
      before you!
3 For when you did awesome things
    that we did not expect,
  you came down, and the
    mountains trembled before
      you.
4 Since ancient times no one has heard,
    no ear has perceived,
  no eye has seen any God besides
    you,
    who acts on behalf of those who
      wait for him.
5 You come to the help of those who
    gladly do right,
    who remember your ways.
  But when we continued to sin against
    them,
    you were angry.
  How then can we be saved?
6 All of us have become like one who is
    unclean,
    and all our righteous acts are like
      filthy rags;
  we all shrivel up like a leaf,
    and like the wind our sins sweep
      us away.

⁷No one calls on your name
   or strives to lay hold of you;
for you have hidden your face from
      us
   and made us waste away because
      of our sins.

⁸Yet, O Lord, you are our Father.
   We are the clay, you are the potter;
   we are all the work of your hand.
⁹Do not be angry beyond measure,
      O Lord;
   do not remember our sins forever.
Oh, look upon us, we pray,
   for we are all your people.
¹⁰Your sacred cities have become a
      desert;
   even Zion is a desert, Jerusalem a
      desolation.
¹¹Our holy and glorious temple, where
      our fathers praised you,
   has been burned with fire,
   and all that we treasured lies in
      ruins.
¹²After all this, O Lord, will you hold
      yourself back?
   Will you keep silent and punish us
      beyond measure?

65:1"I revealed myself to those who did
      not ask for me;
   I was found by those who did not
      seek me.
To a nation that did not call on my
      name,
   I said, 'Here am I, here am I.'
²All day long I have held out my hands
   to an obstinate people,
who walk in ways not good,
   pursuing their own imaginations—
³a people who continually provoke me
      to my very face,
   offering sacrifices in gardens
      and burning incense on altars of
      brick;
⁴who sit among the graves
   and spend their nights keeping
      secret vigil;
who eat the flesh of pigs,
   and whose pots hold broth of
      unclean meat;

⁵who say, 'Keep away; don't come near
      me,
   for I am too sacred for you!'
Such people are smoke in my
      nostrils,
   a fire that keeps burning all day.

⁶"See, it stands written before me:
   I will not keep silent but will pay
      back in full;
   I will pay it back into their laps—
⁷both your sins and the sins of your
      fathers,"
      says the Lord.
"Because they burned sacrifices on
      the mountains
   and defied me on the hills,
I will measure into their laps
   the full payment for their former
      deeds."

⁸This is what the Lord says:

"As when juice is still found in a
      cluster of grapes
   and men say, 'Don't destroy it,
      there is yet some good in it,'
so will I do in behalf of my servants;
   I will not destroy them all.
⁹I will bring forth descendants from
      Jacob,
   and from Judah those who will
      possess my mountains;
my chosen people will inherit them,
   and there will my servants live.
¹⁰Sharon will become a pasture for
      flocks,
   and the Valley of Achor a resting
      place for herds,
   for my people who seek me.

¹¹"But as for you who forsake the Lord
   and forget my holy mountain,
who spread a table for Fortune
   and fill bowls of mixed wine for
      Destiny,
¹²I will destine you for the sword,
   and you will all bend down for the
      slaughter;
for I called but you did not answer,
   I spoke but you did not listen.
You did evil in my sight
   and chose what displeases me."

13 Therefore this is what the Sovereign LORD says:

"My servants will eat,
  but you will go hungry;
my servants will drink,
  but you will go thirsty;
my servants will rejoice,
  but you will be put to shame.
14 My servants will sing
  out of the joy of their hearts,
but you will cry out
  from anguish of heart
  and wail in brokenness of spirit.
15 You will leave your name
  to my chosen ones as a curse;
the Sovereign LORD will put you to
  death,
  but to his servants he will give
  another name.
16 Whoever invokes a blessing in the
  land
  will do so by the God of truth;
he who takes an oath in the land
  will swear by the God of truth.
For the past troubles will be
  forgotten
  and hidden from my eyes.

17 "Behold, I will create
  new heavens and a new earth.
The former things will not be
  remembered,
  nor will they come to mind.
18 But be glad and rejoice forever
  in what I will create,
for I will create Jerusalem to be a
  delight
  and its people a joy.
19 I will rejoice over Jerusalem
  and take delight in my people;
the sound of weeping and of crying
  will be heard in it no more.

20 "Never again will there be in it
  an infant who lives but a few days,
  or an old man who does not live
    out his years;
he who dies at a hundred
  will be thought a mere youth;
he who fails to reach[c] a hundred
  will be considered accursed.

21 They will build houses and dwell in
    them;
  they will plant vineyards and eat
    their fruit.
22 No longer will they build houses and
    others live in them,
  or plant and others eat.
For as the days of a tree,
  so will be the days of my people;
my chosen ones will long enjoy
  the works of their hands.
23 They will not toil in vain
  or bear children doomed to
    misfortune;
for they will be a people blessed by
  the LORD,
  they and their descendants with
    them.
24 Before they call I will answer;
  while they are still speaking I will
    hear.
25 The wolf and the lamb will feed
    together,
  and the lion will eat straw like the
    ox,
  but dust will be the serpent's food.
They will neither harm nor destroy
  on all my holy mountain,"
                                        says the LORD.

a11 Or *But may he recall*   b19 Or *We are like those you*
have never ruled, / like those never called by your name
c20 Or / *the sinner who reaches*

PHILIPPIANS 2:19–3:4A

I hope in the Lord Jesus to send Timothy to you soon, that I also may be cheered when I receive news about you. 20 I have no one else like him, who takes a genuine interest in your welfare. 21 For everyone looks out for his own interests, not those of Jesus Christ. 22 But you know that Timothy has proved himself, because as a son with his father he has served with me in the work of the gospel. 23 I hope, therefore, to send him as soon as I see how things go with me. 24 And I am confident in the Lord that I myself will come soon.

25 But I think it is necessary to send back to you Epaphroditus, my brother, fellow worker and fellow soldier, who is also your messenger, whom you sent to

take care of my needs. 26 For he longs for all of you and is distressed because you heard he was ill. 27 Indeed he was ill, and almost died. But God had mercy on him, and not on him only but also on me, to spare me sorrow upon sorrow. 28 Therefore I am all the more eager to send him, so that when you see him again you may be glad and I may have less anxiety. 29 Welcome him in the Lord with great joy, and honor men like him, 30 because he almost died for the work of Christ, risking his life to make up for the help you could not give me.

3:1 FINALLY, my brothers, rejoice in the Lord! It is no trouble for me to write the same things to you again, and it is a safeguard for you.

2 Watch out for those dogs, those men who do evil, those mutilators of the flesh. 3 For it is we who are the circumcision, we who worship by the Spirit of God, who glory in Christ Jesus, and who put no confidence in the flesh— 4 though I myself have reasons for such confidence.

PSALM 73:1-28
A psalm of Asaph.

1 **S**urely God is good to Israel,
  to those who are pure in heart.

2 But as for me, my feet had almost
    slipped;
  I had nearly lost my foothold.
3 For I envied the arrogant
  when I saw the prosperity of the
    wicked.

4 They have no struggles;
  their bodies are healthy and
    strong.a
5 They are free from the burdens
    common to man;
  they are not plagued by human
    ills.
6 Therefore pride is their necklace;
  they clothe themselves with
    violence.
7 From their callous hearts comes
    iniquityb;
  the evil conceits of their minds
    know no limits.

8 They scoff, and speak with malice;
  in their arrogance they threaten
    oppression.
9 Their mouths lay claim to heaven,
  and their tongues take possession
    of the earth.
10 Therefore their people turn to them
  and drink up waters in
    abundance.c
11 They say, "How can God know?
  Does the Most High have
    knowledge?"

12 This is what the wicked are like—
  always carefree, they increase in
    wealth.

13 Surely in vain have I kept my heart
    pure;
  in vain have I washed my hands in
    innocence.
14 All day long I have been plagued;
  I have been punished every
    morning.

15 If I had said, "I will speak thus,"
  I would have betrayed your
    children.
16 When I tried to understand all this,
  it was oppressive to me
17 till I entered the sanctuary of God;
  then I understood their final
    destiny.

18 Surely you place them on slippery
    ground;
  you cast them down to ruin.
19 How suddenly are they destroyed,
  completely swept away by terrors!
20 As a dream when one awakes,
  so when you arise, O Lord,
  you will despise them as
    fantasies.

21 When my heart was grieved
  and my spirit embittered,
22 I was senseless and ignorant;
  I was a brute beast before you.

23 Yet I am always with you;
  you hold me by my right hand.
24 You guide me with your counsel,
  and afterward you will take me
    into glory.

25 Whom have I in heaven but you?
And earth has nothing I desire
besides you.
26 **My flesh and my heart may fail,
but God is the strength of my
heart
and my portion forever.**

27 Those who are far from you will
perish;
you destroy all who are unfaithful
to you.
28 But as for me, it is good to be near
God.
I have made the Sovereign Lord
my refuge;
I will tell of all your deeds.

a4 With a different word division of the Hebrew; Masoretic
Text *struggles at their death; / their bodies are healthy*
b7 Syriac (see also Septuagint); Hebrew *Their eyes bulge
with fat*   *c10* The meaning of the Hebrew for this verse
is uncertain.

PROVERBS 24:13-14

13 Eat honey, my son, for it is good;
honey from the comb is sweet to
your taste.
14 Know also that wisdom is sweet to
your soul;
if you find it, there is a future hope
for you,
and your hope will not be cut off.

□ DAY 275

GOD SIGHTINGS

October 2

ISAIAH 66:1-24
This is what the Lord says:

"Heaven is my throne,
and the earth is my footstool.
Where is the house you will build for
me?
Where will my resting place be?
2 Has not my hand made all these
things,
and so they came into being?"
declares the Lord.

"This is the one I esteem:
he who is humble and contrite in
spirit,
and trembles at my word.
3 But whoever sacrifices a bull
is like one who kills a man,
and whoever offers a lamb,
like one who breaks a dog's neck;
whoever makes a grain offering
is like one who presents pig's
blood,
and whoever burns memorial
incense,
like one who worships an idol.
They have chosen their own ways,
and their souls delight in their
abominations;
4 so I also will choose harsh treatment
for them
and will bring upon them what
they dread.
For when I called, no one answered,
when I spoke, no one listened.
They did evil in my sight
and chose what displeases me."

5 Hear the word of the Lord,
you who tremble at his word:
"Your brothers who hate you,
and exclude you because of my
name, have said,
'Let the Lord be glorified,
that we may see your joy!'
Yet they will be put to shame.
6 Hear that uproar from the city,
hear that noise from the temple!
It is the sound of the Lord
repaying his enemies all they
deserve.

7 "Before she goes into labor,
she gives birth;
before the pains come upon her,
she delivers a son.
8 Who has ever heard of such a thing?
Who has ever seen such things?
Can a country be born in a day
or a nation be brought forth in a
moment?
Yet no sooner is Zion in labor
than she gives birth to her
children.

⁹Do I bring to the moment of birth
   and not give delivery?" says the
   LORD.
"Do I close up the womb
   when I bring to delivery?" says
   your God.
¹⁰"Rejoice with Jerusalem and be glad
      for her,
   all you who love her;
rejoice greatly with her,
   all you who mourn over her.
¹¹For you will nurse and be satisfied
   at her comforting breasts;
you will drink deeply
   and delight in her overflowing
      abundance."

¹²For this is what the LORD says:

"I will extend peace to her like a
      river,
   and the wealth of nations like a
      flooding stream;
you will nurse and be carried on her
      arm
   and dandled on her knees.
¹³As a mother comforts her child,
   so will I comfort you;
   and you will be comforted over
      Jerusalem."

¹⁴When you see this, your heart will
      rejoice
   and you will flourish like grass;
the hand of the LORD will be made
      known to his servants,
   but his fury will be shown to his
      foes.
¹⁵See, the LORD is coming with fire,
   and his chariots are like a
      whirlwind;
he will bring down his anger with
      fury,
   and his rebuke with flames of fire.
¹⁶For with fire and with his sword
   the LORD will execute judgment
      upon all men,
   and many will be those slain by
      the LORD.

¹⁷"Those who consecrate and purify
themselves to go into the gardens, following the one in the midst of ᵃ those

who eat the flesh of pigs and rats and
other abominable things—they will meet
their end together," declares the LORD.

¹⁸"And I, because of their actions and
their imaginations, am about to come ᵇ
and gather all nations and tongues, and
they will come and see my glory.

¹⁹"I will set a sign among them, and I
will send some of those who survive to
the nations—to Tarshish, to the Libyans ᶜ
and Lydians (famous as archers), to Tubal
and Greece, and to the distant islands
that have not heard of my fame or seen
my glory. They will proclaim my glory
among the nations. ²⁰And they will bring
all your brothers, from all the nations, to
my holy mountain in Jerusalem as an offering to the LORD—on horses, in chariots
and wagons, and on mules and camels,"
says the LORD. "They will bring them, as
the Israelites bring their grain offerings,
to the temple of the LORD in ceremonially
clean vessels. ²¹And I will select some of
them also to be priests and Levites," says
the LORD.

²²"As the new heavens and the new
earth that I make will endure before
me," declares the LORD, "so will your
name and descendants endure. ²³From
one New Moon to another and from one
Sabbath to another, all mankind will
come and bow down before me," says
the LORD. ²⁴"And they will go out and
look upon the dead bodies of those who
rebelled against me; their worm will not
die, nor will their fire be quenched, and
they will be loathsome to all mankind."

ᵃ17 Or gardens behind one of your temples, and   ᵇ18 The
meaning of the Hebrew for this clause is uncertain.   ᶜ19 Some
Septuagint manuscripts Put (Libyans); Hebrew Pul

PHILIPPIANS 3:4B-21

If anyone else thinks he has reasons to
put confidence in the flesh, I have more:
⁵circumcised on the eighth day, of the
people of Israel, of the tribe of Benjamin, a Hebrew of Hebrews; in regard to
the law, a Pharisee; ⁶as for zeal, persecuting the church; as for legalistic righteousness, faultless.
⁷But whatever was to my profit I now
consider loss for the sake of Christ.

⁸What is more, I consider everything a loss compared to the surpassing greatness of knowing Christ Jesus my Lord, for whose sake I have lost all things. I consider them rubbish, that I may gain Christ ⁹and be found in him, not having a righteousness of my own that comes from the law, but that which is through faith in Christ—the righteousness that comes from God and is by faith. ¹⁰I want to know Christ and the power of his resurrection and the fellowship of sharing in his sufferings, becoming like him in his death, ¹¹and so, somehow, to attain to the resurrection from the dead.

¹²Not that I have already obtained all this, or have already been made perfect, but I press on to take hold of that for which Christ Jesus took hold of me. **¹³Brothers, I do not consider myself yet to have taken hold of it. But one thing I do: Forgetting what is behind and straining toward what is ahead, ¹⁴I press on toward the goal to win the prize for which God has called me heavenward in Christ Jesus.**

¹⁵All of us who are mature should take such a view of things. And if on some point you think differently, that too God will make clear to you. ¹⁶Only let us live up to what we have already attained.

¹⁷Join with others in following my example, brothers, and take note of those who live according to the pattern we gave you. ¹⁸For, as I have often told you before and now say again even with tears, many live as enemies of the cross of Christ. ¹⁹Their destiny is destruction, their god is their stomach, and their glory is in their shame. Their mind is on earthly things. ²⁰But our citizenship is in heaven. And we eagerly await a Savior from there, the Lord Jesus Christ, ²¹who, by the power that enables him to bring everything under his control, will transform our lowly bodies so that they will be like his glorious body.

PSALM 74:1-23

A *maskil*[a] of Asaph.

¹**W**hy have you rejected us forever,
O God?

Why does your anger smolder
against the sheep of your
pasture?
²Remember the people you
purchased of old,
the tribe of your inheritance,
whom you redeemed—
Mount Zion, where you dwelt.
³Turn your steps toward these
everlasting ruins,
all this destruction the enemy has
brought on the sanctuary.

⁴Your foes roared in the place where
you met with us;
they set up their standards as
signs.
⁵They behaved like men wielding axes
to cut through a thicket of trees.
⁶They smashed all the carved
paneling
with their axes and hatchets.
⁷They burned your sanctuary to the
ground;
they defiled the dwelling place of
your Name.
⁸They said in their hearts, "We will
crush them completely!"
They burned every place where God
was worshiped in the land.
⁹We are given no miraculous signs;
no prophets are left,
and none of us knows how long
this will be.

¹⁰How long will the enemy mock you,
O God?
Will the foe revile your name
forever?
¹¹Why do you hold back your hand,
your right hand?
Take it from the folds of your
garment and destroy them!

¹²But you, O God, are my king from of
old;
you bring salvation upon the
earth.
¹³It was you who split open the sea by
your power;
you broke the heads of the
monster in the waters.

¹⁴It was you who crushed the heads of
      Leviathan
   and gave him as food to the
      creatures of the desert.
¹⁵It was you who opened up springs
      and streams;
   you dried up the ever flowing
      rivers.
¹⁶The day is yours, and yours also the
      night;
   you established the sun and
      moon.
¹⁷It was you who set all the boundaries
      of the earth;
   you made both summer and
      winter.

¹⁸Remember how the enemy has
      mocked you, O Lᴏʀᴅ,
   how foolish people have reviled
      your name.
¹⁹Do not hand over the life of your
      dove to wild beasts;
   do not forget the lives of your
      afflicted people forever.
²⁰Have regard for your covenant,
   because haunts of violence fill the
      dark places of the land.
²¹Do not let the oppressed retreat in
      disgrace;
   may the poor and needy praise
      your name.

²²Rise up, O God, and defend your
      cause;
   remember how fools mock you all
      day long.
²³Do not ignore the clamor of your
      adversaries,
   the uproar of your enemies, which
      rises continually.

ᵃTitle: Probably a literary or musical term

PROVERBS 24:15-16
¹⁵Do not lie in wait like an outlaw
      against a righteous man's
      house,
   do not raid his dwelling place;
¹⁶for though a righteous man falls
      seven times, he rises again,
   but the wicked are brought down
      by calamity.

□ D A Y 2 7 6

GOD SIGHTINGS

October 3

JEREMIAH 1:1-2:30
The words of Jeremiah son of Hilkiah,
one of the priests at Anathoth in the territory of Benjamin. ²The word of the
Lᴏʀᴅ came to him in the thirteenth year
of the reign of Josiah son of Amon king
of Judah, ³and through the reign of Jehoiakim son of Josiah king of Judah,
down to the fifth month of the eleventh
year of Zedekiah son of Josiah king of
Judah, when the people of Jerusalem
went into exile.

⁴The word of the Lᴏʀᴅ came to me,
saying,

⁵"Before I formed you in the womb I
      knewᵃ you,
   before you were born I set you
      apart;
   I appointed you as a prophet to the
      nations."

⁶"Ah, Sovereign Lᴏʀᴅ," I said, "I do not
know how to speak; I am only a child."
⁷But the Lᴏʀᴅ said to me, "Do not say,
'I am only a child.' You must go to everyone I send you to and say whatever I
command you. ⁸Do not be afraid of
them, for I am with you and will rescue
you," declares the Lᴏʀᴅ.
⁹Then the Lᴏʀᴅ reached out his hand
and touched my mouth and said to me,
"Now, I have put my words in your
mouth. ¹⁰See, today I appoint you over
nations and kingdoms to uproot and
tear down, to destroy and overthrow, to
build and to plant."
¹¹The word of the Lᴏʀᴅ came to me:
"What do you see, Jeremiah?"
"I see the branch of an almond tree," I
replied.
¹²The Lᴏʀᴅ said to me, "You have
seen correctly, for I am watchingᵇ to see
that my word is fulfilled."
¹³The word of the Lᴏʀᴅ came to me
again: "What do you see?"

"I see a boiling pot, tilting away from the north," I answered.

¹⁴The Lᴏʀᴅ said to me, "From the north disaster will be poured out on all who live in the land. ¹⁵I am about to summon all the peoples of the northern kingdoms," declares the Lᴏʀᴅ.

"Their kings will come and set up
    their thrones
    in the entrance of the gates of
        Jerusalem;
they will come against all her
    surrounding walls
and against all the towns of Judah.
¹⁶I will pronounce my judgments on
    my people
    because of their wickedness in
        forsaking me,
in burning incense to other gods
    and in worshiping what their
        hands have made.

¹⁷"Get yourself ready! Stand up and say to them whatever I command you. Do not be terrified by them, or I will terrify you before them. ¹⁸Today I have made you a fortified city, an iron pillar and a bronze wall to stand against the whole land—against the kings of Judah, its officials, its priests and the people of the land. ¹⁹They will fight against you but will not overcome you, for I am with you and will rescue you," declares the Lᴏʀᴅ.

²:¹The word of the Lᴏʀᴅ came to me: ²"Go and proclaim in the hearing of Jerusalem:

"'I remember the devotion of your
    youth,
    how as a bride you loved me
and followed me through the desert,
    through a land not sown.
³Israel was holy to the Lᴏʀᴅ,
    the firstfruits of his harvest;
all who devoured her were held guilty,
    and disaster overtook them,'"
                    declares the Lᴏʀᴅ.

⁴Hear the word of the Lᴏʀᴅ, O house
    of Jacob,
    all you clans of the house of Israel.

⁵This is what the Lᴏʀᴅ says:

"What fault did your fathers find in
    me,
    that they strayed so far from me?
They followed worthless idols
    and became worthless themselves.
⁶They did not ask, 'Where is the Lᴏʀᴅ,
    who brought us up out of Egypt
and led us through the barren
        wilderness,
    through a land of deserts and rifts,
a land of drought and darkness,ᶜ
    a land where no one travels and no
        one lives?'
⁷I brought you into a fertile land
    to eat its fruit and rich produce.
But you came and defiled my land
    and made my inheritance
        detestable.
⁸The priests did not ask,
    'Where is the Lᴏʀᴅ?'
Those who deal with the law did not
        know me;
    the leaders rebelled against me.
The prophets prophesied by Baal,
    following worthless idols.

⁹"Therefore I bring charges against
        you again,"
                    declares the Lᴏʀᴅ.
"And I will bring charges against
        your children's children.
¹⁰Cross over to the coasts of Kittimᵈ
        and look,
    send to Kedarᵉ and observe closely;
    see if there has ever been anything
        like this:
¹¹Has a nation ever changed its gods?
    (Yet they are not gods at all.)
But my people have exchanged theirᶠ
        Glory
    for worthless idols.
¹²Be appalled at this, O heavens,
    and shudder with great horror,"
                    declares the Lᴏʀᴅ.
¹³"My people have committed two sins:
They have forsaken me,
    the spring of living water,
and have dug their own cisterns,
    broken cisterns that cannot hold
        water.

14 Is Israel a servant, a slave by birth?
  Why then has he become
      plunder?
15 Lions have roared;
    they have growled at him.
  They have laid waste his land;
    his towns are burned and
      deserted.
16 Also, the men of Memphis*g* and
      Tahpanhes
    have shaved the crown of your
      head.*h*
17 Have you not brought this on
      yourselves
    by forsaking the LORD your God
    when he led you in the way?
18 Now why go to Egypt
    to drink water from the Shihor*i*?
  And why go to Assyria
    to drink water from the River*j*?
19 Your wickedness will punish you;
    your backsliding will rebuke you.
  Consider then and realize
    how evil and bitter it is for you
  when you forsake the LORD your God
    and have no awe of me,"
                    declares the Lord,
                    the LORD Almighty.

20 "Long ago you broke off your yoke
    and tore off your bonds;
    you said, 'I will not serve you!'
  Indeed, on every high hill
    and under every spreading tree
    you lay down as a prostitute.
21 I had planted you like a choice vine
    of sound and reliable stock.
  How then did you turn against me
    into a corrupt, wild vine?
22 Although you wash yourself with
      soda
    and use an abundance of soap,
    the stain of your guilt is still before
      me,"
            declares the Sovereign LORD.
23 "How can you say, 'I am not defiled;
    I have not run after the Baals'?
  See how you behaved in the valley;
    consider what you have done.
  You are a swift she-camel
    running here and there,

24 a wild donkey accustomed to the
      desert,
    sniffing the wind in her craving—
    in her heat who can restrain her?
  Any males that pursue her need not
      tire themselves;
    at mating time they will find her.
25 Do not run until your feet are bare
    and your throat is dry.
  But you said, 'It's no use!
    I love foreign gods,
    and I must go after them.'

26 "As a thief is disgraced when he is
      caught,
    so the house of Israel is
      disgraced—
  they, their kings and their officials,
    their priests and their prophets.
27 They say to wood, 'You are my
      father,'
    and to stone, 'You gave me birth.'
  They have turned their backs to me
    and not their faces;
  yet when they are in trouble, they say,
    'Come and save us!'
28 Where then are the gods you made
      for yourselves?
  Let them come if they can save
      you
    when you are in trouble!
  For you have as many gods
    as you have towns, O Judah.

29 "Why do you bring charges against
      me?
  You have all rebelled against me,"
                    declares the LORD.
30 "In vain I punished your people;
    they did not respond to correction.
  Your sword has devoured your
      prophets
    like a ravening lion."

*a*5 Or *chose*   *b*12 The Hebrew for *watching* sounds like the
Hebrew for *almond tree.*   *c*6 Or *and the shadow of death*
*d*10 That is, Cyprus and western coastlands   *e*10 The home
of Bedouin tribes in the Syro-Arabian desert   *f*11 Masoretic
Text; an ancient Hebrew scribal tradition *my*   *g*16 Hebrew
Noph   *h*16 Or *have cracked your skull*   *i*18 That is, a
branch of the Nile   *j*18 That is, the Euphrates

PHILIPPIANS 4:1-23

Therefore, my brothers, you whom I
love and long for, my joy and crown, that

is how you should stand firm in the Lord, dear friends!

[2]I plead with Euodia and I plead with Syntyche to agree with each other in the Lord. [3]Yes, and I ask you, loyal yokefellow,[a] help these women who have contended at my side in the cause of the gospel, along with Clement and the rest of my fellow workers, whose names are in the book of life.

[4]Rejoice in the Lord always. I will say it again: Rejoice! [5]Let your gentleness be evident to all. The Lord is near. [6]Do not be anxious about anything, but in everything, by prayer and petition, with thanksgiving, present your requests to God. [7]And the peace of God, which transcends all understanding, will guard your hearts and your minds in Christ Jesus.

[8]**Finally, brothers, whatever is true, whatever is noble, whatever is right, whatever is pure, whatever is lovely, whatever is admirable—if anything is excellent or praiseworthy—think about such things.** [9]Whatever you have learned or received or heard from me, or seen in me—put it into practice. And the God of peace will be with you.

[10]I rejoice greatly in the Lord that at last you have renewed your concern for me. Indeed, you have been concerned, but you had no opportunity to show it. [11]I am not saying this because I am in need, for I have learned to be content whatever the circumstances. [12]I know what it is to be in need, and I know what it is to have plenty. I have learned the secret of being content in any and every situation, whether well fed or hungry, whether living in plenty or in want. [13]I can do everything through him who gives me strength.

[14]Yet it was good of you to share in my troubles. [15]Moreover, as you Philippians know, in the early days of your acquaintance with the gospel, when I set out from Macedonia, not one church shared with me in the matter of giving and receiving, except you only; [16]for even when I was in Thessalonica, you sent me aid again and again when I was in need. [17]Not that I am looking for a gift, but I am looking for what may be credited to your account. [18]I have received full payment and even more; I am amply supplied, now that I have received from Epaphroditus the gifts you sent. They are a fragrant offering, an acceptable sacrifice, pleasing to God. [19]And my God will meet all your needs according to his glorious riches in Christ Jesus.

[20]To our God and Father be glory for ever and ever. Amen.

[21]Greet all the saints in Christ Jesus. The brothers who are with me send greetings. [22]All the saints send you greetings, especially those who belong to Caesar's household.

[23]The grace of the Lord Jesus Christ be with your spirit. Amen.[b]

a3 Or loyal Syzygus   b23 Some manuscripts do not have Amen.

PSALM 75:1-10

For the director of music. ⌊To the tune of⌋ "Do Not Destroy." A psalm of Asaph. A song.

[1]**W**e give thanks to you, O God,
      we give thanks, for your Name is near;
      men tell of your wonderful deeds.

[2]You say, "I choose the appointed time;
      it is I who judge uprightly.
[3]When the earth and all its people quake,
      it is I who hold its pillars firm. *Selah*
[4]To the arrogant I say, 'Boast no more,'
      and to the wicked, 'Do not lift up your horns.
[5]Do not lift your horns against heaven;
      do not speak with outstretched neck.'"

[6]No one from the east or the west
      or from the desert can exalt a man.
[7]But it is God who judges:
      He brings one down, he exalts another.

⁸ In the hand of the LORD is a cup
full of foaming wine mixed with
spices;
he pours it out, and all the wicked of
the earth
drink it down to its very dregs.

⁹ As for me, I will declare this forever;
I will sing praise to the God of
Jacob.
¹⁰ I will cut off the horns of all the
wicked,
but the horns of the righteous will
be lifted up.

PROVERBS 24:17-20
¹⁷ **D**o not gloat when your enemy falls;
when he stumbles, do not let your
heart rejoice,
¹⁸ or the LORD will see and disapprove
and turn his wrath away from him.

¹⁹ Do not fret because of evil men
or be envious of the wicked,
²⁰ for the evil man has no future hope,
and the lamp of the wicked will be
snuffed out.

□ D A Y 2 7 7

GOD SIGHTINGS

October 4

JEREMIAH 2:31–4:18
"**Y**ou of this generation, consider the
word of the LORD:

"Have I [the LORD] been a desert to
Israel
or a land of great darkness?
Why do my people say, 'We are free
to roam;
we will come to you no more'?
³² Does a maiden forget her jewelry,
a bride her wedding ornaments?
Yet my people have forgotten me,
days without number.
³³ How skilled you are at pursuing love!
Even the worst of women can
learn from your ways.

³⁴ On your clothes men find
the lifeblood of the innocent poor,
though you did not catch them
breaking in.
Yet in spite of all this
³⁵   you say, 'I am innocent;
he is not angry with me.'
But I will pass judgment on you
because you say, 'I have not sinned.'
³⁶ Why do you go about so much,
changing your ways?
You will be disappointed by Egypt
as you were by Assyria.
³⁷ You will also leave that place
with your hands on your head,
for the LORD has rejected those you
trust;
you will not be helped by them.

^{3:1} "IF a man divorces his wife
and she leaves him and marries
another man,
should he return to her again?
Would not the land be completely
defiled?
But you have lived as a prostitute
with many lovers—
would you now return to me?"
declares the LORD.
² "Look up to the barren heights and
see.
Is there any place where you have
not been ravished?
By the roadside you sat waiting for
lovers,
sat like a nomad^a in the desert.
You have defiled the land
with your prostitution and
wickedness.
³ Therefore the showers have been
withheld,
and no spring rains have fallen.
Yet you have the brazen look of a
prostitute;
you refuse to blush with shame.
⁴ Have you not just called to me:
'My Father, my friend from my
youth,
⁵ will you always be angry?
Will your wrath continue forever?'
This is how you talk,
but you do all the evil you can."

⁶During the reign of King Josiah, the Lord said to me, "Have you seen what faithless Israel has done? She has gone up on every high hill and under every spreading tree and has committed adultery there. ⁷I thought that after she had done all this she would return to me but she did not, and her unfaithful sister Judah saw it. ⁸I gave faithless Israel her certificate of divorce and sent her away because of all her adulteries. Yet I saw that her unfaithful sister Judah had no fear; she also went out and committed adultery. ⁹Because Israel's immorality mattered so little to her, she defiled the land and committed adultery with stone and wood. ¹⁰In spite of all this, her unfaithful sister Judah did not return to me with all her heart, but only in pretense," declares the Lord.

¹¹The Lord said to me, "Faithless Israel is more righteous than unfaithful Judah. ¹²Go, proclaim this message toward the north:

"'Return, faithless Israel,' declares
      the Lord,
   'I will frown on you no longer,
   for I am merciful,' declares the Lord,
   'I will not be angry forever.
¹³Only acknowledge your guilt—
   you have rebelled against the Lord
      your God,
   you have scattered your favors to
      foreign gods
   under every spreading tree,
   and have not obeyed me,'"
                  declares the Lord.

¹⁴"Return, faithless people," declares the Lord, "for I am your husband. I will choose you—one from a town and two from a clan—and bring you to Zion. ¹⁵Then I will give you shepherds after my own heart, who will lead you with knowledge and understanding. ¹⁶In those days, when your numbers have increased greatly in the land," declares the Lord, "men will no longer say, 'The ark of the covenant of the Lord.' It will never enter

their minds or be remembered; it will not be missed, nor will another one be made. ¹⁷At that time they will call Jerusalem The Throne of the Lord, and all nations will gather in Jerusalem to honor the name of the Lord. No longer will they follow the stubbornness of their evil hearts. ¹⁸In those days the house of Judah will join the house of Israel, and together they will come from a northern land to the land I gave your forefathers as an inheritance.

¹⁹"I myself said,

"'How gladly would I treat you like
      sons
   and give you a desirable land,
   the most beautiful inheritance of
      any nation.'
I thought you would call me 'Father'
   and not turn away from following
      me.
²⁰But like a woman unfaithful to her
      husband,
   so you have been unfaithful to me,
      O house of Israel,"
                  declares the Lord.

²¹A cry is heard on the barren heights,
   the weeping and pleading of the
      people of Israel,
   because they have perverted their
      ways
   and have forgotten the Lord their
      God.

²²"Return, faithless people;
   I will cure you of backsliding."

"Yes, we will come to you,
   for you are the Lord our God.
²³Surely the ⌊idolatrous⌋ commotion
      on the hills
   and mountains is a deception;
   surely in the Lord our God
   is the salvation of Israel.
²⁴From our youth shameful gods have
      consumed
   the fruits of our fathers' labor—
   their flocks and herds,
   their sons and daughters.
²⁵Let us lie down in our shame,
   and let our disgrace cover us.

We have sinned against the LORD our
God,
  both we and our fathers;
from our youth till this day
  we have not obeyed the LORD our
  God."

⁴:¹ "IF you will return, O Israel,
  return to me,"
                    declares the LORD.
"If you put your detestable idols out
  of my sight
  and no longer go astray,
² and if in a truthful, just and righteous
  way
  you swear, 'As surely as the LORD
  lives,'
then the nations will be blessed by
  him
  and in him they will glory."

³ This is what the LORD says to the
men of Judah and to Jerusalem:

"Break up your unplowed ground
  and do not sow among thorns.
⁴ Circumcise yourselves to the LORD,
  circumcise your hearts,
  you men of Judah and people of
  Jerusalem,
or my wrath will break out and burn
  like fire
  because of the evil you have done—
  burn with no one to quench it.

⁵ "Announce in Judah and proclaim in
  Jerusalem and say:
  'Sound the trumpet throughout
  the land!'
Cry aloud and say:
  'Gather together!
  Let us flee to the fortified cities!'
⁶ Raise the signal to go to Zion!
  Flee for safety without delay!
For I am bringing disaster from the
  north,
  even terrible destruction."

⁷ A lion has come out of his lair;
  a destroyer of nations has set out.
He has left his place
  to lay waste your land.
Your towns will lie in ruins
  without inhabitant.

⁸ So put on sackcloth,
  lament and wail,
for the fierce anger of the LORD
  has not turned away from us.

⁹ "In that day," declares the LORD,
  "the king and the officials will lose
  heart,
the priests will be horrified,
  and the prophets will be appalled."

¹⁰ Then I said, "Ah, Sovereign LORD,
how completely you have deceived this
people and Jerusalem by saying, 'You
will have peace,' when the sword is at
our throats."

¹¹ At that time this people and Jerusalem will be told, "A scorching wind from
the barren heights in the desert blows
toward my people, but not to winnow or
cleanse; ¹² a wind too strong for that
comes from me.ᵇ Now I pronounce my
judgments against them."

¹³ Look! He advances like the clouds,
  his chariots come like a whirlwind,
his horses are swifter than eagles.
  Woe to us! We are ruined!
¹⁴ O Jerusalem, wash the evil from your
  heart and be saved.
  How long will you harbor wicked
  thoughts?
¹⁵ A voice is announcing from Dan,
  proclaiming disaster from the hills
  of Ephraim.
¹⁶ "Tell this to the nations,
  proclaim it to Jerusalem:
'A besieging army is coming from a
  distant land,
  raising a war cry against the cities
  of Judah.
¹⁷ They surround her like men
  guarding a field,
  because she has rebelled against
  me,'"
                    declares the LORD.
¹⁸ "Your own conduct and actions
  have brought this upon you.
This is your punishment.
  How bitter it is!
  How it pierces to the heart!"

ᵃ2 Or *an Arab* ᵇ12 Or *comes at my command*

COLOSSIANS 1:1-20

Paul, an apostle of Christ Jesus by the will of God, and Timothy our brother,

2 To the holy and faithful*a* brothers in Christ at Colosse:

Grace and peace to you from God our Father.*b*

3 We always thank God, the Father of our Lord Jesus Christ, when we pray for you, 4 because we have heard of your faith in Christ Jesus and of the love you have for all the saints— 5 the faith and love that spring from the hope that is stored up for you in heaven and that you have already heard about in the word of truth, the gospel 6 that has come to you. All over the world this gospel is bearing fruit and growing, just as it has been doing among you since the day you heard it and understood God's grace in all its truth. 7 You learned it from Epaphras, our dear fellow servant, who is a faithful minister of Christ on our*c* behalf, 8 and who also told us of your love in the Spirit.

9 For this reason, since the day we heard about you, we have not stopped praying for you and asking God to fill you with the knowledge of his will through all spiritual wisdom and understanding. 10 And we pray this in order that you may live a life worthy of the Lord and may please him in every way: bearing fruit in every good work, growing in the knowledge of God, 11 being strengthened with all power according to his glorious might so that you may have great endurance and patience, and joyfully 12 giving thanks to the Father, who has qualified you*d* to share in the inheritance of the saints in the kingdom of light. 13 **For he has rescued us from the dominion of darkness and brought us into the kingdom of the Son he loves, 14 in whom we have redemption,*e* the forgiveness of sins.**

15 He is the image of the invisible God, the firstborn over all creation. 16 For by him all things were created: things in heaven and on earth, visible and invisible, whether thrones or powers or rulers or authorities; all things were created by him and for him. 17 He is before all things, and in him all things hold together. 18 And he is the head of the body, the church; he is the beginning and the firstborn from among the dead, so that in everything he might have the supremacy. 19 For God was pleased to have all his fullness dwell in him, 20 and through him to reconcile to himself all things, whether things on earth or things in heaven, by making peace through his blood, shed on the cross.

a2 Or believing   b2 Some manuscripts Father and the Lord Jesus Christ   c7 Some manuscripts your   d12 Some manuscripts us   e14 A few late manuscripts redemption through his blood

PSALM 76:1-12

For the director of music. With stringed instruments. A psalm of Asaph. A song.

1 In Judah God is known;
　　his name is great in Israel.
2 His tent is in Salem,
　　his dwelling place in Zion.
3 There he broke the flashing arrows,
　　the shields and the swords, the
　　　　weapons of war.   *Selah*

4 You are resplendent with light,
　　more majestic than mountains
　　　　rich with game.
5 Valiant men lie plundered,
　　they sleep their last sleep;
not one of the warriors
　　can lift his hands.
6 At your rebuke, O God of Jacob,
　　both horse and chariot lie still.
7 You alone are to be feared.
　　Who can stand before you when
　　　　you are angry?
8 From heaven you pronounced
　　judgment,
　　and the land feared and was
　　　　quiet—
9 when you, O God, rose up to judge,
　　to save all the afflicted of the land.
　　　　　　　　　　　　　　Selah
10 Surely your wrath against men brings
　　you praise,
　　and the survivors of your wrath are
　　　　restrained.*a*

¹¹Make vows to the Lord your God and
fulfill them;
let all the neighboring lands
bring gifts to the One to be feared.
¹²He breaks the spirit of rulers;
he is feared by the kings of the
earth.

*a 10 Or Surely the wrath of men brings you praise, / and
with the remainder of wrath you arm yourself*

PROVERBS 24:21-22
²¹Fear the Lord and the king, my son,
and do not join with the rebellious,
²²for those two will send sudden
destruction upon them,
and who knows what calamities
they can bring?

☐ D A Y 2 7 8

GOD SIGHTINGS

October 5

JEREMIAH 4:19–6:14
¹⁹Oh, my [the Lord's] anguish, my
anguish!
I writhe in pain.
Oh, the agony of my heart!
My heart pounds within me,
I cannot keep silent.
For I have heard the sound of the
trumpet;
I have heard the battle cry.
²⁰Disaster follows disaster;
the whole land lies in ruins.
In an instant my tents are destroyed,
my shelter in a moment.
²¹How long must I see the battle
standard
and hear the sound of the
trumpet?

²²"My people are fools;
they do not know me.
They are senseless children;
they have no understanding.
They are skilled in doing evil;
they know not how to do good."

²³I looked at the earth,
and it was formless and empty;
and at the heavens,
and their light was gone.
²⁴I looked at the mountains,
and they were quaking;
all the hills were swaying.
²⁵I looked, and there were no people;
every bird in the sky had flown
away.
²⁶I looked, and the fruitful land was a
desert;
all its towns lay in ruins
before the Lord, before his fierce
anger.

²⁷This is what the Lord says:

"The whole land will be ruined,
though I will not destroy it
completely.
²⁸Therefore the earth will mourn
and the heavens above grow dark,
because I have spoken and will not
relent,
I have decided and will not turn
back."

²⁹At the sound of horsemen and archers
every town takes to flight.
Some go into the thickets;
some climb up among the rocks.
All the towns are deserted;
no one lives in them.

³⁰What are you doing, O devastated
one?
Why dress yourself in scarlet
and put on jewels of gold?
Why shade your eyes with paint?
You adorn yourself in vain.
Your lovers despise you;
they seek your life.

³¹I hear a cry as of a woman in labor,
a groan as of one bearing her first
child—
the cry of the Daughter of Zion
gasping for breath,
stretching out her hands and
saying,
"Alas! I am fainting;
my life is given over to
murderers."

5:1"Go up and down the streets of
    Jerusalem,
    look around and consider,
    search through her squares.
If you can find but one person
    who deals honestly and seeks the
        truth,
    I will forgive this city.
2 Although they say, 'As surely as the
        Lord lives,'
    still they are swearing falsely."

3 O Lord, do not your eyes look for
        truth?
    You struck them, but they felt no
        pain;
    you crushed them, but they
        refused correction.
They made their faces harder than
        stone
    and refused to repent.
4 I thought, "These are only the poor;
        they are foolish,
    for they do not know the way of the
        Lord,
    the requirements of their God.
5 So I will go to the leaders
    and speak to them;
    surely they know the way of the Lord,
    the requirements of their God."
But with one accord they too had
        broken off the yoke
    and torn off the bonds.
6 Therefore a lion from the forest will
        attack them,
    a wolf from the desert will ravage
        them,
    a leopard will lie in wait near their
        towns
    to tear to pieces any who venture
        out,
    for their rebellion is great
    and their backslidings many.

7 "Why should I forgive you?
    Your children have forsaken me
    and sworn by gods that are not
        gods.
I supplied all their needs,
    yet they committed adultery
    and thronged to the houses of
        prostitutes.

8 They are well-fed, lusty stallions,
    each neighing for another man's
        wife.
9 Should I not punish them for this?"
    declares the Lord.
"Should I not avenge myself
    on such a nation as this?

10 "Go through her vineyards and
        ravage them,
    but do not destroy them
        completely.
Strip off her branches,
    for these people do not belong to
        the Lord.
11 The house of Israel and the house of
        Judah
    have been utterly unfaithful to
        me,"
                        declares the Lord.

12 They have lied about the Lord;
    they said, "He will do nothing!
No harm will come to us;
    we will never see sword or
        famine.
13 The prophets are but wind
    and the word is not in them;
    so let what they say be done to
        them."

14 Therefore this is what the Lord God
Almighty says:

"Because the people have spoken
        these words,
    I will make my words in your
        mouth a fire
    and these people the wood it
        consumes.
15 O house of Israel," declares the Lord,
    "I am bringing a distant nation
        against you—
    an ancient and enduring nation,
    a people whose language you do
        not know,
    whose speech you do not
        understand.
16 Their quivers are like an open grave;
    all of them are mighty warriors.
17 They will devour your harvests and
        food,
    devour your sons and daughters;

they will devour your flocks and herds,
    devour your vines and fig trees.
With the sword they will destroy
    the fortified cities in which you
        trust.

¹⁸ "Yet even in those days," declares the LORD, "I will not destroy you completely. ¹⁹ And when the people ask, 'Why has the LORD our God done all this to us?' you will tell them, 'As you have forsaken me and served foreign gods in your own land, so now you will serve foreigners in a land not your own.'

²⁰ "Announce this to the house of Jacob
    and proclaim it in Judah:
²¹ Hear this, you foolish and senseless
        people,
    who have eyes but do not see,
    who have ears but do not hear:
²² Should you not fear me?" declares
        the LORD.
    "Should you not tremble in my
        presence?
I made the sand a boundary for the
        sea,
    an everlasting barrier it cannot
        cross.
The waves may roll, but they cannot
        prevail;
    they may roar, but they cannot
        cross it.
²³ But these people have stubborn and
        rebellious hearts;
    they have turned aside and gone
        away.
²⁴ They do not say to themselves,
    'Let us fear the LORD our God,
who gives autumn and spring rains
        in season,
    who assures us of the regular
        weeks of harvest.'
²⁵ Your wrongdoings have kept these
        away;
    your sins have deprived you of
        good.

²⁶ "Among my people are wicked men
    who lie in wait like men who snare
        birds
    and like those who set traps to
        catch men.

²⁷ Like cages full of birds,
    their houses are full of deceit;
they have become rich and
        powerful
²⁸   and have grown fat and sleek.
Their evil deeds have no limit;
    they do not plead the case of the
        fatherless to win it,
    they do not defend the rights of
        the poor.
²⁹ Should I not punish them for this?"
    declares the LORD.
    "Should I not avenge myself
        on such a nation as this?

³⁰ "A horrible and shocking thing
    has happened in the land:
³¹ The prophets prophesy lies,
    the priests rule by their own
        authority,
and my people love it this way.
    But what will you do in the end?

⁶:¹ "FLEE for safety, people of
        Benjamin!
    Flee from Jerusalem!
Sound the trumpet in Tekoa!
    Raise the signal over Beth
        Hakkerem!
For disaster looms out of the north,
    even terrible destruction.
² I will destroy the Daughter of Zion,
    so beautiful and delicate.
³ Shepherds with their flocks will
        come against her;
    they will pitch their tents around
        her,
    each tending his own portion."

⁴ "Prepare for battle against her!
    Arise, let us attack at noon!
But, alas, the daylight is fading,
    and the shadows of evening grow
        long.
⁵ So arise, let us attack at night
    and destroy her fortresses!"

⁶ This is what the LORD Almighty says:

"Cut down the trees
    and build siege ramps against
        Jerusalem.
This city must be punished;
    it is filled with oppression.

7 As a well pours out its water,
  so she pours out her wickedness.
Violence and destruction resound in
    her;
  her sickness and wounds are ever
    before me.
8 Take warning, O Jerusalem,
  or I will turn away from you
and make your land desolate
  so no one can live in it."

9 This is what the LORD Almighty says:

"Let them glean the remnant of
    Israel
  as thoroughly as a vine;
pass your hand over the branches
    again,
  like one gathering grapes."

10 To whom can I speak and give
    warning?
  Who will listen to me?
Their ears are closed[a]
  so they cannot hear.
The word of the LORD is offensive to
    them;
  they find no pleasure in it.
11 But I am full of the wrath of the
    LORD,
  and I cannot hold it in.

"Pour it out on the children in the
    street
  and on the young men gathered
    together;
both husband and wife will be
    caught in it,
  and the old, those weighed down
    with years.
12 Their houses will be turned over to
    others,
  together with their fields and their
    wives,
when I stretch out my hand
  against those who live in the land,"
                        declares the LORD.
13 "From the least to the greatest,
  all are greedy for gain;
prophets and priests alike,
  all practice deceit.
14 They dress the wound of my people
  as though it were not serious.

'Peace, peace,' they say,
  when there is no peace."

[a] 10 Hebrew *uncircumcised*

COLOSSIANS 1:21–2:7

Once you were alienated from God and
were enemies in your minds because
of[a] your evil behavior. 22 But now he has
reconciled you by Christ's physical body
through death to present you holy in his
sight, without blemish and free from accusation— 23 if you continue in your
faith, established and firm, not moved
from the hope held out in the gospel.
This is the gospel that you heard and
that has been proclaimed to every creature under heaven, and of which I, Paul,
have become a servant.

24 Now I rejoice in what was suffered
for you, and I fill up in my flesh what is
still lacking in regard to Christ's afflictions, for the sake of his body, which is
the church. 25 I have become its servant
by the commission God gave me to present to you the word of God in its fullness— 26 the mystery that has been kept
hidden for ages and generations, but is
now disclosed to the saints. 27 To them
God has chosen to make known among
the Gentiles the glorious riches of this
mystery, which is Christ in you, the hope
of glory.

28 We proclaim him, admonishing
and teaching everyone with all wisdom,
so that we may present everyone perfect
in Christ. 29 To this end I labor, struggling with all his energy, which so pow-
erfully works in me.

2:1 I want you to know how much I am
struggling for you and for those at Laodicea, and for all who have not met me
personally. 2 My purpose is that they
may be encouraged in heart and united
in love, so that they may have the full
riches of complete understanding, in
order that they may know the mystery
of God, namely, Christ, 3 in whom are
hidden all the treasures of wisdom and
knowledge. 4 I tell you this so that no
one may deceive you by fine-sounding
arguments. 5 For though I am absent

from you in body, I am present with you in spirit and delight to see how orderly you are and how firm your faith in Christ is.

⁶**So then, just as you received Christ Jesus as Lord, continue to live in him,** ⁷**rooted and built up in him, strengthened in the faith as you were taught, and overflowing with thankfulness.**

ᵃ21 Or *minds, as shown by*

PSALM 77:1-20

For the director of music. For Jeduthun. Of Asaph. A psalm.

¹I cried out to God for help;
  I cried out to God to hear me.
²When I was in distress, I sought the Lord;
    at night I stretched out untiring hands
    and my soul refused to be comforted.

³I remembered you, O God, and I groaned;
  I mused, and my spirit grew faint.   *Selah*

⁴You kept my eyes from closing;
  I was too troubled to speak.
⁵I thought about the former days,
  the years of long ago;
⁶I remembered my songs in the night.
  My heart mused and my spirit inquired:

⁷"Will the Lord reject forever?
  Will he never show his favor again?
⁸Has his unfailing love vanished forever?
  Has his promise failed for all time?
⁹Has God forgotten to be merciful?
  Has he in anger withheld his compassion?"   *Selah*

¹⁰Then I thought, "To this I will appeal:
  the years of the right hand of the Most High."

¹¹I will remember the deeds of the Lord;
  yes, I will remember your miracles of long ago.
¹²I will meditate on all your works
  and consider all your mighty deeds.

¹³Your ways, O God, are holy.
  What god is so great as our God?
¹⁴You are the God who performs miracles;
  you display your power among the peoples.
¹⁵With your mighty arm you redeemed your people,
    the descendants of Jacob and Joseph.   *Selah*

¹⁶The waters saw you, O God,
  the waters saw you and writhed;
  the very depths were convulsed.
¹⁷The clouds poured down water,
  the skies resounded with thunder;
  your arrows flashed back and forth.
¹⁸Your thunder was heard in the whirlwind,
  your lightning lit up the world;
  the earth trembled and quaked.
¹⁹Your path led through the sea,
  your way through the mighty waters,
  though your footprints were not seen.

²⁰You led your people like a flock
  by the hand of Moses and Aaron.

PROVERBS 24:23-25

These also are sayings of the wise:

To show partiality in judging is not good:
²⁴Whoever says to the guilty, "You are innocent"—
  peoples will curse him and nations denounce him.
²⁵But it will go well with those who convict the guilty,
  and rich blessing will come upon them.

☐ DAY 279

GOD SIGHTINGS

October 6

JEREMIAH 6:15–8:7

15 "Are they [the prophets and priests]
      ashamed of their loathsome
      conduct?
   No, they have no shame at all;
      they do not even know how to blush.
   So they will fall among the fallen;
      they will be brought down when I
      punish them,"
                              says the LORD.

16 This is what the LORD says:

   "Stand at the crossroads and look;
      ask for the ancient paths,
   ask where the good way is, and walk
      in it,
      and you will find rest for your
         souls.
   But you said, 'We will not walk in it.'
17 I appointed watchmen over you and
      said,
   'Listen to the sound of the
      trumpet!'
   But you said, 'We will not listen.'
18 Therefore hear, O nations;
      observe, O witnesses,
      what will happen to them.
19 Hear, O earth:
   I am bringing disaster on this people,
      the fruit of their schemes,
   because they have not listened to my
      words
      and have rejected my law.
20 What do I care about incense from
      Sheba
      or sweet calamus from a distant
         land?
   Your burnt offerings are not acceptable;
      your sacrifices do not please me."

21 Therefore this is what the LORD says:

   "I will put obstacles before this people.
      Fathers and sons alike will stumble
         over them;
      neighbors and friends will perish."

22 This is what the LORD says:

   "Look, an army is coming
      from the land of the north;
   a great nation is being stirred up
      from the ends of the earth.
23 They are armed with bow and spear;
      they are cruel and show no mercy.
   They sound like the roaring sea
      as they ride on their horses;
   they come like men in battle
      formation
      to attack you, O Daughter of Zion."

24 We have heard reports about them,
      and our hands hang limp.
   Anguish has gripped us,
      pain like that of a woman in labor.
25 Do not go out to the fields
      or walk on the roads,
   for the enemy has a sword,
      and there is terror on every side.
26 O my people, put on sackcloth
      and roll in ashes;
   mourn with bitter wailing
      as for an only son,
   for suddenly the destroyer
      will come upon us.

27 "I have made you a tester of metals
      and my people the ore,
   that you may observe
      and test their ways.
28 They are all hardened rebels,
      going about to slander.
   They are bronze and iron;
      they all act corruptly.
29 The bellows blow fiercely
      to burn away the lead with fire,
   but the refining goes on in vain;
      the wicked are not purged out.
30 They are called rejected silver,
      because the LORD has rejected
         them."

7:1 THIS is the word that came to Jeremiah from the LORD: 2 "Stand at the gate
of the LORD's house and there proclaim
this message:

   " 'Hear the word of the LORD, all you
people of Judah who come through
these gates to worship the LORD. 3 This is
what the LORD Almighty, the God of Is-

rael, says: Reform your ways and your actions, and I will let you live in this place. ⁴Do not trust in deceptive words and say, "This is the temple of the Lord, the temple of the Lord, the temple of the Lord!" ⁵If you really change your ways and your actions and deal with each other justly, ⁶if you do not oppress the alien, the fatherless or the widow and do not shed innocent blood in this place, and if you do not follow other gods to your own harm, ⁷then I will let you live in this place, in the land I gave your forefathers for ever and ever. ⁸But look, you are trusting in deceptive words that are worthless.

⁹"'Will you steal and murder, commit adultery and perjury,ᵃ burn incense to Baal and follow other gods you have not known, ¹⁰and then come and stand before me in this house, which bears my Name, and say, "We are safe"—safe to do all these detestable things? ¹¹Has this house, which bears my Name, become a den of robbers to you? But I have been watching! declares the Lord.

¹²"'Go now to the place in Shiloh where I first made a dwelling for my Name, and see what I did to it because of the wickedness of my people Israel. ¹³While you were doing all these things, declares the Lord, I spoke to you again and again, but you did not listen; I called you, but you did not answer. ¹⁴Therefore, what I did to Shiloh I will now do to the house that bears my Name, the temple you trust in, the place I gave to you and your fathers. ¹⁵I will thrust you from my presence, just as I did all your brothers, the people of Ephraim.'

¹⁶"So do not pray for this people nor offer any plea or petition for them; do not plead with me, for I will not listen to you. ¹⁷Do you not see what they are doing in the towns of Judah and in the streets of Jerusalem? ¹⁸The children gather wood, the fathers light the fire, and the women knead the dough and make cakes of bread for the Queen of Heaven. They pour out drink offerings to other gods to provoke me to anger. ¹⁹But am I the one they are provoking?

declares the Lord. Are they not rather harming themselves, to their own shame?

²⁰"'Therefore this is what the Sovereign Lord says: My anger and my wrath will be poured out on this place, on man and beast, on the trees of the field and on the fruit of the ground, and it will burn and not be quenched.

²¹"'This is what the Lord Almighty, the God of Israel, says: Go ahead, add your burnt offerings to your other sacrifices and eat the meat yourselves! ²²For when I brought your forefathers out of Egypt and spoke to them, I did not just give them commands about burnt offerings and sacrifices, ²³but I gave them this command: Obey me, and I will be your God and you will be my people. Walk in all the ways I command you, that it may go well with you. ²⁴But they did not listen or pay attention; instead, they followed the stubborn inclinations of their evil hearts. They went backward and not forward. ²⁵From the time your forefathers left Egypt until now, day after day, again and again I sent you my servants the prophets. ²⁶But they did not listen to me or pay attention. They were stiff-necked and did more evil than their forefathers.'

²⁷"When you tell them all this, they will not listen to you; when you call to them, they will not answer. ²⁸Therefore say to them, 'This is the nation that has not obeyed the Lord its God or responded to correction. Truth has perished; it has vanished from their lips. ²⁹Cut off your hair and throw it away; take up a lament on the barren heights, for the Lord has rejected and abandoned this generation that is under his wrath.

³⁰"'The people of Judah have done evil in my eyes, declares the Lord. They have set up their detestable idols in the house that bears my Name and have defiled it. ³¹They have built the high places of Topheth in the Valley of Ben Hinnom to burn their sons and daughters in the fire—something I did not command, nor did it enter my mind.

32 So beware, the days are coming, declares the LORD, when people will no longer call it Topheth or the Valley of Ben Hinnom, but the Valley of Slaughter, for they will bury the dead in Topheth until there is no more room. 33 Then the carcasses of this people will become food for the birds of the air and the beasts of the earth, and there will be no one to frighten them away. 34 I will bring an end to the sounds of joy and gladness and to the voices of bride and bridegroom in the towns of Judah and the streets of Jerusalem, for the land will become desolate.

8:1 "At that time, declares the LORD, the bones of the kings and officials of Judah, the bones of the priests and prophets, and the bones of the people of Jerusalem will be removed from their graves. 2 They will be exposed to the sun and the moon and all the stars of the heavens, which they have loved and served and which they have followed and consulted and worshiped. They will not be gathered up or buried, but will be like refuse lying on the ground. 3 Wherever I banish them, all the survivors of this evil nation will prefer death to life, declares the LORD Almighty.'

4 "Say to them, 'This is what the LORD says:

"'When men fall down, do they not get up?
When a man turns away, does he not return?
5 Why then have these people turned away?
Why does Jerusalem always turn away?
They cling to deceit;
they refuse to return.
6 I have listened attentively,
but they do not say what is right.
No one repents of his wickedness,
saying, "What have I done?"
Each pursues his own course
like a horse charging into battle.
7 Even the stork in the sky
knows her appointed seasons,

and the dove, the swift and the thrush
observe the time of their migration.
But my people do not know
the requirements of the LORD.

a 9 Or *and swear by false gods*

COLOSSIANS 2:8-23

See to it that no one takes you captive through hollow and deceptive philosophy, which depends on human tradition and the basic principles of this world rather than on Christ.

9 **For in Christ all the fullness of the Deity lives in bodily form,** 10 **and you have been given fullness in Christ, who is the head over every power and authority.** 11 In him you were also circumcised, in the putting off of the sinful nature,*a* not with a circumcision done by the hands of men but with the circumcision done by Christ, 12 having been buried with him in baptism and raised with him through your faith in the power of God, who raised him from the dead.

13 When you were dead in your sins and in the uncircumcision of your sinful nature,*b* God made you*c* alive with Christ. He forgave us all our sins, 14 having canceled the written code, with its regulations, that was against us and that stood opposed to us; he took it away, nailing it to the cross. 15 And having disarmed the powers and authorities, he made a public spectacle of them, triumphing over them by the cross.*d*

16 Therefore do not let anyone judge you by what you eat or drink, or with regard to a religious festival, a New Moon celebration or a Sabbath day. 17 These are a shadow of the things that were to come; the reality, however, is found in Christ. 18 Do not let anyone who delights in false humility and the worship of angels disqualify you for the prize. Such a person goes into great detail about what he has seen, and his unspiritual mind puffs him up with idle notions. 19 He has lost connection with the Head, from whom the whole body, supported and

held together by its ligaments and sinews, grows as God causes it to grow.

²⁰Since you died with Christ to the basic principles of this world, why, as though you still belonged to it, do you submit to its rules: ²¹"Do not handle! Do not taste! Do not touch!"? ²²These are all destined to perish with use, because they are based on human commands and teachings. ²³Such regulations indeed have an appearance of wisdom, with their self-imposed worship, their false humility and their harsh treatment of the body, but they lack any value in restraining sensual indulgence.

PSALM 78:1-31

A *maskil*ᵃ of Asaph.

¹**O** my people, hear my teaching;
  listen to the words of my mouth.
²I will open my mouth in parables,
  I will utter hidden things, things
    from of old—
³what we have heard and known,
  what our fathers have told us.
⁴We will not hide them from their
    children;
  we will tell the next generation
the praiseworthy deeds of the LORD,
  his power, and the wonders he has
    done.
⁵He decreed statutes for Jacob
  and established the law in Israel,
which he commanded our forefathers
  to teach their children,
⁶so the next generation would know
    them,
  even the children yet to be born,
  and they in turn would tell their
    children.
⁷Then they would put their trust in God
  and would not forget his deeds
  but would keep his commands.
⁸They would not be like their
    forefathers—
  a stubborn and rebellious
    generation,
whose hearts were not loyal to God,
  whose spirits were not faithful to
    him.

⁹The men of Ephraim, though armed
    with bows,
  turned back on the day of battle;
¹⁰they did not keep God's covenant
  and refused to live by his law.
¹¹They forgot what he had done,
  the wonders he had shown them.
¹²He did miracles in the sight of their
    fathers
  in the land of Egypt, in the region
    of Zoan.
¹³He divided the sea and led them
    through;
  he made the water stand firm like
    a wall.
¹⁴He guided them with the cloud by day
  and with light from the fire all
    night.
¹⁵He split the rocks in the desert
  and gave them water as abundant
    as the seas;
¹⁶he brought streams out of a rocky
    crag
  and made water flow down like
    rivers.

¹⁷But they continued to sin against
    him,
  rebelling in the desert against the
    Most High.
¹⁸They willfully put God to the test
  by demanding the food they
    craved.
¹⁹They spoke against God, saying,
  "Can God spread a table in the
    desert?
²⁰When he struck the rock, water
    gushed out,
  and streams flowed abundantly.
But can he also give us food?
  Can he supply meat for his
    people?"
²¹When the LORD heard them, he was
    very angry;
  his fire broke out against Jacob,
  and his wrath rose against Israel,
²²for they did not believe in God
  or trust in his deliverance.
²³Yet he gave a command to the skies
    above
  and opened the doors of the
    heavens;

24 he rained down manna for the
   people to eat,
   he gave them the grain of heaven.
25 Men ate the bread of angels;
   he sent them all the food they
   could eat.
26 He let loose the east wind from the
   heavens
   and led forth the south wind by his
   power.
27 He rained meat down on them like
   dust,
   flying birds like sand on the
   seashore.
28 He made them come down inside
   their camp,
   all around their tents.
29 They ate till they had more than
   enough,
   for he had given them what they
   craved.
30 But before they turned from the food
   they craved,
   even while it was still in their
   mouths,
31 God's anger rose against them;
   he put to death the sturdiest
   among them,
   cutting down the young men of
   Israel.

aTitle: Probably a literary or musical term

PROVERBS 24:26
26 **A**n honest answer
   is like a kiss on the lips.

□ D A Y 2 8 0

GOD SIGHTINGS

October 7

JEREMIAH 8:8–9:26
8 "'**H**ow can you [the Lord's people]
   say, "We are wise,
   for we have the law of the Lord,"
   when actually the lying pen of the
   scribes
   has handled it falsely?

9 The wise will be put to shame;
   they will be dismayed and
   trapped.
Since they have rejected the word of
   the Lord,
   what kind of wisdom do they
   have?
10 Therefore I will give their wives to
   other men
   and their fields to new owners.
From the least to the greatest,
   all are greedy for gain;
prophets and priests alike,
   all practice deceit.
11 They dress the wound of my people
   as though it were not serious.
"Peace, peace," they say,
   when there is no peace.
12 Are they ashamed of their loathsome
   conduct?
   No, they have no shame at all;
   they do not even know how to
   blush.
So they will fall among the fallen;
   they will be brought down when
   they are punished,
                              says the Lord.

13 "'I will take away their harvest,
                    declares the Lord.
   There will be no grapes on the
   vine.
There will be no figs on the tree,
   and their leaves will wither.
What I have given them
   will be taken from them.a'"

14 "Why are we sitting here?
   Gather together!
Let us flee to the fortified cities
   and perish there!
For the Lord our God has doomed us
   to perish
   and given us poisoned water to
   drink,
   because we have sinned against
   him.
15 We hoped for peace
   but no good has come,
for a time of healing
   but there was only terror.

16 The snorting of the enemy's
           horses
      is heard from Dan;
   at the neighing of their stallions
      the whole land trembles.
   They have come to devour
      the land and everything in it,
      the city and all who live there."

17 "See, I will send venomous snakes
           among you,
      vipers that cannot be charmed,
      and they will bite you,"
                                    declares the LORD.

18 O my Comforter[b] in sorrow,
      my heart is faint within me.
19 Listen to the cry of my people
      from a land far away:
   "Is the LORD not in Zion?
      Is her King no longer there?"

   "Why have they provoked me to
           anger with their images,
      with their worthless foreign
           idols?"

20 "The harvest is past,
      the summer has ended,
      and we are not saved."

21 Since my people are crushed, I am
           crushed;
      I mourn, and horror grips me.
22 Is there no balm in Gilead?
      Is there no physician there?
   Why then is there no healing
      for the wound of my people?

9:1 Oh, that my head were a spring of
           water
      and my eyes a fountain of tears!
   I would weep day and night
      for the slain of my people.
2 Oh, that I had in the desert
      a lodging place for travelers,
   so that I might leave my people
      and go away from them;
   for they are all adulterers,
      a crowd of unfaithful people.

3 "They make ready their tongue
      like a bow, to shoot lies;
   it is not by truth
      that they triumph[c] in the land.

They go from one sin to another;
      they do not acknowledge me,"
                                    declares the LORD.
4 "Beware of your friends;
      do not trust your brothers.
   For every brother is a deceiver,[d]
      and every friend a slanderer.
5 Friend deceives friend,
      and no one speaks the truth.
   They have taught their tongues to lie;
      they weary themselves with
           sinning.
6 You[e] live in the midst of deception;
      in their deceit they refuse to
           acknowledge me,"
                                    declares the LORD.

7 Therefore this is what the LORD Almighty says:

   "See, I will refine and test them,
      for what else can I do
   because of the sin of my people?
8 Their tongue is a deadly arrow;
      it speaks with deceit.
   With his mouth each speaks
           cordially to his neighbor,
      but in his heart he sets a trap for
           him.
9 Should I not punish them for this?"
      declares the LORD.
   "Should I not avenge myself
      on such a nation as this?"

10 I will weep and wail for the
           mountains
      and take up a lament concerning
           the desert pastures.
   They are desolate and untraveled,
      and the lowing of cattle is not
           heard.
   The birds of the air have fled
      and the animals are gone.

11 "I will make Jerusalem a heap of
           ruins,
      a haunt of jackals;
   and I will lay waste the towns of
           Judah
      so no one can live there."

12 What man is wise enough to understand this? Who has been instructed
by the LORD and can explain it? Why has

the land been ruined and laid waste like a desert that no one can cross?

13 The LORD said, "It is because they have forsaken my law, which I set before them; they have not obeyed me or followed my law. 14 Instead, they have followed the stubbornness of their hearts; they have followed the Baals, as their fathers taught them." 15 Therefore, this is what the LORD Almighty, the God of Israel, says: "See, I will make this people eat bitter food and drink poisoned water. 16 I will scatter them among nations that neither they nor their fathers have known, and I will pursue them with the sword until I have destroyed them."

17 This is what the LORD Almighty says:

"Consider now! Call for the wailing
    women to come;
  send for the most skillful of them.
18 Let them come quickly
  and wail over us
till our eyes overflow with tears
  and water streams from our eyelids.
19 The sound of wailing is heard from
    Zion:
  'How ruined we are!
  How great is our shame!
We must leave our land
  because our houses are in ruins.'"

20 Now, O women, hear the word of the
    LORD;
  open your ears to the words of his
    mouth.
Teach your daughters how to wail;
  teach one another a lament.
21 Death has climbed in through our
    windows
  and has entered our fortresses;
it has cut off the children from the
    streets
  and the young men from the
    public squares.

22 Say, "This is what the LORD declares:

"'The dead bodies of men will lie
  like refuse on the open field,
  like cut grain behind the reaper,
  with no one to gather them.'"

23 This is what the LORD says:

"Let not the wise man boast of his
    wisdom
  or the strong man boast of his
    strength
  or the rich man boast of his riches,
24 but let him who boasts boast about
    this:
  that he understands and knows
    me,
  that I am the LORD, who exercises
    kindness,
  justice and righteousness on
    earth,
  for in these I delight,"
                    declares the LORD.

25 "The days are coming," declares the LORD, "when I will punish all who are circumcised only in the flesh— 26 Egypt, Judah, Edom, Ammon, Moab and all who live in the desert in distant places.f For all these nations are really uncircumcised, and even the whole house of Israel is uncircumcised in heart."

a 13 The meaning of the Hebrew for this sentence is uncertain.   b 18 The meaning of the Hebrew for this word is uncertain.   c 3 Or lies; / they are not valiant for truth   d 4 Or a deceiving Jacob   e 6 That is, Jeremiah (the Hebrew is singular)   f 26 Or desert and who clip the hair by their foreheads

COLOSSIANS 3:1-17

Since, then, you have been raised with Christ, set your hearts on things above, where Christ is seated at the right hand of God. 2 Set your minds on things above, not on earthly things. 3 For you died, and your life is now hidden with Christ in God. 4 When Christ, who is youra life, appears, then you also will appear with him in glory.

5 Put to death, therefore, whatever belongs to your earthly nature: sexual immorality, impurity, lust, evil desires and greed, which is idolatry. 6 Because of these, the wrath of God is coming.b 7 You used to walk in these ways, in the life you once lived. 8 But now you must rid yourselves of all such things as these: anger, rage, malice, slander, and filthy language from your lips. 9 Do not lie to each other, since you have taken

off your old self with its practices ¹⁰and have put on the new self, which is being renewed in knowledge in the image of its Creator. ¹¹Here there is no Greek or Jew, circumcised or uncircumcised, barbarian, Scythian, slave or free, but Christ is all, and is in all.

¹²Therefore, as God's chosen people, holy and dearly loved, clothe yourselves with compassion, kindness, humility, gentleness and patience. ¹³Bear with each other and forgive whatever grievances you may have against one another. Forgive as the Lord forgave you. ¹⁴And over all these virtues put on love, which binds them all together in perfect unity.

¹⁵Let the peace of Christ rule in your hearts, since as members of one body you were called to peace. And be thankful. ¹⁶Let the word of Christ dwell in you richly as you teach and admonish one another with all wisdom, and as you sing psalms, hymns and spiritual songs with gratitude in your hearts to God. ¹⁷**And whatever you do, whether in word or deed, do it all in the name of the Lord Jesus, giving thanks to God the Father through him.**

a4 Some manuscripts our b6 Some early manuscripts coming on those who are disobedient

PSALM 78:32-55

³²In spite of all this, they [Israel] kept
  on sinning;
    in spite of his [the LORD's] wonders,
    they did not believe.
³³So he ended their days in futility
    and their years in terror.
³⁴Whenever God slew them, they
  would seek him;
    they eagerly turned to him again.
³⁵They remembered that God was their
  Rock,
    that God Most High was their
    Redeemer.
³⁶But then they would flatter him with
  their mouths,
    lying to him with their tongues;
³⁷their hearts were not loyal to him,
    they were not faithful to his
    covenant.

³⁸Yet he was merciful;
    he forgave their iniquities
    and did not destroy them.
  Time after time he restrained his
  anger
    and did not stir up his full wrath.
³⁹He remembered that they were but
  flesh,
    a passing breeze that does not return.

⁴⁰How often they rebelled against him
  in the desert
    and grieved him in the wasteland!
⁴¹Again and again they put God to the
  test;
    they vexed the Holy One of Israel.
⁴²They did not remember his power—
    the day he redeemed them from
    the oppressor,
⁴³the day he displayed his miraculous
    signs in Egypt,
    his wonders in the region of Zoan.
⁴⁴He turned their rivers to blood;
    they could not drink from their
    streams.
⁴⁵He sent swarms of flies that
    devoured them,
    and frogs that devastated them.
⁴⁶He gave their crops to the
    grasshopper,
    their produce to the locust.
⁴⁷He destroyed their vines with hail
    and their sycamore-figs with sleet.
⁴⁸He gave over their cattle to the hail,
    their livestock to bolts of
    lightning.
⁴⁹He unleashed against them his hot
  anger,
    his wrath, indignation and
    hostility—
    a band of destroying angels.
⁵⁰He prepared a path for his anger;
    he did not spare them from death
    but gave them over to the plague.
⁵¹He struck down all the firstborn of
    Egypt,
    the firstfruits of manhood in the
    tents of Ham.
⁵²But he brought his people out like a
  flock;
    he led them like sheep through
    the desert.

53 He guided them safely, so they were
unafraid;
but the sea engulfed their
enemies.
54 Thus he brought them to the border
of his holy land,
to the hill country his right hand
had taken.
55 He drove out nations before them
and allotted their lands to them as
an inheritance;
he settled the tribes of Israel in
their homes.

PROVERBS 24:27
27 Finish your outdoor work
and get your fields ready;
after that, build your house.

☐ DAY 281

GOD SIGHTINGS

October 8

JEREMIAH 10:1–11:23
Hear what the LORD says to you, O house
of Israel. 2 This is what the LORD says:

"Do not learn the ways of the nations
or be terrified by signs in the sky,
though the nations are terrified by
them.
3 For the customs of the peoples are
worthless;
they cut a tree out of the forest,
and a craftsman shapes it with his
chisel.
4 They adorn it with silver and gold;
they fasten it with hammer and
nails
so it will not totter.
5 Like a scarecrow in a melon patch,
their idols cannot speak;
they must be carried
because they cannot walk.
Do not fear them;
they can do no harm
nor can they do any good."

6 No one is like you, O LORD;
you are great,
and your name is mighty in power.
7 Who should not revere you,
O King of the nations?
This is your due.
Among all the wise men of the
nations
and in all their kingdoms,
there is no one like you.
8 They are all senseless and foolish;
they are taught by worthless
wooden idols.
9 Hammered silver is brought from
Tarshish
and gold from Uphaz.
What the craftsman and goldsmith
have made
is then dressed in blue and
purple—
all made by skilled workers.
10 But the LORD is the true God;
he is the living God, the eternal
King.
When he is angry, the earth trembles;
the nations cannot endure his
wrath.

11 "Tell them this: 'These gods, who
did not make the heavens and the earth,
will perish from the earth and from under the heavens.'"[a]

12 But God made the earth by his
power;
he founded the world by his
wisdom
and stretched out the heavens by
his understanding.
13 When he thunders, the waters in the
heavens roar;
he makes clouds rise from the
ends of the earth.
He sends lightning with the rain
and brings out the wind from his
storehouses.

14 Everyone is senseless and without
knowledge;
every goldsmith is shamed by his
idols.
His images are a fraud;
they have no breath in them.

¹⁵They are worthless, the objects of mockery;
when their judgment comes, they will perish.
¹⁶He who is the Portion of Jacob is not like these,
for he is the Maker of all things,
including Israel, the tribe of his inheritance—
the LORD Almighty is his name.

¹⁷Gather up your belongings to leave the land,
you who live under siege.
¹⁸For this is what the LORD says:
"At this time I will hurl out those who live in this land;
I will bring distress on them
so that they may be captured."

¹⁹Woe to me because of my injury!
My wound is incurable!
Yet I said to myself,
"This is my sickness, and I must endure it."
²⁰My tent is destroyed;
all its ropes are snapped.
My sons are gone from me and are no more;
no one is left now to pitch my tent
or to set up my shelter.
²¹The shepherds are senseless
and do not inquire of the LORD;
so they do not prosper
and all their flock is scattered.
²²Listen! The report is coming—
a great commotion from the land of the north!
It will make the towns of Judah desolate,
a haunt of jackals.

²³I know, O LORD, that a man's life is not his own;
it is not for man to direct his steps.
²⁴Correct me, LORD, but only with justice—
not in your anger,
lest you reduce me to nothing.
²⁵Pour out your wrath on the nations
that do not acknowledge you,
on the peoples who do not call on your name.
For they have devoured Jacob;
they have devoured him completely
and destroyed his homeland.

¹¹:¹This is the word that came to Jeremiah from the LORD: ²"Listen to the terms of this covenant and tell them to the people of Judah and to those who live in Jerusalem. ³Tell them that this is what the LORD, the God of Israel, says: 'Cursed is the man who does not obey the terms of this covenant— ⁴the terms I commanded your forefathers when I brought them out of Egypt, out of the iron-smelting furnace.' I said, 'Obey me and do everything I command you, and you will be my people, and I will be your God. ⁵Then I will fulfill the oath I swore to your forefathers, to give them a land flowing with milk and honey'—the land you possess today."

I answered, "Amen, LORD."

⁶The LORD said to me, "Proclaim all these words in the towns of Judah and in the streets of Jerusalem: 'Listen to the terms of this covenant and follow them. ⁷From the time I brought your forefathers up from Egypt until today, I warned them again and again, saying, "Obey me." ⁸But they did not listen or pay attention; instead, they followed the stubbornness of their evil hearts. So I brought on them all the curses of the covenant I had commanded them to follow but that they did not keep.'"

⁹Then the LORD said to me, "There is a conspiracy among the people of Judah and those who live in Jerusalem. ¹⁰They have returned to the sins of their forefathers, who refused to listen to my words. They have followed other gods to serve them. Both the house of Israel and the house of Judah have broken the covenant I made with their forefathers. ¹¹Therefore this is what the LORD says: 'I will bring on them a disaster they cannot escape. Although they cry out to me, I will not listen to them. ¹²The towns of Judah and the people of Jerusalem will

go and cry out to the gods to whom they burn incense, but they will not help them at all when disaster strikes. [13]You have as many gods as you have towns, O Judah; and the altars you have set up to burn incense to that shameful god Baal are as many as the streets of Jerusalem.'

[14]"Do not pray for this people nor offer any plea or petition for them, because I will not listen when they call to me in the time of their distress.

[15]"What is my beloved doing in my
    temple
  as she works out her evil schemes
    with many?
  Can consecrated meat avert ⸤your
    punishment⸥?
When you engage in your
    wickedness,
    then you rejoice.[b]"

[16]The LORD called you a thriving olive
    tree
  with fruit beautiful in form.
But with the roar of a mighty storm
  he will set it on fire,
    and its branches will be broken.

[17]The LORD Almighty, who planted you, has decreed disaster for you, because the house of Israel and the house of Judah have done evil and provoked me to anger by burning incense to Baal.

[18]Because the LORD revealed their plot to me, I knew it, for at that time he showed me what they were doing. [19]I had been like a gentle lamb led to the slaughter; I did not realize that they had plotted against me, saying,

  "Let us destroy the tree and its fruit;
    let us cut him off from the land of
      the living,
    that his name be remembered no
      more."
[20]But, O LORD Almighty, you who judge
    righteously
  and test the heart and mind,
  let me see your vengeance upon
    them,
  for to you I have committed my
    cause.

[21]"Therefore this is what the LORD says about the men of Anathoth who are seeking your life and saying, 'Do not prophesy in the name of the LORD or you will die by our hands'— [22]therefore this is what the LORD Almighty says: 'I will punish them. Their young men will die by the sword, their sons and daughters by famine. [23]Not even a remnant will be left to them, because I will bring disaster on the men of Anathoth in the year of their punishment.'"

a11 The text of this verse is in Aramaic.   b15 Or Could consecrated meat avert your punishment? / Then you would rejoice

COLOSSIANS 3:18–4:18

Wives, submit to your husbands, as is fitting in the Lord.

[19]Husbands, love your wives and do not be harsh with them.

[20]Children, obey your parents in everything, for this pleases the Lord.

[21]Fathers, do not embitter your children, or they will become discouraged.

[22]Slaves, obey your earthly masters in everything; and do it, not only when their eye is on you and to win their favor, but with sincerity of heart and reverence for the Lord. [23]**Whatever you do, work at it with all your heart, as working for the Lord, not for men,** [24]**since you know that you will receive an inheritance from the Lord as a reward. It is the Lord Christ you are serving.** [25]Anyone who does wrong will be repaid for his wrong, and there is no favoritism.

[4:1]MASTERS, provide your slaves with what is right and fair, because you know that you also have a Master in heaven.

[2]Devote yourselves to prayer, being watchful and thankful. [3]And pray for us, too, that God may open a door for our message, so that we may proclaim the mystery of Christ, for which I am in chains. [4]Pray that I may proclaim it clearly, as I should. [5]Be wise in the way you act toward outsiders; make the most of every opportunity. [6]Let your conversation be always full of grace,

seasoned with salt, so that you may know how to answer everyone.

[7]Tychicus will tell you all the news about me. He is a dear brother, a faithful minister and fellow servant in the Lord. [8]I am sending him to you for the express purpose that you may know about our[a] circumstances and that he may encourage your hearts. [9]He is coming with Onesimus, our faithful and dear brother, who is one of you. They will tell you everything that is happening here.

[10]My fellow prisoner Aristarchus sends you his greetings, as does Mark, the cousin of Barnabas. (You have received instructions about him; if he comes to you, welcome him.) [11]Jesus, who is called Justus, also sends greetings. These are the only Jews among my fellow workers for the kingdom of God, and they have proved a comfort to me. [12]Epaphras, who is one of you and a servant of Christ Jesus, sends greetings. He is always wrestling in prayer for you, that you may stand firm in all the will of God, mature and fully assured. [13]I vouch for him that he is working hard for you and for those at Laodicea and Hierapolis. [14]Our dear friend Luke, the doctor, and Demas send greetings. [15]Give my greetings to the brothers at Laodicea, and to Nympha and the church in her house.

[16]After this letter has been read to you, see that it is also read in the church of the Laodiceans and that you in turn read the letter from Laodicea.

[17]Tell Archippus: "See to it that you complete the work you have received in the Lord."

[18]I, Paul, write this greeting in my own hand. Remember my chains. Grace be with you.

[a]8 Some manuscripts *that he may know about your*

PSALM 78:56-72

[56]**B**ut they [the LORD's people] put God to the test
and rebelled against the Most High;
they did not keep his statutes.

[57]Like their fathers they were disloyal and faithless,
as unreliable as a faulty bow.
[58]They angered him with their high places;
they aroused his jealousy with their idols.
[59]When God heard them, he was very angry;
he rejected Israel completely.
[60]He abandoned the tabernacle of Shiloh,
the tent he had set up among men.
[61]He sent ⌊the ark of⌋ his might into captivity,
his splendor into the hands of the enemy.
[62]He gave his people over to the sword;
he was very angry with his inheritance.
[63]Fire consumed their young men,
and their maidens had no wedding songs;
[64]their priests were put to the sword,
and their widows could not weep.

[65]Then the Lord awoke as from sleep,
as a man wakes from the stupor of wine.
[66]He beat back his enemies;
he put them to everlasting shame.
[67]Then he rejected the tents of Joseph,
he did not choose the tribe of Ephraim;
[68]but he chose the tribe of Judah,
Mount Zion, which he loved.
[69]He built his sanctuary like the heights,
like the earth that he established forever.
[70]He chose David his servant
and took him from the sheep pens;
[71]from tending the sheep he brought him
to be the shepherd of his people Jacob,
of Israel his inheritance.
[72]And David shepherded them with integrity of heart;
with skillful hands he led them.

PROVERBS 24:28-29

28 **D**o not testify against your neighbor
without cause,
or use your lips to deceive.
29 Do not say, "I'll do to him as he has
done to me;
I'll pay that man back for what he
did."

GOD SIGHTINGS

October 9

JEREMIAH 12:1–14:10

You are always righteous, O LORD,
when I [Jeremiah] bring a case
before you.
Yet I would speak with you about
your justice:
Why does the way of the wicked
prosper?
Why do all the faithless live at
ease?
2 You have planted them, and they
have taken root;
they grow and bear fruit.
You are always on their lips
but far from their hearts.
3 Yet you know me, O LORD;
you see me and test my thoughts
about you.
Drag them off like sheep to be
butchered!
Set them apart for the day of
slaughter!
4 How long will the land lie parched[a]
and the grass in every field be
withered?
Because those who live in it are wicked,
the animals and birds have
perished.
Moreover, the people are saying,
"He will not see what happens to
us."

5 "If you have raced with men on foot
and they have worn you out,
how can you compete with horses?

If you stumble in safe country,[b]
how will you manage in the
thickets by[c] the Jordan?
6 Your brothers, your own family—
even they have betrayed you;
they have raised a loud cry against
you.
Do not trust them,
though they speak well of you.

7 "I will forsake my house,
abandon my inheritance;
I will give the one I love
into the hands of her enemies.
8 My inheritance has become to me
like a lion in the forest.
She roars at me;
therefore I hate her.
9 Has not my inheritance become to
me
like a speckled bird of prey
that other birds of prey surround
and attack?
Go and gather all the wild beasts;
bring them to devour.
10 Many shepherds will ruin my
vineyard
and trample down my field;
they will turn my pleasant field
into a desolate wasteland.
11 It will be made a wasteland,
parched and desolate before me;
the whole land will be laid waste
because there is no one who cares.
12 Over all the barren heights in the
desert
destroyers will swarm,
for the sword of the LORD will devour
from one end of the land to the
other;
no one will be safe.
13 They will sow wheat but reap thorns;
they will wear themselves out but
gain nothing.
So bear the shame of your harvest
because of the LORD's fierce
anger."

14 This is what the LORD says: "As for
all my wicked neighbors who seize the
inheritance I gave my people Israel, I
will uproot them from their lands and I

will uproot the house of Judah from among them. ¹⁵But after I uproot them, I will again have compassion and will bring each of them back to his own inheritance and his own country. ¹⁶And if they learn well the ways of my people and swear by my name, saying, 'As surely as the Lord lives'—even as they once taught my people to swear by Baal—then they will be established among my people. ¹⁷But if any nation does not listen, I will completely uproot and destroy it," declares the Lord.

¹³:¹This is what the Lord said to me: "Go and buy a linen belt and put it around your waist, but do not let it touch water." ²So I bought a belt, as the Lord directed, and put it around my waist.

³Then the word of the Lord came to me a second time: ⁴"Take the belt you bought and are wearing around your waist, and go now to Perath*d* and hide it there in a crevice in the rocks." ⁵So I went and hid it at Perath, as the Lord told me.

⁶Many days later the Lord said to me, "Go now to Perath and get the belt I told you to hide there." ⁷So I went to Perath and dug up the belt and took it from the place where I had hidden it, but now it was ruined and completely useless.

⁸Then the word of the Lord came to me: ⁹"This is what the Lord says: 'In the same way I will ruin the pride of Judah and the great pride of Jerusalem. ¹⁰These wicked people, who refuse to listen to my words, who follow the stubbornness of their hearts and go after other gods to serve and worship them, will be like this belt—completely useless! ¹¹For as a belt is bound around a man's waist, so I bound the whole house of Israel and the whole house of Judah to me,' declares the Lord, 'to be my people for my renown and praise and honor. But they have not listened.'

¹²"Say to them: 'This is what the Lord, the God of Israel, says: Every wineskin should be filled with wine.' And if they say to you, 'Don't we know that every wineskin should be filled with wine?'

¹³then tell them, 'This is what the Lord says: I am going to fill with drunkenness all who live in this land, including the kings who sit on David's throne, the priests, the prophets and all those living in Jerusalem. ¹⁴I will smash them one against the other, fathers and sons alike, declares the Lord. I will allow no pity or mercy or compassion to keep me from destroying them.'"

¹⁵Hear and pay attention,
    do not be arrogant,
    for the Lord has spoken.
¹⁶Give glory to the Lord your God
    before he brings the darkness,
before your feet stumble
    on the darkening hills.
You hope for light,
    but he will turn it to thick darkness
    and change it to deep gloom.
¹⁷But if you do not listen,
    I will weep in secret
    because of your pride;
my eyes will weep bitterly,
    overflowing with tears,
    because the Lord's flock will be
      taken captive.

¹⁸Say to the king and to the queen
      mother,
    "Come down from your thrones,
for your glorious crowns
    will fall from your heads."
¹⁹The cities in the Negev will be shut
      up,
    and there will be no one to open
      them.
All Judah will be carried into exile,
    carried completely away.

²⁰Lift up your eyes and see
    those who are coming from the
      north.
Where is the flock that was
      entrusted to you,
    the sheep of which you boasted?
²¹What will you say when ⌊the Lord⌋
      sets over you
    those you cultivated as your
      special allies?
Will not pain grip you
    like that of a woman in labor?

²²And if you ask yourself,
  "Why has this happened to me?"—
it is because of your many sins
    that your skirts have been torn off
    and your body mistreated.
²³Can the Ethiopian^e change his skin
    or the leopard its spots?
Neither can you do good
    who are accustomed to doing evil.

²⁴"I will scatter you like chaff
    driven by the desert wind.
²⁵This is your lot,
    the portion I have decreed for you,"
        declares the Lord,
  "because you have forgotten me
    and trusted in false gods.
²⁶I will pull up your skirts over your
    face
    that your shame may be seen—
²⁷your adulteries and lustful neighings,
    your shameless prostitution!
I have seen your detestable acts
    on the hills and in the fields.
Woe to you, O Jerusalem!
    How long will you be unclean?"

¹⁴:¹This is the word of the Lord to Jeremiah concerning the drought:

²"Judah mourns,
    her cities languish;
they wail for the land,
    and a cry goes up from Jerusalem.
³The nobles send their servants for
    water;
    they go to the cisterns
    but find no water.
They return with their jars unfilled;
    dismayed and despairing,
    they cover their heads.
⁴The ground is cracked
    because there is no rain in the land;
the farmers are dismayed
    and cover their heads.
⁵Even the doe in the field
    deserts her newborn fawn
    because there is no grass.
⁶Wild donkeys stand on the barren
    heights
    and pant like jackals;
    their eyesight fails
    for lack of pasture."

⁷Although our sins testify against us,
    O Lord, do something for the sake
        of your name.
For our backsliding is great;
    we have sinned against you.
⁸O Hope of Israel,
    its Savior in times of distress,
why are you like a stranger in the
    land,
    like a traveler who stays only a
        night?
⁹Why are you like a man taken by
    surprise,
    like a warrior powerless to save?
You are among us, O Lord,
    and we bear your name;
    do not forsake us!

¹⁰This is what the Lord says about
this people:

  "They greatly love to wander;
    they do not restrain their feet.
So the Lord does not accept them;
    he will now remember their
        wickedness
    and punish them for their sins."

a4 Or *land mourn* *b5* Or *If you put your trust in a land of
safety* *c5* Or *the flooding of* *d4* Or possibly *the Euphrates*;
also in verses 5-7 *e23* Hebrew *Cushite* (probably a person
from the upper Nile region)

1 THESSALONIANS 1:1–2:9
Paul, Silas^a and Timothy,

To the church of the Thessalonians in
God the Father and the Lord Jesus
Christ:

Grace and peace to you.^b

²We always thank God for all of you,
mentioning you in our prayers. ³We
continually remember before our God
and Father your work produced by faith,
your labor prompted by love, and your
endurance inspired by hope in our Lord
Jesus Christ.

⁴For we know, brothers loved by God,
that he has chosen you, ⁵because our
gospel came to you not simply with
words, but also with power, with the
Holy Spirit and with deep conviction.
You know how we lived among you for
your sake. ⁶You became imitators of us

and of the Lord; in spite of severe suffering, you welcomed the message with the joy given by the Holy Spirit. [7]And so you became a model to all the believers in Macedonia and Achaia. [8]The Lord's message rang out from you not only in Macedonia and Achaia—your faith in God has become known everywhere. Therefore we do not need to say anything about it, [9]for they themselves report what kind of reception you gave us. They tell how you turned to God from idols to serve the living and true God, [10]and to wait for his Son from heaven, whom he raised from the dead—Jesus, who rescues us from the coming wrath.

[2:1]You know, brothers, that our visit to you was not a failure. [2]We had previously suffered and been insulted in Philippi, as you know, but with the help of our God we dared to tell you his gospel in spite of strong opposition. [3]For the appeal we make does not spring from error or impure motives, nor are we trying to trick you. [4]On the contrary, we speak as men approved by God to be entrusted with the gospel. We are not trying to please men but God, who tests our hearts. [5]You know we never used flattery, nor did we put on a mask to cover up greed—God is our witness. [6]We were not looking for praise from men, not from you or anyone else.

As apostles of Christ we could have been a burden to you, [7]but we were gentle among you, like a mother caring for her little children. [8]We loved you so much that we were delighted to share with you not only the gospel of God but our lives as well, because you had become so dear to us. [9]Surely you remember, brothers, our toil and hardship; we worked night and day in order not to be a burden to anyone while we preached the gospel of God to you.

[a]1 Greek *Silvanus*, a variant of *Silas* [b]1 Some early manuscripts *you from God our Father and the Lord Jesus Christ*

PSALM 79:1-13
A psalm of Asaph.

[1]O God, the nations have invaded your inheritance;

they have defiled your holy temple,
they have reduced Jerusalem to rubble.
[2]They have given the dead bodies of your servants
as food to the birds of the air,
the flesh of your saints to the beasts of the earth.
[3]They have poured out blood like water
all around Jerusalem,
and there is no one to bury the dead.
[4]We are objects of reproach to our neighbors,
of scorn and derision to those around us.

[5]How long, O Lord? Will you be angry forever?
How long will your jealousy burn like fire?
[6]Pour out your wrath on the nations that do not acknowledge you,
on the kingdoms
that do not call on your name;
[7]for they have devoured Jacob
and destroyed his homeland.
[8]Do not hold against us the sins of the fathers;
may your mercy come quickly to meet us,
for we are in desperate need.

[9]**Help us, O God our Savior,
for the glory of your name;
deliver us and forgive our sins
for your name's sake.**
[10]Why should the nations say,
"Where is their God?"
Before our eyes, make known among the nations
that you avenge the outpoured blood of your servants.
[11]May the groans of the prisoners come before you;
by the strength of your arm
preserve those condemned to die.

[12]Pay back into the laps of our neighbors seven times
the reproach they have hurled at you, O Lord.

13 Then we your people, the sheep of
           your pasture,
       will praise you forever;
   from generation to generation
       we will recount your praise.

PROVERBS 24:30-34

30 I went past the field of the sluggard,
       past the vineyard of the man who
           lacks judgment;
31 thorns had come up everywhere,
       the ground was covered with
           weeds,
       and the stone wall was in ruins.
32 I applied my heart to what I observed
       and learned a lesson from what I
           saw:
33 A little sleep, a little slumber,
       a little folding of the hands to
           rest—
34 and poverty will come on you like a
           bandit
       and scarcity like an armed man.a

a 34 Or like a vagrant / and scarcity like a beggar

☐ D A Y 2 8 3

GOD SIGHTINGS

October 10

JEREMIAH 14:11–16:15

Then the LORD said to me [Jeremiah],
"Do not pray for the well-being of this
people. 12 Although they fast, I will not
listen to their cry; though they offer
burnt offerings and grain offerings, I
will not accept them. Instead, I will destroy them with the sword, famine and
plague."

   13 But I said, "Ah, Sovereign LORD, the
prophets keep telling them, 'You will
not see the sword or suffer famine. Indeed, I will give you lasting peace in this
place.'"

   14 Then the LORD said to me, "The
prophets are prophesying lies in my
name. I have not sent them or appointed them or spoken to them. They

are prophesying to you false visions, divinations, idolatriesa and the delusions
of their own minds. 15 Therefore, this is
what the LORD says about the prophets
who are prophesying in my name: I did
not send them, yet they are saying, 'No
sword or famine will touch this land.'
Those same prophets will perish by
sword and famine. 16 And the people
they are prophesying to will be thrown
out into the streets of Jerusalem because of the famine and sword. There
will be no one to bury them or their
wives, their sons or their daughters. I
will pour out on them the calamity they
deserve.

   17 "Speak this word to them:

   "'Let my eyes overflow with tears
       night and day without ceasing;
   for my virgin daughter—my people—
       has suffered a grievous wound,
       a crushing blow.
18 If I go into the country,
       I see those slain by the sword;
   if I go into the city,
       I see the ravages of famine.
   Both prophet and priest
       have gone to a land they know
           not.'"

19 Have you rejected Judah completely?
       Do you despise Zion?
   Why have you afflicted us
       so that we cannot be healed?
   We hoped for peace
       but no good has come,
   for a time of healing
       but there is only terror.
20 O LORD, we acknowledge our
           wickedness
       and the guilt of our fathers;
       we have indeed sinned against
           you.
21 For the sake of your name do not
           despise us;
       do not dishonor your glorious
           throne.
   Remember your covenant with us
       and do not break it.
22 Do any of the worthless idols of the
       nations bring rain?

Do the skies themselves send
    down showers?
No, it is you, O LORD our God.
    Therefore our hope is in you,
    for you are the one who does all
        this.

15:1 THEN the LORD said to me: "Even if Moses and Samuel were to stand before me, my heart would not go out to this people. Send them away from my presence! Let them go! 2 And if they ask you, 'Where shall we go?' tell them, 'This is what the LORD says:

"'Those destined for death, to death;
those for the sword, to the sword;
those for starvation, to starvation;
those for captivity, to captivity.'

3 "I will send four kinds of destroyers against them," declares the LORD, "the sword to kill and the dogs to drag away and the birds of the air and the beasts of the earth to devour and destroy. 4 I will make them abhorrent to all the kingdoms of the earth because of what Manasseh son of Hezekiah king of Judah did in Jerusalem.

5 "Who will have pity on you,
    O Jerusalem?
    Who will mourn for you?
    Who will stop to ask how you are?
6 You have rejected me," declares the
    LORD.
    "You keep on backsliding.
So I will lay hands on you and destroy
    you;
    I can no longer show compassion.
7 I will winnow them with a
        winnowing fork
    at the city gates of the land.
I will bring bereavement and
        destruction on my people,
    for they have not changed their
        ways.
8 I will make their widows more
        numerous
    than the sand of the sea.
At midday I will bring a destroyer
    against the mothers of their young
        men;

suddenly I will bring down on them
    anguish and terror.
9 The mother of seven will grow faint
    and breathe her last.
Her sun will set while it is still day;
    she will be disgraced and
        humiliated.
I will put the survivors to the sword
    before their enemies,"
            declares the LORD.

10 Alas, my mother, that you gave me
        birth,
    a man with whom the whole land
        strives and contends!
I have neither lent nor borrowed,
    yet everyone curses me.

11 The LORD said,

"Surely I will deliver you for a good
        purpose;
    surely I will make your enemies
        plead with you
    in times of disaster and times of
        distress.

12 "Can a man break iron—
    iron from the north—or bronze?
13 Your wealth and your treasures
    I will give as plunder, without
        charge,
    because of all your sins
    throughout your country.
14 I will enslave you to your enemies
    in*b* a land you do not know,
for my anger will kindle a fire
    that will burn against you."

15 You understand, O LORD;
    remember me and care for me.
    Avenge me on my persecutors.
You are long-suffering—do not take
        me away;
    think of how I suffer reproach for
        your sake.
16 When your words came, I ate them;
    they were my joy and my heart's
        delight,
for I bear your name,
    O LORD God Almighty.
17 I never sat in the company of
        revelers,
    never made merry with them;

I sat alone because your hand was on
   me
   and you had filled me with
     indignation.
18 Why is my pain unending
   and my wound grievous and
     incurable?
Will you be to me like a deceptive
   brook,
   like a spring that fails?

19 Therefore this is what the LORD
says:

"If you repent, I will restore you
   that you may serve me;
if you utter worthy, not worthless,
   words,
you will be my spokesman.
Let this people turn to you,
   but you must not turn to them.
20 I will make you a wall to this people,
   a fortified wall of bronze;
they will fight against you
   but will not overcome you,
for I am with you
   to rescue and save you,"
               declares the LORD.
21 "I will save you from the hands of the
   wicked
   and redeem you from the grasp of
     the cruel."

16:1 Then the word of the LORD came to
me: 2 "You must not marry and have
sons or daughters in this place." 3 For
this is what the LORD says about the sons
and daughters born in this land and
about the women who are their mothers
and the men who are their fathers:
4 "They will die of deadly diseases. They
will not be mourned or buried but will
be like refuse lying on the ground. They
will perish by sword and famine, and
their dead bodies will become food for
the birds of the air and the beasts of the
earth."

5 For this is what the LORD says: "Do not
enter a house where there is a funeral
meal; do not go to mourn or show sympathy, because I have withdrawn my
blessing, my love and my pity from this
people," declares the LORD. 6 "Both high

and low will die in this land. They will not
be buried or mourned, and no one will
cut himself or shave his head for them.
7 No one will offer food to comfort those
who mourn for the dead—not even for a
father or a mother—nor will anyone give
them a drink to console them.

8 "And do not enter a house where
there is feasting and sit down to eat and
drink. 9 For this is what the LORD Almighty, the God of Israel, says: Before
your eyes and in your days I will bring an
end to the sounds of joy and gladness
and to the voices of bride and bridegroom in this place.

10 "When you tell these people all this
and they ask you, 'Why has the LORD decreed such a great disaster against us?
What wrong have we done? What sin
have we committed against the LORD
our God?' 11 then say to them, 'It is because your fathers forsook me,' declares
the LORD, 'and followed other gods and
served and worshiped them. They forsook me and did not keep my law. 12 But
you have behaved more wickedly than
your fathers. See how each of you is following the stubbornness of his evil
heart instead of obeying me. 13 So I will
throw you out of this land into a land
neither you nor your fathers have
known, and there you will serve other
gods day and night, for I will show you
no favor.'

14 "However, the days are coming," declares the LORD, "when men will no longer say, 'As surely as the LORD lives, who
brought the Israelites up out of Egypt,'
15 but they will say, 'As surely as the LORD
lives, who brought the Israelites up out
of the land of the north and out of all the
countries where he had banished them.'
For I will restore them to the land I gave
their forefathers."

*a 14 Or visions, worthless divinations   b 14 Some Hebrew
manuscripts, Septuagint and Syriac (see also Jer. 17:4);
most Hebrew manuscripts I will cause your enemies to
bring you / into*

1 THESSALONIANS 2:10–3:13

You are witnesses, and so is God, of
how holy, righteous and blameless we
were among you who believed. 11 For

you know that we dealt with each of you as a father deals with his own children, [12]encouraging, comforting and urging you to live lives worthy of God, who calls you into his kingdom and glory.

[13]And we also thank God continually because, when you received the word of God, which you heard from us, you accepted it not as the word of men, but as it actually is, the word of God, which is at work in you who believe. [14]For you, brothers, became imitators of God's churches in Judea, which are in Christ Jesus: You suffered from your own countrymen the same things those churches suffered from the Jews, [15]who killed the Lord Jesus and the prophets and also drove us out. They displease God and are hostile to all men [16]in their effort to keep us from speaking to the Gentiles so that they may be saved. In this way they always heap up their sins to the limit. The wrath of God has come upon them at last.[a]

[17]But, brothers, when we were torn away from you for a short time (in person, not in thought), out of our intense longing we made every effort to see you. [18]For we wanted to come to you—certainly I, Paul, did, again and again—but Satan stopped us. [19]For what is our hope, our joy, or the crown in which we will glory in the presence of our Lord Jesus when he comes? Is it not you? [20]Indeed, you are our glory and joy.

[3:1]So when we could stand it no longer, we thought it best to be left by ourselves in Athens. [2]We sent Timothy, who is our brother and God's fellow worker[b] in spreading the gospel of Christ, to strengthen and encourage you in your faith, [3]so that no one would be unsettled by these trials. You know quite well that we were destined for them. [4]In fact, when we were with you, we kept telling you that we would be persecuted. And it turned out that way, as you well know. [5]For this reason, when I could stand it no longer, I sent to find out about your faith. I was afraid that in some way the tempter might have

tempted you and our efforts might have been useless.

[6]But Timothy has just now come to us from you and has brought good news about your faith and love. He has told us that you always have pleasant memories of us and that you long to see us, just as we also long to see you. [7]Therefore, brothers, in all our distress and persecution we were encouraged about you because of your faith. [8]For now we really live, since you are standing firm in the Lord. [9]How can we thank God enough for you in return for all the joy we have in the presence of our God because of you? [10]Night and day we pray most earnestly that we may see you again and supply what is lacking in your faith.

[11]Now may our God and Father himself and our Lord Jesus clear the way for us to come to you. [12]**May the Lord make your love increase and overflow for each other and for everyone else, just as ours does for you.** [13]May he strengthen your hearts so that you will be blameless and holy in the presence of our God and Father when our Lord Jesus comes with all his holy ones.

[a]16 Or *them fully*   [b]2 Some manuscripts *brother and fellow worker*; other manuscripts *brother and God's servant*

PSALM 80:1-19

For the director of music. To ⌐the tune of⌐ "The Lilies of the Covenant." Of Asaph. A psalm.

[1] **H**ear us, O Shepherd of Israel,
  you who lead Joseph like a flock;
  you who sit enthroned between the
      cherubim, shine forth
[2]   before Ephraim, Benjamin and
      Manasseh.
  Awaken your might;
    come and save us.

[3]Restore us, O God;
    make your face shine upon us,
    that we may be saved.

[4]O Lord God Almighty,
    how long will your anger smolder
    against the prayers of your
        people?

5 You have fed them with the bread of
   tears;
   you have made them drink tears
      by the bowlful.
6 You have made us a source of
   contention to our neighbors,
   and our enemies mock us.

7 Restore us, O God Almighty;
   make your face shine upon us,
   that we may be saved.

8 You brought a vine out of Egypt;
   you drove out the nations and
      planted it.
9 You cleared the ground for it,
   and it took root and filled the land.
10 The mountains were covered with its
      shade,
   the mighty cedars with its
      branches.
11 It sent out its boughs to the Sea,[a]
   its shoots as far as the River.[b]

12 Why have you broken down its walls
   so that all who pass by pick its
      grapes?
13 Boars from the forest ravage it
   and the creatures of the field feed
      on it.
14 Return to us, O God Almighty!
   Look down from heaven and see!
   Watch over this vine,
15   the root your right hand has
         planted,
     the son[c] you have raised up for
         yourself.

16 Your vine is cut down, it is burned
      with fire;
   at your rebuke your people perish.
17 Let your hand rest on the man at your
      right hand,
   the son of man you have raised up
      for yourself.
18 Then we will not turn away from you;
   revive us, and we will call on your
      name.

19 Restore us, O LORD God Almighty;
   make your face shine upon us,
   that we may be saved.

a11 Probably the Mediterranean   b11 That is, the Euphrates
c15 Or branch

PROVERBS 25:1-5

These are more proverbs of Solomon,
copied by the men of Hezekiah king of
Judah:

2 It is the glory of God to conceal a
      matter;
   to search out a matter is the glory
      of kings.

3 As the heavens are high and the earth
      is deep,
   so the hearts of kings are
      unsearchable.

4 Remove the dross from the silver,
   and out comes material for[a] the
      silversmith;
5 remove the wicked from the king's
      presence,
   and his throne will be established
      through righteousness.

a4 Or comes a vessel from

□ DAY 284

GOD SIGHTINGS

October 11

JEREMIAH 16:16-18:23

"But now I will send for many fishermen," declares the LORD, "and they will
catch them. After that I will send for
many hunters, and they will hunt them
down on every mountain and hill and
from the crevices of the rocks. 17 My
eyes are on all their ways; they are not
hidden from me, nor is their sin concealed from my eyes. 18 I will repay them
double for their wickedness and their
sin, because they have defiled my land
with the lifeless forms of their vile images and have filled my inheritance
with their detestable idols."

19 O LORD, my strength and my fortress,
   my refuge in time of distress,
   to you the nations will come
   from the ends of the earth and
      say,

"Our fathers possessed nothing but
    false gods,
  worthless idols that did them no
    good.
20 Do men make their own gods?
  Yes, but they are not gods!"

21 "Therefore I will teach them—
  this time I will teach them
  my power and might.
Then they will know
  that my name is the LORD.

17:1 "JUDAH's sin is engraved with an iron
    tool,
  inscribed with a flint point,
on the tablets of their hearts
  and on the horns of their altars.
2 Even their children remember
  their altars and Asherah poles*a*
beside the spreading trees
  and on the high hills.
3 My mountain in the land
  and your*b* wealth and all your
    treasures
I will give away as plunder,
  together with your high places,
  because of sin throughout your
    country.
4 Through your own fault you will lose
  the inheritance I gave you.
I will enslave you to your enemies
  in a land you do not know,
for you have kindled my anger,
  and it will burn forever."

5 This is what the LORD says:

"Cursed is the one who trusts in man,
  who depends on flesh for his
    strength
  and whose heart turns away from
    the LORD.
6 He will be like a bush in the
    wastelands;
  he will not see prosperity when it
    comes.
He will dwell in the parched places
    of the desert,
  in a salt land where no one lives.

7 "But blessed is the man who trusts in
    the LORD,
  whose confidence is in him.

8 He will be like a tree planted by the
    water
  that sends out its roots by the
    stream.
It does not fear when heat comes;
  its leaves are always green.
It has no worries in a year of drought
  and never fails to bear fruit."

9 The heart is deceitful above all things
  and beyond cure.
  Who can understand it?

10 "I the LORD search the heart
  and examine the mind,
to reward a man according to his
    conduct,
  according to what his deeds
    deserve."

11 Like a partridge that hatches eggs it
    did not lay
  is the man who gains riches by
    unjust means.
When his life is half gone, they will
    desert him,
  and in the end he will prove to be a
    fool.

12 A glorious throne, exalted from the
    beginning,
  is the place of our sanctuary.
13 O LORD, the hope of Israel,
  all who forsake you will be put to
    shame.
Those who turn away from you will
    be written in the dust
  because they have forsaken the
    LORD,
  the spring of living water.

14 Heal me, O LORD, and I will be
    healed;
  save me and I will be saved,
  for you are the one I praise.
15 They keep saying to me,
  "Where is the word of the LORD?
  Let it now be fulfilled!"
16 I have not run away from being your
    shepherd;
  you know I have not desired the
    day of despair.
What passes my lips is open
    before you.

17 Do not be a terror to me;
     you are my refuge in the day of
          disaster.
18 Let my persecutors be put to shame,
     but keep me from shame;
   let them be terrified,
     but keep me from terror.
   Bring on them the day of disaster;
     destroy them with double
          destruction.

19 This is what the LORD said to me:
"Go and stand at the gate of the people,
through which the kings of Judah go in
and out; stand also at all the other gates
of Jerusalem. 20 Say to them, 'Hear the
word of the LORD, O kings of Judah and
all people of Judah and everyone living
in Jerusalem who come through these
gates. 21 This is what the LORD says: Be
careful not to carry a load on the Sabbath day or bring it through the gates of
Jerusalem. 22 Do not bring a load out of
your houses or do any work on the Sabbath, but keep the Sabbath day holy, as I
commanded your forefathers. 23 Yet
they did not listen or pay attention; they
were stiff-necked and would not listen
or respond to discipline. 24 But if you are
careful to obey me, declares the LORD,
and bring no load through the gates of
this city on the Sabbath, but keep the
Sabbath day holy by not doing any work
on it, 25 then kings who sit on David's
throne will come through the gates of
this city with their officials. They and
their officials will come riding in chariots and on horses, accompanied by the
men of Judah and those living in Jerusalem, and this city will be inhabited forever. 26 People will come from the towns
of Judah and the villages around Jerusalem, from the territory of Benjamin and
the western foothills, from the hill
country and the Negev, bringing burnt
offerings and sacrifices, grain offerings,
incense and thank offerings to the
house of the LORD. 27 But if you do not
obey me to keep the Sabbath day holy by
not carrying any load as you come
through the gates of Jerusalem on
the Sabbath day, then I will kindle an
unquenchable fire in the gates of Jerusalem that will consume her fortresses.'"

18:1 THIS is the word that came to Jeremiah from the LORD: 2 "Go down to the
potter's house, and there I will give you
my message." 3 So I went down to the
potter's house, and I saw him working at
the wheel. 4 But the pot he was shaping
from the clay was marred in his hands;
so the potter formed it into another pot,
shaping it as seemed best to him.

5 Then the word of the LORD came to
me: 6 "O house of Israel, can I not do with
you as this potter does?" declares the
LORD. "Like clay in the hand of the potter, so are you in my hand, O house of Israel. 7 If at any time I announce that a
nation or kingdom is to be uprooted,
torn down and destroyed, 8 and if that
nation I warned repents of its evil, then I
will relent and not inflict on it the disaster I had planned. 9 And if at another
time I announce that a nation or kingdom is to be built up and planted, 10 and
if it does evil in my sight and does not
obey me, then I will reconsider the good
I had intended to do for it.

11 "Now therefore say to the people of
Judah and those living in Jerusalem,
'This is what the LORD says: Look! I am
preparing a disaster for you and devising
a plan against you. So turn from your evil
ways, each one of you, and reform your
ways and your actions.' 12 But they will reply, 'It's no use. We will continue with our
own plans; each of us will follow the
stubbornness of his evil heart.'"

13 Therefore this is what the LORD
says:

"Inquire among the nations:
     Who has ever heard anything like
          this?
   A most horrible thing has been done
     by Virgin Israel.
14 Does the snow of Lebanon
     ever vanish from its rocky slopes?
   Do its cool waters from distant
          sources
     ever cease to flow? c

15 Yet my people have forgotten me;
　　they burn incense to worthless
　　　idols,
　which made them stumble in their
　　　ways
　and in the ancient paths.
　They made them walk in bypaths
　　and on roads not built up.
16 Their land will be laid waste,
　　an object of lasting scorn;
　all who pass by will be appalled
　　and will shake their heads.
17 Like a wind from the east,
　　I will scatter them before their
　　　enemies;
　I will show them my back and not my
　　　face
　　in the day of their disaster."

18 They said, "Come, let's make plans
against Jeremiah; for the teaching of the
law by the priest will not be lost, nor will
counsel from the wise, nor the word
from the prophets. So come, let's attack
him with our tongues and pay no attention to anything he says."

19 Listen to me, O LORD;
　　hear what my accusers are saying!
20 Should good be repaid with evil?
　　Yet they have dug a pit for me.
　Remember that I stood before you
　　and spoke in their behalf
　to turn your wrath away from
　　　them.
21 So give their children over to
　　　famine;
　hand them over to the power of
　　　the sword.
　Let their wives be made childless and
　　　widows;
　let their men be put to death,
　their young men slain by the
　　　sword in battle.
22 Let a cry be heard from their houses
　　when you suddenly bring invaders
　　　against them,
　for they have dug a pit to capture me
　and have hidden snares for my
　　　feet.
23 But you know, O LORD,
　　all their plots to kill me.

Do not forgive their crimes
　or blot out their sins from your
　　　sight.
Let them be overthrown before you;
　deal with them in the time of your
　　　anger.

a2 That is, symbols of the goddess Asherah   *b2,3* Or *hills /*
3 and the mountains of the land. / Your   *c14* The meaning of
the Hebrew for this sentence is uncertain.

1 THESSALONIANS 4:1–5:3

Finally, brothers, we instructed you how
to live in order to please God, as in fact
you are living. Now we ask you and urge
you in the Lord Jesus to do this more and
more. 2 For you know what instructions
we gave you by the authority of the Lord
Jesus.

3 It is God's will that you should be
sanctified: that you should avoid sexual
immorality; 4 that each of you should
learn to control his own body*a* in a way
that is holy and honorable, 5 not in pas-
sionate lust like the heathen, who do not
know God; 6 and that in this matter no
one should wrong his brother or take
advantage of him. The Lord will punish
men for all such sins, as we have already
told you and warned you. 7 For God did
not call us to be impure, but to live a holy
life. 8 Therefore, he who rejects this instruction does not reject man but God,
who gives you his Holy Spirit.

9 Now about brotherly love we do not
need to write to you, for you yourselves
have been taught by God to love each
other. 10 And in fact, you do love all the
brothers throughout Macedonia. Yet we
urge you, brothers, to do so more and
more.

11 Make it your ambition to lead a
quiet life, to mind your own business
and to work with your hands, just as we
told you, 12 so that your daily life may
win the respect of outsiders and so that
you will not be dependent on anybody.

13 **Brothers, we do not want you to
be ignorant about those who fall
asleep, or to grieve like the rest of
men, who have no hope. 14 We believe
that Jesus died and rose again and so
we believe that God will bring with**

Jesus those who have fallen asleep in him. ¹⁵According to the Lord's own word, we tell you that we who are still alive, who are left till the coming of the Lord, will certainly not precede those who have fallen asleep. ¹⁶For the Lord himself will come down from heaven, with a loud command, with the voice of the archangel and with the trumpet call of God, and the dead in Christ will rise first. ¹⁷After that, we who are still alive and are left will be caught up together with them in the clouds to meet the Lord in the air. And so we will be with the Lord forever. ¹⁸Therefore encourage each other with these words.

⁵:¹Now, brothers, about times and dates we do not need to write to you, ²for you know very well that the day of the Lord will come like a thief in the night. ³While people are saying, "Peace and safety," destruction will come on them suddenly, as labor pains on a pregnant woman, and they will not escape.

a4 Or learn to live with his own wife; or learn to acquire a wife

PSALM 81:1-16
For the director of music. According to *gittith.ᵃ* Of Asaph.

¹ **S**ing for joy to God our strength;
    shout aloud to the God of Jacob!
² Begin the music, strike the
        tambourine,
    play the melodious harp and lyre.

³ Sound the ram's horn at the New
        Moon,
    and when the moon is full, on the
        day of our Feast;
⁴ this is a decree for Israel,
    an ordinance of the God of Jacob.
⁵ He established it as a statute for
        Joseph
    when he went out against Egypt,
    where we heard a language we did
        not understand.ᵇ

⁶ He says, "I removed the burden from
        their shoulders;
    their hands were set free from the
        basket.

⁷ In your distress you called and I
        rescued you,
    I answered you out of a
        thundercloud;
    I tested you at the waters of
        Meribah.   *Selah*

⁸ "Hear, O my people, and I will warn
        you—
    if you would but listen to me,
        O Israel!
⁹ You shall have no foreign god among
        you;
    you shall not bow down to an alien
        god.
¹⁰ I am the Lᴏʀᴅ your God,
    who brought you up out of Egypt.
    Open wide your mouth and I will
        fill it.

¹¹ "But my people would not listen to
        me;
    Israel would not submit to me.
¹² So I gave them over to their stubborn
        hearts
    to follow their own devices.

¹³ "If my people would but listen to me,
    if Israel would follow my ways,
¹⁴ how quickly would I subdue their
        enemies
    and turn my hand against their
        foes!
¹⁵ Those who hate the Lᴏʀᴅ would
        cringe before him,
    and their punishment would last
        forever.
¹⁶ But you would be fed with the finest
        of wheat;
    with honey from the rock I would
        satisfy you."

aTitle: Probably a musical term   b5 Or / and we heard a voice we had not known

PROVERBS 25:6-7A
⁶ **D**o not exalt yourself in the king's
        presence,
    and do not claim a place among
        great men;
⁷ it is better for him to say to you,
        "Come up here,"
    than for him to humiliate you
        before a nobleman.

GOD SIGHTINGS

October 12

JEREMIAH 19:1–21:14

This is what the LORD says: "Go and buy a clay jar from a potter. Take along some of the elders of the people and of the priests 2 and go out to the Valley of Ben Hinnom, near the entrance of the Potsherd Gate. There proclaim the words I tell you, 3 and say, 'Hear the word of the LORD, O kings of Judah and people of Jerusalem. This is what the LORD Almighty, the God of Israel, says: Listen! I am going to bring a disaster on this place that will make the ears of everyone who hears of it tingle. 4 For they have forsaken me and made this a place of foreign gods; they have burned sacrifices in it to gods that neither they nor their fathers nor the kings of Judah ever knew, and they have filled this place with the blood of the innocent. 5 They have built the high places of Baal to burn their sons in the fire as offerings to Baal—something I did not command or mention, nor did it enter my mind. 6 So beware, the days are coming, declares the LORD, when people will no longer call this place Topheth or the Valley of Ben Hinnom, but the Valley of Slaughter.

7 "'In this place I will ruina the plans of Judah and Jerusalem. I will make them fall by the sword before their enemies, at the hands of those who seek their lives, and I will give their carcasses as food to the birds of the air and the beasts of the earth. 8 I will devastate this city and make it an object of scorn; all who pass by will be appalled and will scoff because of all its wounds. 9 I will make them eat the flesh of their sons and daughters, and they will eat one another's flesh during the stress of the siege imposed on them by the enemies who seek their lives.'

10 "Then break the jar while those who go with you are watching, 11 and say

to them, 'This is what the LORD Almighty says: I will smash this nation and this city just as this potter's jar is smashed and cannot be repaired. They will bury the dead in Topheth until there is no more room. 12 This is what I will do to this place and to those who live here, declares the LORD. I will make this city like Topheth. 13 The houses in Jerusalem and those of the kings of Judah will be defiled like this place, Topheth—all the houses where they burned incense on the roofs to all the starry hosts and poured out drink offerings to other gods.'"

14 Jeremiah then returned from Topheth, where the LORD had sent him to prophesy, and stood in the court of the LORD's temple and said to all the people, 15 "This is what the LORD Almighty, the God of Israel, says: 'Listen! I am going to bring on this city and the villages around it every disaster I pronounced against them, because they were stiffnecked and would not listen to my words.'"

20:1 WHEN the priest Pashhur son of Immer, the chief officer in the temple of the LORD, heard Jeremiah prophesying these things, 2 he had Jeremiah the prophet beaten and put in the stocks at the Upper Gate of Benjamin at the LORD's temple. 3 The next day, when Pashhur released him from the stocks, Jeremiah said to him, "The LORD's name for you is not Pashhur, but Magor-Missabib.b 4 For this is what the LORD says: 'I will make you a terror to yourself and to all your friends; with your own eyes you will see them fall by the sword of their enemies. I will hand all Judah over to the king of Babylon, who will carry them away to Babylon or put them to the sword. 5 I will hand over to their enemies all the wealth of this city—all its products, all its valuables and all the treasures of the kings of Judah. They will take it away as plunder and carry it off to Babylon. 6 And you, Pashhur, and all who live in your house will go into exile to Babylon. There you will die and be buried, you and all your friends to whom you have prophesied lies.'"

7 O Lord, you deceived[c] me, and I was deceived[c];
   you overpowered me and prevailed.
I am ridiculed all day long;
   everyone mocks me.
8 Whenever I speak, I cry out
   proclaiming violence and destruction.
So the word of the Lord has brought me
   insult and reproach all day long.
9 But if I say, "I will not mention him
   or speak any more in his name,"
his word is in my heart like a fire,
   a fire shut up in my bones.
I am weary of holding it in;
   indeed, I cannot.
10 I hear many whispering,
   "Terror on every side!
   Report him! Let's report him!"
All my friends
   are waiting for me to slip, saying,
"Perhaps he will be deceived;
   then we will prevail over him
   and take our revenge on him."

11 But the Lord is with me like a mighty warrior;
   so my persecutors will stumble and not prevail.
They will fail and be thoroughly disgraced;
   their dishonor will never be forgotten.
12 O Lord Almighty, you who examine the righteous
   and probe the heart and mind,
let me see your vengeance upon them,
   for to you I have committed my cause.

13 Sing to the Lord!
   Give praise to the Lord!
He rescues the life of the needy
   from the hands of the wicked.

14 Cursed be the day I was born!
   May the day my mother bore me not be blessed!
15 Cursed be the man who brought my father the news,
   who made him very glad, saying,
   "A child is born to you—a son!"
16 May that man be like the towns
   the Lord overthrew without pity.
May he hear wailing in the morning,
   a battle cry at noon.
17 For he did not kill me in the womb,
   with my mother as my grave,
   her womb enlarged forever.
18 Why did I ever come out of the womb
   to see trouble and sorrow
   and to end my days in shame?

21:1 The word came to Jeremiah from the Lord when King Zedekiah sent to him Pashhur son of Malkijah and the priest Zephaniah son of Maaseiah. They said: 2 "Inquire now of the Lord for us because Nebuchadnezzar[d] king of Babylon is attacking us. Perhaps the Lord will perform wonders for us as in times past so that he will withdraw from us."

3 But Jeremiah answered them, "Tell Zedekiah, 4 'This is what the Lord, the God of Israel, says: I am about to turn against you the weapons of war that are in your hands, which you are using to fight the king of Babylon and the Babylonians[e] who are outside the wall besieging you. And I will gather them inside this city. 5 I myself will fight against you with an outstretched hand and a mighty arm in anger and fury and great wrath. 6 I will strike down those who live in this city—both men and animals—and they will die of a terrible plague. 7 After that, declares the Lord, I will hand over Zedekiah king of Judah, his officials and the people in this city who survive the plague, sword and famine, to Nebuchadnezzar king of Babylon and to their enemies who seek their lives. He will put them to the sword; he will show them no mercy or pity or compassion.'

8 "Furthermore, tell the people, 'This is what the Lord says: See, I am setting before you the way of life and the way of death. 9 Whoever stays in this city will die by the sword, famine or plague. But

whoever goes out and surrenders to the Babylonians who are besieging you will live; he will escape with his life. [10]I have determined to do this city harm and not good, declares the LORD. It will be given into the hands of the king of Babylon, and he will destroy it with fire.'

[11]"Moreover, say to the royal house of Judah, 'Hear the word of the LORD; [12]O house of David, this is what the LORD says:

"'Administer justice every morning;
    rescue from the hand of his
        oppressor
the one who has been robbed,
or my wrath will break out and burn
        like fire
    because of the evil you have
        done—
    burn with no one to quench it.
[13]I am against you, Jerusalem[b]
    you who live above this valley
    on the rocky plateau,
                    declares the LORD—
you who say, "Who can come against
        us?
    Who can enter our refuge?"
[14]I will punish you as your deeds
        deserve,
                    declares the LORD.
I will kindle a fire in your forests
    that will consume everything
        around you.'"

a7 The Hebrew for ruin sounds like the Hebrew for jar (see verses 1 and 10).   b3 Magor-Missabib means terror on every side.   c7 Or persuaded   d2 Hebrew Nebuchadrezzar, of which Nebuchadnezzar is a variant; here and often in Jeremiah and Ezekiel   e4 Or Chaldeans; also in verse 9

1 THESSALONIANS 5:4-28

But you, brothers, are not in darkness so that this day should surprise you like a thief. [5]You are all sons of the light and sons of the day. We do not belong to the night or to the darkness. [6]So then, let us not be like others, who are asleep, but let us be alert and self-controlled. [7]For those who sleep, sleep at night, and those who get drunk, get drunk at night. [8]But since we belong to the day, let us be self-controlled, putting on faith and love as a breastplate, and the hope of salvation as

a helmet. [9]**For God did not appoint us to suffer wrath but to receive salvation through our Lord Jesus Christ.** [10]**He died for us so that, whether we are awake or asleep, we may live together with him.** [11]Therefore encourage one another and build each other up, just as in fact you are doing.

[12]Now we ask you, brothers, to respect those who work hard among you, who are over you in the Lord and who admonish you. [13]Hold them in the highest regard in love because of their work. Live in peace with each other. [14]And we urge you, brothers, warn those who are idle, encourage the timid, help the weak, be patient with everyone. [15]Make sure that nobody pays back wrong for wrong, but always try to be kind to each other and to everyone else.

[16]Be joyful always; [17]pray continually; [18]give thanks in all circumstances, for this is God's will for you in Christ Jesus.

[19]Do not put out the Spirit's fire; [20]do not treat prophecies with contempt. [21]Test everything. Hold on to the good. [22]Avoid every kind of evil.

[23]May God himself, the God of peace, sanctify you through and through. May your whole spirit, soul and body be kept blameless at the coming of our Lord Jesus Christ. [24]The one who calls you is faithful and he will do it.

[25]Brothers, pray for us. [26]Greet all the brothers with a holy kiss. [27]I charge you before the Lord to have this letter read to all the brothers.

[28]The grace of our Lord Jesus Christ be with you.

PSALM 82:1-8
A psalm of Asaph.

[1]God presides in the great assembly;
    he gives judgment among the
        "gods":

[2]"How long will you[a] defend the
        unjust
    and show partiality to the wicked?
                            Selah

3 Defend the cause of the weak and
    fatherless;
  maintain the rights of the poor
    and oppressed.
4 Rescue the weak and needy;
  deliver them from the hand of the
    wicked.

5 "They know nothing, they
    understand nothing.
  They walk about in darkness;
  all the foundations of the earth are
    shaken.

6 "I said, 'You are "gods";
  you are all sons of the Most High.'
7 But you will die like mere men;
  you will fall like every other ruler."

8 Rise up, O God, judge the earth,
  for all the nations are your
    inheritance.

a2 The Hebrew is plural.

PROVERBS 25:7B-10

7 **W**hat you have seen with your eyes
8   do not bring*a* hastily to court,
  for what will you do in the end
    if your neighbor puts you to
      shame?

9 If you argue your case with a
    neighbor,
  do not betray another man's
    confidence,
10 or he who hears it may shame you
  and you will never lose your bad
    reputation.

a 7,8 Or nobleman / on whom you had set your eyes. / 8Do
not go

□ DAY 286

GOD SIGHTINGS

October 13

JEREMIAH 22:1–23:20

This is what the LORD says: "Go down to
the palace of the king of Judah and proclaim this message there: 2'Hear the

word of the LORD, O king of Judah, you
who sit on David's throne—you, your officials and your people who come
through these gates. 3 This is what the
LORD says: Do what is just and right. Rescue from the hand of his oppressor the
one who has been robbed. Do no wrong
or violence to the alien, the fatherless or
the widow, and do not shed innocent
blood in this place. 4For if you are careful to carry out these commands, then
kings who sit on David's throne will
come through the gates of this palace,
riding in chariots and on horses, accompanied by their officials and their people. 5But if you do not obey these
commands, declares the LORD, I swear
by myself that this palace will become a
ruin.'".

6 For this is what the LORD says about
the palace of the king of Judah:

"Though you are like Gilead to me,
  like the summit of Lebanon,
I will surely make you like a desert,
  like towns not inhabited.
7 I will send destroyers against you,
  each man with his weapons,
  and they will cut up your fine cedar
    beams
  and throw them into the fire.

8 "People from many nations will pass
by this city and will ask one another,
'Why has the LORD done such a thing to
this great city?' 9And the answer will be:
'Because they have forsaken the covenant of the LORD their God and have
worshiped and served other gods.'"

10 Do not weep for the dead ⌊king⌋ or
    mourn his loss;
  rather, weep bitterly for him who
    is exiled,
  because he will never return
    nor see his native land again.

11 For this is what the LORD says about
Shallum*a* son of Josiah, who succeeded
his father as king of Judah but has gone
from this place: "He will never return.
12 He will die in the place where they
have led him captive; he will not see this
land again."

¹³"Woe to him who builds his palace
  by unrighteousness,
  his upper rooms by injustice,
making his countrymen work for
    nothing,
  not paying them for their labor.
¹⁴He says, 'I will build myself a great
    palace
  with spacious upper rooms.'
So he makes large windows in it,
  panels it with cedar
  and decorates it in red.

¹⁵"Does it make you a king
  to have more and more cedar?
Did not your father have food and
    drink?
  He did what was right and just,
  so all went well with him.
¹⁶He defended the cause of the poor
    and needy,
  and so all went well.
Is that not what it means to know
    me?"
  declares the LORD.
¹⁷"But your eyes and your heart
  are set only on dishonest gain,
  on shedding innocent blood
  and on oppression and extortion."

¹⁸Therefore this is what the LORD says
about Jehoiakim son of Josiah king of
Judah:

"They will not mourn for him:
  'Alas, my brother! Alas, my sister!'
They will not mourn for him:
  'Alas, my master! Alas, his
    splendor!'
¹⁹He will have the burial of a donkey—
  dragged away and thrown
  outside the gates of Jerusalem."

²⁰"Go up to Lebanon and cry out,
  let your voice be heard in Bashan,
cry out from Abarim,
  for all your allies are crushed.
²¹I warned you when you felt secure,
  but you said, 'I will not listen!'
This has been your way from your
    youth;
  you have not obeyed me.

²²The wind will drive all your
    shepherds away,
  and your allies will go into exile.
Then you will be ashamed and
    disgraced
  because of all your wickedness.
²³You who live in 'Lebanon,'ᵇ
  who are nestled in cedar
    buildings,
how you will groan when pangs
    come upon you,
  pain like that of a woman in labor!

²⁴"As surely as I live," declares the
LORD, "even if you, Jehoiachinᶜ son of Jehoiakim king of Judah, were a signet
ring on my right hand, I would still pull
you off. ²⁵I will hand you over to those
who seek your life, those you fear—to
Nebuchadnezzar king of Babylon and
to the Babylonians.ᵈ ²⁶I will hurl you
and the mother who gave you birth into
another country, where neither of you
was born, and there you both will die.
²⁷You will never come back to the land
you long to return to."

²⁸Is this man Jehoiachin a despised,
    broken pot,
  an object no one wants?
Why will he and his children be
    hurled out,
  cast into a land they do not know?
²⁹O land, land, land,
  hear the word of the LORD!
³⁰This is what the LORD says:
"Record this man as if childless,
  a man who will not prosper in his
    lifetime,
for none of his offspring will prosper,
  none will sit on the throne of David
  or rule anymore in Judah."

²³:¹"WOE to the shepherds who are destroying and scattering the sheep of my
pasture!" declares the LORD. ²Therefore
this is what the LORD, the God of Israel,
says to the shepherds who tend my people: "Because you have scattered my
flock and driven them away and have
not bestowed care on them, I will bestow punishment on you for the evil
you have done," declares the LORD. ³"I

myself will gather the remnant of my flock out of all the countries where I have driven them and will bring them back to their pasture, where they will be fruitful and increase in number. ⁴I will place shepherds over them who will tend them, and they will no longer be afraid or terrified, nor will any be missing," declares the LORD.

⁵"The days are coming," declares the
    LORD,
        "when I will raise up to David* a
            righteous Branch,
    a King who will reign wisely
        and do what is just and right in the
            land.
⁶In his days Judah will be saved
    and Israel will live in safety.
This is the name by which he will be
    called:
        The LORD Our Righteousness.

⁷"So then, the days are coming," declares the LORD, "when people will no longer say, 'As surely as the LORD lives, who brought the Israelites up out of Egypt,' ⁸but they will say, 'As surely as the LORD lives, who brought the descendants of Israel up out of the land of the north and out of all the countries where he had banished them.' Then they will live in their own land."

⁹Concerning the prophets:

My heart is broken within me;
    all my bones tremble.
I am like a drunken man,
    like a man overcome by wine,
because of the LORD
    and his holy words.
¹⁰The land is full of adulterers;
    because of the curse' the land lies
        parched⁹
    and the pastures in the desert are
        withered.
The ⌐prophets⌐ follow an evil course
    and use their power unjustly.

¹¹"Both prophet and priest are godless;
    even in my temple I find their
        wickedness,"
            declares the LORD.

¹²"Therefore their path will become
    slippery;
    they will be banished to darkness
    and there they will fall.
I will bring disaster on them
    in the year they are punished,"
            declares the LORD.

¹³"Among the prophets of Samaria
    I saw this repulsive thing:
They prophesied by Baal
    and led my people Israel astray.
¹⁴And among the prophets of
    Jerusalem
    I have seen something horrible:
    They commit adultery and live a lie.
They strengthen the hands of
    evildoers,
    so that no one turns from his
        wickedness.
They are all like Sodom to me;
    the people of Jerusalem are like
        Gomorrah."

¹⁵Therefore, this is what the LORD Almighty says concerning the prophets:

"I will make them eat bitter food
    and drink poisoned water,
because from the prophets of
    Jerusalem
    ungodliness has spread
        throughout the land."

¹⁶This is what the LORD Almighty says:

"Do not listen to what the prophets
    are prophesying to you;
    they fill you with false hopes.
They speak visions from their own
    minds,
    not from the mouth of the LORD.
¹⁷They keep saying to those who
    despise me,
    'The LORD says: You will have
        peace.'
And to all who follow the
    stubbornness of their hearts
    they say, 'No harm will come to you.'
¹⁸But which of them has stood in the
    council of the LORD
    to see or to hear his word?
    Who has listened and heard his
        word?

[19] See, the storm of the Lord
  will burst out in wrath,
a whirlwind swirling down
  on the heads of the wicked.
[20] The anger of the Lord will not turn
      back
  until he fully accomplishes
  the purposes of his heart.
In days to come
  you will understand it clearly."

[a]11 Also called *Jehoahaz* [b]23 That is, the palace in
Jerusalem (see 1 Kings 7:2) [c]24 Hebrew *Coniah,* a variant
of *Jehoiachin;* also in verse 28 [d]25 Or *Chaldeans* [e]5 Or *up
from David's line* [f]10 Or *because of these things* [g]10 Or
land mourns

2 THESSALONIANS 1:1-12

Paul, Silas[a] and Timothy,

To the church of the Thessalonians in
God our Father and the Lord Jesus
Christ:

[2] Grace and peace to you from God the
Father and the Lord Jesus Christ.

[3] We ought always to thank God for you,
brothers, and rightly so, because your
faith is growing more and more, and the
love every one of you has for each other is
increasing. [4] Therefore, among God's
churches we boast about your perseverance and faith in all the persecutions and
trials you are enduring.

[5] All this is evidence that God's judgment is right, and as a result you will be
counted worthy of the kingdom of God,
for which you are suffering. [6] God is just:
He will pay back trouble to those who
trouble you [7] and give relief to you who
are troubled, and to us as well. This will
happen when the Lord Jesus is revealed
from heaven in blazing fire with his
powerful angels. [8] He will punish those
who do not know God and do not obey
the gospel of our Lord Jesus. [9] They will
be punished with everlasting destruction and shut out from the presence of
the Lord and from the majesty of his
power [10] on the day he comes to be glorified in his holy people and to be marveled at among all those who have
believed. This includes you, because
you believed our testimony to you.

[11] **With this in mind, we constantly
pray for you, that our God may count
you worthy of his calling, and that by
his power he may fulfill every good
purpose of yours and every act
prompted by your faith.** [12] We pray
this so that the name of our Lord Jesus
may be glorified in you, and you in him,
according to the grace of our God and
the Lord Jesus Christ.[b]

[a]1 Greek *Silvanus,* a variant of *Silas* [b]12 Or *God and Lord,
Jesus Christ*

PSALM 83:1-18

A song. A psalm of Asaph.

[1] **◯** God, do not keep silent;
  be not quiet, O God, be not still.
[2] See how your enemies are astir,
  how your foes rear their heads.
[3] With cunning they conspire against
      your people;
  they plot against those you
      cherish.
[4] "Come," they say, "let us destroy them
      as a nation,
  that the name of Israel be
      remembered no more."

[5] With one mind they plot together;
  they form an alliance against you—
[6] the tents of Edom and the
      Ishmaelites,
  of Moab and the Hagrites,
[7] Gebal,[a] Ammon and Amalek,
  Philistia, with the people of Tyre.
[8] Even Assyria has joined them
  to lend strength to the
      descendants of Lot.   *Selah*

[9] Do to them as you did to Midian,
  as you did to Sisera and Jabin at
      the river Kishon,
[10] who perished at Endor
  and became like refuse on the
      ground.
[11] Make their nobles like Oreb and
      Zeeb,
  all their princes like Zebah and
      Zalmunna,
[12] who said, "Let us take possession
  of the pasturelands of God."

13 Make them like tumbleweed, O my
    God,
    like chaff before the wind.
14 As fire consumes the forest
    or a flame sets the mountains ablaze,
15 so pursue them with your tempest
    and terrify them with your storm.
16 Cover their faces with shame
    so that men will seek your name,
    O Lord.

17 May they ever be ashamed and ·
    dismayed;
    may they perish in disgrace.
18 Let them know that you, whose name
    is the Lord—
    that you alone are the Most High
    over all the earth.

a7 That is, Byblos

PROVERBS 25:11-14

11 **A** word aptly spoken
    is like apples of gold in settings of
    silver.

12 Like an earring of gold or an
            ornament of fine gold
    is a wise man's rebuke to a
            listening ear.

13 Like the coolness of snow at harvest
            time
    is a trustworthy messenger to
            those who send him;
    he refreshes the spirit of his masters.

14 Like clouds and wind without rain
    is a man who boasts of gifts he
            does not give.

□ DAY 287

GOD SIGHTINGS

October 14

JEREMIAH 23:21–25:38

21 ❚ [the Lord] did not send these
    prophets,
    yet they have run with their
    message;

I did not speak to them,
    yet they have prophesied.
22 But if they had stood in my council,
    they would have proclaimed my
        words to my people
and would have turned them from
        their evil ways
and from their evil deeds.

23 "Am I only a God nearby,"
                    declares the Lord,
    "and not a God far away?
24 Can anyone hide in secret places
    so that I cannot see him?"
                    declares the Lord.
    "Do not I fill heaven and earth?"
                    declares the Lord.

25 "I have heard what the prophets say
who prophesy lies in my name. They say,
'I had a dream! I had a dream!' 26 How
long will this continue in the hearts of
these lying prophets, who prophesy the
delusions of their own minds? 27 They
think the dreams they tell one another
will make my people forget my name,
just as their fathers forgot my name
through Baal worship. 28 Let the prophet
who has a dream tell his dream, but let
the one who has my word speak it faithfully. For what has straw to do with
grain?" declares the Lord. 29 "Is not my
word like fire," declares the Lord, "and
like a hammer that breaks a rock in
pieces?

30 "Therefore," declares the Lord, "I
am against the prophets who steal from
one another words supposedly from
me. 31 Yes," declares the Lord, "I am
against the prophets who wag their own
tongues and yet declare, 'The Lord declares.' 32 Indeed, I am against those who
prophesy false dreams," declares the
Lord. "They tell them and lead my people astray with their reckless lies, yet I
did not send or appoint them. They do
not benefit these people in the least,"
declares the Lord.

33 "When these people, or a prophet or
a priest, ask you, 'What is the oracle a of
the Lord?' say to them, 'What oracle? b I
will forsake you, declares the Lord.' 34 If

a prophet or a priest or anyone else claims, 'This is the oracle of the LORD,' I will punish that man and his household. ³⁵This is what each of you keeps on saying to his friend or relative: 'What is the LORD's answer?' or 'What has the LORD spoken?' ³⁶But you must not mention 'the oracle of the LORD' again, because every man's own word becomes his oracle and so you distort the words of the living God, the LORD Almighty, our God. ³⁷This is what you keep saying to a prophet: 'What is the LORD's answer to you?' or 'What has the LORD spoken?' ³⁸Although you claim, 'This is the oracle of the LORD,' this is what the LORD says: You used the words, 'This is the oracle of the LORD,' even though I told you that you must not claim, 'This is the oracle of the LORD.' ³⁹Therefore, I will surely forget you and cast you out of my presence along with the city I gave to you and your fathers. ⁴⁰I will bring upon you everlasting disgrace—everlasting shame that will not be forgotten."

²⁴:¹AFTER Jehoiachinᶜ son of Jehoiakim king of Judah and the officials, the craftsmen and the artisans of Judah were carried into exile from Jerusalem to Babylon by Nebuchadnezzar king of Babylon, the LORD showed me two baskets of figs placed in front of the temple of the LORD. ²One basket had very good figs, like those that ripen early; the other basket had very poor figs, so bad they could not be eaten.

³Then the LORD asked me, "What do you see, Jeremiah?"

"Figs," I answered. "The good ones are very good, but the poor ones are so bad they cannot be eaten."

⁴Then the word of the LORD came to me: ⁵"This is what the LORD, the God of Israel, says: 'Like these good figs, I regard as good the exiles from Judah, whom I sent away from this place to the land of the Babylonians.ᵈ ⁶My eyes will watch over them for their good, and I will bring them back to this land. I will build them up and not tear them down; I will plant them and not uproot them. ⁷I will give

them a heart to know me, that I am the LORD. They will be my people, and I will be their God, for they will return to me with all their heart.

⁸"'But like the poor figs, which are so bad they cannot be eaten,' says the LORD, 'so will I deal with Zedekiah king of Judah, his officials and the survivors from Jerusalem, whether they remain in this land or live in Egypt. ⁹I will make them abhorrent and an offense to all the kingdoms of the earth, a reproach and a byword, an object of ridicule and cursing, wherever I banish them. ¹⁰I will send the sword, famine and plague against them until they are destroyed from the land I gave to them and their fathers.'"

²⁵:¹THE word came to Jeremiah concerning all the people of Judah in the fourth year of Jehoiakim son of Josiah king of Judah, which was the first year of Nebuchadnezzar king of Babylon. ²So Jeremiah the prophet said to all the people of Judah and to all those living in Jerusalem: ³For twenty-three years—from the thirteenth year of Josiah son of Amon king of Judah until this very day— the word of the LORD has come to me and I have spoken to you again and again, but you have not listened.

⁴And though the LORD has sent all his servants the prophets to you again and again, you have not listened or paid any attention. ⁵They said, "Turn now, each of you, from your evil ways and your evil practices, and you can stay in the land the LORD gave to you and your fathers for ever and ever. ⁶Do not follow other gods to serve and worship them; do not provoke me to anger with what your hands have made. Then I will not harm you."

⁷"But you did not listen to me," declares the LORD, "and you have provoked me with what your hands have made, and you have brought harm to yourselves."

⁸Therefore the LORD Almighty says this: "Because you have not listened to my words, ⁹I will summon all the peoples of the north and my servant Nebuchadnezzar king of Babylon," declares the LORD,

"and I will bring them against this land and its inhabitants and against all the surrounding nations. I will completely destroy[e] them and make them an object of horror and scorn, and an everlasting ruin. [10]I will banish from them the sounds of joy and gladness, the voices of bride and bridegroom, the sound of millstones and the light of the lamp. [11]This whole country will become a desolate wasteland, and these nations will serve the king of Babylon seventy years.

[12]"But when the seventy years are fulfilled, I will punish the king of Babylon and his nation, the land of the Babylonians,[d] for their guilt," declares the LORD, "and will make it desolate forever. [13]I will bring upon that land all the things I have spoken against it, all that are written in this book and prophesied by Jeremiah against all the nations. [14]They themselves will be enslaved by many nations and great kings; I will repay them according to their deeds and the work of their hands."

[15]This is what the LORD, the God of Israel, said to me: "Take from my hand this cup filled with the wine of my wrath and make all the nations to whom I send you drink it. [16]When they drink it, they will stagger and go mad because of the sword I will send among them."

[17]So I took the cup from the LORD's hand and made all the nations to whom he sent me drink it: [18]Jerusalem and the towns of Judah, its kings and officials, to make them a ruin and an object of horror and scorn and cursing, as they are today; [19]Pharaoh king of Egypt, his attendants, his officials and all his people, [20]and all the foreign people there; all the kings of Uz; all the kings of the Philistines (those of Ashkelon, Gaza, Ekron, and the people left at Ashdod); [21]Edom, Moab and Ammon; [22]all the kings of Tyre and Sidon; the kings of the coastlands across the sea; [23]Dedan, Tema, Buz and all who are in distant places[f]; [24]all the kings of Arabia and all the kings of the foreign people who live in the desert; [25]all the kings of Zimri, Elam and Media; [26]and all the kings of the

north, near and far, one after the other—all the kingdoms on the face of the earth. And after all of them, the king of Sheshach[g] will drink it too.

[27]"Then tell them, 'This is what the LORD Almighty, the God of Israel, says: Drink, get drunk and vomit, and fall to rise no more because of the sword I will send among you.' [28]But if they refuse to take the cup from your hand and drink, tell them, 'This is what the LORD Almighty says: You must drink it! [29]See, I am beginning to bring disaster on the city that bears my Name, and will you indeed go unpunished? You will not go unpunished, for I am calling down a sword upon all who live on the earth, declares the LORD Almighty.'

[30]"Now prophesy all these words against them and say to them:

"'The LORD will roar from on high;
    he will thunder from his holy
        dwelling
    and roar mightily against his land.
He will shout like those who tread
        the grapes,
    shout against all who live on the
        earth.
[31]The tumult will resound to the ends
        of the earth,
    for the LORD will bring charges
        against the nations;
he will bring judgment on all
        mankind
    and put the wicked to the sword,'"
                            declares the LORD.

[32]This is what the LORD Almighty says:

"Look! Disaster is spreading
    from nation to nation;
a mighty storm is rising
    from the ends of the earth."

[33]At that time those slain by the LORD will be everywhere—from one end of the earth to the other. They will not be mourned or gathered up or buried, but will be like refuse lying on the ground.

[34]Weep and wail, you shepherds;
    roll in the dust, you leaders of the
        flock.

For your time to be slaughtered has
come;
  you will fall and be shattered like
  fine pottery.
³⁵The shepherds will have nowhere to
flee,
  the leaders of the flock no place to
  escape.
³⁶Hear the cry of the shepherds,
  the wailing of the leaders of the
  flock,
  for the Lord is destroying their
  pasture.
³⁷The peaceful meadows will be laid
waste
  because of the fierce anger of the
  Lord.
³⁸Like a lion he will leave his lair,
  and their land will become
  desolate
because of the sword[h] of the
  oppressor
  and because of the Lord's fierce
  anger.

*a33 Or burden (see Septuagint and Vulgate)   b33 Hebrew;
Septuagint and Vulgate 'You are the burden. (The Hebrew for
oracle and burden is the same.)   c1 Hebrew Jeconiah, a
variant of Jehoiachin   d5,12 Or Chaldeans   e9 The Hebrew
term refers to the irrevocable giving over of things or
persons to the Lord, often by totally destroying them.
f23 Or who clip the hair by their foreheads   g26 Sheshach is
a cryptogram for Babylon.   h38 Some Hebrew manuscripts
and Septuagint (see also Jer. 46:16 and 50:16); most Hebrew
manuscripts anger*

2 THESSALONIANS 2:1-17

Concerning the coming of our Lord
Jesus Christ and our being gathered to
him, we ask you, brothers, ²not to become easily unsettled or alarmed by
some prophecy, report or letter supposed to have come from us, saying that
the day of the Lord has already come.
³Don't let anyone deceive you in any
way, for ⌊that day will not come⌋ until
the rebellion occurs and the man of lawlessness[a] is revealed, the man doomed
to destruction. ⁴He will oppose and will
exalt himself over everything that is
called God or is worshiped, so that he
sets himself up in God's temple, proclaiming himself to be God.
  ⁵Don't you remember that when I was
with you I used to tell you these things?
⁶And now you know what is holding him

back, so that he may be revealed at the
proper time. ⁷For the secret power of
lawlessness is already at work; but the
one who now holds it back will continue
to do so till he is taken out of the way.
⁸And then the lawless one will be re-
vealed, whom the Lord Jesus will overthrow with the breath of his mouth and
destroy by the splendor of his coming.
⁹The coming of the lawless one will be in
accordance with the work of Satan displayed in all kinds of counterfeit miracles, signs and wonders, ¹⁰and in every
sort of evil that deceives those who are
perishing. They perish because they refused to love the truth and so be saved.
¹¹For this reason God sends them a pow-
erful delusion so that they will believe
the lie ¹²and so that all will be condemned who have not believed the truth
but have delighted in wickedness.
  ¹³But we ought always to thank God
for you, brothers loved by the Lord, because from the beginning God chose
you[b] to be saved through the sanctifying work of the Spirit and through belief
in the truth. ¹⁴He called you to this
through our gospel, that you might
share in the glory of our Lord Jesus
Christ. ¹⁵So then, brothers, stand firm
and hold to the teachings[c] we passed on
to you, whether by word of mouth or by
letter.
  **¹⁶May our Lord Jesus Christ him-
self and God our Father, who loved us
and by his grace gave us eternal encouragement and good hope, ¹⁷en-
courage your hearts and strengthen
you in every good deed and word.**

*a3 Some manuscripts sin   b13 Some manuscripts because
God chose you as his firstfruits   c15 Or traditions*

PSALM 84:1-12

For the director of music. According to
gittith.[a] Of the Sons of Korah. A psalm.

  ¹**H**ow lovely is your dwelling place,
    O Lord Almighty!
  ²My soul yearns, even faints,
    for the courts of the Lord;
  my heart and my flesh cry out
    for the living God.

3 Even the sparrow has found a home,
and the swallow a nest for herself,
where she may have her young—
a place near your altar,
O Lord Almighty, my King and my
God.
4 Blessed are those who dwell in your
house;
they are ever praising you.   *Selah*

5 Blessed are those whose strength is
in you,
who have set their hearts on
pilgrimage.
6 As they pass through the Valley of
Baca,
they make it a place of springs;
the autumn rains also cover it with
pools.*b*
7 They go from strength to strength,
till each appears before God in
Zion.

8 Hear my prayer, O Lord God
Almighty;
listen to me, O God of Jacob.   *Selah*
9 Look upon our shield,*c* O God;
look with favor on your anointed
one.

10 Better is one day in your courts
than a thousand elsewhere;
I would rather be a doorkeeper in the
house of my God
than dwell in the tents of the
wicked.
11 For the Lord God is a sun and shield;
the Lord bestows favor and honor;
no good thing does he withhold
from those whose walk is
blameless.

12 O Lord Almighty,
blessed is the man who trusts in
you.

a Title: Probably a musical term   *b6* Or *blessings*   *c9* Or
sovereign

PROVERBS 25:15

15 Through patience a ruler can be
persuaded,
and a gentle tongue can break a
bone.

☐ D A Y   2 8 8

GOD SIGHTINGS

October 15

JEREMIAH 26:1–27:22

Early in the reign of Jehoiakim son of Josiah king of Judah, this word came from the Lord: 2"This is what the Lord says: Stand in the courtyard of the Lord's house and speak to all the people of the towns of Judah who come to worship in the house of the Lord. Tell them everything I command you; do not omit a word. 3 Perhaps they will listen and each will turn from his evil way. Then I will relent and not bring on them the disaster I was planning because of the evil they have done. 4 Say to them, 'This is what the Lord says: If you do not listen to me and follow my law, which I have set before you, 5 and if you do not listen to the words of my servants the prophets, whom I have sent to you again and again (though you have not listened), 6 then I will make this house like Shiloh and this city an object of cursing among all the nations of the earth.'"

7 The priests, the prophets and all the people heard Jeremiah speak these words in the house of the Lord. 8 But as soon as Jeremiah finished telling all the people everything the Lord had commanded him to say, the priests, the prophets and all the people seized him and said, "You must die! 9 Why do you prophesy in the Lord's name that this house will be like Shiloh and this city will be desolate and deserted?" And all the people crowded around Jeremiah in the house of the Lord.

10 When the officials of Judah heard about these things, they went up from the royal palace to the house of the Lord and took their places at the entrance of the New Gate of the Lord's house. 11 Then the priests and the prophets said to the officials and all the people, "This man should be sentenced to death because he has prophesied against this

city. You have heard it with your own ears!"

¹²Then Jeremiah said to all the officials and all the people: "The Lord sent me to prophesy against this house and this city all the things you have heard. ¹³Now reform your ways and your actions and obey the Lord your God. Then the Lord will relent and not bring the disaster he has pronounced against you. ¹⁴As for me, I am in your hands; do with me whatever you think is good and right. ¹⁵Be assured, however, that if you put me to death, you will bring the guilt of innocent blood on yourselves and on this city and on those who live in it, for in truth the Lord has sent me to you to speak all these words in your hearing."

¹⁶Then the officials and all the people said to the priests and the prophets, "This man should not be sentenced to death! He has spoken to us in the name of the Lord our God."

¹⁷Some of the elders of the land stepped forward and said to the entire assembly of people, ¹⁸"Micah of Moresheth prophesied in the days of Hezekiah king of Judah. He told all the people of Judah, 'This is what the Lord Almighty says:

"'Zion will be plowed like a field,
    Jerusalem will become a heap of
        rubble,
    the temple hill a mound
        overgrown with thickets.'ᵃ

¹⁹"Did Hezekiah king of Judah or anyone else in Judah put him to death? Did not Hezekiah fear the Lord and seek his favor? And did not the Lord relent, so that he did not bring the disaster he pronounced against them? We are about to bring a terrible disaster on ourselves!"

²⁰(Now Uriah son of Shemaiah from Kiriath Jearim was another man who prophesied in the name of the Lord; he prophesied the same things against this city and this land as Jeremiah did. ²¹When King Jehoiakim and all his officers and officials heard his words, the king sought to put him to death. But Uriah heard of it and fled in fear to Egypt. ²²King Jehoiakim, however, sent Elnathan son of Acbor to Egypt, along with some other men. ²³They brought Uriah out of Egypt and took him to King Jehoiakim, who had him struck down with a sword and his body thrown into the burial place of the common people.)

²⁴Furthermore, Ahikam son of Shaphan supported Jeremiah, and so he was not handed over to the people to be put to death.

²⁷:¹Early in the reign of Zedekiahᵇ son of Josiah king of Judah, this word came to Jeremiah from the Lord: ²This is what the Lord said to me: "Make a yoke out of straps and crossbars and put it on your neck. ³Then send word to the kings of Edom, Moab, Ammon, Tyre and Sidon through the envoys who have come to Jerusalem to Zedekiah king of Judah. ⁴Give them a message for their masters and say, 'This is what the Lord Almighty, the God of Israel, says: "Tell this to your masters: ⁵With my great power and outstretched arm I made the earth and its people and the animals that are on it, and I give it to anyone I please. ⁶Now I will hand all your countries over to my servant Nebuchadnezzar king of Babylon; I will make even the wild animals subject to him. ⁷All nations will serve him and his son and his grandson until the time for his land comes; then many nations and great kings will subjugate him.

⁸"'"If, however, any nation or kingdom will not serve Nebuchadnezzar king of Babylon or bow its neck under his yoke, I will punish that nation with the sword, famine and plague, declares the Lord, until I destroy it by his hand. ⁹So do not listen to your prophets, your diviners, your interpreters of dreams, your mediums or your sorcerers who tell you, 'You will not serve the king of Babylon.' ¹⁰They prophesy lies to you that will only serve to remove you far from your lands; I will banish you and you will perish. ¹¹But if any nation will bow its neck under the yoke of the king

of Babylon and serve him, I will let that nation remain in its own land to till it and to live there, declares the LORD."'"

12I gave the same message to Zedekiah king of Judah. I said, "Bow your neck under the yoke of the king of Babylon; serve him and his people, and you will live. 13Why will you and your people die by the sword, famine and plague with which the LORD has threatened any nation that will not serve the king of Babylon? 14Do not listen to the words of the prophets who say to you, 'You will not serve the king of Babylon,' for they are prophesying lies to you. 15'I have not sent them,' declares the LORD. 'They are prophesying lies in my name. Therefore, I will banish you and you will perish, both you and the prophets who prophesy to you.'"

16Then I said to the priests and all these people, "This is what the LORD says: Do not listen to the prophets who say, 'Very soon now the articles from the LORD's house will be brought back from Babylon.' They are prophesying lies to you. 17Do not listen to them. Serve the king of Babylon, and you will live. Why should this city become a ruin? 18If they are prophets and have the word of the LORD, let them plead with the LORD Almighty that the furnishings remaining in the house of the LORD and in the palace of the king of Judah and in Jerusalem not be taken to Babylon. 19For this is what the LORD Almighty says about the pillars, the Sea, the movable stands and the other furnishings that are left in this city, 20which Nebuchadnezzar king of Babylon did not take away when he carried Jehoiachin*c* son of Jehoiakim king of Judah into exile from Jerusalem to Babylon, along with all the nobles of Judah and Jerusalem— 21yes, this is what the LORD Almighty, the God of Israel, says about the things that are left in the house of the LORD and in the palace of the king of Judah and in Jerusalem: 22'They will be taken to Babylon and there they will remain until the day I come for them,' declares the LORD.

'Then I will bring them back and restore them to this place.'"

a 18 Micah 3:12   *b 1* A few Hebrew manuscripts and Syriac (see also Jer. 27:3, 12 and 28:1); most Hebrew manuscripts *Jehoiakim* (Most Septuagint manuscripts do not have this verse.)   *c 20* Hebrew *Jeconiah*, a variant of *Jehoiachin*

2 THESSALONIANS 3:1-18

Finally, brothers, pray for us that the message of the Lord may spread rapidly and be honored, just as it was with you. 2And pray that we may be delivered from wicked and evil men, for not everyone has faith. 3But the Lord is faithful, and he will strengthen and protect you from the evil one. 4We have confidence in the Lord that you are doing and will continue to do the things we command. 5May the Lord direct your hearts into God's love and Christ's perseverance.

6In the name of the Lord Jesus Christ, we command you, brothers, to keep away from every brother who is idle and does not live according to the teaching*a* you received from us. 7For you yourselves know how you ought to follow our example. We were not idle when we were with you, 8nor did we eat anyone's food without paying for it. On the contrary, we worked night and day, laboring and toiling so that we would not be a burden to any of you. 9We did this, not because we do not have the right to such help, but in order to make ourselves a model for you to follow. 10For even when we were with you, we gave you this rule: "If a man will not work, he shall not eat."

11We hear that some among you are idle. They are not busy; they are busybodies. 12Such people we command and urge in the Lord Jesus Christ to settle down and earn the bread they eat. 13And as for you, brothers, never tire of doing what is right.

14If anyone does not obey our instruction in this letter, take special note of him. Do not associate with him, in order that he may feel ashamed. 15Yet do not regard him as an enemy, but warn him as a brother.

16Now may the Lord of peace himself give you peace at all times and in every way. The Lord be with all of you.

17I, Paul, write this greeting in my own hand, which is the distinguishing mark in all my letters. This is how I write.

18The grace of our Lord Jesus Christ be with you all.

a6 Or *tradition*

PSALM 85:1-13

For the director of music. Of the Sons of Korah. A psalm.

1 You showed favor to your land,
　　O LORD;
　　you restored the fortunes of Jacob.
2 You forgave the iniquity of your
　　people
　　and covered all their sins.　　*Selah*
3 You set aside all your wrath
　　and turned from your fierce anger.

4 Restore us again, O God our Savior,
　　and put away your displeasure
　　　toward us.
5 Will you be angry with us forever?
　　Will you prolong your anger
　　　through all generations?
6 Will you not revive us again,
　　that your people may rejoice in
　　　you?
7 Show us your unfailing love, O LORD,
　　and grant us your salvation.

8 I will listen to what God the LORD will
　　say;
　　he promises peace to his people,
　　　his saints—
　　but let them not return to folly.
9 Surely his salvation is near those who
　　fear him,
　　that his glory may dwell in our land.

10 Love and faithfulness meet
　　　together;
　　righteousness and peace kiss
　　　each other.
11 Faithfulness springs forth from
　　　the earth,
　　and righteousness looks down
　　　from heaven.

12 The LORD will indeed give what is
　　good,
　　and our land will yield its harvest.
13 Righteousness goes before him
　　and prepares the way for his steps.

PROVERBS 25:16

16 If you find honey, eat just enough—
　　too much of it, and you will vomit.

□ D A Y 2 8 9

GOD SIGHTINGS

October 16

JEREMIAH 28:1-29:32

In the fifth month of that same year, the fourth year, early in the reign of Zedekiah king of Judah, the prophet Hananiah son of Azzur, who was from Gibeon, said to me in the house of the LORD in the presence of the priests and all the people: 2"This is what the LORD Almighty, the God of Israel, says: 'I will break the yoke of the king of Babylon. 3Within two years I will bring back to this place all the articles of the LORD's house that Nebuchadnezzar king of Babylon removed from here and took to Babylon. 4I will also bring back to this place Jehoiachina son of Jehoiakim king of Judah and all the other exiles from Judah who went to Babylon,' declares the LORD, 'for I will break the yoke of the king of Babylon.'"

5Then the prophet Jeremiah replied to the prophet Hananiah before the priests and all the people who were standing in the house of the LORD. 6He said, "Amen! May the LORD do so! May the LORD fulfill the words you have prophesied by bringing the articles of the LORD's house and all the exiles back to this place from Babylon. 7Nevertheless, listen to what I have to say in your hearing and in the hearing of all the people: 8From early times the prophets who preceded you and me have prophesied war, disaster and plague against many countries and great kingdoms. 9But the prophet who prophesies peace will be recognized as one truly sent by the LORD only if his prediction comes true."

10Then the prophet Hananiah took the yoke off the neck of the prophet Jeremiah and broke it, 11and he said before all the people, "This is what the LORD says: 'In the same way will I break the yoke of Nebuchadnezzar king of Babylon off the neck of all the nations within two years.'" At this, the prophet Jeremiah went on his way.

12Shortly after the prophet Hananiah had broken the yoke off the neck of the prophet Jeremiah, the word of the LORD came to Jeremiah: 13"Go and tell Hananiah, 'This is what the LORD says: You have broken a wooden yoke, but in its place you will get a yoke of iron. 14This is what the LORD Almighty, the God of Israel, says: I will put an iron yoke on the necks of all these nations to make them serve Nebuchadnezzar king of Babylon, and they will serve him. I will even give him control over the wild animals.'"

15Then the prophet Jeremiah said to Hananiah the prophet, "Listen, Hananiah! The LORD has not sent you, yet you have persuaded this nation to trust in lies. 16Therefore, this is what the LORD says: 'I am about to remove you from the face of the earth. This very year you are going to die, because you have preached rebellion against the LORD.'"

17In the seventh month of that same year, Hananiah the prophet died.

29:1This is the text of the letter that the prophet Jeremiah sent from Jerusalem to the surviving elders among the exiles and to the priests, the prophets and all the other people Nebuchadnezzar had carried into exile from Jerusalem to Babylon. 2(This was after King Jehoiachina and the queen mother, the court officials and the leaders of Judah and Jerusalem, the craftsmen and the artisans had gone into exile from Jerusalem.) 3He entrusted the letter to Elasah son of Shaphan and to Gemariah son of Hilkiah, whom Zedekiah king of Judah sent to King Nebuchadnezzar in Babylon. It said:

4This is what the LORD Almighty, the God of Israel, says to all those I carried into exile from Jerusalem to Babylon: 5"Build houses and settle down; plant gardens and eat what they produce. 6Marry and have sons and daughters; find wives for your sons and give your daughters in marriage, so that they too may have sons and daughters. Increase in number there; do not decrease. 7Also, seek the peace and prosperity of the city to which I have carried you into exile. Pray to the LORD for it, because if it prospers, you too will prosper." 8Yes, this is what the LORD Almighty, the God of Israel, says: "Do not let the prophets and diviners among you deceive you. Do not listen to the dreams you encourage them to have. 9They are prophesying lies to you in my name. I have not sent them," declares the LORD.

10This is what the LORD says: "When seventy years are completed for Babylon, I will come to you and fulfill my gracious promise to bring you back to this place. 11For I know the plans I have for you," declares the LORD, "plans to prosper you and not to harm you, plans to give you hope and a future. 12Then you will call upon me and come and pray to me, and I will listen to you. 13You will seek me and find me when you seek me with all your heart. 14I will be found by you," declares the LORD, "and will bring you back from captivity.b I will gather you from all the nations and places where I have banished you," declares the LORD, "and will bring you back to the place from which I carried you into exile."

15You may say, "The LORD has raised up prophets for us in Babylon," ¹⁶but this is what the Lᴏʀᴅ says about the king who sits on David's throne and all the people who remain in this city, your countrymen who did not go with you into exile— ¹⁷yes, this is what the Lᴏʀᴅ Almighty says: "I will send the sword, famine and plague against them and I will make them like poor figs that are so bad they cannot be eaten. ¹⁸I will pursue them with the sword, famine and plague and will make them abhorrent to all the kingdoms of the earth and an object of cursing and horror, of scorn and reproach, among all the nations where I drive them. ¹⁹For they have not listened to my words," declares the Lᴏʀᴅ, "words that I sent to them again and again by my servants the prophets. And you exiles have not listened either," declares the Lᴏʀᴅ.

²⁰Therefore, hear the word of the Lᴏʀᴅ, all you exiles whom I have sent away from Jerusalem to Babylon. ²¹This is what the Lᴏʀᴅ Almighty, the God of Israel, says about Ahab son of Kolaiah and Zedekiah son of Maaseiah, who are prophesying lies to you in my name: "I will hand them over to Nebuchadnezzar king of Babylon, and he will put them to death before your very eyes. ²²Because of them, all the exiles from Judah who are in Babylon will use this curse: 'The Lᴏʀᴅ treat you like Zedekiah and Ahab, whom the king of Babylon burned in the fire.' ²³For they have done outrageous things in Israel; they have committed adultery with their neighbors' wives and in my name have spoken lies, which I did not tell them to do. I know it and am a witness to it," declares the Lᴏʀᴅ.

²⁴Tell Shemaiah the Nehelamite, ²⁵"This is what the Lᴏʀᴅ Almighty, the God of Israel, says: You sent letters in your own name to all the people in Jeru-salem, to Zephaniah son of Maaseiah the priest, and to all the other priests. You said to Zephaniah, ²⁶'The Lᴏʀᴅ has appointed you priest in place of Jehoiada to be in charge of the house of the Lᴏʀᴅ; you should put any madman who acts like a prophet into the stocks and neck-irons. ²⁷So why have you not reprimanded Jeremiah from Anathoth, who poses as a prophet among you? ²⁸He has sent this message to us in Babylon: It will be a long time. Therefore build houses and settle down; plant gardens and eat what they produce.'"

²⁹Zephaniah the priest, however, read the letter to Jeremiah the prophet. ³⁰Then the word of the Lᴏʀᴅ came to Jeremiah: ³¹"Send this message to all the exiles: 'This is what the Lᴏʀᴅ says about Shemaiah the Nehelamite: Because Shemaiah has prophesied to you, even though I did not send him, and has led you to believe a lie, ³²this is what the Lᴏʀᴅ says: I will surely punish Shemaiah the Nehelamite and his descendants. He will have no one left among this people, nor will he see the good things I will do for my people, declares the Lᴏʀᴅ, because he has preached rebellion against me.'"

ᵃ4,2 Hebrew *Jeconiah*, a variant of *Jehoiachin*   ᵇ14 Or *will restore your fortunes*

1 TIMOTHY 1:1-20

Paul, an apostle of Christ Jesus by the command of God our Savior and of Christ Jesus our hope,

²To Timothy my true son in the faith:

Grace, mercy and peace from God the Father and Christ Jesus our Lord.

³As I urged you when I went into Macedonia, stay there in Ephesus so that you may command certain men not to teach false doctrines any longer ⁴nor to devote themselves to myths and endless genealogies. These promote controversies rather than God's work—which is by faith. ⁵The goal of this command is love, which comes from a pure heart and a good conscience and a

sincere faith. [6]Some have wandered away from these and turned to meaningless talk. [7]They want to be teachers of the law, but they do not know what they are talking about or what they so confidently affirm.

[8]We know that the law is good if one uses it properly. [9]We also know that law[a] is made not for the righteous but for lawbreakers and rebels, the ungodly and sinful, the unholy and irreligious; for those who kill their fathers or mothers, for murderers, [10]for adulterers and perverts, for slave traders and liars and perjurers—and for whatever else is contrary to the sound doctrine [11]that conforms to the glorious gospel of the blessed God, which he entrusted to me.

[12]I thank Christ Jesus our Lord, who has given me strength, that he considered me faithful, appointing me to his service. [13]Even though I was once a blasphemer and a persecutor and a violent man, I was shown mercy because I acted in ignorance and unbelief. [14]The grace of our Lord was poured out on me abundantly, along with the faith and love that are in Christ Jesus.

[15]Here is a trustworthy saying that deserves full acceptance: Christ Jesus came into the world to save sinners—of whom I am the worst. [16]But for that very reason I was shown mercy so that in me, the worst of sinners, Christ Jesus might display his unlimited patience as an example for those who would believe on him and receive eternal life. [17]Now to the King eternal, immortal, invisible, the only God, be honor and glory for ever and ever. Amen.

[18]Timothy, my son, I give you this instruction in keeping with the prophecies once made about you, so that by following them you may fight the good fight, [19]holding on to faith and a good conscience. Some have rejected these and so have shipwrecked their faith. [20]Among them are Hymenaeus and Alexander, whom I have handed over to Satan to be taught not to blaspheme.

[a]9 Or that the law

PSALM 86:1-17

A prayer of David.

[1]**H**ear, O LORD, and answer me,
    for I am poor and needy.
[2]Guard my life, for I am devoted to you.
    You are my God; save your servant
    who trusts in you.
[3]Have mercy on me, O Lord,
    for I call to you all day long.
[4]Bring joy to your servant,
    for to you, O Lord,
    I lift up my soul.

[5]**You are forgiving and good,
        O Lord,
    abounding in love to all who call
        to you.**
[6]**Hear my prayer, O LORD;
    listen to my cry for mercy.**
[7]**In the day of my trouble I will call
        to you,
    for you will answer me.**

[8]Among the gods there is none like
        you, O Lord;
    no deeds can compare with yours.
[9]All the nations you have made
    will come and worship before you,
        O Lord;
    they will bring glory to your name.
[10]For you are great and do marvelous
        deeds;
    you alone are God.

[11]Teach me your way, O LORD,
    and I will walk in your truth;
    give me an undivided heart,
    that I may fear your name.
[12]I will praise you, O Lord my God, with
        all my heart;
    I will glorify your name forever.
[13]For great is your love toward me;
    you have delivered me from the
        depths of the grave.[a]

[14]The arrogant are attacking me, O God;
    a band of ruthless men seeks my
        life—
    men without regard for you.
[15]But you, O Lord, are a compassionate
        and gracious God,
    slow to anger, abounding in love
        and faithfulness.

16 Turn to me and have mercy on me;
   grant your strength to your servant
   and save the son of your
      maidservant.*b*
17 Give me a sign of your goodness,
   that my enemies may see it and be
      put to shame,
   for you, O Lord, have helped me
      and comforted me.

a 13 Hebrew Sheol   b 16 Or save your faithful son

PROVERBS 25:17

17 Seldom set foot in your neighbor's
      house—
   too much of you, and he will hate
      you.

☐ D A Y   2 9 0

GOD SIGHTINGS

October **17**

JEREMIAH 30:1–31:26

This is the word that came to Jeremiah from the Lord: 2 "This is what the Lord, the God of Israel, says: 'Write in a book all the words I have spoken to you. 3 The days are coming,' declares the Lord, 'when I will bring my people Israel and Judah back from captivity*a* and restore them to the land I gave their forefathers to possess,' says the Lord."

4 These are the words the Lord spoke concerning Israel and Judah: 5 "This is what the Lord says:

"'Cries of fear are heard—
   terror, not peace.
6 Ask and see:
   Can a man bear children?
Then why do I see every strong man
   with his hands on his stomach like
      a woman in labor,
   every face turned deathly pale?
7 How awful that day will be!
   None will be like it.
It will be a time of trouble for Jacob,
   but he will be saved out of it.

8 "'In that day,' declares the Lord
      Almighty,
   'I will break the yoke off their
      necks
and will tear off their bonds;
   no longer will foreigners enslave
      them.
9 Instead, they will serve the Lord their
      God
   and David their king,
   whom I will raise up for them.

10 "'So do not fear, O Jacob my servant;
   do not be dismayed, O Israel,'
                  declares the Lord.
'I will surely save you out of a distant
      place,
   your descendants from the land of
      their exile.
Jacob will again have peace and
      security,
   and no one will make him afraid.
11 I am with you and will save you,'
   declares the Lord.
'Though I completely destroy all the
      nations
   among which I scatter you,
   I will not completely destroy you.
I will discipline you but only with
      justice;
   I will not let you go entirely
      unpunished.'

12 "This is what the Lord says:

"'Your wound is incurable,
   your injury beyond healing.
13 There is no one to plead your cause,
   no remedy for your sore,
   no healing for you.
14 All your allies have forgotten you;
   they care nothing for you.
I have struck you as an enemy would
   and punished you as would the
      cruel,
because your guilt is so great
   and your sins so many.
15 Why do you cry out over your wound,
   your pain that has no cure?
Because of your great guilt and many
      sins
   I have done these things to you.

16 "'But all who devour you will be
        devoured;
    all your enemies will go into exile.
    Those who plunder you will be
        plundered;
    all who make spoil of you I will
        despoil.
17 But I will restore you to health
        and heal your wounds,'
                        declares the LORD,
    'because you are called an outcast,
    Zion for whom no one cares.'

18 "This is what the LORD says:

    "'I will restore the fortunes of Jacob's
        tents
    and have compassion on his
        dwellings;
    the city will be rebuilt on her ruins,
    and the palace will stand in its
        proper place.
19 From them will come songs of
        thanksgiving
    and the sound of rejoicing.
    I will add to their numbers,
        and they will not be decreased;
    I will bring them honor,
        and they will not be disdained.
20 Their children will be as in days
        of old,
    and their community will be
        established before me;
    I will punish all who oppress them.
21 Their leader will be one of their own;
    their ruler will arise from among
        them.
    I will bring him near and he will
        come close to me,
    for who is he who will devote himself
        to be close to me?'
                        declares the LORD.
22 "'So you will be my people,
    and I will be your God.'"

23 See, the storm of the LORD
    will burst out in wrath,
    a driving wind swirling down
    on the heads of the wicked.
24 The fierce anger of the LORD will not
        turn back
    until he fully accomplishes
    the purposes of his heart.

In days to come
    you will understand this.

31:1 "At that time," declares the LORD, "I
will be the God of all the clans of Israel,
and they will be my people."
    2 This is what the LORD says:

    "The people who survive the sword
        will find favor in the desert;
    I will come to give rest to Israel."

    3 The LORD appeared to us in the
past,*b* saying:

    "I have loved you with an everlasting
        love;
    I have drawn you with loving-
        kindness.
4 I will build you up again
    and you will be rebuilt, O Virgin
        Israel.
    Again you will take up your
        tambourines
    and go out to dance with the joyful.
5 Again you will plant vineyards
    on the hills of Samaria;
    the farmers will plant them
    and enjoy their fruit.
6 There will be a day when watchmen
        cry out
    on the hills of Ephraim,
    'Come, let us go up to Zion,
    to the LORD our God.'"

    7 This is what the LORD says:

    "Sing with joy for Jacob;
    shout for the foremost of the nations.
    Make your praises heard, and say,
    'O LORD, save your people,
    the remnant of Israel.'
8 See, I will bring them from the land
        of the north
    and gather them from the ends of
        the earth.
    Among them will be the blind and
        the lame,
    expectant mothers and women in
        labor;
    a great throng will return.
9 They will come with weeping;
    they will pray as I bring them
        back.

I will lead them beside streams of
water
   on a level path where they will not
   stumble,
because I am Israel's father,
   and Ephraim is my firstborn son.

¹⁰"Hear the word of the Lord,
   O nations;
proclaim it in distant coastlands:
   'He who scattered Israel will gather
   them
   and will watch over his flock like a
   shepherd.'
¹¹For the Lord will ransom Jacob
   and redeem them from the hand
   of those stronger than they.
¹²They will come and shout for joy on
   the heights of Zion;
they will rejoice in the bounty of
   the Lord—
the grain, the new wine and the oil,
   the young of the flocks and herds.
They will be like a well-watered
   garden,
and they will sorrow no more.
¹³Then maidens will dance and be
   glad,
   young men and old as well.
I will turn their mourning into
   gladness;
I will give them comfort and joy
   instead of sorrow.
¹⁴I will satisfy the priests with
   abundance,
and my people will be filled with
   my bounty,"
                declares the Lord.

¹⁵This is what the Lord says:

"A voice is heard in Ramah,
   mourning and great weeping,
Rachel weeping for her children
   and refusing to be comforted,
   because her children are no
   more."

¹⁶This is what the Lord says:

"Restrain your voice from weeping
   and your eyes from tears,
for your work will be rewarded,"
                declares the Lord.

"They will return from the land of
   the enemy.
¹⁷So there is hope for your future,"
                declares the Lord.
"Your children will return to their
   own land.

¹⁸"I have surely heard Ephraim's
   moaning:
'You disciplined me like an unruly
   calf,
   and I have been disciplined.
Restore me, and I will return,
   because you are the Lord my God.
¹⁹After I strayed,
   I repented;
after I came to understand,
   I beat my breast.
I was ashamed and humiliated
   because I bore the disgrace of my
   youth.'
²⁰Is not Ephraim my dear son,
   the child in whom I delight?
Though I often speak against him,
   I still remember him.
Therefore my heart yearns for him;
   I have great compassion for him,"
                declares the Lord.

²¹"Set up road signs;
   put up guideposts.
Take note of the highway,
   the road that you take.
Return, O Virgin Israel,
   return to your towns.
²²How long will you wander,
   O unfaithful daughter?
The Lord will create a new thing on
   earth—
   a woman will surround^c a man."

²³This is what the Lord Almighty, the
God of Israel, says: "When I bring them
back from captivity,^d the people in the
land of Judah and in its towns will once
again use these words: 'The Lord bless
you, O righteous dwelling, O sacred
mountain.' ²⁴People will live together in
Judah and all its towns—farmers and
those who move about with their flocks.
²⁵I will refresh the weary and satisfy the
faint."

26At this I awoke and looked around. My sleep had been pleasant to me.

a3 Or *will restore the fortunes of my people Israel and Judah*   *b3* Or *Lord has appeared to us from afar*   *c22* Or *will go about* ⌊*seeking*⌋; or *will protect*   *d23* Or *I restore their fortunes*

1 TIMOTHY 2:1-15

I urge, then, first of all, that requests, prayers, intercession and thanksgiving be made for everyone— 2for kings and all those in authority, that we may live peaceful and quiet lives in all godliness and holiness. 3This is good, and pleases God our Savior, 4who wants all men to be saved and to come to a knowledge of the truth. 5**For there is one God and one mediator between God and men, the man Christ Jesus, 6who gave himself as a ransom for all men—the testimony given in its proper time.** 7And for this purpose I was appointed a herald and an apostle—I am telling the truth, I am not lying—and a teacher of the true faith to the Gentiles.

8I want men everywhere to lift up holy hands in prayer, without anger or disputing.

9I also want women to dress modestly, with decency and propriety, not with braided hair or gold or pearls or expensive clothes, 10but with good deeds, appropriate for women who profess to worship God.

11A woman should learn in quietness and full submission. 12I do not permit a woman to teach or to have authority over a man; she must be silent. 13For Adam was formed first, then Eve. 14And Adam was not the one deceived; it was the woman who was deceived and became a sinner. 15But women*a* will be saved*b* through childbearing—if they continue in faith, love and holiness with propriety.

a15 Greek *she*   *b15* Or *restored*

PSALM 87:1-7

Of the Sons of Korah. A psalm. A song.

1 He has set his foundation on the
        holy mountain;
2   the Lord loves the gates of Zion
        more than all the dwellings of
        Jacob.

3 Glorious things are said of you,
    O city of God: *Selah*
4 "I will record Rahab*a* and Babylon
        among those who acknowledge
        me—
Philistia too, and Tyre, along with
        Cush*b*—
    and will say, 'This*c* one was born in
        Zion.'"

5 Indeed, of Zion it will be said,
    "This one and that one were born
        in her,
    and the Most High himself will
        establish her."
6 The Lord will write in the register of
        the peoples:
    "This one was born in Zion." *Selah*
7 As they make music they will sing,
    "All my fountains are in you."

a4 A poetic name for Egypt   *b4* That is, the upper Nile region   *c4* Or *"O Rahab and Babylon, / Philistia, Tyre and Cush, / I will record concerning those who acknowledge me: / 'This*

PROVERBS 25:18-19

18 Like a club or a sword or a sharp
        arrow
    is the man who gives false testimony
        against his neighbor.

19 Like a bad tooth or a lame foot
    is reliance on the unfaithful in
        times of trouble.

☐ D A Y 2 9 1

October 18

JEREMIAH 31:27-32:44

"The days are coming," declares the Lord, "when I will plant the house of Israel and the house of Judah with the offspring of men and of animals. 28Just as I watched over them to uproot and tear down, and to overthrow, destroy and bring disaster, so I will watch over them to build and to plant," declares the Lord. 29"In those days people will no longer say,

'The fathers have eaten sour grapes,
    and the children's teeth are set on
    edge.'

30Instead, everyone will die for his own
sin; whoever eats sour grapes—his own
teeth will be set on edge.

31"The time is coming," declares the
    LORD,
  "when I will make a new covenant
    with the house of Israel
    and with the house of Judah.
32It will not be like the covenant
    I made with their forefathers
  when I took them by the hand
    to lead them out of Egypt,
  because they broke my covenant,
    though I was a husband to*a*
    them,*b*"
                            declares the LORD.
33**" This is the covenant I will make**
    with the house of Israel
    after that time," declares the
    LORD.
  "I will put my law in their minds
    and write it on their hearts.
  I will be their God,
    and they will be my people.
34No longer will a man teach his
    neighbor,
  or a man his brother, saying, 'Know
    the LORD,'
  because they will all know me,
    from the least of them to the
    greatest,"
                            declares the LORD.
  "For I will forgive their wickedness
    and will remember their sins no
    more."

35This is what the LORD says,

  he who appoints the sun
    to shine by day,
  who decrees the moon and stars
    to shine by night,
  who stirs up the sea
    so that its waves roar—
    the LORD Almighty is his name:
36"Only if these decrees vanish from
    my sight,"
                            declares the LORD,

"will the descendants of Israel ever
    cease
    to be a nation before me."

37This is what the LORD says:

"Only if the heavens above can be
    measured
  and the foundations of the earth
    below be searched out
  will I reject all the descendants of
    Israel
  because of all they have done,"
                            declares the LORD.

38"The days are coming," declares the
LORD, "when this city will be rebuilt for
me from the Tower of Hananel to the
Corner Gate. 39The measuring line will
stretch from there straight to the hill of
Gareb and then turn to Goah. 40The
whole valley where dead bodies and
ashes are thrown, and all the terraces out
to the Kidron Valley on the east as far as
the corner of the Horse Gate, will be holy
to the LORD. The city will never again be
uprooted or demolished."

32:1THIS is the word that came to Jeremiah from the LORD in the tenth year of
Zedekiah king of Judah, which was the
eighteenth year of Nebuchadnezzar.
2The army of the king of Babylon was
then besieging Jerusalem, and Jeremiah
the prophet was confined in the courtyard of the guard in the royal palace of
Judah.

3Now Zedekiah king of Judah had imprisoned him there, saying, "Why do
you prophesy as you do? You say, 'This is
what the LORD says: I am about to hand
this city over to the king of Babylon, and
he will capture it. 4Zedekiah king of Judah will not escape out of the hands of
the Babylonians*c* but will certainly be
handed over to the king of Babylon, and
will speak with him face to face and see
him with his own eyes. 5He will take
Zedekiah to Babylon, where he will remain until I deal with him, declares the
LORD. If you fight against the Babylonians, you will not succeed.'"

6Jeremiah said, "The word of the

LORD came to me: [7]Hanamel son of Shallum your uncle is going to come to you and say, 'Buy my field at Anathoth, because as nearest relative it is your right and duty to buy it.'

[8]"Then, just as the LORD had said, my cousin Hanamel came to me in the courtyard of the guard and said, 'Buy my field at Anathoth in the territory of Benjamin. Since it is your right to redeem it and possess it, buy it for yourself.'

"I knew that this was the word of the LORD; [9]so I bought the field at Anathoth from my cousin Hanamel and weighed out for him seventeen shekels[d] of silver. [10]I signed and sealed the deed, had it witnessed, and weighed out the silver on the scales. [11]I took the deed of purchase—the sealed copy containing the terms and conditions, as well as the unsealed copy— [12]and I gave this deed to Baruch son of Neriah, the son of Mahseiah, in the presence of my cousin Hanamel and of the witnesses who had signed the deed and of all the Jews sitting in the courtyard of the guard.

[13]"In their presence I gave Baruch these instructions: [14]'This is what the LORD Almighty, the God of Israel, says: Take these documents, both the sealed and unsealed copies of the deed of purchase, and put them in a clay jar so they will last a long time. [15]For this is what the LORD Almighty, the God of Israel, says: Houses, fields and vineyards will again be bought in this land.'

[16]"After I had given the deed of purchase to Baruch son of Neriah, I prayed to the LORD:

[17]"Ah, Sovereign LORD, you have made the heavens and the earth by your great power and outstretched arm. Nothing is too hard for you. [18]You show love to thousands but bring the punishment for the fathers' sins into the laps of their children after them. O great and powerful God, whose name is the LORD Almighty, [19]great are your purposes and mighty are your deeds.

Your eyes are open to all the ways of men; you reward everyone according to his conduct and as his deeds deserve. [20]You performed miraculous signs and wonders in Egypt and have continued them to this day, both in Israel and among all mankind, and have gained the renown that is still yours. [21]You brought your people Israel out of Egypt with signs and wonders, by a mighty hand and an outstretched arm and with great terror. [22]You gave them this land you had sworn to give their forefathers, a land flowing with milk and honey. [23]They came in and took possession of it, but they did not obey you or follow your law; they did not do what you commanded them to do. So you brought all this disaster upon them.

[24]"See how the siege ramps are built up to take the city. Because of the sword, famine and plague, the city will be handed over to the Babylonians who are attacking it. What you said has happened, as you now see. [25]And though the city will be handed over to the Babylonians, you, O Sovereign LORD, say to me, 'Buy the field with silver and have the transaction witnessed.'"

[26]Then the word of the LORD came to Jeremiah: [27]"I am the LORD, the God of all mankind. Is anything too hard for me? [28]Therefore, this is what the LORD says: I am about to hand this city over to the Babylonians and to Nebuchadnezzar king of Babylon, who will capture it. [29]The Babylonians who are attacking this city will come in and set it on fire; they will burn it down, along with the houses where the people provoked me to anger by burning incense on the roofs to Baal and by pouring out drink offerings to other gods.

[30]"The people of Israel and Judah have done nothing but evil in my sight from their youth; indeed, the people of Israel have done nothing but provoke me with what their hands have made, declares the LORD. [31]From the day it was

built until now, this city has so aroused my anger and wrath that I must remove it from my sight. 32The people of Israel and Judah have provoked me by all the evil they have done—they, their kings and officials, their priests and prophets, the men of Judah and the people of Jerusalem. 33They turned their backs to me and not their faces; though I taught them again and again, they would not listen or respond to discipline. 34They set up their abominable idols in the house that bears my Name and defiled it. 35They built high places for Baal in the Valley of Ben Hinnom to sacrifice their sons and daughters^e to Molech, though I never commanded, nor did it enter my mind, that they should do such a detestable thing and so make Judah sin.

36"You are saying about this city, 'By the sword, famine and plague it will be handed over to the king of Babylon'; but this is what the Lord, the God of Israel, says: 37I will surely gather them from all the lands where I banish them in my furious anger and great wrath; I will bring them back to this place and let them live in safety. 38They will be my people, and I will be their God. 39I will give them singleness of heart and action, so that they will always fear me for their own good and the good of their children after them. 40I will make an everlasting covenant with them: I will never stop doing good to them, and I will inspire them to fear me, so that they will never turn away from me. 41I will rejoice in doing them good and will assuredly plant them in this land with all my heart and soul.

42"This is what the Lord says: As I have brought all this great calamity on this people, so I will give them all the prosperity I have promised them. 43Once more fields will be bought in this land of which you say, 'It is a desolate waste, without men or animals, for it has been handed over to the Babylonians.' 44Fields will be bought for silver, and deeds will be signed, sealed and witnessed in the territory of Benjamin, in the villages around Jerusalem, in the towns of Judah and in the towns of the

hill country, of the western foothills and of the Negev, because I will restore their fortunes,^f declares the Lord."

a32 Hebrew; Septuagint and Syriac / and I turned away from   b32 Or was their master   c4 Or Chaldeans; also in verses 5, 24, 25, 28, 29 and 43   d9 That is, about 7 ounces (about 200 grams)   e35 Or to make their sons and daughters pass through ⌊the fire⌋   f44 Or will bring them back from captivity

1 TIMOTHY 3:1-16

Here is a trustworthy saying: If anyone sets his heart on being an overseer,^a he desires a noble task. 2Now the overseer must be above reproach, the husband of but one wife, temperate, self-controlled, respectable, hospitable, able to teach, 3not given to drunkenness, not violent but gentle, not quarrelsome, not a lover of money. 4He must manage his own family well and see that his children obey him with proper respect. 5(If anyone does not know how to manage his own family, how can he take care of God's church?) 6He must not be a recent convert, or he may become conceited and fall under the same judgment as the devil. 7He must also have a good reputation with outsiders, so that he will not fall into disgrace and into the devil's trap.

8Deacons, likewise, are to be men worthy of respect, sincere, not indulging in much wine, and not pursuing dishonest gain. 9They must keep hold of the deep truths of the faith with a clear conscience. 10They must first be tested; and then if there is nothing against them, let them serve as deacons.

11In the same way, their wives^b are to be women worthy of respect, not malicious talkers but temperate and trustworthy in everything.

12A deacon must be the husband of but one wife and must manage his children and his household well. 13Those who have served well gain an excellent standing and great assurance in their faith in Christ Jesus.

14Although I hope to come to you soon, I am writing you these instructions so that, 15if I am delayed, you will know how people ought to conduct themselves in God's household, which is the church of the living God, the pillar and foundation of the truth. ¹⁶Beyond all question, the mystery of godliness is great:

He*c* appeared in a body,*d*
  was vindicated by the Spirit,
was seen by angels,
  was preached among the nations,
was believed on in the world,
  was taken up in glory.

a1 Traditionally *bishop;* also in verse 2   *b11* Or *way, deaconesses*   *c16* Some manuscripts *God*   *d16* Or *in the flesh*

PSALM 88:1-18

A song. A psalm of the Sons of Korah. For the director of music. According to *mahalath leannoth.ᵃ* A *maskilᵇ* of Heman the Ezrahite.

¹ **O** Lord, the God who saves me,
    day and night I cry out before you.
² May my prayer come before you;
    turn your ear to my cry.

³ For my soul is full of trouble
    and my life draws near the grave.*c*
⁴ I am counted among those who go
      down to the pit;
    I am like a man without strength.
⁵ I am set apart with the dead,
    like the slain who lie in the grave,
  whom you remember no more,
    who are cut off from your care.

⁶ You have put me in the lowest pit,
    in the darkest depths.
⁷ Your wrath lies heavily upon me;
    you have overwhelmed me with all
      your waves.   *Selah*
⁸ You have taken from me my closest
      friends
    and have made me repulsive to
      them.
  I am confined and cannot escape;
⁹   my eyes are dim with grief.

  I call to you, O Lord, every day;
    I spread out my hands to you.
¹⁰ Do you show your wonders to the
      dead?
    Do those who are dead rise up and
      praise you?   *Selah*
¹¹ Is your love declared in the grave,
    your faithfulness in Destruction*d*?

¹² Are your wonders known in the place
      of darkness,
    or your righteous deeds in the
      land of oblivion?
¹³ But I cry to you for help, O Lord;
    in the morning my prayer comes
      before you.
¹⁴ Why, O Lord, do you reject me
    and hide your face from me?

¹⁵ From my youth I have been afflicted
      and close to death;
    I have suffered your terrors and
      am in despair.
¹⁶ Your wrath has swept over me;
    your terrors have destroyed me.
¹⁷ All day long they surround me like a
      flood;
    they have completely engulfed me.
¹⁸ You have taken my companions and
      loved ones from me;
    the darkness is my closest friend.

aTitle: Possibly a tune, "The Suffering of Affliction"   *bTitle:* Probably a literary or musical term   *c3* Hebrew *Sheol*   *d11* Hebrew *Abaddon*

PROVERBS 25:20-22

²⁰ **L**ike one who takes away a garment
      on a cold day,
    or like vinegar poured on soda,
  is one who sings songs to a heavy
      heart.

²¹ If your enemy is hungry, give him
      food to eat;
    if he is thirsty, give him water to
      drink.
²² In doing this, you will heap burning
      coals on his head,
    and the Lord will reward you.

☐ D A Y 2 9 2

GOD SIGHTINGS

October 19

JEREMIAH 33:1-34:22

While Jeremiah was still confined in the courtyard of the guard, the word of the Lord came to him a second time: ²"This is what the Lord says, he who made the earth, the Lord who formed it and established it—the Lord is his name: ³'Call to me and I will answer you and tell you great and unsearchable things you do not know.' ⁴For this is what the Lord, the God of Israel, says about the houses in this city and the royal palaces of Judah that have been torn down to be used against the siege ramps and the sword ⁵in the fight with the Babylonians*ᵃ*: 'They will be filled with the dead bodies of the men I will slay in my anger and wrath. I will hide my face from this city because of all its wickedness.

⁶" 'Nevertheless, I will bring health and healing to it; I will heal my people and will let them enjoy abundant peace and security. ⁷I will bring Judah and Israel back from captivity*ᵇ* and will rebuild them as they were before. ⁸I will cleanse them from all the sin they have committed against me and will forgive all their sins of rebellion against me. ⁹Then this city will bring me renown, joy, praise and honor before all nations on earth that hear of all the good things I do for it; and they will be in awe and will tremble at the abundant prosperity and peace I provide for it.'

¹⁰"This is what the Lord says: 'You say about this place, "It is a desolate waste, without men or animals." Yet in the towns of Judah and the streets of Jerusalem that are deserted, inhabited by neither men nor animals, there will be heard once more ¹¹the sounds of joy and gladness, the voices of bride and bridegroom, and the voices of those who bring thank offerings to the house of the Lord, saying,

"Give thanks to the Lord Almighty,
    for the Lord is good;
    his love endures forever."

For I will restore the fortunes of the land as they were before,' says the Lord.

¹²"This is what the Lord Almighty says: 'In this place, desolate and without

men or animals—in all its towns there will again be pastures for shepherds to rest their flocks. ¹³In the towns of the hill country, of the western foothills and of the Negev, in the territory of Benjamin, in the villages around Jerusalem and in the towns of Judah, flocks will again pass under the hand of the one who counts them,' says the Lord.

¹⁴" 'The days are coming,' declares the Lord, 'when I will fulfill the gracious promise I made to the house of Israel and to the house of Judah.

¹⁵" 'In those days and at that time
    I will make a righteous Branch
        sprout from David's line;
    he will do what is just and right in
        the land.
¹⁶In those days Judah will be saved
    and Jerusalem will live in safety.
This is the name by which it*ᶜ* will be
        called:
    The Lord Our Righteousness.'

¹⁷For this is what the Lord says: 'David will never fail to have a man to sit on the throne of the house of Israel, ¹⁸nor will the priests, who are Levites, ever fail to have a man to stand before me continually to offer burnt offerings, to burn grain offerings and to present sacrifices.'"

¹⁹The word of the Lord came to Jeremiah: ²⁰"This is what the Lord says: 'If you can break my covenant with the day and my covenant with the night, so that day and night no longer come at their appointed time, ²¹then my covenant with David my servant—and my covenant with the Levites who are priests ministering before me—can be broken and David will no longer have a descendant to reign on his throne. ²²I will make the descendants of David my servant and the Levites who minister before me as countless as the stars of the sky and as measureless as the sand on the seashore.'"

²³The word of the Lord came to Jeremiah: ²⁴"Have you not noticed that these people are saying, 'The Lord has rejected the two kingdoms*ᵈ* he chose'?

So they despise my people and no longer regard them as a nation. 25 This is what the LORD says: 'If I have not established my covenant with day and night and the fixed laws of heaven and earth, 26 then I will reject the descendants of Jacob and David my servant and will not choose one of his sons to rule over the descendants of Abraham, Isaac and Jacob. For I will restore their fortunes*e* and have compassion on them.'"

34:1 WHILE Nebuchadnezzar king of Babylon and all his army and all the kingdoms and peoples in the empire he ruled were fighting against Jerusalem and all its surrounding towns, this word came to Jeremiah from the LORD: 2 "This is what the LORD, the God of Israel, says: Go to Zedekiah king of Judah and tell him, 'This is what the LORD says: I am about to hand this city over to the king of Babylon, and he will burn it down. 3 You will not escape from his grasp but will surely be captured and handed over to him. You will see the king of Babylon with your own eyes, and he will speak with you face to face. And you will go to Babylon.

4 "'Yet hear the promise of the LORD, O Zedekiah king of Judah. This is what the LORD says concerning you: You will not die by the sword; 5 you will die peacefully. As people made a funeral fire in honor of your fathers, the former kings who preceded you, so they will make a fire in your honor and lament, "Alas, O master!" I myself make this promise, declares the LORD.'"

6 Then Jeremiah the prophet told all this to Zedekiah king of Judah, in Jerusalem, 7 while the army of the king of Babylon was fighting against Jerusalem and the other cities of Judah that were still holding out—Lachish and Azekah. These were the only fortified cities left in Judah.

8 The word came to Jeremiah from the LORD after King Zedekiah had made a covenant with all the people in Jerusalem to proclaim freedom for the slaves. 9 Everyone was to free his Hebrew slaves, both male and female; no one was to hold a fellow Jew in bondage. 10 So all the officials and people who entered into this covenant agreed that they would free their male and female slaves and no longer hold them in bondage. They agreed, and set them free. 11 But afterward they changed their minds and took back the slaves they had freed and enslaved them again.

12 Then the word of the LORD came to Jeremiah: 13 "This is what the LORD, the God of Israel, says: I made a covenant with your forefathers when I brought them out of Egypt, out of the land of slavery. I said, 14 'Every seventh year each of you must free any fellow Hebrew who has sold himself to you. After he has served you six years, you must let him go free.'*f* Your fathers, however, did not listen to me or pay attention to me. 15 Recently you repented and did what is right in my sight: Each of you proclaimed freedom to his countrymen. You even made a covenant before me in the house that bears my Name. 16 But now you have turned around and profaned my name; each of you has taken back the male and female slaves you had set free to go where they wished. You have forced them to become your slaves again.

17 "Therefore, this is what the LORD says: You have not obeyed me; you have not proclaimed freedom for your fellow countrymen. So I now proclaim 'freedom' for you, declares the LORD—'freedom' to fall by the sword, plague and famine. I will make you abhorrent to all the kingdoms of the earth. 18 The men who have violated my covenant and have not fulfilled the terms of the covenant they made before me, I will treat like the calf they cut in two and then walked between its pieces. 19 The leaders of Judah and Jerusalem, the court officials, the priests and all the people of the land who walked between the pieces of the calf, 20 I will hand over to their enemies who seek their lives. Their dead bodies will become food for the birds of the air and the beasts of the earth.

21 "I will hand Zedekiah king of Judah

and his officials over to their enemies who seek their lives, to the army of the king of Babylon, which has withdrawn from you. 22I am going to give the order, declares the LORD, and I will bring them back to this city. They will fight against it, take it and burn it down. And I will lay waste the towns of Judah so no one can live there."

a5 Or Chaldeans b7 Or will restore the fortunes of Judah and Israel c16 Or he d24 Or families e26 Or will bring them back from captivity f14 Deut. 15:12

1 TIMOTHY 4:1-16

The Spirit clearly says that in later times some will abandon the faith and follow deceiving spirits and things taught by demons. 2Such teachings come through hypocritical liars, whose consciences have been seared as with a hot iron. 3They forbid people to marry and order them to abstain from certain foods, which God created to be received with thanksgiving by those who believe and who know the truth. 4For everything God created is good, and nothing is to be rejected if it is received with thanksgiving, 5because it is consecrated by the word of God and prayer.

6If you point these things out to the brothers, you will be a good minister of Christ Jesus, brought up in the truths of the faith and of the good teaching that you have followed. 7Have nothing to do with godless myths and old wives' tales; rather, train yourself to be godly. 8For physical training is of some value, but godliness has value for all things, holding promise for both the present life and the life to come. 9This is a trustworthy saying that deserves full acceptance 10(and for this we labor and strive), that we have put our hope in the living God, who is the Savior of all men, and especially of those who believe.

11Command and teach these things. 12Don't let anyone look down on you because you are young, but set an example for the believers in speech, in life, in love, in faith and in purity. 13Until I come, devote yourself to the public reading of Scripture, to preaching and to teaching. 14Do not neglect your gift, which was given you through a prophetic message when the body of elders laid their hands on you.

15Be diligent in these matters; give yourself wholly to them, so that everyone may see your progress. 16Watch your life and doctrine closely. Persevere in them, because if you do, you will save both yourself and your hearers.

PSALM 89:1-13
A maskila of Ethan the Ezrahite.

1 I will sing of the LORD's great love forever;
　with my mouth I will make your faithfulness known through all generations.
2 I will declare that your love stands firm forever,
　that you established your faithfulness in heaven itself.

3 You said, "I have made a covenant with my chosen one,
　I have sworn to David my servant,
4 'I will establish your line forever
　and make your throne firm through all generations.'" Selah

5 The heavens praise your wonders, O LORD,
　your faithfulness too, in the assembly of the holy ones.
6 For who in the skies above can compare with the LORD?
　Who is like the LORD among the heavenly beings?
7 In the council of the holy ones God is greatly feared;
　he is more awesome than all who surround him.
8 O LORD God Almighty, who is like you?
　You are mighty, O LORD, and your faithfulness surrounds you.

9 You rule over the surging sea;
　when its waves mount up, you still them.
10 You crushed Rahab like one of the slain;
　with your strong arm you scattered your enemies.

11 The heavens are yours, and yours also
        the earth;
    you founded the world and all that
        is in it.
12 You created the north and the south;
    Tabor and Hermon sing for joy at
        your name.
13 Your arm is endued with power;
    your hand is strong, your right
        hand exalted.

aTitle: Probably a literary or musical term

PROVERBS 25:23-24
23 As a north wind brings rain,
    so a sly tongue brings angry looks.

24 Better to live on a corner of the roof
    than share a house with a
        quarrelsome wife.

□ DAY 293

GOD SIGHTINGS

October 20

JEREMIAH 35:1–36:32
This is the word that came to Jeremiah
from the LORD during the reign of Jehoiakim son of Josiah king of Judah: 2 "Go to
the Recabite family and invite them to
come to one of the side rooms of the
house of the LORD and give them wine to
drink."

3 So I went to get Jaazaniah son of Jeremiah, the son of Habazziniah, and his
brothers and all his sons—the whole
family of the Recabites. 4 I brought them
into the house of the LORD, into the
room of the sons of Hanan son of Igda-
liah the man of God. It was next to the
room of the officials, which was over
that of Maaseiah son of Shallum the
doorkeeper. 5 Then I set bowls full of
wine and some cups before the men of
the Recabite family and said to them,
"Drink some wine."

6 But they replied, "We do not drink
wine, because our forefather Jonadab son
of Recab gave us this command: 'Neither

you nor your descendants must ever drink
wine. 7 Also you must never build houses,
sow seed or plant vineyards; you must
never have any of these things, but must always live in tents. Then you will live a long
time in the land where you are nomads.'
8 We have obeyed everything our forefather Jonadab son of Recab commanded
us. Neither we nor our wives nor our sons
and daughters have ever drunk wine 9 or
built houses to live in or had vineyards,
fields or crops. 10 We have lived in tents
and have fully obeyed everything our forefather Jonadab commanded us. 11 But
when Nebuchadnezzar king of Babylon
invaded this land, we said, 'Come, we must
go to Jerusalem to escape the Babylonian a
and Aramean armies.' So we have remained in Jerusalem."

12 Then the word of the LORD came to
Jeremiah, saying: 13 "This is what the
LORD Almighty, the God of Israel, says:
Go and tell the men of Judah and the
people of Jerusalem, 'Will you not learn
a lesson and obey my words?' declares
the LORD. 14 'Jonadab son of Recab ordered his sons not to drink wine and
this command has been kept. To this
day they do not drink wine, because
they obey their forefather's command.
But I have spoken to you again and
again, yet you have not obeyed me.
15 Again and again I sent all my servants
the prophets to you. They said, "Each of
you must turn from your wicked ways
and reform your actions; do not follow
other gods to serve them. Then you will
live in the land I have given to you and
your fathers." But you have not paid attention or listened to me. 16 The descendants of Jonadab son of Recab have
carried out the command their forefather gave them, but these people have
not obeyed me.'

17 "Therefore, this is what the LORD
God Almighty, the God of Israel, says:
'Listen! I am going to bring on Judah and
on everyone living in Jerusalem every
disaster I pronounced against them. I
spoke to them, but they did not listen; I
called to them, but they did not answer.'"

¹⁸Then Jeremiah said to the family of the Recabites, "This is what the Lord Almighty, the God of Israel, says: 'You have obeyed the command of your forefather Jonadab and have followed all his instructions and have done everything he ordered.' ¹⁹Therefore, this is what the Lord Almighty, the God of Israel, says: 'Jonadab son of Recab will never fail to have a man to serve me.'"

³⁶:¹In the fourth year of Jehoiakim son of Josiah king of Judah, this word came to Jeremiah from the Lord: ²"Take a scroll and write on it all the words I have spoken to you concerning Israel, Judah and all the other nations from the time I began speaking to you in the reign of Josiah till now. ³Perhaps when the people of Judah hear about every disaster I plan to inflict on them, each of them will turn from his wicked way; then I will forgive their wickedness and their sin."

⁴So Jeremiah called Baruch son of Neriah, and while Jeremiah dictated all the words the Lord had spoken to him, Baruch wrote them on the scroll. ⁵Then Jeremiah told Baruch, "I am restricted; I cannot go to the Lord's temple. ⁶So you go to the house of the Lord on a day of fasting and read to the people from the scroll the words of the Lord that you wrote as I dictated. Read them to all the people of Judah who come in from their towns. ⁷Perhaps they will bring their petition before the Lord, and each will turn from his wicked ways, for the anger and wrath pronounced against this people by the Lord are great."

⁸Baruch son of Neriah did everything Jeremiah the prophet told him to do; at the Lord's temple he read the words of the Lord from the scroll. ⁹In the ninth month of the fifth year of Jehoiakim son of Josiah king of Judah, a time of fasting before the Lord was proclaimed for all the people in Jerusalem and those who had come from the towns of Judah. ¹⁰From the room of Gemariah son of Shaphan the secretary, which was in the upper courtyard at the entrance of the New Gate of the temple, Baruch read to all the people at the Lord's temple the words of Jeremiah from the scroll.

¹¹When Micaiah son of Gemariah, the son of Shaphan, heard all the words of the Lord from the scroll, ¹²he went down to the secretary's room in the royal palace, where all the officials were sitting: Elishama the secretary, Delaiah son of Shemaiah, Elnathan son of Acbor, Gemariah son of Shaphan, Zedekiah son of Hananiah, and all the other officials. ¹³After Micaiah told them everything he had heard Baruch read to the people from the scroll, ¹⁴all the officials sent Jehudi son of Nethaniah, the son of Shelemiah, the son of Cushi, to say to Baruch, "Bring the scroll from which you have read to the people and come." So Baruch son of Neriah went to them with the scroll in his hand. ¹⁵They said to him, "Sit down, please, and read it to us."

So Baruch read it to them. ¹⁶When they heard all these words, they looked at each other in fear and said to Baruch, "We must report all these words to the king." ¹⁷Then they asked Baruch, "Tell us, how did you come to write all this? Did Jeremiah dictate it?"

¹⁸"Yes," Baruch replied, "he dictated all these words to me, and I wrote them in ink on the scroll."

¹⁹Then the officials said to Baruch, "You and Jeremiah, go and hide. Don't let anyone know where you are."

²⁰After they put the scroll in the room of Elishama the secretary, they went to the king in the courtyard and reported everything to him. ²¹The king sent Jehudi to get the scroll, and Jehudi brought it from the room of Elishama the secretary and read it to the king and all the officials standing beside him. ²²It was the ninth month and the king was sitting in the winter apartment, with a fire burning in the firepot in front of him. ²³Whenever Jehudi had read three or four columns of the scroll, the king cut them off with a scribe's knife and threw them into the firepot, until the entire scroll was burned in the fire. ²⁴The king and all his attendants who heard all

these words showed no fear, nor did they tear their clothes. ²⁵Even though Elnathan, Delaiah and Gemariah urged the king not to burn the scroll, he would not listen to them. ²⁶Instead, the king commanded Jerahmeel, a son of the king, Seraiah son of Azriel and Shelemiah son of Abdeel to arrest Baruch the scribe and Jeremiah the prophet. But the Lord had hidden them.

²⁷After the king burned the scroll containing the words that Baruch had written at Jeremiah's dictation, the word of the Lord came to Jeremiah: ²⁸"Take another scroll and write on it all the words that were on the first scroll, which Jehoiakim king of Judah burned up. ²⁹Also tell Jehoiakim king of Judah, 'This is what the Lord says: You burned that scroll and said, "Why did you write on it that the king of Babylon would certainly come and destroy this land and cut off both men and animals from it?" ³⁰Therefore, this is what the Lord says about Jehoiakim king of Judah: He will have no one to sit on the throne of David; his body will be thrown out and exposed to the heat by day and the frost by night. ³¹I will punish him and his children and his attendants for their wickedness; I will bring on them and those living in Jerusalem and the people of Judah every disaster I pronounced against them, because they have not listened.'"

³²So Jeremiah took another scroll and gave it to the scribe Baruch son of Neriah, and as Jeremiah dictated, Baruch wrote on it all the words of the scroll that Jehoiakim king of Judah had burned in the fire. And many similar words were added to them.

a 11 Or Chaldean

1 TIMOTHY 5:1-25

Do not rebuke an older man harshly, but exhort him as if he were your father. Treat younger men as brothers, ²older women as mothers, and younger women as sisters, with absolute purity.

³Give proper recognition to those widows who are really in need. ⁴But if a widow has children or grandchildren, these should learn first of all to put their religion into practice by caring for their own family and so repaying their parents and grandparents, for this is pleasing to God. ⁵The widow who is really in need and left all alone puts her hope in God and continues night and day to pray and to ask God for help. ⁶But the widow who lives for pleasure is dead even while she lives. ⁷Give the people these instructions, too, so that no one may be open to blame. ⁸If anyone does not provide for his relatives, and especially for his immediate family, he has denied the faith and is worse than an unbeliever.

⁹No widow may be put on the list of widows unless she is over sixty, has been faithful to her husband,*a* ¹⁰and is well known for her good deeds, such as bringing up children, showing hospitality, washing the feet of the saints, helping those in trouble and devoting herself to all kinds of good deeds.

¹¹As for younger widows, do not put them on such a list. For when their sensual desires overcome their dedication to Christ, they want to marry. ¹²Thus they bring judgment on themselves, because they have broken their first pledge. ¹³Besides, they get into the habit of being idle and going about from house to house. And not only do they become idlers, but also gossips and busybodies, saying things they ought not to. ¹⁴So I counsel younger widows to marry, to have children, to manage their homes and to give the enemy no opportunity for slander. ¹⁵Some have in fact already turned away to follow Satan.

¹⁶If any woman who is a believer has widows in her family, she should help them and not let the church be burdened with them, so that the church can help those widows who are really in need.

¹⁷The elders who direct the affairs of the church well are worthy of double honor, especially those whose work is preaching and teaching. ¹⁸For the Scripture says, "Do not muzzle the ox

while it is treading out the grain,"*b* and "The worker deserves his wages."*c* ¹⁹Do not entertain an accusation against an elder unless it is brought by two or three witnesses. ²⁰Those who sin are to be rebuked publicly, so that the others may take warning.

²¹I charge you, in the sight of God and Christ Jesus and the elect angels, to keep these instructions without partiality, and to do nothing out of favoritism.

²²Do not be hasty in the laying on of hands, and do not share in the sins of others. Keep yourself pure.

²³Stop drinking only water, and use a little wine because of your stomach and your frequent illnesses.

²⁴**The sins of some men are obvious, reaching the place of judgment ahead of them; the sins of others trail behind them. ²⁵In the same way, good deeds are obvious, and even those that are not cannot be hidden.**

a9 Or *has had but one husband*   *b18* Deut. 25:4
c18 Luke 10:7

PSALM 89:14-37

¹⁴**R**ighteousness and justice are the
　　foundation of your [the
　　Lᴏʀᴅ's] throne;
　　love and faithfulness go before
　　you.
¹⁵Blessed are those who have learned
　　to acclaim you,
　　who walk in the light of your
　　presence, O Lᴏʀᴅ.
¹⁶They rejoice in your name all day
　　long;
　　they exult in your righteousness.
¹⁷For you are their glory and strength,
　　and by your favor you exalt our
　　horn.*a*
¹⁸Indeed, our shield*b* belongs to the
　　Lᴏʀᴅ,
　　our king to the Holy One of Israel.

¹⁹Once you spoke in a vision,
　　to your faithful people you said:
　　"I have bestowed strength on a
　　warrior;
　　I have exalted a young man from
　　among the people.

²⁰I have found David my servant;
　　with my sacred oil I have anointed
　　him.
²¹My hand will sustain him;
　　surely my arm will strengthen him.
²²No enemy will subject him to tribute;
　　no wicked man will oppress him.
²³I will crush his foes before him
　　and strike down his adversaries.
²⁴My faithful love will be with him,
　　and through my name his horn*c*
　　will be exalted.
²⁵I will set his hand over the sea,
　　his right hand over the rivers.
²⁶He will call out to me, 'You are my
　　Father,
　　my God, the Rock my Savior.'
²⁷I will also appoint him my firstborn,
　　the most exalted of the kings of
　　the earth.
²⁸I will maintain my love to him
　　forever,
　　and my covenant with him will
　　never fail.
²⁹I will establish his line forever,
　　his throne as long as the heavens
　　endure.

³⁰"If his sons forsake my law
　　and do not follow my statutes,
³¹if they violate my decrees
　　and fail to keep my commands,
³²I will punish their sin with the rod,
　　their iniquity with flogging;
³³but I will not take my love from him,
　　nor will I ever betray my
　　faithfulness.
³⁴I will not violate my covenant
　　or alter what my lips have uttered.
³⁵Once for all, I have sworn by my
　　holiness—
　　and I will not lie to David—
³⁶that his line will continue forever
　　and his throne endure before me
　　like the sun;
³⁷it will be established forever like the
　　moon,
　　the faithful witness in the sky."
　　　　　　　　　　　　　　　　Selah

a17 Horn here symbolizes strong one.   *b18* Or *sovereign*
c24 Horn here symbolizes strength.

PROVERBS 25:25-27

25 Like cold water to a weary soul
   is good news from a distant land.

26 Like a muddied spring or a polluted
      well
   is a righteous man who gives way
      to the wicked.

27 It is not good to eat too much honey,
   nor is it honorable to seek one's
      own honor.

□ DAY 294

GOD SIGHTINGS

October 21

JEREMIAH 37:1-38:28

Zedekiah son of Josiah was made king of Judah by Nebuchadnezzar king of Babylon; he reigned in place of Jehoiachina son of Jehoiakim. 2Neither he nor his attendants nor the people of the land paid any attention to the words the Lord had spoken through Jeremiah the prophet.

3King Zedekiah, however, sent Jehucal son of Shelemiah with the priest Zephaniah son of Maaseiah to Jeremiah the prophet with this message: "Please pray to the Lord our God for us."

4Now Jeremiah was free to come and go among the people, for he had not yet been put in prison. 5Pharaoh's army had marched out of Egypt, and when the Babyloniansb who were besieging Jerusalem heard the report about them, they withdrew from Jerusalem.

6Then the word of the Lord came to Jeremiah the prophet: 7"This is what the Lord, the God of Israel, says: Tell the king of Judah, who sent you to inquire of me, 'Pharaoh's army, which has marched out to support you, will go back to its own land, to Egypt. 8Then the Babylonians will return and attack this city; they will capture it and burn it down.'

9"This is what the Lord says: Do not deceive yourselves, thinking, 'The Bab-

ylonians will surely leave us.' They will not! 10Even if you were to defeat the entire Babylonianc army that is attacking you and only wounded men were left in their tents, they would come out and burn this city down."

11After the Babylonian army had withdrawn from Jerusalem because of Pharaoh's army, 12Jeremiah started to leave the city to go to the territory of Benjamin to get his share of the property among the people there. 13But when he reached the Benjamin Gate, the captain of the guard, whose name was Irijah son of Shelemiah, the son of Hananiah, arrested him and said, "You are deserting to the Babylonians!"

14"That's not true!" Jeremiah said. "I am not deserting to the Babylonians." But Irijah would not listen to him; instead, he arrested Jeremiah and brought him to the officials. 15They were angry with Jeremiah and had him beaten and imprisoned in the house of Jonathan the secretary, which they had made into a prison.

16Jeremiah was put into a vaulted cell in a dungeon, where he remained a long time. 17Then King Zedekiah sent for him and had him brought to the palace, where he asked him privately, "Is there any word from the Lord?"

"Yes," Jeremiah replied, "you will be handed over to the king of Babylon."

18Then Jeremiah said to King Zedekiah, "What crime have I committed against you or your officials or this people, that you have put me in prison? 19Where are your prophets who prophesied to you, 'The king of Babylon will not attack you or this land'? 20But now, my lord the king, please listen. Let me bring my petition before you: Do not send me back to the house of Jonathan the secretary, or I will die there."

21King Zedekiah then gave orders for Jeremiah to be placed in the courtyard of the guard and given bread from the street of the bakers each day until all the bread in the city was gone. So Jeremiah remained in the courtyard of the guard.

38:1SHEPHATIAH son of Mattan, Gedaliah son of Pashhur, Jehucal*d* son of Shelemiah, and Pashhur son of Malkijah heard what Jeremiah was telling all the people when he said, **2**"This is what the LORD says: 'Whoever stays in this city will die by the sword, famine or plague, but whoever goes over to the Babylonians*e* will live. He will escape with his life; he will live.' **3**And this is what the LORD says: 'This city will certainly be handed over to the army of the king of Babylon, who will capture it.'"

4Then the officials said to the king, "This man should be put to death. He is discouraging the soldiers who are left in this city, as well as all the people, by the things he is saying to them. This man is not seeking the good of these people but their ruin."

5"He is in your hands," King Zedekiah answered. "The king can do nothing to oppose you."

6So they took Jeremiah and put him into the cistern of Malkijah, the king's son, which was in the courtyard of the guard. They lowered Jeremiah by ropes into the cistern; it had no water in it, only mud, and Jeremiah sank down into the mud.

7But Ebed-Melech, a Cushite,*f* an official*g* in the royal palace, heard that they had put Jeremiah into the cistern. While the king was sitting in the Benjamin Gate, **8**Ebed-Melech went out of the palace and said to him, **9**"My lord the king, these men have acted wickedly in all they have done to Jeremiah the prophet. They have thrown him into a cistern, where he will starve to death when there is no longer any bread in the city."

10Then the king commanded Ebed-Melech the Cushite, "Take thirty men from here with you and lift Jeremiah the prophet out of the cistern before he dies."

11So Ebed-Melech took the men with him and went to a room under the treasury in the palace. He took some old rags and worn-out clothes from there and let them down with ropes to Jeremiah in the cistern. **12**Ebed-Melech the Cushite said to Jeremiah, "Put these old rags and worn-out clothes under your arms to pad the ropes." Jeremiah did so, **13**and they pulled him up with the ropes and lifted him out of the cistern. And Jeremiah remained in the courtyard of the guard.

14Then King Zedekiah sent for Jeremiah the prophet and had him brought to the third entrance to the temple of the LORD. "I am going to ask you something," the king said to Jeremiah. "Do not hide anything from me."

15Jeremiah said to Zedekiah, "If I give you an answer, will you not kill me? Even if I did give you counsel, you would not listen to me."

16But King Zedekiah swore this oath secretly to Jeremiah: "As surely as the LORD lives, who has given us breath, I will neither kill you nor hand you over to those who are seeking your life."

17Then Jeremiah said to Zedekiah, "This is what the LORD God Almighty, the God of Israel, says: 'If you surrender to the officers of the king of Babylon, your life will be spared and this city will not be burned down; you and your family will live. **18**But if you will not surrender to the officers of the king of Babylon, this city will be handed over to the Babylonians and they will burn it down; you yourself will not escape from their hands.'"

19King Zedekiah said to Jeremiah, "I am afraid of the Jews who have gone over to the Babylonians, for the Babylonians may hand me over to them and they will mistreat me."

20"They will not hand you over," Jeremiah replied. "Obey the LORD by doing what I tell you. Then it will go well with you, and your life will be spared. **21**But if you refuse to surrender, this is what the LORD has revealed to me: **22**All the women left in the palace of the king of Judah will be brought out to the officials of the king of Babylon. Those women will say to you:

"'They misled you and overcame you—
those trusted friends of yours.
Your feet are sunk in the mud;
your friends have deserted you.'

23 "All your wives and children will be brought out to the Babylonians. You yourself will not escape from their hands but will be captured by the king of Babylon; and this city will[h] be burned down."

24 Then Zedekiah said to Jeremiah, "Do not let anyone know about this conversation, or you may die. 25 If the officials hear that I talked with you, and they come to you and say, 'Tell us what you said to the king and what the king said to you; do not hide it from us or we will kill you,' 26 then tell them, 'I was pleading with the king not to send me back to Jonathan's house to die there.'"

27 All the officials did come to Jeremiah and question him, and he told them everything the king had ordered him to say. So they said no more to him, for no one had heard his conversation with the king.

28 And Jeremiah remained in the courtyard of the guard until the day Jerusalem was captured.

1 TIMOTHY 6:1-21

All who are under the yoke of slavery should consider their masters worthy of full respect, so that God's name and our teaching may not be slandered. 2 Those who have believing masters are not to show less respect for them because they are brothers. Instead, they are to serve them even better, because those who benefit from their service are believers, and dear to them. These are the things you are to teach and urge on them.

3 If anyone teaches false doctrines and does not agree to the sound instruction of our Lord Jesus Christ and to godly teaching, 4 he is conceited and un-derstands nothing. He has an unhealthy interest in controversies and quarrels about words that result in envy, strife, malicious talk, evil suspicions 5 and constant friction between men of corrupt mind, who have been robbed of the truth and who think that godliness is a means to financial gain.

6 But godliness with contentment is great gain. 7 For we brought nothing into the world, and we can take nothing out of it. 8 But if we have food and clothing, we will be content with that. 9 People who want to get rich fall into temptation and a trap and into many foolish and harmful desires that plunge men into ruin and destruction. 10 For the love of money is a root of all kinds of evil. Some people, eager for money, have wandered from the faith and pierced themselves with many griefs.

11 But you, man of God, flee from all this, and pursue righteousness, godliness, faith, love, endurance and gentleness. 12 Fight the good fight of the faith. Take hold of the eternal life to which you were called when you made your good confession in the presence of many witnesses. 13 In the sight of God, who gives life to everything, and of Christ Jesus, who while testifying before Pontius Pilate made the good confession, I charge you 14 to keep this command without spot or blame until the appearing of our Lord Jesus Christ, 15 which God will bring about in his own time—God, the blessed and only Ruler, the King of kings and Lord of lords, 16 who alone is immortal and who lives in unapproachable light, whom no one has seen or can see. To him be honor and might forever. Amen.

17 Command those who are rich in this present world not to be arrogant nor to put their hope in wealth, which is so uncertain, but to put their hope in God, who richly provides us with everything for our enjoyment. 18 Command them to do good, to be rich in good deeds, and to be generous and willing to share. 19 In this way they will lay up treasure for them-

selves as a firm foundation for the coming age, so that they may take hold of the life that is truly life.

20Timothy, guard what has been entrusted to your care. Turn away from godless chatter and the opposing ideas of what is falsely called knowledge, 21which some have professed and in so doing have wandered from the faith.

Grace be with you.

PSALM 89:38-52

38**B**ut you have rejected, you [the Lord] have spurned,
you have been very angry with your anointed one.
39You have renounced the covenant with your servant
and have defiled his crown in the dust.
40You have broken through all his walls
and reduced his strongholds to ruins.
41All who pass by have plundered him;
he has become the scorn of his neighbors.
42You have exalted the right hand of his foes;
you have made all his enemies rejoice.
43You have turned back the edge of his sword
and have not supported him in battle.
44You have put an end to his splendor
and cast his throne to the ground.
45You have cut short the days of his youth;
you have covered him with a mantle of shame.   *Selah*

46How long, O Lord? Will you hide yourself forever?
How long will your wrath burn like fire?
47Remember how fleeting is my life.
For what futility you have created all men!
48What man can live and not see death,
or save himself from the power of the grave*a*?   *Selah*

49O Lord, where is your former great love,
which in your faithfulness you swore to David?
50Remember, Lord, how your servant has*b* been mocked,
how I bear in my heart the taunts of all the nations,
51the taunts with which your enemies have mocked, O Lord,
with which they have mocked every step of your anointed one.

52Praise be to the Lord forever!
Amen and Amen.

a48 Hebrew *Sheol*   *b50* Or *your servants have*

PROVERBS 25:28

28**L**ike a city whose walls are broken down
is a man who lacks self-control.

☐ D A Y 2 9 5

GOD SIGHTINGS

October 22

JEREMIAH 39:1–41:18

This is how Jerusalem was taken: 1In the ninth year of Zedekiah king of Judah, in the tenth month, Nebuchadnezzar king of Babylon marched against Jerusalem with his whole army and laid siege to it. 2And on the ninth day of the fourth month of Zedekiah's eleventh year, the city wall was broken through. 3Then all the officials of the king of Babylon came and took seats in the Middle Gate: Nergal-Sharezer of Samgar, Nebo-Sarsekim*a* a chief officer, Nergal-Sharezer a high official and all the other officials of the king of Babylon. 4When Zedekiah king of Judah and all the soldiers saw them, they fled; they left the city at night by way of the king's garden, through the gate between the two walls, and headed toward the Arabah.*b*

5But the Babylonian*c* army pursued them and overtook Zedekiah in the plains of Jericho. They captured him and took him to Nebuchadnezzar king of Babylon at Riblah in the land of Hamath, where he pronounced sentence on him. ⁶There at Riblah the king of Babylon slaughtered the sons of Zedekiah before his eyes and also killed all the nobles of Judah. ⁷Then he put out Zedekiah's eyes and bound him with bronze shackles to take him to Babylon.

⁸The Babylonians*ᵈ* set fire to the royal palace and the houses of the people and broke down the walls of Jerusalem. ⁹Nebuzaradan commander of the imperial guard carried into exile to Babylon the people who remained in the city, along with those who had gone over to him, and the rest of the people. ¹⁰But Nebuzaradan the commander of the guard left behind in the land of Judah some of the poor people, who owned nothing; and at that time he gave them vineyards and fields.

¹¹Now Nebuchadnezzar king of Babylon had given these orders about Jeremiah through Nebuzaradan commander of the imperial guard: ¹²"Take him and look after him; don't harm him but do for him whatever he asks." ¹³So Nebuzaradan the commander of the guard, Nebushazban a chief officer, Nergal-Sharezer a high official and all the other officers of the king of Babylon ¹⁴sent and had Jeremiah taken out of the courtyard of the guard. They turned him over to Gedaliah son of Ahikam, the son of Shaphan, to take him back to his home. So he remained among his own people.

¹⁵While Jeremiah had been confined in the courtyard of the guard, the word of the LORD came to him: ¹⁶"Go and tell Ebed-Melech the Cushite, 'This is what the LORD Almighty, the God of Israel, says: I am about to fulfill my words against this city through disaster, not prosperity. At that time they will be fulfilled before your eyes. ¹⁷But I will rescue you on that day, declares the LORD; you will not be handed over to those you fear. ¹⁸I will save you; you will not fall by the sword but will escape with your life, because you trust in me, declares the LORD.'"

⁴⁰:¹THE word came to Jeremiah from the LORD after Nebuzaradan commander of the imperial guard had released him at Ramah. He had found Jeremiah bound in chains among all the captives from Jerusalem and Judah who were being carried into exile to Babylon. ²When the commander of the guard found Jeremiah, he said to him, "The LORD your God decreed this disaster for this place. ³And now the LORD has brought it about; he has done just as he said he would. All this happened because you people sinned against the LORD and did not obey him. ⁴But today I am freeing you from the chains on your wrists. Come with me to Babylon, if you like, and I will look after you; but if you do not want to, then don't come. Look, the whole country lies before you; go wherever you please." ⁵However, before Jeremiah turned to go,*ᵉ* Nebuzaradan added, "Go back to Gedaliah son of Ahikam, the son of Shaphan, whom the king of Babylon has appointed over the towns of Judah, and live with him among the people, or go anywhere else you please."

Then the commander gave him provisions and a present and let him go. ⁶So Jeremiah went to Gedaliah son of Ahikam at Mizpah and stayed with him among the people who were left behind in the land.

⁷When all the army officers and their men who were still in the open country heard that the king of Babylon had appointed Gedaliah son of Ahikam as governor over the land and had put him in charge of the men, women and children who were the poorest in the land and who had not been carried into exile to Babylon, ⁸they came to Gedaliah at Mizpah—Ishmael son of Nethaniah, Johanan and Jonathan the sons of Kareah, Seraiah son of Tanhumeth, the sons of Ephai the Netophathite, and Jaazaniah*ᶠ* the son of the Maacathite, and their men. ⁹Gedaliah son of Ahikam, the son of Shaphan, took an oath to reassure them and their men. "Do not be afraid to serve the Babylonians,*ᵍ*" he said. "Settle down in the land and serve the king

of Babylon, and it will go well with you. ¹⁰I myself will stay at Mizpah to represent you before the Babylonians who come to us, but you are to harvest the wine, summer fruit and oil, and put them in your storage jars, and live in the towns you have taken over."

¹¹When all the Jews in Moab, Ammon, Edom and all the other countries heard that the king of Babylon had left a remnant in Judah and had appointed Gedaliah son of Ahikam, the son of Shaphan, as governor over them, ¹²they all came back to the land of Judah, to Gedaliah at Mizpah, from all the countries where they had been scattered. And they harvested an abundance of wine and summer fruit.

¹³Johanan son of Kareah and all the army officers still in the open country came to Gedaliah at Mizpah ¹⁴and said to him, "Don't you know that Baalis king of the Ammonites has sent Ishmael son of Nethaniah to take your life?" But Gedaliah son of Ahikam did not believe them.

¹⁵Then Johanan son of Kareah said privately to Gedaliah in Mizpah, "Let me go and kill Ishmael son of Nethaniah, and no one will know it. Why should he take your life and cause all the Jews who are gathered around you to be scattered and the remnant of Judah to perish?"

¹⁶But Gedaliah son of Ahikam said to Johanan son of Kareah, "Don't do such a thing! What you are saying about Ishmael is not true."

⁴¹:¹In the seventh month Ishmael son of Nethaniah, the son of Elishama, who was of royal blood and had been one of the king's officers, came with ten men to Gedaliah son of Ahikam at Mizpah. While they were eating together there, ²Ishmael son of Nethaniah and the ten men who were with him got up and struck down Gedaliah son of Ahikam, the son of Shaphan, with the sword, killing the one whom the king of Babylon had appointed as governor over the land. ³Ishmael also killed all the Jews who were with Gedaliah at Mizpah, as well as the Babylonian soldiers who were there.

⁴The day after Gedaliah's assassination, before anyone knew about it, ⁵eighty men who had shaved off their beards, torn their clothes and cut themselves came from Shechem, Shiloh and Samaria, bringing grain offerings and incense with them to the house of the LORD. ⁶Ishmael son of Nethaniah went out from Mizpah to meet them, weeping as he went. When he met them, he said, "Come to Gedaliah son of Ahikam." ⁷When they went into the city, Ishmael son of Nethaniah and the men who were with him slaughtered them and threw them into a cistern. ⁸But ten of them said to Ishmael, "Don't kill us! We have wheat and barley, oil and honey, hidden in a field." So he let them alone and did not kill them with the others. ⁹Now the cistern where he threw all the bodies of the men he had killed along with Gedaliah was the one King Asa had made as part of his defense against Baasha king of Israel. Ishmael son of Nethaniah filled it with the dead.

¹⁰Ishmael made captives of all the rest of the people who were in Mizpah—the king's daughters along with all the others who were left there, over whom Nebuzaradan commander of the imperial guard had appointed Gedaliah son of Ahikam. Ishmael son of Nethaniah took them captive and set out to cross over to the Ammonites.

¹¹When Johanan son of Kareah and all the army officers who were with him heard about all the crimes Ishmael son of Nethaniah had committed, ¹²they took all their men and went to fight Ishmael son of Nethaniah. They caught up with him near the great pool in Gibeon. ¹³When all the people Ishmael had with him saw Johanan son of Kareah and the army officers who were with him, they were glad. ¹⁴All the people Ishmael had taken captive at Mizpah turned and went over to Johanan son of Kareah. ¹⁵But Ishmael son of Nethaniah and eight of his men escaped from Johanan and fled to the Ammonites.

16Then Johanan son of Kareah and all the army officers who were with him led away all the survivors from Mizpah whom he had recovered from Ishmael son of Nethaniah after he had assassinated Gedaliah son of Ahikam: the soldiers, women, children and court officials he had brought from Gibeon. 17And they went on, stopping at Geruth Kimham near Bethlehem on their way to Egypt 18to escape the Babylonians.*d* They were afraid of them because Ishmael son of Nethaniah had killed Gedaliah son of Ahikam, whom the king of Babylon had appointed as governor over the land.

a3 Or Nergal-Sharezer, Samgar-Nebo, Sarsekim　b4 Or the Jordan Valley　c5,3 Or Chaldean　d8,18 Or Chaldeans　e5 Or Jeremiah answered　f8 Hebrew Jezaniah, a variant of Jaazaniah　g9 Or Chaldeans; also in verse 10

2 TIMOTHY 1:1-18

Paul, an apostle of Christ Jesus by the will of God, according to the promise of life that is in Christ Jesus,

2To Timothy, my dear son:

Grace, mercy and peace from God the Father and Christ Jesus our Lord.

3I thank God, whom I serve, as my forefathers did, with a clear conscience, as night and day I constantly remember you in my prayers. 4Recalling your tears, I long to see you, so that I may be filled with joy. 5I have been reminded of your sincere faith, which first lived in your grandmother Lois and in your mother Eunice and, I am persuaded, now lives in you also. 6For this reason I remind you to fan into flame the gift of God, which is in you through the laying on of my hands. 7For God did not give us a spirit of timidity, but a spirit of power, of love and of self-discipline.

8So do not be ashamed to testify about our Lord, or ashamed of me his prisoner. But join with me in suffering for the gospel, by the power of God, 9who has saved us and called us to a holy life—not because of anything we have done but because of his own purpose and grace. This grace was given us in Christ Jesus before the beginning of time, 10but it has now been revealed through the appearing of our Savior, Christ Jesus, who has destroyed death and has brought life and immortality to light through the gospel. 11And of this gospel I was appointed a herald and an apostle and a teacher. 12**That is why I am suffering as I am. Yet I am not ashamed, because I know whom I have believed, and am convinced that he is able to guard what I have entrusted to him for that day.**

13What you heard from me, keep as the pattern of sound teaching, with faith and love in Christ Jesus. 14Guard the good deposit that was entrusted to you—guard it with the help of the Holy Spirit who lives in us.

15You know that everyone in the province of Asia has deserted me, including Phygelus and Hermogenes.

16May the Lord show mercy to the household of Onesiphorus, because he often refreshed me and was not ashamed of my chains. 17On the contrary, when he was in Rome, he searched hard for me until he found me. 18May the Lord grant that he will find mercy from the Lord on that day! You know very well in how many ways he helped me in Ephesus.

PSALMS 90:1-91:16

A prayer of Moses the man of God.

1Lord, you have been our dwelling
    place
　throughout all generations.
2Before the mountains were born
　or you brought forth the earth and
    　the world,
　from everlasting to everlasting you
    　are God.

3You turn men back to dust,
　saying, "Return to dust, O sons of
    　men."
4For a thousand years in your sight
　are like a day that has just gone by,
　or like a watch in the night.

5 You sweep men away in the sleep of
  death;
   they are like the new grass of the
     morning—
6 though in the morning it springs up
  new,
   by evening it is dry and withered.

7 We are consumed by your anger
   and terrified by your indignation.
8 You have set our iniquities before
  you,
   our secret sins in the light of your
     presence.
9 All our days pass away under your
  wrath;
   we finish our years with a moan.
10 The length of our days is seventy
   years—
   or eighty, if we have the strength;
   yet their span*a* is but trouble and
     sorrow,
   for they quickly pass, and we fly
     away.

11 Who knows the power of your anger?
   For your wrath is as great as the
     fear that is due you.
12 Teach us to number our days aright,
   that we may gain a heart of
     wisdom.

13 Relent, O LORD! How long will it be?
   Have compassion on your
     servants.
14 Satisfy us in the morning with your
   unfailing love,
   that we may sing for joy and be
     glad all our days.
15 Make us glad for as many days as you
   have afflicted us,
   for as many years as we have seen
     trouble.
16 May your deeds be shown to your
   servants,
   your splendor to their children.

17 May the favor*b* of the Lord our God
   rest upon us;
   establish the work of our hands
     for us—
   yes, establish the work of our
     hands.

91:1 HE who dwells in the shelter of the
   Most High
   will rest in the shadow of the
     Almighty.*c*
2 I will say*d* of the LORD, "He is my
   refuge and my fortress,
   my God, in whom I trust."

3 Surely he will save you from the
   fowler's snare
   and from the deadly pestilence.
4 He will cover you with his feathers,
   and under his wings you will find
     refuge;
   his faithfulness will be your shield
     and rampart.
5 You will not fear the terror of night,
   nor the arrow that flies by day,
6 nor the pestilence that stalks in the
   darkness,
   nor the plague that destroys at
     midday.
7 A thousand may fall at your side,
   ten thousand at your right hand,
   but it will not come near you.
8 You will only observe with your eyes
   and see the punishment of the
     wicked.

9 If you make the Most High your
   dwelling—
   even the LORD, who is my refuge—
10 then no harm will befall you,
   no disaster will come near your tent.
11 For he will command his angels
   concerning you
   to guard you in all your ways;
12 they will lift you up in their hands,
   so that you will not strike your foot
     against a stone.
13 You will tread upon the lion and the
   cobra;
   you will trample the great lion and
     the serpent.

14 "Because he loves me," says the LORD,
   "I will rescue him;
   I will protect him, for he
     acknowledges my name.
15 He will call upon me, and I will
   answer him;
   I will be with him in trouble,
   I will deliver him and honor him.

16 With long life will I satisfy him
   and show him my salvation."

a 10 Or *yet the best of them* b 17 Or *beauty* c 1 Hebrew
Shaddai d 2 Or *He says*

PROVERBS 26:1-2

Like snow in summer or rain in
harvest,
    honor is not fitting for a fool.

2 Like a fluttering sparrow or a darting
   swallow,
    an undeserved curse does not
    come to rest.

□ DAY 296

GOD SIGHTINGS

October 23

JEREMIAH 42:1–44:23

Then all the army officers, including Johanan son of Kareah and Jezaniah*a* son of Hoshaiah, and all the people from the least to the greatest approached 2 Jeremiah the prophet and said to him, "Please hear our petition and pray to the LORD your God for this entire remnant. For as you now see, though we were once many, now only a few are left. 3 Pray that the LORD your God will tell us where we should go and what we should do."

4 "I have heard you," replied Jeremiah the prophet. "I will certainly pray to the LORD your God as you have requested; I will tell you everything the LORD says and will keep nothing back from you."

5 Then they said to Jeremiah, "May the LORD be a true and faithful witness against us if we do not act in accordance with everything the LORD your God sends you to tell us. 6 Whether it is favorable or unfavorable, we will obey the LORD our God, to whom we are sending you, so that it will go well with us, for we will obey the LORD our God."

7 Ten days later the word of the LORD came to Jeremiah. 8 So he called together Johanan son of Kareah and all the army officers who were with him and all the people from the least to the greatest. 9 He said to them, "This is what the LORD, the God of Israel, to whom you sent me to present your petition, says: 10 'If you stay in this land, I will build you up and not tear you down; I will plant you and not uproot you, for I am grieved over the disaster I have inflicted on you. 11 Do not be afraid of the king of Babylon, whom you now fear. Do not be afraid of him, declares the LORD, for I am with you and will save you and deliver you from his hands. 12 I will show you compassion so that he will have compassion on you and restore you to your land.'

13 "However, if you say, 'We will not stay in this land,' and so disobey the LORD your God, 14 and if you say, 'No, we will go and live in Egypt, where we will not see war or hear the trumpet or be hungry for bread,' 15 then hear the word of the LORD, O remnant of Judah. This is what the LORD Almighty, the God of Israel, says: 'If you are determined to go to Egypt and you do go to settle there, 16 then the sword you fear will overtake you there, and the famine you dread will follow you into Egypt, and there you will die. 17 Indeed, all who are determined to go to Egypt to settle there will die by the sword, famine and plague; not one of them will survive or escape the disaster I will bring on them.' 18 This is what the LORD Almighty, the God of Israel, says: 'As my anger and wrath have been poured out on those who lived in Jerusalem, so will my wrath be poured out on you when you go to Egypt. You will be an object of cursing and horror, of condemnation and reproach; you will never see this place again.'

19 "O remnant of Judah, the LORD has told you, 'Do not go to Egypt.' Be sure of this: I warn you today 20 that you made a fatal mistake*b* when you sent me to the LORD your God and said, 'Pray to the LORD our God for us; tell us everything he says and we will do it.' 21 I have told you today, but you still have not obeyed the LORD your God in all he sent me to tell you.

22So now, be sure of this: You will die by the sword, famine and plague in the place where you want to go to settle."

43:1WHEN Jeremiah finished telling the people all the words of the LORD their God—everything the LORD had sent him to tell them— 2Azariah son of Hoshaiah and Johanan son of Kareah and all the arrogant men said to Jeremiah, "You are lying! The LORD our God has not sent you to say, 'You must not go to Egypt to settle there.' 3But Baruch son of Neriah is inciting you against us to hand us over to the Babylonians,c so they may kill us or carry us into exile to Babylon."

4So Johanan son of Kareah and all the army officers and all the people disobeyed the LORD's command to stay in the land of Judah. 5Instead, Johanan son of Kareah and all the army officers led away all the remnant of Judah who had come back to live in the land of Judah from all the nations where they had been scattered. 6They also led away all the men, women and children and the king's daughters whom Nebuzaradan commander of the imperial guard had left with Gedaliah son of Ahikam, the son of Shaphan, and Jeremiah the prophet and Baruch son of Neriah. 7So they entered Egypt in disobedience to the LORD and went as far as Tahpanhes.

8In Tahpanhes the word of the LORD came to Jeremiah: 9"While the Jews are watching, take some large stones with you and bury them in clay in the brick pavement at the entrance to Pharaoh's palace in Tahpanhes. 10Then say to them, 'This is what the LORD Almighty, the God of Israel, says: I will send for my servant Nebuchadnezzar king of Babylon, and I will set his throne over these stones I have buried here; he will spread his royal canopy above them. 11He will come and attack Egypt, bringing death to those destined for death, captivity to those destined for captivity, and the sword to those destined for the sword. 12Hed will set fire to the temples of the gods of Egypt; he will burn their temples and take their gods captive. As a shepherd

wraps his garment around him, so will he wrap Egypt around himself and depart from there unscathed. 13There in the temple of the sune in Egypt he will demolish the sacred pillars and will burn down the temples of the gods of Egypt.'"

44:1THIS word came to Jeremiah concerning all the Jews living in Lower Egypt—in Migdol, Tahpanhes and Memphisf—and in Upper Egyptg: 2"This is what the LORD Almighty, the God of Israel, says: You saw the great disaster I brought on Jerusalem and on all the towns of Judah. Today they lie deserted and in ruins 3because of the evil they have done. They provoked me to anger by burning incense and by worshiping other gods that neither they nor you nor your fathers ever knew. 4Again and again I sent my servants the prophets, who said, 'Do not do this detestable thing that I hate!' 5But they did not listen or pay attention; they did not turn from their wickedness or stop burning incense to other gods. 6Therefore, my fierce anger was poured out; it raged against the towns of Judah and the streets of Jerusalem and made them the desolate ruins they are today.

7"Now this is what the LORD God Almighty, the God of Israel, says: Why bring such great disaster on yourselves by cutting off from Judah the men and women, the children and infants, and so leave yourselves without a remnant? 8Why provoke me to anger with what your hands have made, burning incense to other gods in Egypt, where you have come to live? You will destroy yourselves and make yourselves an object of cursing and reproach among all the nations on earth. 9Have you forgotten the wickedness committed by your fathers and by the kings and queens of Judah and the wickedness committed by you and your wives in the land of Judah and the streets of Jerusalem? 10To this day they have not humbled themselves or shown reverence, nor have they followed my law and the decrees I set before you and your fathers.

11"Therefore, this is what the LORD Almighty, the God of Israel, says: I am determined to bring disaster on you and to destroy all Judah. 12I will take away the remnant of Judah who were determined to go to Egypt to settle there. They will all perish in Egypt; they will fall by the sword or die from famine. From the least to the greatest, they will die by sword or famine. They will become an object of cursing and horror, of condemnation and reproach. 13I will punish those who live in Egypt with the sword, famine and plague, as I punished Jerusalem. 14None of the remnant of Judah who have gone to live in Egypt will escape or survive to return to the land of Judah, to which they long to return and live; none will return except a few fugitives."

15Then all the men who knew that their wives were burning incense to other gods, along with all the women who were present—a large assembly—and all the people living in Lower and Upper Egypt,*h* said to Jeremiah, 16"We will not listen to the message you have spoken to us in the name of the LORD! 17We will certainly do everything we said we would: We will burn incense to the Queen of Heaven and will pour out drink offerings to her just as we and our fathers, our kings and our officials did in the towns of Judah and in the streets of Jerusalem. At that time we had plenty of food and were well off and suffered no harm. 18But ever since we stopped burning incense to the Queen of Heaven and pouring out drink offerings to her, we have had nothing and have been perishing by sword and famine."

19The women added, "When we burned incense to the Queen of Heaven and poured out drink offerings to her, did not our husbands know that we were making cakes like her image and pouring out drink offerings to her?"

20Then Jeremiah said to all the people, both men and women, who were answering him, 21"Did not the LORD remember and think about the incense burned in the towns of Judah and the

streets of Jerusalem by you and your fathers, your kings and your officials and the people of the land? 22When the LORD could no longer endure your wicked actions and the detestable things you did, your land became an object of cursing and a desolate waste without inhabitants, as it is today. 23Because you have burned incense and have sinned against the LORD and have not obeyed him or followed his law or his decrees or his stipulations, this disaster has come upon you, as you now see."

a1 Hebrew; Septuagint (see also 43:2) *Azariah*   *b20* Or *you erred in your hearts*   *c3* Or *Chaldeans*   *d12* Or *I*   *e13* Or *in Heliopolis*   *f1* Hebrew *Noph*   *g1* Hebrew *in Pathros*   *h15* Hebrew *in Egypt and Pathros*

2 TIMOTHY 2:1-21

You then, my son, be strong in the grace that is in Christ Jesus. 2And the things you have heard me say in the presence of many witnesses entrust to reliable men who will also be qualified to teach others. 3Endure hardship with us like a good soldier of Christ Jesus. 4No one serving as a soldier gets involved in civilian affairs—he wants to please his commanding officer. 5Similarly, if anyone competes as an athlete, he does not receive the victor's crown unless he competes according to the rules. 6The hardworking farmer should be the first to receive a share of the crops. 7Reflect on what I am saying, for the Lord will give you insight into all this.

8Remember Jesus Christ, raised from the dead, descended from David. This is my gospel, 9for which I am suffering even to the point of being chained like a criminal. But God's word is not chained. 10Therefore I endure everything for the sake of the elect, that they too may obtain the salvation that is in Christ Jesus, with eternal glory.

11Here is a trustworthy saying:

If we died with him,
  we will also live with him;
12if we endure,
  we will also reign with him.
If we disown him,
  he will also disown us;

13 if we are faithless,
  he will remain faithful,
  for he cannot disown himself.

14 Keep reminding them of these things. Warn them before God against quarreling about words; it is of no value, and only ruins those who listen. 15 **Do your best to present yourself to God as one approved, a workman who does not need to be ashamed and who correctly handles the word of truth.** 16 Avoid godless chatter, because those who indulge in it will become more and more ungodly. 17 Their teaching will spread like gangrene. Among them are Hymenaeus and Philetus, 18 who have wandered away from the truth. They say that the resurrection has already taken place, and they destroy the faith of some. 19 Nevertheless, God's solid foundation stands firm, sealed with this inscription: "The Lord knows those who are his,"*a* and, "Everyone who confesses the name of the Lord must turn away from wickedness."

20 In a large house there are articles not only of gold and silver, but also of wood and clay; some are for noble purposes and some for ignoble. 21 If a man cleanses himself from the latter, he will be an instrument for noble purposes, made holy, useful to the Master and prepared to do any good work.

a 19 Num. 16:5 (see Septuagint)

PSALMS 92:1–93:5
A psalm. A song. For the Sabbath day.

1 It is good to praise the LORD
  and make music to your name, O
    Most High,
2 to proclaim your love in the morning
  and your faithfulness at night,
3 to the music of the ten-stringed lyre
  and the melody of the harp.

4 For you make me glad by your deeds,
    O LORD;
  I sing for joy at the works of your
    hands.
5 How great are your works, O LORD,
  how profound your thoughts!

6 The senseless man does not know,
  fools do not understand,
7 that though the wicked spring up
    like grass
  and all evildoers flourish,
  they will be forever destroyed.

8 But you, O LORD, are exalted forever.

9 For surely your enemies, O LORD,
  surely your enemies will perish;
  all evildoers will be scattered.
10 You have exalted my horn*a* like that
    of a wild ox;
  fine oils have been poured upon
    me.
11 My eyes have seen the defeat of my
    adversaries;
  my ears have heard the rout of my
    wicked foes.

12 The righteous will flourish like a
    palm tree,
  they will grow like a cedar of
    Lebanon;
13 planted in the house of the LORD,
  they will flourish in the courts of
    our God.
14 They will still bear fruit in old age,
  they will stay fresh and green,
15 proclaiming, "The LORD is upright;
  he is my Rock, and there is no
    wickedness in him."

93:1 THE LORD reigns, he is robed in
    majesty;
  the LORD is robed in majesty
  and is armed with strength.
  The world is firmly established;
  it cannot be moved.
2 Your throne was established long
    ago;
  you are from all eternity.

3 The seas have lifted up, O LORD,
  the seas have lifted up their
    voice;
  the seas have lifted up their
    pounding waves.
4 Mightier than the thunder of the
    great waters,
  mightier than the breakers of the
    sea—
  the LORD on high is mighty.

5 Your statutes stand firm;
   holiness adorns your house
   for endless days, O LORD.

a 10 *Horn* here symbolizes strength.

PROVERBS 26:3-5

3 **A** whip for the horse, a halter for the
   donkey,
   and a rod for the backs of fools!

4 Do not answer a fool according to his
   folly,
   or you will be like him yourself.

5 Answer a fool according to his folly,
   or he will be wise in his own eyes.

□ D A Y   2 9 7

GOD SIGHTINGS

October 24

JEREMIAH 44:24–47:7

Then Jeremiah said to all the people, including the women, "Hear the word of
the LORD, all you people of Judah in
Egypt. 25 This is what the LORD Almighty,
the God of Israel, says: You and your
wives have shown by your actions what
you promised when you said, 'We will
certainly carry out the vows we made to
burn incense and pour out drink offerings to the Queen of Heaven.'

"Go ahead then, do what you promised! Keep your vows! 26 But hear the
word of the LORD, all Jews living in
Egypt: 'I swear by my great name,' says
the LORD, 'that no one from Judah living
anywhere in Egypt will ever again invoke my name or swear, "As surely as
the Sovereign LORD lives." 27 For I am
watching over them for harm, not for
good; the Jews in Egypt will perish by
sword and famine until they are all destroyed. 28 Those who escape the sword
and return to the land of Judah from
Egypt will be very few. Then the whole
remnant of Judah who came to live in

Egypt will know whose word will
stand—mine or theirs.

29 "'This will be the sign to you that I
will punish you in this place,' declares
the LORD, 'so that you will know that my
threats of harm against you will surely
stand.' 30 This is what the LORD says: 'I
am going to hand Pharaoh Hophra king
of Egypt over to his enemies who seek
his life, just as I handed Zedekiah king
of Judah over to Nebuchadnezzar king
of Babylon, the enemy who was seeking
his life.'"

45:1 THIS is what Jeremiah the prophet
told Baruch son of Neriah in the fourth
year of Jehoiakim son of Josiah king of
Judah, after Baruch had written on a
scroll the words Jeremiah was then dic-
tating: 2 "This is what the LORD, the God
of Israel, says to you, Baruch: 3 You said,
'Woe to me! The LORD has added sorrow
to my pain; I am worn out with groaning
and find no rest.'"

4 The LORD said, "Say this to him:
'This is what the LORD says: I will overthrow what I have built and uproot what
I have planted, throughout the land.
5 Should you then seek great things for
yourself? Seek them not. For I will bring
disaster on all people, declares the LORD,
but wherever you go I will let you escape
with your life.'"

46:1 THIS is the word of the LORD that
came to Jeremiah the prophet concerning the nations:

2 Concerning Egypt:

This is the message against the army
of Pharaoh Neco king of Egypt, which
was defeated at Carchemish on the Euphrates River by Nebuchadnezzar king
of Babylon in the fourth year of Jehoiakim son of Josiah king of Judah:

3 "Prepare your shields, both large and
   small,
   and march out for battle!
4 Harness the horses,
   mount the steeds!
Take your positions
   with helmets on!

Polish your spears,
   put on your armor!
5 What do I see?
   They are terrified,
 they are retreating,
   their warriors are defeated.
 They flee in haste
   without looking back,
   and there is terror on every side,"
                   declares the Lord.
6 "The swift cannot flee
   nor the strong escape.
 In the north by the River Euphrates
   they stumble and fall.

7 "Who is this that rises like the Nile,
   like rivers of surging waters?
8 Egypt rises like the Nile,
   like rivers of surging waters.
 She says, 'I will rise and cover the
       earth;
   I will destroy cities and their
       people.'
9 Charge, O horses!
   Drive furiously, O charioteers!
 March on, O warriors—
   men of Cusha and Put who carry
       shields,
   men of Lydia who draw the bow.
10 But that day belongs to the Lord, the
       Lord Almighty—
   a day of vengeance, for vengeance
       on his foes.
 The sword will devour till it is
       satisfied,
   till it has quenched its thirst with
       blood.
 For the Lord, the Lord Almighty, will
       offer sacrifice
   in the land of the north by the
       River Euphrates.

11 "Go up to Gilead and get balm,
   O Virgin Daughter of Egypt.
 But you multiply remedies in vain;
   there is no healing for you.
12 The nations will hear of your
       shame;
   your cries will fill the earth.
 One warrior will stumble over
       another;
   both will fall down together."

13 This is the message the Lord spoke
to Jeremiah the prophet about the coming of Nebuchadnezzar king of Babylon
to attack Egypt:

14 "Announce this in Egypt, and
       proclaim it in Migdol;
   proclaim it also in Memphisb and
       Tahpanhes:
 'Take your positions and get ready,
   for the sword devours those
       around you.'
15 Why will your warriors be laid low?
   They cannot stand, for the Lord
       will push them down.
16 They will stumble repeatedly;
   they will fall over each other.
 They will say, 'Get up, let us go back
   to our own people and our native
       lands,
   away from the sword of the
       oppressor.'
17 There they will exclaim,
   'Pharaoh king of Egypt is only a
       loud noise;
   he has missed his opportunity.'

18 "As surely as I live," declares the
       King,
   whose name is the Lord Almighty,
 "one will come who is like Tabor
       among the mountains,
   like Carmel by the sea.
19 Pack your belongings for exile,
   you who live in Egypt,
 for Memphis will be laid waste
   and lie in ruins without
       inhabitant.

20 "Egypt is a beautiful heifer,
   but a gadfly is coming
   against her from the north.
21 The mercenaries in her ranks
   are like fattened calves.
 They too will turn and flee together,
   they will not stand their ground,
 for the day of disaster is coming
       upon them,
   the time for them to be punished.
22 Egypt will hiss like a fleeing serpent
   as the enemy advances in force;
 they will come against her with axes,
   like men who cut down trees.

23 They will chop down her forest,"
                    declares the LORD,
    "dense though it be.
They are more numerous than
        locusts,
    they cannot be counted.
24 The Daughter of Egypt will be put to
        shame,
        handed over to the people of the
            north."

25 The LORD Almighty, the God of Israel, says: "I am about to bring punishment on Amon god of Thebes,c on
Pharaoh, on Egypt and her gods and her
kings, and on those who rely on Pharaoh. 26 I will hand them over to those
who seek their lives, to Nebuchadnezzar king of Babylon and his officers.
Later, however, Egypt will be inhabited
as in times past," declares the LORD.

27 "Do not fear, O Jacob my servant;
    do not be dismayed, O Israel.
I will surely save you out of a distant
        place,
        your descendants from the land of
            their exile.
Jacob will again have peace and
        security,
    and no one will make him afraid.
28 Do not fear, O Jacob my servant,
    for I am with you," declares the
        LORD.
    "Though I completely destroy all the
        nations
        among which I scatter you,
    I will not completely destroy you.
I will discipline you but only with
        justice;
    I will not let you go entirely
        unpunished."

47:1 THIS is the word of the LORD that
came to Jeremiah the prophet concerning the Philistines before Pharaoh attacked Gaza:

2 This is what the LORD says:

"See how the waters are rising in the
        north;
    they will become an overflowing
        torrent.

They will overflow the land and
        everything in it,
    the towns and those who live in
        them.
The people will cry out;
    all who dwell in the land will wail
3 at the sound of the hoofs of galloping
        steeds,
    at the noise of enemy chariots
    and the rumble of their wheels.
Fathers will not turn to help their
        children;
    their hands will hang limp.
4 For the day has come
    to destroy all the Philistines
and to cut off all survivors
    who could help Tyre and Sidon.
The LORD is about to destroy the
        Philistines,
    the remnant from the coasts of
        Caphtor.d
5 Gaza will shave her head in
        mourning;
    Ashkelon will be silenced.
O remnant on the plain,
    how long will you cut yourselves?

6 "'Ah, sword of the LORD,' ⌐you cry,⌐
    'how long till you rest?
Return to your scabbard;
    cease and be still.'
7 But how can it rest
    when the LORD has commanded it,
when he has ordered it
    to attack Ashkelon and the coast?"

a9 That is, the upper Nile region   b14 Hebrew Noph; also
in verse 19   c25 Hebrew No   d4 That is, Crete

2 TIMOTHY 2:22–3:17

Flee the evil desires of youth, and pursue righteousness, faith, love and
peace, along with those who call on the
Lord out of a pure heart. 23 Don't have
anything to do with foolish and stupid
arguments, because you know they produce quarrels. 24 And the Lord's servant
must not quarrel; instead, he must be
kind to everyone, able to teach, not re-
sentful. 25 Those who oppose him he
must gently instruct, in the hope that
God will grant them repentance leading
them to a knowledge of the truth, 26 and

that they will come to their senses and escape from the trap of the devil, who has taken them captive to do his will.

3:1But mark this: There will be terrible times in the last days. 2People will be lovers of themselves, lovers of money, boastful, proud, abusive, disobedient to their parents, ungrateful, unholy, 3without love, unforgiving, slanderous, without self-control, brutal, not lovers of the good, 4treacherous, rash, conceited, lovers of pleasure rather than lovers of God—5having a form of godliness but denying its power. Have nothing to do with them.

6They are the kind who worm their way into homes and gain control over weak-willed women, who are loaded down with sins and are swayed by all kinds of evil desires, 7always learning but never able to acknowledge the truth. 8Just as Jannes and Jambres opposed Moses, so also these men oppose the truth—men of depraved minds, who, as far as the faith is concerned, are rejected. 9But they will not get very far because, as in the case of those men, their folly will be clear to everyone.

10You, however, know all about my teaching, my way of life, my purpose, faith, patience, love, endurance, 11persecutions, sufferings—what kinds of things happened to me in Antioch, Iconium and Lystra, the persecutions I endured. Yet the Lord rescued me from all of them. 12In fact, everyone who wants to live a godly life in Christ Jesus will be persecuted, 13while evil men and impostors will go from bad to worse, deceiving and being deceived. 14But as for you, continue in what you have learned and have become convinced of, because you know those from whom you learned it, 15and how from infancy you have known the holy Scriptures, which are able to make you wise for salvation through faith in Christ Jesus. 16**All Scripture is God-breathed and is useful for teaching, rebuking, correcting and training in righteousness, 17so that the man of God may be thoroughly equipped for every good work.**

PSALM 94:1-23

1 ● LORD, the God who avenges,
   O God who avenges, shine forth.
2 Rise up, O Judge of the earth;
   pay back to the proud what they
      deserve.
3 How long will the wicked, O LORD,
   how long will the wicked be
      jubilant?

4 They pour out arrogant words;
   all the evildoers are full of
      boasting.
5 They crush your people, O LORD;
   they oppress your inheritance.
6 They slay the widow and the alien;
   they murder the fatherless.
7 They say, "The LORD does not see;
   the God of Jacob pays no heed."

8 Take heed, you senseless ones among
      the people;
   you fools, when will you become
      wise?
9 Does he who implanted the ear not
      hear?
   Does he who formed the eye not
      see?
10 Does he who disciplines nations not
      punish?
   Does he who teaches man lack
      knowledge?
11 The LORD knows the thoughts of man;
   he knows that they are futile.

12 Blessed is the man you discipline,
      O LORD,
   the man you teach from your law;
13 you grant him relief from days of
      trouble,
   till a pit is dug for the wicked.
14 For the LORD will not reject his people;
   he will never forsake his
      inheritance.
15 Judgment will again be founded on
      righteousness,
   and all the upright in heart will
      follow it.

16 Who will rise up for me against the
      wicked?
   Who will take a stand for me
      against evildoers?

17 Unless the LORD had given me help,
    I would soon have dwelt in the
        silence of death.
18 When I said, "My foot is slipping,"
    your love, O LORD, supported me.
19 When anxiety was great within me,
    your consolation brought joy to
        my soul.

20 Can a corrupt throne be allied with
        you—
    one that brings on misery by its
        decrees?
21 They band together against the
        righteous
    and condemn the innocent to
        death.
22 But the LORD has become my fortress,
    and my God the rock in whom I
        take refuge.
23 He will repay them for their sins
    and destroy them for their
        wickedness;
    the LORD our God will destroy them.

PROVERBS 26:6-8

6 Like cutting off one's feet or
        drinking violence
    is the sending of a message by the
        hand of a fool.

7 Like a lame man's legs that hang limp
    is a proverb in the mouth of a fool.

8 Like tying a stone in a sling
    is the giving of honor to a fool.

□ DAY 298

GOD SIGHTINGS

October 25

JEREMIAH 48:1–49:22
Concerning Moab:

This is what the LORD Almighty, the
God of Israel, says:

"Woe to Nebo, for it will be ruined.
    Kiriathaim will be disgraced and
        captured;

the stronghold[a] will be disgraced
    and shattered.
2 Moab will be praised no more;
    in Heshbon[b] men will plot her
        downfall:
    'Come, let us put an end to that
        nation.'
You too, O Madmen,[c] will be
        silenced;
    the sword will pursue you.
3 Listen to the cries from Horonaim,
    cries of great havoc and
        destruction.
4 Moab will be broken;
    her little ones will cry out.[d]
5 They go up the way to Luhith,
    weeping bitterly as they go;
on the road down to Horonaim
    anguished cries over the
        destruction are heard.
6 Flee! Run for your lives;
    become like a bush[e] in the desert.
7 Since you trust in your deeds and
        riches,
    you too will be taken captive,
and Chemosh will go into exile,
    together with his priests and
        officials.
8 The destroyer will come against
        every town,
    and not a town will escape.
The valley will be ruined
    and the plateau destroyed,
    because the LORD has spoken.
9 Put salt on Moab,
    for she will be laid waste[f];
her towns will become desolate,
    with no one to live in them.

10 "A curse on him who is lax in doing
        the LORD's work!
    A curse on him who keeps his
        sword from bloodshed!

11 "Moab has been at rest from youth,
    like wine left on its dregs,
not poured from one jar to another—
    she has not gone into exile.
So she tastes as she did,
    and her aroma is unchanged.
12 But days are coming,"
    declares the LORD,

"when I will send men who pour
        from jars,
    and they will pour her out;
they will empty her jars
    and smash her jugs.
¹³ Then Moab will be ashamed of
        Chemosh,
    as the house of Israel was ashamed
        when they trusted in Bethel.

¹⁴ "How can you say, 'We are warriors,
        men valiant in battle'?
¹⁵ Moab will be destroyed and her
        towns invaded;
    her finest young men will go down
        in the slaughter,"
    declares the King, whose name is
        the LORD Almighty.
¹⁶ "The fall of Moab is at hand;
    her calamity will come quickly.
¹⁷ Mourn for her, all who live around
        her,
    all who know her fame;
    say, 'How broken is the mighty scepter,
        how broken the glorious staff!'

¹⁸ "Come down from your glory
    and sit on the parched ground,
        O inhabitants of the Daughter of
            Dibon,
    for he who destroys Moab
        will come up against you
    and ruin your fortified cities.
¹⁹ Stand by the road and watch,
    you who live in Aroer.
Ask the man fleeing and the woman
        escaping,
    ask them, 'What has happened?'
²⁰ Moab is disgraced, for she is
        shattered.
    Wail and cry out!
Announce by the Arnon
    that Moab is destroyed.
²¹ Judgment has come to the plateau—
    to Holon, Jahzah and Mephaath,
²²   to Dibon, Nebo and Beth
        Diblathaim,
²³   to Kiriathaim, Beth Gamul and
        Beth Meon,
²⁴   to Kerioth and Bozrah—
    to all the towns of Moab, far and
        near.

²⁵ Moab's hornᵍ is cut off;
    her arm is broken,"
                    declares the LORD.

²⁶ "Make her drunk,
    for she has defied the LORD.
Let Moab wallow in her vomit;
    let her be an object of ridicule.
²⁷ Was not Israel the object of your
        ridicule?
    Was she caught among thieves,
that you shake your head in scorn
    whenever you speak of her?
²⁸ Abandon your towns and dwell
        among the rocks,
    you who live in Moab.
Be like a dove that makes its nest
    at the mouth of a cave.

²⁹ "We have heard of Moab's pride—
    her overweening pride and
        conceit,
her pride and arrogance
    and the haughtiness of her heart.
³⁰ I know her insolence but it is futile,"
                    declares the LORD,
    "and her boasts accomplish
        nothing.
³¹ Therefore I wail over Moab,
    for all Moab I cry out,
    I moan for the men of Kir
        Hareseth.
³² I weep for you, as Jazer weeps,
    O vines of Sibmah.
Your branches spread as far as the
        sea;
    they reached as far as the sea of
        Jazer.
The destroyer has fallen
    on your ripened fruit and grapes.
³³ Joy and gladness are gone
    from the orchards and fields of
        Moab.
I have stopped the flow of wine from
        the presses;
    no one treads them with shouts
        of joy.
Although there are shouts,
    they are not shouts of joy.

³⁴ "The sound of their cry rises
    from Heshbon to Elealeh and
        Jahaz,

from Zoar as far as Horonaim and
Eglath Shelishiyah,
for even the waters of Nimrim are
dried up.
35 In Moab I will put an end
to those who make offerings on
the high places
and burn incense to their gods,"
declares the LORD.
36 "So my heart laments for Moab like a
flute;
it laments like a flute for the men
of Kir Hareseth.
The wealth they acquired is gone.
37 Every head is shaved
and every beard cut off;
every hand is slashed
and every waist is covered with
sackcloth.
38 On all the roofs in Moab
and in the public squares
there is nothing but mourning,
for I have broken Moab
like a jar that no one wants,"
declares the LORD.
39 "How shattered she is! How they
wail!
How Moab turns her back in shame!
Moab has become an object of
ridicule,
an object of horror to all those
around her."

40 This is what the LORD says:

"Look! An eagle is swooping down,
spreading its wings over Moab.
41 Kerioth h will be captured
and the strongholds taken.
In that day the hearts of Moab's
warriors
will be like the heart of a woman
in labor.
42 Moab will be destroyed as a nation
because she defied the LORD.
43 Terror and pit and snare await you,
O people of Moab,"
declares the LORD.
44 "Whoever flees from the terror
will fall into a pit,
whoever climbs out of the pit
will be caught in a snare;

for I will bring upon Moab
the year of her punishment,"
declares the LORD.
45 "In the shadow of Heshbon
the fugitives stand helpless,
for a fire has gone out from
Heshbon,
a blaze from the midst of Sihon;
it burns the foreheads of Moab,
the skulls of the noisy boasters.
46 Woe to you, O Moab!
The people of Chemosh are
destroyed;
your sons are taken into exile
and your daughters into captivity.

47 "Yet I will restore the fortunes of
Moab
in days to come,"
declares the LORD.

Here ends the judgment on Moab.

49:1 CONCERNING the Ammonites:

This is what the LORD says:

"Has Israel no sons?
Has she no heirs?
Why then has Molech j taken
possession of Gad?
Why do his people live in its towns?
2 But the days are coming,"
declares the LORD,
"when I will sound the battle cry
against Rabbah of the Ammonites;
it will become a mound of ruins,
and its surrounding villages will be
set on fire.
Then Israel will drive out
those who drove her out,"
says the LORD.
3 "Wail, O Heshbon, for Ai is
destroyed!
Cry out, O inhabitants of Rabbah!
Put on sackcloth and mourn;
rush here and there inside the
walls,
for Molech will go into exile,
together with his priests and
officials.
4 Why do you boast of your valleys,
boast of your valleys so fruitful?

O unfaithful daughter,
　you trust in your riches and say,
　'Who will attack me?'
⁵I will bring terror on you
　from all those around you,"
　　　　　　　declares the Lord,
　　　　　　　the LORD Almighty.
"Every one of you will be driven
　away,
　and no one will gather the
　fugitives.

⁶"Yet afterward, I will restore the
　fortunes of the Ammonites,"
　　　　　　　declares the LORD.

⁷Concerning Edom:

This is what the LORD Almighty says:

"Is there no longer wisdom in
　Teman?
　Has counsel perished from the
　prudent?
　Has their wisdom decayed?
⁸Turn and flee, hide in deep caves,
　you who live in Dedan,
　for I will bring disaster on Esau
　at the time I punish him.
⁹If grape pickers came to you,
　would they not leave a few grapes?
　If thieves came during the night,
　would they not steal only as much
　as they wanted?
¹⁰But I will strip Esau bare;
　I will uncover his hiding places,
　so that he cannot conceal himself.
　His children, relatives and neighbors
　will perish,
　and he will be no more.
¹¹Leave your orphans; I will protect
　their lives.
　Your widows too can trust in me."

¹²This is what the LORD says: "If those
who do not deserve to drink the cup
must drink it, why should you go unpunished? You will not go unpunished,
but must drink it. ¹³I swear by myself,"
declares the LORD, "that Bozrah will become a ruin and an object of horror, of
reproach and of cursing; and all its
towns will be in ruins forever."

¹⁴I have heard a message from the
　LORD:
　An envoy was sent to the nations
　to say,
　"Assemble yourselves to attack it!
　Rise up for battle!"

¹⁵"Now I will make you small among
　the nations,
　despised among men.
¹⁶The terror you inspire
　and the pride of your heart have
　deceived you,
　you who live in the clefts of the
　rocks,
　who occupy the heights of the hill.
　Though you build your nest as high
　as the eagle's,
　from there I will bring you down,"
　　　　　　　declares the LORD.
¹⁷"Edom will become an object of
　horror;
　all who pass by will be appalled
　and will scoff
　because of all its wounds.
¹⁸As Sodom and Gomorrah were
　overthrown,
　along with their neighboring
　towns,"
　　　　　　　says the LORD,
"so no one will live there;
　no man will dwell in it.

¹⁹"Like a lion coming up from Jordan's
　thickets
　to a rich pastureland,
　I will chase Edom from its land in an
　instant.
　Who is the chosen one I will
　appoint for this?
　Who is like me and who can
　challenge me?
　And what shepherd can stand
　against me?"
²⁰Therefore, hear what the LORD has
　planned against Edom,
　what he has purposed against
　those who live in Teman:
The young of the flock will be
　dragged away;
　he will completely destroy their
　pasture because of them.

21 At the sound of their fall the earth
    will tremble;
  their cry will resound to the Red
    Sea.*j*
22 Look! An eagle will soar and swoop
    down,
  spreading its wings over Bozrah.
  In that day the hearts of Edom's
    warriors
  will be like the heart of a woman
    in labor.

*a1 Or / Misgab   b2 The Hebrew for Heshbon sounds like the
Hebrew for plot.   c2 The name of the Moabite town
Madmen sounds like the Hebrew for be silenced.
d4 Hebrew; Septuagint / proclaim it to Zoar   e6 Or like Aroer
f9 Or Give wings to Moab, / for she will fly away   g25 Horn
here symbolizes strength.   h41 Or The cities   i1 Or their
king; Hebrew malcam; also in verse 3   j21 Hebrew Yam
Suph; that is, Sea of Reeds*

2 TIMOTHY 4:1-22

In the presence of God and of Christ
Jesus, who will judge the living and the
dead, and in view of his appearing and
his kingdom, I give you this charge:
²**Preach the Word; be prepared in season and out of season; correct, rebuke
and encourage—with great patience
and careful instruction.** ³For the time
will come when men will not put up with
sound doctrine. Instead, to suit their own
desires, they will gather around them a
great number of teachers to say what
their itching ears want to hear. ⁴They will
turn their ears away from the truth and
turn aside to myths. ⁵But you, keep your
head in all situations, endure hardship,
do the work of an evangelist, discharge
all the duties of your ministry.

⁶For I am already being poured out
like a drink offering, and the time has
come for my departure. ⁷I have fought
the good fight, I have finished the race, I
have kept the faith. ⁸Now there is in
store for me the crown of righteousness,
which the Lord, the righteous Judge, will
award to me on that day—and not only
to me, but also to all who have longed for
his appearing.

⁹Do your best to come to me quickly,
¹⁰for Demas, because he loved this
world, has deserted me and has gone to
Thessalonica. Crescens has gone to Galatia, and Titus to Dalmatia. ¹¹Only Luke

is with me. Get Mark and bring him with
you, because he is helpful to me in my
ministry. ¹²I sent Tychicus to Ephesus.
¹³When you come, bring the cloak that I
left with Carpus at Troas, and my scrolls,
especially the parchments.

¹⁴Alexander the metalworker did me a
great deal of harm. The Lord will repay
him for what he has done. ¹⁵You too
should be on your guard against him, because he strongly opposed our message.

¹⁶At my first defense, no one came to
my support, but everyone deserted me.
May it not be held against them. ¹⁷But
the Lord stood at my side and gave me
strength, so that through me the message
might be fully proclaimed and all the
Gentiles might hear it. And I was delivered from the lion's mouth. ¹⁸The Lord
will rescue me from every evil attack and
will bring me safely to his heavenly kingdom. To him be glory for ever and ever.
Amen.

¹⁹Greet Priscilla*a* and Aquila and the
household of Onesiphorus. ²⁰Erastus
stayed in Corinth, and I left Trophimus
sick in Miletus. ²¹Do your best to get
here before winter. Eubulus greets you,
and so do Pudens, Linus, Claudia and all
the brothers.

²²The Lord be with your spirit. Grace
be with you.

a19 Greek Prisca, a variant of Priscilla

PSALMS 95:1-96:13

¹ **C**ome, let us sing for joy to the LORD;
    let us shout aloud to the Rock of
      our salvation.
² Let us come before him with
      thanksgiving
    and extol him with music and song.

³ For the LORD is the great God,
    the great King above all gods.
⁴ In his hand are the depths of the earth,
    and the mountain peaks belong to
      him.
⁵ The sea is his, for he made it,
    and his hands formed the dry land.

⁶ Come, let us bow down in worship,
    let us kneel before the LORD our
      Maker;

7 for he is our God
and we are the people of his pasture,
the flock under his care.

Today, if you hear his voice,
8   do not harden your hearts as you
did at Meribah,*a*
as you did that day at Massah*b* in
the desert,
9 where your fathers tested and tried
me,
though they had seen what I did.
10 For forty years I was angry with that
generation;
I said, "They are a people whose
hearts go astray,
and they have not known my
ways."
11 So I declared on oath in my anger,
"They shall never enter my rest."

96:1 SING to the LORD a new song;
sing to the LORD, all the earth.
2 Sing to the LORD, praise his name;
proclaim his salvation day after
day.
3 Declare his glory among the nations,
his marvelous deeds among all
peoples.
4 For great is the LORD and most
worthy of praise;
he is to be feared above all gods.
5 For all the gods of the nations are
idols,
but the LORD made the heavens.
6 Splendor and majesty are before him;
strength and glory are in his
sanctuary.

7 Ascribe to the LORD, O families of
nations,
ascribe to the LORD glory and
strength.
8 Ascribe to the LORD the glory due his
name;
bring an offering and come into
his courts.
9 Worship the LORD in the splendor of
his*c* holiness;
tremble before him, all the earth.

10 Say among the nations, "The LORD
reigns."

The world is firmly established, it
cannot be moved;
he will judge the peoples with
equity.
11 Let the heavens rejoice, let the earth
be glad;
let the sea resound, and all that is
in it;
12   let the fields be jubilant, and
everything in them.
Then all the trees of the forest will
sing for joy;
13   they will sing before the LORD, for
he comes,
he comes to judge the earth.
He will judge the world in
righteousness
and the peoples in his truth.

a8 Meribah means *quarreling.*   *b8 Massah* means *testing.*
c9 Or LORD *with the splendor of*

PROVERBS 26:9-12

9 Like a thornbush in a drunkard's
hand
is a proverb in the mouth of a fool.

10 Like an archer who wounds at random
is he who hires a fool or any
passer-by.

11 As a dog returns to its vomit,
so a fool repeats his folly.

12 Do you see a man wise in his own
eyes?
There is more hope for a fool than
for him.

☐ D A Y   2 9 9

October 26

JEREMIAH 49:23–50:46
Concerning Damascus:

"Hamath and Arpad are dismayed,
for they have heard bad news.
They are disheartened,
troubled like*a* the restless sea.

²⁴Damascus has become feeble,
　　she has turned to flee
　　and panic has gripped her;
　anguish and pain have seized her,
　　pain like that of a woman in labor.
²⁵Why has the city of renown not been
　　abandoned,
　　the town in which I delight?
²⁶Surely, her young men will fall in the
　　streets;
　　all her soldiers will be silenced in
　　　that day,"
　　　　　　declares the LORD Almighty.
²⁷"I will set fire to the walls of
　　Damascus;
　　it will consume the fortresses of
　　Ben-Hadad."

²⁸Concerning Kedar and the kingdoms of Hazor, which Nebuchadnezzar
king of Babylon attacked:

This is what the LORD says:

"Arise, and attack Kedar
　　and destroy the people of the East.
²⁹Their tents and their flocks will be
　　taken;
　　their shelters will be carried off
　　with all their goods and camels.
Men will shout to them,
　　'Terror on every side!'

³⁰"Flee quickly away!
　　Stay in deep caves, you who live in
　　Hazor,"
　　　　　　declares the LORD.
"Nebuchadnezzar king of Babylon
　　has plotted against you;
　　he has devised a plan against you.

³¹"Arise and attack a nation at ease,
　　which lives in confidence,"
　　　　　　declares the LORD,
　"a nation that has neither gates nor
　　bars;
　　its people live alone.
³²Their camels will become plunder,
　　and their large herds will be booty.
I will scatter to the winds those who
　　are in distant places[b]
　　and will bring disaster on them
　　from every side,"
　　　　　　declares the LORD.

³³"Hazor will become a haunt of
　　jackals,
　　a desolate place forever.
No one will live there;
　　no man will dwell in it."

³⁴This is the word of the LORD that
came to Jeremiah the prophet concerning Elam, early in the reign of Zedekiah
king of Judah:

³⁵This is what the LORD Almighty
says:

"See, I will break the bow of Elam,
　　the mainstay of their might.
³⁶I will bring against Elam the four
　　winds
　　from the four quarters of the
　　　heavens;
I will scatter them to the four winds,
　　and there will not be a nation
　　where Elam's exiles do not go.
³⁷I will shatter Elam before their foes,
　　before those who seek their lives;
I will bring disaster upon them,
　　even my fierce anger,"
　　　　　　declares the LORD.
"I will pursue them with the sword
　　until I have made an end of them.
³⁸I will set my throne in Elam
　　and destroy her king and
　　officials,"
　　　　　　declares the LORD.

³⁹"Yet I will restore the fortunes of
　　Elam
　　in days to come,"
　　　　　　declares the LORD.

⁵⁰:¹THIS is the word the LORD spoke
through Jeremiah the prophet concerning Babylon and the land of the Babylonians[c]:

²"Announce and proclaim among the
　　nations,
　　lift up a banner and proclaim it;
　　keep nothing back, but say,
'Babylon will be captured;
　　Bel will be put to shame,
　　Marduk filled with terror.
Her images will be put to shame
　　and her idols filled with terror.'

³A nation from the north will attack
          her
     and lay waste her land.
No one will live in it;
     both men and animals will flee
          away.

⁴"In those days, at that time,"
     declares the LORD,
"the people of Israel and the people
          of Judah together
will go in tears to seek the LORD
          their God.
⁵They will ask the way to Zion
     and turn their faces toward it.
They will come and bind themselves
          to the LORD
     in an everlasting covenant
     that will not be forgotten.

⁶"My people have been lost sheep;
     their shepherds have led them
          astray
     and caused them to roam on the
          mountains.
They wandered over mountain and
          hill
     and forgot their own resting
          place.
⁷Whoever found them devoured
          them;
     their enemies said, 'We are not
          guilty,
for they sinned against the LORD,
          their true pasture,
     the LORD, the hope of their
          fathers.'

⁸"Flee out of Babylon;
     leave the land of the Babylonians,
     and be like the goats that lead the
          flock.
⁹For I will stir up and bring against
          Babylon
     an alliance of great nations from
          the land of the north.
They will take up their positions
          against her,
     and from the north she will be
          captured.
Their arrows will be like skilled
          warriors
     who do not return empty-handed.

¹⁰So Babylonia^d will be plundered;
     all who plunder her will have their
          fill,"

                         declares the LORD.

¹¹"Because you rejoice and are glad,
     you who pillage my inheritance,
because you frolic like a heifer
          threshing grain
     and neigh like stallions,
¹²your mother will be greatly ashamed;
     she who gave you birth will be
          disgraced.
She will be the least of the nations—
     a wilderness, a dry land, a desert.
¹³Because of the LORD's anger she will
          not be inhabited
     but will be completely desolate.
All who pass Babylon will be
          horrified and scoff
     because of all her wounds.

¹⁴"Take up your positions around
          Babylon,
     all you who draw the bow.
Shoot at her! Spare no arrows,
     for she has sinned against the
          LORD.
¹⁵Shout against her on every side!
     She surrenders, her towers fall,
     her walls are torn down.
Since this is the vengeance of the
          LORD,
     take vengeance on her;
     do to her as she has done to
          others.
¹⁶Cut off from Babylon the sower,
     and the reaper with his sickle at
          harvest.
Because of the sword of the
          oppressor
     let everyone return to his own
          people,
     let everyone flee to his own land.

¹⁷"Israel is a scattered flock
     that lions have chased away.
The first to devour him
     was the king of Assyria;
the last to crush his bones
     was Nebuchadnezzar king of
          Babylon."

¹⁸Therefore this is what the Lord Almighty, the God of Israel, says:

"I will punish the king of Babylon
     and his land
  as I punished the king of Assyria.
¹⁹But I will bring Israel back to his own
          pasture
  and he will graze on Carmel and
          Bashan;
  his appetite will be satisfied
     on the hills of Ephraim and
          Gilead.
²⁰In those days, at that time,"
     declares the Lord,
  "search will be made for Israel's
          guilt,
     but there will be none,
  and for the sins of Judah,
     but none will be found,
  for I will forgive the remnant I
          spare.

²¹"Attack the land of Merathaim
     and those who live in Pekod.
  Pursue, kill and completely destroy^e
          them,"
                    declares the Lord.
     "Do everything I have commanded
          you.
²²The noise of battle is in the land,
     the noise of great destruction!
²³How broken and shattered
     is the hammer of the whole earth!
  How desolate is Babylon
     among the nations!
²⁴I set a trap for you, O Babylon,
     and you were caught before you
          knew it;
  you were found and captured
     because you opposed the Lord.
²⁵The Lord has opened his arsenal
     and brought out the weapons of
          his wrath,
  for the Sovereign Lord Almighty has
          work to do
     in the land of the Babylonians.
²⁶Come against her from afar.
  Break open her granaries;
     pile her up like heaps of grain.
  Completely destroy her
     and leave her no remnant.

²⁷Kill all her young bulls;
     let them go down to the slaughter!
  Woe to them! For their day has
          come,
     the time for them to be punished.
²⁸Listen to the fugitives and refugees
          from Babylon
  declaring in Zion
  how the Lord our God has taken
          vengeance,
     vengeance for his temple.

²⁹"Summon archers against Babylon,
     all those who draw the bow.
  Encamp all around her;
     let no one escape.
  Repay her for her deeds;
     do to her as she has done.
  For she has defied the Lord,
     the Holy One of Israel.
³⁰Therefore, her young men will fall in
          the streets;
  all her soldiers will be silenced in
          that day,"
                    declares the Lord.
³¹"See, I am against you, O arrogant
          one,"
     declares the Lord, the Lord
          Almighty,
  "for your day has come,
     the time for you to be punished.
³²The arrogant one will stumble and
          fall
     and no one will help her up;
  I will kindle a fire in her towns
     that will consume all who are
          around her."

³³This is what the Lord Almighty
says:

"The people of Israel are oppressed,
     and the people of Judah as well.
  All their captors hold them fast,
     refusing to let them go.
³⁴Yet their Redeemer is strong;
     the Lord Almighty is his name.
  He will vigorously defend their cause
     so that he may bring rest to their
          land,
     but unrest to those who live in
          Babylon.

35 "A sword against the Babylonians!"
    declares the LORD—
  "against those who live in Babylon
    and against her officials and wise
      men!
36 A sword against her false prophets!
    They will become fools.
  A sword against her warriors!
    They will be filled with terror.
37 A sword against her horses and
    chariots
    and all the foreigners in her ranks!
    They will become women.
  A sword against her treasures!
    They will be plundered.
38 A drought on[f] her waters!
    They will dry up.
  For it is a land of idols,
    idols that will go mad with terror.

39 "So desert creatures and hyenas will
    live there,
    and there the owl will dwell.
  It will never again be inhabited
    or lived in from generation to
      generation.
40 As God overthrew Sodom and
    Gomorrah
    along with their neighboring towns,"
          declares the LORD,
  "so no one will live there;
    no man will dwell in it.

41 "Look! An army is coming from the
    north;
    a great nation and many kings
    are being stirred up from the ends
      of the earth.
42 They are armed with bows and
    spears;
    they are cruel and without mercy.
  They sound like the roaring sea
    as they ride on their horses;
  they come like men in battle
    formation
    to attack you, O Daughter of
      Babylon.
43 The king of Babylon has heard
    reports about them,
    and his hands hang limp.
  Anguish has gripped him,
    pain like that of a woman in labor.

44 Like a lion coming up from Jordan's
    thickets
  to a rich pastureland,
  I will chase Babylon from its land in
    an instant.
  Who is the chosen one I will
    appoint for this?
  Who is like me and who can
    challenge me?
  And what shepherd can stand
    against me?"
45 Therefore, hear what the LORD has
    planned against Babylon,
  what he has purposed against the
    land of the Babylonians:
  The young of the flock will be
    dragged away;
  he will completely destroy their
    pasture because of them.
46 At the sound of Babylon's capture the
    earth will tremble;
  its cry will resound among the
    nations.

a 23 Hebrew *on* or *by*   b 32 Or *who clip the hair by their
foreheads*   c 1 Or *Chaldeans*; also in verses 8, 25, 35 and 45
d 10 Or *Chaldea*   e 21 The Hebrew term refers to the
irrevocable giving over of things or persons to the LORD,
often by totally destroying them; also in verse 26.   f 38 Or *A
sword against*

TITUS 1:1-16

Paul, a servant of God and an apostle of
Jesus Christ for the faith of God's elect
and the knowledge of the truth that
leads to godliness— 2 a faith and knowledge resting on the hope of eternal life,
which God, who does not lie, promised
before the beginning of time, 3 and at his
appointed season he brought his word
to light through the preaching entrusted to me by the command of God
our Savior,

4 To Titus, my true son in our common
faith:

Grace and peace from God the Father
and Christ Jesus our Savior.

5 The reason I left you in Crete was
that you might straighten out what was
left unfinished and appoint[a] elders in
every town, as I directed you. 6 An elder
must be blameless, the husband of but
one wife, a man whose children believe

and are not open to the charge of being wild and disobedient. [7]Since an overseer[b] is entrusted with God's work, he must be blameless—not overbearing, not quick-tempered, not given to drunkenness, not violent, not pursuing dishonest gain. [8]Rather he must be hospitable, one who loves what is good, who is self-controlled, upright, holy and disciplined. [9]He must hold firmly to the trustworthy message as it has been taught, so that he can encourage others by sound doctrine and refute those who oppose it.

[10]For there are many rebellious people, mere talkers and deceivers, especially those of the circumcision group. [11]They must be silenced, because they are ruining whole households by teaching things they ought not to teach—and that for the sake of dishonest gain. [12]Even one of their own prophets has said, "Cretans are always liars, evil brutes, lazy gluttons." [13]This testimony is true. Therefore, rebuke them sharply, so that they will be sound in the faith [14]and will pay no attention to Jewish myths or to the commands of those who reject the truth. [15]To the pure, all things are pure, but to those who are corrupted and do not believe, nothing is pure. In fact, both their minds and consciences are corrupted. [16]They claim to know God, but by their actions they deny him. They are detestable, disobedient and unfit for doing anything good.

[a]5 Or ordain   [b]7 Traditionally bishop

PSALMS 97:1–98:9

[1]The Lord reigns, let the earth be
        glad;
    let the distant shores rejoice.

[2]Clouds and thick darkness surround
        him;
    righteousness and justice are the
        foundation of his throne.
[3]Fire goes before him
    and consumes his foes on every
        side.
[4]His lightning lights up the world;
    the earth sees and trembles.

[5]The mountains melt like wax before
        the Lord,
    before the Lord of all the earth.
[6]The heavens proclaim his
        righteousness,
    and all the peoples see his glory.

[7]All who worship images are put to
        shame,
    those who boast in idols—
    worship him, all you gods!

[8]Zion hears and rejoices
    and the villages of Judah are glad
    because of your judgments,
        O Lord.
[9]For you, O Lord, are the Most High
        over all the earth;
    you are exalted far above all gods.

[10]Let those who love the Lord hate evil,
    for he guards the lives of his
        faithful ones
    and delivers them from the hand
        of the wicked.
[11]Light is shed upon the righteous
    and joy on the upright in heart.
[12]Rejoice in the Lord, you who are
        righteous,
    and praise his holy name.

        A psalm.

[98:1]Sing to the Lord a new song,
    for he has done marvelous things;
    his right hand and his holy arm
    have worked salvation for him.
[2]**The Lord has made his salvation
        known**
    and revealed his righteousness
        to the nations.
[3]He has remembered his love
    and his faithfulness to the house
        of Israel;
    all the ends of the earth have seen
    the salvation of our God.

[4]Shout for joy to the Lord, all the
        earth,
    burst into jubilant song with music;
[5]make music to the Lord with the
        harp,
    with the harp and the sound of
        singing,

6 with trumpets and the blast of the
        ram's horn—
    shout for joy before the Lord, the
        King.

7 Let the sea resound, and everything
        in it,
    the world, and all who live in it.
8 Let the rivers clap their hands,
    let the mountains sing together for
        joy;
9 let them sing before the Lord,
    for he comes to judge the earth.
He will judge the world in
        righteousness
    and the peoples with equity.

PROVERBS 26:13-16
13 The sluggard says, "There is a lion in
        the road,
    a fierce lion roaming the streets!"

14 As a door turns on its hinges,
    so a sluggard turns on his bed.

15 The sluggard buries his hand in the
        dish;
    he is too lazy to bring it back to his
        mouth.

16 The sluggard is wiser in his own eyes
    than seven men who answer
        discreetly.

☐ D A Y   3 0 0

GOD SIGHTINGS

October 27

JEREMIAH 51:1-53
This is what the Lord says:

    "See, I will stir up the spirit of a
        destroyer
    against Babylon and the people of
        Leb Kamai.ᵃ
2 I will send foreigners to Babylon
    to winnow her and to devastate
        her land;
they will oppose her on every side
    in the day of her disaster.

3 Let not the archer string his bow,
    nor let him put on his armor.
Do not spare her young men;
    completely destroyᵇ her army.
4 They will fall down slain in Babylon,ᶜ
    fatally wounded in her streets.
5 For Israel and Judah have not been
        forsaken
    by their God, the Lord Almighty,
though their landᵈ is full of guilt
    before the Holy One of Israel.

6 "Flee from Babylon!
    Run for your lives!
    Do not be destroyed because of
        her sins.
It is time for the Lord's vengeance;
    he will pay her what she deserves.
7 Babylon was a gold cup in the Lord's
        hand;
    she made the whole earth drunk.
The nations drank her wine;
    therefore they have now gone
        mad.
8 Babylon will suddenly fall and be
        broken.
    Wail over her!
Get balm for her pain;
    perhaps she can be healed.

9 "'We would have healed Babylon,
    but she cannot be healed;
let us leave her and each go to his
        own land,
    for her judgment reaches to the
        skies,
    it rises as high as the clouds.'

10 "'The Lord has vindicated us;
    come, let us tell in Zion
    what the Lord our God has done.'

11 "Sharpen the arrows,
    take up the shields!
The Lord has stirred up the kings of
        the Medes,
    because his purpose is to destroy
        Babylon.
The Lord will take vengeance,
    vengeance for his temple.
12 Lift up a banner against the walls of
        Babylon!
    Reinforce the guard,

station the watchmen,
    prepare an ambush!
The LORD will carry out his purpose,
    his decree against the people of
        Babylon.
13 You who live by many waters
    and are rich in treasures,
your end has come,
    the time for you to be cut off.
14 The LORD Almighty has sworn by
        himself:
    I will surely fill you with men, as
        with a swarm of locusts,
    and they will shout in triumph
        over you.

15 "He made the earth by his power;
    he founded the world by his
        wisdom
    and stretched out the heavens by
        his understanding.
16 When he thunders, the waters in the
        heavens roar;
    he makes clouds rise from the
        ends of the earth.
He sends lightning with the rain
    and brings out the wind from his
        storehouses.

17 "Every man is senseless and without
        knowledge;
    every goldsmith is shamed by his
        idols.
His images are a fraud;
    they have no breath in them.
18 They are worthless, the objects of
        mockery;
    when their judgment comes, they
        will perish.
19 He who is the Portion of Jacob is not
        like these,
    for he is the Maker of all things,
including the tribe of his
        inheritance—
    the LORD Almighty is his name.

20 "You are my war club,
    my weapon for battle—
with you I shatter nations,
    with you I destroy kingdoms,
21 with you I shatter horse and rider,
    with you I shatter chariot and
        driver,

22 with you I shatter man and woman,
    with you I shatter old man and
        youth,
    with you I shatter young man and
        maiden,
23 with you I shatter shepherd and
        flock,
    with you I shatter farmer and
        oxen,
    with you I shatter governors and
        officials.

24 "Before your eyes I will repay Babylon and all who live in Babylonia^e for
all the wrong they have done in Zion,"
declares the LORD.

25 "I am against you, O destroying
        mountain,
    you who destroy the whole earth,"
            declares the LORD.
    "I will stretch out my hand against
        you,
    roll you off the cliffs,
    and make you a burned-out
        mountain.
26 No rock will be taken from you for a
        cornerstone,
    nor any stone for a foundation,
    for you will be desolate forever,"
            declares the LORD.

27 "Lift up a banner in the land!
    Blow the trumpet among the
        nations!
Prepare the nations for battle against
        her;
    summon against her these
        kingdoms:
    Ararat, Minni and Ashkenaz.
Appoint a commander against her;
    send up horses like a swarm of
        locusts.
28 Prepare the nations for battle against
        her—
    the kings of the Medes,
    their governors and all their officials,
    and all the countries they rule.
29 The land trembles and writhes,
    for the LORD's purposes against
        Babylon stand—
to lay waste the land of Babylon
    so that no one will live there.

³⁰Babylon's warriors have stopped
        fighting;
    they remain in their
        strongholds.
Their strength is exhausted;
    they have become like women.
Her dwellings are set on fire;
    the bars of her gates are broken.
³¹One courier follows another
    and messenger follows
        messenger
to announce to the king of Babylon
    that his entire city is captured,
³²the river crossings seized,
    the marshes set on fire,
    and the soldiers terrified."

³³This is what the LORD Almighty, the
God of Israel, says:

"The Daughter of Babylon is like a
        threshing floor
    at the time it is trampled;
    the time to harvest her will soon
        come."

³⁴"Nebuchadnezzar king of Babylon
        has devoured us,
    he has thrown us into confusion,
    he has made us an empty jar.
Like a serpent he has swallowed us
    and filled his stomach with our
        delicacies,
    and then has spewed us out.
³⁵May the violence done to our flesh ᶠ
        be upon Babylon,"
    say the inhabitants of Zion.
"May our blood be on those who live
        in Babylonia,"
    says Jerusalem.

³⁶Therefore, this is what the LORD
says:

"See, I will defend your cause
    and avenge you;
I will dry up her sea
    and make her springs dry.
³⁷Babylon will be a heap of ruins,
    a haunt of jackals,
an object of horror and scorn,
    a place where no one lives.
³⁸Her people all roar like young lions,
    they growl like lion cubs.

³⁹But while they are aroused,
    I will set out a feast for them
    and make them drunk,
so that they shout with laughter—
    then sleep forever and not awake,"
            declares the LORD.
⁴⁰"I will bring them down
    like lambs to the slaughter,
    like rams and goats.

⁴¹"How Sheshach ᵍ will be captured,
    the boast of the whole earth
        seized!
What a horror Babylon will be
    among the nations!
⁴²The sea will rise over Babylon;
    its roaring waves will cover her.
⁴³Her towns will be desolate,
    a dry and desert land,
a land where no one lives,
    through which no man travels.
⁴⁴I will punish Bel in Babylon
    and make him spew out what he
        has swallowed.
The nations will no longer stream to
        him.
    And the wall of Babylon will fall.

⁴⁵"Come out of her, my people!
    Run for your lives!
    Run from the fierce anger of the
        LORD.
⁴⁶Do not lose heart or be afraid
    when rumors are heard in the
        land;
one rumor comes this year, another
        the next,
    rumors of violence in the land
    and of ruler against ruler.
⁴⁷For the time will surely come
    when I will punish the idols of
        Babylon;
her whole land will be disgraced
    and her slain will all lie fallen
        within her.
⁴⁸Then heaven and earth and all that is
        in them
    will shout for joy over Babylon,
for out of the north
    destroyers will attack her,"
            declares the LORD.

⁴⁹"Babylon must fall because of Israel's
slain,
just as the slain in all the earth
have fallen because of Babylon.
⁵⁰You who have escaped the sword,
leave and do not linger!
Remember the Lᴏʀᴅ in a distant
land,
and think on Jerusalem."

⁵¹"We are disgraced,
for we have been insulted
and shame covers our faces,
because foreigners have entered
the holy places of the Lᴏʀᴅ's
house."

⁵²"But days are coming," declares the
Lᴏʀᴅ,
"when I will punish her idols,
and throughout her land
the wounded will groan.
⁵³Even if Babylon reaches the sky
and fortifies her lofty stronghold,
I will send destroyers against her,"
declares the Lᴏʀᴅ.

a1 Leb Kamai is a cryptogram for Chaldea, that is, Babylonia.
b3 The Hebrew term refers to the irrevocable giving over of
things or persons to the Lᴏʀᴅ, often by totally destroying them.
c4 Or *Chaldea*   *d5* Or */ and the land ⌊of the Babylonians⌋*
e24 Or *Chaldea*; also in verse 35   *f35* Or *done to us and to
our children*   *g41 Sheshach* is a cryptogram for Babylon.

TITUS 2:1-15

You must teach what is in accord with
sound doctrine. ²Teach the older men
to be temperate, worthy of respect, self-
controlled, and sound in faith, in love
and in endurance.

³Likewise, teach the older women to
be reverent in the way they live, not to be
slanderers or addicted to much wine,
but to teach what is good. ⁴Then they
can train the younger women to love
their husbands and children, ⁵to be self-
controlled and pure, to be busy at home,
to be kind, and to be subject to their
husbands, so that no one will malign the
word of God.

⁶Similarly, encourage the young men
to be self-controlled. ⁷In everything set
them an example by doing what is good.
In your teaching show integrity, serious-
ness ⁸and soundness of speech that

cannot be condemned, so that those
who oppose you may be ashamed because they have nothing bad to say
about us.

⁹Teach slaves to be subject to their
masters in everything, to try to please
them, not to talk back to them, ¹⁰and
not to steal from them, but to show that
they can be fully trusted, so that in every
way they will make the teaching about
God our Savior attractive.

¹¹For the grace of God that brings salvation has appeared to all men. ¹²It
teaches us to say "No" to ungodliness
and worldly passions, and to live self-
controlled, upright and godly lives in
this present age, ¹³while we wait for the
blessed hope—the glorious appearing
of our great God and Savior, Jesus Christ,
¹⁴who gave himself for us to redeem us
from all wickedness and to purify for
himself a people that are his very own,
eager to do what is good.

¹⁵These, then, are the things you
should teach. Encourage and rebuke
with all authority. Do not let anyone despise you.

PSALM 99:1-9

¹The Lᴏʀᴅ reigns,
let the nations tremble;
he sits enthroned between the
cherubim,
let the earth shake.
²Great is the Lᴏʀᴅ in Zion;
he is exalted over all the nations.
³Let them praise your great and
awesome name—
he is holy.

⁴The King is mighty, he loves
justice—
you have established equity;
in Jacob you have done
what is just and right.
⁵Exalt the Lᴏʀᴅ our God
and worship at his footstool;
he is holy.

⁶Moses and Aaron were among his
priests,

Samuel was among those who
    called on his name;
they called on the LORD
    and he answered them.
[7] He spoke to them from the pillar of
    cloud;
they kept his statutes and the
    decrees he gave them.

[8] O LORD our God,
    you answered them;
you were to Israel[a] a forgiving God,
    though you punished their
        misdeeds.[b]
[9] Exalt the LORD our God
    and worship at his holy mountain,
for the LORD our God is holy.

*a8 Hebrew them   b8 Or / an avenger of the wrongs done
to them*

PROVERBS 26:17
[17] Like one who seizes a dog by the
    ears
        is a passer-by who meddles in a
            quarrel not his own.

□ DAY 301

GOD SIGHTINGS

October 28

JEREMIAH 51:54–52:34
[54] "The sound of a cry comes from
    Babylon,
        the sound of great destruction
        from the land of the Babylonians.[a]
[55] The LORD will destroy Babylon;
    he will silence her noisy din.
Waves ⌊of enemies⌋ will rage like
    great waters;
        the roar of their voices will
            resound.
[56] A destroyer will come against
    Babylon;
        her warriors will be captured,
        and their bows will be broken.
For the LORD is a God of retribution;
    he will repay in full.

[57] I will make her officials and wise
    men drunk,
        her governors, officers and
            warriors as well;
they will sleep forever and not
    awake,"
        declares the King, whose name is
            the LORD Almighty.

[58] This is what the LORD Almighty
says:

"Babylon's thick wall will be leveled
    and her high gates set on fire;
the peoples exhaust themselves for
    nothing,
        the nations' labor is only fuel for
            the flames."

[59] This is the message Jeremiah gave
to the staff officer Seraiah son of Neriah, the son of Mahseiah, when he went
to Babylon with Zedekiah king of Judah
in the fourth year of his reign. [60] Jeremiah had written on a scroll about all
the disasters that would come upon
Babylon—all that had been recorded
concerning Babylon. [61] He said to Seraiah, "When you get to Babylon, see that
you read all these words aloud. [62] Then
say, 'O LORD, you have said you will destroy this place, so that neither man nor
animal will live in it; it will be desolate
forever.' [63] When you finish reading this
scroll, tie a stone to it and throw it into
the Euphrates. [64] Then say, 'So will Babylon sink to rise no more because of the
disaster I will bring upon her. And her
people will fall.'"

The words of Jeremiah end here.

[52:1] ZEDEKIAH was twenty-one years old
when he became king, and he reigned in
Jerusalem eleven years. His mother's
name was Hamutal daughter of Jeremiah; she was from Libnah. [2] He did evil
in the eyes of the LORD, just as Jehoiakim
had done. [3] It was because of the LORD's
anger that all this happened to Jerusalem and Judah, and in the end he thrust
them from his presence.
    Now Zedekiah rebelled against the
king of Babylon.

⁴So in the ninth year of Zedekiah's reign, on the tenth day of the tenth month, Nebuchadnezzar king of Babylon marched against Jerusalem with his whole army. They camped outside the city and built siege works all around it. ⁵The city was kept under siege until the eleventh year of King Zedekiah.

⁶By the ninth day of the fourth month the famine in the city had become so severe that there was no food for the people to eat. ⁷Then the city wall was broken through, and the whole army fled. They left the city at night through the gate between the two walls near the king's garden, though the Babylonians*b* were surrounding the city. They fled toward the Arabah,*c* ⁸but the Babylonian*d* army pursued King Zedekiah and overtook him in the plains of Jericho. All his soldiers were separated from him and scattered, ⁹and he was captured.

He was taken to the king of Babylon at Riblah in the land of Hamath, where he pronounced sentence on him. ¹⁰There at Riblah the king of Babylon slaughtered the sons of Zedekiah before his eyes; he also killed all the officials of Judah. ¹¹Then he put out Zedekiah's eyes, bound him with bronze shackles and took him to Babylon, where he put him in prison till the day of his death.

¹²On the tenth day of the fifth month, in the nineteenth year of Nebuchadnezzar king of Babylon, Nebuzaradan commander of the imperial guard, who served the king of Babylon, came to Jerusalem. ¹³He set fire to the temple of the Lord, the royal palace and all the houses of Jerusalem. Every important building he burned down. ¹⁴The whole Babylonian army under the commander of the imperial guard broke down all the walls around Jerusalem. ¹⁵Nebuzaradan the commander of the guard carried into exile some of the poorest people and those who remained in the city, along with the rest of the craftsmen*e* and those who had gone over to the king of Babylon. ¹⁶But Nebuzaradan left behind the rest of the poor-

est people of the land to work the vineyards and fields.

¹⁷The Babylonians broke up the bronze pillars, the movable stands and the bronze Sea that were at the temple of the Lord and they carried all the bronze to Babylon. ¹⁸They also took away the pots, shovels, wick trimmers, sprinkling bowls, dishes and all the bronze articles used in the temple service. ¹⁹The commander of the imperial guard took away the basins, censers, sprinkling bowls, pots, lampstands, dishes and bowls used for drink offerings—all that were made of pure gold or silver.

²⁰The bronze from the two pillars, the Sea and the twelve bronze bulls under it, and the movable stands, which King Solomon had made for the temple of the Lord, was more than could be weighed. ²¹Each of the pillars was eighteen cubits high and twelve cubits in circumference*f*; each was four fingers thick, and hollow. ²²The bronze capital on top of the one pillar was five cubits*g* high and was decorated with a network and pomegranates of bronze all around. The other pillar, with its pomegranates, was similar. ²³There were ninety-six pomegranates on the sides; the total number of pomegranates above the surrounding network was a hundred.

²⁴The commander of the guard took as prisoners Seraiah the chief priest, Zephaniah the priest next in rank and the three doorkeepers. ²⁵Of those still in the city, he took the officer in charge of the fighting men, and seven royal advisers. He also took the secretary who was chief officer in charge of conscripting the people of the land and sixty of his men who were found in the city. ²⁶Nebuzaradan the commander took them all and brought them to the king of Babylon at Riblah. ²⁷There at Riblah, in the land of Hamath, the king had them executed.

So Judah went into captivity, away from her land. ²⁸This is the number of the people Nebuchadnezzar carried into exile:

in the seventh year, 3,023 Jews;
[29]in Nebuchadnezzar's eighteenth year,
832 people from Jerusalem;
[30]in his twenty-third year,
745 Jews taken into exile by Nebuzaradan the commander of the imperial guard.
There were 4,600 people in all.

[31]In the thirty-seventh year of the exile of Jehoiachin king of Judah, in the year Evil-Merodach[h] became king of Babylon, he released Jehoiachin king of Judah and freed him from prison on the twenty-fifth day of the twelfth month. [32]He spoke kindly to him and gave him a seat of honor higher than those of the other kings who were with him in Babylon. [33]So Jehoiachin put aside his prison clothes and for the rest of his life ate regularly at the king's table. [34]Day by day the king of Babylon gave Jehoiachin a regular allowance as long as he lived, till the day of his death.

a54 Or *Chaldeans*   *b7* Or *Chaldeans;* also in verse 17
c7 Or *the Jordan Valley*   *d8* Or *Chaldean;* also in verse 14
e15 Or *populace*   *f21* That is, about 27 feet (about 8.1 meters) high and 18 feet (about 5.4 meters) in circumference
g22 That is, about 7 1/2 feet (about 2.3 meters)   *h31* Also called *Amel-Marduk*

TITUS 3:1-15

Remind the people to be subject to rulers and authorities, to be obedient, to be ready to do whatever is good, [2]to slander no one, to be peaceable and considerate, and to show true humility toward all men.

[3]At one time we too were foolish, disobedient, deceived and enslaved by all kinds of passions and pleasures. We lived in malice and envy, being hated and hating one another. [4]But when the kindness and love of God our Savior appeared, [5]he saved us, not because of righteous things we had done, but because of his mercy. He saved us through the washing of rebirth and renewal by the Holy Spirit, [6]whom he poured out on us generously through Jesus Christ

our Savior, [7]so that, having been justified by his grace, we might become heirs having the hope of eternal life. [8]This is a trustworthy saying. And I want you to stress these things, so that those who have trusted in God may be careful to devote themselves to doing what is good. These things are excellent and profitable for everyone.

[9]But avoid foolish controversies and genealogies and arguments and quarrels about the law, because these are unprofitable and useless. [10]Warn a divisive person once, and then warn him a second time. After that, have nothing to do with him. [11]You may be sure that such a man is warped and sinful; he is self-condemned.

[12]As soon as I send Artemas or Tychicus to you, do your best to come to me at Nicopolis, because I have decided to winter there. [13]Do everything you can to help Zenas the lawyer and Apollos on their way and see that they have everything they need. [14]Our people must learn to devote themselves to doing what is good, in order that they may provide for daily necessities and not live unproductive lives.

[15]Everyone with me sends you greetings. Greet those who love us in the faith.

Grace be with you all.

PSALM 100:1-5
A psalm. For giving thanks.

[1]Shout for joy to the LORD, all the earth.
[2]   Worship the LORD with gladness;
   come before him with joyful songs.
[3]Know that the LORD is God.
   It is he who made us, and we are his[a];
   we are his people, the sheep of his pasture.

**[4]Enter his gates with thanksgiving and his courts with praise;
   give thanks to him and praise his name.**

⁵**For the Lᴏʀᴅ is good and his love**
     endures forever;
  his faithfulness continues
     through all generations.

ᵃ3 Or *and not we ourselves*

PROVERBS 26:18-19
¹⁸**L**ike a madman shooting
     firebrands or deadly arrows
¹⁹is a man who deceives his neighbor
     and says, "I was only joking!"

□ D A Y   3 0 2

GOD SIGHTINGS

October **29**

LAMENTATIONS 1:1–2:19
  ᵃ**H**ow deserted lies the city,
     once so full of people!
How like a widow is she,
     who once was great among the
          nations!
She who was queen among the
          provinces
     has now become a slave.

²Bitterly she weeps at night,
     tears are upon her cheeks.
Among all her lovers
     there is none to comfort her.
All her friends have betrayed her;
     they have become her enemies.

³After affliction and harsh labor,
     Judah has gone into exile.
She dwells among the nations;
     she finds no resting place.
All who pursue her have overtaken
          her
     in the midst of her distress.

⁴The roads to Zion mourn,
     for no one comes to her appointed
          feasts.
All her gateways are desolate,
     her priests groan,
her maidens grieve,
     and she is in bitter anguish.

⁵Her foes have become her masters;
     her enemies are at ease.
The Lᴏʀᴅ has brought her grief
     because of her many sins.
Her children have gone into exile,
     captive before the foe.

⁶All the splendor has departed
     from the Daughter of Zion.
Her princes are like deer
     that find no pasture;
in weakness they have fled
     before the pursuer.

⁷In the days of her affliction and
          wandering
     Jerusalem remembers all the
          treasures
     that were hers in days of old.
When her people fell into enemy
          hands,
     there was no one to help her.
Her enemies looked at her
     and laughed at her destruction.

⁸Jerusalem has sinned greatly
     and so has become unclean.
All who honored her despise her,
     for they have seen her nakedness;
she herself groans
     and turns away.

⁹Her filthiness clung to her skirts;
     she did not consider her future.
Her fall was astounding;
     there was none to comfort her.
"Look, O Lᴏʀᴅ, on my affliction,
     for the enemy has triumphed."

¹⁰The enemy laid hands
     on all her treasures;
she saw pagan nations
     enter her sanctuary—
those you had forbidden
     to enter your assembly.

¹¹All her people groan
     as they search for bread;
they barter their treasures for food
     to keep themselves alive.
"Look, O Lᴏʀᴅ, and consider,
     for I am despised."

¹²"Is it nothing to you, all you who
          pass by?
     Look around and see.

Is any suffering like my suffering
that was inflicted on me,
that the LORD brought on me
in the day of his fierce anger?

13 "From on high he sent fire,
sent it down into my bones.
He spread a net for my feet
and turned me back.
He made me desolate,
faint all the day long.

14 "My sins have been bound into a
yoke*b*;
by his hands they were woven
together.
They have come upon my neck
and the Lord has sapped my
strength.
He has handed me over
to those I cannot withstand.

15 "The Lord has rejected
all the warriors in my midst;
he has summoned an army against
me
to*c* crush my young men.
In his winepress the Lord has
trampled
the Virgin Daughter of Judah.

16 "This is why I weep
and my eyes overflow with tears.
No one is near to comfort me,
no one to restore my spirit.
My children are destitute
because the enemy has prevailed."

17 Zion stretches out her hands,
but there is no one to comfort her.
The LORD has decreed for Jacob
that his neighbors become his
foes;
Jerusalem has become
an unclean thing among them.

18 "The LORD is righteous,
yet I rebelled against his command.
Listen, all you peoples;
look upon my suffering.
My young men and maidens
have gone into exile.

19 "I called to my allies
but they betrayed me.

My priests and my elders
perished in the city
while they searched for food
to keep themselves alive.

20 "See, O LORD, how distressed I am!
I am in torment within,
and in my heart I am disturbed,
for I have been most rebellious.
Outside, the sword bereaves;
inside, there is only death.

21 "People have heard my groaning,
but there is no one to comfort me.
All my enemies have heard of my
distress;
they rejoice at what you have done.
May you bring the day you have
announced
so they may become like me.

22 "Let all their wickedness come
before you;
deal with them
as you have dealt with me
because of all my sins.
My groans are many
and my heart is faint."

2:1*a* How the Lord has covered the
Daughter of Zion
with the cloud of his anger*d*!
He has hurled down the splendor of
Israel
from heaven to earth;
he has not remembered his footstool
in the day of his anger.

2 Without pity the Lord has swallowed
up
all the dwellings of Jacob;
in his wrath he has torn down
the strongholds of the Daughter of
Judah.
He has brought her kingdom and its
princes
down to the ground in dishonor.

3 In fierce anger he has cut off
every horn*e* of Israel.
He has withdrawn his right hand
at the approach of the enemy.
He has burned in Jacob like a
flaming fire
that consumes everything around it.

4 Like an enemy he has strung his bow;
  his right hand is ready.
Like a foe he has slain
  all who were pleasing to the eye;
he has poured out his wrath like fire
  on the tent of the Daughter of
  Zion.

5 The Lord is like an enemy;
  he has swallowed up Israel.
He has swallowed up all her palaces
  and destroyed her strongholds.
He has multiplied mourning and
  lamentation
  for the Daughter of Judah.

6 He has laid waste his dwelling like a
  garden;
  he has destroyed his place of
  meeting.
The Lord has made Zion forget
  her appointed feasts and her
  Sabbaths;
in his fierce anger he has spurned
  both king and priest.

7 The Lord has rejected his altar
  and abandoned his sanctuary.
He has handed over to the enemy
  the walls of her palaces;
they have raised a shout in the house
  of the Lord
  as on the day of an appointed
  feast.

8 The Lord determined to tear down
  the wall around the Daughter of
  Zion.
He stretched out a measuring line
  and did not withhold his hand
  from destroying.
He made ramparts and walls lament;
  together they wasted away.

9 Her gates have sunk into the
  ground;
  their bars he has broken and
  destroyed.
Her king and her princes are exiled
  among the nations,
  the law is no more,
and her prophets no longer find
  visions from the Lord.

10 The elders of the Daughter of Zion
  sit on the ground in silence;
they have sprinkled dust on their
  heads
  and put on sackcloth.
The young women of Jerusalem
  have bowed their heads to the
  ground.

11 My eyes fail from weeping,
  I am in torment within,
my heart is poured out on the ground
  because my people are destroyed,
because children and infants faint
  in the streets of the city.

12 They say to their mothers,
  "Where is bread and wine?"
as they faint like wounded men
  in the streets of the city,
as their lives ebb away
  in their mothers' arms.

13 What can I say for you?
  With what can I compare you,
  O Daughter of Jerusalem?
To what can I liken you,
  that I may comfort you,
  O Virgin Daughter of Zion?
Your wound is as deep as the sea.
  Who can heal you?

14 The visions of your prophets
  were false and worthless;
they did not expose your sin
  to ward off your captivity.
The oracles they gave you
  were false and misleading.

15 All who pass your way
  clap their hands at you;
they scoff and shake their heads
  at the Daughter of Jerusalem:
"Is this the city that was called
  the perfection of beauty,
  the joy of the whole earth?"

16 All your enemies open their mouths
  wide against you;
they scoff and gnash their teeth
  and say, "We have swallowed her
  up.
This is the day we have waited for;
  we have lived to see it."

1727

OCTOBER 29

17 The Lord has done what he planned;
he has fulfilled his word,
which he decreed long ago.
He has overthrown you without pity,
he has let the enemy gloat over
you,
he has exalted the horn*e* of your
foes.

18 The hearts of the people
cry out to the Lord.
O wall of the Daughter of Zion,
let your tears flow like a river
day and night;
give yourself no relief,
your eyes no rest.

19 Arise, cry out in the night,
as the watches of the night begin;
pour out your heart like water
in the presence of the Lord.
Lift up your hands to him
for the lives of your children,
who faint from hunger
at the head of every street.

aThis chapter is an acrostic poem, the verses of which begin with the successive letters of the Hebrew alphabet. b14 Most Hebrew manuscripts; Septuagint He kept watch over my sins c15 Or has set a time for me / when he will d1 Or How the Lord in his anger / has treated the Daughter of Zion with contempt e3 Or / all the strength; or every king; horn here symbolizes strength. f17 Horn here symbolizes strength.

PHILEMON 1:1-25

Paul, a prisoner of Christ Jesus, and Timothy our brother,

To Philemon our dear friend and fellow worker, 2 to Apphia our sister, to Archippus our fellow soldier and to the church that meets in your home:

3 Grace to you and peace from God our Father and the Lord Jesus Christ.

4 I always thank my God as I remember you in my prayers, 5 because I hear about your faith in the Lord Jesus and your love for all the saints. 6 I pray that you may be active in sharing your faith, so that you will have a full understanding of every good thing we have in Christ. 7 Your love has given me great joy and encouragement, because you,

brother, have refreshed the hearts of the saints.

8 Therefore, although in Christ I could be bold and order you to do what you ought to do, 9 yet I appeal to you on the basis of love. I then, as Paul—an old man and now also a prisoner of Christ Jesus— 10 I appeal to you for my son Onesimus,*a* who became my son while I was in chains. 11 Formerly he was useless to you, but now he has become useful both to you and to me.

12 I am sending him—who is my very heart—back to you. 13 I would have liked to keep him with me so that he could take your place in helping me while I am in chains for the gospel. 14 But I did not want to do anything without your consent, so that any favor you do will be spontaneous and not forced. 15 Perhaps the reason he was separated from you for a little while was that you might have him back for good— 16 no longer as a slave, but better than a slave, as a dear brother. He is very dear to me but even dearer to you, both as a man and as a brother in the Lord.

17 So if you consider me a partner, welcome him as you would welcome me. 18 If he has done you any wrong or owes you anything, charge it to me. 19 I, Paul, am writing this with my own hand. I will pay it back—not to mention that you owe me your very self. 20 I do wish, brother, that I may have some benefit from you in the Lord; refresh my heart in Christ. 21 Confident of your obedience, I write to you, knowing that you will do even more than I ask.

22 And one thing more: Prepare a guest room for me, because I hope to be restored to you in answer to your prayers.

23 Epaphras, my fellow prisoner in Christ Jesus, sends you greetings. 24 And so do Mark, Aristarchus, Demas and Luke, my fellow workers.

25 The grace of the Lord Jesus Christ be with your spirit.

a10 Onesimus means useful.

PSALM 101:1-8
Of David. A psalm.

¹ I will sing of your love and justice;
to you, O Lord, I will sing
praise.
² I will be careful to lead a
blameless life—
when will you come to me?

I will walk in my house
with blameless heart.
³ I will set before my eyes
no vile thing.

The deeds of faithless men I hate;
they will not cling to me.
⁴ Men of perverse heart shall be far
from me;
I will have nothing to do with evil.

⁵ Whoever slanders his neighbor in
secret,
him will I put to silence;
whoever has haughty eyes and a
proud heart,
him will I not endure.

⁶ My eyes will be on the faithful in the
land,
that they may dwell with me;
he whose walk is blameless
will minister to me.

⁷ No one who practices deceit
will dwell in my house;
no one who speaks falsely
will stand in my presence.

⁸ Every morning I will put to silence
all the wicked in the land;
I will cut off every evildoer
from the city of the Lord.

PROVERBS 26:20
²⁰ Without wood a fire goes out;
without gossip a quarrel dies
down.

☐ DAY 303

GOD SIGHTINGS

October 30

LAMENTATIONS 2:20–3:66
²⁰ "Look, O Lord, and consider:
Whom have you ever treated like
this?
Should women eat their offspring,
the children they have cared for?
Should priest and prophet be killed
in the sanctuary of the Lord?

²¹ "Young and old lie together
in the dust of the streets;
my young men and maidens
have fallen by the sword.
You have slain them in the day of
your anger;
you have slaughtered them
without pity.

²² "As you summon to a feast day,
so you summoned against me
terrors on every side.
In the day of the Lord's anger
no one escaped or survived;
those I cared for and reared,
my enemy has destroyed."

³:¹ᵃ I AM the man who has seen affliction
by the rod of his wrath.
² He has driven me away and made me
walk
in darkness rather than light;
³ indeed, he has turned his hand
against me
again and again, all day long.

⁴ He has made my skin and my flesh
grow old
and has broken my bones.
⁵ He has besieged me and surrounded
me
with bitterness and hardship.
⁶ He has made me dwell in darkness
like those long dead.

⁷ He has walled me in so I cannot escape;
he has weighed me down with
chains.

⁸Even when I call out or cry for help,
   he shuts out my prayer.
⁹He has barred my way with blocks of
   stone;
   he has made my paths crooked.

¹⁰Like a bear lying in wait,
   like a lion in hiding,
¹¹he dragged me from the path and
   mangled me
   and left me without help.
¹²He drew his bow
   and made me the target for his
   arrows.

¹³He pierced my heart
   with arrows from his quiver.
¹⁴I became the laughingstock of all my
   people;
   they mock me in song all day long.
¹⁵He has filled me with bitter herbs
   and sated me with gall.

¹⁶He has broken my teeth with gravel;
   he has trampled me in the dust.
¹⁷I have been deprived of peace;
   I have forgotten what prosperity is.
¹⁸So I say, "My splendor is gone
   and all that I had hoped from the
   LORD."

¹⁹I remember my affliction and my
   wandering,
   the bitterness and the gall.
²⁰I well remember them,
   and my soul is downcast within me.
²¹Yet this I call to mind
   and therefore I have hope:

²²Because of the LORD's great love we
   are not consumed,
   for his compassions never fail.
²³They are new every morning;
   great is your faithfulness.
²⁴I say to myself, "The LORD is my
   portion;
   therefore I will wait for him."

²⁵The LORD is good to those whose
   hope is in him,
   to the one who seeks him;
²⁶it is good to wait quietly
   for the salvation of the LORD.

²⁷It is good for a man to bear the yoke
   while he is young.

²⁸Let him sit alone in silence,
   for the LORD has laid it on him.
²⁹Let him bury his face in the dust—
   there may yet be hope.
³⁰Let him offer his cheek to one who
   would strike him,
   and let him be filled with disgrace.

³¹For men are not cast off
   by the Lord forever.
³²Though he brings grief, he will show
   compassion,
   so great is his unfailing love.
³³For he does not willingly bring
   affliction
   or grief to the children of men.

³⁴To crush underfoot
   all prisoners in the land,
³⁵to deny a man his rights
   before the Most High,
³⁶to deprive a man of justice—
   would not the Lord see such
   things?

³⁷Who can speak and have it happen
   if the Lord has not decreed it?
³⁸Is it not from the mouth of the Most
   High
   that both calamities and good
   things come?
³⁹Why should any living man complain
   when punished for his sins?

⁴⁰Let us examine our ways and test
   them,
   and let us return to the LORD.
⁴¹Let us lift up our hearts and our
   hands
   to God in heaven, and say:
⁴²"We have sinned and rebelled
   and you have not forgiven.

⁴³"You have covered yourself with
   anger and pursued us;
   you have slain without pity.
⁴⁴You have covered yourself with a
   cloud
   so that no prayer can get through.
⁴⁵You have made us scum and refuse
   among the nations.

46 "All our enemies have opened their
  mouths
    wide against us.
47 We have suffered terror and pitfalls,
    ruin and destruction."
48 Streams of tears flow from my eyes
    because my people are destroyed.

49 My eyes will flow unceasingly,
    without relief,
50 until the LORD looks down
    from heaven and sees.
51 What I see brings grief to my soul
    because of all the women of my
      city.

52 Those who were my enemies without
  cause
    hunted me like a bird.
53 They tried to end my life in a pit
    and threw stones at me;
54 the waters closed over my head,
    and I thought I was about to be cut
      off.

55 I called on your name, O LORD,
    from the depths of the pit.
56 You heard my plea: "Do not close
      your ears
    to my cry for relief."
57 You came near when I called you,
    and you said, "Do not fear."

58 O Lord, you took up my case;
    you redeemed my life.
59 You have seen, O LORD, the wrong
      done to me.
    Uphold my cause!
60 You have seen the depth of their
      vengeance,
    all their plots against me.

61 O LORD, you have heard their insults,
    all their plots against me—
62 what my enemies whisper and mutter
    against me all day long.
63 Look at them! Sitting or standing,
    they mock me in their songs.

64 Pay them back what they deserve,
      O LORD,
    for what their hands have done.
65 Put a veil over their hearts,
    and may your curse be on them!

66 Pursue them in anger and destroy
      them
    from under the heavens of the LORD.

*aThis chapter is an acrostic poem; the verses of each stanza
begin with the successive letters of the Hebrew alphabet,
and the verses within each stanza begin with the same letter.*

HEBREWS 1:1-14

In the past God spoke to our forefathers
through the prophets at many times and
in various ways, 2 but in these last days he
has spoken to us by his Son, whom he appointed heir of all things, and through
whom he made the universe. 3 **The Son
is the radiance of God's glory and the
exact representation of his being, sus-
taining all things by his powerful
word. After he had provided purification for sins, he sat down at the right
hand of the Majesty in heaven.** 4 So he
became as much superior to the angels
as the name he has inherited is superior
to theirs.

5 For to which of the angels did God
ever say,

  "You are my Son;
    today I have become your
      Father*a*"*b*?

Or again,

  "I will be his Father,
    and he will be my Son"*c*?

6 And again, when God brings his firstborn into the world, he says,

  "Let all God's angels worship him."*d*

7 In speaking of the angels he says,

  "He makes his angels winds,
    his servants flames of fire."*e*

8 But about the Son he says,

  "Your throne, O God, will last for ever
      and ever,
    and righteousness will be the
      scepter of your kingdom.
9 You have loved righteousness and
      hated wickedness;
    therefore God, your God, has set
      you above your companions
    by anointing you with the oil of
      joy."*f*

¹⁰He also says,

"In the beginning, O Lord, you laid
the foundations of the earth,
and the heavens are the work of
your hands.
¹¹They will perish, but you remain;
they will all wear out like a
garment.
¹²You will roll them up like a robe;
like a garment they will be changed.
But you remain the same,
and your years will never end."^g

¹³To which of the angels did God ever
say,

"Sit at my right hand
until I make your enemies
a footstool for your feet"^h?

¹⁴Are not all angels ministering spirits
sent to serve those who will inherit salvation?

^a5 Or *have begotten you* ^b5 Psalm 2:7 ^c5 2 Samuel 7:14;
1 Chron. 17:13 ^d6 Deut. 32:43 (see Dead Sea Scrolls and
Septuagint) ^e7 Psalm 104:4 ^f9 Psalm 45:6,7 ^g12 Psalm
102:25-27 ^h13 Psalm 110:1

PSALM 102:1-28

A prayer of an afflicted man. When he is
faint and pours out his lament before the
LORD.

¹Hear my prayer, O LORD;
let my cry for help come to you.
²Do not hide your face from me
when I am in distress.
Turn your ear to me;
when I call, answer me quickly.

³For my days vanish like smoke;
my bones burn like glowing
embers.
⁴My heart is blighted and withered
like grass;
I forget to eat my food.
⁵Because of my loud groaning
I am reduced to skin and bones.
⁶I am like a desert owl,
like an owl among the ruins.
⁷I lie awake; I have become
like a bird alone on a roof.
⁸All day long my enemies taunt me;
those who rail against me use my
name as a curse.

⁹For I eat ashes as my food
and mingle my drink with tears
¹⁰because of your great wrath,
for you have taken me up and
thrown me aside.
¹¹My days are like the evening shadow;
I wither away like grass.

¹²But you, O LORD, sit enthroned
forever;
your renown endures through all
generations.
¹³You will arise and have compassion
on Zion,
for it is time to show favor to her;
the appointed time has come.
¹⁴For her stones are dear to your
servants;
her very dust moves them to pity.
¹⁵The nations will fear the name of the
LORD,
all the kings of the earth will
revere your glory.
¹⁶For the LORD will rebuild Zion
and appear in his glory.
¹⁷He will respond to the prayer of the
destitute;
he will not despise their plea.

¹⁸Let this be written for a future
generation,
that a people not yet created may
praise the LORD:
¹⁹"The LORD looked down from his
sanctuary on high,
from heaven he viewed the earth,
²⁰to hear the groans of the prisoners
and release those condemned to
death."
²¹So the name of the LORD will be
declared in Zion
and his praise in Jerusalem
²²when the peoples and the kingdoms
assemble to worship the LORD.

²³In the course of my life^a he broke my
strength;
he cut short my days.
²⁴So I said:
"Do not take me away, O my God,
in the midst of my days;
your years go on through all
generations.

²⁵ In the beginning you laid the
      foundations of the earth,
   and the heavens are the work of
      your hands.
²⁶ They will perish, but you remain;
      they will all wear out like a
         garment.
   Like clothing you will change them
      and they will be discarded.
²⁷ But you remain the same,
      and your years will never end.
²⁸ The children of your servants will
      live in your presence;
   their descendants will be
      established before you."

a23 Or *By his power*

PROVERBS 26:21-22

²¹ **A**s charcoal to embers and as wood
      to fire,
   so is a quarrelsome man for
      kindling strife.

²² The words of a gossip are like choice
      morsels;
   they go down to a man's inmost
      parts.

☐ DAY 304

GOD SIGHTINGS

October 31

LAMENTATIONS 4:1-5:22

How the gold has lost its luster,
   the fine gold become dull!
The sacred gems are scattered
   at the head of every street.

² How the precious sons of Zion,
      once worth their weight in gold,
   are now considered as pots of clay,
      the work of a potter's hands!

³ Even jackals offer their breasts
      to nurse their young,
   but my people have become
         heartless
      like ostriches in the desert.

⁴ Because of thirst the infant's tongue
      sticks to the roof of its mouth;
   the children beg for bread,
      but no one gives it to them.

⁵ Those who once ate delicacies
      are destitute in the streets.
   Those nurtured in purple
      now lie on ash heaps.

⁶ The punishment of my people
      is greater than that of Sodom,
   which was overthrown in a moment
      without a hand turned to help her.

⁷ Their princes were brighter than
         snow
      and whiter than milk,
   their bodies more ruddy than rubies,
      their appearance like sapphires.ᵇ

⁸ But now they are blacker than soot;
      they are not recognized in the
         streets.
   Their skin has shriveled on their
         bones;
      it has become as dry as a stick.

⁹ Those killed by the sword are better
         off
      than those who die of famine;
   racked with hunger, they waste away
      for lack of food from the field.

¹⁰ With their own hands
         compassionate women
      have cooked their own children,
   who became their food
      when my people were destroyed.

¹¹ The LORD has given full vent to his
         wrath;
      he has poured out his fierce anger.
   He kindled a fire in Zion
      that consumed her foundations.

¹² The kings of the earth did not believe,
      nor did any of the world's people,
   that enemies and foes could enter
      the gates of Jerusalem.

¹³ But it happened because of the sins
         of her prophets
      and the iniquities of her priests,
   who shed within her
      the blood of the righteous.

14 Now they grope through the streets
  like men who are blind.
 They are so defiled with blood
   that no one dares to touch their
     garments.

15 "Go away! You are unclean!" men cry
   to them.
  "Away! Away! Don't touch us!"
 When they flee and wander about,
  people among the nations say,
  "They can stay here no longer."

16 The LORD himself has scattered them;
   he no longer watches over them.
 The priests are shown no honor,
   the elders no favor.

17 Moreover, our eyes failed,
   looking in vain for help;
 from our towers we watched
   for a nation that could not save us.

18 Men stalked us at every step,
   so we could not walk in our
     streets.
 Our end was near, our days were
   numbered,
   for our end had come.

19 Our pursuers were swifter
   than eagles in the sky;
 they chased us over the mountains
   and lay in wait for us in the desert.

20 The LORD's anointed, our very life
     breath,
   was caught in their traps.
 We thought that under his shadow
   we would live among the nations.

21 Rejoice and be glad, O Daughter of
     Edom,
   you who live in the land of Uz.
 But to you also the cup will be
     passed;
   you will be drunk and stripped
     naked.

22 O Daughter of Zion, your
     punishment will end;
   he will not prolong your exile.
 But, O Daughter of Edom, he will
     punish your sin
   and expose your wickedness.

5:1 REMEMBER, O LORD, what has
     happened to us;
   look, and see our disgrace.
2 Our inheritance has been turned
     over to aliens,
   our homes to foreigners.
3 We have become orphans and
     fatherless,
   our mothers like widows.
4 We must buy the water we drink;
   our wood can be had only at a
     price.
5 Those who pursue us are at our
     heels;
   we are weary and find no rest.
6 We submitted to Egypt and Assyria
   to get enough bread.
7 Our fathers sinned and are no more,
   and we bear their punishment.
8 Slaves rule over us,
   and there is none to free us from
     their hands.
9 We get our bread at the risk of our
     lives
   because of the sword in the
     desert.
10 Our skin is hot as an oven,
   feverish from hunger.
11 Women have been ravished in Zion,
   and virgins in the towns of Judah.
12 Princes have been hung up by their
     hands;
   elders are shown no respect.
13 Young men toil at the millstones;
   boys stagger under loads of
     wood.
14 The elders are gone from the city
     gate;
   the young men have stopped their
     music.
15 Joy is gone from our hearts;
   our dancing has turned to
     mourning.
16 The crown has fallen from our
     head.
 Woe to us, for we have sinned!
17 Because of this our hearts are faint,
   because of these things our eyes
     grow dim
18 for Mount Zion, which lies desolate,
   with jackals prowling over it.

¹⁹You, O Lᴏʀᴅ, reign forever;
  your throne endures from
      generation to generation.
²⁰Why do you always forget us?
  Why do you forsake us so long?
²¹Restore us to yourself, O Lᴏʀᴅ, that
      we may return;
  renew our days as of old
²²unless you have utterly rejected us
  and are angry with us beyond
      measure.

^aThis chapter is an acrostic poem, the verses of which begin with the successive letters of the Hebrew alphabet. ^b7 Or *lapis lazuli*

HEBREWS 2:1-18
We must pay more careful attention, therefore, to what we have heard, so that we do not drift away. ²For if the message spoken by angels was binding, and every violation and disobedience received its just punishment, ³how shall we escape if we ignore such a great salvation? This salvation, which was first announced by the Lord, was confirmed to us by those who heard him. ⁴God also testified to it by signs, wonders and various miracles, and gifts of the Holy Spirit distributed according to his will.

⁵It is not to angels he has subjected the world to come, about which we are speaking. ⁶But there is a place where someone has testified:

"What is man that you are mindful
      of him,
  the son of man that you care for
      him?
⁷You made him a little^a lower than the
      angels;
  you crowned him with glory and
      honor
⁸ and put everything under his feet."^b

In putting everything under him, God left nothing that is not subject to him. Yet at present we do not see everything subject to him. ⁹**But we see Jesus, who was made a little lower than the angels, now crowned with glory and honor because he suffered death, so that by the grace of God he might taste death for everyone.**

¹⁰In bringing many sons to glory, it was fitting that God, for whom and through whom everything exists, should make the author of their salvation perfect through suffering. ¹¹Both the one who makes men holy and those who are made holy are of the same family. So Jesus is not ashamed to call them brothers. ¹²He says,

"I will declare your name to my
      brothers;
  in the presence of the
      congregation I will sing your
      praises."^c

¹³And again,

"I will put my trust in him."^d

And again he says,

"Here am I, and the children God has
      given me."^e

¹⁴Since the children have flesh and blood, he too shared in their humanity so that by his death he might destroy him who holds the power of death—that is, the devil— ¹⁵and free those who all their lives were held in slavery by their fear of death. ¹⁶For surely it is not angels he helps, but Abraham's descendants. ¹⁷For this reason he had to be made like his brothers in every way, in order that he might become a merciful and faithful high priest in service to God, and that he might make atonement for^f the sins of the people. ¹⁸Because he himself suffered when he was tempted, he is able to help those who are being tempted.

^a7 Or *him for a little while*; also in verse 9   ^b8 Psalm 8:4-6
^c12 Psalm 22:22   ^d13 Isaiah 8:17   ^e13 Isaiah 8:18
^f17 Or *and that he might turn aside God's wrath, taking away*

PSALM 103:1-22
Of David.

¹**P**raise the Lᴏʀᴅ, O my soul;
  all my inmost being, praise his
      holy name.
²Praise the Lᴏʀᴅ, O my soul,
  and forget not all his benefits—
³who forgives all your sins
  and heals all your diseases,

4 who redeems your life from the pit
   and crowns you with love and
      compassion,
5 who satisfies your desires with good
      things
   so that your youth is renewed like
      the eagle's.

6 The LORD works righteousness
   and justice for all the oppressed.

7 He made known his ways to Moses,
   his deeds to the people of Israel:
8 The LORD is compassionate and
      gracious,
   slow to anger, abounding in love.
9 He will not always accuse,
   nor will he harbor his anger
      forever;
10 he does not treat us as our sins
      deserve
   or repay us according to our
      iniquities.
11 For as high as the heavens are above
      the earth,
   so great is his love for those who
      fear him;
12 as far as the east is from the west,
   so far has he removed our
      transgressions from us.
13 As a father has compassion on his
      children,
   so the LORD has compassion on
      those who fear him;
14 for he knows how we are formed,
   he remembers that we are dust.

15 As for man, his days are like grass,
   he flourishes like a flower of the
      field;
16 the wind blows over it and it is gone,
   and its place remembers it no
      more.
17 But from everlasting to everlasting
   the LORD's love is with those who
      fear him,
   and his righteousness with their
      children's children—
18 with those who keep his covenant
   and remember to obey his
      precepts.

19 The LORD has established his throne
      in heaven,
   and his kingdom rules over all.

20 Praise the LORD, you his angels,
   you mighty ones who do his
      bidding,
   who obey his word.
21 Praise the LORD, all his heavenly hosts,
   you his servants who do his will.
22 Praise the LORD, all his works
   everywhere in his dominion.

   Praise the LORD, O my soul.

PROVERBS 26:23

23 Like a coating of glaze*a* over
      earthenware
   are fervent lips with an evil heart.

a23 With a different word division of the Hebrew; Masoretic
Text *of silver dross*

GOD SIGHTINGS

November 1

EZEKIEL 1:1–3:15

In the[a] thirtieth year, in the fourth month on the fifth day, while I was among the exiles by the Kebar River, the heavens were opened and I saw visions of God.

[2]On the fifth of the month—it was the fifth year of the exile of King Jehoiachin— [3]the word of the LORD came to Ezekiel the priest, the son of Buzi,[b] by the Kebar River in the land of the Babylonians.[c] There the hand of the LORD was upon him.

[4]I looked, and I saw a windstorm coming out of the north—an immense cloud with flashing lightning and surrounded by brilliant light. The center of the fire looked like glowing metal, [5]and in the fire was what looked like four living creatures. In appearance their form was that of a man, [6]but each of them had four faces and four wings. [7]Their legs were straight; their feet were like those of a calf and gleamed like burnished bronze. [8]Under their wings on their four sides they had the hands of a man. All four of them had faces and wings, [9]and their wings touched one another. Each one went straight ahead; they did not turn as they moved.

[10]Their faces looked like this: Each of the four had the face of a man, and on the right side each had the face of a lion, and on the left the face of an ox; each also had the face of an eagle. [11]Such were their faces. Their wings were spread out upward; each had two wings, one touching the wing of another creature on either side, and two wings covering its body. [12]Each one went straight ahead. Wherever the spirit would go, they would go, without turning as they went. [13]The appearance of the living creatures was like burning coals of fire or like torches. Fire moved back and forth among the creatures; it was bright, and lightning flashed out of it. [14]The creatures sped back and forth like flashes of lightning.

[15]As I looked at the living creatures, I saw a wheel on the ground beside each creature with its four faces. [16]This was the appearance and structure of the wheels: They sparkled like chrysolite, and all four looked alike. Each appeared to be made like a wheel intersecting a wheel. [17]As they moved, they would go in any one of the four directions the creatures faced; the wheels did not turn about[d] as the creatures went. [18]Their rims were high and awesome, and all four rims were full of eyes all around.

[19]When the living creatures moved, the wheels beside them moved; and when the living creatures rose from the ground, the wheels also rose. [20]Wherever the spirit would go, they would go, and the wheels would rise along with them, because the spirit of the living creatures was in the wheels. [21]When the creatures moved, they also moved; when the creatures stood still, they also stood still; and when the creatures rose from the ground, the wheels rose along with them, because the spirit of the living creatures was in the wheels.

[22]Spread out above the heads of the living creatures was what looked like an expanse, sparkling like ice, and awesome. [23]Under the expanse their wings were stretched out one toward the other, and each had two wings covering its body. [24]When the creatures moved, I heard the sound of their wings, like the roar of rushing waters, like the voice of the Almighty,[e] like the tumult of an army. When they stood still, they lowered their wings.

[25]Then there came a voice from above the expanse over their heads as they stood with lowered wings. [26]Above the expanse over their heads was what looked like a throne of sapphire,[f] and

high above on the throne was a figure like that of a man. 27 I saw that from what appeared to be his waist up he looked like glowing metal, as if full of fire, and that from there down he looked like fire; and brilliant light surrounded him. 28Like the appearance of a rainbow in the clouds on a rainy day, so was the radiance around him.

This was the appearance of the likeness of the glory of the Lord. When I saw it, I fell facedown, and I heard the voice of one speaking.

2:1He said to me, "Son of man, stand up on your feet and I will speak to you." 2As he spoke, the Spirit came into me and raised me to my feet, and I heard him speaking to me.

3He said: "Son of man, I am sending you to the Israelites, to a rebellious nation that has rebelled against me; they and their fathers have been in revolt against me to this very day. 4The people to whom I am sending you are obstinate and stubborn. Say to them, 'This is what the Sovereign Lord says.' 5And whether they listen or fail to listen—for they are a rebellious house—they will know that a prophet has been among them. 6And you, son of man, do not be afraid of them or their words. Do not be afraid, though briers and thorns are all around you and you live among scorpions. Do not be afraid of what they say or terrified by them, though they are a rebellious house. 7You must speak my words to them, whether they listen or fail to listen, for they are rebellious. 8But you, son of man, listen to what I say to you. Do not rebel like that rebellious house; open your mouth and eat what I give you."

9Then I looked, and I saw a hand stretched out to me. In it was a scroll, 10which he unrolled before me. On both sides of it were written words of lament and mourning and woe.

3:1And he said to me, "Son of man, eat what is before you, eat this scroll; then go and speak to the house of Israel." 2So

I opened my mouth, and he gave me the scroll to eat.

3Then he said to me, "Son of man, eat this scroll I am giving you and fill your stomach with it." So I ate it, and it tasted as sweet as honey in my mouth.

4He then said to me: "Son of man, go now to the house of Israel and speak my words to them. 5You are not being sent to a people of obscure speech and difficult language, but to the house of Israel— 6not to many peoples of obscure speech and difficult language, whose words you cannot understand. Surely if I had sent you to them, they would have listened to you. 7But the house of Israel is not willing to listen to you because they are not willing to listen to me, for the whole house of Israel is hardened and obstinate. 8But I will make you as unyielding and hardened as they are. 9I will make your forehead like the hardest stone, harder than flint. Do not be afraid of them or terrified by them, though they are a rebellious house."

10And he said to me, "Son of man, listen carefully and take to heart all the words I speak to you. 11Go now to your countrymen in exile and speak to them. Say to them, 'This is what the Sovereign Lord says,' whether they listen or fail to listen."

12Then the Spirit lifted me up, and I heard behind me a loud rumbling sound—May the glory of the Lord be praised in his dwelling place!— 13the sound of the wings of the living creatures brushing against each other and the sound of the wheels beside them, a loud rumbling sound. 14The Spirit then lifted me up and took me away, and I went in bitterness and in the anger of my spirit, with the strong hand of the Lord upon me. 15I came to the exiles who lived at Tel Abib near the Kebar River. And there, where they were living, I sat among them for seven days— overwhelmed.

a 1 Or my   b 3 Or Ezekiel son of Buzi the priest
c 3 Or Chaldeans   d 17 Or aside   e 24 Hebrew Shaddai
f 26 Or lapis lazuli

HEBREWS 3:1-19

Therefore, holy brothers, who share in the heavenly calling, fix your thoughts on Jesus, the apostle and high priest whom we confess. ²He was faithful to the one who appointed him, just as Moses was faithful in all God's house. ³Jesus has been found worthy of greater honor than Moses, just as the builder of a house has greater honor than the house itself. ⁴For every house is built by someone, but God is the builder of everything. ⁵Moses was faithful as a servant in all God's house, testifying to what would be said in the future. ⁶But Christ is faithful as a son over God's house. And we are his house, if we hold on to our courage and the hope of which we boast.

⁷So, as the Holy Spirit says:

"Today, if you hear his voice,
⁸ do not harden your hearts
as you did in the rebellion,
during the time of testing in the desert,
⁹where your fathers tested and tried me
and for forty years saw what I did.
¹⁰That is why I was angry with that generation,
and I said, 'Their hearts are always going astray,
and they have not known my ways.'
¹¹So I declared on oath in my anger,
'They shall never enter my rest.'"ᵃ

¹²**See to it, brothers, that none of you has a sinful, unbelieving heart that turns away from the living God.** ¹³**But encourage one another daily, as long as it is called Today, so that none of you may be hardened by sin's deceitfulness.** ¹⁴We have come to share in Christ if we hold firmly till the end the confidence we had at first. ¹⁵As has just been said:

"Today, if you hear his voice,
do not harden your hearts
as you did in the rebellion."ᵇ

¹⁶Who were they who heard and rebelled? Were they not all those Moses led out of Egypt? ¹⁷And with whom was he angry for forty years? Was it not with those who sinned, whose bodies fell in the desert? ¹⁸And to whom did God swear that they would never enter his rest if not to those who disobeyedᶜ? ¹⁹So we see that they were not able to enter, because of their unbelief.

a11 Psalm 95:7-11   *b15* Psalm 95:7,8   *c18* Or *disbelieved*

PSALM 104:1-23

¹ **P**raise the Lord, O my soul.

O Lord my God, you are very great;
you are clothed with splendor and majesty.
² He wraps himself in light as with a garment;
he stretches out the heavens like a tent
³ and lays the beams of his upper chambers on their waters.
He makes the clouds his chariot
and rides on the wings of the wind.
⁴ He makes winds his messengers,ᵃ
flames of fire his servants.
⁵ He set the earth on its foundations;
it can never be moved.
⁶ You covered it with the deep as with a garment;
the waters stood above the mountains.
⁷ But at your rebuke the waters fled,
at the sound of your thunder they took to flight;
⁸ they flowed over the mountains,
they went down into the valleys,
to the place you assigned for them.
⁹ You set a boundary they cannot cross;
never again will they cover the earth.
¹⁰ He makes springs pour water into the ravines;
it flows between the mountains.
¹¹ They give water to all the beasts of the field;
the wild donkeys quench their thirst.

12 The birds of the air nest by the waters;
    they sing among the branches.
13 He waters the mountains from his
        upper chambers;
    the earth is satisfied by the fruit of
        his work.
14 He makes grass grow for the cattle,
    and plants for man to cultivate—
        bringing forth food from the earth:
15 wine that gladdens the heart of man,
    oil to make his face shine,
    and bread that sustains his heart.
16 The trees of the Lord are well
        watered,
    the cedars of Lebanon that he
        planted.
17 There the birds make their nests;
    the stork has its home in the pine
        trees.
18 The high mountains belong to the
        wild goats;
    the crags are a refuge for the
        coneys.*b*

19 The moon marks off the seasons,
    and the sun knows when to go
        down.
20 You bring darkness, it becomes
        night,
    and all the beasts of the forest
        prowl.
21 The lions roar for their prey
    and seek their food from God.
22 The sun rises, and they steal away;
    they return and lie down in their
        dens.
23 Then man goes out to his work,
    to his labor until evening.

a4 Or *angels*   *b18* That is, the hyrax or rock badger

PROVERBS 26:24-26

24 **A** malicious man disguises himself
        with his lips,
    but in his heart he harbors deceit.
25 Though his speech is charming, do
        not believe him,
    for seven abominations fill his
        heart.
26 His malice may be concealed by
        deception,
    but his wickedness will be
        exposed in the assembly.

□ DAY 306

GOD SIGHTINGS

November 2

EZEKIEL 3:16-6:14

At the end of seven days the word of the Lord came to me [Ezekiel]: 17 "Son of man, I have made you a watchman for the house of Israel; so hear the word I speak and give them warning from me. 18 When I say to a wicked man, 'You will surely die,' and you do not warn him or speak out to dissuade him from his evil ways in order to save his life, that wicked man will die for*a* his sin, and I will hold you accountable for his blood. 19 But if you do warn the wicked man and he does not turn from his wickedness or from his evil ways, he will die for his sin; but you will have saved yourself.

20 "Again, when a righteous man turns from his righteousness and does evil, and I put a stumbling block before him, he will die. Since you did not warn him, he will die for his sin. The righteous things he did will not be remembered, and I will hold you accountable for his blood. 21 But if you do warn the righteous man not to sin and he does not sin, he will surely live because he took warning, and you will have saved yourself."

22 The hand of the Lord was upon me there, and he said to me, "Get up and go out to the plain, and there I will speak to you." 23 So I got up and went out to the plain. And the glory of the Lord was standing there, like the glory I had seen by the Kebar River, and I fell facedown.

24 Then the Spirit came into me and raised me to my feet. He spoke to me and said: "Go, shut yourself inside your house. 25 And you, son of man, they will tie with ropes; you will be bound so that you cannot go out among the people. 26 I will make your tongue stick to the roof of your mouth so that you will be silent and unable to rebuke them, though they are a rebellious house. 27 But when I speak to you, I will open your mouth

and you shall say to them, 'This is what the Sovereign LORD says.' Whoever will listen let him listen, and whoever will refuse let him refuse; for they are a rebellious house.

4:1"Now, son of man, take a clay tablet, put it in front of you and draw the city of Jerusalem on it. 2 Then lay siege to it: Erect siege works against it, build a ramp up to it, set up camps against it and put battering rams around it. 3 Then take an iron pan, place it as an iron wall between you and the city and turn your face toward it. It will be under siege, and you shall besiege it. This will be a sign to the house of Israel.

4"Then lie on your left side and put the sin of the house of Israel upon yourself.b You are to bear their sin for the number of days you lie on your side. 5 I have assigned you the same number of days as the years of their sin. So for 390 days you will bear the sin of the house of Israel.

6"After you have finished this, lie down again, this time on your right side, and bear the sin of the house of Judah. I have assigned you 40 days, a day for each year. 7 Turn your face toward the siege of Jerusalem and with bared arm prophesy against her. 8 I will tie you up with ropes so that you cannot turn from one side to the other until you have finished the days of your siege.

9"Take wheat and barley, beans and lentils, millet and spelt; put them in a storage jar and use them to make bread for yourself. You are to eat it during the 390 days you lie on your side. 10Weigh out twenty shekelsc of food to eat each day and eat it at set times. 11Also measure out a sixth of a hind of water and drink it at set times. 12Eat the food as you would a barley cake; bake it in the sight of the people, using human excrement for fuel." 13The LORD said, "In this way the people of Israel will eat defiled food among the nations where I will drive them."

14Then I said, "Not so, Sovereign LORD! I have never defiled myself. From my youth until now I have never eaten anything found dead or torn by wild animals. No unclean meat has ever entered my mouth."

15"Very well," he said, "I will let you bake your bread over cow manure instead of human excrement."

16He then said to me: "Son of man, I will cut off the supply of food in Jerusalem. The people will eat rationed food in anxiety and drink rationed water in despair, 17 for food and water will be scarce. They will be appalled at the sight of each other and will waste away because ofe their sin.

5:1"Now, son of man, take a sharp sword and use it as a barber's razor to shave your head and your beard. Then take a set of scales and divide up the hair. 2 When the days of your siege come to an end, burn a third of the hair with fire inside the city. Take a third and strike it with the sword all around the city. And scatter a third to the wind. For I will pursue them with drawn sword. 3 But take a few strands of hair and tuck them away in the folds of your garment. 4 Again, take a few of these and throw them into the fire and burn them up. A fire will spread from there to the whole house of Israel.

5"This is what the Sovereign LORD says: This is Jerusalem, which I have set in the center of the nations, with countries all around her. 6 Yet in her wickedness she has rebelled against my laws and decrees more than the nations and countries around her. She has rejected my laws and has not followed my decrees.

7"Therefore this is what the Sovereign LORD says: You have been more unruly than the nations around you and have not followed my decrees or kept my laws. You have not evenf conformed to the standards of the nations around you.

8"Therefore this is what the Sovereign LORD says: I myself am against you, Jerusalem, and I will inflict punishment on you in the sight of the nations. 9 Because of all your detestable idols, I will do to you what I have never done before and will never do again. [10]Therefore in your midst fathers will eat their children, and children will eat their fathers. I will inflict punishment on you and will scatter all your survivors to the winds. [11]Therefore as surely as I live, declares the Sovereign Lord, because you have defiled my sanctuary with all your vile images and detestable practices, I myself will withdraw my favor; I will not look on you with pity or spare you. [12]A third of your people will die of the plague or perish by famine inside you; a third will fall by the sword outside your walls; and a third I will scatter to the winds and pursue with drawn sword.

[13]"Then my anger will cease and my wrath against them will subside, and I will be avenged. And when I have spent my wrath upon them, they will know that I the Lord have spoken in my zeal.

[14]"I will make you a ruin and a reproach among the nations around you, in the sight of all who pass by. [15]You will be a reproach and a taunt, a warning and an object of horror to the nations around you when I inflict punishment on you in anger and in wrath and with stinging rebuke. I the Lord have spoken. [16]When I shoot at you with my deadly and destructive arrows of famine, I will shoot to destroy you. I will bring more and more famine upon you and cut off your supply of food. [17]I will send famine and wild beasts against you, and they will leave you childless. Plague and bloodshed will sweep through you, and I will bring the sword against you. I the Lord have spoken."

[6:1]The word of the Lord came to me: [2]"Son of man, set your face against the mountains of Israel; prophesy against them [3]and say: 'O mountains of Israel, hear the word of the Sovereign Lord. This is what the Sovereign Lord says to the mountains and hills, to the ravines and valleys: I am about to bring a sword against you, and I will destroy your high places. [4]Your altars will be demolished and your incense altars will be smashed; and I will slay your people in front of your idols. [5]I will lay the dead bodies of the Israelites in front of their idols, and I will scatter your bones around your altars. [6]Wherever you live, the towns will be laid waste and the high places demolished, so that your altars will be laid waste and devastated, your idols smashed and ruined, your incense altars broken down, and what you have made wiped out. [7]Your people will fall slain among you, and you will know that I am the Lord.

[8]" 'But I will spare some, for some of you will escape the sword when you are scattered among the lands and nations. [9]Then in the nations where they have been carried captive, those who escape will remember me—how I have been grieved by their adulterous hearts, which have turned away from me, and by their eyes, which have lusted after their idols. They will loathe themselves for the evil they have done and for all their detestable practices. [10]And they will know that I am the Lord; I did not threaten in vain to bring this calamity on them.

[11]" 'This is what the Sovereign Lord says: Strike your hands together and stamp your feet and cry out "Alas!" because of all the wicked and detestable practices of the house of Israel, for they will fall by the sword, famine and plague. [12]He that is far away will die of the plague, and he that is near will fall by the sword, and he that survives and is spared will die of famine. So will I spend my wrath upon them. [13]And they will know that I am the Lord, when their people lie slain among their idols around their altars, on every high hill and on all the mountaintops, under every spreading tree and every leafy oak—places where they offered fragrant incense to all their idols. [14]And I will stretch out my hand against them and make the land a desolate waste from the desert to Diblah*g*—wherever they live. Then they will know that I am the Lord.'"

a18 Or *in*; also in verses 19 and 20   *b4* Or *your side*   *c10* That is, about 8 ounces (about 0.2 kilogram)   *d11* That is, about 2/3 quart (about 0.6 liter)   *e17* Or *away in*   *f7* Most Hebrew manuscripts; some Hebrew manuscripts and Syriac *You have*   *g14* Most Hebrew manuscripts; a few Hebrew manuscripts *Riblah*

HEBREWS 4:1-16

Therefore, since the promise of entering his [God's] rest still stands, let us be careful that none of you be found to have fallen short of it. ²For we also have had the gospel preached to us, just as they did; but the message they heard was of no value to them, because those who heard did not combine it with faith.ᵃ ³Now we who have believed enter that rest, just as God has said,

"So I declared on oath in my anger,
'They shall never enter my rest.'"ᵇ

And yet his work has been finished since the creation of the world. ⁴For somewhere he has spoken about the seventh day in these words: "And on the seventh day God rested from all his work."ᶜ ⁵And again in the passage above he says, "They shall never enter my rest."

⁶It still remains that some will enter that rest, and those who formerly had the gospel preached to them did not go in, because of their disobedience. ⁷Therefore God again set a certain day, calling it Today, when a long time later he spoke through David, as was said before:

"Today, if you hear his voice,
do not harden your hearts."ᵈ

⁸For if Joshua had given them rest, God would not have spoken later about another day. ⁹There remains, then, a Sabbath-rest for the people of God; ¹⁰for anyone who enters God's rest also rests from his own work, just as God did from his. ¹¹Let us, therefore, make every effort to enter that rest, so that no one will fall by following their example of disobedience.

¹²**For the word of God is living and active. Sharper than any double-edged sword, it penetrates even to dividing soul and spirit, joints and marrow; it judges the thoughts and attitudes of the heart.** ¹³Nothing in all creation is hidden from God's sight. Everything is uncovered and laid bare before the eyes of him to whom we must give account.

¹⁴Therefore, since we have a great high priest who has gone through the heavens,ᵉ Jesus the Son of God, let us hold firmly to the faith we profess. ¹⁵For we do not have a high priest who is unable to sympathize with our weaknesses, but we have one who has been tempted in every way, just as we are—yet was without sin. ¹⁶Let us then approach the throne of grace with confidence, so that we may receive mercy and find grace to help us in our time of need.

ᵃ2 Many manuscripts *because they did not share in the faith of those who obeyed* ᵇ3 Psalm 95:11; also in verse 5 ᶜ4 Gen. 2:2 ᵈ7 Psalm 95:7,8 ᵉ14 Or *gone into heaven*

PSALM 104:24-35

²⁴**H**ow many are your works, O Lᴏʀᴅ!
In wisdom you made them all;
the earth is full of your creatures.
²⁵There is the sea, vast and spacious,
teeming with creatures beyond
number—
living things both large and small.
²⁶There the ships go to and fro,
and the leviathan, which you
formed to frolic there.

²⁷These all look to you
to give them their food at the
proper time.
²⁸When you give it to them,
they gather it up;
when you open your hand,
they are satisfied with good
things.
²⁹When you hide your face,
they are terrified;
when you take away their breath,
they die and return to the dust.
³⁰When you send your Spirit,
they are created,
and you renew the face of the
earth.

³¹May the glory of the Lᴏʀᴅ endure
forever;
may the Lᴏʀᴅ rejoice in his
works—
³²he who looks at the earth, and it
trembles,
who touches the mountains, and
they smoke.

³³I will sing to the Lord all my life;
   I will sing praise to my God as long
      as I live.
³⁴May my meditation be pleasing to
      him,
   as I rejoice in the Lord.
³⁵But may sinners vanish from the
      earth
   and the wicked be no more.

Praise the Lord, O my soul.

Praise the Lord.^a

^a35 Hebrew *Hallelu Yah*; in the Septuagint this line stands at
the beginning of Psalm 105.

PROVERBS 26:27

²⁷ If a man digs a pit, he will fall into it;
   if a man rolls a stone, it will roll
      back on him.

□ D A Y   3 0 7

GOD SIGHTINGS

November 3

EZEKIEL 7:1–9:11

The word of the Lord came to me
[Ezekiel]: ²"Son of man, this is what the
Sovereign Lord says to the land of Israel:
The end! The end has come upon the
four corners of the land. ³The end is
now upon you and I will unleash my anger against you. I will judge you according to your conduct and repay you for all
your detestable practices. ⁴I will not
look on you with pity or spare you; I will
surely repay you for your conduct and
the detestable practices among you.
Then you will know that I am the Lord.

⁵"This is what the Sovereign Lord
says: Disaster! An unheard-of^a disaster
is coming. ⁶The end has come! The end
has come! It has roused itself against
you. It has come! ⁷Doom has come upon
you—you who dwell in the land. The
time has come, the day is near; there is
panic, not joy, upon the mountains. ⁸I
am about to pour out my wrath on you

and spend my anger against you; I will
judge you according to your conduct
and repay you for all your detestable
practices. ⁹I will not look on you with
pity or spare you; I will repay you in accordance with your conduct and the detestable practices among you. Then you
will know that it is I the Lord who
strikes the blow.

¹⁰"The day is here! It has come!
Doom has burst forth, the rod has budded, arrogance has blossomed! ¹¹Vio-
lence has grown into^b a rod to punish
wickedness; none of the people will be
left, none of that crowd—no wealth,
nothing of value. ¹²The time has come,
the day has arrived. Let not the buyer rejoice nor the seller grieve, for wrath is
upon the whole crowd. ¹³The seller will
not recover the land he has sold as long
as both of them live, for the vision concerning the whole crowd will not be re-
versed. Because of their sins, not one of
them will preserve his life. ¹⁴Though
they blow the trumpet and get everything ready, no one will go into battle,
for my wrath is upon the whole crowd.

¹⁵"Outside is the sword, inside are
plague and famine; those in the country
will die by the sword, and those in the
city will be devoured by famine and
plague. ¹⁶All who survive and escape
will be in the mountains, moaning like
doves of the valleys, each because of his
sins. ¹⁷Every hand will go limp, and every knee will become as weak as water.
¹⁸They will put on sackcloth and be
clothed with terror. Their faces will be
covered with shame and their heads
will be shaved. ¹⁹They will throw their
silver into the streets, and their gold will
be an unclean thing. Their silver and
gold will not be able to save them in the
day of the Lord's wrath. They will not
satisfy their hunger or fill their stom-
achs with it, for it has made them stumble into sin. ²⁰They were proud of their
beautiful jewelry and used it to make
their detestable idols and vile images.
Therefore I will turn these into an unclean thing for them. ²¹I will hand it all
over as plunder to foreigners and as loot

to the wicked of the earth, and they will defile it. 22I will turn my face away from them, and they will desecrate my treasured place; robbers will enter it and desecrate it.

23"Prepare chains, because the land is full of bloodshed and the city is full of violence. 24I will bring the most wicked of the nations to take possession of their houses; I will put an end to the pride of the mighty, and their sanctuaries will be desecrated. 25When terror comes, they will seek peace, but there will be none. 26Calamity upon calamity will come, and rumor upon rumor. They will try to get a vision from the prophet; the teaching of the law by the priest will be lost, as will the counsel of the elders. 27The king will mourn, the prince will be clothed with despair, and the hands of the people of the land will tremble. I will deal with them according to their conduct, and by their own standards I will judge them. Then they will know that I am the LORD."

8:1IN the sixth year, in the sixth month on the fifth day, while I was sitting in my house and the elders of Judah were sitting before me, the hand of the Sovereign LORD came upon me there. 2I looked, and I saw a figure like that of a man.c From what appeared to be his waist down he was like fire, and from there up his appearance was as bright as glowing metal. 3He stretched out what looked like a hand and took me by the hair of my head. The Spirit lifted me up between earth and heaven and in visions of God he took me to Jerusalem, to the entrance to the north gate of the inner court, where the idol that provokes to jealousy stood. 4And there before me was the glory of the God of Israel, as in the vision I had seen in the plain.

5Then he said to me, "Son of man, look toward the north." So I looked, and in the entrance north of the gate of the altar I saw this idol of jealousy.

6And he said to me, "Son of man, do you see what they are doing—the utterly detestable things the house of Israel is

doing here, things that will drive me far from my sanctuary? But you will see things that are even more detestable."

7Then he brought me to the entrance to the court. I looked, and I saw a hole in the wall. 8He said to me, "Son of man, now dig into the wall." So I dug into the wall and saw a doorway there.

9And he said to me, "Go in and see the wicked and detestable things they are doing here." 10So I went in and looked, and I saw portrayed all over the walls all kinds of crawling things and detestable animals and all the idols of the house of Israel. 11In front of them stood seventy elders of the house of Israel, and Jaazaniah son of Shaphan was standing among them. Each had a censer in his hand, and a fragrant cloud of incense was rising.

12He said to me, "Son of man, have you seen what the elders of the house of Israel are doing in the darkness, each at the shrine of his own idol? They say, 'The LORD does not see us; the LORD has forsaken the land.' " 13Again, he said, "You will see them doing things that are even more detestable."

14Then he brought me to the entrance to the north gate of the house of the LORD, and I saw women sitting there, mourning for Tammuz. 15He said to me, "Do you see this, son of man? You will see things that are even more detestable than this."

16He then brought me into the inner court of the house of the LORD, and there at the entrance to the temple, between the portico and the altar, were about twenty-five men. With their backs toward the temple of the LORD and their faces toward the east, they were bowing down to the sun in the east.

17He said to me, "Have you seen this, son of man? Is it a trivial matter for the house of Judah to do the detestable things they are doing here? Must they also fill the land with violence and continually provoke me to anger? Look at them putting the branch to their nose! 18Therefore I will deal with them in anger; I will not look on them with pity or spare them. Although they shout in my ears, I will not listen to them."

9:1Then I heard him call out in a loud voice, "Bring the guards of the city here, each with a weapon in his hand." 2And I saw six men coming from the direction of the upper gate, which faces north, each with a deadly weapon in his hand. With them was a man clothed in linen who had a writing kit at his side. They came in and stood beside the bronze altar.

3Now the glory of the God of Israel went up from above the cherubim, where it had been, and moved to the threshold of the temple. Then the Lord called to the man clothed in linen who had the writing kit at his side 4and said to him, "Go throughout the city of Jerusalem and put a mark on the foreheads of those who grieve and lament over all the detestable things that are done in it."

5As I listened, he said to the others, "Follow him through the city and kill, without showing pity or compassion. 6Slaughter old men, young men and maidens, women and children, but do not touch anyone who has the mark. Begin at my sanctuary." So they began with the elders who were in front of the temple.

7Then he said to them, "Defile the temple and fill the courts with the slain. Go!" So they went out and began killing throughout the city. 8While they were killing and I was left alone, I fell facedown, crying out, "Ah, Sovereign Lord! Are you going to destroy the entire remnant of Israel in this outpouring of your wrath on Jerusalem?"

9He answered me, "The sin of the house of Israel and Judah is exceedingly great; the land is full of bloodshed and the city is full of injustice. They say, 'The Lord has forsaken the land; the Lord does not see.' 10So I will not look on them with pity or spare them, but I will bring down on their own heads what they have done."

11Then the man in linen with the writing kit at his side brought back

word, saying, "I have done as you commanded."

a5 Most Hebrew manuscripts; some Hebrew manuscripts and Syriac *Disaster after*   b11 Or *The violent one has become*   c2 Or *saw a fiery figure*

HEBREWS 5:1-14

Every high priest is selected from among men and is appointed to represent them in matters related to God, to offer gifts and sacrifices for sins. 2He is able to deal gently with those who are ignorant and are going astray, since he himself is subject to weakness. 3This is why he has to offer sacrifices for his own sins, as well as for the sins of the people.

4No one takes this honor upon himself; he must be called by God, just as Aaron was. 5So Christ also did not take upon himself the glory of becoming a high priest. But God said to him,

"You are my Son;
    today I have become your
        Father.*a"b*

6And he says in another place,

"You are a priest forever,
    in the order of Melchizedek."*c*

7During the days of Jesus' life on earth, he offered up prayers and petitions with loud cries and tears to the one who could save him from death, and he was heard because of his reverent submission. **8Although he was a son, he learned obedience from what he suffered 9and, once made perfect, he became the source of eternal salvation for all who obey him** 10and was designated by God to be high priest in the order of Melchizedek.

11We have much to say about this, but it is hard to explain because you are slow to learn. 12In fact, though by this time you ought to be teachers, you need someone to teach you the elementary truths of God's word all over again. You need milk, not solid food! 13Anyone who lives on milk, being still an infant, is not acquainted with the teaching about righteousness. 14But solid food is for the mature, who by constant use have trained themselves to distinguish good from evil.

a5 Or have begotten you   b5 Psalm 2:7   c6 Psalm 110:4

PSALM 105:1-15

¹**G**ive thanks to the Lord, call on his
    name;
  make known among the nations
    what he has done.
²Sing to him, sing praise to him;
  tell of all his wonderful acts.
³Glory in his holy name;
  let the hearts of those who seek
    the Lord rejoice.
⁴Look to the Lord and his strength;
  seek his face always.

⁵Remember the wonders he has done,
  his miracles, and the judgments he
    pronounced,
⁶O descendants of Abraham his
    servant,
  O sons of Jacob, his chosen ones.
⁷He is the Lord our God;
  his judgments are in all the earth.

⁸He remembers his covenant forever,
  the word he commanded, for a
    thousand generations,
⁹the covenant he made with Abraham,
  the oath he swore to Isaac.
¹⁰He confirmed it to Jacob as a decree,
  to Israel as an everlasting
    covenant:
¹¹"To you I will give the land of Canaan
  as the portion you will inherit."

¹²When they were but few in number,
  few indeed, and strangers in it,
¹³they wandered from nation to nation,
  from one kingdom to another.
¹⁴He allowed no one to oppress them;
  for their sake he rebuked kings:
¹⁵"Do not touch my anointed ones;
  do my prophets no harm."

PROVERBS 26:28

²⁸**A** lying tongue hates those it hurts,
  and a flattering mouth works ruin.

□ DAY 308

GOD SIGHTINGS

November 4

EZEKIEL 10:1–11:25

1 [Ezekiel] looked, and I saw the likeness of a throne of sapphire[a] above the expanse that was over the heads of the cherubim. ²The Lord said to the man clothed in linen, "Go in among the wheels beneath the cherubim. Fill your hands with burning coals from among the cherubim and scatter them over the city." And as I watched, he went in.

³Now the cherubim were standing on the south side of the temple when the man went in, and a cloud filled the inner court. ⁴Then the glory of the Lord rose from above the cherubim and moved to the threshold of the temple. The cloud filled the temple, and the court was full of the radiance of the glory of the Lord. ⁵The sound of the wings of the cherubim could be heard as far away as the outer court, like the voice of God Almighty[b] when he speaks.

⁶When the Lord commanded the man in linen, "Take fire from among the wheels, from among the cherubim," the man went in and stood beside a wheel. ⁷Then one of the cherubim reached out his hand to the fire that was among them. He took up some of it and put it into the hands of the man in linen, who took it and went out. ⁸(Under the wings of the cherubim could be seen what looked like the hands of a man.)

⁹I looked, and I saw beside the cherubim four wheels, one beside each of the cherubim; the wheels sparkled like chrysolite. ¹⁰As for their appearance, the four of them looked alike; each was like a wheel intersecting a wheel. ¹¹As they moved, they would go in any one of the four directions the cherubim faced; the wheels did not turn about[c] as the cherubim went. The cherubim went in whatever direction the head faced, without turning as they went. ¹²Their

entire bodies, including their backs, their hands and their wings, were completely full of eyes, as were their four wheels. ¹³I heard the wheels being called "the whirling wheels." ¹⁴Each of the cherubim had four faces: One face was that of a cherub, the second the face of a man, the third the face of a lion, and the fourth the face of an eagle.

¹⁵Then the cherubim rose upward. These were the living creatures I had seen by the Kebar River. ¹⁶When the cherubim moved, the wheels beside them moved; and when the cherubim spread their wings to rise from the ground, the wheels did not leave their side. ¹⁷When the cherubim stood still, they also stood still; and when the cherubim rose, they rose with them, because the spirit of the living creatures was in them.

¹⁸Then the glory of the LORD departed from over the threshold of the temple and stopped above the cherubim. ¹⁹While I watched, the cherubim spread their wings and rose from the ground, and as they went, the wheels went with them. They stopped at the entrance to the east gate of the LORD's house, and the glory of the God of Israel was above them.

²⁰These were the living creatures I had seen beneath the God of Israel by the Kebar River, and I realized that they were cherubim. ²¹Each had four faces and four wings, and under their wings was what looked like the hands of a man. ²²Their faces had the same appearance as those I had seen by the Kebar River. Each one went straight ahead.

¹¹:¹THEN the Spirit lifted me up and brought me to the gate of the house of the LORD that faces east. There at the entrance to the gate were twenty-five men, and I saw among them Jaazaniah son of Azzur and Pelatiah son of Benaiah, leaders of the people. ²The LORD said to me, "Son of man, these are the men who are plotting evil and giving wicked advice in this city. ³They say, 'Will it not soon be time to build houses?ᵈ This city is a cooking pot, and

we are the meat.' ⁴Therefore prophesy against them; prophesy, son of man."

⁵Then the Spirit of the LORD came upon me, and he told me to say: "This is what the LORD says: That is what you are saying, O house of Israel, but I know what is going through your mind. ⁶You have killed many people in this city and filled its streets with the dead.

⁷"Therefore this is what the Sovereign LORD says: The bodies you have thrown there are the meat and this city is the pot, but I will drive you out of it. ⁸You fear the sword, and the sword is what I will bring against you, declares the Sovereign LORD. ⁹I will drive you out of the city and hand you over to foreigners and inflict punishment on you. ¹⁰You will fall by the sword, and I will execute judgment on you at the borders of Israel. Then you will know that I am the LORD. ¹¹This city will not be a pot for you, nor will you be the meat in it; I will execute judgment on you at the borders of Israel. ¹²And you will know that I am the LORD, for you have not followed my decrees or kept my laws but have conformed to the standards of the nations around you."

¹³Now as I was prophesying, Pelatiah son of Benaiah died. Then I fell facedown and cried out in a loud voice, "Ah, Sovereign LORD! Will you completely destroy the remnant of Israel?"

¹⁴The word of the LORD came to me: ¹⁵"Son of man, your brothers—your brothers who are your blood relativesᵉ and the whole house of Israel—are those of whom the people of Jerusalem have said, 'They areᶠ far away from the LORD; this land was given to us as our possession.'

¹⁶"Therefore say: 'This is what the Sovereign LORD says: Although I sent them far away among the nations and scattered them among the countries, yet for a little while I have been a sanctuary for them in the countries where they have gone.'

¹⁷"Therefore say: 'This is what the Sovereign LORD says: I will gather you from the nations and bring you back

from the countries where you have been scattered, and I will give you back the land of Israel again.'

¹⁸"They will return to it and remove all its vile images and detestable idols. ¹⁹I will give them an undivided heart and put a new spirit in them; I will remove from them their heart of stone and give them a heart of flesh. ²⁰Then they will follow my decrees and be careful to keep my laws. They will be my people, and I will be their God. ²¹But as for those whose hearts are devoted to their vile images and detestable idols, I will bring down on their own heads what they have done, declares the Sovereign LORD."

²²Then the cherubim, with the wheels beside them, spread their wings, and the glory of the God of Israel was above them. ²³The glory of the LORD went up from within the city and stopped above the mountain east of it. ²⁴The Spirit lifted me up and brought me to the exiles in Babyloniaᵍ in the vision given by the Spirit of God.

Then the vision I had seen went up from me, ²⁵and I told the exiles everything the LORD had shown me.

a1 Or lapis lazuli   b5 Hebrew El-Shaddai   c11 Or aside   d3 Or This is not the time to build houses.   e15 Or are in exile with you (see Septuagint and Syriac)   f15 Or those to whom the people of Jerusalem have said, 'Stay   g24 Or Chaldea

HEBREWS 6:1-20

Therefore let us leave the elementary teachings about Christ and go on to maturity, not laying again the foundation of repentance from acts that lead to death,ᵃ and of faith in God, ²instruction about baptisms, the laying on of hands, the resurrection of the dead, and eternal judgment. ³And God permitting, we will do so.

⁴It is impossible for those who have once been enlightened, who have tasted the heavenly gift, who have shared in the Holy Spirit, ⁵who have tasted the goodness of the word of God and the powers of the coming age, ⁶if they fall away, to be brought back to repentance, becauseᵇ to their loss they are crucify-

ing the Son of God all over again and subjecting him to public disgrace.

⁷Land that drinks in the rain often falling on it and that produces a crop useful to those for whom it is farmed receives the blessing of God. ⁸But land that produces thorns and thistles is worthless and is in danger of being cursed. In the end it will be burned.

⁹Even though we speak like this, dear friends, we are confident of better things in your case—things that accompany salvation. ¹⁰**God is not unjust; he will not forget your work and the love you have shown him as you have helped his people and continue to help them.** ¹¹We want each of you to show this same diligence to the very end, in order to make your hope sure. ¹²We do not want you to become lazy, but to imitate those who through faith and patience inherit what has been promised.

¹³When God made his promise to Abraham, since there was no one greater for him to swear by, he swore by himself, ¹⁴saying, "I will surely bless you and give you many descendants."ᶜ ¹⁵And so after waiting patiently, Abraham received what was promised.

¹⁶Men swear by someone greater than themselves, and the oath confirms what is said and puts an end to all argument. ¹⁷Because God wanted to make the unchanging nature of his purpose very clear to the heirs of what was promised, he confirmed it with an oath. ¹⁸God did this so that, by two unchangeable things in which it is impossible for God to lie, we who have fled to take hold of the hope offered to us may be greatly encouraged. ¹⁹We have this hope as an anchor for the soul, firm and secure. It enters the inner sanctuary behind the curtain, ²⁰where Jesus, who went before us, has entered on our behalf. He has become a high priest forever, in the order of Melchizedek.

a1 Or from useless rituals   b6 Or repentance while   c14 Gen. 22:17

PSALM 105:16-36

16 He [the LORD] called down famine on
    the land
    and destroyed all their supplies of
      food;
17 and he sent a man before them—
    Joseph, sold as a slave.
18 They bruised his feet with shackles,
    his neck was put in irons,
19 till what he foretold came to pass,
    till the word of the LORD proved
      him true.
20 The king sent and released him,
    the ruler of peoples set him free.
21 He made him master of his
      household,
    ruler over all he possessed,
22 to instruct his princes as he pleased
    and teach his elders wisdom.

23 Then Israel entered Egypt;
    Jacob lived as an alien in the land
      of Ham.
24 The LORD made his people very
      fruitful;
    he made them too numerous for
      their foes,
25 whose hearts he turned to hate his
      people,
    to conspire against his servants.
26 He sent Moses his servant,
    and Aaron, whom he had chosen.
27 They performed his miraculous signs
      among them,
    his wonders in the land of Ham.
28 He sent darkness and made the land
      dark—
    for had they not rebelled against
      his words?
29 He turned their waters into blood,
    causing their fish to die.
30 Their land teemed with frogs,
    which went up into the bedrooms
      of their rulers.
31 He spoke, and there came swarms of
      flies,
    and gnats throughout their
      country.
32 He turned their rain into hail,
    with lightning throughout their
      land;

33 he struck down their vines and fig
      trees
    and shattered the trees of their
      country.
34 He spoke, and the locusts came,
    grasshoppers without number;
35 they ate up every green thing in their
      land,
    ate up the produce of their soil.
36 Then he struck down all the
      firstborn in their land,
    the firstfruits of all their
      manhood.

PROVERBS 27:1-2

Do not boast about tomorrow,
    for you do not know what a day
      may bring forth.

2 Let another praise you, and not your
      own mouth;
    someone else, and not your own
      lips.

☐ D A Y 3 0 9

GOD SIGHTINGS

November 5

EZEKIEL 12:1–14:11

The word of the LORD came to me
[Ezekiel]: 2 "Son of man, you are living
among a rebellious people. They have
eyes to see but do not see and ears to
hear but do not hear, for they are a rebellious people.

3 "Therefore, son of man, pack your
belongings for exile and in the daytime,
as they watch, set out and go from where
you are to another place. Perhaps they
will understand, though they are a rebellious house. 4 During the daytime,
while they watch, bring out your belongings packed for exile. Then in the
evening, while they are watching, go out
like those who go into exile. 5 While
they watch, dig through the wall and
take your belongings out through it.
6 Put them on your shoulder as they are

watching and carry them out at dusk. Cover your face so that you cannot see the land, for I have made you a sign to the house of Israel."

7So I did as I was commanded. During the day I brought out my things packed for exile. Then in the evening I dug through the wall with my hands. I took my belongings out at dusk, carrying them on my shoulders while they watched.

8In the morning the word of the Lord came to me: 9"Son of man, did not that rebellious house of Israel ask you, 'What are you doing?'

10"Say to them, 'This is what the Sovereign Lord says: This oracle concerns the prince in Jerusalem and the whole house of Israel who are there.' 11Say to them, 'I am a sign to you.'

"As I have done, so it will be done to them. They will go into exile as captives.

12"The prince among them will put his things on his shoulder at dusk and leave, and a hole will be dug in the wall for him to go through. He will cover his face so that he cannot see the land. 13I will spread my net for him, and he will be caught in my snare; I will bring him to Babylonia, the land of the Chaldeans, but he will not see it, and there he will die. 14I will scatter to the winds all those around him—his staff and all his troops—and I will pursue them with drawn sword.

15"They will know that I am the Lord, when I disperse them among the nations and scatter them through the countries. 16But I will spare a few of them from the sword, famine and plague, so that in the nations where they go they may acknowledge all their detestable practices. Then they will know that I am the Lord."

17The word of the Lord came to me: 18"Son of man, tremble as you eat your food, and shudder in fear as you drink your water. 19Say to the people of the land: 'This is what the Sovereign Lord says about those living in Jerusalem and in the land of Israel: They will eat their food in anxiety and drink their water in despair, for their land will be stripped of everything in it because of the violence of all who live there. 20The inhabited towns will be laid waste and the land will be desolate. Then you will know that I am the Lord.'"

21The word of the Lord came to me: 22"Son of man, what is this proverb you have in the land of Israel: 'The days go by and every vision comes to nothing'? 23Say to them, 'This is what the Sovereign Lord says: I am going to put an end to this proverb, and they will no longer quote it in Israel.' Say to them, 'The days are near when every vision will be fulfilled. 24For there will be no more false visions or flattering divinations among the people of Israel. 25But I the Lord will speak what I will, and it shall be fulfilled without delay. For in your days, you rebellious house, I will fulfill whatever I say, declares the Sovereign Lord.'"

26The word of the Lord came to me: 27"Son of man, the house of Israel is saying, 'The vision he sees is for many years from now, and he prophesies about the distant future.'

28"Therefore say to them, 'This is what the Sovereign Lord says: None of my words will be delayed any longer; whatever I say will be fulfilled, declares the Sovereign Lord.'"

13:1The word of the Lord came to me: 2"Son of man, prophesy against the prophets of Israel who are now prophesying. Say to those who prophesy out of their own imagination: 'Hear the word of the Lord! 3This is what the Sovereign Lord says: Woe to the foolisha prophets who follow their own spirit and have seen nothing! 4Your prophets, O Israel, are like jackals among ruins. 5You have not gone up to the breaks in the wall to repair it for the house of Israel so that it will stand firm in the battle on the day of the Lord. 6Their visions are false and their divinations a lie. They say, "The Lord declares," when the Lord has not sent them; yet they expect their words to be fulfilled. 7Have you not seen false visions and uttered lying divinations when you say, "The LORD declares," though I have not spoken?

8 " 'Therefore this is what the Sovereign LORD says: Because of your false words and lying visions, I am against you, declares the Sovereign LORD. 9My hand will be against the prophets who see false visions and utter lying divinations. They will not belong to the council of my people or be listed in the records of the house of Israel, nor will they enter the land of Israel. Then you will know that I am the Sovereign LORD.

10 " 'Because they lead my people astray, saying, "Peace," when there is no peace, and because, when a flimsy wall is built, they cover it with whitewash, 11 therefore tell those who cover it with whitewash that it is going to fall. Rain will come in torrents, and I will send hailstones hurtling down, and violent winds will burst forth. 12 When the wall collapses, will people not ask you, "Where is the whitewash you covered it with?"

13 " 'Therefore this is what the Sovereign LORD says: In my wrath I will unleash a violent wind, and in my anger hailstones and torrents of rain will fall with destructive fury. 14 I will tear down the wall you have covered with whitewash and will level it to the ground so that its foundation will be laid bare. When it*b* falls, you will be destroyed in it; and you will know that I am the LORD. 15 So I will spend my wrath against the wall and against those who covered it with whitewash. I will say to you, "The wall is gone and so are those who whitewashed it, 16 those prophets of Israel who prophesied to Jerusalem and saw visions of peace for her when there was no peace, declares the Sovereign LORD."'

17 "Now, son of man, set your face against the daughters of your people who prophesy out of their own imagination. Prophesy against them 18 and say, 'This is what the Sovereign LORD says: Woe to the women who sew magic charms on all their wrists and make veils of various lengths for their heads in order to ensnare people. Will you ensnare the lives of my people but preserve your own? 19 You have profaned me among my people for a few handfuls of barley and scraps of bread. By lying to my people, who listen to lies, you have killed those who should not have died and have spared those who should not live.

20 " 'Therefore this is what the Sovereign LORD says: I am against your magic charms with which you ensnare people like birds and I will tear them from your arms; I will set free the people that you ensnare like birds. 21 I will tear off your veils and save my people from your hands, and they will no longer fall prey to your power. Then you will know that I am the LORD. 22 Because you disheartened the righteous with your lies, when I had brought them no grief, and because you encouraged the wicked not to turn from their evil ways and so save their lives, 23 therefore you will no longer see false visions or practice divination. I will save my people from your hands. And then you will know that I am the LORD.'"

14:1 SOME of the elders of Israel came to me and sat down in front of me. 2 Then the word of the LORD came to me: 3 "Son of man, these men have set up idols in their hearts and put wicked stumbling blocks before their faces. Should I let them inquire of me at all? 4 Therefore speak to them and tell them, 'This is what the Sovereign LORD says: When any Israelite sets up idols in his heart and puts a wicked stumbling block before his face and then goes to a prophet, I the LORD will answer him myself in keeping with his great idolatry. 5 I will do this to recapture the hearts of the people of Israel, who have all deserted me for their idols.'

6 "Therefore say to the house of Israel, 'This is what the Sovereign LORD says: Repent! Turn from your idols and renounce all your detestable practices!

7 " 'When any Israelite or any alien living in Israel separates himself from me and sets up idols in his heart and puts a wicked stumbling block before his face and then goes to a prophet to inquire of

me, I the Lord will answer him myself. [8]I will set my face against that man and make him an example and a byword. I will cut him off from my people. Then you will know that I am the Lord.

[9]"'And if the prophet is enticed to utter a prophecy, I the Lord have enticed that prophet, and I will stretch out my hand against him and destroy him from among my people Israel. [10]They will bear their guilt—the prophet will be as guilty as the one who consults him. [11]Then the people of Israel will no longer stray from me, nor will they defile themselves anymore with all their sins. They will be my people, and I will be their God, declares the Sovereign Lord.'"

a3 Or wicked   b14 Or the city

HEBREWS 7:1-17

This Melchizedek was king of Salem and priest of God Most High. He met Abraham returning from the defeat of the kings and blessed him, [2]and Abraham gave him a tenth of everything. First, his name means "king of righteousness"; then also, "king of Salem" means "king of peace." [3]Without father or mother, without genealogy, without beginning of days or end of life, like the Son of God he remains a priest forever.

[4]Just think how great he was: Even the patriarch Abraham gave him a tenth of the plunder! [5]Now the law requires the descendants of Levi who become priests to collect a tenth from the people—that is, their brothers—even though their brothers are descended from Abraham. [6]This man, however, did not trace his descent from Levi, yet he collected a tenth from Abraham and blessed him who had the promises. [7]And without doubt the lesser person is blessed by the greater. [8]In the one case, the tenth is collected by men who die; but in the other case, by him who is declared to be living. [9]One might even say that Levi, who collects the tenth, paid the tenth through Abraham, [10]because when Melchizedek met Abraham, Levi was still in the body of his ancestor.

[11]If perfection could have been attained through the Levitical priesthood (for on the basis of it the law was given to the people), why was there still need for another priest to come—one in the order of Melchizedek, not in the order of Aaron? [12]For when there is a change of the priesthood, there must also be a change of the law. [13]He of whom these things are said belonged to a different tribe, and no one from that tribe has ever served at the altar. [14]For it is clear that our Lord descended from Judah, and in regard to that tribe Moses said nothing about priests. [15]And what we have said is even more clear if another priest like Melchizedek appears, [16]one who has become a priest not on the basis of a regulation as to his ancestry but on the basis of the power of an indestructible life. [17]For it is declared:

"You are a priest forever,
    in the order of Melchizedek."a

a17 Psalm 110:4

PSALM 105:37-45

[37]He [the Lord] brought out Israel,
        laden with silver and gold,
    and from among their tribes no
        one faltered.
[38]Egypt was glad when they left,
        because dread of Israel had fallen
        on them.
[39]He spread out a cloud as a
        covering,
    and a fire to give light at night.
[40]They asked, and he brought them
        quail
    and satisfied them with the
        bread of heaven.
[41]He opened the rock, and water
        gushed out;
    like a river it flowed in the desert.

[42]For he remembered his holy promise
        given to his servant Abraham.
[43]He brought out his people with
        rejoicing,
    his chosen ones with shouts of joy;
[44]he gave them the lands of the
        nations,
    and they fell heir to what others
        had toiled for—

⁴⁵that they might keep his precepts
and observe his laws.

Praise the LORD.ᵃ

ᵃ45 Hebrew *Hallelu Yah*

PROVERBS 27:3
³**S**tone is heavy and sand a burden,
but provocation by a fool is
heavier than both.

□ DAY 310

GOD SIGHTINGS

November 6

EZEKIEL 14:12–16:42

The word of the LORD came to me
[Ezekiel]: ¹³"Son of man, if a country
sins against me by being unfaithful and
I stretch out my hand against it to cut off
its food supply and send famine upon it
and kill its men and their animals,
¹⁴even if these three men—Noah, Dan-
ielᵃ and Job—were in it, they could save
only themselves by their righteousness,
declares the Sovereign LORD.

¹⁵"Or if I send wild beasts through
that country and they leave it childless
and it becomes desolate so that no one
can pass through it because of the
beasts, ¹⁶as surely as I live, declares the
Sovereign LORD, even if these three men
were in it, they could not save their own
sons or daughters. They alone would be
saved, but the land would be desolate.

¹⁷"Or if I bring a sword against that
country and say, 'Let the sword pass
throughout the land,' and I kill its men
and their animals, ¹⁸as surely as I live,
declares the Sovereign LORD, even if
these three men were in it, they could
not save their own sons or daughters.
They alone would be saved.

¹⁹"Or if I send a plague into that land
and pour out my wrath upon it through
bloodshed, killing its men and their animals, ²⁰as surely as I live, declares the
Sovereign LORD, even if Noah, Daniel

and Job were in it, they could save neither son nor daughter. They would save
only themselves by their righteousness.

²¹"For this is what the Sovereign LORD
says: How much worse will it be when I
send against Jerusalem my four dreadful judgments—sword and famine and
wild beasts and plague—to kill its men
and their animals! ²²Yet there will be
some survivors—sons and daughters
who will be brought out of it. They will
come to you, and when you see their
conduct and their actions, you will be
consoled regarding the disaster I have
brought upon Jerusalem—every disaster I have brought upon it. ²³You will be
consoled when you see their conduct
and their actions, for you will know that
I have done nothing in it without cause,
declares the Sovereign LORD."

¹⁵:¹THE word of the LORD came to me:
²"Son of man, how is the wood of a vine
better than that of a branch on any of
the trees in the forest? ³Is wood ever
taken from it to make anything useful?
Do they make pegs from it to hang
things on? ⁴And after it is thrown on the
fire as fuel and the fire burns both ends
and chars the middle, is it then useful
for anything? ⁵If it was not useful for
anything when it was whole, how much
less can it be made into something useful when the fire has burned it and it is
charred?

⁶"Therefore this is what the Sovereign
LORD says: As I have given the wood of the
vine among the trees of the forest as fuel
for the fire, so will I treat the people living
in Jerusalem. ⁷I will set my face against
them. Although they have come out of
the fire, the fire will yet consume them.
And when I set my face against them, you
will know that I am the LORD. ⁸I will make
the land desolate because they have
been unfaithful, declares the Sovereign
LORD."

¹⁶:¹THE word of the LORD came to me:
²"Son of man, confront Jerusalem with
her detestable practices ³and say, 'This
is what the Sovereign LORD says to Jeru-

salem: Your ancestry and birth were in the land of the Canaanites; your father was an Amorite and your mother a Hittite. [4]On the day you were born your cord was not cut, nor were you washed with water to make you clean, nor were you rubbed with salt or wrapped in cloths. [5]No one looked on you with pity or had compassion enough to do any of these things for you. Rather, you were thrown out into the open field, for on the day you were born you were despised.

[6]" 'Then I passed by and saw you kicking about in your blood, and as you lay there in your blood I said to you, "Live!"[b] [7]I made you grow like a plant of the field. You grew up and developed and became the most beautiful of jewels.[c] Your breasts were formed and your hair grew, you who were naked and bare.

[8]" 'Later I passed by, and when I looked at you and saw that you were old enough for love, I spread the corner of my garment over you and covered your nakedness. I gave you my solemn oath and entered into a covenant with you, declares the Sovereign LORD, and you became mine.

[9]" 'I bathed[d] you with water and washed the blood from you and put ointments on you. [10]I clothed you with an embroidered dress and put leather sandals on you. I dressed you in fine linen and covered you with costly garments. [11]I adorned you with jewelry: I put bracelets on your arms and a necklace around your neck, [12]and I put a ring on your nose, earrings on your ears and a beautiful crown on your head. [13]So you were adorned with gold and silver; your clothes were of fine linen and costly fabric and embroidered cloth. Your food was fine flour, honey and olive oil. You became very beautiful and rose to be a queen. [14]And your fame spread among the nations on account of your beauty, because the splendor I had given you made your beauty perfect, declares the Sovereign LORD.

[15]" 'But you trusted in your beauty and used your fame to become a prostitute. You lavished your favors on anyone who passed by and your beauty became his.[e] [16]You took some of your garments to make gaudy high places, where you carried on your prostitution. Such things should not happen, nor should they ever occur. [17]You also took the fine jewelry I gave you, the jewelry made of my gold and silver, and you made for yourself male idols and engaged in prostitution with them. [18]And you took your embroidered clothes to put on them, and you offered my oil and incense before them. [19]Also the food I provided for you—the fine flour, olive oil and honey I gave you to eat—you offered as fragrant incense before them. That is what happened, declares the Sovereign LORD.

[20]" 'And you took your sons and daughters whom you bore to me and sacrificed them as food to the idols. Was your prostitution not enough? [21]You slaughtered my children and sacrificed them[f] to the idols. [22]In all your detestable practices and your prostitution you did not remember the days of your youth, when you were naked and bare, kicking about in your blood.

[23]" 'Woe! Woe to you, declares the Sovereign LORD. In addition to all your other wickedness, [24]you built a mound for yourself and made a lofty shrine in every public square. [25]At the head of every street you built your lofty shrines and degraded your beauty, offering your body with increasing promiscuity to anyone who passed by. [26]You engaged in prostitution with the Egyptians, your lustful neighbors, and provoked me to anger with your increasing promiscuity. [27]So I stretched out my hand against you and reduced your territory; I gave you over to the greed of your enemies, the daughters of the Philistines, who were shocked by your lewd conduct. [28]You engaged in prostitution with the Assyrians too, because you were insatiable; and even after that, you still were not satisfied. [29]Then you increased your

promiscuity to include Babylonia,*g* a land of merchants, but even with this you were not satisfied.

30 "How weak-willed you are, declares the Sovereign LORD, when you do all these things, acting like a brazen prostitute! 31 When you built your mounds at the head of every street and made your lofty shrines in every public square, you were unlike a prostitute, because you scorned payment.

32 " 'You adulterous wife! You prefer strangers to your own husband! 33 Every prostitute receives a fee, but you give gifts to all your lovers, bribing them to come to you from everywhere for your illicit favors. 34 So in your prostitution you are the opposite of others; no one runs after you for your favors. You are the very opposite, for you give payment and none is given to you.

35 " 'Therefore, you prostitute, hear the word of the LORD! 36 This is what the Sovereign LORD says: Because you poured out your wealth*h* and exposed your nakedness in your promiscuity with your lovers, and because of all your detestable idols, and because you gave them your children's blood, 37 therefore I am going to gather all your lovers, with whom you found pleasure, those you loved as well as those you hated. I will gather them against you from all around and will strip you in front of them, and they will see all your nakedness. 38 I will sentence you to the punishment of women who commit adultery and who shed blood; I will bring upon you the blood vengeance of my wrath and jealous anger. 39 Then I will hand you over to your lovers, and they will tear down your mounds and destroy your lofty shrines. They will strip you of your clothes and take your fine jewelry and leave you naked and bare. 40 They will bring a mob against you, who will stone you and hack you to pieces with their swords. 41 They will burn down your houses and inflict punishment on you in the sight of many women. I will put a stop to your prostitution,

and you will no longer pay your lovers. 42 Then my wrath against you will subside and my jealous anger will turn away from you; I will be calm and no longer angry.' "

a 14 Or Danel; the Hebrew spelling may suggest a person other than the prophet Daniel; also in verse 20. b 6 A few Hebrew manuscripts, Septuagint and Syriac; most Hebrew manuscripts "Live!" And as you lay there in your blood I said to you, "Live!" c 7 Or became mature d 9 Or I had bathed e 15 Most Hebrew manuscripts; one Hebrew manuscript (see some Septuagint manuscripts) by. Such a thing should not happen f 21 Or and made them pass through ⌊the fire⌋ g 29 Or Chaldea h 36 Or lust

HEBREWS 7:18-28

The former regulation is set aside because it was weak and useless 19 (for the law made nothing perfect), and a better hope is introduced, by which we draw near to God.

20 And it was not without an oath! Others became priests without any oath, 21 but he became a priest with an oath when God said to him:

"The Lord has sworn
    and will not change his mind:
    'You are a priest forever.' "*a*

22 Because of this oath, Jesus has become the guarantee of a better covenant.

23 Now there have been many of those priests, since death prevented them from continuing in office; 24 but because Jesus lives forever, he has a permanent priesthood. 25 Therefore he is able to save completely*b* those who come to God through him, because he always lives to intercede for them.

26 Such a high priest meets our need—one who is holy, blameless, pure, set apart from sinners, exalted above the heavens. 27 Unlike the other high priests, he does not need to offer sacrifices day after day, first for his own sins, and then for the sins of the people. He sacrificed for their sins once for all when he offered himself. 28 **For the law appoints as high priests men who are weak; but the oath, which came after the law, appointed the Son, who has been made perfect forever.**

a 21 Psalm 110:4 b 25 Or forever

PSALM 106:1-12

¹ **P**raise the LORD.ᵃ

Give thanks to the LORD, for he is
good;
his love endures forever.
² Who can proclaim the mighty acts of
the LORD
or fully declare his praise?
³ Blessed are they who maintain
justice,
who constantly do what is right.
⁴ Remember me, O LORD, when you
show favor to your people,
come to my aid when you save
them,
⁵ that I may enjoy the prosperity of
your chosen ones,
that I may share in the joy of your
nation
and join your inheritance in giving
praise.

⁶ We have sinned, even as our fathers
did;
we have done wrong and acted
wickedly.
⁷ When our fathers were in Egypt,
they gave no thought to your
miracles;
they did not remember your many
kindnesses,
and they rebelled by the sea, the
Red Sea.ᵇ
⁸ Yet he saved them for his name's
sake,
to make his mighty power known.
⁹ He rebuked the Red Sea, and it dried
up;
he led them through the depths as
through a desert.
¹⁰ He saved them from the hand of the
foe;
from the hand of the enemy he
redeemed them.
¹¹ The waters covered their adversaries;
not one of them survived.
¹² Then they believed his promises
and sang his praise.

ᵃ1 Hebrew *Hallelu Yah*; also in verse 48   ᵇ7 Hebrew *Yam Suph*; that is, Sea of Reeds; also in verses 9 and 22

PROVERBS 27:4-6

⁴ **A**nger is cruel and fury
overwhelming,
but who can stand before
jealousy?

⁵ Better is open rebuke
than hidden love.

⁶ Wounds from a friend can be
trusted,
but an enemy multiplies kisses.

☐ D A Y   3 1 1

GOD SIGHTINGS

November 7

EZEKIEL 16:43–17:24

"'**B**ecause you [the people of Jerusalem] did not remember the days of your youth but enraged me [the LORD] with all these things, I will surely bring down on your head what you have done, declares the Sovereign LORD. Did you not add lewdness to all your other detestable practices?

⁴⁴"'Everyone who quotes proverbs will quote this proverb about you: "Like mother, like daughter." ⁴⁵ You are a true daughter of your mother, who despised her husband and her children; and you are a true sister of your sisters, who despised their husbands and their children. Your mother was a Hittite and your father an Amorite. ⁴⁶ Your older sister was Samaria, who lived to the north of you with her daughters; and your younger sister, who lived to the south of you with her daughters, was Sodom. ⁴⁷ You not only walked in their ways and copied their detestable practices, but in all your ways you soon became more depraved than they. ⁴⁸ As surely as I live, declares the Sovereign LORD, your sister Sodom and her daughters never did what you and your daughters have done.

⁴⁹"'Now this was the sin of your sister Sodom: She and her daughters were

arrogant, overfed and unconcerned; they did not help the poor and needy. 50They were haughty and did detestable things before me. Therefore I did away with them as you have seen. 51Samaria did not commit half the sins you did. You have done more detestable things than they, and have made your sisters seem righteous by all these things you have done. 52Bear your disgrace, for you have furnished some justification for your sisters. Because your sins were more vile than theirs, they appear more righteous than you. So then, be ashamed and bear your disgrace, for you have made your sisters appear righteous.

53" 'However, I will restore the fortunes of Sodom and her daughters and of Samaria and her daughters, and your fortunes along with them, 54so that you may bear your disgrace and be ashamed of all you have done in giving them comfort. 55And your sisters, Sodom with her daughters and Samaria with her daughters, will return to what they were before; and you and your daughters will return to what you were before. 56You would not even mention your sister Sodom in the day of your pride, 57before your wickedness was uncovered. Even so, you are now scorned by the daughters of Edom*a* and all her neighbors and the daughters of the Philistines—all those around you who despise you. 58You will bear the consequences of your lewdness and your detestable practices, declares the LORD.

59" 'This is what the Sovereign LORD says: I will deal with you as you deserve, because you have despised my oath by breaking the covenant. 60Yet I will remember the covenant I made with you in the days of your youth, and I will establish an everlasting covenant with you. 61Then you will remember your ways and be ashamed when you receive your sisters, both those who are older than you and those who are younger. I will give them to you as daughters, but not on the basis of my covenant with you. 62So I will establish my covenant with you, and you will know that I am

the LORD. 63Then, when I make atonement for you for all you have done, you will remember and be ashamed and never again open your mouth because of your humiliation, declares the Sovereign LORD.'"

17:1THE word of the LORD came to me: 2"Son of man, set forth an allegory and tell the house of Israel a parable. 3Say to them, 'This is what the Sovereign LORD says: A great eagle with powerful wings, long feathers and full plumage of varied colors came to Lebanon. Taking hold of the top of a cedar, 4he broke off its topmost shoot and carried it away to a land of merchants, where he planted it in a city of traders.

5" 'He took some of the seed of your land and put it in fertile soil. He planted it like a willow by abundant water, 6and it sprouted and became a low, spreading vine. Its branches turned toward him, but its roots remained under it. So it became a vine and produced branches and put out leafy boughs.

7" 'But there was another great eagle with powerful wings and full plumage. The vine now sent out its roots toward him from the plot where it was planted and stretched out its branches to him for water. 8It had been planted in good soil by abundant water so that it would produce branches, bear fruit and become a splendid vine.'

9"Say to them, 'This is what the Sovereign LORD says: Will it thrive? Will it not be uprooted and stripped of its fruit so that it withers? All its new growth will wither. It will not take a strong arm or many people to pull it up by the roots. 10Even if it is transplanted, will it thrive? Will it not wither completely when the east wind strikes it—wither away in the plot where it grew?'"

11Then the word of the LORD came to me: 12"Say to this rebellious house, 'Do you not know what these things mean?' Say to them: 'The king of Babylon went to Jerusalem and carried off her king and her nobles, bringing them back with him to Babylon. 13Then he took a member of the royal family and made a treaty with him, putting him under oath. He also carried away the leading men of the land, [14]so that the kingdom would be brought low, unable to rise again, surviving only by keeping his treaty. [15]But the king rebelled against him by sending his envoys to Egypt to get horses and a large army. Will he succeed? Will he who does such things escape? Will he break the treaty and yet escape?

[16]"'As surely as I live, declares the Sovereign LORD, he shall die in Babylon, in the land of the king who put him on the throne, whose oath he despised and whose treaty he broke. [17]Pharaoh with his mighty army and great horde will be of no help to him in war, when ramps are built and siege works erected to destroy many lives. [18]He despised the oath by breaking the covenant. Because he had given his hand in pledge and yet did all these things, he shall not escape.

[19]"'Therefore this is what the Sovereign LORD says: As surely as I live, I will bring down on his head my oath that he despised and my covenant that he broke. [20]I will spread my net for him, and he will be caught in my snare. I will bring him to Babylon and execute judgment upon him there because he was unfaithful to me. [21]All his fleeing troops will fall by the sword, and the survivors will be scattered to the winds. Then you will know that I the LORD have spoken.

[22]"'This is what the Sovereign LORD says: I myself will take a shoot from the very top of a cedar and plant it; I will break off a tender sprig from its topmost shoots and plant it on a high and lofty mountain. [23]On the mountain heights of Israel I will plant it; it will produce branches and bear fruit and become a splendid cedar. Birds of every kind will nest in it; they will find shelter in the shade of its branches. [24]**All the trees of the field will know that I the LORD bring down the tall tree and make the low tree grow tall. I dry up**

the green tree and make the dry tree flourish.

"'I the LORD have spoken, and I will do it.'"

[a]57 Many Hebrew manuscripts and Syriac; most Hebrew manuscripts, Septuagint and Vulgate *Aram*

HEBREWS 8:1-13

The point of what we are saying is this: We do have such a high priest, who sat down at the right hand of the throne of the Majesty in heaven, [2]and who serves in the sanctuary, the true tabernacle set up by the Lord, not by man.

[3]Every high priest is appointed to offer both gifts and sacrifices, and so it was necessary for this one also to have something to offer. [4]If he were on earth, he would not be a priest, for there are already men who offer the gifts prescribed by the law. [5]They serve at a sanctuary that is a copy and shadow of what is in heaven. This is why Moses was warned when he was about to build the tabernacle: "See to it that you make everything according to the pattern shown you on the mountain."[a] [6]But the ministry Jesus has received is as superior to theirs as the covenant of which he is mediator is superior to the old one, and it is founded on better promises.

[7]For if there had been nothing wrong with that first covenant, no place would have been sought for another. [8]But God found fault with the people and said[b]:

"The time is coming, declares the
        Lord,
    when I will make a new covenant
  with the house of Israel
    and with the house of Judah.
[9]It will not be like the covenant
    I made with their forefathers
  when I took them by the hand
    to lead them out of Egypt,
  because they did not remain faithful
        to my covenant,
    and I turned away from them,
                declares the Lord.
[10]This is the covenant I will make with
        the house of Israel
    after that time, declares the Lord.

I will put my laws in their minds
   and write them on their hearts.
I will be their God,
   and they will be my people.
11 No longer will a man teach his
     neighbor,
   or a man his brother, saying, 'Know
     the Lord,'
because they will all know me,
   from the least of them to the
     greatest.
12 For I will forgive their wickedness
   and will remember their sins no
     more."c

13 By calling this covenant "new," he
has made the first one obsolete; and
what is obsolete and aging will soon disappear.

a5 Exodus 25:40   b8 Some manuscripts may be translated
fault and said to the people.   c12 Jer. 31:31-34

PSALM 106:13-31

13 But they [the Israelites] soon forgot
     what he [the Lord] had done
   and did not wait for his counsel.
14 In the desert they gave in to their
     craving;
   in the wasteland they put God to
     the test.
15 So he gave them what they asked for,
   but sent a wasting disease upon
     them.

16 In the camp they grew envious of
     Moses
   and of Aaron, who was
     consecrated to the Lord.
17 The earth opened up and swallowed
     Dathan;
   it buried the company of Abiram.
18 Fire blazed among their followers;
   a flame consumed the wicked.

19 At Horeb they made a calf
   and worshiped an idol cast from
     metal.
20 They exchanged their Glory
   for an image of a bull, which eats
     grass.
21 They forgot the God who saved them,
   who had done great things in
     Egypt,

22 miracles in the land of Ham
   and awesome deeds by the Red
     Sea.
23 So he said he would destroy them—
   had not Moses, his chosen one,
stood in the breach before him
   to keep his wrath from destroying
     them.

24 Then they despised the pleasant
     land;
   they did not believe his promise.
25 They grumbled in their tents
   and did not obey the Lord.
26 So he swore to them with uplifted
     hand
   that he would make them fall in
     the desert,
27 make their descendants fall among
     the nations
   and scatter them throughout the
     lands.

28 They yoked themselves to the Baal of
     Peor
   and ate sacrifices offered to
     lifeless gods;
29 they provoked the Lord to anger by
     their wicked deeds,
   and a plague broke out among
     them.
30 But Phinehas stood up and
     intervened,
   and the plague was checked.
31 This was credited to him as
     righteousness
   for endless generations to come.

PROVERBS 27:7-9

7 He who is full loathes honey,
   but to the hungry even what is
     bitter tastes sweet.

8 Like a bird that strays from its nest
   is a man who strays from his
     home.

9 Perfume and incense bring joy to the
     heart,
   and the pleasantness of one's
     friend springs from his
     earnest counsel.

GOD SIGHTINGS

November 8

EZEKIEL 18:1–19:14

The word of the Lord came to me [Ezekiel]: 2"What do you people mean by quoting this proverb about the land of Israel:

"'The fathers eat sour grapes,
and the children's teeth are set on edge'?

3"As surely as I live, declares the Sovereign Lord, you will no longer quote this proverb in Israel. 4For every living soul belongs to me, the father as well as the son—both alike belong to me. The soul who sins is the one who will die.

5"Suppose there is a righteous man
who does what is just and right.
6He does not eat at the mountain shrines
or look to the idols of the house of Israel.
He does not defile his neighbor's wife
or lie with a woman during her period.
7He does not oppress anyone,
but returns what he took in pledge for a loan.
He does not commit robbery
but gives his food to the hungry
and provides clothing for the naked.
8He does not lend at usury
or take excessive interest.*a*
He withholds his hand from doing wrong
and judges fairly between man and man.
9He follows my decrees
and faithfully keeps my laws.
That man is righteous;
he will surely live,
declares the Sovereign Lord.

10"Suppose he has a violent son, who sheds blood or does any of these other

things*b* 11(though the father has done none of them):

"He eats at the mountain shrines.
He defiles his neighbor's wife.
12He oppresses the poor and needy.
He commits robbery.
He does not return what he took in pledge.
He looks to the idols.
He does detestable things.
13He lends at usury and takes excessive interest.

Will such a man live? He will not! Because he has done all these detestable things, he will surely be put to death and his blood will be on his own head.

14"But suppose this son has a son who sees all the sins his father commits, and though he sees them, he does not do such things:

15"He does not eat at the mountain shrines
or look to the idols of the house of Israel.
He does not defile his neighbor's wife.
16He does not oppress anyone
or require a pledge for a loan.
He does not commit robbery
but gives his food to the hungry
and provides clothing for the naked.
17He withholds his hand from sin*c*
and takes no usury or excessive interest.
He keeps my laws and follows my decrees.

He will not die for his father's sin; he will surely live. 18But his father will die for his own sin, because he practiced extortion, robbed his brother and did what was wrong among his people.

19"Yet you ask, 'Why does the son not share the guilt of his father?' Since the son has done what is just and right and has been careful to keep all my decrees, he will surely live. 20The soul who sins is the one who will die. The son will not share the guilt of the father, nor will the father share the guilt of the son. The righteousness of the righteous man will be credited to him, and the wickedness of the wicked will be charged against him.

²¹"But if a wicked man turns away from all the sins he has committed and keeps all my decrees and does what is just and right, he will surely live; he will not die. ²²None of the offenses he has committed will be remembered against him. Because of the righteous things he has done, he will live. ²³Do I take any pleasure in the death of the wicked? declares the Sovereign Lord. Rather, am I not pleased when they turn from their ways and live?

²⁴"But if a righteous man turns from his righteousness and commits sin and does the same detestable things the wicked man does, will he live? None of the righteous things he has done will be remembered. Because of the unfaithfulness he is guilty of and because of the sins he has committed, he will die.

²⁵"Yet you say, 'The way of the Lord is not just.' Hear, O house of Israel: Is my way unjust? Is it not your ways that are unjust? ²⁶If a righteous man turns from his righteousness and commits sin, he will die for it; because of the sin he has committed he will die. ²⁷But if a wicked man turns away from the wickedness he has committed and does what is just and right, he will save his life. ²⁸Because he considers all the offenses he has committed and turns away from them, he will surely live; he will not die. ²⁹Yet the house of Israel says, 'The way of the Lord is not just.' Are my ways unjust, O house of Israel? Is it not your ways that are unjust?

³⁰"Therefore, O house of Israel, I will judge you, each one according to his ways, declares the Sovereign Lord. Repent! Turn away from all your offenses; then sin will not be your downfall. ³¹**Rid yourselves of all the offenses you have committed, and get a new heart and a new spirit. Why will you die, O house of Israel? ³²For I take no pleasure in the death of anyone, declares the Sovereign Lord. Repent and live!**

¹⁹:¹"Take up a lament concerning the princes of Israel ²and say:

"'What a lioness was your mother
   among the lions!
She lay down among the young lions
   and reared her cubs.
³She brought up one of her cubs,
   and he became a strong lion.
He learned to tear the prey
   and he devoured men.
⁴The nations heard about him,
   and he was trapped in their pit.
They led him with hooks
   to the land of Egypt.

⁵"'When she saw her hope unfulfilled,
   her expectation gone,
she took another of her cubs
   and made him a strong lion.
⁶He prowled among the lions,
   for he was now a strong lion.
He learned to tear the prey
   and he devoured men.
⁷He broke down*d* their strongholds
   and devastated their towns.
The land and all who were in it
   were terrified by his roaring.
⁸Then the nations came against him,
   those from regions round about.
They spread their net for him,
   and he was trapped in their pit.
⁹With hooks they pulled him into a
      cage
   and brought him to the king of
      Babylon.
They put him in prison,
   so his roar was heard no longer
      on the mountains of Israel.

¹⁰"'Your mother was like a vine in your
      vineyard*e*
   planted by the water;
it was fruitful and full of branches
   because of abundant water.
¹¹Its branches were strong,
   fit for a ruler's scepter.
It towered high
   above the thick foliage,
conspicuous for its height
   and for its many branches.
¹²But it was uprooted in fury
   and thrown to the ground.

The east wind made it shrivel,
  it was stripped of its fruit;
its strong branches withered
  and fire consumed them.
¹³Now it is planted in the desert,
  in a dry and thirsty land.
¹⁴Fire spread from one of its main^f
  branches
  and consumed its fruit.
No strong branch is left on it
  fit for a ruler's scepter.'

This is a lament and is to be used as a lament."

^a8 Or *take interest*; similarly in verses 13 and 17   ^b10 Or
things to a brother   ^c17 Septuagint (see also verse 8);
Hebrew *from the poor*   ^d7 Targum (see Septuagint); Hebrew
He knew   ^e10 Two Hebrew manuscripts; most Hebrew
manuscripts *your blood*   ^f14 Or *from under its*

HEBREWS 9:1-10

Now the first covenant had regulations
for worship and also an earthly sanctu-
ary. ²A tabernacle was set up. In its first
room were the lampstand, the table and
the consecrated bread; this was called
the Holy Place. ³Behind the second curtain was a room called the Most Holy
Place, ⁴which had the golden altar of incense and the gold-covered ark of the
covenant. This ark contained the gold
jar of manna, Aaron's staff that had budded, and the stone tablets of the covenant. ⁵Above the ark were the cherubim
of the Glory, overshadowing the atonement cover.^a But we cannot discuss
these things in detail now.

⁶When everything had been ar-
ranged like this, the priests entered regularly into the outer room to carry on
their ministry. ⁷But only the high priest
entered the inner room, and that only
once a year, and never without blood,
which he offered for himself and for the
sins the people had committed in ignorance. ⁸The Holy Spirit was showing by
this that the way into the Most Holy
Place had not yet been disclosed as long
as the first tabernacle was still standing.
⁹This is an illustration for the present
time, indicating that the gifts and sacrifices being offered were not able to
clear the conscience of the worshiper.

¹⁰They are only a matter of food and
drink and various ceremonial wash-
ings—external regulations applying until the time of the new order.

^a5 Traditionally *the mercy seat*

PSALM 106:32-48

³²**B**y the waters of Meribah they [the
    Israelites] angered the LORD,
  and trouble came to Moses
    because of them;
³³for they rebelled against the Spirit of
    God,
  and rash words came from Moses'
    lips.^a

³⁴They did not destroy the peoples
    as the LORD had commanded
    them,
³⁵but they mingled with the nations
    and adopted their customs.
³⁶They worshiped their idols,
    which became a snare to them.
³⁷They sacrificed their sons
    and their daughters to demons.
³⁸They shed innocent blood,
    the blood of their sons and
    daughters,
  whom they sacrificed to the idols of
    Canaan,
    and the land was desecrated by
    their blood.
³⁹They defiled themselves by what
    they did;
  by their deeds they prostituted
    themselves.

⁴⁰Therefore the LORD was angry with
    his people
  and abhorred his inheritance.
⁴¹He handed them over to the nations,
    and their foes ruled over them.
⁴²Their enemies oppressed them
    and subjected them to their
    power.
⁴³Many times he delivered them,
    but they were bent on rebellion
    and they wasted away in their sin.

⁴⁴But he took note of their distress
    when he heard their cry;
⁴⁵for their sake he remembered his
    covenant

and out of his great love he
relented.
46 He caused them to be pitied
by all who held them captive.

47 Save us, O Lord our God,
and gather us from the nations,
that we may give thanks to your holy
name
and glory in your praise.

48 Praise be to the Lord, the God of
Israel,
from everlasting to everlasting.
Let all the people say, "Amen!"

Praise the Lord.

a 33 Or against his spirit, / and rash words came from his lips

PROVERBS 27:10
10 Do not forsake your friend and the
friend of your father,
and do not go to your brother's
house when disaster strikes
you—
better a neighbor nearby than a
brother far away.

☐ DAY 313

GOD SIGHTINGS

November 9

EZEKIEL 20:1-49
In the seventh year, in the fifth month
on the tenth day, some of the elders of
Israel came to inquire of the Lord, and
they sat down in front of me.

2 Then the word of the Lord came to
me: 3 "Son of man, speak to the elders of
Israel and say to them, 'This is what the
Sovereign Lord says: Have you come to
inquire of me? As surely as I live, I will
not let you inquire of me, declares the
Sovereign Lord.'

4 "Will you judge them? Will you
judge them, son of man? Then confront
them with the detestable practices of
their fathers 5 and say to them: 'This is
what the Sovereign Lord says: On the

day I chose Israel, I swore with uplifted
hand to the descendants of the house of
Jacob and revealed myself to them in
Egypt. With uplifted hand I said to
them, "I am the Lord your God." 6 On
that day I swore to them that I would
bring them out of Egypt into a land I had
searched out for them, a land flowing
with milk and honey, the most beautiful
of all lands. 7 And I said to them, "Each of
you, get rid of the vile images you have
set your eyes on, and do not defile yourselves with the idols of Egypt. I am the
Lord your God."

8 " 'But they rebelled against me and
would not listen to me; they did not get
rid of the vile images they had set their
eyes on, nor did they forsake the idols of
Egypt. So I said I would pour out my
wrath on them and spend my anger
against them in Egypt. 9 But for the sake
of my name I did what would keep it
from being profaned in the eyes of the
nations they lived among and in whose
sight I had revealed myself to the Israelites by bringing them out of Egypt.
10 Therefore I led them out of Egypt and
brought them into the desert. 11 I gave
them my decrees and made known to
them my laws, for the man who obeys
them will live by them. 12 Also I gave
them my Sabbaths as a sign between us,
so they would know that I the Lord
made them holy.

13 " 'Yet the people of Israel rebelled
against me in the desert. They did not
follow my decrees but rejected my
laws—although the man who obeys
them will live by them—and they utterly
desecrated my Sabbaths. So I said I
would pour out my wrath on them and
destroy them in the desert. 14 But for the
sake of my name I did what would keep
it from being profaned in the eyes of the
nations in whose sight I had brought
them out. 15 Also with uplifted hand I
swore to them in the desert that I would
not bring them into the land I had given
them—a land flowing with milk and
honey, most beautiful of all lands—
16 because they rejected my laws and did
not follow my decrees and desecrated

my Sabbaths. For their hearts were devoted to their idols. [17]Yet I looked on them with pity and did not destroy them or put an end to them in the desert. [18]I said to their children in the desert, "Do not follow the statutes of your fathers or keep their laws or defile yourselves with their idols. [19]I am the LORD your God; follow my decrees and be careful to keep my laws. [20]Keep my Sabbaths holy, that they may be a sign between us. Then you will know that I am the LORD your God."

[21]" 'But the children rebelled against me: They did not follow my decrees, they were not careful to keep my laws—although the man who obeys them will live by them—and they desecrated my Sabbaths. So I said I would pour out my wrath on them and spend my anger against them in the desert. [22]But I withheld my hand, and for the sake of my name I did what would keep it from being profaned in the eyes of the nations in whose sight I had brought them out. [23]Also with uplifted hand I swore to them in the desert that I would disperse them among the nations and scatter them through the countries, [24]because they had not obeyed my laws but had rejected my decrees and desecrated my Sabbaths, and their eyes lusted after their fathers' idols. [25]I also gave them over to statutes that were not good and laws they could not live by; [26]I let them become defiled through their gifts—the sacrifice of every firstborn[a]—that I might fill them with horror so they would know that I am the LORD.'

[27]"Therefore, son of man, speak to the people of Israel and say to them, 'This is what the Sovereign LORD says: In this also your fathers blasphemed me by forsaking me: [28]When I brought them into the land I had sworn to give them and they saw any high hill or any leafy tree, there they offered their sacrifices, made offerings that provoked me to anger, presented their fragrant incense and poured out their drink offerings. [29]Then I said to them: What is this high place you go to?' " (It is called Bamah[b] to this day.)

[30]"Therefore say to the house of Israel: 'This is what the Sovereign LORD says: Will you defile yourselves the way your fathers did and lust after their vile images? [31]When you offer your gifts—the sacrifice of your sons in[c] the fire—you continue to defile yourselves with all your idols to this day. Am I to let you inquire of me, O house of Israel? As surely as I live, declares the Sovereign LORD, I will not let you inquire of me.

[32]" 'You say, "We want to be like the nations, like the peoples of the world, who serve wood and stone." But what you have in mind will never happen. [33]As surely as I live, declares the Sovereign LORD, I will rule over you with a mighty hand and an outstretched arm and with outpoured wrath. [34]I will bring you from the nations and gather you from the countries where you have been scattered—with a mighty hand and an outstretched arm and with outpoured wrath. [35]I will bring you into the desert of the nations and there, face to face, I will execute judgment upon you. [36]As I judged your fathers in the desert of the land of Egypt, so I will judge you, declares the Sovereign LORD. [37]I will take note of you as you pass under my rod, and I will bring you into the bond of the covenant. [38]I will purge you of those who revolt and rebel against me. Although I will bring them out of the land where they are living, yet they will not enter the land of Israel. Then you will know that I am the LORD.

[39]"As for you, O house of Israel, this is what the Sovereign LORD says: Go and serve your idols, every one of you! But afterward you will surely listen to me and no longer profane my holy name with your gifts and idols. [40]For on my holy mountain, the high mountain of Israel, declares the Sovereign LORD, there in the land the entire house of Israel will serve me, and there I will accept them. There I will require your offerings and your choice gifts,[d] along with all your holy sacrifices. [41]I will accept you as fragrant incense when I bring you out from the nations and gather you from the countries

where you have been scattered, and I will show myself holy among you in the sight of the nations. [42]Then you will know that I am the LORD, when I bring you into the land of Israel, the land I had sworn with uplifted hand to give to your fathers. [43]There you will remember your conduct and all the actions by which you have defiled yourselves, and you will loathe yourselves for all the evil you have done. [44]You will know that I am the LORD, when I deal with you for my name's sake and not according to your evil ways and your corrupt practices, O house of Israel, declares the Sovereign LORD.'"

[45]The word of the LORD came to me: [46]"Son of man, set your face toward the south; preach against the south and prophesy against the forest of the southland. [47]Say to the southern forest: 'Hear the word of the LORD. This is what the Sovereign LORD says: I am about to set fire to you, and it will consume all your trees, both green and dry. The blazing flame will not be quenched, and every face from south to north will be scorched by it. [48]Everyone will see that I the LORD have kindled it; it will not be quenched.'"

[49]Then I said, "Ah, Sovereign LORD! They are saying of me, 'Isn't he just telling parables?'"

a26 Or —making every firstborn pass through ⌊the fire⌋
b29 Bamah means high place.   c31 Or —making your sons pass through   d40 Or and the gifts of your firstfruits

HEBREWS 9:11-28

When Christ came as high priest of the good things that are already here,[a] he went through the greater and more perfect tabernacle that is not man-made, that is to say, not a part of this creation. [12]He did not enter by means of the blood of goats and calves; but he entered the Most Holy Place once for all by his own blood, having obtained eternal redemption. [13]The blood of goats and bulls and the ashes of a heifer sprinkled on those who are ceremonially unclean sanctify them so that they are outwardly clean. [14]How much more, then, will the blood of Christ, who through the eternal Spirit

offered himself unblemished to God, cleanse our consciences from acts that lead to death,[b] so that we may serve the living God!

[15]For this reason Christ is the mediator of a new covenant, that those who are called may receive the promised eternal inheritance—now that he has died as a ransom to set them free from the sins committed under the first covenant.

[16]In the case of a will,[c] it is necessary to prove the death of the one who made it, [17]because a will is in force only when somebody has died; it never takes effect while the one who made it is living. [18]This is why even the first covenant was not put into effect without blood. [19]When Moses had proclaimed every commandment of the law to all the people, he took the blood of calves, together with water, scarlet wool and branches of hyssop, and sprinkled the scroll and all the people. [20]He said, "This is the blood of the covenant, which God has commanded you to keep."[d] [21]In the same way, he sprinkled with the blood both the tabernacle and everything used in its ceremonies. [22]In fact, the law requires that nearly everything be cleansed with blood, and without the shedding of blood there is no forgiveness.

[23]It was necessary, then, for the copies of the heavenly things to be purified with these sacrifices, but the heavenly things themselves with better sacrifices than these. [24]For Christ did not enter a man-made sanctuary that was only a copy of the true one; he entered heaven itself, now to appear for us in God's presence. [25]Nor did he enter heaven to offer himself again and again, the way the high priest enters the Most Holy Place every year with blood that is not his own. [26]Then Christ would have had to suffer many times since the creation of the world. But now he has appeared once for all at the end of the ages to do away with sin by the sacrifice of himself. [27]**Just as man is destined to die once, and after that to face judgment,** [28]**so Christ was sacrificed once to take away the sins of many people;**

and he will appear a second time, not to bear sin, but to bring salvation to those who are waiting for him.

a 11 Some early manuscripts *are to come* b 14 Or *from useless rituals* c 16 Same Greek word as *covenant*; also in verse 17 d 20 Exodus 24:8

PSALM 107:1-43

1 Give thanks to the Lord, for he is good;
    his love endures forever.
2 Let the redeemed of the Lord say this—
    those he redeemed from the hand of the foe,
3 those he gathered from the lands,
    from east and west, from north and south.a

4 Some wandered in desert wastelands,
    finding no way to a city where they could settle.
5 They were hungry and thirsty,
    and their lives ebbed away.
6 Then they cried out to the Lord in their trouble,
    and he delivered them from their distress.
7 He led them by a straight way
    to a city where they could settle.
8 Let them give thanks to the Lord for his unfailing love
    and his wonderful deeds for men,
9 for he satisfies the thirsty
    and fills the hungry with good things.

10 Some sat in darkness and the deepest gloom,
    prisoners suffering in iron chains,
11 for they had rebelled against the words of God
    and despised the counsel of the Most High.
12 So he subjected them to bitter labor;
    they stumbled, and there was no one to help.
13 Then they cried to the Lord in their trouble,
    and he saved them from their distress.

14 He brought them out of darkness and the deepest gloom
    and broke away their chains.
15 Let them give thanks to the Lord for his unfailing love
    and his wonderful deeds for men,
16 for he breaks down gates of bronze
    and cuts through bars of iron.

17 Some became fools through their rebellious ways
    and suffered affliction because of their iniquities.
18 They loathed all food
    and drew near the gates of death.
19 Then they cried to the Lord in their trouble,
    and he saved them from their distress.
20 He sent forth his word and healed them;
    he rescued them from the grave.
21 Let them give thanks to the Lord for his unfailing love
    and his wonderful deeds for men.
22 Let them sacrifice thank offerings
    and tell of his works with songs of joy.

23 Others went out on the sea in ships;
    they were merchants on the mighty waters.
24 They saw the works of the Lord,
    his wonderful deeds in the deep.
25 For he spoke and stirred up a tempest
    that lifted high the waves.
26 They mounted up to the heavens and went down to the depths;
    in their peril their courage melted away.
27 They reeled and staggered like drunken men;
    they were at their wits' end.
28 Then they cried out to the Lord in their trouble,
    and he brought them out of their distress.
29 He stilled the storm to a whisper;
    the waves of the sea were hushed.

30 They were glad when it grew calm,
    and he guided them to their
        desired haven.
31 Let them give thanks to the LORD for
        his unfailing love
    and his wonderful deeds for men.
32 Let them exalt him in the assembly
        of the people
    and praise him in the council of
        the elders.

33 He turned rivers into a desert,
    flowing springs into thirsty
        ground,
34 and fruitful land into a salt waste,
    because of the wickedness of
        those who lived there.
35 He turned the desert into pools of
        water
    and the parched ground into
        flowing springs;
36 there he brought the hungry to live,
    and they founded a city where
        they could settle.
37 They sowed fields and planted
        vineyards
    that yielded a fruitful harvest;
38 he blessed them, and their numbers
        greatly increased,
    and he did not let their herds
        diminish.

39 Then their numbers decreased, and
        they were humbled
    by oppression, calamity and
        sorrow;
40 he who pours contempt on nobles
    made them wander in a trackless
        waste.
41 But he lifted the needy out of their
        affliction
    and increased their families like
        flocks.
42 The upright see and rejoice,
    but all the wicked shut their mouths.

43 Whoever is wise, let him heed these
        things
    and consider the great love of the
        LORD.

a3 Hebrew *north and the sea*

PROVERBS 27:11
11 Be wise, my son, and bring joy to my
        heart;
    then I can answer anyone who
        treats me with contempt.

☐ DAY 314

GOD SIGHTINGS

November 10

EZEKIEL 21:1–22:31
The word of the LORD came to me
[Ezekiel]: 2 "Son of man, set your face
against Jerusalem and preach against
the sanctuary. Prophesy against the land
of Israel 3 and say to her: 'This is what
the LORD says: I am against you. I will
draw my sword from its scabbard and
cut off from you both the righteous and
the wicked. 4 Because I am going to cut
off the righteous and the wicked, my
sword will be unsheathed against everyone from south to north. 5 Then all people will know that I the LORD have drawn
my sword from its scabbard; it will not
return again.'

6 "Therefore groan, son of man!
Groan before them with broken heart
and bitter grief. 7 And when they ask
you, 'Why are you groaning?' you shall
say, 'Because of the news that is coming.
Every heart will melt and every hand go
limp; every spirit will become faint and
every knee become as weak as water.' It
is coming! It will surely take place, declares the Sovereign LORD."

8 The word of the LORD came to me:
9 "Son of man, prophesy and say, 'This is
what the Lord says:

"'A sword, a sword,
    sharpened and polished—
10 sharpened for the slaughter,
    polished to flash like lightning!

"'Shall we rejoice in the scepter of my
son ⌊Judah⌋? The sword despises every
such stick.

¹¹"'The sword is appointed to be
        polished,
    to be grasped with the hand;
it is sharpened and polished,
        made ready for the hand of the
        slayer.
¹²Cry out and wail, son of man,
    for it is against my people;
    it is against all the princes of
        Israel.
They are thrown to the sword
    along with my people.
Therefore beat your breast.

¹³" 'Testing will surely come. And
what if the scepter ⌊of Judah⌋, which the
sword despises, does not continue? declares the Sovereign Lᴏʀᴅ.'

¹⁴"So then, son of man, prophesy
    and strike your hands together.
Let the sword strike twice,
    even three times.
It is a sword for slaughter—
    a sword for great slaughter,
    closing in on them from every
        side.
¹⁵So that hearts may melt
    and the fallen be many,
I have stationed the sword for
        slaughterᵃ
    at all their gates.
Oh! It is made to flash like lightning,
    it is grasped for slaughter.
¹⁶O sword, slash to the right,
    then to the left,
    wherever your blade is turned.
¹⁷I too will strike my hands together,
    and my wrath will subside.
I the Lᴏʀᴅ have spoken."

¹⁸The word of the Lᴏʀᴅ came to me:
¹⁹"Son of man, mark out two roads for
the sword of the king of Babylon to take,
both starting from the same country.
Make a signpost where the road branches
off to the city. ²⁰Mark out one road for
the sword to come against Rabbah of the
Ammonites and another against Judah
and fortified Jerusalem. ²¹For the king of
Babylon will stop at the fork in the road,
at the junction of the two roads, to seek
an omen: He will cast lots with arrows,

he will consult his idols, he will examine
the liver. ²²Into his right hand will come
the lot for Jerusalem, where he is to set
up battering rams, to give the command
to slaughter, to sound the battle cry, to set
battering rams against the gates, to build
a ramp and to erect siege works. ²³It will
seem like a false omen to those who have
sworn allegiance to him, but he will remind them of their guilt and take them
captive.

²⁴"Therefore this is what the Sovereign Lᴏʀᴅ says: 'Because you people
have brought to mind your guilt by your
open rebellion, revealing your sins in all
that you do—because you have done
this, you will be taken captive.

²⁵"'O profane and wicked prince of Israel, whose day has come, whose time of
punishment has reached its climax,
²⁶this is what the Sovereign Lᴏʀᴅ says:
Take off the turban, remove the crown. It
will not be as it was: The lowly will be exalted and the exalted will be brought low.
²⁷A ruin! A ruin! I will make it a ruin! It
will not be restored until he comes to
whom it rightfully belongs; to him I will
give it.'

²⁸"And you, son of man, prophesy and
say, 'This is what the Sovereign Lᴏʀᴅ
says about the Ammonites and their
insults:

"'A sword, a sword,
    drawn for the slaughter,
polished to consume
    and to flash like lightning!
²⁹Despite false visions concerning you
    and lying divinations about you,
it will be laid on the necks
    of the wicked who are to be slain,
whose day has come,
    whose time of punishment has
        reached its climax.
³⁰Return the sword to its scabbard.
    In the place where you were
        created,
in the land of your ancestry,
    I will judge you.
³¹I will pour out my wrath upon you
    and breathe out my fiery anger
        against you;

I will hand you over to brutal men,
  men skilled in destruction.
³²You will be fuel for the fire,
  your blood will be shed in your
    land,
you will be remembered no more;
  for I the LORD have spoken.'"

22:1THE word of the LORD came to me:
²"Son of man, will you judge her? Will you
judge this city of bloodshed? Then confront her with all her detestable practices
³and say: 'This is what the Sovereign LORD
says: O city that brings on herself doom by
shedding blood in her midst and defiles
herself by making idols, ⁴you have become guilty because of the blood you
have shed and have become defiled by
the idols you have made. You have
brought your days to a close, and the end
of your years has come. Therefore I will
make you an object of scorn to the nations
and a laughingstock to all the countries.
⁵Those who are near and those who are
far away will mock you, O infamous city,
full of turmoil.

⁶"'See how each of the princes of Israel who are in you uses his power to
shed blood. ⁷In you they have treated
father and mother with contempt; in
you they have oppressed the alien and
mistreated the fatherless and the
widow. ⁸You have despised my holy
things and desecrated my Sabbaths. ⁹In
you are slanderous men bent on shedding blood; in you are those who eat at
the mountain shrines and commit lewd
acts. ¹⁰In you are those who dishonor
their fathers' bed; in you are those who
violate women during their period,
when they are ceremonially unclean.
¹¹In you one man commits a detestable
offense with his neighbor's wife, another shamefully defiles his daughter-
in-law, and another violates his sister,
his own father's daughter. ¹²In you men
accept bribes to shed blood; you take
usury and excessive interest*b* and make
unjust gain from your neighbors by extortion. And you have forgotten me, declares the Sovereign LORD.

¹³"'I will surely strike my hands together at the unjust gain you have made
and at the blood you have shed in your
midst. ¹⁴Will your courage endure or
your hands be strong in the day I deal
with you? I the LORD have spoken, and I
will do it. ¹⁵I will disperse you among
the nations and scatter you through the
countries; and I will put an end to your
uncleanness. ¹⁶When you have been
defiled*c* in the eyes of the nations, you
will know that I am the LORD.'"

¹⁷Then the word of the LORD came to
me: ¹⁸"Son of man, the house of Israel
has become dross to me; all of them are
the copper, tin, iron and lead left inside
a furnace. They are but the dross of silver. ¹⁹Therefore this is what the Sovereign LORD says: 'Because you have all
become dross, I will gather you into Jerusalem. ²⁰As men gather silver, copper,
iron, lead and tin into a furnace to melt
it with a fiery blast, so will I gather you in
my anger and my wrath and put you inside the city and melt you. ²¹I will gather
you and I will blow on you with my fiery
wrath, and you will be melted inside her.
²²As silver is melted in a furnace, so you
will be melted inside her, and you will
know that I the LORD have poured out
my wrath upon you.'"

²³Again the word of the LORD came to
me: ²⁴"Son of man, say to the land, 'You
are a land that has had no rain or showers*d* in the day of wrath.' ²⁵There is a conspiracy of her princes*e* within her like a
roaring lion tearing its prey; they devour
people, take treasures and precious
things and make many widows within
her. ²⁶Her priests do violence to my law
and profane my holy things; they do not
distinguish between the holy and the
common; they teach that there is no difference between the unclean and the
clean; and they shut their eyes to the
keeping of my Sabbaths, so that I am profaned among them. ²⁷Her officials
within her are like wolves tearing their
prey; they shed blood and kill people to
make unjust gain. ²⁸Her prophets whitewash these deeds for them by false visions and lying divinations. They say,
'This is what the Sovereign LORD says'—

when the LORD has not spoken. ²⁹The people of the land practice extortion and commit robbery; they oppress the poor and needy and mistreat the alien, denying them justice.

³⁰"I looked for a man among them who would build up the wall and stand before me in the gap on behalf of the land so I would not have to destroy it, but I found none. ³¹So I will pour out my wrath on them and consume them with my fiery anger, bringing down on their own heads all they have done, declares the Sovereign LORD."

a15 Septuagint; the meaning of the Hebrew for this word is uncertain.   *b12* Or *usury and interest*   *c16* Or *When I have allotted you your inheritance*   *d24* Septuagint; Hebrew *has not been cleansed or rained on*   *e25* Septuagint; Hebrew *prophets*

HEBREWS 10:1-17

The law is only a shadow of the good things that are coming—not the realities themselves. For this reason it can never, by the same sacrifices repeated endlessly year after year, make perfect those who draw near to worship. ²If it could, would they not have stopped being offered? For the worshipers would have been cleansed once for all, and would no longer have felt guilty for their sins. ³But those sacrifices are an annual reminder of sins, ⁴because it is impossible for the blood of bulls and goats to take away sins.

⁵Therefore, when Christ came into the world, he said:

"Sacrifice and offering you did not
      desire,
   but a body you prepared for me;
⁶with burnt offerings and sin
      offerings
   you were not pleased.
⁷Then I said, 'Here I am—it is written
      about me in the scroll—
   I have come to do your will,
      O God.'"*a*

⁸First he said, "Sacrifices and offerings, burnt offerings and sin offerings you did not desire, nor were you pleased with them" (although the law required them to be made). ⁹Then he said, "Here

I am, I have come to do your will." He sets aside the first to establish the second. ¹⁰And by that will, we have been made holy through the sacrifice of the body of Jesus Christ once for all.

¹¹Day after day every priest stands and performs his religious duties; again and again he offers the same sacrifices, which can never take away sins. ¹²**But when this priest had offered for all time one sacrifice for sins, he sat down at the right hand of God.** ¹³Since that time he waits for his enemies to be made his footstool, ¹⁴because by one sacrifice he has made perfect forever those who are being made holy.

¹⁵The Holy Spirit also testifies to us about this. First he says:

¹⁶"This is the covenant I will make
      with them
   after that time, says the Lord.
I will put my laws in their hearts,
   and I will write them on their
      minds."*b*

¹⁷Then he adds:

"Their sins and lawless acts
   I will remember no more."*c*

a7 Psalm 40:6-8 (see Septuagint)   *b16* Jer. 31:33   *c17* Jer. 31:34

PSALM 108:1-13

A song. A psalm of David.

¹ My heart is steadfast, O God;
   I will sing and make music with all
      my soul.
² Awake, harp and lyre!
   I will awaken the dawn.
³ I will praise you, O LORD, among the
      nations;
   I will sing of you among the
      peoples.
⁴ For great is your love, higher than the
      heavens;
   your faithfulness reaches to the
      skies.
⁵ Be exalted, O God, above the
      heavens,
   and let your glory be over all the
      earth.

6 Save us and help us with your right
  hand,
  that those you love may be
    delivered.
7 God has spoken from his sanctuary:
  "In triumph I will parcel out
    Shechem
  and measure off the Valley of
    Succoth.
8 Gilead is mine, Manasseh is mine;
  Ephraim is my helmet,
  Judah my scepter.
9 Moab is my washbasin,
  upon Edom I toss my sandal;
  over Philistia I shout in triumph."

10 Who will bring me to the fortified
    city?
  Who will lead me to Edom?
11 Is it not you, O God, you who have
    rejected us
  and no longer go out with our
    armies?
12 Give us aid against the enemy,
  for the help of man is worthless.
13 With God we will gain the victory,
  and he will trample down our
    enemies.

PROVERBS 27:12
12 The prudent see danger and take
    refuge,
  but the simple keep going and
    suffer for it.

□ D A Y   3 1 5

GOD SIGHTINGS

November 11

EZEKIEL 23:1-49
The word of the LORD came to me
[Ezekiel]: 2 "Son of man, there were two
women, daughters of the same mother.
3 They became prostitutes in Egypt, en-
gaging in prostitution from their youth.
In that land their breasts were fondled
and their virgin bosoms caressed. 4 The
older was named Oholah, and her sister

was Oholibah. They were mine and gave
birth to sons and daughters. Oholah is
Samaria, and Oholibah is Jerusalem.

5 "Oholah engaged in prostitution
while she was still mine; and she lusted
after her lovers, the Assyrians—warriors
6 clothed in blue, governors and commanders, all of them handsome young
men, and mounted horsemen. 7 She
gave herself as a prostitute to all the elite
of the Assyrians and defiled herself with
all the idols of everyone she lusted after.
8 She did not give up the prostitution she
began in Egypt, when during her youth
men slept with her, caressed her virgin
bosom and poured out their lust upon
her.

9 "Therefore I handed her over to her
lovers, the Assyrians, for whom she
lusted. 10 They stripped her naked, took
away her sons and daughters and killed
her with the sword. She became a byword among women, and punishment
was inflicted on her.

11 "Her sister Oholibah saw this, yet in
her lust and prostitution she was more
depraved than her sister. 12 She too
lusted after the Assyrians—governors
and commanders, warriors in full dress,
mounted horsemen, all handsome
young men. 13 I saw that she too defiled
herself; both of them went the same way.

14 "But she carried her prostitution
still further. She saw men portrayed on
a wall, figures of Chaldeans^a portrayed
in red, 15 with belts around their waists
and flowing turbans on their heads; all
of them looked like Babylonian chariot
officers, natives of Chaldea.^b 16 As soon
as she saw them, she lusted after them
and sent messengers to them in Chaldea. 17 Then the Babylonians came to
her, to the bed of love, and in their lust
they defiled her. After she had been defiled by them, she turned away from
them in disgust. 18 When she carried on
her prostitution openly and exposed
her nakedness, I turned away from her
in disgust, just as I had turned away
from her sister. 19 Yet she became more
and more promiscuous as she recalled
the days of her youth, when she was a

prostitute in Egypt. [20]There she lusted after her lovers, whose genitals were like those of donkeys and whose emission was like that of horses. [21]So you longed for the lewdness of your youth, when in Egypt your bosom was caressed and your young breasts fondled.[c]

[22]"Therefore, Oholibah, this is what the Sovereign Lord says: I will stir up your lovers against you, those you turned away from in disgust, and I will bring them against you from every side— [23]the Babylonians and all the Chaldeans, the men of Pekod and Shoa and Koa, and all the Assyrians with them, handsome young men, all of them governors and commanders, chariot officers and men of high rank, all mounted on horses. [24]They will come against you with weapons,[d] chariots and wagons and with a throng of people; they will take up positions against you on every side with large and small shields and with helmets. I will turn you over to them for punishment, and they will punish you according to their standards. [25]I will direct my jealous anger against you, and they will deal with you in fury. They will cut off your noses and your ears, and those of you who are left will fall by the sword. They will take away your sons and daughters, and those of you who are left will be consumed by fire. [26]They will also strip you of your clothes and take your fine jewelry. [27]So I will put a stop to the lewdness and prostitution you began in Egypt. You will not look on these things with longing or remember Egypt anymore.

[28]"For this is what the Sovereign Lord says: I am about to hand you over to those you hate, to those you turned away from in disgust. [29]They will deal with you in hatred and take away everything you have worked for. They will leave you naked and bare, and the shame of your prostitution will be exposed. Your lewdness and promiscuity [30]have brought this upon you, because you lusted after the nations and defiled yourself with their idols. [31]You have gone the way of your sister; so I will put her cup into your hand.

[32]"This is what the Sovereign Lord says:

"You will drink your sister's cup,
    a cup large and deep;
it will bring scorn and derision,
    for it holds so much.
[33]You will be filled with drunkenness
        and sorrow,
    the cup of ruin and desolation,
    the cup of your sister Samaria.
[34]You will drink it and drain it dry;
    you will dash it to pieces
    and tear your breasts.

I have spoken, declares the Sovereign Lord.

[35]"Therefore this is what the Sovereign Lord says: Since you have forgotten me and thrust me behind your back, you must bear the consequences of your lewdness and prostitution."

[36]The Lord said to me: "Son of man, will you judge Oholah and Oholibah? Then confront them with their detestable practices, [37]for they have committed adultery and blood is on their hands. They committed adultery with their idols; they even sacrificed their children, whom they bore to me,[e] as food for them. [38]They have also done this to me: At that same time they defiled my sanctuary and desecrated my Sabbaths. [39]On the very day they sacrificed their children to their idols, they entered my sanctuary and desecrated it. That is what they did in my house.

[40]"They even sent messengers for men who came from far away, and when they arrived you bathed yourself for them, painted your eyes and put on your jewelry. [41]You sat on an elegant couch, with a table spread before it on which you had placed the incense and oil that belonged to me.

[42]"The noise of a carefree crowd was around her; Sabeans[f] were brought from the desert along with men from the rabble, and they put bracelets on the arms of the woman and her sister and beautiful crowns on their heads. [43]Then I said about the one worn out by adultery, 'Now

let them use her as a prostitute, for that is all she is.' 44And they slept with her. As men sleep with a prostitute, so they slept with those lewd women, Oholah and Oholibah. 45But righteous men will sentence them to the punishment of women who commit adultery and shed blood, because they are adulterous and blood is on their hands.

46"This is what the Sovereign LORD says: Bring a mob against them and give them over to terror and plunder. 47The mob will stone them and cut them down with their swords; they will kill their sons and daughters and burn down their houses.

48"So I will put an end to lewdness in the land, that all women may take warning and not imitate you. 49You will suffer the penalty for your lewdness and bear the consequences of your sins of idolatry. Then you will know that I am the Sovereign LORD."

a14 Or *Babylonians*   b15 Or *Babylonia*; also in verse 16
c21 Syriac (see also verse 3); Hebrew *caressed because of your young breasts*   d24 The meaning of the Hebrew for this word is uncertain.   e37 Or *even made the children they bore to me pass through ⌊the fire⌋*   f42 Or *drunkards*

HEBREWS 10:18-39

And where these [the sins and lawless acts of God's people] have been forgiven, there is no longer any sacrifice for sin.

19Therefore, brothers, since we have confidence to enter the Most Holy Place by the blood of Jesus, 20by a new and living way opened for us through the curtain, that is, his body, 21and since we have a great priest over the house of God, 22let us draw near to God with a sincere heart in full assurance of faith, having our hearts sprinkled to cleanse us from a guilty conscience and having our bodies washed with pure water. 23**Let us hold unswervingly to the hope we profess, for he who promised is faithful.** 24**And let us consider how we may spur one another on toward love and good deeds.** 25Let us not give up meeting together, as some are in the habit of doing, but let us en-

courage one another—and all the more as you see the Day approaching.

26If we deliberately keep on sinning after we have received the knowledge of the truth, no sacrifice for sins is left, 27but only a fearful expectation of judgment and of raging fire that will consume the enemies of God. 28Anyone who rejected the law of Moses died without mercy on the testimony of two or three witnesses. 29How much more severely do you think a man deserves to be punished who has trampled the Son of God under foot, who has treated as an unholy thing the blood of the covenant that sanctified him, and who has insulted the Spirit of grace? 30For we know him who said, "It is mine to avenge; I will repay,"a and again, "The Lord will judge his people."b 31It is a dreadful thing to fall into the hands of the living God.

32Remember those earlier days after you had received the light, when you stood your ground in a great contest in the face of suffering. 33Sometimes you were publicly exposed to insult and persecution; at other times you stood side by side with those who were so treated. 34You sympathized with those in prison and joyfully accepted the confiscation of your property, because you knew that you yourselves had better and lasting possessions.

35So do not throw away your confidence; it will be richly rewarded. 36You need to persevere so that when you have done the will of God, you will receive what he has promised. 37For in just a very little while,

> "He who is coming will come and
>   will not delay.
> 38   But my righteous onec will live by
>   faith.
> And if he shrinks back,
>   I will not be pleased with him."d

39But we are not of those who shrink back and are destroyed, but of those who believe and are saved.

a30 Deut. 32:35   b30 Deut. 32:36; Psalm 135:14   c38 One early manuscript *But the righteous*   d38 Hab. 2:3,4

PSALM 109:1-31
For the director of music. Of David.
A psalm.

1 ◐ God, whom I praise,
   do not remain silent,
2 for wicked and deceitful men
   have opened their mouths against
      me;
   they have spoken against me with
      lying tongues.
3 With words of hatred they surround
      me;
   they attack me without cause.
4 In return for my friendship they
      accuse me,
   but I am a man of prayer.
5 They repay me evil for good,
   and hatred for my friendship.

6 Appoint*a* an evil man*b* to oppose him;
   let an accuser*c* stand at his right
      hand.
7 When he is tried, let him be found
      guilty,
   and may his prayers condemn
      him.
8 May his days be few;
   may another take his place of
      leadership.
9 May his children be fatherless
   and his wife a widow.
10 May his children be wandering
      beggars;
   may they be driven*d* from their
      ruined homes.
11 May a creditor seize all he has;
   may strangers plunder the fruits of
      his labor.
12 May no one extend kindness to him
   or take pity on his fatherless
      children.
13 May his descendants be cut off,
   their names blotted out from the
      next generation.
14 May the iniquity of his fathers be
      remembered before the LORD;
   may the sin of his mother never be
      blotted out.
15 May their sins always remain before
      the LORD,
   that he may cut off the memory of
      them from the earth.

16 For he never thought of doing a
      kindness,
   but hounded to death the poor
   and the needy and the
      brokenhearted.
17 He loved to pronounce a curse—
   may it*e* come on him;
   he found no pleasure in blessing—
   may it be*f* far from him.
18 He wore cursing as his garment;
   it entered into his body like water,
   into his bones like oil.
19 May it be like a cloak wrapped about
      him,
   like a belt tied forever around him.
20 May this be the LORD's payment to
      my accusers,
   to those who speak evil of me.

21 But you, O Sovereign LORD,
   deal well with me for your name's
      sake;
   out of the goodness of your love,
      deliver me.
22 For I am poor and needy,
   and my heart is wounded within
      me.
23 I fade away like an evening shadow;
   I am shaken off like a locust.
24 My knees give way from fasting;
   my body is thin and gaunt.
25 I am an object of scorn to my
      accusers;
   when they see me, they shake their
      heads.

26 Help me, O LORD my God;
   save me in accordance with your
      love.
27 Let them know that it is your hand,
   that you, O LORD, have done it.
28 They may curse, but you will bless;
   when they attack they will be put
      to shame,
   but your servant will rejoice.
29 My accusers will be clothed with
      disgrace
   and wrapped in shame as in a cloak.

30 With my mouth I will greatly extol
      the LORD;
   in the great throng I will praise
      him.

31 For he stands at the right hand of the
    needy one,
  to save his life from those who
    condemn him.

*a6 Or They say: "Appoint (with quotation marks at the
end of verse 19)   b6 Or the Evil One   c6 Or let Satan
d10 Septuagint; Hebrew sought   e17 Or curse, / and it has
f17 Or blessing, / and it is*

PROVERBS 27:13

13 Take the garment of one who puts up
    security for a stranger;
  hold it in pledge if he does it for a
    wayward woman.

□ DAY 316

GOD SIGHTINGS

November 12

EZEKIEL 24:1–26:21

In the ninth year, in the tenth month on
the tenth day, the word of the LORD came
to me [Ezekiel]: 2 "Son of man, record
this date, this very date, because the
king of Babylon has laid siege to Jerusalem this very day. 3 Tell this rebellious
house a parable and say to them: 'This is
what the Sovereign LORD says:

  "'Put on the cooking pot; put it on
    and pour water into it.
4 Put into it the pieces of meat,
    all the choice pieces—the leg and
      the shoulder.
  Fill it with the best of these bones;
5   take the pick of the flock.
  Pile wood beneath it for the bones;
    bring it to a boil
    and cook the bones in it.

6 " 'For this is what the Sovereign LORD
says:

  "'Woe to the city of bloodshed,
    to the pot now encrusted,
    whose deposit will not go away!
  Empty it piece by piece
    without casting lots for them.

7 "'For the blood she shed is in her
    midst:
  She poured it on the bare rock;
  she did not pour it on the ground,
    where the dust would cover it.
8 To stir up wrath and take revenge
  I put her blood on the bare rock,
    so that it would not be covered.

9 "'Therefore this is what the Sovereign
LORD says:

  "'Woe to the city of bloodshed!
    I, too, will pile the wood high.
10 So heap on the wood
    and kindle the fire.
  Cook the meat well,
    mixing in the spices;
    and let the bones be charred.
11 Then set the empty pot on the coals
    till it becomes hot and its copper
      glows
  so its impurities may be melted
    and its deposit burned away.
12 It has frustrated all efforts;
    its heavy deposit has not been
      removed,
    not even by fire.

13 " 'Now your impurity is lewdness.
Because I tried to cleanse you but you
would not be cleansed from your impurity, you will not be clean again until my
wrath against you has subsided.

14 " 'I the LORD have spoken. The time
has come for me to act. I will not hold
back; I will not have pity, nor will I relent. You will be judged according to
your conduct and your actions, declares
the Sovereign LORD.' "

15 The word of the LORD came to me:
16 "Son of man, with one blow I am
about to take away from you the delight
of your eyes. Yet do not lament or weep
or shed any tears. 17 Groan quietly; do
not mourn for the dead. Keep your turban fastened and your sandals on your
feet; do not cover the lower part of your
face or eat the customary food of
mourners ."

18 So I spoke to the people in the
morning, and in the evening my wife

died. The next morning I did as I had been commanded.

¹⁹Then the people asked me, "Won't you tell us what these things have to do with us?"

²⁰So I said to them, "The word of the LORD came to me: ²¹Say to the house of Israel, 'This is what the Sovereign LORD says: I am about to desecrate my sanctuary—the stronghold in which you take pride, the delight of your eyes, the object of your affection. The sons and daughters you left behind will fall by the sword. ²²And you will do as I have done. You will not cover the lower part of your face or eat the customary food ⸀of mourners⸢. ²³You will keep your turbans on your heads and your sandals on your feet. You will not mourn or weep but will waste away because of⸺ your sins and groan among yourselves. ²⁴Ezekiel will be a sign to you; you will do just as he has done. When this happens, you will know that I am the Sovereign LORD.'

²⁵"And you, son of man, on the day I take away their stronghold, their joy and glory, the delight of their eyes, their heart's desire, and their sons and daughters as well— ²⁶on that day a fugitive will come to tell you the news. ²⁷At that time your mouth will be opened; you will speak with him and will no longer be silent. So you will be a sign to them, and they will know that I am the LORD."

²⁵:¹THE word of the LORD came to me: ²"Son of man, set your face against the Ammonites and prophesy against them. ³Say to them, 'Hear the word of the Sovereign LORD. This is what the Sovereign LORD says: Because you said "Aha!" over my sanctuary when it was desecrated and over the land of Israel when it was laid waste and over the people of Judah when they went into exile, ⁴therefore I am going to give you to the people of the East as a possession. They will set up their camps and pitch their tents among you; they will eat your fruit and drink your milk. ⁵I will turn Rabbah into a

pasture for camels and Ammon into a resting place for sheep. Then you will know that I am the LORD. ⁶For this is what the Sovereign LORD says: Because you have clapped your hands and stamped your feet, rejoicing with all the malice of your heart against the land of Israel, ⁷therefore I will stretch out my hand against you and give you as plunder to the nations. I will cut you off from the nations and exterminate you from the countries. I will destroy you, and you will know that I am the LORD.'"

⁸"This is what the Sovereign LORD says: 'Because Moab and Seir said, "Look, the house of Judah has become like all the other nations," ⁹therefore I will expose the flank of Moab, beginning at its frontier towns—Beth Jeshimoth, Baal Meon and Kiriathaim—the glory of that land. ¹⁰I will give Moab along with the Ammonites to the people of the East as a possession, so that the Ammonites will not be remembered among the nations; ¹¹and I will inflict punishment on Moab. Then they will know that I am the LORD.'"

¹²"This is what the Sovereign LORD says: 'Because Edom took revenge on the house of Judah and became very guilty by doing so, ¹³therefore this is what the Sovereign LORD says: I will stretch out my hand against Edom and kill its men and their animals. I will lay it waste, and from Teman to Dedan they will fall by the sword. ¹⁴I will take vengeance on Edom by the hand of my people Israel, and they will deal with Edom in accordance with my anger and my wrath; they will know my vengeance, declares the Sovereign LORD.'"

¹⁵"This is what the Sovereign LORD says: 'Because the Philistines acted in vengeance and took revenge with malice in their hearts, and with ancient hostility sought to destroy Judah, ¹⁶therefore this is what the Sovereign LORD says: I am about to stretch out my hand against the Philistines, and I will cut off the Kerethites and destroy those remaining along the coast. ¹⁷I will carry out great vengeance on them and punish them in my

wrath. Then they will know that I am the Lord, when I take vengeance on them.'"

26:1 In the eleventh year, on the first day of the month, the word of the Lord came to me: 2 "Son of man, because Tyre has said of Jerusalem, 'Aha! The gate to the nations is broken, and its doors have swung open to me; now that she lies in ruins I will prosper,' 3 therefore this is what the Sovereign Lord says: I am against you, O Tyre, and I will bring many nations against you, like the sea casting up its waves. 4 They will destroy the walls of Tyre and pull down her towers; I will scrape away her rubble and make her a bare rock. 5 Out in the sea she will become a place to spread fishnets, for I have spoken, declares the Sovereign Lord. She will become plunder for the nations, 6 and her settlements on the mainland will be ravaged by the sword. Then they will know that I am the Lord.

7 "For this is what the Sovereign Lord says: From the north I am going to bring against Tyre Nebuchadnezzar[b] king of Babylon, king of kings, with horses and chariots, with horsemen and a great army. 8 He will ravage your settlements on the mainland with the sword; he will set up siege works against you, build a ramp up to your walls and raise his shields against you. 9 He will direct the blows of his battering rams against your walls and demolish your towers with his weapons. 10 His horses will be so many that they will cover you with dust. Your walls will tremble at the noise of the war horses, wagons and chariots when he enters your gates as men enter a city whose walls have been broken through. 11 The hoofs of his horses will trample all your streets; he will kill your people with the sword, and your strong pillars will fall to the ground. 12 They will plunder your wealth and loot your merchandise; they will break down your walls and demolish your fine houses and throw your stones, timber and rubble into the sea. 13 I will put an end to your noisy songs, and the music of your harps will be heard no more. 14 I will

make you a bare rock, and you will become a place to spread fishnets. You will never be rebuilt, for I the Lord have spoken, declares the Sovereign Lord.

15 "This is what the Sovereign Lord says to Tyre: Will not the coastlands tremble at the sound of your fall, when the wounded groan and the slaughter takes place in you? 16 Then all the princes of the coast will step down from their thrones and lay aside their robes and take off their embroidered garments. Clothed with terror, they will sit on the ground, trembling every moment, appalled at you. 17 Then they will take up a lament concerning you and say to you:

"'How you are destroyed, O city of
    renown,
    peopled by men of the sea!
You were a power on the seas,
    you and your citizens;
you put your terror
    on all who lived there.
18 Now the coastlands tremble
    on the day of your fall;
    the islands in the sea
    are terrified at your collapse.'

19 "This is what the Sovereign Lord says: When I make you a desolate city, like cities no longer inhabited, and when I bring the ocean depths over you and its vast waters cover you, 20 then I will bring you down with those who go down to the pit, to the people of long ago. I will make you dwell in the earth below, as in ancient ruins, with those who go down to the pit, and you will not return or take your place[c] in the land of the living. 21 I will bring you to a horrible end and you will be no more. You will be sought, but you will never again be found, declares the Sovereign Lord."

a 23 Or *away in*   b 7 Hebrew *Nebuchadrezzar*, of which *Nebuchadnezzar* is a variant; here and often in Ezekiel and Jeremiah   c 20 Septuagint; Hebrew *return, and I will give glory*

HEBREWS 11:1-16
Now faith is being sure of what we hope for and certain of what we do not see. 2 This is what the ancients were commended for.

³By faith we understand that the universe was formed at God's command, so that what is seen was not made out of what was visible.

⁴By faith Abel offered God a better sacrifice than Cain did. By faith he was commended as a righteous man, when God spoke well of his offerings. And by faith he still speaks, even though he is dead.

⁵By faith Enoch was taken from this life, so that he did not experience death; he could not be found, because God had taken him away. For before he was taken, he was commended as one who pleased God. ⁶And without faith it is impossible to please God, because anyone who comes to him must believe that he exists and that he rewards those who earnestly seek him.

⁷By faith Noah, when warned about things not yet seen, in holy fear built an ark to save his family. By his faith he condemned the world and became heir of the righteousness that comes by faith.

⁸By faith Abraham, when called to go to a place he would later receive as his inheritance, obeyed and went, even though he did not know where he was going. ⁹By faith he made his home in the promised land like a stranger in a foreign country; he lived in tents, as did Isaac and Jacob, who were heirs with him of the same promise. ¹⁰For he was looking forward to the city with foundations, whose architect and builder is God.

¹¹By faith Abraham, even though he was past age—and Sarah herself was barren—was enabled to become a father because heᵃ considered him faithful who had made the promise. ¹²And so from this one man, and he as good as dead, came descendants as numerous as the stars in the sky and as countless as the sand on the seashore.

¹³All these people were still living by faith when they died. They did not receive the things promised; they only saw them and welcomed them from a distance. And they admitted that they were aliens and strangers on earth.

¹⁴People who say such things show that they are looking for a country of their own. ¹⁵If they had been thinking of the country they had left, they would have had opportunity to return. ¹⁶Instead, they were longing for a better country—a heavenly one. Therefore God is not ashamed to be called their God, for he has prepared a city for them.

ᵃ11 Or *By faith even Sarah, who was past age, was enabled to bear children because she*

PSALM 110:1-7
Of David. A psalm.

¹ The Lᴏʀᴅ says to my Lord:
    "Sit at my right hand
until I make your enemies
    a footstool for your feet."

² The Lᴏʀᴅ will extend your mighty
        scepter from Zion;
    you will rule in the midst of your
        enemies.
³ Your troops will be willing
    on your day of battle.
Arrayed in holy majesty,
    from the womb of the dawn
    you will receive the dew of your
        youth.ᵃ

⁴ The Lᴏʀᴅ has sworn
    and will not change his mind:
"You are a priest forever,
    in the order of Melchizedek."

⁵ The Lord is at your right hand;
    he will crush kings on the day of
        his wrath.
⁶ He will judge the nations, heaping up
        the dead
    and crushing the rulers of the
        whole earth.
⁷ He will drink from a brook beside
        the wayᵇ;
    therefore he will lift up his head.

ᵃ3 Or / *your young men will come to you like the dew*
ᵇ7 Or / *The One who grants succession will set him in authority*

PROVERBS 27:14
¹⁴ If a man loudly blesses his neighbor
        early in the morning,
    it will be taken as a curse.

☐ DAY 317

GOD SIGHTINGS

November 13

EZEKIEL 27:1–28:26

The word of the LORD came to me [Ezekiel]: 2"Son of man, take up a lament concerning Tyre. 3 Say to Tyre, situated at the gateway to the sea, merchant of peoples on many coasts, 'This is what the Sovereign LORD says:

"'You say, O Tyre,
    "I am perfect in beauty."
4 Your domain was on the high seas;
    your builders brought your beauty
        to perfection.
5 They made all your timbers
    of pine trees from Senir[a];
they took a cedar from Lebanon
    to make a mast for you.
6 Of oaks from Bashan
    they made your oars;
of cypress wood[b] from the coasts of
        Cyprus[c]
    they made your deck, inlaid with
        ivory.
7 Fine embroidered linen from Egypt
        was your sail
    and served as your banner;
your awnings were of blue and purple
    from the coasts of Elishah.
8 Men of Sidon and Arvad were your
        oarsmen;
    your skilled men, O Tyre, were
        aboard as your seamen.
9 Veteran craftsmen of Gebal[d] were on
        board
    as shipwrights to caulk your
        seams.
All the ships of the sea and their
        sailors
    came alongside to trade for your
        wares.

10 "'Men of Persia, Lydia and Put
    served as soldiers in your army.
They hung their shields and helmets
        on your walls,
    bringing you splendor.

11 Men of Arvad and Helech
    manned your walls on every side;
men of Gammad
    were in your towers.
They hung their shields around your
        walls;
    they brought your beauty to
        perfection.

12 "'Tarshish did business with you because of your great wealth of goods; they exchanged silver, iron, tin and lead for your merchandise.

13 "'Greece, Tubal and Meshech traded with you; they exchanged slaves and articles of bronze for your wares.

14 "'Men of Beth Togarmah exchanged work horses, war horses and mules for your merchandise.

15 "'The men of Rhodes[e] traded with you, and many coastlands were your customers; they paid you with ivory tusks and ebony.

16 "'Aram[f] did business with you because of your many products; they exchanged turquoise, purple fabric, embroidered work, fine linen, coral and rubies for your merchandise.

17 "'Judah and Israel traded with you; they exchanged wheat from Minnith and confections,[g] honey, oil and balm for your wares.

18 "'Damascus, because of your many products and great wealth of goods, did business with you in wine from Helbon and wool from Zahar.

19 "'Danites and Greeks from Uzal bought your merchandise; they exchanged wrought iron, cassia and calamus for your wares.

20 "'Dedan traded in saddle blankets with you.

21 "'Arabia and all the princes of Kedar were your customers; they did business with you in lambs, rams and goats.

22 "'The merchants of Sheba and Raamah traded with you; for your merchandise they exchanged the finest of all kinds of spices and precious stones, and gold.

23 "'Haran, Canneh and Eden and merchants of Sheba, Asshur and Kil-

mad traded with you. ²⁴In your marketplace they traded with you beautiful garments, blue fabric, embroidered work and multicolored rugs with cords twisted and tightly knotted.

²⁵"'The ships of Tarshish serve
    as carriers for your wares.
  You are filled with heavy cargo
    in the heart of the sea.
²⁶Your oarsmen take you
    out to the high seas.
  But the east wind will break you to
        pieces
    in the heart of the sea.
²⁷Your wealth, merchandise and wares,
    your mariners, seamen and
        shipwrights,
  your merchants and all your soldiers,
    and everyone else on board
  will sink into the heart of the sea
    on the day of your shipwreck.
²⁸The shorelands will quake
    when your seamen cry out.
²⁹All who handle the oars
    will abandon their ships;
  the mariners and all the seamen
    will stand on the shore.
³⁰They will raise their voice
    and cry bitterly over you;
  they will sprinkle dust on their heads
    and roll in ashes.
³¹They will shave their heads because
        of you
    and will put on sackcloth.
  They will weep over you with
        anguish of soul
    and with bitter mourning.
³²As they wail and mourn over you,
    they will take up a lament
        concerning you:
  "Who was ever silenced like Tyre,
    surrounded by the sea?"
³³When your merchandise went out on
        the seas,
    you satisfied many nations;
  with your great wealth and your wares
    you enriched the kings of the earth.
³⁴Now you are shattered by the sea
    in the depths of the waters;
  your wares and all your company
    have gone down with you.

³⁵All who live in the coastlands
    are appalled at you;
  their kings shudder with horror
    and their faces are distorted with
        fear.
³⁶The merchants among the nations
        hiss at you;
    you have come to a horrible end
    and will be no more.'"

28:1The word of the Lord came to me: ²"Son of man, say to the ruler of Tyre, 'This is what the Sovereign Lord says:

  "'In the pride of your heart
    you say, "I am a god;
  I sit on the throne of a god
    in the heart of the seas."
  But you are a man and not a god,
    though you think you are as wise
        as a god.
³Are you wiser than Danielʰ?
    Is no secret hidden from you?
⁴By your wisdom and understanding
    you have gained wealth for yourself
  and amassed gold and silver
    in your treasuries.
⁵By your great skill in trading
    you have increased your wealth,
  and because of your wealth
    your heart has grown proud.

⁶"'Therefore this is what the Sovereign Lord says:

  "'Because you think you are wise,
    as wise as a god,
⁷I am going to bring foreigners
        against you,
    the most ruthless of nations;
  they will draw their swords against
        your beauty and wisdom
    and pierce your shining splendor.
⁸They will bring you down to the pit,
    and you will die a violent death
    in the heart of the seas.
⁹Will you then say, "I am a god,"
    in the presence of those who kill
        you?
  You will be but a man, not a god,
    in the hands of those who slay
        you.

¹⁰You will die the death of the
    uncircumcised
  at the hands of foreigners.

I have spoken, declares the Sovereign
LORD.'"

¹¹The word of the LORD came to me:
¹²"Son of man, take up a lament concerning the king of Tyre and say to him:
'This is what the Sovereign LORD says:

"'You were the model of perfection,
    full of wisdom and perfect in
    beauty.
¹³You were in Eden,
    the garden of God;
  every precious stone adorned you:
    ruby, topaz and emerald,
    chrysolite, onyx and jasper,
    sapphire,ⁱ turquoise and beryl.ʲ
  Your settings and mountingsᵏ were
    made of gold;
  on the day you were created they
    were prepared.
¹⁴You were anointed as a guardian
    cherub,
    for so I ordained you.
  You were on the holy mount of God;
    you walked among the fiery
    stones.
¹⁵You were blameless in your ways
    from the day you were created
    till wickedness was found in you.
¹⁶Through your widespread trade
    you were filled with violence,
    and you sinned.
  So I drove you in disgrace from the
    mount of God,
  and I expelled you, O guardian
    cherub,
    from among the fiery stones.
¹⁷Your heart became proud
    on account of your beauty,
  and you corrupted your wisdom
    because of your splendor.
  So I threw you to the earth;
    I made a spectacle of you before
    kings.
¹⁸By your many sins and dishonest
    trade
  you have desecrated your
    sanctuaries.

So I made a fire come out from you,
    and it consumed you,
  and I reduced you to ashes on the
    ground
  in the sight of all who were watching.
¹⁹All the nations who knew you
    are appalled at you;
  you have come to a horrible end
    and will be no more.'"

²⁰The word of the LORD came to me:
²¹"Son of man, set your face against Sidon; prophesy against her ²²and say:
'This is what the Sovereign LORD says:

"'I am against you, O Sidon,
    and I will gain glory within you.
  They will know that I am the LORD,
    when I inflict punishment on her
    and show myself holy within her.
²³I will send a plague upon her
    and make blood flow in her
    streets.
  The slain will fall within her,
    with the sword against her on
    every side.
  Then they will know that I am the
    LORD.

²⁴"'No longer will the people of Israel
have malicious neighbors who are painful briers and sharp thorns. Then they
will know that I am the Sovereign LORD.

²⁵"'This is what the Sovereign LORD
says: When I gather the people of Israel
from the nations where they have been
scattered, I will show myself holy among
them in the sight of the nations. Then
they will live in their own land, which I
gave to my servant Jacob. ²⁶They will
live there in safety and will build houses
and plant vineyards; they will live in
safety when I inflict punishment on all
their neighbors who maligned them.
Then they will know that I am the LORD
their God.'"

ᵃ5 That is, Hermon   ᵇ6 Targum; the Masoretic Text has a
different division of the consonants.   ᶜ6 Hebrew Kittim
ᵈ9 That is, Byblos   ᵉ15 Septuagint; Hebrew Dedan
ᶠ16 Most Hebrew manuscripts; some Hebrew manuscripts
and Syriac Edom   ᵍ17 The meaning of the Hebrew for
this word is uncertain.   ʰ3 Or Danel; the Hebrew spelling
may suggest a person other than the prophet Daniel.
ⁱ13 Or lapis lazuli   ʲ13 The precise identification of some
of these precious stones is uncertain.   ᵏ13 The meaning
of the Hebrew for this phrase is uncertain.

HEBREWS 11:17-31

By faith Abraham, when God tested him, offered Isaac as a sacrifice. He who had received the promises was about to sacrifice his one and only son, [18] even though God had said to him, "It is through Isaac that your offspring[a] will be reckoned."[b] [19] Abraham reasoned that God could raise the dead, and figuratively speaking, he did receive Isaac back from death.

[20] By faith Isaac blessed Jacob and Esau in regard to their future.

[21] By faith Jacob, when he was dying, blessed each of Joseph's sons, and worshiped as he leaned on the top of his staff.

[22] By faith Joseph, when his end was near, spoke about the exodus of the Israelites from Egypt and gave instructions about his bones.

[23] By faith Moses' parents hid him for three months after he was born, because they saw he was no ordinary child, and they were not afraid of the king's edict.

[24] By faith Moses, when he had grown up, refused to be known as the son of Pharaoh's daughter. [25] He chose to be mistreated along with the people of God rather than to enjoy the pleasures of sin for a short time. [26] He regarded disgrace for the sake of Christ as of greater value than the treasures of Egypt, because he was looking ahead to his reward. [27] By faith he left Egypt, not fearing the king's anger; he persevered because he saw him who is invisible. [28] By faith he kept the Passover and the sprinkling of blood, so that the destroyer of the firstborn would not touch the firstborn of Israel.

[29] By faith the people passed through the Red Sea[c] as on dry land; but when the Egyptians tried to do so, they were drowned.

[30] By faith the walls of Jericho fell, after the people had marched around them for seven days.

[31] By faith the prostitute Rahab, because she welcomed the spies, was not killed with those who were disobedient.[d]

a18 Greek seed   b18 Gen. 21:12   c29 That is, Sea of Reeds   d31 Or unbelieving

PSALM 111:1-10[a]
[1] **P**raise the LORD.[b]

I will extol the LORD with all my heart
    in the council of the upright and
        in the assembly.

[2] **Great are the works of the LORD;**
    they are pondered by all who
        delight in them.
[3] **Glorious and majestic are his**
    deeds,
    and his righteousness endures
        forever.
[4] He has caused his wonders to be
    remembered;
    the LORD is gracious and
        compassionate.
[5] He provides food for those who fear
    him;
    he remembers his covenant
        forever.
[6] He has shown his people the power
    of his works,
    giving them the lands of other
        nations.
[7] The works of his hands are faithful
    and just;
    all his precepts are trustworthy.
[8] They are steadfast for ever and ever,
    done in faithfulness and
        uprightness.
[9] He provided redemption for his
    people;
    he ordained his covenant
        forever—
    holy and awesome is his name.

[10] The fear of the LORD is the beginning
    of wisdom;
    all who follow his precepts have
        good understanding.
    To him belongs eternal praise.

aThis psalm is an acrostic poem, the lines of which begin with the successive letters of the Hebrew alphabet.
b1 Hebrew Hallelu Yah

PROVERBS 27:15-16
[15] **A** quarrelsome wife is like
    a constant dripping on a rainy day;
[16] restraining her is like restraining the
    wind
    or grasping oil with the hand.

☐ DAY 318

GOD SIGHTINGS

November 14

EZEKIEL 29:1–30:26

In the tenth year, in the tenth month on the twelfth day, the word of the LORD came to me [Ezekiel]: 2"Son of man, set your face against Pharaoh king of Egypt and prophesy against him and against all Egypt. 3Speak to him and say: 'This is what the Sovereign LORD says:

"'I am against you, Pharaoh king of
    Egypt,
  you great monster lying among
    your streams.
You say, "The Nile is mine;
  I made it for myself."
4But I will put hooks in your jaws
    and make the fish of your streams
      stick to your scales.
I will pull you out from among your
    streams,
  with all the fish sticking to your
    scales.
5I will leave you in the desert,
  you and all the fish of your
    streams.
You will fall on the open field
  and not be gathered or picked up.
I will give you as food
  to the beasts of the earth and the
    birds of the air.

6Then all who live in Egypt will know that I am the LORD.

"'You have been a staff of reed for the house of Israel. 7When they grasped you with their hands, you splintered and you tore open their shoulders; when they leaned on you, you broke and their backs were wrenched.ª

8" 'Therefore this is what the Sovereign LORD says: I will bring a sword against you and kill your men and their animals. 9Egypt will become a desolate wasteland. Then they will know that I am the LORD.

"'Because you said, "The Nile is mine; I made it," 10therefore I am against you and against your streams, and I will make the land of Egypt a ruin and a desolate waste from Migdol to Aswan, as far as the border of Cush.ᵇ 11No foot of man or animal will pass through it; no one will live there for forty years. 12I will make the land of Egypt desolate among devastated lands, and her cities will lie desolate forty years among ruined cities. And I will disperse the Egyptians among the nations and scatter them through the countries.

13"'Yet this is what the Sovereign LORD says: At the end of forty years I will gather the Egyptians from the nations where they were scattered. 14I will bring them back from captivity and return them to Upper Egypt,ᶜ the land of their ancestry. There they will be a lowly kingdom. 15It will be the lowliest of kingdoms and will never again exalt itself above the other nations. I will make it so weak that it will never again rule over the nations. 16Egypt will no longer be a source of confidence for the people of Israel but will be a reminder of their sin in turning to her for help. Then they will know that I am the Sovereign LORD.'"

17In the twenty-seventh year, in the first month on the first day, the word of the LORD came to me: 18"Son of man, Nebuchadnezzar king of Babylon drove his army in a hard campaign against Tyre; every head was rubbed bare and every shoulder made raw. Yet he and his army got no reward from the campaign he led against Tyre. 19Therefore this is what the Sovereign LORD says: I am going to give Egypt to Nebuchadnezzar king of Babylon, and he will carry off its wealth. He will loot and plunder the land as pay for his army. 20I have given him Egypt as a reward for his efforts because he and his army did it for me, declares the Sovereign LORD. 21"On that day I will make a hornᵈ grow for the house of Israel, and I will open your mouth among them. Then they will know that I am the LORD."

30:1THE word of the LORD came to me:
2"Son of man, prophesy and say: 'This is
what the Sovereign LORD says:

"'Wail and say,
    "Alas for that day!"
3For the day is near,
    the day of the LORD is near—
a day of clouds,
    a time of doom for the nations.
4A sword will come against Egypt,
    and anguish will come upon Cush.*e*
When the slain fall in Egypt,
    her wealth will be carried away
    and her foundations torn down.

5Cush and Put, Lydia and all Arabia,
Libya*f* and the people of the covenant
land will fall by the sword along with
Egypt.
    6"'This is what the LORD says:

"'The allies of Egypt will fall
    and her proud strength will fail.
From Migdol to Aswan
    they will fall by the sword within
    her,
        declares the Sovereign LORD.
7"'They will be desolate
    among desolate lands,
    and their cities will lie
    among ruined cities.
8Then they will know that I am the
    LORD,
        when I set fire to Egypt
        and all her helpers are crushed.

9"'On that day messengers will go out
from me in ships to frighten Cush out of
her complacency. Anguish will take
hold of them on the day of Egypt's
doom, for it is sure to come.

10"'This is what the Sovereign LORD
says:

"'I will put an end to the hordes of
    Egypt
    by the hand of Nebuchadnezzar
    king of Babylon.
11He and his army—the most ruthless
    of nations—
    will be brought in to destroy the
    land.

They will draw their swords against
    Egypt
    and fill the land with the slain.
12I will dry up the streams of the Nile
    and sell the land to evil men;
by the hand of foreigners
    I will lay waste the land and
    everything in it.

I the LORD have spoken.

    13"'This is what the Sovereign LORD
says:

"'I will destroy the idols
    and put an end to the images in
    Memphis.*g*
No longer will there be a prince in
    Egypt,
    and I will spread fear throughout
    the land.
14I will lay waste Upper Egypt,*h*
    set fire to Zoan
    and inflict punishment on
    Thebes.*i*
15I will pour out my wrath on
    Pelusium,*j*
    the stronghold of Egypt,
    and cut off the hordes of Thebes.
16I will set fire to Egypt;
    Pelusium will writhe in agony.
Thebes will be taken by storm;
    Memphis will be in constant
    distress.
17The young men of Heliopolis*k* and
    Bubastis*l*
    will fall by the sword,
    and the cities themselves will go
    into captivity.
18Dark will be the day at Tahpanhes
    when I break the yoke of Egypt;
    there her proud strength will come
    to an end.
She will be covered with clouds,
    and her villages will go into
    captivity.
19So I will inflict punishment on Egypt,
    and they will know that I am the
    LORD.'"

20In the eleventh year, in the first
month on the seventh day, the word of
the LORD came to me: 21"Son of man, I

have broken the arm of Pharaoh king of Egypt. It has not been bound up for healing or put in a splint so as to become strong enough to hold a sword. ²²Therefore this is what the Sovereign Lᴏʀᴅ says: I am against Pharaoh king of Egypt. I will break both his arms, the good arm as well as the broken one, and make the sword fall from his hand. ²³I will disperse the Egyptians among the nations and scatter them through the countries. ²⁴I will strengthen the arms of the king of Babylon and put my sword in his hand, but I will break the arms of Pharaoh, and he will groan before him like a mortally wounded man. ²⁵I will strengthen the arms of the king of Babylon, but the arms of Pharaoh will fall limp. Then they will know that I am the Lᴏʀᴅ, when I put my sword into the hand of the king of Babylon and he brandishes it against Egypt. ²⁶I will disperse the Egyptians among the nations and scatter them through the countries. Then they will know that I am the Lᴏʀᴅ."

a 7 Syriac (see also Septuagint and Vulgate); Hebrew *and you caused their backs to stand*   b 10 That is, the upper Nile region   c 14 Hebrew *to Pathros*   d 21 Horn here symbolizes strength.   e 4 That is, the upper Nile region; also in verses 5 and 9   f 5 Hebrew *Cub*   g 13 Hebrew *Noph*; also in verse 16   h 14 Hebrew *waste Pathros*   i 14 Hebrew *No*; also in verses 15 and 16   j 15 Hebrew *Sin*; also in verse 16   k 17 Hebrew *Awen* (or *On*)   l 17 Hebrew *Pi Beseth*

HEBREWS 11:32–12:13

And what more shall I say? I do not have time to tell about Gideon, Barak, Samson, Jephthah, David, Samuel and the prophets, ³³who through faith conquered kingdoms, administered justice, and gained what was promised; who shut the mouths of lions, ³⁴quenched the fury of the flames, and escaped the edge of the sword; whose weakness was turned to strength; and who became powerful in battle and routed foreign armies. ³⁵Women received back their dead, raised to life again. Others were tortured and refused to be released, so that they might gain a better resurrection. ³⁶Some faced jeers and flogging, while still others were chained and put in prison. ³⁷They were stonedᵃ; they were sawed in two; they were put to death by the sword. They went about in sheepskins and goatskins, destitute, persecuted and mistreated— ³⁸the world was not worthy of them. They wandered in deserts and mountains, and in caves and holes in the ground.

³⁹These were all commended for their faith, yet none of them received what had been promised. ⁴⁰God had planned something better for us so that only together with us would they be made perfect.

12:1**Therefore, since we are surrounded by such a great cloud of witnesses, let us throw off everything that hinders and the sin that so easily entangles, and let us run with perseverance the race marked out for us.** ²Let us fix our eyes on Jesus, the author and perfecter of our faith, who for the joy set before him endured the cross, scorning its shame, and sat down at the right hand of the throne of God. ³Consider him who endured such opposition from sinful men, so that you will not grow weary and lose heart.

⁴In your struggle against sin, you have not yet resisted to the point of shedding your blood. ⁵And you have forgotten that word of encouragement that addresses you as sons:

> "My son, do not make light of the
>   Lord's discipline,
>   and do not lose heart when he
>   rebukes you,
> ⁶because the Lord disciplines those
>   he loves,
>   and he punishes everyone he
>   accepts as a son."ᵇ

⁷Endure hardship as discipline; God is treating you as sons. For what son is not disciplined by his father? ⁸If you are not disciplined (and everyone undergoes discipline), then you are illegitimate children and not true sons. ⁹Moreover, we have all had human fathers who disciplined us and we respected them for it. How much more should we submit to the Father of our spirits and live! ¹⁰Our fathers disciplined us for a little while as

they thought best; but God disciplines us for our good, that we may share in his holiness. [11]No discipline seems pleasant at the time, but painful. Later on, however, it produces a harvest of righteousness and peace for those who have been trained by it.

[12]Therefore, strengthen your feeble arms and weak knees. [13]"Make level paths for your feet,"*c* so that the lame may not be disabled, but rather healed.

a37 Some early manuscripts *stoned; they were put to the test;* *b6* Prov. 3:11,12 *c13* Prov. 4:26

PSALM 112:1-10*a*

[1]**P**raise the LORD.*b*

Blessed is the man who fears the
  LORD,
    who finds great delight in his
      commands.
[2]His children will be mighty in the
  land;
    the generation of the upright will
      be blessed.
[3]Wealth and riches are in his house,
    and his righteousness endures
      forever.
[4]Even in darkness light dawns for the
  upright,
    for the gracious and
      compassionate and righteous
        man.*c*
[5]Good will come to him who is
  generous and lends freely,
    who conducts his affairs with
      justice.
[6]Surely he will never be shaken;
    a righteous man will be
      remembered forever.
[7]He will have no fear of bad news;
    his heart is steadfast, trusting in
      the LORD.
[8]His heart is secure, he will have no
  fear;
    in the end he will look in triumph
      on his foes.
[9]He has scattered abroad his gifts to
  the poor,
    his righteousness endures forever;
    his horn*d* will be lifted high in
      honor.

[10]The wicked man will see and be
  vexed,
    he will gnash his teeth and waste
      away;
    the longings of the wicked will
      come to nothing.

*a*This psalm is an acrostic poem, the lines of which begin with the successive letters of the Hebrew alphabet. *b1* Hebrew *Hallelu Yah* *c4* Or */ for* ⌊*the* LORD⌋ *is gracious and compassionate and righteous* *d9* Horn here symbolizes dignity.

PROVERBS 27:17

[17]**A**s iron sharpens iron,
    so one man sharpens another.

□ D A Y   3 1 9

GOD SIGHTINGS

November 15

EZEKIEL 31:1–32:32

In the eleventh year, in the third month on the first day, the word of the LORD came to me [Ezekiel]: [2]"Son of man, say to Pharaoh king of Egypt and to his hordes:

"'Who can be compared with you in
  majesty?
[3]Consider Assyria, once a cedar in
  Lebanon,
    with beautiful branches
      overshadowing the forest;
    it towered on high,
      its top above the thick foliage.
[4]The waters nourished it,
    deep springs made it grow tall;
    their streams flowed
      all around its base
    and sent their channels
      to all the trees of the field.
[5]So it towered higher
    than all the trees of the field;
    its boughs increased
      and its branches grew long,
      spreading because of abundant
        waters.
[6]All the birds of the air
    nested in its boughs,

all the beasts of the field
    gave birth under its branches;
all the great nations
    lived in its shade.
[7] It was majestic in beauty,
    with its spreading boughs,
for its roots went down
    to abundant waters.
[8] The cedars in the garden of God
    could not rival it,
nor could the pine trees
    equal its boughs,
nor could the plane trees
    compare with its branches—
no tree in the garden of God
    could match its beauty.
[9] I made it beautiful
    with abundant branches,
the envy of all the trees of Eden
    in the garden of God.

[10] " 'Therefore this is what the Sovereign LORD says: Because it towered on high, lifting its top above the thick foliage, and because it was proud of its height, [11] I handed it over to the ruler of the nations, for him to deal with according to its wickedness. I cast it aside, [12] and the most ruthless of foreign nations cut it down and left it. Its boughs fell on the mountains and in all the valleys; its branches lay broken in all the ravines of the land. All the nations of the earth came out from under its shade and left it. [13] All the birds of the air settled on the fallen tree, and all the beasts of the field were among its branches. [14] Therefore no other trees by the waters are ever to tower proudly on high, lifting their tops above the thick foliage. No other trees so well-watered are ever to reach such a height; they are all destined for death, for the earth below, among mortal men, with those who go down to the pit.

[15] " 'This is what the Sovereign LORD says: On the day it was brought down to the grave[a] I covered the deep springs with mourning for it; I held back its streams, and its abundant waters were restrained. Because of it I clothed Lebanon with gloom, and all the trees of the field withered away. [16] I made the na-

tions tremble at the sound of its fall when I brought it down to the grave with those who go down to the pit. Then all the trees of Eden, the choicest and best of Lebanon, all the trees that were well-watered, were consoled in the earth below. [17] Those who lived in its shade, its allies among the nations, had also gone down to the grave with it, joining those killed by the sword.

[18] " 'Which of the trees of Eden can be compared with you in splendor and majesty? Yet you, too, will be brought down with the trees of Eden to the earth below; you will lie among the uncircumcised, with those killed by the sword.

" 'This is Pharaoh and all his hordes, declares the Sovereign LORD.' "

[32:1] In the twelfth year, in the twelfth month on the first day, the word of the LORD came to me: [2] "Son of man, take up a lament concerning Pharaoh king of Egypt and say to him:

" 'You are like a lion among the
    nations;
you are like a monster in the seas
thrashing about in your streams,
    churning the water with your feet
    and muddying the streams.

[3] " 'This is what the Sovereign LORD says:

" 'With a great throng of people
    I will cast my net over you,
    and they will haul you up in my net.
[4] I will throw you on the land
    and hurl you on the open field.
I will let all the birds of the air settle
    on you
    and all the beasts of the earth
        gorge themselves on you.
[5] I will spread your flesh on the
        mountains
    and fill the valleys with your
        remains.
[6] I will drench the land with your
        flowing blood
all the way to the mountains,
    and the ravines will be filled with
        your flesh.

7 When I snuff you out, I will cover the
heavens
and darken their stars;
I will cover the sun with a cloud,
and the moon will not give its
light.
8 All the shining lights in the heavens
I will darken over you;
I will bring darkness over your
land,
declares the Sovereign LORD.
9 I will trouble the hearts of many
peoples
when I bring about your destruction
among the nations,
among[b] lands you have not
known.
10 I will cause many peoples to be
appalled at you,
and their kings will shudder with
horror because of you
when I brandish my sword before
them.
On the day of your downfall
each of them will tremble
every moment for his life.

11 " 'For this is what the Sovereign
LORD says:

" 'The sword of the king of Babylon
will come against you.
12 I will cause your hordes to fall
by the swords of mighty men—
the most ruthless of all nations.
They will shatter the pride of Egypt,
and all her hordes will be
overthrown.
13 I will destroy all her cattle
from beside abundant waters
no longer to be stirred by the foot of
man
or muddied by the hoofs of cattle.
14 Then I will let her waters settle
and make her streams flow like oil,
declares the Sovereign LORD.
15 When I make Egypt desolate
and strip the land of everything
in it,
when I strike down all who live there,
then they will know that I am the
LORD.'

16 "This is the lament they will chant
for her. The daughters of the nations
will chant it; for Egypt and all her hordes
they will chant it, declares the Sovereign
LORD."

17 In the twelfth year, on the fifteenth
day of the month, the word of the LORD
came to me: 18 "Son of man, wail for the
hordes of Egypt and consign to the
earth below both her and the daughters
of mighty nations, with those who go
down to the pit. 19 Say to them, 'Are you
more favored than others? Go down and
be laid among the uncircumcised.'
20 They will fall among those killed by
the sword. The sword is drawn; let her
be dragged off with all her hordes.
21 From within the grave[c] the mighty
leaders will say of Egypt and her allies,
'They have come down and they lie with
the uncircumcised, with those killed by
the sword.'

22 "Assyria is there with her whole
army; she is surrounded by the graves of
all her slain, all who have fallen by the
sword. 23 Their graves are in the depths
of the pit and her army lies around her
grave. All who had spread terror in the
land of the living are slain, fallen by the
sword.

24 "Elam is there, with all her hordes
around her grave. All of them are slain,
fallen by the sword. All who had spread
terror in the land of the living went
down uncircumcised to the earth below.
They bear their shame with those who
go down to the pit. 25 A bed is made for
her among the slain, with all her hordes
around her grave. All of them are uncircumcised, killed by the sword. Because
their terror had spread in the land of the
living, they bear their shame with those
who go down to the pit; they are laid
among the slain.

26 "Meshech and Tubal are there, with
all their hordes around their graves. All
of them are uncircumcised, killed by the
sword because they spread their terror in
the land of the living. 27 Do they not lie
with the other uncircumcised warriors
who have fallen, who went down to the

grave with their weapons of war, whose swords were placed under their heads? The punishment for their sins rested on their bones, though the terror of these warriors had stalked through the land of the living.

28 "You too, O Pharaoh, will be broken and will lie among the uncircumcised, with those killed by the sword.

29 "Edom is there, her kings and all her princes; despite their power, they are laid with those killed by the sword. They lie with the uncircumcised, with those who go down to the pit.

30 "All the princes of the north and all the Sidonians are there; they went down with the slain in disgrace despite the terror caused by their power. They lie uncircumcised with those killed by the sword and bear their shame with those who go down to the pit.

31 "Pharaoh—he and all his army— will see them and he will be consoled for all his hordes that were killed by the sword, declares the Sovereign LORD. 32 Although I had him spread terror in the land of the living, Pharaoh and all his hordes will be laid among the uncircumcised, with those killed by the sword, declares the Sovereign LORD."

a 15 Hebrew *Sheol*; also in verses 16 and 17   b 9 Hebrew; Septuagint *bring you into captivity among the nations, / to* c 21 Hebrew *Sheol*; also in verse 27

HEBREWS 12:14-29

Make every effort to live in peace with all men and to be holy; without holiness no one will see the Lord. 15 See to it that no one misses the grace of God and that no bitter root grows up to cause trouble and defile many. 16 See that no one is sexually immoral, or is godless like Esau, who for a single meal sold his inheritance rights as the oldest son. 17 Afterward, as you know, when he wanted to inherit this blessing, he was rejected. He could bring about no change of mind, though he sought the blessing with tears.

18 You have not come to a mountain that can be touched and that is burning with fire; to darkness, gloom and storm;

19 to a trumpet blast or to such a voice speaking words that those who heard it begged that no further word be spoken to them, 20 because they could not bear what was commanded: "If even an animal touches the mountain, it must be stoned."a 21 The sight was so terrifying that Moses said, "I am trembling with fear."b

22 But you have come to Mount Zion, to the heavenly Jerusalem, the city of the living God. You have come to thousands upon thousands of angels in joyful assembly, 23 to the church of the firstborn, whose names are written in heaven. You have come to God, the judge of all men, to the spirits of righteous men made perfect, 24 to Jesus the mediator of a new covenant, and to the sprinkled blood that speaks a better word than the blood of Abel.

25 See to it that you do not refuse him who speaks. If they did not escape when they refused him who warned them on earth, how much less will we, if we turn away from him who warns us from heaven? 26 At that time his voice shook the earth, but now he has promised, "Once more I will shake not only the earth but also the heavens."c 27 The words "once more" indicate the removing of what can be shaken—that is, created things—so that what cannot be shaken may remain.

28 Therefore, since we are receiving a kingdom that cannot be shaken, let us be thankful, and so worship God acceptably with reverence and awe, 29 for our "God is a consuming fire."d

a 20 Exodus 19:12,13   b 21 Deut. 9:19   c 26 Haggai 2:6 d 29 Deut. 4:24

PSALMS 113:1–114:8

1 Praise the LORD.a

Praise, O servants of the LORD,
  praise the name of the LORD.
2 Let the name of the LORD be praised,
  both now and forevermore.
3 From the rising of the sun to the
  place where it sets,
  the name of the LORD is to be
  praised.

4 **The Lord is exalted over all the
nations,**
his glory above the heavens.

5 Who is like the Lord our God,
the One who sits enthroned on
high,
6 who stoops down to look
on the heavens and the earth?

7 He raises the poor from the dust
and lifts the needy from the ash
heap;
8 he seats them with princes,
with the princes of their people.
9 He settles the barren woman in her
home
as a happy mother of children.

Praise the Lord.

114:1 When Israel came out of Egypt,
the house of Jacob from a people
of foreign tongue,
2 Judah became God's sanctuary,
Israel his dominion.

3 The sea looked and fled,
the Jordan turned back;
4 the mountains skipped like rams,
the hills like lambs.

5 Why was it, O sea, that you fled,
O Jordan, that you turned back,
6 you mountains, that you skipped like
rams,
you hills, like lambs?

7 Tremble, O earth, at the presence of
the Lord,
at the presence of the God of
Jacob,
8 who turned the rock into a pool,
the hard rock into springs of
water.

a1 Hebrew Hallelu Yah; also in verse 9

PROVERBS 27:18-20

18 He who tends a fig tree will eat its
fruit,
and he who looks after his master
will be honored.

19 As water reflects a face,
so a man's heart reflects the man.

20 Death and Destruction*a* are never
satisfied,
and neither are the eyes of man.

a20 Hebrew Sheol and Abaddon

☐ D A Y 3 2 0

GOD SIGHTINGS

November 16

EZEKIEL 33:1–34:31

The word of the Lord came to me
[Ezekiel]: 2 "Son of man, speak to your
countrymen and say to them: 'When I
bring the sword against a land, and the
people of the land choose one of their
men and make him their watchman, 3 and
he sees the sword coming against the land
and blows the trumpet to warn the people, 4 then if anyone hears the trumpet but
does not take warning and the sword
comes and takes his life, his blood will be
on his own head. 5 Since he heard the
sound of the trumpet but did not take
warning, his blood will be on his own
head. If he had taken warning, he would
have saved himself. 6 But if the watchman
sees the sword coming and does not blow
the trumpet to warn the people and the
sword comes and takes the life of one of
them, that man will be taken away because of his sin, but I will hold the watchman accountable for his blood.'

7 "Son of man, I have made you a
watchman for the house of Israel; so
hear the word I speak and give them
warning from me. 8 When I say to the
wicked, 'O wicked man, you will surely
die,' and you do not speak out to dissuade him from his ways, that wicked
man will die for*a* his sin, and I will hold
you accountable for his blood. 9 But if
you do warn the wicked man to turn
from his ways and he does not do so, he
will die for his sin, but you will have
saved yourself.

10 "Son of man, say to the house of Israel, 'This is what you are saying: "Our

offenses and sins weigh us down, and we are wasting away because of[b] them. How then can we live?"' 11Say to them, 'As surely as I live, declares the Sovereign LORD, I take no pleasure in the death of the wicked, but rather that they turn from their ways and live. Turn! Turn from your evil ways! Why will you die, O house of Israel?'

12"Therefore, son of man, say to your countrymen, 'The righteousness of the righteous man will not save him when he disobeys, and the wickedness of the wicked man will not cause him to fall when he turns from it. The righteous man, if he sins, will not be allowed to live because of his former righteousness.' 13If I tell the righteous man that he will surely live, but then he trusts in his righteousness and does evil, none of the righteous things he has done will be remembered; he will die for the evil he has done. 14And if I say to the wicked man, 'You will surely die,' but he then turns away from his sin and does what is just and right— 15if he gives back what he took in pledge for a loan, returns what he has stolen, follows the decrees that give life, and does no evil, he will surely live; he will not die. 16None of the sins he has committed will be remembered against him. He has done what is just and right; he will surely live.

17"Yet your countrymen say, 'The way of the Lord is not just.' But it is their way that is not just. 18If a righteous man turns from his righteousness and does evil, he will die for it. 19And if a wicked man turns away from his wickedness and does what is just and right, he will live by doing so. 20Yet, O house of Israel, you say, 'The way of the Lord is not just.' But I will judge each of you according to his own ways."

21In the twelfth year of our exile, in the tenth month on the fifth day, a man who had escaped from Jerusalem came to me and said, "The city has fallen!" 22Now the evening before the man arrived, the hand of the LORD was upon me, and he opened my mouth before the man came to me in the morning. So my mouth was opened and I was no longer silent.

23Then the word of the LORD came to me: 24"Son of man, the people living in those ruins in the land of Israel are saying, 'Abraham was only one man, yet he possessed the land. But we are many; surely the land has been given to us as our possession.' 25Therefore say to them, 'This is what the Sovereign LORD says: Since you eat meat with the blood still in it and look to your idols and shed blood, should you then possess the land? 26You rely on your sword, you do detestable things, and each of you defiles his neighbor's wife. Should you then possess the land?'

27"Say this to them: 'This is what the Sovereign LORD says: As surely as I live, those who are left in the ruins will fall by the sword, those out in the country I will give to the wild animals to be devoured, and those in strongholds and caves will die of a plague. 28I will make the land a desolate waste, and her proud strength will come to an end, and the mountains of Israel will become desolate so that no one will cross them. 29Then they will know that I am the LORD, when I have made the land a desolate waste because of all the detestable things they have done.'

30"As for you, son of man, your countrymen are talking together about you by the walls and at the doors of the houses, saying to each other, 'Come and hear the message that has come from the LORD.' 31My people come to you, as they usually do, and sit before you to listen to your words, but they do not put them into practice. With their mouths they express devotion, but their hearts are greedy for unjust gain. 32Indeed, to them you are nothing more than one who sings love songs with a beautiful voice and plays an instrument well, for they hear your words but do not put them into practice.

33"When all this comes true—and it surely will—then they will know that a prophet has been among them."

34:1THE word of the LORD came to me:
2"Son of man, prophesy against the
shepherds of Israel; prophesy and say to
them: 'This is what the Sovereign LORD
says: Woe to the shepherds of Israel
who only take care of themselves!
Should not shepherds take care of the
flock? 3You eat the curds, clothe yourselves with the wool and slaughter the
choice animals, but you do not take care
of the flock. 4You have not strengthened
the weak or healed the sick or bound up
the injured. You have not brought back
the strays or searched for the lost. You
have ruled them harshly and brutally.
5So they were scattered because there
was no shepherd, and when they were
scattered they became food for all the
wild animals. 6My sheep wandered over
all the mountains and on every high hill.
They were scattered over the whole
earth, and no one searched or looked for
them.

7" 'Therefore, you shepherds, hear
the word of the LORD: 8As surely as I
live, declares the Sovereign LORD, because my flock lacks a shepherd and so
has been plundered and has become
food for all the wild animals, and because my shepherds did not search for
my flock but cared for themselves
rather than for my flock, 9therefore, O
shepherds, hear the word of the LORD:
10This is what the Sovereign LORD says:
I am against the shepherds and will
hold them accountable for my flock. I
will remove them from tending the
flock so that the shepherds can no longer feed themselves. I will rescue my
flock from their mouths, and it will no
longer be food for them.

11" 'For this is what the Sovereign
LORD says: I myself will search for my
sheep and look after them. 12As a shepherd looks after his scattered flock
when he is with them, so will I look after
my sheep. I will rescue them from all the
places where they were scattered on a
day of clouds and darkness. 13I will
bring them out from the nations and
gather them from the countries, and I
will bring them into their own land. I

will pasture them on the mountains of
Israel, in the ravines and in all the settlements in the land. 14I will tend them in a
good pasture, and the mountain heights
of Israel will be their grazing land.
There they will lie down in good grazing
land, and there they will feed in a rich
pasture on the mountains of Israel. 15I
myself will tend my sheep and have
them lie down, declares the Sovereign
LORD. 16I will search for the lost and
bring back the strays. I will bind up the
injured and strengthen the weak, but
the sleek and the strong I will destroy. I
will shepherd the flock with justice.

17" 'As for you, my flock, this is what
the Sovereign LORD says: I will judge between one sheep and another, and between rams and goats. 18Is it not enough
for you to feed on the good pasture?
Must you also trample the rest of your
pasture with your feet? Is it not enough
for you to drink clear water? Must you
also muddy the rest with your feet?
19Must my flock feed on what you have
trampled and drink what you have muddied with your feet?

20" 'Therefore this is what the Sovereign LORD says to them: See, I myself will
judge between the fat sheep and the
lean sheep. 21Because you shove with
flank and shoulder, butting all the weak
sheep with your horns until you have
driven them away, 22I will save my flock,
and they will no longer be plundered. I
will judge between one sheep and another. 23I will place over them one shepherd, my servant David, and he will tend
them; he will tend them and be their
shepherd. 24I the LORD will be their God,
and my servant David will be prince
among them. I the LORD have spoken.

25" 'I will make a covenant of peace
with them and rid the land of wild
beasts so that they may live in the desert
and sleep in the forests in safety. 26I will
bless them and the places surrounding
my hill.c I will send down showers in
season; there will be showers of blessing. 27The trees of the field will yield
their fruit and the ground will yield its
crops; the people will be secure in their

land. They will know that I am the LORD, when I break the bars of their yoke and rescue them from the hands of those who enslaved them. [28]They will no longer be plundered by the nations, nor will wild animals devour them. They will live in safety, and no one will make them afraid. [29]I will provide for them a land renowned for its crops, and they will no longer be victims of famine in the land or bear the scorn of the nations. [30]Then they will know that I, the LORD their God, am with them and that they, the house of Israel, are my people, declares the Sovereign LORD. [31]You my sheep, the sheep of my pasture, are people, and I am your God, declares the Sovereign LORD.'"

[a]8 Or in; also in verse 9   [b]10 Or away in   [c]26 Or I will make them and the places surrounding my hill a blessing

HEBREWS 13:1-25

Keep on loving each other as brothers. [2]Do not forget to entertain strangers, for by so doing some people have entertained angels without knowing it. [3]Remember those in prison as if you were their fellow prisoners, and those who are mistreated as if you yourselves were suffering.

[4]Marriage should be honored by all, and the marriage bed kept pure, for God will judge the adulterer and all the sexually immoral. [5]Keep your lives free from the love of money and be content with what you have, because God has said,

"Never will I leave you;
    never will I forsake you."[a]

[6]So we say with confidence,

"The Lord is my helper; I will not be afraid.
    What can man do to me?"[b]

[7]Remember your leaders, who spoke the word of God to you. Consider the outcome of their way of life and imitate their faith. [8]Jesus Christ is the same yesterday and today and forever.

[9]Do not be carried away by all kinds of strange teachings. It is good for our hearts to be strengthened by grace, not by ceremonial foods, which are of no value to those who eat them. [10]We have an altar from which those who minister at the tabernacle have no right to eat.

[11]The high priest carries the blood of animals into the Most Holy Place as a sin offering, but the bodies are burned outside the camp. [12]And so Jesus also suffered outside the city gate to make the people holy through his own blood. [13]Let us, then, go to him outside the camp, bearing the disgrace he bore. [14]For here we do not have an enduring city, but we are looking for the city that is to come.

[15]**Through Jesus, therefore, let us continually offer to God a sacrifice of praise—the fruit of lips that confess his name. [16]And do not forget to do good and to share with others, for with such sacrifices God is pleased.**

[17]Obey your leaders and submit to their authority. They keep watch over you as men who must give an account. Obey them so that their work will be a joy, not a burden, for that would be of no advantage to you.

[18]Pray for us. We are sure that we have a clear conscience and desire to live honorably in every way. [19]I particularly urge you to pray so that I may be restored to you soon.

[20]May the God of peace, who through the blood of the eternal covenant brought back from the dead our Lord Jesus, that great Shepherd of the sheep, [21]equip you with everything good for doing his will, and may he work in us what is pleasing to him, through Jesus Christ, to whom be glory for ever and ever. Amen.

[22]Brothers, I urge you to bear with my word of exhortation, for I have written you only a short letter.

[23]I want you to know that our brother Timothy has been released. If he arrives soon, I will come with him to see you.

[24]Greet all your leaders and all God's people. Those from Italy send you their greetings.

[25]Grace be with you all.

[a]5 Deut. 31:6   [b]6 Psalm 118:6,7

PSALM 115:1-18

[1] Not to us, O Lord, not to us
      but to your name be the glory,
      because of your love and
         faithfulness.

[2] Why do the nations say,
      "Where is their God?"
[3] Our God is in heaven;
      he does whatever pleases him.
[4] But their idols are silver and gold,
      made by the hands of men.
[5] They have mouths, but cannot speak,
      eyes, but they cannot see;
[6] they have ears, but cannot hear,
      noses, but they cannot smell;
[7] they have hands, but cannot feel,
      feet, but they cannot walk;
      nor can they utter a sound with
         their throats.
[8] Those who make them will be like
      them,
      and so will all who trust in them.

[9] O house of Israel, trust in the Lord—
      he is their help and shield.
[10] O house of Aaron, trust in the Lord—
      he is their help and shield.
[11] You who fear him, trust in the Lord—
      he is their help and shield.

[12] The Lord remembers us and will
         bless us:
      He will bless the house of Israel,
      he will bless the house of Aaron,
[13] he will bless those who fear the Lord—
      small and great alike.

[14] May the Lord make you increase,
      both you and your children.
[15] May you be blessed by the Lord,
      the Maker of heaven and earth.

[16] The highest heavens belong to the
         Lord,
      but the earth he has given to man.
[17] It is not the dead who praise the
         Lord,
      those who go down to silence;
[18] it is we who extol the Lord,
      both now and forevermore.

   Praise the Lord.[a]

[a] 18 Hebrew Hallelu Yah

PROVERBS 27:21-22

[21] The crucible for silver and the
         furnace for gold,
      but man is tested by the praise he
         receives.

[22] Though you grind a fool in a mortar,
      grinding him like grain with a
         pestle,
      you will not remove his folly from
         him.

☐ DAY 321

GOD SIGHTINGS

November 17

EZEKIEL 35:1–36:38

The word of the Lord came to me
[Ezekiel]: [2] "Son of man, set your face
against Mount Seir; prophesy against it
[3] and say: 'This is what the Sovereign
Lord says: I am against you, Mount Seir,
and I will stretch out my hand against
you and make you a desolate waste. [4] I
will turn your towns into ruins and you
will be desolate. Then you will know
that I am the Lord.

[5] "'Because you harbored an ancient
hostility and delivered the Israelites over
to the sword at the time of their calamity,
the time their punishment reached its
climax, [6] therefore as surely as I live, declares the Sovereign Lord, I will give you
over to bloodshed and it will pursue you.
Since you did not hate bloodshed, bloodshed will pursue you. [7] I will make Mount
Seir a desolate waste and cut off from it
all who come and go. [8] I will fill your
mountains with the slain; those killed by
the sword will fall on your hills and in
your valleys and in all your ravines. [9] I will
make you desolate forever; your towns
will not be inhabited. Then you will
know that I am the Lord.

[10] "'Because you have said, "These two
nations and countries will be ours and
we will take possession of them," even
though I the Lord was there, [11] therefore

as surely as I live, declares the Sovereign LORD, I will treat you in accordance with the anger and jealousy you showed in your hatred of them and I will make myself known among them when I judge you. 12Then you will know that I the LORD have heard all the contemptible things you have said against the mountains of Israel. You said, "They have been laid waste and have been given over to us to devour." 13You boasted against me and spoke against me without restraint, and I heard it. 14This is what the Sovereign LORD says: While the whole earth rejoices, I will make you desolate. 15Because you rejoiced when the inheritance of the house of Israel became desolate, that is how I will treat you. You will be desolate, O Mount Seir, you and all of Edom. Then they will know that I am the LORD.'"

36:1"SON of man, prophesy to the mountains of Israel and say, 'O mountains of Israel, hear the word of the LORD. 2This is what the Sovereign LORD says: The enemy said of you, "Aha! The ancient heights have become our possession."' 3Therefore prophesy and say, 'This is what the Sovereign LORD says: Because they ravaged and hounded you from every side so that you became the possession of the rest of the nations and the object of people's malicious talk and slander, 4therefore, O mountains of Israel, hear the word of the Sovereign LORD: This is what the Sovereign LORD says to the mountains and hills, to the ravines and valleys, to the desolate ruins and the deserted towns that have been plundered and ridiculed by the rest of the nations around you— 5this is what the Sovereign LORD says: In my burning zeal I have spoken against the rest of the nations, and against all Edom, for with glee and with malice in their hearts they made my land their own possession so that they might plunder its pastureland.' 6Therefore prophesy concerning the land of Israel and say to the mountains and hills, to the ravines and valleys: 'This is what the Sovereign LORD says: I speak

in my jealous wrath because you have suffered the scorn of the nations. 7Therefore this is what the Sovereign LORD says: I swear with uplifted hand that the nations around you will also suffer scorn.

8"'But you, O mountains of Israel, will produce branches and fruit for my people Israel, for they will soon come home. 9I am concerned for you and will look on you with favor; you will be plowed and sown, 10and I will multiply the number of people upon you, even the whole house of Israel. The towns will be inhabited and the ruins rebuilt. 11I will increase the number of men and animals upon you, and they will be fruitful and become numerous. I will settle people on you as in the past and will make you prosper more than before. Then you will know that I am the LORD. 12I will cause people, my people Israel, to walk upon you. They will possess you, and you will be their inheritance; you will never again deprive them of their children.

13"'This is what the Sovereign LORD says: Because people say to you, "You devour men and deprive your nation of its children," 14therefore you will no longer devour men or make your nation childless, declares the Sovereign LORD. 15No longer will I make you hear the taunts of the nations, and no longer will you suffer the scorn of the peoples or cause your nation to fall, declares the Sovereign LORD.'"

16Again the word of the LORD came to me: 17"Son of man, when the people of Israel were living in their own land, they defiled it by their conduct and their actions. Their conduct was like a woman's monthly uncleanness in my sight. 18So I poured out my wrath on them because they had shed blood in the land and because they had defiled it with their idols. 19I dispersed them among the nations, and they were scattered through the countries; I judged them according to their conduct and their actions. 20And wherever they went among the nations they profaned my holy name, for it was said of them, 'These are the

Lord's people, and yet they had to leave his land.' 21I had concern for my holy name, which the house of Israel profaned among the nations where they had gone.

22"Therefore say to the house of Israel, 'This is what the Sovereign Lord says: It is not for your sake, O house of Israel, that I am going to do these things, but for the sake of my holy name, which you have profaned among the nations where you have gone. 23I will show the holiness of my great name, which has been profaned among the nations, the name you have profaned among them. Then the nations will know that I am the Lord, declares the Sovereign Lord, when I show myself holy through you before their eyes.

24" 'For I will take you out of the nations; I will gather you from all the countries and bring you back into your own land. 25I will sprinkle clean water on you, and you will be clean; I will cleanse you from all your impurities and from all your idols. 26I will give you a new heart and put a new spirit in you; I will remove from you your heart of stone and give you a heart of flesh. 27And I will put my Spirit in you and move you to follow my decrees and be careful to keep my laws. 28You will live in the land I gave your forefathers; you will be my people, and I will be your God. 29I will save you from all your uncleanness. I will call for the grain and make it plentiful and will not bring famine upon you. 30I will increase the fruit of the trees and the crops of the field, so that you will no longer suffer disgrace among the nations because of famine. 31Then you will remember your evil ways and wicked deeds, and you will loathe yourselves for your sins and detestable practices. 32I want you to know that I am not doing this for your sake, declares the Sovereign Lord. Be ashamed and disgraced for your conduct, O house of Israel!

33" 'This is what the Sovereign Lord says: On the day I cleanse you from all your sins, I will resettle your towns, and the ruins will be rebuilt. 34The desolate land will be cultivated instead of lying desolate in the sight of all who pass through it. 35They will say, "This land that was laid waste has become like the garden of Eden; the cities that were lying in ruins, desolate and destroyed, are now fortified and inhabited." 36Then the nations around you that remain will know that I the Lord have rebuilt what was destroyed and have replanted what was desolate. I the Lord have spoken, and I will do it.'

37"This is what the Sovereign Lord says: Once again I will yield to the plea of the house of Israel and do this for them: I will make their people as numerous as sheep, 38as numerous as the flocks for offerings at Jerusalem during her appointed feasts. So will the ruined cities be filled with flocks of people. Then they will know that I am the Lord."

JAMES 1:1-18

James, a servant of God and of the Lord Jesus Christ,

To the twelve tribes scattered among the nations:

Greetings.

2Consider it pure joy, my brothers, whenever you face trials of many kinds, 3because you know that the testing of your faith develops perseverance. 4Perseverance must finish its work so that you may be mature and complete, not lacking anything. 5If any of you lacks wisdom, he should ask God, who gives generously to all without finding fault, and it will be given to him. 6But when he asks, he must believe and not doubt, because he who doubts is like a wave of the sea, blown and tossed by the wind. 7That man should not think he will receive anything from the Lord; 8he is a double-minded man, unstable in all he does.

9The brother in humble circumstances ought to take pride in his high position. 10But the one who is rich should take pride in his low position, because he will pass away like a wild flower. 11For the sun rises with scorching heat and withers the plant; its blossom falls and its beauty is destroyed. In the same way, the rich man will fade away even while he goes about his business.

12**Blessed is the man who perseveres under trial, because when he has stood the test, he will receive the crown of life that God has promised to those who love him.**

13When tempted, no one should say, "God is tempting me." For God cannot be tempted by evil, nor does he tempt anyone; 14but each one is tempted when, by his own evil desire, he is dragged away and enticed. 15Then, after desire has conceived, it gives birth to sin; and sin, when it is full-grown, gives birth to death.

16Don't be deceived, my dear brothers. 17Every good and perfect gift is from above, coming down from the Father of the heavenly lights, who does not change like shifting shadows. 18He chose to give us birth through the word of truth, that we might be a kind of firstfruits of all he created.

PSALM 116:1-19

1 I love the LORD, for he heard my
     voice;
  he heard my cry for mercy.
2 Because he turned his ear to me,
  I will call on him as long as I live.

3 The cords of death entangled me,
    the anguish of the grave*a* came
        upon me;
  I was overcome by trouble and
        sorrow.
4 Then I called on the name of the
    LORD:
  "O LORD, save me!"

5 The LORD is gracious and righteous;
  our God is full of compassion.
6 The LORD protects the
        simplehearted;
  when I was in great need, he saved
        me.

7 Be at rest once more, O my soul,
  for the LORD has been good to you.

8 For you, O LORD, have delivered my
        soul from death,
  my eyes from tears,
  my feet from stumbling,
9 that I may walk before the LORD
  in the land of the living.
10 I believed; therefore*b* I said,
  "I am greatly afflicted."
11 And in my dismay I said,
  "All men are liars."

12 How can I repay the LORD
  for all his goodness to me?
13 I will lift up the cup of salvation
  and call on the name of the LORD.
14 I will fulfill my vows to the LORD
  in the presence of all his people.

15 Precious in the sight of the LORD
  is the death of his saints.

16 O LORD, truly I am your servant;
    I am your servant, the son of your
        maidservant*c*;
  you have freed me from my chains.

17 I will sacrifice a thank offering to
        you
  and call on the name of the LORD.
18 I will fulfill my vows to the LORD
  in the presence of all his people,
19 in the courts of the house of the
        LORD—
  in your midst, O Jerusalem.

  Praise the LORD.*d*

a3 Hebrew *Sheol*   *b10* Or *believed even when*
c16 Or *servant, your faithful son*   *d19* Hebrew *Hallelu Yah*

PROVERBS 27:23-27

23 Be sure you know the condition of
        your flocks,
  give careful attention to your
        herds;
24 for riches do not endure forever,
  and a crown is not secure for all
        generations.
25 When the hay is removed and new
        growth appears
  and the grass from the hills is
        gathered in,
26 the lambs will provide you with
        clothing,
  and the goats with the price of a
        field.

²⁷ You will have plenty of goats' milk
     to feed you and your family
     and to nourish your servant girls.

☐ DAY 322

GOD SIGHTINGS

November 18

EZEKIEL 37:1–38:23

The hand of the LORD was upon me [Ezekiel], and he brought me out by the Spirit of the LORD and set me in the middle of a valley; it was full of bones. ²He led me back and forth among them, and I saw a great many bones on the floor of the valley, bones that were very dry. ³He asked me, "Son of man, can these bones live?"

I said, "O Sovereign LORD, you alone know."

⁴Then he said to me, "Prophesy to these bones and say to them, 'Dry bones, hear the word of the LORD! ⁵This is what the Sovereign LORDᵃ says to these bones: I will make breathᵃ enter you, and you will come to life. ⁶I will attach tendons to you and make flesh come upon you and cover you with skin; I will put breath in you, and you will come to life. Then you will know that I am the LORD.'"

⁷So I prophesied as I was commanded. And as I was prophesying, there was a noise, a rattling sound, and the bones came together, bone to bone. ⁸I looked, and tendons and flesh appeared on them and skin covered them, but there was no breath in them.

⁹Then he said to me, "Prophesy to the breath; prophesy, son of man, and say to it, 'This is what the Sovereign LORD says: Come from the four winds, O breath, and breathe into these slain, that they may live.'" ¹⁰So I prophesied as he commanded me, and breath entered them; they came to life and stood up on their feet—a vast army.

¹¹Then he said to me: "Son of man,

these bones are the whole house of Israel. They say, 'Our bones are dried up and our hope is gone; we are cut off.' ¹²Therefore prophesy and say to them: 'This is what the Sovereign LORD says: O my people, I am going to open your graves and bring you up from them; I will bring you back to the land of Israel. ¹³Then you, my people, will know that I am the LORD, when I open your graves and bring you up from them. ¹⁴I will put my Spirit in you and you will live, and I will settle you in your own land. Then you will know that I the LORD have spoken, and I have done it, declares the LORD.'"

¹⁵The word of the LORD came to me: ¹⁶"Son of man, take a stick of wood and write on it, 'Belonging to Judah and the Israelites associated with him.' Then take another stick of wood, and write on it, 'Ephraim's stick, belonging to Joseph and all the house of Israel associated with him.' ¹⁷Join them together into one stick so that they will become one in your hand.

¹⁸"When your countrymen ask you, 'Won't you tell us what you mean by this?' ¹⁹say to them, 'This is what the Sovereign LORD says: I am going to take the stick of Joseph—which is in Ephraim's hand—and of the Israelite tribes associated with him, and join it to Judah's stick, making them a single stick of wood, and they will become one in my hand.' ²⁰Hold before their eyes the sticks you have written on ²¹and say to them, 'This is what the Sovereign LORD says: I will take the Israelites out of the nations where they have gone. I will gather them from all around and bring them back into their own land. ²²I will make them one nation in the land, on the mountains of Israel. There will be one king over all of them and they will never again be two nations or be divided into two kingdoms. ²³They will no longer defile themselves with their idols and vile images or with any of their offenses, for I will save them from all their sinful backsliding,ᵇ and I will

cleanse them. They will be my people, and I will be their God.

24 "'My servant David will be king over them, and they will all have one shepherd. They will follow my laws and be careful to keep my decrees. 25 They will live in the land I gave to my servant Jacob, the land where your fathers lived. They and their children and their children's children will live there forever, and David my servant will be their prince forever. 26 I will make a covenant of peace with them; it will be an everlasting covenant. I will establish them and increase their numbers, and I will put my sanctuary among them forever. 27 My dwelling place will be with them; I will be their God, and they will be my people. 28 Then the nations will know that I the LORD make Israel holy, when my sanctuary is among them forever.'"

38:1 THE word of the LORD came to me: 2 "Son of man, set your face against Gog, of the land of Magog, the chief prince of c Meshech and Tubal; prophesy against him 3 and say: 'This is what the Sovereign LORD says: I am against you, O Gog, chief prince of d Meshech and Tubal. 4 I will turn you around, put hooks in your jaws and bring you out with your whole army—your horses, your horsemen fully armed, and a great horde with large and small shields, all of them brandishing their swords. 5 Persia, Cush e and Put will be with them, all with shields and helmets, 6 also Gomer with all its troops, and Beth Togarmah from the far north with all its troops—the many nations with you.

7 "'Get ready; be prepared, you and all the hordes gathered about you, and take command of them. 8 After many days you will be called to arms. In future years you will invade a land that has recovered from war, whose people were gathered from many nations to the mountains of Israel, which had long been desolate. They had been brought out from the nations, and now all of them live in safety. 9 You and all your troops and the many nations with you

will go up, advancing like a storm; you will be like a cloud covering the land.

10 "'This is what the Sovereign LORD says: On that day thoughts will come into your mind and you will devise an evil scheme. 11 You will say, "I will invade a land of unwalled villages; I will attack a peaceful and unsuspecting people—all of them living without walls and without gates and bars. 12 I will plunder and loot and turn my hand against the resettled ruins and the people gathered from the nations, rich in livestock and goods, living at the center of the land." 13 Sheba and Dedan and the merchants of Tarshish and all her villages f will say to you, "Have you come to plunder? Have you gathered your hordes to loot, to carry off silver and gold, to take away livestock and goods and to seize much plunder?"'

14 "Therefore, son of man, prophesy and say to Gog: 'This is what the Sovereign LORD says: In that day, when my people Israel are living in safety, will you not take notice of it? 15 You will come from your place in the far north, you and many nations with you, all of them riding on horses, a great horde, a mighty army. 16 You will advance against my people Israel like a cloud that covers the land. In days to come, O Gog, I will bring you against my land, so that the nations may know me when I show myself holy through you before their eyes.

17 "'This is what the Sovereign LORD says: Are you not the one I spoke of in former days by my servants the prophets of Israel? At that time they prophesied for years that I would bring you against them. 18 This is what will happen in that day: When Gog attacks the land of Israel, my hot anger will be aroused, declares the Sovereign LORD. 19 In my zeal and fiery wrath I declare that at that time there shall be a great earthquake in the land of Israel. 20 The fish of the sea, the birds of the air, the beasts of the field, every creature that moves along the ground, and all the people on the face of the earth will tremble at my presence. The mountains will be overturned, the cliffs will crum-

ble and every wall will fall to the ground. [21]I will summon a sword against Gog on all my mountains, declares the Sovereign Lord. Every man's sword will be against his brother. [22]I will execute judgment upon him with plague and bloodshed; I will pour down torrents of rain, hailstones and burning sulfur on him and on his troops and on the many nations with him. [23]And so I will show my greatness and my holiness, and I will make myself known in the sight of many nations. Then they will know that I am the Lord.'"

[a]5 The Hebrew for this word can also mean *wind* or *spirit* (see verses 6-14). [b]23 Many Hebrew manuscripts (see also Septuagint); most Hebrew manuscripts *all their dwelling places where they sinned* [c]2 Or *the prince of Rosh,* [d]3 Or *Gog, prince of Rosh,* [e]5 That is, the upper Nile region [f]13 Or *her strong lions*

JAMES 1:19–2:17

My dear brothers, take note of this: Everyone should be quick to listen, slow to speak and slow to become angry, [20]for man's anger does not bring about the righteous life that God desires. [21]Therefore, get rid of all moral filth and the evil that is so prevalent and humbly accept the word planted in you, which can save you.

[22]Do not merely listen to the word, and so deceive yourselves. Do what it says. [23]Anyone who listens to the word but does not do what it says is like a man who looks at his face in a mirror [24]and, after looking at himself, goes away and immediately forgets what he looks like. [25]But the man who looks intently into the perfect law that gives freedom, and continues to do this, not forgetting what he has heard, but doing it—he will be blessed in what he does.

[26]If anyone considers himself religious and yet does not keep a tight rein on his tongue, he deceives himself and his religion is worthless. [27]**Religion that God our Father accepts as pure and faultless is this: to look after orphans and widows in their distress and to keep oneself from being polluted by the world.**

[2:1]My brothers, as believers in our glorious Lord Jesus Christ, don't show favor-

itism. [2]Suppose a man comes into your meeting wearing a gold ring and fine clothes, and a poor man in shabby clothes also comes in. [3]If you show special attention to the man wearing fine clothes and say, "Here's a good seat for you," but say to the poor man, "You stand there" or "Sit on the floor by my feet," [4]have you not discriminated among yourselves and become judges with evil thoughts?

[5]Listen, my dear brothers: Has not God chosen those who are poor in the eyes of the world to be rich in faith and to inherit the kingdom he promised those who love him? [6]But you have insulted the poor. Is it not the rich who are exploiting you? Are they not the ones who are dragging you into court? [7]Are they not the ones who are slandering the noble name of him to whom you belong?

[8]If you really keep the royal law found in Scripture, "Love your neighbor as yourself,"[a] you are doing right. [9]But if you show favoritism, you sin and are convicted by the law as lawbreakers. [10]For whoever keeps the whole law and yet stumbles at just one point is guilty of breaking all of it. [11]For he who said, "Do not commit adultery,"[b] also said, "Do not murder."[c] If you do not commit adultery but do commit murder, you have become a lawbreaker.

[12]Speak and act as those who are going to be judged by the law that gives freedom, [13]because judgment without mercy will be shown to anyone who has not been merciful. Mercy triumphs over judgment!

[14]What good is it, my brothers, if a man claims to have faith but has no deeds? Can such faith save him? [15]Suppose a brother or sister is without clothes and daily food. [16]If one of you says to him, "Go, I wish you well; keep warm and well fed," but does nothing about his physical needs, what good is it? [17]In the same way, faith by itself, if it is not accompanied by action, is dead.

[a]8 Lev. 19:18 [b]11 Exodus 20:14; Deut. 5:18 [c]11 Exodus 20:13; Deut. 5:17

PSALM 117:1-2

¹ Praise the LORD, all you nations;
   extol him, all you peoples.
² For great is his love toward us,
   and the faithfulness of the LORD
   endures forever.

Praise the LORD.ᵃ

ᵃ 2 Hebrew Hallelu Yah

PROVERBS 28:1

The wicked man flees though no one
   pursues,
   but the righteous are as bold as a
   lion.

☐ D A Y   3 2 3

GOD SIGHTINGS

November 19

EZEKIEL 39:1–40:27

"Son of man, prophesy against Gog and
say: 'This is what the Sovereign LORD
says: I am against you, O Gog, chief
prince ofᵃ Meshech and Tubal. ²I will
turn you around and drag you along. I
will bring you from the far north and
send you against the mountains of Israel. ³Then I will strike your bow from
your left hand and make your arrows
drop from your right hand. ⁴On the
mountains of Israel you will fall, you and
all your troops and the nations with you.
I will give you as food to all kinds of car-
rion birds and to the wild animals. ⁵You
will fall in the open field, for I have spoken, declares the Sovereign LORD. ⁶I will
send fire on Magog and on those who
live in safety in the coastlands, and they
will know that I am the LORD.

⁷" 'I will make known my holy name
among my people Israel. I will no longer
let my holy name be profaned, and the
nations will know that I the LORD am the
Holy One in Israel. ⁸It is coming! It will
surely take place, declares the Sovereign
LORD. This is the day I have spoken of.

⁹" 'Then those who live in the towns
of Israel will go out and use the weapons
for fuel and burn them up—the small
and large shields, the bows and arrows,
the war clubs and spears. For seven
years they will use them for fuel. ¹⁰They
will not need to gather wood from the
fields or cut it from the forests, because
they will use the weapons for fuel. And
they will plunder those who plundered
them and loot those who looted them,
declares the Sovereign LORD.

¹¹" 'On that day I will give Gog a burial
place in Israel, in the valley of those who
travel east towardᵇ the Sea.ᶜ It will block
the way of travelers, because Gog and all
his hordes will be buried there. So it will
be called the Valley of Hamon Gog.ᵈ

¹²" 'For seven months the house of Israel will be burying them in order to
cleanse the land. ¹³All the people of the
land will bury them, and the day I am
glorified will be a memorable day for
them, declares the Sovereign LORD.

¹⁴" 'Men will be regularly employed to
cleanse the land. Some will go throughout the land and, in addition to them,
others will bury those that remain on the
ground. At the end of the seven months
they will begin their search. ¹⁵As they go
through the land and one of them sees a
human bone, he will set up a marker beside it until the gravediggers have buried
it in the Valley of Hamon Gog. ¹⁶(Also a
town called Hamonahᵉ will be there.)
And so they will cleanse the land.'

¹⁷"Son of man, this is what the Sovereign LORD says: Call out to every kind of
bird and all the wild animals: 'Assemble
and come together from all around to
the sacrifice I am preparing for you, the
great sacrifice on the mountains of Israel. There you will eat flesh and drink
blood. ¹⁸You will eat the flesh of mighty
men and drink the blood of the princes
of the earth as if they were rams and
lambs, goats and bulls—all of them fattened animals from Bashan. ¹⁹At the
sacrifice I am preparing for you, you will
eat fat till you are glutted and drink
blood till you are drunk. ²⁰At my table
you will eat your fill of horses and riders,

mighty men and soldiers of every kind,' declares the Sovereign LORD.

21"I will display my glory among the nations, and all the nations will see the punishment I inflict and the hand I lay upon them. 22From that day forward the house of Israel will know that I am the LORD their God. 23And the nations will know that the people of Israel went into exile for their sin, because they were unfaithful to me. So I hid my face from them and handed them over to their enemies, and they all fell by the sword. 24I dealt with them according to their uncleanness and their offenses, and I hid my face from them.

25"Therefore this is what the Sovereign LORD says: I will now bring Jacob back from captivity*f* and will have compassion on all the people of Israel, and I will be zealous for my holy name. 26They will forget their shame and all the unfaithfulness they showed toward me when they lived in safety in their land with no one to make them afraid. 27When I have brought them back from the nations and have gathered them from the countries of their enemies, I will show myself holy through them in the sight of many nations. 28Then they will know that I am the LORD their God, for though I sent them into exile among the nations, I will gather them to their own land, not leaving any behind. 29I will no longer hide my face from them, for I will pour out my Spirit on the house of Israel, declares the Sovereign LORD."

40:1IN the twenty-fifth year of our exile, at the beginning of the year, on the tenth of the month, in the fourteenth year after the fall of the city—on that very day the hand of the LORD was upon me and he took me there. 2In visions of God he took me to the land of Israel and set me on a very high mountain, on whose south side were some buildings that looked like a city. 3He took me there, and I saw a man whose appearance was like bronze; he was standing in the gateway with a linen cord and a measuring rod in his hand. 4The man said to me, "Son of man, look with your eyes and hear with your ears

and pay attention to everything I am going to show you, for that is why you have been brought here. Tell the house of Israel everything you see."

5I saw a wall completely surrounding the temple area. The length of the measuring rod in the man's hand was six long cubits, each of which was a cubit*g* and a handbreadth.*h* He measured the wall; it was one measuring rod thick and one rod high.

6Then he went to the gate facing east. He climbed its steps and measured the threshold of the gate; it was one rod deep.*i* 7The alcoves for the guards were one rod long and one rod wide, and the projecting walls between the alcoves were five cubits thick. And the threshold of the gate next to the portico facing the temple was one rod deep.

8Then he measured the portico of the gateway; 9it*j* was eight cubits deep and its jambs were two cubits thick. The portico of the gateway faced the temple.

10Inside the east gate were three alcoves on each side; the three had the same measurements; and the faces of the projecting walls on each side had the same measurements. 11Then he measured the width of the entrance to the gateway; it was ten cubits and its length was thirteen cubits. 12In front of each alcove was a wall one cubit high, and the alcoves were six cubits square. 13Then he measured the gateway from the top of the rear wall of one alcove to the top of the opposite one; the distance was twenty-five cubits from one parapet opening to the opposite one. 14He measured along the faces of the projecting walls all around the inside of the gateway—sixty cubits. The measurement was up to the portico*k* facing the courtyard.*l* 15The distance from the entrance of the gateway to the far end of its portico was fifty cubits. 16The alcoves and the projecting walls inside the gateway were surmounted by narrow parapet openings all around, as was the portico; the openings all around faced inward. The faces of the projecting walls were decorated with palm trees.

17 Then he brought me into the outer court. There I saw some rooms and a pavement that had been constructed all around the court; there were thirty rooms along the pavement. 18 It abutted the sides of the gateways and was as wide as they were long; this was the lower pavement. 19 Then he measured the distance from the inside of the lower gateway to the outside of the inner court; it was a hundred cubits on the east side as well as on the north.

20 Then he measured the length and width of the gate facing north, leading into the outer court. 21 Its alcoves—three on each side—its projecting walls and its portico had the same measurements as those of the first gateway. It was fifty cubits long and twenty-five cubits wide. 22 Its openings, its portico and its palm tree decorations had the same measurements as those of the gate facing east. Seven steps led up to it, with its portico opposite them. 23 There was a gate to the inner court facing the north gate, just as there was on the east. He measured from one gate to the opposite one; it was a hundred cubits.

24 Then he led me to the south side and I saw a gate facing south. He measured its jambs and its portico, and they had the same measurements as the others. 25 The gateway and its portico had narrow openings all around, like the openings of the others. It was fifty cubits long and twenty-five cubits wide. 26 Seven steps led up to it, with its portico opposite them; it had palm tree decorations on the faces of the projecting walls on each side. 27 The inner court also had a gate facing south, and he measured from this gate to the outer gate on the south side; it was a hundred cubits.

a 1 Or Gog, prince of Rosh, b 11 Or of c 11 That is, the Dead Sea d 11 Hamon Gog means hordes of Gog. e 16 Hamonah means horde. f 25 Or now restore the fortunes of Jacob g 5 The common cubit was about 1 1/2 feet (about 0.5 meter). h 5 That is, about 3 inches (about 8 centimeters) i 6 Septuagint; Hebrew deep, the first threshold, one rod deep j 8,9 Many Hebrew manuscripts, Septuagint, Vulgate and Syriac; most Hebrew manuscripts gateway facing the temple; it was one rod deep. g Then he measured the portico of the gateway; it k 14 Septuagint; Hebrew projecting wall l 14 The meaning of the Hebrew for this verse is uncertain.

JAMES 2:18–3:18

But someone will say, "You have faith; I have deeds."

Show me your faith without deeds, and I will show you my faith by what I do. 19 You believe that there is one God. Good! Even the demons believe that— and shudder.

20 You foolish man, do you want evidence that faith without deeds is useless*a* ? 21 Was not our ancestor Abraham considered righteous for what he did when he offered his son Isaac on the altar? 22 You see that his faith and his actions were working together, and his faith was made complete by what he did. 23 And the scripture was fulfilled that says, "Abraham believed God, and it was credited to him as righteousness,"*b* and he was called God's friend. 24 You see that a person is justified by what he does and not by faith alone.

25 In the same way, was not even Rahab the prostitute considered righteous for what she did when she gave lodging to the spies and sent them off in a different direction? 26 As the body without the spirit is dead, so faith without deeds is dead.

3:1 Not many of you should presume to be teachers, my brothers, because you know that we who teach will be judged more strictly. 2 We all stumble in many ways. If anyone is never at fault in what he says, he is a perfect man, able to keep his whole body in check.

3 When we put bits into the mouths of horses to make them obey us, we can turn the whole animal. 4 Or take ships as an example. Although they are so large and are driven by strong winds, they are steered by a very small rudder wherever the pilot wants to go. 5 Likewise the tongue is a small part of the body, but it makes great boasts. Consider what a great forest is set on fire by a small spark. 6 The tongue also is a fire, a world of evil among the parts of the body. It corrupts the whole person, sets the whole course of his life on fire, and is itself set on fire by hell.

7All kinds of animals, birds, reptiles and creatures of the sea are being tamed and have been tamed by man, 8but no man can tame the tongue. It is a restless evil, full of deadly poison.

9With the tongue we praise our Lord and Father, and with it we curse men, who have been made in God's likeness. 10Out of the same mouth come praise and cursing. My brothers, this should not be. 11Can both fresh water and salt*c* water flow from the same spring? 12My brothers, can a fig tree bear olives, or a grapevine bear figs? Neither can a salt spring produce fresh water.

13Who is wise and understanding among you? Let him show it by his good life, by deeds done in the humility that comes from wisdom. 14But if you harbor bitter envy and selfish ambition in your hearts, do not boast about it or deny the truth. 15Such "wisdom" does not come down from heaven but is earthly, unspiritual, of the devil. 16For where you have envy and selfish ambition, there you find disorder and every evil practice.

17But the wisdom that comes from heaven is first of all pure; then peace-loving, considerate, submissive, full of mercy and good fruit, impartial and sincere. 18Peacemakers who sow in peace raise a harvest of righteousness.

a20 Some early manuscripts *dead*   *b23* Gen. 15:6
c11 Greek *bitter* (see also verse 14)

PSALM 118:1-18
1Give thanks to the Lord, for he is good;
his love endures forever.

2Let Israel say:
"His love endures forever."
3Let the house of Aaron say:
"His love endures forever."
4Let those who fear the Lord say:
"His love endures forever."

5In my anguish I cried to the Lord,
and he answered by setting me free.

6The Lord is with me; I will not be afraid.
What can man do to me?
7The Lord is with me; he is my helper.
I will look in triumph on my enemies.

8It is better to take refuge in the Lord
than to trust in man.
9It is better to take refuge in the Lord
than to trust in princes.

10All the nations surrounded me,
but in the name of the Lord I cut them off.
11They surrounded me on every side,
but in the name of the Lord I cut them off.
12They swarmed around me like bees,
but they died out as quickly as burning thorns;
in the name of the Lord I cut them off.

13I was pushed back and about to fall,
but the Lord helped me.
14The Lord is my strength and my song;
he has become my salvation.

15Shouts of joy and victory
resound in the tents of the righteous:
"The Lord's right hand has done mighty things!
16The Lord's right hand is lifted high;
the Lord's right hand has done mighty things!"

17I will not die but live,
and will proclaim what the Lord has done.
18The Lord has chastened me severely,
but he has not given me over to death.

PROVERBS 28:2
2When a country is rebellious, it has many rulers,
but a man of understanding and knowledge maintains order.

☐ DAY 324

GOD SIGHTINGS

November 20

EZEKIEL 40:28–41:26

Then he [the LORD] brought me [Ezekiel] into the inner court through the south gate, and he measured the south gate; it had the same measurements as the others. 29 Its alcoves, its projecting walls and its portico had the same measurements as the others. The gateway and its portico had openings all around. It was fifty cubits long and twenty-five cubits wide. 30 (The porticoes of the gateways around the inner court were twenty-five cubits wide and five cubits deep.) 31 Its portico faced the outer court; palm trees decorated its jambs, and eight steps led up to it.

32 Then he brought me to the inner court on the east side, and he measured the gateway; it had the same measurements as the others. 33 Its alcoves, its projecting walls and its portico had the same measurements as the others. The gateway and its portico had openings all around. It was fifty cubits long and twenty-five cubits wide. 34 Its portico faced the outer court; palm trees decorated the jambs on either side, and eight steps led up to it.

35 Then he brought me to the north gate and measured it. It had the same measurements as the others, 36 as did its alcoves, its projecting walls and its portico, and it had openings all around. It was fifty cubits long and twenty-five cubits wide. 37 Its portico a faced the outer court; palm trees decorated the jambs on either side, and eight steps led up to it.

38 A room with a doorway was by the portico in each of the inner gateways, where the burnt offerings were washed. 39 In the portico of the gateway were two tables on each side, on which the burnt offerings, sin offerings and guilt offerings were slaughtered. 40 By the outside wall of the portico of the gateway, near the steps at the entrance to the north gateway were two tables, and on the other side of the steps were two tables. 41 So there were four tables on one side of the gateway and four on the other—eight tables in all—on which the sacrifices were slaughtered. 42 There were also four tables of dressed stone for the burnt offerings, each a cubit and a half long, a cubit and a half wide and a cubit high. On them were placed the utensils for slaughtering the burnt offerings and the other sacrifices. 43 And double-pronged hooks, each a handbreadth long, were attached to the wall all around. The tables were for the flesh of the offerings.

44 Outside the inner gate, within the inner court, were two rooms, one b at the side of the north gate and facing south, and another at the side of the south c gate and facing north. 45 He said to me, "The room facing south is for the priests who have charge of the temple, 46 and the room facing north is for the priests who have charge of the altar. These are the sons of Zadok, who are the only Levites who may draw near to the LORD to minister before him."

47 Then he measured the court: It was square—a hundred cubits long and a hundred cubits wide. And the altar was in front of the temple.

48 He brought me to the portico of the temple and measured the jambs of the portico; they were five cubits wide on either side. The width of the entrance was fourteen cubits and its projecting walls were d three cubits wide on either side. 49 The portico was twenty cubits wide, and twelve e cubits from front to back. It was reached by a flight of stairs, f and there were pillars on each side of the jambs.

41:1 THEN the man brought me to the outer sanctuary and measured the jambs; the width of the jambs was six cubits g on each side. h 2 The entrance was ten cubits wide, and the projecting walls on each side of it were five cubits wide. He also measured the outer sanctuary; it was forty cubits long and twenty cubits wide.

³Then he went into the inner sanctuary and measured the jambs of the entrance; each was two cubits wide. The entrance was six cubits wide, and the projecting walls on each side of it were seven cubits wide. ⁴And he measured the length of the inner sanctuary; it was twenty cubits, and its width was twenty cubits across the end of the outer sanctuary. He said to me, "This is the Most Holy Place."

⁵Then he measured the wall of the temple; it was six cubits thick, and each side room around the temple was four cubits wide. ⁶The side rooms were on three levels, one above another, thirty on each level. There were ledges all around the wall of the temple to serve as supports for the side rooms, so that the supports were not inserted into the wall of the temple. ⁷The side rooms all around the temple were wider at each successive level. The structure surrounding the temple was built in ascending stages, so that the rooms widened as one went upward. A stairway went up from the lowest floor to the top floor through the middle floor.

⁸I saw that the temple had a raised base all around it, forming the foundation of the side rooms. It was the length of the rod, six long cubits. ⁹The outer wall of the side rooms was five cubits thick. The open area between the side rooms of the temple ¹⁰and the ⌐priests'⌐ rooms was twenty cubits wide all around the temple. ¹¹There were entrances to the side rooms from the open area, one on the north and another on the south; and the base adjoining the open area was five cubits wide all around.

¹²The building facing the temple courtyard on the west side was seventy cubits wide. The wall of the building was five cubits thick all around, and its length was ninety cubits.

¹³Then he measured the temple; it was a hundred cubits long, and the temple courtyard and the building with its walls were also a hundred cubits long. ¹⁴The width of the temple courtyard on the east, including the front of the temple, was a hundred cubits.

¹⁵Then he measured the length of the building facing the courtyard at the rear of the temple, including its galleries on each side; it was a hundred cubits.

The outer sanctuary, the inner sanctuary and the portico facing the court, ¹⁶as well as the thresholds and the narrow windows and galleries around the three of them—everything beyond and including the threshold was covered with wood. The floor, the wall up to the windows, and the windows were covered. ¹⁷In the space above the outside of the entrance to the inner sanctuary and on the walls at regular intervals all around the inner and outer sanctuary ¹⁸were carved cherubim and palm trees. Palm trees alternated with cherubim. Each cherub had two faces: ¹⁹the face of a man toward the palm tree on one side and the face of a lion toward the palm tree on the other. They were carved all around the whole temple. ²⁰From the floor to the area above the entrance, cherubim and palm trees were carved on the wall of the outer sanctuary.

²¹The outer sanctuary had a rectangular doorframe, and the one at the front of the Most Holy Place was similar. ²²There was a wooden altar three cubits high and two cubits square*ⁱ*; its corners, its base*ʲ* and its sides were of wood. The man said to me, "This is the table that is before the LORD." ²³Both the outer sanctuary and the Most Holy Place had double doors. ²⁴Each door had two leaves—two hinged leaves for each door. ²⁵And on the doors of the outer sanctuary were carved cherubim and palm trees like those carved on the walls, and there was a wooden overhang on the front of the portico. ²⁶On the sidewalls of the portico were narrow windows with palm trees carved on each side. The side rooms of the temple also had overhangs.

a37 Septuagint (see also verses 31 and 34); Hebrew *jambs*
b44 Septuagint; Hebrew *were rooms for singers, which were*
c44 Septuagint; Hebrew *east*   *d48* Septuagint; Hebrew *entrance was*   *e49* Septuagint; Hebrew *eleven*   *f49* Hebrew; Septuagint *Ten steps led up to it*   *g1* The common cubit was about 1 1/2 feet (about 0.5 meter).   *h1* One Hebrew manuscript and Septuagint; most Hebrew manuscripts *side, the width of the tent*   *i22* Septuagint; Hebrew *long*
j22 Septuagint; Hebrew *length*

JAMES 4:1-17

What causes fights and quarrels among you? Don't they come from your desires that battle within you? ²You want something but don't get it. You kill and covet, but you cannot have what you want. You quarrel and fight. You do not have, because you do not ask God. ³When you ask, you do not receive, because you ask with wrong motives, that you may spend what you get on your pleasures.

⁴You adulterous people, don't you know that friendship with the world is hatred toward God? Anyone who chooses to be a friend of the world becomes an enemy of God. ⁵Or do you think Scripture says without reason that the spirit he caused to live in us envies intensely?*a* ⁶But he gives us more grace. That is why Scripture says:

"God opposes the proud
    but gives grace to the humble."*b*

⁷**Submit yourselves, then, to God. Resist the devil, and he will flee from you.** ⁸**Come near to God and he will come near to you. Wash your hands, you sinners, and purify your hearts, you double-minded.** ⁹Grieve, mourn and wail. Change your laughter to mourning and your joy to gloom. ¹⁰Humble yourselves before the Lord, and he will lift you up.

¹¹Brothers, do not slander one another. Anyone who speaks against his brother or judges him speaks against the law and judges it. When you judge the law, you are not keeping it, but sitting in judgment on it. ¹²There is only one Lawgiver and Judge, the one who is able to save and destroy. But you—who are you to judge your neighbor?

¹³Now listen, you who say, "Today or tomorrow we will go to this or that city, spend a year there, carry on business and make money." ¹⁴Why, you do not even know what will happen tomorrow. What is your life? You are a mist that appears for a little while and then vanishes. ¹⁵Instead, you ought to say, "If it is the Lord's will, we will live and do this

or that." ¹⁶As it is, you boast and brag. All such boasting is evil. ¹⁷Anyone, then, who knows the good he ought to do and doesn't do it, sins.

a5 Or that God jealously longs for the spirit that he made to live in us; or that the Spirit he caused to live in us longs jealously   b6 Prov. 3:34

PSALM 118:19-29

¹⁹**O**pen for me the gates of
        righteousness;
    I will enter and give thanks to the
        Lord.
²⁰This is the gate of the Lord
    through which the righteous may
        enter.
²¹I will give you thanks, for you
        answered me;
    you have become my salvation.

²²The stone the builders rejected
    has become the capstone;
²³the Lord has done this,
    and it is marvelous in our eyes.
²⁴This is the day the Lord has made;
    let us rejoice and be glad in it.

²⁵O Lord, save us;
    O Lord, grant us success.
²⁶Blessed is he who comes in the name
        of the Lord.
    From the house of the Lord we
        bless you.*a*
²⁷The Lord is God,
    and he has made his light shine
        upon us.
    With boughs in hand, join in the
        festal procession
    up*b* to the horns of the altar.

²⁸You are my God, and I will give you
        thanks;
    you are my God, and I will exalt
        you.

²⁹Give thanks to the Lord, for he is
        good;
    his love endures forever.

a26 The Hebrew is plural.   b27 Or Bind the festal sacrifice with ropes / and take it

PROVERBS 28:3-5

³**A** ruler*a* who oppresses the poor
    is like a driving rain that leaves no
        crops.

⁴Those who forsake the law praise the wicked,
  but those who keep the law resist them.

⁵Evil men do not understand justice,
  but those who seek the LORD understand it fully.

ᵃ3 Or *A poor man*

□ D A Y 3 2 5

GOD SIGHTINGS

November 21

EZEKIEL 42:1–43:27

Then the man led me [Ezekiel] northward into the outer court and brought me to the rooms opposite the temple courtyard and opposite the outer wall on the north side. ²The building whose door faced north was a hundred cubitsᵃ long and fifty cubits wide. ³Both in the section twenty cubits from the inner court and in the section opposite the pavement of the outer court, gallery faced gallery at the three levels. ⁴In front of the rooms was an inner passageway ten cubits wide and a hundred cubitsᵇ long. Their doors were on the north. ⁵Now the upper rooms were narrower, for the galleries took more space from them than from the rooms on the lower and middle floors of the building. ⁶The rooms on the third floor had no pillars, as the courts had; so they were smaller in floor space than those on the lower and middle floors. ⁷There was an outer wall parallel to the rooms and the outer court; it extended in front of the rooms for fifty cubits. ⁸While the row of rooms on the side next to the outer court was fifty cubits long, the row on the side nearest the sanctuary was a hundred cubits long. ⁹The lower rooms had an entrance on the east side as one enters them from the outer court.
¹⁰On the south sideᶜ along the length

of the wall of the outer court, adjoining the temple courtyard and opposite the outer wall, were rooms ¹¹with a passageway in front of them. These were like the rooms on the north; they had the same length and width, with similar exits and dimensions. Similar to the doorways on the north ¹²were the doorways of the rooms on the south. There was a doorway at the beginning of the passageway that was parallel to the corresponding wall extending eastward, by which one enters the rooms.

¹³Then he said to me, "The north and south rooms facing the temple courtyard are the priests' rooms, where the priests who approach the LORD will eat the most holy offerings. There they will put the most holy offerings—the grain offerings, the sin offerings and the guilt offerings—for the place is holy. ¹⁴Once the priests enter the holy precincts, they are not to go into the outer court until they leave behind the garments in which they minister, for these are holy. They are to put on other clothes before they go near the places that are for the people."

¹⁵When he had finished measuring what was inside the temple area, he led me out by the east gate and measured the area all around: ¹⁶He measured the east side with the measuring rod; it was five hundred cubits.ᵈ ¹⁷He measured the north side; it was five hundred cubitsᵉ by the measuring rod. ¹⁸He measured the south side; it was five hundred cubits by the measuring rod. ¹⁹Then he turned to the west side and measured; it was five hundred cubits by the measuring rod. ²⁰So he measured the area on all four sides. It had a wall around it, five hundred cubits long and five hundred cubits wide, to separate the holy from the common.

⁴³:¹THEN the man brought me to the gate facing east, ²and I saw the glory of the God of Israel coming from the east. His voice was like the roar of rushing waters, and the land was radiant with his glory. ³The vision I saw was like the

vision I had seen when he*f* came to destroy the city and like the visions I had seen by the Kebar River, and I fell facedown. ⁴The glory of the LORD entered the temple through the gate facing east. ⁵Then the Spirit lifted me up and brought me into the inner court, and the glory of the LORD filled the temple.

⁶While the man was standing beside me, I heard someone speaking to me from inside the temple. ⁷He said: "Son of man, this is the place of my throne and the place for the soles of my feet. This is where I will live among the Israelites forever. The house of Israel will never again defile my holy name—neither they nor their kings—by their prostitution*g* and the lifeless idols*h* of their kings at their high places. ⁸When they placed their threshold next to my threshold and their doorposts beside my doorposts, with only a wall between me and them, they defiled my holy name by their detestable practices. So I destroyed them in my anger. ⁹Now let them put away from me their prostitution and the lifeless idols of their kings, and I will live among them forever.

¹⁰"Son of man, describe the temple to the people of Israel, that they may be ashamed of their sins. Let them consider the plan, ¹¹and if they are ashamed of all they have done, make known to them the design of the temple—its arrangement, its exits and entrances—its whole design and all its regulations*i* and laws. Write these down before them so that they may be faithful to its design and follow all its regulations.

¹²"This is the law of the temple: All the surrounding area on top of the mountain will be most holy. Such is the law of the temple.

¹³"These are the measurements of the altar in long cubits, that cubit being a cubit*j* and a handbreadth*k*: Its gutter is a cubit deep and a cubit wide, with a rim of one span*l* around the edge. And this is the height of the altar: ¹⁴From the gutter on the ground up to the lower ledge it is two cubits high and a cubit wide, and from the smaller ledge up to the larger ledge it is four cubits high and a cubit wide. ¹⁵The altar hearth is four cubits high, and four horns project upward from the hearth. ¹⁶The altar hearth is square, twelve cubits long and twelve cubits wide. ¹⁷The upper ledge also is square, fourteen cubits long and fourteen cubits wide, with a rim of half a cubit and a gutter of a cubit all around. The steps of the altar face east."

¹⁸Then he said to me, "Son of man, this is what the Sovereign LORD says: These will be the regulations for sacrificing burnt offerings and sprinkling blood upon the altar when it is built: ¹⁹You are to give a young bull as a sin offering to the priests, who are Levites, of the family of Zadok, who come near to minister before me, declares the Sovereign LORD. ²⁰You are to take some of its blood and put it on the four horns of the altar and on the four corners of the upper ledge and all around the rim, and so purify the altar and make atonement for it. ²¹You are to take the bull for the sin offering and burn it in the designated part of the temple area outside the sanctuary.

²²"On the second day you are to offer a male goat without defect for a sin offering, and the altar is to be purified as it was purified with the bull. ²³When you have finished purifying it, you are to offer a young bull and a ram from the flock, both without defect. ²⁴You are to offer them before the LORD, and the priests are to sprinkle salt on them and sacrifice them as a burnt offering to the LORD.

²⁵"For seven days you are to provide a male goat daily for a sin offering; you are also to provide a young bull and a ram from the flock, both without defect. ²⁶For seven days they are to make atonement for the altar and cleanse it; thus they will dedicate it. ²⁷At the end of these days, from the eighth day on, the priests are to present your burnt offerings and fellowship offerings*m* on the

altar. Then I will accept you, declares the Sovereign LORD."

a2 The common cubit was about 1 1/2 feet (about 0.5 meter). *b4* Septuagint and Syriac; Hebrew *and one cubit* *c10* Septuagint; Hebrew *Eastward* *d16* See Septuagint of verse 17; Hebrew *rods*; also in verses 18 and 19. *e17* Septuagint; Hebrew *rods* *f3* Some Hebrew manuscripts and Vulgate; most Hebrew manuscripts *I* *g7* Or *their spiritual adultery*; also in verse 9 *h7* Or *the corpses*; also in verse 9 *i11* Some Hebrew manuscripts and Septuagint; most Hebrew manuscripts *regulations and its whole design* *j13* The common cubit was about 1 1/2 feet (about 0.5 meter). *k13* That is, about 3 inches (about 8 centimeters) *l13* That is, about 9 inches (about 22 centimeters) *m27* Traditionally *peace offerings*

JAMES 5:1-20

Now listen, you rich people, weep and wail because of the misery that is coming upon you. ²Your wealth has rotted, and moths have eaten your clothes. ³Your gold and silver are corroded. Their corrosion will testify against you and eat your flesh like fire. You have hoarded wealth in the last days. ⁴Look! The wages you failed to pay the workmen who mowed your fields are crying out against you. The cries of the harvesters have reached the ears of the Lord Almighty. ⁵You have lived on earth in luxury and self-indulgence. You have fattened yourselves in the day of slaughter.*a* ⁶You have condemned and murdered innocent men, who were not opposing you.

⁷Be patient, then, brothers, until the Lord's coming. See how the farmer waits for the land to yield its valuable crop and how patient he is for the autumn and spring rains. ⁸You too, be patient and stand firm, because the Lord's coming is near. ⁹Don't grumble against each other, brothers, or you will be judged. The Judge is standing at the door!

¹⁰Brothers, as an example of patience in the face of suffering, take the prophets who spoke in the name of the Lord. ¹¹As you know, we consider blessed those who have persevered. You have heard of Job's perseverance and have seen what the Lord finally brought about. The Lord is full of compassion and mercy.

¹²Above all, my brothers, do not swear—not by heaven or by earth or by anything else. Let your "Yes" be yes, and your "No," no, or you will be condemned.

¹³Is any one of you in trouble? He should pray. Is anyone happy? Let him sing songs of praise. ¹⁴Is any one of you sick? He should call the elders of the church to pray over him and anoint him with oil in the name of the Lord. ¹⁵And the prayer offered in faith will make the sick person well; the Lord will raise him up. If he has sinned, he will be forgiven. ¹⁶Therefore confess your sins to each other and pray for each other so that you may be healed. The prayer of a righteous man is powerful and effective.

¹⁷Elijah was a man just like us. He prayed earnestly that it would not rain, and it did not rain on the land for three and a half years. ¹⁸Again he prayed, and the heavens gave rain, and the earth produced its crops.

¹⁹My brothers, if one of you should wander from the truth and someone should bring him back, ²⁰remember this: Whoever turns a sinner from the error of his way will save him from death and cover over a multitude of sins.

a5 Or *yourselves as in a day of feasting*

PSALM 119:1-16

א Aleph*a*

¹ **B**lessed are they whose ways are
   blameless,
  who walk according to the law of
   the LORD.
² Blessed are they who keep his statutes
  and seek him with all their heart.
³ They do nothing wrong;
  they walk in his ways.
⁴ You have laid down precepts
  that are to be fully obeyed.
⁵ Oh, that my ways were steadfast
  in obeying your decrees!
⁶ Then I would not be put to shame
  when I consider all your commands.
⁷ I will praise you with an upright heart
  as I learn your righteous laws.
⁸ I will obey your decrees;
  do not utterly forsake me.

ב Beth

⁹ How can a young man keep his way
   pure?
  By living according to your word.

10 I seek you with all my heart;
    do not let me stray from your
      commands.
11 I have hidden your word in my
    heart
    that I might not sin against you.
12 Praise be to you, O LORD;
    teach me your decrees.
13 With my lips I recount
    all the laws that come from your
      mouth.
14 I rejoice in following your statutes
    as one rejoices in great riches.
15 I meditate on your precepts
    and consider your ways.
16 I delight in your decrees;
    I will not neglect your word.

aThis psalm is an acrostic poem; the verses of each stanza
begin with the same letter of the Hebrew alphabet.

PROVERBS 28:6-7
6 Better a poor man whose walk is
    blameless
    than a rich man whose ways are
      perverse.

7 He who keeps the law is a discerning
    son,
    but a companion of gluttons
      disgraces his father.

□ D A Y   3 2 6

GOD SIGHTINGS

November 22

EZEKIEL 44:1–45:12
Then the man brought me [Ezekiel]
back to the outer gate of the sanctuary,
the one facing east, and it was shut.
2 The LORD said to me, "This gate is to remain shut. It must not be opened; no
one may enter through it. It is to remain
shut because the LORD, the God of Israel,
has entered through it. 3 The prince
himself is the only one who may sit inside the gateway to eat in the presence
of the LORD. He is to enter by way of the

portico of the gateway and go out the
same way."

4 Then the man brought me by way of
the north gate to the front of the temple.
I looked and saw the glory of the LORD
filling the temple of the LORD, and I fell
facedown.

5 The LORD said to me, "Son of man,
look carefully, listen closely and give attention to everything I tell you concerning
all the regulations regarding the temple of
the LORD. Give attention to the entrance of
the temple and all the exits of the sanctuary. 6 Say to the rebellious house of Israel,
'This is what the Sovereign LORD says:
Enough of your detestable practices, O
house of Israel! 7 In addition to all your
other detestable practices, you brought
foreigners uncircumcised in heart and
flesh into my sanctuary, desecrating my
temple while you offered me food, fat and
blood, and you broke my covenant. 8 Instead of carrying out your duty in regard
to my holy things, you put others in
charge of my sanctuary. 9 This is what the
Sovereign LORD says: No foreigner uncircumcised in heart and flesh is to enter my
sanctuary, not even the foreigners who
live among the Israelites.

10 " 'The Levites who went far from
me when Israel went astray and who
wandered from me after their idols
must bear the consequences of their
sin. 11 They may serve in my sanctuary,
having charge of the gates of the temple and serving in it; they may slaughter
the burnt offerings and sacrifices for
the people and stand before the people
and serve them. 12 But because they
served them in the presence of their
idols and made the house of Israel fall
into sin, therefore I have sworn with
uplifted hand that they must bear the
consequences of their sin, declares the
Sovereign LORD. 13 They are not to
come near to serve me as priests or
come near any of my holy things or my
most holy offerings; they must bear the
shame of their detestable practices.
14 Yet I will put them in charge of the
duties of the temple and all the work
that is to be done in it.

15 "'But the priests, who are Levites and descendants of Zadok and who faithfully carried out the duties of my sanctuary when the Israelites went astray from me, are to come near to minister before me; they are to stand before me to offer sacrifices of fat and blood, declares the Sovereign LORD. 16They alone are to enter my sanctuary; they alone are to come near my table to minister before me and perform my service.

17 "'When they enter the gates of the inner court, they are to wear linen clothes; they must not wear any woolen garment while ministering at the gates of the inner court or inside the temple. 18They are to wear linen turbans on their heads and linen undergarments around their waists. They must not wear anything that makes them perspire. 19When they go out into the outer court where the people are, they are to take off the clothes they have been ministering in and are to leave them in the sacred rooms, and put on other clothes, so that they do not consecrate the people by means of their garments.

20 "'They must not shave their heads or let their hair grow long, but they are to keep the hair of their heads trimmed. 21No priest is to drink wine when he enters the inner court. 22They must not marry widows or divorced women; they may marry only virgins of Israelite descent or widows of priests. 23They are to teach my people the difference between the holy and the common and show them how to distinguish between the unclean and the clean.

24 "'In any dispute, the priests are to serve as judges and decide it according to my ordinances. They are to keep my laws and my decrees for all my appointed feasts, and they are to keep my Sabbaths holy.

25 "'A priest must not defile himself by going near a dead person; however, if the dead person was his father or mother, son or daughter, brother or unmarried sister, then he may defile himself. 26After he is cleansed, he must wait seven days. 27On the day he goes into the inner court of the sanctuary to minister in the sanctuary, he is to offer a sin offering for himself, declares the Sovereign LORD.

28 "'I am to be the only inheritance the priests have. You are to give them no possession in Israel; I will be their possession. 29They will eat the grain offerings, the sin offerings and the guilt offerings; and everything in Israel devoted[a] to the LORD will belong to them. 30The best of all the firstfruits and of all your special gifts will belong to the priests. You are to give them the first portion of your ground meal so that a blessing may rest on your household. 31The priests must not eat anything, bird or animal, found dead or torn by wild animals.

45:1 "'WHEN you allot the land as an inheritance, you are to present to the LORD a portion of the land as a sacred district, 25,000 cubits long and 20,000[b] cubits wide; the entire area will be holy. 2Of this, a section 500 cubits square is to be for the sanctuary, with 50 cubits around it for open land. 3In the sacred district, measure off a section 25,000 cubits[c] long and 10,000 cubits[d] wide. In it will be the sanctuary, the Most Holy Place. 4It will be the sacred portion of the land for the priests, who minister in the sanctuary and who draw near to minister before the LORD. It will be a place for their houses as well as a holy place for the sanctuary. 5An area 25,000 cubits long and 10,000 cubits wide will belong to the Levites, who serve in the temple, as their possession for towns to live in.[e]

6 "'You are to give the city as its property an area 5,000 cubits wide and 25,000 cubits long, adjoining the sacred portion; it will belong to the whole house of Israel.

7 "'The prince will have the land bordering each side of the area formed by the sacred district and the property of the city. It will extend westward from the west side and eastward from the east side, running lengthwise from the

western to the eastern border parallel to one of the tribal portions. ⁸This land will be his possession in Israel. And my princes will no longer oppress my people but will allow the house of Israel to possess the land according to their tribes.

⁹"'This is what the Sovereign LORD says: You have gone far enough, O princes of Israel! Give up your violence and oppression and do what is just and right. Stop dispossessing my people, declares the Sovereign LORD. ¹⁰You are to use accurate scales, an accurate ephah*f* and an accurate bath.*g* ¹¹The ephah and the bath are to be the same size, the bath containing a tenth of a homer*h* and the ephah a tenth of a homer; the homer is to be the standard measure for both. ¹²The shekel*i* is to consist of twenty gerahs. Twenty shekels plus twenty-five shekels plus fifteen shekels equal one mina.*j*'"

a29 The Hebrew term refers to the irrevocable giving over of things or persons to the LORD.   *b1* Septuagint (see also verses 3 and 5 and 48:9); Hebrew *10,000*   *c3* That is, about 7 miles (about 12 kilometers)   *d3* That is, about 3 miles (about 5 kilometers)   *e5* Septuagint; Hebrew *temple; they will have as their possession 20 rooms*   *f10* An ephah was a dry measure.   *g10* A bath was a liquid measure.   *h11* A homer was a dry measure.   *i12* A shekel weighed about 2/5 ounce (about 11.5 grams).   *j12* That is, 60 shekels; the common mina was 50 shekels.

1 PETER 1:1-12
Peter, an apostle of Jesus Christ,

To God's elect, strangers in the world, scattered throughout Pontus, Galatia, Cappadocia, Asia and Bithynia, ²who have been chosen according to the foreknowledge of God the Father, through the sanctifying work of the Spirit, for obedience to Jesus Christ and sprinkling by his blood:

Grace and peace be yours in abundance.

³Praise be to the God and Father of our Lord Jesus Christ! In his great mercy he has given us new birth into a living hope through the resurrection of Jesus Christ from the dead, ⁴and into an inheritance that can never perish, spoil or fade—kept in heaven for you, ⁵who through faith are shielded by God's power until the coming of the salvation that is ready to be revealed in the last time. ⁶In this you greatly rejoice, though now for a little while you may have had to suffer grief in all kinds of trials. ⁷These have come so that your faith—of greater worth than gold, which perishes even though refined by fire—may be proved genuine and may result in praise, glory and honor when Jesus Christ is revealed. ⁸Though you have not seen him, you love him; and even though you do not see him now, you believe in him and are filled with an inexpressible and glorious joy, ⁹for you are receiving the goal of your faith, the salvation of your souls.

¹⁰Concerning this salvation, the prophets, who spoke of the grace that was to come to you, searched intently and with the greatest care, ¹¹trying to find out the time and circumstances to which the Spirit of Christ in them was pointing when he predicted the sufferings of Christ and the glories that would follow. ¹²It was revealed to them that they were not serving themselves but you, when they spoke of the things that have now been told you by those who have preached the gospel to you by the Holy Spirit sent from heaven. Even angels long to look into these things.

PSALM 119:17-32

ג Gimel

¹⁷Do good to your [the LORD'S] servant,
     and I will live;
   I will obey your word.
¹⁸Open my eyes that I may see
     wonderful things in your law.
¹⁹I am a stranger on earth;
     do not hide your commands
     from me.
²⁰My soul is consumed with longing
     for your laws at all times.
²¹You rebuke the arrogant, who are
     cursed
     and who stray from your
     commands.
²²Remove from me scorn and contempt,
     for I keep your statutes.

23 Though rulers sit together and
        slander me,
    your servant will meditate on your
        decrees.
24 Your statutes are my delight;
    they are my counselors.

              ‫ד‬   Daleth

25 I am laid low in the dust;
    preserve my life according to your
        word.
26 I recounted my ways and you
        answered me;
    teach me your decrees.
27 Let me understand the teaching of
        your precepts;
    then I will meditate on your
        wonders.
28 My soul is weary with sorrow;
    strengthen me according to your
        word.
29 Keep me from deceitful ways;
    be gracious to me through your
        law.
30 **I have chosen the way of truth;**
    I have set my heart on your
        laws.
31 **I hold fast to your statutes,**
        O Lord;
    do not let me be put to shame.
32 **I run in the path of your**
        commands,
    for you have set my heart free.

PROVERBS 28:8-10
8 **H**e who increases his wealth by
        exorbitant interest
    amasses it for another, who will be
        kind to the poor.

9 If anyone turns a deaf ear to the law,
    even his prayers are detestable.

10 He who leads the upright along an
        evil path
    will fall into his own trap,
    but the blameless will receive a
        good inheritance.

GOD SIGHTINGS

November 23

EZEKIEL 45:13–46:24
" "**T**his is the special gift you [the princes
of Israel] are to offer: a sixth of an ephah
from each homer of wheat and a sixth of
an ephah from each homer of barley.
14 The prescribed portion of oil, measured by the bath, is a tenth of a bath
from each cor (which consists of ten
baths or one homer, for ten baths are
equivalent to a homer). 15 Also one
sheep is to be taken from every flock of
two hundred from the well-watered
pastures of Israel. These will be used for
the grain offerings, burnt offerings and
fellowship offerings*a* to make atonement for the people, declares the Sovereign Lord. 16 All the people of the land
will participate in this special gift for
the use of the prince in Israel. 17 It will
be the duty of the prince to provide the
burnt offerings, grain offerings and
drink offerings at the festivals, the New
Moons and the Sabbaths—at all the appointed feasts of the house of Israel. He
will provide the sin offerings, grain offerings, burnt offerings and fellowship
offerings to make atonement for the
house of Israel.

18 " 'This is what the Sovereign Lord
says: In the first month on the first day
you are to take a young bull without defect and purify the sanctuary. 19 The
priest is to take some of the blood of the
sin offering and put it on the doorposts
of the temple, on the four corners of the
upper ledge of the altar and on the gate-
posts of the inner court. 20 You are to do
the same on the seventh day of the
month for anyone who sins unintentionally or through ignorance; so you
are to make atonement for the temple.

21 " 'In the first month on the fourteenth day you are to observe the Passover, a feast lasting seven days, during
which you shall eat bread made without

yeast. ²²On that day the prince is to provide a bull as a sin offering for himself and for all the people of the land. ²³Every day during the seven days of the Feast he is to provide seven bulls and seven rams without defect as a burnt offering to the LORD, and a male goat for a sin offering. ²⁴He is to provide as a grain offering an ephah for each bull and an ephah for each ram, along with a hin*b* of oil for each ephah.

²⁵"'During the seven days of the Feast, which begins in the seventh month on the fifteenth day, he is to make the same provision for sin offerings, burnt offerings, grain offerings and oil.

⁴⁶:¹" 'THIS is what the Sovereign LORD says: The gate of the inner court facing east is to be shut on the six working days, but on the Sabbath day and on the day of the New Moon it is to be opened. ²The prince is to enter from the outside through the portico of the gateway and stand by the gatepost. The priests are to sacrifice his burnt offering and his fellowship offerings.*c* He is to worship at the threshold of the gateway and then go out, but the gate will not be shut until evening. ³On the Sabbaths and New Moons the people of the land are to worship in the presence of the LORD at the entrance to that gateway. ⁴The burnt offering the prince brings to the LORD on the Sabbath day is to be six male lambs and a ram, all without defect. ⁵The grain offering given with the ram is to be an ephah,*d* and the grain offering with the lambs is to be as much as he pleases, along with a hin*e* of oil for each ephah. ⁶On the day of the New Moon he is to offer a young bull, six lambs and a ram, all without defect. ⁷He is to provide as a grain offering one ephah with the bull, one ephah with the ram, and with the lambs as much as he wants to give, along with a hin of oil with each ephah. ⁸When the prince enters, he is to go in through the portico of the gateway, and he is to come out the same way.

⁹"'When the people of the land come before the LORD at the appointed feasts, whoever enters by the north gate to worship is to go out the south gate; and whoever enters by the south gate is to go out the north gate. No one is to return through the gate by which he entered, but each is to go out the opposite gate. ¹⁰The prince is to be among them, going in when they go in and going out when they go out.

¹¹" 'At the festivals and the appointed feasts, the grain offering is to be an ephah with a bull, an ephah with a ram, and with the lambs as much as one pleases, along with a hin of oil for each ephah. ¹²When the prince provides a freewill offering to the LORD—whether a burnt offering or fellowship offerings—the gate facing east is to be opened for him. He shall offer his burnt offering or his fellowship offerings as he does on the Sabbath day. Then he shall go out, and after he has gone out, the gate will be shut.

¹³" 'Every day you are to provide a year-old lamb without defect for a burnt offering to the LORD; morning by morning you shall provide it. ¹⁴You are also to provide with it morning by morning a grain offering, consisting of a sixth of an ephah with a third of a hin of oil to moisten the flour. The presenting of this grain offering to the LORD is a lasting ordinance. ¹⁵So the lamb and the grain offering and the oil shall be provided morning by morning for a regular burnt offering.

¹⁶" 'This is what the Sovereign LORD says: If the prince makes a gift from his inheritance to one of his sons, it will also belong to his descendants; it is to be their property by inheritance. ¹⁷If, however, he makes a gift from his inheritance to one of his servants, the servant may keep it until the year of freedom; then it will revert to the prince. His inheritance belongs to his sons only; it is theirs. ¹⁸The prince must not take any of the inheritance of the people, driving them off their property. He is to give his sons their inheritance out of his own property, so that none of my people will be separated from his property.'"

¹⁹Then the man brought me through

the entrance at the side of the gate to the sacred rooms facing north, which belonged to the priests, and showed me a place at the western end. 20He said to me, "This is the place where the priests will cook the guilt offering and the sin offering and bake the grain offering, to avoid bringing them into the outer court and consecrating the people."

21He then brought me to the outer court and led me around to its four corners, and I saw in each corner another court. 22In the four corners of the outer court were enclosed[f] courts, forty cubits long and thirty cubits wide; each of the courts in the four corners was the same size. 23Around the inside of each of the four courts was a ledge of stone, with places for fire built all around under the ledge. 24He said to me, "These are the kitchens where those who minister at the temple will cook the sacrifices of the people."

1 PETER 1:13–2:10

Therefore, prepare your minds for action; be self-controlled; set your hope fully on the grace to be given you when Jesus Christ is revealed. 14As obedient children, do not conform to the evil desires you had when you lived in ignorance. 15But just as he who called you is holy, so be holy in all you do; 16for it is written: "Be holy, because I am holy."[a]

17Since you call on a Father who judges each man's work impartially, live your lives as strangers here in reverent fear. 18For you know that it was not with perishable things such as silver or gold that you were redeemed from the empty way of life handed down to you from your forefathers, 19but with the precious blood of Christ, a lamb without blemish or defect. 20He was chosen before the creation of the world, but was revealed in these last times for your sake. 21Through him you believe in God, who raised him from the

dead and glorified him, and so your faith and hope are in God.

22Now that you have purified yourselves by obeying the truth so that you have sincere love for your brothers, love one another deeply, from the heart.[b] 23For you have been born again, not of perishable seed, but of imperishable, through the living and enduring word of God. 24For,

"All men are like grass,
    and all their glory is like the
        flowers of the field;
the grass withers and the flowers fall,
25   but the word of the Lord stands
        forever."[c]

And this is the word that was preached to you.

2:1Therefore, rid yourselves of all malice and all deceit, hypocrisy, envy, and slander of every kind. 2Like newborn babies, crave pure spiritual milk, so that by it you may grow up in your salvation, 3now that you have tasted that the Lord is good.

4As you come to him, the living Stone—rejected by men but chosen by God and precious to him— 5you also, like living stones, are being built into a spiritual house to be a holy priesthood, offering spiritual sacrifices acceptable to God through Jesus Christ. 6For in Scripture it says:

"See, I lay a stone in Zion,
    a chosen and precious
        cornerstone,
and the one who trusts in him
    will never be put to shame."[d]

7Now to you who believe, this stone is precious. But to those who do not believe,

"The stone the builders rejected
    has become the capstone,[e]"[f]

8and,

"A stone that causes men to stumble
    and a rock that makes them fall."[g]

They stumble because they disobey the message—which is also what they were destined for.

9But you are a chosen people, a royal priesthood, a holy nation, a people belonging to God, that you may declare the praises of him who called you out of darkness into his wonderful light. 10Once you were not a people, but now you are the people of God; once you had not received mercy, but now you have received mercy.

a16 Lev. 11:44,45; 19:2   b22 Some early manuscripts from a pure heart   c25 Isaiah 40:6-8   d6 Isaiah 28:16   e7 Or cornerstone   f7 Psalm 118:22   98 Isaiah 8:14

PSALM 119:33-48

ה He

33 Teach me, O LORD, to follow your decrees;
  then I will keep them to the end.
34 Give me understanding, and I will keep your law
  and obey it with all my heart.
35 Direct me in the path of your commands,
  for there I find delight.
36 Turn my heart toward your statutes
  and not toward selfish gain.
37 Turn my eyes away from worthless things;
  preserve my life according to your word.a
38 Fulfill your promise to your servant,
  so that you may be feared.
39 Take away the disgrace I dread,
  for your laws are good.
40 How I long for your precepts!
  Preserve my life in your righteousness.

ו Waw

41 May your unfailing love come to me,
  O LORD,
  your salvation according to your promise;
42 then I will answer the one who taunts me,
  for I trust in your word.
43 Do not snatch the word of truth from my mouth,
  for I have put my hope in your laws.
44 I will always obey your law,
  for ever and ever.

45 I will walk about in freedom,
  for I have sought out your precepts.
46 I will speak of your statutes before kings
  and will not be put to shame,
47 for I delight in your commands
  because I love them.
48 I lift up my hands tob your commands, which I love,
  and I meditate on your decrees.

a37 Two manuscripts of the Masoretic Text and Dead Sea Scrolls; most manuscripts of the Masoretic Text life in your way   b48 Or for

PROVERBS 28:11

11 A rich man may be wise in his own eyes,
  but a poor man who has discernment sees through him.

□ D A Y   3 2 8

GOD SIGHTINGS

November 24

EZEKIEL 47:1–48:35

The man brought me [Ezekiel] back to the entrance of the temple, and I saw water coming out from under the threshold of the temple toward the east (for the temple faced east). The water was coming down from under the south side of the temple, south of the altar. 2He then brought me out through the north gate and led me around the outside to the outer gate facing east, and the water was flowing from the south side.

3As the man went eastward with a measuring line in his hand, he measured off a thousand cubitsa and then led me through water that was ankle-deep. 4He measured off another thousand cubits and led me through water that was knee-deep. He measured off another thousand and led me through water that was up to the waist. 5He measured off another thousand, but now it was a river that I could not cross, because the water had risen and was deep enough to swim in—a river that no one could cross. ⁶He asked me, "Son of man, do you see this?"

Then he led me back to the bank of the river. ⁷When I arrived there, I saw a great number of trees on each side of the river. ⁸He said to me, "This water flows toward the eastern region and goes down into the Arabah,ᵇ where it enters the Sea.ᶜ When it empties into the Sea,ᶜ the water there becomes fresh. ⁹Swarms of living creatures will live wherever the river flows. There will be large numbers of fish, because this water flows there and makes the salt water fresh; so where the river flows everything will live. ¹⁰Fishermen will stand along the shore; from En Gedi to En Eglaim there will be places for spreading nets. The fish will be of many kinds—like the fish of the Great Sea.ᵈ ¹¹But the swamps and marshes will not become fresh; they will be left for salt. ¹²Fruit trees of all kinds will grow on both banks of the river. Their leaves will not wither, nor will their fruit fail. Every month they will bear, because the water from the sanctuary flows to them. Their fruit will serve for food and their leaves for healing."

¹³This is what the Sovereign Lᴏʀᴅ says: "These are the boundaries by which you are to divide the land for an inheritance among the twelve tribes of Israel, with two portions for Joseph. ¹⁴You are to divide it equally among them. Because I swore with uplifted hand to give it to your forefathers, this land will become your inheritance.

¹⁵"This is to be the boundary of the land:

"On the north side it will run from the Great Sea by the Hethlon road past Leboᵉ Hamath to Zedad, ¹⁶Berothahᶠ and Sibraim (which lies on the border between Damascus and Hamath), as far as Hazer Hatticon, which is on the border of Hauran. ¹⁷The boundary will extend from the sea to Hazar Enan,ᵍ along the northern border of Damascus, with the border of Hamath to the north. This will be the north boundary.

¹⁸"On the east side the boundary will run between Hauran and Damascus, along the Jordan between Gilead and the land of Israel, to the eastern sea and as far as Tamar.ʰ This will be the east boundary.

¹⁹"On the south side it will run from Tamar as far as the waters of Meribah Kadesh, then along the Wadi of Egypt to the Great Sea. This will be the south boundary.

²⁰"On the west side, the Great Sea will be the boundary to a point opposite Leboʲ Hamath. This will be the west boundary.

²¹"You are to distribute this land among yourselves according to the tribes of Israel. ²²You are to allot it as an inheritance for yourselves and for the aliens who have settled among you and who have children. You are to consider them as native-born Israelites; along with you they are to be allotted an inheritance among the tribes of Israel. ²³In whatever tribe the alien settles, there you are to give him his inheritance," declares the Sovereign Lᴏʀᴅ.

⁴⁸:¹"Tʜᴇsᴇ are the tribes, listed by name: At the northern frontier, Dan will have one portion; it will follow the Hethlon road to Leboʲ Hamath; Hazar Enan and the northern border of Damascus next to Hamath will be part of its border from the east side to the west side.

²"Asher will have one portion; it will border the territory of Dan from east to west.

³"Naphtali will have one portion; it will border the territory of Asher from east to west.

⁴"Manasseh will have one portion; it will border the territory of Naphtali from east to west.

⁵"Ephraim will have one portion; it will border the territory of Manasseh from east to west.

⁶"Reuben will have one portion; it will border the territory of Ephraim from east to west.

7 "Judah will have one portion; it will border the territory of Reuben from east to west.

8 "Bordering the territory of Judah from east to west will be the portion you are to present as a special gift. It will be 25,000 cubits[k] wide, and its length from east to west will equal one of the tribal portions; the sanctuary will be in the center of it.

9 "The special portion you are to offer to the LORD will be 25,000 cubits long and 10,000 cubits[l] wide. 10 This will be the sacred portion for the priests. It will be 25,000 cubits long on the north side, 10,000 cubits wide on the west side, 10,000 cubits wide on the east side and 25,000 cubits long on the south side. In the center of it will be the sanctuary of the LORD. 11 This will be for the consecrated priests, the Zadokites, who were faithful in serving me and did not go astray as the Levites did when the Israelites went astray. 12 It will be a special gift to them from the sacred portion of the land, a most holy portion, bordering the territory of the Levites.

13 "Alongside the territory of the priests, the Levites will have an allotment 25,000 cubits long and 10,000 cubits wide. Its total length will be 25,000 cubits and its width 10,000 cubits. 14 They must not sell or exchange any of it. This is the best of the land and must not pass into other hands, because it is holy to the LORD.

15 "The remaining area, 5,000 cubits wide and 25,000 cubits long, will be for the common use of the city, for houses and for pastureland. The city will be in the center of it 16 and will have these measurements: the north side 4,500 cubits, the south side 4,500 cubits, the east side 4,500 cubits, and the west side 4,500 cubits. 17 The pastureland for the city will be 250 cubits on the north, 250 cubits on the south, 250 cubits on the east, and 250 cubits on the west. 18 What remains of the area, bordering on the sacred portion and running the length of it, will be 10,000 cubits on the east side and 10,000 cubits on the west

side. Its produce will supply food for the workers of the city. 19 The workers from the city who farm it will come from all the tribes of Israel. 20 The entire portion will be a square, 25,000 cubits on each side. As a special gift you will set aside the sacred portion, along with the property of the city.

21 "What remains on both sides of the area formed by the sacred portion and the city property will belong to the prince. It will extend eastward from the 25,000 cubits of the sacred portion to the eastern border, and westward from the 25,000 cubits to the western border. Both these areas running the length of the tribal portions will belong to the prince, and the sacred portion with the temple sanctuary will be in the center of them. 22 So the property of the Levites and the property of the city will lie in the center of the area that belongs to the prince. The area belonging to the prince will lie between the border of Judah and the border of Benjamin.

23 "As for the rest of the tribes: Benjamin will have one portion; it will extend from the east side to the west side.

24 "Simeon will have one portion; it will border the territory of Benjamin from east to west.

25 "Issachar will have one portion; it will border the territory of Simeon from east to west.

26 "Zebulun will have one portion; it will border the territory of Issachar from east to west.

27 "Gad will have one portion; it will border the territory of Zebulun from east to west.

28 "The southern boundary of Gad will run south from Tamar to the waters of Meribah Kadesh, then along the Wadi of Egypt to the Great Sea.[m]

29 "This is the land you are to allot as an inheritance to the tribes of Israel, and these will be their portions," declares the Sovereign LORD.

30 "These will be the exits of the city: Beginning on the north side, which is 4,500 cubits long, 31 the gates of the city

will be named after the tribes of Israel. The three gates on the north side will be the gate of Reuben, the gate of Judah and the gate of Levi.

32"On the east side, which is 4,500 cubits long, will be three gates: the gate of Joseph, the gate of Benjamin and the gate of Dan.

33"On the south side, which measures 4,500 cubits, will be three gates: the gate of Simeon, the gate of Issachar and the gate of Zebulun.

34"On the west side, which is 4,500 cubits long, will be three gates: the gate of Gad, the gate of Asher and the gate of Naphtali.

35"The distance all around will be 18,000 cubits.

"And the name of the city from that time on will be:

THE LORD IS THERE."

a3 That is, about 1,500 feet (about 450 meters)   b8 Or the Jordan Valley   c8 That is, the Dead Sea   d10 That is, the Mediterranean; also in verses 15, 19 and 20   e15 Or past the entrance to   f15,16 See Septuagint and Ezekiel 48:1; Hebrew road to go into Zedad,   16Hamath, Berothah   g17 Hebrew Enon, a variant of Enan   h18 Septuagint and Syriac; Hebrew Israel. You will measure to the eastern sea   i20 Or opposite the entrance to   j1 Or to the entrance to   k8 That is, about 7 miles (about 12 kilometers)   l9 That is, about 3 miles (about 5 kilometers)   m28 That is, the Mediterranean

1 PETER 2:11–3:7

Dear friends, I urge you, as aliens and strangers in the world, to abstain from sinful desires, which war against your soul. 12Live such good lives among the pagans that, though they accuse you of doing wrong, they may see your good deeds and glorify God on the day he visits us.

13Submit yourselves for the Lord's sake to every authority instituted among men: whether to the king, as the supreme authority, 14or to governors, who are sent by him to punish those who do wrong and to commend those who do right. 15For it is God's will that by doing good you should silence the ignorant talk of foolish men. 16Live as free men, but do not use your freedom as a cover-up for evil; live as servants of God. 17Show proper respect to everyone: Love the brotherhood of believers, fear God, honor the king.

18Slaves, submit yourselves to your masters with all respect, not only to those who are good and considerate, but also to those who are harsh. 19For it is commendable if a man bears up under the pain of unjust suffering because he is conscious of God. 20But how is it to your credit if you receive a beating for doing wrong and endure it? But if you suffer for doing good and you endure it, this is commendable before God. 21To this you were called, because Christ suffered for you, leaving you an example, that you should follow in his steps.

22"He committed no sin,
    and no deceit was found in his
        mouth."a

23When they hurled their insults at him, he did not retaliate; when he suffered, he made no threats. Instead, he entrusted himself to him who judges justly. 24He himself bore our sins in his body on the tree, so that we might die to sins and live for righteousness; by his wounds you have been healed. 25For you were like sheep going astray, but now you have returned to the Shepherd and Overseer of your souls.

3:1Wives, in the same way be submissive to your husbands so that, if any of them do not believe the word, they may be won over without words by the behavior of their wives, 2when they see the purity and reverence of your lives. 3Your beauty should not come from outward adornment, such as braided hair and the wearing of gold jewelry and fine clothes. 4Instead, it should be that of your inner self, the unfading beauty of a gentle and quiet spirit, which is of great worth in God's sight. 5For this is the way the holy women of the past who put their hope in God used to make themselves beautiful. They were submissive to their own husbands, 6like Sarah, who obeyed Abraham and called him her master. You are her daughters if you do what is right and do not give way to fear.

7Husbands, in the same way be considerate as you live with your wives, and treat them with respect as the weaker partner and as heirs with you of the gracious gift of life, so that nothing will hinder your prayers.

a22 Isaiah 53:9

PSALM 119:49-64

֏   Zayin

49 **R**emember your [the LORD's] word to your servant,
for you have given me hope.
50 My comfort in my suffering is this:
Your promise preserves my life.
51 The arrogant mock me without restraint,
but I do not turn from your law.
52 I remember your ancient laws, O LORD,
and I find comfort in them.
53 Indignation grips me because of the wicked,
who have forsaken your law.
54 **Your decrees are the theme of my song**
wherever I lodge.
55 **In the night I remember your name, O LORD,**
and I will keep your law.
56 **This has been my practice:**
I obey your precepts.

ח   Heth

57 You are my portion, O LORD;
I have promised to obey your words.
58 I have sought your face with all my heart;
be gracious to me according to your promise.
59 I have considered my ways
and have turned my steps to your statutes.
60 I will hasten and not delay
to obey your commands.
61 Though the wicked bind me with ropes,
I will not forget your law.
62 At midnight I rise to give you thanks
for your righteous laws.
63 I am a friend to all who fear you,
to all who follow your precepts.
64 The earth is filled with your love, O LORD;
teach me your decrees.

PROVERBS 28:12-13

12 **W**hen the righteous triumph, there is great elation;
but when the wicked rise to power, men go into hiding.

13 He who conceals his sins does not prosper,
but whoever confesses and renounces them finds mercy.

☐ DAY 329

November 25

DANIEL 1:1–2:23

In the third year of the reign of Jehoiakim king of Judah, Nebuchadnezzar king of Babylon came to Jerusalem and besieged it. 2 And the Lord delivered Jehoiakim king of Judah into his hand, along with some of the articles from the temple of God. These he carried off to the temple of his god in Babylonia a and put in the treasure house of his god.

3 Then the king ordered Ashpenaz, chief of his court officials, to bring in some of the Israelites from the royal family and the nobility— 4 young men without any physical defect, handsome, showing aptitude for every kind of learning, well informed, quick to understand, and qualified to serve in the king's palace. He was to teach them the language and literature of the Babylonians. b 5 The king assigned them a daily amount of food and wine from the king's table. They were to be trained for three years, and after that they were to enter the king's service.

6 Among these were some from Judah: Daniel, Hananiah, Mishael and Azariah. 7 The chief official gave them new names: to Daniel, the name Belteshazzar; to Hananiah, Shadrach; to Mishael, Meshach; and to Azariah, Abednego.

8 But Daniel resolved not to defile himself with the royal food and wine, and he

asked the chief official for permission not to defile himself this way. [9]Now God had caused the official to show favor and sympathy to Daniel, [10]but the official told Daniel, "I am afraid of my lord the king, who has assigned your[c] food and drink. Why should he see you looking worse than the other young men your age? The king would then have my head because of you."

[11]Daniel then said to the guard whom the chief official had appointed over Daniel, Hananiah, Mishael and Azariah, [12]"Please test your servants for ten days: Give us nothing but vegetables to eat and water to drink. [13]Then compare our appearance with that of the young men who eat the royal food, and treat your servants in accordance with what you see." [14]So he agreed to this and tested them for ten days.

[15]At the end of the ten days they looked healthier and better nourished than any of the young men who ate the royal food. [16]So the guard took away their choice food and the wine they were to drink and gave them vegetables instead.

[17]To these four young men God gave knowledge and understanding of all kinds of literature and learning. And Daniel could understand visions and dreams of all kinds.

[18]At the end of the time set by the king to bring them in, the chief official presented them to Nebuchadnezzar. [19]The king talked with them, and he found none equal to Daniel, Hananiah, Mishael and Azariah; so they entered the king's service. [20]In every matter of wisdom and understanding about which the king questioned them, he found them ten times better than all the magicians and enchanters in his whole kingdom.

[21]And Daniel remained there until the first year of King Cyrus.

[2:1]IN the second year of his reign, Nebuchadnezzar had dreams; his mind was troubled and he could not sleep. [2]So the king summoned the magicians, enchanters, sorcerers and astrologers[d] to tell him what he had dreamed. When they came in and stood before the king, [3]he said to them, "I have had a dream that troubles me and I want to know what it means.[e]"

[4]Then the astrologers answered the king in Aramaic,[f] "O king, live forever! Tell your servants the dream, and we will interpret it."

[5]The king replied to the astrologers, "This is what I have firmly decided: If you do not tell me what my dream was and interpret it, I will have you cut into pieces and your houses turned into piles of rubble. [6]But if you tell me the dream and explain it, you will receive from me gifts and rewards and great honor. So tell me the dream and interpret it for me."

[7]Once more they replied, "Let the king tell his servants the dream, and we will interpret it."

[8]Then the king answered, "I am certain that you are trying to gain time, because you realize that this is what I have firmly decided: [9]If you do not tell me the dream, there is just one penalty for you. You have conspired to tell me misleading and wicked things, hoping the situation will change. So then, tell me the dream, and I will know that you can interpret it for me."

[10]The astrologers answered the king, "There is not a man on earth who can do what the king asks! No king, however great and mighty, has ever asked such a thing of any magician or enchanter or astrologer. [11]What the king asks is too difficult. No one can reveal it to the king except the gods, and they do not live among men."

[12]This made the king so angry and furious that he ordered the execution of all the wise men of Babylon. [13]So the decree was issued to put the wise men to death, and men were sent to look for Daniel and his friends to put them to death.

[14]When Arioch, the commander of the king's guard, had gone out to put to death the wise men of Babylon, Daniel spoke to him with wisdom and tact.

15He asked the king's officer, "Why did the king issue such a harsh decree?" Arioch then explained the matter to Daniel. 16At this, Daniel went in to the king and asked for time, so that he might interpret the dream for him.

17Then Daniel returned to his house and explained the matter to his friends Hananiah, Mishael and Azariah. 18He urged them to plead for mercy from the God of heaven concerning this mystery, so that he and his friends might not be executed with the rest of the wise men of Babylon. 19During the night the mystery was revealed to Daniel in a vision. Then Daniel praised the God of heaven 20and said:

"Praise be to the name of God for
        ever and ever;
    wisdom and power are his.
21He changes times and seasons;
    he sets up kings and deposes them.
He gives wisdom to the wise
    and knowledge to the discerning.
22He reveals deep and hidden things;
    he knows what lies in darkness,
    and light dwells with him.
23I thank and praise you, O God of my
        fathers:
    You have given me wisdom and
        power,
you have made known to me what we
        asked of you,
    you have made known to us the
        dream of the king."

a2 Hebrew Shinar   b4 Or Chaldeans   c10 The Hebrew for your and you in this verse is plural.   d2 Or Chaldeans; also in verses 4, 5 and 10   e3 Or was   f4 The text from here through chapter 7 is in Aramaic.

1 PETER 3:8–4:6

Finally, all of you, live in harmony with one another; be sympathetic, love as brothers, be compassionate and humble. 9Do not repay evil with evil or insult with insult, but with blessing, because to this you were called so that you may inherit a blessing. 10For,

"Whoever would love life
    and see good days
must keep his tongue from evil
    and his lips from deceitful speech.

11He must turn from evil and do good;
    he must seek peace and pursue it.
12For the eyes of the Lord are on the
        righteous
    and his ears are attentive to their
        prayer,
but the face of the Lord is against
    those who do evil."a

13Who is going to harm you if you are eager to do good? 14But even if you should suffer for what is right, you are blessed. "Do not fear what they fearb; do not be frightened."c 15But in your hearts set apart Christ as Lord. Always be prepared to give an answer to everyone who asks you to give the reason for the hope that you have. But do this with gentleness and respect, 16keeping a clear conscience, so that those who speak maliciously against your good behavior in Christ may be ashamed of their slander. 17It is better, if it is God's will, to suffer for doing good than for doing evil. 18For Christ died for sins once for all, the righteous for the unrighteous, to bring you to God. He was put to death in the body but made alive by the Spirit, 19through whomd also he went and preached to the spirits in prison 20who disobeyed long ago when God waited patiently in the days of Noah while the ark was being built. In it only a few people, eight in all, were saved through water, 21and this water symbolizes baptism that now saves you also—not the removal of dirt from the body but the pledgee of a good conscience toward God. It saves you by the resurrection of Jesus Christ, 22who has gone into heaven and is at God's right hand—with angels, authorities and powers in submission to him.

4:1Therefore, since Christ suffered in his body, arm yourselves also with the same attitude, because he who has suffered in his body is done with sin. 2As a result, he does not live the rest of his earthly life for evil human desires, but rather for the will of God. 3For you have spent enough time in the past doing what pagans choose to do—living in debauchery, lust, drunkenness, orgies, carousing and detestable idolatry. ⁴They think it strange that you do not plunge with them into the same flood of dissipation, and they heap abuse on you. ⁵But they will have to give account to him who is ready to judge the living and the dead. ⁶For this is the reason the gospel was preached even to those who are now dead, so that they might be judged according to men in regard to the body, but live according to God in regard to the spirit.

a12 Psalm 34:12-16 *b14* Or *not fear their threats*
c14 Isaiah 8:12 *d18,19* Or *alive in the spirit,* ¹⁹*through which* *e21* Or *response*

PSALM 119:65-80

ט Teth

⁶⁵ **D**o good to your servant
        according to your word, O LORD.
⁶⁶ Teach me knowledge and good
        judgment,
    for I believe in your commands.
⁶⁷ Before I was afflicted I went astray,
    but now I obey your word.
⁶⁸ You are good, and what you do is good;
    teach me your decrees.
⁶⁹ Though the arrogant have smeared
        me with lies,
    I keep your precepts with all my
        heart.
⁷⁰ Their hearts are callous and unfeeling,
    but I delight in your law.
⁷¹ It was good for me to be afflicted
    so that I might learn your decrees.
⁷² The law from your mouth is more
        precious to me
    than thousands of pieces of silver
        and gold.

י Yodh

⁷³ Your hands made me and formed me;
    give me understanding to learn
        your commands.
⁷⁴ May those who fear you rejoice when
        they see me,
    for I have put my hope in your word.
⁷⁵ I know, O LORD, that your laws are
        righteous,
    and in faithfulness you have
        afflicted me.

⁷⁶ May your unfailing love be my
        comfort,
    according to your promise to your
        servant.
⁷⁷ Let your compassion come to me
        that I may live,
    for your law is my delight.
⁷⁸ May the arrogant be put to shame for
        wronging me without cause;
    but I will meditate on your
        precepts.
⁷⁹ May those who fear you turn to me,
    those who understand your
        statutes.
⁸⁰ May my heart be blameless toward
        your decrees,
    that I may not be put to shame.

PROVERBS 28:14

¹⁴ **B**lessed is the man who always fears
        the LORD,
    but he who hardens his heart falls
        into trouble.

□ D A Y   3 3 0

GOD SIGHTINGS

November 26

DANIEL 2:24–3:30

Then Daniel went to Arioch, whom the king had appointed to execute the wise men of Babylon, and said to him, "Do not execute the wise men of Babylon. Take me to the king, and I will interpret his dream for him."

²⁵ Arioch took Daniel to the king at once and said, "I have found a man among the exiles from Judah who can tell the king what his dream means."

²⁶ The king asked Daniel (also called Belteshazzar), "Are you able to tell me what I saw in my dream and interpret it?"

²⁷ Daniel replied, "No wise man, enchanter, magician or diviner can explain to the king the mystery he has asked about, ²⁸ but there is a God in heaven who reveals mysteries. He has shown

King Nebuchadnezzar what will happen in days to come. Your dream and the visions that passed through your mind as you lay on your bed are these:

29"As you were lying there, O king, your mind turned to things to come, and the revealer of mysteries showed you what is going to happen. 30As for me, this mystery has been revealed to me, not because I have greater wisdom than other living men, but so that you, O king, may know the interpretation and that you may understand what went through your mind.

31"You looked, O king, and there before you stood a large statue—an enormous, dazzling statue, awesome in appearance. 32The head of the statue was made of pure gold, its chest and arms of silver, its belly and thighs of bronze, 33its legs of iron, its feet partly of iron and partly of baked clay. 34While you were watching, a rock was cut out, but not by human hands. It struck the statue on its feet of iron and clay and smashed them. 35Then the iron, the clay, the bronze, the silver and the gold were broken to pieces at the same time and became like chaff on a threshing floor in the summer. The wind swept them away without leaving a trace. But the rock that struck the statue became a huge mountain and filled the whole earth.

36"This was the dream, and now we will interpret it to the king. 37You, O king, are the king of kings. The God of heaven has given you dominion and power and might and glory; 38in your hands he has placed mankind and the beasts of the field and the birds of the air. Wherever they live, he has made you ruler over them all. You are that head of gold.

39"After you, another kingdom will rise, inferior to yours. Next, a third kingdom, one of bronze, will rule over the whole earth. 40Finally, there will be a fourth kingdom, strong as iron—for iron breaks and smashes everything—and as iron breaks things to pieces, so it will crush and break all the others. 41Just as you saw that the feet and toes were partly of baked clay and partly of

iron, so this will be a divided kingdom; yet it will have some of the strength of iron in it, even as you saw iron mixed with clay. 42As the toes were partly iron and partly clay, so this kingdom will be partly strong and partly brittle. 43And just as you saw the iron mixed with baked clay, so the people will be a mixture and will not remain united, any more than iron mixes with clay.

44"In the time of those kings, the God of heaven will set up a kingdom that will never be destroyed, nor will it be left to another people. It will crush all those kingdoms and bring them to an end, but it will itself endure forever. 45This is the meaning of the vision of the rock cut out of a mountain, but not by human hands—a rock that broke the iron, the bronze, the clay, the silver and the gold to pieces.

"The great God has shown the king what will take place in the future. The dream is true and the interpretation is trustworthy."

46Then King Nebuchadnezzar fell prostrate before Daniel and paid him honor and ordered that an offering and incense be presented to him. 47The king said to Daniel, "Surely your God is the God of gods and the Lord of kings and a revealer of mysteries, for you were able to reveal this mystery."

48Then the king placed Daniel in a high position and lavished many gifts on him. He made him ruler over the entire province of Babylon and placed him in charge of all its wise men. 49Moreover, at Daniel's request the king appointed Shadrach, Meshach and Abednego administrators over the province of Babylon, while Daniel himself remained at the royal court.

3:1KING Nebuchadnezzar made an image of gold, ninety feet high and nine feet[a] wide, and set it up on the plain of Dura in the province of Babylon. 2He then summoned the satraps, prefects, governors, advisers, treasurers, judges, magistrates and all the other provincial officials to come to the dedication of the image he had set up. 3So the satraps, prefects, governors, advisers, treasurers, judges, magistrates and all the other provincial officials assembled for the dedication of the image that King Nebuchadnezzar had set up, and they stood before it.

⁴Then the herald loudly proclaimed, "This is what you are commanded to do, O peoples, nations and men of every language: ⁵As soon as you hear the sound of the horn, flute, zither, lyre, harp, pipes and all kinds of music, you must fall down and worship the image of gold that King Nebuchadnezzar has set up. ⁶Whoever does not fall down and worship will immediately be thrown into a blazing furnace."

⁷Therefore, as soon as they heard the sound of the horn, flute, zither, lyre, harp and all kinds of music, all the peoples, nations and men of every language fell down and worshiped the image of gold that King Nebuchadnezzar had set up.

⁸At this time some astrologersᵇ came forward and denounced the Jews. ⁹They said to King Nebuchadnezzar, "O king, live forever! ¹⁰You have issued a decree, O king, that everyone who hears the sound of the horn, flute, zither, lyre, harp, pipes and all kinds of music must fall down and worship the image of gold, ¹¹and that whoever does not fall down and worship will be thrown into a blazing furnace. ¹²But there are some Jews whom you have set over the affairs of the province of Babylon—Shadrach, Meshach and Abednego—who pay no attention to you, O king. They neither serve your gods nor worship the image of gold you have set up."

¹³Furious with rage, Nebuchadnezzar summoned Shadrach, Meshach and Abednego. So these men were brought before the king, ¹⁴and Nebuchadnezzar said to them, "Is it true, Shadrach, Meshach and Abednego, that you do not serve my gods or worship the image of gold I have set up? ¹⁵Now when you hear the sound of the horn, flute, zither, lyre, harp, pipes and all kinds of music, if you are ready to fall down and worship the image I made, very good. But if you do not worship it, you will be

thrown immediately into a blazing furnace. Then what god will be able to rescue you from my hand?"

¹⁶Shadrach, Meshach and Abednego replied to the king, "O Nebuchadnezzar, we do not need to defend ourselves before you in this matter. ¹⁷If we are thrown into the blazing furnace, the God we serve is able to save us from it, and he will rescue us from your hand, O king. ¹⁸But even if he does not, we want you to know, O king, that we will not serve your gods or worship the image of gold you have set up."

¹⁹Then Nebuchadnezzar was furious with Shadrach, Meshach and Abednego, and his attitude toward them changed. He ordered the furnace heated seven times hotter than usual ²⁰and commanded some of the strongest soldiers in his army to tie up Shadrach, Meshach and Abednego and throw them into the blazing furnace. ²¹So these men, wearing their robes, trousers, turbans and other clothes, were bound and thrown into the blazing furnace. ²²The king's command was so urgent and the furnace so hot that the flames of the fire killed the soldiers who took up Shadrach, Meshach and Abednego, ²³and these three men, firmly tied, fell into the blazing furnace.

²⁴Then King Nebuchadnezzar leaped to his feet in amazement and asked his advisers, "Weren't there three men that we tied up and threw into the fire?"

They replied, "Certainly, O king."

²⁵He said, "Look! I see four men walking around in the fire, unbound and unharmed, and the fourth looks like a son of the gods."

²⁶Nebuchadnezzar then approached the opening of the blazing furnace and shouted, "Shadrach, Meshach and Abednego, servants of the Most High God, come out! Come here!"

So Shadrach, Meshach and Abednego came out of the fire, ²⁷and the satraps, prefects, governors and royal advisers crowded around them. They saw that the fire had not harmed their bodies, nor was a hair of their heads singed; their robes were not scorched, and there was no smell of fire on them.

28Then Nebuchadnezzar said, "Praise be to the God of Shadrach, Meshach and Abednego, who has sent his angel and rescued his servants! They trusted in him and defied the king's command and were willing to give up their lives rather than serve or worship any god except their own God. 29Therefore I decree that the people of any nation or language who say anything against the God of Shadrach, Meshach and Abednego be cut into pieces and their houses be turned into piles of rubble, for no other god can save in this way."

30Then the king promoted Shadrach, Meshach and Abednego in the province of Babylon.

a1 Aramaic sixty cubits high and six cubits wide (about 27 meters high and 2.7 meters wide) b8 Or Chaldeans

1 PETER 4:7–5:14

The end of all things is near. Therefore be clear minded and self-controlled so that you can pray. 8Above all, love each other deeply, because love covers over a multitude of sins. 9Offer hospitality to one another without grumbling. 10Each one should use whatever gift he has received to serve others, faithfully administering God's grace in its various forms. 11If anyone speaks, he should do it as one speaking the very words of God. If anyone serves, he should do it with the strength God provides, so that in all things God may be praised through Jesus Christ. To him be the glory and the power for ever and ever. Amen.

12Dear friends, do not be surprised at the painful trial you are suffering, as though something strange were happening to you. 13But rejoice that you participate in the sufferings of Christ, so that you may be overjoyed when his glory is revealed. 14If you are insulted because of the name of Christ, you are blessed, for the Spirit of glory and of God rests on you. 15If you suffer, it should not be as a murderer or thief or any other kind of criminal, or even as a meddler. 16However, if you suffer as a

Christian, do not be ashamed, but praise God that you bear that name. 17For it is time for judgment to begin with the family of God; and if it begins with us, what will the outcome be for those who do not obey the gospel of God? 18And,

> "If it is hard for the righteous to be
> saved,
> what will become of the ungodly
> and the sinner?"*a*

19So then, those who suffer according to God's will should commit themselves to their faithful Creator and continue to do good.

5:1To the elders among you, I appeal as a fellow elder, a witness of Christ's sufferings and one who also will share in the glory to be revealed: 2Be shepherds of God's flock that is under your care, serving as overseers—not because you must, but because you are willing, as God wants you to be; not greedy for money, but eager to serve; 3not lording it over those entrusted to you, but being examples to the flock. 4And when the Chief Shepherd appears, you will receive the crown of glory that will never fade away.

5Young men, in the same way be submissive to those who are older. All of you, clothe yourselves with humility toward one another, because,

> "God opposes the proud
> but gives grace to the humble."*b*

6Humble yourselves, therefore, under God's mighty hand, that he may lift you up in due time. 7Cast all your anxiety on him because he cares for you.

8Be self-controlled and alert. Your enemy the devil prowls around like a roaring lion looking for someone to devour. 9Resist him, standing firm in the faith, because you know that your brothers throughout the world are undergoing the same kind of sufferings.

10And the God of all grace, who called you to his eternal glory in Christ, after you have suffered a little while, will himself restore you and make you

strong, firm and steadfast. ¹¹To him be
the power for ever and ever. Amen.

¹²With the help of Silas,ᶜ whom I regard as a faithful brother, I have written
to you briefly, encouraging you and testifying that this is the true grace of God.
Stand fast in it.

¹³She who is in Babylon, chosen together with you, sends you her greetings, and so does my son Mark. ¹⁴Greet
one another with a kiss of love.

Peace to all of you who are in Christ.

a18 Prov. 11:31   *b5* Prov. 3:34   *c12* Greek *Silvanus,* a
variant of *Silas*

PSALM 119:81-96

כ Kaph

⁸¹**M**y soul faints with longing for your
        [the Lᴏʀᴅ's] salvation,
    but I have put my hope in your
        word.
⁸²My eyes fail, looking for your promise;
    I say, "When will you comfort
        me?"
⁸³Though I am like a wineskin in the
        smoke,
    I do not forget your decrees.
⁸⁴How long must your servant wait?
    When will you punish my
        persecutors?
⁸⁵The arrogant dig pitfalls for me,
    contrary to your law.
⁸⁶All your commands are trustworthy;
    help me, for men persecute me
        without cause.
⁸⁷They almost wiped me from the earth,
    but I have not forsaken your
        precepts.
⁸⁸Preserve my life according to your
        love,
    and I will obey the statutes of your
        mouth.

ל Lamedh

⁸⁹Your word, O Lᴏʀᴅ, is eternal;
    it stands firm in the heavens.
⁹⁰Your faithfulness continues through
        all generations;
    you established the earth, and it
        endures.

⁹¹Your laws endure to this day,
    for all things serve you.
⁹²If your law had not been my delight,
    I would have perished in my
        affliction.
⁹³I will never forget your precepts,
    for by them you have preserved my
        life.
⁹⁴Save me, for I am yours;
    I have sought out your precepts.
⁹⁵The wicked are waiting to destroy
        me,
    but I will ponder your statutes.
⁹⁶To all perfection I see a limit;
    but your commands are
        boundless.

PROVERBS 28:15-16

¹⁵**L**ike a roaring lion or a charging bear
    is a wicked man ruling over a
        helpless people.

¹⁶A tyrannical ruler lacks judgment,
    but he who hates ill-gotten gain
        will enjoy a long life.

□ DAY 331

GOD SIGHTINGS

November 27

DANIEL 4:1-37

King Nebuchadnezzar,

    To the peoples, nations and men
of every language, who live in all
the world:

    May you prosper greatly!

²It is my pleasure to tell you
about the miraculous signs and
wonders that the Most High God
has performed for me.

³ How great are his signs,
    how mighty his wonders!
His kingdom is an eternal
        kingdom;
    his dominion endures from
        generation to generation.

⁴I, Nebuchadnezzar, was at home in my palace, contented and prosperous. ⁵I had a dream that made me afraid. As I was lying in my bed, the images and visions that passed through my mind terrified me. ⁶So I commanded that all the wise men of Babylon be brought before me to interpret the dream for me. ⁷When the magicians, enchanters, astrologers*a* and diviners came, I told them the dream, but they could not interpret it for me. ⁸Finally, Daniel came into my presence and I told him the dream. (He is called Belteshazzar, after the name of my god, and the spirit of the holy gods is in him.)

⁹I said, "Belteshazzar, chief of the magicians, I know that the spirit of the holy gods is in you, and no mystery is too difficult for you. Here is my dream; interpret it for me. ¹⁰These are the visions I saw while lying in my bed: I looked, and there before me stood a tree in the middle of the land. Its height was enormous. ¹¹The tree grew large and strong and its top touched the sky; it was visible to the ends of the earth. ¹²Its leaves were beautiful, its fruit abundant, and on it was food for all. Under it the beasts of the field found shelter, and the birds of the air lived in its branches; from it every creature was fed.

¹³"In the visions I saw while lying in my bed, I looked, and there before me was a messenger,*b* a holy one, coming down from heaven. ¹⁴He called in a loud voice: 'Cut down the tree and trim off its branches; strip off its leaves and scatter its fruit. Let the animals flee from under it and the birds from its branches. ¹⁵But let the stump and its roots, bound with iron and bronze, remain in the ground, in the grass of the field.

"'Let him be drenched with the dew of heaven, and let him live with the animals among the plants of the

earth. ¹⁶Let his mind be changed from that of a man and let him be given the mind of an animal, till seven times*c* pass by for him.

¹⁷"'The decision is announced by messengers, the holy ones declare the verdict, so that the living may know that the Most High is sovereign over the kingdoms of men and gives them to anyone he wishes and sets over them the lowliest of men.'

¹⁸"This is the dream that I, King Nebuchadnezzar, had. Now, Belteshazzar, tell me what it means, for none of the wise men in my kingdom can interpret it for me. But you can, because the spirit of the holy gods is in you."

¹⁹Then Daniel (also called Belteshazzar) was greatly perplexed for a time, and his thoughts terrified him. So the king said, "Belteshazzar, do not let the dream or its meaning alarm you."

Belteshazzar answered, "My lord, if only the dream applied to your enemies and its meaning to your adversaries! ²⁰The tree you saw, which grew large and strong, with its top touching the sky, visible to the whole earth, ²¹with beautiful leaves and abundant fruit, providing food for all, giving shelter to the beasts of the field, and having nesting places in its branches for the birds of the air— ²²you, O king, are that tree! You have become great and strong; your greatness has grown until it reaches the sky, and your dominion extends to distant parts of the earth.

²³"You, O king, saw a messenger, a holy one, coming down from heaven and saying, 'Cut down the tree and destroy it, but leave the stump, bound with iron and bronze, in the grass of the field, while its roots remain in the ground. Let him be drenched with the dew of heaven; let him live like

the wild animals, until seven times pass by for him.'

24"This is the interpretation, O king, and this is the decree the Most High has issued against my lord the king: 25 You will be driven away from people and will live with the wild animals; you will eat grass like cattle and be drenched with the dew of heaven. Seven times will pass by for you until you acknowledge that the Most High is sovereign over the kingdoms of men and gives them to anyone he wishes. 26The command to leave the stump of the tree with its roots means that your kingdom will be restored to you when you acknowledge that Heaven rules. 27Therefore, O king, be pleased to accept my advice: Renounce your sins by doing what is right, and your wickedness by being kind to the oppressed. It may be that then your prosperity will continue."

28All this happened to King Nebuchadnezzar. 29Twelve months later, as the king was walking on the roof of the royal palace of Babylon, 30he said, "Is not this the great Babylon I have built as the royal residence, by my mighty power and for the glory of my majesty?"

31The words were still on his lips when a voice came from heaven, "This is what is decreed for you, King Nebuchadnezzar: Your royal authority has been taken from you. 32You will be driven away from people and will live with the wild animals; you will eat grass like cattle. Seven times will pass for you until you acknowledge that the Most High is sovereign over the kingdoms of men and gives them to anyone he wishes."

33Immediately what had been said about Nebuchadnezzar was fulfilled. He was driven away from people and ate grass like cattle. His body was drenched with the dew of heaven until his hair grew like the feathers of an eagle and his nails like the claws of a bird.

34At the end of that time, I, Nebuchadnezzar, raised my eyes toward heaven, and my sanity was restored. Then I praised the Most High; I honored and glorified him who lives forever.

His dominion is an eternal dominion;
    his kingdom endures from generation to generation.
35All the peoples of the earth are regarded as nothing.
He does as he pleases with the powers of heaven and the peoples of the earth.
No one can hold back his hand or say to him: "What have you done?"

36At the same time that my sanity was restored, my honor and splendor were returned to me for the glory of my kingdom. My advisers and nobles sought me out, and I was restored to my throne and became even greater than before. 37Now I, Nebuchadnezzar, praise and exalt and glorify the King of heaven, because everything he does is right and all his ways are just. And those who walk in pride he is able to humble.

a7 Or *Chaldeans*   b13 Or *watchman*; also in verses 17 and 23   c16 Or *years*; also in verses 23, 25 and 32

2 PETER 1:1-21

Simon Peter, a servant and apostle of Jesus Christ,

To those who through the righteousness of our God and Savior Jesus Christ have received a faith as precious as ours:

2Grace and peace be yours in abundance through the knowledge of God and of Jesus our Lord.

3His divine power has given us everything we need for life and godliness through our knowledge of him who called us by his own glory and goodness. [4]Through these he has given us his very great and precious promises, so that through them you may participate in the divine nature and escape the corruption in the world caused by evil desires.

[5]For this very reason, make every effort to add to your faith goodness; and to goodness, knowledge; [6]and to knowledge, self-control; and to self-control, perseverance; and to perseverance, godliness; [7]and to godliness, brotherly kindness; and to brotherly kindness, love. [8]For if you possess these qualities in increasing measure, they will keep you from being ineffective and unproductive in your knowledge of our Lord Jesus Christ. [9]But if anyone does not have them, he is nearsighted and blind, and has forgotten that he has been cleansed from his past sins.

[10]Therefore, my brothers, be all the more eager to make your calling and election sure. For if you do these things, you will never fall, [11]and you will receive a rich welcome into the eternal kingdom of our Lord and Savior Jesus Christ.

[12]So I will always remind you of these things, even though you know them and are firmly established in the truth you now have. [13]I think it is right to refresh your memory as long as I live in the tent of this body, [14]because I know that I will soon put it aside, as our Lord Jesus Christ has made clear to me. [15]And I will make every effort to see that after my departure you will always be able to remember these things.

[16]We did not follow cleverly invented stories when we told you about the power and coming of our Lord Jesus Christ, but we were eyewitnesses of his majesty. [17]For he received honor and glory from God the Father when the voice came to him from the Majestic Glory, saying, "This is my Son, whom I love; with him I am well pleased."[a] [18]We ourselves heard this voice that came from heaven when we were with him on the sacred mountain.

[19]And we have the word of the prophets made more certain, and you will do well to pay attention to it, as to a light shining in a dark place, until the day dawns and the morning star rises in your hearts. **[20]Above all, you must understand that no prophecy of Scripture came about by the prophet's own interpretation. [21]For prophecy never had its origin in the will of man, but men spoke from God as they were carried along by the Holy Spirit.**

*a*17 Matt. 17:5; Mark 9:7; Luke 9:35

PSALM 119:97-112

מ Mem

[97] **O**h, how I love your [the Lord's] law!
　　I meditate on it all day long.
[98] Your commands make me wiser than
　　　my enemies,
　　for they are ever with me.
[99] I have more insight than all my
　　　teachers,
　　for I meditate on your statutes.
[100] I have more understanding than the
　　　elders,
　　for I obey your precepts.
[101] I have kept my feet from every evil
　　　path
　　so that I might obey your word.
[102] I have not departed from your laws,
　　for you yourself have taught me.
[103] How sweet are your words to my taste,
　　sweeter than honey to my mouth!
[104] I gain understanding from your
　　　precepts;
　　therefore I hate every wrong path.

נ Nun

[105] Your word is a lamp to my feet
　　and a light for my path.
[106] I have taken an oath and confirmed it,
　　that I will follow your righteous laws.
[107] I have suffered much;
　　preserve my life, O Lord, according
　　　to your word.
[108] Accept, O Lord, the willing praise of
　　　my mouth,
　　and teach me your laws.
[109] Though I constantly take my life in
　　　my hands,
　　I will not forget your law.

110 The wicked have set a snare for me,
　　but I have not strayed from your
　　　precepts.
111 Your statutes are my heritage
　　forever;
　　they are the joy of my heart.
112 My heart is set on keeping your
　　decrees
　　to the very end.

PROVERBS 28:17-18

17 **A** man tormented by the guilt of
　　murder
　　will be a fugitive till death;
　　let no one support him.

18 He whose walk is blameless is kept
　　safe,
　　but he whose ways are perverse
　　will suddenly fall.

☐ D A Y 3 3 2

GOD SIGHTINGS

November 28

DANIEL 5:1-31

King Belshazzar gave a great banquet
for a thousand of his nobles and drank
wine with them. 2 While Belshazzar was
drinking his wine, he gave orders to
bring in the gold and silver goblets that
Nebuchadnezzar his father*a* had taken
from the temple in Jerusalem, so that
the king and his nobles, his wives and
his concubines might drink from them.
3 So they brought in the gold goblets
that had been taken from the temple of
God in Jerusalem, and the king and his
nobles, his wives and his concubines
drank from them. 4 As they drank the
wine, they praised the gods of gold and
silver, of bronze, iron, wood and stone.

5 Suddenly the fingers of a human
hand appeared and wrote on the plaster
of the wall, near the lampstand in the
royal palace. The king watched the
hand as it wrote. 6 His face turned pale

and he was so frightened that his knees
knocked together and his legs gave way.

7 The king called out for the enchanters, astrologers*b* and diviners to be
brought and said to these wise men of
Babylon, "Whoever reads this writing and
tells me what it means will be clothed in
purple and have a gold chain placed
around his neck, and he will be made the
third highest ruler in the kingdom."

8 Then all the king's wise men came
in, but they could not read the writing or
tell the king what it meant. 9 So King
Belshazzar became even more terrified
and his face grew more pale. His nobles
were baffled.

10 The queen,*c* hearing the voices of
the king and his nobles, came into the
banquet hall. "O king, live forever!" she
said. "Don't be alarmed! Don't look so
pale! 11 There is a man in your kingdom
who has the spirit of the holy gods in
him. In the time of your father he was
found to have insight and intelligence
and wisdom like that of the gods. King
Nebuchadnezzar your father—your father the king, I say—appointed him
chief of the magicians, enchanters, astrologers and diviners. 12 This man Daniel, whom the king called Belteshazzar,
was found to have a keen mind and
knowledge and understanding, and also
the ability to interpret dreams, explain
riddles and solve difficult problems.
Call for Daniel, and he will tell you what
the writing means."

13 So Daniel was brought before the
king, and the king said to him, "Are you
Daniel, one of the exiles my father the
king brought from Judah? 14 I have
heard that the spirit of the gods is in you
and that you have insight, intelligence
and outstanding wisdom. 15 The wise
men and enchanters were brought before me to read this writing and tell me
what it means, but they could not explain it. 16 Now I have heard that you are
able to give interpretations and to solve
difficult problems. If you can read this
writing and tell me what it means, you
will be clothed in purple and have a gold
chain placed around your neck, and you

will be made the third highest ruler in the kingdom."

17 Then Daniel answered the king, "You may keep your gifts for yourself and give your rewards to someone else. Nevertheless, I will read the writing for the king and tell him what it means.

18 "O king, the Most High God gave your father Nebuchadnezzar sovereignty and greatness and glory and splendor. 19 Because of the high position he gave him, all the peoples and nations and men of every language dreaded and feared him. Those the king wanted to put to death, he put to death; those he wanted to spare, he spared; those he wanted to promote, he promoted; and those he wanted to humble, he humbled. 20 But when his heart became arrogant and hardened with pride, he was deposed from his royal throne and stripped of his glory. 21 He was driven away from people and given the mind of an animal; he lived with the wild donkeys and ate grass like cattle; and his body was drenched with the dew of heaven, until he acknowledged that the Most High God is sovereign over the kingdoms of men and sets over them anyone he wishes.

22 "But you his son,*d* O Belshazzar, have not humbled yourself, though you knew all this. 23 Instead, you have set yourself up against the Lord of heaven. You had the goblets from his temple brought to you, and you and your nobles, your wives and your concubines drank wine from them. You praised the gods of silver and gold, of bronze, iron, wood and stone, which cannot see or hear or understand. But you did not honor the God who holds in his hand your life and all your ways. 24 Therefore he sent the hand that wrote the inscription.

25 "This is the inscription that was written:

MENE, MENE, TEKEL, PARSIN*e*

26 "This is what these words mean:

*Mene*f: God has numbered the days of your reign and brought it to an end.

27 *Tekel*g: You have been weighed on the scales and found wanting.

28 *Peres*h: Your kingdom is divided and given to the Medes and Persians."

29 Then at Belshazzar's command, Daniel was clothed in purple, a gold chain was placed around his neck, and he was proclaimed the third highest ruler in the kingdom.

30 That very night Belshazzar, king of the Babylonians,*i* was slain, 31 and Darius the Mede took over the kingdom, at the age of sixty-two.

a2 Or *ancestor;* or *predecessor;* also in verses 11, 13 and 18 *b7* Or *Chaldeans;* also in verse 11 *c10* Or *queen mother* *d22* Or *descendant;* or *successor* *e25* Aramaic *UPARSIN* (that is, *AND PARSIN*) *f26 Mene* can mean *numbered* or *mina* (a unit of money). *g27 Tekel* can mean *weighed* or *shekel.* *h28 Peres* (the singular of *Parsin*) can mean *divided* or *Persia* or *a half mina* or *a half shekel.* *i30* Or *Chaldeans*

2 PETER 2:1-22

But there were also false prophets among the people, just as there will be false teachers among you. They will secretly introduce destructive heresies, even denying the sovereign Lord who bought them—bringing swift destruction on themselves. 2 Many will follow their shameful ways and will bring the way of truth into disrepute. 3 In their greed these teachers will exploit you with stories they have made up. Their condemnation has long been hanging over them, and their destruction has not been sleeping.

4 For if God did not spare angels when they sinned, but sent them to hell,*a* putting them into gloomy dungeons*b* to be held for judgment; 5 if he did not spare the ancient world when he brought the flood on its ungodly people, but protected Noah, a preacher of righteousness, and seven others; 6 if he condemned the cities of Sodom and Gomorrah by burning them to ashes, and made them an example of what is going to happen to the ungodly; 7 and if he rescued Lot, a righteous man, who was distressed by the filthy lives of lawless men 8 (for that righteous man, living among them day after day, was tormented in his righteous soul

by the lawless deeds he saw and heard)—
[9] if this is so, then the Lord knows how to rescue godly men from trials and to hold the unrighteous for the day of judgment, while continuing their punishment.[c] [10] This is especially true of those who follow the corrupt desire of the sinful nature[d] and despise authority.

Bold and arrogant, these men are not afraid to slander celestial beings; [11] yet even angels, although they are stronger and more powerful, do not bring slanderous accusations against such beings in the presence of the Lord. [12] But these men blaspheme in matters they do not understand. They are like brute beasts, creatures of instinct, born only to be caught and destroyed, and like beasts they too will perish.

[13] They will be paid back with harm for the harm they have done. Their idea of pleasure is to carouse in broad daylight. They are blots and blemishes, reveling in their pleasures while they feast with you.[e] [14] With eyes full of adultery, they never stop sinning; they seduce the unstable; they are experts in greed—an accursed brood! [15] They have left the straight way and wandered off to follow the way of Balaam son of Beor, who loved the wages of wickedness. [16] But he was rebuked for his wrongdoing by a donkey—a beast without speech—who spoke with a man's voice and restrained the prophet's madness.

[17] These men are springs without water and mists driven by a storm. Blackest darkness is reserved for them. [18] For they mouth empty, boastful words and, by appealing to the lustful desires of sinful human nature, they entice people who are just escaping from those who live in error. [19] They promise them freedom, while they themselves are slaves of depravity—for a man is a slave to whatever has mastered him. [20] If they have escaped the corruption of the world by knowing our Lord and Savior Jesus Christ and are again entangled in it and overcome, they are worse off at the end than they were at the beginning. [21] It would have been better for them not to have known the way of righteousness, than to have known it and then to turn their backs on the sacred command that was passed on to them. [22] Of them the proverbs are true: "A dog returns to its vomit,"[f] and, "A sow that is washed goes back to her wallowing in the mud."

a4 Greek *Tartarus*   *b4* Some manuscripts *into chains of darkness*   *c9* Or *unrighteous for punishment until the day of judgment*   *d10* Or *the flesh*   *e13* Some manuscripts *in their love feasts*   *f22* Prov. 26:11

PSALM 119:113-128

ס   Samekh

[113] I hate double-minded men,
    but I love your [the LORD's] law.
[114] You are my refuge and my shield;
    I have put my hope in your word.
[115] Away from me, you evildoers,
    that I may keep the commands of
        my God!
[116] Sustain me according to your
        promise, and I will live;
    do not let my hopes be dashed.
[117] Uphold me, and I will be delivered;
    I will always have regard for your
        decrees.
[118] You reject all who stray from your
        decrees,
    for their deceitfulness is in vain.
[119] All the wicked of the earth you
        discard like dross;
    therefore I love your statutes.
[120] My flesh trembles in fear of you;
    I stand in awe of your laws.

ע   Ayin

[121] I have done what is righteous and just;
    do not leave me to my oppressors.
[122] Ensure your servant's well-being;
    let not the arrogant oppress me.
[123] **My eyes fail, looking for your
        salvation,
    looking for your righteous
        promise.**
[124] **Deal with your servant according
        to your love
    and teach me your decrees.**
[125] I am your servant; give me
        discernment
    that I may understand your statutes.

126 It is time for you to act, O Lord;
     your law is being broken.
127 Because I love your commands
     more than gold, more than pure gold,
128 and because I consider all your
     precepts right,
     I hate every wrong path.

PROVERBS 28:19-20

19 He who works his land will have
     abundant food,
     but the one who chases fantasies
     will have his fill of poverty.

20 A faithful man will be richly blessed,
     but one eager to get rich will not
     go unpunished.

□ DAY 333

GOD SIGHTINGS

November 29

DANIEL 6:1-28

It pleased Darius to appoint 120 satraps to rule throughout the kingdom, 2 with three administrators over them, one of whom was Daniel. The satraps were made accountable to them so that the king might not suffer loss. 3 Now Daniel so distinguished himself among the administrators and the satraps by his exceptional qualities that the king planned to set him over the whole kingdom. 4 At this, the administrators and the satraps tried to find grounds for charges against Daniel in his conduct of government affairs, but they were unable to do so. They could find no corruption in him, because he was trustworthy and neither corrupt nor negligent. 5 Finally these men said, "We will never find any basis for charges against this man Daniel unless it has something to do with the law of his God."

6 So the administrators and the satraps went as a group to the king and said: "O King Darius, live forever! 7 The royal administrators, prefects, satraps, advisers and governors have all agreed that the king should issue an edict and enforce the decree that anyone who prays to any god or man during the next thirty days, except to you, O king, shall be thrown into the lions' den. 8 Now, O king, issue the decree and put it in writing so that it cannot be altered—in accordance with the laws of the Medes and Persians, which cannot be repealed." 9 So King Darius put the decree in writing.

10 Now when Daniel learned that the decree had been published, he went home to his upstairs room where the windows opened toward Jerusalem. Three times a day he got down on his knees and prayed, giving thanks to his God, just as he had done before. 11 Then these men went as a group and found Daniel praying and asking God for help. 12 So they went to the king and spoke to him about his royal decree: "Did you not publish a decree that during the next thirty days anyone who prays to any god or man except to you, O king, would be thrown into the lions' den?"

The king answered, "The decree stands—in accordance with the laws of the Medes and Persians, which cannot be repealed."

13 Then they said to the king, "Daniel, who is one of the exiles from Judah, pays no attention to you, O king, or to the decree you put in writing. He still prays three times a day." 14 When the king heard this, he was greatly distressed; he was determined to rescue Daniel and made every effort until sundown to save him.

15 Then the men went as a group to the king and said to him, "Remember, O king, that according to the law of the Medes and Persians no decree or edict that the king issues can be changed."

16 So the king gave the order, and they brought Daniel and threw him into the lions' den. The king said to Daniel, "May your God, whom you serve continually, rescue you!"

17 A stone was brought and placed over the mouth of the den, and the king sealed it with his own signet ring and with the rings of his nobles, so that Daniel's situation might not be changed.

¹⁸Then the king returned to his palace and spent the night without eating and without any entertainment being brought to him. And he could not sleep.

¹⁹At the first light of dawn, the king got up and hurried to the lions' den. ²⁰When he came near the den, he called to Daniel in an anguished voice, "Daniel, servant of the living God, has your God, whom you serve continually, been able to rescue you from the lions?"

²¹Daniel answered, "O king, live forever! ²²My God sent his angel, and he shut the mouths of the lions. They have not hurt me, because I was found innocent in his sight. Nor have I ever done any wrong before you, O king."

²³The king was overjoyed and gave orders to lift Daniel out of the den. And when Daniel was lifted from the den, no wound was found on him, because he had trusted in his God.

²⁴At the king's command, the men who had falsely accused Daniel were brought in and thrown into the lions' den, along with their wives and children. And before they reached the floor of the den, the lions overpowered them and crushed all their bones.

²⁵Then King Darius wrote to all the peoples, nations and men of every language throughout the land:

"May you prosper greatly!

²⁶"I issue a decree that in every part of my kingdom people must fear and reverence the God of Daniel.

"For he is the living God
  and he endures forever;
his kingdom will not be destroyed,
  his dominion will never end.
²⁷He rescues and he saves;
  he performs signs and wonders
  in the heavens and on the earth.
He has rescued Daniel
  from the power of the lions."

²⁸So Daniel prospered during the reign of Darius and the reign of Cyrus*a* the Persian.

a28 Or Darius, that is, the reign of Cyrus

2 PETER 3:1-18

Dear friends, this is now my second letter to you. I have written both of them as reminders to stimulate you to wholesome thinking. ²I want you to recall the words spoken in the past by the holy prophets and the command given by our Lord and Savior through your apostles.

³First of all, you must understand that in the last days scoffers will come, scoffing and following their own evil desires. ⁴They will say, "Where is this 'coming' he promised? Ever since our fathers died, everything goes on as it has since the beginning of creation." ⁵But they deliberately forget that long ago by God's word the heavens existed and the earth was formed out of water and by water. ⁶By these waters also the world of that time was deluged and destroyed. ⁷By the same word the present heavens and earth are reserved for fire, being kept for the day of judgment and destruction of ungodly men.

⁸But do not forget this one thing, dear friends: With the Lord a day is like a thousand years, and a thousand years are like a day. ⁹**The Lord is not slow in keeping his promise, as some understand slowness. He is patient with you, not wanting anyone to perish, but everyone to come to repentance.**

¹⁰But the day of the Lord will come like a thief. The heavens will disappear with a roar; the elements will be destroyed by fire, and the earth and everything in it will be laid bare.*a*

¹¹Since everything will be destroyed in this way, what kind of people ought you to be? You ought to live holy and godly lives ¹²as you look forward to the day of God and speed its coming.*b* That day will bring about the destruction of the heavens by fire, and the elements will melt in the heat. ¹³But in keeping with his promise we are looking forward to a new heaven and a new earth, the home of righteousness.

¹⁴So then, dear friends, since you are looking forward to this, make every effort to be found spotless, blameless and at peace with him. ¹⁵Bear in mind

that our Lord's patience means salvation, just as our dear brother Paul also wrote you with the wisdom that God gave him. [16]He writes the same way in all his letters, speaking in them of these matters. His letters contain some things that are hard to understand, which ignorant and unstable people distort, as they do the other Scriptures, to their own destruction.

[17]Therefore, dear friends, since you already know this, be on your guard so that you may not be carried away by the error of lawless men and fall from your secure position. [18]But grow in the grace and knowledge of our Lord and Savior Jesus Christ. To him be glory both now and forever! Amen.

a10 Some manuscripts *be burned up*   b12 Or *as you wait eagerly for the day of God to come*

PSALM 119:129-152

פ Pe

[129]**Y**our [the LORD's] statutes are wonderful;
therefore I obey them.
[130]The unfolding of your words gives light;
it gives understanding to the simple.
[131]I open my mouth and pant,
longing for your commands.
[132]Turn to me and have mercy on me,
as you always do to those who love your name.
[133]Direct my footsteps according to your word;
let no sin rule over me.
[134]Redeem me from the oppression of men,
that I may obey your precepts.
[135]Make your face shine upon your servant
and teach me your decrees.
[136]Streams of tears flow from my eyes,
for your law is not obeyed.

צ Tsadhe

[137]Righteous are you, O LORD,
and your laws are right.

[138]The statutes you have laid down are righteous;
they are fully trustworthy.
[139]My zeal wears me out,
for my enemies ignore your words.
[140]Your promises have been thoroughly tested,
and your servant loves them.
[141]Though I am lowly and despised,
I do not forget your precepts.
[142]Your righteousness is everlasting
and your law is true.
[143]Trouble and distress have come upon me,
but your commands are my delight.
[144]Your statutes are forever right;
give me understanding that I may live.

ק Qoph

[145]I call with all my heart; answer me, O LORD,
and I will obey your decrees.
[146]I call out to you; save me
and I will keep your statutes.
[147]I rise before dawn and cry for help;
I have put my hope in your word.
[148]My eyes stay open through the watches of the night,
that I may meditate on your promises.
[149]Hear my voice in accordance with your love;
preserve my life, O LORD, according to your laws.
[150]Those who devise wicked schemes are near,
but they are far from your law.
[151]Yet you are near, O LORD,
and all your commands are true.
[152]Long ago I learned from your statutes
that you established them to last forever.

PROVERBS 28:21-22

[21]**T**o show partiality is not good—
yet a man will do wrong for a piece of bread.

[22]A stingy man is eager to get rich
and is unaware that poverty awaits him.

GOD SIGHTINGS

November 30

DANIEL 7:1-28

In the first year of Belshazzar king of Babylon, Daniel had a dream, and visions passed through his mind as he was lying on his bed. He wrote down the substance of his dream.

²Daniel said: "In my vision at night I looked, and there before me were the four winds of heaven churning up the great sea. ³Four great beasts, each different from the others, came up out of the sea.

⁴"The first was like a lion, and it had the wings of an eagle. I watched until its wings were torn off and it was lifted from the ground so that it stood on two feet like a man, and the heart of a man was given to it.

⁵"And there before me was a second beast, which looked like a bear. It was raised up on one of its sides, and it had three ribs in its mouth between its teeth. It was told, 'Get up and eat your fill of flesh!'

⁶"After that, I looked, and there before me was another beast, one that looked like a leopard. And on its back it had four wings like those of a bird. This beast had four heads, and it was given authority to rule.

⁷"After that, in my vision at night I looked, and there before me was a fourth beast—terrifying and frightening and very powerful. It had large iron teeth; it crushed and devoured its victims and trampled underfoot whatever was left. It was different from all the former beasts, and it had ten horns.

⁸"While I was thinking about the horns, there before me was another horn, a little one, which came up among them; and three of the first horns were uprooted before it. This horn had eyes like the eyes of a man and a mouth that spoke boastfully.

⁹"As I looked,

"thrones were set in place,
    and the Ancient of Days took his
        seat.
His clothing was as white as snow;
    the hair of his head was white like
        wool.
His throne was flaming with fire,
    and its wheels were all ablaze.
¹⁰A river of fire was flowing,
    coming out from before him.
Thousands upon thousands attended
        him;
    ten thousand times ten thousand
        stood before him.
The court was seated,
    and the books were opened.

¹¹"Then I continued to watch because of the boastful words the horn was speaking. I kept looking until the beast was slain and its body destroyed and thrown into the blazing fire. ¹²(The other beasts had been stripped of their authority, but were allowed to live for a period of time.)

¹³"In my vision at night I looked, and there before me was one like a son of man, coming with the clouds of heaven. He approached the Ancient of Days and was led into his presence. ¹⁴He was given authority, glory and sovereign power; all peoples, nations and men of every language worshiped him. His dominion is an everlasting dominion that will not pass away, and his kingdom is one that will never be destroyed.

¹⁵"I, Daniel, was troubled in spirit, and the visions that passed through my mind disturbed me. ¹⁶I approached one of those standing there and asked him the true meaning of all this.

"So he told me and gave me the interpretation of these things: ¹⁷'The four great beasts are four kingdoms that will rise from the earth. ¹⁸But the saints of the Most High will receive the kingdom and will possess it forever—yes, for ever and ever.'

¹⁹"Then I wanted to know the true meaning of the fourth beast, which was

different from all the others and most terrifying, with its iron teeth and bronze claws—the beast that crushed and devoured its victims and trampled underfoot whatever was left. 20I also wanted to know about the ten horns on its head and about the other horn that came up, before which three of them fell—the horn that looked more imposing than the others and that had eyes and a mouth that spoke boastfully. 21As I watched, this horn was waging war against the saints and defeating them, 22until the Ancient of Days came and pronounced judgment in favor of the saints of the Most High, and the time came when they possessed the kingdom.

23"He gave me this explanation: 'The fourth beast is a fourth kingdom that will appear on earth. It will be different from all the other kingdoms and will devour the whole earth, trampling it down and crushing it. 24The ten horns are ten kings who will come from this kingdom. After them another king will arise, different from the earlier ones; he will subdue three kings. 25He will speak against the Most High and oppress his saints and try to change the set times and the laws. The saints will be handed over to him for a time, times and half a time.a

26" 'But the court will sit, and his power will be taken away and completely destroyed forever. 27Then the sovereignty, power and greatness of the kingdoms under the whole heaven will be handed over to the saints, the people of the Most High. His kingdom will be an everlasting kingdom, and all rulers will worship and obey him.'

28"This is the end of the matter. I, Daniel, was deeply troubled by my thoughts, and my face turned pale, but I kept the matter to myself."

a25 Or for a year, two years and half a year

1 JOHN 1:1-10

That which was from the beginning, which we have heard, which we have seen with our eyes, which we have looked at and our hands have touched— this we proclaim concerning the Word

of life. 2The life appeared; we have seen it and testify to it, and we proclaim to you the eternal life, which was with the Father and has appeared to us. 3We proclaim to you what we have seen and heard, so that you also may have fellowship with us. And our fellowship is with the Father and with his Son, Jesus Christ. 4We write this to make oura joy complete.

5This is the message we have heard from him and declare to you: God is light; in him there is no darkness at all. 6If we claim to have fellowship with him yet walk in the darkness, we lie and do not live by the truth. 7**But if we walk in the light, as he is in the light, we have fellowship with one another, and the blood of Jesus, his Son, purifies us from all**b **sin.**

8If we claim to be without sin, we deceive ourselves and the truth is not in us. 9If we confess our sins, he is faithful and just and will forgive us our sins and purify us from all unrighteousness. 10If we claim we have not sinned, we make him out to be a liar and his word has no place in our lives.

a4 Some manuscripts your   b7 Or every

PSALM 119:153-176

ר   Resh

153 Look upon my suffering and deliver me,
    for I have not forgotten your [the
    LORD'S] law.
154 Defend my cause and redeem me;
    preserve my life according to your
    promise.
155 Salvation is far from the wicked,
    for they do not seek out your
    decrees.
156 Your compassion is great, O LORD;
    preserve my life according to your
    laws.
157 Many are the foes who persecute me,
    but I have not turned from your
    statutes.
158 I look on the faithless with
    loathing,
    for they do not obey your word.

159 See how I love your precepts;
preserve my life, O LORD, according
to your love.
160 All your words are true;
all your righteous laws are eternal.

ש Sin and Shin

161 Rulers persecute me without cause,
but my heart trembles at your word.
162 I rejoice in your promise
like one who finds great spoil.
163 I hate and abhor falsehood
but I love your law.
164 Seven times a day I praise you
for your righteous laws.
165 Great peace have they who love your
law,
and nothing can make them
stumble.
166 I wait for your salvation, O LORD,
and I follow your commands.
167 I obey your statutes,
for I love them greatly.
168 I obey your precepts and your
statutes,
for all my ways are known to you.

ת Taw

169 May my cry come before you,
O LORD;

give me understanding according
to your word.
170 May my supplication come before
you;
deliver me according to your
promise.
171 May my lips overflow with praise,
for you teach me your decrees.
172 May my tongue sing of your word,
for all your commands are
righteous.
173 May your hand be ready to help me,
for I have chosen your precepts.
174 I long for your salvation, O LORD,
and your law is my delight.
175 Let me live that I may praise you,
and may your laws sustain me.
176 I have strayed like a lost sheep.
Seek your servant,
for I have not forgotten your
commands.

PROVERBS 28:23-24
23 He who rebukes a man will in the
end gain more favor
than he who has a flattering
tongue.

24 He who robs his father or mother
and says, "It's not wrong"—
he is partner to him who destroys.

GOD SIGHTINGS

December 1

DANIEL 8:1-27

In the third year of King Belshazzar's reign, I, Daniel, had a vision, after the one that had already appeared to me. ²In my vision I saw myself in the citadel of Susa in the province of Elam; in the vision I was beside the Ulai Canal. ³I looked up, and there before me was a ram with two horns, standing beside the canal, and the horns were long. One of the horns was longer than the other but grew up later. ⁴I watched the ram as he charged toward the west and the north and the south. No animal could stand against him, and none could rescue from his power. He did as he pleased and became great.

⁵As I was thinking about this, suddenly a goat with a prominent horn between his eyes came from the west, crossing the whole earth without touching the ground. ⁶He came toward the two-horned ram I had seen standing beside the canal and charged at him in great rage. ⁷I saw him attack the ram furiously, striking the ram and shattering his two horns. The ram was powerless to stand against him; the goat knocked him to the ground and trampled on him, and none could rescue the ram from his power. ⁸The goat became very great, but at the height of his power his large horn was broken off, and in its place four prominent horns grew up toward the four winds of heaven.

⁹Out of one of them came another horn, which started small but grew in power to the south and to the east and toward the Beautiful Land. ¹⁰It grew until it reached the host of the heavens, and it threw some of the starry host down to the earth and trampled on them. ¹¹It set itself up to be as great as the Prince of the host; it took away the daily sacrifice from him, and the place of his sanctuary was brought low. ¹²Because of rebellion, the host ⌊of the saints⌋ᵃ and the daily sacrifice were given over to it. It prospered in everything it did, and truth was thrown to the ground.

¹³Then I heard a holy one speaking, and another holy one said to him, "How long will it take for the vision to be fulfilled—the vision concerning the daily sacrifice, the rebellion that causes desolation, and the surrender of the sanctuary and of the host that will be trampled underfoot?"

¹⁴He said to me, "It will take 2,300 evenings and mornings; then the sanctuary will be reconsecrated."

¹⁵While I, Daniel, was watching the vision and trying to understand it, there before me stood one who looked like a man. ¹⁶And I heard a man's voice from the Ulai calling, "Gabriel, tell this man the meaning of the vision."

¹⁷As he came near the place where I was standing, I was terrified and fell prostrate. "Son of man," he said to me, "understand that the vision concerns the time of the end."

¹⁸While he was speaking to me, I was in a deep sleep, with my face to the ground. Then he touched me and raised me to my feet.

¹⁹He said: "I am going to tell you what will happen later in the time of wrath, because the vision concerns the appointed time of the end.ᵇ ²⁰The two-horned ram that you saw represents the kings of Media and Persia. ²¹The shaggy goat is the king of Greece, and the large horn between his eyes is the first king. ²²The four horns that replaced the one that was broken off represent four kingdoms that will emerge from his nation but will not have the same power.

²³"In the latter part of their reign, when rebels have become completely wicked, a stern-faced king, a master of

intrigue, will arise. 24He will become very strong, but not by his own power. He will cause astounding devastation and will succeed in whatever he does. He will destroy the mighty men and the holy people. 25He will cause deceit to prosper, and he will consider himself superior. When they feel secure, he will destroy many and take his stand against the Prince of princes. Yet he will be destroyed, but not by human power.

26"The vision of the evenings and mornings that has been given you is true, but seal up the vision, for it concerns the distant future."

27I, Daniel, was exhausted and lay ill for several days. Then I got up and went about the king's business. I was appalled by the vision; it was beyond understanding.

a12 Or rebellion, the armies b19 Or because the end will be at the appointed time

1 JOHN 2:1-17

My dear children, I write this to you so that you will not sin. But if anybody does sin, we have one who speaks to the Father in our defense—Jesus Christ, the Righteous One. 2He is the atoning sacrifice for our sins, and not only for ours but also for*a* the sins of the whole world.

3We know that we have come to know him if we obey his commands. 4The man who says, "I know him," but does not do what he commands is a liar, and the truth is not in him. 5**But if anyone obeys his word, God's love*b* is truly made complete in him. This is how we know we are in him: 6Whoever claims to live in him must walk as Jesus did.**

7Dear friends, I am not writing you a new command but an old one, which you have had since the beginning. This old command is the message you have heard. 8Yet I am writing you a new command; its truth is seen in him and you, because the darkness is passing and the true light is already shining.

9Anyone who claims to be in the light but hates his brother is still in the darkness. 10Whoever loves his brother lives

in the light, and there is nothing in him*c* to make him stumble. 11But whoever hates his brother is in the darkness and walks around in the darkness; he does not know where he is going, because the darkness has blinded him.

12I write to you, dear children,
  because your sins have been
    forgiven on account of his
    name.
13I write to you, fathers,
  because you have known him who
    is from the beginning.
I write to you, young men,
  because you have overcome the
    evil one.
I write to you, dear children,
  because you have known the
    Father.
14I write to you, fathers,
  because you have known him who
    is from the beginning.
I write to you, young men,
  because you are strong,
  and the word of God lives in you,
  and you have overcome the evil
    one.

15Do not love the world or anything in the world. If anyone loves the world, the love of the Father is not in him. 16For everything in the world—the cravings of sinful man, the lust of his eyes and the boasting of what he has and does—comes not from the Father but from the world. 17The world and its desires pass away, but the man who does the will of God lives forever.

a2 Or He is the one who turns aside God's wrath, taking away our sins, and not only ours but also b5 Or word, love for God c10 Or it

PSALM 120:1-7
A song of ascents.

1I call on the LORD in my distress,
  and he answers me.
2Save me, O LORD, from lying lips
  and from deceitful tongues.

3What will he do to you,
  and what more besides,
    O deceitful tongue?

4 He will punish you with a warrior's
  sharp arrows,
    with burning coals of the broom
    tree.

5 Woe to me that I dwell in Meshech,
    that I live among the tents of
    Kedar!
6 Too long have I lived
    among those who hate peace.
7 I am a man of peace;
    but when I speak, they are for war.

PROVERBS 28:25-26

25 **A** greedy man stirs up dissension,
    but he who trusts in the LORD will
    prosper.

26 He who trusts in himself is a fool,
    but he who walks in wisdom is
    kept safe.

☐ D A Y 3 3 6

GOD SIGHTINGS

December 2

DANIEL 9:1–11:1

In the first year of Darius son of Xerxes*a*
(a Mede by descent), who was made ruler
over the Babylonian*b* kingdom— 2 in the
first year of his reign, I, Daniel, understood from the Scriptures, according to
the word of the LORD given to Jeremiah
the prophet, that the desolation of Jerusalem would last seventy years. 3 So I
turned to the Lord God and pleaded with
him in prayer and petition, in fasting,
and in sackcloth and ashes.

4 I prayed to the LORD my God and
confessed:

"O Lord, the great and awesome
God, who keeps his covenant of
love with all who love him and
obey his commands, 5 we have
sinned and done wrong. We have
been wicked and have rebelled; we
have turned away from your commands and laws. 6 We have not lis-

tened to your servants the prophets, who spoke in your name to our
kings, our princes and our fathers,
and to all the people of the land.

7 "Lord, you are righteous, but
this day we are covered with shame—
the men of Judah and people of Jerusalem and all Israel, both near
and far, in all the countries where
you have scattered us because of
our unfaithfulness to you. 8 O LORD,
we and our kings, our princes and
our fathers are covered with shame
because we have sinned against
you. 9 The Lord our God is merciful
and forgiving, even though we have
rebelled against him; 10 we have not
obeyed the LORD our God or kept
the laws he gave us through his servants the prophets. 11 All Israel has
transgressed your law and turned
away, refusing to obey you.

"Therefore the curses and
sworn judgments written in the
Law of Moses, the servant of God,
have been poured out on us, because we have sinned against you.
12 You have fulfilled the words spoken against us and against our rulers by bringing upon us great
disaster. Under the whole heaven
nothing has ever been done like
what has been done to Jerusalem.
13 Just as it is written in the Law of
Moses, all this disaster has come
upon us, yet we have not sought the
favor of the LORD our God by turning from our sins and giving attention to your truth. 14 The LORD did
not hesitate to bring the disaster
upon us, for the LORD our God is
righteous in everything he does;
yet we have not obeyed him.

15 "Now, O Lord our God, who
brought your people out of Egypt
with a mighty hand and who made
for yourself a name that endures
to this day, we have sinned, we
have done wrong. 16 O Lord, in
keeping with all your righteous
acts, turn away your anger and
your wrath from Jerusalem, your

city, your holy hill. Our sins and the iniquities of our fathers have made Jerusalem and your people an object of scorn to all those around us.

17 "Now, our God, hear the prayers and petitions of your servant. For your sake, O Lord, look with favor on your desolate sanctuary. 18 Give ear, O God, and hear; open your eyes and see the desolation of the city that bears your Name. We do not make requests of you because we are righteous, but because of your great mercy. 19 O Lord, listen! O Lord, forgive! O Lord, hear and act! For your sake, O my God, do not delay, because your city and your people bear your Name."

20 While I was speaking and praying, confessing my sin and the sin of my people Israel and making my request to the LORD my God for his holy hill— 21 while I was still in prayer, Gabriel, the man I had seen in the earlier vision, came to me in swift flight about the time of the evening sacrifice. 22 He instructed me and said to me, "Daniel, I have now come to give you insight and understanding. 23 As soon as you began to pray, an answer was given, which I have come to tell you, for you are highly esteemed. Therefore, consider the message and understand the vision:

24 "Seventy 'sevens'c are decreed for your people and your holy city to finishd transgression, to put an end to sin, to atone for wickedness, to bring in everlasting righteousness, to seal up vision and prophecy and to anoint the most holy.e

25 "Know and understand this: From the issuing of the decreef to restore and rebuild Jerusalem until the Anointed One,g the ruler, comes, there will be seven 'sevens,' and sixty-two 'sevens.' It will be rebuilt with streets and a trench, but in times of trouble. 26 After the sixty-two 'sevens,' the Anointed One will be cut off and will have nothing.h The peo-

ple of the ruler who will come will destroy the city and the sanctuary. The end will come like a flood: War will continue until the end, and desolations have been decreed. 27 He will confirm a covenant with many for one 'seven.'i In the middle of the 'seven'i he will put an end to sacrifice and offering. And on a wing ⌊of the temple⌋ he will set up an abomination that causes desolation, until the end that is decreed is poured out on him.j "k

10:1 IN the third year of Cyrus king of Persia, a revelation was given to Daniel (who was called Belteshazzar). Its message was true and it concerned a great war.l The understanding of the message came to him in a vision.

2 At that time I, Daniel, mourned for three weeks. 3 I ate no choice food; no meat or wine touched my lips; and I used no lotions at all until the three weeks were over.

4 On the twenty-fourth day of the first month, as I was standing on the bank of the great river, the Tigris, 5 I looked up and there before me was a man dressed in linen, with a belt of the finest gold around his waist. 6 His body was like chrysolite, his face like lightning, his eyes like flaming torches, his arms and legs like the gleam of burnished bronze, and his voice like the sound of a multitude.

7 I, Daniel, was the only one who saw the vision; the men with me did not see it, but such terror overwhelmed them that they fled and hid themselves. 8 So I was left alone, gazing at this great vision; I had no strength left, my face turned deathly pale and I was helpless. 9 Then I heard him speaking, and as I listened to him, I fell into a deep sleep, my face to the ground.

10 A hand touched me and set me trembling on my hands and knees. 11 He said, "Daniel, you who are highly esteemed, consider carefully the words I am about to speak to you, and stand up, for I have now been sent to you." And when he said this to me, I stood up trembling.

¹²Then he continued, "Do not be afraid, Daniel. Since the first day that you set your mind to gain understanding and to humble yourself before your God, your words were heard, and I have come in response to them. ¹³But the prince of the Persian kingdom resisted me twenty-one days. Then Michael, one of the chief princes, came to help me, because I was detained there with the king of Persia. ¹⁴Now I have come to explain to you what will happen to your people in the future, for the vision concerns a time yet to come."

¹⁵While he was saying this to me, I bowed with my face toward the ground and was speechless. ¹⁶Then one who looked like a man^m touched my lips, and I opened my mouth and began to speak. I said to the one standing before me, "I am overcome with anguish because of the vision, my lord, and I am helpless. ¹⁷How can I, your servant, talk with you, my lord? My strength is gone and I can hardly breathe."

¹⁸Again the one who looked like a man touched me and gave me strength. ¹⁹"Do not be afraid, O man highly esteemed," he said. "Peace! Be strong now; be strong."

When he spoke to me, I was strengthened and said, "Speak, my lord, since you have given me strength."

²⁰So he said, "Do you know why I have come to you? Soon I will return to fight against the prince of Persia, and when I go, the prince of Greece will come; ²¹but first I will tell you what is written in the Book of Truth. (No one supports me against them except Michael, your prince." ¹¹:¹AND in the first year of Darius the Mede, I took my stand to support and protect him.)

a 1 Hebrew *Ahasuerus* *b 1* Or *Chaldean* *c 24* Or *'weeks'*; also in verses 25 and 26 *d 24* Or *restrain* *e 24* Or *Most Holy Place*; or *most holy One* *f 25* Or *word* *g 25* Or *an anointed one*; also in verse 26 *h 26* Or *off and will have no one*; or *off, but not for himself* *i 27* Or *'week'* *j 27* Or *it* *k 27* Or *And one who causes desolation will come upon the pinnacle of the abominable* ⌊*temple*⌋, *until the end that is decreed is poured out on the desolated* ⌊*city*⌋ *l 1* Or *true and burdensome* *m 16* Most manuscripts of the Masoretic Text; one manuscript of the Masoretic Text, Dead Sea Scrolls and Septuagint *Then something that looked like a man's hand*

1 JOHN 2:18–3:6

Dear children, this is the last hour; and as you have heard that the antichrist is coming, even now many antichrists have come. This is how we know it is the last hour. ¹⁹They went out from us, but they did not really belong to us. For if they had belonged to us, they would have remained with us; but their going showed that none of them belonged to us.

²⁰But you have an anointing from the Holy One, and all of you know the truth.^{a} ²¹I do not write to you because you do not know the truth, but because you do know it and because no lie comes from the truth. ²²Who is the liar? It is the man who denies that Jesus is the Christ. Such a man is the antichrist—he denies the Father and the Son. ²³No one who denies the Son has the Father; whoever acknowledges the Son has the Father also.

²⁴See that what you have heard from the beginning remains in you. If it does, you also will remain in the Son and in the Father. ²⁵And this is what he promised us—even eternal life.

²⁶I am writing these things to you about those who are trying to lead you astray. ²⁷As for you, the anointing you received from him remains in you, and you do not need anyone to teach you. But as his anointing teaches you about all things and as that anointing is real, not counterfeit—just as it has taught you, remain in him.

²⁸And now, dear children, continue in him, so that when he appears we may be confident and unashamed before him at his coming.

²⁹If you know that he is righteous, you know that everyone who does what is right has been born of him.

³:¹**How great is the love the Father has lavished on us, that we should be called children of God! And that is what we are! The reason the world does not know us is that it did not know him.** ²Dear friends, now we are children of God, and what we will be has not yet been made known. But we know

that when he appears,*b* we shall be like him, for we shall see him as he is. [3]Everyone who has this hope in him purifies himself, just as he is pure.

[4]Everyone who sins breaks the law; in fact, sin is lawlessness. [5]But you know that he appeared so that he might take away our sins. And in him is no sin. [6]No one who lives in him keeps on sinning. No one who continues to sin has either seen him or known him.

a20 Some manuscripts and you know all things   b2 Or when it is made known

PSALM 121:1-8
A song of ascents.

[1]I lift up my eyes to the hills—
    where does my help come from?
[2]My help comes from the Lord,
    the Maker of heaven and earth.

[3]He will not let your foot slip—
    he who watches over you will not
        slumber;
[4]indeed, he who watches over Israel
    will neither slumber nor sleep.

[5]The Lord watches over you—
    the Lord is your shade at your
        right hand;
[6]the sun will not harm you by day,
    nor the moon by night.

[7]The Lord will keep you from all
        harm—
    he will watch over your life;
[8]the Lord will watch over your
        coming and going
    both now and forevermore.

PROVERBS 28:27-28
[27]He who gives to the poor will lack
        nothing,
    but he who closes his eyes to them
        receives many curses.

[28]When the wicked rise to power,
        people go into hiding;
    but when the wicked perish, the
        righteous thrive.

□ DAY 337

GOD SIGHTINGS

December 3

DANIEL 11:2-35
"Now then, I [the one sent to Daniel] tell you [Daniel] the truth: Three more kings will appear in Persia, and then a fourth, who will be far richer than all the others. When he has gained power by his wealth, he will stir up everyone against the kingdom of Greece. [3]Then a mighty king will appear, who will rule with great power and do as he pleases. [4]After he has appeared, his empire will be broken up and parceled out toward the four winds of heaven. It will not go to his descendants, nor will it have the power he exercised, because his empire will be uprooted and given to others.

[5]"The king of the South will become strong, but one of his commanders will become even stronger than he and will rule his own kingdom with great power. [6]After some years, they will become allies. The daughter of the king of the South will go to the king of the North to make an alliance, but she will not retain her power, and he and his power*a* will not last. In those days she will be handed over, together with her royal escort and her father*b* and the one who supported her.

[7]"One from her family line will arise to take her place. He will attack the forces of the king of the North and enter his fortress; he will fight against them and be victorious. [8]He will also seize their gods, their metal images and their valuable articles of silver and gold and carry them off to Egypt. For some years he will leave the king of the North alone. [9]Then the king of the North will invade the realm of the king of the South but will retreat to his own country. [10]His sons will prepare for war and assemble a great army, which will sweep on like an irresistible flood and carry the battle as far as his fortress.

[11]"Then the king of the South will march out in a rage and fight against the king of the North, who will raise a large army, but it will be defeated. [12]When the army is carried off, the king of the South will be filled with pride and will slaughter many thousands, yet he will not remain triumphant. [13]For the king of the North will muster another army, larger than the first; and after several years, he will advance with a huge army fully equipped.

[14]"In those times many will rise against the king of the South. The violent men among your own people will rebel in fulfillment of the vision, but without success. [15]Then the king of the North will come and build up siege ramps and will capture a fortified city. The forces of the South will be powerless to resist; even their best troops will not have the strength to stand. [16]The invader will do as he pleases; no one will be able to stand against him. He will establish himself in the Beautiful Land and will have the power to destroy it. [17]He will determine to come with the might of his entire kingdom and will make an alliance with the king of the South. And he will give him a daughter in marriage in order to overthrow the kingdom, but his plans[c] will not succeed or help him. [18]Then he will turn his attention to the coastlands and will take many of them, but a commander will put an end to his insolence and turn his insolence back upon him. [19]After this, he will turn back toward the fortresses of his own country but will stumble and fall, to be seen no more.

[20]"His successor will send out a tax collector to maintain the royal splendor. In a few years, however, he will be destroyed, yet not in anger or in battle.

[21]"He will be succeeded by a contemptible person who has not been given the honor of royalty. He will invade the kingdom when its people feel secure, and he will seize it through intrigue. [22]Then an overwhelming army will be swept away before him; both it and a prince of the covenant will be destroyed. [23]After coming to an agreement with him, he will act deceitfully, and with only a few people he will rise to power. [24]When the richest provinces feel secure, he will invade them and will achieve what neither his fathers nor his forefathers did. He will distribute plunder, loot and wealth among his followers. He will plot the overthrow of fortresses—but only for a time.

[25]"With a large army he will stir up his strength and courage against the king of the South. The king of the South will wage war with a large and very powerful army, but he will not be able to stand because of the plots devised against him. [26]Those who eat from the king's provisions will try to destroy him; his army will be swept away, and many will fall in battle. [27]The two kings, with their hearts bent on evil, will sit at the same table and lie to each other, but to no avail, because an end will still come at the appointed time. [28]The king of the North will return to his own country with great wealth, but his heart will be set against the holy covenant. He will take action against it and then return to his own country.

[29]"At the appointed time he will invade the South again, but this time the outcome will be different from what it was before. [30]Ships of the western coastlands[d] will oppose him, and he will lose heart. Then he will turn back and vent his fury against the holy covenant. He will return and show favor to those who forsake the holy covenant.

[31]"His armed forces will rise up to desecrate the temple fortress and will abolish the daily sacrifice. Then they will set up the abomination that causes desolation. [32]With flattery he will corrupt those who have violated the covenant, but the people who know their God will firmly resist him.

[33]"Those who are wise will instruct many, though for a time they will fall by the sword or be burned or captured or plundered. [34]When they fall, they will receive a little help, and many who are not sincere will join them. [35]Some of

the wise will stumble, so that they may be refined, purified and made spotless until the time of the end, for it will still come at the appointed time."

a6 Or *offspring* b6 Or *child* (see Vulgate and Syriac)
c17 Or *but she* d30 Hebrew *of Kittim*

1 JOHN 3:7-24

Dear children, do not let anyone lead you astray. He who does what is right is righteous, just as he is righteous. 8He who does what is sinful is of the devil, because the devil has been sinning from the beginning. The reason the Son of God appeared was to destroy the devil's work. 9No one who is born of God will continue to sin, because God's seed remains in him; he cannot go on sinning, because he has been born of God. 10This is how we know who the children of God are and who the children of the devil are: Anyone who does not do what is right is not a child of God; nor is anyone who does not love his brother.

11This is the message you heard from the beginning: We should love one another. 12Do not be like Cain, who belonged to the evil one and murdered his brother. And why did he murder him? Because his own actions were evil and his brother's were righteous. 13Do not be surprised, my brothers, if the world hates you. 14We know that we have passed from death to life, because we love our brothers. Anyone who does not love remains in death. 15Anyone who hates his brother is a murderer, and you know that no murderer has eternal life in him.

16**This is how we know what love is: Jesus Christ laid down his life for us. And we ought to lay down our lives for our brothers.** 17If anyone has material possessions and sees his brother in need but has no pity on him, how can the love of God be in him? 18Dear children, let us not love with words or tongue but with actions and in truth. 19This then is how we know that we belong to the truth, and how we set our hearts at rest in his presence 20whenever our hearts condemn us. For God is

greater than our hearts, and he knows everything.

21Dear friends, if our hearts do not condemn us, we have confidence before God 22and receive from him anything we ask, because we obey his commands and do what pleases him. 23And this is his command: to believe in the name of his Son, Jesus Christ, and to love one another as he commanded us. 24Those who obey his commands live in him, and he in them. And this is how we know that he lives in us: We know it by the Spirit he gave us.

PSALM 122:1-9
A song of ascents. Of David.

1 **I** rejoiced with those who said to me,
  "Let us go to the house of the
    LORD."
2 Our feet are standing
  in your gates, O Jerusalem.

3 Jerusalem is built like a city
  that is closely compacted together.
4 That is where the tribes go up,
  the tribes of the LORD,
 to praise the name of the LORD
  according to the statute given to
    Israel.
5 There are the thrones for judgment
    stand,
  the thrones of the house of David.

6 Pray for the peace of Jerusalem:
  "May those who love you be
    secure.
7 May there be peace within your walls
  and security within your citadels."
8 For the sake of my brothers and
    friends,
  I will say, "Peace be within you."
9 For the sake of the house of the LORD
    our God,
  I will seek your prosperity.

PROVERBS 29:1
  A man who remains stiff-necked
    after many rebukes
  will suddenly be destroyed—
    without remedy.

☐ DAY 338

GOD SIGHTINGS

December 4

DANIEL 11:36–12:13

"The king will do as he pleases. He will exalt and magnify himself above every god and will say unheard-of things against the God of gods. He will be successful until the time of wrath is completed, for what has been determined must take place. ³⁷He will show no regard for the gods of his fathers or for the one desired by women, nor will he regard any god, but will exalt himself above them all. ³⁸Instead of them, he will honor a god of fortresses; a god unknown to his fathers he will honor with gold and silver, with precious stones and costly gifts. ³⁹He will attack the mightiest fortresses with the help of a foreign god and will greatly honor those who acknowledge him. He will make them rulers over many people and will distribute the land at a price.ª

⁴⁰"At the time of the end the king of the South will engage him in battle, and the king of the North will storm out against him with chariots and cavalry and a great fleet of ships. He will invade many countries and sweep through them like a flood. ⁴¹He will also invade the Beautiful Land. Many countries will fall, but Edom, Moab and the leaders of Ammon will be delivered from his hand. ⁴²He will extend his power over many countries; Egypt will not escape. ⁴³He will gain control of the treasures of gold and silver and all the riches of Egypt, with the Libyans and Nubians in submission. ⁴⁴But reports from the east and the north will alarm him, and he will set out in a great rage to destroy and annihilate many. ⁴⁵He will pitch his royal tents between the seas atᵇ the beautiful holy mountain. Yet he will come to his end, and no one will help him.

¹²:¹"At that time Michael, the great prince who protects your people, will arise. There will be a time of distress such as has not happened from the beginning of nations until then. But at that time your people—everyone whose name is found written in the book—will be delivered. ²Multitudes who sleep in the dust of the earth will awake: some to everlasting life, others to shame and everlasting contempt. ³Those who are wiseᶜ will shine like the brightness of the heavens, and those who lead many to righteousness, like the stars for ever and ever. ⁴But you, Daniel, close up and seal the words of the scroll until the time of the end. Many will go here and there to increase knowledge."

⁵Then I, Daniel, looked, and there before me stood two others, one on this bank of the river and one on the opposite bank. ⁶One of them said to the man clothed in linen, who was above the waters of the river, "How long will it be before these astonishing things are fulfilled?"

⁷The man clothed in linen, who was above the waters of the river, lifted his right hand and his left hand toward heaven, and I heard him swear by him who lives forever, saying, "It will be for a time, times and half a time.ᵈ When the power of the holy people has been finally broken, all these things will be completed."

⁸I heard, but I did not understand. So I asked, "My lord, what will the outcome of all this be?"

⁹He replied, "Go your way, Daniel, because the words are closed up and sealed until the time of the end. ¹⁰Many will be purified, made spotless and refined, but the wicked will continue to be wicked. None of the wicked will understand, but those who are wise will understand.

¹¹"From the time that the daily sacrifice is abolished and the abomination that causes desolation is set up, there will be 1,290 days. ¹²Blessed is the one who waits for and reaches the end of the 1,335 days.

¹³"As for you, go your way till the end. You will rest, and then at the end of the

days you will rise to receive your allotted inheritance."

a39 Or land for a reward b45 Or the sea and c3 Or who impart wisdom d7 Or a year, two years and half a year

1 JOHN 4:1-21

Dear friends, do not believe every spirit, but test the spirits to see whether they are from God, because many false prophets have gone out into the world. [2] This is how you can recognize the Spirit of God: Every spirit that acknowledges that Jesus Christ has come in the flesh is from God, [3] but every spirit that does not acknowledge Jesus is not from God. This is the spirit of the antichrist, which you have heard is coming and even now is already in the world.

[4] You, dear children, are from God and have overcome them, because the one who is in you is greater than the one who is in the world. [5] They are from the world and therefore speak from the viewpoint of the world, and the world listens to them. [6] We are from God, and whoever knows God listens to us; but whoever is not from God does not listen to us. This is how we recognize the Spirit[a] of truth and the spirit of falsehood.

[7] Dear friends, let us love one another, for love comes from God. Everyone who loves has been born of God and knows God. [8] Whoever does not love does not know God, because God is love. [9] This is how God showed his love among us: He sent his one and only Son[b] into the world that we might live through him. [10] **This is love: not that we loved God, but that he loved us and sent his Son as an atoning sacrifice for[c] our sins.** [11] **Dear friends, since God so loved us, we also ought to love one another.** [12] No one has ever seen God; but if we love one another, God lives in us and his love is made complete in us.

[13] We know that we live in him and he in us, because he has given us of his Spirit. [14] And we have seen and testify that the Father has sent his Son to be the Savior of the world. [15] If anyone acknowledges that Jesus is the Son of God, God lives in him and he in God. [16] And so

we know and rely on the love God has for us.

God is love. Whoever lives in love lives in God, and God in him. [17] In this way, love is made complete among us so that we will have confidence on the day of judgment, because in this world we are like him. [18] There is no fear in love. But perfect love drives out fear, because fear has to do with punishment. The one who fears is not made perfect in love.

[19] We love because he first loved us. [20] If anyone says, "I love God," yet hates his brother, he is a liar. For anyone who does not love his brother, whom he has seen, cannot love God, whom he has not seen. [21] And he has given us this command: Whoever loves God must also love his brother.

a6 Or spirit b9 Or his only begotten Son c10 Or as the one who would turn aside his wrath, taking away

PSALM 123:1-4

A song of ascents.

[1] **I** lift up my eyes to you,
    to you whose throne is in heaven.
[2] As the eyes of slaves look to the hand
        of their master,
    as the eyes of a maid look to the
        hand of her mistress,
  so our eyes look to the LORD our
        God,
    till he shows us his mercy.

[3] Have mercy on us, O LORD, have
        mercy on us,
    for we have endured much
        contempt.
[4] We have endured much ridicule
        from the proud,
    much contempt from the
        arrogant.

PROVERBS 29:2-4

[2] **W**hen the righteous thrive, the
        people rejoice;
    when the wicked rule, the people
        groan.

[3] A man who loves wisdom brings joy
        to his father,
    but a companion of prostitutes
        squanders his wealth.

⁴By justice a king gives a country
 stability,
   but one who is greedy for bribes
   tears it down.

□ DAY 339

GOD SIGHTINGS

December 5

HOSEA 1:1–3:5

The word of the Lᴏʀᴅ that came to Hosea son of Beeri during the reigns of Uzziah, Jotham, Ahaz and Hezekiah, kings
of Judah, and during the reign of Jeroboam son of Jehoashᵃ king of Israel:

²When the Lᴏʀᴅ began to speak
through Hosea, the Lᴏʀᴅ said to him,
"Go, take to yourself an adulterous wife
and children of unfaithfulness, because
the land is guilty of the vilest adultery in
departing from the Lᴏʀᴅ." ³So he married Gomer daughter of Diblaim, and
she conceived and bore him a son.

⁴Then the Lᴏʀᴅ said to Hosea, "Call
him Jezreel, because I will soon punish
the house of Jehu for the massacre at
Jezreel, and I will put an end to the kingdom of Israel. ⁵In that day I will break
Israel's bow in the Valley of Jezreel."

⁶Gomer conceived again and gave
birth to a daughter. Then the Lᴏʀᴅ said
to Hosea, "Call her Lo-Ruhamah,ᵇ for I
will no longer show love to the house of
Israel, that I should at all forgive them.
⁷Yet I will show love to the house of Judah; and I will save them—not by bow,
sword or battle, or by horses and horsemen, but by the Lᴏʀᴅ their God."

⁸After she had weaned Lo-Ruhamah,
Gomer had another son. ⁹Then the
Lᴏʀᴅ said, "Call him Lo-Ammi,ᶜ for you
are not my people, and I am not your
God.

¹⁰"Yet the Israelites will be like the
sand on the seashore, which cannot be
measured or counted. In the place
where it was said to them, 'You are not

my people,' they will be called 'sons of
the living God.' ¹¹The people of Judah
and the people of Israel will be reunited,
and they will appoint one leader and
will come up out of the land, for great
will be the day of Jezreel.

²:¹"Sᴀʏ of your brothers, 'My people,'
and of your sisters, 'My loved one.'

²"Rebuke your mother, rebuke her,
   for she is not my wife,
   and I am not her husband.
 Let her remove the adulterous look
   from her face
 and the unfaithfulness from
   between her breasts.
³Otherwise I will strip her naked
   and make her as bare as on the day
   she was born;
 I will make her like a desert,
   turn her into a parched land,
   and slay her with thirst.
⁴I will not show my love to her
   children,
   because they are the children of
   adultery.
⁵Their mother has been unfaithful
   and has conceived them in
   disgrace.
 She said, 'I will go after my lovers,
   who give me my food and my
   water,
   my wool and my linen, my oil and
   my drink.'
⁶Therefore I will block her path with
   thornbushes;
   I will wall her in so that she cannot
   find her way.
⁷She will chase after her lovers but
   not catch them;
   she will look for them but not find
   them.
 Then she will say,
   'I will go back to my husband as at
   first,
   for then I was better off than now.'
⁸She has not acknowledged that I was
   the one
   who gave her the grain, the new
   wine and oil,

who lavished on her the silver and
    gold—
    which they used for Baal.

9"Therefore I will take away my grain
    when it ripens,
    and my new wine when it is ready.
I will take back my wool and my
    linen,
    intended to cover her nakedness.
10So now I will expose her lewdness
    before the eyes of her lovers;
    no one will take her out of my
        hands.
11I will stop all her celebrations:
    her yearly festivals, her New Moons,
    her Sabbath days—all her
        appointed feasts.
12I will ruin her vines and her fig trees,
    which she said were her pay from
        her lovers;
I will make them a thicket,
    and wild animals will devour them.
13I will punish her for the days
    she burned incense to the Baals;
she decked herself with rings and
    jewelry,
    and went after her lovers,
    but me she forgot,"
                    declares the LORD.

14"Therefore I am now going to allure
    her;
I will lead her into the desert
    and speak tenderly to her.
15There I will give her back her
    vineyards,
    and will make the Valley of Achor*d*
        a door of hope.
There she will sing*e* as in the days of
    her youth,
    as in the day she came up out of
        Egypt.

16"In that day," declares the LORD,
    "you will call me 'my husband';
    you will no longer call me 'my
        master.'*f*'
17I will remove the names of the Baals
    from her lips;
    no longer will their names be
        invoked.

18In that day I will make a covenant for
    them
    with the beasts of the field and the
        birds of the air
    and the creatures that move along
        the ground.
Bow and sword and battle
    I will abolish from the land,
    so that all may lie down in safety.
19I will betroth you to me forever;
    I will betroth you in*g*
        righteousness and justice,
    in*h* love and compassion.
20I will betroth you in faithfulness,
    and you will acknowledge the
        LORD.

21"In that day I will respond,"
    declares the LORD—
"I will respond to the skies,
    and they will respond to the earth;
22and the earth will respond to the
    grain,
    the new wine and oil,
    and they will respond to Jezreel.*i*
23I will plant her for myself in the land;
    I will show my love to the one I
        called 'Not my loved one.*j*'
I will say to those called 'Not my
    people,*k*' 'You are my people';
    and they will say, 'You are my
        God.'"

3:1THE LORD said to me, "Go, show your
love to your wife again, though she is
loved by another and is an adulteress.
Love her as the LORD loves the Israelites,
though they turn to other gods and love
the sacred raisin cakes."

2So I bought her for fifteen shekels*l*
of silver and about a homer and a le-
thek*m* of barley. 3Then I told her, "You
are to live with*n* me many days; you must
not be a prostitute or be intimate with
any man, and I will live with*n* you."

4For the Israelites will live many days
without king or prince, without sacrifice or sacred stones, without ephod or
idol. 5Afterward the Israelites will return and seek the LORD their God and
David their king. They will come trem-

bling to the Lord and to his blessings in the last days.

a 1 Hebrew Joash, a variant of Jehoash b 6 Lo-Ruhamah means not loved. c 9 Lo-Ammi means not my people. d 15 Achor means trouble. e 15 Or respond f 16 Hebrew baal g 19 Or with; also in verse 20 h 19 Or with i 22 Jezreel means God plants. j 23 Hebrew Lo-Ruhamah k 23 Hebrew Lo-Ammi l 2 That is, about 6 ounces (about 170 grams) m 2 That is, probably about 10 bushels (about 330 liters) n 3 Or wait for

1 JOHN 5:1-21

Everyone who believes that Jesus is the Christ is born of God, and everyone who loves the father loves his child as well. ²This is how we know that we love the children of God: by loving God and carrying out his commands. ³This is love for God: to obey his commands. And his commands are not burdensome, ⁴for everyone born of God overcomes the world. This is the victory that has overcome the world, even our faith. ⁵Who is it that overcomes the world? Only he who believes that Jesus is the Son of God.

⁶This is the one who came by water and blood—Jesus Christ. He did not come by water only, but by water and blood. And it is the Spirit who testifies, because the Spirit is the truth. ⁷For there are three that testify: ⁸the*a* Spirit, the water and the blood; and the three are in agreement. ⁹We accept man's testimony, but God's testimony is greater because it is the testimony of God, which he has given about his Son. ¹⁰Anyone who believes in the Son of God has this testimony in his heart. Anyone who does not believe God has made him out to be a liar, because he has not believed the testimony God has given about his Son. ¹¹**And this is the testimony: God has given us eternal life, and this life is in his Son. ¹²He who has the Son has life; he who does not have the Son of God does not have life.**

¹³I write these things to you who believe in the name of the Son of God so that you may know that you have eternal life. ¹⁴This is the confidence we have in approaching God: that if we ask anything according to his will, he hears us. ¹⁵And if we know that he hears us—

whatever we ask—we know that we have what we asked of him.

¹⁶If anyone sees his brother commit a sin that does not lead to death, he should pray and God will give him life. I refer to those whose sin does not lead to death. There is a sin that leads to death. I am not saying that he should pray about that. ¹⁷All wrongdoing is sin, and there is sin that does not lead to death.

¹⁸We know that anyone born of God does not continue to sin; the one who was born of God keeps him safe, and the evil one cannot harm him. ¹⁹We know that we are children of God, and that the whole world is under the control of the evil one. ²⁰We know also that the Son of God has come and has given us understanding, so that we may know him who is true. And we are in him who is true—even in his Son Jesus Christ. He is the true God and eternal life.

²¹Dear children, keep yourselves from idols.

a 7,8 Late manuscripts of the Vulgate testify in heaven: the Father, the Word and the Holy Spirit, and these three are one. 8 And there are three that testify on earth: the (not found in any Greek manuscript before the fourteenth century)

PSALM 124:1-8
A song of ascents. Of David.

¹ **I**f the Lord had not been on our
        side—
    let Israel say—
²if the Lord had not been on our side
    when men attacked us,
³when their anger flared against us,
    they would have swallowed us alive;
⁴the flood would have engulfed us,
    the torrent would have swept over
        us,
⁵the raging waters
    would have swept us away.

⁶Praise be to the Lord,
    who has not let us be torn by their
        teeth.
⁷We have escaped like a bird
    out of the fowler's snare;
  the snare has been broken,
    and we have escaped.
⁸Our help is in the name of the Lord,
    the Maker of heaven and earth.

PROVERBS 29:5-8

⁵ **W**hoever flatters his neighbor
is spreading a net for his feet.

⁶ An evil man is snared by his own sin,
but a righteous one can sing and
be glad.

⁷ The righteous care about justice for
the poor,
but the wicked have no such
concern.

⁸ Mockers stir up a city,
but wise men turn away anger.

□ DAY 340

GOD SIGHTINGS

December 6

HOSEA 4:1–5:15

Hear the word of the Lᴏʀᴅ, you
Israelites,
because the Lᴏʀᴅ has a charge to
bring
against you who live in the land:
"There is no faithfulness, no love,
no acknowledgment of God in the
land.
² There is only cursing,ᵃ lying and
murder,
stealing and adultery;
they break all bounds,
and bloodshed follows bloodshed.
³ Because of this the land mourns,ᵇ
and all who live in it waste away;
the beasts of the field and the birds
of the air
and the fish of the sea are dying.

⁴ "But let no man bring a charge,
let no man accuse another,
for your people are like those
who bring charges against a priest.
⁵ You stumble day and night,
and the prophets stumble with
you.
So I will destroy your mother—

⁶ my people are destroyed from lack
of knowledge.

"Because you have rejected
knowledge,
I also reject you as my priests;
because you have ignored the law of
your God,
I also will ignore your children.
⁷ The more the priests increased,
the more they sinned against me;
they exchangedᶜ theirᵈ Glory for
something disgraceful.
⁸ They feed on the sins of my people
and relish their wickedness.
⁹ And it will be: Like people, like priests.
I will punish both of them for their
ways
and repay them for their deeds.

¹⁰ "They will eat but not have enough;
they will engage in prostitution
but not increase,
because they have deserted the Lᴏʀᴅ
to give themselves ¹¹ to prostitution,
to old wine and new,
which take away the understanding
¹² of my people.
They consult a wooden idol
and are answered by a stick of
wood.
A spirit of prostitution leads them
astray;
they are unfaithful to their God.
¹³ They sacrifice on the mountaintops
and burn offerings on the hills,
under oak, poplar and terebinth,
where the shade is pleasant.
Therefore your daughters turn to
prostitution
and your daughters-in-law to
adultery.

¹⁴ "I will not punish your daughters
when they turn to prostitution,
nor your daughters-in-law
when they commit adultery,
because the men themselves consort
with harlots
and sacrifice with shrine
prostitutes—
a people without understanding
will come to ruin!

15 "Though you commit adultery,
  O Israel,
  let not Judah become guilty.

"Do not go to Gilgal;
  do not go up to Beth Aven.*e*
And do not swear, 'As surely as the
  LORD lives!'
16 The Israelites are stubborn,
  like a stubborn heifer.
How then can the LORD pasture them
  like lambs in a meadow?
17 Ephraim is joined to idols;
  leave him alone!
18 Even when their drinks are gone,
  they continue their prostitution;
  their rulers dearly love shameful
    ways.
19 A whirlwind will sweep them away,
  and their sacrifices will bring
    them shame.

5:1 "HEAR this, you priests!
  Pay attention, you Israelites!
Listen, O royal house!
  This judgment is against you:
You have been a snare at Mizpah,
  a net spread out on Tabor.
2 The rebels are deep in slaughter.
  I will discipline all of them.
3 I know all about Ephraim;
  Israel is not hidden from me.
Ephraim, you have now turned to
    prostitution;
  Israel is corrupt.

4 "Their deeds do not permit them
  to return to their God.
A spirit of prostitution is in their
    heart;
  they do not acknowledge the
    LORD.
5 Israel's arrogance testifies against
    them;
  the Israelites, even Ephraim,
    stumble in their sin;
  Judah also stumbles with them.
6 When they go with their flocks and
    herds
  to seek the LORD,
they will not find him;
  he has withdrawn himself from
    them.

7 They are unfaithful to the LORD;
  they give birth to illegitimate
    children.
Now their New Moon festivals
  will devour them and their fields.

8 "Sound the trumpet in Gibeah,
  the horn in Ramah.
Raise the battle cry in Beth Aven*e*;
  lead on, O Benjamin.
9 Ephraim will be laid waste
  on the day of reckoning.
Among the tribes of Israel
  I proclaim what is certain.
10 Judah's leaders are like those
  who move boundary stones.
I will pour out my wrath on them
  like a flood of water.
11 Ephraim is oppressed,
  trampled in judgment,
  intent on pursuing idols.*f*
12 I am like a moth to Ephraim,
  like rot to the people of Judah.

13 "When Ephraim saw his sickness,
  and Judah his sores,
then Ephraim turned to Assyria,
  and sent to the great king for
    help.
But he is not able to cure you,
  not able to heal your sores.
14 For I will be like a lion to Ephraim,
  like a great lion to Judah.
I will tear them to pieces and go
    away;
  I will carry them off, with no one
    to rescue them.
15 Then I will go back to my place
  until they admit their guilt.
And they will seek my face;
  in their misery they will earnestly
    seek me."

a2 That is, to pronounce a curse upon *b3* Or *dries up*
c7 Syriac and an ancient Hebrew scribal tradition; Masoretic
Text *I will exchange* *d7* Masoretic Text; an ancient Hebrew
scribal tradition *my* *e15,8 Beth Aven* means *house of
wickedness* (a name for Bethel, which means *house of God*).
f11 The meaning of the Hebrew for this word is uncertain.

2 JOHN 1:1-13

The elder,

To the chosen lady and her children,
whom I love in the truth—and not I
only, but also all who know the truth—

²because of the truth, which lives in us and will be with us forever:

³Grace, mercy and peace from God the Father and from Jesus Christ, the Father's Son, will be with us in truth and love.

⁴It has given me great joy to find some of your children walking in the truth, just as the Father commanded us. ⁵And now, dear lady, I am not writing you a new command but one we have had from the beginning. I ask that we love one another. ⁶And this is love: that we walk in obedience to his commands. As you have heard from the beginning, his command is that you walk in love.

⁷Many deceivers, who do not acknowledge Jesus Christ as coming in the flesh, have gone out into the world. Any such person is the deceiver and the antichrist. ⁸Watch out that you do not lose what you have worked for, but that you may be rewarded fully. ⁹Anyone who runs ahead and does not continue in the teaching of Christ does not have God; whoever continues in the teaching has both the Father and the Son. ¹⁰If anyone comes to you and does not bring this teaching, do not take him into your house or welcome him. ¹¹Anyone who welcomes him shares in his wicked work.

¹²I have much to write to you, but I do not want to use paper and ink. Instead, I hope to visit you and talk with you face to face, so that our joy may be complete.

¹³The children of your chosen sister send their greetings.

PSALM 125:1-5
A song of ascents.

¹Those who trust in the LORD are
    like Mount Zion,
    which cannot be shaken but
        endures forever.
²As the mountains surround
        Jerusalem,
    so the LORD surrounds his
        people
    both now and forevermore.

³The scepter of the wicked will not
        remain
    over the land allotted to the
        righteous,
for then the righteous might use
    their hands to do evil.

⁴Do good, O LORD, to those who are
        good,
    to those who are upright in heart.
⁵But those who turn to crooked ways
    the LORD will banish with the
        evildoers.

Peace be upon Israel.

PROVERBS 29:9-11
⁹If a wise man goes to court with a
        fool,
    the fool rages and scoffs, and there
        is no peace.

¹⁰Bloodthirsty men hate a man of
        integrity
    and seek to kill the upright.

¹¹A fool gives full vent to his anger,
    but a wise man keeps himself
        under control.

☐ DAY 341

GOD SIGHTINGS

December 7

HOSEA 6:1-9:17
"Come, let us [Israel and Judah]
        return to the LORD.
He has torn us to pieces
    but he will heal us;
he has injured us
    but he will bind up our wounds.
²After two days he will revive us;
    on the third day he will restore us,
    that we may live in his presence.
³Let us acknowledge the LORD;
    let us press on to acknowledge
        him.
As surely as the sun rises,
    he will appear;

he will come to us like the winter
        rains,
    like the spring rains that water the
        earth."

⁴"What can I do with you, Ephraim?
    What can I do with you, Judah?
Your love is like the morning mist,
    like the early dew that disappears.
⁵Therefore I cut you in pieces with my
        prophets,
    I killed you with the words of my
        mouth;
    my judgments flashed like
        lightning upon you.
⁶For I desire mercy, not sacrifice,
    and acknowledgment of God
        rather than burnt offerings.
⁷Like Adam,ᵃ they have broken the
        covenant—
    they were unfaithful to me there.
⁸Gilead is a city of wicked men,
    stained with footprints of blood.
⁹As marauders lie in ambush for a
        man,
    so do bands of priests;
    they murder on the road to
        Shechem,
    committing shameful crimes.
¹⁰I have seen a horrible thing
    in the house of Israel.
There Ephraim is given to
        prostitution
    and Israel is defiled.

¹¹"Also for you, Judah,
    a harvest is appointed.

    "Whenever I would restore the
        fortunes of my people,
⁷:¹   whenever I would heal Israel,
    the sins of Ephraim are exposed
    and the crimes of Samaria
        revealed.
They practice deceit,
    thieves break into houses,
    bandits rob in the streets;
²but they do not realize
    that I remember all their evil
        deeds.
Their sins engulf them;
    they are always before me.

³"They delight the king with their
        wickedness,
    the princes with their lies.
⁴They are all adulterers,
    burning like an oven
whose fire the baker need not stir
    from the kneading of the dough
        till it rises.
⁵On the day of the festival of our king
    the princes become inflamed with
        wine,
    and he joins hands with the
        mockers.
⁶Their hearts are like an oven;
    they approach him with intrigue.
Their passion smolders all night;
    in the morning it blazes like a
        flaming fire.
⁷All of them are hot as an oven;
    they devour their rulers.
All their kings fall,
    and none of them calls on me.

⁸"Ephraim mixes with the nations;
    Ephraim is a flat cake not turned
        over.
⁹Foreigners sap his strength,
    but he does not realize it.
His hair is sprinkled with gray,
    but he does not notice.
¹⁰Israel's arrogance testifies against him,
    but despite all this
he does not return to the Lᴏʀᴅ his God
    or search for him.

¹¹"Ephraim is like a dove,
    easily deceived and senseless—
now calling to Egypt,
    now turning to Assyria.
¹²When they go, I will throw my net
        over them;
    I will pull them down like birds of
        the air.
When I hear them flocking together,
    I will catch them.
¹³Woe to them,
    because they have strayed from me!
Destruction to them,
    because they have rebelled against
        me!
I long to redeem them
    but they speak lies against me.

14 They do not cry out to me from their
   hearts
      but wail upon their beds.
   They gather together^b for grain and
      new wine
      but turn away from me.
15 I trained them and strengthened
   them,
      but they plot evil against me.
16 They do not turn to the Most High;
      they are like a faulty bow.
   Their leaders will fall by the sword
      because of their insolent words.
   For this they will be ridiculed
      in the land of Egypt.

8:1 "PUT the trumpet to your lips!
      An eagle is over the house of the
      LORD
   because the people have broken my
      covenant
      and rebelled against my law.
2 Israel cries out to me,
      'O our God, we acknowledge you!'
3 But Israel has rejected what is good;
      an enemy will pursue him.
4 They set up kings without my
      consent;
      they choose princes without my
      approval.
   With their silver and gold
      they make idols for themselves
      to their own destruction.
5 Throw out your calf-idol, O Samaria!
      My anger burns against them.
   How long will they be incapable of
      purity?
6   They are from Israel!
   This calf—a craftsman has made it;
      it is not God.
   It will be broken in pieces,
      that calf of Samaria.

7 "They sow the wind
      and reap the whirlwind.
   The stalk has no head;
      it will produce no flour.
   Were it to yield grain,
      foreigners would swallow it up.
8 Israel is swallowed up;
      now she is among the nations
      like a worthless thing.

9 For they have gone up to Assyria
      like a wild donkey wandering
      alone.
   Ephraim has sold herself to lovers.
10 Although they have sold themselves
      among the nations,
      I will now gather them together.
   They will begin to waste away
      under the oppression of the
      mighty king.

11 "Though Ephraim built many altars
      for sin offerings,
      these have become altars for
      sinning.
12 I wrote for them the many things of
      my law,
      but they regarded them as
      something alien.
13 They offer sacrifices given to me
      and they eat the meat,
      but the LORD is not pleased with
      them.
   Now he will remember their
      wickedness
      and punish their sins:
      They will return to Egypt.
14 Israel has forgotten his Maker
      and built palaces;
      Judah has fortified many towns.
   But I will send fire upon their cities
      that will consume their
      fortresses."

9:1 Do not rejoice, O Israel;
      do not be jubilant like the other
      nations.
   For you have been unfaithful to your
      God;
      you love the wages of a prostitute
      at every threshing floor.
2 Threshing floors and winepresses
      will not feed the people;
      the new wine will fail them.
3 They will not remain in the LORD's
      land;
      Ephraim will return to Egypt
      and eat unclean^c food in Assyria.
4 They will not pour out wine offerings
      to the LORD,
      nor will their sacrifices please
      him.

Such sacrifices will be to them like
  the bread of mourners;
all who eat them will be unclean.
This food will be for themselves;
  it will not come into the temple of
    the Lord.

⁵What will you do on the day of your
    appointed feasts,
  on the festival days of the Lord?
⁶Even if they escape from
    destruction,
  Egypt will gather them,
  and Memphis will bury them.
Their treasures of silver will be taken
    over by briers,
  and thorns will overrun their
    tents.
⁷The days of punishment are coming,
  the days of reckoning are at hand.
  Let Israel know this.
Because your sins are so many
  and your hostility so great,
the prophet is considered a fool,
  the inspired man a maniac.
⁸The prophet, along with my God,
  is the watchman over Ephraim,ᵈ
yet snares await him on all his paths,
  and hostility in the house of his
    God.
⁹They have sunk deep into
    corruption,
  as in the days of Gibeah.
God will remember their
    wickedness
  and punish them for their sins.

¹⁰"When I found Israel,
  it was like finding grapes in the
    desert;
when I saw your fathers,
  it was like seeing the early fruit on
    the fig tree.
But when they came to Baal Peor,
  they consecrated themselves to
    that shameful idol
and became as vile as the thing
    they loved.
¹¹Ephraim's glory will fly away like a
    bird—
  no birth, no pregnancy, no
    conception.

¹²Even if they rear children,
  I will bereave them of every one.
Woe to them
  when I turn away from them!
¹³I have seen Ephraim, like Tyre,
  planted in a pleasant place.
But Ephraim will bring out
  their children to the slayer."

¹⁴Give them, O Lord—
  what will you give them?
Give them wombs that miscarry
  and breasts that are dry.

¹⁵"Because of all their wickedness in
    Gilgal,
  I hated them there.
Because of their sinful deeds,
  I will drive them out of my house.
I will no longer love them;
  all their leaders are rebellious.
¹⁶Ephraim is blighted,
  their root is withered,
    they yield no fruit.
Even if they bear children,
  I will slay their cherished
    offspring."

¹⁷My God will reject them
  because they have not obeyed
    him;
  they will be wanderers among the
    nations.

ᵃ7 Or As at Adam; or Like men   ᵇ14 Most Hebrew
manuscripts; some Hebrew manuscripts and Septuagint
They slash themselves   ᶜ3 That is, ceremonially unclean
ᵈ8 Or The prophet is the watchman over Ephraim, / the
people of my God

3 JOHN 1:1-14

The elder,

To my dear friend Gaius, whom I love
in the truth.

²Dear friend, I pray that you may enjoy good health and that all may go well
with you, even as your soul is getting
along well. ³It gave me great joy to have
some brothers come and tell about your
faithfulness to the truth and how you
continue to walk in the truth. ⁴I have no
greater joy than to hear that my children
are walking in the truth.
⁵Dear friend, you are faithful in what

you are doing for the brothers, even though they are strangers to you. ⁶They have told the church about your love. You will do well to send them on their way in a manner worthy of God. ⁷It was for the sake of the Name that they went out, receiving no help from the pagans. ⁸We ought therefore to show hospitality to such men so that we may work together for the truth.

⁹I wrote to the church, but Diotrephes, who loves to be first, will have nothing to do with us. ¹⁰So if I come, I will call attention to what he is doing, gossiping maliciously about us. Not satisfied with that, he refuses to welcome the brothers. He also stops those who want to do so and puts them out of the church.

¹¹Dear friend, do not imitate what is evil but what is good. Anyone who does what is good is from God. Anyone who does what is evil has not seen God. ¹²Demetrius is well spoken of by everyone—and even by the truth itself. We also speak well of him, and you know that our testimony is true.

¹³I have much to write you, but I do not want to do so with pen and ink. ¹⁴I hope to see you soon, and we will talk face to face.

Peace to you. The friends here send their greetings. Greet the friends there by name.

PSALM 126:1-6
A song of ascents.

¹ **W**hen the Lord brought back the captives to*a* Zion,
   we were like men who dreamed.*b*
² Our mouths were filled with laughter,
   our tongues with songs of joy.
Then it was said among the nations,
   "The Lord has done great things for them."
³ The Lord has done great things for us,
   and we are filled with joy.

⁴ **Restore our fortunes,*c* O Lord,
   like streams in the Negev.**

⁵ **Those who sow in tears
   will reap with songs of joy.**
⁶ **He who goes out weeping,
   carrying seed to sow,
will return with songs of joy,
   carrying sheaves with him.**

a1 Or Lord *restored the fortunes of*   *b1* Or *men restored to
health*   *c4* Or *Bring back our captives*

PROVERBS 29:12-14
¹² **I**f a ruler listens to lies,
   all his officials become wicked.

¹³ The poor man and the oppressor
   have this in common:
   The Lord gives sight to the eyes of
      both.

¹⁴ If a king judges the poor with
      fairness,
   his throne will always be secure.

☐ D A Y   3 4 2

GOD SIGHTINGS

December 8

HOSEA 10:1–14:9
Israel was a spreading vine;
   he brought forth fruit for himself.
As his fruit increased,
   he built more altars;
as his land prospered,
   he adorned his sacred stones.
² Their heart is deceitful,
   and now they must bear their
      guilt.
The Lord will demolish their altars
   and destroy their sacred stones.

³ Then they will say, "We have no king
   because we did not revere the Lord.
But even if we had a king,
   what could he do for us?"
⁴ They make many promises,
   take false oaths
   and make agreements;
therefore lawsuits spring up
   like poisonous weeds in a plowed
      field.

⁵The people who live in Samaria
fear
    for the calf-idol of Beth Aven.ᵃ
Its people will mourn over it,
    and so will its idolatrous priests,
those who had rejoiced over its
splendor,
    because it is taken from them into
exile.
⁶It will be carried to Assyria
    as tribute for the great king.
Ephraim will be disgraced;
    Israel will be ashamed of its
wooden idols.ᵇ
⁷Samaria and its king will float away
    like a twig on the surface of the
waters.
⁸The high places of wicknessᶜ will
be destroyed—
    it is the sin of Israel.
Thorns and thistles will grow up
    and cover their altars.
Then they will say to the mountains,
    "Cover us!"
    and to the hills, "Fall on us!"

⁹"Since the days of Gibeah, you have
sinned, O Israel,
    and there you have remained.ᵈ
Did not war overtake
    the evildoers in Gibeah?
¹⁰When I please, I will punish them;
    nations will be gathered against
them
    to put them in bonds for their
double sin.
¹¹Ephraim is a trained heifer
    that loves to thresh;
so I will put a yoke
    on her fair neck.
I will drive Ephraim,
    Judah must plow,
    and Jacob must break up the
ground.
¹²Sow for yourselves righteousness,
    reap the fruit of unfailing love,
and break up your unplowed
ground;
    for it is time to seek the LORD,
until he comes
    and showers righteousness on
you.

¹³But you have planted wickedness,
    you have reaped evil,
    you have eaten the fruit of
deception.
Because you have depended on your
own strength
    and on your many warriors,
¹⁴the roar of battle will rise against
your people,
    so that all your fortresses will be
devastated—
as Shalman devastated Beth Arbel on
the day of battle,
    when mothers were dashed to the
ground with their children.
¹⁵Thus will it happen to you, O Bethel,
    because your wickedness is great.
When that day dawns,
    the king of Israel will be
completely destroyed.

11:1"WHEN Israel was a child, I loved
him,
    and out of Egypt I called my son.
²But the more Iᵉ called Israel,
    the further they went from me.ᶠ
They sacrificed to the Baals
    and they burned incense to images.
³It was I who taught Ephraim to walk,
    taking them by the arms;
but they did not realize
    it was I who healed them.
⁴I led them with cords of human
kindness,
    with ties of love;
I lifted the yoke from their neck
    and bent down to feed them.

⁵"Will they not return to Egypt
    and will not Assyria rule over them
    because they refuse to repent?
⁶Swords will flash in their cities,
    will destroy the bars of their gates
    and put an end to their plans.
⁷My people are determined to turn
from me.
    Even if they call to the Most High,
    he will by no means exalt them.

⁸"How can I give you up, Ephraim?
    How can I hand you over, Israel?
How can I treat you like Admah?
    How can I make you like Zeboiim?

My heart is changed within me;
　all my compassion is aroused.
⁹ I will not carry out my fierce anger,
　nor will I turn and devastate
　　Ephraim.
For I am God, and not man—
　the Holy One among you.
I will not come in wrath.⁹
¹⁰ They will follow the LORD;
　he will roar like a lion.
When he roars,
　his children will come trembling
　　from the west.
¹¹ They will come trembling
　like birds from Egypt,
　like doves from Assyria.
I will settle them in their homes,"
　declares the LORD.

¹² Ephraim has surrounded me with
　　lies,
　the house of Israel with deceit.
And Judah is unruly against God,
　even against the faithful Holy
　　One.

¹²:¹ EPHRAIM feeds on the wind;
　he pursues the east wind all day
　and multiplies lies and violence.
He makes a treaty with Assyria
　and sends olive oil to Egypt.
² The LORD has a charge to bring
　　against Judah;
　he will punish Jacobʰ according to
　　his ways
　and repay him according to his
　　deeds.
³ In the womb he grasped his brother's
　　heel;
　as a man he struggled with God.
⁴ He struggled with the angel and
　　overcame him;
　he wept and begged for his favor.
He found him at Bethel
　and talked with him there—
⁵ the LORD God Almighty,
　the LORD is his name of renown!
⁶ But you must return to your God;
　maintain love and justice,
　and wait for your God always.

⁷ The merchant uses dishonest scales;
　he loves to defraud.

⁸ Ephraim boasts,
　"I am very rich; I have become
　　wealthy.
With all my wealth they will not find
　　in me
　any iniquity or sin."

⁹ "I am the LORD your God,
　⌊who brought you⌋ out ofⁱ Egypt;
I will make you live in tents again,
　as in the days of your appointed
　　feasts.
¹⁰ I spoke to the prophets,
　gave them many visions
　and told parables through them."

¹¹ Is Gilead wicked?
　Its people are worthless!
Do they sacrifice bulls in Gilgal?
　Their altars will be like piles of stones
　　on a plowed field.
¹² Jacob fled to the country of Aramʲ;
　Israel served to get a wife,
　and to pay for her he tended sheep.
¹³ The LORD used a prophet to bring
　　Israel up from Egypt,
　by a prophet he cared for him.
¹⁴ But Ephraim has bitterly provoked
　　him to anger;
　his Lord will leave upon him the
　　guilt of his bloodshed
　and will repay him for his contempt.

¹³:¹ WHEN Ephraim spoke, men
　　trembled;
　he was exalted in Israel.
But he became guilty of Baal
　worship and died.
² Now they sin more and more;
　they make idols for themselves
　　from their silver,
cleverly fashioned images,
　all of them the work of craftsmen.
It is said of these people,
　"They offer human sacrifice
　and kissᵏ the calf-idols."
³ Therefore they will be like the
　　morning mist,
　like the early dew that disappears,
　like chaff swirling from a
　　threshing floor,
　like smoke escaping through a
　　window.

4"But I am the LORD your God,
⌊who brought you⌋ out of[f] Egypt.
You shall acknowledge no God but me,
no Savior except me.
5 I cared for you in the desert,
in the land of burning heat.
6 When I fed them, they were
satisfied;
when they were satisfied, they
became proud;
then they forgot me.
7 So I will come upon them like a lion,
like a leopard I will lurk by the path.
8 Like a bear robbed of her cubs,
I will attack them and rip them
open.
Like a lion I will devour them;
a wild animal will tear them apart.

9 "You are destroyed, O Israel,
because you are against me,
against your helper.
10 Where is your king, that he may save
you?
Where are your rulers in all your
towns,
of whom you said,
'Give me a king and princes'?
11 So in my anger I gave you a king,
and in my wrath I took him away.
12 The guilt of Ephraim is stored up,
his sins are kept on record.
13 Pains as of a woman in childbirth
come to him,
but he is a child without wisdom;
when the time arrives,
he does not come to the opening
of the womb.

14 "I will ransom them from the power
of the grave[l];
I will redeem them from death.
Where, O death, are your plagues?
Where, O grave,[m] is your
destruction?

"I will have no compassion,
15   even though he thrives among his
brothers.
An east wind from the LORD will come,
blowing in from the desert;
his spring will fail
and his well dry up.

His storehouse will be plundered
of all its treasures.
16 The people of Samaria must bear
their guilt,
because they have rebelled against
their God.
They will fall by the sword;
their little ones will be dashed to
the ground,
their pregnant women ripped
open."

14:1 RETURN, O Israel, to the LORD your
God.
Your sins have been your downfall!
2 Take words with you
and return to the LORD.
Say to him:
"Forgive all our sins
and receive us graciously,
that we may offer the fruit of our
lips.[n]
3 Assyria cannot save us;
we will not mount war-horses.
We will never again say 'Our gods'
to what our own hands have made,
for in you the fatherless find
compassion."

4 "I will heal their waywardness
and love them freely,
for my anger has turned away
from them.
5 I will be like the dew to Israel;
he will blossom like a lily.
Like a cedar of Lebanon
he will send down his roots;
6   his young shoots will grow.
His splendor will be like an olive tree,
his fragrance like a cedar of
Lebanon.
7 Men will dwell again in his shade.
He will flourish like the grain.
He will blossom like a vine,
and his fame will be like the wine
from Lebanon.
8 O Ephraim, what more have I[o] to do
with idols?
I will answer him and care for him.
I am like a green pine tree;
your fruitfulness comes from me."

⁹Who is wise? He will realize these
    things.
  Who is discerning? He will
    understand them.
  The ways of the LORD are right;
    the righteous walk in them,
    but the rebellious stumble in
      them.

JUDE 1:1-25

Jude, a servant of Jesus Christ and a
brother of James,

To those who have been called, who
are loved by God the Father and kept byᵃ
Jesus Christ:

²Mercy, peace and love be yours in
abundance.

³Dear friends, although I was very eager to write to you about the salvation we
share, I felt I had to write and urge you to
contend for the faith that was once for all
entrusted to the saints. ⁴For certain men
whose condemnation was written
aboutᵇ long ago have secretly slipped in
among you. They are godless men, who
change the grace of our God into a li-
cense for immorality and deny Jesus
Christ our only Sovereign and Lord.

⁵Though you already know all this, I
want to remind you that the Lordᶜ delivered his people out of Egypt, but later
destroyed those who did not believe.
⁶And the angels who did not keep their
positions of authority but abandoned
their own home—these he has kept in
darkness, bound with everlasting
chains for judgment on the great Day.
⁷In a similar way, Sodom and Gomorrah
and the surrounding towns gave themselves up to sexual immorality and perversion. They serve as an example of
those who suffer the punishment of
eternal fire.

⁸In the very same way, these dreamers
pollute their own bodies, reject authority and slander celestial beings. ⁹But
even the archangel Michael, when he
was disputing with the devil about the
body of Moses, did not dare to bring a
slanderous accusation against him, but
said, "The Lord rebuke you!" ¹⁰Yet these
men speak abusively against whatever
they do not understand; and what
things they do understand by instinct,
like unreasoning animals—these are the
very things that destroy them.

¹¹Woe to them! They have taken the
way of Cain; they have rushed for profit
into Balaam's error; they have been destroyed in Korah's rebellion.

¹²These men are blemishes at your
love feasts, eating with you without the
slightest qualm—shepherds who feed
only themselves. They are clouds without rain, blown along by the wind; autumn trees, without fruit and uprooted—
twice dead. ¹³They are wild waves of the
sea, foaming up their shame; wandering
stars, for whom blackest darkness has
been reserved forever.

¹⁴Enoch, the seventh from Adam,
prophesied about these men: "See, the
Lord is coming with thousands upon
thousands of his holy ones ¹⁵to judge
everyone, and to convict all the ungodly
of all the ungodly acts they have done in
the ungodly way, and of all the harsh
words ungodly sinners have spoken
against him." ¹⁶These men are grum-
blers and faultfinders; they follow their
own evil desires; they boast about themselves and flatter others for their own
advantage.

¹⁷But, dear friends, remember what
the apostles of our Lord Jesus Christ
foretold. ¹⁸They said to you, "In the last
times there will be scoffers who will follow their own ungodly desires." ¹⁹These
are the men who divide you, who follow
mere natural instincts and do not have
the Spirit.

²⁰**But you, dear friends, build yourselves up in your most holy faith and**

pray in the Holy Spirit. [21]Keep yourselves in God's love as you wait for the mercy of our Lord Jesus Christ to bring you to eternal life.

[22]Be merciful to those who doubt; [23]snatch others from the fire and save them; to others show mercy, mixed with fear—hating even the clothing stained by corrupted flesh.

[24]To him who is able to keep you from falling and to present you before his glorious presence without fault and with great joy— [25]to the only God our Savior be glory, majesty, power and authority, through Jesus Christ our Lord, before all ages, now and forevermore! Amen.

[a]1 Or *for; or in* [b]4 Or *men who were marked out for condemnation* [c]5 Some early manuscripts *Jesus*

PSALM 127:1-5
A song of ascents. Of Solomon.

[1]**U**nless the LORD builds the house,
  its builders labor in vain.
Unless the LORD watches over the city,
  the watchmen stand guard in vain.
[2]In vain you rise early
  and stay up late,
toiling for food to eat—
  for he grants sleep to[a] those he loves.

[3]Sons are a heritage from the LORD,
  children a reward from him.
[4]Like arrows in the hands of a warrior
  are sons born in one's youth.
[5]Blessed is the man
  whose quiver is full of them.
They will not be put to shame
  when they contend with their enemies in the gate.

[a]2 Or *eat—/ for while they sleep he provides for*

PROVERBS 29:15-17
[15]**T**he rod of correction imparts wisdom,
  but a child left to himself disgraces his mother.

[16]When the wicked thrive, so does sin,
  but the righteous will see their downfall.

[17]Discipline your son, and he will give you peace;
  he will bring delight to your soul.

□ DAY 343

GOD SIGHTINGS

December 9

JOEL 1:1–3:21
The word of the LORD that came to Joel son of Pethuel.

[2]Hear this, you elders;
  listen, all who live in the land.
Has anything like this ever happened
    in your days
  or in the days of your
      forefathers?
[3]Tell it to your children,
  and let your children tell it to their children,
  and their children to the next generation.
[4]What the locust swarm has left
  the great locusts have eaten;
what the great locusts have left
  the young locusts have eaten;
what the young locusts have left
  other locusts[a] have eaten.

[5]Wake up, you drunkards, and weep!
  Wail, all you drinkers of wine;
wail because of the new wine,
  for it has been snatched from
      your lips.
[6]A nation has invaded my land,
  powerful and without number;
it has the teeth of a lion,
  the fangs of a lioness.
[7]It has laid waste my vines
  and ruined my fig trees.
It has stripped off their bark
  and thrown it away,
  leaving their branches white.

[8]Mourn like a virgin[b] in sackcloth
  grieving for the husband[c] of her youth.

⁹Grain offerings and drink offerings
  are cut off from the house of the
    LORD.
The priests are in mourning,
  those who minister before the
    LORD.
¹⁰The fields are ruined,
  the ground is dried up*d*;
the grain is destroyed,
  the new wine is dried up,
  the oil fails.
¹¹Despair, you farmers,
  wail, you vine growers;
grieve for the wheat and the barley,
  because the harvest of the field is
    destroyed.
¹²The vine is dried up
  and the fig tree is withered;
the pomegranate, the palm and the
    apple tree—
  all the trees of the field—are dried
    up.
Surely the joy of mankind
  is withered away.

¹³Put on sackcloth, O priests, and
    mourn;
  wail, you who minister before the
    altar.
Come, spend the night in sackcloth,
  you who minister before my God;
for the grain offerings and drink
    offerings
  are withheld from the house of
    your God.
¹⁴Declare a holy fast;
  call a sacred assembly.
Summon the elders
  and all who live in the land
to the house of the LORD your God,
  and cry out to the LORD.

¹⁵Alas for that day!
  For the day of the LORD is near;
  it will come like destruction from
    the Almighty.*e*

¹⁶Has not the food been cut off
  before our very eyes—
joy and gladness
  from the house of our God?
¹⁷The seeds are shriveled
  beneath the clods.*f*

The storehouses are in ruins,
  the granaries have been broken
    down,
  for the grain has dried up.
¹⁸How the cattle moan!
  The herds mill about
because they have no pasture;
  even the flocks of sheep are
    suffering.

¹⁹To you, O LORD, I call,
  for fire has devoured the open
    pastures
  and flames have burned up all the
    trees of the field.
²⁰Even the wild animals pant for you;
  the streams of water have dried up
  and fire has devoured the open
    pastures.

²·¹BLOW the trumpet in Zion;
  sound the alarm on my holy hill.
Let all who live in the land tremble,
  for the day of the LORD is coming.
It is close at hand—
² a day of darkness and gloom,
  a day of clouds and blackness.
Like dawn spreading across the
    mountains
  a large and mighty army comes,
such as never was of old
  nor ever will be in ages to come.

³Before them fire devours,
  behind them a flame blazes.
Before them the land is like the
    garden of Eden,
  behind them, a desert waste—
  nothing escapes them.
⁴They have the appearance of horses;
  they gallop along like cavalry.
⁵With a noise like that of chariots
  they leap over the mountaintops,
like a crackling fire consuming
    stubble,
  like a mighty army drawn up for
    battle.

⁶At the sight of them, nations are in
    anguish;
  every face turns pale.
⁷They charge like warriors;
  they scale walls like soldiers.

They all march in line,
  not swerving from their course.
⁸They do not jostle each other;
  each marches straight ahead.
They plunge through defenses
  without breaking ranks.
⁹They rush upon the city;
  they run along the wall.
They climb into the houses;
  like thieves they enter through the
    windows.

¹⁰Before them the earth shakes,
  the sky trembles,
the sun and moon are darkened,
  and the stars no longer shine.
¹¹The Lord thunders
  at the head of his army;
his forces are beyond number,
  and mighty are those who obey his
    command.
The day of the Lord is great;
  it is dreadful.
Who can endure it?

¹²"Even now," declares the Lord,
  "return to me with all your heart,
  with fasting and weeping and
    mourning."

¹³Rend your heart
  and not your garments.
Return to the Lord your God,
  for he is gracious and
    compassionate,
slow to anger and abounding in
  love,
  and he relents from sending
    calamity.
¹⁴Who knows? He may turn and have
    pity
  and leave behind a blessing—
grain offerings and drink offerings
  for the Lord your God.

¹⁵Blow the trumpet in Zion,
  declare a holy fast,
  call a sacred assembly.
¹⁶Gather the people,
  consecrate the assembly;
  bring together the elders,
  gather the children,
    those nursing at the breast.

Let the bridegroom leave his room
  and the bride her chamber.
¹⁷Let the priests, who minister before
    the Lord,
  weep between the temple porch
    and the altar.
Let them say, "Spare your people,
    O Lord.
  Do not make your inheritance an
    object of scorn,
  a byword among the nations.
Why should they say among the
    peoples,
  'Where is their God?'"

¹⁸Then the Lord will be jealous for his
    land
  and take pity on his people.
¹⁹The Lord will reply*ᵍ* to them:

"I am sending you grain, new wine
    and oil,
  enough to satisfy you fully;
never again will I make you
  an object of scorn to the nations.

²⁰"I will drive the northern army far
    from you,
  pushing it into a parched and
    barren land,
with its front columns going into the
    eastern sea*ʰ*
  and those in the rear into the
    western sea.*ⁱ*
And its stench will go up;
  its smell will rise."

Surely he has done great things.*ʲ*
²¹ Be not afraid, O land;
    be glad and rejoice.
Surely the Lord has done great
    things.
²² Be not afraid, O wild animals,
    for the open pastures are
      becoming green.
The trees are bearing their fruit;
    the fig tree and the vine yield their
      riches.
²³Be glad, O people of Zion,
    rejoice in the Lord your God,
  for he has given you
    the autumn rains in
      righteousness.*ᵏ*

He sends you abundant showers,
   both autumn and spring rains, as
      before.
²⁴ The threshing floors will be filled
      with grain;
   the vats will overflow with new
      wine and oil.

²⁵ "I will repay you for the years the
      locusts have eaten—
   the great locust and the young
      locust,
   the other locusts and the locust
      swarm*ᵃ*—
my great army that I sent among you.
²⁶ You will have plenty to eat, until you
      are full,
   and you will praise the name of
      the Lᴏʀᴅ your God,
   who has worked wonders for you;
never again will my people be shamed.
²⁷ Then you will know that I am in Israel,
   that I am the Lᴏʀᴅ your God,
   and that there is no other;
never again will my people be shamed.

²⁸ **"And afterward,**
   I will pour out my Spirit on all
      people.
   Your sons and daughters will
      prophesy,
   your old men will dream dreams,
   your young men will see visions.
²⁹ **Even on my servants, both men**
      and women,
   I will pour out my Spirit in those
      days.
³⁰ I will show wonders in the heavens
      and on the earth,
   blood and fire and billows of smoke.
³¹ The sun will be turned to darkness
      and the moon to blood
   before the coming of the great and
      dreadful day of the Lᴏʀᴅ.
³² And everyone who calls
   on the name of the Lᴏʀᴅ will be
      saved;
   for on Mount Zion and in Jerusalem
      there will be deliverance,
   as the Lᴏʀᴅ has said,
among the survivors
   whom the Lᴏʀᴅ calls.

³:¹ "Iɴ those days and at that time,
   when I restore the fortunes of
      Judah and Jerusalem,
² I will gather all nations
   and bring them down to the Valley
      of Jehoshaphat.*ⁱ*
There I will enter into judgment
      against them
   concerning my inheritance, my
      people Israel,
for they scattered my people among
      the nations
   and divided up my land.
³ They cast lots for my people
   and traded boys for prostitutes;
they sold girls for wine
   that they might drink.

⁴ "Now what have you against me, O Tyre
and Sidon and all you regions of Philistia? Are you repaying me for something
I have done? If you are paying me back, I
will swiftly and speedily return on your
own heads what you have done. ⁵ For you
took my silver and my gold and carried
off my finest treasures to your temples.
⁶ You sold the people of Judah and Jerusalem to the Greeks, that you might
send them far from their homeland.

⁷ "See, I am going to rouse them out
of the places to which you sold them,
and I will return on your own heads
what you have done. ⁸ I will sell your
sons and daughters to the people of Judah, and they will sell them to the Sabeans, a nation far away." The Lᴏʀᴅ has
spoken.

⁹ Proclaim this among the nations:
   Prepare for war!
Rouse the warriors!
   Let all the fighting men draw near
      and attack.
¹⁰ Beat your plowshares into swords
   and your pruning hooks into spears.
Let the weakling say,
   "I am strong!"
¹¹ Come quickly, all you nations from
      every side,
   and assemble there.

Bring down your warriors, O Lᴏʀᴅ!

¹²"Let the nations be roused;
    let them advance into the Valley of
        Jehoshaphat,
for there I will sit
    to judge all the nations on every
        side.
¹³Swing the sickle,
    for the harvest is ripe.
Come, trample the grapes,
    for the winepress is full
    and the vats overflow—
so great is their wickedness!"

¹⁴Multitudes, multitudes
    in the valley of decision!
For the day of the Lᴏʀᴅ is near
    in the valley of decision.
¹⁵The sun and moon will be darkened,
    and the stars no longer shine.
¹⁶The Lᴏʀᴅ will roar from Zion
    and thunder from Jerusalem;
    the earth and the sky will tremble.
But the Lᴏʀᴅ will be a refuge for his
        people,
    a stronghold for the people of
        Israel.
¹⁷"Then you will know that I, the Lᴏʀᴅ
        your God,
    dwell in Zion, my holy hill.
Jerusalem will be holy;
    never again will foreigners invade
        her.

¹⁸"In that day the mountains will drip
        new wine,
    and the hills will flow with milk;
    all the ravines of Judah will run
        with water.
A fountain will flow out of the Lᴏʀᴅ's
        house
    and will water the valley of
        acacias.ᵐ
¹⁹But Egypt will be desolate,
    Edom a desert waste,
because of violence done to the
        people of Judah,
    in whose land they shed innocent
        blood.
²⁰Judah will be inhabited forever
    and Jerusalem through all
        generations.

²¹Their bloodguilt, which I have not
        pardoned,
    I will pardon."

The Lᴏʀᴅ dwells in Zion!

ᵃ4,25 The precise meaning of the four Hebrew words used here for locusts is uncertain.   ᵇ8 Or *young woman*   ᶜ8 Or *betrothed*   ᵈ10 Or *ground mourns*   ᵉ15 Hebrew *Shaddai*   ᶠ17 The meaning of the Hebrew for this word is uncertain.   ᵍ18,19 Or Lᴏʀᴅ *was jealous… / and took pity… /*   ᵍ19 The Lᴏʀᴅ *replied*   ʰ20 That is, the Dead Sea   ⁱ20 That is, the Mediterranean   ʲ20 Or *rise. / Surely it has done great things."*   ᵏ23 Or */ the teacher for righteousness:*   ˡ2 *Jehoshaphat* means the Lᴏʀᴅ *judges*; also in verse 12.   ᵐ18 Or *Valley of Shittim*

REVELATION 1:1-20

Tʜe revelation of Jesus Christ, which God gave him to show his servants what must soon take place. He made it known by sending his angel to his servant John, ²who testifies to everything he saw—that is, the word of God and the testimony of Jesus Christ. ³Blessed is the one who reads the words of this prophecy, and blessed are those who hear it and take to heart what is written in it, because the time is near.

⁴John,

To the seven churches in the province of Asia:

Grace and peace to you from him who is, and who was, and who is to come, and from the seven spiritsᵃ before his throne, ⁵and from Jesus Christ, who is the faithful witness, the firstborn from the dead, and the ruler of the kings of the earth.

To him who loves us and has freed us from our sins by his blood, ⁶and has made us to be a kingdom and priests to serve his God and Father—to him be glory and power for ever and ever! Amen.

⁷Look, he is coming with the clouds,
    and every eye will see him,
even those who pierced him;
    and all the peoples of the earth
        will mourn because of him.
        So shall it be! Amen.

⁸"I am the Alpha and the Omega," says the Lord God, "who is, and who was, and who is to come, the Almighty."

⁹I, John, your brother and companion in the suffering and kingdom and patient endurance that are ours in Jesus, was on the island of Patmos because of the word of God and the testimony of Jesus. ¹⁰On the Lord's Day I was in the Spirit, and I heard behind me a loud voice like a trumpet, ¹¹which said: "Write on a scroll what you see and send it to the seven churches: to Ephesus, Smyrna, Pergamum, Thyatira, Sardis, Philadelphia and Laodicea."

¹²I turned around to see the voice that was speaking to me. And when I turned I saw seven golden lampstands, ¹³and among the lampstands was someone "like a son of man,"ᵇ dressed in a robe reaching down to his feet and with a golden sash around his chest. ¹⁴His head and hair were white like wool, as white as snow, and his eyes were like blazing fire. ¹⁵His feet were like bronze glowing in a furnace, and his voice was like the sound of rushing waters. ¹⁶In his right hand he held seven stars, and out of his mouth came a sharp double-edged sword. His face was like the sun shining in all its brilliance.

¹⁷When I saw him, I fell at his feet as though dead. Then he placed his right hand on me and said: "Do not be afraid. I am the First and the Last. ¹⁸I am the Living One; I was dead, and behold I am alive for ever and ever! And I hold the keys of death and Hades.

¹⁹"Write, therefore, what you have seen, what is now and what will take place later. ²⁰The mystery of the seven stars that you saw in my right hand and of the seven golden lampstands is this: The seven stars are the angelsᶜ of the seven churches, and the seven lampstands are the seven churches."

ᵃ4 Or *the sevenfold Spirit* ᵇ13 Daniel 7:13 ᶜ20 Or *messengers*

PSALM 128:1-6
A song of ascents.

¹Blessed are all who fear the LORD, who walk in his ways.
²You will eat the fruit of your labor; blessings and prosperity will be yours.

³Your wife will be like a fruitful vine within your house;
your sons will be like olive shoots around your table.
⁴Thus is the man blessed who fears the LORD.

⁵May the LORD bless you from Zion all the days of your life;
may you see the prosperity of Jerusalem,
⁶ and may you live to see your children's children.

Peace be upon Israel.

PROVERBS 29:18
¹⁸Where there is no revelation, the people cast off restraint;
but blessed is he who keeps the law.

□ DAY 344

GOD SIGHTINGS

December 10

AMOS 1:1–3:15
The words of Amos, one of the shepherds of Tekoa—what he saw concerning Israel two years before the earthquake, when Uzziah was king of Judah and Jeroboam son of Jehoashᵃ was king of Israel.
²He said:

"The LORD roars from Zion and thunders from Jerusalem;
the pastures of the shepherds dry up,ᵇ
and the top of Carmel withers."

³This is what the LORD says:

"For three sins of Damascus, even for four, I will not turn back ⌐my wrath⌐.
Because she threshed Gilead with sledges having iron teeth,
⁴I will send fire upon the house of Hazael
that will consume the fortresses of Ben-Hadad.

⁵I will break down the gate of
    Damascus;
  I will destroy the king who is inᶜ
    the Valley of Avenᵈ
and the one who holds the scepter in
    Beth Eden.
  The people of Aram will go into
    exile to Kir,"
                            says the LORD.

⁶This is what the LORD says:

"For three sins of Gaza,
    even for four, I will not turn back
    ˌmy wrathˌ.
Because she took captive whole
    communities
  and sold them to Edom,
⁷I will send fire upon the walls of Gaza
    that will consume her fortresses.
⁸I will destroy the kingᵉ of Ashdod
    and the one who holds the scepter
    in Ashkelon.
  I will turn my hand against Ekron,
    till the last of the Philistines is
    dead,"
                    says the Sovereign LORD.

⁹This is what the LORD says:

"For three sins of Tyre,
    even for four, I will not turn back
    ˌmy wrathˌ.
Because she sold whole communities
    of captives to Edom,
  disregarding a treaty of
    brotherhood,
¹⁰I will send fire upon the walls of
    Tyre
  that will consume her fortresses."

¹¹This is what the LORD says:

"For three sins of Edom,
    even for four, I will not turn back
    ˌmy wrathˌ.
Because he pursued his brother with
    a sword,
  stifling all compassion,ᶠ
because his anger raged continually
    and his fury flamed unchecked,
¹²I will send fire upon Teman
    that will consume the fortresses of
    Bozrah."

¹³This is what the LORD says:

"For three sins of Ammon,
    even for four, I will not turn back
    ˌmy wrathˌ.
Because he ripped open the pregnant
    women of Gilead
  in order to extend his borders,
¹⁴I will set fire to the walls of Rabbah
    that will consume her fortresses
amid war cries on the day of battle,
    amid violent winds on a stormy
    day.
¹⁵Her kingᵍ will go into exile,
    he and his officials together,"
                            says the LORD.

²:¹THIS is what the LORD says:

"For three sins of Moab,
    even for four, I will not turn back
    ˌmy wrathˌ.
Because he burned, as if to lime,
    the bones of Edom's king,
²I will send fire upon Moab
    that will consume the fortresses of
    Kerioth.ʰ
Moab will go down in great tumult
    amid war cries and the blast of the
    trumpet.
³I will destroy her ruler
    and kill all her officials with him,"
                            says the LORD.

⁴This is what the LORD says:

"For three sins of Judah,
    even for four, I will not turn back
    ˌmy wrathˌ.
Because they have rejected the law of
    the LORD
  and have not kept his decrees,
because they have been led astray by
    false gods,ⁱ
  the godsʲ their ancestors
    followed,
⁵I will send fire upon Judah
    that will consume the fortresses of
    Jerusalem."

⁶This is what the LORD says:

"For three sins of Israel,
    even for four, I will not turn back
    ˌmy wrathˌ.

They sell the righteous for silver,
  and the needy for a pair of sandals.
[7] They trample on the heads of the
      poor
    as upon the dust of the ground
    and deny justice to the
      oppressed.
  Father and son use the same girl
    and so profane my holy name.
[8] They lie down beside every altar
    on garments taken in pledge.
  In the house of their god
    they drink wine taken as fines.

[9] "I destroyed the Amorite before
      them,
    though he was tall as the cedars
    and strong as the oaks.
  I destroyed his fruit above
    and his roots below.

[10] "I brought you up out of Egypt,
    and I led you forty years in the
      desert
    to give you the land of the Amorites.
[11] I also raised up prophets from
      among your sons
    and Nazirites from among your
      young men.
  Is this not true, people of Israel?"
                    declares the LORD.
[12] "But you made the Nazirites drink
      wine
    and commanded the prophets not
      to prophesy.

[13] "Now then, I will crush you
    as a cart crushes when loaded with
      grain.
[14] The swift will not escape,
    the strong will not muster their
      strength,
    and the warrior will not save his
      life.
[15] The archer will not stand his ground,
    the fleet-footed soldier will not get
      away,
    and the horseman will not save his
      life.
[16] Even the bravest warriors
    will flee naked on that day,"
                    declares the LORD.

[3:1] HEAR this word the LORD has spoken
against you, O people of Israel—against
the whole family I brought up out of
Egypt:

[2] "You only have I chosen
    of all the families of the earth;
  therefore I will punish you
    for all your sins."

[3] Do two walk together
    unless they have agreed to do so?
[4] Does a lion roar in the thicket
    when he has no prey?
  Does he growl in his den
    when he has caught nothing?
[5] Does a bird fall into a trap on the
      ground
    where no snare has been set?
  Does a trap spring up from the earth
    when there is nothing to catch?
[6] When a trumpet sounds in a city,
    do not the people tremble?
  When disaster comes to a city,
    has not the LORD caused it?

[7] Surely the Sovereign LORD does
      nothing
    without revealing his plan
    to his servants the prophets.

[8] The lion has roared—
    who will not fear?
  The Sovereign LORD has spoken—
    who can but prophesy?

[9] Proclaim to the fortresses of Ashdod
    and to the fortresses of Egypt:
  "Assemble yourselves on the
      mountains of Samaria;
    see the great unrest within her
    and the oppression among her
      people."

[10] "They do not know how to do right,"
                    declares the LORD,
  "who hoard plunder and loot in
    their fortresses."

[11] Therefore this is what the Sovereign LORD says:

  "An enemy will overrun the land;
    he will pull down your strongholds
    and plunder your fortresses."

12 This is what the LORD says:

"As a shepherd saves from the lion's
      mouth
   only two leg bones or a piece of an
      ear,
   so will the Israelites be saved,
those who sit in Samaria
   on the edge of their beds
   and in Damascus on their couches.*"

13 "Hear this and testify against the
house of Jacob," declares the Lord, the
LORD God Almighty.

14 "On the day I punish Israel for her
      sins,
   I will destroy the altars of Bethel;
the horns of the altar will be cut off
   and fall to the ground.
15 I will tear down the winter house
   along with the summer house;
the houses adorned with ivory will be
      destroyed
   and the mansions will be
      demolished,"
                        declares the LORD.

a1 Hebrew *Joash*, a variant of *Jehoash*   b2 Or *shepherds mourn*
c5 Or *the inhabitants of*   d5 *Aven* means *wickedness*.
e8 Or *inhabitants*   f11 Or *sword / and destroyed his allies*
g15 Or / *Molech*; Hebrew *malcam*   h2 Or *of her cities*
i4 Or *by lies*   j4 Or *lies*   k12 The meaning of the Hebrew
for this line is uncertain.

REVELATION 2:1-17

"To the angel*a* of the church in Ephesus
write:

These are the words of him who
holds the seven stars in his right
hand and walks among the seven
golden lampstands: 2 I know your
deeds, your hard work and your
perseverance. I know that you cannot tolerate wicked men, that you
have tested those who claim to be
apostles but are not, and have
found them false. 3 You have persevered and have endured hardships
for my name, and have not grown
weary.
   4 Yet I hold this against you: You
have forsaken your first love. 5 Remember the height from which you
have fallen! Repent and do the

things you did at first. If you do not
repent, I will come to you and remove your lampstand from its
place. 6 But you have this in your favor: You hate the practices of the
Nicolaitans, which I also hate.
   7 He who has an ear, let him hear
what the Spirit says to the churches.
To him who overcomes, I will give
the right to eat from the tree of life,
which is in the paradise of God.

8 "To the angel of the church in Smyrna
write:

These are the words of him who
is the First and the Last, who died
and came to life again. 9 I know
your afflictions and your poverty—
yet you are rich! I know the slander
of those who say they are Jews and
are not, but are a synagogue of Satan. 10 **Do not be afraid of what
you are about to suffer. I tell you,
the devil will put some of you in
prison to test you, and you will
suffer persecution for ten days.
Be faithful, even to the point of
death, and I will give you the
crown of life.**
   11 He who has an ear, let him
hear what the Spirit says to the
churches. He who overcomes will
not be hurt at all by the second
death.

12 "To the angel of the church in Pergamum write:

These are the words of him who
has the sharp, double-edged sword.
13 I know where you live—where Satan has his throne. Yet you remain
true to my name. You did not renounce your faith in me, even in the
days of Antipas, my faithful witness,
who was put to death in your city—
where Satan lives.
   14 Nevertheless, I have a few things
against you: You have people there
who hold to the teaching of Balaam,
who taught Balak to entice the Israelites to sin by eating food sacrificed to

idols and by committing sexual immorality. 15Likewise you also have those who hold to the teaching of the Nicolaitans. 16Repent therefore! Otherwise, I will soon come to you and will fight against them with the sword of my mouth.

17He who has an ear, let him hear what the Spirit says to the churches. To him who overcomes, I will give some of the hidden manna. I will also give him a white stone with a new name written on it, known only to him who receives it."

a 1 Or messenger; also in verses 8, 12 and 18

PSALM 129:1-8
A song of ascents.

1They have greatly oppressed me
    from my youth—
    let Israel say—
2they have greatly oppressed me from
    my youth,
    but they have not gained the
    victory over me.
3Plowmen have plowed my back
    and made their furrows long.
4But the Lord is righteous;
    he has cut me free from the cords
    of the wicked.

5May all who hate Zion
    be turned back in shame.
6May they be like grass on the roof,
    which withers before it can grow;
7with it the reaper cannot fill his
    hands,
    nor the one who gathers fill his
    arms.
8May those who pass by not say,
    "The blessing of the Lord be upon
    you;
    we bless you in the name of the
    Lord."

PROVERBS 29:19-20
19A servant cannot be corrected by
    mere words;
    though he understands, he will not
    respond.

20Do you see a man who speaks in
    haste?
    There is more hope for a fool than
    for him.

☐ D A Y   3 4 5

GOD SIGHTINGS

December 11

AMOS 4:1–6:14
Hear this word, you cows of Bashan
    on Mount Samaria,
    you women who oppress the poor
    and crush the needy
    and say to your husbands, "Bring
    us some drinks!"
2The Sovereign Lord has sworn by his
    holiness:
    "The time will surely come
when you will be taken away with
    hooks,
    the last of you with fishhooks.
3You will each go straight out
    through breaks in the wall,
    and you will be cast out toward
    Harmon,a"
                    declares the Lord.
4"Go to Bethel and sin;
    go to Gilgal and sin yet more.
Bring your sacrifices every morning,
    your tithes every three years.b
5Burn leavened bread as a thank
    offering
    and brag about your freewill
    offerings—
boast about them, you Israelites,
    for this is what you love to do,"
                declares the Sovereign Lord.

6"I gave you empty stomachsc in every
    city
    and lack of bread in every town,
    yet you have not returned to me,"
                    declares the Lord.

7"I also withheld rain from you
    when the harvest was still three
    months away.

I sent rain on one town,
    but withheld it from another.
One field had rain;
    another had none and dried up.
8 People staggered from town to town
        for water
    but did not get enough to drink,
    yet you have not returned to me,"
                declares the LORD.

9 "Many times I struck your gardens
        and vineyards,
    I struck them with blight and
        mildew.
Locusts devoured your fig and olive
        trees,
    yet you have not returned to me,"
                declares the LORD.

10 "I sent plagues among you
        as I did to Egypt.
I killed your young men with the
        sword,
    along with your captured horses.
I filled your nostrils with the stench
        of your camps,
    yet you have not returned to me,"
                declares the LORD.

11 "I overthrew some of you
        as I*d* overthrew Sodom and
        Gomorrah.
You were like a burning stick
        snatched from the fire,
    yet you have not returned to me,"
                declares the LORD.

12 "Therefore this is what I will do to
        you, Israel,
    and because I will do this to you,
    prepare to meet your God, O Israel."

13 He who forms the mountains,
        creates the wind,
    and reveals his thoughts to man,
he who turns dawn to darkness,
    and treads the high places of the
        earth—
    the LORD God Almighty is his name.

5:1 HEAR this word, O house of Israel, this
lament I take up concerning you:

2 "Fallen is Virgin Israel,
    never to rise again,

deserted in her own land,
    with no one to lift her up."

3 This is what the Sovereign LORD
says:

"The city that marches out a
        thousand strong for Israel
    will have only a hundred left;
the town that marches out a hundred
        strong
    will have only ten left."

4 This is what the LORD says to the
house of Israel:

"Seek me and live;
5   do not seek Bethel,
    do not go to Gilgal,
        do not journey to Beersheba.
For Gilgal will surely go into exile,
    and Bethel will be reduced to
        nothing.*e*"
6 Seek the LORD and live,
    or he will sweep through the
        house of Joseph like a fire;
    it will devour,
    and Bethel will have no one to
        quench it.

7 You who turn justice into bitterness
    and cast righteousness to the
        ground
8 (he who made the Pleiades and
        Orion,
    who turns blackness into dawn
    and darkens day into night,
who calls for the waters of the sea
    and pours them out over the face
        of the land—
    the LORD is his name—
9 he flashes destruction on the
        stronghold
    and brings the fortified city to
        ruin),
10 you hate the one who reproves in
        court
    and despise him who tells the truth.

11 You trample on the poor
    and force him to give you grain.
Therefore, though you have built
        stone mansions,
    you will not live in them;

though you have planted lush
    vineyards,
you will not drink their wine.
¹²For I know how many are your
        offenses
    and how great your sins.

You oppress the righteous and take
        bribes
    and you deprive the poor of justice
        in the courts.
¹³Therefore the prudent man keeps
        quiet in such times,
    for the times are evil.

¹⁴Seek good, not evil,
    that you may live.
Then the LORD God Almighty will be
        with you,
    just as you say he is.
¹⁵Hate evil, love good;
    maintain justice in the courts.
Perhaps the LORD God Almighty will
        have mercy
    on the remnant of Joseph.

¹⁶Therefore this is what the Lord, the
LORD God Almighty, says:

"There will be wailing in all the
        streets
    and cries of anguish in every
        public square.
The farmers will be summoned to
        weep
    and the mourners to wail.
¹⁷There will be wailing in all the
        vineyards,
    for I will pass through your
        midst,"
                        says the LORD.

¹⁸Woe to you who long
    for the day of the LORD!
Why do you long for the day of the
        LORD?
    That day will be darkness, not
        light.
¹⁹It will be as though a man fled from a
        lion
    only to meet a bear,
as though he entered his house
    and rested his hand on the wall
    only to have a snake bite him.

²⁰Will not the day of the LORD be
        darkness, not light—
    pitch-dark, without a ray of
        brightness?

²¹"I hate, I despise your religious
        feasts;
    I cannot stand your assemblies.
²²Even though you bring me burnt
        offerings and grain
        offerings,
    I will not accept them.
Though you bring choice fellowship
        offerings,ᶠ
    I will have no regard for them.
²³Away with the noise of your songs!
    I will not listen to the music of
        your harps.
²⁴But let justice roll on like a river,
    righteousness like a never-failing
        stream!

²⁵"Did you bring me sacrifices and
        offerings
    forty years in the desert, O house
        of Israel?
²⁶You have lifted up the shrine of your
        king,
    the pedestal of your idols,
    the star of your godᵍ—
    which you made for yourselves.
²⁷Therefore I will send you into exile
        beyond Damascus,"
    says the LORD, whose name is God
        Almighty.

⁶:¹WOE to you who are complacent in
        Zion,
    and to you who feel secure on
        Mount Samaria,
you notable men of the foremost
        nation,
    to whom the people of Israel
        come!
²Go to Calneh and look at it;
    go from there to great Hamath,
    and then go down to Gath in
        Philistia.
Are they better off than your two
        kingdoms?
    Is their land larger than yours?
³You put off the evil day
    and bring near a reign of terror.

4 You lie on beds inlaid with ivory
  and lounge on your couches.
You dine on choice lambs
  and fattened calves.
5 You strum away on your harps like
    David
  and improvise on musical
    instruments.
6 You drink wine by the bowlful
  and use the finest lotions,
  but you do not grieve over the ruin
    of Joseph.
7 Therefore you will be among the first
    to go into exile;
  your feasting and lounging will end.

8 The Sovereign Lord has sworn by
himself—the Lord God Almighty declares:

"I abhor the pride of Jacob
  and detest his fortresses;
I will deliver up the city
  and everything in it."

9 If ten men are left in one house, they
too will die. 10 And if a relative who is to
burn the bodies comes to carry them
out of the house and asks anyone still
hiding there, "Is anyone with you?" and
he says, "No," then he will say, "Hush! We
must not mention the name of the
Lord."

11 For the Lord has given the command,
  and he will smash the great house
    into pieces
  and the small house into bits.

12 Do horses run on the rocky crags?
  Does one plow there with oxen?
But you have turned justice into
    poison
  and the fruit of righteousness into
    bitterness—
13 you who rejoice in the conquest of Lo
    Debar[h]
  and say, "Did we not take
    Karnaim[i] by our own
    strength?"

14 For the Lord God Almighty declares,
  "I will stir up a nation against you,
    O house of Israel,

that will oppress you all the way
  from Lebo/ Hamath to the valley of
    the Arabah."

[a]3 Masoretic Text; with a different word division of the
Hebrew (see Septuagint) out, O mountain of oppression
[b]4 Or tithes on the third day   [c]6 Hebrew you cleanness
of teeth   [d]11 Hebrew God   [e]5 Or grief; or wickedness;
Hebrew aven, a reference to Beth Aven (a derogatory name
for Bethel)   [f]22 Traditionally peace offerings   [g]26 Or lifted
up Sakkuth your king / and Kaiwan your idols, / your star-
gods; Septuagint lifted up the shrine of Molech / and the star
of your god Rephan, / their idols   [h]13 Lo Debar means
nothing.   [i]13 Karnaim means horns; horn here symbolizes
strength.   [j]14 Or from the entrance to

REVELATION 2:18–3:6

"To the angel of the church in Thyatira
write:

These are the words of the Son of
God, whose eyes are like blazing fire
and whose feet are like burnished
bronze. 19 I know your deeds, your
love and faith, your service and perseverance, and that you are now doing more than you did at first.

20 Nevertheless, I have this
against you: You tolerate that
woman Jezebel, who calls herself a
prophetess. By her teaching she
misleads my servants into sexual
immorality and the eating of food
sacrificed to idols. 21 I have given
her time to repent of her immorality, but she is unwilling. 22 So I will
cast her on a bed of suffering, and I
will make those who commit adultery with her suffer intensely, unless they repent of her ways. 23 I will
strike her children dead. Then all
the churches will know that I am he
who searches hearts and minds,
and I will repay each of you according to your deeds. 24 Now I say to the
rest of you in Thyatira, to you who
do not hold to her teaching and
have not learned Satan's so-called
deep secrets (I will not impose any
other burden on you): 25 Only hold
on to what you have until I come.

26 To him who overcomes and
does my will to the end, I will give
authority over the nations—

27 'He will rule them with an iron
    scepter;

he will dash them to pieces like pottery'ᵃ—

just as I have received authority from my Father. 28I will also give him the morning star. 29He who has an ear, let him hear what the Spirit says to the churches.

3:1"To the angelᵇ of the church in Sardis write:

These are the words of him who holds the seven spiritsᶜ of God and the seven stars. I know your deeds; you have a reputation of being alive, but you are dead. 2Wake up! Strengthen what remains and is about to die, for I have not found your deeds complete in the sight of my God. 3Remember, therefore, what you have received and heard; obey it, and repent. But if you do not wake up, I will come like a thief, and you will not know at what time I will come to you.

4Yet you have a few people in Sardis who have not soiled their clothes. They will walk with me, dressed in white, for they are worthy. 5**He who overcomes will, like them, be dressed in white. I will never blot out his name from the book of life, but will acknowledge his name before my Father and his angels.** 6He who has an ear, let him hear what the Spirit says to the churches."

ᵃ27 Psalm 2:9   ᵇ1 Or *messenger*; also in verses 7 and 14
ᶜ1 Or *the sevenfold Spirit*

PSALM 130:1-8
A song of ascents.

1 **O**ut of the depths I cry to you,
   O LORD;
2   O Lord, hear my voice.
Let your ears be attentive
   to my cry for mercy.

3 If you, O LORD, kept a record of sins,
   O Lord, who could stand?
4 But with you there is forgiveness;
   therefore you are feared.

5 I wait for the LORD, my soul waits,
   and in his word I put my hope.
6 My soul waits for the Lord
   more than watchmen wait for the
      morning,
   more than watchmen wait for the
      morning.

7 O Israel, put your hope in the LORD,
   for with the LORD is unfailing love
   and with him is full redemption.
8 He himself will redeem Israel
   from all their sins.

PROVERBS 29:21-22
21 **I**f a man pampers his servant from
      youth,
   he will bring griefᵃ in the end.

22 An angry man stirs up dissension,
   and a hot-tempered one commits
      many sins.

ᵃ21 The meaning of the Hebrew for this word is uncertain.

□ DAY 346

GOD SIGHTINGS

December 12

AMOS 7:1–9:15
This is what the Sovereign LORD showed me [Amos]: He was preparing swarms of locusts after the king's share had been harvested and just as the second crop was coming up. 2When they had stripped the land clean, I cried out, "Sovereign LORD, forgive! How can Jacob survive? He is so small!"

3So the LORD relented.

"This will not happen," the LORD said.

4This is what the Sovereign LORD showed me: The Sovereign LORD was calling for judgment by fire; it dried up the great deep and devoured the land. 5Then I cried out, "Sovereign LORD, I beg you, stop! How can Jacob survive? He is so small!"

6So the LORD relented.

"This will not happen either," the Sovereign LORD said.

7 This is what he showed me: The Lord was standing by a wall that had been built true to plumb, with a plumb line in his hand. 8 And the LORD asked me, "What do you see, Amos?"

"A plumb line," I replied.

Then the Lord said, "Look, I am setting a plumb line among my people Israel; I will spare them no longer.

9 "The high places of Isaac will be destroyed
    and the sanctuaries of Israel will be ruined;
    with my sword I will rise against the house of Jeroboam."

10 Then Amaziah the priest of Bethel sent a message to Jeroboam king of Israel: "Amos is raising a conspiracy against you in the very heart of Israel. The land cannot bear all his words. 11 For this is what Amos is saying:

"'Jeroboam will die by the sword,
    and Israel will surely go into exile,
    away from their native land.'"

12 Then Amaziah said to Amos, "Get out, you seer! Go back to the land of Judah. Earn your bread there and do your prophesying there. 13 Don't prophesy anymore at Bethel, because this is the king's sanctuary and the temple of the kingdom."

14 Amos answered Amaziah, "I was neither a prophet nor a prophet's son, but I was a shepherd, and I also took care of sycamore-fig trees. 15 But the LORD took me from tending the flock and said to me, 'Go, prophesy to my people Israel.' 16 Now then, hear the word of the LORD. You say,

"'Do not prophesy against Israel,
    and stop preaching against the house of Isaac.'

17 "Therefore this is what the LORD says:

"'Your wife will become a prostitute in the city,

and your sons and daughters will fall by the sword.
Your land will be measured and divided up,
    and you yourself will die in a pagan*a* country.
And Israel will certainly go into exile,
    away from their native land.'"

8:1 THIS is what the Sovereign LORD showed me: a basket of ripe fruit. 2 "What do you see, Amos?" he asked.

"A basket of ripe fruit," I answered.

Then the LORD said to me, "The time is ripe for my people Israel; I will spare them no longer.

3 "In that day," declares the Sovereign LORD, "the songs in the temple will turn to wailing.*b* Many, many bodies—flung everywhere! Silence!"

4 Hear this, you who trample the needy
    and do away with the poor of the land,

5 saying,

"When will the New Moon be over
    that we may sell grain,
and the Sabbath be ended
    that we may market wheat?"—
skimping the measure,
    boosting the price
    and cheating with dishonest scales,
6 buying the poor with silver
    and the needy for a pair of sandals,
    selling even the sweepings with the wheat.

7 The LORD has sworn by the Pride of Jacob: "I will never forget anything they have done.

8 "Will not the land tremble for this,
    and all who live in it mourn?
The whole land will rise like the Nile;
    it will be stirred up and then sink
    like the river of Egypt.

9 "In that day," declares the Sovereign LORD,

"I will make the sun go down at noon
    and darken the earth in broad
        daylight.
¹⁰I will turn your religious feasts into
        mourning
    and all your singing into weeping.
I will make all of you wear sackcloth
    and shave your heads.
I will make that time like mourning
        for an only son
    and the end of it like a bitter day.

¹¹"The days are coming," declares the
        Sovereign LORD,
    "when I will send a famine
        through the land—
not a famine of food or a thirst for
        water,
    but a famine of hearing the words
        of the LORD.
¹²Men will stagger from sea to sea
    and wander from north to east,
searching for the word of the LORD,
    but they will not find it.

¹³"In that day

"the lovely young women and strong
        young men
    will faint because of thirst.
¹⁴They who swear by the shameᶜ of
        Samaria,
    or say, 'As surely as your god lives,
        O Dan,'
    or, 'As surely as the godᵈ of
        Beersheba lives'—
they will fall,
    never to rise again."

⁹:¹I saw the Lord standing by the altar,
and he said:

"Strike the tops of the pillars
    so that the thresholds shake.
Bring them down on the heads of all
        the people;
    those who are left I will kill with
        the sword.
Not one will get away,
    none will escape.
²Though they dig down to the depths
        of the grave,ᵉ
    from there my hand will take
        them.

Though they climb up to the
        heavens,
    from there I will bring them down.
³Though they hide themselves on the
        top of Carmel,
    there I will hunt them down and
        seize them.
Though they hide from me at the
        bottom of the sea,
    there I will command the serpent
        to bite them.
⁴Though they are driven into exile by
        their enemies,
    there I will command the sword to
        slay them.
I will fix my eyes upon them
    for evil and not for good."

⁵The Lord, the LORD Almighty,
    he who touches the earth and it
        melts,
    and all who live in it mourn—
the whole land rises like the Nile,
    then sinks like the river of Egypt—
⁶he who builds his lofty palaceᶠ in the
        heavens
    and sets its foundationᵍ on the
        earth,
who calls for the waters of the sea
    and pours them out over the face
        of the land—
    the LORD is his name.

⁷"Are not you Israelites
    the same to me as the Cushitesʰ?"
                    declares the LORD.
"Did I not bring Israel up from Egypt,
    the Philistines from Caphtorⁱ
    and the Arameans from Kir?

⁸"Surely the eyes of the Sovereign LORD
    are on the sinful kingdom.
I will destroy it
    from the face of the earth—
yet I will not totally destroy
    the house of Jacob,"
                    declares the LORD.
⁹"For I will give the command,
    and I will shake the house of Israel
        among all the nations
as grain is shaken in a sieve,
    and not a pebble will reach the
        ground.

¹⁰All the sinners among my people
will die by the sword,
all those who say,
'Disaster will not overtake or
meet us.'

¹¹"In that day I will restore
David's fallen tent.
I will repair its broken places,
restore its ruins,
and build it as it used to be,
¹²so that they may possess the remnant
of Edom
and all the nations that bear my
name,^j"
declares the LORD,
who will do these things.

¹³" The days are coming," declares
the LORD,

"when the reaper will be
overtaken by the plowman
and the planter by the one
treading grapes.
New wine will drip from the
mountains
and flow from all the hills.
¹⁴I will bring back my exiled^k people
Israel;
they will rebuild the ruined
cities and live in them.
They will plant vineyards and
drink their wine;
they will make gardens and eat
their fruit.
¹⁵I will plant Israel in their own land,
never again to be uprooted
from the land I have given them,"
says the LORD your God.

^a17 Hebrew an unclean   ^b3 Or "the temple singers will wail
^c14 Or by Ashima; or by the idol   ^d14 Or power   ^e2 Hebrew
to Sheol   ^f6 The meaning of the Hebrew for this phrase
is uncertain.   ^g6 The meaning of the Hebrew for this word
is uncertain.   ^h7 That is, people from the upper Nile region
ⁱ7 That is, Crete   ^j12 Hebrew; Septuagint so that the
remnant of men / and all the nations that bear my name
may seek ⌊the Lord⌋   ^k14 Or will restore the fortunes of my

REVELATION 3:7-22

"To the angel of the church in Philadelphia write:

These are the words of him who
is holy and true, who holds the key
of David. What he opens no one

can shut, and what he shuts no one
can open. ⁸I know your deeds. See,
I have placed before you an open
door that no one can shut. I know
that you have little strength, yet
you have kept my word and have
not denied my name. ⁹I will make
those who are of the synagogue of
Satan, who claim to be Jews though
they are not, but are liars—I will
make them come and fall down at
your feet and acknowledge that I
have loved you. ¹⁰Since you have
kept my command to endure patiently, I will also keep you from the
hour of trial that is going to come
upon the whole world to test those
who live on the earth.

¹¹I am coming soon. Hold on to
what you have, so that no one will
take your crown. ¹²Him who overcomes I will make a pillar in the
temple of my God. Never again will
he leave it. I will write on him the
name of my God and the name of
the city of my God, the new Jerusalem, which is coming down out of
heaven from my God; and I will also
write on him my new name. ¹³He
who has an ear, let him hear what
the Spirit says to the churches.

¹⁴"To the angel of the church in Laodicea write:

These are the words of the Amen,
the faithful and true witness, the
ruler of God's creation. ¹⁵I know
your deeds, that you are neither
cold nor hot. I wish you were either
one or the other! ¹⁶So, because you
are lukewarm—neither hot nor
cold—I am about to spit you out of
my mouth. ¹⁷You say, 'I am rich; I
have acquired wealth and do not
need a thing.' But you do not realize
that you are wretched, pitiful, poor,
blind and naked. ¹⁸I counsel you to
buy from me gold refined in the
fire, so you can become rich; and
white clothes to wear, so you can
cover your shameful nakedness;

and salve to put on your eyes, so you can see.

¹⁹Those whom I love I rebuke and discipline. So be earnest, and repent. ²⁰Here I am! I stand at the door and knock. If anyone hears my voice and opens the door, I will come in and eat with him, and he with me.

²¹To him who overcomes, I will give the right to sit with me on my throne, just as I overcame and sat down with my Father on his throne. ²²He who has an ear, let him hear what the Spirit says to the churches."

PSALM 131:1-3
A song of ascents. Of David.

¹ **M**y heart is not proud, O Lord,
  my eyes are not haughty;
 I do not concern myself with great matters
  or things too wonderful for me.
² But I have stilled and quieted my soul;
  like a weaned child with its mother,
  like a weaned child is my soul within me.

³ O Israel, put your hope in the Lord
  both now and forevermore.

PROVERBS 29:23
²³**A** man's pride brings him low,
  but a man of lowly spirit gains honor.

☐ DAY 347

GOD SIGHTINGS

December 13

OBADIAH 1:1-21
The vision of Obadiah.

This is what the Sovereign Lord says about Edom—

We have heard a message from the Lord:

An envoy was sent to the nations to say,
"Rise, and let us go against her for battle"—

² "See, I will make you small among the nations;
  you will be utterly despised.
³ The pride of your heart has deceived you,
  you who live in the clefts of the rocks*a*
  and make your home on the heights,
 you who say to yourself,
  'Who can bring me down to the ground?'
⁴ Though you soar like the eagle
  and make your nest among the stars,
  from there I will bring you down,"
                declares the Lord.
⁵ "If thieves came to you,
  if robbers in the night—
 Oh, what a disaster awaits you—
  would they not steal only as much as they wanted?
 If grape pickers came to you,
  would they not leave a few grapes?
⁶ But how Esau will be ransacked,
  his hidden treasures pillaged!
⁷ All your allies will force you to the border;
  your friends will deceive and overpower you;
 those who eat your bread will set a trap for you,*b*
  but you will not detect it.

⁸ "In that day," declares the Lord,
  "will I not destroy the wise men of Edom,
  men of understanding in the mountains of Esau?
⁹ Your warriors, O Teman, will be terrified,
  and everyone in Esau's mountains will be cut down in the slaughter.
¹⁰Because of the violence against your brother Jacob,
  you will be covered with shame;
  you will be destroyed forever.

¹¹On the day you stood aloof
  while strangers carried off his
    wealth
and foreigners entered his gates
  and cast lots for Jerusalem,
  you were like one of them.
¹²You should not look down on your
    brother
  in the day of his misfortune,
  nor rejoice over the people of Judah
    in the day of their destruction,
  nor boast so much
    in the day of their trouble.
¹³You should not march through the
    gates of my people
  in the day of their disaster,
  nor look down on them in their
    calamity
    in the day of their disaster,
  nor seize their wealth
    in the day of their disaster.
¹⁴ You should not wait at the
    crossroads
  to cut down their fugitives,
  nor hand over their survivors
    in the day of their trouble.

¹⁵"The day of the LORD is near
  for all nations.
As you have done, it will be done to
    you;
  your deeds will return upon your
    own head.
¹⁶Just as you drank on my holy hill,
  so all the nations will drink
    continually;
  they will drink and drink
  and be as if they had never been.
¹⁷But on Mount Zion will be
    deliverance;
  it will be holy,
and the house of Jacob
  will possess its inheritance.
¹⁸The house of Jacob will be a fire
  and the house of Joseph a flame;
the house of Esau will be stubble,
  and they will set it on fire and
    consume it.
There will be no survivors
  from the house of Esau."
          The LORD has spoken.

¹⁹People from the Negev will occupy
  the mountains of Esau,
and people from the foothills will
    possess
  the land of the Philistines.
They will occupy the fields of
    Ephraim and Samaria,
  and Benjamin will possess Gilead.
²⁰This company of Israelite exiles who
    are in Canaan
will possess ⸢the land⸣ as far as
    Zarephath;
the exiles from Jerusalem who are in
    Sepharad
will possess the towns of the
    Negev.
²¹Deliverers will go up on^c Mount Zion
  to govern the mountains of Esau.
And the kingdom will be the
    LORD's.

^a3 Or of Sela ^b7 The meaning of the Hebrew for this clause
is uncertain. ^c21 Or from

REVELATION 4:1-11

After this I [John] looked, and there before me was a door standing open in heaven. And the voice I had first heard speaking to me like a trumpet said, "Come up here, and I will show you what must take place after this." ²At once I was in the Spirit, and there before me was a throne in heaven with someone sitting on it. ³And the one who sat there had the appearance of jasper and carnelian. A rainbow, resembling an emerald, encircled the throne. ⁴Surrounding the throne were twenty-four other thrones, and seated on them were twenty-four elders. They were dressed in white and had crowns of gold on their heads. ⁵From the throne came flashes of lightning, rumblings and peals of thunder. Before the throne, seven lamps were blazing. These are the seven spirits^a of God. ⁶Also before the throne there was what looked like a sea of glass, clear as crystal.

In the center, around the throne, were four living creatures, and they were covered with eyes, in front and in back. ⁷The first living creature was like a lion, the second was like an ox, the third had a face like a man, the fourth was like a flying eagle. [8]Each of the four living creatures had six wings and was covered with eyes all around, even under his wings. Day and night they never stop saying:

> "Holy, holy, holy
> is the Lord God Almighty,
> who was, and is, and is to come."

[9]Whenever the living creatures give glory, honor and thanks to him who sits on the throne and who lives for ever and ever, [10]the twenty-four elders fall down before him who sits on the throne, and worship him who lives for ever and ever. They lay their crowns before the throne and say:

[11]" You are worthy, our Lord and God,
     to receive glory and honor and power,
   for you created all things,
     and by your will they were created
     and have their being."

[a]5 Or *the sevenfold Spirit*

PSALM 132:1-18
A song of ascents.

[1]◉ Lord, remember David
   and all the hardships he endured.

[2]He swore an oath to the Lord
   and made a vow to the Mighty One of Jacob:
[3]"I will not enter my house
   or go to my bed—
[4]I will allow no sleep to my eyes,
   no slumber to my eyelids,
[5]till I find a place for the Lord,
   a dwelling for the Mighty One of Jacob."

[6]We heard it in Ephrathah,
   we came upon it in the fields of Jaar[a;b]
[7]"Let us go to his dwelling place;
   let us worship at his footstool—
[8]arise, O Lord, and come to your resting place,
   you and the ark of your might.

[9]May your priests be clothed with righteousness;
   may your saints sing for joy."

[10]For the sake of David your servant,
   do not reject your anointed one.

[11]The Lord swore an oath to David,
   a sure oath that he will not revoke:
  "One of your own descendants
   I will place on your throne—
[12]if your sons keep my covenant
   and the statutes I teach them,
  then their sons will sit
   on your throne for ever and ever."

[13]For the Lord has chosen Zion,
   he has desired it for his dwelling:
[14]"This is my resting place for ever and ever;
   here I will sit enthroned, for I have desired it—
[15]I will bless her with abundant provisions;
   her poor will I satisfy with food.
[16]I will clothe her priests with salvation,
   and her saints will ever sing for joy.

[17]"Here I will make a horn[c] grow for David
   and set up a lamp for my anointed one.
[18]I will clothe his enemies with shame,
   but the crown on his head will be resplendent."

[a]6 That is, Kiriath Jearim   [b]6 Or *heard of it in Ephrathah, / we found it in the fields of Jaar.* (And no quotes around verses 7-9)   [c]17 *Horn* here symbolizes strong one, that is, king.

PROVERBS 29:24-25
[24]The accomplice of a thief is his own enemy;
   he is put under oath and dare not testify.

[25]Fear of man will prove to be a snare,
   but whoever trusts in the Lord is kept safe.

GOD SIGHTINGS

December 14

JONAH 1:1–4:11

The word of the LORD came to Jonah son of Amittai: 2 "Go to the great city of Nineveh and preach against it, because its wickedness has come up before me."

3 But Jonah ran away from the LORD and headed for Tarshish. He went down to Joppa, where he found a ship bound for that port. After paying the fare, he went aboard and sailed for Tarshish to flee from the LORD.

4 Then the LORD sent a great wind on the sea, and such a violent storm arose that the ship threatened to break up. 5 All the sailors were afraid and each cried out to his own god. And they threw the cargo into the sea to lighten the ship.

But Jonah had gone below deck, where he lay down and fell into a deep sleep. 6 The captain went to him and said, "How can you sleep? Get up and call on your god! Maybe he will take notice of us, and we will not perish."

7 Then the sailors said to each other, "Come, let us cast lots to find out who is responsible for this calamity." They cast lots and the lot fell on Jonah.

8 So they asked him, "Tell us, who is responsible for making all this trouble for us? What do you do? Where do you come from? What is your country? From what people are you?"

9 He answered, "I am a Hebrew and I worship the LORD, the God of heaven, who made the sea and the land."

10 This terrified them and they asked, "What have you done?" (They knew he was running away from the LORD, because he had already told them so.)

11 The sea was getting rougher and rougher. So they asked him, "What should we do to you to make the sea calm down for us?"

12 "Pick me up and throw me into the sea," he replied, "and it will become calm. I know that it is my fault that this great storm has come upon you."

13 Instead, the men did their best to row back to land. But they could not, for the sea grew even wilder than before. 14 Then they cried to the LORD, "O LORD, please do not let us die for taking this man's life. Do not hold us accountable for killing an innocent man, for you, O LORD, have done as you pleased." 15 Then they took Jonah and threw him overboard, and the raging sea grew calm. 16 At this the men greatly feared the LORD, and they offered a sacrifice to the LORD and made vows to him.

17 But the LORD provided a great fish to swallow Jonah, and Jonah was inside the fish three days and three nights.

2:1 FROM inside the fish Jonah prayed to the LORD his God. 2 He said:

"In my distress I called to the LORD,
    and he answered me.
From the depths of the grave*a* I
        called for help,
    and you listened to my cry.
3 You hurled me into the deep,
    into the very heart of the seas,
    and the currents swirled about me;
all your waves and breakers
    swept over me.
4 I said, 'I have been banished
    from your sight;
yet I will look again
    toward your holy temple.'
5 The engulfing waters threatened me,*b*
    the deep surrounded me;
    seaweed was wrapped around my
        head.
6 To the roots of the mountains I sank
        down;
    the earth beneath barred me in
        forever.
But you brought my life up from the
        pit,
    O LORD my God.

7 "When my life was ebbing away,
    I remembered you, LORD,
and my prayer rose to you,
    to your holy temple.

8"Those who cling to worthless idols
  forfeit the grace that could be theirs.
9But I, with a song of thanksgiving,
  will sacrifice to you.
What I have vowed I will make good.
  Salvation comes from the Lord."

10And the Lord commanded the fish, and it vomited Jonah onto dry land.

3:1Then the word of the Lord came to Jonah a second time: 2"Go to the great city of Nineveh and proclaim to it the message I give you."

3Jonah obeyed the word of the Lord and went to Nineveh. Now Nineveh was a very important city—a visit required three days. 4On the first day, Jonah started into the city. He proclaimed: "Forty more days and Nineveh will be overturned." 5The Ninevites believed God. They declared a fast, and all of them, from the greatest to the least, put on sackcloth.

6When the news reached the king of Nineveh, he rose from his throne, took off his royal robes, covered himself with sackcloth and sat down in the dust. 7Then he issued a proclamation in Nineveh:

"By the decree of the king and his nobles:

Do not let any man or beast, herd or flock, taste anything; do not let them eat or drink. 8But let man and beast be covered with sackcloth. Let everyone call urgently on God. Let them give up their evil ways and their violence. 9Who knows? God may yet relent and with compassion turn from his fierce anger so that we will not perish."

10When God saw what they did and how they turned from their evil ways, he had compassion and did not bring upon them the destruction he had threatened.

4:1But Jonah was greatly displeased and became angry. 2He prayed to the Lord, "O Lord, is this not what I said when I was

still at home? That is why I was so quick to flee to Tarshish. I knew that you are a gracious and compassionate God, slow to anger and abounding in love, a God who relents from sending calamity. 3Now, O Lord, take away my life, for it is better for me to die than to live."

4But the Lord replied, "Have you any right to be angry?"

5Jonah went out and sat down at a place east of the city. There he made himself a shelter, sat in its shade and waited to see what would happen to the city. 6Then the Lord God provided a vine and made it grow up over Jonah to give shade for his head to ease his discomfort, and Jonah was very happy about the vine. 7But at dawn the next day God provided a worm, which chewed the vine so that it withered. 8When the sun rose, God provided a scorching east wind, and the sun blazed on Jonah's head so that he grew faint. He wanted to die, and said, "It would be better for me to die than to live."

9But God said to Jonah, "Do you have a right to be angry about the vine?"

"I do," he said. "I am angry enough to die."

10But the Lord said, "You have been concerned about this vine, though you did not tend it or make it grow. It sprang up overnight and died overnight. 11But Nineveh has more than a hundred and twenty thousand people who cannot tell their right hand from their left, and many cattle as well. Should I not be concerned about that great city?"

a2 Hebrew Sheol   b5 Or waters were at my throat

REVELATION 5:1-14
Then I [John] saw in the right hand of him who sat on the throne a scroll with writing on both sides and sealed with seven seals. 2And I saw a mighty angel proclaiming in a loud voice, "Who is worthy to break the seals and open the scroll?" 3But no one in heaven or on earth or under the earth could open the scroll or even look inside it. 4I wept and wept because no one was found who was worthy to open the scroll or look inside. 5Then one of the elders said to me,

"Do not weep! See, the Lion of the tribe of Judah, the Root of David, has triumphed. He is able to open the scroll and its seven seals."

⁶Then I saw a Lamb, looking as if it had been slain, standing in the center of the throne, encircled by the four living creatures and the elders. He had seven horns and seven eyes, which are the seven spirits*a* of God sent out into all the earth. ⁷He came and took the scroll from the right hand of him who sat on the throne. ⁸And when he had taken it, the four living creatures and the twenty-four elders fell down before the Lamb. Each one had a harp and they were holding golden bowls full of incense, which are the prayers of the saints. ⁹And they sang a new song:

> "You are worthy to take the scroll
>   and to open its seals,
> because you were slain,
>   and with your blood you
>   purchased men for God
>   from every tribe and language and
>   people and nation.
> ¹⁰You have made them to be a
>   kingdom and priests to serve
>   our God,
>   and they will reign on the earth."

¹¹Then I looked and heard the voice of many angels, numbering thousands upon thousands, and ten thousand times ten thousand. They encircled the throne and the living creatures and the elders. ¹²In a loud voice they sang:

> "Worthy is the Lamb, who was slain,
> to receive power and wealth and
>   wisdom and strength
> and honor and glory and praise!"

¹³Then I heard every creature in heaven and on earth and under the earth and on the sea, and all that is in them, singing:

> "To him who sits on the throne and
>   to the Lamb
> be praise and honor and glory and
>   power,
>   for ever and ever!"

¹⁴The four living creatures said, "Amen," and the elders fell down and worshiped.

a6 Or the sevenfold Spirit

PSALM 133:1-3
A song of ascents. Of David.

> ¹How good and pleasant it is
>   when brothers live together in
>   unity!
> ²It is like precious oil poured on the
>   head,
>   running down on the beard,
> running down on Aaron's beard,
>   down upon the collar of his
>   robes.
> ³It is as if the dew of Hermon
>   were falling on Mount Zion.
> For there the LORD bestows his
>   blessing,
>   even life forevermore.

PROVERBS 29:26-27
> ²⁶Many seek an audience with a ruler,
>   but it is from the LORD that man
>   gets justice.

> ²⁷The righteous detest the dishonest;
>   the wicked detest the upright.

□ DAY 349

GOD SIGHTINGS

December 15

MICAH 1:1–4:13
The word of the LORD that came to Micah of Moresheth during the reigns of Jotham, Ahaz and Hezekiah, kings of Judah—the vision he saw concerning Samaria and Jerusalem.

> ²Hear, O peoples, all of you,
>   listen, O earth and all who are in it,
> that the Sovereign LORD may witness
>   against you,
>   the Lord from his holy temple.
> ³Look! The LORD is coming from his
>   dwelling place;

he comes down and treads the
high places of the earth.
4 The mountains melt beneath him
and the valleys split apart,
like wax before the fire,
like water rushing down a slope.
5 All this is because of Jacob's
transgression,
because of the sins of the house
of Israel.
What is Jacob's transgression?
Is it not Samaria?
What is Judah's high place?
Is it not Jerusalem?

6 "Therefore I will make Samaria a
heap of rubble,
a place for planting vineyards.
I will pour her stones into the valley
and lay bare her foundations.
7 All her idols will be broken to pieces;
all her temple gifts will be burned
with fire;
I will destroy all her images.
Since she gathered her gifts from the
wages of prostitutes,
as the wages of prostitutes they
will again be used."

8 Because of this I will weep and wail;
I will go about barefoot and naked.
I will howl like a jackal
and moan like an owl.
9 For her wound is incurable;
it has come to Judah.
It*a* has reached the very gate of my
people,
even to Jerusalem itself.
10 Tell it not in Gath*b*;
weep not at all.*c*
In Beth Ophrah*d*
roll in the dust.
11 Pass on in nakedness and shame,
you who live in Shaphir.*e*
Those who live in Zaanan*f*
will not come out.
Beth Ezel is in mourning;
its protection is taken from you.
12 Those who live in Maroth*g* writhe in
pain,
waiting for relief,

because disaster has come from the
LORD,
even to the gate of Jerusalem.
13 You who live in Lachish,*h*
harness the team to the chariot.
You were the beginning of sin
to the Daughter of Zion,
for the transgressions of Israel
were found in you.
14 Therefore you will give parting gifts
to Moresheth Gath.
The town of Aczib*i* will prove
deceptive
to the kings of Israel.
15 I will bring a conqueror against you
who live in Mareshah.*j*
He who is the glory of Israel
will come to Adullam.
16 Shave your heads in mourning
for the children in whom you
delight;
make yourselves as bald as the
vulture,
for they will go from you into
exile.

2:1 WOE to those who plan iniquity,
to those who plot evil on their
beds!
At morning's light they carry it out
because it is in their power to do it.
2 They covet fields and seize them,
and houses, and take them.
They defraud a man of his home,
a fellowman of his inheritance.

3 Therefore, the LORD says:

"I am planning disaster against this
people,
from which you cannot save
yourselves.
You will no longer walk proudly,
for it will be a time of calamity.
4 In that day men will ridicule you;
they will taunt you with this
mournful song:
'We are utterly ruined;
my people's possession is divided
up.
He takes it from me!
He assigns our fields to traitors.'"

⁵Therefore you will have no one in the
  assembly of the LORD
    to divide the land by lot.

⁶"Do not prophesy," their prophets say.
  "Do not prophesy about these
    things;
  disgrace will not overtake us."
⁷Should it be said, O house of Jacob:
  "Is the Spirit of the LORD angry?
  Does he do such things?"

  "Do not my words do good
    to him whose ways are upright?
⁸Lately my people have risen up
  like an enemy.
You strip off the rich robe
  from those who pass by without a
    care,
  like men returning from battle.
⁹You drive the women of my people
  from their pleasant homes.
You take away my blessing
  from their children forever.
¹⁰Get up, go away!
  For this is not your resting place,
because it is defiled,
  it is ruined, beyond all remedy.
¹¹If a liar and deceiver comes and says,
  'I will prophesy for you plenty of
    wine and beer,'
  he would be just the prophet for
    this people!

¹²"I will surely gather all of you, O Jacob;
  I will surely bring together the
    remnant of Israel.
I will bring them together like sheep
    in a pen,
  like a flock in its pasture;
  the place will throng with people.
¹³One who breaks open the way will go
    up before them;
  they will break through the gate
    and go out.
Their king will pass through before
    them,
  the LORD at their head."

3:1THEN I said,

"Listen, you leaders of Jacob,
  you rulers of the house of Israel.
Should you not know justice,

² you who hate good and love evil;
  who tear the skin from my people
    and the flesh from their bones;
³who eat my people's flesh,
  strip off their skin
  and break their bones in pieces;
  who chop them up like meat for the
    pan,
  like flesh for the pot?"

⁴Then they will cry out to the LORD,
  but he will not answer them.
At that time he will hide his face
    from them
  because of the evil they have
    done.

⁵This is what the LORD says:

"As for the prophets
  who lead my people astray,
if one feeds them,
  they proclaim 'peace';
if he does not,
  they prepare to wage war against
    him.
⁶Therefore night will come over you,
    without visions,
  and darkness, without divination.
The sun will set for the prophets,
  and the day will go dark for them.
⁷The seers will be ashamed
  and the diviners disgraced.
They will all cover their faces
  because there is no answer from
    God."

⁸But as for me, I am filled with power,
  with the Spirit of the LORD,
  and with justice and might,
to declare to Jacob his transgression,
  to Israel his sin.
⁹Hear this, you leaders of the house of
    Jacob,
  you rulers of the house of Israel,
who despise justice
  and distort all that is right;
¹⁰who build Zion with bloodshed,
  and Jerusalem with wickedness.
¹¹Her leaders judge for a bribe,
  her priests teach for a price,
  and her prophets tell fortunes for
    money.

Yet they lean upon the L ORD and say,
  "Is not the L ORD among us?
  No disaster will come upon us."
¹²Therefore because of you,
  Zion will be plowed like a field,
  Jerusalem will become a heap of
      rubble,
  the temple hill a mound
      overgrown with thickets.

⁴:¹I N the last days

the mountain of the L ORD 's temple
    will be established
  as chief among the mountains;
it will be raised above the hills,
  and peoples will stream to it.

²Many nations will come and say,

"Come, let us go up to the mountain
    of the L ORD ,
  to the house of the God of Jacob.
He will teach us his ways,
  so that we may walk in his paths."
The law will go out from Zion,
  the word of the L ORD from
      Jerusalem.
³**He will judge between many
    peoples
  and will settle disputes for
      strong nations far and wide.
They will beat their swords into
    plowshares
  and their spears into pruning
      hooks.
Nation will not take up sword
    against nation,
  nor will they train for war
      anymore.**
⁴Every man will sit under his own vine
  and under his own fig tree,
and no one will make them afraid,
  for the L ORD Almighty has spoken.
⁵All the nations may walk
  in the name of their gods;
we will walk in the name of the L ORD
  our God for ever and ever.

⁶"In that day," declares the L ORD ,

"I will gather the lame;
  I will assemble the exiles
  and those I have brought to grief.

⁷I will make the lame a remnant,
  those driven away a strong nation.
The L ORD will rule over them in
      Mount Zion
  from that day and forever.
⁸As for you, O watchtower of the flock,
  O stronghold ᵏ of the Daughter of
      Zion,
the former dominion will be restored
    to you;
  kingship will come to the
      Daughter of Jerusalem."

⁹Why do you now cry aloud—
  have you no king?
Has your counselor perished,
  that pain seizes you like that of a
      woman in labor?
¹⁰Writhe in agony, O Daughter of Zion,
  like a woman in labor,
for now you must leave the city
  to camp in the open field.
You will go to Babylon;
  there you will be rescued.
There the L ORD will redeem you
  out of the hand of your enemies.

¹¹But now many nations
  are gathered against you.
They say, "Let her be defiled,
  let our eyes gloat over Zion!"
¹²But they do not know
  the thoughts of the L ORD ;
they do not understand his plan,
  he who gathers them like sheaves
      to the threshing floor.

¹³"Rise and thresh, O Daughter of Zion,
  for I will give you horns of iron;
I will give you hoofs of bronze
  and you will break to pieces many
      nations."

You will devote their ill-gotten gains
    to the L ORD ,
  their wealth to the Lord of all the
      earth.

*a9*Or *He*   *b10Gath* sounds like the Hebrew for *tell.*
*c10*Hebrew; Septuagint may suggest *not in Acco.* The
Hebrew for *in Acco* sounds like the Hebrew for *weep.*
d10Beth Ophrah means *house of dust.*   *e11Shaphir* means
pleasant.   *f11Zaanan* sounds like the Hebrew for *come out.*
g12Maroth sounds like the Hebrew for *bitter.*   *h13Lachish*
sounds like the Hebrew for *team.*   *i14Aczib* means *deception.*
j15Mareshah sounds like the Hebrew for *conqueror.*
*k8*Or *hill*

REVELATION 6:1-17

❚ [John] watched as the Lamb opened the first of the seven seals. Then I heard one of the four living creatures say in a voice like thunder, "Come!" ²I looked, and there before me was a white horse! Its rider held a bow, and he was given a crown, and he rode out as a conqueror bent on conquest.

³When the Lamb opened the second seal, I heard the second living creature say, "Come!" ⁴Then another horse came out, a fiery red one. Its rider was given power to take peace from the earth and to make men slay each other. To him was given a large sword.

⁵When the Lamb opened the third seal, I heard the third living creature say, "Come!" I looked, and there before me was a black horse! Its rider was holding a pair of scales in his hand. ⁶Then I heard what sounded like a voice among the four living creatures, saying, "A quart*a* of wheat for a day's wages,*b* and three quarts of barley for a day's wages,*b* and do not damage the oil and the wine!"

⁷When the Lamb opened the fourth seal, I heard the voice of the fourth living creature say, "Come!" ⁸I looked, and there before me was a pale horse! Its rider was named Death, and Hades was following close behind him. They were given power over a fourth of the earth to kill by sword, famine and plague, and by the wild beasts of the earth.

⁹When he opened the fifth seal, I saw under the altar the souls of those who had been slain because of the word of God and the testimony they had maintained. ¹⁰They called out in a loud voice, "How long, Sovereign Lord, holy and true, until you judge the inhabitants of the earth and avenge our blood?" ¹¹Then each of them was given a white robe, and they were told to wait a little longer, until the number of their fellow servants and brothers who were to be killed as they had been was completed.

¹²I watched as he opened the sixth seal. There was a great earthquake. The sun turned black like sackcloth made of goat hair, the whole moon turned blood red, ¹³and the stars in the sky fell to earth, as late figs drop from a fig tree when shaken by a strong wind. ¹⁴The sky receded like a scroll, rolling up, and every mountain and island was removed from its place.

¹⁵Then the kings of the earth, the princes, the generals, the rich, the mighty, and every slave and every free man hid in caves and among the rocks of the mountains. ¹⁶They called to the mountains and the rocks, "Fall on us and hide us from the face of him who sits on the throne and from the wrath of the Lamb! ¹⁷For the great day of their wrath has come, and who can stand?"

*a*6 Greek *a choinix* (probably about a liter)   *b*6 Greek *a denarius*

PSALM 134:1-3

A song of ascents.

¹ **P**raise the Lᴏʀᴅ, all you servants of the Lᴏʀᴅ
  who minister by night in the house of the Lᴏʀᴅ.
²Lift up your hands in the sanctuary and praise the Lᴏʀᴅ.

³May the Lᴏʀᴅ, the Maker of heaven and earth,
  bless you from Zion.

PROVERBS 30:1-4

❚he sayings of Agur son of Jakeh—an oracle*a*:

This man declared to Ithiel,
  to Ithiel and to Ucal:*b*

²"I am the most ignorant of men;
  I do not have a man's understanding.
³I have not learned wisdom,
  nor have I knowledge of the Holy One.
⁴Who has gone up to heaven and come down?
  Who has gathered up the wind in the hollow of his hands?
  Who has wrapped up the waters in his cloak?
  Who has established all the ends of the earth?

What is his name, and the name of
   his son?
   Tell me if you know!"

a 1 Or *Jakeh of Massa*   *b 1* Masoretic Text; with a different
word division of the Hebrew *declared, "I am weary, O God;
/ I am weary, O God, and faint.*

☐ D A Y   3 5 0

GOD SIGHTINGS

December 16

MICAH 5:1–7:20
Marshal your troops, O city of troops,*a*
   for a siege is laid against us.
They will strike Israel's ruler
   on the cheek with a rod.

² "But you, Bethlehem Ephrathah,
   though you are small among the
      clans*b* of Judah,
out of you will come for me
   one who will be ruler over Israel,
   whose origins*c* are from of old,
      from ancient times.*d* "

³ Therefore Israel will be abandoned
   until the time when she who is in
      labor gives birth
and the rest of his brothers return
   to join the Israelites.

⁴ He will stand and shepherd his flock
   in the strength of the LORD,
   in the majesty of the name of the
      LORD his God.
And they will live securely, for then
   his greatness
   will reach to the ends of the earth.
⁵   And he will be their peace.

When the Assyrian invades our land
   and marches through our
      fortresses,
we will raise against him seven
   shepherds,
   even eight leaders of men.
⁶ They will rule*e* the land of Assyria
   with the sword,
   the land of Nimrod with drawn
      sword.*f*

He will deliver us from the Assyrian
   when he invades our land
   and marches into our borders.

⁷ The remnant of Jacob will be
   in the midst of many peoples
like dew from the LORD,
   like showers on the grass,
which do not wait for man
   or linger for mankind.
⁸ The remnant of Jacob will be
      among the nations,
   in the midst of many peoples,
like a lion among the beasts of the
      forest,
   like a young lion among flocks
      of sheep,
which mauls and mangles as it
      goes,
   and no one can rescue.
⁹ Your hand will be lifted up in
      triumph over your enemies,
   and all your foes will be destroyed.

¹⁰ "In that day," declares the LORD,

"I will destroy your horses from
      among you
   and demolish your chariots.
¹¹ I will destroy the cities of your land
   and tear down all your
      strongholds.
¹² I will destroy your witchcraft
   and you will no longer cast spells.
¹³ I will destroy your carved images
   and your sacred stones from
      among you;
you will no longer bow down
   to the work of your hands.
¹⁴ I will uproot from among you your
      Asherah poles*g*
   and demolish your cities.
¹⁵ I will take vengeance in anger and
      wrath
   upon the nations that have not
      obeyed me."

6:1 LISTEN to what the LORD says:

"Stand up, plead your case before the
      mountains;
   let the hills hear what you have
      to say.

² Hear, O mountains, the Lord's
    accusation;
    listen, you everlasting foundations
        of the earth.
For the Lord has a case against his
    people;
    he is lodging a charge against
        Israel.

³ "My people, what have I done to
    you?
    How have I burdened you? Answer
        me.
⁴ I brought you up out of Egypt
    and redeemed you from the land
        of slavery.
I sent Moses to lead you,
    also Aaron and Miriam.
⁵ My people, remember
    what Balak king of Moab counseled
    and what Balaam son of Beor
        answered.
Remember ⌐your journey⌐ from
        Shittim to Gilgal,
    that you may know the righteous
        acts of the Lord."

⁶ With what shall I come before the Lord
    and bow down before the exalted
        God?
Shall I come before him with burnt
    offerings,
    with calves a year old?
⁷ Will the Lord be pleased with
        thousands of rams,
    with ten thousand rivers of oil?
Shall I offer my firstborn for my
    transgression,
    the fruit of my body for the sin of
        my soul?
⁸ He has showed you, O man, what is
    good.
    And what does the Lord require of
        you?
To act justly and to love mercy
    and to walk humbly with your
        God.

⁹ Listen! The Lord is calling to the
    city—
    and to fear your name is wisdom—
    "Heed the rod and the One who
        appointed it.ʰ

¹⁰ Am I still to forget, O wicked house,
    your ill-gotten treasures
    and the short ephah,ⁱ which is
        accursed?
¹¹ Shall I acquit a man with dishonest
        scales,
    with a bag of false weights?
¹² Her rich men are violent;
    her people are liars
    and their tongues speak
        deceitfully.
¹³ Therefore, I have begun to destroy
        you,
    to ruin you because of your sins.
¹⁴ You will eat but not be satisfied;
    your stomach will still be empty.ʲ
You will store up but save nothing,
    because what you save I will give
        to the sword.
¹⁵ You will plant but not harvest;
    you will press olives but not use
        the oil on yourselves,
    you will crush grapes but not drink
        the wine.
¹⁶ You have observed the statutes of
        Omri
    and all the practices of Ahab's
        house,
    and you have followed their
        traditions.
Therefore I will give you over to ruin
    and your people to derision;
    you will bear the scorn of the
        nations.ᵏ"

7:1 WHAT misery is mine!
    I am like one who gathers summer
        fruit
    at the gleaning of the vineyard;
    there is no cluster of grapes to eat,
    none of the early figs that I crave.
² The godly have been swept from the
        land;
    not one upright man remains.
All men lie in wait to shed blood;
    each hunts his brother with a net.
³ Both hands are skilled in doing evil;
    the ruler demands gifts,
    the judge accepts bribes,
    the powerful dictate what they
        desire—
    they all conspire together.

⁴The best of them is like a brier,
 the most upright worse than a
  thorn hedge.
The day of your watchmen has come,
 the day God visits you.
Now is the time of their confusion.
⁵Do not trust a neighbor;
 put no confidence in a friend.
Even with her who lies in your
  embrace
 be careful of your words.
⁶For a son dishonors his father,
 a daughter rises up against her
  mother,
a daughter-in-law against her
  mother-in-law—
 a man's enemies are the members
  of his own household.

⁷But as for me, I watch in hope for the
  LORD,
 I wait for God my Savior;
 my God will hear me.

⁸Do not gloat over me, my enemy!
 Though I have fallen, I will rise.
Though I sit in darkness,
 the LORD will be my light.
⁹Because I have sinned against him,
 I will bear the LORD's wrath,
until he pleads my case
 and establishes my right.
He will bring me out into the light;
 I will see his righteousness.
¹⁰Then my enemy will see it
 and will be covered with shame,
she who said to me,
 "Where is the LORD your God?"
My eyes will see her downfall;
 even now she will be trampled
  underfoot
 like mire in the streets.

¹¹The day for building your walls will
  come,
 the day for extending your
  boundaries.
¹²In that day people will come to you
 from Assyria and the cities of Egypt,
even from Egypt to the Euphrates
 and from sea to sea
 and from mountain to mountain.

¹³The earth will become desolate
 because of its inhabitants,
 as the result of their deeds.

¹⁴Shepherd your people with your staff,
 the flock of your inheritance,
which lives by itself in a forest,
 in fertile pasturelands.ʲ
Let them feed in Bashan and Gilead
 as in days long ago.

¹⁵"As in the days when you came out of
  Egypt,
 I will show them my wonders."

¹⁶Nations will see and be ashamed,
 deprived of all their power.
They will lay their hands on their mouths
 and their ears will become deaf.
¹⁷They will lick dust like a snake,
 like creatures that crawl on the
  ground.
They will come trembling out of
  their dens;
 they will turn in fear to the LORD
  our God
 and will be afraid of you.
¹⁸Who is a God like you,
 who pardons sin and forgives the
  transgression
 of the remnant of his inheritance?
You do not stay angry forever
 but delight to show mercy.
¹⁹You will again have compassion on us;
 you will tread our sins underfoot
 and hurl all our iniquities into the
  depths of the sea.
²⁰You will be true to Jacob,
 and show mercy to Abraham,
 as you pledged on oath to our fathers
  in days long ago.

*a 1 Or Strengthen your walls, O walled city   b 2 Or rulers
c 2 Hebrew goings out   d 2 Or from days of eternity
e 6 Or crush   f 6 Or Nimrod in its gates   g 14 That is, symbols
of the goddess Asherah   h 9 The meaning of the Hebrew for
this line is uncertain.   i 10 An ephah was a dry
measure.   j 14 The meaning of the Hebrew for this word is
uncertain.   k 16 Septuagint; Hebrew scorn due my people
l 14 Or in the middle of Carmel*

REVELATION 7:1-17

After this I [John] saw four angels
standing at the four corners of the
earth, holding back the four winds of
the earth to prevent any wind from

blowing on the land or on the sea or on any tree. ²Then I saw another angel coming up from the east, having the seal of the living God. He called out in a loud voice to the four angels who had been given power to harm the land and the sea: ³"Do not harm the land or the sea or the trees until we put a seal on the foreheads of the servants of our God." ⁴Then I heard the number of those who were sealed: 144,000 from all the tribes of Israel.

⁵From the tribe of Judah 12,000 were sealed,
from the tribe of Reuben 12,000,
from the tribe of Gad 12,000,
⁶from the tribe of Asher 12,000,
from the tribe of Naphtali 12,000,
from the tribe of Manasseh 12,000,
⁷from the tribe of Simeon 12,000,
from the tribe of Levi 12,000,
from the tribe of Issachar 12,000,
⁸from the tribe of Zebulun 12,000,
from the tribe of Joseph 12,000,
from the tribe of Benjamin 12,000.

⁹After this I looked and there before me was a great multitude that no one could count, from every nation, tribe, people and language, standing before the throne and in front of the Lamb. They were wearing white robes and were holding palm branches in their hands. ¹⁰And they cried out in a loud voice:

"Salvation belongs to our God,
who sits on the throne,
and to the Lamb."

¹¹All the angels were standing around the throne and around the elders and the four living creatures. They fell down on their faces before the throne and worshiped God, ¹²saying:

"Amen!
Praise and glory
and wisdom and thanks and honor
and power and strength
be to our God for ever and ever.
Amen!"

¹³Then one of the elders asked me, "These in white robes—who are they, and where did they come from?"

¹⁴I answered, "Sir, you know."

And he said, "These are they who have come out of the great tribulation; they have washed their robes and made them white in the blood of the Lamb. ¹⁵Therefore,

"they are before the throne of God
and serve him day and night in his temple;
and he who sits on the throne will spread his tent over them.
¹⁶Never again will they hunger;
never again will they thirst.
The sun will not beat upon them,
nor any scorching heat.
¹⁷For the Lamb at the center of the throne will be their shepherd;
he will lead them to springs of living water.
And God will wipe away every tear from their eyes."

PSALM 135:1-21

¹Praise the LORD.ᵃ

Praise the name of the LORD;
praise him, you servants of the LORD,
²you who minister in the house of the LORD,
in the courts of the house of our God.

³Praise the LORD, for the LORD is good;
sing praise to his name, for that is pleasant.
⁴For the LORD has chosen Jacob to be his own,
Israel to be his treasured possession.

⁵I know that the LORD is great,
that our Lord is greater than all gods.
⁶The LORD does whatever pleases him,
in the heavens and on the earth,
in the seas and all their depths.
⁷He makes clouds rise from the ends of the earth;
he sends lightning with the rain
and brings out the wind from his storehouses.

⁸He struck down the firstborn of
     Egypt,
    the firstborn of men and animals.
⁹He sent his signs and wonders into
     your midst, O Egypt,
    against Pharaoh and all his
     servants.
¹⁰He struck down many nations
    and killed mighty kings—
¹¹Sihon king of the Amorites,
    Og king of Bashan
    and all the kings of Canaan—
¹²and he gave their land as an
     inheritance,
    an inheritance to his people Israel.

¹³Your name, O Lord, endures forever,
    your renown, O Lord, through all
     generations.
¹⁴For the Lord will vindicate his people
    and have compassion on his
     servants.

¹⁵The idols of the nations are silver
     and gold,
    made by the hands of men.
¹⁶They have mouths, but cannot
     speak,
    eyes, but they cannot see;
¹⁷they have ears, but cannot hear,
    nor is there breath in their mouths.
¹⁸Those who make them will be like
     them,
    and so will all who trust in them.

¹⁹O house of Israel, praise the Lord;
    O house of Aaron, praise the Lord;
²⁰O house of Levi, praise the Lord;
    you who fear him, praise the Lord.
²¹Praise be to the Lord from Zion,
    to him who dwells in Jerusalem.

    Praise the Lord.

a 1 Hebrew Hallelu Yah; also in verses 3 and 21

PROVERBS 30:5-6

⁵"Every word of God is flawless;
    he is a shield to those who take
     refuge in him.
⁶Do not add to his words,
    or he will rebuke you and prove
     you a liar."

☐ D A Y 3 5 1

GOD SIGHTINGS

December 17

NAHUM 1:1–3:19

An oracle concerning Nineveh. The book of the vision of Nahum the Elkoshite.

²The Lord is a jealous and avenging
     God;
    the Lord takes vengeance and is
     filled with wrath.
The Lord takes vengeance on his foes
    and maintains his wrath against
     his enemies.
**³The Lord is slow to anger and
     great in power;
    the Lord will not leave the
     guilty unpunished.
His way is in the whirlwind and
     the storm,
    and clouds are the dust of his
     feet.**
⁴He rebukes the sea and dries it up;
    he makes all the rivers run dry.
Bashan and Carmel wither
    and the blossoms of Lebanon fade.
⁵The mountains quake before him
    and the hills melt away.
The earth trembles at his presence,
    the world and all who live in it.
⁶Who can withstand his indignation?
    Who can endure his fierce anger?
His wrath is poured out like fire;
    the rocks are shattered before him.

⁷The Lord is good,
    a refuge in times of trouble.
He cares for those who trust in him,
⁸   but with an overwhelming flood
he will make an end of ⌊Nineveh⌋;
    he will pursue his foes into darkness.

⁹Whatever they plot against the Lord
    he^a will bring to an end;
    trouble will not come a second
     time.
¹⁰They will be entangled among thorns
    and drunk from their wine;

they will be consumed like dry
stubble.*b*

11 From you, ⌐O Nineveh,⌐ has one
come forth
who plots evil against the LORD
and counsels wickedness.

12 This is what the LORD says:

"Although they have allies and are
numerous,
they will be cut off and pass away.
Although I have afflicted you,
⌐O Judah,⌐
I will afflict you no more.
13 Now I will break their yoke from your
neck
and tear your shackles away."

14 The LORD has given a command
concerning you, ⌐Nineveh⌐:
"You will have no descendants to
bear your name.
I will destroy the carved images and
cast idols
that are in the temple of your
gods.
I will prepare your grave,
for you are vile."

15 Look, there on the mountains,
the feet of one who brings good
news,
who proclaims peace!
Celebrate your festivals, O Judah,
and fulfill your vows.
No more will the wicked invade you;
they will be completely destroyed.

2:1 AN attacker advances against you,
⌐Nineveh⌐.
Guard the fortress,
watch the road,
brace yourselves,
marshal all your strength!

2 The LORD will restore the splendor of
Jacob
like the splendor of Israel,
though destroyers have laid them
waste
and have ruined their vines.

3 The shields of his soldiers are red;
the warriors are clad in scarlet.

The metal on the chariots flashes
on the day they are made ready;
the spears of pine are
brandished.*c*
4 The chariots storm through the
streets,
rushing back and forth through
the squares.
They look like flaming torches;
they dart about like lightning.

5 He summons his picked troops,
yet they stumble on their way.
They dash to the city wall;
the protective shield is put in
place.
6 The river gates are thrown open
and the palace collapses.
7 It is decreed*d* that ⌐the city⌐
be exiled and carried away.
Its slave girls moan like doves
and beat upon their breasts.
8 Nineveh is like a pool,
and its water is draining away.
"Stop! Stop!" they cry,
but no one turns back.
9 Plunder the silver!
Plunder the gold!
The supply is endless,
the wealth from all its treasures!
10 She is pillaged, plundered, stripped!
Hearts melt, knees give way,
bodies tremble, every face grows
pale.

11 Where now is the lions' den,
the place where they fed their
young,
where the lion and lioness went,
and the cubs, with nothing to fear?
12 The lion killed enough for his cubs
and strangled the prey for his mate,
filling his lairs with the kill
and his dens with the prey.

13 "I am against you,"
declares the LORD Almighty.
"I will burn up your chariots in
smoke,
and the sword will devour your
young lions.
I will leave you no prey on the
earth.

The voices of your messengers
 will no longer be heard."

3:1 WOE to the city of blood,
 full of lies,
full of plunder,
 never without victims!
2 The crack of whips,
 the clatter of wheels,
galloping horses
 and jolting chariots!
3 Charging cavalry,
 flashing swords
 and glittering spears!
Many casualties,
 piles of dead,
bodies without number,
 people stumbling over the corpses—
4 all because of the wanton lust of a
  harlot,
 alluring, the mistress of sorceries,
who enslaved nations by her
  prostitution
 and peoples by her witchcraft.

5 "I am against you," declares the LORD
  Almighty.
 "I will lift your skirts over your
  face.
I will show the nations your
  nakedness
 and the kingdoms your shame.
6 I will pelt you with filth,
 I will treat you with contempt
 and make you a spectacle.
7 All who see you will flee from you
 and say,
 'Nineveh is in ruins—who will
  mourn for her?'
 Where can I find anyone to
  comfort you?"

8 Are you better than Thebes,*e*
 situated on the Nile,
 with water around her?
The river was her defense,
 the waters her wall.
9 Cush*f* and Egypt were her boundless
  strength;
 Put and Libya were among her
  allies.
10 Yet she was taken captive
 and went into exile.

Her infants were dashed to pieces
 at the head of every street.
Lots were cast for her nobles,
 and all her great men were put in
  chains.
11 You too will become drunk;
 you will go into hiding
 and seek refuge from the enemy.

12 All your fortresses are like fig trees
 with their first ripe fruit;
when they are shaken,
 the figs fall into the mouth of the
  eater.
13 Look at your troops—
 they are all women!
The gates of your land
 are wide open to your enemies;
 fire has consumed their bars.

14 Draw water for the siege,
 strengthen your defenses!
Work the clay,
 tread the mortar,
 repair the brickwork!
15 There the fire will devour you;
 the sword will cut you down
 and, like grasshoppers, consume
  you.
Multiply like grasshoppers,
 multiply like locusts!
16 You have increased the number of
  your merchants
 till they are more than the stars of
  the sky,
but like locusts they strip the land
 and then fly away.
17 Your guards are like locusts,
 your officials like swarms of locusts
 that settle in the walls on a cold
  day—
but when the sun appears they fly
  away,
 and no one knows where.

18 O king of Assyria, your shepherds*g*
  slumber;
 your nobles lie down to rest.
Your people are scattered on the
  mountains
 with no one to gather them.
19 Nothing can heal your wound;
 your injury is fatal.

Everyone who hears the news about
    you
    claps his hands at your fall,
for who has not felt
    your endless cruelty?

a9 Or *What do you foes plot against the Lord? / He*
b10 The meaning of the Hebrew for this verse is uncertain.
c3 Hebrew; Septuagint and Syriac / *the horsemen rush to
and fro* d7 The meaning of the Hebrew for this word is
uncertain. e8 Hebrew *No Amon* f9 That is, the upper Nile
region g18 Or *rulers*

REVELATION 8:1-13

When he [the Lamb] opened the seventh seal, there was silence in heaven
for about half an hour.

²And I saw the seven angels who
stand before God, and to them were
given seven trumpets.

³Another angel, who had a golden
censer, came and stood at the altar. He
was given much incense to offer, with
the prayers of all the saints, on the
golden altar before the throne. ⁴The
smoke of the incense, together with the
prayers of the saints, went up before
God from the angel's hand. ⁵Then the
angel took the censer, filled it with fire
from the altar, and hurled it on the
earth; and there came peals of thunder,
rumblings, flashes of lightning and an
earthquake.

⁶Then the seven angels who had the
seven trumpets prepared to sound
them.

⁷The first angel sounded his trumpet, and there came hail and fire mixed
with blood, and it was hurled down
upon the earth. A third of the earth was
burned up, a third of the trees were
burned up, and all the green grass was
burned up.

⁸The second angel sounded his trumpet, and something like a huge mountain, all ablaze, was thrown into the sea.
A third of the sea turned into blood, ⁹a
third of the living creatures in the sea
died, and a third of the ships were destroyed.

¹⁰The third angel sounded his trumpet, and a great star, blazing like a torch,
fell from the sky on a third of the rivers
and on the springs of water— ¹¹the

name of the star is Wormwood.ᵃ A
third of the waters turned bitter, and
many people died from the waters that
had become bitter.

¹²The fourth angel sounded his trumpet, and a third of the sun was struck, a
third of the moon, and a third of the
stars, so that a third of them turned dark.
A third of the day was without light, and
also a third of the night.

¹³As I watched, I heard an eagle that
was flying in midair call out in a loud
voice: "Woe! Woe! Woe to the inhabitants of the earth, because of the trumpet blasts about to be sounded by the
other three angels!"

a11 That is, Bitterness

PSALM 136:1-26

¹**G**ive thanks to the Lord, for he is
    good.
        His love endures forever.
²Give thanks to the God of gods.
        His love endures forever.
³Give thanks to the Lord of lords:
        His love endures forever.

⁴to him who alone does great
    wonders,
        His love endures forever.
⁵who by his understanding made the
    heavens,
        His love endures forever.
⁶who spread out the earth upon the
    waters,
        His love endures forever.
⁷who made the great lights—
        His love endures forever.
⁸the sun to govern the day,
        His love endures forever.
⁹the moon and stars to govern the
    night;
        His love endures forever.

¹⁰to him who struck down the
    firstborn of Egypt
        His love endures forever.
¹¹and brought Israel out from among
    them
        His love endures forever.
¹²with a mighty hand and outstretched
    arm;
        His love endures forever.

¹³to him who divided the Red Sea^a
     asunder
          His love endures forever.
¹⁴and brought Israel through the midst
     of it,
          His love endures forever.
¹⁵but swept Pharaoh and his army into
     the Red Sea;
          His love endures forever.

¹⁶to him who led his people through
     the desert,
          His love endures forever.
¹⁷who struck down great kings,
          His love endures forever.
¹⁸and killed mighty kings—
          His love endures forever.
¹⁹Sihon king of the Amorites
          His love endures forever.
²⁰and Og king of Bashan—
          His love endures forever.
²¹and gave their land as an inheritance,
          His love endures forever.
²²an inheritance to his servant Israel;
          His love endures forever.

²³to the One who remembered us in
     our low estate
          His love endures forever.
²⁴and freed us from our enemies,
          His love endures forever.
²⁵and who gives food to every creature.
          His love endures forever.

²⁶Give thanks to the God of heaven.
          His love endures forever.

^a13 Hebrew *Yam Suph;* that is, Sea of Reeds; also in verse 15

PROVERBS 30:7-9

⁷"Two things I ask of you, O Lord;
     do not refuse me before I die:
⁸Keep falsehood and lies far from
     me;
     give me neither poverty nor
          riches,
     but give me only my daily bread.
⁹Otherwise, I may have too much and
          disown you
     and say, 'Who is the Lord?'
Or I may become poor and steal,
     and so dishonor the name of my
          God."

□ DAY 352

GOD SIGHTINGS

December 18

HABAKKUK 1:1–3:19
The oracle that Habakkuk the prophet
received.

²How long, O Lord, must I call for help,
     but you do not listen?
Or cry out to you, "Violence!"
     but you do not save?
³Why do you make me look at
          injustice?
     Why do you tolerate wrong?
Destruction and violence are before
     me;
     there is strife, and conflict
          abounds.
⁴Therefore the law is paralyzed,
     and justice never prevails.
The wicked hem in the righteous,
     so that justice is perverted.

⁵"Look at the nations and watch—
     and be utterly amazed.
For I am going to do something in
          your days
     that you would not believe,
     even if you were told.
⁶I am raising up the Babylonians,^a
     that ruthless and impetuous
          people,
who sweep across the whole earth
     to seize dwelling places not their
          own.
⁷They are a feared and dreaded people;
     they are a law to themselves
     and promote their own honor.
⁸Their horses are swifter than
          leopards,
     fiercer than wolves at dusk.
Their cavalry gallops headlong;
     their horsemen come from afar.
They fly like a vulture swooping to
          devour;
⁹   they all come bent on violence.
Their hordes^b advance like a desert
          wind
     and gather prisoners like sand.

10 They deride kings
    and scoff at rulers.
  They laugh at all fortified cities;
    they build earthen ramps and
      capture them.
11 Then they sweep past like the wind
    and go on—
  guilty men, whose own strength is
    their god."

12 O Lord, are you not from everlasting?
  My God, my Holy One, we will not
    die.
  O Lord, you have appointed them to
    execute judgment;
  O Rock, you have ordained them
    to punish.
13 Your eyes are too pure to look on evil;
    you cannot tolerate wrong.
  Why then do you tolerate the
    treacherous?
  Why are you silent while the
    wicked
  swallow up those more righteous
    than themselves?
14 You have made men like fish in the
    sea,
  like sea creatures that have no
    ruler.
15 The wicked foe pulls all of them up
    with hooks,
  he catches them in his net,
  he gathers them up in his dragnet;
    and so he rejoices and is glad.
16 Therefore he sacrifices to his net
    and burns incense to his dragnet,
  for by his net he lives in luxury
    and enjoys the choicest food.
17 Is he to keep on emptying his net,
    destroying nations without mercy?

2:1 I will stand at my watch
    and station myself on the ramparts;
  I will look to see what he will say to
    me,
  and what answer I am to give to
    this complaint.c

2 Then the Lord replied:

"Write down the revelation
  and make it plain on tablets
  so that a heraldd may run with it.

3 For the revelation awaits an
    appointed time;
  it speaks of the end
    and will not prove false.
  Though it linger, wait for it;
    ite will certainly come and will not
      delay.

4 "See, he is puffed up;
  his desires are not upright—
  but the righteous will live by his
    faithf—
5 indeed, wine betrays him;
  he is arrogant and never at rest.
  Because he is as greedy as the graveg
    and like death is never satisfied,
  he gathers to himself all the nations
    and takes captive all the peoples.

6 "Will not all of them taunt him with
  ridicule and scorn, saying,

"'Woe to him who piles up stolen
    goods
  and makes himself wealthy by
    extortion!
  How long must this go on?'
7 Will not your debtorsh suddenly arise?
  Will they not wake up and make
    you tremble?
  Then you will become their victim.
8 Because you have plundered many
    nations,
  the peoples who are left will
    plunder you.
  For you have shed man's blood;
    you have destroyed lands and
    cities and everyone in them.

9 "Woe to him who builds his realm by
    unjust gain
  to set his nest on high,
  to escape the clutches of ruin!
10 You have plotted the ruin of many
    peoples,
  shaming your own house and
    forfeiting your life.
11 The stones of the wall will cry out,
  and the beams of the woodwork
    will echo it.

12 "Woe to him who builds a city with
    bloodshed
  and establishes a town by crime!

13 Has not the LORD Almighty
        determined
    that the people's labor is only fuel
        for the fire,
    that the nations exhaust
        themselves for nothing?
14 For the earth will be filled with the
        knowledge of the glory of the
        LORD,
    as the waters cover the sea.

15 "Woe to him who gives drink to his
        neighbors,
    pouring it from the wineskin till
        they are drunk,
    so that he can gaze on their naked
        bodies.
16 You will be filled with shame instead
        of glory.
    Now it is your turn! Drink and be
        exposed[i]!
    The cup from the LORD's right hand
        is coming around to you,
    and disgrace will cover your glory.
17 The violence you have done to
        Lebanon will overwhelm you,
    and your destruction of animals
        will terrify you.
    For you have shed man's blood;
        you have destroyed lands and
        cities and everyone in them.

18 "Of what value is an idol, since a man
        has carved it?
    Or an image that teaches lies?
    For he who makes it trusts in his own
        creation;
    he makes idols that cannot speak.
19 Woe to him who says to wood, 'Come
        to life!'
    Or to lifeless stone, 'Wake up!'
    Can it give guidance?
    It is covered with gold and silver;
        there is no breath in it.
20 But the LORD is in his holy temple;
    let all the earth be silent before him."

3:1 A prayer of Habakkuk the prophet.
On *shigionoth*.[j]

2 LORD, I have heard of your fame;
    I stand in awe of your deeds,
        O LORD

Renew them in our day,
    in our time make them known;
    in wrath remember mercy.

3 God came from Teman,
    the Holy One from Mount Paran.
                                    Selah[k]
    His glory covered the heavens
        and his praise filled the earth.
4 His splendor was like the sunrise;
        rays flashed from his hand,
    where his power was hidden.
5 Plague went before him;
        pestilence followed his steps.
6 He stood, and shook the earth;
    he looked, and made the nations
        tremble.
    The ancient mountains crumbled
        and the age-old hills collapsed.
    His ways are eternal.
7 I saw the tents of Cushan in distress,
    the dwellings of Midian in anguish.

8 Were you angry with the rivers,
        O LORD?
    Was your wrath against the
        streams?
    Did you rage against the sea
        when you rode with your horses
    and your victorious chariots?
9 You uncovered your bow,
    you called for many arrows. *Selah*
    You split the earth with rivers;
10   the mountains saw you and writhed.
    Torrents of water swept by;
        the deep roared
    and lifted its waves on high.

11 Sun and moon stood still in the
        heavens
    at the glint of your flying arrows,
    at the lightning of your flashing
        spear.
12 In wrath you strode through the
        earth
    and in anger you threshed the
        nations.
13 You came out to deliver your people,
    to save your anointed one.
    You crushed the leader of the land of
        wickedness,
    you stripped him from head to
        foot.   *Selah*

¹⁴With his own spear you pierced his
head
when his warriors stormed out to
scatter us,
gloating as though about to devour
the wretched who were in hiding.
¹⁵You trampled the sea with your
horses,
churning the great waters.

¹⁶I heard and my heart pounded,
my lips quivered at the sound;
decay crept into my bones,
and my legs trembled.
Yet I will wait patiently for the day of
calamity
to come on the nation invading us.
¹⁷Though the fig tree does not bud
and there are no grapes on the
vines,
though the olive crop fails
and the fields produce no food,
though there are no sheep in the pen
and no cattle in the stalls,
¹⁸yet I will rejoice in the LORD,
I will be joyful in God my Savior.

¹⁹The Sovereign LORD is my strength;
he makes my feet like the feet of a
deer,
he enables me to go on the
heights.

For the director of music. On my
stringed instruments.

^a6 Or *Chaldeans*   ^b9 The meaning of the Hebrew for this
word is uncertain.   ^c1 Or *and what to answer when I am
rebuked*   ^d2 Or *so that whoever reads it*   ^e3 Or *Though he
linger, wait for him; / he*   ^f4 Or *faithfulness*   ^g5 Hebrew
Sheol   ^h7 Or *creditors*   ⁱ16 Masoretic Text; Dead Sea
Scrolls, Aquila, Vulgate and Syriac (see also Septuagint) *and
stagger*   ^j1 Probably a literary or musical term   ^k3 A word
of uncertain meaning; possibly a musical term; also in verses
9 and 13

REVELATION 9:1-21

The fifth angel sounded his trumpet,
and I [John] saw a star that had fallen
from the sky to the earth. The star was
given the key to the shaft of the Abyss.
²When he opened the Abyss, smoke
rose from it like the smoke from a gi-
gantic furnace. The sun and sky were
darkened by the smoke from the Abyss.
³And out of the smoke locusts came
down upon the earth and were given
power like that of scorpions of the
earth. ⁴They were told not to harm the
grass of the earth or any plant or tree,
but only those people who did not have
the seal of God on their foreheads.
⁵They were not given power to kill
them, but only to torture them for five
months. And the agony they suffered
was like that of the sting of a scorpion
when it strikes a man. ⁶During those
days men will seek death, but will not
find it; they will long to die, but death
will elude them.

⁷The locusts looked like horses pre-
pared for battle. On their heads they
wore something like crowns of gold, and
their faces resembled human faces.
⁸Their hair was like women's hair, and
their teeth were like lions' teeth. ⁹They
had breastplates like breastplates of
iron, and the sound of their wings was
like the thundering of many horses and
chariots rushing into battle. ¹⁰They had
tails and stings like scorpions, and in
their tails they had power to torment
people for five months. ¹¹They had as
king over them the angel of the Abyss,
whose name in Hebrew is Abaddon, and
in Greek, Apollyon.^a

¹²The first woe is past; two other
woes are yet to come.

¹³The sixth angel sounded his trum-
pet, and I heard a voice coming from the
horns^b of the golden altar that is before
God. ¹⁴It said to the sixth angel who had
the trumpet, "Release the four angels
who are bound at the great river Euphrates." ¹⁵And the four angels who had
been kept ready for this very hour and
day and month and year were released
to kill a third of mankind. ¹⁶The number of the mounted troops was two hundred million. I heard their number.

¹⁷The horses and riders I saw in my
vision looked like this: Their breastplates were fiery red, dark blue, and yellow as sulfur. The heads of the horses
resembled the heads of lions, and out of
their mouths came fire, smoke and sulfur. ¹⁸A third of mankind was killed by
the three plagues of fire, smoke and sulfur that came out of their mouths.

¹⁹The power of the horses was in their mouths and in their tails; for their tails were like snakes, having heads with which they inflict injury.

²⁰The rest of mankind that were not killed by these plagues still did not repent of the work of their hands; they did not stop worshiping demons, and idols of gold, silver, bronze, stone and wood—idols that cannot see or hear or walk. ²¹Nor did they repent of their murders, their magic arts, their sexual immorality or their thefts.

a11 Abaddon and *Apollyon* mean *Destroyer.*   *b13* That is, projections

PSALM 137:1-9

¹ By the rivers of Babylon we sat and wept
  when we remembered Zion.
² There on the poplars
  we hung our harps,
³ for there our captors asked us for songs,
  our tormentors demanded songs of joy;
  they said, "Sing us one of the songs of Zion!"

⁴ How can we sing the songs of the LORD
  while in a foreign land?
⁵ If I forget you, O Jerusalem,
  may my right hand forget ˌits skillˌ.
⁶ May my tongue cling to the roof of my mouth
  if I do not remember you,
  if I do not consider Jerusalem
  my highest joy.

⁷ Remember, O LORD, what the Edomites did
  on the day Jerusalem fell.
 "Tear it down," they cried,
  "tear it down to its foundations!"

⁸ O Daughter of Babylon, doomed to destruction,
  happy is he who repays you
  for what you have done to us—
⁹ he who seizes your infants
  and dashes them against the rocks.

PROVERBS 30:10

¹⁰"Do not slander a servant to his master,
  or he will curse you, and you will pay for it."

□ DAY 353

GOD SIGHTINGS

December 19

ZEPHANIAH 1:1-3:20

The word of the LORD that came to Zephaniah son of Cushi, the son of Gedaliah, the son of Amariah, the son of Hezekiah, during the reign of Josiah son of Amon king of Judah:

²"I will sweep away everything
  from the face of the earth,"
                    declares the LORD.
³"I will sweep away both men and animals;
  I will sweep away the birds of the air
  and the fish of the sea.
The wicked will have only heaps of rubble*a*
  when I cut off man from the face of the earth,"
                    declares the LORD.

⁴"I will stretch out my hand against Judah
  and against all who live in Jerusalem.
I will cut off from this place every remnant of Baal,
  the names of the pagan and the idolatrous priests—
⁵those who bow down on the roofs
  to worship the starry host,
  those who bow down and swear by the LORD
  and who also swear by Molech,*b*
⁶those who turn back from following the LORD
  and neither seek the LORD nor inquire of him.

⁷Be silent before the Sovereign Lord,
  for the day of the Lord is near.
The Lord has prepared a sacrifice;
  he has consecrated those he has
    invited.
⁸On the day of the Lord's sacrifice
  I will punish the princes
  and the king's sons
and all those clad
  in foreign clothes.
⁹On that day I will punish
  all who avoid stepping on the
    threshold,ᶜ
who fill the temple of their gods
  with violence and deceit.

¹⁰"On that day," declares the Lord,
  "a cry will go up from the Fish
    Gate,
    wailing from the New Quarter,
    and a loud crash from the hills.
¹¹Wail, you who live in the market
    districtᵈ;
  all your merchants will be wiped
    out,
  all who trade withᵉ silver will be
    ruined.
¹²At that time I will search Jerusalem
    with lamps
  and punish those who are
    complacent,
  who are like wine left on its dregs,
who think, 'The Lord will do
    nothing,
    either good or bad.'
¹³Their wealth will be plundered,
    their houses demolished.
They will build houses
  but not live in them;
they will plant vineyards
  but not drink the wine.

¹⁴"The great day of the Lord is near—
    near and coming quickly.
Listen! The cry on the day of the
    Lord will be bitter,
    the shouting of the warrior there.
¹⁵That day will be a day of wrath,
  a day of distress and anguish,
a day of trouble and ruin,
  a day of darkness and gloom,
  a day of clouds and blackness,

¹⁶a day of trumpet and battle cry
  against the fortified cities
  and against the corner towers.
¹⁷I will bring distress on the people
  and they will walk like blind men,
  because they have sinned against
    the Lord.
Their blood will be poured out like
    dust
  and their entrails like filth.
¹⁸Neither their silver nor their gold
  will be able to save them
  on the day of the Lord's wrath.
In the fire of his jealousy
  the whole world will be
    consumed,
for he will make a sudden end
  of all who live in the earth."

²:¹Gather together, gather together,
  O shameful nation,
  ²before the appointed time arrives
    and that day sweeps on like chaff,
before the fierce anger of the Lord
    comes upon you,
  before the day of the Lord's wrath
    comes upon you.
³Seek the Lord, all you humble of the
    land,
  you who do what he commands.
Seek righteousness, seek humility;
  perhaps you will be sheltered
  on the day of the Lord's anger.

⁴Gaza will be abandoned
  and Ashkelon left in ruins.
At midday Ashdod will be emptied
  and Ekron uprooted.
⁵Woe to you who live by the sea,
  O Kerethite people;
the word of the Lord is against you,
  O Canaan, land of the Philistines.

"I will destroy you,
  and none will be left."

⁶The land by the sea, where the
    Kerethitesᶠ dwell,
  will be a place for shepherds and
    sheep pens.
⁷It will belong to the remnant of the
    house of Judah;
  there they will find pasture.

In the evening they will lie down
   in the houses of Ashkelon.
The Lord their God will care for them;
   he will restore their fortunes.*g*

8"I have heard the insults of Moab
   and the taunts of the Ammonites,
who insulted my people
   and made threats against their
      land.
9Therefore, as surely as I live,"
   declares the Lord Almighty, the
      God of Israel,
"surely Moab will become like
      Sodom,
   the Ammonites like Gomorrah—
a place of weeds and salt pits,
   a wasteland forever.
The remnant of my people will
      plunder them;
   the survivors of my nation will
      inherit their land."

10This is what they will get in return
      for their pride,
   for insulting and mocking the
      people of the Lord Almighty.
11The Lord will be awesome to them
   when he destroys all the gods of
      the land.
The nations on every shore will
      worship him,
   every one in its own land.

12"You too, O Cushites,*h*
   will be slain by my sword."

13He will stretch out his hand against
      the north
   and destroy Assyria,
leaving Nineveh utterly desolate
   and dry as the desert.
14Flocks and herds will lie down there,
   creatures of every kind.
The desert owl and the screech owl
   will roost on her columns.
Their calls will echo through the
      windows,
   rubble will be in the doorways,
   the beams of cedar will be
      exposed.
15This is the carefree city
   that lived in safety.

She said to herself,
   "I am, and there is none besides
      me."
What a ruin she has become,
   a lair for wild beasts!
All who pass by her scoff
   and shake their fists.

3:1Woe to the city of oppressors,
   rebellious and defiled!
2She obeys no one,
   she accepts no correction.
She does not trust in the Lord,
   she does not draw near to her God.
3Her officials are roaring lions,
   her rulers are evening wolves,
   who leave nothing for the
      morning.
4Her prophets are arrogant;
   they are treacherous men.
Her priests profane the sanctuary
   and do violence to the law.
5The Lord within her is righteous;
   he does no wrong.
Morning by morning he dispenses
      his justice,
   and every new day he does not fail,
   yet the unrighteous know no
      shame.

6"I have cut off nations;
   their strongholds are demolished.
I have left their streets deserted,
   with no one passing through.
Their cities are destroyed;
   no one will be left—no one at all.
7I said to the city,
   'Surely you will fear me
   and accept correction!'
Then her dwelling would not be cut
      off,
   nor all my punishments come
      upon her.
But they were still eager
   to act corruptly in all they did.
8Therefore wait for me," declares the
      Lord,
   "for the day I will stand up to
      testify.*i*
I have decided to assemble the
      nations,
   to gather the kingdoms

and to pour out my wrath on them—
all my fierce anger.
The whole world will be consumed
by the fire of my jealous anger.

9 "Then will I purify the lips of the
peoples,
that all of them may call on the
name of the LORD
and serve him shoulder to
shoulder.
10 From beyond the rivers of Cush*j*
my worshipers, my scattered
people,
will bring me offerings.
11 On that day you will not be put to
shame
for all the wrongs you have done
to me,
because I will remove from this city
those who rejoice in their pride.
Never again will you be haughty
on my holy hill.
12 But I will leave within you
the meek and humble,
who trust in the name of the LORD.
13 The remnant of Israel will do no
wrong;
they will speak no lies,
nor will deceit be found in their
mouths.
They will eat and lie down
and no one will make them afraid."

14 Sing, O Daughter of Zion;
shout aloud, O Israel!
Be glad and rejoice with all your
heart,
O Daughter of Jerusalem!
15 The LORD has taken away your
punishment,
he has turned back your enemy.
The LORD, the King of Israel, is with
you;
never again will you fear any
harm.
16 On that day they will say to
Jerusalem,
"Do not fear, O Zion;
do not let your hands hang limp.
17 The LORD your God is with you,
he is mighty to save.

He will take great delight in you,
he will quiet you with his love,
he will rejoice over you with
singing."

18 "The sorrows for the appointed
feasts
I will remove from you;
they are a burden and a reproach
to you.*k*
19 At that time I will deal
with all who oppressed you;
I will rescue the lame
and gather those who have been
scattered.
I will give them praise and honor
in every land where they were put
to shame.
20 At that time I will gather you;
at that time I will bring you home.
I will give you honor and praise
among all the peoples of the earth
when I restore your fortunes*l*
before your very eyes,"

says the LORD.

a3 The meaning of the Hebrew for this line is uncertain.
b5 Hebrew *Malcam,* that is, Milcom   *c9* See 1 Samuel 5:5.
d11 Or *the Mortar*   *e11* Or *in*   *f6* The meaning of the
Hebrew for this word is uncertain.   *g7* Or *will bring
back their captives*   *h12* That is, people from the upper
Nile region   *i8* Septuagint and Syriac; Hebrew *will rise up
to plunder*   *j10* That is, the upper Nile region   *k18* Or *"I will
gather you who mourn for the appointed feasts; / your
reproach is a burden to you*   *l20* Or *I bring back your captives*

REVELATION 10:1-11

Then I [John] saw another mighty angel
coming down from heaven. He was
robed in a cloud, with a rainbow above
his head; his face was like the sun, and
his legs were like fiery pillars. 2 He was
holding a little scroll, which lay open in
his hand. He planted his right foot on
the sea and his left foot on the land,
3 and he gave a loud shout like the roar
of a lion. When he shouted, the voices
of the seven thunders spoke. 4 And
when the seven thunders spoke, I was
about to write; but I heard a voice from
heaven say, "Seal up what the seven
thunders have said and do not write it
down."

5 Then the angel I had seen standing
on the sea and on the land raised his
right hand to heaven. 6 And he swore by

him who lives for ever and ever, who created the heavens and all that is in them, the earth and all that is in it, and the sea and all that is in it, and said, "There will be no more delay! ⁷But in the days when the seventh angel is about to sound his trumpet, the mystery of God will be accomplished, just as he announced to his servants the prophets."

⁸Then the voice that I had heard from heaven spoke to me once more: "Go, take the scroll that lies open in the hand of the angel who is standing on the sea and on the land."

⁹So I went to the angel and asked him to give me the little scroll. He said to me, "Take it and eat it. It will turn your stomach sour, but in your mouth it will be as sweet as honey." ¹⁰I took the little scroll from the angel's hand and ate it. It tasted as sweet as honey in my mouth, but when I had eaten it, my stomach turned sour. ¹¹Then I was told, "You must prophesy again about many peoples, nations, languages and kings."

PSALM 138:1-8
Of David.

¹I will praise you, O LORD, with all my
    heart;
  before the "gods" I will sing your
    praise.
²I will bow down toward your holy
    temple
  and will praise your name
  for your love and your
    faithfulness,
 for you have exalted above all things
  your name and your word.
³When I called, you answered me;
  you made me bold and
    stouthearted.

⁴May all the kings of the earth praise
    you, O LORD,
  when they hear the words of your
    mouth.
⁵May they sing of the ways of the
    LORD,
  for the glory of the LORD is great.

⁶Though the LORD is on high, he
    looks upon the lowly,
  but the proud he knows from
    afar.
⁷Though I walk in the midst of
    trouble,
  you preserve my life;
 you stretch out your hand against the
    anger of my foes,
  with your right hand you save me.
⁸The LORD will fulfill ⌊his purpose⌋ for
    me;
  your love, O LORD, endures
    forever—
  do not abandon the works of your
    hands.

PROVERBS 30:11-14

¹¹There are those who curse their
    fathers
  and do not bless their mothers;
¹²those who are pure in their own eyes
  and yet are not cleansed of their
    filth;
¹³those whose eyes are ever so
    haughty,
  whose glances are so disdainful;
¹⁴those whose teeth are swords
  and whose jaws are set with knives
 to devour the poor from the earth,
  the needy from among mankind."

□ DAY 354

GOD SIGHTINGS

December 20

HAGGAI 1:1–2:23

In the second year of King Darius, on the first day of the sixth month, the word of the LORD came through the prophet Haggai to Zerubbabel son of Shealtiel, governor of Judah, and to Joshuaᵃ son of Jehozadak, the high priest:

²This is what the LORD Almighty says: "These people say, 'The time has not yet come for the LORD's house to be built.'"

³Then the word of the Lᴏʀᴅ came through the prophet Haggai: ⁴"Is it a time for you yourselves to be living in your paneled houses, while this house remains a ruin?"

⁵Now this is what the Lᴏʀᴅ Almighty says: "Give careful thought to your ways. ⁶You have planted much, but have harvested little. You eat, but never have enough. You drink, but never have your fill. You put on clothes, but are not warm. You earn wages, only to put them in a purse with holes in it."

⁷This is what the Lᴏʀᴅ Almighty says: "Give careful thought to your ways. ⁸Go up into the mountains and bring down timber and build the house, so that I may take pleasure in it and be honored," says the Lᴏʀᴅ. ⁹"You expected much, but see, it turned out to be little. What you brought home, I blew away. Why?" declares the Lᴏʀᴅ Almighty. "Because of my house, which remains a ruin, while each of you is busy with his own house. ¹⁰Therefore, because of you the heavens have withheld their dew and the earth its crops. ¹¹I called for a drought on the fields and the mountains, on the grain, the new wine, the oil and whatever the ground produces, on men and cattle, and on the labor of your hands."

¹²Then Zerubbabel son of Shealtiel, Joshua son of Jehozadak, the high priest, and the whole remnant of the people obeyed the voice of the Lᴏʀᴅ their God and the message of the prophet Haggai, because the Lᴏʀᴅ their God had sent him. And the people feared the Lᴏʀᴅ.

¹³Then Haggai, the Lᴏʀᴅ's messenger, gave this message of the Lᴏʀᴅ to the people: "I am with you," declares the Lᴏʀᴅ. ¹⁴So the Lᴏʀᴅ stirred up the spirit of Zerubbabel son of Shealtiel, governor of Judah, and the spirit of Joshua son of Jehozadak, the high priest, and the spirit of the whole remnant of the people. They came and began to work on the house of the Lᴏʀᴅ Almighty, their God, ¹⁵on the twenty-fourth day of the sixth month in the second year of King Darius.

²:¹Oɴ the twenty-first day of the seventh month, the word of the Lᴏʀᴅ came through the prophet Haggai: ²"Speak to Zerubbabel son of Shealtiel, governor of Judah, to Joshua son of Jehozadak, the high priest, and to the remnant of the people. Ask them, ³'Who of you is left who saw this house in its former glory? How does it look to you now? Does it not seem to you like nothing? ⁴But now be strong, O Zerubbabel,' declares the Lᴏʀᴅ. 'Be strong, O Joshua son of Jehozadak, the high priest. Be strong, all you people of the land,' declares the Lᴏʀᴅ, 'and work. For I am with you,' declares the Lᴏʀᴅ Almighty. ⁵'This is what I covenanted with you when you came out of Egypt. And my Spirit remains among you. Do not fear.'

⁶"This is what the Lᴏʀᴅ Almighty says: 'In a little while I will once more shake the heavens and the earth, the sea and the dry land. ⁷I will shake all nations, and the desired of all nations will come, and I will fill this house with glory,' says the Lᴏʀᴅ Almighty. ⁸'The silver is mine and the gold is mine,' declares the Lᴏʀᴅ Almighty. ⁹'The glory of this present house will be greater than the glory of the former house,' says the Lᴏʀᴅ Almighty. 'And in this place I will grant peace,' declares the Lᴏʀᴅ Almighty."

¹⁰On the twenty-fourth day of the ninth month, in the second year of Darius, the word of the Lᴏʀᴅ came to the prophet Haggai: ¹¹"This is what the Lᴏʀᴅ Almighty says: 'Ask the priests what the law says: ¹²If a person carries consecrated meat in the fold of his garment, and that fold touches some bread or stew, some wine, oil or other food, does it become consecrated?'"

The priests answered, "No."

¹³Then Haggai said, "If a person defiled by contact with a dead body touches one of these things, does it become defiled?"

"Yes," the priests replied, "it becomes defiled."

¹⁴Then Haggai said, "'So it is with this people and this nation in my sight,'

declares the LORD. 'Whatever they do and whatever they offer there is defiled.

15 " 'Now give careful thought to this from this day on[b]—consider how things were before one stone was laid on another in the LORD's temple. 16 When anyone came to a heap of twenty measures, there were only ten. When anyone went to a wine vat to draw fifty measures, there were only twenty. 17 I struck all the work of your hands with blight, mildew and hail, yet you did not turn to me,' declares the LORD. 18 'From this day on, from this twenty-fourth day of the ninth month, give careful thought to the day when the foundation of the LORD's temple was laid. Give careful thought: 19 Is there yet any seed left in the barn? Until now, the vine and the fig tree, the pomegranate and the olive tree have not borne fruit.

" 'From this day on I will bless you.' "

20 The word of the LORD came to Haggai a second time on the twenty-fourth day of the month: 21 "Tell Zerubbabel governor of Judah that I will shake the heavens and the earth. 22 I will overturn royal thrones and shatter the power of the foreign kingdoms. I will overthrow chariots and their drivers; horses and their riders will fall, each by the sword of his brother.

23 "'On that day,' declares the LORD Almighty, 'I will take you, my servant Zerubbabel son of Shealtiel,' declares the LORD, 'and I will make you like my signet ring, for I have chosen you,' declares the LORD Almighty."

a 1 A variant of *Jeshua;* here and elsewhere in Haggai
b 15 Or *to the days past*

REVELATION 11:1-19

❚ [John] was given a reed like a measuring rod and was told, "Go and measure the temple of God and the altar, and count the worshipers there. 2 But exclude the outer court; do not measure it, because it has been given to the Gentiles. They will trample on the holy city for 42 months. 3 And I will give power to my two witnesses, and they will prophesy for 1,260 days, clothed in sackcloth." 4 These are the two olive trees and the two lampstands that stand before the Lord of the earth. 5 If anyone tries to harm them, fire comes from their mouths and devours their enemies. This is how anyone who wants to harm them must die. 6 These men have power to shut up the sky so that it will not rain during the time they are prophesying; and they have power to turn the waters into blood and to strike the earth with every kind of plague as often as they want.

7 Now when they have finished their testimony, the beast that comes up from the Abyss will attack them, and overpower and kill them. 8 Their bodies will lie in the street of the great city, which is figuratively called Sodom and Egypt, where also their Lord was crucified. 9 For three and a half days men from every people, tribe, language and nation will gaze on their bodies and refuse them burial. 10 The inhabitants of the earth will gloat over them and will celebrate by sending each other gifts, because these two prophets had tormented those who live on the earth.

11 But after the three and a half days a breath of life from God entered them, and they stood on their feet, and terror struck those who saw them. 12 Then they heard a loud voice from heaven saying to them, "Come up here." And they went up to heaven in a cloud, while their enemies looked on.

13 At that very hour there was a severe earthquake and a tenth of the city collapsed. Seven thousand people were killed in the earthquake, and the survivors were terrified and gave glory to the God of heaven.

14 The second woe has passed; the third woe is coming soon.

15 **The seventh angel sounded his trumpet, and there were loud voices in heaven, which said:**

" **The kingdom of the world has
    become the kingdom of
    our Lord and of his Christ,
    and he will reign for ever and
    ever."**

16And the twenty-four elders, who were seated on their thrones before God, fell on their faces and worshiped God, 17saying:

"We give thanks to you, Lord God Almighty,
    the One who is and who was,
because you have taken your great power
    and have begun to reign.
18The nations were angry;
    and your wrath has come.
The time has come for judging the dead,
    and for rewarding your servants the prophets
and your saints and those who reverence your name,
    both small and great—
and for destroying those who destroy the earth."

19Then God's temple in heaven was opened, and within his temple was seen the ark of his covenant. And there came flashes of lightning, rumblings, peals of thunder, an earthquake and a great hailstorm.

PSALM 139:1-24
For the director of music. Of David. A psalm.

1 O Lord, you have searched me
    and you know me.
2You know when I sit and when I rise;
    you perceive my thoughts from afar.
3You discern my going out and my lying down;
    you are familiar with all my ways.
4Before a word is on my tongue
    you know it completely, O Lord.

5You hem me in—behind and before;
    you have laid your hand upon me.
6Such knowledge is too wonderful for me,
    too lofty for me to attain.

7Where can I go from your Spirit?
    Where can I flee from your presence?

8If I go up to the heavens, you are there;
    if I make my bed in the depths,a you are there.
9If I rise on the wings of the dawn,
    if I settle on the far side of the sea,
10even there your hand will guide me,
    your right hand will hold me fast.
11If I say, "Surely the darkness will hide me
    and the light become night around me,"
12even the darkness will not be dark to you;
    the night will shine like the day,
    for darkness is as light to you.

13For you created my inmost being;
    you knit me together in my mother's womb.
14I praise you because I am fearfully and wonderfully made;
    your works are wonderful,
    I know that full well.
15My frame was not hidden from you
    when I was made in the secret place.
When I was woven together in the depths of the earth,
16   your eyes saw my unformed body.
All the days ordained for me
    were written in your book
    before one of them came to be.

17How precious tob me are your thoughts, O God!
    How vast is the sum of them!
18Were I to count them,
    they would outnumber the grains of sand.
When I awake,
    I am still with you.

19If only you would slay the wicked, O God!
    Away from me, you bloodthirsty men!
20They speak of you with evil intent;
    your adversaries misuse your name.

²¹Do I not hate those who hate you,
O Lᴏʀᴅ,
and abhor those who rise up
against you?
²²I have nothing but hatred for them;
I count them my enemies.

²³Search me, O God, and know my
heart;
test me and know my anxious
thoughts.
²⁴See if there is any offensive way in
me,
and lead me in the way
everlasting.

ᵃ8 Hebrew *Sheol*   ᵇ17 Or *concerning*

PROVERBS 30:15-16
¹⁵"The leech has two daughters.
'Give! Give!' they cry.

"There are three things that are
never satisfied,
four that never say, 'Enough!':
¹⁶the grave,ᵃ the barren womb,
land, which is never satisfied with
water,
and fire, which never says,
'Enough!'"

ᵃ16 Hebrew *Sheol*

□ D A Y   3 5 5

GOD SIGHTINGS

December 21

ZECHARIAH 1:1-21
In the eighth month of the second year
of Darius, the word of the Lᴏʀᴅ came to
the prophet Zechariah son of Berekiah,
the son of Iddo:
²"The Lᴏʀᴅ was very angry with your
forefathers. ³Therefore tell the people:
This is what the Lᴏʀᴅ Almighty says:
'Return to me,' declares the Lᴏʀᴅ Almighty, 'and I will return to you,' says
the Lᴏʀᴅ Almighty. ⁴Do not be like your
forefathers, to whom the earlier prophets proclaimed: This is what the Lᴏʀᴅ

Almighty says: 'Turn from your evil
ways and your evil practices.' But they
would not listen or pay attention to me,
declares the Lᴏʀᴅ. ⁵Where are your
forefathers now? And the prophets, do
they live forever? ⁶But did not my
words and my decrees, which I commanded my servants the prophets,
overtake your forefathers?

"Then they repented and said, 'The
Lᴏʀᴅ Almighty has done to us what our
ways and practices deserve, just as he
determined to do.'"

⁷On the twenty-fourth day of the
eleventh month, the month of Shebat,
in the second year of Darius, the word of
the Lᴏʀᴅ came to the prophet Zechariah
son of Berekiah, the son of Iddo.

⁸During the night I had a vision—and
there before me was a man riding a red
horse! He was standing among the myrtle trees in a ravine. Behind him were
red, brown and white horses.

⁹I asked, "What are these, my lord?"
The angel who was talking with me
answered, "I will show you what they
are."

¹⁰Then the man standing among the
myrtle trees explained, "They are the
ones the Lᴏʀᴅ has sent to go throughout
the earth."

¹¹And they reported to the angel of
the Lᴏʀᴅ, who was standing among the
myrtle trees, "We have gone throughout
the earth and found the whole world at
rest and in peace."

¹²Then the angel of the Lᴏʀᴅ said,
"Lᴏʀᴅ Almighty, how long will you
withhold mercy from Jerusalem and
from the towns of Judah, which you
have been angry with these seventy
years?" ¹³So the Lᴏʀᴅ spoke kind and
comforting words to the angel who
talked with me.

¹⁴Then the angel who was speaking
to me said, "Proclaim this word: This is
what the Lᴏʀᴅ Almighty says: 'I am very
jealous for Jerusalem and Zion, ¹⁵but I
am very angry with the nations that feel
secure. I was only a little angry, but they
added to the calamity.'

¹⁶"Therefore, this is what the Lᴏʀᴅ

says: 'I will return to Jerusalem with mercy, and there my house will be rebuilt. And the measuring line will be stretched out over Jerusalem,' declares the LORD Almighty.

¹⁷"Proclaim further: This is what the LORD Almighty says: 'My towns will again overflow with prosperity, and the LORD will again comfort Zion and choose Jerusalem.'"

¹⁸Then I looked up—and there before me were four horns! ¹⁹I asked the angel who was speaking to me, "What are these?"

He answered me, "These are the horns that scattered Judah, Israel and Jerusalem."

²⁰Then the LORD showed me four craftsmen. ²¹I asked, "What are these coming to do?"

He answered, "These are the horns that scattered Judah so that no one could raise his head, but the craftsmen have come to terrify them and throw down these horns of the nations who lifted up their horns against the land of Judah to scatter its people."

REVELATION 12:1–13:1A

A great and wondrous sign appeared in heaven: a woman clothed with the sun, with the moon under her feet and a crown of twelve stars on her head. ²She was pregnant and cried out in pain as she was about to give birth. ³Then another sign appeared in heaven: an enormous red dragon with seven heads and ten horns and seven crowns on his heads. ⁴His tail swept a third of the stars out of the sky and flung them to the earth. The dragon stood in front of the woman who was about to give birth, so that he might devour her child the moment it was born. ⁵She gave birth to a son, a male child, who will rule all the nations with an iron scepter. And her child was snatched up to God and to his throne. ⁶The woman fled into the desert to a place prepared for her by God, where she might be taken care of for 1,260 days.

⁷And there was war in heaven. Mi-
chael and his angels fought against the dragon, and the dragon and his angels fought back. ⁸But he was not strong enough, and they lost their place in heaven. ⁹The great dragon was hurled down—that ancient serpent called the devil, or Satan, who leads the whole world astray. He was hurled to the earth, and his angels with him.

¹⁰Then I heard a loud voice in heaven say:

"Now have come the salvation and
        the power and the kingdom
        of our God,
    and the authority of his Christ.
For the accuser of our brothers,
    who accuses them before our God
        day and night,
    has been hurled down.
¹¹They overcame him
    by the blood of the Lamb
    and by the word of their
        testimony;
they did not love their lives so much
    as to shrink from death.
¹²Therefore rejoice, you heavens
    and you who dwell in them!
But woe to the earth and the sea,
    because the devil has gone down
        to you!
He is filled with fury,
    because he knows that his time is
        short."

¹³When the dragon saw that he had been hurled to the earth, he pursued the woman who had given birth to the male child. ¹⁴The woman was given the two wings of a great eagle, so that she might fly to the place prepared for her in the desert, where she would be taken care of for a time, times and half a time, out of the serpent's reach. ¹⁵Then from his mouth the serpent spewed water like a river, to overtake the woman and sweep her away with the torrent. ¹⁶But the earth helped the woman by opening its mouth and swallowing the river that the dragon had spewed out of his mouth. ¹⁷Then the dragon was enraged at the woman and went off to make war

against the rest of her offspring—those who obey God's commandments and hold to the testimony of Jesus. ^{13:1}AND the dragon^a stood on the shore of the sea.

^a*1 Some late manuscripts And I*

PSALM 140:1-13
For the director of music. A psalm of David.

¹Rescue me, O LORD, from evil men;
  protect me from men of violence,
²who devise evil plans in their hearts
  and stir up war every day.
³They make their tongues as sharp as
    a serpent's;
  the poison of vipers is on their
    lips.   *Selah*

⁴Keep me, O LORD, from the hands of
    the wicked;
  protect me from men of violence
  who plan to trip my feet.
⁵Proud men have hidden a snare for
    me;
  they have spread out the cords of
    their net
  and have set traps for me along my
    path.   *Selah*

⁶O LORD, I say to you, "You are my
    God."
  Hear, O LORD, my cry for mercy.
⁷O Sovereign LORD, my strong
    deliverer,
  who shields my head in the day of
    battle—
⁸do not grant the wicked their desires,
    O LORD;
  do not let their plans succeed,
  or they will become proud.   *Selah*

⁹Let the heads of those who surround
    me
  be covered with the trouble their
    lips have caused.
¹⁰Let burning coals fall upon them;
  may they be thrown into the fire,
  into miry pits, never to rise.
¹¹Let slanderers not be established in
    the land;
  may disaster hunt down men of
    violence.

¹²I know that the LORD secures
    justice for the poor
  and upholds the cause of the
    needy.
¹³Surely the righteous will praise
    your name
  and the upright will live before
    you.

PROVERBS 30:17
¹⁷"The eye that mocks a father,
  that scorns obedience to a mother,
will be pecked out by the ravens of
    the valley,
  will be eaten by the vultures."

□ DAY 356

GOD SIGHTINGS

December 22

ZECHARIAH 2:1–3:10
Then I [Zechariah] looked up—and there before me was a man with a measuring line in his hand! ²I asked, "Where are you going?"

He answered me, "To measure Jerusalem, to find out how wide and how long it is."

³Then the angel who was speaking to me left, and another angel came to meet him ⁴and said to him: "Run, tell that young man, 'Jerusalem will be a city without walls because of the great number of men and livestock in it. ⁵And I myself will be a wall of fire around it,' declares the LORD, 'and I will be its glory within.'

⁶"Come! Come! Flee from the land of the north," declares the LORD, "for I have scattered you to the four winds of heaven," declares the LORD.

⁷"Come, O Zion! Escape, you who live in the Daughter of Babylon!" ⁸For this is what the LORD Almighty says: "After he has honored me and has sent me against the nations that have plundered you—for whoever touches you touches the apple

of his eye—⁹I will surely raise my hand against them so that their slaves will plunder them.ᵃ Then you will know that the Lᴏʀᴅ Almighty has sent me.

¹⁰"Shout and be glad, O Daughter of Zion. For I am coming, and I will live among you," declares the Lᴏʀᴅ. ¹¹"Many nations will be joined with the Lᴏʀᴅ in that day and will become my people. I will live among you and you will know that the Lᴏʀᴅ Almighty has sent me to you. ¹²The Lᴏʀᴅ will inherit Judah as his portion in the holy land and will again choose Jerusalem. ¹³Be still before the Lᴏʀᴅ, all mankind, because he has roused himself from his holy dwelling."

³:¹Tʜᴇɴ he showed me Joshuaᵇ the high priest standing before the angel of the Lᴏʀᴅ, and Satanᶜ standing at his right side to accuse him. ²The Lᴏʀᴅ said to Satan, "The Lᴏʀᴅ rebuke you, Satan! The Lᴏʀᴅ, who has chosen Jerusalem, rebuke you! Is not this man a burning stick snatched from the fire?"

³Now Joshua was dressed in filthy clothes as he stood before the angel. ⁴The angel said to those who were standing before him, "Take off his filthy clothes."

Then he said to Joshua, "See, I have taken away your sin, and I will put rich garments on you."

⁵Then I said, "Put a clean turban on his head." So they put a clean turban on his head and clothed him, while the angel of the Lᴏʀᴅ stood by.

⁶The angel of the Lᴏʀᴅ gave this charge to Joshua: ⁷"This is what the Lᴏʀᴅ Almighty says: 'If you will walk in my ways and keep my requirements, then you will govern my house and have charge of my courts, and I will give you a place among these standing here.

⁸" 'Listen, O high priest Joshua and your associates seated before you, who are men symbolic of things to come: I am going to bring my servant, the Branch. ⁹See, the stone I have set in front of Joshua! There are seven eyesᵈ on that one stone, and I will engrave an inscription on it,' says the Lᴏʀᴅ Almighty, 'and I will remove the sin of this land in a single day.

¹⁰" 'In that day each of you will invite his neighbor to sit under his vine and fig tree,' declares the Lᴏʀᴅ Almighty."

ᵃ8,9 Or says after... eye: 9"I... plunder them." ᵇ1 A variant of Jeshua; here and elsewhere in Zechariah ᶜ1 Satan means accuser. ᵈ9 Or facets

REVELATION 13:1B-18

Aɴᴅ I [John] saw a beast coming out of the sea. He had ten horns and seven heads, with ten crowns on his horns, and on each head a blasphemous name. ²The beast I saw resembled a leopard, but had feet like those of a bear and a mouth like that of a lion. The dragon gave the beast his power and his throne and great authority. ³One of the heads of the beast seemed to have had a fatal wound, but the fatal wound had been healed. The whole world was astonished and followed the beast. ⁴Men worshiped the dragon because he had given authority to the beast, and they also worshiped the beast and asked, "Who is like the beast? Who can make war against him?"

⁵The beast was given a mouth to utter proud words and blasphemies and to exercise his authority for forty-two months. ⁶He opened his mouth to blaspheme God, and to slander his name and his dwelling place and those who live in heaven. ⁷He was given power to make war against the saints and to conquer them. And he was given authority over every tribe, people, language and nation. ⁸All inhabitants of the earth will worship the beast—all whose names have not been written in the book of life belonging to the Lamb that was slain from the creation of the world.ᵃ

⁹He who has an ear, let him hear.

¹⁰If anyone is to go into captivity,
    into captivity he will go.
If anyone is to be killedᵇ with the
        sword,
    with the sword he will be killed.

This calls for patient endurance and faithfulness on the part of the saints.

¹¹Then I saw another beast, coming out of the earth. He had two horns like a lamb, but he spoke like a dragon. ¹²He exercised all the authority of the first beast on his behalf, and made the earth and its inhabitants worship the first beast, whose fatal wound had been healed. ¹³And he performed great and miraculous signs, even causing fire to come down from heaven to earth in full view of men. ¹⁴Because of the signs he was given power to do on behalf of the first beast, he deceived the inhabitants of the earth. He ordered them to set up an image in honor of the beast who was wounded by the sword and yet lived. ¹⁵He was given power to give breath to the image of the first beast, so that it could speak and cause all who refused to worship the image to be killed. ¹⁶He also forced everyone, small and great, rich and poor, free and slave, to receive a mark on his right hand or on his forehead, ¹⁷so that no one could buy or sell unless he had the mark, which is the name of the beast or the number of his name.

¹⁸This calls for wisdom. If anyone has insight, let him calculate the number of the beast, for it is man's number. His number is 666.

a8 Or written from the creation of the world in the book of life belonging to the Lamb that was slain   b10 Some manuscripts anyone kills

PSALM 141:1-10

A psalm of David.

¹ **O** Lord, I call to you; come quickly to me.
 Hear my voice when I call to you.
² **May my prayer be set before you like incense;**
 may the lifting up of my hands be like the evening sacrifice.

³Set a guard over my mouth, O Lord;
 keep watch over the door of my lips.

⁴Let not my heart be drawn to what is evil,
 to take part in wicked deeds
 with men who are evildoers;
 let me not eat of their delicacies.

⁵Let a righteous man*ᵃ* strike me—it is a kindness;
 let him rebuke me—it is oil on my head.
 My head will not refuse it.

Yet my prayer is ever against the deeds of evildoers;
⁶   their rulers will be thrown down from the cliffs,
 and the wicked will learn that my words were well spoken.
⁷ ˏThey will say,˳ "As one plows and breaks up the earth,
 so our bones have been scattered at the mouth of the grave.*ᵇ*"

⁸But my eyes are fixed on you,
 O Sovereign Lord;
 in you I take refuge—do not give me over to death.
⁹Keep me from the snares they have laid for me,
 from the traps set by evildoers.
¹⁰Let the wicked fall into their own nets,
 while I pass by in safety.

a5 Or Let the Righteous One   b7 Hebrew Sheol

PROVERBS 30:18-20

¹⁸"**T**here are three things that are too amazing for me,
 four that I do not understand:
¹⁹the way of an eagle in the sky,
 the way of a snake on a rock,
 the way of a ship on the high seas,
 and the way of a man with a maiden.

²⁰"This is the way of an adulteress:
 She eats and wipes her mouth
 and says, 'I've done nothing wrong.'"

☐ DAY 357

GOD SIGHTINGS

December 23

ZECHARIAH 4:1–5:11

Then the angel who talked with me [Zechariah] returned and wakened me, as a man is wakened from his sleep. [2]He asked me, "What do you see?"

I answered, "I see a solid gold lampstand with a bowl at the top and seven lights on it, with seven channels to the lights. [3]Also there are two olive trees by it, one on the right of the bowl and the other on its left."

[4]I asked the angel who talked with me, "What are these, my lord?"

[5]He answered, "Do you not know what these are?"

"No, my lord," I replied.

[6]So he said to me, "This is the word of the LORD to Zerubbabel: 'Not by might nor by power, but by my Spirit,' says the LORD Almighty.

[7]"What[a] are you, O mighty mountain? Before Zerubbabel you will become level ground. Then he will bring out the capstone to shouts of 'God bless it! God bless it!'"

[8]Then the word of the LORD came to me: [9]"The hands of Zerubbabel have laid the foundation of this temple; his hands will also complete it. Then you will know that the LORD Almighty has sent me to you.

[10]"Who despises the day of small things? Men will rejoice when they see the plumb line in the hand of Zerubbabel.

"(These seven are the eyes of the LORD, which range throughout the earth.)"

[11]Then I asked the angel, "What are these two olive trees on the right and the left of the lampstand?"

[12]Again I asked him, "What are these two olive branches beside the two gold pipes that pour out golden oil?"

[13]He replied, "Do you not know what these are?"

"No, my lord," I said.

[14]So he said, "These are the two who are anointed to[b] serve the Lord of all the earth."

[5:1]I looked again—and there before me was a flying scroll!

[2]He asked me, "What do you see?"

I answered, "I see a flying scroll, thirty feet long and fifteen feet wide.[c]"

[3]And he said to me, "This is the curse that is going out over the whole land; for according to what it says on one side, every thief will be banished, and according to what it says on the other, everyone who swears falsely will be banished. [4]The LORD Almighty declares, 'I will send it out, and it will enter the house of the thief and the house of him who swears falsely by my name. It will remain in his house and destroy it, both its timbers and its stones.'"

[5]Then the angel who was speaking to me came forward and said to me, "Look up and see what this is that is appearing."

[6]I asked, "What is it?"

He replied, "It is a measuring basket.[d]" And he added, "This is the iniquity[e] of the people throughout the land."

[7]Then the cover of lead was raised, and there in the basket sat a woman! [8]He said, "This is wickedness," and he pushed her back into the basket and pushed the lead cover down over its mouth.

[9]Then I looked up—and there before me were two women, with the wind in their wings! They had wings like those of a stork, and they lifted up the basket between heaven and earth.

[10]"Where are they taking the basket?" I asked the angel who was speaking to me.

[11]He replied, "To the country of Babylonia[f] to build a house for it. When it is ready, the basket will be set there in its place."

a7 Or *Who*   b14 Or *two who bring oil and*   c2 Hebrew *twenty cubits long and ten cubits wide* (about 9 meters long and 4.5 meters wide)   d6 Hebrew *an ephah;* also in verses 7-11   e6 Or *appearance*   f11 Hebrew *Shinar*

REVELATION 14:1-20

Then I [John] looked, and there before me was the Lamb, standing on Mount Zion, and with him 144,000 who had his name and his Father's name written on their foreheads. ²And I heard a sound from heaven like the roar of rushing waters and like a loud peal of thunder. The sound I heard was like that of harpists playing their harps. ³And they sang a new song before the throne and before the four living creatures and the elders. No one could learn the song except the 144,000 who had been redeemed from the earth. ⁴These are those who did not defile themselves with women, for they kept themselves pure. They follow the Lamb wherever he goes. They were purchased from among men and offered as firstfruits to God and the Lamb. ⁵No lie was found in their mouths; they are blameless.

⁶Then I saw another angel flying in midair, and he had the eternal gospel to proclaim to those who live on the earth—to every nation, tribe, language and people. ⁷He said in a loud voice, "Fear God and give him glory, because the hour of his judgment has come. Worship him who made the heavens, the earth, the sea and the springs of water."

⁸A second angel followed and said, "Fallen! Fallen is Babylon the Great, which made all the nations drink the maddening wine of her adulteries."

⁹A third angel followed them and said in a loud voice: "If anyone worships the beast and his image and receives his mark on the forehead or on the hand, ¹⁰he, too, will drink of the wine of God's fury, which has been poured full strength into the cup of his wrath. He will be tormented with burning sulfur in the presence of the holy angels and of the Lamb. ¹¹And the smoke of their torment rises for ever and ever. There is no rest day or night for those who worship the beast and his image, or for anyone who receives the mark of his name." ¹²This calls for patient endurance on the part of the saints who obey God's commandments and remain faithful to Jesus.

¹³Then I heard a voice from heaven say, "Write: Blessed are the dead who die in the Lord from now on."

"Yes," says the Spirit, "they will rest from their labor, for their deeds will follow them."

¹⁴I looked, and there before me was a white cloud, and seated on the cloud was one "like a son of man"ᵃ with a crown of gold on his head and a sharp sickle in his hand. ¹⁵Then another angel came out of the temple and called in a loud voice to him who was sitting on the cloud, "Take your sickle and reap, because the time to reap has come, for the harvest of the earth is ripe." ¹⁶So he who was seated on the cloud swung his sickle over the earth, and the earth was harvested.

¹⁷Another angel came out of the temple in heaven, and he too had a sharp sickle. ¹⁸Still another angel, who had charge of the fire, came from the altar and called in a loud voice to him who had the sharp sickle, "Take your sharp sickle and gather the clusters of grapes from the earth's vine, because its grapes are ripe." ¹⁹The angel swung his sickle on the earth, gathered its grapes and threw them into the great winepress of God's wrath. ²⁰They were trampled in the winepress outside the city, and blood flowed out of the press, rising as high as the horses' bridles for a distance of 1,600 stadia.ᵇ

ᵃ14 Daniel 7:13 ᵇ20 That is, about 180 miles (about 300 kilometers)

PSALM 142:1-7

A maskilᵃ of David. When he was in the cave. A prayer.

¹ I cry aloud to the LORD;
    I lift up my voice to the LORD for mercy.
² I pour out my complaint before him;
    before him I tell my trouble.

³ When my spirit grows faint within me,
    it is you who know my way.
In the path where I walk
    men have hidden a snare for me.

⁴Look to my right and see;
    no one is concerned for me.
I have no refuge;
    no one cares for my life.

⁵I cry to you, O LORD;
    I say, " You are my refuge,
    my portion in the land of the
        living."
⁶Listen to my cry,
    for I am in desperate need;
    rescue me from those who pursue
        me,
    for they are too strong for me.
⁷Set me free from my prison,
    that I may praise your name.

Then the righteous will gather about
    me
    because of your goodness to me.

ᵃTitle: Probably a literary or musical term

PROVERBS 30:21-23

²¹"Under three things the earth
        trembles,
    under four it cannot bear up:
²²a servant who becomes king,
    a fool who is full of food,
²³an unloved woman who is married,
    and a maidservant who displaces
        her mistress."

☐ D A Y 3 5 8

GOD SIGHTINGS

December 24

ZECHARIAH 6:1–7:14

1 [Zechariah] looked up again—and
there before me were four chariots
coming out from between two mountains—mountains of bronze! ²The first
chariot had red horses, the second
black, ³the third white, and the fourth
dappled—all of them powerful. ⁴I asked
the angel who was speaking to me,
"What are these, my lord?"

⁵The angel answered me, "These are
the four spiritsᵃ of heaven, going out

from standing in the presence of the
Lord of the whole world. ⁶The one with
the black horses is going toward the
north country, the one with the white
horses toward the west,ᵇ and the one
with the dappled horses toward the
south."

⁷When the powerful horses went out,
they were straining to go throughout the
earth. And he said, "Go throughout the
earth!" So they went throughout the
earth.

⁸Then he called to me, "Look, those
going toward the north country have
given my Spiritᶜ rest in the land of the
north."

⁹The word of the LORD came to me:
¹⁰"Take ⌞silver and gold⌟ from the exiles
Heldai, Tobijah and Jedaiah, who have arrived from Babylon. Go the same day to
the house of Josiah son of Zephaniah.
¹¹Take the silver and gold and make a
crown, and set it on the head of the high
priest, Joshua son of Jehozadak. ¹²Tell
him this is what the LORD Almighty says:
'Here is the man whose name is the
Branch, and he will branch out from his
place and build the temple of the LORD.
¹³It is he who will build the temple of the
LORD, and he will be clothed with majesty
and will sit and rule on his throne. And
he will be a priest on his throne. And
there will be harmony between the two.'
¹⁴The crown will be given to Heldai,ᵈ Tobijah, Jedaiah and Henᵉ son of Zephaniah as a memorial in the temple of the
LORD. ¹⁵Those who are far away will
come and help to build the temple of the
LORD, and you will know that the LORD Almighty has sent me to you. This will happen if you diligently obey the LORD your
God."

7:1In the fourth year of King Darius, the
word of the LORD came to Zechariah on
the fourth day of the ninth month, the
month of Kislev. ²The people of Bethel
had sent Sharezer and Regem-Melech,
together with their men, to entreat the
LORD ³by asking the priests of the house
of the LORD Almighty and the prophets,
"Should I mourn and fast in the fifth

month, as I have done for so many years?"

[4] Then the word of the Lord Almighty came to me: [5] "Ask all the people of the land and the priests, 'When you fasted and mourned in the fifth and seventh months for the past seventy years, was it really for me that you fasted? [6] And when you were eating and drinking, were you not just feasting for yourselves? [7] Are these not the words the Lord proclaimed through the earlier prophets when Jerusalem and its surrounding towns were at rest and prosperous, and the Negev and the western foothills were settled?'"

[8] And the word of the Lord came again to Zechariah: [9] " This is what the Lord Almighty says: 'Administer true justice; show mercy and compassion to one another. [10] Do not oppress the widow or the fatherless, the alien or the poor. In your hearts do not think evil of each other.'

[11] "But they refused to pay attention; stubbornly they turned their backs and stopped up their ears. [12] They made their hearts as hard as flint and would not listen to the law or to the words that the Lord Almighty had sent by his Spirit through the earlier prophets. So the Lord Almighty was very angry.

[13] "'When I called, they did not listen; so when they called, I would not listen,' says the Lord Almighty. [14] 'I scattered them with a whirlwind among all the nations, where they were strangers. The land was left so desolate behind them that no one could come or go. This is how they made the pleasant land desolate.'"

a5 Or *winds*   *b6* Or *horses after them*   *c8* Or *spirit*
d14 Syriac; Hebrew *Helem*   *e14* Or *and the gracious one, the*

REVELATION 15:1-8

▌[John] saw in heaven another great and marvelous sign: seven angels with the seven last plagues—last, because with them God's wrath is completed. [2] And I saw what looked like a sea of glass mixed with fire and, standing beside the sea, those who had been victorious over the beast and his image and over the number of his name. They held harps given them by God [3] and sang the song of Moses the servant of God and the song of the Lamb:

"Great and marvelous are your deeds,
    Lord God Almighty.
Just and true are your ways,
    King of the ages.
[4] Who will not fear you, O Lord,
    and bring glory to your name?
For you alone are holy.
All nations will come
    and worship before you,
for your righteous acts have been
    revealed."

[5] After this I looked and in heaven the temple, that is, the tabernacle of the Testimony, was opened. [6] Out of the temple came the seven angels with the seven plagues. They were dressed in clean, shining linen and wore golden sashes around their chests. [7] Then one of the four living creatures gave to the seven angels seven golden bowls filled with the wrath of God, who lives for ever and ever. [8] And the temple was filled with smoke from the glory of God and from his power, and no one could enter the temple until the seven plagues of the seven angels were completed.

PSALM 143:1-12
A psalm of David.

[1] ◗ Lord, hear my prayer,
    listen to my cry for mercy;
in your faithfulness and
        righteousness
    come to my relief.
[2] Do not bring your servant into
        judgment,
    for no one living is righteous
        before you.

[3] The enemy pursues me,
    he crushes me to the ground;
he makes me dwell in darkness
    like those long dead.
[4] So my spirit grows faint within me;
    my heart within me is dismayed.

⁵I remember the days of long ago;
   I meditate on all your works
   and consider what your hands
      have done.
⁶I spread out my hands to you;
   my soul thirsts for you like a
      parched land.   *Selah*

⁷Answer me quickly, O LORD;
   my spirit fails.
Do not hide your face from me
   or I will be like those who go down
      to the pit.
⁸Let the morning bring me word of
      your unfailing love,
   for I have put my trust in you.
Show me the way I should go,
   for to you I lift up my soul.
⁹Rescue me from my enemies, O LORD,
   for I hide myself in you.
¹⁰Teach me to do your will,
   for you are my God;
may your good Spirit
   lead me on level ground.

¹¹For your name's sake, O LORD,
      preserve my life;
   in your righteousness, bring me
      out of trouble.
¹²In your unfailing love, silence my
      enemies;
   destroy all my foes,
   for I am your servant.

PROVERBS 30:24-28

²⁴"**F**our things on earth are small,
   yet they are extremely wise:
²⁵Ants are creatures of little strength,
   yet they store up their food in the
      summer;
²⁶coneys*ᵃ* are creatures of little power,
   yet they make their home in the
      crags;
²⁷locusts have no king,
   yet they advance together in
      ranks;
²⁸a lizard can be caught with the
      hand,
   yet it is found in kings' palaces."

a26 That is, the hyrax or rock badger

□ DAY 359

GOD SIGHTINGS

December 25

ZECHARIAH 8:1-23

Again the word of the LORD Almighty came to me [Zechariah]. ²This is what the LORD Almighty says: "I am very jealous for Zion; I am burning with jealousy for her."

³This is what the LORD says: "I will return to Zion and dwell in Jerusalem. Then Jerusalem will be called the City of Truth, and the mountain of the LORD Almighty will be called the Holy Mountain."

⁴This is what the LORD Almighty says: "Once again men and women of ripe old age will sit in the streets of Jerusalem, each with cane in hand because of his age. ⁵The city streets will be filled with boys and girls playing there."

⁶This is what the LORD Almighty says: "It may seem marvelous to the remnant of this people at that time, but will it seem marvelous to me?" declares the LORD Almighty.

⁷This is what the LORD Almighty says: "I will save my people from the countries of the east and the west. ⁸I will bring them back to live in Jerusalem; they will be my people, and I will be faithful and righteous to them as their God."

⁹This is what the LORD Almighty says: "You who now hear these words spoken by the prophets who were there when the foundation was laid for the house of the LORD Almighty, let your hands be strong so that the temple may be built. ¹⁰Before that time there were no wages for man or beast. No one could go about his business safely because of his enemy, for I had turned every man against his neighbor. ¹¹But now I will not deal with the remnant of this people as I did in the past," declares the LORD Almighty.

¹²"The seed will grow well, the vine

will yield its fruit, the ground will produce its crops, and the heavens will drop their dew. I will give all these things as an inheritance to the remnant of this people. [13]As you have been an object of cursing among the nations, O Judah and Israel, so will I save you, and you will be a blessing. Do not be afraid, but let your hands be strong."

[14]This is what the LORD Almighty says: "Just as I had determined to bring disaster upon you and showed no pity when your fathers angered me," says the LORD Almighty, [15]"so now I have determined to do good again to Jerusalem and Judah. Do not be afraid. [16]These are the things you are to do: Speak the truth to each other, and render true and sound judgment in your courts; [17]do not plot evil against your neighbor, and do not love to swear falsely. I hate all this," declares the LORD.

[18]Again the word of the LORD Almighty came to me. [19]This is what the LORD Almighty says: "The fasts of the fourth, fifth, seventh and tenth months will become joyful and glad occasions and happy festivals for Judah. Therefore love truth and peace."

[20]This is what the LORD Almighty says: "Many peoples and the inhabitants of many cities will yet come, [21]and the inhabitants of one city will go to another and say, 'Let us go at once to entreat the LORD and seek the LORD Almighty. I myself am going.' [22]And many peoples and powerful nations will come to Jerusalem to seek the LORD Almighty and to entreat him."

[23]This is what the LORD Almighty says: "In those days ten men from all languages and nations will take firm hold of one Jew by the hem of his robe and say, 'Let us go with you, because we have heard that God is with you.'"

REVELATION 16:1-21

Then I [John] heard a loud voice from the temple saying to the seven angels, "Go, pour out the seven bowls of God's wrath on the earth."

[2]The first angel went and poured out his bowl on the land, and ugly and painful sores broke out on the people who had the mark of the beast and worshiped his image.

[3]The second angel poured out his bowl on the sea, and it turned into blood like that of a dead man, and every living thing in the sea died.

[4]The third angel poured out his bowl on the rivers and springs of water, and they became blood. [5]Then I heard the angel in charge of the waters say:

"You are just in these judgments,
    you who are and who were, the
        Holy One,
    because you have so judged;
[6]for they have shed the blood of your
        saints and prophets,
    and you have given them blood to
        drink as they deserve."

[7]And I heard the altar respond:

"Yes, Lord God Almighty,
    true and just are your judgments."

[8]The fourth angel poured out his bowl on the sun, and the sun was given power to scorch people with fire. [9]They were seared by the intense heat and they cursed the name of God, who had control over these plagues, but they refused to repent and glorify him.

[10]The fifth angel poured out his bowl on the throne of the beast, and his kingdom was plunged into darkness. Men gnawed their tongues in agony [11]and cursed the God of heaven because of their pains and their sores, but they refused to repent of what they had done.

[12]The sixth angel poured out his bowl on the great river Euphrates, and its water was dried up to prepare the way for the kings from the East. [13]Then I saw three evil[a] spirits that looked like frogs; they came out of the mouth of the dragon, out of the mouth of the beast and out of the mouth of the false prophet. [14]They are spirits of demons performing miraculous signs, and they go out to the kings of the whole world,

to gather them for the battle on the great day of God Almighty.

¹⁵"Behold, I come like a thief! Blessed is he who stays awake and keeps his clothes with him, so that he may not go naked and be shamefully exposed."

¹⁶Then they gathered the kings together to the place that in Hebrew is called Armageddon.

¹⁷The seventh angel poured out his bowl into the air, and out of the temple came a loud voice from the throne, saying, "It is done!" ¹⁸Then there came flashes of lightning, rumblings, peals of thunder and a severe earthquake. No earthquake like it has ever occurred since man has been on earth, so tremendous was the quake. ¹⁹The great city split into three parts, and the cities of the nations collapsed. God remembered Babylon the Great and gave her the cup filled with the wine of the fury of his wrath. ²⁰Every island fled away and the mountains could not be found. ²¹From the sky huge hailstones of about a hundred pounds each fell upon men. And they cursed God on account of the plague of hail, because the plague was so terrible.

a13 Greek *unclean*

PSALM 144:1-15

Of David.

¹ **Praise be to the Lord my Rock,**
 who trains my hands for war,
 my fingers for battle.
² **He is my loving God and my**
   fortress,
 my stronghold and my
   deliverer,
 my shield, in whom I take refuge,
 who subdues peoples*a* under
   me.

³ O Lord, what is man that you care for
   him,
 the son of man that you think of
   him?
⁴ Man is like a breath;
 his days are like a fleeting shadow.

⁵ Part your heavens, O Lord, and come
   down;
 touch the mountains, so that they
   smoke.
⁶ Send forth lightning and scatter ⌐the
   enemies⌐;
 shoot your arrows and rout them.
⁷ Reach down your hand from on high;
 deliver me and rescue me
 from the mighty waters,
 from the hands of foreigners
⁸ whose mouths are full of lies,
 whose right hands are deceitful.

⁹ I will sing a new song to you, O God;
 on the ten-stringed lyre I will
   make music to you,
¹⁰ to the One who gives victory to kings,
 who delivers his servant David
 from the deadly sword.

¹¹ Deliver me and rescue me
 from the hands of foreigners
 whose mouths are full of lies,
 whose right hands are deceitful.

¹² Then our sons in their youth
 will be like well-nurtured plants,
 and our daughters will be like pillars
 carved to adorn a palace.
¹³ Our barns will be filled
 with every kind of provision.
 Our sheep will increase by
   thousands,
 by tens of thousands in our fields;
¹⁴   our oxen will draw heavy loads.*b*
 There will be no breaching of walls,
 no going into captivity,
 no cry of distress in our streets.

¹⁵ Blessed are the people of whom this
   is true;
 blessed are the people whose God
 is the Lord.

a2 Many manuscripts of the Masoretic Text, Dead Sea Scrolls, Aquila, Jerome and Syriac; most manuscripts of the Masoretic Text *subdues my people*   *b14* Or *our chieftains will be firmly established*

PROVERBS 30:29-31

²⁹"There are three things that are
   stately in their stride,
 four that move with stately
   bearing:

³⁰a lion, mighty among beasts,
who retreats before nothing;
³¹a strutting rooster, a he-goat,
and a king with his army around
him.ᵃ"

ᵃ31 Or king secure against revolt

□ DAY 360

GOD SIGHTINGS

December 26

ZECHARIAH 9:1-17
An Oracle

THE word of the LORD is against the
land of Hadrach
and will rest upon Damascus—
for the eyes of men and all the tribes
of Israel
are on the LORD—ᵃ
²and upon Hamath too, which
borders on it,
and upon Tyre and Sidon, though
they are very skillful.
³Tyre has built herself a stronghold;
she has heaped up silver like dust,
and gold like the dirt of the streets.
⁴But the Lord will take away her
possessions
and destroy her power on the sea,
and she will be consumed by fire.
⁵Ashkelon will see it and fear;
Gaza will writhe in agony,
and Ekron too, for her hope will
wither.
Gaza will lose her king
and Ashkelon will be deserted.
⁶Foreigners will occupy Ashdod,
and I will cut off the pride of the
Philistines.
⁷I will take the blood from their
mouths,
the forbidden food from between
their teeth.
Those who are left will belong to our
God
and become leaders in Judah,
and Ekron will be like the Jebusites.

⁸But I will defend my house
against marauding forces.
Never again will an oppressor
overrun my people,
for now I am keeping watch.

⁹Rejoice greatly, O Daughter of Zion!
Shout, Daughter of Jerusalem!
See, your kingᵇ comes to you,
righteous and having salvation,
gentle and riding on a donkey,
on a colt, the foal of a donkey.
¹⁰I will take away the chariots from
Ephraim
and the war-horses from
Jerusalem,
and the battle bow will be broken.
He will proclaim peace to the nations.
His rule will extend from sea to
sea
and from the Riverᶜ to the ends of
the earth.ᵈ
¹¹As for you, because of the blood of
my covenant with you,
I will free your prisoners from the
waterless pit.
¹²Return to your fortress, O prisoners
of hope;
even now I announce that I will
restore twice as much to you.
¹³I will bend Judah as I bend my bow
and fill it with Ephraim.
I will rouse your sons, O Zion,
against your sons, O Greece,
and make you like a warrior's
sword.

¹⁴Then the LORD will appear over them;
his arrow will flash like lightning.
The Sovereign LORD will sound the
trumpet;
he will march in the storms of the
south,
¹⁵ and the LORD Almighty will shield
them.
They will destroy
and overcome with slingstones.
They will drink and roar as with
wine;
they will be full like a bowl
used for sprinklingᵉ the corners
of the altar.

16 The Lord their God will save them on
      that day
   as the flock of his people.
   They will sparkle in his land
      like jewels in a crown.
17 How attractive and beautiful they
      will be!
   Grain will make the young men
      thrive,
   and new wine the young women.

*a1 Or Damascus. / For the eye of the Lord is on all mankind,
/ as well as on the tribes of Israel, b9 Or King c10 That is,
the Euphrates d10 Or the end of the land e15 Or bowl, /
like*

REVELATION 17:1-18

One of the seven angels who had the
seven bowls came and said to me [John],
"Come, I will show you the punishment
of the great prostitute, who sits on many
waters. 2 With her the kings of the earth
committed adultery and the inhabitants
of the earth were intoxicated with the
wine of her adulteries."

3 Then the angel carried me away in
the Spirit into a desert. There I saw a
woman sitting on a scarlet beast that
was covered with blasphemous names
and had seven heads and ten horns.
4 The woman was dressed in purple and
scarlet, and was glittering with gold,
precious stones and pearls. She held a
golden cup in her hand, filled with
abominable things and the filth of her
adulteries. 5 This title was written on her
forehead:

MYSTERY
BABYLON THE GREAT
THE MOTHER OF PROSTITUTES
AND OF THE ABOMINATIONS OF THE EARTH.

6 I saw that the woman was drunk with
the blood of the saints, the blood of
those who bore testimony to Jesus.

When I saw her, I was greatly astonished. 7 Then the angel said to me: "Why
are you astonished? I will explain to you
the mystery of the woman and of the
beast she rides, which has the seven
heads and ten horns. 8 The beast, which
you saw, once was, now is not, and will
come up out of the Abyss and go to his
destruction. The inhabitants of the

earth whose names have not been written in the book of life from the creation
of the world will be astonished when
they see the beast, because he once was,
now is not, and yet will come.

9 "This calls for a mind with wisdom.
The seven heads are seven hills on which
the woman sits. 10 They are also seven
kings. Five have fallen, one is, the other
has not yet come; but when he does
come, he must remain for a little while.
11 The beast who once was, and now is
not, is an eighth king. He belongs to the
seven and is going to his destruction.

12 "The ten horns you saw are ten
kings who have not yet received a kingdom, but who for one hour will receive
authority as kings along with the beast.
13 They have one purpose and will give
their power and authority to the beast.
14 They will make war against the Lamb,
but the Lamb will overcome them because he is Lord of lords and King of
kings—and with him will be his called,
chosen and faithful followers."

15 Then the angel said to me, "The waters you saw, where the prostitute sits,
are peoples, multitudes, nations and
languages. 16 The beast and the ten
horns you saw will hate the prostitute.
They will bring her to ruin and leave her
naked; they will eat her flesh and burn
her with fire. 17 For God has put it into
their hearts to accomplish his purpose
by agreeing to give the beast their power
to rule, until God's words are fulfilled.
18 The woman you saw is the great city
that rules over the kings of the earth."

PSALM 145:1-21ª
A psalm of praise. Of David.

1 I will exalt you, my God the King;
   I will praise your name for ever
      and ever.
2 Every day I will praise you
   and extol your name for ever and
      ever.

3 Great is the Lord and most worthy of
      praise;
   his greatness no one can fathom.

4 One generation will commend your
     works to another;
   they will tell of your mighty acts.
5 They will speak of the glorious
     splendor of your majesty,
   and I will meditate on your
     wonderful works.*b*
6 They will tell of the power of your
     awesome works,
   and I will proclaim your great deeds.
7 They will celebrate your abundant
     goodness
   and joyfully sing of your
     righteousness.

8 The LORD is gracious and
     compassionate,
   slow to anger and rich in love.
9 The LORD is good to all;
   he has compassion on all he has
     made.
10 All you have made will praise you,
     O LORD;
   your saints will extol you.
11 They will tell of the glory of your
     kingdom
   and speak of your might,
12 so that all men may know of your
     mighty acts
   and the glorious splendor of your
     kingdom.
13 Your kingdom is an everlasting
     kingdom,
   and your dominion endures
     through all generations.

**The LORD is faithful to all his
   promises
   and loving toward all he has
   made.***c*
14 The LORD upholds all those who
   fall
   and lifts up all who are bowed
   down.
15 The eyes of all look to you,
   and you give them their food at
     the proper time.
16 You open your hand
   and satisfy the desires of every
     living thing.

17 The LORD is righteous in all his ways
   and loving toward all he has made.

18 The LORD is near to all who call on
     him,
   to all who call on him in truth.
19 He fulfills the desires of those who
     fear him;
   he hears their cry and saves
     them.
20 The LORD watches over all who love
     him,
   but all the wicked he will destroy.

21 My mouth will speak in praise of the
     LORD.
   Let every creature praise his holy
     name
   for ever and ever.

*a*This psalm is an acrostic poem, the verses of which
(including verse 13b) begin with the successive letters of the
Hebrew alphabet.   *b*5 Dead Sea Scrolls and Syriac (see also
Septuagint); Masoretic Text *On the glorious splendor of your
majesty / and on your wonderful works I will meditate*
*c*13 One manuscript of the Masoretic Text, Dead Sea Scrolls
and Syriac (see also Septuagint); most manuscripts of the
Masoretic Text do not have the last two lines of verse 13.

PROVERBS 30:32

32 "If you have played the fool and
     exalted yourself,
   or if you have planned evil,
   clap your hand over your mouth!"

□ DAY 361

GOD SIGHTINGS

December 27

ZECHARIAH 10:1–11:17

Ask the LORD for rain in the
     springtime;
   it is the LORD who makes the storm
     clouds.
He gives showers of rain to men,
   and plants of the field to
     everyone.
2 The idols speak deceit,
   diviners see visions that lie;
 they tell dreams that are false,
   they give comfort in vain.
 Therefore the people wander like
     sheep
   oppressed for lack of a shepherd.

3"My anger burns against the
shepherds,
and I will punish the leaders;
for the LORD Almighty will care
for his flock, the house of Judah,
and make them like a proud horse
in battle.
4From Judah will come the cornerstone,
from him the tent peg,
from him the battle bow,
from him every ruler.
5Together they*a* will be like mighty
men
trampling the muddy streets in
battle.
Because the LORD is with them,
they will fight and overthrow the
horsemen.

6"I will strengthen the house of Judah
and save the house of Joseph.
I will restore them
because I have compassion on
them.
They will be as though
I had not rejected them,
for I am the LORD their God
and I will answer them.
7The Ephraimites will become like
mighty men,
and their hearts will be glad as
with wine.
Their children will see it and be
joyful;
their hearts will rejoice in the LORD.
8I will signal for them
and gather them in.
Surely I will redeem them;
they will be as numerous as
before.
9Though I scatter them among the
peoples,
yet in distant lands they will
remember me.
They and their children will survive,
and they will return.
10I will bring them back from Egypt
and gather them from Assyria.
I will bring them to Gilead and
Lebanon,
and there will not be room enough
for them.

11They will pass through the sea of
trouble;
the surging sea will be subdued
and all the depths of the Nile will
dry up.
Assyria's pride will be brought down
and Egypt's scepter will pass away.
12I will strengthen them in the LORD
and in his name they will walk,"
declares the LORD.

11:1OPEN your doors, O Lebanon,
so that fire may devour your
cedars!
2Wail, O pine tree, for the cedar has
fallen;
the stately trees are ruined!
Wail, oaks of Bashan;
the dense forest has been cut
down!
3Listen to the wail of the shepherds;
their rich pastures are destroyed!
Listen to the roar of the lions;
the lush thicket of the Jordan is
ruined!

4This is what the LORD my God says:
"Pasture the flock marked for slaughter.
5Their buyers slaughter them and go unpunished. Those who sell them say,
'Praise the LORD, I am rich!' Their own
shepherds do not spare them. 6For I will
no longer have pity on the people of the
land," declares the LORD. "I will hand everyone over to his neighbor and his king.
They will oppress the land, and I will not
rescue them from their hands."

7So I pastured the flock marked for
slaughter, particularly the oppressed of
the flock. Then I took two staffs and
called one Favor and the other Union,
and I pastured the flock. 8In one month
I got rid of the three shepherds.

The flock detested me, and I grew
weary of them 9and said, "I will not be
your shepherd. Let the dying die, and
the perishing perish. Let those who are
left eat one another's flesh."

10Then I took my staff called Favor
and broke it, revoking the covenant I
had made with all the nations. 11It was
revoked on that day, and so the afflicted

of the flock who were watching me knew it was the word of the Lord.

¹²I told them, "If you think it best, give me my pay; but if not, keep it." So they paid me thirty pieces of silver.

¹³And the Lord said to me, "Throw it to the potter"—the handsome price at which they priced me! So I took the thirty pieces of silver and threw them into the house of the Lord to the potter.

¹⁴Then I broke my second staff called Union, breaking the brotherhood between Judah and Israel.

¹⁵Then the Lord said to me, "Take again the equipment of a foolish shepherd. ¹⁶For I am going to raise up a shepherd over the land who will not care for the lost, or seek the young, or heal the injured, or feed the healthy, but will eat the meat of the choice sheep, tearing off their hoofs.

¹⁷"Woe to the worthless shepherd,
    who deserts the flock!
May the sword strike his arm and his
        right eye!
    May his arm be completely
        withered,
    his right eye totally blinded!"

a4,5 Or ruler, all of them together. / ⁵They

REVELATION 18:1-24

After this I [John] saw another angel coming down from heaven. He had great authority, and the earth was illuminated by his splendor. ²With a mighty voice he shouted:

"Fallen! Fallen is Babylon the Great!
    She has become a home for
        demons
and a haunt for every evil*a* spirit,
    a haunt for every unclean and
        detestable bird.
³For all the nations have drunk
    the maddening wine of her
        adulteries.
The kings of the earth committed
    adultery with her,
    and the merchants of the earth
        grew rich from her excessive
        luxuries."

⁴Then I heard another voice from heaven say:

"Come out of her, my people,
    so that you will not share in her
        sins,
    so that you will not receive any of
        her plagues;
⁵for her sins are piled up to heaven,
    and God has remembered her
        crimes.
⁶Give back to her as she has given;
    pay her back double for what she
        has done.
    Mix her a double portion from her
        own cup.
⁷Give her as much torture and grief
    as the glory and luxury she gave
        herself.
In her heart she boasts,
    'I sit as queen; I am not a widow,
    and I will never mourn.'
⁸Therefore in one day her plagues will
        overtake her:
    death, mourning and famine.
She will be consumed by fire,
    for mighty is the Lord God who
        judges her.

⁹"When the kings of the earth who committed adultery with her and shared her luxury see the smoke of her burning, they will weep and mourn over her. ¹⁰Terrified at her torment, they will stand far off and cry:

"'Woe! Woe, O great city,
    O Babylon, city of power!
In one hour your doom has come!'

¹¹"The merchants of the earth will weep and mourn over her because no one buys their cargoes any more— ¹²cargoes of gold, silver, precious stones and pearls; fine linen, purple, silk and scarlet cloth; every sort of citron wood, and articles of every kind made of ivory, costly wood, bronze, iron and marble; ¹³cargoes of cinnamon and spice, of incense, myrrh and frankincense, of wine and olive oil, of fine flour and wheat; cattle and sheep; horses and carriages; and bodies and souls of men.

14"They will say, 'The fruit you longed for is gone from you. All your riches and splendor have vanished, never to be recovered.' 15The merchants who sold these things and gained their wealth from her will stand far off, terrified at her torment. They will weep and mourn 16and cry out:

"'Woe! Woe, O great city,
    dressed in fine linen, purple and
        scarlet,
    and glittering with gold, precious
        stones and pearls!
17In one hour such great wealth has
        been brought to ruin!'

"Every sea captain, and all who travel by ship, the sailors, and all who earn their living from the sea, will stand far off. 18When they see the smoke of her burning, they will exclaim, 'Was there ever a city like this great city?' 19They will throw dust on their heads, and with weeping and mourning cry out:

"'Woe! Woe, O great city,
    where all who had ships on the sea
        became rich through her wealth!
In one hour she has been brought to
        ruin!
20Rejoice over her, O heaven!
    Rejoice, saints and apostles and
        prophets!
God has judged her for the way she
        treated you.'"

21Then a mighty angel picked up a boulder the size of a large millstone and threw it into the sea, and said:

"With such violence
    the great city of Babylon will be
        thrown down,
    never to be found again.
22The music of harpists and musicians,
        flute players and trumpeters,
    will never be heard in you again.
No workman of any trade
    will ever be found in you again.
The sound of a millstone
    will never be heard in you again.
23The light of a lamp
    will never shine in you again.

The voice of bridegroom and bride
    will never be heard in you again.
Your merchants were the world's
        great men.
    By your magic spell all the nations
        were led astray.
24In her was found the blood of
        prophets and of the saints,
    and of all who have been killed on
        the earth."

a2 Greek unclean

PSALM 146:1-10
1 **P**raise the LORD.*a*

Praise the LORD, O my soul.
2   I will praise the LORD all my life;
    I will sing praise to my God as long
        as I live.

3Do not put your trust in princes,
    in mortal men, who cannot save.
4When their spirit departs, they
        return to the ground;
    on that very day their plans come
        to nothing.

5Blessed is he whose help is the God
        of Jacob,
    whose hope is in the LORD his God,
6the Maker of heaven and earth,
    the sea, and everything in them—
    the LORD, who remains faithful
        forever.
7He upholds the cause of the
        oppressed
    and gives food to the hungry.
The LORD sets prisoners free,
8   the LORD gives sight to the blind,
the LORD lifts up those who are
        bowed down,
    the LORD loves the righteous.
9**The LORD watches over the alien
    and sustains the fatherless and
        the widow,
    but he frustrates the ways of the
        wicked.**

10The LORD reigns forever,
    your God, O Zion, for all
        generations.

Praise the LORD.

a1 Hebrew Hallelu Yah; also in verse 10

PROVERBS 30:33

³³"For as churning the milk produces
   butter,
   and as twisting the nose produces
      blood,
   so stirring up anger produces
      strife."

☐ DAY 362

GOD SIGHTINGS

December 28

ZECHARIAH 12:1–13:9
An Oracle

This is the word of the LORD concerning
Israel. The LORD, who stretches out the
heavens, who lays the foundation of the
earth, and who forms the spirit of man
within him, declares: ²"I am going to
make Jerusalem a cup that sends all the
surrounding peoples reeling. Judah will
be besieged as well as Jerusalem. ³On
that day, when all the nations of the
earth are gathered against her, I will
make Jerusalem an immovable rock for
all the nations. All who try to move it will
injure themselves. ⁴On that day I will
strike every horse with panic and its
rider with madness," declares the LORD.
"I will keep a watchful eye over the
house of Judah, but I will blind all the
horses of the nations. ⁵Then the leaders
of Judah will say in their hearts, 'The
people of Jerusalem are strong, because
the LORD Almighty is their God.'

⁶"On that day I will make the leaders
of Judah like a firepot in a woodpile, like
a flaming torch among sheaves. They
will consume right and left all the surrounding peoples, but Jerusalem will remain intact in her place.

⁷"The LORD will save the dwellings of
Judah first, so that the honor of the
house of David and of Jerusalem's inhabitants may not be greater than that
of Judah. ⁸On that day the LORD will
shield those who live in Jerusalem, so

that the feeblest among them will be
like David, and the house of David will
be like God, like the Angel of the LORD
going before them. ⁹On that day I will
set out to destroy all the nations that attack Jerusalem.

¹⁰"And I will pour out on the house of
David and the inhabitants of Jerusalem
a spirit*a* of grace and supplication. They
will look on*b* me, the one they have
pierced, and they will mourn for him as
one mourns for an only child, and grieve
bitterly for him as one grieves for a firstborn son. ¹¹On that day the weeping in
Jerusalem will be great, like the weeping
of Hadad Rimmon in the plain of Megiddo. ¹²The land will mourn, each clan
by itself, with their wives by themselves:
the clan of the house of David and their
wives, the clan of the house of Nathan
and their wives, ¹³the clan of the house
of Levi and their wives, the clan of
Shimei and their wives, ¹⁴and all the
rest of the clans and their wives.

¹³:¹"On that day a fountain will be
opened to the house of David and the
inhabitants of Jerusalem, to cleanse
them from sin and impurity.

²"On that day, I will banish the names
of the idols from the land, and they will
be remembered no more," declares the
LORD Almighty. "I will remove both the
prophets and the spirit of impurity
from the land. ³And if anyone still
prophesies, his father and mother, to
whom he was born, will say to him, 'You
must die, because you have told lies in
the LORD's name.' When he prophesies,
his own parents will stab him.

⁴"On that day every prophet will be
ashamed of his prophetic vision. He will
not put on a prophet's garment of hair in
order to deceive. ⁵He will say, 'I am not a
prophet. I am a farmer; the land has
been my livelihood since my youth.*c*' ⁶If
someone asks him, 'What are these
wounds on your body*d*?' he will answer,
'The wounds I was given at the house of
my friends.'

7 "Awake, O sword, against my
    shepherd,
   against the man who is close to
    me!"
  declares the LORD Almighty.
"Strike the shepherd,
   and the sheep will be scattered,
   and I will turn my hand against the
    little ones.
8 In the whole land," declares the LORD,
  "two-thirds will be struck down
    and perish;
  yet one-third will be left in it.
9 This third I will bring into the fire;
  I will refine them like silver
   and test them like gold.
They will call on my name
  and I will answer them;
I will say, 'They are my people,'
  and they will say, 'The LORD is our
    God.'"

*a10 Or the Spirit   b10 Or to   c5 Or farmer; a man sold me
in my youth   d6 Or wounds between your hands*

REVELATION 19:1-21

After this I [John] heard what sounded
like the roar of a great multitude in
heaven shouting:

"Hallelujah!
Salvation and glory and power
    belong to our God,
2 for true and just are his
    judgments.
He has condemned the great
    prostitute
  who corrupted the earth by her
    adulteries.
He has avenged on her the blood of
   his servants."

3 And again they shouted:

"Hallelujah!
The smoke from her goes up for ever
   and ever."

4 The twenty-four elders and the four
living creatures fell down and worshiped God, who was seated on the
throne. And they cried:

"Amen, Hallelujah!"

5 Then a voice came from the throne,
saying:

"Praise our God,
  all you his servants,
you who fear him,
  both small and great!"

6 Then I heard what sounded like a
great multitude, like the roar of rushing
waters and like loud peals of thunder,
shouting:

"Hallelujah!
  For our Lord God Almighty reigns.
7 **Let us rejoice and be glad**
  and give him glory!
For the wedding of the Lamb has
  come,
  and his bride has made herself
    ready.
8 Fine linen, bright and clean,
  was given her to wear."
(Fine linen stands for the righteous acts
of the saints.)

9 Then the angel said to me, "Write:
'Blessed are those who are invited to the
wedding supper of the Lamb!'" And he
added, "These are the true words of
God."

10 At this I fell at his feet to worship
him. But he said to me, "Do not do it! I am
a fellow servant with you and with your
brothers who hold to the testimony of
Jesus. Worship God! For the testimony of
Jesus is the spirit of prophecy."

11 I saw heaven standing open and
there before me was a white horse,
whose rider is called Faithful and True.
With justice he judges and makes war.
12 His eyes are like blazing fire, and on
his head are many crowns. He has a
name written on him that no one knows
but he himself. 13 He is dressed in a robe
dipped in blood, and his name is the
Word of God. 14 The armies of heaven
were following him, riding on white
horses and dressed in fine linen, white
and clean. 15 Out of his mouth comes a
sharp sword with which to strike down
the nations. "He will rule them with an
iron scepter."*a* He treads the winepress

of t fury of the wrath of God Almighty.
16 his robe and on his thigh he has
t s name written:

KING OF KINGS AND LORD OF LORDS.

17 And I saw an angel standing in the
sun, who cried in a loud voice to all the
birds flying in midair, "Come, gather together for the great supper of God, 18 so
that you may eat the flesh of kings, generals, and mighty men, of horses and
their riders, and the flesh of all people,
free and slave, small and great."

19 Then I saw the beast and the kings
of the earth and their armies gathered
together to make war against the rider
on the horse and his army. 20 But the
beast was captured, and with him the
false prophet who had performed the
miraculous signs on his behalf. With
these signs he had deluded those who
had received the mark of the beast and
worshiped his image. The two of them
were thrown alive into the fiery lake of
burning sulfur. 21 The rest of them were
killed with the sword that came out of
the mouth of the rider on the horse, and
all the birds gorged themselves on their
flesh.

a 15 Psalm 2:9

PSALM 147:1-20

1 Praise the LORD.a

How good it is to sing praises to our
    God,
  how pleasant and fitting to praise
    him!

2 The LORD builds up Jerusalem;
  he gathers the exiles of Israel.
3 He heals the brokenhearted
  and binds up their wounds.

4 He determines the number of the
    stars
  and calls them each by name.
5 Great is our Lord and mighty in
    power;
  his understanding has no limit.
6 The LORD sustains the humble
  but casts the wicked to the
    ground.

7 Sing to the LORD with thanksgiving;
  make music to our God on the
    harp.
8 He covers the sky with clouds;
  he supplies the earth with rain
  and makes grass grow on the hills.
9 He provides food for the cattle
  and for the young ravens when
    they call.

10 His pleasure is not in the strength of
    the horse,
  nor his delight in the legs of a man;
11 the LORD delights in those who fear
    him,
  who put their hope in his unfailing
    love.

12 Extol the LORD, O Jerusalem;
  praise your God, O Zion,
13 for he strengthens the bars of your
    gates
  and blesses your people within
    you.
14 He grants peace to your borders
  and satisfies you with the finest of
    wheat.

15 He sends his command to the earth;
  his word runs swiftly.
16 He spreads the snow like wool
  and scatters the frost like ashes.
17 He hurls down his hail like pebbles.
  Who can withstand his icy blast?
18 He sends his word and melts them;
  he stirs up his breezes, and the
    waters flow.

19 He has revealed his word to Jacob,
  his laws and decrees to Israel.
20 He has done this for no other nation;
  they do not know his laws.

  Praise the LORD.

a 1 Hebrew Hallelu Yah; also in verse 20

PROVERBS 31:1-7
The sayings of King Lemuel—an oraclea
his mother taught him:

2 "O my son, O son of my womb,
  O son of my vows,b
3 do not spend your strength on women,
  your vigor on those who ruin kings.

4"It is not for kings, O Lemuel—
    not for kings to drink wine,
    not for rulers to crave beer,
5 lest they drink and forget what the
        law decrees,
    and deprive all the oppressed of
        their rights.
6 Give beer to those who are perishing,
    wine to those who are in anguish;
7 let them drink and forget their
        poverty
    and remember their misery no
        more."

*a1 Or of Lemuel king of Massa, which   b2 Or / the answer
to my prayers*

□ DAY 363

GOD SIGHTINGS

December 29

ZECHARIAH 14:1-21

A day of the LORD is coming when your plunder will be divided among you.

2 I will gather all the nations to Jerusalem to fight against it; the city will be captured, the houses ransacked, and the women raped. Half of the city will go into exile, but the rest of the people will not be taken from the city.

3 Then the LORD will go out and fight against those nations, as he fights in the day of battle. 4 On that day his feet will stand on the Mount of Olives, east of Jerusalem, and the Mount of Olives will be split in two from east to west, forming a great valley, with half of the mountain moving north and half moving south. 5 You will flee by my mountain valley, for it will extend to Azel. You will flee as you fled from the earthquake*a* in the days of Uzziah king of Judah. Then the LORD my God will come, and all the holy ones with him.

6 On that day there will be no light, no cold or frost. 7 It will be a unique day, without daytime or nighttime—a day

known to the LORD. When evening comes, there will be light.

8 On that day living water will flow out from Jerusalem, half to the eastern sea*b* and half to the western sea,*c* in summer and in winter.

9 The LORD will be king over the whole earth. On that day there will be one LORD, and his name the only name.

10 The whole land, from Geba to Rimmon, south of Jerusalem, will become like the Arabah. But Jerusalem will be raised up and remain in its place, from the Benjamin Gate to the site of the First Gate, to the Corner Gate, and from the Tower of Hananel to the royal winepresses. 11 It will be inhabited; never again will it be destroyed. Jerusalem will be secure.

12 This is the plague with which the LORD will strike all the nations that fought against Jerusalem: Their flesh will rot while they are still standing on their feet, their eyes will rot in their sockets, and their tongues will rot in their mouths. 13 On that day men will be stricken by the LORD with great panic. Each man will seize the hand of another, and they will attack each other. 14 Judah too will fight at Jerusalem. The wealth of all the surrounding nations will be collected—great quantities of gold and silver and clothing. 15 A similar plague will strike the horses and mules, the camels and donkeys, and all the animals in those camps.

16 Then the survivors from all the nations that have attacked Jerusalem will go up year after year to worship the King, the LORD Almighty, and to celebrate the Feast of Tabernacles. 17 If any of the peoples of the earth do not go up to Jerusalem to worship the King, the LORD Almighty, they will have no rain. 18 If the Egyptian people do not go up and take part, they will have no rain. The LORD*d* will bring on them the plague he inflicts on the nations that do not go up to celebrate the Feast of Tabernacles. 19 This will be the punishment of Egypt and the punishment of all the nations

that do not go up to celebrate the Feast of Tabernacles.

20On that day HOLY TO THE LORD will be inscribed on the bells of the horses, and the cooking pots in the LORD's house will be like the sacred bowls in front of the altar. 21Every pot in Jerusalem and Judah will be holy to the LORD Almighty, and all who come to sacrifice will take some of the pots and cook in them. And on that day there will no longer be a Canaanite*e* in the house of the LORD Almighty.

a5 Or 5My mountain valley will be blocked and will extend to Azel. It will be blocked as it was blocked because of the earthquake b8 That is, the Dead Sea c8 That is, the Mediterranean d18 Or part, then the LORD e21 Or merchant

REVELATION 20:1-15

And I [John] saw an angel coming down out of heaven, having the key to the Abyss and holding in his hand a great chain. 2He seized the dragon, that ancient serpent, who is the devil, or Satan, and bound him for a thousand years. 3He threw him into the Abyss, and locked and sealed it over him, to keep him from deceiving the nations anymore until the thousand years were ended. After that, he must be set free for a short time.

4I saw thrones on which were seated those who had been given authority to judge. And I saw the souls of those who had been beheaded because of their testimony for Jesus and because of the word of God. They had not worshiped the beast or his image and had not received his mark on their foreheads or their hands. They came to life and reigned with Christ a thousand years. 5(The rest of the dead did not come to life until the thousand years were ended.) This is the first resurrection. 6Blessed and holy are those who have part in the first resurrection. The second death has no power over them, but they will be priests of God and of Christ and will reign with him for a thousand years.

7When the thousand years are over, Satan will be released from his prison 8and will go out to deceive the nations

in the four corners of the earth—Gog and Magog—to gather them for battle. In number they are like the sand on the seashore. 9They marched across the breadth of the earth and surrounded the camp of God's people, the city he loves. But fire came down from heaven and devoured them. 10And the devil, who deceived them, was thrown into the lake of burning sulfur, where the beast and the false prophet had been thrown. They will be tormented day and night for ever and ever.

11Then I saw a great white throne and him who was seated on it. Earth and sky fled from his presence, and there was no place for them. 12And I saw the dead, great and small, standing before the throne, and books were opened. Another book was opened, which is the book of life. The dead were judged according to what they had done as recorded in the books. 13The sea gave up the dead that were in it, and death and Hades gave up the dead that were in them, and each person was judged according to what he had done. 14Then death and Hades were thrown into the lake of fire. The lake of fire is the second death. 15If anyone's name was not found written in the book of life, he was thrown into the lake of fire.

PSALM 148:1-14

1**P**raise the LORD.*a*

Praise the LORD from the heavens,
    praise him in the heights above.
2Praise him, all his angels,
    praise him, all his heavenly hosts.
3Praise him, sun and moon,
    praise him, all you shining stars.
4Praise him, you highest heavens
    and you waters above the skies.
5Let them praise the name of the
    LORD,
    for he commanded and they were
        created.
6He set them in place for ever and
    ever;
    he gave a decree that will never
        pass away.

7 Praise the Lord from the earth,
    you great sea creatures and all
        ocean depths,
8 lightning and hail, snow and clouds,
    stormy winds that do his bidding,
9 you mountains and all hills,
    fruit trees and all cedars,
10 wild animals and all cattle,
    small creatures and flying birds,
11 kings of the earth and all nations,
    you princes and all rulers on earth,
12 young men and maidens,
    old men and children.

13 Let them praise the name of the Lord,
    for his name alone is exalted;
    his splendor is above the earth and
        the heavens.
14 He has raised up for his people a
    horn,*b*
    the praise of all his saints,
    of Israel, the people close to his
        heart.

    Praise the Lord.

*a 1 Hebrew Hallelu Yah; also in verse 14   b 14 Horn here
symbolizes strong one, that is, king.*

PROVERBS 31:8-9

8 **S**peak up for those who cannot
        speak for themselves,
    for the rights of all who are
        destitute.
9 Speak up and judge fairly;
    defend the rights of the poor and
        needy."

□ D A Y   3 6 4

GOD SIGHTINGS

December 30

MALACHI 1:1–2:17
An oracle: The word of the Lord to Israel through Malachi.*a*

2 "I have loved you," says the Lord.
    "But you ask, 'How have you loved
us?'
    "Was not Esau Jacob's brother?" the

Lord says. "Yet I have loved Jacob, 3 but
Esau I have hated, and I have turned his
mountains into a wasteland and left his
inheritance to the desert jackals."

4 Edom may say, "Though we have
been crushed, we will rebuild the ruins."
But this is what the Lord Almighty
says: "They may build, but I will demolish. They will be called the Wicked
Land, a people always under the wrath
of the Lord. 5 You will see it with your
own eyes and say, 'Great is the Lord—
even beyond the borders of Israel!'

6 "A son honors his father, and a servant his master. If I am a father, where is
the honor due me? If I am a master,
where is the respect due me?" says the
Lord Almighty. "It is you, O priests, who
show contempt for my name.
    "But you ask, 'How have we shown
contempt for your name?'
    7 "You place defiled food on my altar.
    "But you ask, 'How have we defiled
you?'
    "By saying that the Lord's table is con-
temptible. 8 When you bring blind animals for sacrifice, is that not wrong?
When you sacrifice crippled or diseased animals, is that not wrong? Try offering them to your governor! Would he
be pleased with you? Would he accept
you?" says the Lord Almighty.

9 "Now implore God to be gracious to
us. With such offerings from your
hands, will he accept you?"—says the
Lord Almighty.

10 "Oh, that one of you would shut the
temple doors, so that you would not
light useless fires on my altar! I am not
pleased with you," says the Lord Almighty, "and I will accept no offering
from your hands. 11 My name will be
great among the nations, from the rising
to the setting of the sun. In every place
incense and pure offerings will be
brought to my name, because my name
will be great among the nations," says
the Lord Almighty.

12 "But you profane it by saying of the
Lord's table, 'It is defiled,' and of its
food, 'It is contemptible.' 13 And you say,

'What a burden!' and you sniff at it contemptuously," says the LORD Almighty.

"When you bring injured, crippled or diseased animals and offer them as sacrifices, should I accept them from your hands?" says the LORD. [14]"Cursed is the cheat who has an acceptable male in his flock and vows to give it, but then sacrifices a blemished animal to the Lord. For I am a great king," says the LORD Almighty, "and my name is to be feared among the nations.

[2:1]"AND now this admonition is for you, O priests. [2]If you do not listen, and if you do not set your heart to honor my name," says the LORD Almighty, "I will send a curse upon you, and I will curse your blessings. Yes, I have already cursed them, because you have not set your heart to honor me.

[3]"Because of you I will rebuke[b] your descendants[c]; I will spread on your faces the offal from your festival sacrifices, and you will be carried off with it. [4]And you will know that I have sent you this admonition so that my covenant with Levi may continue," says the LORD Almighty. [5]"My covenant was with him, a covenant of life and peace, and I gave them to him; this called for reverence and he revered me and stood in awe of my name. [6]True instruction was in his mouth and nothing false was found on his lips. He walked with me in peace and uprightness, and turned many from sin.

[7]"For the lips of a priest ought to preserve knowledge, and from his mouth men should seek instruction—because he is the messenger of the LORD Almighty. [8]But you have turned from the way and by your teaching have caused many to stumble; you have violated the covenant with Levi," says the LORD Almighty. [9]"So I have caused you to be despised and humiliated before all the people, because you have not followed my ways but have shown partiality in matters of the law."

[10]Have we not all one Father[d]? Did not one God create us? Why do we profane the covenant of our fathers by breaking faith with one another?

[11]Judah has broken faith. A detestable thing has been committed in Israel and in Jerusalem: Judah has desecrated the sanctuary the LORD loves, by marrying the daughter of a foreign god. [12]As for the man who does this, whoever he may be, may the LORD cut him off from the tents of Jacob[e]—even though he brings offerings to the LORD Almighty.

[13]Another thing you do: You flood the LORD's altar with tears. You weep and wail because he no longer pays attention to your offerings or accepts them with pleasure from your hands. [14]You ask, "Why?" It is because the LORD is acting as the witness between you and the wife of your youth, because you have broken faith with her, though she is your partner, the wife of your marriage covenant.

[15]Has not ⌊the LORD⌋ made them one? In flesh and spirit they are his. And why one? Because he was seeking godly offspring.[f] So guard yourself in your spirit, and do not break faith with the wife of your youth.

[16]"I hate divorce," says the LORD God of Israel, "and I hate a man's covering himself[g] with violence as well as with his garment," says the LORD Almighty. So guard yourself in your spirit, and do not break faith.

[17]You have wearied the LORD with your words.

"How have we wearied him?" you ask.

By saying, "All who do evil are good in the eyes of the LORD, and he is pleased with them" or "Where is the God of justice?"

[a]1 Malachi means my messenger.   [b]3 Or cut off (see Septuagint)   [c]3 Or will blight your grain   [d]10 Or father   [e]12 Or [12]May the LORD cut off from the tents of Jacob anyone who gives testimony in behalf of the man who does this   [f]15 Or [15]But the one ⌊who is our father⌋ did not do this, not as long as life remained in him. And what was he seeking? An offspring from God   [g]16 Or his wife

REVELATION 21:1-27

Then I [John] saw a new heaven and a new earth, for the first heaven and the first earth had passed away, and there was no longer any sea. [2]I saw the Holy

City, the new Jerusalem, coming down out of heaven from God, prepared as a bride beautifully dressed for her husband. ³And I heard a loud voice from the throne saying, "Now the dwelling of God is with men, and he will live with them. They will be his people, and God himself will be with them and be their God. ⁴He will wipe every tear from their eyes. There will be no more death or mourning or crying or pain, for the old order of things has passed away."

⁵He who was seated on the throne said, "I am making everything new!" Then he said, "Write this down, for these words are trustworthy and true."

⁶**He said to me: "It is done. I am the Alpha and the Omega, the Beginning and the End. To him who is thirsty I will give to drink without cost from the spring of the water of life. ⁷He who overcomes will inherit all this, and I will be his God and he will be my son.** ⁸But the cowardly, the unbelieving, the vile, the murderers, the sexually immoral, those who practice magic arts, the idolaters and all liars—their place will be in the fiery lake of burning sulfur. This is the second death."

⁹One of the seven angels who had the seven bowls full of the seven last plagues came and said to me, "Come, I will show you the bride, the wife of the Lamb." ¹⁰And he carried me away in the Spirit to a mountain great and high, and showed me the Holy City, Jerusalem, coming down out of heaven from God. ¹¹It shone with the glory of God, and its brilliance was like that of a very precious jewel, like a jasper, clear as crystal. ¹²It had a great, high wall with twelve gates, and with twelve angels at the gates. On the gates were written the names of the twelve tribes of Israel. ¹³There were three gates on the east, three on the north, three on the south and three on the west. ¹⁴The wall of the city had twelve foundations, and on them were the names of the twelve apostles of the Lamb.

¹⁵The angel who talked with me had a measuring rod of gold to measure the city, its gates and its walls. ¹⁶The city was laid out like a square, as long as it was wide. He measured the city with the rod and found it to be 12,000 stadia*a* in length, and as wide and high as it is long. ¹⁷He measured its wall and it was 144 cubits*b* thick,*c* by man's measurement, which the angel was using. ¹⁸The wall was made of jasper, and the city of pure gold, as pure as glass. ¹⁹The foundations of the city walls were decorated with every kind of precious stone. The first foundation was jasper, the second sapphire, the third chalcedony, the fourth emerald, ²⁰the fifth sardonyx, the sixth carnelian, the seventh chrysolite, the eighth beryl, the ninth topaz, the tenth chrysoprase, the eleventh jacinth, and the twelfth amethyst.*d* ²¹The twelve gates were twelve pearls, each gate made of a single pearl. The great street of the city was of pure gold, like transparent glass.

²²I did not see a temple in the city, because the Lord God Almighty and the Lamb are its temple. ²³The city does not need the sun or the moon to shine on it, for the glory of God gives it light, and the Lamb is its lamp. ²⁴The nations will walk by its light, and the kings of the earth will bring their splendor into it. ²⁵On no day will its gates ever be shut, for there will be no night there. ²⁶The glory and honor of the nations will be brought into it. ²⁷Nothing impure will ever enter it, nor will anyone who does what is shameful or deceitful, but only those whose names are written in the Lamb's book of life.

a16 That is, about 1,400 miles (about 2,200 kilometers) *b17* That is, about 200 feet (about 65 meters) *c17* Or *high* *d20* The precise identification of some of these precious stones is uncertain.

PSALM 149:1-9
¹**P**raise the Lᴏʀᴅ.*a*

Sing to the Lᴏʀᴅ a new song,
   his praise in the assembly of the saints.
²Let Israel rejoice in their Maker;
   let the people of Zion be glad in their King.

³Let them praise his name with
  dancing
and make music to him with
  tambourine and harp.
⁴For the LORD takes delight in his
  people;
he crowns the humble with
  salvation.
⁵Let the saints rejoice in this honor
and sing for joy on their beds.

⁶May the praise of God be in their
  mouths
and a double-edged sword in their
  hands,
⁷to inflict vengeance on the nations
and punishment on the peoples,
⁸to bind their kings with fetters,
  their nobles with shackles of
    iron,
⁹to carry out the sentence written
  against them.
  This is the glory of all his saints.

  Praise the LORD.

a 1 Hebrew *Hallelu Yah*; also in verse 9

PROVERBS 31:10-24

¹⁰ᵃ**A** wife of noble character who can
  find?
  She is worth far more than
    rubies.
¹¹Her husband has full confidence in
  her
and lacks nothing of value.
¹²She brings him good, not harm,
  all the days of her life.
¹³She selects wool and flax
  and works with eager hands.
¹⁴She is like the merchant ships,
  bringing her food from afar.
¹⁵She gets up while it is still dark;
  she provides food for her family
  and portions for her servant girls.
¹⁶She considers a field and buys it;
  out of her earnings she plants a
    vineyard.
¹⁷She sets about her work vigorously;
  her arms are strong for her tasks.
¹⁸She sees that her trading is
    profitable,
  and her lamp does not go out at
    night.

¹⁹In her hand she holds the distaff
  and grasps the spindle with her
    fingers.
²⁰She opens her arms to the poor
  and extends her hands to the
    needy.
²¹When it snows, she has no fear for
    her household;
  for all of them are clothed in
    scarlet.
²²She makes coverings for her bed;
  she is clothed in fine linen and
    purple.
²³Her husband is respected at the city
    gate,
  where he takes his seat among the
    elders of the land.
²⁴She makes linen garments and sells
    them,
  and supplies the merchants with
    sashes.

a 10 Verses 10-31 are an acrostic, each verse beginning with
a successive letter of the Hebrew alphabet.

☐ D A Y   3 6 5

GOD SIGHTINGS

December 31

MALACHI 3:1–4:6

"**S**ee, I [the LORD Almighty] will send my
messenger, who will prepare the way before me. Then suddenly the Lord you are
seeking will come to his temple; the
messenger of the covenant, whom you
desire, will come," says the LORD Almighty.

²But who can endure the day of his
coming? Who can stand when he appears? For he will be like a refiner's fire
or a launderer's soap. ³He will sit as a
refiner and purifier of silver; he will
purify the Levites and refine them like
gold and silver. Then the LORD will have
men who will bring offerings in righteousness, ⁴and the offerings of Judah
and Jerusalem will be acceptable to the

LORD, as in days gone by, as in former years.

⁵"So I will come near to you for judgment. I will be quick to testify against sorcerers, adulterers and perjurers, against those who defraud laborers of their wages, who oppress the widows and the fatherless, and deprive aliens of justice, but do not fear me," says the LORD Almighty.

⁶"I the LORD do not change. So you, O descendants of Jacob, are not destroyed. ⁷Ever since the time of your forefathers you have turned away from my decrees and have not kept them. Return to me, and I will return to you," says the LORD Almighty.

"But you ask, 'How are we to return?'

⁸"Will a man rob God? Yet you rob me.

"But you ask, 'How do we rob you?'

"In tithes and offerings. ⁹You are under a curse—the whole nation of you—because you are robbing me. ¹⁰Bring the whole tithe into the storehouse, that there may be food in my house. Test me in this," says the LORD Almighty, "and see if I will not throw open the floodgates of heaven and pour out so much blessing that you will not have room enough for it. ¹¹I will prevent pests from devouring your crops, and the vines in your fields will not cast their fruit," says the LORD Almighty. ¹²"Then all the nations will call you blessed, for yours will be a delightful land," says the LORD Almighty.

¹³"You have said harsh things against me," says the LORD.

"Yet you ask, 'What have we said against you?'

¹⁴"You have said, 'It is futile to serve God. What did we gain by carrying out his requirements and going about like mourners before the LORD Almighty? ¹⁵But now we call the arrogant blessed. Certainly the evildoers prosper, and even those who challenge God escape.'"

¹⁶Then those who feared the LORD talked with each other, and the LORD listened and heard. A scroll of remembrance was written in his presence

concerning those who feared the LORD and honored his name.

¹⁷"They will be mine," says the LORD Almighty, "in the day when I make up my treasured possession.ᵃ I will spare them, just as in compassion a man spares his son who serves him. ¹⁸And you will again see the distinction between the righteous and the wicked, between those who serve God and those who do not.

⁴:¹"SURELY the day is coming; it will burn like a furnace. All the arrogant and every evildoer will be stubble, and that day that is coming will set them on fire," says the LORD Almighty. "Not a root or a branch will be left to them. ²But for you who revere my name, the sun of righteousness will rise with healing in its wings. And you will go out and leap like calves released from the stall. ³Then you will trample down the wicked; they will be ashes under the soles of your feet on the day when I do these things," says the LORD Almighty.

⁴"Remember the law of my servant Moses, the decrees and laws I gave him at Horeb for all Israel.

⁵"See, I will send you the prophet Elijah before that great and dreadful day of the LORD comes. ⁶He will turn the hearts of the fathers to their children, and the hearts of the children to their fathers; or else I will come and strike the land with a curse."

ᵃ17 Or Almighty, "my treasured possession, in the day when I act

REVELATION 22:1-21

Then the angel showed me [John] the river of the water of life, as clear as crystal, flowing from the throne of God and of the Lamb ²down the middle of the great street of the city. On each side of the river stood the tree of life, bearing twelve crops of fruit, yielding its fruit every month. And the leaves of the tree are for the healing of the nations. ³No longer will there be any curse. The throne of God and of the Lamb will be in the city, and his servants will serve him.

4They will see his face, and his name will be on their foreheads. 5There will be no more night. They will not need the light of a lamp or the light of the sun, for the Lord God will give them light. And they will reign for ever and ever.

6The angel said to me, "These words are trustworthy and true. The Lord, the God of the spirits of the prophets, sent his angel to show his servants the things that must soon take place."

7"Behold, I am coming soon! Blessed is he who keeps the words of the prophecy in this book."

8I, John, am the one who heard and saw these things. And when I had heard and seen them, I fell down to worship at the feet of the angel who had been showing them to me. 9But he said to me, "Do not do it! I am a fellow servant with you and with your brothers the prophets and of all who keep the words of this book. Worship God!"

10Then he told me, "Do not seal up the words of the prophecy of this book, because the time is near. 11Let him who does wrong continue to do wrong; let him who is vile continue to be vile; let him who does right continue to do right; and let him who is holy continue to be holy."

12"Behold, I am coming soon! My reward is with me, and I will give to everyone according to what he has done. 13I am the Alpha and the Omega, the First and the Last, the Beginning and the End.

14"Blessed are those who wash their robes, that they may have the right to the tree of life and may go through the gates into the city. 15Outside are the dogs, those who practice magic arts, the sexually immoral, the murderers, the idolaters and everyone who loves and practices falsehood.

16"I, Jesus, have sent my angel to give youa this testimony for the churches. I am the Root and the Offspring of David, and the bright Morning Star."

17The Spirit and the bride say, "Come!" And let him who hears say, "Come!" Whoever is thirsty, let him come; and whoever wishes, let him take the free gift of the water of life.

18I warn everyone who hears the words of the prophecy of this book: If anyone adds anything to them, God will add to him the plagues described in this book. 19And if anyone takes words away from this book of prophecy, God will take away from him his share in the tree of life and in the holy city, which are described in this book.

20He who testifies to these things says, "Yes, I am coming soon."

Amen. Come, Lord Jesus.

21The grace of the Lord Jesus be with God's people. Amen.

a16 The Greek is plural.

PSALM 150:1-6

1Praise the Lord.a

Praise God in his sanctuary;
    praise him in his mighty heavens.
2Praise him for his acts of power;
    praise him for his surpassing
        greatness.
3Praise him with the sounding of the
        trumpet,
    praise him with the harp and lyre,
4praise him with tambourine and
        dancing,
    praise him with the strings and
        flute,
5praise him with the clash of cymbals,
    praise him with resounding
        cymbals.

6Let everything that has breath praise
        the Lord.

Praise the Lord.

a1 Hebrew Hallelu Yah; also in verse 6

PROVERBS 31:25-31

25She [a wife of noble character] is
        clothed with strength and
        dignity;
    she can laugh at the days to
        come.

26 She speaks with wisdom,
   and faithful instruction is on her
   tongue.
27 She watches over the affairs of her
   household
   and does not eat the bread of
   idleness.
28 Her children arise and call her blessed;
   her husband also, and he praises
   her:

29 "Many women do noble things,
   but you surpass them all."
30 Charm is deceptive, and beauty is
   fleeting;
   but a woman who fears the Lord is
   to be praised.
31 Give her the reward she has
   earned,
   and let her works bring her praise
   at the city gate.